The UNIVERSITY ATLAS

Sixteenth Edition

edited by
Harold Fullard, M.Sc., Cartographic Editor
and
H. C. Darby, O.B.E., Litt.D., Professor of Geography, University of Cambridge

George Philip & Son Limited, London

First Edition	February 1937
Second Edition	August 1940
Third Edition	February 1944
Fourth Edition	July 1945
Fifth Edition	November 1946
Sixth Edition	November 1948
Seventh Edition	January 1953
Eighth Edition	
Completely redesigned. © May 1958	
Ninth Edition	© August 1960
Tenth Edition	© April 1962
Eleventh Edition	© June 1964
Twelfth Edition	
Redesigned.	© March 1967
Thirteenth Edition	© June 1969
Fourteenth Edition	© January 1972
Fifteenth Edition	© February 1973
Sixteenth Edition	© **August 1974**

© 1974 George Philip & Son Ltd.
The entire contents of this atlas are
copyright in all countries signatory to
the Berne and International Copyright
Conventions. Reproduction in part or
in whole is strictly reserved to the
proprietors George Philip & Son, Ltd.

Printed in Great Britain
by George Philip Printers, Ltd., London.

Preface

During the course of nearly forty years since its original publication the University Atlas has been through sixteen editions each of which has in its turn been revised and improved.

For the eighth edition in 1958, the atlas was completely redesigned because it was considered that only an entirely new version would suffice to show the many developments, and incorporate the results of the new surveys of the post-war years. In that edition we made two significant changes: a substantial increase in the scale of the sectional maps, and the re-arrangement of the atlas into an easily portable size, convenient for frequent use, and able to stand on a bookshelf. The present content and format is essentially as then devised.

For the twelfth edition in 1967, the style of colouring of the maps was completely changed to take advantage of new developments in map reproduction and to provide lighter yet clearer layer colours. This in turn made possible an improvement in the cartographical design: the inclusion of a hill-shading to complement the layer colouring and bring out clearly the character of the land and relief features without impairing in the slightest the detail of names, settlement and communications. The opportunity of new reproduction was also taken to carry out another full-scale revision of coastlines and rivers, boundaries and administrative divisions, railways, roads and airports; to effect improvements in features of design and presentation and to include a map of Southern Japan on 1:5M. As in previous editions international boundaries are drawn to show the *de facto* situation where there are rival claims to territory. The preliminary matter, which includes a summary of projections used in the atlas and also climate graphs for over 200 representative stations, has been revised and redesigned using a second colour printing to give greater clarity. The rainfall graphs are on a uniform scale to facilitate true comparison between them. For this edition the wider use of the metric system has been reflected in conversion to, or inclusion of metric measures where they had not already been given in previous editions.

Spellings of names are in the forms given in the latest official lists and generally agree with the rules of the Permanent Committee on Geographical Names and the United States Board on Geographic Names, and a list of changed place names and names for which alternatives are often used appears in the introductory matter. The index contains over 50,000 entries.

We gratefully acknowledge the help of many official organisations and individuals, and especially thank the Meteorological Office for extracting data for the climate graphs.

H. FULLARD
H. C. DARBY

Contents

iii Preface
iv–vi Contents
vii–viii Alternative Spellings
ix Notes on Climatic Graphs
x–xxiii Climatic Graphs of the Continents and the British Isles
xxiv List of Projections used in the Atlas

1 **General Reference**

1 **The World**
Volcanoes and Earthquake Zones, Equatorial Scale 1:220M
Chief Centres of Volcanic Activity 1:50M

2-3 **The World**
Geology 1:100M
Structure 1:140M

4 **The World**
Temperature and Ocean Currents 1:215M
January, July and Annual Temperature

5 **The World**
Isobars and Winds 1:215M
Seasonal and Annual Rainfall
January and July Isobars and Prevailing Winds

6 **The World**
Soil Regions 1:140M

7 **The World**
Natural Vegetation 1:165M
Climatic Regions 1:165M

8–9 **The World**
Density of Population 1:81$\frac{1}{2}$M

10–11 **The World**
Political 1:80M

12–13 **The World in Hemispheres**
Political and Communications—Centred on London and Antipodes 1:100M
Centred on San Francisco, Cape Town, Cairo and Shanghai 1:300M

14–15 **The Polar Regions** 1:35M

16–17 **The Atlantic Ocean**
Equatorial Scale 1:50M

18–19 **Europe**
Physical 1:17$\frac{1}{2}$M
Annual Rainfall 1:40M

20–21 **France and Central Europe**
Geology 1:5M

22 **Europe**
Climate 1:40M
January and July Temperature
Winter and Summer Rainfall, Pressure and Winds

23 **Europe**
Natural Vegetation 1:20M

24 **Europe**
Density of Population 1:20M

25 **Europe**
Political 1:20M

26–27 **The British Isles**
Solid Geology 1:3$\frac{1}{4}$M

28–29 **The British Isles**
Physical 1:3$\frac{1}{4}$M

30–31 **The British Isles**
Climate—Annual Rainfall and Isobars 1:3$\frac{1}{4}$M
January and July Temperature 1:12$\frac{1}{2}$M
Duration of Bright Sunshine 1:12$\frac{1}{2}$M

32 **The British Isles**
Population 1:4M

33 **The British Isles**
Counties 1:4M

34–35 **South and South-East England** 1:1M

36 **South-West England** 1:1M

37 **Wales** 1:1M

38–39 **Northern England** 1:1M

40–41 **Southern Scotland** 1:1M

42–43 **Northern Scotland** 1:1M

44–45 **Southern Ireland** 1:1M

46 **Northern Ireland** 1:1M

47 **France** 1:5M

48–49 **Northern France** 1:2$\frac{1}{2}$M

50–51 **Southern France** 1:2$\frac{1}{2}$M

52–53 **Central Europe** 1:5M
Political 1:25M

54	**The Netherlands, Belgium and Luxembourg**	
		1:2½M
55	**The Sambre-Meuse-Ruhr Region**	1:1M
56–57	**Germany and Switzerland**	1:2½M
58–59	**Austria, Czechoslovakia and Hungary**	1:2½M
60	**Poland**	1:2½M
61	**Spain and Portugal**	1:5M
62–63	**Western Spain and Portugal**	1:2½M
64–65	**Eastern Spain**	1:2½M
66–67	**The Mediterranean Lands**	1:10M
68–69	**Italy and The Balkan States**	1:5M
	S.E. Europe: Political	1:25M
70–71	**Northern Italy and Western Yugoslavia**	1:2½M
72–73	**Southern Italy**	1:2½M
74–75	**Yugoslavia and Bulgaria**	1:2½M
76–77	**Greece and Albania**	1:2½M
78	**Rumania**	1:2½M
79	**Southern Norway**	1:2½M
80–81	**Denmark and Southern Sweden**	1:2½M
82–83	**Scandinavia and the Baltic Lands**	1:5M
	Iceland	1:5M
84–85	**The U.S.S.R. in Europe**	1:10M
86–87	**European Russia** Central	1:5M
88–89	**European Russia** South	1:5M
90–91	**The Union of Soviet Socialist Republics**	1:20M
92–93	**Asia**	
	Physical	1:40M
	Winter Rainfall, Pressure and Winds	1:80M
	Summer Rainfall, Pressure and Winds	1:80M
94–95	**Asia**	
	Political	1:40M
	January Temperature	1:80M
	July Temperature	1:80M
96	**Asia**	
	Annual Rainfall	1:80M
	India: Monsoons, their evolution	
97	**Asia**	
	Natural Vegetation	1:50M
98	**The Holy Land**	1:1M
99	**Arabia and The Horn of Africa**	1:15M
100–1	**The Near and Middle East**	1:10M
102–3	**South Asia**	1:10M
104–5	**The Indo-Gangetic Plain**	1:6M
	S. Asia: Irrigation	1:40M
106	**Southern India and Sri Lanka**	1:6M
107	**Mainland Southeast Asia**	1:10M
	Malaya and Singapore	1:6M
108–9	**The East Indies**	1:12½M
	Java and Madura	1:7½M
110	**Southern and Eastern Asia**	
	Density of Population	1:30M
111	**China**	1:20M
112–13	**Eastern China and Korea**	1:10M
114	**Japan**	1:10M
	Southern Japan	1:5M
115	**Africa**	
	Political	1:40M
	Density of Population	1:80M
116–17	**Africa**	
	Physical	1:30M
	Annual Rainfall	1:80M
118	**Africa**	
	Climate	1:80M
	January and July Temperature	
	Summer and Winter Rainfall, Pressure and Winds	
119	**Africa**	
	Natural Vegetation	1:40M
120–1	**Northern Africa**	1:15M
122–3	**Northwest Africa**	1:8M
124–5	**West Africa**	1:8M

Page	Map	Scale
126–7	**The Nile Valley**	1:8M
	The Nile Delta	1:4M
128–9	**Central and South Africa**	1:15M
130–1	**Central and East Africa**	1:8M
132	**Rhodesia, Zambia and Malawi**	1:8M
133	**The Transvaal**	1:4M
134–5	**Cape Province, Orange Free State and Natal**	1:4M
136–7	**The Pacific Ocean**	
	Equatorial Scale	1:60M
138–9	**Australia**	1:12M
	Australasia: Political	1:80M
140	**Australia**	
	Climate	1:60M
	January and July Temperature	
	Summer and Winter Rainfall, Pressure and Winds	
141	**Australia**	
	Natural Vegetation	1:30M
	Annual Rainfall	1:60M
	Density of Population	1:50M
142	**Western Australia**	1:7½M
143	**Southeast Australia**	1:4½M
144–5	**Eastern Australia**	1:7½M
	The Territory of Papua and New Guinea	1:12M
146	**New Zealand**	
	North Island	1:3½M
	January and July Temperature	1:25M
	Summer and Winter Rainfall	1:25M
	Pressure and Winds	
	Annual Rainfall	1:25M
147	**New Zealand**	
	South Island	1:3½M
	Density of Population	1:15M
	Natural Vegetation	1:15M
148–9	**North America**	
	Physical	1:30M
	Political	1:70M
	Annual Rainfall	1:70M
150	**North America**	
	Climate	1:70M
	January and July Temperature	
	Winter and Summer Rainfall, Pressure and Winds	
151	**North America**	
	Natural Vegetation	1:32M
152–3	**Canada**	1:15M
	Alaska	1:30M
154–5	**Eastern Canada**	1:7M
156–7	**Western Canada**	1:7M
158–9	**The United States**	1:12M
	Hawaii	1:10M
160–1	**Northeastern United States**	1:2½M
162–3	**The Eastern United States**	1:6M
	Density of Population	1:50M
164–5	**The Middle United States**	1:6M
166–7	**The Western United States**	1:6M
	Soils	1:50M
168	**Mexico**	1:12M
	Panama Canal	1:1M
169	**The West Indies**	1:12M
	Bermuda	1:1M
	Leeward Is.	1:8M
	Windward Is.	1:8M
	Trinidad and Tobago	1:8M
	Jamaica	1:8M
170	**South America**	
	Physical	1:30M
	Annual Rainfall	1:80M
171	**South America**	
	Natural Vegetation	1:40M
	Climate	1:80M
	January and July Temperature	
	Summer and Winter Rainfall, Pressure and Winds	
172–3	**Central South America**	1:8M
174–5	**South America**	
	North	1:16M
	Political	1:80M
176	**South America**	
	South	1:16M
	Density of Population	1:80M
	Index	

Alternative Spellings

NOTE: The following list gives the principal places where new names or spellings (given first) have been adopted. Earlier forms still in use are cross referenced to the new form. Place names of which the national spelling varies considerably from the English form, e.g. Livorno—Leghorn, are also included.

Aachen, Aix la Chapelle
Aalst: Alost
Abercorn, see Mbala
Abo, see Turku
Acre, see 'Akko
Adrianople, see Edirne
Affreville, see Khemis Miliana
Agram, see Zagreb
Agrigento: Girgenti
Ahvenanmaa: Åland Is.
Aix la Chapelle, see Aachen
Ain Mokra, see Berrahal
Ain Salah, see In Salah
Ain Touta: MacMahon
Akmolinsk, see Tselinograd
Al Hoceima: Alhucemas,
    Villa Sanjurjo
Al Khalil: Hebron
Al Khums: Homs, Leptis
    Magna
Al Ladhiqiyah: Latakia
Al Marj: Barce
Al Mawsil: Mosul
Al Qasabat: Cussabat
Al Quds: Jerusalem
Åland Is., see Ahvenanmaa
Alashanchih: Bayinhot
Alba Iulia: Karlsburg
Albertville, see Kalemie
Alcazarquivir, see Ksar el Kebir
Aleppo, see Halab
Alexandretta, see Iskenderon
Alexandria, see El Iskandariya
Alhucemas, see Al Hoceima
Allenstein, see Olsztyn
Alost, see Aalst
Amraoti-Amravati
An Geata Mór: Binghamstown
An Nhon: Binh Dinh
An Uaimh: Navan
Angora, see Ankara
Ankara: Angora
Annaba: Bône
Antakya: Antioch
Anvers: Antwerp, Antwerpen
Apollonia, see Marsa Susa
Ar Riyad: Riyadah
Arabian Gulf, see Persian G.
Arkhangelsk: Archangel
Arlon: Aarlen
Artemovsk: Bakhmut
Athinai: Athens
Augusto Cardosa: Matangula
Aumale, see Sour el Ghozlane
Auschwitz, see Oswiecim
Azetfoun: Port Gueydon

Bac Lieu, see Vinh Loi
Bagenalstown, see Muine
    Bheag
Bahia, see Salvador
Baile Etha Cliath: Dublin
Baile Deasmhumhna:
    Ballydesmond
Bakhmut, see Artemovsk
Bakwanga, see Mbuji-Mayi
Ballydesmond, see Baile
    Deasmhumhna
Baltiisk: Pillau
Banaras, see Varanasi
Bancroft, see Chililabombwe
Banda Atjeh: Kutaradja
Bandar, see Masulipatnam
Bandar Maharani, see Muar
Bandar Penggarem, see
    Batu Pahat
Bandundu: Banningville
Banghazi: Benghazi
Bangladesh: East Pakistan
Banhida, see Tatabanya
Barce, see Al Marj
Bayinhot, see Alashanchih
Basel: Basle
Basle, see Basel
Basutoland, see Lesotho
Batavia, see Djakarta
Batu Pahat: Bandar Penggarem
Bhavnagar: Bhaunagar
Bayan Tumen, see Choibalsan
Béchar: Colomb-Béchar
Bechuanaland Prot, see
    Botswana
Bedeau, see Ras el Ma
Beit Nabala, see Nevalat
Bejala: Bougie
Belém: Para
Belgard, see Bialogard
Bellin: Payne Bay

Belogorsk: Kuibyshevka
    Vostochnaya
Benares, see Varanasi
Benghazi: Banghazi
Beograd: Belgrade
Berdyansk: Osipenko
Bern: Berne
Berrahal: Ain Mokra
Beuthen: Bytom
Bezwada, see Vijayavada
Bharat: India
Bhilsa, see Vidisha
Bialogard: Belgard
Binghamstown, see
    An Geata Mór
Binh Dinh. see An Nhon
Bir Mogreïn: Fort Trinquet
Bitolj: Monastir
Björneborg, see Pori
Bolzano: Bozen
Bône, see Annaba
Borgå, see Porvoo
Botswana: Bechuanaland Prot.
Bougie, see Bejaïa
Brahestad, see Raahe
Braniewo: Braunsberg
Bratislava: Pressburg
Braunsberg, see Braniewo
Breslau, see Wroclaw
Bressanone: Brixen
Brest: Brest Litovsk
British Guiana, see Guyana
Brixen, see Bressanone
Brno: Brünn
Broken Hill, see Kabwe
Brugge: Bruges
Brunico: Bruneck
Brünn, see Brno
Brusa, see Bursa
Brussels, see Bruxelles
Bruxelles: Brussel, Brussels
Bucuresti: Bucharest
Budweis, see Ceske
    Budejovice
Bujumbura: Usumbura
Bukavu: Costermansville
Bunclody: Newtownbarry
Bursa: Brusa
Bytom: Beuthen

Ca Mau, see Quang Long
Caesarea, see Qeisari
Cairo, see El Qahira
Calicut: Kozhikode
Cambodia, see
    Khmer Rep.
Candia, see Iraklion
Canicado, see Vila A.
    Chamusca
Canton: Panyu, Punyu
    Kwangchow
Caporetto, see Kobarid
Caribrod: Dimitrovgrad
Carlsbad, see Karlovy Vary
Cattaro, see Kotor
Cawnpore, see Kanpur
Ceanannus Mór: Kells
Ceará, see Fortaleza
Celebes, see Sulawesi
Cerigo, see Kithira
Cernauti, see Chernovtsy
Ceske Budejovice: Budweis
Ceylon, see Sri Lanka
Chad: Tchad
Changan, see Sian
Changchow, see Lungki
Charleville, see Rath Luirc
Chefoo, see Yentai
Cheju-do: Quelpart
Chemnitz, see Karl Marx Stadt
Chemulpho, see Inchon
Cheribon, see Tjirebon
Chernovtsy: Cernauti,
    Czernowitz
Chernyakovsk: Insterberg
Chihli: Pohai
Chilumba: Deep Bay
Chilung: Keelung
Chios, see Khios
Chipata: Fort Jameson
Chisinau, see Kishinev
Chistyakovo, see Thorez
Chitipa: Fort Hill
Chkalov, see Orenburg
Choibalsan: Bayan Tumen
Chongjin: Seishin
Chtimba: Florence Bay
Churchill, R.: Hamilton R.
Cieszyn: Teschen

Cluj: Klausenburg
Coatzacoalcos: Pto. Mexico
Cocanada, see Kakinada
Colomb-Béchar, see Béchar
Cologne: Köln
Congo (Kinshasa), see
    Zaïre
Conjeeveram: Kanchipuram
Constance, see Konstanz
Constanta: Küstenje
Constantinople, see Istanbul
Copenhagen, Köbenhavn
Corfu, see Kerkira
Corunna, see La Coruña
Costermansville, see Bukavu
Courtrai, see Kortrijk
Coquilhatville, see Mbandaka
Craigavon: Lurgan and
    Portadown
Crete, see Kriti
Cuamba, see Novo Freixo
Cussabat, see Al Qasabat
Cyclades, see Kikladhes
Cyrene, see Shahhat
Czernowitz, see Chernovtsy

Dairen, see Lu-ta
Damascus, see Esh Sham
Damietta: Dumyat
Danzig, see Gdansk
Daugavpils: Dvinsk
Deep Bay, see Chilumba
Deutsch Krone, see Walcz
Dimitrovgrad: Caribrod
Dimitrovo, see Pernik
Djakarta: Batavia
Djambi, see Telanaipura
Djerba: Houmt Souk
Djibouti: Jibuti
Dnepropetrovsk:
    Yekaterinoslav
Dobrich, see Tolbukhin
Donetsk: Stalino
Doornik, see Tournai
Dor: Tantura
Dorpat, see Tartu
Drissa, see Verchedvinsk
Droichead Nua: Newbridge
Dublin, see Baile Átha Cliath
Dubrovnik: Ragusa
Dumyat: Damietta
Dunaujvaros: Sztalinvaros
Dunkerque: Dunquerque,
    Dunkirk
Durres: Durazzo
Dushanbe: Stalinabad
Dvinsk, see Daugavpils
Dzaudzhikau, see
    Ordzhonikidze
Dzhargalantu, see Hovd
Dzhibkhalantu, see Ulyasutay

East Pakistan, see
    Bangladesh
Edirne: Adrianople
Eisenhuttenstadt:
    Stalinstadt, Furstenberg
El Asnam: Orléansville
El Bayadh: Géryville
El Eulma: St. Arnaud
El Harrach: Maison Carrée
El Iskandariya: Alexandria
El Jadida: Mazagan
El Kala: La Calle
El Qahira: Cairo
El Suweis: Suez
Elblag: Elbing
Elizabethville, see Lubumbashi
Ellore: Eluru, Elluru
Escaut, see Schelde
Esfahan: Isfahan
Esh Sham: Damascus
Essaouira: Mogador
Evvoia: Euboea

Faizabad: Fyzabad
F'Dérik: Fort Gouraud
Felsogalla, see Tatabanya
Fengtien, see Mukden
Ferdinand, see Mikhailovgrad
Firenze, see Florence
Fiume, see Rijeka
Flanders: Vlaanderen
Florence Bay, see Chtimba
Florence: Firenze
Flushing, see Vlissingen
Foochow: Minhow
Formosa, see Taiwan
Fort de Polignac, see Illizi

Fort Flatters, see
    Zaouiet El-Kahla
Fort Gouraud, see F'Dérik
Fort Hall, see Muranga
Fort Jameson, see Chipata
Fort Rosebery, see Mansa
Fort Rupert: Rupert House
Fort Hill, see Chitipa
Fort Manning, see Mchinji
Fort Trinquet, see Bir Mogreïn
Fortaleza: Ceará
Fredrikshald, see Halden
French Terr. of the Afars & the
    Issas: Fr. Somaliland
Fribourg: Freiburg
Frunze: Pishpek
Fünfkirchen, see Pécs
Fyzabad, see Faizabad

Gagarin: Gzhatsk
Gallipoli, see Gelibolu
Gamlakarleby, see Kokkola
Gand, see Gent
Gävle: Gefle
Gzhatsk, see Gagarin
Gdansk: Danzig
Gelibolu: Gallipoli
Geneva (Lake), see Leman
Genève: Geneva (Town)
Genoa: Genova
Gent: Gand, Ghent
George River,
    see Port Nouveau-Québec
Géryville, see El Bayadh
Ghazaouet: Nemours
Ghent, see Gent
Girgenti, see Agrigento
Glatz, see Klodzko
Gliwice: Gleiwitz
Glorenza: Glurns
Glubczyce: Leobschütz
Goleniow: Gollnow
Gorki: Nijni Novgorod
Gorodok, see Zakamensk
Göteborg: Gothenburg
Gottwaldov: Zlin
Great Whale River,
    see Poste de la Baleine
Grosswardein, see Oradea
Grünberg, see Zielona
    Góra
Guardaful, C. see Ras Asir
Guyana: British Guiana

Haeju: Haiju
Hailar: Hulun
Halab: Haleb, Aleppo
Halden: Fredrikshald
Haleb, see Halab
Halq el Qued: La Goulette
Hamadia: Victor Hugo
Hamilton R., see Churchill R.
Hämeenlinna: Tavastehus
Hannover: Hanover
Harbin: Pinkiang
Hebron, see Al Khalih
Heijo, see Pyong-yang
Helsinki: Helsingfors
Hermannstadt, see Sibiu
Hirschberg, see Jelenia Góra
Hollandia, see Sukarnapura
Homs (Libya), see Al Khums
Hot Springs, see Truth or
    Consequences
Hotien: Khotan
Houmt Souk, see Djerba
Hovd: Jargalant,
    Dzhargalantu, Kobdo
Hulun, see Hailar

Iasi: Jassy
Ibiza: Iviza
Ieper: Ypres
Ighil Izane: Relizane
Ilebo: Port Francqui
Illizi: Fort de Polignac
In Salah: Ain Salah
Inchon: Chemulpho
India: Bharat
Inoucdjouac: Port Harrison
Insterberg, see Chernyakovsk
Iraklion: Candia
Iran: Persia
Isfahan, see Esfahan
Iskenderon: Alexandretta
Isoro: Paulis
Istanbul: Constantinople
Ivano-Frankovsk: Stanislav
Iviza, see Ibiza

Izmir: Smyrna

Jabalpur: Jubbulpore
Jadotville, see Likasi
Jaffa, see Tel Aviv-Jaffa
Jamnagar: Navanagar
Jargalant, see Hovd
Jassey, see Iasi
Javhlant, see Ulyasufay
Jelenia Góra: Hirschberg
Jelgave: Mitau
Jerusalem: Al Quds
Jesselton, see Kota Kinabalu
Jibuti, see Djibouti
João Pessoa: Paraiba
Jogiakarta: Djokjakarta
Jubbulpore, see Jabalpur

Kabwe: Broken Hill
Kakinada: Cocanada
Kalamata: Kalámal
Kalemie: Albertville
Kalgan: Wanchüan
Kalinin: Tver
Kaliningrad: Königsberg
Kananga: Luluabourg
Kanchipuram, see
    Conjeeveram
Kanchow: Kanhsien
Kanpur: Cawnpore
Kaolan, see Lanchow
Karl Marx Stadt: Chemnitz
Karlovac: Karlstadt
Karlsburg, see Alba Iulia
Karlstadt, see Karlovac
Karlovy Vary: Carlsbad
Kaschau, see Kosice
Kaskinen: Kaskö
Katowice: Stalinogrod
Kaunas: Kovno
Keelung, see Chilung
Keijo, see Seoul
Kells, see Ceanannus Mór
Kendrapara: Kendlapara
Kenitra: Port Lyautey
Kerkira: Corfu
Khanh Hung: Soc Trang
Khemis Miliana: Affreville
Khios: Chios
Khmelnitski: Proskurov
Khmer Rep.: Cambodia
Khodzhent, see Leninabad
Khotan, see Hotien
Kikladhes: Cyclades
Kinshasa: Leopoldville
Kirin: Yungki
Kirov: Viatka, Vyatka
Kirovgrad: Kirovo
    Yelisavetgrad, Zinovyevsk
Kisangani: Stanleyville
Kishinev: Chisinau
Kitakyushu: Kokura,
    Moji, Tobata,
    Wakamatsu & Yawata
Kithira: Cerigo
Klaipeda: Memel
Klausenburg, see Cluj
Klodzko: Glatz
Kobarid: Caporetto
Kobdo, see Hovd
Köbenhavn, see Copenhagen
Kokkola: Gamlakarleby
Kokura, see Kitakyushu
Kolarovgrad, see Šumen
Kolchugino, see Leninsk
    Kuznetski
Köln, see Cologne
Kolobrzeg: Kolberg
Kommunarsk: Voroshilovsk,
    Stavropol
Königsberg, see Kaliningrad
Konstanz: Constance
Kortrijk: Courtrai
Kosice: Kaschau
Koszalin: Köslin
Kota Baru, see Sukarnapura
Kota Kinabalu: Jesselton
Kotor: Cattaro
Kovna, see kaunas
Kozhikode, see Calicut
Krasnodar: Yekaterinodar
Kristinankaupunki:
    Kristinestad
Kriti: Krete, Crete
Kropotkin: Romanovsk
Ksar Chellala: Reibell
Ksar el Kebir: Alcazarquivir
Kucove, see Qytet Stalin
Kuibyshev: Samara

Kuibyshevka Vostochnaya, *see* Belogorsk
Kunming: Yunnan
Küstenje, *see* Constanta
Kutaradja, *see* Banda Atjeh
Kwangchow, *see* Canton

La Calle, *see* El Kala
La Coruña: Corunna
La Goulette, *see* Halq el Qued
Laibach, *see* Ljubljana
Lanchow: Kaolan
Lappeenranta: Villmanstrand
Latakia, *see* Al Ladhiqiyah
Lauenburg, *see* Lebork
Lebork: Lauenburg
Leeu-Gamka: Fraserburg Road
Leghorn: Livorno
Legnica: Liegnitz
Léman, Lake: Geneva, Lake
Lemberg, *see* Lvov
Leninabad: Khodzhent
Leninsk Kuznetski: Lenino, Kolchugino
Lensk: Mukhtuya
Leobschütz, *see* Glubczyce
Leopoldville, *see* Kinshasa
Leptis Magna, *see* Al Khums
Lesotho: Basutoland
Leuven: Louvain
Libau, *see* Liepaja
Liberec: Reichenberg
Liegnitz, *see* Legnica
Liepaja: Libau
Likasi: Jadotville
Lisbon: Lisboa
Livorno, *see* Leghorn
Llanelli: Llanelly
Ljubljana: Laibach
Lod: Lydda
Louvain, *see* Leuven
Lubumbashi: Elizabethville
Lucerne: Luzern
Lugansk, *see* Voroshilovgrad
Luluabourg, *see* Kananga
Lungki: Changchow, Lunki
Luofu: Lubero
Lurgan, *see* Craigavon
Lungkiang, *see* Tsitsihar
Lu-ta: Port Arthur and Dairen
Luxembourg: Luxemburg
Lvov: Lwow, Lemberg
Lwow, *see* Lvov
Lydda, *see* Lod
Lyons: Lyon

Maas, *see* Meuse
MacMahon, *see* Ain Touta
Madurai: Madura
Magallanes, *see* Punta Arenas
Maghnia: Marnia
Maison Carrée, *see* El Harrach
Majorca, *see* Mallorca
Malawi: Nyasaland
Malawi, L.: L. Nyasa
Malbork: Marienburg
Malines, *see* Mechelen
Mallorca: Majorca
Mandsaur: Mandasor
Mansa: Fort Rosebery
Mantes-la-Jolie: Mantes Gassicourt
Mantova: Mantua
Maranhão, *see* São Luis
Marburg, *see* Maribor
Marchand, *see* Rommani
Maricourt: Wakeham Bay
Marek, *see* Stanke Dimitrov
Maria Theresiopel, *see* Subotica
Mariánske Lánské: Marienbad
Maribor: Marburg
Marienburg, *see* Malbork
Mariupol, *see* Zhdanov
Marnia, *see* Maghnia
Marrakech: Morocco
Marsa Susa: Apollonia
Marseille: Marseilles
Masulipatnam: Bandar
Mathura: Muttra
Matangula, *see* Augusto Cardoso
Mayuram: Mayavaram
Mazagan: El Jadida
Mbala: Abercorn
Mbandaka: Coquilhatville
Mbuji-Mayi: Bakwanga
Mchinji: Fort Manning
Meathas Truim: Edgeworthstown
Mechelen: Malines
Memel, *see* Klaipeda
Menorca: Minorca
Me'ona: Tarshiha
Merano: Meran
Meuse: Maas
Mikhailovgrad: Ferdinand
Mikkeli: Sankt Michel
Milano: Milan
Minhow, *see* Foochow
Minorca, *see* Menorca
Misratah: Misurata
Mitau, *see* Jelgava
Mocha, *see* Mukha

Mogador, *see* Essaouira
Mohammadia: Perrégaux
Moji, *see* Kitakyushu
Molotov, *see* Perm
Molotovsk, *see* Severodvinsk
Monastir, *see* Bitolj
Montagnac, *see* Remchi
Montgomery, *see* Sahiwal
Moskva: Moscow
Mosul, *see* Al Mawsil
Muar: Bandar Maharani
Mukden: Shenyang, Fengtien
Mukha: Mocha
Muine Bheag: Bagenalstown
Mukhtuya, *see* Lensk
Munich: München
Muranga: Fort Hall
Muttra, *see* Mathura
Mymensingh, *see* Nasirabad

Najin: Rashin
Namen, *see* Namur
Namur: Namen
Nanning: Yungning
Naples: Napoli
Nasirabad: Mymensingh
Navan, *see* An Uaimh
Navanagar, *see* Jamnagar
Neemuch: Nimach
Neisse, *see* Nysa
Nemours, *see* Ghazaouet
Netherlands Guiana, *see* Surinam(e)
Neusatz, *see* Novi Sad
Neustettin, *see* Szczecinek
Nevalat: Beit Nabala
Newbridge (Ire.), *see* Droichead Nua
Newtonbarry, *see* Bunclody
Nictheroy, *see* Niteroi
Nieuwport: Nieuport
Nijni Novgorod, *see* Gorki
Nikolaistad, *see* Vaasa
Nimach, *see* Neemuch
Nisa, *see* Nysa
Niteroi: Nictheroy
Northern Rhodesia, *see* Zambia
Nouadhibou: Port Etienne
Nouveau Comptoir: Paint Hills
Nova Freixo: Cuamba
Novi Becej: Volosinovo
Novi Sad: Neusatz
Novokuznetsk: Stalinsk
Novomoskovsk: Stalinogorsk
Novosibirsk: Novo Nikolaevsk
Nsanje: Port Herald
Nukha, *see* Sheki
Nürnberg: Nuremberg
Nusaybin: Nisibin
Nyasa, L., *see* Malawi, L.
Nyasaland, *see* Malawi
Nykarleby, *see* Uusikaarlepyy
Nysa: Nisa, Neisse
Nyslott, *see* Savonlinna
Nystad, *see* Uusikaupunki

Odenburg, *see* Sopron
Olomouc: Olmutz
Olsztyn: Allenstein
Opava: Troppau
Opole: Oppeln
Oporto, *see* Pôrto
Oradea: Grosswardein
Ordzhonikidze: Dzaudzihikau
Orléansville, *see* El Asnam
Orenburg: Chkalov
Osipenko, *see* Berdyansk
Ostende: Oostende, Ostend
Oswiecim: Auschwitz
Ouagadougou, *see* Wagadugu
Ouahran: Oran, Wahran
Ourgla: Wargla
Oulu: Uleåborg

Paint Hills, *see* Nouveau Comptoir
Palanka Raya: Pahandut
Panyu, *see* Canton
Paoshan: Yungchang
Paoting: Tsingyuan
Para, *see* Belem
Paraiba, *see* João Pessoa
Patrai: Patras
Paulis, *see* Isiro
Payne Bay, *see* Bellin
Pécs: Fünfkirchen
Peking: Peiping, Pekin
Perm: Molotov
Pernambuco, *see* Recife
Pernik: Dimitrovo
Perrégaux, *see* Mohammadia
Persia, *see* Iran
Persian Gulf: Arabian G.
Philippeville, *see* Skikda
Philippopolis, *see* Plovdiv
Pillau, *see* Baltisk
Pilsen, *see* Pizen
Pinkiang, *see* Harbin
Piraevis: Piraeus, Peiraieus, Pireets
Pishpek, *see* Frunze
Plovdiv: Philippopolis
Pizen, Pilsen

Podgorica, *see* Titograd
Pohai, *see* Chihli
Pola, *see* Pula
Ponthierville, *see* Ubundi
Pori: Björneborg
Port Arthur, *see* Lu-ta
Port Etienne, *see* Nouadhibou
Port Francqui, *see* Ilebo
Port Gueydon, *see* Azetfoun
Port Harrison, *see* Inoucdjouac
Port Herald, *see* Nsanje
Port Lyautey, *see* Kenitra
Port Nouveau-Québec: George River
Portadown, *see* Craigavon
Pôrto: Oporto
Porvoo: Borgå
Poste de la Baleine: Great Whale River
Poznan: Posen
Praha: Prague
Pressburg, *see* Bratislava
Proskurov, *see* Khmelnitski
Puerto Mexico, *see* Coatzacoalcos
Pula: Pola
Punta Arenas: Magallanes
Pyong-yang: Heijo

Qeisari: Caesarea
Quang Long: Ca Mau
Quelpart, *see* Cheju-do
Qytet Stalin: Kucove

Raahe: Brahestad
Raciborz: Ratibor
Ragusa, *see* Dubrovnik
Raheng, *see* Tak
Rankovicevo: Kraljevo
Ras Asir: Cape Guardafui
Ras el Ma: Bedeau
Rashid: Rosetta
Rashin, *see* Najin
Rass el Oued: Tocqueville
Rath Luitc: Charleville
Ratibor, *see* Raciborz
Ratisbon, *see* Regensburg
Recife: Pernambuco
Regensburg: Ratisbon
Reibell, *see* Ksar Chellala
Reichenberg, *see* Liberec
Relizane, *see* Ighil Izane
Remchi: Montagnac
Revel, *see* Tallinn
Rezâiyeh, L.: Urmia, L.
Rhodes, *see* Rodhós
Rhodesia: Southern Rhodesia
Rijeka: Fiume
Riyadah, *see* Ar Riyad
Rodhós: Rhodes
Roeselare: Roulers
Roma: Rome
Romanovsk, *see* Kropotkin
Rommani: Marchand
Roraima: Rio Branco
Rosetta: Rashid
Roulers, *see* Roeselare
Rovinj: Rovigno
Rupert House, *see* Fort Rupert
Ruse: Ruschuk
Rybinsk: Schcherbakov

Saglouc: Sugluk
Sahiwal: Montgomery
Saida: Sidon
Saint Arnaud, *see* El Eulma
Saint Denis, *see* Sig
Saint Gall: Sankt Gallen
Saint Nicolas, *see* Sint Niklaas
Salonika, *see* Thessaloniki
Salvador: Baia, Bahia
Sandan: Sanbor
Samara, *see* Kuibyshev
Sankt Gallen, *see* Saint Gall
Sankt Michel: Mikkeli
Santo Domingo: Ciudad Trujillo
São Luis: Maranhão
Saragossa, *see* Zaragoza
Savonlinna: Nyslott
Schässburg, *see* Sighisoara
Schelde: Escaut, Scheldt
Schweidnitz, *see* Swidnica
Scutari (Albania), *see* Shkodër
Scutari (Turkey), *see* Usküdar
Sedom: Sodom
Seishin, *see* Chongjin
Semlin, *see* Zemun
Seoul: Keijo
Sept Iles: Seven Islands
Severodvinsk: Molotovsk
Sevilla: Seville
's Gravenhage: The Hague
Shahhat: Cyrene
Shcherbakov, *see* Rybinsk
Sheki: Nukha
Shenyang, *see* Mukden
Shetland: Zetland
Shkodër: Scutari, Shkodra
Shumen, *see* Šumen
Siam, *see* Thailand
Sian: Changan
Sibiu: Hermannstadt

Sidon, *see* Saida
Sig: St. Denis
Sighisoara: Schässburg
Simbirsk, *see* Ulyanovsk
Singora, *see* Songkhla
Sint Niklaas: Saint Nicolas
Siracusa: Syracuse
Skikda: Philippeville
Skopje: Skoplje, Usküb
Sliten, *see* Zliten
Slupsk: Stolp
Smyrna, *see* Izmir
Soc Trang, *see* Khanh Hung
Soche: Yarkand
Sodom, *see* Sedom
Sofiya: Sofia
Sombor: Zombor
Songkhla: Singora
Soochow: Wuhsien
Sorpon: Odenburg
Sour el Ghozlane: Aumale
Sousse: Susa
South Yemen: South Arabia
Southern Rhodesia, *see* Rhodesia
Sovetsk: Tilsit
Split: Spalato
Sri Lanka: Ceylon
Stalin, *see* Varna
Stalin (Qytet): Kucove
Stalinabad, *see* Dushanbe
Stalingrad, *see* Volgograd
Staliniri, *see* Tskhinvali
Stalino, *see* Donetsk
Stalinogorsk, *see* Novomoskovsk
Stalinograd, *see* Katowice
Stalinsk, *see* Novokuznetsk
Stalinstad, *see* Eisenhuttenstadt
Stanislav, *see* Ivano-Frankovsk
Stanke Dimilrov: Marek
Stanleyville, *see* Kisangani
Stettin, *see* Szczecin
Sterzing: Vipiteno
Stolp, *see* Slôpsk
Stolpmünde, *see* Ustka
Stuhlweissenburg, *see* Székesfehérvár
Subotica: Maria Theresiopel
Suez, *see* El Suweis
Sugluk, *see* Saglouc
Sukarnapura: Kota Baru, Hollandia
Sulawesi: Celebes
Sur: Tyre
Surinam(e): Netherlands Guiana
Susa, *see* Sousse
Sverdlovsk: Yekaterinburg
Swidnica: Schweidnitz
Syracuse, *see* Siracusa
Szczecin: Stettin
Szczecinek: Neustettin
Székesfehérvár: Stuhlweissenburg
Sztalinvarose, *see* Dunaujvaros

Tagdempt: Tiaret
Taihoku, *see* Taipei
Taiwan: Formosa
Taiyüan: Yangku
Tak: Raheng, Rehaeng
Tallinn: Revel, Reval
Tammefors, *see* Tampere
Tampere: Tammefors
Tanganyika, *see* Tanzania
Tantura, *see* Dor
Tanzania: Tanganyika and Zanzibar
Tarabulus, *see* Tripoli
Tarshiha, *see* Me'ona
Tartu: Dorpat
Tatabanya: Banhida and Felsogalla
Tavastehus, *see* Hämeenlinna
Tbilisi: Tiflis
Tchad, *see* Chad
Tel Aviv-Jaffa: Jaffa, Tel Aviv
Telanaipura: Djambi
Tende: Tenda
Teschen, *see* Cieszyn
Thailand: Siam
Thebes, *see* Thivai
The Hague, *see* 's Gravenhage
Thessaloniki: Salonika
Tiaret, *see* Tagdempt
Thivai: Thebes
Thorez: Christyakovo
Tiflis, *see* Tbilisi
Tihwa, *see* Urumchi
Tilsit, *see* Sovetsk
Timbuktu, *see* Tombouctou
Tiruchchirappalli: Trichinopoly
Tissemsilt: Vialar
Titograd: Podgorica
Tjirebon: Cheribon
Tobata, *see* Kitakyushu
Tocqueville, *see* Rass el Oued
Tolbukhin: Dobrich
Tombouctou: Timbuktu
Tornio: Tornea
Tournai: Doornik
Trèves: Trier

Trichinopoly, *see* Tiruchchirappalli
Tripoli: Tarabulus
Troppau, *see* Opava
Truth or Consequences: Hot Springs
Tselinograd: Akmolinsk
Tsingyuan, *see* Paoting
Tsitsihar: Lungkiang
Tskhinvali: Staliniri
Turin: Torino
Turku: Abo
Turnovo, *see* Veliko Tarnovo
Tver, *see* Kalinin
Tyre, *see* Sur

Ubundi: Ponthierville
Ulan Ude: Verkhneudinsk
Uleåborg, *see* Oulu
Ulyanovsk: Simbitsk
Ulyasutay: Javhlant, Dzhibkhalantu
Urmia, L., *see* Rezâiyeh, L.
Urumchi: Tihwa
Usküb, *see* Skopje
Usküdar: Scutari
Ussurysk: Voroshilov
Ustka: Stolpmünde
Usumbura, *see* Bujumbura
Uusikaarlepyy: Nykarleby
Uusikaupunki: Nustad

Vassa: Nikolaistad
Varanasi: Banaras, Benares
Varna: Stalin
Veliko Tarnoyo: Turnovo
Venice: Venezia
Ventspils: Windau, Vindava
Verchnevdinsk: Drissa
Verkhneudinsk, *see* Ulan Ude
Vialar, *see* Tissemsilt
Victor Hugo, *see* Hamadia
Viborg: Viipuri, Vyborg
Vidisha: Bhilsa
Vienna: Wien
Vijayavada: Bezwada
Vila A, Chamusca: Canicado
Villa Sanjurjo, *see* Al Hoceima
Villamstrand, *see* Lappeenranta
Vilnius: Vilna, Vilno
Vilnyus, Wilno
Vinh Loi: Bac Lieu
Vindava, *see* Ventspils
Vipteno: Sterzing
Vishakhapatnam: Vizagapatam, Visakakhapatnam
Vlaanderen, *see* Flanders
Vlissingen: Flushing
Volgograd: Stalingrad
Volosinovo, *see* Novi Becej
Voroshilov: Ussurysk
Voroshilovgrad: Lugansk
Voroshilovsk, *see* Kommunarsk
Vyatka, *see* Kirov

Wagadugu, *see* Ougadougou
Wakamatsu, *see* Kitakyushu
Wakeham Bay, *see* Maricourt
Walbrzych: Waldenburg
Walcz: Deutsch Krone
Wanchüan, *see* Kalgan
Warszawa: Warsaw
Wenchow: Yungkia
Wien, *see* Vienna
Wilno, *see* Vilnius
Windau, *see* Ventspils
Wroclaw: Breslau
Wuhsien, *see* Soochow

Yanam: Yanaon
Yangku, *see* Taiyüan
Yarkand, *see* Soche
Yawata, *see* Kitakyushu
Yekaterinburg, *see* Sverdlovsk
Yekaterinodar, *see* Krasnodar
Yekaterinoslav, *see* Dnepropetrovsk
Yelisavetgrad, *see* Kirovgrad
Yentai: Chéfoo
Ypres, *see* Ieper
Yungchang, *see* Paoshan
Yungki, *see* Kirin
Yungkia, *see* Wenchow
Yungning, *see* Nanning
Yunnan, *see* Kunming

Zadar: Zara
Zaïre: Congo (Kinshasa)
Zegreb: Agram
Zakamensk: Gotodok
Zambia: Northern Rhodesia
Zaouiet El-Kahla: Fort Flatters
Zaragoza: Saragossa
Zemun: Semlin
Zetland: Shetland
Zhdanov: Mariupol
Zielona Góra: Grünberg
Zinovyevsk, *see* Kirovgrad
Zlin, *see* Gottwaldov
Zliten: Sliten
Zombor, *see* Sombor

The climate graphs should be used in conjunction with the maps illustrating the climate of the World, and also the more detailed maps of the climates of the Continents and the British Isles. For each of the Continents and the British Isles about thirty different stations have been selected so that practically every type of climate throughout the world is covered by the graphs. Complete temperature, pressure and rainfall statistics have been obtained for all except a few stations where pressure statistics were not available. Wherever possible the graphs show average observations based upon long period means, and in all other cases over as long a period as possible. The latest available statistics have been consulted throughout.

Small maps are given on each sheet of graphs showing the location of every station. The figure after the name of the station gives the height in metres of the station above sea-level, so that comparisons between stations can be made after allowing for elevation. For temperature, measurements are given in degrees Fahrenheit and Centigrade*; for pressure, inches and millibars; and for rainfall, in inches and centimetres. The temperature graphs show the monthly means of daily maximum and minimum actual temperatures: from these the mean monthly actual temperatures can easily be determined. The mean annual range of temperature is given above the temperature graphs. The pressure graphs show the mean monthly pressure at sea-level, except in cases of high-level stations, where the height to which the pressure has been reduced is noted. For both temperature and pressure graphs a uniform scale has been employed throughout.

The rainfall graphs show the average monthly rainfall, and above them is given the average total annual rainfall. These graphs have been drawn to show the rainfall on the same scale for all stations to facilitate true comparisons between them. Where the rainfall graph extends over to the temperature graph the rainfall scale has been continued at the side of the graph.

On the temperature maps the actual temperatures and sea-level isotherms for the two extreme months of the year, January and July, are given. This information is supplemented by the graphs so that a far more complete picture of temperature changes can now be visualized. A comparison of stations in high latitudes with those in low latitudes renders apparent the importance of the seasonal changes due to insolation. In high latitudes the annual range of temperature is considerable. It decreases gradually as the equator is approached where there is scarcely any variation throughout the year. Another important factor in determining the range is the position of a station in relation to the sea, which exercises a strong moderating influence. The graphs for Africa illustrate the differences in seasons in the northern and southern hemispheres. The influence of the sea also shows itself in the small differences between the mean daily maxima and minima of seaside stations as compared with inland stations. Those most remote from the sea experience a large diurnal range.

The graphs reveal very clearly the intimate connection existing between temperature and pressure. This is perhaps nowhere more clearly indicated than in Asia, where the intense winter cold of the interior coincides with a high pressure system, and the warmth of summer with a low pressure system. As the graphs deal only with land stations all the great pressure systems of the world cannot be demonstrated. Their influence is discernible however in the pressure graphs for many of the stations, e.g., the permanent low pressure system centred on Iceland and the permanent high pressure system based on the Azores, seen in the graphs for Reykjavik and Lisbon respectively, and the permanent equatorial low pressures. One further factor having an important bearing on local climate in high mountain regions deserves mention, namely, the influence of height in reducing pressure. Reduced to sea-level, the pressures for Quito and Guayaquil would appear to be the same, but the graphs reveal the differences which actually exist.

The rainfall maps in the atlas show broadly seasonal rainfall for summer and winter. These are now supplemented by the rainfall graphs, a study of which enables greater distinctions to be drawn between the various rainfall regions, by showing both the amount of precipitation and the months in which it occurs—factors of prime significance for vegetation. In classifying the different rainfall regimes attention should be paid to the factor of relief and the connection noted between the low pressures and convectional rains of equatorial regions.

*In the Absolute scale of temperature the freezing point of water is assumed to be 273°. The formula for converting degrees Fahrenheit (F) to degrees Absolute (A) is $A = 273 + \frac{5}{9}(F-32)$.

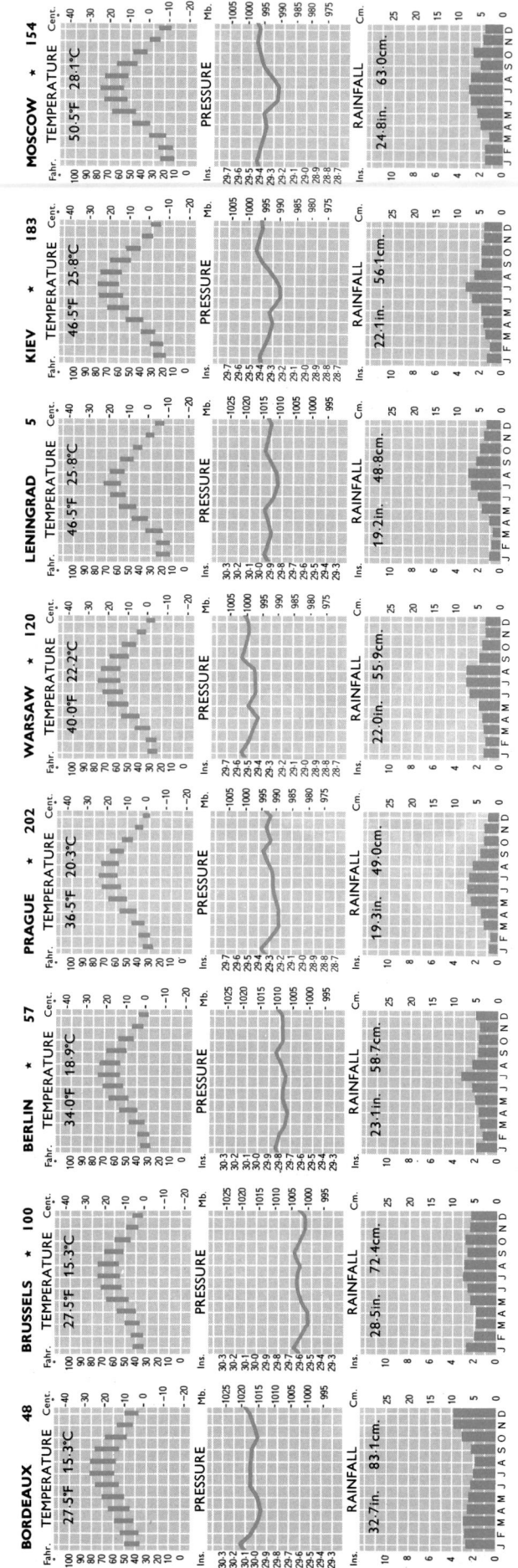

See Climatic Maps in Atlas, pages 18 and 22

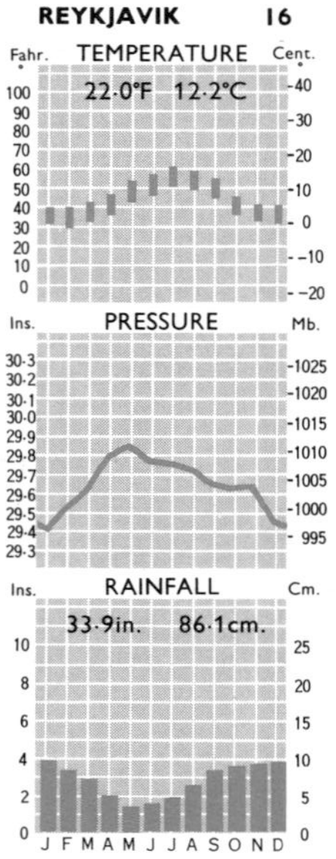

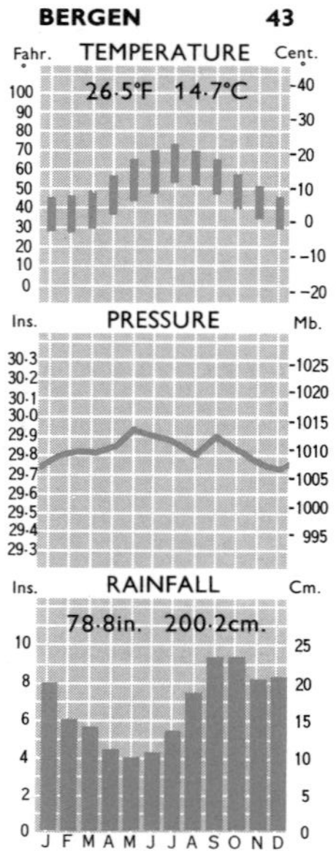

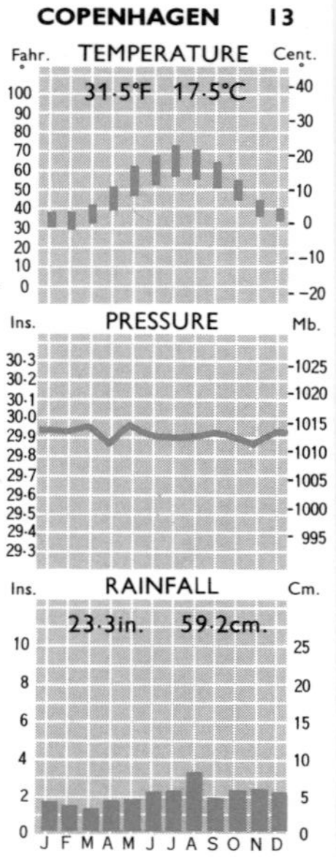

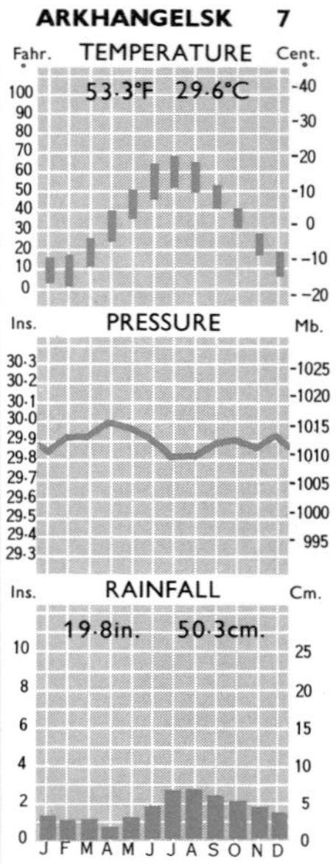

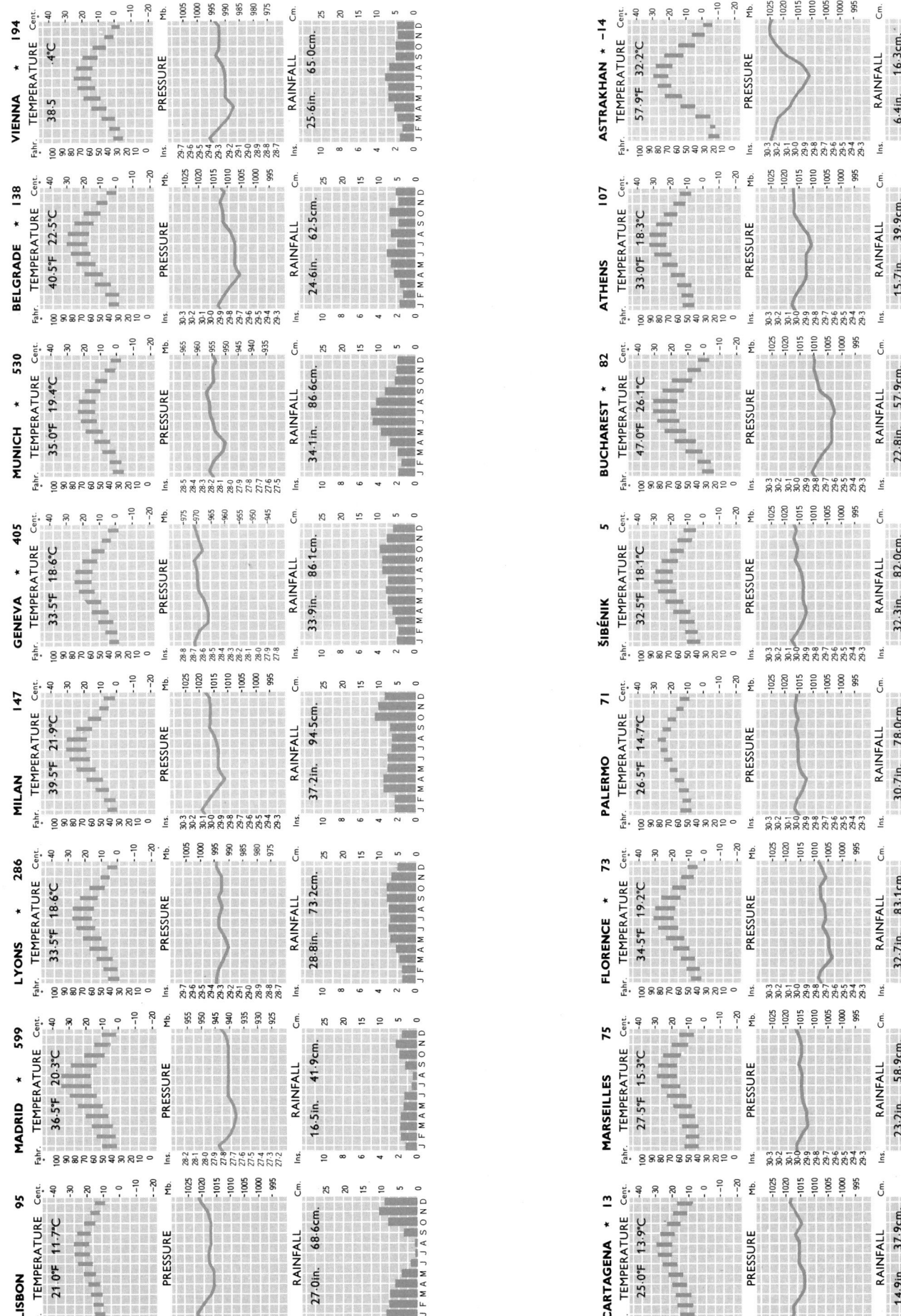

Copyright, George Philip & Son, Ltd

* Pressure at station level

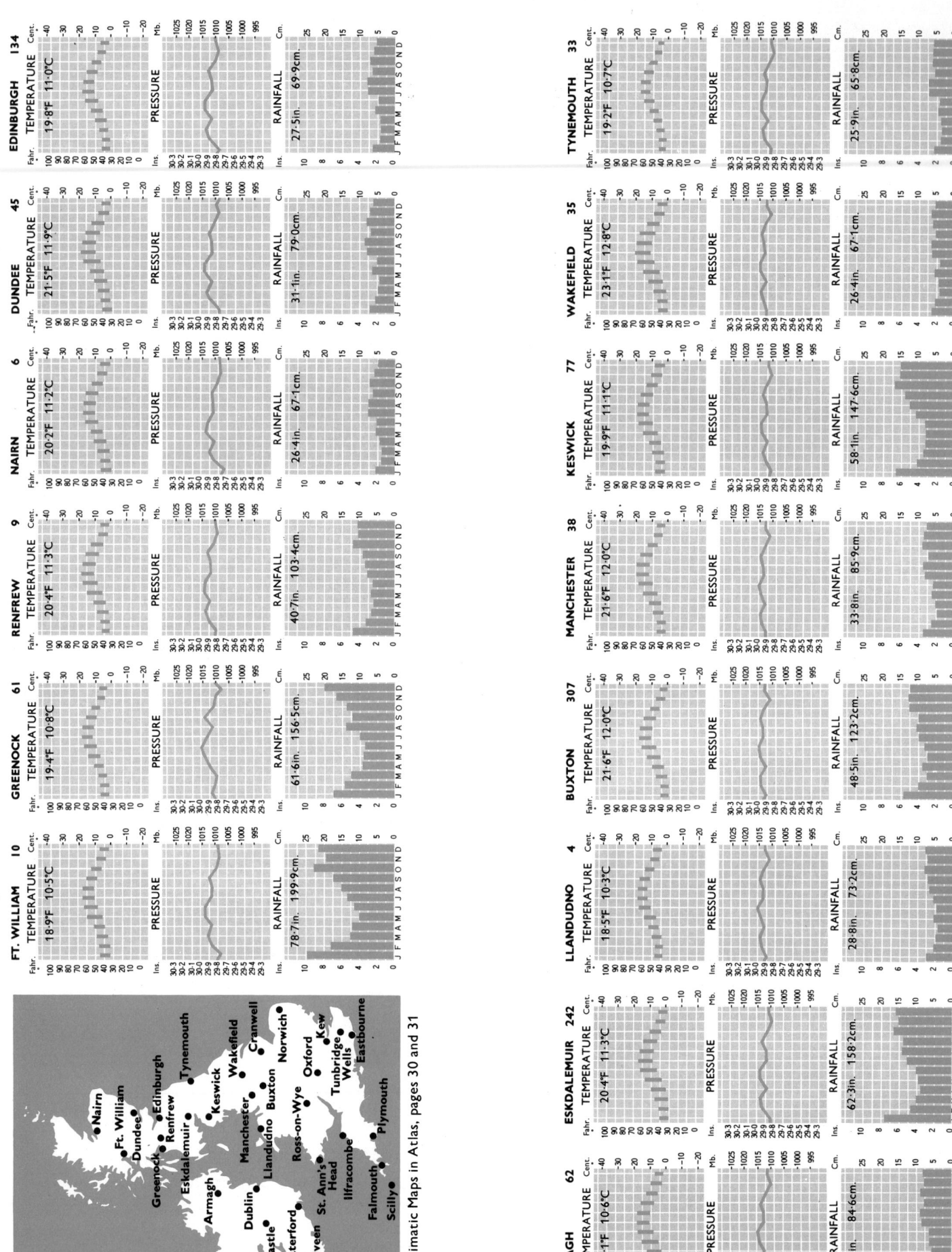
Nairn
Ft. William
Dundee
Edinburgh
Greenock
Renfrew
Eskdalemuir
Tynemouth
Armagh
Keswick
Wakefield
Manchester
Dublin
Cranwell
Birr Castle
Llandudno
Buxton
Norwich
Waterford
Ross-on-Wye
Oxford
Cahirciveen
St. Ann's Head
Kew
Tunbridge Wells
Ilfracombe
Eastbourne
Falmouth
Plymouth
Scilly
FT. WILLIAM 10
TEMPERATURE 18·9°F 10·5°C
PRESSURE
RAINFALL 78·7in. 199·9cm.
GREENOCK 61
TEMPERATURE 19·4°F 10·8°C
PRESSURE
RAINFALL 61·6in. 156·5cm.
RENFREW 9
TEMPERATURE 20·4°F 11·3°C
PRESSURE
RAINFALL 40·7in. 103·4cm.
NAIRN 6
TEMPERATURE 20·2°F 11·2°C
PRESSURE
RAINFALL 26·4in. 67·1cm.
DUNDEE 45
TEMPERATURE 21·5°F 11·9°C
PRESSURE
RAINFALL 31·1in. 79·0cm.
EDINBURGH 134
TEMPERATURE 19·8°F 11·0°C
PRESSURE
RAINFALL 27·5in. 69·9cm.
ARMAGH 62
TEMPERATURE 19·1°F 10·6°C
PRESSURE
RAINFALL 33·3in. 84·6cm.
ESKDALEMUIR 242
TEMPERATURE 20·4°F 11·3°C
PRESSURE
RAINFALL 62·3in. 158·2cm.
LLANDUDNO 4
TEMPERATURE 18·5°F 10·3°C
PRESSURE
RAINFALL 28·8in. 73·2cm.
BUXTON 307
TEMPERATURE 21·6°F 12·0°C
PRESSURE
RAINFALL 48·5in. 123·2cm.
MANCHESTER 38
TEMPERATURE 21·6°F 12·0°C
PRESSURE
RAINFALL 33·8in. 85·9cm.
KESWICK 77
TEMPERATURE 19·9°F 11·1°C
PRESSURE
RAINFALL 58·1in. 147·6cm.
WAKEFIELD 35
TEMPERATURE 23·1°F 12·8°C
PRESSURE
RAINFALL 26·4in. 67·1cm.
TYNEMOUTH 33
TEMPERATURE 19·2°F 10·7°C
PRESSURE
RAINFALL 25·9in. 65·8cm.
Fahr.
Cent.
Ins.
Mb.
Cm.
J F M A M J J A S O N D

See Climatic Maps in Atlas, pages 30 and 31

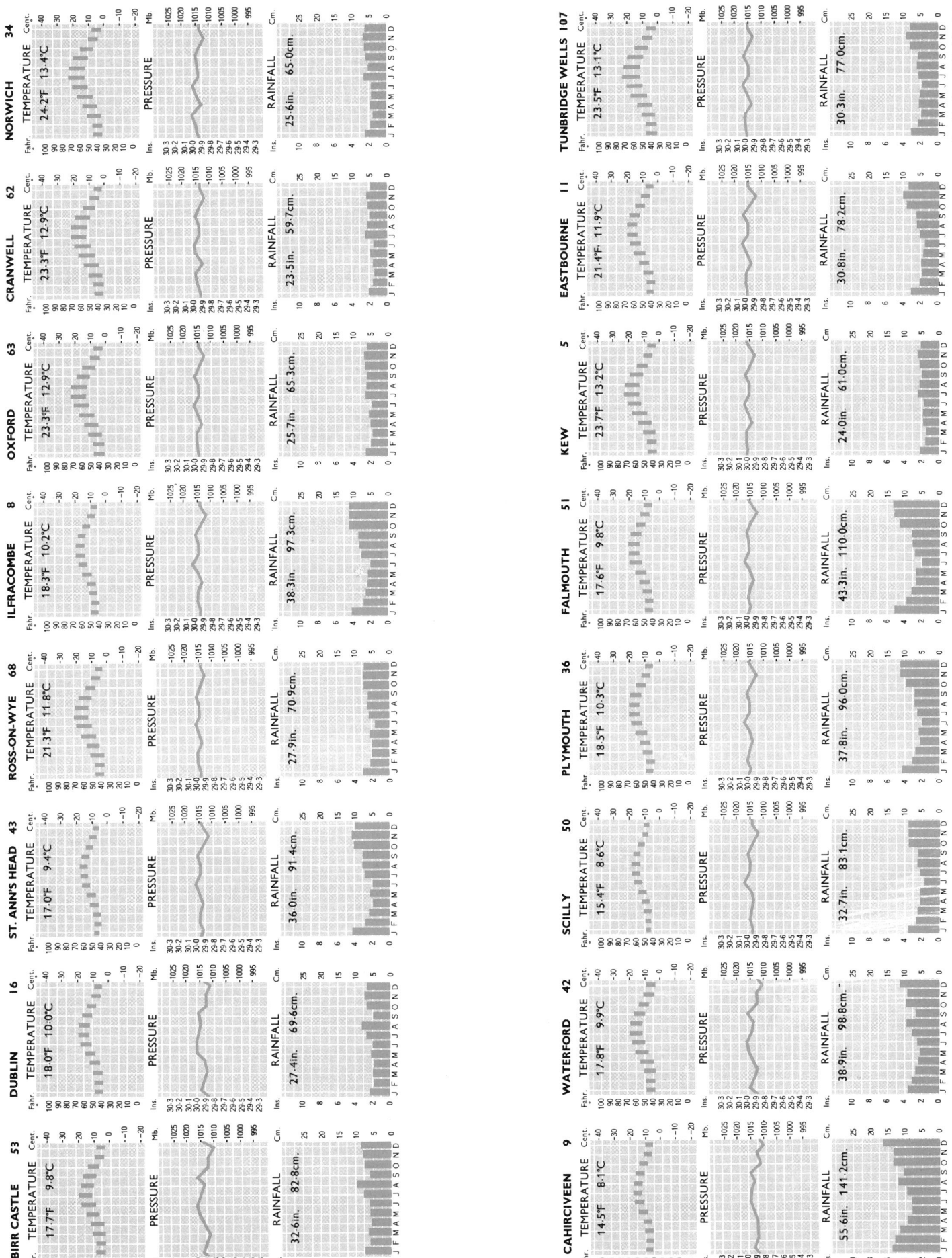

BIRR CASTLE 53
TEMPERATURE 17·7°F 9·8°C
PRESSURE
RAINFALL 32·6in. 82·8cm.
DUBLIN 16
TEMPERATURE 18·0°F 10·0°C
PRESSURE
RAINFALL 27·4in. 69·6cm.
ST. ANN'S HEAD 43
TEMPERATURE 17·0°F 9·4°C
PRESSURE
RAINFALL 36·0in. 91·4cm.
ROSS-ON-WYE 68
TEMPERATURE 21·3°F 11·8°C
PRESSURE
RAINFALL 27·9in. 70·9cm.
ILFRACOMBE 8
TEMPERATURE 18·3°F 10·2°C
PRESSURE
RAINFALL 38·3in. 97·3cm.
OXFORD 63
TEMPERATURE 23·3°F 12·9°C
PRESSURE
RAINFALL 25·7in. 65·3cm.
CRANWELL 62
TEMPERATURE 23·3°F 12·9°C
PRESSURE
RAINFALL 23·5in. 59·7cm.
NORWICH 34
TEMPERATURE 24·2°F 13·4°C
PRESSURE
RAINFALL 25·6in. 65·0cm.
CAHIRCIVEEN 9
TEMPERATURE 14·5°F 8·1°C
PRESSURE
RAINFALL 55·6in. 141·2cm.
WATERFORD 42
TEMPERATURE 17·8°F 9·9°C
PRESSURE
RAINFALL 38·9in. 98·8cm.
SCILLY 50
TEMPERATURE 15·4°F 8·6°C
PRESSURE
RAINFALL 32·7in. 83·1cm.
PLYMOUTH 36
TEMPERATURE 18·5°F 10·3°C
PRESSURE
RAINFALL 37·8in. 96·0cm.
FALMOUTH 51
TEMPERATURE 17·6°F 9·8°C
PRESSURE
RAINFALL 43·3in. 110·0cm.
KEW 5
TEMPERATURE 23·7°F 13·2°C
PRESSURE
RAINFALL 24·0in. 61·0cm.
EASTBOURNE 11
TEMPERATURE 21·4°F 11·9°C
PRESSURE
RAINFALL 30·8in. 78·2cm.
TUNBRIDGE WELLS 107
TEMPERATURE 23·5°F 13·1°C
PRESSURE
RAINFALL 30·3in. 77·0cm.
Fahr. Cent. Ins. Mb. Cm.
J F M A M J J A S O N D

Copyright, George Philip & Son, Ltd.

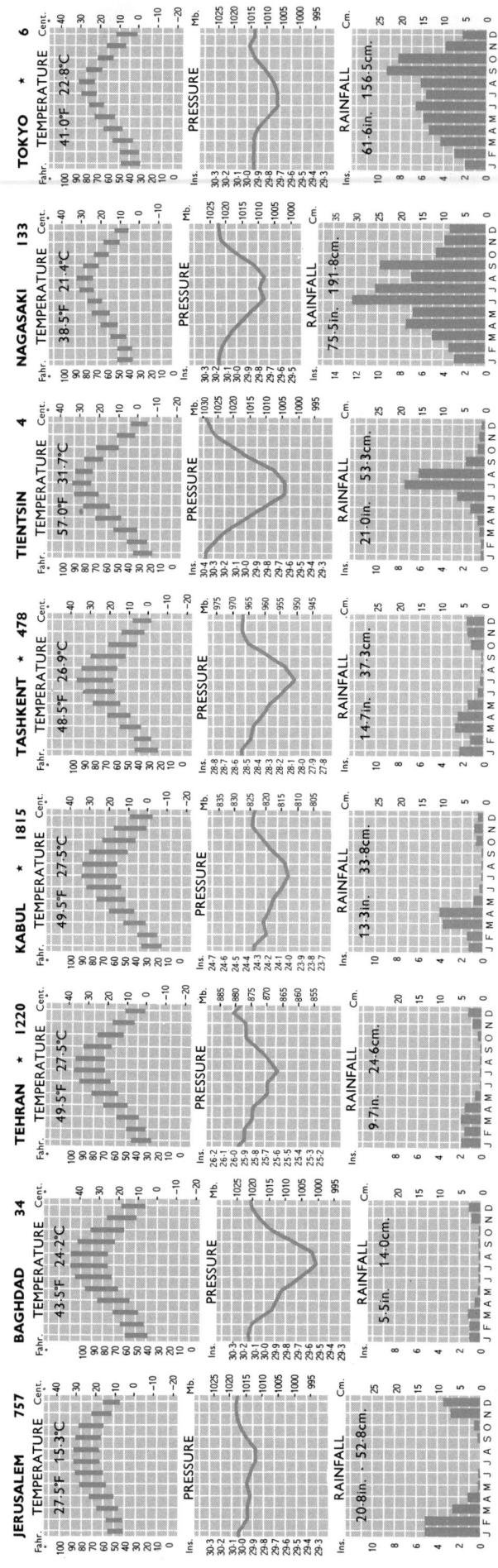

VLADIVOSTOK 29 — TEMPERATURE 63·0°F 35·0°C — PRESSURE — RAINFALL 23·6in. 59·9cm.

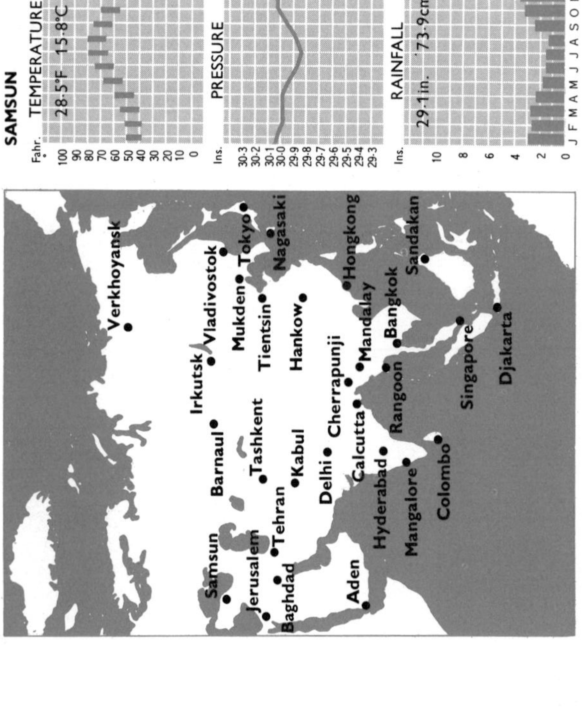

MUKDEN 43 — TEMPERATURE 67·5°F 37·5°C — PRESSURE — RAINFALL 27·9in. 70·9cm.

VERKHOYANSK 100 — TEMPERATURE 121·8°F 67·7°C — PRESSURE — RAINFALL 5·3in. 13·5cm.

IRKUTSK 467 — TEMPERATURE 59·9°F 33·3°C — PRESSURE — RAINFALL 14·9in. 37·9cm.

BARNAUL ★ 162 — TEMPERATURE 68·4°F 38·0°C — PRESSURE — RAINFALL 13·8in. 35·1cm.

SAMSUN 40 — TEMPERATURE 28·5°F 15·8°C — PRESSURE — RAINFALL 29·1in. 73·9cm.

TOKYO ★ 6 — TEMPERATURE 41·0°F 22·8°C — PRESSURE — RAINFALL 61·6in. 156·5cm.

NAGASAKI 133 — TEMPERATURE 38·5°F 21·4°C — PRESSURE — RAINFALL 75·5in. 191·8cm.

TIENTSIN 4 — TEMPERATURE 57·0°F 31·7°C — PRESSURE — RAINFALL 21·0in. 53·3cm.

TASHKENT ★ 478 — TEMPERATURE 48·5°F 26·9°C — PRESSURE — RAINFALL 14·7in. 37·3cm.

KABUL ★ 1815 — TEMPERATURE 49·5°F 27·5°C — PRESSURE — RAINFALL 13·3in. 33·8cm.

TEHRAN ★ 1220 — TEMPERATURE 49·5°F 27·5°C — PRESSURE — RAINFALL 9·7in. 24·6cm.

BAGHDAD 34 — TEMPERATURE 43·5°F 24·2°C — PRESSURE — RAINFALL 5·5in. 14·0cm.

JERUSALEM 757 — TEMPERATURE 27·5°F 15·3°C — PRESSURE — RAINFALL 20·8in. 52·8cm.

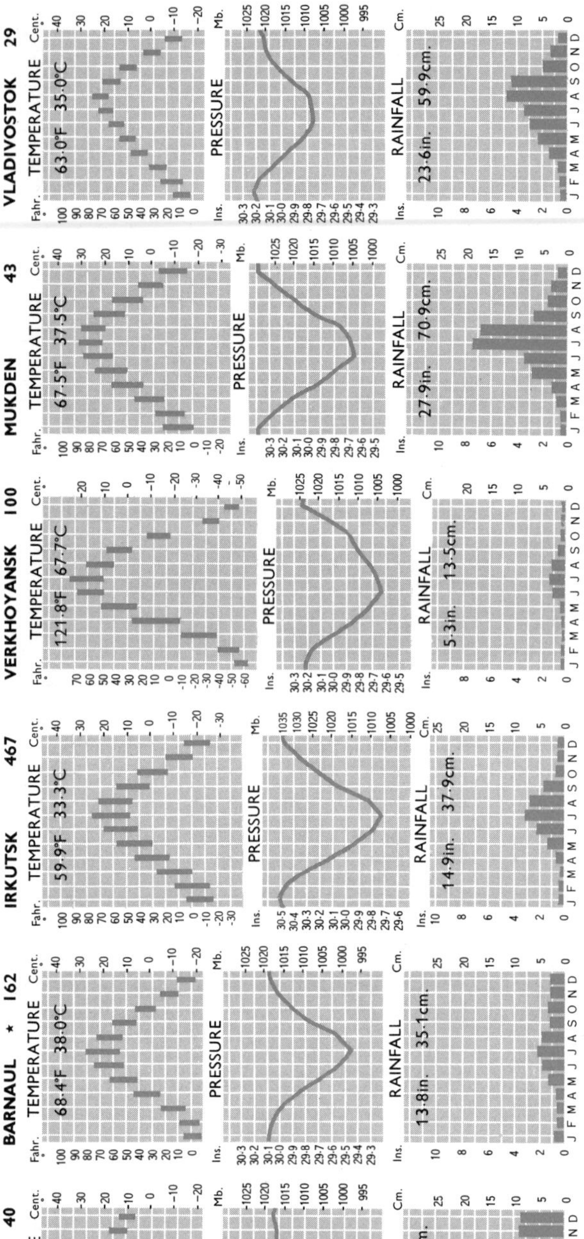

See Climatic Maps in Atlas, pages 92, 94 and 96

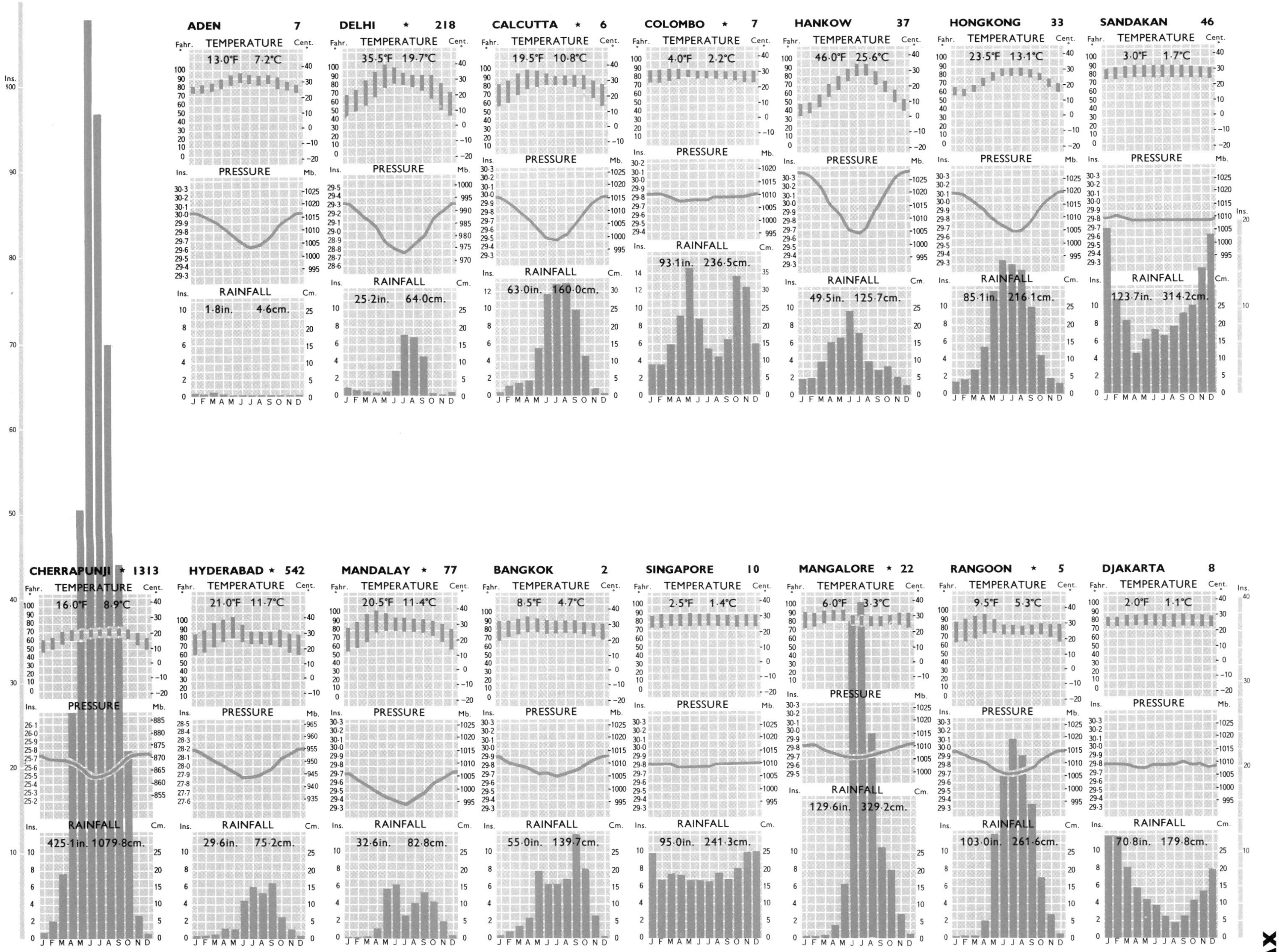

Copyright, George Philip & Son, Ltd.

SANDAKAN 46
TEMPERATURE 1·7°C — 3·0°F
PRESSURE
RAINFALL 314·2cm. — 123·7in.

HONGKONG 33
TEMPERATURE 13·1°C — 23·5°F
PRESSURE
RAINFALL 216·1cm. — 85·1in.

HANKOW 37
TEMPERATURE 25·6°C — 46·0°F
PRESSURE
RAINFALL 125·7cm. — 49·5in.

COLOMBO ★ 7
TEMPERATURE 2·2°C — 4·0°F
PRESSURE
RAINFALL 236·5cm. — 93·1in.

CALCUTTA ★ 6
TEMPERATURE 10·8°C — 19·5°F
PRESSURE
RAINFALL 160·0cm. — 63·0in.

DELHI ★ 218
TEMPERATURE 19·7°C — 35·5°F
PRESSURE
RAINFALL 64·0cm. — 25·2in.

ADEN 7
TEMPERATURE 7·2°C — 13·0°F
PRESSURE
RAINFALL 4·6cm. — 1·8in.

DJAKARTA 8
TEMPERATURE 1·1°C — 2·0°F
PRESSURE
RAINFALL 179·8cm. — 70·8in.

RANGOON ★ 5
TEMPERATURE 5·3°C — 9·5°F
PRESSURE
RAINFALL 261·6cm. — 103·0in.

MANGALORE ★ 22
TEMPERATURE 3·3°C — 6·0°F
PRESSURE
RAINFALL 329·2cm. — 129·6in.

SINGAPORE 10
TEMPERATURE 1·4°C — 2·5°F
PRESSURE
RAINFALL 241·3cm. — 95·0in.

BANGKOK 2
TEMPERATURE 4·7°C — 8·5°F
PRESSURE
RAINFALL 139·7cm. — 55·0in.

MANDALAY ★ 77
TEMPERATURE 11·4°C — 20·5°F
PRESSURE
RAINFALL 82·8cm. — 32·6in.

HYDERABAD ★ 542
TEMPERATURE 11·7°C — 21·0°F
PRESSURE
RAINFALL 75·2cm. — 29·6in.

CHERRAPUNJI ★ 1313
TEMPERATURE 8·9°C — 16·0°F
PRESSURE
RAINFALL 1079·8cm. — 425·1in.

★ Pressure at station level

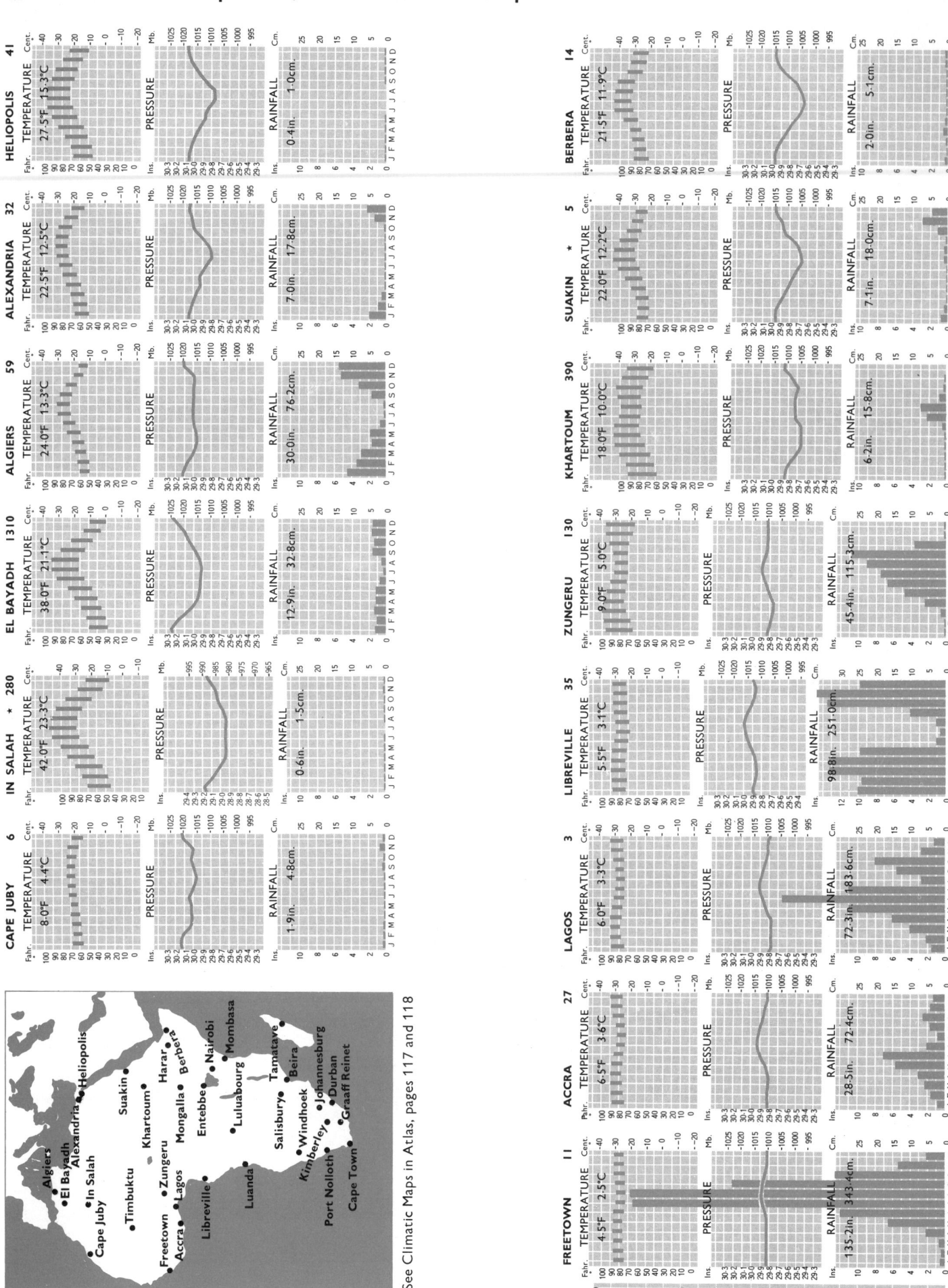
Algiers
El Bayadh
Alexandria
Heliopolis
In Salah
Cape Juby
Suakin
Timbuktu
Khartoum
Freetown
Zungeru
Harar
Accra
Lagos
Mongalla
Berbera
Libreville
Entebbe
Nairobi
Mombasa
Luluabourg
Luanda
Salisbury
Tamatave
Beira
Windhoek
Kimberley
Johannesburg
Port Nolloth
Durban
Cape Town
Graaff Reinet
CAPE JUBY 6
TEMPERATURE 8·0°F 4·4°C
PRESSURE
RAINFALL 1·9in. 4·8cm.
IN SALAH * 280
TEMPERATURE 42·0°F 23·3°C
PRESSURE
RAINFALL 0·6in. 1·5cm.
EL BAYADH 1310
TEMPERATURE 38·0°F 21·1°C
PRESSURE
RAINFALL 12·9in. 32·8cm.
ALGIERS 59
TEMPERATURE 24·0°F 13·3°C
PRESSURE
RAINFALL 30·0in. 76·2cm.
ALEXANDRIA 32
TEMPERATURE 22·5°F 12·5°C
PRESSURE
RAINFALL 7·0in. 17·8cm.
HELIOPOLIS 41
TEMPERATURE 27·5°F 15·3°C
PRESSURE
RAINFALL 0·4in. 1·0cm.
FREETOWN 11
TEMPERATURE 4·5°F 2·5°C
PRESSURE
RAINFALL 135·2in. 343·4cm.
ACCRA 27
TEMPERATURE 6·5°F 3·6°C
PRESSURE
RAINFALL 28·5in. 72·4cm.
LAGOS 3
TEMPERATURE 6·0°F 3·3°C
PRESSURE
RAINFALL 72·3in. 183·6cm.
LIBREVILLE 35
TEMPERATURE 5·5°F 3·1°C
PRESSURE
RAINFALL 98·8in. 251·0cm.
ZUNGERU 130
TEMPERATURE 9·0°F 5·0°C
PRESSURE
RAINFALL 45·4in. 115·3cm.
KHARTOUM 390
TEMPERATURE 18·0°F 10·0°C
PRESSURE
RAINFALL 6·2in. 15·8cm.
SUAKIN * 5
TEMPERATURE 22·0°F 12·2°C
PRESSURE
RAINFALL 7·1in. 18·0cm.
BERBERA 14
TEMPERATURE 21·5°F 11·9°C
PRESSURE
RAINFALL 2·0in. 5·1cm.
Fahr.
Cent.
Ins.
Mb.
Cm.
J F M A M J J A S O N D

See Climatic Maps in Atlas, pages 117 and 118

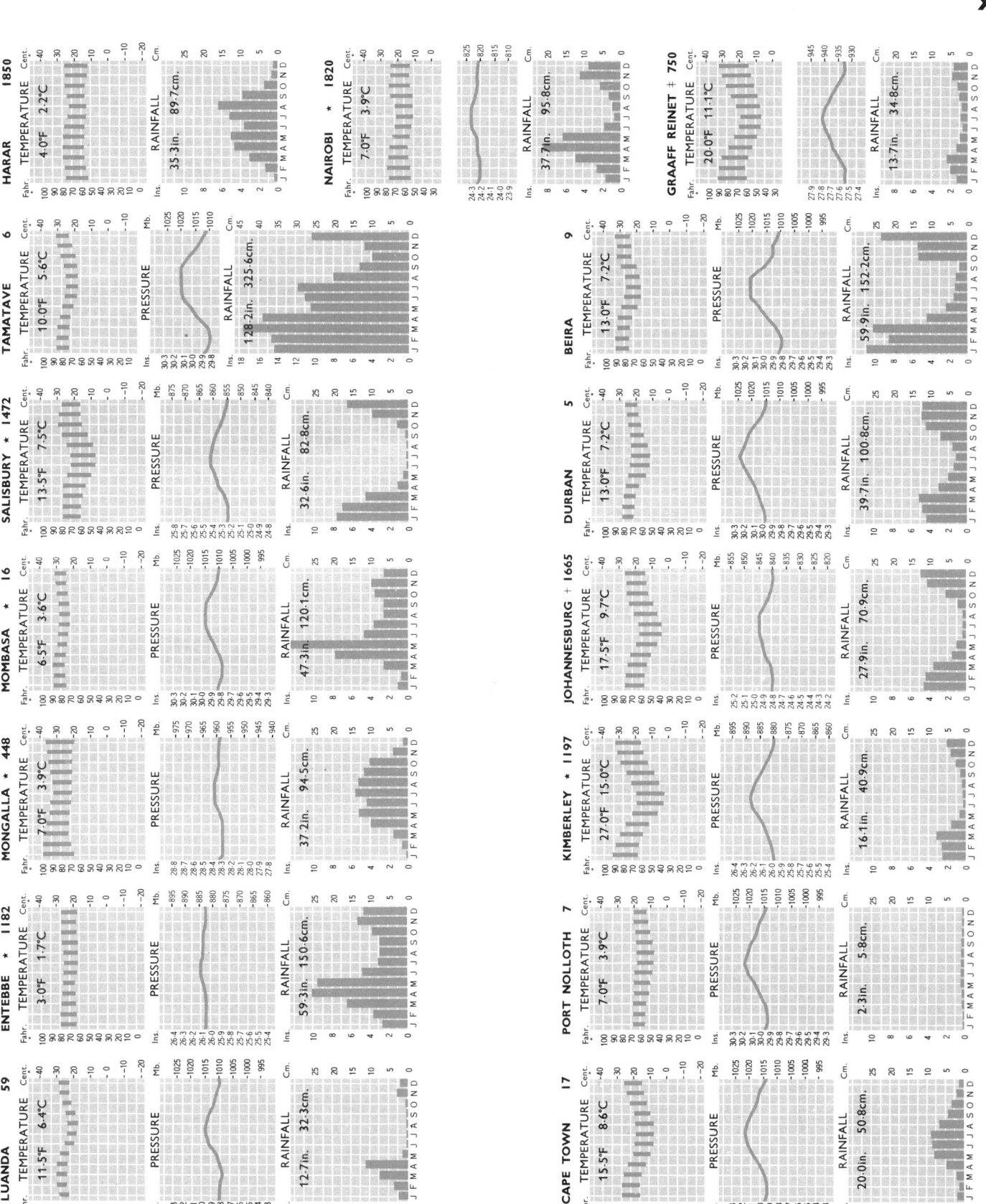

HARAR 1850
TEMPERATURE 22°C
RAINFALL 89.7cm.
35.3in.

NAIROBI ★ 1820
TEMPERATURE 3.9°C
RAINFALL 95.8cm.
37.7in.

GRAAFF REINET ‡ 750
TEMPERATURE 11.1°C
RAINFALL 34.8cm.
13.7in.

TAMATAVE 6
TEMPERATURE 25.6°C
PRESSURE
RAINFALL 325.6cm.
128.2in.

BEIRA 9
TEMPERATURE 7.2°C
PRESSURE
RAINFALL 152.2cm.
59.9in.

SALISBURY ★ 1472
TEMPERATURE 7.5°C
PRESSURE
RAINFALL 82.8cm.
32.6in.

DURBAN 5
TEMPERATURE 7.2°C
PRESSURE
RAINFALL 100.8cm.
39.7in.

MOMBASA ★ 16
TEMPERATURE 3.6°C
PRESSURE
RAINFALL 120.1cm.
47.3in.

JOHANNESBURG + 1665
TEMPERATURE 9.7°C
PRESSURE
RAINFALL 70.9cm.
27.9in.

MONGALLA ★ 448
TEMPERATURE 3.9°C
PRESSURE
RAINFALL 94.5cm.
37.2in.

KIMBERLEY ★ 1197
TEMPERATURE 15.0°C
PRESSURE
RAINFALL 40.9cm.
16.1in.

ENTEBBE ★ 1182
TEMPERATURE 1.7°C
PRESSURE
RAINFALL 150.6cm.
59.3in.

PORT NOLLOTH 7
TEMPERATURE 3.9°C
PRESSURE
RAINFALL 5.8cm.
2.3in.

LUANDA 59
TEMPERATURE 6.4°C
PRESSURE
RAINFALL 32.3cm.
12.7in.

CAPE TOWN 17
TEMPERATURE 8.6°C
PRESSURE
RAINFALL 50.8cm.
20.0in.

TIMBUKTU 301
TEMPERATURE 13.1°C
RAINFALL 23.1cm.
9.1in.

LULUABOURG 670
TEMPERATURE 1.9°C
RAINFALL 158.2cm.
62.3in.

WINDHOEK 1728
TEMPERATURE 10.3°C
RAINFALL 36.3cm.
14.3in.

★ Pressure at station level.
+ Pressure reduced to a level of 1600 geodynamic metres.
‡ Pressure reduced to a level of 700 geodynamic metres.

The Pressure figures for Timbuktu, Luluabourg, Windhoek and Harar, are unavailable owing to lack of reliable data.

Copyright, George Philip & Son, Ltd.

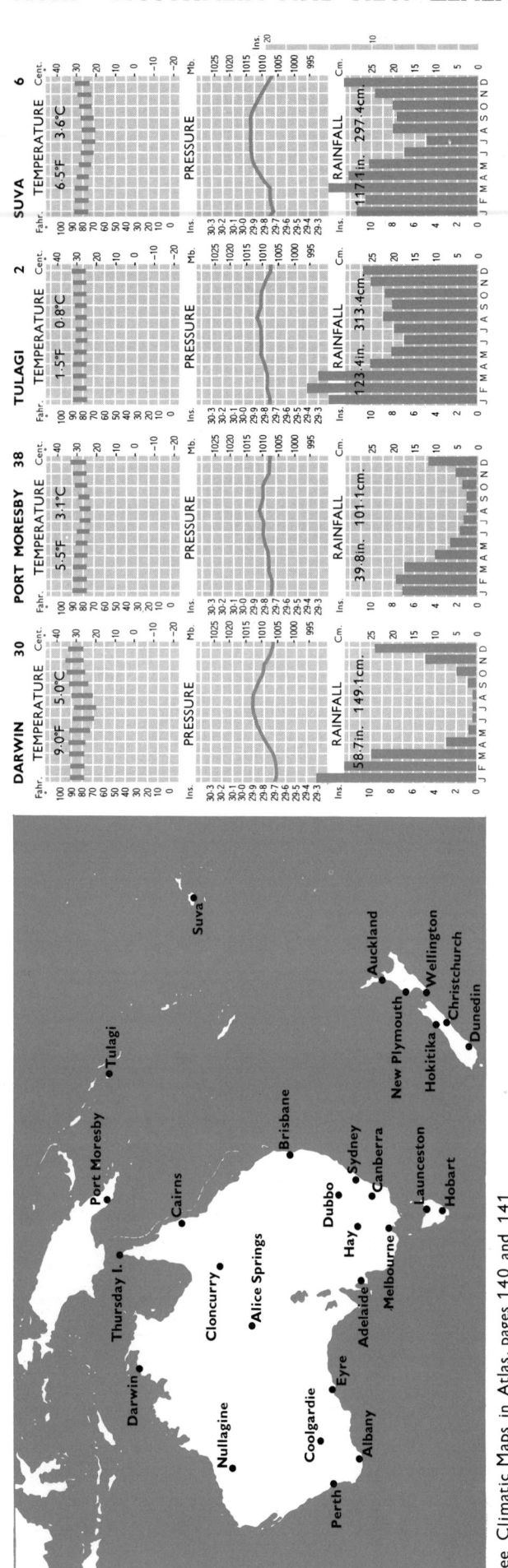

See Climatic Maps in Atlas, pages 140 and 141

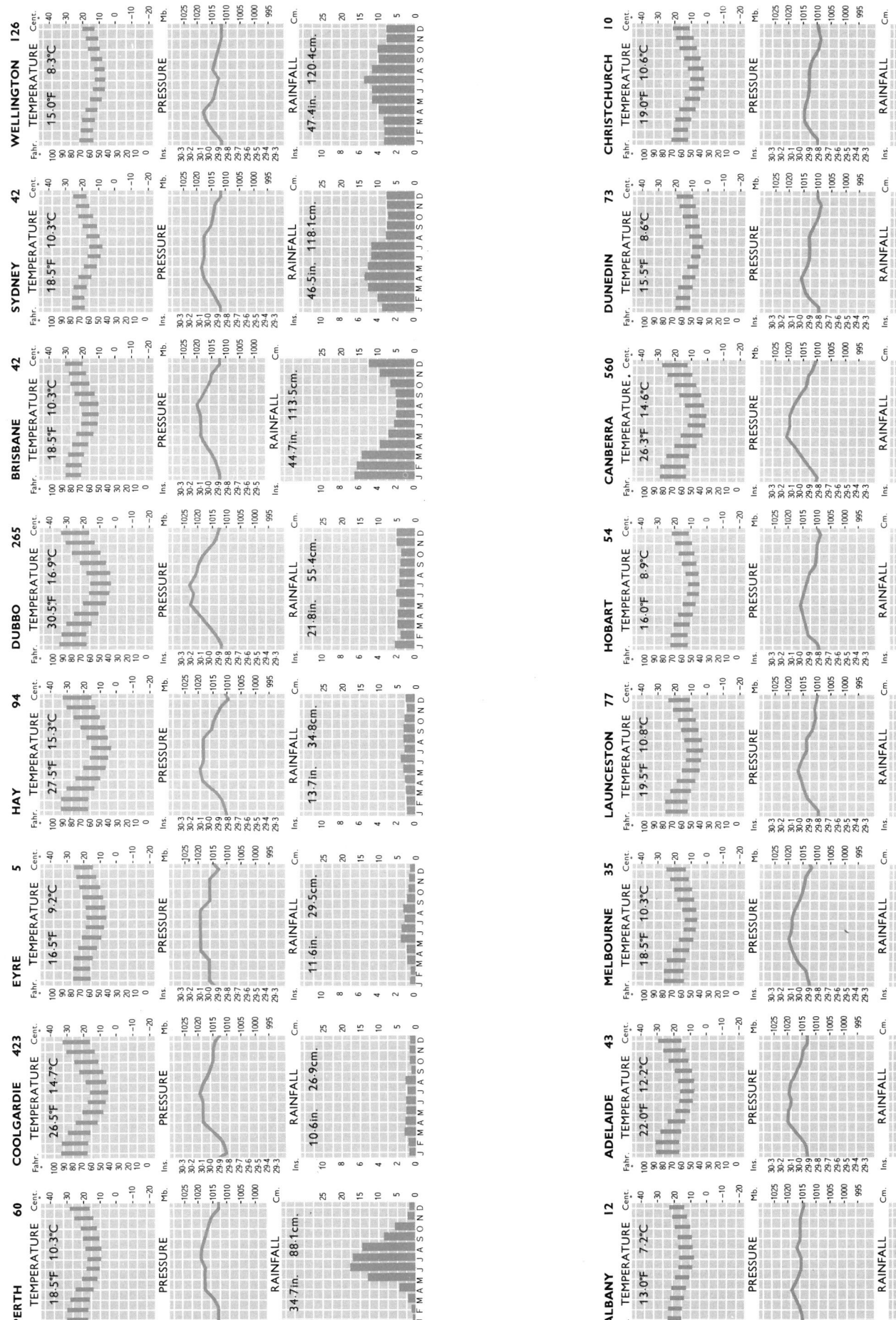

Copyright, George Philip & Son, Ltd.

★ Pressure at station level

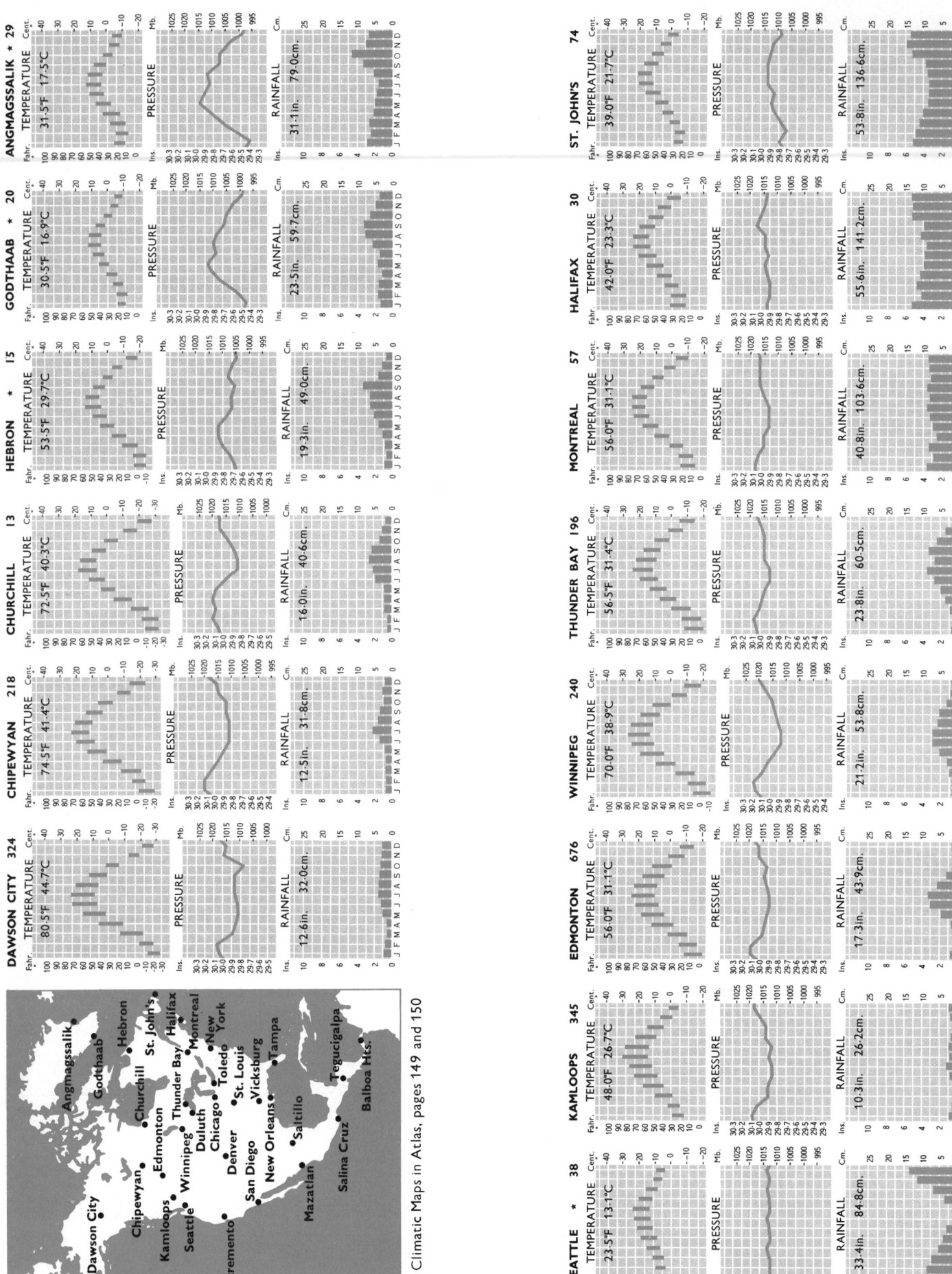
Angmagssalik
Dawson City
Godthaab
Hebron
Chipewyan
Churchill
St. John's
Kamloops
Edmonton
Halifax
Seattle
Winnipeg
Thunder Bay
Montreal
Duluth
Chicago
New York
Sacremento
Denver
Toledo
St. Louis
San Diego
Vicksburg
New Orleans
Tampa
Saltillo
Mazatlan
Tegucigalpa
Salina Cruz
Balboa Hts.
DAWSON CITY 324
TEMPERATURE 80.5°F 44.7°C
PRESSURE
RAINFALL 12.6in. 32.0cm.
CHIPEWYAN 218
TEMPERATURE 74.5°F 41.4°C
PRESSURE
RAINFALL 12.5in. 31.8cm.
CHURCHILL 13
TEMPERATURE 72.5°F 40.3°C
PRESSURE
RAINFALL 16.0in. 40.6cm.
HEBRON * 15
TEMPERATURE 53.5°F 29.7°C
PRESSURE
RAINFALL 19.3in. 49.0cm.
GODTHAAB * 20
TEMPERATURE 30.5°F 16.9°C
PRESSURE
RAINFALL 23.5in. 59.7cm.
ANGMAGSSALIK * 29
TEMPERATURE 31.5°F 17.5°C
PRESSURE
RAINFALL 31.1in. 79.0cm.
SEATTLE * 38
TEMPERATURE 23.5°F 13.1°C
PRESSURE
RAINFALL 33.4in. 84.8cm.
KAMLOOPS 345
TEMPERATURE 48.0°F 26.7°C
PRESSURE
RAINFALL 10.3in. 26.2cm.
EDMONTON 676
TEMPERATURE 56.0°F 31.1°C
PRESSURE
RAINFALL 17.3in. 43.9cm.
WINNIPEG 240
TEMPERATURE 70.0°F 38.9°C
PRESSURE
RAINFALL 21.2in. 53.8cm.
THUNDER BAY 196
TEMPERATURE 56.5°F 31.4°C
PRESSURE
RAINFALL 23.8in. 60.5cm.
MONTREAL 57
TEMPERATURE 56.0°F 31.1°C
PRESSURE
RAINFALL 40.8in. 103.6cm.
HALIFAX 30
TEMPERATURE 42.0°F 23.3°C
PRESSURE
RAINFALL 55.6in. 141.2cm.
ST. JOHN'S 74
TEMPERATURE 39.0°F 21.7°C
PRESSURE
RAINFALL 53.8in. 136.6cm.
J F M A M J J A S O N D

See Climatic Maps in Atlas, pages 149 and 150

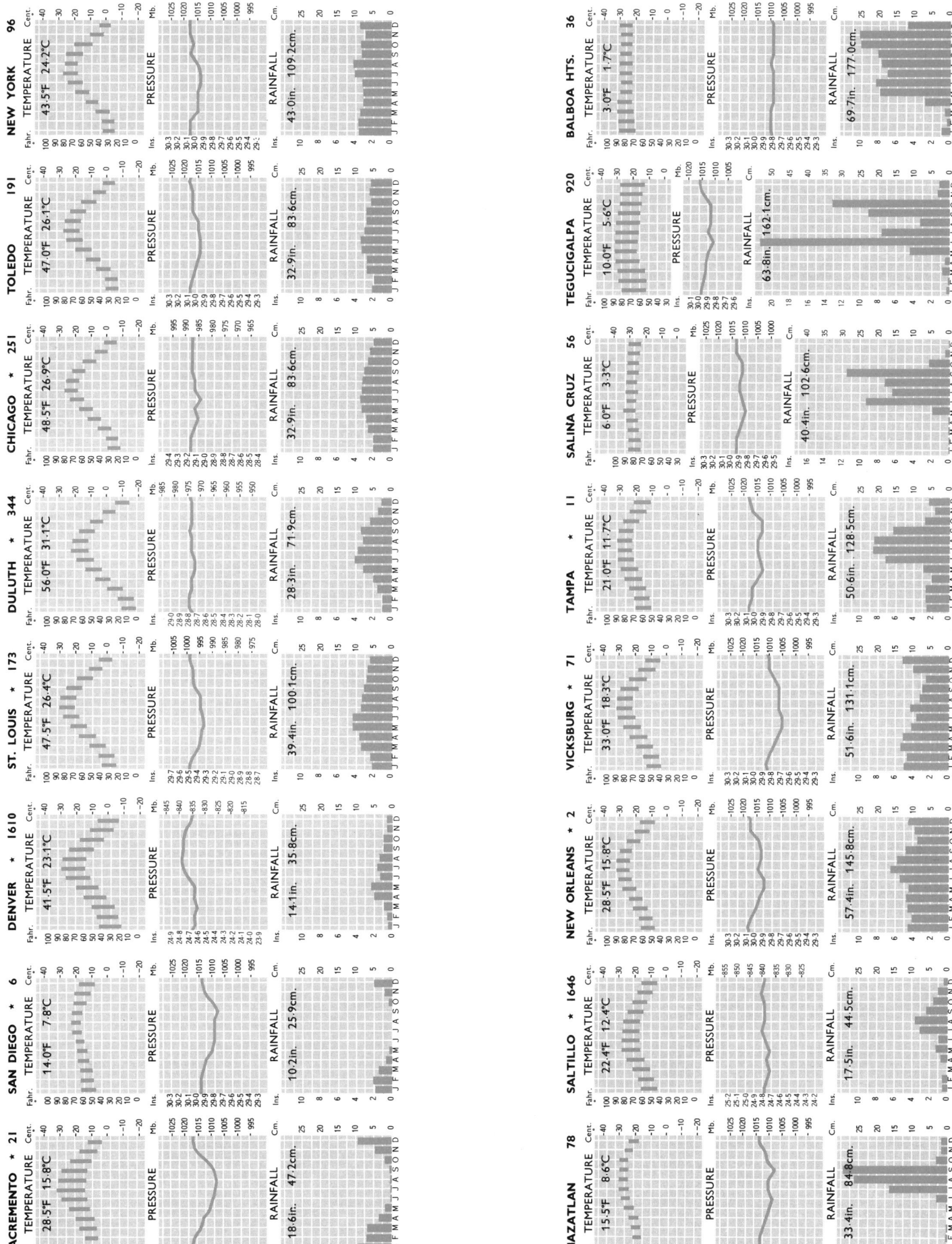

Copyright, George Philip & Son, Ltd.

★ Pressure at station level

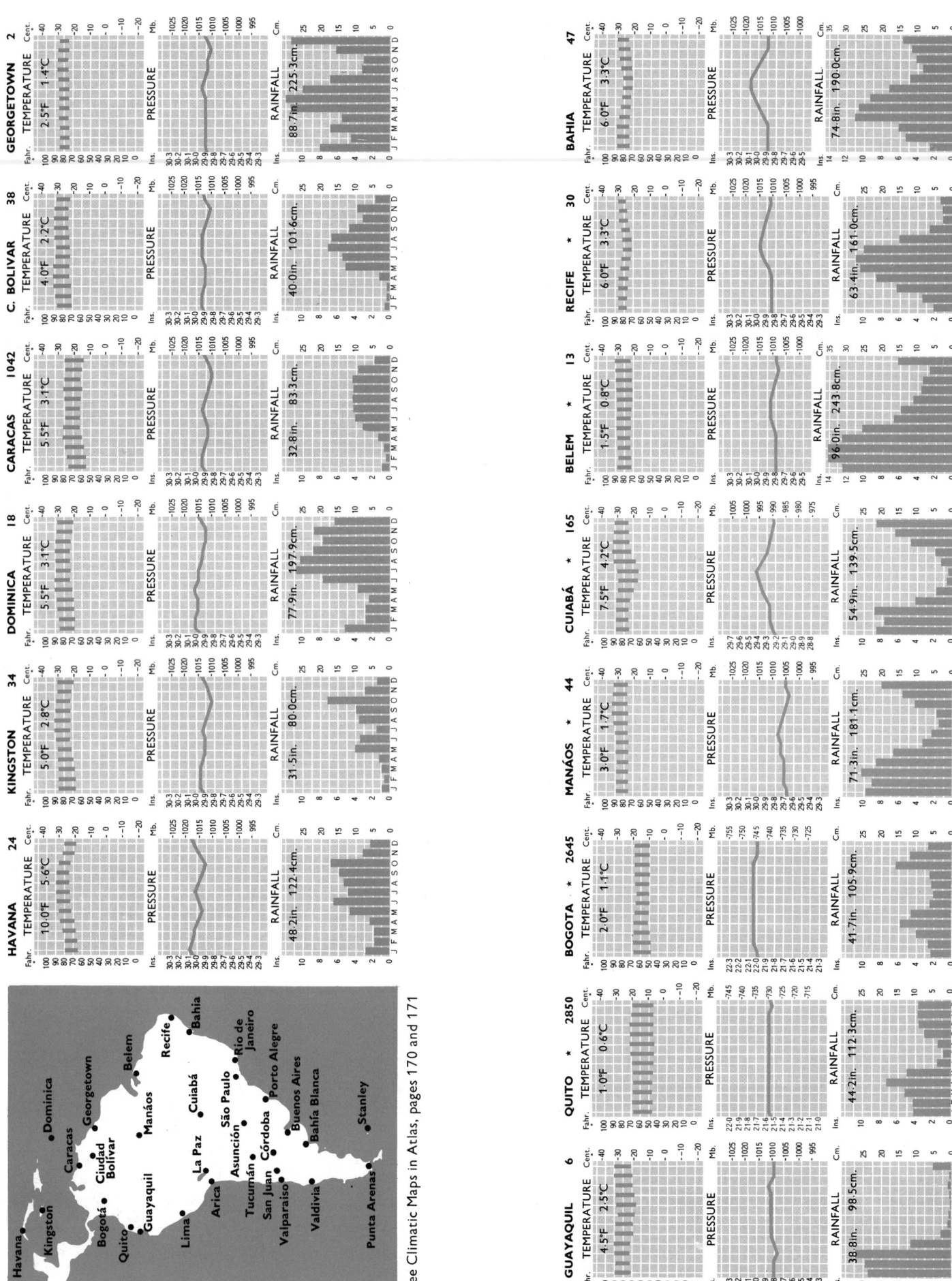

See Climatic Maps in Atlas, pages 170 and 171

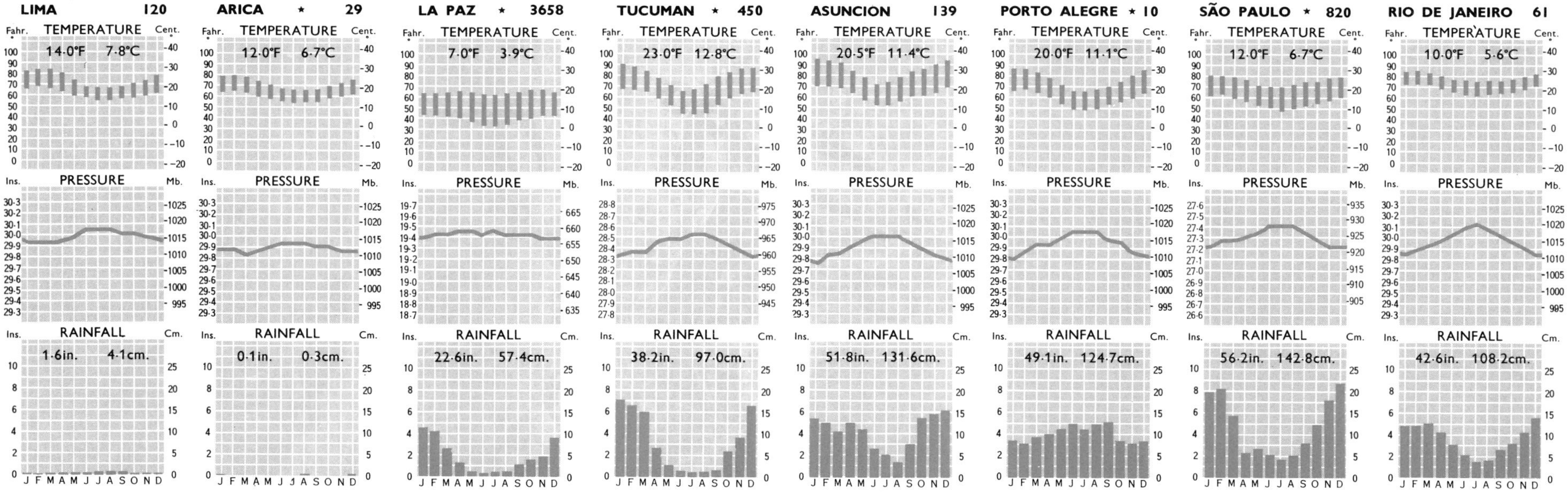

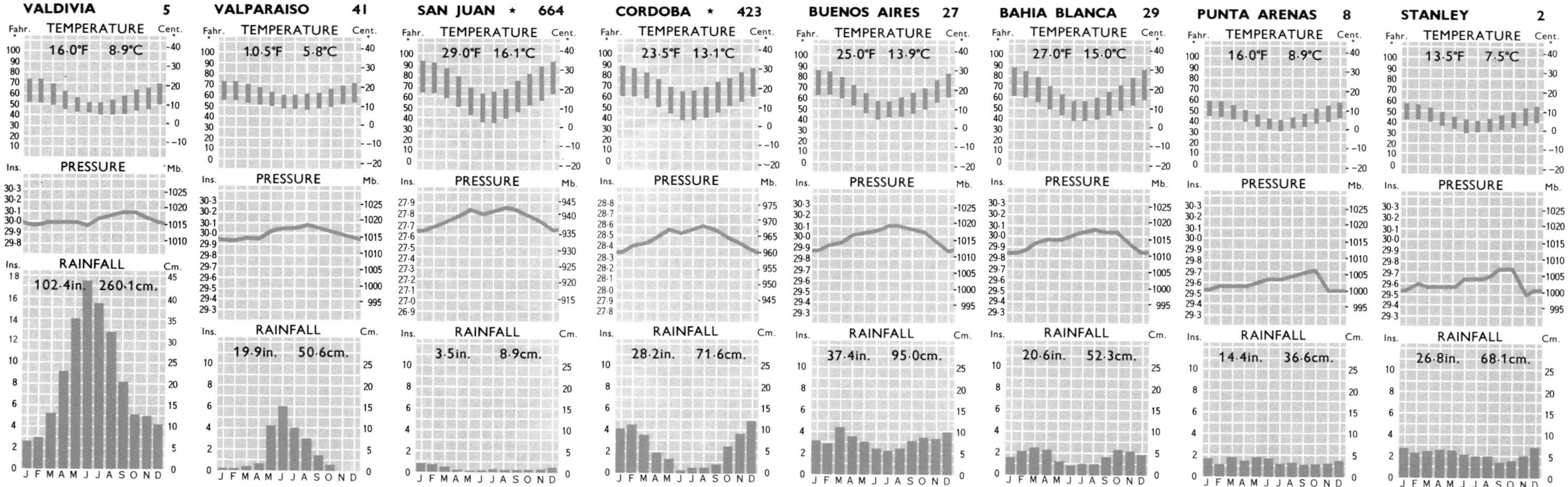

Climate graphs — temperature, pressure and rainfall (monthly, J F M A M J J A S O N D) for selected stations. Each station label lists its elevation and mean annual temperature range.

Station	Elevation	Temperature (range / mean)	Rainfall (annual)
RIO DE JANEIRO	61	10.0°F / 5.6°C	42.6 in. / 108.2 cm.
SÃO PAULO ★	820	12.0°F / 6.7°C	56.2 in. / 142.8 cm.
PORTO ALEGRE ★	10	20.0°F / 11.1°C	49.1 in. / 124.7 cm.
ASUNCION	139	20.5°F / 11.4°C	51.8 in. / 131.6 cm.
TUCUMAN ★	450	23.0°F / 12.8°C	38.2 in. / 97.0 cm.
LA PAZ ★	3658	7.0°F / 3.9°C	22.6 in. / 57.4 cm.
ARICA ★	29	12.0°F / 6.7°C	0.1 in. / 0.3 cm.
LIMA	120	14.0°F / 7.8°C	1.6 in. / 4.1 cm.
STANLEY	2	13.5°F / 7.5°C	26.8 in. / 68.1 cm.
PUNTA ARENAS	8	16.0°F / 8.9°C	14.4 in. / 36.6 cm.
BAHIA BLANCA	29	27.0°F / 15.0°C	20.6 in. / 52.3 cm.
BUENOS AIRES	27	25.0°F / 13.9°C	37.4 in. / 95.0 cm.
CORDOBA ★	423	23.5°F / 13.1°C	28.2 in. / 71.6 cm.
SAN JUAN ★	664	29.0°F / 16.1°C	3.5 in. / 8.9 cm.
VALPARAISO	41	10.5°F / 5.8°C	19.9 in. / 50.6 cm.
VALDIVIA	5	16.0°F / 8.9°C	102.4 in. / 260.1 cm.

★ Pressure at station level

Copyright, George Philip & Son, Ltd.

Projections Used

Mercator
1 The World: Volcanoes and Earthquake Zones, 1:220M
108–9 The East Indies, 1:12½M. Java and Madura, 1:7½M
144 The Territory of Papua and New Guinea, 1:12M
107 Malaya and Singapore, 1:6M

Mollweide's Homolographic
16–17 The Atlantic Ocean: Equatorial Scale, 1:50M
136–7 The Pacific Ocean. Equatorial Scale 1:60M
140 Australia: Climate, 1:60M
141 Australia: Density of Population, 1:50M
Australia: Annual Rainfall, 1:60M

Mollweide's Interrupted Homolographic
2–3 The World: Geology, 1:100M
The World: Structure, 1:140M
4 The World: Temperature and Ocean Currents, 1:215M
5 The World: Rainfall, Isobars and Winds, 1:215M
6 The World: Soil Regions, 1:140M
7 The World: Natural Vegetation, 1:165M
The World: Climatic Regions, 1:165M
8–9 The World: Density of Population, 1:81½M

Oblique Azimuthal Equidistant
12–13 The World in Hemispheres: Political and Communications 1:100M
and 1:300M

Zenithal Equidistant
14–15 The Polar Regions, 1:35M
115 Africa: Political, 1:40M
Africa: Density of Population, 1:80M
116–17 Africa: Physical, 1:30M
Africa: Annual Rainfall, 1:80M
119 Africa: Natural Vegetation, 1:40M

Lambert's Equivalent Azimuthal or Zenithal Equal Area
96 Asia: Annual Rainfall, 1:80M
112–13 Eastern China and Korea, 1:10M
122–3 Northwest Africa, 1:8M
124–5 West Africa, 1:8M
126–7 The Nile Valley, 1:8M
130–1 Central and East Africa, 1:8M
132 Rhodesia, Zambia and Malawi, 1:8M
150 North America: Climate, 1:70M
154–5 Eastern Canada, 1:7M
156–7 Western Canada, 1:7M
170 South America: Physical, 1:30M
171 South America: Natural Vegetation, 1:40M
South America: Climate, 1:80M
172–3 Central South America, 1:8M
175 South America: Political, 1:80M
176 South America: Density of Population, 1:80M

Conical with two standard parallels
20–21 France and Central Europe: Geology, 1:5M
26–27 The British Isles: Solid Geology, 1:3¼M
28–29 The British Isles: Physical, 1:3¼M
30–31 The British Isles: Climate, 1:3¼M
32 The British Isles: Population, 1:4M
33 The British Isles: Counties, 1:4M
34–35 South and South-East England, 1:1M
36 South-West England, 1:1M
37 Wales, 1:1M
38–39 Northern England, 1:1M
40–41 Scotland: South, 1:1M
42–43 Scotland: North, 1:1M
44–45 Ireland: South, 1:1M
46 Ireland: North, 1:1M
47 France, 1:5M
48–49 Northern France, 1:2½M
50–51 Southern France, 1:2½M
52–53 Central Europe, 1:5M. Central Europe, Political, 1:25M
54 The Netherlands, Belgium and Luxembourg, 1:2½M
55 The Sambre-Meuse-Ruhr Region, 1:1M
56–57 Germany and Switzerland, 1:2½M
58–59 Austria, Czechoslovakia and Hungary, 1:2½M
60 Poland, 1:2½M
61 Spain and Portugal, 1:5M
62–63 Western Spain and Portugal, 1:2½M
64–65 Eastern Spain, 1:2½M
66–67 The Mediterranean Lands, 1:10M
68–69 Italy and the Balkan States, 1:5M
S.E. Europe, Political, 1:25M
70–71 Northern Italy and Western Yugoslavia, 1:2½M
72–73 Southern Italy, 1:2½M
74–75 Yugoslavia and Bulgaria, 1:2½M
76–77 Greece and Albania, 1:2½M
78 Rumania, 1:2½M
79 Southern Norway, 1:2½M
80–81 Denmark and Southern Sweden, 1:2½M
82–83 Scandinavia, the Baltic Lands, and Iceland, 1:5M
84–85 The U.S.S.R. in Europe, 1:10M
86–87 European Russia: Central, 1:5M
88–89 European Russia: South, 1:5M
98 The Holy Land, 1:1M
102–3 South Asia, 1:10M
104–5 The Indo-Gangetic Plain, 1:6M
106 Southern India and Sri Lanka, 1:6M
107 Mainland Southeast Asia, 1:10M
114 Japan, 1:5M
126 The Nile Delta, 1:4M
133 The Transvaal, 1:4M
134–5 Cape Province, Orange Free State and Natal, 1:4M
146 New Zealand: North Island, 1:3½M
147 New Zealand: South Island, 1:3½M
152 Alaska, 1:30M

Conical Orthomorphic with two standard parallels
90–91 The Union of Soviet Socialist Republics, 1:20M
100–1 The Near and Middle East, 1:10M

Bi-Polar Oblique Conical Orthomorphic
168 Mexico, 1:12M
169 The West Indies, 1:12M

Albers' Equal Area with two standard parallels
143 Southeast Australia, 1:4½M
158–9 The United States 1:12M
162–3 The Eastern United States, 1:6M
164–5 The Middle United States, 1:6M
166–7 The Western United States, 1:6M

Bonne
18–19 Europe: Physical, 1:17½M. Annual Rainfall, 1:40M
22 Europe: Climate, 1:40M
23 Europe: Natural Vegetation, 1:20M
24 Europe: Density of Population, 1:20M
25 Europe: Political, 1:20M
92–93 Asia: Physical, 1:40M
Asia: Rainfall, Pressure and Winds, 1:80M
94–95 Asia: Political, 1:40M
Asia: Temperature, 1:80M
97 Asia: Natural Vegetation, 1:50M
110 Southern and Eastern Asia: Density of Population, 1:30M
111 China, 1:20M
114 Japan, 1:10M
138–9 Australia, 1:12M. Australasia: Political, 1:80M
141 Australia: Natural Vegetation, 1:30M
142 Western Australia, 1:7½M
144–5 Eastern Australia, 1:7½M
148–9 North America: Physical, 1:30M
152–3 Canada, 1:15M
160–1 The Northeastern United States, 1:2½M
163 United States: Density of Population, 1:50M
167 United States: Soils, 1:50M

Sanson-Flamsteed's Sinusoidal
99 Arabia and the Horn of Africa, 1:15M
118 Africa: Climate, 1:80M
120–1 Northern Africa, 1:15M
128–9 Central and South Africa, 1:15M
170 South America: Annual Rainfall, 1:80M
174–5 South America: North, 1:16M
176 South America: South, 1:16M

Polyconic
151 North America: Natural Vegetation, 1:32M

Hammer Equal Area
10–11 The World: Political, 1:80M

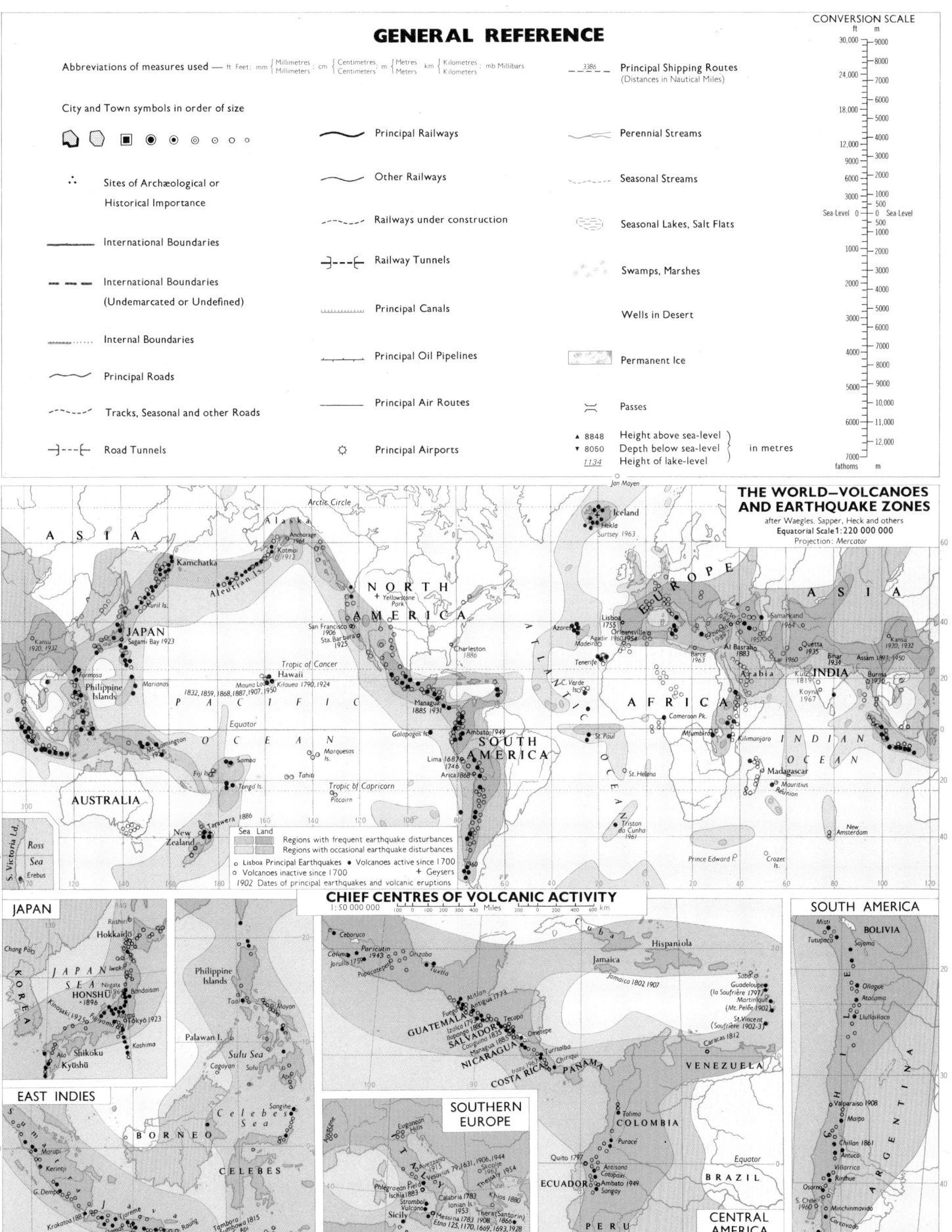

GENERAL REFERENCE

Abbreviations of measures used — ft Feet: mm {Millimetres / Millimeters} cm {Centimetres / Centimeters} m {Metres / Meters} km {Kilometres / Kilometers} mb Millibars

City and Town symbols in order of size

Sites of Archæological or Historical Importance

International Boundaries

International Boundaries (Undemarcated or Undefined)

Internal Boundaries

Principal Roads

Tracks, Seasonal and other Roads

Road Tunnels

Principal Railways

Other Railways

Railways under construction

Railway Tunnels

Principal Canals

Principal Oil Pipelines

Principal Air Routes

Principal Airports

Principal Shipping Routes (Distances in Nautical Miles)

Perennial Streams

Seasonal Streams

Seasonal Lakes, Salt Flats

Swamps, Marshes

Wells in Desert

Permanent Ice

Passes

▲ 8848 Height above sea-level
▼ 8050 Depth below sea-level   in metres
1134 Height of lake-level

CONVERSION SCALE

THE WORLD—VOLCANOES AND EARTHQUAKE ZONES
after Waegles, Sapper, Heck and others
Equatorial Scale 1:220 000 000
Projection: Mercator

Sea Land
Regions with frequent earthquake disturbances
Regions with occasional earthquake disturbances
○ Lisboa Principal Earthquakes
● Volcanoes active since 1700
○ Volcanoes inactive since 1700
+ Geysers
1902 Dates of principal earthquakes and volcanic eruptions

CHIEF CENTRES OF VOLCANIC ACTIVITY
1:50 000 000

JAPAN

EAST INDIES

SOUTHERN EUROPE

CENTRAL AMERICA

SOUTH AMERICA

COPYRIGHT. GEORGE PHILIP & SON. LTD.

GEOLOGY

after
Beyschlag, Nalivkin and others

1:100 000 000

Ⓐ

Arctic Circle

Tropic of Cancer

Equator

Tropic of Capricorn

Antarctic Circle

Projections: *Interrupted Mollweide's Homolographic*

Ⓒ GEOLOGICAL CYCLES

Quaternary	Recent		
Tertiary (Cainozoic)	Pliocene		
	Miocene		
	Oligocene	Alpine Folding	
	Eocene		
Secondary (Mesozoic)	Cretaceous	Laramide Folding	
	Jurassic		
	Triassic		
	Permian		
Primary Upper (Palæozoic)	Carboniferous	Hercynian Folding	
	Devonian		
Primary Lower (Palæozoic)	Silurian	Caledonian Folding	
	Ordovician		
	Cambrian		
Archaean	Pre-Cambrian		

Ⓑ An Interpretation of STRUCTURE
showing
the distribution of rigid masses and folded regions
after L. Kober and others

Pre-Cambrian tables composite in structure, rigid since the Cambrian period and forming stable elements separating the geo-synclines of later times.

Regions of Caledonian folding; Siluro-Devonian earth movements.

Regions of Hercynian folding; Carbo-Permian earth movements.

Regions of Tertiary folding; Cretaceo-Tertiary earth movements.

The Great Rift Valley

Main Trend lines

LAURENTIA

G

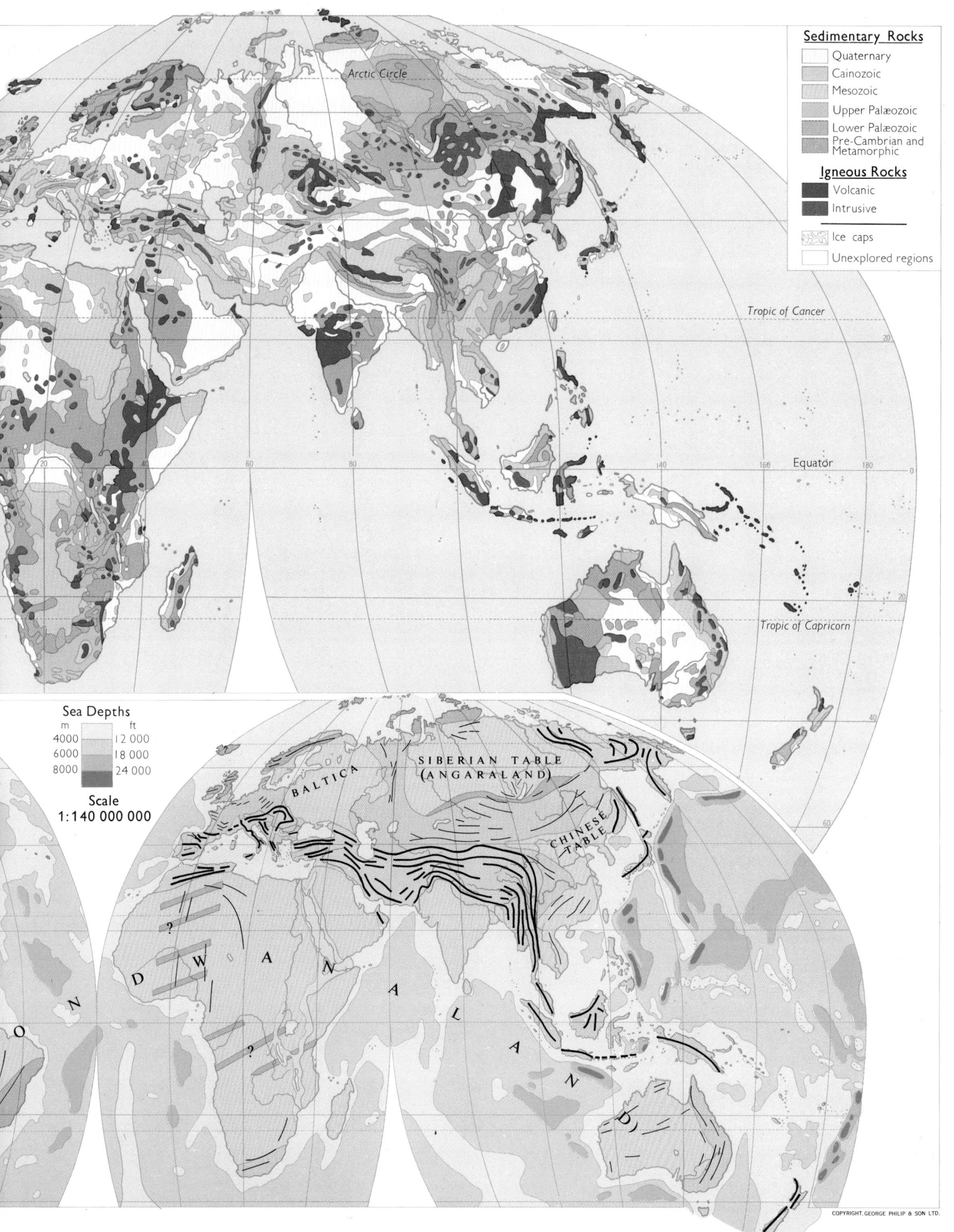

3

Sedimentary Rocks
- Quaternary
- Cainozoic
- Mesozoic
- Upper Palæozoic
- Lower Palæozoic
- Pre-Cambrian and Metamorphic

Igneous Rocks
- Volcanic
- Intrusive

- Ice caps
- Unexplored regions

Arctic Circle

Tropic of Cancer

Equator

Tropic of Capricorn

20

60

20

140

160

180

0

20

40

60

Sea Depths

m		ft
4000		12 000
6000		18 000
8000		24 000

Scale
1:140 000 000

BALTICA

SIBERIAN TABLE
(ANGARALAND)

CHINESE
TABLE

G O N D W A N A L A N D

?

?

60

COPYRIGHT. GEORGE PHILIP & SON LTD.

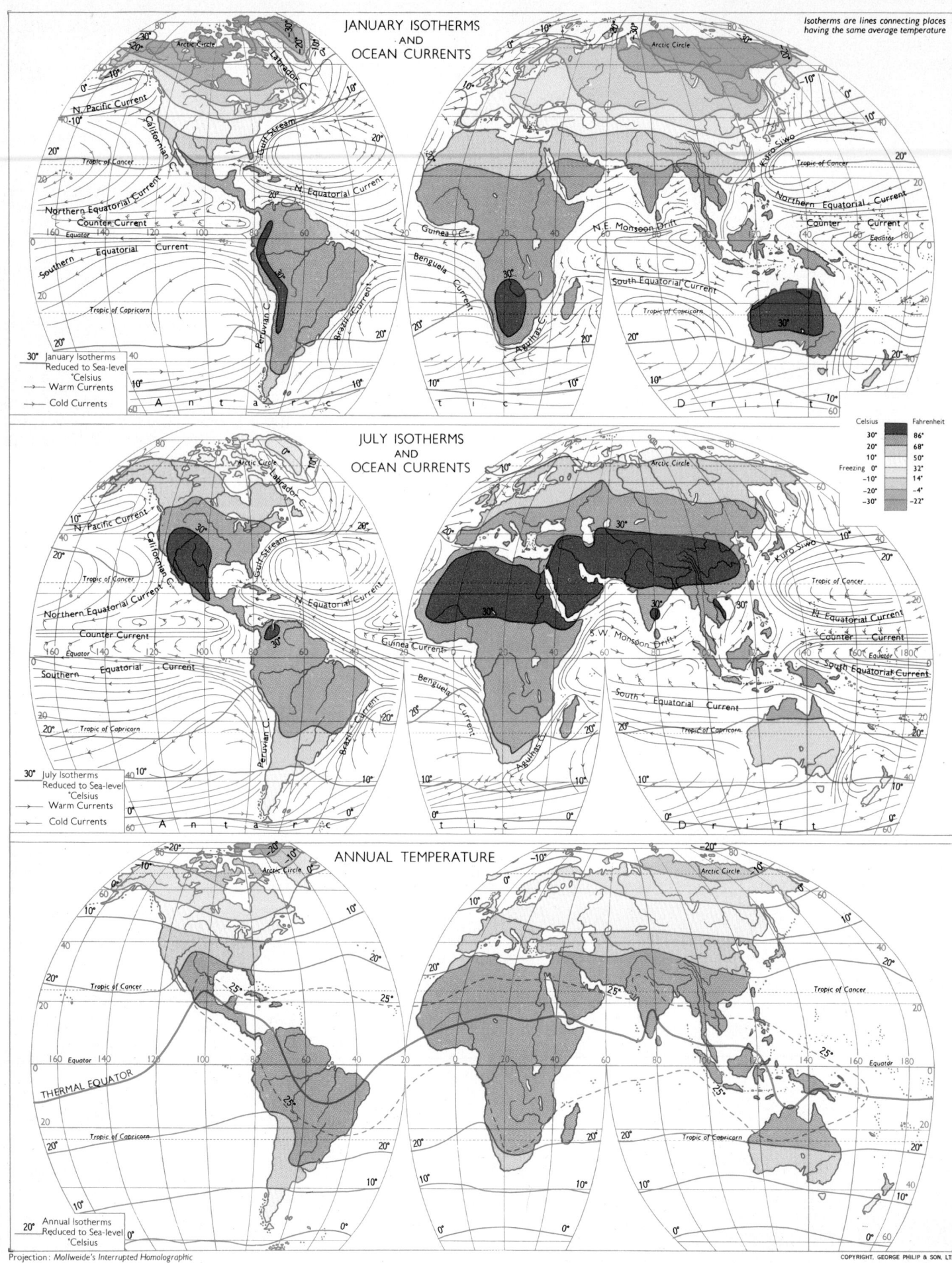

JANUARY ISOTHERMS
AND
OCEAN CURRENTS

Isotherms are lines connecting places
having the same average temperature

30° January Isotherms
Reduced to Sea-level
°Celsius
→ Warm Currents
→ Cold Currents

JULY ISOTHERMS
AND
OCEAN CURRENTS

Celsius	Fahrenheit
30°	86°
20°	68°
10°	50°
Freezing 0°	32°
-10°	14°
-20°	-4°
-30°	-22°

30° July Isotherms
Reduced to Sea-level
°Celsius
→ Warm Currents
→ Cold Currents

ANNUAL TEMPERATURE

THERMAL EQUATOR

20° Annual Isotherms
Reduced to Sea-level
°Celsius

Projection: Mollweide's Interrupted Homolographic

COPYRIGHT. GEORGE PHILIP & SON. LTD.

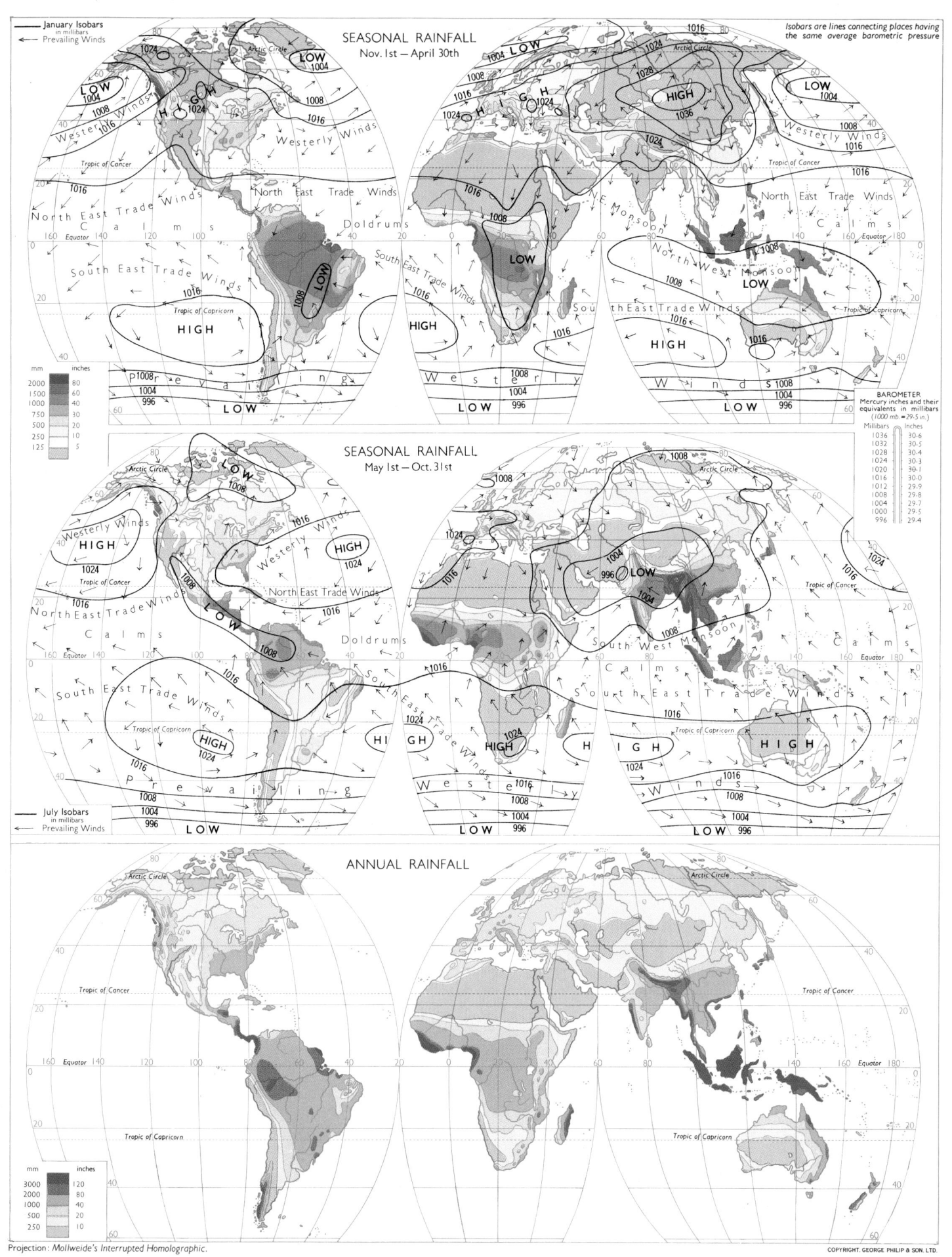

SEASONAL RAINFALL
Nov. 1st — April 30th

January Isobars
in millibars
Prevailing Winds

Isobars are lines connecting places having
the same average barometric pressure

SEASONAL RAINFALL
May 1st — Oct. 31st

July Isobars
in millibars
Prevailing Winds

ANNUAL RAINFALL

BAROMETER
Mercury inches and their
equivalents in millibars
(1000 mb.=29.5 in.)

Millibars	Inches
1036	30.6
1032	30.5
1028	30.4
1024	30.3
1020	30.1
1016	30.0
1012	29.9
1008	29.8
1004	29.7
1000	29.5
996	29.4

Projection: Mollweide's Interrupted Homolographic.

COPYRIGHT. GEORGE PHILIP & SON LTD.

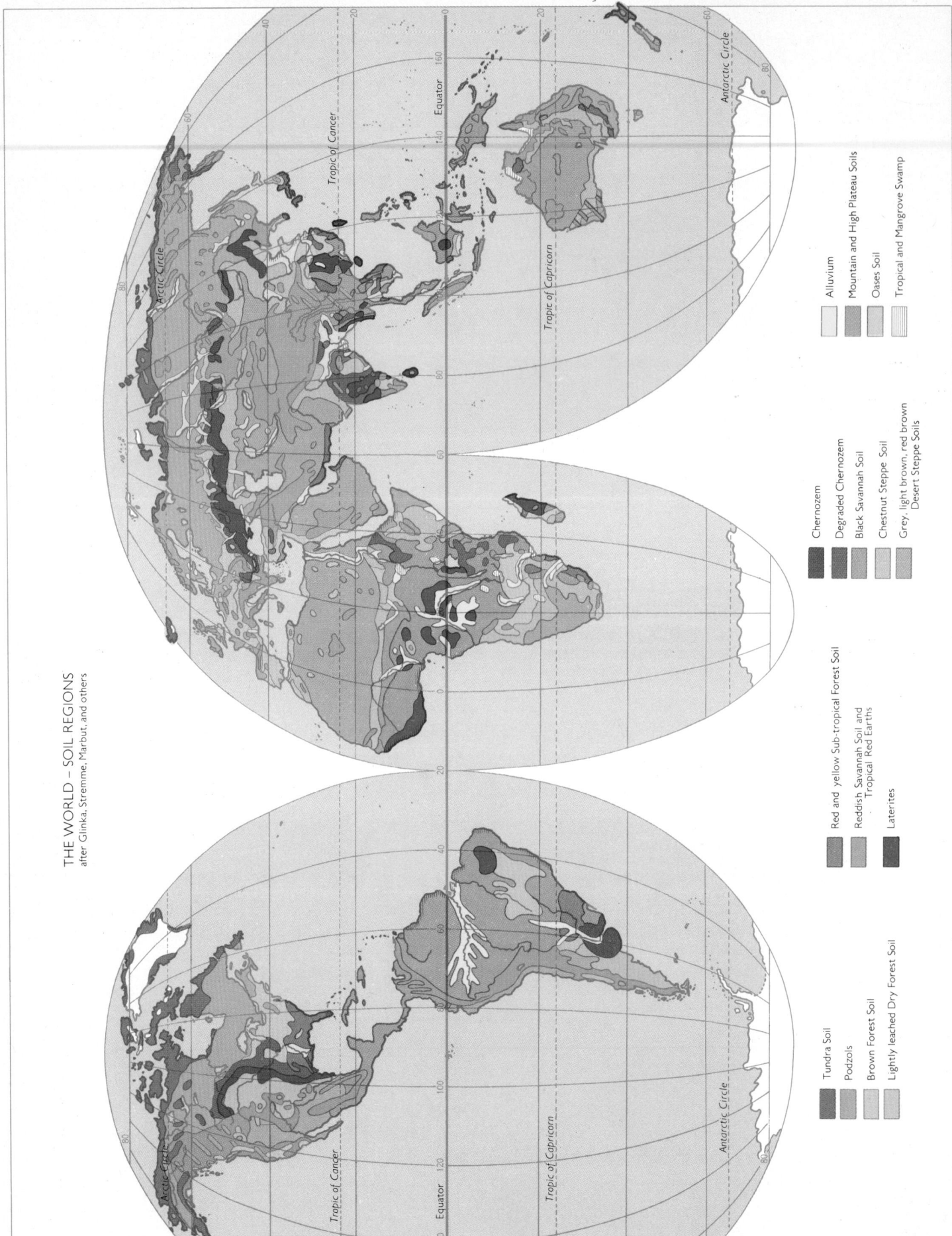

THE WORLD – SOIL REGIONS
after Glinka, Stremme, Marbut, and others

Chernozem

Degraded Chernozem

Black Savannah Soil

Chestnut Steppe Soil

Grey, light brown, red brown
Desert Steppe Soils

Red and yellow Sub-tropical Forest Soil

Reddish Savannah Soil and
Tropical Red Earths

Laterites

Alluvium

Mountain and High Plateau Soils

Oases Soil

Tropical and Mangrove Swamp

Tundra Soil

Podzols

Brown Forest Soil

Lightly leached Dry Forest Soil

COPYRIGHT GEORGE PHILIP & SON LTD.

Projection: Interrupted Mollweide's Homolographic

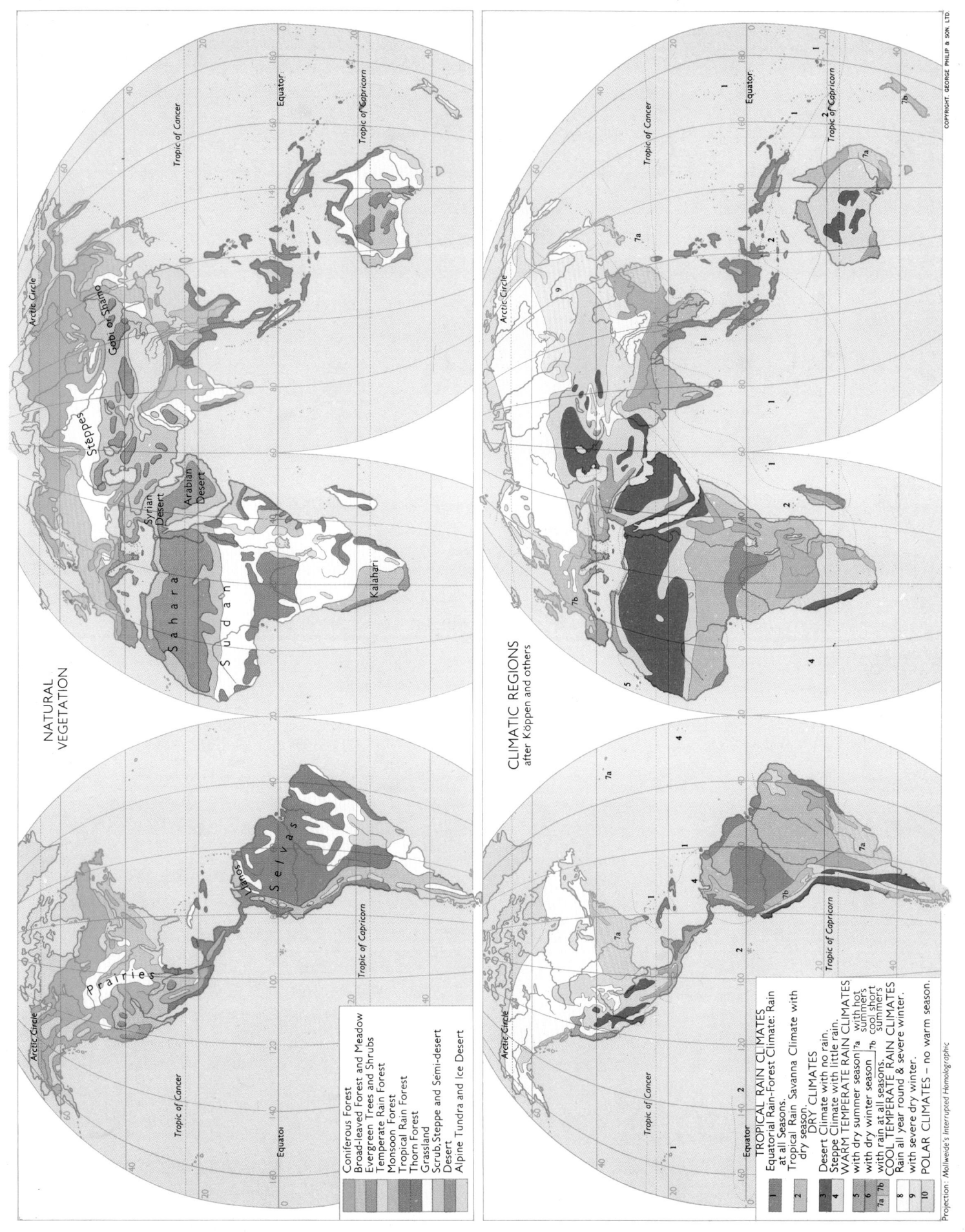

NATURAL
VEGETATION

Steppes

Gobi or Shamo

Syrian
Desert

Arabian
Desert

Sahara

Sudan

Kalahari

Arctic Circle

Tropic of Cancer

Equator

Tropic of Capricorn

Selvas

Llanos

Prairies

Arctic Circle

Coniferous Forest
Broad-leaved Forest and Meadow
Evergreen Trees and Shrubs
Temperate Rain Forest
Monsoon Forest
Tropical Rain Forest
Thorn Forest
Grassland
Scrub, Steppe and Semi-desert
Desert
Alpine Tundra and Ice Desert

CLIMATIC REGIONS
after Köppen and others

Arctic Circle

TROPICAL RAIN CLIMATES
Equatorial Rain-Forest Climate: Rain
at all Seasons.
Tropical Rain Savanna Climate with
dry season.
DRY CLIMATES
Desert Climate with no rain.
Steppe Climate with little rain.
WARM TEMPERATE RAIN CLIMATES
with dry summer season 7a with hot
7b summers
with dry winter season   cool short
with rain at all seasons.   summers
COOL TEMPERATE RAIN CLIMATES
Rain all year round & severe winter.
with severe dry winter.
POLAR CLIMATES – no warm season.

COPYRIGHT. GEORGE PHILIP & SON. LTD.

Projection: Mollweide's Interrupted Homolographic

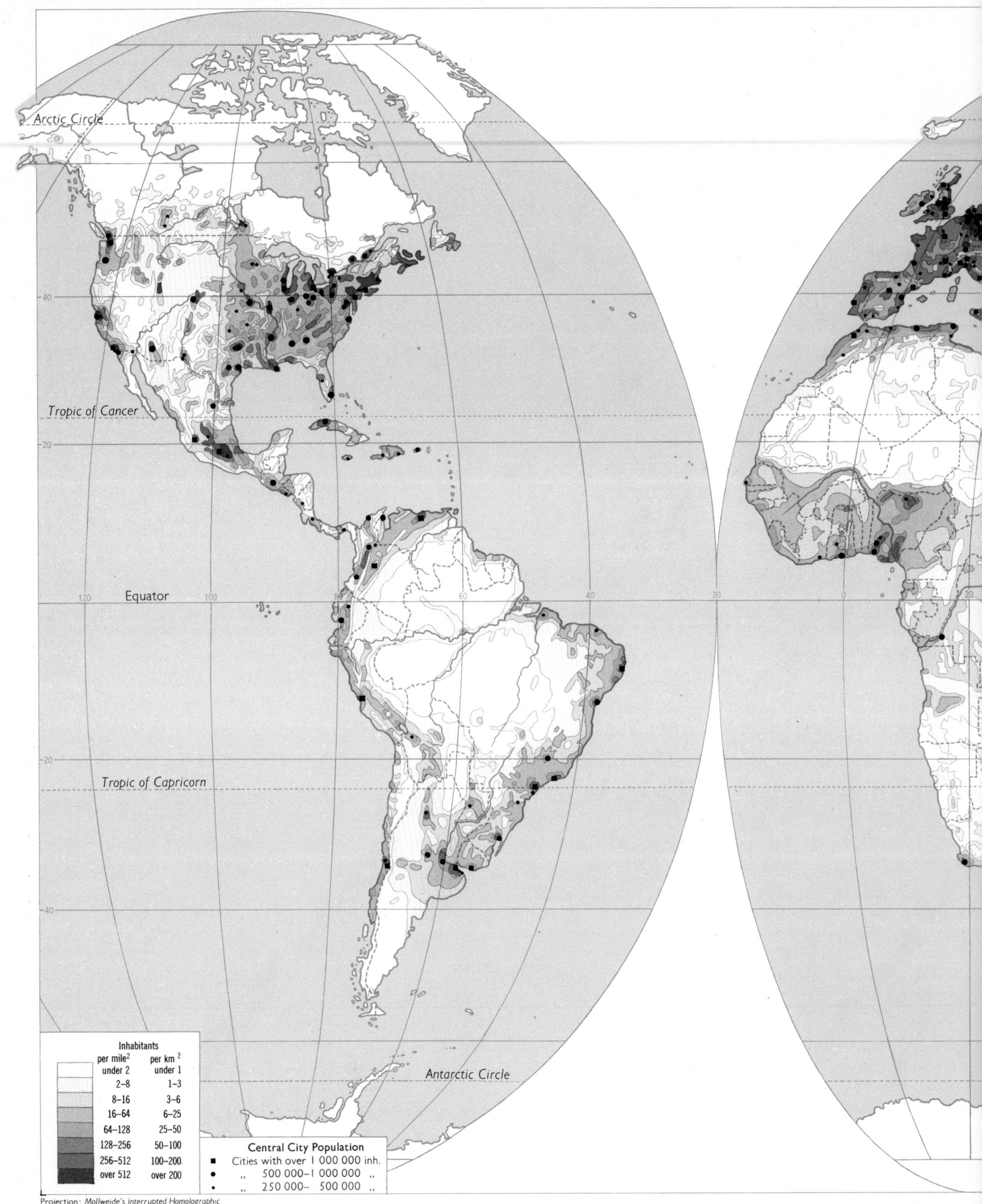

Arctic Circle

Tropic of Cancer

Equator

Tropic of Capricorn

Antarctic Circle

Inhabitants	
per mile²	per km²
under 2	under 1
2–8	1–3
8–16	3–6
16–64	6–25
64–128	25–50
128–256	50–100
256–512	100–200
over 512	over 200

Central City Population
■ Cities with over 1 000 000 inh.
●   ,,   500 000– 1 000 000 ,,
•   ,,   250 000– 500 000 ,,

Projection: Mollweide's Interrupted Homolographic

Arctic Circle

60

40

Tropic of Cancer

20

Equator

Tropic of Capricorn

40

60

Antarctic Circle

COPYRIGHT. GEORGE PHILIP & SON. LTD.

GREENLAND
ICELAND
CANADA
UNITED STATES
MEXICO
ATLANTIC OCEAN
PACIFIC OCEAN
BRAZIL
PERU
BOLIVIA
ARGENTINA
COLOMBIA
VENEZUELA
ECUADOR
PARAGUAY
URUGUAY
GUYANA
SURINAM
FR. GUIANA
CUBA
HAITI
DOM. REP.
JAMAICA
BAHAMAS
BELIZE
GUATEMALA
HONDURAS
EL SALVADOR
NICARAGUA
COSTA RICA
PANAMA
TRINIDAD & TOBAGO
BARBADOS
UNITED KINGDOM
IRELAND
PORTUGAL
SPAIN
MOROCCO
MAURITANIA
SENEGAL
GAMBIA
PORT. GUINEA
GUINEA
SIERRA LEONE
LIBERIA
IVORY COAST
Beaufort Sea
Amundsen G.
Queen Elizabeth Is.
Ellesmere I.
Baffin Bay
Davis Strait
Hudson Bay
Hudson Str.
Foxe Basin
Gulf of Alaska
Bristol Bay
Bering Str.
Chukchi Sea
Wrangel I.
Aleutian Islands
ALASKA
Denmark Strait
Gulf of Mexico
Caribbean Sea
West Indies
Leeward Is.
Windward Is.
Hispaniola
Gulf of California
Tropic of Cancer
Equator
Tropic of Capricorn
Antarctic Circle
Arctic Circle
International Date Line
Hawaiian Islands (U.S.)
Honolulu
Hawaii
Galapagos Is. (Ecuador)
Marquesas Is. (Fr.)
Tuamotu Archipelago (Fr.)
Society Is. (Fr.)
Tahiti
Cook Is. (N.Z.)
Tonga Is. (Friendly Is.)
W. Samoa
Phoenix Is. (Br.)
Tokelau Is.
Tubuai Is. (Fr.)
Pitcairn I. (Br.)
Easter I. (Chile)
Kermadec Is. (N.Z.)
Chatham Is. (N.Z.)
Azores (Port.)
Bermuda (Br.)
Madeira (Port.)
Canary Is. (Span.)
C. Verde Is. (Port.)
Ascension (Br.)
St. Helena (Br.)
Tristan da Cunha (Br.)
Gough I. (Br.)
Falkland Is. (Br.)
S. Georgia
S. Sandwich Is.
South Orkney Is.
South Shetland Is.
Scotia Sea
Drake Passage
Magellan's Str.
Tierra del Fuego
C. Horn
FALKLAND IS. DEPENDENCIES
Antarctic Peninsula
Graham Land
Palmer Land
Weddell Sea
Bellingshausen Sea
Amundsen Sea
Ellsworth Land
Byrd Land
BRITISH ANTARCTIC TERRITORY
ROSS DEPENDENCY
Patagonia
G. of San Matias
G. of San Jorge
Newfoundland
G. of St. Lawrence
Anchorage
Edmonton
Calgary
Vancouver
Seattle
Portland
Winnipeg
Montréal
Québec
Ottawa
Toronto
Chicago
Detroit
Boston
New York
Philadelphia
Washington
San Francisco
Los Angeles
San Diego
Denver
St. Louis
Dallas
Houston
New Orleans
Atlanta
Miami
Monterrey
Guadalajara
México
La Habana
Port-au-Prince
Santo Domingo
Kingston
Caracas
Bogotá
Medellín
Cali
Quito
Guayaquil
Lima
La Paz
Belém
Manaus
Fortaleza
Recife
Salvador
Brasília
Belo Horizonte
Rio de Janeiro
São Paulo
Asunción
Pôrto Alegre
Montevideo
Buenos Aires
Rosario
Córdoba
Santiago
Valparaíso
Amazon
West from Greenwich

Projection: *Hammer Equal Area*

ARCTIC OCEAN
Franz Joseph Ld.
Severnaya Zemlya
New Siberian Is.
East Siberian Sea
Laptev Sea
Kara Sea
Barents Sea
Novaya Zemlya
Svalbard (Norway)
Taymyr Pen.
UNION OF SOVIET SOCIALIST REPUBLICS
RUSSIAN SOVIET FEDERAL SOCIALIST REPUBLIC
Siberia
Bering Sea
Sea of Okhotsk
Kamchatka
Sakhalin
Kuril Islands
Arctic Circle
Leningrad
Moskva
Stockholm
Helsinki
Sverdlovsk
Novosibirsk
Omsk
Tomsk
Krasnoyarsk
Chelyabinsk
Magnitogorsk
Gorkiy
Kazan
Kuybyshev
Kharkov
Kiyev
Volgograd
Rostov
Odessa
Baku
Tbilisi
Tashkent
Alma Ata
Dushanbe
Irkutsk
Ulan Ude
Khabarovsk
Vladivostok
Berlin
Warszawa
Praha
Wien
Budapest
Bucuresti
Istanbul
Ankara
Roma
Napoli
Paris
Barcelona
Milano
Athinai
Mediterranean Sea
Black Sea
Caspian Sea
Aral Sea
KAZAKHSTAN
UZBEKISTAN
TURKMENISTAN
KIRGIZIA
MONGOLIA
CHINA
Tibet
Peiping
Tientsin
Shenyang
Harbin
Changchun
Taiyuan
Tsinan
Sian
Lanchow
Chengtu
Chungking
Wuhan
Nanking
Shanghai
Changsha
Kunming
Kwangchow
Hong Kong
Taipei
TAIWAN (FORMOSA)
Sea of Japan
JAPAN
Tōkyō
Yokohama
Nagoya
Kyōto
Kōbe
Ōsaka
Kitakyūshū
Sapporo
Sŏul
Pusan
Pyŏngyang
East China Sea
PACIFIC OCEAN
Tropic of Cancer
TURKEY
IRAN (PERSIA)
Tehrān
Baghdād
IRAQ
SYRIA
CYPRUS
Halab
Dimashq
Bayrūt
Tel Aviv-Yafo
'Ammān
Al Qāhira
Iskandariya
EGYPT
LIBYA
SAUDI ARABIA
Makkah
Nejd
Ar Riyād
Persian Gulf
Red Sea
OMAN
SOUTH YEMEN
YEMEN
G. of Aden
Arabian Sea
AFGHANISTAN
Kabul
PAKISTAN
Karachi
Lahore
INDIA
Delhi
Agra
Kanpur
Lucknow
Calcutta
Ahmadabad
Bombay
Poona
Nagpur
Hyderabad
Madras
Bangalore
NEPAL
Bay of Bengal
SRI LANKA (CEYLON)
Colombo
BURMA
Rangoon
THAILAND (SIAM)
Krung Thep
Saigon
Hanoi
South China Sea
PHILIPPINES
Manila
Quezon City
MALAYSIA
Kuala Lumpur
Singapore
Borneo
Sumatra
Sulawesi
Moluccas
INDONESIA
Djakarta
Surabaja
Sunda Islands
Timor
New Guinea
PAPUA NEW GUINEA
Arafura Sea
INDIAN OCEAN
Equator
Maldive Is.
Seychelles
Chagos Arch.
BRITISH INDIAN OCEAN TERR.
MALAGASY REPUBLIC
Madagascar
Mozambique Chan.
Tropic of Capricorn
Mauritius
Réunion
SUDAN
Khartūm
ETHIOPIA
Addis Abeba
KENYA
Nairobi
UGANDA
TANZANIA
Dar es Salaam
Zanzibar
Mogadishu
SOMALI REP.
CHAD
NIGER
NIGERIA
Lagos
CENTRAL AFRICA
ZAÏRE (CONGO)
Kinshasa
CONGO
GABON
ANGOLA
Luanda
ZAMBIA
RHODESIA
Salisbury
MOZAMBIQUE
Malawi
SOUTH WEST AFRICA (NAMIBIA)
BOTSWANA
Johannesburg
Pretoria
SOUTH AFRICA
Durban
Cape Town
C. of Good Hope
Port Elizabeth
East London
AUSTRALIA
NORTHERN TERRITORY
QUEENSLAND
WESTERN AUSTRALIA
SOUTH AUSTRALIA
NEW SOUTH WALES
VICTORIA
TASMANIA
Perth
Adelaide
Melbourne
Sydney
Brisbane
Canberra
Great Australian Bight
Tasman Sea
NEW ZEALAND
North I.
South I.
Auckland
Wellington
Christchurch
New Caledonia
New Hebrides
Fiji Is.
Solomon Is.
Marshall Is.
Caroline Is.
Mariana or Ladrone Is.
Gilbert Is.
(U. S. Trust Territory)
SOUTHERN OCEAN
Kerguelen (Fr.)
Antarctic Circle
Enderby Land
Wilkes Land
AUSTRALIAN DEPENDENCY
Ross Sea
East from Greenwich

COPYRIGHT. GEORGE PHILIP & SON. LTD.

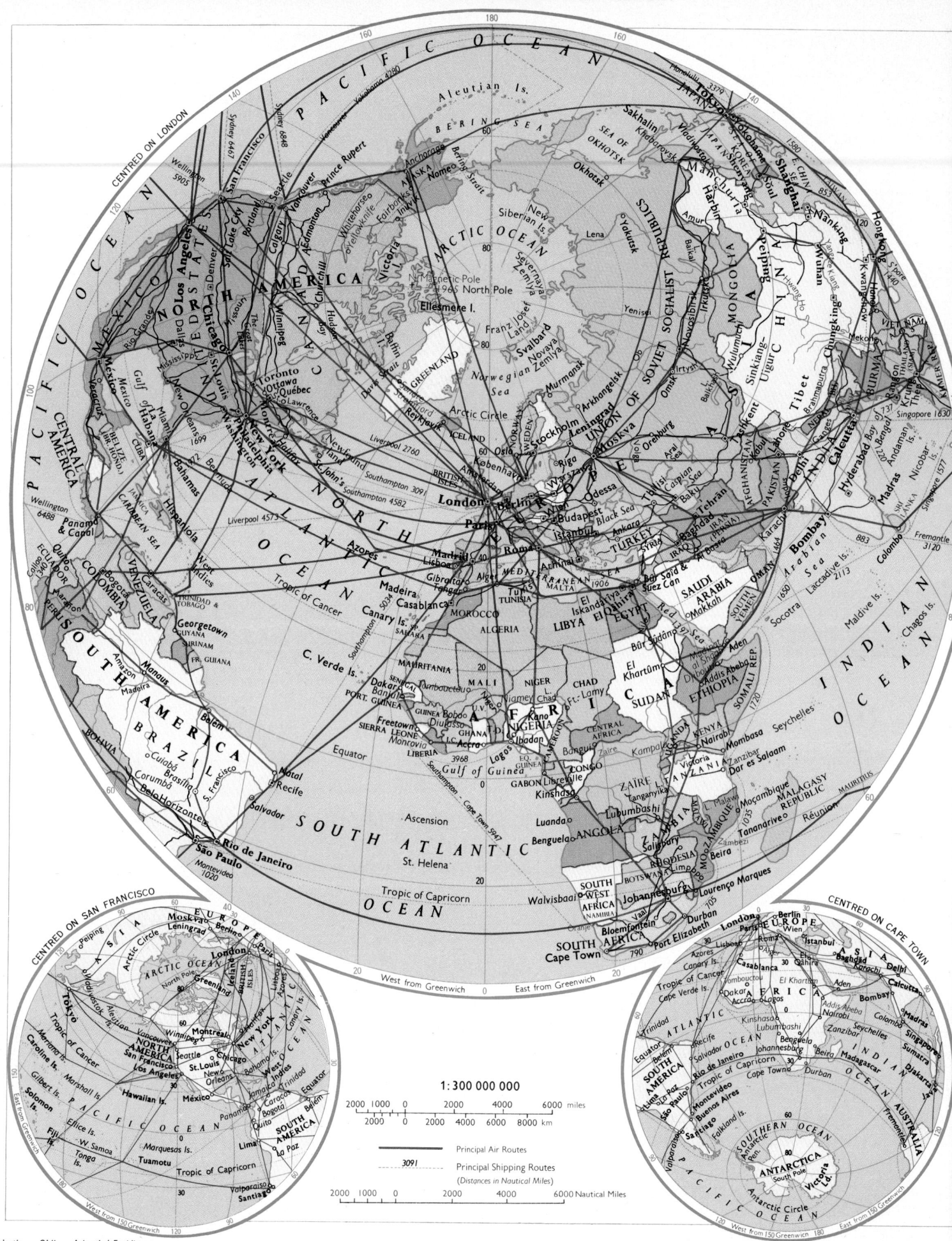

1 : 300 000 000

2000 1000 0   2000   4000   6000 miles

2000   0   2000   4000   6000   8000 km

————— Principal Air Routes

------ 3091 Principal Shipping Routes
(Distances in Nautical Miles)

2000 1000 0   2000   4000   6000 Nautical Miles

Projection : *Oblique Azimuthal Equidistant*

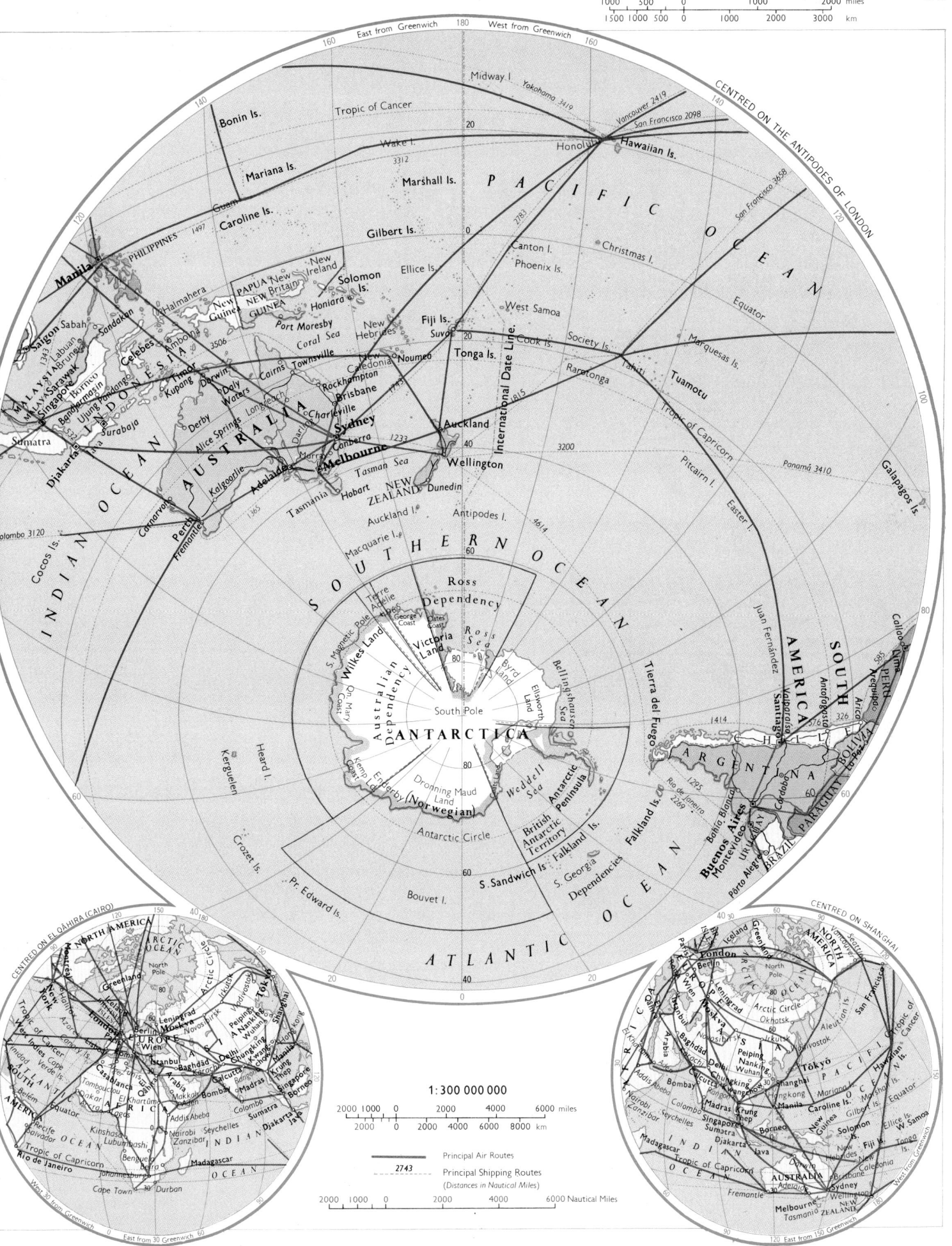
1:100 000 000
1000 500 0 1000 2000 miles
1500 1000 500 0 1000 2000 3000 km
East from Greenwich
West from Greenwich
CENTRED ON THE ANTIPODES OF LONDON
Tropic of Cancer
Midway I.
Yokohama 3419
Vancouver 2419
San Francisco 2098
Honolulu
Hawaiian Is.
Bonin Is.
Wake I.
Mariana Is.
Marshall Is.
Guam
Caroline Is.
Gilbert Is.
PACIFIC OCEAN
San Francisco 3658
San Francisco
Canton I.
Phoenix Is.
Christmas I.
Equator
PHILIPPINES
Manila
New Ireland
PAPUA New
NEW Britain
GUINEA
New Guinea
Halmahera
Solomon Is.
Honiara
Ellice Is.
West Samoa
Port Moresby
Coral Sea
New Hebrides
Fiji Is.
Suva
Cook Is.
Society Is.
Marquesas Is.
Saigon
Sabah
Sandakan
Labuan
Brunei
MALAYSIA
Sarawak
Singapore
Borneo
Celebes
Ambon
INDONESIA
Timor
Kupang
Darwin
Daly Waters
Cairns
Townsville
New Caledonia
Noumea
Tonga Is.
Rarotonga
Tahiti
Tuamotu
Bandjarmasin
Ujung Pandang
Surabaja
Sumatra
Djakarta
Derby
Alice Springs
Longreach
Rockhampton
Brisbane
Charleville
Sydney
Auckland
International Date Line
Tropic of Capricorn
Darling
Canberra
Murray
Melbourne
Wellington
Tasman Sea
AUSTRALIA
Kalgoorlie
Adelaide
Hobart
Tasmania
NEW ZEALAND
Dunedin
Panamá 3410
Pitcairn I.
Galapagos Is.
Easter I.
INDIAN OCEAN
Carnarvon
Perth
Fremantle
Colombo 3120
Cocos Is.
Auckland I.
Antipodes I.
Macquarie I.
SOUTHERN OCEAN
Ross Dependency
Terre Adélie
George V Coast
Oates Coast
S. Magnetic Pole
Wilkes Land
Victoria Land
Ross Sea
Byrd Land
Bellingshausen Sea
Ellsworth Land
Australian Dependency
Qn. Mary Coast
South Pole
ANTARCTICA
Juan Fernández
Tierra del Fuego
SOUTH AMERICA
Callao
Lima
PERU
Arequipa
Antofagasta
Arica
Valparaiso
Santiago
CHILE
ARGENTINA
Córdoba
BOLIVIA
La Paz
PARAGUAY
Heard I.
Kerguelen
Kemp Coast
Enderby Ld.
Dronning Maud Land (Norwegian)
Coats Land
Weddell Sea
Antarctic Peninsula
Antarctic Circle
British Antarctic Territory
Falkland Is.
Rio de Janeiro
Bahía Blanca
Buenos Aires
Montevideo
URUGUAY
Pôrto Alegre
BRAZIL
Crozet Is.
Pr. Edward Is.
Bouvet I.
S. Sandwich Is.
S. Georgia
Falkland Is. Dependencies
ATLANTIC OCEAN
CENTRED ON EL QÂHIRA (CAIRO)
NORTH AMERICA
ARCTIC OCEAN
North Pole
Greenland
Arctic Circle
Montreal
New York
London
Leningrad
Moskva
Berlin
EUROPE
Wien
Istanbul
Roma
Novosibirsk
Irkutsk
Vladivostok
Tôkyô
Shanghai
Peiping
Nanking
Wuhan
Chungking
Hong Kong
Manila
Tropic of Cancer
West Indies
Canary Is.
Cape Verde Is.
Casablanca
Tombouctou
Dakar
Accra
Lagos
El Qâhira
El Khartûm
Baghdâd
Karachi
Delhi
Calcutta
Rangoon
Krung Thep
Singapore
Borneo
Bombay
Madras
Colombo
Aden
Arabia
AFRICA
Addis Abeba
Nairobi
Zanzibar
Seychelles
Sumatra
Djakarta
Java
Belém
Recife
Salvador
Equator
Kinshasa
Lubumbashi
Benguela
Beira
Madagascar
Johannesburg
Durban
Cape Town
Rio de Janeiro
Tropic of Capricorn
INDIAN OCEAN
West 30 from Greenwich
East from 30 Greenwich
1:300 000 000
2000 1000 0 2000 4000 6000 miles
2000 0 2000 4000 6000 8000 km
Principal Air Routes
2743
Principal Shipping Routes
(Distances in Nautical Miles)
2000 1000 0 2000 4000 6000 Nautical Miles
CENTRED ON SHANGHAI
Iceland
Greenland
NORTH AMERICA
Vancouver
Seattle
San Francisco
London
Paris
Berlin
Wien
Leningrad
Moskva
EUROPE
ASIA
Istanbul
Arctic Circle
Okhotsk
Aleutian Is.
Novosibirsk
Irkutsk
Vladivostok
Baghdâd
Arabia
Karachi
Delhi
Peiping
Nanking
Wuhan
Tôkyô
Hawaiian Is.
Tropic of Cancer
PACIFIC OCEAN
Addis Abeba
Bombay
Calcutta
Chungking
Shanghai
Hongkong
Mariana Is.
Marshall Is.
Nairobi
Zanzibar
Colombo
Madras
Krung Thep
Manila
Caroline Is.
Gilbert Is.
Equator
Seychelles
Singapore
Sumatra
Borneo
New Guinea
Solomon Is.
Ellice Is.
W. Samoa
INDIAN OCEAN
Djakarta
Java
Fiji Is.
Tonga Is.
Madagascar
Tropic of Capricorn
Darwin
New Hebrides
New Caledonia
AUSTRALIA
Brisbane
Adelaide
Fremantle
Sydney
Wellington
Melbourne
Tasmania
NEW ZEALAND
West from Greenwich
Greenwich
East from 150

COPYRIGHT. GEORGE PHILIP & SON. LTD.

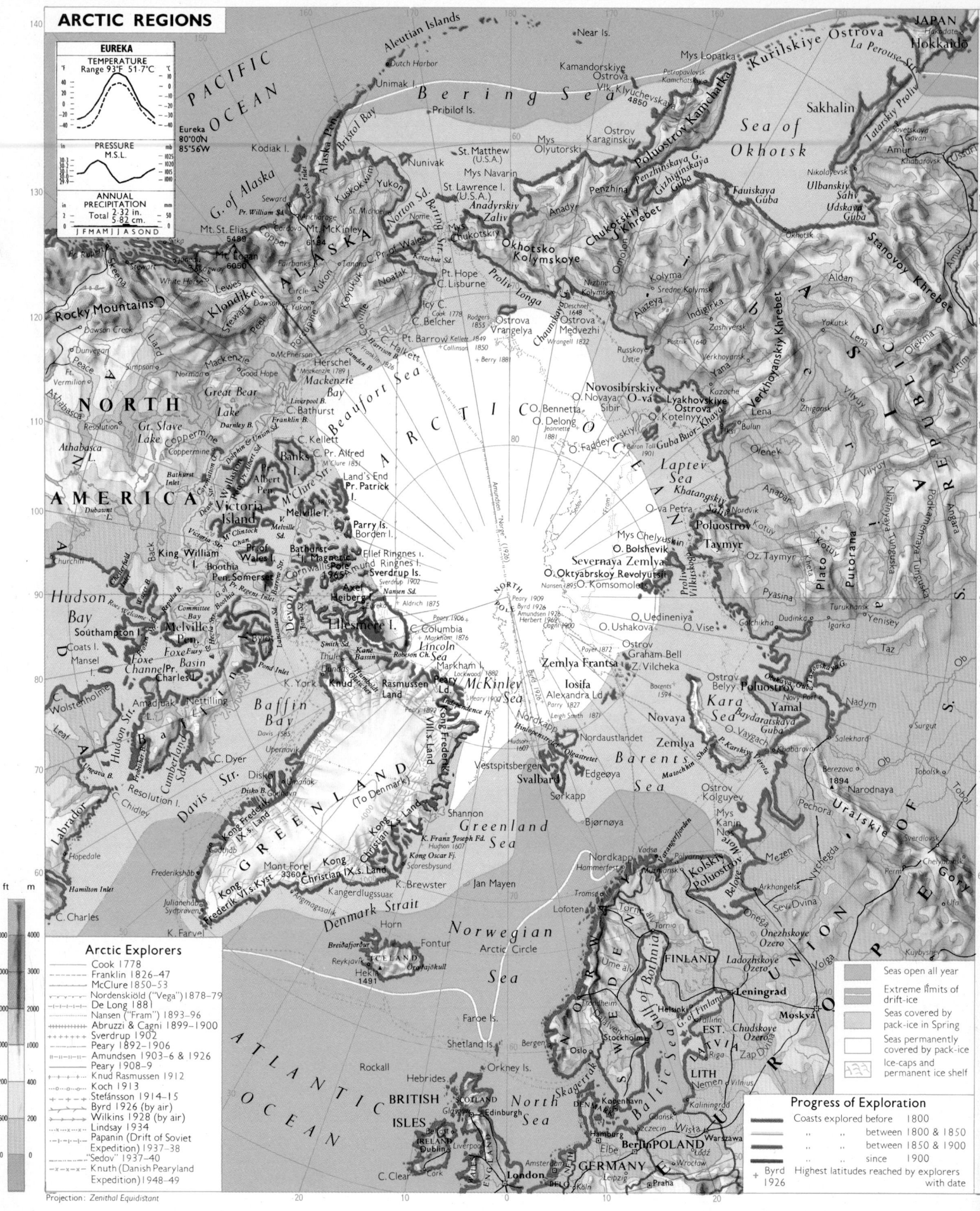

ARCTIC REGIONS

EUREKA

TEMPERATURE
Range 93°F 51.7°C

Eureka
80°00'N
85°56'W

PRESSURE
M.S.L.

ANNUAL
PRECIPITATION
Total 2·32 in.
5·82 cm.

J F M A M J J A S O N D

Arctic Explorers

Cook 1778
Franklin 1826–47
McClure 1850–53
Nordenskiöld ("Vega")1878–79
De Long 1881
Nansen ("Fram") 1893–96
Abruzzi & Cagni 1899–1900
Sverdrup 1902
Peary 1892–1906
Amundsen 1903–6 & 1926
Peary 1908–9
Knud Rasmussen 1912
Koch 1913
Stefánsson 1914–15
Byrd 1926 (by air)
Wilkins 1928 (by air)
Lindsay 1934
Papanin (Drift of Soviet
Expedition) 1937–38
"Sedov" 1937–40
Knuth (Danish Pearyland
Expedition) 1948–49

Projection: Zenithal Equidistant

Seas open all year
Extreme limits of
drift-ice
Seas covered by
pack-ice in Spring
Seas permanently
covered by pack-ice
Ice-caps and
permanent ice shelf

Progress of Exploration

Coasts explored before 1800
„   „   „ between 1800 & 1850
„   „   „ between 1850 & 1900
„   „   „ since 1900
+ Byrd Highest latitudes reached by explorers
1926   with date

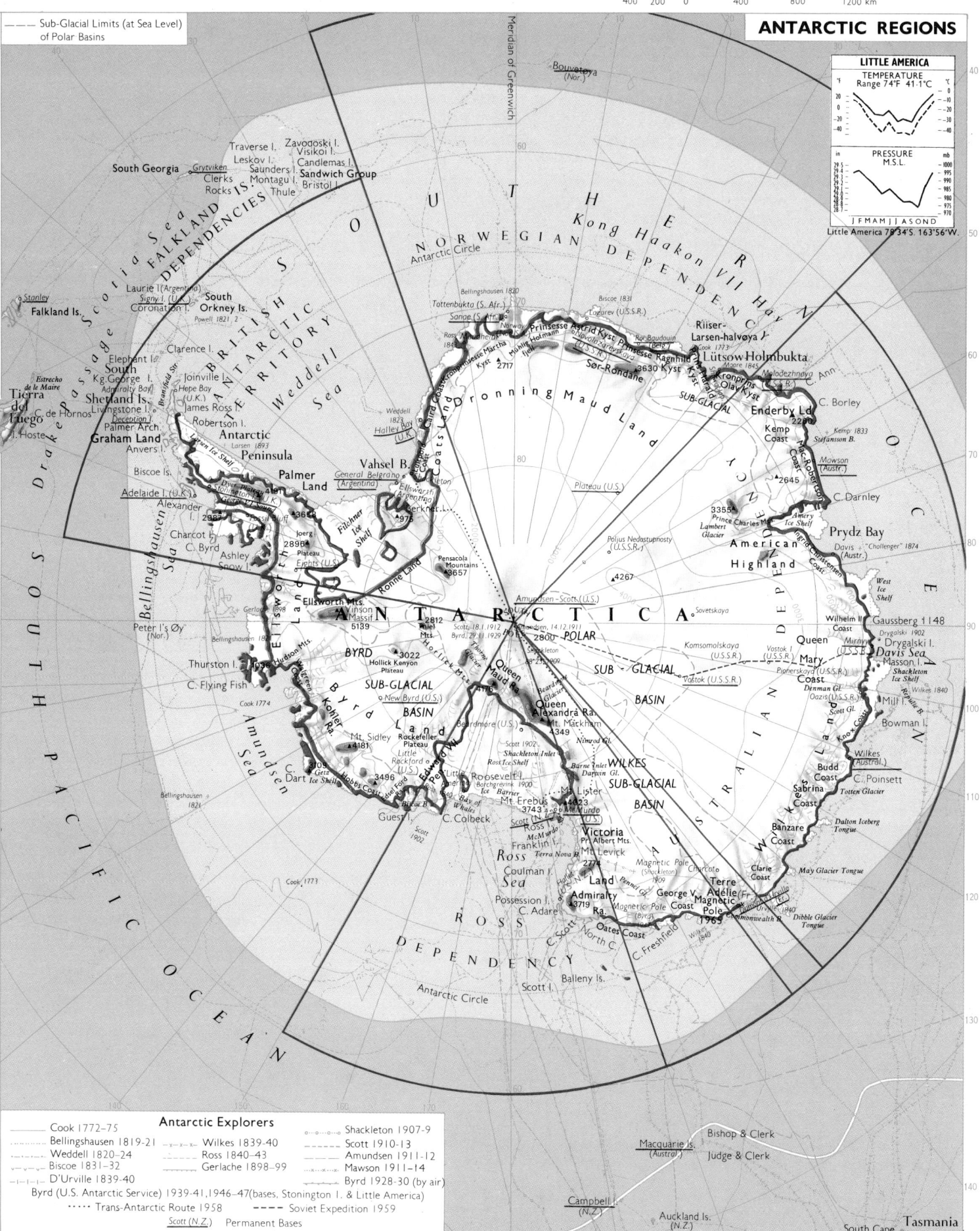

ANTARCTIC REGIONS

1:35 000 000

400 200 0 400 800 1200 km

15

LITTLE AMERICA
TEMPERATURE
Range 74°F 41.1°C

PRESSURE
M.S.L.

J F M A M J J A S O N D
Little America 78°34'S. 163°56'W.

Sub-Glacial Limits (at Sea Level) of Polar Basins

Antarctic Explorers

Cook 1772–75
Bellingshausen 1819–21
Weddell 1820–24
Biscoe 1831–32
D'Urville 1839–40
Wilkes 1839–40
Ross 1840–43
Gerlache 1898–99
Shackleton 1907–9
Scott 1910–13
Amundsen 1911–12
Mawson 1911–14
Byrd 1928–30 (by air)
Byrd (U.S. Antarctic Service) 1939–41,1946–47(bases, Stonington I. & Little America)
Trans-Antarctic Route 1958
Soviet Expedition 1959
Scott (N.Z.) Permanent Bases

COPYRIGHT. GEORGE PHILIP & SON. LTD.

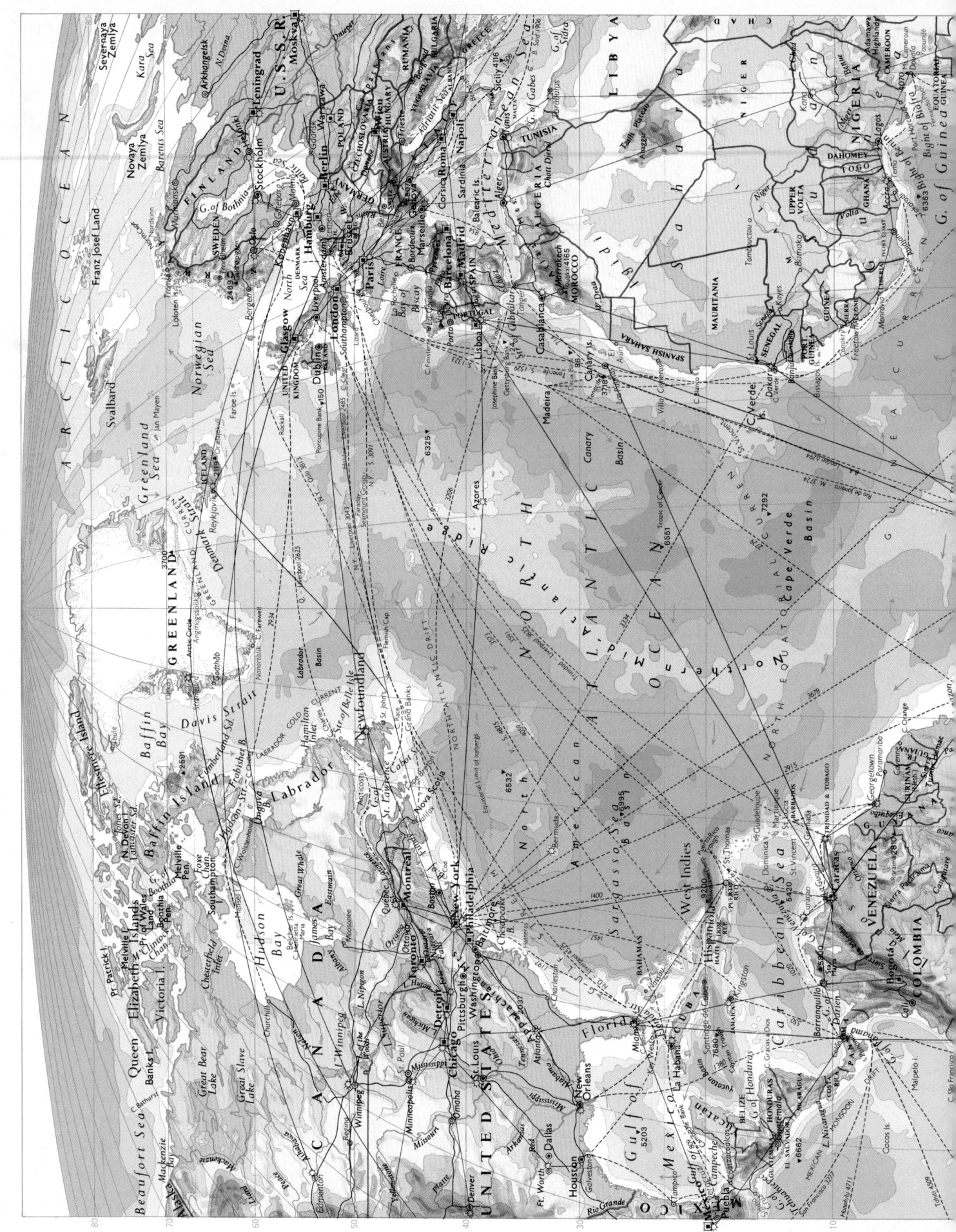

ARCTIC OCEAN
NORTH ATLANTIC OCEAN
Greenland Sea
Norwegian Sea
Barents Sea
Kara Sea
Baffin Bay
Davis Strait
Denmark Strait
Labrador Basin
Hudson Bay
Beaufort Sea
Gulf of Mexico
Caribbean Sea
Sargasso Sea
North American Basin
Canary Basin
Cape Verde Basin
Mediterranean Sea
G. of Guinea
GREENLAND
ICELAND
Svalbard
Franz Josef Land
Novaya Zemlya
Severnaya Zemlya
Baffin Island
Ellesmere Island
Queen Elizabeth Islands
Victoria I.
Newfoundland
Labrador
CANADA
UNITED STATES
MEXICO
CUBA
West Indies
BAHAMAS
VENEZUELA
COLOMBIA
UNITED KINGDOM
IRELAND
FRANCE
SPAIN
PORTUGAL
SWEDEN
FINLAND
POLAND
GERMANY
U.S.S.R.
MOROCCO
ALGERIA
TUNISIA
LIBYA
MAURITANIA
SPANISH SAHARA
SENEGAL
NIGER
NIGERIA
Sahara
Azores
Madeira
Canary Is.
Cape Verde Is.
Bermuda
Tropic of Cancer
London
Paris
New York
Montreal
Chicago
Washington
Philadelphia
Boston
Moskva
Leningrad
Stockholm
Berlin
Madrid
Lisboa
Roma
Dakar
Caracas

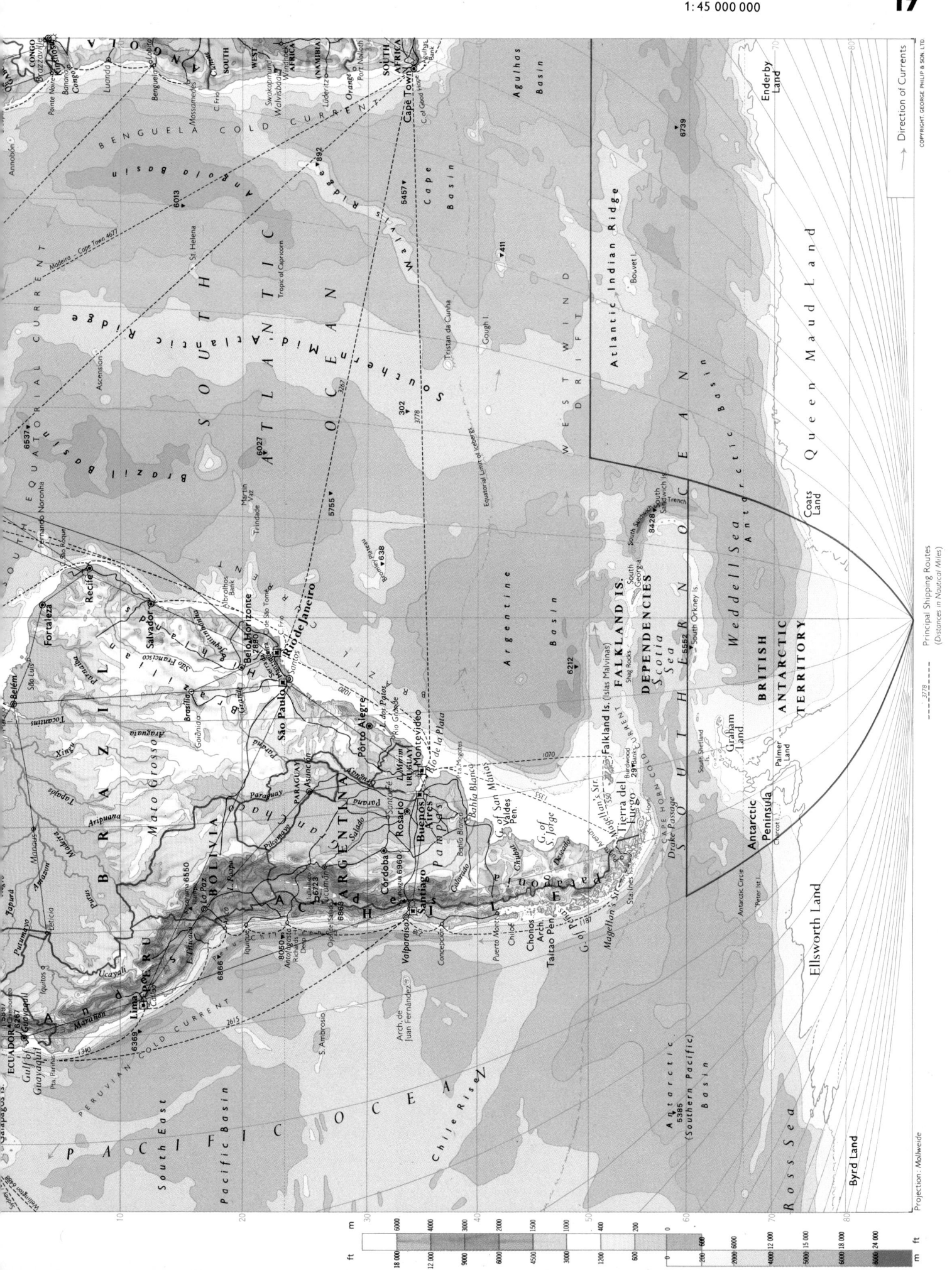

Direction of Currents

COPYRIGHT GEORGE PHILIP & SON, LTD.

Principal Shipping Routes
(Distances in Nautical Miles)

Projection : Mollweide

PACIFIC OCEAN

SOUTH ATLANTIC OCEAN

SOUTHERN OCEAN

Queen Maud Land

Enderby Land

Coats Land

BRITISH ANTARCTIC TERRITORY

Ellsworth Land

Byrd Land

Ross Sea

Weddell Sea

Atlantic Indian Ridge

Agulhas Basin

Cape Basin

Angola Basin

Brazil Basin

Argentine Basin

Chile Rise

Antarctic (Southern Pacific) Basin

BRAZIL

ARGENTINA

BOLIVIA

PERU

CHILE

PARAGUAY

URUGUAY

ECUADOR

Andes

FALKLAND IS.
DEPENDENCIES

ANGOLA

SOUTH AFRICA

SOUTH WEST AFRICA (NAMIBIA)

CONGO

BENGUELA COLD CURRENT

PERUVIAN COLD CURRENT

SOUTH EQUATORIAL CURRENT

WEST WIND DRIFT

CAPE HORN COLD CURRENT

m   ft
6000 18 000
4000 12 000
3000 9000
2000 6000
1500 4500
1000 3000
400   1200
200   600
0
200   2000
600   6000
2000 12 000
4000 15 000
5000 18 000
8000 24 000
m   ft

ANNUAL RAINFALL
1:40 000 000

mm	inches
1500	60
1000	40
750	30
500	20
250	10

Arctic Circle

3734▼

Iceland
Reykjavik
Hekla
1491
Öræfajökull
2119

Arctic Circle

N O R W E G I A N   S E A

Faroe Is.

Rockall

Shetland Is.

St. Kilda

Hebrides

Orkney Is.

Lindesnes

British Isles

Ben Nevis
▲1343

N O R T H   S E A

Jutla

Edinburgh

Ireland
Belfast
Irish Sea
Dublin

Great Britain

C. Clear
St. George's Channel
Snowdon
1085

Frisian Is.

Amsterdam
Netherlands

Cardiff

Lands End
Scilly Is.

Thames
London

English Channel
Channel Is.
Str. of Dover

Brussel
Westerwald

Paris
Seine
Ardennes
Meuse
Eifel
Taunus

A T L A N T I C

Flores

O C E A N

Terceira
Pico
Azores
São Miguel

Brittany

Loire

B a y   o f
B i s c a y

4861▼
Gironde

Vosges
Black Forest
Rhine
Zürich

Massif
Central
Mt. Dore
1886

Saône
Jura

Mt. Blanc
4807▲

A L P

C. Finisterre

Cantabrian Mts.

Old Castile
Iberian

Pyrenees
Maladetta
3404

Garonne
Cévennes
Rhône

Po
Riv
Ligurian
Sea

Lisboa
C. da Roca

Madrid

Ebro

G. of Lion

Corsica

Tagus
New
Castile

P e n i n s u l a
Guadiana
Sierra Morena

Str. of
Bonifacio

C. St. Vincent

Sardinia

Balearic
Is.

Guadalquivir
Andalusia Mulhacen
3478
Sa. Nevada

Madeira

6293

Str. of Gibraltar
C. Trafalgar
Gibraltar

M E D I T E R

Casablanca

Er Rif

Alger
Maritime Atlas

Tunis

C.

Great Atlas
Plateau of the Shotts
Saharan Atlas

Gulf of
Gabes

Palma

Canary Is.
Tenerife

Toubkal
4165

S a h a r a

Gran
Canaria
Fuerteventura

Tropic of Cancer

ft	m
12 000	4000
6000	2000
3000	1000
1200	400
600	200
0	0
200	600
2000	6000
4000	12 000
m	ft

Projection: Bonne.   20   15   10   5   West from Greenwich   0   East from Greenwich   5   10

1:17 500 000

100   0   100   200   300   400   500 miles
100   0   200   400   600   800 km

Nordkapp   Nordkinn

Lofoten

L. Inari

Lappland

Kanin Peninsula

Pechora

Tundra

Ural Mountains

Narodnaya 1894

West Siberian Plain

Ob

Kebnekaise 2123

Torne älv

Kola Peninsula

White Sea

Telpos Iz. 1617

Mezen

Irtysh

Scandinavia

Indalsälven

Umeälv

Gulf of Bothnia

Finland

N. Dvina

Mezen

Galdhøpiggen 2469

Oslo

Stockholm

Vänern

Mälaren

Vättern

Gotland

Åland Is.

Helsinki

Lake Ladoga

Svir

L. Onega

Onega

Omega

Rybinsk Res.

Kama

Volga

Tobol

55

Skaw

Katte-gat

København

Gulf of Finland

Neva

Leningrad

L. Chudskoye

Valdai Hills

European

Plain

Moskva

Gorkiy

Volga

Oka

Volga

Obshchi Syrt

Ural

Volga Heights

50

Berlin

Oder

Elbe

Neman

Vistula

Warszawa

Dvina

Pripet

Pripet Marshes

Central Russian Uplands

Ukraine

Kiyevo

Dnieper

Tsimlyansk Res.

Volga

Kirgiz Steppe

Ust Urt Plateau

Ural

45

North

European

Plain

Ore Mts.

Praha

Sudetes

Bohemian Forest

Moravia Hts.

Tatra 2655

Carpathians

Dnieper

Don

Karagiye Depression -132

Kara Bogaz

Inn

Wien

Danube

Bakony Forest

Budapest

Plain of Hungary

Drava

Sava

Tisza

Mures

Transylvanian Alps

Dniester

Prut

Bug

Odessa

Dnieper

Sea of Azov

Crimea

Kuban

Strait of Kerch

Terek

Caucasus

Elbrus 5633

Transcaucasia

Kura

Baku

Caspian Sea

40

Adriatic Sea

Dinaric Alps

Dalmatia

Beograd

Morava

Wallachia

Bucureşti

Danube

Mouths of the Danube

Black Sea

2211

Ararat 5165

L. Van

Kura

Araks

L. Urmia

Elburz Mts. Tehran

Apennines

Gran Sasso 2914

Roma

Sofiya

Balkans

Rhodope

Balkan Peninsula

Istanbul

Bosporus

Sea of Marmara

Pontine Mts.

Kurdistan

Str. of Otranto

Pindus

Dardanelles

Ankara

Kizil

Anatolia

L. Tuz

Erciyas 3770

Taurus Mts.

Mesopotamia

Tigris

Baghdād

Strait of Messina

Calabria

Ionian Sea

Ionian Is.

Morea

Athinai

Aegean Sea

Halab

Euphrates

Etna 3263

Sicily

C. Spartivento

5121

C. Matapan

Crete

Rhodes

Cyprus

Levant

Bayrūt

Syrian Desert

Persian Gulf

telleria

Malta

Tel Aviv-Yafo

Nile Delta

Dead Sea -395

30

Tripoli

N

SEA

Gulf of Sidra

15   20   25   30   35   40   45

COPYRIGHT. GEORGE PHILIP & SON. LTD.

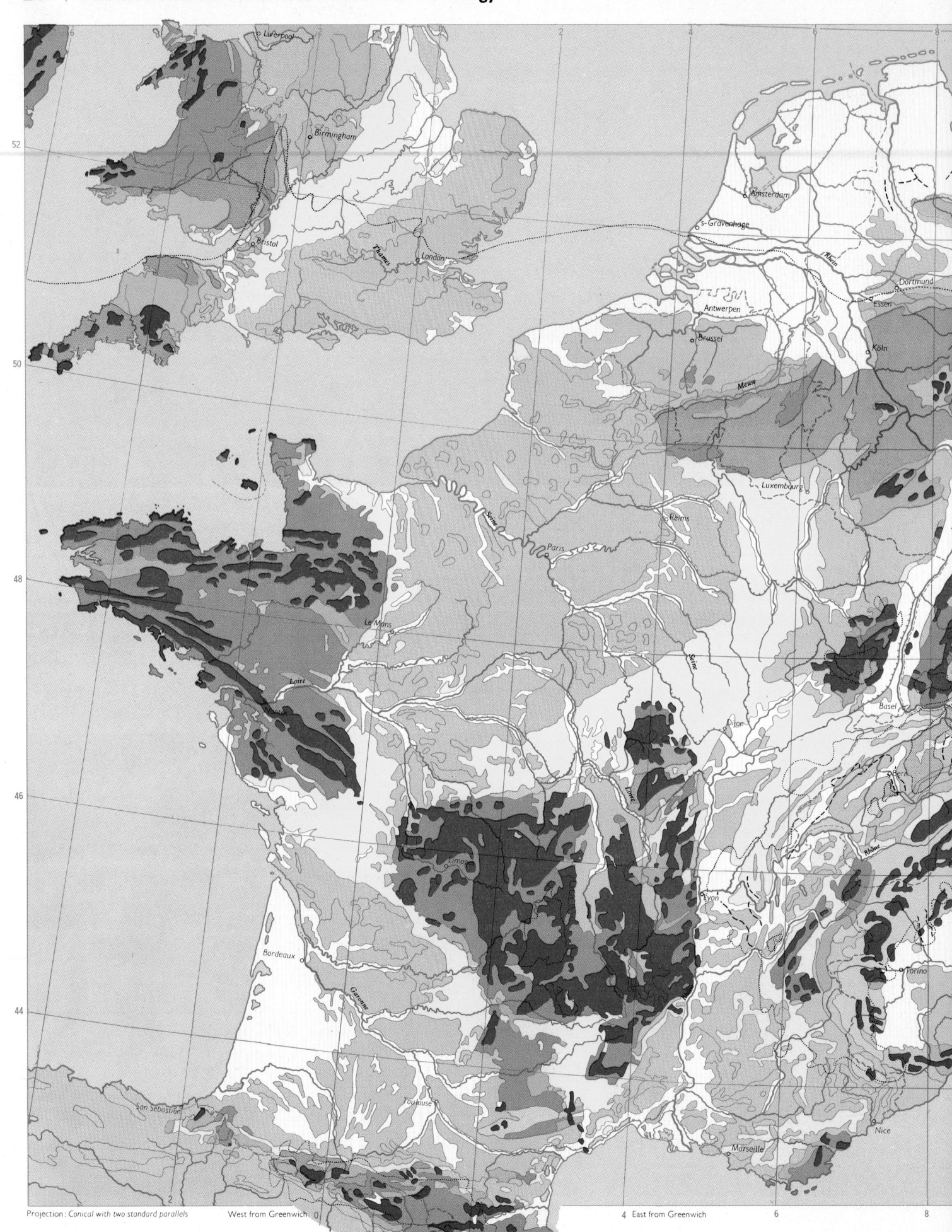

Liverpool
Birmingham
Bristol
Thames
London
Amsterdam
's-Gravenhage
Rhein
Dortmund
Essen
Antwerpen
Brussel
Köln
Meuse
Luxembourg
Reims
Seine
Paris
Le Mans
Loire
Nantes
Dijon
Basel
Bern
Limoges
Lyon
Rhône
Bordeaux
Garonne
Torino
San Sebastian
Toulouse
Nice
Marseille
52
50
48
46
44
Projection: *Conical with two standard parallels*
West from Greenwich
East from Greenwich

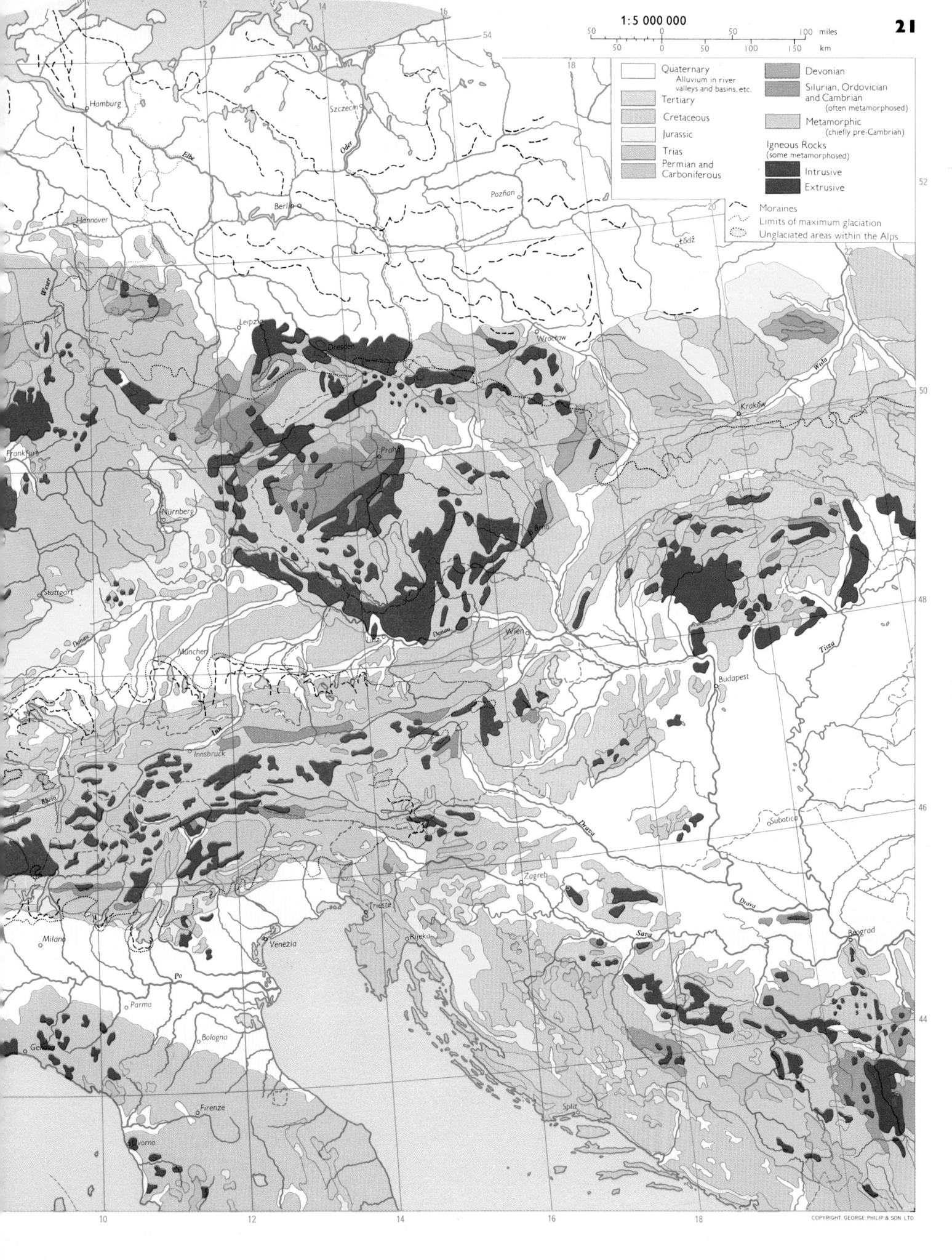

1:5 000 000

Quaternary
Alluvium in river valleys and basins, etc.
Tertiary
Cretaceous
Jurassic
Trias
Permian and Carboniferous

Devonian
Silurian, Ordovician and Cambrian (often metamorphosed)
Metamorphic (chiefly pre-Cambrian)

Igneous Rocks
(some metamorphosed)
Intrusive
Extrusive

Moraines
Limits of maximum glaciation
Unglaciated areas within the Alps

Hamburg
Szczecin
Hannover
Berlin
Poznań
Łódź
Weser
Elbe
Oder
Wisła
Leipzig
Dresden
Wrocław
Kraków
Praha
Frankfurt
Nürnberg
Brno
Stuttgart
Linz
Donau
Wien
München
Budapest
Donau
Innsbruck
Tisza
Inn
Rhein
Drava
Subotica
Milano
Zagreb
Po
Trieste
Drava
Parma
Venezia
Rijeka
Sava
Beograd
Bologna
Genova
Firenze
Split
Livorno

COPYRIGHT. GEORGE PHILIP & SON LTD

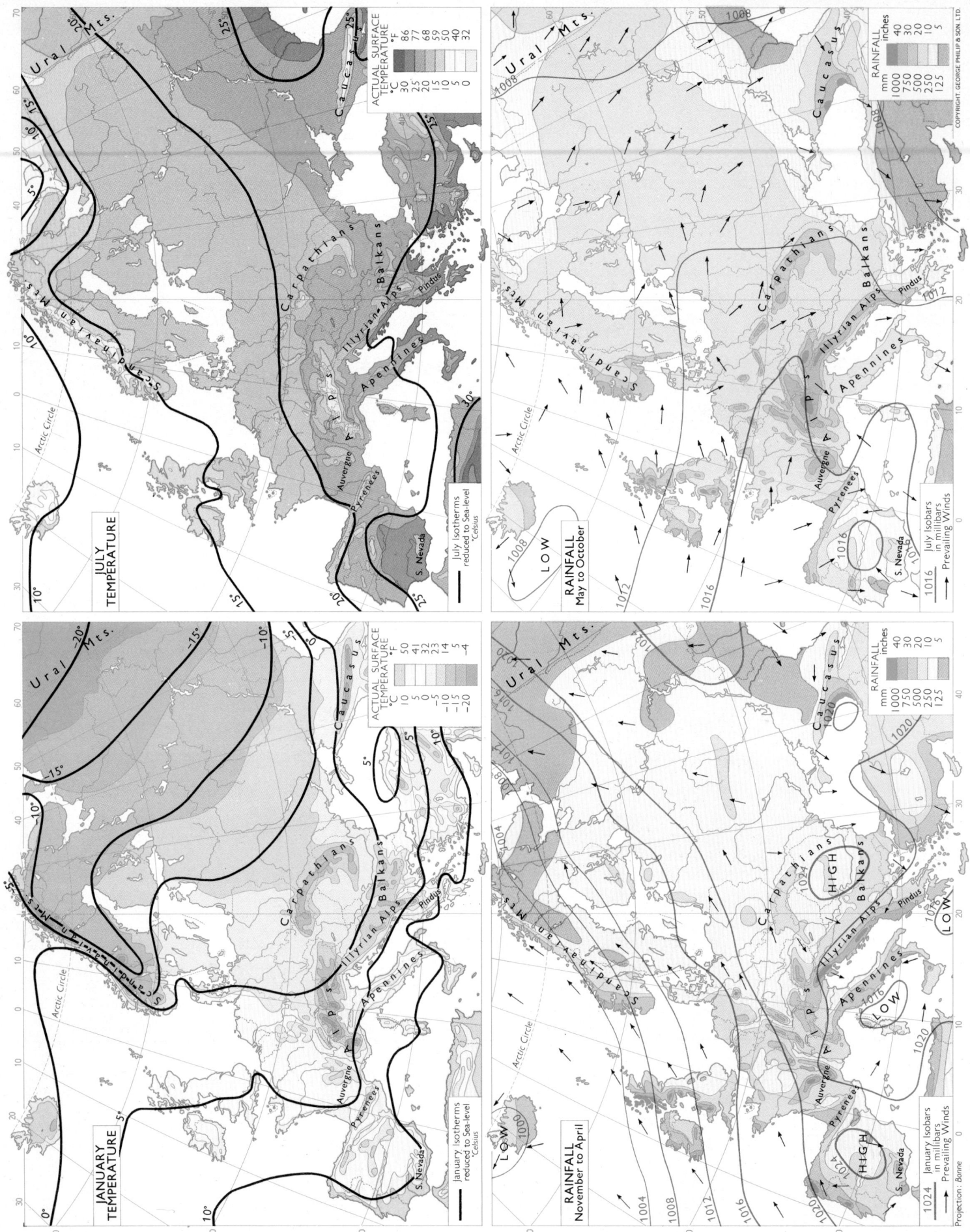

1 : 40 000 000

ACTUAL SURFACE TEMPERATURE

°C	°F
30	86
25	77
20	68
15	59
10	50
5	40
0	32

JULY TEMPERATURE

July Isotherms reduced to Sea-level °Celsius

RAINFALL May to October

RAINFALL
mm	inches
1000	40
750	30
500	20
250	10
125	5

July Isobars in millibars Prevailing Winds

ACTUAL SURFACE TEMPERATURE

°C	°F
10	50
5	41
0	32
-5	23
-10	14
-15	5
-20	-4

JANUARY TEMPERATURE

January Isotherms reduced to Sea-level °Celsius

RAINFALL November to April

RAINFALL
mm	inches
1000	40
750	30
500	20
250	10
125	5

January Isobars in millibars Prevailing Winds

COPYRIGHT GEORGE PHILIP & SON LTD.

Projection: Bonne

COPYRIGHT GEORGE PHILIP & SON, LTD.

1:20 000 000

100   0   500 miles
100   0   100   200   300   400
          0   200   400   600   800 km

FOREST VEGETATION

Northern Coniferous Forest—
  a. Fenno-Scandian Forest (pine, spruce, birch)
  b. Taiga (Siberian larch, fir, spruce)

Mountain Forest, mainly Coniferous (fir, pine, spruce), sometimes with (oak, beech, fir, etc.)
lower belt of Broad-leaved Forest (oak, beech, chestnut)

Mixed Broad-leaved and Coniferous Forest
Mixed Broad-leaved and Coniferous Woodland and Meadow } (oak, beech, fir, etc.)

Mediterranean Evergreen Forest (evergreen oak, stone pine, cork—in S.W. Europe)

Mediterranean Evergreen Maquis and Meadow (myrtle and other aromatic shrubs, olive)

Tundra (moss, lichen, heather bog, dwarf willow, birch and alder)

GRASS VEGETATION
  Grassland
  Steppe
  Salt Steppe and Semi-Desert
  Heath, Moor and Sandy Coastal Wastes
  Swamp Vegetation (liable to inundation)

DESERT VEGETATION
  Desert
  Alpine (above Timber line)

a
b

North limit of Oak (quercus robur)
Limits of Beech (fagus silvatica)
North limit of Olive (olea europaea)
East limit of Evergreen Oak (quercus ilex)
Seas and Lakes frozen in Winter

Arctic Circle

East from Greenwich

Projection: Bonne.

1 : 20 000 000

100   0   100   200   300   400   500 miles

100   0   200   400   600   800 km

Inhabitants

per mile²	per km²
under 16	under 6
16–32	6–12
32–64	12–25
64–128	25–50
128–256	50–100
256–512	100–200
over 512	over 200

Cities with over
1 000 000 inhabitants

Cities with 500 000 to
1 000 000 inhabitants

Cities with 200 000 to
500 000 inhabitants

COPYRIGHT. GEORGE PHILIP & SON, LTD.

Arctic Circle

Projection: Bonne   West from Greenwich 0 East from Greenwich

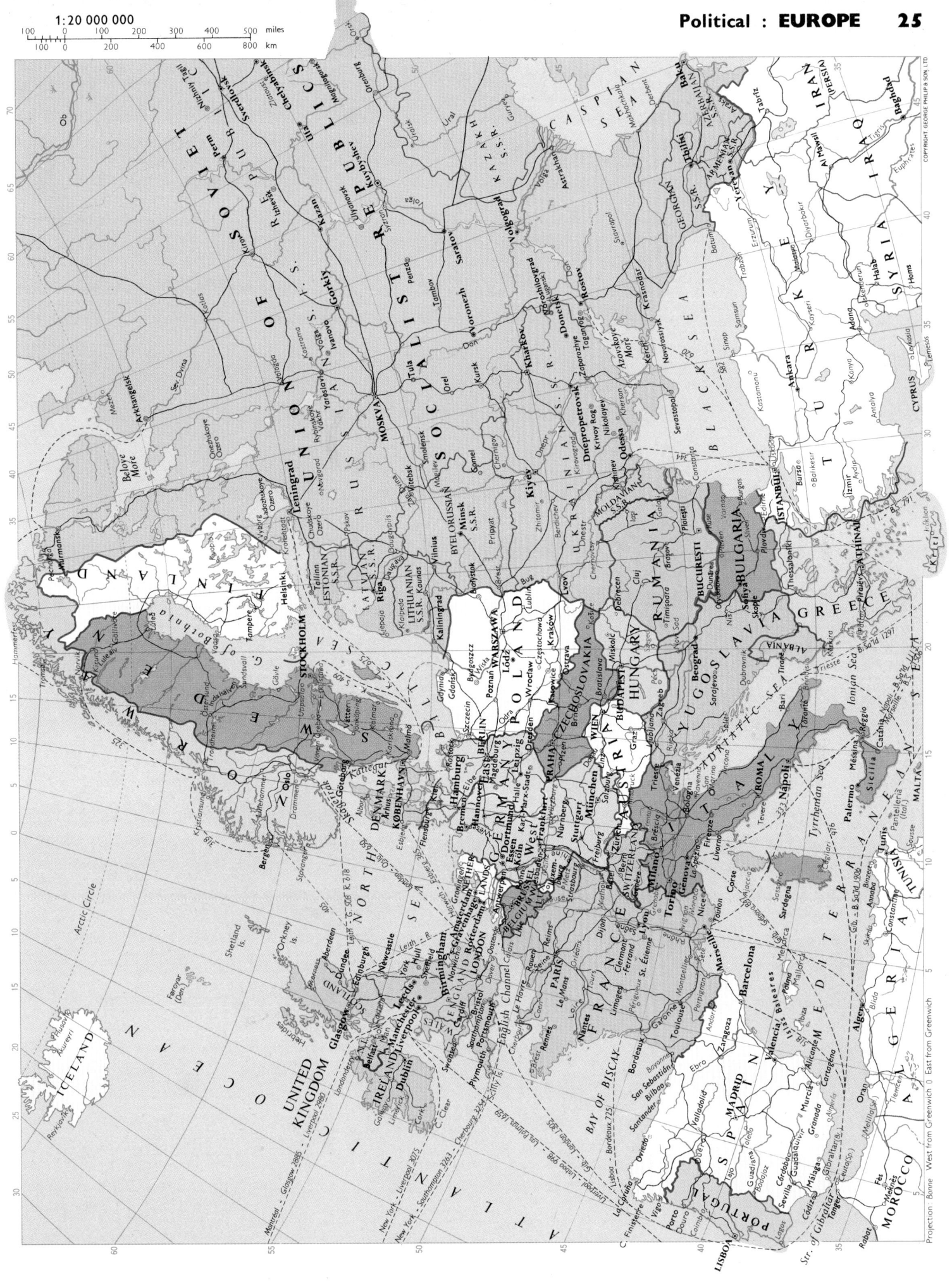
1:20 000 000
miles 100 0 100 200 300 400 500
km 100 0 200 400 600 800
UNION OF SOVIET SOCIALIST REPUBLICS
R. S. F. S. R.
FINLAND
SWEDEN
NORWAY
ESTONIAN S.S.R.
LATVIAN S.S.R.
LITHUANIAN S.S.R.
BYELORUSSIAN S.S.R.
UKRAINIAN S.S.R.
MOLDAVIAN S.S.R.
GEORGIAN S.S.R.
ARMENIAN S.S.R.
AZERBAIJAN S.S.R.
KAZAKH S.S.R.
POLAND
GERMANY
CZECHOSLOVAKIA
AUSTRIA
HUNGARY
RUMANIA
BULGARIA
YUGOSLAVIA
GREECE
ALBANIA
ITALY
SWITZERLAND
FRANCE
SPAIN
PORTUGAL
UNITED KINGDOM
IRELAND
ICELAND
DENMARK
TURKEY
SYRIA
IRAQ
IRAN (PERSIA)
CYPRUS
MALTA
TUNISIA
ALGERIA
MOROCCO
ATLANTIC OCEAN
NORTH SEA
BALTIC SEA
BLACK SEA
CASPIAN SEA
MEDITERRANEAN SEA
ADRIATIC SEA
Tyrrhenian Sea
Ionian Sea
BAY OF BISCAY
English Channel
G. of Bothnia
Arctic Circle
MOSKVA
Leningrad
STOCKHOLM
Oslo
KØBENHAVN
BERLIN
WARSZAWA
PRAHA
WIEN
BUDAPEST
BUCUREŞTI
Beograd
Sofiya
ATHÍNAI
ISTANBUL
ROMA
MADRID
LISBOA
PARIS
LONDON
Dublin
Projection: Bonne West from Greenwich 0 East from Greenwich
COPYRIGHT, GEORGE PHILIP & SON, LTD.

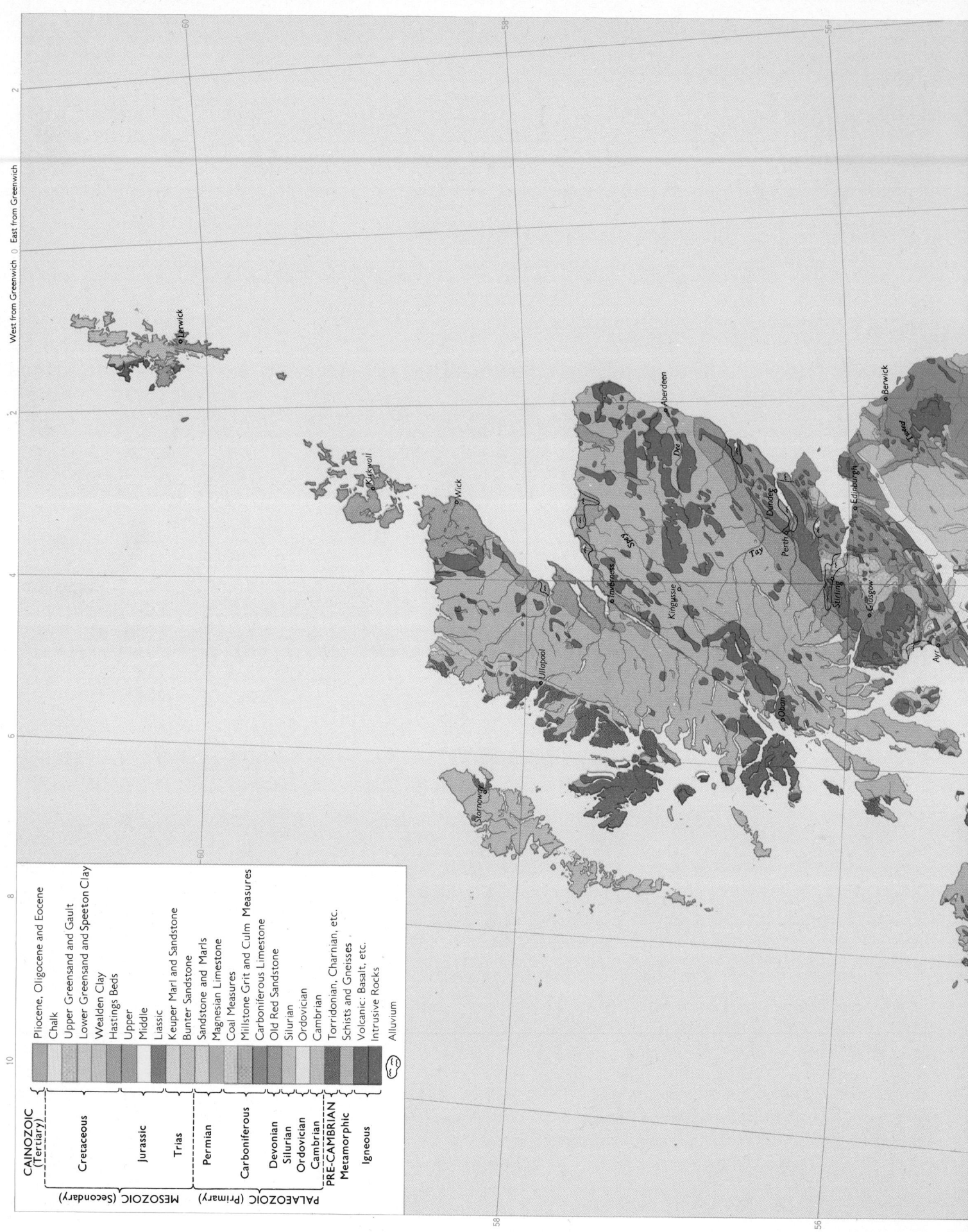

West from Greenwich | East from Greenwich

Lerwick

Kirkwall

Wick

Stornoway

Ullapool

Inverness

Kingussie

Oban

Dee

Spey

Tay

Perth

Dundee

Aberdeen

Stirling

Edinburgh

Glasgow

Tweed

Berwick

Ayr

CAINOZOIC (Tertiary)
- Pliocene, Oligocene and Eocene

Cretaceous (MESOZOIC (Secondary))
- Chalk
- Upper Greensand and Gault
- Lower Greensand and Speeton Clay
- Wealden Clay
- Hastings Beds

Jurassic
- Upper
- Middle
- Liassic

Trias
- Keuper Marl and Sandstone
- Bunter Sandstone

Permian
- Sandstone and Marls
- Magnesian Limestone

Carboniferous (PALAEOZOIC (Primary))
- Coal Measures
- Millstone Grit and Culm Measures
- Carboniferous Limestone

Devonian
- Old Red Sandstone

Silurian
- Silurian

Ordovician
- Ordovician

Cambrian
- Cambrian

PRE-CAMBRIAN
Metamorphic
- Torridonian, Charnian, etc.
- Schists and Gneisses

Igneous
- Volcanic: Basalt, etc.
- Intrusive Rocks

Alluvium

1:3 250 000

20 10   0   20   40   60   miles

20 10 0   20   40   60   80   100   km

COPYRIGHT GEORGE PHILIP & SON, LTD.

Projection : *Conical with two standard parallels*

Newcastle

Tyne

Carlisle

Eden

Appleby

Lancaster

Wigtown

Douglas

Middlesbrough

Tees

York

Leeds

Manchester

Liverpool

Chester

Stoke

Hull

Lincoln

Sheffield

Ouse

Trent

Nottingham

Leicester

Dee

Shrewsbury

Aberystwyth

Teifi

Birmingham

Avon

Peterborough

Ouse

Nene

Norwich

Ipswich

Cambridge

London

Thames

Oxford

Reading

Severn

Gloucester

Wye

Cardiff

Swansea

Bristol

Salisbury

Southampton

Brighton

Dover

Barnstaple

Exeter

Plymouth

Le Havre

Dieppe

Rouen

Seine

Cherbourg

St. Helier

Belfast

Londonderry

Omagh

Donegal

Dundalk

Dublin

Athlone

Shannon

Limerick

Galway

Kilkenny

Barrow

Wexford

Waterford

Suir

Blackwater

Cork

LIMIT OF MAXIMUM GLACIATION

54

52

50

54

52

50

0

2

4

6

8

West from Greenwich 0 East from Greenwich

N O R T H

S E A

Devil's Hole ▾238

Unst
Fetlar
Out Skerries
Whalsay
Yell
Mainland
Bressay
St. Magnus B.
Shetland Is.
Foula
Sumburgh Hd.
Fair Isle

N Ronaldsay
Start Point
Sanday
Stronsay
Orkney Is.
Mull Head
Rousay
Westray
Mainland
Hoy
S. Ronaldsay
Hoy Sound
Penland Firth
Stroma Duncansby Hd.
Dunnet Hd.
John o'Groats
Wick

Sule Skerry
Stack Skerry
Thurso
Helmsdale

Kinnairds Hd.
Aberdeen
Girdle Ness

Ythan
Deveron
Don
Dee
Lochnagar ▲1154
North Esk
South Esk
Ben Macdhui ▲1311
Cairn Gorm ▲1245
P. of Killiecrankie
Ida
Strathmore
Sidlaw Hills
Dundee
Firth of Tay
Fife Ness
Hay I.
Bass Rock
Firth of Forth
St. Abb's Hd.
Berwick
Holy I.
Farne Is.
Tweed
The Cheviot ▲816
Coquet
Cheviot Hills

Ben More Assynt ▲998
Maven
Ben Hope ▲927
▲706
Dornoch Firth
Tarbat Ness
Beauly Firth
Conon Firth
Shin
L. Shin
Ben Wyvis ▲1045
Inverness
Strath Spey
Spey
Schiehallion ▲1081
L. Tay
L. Tummel
L. Earn
Crieff
Perth
Ochil Hills
Forth
Campsie Fells
Lammermuir Hills
Moorfoot Hills
Broad Law ▲830
Pentland Hills
Edinburgh
Lammermuir

L. Erboll
Kyle of Tongue
C. Wrath
Burt of Lewis
H I G H L A N D S
Ben Dearg ▲1081
Beinn Attow ▲998
Moray Firth
Ben Nevis ▲1345
Loch Ness
Glen More
Ben Lawers ▲1214
G R A M P I A N   M O U N T A I N S
L. Katrine
The Trossachs
L. Lomond ▲974
L. Awe
Campsie Fells
Glasgow
Clyde
Ayr
Doon

N O R T H
W E S T
Eddrachillis B.
L. Assynt
L. More Assynt
B. Broom
L. Broom
L. Maree
L. Torridon
L. Garioch
L. Etive
Ben Cruachan ▲1109
Glen Coe
Carn Eige ▲1182
Glen Affric
Ben More ▲966
Morar
Sound of Sleat
Glen Garry
Spean
L. Linnhe
Oban
Lorn
Bute
Goat Fell ▲874
Arran
Firth of Clyde
Kintyre
Ailsa Craig

N O R T H   M I N C H
Lewis
▲799
L. Langavat
Harris
L. Etive
Skye ▲1009
Cuillin Hills
Rhum
Canna
Eigg
Muck
Pt. of Ardnamurchan
Coll
Staffa
Iona
Mull
Ben More ▲966
Firth of Lorn
Sound of Jura
Jura
Colonsay
Islay
Gigha
Rathlin I.
Fair Hd.
Mull of Kintyre

I N N E R   H E B R I D E S
Little Minch
Tiree
Giant's Causeway

Flannan Is.
North Uist
Benbecula
South Uist
Barra
Barra Hd.
O U T E R   H E B R I D E S
Malin Hd.
Lough Swilly
Sheep Haven
Tory I.
Bloody Foreland

St. Kilda

A T L A N T I C   O C E A N

Sydero Bank

Faeroe Bank

Rosemary Bank

Bill Baileys Bank

Rona
Sula Sgeir
1159 ▾

1:3 250 000

20   0   20   40   60 miles

20   0   20   40   60   80   100 km

COPYRIGHT GEORGE PHILIP & SON LTD.

Projection: Conical with two standard parallels

Dogger Bank

ENGLISH CHANNEL

IRISH SEA

St. George's Channel

North Channel

PENNINES

Vale of York

Cumbrian Mts.
Lake District

Cambrian Mountains

Central Plain

m   ft
3000   1000
1200   400
600   200
300   100
0   50
0

ft   m
1000   150
400   50
200
100
50   0
0

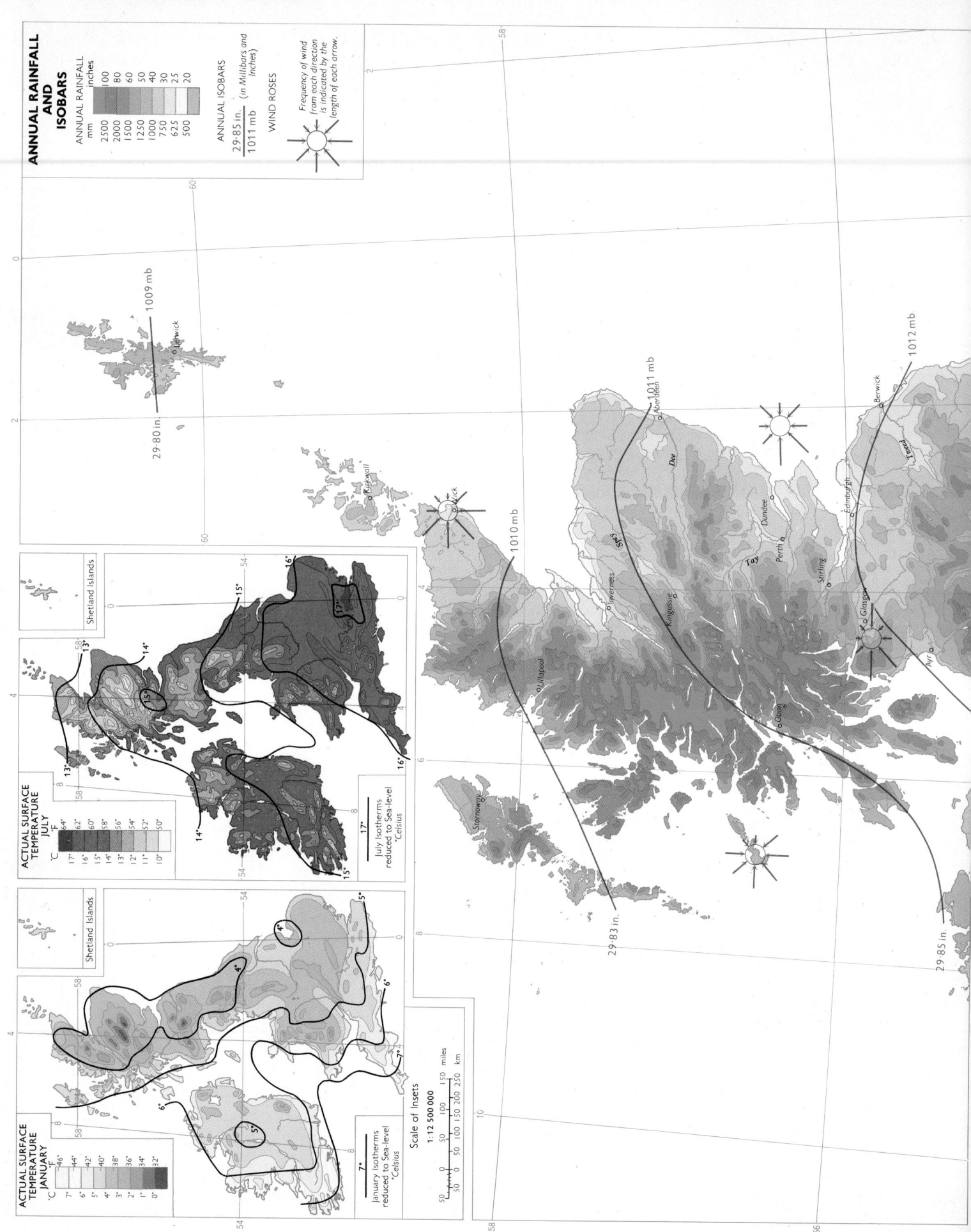

ANNUAL RAINFALL AND ISOBARS

ANNUAL RAINFALL
mm / inches
2500 / 100
2000 / 80
1500 / 60
1250 / 50
1000 / 40
750 / 30
625 / 25
500 / 20

ANNUAL ISOBARS (in Millibars and Inches)
29·85 in.
1011 mb

WIND ROSES
Frequency of wind from each direction is indicated by the length of each arrow.

ACTUAL SURFACE TEMPERATURE
JULY
°C / °F
17° / 64°
16° / 62°
15° / 60°
14° / 58°
13° / 56°
12° / 54°
11° / 52°
10° / 50°

17°
July Isotherms reduced to Sea-level °Celsius

Shetland Islands

ACTUAL SURFACE TEMPERATURE
JANUARY
°C / °F
7° / 46°
6° / 44°
5° / 42°
4° / 40°
3° / 38°
2° / 36°
1° / 34°
0° / 32°

7°
January Isotherms reduced to Sea-level °Celsius

Shetland Islands

Scale of Insets
1:12 500 000
miles
km

1009 mb
29·80 in.

Lerwick
Kirkwall
Wick
Ullapool
Stornoway
Oban
Inverness
Kingussie
Aberdeen
Dee
Dundee
Tay
Perth
Stirling
Glasgow
Ayr
Edinburgh
Berwick
Tweed

1010 mb
1011 mb
1012 mb
29·83 in.
29·85 in.

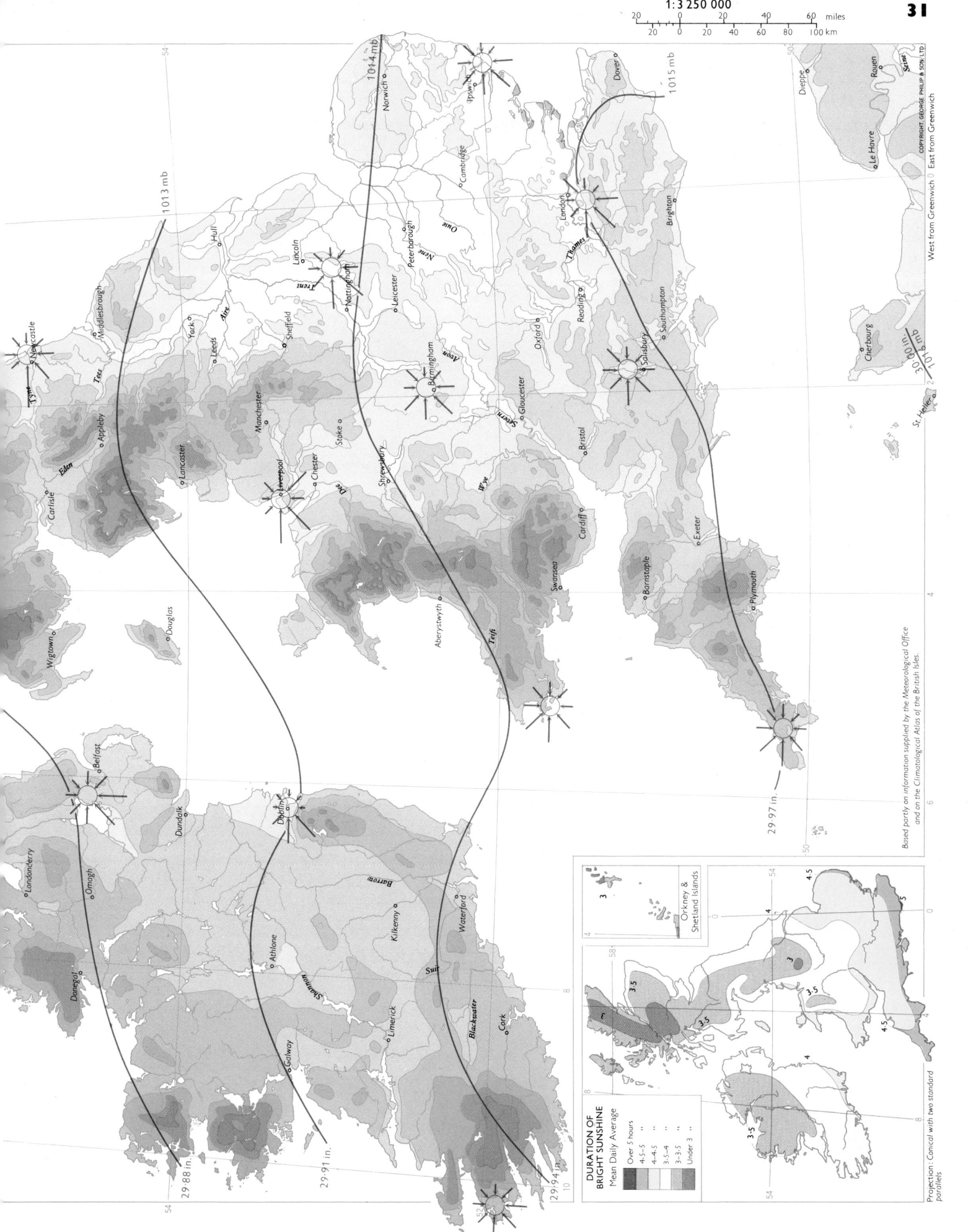

1 : 3 250 000

20   20   40   60   miles

20   0   20   40   60   80   100 km

31

1014 mb

1015 mb

1013 mb

Norwich
Ipswich
Dover
Dieppe
Rouen
Seine
Le Havre
Cambridge
Cherbourg
St. Helier

Hull
Lincoln
Nottingham
Peterborough
Nene
Ouse
Trent
London
Thames
Reading
Oxford
Brighton
Southampton
Salisbury

Newcastle
Tyne
Tees
Middlesbrough
York
Leeds
Aire
Sheffield
Manchester
Leicester
Birmingham
Avon
Gloucester
Severn
Bristol
30·00 in.
1016 mb

Appleby
Eden
Carlisle
Lancaster
Liverpool
Chester
Stoke
Dee
Shrewsbury
Wye
Cardiff
Swansea
Barnstaple
Exeter
Plymouth
29·97 in.

Wigtown
Douglas
Aberystwyth
Teifi

Belfast
Londonderry
Omagh
Dundalk
Dublin
Donegal
Athlone
Shannon
Galway
Limerick
Barrow
Kilkenny
Suir
Waterford
Blackwater
Cork
29·88 in.
29·91 in.
29·94 in.

West from Greenwich 0 East from Greenwich 2

Based partly on information supplied by the Meteorological Office and on the Climatological Atlas of the British Isles.

COPYRIGHT. GEORGE PHILIP & SON. LTD.

Projection : Conical with two standard parallels

DURATION OF BRIGHT SUNSHINE

Mean Daily Average

Over 5 hours
4·5–5   ,,
4–4·5   ,,
3·5–4   ,,
3–3·5   ,,
Under 3   ,,

Orkney &
Shetland Islands

3
3·5
4
4·5
5

1 : 4 000 000

20   20   40   60   80 miles
20   0   20 40 60 80 100 120 km

West from Greenwich   0   East from Greenwich

Inhabitants

per mile²	per km²
under 16	under 6
16–32	6–12
32–64	12–25
64–128	25–50
128–256	50–100
256–512	100–200
over 512	over 200

■ Cities with over 500 000 inhabitants

● Cities with 100 000 – 500 000 inhabitants

Projection: *Conical with two standard parallels*

COPYRIGHT. GEORGE PHILIP & SON. LTD.

1 : 4 000 000

The DISTRICTS of Northern Ireland have been numbered
and can be identified by reference to this table.

1	Londonderry	14	Craigavon
2	Limavady	15	Armagh
3	Coleraine	16	Newry & Mourne
4	Ballymoney	17	Banbridge
5	Moyle	18	Down
6	Larne	19	Lisburn
7	Ballymena	20	Antrim
8	Magherafelt	21	Newtownabbey
9	Cookstown	22	Carrickfergus
10	Strabane	23	North Down
11	Omagh	24	Ards
12	Fermanagh	25	Castlereagh
13	Dungannon	26	Belfast

1 Merseyside
2 Greater Manchester
3 West Yorkshire
4 South Yorkshire
5 West Glamorgan
6 Mid Glamorgan
7 South Glamorgan

This map shows the counties in England and Wales,
effective April 1974, the new districts in Northern Ireland,
effective October 1973 and the new counties and island
authorities of Scotland, effective April 1975. The maps of these
areas in the following pages show the county boundaries
prior to these changes.

West from Greenwich   0   East from Greenwich
COPYRIGHT. GEORGE PHILIP & SON. LTD.

Projection: Conical with two
standard parallels

1:1 000 000

Motorways
Motorways under construction

West from Greenwich
East from Greenwich

COPYRIGHT. GEORGE PHILIP & SON. LTD.

1:1 000 000

10   0   10   20 miles
10   0   10   20   30 km

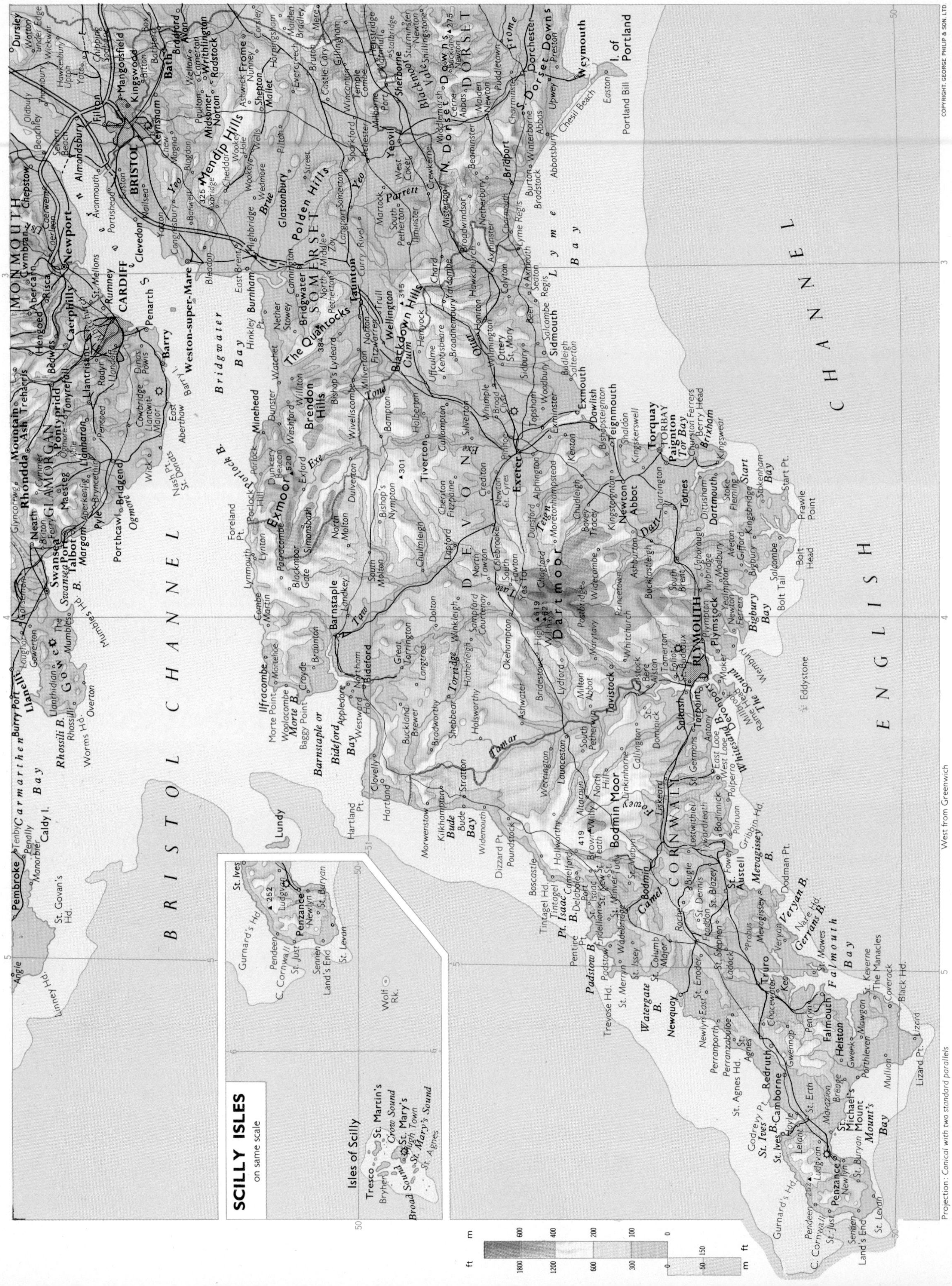

SCILLY ISLES
on same scale

Isles of Scilly

Tresco · St. Martin's
Bryher · St. Mary's
Broad Sound · St. Agnes
St. Mary's Sound

Crow Sound
Gurnard's Hd. · Ludgvan · Penzance · Newlyn
C. Cornwall · St. Just · St. Buryan
Land's End · Sennen · St. Levan

Wolf Rk.

BRISTOL CHANNEL

ENGLISH CHANNEL

MONMOUTH · GLAMORGAN · SOMERSET · DORSET · DEVON · CORNWALL

Projection: Conical with two standard parallels

West from Greenwich

Motorways

Motorways under construction

COPYRIGHT. GEORGE PHILIP & SON, LTD.

ft   m   m   ft
1800 600 0 0
1200 400 150
600   200 300
0   100

Dartmoor · Exmoor · Bodmin Moor · Mendip Hills · Blackdown Hills · Brendon Hills · The Quantocks · Polden Hills

Bristol · Cardiff · Newport · Swansea · Plymouth · Exeter · Torquay · Weymouth · Dorchester · Bridport · Yeovil · Taunton · Tiverton · Barnstaple · Bideford · Truro · Falmouth · Penzance · St. Ives · Newquay · Redruth · Camborne · Helston

Lundy

Lyme Bay · Bridgwater Bay · Barnstaple or Bideford Bay · Falmouth Bay · St. Ives Bay · Tor Bay · Start Bay · Bigbury Bay · Veryan B.

Land's End · Lizard Pt. · Start Pt. · Bolt Head · Hartland Pt. · Trevose Hd. · I. of Portland · Portland Bill · Chesil Beach

1:1 000 000

10   0   10   20 miles
10 0 10 20 30 km

Cardigan

Bay

BRISTOL CHANNEL

ANGLESEY
The Skerries
Carmel Head
Holyhead B.
Holyhead
Holy I.
Parys Mt. 128
Cemaes Bay
Amlwch
Wylfa Head
Dulas B.
Moelfre
Red Wharf B.
Llanfechell
Llanerchymedd
Pentraeth
Bodedern
Valley
Gwalchmai
Llanfaelog
Llangefni
Aberffraw
Gaerwen
Newborough
Menai Str.
Malltraeth B.
Beaumaris
Menai Bridge
Bangor
Port Dinorwic
Caernarvon
Waenfawr
Llanberis 1062
Carnedd Llewelyn
Rhaeadr Ogwen
Bethesda
Capel Curig
Dolgarrog
Penmaenmawr
Conway
Deganwy
Conwy
Gt. Ormes Hd.
Llandudno
Lit. Ormes Hd.
Rhos on Sea
Colwyn Bay
Colwyn
Abergele
Rhyl
Prestatyn
Rhuddlan
Mostyn
Holywell
St. Asaph
Trefriw
Betws-y-coed
Penmachno
Dolwyddelan
Snowdon 1085
Tal-y-sarn
Pen-y-groes
Clynnog-fawr
Llanllyfni
Beddgelert
Ffestiniog
Blaenau Ffestiniog
Maentwrog
Tremadoc
Porthmadog
Criccieth
Pwllheli
Llanystumdwy
Llanbedrog
564
Nefyn
Tudweiliog
Llyn Peninsula
Llanaelhaiarn
Rhiw
Aberdaron
Braich-y-pwll
Bardsey Sd.
Bardsey I.
Trwyn Cilan
Porth Neigwl
Aber-soch
St. Tudwal's Is.
Llanbedr
Harlech
Tremadoc Bay
Llanendwyn
Barmouth
Llanaber
Arthog
754 Llethr
Dyffryn
Fairbourne
Llwyngwril
Llangelynin
892 Cader Idris
Tal-y-llyn
Dolgellau (Dolgelley)
Corris
Abergynolwyn
Cemmes Road
Tywyn
Aberdovey
Dovey
Borth
Aberystwyth
Rheidol
Devil's Bridge
Ystwyth
Llanfihangel
Llanrhystyd
Llanon
Aberaeron
New Quay
Llanarth
Aberporth
Cemaes Hd.
Cardigan
Llangranog
Llanddewi-Brefi
Tregaron
Mynydd Bach
645
Pontrhydfendigaid
361
Reservoirs
Drygarn Fawr 645
Llanafan-fawr
Newbridge on Wye

DENBIGH
Llanfair Talhaiarn
Henllan
Denbigh
Llandyrnog
Llansannan
Bylchau
Cerrigydrudion
Pentrefoelas
Gwyddelwern
Corwen
Llandrillo
Bala
Aran Benllyn
Berwyn Mts.
Glyn Ceiriog
Llangollen
Llanarmon
Dyffryn Ceiriog 827
Llanrhaeadr-ym-Mochnant
Llanfyllin
Llanfihangel
Llanymynech
Llanblodwel

MERIONETH
Aran Fawddwy 905
Arenig Fawr 853
Trawsfynydd
Llanuwchllyn
L. Tegid (Bala L.)
Llangynog
Dinas Mawddwy
Mallwyd
Vyrnwy
L. Vyrnwy
Guilsfield
Welshpool
MONTGOMERY
Wynnstay
Berriew
Tregynon
Carno
Caersws
Newtown
Trefeglwys
Kerry
Llanfair Caereinion
Llanidloes
752 Plynlimon (Plumlimon)
Talybont
Severn
Llangurig
Rhayader
CARDIGAN
Ystbyty Ystwyth
Elan Village
Elan
RADNOR
St. Harmon
Llanbister
Llanidloes
Penybont
660 Radnor
Radnor Forest
New Radnor
Old Radnor
Presteigne
Llandrindod Wells
Hundred House
Newchurch
Builth Wells
Llandewi
Bettws Bledrws
Llanwrtyd Wells
Painscastle
Hay
Llanwddyn
Lampeter
Llanybyther
Pumsaint
Llandovery
Llanwrda
Llandeilo
Llangadog
Cilgerran
Cardigan
St. Dogmaels
Newcastle Emlyn
Cenarth
Llandysul
Llandyfriog
Adpar

CARMARTHEN
Whitland
Llandissilio
Meidrim
Carmarthen
Abergwili
Llanarthney
Llandybie
Ammanford
Cross Hands
Penygroes
Kidwelly
Llanelli
Burry Port
Pembrey
Llangennech
Pontardulais
Clydach
Gorseinon
Gowerton
Llanrhidian
Rhossili B.
Worms Hd.
Porteynon
Mumbles Hd.
Gower

PEMBROKE
St. David's Hd.
St. David's
Ramsey I.
St. Brides Bay
Solva
Camrose
Wolf's Castle
Letterston
Mathry
Strumble Hd.
Goodwick
Fishguard
Fishguard B.
Dinas Hd.
Nevern
Newport
Crymmych
Mynydd Prescelly 536
Preseli
Haverfordwest
Narberth
Templeton
Clynderwen
Llawhaden
Johnston
Milford Haven
Neyland
Pembroke Dock
Pembroke
Angle
St. Ann's Head
Dale
Skomer I.
Skokholm I.
Broad Haven
Sageston
Saundersfoot
Tenby
Penally
Manorbier
Caldy I.
St. Govan's Hd.
Laugharne
Pendine
Carmarthen Bay
Linney Hd.

GLAMORGAN
Swansea
Port Talbot
Neath
Aberdulais
Resolven
Glyn Neath
Seven Sisters
Ystradgynlais
Abercrave
Glanrhyd
Ystalyfera
Pontardawe
Glyncorrwg
Rhondda
Treorchy
Mountain Ash
Aberdare
Merthyr Tydfil
Treharris
Maesteg
Margam
Kenfig
Pyle
Bridgend
Porthcawl
Ogmore
Cowbridge
Llantwit Major
Pencoed
Llanharan
Bryncethin
Brynaman
Llandough
Penarth
Barry
Barry I.
St. Donats
Nash Pt.
Aberthaw
Dinas Powis
Llantrisant
Radyr
Llandaff
CARDIFF
Rumney
Caerphilly
Newport
Pontypridd
Taff
Taff's Well
Caerleon

BRECKNOCK
Brecon
Brecon Beacons 886
Forest Fawr
Mynydd Du (Black Mt.)
Senny Bridge
Upper Chapel
Mynydd Eppynt
Talgarth 811
Black Mountains
Crickhowell
Tretower
Llyswen

MONMOUTH
Abergavenny
Monmouth
Pontypool
Cwmbran
Blaenavon
Abertillery
Ebbw Vale
Blaina
Brynmawr
Tredegar
Rhymney
Bargoed
Hengoed
Bedwas
Risca
Abercarn
Abersychan
Crumlin
Chepstow
Raglan
Tintern
Trellech
Forest of Dean
Coleford
Mitchel Troy
Llandogo
St. Briavels

CHESHIRE
Chester
Northwich
Winsford
Tarporley
Kelsall
Tattenhall
Malpas
Nantwich
Audlem
Market Drayton
Whitchurch
Wem
Prees
Ellesmere
Overton
Chirk
Oswestry
Shawbury
Myddle
Wellington
The Wrekin 407
Shrewsbury
Westbury
Minsterley
Stiperstones 528
Pontesbury
Church Stretton
Long Mynd
The Long Mynd
Wenlock Edge
Much Wenlock
Brosely
Coalbrookdale
Ironbridge
SHROPSHIRE
Clun Forest
Clun
Clunbury
Bishop's Castle
Beguildy
Craven Arms
Bromfield
Ludlow
Wigmore
Leintwardine
Clee Hills
Ditton Priors
Corve
Tenbury
Clungunford
Leominster
Kington
Pembridge
Eardisland
Weobley
HEREFORD
Hereford
Credenhill
Dorstone
Peterchurch
Madley
Marden
Bodenham
Fownhope
Ross on Wye
Goodrich
Symonds Yat

LIVERPOOL
Bootle
St. Helens
Newton le Willows
Prescot
Wallasey
New Brighton
Huyton
Whiston
Warrington
West Kirby
Hoylake
Birkenhead
Bebington
Port Sunlight
Bromborough
Neston
Ellesmere Port
Runcorn
Widnes
Garston
Speke
Frodsham
FLINT
Flint
Connah's Quay
Mold
Buckley
Hawarden
Holt
Wrexham
Ruabon
Rhosllanerchrugog

Milford Haven
St. Brides Bay
Carmarthen Bay
Bristol Channel
Bridgwater Bay

Mersey

113

325 Mendip Hills
Weston-super-Mare
Bristol
Avonmouth
Portishead
Clevedon
Nailsea
Filton
Almondsbury
Severn Beach
Aust

ft	m
3000	1000
2400	800
1800	600
1200	400
600	200
300	100
0	0
50	150
100	300
m	ft

Projection: Conical with two standard parallels

COPYRIGHT. GEORGE PHILIP & SON LTD.

West from Greenwich

———— Motorways
==== Motorways under construction

Projection: Conical with two standard parallels

══════ Motorways
══════ Motorways under construction

1:1 000 000

Continuation
Northwards
on same scale

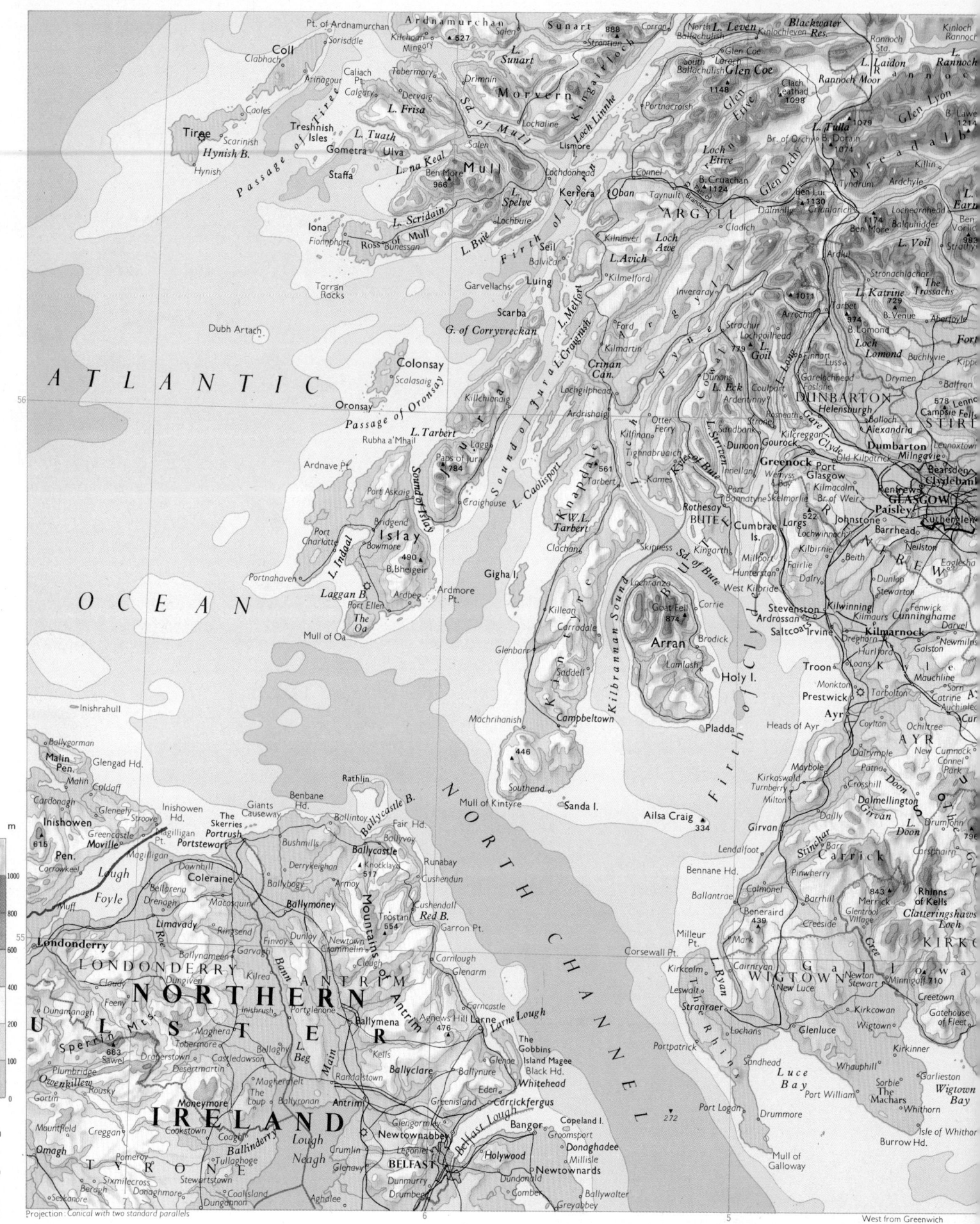

Projection: Conical with two standard parallels

West from Greenwich

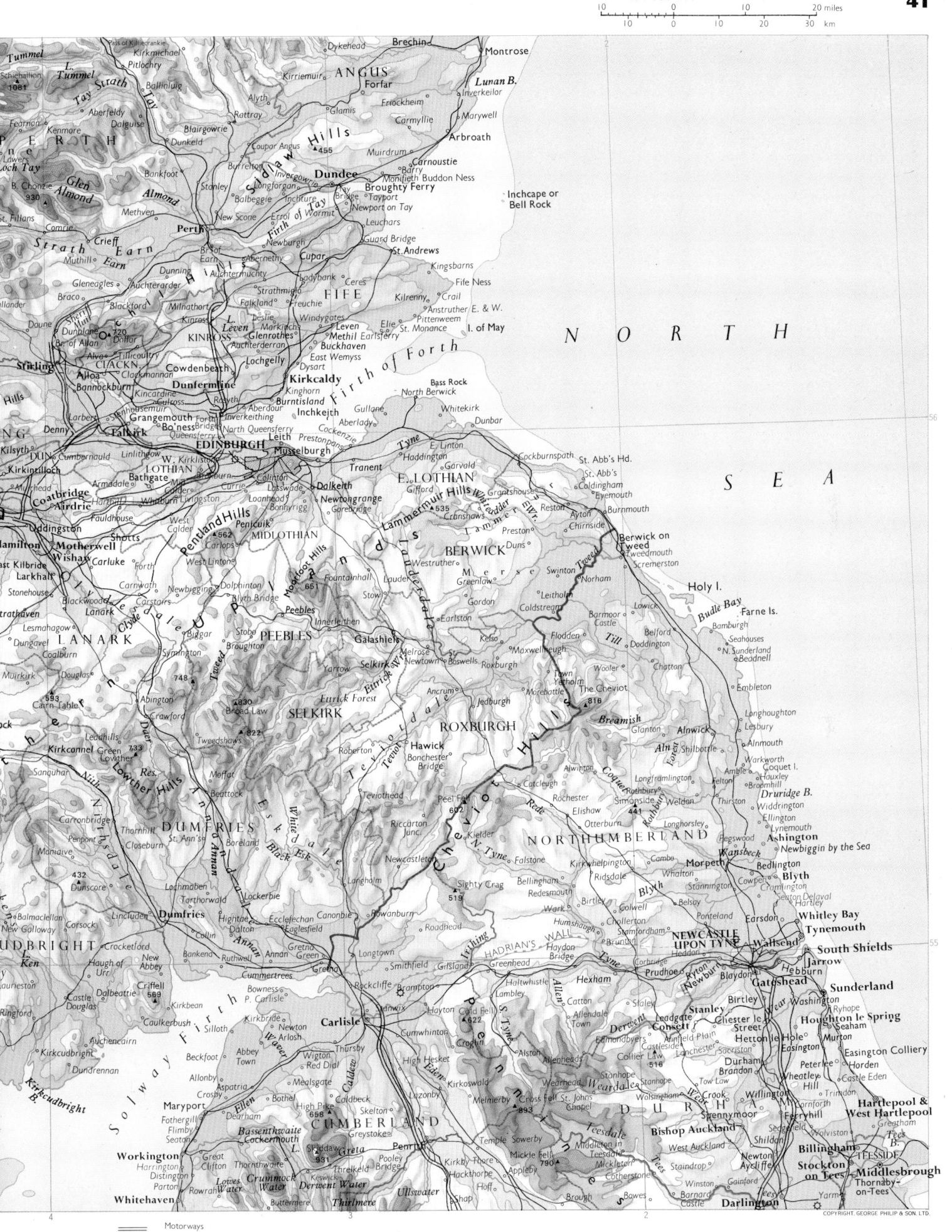

1:1 000 000

10   0   10   20 miles

10   0   10   20   30 km

NORTH

SEA

Motorways

Motorways under construction

COPYRIGHT. GEORGE PHILIP & SON. LTD.

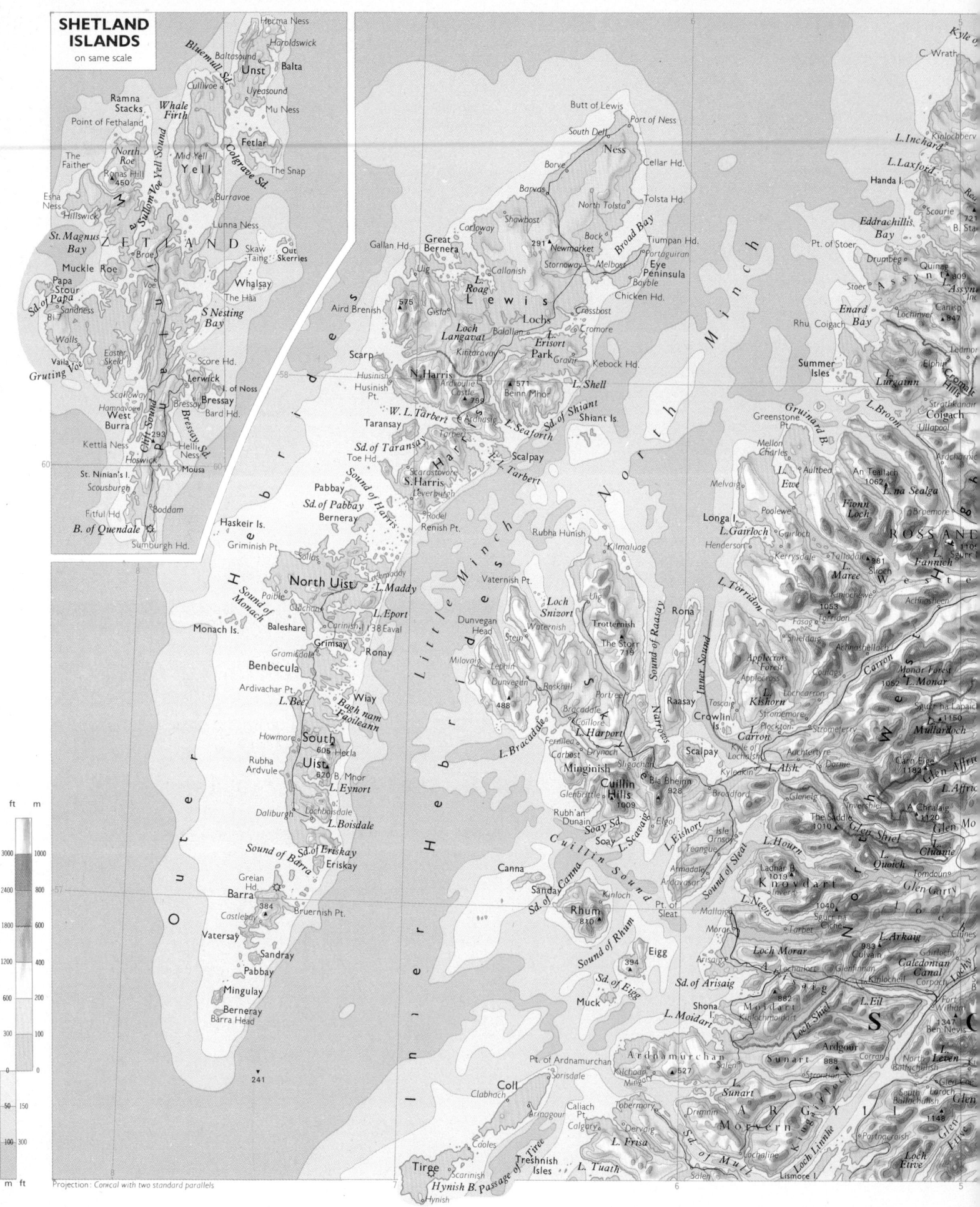

SHETLAND ISLANDS
on same scale

Hecma Ness
Haroldswick
Balta
Baltasound
Unst
Balta
Bluemull Sd.
Cullivoe
Uyeasound
Mu Ness
Ramna Stacks
Whale Firth
Fetlar
Point of Fethaland
Mid Yell
The Snap
The Faither
North Roe
Colgrave Sd.
Yell
Ronas Hill ▲450
Esha Ness
Burravoe
Hillswick
Lunna Ness
St. Magnus Bay
Brae
Skaw Taing
Out Skerries
Muckle Roe
Voe
Whalsay
Papa Stour
The Häa
Sd. of Papa
Sandness
Bl.7
S Nesting Bay
Walls
Vaila
Easter Skeld
Score Hd.
Gruting Voe
I. of Noss
Lerwick
Bressay
Scalloway
Bressay
Hamnavoe
Bard Hd.
West Burra
Helli Ness
Kettla Ness
Clift Sound
Mousa
Hoswick
St. Ninian's I.
Scousburgh
Boddam
Fitful Hd.
B. of Quendale
Sumburgh Hd.

Butt of Lewis
South Dell
Port of Ness
Ness
Borve
Cellar Hd.
Barvas
North Tolsta
Tolsta Hd.
Shawbost
Back
Broad Bay
Gallan Hd.
Great Bernera
Coruway
291▲ Newmarket
Tiumpan Hd.
Uig
Callanish
Portaguiran
Eye Peninsula
Aird Brenish
L. Roag
Stornoway
Melbost
Bayble
575▲
Gisla
Lewis
Lochs
Chicken Hd.
Scarp
Loch Langavat
Balallan
L. Erisort
Crossbost
Park
Cromore
Husinish
Kintaravay
Gravir
Kebock Hd.
N. Harris
Ardvoulie Castle
571▲
L. Shell
Husinish Pt.
789▲
Beinn Mhor
W. L. Tarbert
Ardhasig
L. Seaforth
Sd. of Shiant
Taransay
Tarbert
Shiant Is.
Sd. of Taransay
E. L. Tarbert
Toe Hd.
Harris
Scalpay
Scarastavore
S. Harris
Leverburgh
Pabbay
Rodel
Sd. of Pabbay
Renish Pt.
Berneray
Rubha Hunish
Haskeir Is.
Griminish Pt.
Kilmaluag
Sollas
Vaternish Pt.
North Uist
Lochmaddy
L. Maddy
Vaternish Pt.
Paible
Clachan
Loch Snizort
Uig
Trotternish
Rona
Sound of Monach
L. Eport
138 Eaval
Dunvegan Head
Waternish
The Storr 719
Monach Is.
Baleshare
Carinish
Stein
Sound of Raasay
Gramisdale
Grimsay
Ronay
Milovaig
Lephin
Roskhill
Benbecula
Wiay
Bagh nam Faoileann
Dunvegan
488
Bracadale
Portree
Raasay
Ardivachar Pt.
Coillore
Crowlin Is.
L. Bee
S K Y E
L. Harport
Scalpay
Howmore
Bracadale
Carbost
Kyle of Lochalsh
South Uist
605 Hecla
Drynoch
Sligachan
L. Carron
L. Eynort
Minginish
Bla Bheinn 928
820 B. Mhor
Cuillin Hills 1009
Broadford
Daliburgh
Lochboisdale
Glenbrittle
Elgol
L. Boisdale
Rubh'an Dunain
Soay Sd.
L. Scavaig
Soay
L. Eishort
Isle Ornsay
Sound of Barra
Sd. of Eriskay
Eriskay
Canna
Sanday
Teangue
Greian Hd.
Armadale
Barra
Kinloch
Ardvasar
Sound of Sleat
Castlebay
384
Rhum 810
Pt. of Sleat
Vatersay
Sd. of Canna
Mallaig
Sandray
Canna Sound
Pabbay
Eigg
394
Mingulay
Sd. of Eigg
Berneray
Barra Head
Muck
Sd. of Arisaig
Sorisdale
Coll
241
Pt. of Ardnamurchan
Kilchoan
Ardnamurchan
527
Mingary
Clabhach
Salen
Caliach Pt.
Calgary
Shona
L. Moidart
Sunart
Ardgour
Arinagour
Tobermory
Sunart
Morvern
Tiree
Dervaig
L. Frisa
Scarinish
Treshnish Isles
L. Tuath
Caoles
Hynish B.
passage of Tiree
Hynish

C. Wrath
Kyle of
Kinlochbervie
L. Inchard
L. Laxford
Handa I.
Scourie
Eddrachillis Bay
Drumbeg
Quinag
Stoer
Pt. of Stoer
Assynt
809
Assynt
Canisp 847▲
Rhu Coigach
Lochinver
Enard Bay
Elphin
Coigach Hills
Summer Isles
Ullapool
L. Lurgainn
L. Broom
Greenstone Pt.
Gruinard B.
Coigach
Mellon Charles
Mellon Udrigle
An Teallach 1062▲
Aultbea
L. na Sealga
Longa I.
L. Ewe
Poolewe
ROSS AND
Gairloch
Bruachmore
L. Gairloch
Fionn Loch
Kerrysdale
981▲
Talladale
Slioch
Fannich
L. Maree
1053
Kinlochewe
Torridon
W E S T E R
L. Torridon
Shieldag
Achnasheen
Applecross Forest
Coulags
1052
Monar Forest
Applecross
Carron
L. Monar
Toscaig
L. Kishorn
Lochcarron
Kishorn
Stromemore
1150
Strome ferry
Mullardoch
Plockton
L. Carron
Carn Eige 1183
Glen Affric
Kyle of Lochalsh
L. Affric
Kyleakin
Auchtertyre
L. Alsh
Dornie
Glenelg
Glen Mo
A' Chralaig 1120
Glen Shiel
The Saddle 1010
Glen Mo
L. Hourn
Inverie
Knoydart
953▲
L. Quoich
Ladhar B. 1019
Tomdoun
Glen Garry
1040
L. Arkaig
L. Nevis
Sgurr na Ciche
Colvin
Tarbet
Glenfinnan
Caledonian Canal
Arisaig
Loch Morar
Kinlocharloch
Glenfinnan
Corpach
L. Lochy
Kinlochen
L. Shiel
862
L. Eil
Moidart
Kinlochmoidart
Fort Will
1347
Ben Nevis
Corran
888
Strontian
Ardgour
North Ballachulish
Leven
L. Sunart
Argyll
L. Linnhe
Lochaline
1148
Drimnin
Sd. of Mull
South Ballachulish
Loch Leven
Portnacroish
Lismore I.
Loch Etive

Scale (ft / m):
3000 / 1000
2400 / 800
1800 / 600
1200 / 400
600 / 200
300 / 100
0 / 0
50 / 150
100 / 300
m / ft

1:1 000 000

10   0   10   20 miles

10   0   10   20   30 km

ORKNEY ISLANDS
on same scale

Pentland Firth

Stroma

Mull Hd.   Papa   Hollandstoun   Dennis Hd.

Noup Hd.   Pierowall   Westray   N. Ronaldsay

Westray   The North Sound   N. Ronaldsay Firth

Berst Ness   Rapness   Overbister   Start Pt.

Sacquoy Hd.   Westray Firth   Eday   Sanday

Wasbister   Rousay   Sanday Sound

Brough Hd.   Eynhallow Sd.   Brinyan   Papa Stronsay

Twatt   Egilsay   Whitehall   Stronsay

Redland   Wyre   Stronsay   Auskerry

L. of Harray   Dounby   Gairsay   Lamb Hd.

Voy   Finstown   Shapinsay   Y Firth

O R K   Wide Firth   N. Y

L. of Stenness   Kirkwall   Shapinsay Sd.

Stromness   Mainland   Deer Sd.   Mull Hd.

Graemsay   Hoy   St. Mary's   Deerness

Old Man   Ward Hill   Orphir   Gritley

of Hoy   477   Pt. of Ayre

Rora Hd.   Scapa Flow   Copinsay

Rackwick   Hoy   Burray   Rose Ness

Flotta   St. Margaret's Hope

Lyness   South Ronaldsay

Hurliness   S. Walls

Tor Ness   Swona   Cleat

Pentland Firth

Dunnet Hd.   Stroma   Pentland Skerries

Mey   John o'Groats   Duncansby Hd.

Canisbay

58

59

57

SUTHERLAND

CAITHNESS

Pentland Firth

Stroma

Holborn Hd.   Dunnet B.   Mey   John o'   Duncansby Hd.

Scrabster   Dunnet   Groats   Duncansby

Strathy Pt.   Thurso B.   Castletown   Freswick

Portskerra   Thurso   Sortat   Nybster

Strathy   Reay   Dounreay   Halkirk   Keiss

Melvich   Dalhalvaig   Olgrinmore   Hastigrow   Sinclair's B.

Bettyhill   Craigtown   Watten   Wick   Reiss   Noss Head

Forsinain   Staxigoe

Forsinard   Wick

Strath Halladale   Mybster   Thrumster

Kyle of Tongue   Strathy   Achavanich   Ulbster

Whiten Hd.   Faraid Hd.   Durness   Lybster

L. Eriboll   Heilam   Tongue   Braemore   705   Lybster

Loch Hope   Bogie   Loch Loyal   Marven   Dunbeath

927   B. 763   Berriedale

908   Ben Hope   B. Loyal   Kildonan   628   Ord of Caithness

Strathmore   L. Naver   L. nan Clar   B. Dhorain   Ousdale

L. Hee   B. Klibreck   Kinbrace   Helmsdale

Altnaharra   961

998   Loch   Brora

Ben More   Shin   Brora

Assynt   L. Brora

Kinloch   Lairg   Golspie

Rosehall   Shin   Fleet   L. Fleet   Embo

Oykel Br.   Auchness   Torroboll   Dornoch

Invershin   Culrain   Clashmore   Dornoch Firth

Bonarbridge   Tarbat Ness

Kincardine   Portmahomack

EASTER ROSS

Freevater Forest   Garron   Edderton   Tain   Balintore

Rosehall   B. Tharsuinn   Fearn

1081   692   Balnapaling

CROMARTY

B. Wyvis   Alness   Nigg   Moray Firth

1045   Evanton   Invergordon B.

ROSS   Strathpeffer   Cromarty Firth

L. Luichart   Dingwall   Balblair   Cromarty

Contin   Black   Rosemarkie

Isle   Fortrose   Campbeltown   Nairn

Glen Orrin   Muir of Ord   Avoch   Auldearn   Forres

Beauly F.   Nth. Kessock   Littlemill

Beauly   Culloden   **NAIRN**   Dallas   Rothes

1083   Stray   Moor   Cawdor   Kellas   Craigellachie

The Aird   **Inverness**   Ferness   **MORAY**

Caledonian Canal   Nairn   Findhorn   Archiestown

Cannich   Strath Glass   Dores   Cragga   Lettoch

Affric   Milton   Farr   Carn

Lewiston   L.   Moy   Glas-choire

Mealfuarvonie   Duntelchaig   Tomatin   659   Dulnain Bridge

696   Foyers   Torness   Carrbridge

Invermoriston   Errogie   Carn na   Boat of

Saobhaidhe   Garten   Nethy Bridge

Fort Augustus   810   White Bridge   Aviemore

Monadhliath Mts.   Alvie

Carn Ban   Kincraig   Cairn Gorm

941   Kingussie   1245

Newtonmore   **Cairngorm Mts.**

INVERNESS   Ruthven   1295   1311

L. Garry   Laggan   Braeriach   B. Macdhui

Invergarry   Lochloggan Hotel

Creag Meagaidh   Dalwhinnie

L. Lochy   1128   **Grampian**

Roybridge   Glen   **Mountains**   B. Dearg   1008

Laggan   Spean   Forest of Atholl   Beinn a' Ghlo   1121

L. Treig   B. Alder   1148   Glen Garry   Blair Atholl

Blackwater Res.   L. Ericht   Errochty

Kinloch   Pass of   Killiecrankie

Clach   Rannoch   Tummel   Kirkmichael

Leathad   L. Laidon   L. Rannoch   Tummel   Pitlochry

1098   Rannoch Sta.   Schiehallion   Ballinluig

Coe   Rannoch Moor   1081   Tummel   **PERTH**

1079   B. Lawers   Tay Strath   Aberfeldy   Dalguise

Br. of Orchy   Tulla   1214   Dunkeld

1074   Glen Lyon   Kenmore   Blairgowrie

Breadalbane   L. Tay   Bankfoot

Moray Firth

Branderburgh   Spey B.   Findochty   Portknockie   Troup Hd.   Rosehearty   Kinnairds Hd.

Lossiemouth   Buckie   Cullen   Portsoy   Rosehearty   Fraserburgh

Burghead   Hopeman   Spey Bay   Banff   Macduff   Gardenstown   Inverallochy

Burghead B.   Garmouth   Portgordon   Fordyce   New   St. Combs

Findhorn   Shanbryde   Aberdour

Kinloss   Elgin   Fochabers   Witchburn   Newbyth   New   Rathen   Crimond

Forres   Newmill   Aberchirder   Pitsligo   Rattray Hd.

Keith   Fortie   **Buchan**   Strichen   St. Fergus

840   Deveron   Turriff   New Aberdour   Mintlaw   Peterhead

Dufftown   Loggie   Rothienorman   Maud   Old Deer   Longside

Charlestown of Aberlour   Huntly   Fyvie   New Deer   Boddam

Hills of Cromdale   **Strathbogie**   Badenscoth   Methlick   Buchan Ness

Cabrach   Rhynie   Colpy   Ythan   Hatton   Port Erroll

Grantown-on-Spey   **Strath Avon**   722   Lumsden   Insch   **Formartine**

Spey   Tomnavoulin   The Buck   Oldmeldrum   Newburgh

Tomintoul   Kenmay   **Aberdeen**

863   Strathdon   Alford   Inverurie

Carn Mor   Ardwell   Monymusk   Kintore   Dyce   Balmedie

Ladder Hills   **BANFF**   Don   Ordhead   Bankhead   Bridge of Don

Avon   Don   **Mar**   Torphins   Buckstown   **Aberdeen**

Morven   Tarland   Lumphanan   Echt   Cults   Girdle Ness

872   Ordie   Aboyne   Banchory   Peterculter   Cove Bay

B. Avon   Crathie   **Braemar**   Ballater   Dee   Strachan   Cammachmore

1171   Dee   Balmoral Castle   Muchalls

Braemar   Balmoral Forest   Mt. Keen   **KINCARDINE**   Skatterare   Stonehaven

1154   Lochnagar   938   Spitalburn   57

Glas Maol   **Braes of Angus**   North Esk   Auchenblae

1067   Glen Esk   Howe of the Mearns   Inverbervie

Mountains   Clova   Fettercairn   Laurencekirk   Gourdon

Glen Shee   South Esk   Rottal   Edzell   Johnshaven

Grampian   Isla   Glen Esk   Marykirk   St. Cyrus

LOWLAND   Kirriemuir   Brechin   **NORTH**

Alyth   **ANGUS**   Dykehead   Friockheim   Lunan B.   Inverkeilor

Rattray   Forfar   Marywell

Glamis   **SEA**

Coupar Angus   **Sidlaw Hills**   455   Muirdrum   Carmyllie   Arbroath

Burrelton   Carnoustie

West from Greenwich   3   Monifieth Buddon Ness

Dundee   Broughty Ferry

COPYRIGHT GEORGE PHILIP & SON LTD.

4

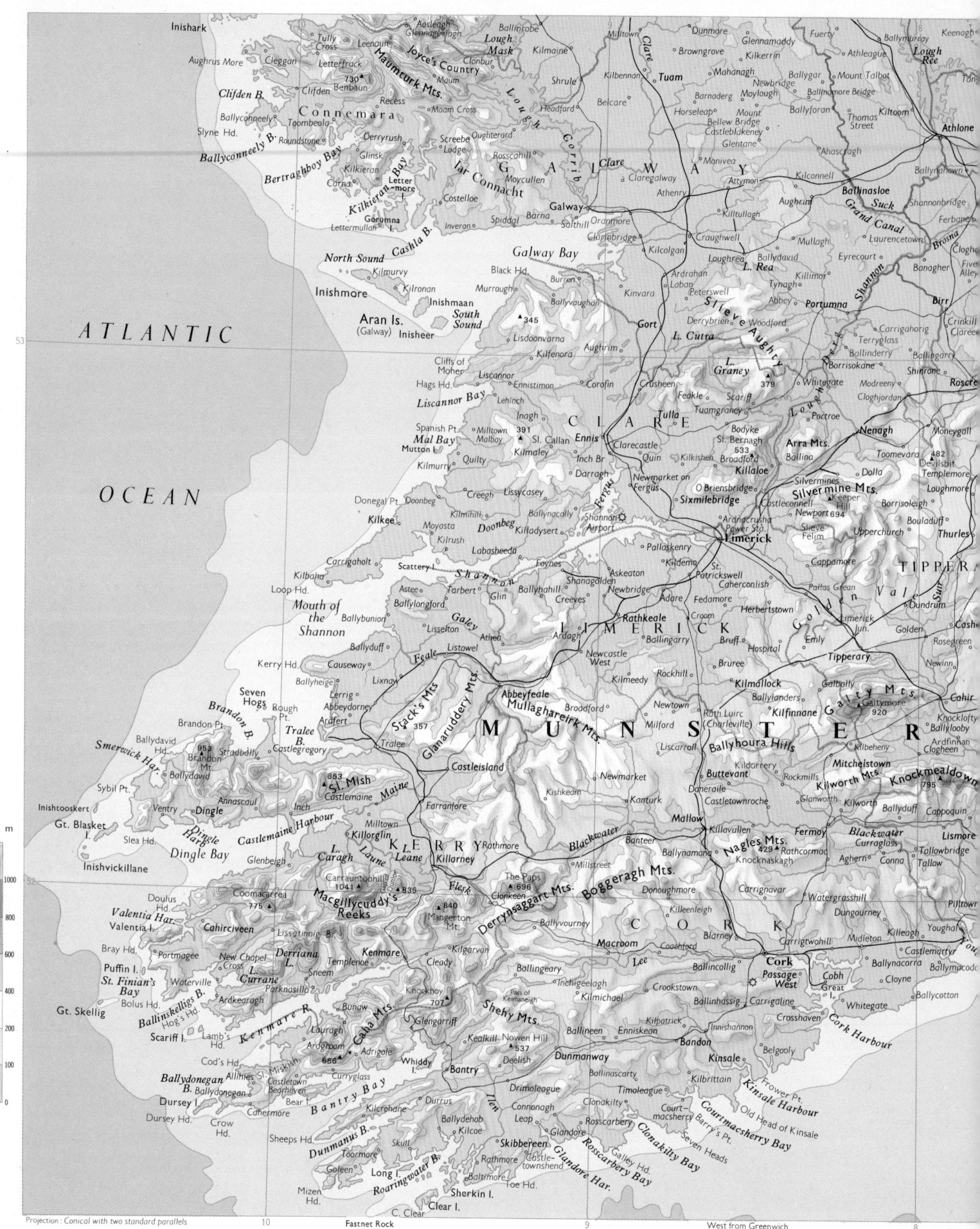
ATLANTIC
OCEAN
Inishark
Aughrus More
Cleggan
Clifden B.
Clifden
Ballyconneely
Slyne Hd.
Ballyconneely B.
Roundstone
Toombeola
Connemara
Bertraghboy Bay
Derryrush
Glinsk
Kilkieran
Carna
Kilkieran Bay
Letter-more
Gorumna I.
Lettermullan
Cashla B.
North Sound
Kilmurvy
Kilronan
Inishmore
Inishmaan
Aran Is. (Galway)
Inisheer
South Sound
Tully Cross
Letterfrack
Leenaun
Benbaun
Maumturk Mts.
Joyce's Country
Maum
Recess
Maam Cross
Screebe Lodge
Oughterard
Rosscahill
Iar Connacht
Moycullen
Costelloe
Inverin
Spiddal
Barna
Salthill
Galway
Lough Corrib
Lough Mask
Ballinrobe
Kilmaine
Clonbur
Shrule
Headford
Aasleagh
Glennagevlagh
Milltown
Clare
Kilbennan
Tuam
Belcare
Dunmore
Brownsgrove
Glennamaddy
Kilkerrin
Mahanagh
Newbridge
Moylough
Barnaderg
Horseleap
Mount Bellew Bridge
Castleblakeney
Glentane
Ballygar
Mount Talbot
Ballinmore Bridge
Ballyforan
Thomas Street
Kiltoom
Fuerty
Athleague
Ballymurray
Lough Ree
Keenagh
Athlone
Ahascragh
Monivea
G A L W A Y
Claregalway
Athenry
Attymon
Kilconnell
Ballinasloe
Suck
Grand Canal
Aughrim
Shannonbridge
Ferbane
Kiltullagh
Oranmore
Clarinbridge
Kilcolgan
Craughwell
Mullagh
Laurencetown
Brosna
Galway Bay
Black Hd.
Burren
Kinvara
Ardrahan
Labane
Loughrea
L. Rea
Ballydavid
Eyrecourt
Killimor
Tynagh
Banagher
Peterswell
Slieve Aughty
Abbey
Portumna
Shannon
Birr
Murrough
Ballyvaughan
345
Lisdoonvarna
Kilfenora
Aughrim
Gort
L. Cutra
Derrybrien
Woodford
Carrigahorig
Terryglass
Ballinderry
Borrisokane
Lough Derg
Shinrone
Roscrea
Cliffs of Moher
Liscannor
Hags Hd.
Ennistimon
Corofin
Liscannor Bay
Lehinch
Crusheen
L. Graney
379
Feakle
Scarriff
Tulla
Tuamgraney
Whitegate
Modreeny
Cloghjordan
Portroe
Spanish Pt.
Mal Bay
Mutton I.
Milltown Malbay
Inagh
391
Sl. Callan
Kilmaley
CLARE
Ennis
Clarecastle
Quin
Inch Br
Kilkishen
Bodyke
Sl. Bernagh
533
Broadford
Killaloe
Arra Mts.
Ballina
Nenagh
Moneygall
Toomevara
482
Devilsbit
Templemore
Kilmurry
Quilty
Darragh
Newmarket on Fergus
O'Briensbridge
Sixmilebridge
Silvermines
Silvermine Mts.
Keeper Hill
694
Loughmore
Castleconnell
Newport
Borrisoleigh
Donegal Pt.
Doonbeg
Creegh
Lissycasey
Kilkee
Kilmihil
Moyasta
Kilrush
Doonbeg
Ballynacally
Killadysert
Fergus
Shannon Airport
Ardnacrusha Power Sta.
Limerick
Slieve Felim
Upperchurch
Bouladuff
Thurles
Labasheeda
Pallaskenry
Kildemo
Carrigaholt
Scattery I.
Shannon
Foynes
Askeaton
Kilbaha
Loop Hd.
Astee
Tarbert
Glin
Ballyhahill
Shanagolden
Newbridge
St. Patrickswell
Caherconlish
Cappamore
TIPPERA
Ballylongford
Creeves
Adare
Fedamore
Pallas Grean
Vale
Golden
Mouth of the Shannon
Ballybunion
Galey
Lisselton
Athea
Rathkeale
LIMERICK
Ardagh
Ballingarry
Croom
Herbertstown
Limerick Jn.
Dundrum
Suir
Ballyduff
Listowel
Feale
Newcastle West
Bruff
Hospital
Emly
Golden
Cashel
Rosegreen
Tipperary
Newinn
Kerry Hd.
Causeway
Ballyheige
Lixnaw
Kilmeedy
Rockhill
Bruree
Kilmallock
Galbally
Galty Mts.
Galtymore
920
Cahir
Seven Hogs
Rough Pt.
Lerrig
Abbeydorney
Ardfert
Stack's Mts.
357
Glanaruddery Mts.
Abbeyfeale
Mullaghareirk Mts.
Broadford
Newtown
Ballylanders
Kilfinnane
Knocklofty
Ballylooby
Brandon B.
Brandon Pt.
Ballydavid Hd.
Tralee B.
Tralee
Castlegregory
MUNSTER
Milford
Rath Luirc (Charleville)
Ardfinnan
Clogheen
Smerwick Har.
953
Brandon Mt.
Stradbally
Liscarroll
Ballyhoura Hills
Kilbeheny
Mitchelstown
Ballydavid
Castleisland
Kildorrery
Buttevant
Rockmills
Kilworth Mts.
Knockmealdown
795
Sybil Pt.
853
Sl. Mish
Castlemaine
Maine
Newmarket
Doneraile
Castletownroche
Glanworth
Kilworth
Ballyduff
Cappoquin
Inishtooskert
Ventry
Dingle
Annascaul
Inch
Farranfore
Kishkeam
Kanturk
Gt. Blasket I.
Castlemaine Harbour
Milltown
Killorglin
Mallow
Killavullen
Fermoy
Blackwater
Curraglass
Lismore
Slea Hd.
Dingle Har.
Dingle Bay
KERRY
Rathmore
Blackwater
Banteer
Nagles Mts.
429
Rathcormac
Tallowbridge
Inishvickillane
Glenbeigh
L. Caragh
Laune
L. Leane
Killarney
Millstreet
Ballynamona
Knocknaskagh
Aghern
Conna
Tallow
Carrauntoohill
1041
835
Macgillycuddy's Reeks
Flesk
The Paps
696
Clonkeen
Boggeragh Mts.
Donoughmore
Carrignavar
Watergrasshill
Piltown
Doulus Hd.
Coomacarrea
775
840
Mangerton Mt.
Derrynasaggart Mts.
Killeenleigh
Dungourney
Valentia Har.
Valentia I.
Cahirciveen
Lissatinnig Br.
Ballyvourney
CORK
Carrigtwohill
Midleton
Killeagh
Youghal
Bray Hd.
Portmagee
New Chapel Cross
Derriana L.
Kenmare
Kilgarvan
Macroom
Coachford
Blarney
Cork
Castlemartyr
Puffin I.
St. Finian's Bay
Waterville
L. Currane
Templenoe
Sneem
Parknasilla
Cleady
Ballingeary
Inchigeelagh
Lee
Ballincollig
Passage West
Cobh
Great I.
Ballynacorra
Ballymacoda
Cloyne
Ballycotton
Bolus Hd.
Ballinskelligs B.
Hog's Hd.
Ardkearagh
Knockboy
707
Pass of Keimaneigh
Kilmichael
Crookstown
Ballinhassig
Carrigaline
Whitegate
Gt. Skellig
Kenmare R.
Bunaw
Caha Mts.
Glengarriff
Shehy Mts.
Crosshaven
Cork Harbour
Scariff I.
Lamb's Hd.
Lauragh
Ardgroom
686
Adrigole
Kealkill
Nowen Hill
537
Ballineen
Enniskean
Kilpatrick
Innishannon
Bandon
Cod's Hd.
Whiddy I.
Deelish
Dunmanway
Kinsale
Belgooly
Ballydonegan B.
Ballydonegan
Allihies
Sl. Miskish
Castletown Bearhaven
Curryglass
Bantry
Ballinascarty
Kilbrittain
Kinsale Harbour
Dursey I.
Dursey Hd.
Cahermore
Bear I.
Bantry Bay
Kilcrohane
Durrus
Drimoleague
Timoleague
Frower Pt.
Connonagh
Clonakilty
Court-macsherry
Old Head of Kinsale
Courtmacsherry Bay
Crow Hd.
Sheeps Hd.
Dunmanus B.
Ballydehob
Kilcoe
Leap
Rosscarbery
Barry's Pt.
Seven Heads
Ilen
Skull
Skibbereen
Glandore
Clonakilty Bay
Toormore
Goleen
Long I.
Roaringwater B.
Rathmore
Castle-townshend
Rosscarbery Bay
Glandore Har.
Galley Hd.
Mizen Hd.
Baltimore
Toe Hd.
Sherkin I.
Clear I.
C. Clear
Fastnet Rock
Projection: Conical with two standard parallels
West from Greenwich
53
52
10
9
8
ft
m
3000
2400
1800
1200
600
300
1000
800
600
400
200
100
0
50
150
100
300
m
ft

1:1 000 000

10   0   10   20 miles
10   0   10   20   30 km

IRISH SEA

WESTMEATH

OFFALY

LEINSTER

LAOIS

KILDARE

WICKLOW

CARLOW

KILKENNY

WEXFORD

WATERFORD

DUBLIN (Baile Atha Cliath)

Dún Laoghaire (Dunleary)

Mullingar
Tullamore
Port Laoise
Kilkenny
Carlow
Wicklow
Arklow
Wexford
Waterford
New Ross
Enniscorthy
Clonmel

Grand Canal
Royal Canal
Bog of Allen
Slieve Bloom
Wicklow Mountains
Blackstairs Mt.
Mt. Leinster 796
Lugnaquillia 926
Comeragh Mts.
Monavullagh Mts.

Rosslare Harbour
Carnsore Pt.
Saltee Is.
Hook Hd.
Tramore Bay
Dungarvan Harbour

Continuation North-West on same scale

CONNACHT
MAYO

Achill I.
Clare I.
Clew Bay
Westport
Newport
Castlebar
Croaghpatrick
NephinBeg Range
Carrowmore L.
L. Conn
L. Cullin
Belmullet
Erris Hd.
Broad Haven
Downpatrick Hd.
Killala B.
Ballina
Killary Har.
Lough Mask
Lough Corrib
Maumturk Mts.
Joyce's Country
Partry Mts.
Clifden B.

COPYRIGHT GEORGE PHILIP & SON LTD

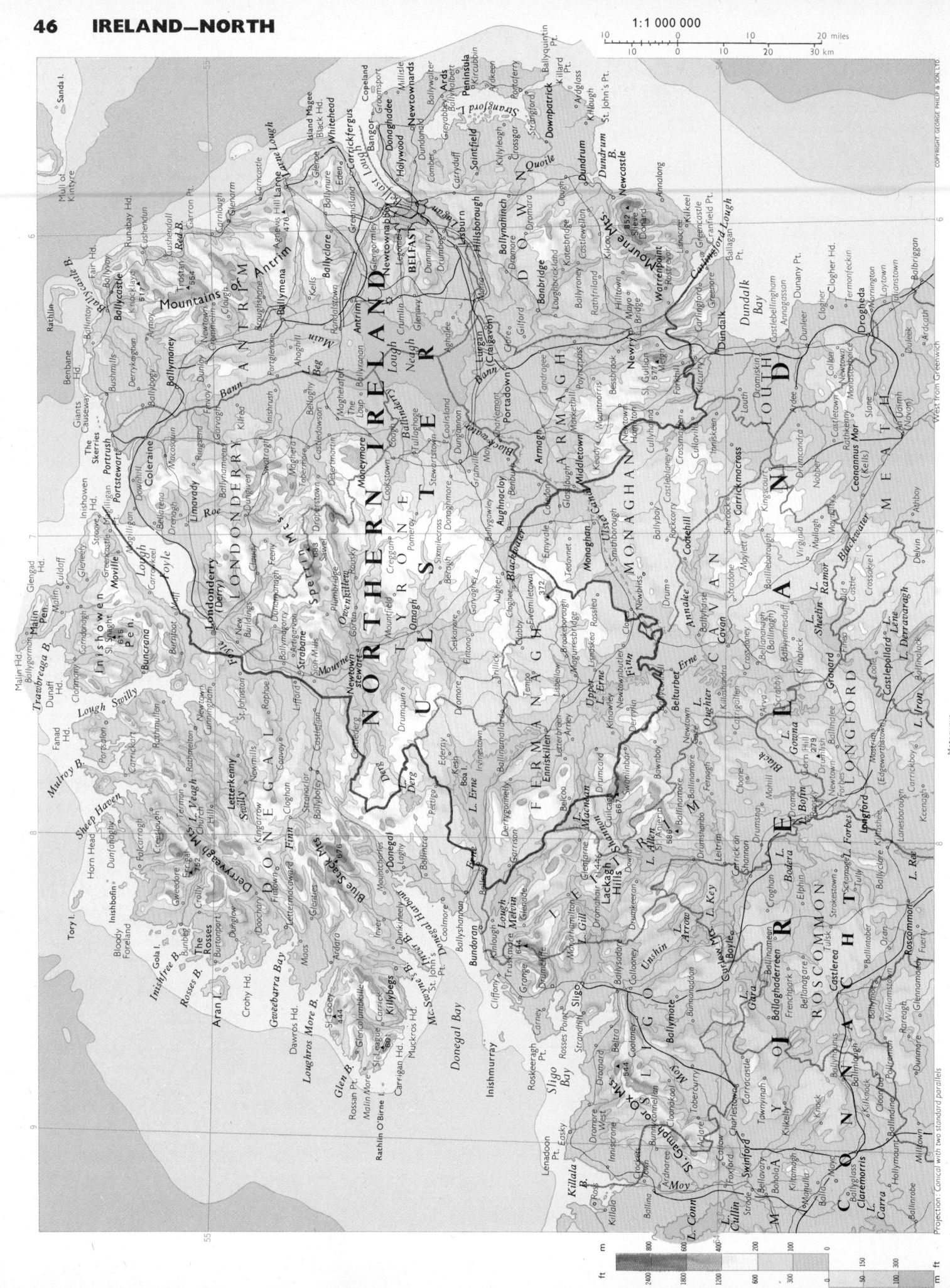
1:1 000 000
20 miles
30 km
NORTHERN IRELAND
ULSTER
IRELAND
CONNACHT
LEINSTER
DONEGAL
LONDONDERRY
ANTRIM
TYRONE
FERMANAGH
ARMAGH
DOWN
MONAGHAN
CAVAN
LEITRIM
SLIGO
MAYO
ROSCOMMON
LONGFORD
LOUTH
MEATH
BELFAST
Londonderry (Derry)
Lough Neagh
Sperrin Mts.
Mourne Mts.
Blue Stack Mts.
Derryveagh Mts.
Donegal Bay
Sligo Bay
Dundalk Bay
Motorways
Motorways under construction
Projection: Conical with two standard parallels
West from Greenwich
COPYRIGHT GEORGE PHILIP & SON, LTD.

1:5 000 000

20 10 0 20 40 60 80 100 miles
40 20 0 40 80 120 160 km

FRENCH DEPARTMENTS

Abbr.	Department	No.
A.	Ain	01
Ai.	Aisne	02
A.H.P.	Alpes-de-Haute-Provence	04
H.A.	Hautes-Alpes	05
A.M.	Alpes-Maritimes	06
Ard.	Ardèche	07
Ard.	Ardennes	08
Ar.	Ariège	09
Aub.	Aube	10
Aud.	Aude	11
Av.	Aveyron	12
B.R.	Bouches-du-Rhône	13
Cv.	Calvados	14
Ch.	Cantal	15
Ch.	Charente	16
Ch.M.	Charente-Maritime	17
Che.	Cher	18
Co.	Corrèze	19
C.O.	Côte-d'Or	21
Cô.N.	Côtes-du-Nord	22
Cr.	Creuse	23
D.	Dordogne	24
Do.	Doubs	25
Dr.	Drôme	26
E.	Eure	27
E.L.	Eure-et-Loir	28
F.	Finistère Nord et Sud	29
Ga.	Gard	30
H.G.	Haute-Garonne	31
Ge.	Gers	32
Gi.	Gironde	33
H.	Hérault	34
I.V.	Ille-et-Vilaine	35
I.	Indre	36
I.L.	Indre-et-Loire	37
Is.	Isère	38
J.	Jura	39
L.	Landes	40
L.C.	Loir-et-Cher	41
Loi.	Loire	42
H.L.	Haute-Loire	43
L.A.	Loire-Atlantique	44
Loi.	Loiret	45
Lot	Lot	46
L.G.	Lot-et-Garonne	47
Loz.	Lozère	48
M.L.	Maine-et-Loire	49
Ma.	Manche	50
	Marne	51
H.M.	Haute-Marne	52
May.	Mayenne	53
M.M.	Meurthe-et-Moselle	54
Me.	Meuse	55
Mo.	Morbihan	56
Mos.	Moselle	57
N.	Nièvre	58
No.	Nord	59
Oi.	Oise	60
Or.	Orne	61
P.C.	Pas-de-Calais	62
P.D.	Puy-de-Dôme	63
P.A.	Pyrénées Atlantiques	64
H.P.	Hautes Pyrénées	65
P.O.	Pyrénées (Orientales)	66
B.R.	Bas Rhin	67
H.R.	Haut Rhin	68
Rh.	Rhône	69
H.S.	Haute Saône	70
S.L.	Saône-et-Loire	71
Sa.	Sarthe	72
	Savoie	73
H.Sa.	Haute-Savoie	74
	Paris	75
S.M.	Seine-Maritime	76
S.M.	Seine-et-Marne	77
Y.	Yvelines	78
D.S.	Deux-Sèvres	79
So.	Somme	80
T.	Tarn	81
T.G.	Tarn-et-Garonne	82
Va.	Vaucluse	84
V.	Vendée	85
Vi.	Vienne	86
H.V.	Haute-Vienne	87
Vo.	Vosges	88
Y.	Yonne	89
B.S.	Belfort	90
Es.	Essonne	91
H.S.S.	Hauts-de-Seine	92
S.S.D.	Seine-St-Denis	93
V.M.	Val-de-Marne	94
V.O.	Val-d'Oise	95

CORSICA On same scale

Corse

COPYRIGHT GEORGE PHILIP & SON LTD

MEDITERRANEAN SEA

BAY OF BISCAY

ENGLISH CHANNEL

Projection: Conical with two standard parallels

East from Greenwich — West from Greenwich

E N G L A N D
English Channel
CHANNEL ISLANDS
Alderney
Guernsey
St. Peter Port
Sark
Herm
Jersey
St. Helier
Golfe de St. Malo
Baie de la Seine
BAY OF BISCAY
Baie de Bourgneuf
Lyme Bay
Exeter
Plymouth
Southampton
Portsmouth
Bournemouth
Brighton
Hastings
Eastbourne
Cherbourg
Le Havre
Rouen
Caen
Dieppe
Brest
Quimper
Lorient
Vannes
St. Brieuc
St. Malo
Rennes
Laval
Le Mans
Alençon
Angers
Nantes
St. Nazaire
Cholet
Tours
Poitiers
Niort
La Rochelle
Rochefort
Angoulême
La Roche-sur-Yon
Île d'Ouessant (Ushant)
Belle Île
Île de Noirmoutier
Île d'Yeu
Île de Ré
Île d'Oléron
ft
m
12 000
4000
9000
3000
6000
2000
4500
1500
3000
1000
1200
400
600
200
0
0
200
600
2000
6000
m
ft
DÉPARTEMENTS IN THE PARIS AREA
1 Ville de Paris
2 Seine-St. Denis
3 Val-de-Marne
4 Hauts-de-Seine
Projection: Conical with two standard parallels
West from Greenwich
East from Greenwich

1:2 500 000

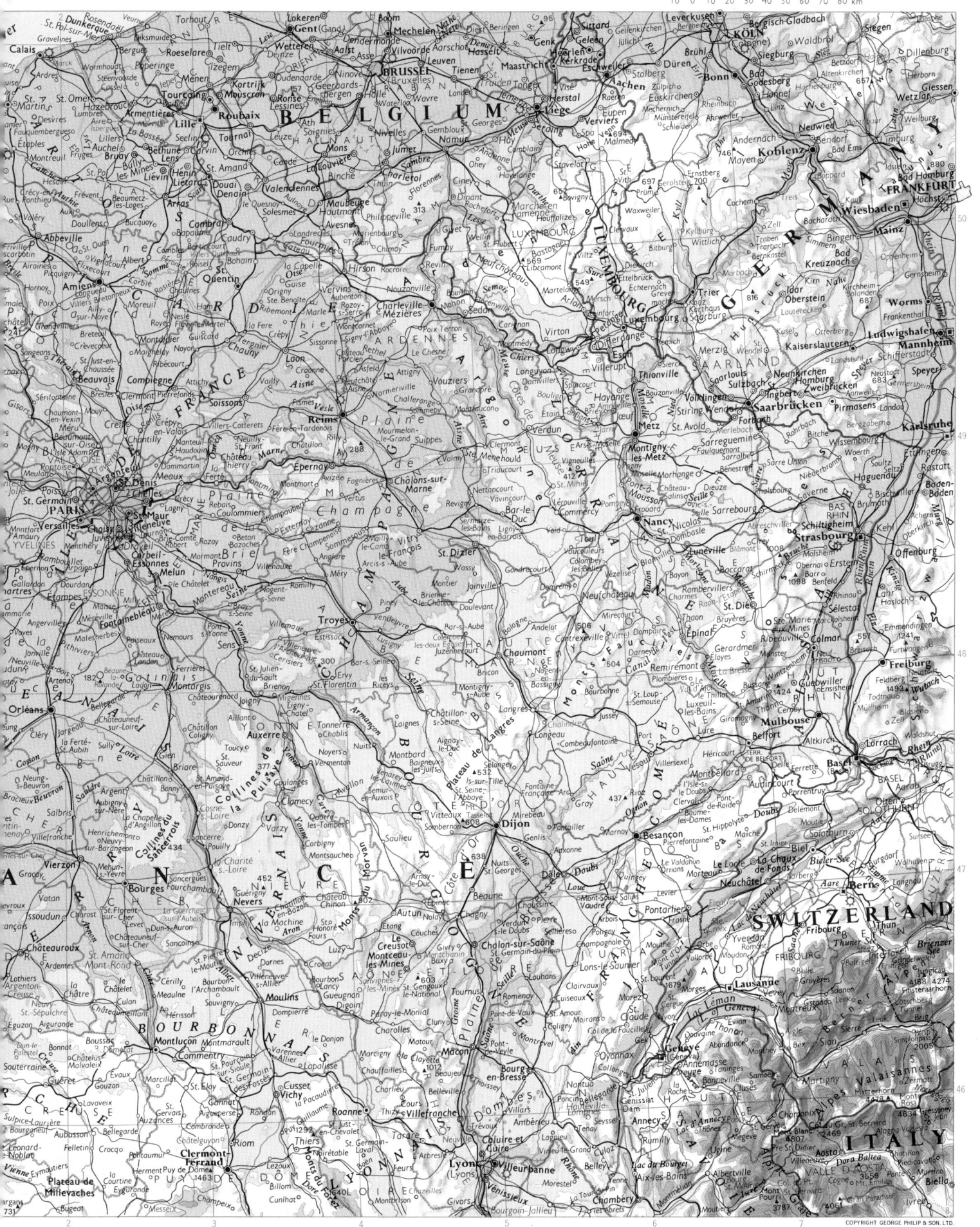
BELGIUM
FRANCE
LUXEMBOURG
GERMANY
SWITZERLAND
ITALY
PARIS
BRUSSEL (Bruxelles)
Lille
Reims
Metz
Nancy
Strasbourg
Dijon
Besançon
Lyon
Genève
Lausanne
Bern
Basel
Freiburg
Karlsruhe
Saarbrücken
Koblenz
Köln
Frankfurt
Luxembourg
Liège
Orléans
Bourges
Clermont-Ferrand
Champagne
Bourgogne
Lorraine
Picardie
Nivernais
Bourbonnais
Lyonnais
Savoie
Franche-Comté

COPYRIGHT GEORGE PHILIP & SON, LTD.

BAY OF BISCAY
Golfe de Gascogne
FRANCE
SPAIN
ANDORRA
Île de Noirmoutier
Île d' Yeu
Île de Ré
Île d'Oléron
Pertuis Breton
Pertuis d'Antioche
Cholet
La Roche-sur-Yon
les Sables d'Olonne
Poitiers
Châtellerault
Niort
La Rochelle
Rochefort
Saintes
Cognac
Angoulême
Limoges
Châteauroux
Bourges
Nevers
Moulins
Montluçon
Vichy
Clermont-Ferrand
Périgueux
Brive-la-Gaillarde
Tulle
Aurillac
Bordeaux
Libourne
Bergerac
Arcachon
Agen
Cahors
Montauban
Rodez
Millau
Albi
Castres
Toulouse
Tarbes
Pau
Bayonne
Biarritz
Dax
Mont-de-Marsan
Carcassonne
Narbonne
Béziers
Sète
Perpignan
Foix
San Sebastián
Pamplona
Huesca
Zaragoza (Saragossa)
Lérida
Gerona
Figueras
POITOU
ANGOUMOIS
LIMOUSIN
MARCHE
BERRY
BOURBONNAIS
AUVERGNE
SAINTONGE
AUNIS
PÉRIGORD
GUYENNE
GASCOGNE
LANDES
BÉARN
NAVARRE
LANGUEDOC
ROUSSILLON
Massif Central
Plateau de Millevaches
Causse Méjean
Mts. de Lacaune
Pyrénées
Sierra de la Peña
Sierra de Guara
Sierra del Cadí
Golfe du Lion
Projection: Conical with two standard parallels
West from Greenwich
East from Greenwich

NORTH SEA

BALTIC

NETHERLANDS

BELGIUM

LUX

FRANCE

WEST GERMANY

EAST GERMANY

CZECHOSL

SWITZERLAND

ITALY

ÖSTERREICH

ADRIATIC SEA

Berlin

Hamburg

München (Munich)

Praha (Prague)

Wien (Vienna)

Amsterdam

Rotterdam

Brussel (Bruxelles)

Köln (Cologne)

Frankfurt

Stuttgart

Zürich

Milano (Milan)

Venézia (Venice)

Marseille

Projection: Conical with two standard parallels

East from Greenwich

1:5 000 000

50   50   100 miles
50   50   100   150 km

CENTRAL EUROPE POLITICAL
1:25 000 000

COPYRIGHT. GEORGE PHILIP & SON. LTD.

1:2 500 000

NORTH SEA

ENGLAND

NETHERLANDS

BELGIUM

LUXEMBOURG

FRANCE

GERMANY

AMSTERDAM · 's-GRAVENHAGE (The Hague) · ROTTERDAM · Utrecht · Groningen · BRUSSEL (Bruxelles) · Antwerpen · Gent · Liège · Luxembourg · PARIS · Strasbourg

Projection: Conical with two standard parallels   East from Greenwich   COPYRIGHT. GEORGE PHILIP & SON, LTD.

1:1 000 000
5 0 10 20 30 miles
10 0 10 20 30 40 50 km.
NETHERLANDS
BELGIUM
GERMANY
LUXEMBOURG
DÜSSELDORF
DORTMUND
ESSEN
DUISBURG
KÖLN (COLOGNE)
ROTTERDAM
BRUSSEL
Antwerpen
Maastricht
Liège
Aachen
Eindhoven
Bonn
Koblenz
East from Greenwich
Projection: Conical with two standard parallels
COPYRIGHT, GEORGE PHILIP & SON, LTD.
ft m
1800 600
1200 400
600 200
300 100
0 0

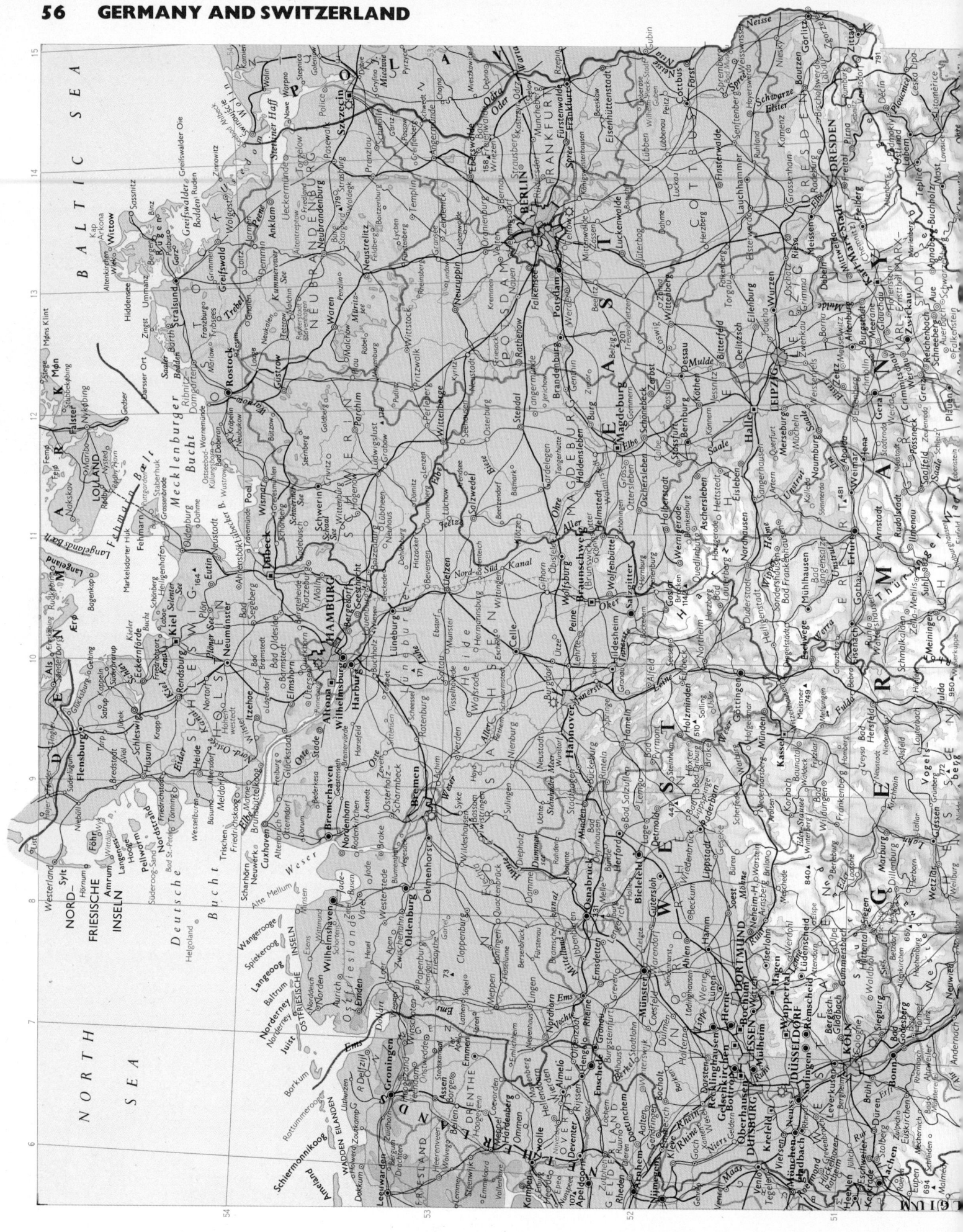
NORTH SEA
BALTIC SEA
BERLIN
HAMBURG
DRESDEN
LEIPZIG
Magdeburg
Hannover
Bremen
Kiel
Rostock
Lübeck
Szczecin
FRANKFURT
Potsdam
DORTMUND
ESSEN
DÜSSELDORF
KÖLN
Mecklenburger Bucht
Deutsche Bucht
NORD-FRIESISCHE INSELN
OSTFRIESISCHE INSELN
WADDEN EILANDEN

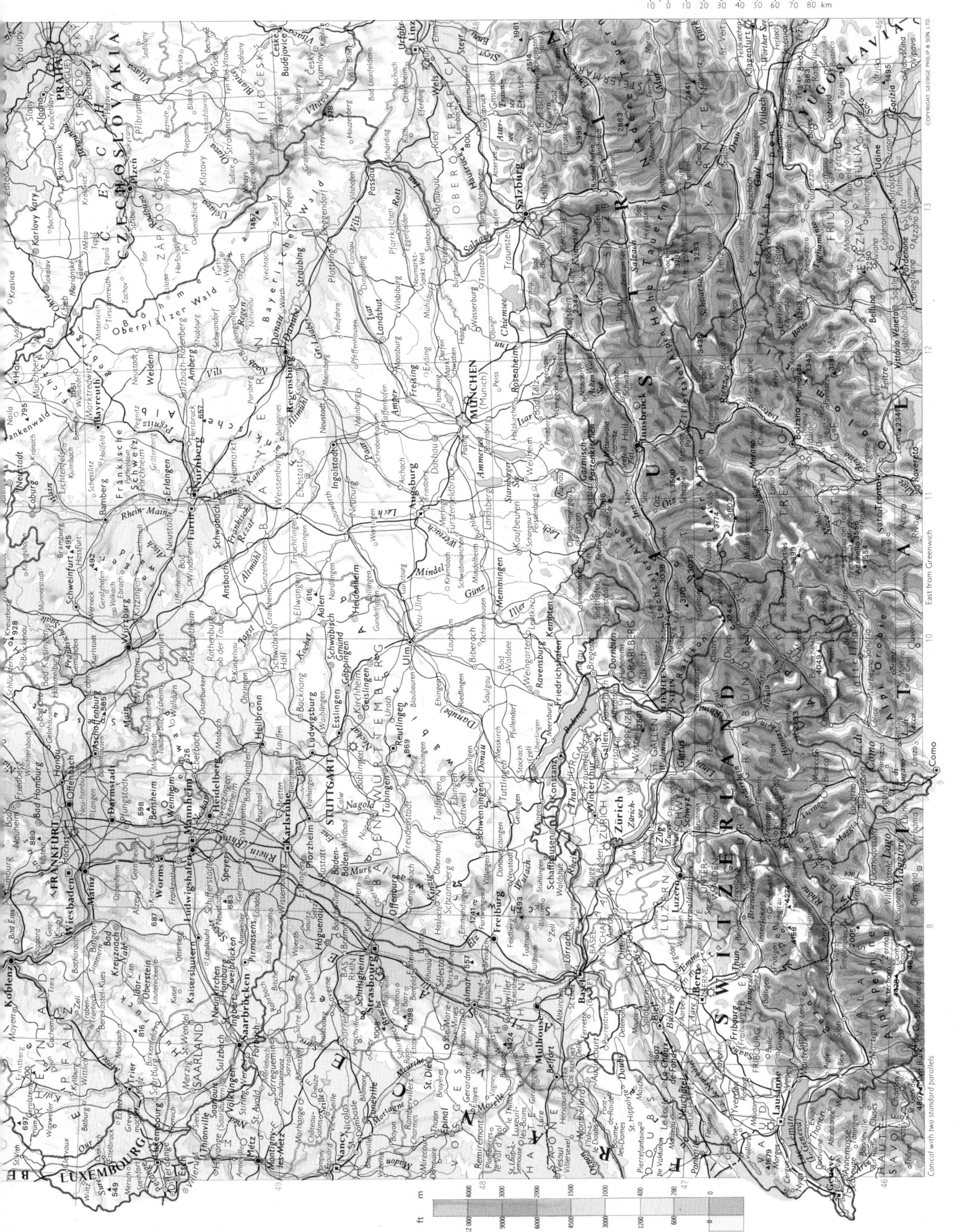
1:2 500 000
10 0 10 20 30 40 50 miles
10 0 10 20 30 40 50 60 70 80 km
COPYRIGHT, GEORGE PHILIP & SON, LTD.
Conical with two standard parallels
East from Greenwich
SWITZERLAND
LUXEMBOURG
CZECHOSLOVAKIA
YUGOSLAVIA
SAARLAND
BADEN-WÜRTTEMBERG
STUTTGART
MÜNCHEN (Munich)
Innsbruck
Zürich
Salzburg
Nürnberg
FRANKFURT
Strasbourg
Basel
Bern
Lausanne
Genève
Como
Bolzano
Udine
Linz
Passau
Regensburg
Augsburg
Ulm
Mannheim
Karlsruhe
Saarbrücken
Metz
Nancy
Koblenz
Plzeň
PRAHA (PRAGUE)
Klagenfurt
Villach
ft
m

DRESDEN
Karl-Marx-Stadt
Erfurt
Weimar
Jena
Gera
Zwickau
Plauen
Hof
Bayreuth
Bamberg
Würzburg
Nürnberg
Fürth
Erlangen
Regensburg
Ingolstadt
Augsburg
MÜNCHEN
(Munich)
Ulm
STUTTGART
Heilbronn
Ludwigsburg
Esslingen
Göppingen
Memmingen
Kempten
Friedrichshafen
Rosenheim
Landshut
Passau
Salzburg
Linz
Urfahr
Wels
Steyr
Krems
St. Pölten
Innsbruck
Graz
Klagenfurt
Villach
Leoben
Kapfenberg
Maribor
Ljubljana
Zagreb
Trieste
Udine
Bolzano
Trento
Belluno
Treviso
Vicenza
Brescia
Bergamo
PRAHA
(PRAGUE)
Plzeň
Karlovy Vary
Cheb
Chomutov
Most
Teplice
Ústí nad Labem
Liberec
České Budějovice
Jihlava
Kladno
Kolín
Pardubice
AUSTRIA
ITALY
SWITZERLAND
LIECHTENSTEIN
VORARLBERG
BADEN-WÜRTTEMBERG
HESSEN
BAYERN
Donau (Danube)
Labe (Elbe)
Vltava
Inn
Salzach
Enns
Drau
Mur
Chiemsee
Ammersee
Starnberger See
Bodensee
Hohe Tauern
Niedere Tauern
Zillertaler Alpen
Ötztaler Alpen
Lechtaler Alpen
Karnische Alpen
Dolomiti
Böhmer Wald
Bayerischer Wald
Oberpfälzer Wald
Thüringer Wald
Frankenwald
Fichtelgebirge
Schwäbische Alb
Fränkische Alb

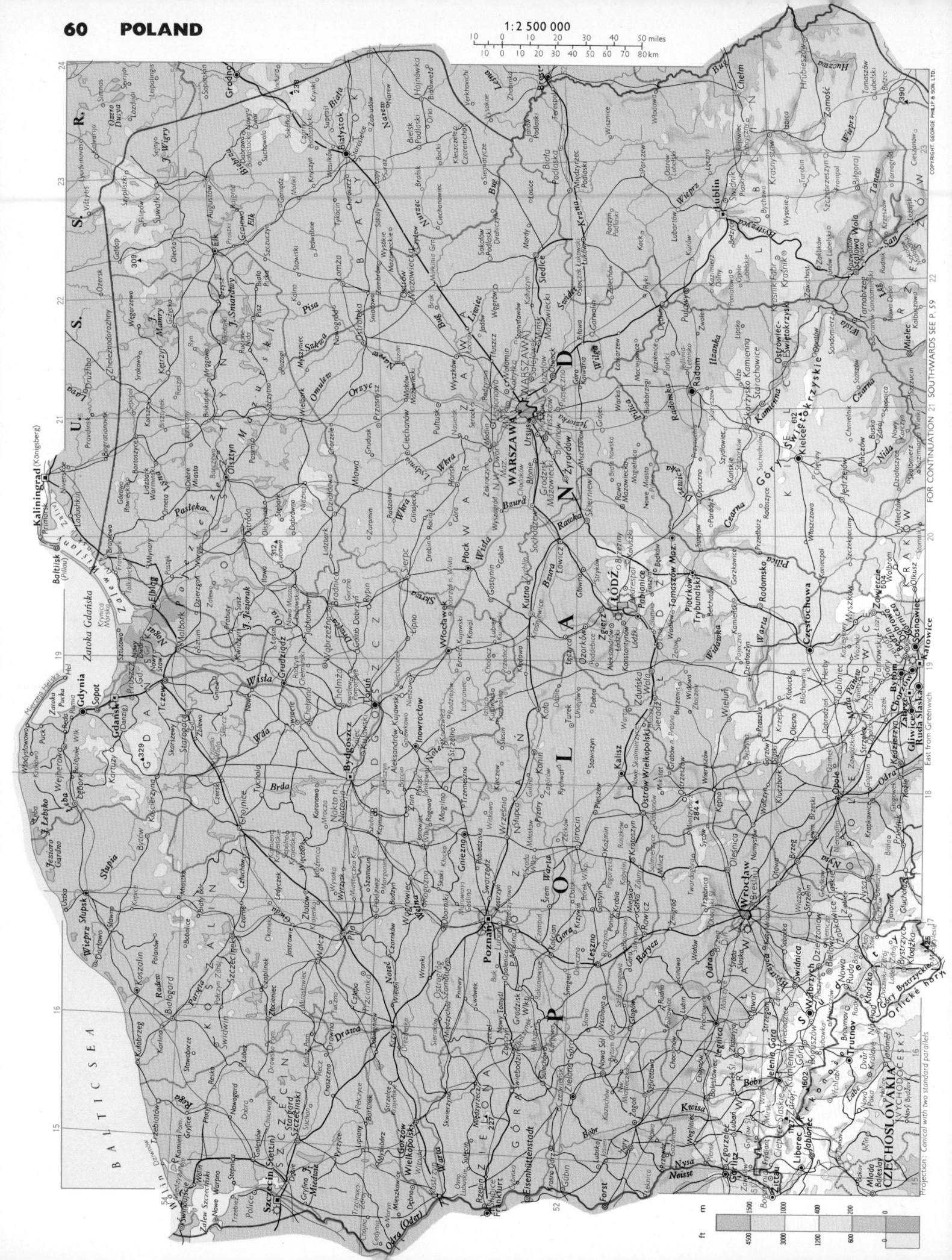
1:2 500 000
10 0 10 20 30 40 50 miles
10 0 10 20 30 40 50 60 70 80 km
BALTIC SEA
U. S. S. R.
POLAND
CZECHOSLOVAKIA
WARSZAWA
Kaliningrad (Königsberg)
Zatoka Gdańska
Gdańsk (Danzig)
Gdynia
Sopot
Szczecin (Stettin)
Poznań
Wrocław (Breslau)
ŁÓDŹ
Katowice
Lublin
Białystok
Bydgoszcz
Toruń
Olsztyn
Kielce
Radom
Częstochowa
ft
m
4500
1500
3000
1000
1200
400
600
200
0
0
Projection: Conical with two standard parallels
East from Greenwich
FOR CONTINUATION SOUTHWARDS SEE P. 59
COPYRIGHT. GEORGE PHILIP & SON. LTD.

1:5 000 000

50   50   100 miles
50   0   50   100   150 km

COPYRIGHT GEORGE PHILIP & SON LTD.

East from Greenwich

West from Greenwich

Projection : Conical with two standard parallels

FRANCE

Toulouse
Montpellier
Béziers
Narbonne
Golfe du Lion
Agde
Sète
Port St. Louis
Castres
Mont-de-Marsan
Condom
Orthez
Adour
Bayonne
Biarritz
Hendaye
San Sebastián
Bay of Biscay

Perpignan
Port Bou
Port Vendres
Golfe de Rosas
Rosas
C. Creus
Gerona
S. Feliú de Guixols
Blanes

Pyrénées
ANDORRA
Andorra
3404

Barcelona
Badalona
Sabadell
Tarrasa
Hospitalet
Mataró

NAVARRA
Pamplona
Logroño
Zaragoza
Huesca
Lérida
Tarragona
C. de Tortosa
Tortosa
Golfo de San Jorge

Bilbao
Vitoria
Burgos
Soria
ARAGON
Teruel

Mts. de Maestrazgo

Sierra de la Demanda
La Rioja
Sierra de Albarracín

Castellón de la Plana
Islas Columbretes

Sagunto
Valencia
Albufera de Valencia
Cullera

SPAIN
MADRID
Guadalajara
Alcalá de Henares
Cuenca
Serranía de Cuenca

Segovia
Ávila
Sierra de Gredos
Valladolid
Palencia
Salamanca
Zamora
León

CASTILLA LA VIEJA
CASTILLA LA NUEVA

Toledo
Montes de Toledo
Ciudad Real

Albacete
MURCIA
Murcia
Alicante
Elche
Cartagena
Lorca

Gijón
Oviedo
Mieres
Cordillera Cantábrica
ASTURIAS

GALICIA
La Coruña
El Ferrol
Santiago de Compostela
Lugo
Pontevedra
Vigo
Orense

PORTUGAL
Porto
Coimbra
Lisboa
Setúbal
Évora
BEIRA-ALTA
BEIRA-BAIXA
BEIRA LITORAL
DOURO LITORAL
MINHO
TRAS-OS-MONTES
ALTO DOURO
ESTREMADURA
RIBATEJO
ALTO ALENTEJO
BAIXO ALENTEJO
ALGARVE
C. de S. Vicente

EXTREMADURA
Cáceres
Badajoz
Mérida

Sierra Morena
Córdoba
Linares
Jaén
ANDALUCIA
Sevilla
Huelva
Cádiz
Jerez
Málaga
Granada
Sierra Nevada
3478
Almería
Guadix

Strait of Gibraltar
Gibraltar (Br.)
La Línea de la Concepción
Algeciras
Ceuta (Sp.)
Tánger
Tetuán
MOROCCO

MEDITERRANEAN SEA

Balearic Islands
Menorca
Mallorca
Palma
Ibiza
Formentera
Cabrera

ALGERIA
Alger
Blida
Oran
Mostaganem

ATLANTIC OCEAN

m
ft
5000
4000

BAY OF BISCAY
ATLANTIC OCEAN
SPAIN
San Sebastián
Bilbao
Santander
Gijón
Oviedo
León
Burgos
Logroño
Vitoria
Palencia
Valladolid
Salamanca
Zamora
Segovia
Avila
MADRID
Chamartín de la Rosa
Guadalajara
Alcalá de Henares
Soria
Lugo
Orense
Vigo
La Coruña (Corunna)
El Ferrol
Santiago de Compostela
Pontevedra
Porto (Oporto)
Vila Nova de Gaia
Braga
Coimbra
Aveiro
Figueira da Foz
Picos de Europa
Sierra de Gredos
Sierra de Guadarrama
Sierra de la Culebra
Sierra de Gata
Sierra da Estrêla
Sierra de la Demanda
Montañas de León

1:2 500 000

10 0 10 20 30 40 50 miles

10 0 10 20 30 40 50 60 70 80 km

MEDITERRANEAN SEA
Golfo de Cádiz
Strait of Gibraltar
MOROCCO
LISBOA (LISBON)
Setúbal
Évora
Faro
Badajoz
Mérida
Cáceres
Sevilla
Huelva
Cádiz
Jerez de la Frontera
Córdoba
Jaén
Granada
Málaga
Almería
Algeciras
Gibraltar (Br.)
Ceuta (Sp.)
Tanger (Tangier)
Tetouan
Melilla (Sp.)
Alborán (Sp.)
Ciudad Real
Sierra Nevada
Montes de Toledo
Guadiana
Guadalquivir
Tejo
Algarve
Costa del Sol
West from Greenwich
Projection: Conical with two standard parallels
COPYRIGHT, GEORGE PHILIP & SON, LTD.
ft m
9000 3000
6000 2000
4500 1500
3000 1000
1200 400
600 200
0 0
200 600
2000 6000
m ft

BAY OF BISCAY
Golfe de Gascogne
FRANCE
SPAIN
BARCELONA
MADRID
Zaragoza
(Saragossa)
Pamplona
Bilbao
San Sebastián
Toulouse
Perpignan
Tarragona
Lérida
Gerona
Huesca
Logroño
Vitoria
Burgos
Soria
Teruel
Cuenca
Guadalajara
Castellón de la Plana
Carcassonne
Narbonne
Béziers
Sète
Montauban
Tarbes
Pau
Bayonne
Biarritz
Santander
ANDORRA
ROUSSILLON
NAVARRE
BÉARN
PYRÉNÉES ATLANTIQUES
HAUTES PYRÉNÉES
PYRÉNÉES ORIENTALES
Menorca (Minorca)
Mallorca (Majorca)
Palma
Mahón
Ciudadela
BALEARES (ISLANDS)
Costa Brava
Costa Dorada
Sierra de la Peña
Sierra de Guara
Sa. de Alcubierre
Los Monegros
Montes Universales
Mts. del Maestrazgo
Sa. del Moncayo
Sa. de Cebollera
Sierra de la Demanda
Sa. del Montsech
Sa. de Montsant
Sierra del Cadí
Ebro
Golfo de San Jorge
Islas Columbretes
Golfo

1:2 500 000

10   0   10   20   30   40   50 miles
10   0   10   20   30   40   50   60   70   80 km

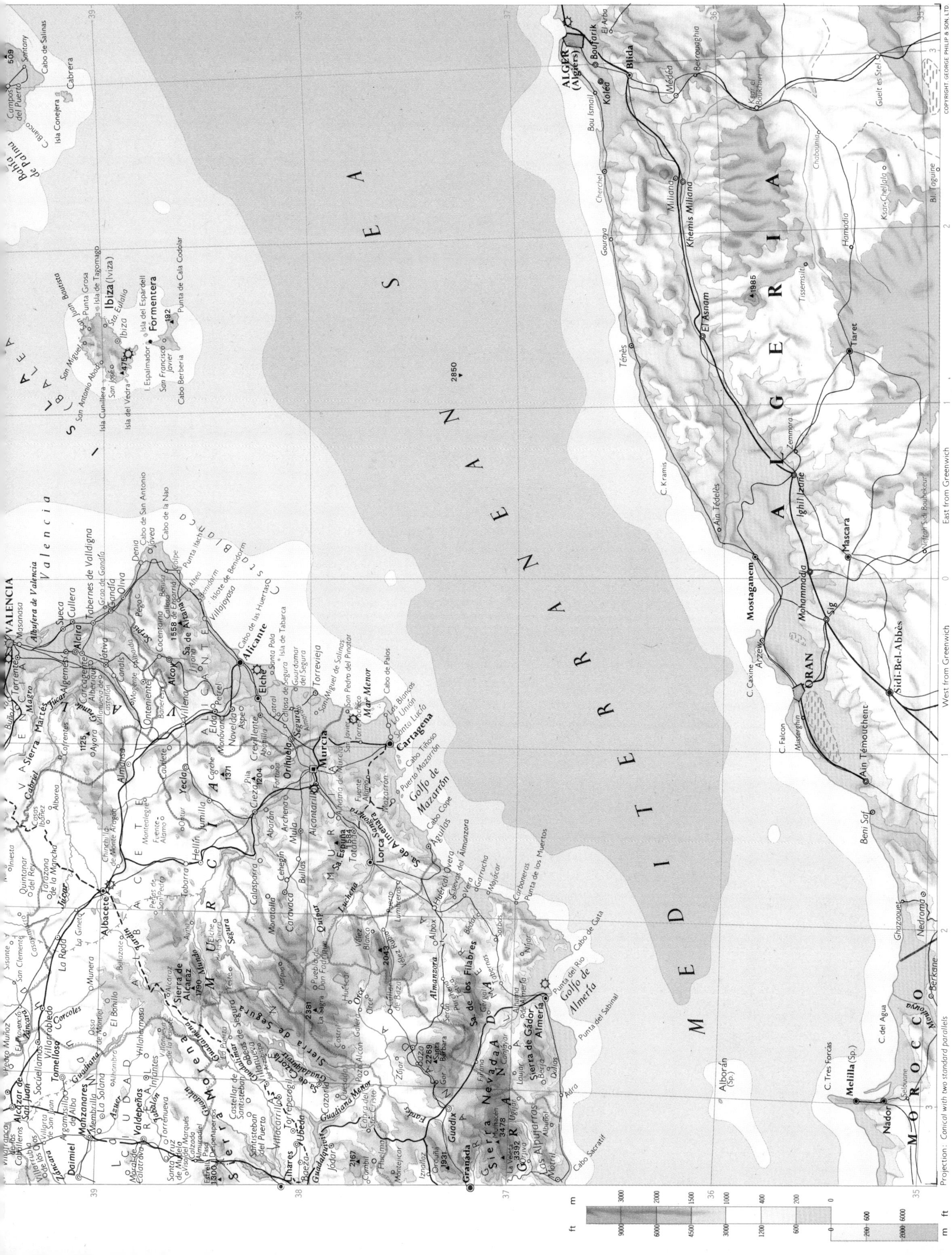

COPYRIGHT GEORGE PHILIP & SON, LTD.

East from Greenwich

West from Greenwich

M E D I T E R R A N E A N   S E A

ALGERIA

ALGER (Algiers)
Bou Ismail
Boufarik   El Arba
Koléa
Blida   Médéa
El Affroun   Berrouaghia
Cherchel
Miliana
Khemis Miliana
El Asnam
Ténès
Gouraya
C. Kramis
Ain Tédélès
Mostaganem
Arzeu
Mohammadia
Sig
ORAN
C. Caxine
C. Falcon
Mascara
Ighil Izane
Tiaret
Tissemsilt
Sidi-Bel-Abbès
Ain Témouchent
Beni Saf
Musserghin
1985
2850

Chabounia
Hamadia
Zemmora

MOROCCO
Nedroma
Ghazaouet
Nador
Melilla (Sp.)
C. Tres Forcas
Seloune
C. del Agua
Berkane

Alborán (Sp.)

BALEARIC IS.
I S L A S   B A L E A R E S

Cabo de Salinas
Isla Conejera
Campos del Puerto
Cabo de Cabrera
C. Blanco
Bahía de Palma
509

San Miguel
San Juan Bautista
San Antonio Abad
Isla de Tagomago
Santa Eulalia
Ibiza (Iviza)
Isla del Espardell
I. Espalmador
San José
San Francisco Javier
Formentera
Punta de Cala Codolar
Cabo Berbería
192
475
Isla de Vedra
Isla Cunillera

VALENCIA
VALENCIA
Albufera de Valencia
Manises
Torrente
Mislata
Masanosa
Sueca
Alcira   Cullera
Algemesí
Carcagente
Tabernes de Valldigna
Gandía
Grao de Gandía
Oliva
Pego
Denia
Javea
Cabo de San Antonio
Cabo de la Nao
Cabo de San Martín
Benisa
Calpe
Altea
Benidorm
Villajoyosa
Istope de Benidorm
Cocentaina
Alcoy
Jijona
Muchamiel
ALICANTE
Santa Pola
Isla de Tabarca
Elche
Crevillente
Aspe
Novelda
Monóvar
Eldo
Petrel
Villena
Sax
Orihuela
Callosa de Segura
Guardamar del Segura
Torrevieja
San Pedro del Pinatar
San Javier
Los Alcázares
Torre del Rame
Mar Menor
Cabo de Palos
La Unión
Santa Lucía
Cartagena
Cabo Tiñoso

MURCIA
Murcia
Alcantarilla
Molina
Fortuna
Archena
Cieza
Mula
Bullas
Cehegín
Caravaca
Calasparra
Moratalla
Fuente Álamo
Mazarrón
Puerto Mazarrón
Águilas
Golfo de Mazarrón
Cabo Cope

Jumilla
Yecla
Montealegre
Hellín
Tobarra
Almansa
Ayora
Cofrentes
Requena
Utiel

VALENCIA
Buñol
Chiva

Albacete
La Roda
Quintanar del Rey
Tarazona de la Mancha
Casas Ibáñez

Lorca
Totana
Alhama
Vélez Rubio
Vélez Blanco
Huércal Overa
Cuevas del Almanzora
Vera
Garrucha
Mojácar
Carboneras
Punta de los Muertos
Cabo de Gata
Níjar
Sorbas
Tabernas
Gérgal
Sierra de los Filabres
Sierra Nevada
Guadix
Baza
Cúllar
Huéscar
Orce
Galera
Orcera
La Sagra
Pozo Alcón
Sierra de Cazorla
Cazorla
Úbeda
Baeza
Linares
Villacarrillo
Villanueva del Arzobispo
Santisteban del Puerto
Castellar de Santisteban

Granada
Sierra Nevada
3478
3392
Sierra de Gádor
Almería
Golfo de Almería
Gádor
Punta del Río
Punta Entinas
Punta del Sabinal
Adra
Motril
Cabo Sacratif

Sierra de Gúdar
Benamaurel
Cúllar
Caniles

Daimiel
Manzanares
Valdepeñas
Membrilla
La Solana
Tomelloso
Socuéllamos
Alcázar de San Juan
Villarrobledo
Munera
El Bonillo
Alcaraz
Riópar
Sierra de Alcaraz
1790
Sierra de Segura
Segura de la Sierra
Beas de Segura

Jaén
Jódar
Guadalquivir
Mengíbar
Bailén
La Carolina

C. del Río
Punta del Río

MEDITERRANEAN   SEA
OCEAN

Projection: Conical with two standard parallels

m   ft
ft   m
3000   9000
2000   6000
1500   4500
1000   3000
600   1800
400   1200
200   600
0   0
0   0
200   600
600   1800
2000   6000
6000   18000

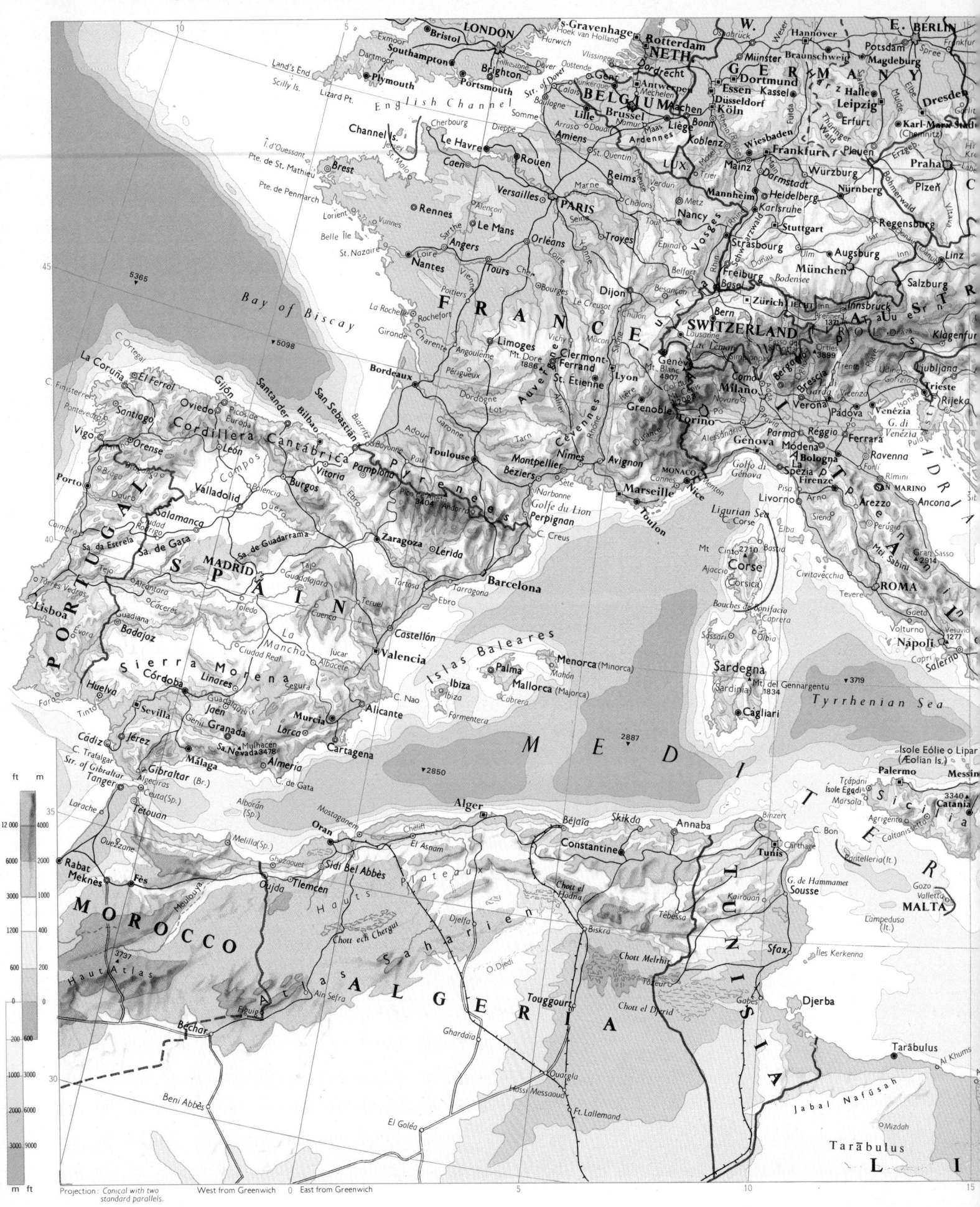

LONDON
Bristol
Southampton
Brighton
Portsmouth
Plymouth
Land's End
Scilly Is.
Lizard Pt.
English Channel
Channel Is.
Str. of Dover
's-Gravenhage
Rotterdam
NETH.
Dordrecht
Antwerpen
BELGIUM
Brussel
Gent
Lille
Liège
Aachen
Köln
Bonn
Düsseldorf
Essen
Dortmund
Münster
Kassel
Hannover
Braunschweig
Magdeburg
Potsdam
BERLIN
W.
E.
GERMANY
Halle
Leipzig
Dresden
Erfurt
Karl-Marx-Stadt (Chemnitz)
Praha
Plzeň
Frankfurt
Wiesbaden
Mainz
Koblenz
Darmstadt
Mannheim
Heidelberg
Karlsruhe
Stuttgart
Würzburg
Nürnberg
Regensburg
Augsburg
München
Linz
Salzburg
Innsbruck
Klagenfurt
LUX.
Cherbourg
Le Havre
Rouen
Caen
Amiens
Reims
St. Quentin
Brest
Rennes
Le Mans
Versailles
PARIS
Nancy
Strasbourg
Vosges
Troyes
Orléans
Angers
Tours
Nantes
St. Nazaire
Lorient
Belle Île
Bay of Biscay
FRANCE
La Rochelle
Rochefort
Poitiers
Limoges
Dijon
Besançon
Freiburg
Basel
Zürich
Bern
SWITZERLAND
Lausanne
Genève
Lac Léman
Mt. Blanc 4807
Lyon
Clermont-Ferrand
St. Étienne
Bordeaux
Grenoble
Torino
Milano
Como
Bergamo
Brescia
Verona
Padova
Venezia
Trieste
Rijeka
Ljubljana
Genova
Parma
Modena
Bologna
Ferrara
Ravenna
Rimini
SAN MARINO
Firenze
La Spezia
Livorno
Pisa
Ancona
Arezzo
Perugia
Gran Sasso 2914
ROMA
Civitavecchia
Nápoli
Salerno
Vesuvio 1277
Toulouse
Montpellier
Nîmes
Béziers
Avignon
Marseille
Toulon
Nice
MONACO
Cannes
Narbonne
Golfe du Lion
Perpignan
C. Creus
Cévennes
Auvergne
Pyrenees
Pamplona
Andorra
Pico de Aneto 3404
Biarritz
Bayonne
San Sebastián
Bilbao
Santander
Vitoria
Burgos
Gijón
Oviedo
Cordillera Cantábrica
La Coruña
El Ferrol
Santiago
Vigo
Orense
León
Valladolid
Palencia
Salamanca
Porto
PORTUGAL
Coimbra
Sa. da Estrela
Sa. de Gata
Sa. de Guadarrama
MADRID
SPAIN
Guadalajara
Toledo
Zaragoza
Lérida
Barcelona
Tarragona
Tortosa
Teruel
Cuenca
Castellón
Valencia
Lisboa
Évora
Badajoz
Cáceres
Ciudad Real
La Mancha
Albacete
Sierra Morena
Córdoba
Linares
Jaén
Granada
Sevilla
Huelva
Faro
Cádiz
Jérez
Málaga
Almería
Murcia
Lorca
Cartagena
Alicante
C. Nao
Sa. Nevada
Mulhacén 3478
C. Trafalgar
Str. of Gibraltar
Gibraltar (Br.)
Algeciras
Ceuta (Sp.)
Tanger
Tétouan
Larache
Islas Baleares
Ibiza
Formentera
Palma
Mallorca (Majorca)
Menorca (Minorca)
Mahón
Cabrera
C. de Gata
Alborán (Sp.)
Ligurian Sea
C. Corse
Corse (Corsica)
Mt Cinto 2710
Ajaccio
Bastia
Elba
Bouches de Bonifacio
Sardegna (Sardinia)
Mt del Gennargentu 1834
Sássari
Cagliari
Tyrrhenian Sea
MEDITERRANEAN
Isole Eólie o Lipari (Æolian Is.)
Palermo
Trápani
Isole Egadi
Marsala
Agrigento
Caltanissetta
Catania 3340
Sicilia
C. Bon
Pantelleria (It.)
Gozo
Valletta
MALTA
Lampedusa (It.)
Alger
Oran
Mostaganem
Chéliff
El Asnam
Béjaïa
Skikda
Annaba
Constantine
Bizerte
Tunis
Carthage
Sousse
G. de Hammamet
Kairouan
Tébessa
Sfax
Îles Kerkenna
Gabès
Djerba
Tarābulus
Al Khums
Jabal Nafūsah
Mizdah
LI
Melilla (Sp.)
Rabat
Meknès
Fès
Ouezzane
Oujda
Tlemcen
Sidi Bel Abbès
Ghazaouet
MOROCCO
Haut Atlas
3737
Hauts Plateaux
Atlas Saharien
Chott ech Chergui
Chott el Hodna
Biskra
Djelfa
Chott Melrhir
Chott el Djerid
Tozeur
Touggourt
ALGERIA
TUNISIA
Aïn Sefra
Figuig
Béchar
Ghardaïa
Ouargla
Hassi Messaoud
Ft. Lallemand
El Goléa
Beni Abbès
O. Djedi
5365
5098
2850
2887
3719
ft
m
12 000
4000
6000
2000
3000
1000
1200
400
600
200
0
200
600
1000
3000
2000
6000
3000
9000
Projection: Conical with two standard parallels.
West from Greenwich
East from Greenwich

1:10 000 000

COPYRIGHT. GEORGE PHILIP & SON. LTD

SWITZERLAND
Passo del S. Gottardo
Brenner
Genève
Lyon
Villeurbanne
Grenoble
Torino (Turin)
Milano (Milan)
Como
Bergamo
Brescia
Verona
Vicenza
Padova (Padua)
Venézia (Venice)
Treviso
Trento
Bolzano
Udine
Trieste
Ljubljana
Klagenfurt
Maribor
Zagreb
Rijeka (Fiume)
Pula (Pola)
Istra
Golfo di Venézia
LOMBARDIA
PIEMONTE
DAUPHINÉ
PROVENCE
Alessándria
Piacenza
Cremona
Mántova (Mantua)
Parma
Réggio
Módena
Bologna
Ferrara
Ravenna
Genova (Genoa)
Savona
Golfo di Génova
La Spézia
Avignon
Aix
Marseille
Toulon
Nice
Cannes
MONACO
LIGURIAN SEA
Îles d'Hyères
Pisa
Lucca
Prato
Firenze (Florence)
Livorno (Leghorn)
TOSCANA
Siena
Arezzo
Perúgia
UMBRIA
Terni
Ancona
Pésaro
Rímini
SAN MARINO
Pescara
L'Aquila
ROMA (Rome)
ADRIATIC SEA
CORSE (CORSICA) (Fr.)
Ajaccio
Bastia
Elba
Bouches de Bonifacio
Sássari
SARDEGNA (SARDINIA)
Cágliari
TYRRHENIAN SEA
MOLISE
Fóggia
Bari
Barletta
Napoli (Naples)
Salerno
BASILICATA
Taranto
Golfo di Táranto
Cosenza
Catanzaro
Réggio
Isole Eólie o Lípari
Palermo
Trápani
Messina
Catánia
Siracusa (Syracuse)
Ragusa
Caltanissetta
Etna 3340
Pantelleria (Ital.)
Lampedusa (Ital.)
AFRICA
MEDITE
MALTA
Gozo
Comino
Valletta
Split
Zadar
Dugi Otok
MALTA 1:1 000 000
Gozo (Ghawdex)
Comino (Kemmuna)
Victoria (Rabat)
St. Pauls Bay
Mosta
Valletta
Mdina
Rabat
S.E. EUROPE POLITICAL 1:25 000 000
SWITZ.
AUSTRIA
HUNGARY
RUMANIA
U.S.S.R.
YUGOSLAVIA
BULGARIA
ALBANIA
GREECE
TURKEY
ITALY
FRANCE
SAN MARINO
Corse (Fr.)
Sicilia
ADRIATIC SEA
AEGEAN SEA
MEDITERRANEAN SEA
Projection: Conical with two standard parallels

SWITZERLAND
FRANCE
LIGURIAN SEA
Golfo di Génova
CORSE
(CORSICA)
Arcipelago
Toscano
ILES D'HYERES
Côte d'Azur
MILANO
TORINO
GENOVA
MARSEILLE
(Marseilles)
Lyon
(Lyons)
Grenoble
Nice
MONACO
Bern
Lausanne
Genève
Bergamo
Bréscia
Cremona
Parma
Reggio
Módena
Pavia
Piacenza
Alessándria
Asti
Novara
Vercelli
Savona
La Spezia
Livorno
(Leghorn)
Pisa
Lucca
Bastia
Ajaccio
Elba
Capraia
Gorgona
Pianosa
Montecristo
Avignon
Toulon
Aix-en-Provence
Valence
Chambéry
Annecy
Aosta
Cúneo
Sanremo
Impéria
Lago Maggiore
L. di Como
Lago di Garda
PROVENCE
DAUPHINÉ
SAVOIE
ALPES MARITIMES
VAUCLUSE
BOUCHES DU RHÔNE
FRANCHE-COMTÉ
GRAUBÜNDEN
TICINO
VALAIS
LOMBARDIA
PIEMONTE
EMILIA-ROMAGNA
LIGURIA
ft
m
12 000
4000
9000
3000
6000
2000
4500
1500
3000
1000
1200
400
600
200
0
200
600
2000
6000
m ft
Projection: Conical with two standard parallels
East from Greenwich
6
7
8
9
10
11
47
46
45
44
43
42

1:2 500 000

COPYRIGHT. GEORGE PHILIP & SON. LTD.

CORSICA
CORSE
Iles Sanguinaires
G.d'Ajaccio
G. de Valinco
Sartène
Porto-Vecchio
Solenzara
Favone
Iles Cerbicales
Bonifacio
I. de Cavallo
Bouches de Bonifacio
Santa Teresa Gallura
Maddalena
La Maddalena
Caprera
Costa Smeralda
Punta dello Scorno
Asinara
Golfo dell' Asinara
Coghinas
Tempio Pausania
Calangianus
M. Limbara
G.di Ólbia
Golfo Aranci
Tavolara
Ólbia
Porto Tórres
Sénnori
Sássari
C. dell' Argentiera
Osilo
L. di Coghinas
Ozieri
Pattada
Buddusò
Posada
Tanaunella
Alghero
Villanova Monteleone
Bonorva
Tirso
Bitti
Siniscola
Orune
C. Comino
Temo
Bosa
Nùoro
Macomer
Dorgali
Oliena
Golfo di Orosei
SARDEGNA
SARDINIA
C. Mannu
Ghilarza
L. del Tirso
Fonni
Monti del Gennargentu
1834
Baunei
C. di Monte Santu
Cábras
Oristano
Golfo di Oristano
M. Arci
812
Laconi
Arbatax
Lanusei
Tortolì
Arborea
Terralba
Nurri
Mandas
Flumendosa
Guspini
Arbus
S. Gavino Monreale
Sanluri
C. Pecora
Fluminimaggiore
M. Linas
1236
Villacidro
Serramanna
Senorbì
S. Vito
Muravera
Iglesias
Cixerri
Dolianova
Sinnai
1069
Portoscuso
Gonnesa
Siliqua
Assemini
Selargius
Quartu Sant'Elena
C. Ferrato
Carloforte
Carbonia
1116
Santadi
San Pietro
Sant' Antíoco
Porto Botte
Cágliari
Golfo di Cágliari
Pula
Teulada
Serpentara
C. Carbonara
G. di Palmas
C. Spartivento
ROMA
(Rome)
Vatican City
Fregene
Tivoli
Subiaco
Palestrina
Valmontone
Lido di Óstia
(Lido di Roma)
Tevere (Tiber)
Frascati
Velletri
Albano Laziale
Anagni
Alatri
Veroli
Sora
Isola del Liri
Arpino
Frosinone
Ferentino
Cisterna di Latina
Latina
Ceccano
Priverno
Sezze
Cassino
Pontecorvo
Anzio
Nettuno
Pontinia
Sabaudia
Monte Circeo
541
Terracina
Fondi
1533
Formia
Liri
Gaeta
Minturno
Garigliano
Golfo di Gaeta
Zannone
Palmarola
Ponza
283
Ísole Ponziane
Ventotene
Íschia
788
(Naples)
Mondragone
Volturno
TYRRHENIAN SEA
3719
3589
Ustica
C. San Vito
C. Gallo
G. di Castellammare
Castellammare del Golfo
Terrasini Favarotta
PALERMO
Monreale
Bagheria
Termini Imerese
Carini
Misilmeri
Partinico
Levanzo
Trápani
Érice
1110
Alcamo
Maréttimo
Ísole Égadi
Favignana
Paceco
Calatafimi
Salemi
Stagnone
Marsala
Corleone
1613
Partanna
Castelvetrano
Gibellina
Bisacquino
Prizzi
Mazara del Vallo
Sambuca di Sicilia
Menfi
Campobello di Mazara
Belice
Sciacca
Caltabellotta
Ribera
Burgio
Mussomeli
Casteltermini
Platani
San Cataldo
Caltanissetta
Racalmuto
Canicattì
Cattólica Eraclea
Raffadali
Aragona
Siculiana
Porto Empédocle
Agrigento
Favara
Naro
Palma di Montechiaro
Campobello di Licata
Licata
Sicilian Channel
Malta
Iles de la Galite
C. Serrat
C. Blanc
Cani
Bizerte (Binzert)
Menzel-Bourguiba
Plane
Zembra
Golfe de Tunis
C. Bon
El Kala
ALGERIA
Tabarka
Mateur
Tébourba
TUNIS
Halq el Oued (La Goulette)
Kelibia
Menzel Temime
Bou Salem
Béja
Medjerda
Soliman
TUNISIA
Téboursouk
Nabeul
Zaghouan
Hammamet
Pantelleria
Pantelleria (It.)
836
1319
MEDITE
ft
m
9000
3000
6000
2000
4500
1500
3000
1000
1200
400
600
200
37
0
200
600
2000
6000
4000
12 000
m
ft
Projection: Conical with two standard parallels
East from Greenwich
8
9
10
11
12
13
41
40
39
38

1:2 500 000

10   0   10   20   30   40   50 miles
10   0   10   20   30   40   50   60   70   80 km

A D R I A T I C

S E A

Strait of Otranto

I O N I A N

S E A

Golfo di Táranto

Golfo di
Sant'Eufémia

Golfo di Squillace

Isole Eólie o Lípari (Æolian Is.)

A L B A N I A

Drini

Durrës
(Durazzo)

Tirana

Shkumbini

Vlora

Kérkira
(Corfu)

R A N E A N   S E A

Channel

COPYRIGHT, GEORGE PHILIP & SON LTD.

HUNGARY
YUGOSLAVIA
ALBANIA
ADRIATIC SEA
TOLNA
CSONGRÁD
SOMOGY
BARANYA
BIHOR
ARAD
TIMIŞ
CARAŞ SEVERIN
Autonomna Pokrajina Vojvodina
Socijalisticka Autonomna Pokrajina Kosovo
BOSNA
HERCEGOVINA
CRNA GORA (MONTENEGRO)
SRBIJA
MAKEDONIJA
DALMACIJA
SHKODRA
TIRANA-DURRËSI
Nagykanizsa
Kaposvár
Szekszárd
Baja
Pécs
Mohács
Kiskunhalas
Kiskunmajsa
Hódmezővásárhely
Szeged
Makó
Orosháza
Gyula
Arad
Timişoara
Lugoj
Hunedoara
Reşiţa
Caransebeş
Turnu-Severin
Subotica
Sombor
Kikinda
Zrenjanin
Novi Sad
Vršac
Pančevo
Beograd (Belgrade)
Zemun
Smederevo
Požarevac
Osijek
Vukovar
Vinkovci
Slavonski Brod
Banja Luka
Tuzla
Zenica
Sarajevo
Mostar
Dubrovnik
Kotor
Cetinje
Titograd
Nikšić
Valjevo
Šabac
Kragujevac
Čačak
Kraljevo
Kruševac
Niš
Leskovac
Priština
Peć
Prizren
Skopje
Kumanovo
Tetovo
Titov Veles
Prilep
Bitola
Ohrid
Štip
Strumica
Shkodra (Shkodër)
Durrësi (Durazzo)
Tirana (Tiranë)
Elbasani
Korčula
Lastovo
Mljet
Hvar
Vidin
Pernik
Kyustendil
Blagoevgrad
Dunav (Danube)
Drava
Sava
Tisa
Morava
Drina
Timok
Ohridsko Jezero (L. Ohrid)
Prespansko Jezero (L. Prespa)
Skadarsko Jezero
Dojransko Jezero (L. Doiran)
Fruška Gora
Šar Planina
Kopaonik
Prokletije
Suva Planina
Plakenska Planina
ft
m
9000
3000
6000
2000
4500
1500
3000
1000
1200
400
600
200
0
0
200
600
2000
6000
m
ft
Projection: Conical with two standard parallels
East from Greenwich
19
20
21
22
23
46
45
44
43
42
41

FOR CONTINUATION SEE PAGE 71

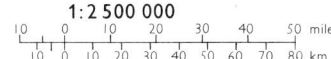

1 : 2 500 000

10   0   10   20   30   40   50 miles
10   0   10   20   30   40   50   60   70   80 km

U. S. S. R.

IZMAIL

UKRAINIAN S.S.R.

Ozero Kitai   Ozero Sasyk

Kiliya   Vilkovo

Bratul Chilia

Bratul Sulina

Ostrov Letea

Sulina

Sfintu Gheorghe

Bratul Sfintu Gheorghe

R O M A N I A

TRANSILVANIA

Cluj   Turda   Lugoj   Band   Tirgu   Sovata   Praid   Bacău   Princesa   VASLUI   Leovo   Volontirovka

Mures   Harghita   Muntii Harghita   Bessarabka   Komrat   Tarutino

Aiud   Odorhei   Gheorghe   Gheorghiu-Dej   Birlad   Berest

Medias   Sighisoara   Tirgu Ocna   Panciu   Galați   Dunay (Danube)   Ismail

Sibiu   Brasov   Focsani   Braila   Macin   Tulcea   Lacul Razelm

VALAHIA (WALACHIA)

Craiova   Pitesti   Ploiesti   Buzău   Constanța

BUCUREȘTI (Bucharest)

IALOMIȚA

Giurgiu   Ruse (Ruschuk)   Silistra   Dunărea (Danube)

TELEORMAN   Alexandria

Constanța

DOBRUJA

B U L G A R I A

Balkan Mountains (Chatal Balkan)

Sofiya (Sofia)   Plovdiv   Stara Zagora   Nova Zagora   Yambol   Burgas

Pleven   Turgovishte   Varna

Tolbukhin   Dobrich Bazargic

B L A C K   S E A

T U R K E Y

Edirne (Adrianople)   KIRKLARELI

TEKIRDAG   İSTANBUL   Üsküdar

Karadeniz Boğazı (Bosporus)

G R E E C E

Drama   Xanthi   Komotini

COPYRIGHT GEORGE PHILIP & SON LTD.

Sofiya
Skopje
Tirana
Thessaloníki
Plovdiv
Thásos
Límnos
Samothráki
Saros Körfezi
Thermaïkós Kólpos
Strimonikós Kólpos

1:2 500 000

10   20   30   40   50 miles

10   0   10   20   30   40   50   60   70   80 km

COPYRIGHT GEORGE PHILIP & SON, LTD

(LÉSVOS)

Mithíni

Ayíasós

968 ▲

1212 ▲

Karábúrun

Plomárion

Karádhámila

Oinoúsa

Volissós

Vrondádhos

Khios ⊙

Khíos (Chios)

Akra Mastíka

Akra Mestá

Psará

Psará

Andípsara

Skópelos

Kaloyeroi

VORIAI SPORÁDHES (Northern Sporades)

Skántzoúra

Perístera

Skiros ⊙

792 ▲

Skiropoúla

Valáxa

Skópelos

Pélion Tríkeri

Skiáthos

Skíros

1262 ▲

Foúrnoi

Foúrnoi

Ródhikni

Ikaría

Melíssa

957 ▲

1297 ▲

822 ▲

Levítha

Kínaros

Líadhoi

Kínaros

Dhenoúsa

Mikonos

Dhragonísi

Náxos

957 ▲

Koufonísia

Káros

Skhoinoúsa

Astipálaia

Astipálaia

Ofidhoúsa

Áyios Yeóryios

Ándhros

Anáfi

Khamilónísion

S P O R A D H E S

A E G E A N   S E A

(Cyclades)

KIKLÁDHES (CYCLADES)

Andíros

Akra Kafir̂évs

OKHI OROS

Mikonos

Tínos

Síros

Síros (Ermoúpolis)

Rínia

Dhílos

Páros

Náxos

1001 ▲

706 ▲

Iráklia

Irakliá

Ios

Ios

Thíra

Thirasía

Khristianá

SEA OF CRETE

(Sea of Candia)

Khersónisos

Akrotíri

Spáthou

Kólpos Soúdhas

Kólpos Khanión

KHANIÁ

2456 ▲

Réthimnon

2453 ▲

IRÁKLION

Iráklion (Candia)

Dia

Ano Viánnos

IERÁPETRA

LASÍTHI

2148 ▲

Sitía

Palaiókhora

Gávdhos

Gavdhopoúla

Kólpos Kisámou

Akra Vódxai

Kólpos Mesarás

Paxmádhia

Akra Líthinon

Timbákion

Áyios Yeóryios

East from Greenwich

Projection: Conical with two standard parallels

Continuation Eastwards on same scale

m ____ ft

9000 6000 4500 3000 1500 1200 600 400 200 0

m ____ ft

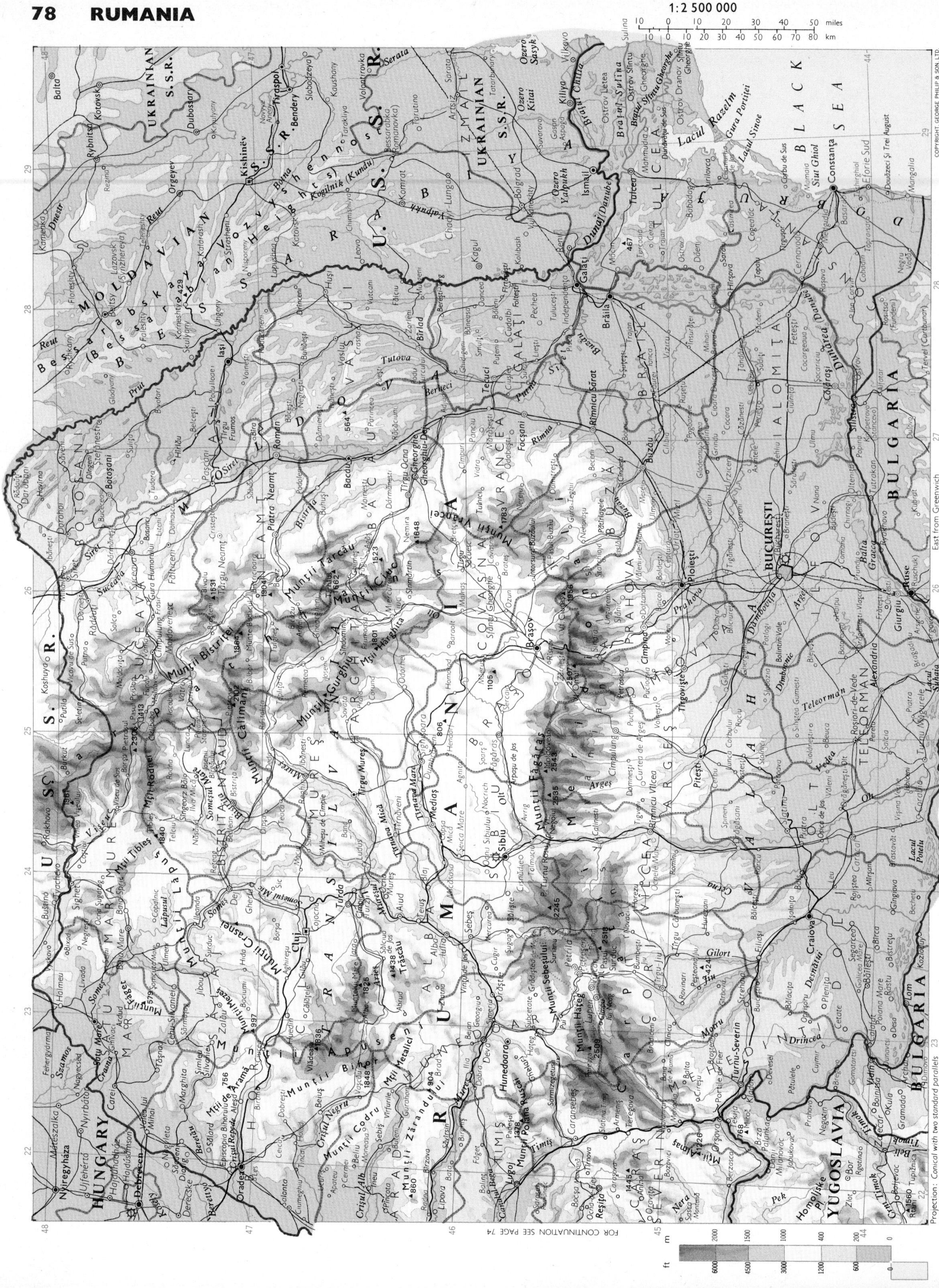

1:2 500 000

miles
km

BLACK SEA

HUNGARY

YUGOSLAVIA

BULGARIA

U.S.S.R.

UKRAINIAN S.S.R.

MOLDAVIAN S.S.R.

TRANSILVANIA

CARPATII MERIDIONALI

East from Greenwich

COPYRIGHT GEORGE PHILIP & SON, LTD.

Projection: Conical with two standard parallels

FOR CONTINUATION SEE PAGE 74

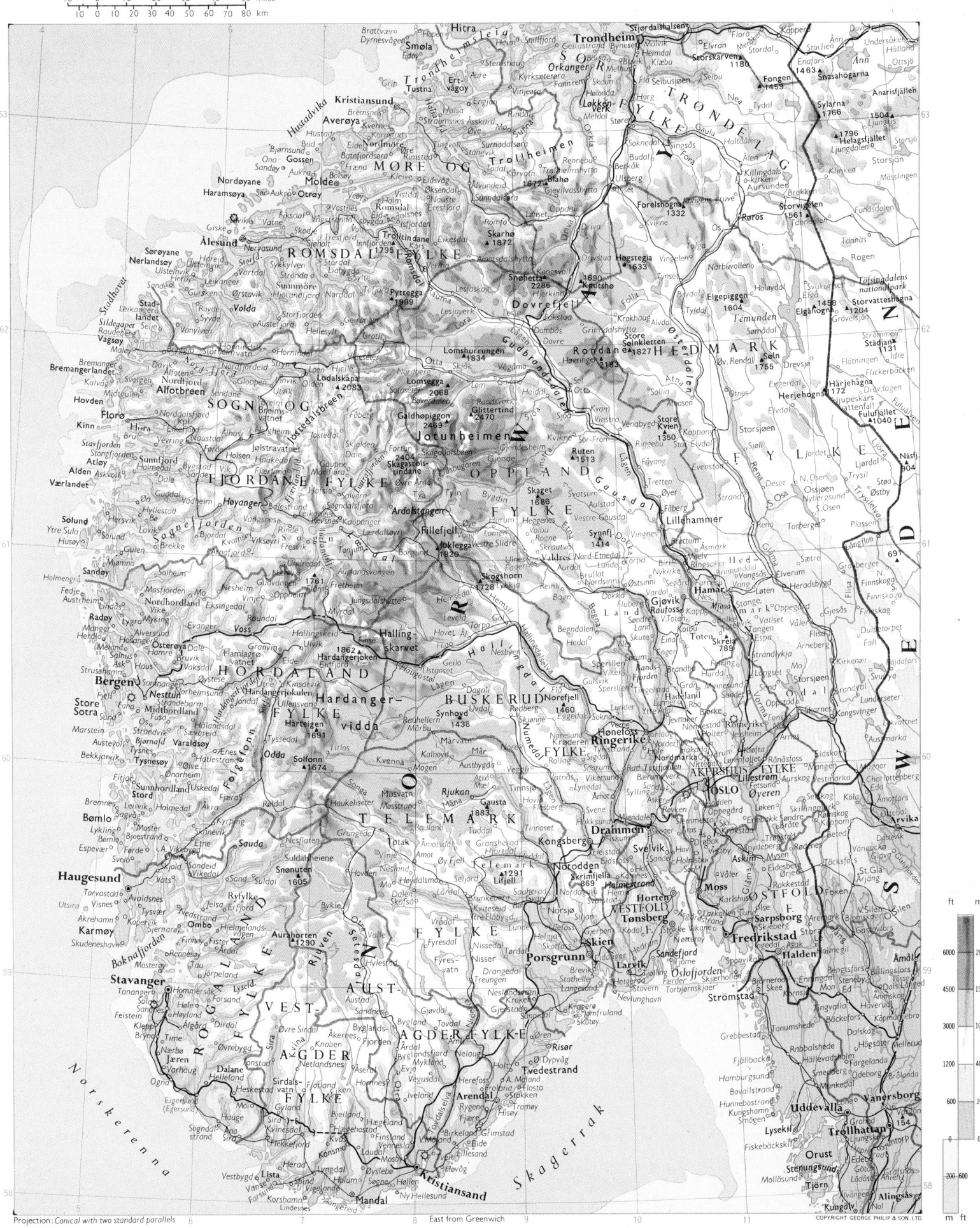

1:2 500 000

10   0   10   20   30   40   50 miles
10   0   10   20   30   40   50   60   70   80 km

Projection: Conical with two standard parallels

East from Greenwich

COPYRIGHT GEORGE PHILIP & SON, LTD.

Gulf of Bothnia

Örnsköldsvik · Härnösand · Sundsvall · Söderhamn · Gävle · Uppsala · STOCKHOLM · Södertälje · Nacka

Östersund · Sveg · Ljusdal · Bollnäs · Falun · Borlänge · Örebro · Eskilstuna · Västerås · Köping · Arboga

VÄSTERNORRLANDS LÄN · GÄVLEBORGS LÄN · KOPPARBERGS LÄN · VÄSTMANLANDS LÄN · SÖDERMANLANDS LÄN · UPPSALA LÄN · STOCKHOLMS LÄN · ÖREBRO LÄN

JÄMTLANDS LÄN · Mora · Orsa · Malung · Sälen

Trondheim · Røros · Lillehammer · Hamar · Gjøvik · Oslo · Drammen · Kongsberg · Skien · Porsgrunn · Fredrikstad · Sarpsborg · Moss · Horten · Tønsberg

TRØNDELAG FYLKE · MØRE OG ROMSDAL FYLKE · HEDMARK FYLKE · OPPLAND FYLKE · BUSKERUD FYLKE · AKERSHUS · ØSTFOLD · VESTFOLD · TELEMARK FYLKE · VÄRMLANDS LÄN

Kristiansund · Karlstad · Säffle · Arvika · Sunne

Snøhetta 2286 · Galdhøpiggen 2469 · Glittertind 2470 · Jotunheimen · Dovrefjell · Rondane · Gausta 1883 · Gudbrandsdalen · Hallingdal · Numedal

1:2 500 000

COPYRIGHT GEORGE PHILIP & SON, LTD.

Projection: Conical with two standard parallels

East from Greenwich

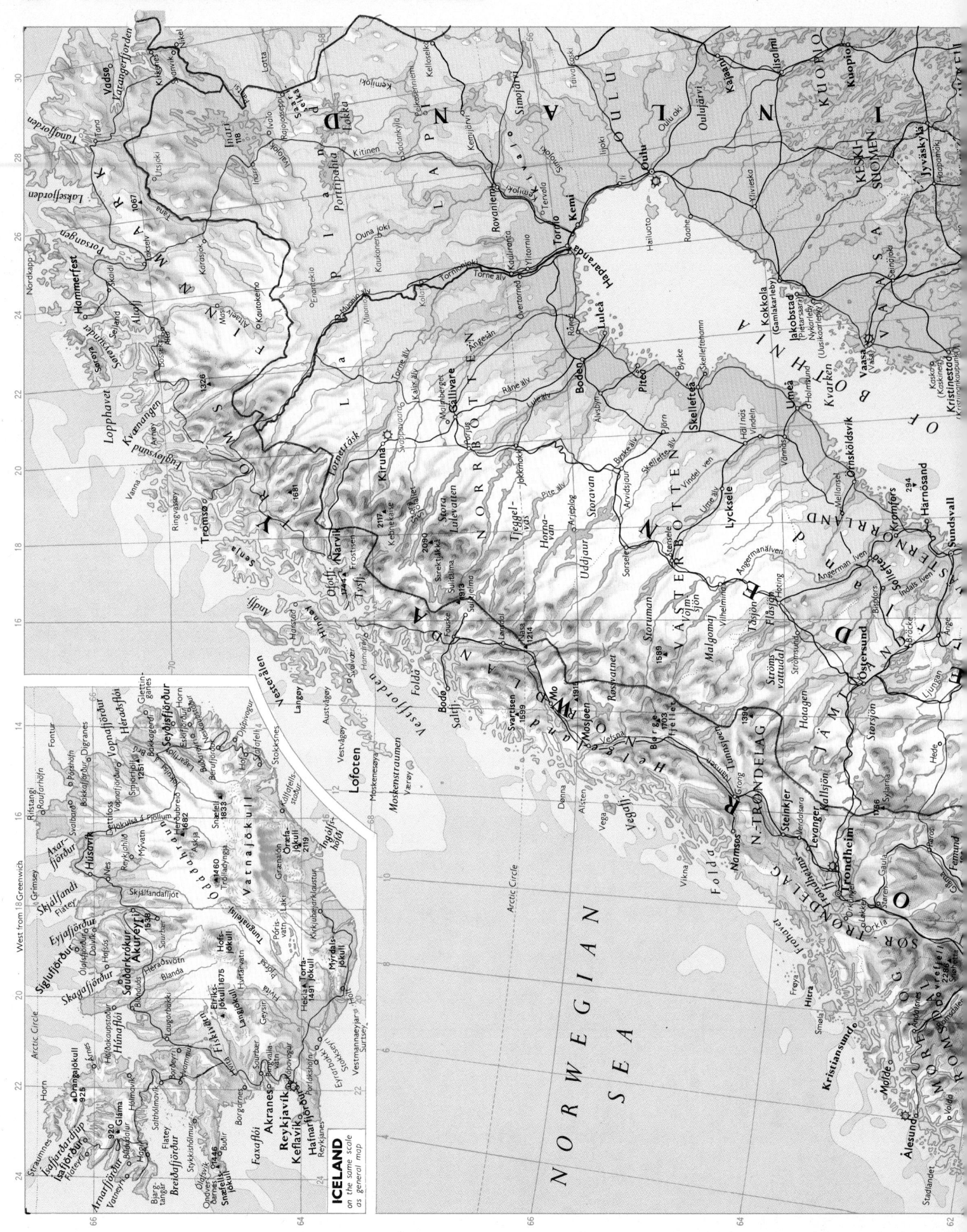
ICELAND
on the same scale
as general map
West from 18 Greenwich
Arctic Circle
NORWEGIAN SEA
GULF OF BOTHNIA
Lofoten
Vesterålen
Vestfjorden
Moskenstraumen
Tromsø
Narvik
Kiruna
Gällivare
Boden
Luleå
Piteå
Skellefteå
Umeå
Haparanda
Tornio
Kemi
Oulu
Rovaniemi
Kokkola
Jakobstad
Vaasa
Kristinestad
Jyväskylä
Kuopio
Iisalmi
Kajaani
Hammerfest
Vadsø
Inari
Bodø
Mo
Mosjøen
Namsos
Steinkjer
Levanger
Trondheim
Kristiansund
Molde
Ålesund
Östersund
Sundsvall
Härnösand
Kramfors
Örnsköldsvik
Lycksele
NORRBOTTEN
VÄSTERBOTTEN
N.-TRØNDELAG
Reykjavík
Keflavík
Akranes
Akureyri
Húsavík
Siglufjörður
Sauðárkrókur
Seyðisfjörður
Ísafjörður
Vatnajökull
Hafnarfjörður
Faxaflói

1:5 000 000

20 10 0   60   80   100 miles
40 20 0   40   80   120   160 km

COPYRIGHT GEORGE PHILIP & SON, LTD.

BALTIC SEA

GULF OF FINLAND

GULF OF RIGA

East from Greenwich

Projection. Conical with two standard parallels

Ural'skiye Gory
Timanskiy Kryazh
Bolshezemelskaya Tundra
Malozemelskaya Tundra
Pechorskaya Guba
Kolguyev
P-ov. Kanin
Cheshskaya Guba
Ostrov Morzhovets
M. Kanin Nos
Kolskiy Poluostrov
P-ov. Rybachiy
Murmansk
Beloye More (White Sea)
Kandalakshskiy Zaliv
Dvinskaya Guba
Onezhskaya Guba
Arkhangelsk (Archangel)
Severodvinsk (Molotovsk)
Severnyye Uvaly
Syktyvkar
Kotlas
Kirov
Vologda
Perm
Sverdlovsk
Nizhniy Tagil
Zlatoust
Magnitogorsk
Orenburg
Ufa
Kuybyshev
Togliatti
Izhevsk
Kazan
Udmurt A.S.S.R.
Tatar A.S.S.R.
Bashkir A.S.S.R.
Mari A.S.S.R.
Chuvash
Mordovian A.S.S.R.
Gorkiy
Cheboksary
Yoshkar Ola
Ulyanovsk
Penza
Russian Soviet Federal Socialist Republic
Moskva (Moscow)
Yaroslavl
Kostroma
Ivanovo
Vladimir
Kalinin
Rybinsk
Ryazan
Tula
Kaluga
Tambov
Lipetsk
Orel
Bryansk
Smolensk
Leningrad
Kronshtadt
Ladozhskoye Ozero
Onezhskoye Ozero
Petrozavodsk
Karelian A.S.S.R.
Novgorod
Pskov
Valdayskaya Vozvyshennost
Estonian S.S.R.
Tallinn
Tartu
Latvian S.S.R.
Riga
Lithuanian S.S.R.
Vilnius
Kaunas
Kaliningrad (Königsberg)
Byelorussian S.S.R. (White Russia)
Minsk
Vitebsk
Mogilev
Gomel
Bobruysk
Polesye (Pripet-Marshes)
Brest
Grodno
Poland
Warszawa (Warsaw)
Finland
Helsinki
Tampere
Turku
Oulu
Lappland
Sweden
Norway
Stockholm
Gulf of Bothnia
G. of Finland
Aland (Ahvenanmaa)
Saaremaa (Osel)
Hiiumaa (Dagö)
Rigas Juras Licis

85

1:10 000 000

Projection: Conical with two standard parallels

East from Greenwich

COPYRIGHT GEORGE PHILIP & SON LTD.

Kabardino-Balkar A.S.S.R.
North Ossetian A.S.S.R. (Azer.)
Nakhichevan A.S.S.R. (Azer.)
Checheno-Ingush A.S.S.R.
Karagiye Depression

1:5 000 000

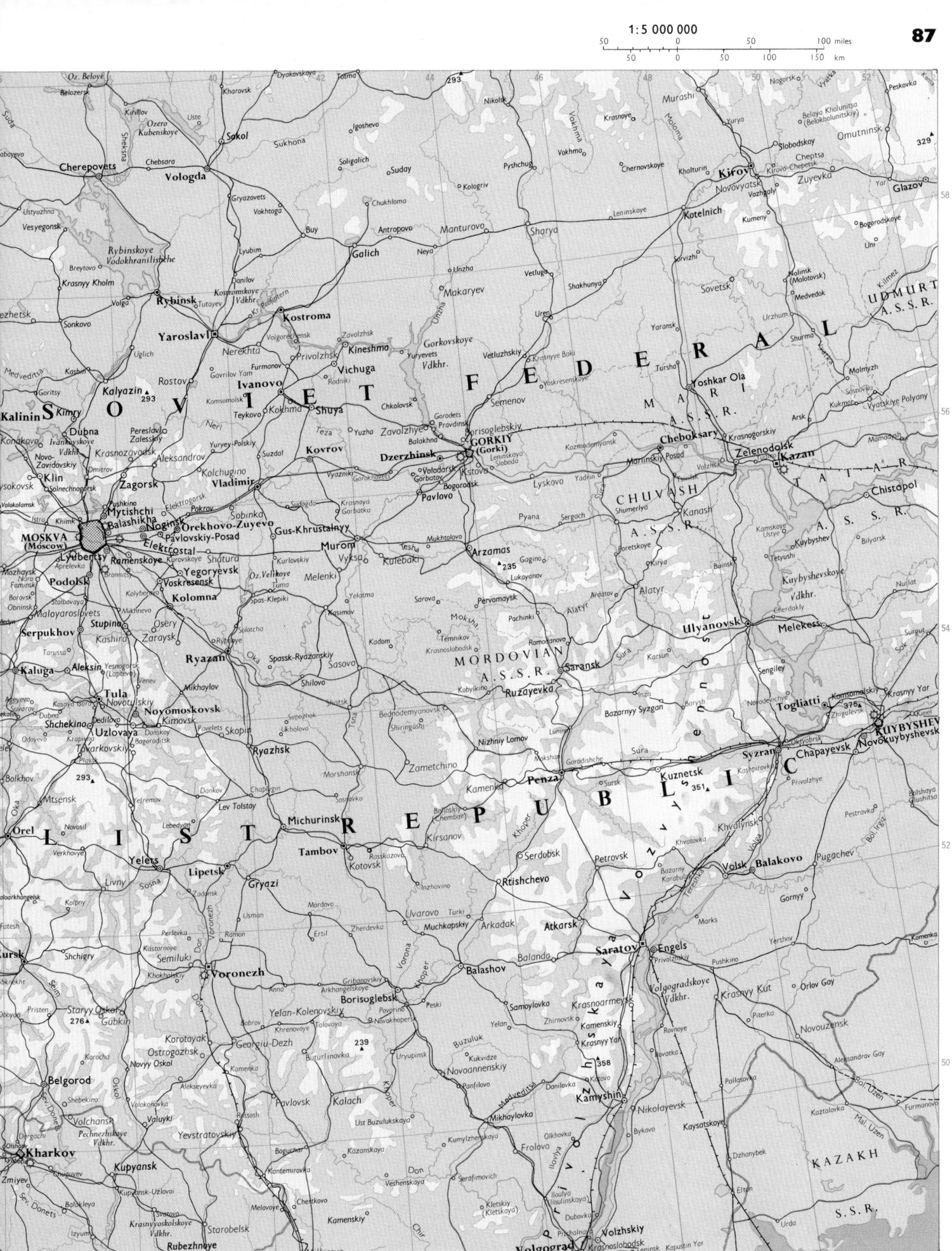
50 0 50 100 miles
50 0 50 100 150 km
SOVIET FEDERAL SOCIALIST REPUBLIC
MARI A.S.S.R.
CHUVASH A.S.S.R.
TATAR A.S.S.R.
MORDOVIAN A.S.S.R.
UDMURT A.S.S.R.
KAZAKH S.S.R.
Privolzhskaya Vozvyshennost
Oz. Beloye
Belozersk
Kirillov
Ozero Kubenskoye
Sheksna
Sokol
Kharovsk
Dyakovskoye
Totma
Nikolsk
Murashi
Vokhma
Molema
Krasnoye
Yurya
Nagorsk
Vyatka
Peskovka
Kama
Belaya Kholunitsa (Belokholunitskiy)
Omutninsk
Slobodskoy
Kirov
Kirovo-Chepetsk
Cheptsa
Zuyevka
Glazov
Yar
Khalturin
Novovyatsk
Vozhgaly
Chernovskoye
Vokhma
Pyshchug
Sukhona
Igoshevo
Soligalich
Suday
Kologriv
Cherepovets
Chebsara
Vologda
Uste
Ustyuzhna
Vesyegonsk
Gryazovets
Vokhtoga
Chukhloma
Buy
Antropovo
Manturovo
Sharya
Leninskoye
Kotelnich
Kumeny
Bogorodskoye
Uni
Rybinskoye Vodokhranilishche
Lyubim
Galich
Neya
Breytovo
Krasnyy Kholm
Danilov
Unzha
Makaryev
Vetluga
Shakhunya
Sovetsk
Nolinsk (Molotovsk)
Medvedok
Kilmez
Rybinsk
Tutayev
Kostromskoye Vdkhr.
Kostroma
Uren
Urzhum
Sonkovo
Yaroslavl
Volgorechensk
Zavolzhsk
Gorkovskoye Vdkhr.
Yuryevets
Vetluzhskiy
Krasnyye Baki
Yaransk
Shurma
Malmyzh
Uglich
Nerekhta
Privolzhsk
Kineshma
Vichuga
Rodniki
Medveditsa
Kashin
Goritsy
Kalyazin
Rostov
Gavrilov Yam
Furmanov
Ivanovo
Yoshkar Ola
Tursha
Sosnovka
Kukmor
Vyatskiye Polyany
Kalinin
Kimry
Dubna
Komsomolsk
Teykovo
Kokhma
Shuya
Chkalovsk
Gorodets
Pravdinsk
Semenov
Arsk
Konakovo
Ivankovskoye Vdkhr.
Pereslavl Zalesskiy
Neri
Teza
Yuzha
Zavolzhye
Balakhna
Borisoglebskiy
GORKIY (Gorki)
Cheboksary
Krasnogorskiy
Zelenodolsk
Kazan
Mamadysh
Novo-Zavidovskiy
Krasnozavodsk
Aleksandrov
Yuryev-Polskiy
Suzdal
Kovrov
Dzerzhinsk
Kozmodemyansk
Mariinskiy Posad
Klin
Dmitrov
Kolchugino
Vyazniki
Gorokhovets
Volodarsk
Gorbatov
Kstovo
Leninskaya Sloboda
Yadrin
Tsivilsk
Volzhsk
Solnechnogorsk
Zagorsk
Vladimir
Bogorodsk
Lyskovo
Chistopol
Volokolamsk
Pushkino
Mytishchi
Elektrogorsk
Pokrov
Sobinka
Sudogda
Krasnaya Gorbatka
Pavlovo
Shumerlya
Kanash
Istra
Khimki
Balashikha
Noginsk
Orekhovo-Zuyevo
Pyana
Sergach
MOSKVA (Moscow)
Pavlovskiy-Posad
Elektrostal
Gus-Khrustalnyy
Murom
Mukhtolovo
Tesha
Arzamas
Poretskoye
Kamskoye Ustye
Kuybyshev
Bilyarsk
Lyubertsy
Ramenskoye
Kurovskoye
Shatura
Vyksa
Kulebaki
Kurlovskiy
Gagino
Kirya
Tetyushi
Mozhaysk
Aprelevka
Bronnitsy
Yegoryevsk
Oz. Velikoye
Melenki
Lukoyanov
Buinsk
Kuybyshevskoye Vdkhr.
Naro Fominsk
Podolsk
Voskresensk
Tuma
Nurlat
Borovsk
Obninsk
Kolybelka
Kolomna
Spas-Klepiki
Yelatma
Sarova
Pervomaysk
Ardatov
Alatyr
Maloyaroslavets
Mikhnevo
Kasimov
Moksha
Pachinki
Cherdakly
Serpukhov
Stupino
Kashira
Ozery
Zaraysk
Splotcha
Rybnoye
Kodom
Temnikov
Krasnoslobodsk
Romodanovo
Ulyanovsk
Melekess
Surgut
Tarussa
Aleksin
Yasnogorsk (Laptevo)
Ryazan
Oka
Spassk-Ryazanskiy
Sasovo
MORDOVIAN A.S.S.R.
Saransk
Sura
Karsun
Sok
Kaluga
Venev
Shilovo
Kobylkino
Ruzayevka
Inza
Sengiley
Novodevichye
Komsomolskiy
Krasnyy Yar
Tula
Novotulskiy
Mikhaylov
Shatsk
Bazarnyy Syzgan
Barysh
Togliatti
Zhigulevsk
375
Kinel
Kosaya Gora
Dubna
Novomoskovsk
Sapozhok
Ukholovo
Bednodemyanovsk
Tsna
Shchekino
Uzlovaya
Kimovsk
Dedilovo
Povelets
Skopin
Shiringushi
KUYBYSHEV
Novokuybyshevsk
Odoyevo
Krapivna
Donskoy
Bogoroditsk
Tovarkovskiy
Ryazhsk
Nizhniy Lomov
Lunino
Oktyabrsk
Chapayevsk
Plavsk
Zametchino
Mokshan
Gorodishche
Syzran
293
Bolkhov
Morshansk
Penza
Kuznetsk
Kashpirovka
Privolzhye
Mtsensk
Dankov
Chaplygin
Sosnovka
Kamenka
Sursk
351
Bolshaya Glushitsa
Yefremov
Lev Tolstoy
Belinskiy (Chembar)
Pestravka
Oka
Orel
Novosil
Lebedyan
Michurinsk
Khoper
Khvalynsk
Bol. Irgiz
Verkhovye
Yelets
Tambov
Rasskazovo
Kirsanov
Serdobsk
Petrovsk
Khvatovka
Volga
Livny
Lipetsk
Kotovsk
Volsk
Balakovo
Pugachev
Sosna
Gryazi
Inzhavino
Rtishchevo
Bazarny Karabulak
Tereshka
Kolpny
Zadonsk
Mordovo
Gornyy
Usman
Uvarovo
Turki
Fatezh
Voronezh
Perlevka
Ertil
Zherdevka
Muchkapskiy
Arkadak
Atkarsk
Marks
Ramon
Kastornoye
Vorona
Kamenka
Kursk
Shchigry
Semiluki
Saratov
Engels
Yershov
Don
Balanda
Privolzhskiy
Pushkino
Khokholskiy
Voronezh
Balashov
Gribanovskiy
Arkhangelskoye
Anna
Borisoglebsk
Volgogradskoye Vdkhr.
Krasnyy Kut
Orlov Gay
Seim
Peski
Samoylovka
Krasnoarmeysk
Staryy Oskol
Pristen
Gubkin
276
Yelan-Kolenovskiy
Povorino
Novokhopersk
Bobrov
Khrenovoye
Talovaya
Zhirnovsk
Piterka
Yelan
Kamenskiy
Rovnoye
Novouzensk
Korotoyak
Ostrogozhsk
Georgiu-Dezh
239
Buzuluk
Kukvidze
Krasnyy Yar
Korocha
Novyy Oskol
Kamenka
Buturlinovka
Uryupinsk
Novoannenskiy
358
Novatka
Aleksandrov Gay
Belgorod
Alekseyevka
Panfilovo
Kotovo
Pallasovka
Oskol
Shebekino
Volokonovka
Pavlovsk
Kalach
Medveditsa
Danilovka
Kamyshin
Bol. Uzen
Furmanov
Sev. Donets
Rossosh
Nikolayevsk
Volchansk
Valuyki
Ust Buzulukskaya
Mikhaylovka
Kaztalovka
Mal. Uzen
Pechenezhskoye Vdkhr.
Dergachi
Yevstratovskiy
Kumylzhenskaya
Olkhovka
Bykovo
Kaysatskoye
Kharkov
Boguchar
Kazanskaya
Frolovo
Dzhanybek
Kupyansk
Chuguyev
Kantemirovka
Don
Ilovlya
Zmiyev
Kupyansk-Uzlovoi
Veshenskaya
Serafimovich
Elton
Balakleya
Svatovo
Chertkovo
Melovoye
Kletskiy (Kletskaya)
Ilovlya (Iloulinskaya)
Dubovka
Sev. Donets
Krasnyyoskolskoye Vdkhr.
Starobelsk
Kamenskiy
Chir
Urda
Izyum
Rubezhnoye
Millerovo
Volzhskiy
Prishibinsk
Volgograd (Stalingrad)
Krasnoslobodsk
Leninsk
Kapustin Yar
36
38
40
42
44
46
48
50
52
54
56
58
293
329

COPYRIGHT. GEORGE PHILIP & SON. LTD.

RUMANIA
BULGARIA
BLACK SEA
AZOVSKOYE MORE
(Sea of Azov)
Rovno
Zhitomir
KIYEV
(Kiev)
Nezhin
Bakhmach
Sumy
Belgorod
Lvov
Berdichev
Belaya Tserkov
Khmelnitskiy
Vinnitsa
Priluki
Kharkov
Poltava
Kremenchug
Cherkassy
Kirovograd
Dnepropetrovsk
Zaporozhye
Krivoy Rog
Nikopol
Donetsk
(Stalino)
Makeyevka
Gorlovka
Zhdanov
Melitopol
Berdyansk
Nikolayev
Kherson
Odessa
Kishinev
Tiraspol
Bendery
Iasi
Bacău
Galaţi
Braila
Ploeşti
BUCUREŞTI
(Bucharest)
Constanţa
Ruse
Varna
Burgas
Edirne
Kirklareli
İstanbul
Üsküdar
İzmit
Adapazari
Bursa
Ankara
Zonguldak
Kastamonu
Samsun
Amasya
Çorum
Sinop
Ince-Burnu
Karadeniz Boğazi
(Bosporus)
MARMARA DENIZI
(Sea of Marmara)
Karkinitskiy Zaliv
Dzhankoi
Krymskiy P.-ov
(Crimea)
Yevpatoriya
Simferopol
Sevastopol
Yalta
Feodosiya
Kerch
Novorossiysk
Taganrogski
Yeysk
Kakhovskoye Vdkhr.
Kremenchugskoye Vdkhr.
Dneprodzerzhinskoye Vdkhr.
Projection: Conical with two standard parallels

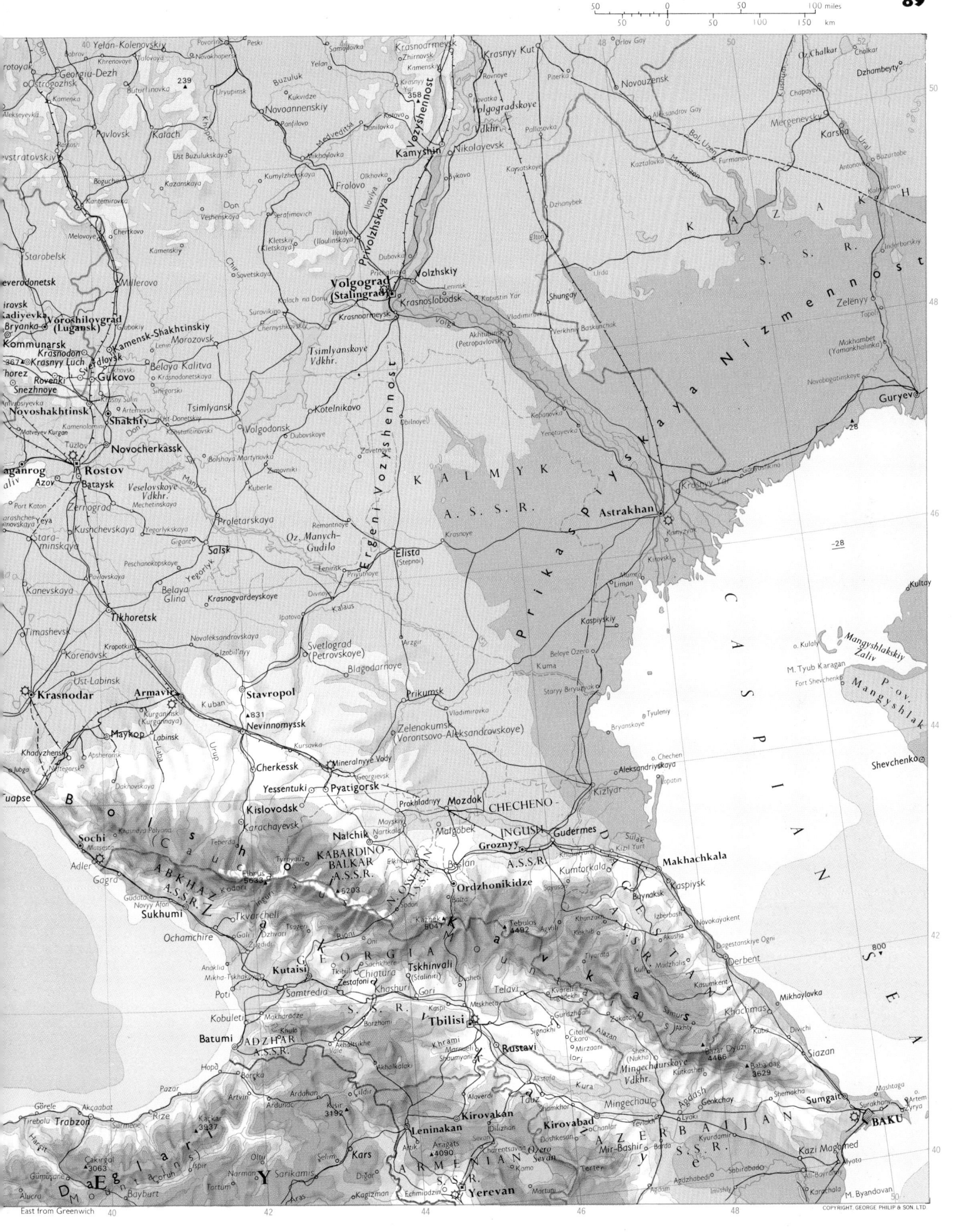

1 : 5 000 000

50   0   50   100 miles

50   0   50   100   150 km

East from Greenwich   40

COPYRIGHT. GEORGE PHILIP & SON. LTD

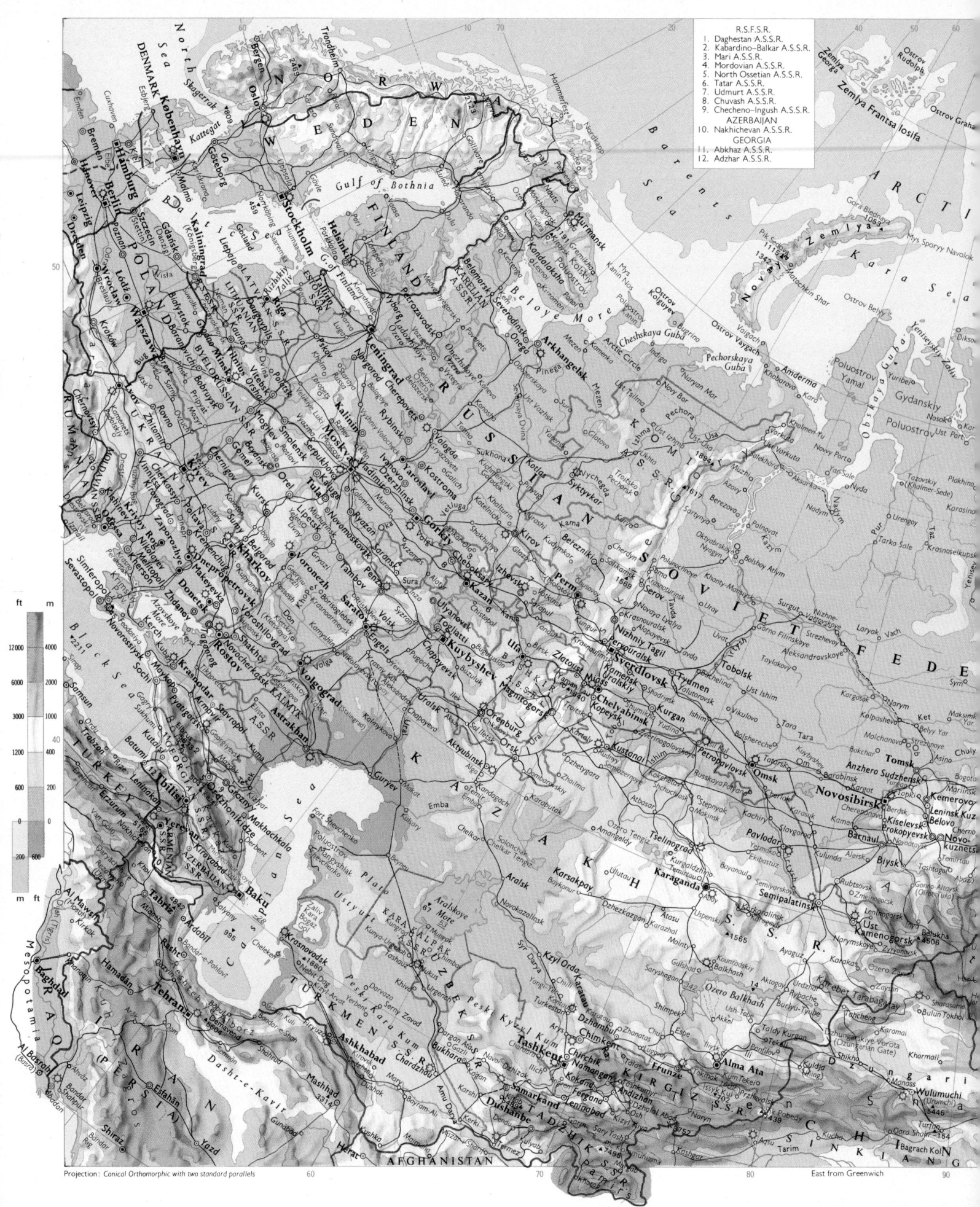

Projection: Conical Orthomorphic with two standard parallels

East from Greenwich

1:20 000 000

100   0   100   200   300   400   500 miles
100   0   200   400   600   800 km

OCEAN

Mys Dezhneva
(East C.)

St. Lawrence I.
(U.S.A.)

Laptev Sea

East Siberian Sea

Severnaya Zemlya

Ostrov Komsomolets

Ostrov Oktyabrskoy Revolyutsii

Bering Sea

Poluostrov Kamchatka

Petropavlovsk-Kamchatskiy

Sea of Okhotsk

Chukotskiy Khrebet

Koryakskiy Khrebet

Sredinnyy Khrebet

Poluostrov Pyrranga Goryuostrov Taymyr

Nordvik

Tiksi

Verkhoyansk

Khrebet Cherskogo

Magadan

Okhotsk

Khrebet Dzhugdzur

Kolyma

Zaliv Shelikhova

Gizhiginskaya Guba

Penzhinskaya Guba

Yakutsk

Olekminsk

Igarka

Norilsk

Gory Putorana

Severnaya Zemlya

Yenisey

A. S. S. R.

Sredinny Khrebet

Ostrov Shantar

Nikolayevsk-na-Am.

Sakhalin

Sovetskaya Gavan

Yuzhno-Sakhalinsk

Kirensk

Bratsk

Achinsk

Krasnoyarsk

Nizhneudinsk

Stanovoy Khrebet

Khrebet Sikhote Alin

Komsomolsk

Khabarovsk

Birobidzhan

Blagoveshchensk

Amur

Kiamusze

Cheremkhovo

Angarsk

Ulan Ude

Irkutsk

Chita

Zapadnyy Sayan

Munku Sardyk
3491

TUVA A.S.S.R.

Hovsgol Nuur

Tsitsihar

Harbin

Ussurisk

Vladivostok

Nakhodka

MONGOLIA

Hangayn Nuruu

Hentiyn Nuruu

Ulaanbaatar
(Ulan Bator)

Tung Pei
(Manchuria)

Kirin

Changchun

Szeping

Hokkaido

Sapporo

Hakodate

Sea of JAPAN

Honshū

Nii-gata

To-yama

Kanazawa

Shenyang

Anshan

Fushun

Antung

North

Wŏnsan

Pyongyang

Sŏul

Inch'ŏn

South

Taejŏn

Pusan

Edrengiyn Nuruu

Hami

Gashiun Nor

Mingshui

Paotow

Changkiakow
(Kalgan)

Peiping
(Peking)

Lu-ta

Yingkow

GOBI

INNER MONGOLIA REPUBLIC

	Boundaries of U.S.S.R.
	Boundaries of S.S.R.
	Boundaries of A.S.S.R.

COPYRIGHT. GEORGE PHILIP & SON. LTD.

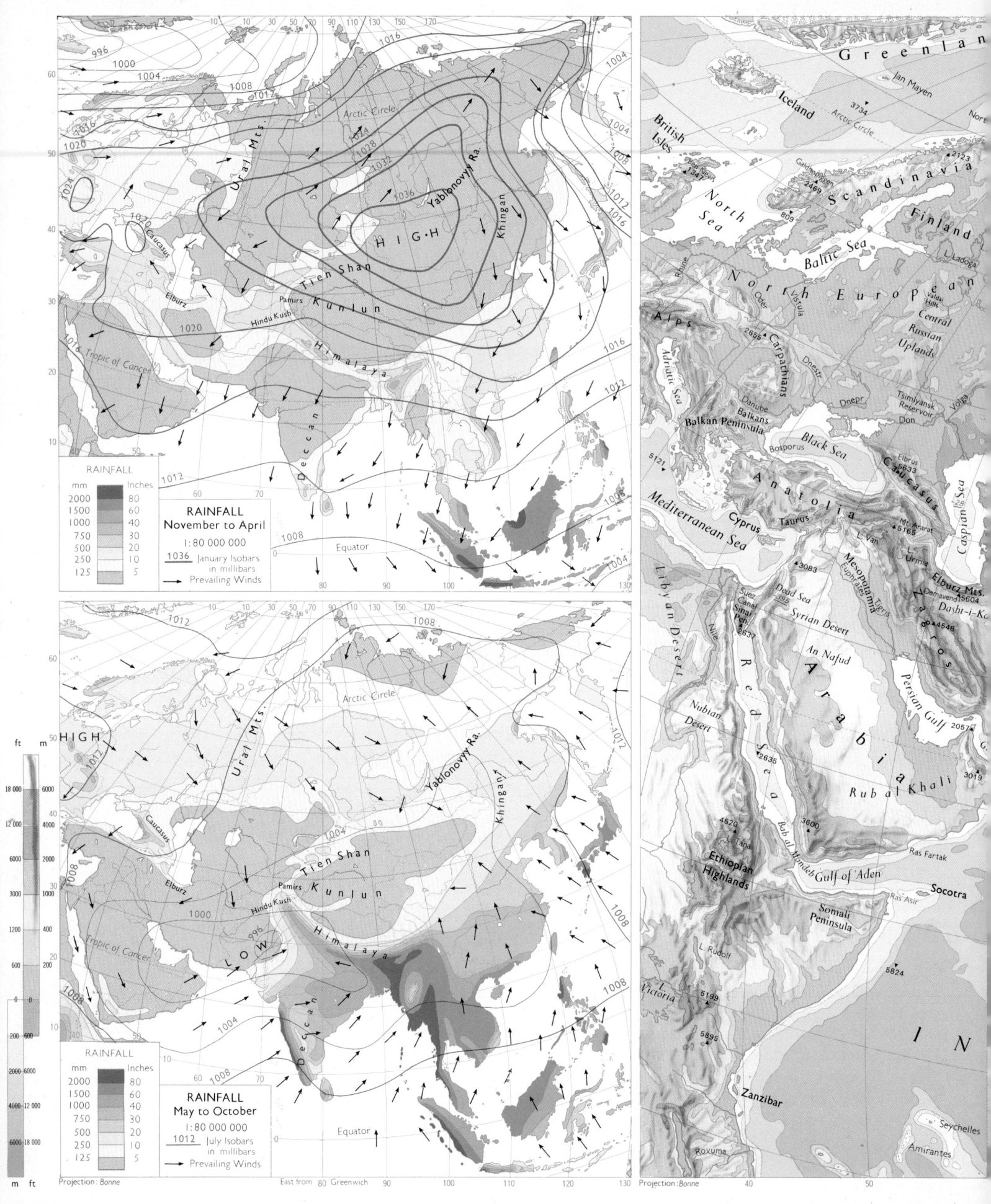

RAINFALL

mm		Inches
2000		80
1500		60
1000		40
750		30
500		20
250		10
125		5

RAINFALL
November to April
1:80 000 000
<u>1036</u> January Isobars in millibars
→ Prevailing Winds

RAINFALL

mm		Inches
2000		80
1500		60
1000		40
750		30
500		20
250		10
125		5

RAINFALL
May to October
1:80 000 000
<u>1012</u> July Isobars in millibars
→ Prevailing Winds

ft	m
18 000	6000
12 000	4000
6000	2000
3000	1000
1200	400
600	200
0	0
200	600
2000	6000
4000	12 000
6000	18 000

m ft

Projection: Bonne

East from 80 Greenwich

Projection: Bonne

1:40 000 000

200   0   200   400   600   800   1000 miles
200   0   400   800   1200   1600 km

ARCTIC OCEAN

Svalbard
Fr. Josef Land
Severnaya Zemlya
Bear I.
Cape
C. Chelyuskin
Taimyr Peninsula
Byrrang Mts.
Laptev Sea
Foddeyev
New Siberian Is.
Lyakhov Is.
Kotelny
Wrangel I.
Bear Is.
C. Dezhneva (East C.)
Bering Str.

Barents Sea
Novaya Zemlya
Kara Sea
Kolguyev
Kola Pen.
White Sea
Onega
N. Dvina
Yamal Pen.
Gydan Pen.
Ob
Yenisey
Koтuy
Olenek
Putoran Mts.
Central
Siberian
Plateau
Lower Tunguska
Stony Tunguska
Lena
Verkhoyansk Ra.
Indigirka
Kolyma Plain
Kolyma
Cherskiy Ra.
3147
2959
Chukot Ra.
G. of Anadyr
Gyda Ra.
Koryak Ra.
2562
Bering Sea
Kamchatka Peninsula
4750
Komandorskiye
Sredinny Ra.
C. Lopatka
7999
Kuril Is.
Spurilisland

Ural Mountains
Narodnaya 1894
West
Siberian
Plain
Kama
Yaman Tau 1640
Tobol
Ob
Irtysh
Ural

Sea of Okhotsk
Shantar Is.
Shelekhov Bay
Sakhalin
Tartary Str.
La Pérouse Str.
10.542
Hokkaido
2290

Angara
Selenga
Stanovoy Ra. 2482
Dzhugdzhur Ra.
Amur
Hsiao Khingan Shan
Ta Khingan Shan
Manchurian Plain
Khanka
Hsi-liao
Sikhote Alin Ra.
Tsugaru Str.
Sea of Japan
2744 Sungari Reservoir

Kirgiz Steppe
L. Balkhash 342
Muyun Kum
53
Syr Darya
Ili
Chu
Belukha 4506
A l t a i
Western Sayan
Eastern Sayan
Yenisey
L. Baikal 456
Yablonovy Ra.
2999

Ust-Urt Plateau
Aral Sea
Turanian Plain
Kyzyl Kum
Kara Kum
Amu Darya
Tien Shan
Issyk-Kul
7439
Turfan Basin
-154
Tarim
Lop Nor
Tarim Basin
Ala Shan
3015 Ordos Plateau
2894
Shantung Pen.
Hwang Ho
Great Plain of China
Yangtze-kiang

Plateau of Mongolia
G o b i
Koko Nor

Korea
Yellow Sea
G. of Chihli
Korea Str.
Honshu
3776
Shikoku
Kyushu
10.554
East China Sea
Ryukyu Islands
7507
Tropic of Cancer

Communism Pk. 7495
Pamirs
Hindu Kush 7789
8611
Karakoram Ra. 8126
5143
Saihan Ra.
4419
Helmand
Dasht-i-Lut
Sulaiman Ra.
Chenab
Sutlej
Takla Makan
Altyn Tagh
7723
Kunlun Shan
Plateau of Tibet
Bayan Kara Shan
Nan Shan 6346
Tsaidam
Himalaya
8221
Mt. Everest 8848
Kanchenjunga 8598
Brahmaputra
Nam Tso
Tsangpo 7756
Naga Hills
Khasi Hills
Nam Shan
Chinling Shan
4107
Minya Konka 7590
Ta Liang Shan
Red Basin
Yangtze-kiang
2710
Nan Shan
Tung Ting
Poyang
Si-kiang
3997
Formosa
Bushi Chan.
Formosa Str.
7559

Thar
Aravalli Ra.
Chambal
Yamuna
Ganges
Indo-Gangetic Plain
India
Vindhya Mts.
Narmada
Satpura Ra.
Godavari
Indus
Saihan Ra.

Arabian Sea
of Oman
Ras al Hadd

Laccadive Is.
5875
Maldive Is.
Western Ghats
Malabar Coast
Deccan
Krishna
Eastern Ghats
Coromandel Coast
Anai Mudi 2698
C. Comorin
G. of Mannar
Pulk Str.
Ceylon
Pidurutalagala 2624
Dondra Head

Ganges Delta
Arakan Yoma
Mt. Victoria 3053
Irrawaddy
Salween
3143
G. of Martaban
Andaman Sea
Andaman Is.
Isthmus of Kra
Nicobar Is.

Bay of Bengal

G. of Tongking
Hainan
Mekong
3280
Bilauk Taung Ra.
Phanom Dong Rak
Tonle Sap
G. of Siam
Ca Mau Pt.
South China Sea
Malay Peninsula
Natuna Is.

Philippine Islands
2928
Luzon
5245
Mindoro
Samar
Leyte
Cape Johnson Deep 10.497
8054
Mindanao
2954
5842
Sulu Sea
Negros
Panay
Palawan
Kinabalu 4101
Celebes Sea
Morotai
Halmahera
New Guinea
Molucca
Celebes
7440
Buru
Ceram
Banda Sea
3455

PACIFIC OCEAN

INDIAN OCEAN
Equator
Chagos Arch.
Sumatra
3466
3800
6073
Sunda Islands
Java
Java Sea
Bali
Lombok
Semeru 3676
3716
Sumbawa 5123
Flores
Sumba
Timor
Arafura Sea
East Indies
Borneo
Makassar Str.

Australia

East from 80 Greenwich

COPYRIGHT. GEORGE PHILIP & SON, LTD.

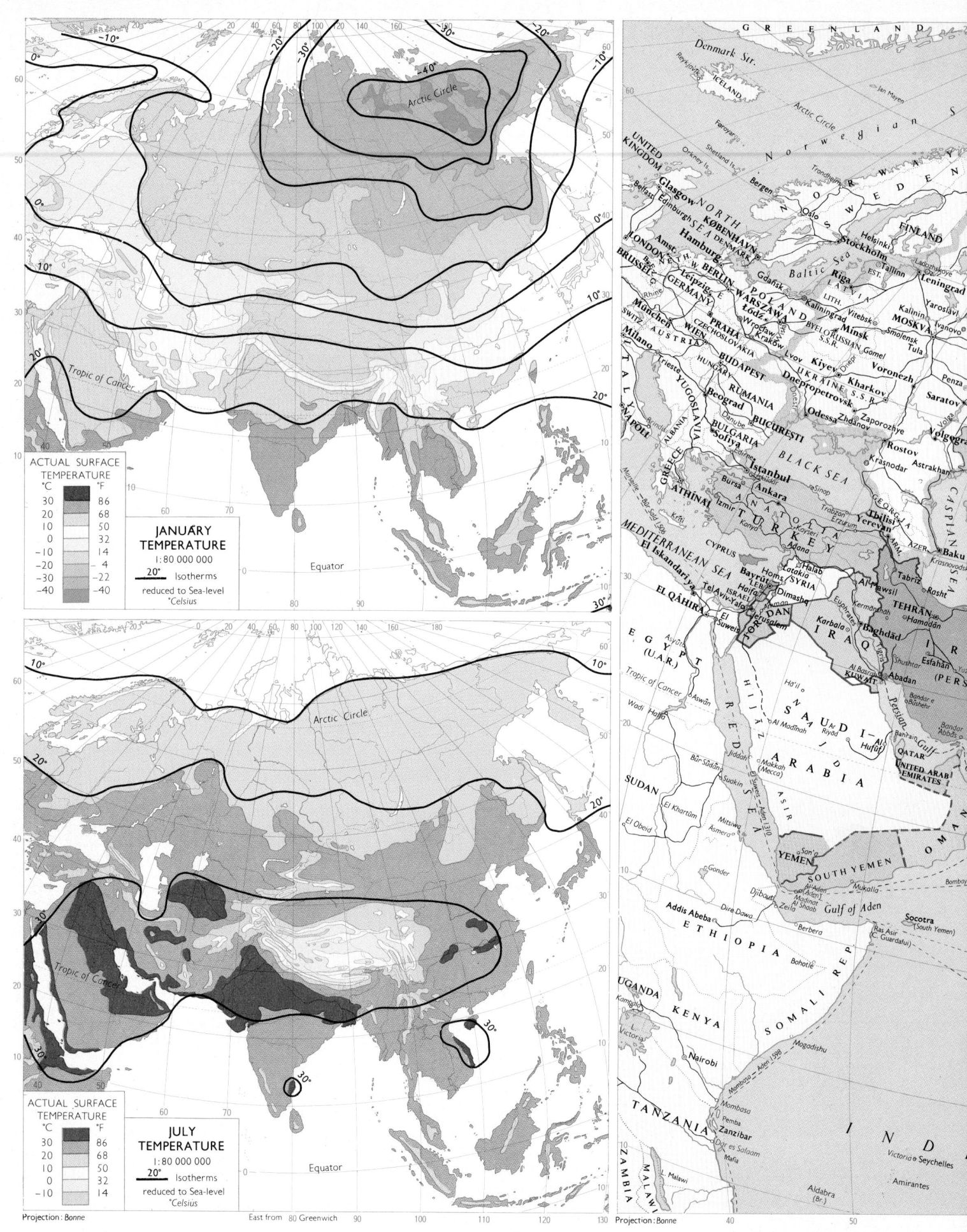

ACTUAL SURFACE
TEMPERATURE
°C   °F
30   86
20   68
10   50
0   32
-10   14
-20   - 4
-30   -22
-40   -40

JANUARY
TEMPERATURE
1:80 000 000
20°   Isotherms
reduced to Sea-level
°Celsius

ACTUAL SURFACE
TEMPERATURE
°C   °F
30   86
20   68
10   50
0   32
-10   14

JULY
TEMPERATURE
1:80 000 000
20°   Isotherms
reduced to Sea-level
°Celsius

Projection: Bonne   East from 80 Greenwich   Projection: Bonne

1 : 40 000 000

200   0   200   400   600   800   1000   miles
200   0   200 400 600 800 1000 1200 1400 1600   km

ARCTIC OCEAN

Svalbard
Bear I.
Nord Kapp
Barents Sea
Zemlya Frantsa Iosifa
Novaya Zemlya
Severnaya Zemlya
Laptev Sea
Novosibirskiye Ostrova
Lyakhovskiye Ostrova
East Siberian Sea
Ostrov Vrangelya
Mys Chukotskiy
Anadyrskiy Zaliv
BERING SEA

Murmansk
Beloje More
Arkhangelsk
Kara Sea
Obskaya Guba
Dikson
Khatanga
Nordvik
Bulun
Tiksi
Verkhoyansk
Sredne Kolymsk
Nizhne Kolymsk
Kolyma
Gizhiga
Provideniya
Anadyr

Naryan Mar
Kotlas
Vorkuta
Novyy Port
Salekhard
Igarka
Dudinka
Norilsk
Yenisey
Podkamennaya Tunguska
Yakutsk
Olekminsk
Aldan
Magadan
Okhotsk
Petropavlovsk-Kamchatskiy
Mys Lopatka

RUSSIAN S.F.S.R.
SOVIET SOCIALIST REPUBLICS
UNION OF

Gorkiy
Kirov
Serov
Perm
Nizhniy Tagil
Sverdlovsk
Tyumen
Tobolsk
Omsk
Petropavlovsk
Kazan
Ufa
Kuybyshev
Magnitogorsk
Orenburg
Orsk
Uralsk
Chelyabinsk
Kokchetav
Pavlodar
Tselinograd
Novosibirsk
Tomsk
Kemerovo
Novokuznetsk
Prokopyevsk
Barnaul
Biysk
Krasnoyarsk
Nizhneudinsk
Kansk
Cheremkhovo
Irkutsk
Ozero Baykal
Ulan Ude
Chita
Skovorodino
Blagoveshchensk
Amur
Khabarovsk
Komsomolsk
Sakhalin
Nikolayevsk
Aleksandrovsk
Tatarskiy Proliv
SEA OF OKHOTSK
Mys Yelizavety

KAZAKH S.S.R.
Karsakpai
Karaganda
Aralsk
Ozero Balkhash
Balkhash
Semipalatinsk
Ulaanbaatar (Ulan Bator)
Hovd (Jargalant)
Ulyasutay
MONGOLIA
INNER MONGOLIA
Hailar
Tsitsihar
Harbin
Changchun
Kirin
Vladivostok
Ussuriysk
SEA OF JAPAN
Otaru
Sapporo
HOKKAIDO
Hakodate
Aomori
Sendai

Aralskoye More
Kzyl Orda
Dzhambul
Alma Ata
Wulumuchi (Urumchi)
Hami
Huhehot
Changkiakow
Chinwangtao
Antung
Mukden (Shenyang)
Lu-ta
Pyongyang
KOREA
N.
S.
Chongjin
Akita
Niigata
HONSHU
TOKYO
Yokohama

UZBEK S.S.R.
KIRGIZIA
Tashkent
Chimkent
Namangan
Frunze
Andizhan
Kokand
TADZHIKISTAN
Dushanbe
Samarkand
Bukhara
Chardzhou
Amu Darya
Kashgar
Soche
Khotan
SINKIANG-UIGUR
Lop Nor
Koko Nor
CHINESE REPUBLIC
NINGSIA HUI
Lanchow
Tsinan
PEIPING
Tientsin
YELLOW SEA
Tsingtao
Taiyuan
Pusan
Taegu
Inchon
SEOUL
Hiroshima
Kitakyushu
Fukuoka
KYUSHU
Nagasaki
Kagoshima
Kanazawa
Nagoya
Kyoto
Kobe
Osaka
SHIKOKU
Shizuoka

TURKMEN S.S.R.
Mashhad
Herat
Mary
Mazar-i-sharif
Kabul
AFGHANISTAN
Kandahar
Quetta
Zahedan
PAKISTAN
Peshawar
Islamabad
Rawalpindi
KASHMIR
Srinagar
Gilgit
Amritsar
Lahore
Multan
Indus
TIBET
Lhasa
Shigatse
Tsangpo
NEPAL
Katmandu
BHUTAN
Brahmaputra
Sian
Tienshui
Chowkiakow
Kaifeng
Hwang Ho
Suchow
Hwai
Chengchow
Nantung
Nanking
Wuhu
Shanghai
Hangchow
Ningpo
EAST CHINA SEA
Wanhsien
Chengtu
Chungking
Ipin
Yangtze
Ichang
Shasi
Wuhan
Nanchang
Tsinkiang
Wenchow
Foochow
CHINA
TAIWAN (FORMOSA)
Taipei
Ryukyu-retto
Okinawa

DELHI
Meerut
Agra
Jaipur
Jodhpur
Ajmer
Lucknow
Kanpur
Patna
Allahabad
Varanasi
Ganga
Dacca
BANGLADESH
Chittagong
Akyab
Myitkyina
BURMA
Mandalay
Luang Prabang
Chieng-mai
Chengtu
Chungking
Changsha
Hengyang
Kweiyang
Kunming
Kweilin
Kanchow
Changchow
Shantow
Kwangchow
Wuchow
Liuchow
Nanning
Hong Kong
Macau (Port.)
Hainan
Hanoi
Tongking
Da Nang
Paracel Is.
Batan Is.
Babuyan Is.
Luzon
MANILA
PHILIPPINES
Mindoro
Samar

KARACHI
G. of Kutch
Hyderabad
INDIA
Ahmadabad
Indore
Jabalpur
Nagpur
Raipur
Cuttack
Howrah
Calcutta
Pakokku
Basseini
Rangoon (Rangoon)
THAILAND (SIAM)
KRUNG THEP (Bangkok)
Ayutthaya
KHMER REP.
Phnom Penh
SAIGON
Long Xuyen
Iloilo
Cebu
Negros
Palawan
Mindanao
Davao
Sulu Sea
Kepulauan Talaud

Bombay
Poona
Sholapur
Hyderabad
Kolhapur
Goa
Hubli
Bellary
Bangalore
Madras
Pondicherry
Nellore
BAY OF BENGAL
Andaman Is. (Ind.)
Tavoy
Myeik (Mergui)
Gulf of Siam
Nicobar Is. (Ind.)
SOUTH CHINA SEA
SABAH
N. BORNEO
Brunei
SARAWAK
Kuching
Pontianak
KALIMANTAN
Celebes Sea
Sandakan
Sulawesi
Makasar
Bonthain
Sangihe
Halmahera
NEW GUINEA
Vogelkop

ARABIAN SEA
Laccadive Is. (Ind.)
Calicut (Kozhikode)
Kandy
Madurai
Trivandrum
C. Comorin
SRI LANKA
Jaffna
Colombo
Dondra Hd.
MALAYA
Penang
Ipoh
Kuala Lumpur
Johor Baharu
SINGAPORE
Kota Baharu
MALAYSIA
Medan
Sumatra
Labuan
Padang
Borneo
Belitung
Bangka
Palembang
Balikpapan
Bandjarmasin
Banda Sea
Buru
Ceram
Buton
Flores
Timor (Port.)
Kepulauan Tanimbar
Arafura Sea
Darwin
AUSTRALIA

Maldive Is.
Male
Suvadiva Atoll
Addu Atoll
INDIAN OCEAN
Equator
Kepulauan Mentawai
JAVA
JAKARTA
DJAKARTA
Bandung
Semarang
Surabaja
Bogor
Jogjakarta
Malang
Madura
Bali
Sumbawa
Sumba
Sunda Sea
Timor Sea

PACIFIC OCEAN

COPYRIGHT. GEORGE PHILIP & SON. LTD.

East from Greenwich

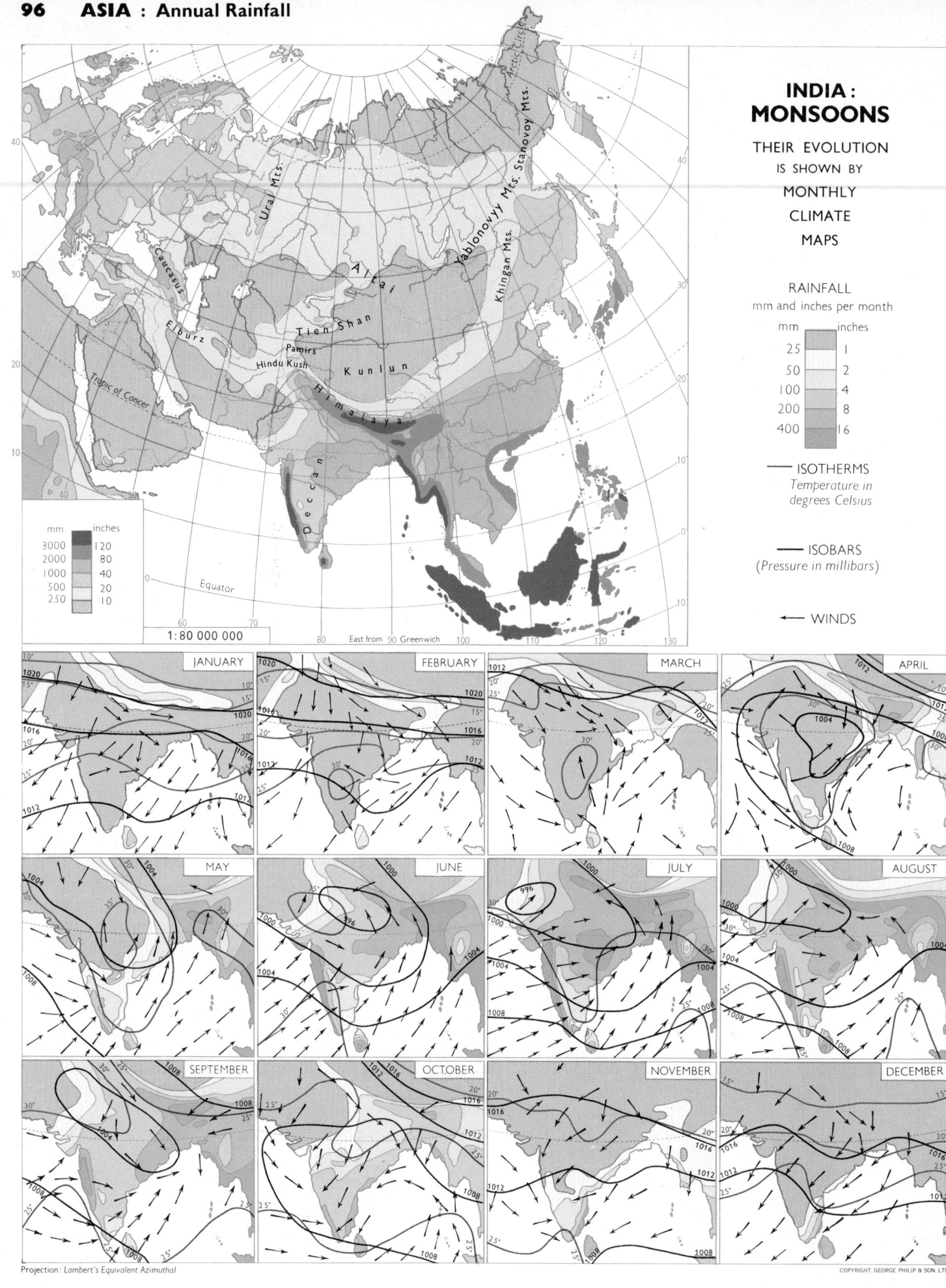

INDIA: MONSOONS

THEIR EVOLUTION

IS SHOWN BY

MONTHLY

CLIMATE

MAPS

RAINFALL
mm and inches per month

mm	inches
25	1
50	2
100	4
200	8
400	16

——— ISOTHERMS
Temperature in degrees Celsius

——— ISOBARS
(Pressure in millibars)

←—— WINDS

mm	inches
3000	120
2000	80
1000	40
500	20
250	10

1 : 80 000 000

East from Greenwich

JANUARY

FEBRUARY

MARCH

APRIL

MAY

JUNE

JULY

AUGUST

SEPTEMBER

OCTOBER

NOVEMBER

DECEMBER

Projection: *Lambert's Equivalent Azimuthal*

COPYRIGHT. GEORGE PHILIP & SON. LTD.

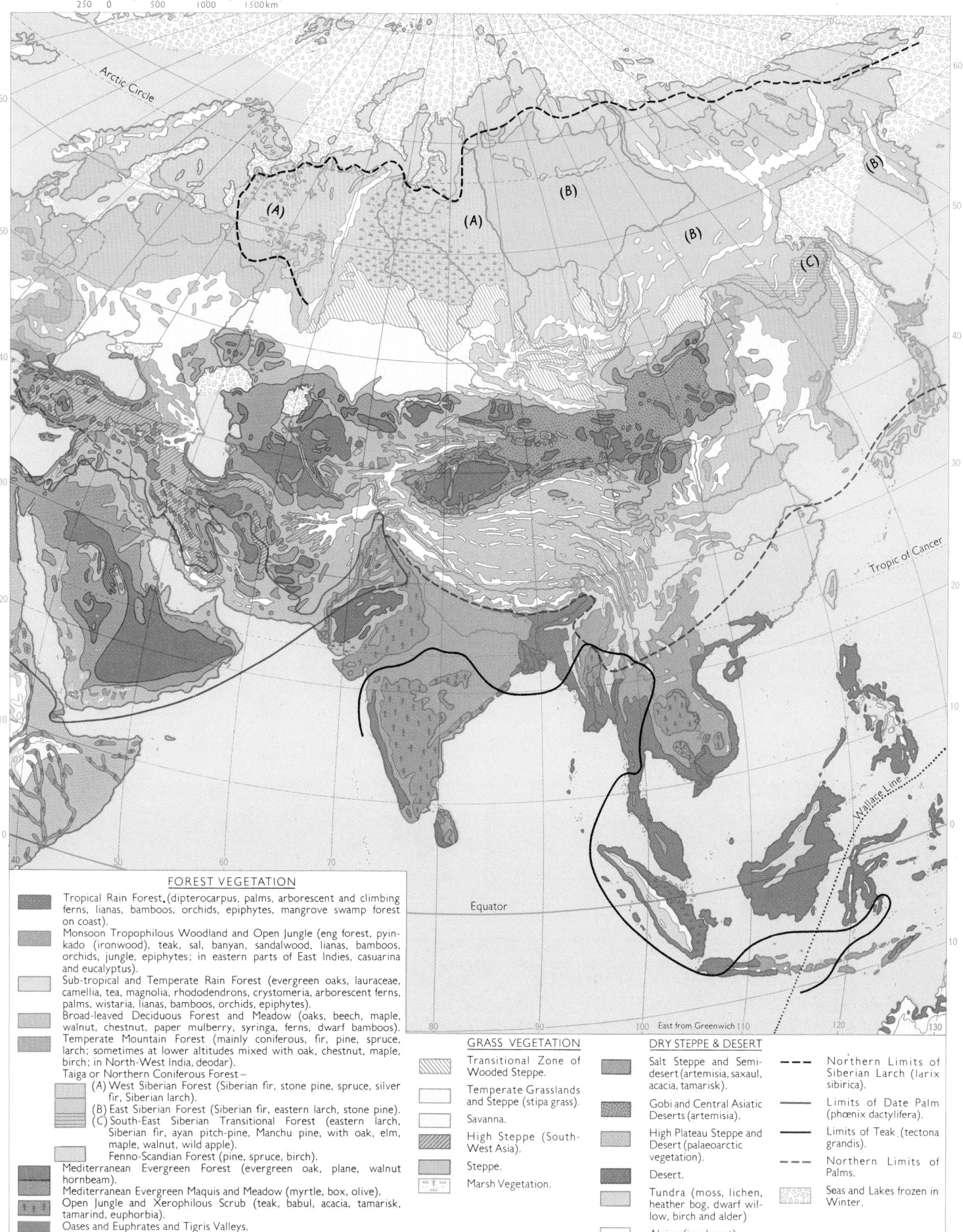

1:50 000 000

Arctic Circle

Equator

Tropic of Cancer

Wallace Line

East from Greenwich

Projection: Bonne

COPYRIGHT. GEORGE PHILIP & SON. LTD.

FOREST VEGETATION

Tropical Rain Forest. (dipterocarpus, palms, arborescent and climbing ferns, lianas, bamboos, orchids, epiphytes, mangrove swamp forest on coast).

Monsoon Tropophilous Woodland and Open Jungle (eng forest, pyinkado (ironwood), teak, sal, banyan, sandalwood, lianas, bamboos, orchids, jungle, epiphytes; in eastern parts of East Indies, casuarina and eucalyptus).

Sub-tropical and Temperate Rain Forest (evergreen oaks, lauraceae, camellia, tea, magnolia, rhododendrons, crystomeria, arborescent ferns, palms, wistaria, lianas, bamboos, orchids, epiphytes).

Broad-leaved Deciduous Forest and Meadow (oaks, beech, maple, walnut, chestnut, paper mulberry, syringa, ferns, dwarf bamboos).

Temperate Mountain Forest (mainly coniferous, fir, pine, spruce, larch; sometimes at lower altitudes mixed with oak, chestnut, maple, birch; in North-West India, deodar).

Taiga or Northern Coniferous Forest –

(A) West Siberian Forest (Siberian fir, stone pine, spruce, silver fir, Siberian larch).

(B) East Siberian Forest (Siberian fir, eastern larch, stone pine).

(C) South-East Siberian Transitional Forest (eastern larch, Siberian fir, ayan pitch-pine, Manchu pine, with oak, elm, maple, walnut, wild apple).

Fenno-Scandian Forest (pine, spruce, birch).

Mediterranean Evergreen Forest (evergreen oak, plane, walnut hornbeam).

Mediterranean Evergreen Maquis and Meadow (myrtle, box, olive).

Open Jungle and Xerophilous Scrub (teak, babul, acacia, tamarisk, tamarind, euphorbia).

Oases and Euphrates and Tigris Valleys.

GRASS VEGETATION

Transitional Zone of Wooded Steppe.

Temperate Grasslands and Steppe (stipa grass).

Savanna.

High Steppe (South-West Asia).

Steppe.

Marsh Vegetation.

DRY STEPPE & DESERT

Salt Steppe and Semi-desert (artemisia, saxaul, acacia, tamarisk).

Gobi and Central Asiatic Deserts (artemisia).

High Plateau Steppe and Desert (palaeoarctic vegetation).

Desert.

Tundra (moss, lichen, heather bog, dwarf willow, birch and alder).

Alpine (ice desert).

- - - Northern Limits of Siberian Larch (larix sibirica).

——— Limits of Date Palm (phœnix dactylifera).

——— Limits of Teak (tectona grandis).

- - - Northern Limits of Palms.

Seas and Lakes frozen in Winter.

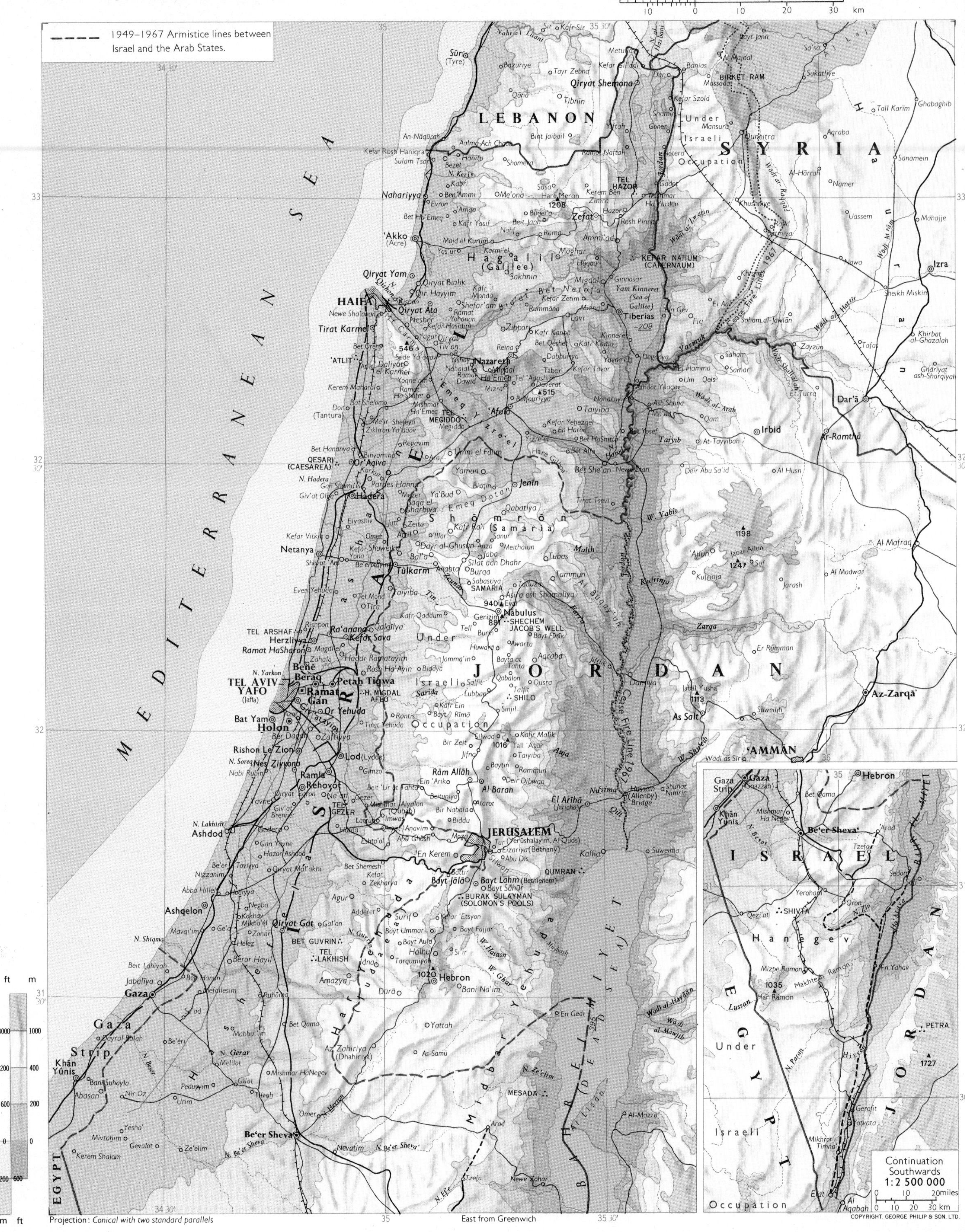

1:1 000 000

10 5 0 10 20 miles
10 0 10 20 30 km

_____ 1949–1967 Armistice lines between
Israel and the Arab States.

LEBANON

SYRIA

MEDITERRANEAN SEA

ISRAEL

JORDAN

EGYPT

Place names (north to south, as labelled):

Sūr (Tyre), Nahr al Lītānī, Sir, Kafr Sir, Bayt Jann, Tall Karim, Ghabaghib, Qiryat Shemona, Tibnīn, Tayr Zebna, Kefar Gil'adi, Dan, Bāniyās, Al Majdal, Sa'sa', Sukatiye, Aqraba

Qānā, An-Nāqūrah, Aalma-Ach Cha'b, Bint Jbail, Yiftah, Kefar Rosh Haniqra, 'Itah, Gonen, Nahariyya, Evron, Ben 'Ammi, N. Keziv, Ḥanita, Shomera, Ramot Naftali, BIRKET RAM, Neqarot, Qureitra

Under Israeli Occupation

Akko (Acre), Kefar Yasif, Bet Ha'Emeq, Majd el Kurūm, Nahf, Rama, Ammi'ad, Qiryat Yam, Qiryat Bialik, Qir. Hayyim, Kafr Manda, Sakhnin, Bet Netofa, Tel HAZOR, Hazor, Rosh Pinna, HAIFA, Qiryat Ata, Nesher, Shefar'am, Zippori, Reina, Kefar Kanna, Yam Kinneret (Sea of Galilee), Tiberias –209, En Gev, El Āl, Saham al-Jawlān

HAGALIL (GALILEE), KEFAR NAHUM (CAPERNAUM)

Tirat Karmel, Yagur, Kefar Hasidim, Nazareth, 'Atlit, Daliyōt, Tel Karmel, Kerem Maharal, Mizra, Tabor, Kefar Tavor, Degavia, El Hamma, Um Qeis, Irbid, Ar-Ramthā, Dar'ā

MEGIDDO, EMEQ YIZRE'EL, 'Afula, En Harod, Bet HaShitta

QESARI (CAESAREA), Or 'Aqiva, Karkur, Pardes Hanna, Yamun, Bet She'an, New Zan, Tirat Tsevi, Taiyiba, Deir Abu Sa'id, Al Husn, Al Hamma

Hadera, Gan Shemu'el, Bisqina, Jenin, SHOMRON (SAMARIA), Al Mafraq

Netanya, Kefar Vitkin, 'Omez, Tulkarm, Qabatiya, Tubas, 1198, 'Ajlun, Jabal 'Ajlun, 1247, Suf, Al Madwar, Jarash

Even Yehuda, Kefar Qaddum, Silat adh Dhahr, Burqa, Tammun, Er Rimmin, SAMARIA, 940 Eval, Nabulus, SHECHEM, JACOB'S WELL, Bayt Furik, Awarta, Zarqa

TEL ARSHAF, Herzliyya, Ra'anana, Kefar Sava, Qalqilya, Under Israeli Occupation, Huwara, Bayta, 'Aqraba, Qusra, Damiya, Az-Zarqā'

Ramat HaSharon, Hodar Ramatayim, Rosh Ha'Ayin, Biddya, SHILO, Jabal Yusha', 1113, AMMĀN

TEL AVIV–YAFO (Jaffa), Bene Beraq, Petah Tiqwa, H. MIGDAL AFEQ, Sarida, Lubban, Sinjil, As Salt

Ramat Gan, Or Yehuda, Rantis, Bayt Rima, Qabalon, Suweileh

Bat Yam, Holon, Zafriyya, Tirat Yehuda, 'Ein, Bīr Zeit, Kafr Malik, 1016, Tall 'Asur, Taiyiba, 'Awja, W. Shu'ayb, Wādi as Sir

Rishon Le Zion, Nes Ziyyona, Lod (Lydda), Ginzua, Rām Allāh, Baytin, Rammun

N. Soreq, Nabi Rubin, Ramla, 'Anavim, Beit Ur et Tahta, 'Ein 'Arik, Beitunya, Deir Dibwan, El Arīḥā (Jericho), Suweima

Rehovot, Giv'at Brenner, Gezer, TEL GEZER, Laṭrun, 'Imwas, Biddu, Mevo Betar, Abu Ghosh, Mozo, JERUSALEM (Yerushalayim, Al Quds), Al 'Aziziya (Bethany), Abu Dis, Kalha

Ashdod, Yavne, Hazor Ashdod, Qiryat Mal'akhi, Bet Shemesh, En Kerem, Tur, Qumran

Ashqelon, Kokhav, Mikha'el, Zohar, Qiryat Gat, Adderet, Surif, Bayt Ummar, Bayt Fajjar, En Gedi

BET GUVRIN, TEL LAKHISH, N. Guvrin, Gal'on, Bayt Jala, Bayt Lahm (Bethlehem), Bayt Sahur, BURAK SULAYMAN (SOLOMON'S POOLS), Si'ir

Beit Lahiya, Jabaliya, Gaza, Gaza Strip, Dayr al Balah, Khān Yūnis, Banī Suhayla, Abasan, Nir Oz, Ze'elim, Kerem Shalom, Be'er Hayil, Amazya, Dūrā, Hebron 1022, Bani Na'im, 'Arad, Al-Mazra'

Mishmar HaNegev, As-Samū', Yattah, Az Zahiriya (Dhahriya), MESADA, Be'er Sheva'

Inset (Continuation Southwards 1:2 500 000):

Gaza Strip, Gaza (Ghazzah), Hebron, Khān Yūnis, Bet Qama, ISRAEL, Be'er Sheva', Arad, Yeroham, SHIVTA, Qezi'ot, HaNegev, Mizpe Ramon, Makhtesh Ramon, 1035, Har Ramon, En Yahav, Under Jordan, Hiyy, 1727, Egypt, PETRA, Gerofit, Yotvata, Mikhrot Timna, Al 'Aqabah, Eilat, Israeli Occupation

Continuation Southwards
1:2 500 000
0 10 20 miles
0 10 20 30 km

Elevation scale (left):

ft m
3000 1000
1200 400
600 200
0 0
200 600
m ft

Projection: Conical with two standard parallels

East from Greenwich

COPYRIGHT. GEORGE PHILIP & SON, LTD.

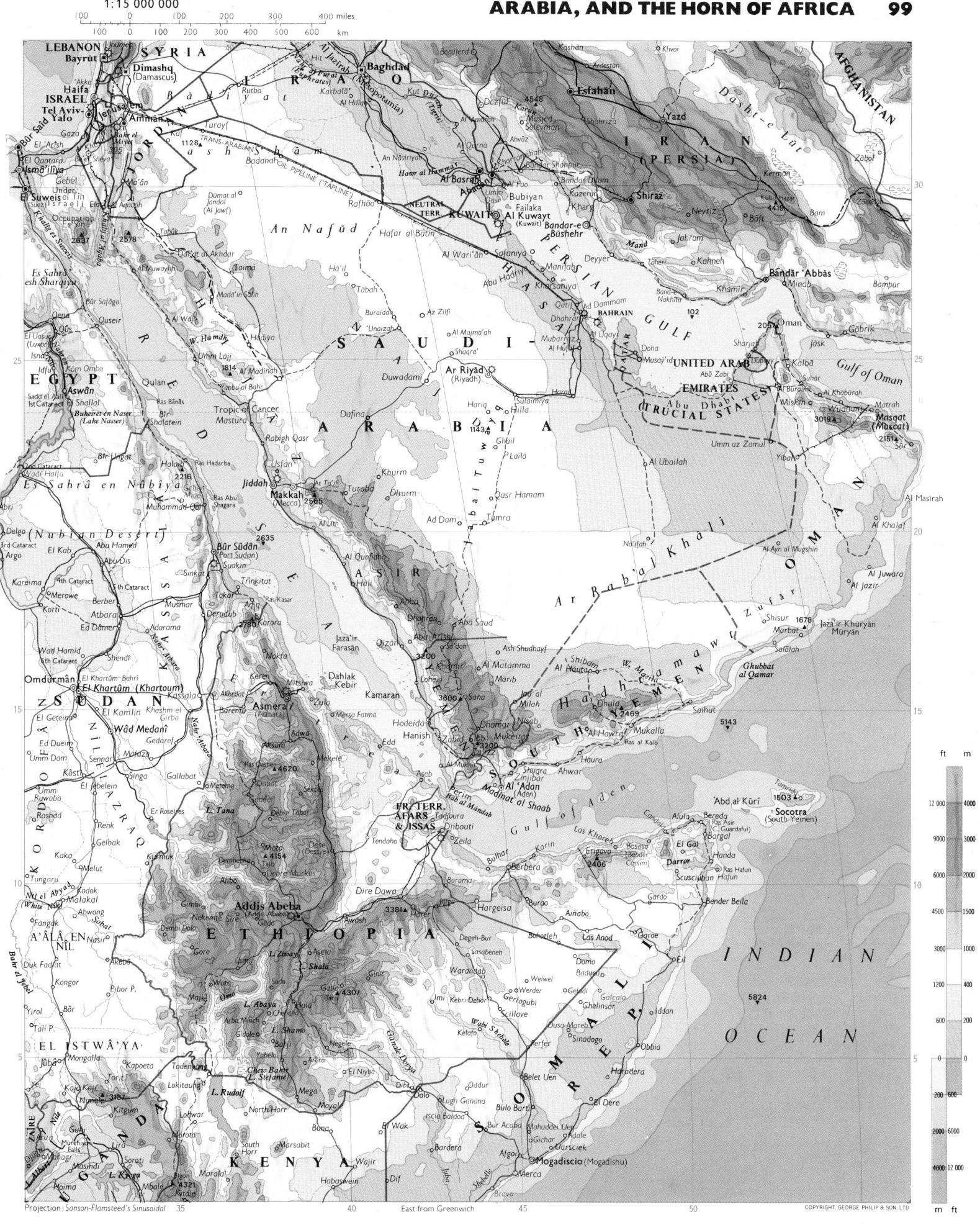
1:15 000 000
miles
km
SAUDI ARABIA
ETHIOPIA
SUDAN
EGYPT
IRAN (PERSIA)
IRAQ
SYRIA
JORDAN
LEBANON
ISRAEL
KUWAIT
BAHRAIN
QATAR
UNITED ARAB EMIRATES (TRUCIAL STATES)
OMAN
YEMEN
SOUTH YEMEN
FR. TERR. AFARS & ISSAS
SOMALI REP.
KENYA
UGANDA
AFGHANISTAN
INDIAN OCEAN
PERSIAN GULF
Gulf of Oman
Gulf of Aden
RED SEA
An Nafūd
Ar Rab'al Khali
Ar Riyāḍ (Riyadh)
Makkah (Mecca)
Jiddah
Baghdad
Addis Abeba
El Khartûm (Khartoum)
Mogadiscio (Mogadishu)
Tropic of Cancer
Projection: Sanson-Flamsteed's Sinusoidal
East from Greenwich
ft
m
COPYRIGHT, GEORGE PHILIP & SON, LTD

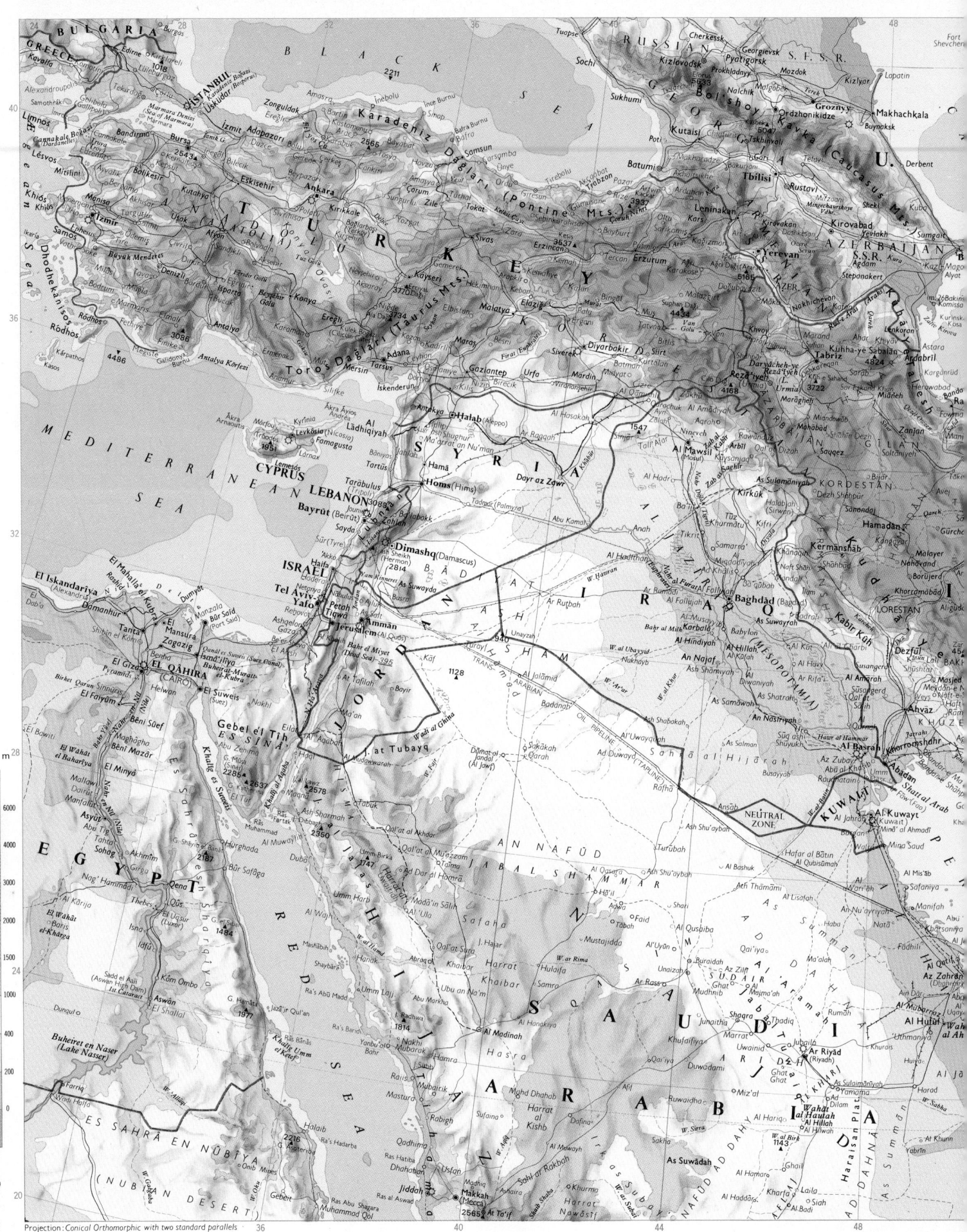

Projection: Conical Orthomorphic with two standard parallels

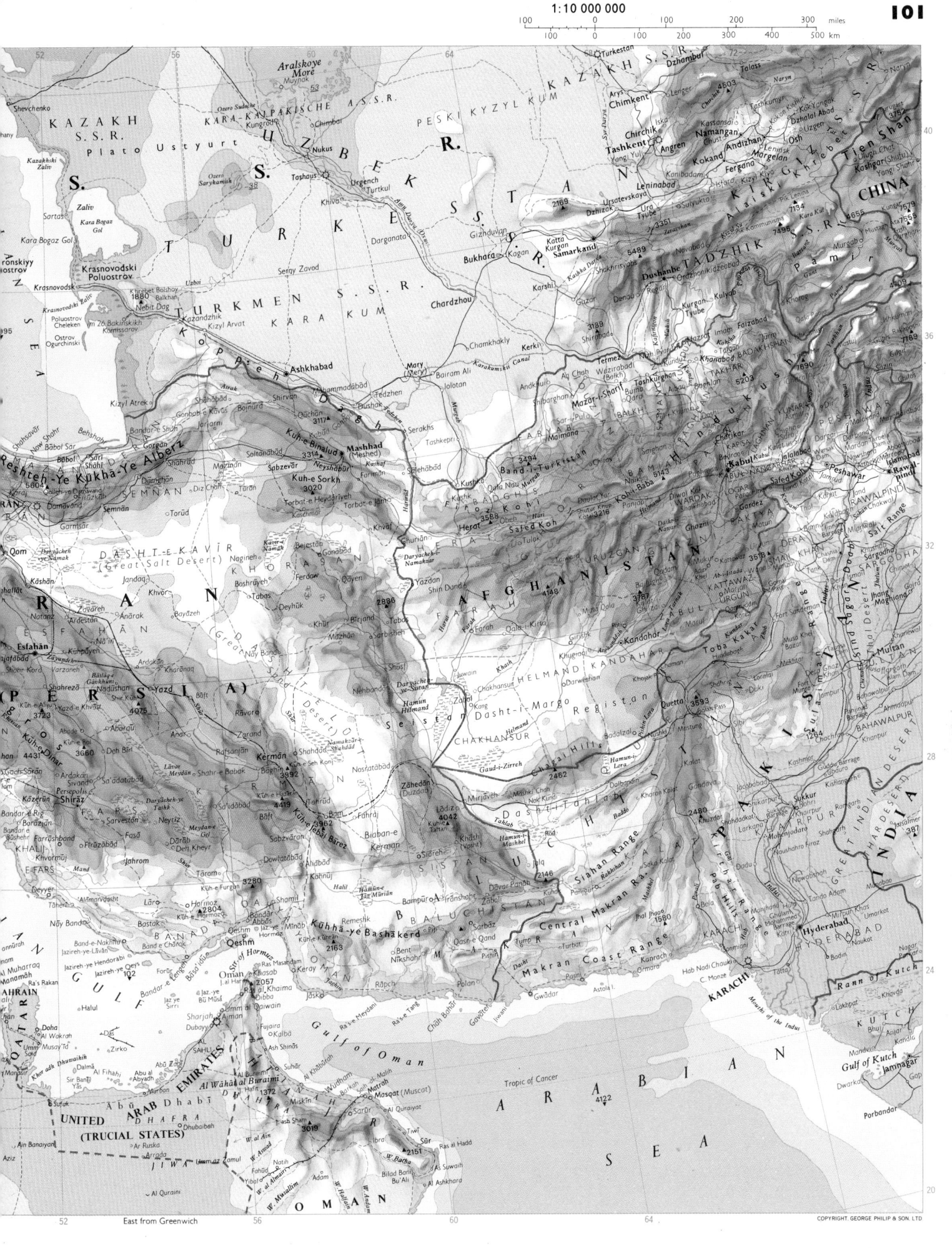

1:10 000 000

100   0   100   200   300   miles
100   0   100   200   300   400   500   km

KAZAKH S.S.R.
Plato Ustyurt
Kara-Kalpakische A.S.S.R.
UZBEK S.S.R.
PESKI KYZYL KUM
KAZAKH S.S.R.

TURKMEN S.S.R.
KARA KUM
Ashkhabad

TADZHIK S.S.R.
DUSHANBE
KIRGIZ S.S.R.
CHINA
Tien Shan
Pamir

IRAN (PERSIA)
DASHT-E KAVIR
(Great Salt Desert)
KHORASAN
Mashhad (Meshed)
Herat

AFGHANISTAN
Hindu Kush
Kabul
Peshawar
RAWALPINDI

Kandahar
HELMAND
KANDAHAR
Registan
Quetta

BALUCHISTAN
Makran Coast Range

Kerman
FARS
Shiraz

GULF
Gulf of Oman
UNITED ARAB EMIRATES
(TRUCIAL STATES)
OMAN
Masqat (Muscat)

ARABIAN SEA

Tropic of Cancer

KARACHI
INDIA
GREAT INDIAN DESERT
Hyderabad
Gulf of Kutch
Rann of Kutch

COPYRIGHT. GEORGE PHILIP & SON. LTD

U.S.S.R.

SAMANGAN
FARYAB
BALKH
BADGHIS
BAGHLAN
TAKHAR
BADAKHSHAN
HERAT
GHOR
BAMIAN
PARWAN
KAPISA
LAGHMAN
KUNAR
NANGARHAR
KABUL
WARDAK
LOGAR
PAKTYA
GHAZNI
URUZGAN
ZABUL
KATTAWAZ-URGUN
HELMAND
KANDAHAR
CHAKHANSUR
FARAH

AFGHANISTAN
PERSIA

Herat
Kabul
Kandahar
Quetta

PESHAWAR
Peshawar
Rawalpindi
Islamabad
Srinagar
KASHMIR
JAMMU
HIMACHAL PRADESH

Lahore
Amritsar
PUNJAB
Jullundur
Ludhiana
Simla
Chandigarh
Ambala
Dehra Dun
Saharanpur
Hardwar

Multan
BAHAWALPUR
BIKANER
HARYANA
DELHI
Meerut
Moradabad
Rampur
Bareilly

SIND
KHAIRPUR
Sukkur
Hyderabad
KARACHI
Karachi

RAJASTHAN
Jodhpur
Ajmer
Jaipur
Agra
Gwalior
Kanpur
Jhansi

ARABIAN SEA

Tropic of Cancer

Mouths of the Indus

Rann of Kutch
Gulf of Kutch
GUJARAT
Ahmadabad
Baroda
Rajkot
Jamnagar
Surat

BHARAT
MADHYA PRADESH
Indore
Bhopal
Jabalpur
Nagpur

Satpura Range
Ajanta Range
MAHARASHTRA
Nasik
Aurangabad
BOMBAY
Poona
Sholapur
Kolhapur

ANDHRA PRADESH
Hyderabad
Gulbarga
Bijapur
Raichur

GOA

Projection: Conical with two standard parallels

Inset map (Continuation Southwards on same scale):

GOA
Dharwar
Gadag
Hubli
Bellary
MYSORE
Bangalore
Mangalore
Mysore
Kolar Gold Fields
Vellore
MADRAS
Coimbatore
Salem
TAMIL NADU
Pondicherry
Cuddalore
Trichur
Calicut (Kozhikode)
Madurai
Trichy (Tiruchirappalli)
Thanjavur
Nagappattinam
Quilon
Trivandrum
Nagercoil
Cape Comorin
Palk Strait
Palk Bay
Gulf of Mannar
Adam's Bridge
Jaffna
Trincomalee
SRI LANKA (CEYLON)
Anuradhapura
Kandy
Colombo
Moratuwa
Galle
Dondra Head

Elevation scale:

ft	m
18 000	6000
12 000	4000
9000	3000
6000	2000
4500	1500
3000	1000
1200	400
600	200
0	0
600	200

Continuation Southwards on same scale

AFGHANISTAN
PAKISTAN
KASHMIR
JAMMU
HIMACHAL PRADESH
PUNJAB
HARYANA
DELHI
RAJASTHAN
MADHYA
GREAT INDIAN DESERT
THAL DESERT
BAHAWALPUR
KHAIRPUR
HYDERABAD
QUETTA
Toba Kakar
Salt Range
Sulaiman Range
Kirthar Range
Rann of Kutch
Mouths of the Indus
Gulf of Kutch
Gulf of Cambay
ARABIAN SEA
Little Rann
Tropic of Cancer
Gir Hills
Satmala Hills
Ajanta Range
Gawilgarh Hills
Mahadeo Hills
Satpura
Vindhya
KARACHI
Hyderabad
Quetta
Multan
Lahore
Amritsar
Jullundur
Ludhiana
Ambala
Sialkot
Jammu
Gujranwala
Sargodha
Lyallpur
Bahawalpur
Sukkur
Jacobabad
Bikaner
Jodhpur
Jaipur
Ajmer
Agra
Mathura
Aligarh
Meerut
Gwalior
Jhansi
Bhopal
Indore
Ujjain
Ahmadabad
Baroda
Surat
Rajkot
Jamnagar
Bhavnagar
Porbandar
Nasik
Malegaon
Aurangabad
Akola
Amraoti
Nagpur
Burhanpur
Kota
Udaipur
Saharanpur
Dehra Dun
Patiala
Hissar
Rohtak
Sagar
Projection: Conical with two standard parallels
ft m
18 000 6000
12 000 4000
9000 3000
6000 2000
4500 1500
3000 1000
1200 400
600 200
0 0
200 600
2000 6000
m ft

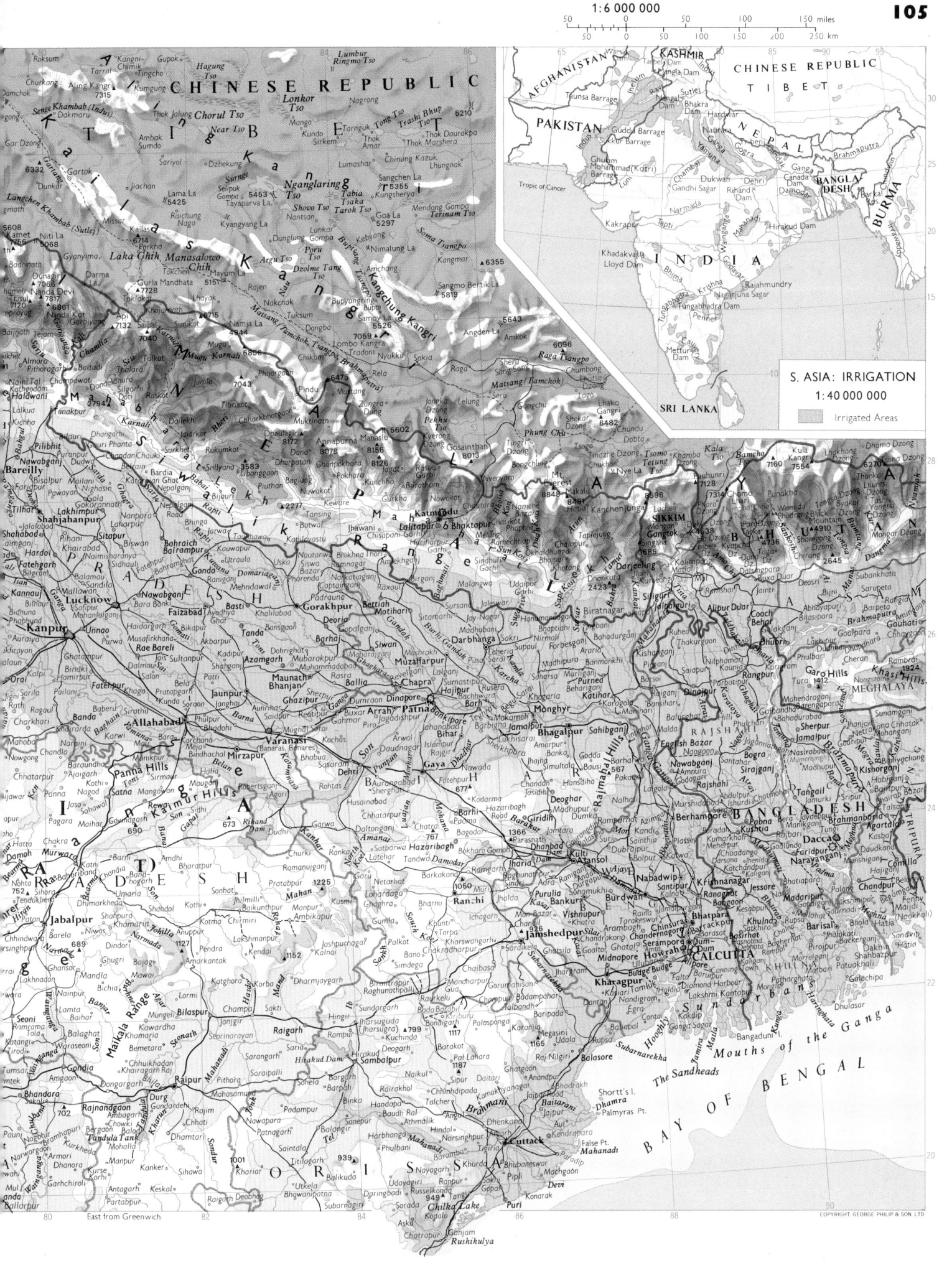

1:6 000 000

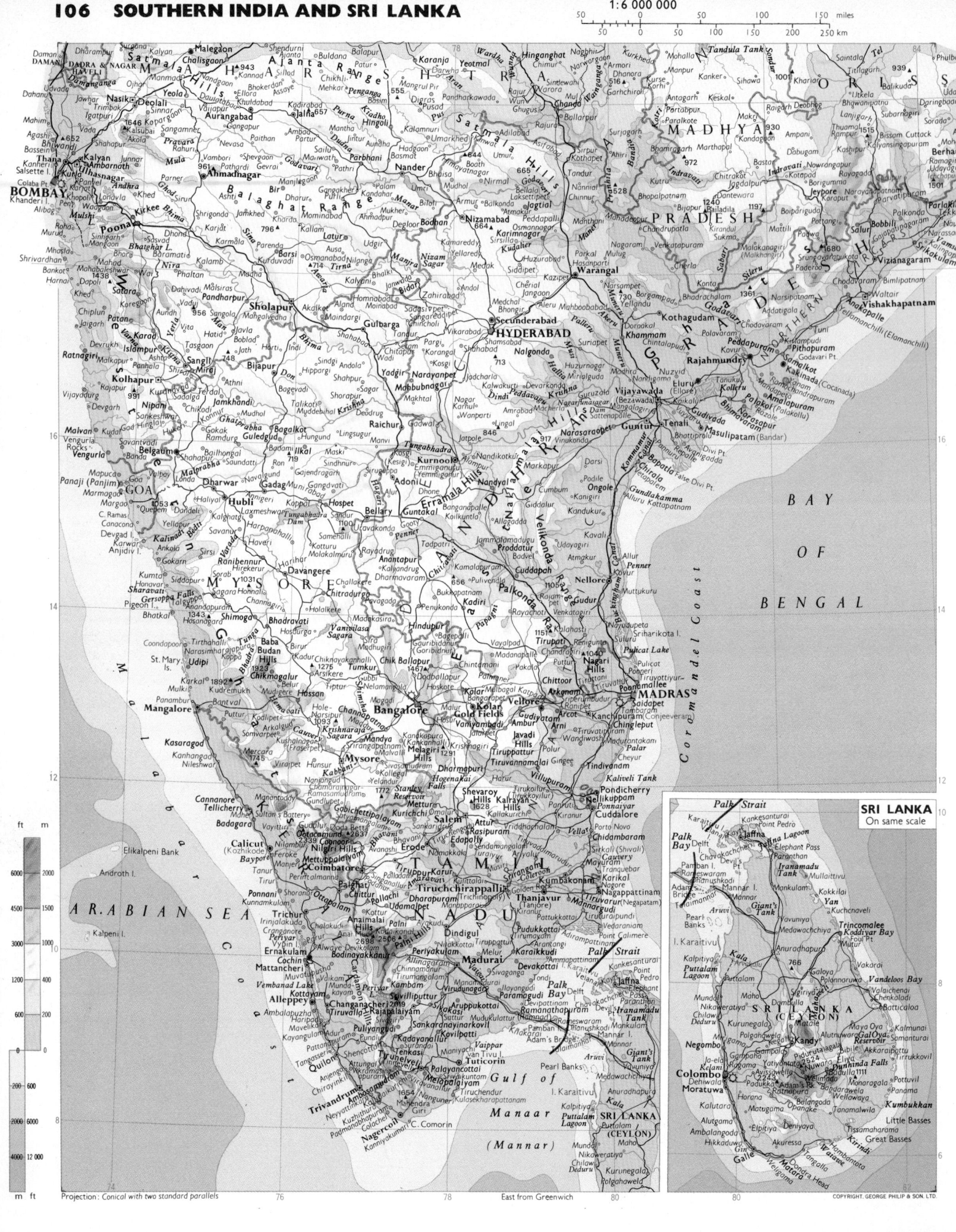
BAY OF BENGAL
ARABIAN SEA
SRI LANKA
On same scale
MYSORE
TAMIL NADU
ANDHRA PRADESH
MADHYA PRADESH
BOMBAY
MADRAS
HYDERABAD
Bangalore
Mysore
Madurai
Colombo
Coromandel Coast
Malabar Coast
Gulf of Manaar (Mannar)
Palk Strait
Projection: Conical with two standard parallels
East from Greenwich

COPYRIGHT, GEORGE PHILIP & SON, LTD.

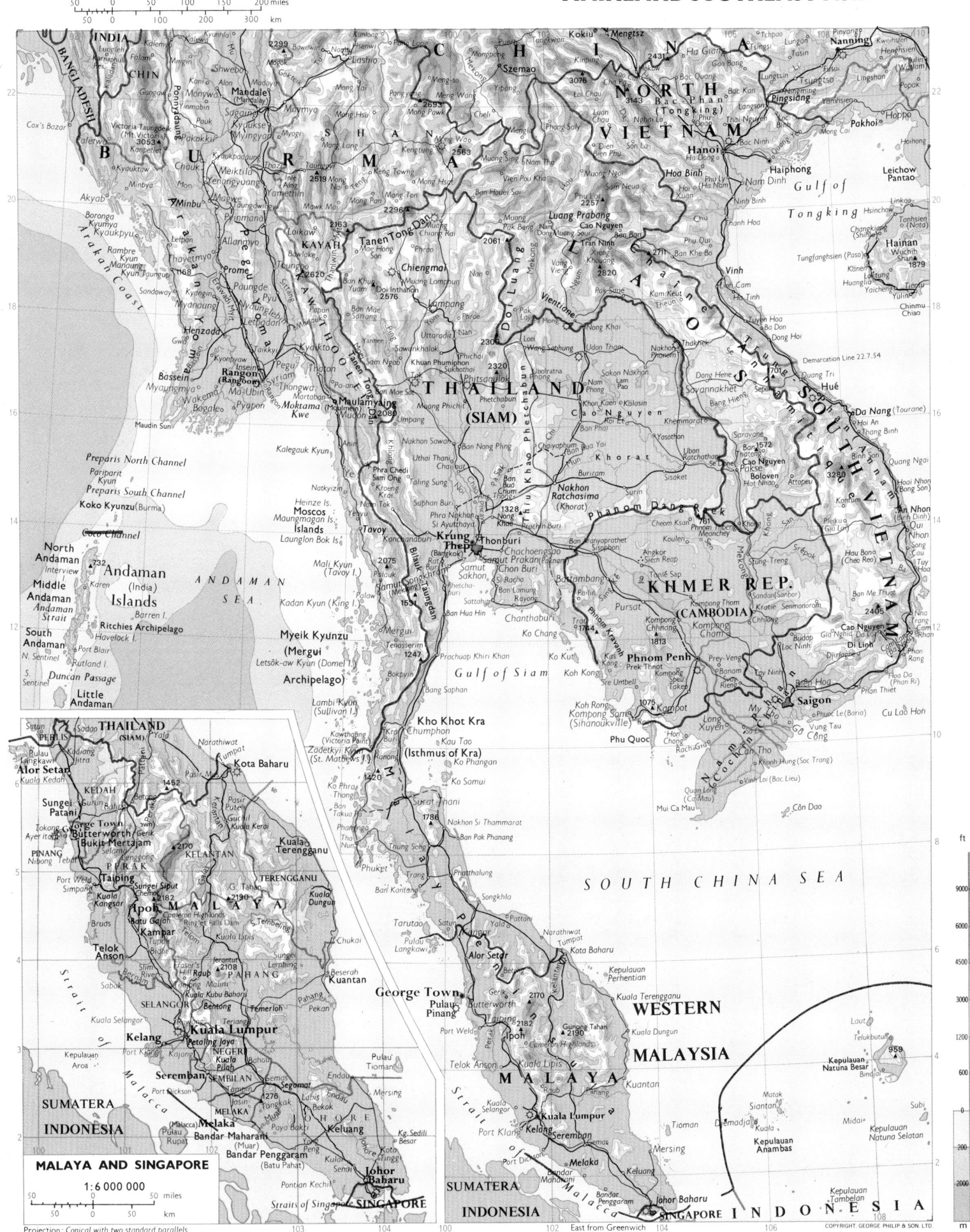

1:10 000 000

MALAYA AND SINGAPORE

1:6 000 000

Projection: Conical with two standard parallels

East from Greenwich

COPYRIGHT. GEORGE PHILIP & SON. LTD.

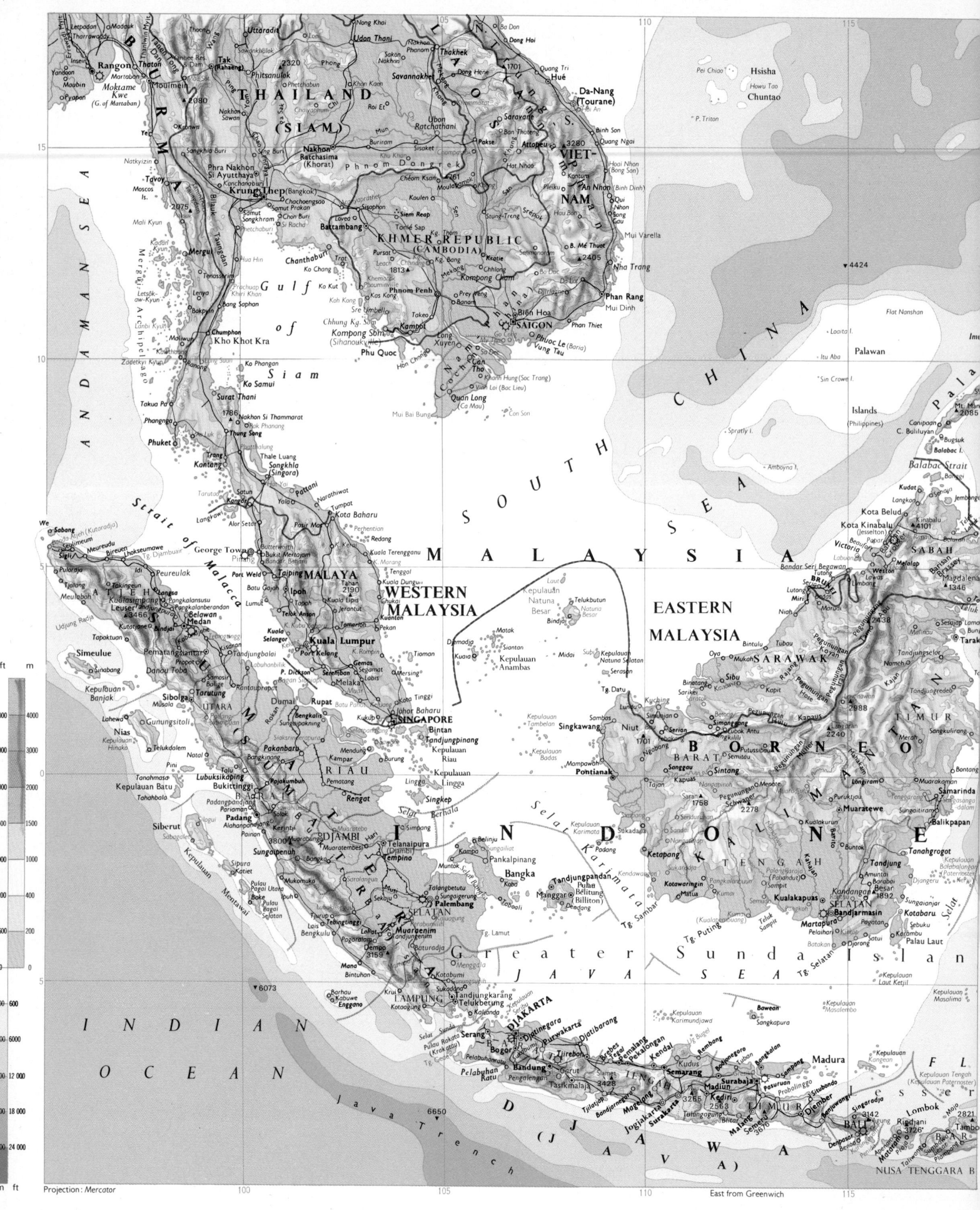
BURMA
THAILAND
(SIAM)
LAOS
N. VIET-NAM
S. VIET-NAM
KHMER REPUBLIC
(CAMBODIA)
Gulf of Siam
ANDAMAN SEA
SOUTH CHINA SEA
MALAYSIA
WESTERN MALAYSIA
EASTERN MALAYSIA
MALAYA
SARAWAK
SABAH
BRUNEI
BORNEO
INDONESIA
KALIMANTAN
SUMATERA
JAWA
(JAVA)
JAVA SEA
Greater Sunda Islands
INDIAN OCEAN
Java Trench
Strait of Malacca
Rangon
Moulmein
Moktame Kwe
(G. of Martaban)
Tavoy
Mergui
Mergui Archipelago
Krung Thep (Bangkok)
Phitsanulok
Nakhon Ratchasima (Khorat)
Ubon Ratchathani
Udon Thani
Savannakhet
Hué
Da-Nang (Tourane)
Qui Nhon
Nha Trang
Phan Rang
Phnom Penh
SAIGON
Vung Tau
Can Tho
Kompong Som (Sihanoukville)
Phu Quoc
Kho Khot Kra
Ko Samui
Surat Thani
Phuket
Songkhla (Singora)
Kota Baharu
George Town
Pinang
Ipoh
Kuala Lumpur
Port Kelang
Melaka
SINGAPORE
Johor Baharu
Tioman
Kepulauan Anambas
Kepulauan Natuna
Kepulauan Riau
Kepulauan Lingga
Bintan
Medan
Sibolga
Padang
Pakanbaru
Djambi
Palembang
Bengkulu
Telukbetung
Bangka
Pangkalpinang
Belitung (Billiton)
Selat Karimata
Pontianak
Kuching
Sibu
Miri
Bandar Seri Begawan
Kota Kinabalu (Jesselton)
Kinabalu 4101
Balikpapan
Samarinda
Bandjarmasin
DJAKARTA
Bogor
Bandung
Semarang
Surabaja
Jogjakarta
Surakarta
Malang
Madura
BALI
Lombok
Simeulue
Nias
Siberut
Kepulauan Mentawai
Enggano
Hsisha
Chuntao
Palawan
Spratly I.
NUSA TENGGARA
Projection: Mercator
East from Greenwich

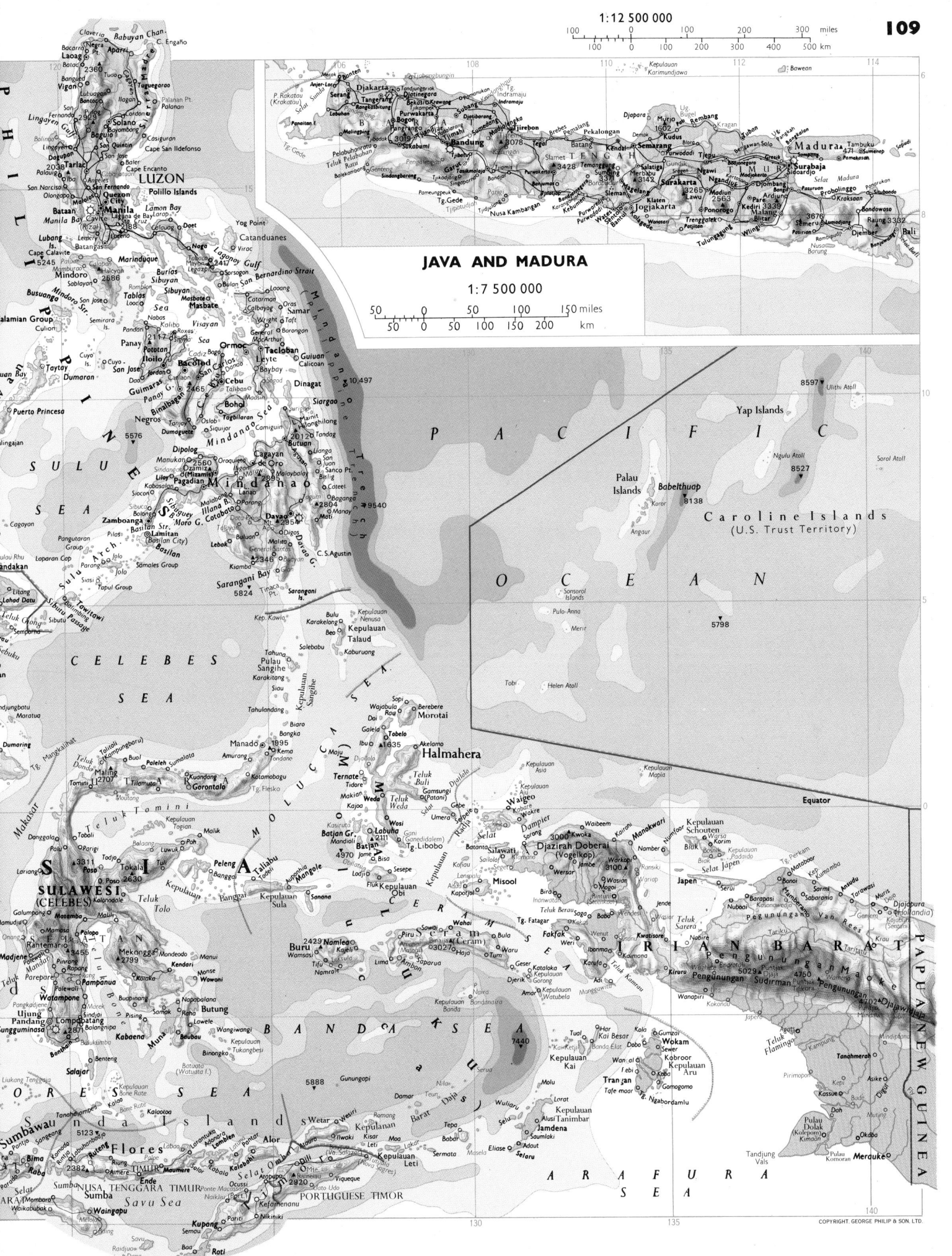
1:12 500 000
miles
km
JAVA AND MADURA
1:7 500 000
miles
km
PHILIPPINES
LUZON
Manila
Quezon City
Mindoro
Mindanao
Samar
Leyte
Cebu
Negros
Panay
Bohol
SULU SEA
CELEBES SEA
Mindanao Trench
Philippine Trench
PACIFIC OCEAN
Caroline Islands
(U.S. Trust Territory)
Palau Islands
Yap Islands
Equator
Halmahera
MOLUCCA SEA
SULAWESI
(CELEBES)
BANDA SEA
FLORES SEA
Flores
Sumbawa
Sumba
Savu Sea
PORTUGUESE TIMOR
NUSA TENGGARA TIMUR
ARAFURA SEA
IRIAN BARAT
PAPUA NEW GUINEA
Pegunungan Sudirman
Djazirah Doberai
(Vogelkop)
Seram (Ceram)
Buru
Kepulauan Aru
Kepulauan Kai
Kepulauan Tanimbar
Madura
Surabaja
Djakarta
Bandung
Semarang
Jogjakarta
Bali
Merauke
Djajapura

COPYRIGHT, GEORGE PHILIP & SON, LTD.

1:30 000 000

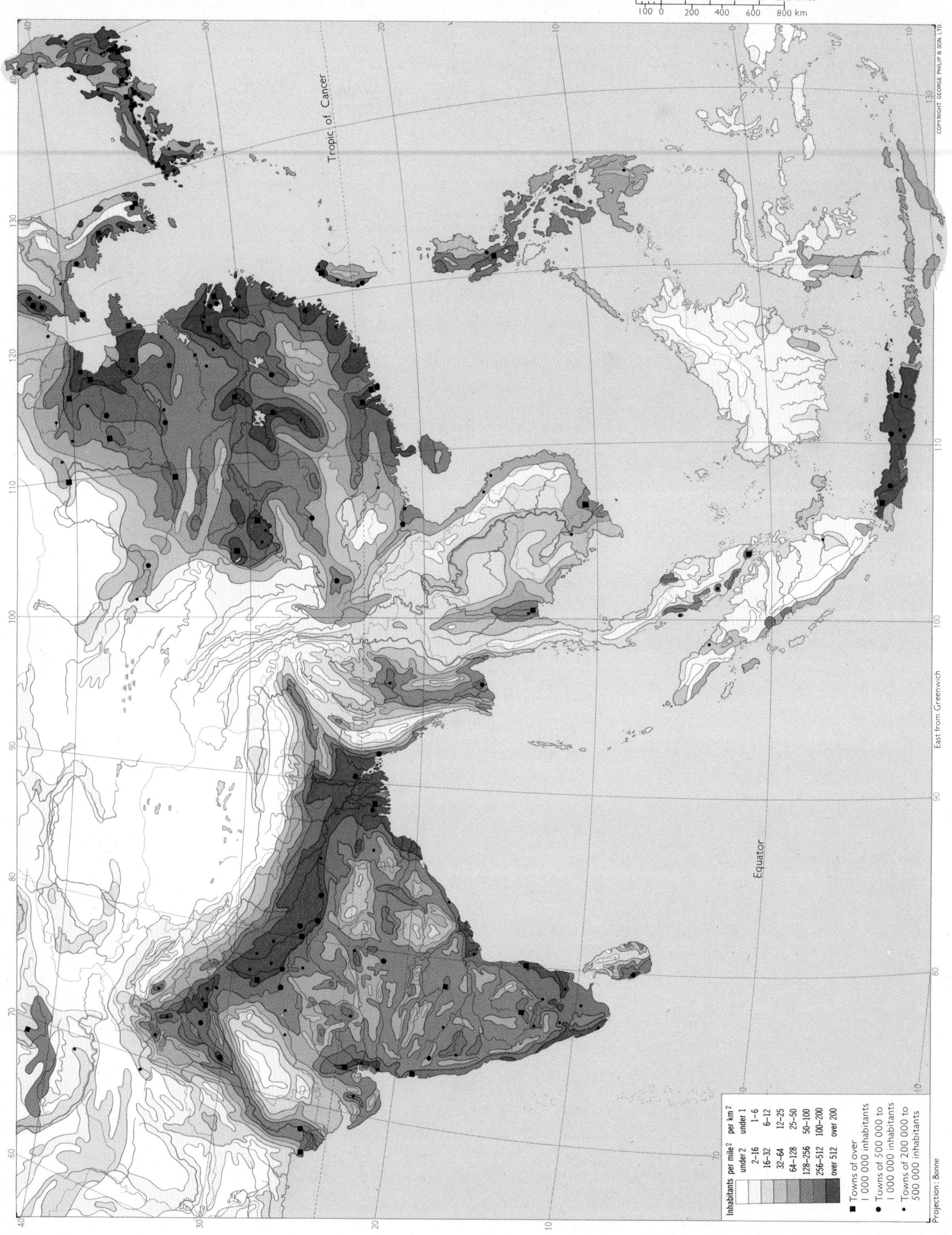

Tropic of Cancer

East from Greenwich

Equator

COPYRIGHT GEORGE PHILIP & SON LTD.

Inhabitants per mile²	per km²
under 2	under 1
2–16	1–6
16–32	6–12
32–64	12–25
64–128	25–50
128–256	50–100
256–512	100–200
over 512	over 200

■ Towns of over 1 000 000 inhabitants
● Towns of 500 000 to 1 000 000 inhabitants
● Towns of 200 000 to 500 000 inhabitants

Projection: Bonne

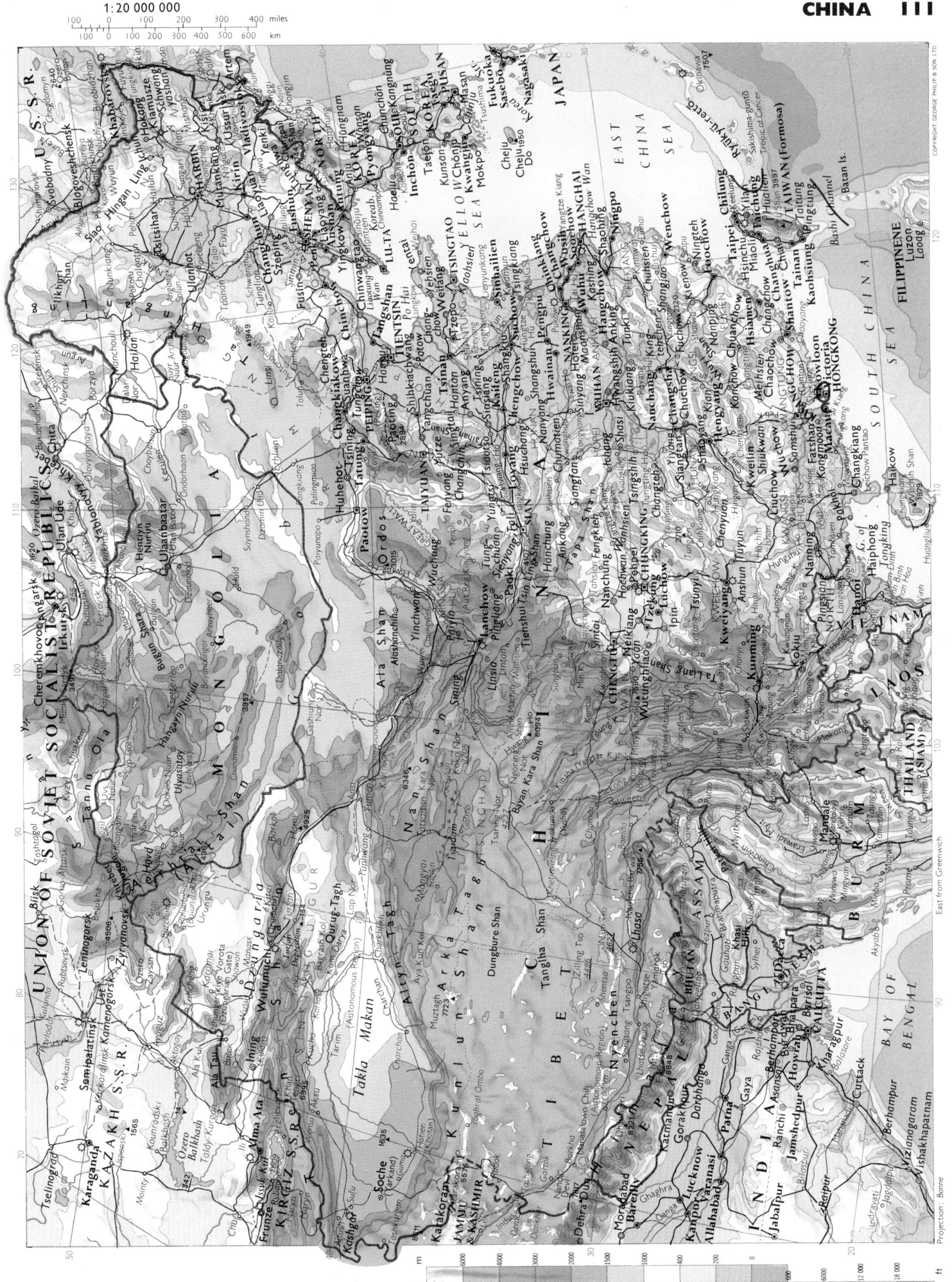

1 : 20 000 000

100   0   100   200   300   400 miles
100   0   100   200   300   400   500   600 km

COPYRIGHT GEORGE PHILIP & SON LTD

East from Greenwich

Projection : Borne

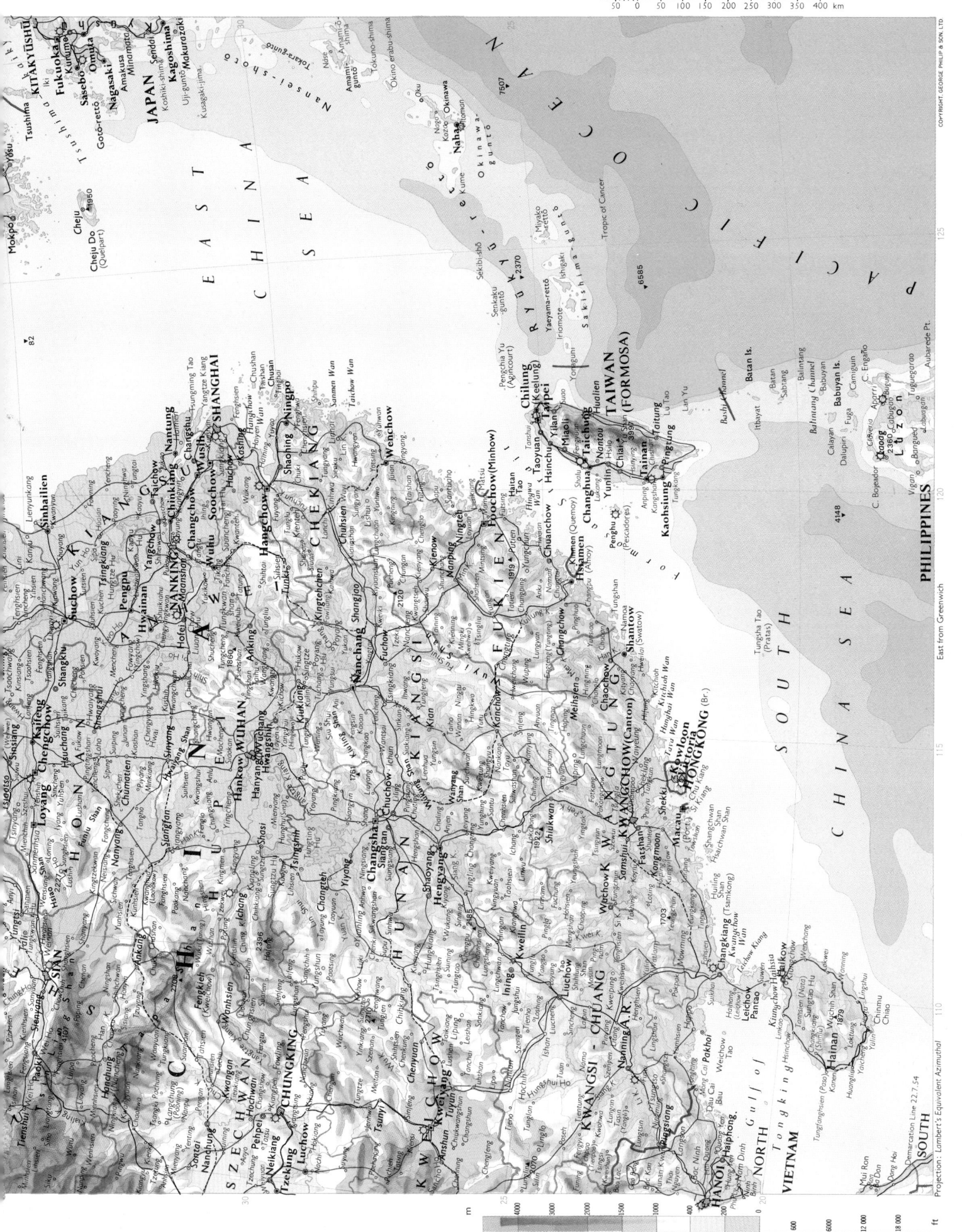

1:10 000 000

50   0   50   100   150   200   250 miles

50   0   50   100   150   200   250   300   350   400 km

PACIFIC OCEAN

RYUKYU

Tropic of Cancer

JAPAN

KITAKYUSHU
Fukuoka
Kurume
Omuta
Sasebo
Nagasaki
Kagoshima
Makurazaki
Amakusa
Minamata
Sendai

Mokpo

Cheju
Cheju Do
(Quelpart)

EAST

CHINA

SEA

Nansei-shotō

Tokara-guntō

Amami-ō-shima
Amami guntō
Tokuno-shima
Okino erabu-shima

Oku

Okinawa

Naha
Okinawa-guntō

Kume

Miyako
rettō

Ishigaki

Sakishima-guntō
Yaeyama-guntō

6585

Senkaku
guntō

Pengchia Yu
(Agincourt)

2370

Keelung
Chilung
(Keelung)
Taipei

TAIWAN
(FORMOSA)

SHANGHAI

CHEKIANG

Hangchow

Ningpo
Wenchow

FUKIEN

Foochow(Minhow)

Amoy
Hsiamen
(Amoy)

Chuanchow

KIANGSI

Nanchang

Shantow
(Swatow)

Chaochow

KWANGTUNG

KWANGCHOW
(Canton)

Macau
(Port.)

Kowloon
Victoria
HONGKONG (Br.)

PHILIPPINES

Luzon

Batan Is.

SOUTH

CHINA

SEA

HONAN

Kaifeng

ANHWEI

NANKING

WUHAN
Hankow
Hanyang Wuchang

HUNAN

Changsha

Hengyang

KWEICHOW

Kweiyang

KWANGSI-CHUANG A.R.

Nanning

Liuchow

Kweilin

HAINAN

Haikow

SZECHWAN

CHUNGKING

SHENSI

HANOI

VIETNAM

Haiphong

Gulf of
Tongking

NORTH

SOUTH

COPYRIGHT. GEORGE PHILIP & SON. LTD.

East from Greenwich

Projection: Lambert's Equivalent Azimuthal

Demarcation Line 22.7.54

m
ft
4000   12 000
9000
6000
4500
3000
2000
1500
1000
600
200   600
0
2000   6000
4000   12 000
6000   18 000

SEA OF JAPAN

CHŪGOKU

PACIFIC OCEAN

SEA OF JAPAN

KYŪSHŪ

SHIKOKU

HOKKAIDŌ

Sea of Okhotsk

TŌHOKU

CHŪBU

KANTŌ

KINKI

SOUTH KOREA

1:5 000 000
25   0   25   50   75   100 miles
25   0   50   100   150 km
Projection: Conical with two standard parallels

East from Greenwich

1:10 000 000
100   50   0   50   100   150   200 miles
100   0   100   200   300 km
Projection: Bonne

East from Greenwich

Continuation Southwards on same scale

ft   m

9000   3000
6000   2000
4500   1500
3000   1000
1200   400
600   200
0

200   600
2000   6000
4000   12 000
6000   18 000
8000   24 000

m   ft

REFERENCE TO PREFECTURES

HOKKAIDŌ DISTRICT	KINKI DISTRICT
1 Hokkaidō	24 Hyogo
TŌHOKU DISTRICT	25 Kyōto
2 Aomori	26 Shiga
3 Akita	27 Ōsaka
4 Iwate	28 Nara
5 Yamagata	29 Mie
6 Miyagi	30 Wakayama
7 Fukushima	**CHŪGOKU DISTRICT**
CHŪBU DISTRICT	31 Tottori
8 Niigata	32 Okayama
9 Ishikawa	33 Shimane
10 Toyama	34 Hiroshima
11 Fukui	35 Yamaguchi
12 Gifu	**SHIKOKU DISTRICT**
13 Nagano	36 Kagawa
14 Yamanashi	37 Tokushima
15 Aichi	38 Ehime
16 Shizuoka	39 Kōchi
KANTŌ DISTRICT	**KYŪSHŪ DISTRICT**
17 Gumma	40 Fukuoka
18 Tochigi	41 Saga
19 Saitama	42 Nagasaki
20 Ibaraki	43 Kumamoto
21 Tōkyō	44 Ōita
22 Chiba	45 Miyazaki
23 Kanagawa	46 Kagoshima

COPYRIGHT. GEORGE PHILIP & SON, LTD.

1 : 40 000 000

200 0 200 400 600 800 1000 miles
200 0 200 400 600 800 1000 1200 1400 1600 km

SPAIN

Main map labels

Madeira (Port.)
Islas Canarias
Tenerife
Villa Cisneros
C. Blanc
St. Louis
Dakar
GAMBIA
Banjul
PORT. GUINEA
Bissau
GUINEA
Conakry
Freetown
SIERRA LEONE
LIBERIA
Monrovia

Tanger
Tetouan
Gibraltar (Br.)
Casablanca
Rabat Fès
Oran
MOROCCO
Marrakech
Essaouira
Ifni
El Aaiun
SPANISH SAHARA
F. Dérik

Alger
Constantine
Annaba
Bizerte
Tunis
TUNISIA
Sfax
Djerba
ALGERIA
Ghardaia
In Salah
Ghadames
Ghat

Sicilia
MALTA
Tarābulus
Banghāzī
LIBYA
Sahrā'
Marzuq
Al Jawf

TURKEY
Athínai
Kriti
CYPRUS
SYRIA
Halab
Tel Aviv-Yafo
Jerusalem
ISRAEL
JORDAN
LEBANON
El Iskandarîya
Bûr Sa'id
El Suweis
El QAHIRA
El Faiyûm
Asyût
EGYPT (UNITED ARAB REPUBLIC)
Aswân
Wadi-Halfa
Es Sahrâ En Nûbiya

Al Mawsil
Baghdâd
Tehrān
Esfahān
IRAN
Al Basrah
KUWAIT
Persian Gulf
Bahrain
QATAR
SAUDI-ARABIA
Al Madînah
Tropic of Cancer
Makkah
'Asir
Bûr Sûdân

MAURITANIA
Nouakchott
Tombouctou
MALI
Kayes
SENEGAL
Bamako
Kankan
Kumasi
IVORY COAST
GHANA
Accra
Abidjan
Sekondi-Takoradi

UPPER VOLTA
Ouagadougou
Niamey
Sokoto
Kano
Kaduna
Bauchi
NIGERIA
Ibadan
Lagos
Porto Novo
TOGO
DAHOMEY
Tamale

NIGER
Agades
Maiduguri
Ngeru
Lac Tchad
Ft.-Lamy
CHAD
Abéché
El Fâsher
DARFÛR
Kordofân
El Obeid
Omdurmân
El Khartûm
SUDAN
Dongola
Esh Shimâliya
Atbara
Kassala
Asmera
Mitsiwa
Massawa

YEMEN
SOUTH YEMEN
Madinat al Shaab
Al 'Adan (Aden)
Djibouti
Berbera
Ras Asir
Socotra (South Yemen)
Gulf of Aden

CAMEROON
Douala
Yaoundé
EQUATORIAL GUINEA
Rio Muni
Fernando Póo
Sta. Isabel
Principe (Port.)
São Tomé (Port.)
Annobón
GABON
Libreville
C. Lopez

CENTRAL AFRICAN REPUBLIC
Bangui
Oubangi
Bahr el Ghazâl
Wâw
Mongalla
El Istwâ'ya
Bahr el Jebel
A'Âli en Nil
Malakâl
Nil el Azraq
Nil el Abyad
L. Tana
Addis Abeba
Harer
ETHIOPIA
Shebele
SOMALI REP.
Mogadishu

Gulf of Guinea
Bight of Benin
Enugu
Benue
Port Harcourt

CONGO
Brazzaville
Pointe Noire
Kinshasa
Cabinda
Boma
ZAÏRE (Congo)
Mbandaka
Kisangani
Zaïre (Congo)
Ilebo
Kasai
Katanga
Bukama
Lubumbashi
Mweru

L. Albert
L. Edward
L. Kivu
UGANDA
Kampala
RWANDA
BURUNDI
Bujumbura
Kigoma
L. Victoria
Mwanza
Kigali
Kisumu
KENYA
Nairobi
Equator
Tana
L. Rudolf
Mombasa
Pemba
Zanzibar
Dar-es-Salaam
Tabora
TANZANIA
L. Tanganyika
Ruvuma
Cabo Delgado
Arch. des Comores (Fr.)
Aldabra Is. (Br.)
Diego-Suarez

ATLANTIC OCEAN
Ascension (Br.)

ANGOLA
Luanda
Cuanza
Benguela
Lobito
Nova Lisboa
Moçâmedes
Cunene
C. Frio
ZAMBIA
Lusaka
Livingstone
Lilongwe
Kafue
Zambezi
MALAWI
L. Malawi
Zomba
Blantyre
MOZAMBIQUE
Moçambique
Quelimane
Chinde
Beira
Majunga
Diego-Suarez
MALAGASY REPUBLIC
Tamatave
Tananarive
MAURITIUS
Réunion (Fr.)
Fianarantsoa
Tuléar
Mozambique Channel

SOUTH WEST AFRICA (NAMIBIA)
Windhoek
Swakopmund
Walvis baai
Lüderitz
BOTSWANA
Kalahari
Gaborone
Orange
RHODESIA
Salisbury
Bulawayo
Limpopo
TRANSVAAL
Pretoria
Johannesburg
Vaal
Kimberley
O.V.S.
Bloemfontein
NATAL
Durban
SOUTH AFRICA
CAPE PROVINCE
Cape Town
Kaap die Goeie Hoop (Cape of Good Hope)
East London
Port Elizabeth
SWAZ
LES
Lourenço Marques
Tropic of Capricorn

Pr. Edward Is. (S.A.)

Inset map — Density of Population

DENSITY OF POPULATION
1 : 80 000 000
Inhabitants

per mile²	per km²	per mile²	per km²
under 2	under 1	32–64	12–25
2–8	1–3	64–128	25–50
8–16	3–6	128–256	50–100
16–32	6–12	over 256	over 100

■ Towns of over 200 000 inhabitants

Projection: Zenithal Equidistant

COPYRIGHT. GEORGE. PHILIP & SON. LTD.

LES.   Lesotho
O.F.S. Orange Free State
SWAZ. Swaziland
T.A.I. Territory of Afars & Issas

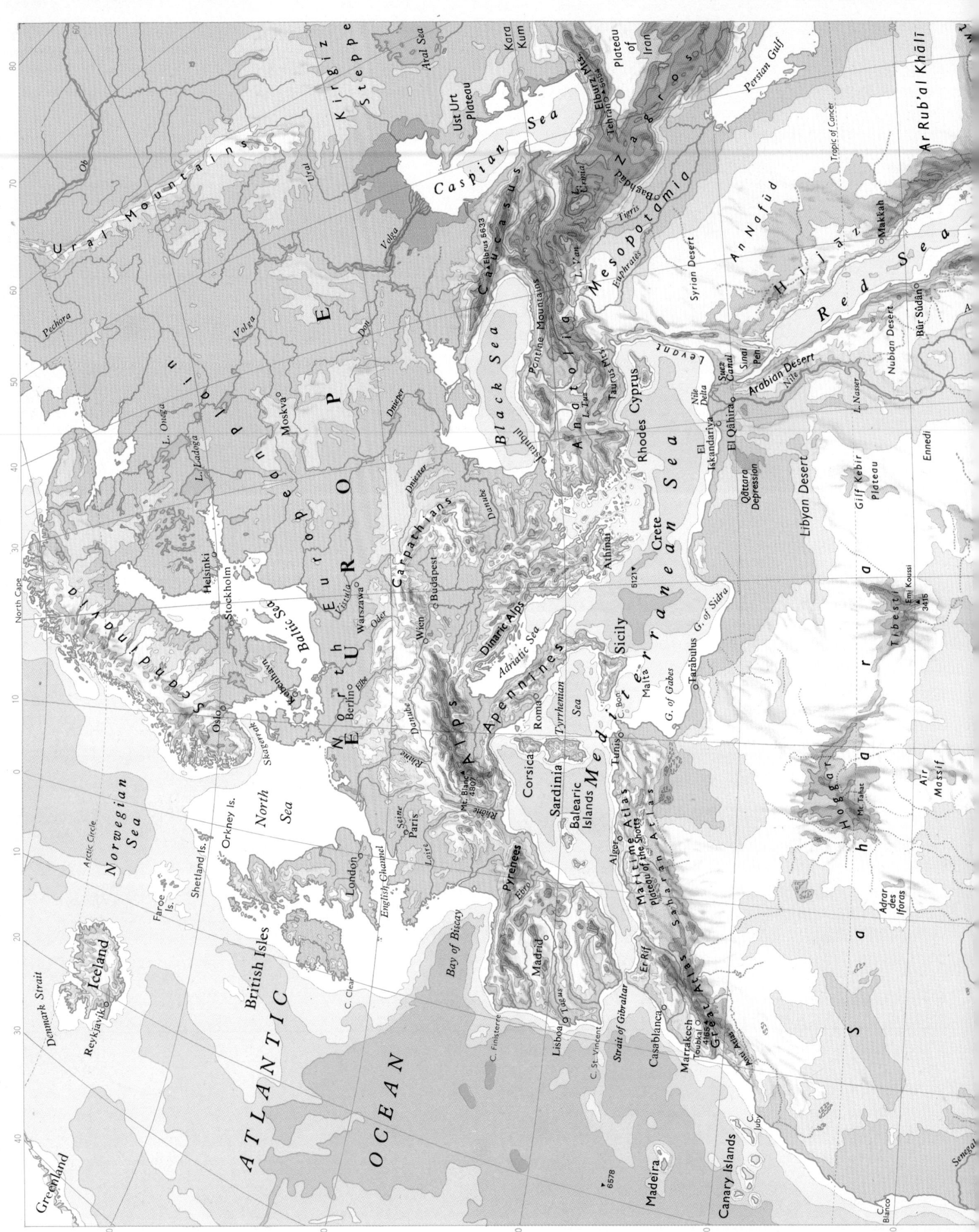

Greenland
Denmark Strait
Iceland
Reykjavik
Arctic Circle
Norwegian Sea
Faroe Is.
Shetland Is.
Orkney Is.
North Cape
Scandinavia
Oslo
Stockholm
Helsinki
København
Skagerrak
Baltic Sea
North Sea
ATLANTIC OCEAN
British Isles
C. Clear
London
English Channel
Paris
Seine
Loire
Rhine
Danube
Elbe
Oder
Vistula
Berlin
Warszawa
Wien
Budapest
Carpathians
Dniester
Dnieper
Don
Volga
Pechora
Ob
Ural
Ural Mountains
Kirgiz Steppe
Aral Sea
Kara Kum
Ust Urt Plateau
Caspian Sea
Caucasus
Elbrus 5633
Elburz Mts.
Tehran
5604
Plateau of Iran
Zagros
Persian Gulf
L. Urmia
L. Van
Baghdad
Tigris
Euphrates
Mesopotamia
Syrian Desert
An Nafūd
Hijaz
Makkah
Ar Rub'al Khālī
Tropic of Cancer
L. Onega
L. Ladoga
Moskva
North European Plain
EUROPE
Black Sea
Istanbul
Pontine Mountains
Anatolia
L. Tuz
Taurus Mts.
Cyprus
Levant
Rhodes
Crete
Athinai
5121
Dinaric Alps
Adriatic Sea
Apennines
Alps
Mt. Blanc 4807
Rhône
Roma
Tyrrhenian Sea
Corsica
Sardinia
Sicily
Malta
Balearic Islands
Mediterranean Sea
G. of Gabes
G. of Sidra
Tunis
C. Bon
Tarābulus
Alger
Maritime Atlas
Plateau of the Shotts
Saharan Atlas
Great Atlas
Anti Atlas
Er Rif
Toubkal 4165
Marrakech
Casablanca
Strait of Gibraltar
C. St. Vincent
Lisboa
Tagus
Madrid
Ebro
Pyrenees
Bay of Biscay
C. Finisterre
6578
Madeira
Canary Islands
C. Juby
C. Blanco
Senegal
El Iskandariya
El Qâhira
Nile Delta
Suez Canal
Sinai Pen.
Arabian Desert
Nile
Nubian Desert
Bûr Sûdân
Red Sea
L. Nasser
Qâttara Depression
Libyan Desert
Gilf Kebir Plateau
Ennedi
Tibesti
Emi Koussi 3415
Hoggar
Mt. Tahat
Aïr Massif
Adrar des Iforas
Sahara

1:30 000 000

100   0   100   200   300   400   500   600   miles
100   0   200   400   600   800   1000   km

COPYRIGHT GEORGE PHILIP & SON LTD

Ras Asir
(C. Guardafui)

Bay of Aden

Somali Peninsula

Hadhramaut

Bab al Mandab
Perim I.

5340

INDIAN OCEAN

Mogadishu

C. Amber
Comoro Is.
Aldabra

Madagascar

Tananarive

Madagascar Plateau

C. St. Mary

50

Shabelle
Juba
Zanzibar
Dar-es-Salaam

El Khartûm
Asmera
L. Tana
Ras Dashen 4620
Chew Bahir/L. Stefanie
Ethiopian Highlands
Addis Abeba
Blue Nile
White Nile
Omo
L. Rudolf
Sobat
Bahr el Ghazal
Sudd
Bahr el Jebel

Eastern Rift Valley
Kenya 5199
Nairobi
Kilimanjaro 5895
Elgon 4321
Kioga
Kampala
L. Albert
Ruwenzori 5109
L. Edward
L. Kivu
L. Victoria
Western Rift Valley
Tabora
L. Tanganyika

Mozambique
Mozambique Channel

Rufiji
Ruvuma

40

Bahr el Arab
Tur
Bahr el Jebel

Darfûr
Jabal Marra
Mongos Plateau
Uele
Ubangi
Congo (Zaïre)
Chutes Boyoma

Lualaba
Congo Basin
Kasai
L. Mai-Ndombe

L. Malawi
Shire
Blantyre
L. Bangweulu
L. Mweru
Mitumba Mts.
Katanga
Muchinga Mts.
Luangwa
Zambezi

Beira
Save
Sabi

Salisbury
Kafue
L. Kariba
Victoria Falls
Bulawayo

Lourenço Marques
Pretoria
Vaal
Johannesburg
High Veld
Drakensberg
Thaban Ntlenyana 3482
Durban
Orange
Great Karoo
Swartberg
Nieuweld
Port Elizabeth

30

L. Chad
Chari

The Sudan

Kano
Jos Plateau
Benue
Adamawa Highlands
Mt. Cameroun 4070
Niger

Ogowe
Ouesso
Brazzaville
Kinshasa (Léopoldville)
Pool Malebo
Congo
Cuango

Luanda
Cuanza
Cuango
Bié
Nova Lisboa
Plateau
Benguela

Makarikari Salt Pan
Limpopo
Marico
Cuando
Cubango

Okavango
Etosha Pan
Ovamboland
Windhoek
Damaraland
Great Namaqualand
Kalahari
Orange

Cape Town
C. of Good Hope
Agulhas Bank

East from Greenwich

40

5283

Namib Desert
Walvisbaai
C. Frio
Cunene

20

Fouta Djalon
Freetown

Guinea

Ivory Coast
Grain Coast
C. Palmas
Gold Coast
Accra
L. Volta
Slave Coast
Bight of Benin
Lagos
Ibadan

Fernando Póo
Bight of Biafra
Príncipe
São Tomé
Annobón
6363

Gulf of Guinea
Guinea Basin

ATLANTIC OCEAN

Equator

10

ANNUAL RAINFALL
1:80 000 000

mm	inches
3000	120
2000	80
1000	40
500	20
250	10

Tropic of Cancer
Equator
Tropic of Capricorn

Projection Zenithal Equidistant

ft   m
12 000
9000
6000
4500
3000
1200
600
0
−200 −600

4000
3000
2000
1500
1000
400
200
0

2000 6000
4000 12 000
6000 18 000

ft   m

1 : 80 000 000

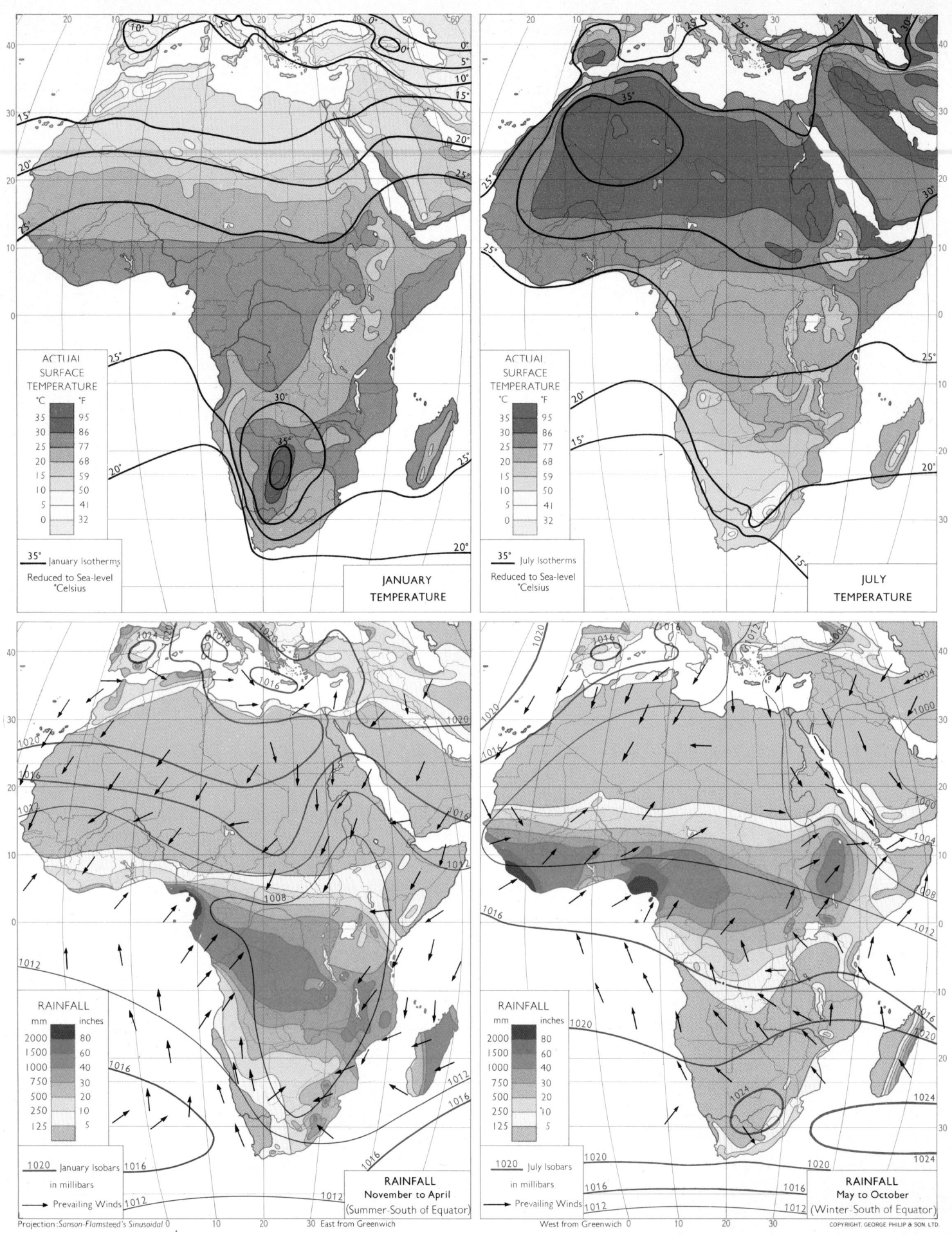

ACTUAL
SURFACE
TEMPERATURE

°C	°F
35	95
30	86
25	77
20	68
15	59
10	50
5	41
0	32

35° January Isotherms

Reduced to Sea-level
°Celsius

JANUARY
TEMPERATURE

ACTUAL
SURFACE
TEMPERATURE

°C	°F
35	95
30	86
25	77
20	68
15	59
10	50
5	41
0	32

35° July Isotherms

Reduced to Sea-level
°Celsius

JULY
TEMPERATURE

RAINFALL

mm	inches
2000	80
1500	60
1000	40
750	30
500	20
250	10
125	5

1020 January Isobars 1016

in millibars

→ Prevailing Winds

RAINFALL
November to April
(Summer-South of Equator)

RAINFALL

mm	inches
2000	80
1500	60
1000	40
750	30
500	20
250	10
125	5

1020 July Isobars

in millibars

→ Prevailing Winds

RAINFALL
May to October
(Winter-South of Equator)

Projection:Sanson-Flamsteed's Sinusoidal 0   10   20   30 East from Greenwich

West from Greenwich 0   10   20   30

COPYRIGHT. GEORGE PHILIP & SON. LTD

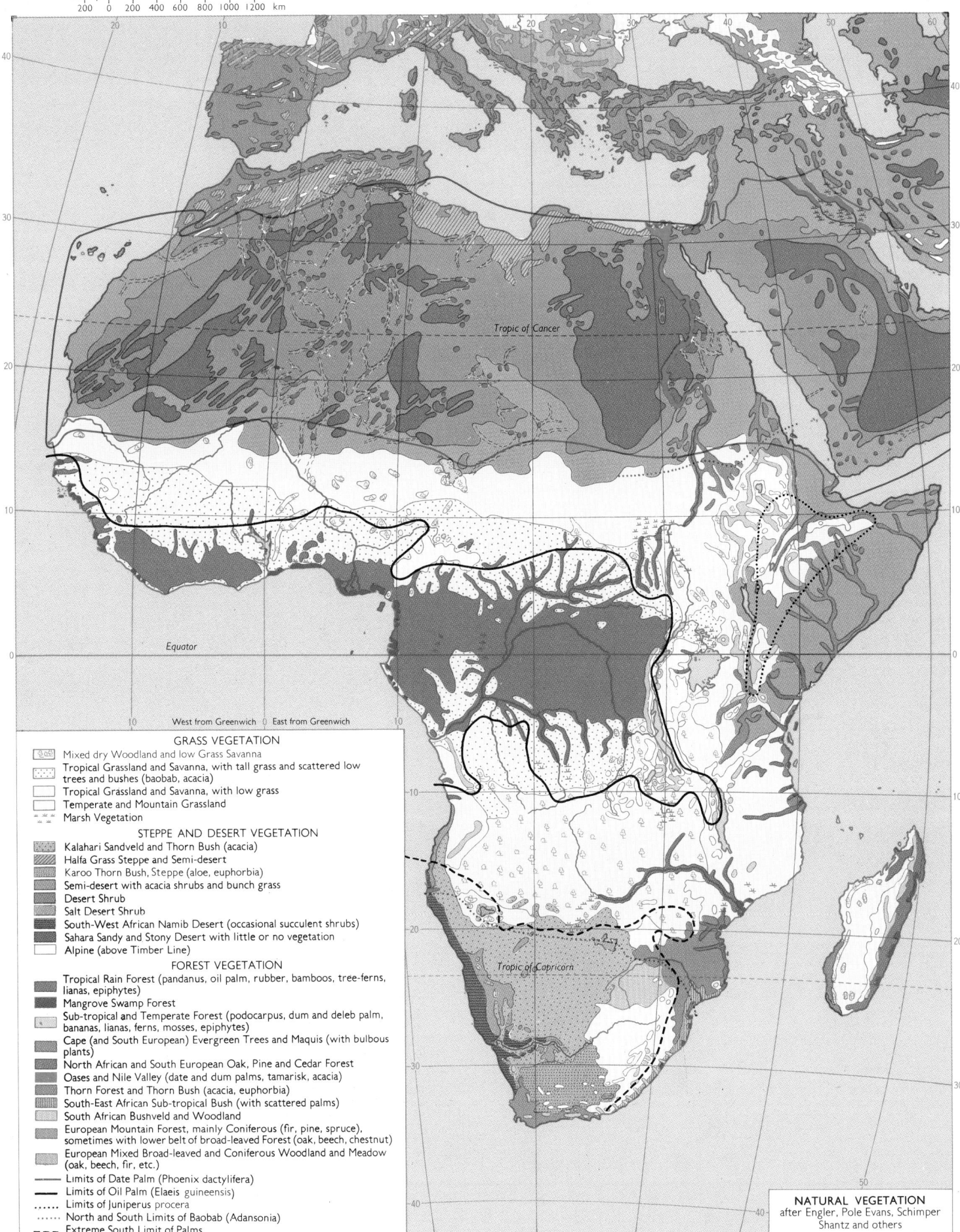

1:40 000 000

| 200 | 0 | 200 | 400 | 600 | 800 miles |
| 200 | 0 | 200 | 400 | 600 | 800 | 1000 | 1200 km |

Tropic of Cancer

Equator

West from Greenwich   East from Greenwich

Tropic of Capricorn

GRASS VEGETATION
Mixed dry Woodland and low Grass Savanna
Tropical Grassland and Savanna, with tall grass and scattered low trees and bushes (baobab, acacia)
Tropical Grassland and Savanna, with low grass
Temperate and Mountain Grassland
Marsh Vegetation

STEPPE AND DESERT VEGETATION
Kalahari Sandveld and Thorn Bush (acacia)
Halfa Grass Steppe and Semi-desert
Karoo Thorn Bush, Steppe (aloe, euphorbia)
Semi-desert with acacia shrubs and bunch grass
Desert Shrub
Salt Desert Shrub
South-West African Namib Desert (occasional succulent shrubs)
Sahara Sandy and Stony Desert with little or no vegetation
Alpine (above Timber Line)

FOREST VEGETATION
Tropical Rain Forest (pandanus, oil palm, rubber, bamboos, tree-ferns, lianas, epiphytes)
Mangrove Swamp Forest
Sub-tropical and Temperate Forest (podocarpus, dum and deleb palm, bananas, lianas, ferns, mosses, epiphytes)
Cape (and South European) Evergreen Trees and Maquis (with bulbous plants)
North African and South European Oak, Pine and Cedar Forest
Oases and Nile Valley (date and dum palms, tamarisk, acacia)
Thorn Forest and Thorn Bush (acacia, euphorbia)
South-East African Sub-tropical Bush (with scattered palms)
South African Bushveld and Woodland
European Mountain Forest, mainly Coniferous (fir, pine, spruce), sometimes with lower belt of broad-leaved Forest (oak, beech, chestnut)
European Mixed Broad-leaved and Coniferous Woodland and Meadow (oak, beech, fir, etc.)
—— Limits of Date Palm (Phoenix dactylifera)
—— Limits of Oil Palm (Elaeis guineensis)
······ Limits of Juniperus procera
········ North and South Limits of Baobab (Adansonia)
– – – Extreme South Limit of Palms

NATURAL VEGETATION
after Engler, Pole Evans, Schimper
Shantz and others

Projection: Zenithal Equidistant

COPYRIGHT. GEORGE PHILIP & SON. LTD.

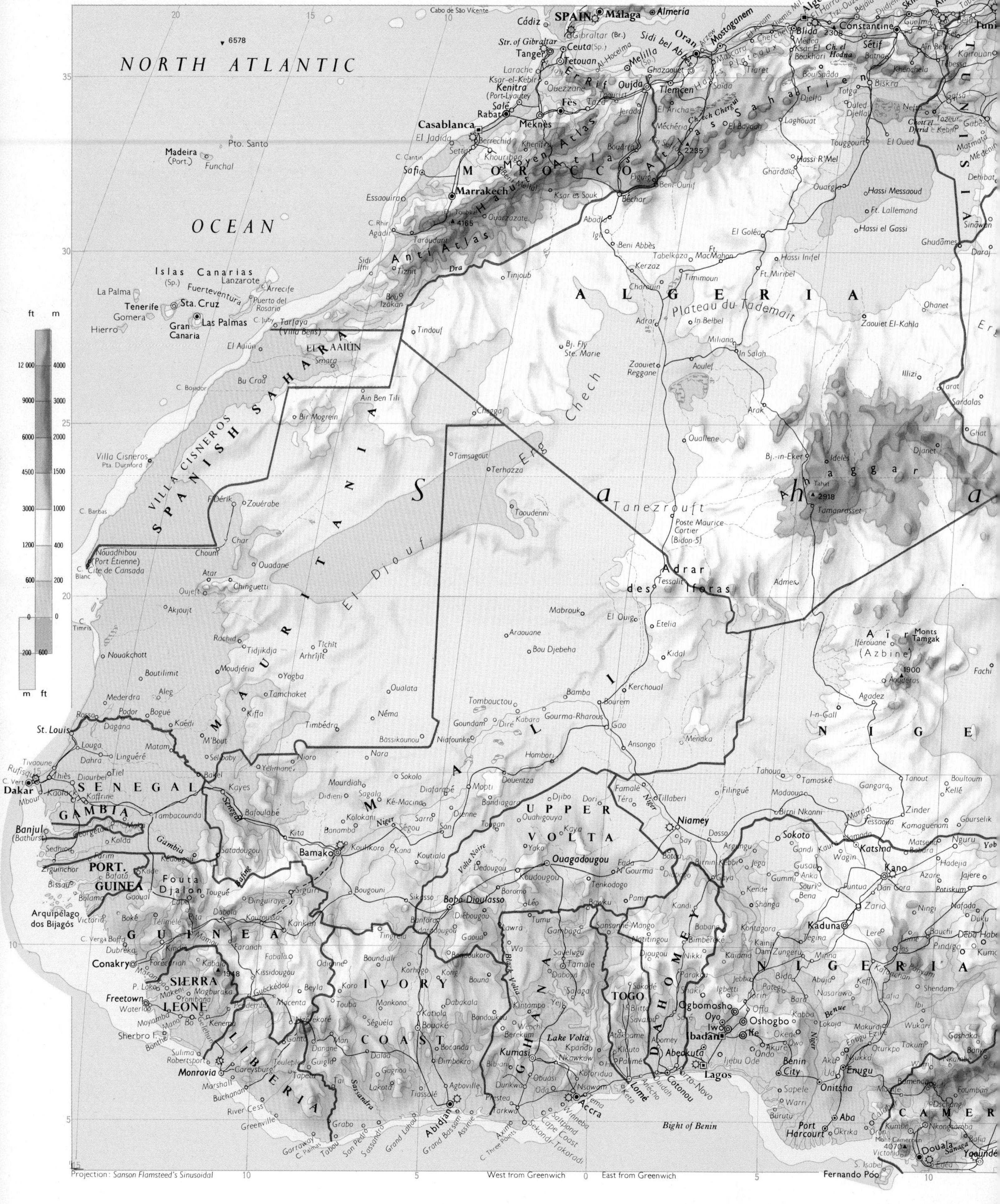

NORTH ATLANTIC

OCEAN

▼ 6578

Madeira (Port.)
Pto. Santo
Funchal

Cabo de São Vicente
Cádiz
SPAIN ● Málaga Almería
Str. of Gibraltar Gibraltar (Br.) Sidi bel Abbès Oran Mostaganem Blida 2308 Constantine Guelma Skikda Annaba Tuni
Tanger Ceuta (Sp.) Melilla Ghazaouet Tlemcen Mascara Aïn Beïda Tabarka
Larache Al-Hoceima Médéa Ksar El Hodna Sétif Batna Khenchela Biskra
Ksar-el-Kebir Tetouan Er Rif Oujda El Aricha Saïda Tiaret Oued Djellal Chott el Hodna Tozeur Gabès
Kenitra (Port-Lyautey) Fès Taza Taourirt Méchéria El Bayadh Laghouat Djelfa Chott el Djerid Médenine
Salé Rabat Meknès
Casablanca Berrechid Khouribga Moyen Atlas Aïn Sefra 2235 Ghardaïa Hassi R'Mel Ouargla Matmata
El Jadida Settat Khenifra Haut Atlas Béni Ounif El Goléa Hassi Messaoud El Oued Dehibat
Safi Beni Mellal Béchar Touggourt Ft. Lallemand Ghudāmes
Essaouira Marrakech Ksar es Souk Abadla Igli Kerzaz Tabelkoza Hassi el Gassi Daraj
C. Rhir Toubkal ▲ 4165 Ouarzazate Ft. MacMahon Hassi Inifel Ghudāmes
Agadir Taroudant Anti Atlas Dra Tinjoub Timimoun Zaouiet El-Kahla Ohanet
Sidi Ifni Tiznit Charouin In-Belbel Miliana In Salah Illizi
Bou Izakarn Plateau du Tademaït Adrar Tarat Sardalas
A L G E R I A Aoulef Sdawan Ghat

Islas Canarias (Sp.)
Lanzarote
La Palma Fuerteventura Arrecife
Tenerife ● Sta. Cruz Puerto del Rosario
Gomera Gran Las Palmas
Hierro Canaria C. Juby
El Aaiún Tarfaya (Villa Bens)
EL AAIÚN
Smara
Bu Craa
C. Bojador
Villa Cisneros
Pta. Durnford
Bir Mogrein
Ain Ben Tili
Zaouiet Reggane Arak
Chegga Bj.-in-Eket Idelès Djanet
Tamsagout H a g g a r
Terhazza Tanezrouft Tahat ▲ 2918 Tamanrasset
Taoudenni Poste Maurice Cortier (Bidon 5)
C. Barbas
F'Dérik Zouérate
Nouadhibou (Port Étienne) Choum
Cité de Cansado
C. Blanc Char El Djouf
Atar Chinguetti
Ouadane
Timiris Oujeft Adrar des Iforas
Akjoujt Tessalit Admer
Nouakchott Rachid Tidjikdja Tichît Mabrouk El Ouig Etelia Aïr Monts Tamgak
Boutilimit Moudjéria Arhrîjit (Azbine) 1900
Aleg Yogba Tamchaket Araouane Kidal Iférouane Fachi
Mederdra M'Bout Kiffa Ouallata Bou Djebeha Anderaras
Rosso Podor Kaédi Tamchaket Néma Bou Djebeha Agadez
St. Louis Dagana Timbédra Bâssikounou Tombouctou Bamba Bourem I-n-Gall
Louga Matam Nioro Goundam Diré Kabara Gao N I G E
Tivaouane Dahra Linguère Nara Niafounke Gourma-Rharous Ansongo Menaka Tahoua Tamaské Gangara
Rufisque Thiès Yélimané Sokolo Hombori Tillaberi Filingué Madaoua Zinder
C. Vert Diourbel Baïel Mourdiah Diafarabé Mopti Djibo Dori Téra Niamey Tessaoua Nkonni Maradi Gourselik
Dakar Kaolack Kaffrine Didieni Sagala Djenné Bandiagara Ouahigouya Dosso Argungu Gandi Sokoto Gusau Matseka Yob
Mbour Tambacounda Bafoulabé Kolokani Ségou Sarro San Tougan Yako Say Birnin Kebbi Katsina Nguru
SENEGAL Kita Banamba Niger Koutiala M A L I UPPER VOLTA Dedougou Fada N'Gourma Botou Gaya Dan Gora Kano Hadejia
GAMBIA Kayes Koulikoro Kana Bobo-Dioulasso Koudougou Ouagadougou Kende Shanga Kaduna Azare
Banjul (Bathurst) Satadougou Bamako Sikasso Bawku Tenkodogo Kandi Puntua Bena Ningi Patiskum
Sedhiou Forim Tambacounda Bougouni Diébougou Léo Tumu Wa Birnin Kudu Ilega Kontagora Zaria Nguru Mafada
Ziguinchor Kolda Siguiri Bonfora Tingréla Gaoua Gambaga Natitingou Nikki Kaiama Dam Zungeru Minna Nguru Kumo
PORT. Bafatá Kouroussa Banfora Bouna Sansanné-Mango Dabola Bimbéréke Kainji Leré Pindiga Deba Habe
GUINEA Fouta Tougué Odienné Boundiali Korhogo Kong Wenchi Salaga Kabba Bauchi Duku
Bolama Djalon Télimélé Kankan Fabala Séguéla Bouaké Katiola Tamale Djougou Nasarawo Kontagora Lafia Shendam
Arquipélago Boké Dabola Dabakala Yeji Sokode Igbetti Abuja Wukari
dos Bijagós Bissau G U I N E A Dinguiraye Bondoukou Lawra Yendi Salaga Oyo Offa Lokoja Makurdi Ibi Gashaka
Victoria Faranah Mankono TOGO Ilorin Oshogbo Kabba Benue Enugu Oturkpo Takum
Conakry Kissidougou Macenta Séguéla I V O R Y Kintampo Abomey DAHOMEY Iwo Oyo Ife Benin Udi
SIERRA 1948 Beyla Toubu Dabakala Bondoukro Sunyani Pama Lomé Ibadan Ondo City Akure Enugu Aba
P. Loko Makeni Magburaka Guéckédou Gbarnga Kumasi Obuasi G H A N A Abeokuta Ijebu Ode Sapele Onitsha
LEONE Freetown Moyamba Man C O A S T Ségbwema Kpandu Koforidua Lagos Warri CAMER
Waterloo Bo Kenema Gagnoa Bibiani Nkawkaw Cotonou Porto-Novo Benin City Bamenda Kumba
Sherbro I. Zimmi Danané Guiglo Dimbokro Oda Nsawam Keta Aného Buruti CAMER
Sulima Kenema Touba Bondoukou Anyama Accra Bight of Benin Port Harcourt Okrika Mt. Cameroun ▲ 4070
LIBERIA Monrovia Tapeta Tabou Tiassalé Agboville Tema Port Harcourt Douala Yaoundé
Marshall River Cess Lakota Dunkwa Takoradi Fernando Póo
Robertsport Buchanan Sassandra Grand Bassam Cape Coast Sekondi-Takoradi St. Isabel
Greenville San Pedro Abidjan Axim C. Three Points

SPANISH SAHARA

MAURITANIA

M A L I

Chech

Erg

El Djouf

Tanezrouft

Bight of Benin

Projection: Sanson Flamsteed's Sinusoidal
West from Greenwich   East from Greenwich

ft m
12 000 4000
9000 3000
6000 2000
4500 1500
3000 1000
1200 400
600 200
0 0
200 600
m ft

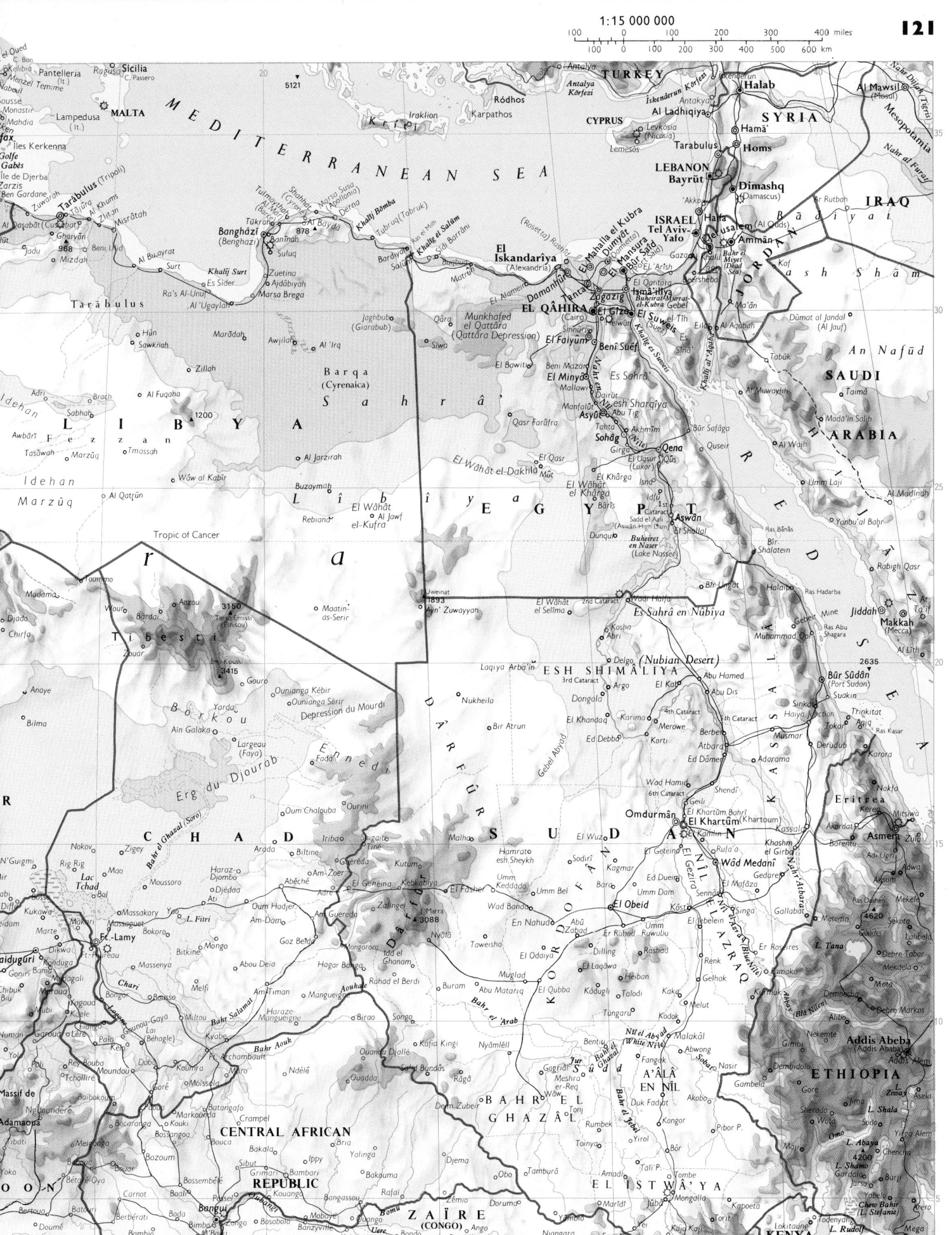

1:15 000 000

100   0   100   200   300   400 miles
100   0   100   200   300   400   500   600 km

MEDITERRANEAN SEA

TURKEY

MALTA

CYPRUS

SYRIA

Halab

Al Mawsil (Mosul)

Mesopotamia

Antalya
Ródhos

Iraklion
Kriti
Karpathos

Al Ladhiqiya
Levkosía
(Nicosia)
Lemesós
Tarabulus
Hamā

Homs

İskenderun Körfezi

IRAQ

LEBANON
Bayrūt

Dimashq
(Damascus)

ISRAEL
Tel Aviv-
Yafo
Jerusalem (Al Quds)
Amman

JORDAN

Ar Rutbah

Bādiyat
ash Shām

LIBYA

Tarabulus (Tripoli)

Banghāzi
(Benghazi)

Barqa
(Cyrenaica)

Sahrâ'

El Iskandarîya
(Alexandria)

El Qâhira
(Cairo)

Munkhafed
el Qattâra
(Qattâra Depression)

EGYPT

SAUDI
ARABIA

An Nafūd

Makkah
(Mecca)

Jiddah

RED SEA

Tropic of Cancer

Tibesti

CHAD

Lac
Tchad

Ft.-Lamy

ESH SHIMÂLIYA

SUDAN

El Khartûm
(Khartoum)
Omdurmân

KORDOFAN

DÂRFÛR

Eritrea

Asmera

BAHR EL
GHAZÂL

CENTRAL AFRICAN
REPUBLIC

Bangui

ZAÏRE
(CONGO)

ETHIOPIA

Addis Abeba
(Addis Ababa)

EL ISTWÂ'YA

KENYA

COPYRIGHT. GEORGE PHILIP & SON, LTD.

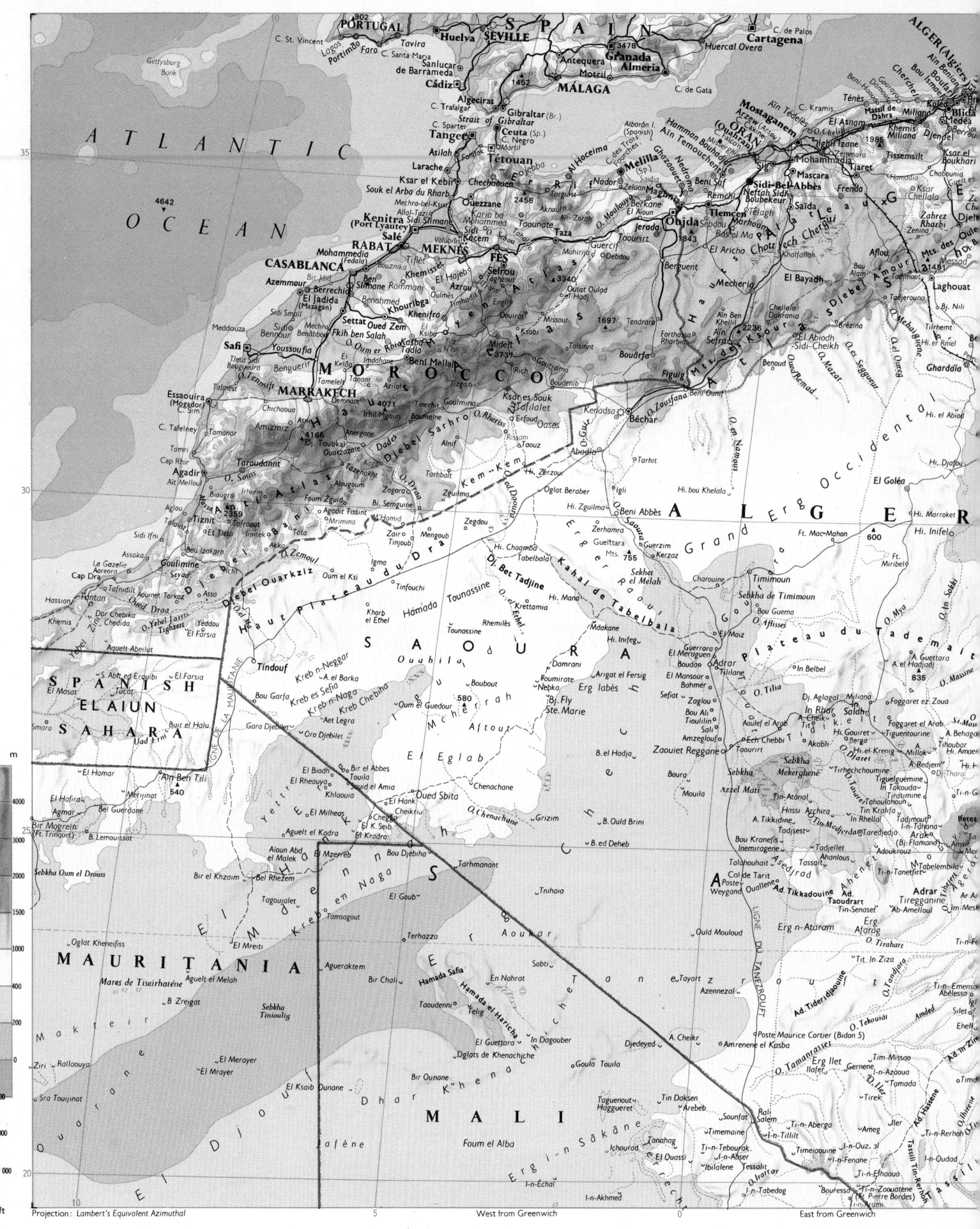
PORTUGAL
SPAIN
C. St. Vincent
Lagos
Portimão
Faro
Tavira
C. Santa Maria
Huelva
SEVILLE
Sanlucar de Barrameda
Cádiz
Granada
Almeria
Antequera
Motril
MÁLAGA
Cartagena
Huercal Overa
C. de Palos
C. de Gata
Algeciras
C. Trafalgar
Gibraltar (Br.)
Strait of Gibraltar
C. Spartel
Ceuta (Sp.)
C. Negro
Tanger
Asilah
Tétouan
Larache
Ksar el Kebir
Chechaouen
Souk el Arba du Rharb
Ouezzane
Kenitra (Port Lyautey)
Salé
RABAT
MEKNÈS
FÈS
Sefrou
CASABLANCA
Mohammedia (Fedala)
Azemmour
El Jadida (Mazagan)
Settat
Oued Zem
Khouribga
Safi
Youssoufia
MARRAKECH
MOROCCO
Essaouira (Mogador)
C. Sim
C. Tafelney
Agadir
Taroudannt
Tiznit
Sidi Ifni
Goulimine
Cap Dra
Tan-Tan
Al Hoceima
Melilla (Sp.)
Nador
Taza
Oujda
Tlemcen
Taourirt
Jerada
Berguent
Figuig
Bouarfa
Midelt
Missour
Ksar es Souk
Tafilalet
Erfoud
Rissani
Goulmima
Tinerhir
Boulmalne
Ouarzazate
Zagora
Beni Mellal
Kasba Tadla
Fkih ben Salah
Djebel Sarhro
Anti Atlas
Haut Atlas
Moyen Atlas
Djebel Bani
Djebel Ouarkziz
Oued Draa
Hamada du Draa
Haut Plateau du Dra
ALGER (Algiers)
Blida
Médéa
Cherchell
Ténès
Miliana
Mostaganem
Arzew
ORAN (Ouahran)
Sidi-Bel-Abbès
Mascara
Saïda
Tiaret
Frenda
Mohammadia
Relizane
Tissemsilt
Aflou
Laghouat
El Bayadh
Mecheria
Aïn Sefra
Djebel Amour
Mts. des Ksour
Chott ech Chergui
Ghardaïa
Béchar
Kenadsa
Abadla
Beni Abbès
Grand Erg Occidental
Erg er Raoui
Kahal de Tabelbala
Tabelbalat
Timimoun
Sebkha de Timimoun
Adrar
Reggane
Zaouiet Reggane
Tidikelt
In Salah
Aoulef el Arab
Plateau du Tademait
El Goléa
ALGERIA
Tindouf
SAOURA
Hamada Tounassine
Ouahila
Iguidi
El Eglab
Erg Chech
Tanezrouft
Hank
Oglat Kheneifiss
SPANISH SAHARA
ELAIUN
Smara
Aïn Ben Tili
Bir Mogrein (Ft. Trinquet)
MAURITANIA
Makteir
El Djouf
Ouarane
Taoudenni
Hamada Safia
Aoukar
MALI
Erg-i-n Sakane
Foum el Alba
Poste Maurice Cortier (Bidon 5)
Erg n-Ataram
Tamanrasset
Ahnet
Tassili Tin-Rerhoh
ATLANTIC OCEAN
Gettysburg Bank
Projection: Lambert's Equivalent Azimuthal
West from Greenwich
East from Greenwich

1:8 000 000

50 0 50 100 150 200 miles

50 0 50 100 150 200 250 300 km

MEDITERRANEAN SEA

SICILY

Marsala
Agrigento
Caltanissetta
CATANIA
Siracusa
Ragusa
Etna 3340
C. Spartivento
C. Passero
Pantelleria (Italian)
Linosa I. (Italian)
Lampione I. (Italian)
Lampedusa (Italian)
Gozo
Valletta
MALTA

Galite Is.
C. Serrat
C. Blanc
Menzel Bourguiba
Bizerte (Binzert)
Mateur
C. Farina
Golfe de Tunis
Zembra I.
C. Bon
Ariana
Tabarka
Halq el Oued
Kelibia
Béja
Téboursouk
Soliman
R. Mostefa
Bou Salem
TUNIS
Menzel-Temime
Jendouba
Nabeul
Hammamet
G. de Hammamet
Zaghouan
Enfida
Kalaa-Kebira
Maktar
Kairouan
Sousse
Monastir
Moknine
Mahdia
Thala
Msaken
El Kef
Souk Ahras
Sbeitla
Hadjeb El Aïoun
Djem
Rass Kaboudia
Djebiniana
Sidi Bou Zid
Menzel Chaker
Fériana
Sfax
Graiba
Iles Kerkenna
Maharès
Kneiss Is.
Gafsa
Metlaoui
Tamerza
Cekhira
1165
G. de Gabès
Nefta
Tozeur
Chott Djerid
Chott el Fedjadj
El Hamma
Gabès
Djerba
Djerba I.
Adjim
El Kantara
Kebili
Douz
Sabria
Matmata
Zarzis
Médenine
Ksar Rhilane
Bahiret el Bibane
Ben Gardane
Tatahouine
B. Aouine
Bj. Bourguiba
Dehibat
TUNISIA

Collo
C. Bougaroun
Skikda
Ile Fer
Chetaibi
C. de Fer
Annaba
C. Rosa
El Kala
Djidjelli
Bejaia
El Kseur
Azeffoun
Tizi-Ouzou
Dellys
Bordj Menaiel
Azazga
El Milia
Azzaba
Guelma
Medjerda
Dj. Babor
Kherrata
El Arrouch
CONSTANTINE
Akbou
2004
Bordj bou Arreridj
El Eulma
Sedrata
Ouenza
Sétif
Aïn M'lila
El Kroubs
Ras el Oued
Ampere
Oum-el-Bouaghi
Aïn Beïda
Mts. du Hodna
1863
M'sila
Chott el Hodna
Batna
Tazoult
2328
Khenchela
Tébessa
Aïn Touta
Aurès
Babar
Bou Saâda
Kantara
Biskra
Monts du Zab
1338
Bir el Ater
Aïn Rich
Tolga
Ferkane
Négrine
Ouled Djellal
Chott Melrhir
El Guettar
El Meghaier
Hi. Berrekrem
O. er Retem
O. Attar
Djamâa
Guemar
El Oued
Dzioua
Megarine
Hassi Daoula
Touggourt
Blidet Amor
Guerrara
Bir Gueboussa
Bj. Zelfana
O. en Nsa
Msab
El Hadjira
Bj. el Hobra
Ouargla
Hassi Rhénami
Hassi Messaoud
B. Lahrache
Ft. Lallemand
B. Sif Fatima
Hi. Rhourde ex Zina
Hi. ben Hamra
Hi. el Gassi
O. Mya
Ain Taiba
Hi. Tartrat
Grand Erg Oriental
Hi. Imoulaye
Hi. Larchuy
Timellouline
Plateau du Tinrhert
Ohanet
Hi. el Biod
Hi. Tanezrouft
O. ben Abbou
O. el Hadjadj
O. el Melah
Zaouiet El-Kala (Ft. Flatters)
El Bir
Gara Kranfoussa
Ta-n-elak
Irhârharene
Tabelbalet
A el Hadjadj
O. Isekfaf
Tarat
In Amenas
Tiguentourine
El Adeb Larache
Hi. Bourarhet
Oubarakat
Edjeleh
Zarzaïtine
Hi. Souguerd
Tan Esekeb
Tan Iddah
I-n-Isendjel
Illizi
Menkrour
Ahelledjem
Tanarine
Ims el Puits
Tamelelt
In-Dekkak
I-n-Kelemet
O. Irharhar
Dj. Iraouene
Amguid
Ebeggui
I-n-Azaoua
Tassili n Ajjer
Tarz Ulli
Aoussedjine
Bj. Tarat
O. Tadjerdjeri
O. Imirhou
Dunes de Tihodaine
Tedjedi
Adrar 2254
Ouranene
Dj. Ounane
Ahohene
Ahelledjem
Zaouatalaz
Toukmatine
Garet el Djenoun
2327
Ouket
Ti-n-Tirès
Tesnou
Rhans
Ti-n-ebarik
Asekseme
Tanombelia
O. Amadror
Serouenout
Erg d'Admer
Djanet
Efeni
Amiok
Tin Alkoum
Adjiri
Erg Tin Merzouga
Tamessouet
I-n-Ezzane
I-n-Afaleleh
Tiririne
Abezzou
Denine
Gif Amane
Bj.-in-Eker
Idelès
Ad. Edekel
Mt. Serkout
Tekch
Hirhafok
Ad. Tendjedj
Ahaggar
Mt. Tahat 2918
Assekrem
Afilal
Tanoumrout
Temasint
Tit
Tadjenout
B. el Garama
Tamanrasset
Katelet
Amsel
Tarahouahout
Isalene
I-n-Abalas
Anfeg
O. Tadent
O. Tafassasset
O. Zazir
O. Tadjetaret
I-n-Abeggr
O. Ti-n-Tarabine
Tedjert
Assiou
Abalemma
Ouan-n-Ahaggar
O. Tiferrer
In Atei
I-n-Azaoua
Izileg
Tadéra
Touaret
Massif de Terazit
Idikel
Admer
Yeggert
Ghat
1428
Al Barkât
Mesach Mellet
Sardalas
945
Wadi Tanezzuft
ALGERIA
I A G H O A S I S

Tarâbulus (Tripoli)
Suq al Jum'ah
Tâjûrâ
Homs (Al Khums)
Leptis Magna (Labdah)
Zaltan
Zuwârah
Al 'Ujaylat
Sabrâtah
Az Zâwiyah
Zanzur
Al Wâtiyah
Al 'Azîzîyah
Al Qasabât
Zlîtan
Misurata
Jabal Nafûsah
Tarhûnah
Tâwurghâ
Nâlût
Tiji
Yafran
Gharyân
968
Bi'r Dbu'lân
Bani Walid
Wâzin
Jâdû
Az Zintân
716
Djenefene
B. Zâr
Mizdah
Wadi Sawfajjin
Al Qaddâhîyah
AL KHUMS
Shumaykh
W. Zamzam
Qirzah
Bi'r al Malfa
Sabkhat Tâwurghâ'
Khalij Surt (Gulf of Sidra)
Al Bu'ayrât
Surt
Sîdî Miftâh
Qasr Bû Hadi
As Sultân
Sîdî Yahyâ
An Nowfalîyah
W. Thâmit
Ra's Al-Unuf
Siwan
AL JABAL AL GHARB
Al Qaryah ash Sharqîyah
W. Qirzah
W. Zâramt
W. Ruaus
Bu Nujaym
W. Bay al Kabir
Bû Athlah
Quwayrât al Milh
Al Hammadah al Surt
MISRÂTAH
Dahra
Ash Shuwayrif
Tfalfalt
Ft. Saint
Bordj Messouda
Ghudâmis
Daraj
Al Hammâdah al Hamrâ'
Bi'r al Ghaylânîyah
W. Nânâ
Waddân
Hûn
Jabal Waddân
Taghrifat
Al Jufrah
Jabal as Sawdâ'
840
Zillah
Al Harûj al Aswad
SABHAH
Hasy Tissan
Bi'r al Qâf
Bi'r al Ghazâl
Adrî
Tmîsân
Barqîn
Wanzarik
Brach
Wadi ash Shâti
Umm al 'Abîd
Samnû
Sabhah (Sebha)
1200
Hasy 'Atshân
Idehan
Al Abyad
Awbârî
Bi'r Tin Abunda
B. 'Umrân
Bi'r al Hajj 'Alî
Goddua
Umm al Arânib
Tmassah
Hatîyat al Ma'bus
Tasâwah
Marzûq
Trâghan
Tarbû
Ma'lân
Majdûl
Marqa
Al Hufrah
Bi'r al Mastûtah
W. Barjîj
AWBÂRÎ
B. Umm al 'Izâm
Wâw al Kabîr
Qurârat al Manâsîr
Ghadîr 'Odhirah
Thamad 'Ulaywah
Ideham Marzûq
Madrusah
Al Qatrûn
Tajarhi
B. Zâmûs
583
Al Quttîn
B. al Ma'rûf
Wâw an Nâmûs
Taiga Madema
Tropic of Cancer
LIBYA

Tûkrah
Al Abyâr
Banghâzî (Benghazi)
Bâninah
Suluq
Kurkûrah
Antalât
Zueitina
Ajdâbiyah
Al 'Uqaylah
Marsa Brega
Al Husayyât
Ma'tan Julût
Sabkhat al Muhayrîqah
Marâdah
Al Hufrah
Ayn Zaqqût
Thamad Dukkân Bû Ratam
J. Zaltan
Ramlat Zaltan
Zaltan
Qaltat Bû As Su'ud
Al Wâbirîyah
W. Bû al Hîlân
W. Bû Tummâyim
Ar Ramlah
BANGHÂZI

Hamada Mangueni
El Oumi
Achelouma
Enneri Achelouma
Toummo
Toummo Dhoba
Passe de Kourizo
Massif d'Afafi
Madama
Latouma
Fezzane
Plateau du Djado
Blaka
Kamada
Djado
Orida
Chirfa
Mabrous
Sobozo
Drigana
Sara
Boulélougou
Yat
Agra
Tefi
Dada
Itchoumma
Aguézi-Guém
Séguédine
Cheffadine
Yegguéba
NIGER

Ténéré
Sarîr Tibasti
J. Nugayy
Erissi
Ghelîni
Idd Chiussu
Tuzugu
Pic Bette 2286
Massif de Kemet
E. Arave
E. Yebigué
Yedri
Aozou
M. d'Abo
Tarso Ourari
Omchi
Tarso Emissi 3150
Wour
Bardai
Tiéboro
Yebbi-Souma
Pic Touside 3265
Tibesti
Tarso Tieroko 2910
Zouar
Sherda
Tarso Ahon
Bini Erde
E. Miski
E. Bincom
Emi Koussi 3415
Gouro
CHAD

5 10 15 20
35 30 25 20

COPYRIGHT, GEORGE PHILIP & SON, LTD.

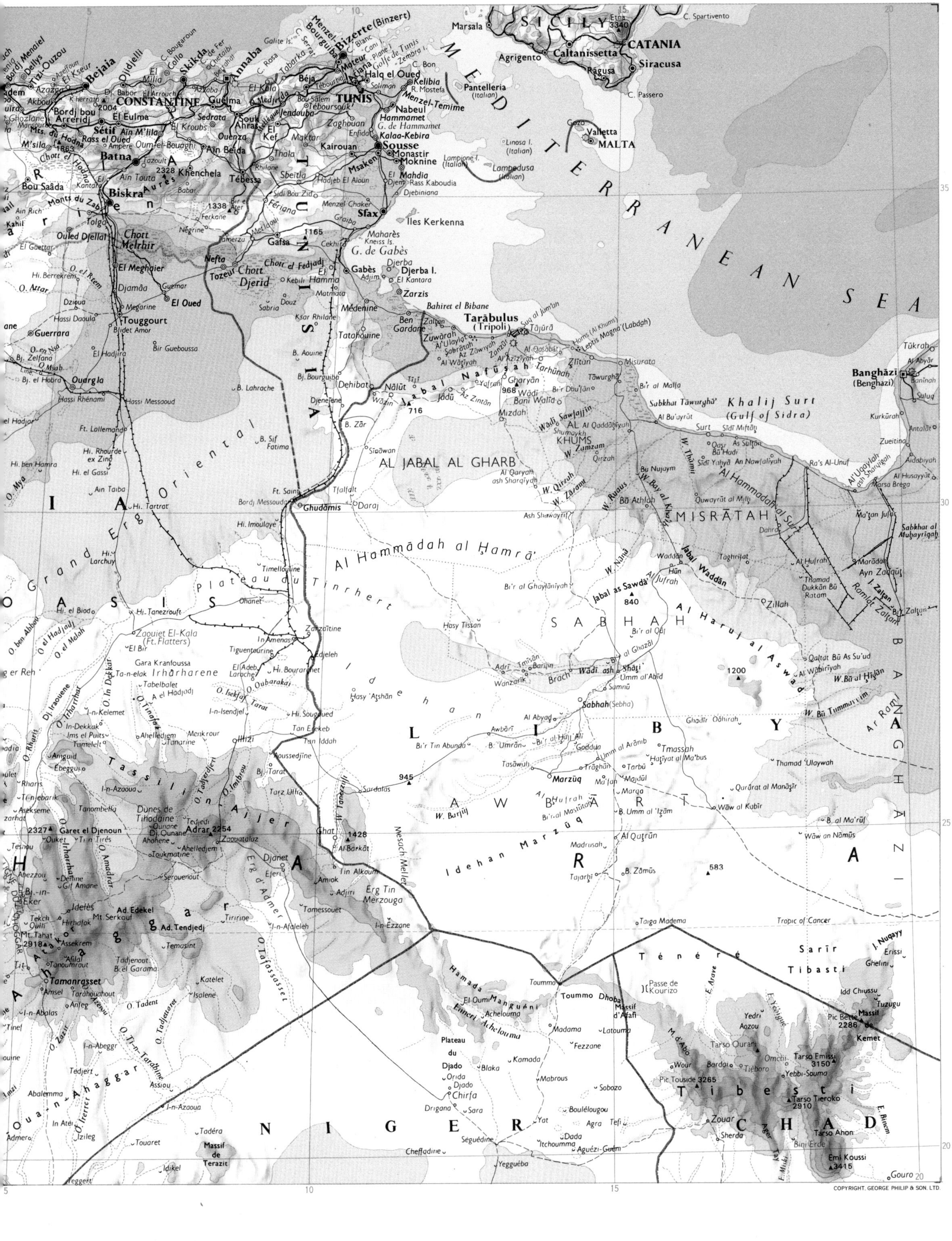

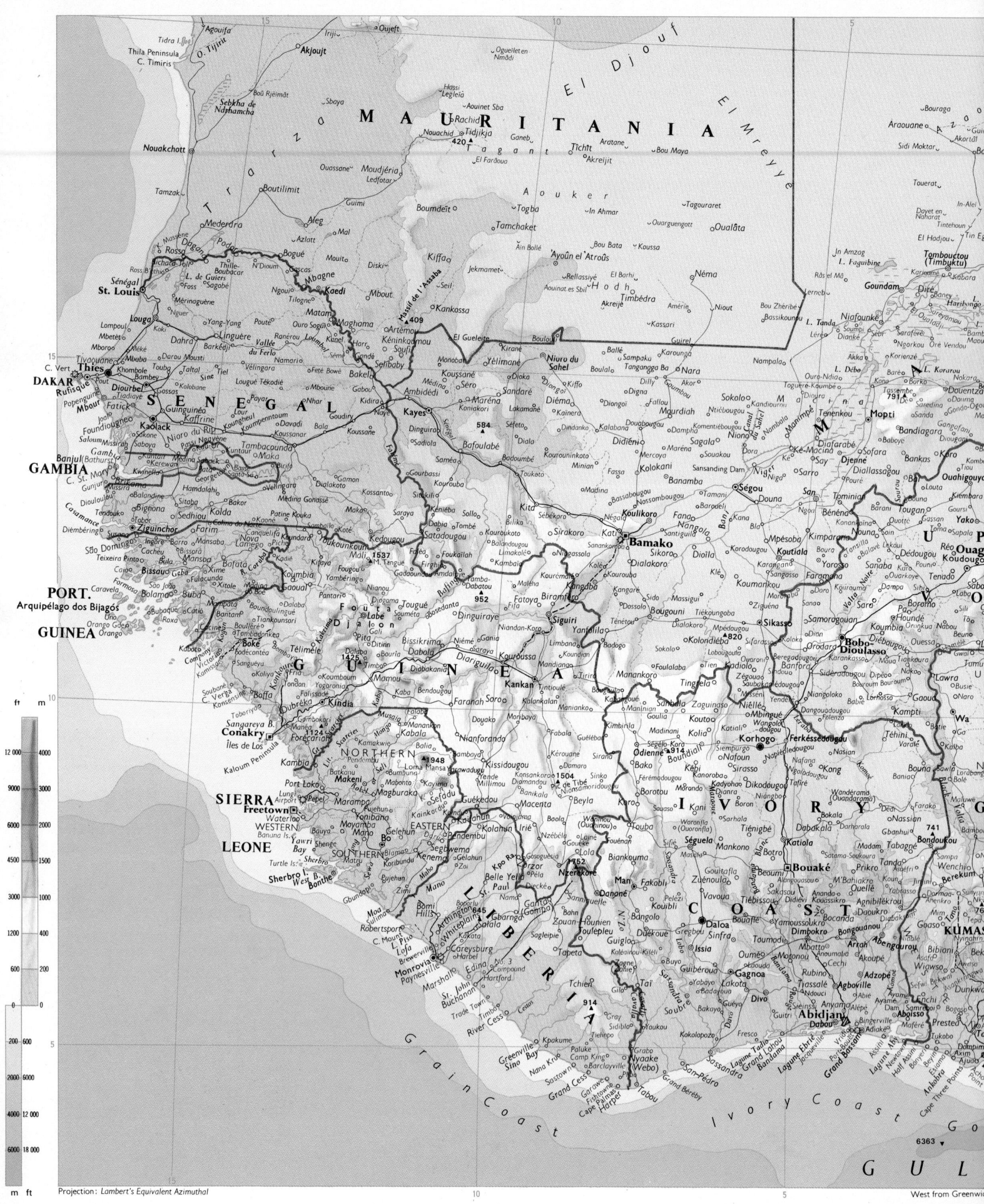

1:8 000 000
50 0 50 100 150 200 miles
50 0 50 100 150 200 250 300 km
A L G E R I A
Adrar des Iforhas
N I G E R
Aïr (Azbine)
Ténéré
Talak
Tahoua
Massif de Terazit
Monts Bagzane 1900
Agadez (Agadès)
Zinder
Maradi
Niamey
Gao
Tillabéri
Dallol Bosso
Dallol Maouri
Birni Nkonni
Tanout
Manga
Nguigmi
Diffa
N.E. NIGERIA
on same scale as general map
NIGER
CHAD
Lac Tchad
Maiduguri
Dikwa
Bama
Mubi
Garoua
CAMEROON
Sokoto
Katsina
Kano
Zaria
Kaduna
Jos
Jos Plateau
Bauchi
Gombe
Potiskum
Nguru
Gashua
NORTH WESTERN
NORTH CENTRAL
NORTH EASTERN
KANO
BENUE PLATEAU
N I G E R I A
Kainji Res.
Kontagora
Minna
Bida
Abuja
Lafia
Makurdi
ILORIN
Ogbomosho
Oshogbo
Iwo
IBADAN
Abeokuta
Ife
Ilesha
Ondo
Akure
Ado-Ekiti
Owo
Ijebu-Ode
LAGOS
Benin City
Sapele
Warri
Onitsha
Enugu
Abakaliki
Aba
Port-Harcourt
Calabar
Okrika
Niger Delta
Bight of Benin
Slave Coast
Bight of Biafra
GULF OF GUINEA
EQUATORIAL GUINEA
FERNANDO PÓO
Santa Isabel
DOUALA
Yaounde
Edea
Kribi
Buea
Victoria
Tiko
Kumba
Nkongsamba
Bamenda
Foumban
Ngaoundéré
DAHOMEY
Porto-Novo
Cotonou
Ouidah
Abomey
Parakou
Natitingou
Kandi
TOGO
Lomé
Sokodé
Anecho
GHANA
ACCRA
Tema
Kumasi
Tamale
Yendi
Bolgatanga
Bawku
Cape Coast
Winneba
Keta
UPPER VOLTA
Ouagadougou
Tenkodogo
Fada N'Gourma
Dori
Djibo
Niger
Benue
East from Greenwich

COPYRIGHT, GEORGE PHILIP & SON, LTD.

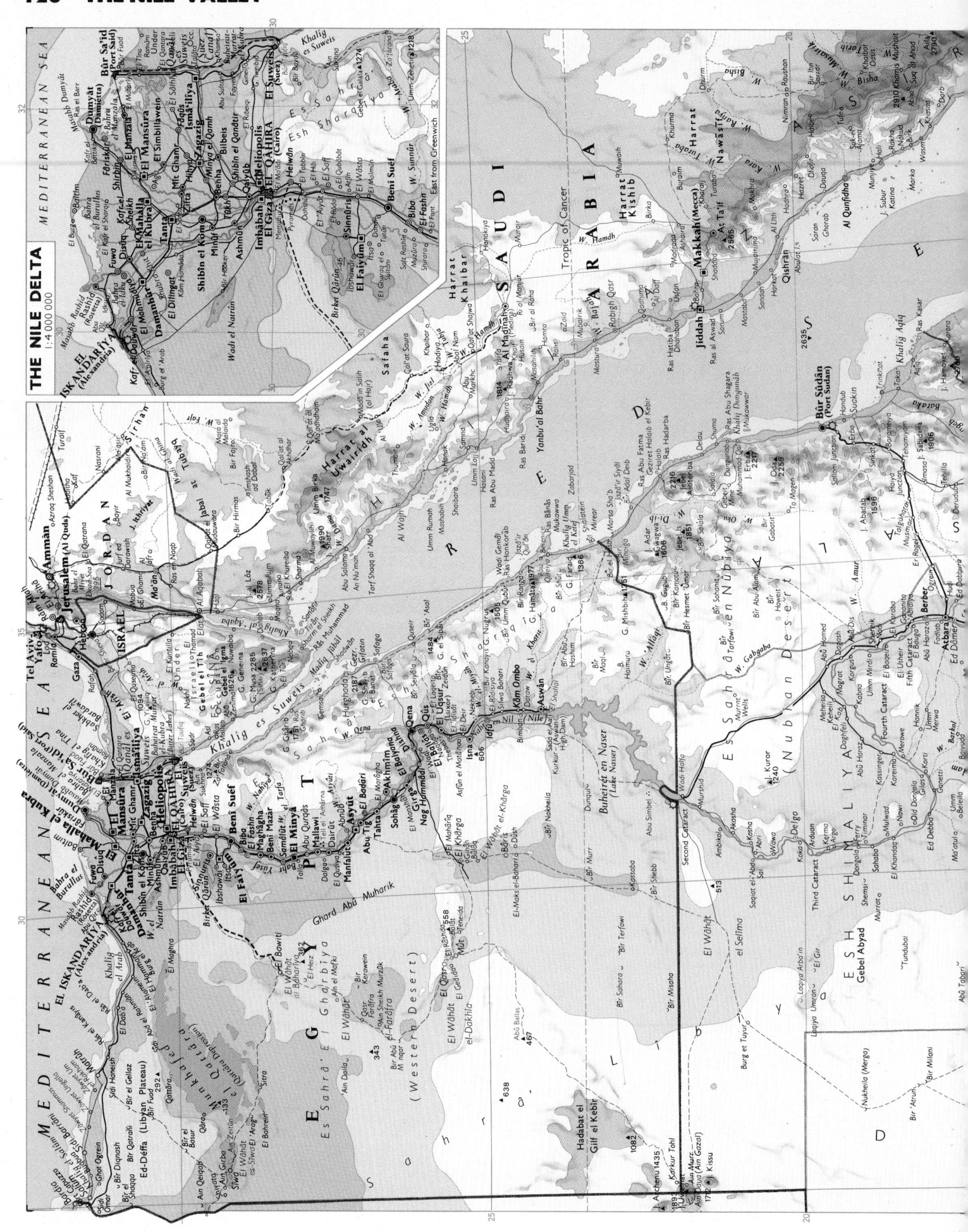
THE NILE DELTA
1:4 000 000
East from Greenwich
MEDITERRANEAN SEA
EL ISKANDARÎYA (Alexandria)
EL QÂHIRA (Cairo)
Bûr Sa'îd (Port Said)
Dumyât (Damietta)
Rashîd (Rosetta)
El Mansûra
Tanta
Zagazig
Ismâ'ilîya
Suweis (Suez)
El Giza
Heliopolis
Helwân
Benî Suêf
El Faiyûm
Birket Qârûn
El Minyâ
Asyût
Sohâg
Qena
El Uqsur (Luxor)
Aswân
Kôm Ombo
Isna
Idfu
Buheirat en Naser (Lake Nasser)
Wadi Halfa
Second Cataract
Third Cataract
Fourth Cataract
Fifth Cataract
Atbara
Berber
Bûr Sûdân (Port Sudan)
Suakin
Tel Aviv Yafo
Jerusalem (Al Quds)
Ammân
JORDAN
ISRAEL
Gaza
Ma'ân
Al Aqabah
Khalig el Aqaba
Khalig es Suweis
SAUDI ARABIA
Al Madinah (Medina)
Jiddah
Makkah (Mecca)
At Ta'if
Yanbu'al Bahr
Tropic of Cancer
EGYPT
Es Sahrâ' el Gharbîya (Western Desert)
Es Sahrâ en Nûbîya (Nubian Desert)
Munkhafed el Qattâra (Qattâra Depression)
Matrûh
Siwa
El Wâhât el-Khârga
El Wâhât el-Dakhla
El Wâhât el-Farâfra
El Wâhât el Bahariya
Hadabat el Gilf el Kebîr
ESH SHIMALIYA
Gebel Abyad

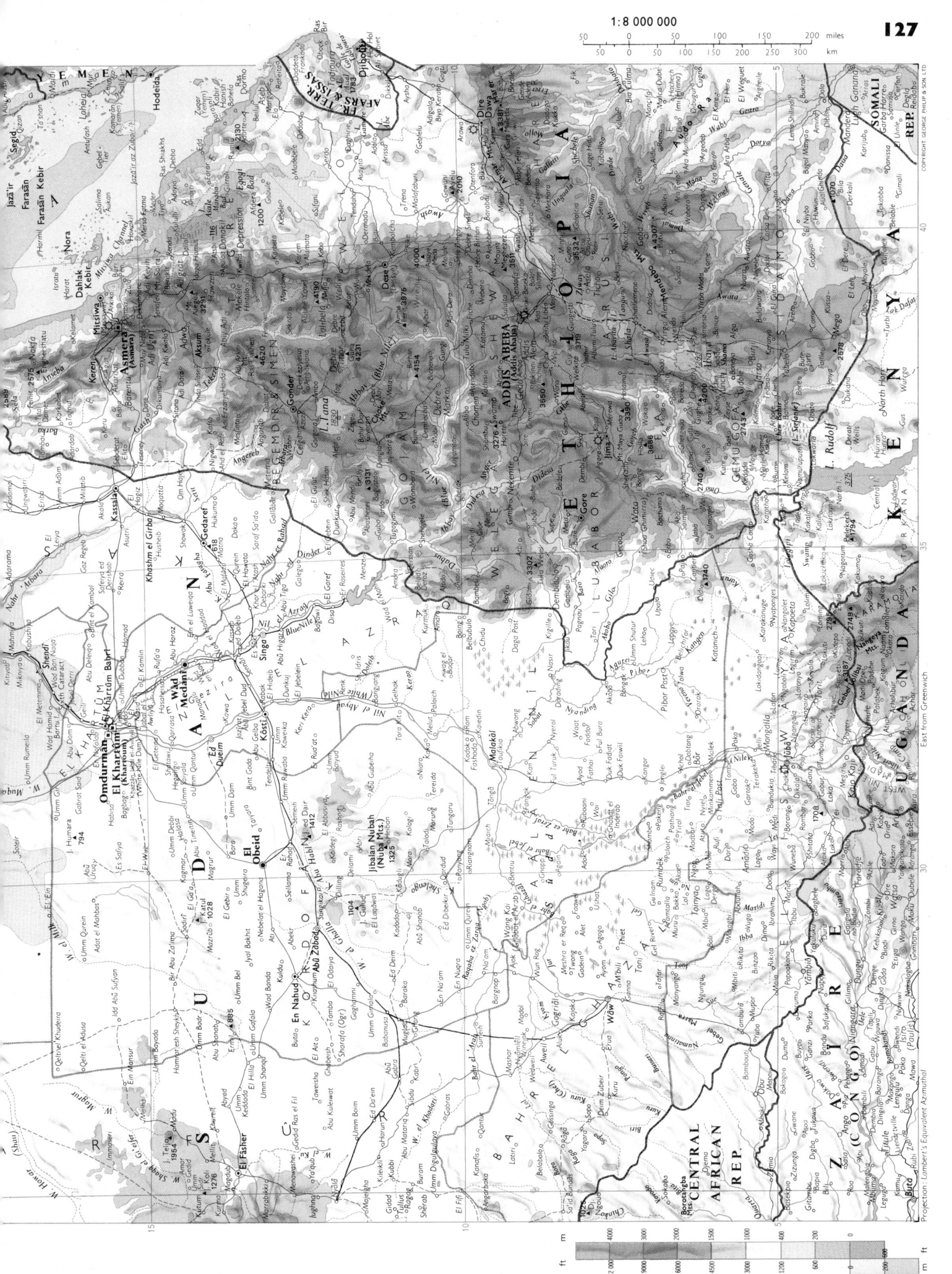
1:8 000 000
50 0 50 100 150 200 miles
50 0 50 100 150 200 250 300 km
YEMEN
FR. TERR. AFARS & ISSAS
Djibouti
ETHIOPIA
ADDIS ABEBA
(Addis Ababa)
Asmera
(Asmara)
Gonder
Dese
Dire Dawa
SOMALI REP.
KENYA
UGANDA
SUDAN
Omdurman
El Khartûm
(Khartoum)
Wad Medani
El Obeid
En Nahud
El Fâsher
Malakâl
Wâw
Jûbâ
ZAIRE (CONGO)
CENTRAL AFRICAN REP.
L. Rudolf
L. Tana
Projection: Lambert's Equivalent Azimuthal
East from Greenwich
COPYRIGHT GEORGE PHILIP & SON LTD.

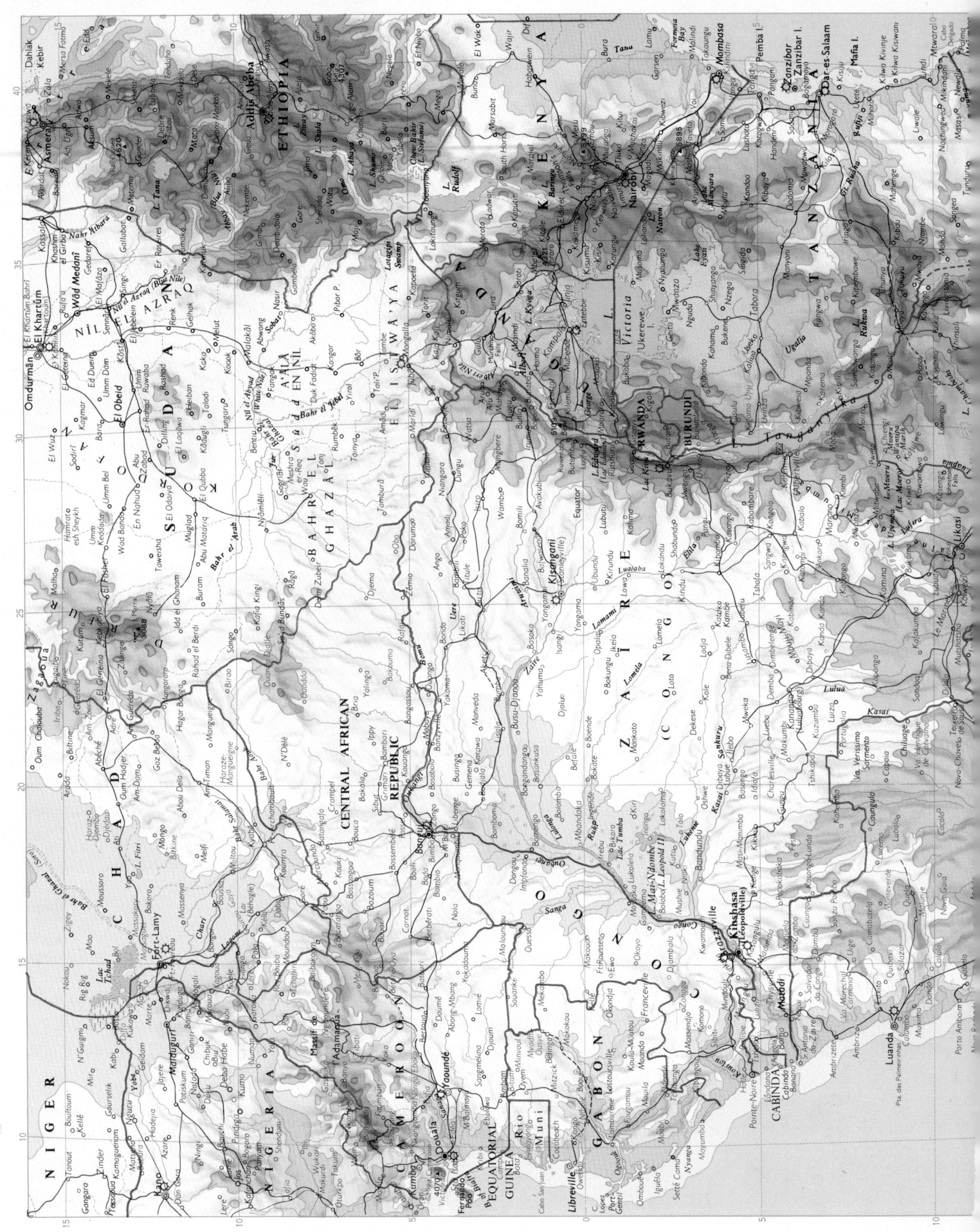
NIGER
CHAD
Lac Tchad
Fort-Lamy
NIGERIA
Kano
CAMEROON
Yaoundé
Douala
EQUATORIAL GUINEA
Rio Muni
GABON
Libreville
CONGO
Brazzaville
Kinshasa (Léopoldville)
CABINDA
Luanda
CENTRAL AFRICAN REPUBLIC
Bangui
SUDAN
Omdurmân
El Khartûm
Wad Medanî
El Obeid
ETHIOPIA
Addis Abeba
Asmera
L. Tana
L. Rudolf
UGANDA
KENYA
Nairobi
Mombasa
Victoria
RWANDA
BURUNDI
TANZANIA
Zanzibar
Dar-es-Salaam
ZAÏRE (CONGO)
Kisangani (Stanleyville)
Likasi

1:15 000 000

100   0   100   200   300   400 miles
100   0   100   200   300   400   500   600 km

MALAGASY REPUBLIC
On same scale as General Map

COPYRIGHT GEORGE PHILIP & SON LTD.

INDIAN OCEAN

ATLANTIC OCEAN

RHODESIA

BOTSWANA

SOUTH WEST AFRICA (NAMIBIA)

SOUTH AFRICA

CAPE PROVINCE

Tropic of Capricorn

Projection: Sanson Flamsteed's Sinusoidal

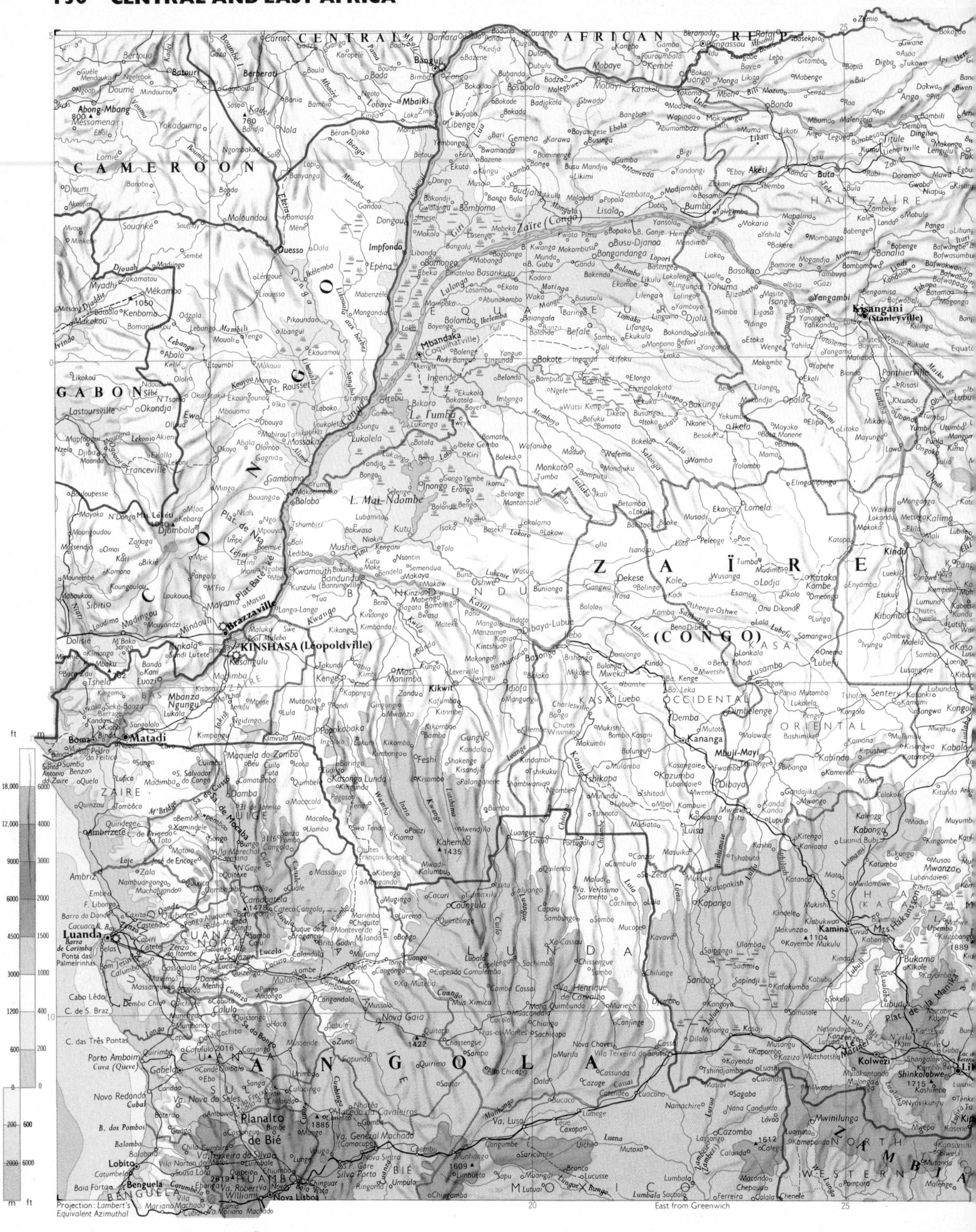
CENTRAL AFRICAN REP.
CAMEROON
GABON
CONGO
ZAÏRE (CONGO)
ANGOLA
ZAMBIA
Bangui
Brazzaville
KINSHASA (Léopoldville)
Kisangani (Stanleyville)
Mbandaka (Coquilhatville)
Luanda
Lobito
Benguela
Nova Lisboa
HUAMBO
Matadi
Boma
Kananga
Mbuji-Mayi
Kolwezi
Kindu
Kamina
Zaïre (Congo)
L. Tumba
L. Mai-Ndombe
Planalto de Bié
LUNDA
HAUT ZAÏRE
EQUATEUR
BANDUNDU
KASAI OCCIDENTAL
KASAI ORIENTAL
SHABA (KATANGA)
CUANZA NORTE
CUANZA SUL
MOXICO
BIÉ
BENGUELA
ZAIRE
UIGE
NORTH WESTERN
Projection: Lambert's Equivalent Azimuthal
East from Greenwich
ft
m
18,000
12,000
9000
6000
4500
3000
1200
600
0
200
2000
6000
4000
3000
2000
1500
1000
400
200
0
600
6000

1:8 000 000

50   0   50   100   150   200 miles

50   0   50   100   150   200   250   300 km

SUDAN

ETHIOPIA

SOMALI REP.

UGANDA

KENYA

RWANDA

BURUNDI

TANZANIA

MOZAMBIQUE

ZAMBIA

Lake Victoria

Lake Nyasa

Lake Rukwa

Lake Mweru

L. Rudolf

L. Albert

L. Kyoga

L. Edward

L. Kivu

L. Eyasi

L. Natron

Nairobi

Mombasa
Kilindini

Dar-es-Salaam

Zanzibar

Zanzibar I.

Pemba I.

Mafia I.

Kampala

Entebbe

Kigali

Bujumbura

Kigoma

Tabora

Mwanza

Dodoma

Mbeya

Lindi

Mtwara

Lubumbashi (Elisabethville)

Mufulira

Kitwe

Ngorongoro Crater

Serengeti Plain

Masai Steppe

COPYRIGHT. GEORGE PHILIP & SON. LTD.

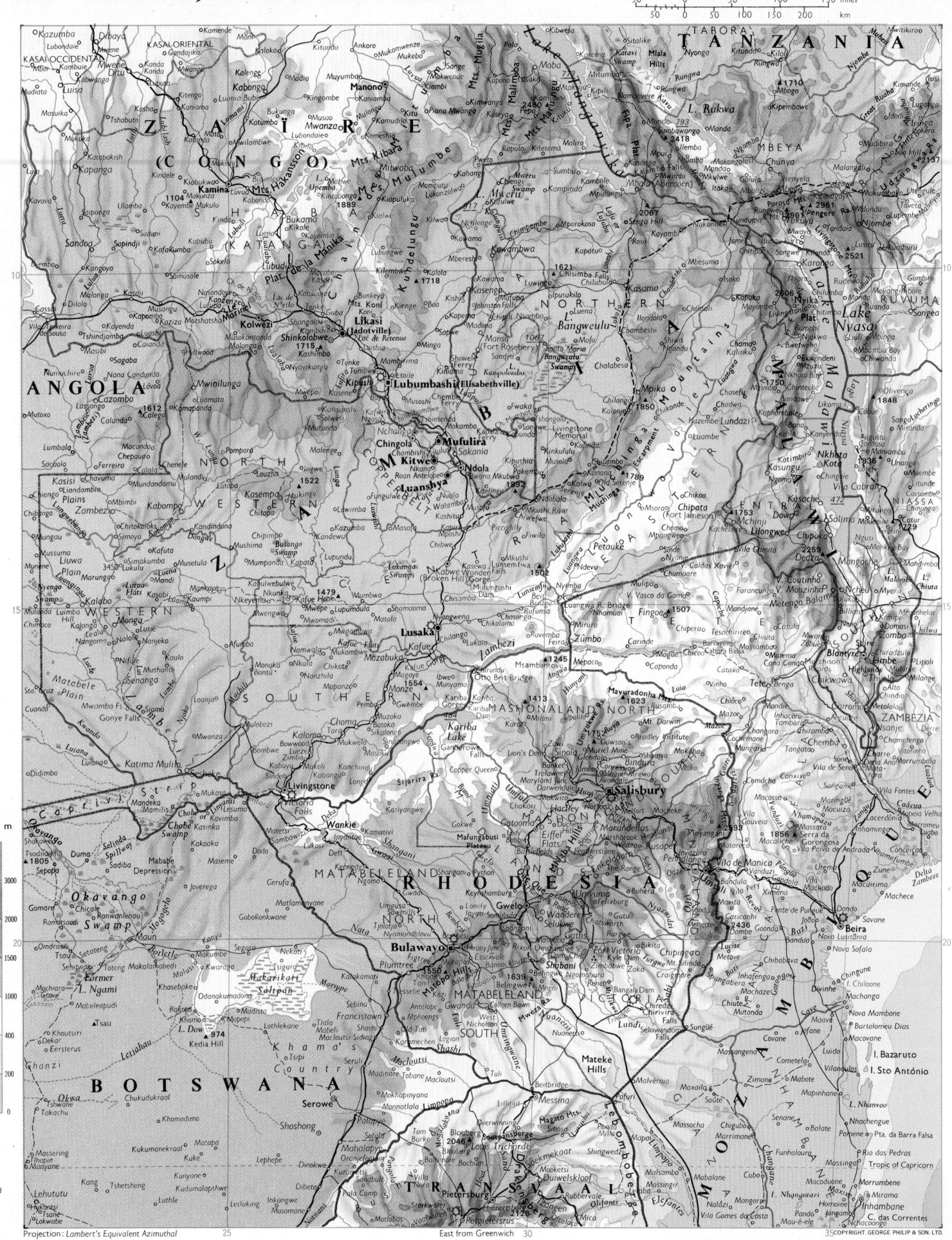

1:8 000 000

1:4 000 000

25 0 25 50 75 100 miles
25 0 25 50 75 100 125 150 km

COPYRIGHT GEORGE PHILIP & SON LTD.

M O Z A M B I Q U E

R H O D E S I A

B O T S W A N A

K a l a h a r i

T R A N S V A A L

SWAZILAND

N A T A L

O R A N J E   V R Y S T A A T   (O.F.S.)

LESOTHO

C A P E   P R O V I N C E

BETSJOEANALAND (BECHUANALAND)

INDIAN OCEAN

KRUGER NATIONAL PARK

Lourenço Marques

JOHANNESBURG

PRETORIA

Pietersburg

Louis Trichardt

Messina

Tzaneen

Nelspruit

Barberton

Carolina

Middelburg

Witbank

Lydenburg

Ermelo

Standerton

Vryheid

Utrecht

Newcastle

Ladysmith

Dundee

Paulpietersburg

Piet Retief

Mbabane

Krugersdorp

Rustenburg

Koster

Lichtenburg

Zeerust

Mafeking

Molepolole

Gaborone

Kanye

Serowe

Warmbad

Nylstroom

Potchefstroom

Klerksdorp

Carletonville

Ventersdorp

Vereeniging

Heidelberg

Nigel

Springs

Benoni

Vryburg

Kuruman

Kimberley

Warrenton

Christiana

Bloemhof

Kroonstad

Welkom

Virginia

Odendaalsrus

Bethlehem

Harrismith

Reitz

Frankfort

Heilbron

Bethal

Amersfoort

Wakkerstroom

Volksrust

Empangeni

Eshowe

Richards B.

Tropic of Capricorn

East from 28 Greenwich

Projection: Conical with two standard parallels

ft m
9000 3000
6000 2000
4500 1500
3000 1000
1200 400
600 200
0 0
m ft

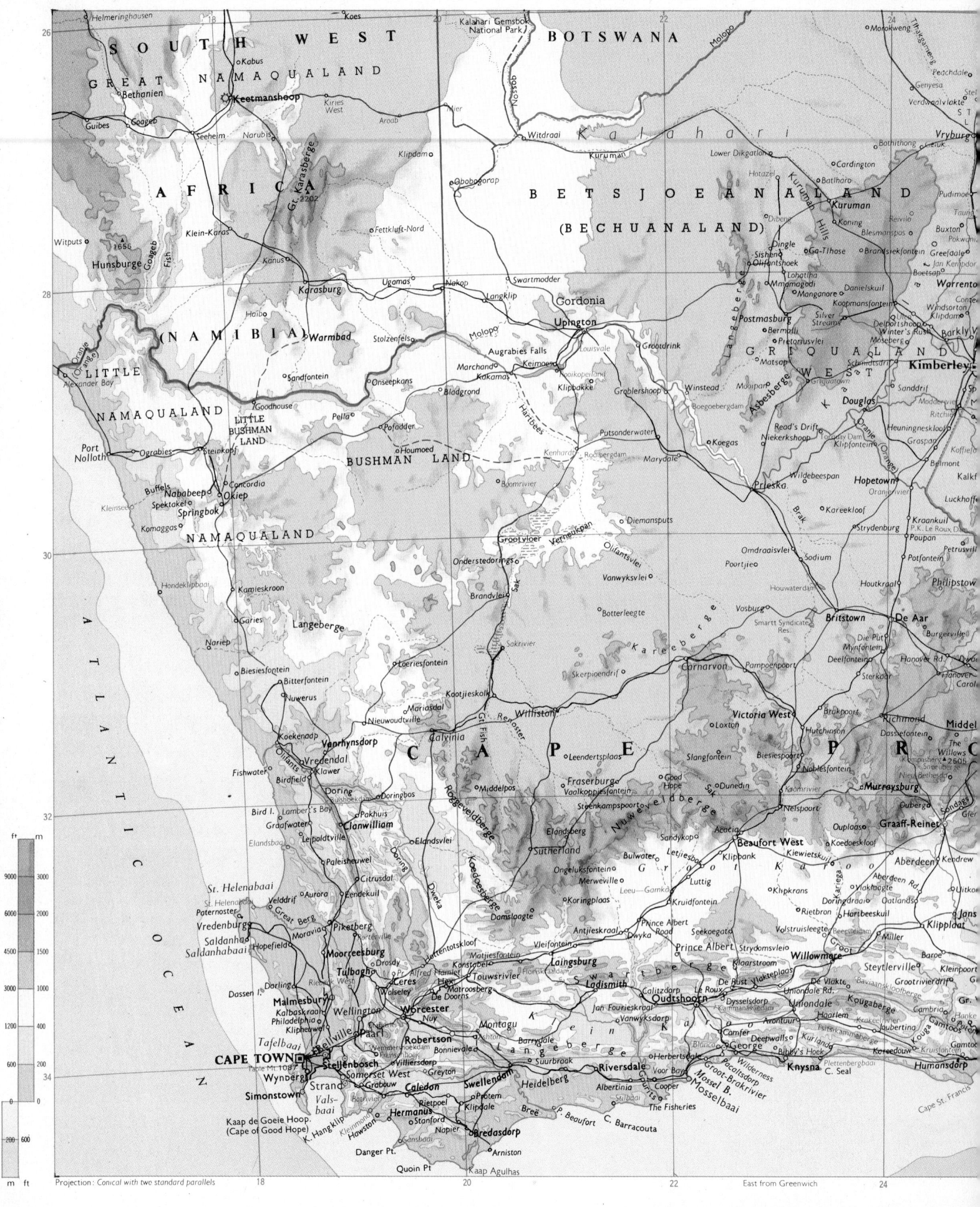
SOUTH WEST
AFRICA
(NAMIBIA)
GREAT NAMAQUALAND
BOTSWANA
BETSJOEANALAND
(BECHUANALAND)
Kalahari
Kalahari Gemsbok National Park
GRIQUALAND WEST
LITTLE NAMAQUALAND
LITTLE BUSHMAN LAND
BUSHMAN LAND
NAMAQUALAND
CAPE PROVINCE
ATLANTIC OCEAN
Helmeringhausen
Koes
Kabus
Bethanien
Keetmanshoop
Kiries West
Aroab
Mier
Nossob
Molopo
Morokweng
Genyesa
Vryburg
Guibes
Goageb
Seeheim
Narubis
Witdraai
Kuruman
Lower Dikgatlon
Bothithong
Cardington
Klipdam
Obobogorap
Gt. Karasberge 2202
Hotazel
Batlharo
Kuruman Hills
Pudimoe
Taung
Klein-Karas
Fettkluft-Nord
Dibeng
Koning
Reivilo
Blesmanspos
Buxton
Witputs
1655
Hunsburge
Fish
Dingle
Sishen
Olifantshoek
Ga-Tlhose
Brandsiekfontein
Greefdale
Kanus
Lohatlha
Mmamagodi
Manganore
Danielskuil
Warrenton
Karasburg
Ugamas
Nakop
Swartmodder
Langklip
Gordonia
Koopmansfontein
Windsorton
Haib
Postmasburg
Silver Streams
Delportshoop
Winter's Rush
Barkly W.
Warmbad
Stolzenfels
Molopo
Upington
Bermolli
Pretoriusvlei
Moseberg
Orange
Augrabies Falls
Louisvale
Grootdrink
Langeberg
Schmidtsdrif
Kimberley
Alexander Bay
Sandfontein
Onseepkans
Marchand
Kakamas
Keimoes
Kopkopeiland
Matsap
Griquatown
Sanddrif
Goodhouse
Bladgrond
Klipbakke
Groblershoop
Winstead
Boegoebergdam
Asbesberge
Douglas
Pella
Pofadder
Hartbees
Putsonderwater
Read's Drift
Niekerkshoop
Klipfontein
Heuningneskloof
Graspan
Port Nolloth
Ograbies
Steinkopf
Houmoed
Kenhardt
Roobergdam
Marydale
Koegas
Belmont
Buffels
Concordia
Nababeep
Okiep
Spektakel
Springbok
Kleinsee
Boomrivier
Prieska
Wildebeespan
Hopetown
Kalkfontein
Kareekloof
Brak
Luckhoff
Komaggas
Diemansputs
Kraankuil
P.K. Le Roux Dam
Strydenburg
Poupan
Grootvloer
Verneukpan
Olifantsvlei
Omdraaisvlei
Poortjie
Sodium
Petrusville
Potfontein
Onderstedorings
Vanwyksvlei
Houwaterdam
Houtkraal
Philipstown
Hondeklipbaai
Kamieskroon
Brandvlei
Sak
Botterleegte
Vosburg
Smartt Syndicate Res.
Britstown
De Aar
Garies
Langeberge
Kareeberge
Burgerville
Die Put
Mynfontein
Deelfontein
Hanover Rd.
Nariep
Sakrivier
Carnarvon
Pampoenpoort
Biesiesfontein
Loeriesfontein
Skerpioendrif
Sterkaar
Hanover
Bitterfontein
Nuwerus
Kootjieskolk
Williston
Renoster
Victoria West
Brakpoort
Richmond
Middelburg
Mariasdal
Nieuwoudtville
Loxton
Hutchinson
Dassiefontein
The Willows 2505
Koekenaap
Vanrhynsdorp
Calvinia
Gt. Fish
Leendertsplaas
Slangfontein
Biesiespoort
Olifants
Vredendal
Klawer
Nobelsfontein
Fishwater
Birdfield
Fraserburg
Good Hope
Dunedin
Vaalkoppiesfontein
Doring
Bulshoekdam
Doringbos
Middelpos
Murraysburg
Roggeveldberge
Steenkampspoort
Nuweveldberge
Nelspoort
Oubergo
Bird I.
Lambert's Bay
Pakhuis
Clanwilliam
Graafwater
Elandsberg
Sandykop
Acacia
Beaufort West
Oupiaas
Graaff-Reinet
Leipoldtville
Elandsvlei
Sutherland
Kiewietskuil
Koedoeskloof
Aberdeen
Kendrew
Elandsbaai
Letjiesbos
Klipbank
Groot Karoo
Paleisheuwel
Ongeluksfontein
Bulwater
Merweville
Luttig
Aberdeen Rd.
Vlaktegte
Citrusdal
Koedoesberge
Dweka
Leeu-Gamka
Klipkrans
Kariega
Doringdraai
Oatlands
St. Helenabaai
St. Helena
Aurora
Velddrif
Zendekuil
Koringplaas
Kruidfontein
Uitkomst
Paternoster
Great Berg
Damslaagte
Prince Albert Road
Rietbron
Hartbeeskuil
Jansenville
Vredenburg
Moravia
Piketberg
Porterville
Antjieskraal
Dwyka
Seekoegat
Volstruisleegte
Beervlei dam
Miller
Klipplaat
Saldanha
Saldanhabaai
Hopefield
Moorreesburg
Hottentotskloof
Matjiesfontein
Vleifontein
Prince Albert
Strydomsvlei
Groot
Baroe
Tulbagh
Drosdy
Pr. Alfred Hamlet
Konstabel
Floriskraaldam
Laingsburg
Swartberge
Klaarstroom
Willowmore
Steytlerville
Kleinpoort
Dassen I.
Darling
Riebeek West
Ceres
Hex
Touwsrivier
Matroosberg
Ladismith
Calitzdorp
Le Roux
De Rust
Vlakteplaas
De Vlakte
Baviaanskloofberge
Grootrivierdrif
Malmesbury
Wolseley
De Doorns
Oudtshoorn
Dysselsdorp
Uniondale Rd.
Kalbaskraal
Philadelphia
Klipheuwel
Wellington
Worcester
Nuy
Montagu
Jan Fourieskraal
Vanwyksdorp
Kammanassiedam
Klein Karoo
Uniondale
Kougaberge
Avontuur
Haarlem
Cambria
Tafelbaai
Bellville
Paarl
Robertson
Ashton
Barrydale
Langeberge
Camfer
Deepwalls
Kurland
Tsitsikammaberge
Joubertina
Gamtoos
Kouga
Wemmershoekdam
Bonnievale
Herbertsdale
George
Bibby's Hoek
Koreedouw
Kruisfontein
CAPE TOWN
Table Mt. 1087
Stellenbosch
Villiersdorp
Greyton
Suurbraak
Riversdale
Voor Baai
Wilderness
Knysna
Plettenbergbaai
C. Seal
Humansdorp
Wynberg
Somerset West
Strand
Grabouw
Caledon
Swellendam
Heidelberg
Albertinia
Gourits
Cooper
Groot-Brakrivier
Pacaltsdorp
Mossel B.
Mosselbaai
Cape St. Francis
Simonstown
Valsbaai
Botrivier
Rietpoel
Protem
Klipdale
Stilbaai
The Fisheries
Kaap de Goeie Hoop
(Cape of Good Hope)
K. Hangklip
Kleinmond
Hawston
Hermanus
Stanford
Napier
Breë
P. Beaufort
C. Barracouta
Bredasdorp
Gansbaai
Danger Pt.
Arniston
Quoin Pt
Kaap Agulhas
ft m
9000 3000
6000 2000
4500 1500
3000 1000
1200 400
600 200
0 0
200 600
m ft
18
20
22
24
26
28
30
32
34
Projection: Conical with two standard parallels
East from Greenwich

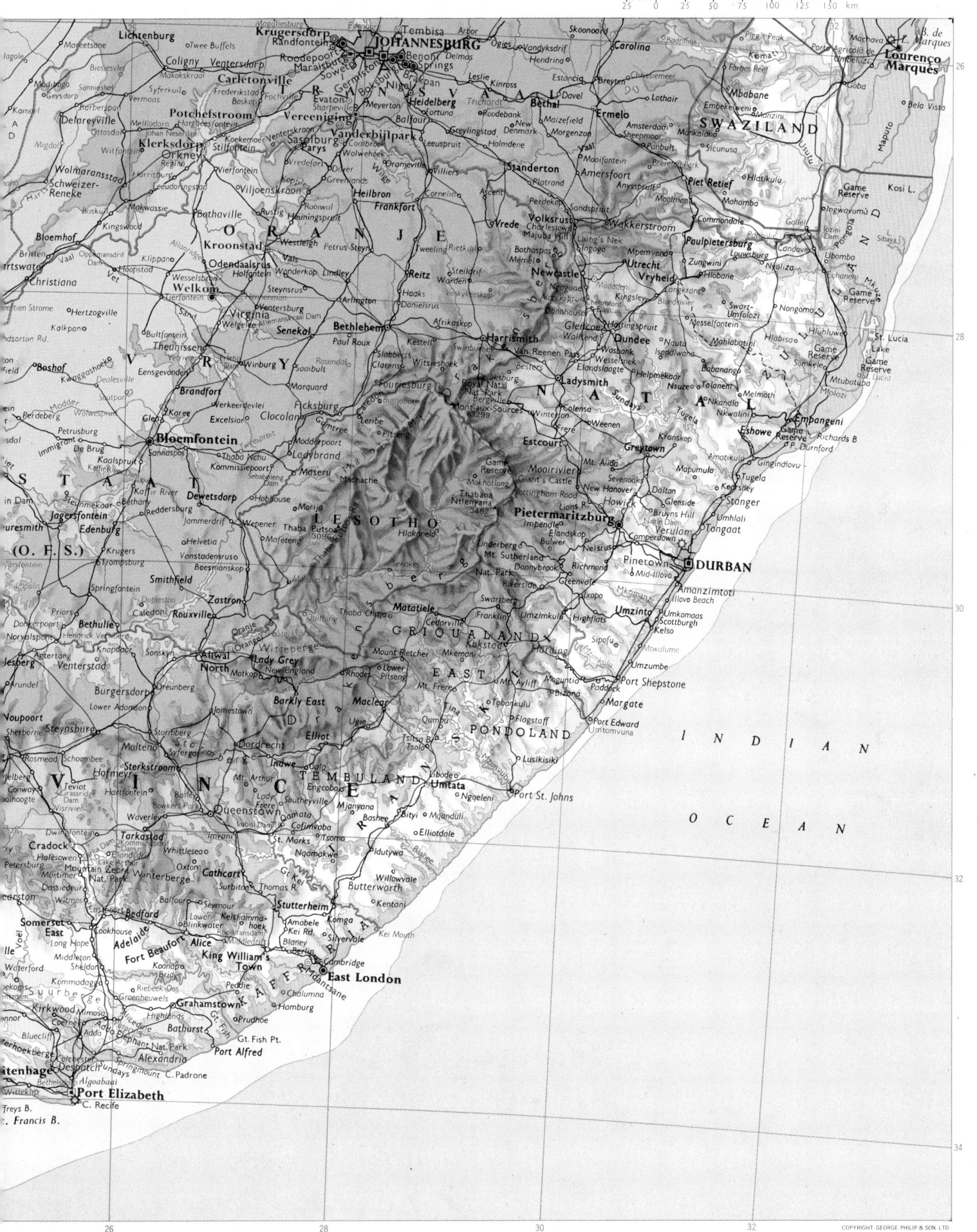

1 : 4 000 000

25   0   25   50   75   100 miles
25   0   25   50   75   100   125   150 km

COPYRIGHT GEORGE PHILIP & SON LTD

-------- 5615 Principal Shipping Routes
(Distances in Nautical Miles)

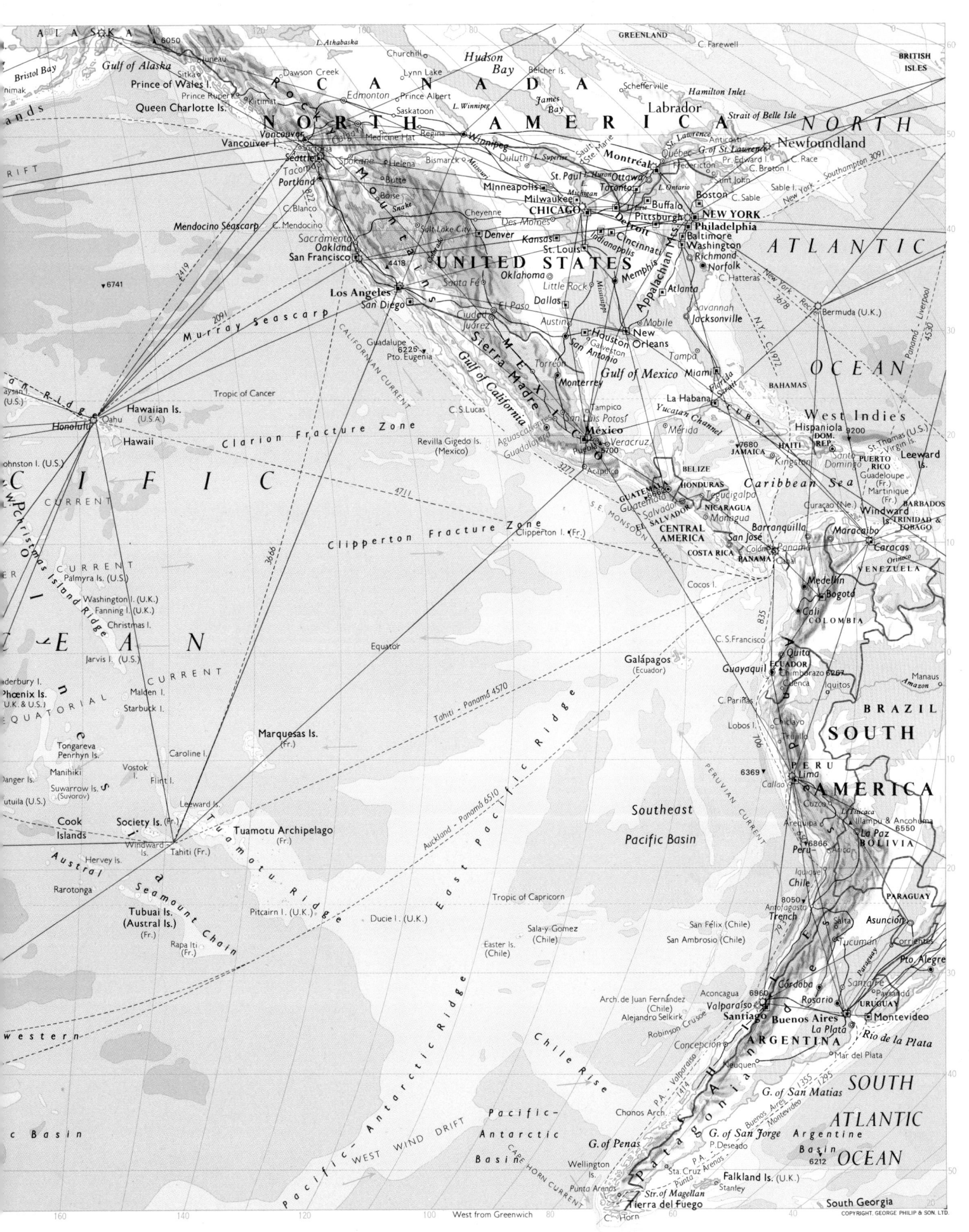
NORTH AMERICA
CANADA
UNITED STATES
ATLANTIC OCEAN
SOUTH AMERICA
SOUTH ATLANTIC OCEAN
Hudson Bay
Gulf of Alaska
Gulf of Mexico
Caribbean Sea
West Indies
Newfoundland
Labrador
NEW YORK
CHICAGO
Philadelphia
Washington
Los Angeles
San Francisco
Hawaiian Is.
Honolulu
Clarion Fracture Zone
Clipperton Fracture Zone
Murray Seascarp
Mendocino Seascarp
Tropic of Cancer
Equator
Tropic of Capricorn
Southeast Pacific Basin
East Pacific Ridge
Pacific-Antarctic Ridge
Pacific-Antarctic Basin
Chile Rise
Argentine Basin
Tuamotu Archipelago
Marquesas Is.
Galápagos (Ecuador)
Easter Is. (Chile)
Falkland Is. (U.K.)
South Georgia
Tierra del Fuego
C. Horn
BRAZIL
ARGENTINA
PERU
BOLIVIA
COLOMBIA
VENEZUELA
CHILE
PARAGUAY
URUGUAY
Buenos Aires
Santiago
Lima
Bogotá
Caracas
México
West from Greenwich
COPYRIGHT, GEORGE PHILIP & SON, LTD.

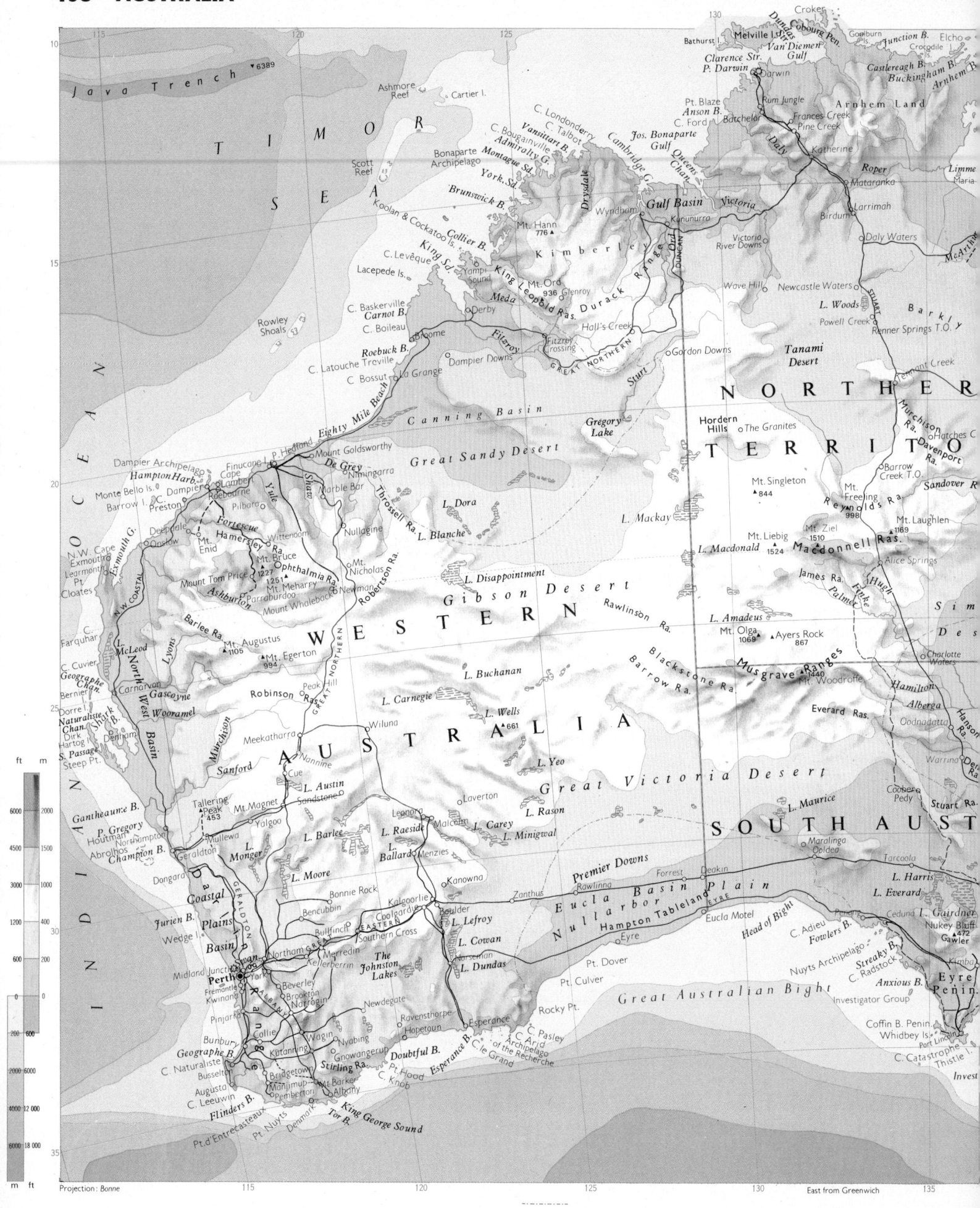
Java Trench
6389
TIMOR SEA
INDIAN OCEAN
Ashmore Reef
Cartier I.
Scott Reef
Bonaparte Archipelago
Rowley Shoals
Lacepede Is.
Melville I.
Bathurst I.
Croker I.
Cobourg Pen.
Dundas Str.
Van Diemen Gulf
Clarence Str.
P. Darwin
Darwin
Goulburn Is.
Junction B.
Elcho I.
Crocodile Is.
Castlereagh B.
Buckingham B.
Arnhem B.
Arnhem Land
Rum Jungle
Batchelor
Pt. Blaze
Anson B.
C. Ford
Frances Creek
Pine Creek
Daly
Katherine
Roper
Mataranka
Larrimah
Birdum
Limmen
Maria
C. Londonderry
C. Talbot
C. Bougainville
Vansittart B.
Admiralty G.
Montague Sd.
York Sd.
Brunswick B.
Jos. Bonaparte Gulf
Cambridge G.
Queens Chan.
Drysdale
Wyndham
Gulf Basin
Victoria
Kununurra
Ord
DUNCAN
Victoria River Downs
Daly Waters
McArthur
Koolan & Cockatoo Is.
Collier B.
King Sd.
C. Levêque
Yampi Sound
Mt. Hann
776
Kimberley
King Leopold Ras.
Mt. Ord
936
Glenroy
Durack Range
Wave Hill
Newcastle Waters
STUART
L. Woods
Powell Creek
Renner Springs T.O.
Barkly
C. Baskerville
Carnot B.
C. Boileau
Meda
Derby
Fitzroy
Fitzroy Crossing
Hall's Creek
GREAT NORTHERN
Gordon Downs
Tanami Desert
Tennant Creek
Broome
Roebuck B.
C. Latouche Treville
C. Bossut
La Grange
Dampier Downs
Sturt
Eighty Mile Beach
Canning Basin
Gregory Lake
NORTHERN TERRITORY
Hordern Hills
The Granites
Murchison Ra.
Hatches Creek
Davenport Ra.
Dampier Archipelago
Hampton Harb.
Finucane I.
P. Hedland
Mount Goldsworthy
De Grey
Nimingarra
Great Sandy Desert
Monte Bello Is.
Barrow I.
C. Preston
Cape Lambert
Dampier
Roebourne
Pilbara
Yule
Shaw
Marble Bar
Throssell Ra.
L. Dora
Barrow Creek T.O.
Sandover R.
Mt. Singleton
844
Mt. Freeling
Reynolds Ra.
998
Fortescue
Deepdale
Onslow
Mt. Enid
Hamersley Ra.
Wittenoom
Nullagine
L. Blanche
L. Mackay
Mt. Laughlen
1169
Mt. Ziel
1510
Mt. Liebig
1524
L. Macdonald
Macdonnell Ras.
Alice Springs
N.W. Cape
Exmouth
Exmouth G.
Learmonth
Pt Cloates
N.W. COASTAL
Mt. Bruce
1227
1251
Ophthalmia Ra.
Mt. Meharry
Mt. Nicholas
Robertson Ra.
Mount Tom Price
Parraburdoo
Ashburton
Mount Whaleback
Newman
L. Disappointment
Gibson Desert
Rawlinson Ra.
James Ra.
Palmer
Finke
Hugh
Simpson Desert
WESTERN AUSTRALIA
Barlee Ra.
Mt. Augustus
1105
Mt. Egerton
994
Lyons
C. Farquhar
L. McLeod
North West Basin
L. Amadeus
Mt. Olga
1069
Ayers Rock
867
Blackstone Ra.
Barrow Ra.
Musgrave Ranges
1440
Mt. Woodroffe
Charlotte Waters
C. Cuvier
Geographe Chan.
Bernier I.
Carnarvon
Gascoyne
Robinson Ras.
Peak Hill
L. Buchanan
L. Carnegie
L. Wells
661
Hamilton
Alberga
Oodnadatta
Everard Ras.
Hanson Ra.
Dorre I.
Naturaliste Chan.
Dirk Hartog I.
Shark B.
Denham
Wooramel
S. Passage
Steep Pt.
Murchison
Meekatharra
Wiluna
Sanford
Nannine
Cue
L. Yeo
Great Victoria Desert
Warrina
L. Austin
Sandstone
Laverton
L. Rason
L. Maurice
Coober Pedy
Stuart Ra.
Gantheaume B.
Tallering Peak
453
Mt. Magnet
Yalgoo
Leonora
Malcolm
L. Carey
L. Minigwal
P. Gregory
Houtman Abrolhos
Northampton
Mullewa
Champion B.
Geraldton
L. Monger
L. Barlee
L. Raeside
L. Ballard
Menzies
SOUTH AUSTRALIA
Maralinga
Ooldea
Tarcoola
Dongara
L. Moore
GERALDTON
Dandaragan
Coastal Plains
Basin
Kanowna
Bonnie Rock
Kalgoorlie
Premier Downs
Rawlinna
Forrest
Deakin
Eucla Basin
Nullarbor Plain
L. Harris
L. Everard
Jurien B.
Wedge I.
Bencubbin
Coolgardie
Boulder
Zanthus
Hampton Tableland
EYRE
Eucla Motel
Head of Bight
Penong
Cedund
L. Gairdner
Nukey Bluff
472
Gawler
Bullfinch
EASTERN
Southern Cross
L. Lefroy
L. Cowan
Norseman
L. Dundas
Eyre
C. Adieu
Fowlers B.
Streaky B.
C. Radstock
Nuyts Archipelago
Kimba
Anxious B.
Eyre Penin.
Midland Junction
Swan
Perth
Fremantle
Kwinana
Northam
Merredin
Kellerberrin
The Johnston Lakes
York
Beverley
Brookton
Narrogin
ALBANY
Pt. Dover
Pt. Culver
Great Australian Bight
Investigator Group
Newdegate
Ravensthorpe
Hopetoun
Esperance
Rocky Pt.
Pinjarra
Collie
Wagin
Nyabing
Katanning
Gnowangerup
Bunbury
Geographe B.
C. Naturaliste
Busselton
Darling Range
Stirling Ra.
Doubtful B.
Esperance B.
C. Arid
C. Pasley
Archipelago of the Recherche
C. le Grand
Pt. Hood
C. Knob
Coffin B. Penin.
Whidbey Is.
Port Lincoln
C. Catastrophe
Thistle I.
Investigator Strait
Bridgetown
Manjimup
Mt. Barker
Pemberton
Albany
Augusta
C. Leeuwin
Flinders B.
Pt. d'Entrecasteaux
Pt. Nuyts
Denmark
Tor B.
King George Sound
ft
m
6000
2000
4500
1500
3000
1000
1200
400
600
200
0
0
200
600
2000
6000
4000
12 000
6000
18 000
m
ft
10
15
20
25
30
35
115
120
125
130
135
Projection: Bonne
East from Greenwich

AUSTRALASIA POLITICAL
1:80 000 000

1:12 000 000

COPYRIGHT. GEORGE PHILIP & SON. LTD

QUEENSLAND

NEW SOUTH WALES

VICTORIA

TASMANIA

Gulf of Carpentaria

CORAL SEA ISLANDS TERRITORY

PACIFIC OCEAN

Tasman Sea

1:60 000 000

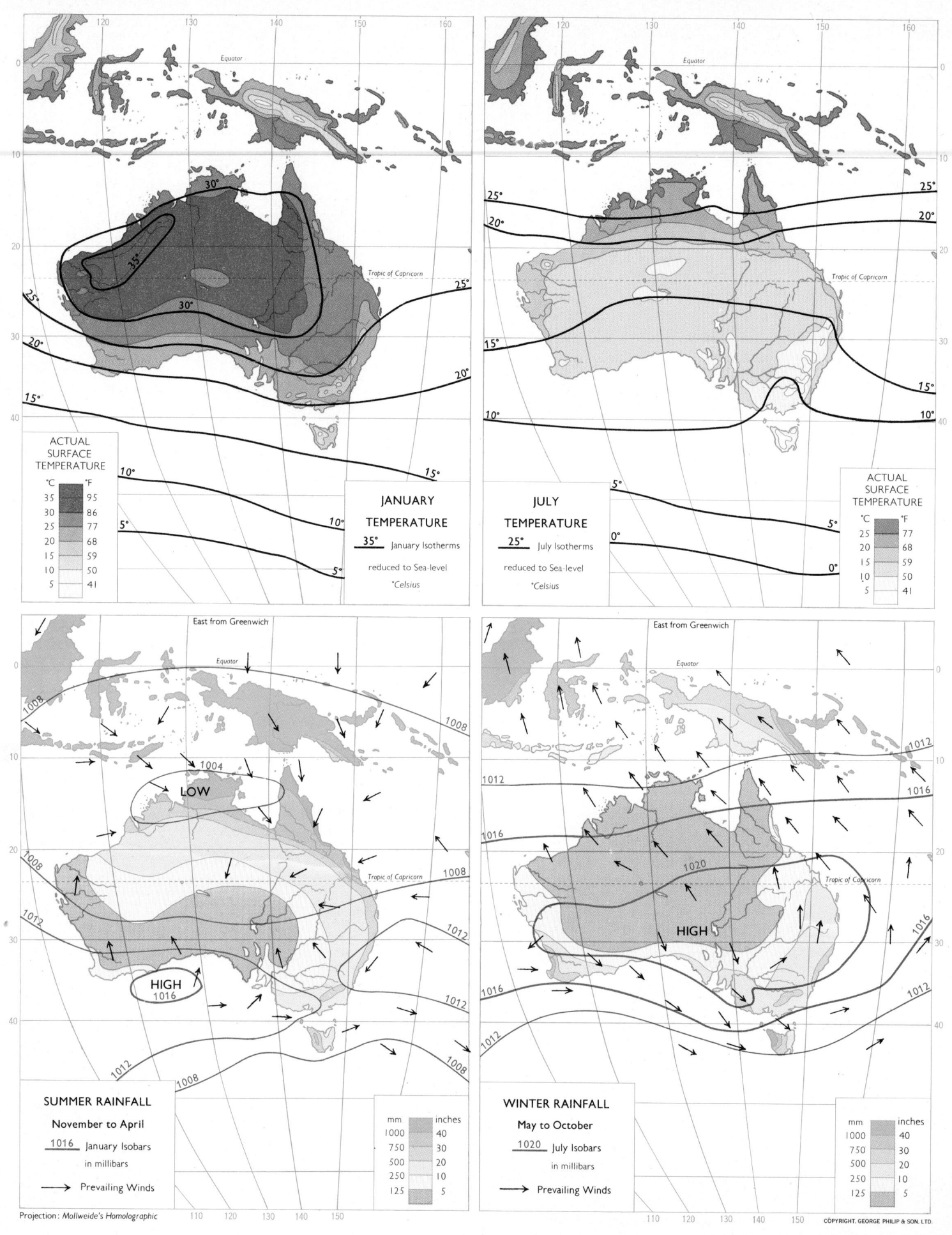

ACTUAL
SURFACE
TEMPERATURE

°C		°F
35		95
30		86
25		77
20		68
15		59
10		50
5		41

JANUARY

TEMPERATURE

35° January Isotherms

reduced to Sea-level

°Celsius

JULY

TEMPERATURE

25° July Isotherms

reduced to Sea-level

°Celsius

ACTUAL
SURFACE
TEMPERATURE

°C		°F
25		77
20		68
15		59
10		50
5		41

East from Greenwich

East from Greenwich

SUMMER RAINFALL

November to April

1016 January Isobars

in millibars

→ Prevailing Winds

WINTER RAINFALL

May to October

1020 July Isobars

in millibars

→ Prevailing Winds

mm		inches
1000		40
750		30
500		20
250		10
125		5

mm		inches
1000		40
750		30
500		20
250		10
125		5

Projection: Mollweide's Homolographic

COPYRIGHT. GEORGE PHILIP & SON. LTD.

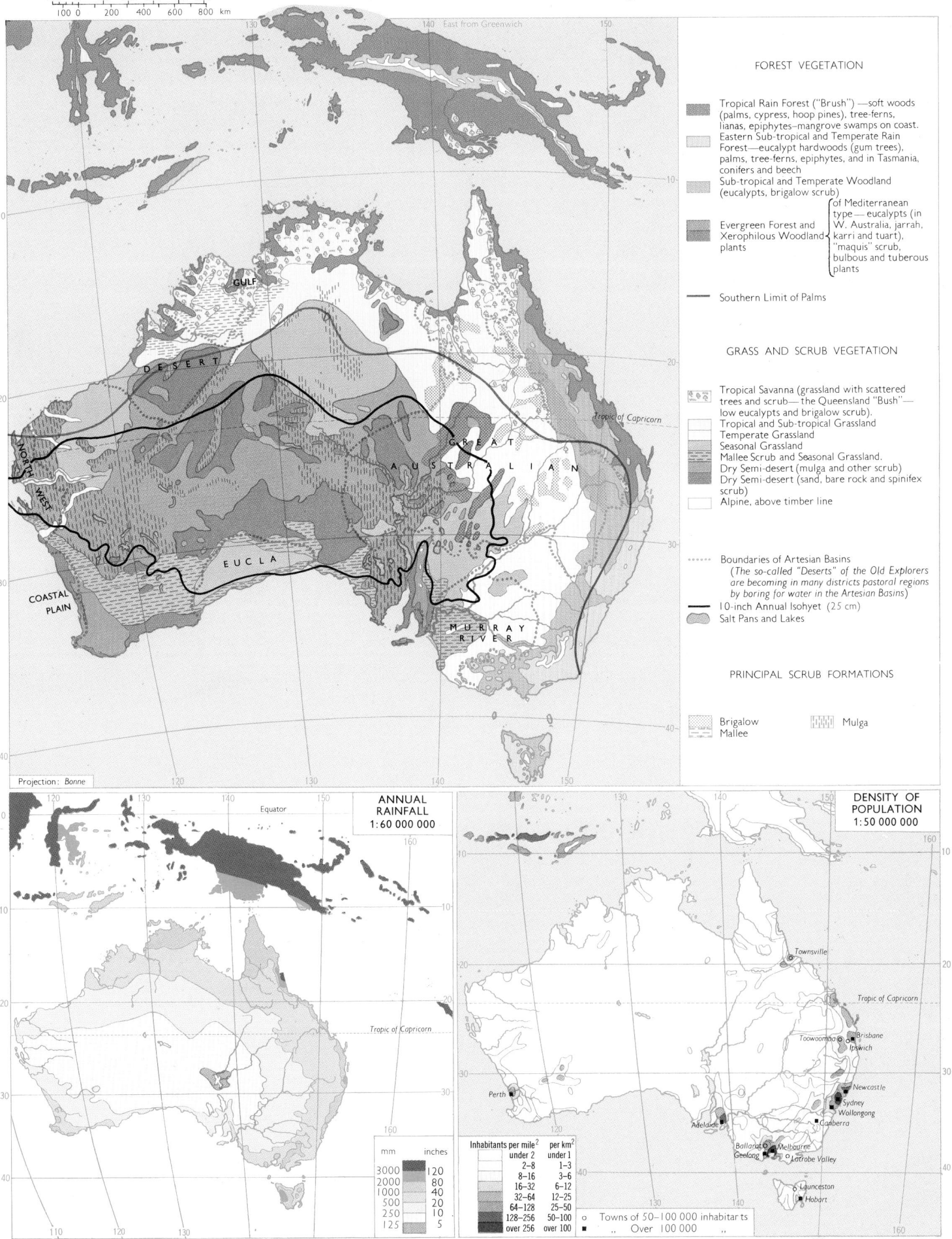

1 : 30 000 000

100   0   100 200 300 400   500   miles
100   0   200   400   600   800   km

FOREST VEGETATION

Tropical Rain Forest ("Brush") —soft woods (palms, cypress, hoop pines), tree-ferns, lianas, epiphytes—mangrove swamps on coast.

Eastern Sub-tropical and Temperate Rain Forest—eucalypt hardwoods (gum trees), palms, tree-ferns, epiphytes, and in Tasmania, conifers and beech

Sub-tropical and Temperate Woodland (eucalypts, brigalow scrub)

Evergreen Forest and Xerophilous Woodland plants
⎧ of Mediterranean
  type — eucalypts (in
  W. Australia, jarrah,
⎨ karri and tuart),
  "maquis" scrub,
  bulbous and tuberous
⎩ plants

——— Southern Limit of Palms

GRASS AND SCRUB VEGETATION

Tropical Savanna (grassland with scattered trees and scrub— the Queensland "Bush"— low eucalypts and brigalow scrub).
Tropical and Sub-tropical Grassland
Temperate Grassland
Seasonal Grassland
Mallee Scrub and Seasonal Grassland.
Dry Semi-desert (mulga and other scrub)
Dry Semi-desert (sand, bare rock and spinifex scrub)
Alpine, above timber line

.... Boundaries of Artesian Basins
(The so-called "Deserts" of the Old Explorers are becoming in many districts pastoral regions by boring for water in the Artesian Basins)
——— 10-inch Annual Isohyet (25 cm)
Salt Pans and Lakes

PRINCIPAL SCRUB FORMATIONS

Brigalow
Mallee   Mulga

Projection: Bonne

ANNUAL RAINFALL
1 : 60 000 000

mm	inches
3000	120
2000	80
1000	40
500	20
250	10
125	5

DENSITY OF POPULATION
1 : 50 000 000

Inhabitants per mile²	per km²
under 2	under 1
2–8	1–3
8–16	3–6
16–32	6–12
32–64	12–25
64–128	25–50
128–256	50–100
over 256	over 100

o Towns of 50–100 000 inhabitants
■ „   „ Over 100 000 „

Townsville
Toowoomba Brisbane
Ipswich
Perth
Newcastle
Sydney
Wollongong
Adelaide Canberra
Ballarat Melbourne
Geelong Latrobe Valley
Launceston
Hobart

Projection of Insets : Mollweide's Homolographic

150   COPYRIGHT. GEORGE PHILIP & SON LTD.

1 : 7 500 000

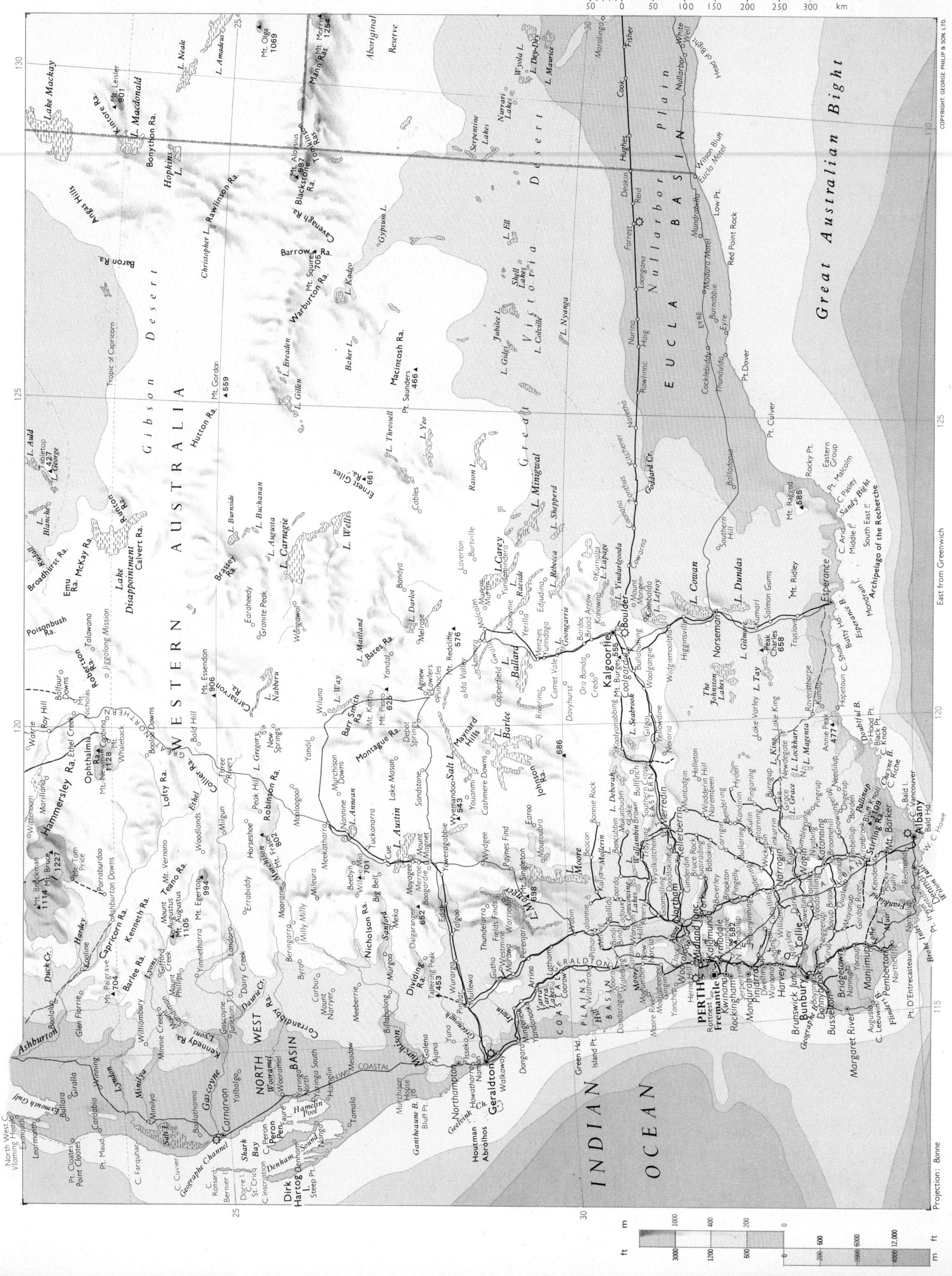

50 0 50 100 150 200 miles
50 0 50 100 150 200 250 300 km

WESTERN AUSTRALIA

GIBSON DESERT

GREAT VICTORIA DESERT

NULLARBOR PLAIN

EUCLA BASIN

GREAT AUSTRALIAN BIGHT

INDIAN OCEAN

NORTH WEST BASIN

COASTAL PLAINS BASIN

PERTH
Fremantle
Albany
Kalgoorlie
Boulder
Geraldton
Bunbury
Esperance
Norseman

East from Greenwich

Projection: Bonne

COPYRIGHT GEORGE PHILIP & SON, LTD.

m 3000 1200 600 200 0 ft
ft 12,000 6000 4000 2000 600 200 0 m

1:4 500 000

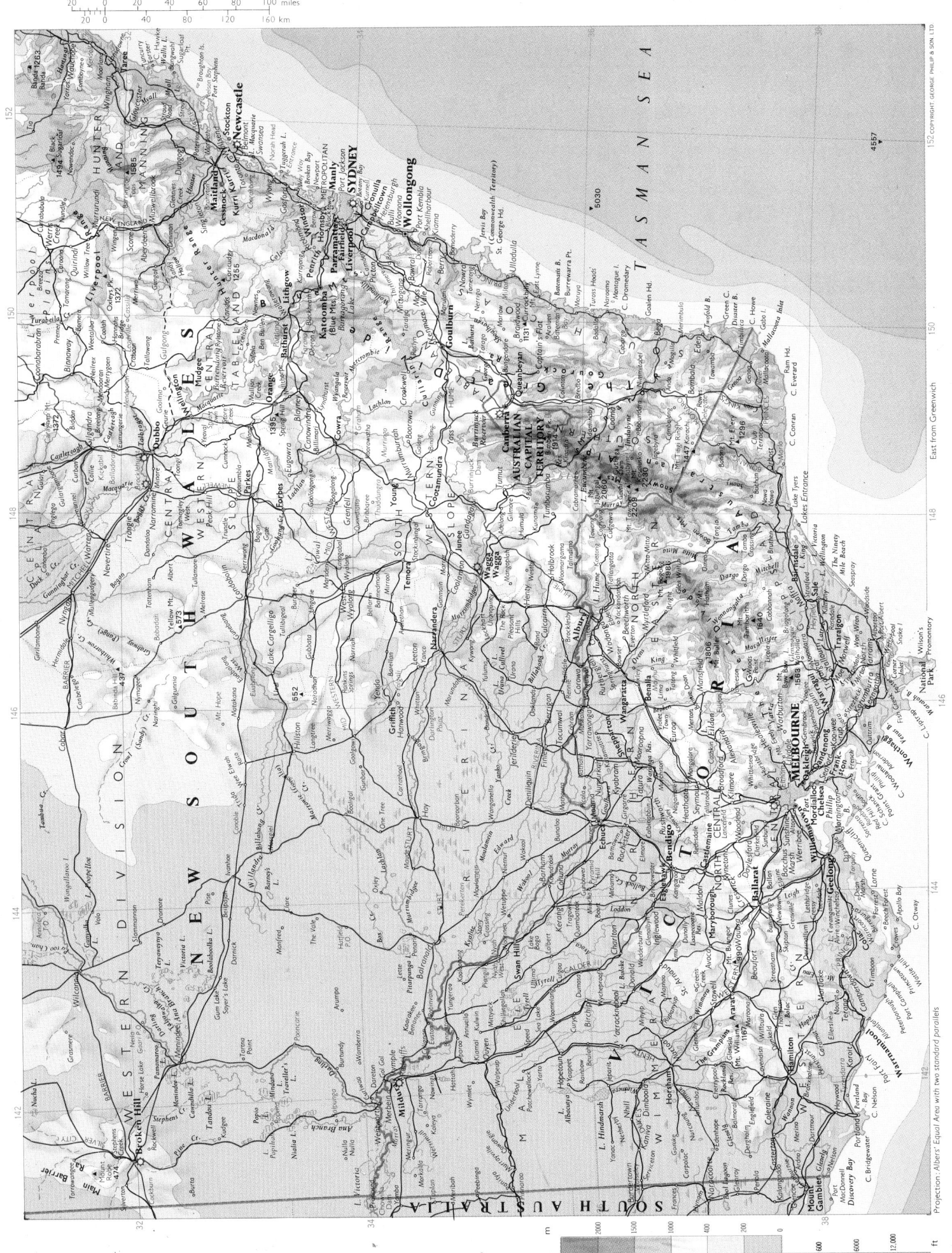

Projection: Albers' Equal Area with two standard parallels

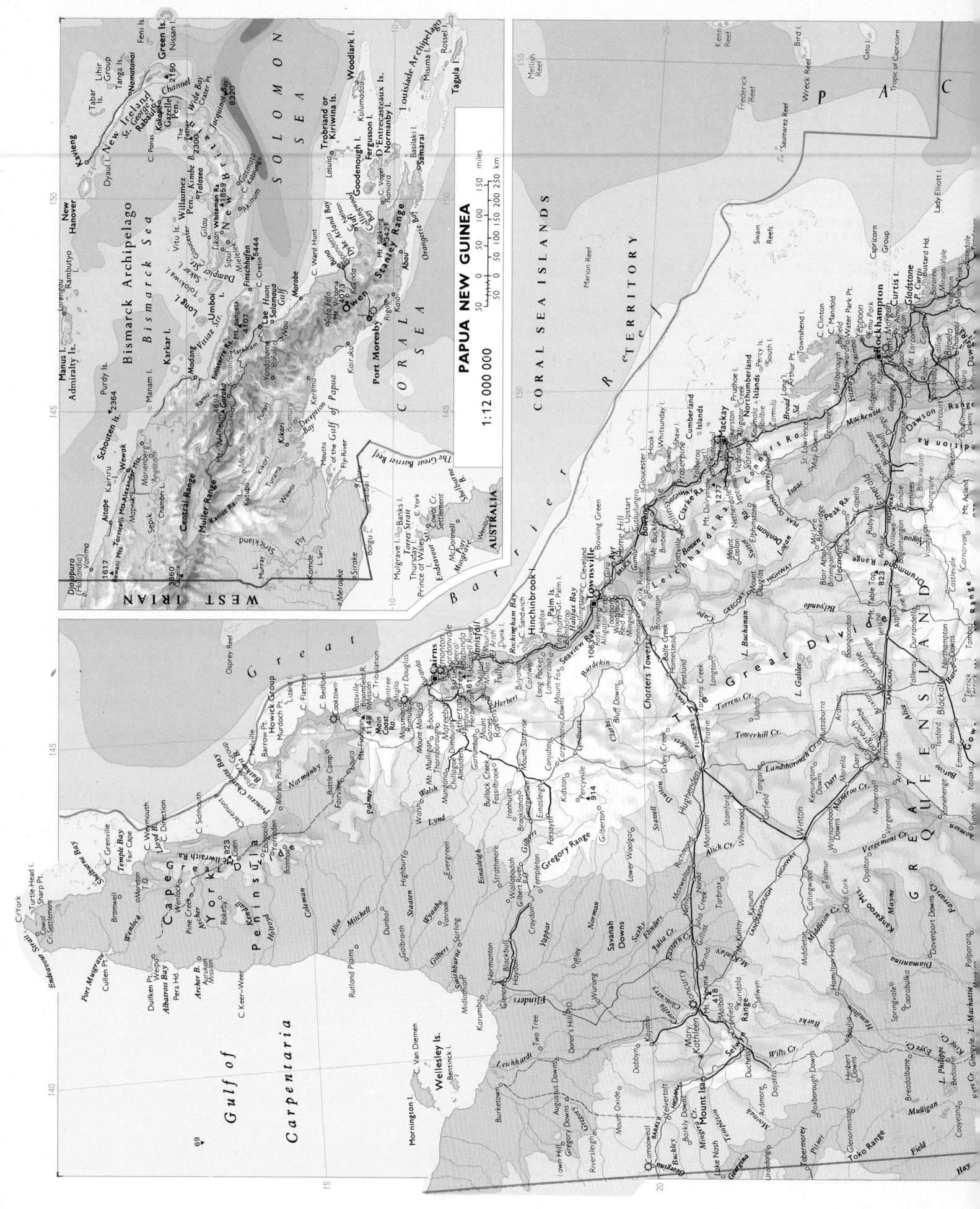
PAPUA NEW GUINEA
1:12 000 000
WEST IRIAN
Bismarck Archipelago
Bismarck Sea
SOLOMON SEA
CORAL SEA
Gulf of Papua
Port Moresby
Owen Stanley Range
New Britain
New Ireland
Louisiade Archipelago
Trobriand or Kiriwina Is.
D'Entrecasteaux Is.
AUSTRALIA
CORAL SEA ISLANDS TERRITORY
Great Barrier Reef
Gulf of Carpentaria
Cape York Peninsula
QUEENSLAND
The Great Divide
Cairns
Townsville
Mackay
Rockhampton
Gladstone
Charters Towers
Hughenden
Winton
Cloncurry
Mount Isa
Mary Kathleen
Normanton
Cooktown
Bowen
Ayr
Innisfail
Wellesley Is.
Mornington I.
Tropic of Capricorn

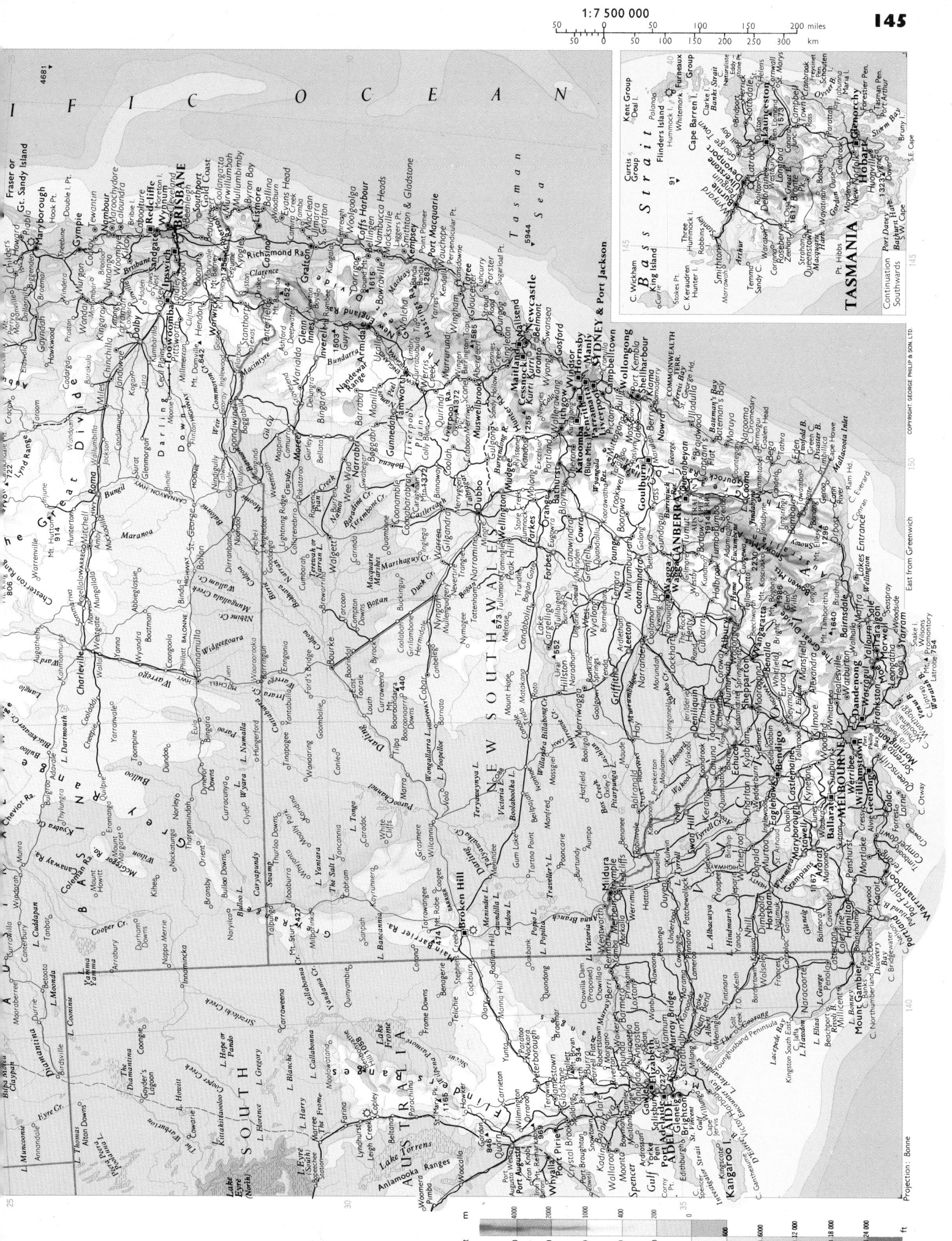
1:7 500 000
miles
km
PACIFIC OCEAN
Tasman Sea
Bass Strait
TASMANIA
NEW SOUTH WALES
SOUTH AUSTRALIA
VICTORIA
BRISBANE
SYDNEY & Port Jackson
CANBERRA
MELBOURNE
ADELAIDE
Hobart
Continuation Southwards
East from Greenwich
Projection: Bonne
COPYRIGHT. GEORGE PHILIP & SON. LTD.

1:3 500 000

10   20   30   40   50   60 miles
20   0   20   40   60   80   100 km

JANUARY TEMPERATURE
1:25 000 000

ACTUAL SURFACE TEMPERATURE
°C   °F
20   68
15   59
10   50
5   41
0   32

20° Isotherms reduced to Sea-level
°Celsius

JULY TEMPERATURE
1:25 000 000

ANNUAL RAINFALL
1:25 000 000

RAINFALL
mm   inches
3000   120
2000   80
1000   40
500   20

SUMMER AND WINTER RAINFALL
mm   inches
1000   40
750   30
500   20
250   10

1012 Isobars in millibars
→ Prevailing Winds

SUMMER RAINFALL
November to April
1:25 000 000

WINTER RAINFALL
May to October
1:25 000 000

TASMAN SEA

Bay of Plenty

Hauraki Gulf

AUCKLAND

Hamilton

Tauranga

Rotorua

Gisborne

Poverty Bay

New Plymouth

Napier

Hawke Bay

Hastings

Wanganui

Palmerston North

Masterton

Nelson

Picton

Blenheim

WELLINGTON

Coromandel Peninsula

Whangarei

Bay of Islands

Ninety Mile Beach

Hokianga Harb.

Dargaville

Lake Taupo

Golden Bay

Tasman Bay

Cook Strait

ft   m
9000 3000
6000 2000
3000 1200
     600
     400
     200
0   0
     200
     600
2000 6000
m   ft

Projection: Conical with two standard parallels

East from Greenwich

COPYRIGHT. GEORGE PHILIP & SON, LTD.

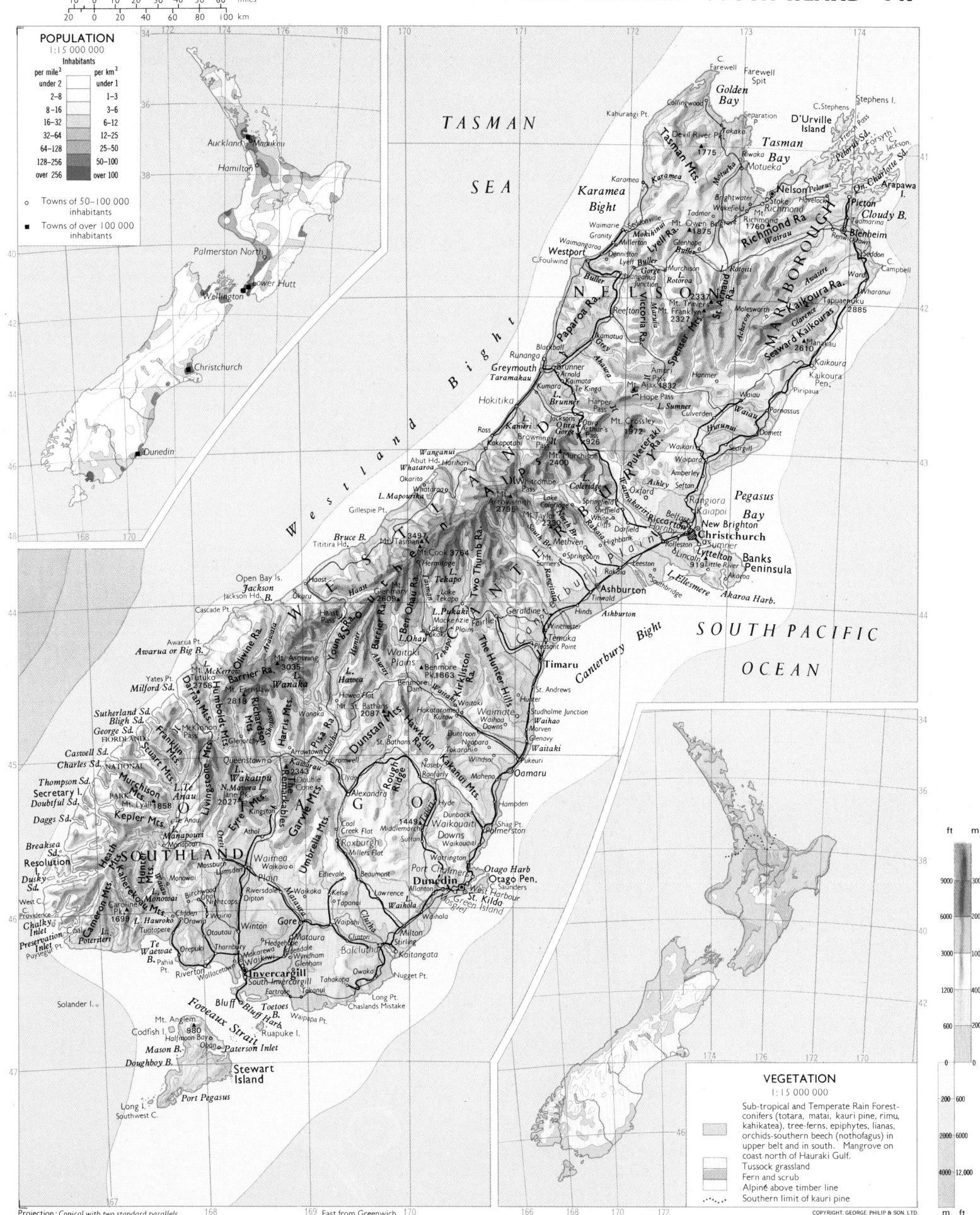

1:3 500 000

10   0   10   20   30   40   50   60 miles
20   0   20   40   60   80   100 km

POPULATION
1:15 000 000

per mile²	Inhabitants	per km²
under 2		under 1
2–8		1–3
8–16		3–6
16–32		6–12
32–64		12–25
64–128		25–50
128–256		50–100
over 256		over 100

○ Towns of 50–100 000 inhabitants

■ Towns of over 100 000 inhabitants

VEGETATION
1:15 000 000

Sub-tropical and Temperate Rain Forest–conifers (totara, matai, kauri pine, rimu, kahikatea), tree-ferns, epiphytes, lianas, orchids–southern beech (nothofagus) in upper belt and in south. Mangrove on coast north of Hauraki Gulf.

Tussock grassland
Fern and scrub
Alpine above timber line
Southern limit of kauri pine

Projection: Conical with two standard parallels

168   169   East from Greenwich   170

COPYRIGHT. GEORGE PHILIP & SON. LTD.

Iceland
Denmark Strait
Greenland Sea
Greenland
Davis Strait
Baffin Bay
Baffin Island
Cumberland Sound
Frobisher Bay
Hudson Strait
Ungava Peninsula
Labrador
Hamilton Inlet
Newfoundland
Belle Isle Strait
Gulf of St. Lawrence
Nova Scotia
Bay of Fundy
Laurentian Plateau
Hudson Bay
James Bay
Southampton I.
Foxe Basin
Foxe Channel
Melville Pen.
Gulf of Boothia
Boothia Pen.
Ellesmere I.
Kane Basin
Nares Str.
Devon I.
Lancaster Sound
Axel Heiberg
Sverdrup Is.
Queen Elizabeth Islands
Parry Is.
Melville I.
Prince of Wales I.
Victoria I.
Banks I.
M'Clure Strait
ARCTIC OCEAN
Beaufort Sea
Great Bear L.
Great Slave L.
Athabasca L.
Reindeer L.
Lake Winnipeg
Mackenzie Mts.
Brooks Range
Alaska Range
Mt. McKinley 6194
Mt. Logan 6050
Mt. St. Elias 5489
Alaska
Gulf of Alaska
Alaska Pen.
Alexander Archipelago
Queen Charlotte Islands
Vancouver I.
Coast Mountains
Rocky Mountains
Selkirk Mts.
Cascade Range
Sierra Nevada
Coast Range
Great Basin
Wasatch Mountains
Colorado Plateau
Great Plains
Appalachian Mts.
Allegheny Mts.
Blue Ridge
Cumberland Plateau
Ozark Plateau
Llano Estacado
Bering Strait
Bering Sea
Aleutian Islands
Asia
Wrangel I.
St. Lawrence I.
Nunivak I.
Kodiak I.
PACIFIC
ATLANTIC OCEAN
Mendocino Seascarp
Murray Seascarp
Tropic of Cancer
Winnipeg
Regina
Edmonton
Calgary
Vancouver
Seattle
Portland
San Francisco
Los Angeles
Denver
Minneapolis
Chicago
Detroit
Toronto
Hamilton
Ottawa
Montreal
Quebec
New York
Philadelphia
Washington
St. Louis
Kansas City
Memphis
Atlanta
Dallas
L. Superior
L. Michigan
L. Huron
L. Erie
L. Ontario
Great Salt Lake
Death Valley
Mt. Whitney 4418
Mt. Shasta 4317
Mt. Rainier 4392
Mt. Robson 3954
Mt. Elbert 4399
Blanca Pk. 4364
Grand Canyon
Mississippi
Missouri
Arkansas
Colorado
Columbia
Snake
Yukon
Mackenzie
Bermuda
C. Hatteras
Chesapeake Bay

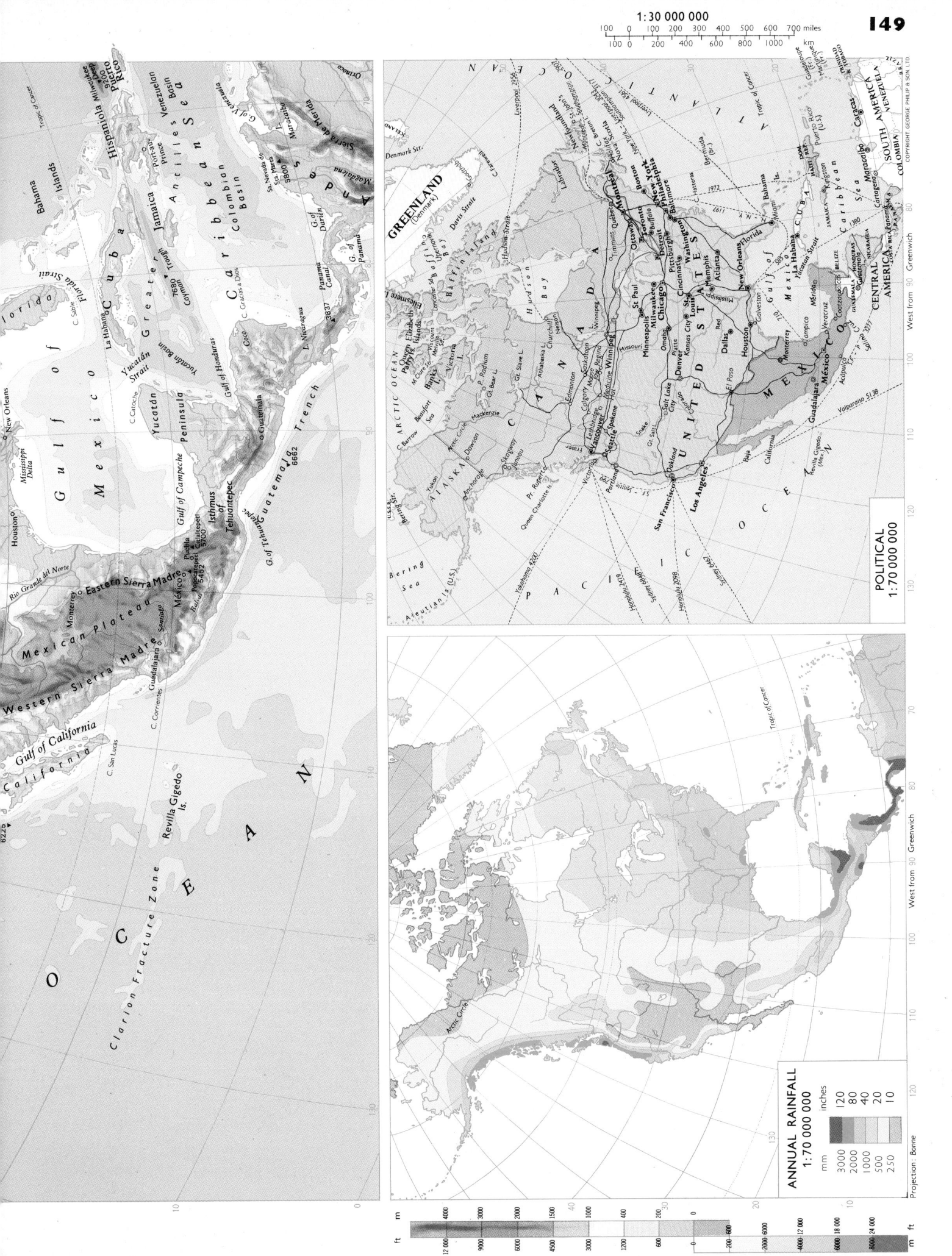

Gulf of Mexico
Caribbean Sea
Greater Antilles
Cuba
Hispaniola
Jamaica
Puerto Rico
Bahama Islands
Yucatán Peninsula
Gulf of California
Mexican Plateau
Western Sierra Madre
Eastern Sierra Madre
Isthmus of Tehuantepec
Guatemala Trench
Clarion Fracture Zone
Revilla Gigedo Is.
Colombian Basin
Venezuelan Basin
Cayman Trough
Yucatán Basin
Gulf of Honduras
Panama Canal
Andes
OCEAN
ANNUAL RAINFALL
1:70 000 000
mm inches
3000 120
2000 80
1000 40
500 20
250 10
Projection: Bonne
West from 90 Greenwich
POLITICAL
1:70 000 000
GREENLAND (Denmark)
CANADA
UNITED STATES
MEXICO
CENTRAL AMERICA
SOUTH AMERICA
ALASKA
ARCTIC OCEAN
Hudson Bay
Baffin Bay
COPYRIGHT GEORGE PHILIP & SON, LTD.

1:30 000 000

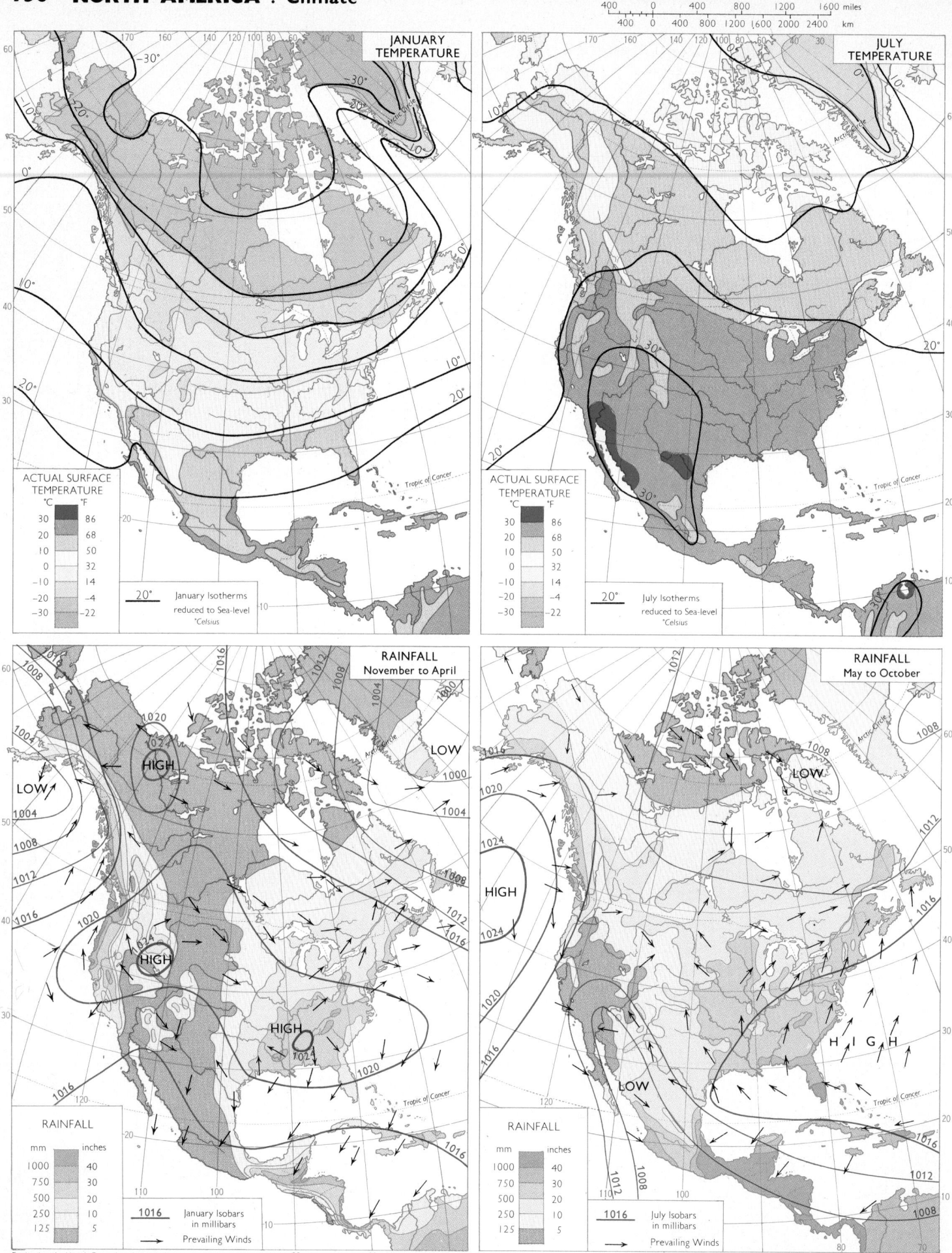

1:70 000 000

JANUARY TEMPERATURE

JULY TEMPERATURE

ACTUAL SURFACE TEMPERATURE

°C	°F
30	86
20	68
10	50
0	32
-10	14
-20	-4
-30	-22

20° January Isotherms reduced to Sea-level °Celsius

20° July Isotherms reduced to Sea-level °Celsius

RAINFALL November to April

RAINFALL May to October

RAINFALL

mm	inches
1000	40
750	30
500	20
250	10
125	5

1016 January Isobars in millibars

Prevailing Winds

1016 July Isobars in millibars

Prevailing Winds

Projection: Lambert's Equivalent Azimuthal

West from 70 Greenwich

COPYRIGHT. GEORGE PHILIP & SON. LTD.

1 : 32 000 000

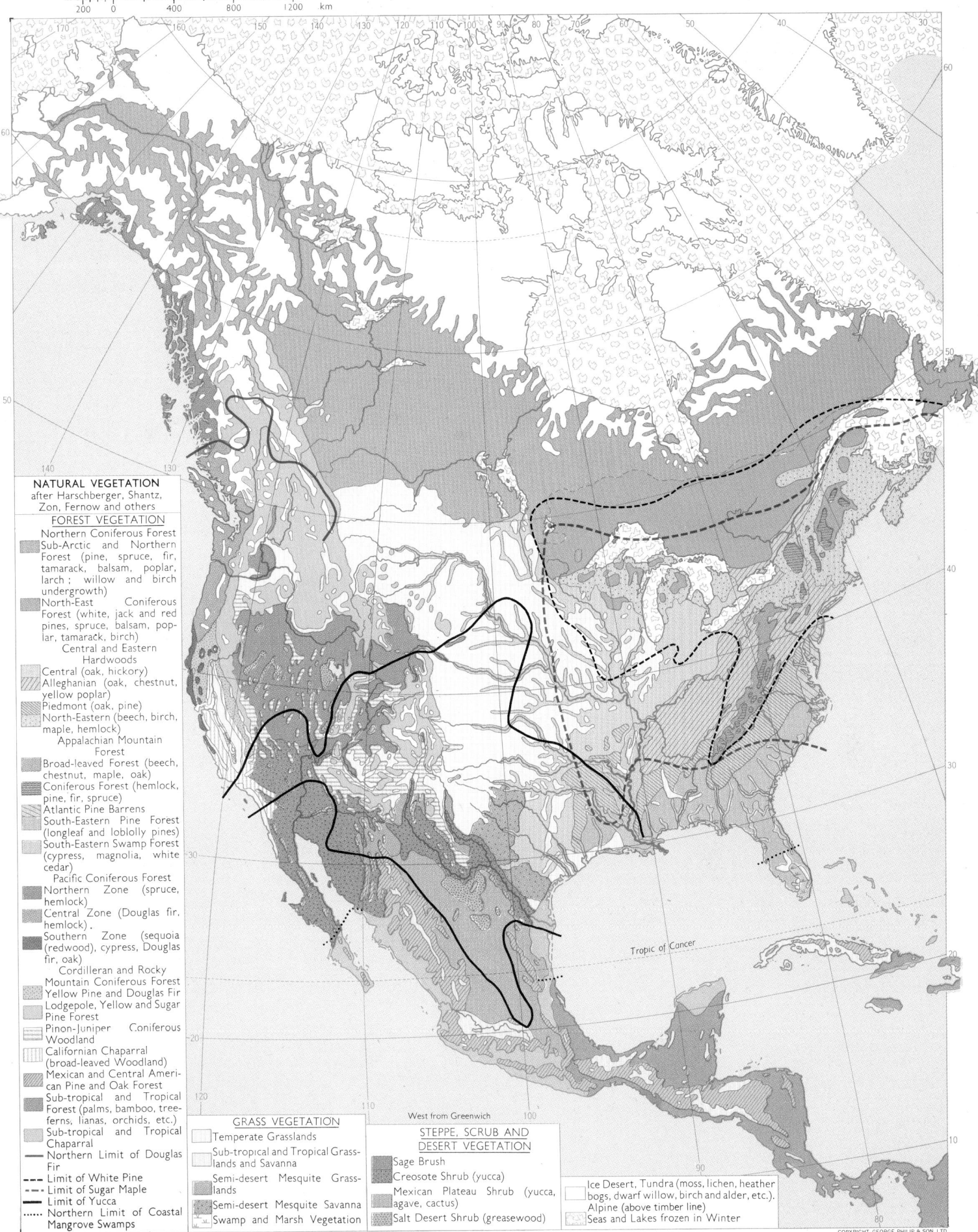

NATURAL VEGETATION
after Harschberger, Shantz, Zon, Fernow and others

FOREST VEGETATION

Northern Coniferous Forest
Sub-Arctic and Northern Forest (pine, spruce, fir, tamarack, balsam, poplar, larch ; willow and birch undergrowth)
North-East Coniferous Forest (white, jack and red pines, spruce, balsam, poplar, tamarack, birch)

Central and Eastern Hardwoods
Central (oak, hickory)
Alleghanian (oak, chestnut, yellow poplar)
Piedmont (oak, pine)
North-Eastern (beech, birch, maple, hemlock)

Appalachian Mountain Forest
Broad-leaved Forest (beech, chestnut, maple, oak)
Coniferous Forest (hemlock, pine, fir, spruce)
Atlantic Pine Barrens
South-Eastern Pine Forest (longleaf and loblolly pines)
South-Eastern Swamp Forest (cypress, magnolia, white cedar)

Pacific Coniferous Forest
Northern Zone (spruce, hemlock)
Central Zone (Douglas fir, hemlock).
Southern Zone (sequoia (redwood), cypress, Douglas fir, oak)

Cordilleran and Rocky Mountain Coniferous Forest
Yellow Pine and Douglas Fir
Lodgepole, Yellow and Sugar Pine Forest
Pinon-Juniper Coniferous Woodland
Californian Chaparral (broad-leaved Woodland)
Mexican and Central American Pine and Oak Forest
Sub-tropical and Tropical Forest (palms, bamboo, tree-ferns, lianas, orchids, etc.)
Sub-tropical and Tropical Chaparral

—— Northern Limit of Douglas Fir
– – – Limit of White Pine
–·–·– Limit of Sugar Maple
—— Limit of Yucca
······· Northern Limit of Coastal Mangrove Swamps

GRASS VEGETATION
Temperate Grasslands
Sub-tropical and Tropical Grasslands and Savanna
Semi-desert Mesquite Grasslands
Semi-desert Mesquite Savanna
Swamp and Marsh Vegetation

STEPPE, SCRUB AND DESERT VEGETATION
Sage Brush
Creosote Shrub (yucca)
Mexican Plateau Shrub (yucca, agave, cactus)
Salt Desert Shrub (greasewood)

Ice Desert, Tundra (moss, lichen, heather bogs, dwarf willow, birch and alder, etc.).
Alpine (above timber line)
Seas and Lakes frozen in Winter

Tropic of Cancer

West from Greenwich

Projection: Polyconic

COPYRIGHT. GEORGE PHILIP & SON LTD

ft m

9000 3000
6000 2000
4500 1500
3000 1000
1200 400
600 200
0 0

m ft
200 600
2000 6000

Projection: Bonne

ALASKA
1:30 000 000

100 0 100 200 300 miles
100 0 200 400 km

1:15 000 000

100 50 0 100 200 300 400 miles
100 0 100 200 300 400 500 600 km

Devon Island
Lancaster Sound
Baffin Bay
GREENLAND
ATLANTIC

Arctic Bay
Brodeur
Peninsula
Bylot I.
1890
Pond Inlet
Milne Inlet
Scott I.
Clyde
C. Hewett
Mary River
Fury & Hecla Str.
Igloolik Island
2136
Svartenhuk Halvø
Angmagssalik
Disko B.
Christianshåb
Disko
Sendre Strømfjord
Kong Frederik VI's Kyst
2850

Gulf of Boothia
Pelly Bay
Melville Peninsula
Hall Lake
Prince Charles I.
Cumberland Peninsula
2591
C. Dyer
Cape Dyer
Davis Strait
Holsteinsborg
Broughton Island
Padloping Island
Home B.
Pangnirtung
Cumberland Sd.
C. Mercy
Godthåb
Frederikshåb
Ivigtut
Julianehåb
Sydprøven
Nanortalik
Kap Farvel

Circle
Rae Isthmus
Repulse Bay
Wager B.
Jager B.
Foxe Basin
Nettilling L.
C. Dorchester
Amadjuak L.
Foxe Penin.
Cape Dorset
Lake Harbour
Frobisher Bay
Resolution I.
3809

Foxe Channel
Southampton I.
Coral Harbour
Bell Pen.
Coats I.
Digges Is.
Mansel I.
Hudson Strait
C. Chidley

Ross Welcome Sd.
Saglouc (Sugluk)
Ivugivik (Notre Dame d'Ivugivic)
Maricourt (Wakeham Bay)
Koartac (Notre Dame de Koartac)
Akpatok I.
Bellin (Payne bay)
Payne L.
Ungava Bay
1676
Port Nouveau-Quebec (George R.)
Hebron
Nutak

Hudson
Ottawa Is.
257
Ungava Peninsula
Portland Promontory
Inoucdjouac (Port Harrison)
Payne
Leaf
Larch
Kaniapiskau
George
Whale
Ft. Chimo
Kok-soak
NEWFOUNDLAND
Nain
Hopedale
Indian Harbour
C. Harrison

Bay
Sleeper Is.
King George Is.
King George I.
Baker's Dozen
Belcher Is.
L. Minto
Lower Seal L.
Lac Bienville
Petitsikapau L.
Schefferville
Lobstick L.
Ashuanipi L.
Wabush City
Michikamau L.
North West R.
Churchill Falls
Churchill
L. Melville
Rigolet
Goose Bay
Cartwright
Battle Hbr.
Belle Isle
LABRADOR

C. Tatnam
Ft. Severn
Severn
Winisk
C. Henrietta Maria
Gr. Whale R.
Poste de la Baleine (Great Whale River)
Fort George
Kaniapiskau
Clearwater
1128
Gagnon
Moisie
QUEBEC
Natashquan
Mingan
St. Augustin
Natashquan
Romaine
Str. of Belle Isle
Notre Dame B.
Twillingate
Lewisporte
Gander
Bonavista
Trinity B.
Grand Falls
Corner Brook
Millertown Jct.
814
Buchans
Harbour Grace
Carbonear
Bell I.
St. John's
Placentia B.
Trepassey
C. Race

Winisk
Big Trout L.
D
Akimiski I.
Nouveau Comptoir (Paint Hills)
Ft. George
East Main
Eastmain
Fort Rupert (Rupert House)
Rupert
Mistassini L.
L. Albanel
Nottaway
Bersimis
Manicouagan
Moisie
Sept Iles
Port Cartier
Anticosti
Gulf of St. Lawrence
Magdalen Is.
Cabot Str.
C. North
Cape Breton I.
C. Race
Cape Ray
Channel
P. aux Basques

Albany
L. St. Joseph
Armstrong
Nakina
Attawapiskat
Moosonee
Charlton
Ft. Albany
Harricanaw
Chibougamau
Baie Comeau
R. St. Lawrence
Matane
Gaspé
Gaspé Pen.
Campbellton
Dalhousie
Bathurst
Chatham
Tignish
Summerside
PR. EDWARD I.
Charlottetown
C. North
Glace Bay
Sydney
Port Hawkesbury
C. Canso

Nipigon
L. Nipigon
Longlac
Longlac
Kenogami
Hearst
Cochrane
Matagami
Senneterre
Val d'Or
Doucet
Weymont
La Tuque
Dolbeau
St. John
Saguenay
Jonquière
Chicoutimi
Roberval
Lac St-Jean
Rimouski
Rivière du Loup
St. Leonard
Edmundston
Newcastle
NEW BRUNSWICK
Moncton
Amherst
Springhill
Pictou L.
New Glasgow
Truro
NOVA SCOTIA
Windsor
Dartmouth

Thunder Bay
(Ft. William, Pt. Arthur)
Michipicoten
Franz
Heron Bay
Oba
Timmins
Norandaa
Rouyn
Kirkland Lake
Haileybury
Cobalt
Timiskaming
Cabonga Reservoir
Gouin Reservoir
Shawinigan
Trois Rivières
Québec
Lévis
Thetford Mines
Woodstock
Fredericton
Saint John
B. of Fundy
Digby
Kentville
Bridgewater
Liverpool
Shelburne
C. Sable
Sable I. (Nova Scotia)
6309

Lake Superior
Calumet
Keweenaw Bay
Bessemer
Ironwood
Sault Ste. Marie
Coppercliff
Sudbury
North Bay
Parry Sound
Pembroke
Ottawa
Hull
Lachine
MONTRÉAL
Granby
Sherbrooke
Sorel
St. Hyacinthe
Joliette
Drummondville
MAINE
Bangor
Augusta
Lewiston
Portland

Marquette
Manistique
Cheboygan
Petoskey
Georgian Bay
Lake Huron
Orillia
Barrie
Belleville
Kingston
Cornwall
Brockville
Cobourg
Watertown
Glens Falls
NEW HAMPSHIRE
Concord
Manchester
Lowell
Boston
C. Cod

WISCONSIN
Wausau
Green Bay
Appleton
Sheboygan
Manitowoc
Traverse City
Cadillac
Ludington
Saginaw
Owen Sound
Oshawa
TORONTO
Guelph
Stratford
Kitchener
Hamilton
St. Catharines
Niagara Falls
Ontario
L. Ontario
Rochester
Syracuse
Utica
Albany
Springfield
Worcester
MASS.
Providence
RHODE I.

Madison
Rockford
Milwaukee
Racine
Kenosha
Kalamazoo
Grand Rapids
London
Brantford
Buffalo
NEW YORK
Elmira
Binghamton
Scranton
Waterbury
Bridgeport
New Haven
VERMONT
1917

ILLINOIS
CHICAGO
Gary
Evanston
South Bend
DETROIT
Windsor
Chatham
Sarnia
Erie
Jamestown
Williamsport
PENNSYLVANIA
Allentown
Reading
Trenton
NEW JERSEY
Jersey City
Newark
NEW YORK
INDIANA
Toledo
OHIO
Cleveland
Akron
Youngstown

90   80   70   West from Greenwich   60   COPYRIGHT. GEORGE PHILIP & SON, LTD.

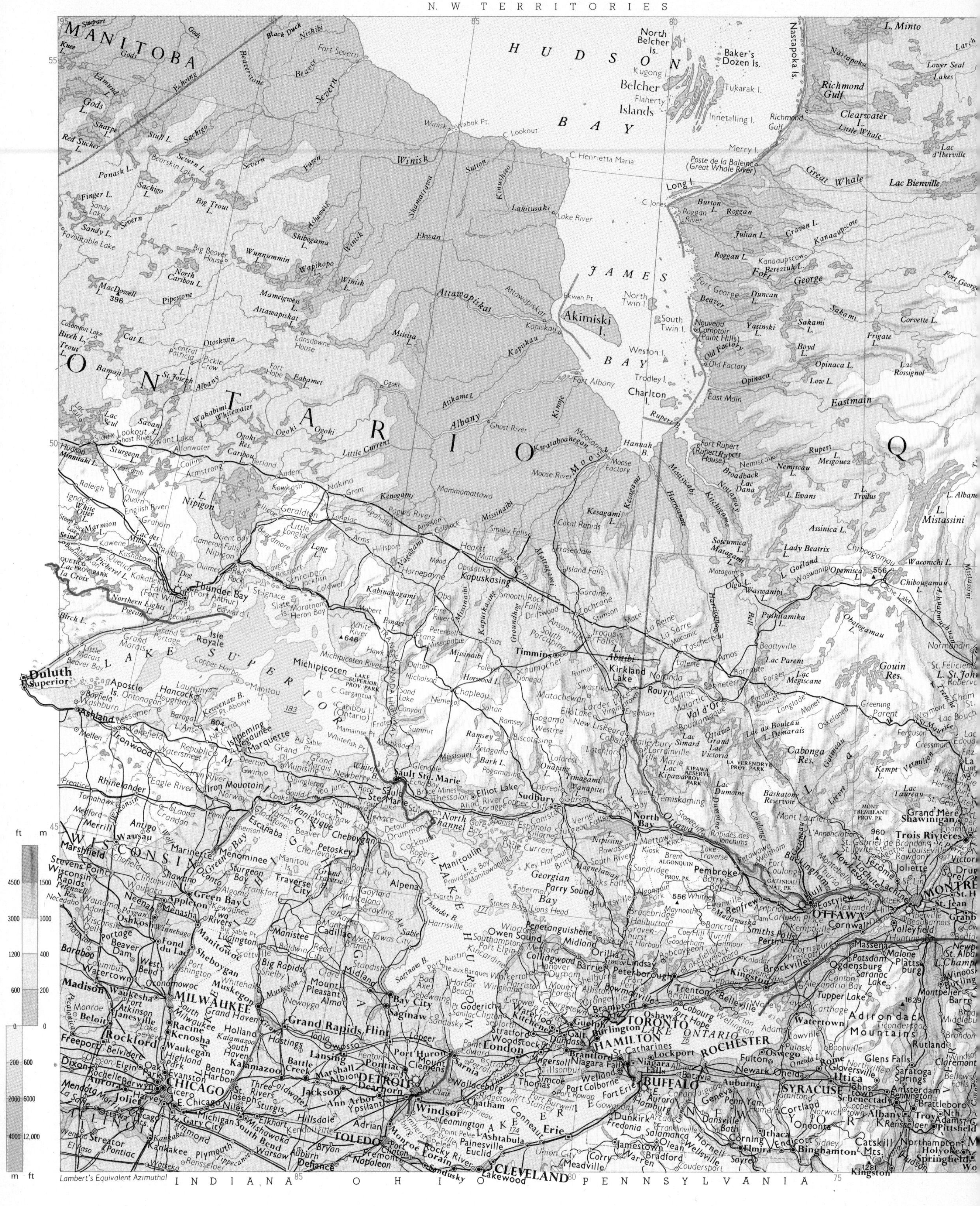

N.W TERRITORIES

MANITOBA

HUDSON BAY

JAMES BAY

ONTARIO

QUEBEC

North Belcher Is.
Kugong I.
Baker's Dozen Is.
Belcher Islands
Flaherty I.
Tukarak I.
Innetalling I.
Richmond Gulf
Clearwater
Lower Seal Lakes
L. Minto
Nastapoka Is.
Larch
Richmond Gulf
Little Whale
Great Whale
Lac d'Iberville
Lac Bienville

Akimiski I.
North Twin I.
South Twin I.
Weston I.
Tradley I.
Fort Albany
Charlton
Hannah B.
Rupert B.
Fort Rupert (Rupert House)
East Main
Eastmain
Nouveau Comptoir (Paint Hills)
Old Factory
Fort George
Duncan
Beaver
Yasinski
Sakami
Corvette L.
Opinaca L.
Lac Rossignol
Nemiscau
Lac Dana
Broadback
L. Evans
Assinica L.
Mistassini
L. Albane

Winisk
Wabuk Pt.
C. Lookout
Sutton
Ekwan
Kinushseo
C. Henrietta Maria
Lake River
Lakitusaki
Merry I.
Roggan L.
Julian L.
Craven L.
Kanaaypscow
Roggan
Berezuik L.
Fort George

Attawapiskat
Attawapiskat
Missa
Kapiskau
Kapiskau
Ekwan Pt.
Moosonee
Moose Factory
Moose River
Kwataboahegan
Coral Rapids
Kesagami L.
Soscumica L.
Matagami
Lady Beatrix
L. Goëland
Waswanipi
Opemisca
Chibougamau
Waconichi L.
Mistassini

Albany
Ghost River
Kapiskan
Kings
Missinaibi
Mattawitchewan
Moose River
Smoky Falls
Fraserdale
Island Falls
Gardiner
Cochrane
Stimson
La Sarre
La Reine
Taschereau
Amos
Barraute
Senneterre
Lac Parent
Louvicourt
Chibougamau
L. aux Dorés

Thunder Bay (Fort William)(Port Arthur)
Nipigon
Lake Nipigon
Geraldton
Long L.
Hearst
Kapuskasing
Hornepayne
Mattice
Opasatika
Smooth Rock Falls
Driftwood
South Porcupine
Timmins
Schumacher
Iroquois Falls
Kirkland Lake
Noranda
Rouyn
Cadillac
Malartic
Val d'Or
Bourlamaque
Louvicourt
Gouin Res.
St. Félicien
St. John
Roberval

LAKE SUPERIOR
Isle Royale
Michipicoten
Sault Ste. Marie
Sudbury
Copper Cliff
Elliot Lake
Blind River
Espanola
North Bay
Mattawa
Pembroke
Ottawa
Hull
Gatineau
Montreal
Trois Rivières
Shawinigan
Grand'Mère
Joliette
Sorel
St. Jean
Valleyfield
Cornwall
Hawkesbury
Arnprior
Renfrew
Smiths Falls
Perth
Brockville
Kingston
Belleville
Trenton
Cobourg
Peterborough
Lindsay
Barrie
Orillia
Owen Sound
Collingwood
Midland
Penetanguishene
Parry Sound
Huntsville
Bracebridge

Georgian Bay
LAKE HURON
Manitoulin I.
Tobermory
Lions Head
Wiarton
Southampton
Kincardine
Goderich
Sarnia
London
Stratford
Woodstock
Kitchener
Guelph
Brampton
TORONTO
Hamilton
St. Catharines
Niagara Falls
Welland
BUFFALO
ROCHESTER
SYRACUSE
Utica
Albany

Duluth
Superior
Ashland
Ironwood
Hancock
Houghton
Marquette
Escanaba
Menominee
Marinette
Green Bay
Appleton
Oshkosh
Fond du Lac
Sheboygan
Manitowoc
MILWAUKEE
Racine
Kenosha
Madison
Beloit
Rockford
Freeport
CHICAGO
Gary
Joliet
Aurora
Elgin

WISCONSIN
MICHIGAN
Traverse City
Cadillac
Manistee
Ludington
Muskegon
Grand Rapids
Flint
Saginaw
Bay City
Lansing
Battle Creek
Kalamazoo
Jackson
Ann Arbor
DETROIT
Dearborn
Pontiac
Port Huron
Windsor
Chatham
Leamington
Pt. Pelee
LAKE ERIE
TOLEDO
Sandusky
CLEVELAND
Lakewood
Lorain
Elyria

ILLINOIS
INDIANA
OHIO
PENNSYLVANIA
NEW YORK
Adirondack Mountains
Catskill Mts.
Binghamton
Elmira
Ithaca
Corning
Olean
Jamestown
Bradford
Warren
Meadville

Lambert's Equivalent Azimuthal

1:7 000 000

50   0   50   100   150   200 miles
50 0 50 100 150 200 250 300 km

COAST OF

LABRADOR

QUEBEC

West from Greenwich

NEWFOUNDLAND

GULF OF ST. LAWRENCE

St. Lawrence

Gaspé Peninsula
Shickshock Mts.
GASPESIAN PROV. PARK

Anticosti I.
Jupiter
Jacques Cartier Passage

NEW BRUNSWICK

PRINCE EDWARD ISLAND
Charlottetown
Summerside

NOVA SCOTIA

Cape Breton Island
Sydney
Glace Bay

Cabot Strait

SAINT-PIERRE ET MIQUELON (Fr.)
Miquelon
Langlade

St. John's
Avalon Peninsula

MAINE

Magdalen Is. (Quebec)

ATLANTIC OCEAN

Sable I. (Nova Scotia)

BOSTON
Portland
Halifax
Dartmouth
Fredericton
Saint John
Bay of Fundy
Moncton
Bathurst
Campbellton
Rimouski
Mont Joli
Quebec
Lévis
Sherbrooke
Bangor
Corner Brook
Bay of Islands

COPYRIGHT. GEORGE PHILIP & SON. LTD.

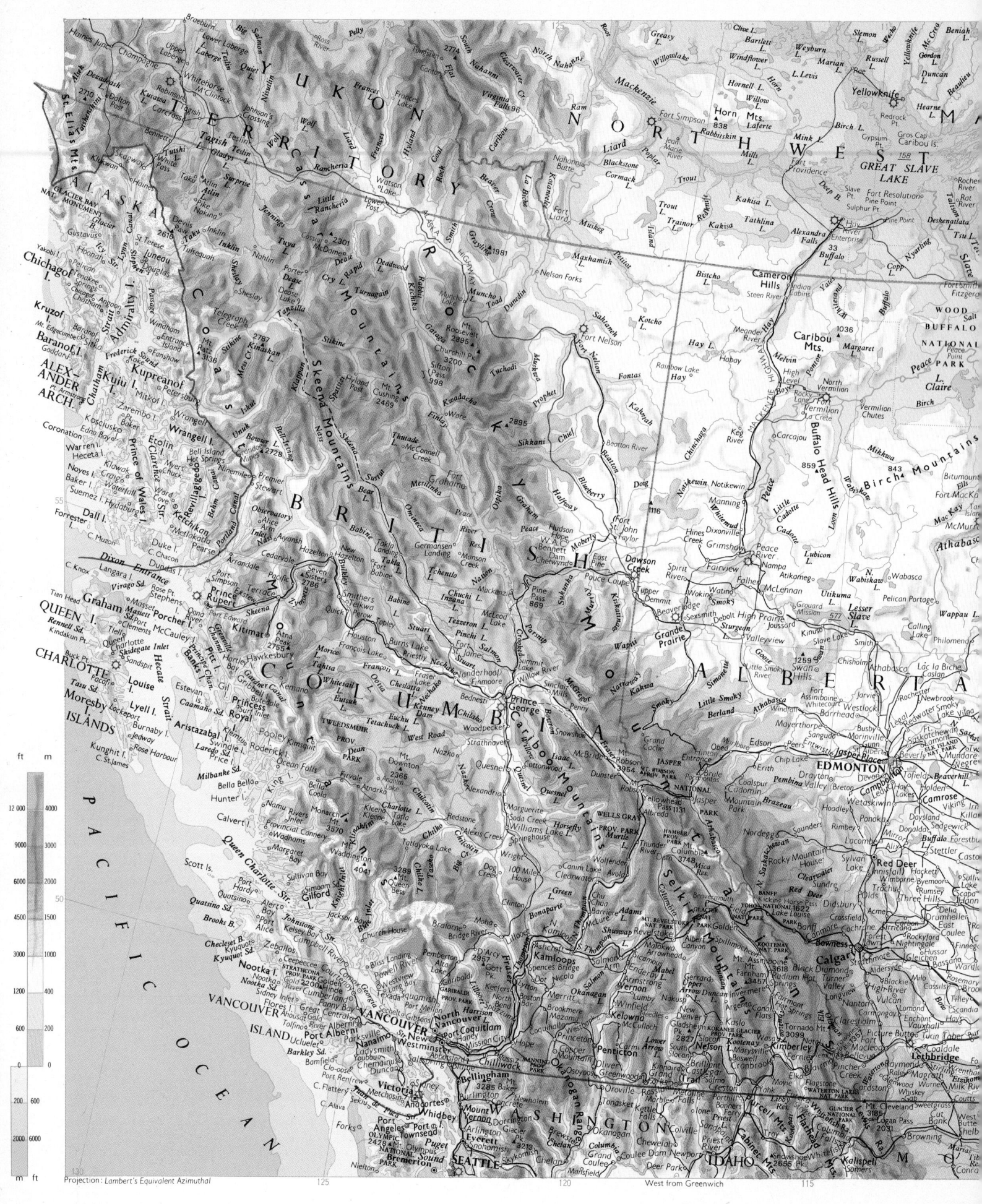
YUKON TERRITORY
NORTHWEST
BRITISH COLUMBIA
ALBERTA
ALASKA
WASHINGTON
IDAHO
PACIFIC OCEAN
QUEEN CHARLOTTE ISLANDS
VANCOUVER ISLAND
ALEXANDER ARCH.
GREAT SLAVE LAKE
Coast Mountains
Rocky Mountains
Skeena Mountains
Cassiar Mountains
Cariboo Mountains
Selkirk Mountains
Purcell Mts.
Birch Mountains
Buffalo Head Hills
Caribou Mts.
Horn Mts.
Cameron Hills
St. Elias Mts.
Whitehorse
Yellowknife
Fort Simpson
Fort Nelson
Fort St. John
Dawson Creek
Grande Prairie
Peace River
Prince George
Prince Rupert
Kitimat
Kamloops
Kelowna
Penticton
VANCOUVER
Victoria
Nanaimo
Port Alberni
Bellingham
SEATTLE
Everett
EDMONTON
Red Deer
Calgary
Lethbridge
Medicine Hat
Jasper
Banff
Juneau
Ketchikan
Skagway
Queen Charlotte Str.
Hecate Strait
Dixon Entrance
Mackenzie
Liard
Peace
Athabasca
Fraser
Columbia
Skeena
Stikine
Mt. Robson 3954
Mt. Waddington 4041
ALASKA HIGHWAY
MACKENZIE HIGHWAY
WOOD BUFFALO NATIONAL PARK
JASPER NATIONAL PARK
BANFF NATIONAL PARK
WELLS GRAY PROV. PARK
TWEEDSMUIR PROV. PARK
GLACIER BAY NAT. MONUMENT
ft
m
12 000
9000
6000
4500
3000
1200
600
0
200
2000
4000
3000
2000
1500
1000
400
200
0
600
6000
Projection: Lambert's Equivalent Azimuthal
West from Greenwich
130
125
120
115
55
50

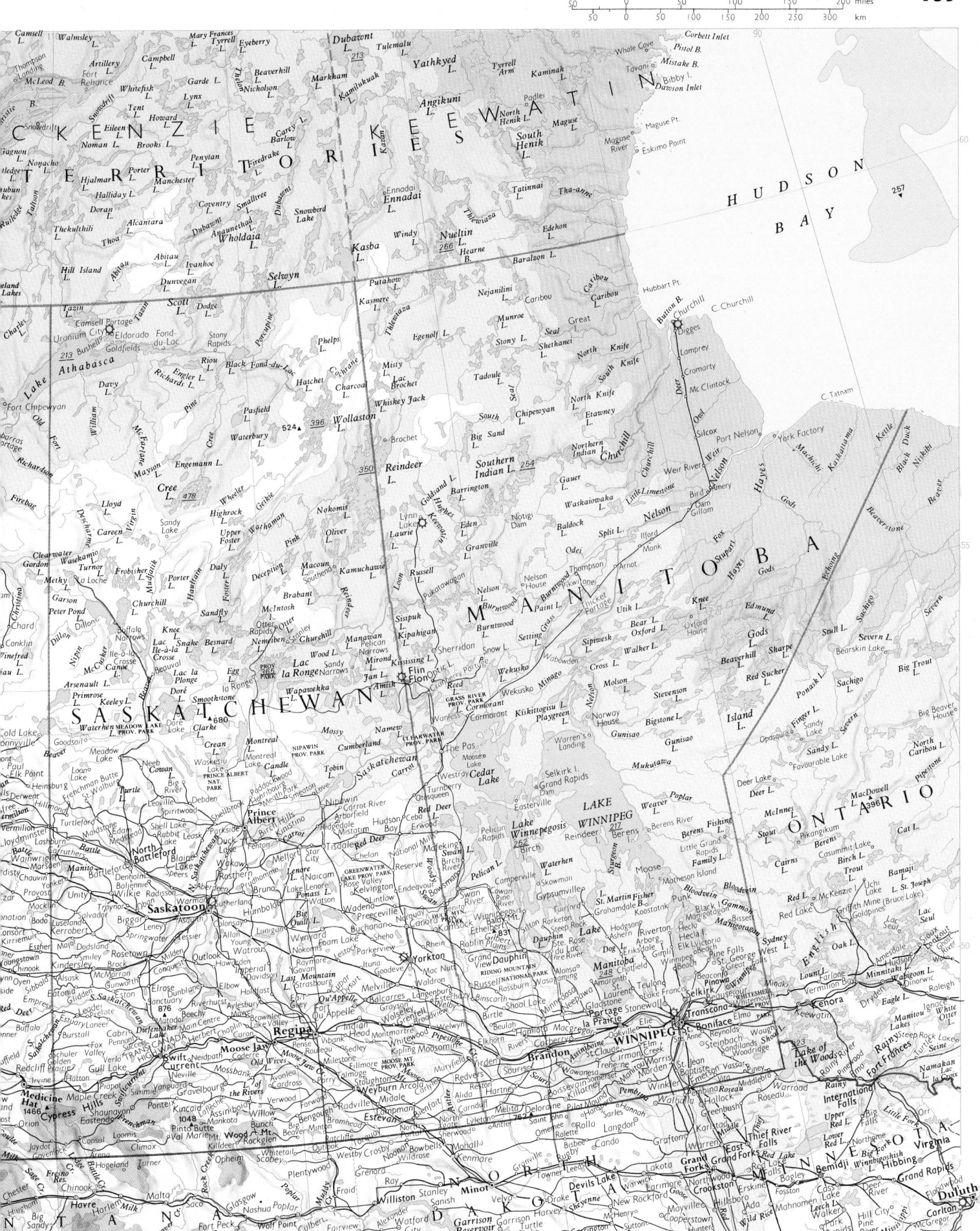

1:7 000 000
50 0 50 100 150 200 miles
50 0 50 100 150 200 250 300 km
MACKENZIE
KEEWATIN
TERRITORIES
HUDSON BAY
SASKATCHEWAN
MANITOBA
ONTARIO
NORTH DAKOTA
MINNESOTA
MONTANA
LAKE WINNIPEG
Lake Winnipegosis
Lake Manitoba
Lake Athabasca
Wollaston L.
Reindeer L.
Southern Indian L.
Cedar Lake
Lake of the Woods
Churchill
Flin Flon
The Pas
Prince Albert
Saskatoon
Regina
Moose Jaw
Swift Current
Medicine Hat
Yorkton
Brandon
WINNIPEG
Kenora
Duluth
Minot
Grand Forks
Thompson
Uranium City
COPYRIGHT, GEORGE PHILIP & SON, LTD.

HAWAII
1:10 000 000

Projection: Albers' Equal Area with two standard parallels

1:12 000 000

50   50   100   150   200   250   300 miles
50   0   50 100 150 200 250 300 350 400 450 km

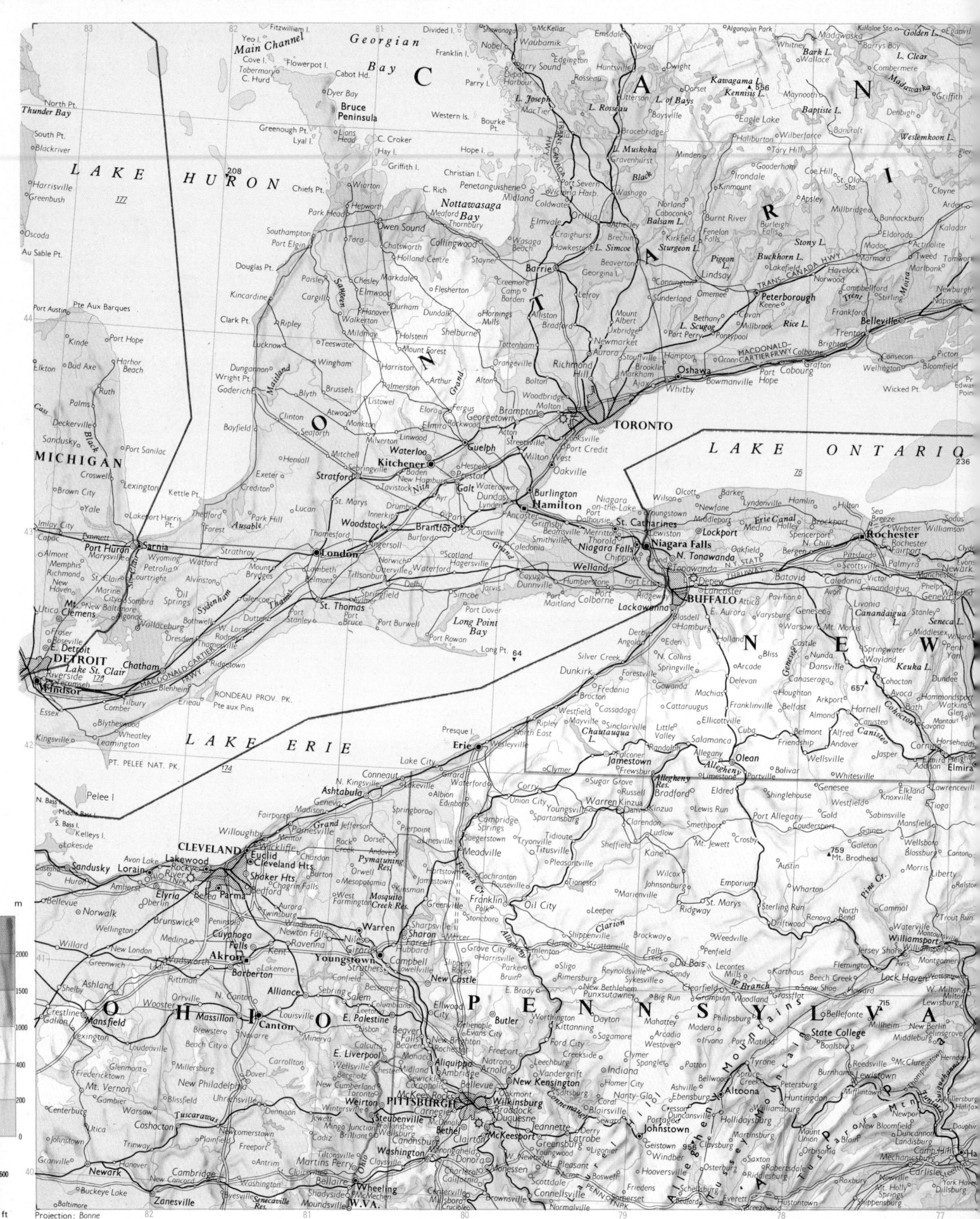

Interstate Highways (U.S.A.), Superhighways (Canada)
Interstate Highways and Superhighways under Construction

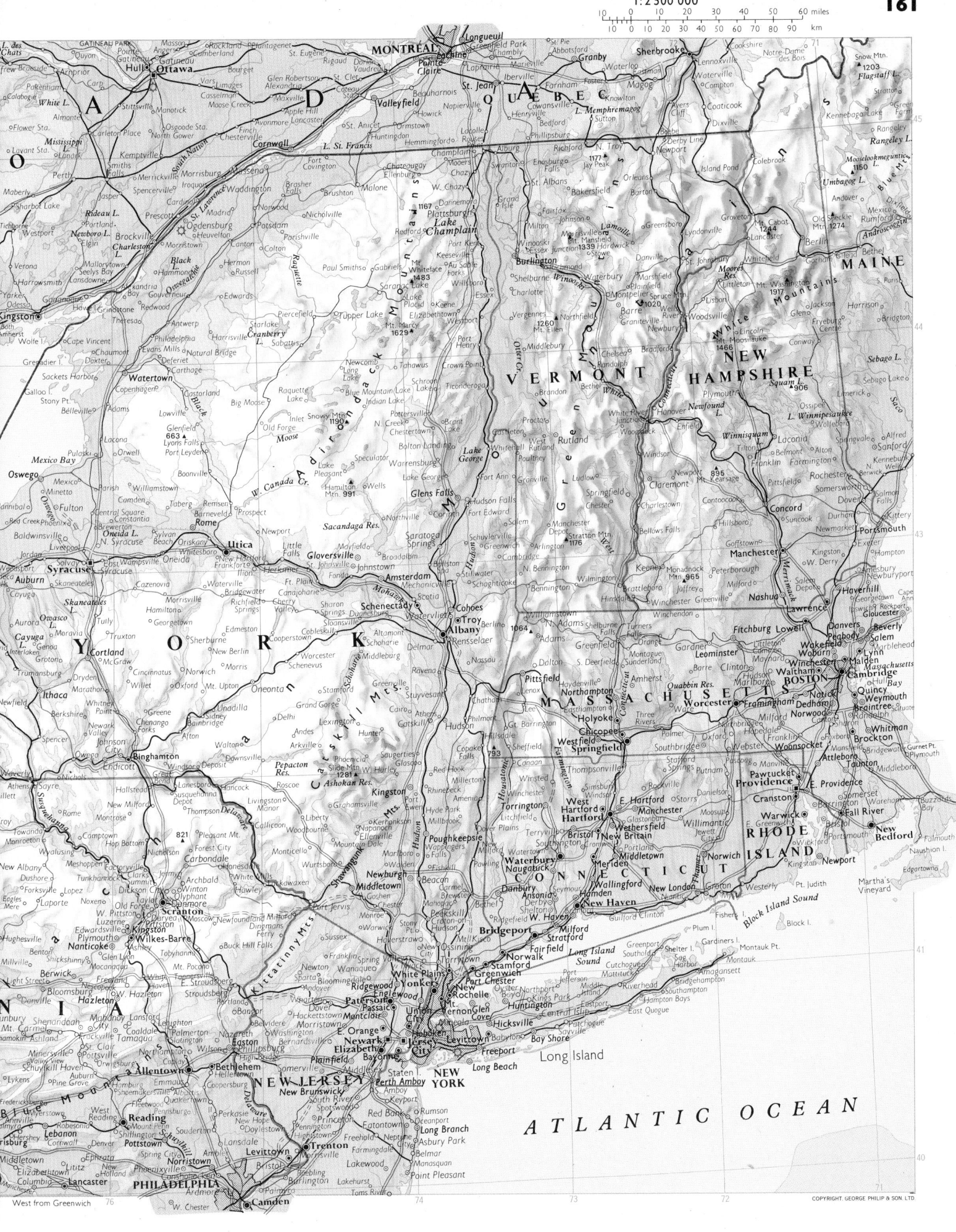

1 : 2 500 000

10   0   10   20   30   40   50   60 miles

10 0 10 20 30 40 50 60 70 80 90 km

ATLANTIC OCEAN

West from Greenwich

COPYRIGHT. GEORGE PHILIP & SON. LTD.

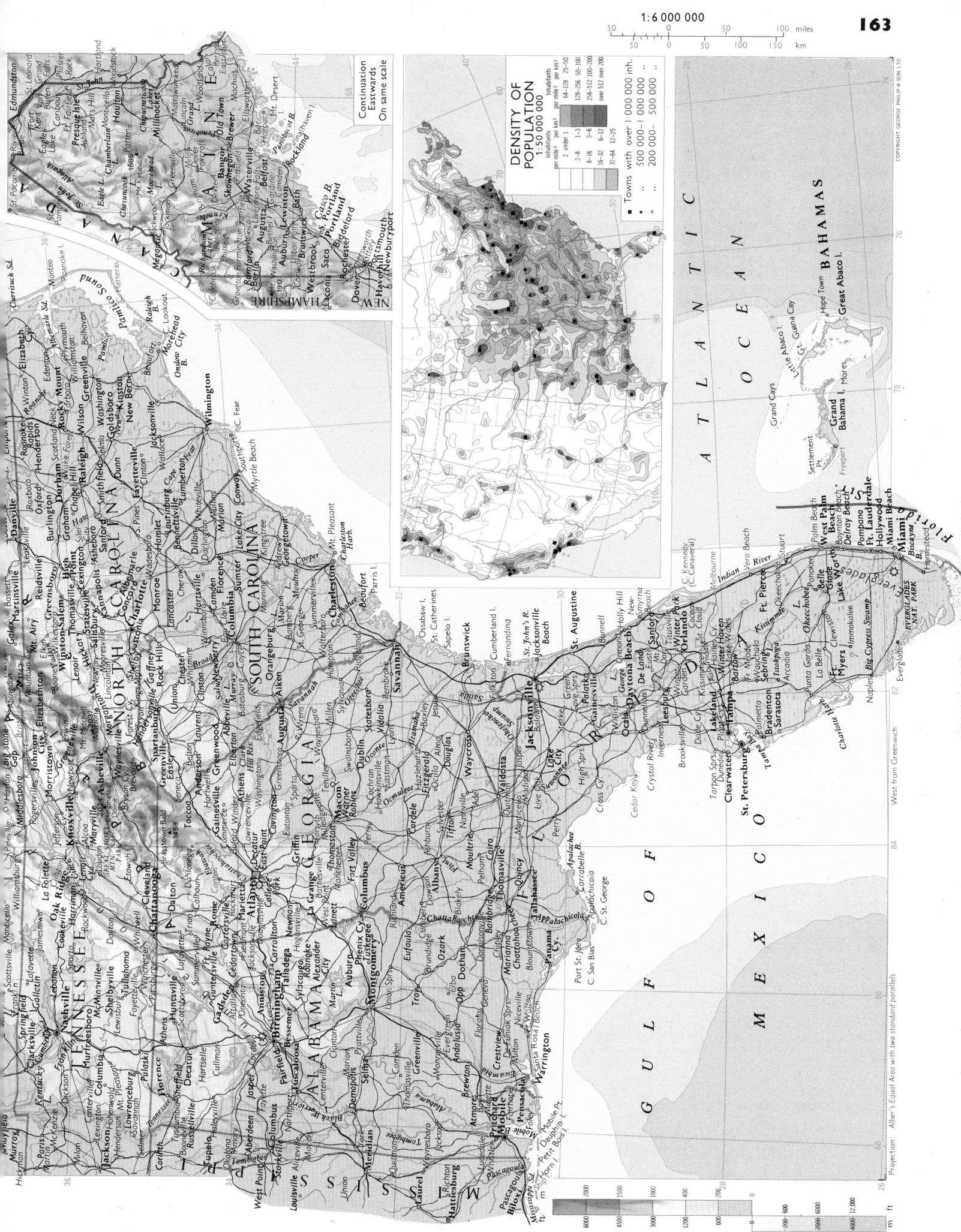

1:6 000 000

50   0   50   100 miles

50   0   50   100   150 km

Continuation
Eastwards
On same scale

DENSITY OF
POPULATION
1:50 000 000

Inhabitants per mile²	per km²
64–128	25–50
128–256	50–100
256–512	100–200
over 512	over 200
2–8	under 1
8–16	1–3
16–32	3–6
32–64	6–12
	12–25

■ Towns with over 1 000 000 inh.
500 000–1 000 000
● 200 000–500 000
○ 500 000

ATLANTIC OCEAN

BAHAMAS

Projection: Alber's Equal Area with two standard parallels

West from Greenwich

COPYRIGHT GEORGE PHILIP & SON LTD

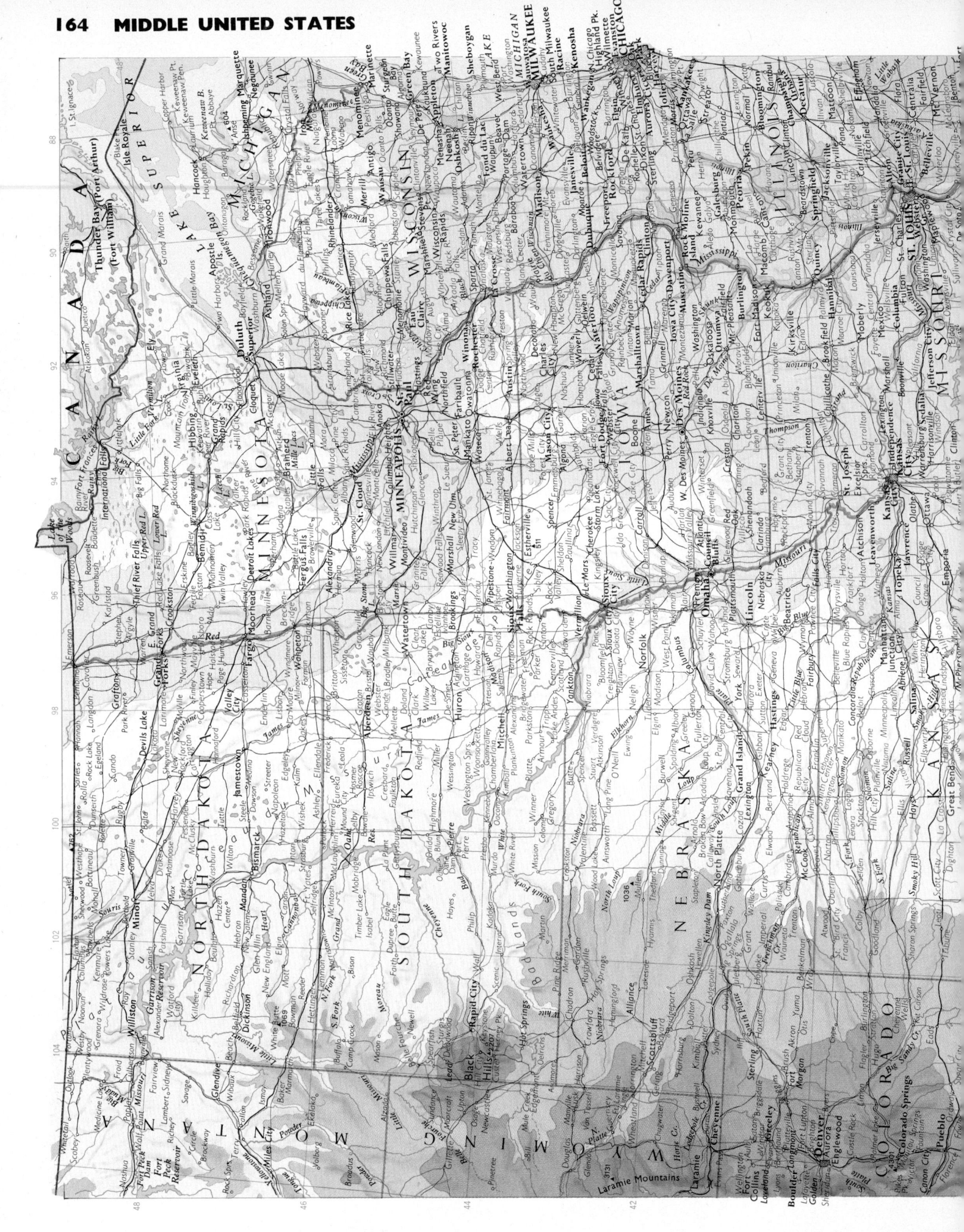
CANADA
LAKE SUPERIOR
LAKE MICHIGAN
MICHIGAN
WISCONSIN
MINNESOTA
NORTH DAKOTA
SOUTH DAKOTA
IOWA
ILLINOIS
NEBRASKA
MISSOURI
KANSAS
COLORADO
WYOMING
MONTANA
MILWAUKEE
CHICAGO
MINNEAPOLIS
St. Paul
Duluth
Superior
Des Moines
Omaha
Council Bluffs
Lincoln
Kansas City
ST. LOUIS
Denver
Colorado Springs
Pueblo
Cheyenne
Laramie Mountains
Black Hills
Bad Lands
Bismarck
Fargo
Sioux Falls
Sioux City
Rapid City
Thunder Bay (Port Arthur)
(Fort William)
Lake of the Woods
Mississippi
Missouri
Red
48
46
44
42
88
90
92
94
96
98
100
102
104

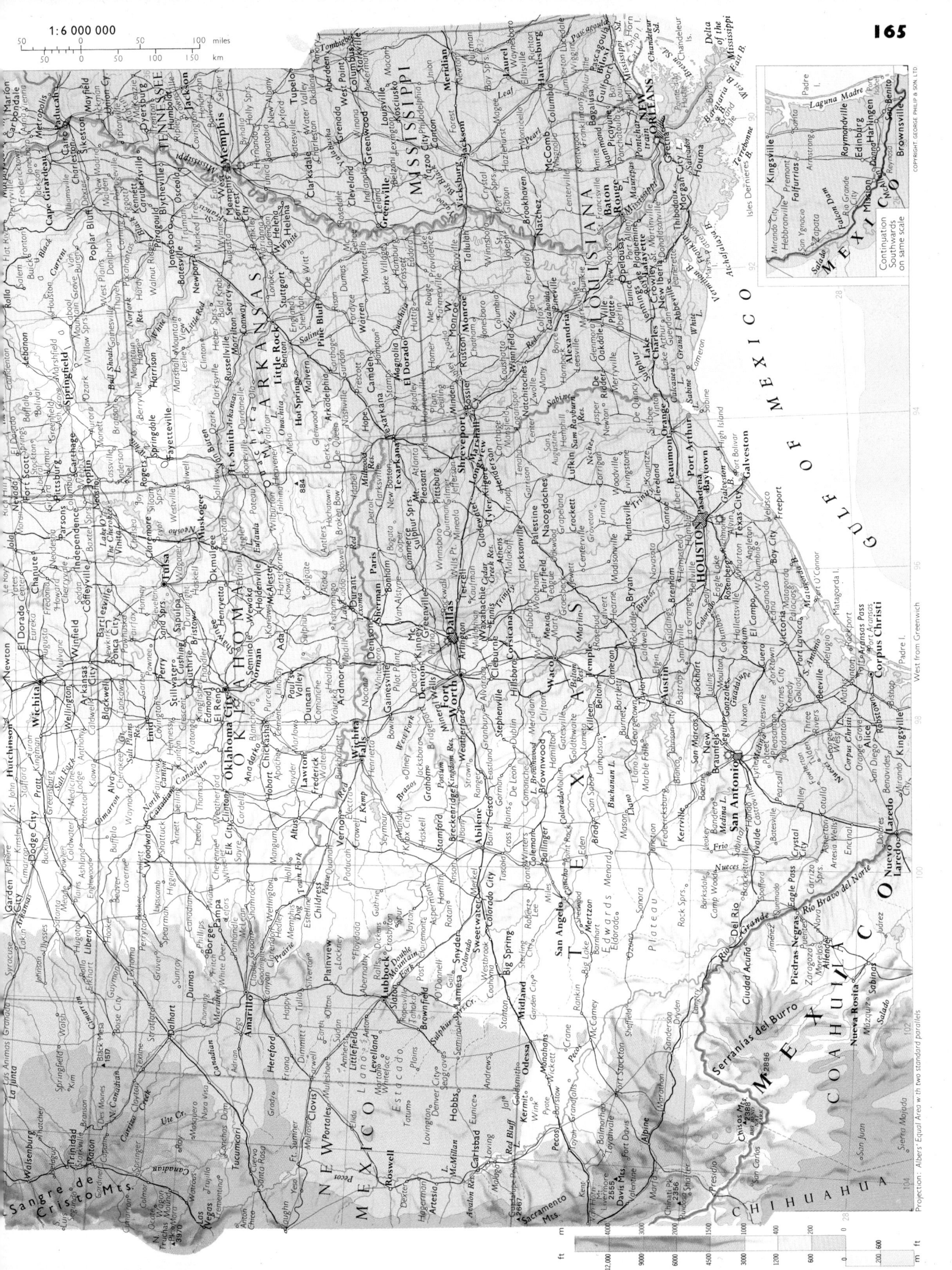
1:6 000 000
50 0 50 100 miles
50 0 50 100 150 km
OKLAHOMA
ARKANSAS
MISSISSIPPI
TENNESSEE
LOUISIANA
TEXAS
NEW MEXICO
MEXICO
COAHUILA
CHIHUAHUA
GULF OF MEXICO
Sangre de Cristo Mts.
Llano Estacado
Edwards Plateau
Serranías del Burro
Wichita
Tulsa
Oklahoma City
Little Rock
Memphis
Dallas
Fort Worth
Houston
San Antonio
Austin
New Orleans
Shreveport
Amarillo
Lubbock
Corpus Christi
Galveston
Beaumont
Baton Rouge
Jackson
Continuation Southwards on same scale
West from Greenwich
Projection: Albers' Equal Area with two standard parallels
COPYRIGHT. GEORGE PHILIP & SON, LTD.

1:6 000 000

50   0   50   100 miles
50   0 50 100 150 km

SASKATCHEWAN

ALBERTA

BRITISH COLUMBIA

MONTANA

WYOMING

IDAHO

Park Range

Medicine Bow Range

Bighorn Mountains

Wind River Range

Uinta Mountains

GREAT SALT LAKE

Salt Lake City

UTAH

NEVADA

Lewis Range

Bitterroot Range

Lemhi Range

Salmon River Mountains

Sapphire Mts.

Cabinet Mountains

Clearwater Mountains

Great Falls

Helena

Butte

Bozeman

Billings

Missoula

Anaconda

Spokane

WASHINGTON

Seattle

Tacoma

Olympia

Bremerton

Everett

Olympic Mts.

VANCOUVER

Juan de Fuca Strait

Yakima

Walla Walla

Pullman

Lewiston

Wenatchee

Pendleton

OREGON

Blue Mountains

Portland

Vancouver

Salem

Albany

Eugene

Bend

Medford

Klamath Falls

Coast Range

Warner

Boise

Nampa

Caldwell

Ontario

Idaho Falls

Pocatello

Twin Falls

Ogden

Provo

Reno

Sparks

Carson City

Lake Tahoe

Sacramento

CALIFORNIA

Independence Mts.

Ruby Mts.

Shoshone Mountains

Casper

Rawlins

Rock Springs

Green River

Sheridan

Yellowstone

Missouri

Columbia

Snake

Columbia R.

Fort Peck Reservoir

Franklin D. Roosevelt L.

Grand Coulee Dam

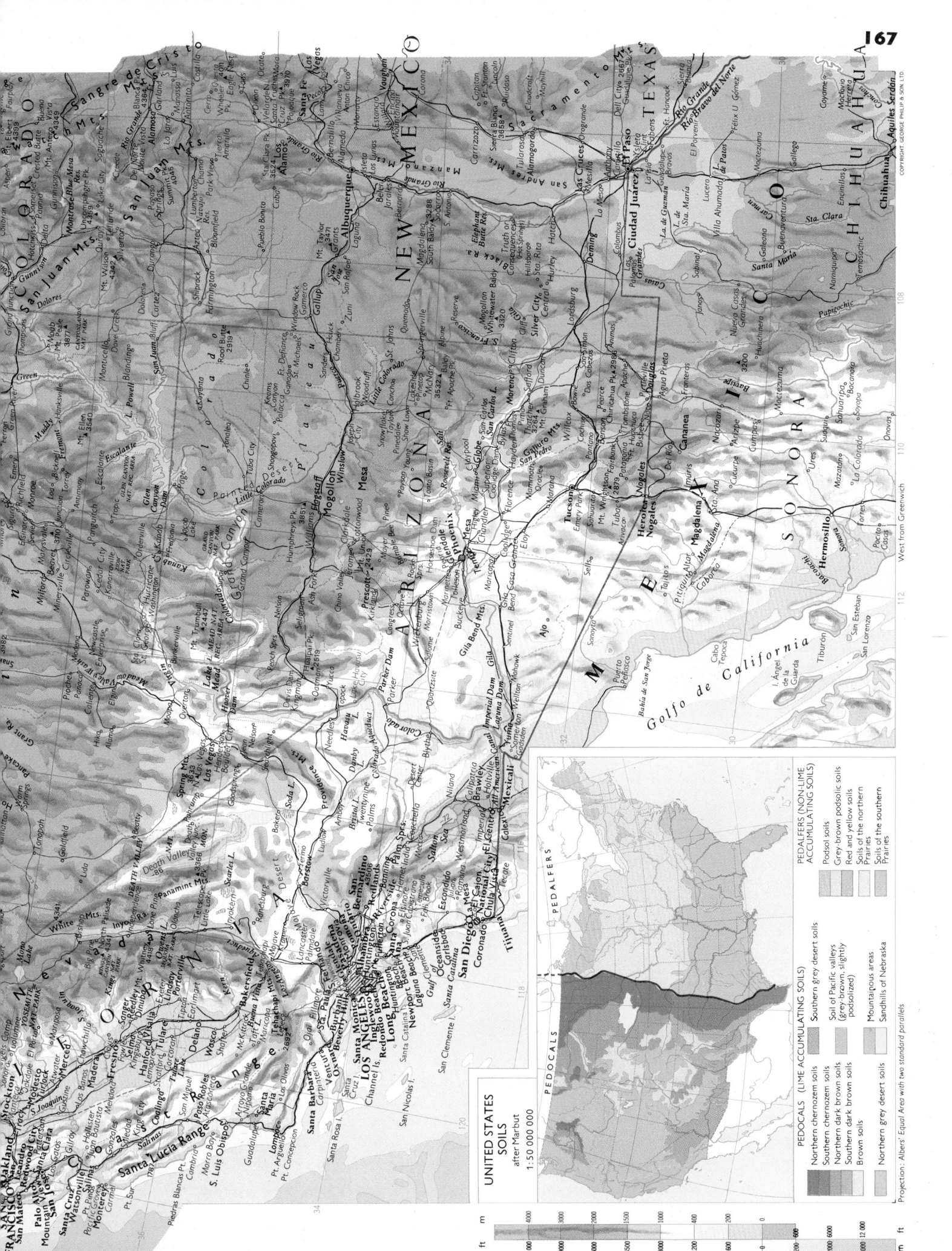

UNITED STATES
SOILS
after Marbut
1:50 000 000

PEDOCALS (LIME ACCUMULATING SOILS)

Northern chernozem soils
Southern chernozem soils
Northern dark brown soils
Southern dark brown soils
Brown soils
Northern grey desert soils

Southern grey desert soils
Soil of Pacific valleys
(grey-brown, slightly
podsolized)
Mountainous areas
Sandhills of Nebraska

PEDALFERS (NON-LIME ACCUMULATING SOILS)

Podsol soils
Grey-brown podsolic soils
Red and yellow soils
Soils of the northern Prairies
Soils of the southern Prairies

Projection: Albers' Equal Area with two standard parallels

COPYRIGHT GEORGE PHILIP & SON, LTD.

West from Greenwich

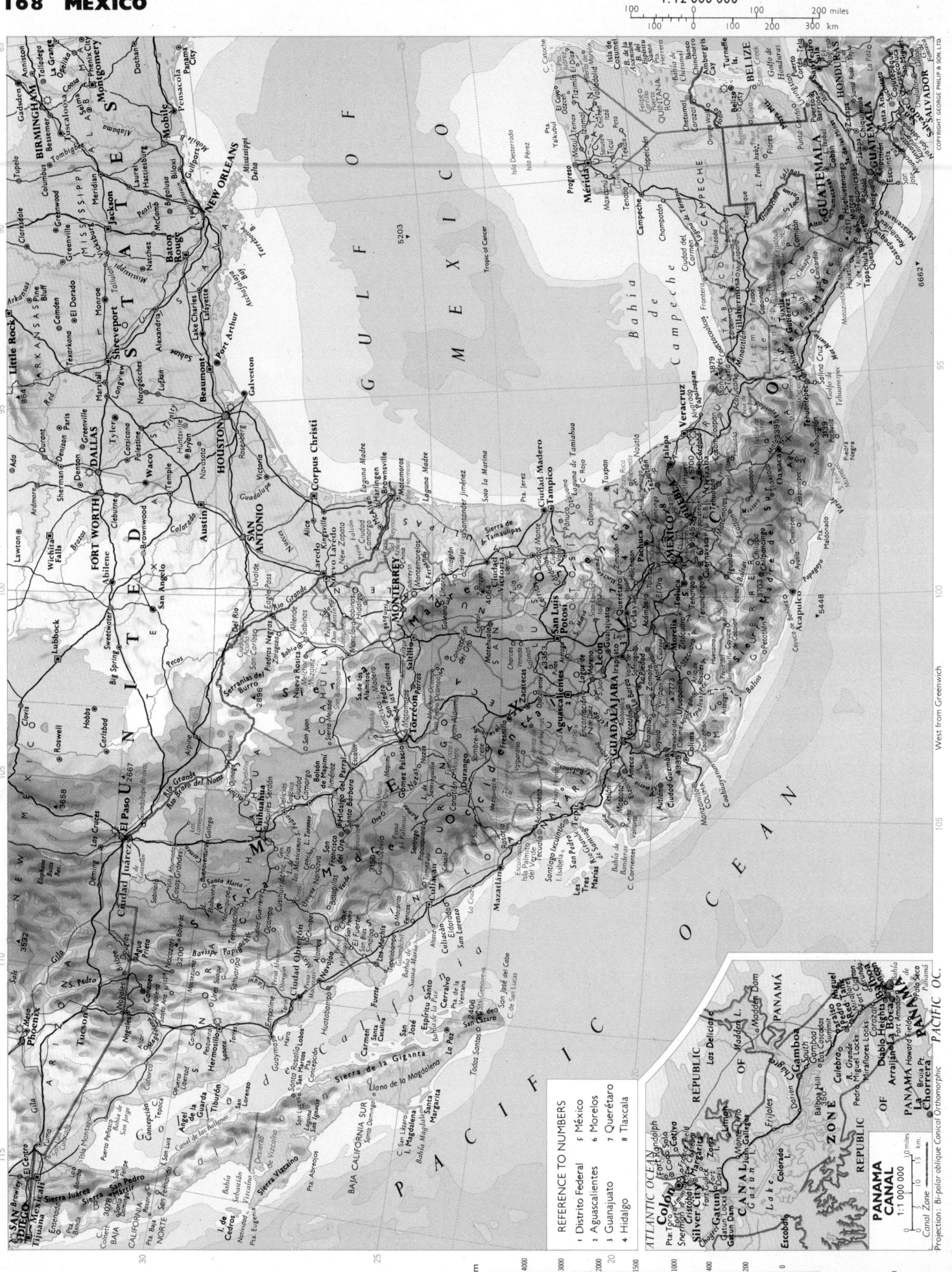

1:12 000 000

REFERENCE TO NUMBERS
1 Distrito Federal   5 México
2 Aguascalientes   6 Morelos
3 Guanajuato   7 Querétaro
4 Hidalgo   8 Tlaxcala

PANAMA
CANAL
1:1 000 000

Projection: Bi-polar oblique Conical Orthomorphic

COPYRIGHT GEORGE PHILIP & SON, LTD.

1:12 000 000

100   0   100   200 miles
100   0   100   200   300 km

WINDWARD ISLANDS 1:8 000 000

TRINIDAD & TOBAGO 1:8 000 000

JAMAICA 1:8 000 000

LEEWARD ISLANDS 1:8 000 000

BERMUDA 1:1 000 000

A T L A N T I C   O C E A N

C A R I B B E A N   S E A

GULF OF MEXICO

PACIFIC OCEAN

G R E A T E R   A N T I L L E S

L E S S E R   A N T I L L E S

WINDWARD ISLANDS

LEEWARD ISLANDS

BAHAMAS

CUBA

HISPANIOLA

HAITI

DOMINICAN REP.

JAMAICA

PUERTO RICO (U.S.A.)

MEXICO

HONDURAS

NICARAGUA

COSTA RICA

PANAMA

CANAL ZONE (U.S.A.)

COLOMBIA

VENEZUELA

GUYANA

La Habana
Santiago de Cuba
Santo Domingo
Port-au-Prince
Kingston
San Juan
Nassau
Port of Spain
Caracas
Maracaibo
Barranquilla
Cartagena
Barquisimeto
Valencia
Managua
Tegucigalpa
San José
Panamá
Bucaramanga

GREAT BAHAMA BANK

Tropic of Cancer

MIAMI
FLORIDA
West Palm Beach
Fort Lauderdale
Key West
Sarasota
Fort Myers

TRINIDAD
TOBAGO
BARBADOS
Bridgetown
GRENADA
St. George's
ST. VINCENT
Kingstown
ST. LUCIA
Castries
MARTINIQUE
Fort-de-France
DOMINICA
Roseau
GUADELOUPE
Basse-Terre
ANTIGUA
St. John's
MONTSERRAT
Plymouth
NEVIS
ST. CHRISTOPHER
Basseterre
BARBUDA
ANGUILLA
St. Martin
St. Barthélemy
St. Eustatius
Saba
St. Croix
St. Thomas
VIRGIN ISLANDS

West from Greenwich

Projection: Bi-polar oblique Conical Orthomorphic

COPYRIGHT GEORGE PHILIP & SON LTD.

m ft (elevation scale)
6000 18 000
4000 12 000
3000 9000
2000 6000
1500 4500
1000 3000
600 1800
400 1200
200 600
0 0

1:30 000 000

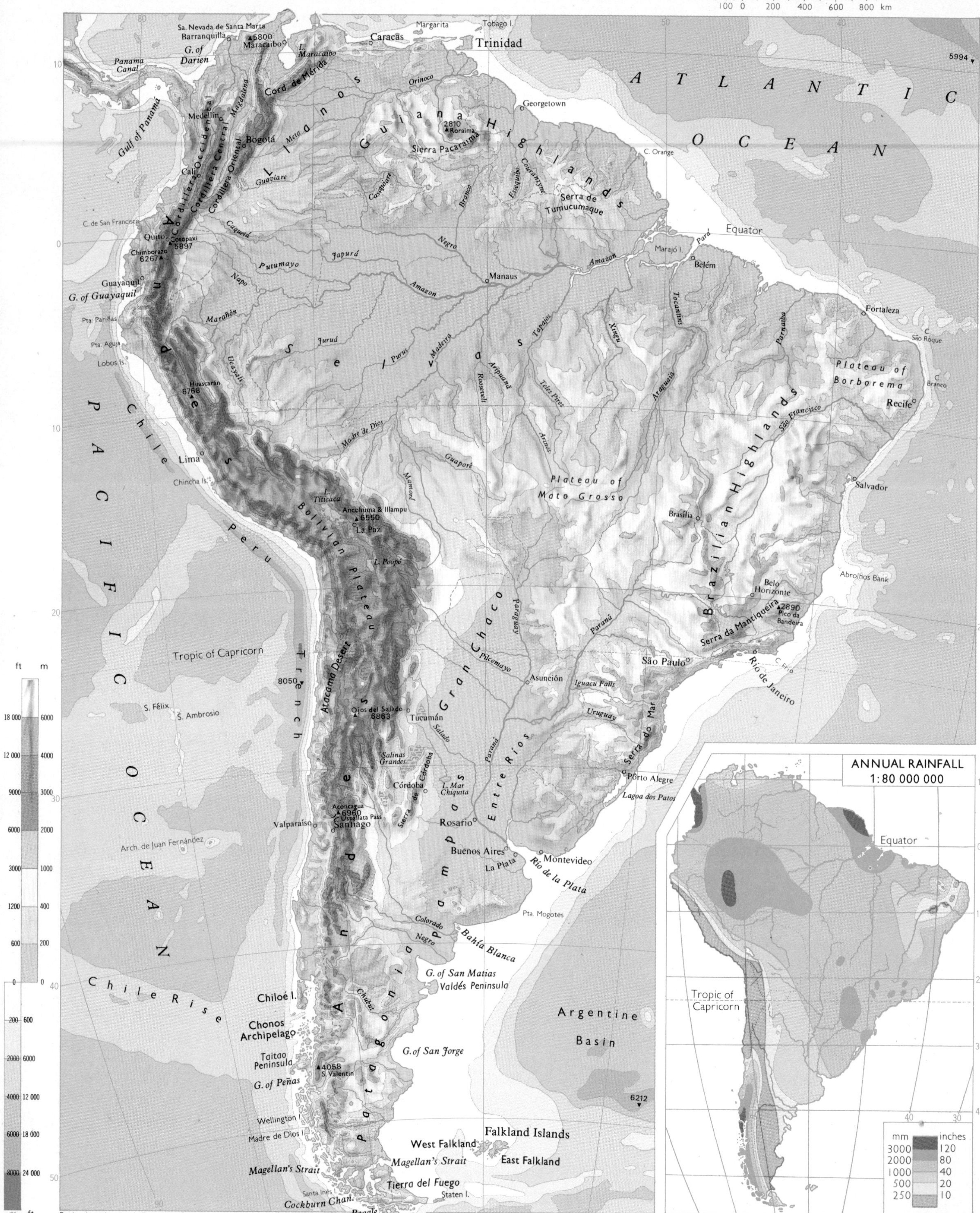

100   0   100   200   300   400   500 miles
100   0   200   400   600   800 km

5994

ATLANTIC OCEAN

Sa. Nevada de Santa Marta
Barranquilla
▲5800
Maracaibo
G. of Darien
Panama Canal
Margarita
Tobago I.
Caracas
Trinidad
L. Maracaibo
Cord. de Mérida
Georgetown
Medellin
Llanos
Orinoco
C. Orange
Cali
Bogotá
Guiana Highlands
2810
Roraima
Sierra Pacaraima
Serra de Tumucumaque
Gulf of Panama
Cordillera Occidental
Cordillera Central
Magdalena
Cordillera Oriental
Meta
Guaviare
Casiquiare
Branco
Cassiquiare
Essequibo
Caratayana
C. de San Francisco
Quito
Cotopaxi
5897
Coqueá
Negro
Equator
Pará
Marajó I.
Belém
Chimborazo
6267
Putumayo
Japurá
Amazon
Manaus
Amazon
Guayaquil
Napo
G. of Guayaquil
Marañón
Amazon
Tocantins
Fortaleza
São Roque
Pta. Pariñas
Juruá
Purus
Madeira
Aripuanã
Xingu
Parnaíba
Pta. Aguja
Ucayali
Roosevelt
Teles Pires
Araguaia
Tapajós
Plateau of Borborema
Lobos Is.
Recife
C. Branco
A   n   d   e   s
S   e   l   v   a   s
Huascarán
6768
Madre de Dios
Guaporé
São Francisco
Arinos
Salvador
Lima
Mamoré
Plateau of Mato Grosso
Titicaca
Ancohuma & Illampu
6550
La Paz
Brasília
Belo Horizonte
2890
Pico da Bandeira
Serra da Mantiqueira
Bolivian Plateau
L. Poopó
Abrolhos Bank
PACIFIC
Chile
Peru
Tropic of Capricorn
Gran Chaco
Paraguay
Paraná
São Paulo
Rio de Janeiro
C. Frio
Serra do Mar
French Trench
8050
Atacama Desert
Ojos del Salado
6863
Tucumán
Salado
Pilcomayo
Asunción
Iguaçu Falls
Uruguay
S. Félix
S. Ambrosio
Salinas Grandes
Entre Rios
Pôrto Alegre
Córdoba
L. Mar Chiquita
Lagoa dos Patos
Arch. de Juan Fernández
Aconcagua
6960
Uspallata Pass
Sierra de Córdoba
Rosario
Equator
Valparaíso
Santiago
Buenos Aires
Montevideo
La Plata
Río de la Plata
Pta. Mogotes
PACIFIC OCEAN
P   a   m   p   a   s
Chile Rise
Colorado
Negro
Bahía Blanca
Tropic of Capricorn
Chiloé I.
G. of San Matias
Valdés Peninsula
Chubut
A   n   d   e   s
Argentine Basin
Chonos Archipelago
Taitao Peninsula
G. of San Jorge
Patagonia
G. of Peñas
4058
S. Valentin
6212
Wellington I.
Madre de Dios I.
Falkland Islands
West Falkland
East Falkland
Santa Inés I.
Magellan's Strait
Magellan's Strait
Tierra del Fuego
Staten I.
Cockburn Chan.
Beagle Chan.
C. Horn

West from Greenwich

Projection: Lambert's Equivalent Azimuthal

COPYRIGHT. GEORGE PHILIP & SON. LTD.

ANNUAL RAINFALL
1:80 000 000

Equator

Tropic of Capricorn

mm	inches
3000	120
2000	80
1000	40
500	20
250	10

ft	m
18 000	6000
12 000	4000
9000	3000
6000	2000
3000	1000
1200	400
600	200
0	0
600	200
6000	2000
12 000	4000
18 000	6000
24 000	8000

m   ft

1:40 000 000

150   0   150 300 450 600 750 900 miles
200   0   200 400 600 800 1000 1200 1400 km

JULY TEMPERATURE
1:80 000 000

Equator
Tropic of Capricorn

25° 20° 20° 15° 10° 5° 0°
30°
25° 20° 15°
10° 5°
15°

JANUARY TEMPERATURE
1:80 000 000

Equator
Tropic of Capricorn

25° 20° 20° 15° 10°
25°
20°
30°
20° 15° 10°
25° 15° 10°

ACTUAL SURFACE TEMPERATURE

°C	°F
30	86
25	77
20	68
15	59
10	50
5	41
0	32

25° Isotherms reduced to Sea-level
30° reduced to Sea-level
Celsius

RAINFALL May to October
1:80,000,000

HIGH
1024 1020
1016
1012
1016
1012
LOW
1008
LOW
1020

1020 July Isobars in millibars
→ Prevailing Winds

COPYRIGHT GEORGE PHILIP & SON LTD

Equator
Tropic of Capricorn

RAINFALL November to April
1:80 000 000

1012
1012
LOW
1008
1004
LOW
1000
1016
HIGH
1020
1012
1008

1020 January Isobars in millibars
→ Prevailing Winds

Equator
Tropic of Capricorn

RAINFALL

mm	inches
1500	60
1000	40
750	30
500	20
250	10
125	5

NATURAL VEGETATION
after Engler, Denis and others

FOREST VEGETATION

- Selvas Tropical Forest (hevea rubber, palms, castanha, lianas)
- Andean Tropical Forest (cinchona, palms, tree-fern, maquis)
- Brazilian Montane Tropical Forest (palms, tree-fern, bamboos)
- Andean Temperate Rain Forest (araucaria, beech, epiphytes)
- Catinga Xerophilous Forest (mimosa, cacti)
- Chilean Sclerophyllous Woodland (cypress, acacias, laurels, cacti)
- Chaco Xerophilous Woodlands (quebracho, mimosa scrub)
- Cerrados Sub-tropical Forest (araucaria—in south)
- North Chaco Savanna
- Marsh subject to inundation
- --- Limit of Araucaria brasiliensis
- —— South Limit of Quebracho
- —— South Limit of Hevea (wild rubber)

GRASS VEGETATION

- Tropical Grasslands (llanos and campos, with gallery woods)
- Sub-tropical and Temperate Grasslands

STEPPE, SCRUB AND DESERT VEGETATION

- Xerophilous Scrub, Steppe (thorn and other drought-resisting plants)
- Patagonian Steppe (thorn bushes)
- Andean Plateau Steppe
- Paramos Steppe
- Dry Puna Steppe
- Arid Tola Steppe
- Atacama Lomas (subject to sea-fogs; occasional pasturage)
- Atacama Desert
- Salt Swamps
- Sub-antarctic Steppe and Andean Ice Desert

Equator
Tropic of Capricorn
West from 60° Greenwich

Projection: Lambert's Equivalent Azimuthal.

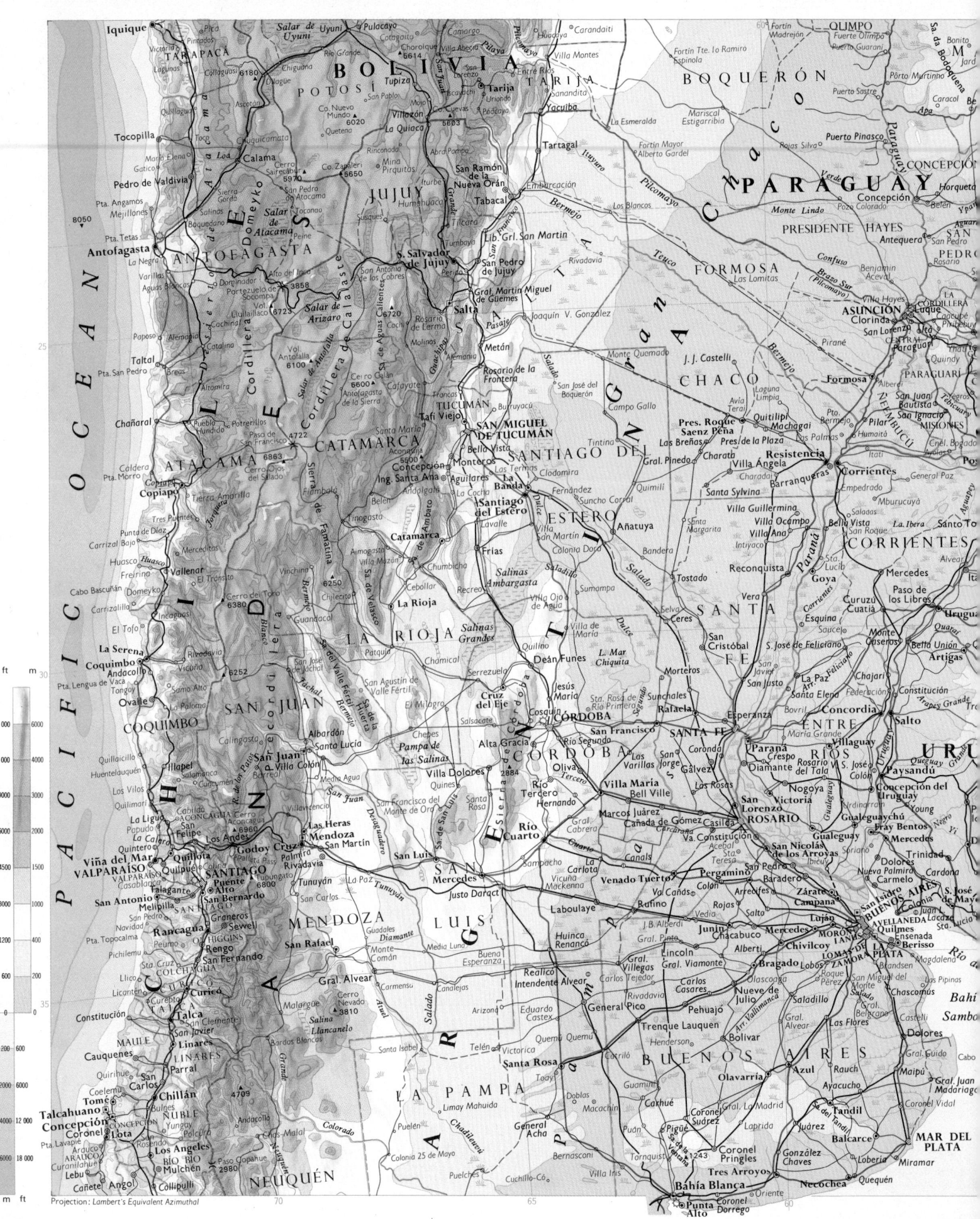
BOLIVIA
PARAGUAY
URU
PACIFIC OCEAN
CHILE
ANDES
ARGENTINA
Gran Chaco
Atacama
Desierto de Atacama
Cordillera Domeyko
POTOSÍ
TARIJA
TARAPACÁ
ANTOFAGASTA
ATACAMA
COQUIMBO
JUJUY
SALTA
CATAMARCA
TUCUMÁN
LA RIOJA
SAN JUAN
MENDOZA
SAN LUIS
CÓRDOBA
SANTIAGO DEL ESTERO
CHACO
FORMOSA
SANTA FE
ENTRE RÍOS
CORRIENTES
BUENOS AIRES
LA PAMPA
NEUQUÉN
BOQUERÓN
PRESIDENTE HAYES
CONCEPCIÓN
Iquique
Tocopilla
Pedro de Valdivia
Calama
Antofagasta
Taltal
Chañaral
Copiapó
Vallenar
La Serena
Coquimbo
Ovalle
Illapel
Viña del Mar
VALPARAÍSO
SANTIAGO
San Antonio
Rancagua
Curicó
Talca
Linares
Cauquenes
Chillán
Talcahuano
Concepción
Los Angeles
Tupiza
Tarija
Villazón
Yacuiba
La Quiaca
S. Salvador de Jujuy
Salta
SAN MIGUEL DE TUCUMÁN
Catamarca
La Rioja
San Juan
Mendoza
San Rafael
San Luis
Río Cuarto
CÓRDOBA
Santiago del Estero
SANTA FE
ROSARIO
Paraná
Resistencia
Corrientes
Formosa
ASUNCIÓN
Concepción
Paysandú
Salto
Concordia
BUENOS AIRES
LA PLATA
MAR DEL PLATA
Bahía Blanca
Tandil
Santa Rosa
Aconcagua 6960
Salar de Uyuni
Salar de Atacama
Salinas Grandes
Projection: Lambert's Equivalent Azimuthal

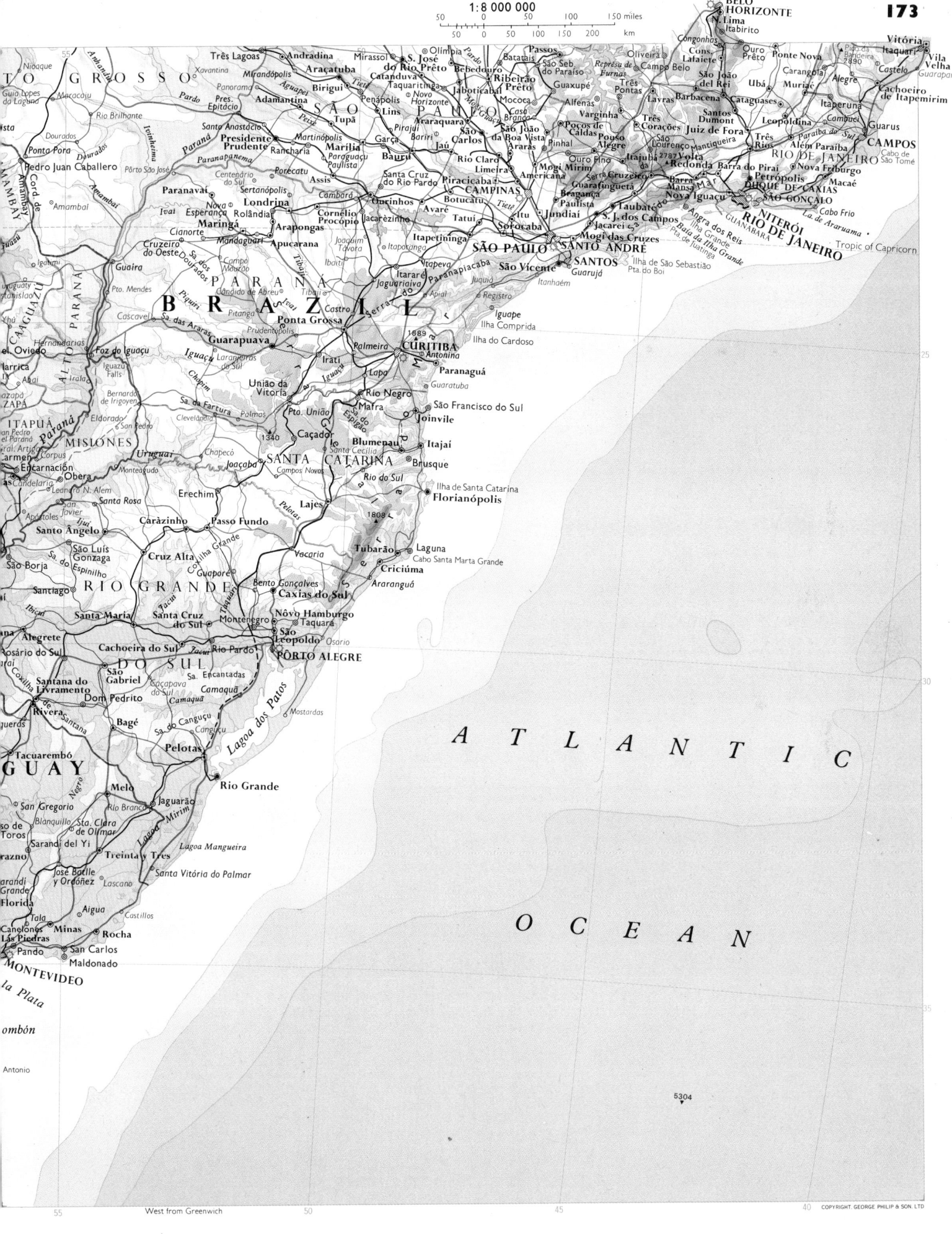

1:8 000 000
50 0 50 100 150 miles
50 0 50 100 150 200 km
BELO HORIZONTE
N. Lima
Itabirito
Vitória
Vila Velha
Guarapari
Castelo
Cachoeiro de Itapemirim
Guarus
CAMPOS
Cabo de São Tomé
Macaé
Cabo Frio
La. de Araruama
Nova Friburgo
Petrópolis
DUQUE DE CAXIAS
SÃO GONÇALO
NITERÓI
RIO DE JANEIRO
GUANABARA
Tropic of Capricorn
Nova Iguaçu
Barra Mansa
Volta Redonda
Barra do Piraí
Três Rios
Além Paraíba
RIO DE JANEIRO
Itaperuna
Cambuci
Leopoldina
Cataguases
Juiz de Fora
Santos Dumont
Barbacena
São João del Rei
Ubá
Muriaé
Carangola
Alegre
Ponte Nova
Ouro Prêto
Cons. Lafaiete
Congonhas
Oliveira
Campo Belo
Represa de Furnas
Lavras
Três Pontas
Três Corações
Varginha
Alfenas
São Lourenço
Mantiqueira
Itajubá
2787
Cruzeiro
Guaratinguetá
Taubaté
S. J. dos Campos
Jacareí
Mogi das Cruzes
Angra dos Reis
Ilha Grande
Baía da Ilha Grande
Pta. de Juatinga
Ilha de São Sebastião
Pta. do Boi
SANTOS
Guarujá
São Vicente
SANTO ANDRÉ
SÃO PAULO
Itanhaém
Sorocaba
Itu
Jundiaí
Bragança Paulista
CAMPINAS
Americana
Limeira
Piracicaba
Mogi Mirim
Ouro Fino
Pouso Alegre
Poços de Caldas
São João da Boa Vista
Pinhal
Araras
Rio Claro
São Carlos
Araraquara
Jaú
Bauru
Garça
Marília
Lins
Penápolis
Birigui
Araçatuba
Andradina
Três Lagoas
Mirassol
S. José do Rio Prêto
Olímpia
Bebedouro
Barretos
Passos
São Seb. do Paraíso
Guaxupé
Ribeirão Prêto
Jaboticabal
Mococa
Casa Branca
Catanduva
Taquaritinga
Novo Horizonte
SÃO PAULO
Tupã
Adamantina
Pres. Epitácio
Presidente Prudente
Rancharia
Paraguaçu Paulista
Assis
Santa Cruz do Rio Pardo
Ourinhos
Avaré
Botucatu
Tatuí
Itapetininga
Itapeva
Itararé
Jaguariaíva
Paranapiacaba
Cornélio Procópio
Jacarèzinho
Londrina
Arapongas
Apucarana
Rolândia
Maringá
Mandaguari
Cianorte
Paranavaí
Nova Esperança
Cruzeiro do Oeste
Campo Mourão
PARANÁ
BRAZIL
Ponta Grossa
Castro
Guarapuava
Cascavel
Foz do Iguaçu
Iguazu Falls
Guaíra
Pto. Mendes
Palmeira
CURITIBA
1889
Antonina
Paranaguá
Guaratuba
Iguape
Ilha Comprida
Ilha do Cardoso
Registro
Irati
Lapa
Rio Negro
Mafra
União da Vitória
Pto. União
São Francisco do Sul
Joinvile
Caçador
1340
Blumenau
Itajaí
Brusque
SANTA CATARINA
Joaçaba
Chapecó
Campos Novos
Rio do Sul
Ilha de Santa Catarina
Florianópolis
Lajes
1808
Tubarão
Laguna
Cabo Santa Marta Grande
Criciúma
Araranguá
Erechim
Passo Fundo
Carazinho
Cruz Alta
Vacaria
Guaporé
Bento Gonçalves
Caxias do Sul
Nôvo Hamburgo
Taquara
São Leopoldo
Osório
PÔRTO ALEGRE
Montenegro
Santa Cruz do Sul
Santa Maria
Cachoeira do Sul
Rio Pardo
RIO GRANDE DO SUL
São Gabriel
Caçapava do Sul
Camaquã
Sa. Encantadas
Mostardas
Lagoa dos Patos
Pelotas
Canguçu
Rio Grande
Bagé
Dom Pedrito
Santana do Livramento
Rivera
Alegrete
Rosário do Sul
Santiago
São Borja
São Luís Gonzaga
Santo Ângelo
Santa Rosa
Obera
Encarnación
Posadas
MISIONES
ITAPUÁ
Eldorado
Tacuarembó
URUGUAY
Melo
Jaguarão
Lagoa Mirim
Lagoa Mangueira
Santa Vitória do Palmar
Treinta y Tres
Sarandí del Yi
San Gregorio
Río Branco
Sta. Clara de Olimar
José Batlle y Ordóñez
Lascano
Aigua
Castillos
Minas
Rocha
San Carlos
Maldonado
Pando
Canelones
Las Piedras
Florida
MONTEVIDEO
la Plata
MATO GROSSO
Ponta Porã
Pedro Juan Caballero
Dourados
Amambaí
ATLANTIC OCEAN
5304
West from Greenwich
55 50 45 40

COPYRIGHT. GEORGE PHILIP & SON. LTD

1:16 000 000

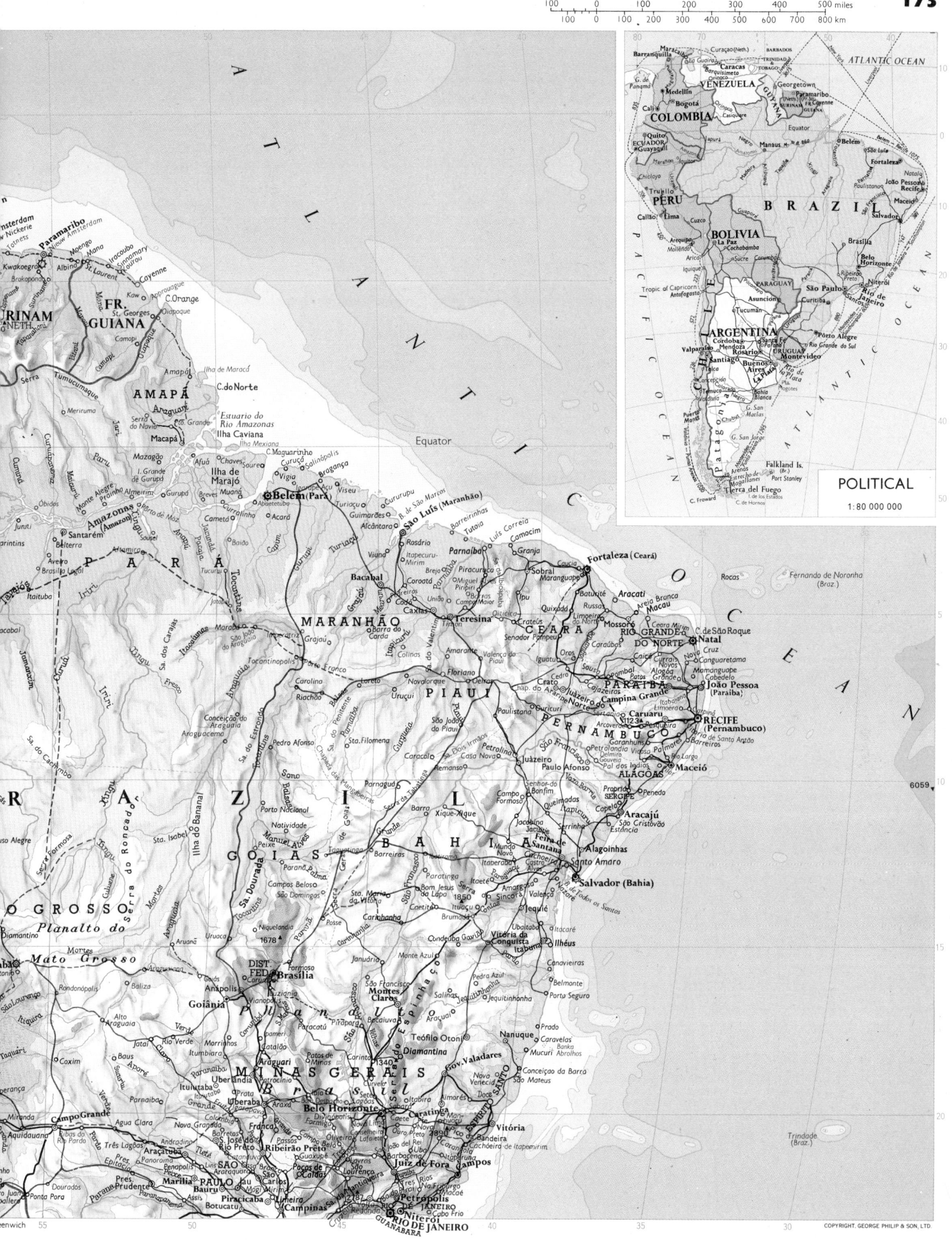

100 0 100 200 300 400 500 miles
100 0 100 200 300 400 500 600 700 800 km
ATLANTIC OCEAN
Equator
BRAZIL
PARÁ
MARANHÃO
PIAUI
CEARÁ
RIO GRANDE DO NORTE
PARAIBA
PERNAMBUCO
ALAGOAS
SERGIPE
BAHIA
GOIAS
MINAS GERAIS
ESPIRITO SANTO
SÃO PAULO
MATO GROSSO
AMAPÁ
FR. GUIANA
SURINAM
NETH.
Paramaribo
Cayenne
Macapá
Belém (Pará)
São Luís (Maranhão)
Fortaleza (Ceará)
Teresina
Natal
João Pessoa (Paraíba)
Campina Grande
RECIFE (Pernambuco)
Maceió
Aracajú
Salvador (Bahia)
Feira de Santana
Ilhéus
Vitória da Conquista
Brasília
DIST. FED.
Goiânia
Anápolis
Belo Horizonte
Montes Claros
Uberlândia
Uberaba
Ribeirão Preto
Juiz de Fora
Vitória
Campos
Petrópolis
Niterói
RIO DE JANEIRO
GUANABARA
Campinas
Campo Grande
Santarém
Ilha de Marajó
Estuario do Rio Amazonas
Ilha Caviana
Amazonas (Amazon)
Tocantins
Araguaia
São Francisco
Planalto do Mato Grosso
Chapada das Mangabeiras
Serra do Espinhaço
Fernando de Noronha (Braz.)
Rocas
Trindade (Braz.)
6059
C. do Norte
C. de São Roque
POLITICAL
1:80 000 000
VENEZUELA
COLOMBIA
GUYANA
SURINAM
FR. GUIANA
ECUADOR
PERU
BOLIVIA
PARAGUAY
BRAZIL
CHILE
ARGENTINA
URUGUAY
PACIFIC OCEAN
ATLANTIC OCEAN
Tropic of Capricorn
Falkland Is. (Br.)
Tierra del Fuego
Patagonia
Caracas
Bogotá
Quito
Lima
La Paz
Asunción
Buenos Aires
Montevideo
Santiago
São Paulo
Rio de Janeiro
Manaus

COPYRIGHT, GEORGE PHILIP & SON, LTD.

1:16 000 000

100 50 0 100 200 300 miles

100 0 100 200 300 400 km

PARAGUAY

PARANÁ

BRAZIL

SANTA CATARINA

RIO GRANDE DO SUL

URUGUAY

Asunción

Curitiba

São Paulo

RIO DE JANEIRO

Santiago

Valparaíso

Viña del Mar

Córdoba

Rosario

BUENOS AIRES

MONTEVIDEO

Mar del Plata

Bahía Blanca

Neuquén

Valdivia

Puerto Montt

Comodoro Rivadavia

Río Gallegos

Tierra del Fuego

Cabo de Hornos (C. Horn)

SOUTH ATLANTIC OCEAN

Tropic of Capricorn

Peru–Chile Trench

FALKLAND ISLANDS (ISLAS MALVINAS) (Br.)

West Falkland

East Falkland

Stanley

Estrecho de Magallanes (Magellan's Str.)

Projection: Sanson-Flamsteed's Sinusoidal

70   65   60 West from Greenwich 55

ft   m

18 000 6000

12 000 4000

9000   3000

4500   1500

3000   1000

1200   400

600   200

0   0

200   600

2000   6000

4000   12 000

6000   18 000

8000   24 000

m   ft

DENSITY OF POPULATION

1:80 000 000

Inhabitants	per mile²	per km²
	under 2	under 1
	2–8	1–3
	8–16	3–6
	16–32	6–12
	32–64	12–25
	64–128	25–50
	over 128	over 50

■ Cities with over 1 000 000 inhabitants

● Cities with 500 000 – 1 000 000 inhabitants

• Cities with 200 000 – 500 000 inhabitants

COPYRIGHT GEORGE PHILIP & SON. LTD

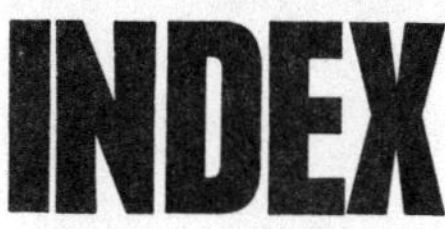

INDEX

Index

ABBREVIATIONS

Afghan. – *Afghanistan*
Afr. – *Africa, African*
Ala. – *Alabama*
Alas. – *Alaska*
Alb. – *Albania*
Alg. – *Algeria*
Alta. – *Alberta*
Amaz. – *Amazonas*
Amer. – *America*
And. P. – *Andhra Pradesh*
Ang. – *Angola*
Ant. – *Antarctica*
Arab. – *Arabia*
Arch. – *Archipelago*
Arg. – *Argentina*
Ariz. – *Arizona*
Ark. – *Arkansas*
A.S.S.R. – *Autonomous Soviet Socialist Republic*
Aust. – *Austria*
Austral. – *Australia*
B. – *Bay, Bight, (Baie, Bahia, Baia)*
B.C. – *British Columbia*
Bav. – *Bavaria (Bayern)*
Beds. – *Bedfordshire*
Belg. – *Belgium*
Beng. – *Bengal*
Berks. – *Berkshire*
Bg. – *Berg.*
Bk. – *Bank*
Bol. – *Bolivia*
Bots. – *Botswana*
Br., Brit. – *British, Britain*
Braz. – *Brazil*
Bucks. – *Buckinghamshire*
Bulg. – *Bulgaria*
C. – *Cape (Cabo), Coast*
Calif. – *California*
Cam. – *Cameroon*
Cambod. – *Cambodia*
Cambs. – *Cambridgeshire & Isle of Ely*
Can. – *Canada, Canal*
Can. Is. – *Canary Islands*
Cant. – *Canton*
Cards. – *Cardiganshire*
Cas. – *Castle*
Cent. – *Central*
Cey. – *Ceylon*
Chan. – *Channel*
Ches. – *Cheshire*
Co. – *County*
Col. – *Colombia, Colony*
Colo. – *Colorado*
Conn. – *Connecticut*
C. Prov. – *Cape Province*
Cr. – *Creek*
C. Rica – *Costa Rica*
Cumb. – *Cumberland*
Cz. – *Czechoslovakia*
D.C. – *District of Columbia*
Del. – *Delaware*
Den. – *Denmark*
Dépt. – *Département, Department*
Des. – *Desert*
Dist. – *District*
Div. – *Division*
Dj. – *Djebel*
Dom. Rep. – *Dominican Republic*
E. – *East*
Ec. – *Ecuador*
Eg. – *Egypt*
Eng. – *England*
Est. – *Estuary*
Eur. – *Europe*
Falk. Is. – *Falkland Islands*
Fd. – *Fiord, Fjord*
Fed. – *Federal, Federation*
Fin. – *Finland*
Fla. – *Florida*
For. – *Forest*
Fr. – *France, French*
Fr. Gui. – *French Guiana*
Fs. – *Falls*
Ft. – *Fort*
G. – *Gulf, Gebel*
Ga. – *Georgia*
Gam. – *Gambia*
Ger. – *Germany*
Gl. – *Glacier*
Glos. – *Gloucestershire*
Gr. – *Greece*
Green. – *Greenland*
Grn. – *Green*
Grp. – *Group*
Gt. – *Great*
Guat. – *Guatemala*
Guin. – *Guinea*
Guy. – *Guyana*
Hants. – *Hampshire*
Hr., Harb. – *Harbor, Harbour*
Hd. – *Head*
Here. – *Herefordshire*
Herts. – *Hertfordshire*
Him. P. – *Himachal Pradesh*
Ho. – *House*
Hond. – *Honduras*
Hs. – *Hills*
Hts. – *Heights*
Hung. – *Hungary*
Hunt. – *Huntingdon & Peterborough*
I.(s) – *Island(s) (Isle, Ile)*
Ice. – *Iceland*
Ill. – *Illinois*
Ind. – *Indiana*
Indon. – *Indonesia*
I. of M. – *Isle of Man*
I. of W. – *Isle of Wight*
Ire. – *Ireland*
Isr. – *Israel*
Isth. – *Isthmus*
It. – *Italy*
J. – *Jebel, Jabal*
Jam. – *Jamaica*
Jap. – *Japan*
Jc., Junc. – *Junction*
Kans. – *Kansas*
King. – *Kingdom*
Ky. – *Kentucky*
L. – *Lake, Lough, Loch, Lago*
La. – *Louisiana*
Lab. – *Labrador*
Lag. – *Lagoon, Laguna, Lagôa*
Lancs. – *Lancashire*
Ld. – *Land*
Leics. – *Leicestershire*
Les. – *Lesotho*
Lib. – *Liberia*
Lim. – *Limerick*
Lincs. – *Lincolnshire*
Lit. – *Little*
Lr. – *Lower*
Lux. – *Luxembourg*
Mad. – *Madras*
Mad. P. – *Madhya Pradesh*
Mal. – *Malawi*
Malag. – *Malagasy Republic*
Malay. – *Malaysia*
Man. – *Manitoba*
Mass. – *Massachusetts*
Maur. – *Mauritania*
Md. – *Maryland*
Me. – *Maine*
Medit. – *Mediterranean*
Mex. – *Mexico*
M. Grosso – *Mato Grosso*
Mich. (U.S.A.) – *Michigan*
Mich. (Mexico) – *Michoacan*
Mid. – *Middle*
Min. Ger. – *Minas Gerais*
Minn. – *Minnesota*
Miss. – *Mississippi*
Mo. – *Missouri*
Mon. – *Monmouthshire*
Mong. – *Mongolia*
Mont. – *Montana*
Mor. – *Morocco*
Mozam. – *Mozambique*
Mt. – *Mountain, Mount*
Mte. – *Monte*
Mth. – *Mouth*
Mti. – *Monti*
Mts. – *Mountains, Monts.*
Mus. & 'O. – *'Oman*
Mys. – *Mysore*
N. – *North, Northern*
Nat. – *Natal, National*
N.B. – *New Brunswick*
N.C. – *North Carolina*
N.D. – *North Dakota*
Neb. – *Nebraska*
Neth. – *Netherlands*
Nev. – *Nevada*
Newf. – *Newfoundland*
N. Guin. – *New Guinea, Terr. of,*
N.H. – *New Hampshire*
Nic. – *Nicaragua*
Nig. – *Nigeria*
N.J. – *New Jersey*
N. Mex. – *New Mexico*
Nor. – *Norway*
Northants. – *Northamptonshire*
Northumb. – *Northumberland*
Notts. – *Nottinghamshire*
N.S. – *Nova Scotia*
N.S.W. – *New South Wales*
N.Y. – *New York*
N.Z. – *New Zealand*
O. – *Oasis*
Oc. – *Ocean*
O.F.S. – *Orange Free State*
Okla. – *Oklahoma*
Ont. – *Ontario*
Oreg. – *Oregon*
P. – *Paso, Pass, Passo*
Pa. – *Pennsylvania*
Pac. – *Pacific*
Pak. – *Pakistan*
Pan. – *Panama*
Par. – *Paraguay*
Pass. – *Passage*
P.E.I. – *Prince Edward Island*
Pen. – *Peninsula*
Phil. – *Philippines*
Pk. – *Peak, Park*
Pl. – *Plain, Planina*
Plat. – *Plateau*
Pol. – *Poland*
Port. – *Portugal, Portuguese*
Préf. – *Préfecture*
P. Rico – *Puerto Rico*
Prom. – *Promontory*
Prot. – *Protectorate*
Prov. – *Province, Provincial*
Pt. – *Point, Port*
Pta. – *Punta (Point)*
Pte. – *Pointe (Point)*
Pto. – *Porto, Puerto (Port)*
Que. – *Quebec*
Queens. – *Queensland*
R. – *River, Rio*
Ra. – *Range*
Raj. – *Rajasthan*
Rd. – *Road*
Reg. – *Region*
Rep. – *Republic*
Res. – *Reserve, Reservoir*
Rf. – *Reef*
Rhod. – *Rhodesia*
R.I. – *Rhode Island*
Rks. – *Rocks*
Rosc. – *Roscommon*
R.S.F.S.R. – *Russian Soviet Federal Socialist Republic*
Rum. – *Rumania*
S. – *Sea, South*
Sa. – *Sierra, Serra*
Sab. – *Sabah*
Sal. – *El Salvador*
Salop. – *Shropshire*
Sar. – *Sarawak*
Sard. – *Sardinia*
Sask. – *Saskatchewan*
S. Afr. – *Rep. of South Africa*
S. Austral. – *South Australia*
S.C. – *South Carolina*
Scot. – *Scotland*
S.D. – *South Dakota*
Sd. – *Sound*
Sen. – *Senegal*
Si. Arab. – *Saudi Arabia*
S. Leone – *Sierra Leone*
Sp., Span. – *Spain, Spanish*
S.S.R. – *Soviet Socialist Republic*
st. – *State*
S. – *San*
St. – *Saint, also see note below*
Sta. – *Santa*
Ste. – *Sainte*
Sto. – *Santo*
Staffs. – *Staffordshire*
Stn. – *Station*
Str. – *Strait*
Sud. – *Sudan*
Sun. (Malay) – *Sungei (River)*
Sur. – *Suriname(e)*
Swazl. – *Swaziland*
Swed. – *Sweden*
Switz. – *Switzerland*
Tanz. – *Tanzania*
Tas. – *Tasmania*
Tenn. – *Tennessee*
Terr. – *Territory*
Tex. – *Texas*
Thai. – *Thailand*
Tipp. – *Tipperary*
tn. – *Town*
Trans. – *Transvaal*
Tr. States – *Trucial States*
Tun. – *Tunisia*
Tur. – *Turkey*
U.A.R. – *United Arab Republic*
Ugan. – *Uganda*
Ukr. – *Ukraine*
U.K. – *United Kingdom of Great Britain and Northern Ireland*
Ut. P. – *Uttar Pradesh*
Urug. – *Uruguay*
U.S.A. – *United States of America*
U.S.S.R. – *Union of Soviet Socialist Republics*
Va. – *Virginia*
Val. – *Valley*
Ven. – *Venezuela*
Vic. – *Victoria*
Viet. – *Vietnam*
Vil. – *Village, Vilayet*
Vol. – *Volcano*
Vt. – *Vermont*
W. – *West, Wadi, Wady*
War. – *Warwickshire*
Wash. – *Washington*
W. I. – *West Indies*
Wick. – *Wicklow*
Wilts. – *Wiltshire*
Wind. Is. – *Windward Islands*
Wis. – *Wisconsin*
Worcs. – *Worcestershire*
W. A. – *Western Australia*
W. Va. – *West Virginia*
Wyo. – *Wyoming*
Yorks. – *Yorkshire*
Y.-slav. – *Yugoslavia*
Zam. – *Zambia*

Names beginning with M', Mc, M'c are indexed under Mac. The following names meaning Saint are indexed under St. (Saint):—Saint, Sanct, Sankt, Sant', Sent, Sint, Svaty, Sveti. Svety, Szent.
The latitudes and longitudes given below are primarily intended as a guide to finding the places on the map, and in some cases are only approximate.
Congo denotes the former Belgian Congo, now Zaïre: Congo (Fr.) the Republic of Congo formerly part of French Equatorial Africa. East Pakistan is now named Bangladesh, Ceylon is Sri Lanka, Cambodia is the Khmer Republic, British Honduras is Belize, the Bahamas are an independent state and Papua and the Territory of New Guinea are independent with the name Papua New Guinea.

MAP
81 Aabenraa, Denmark ...55 4N 9 25E
81 Aabenraa–Sönderborg Amt, Denmark 55 0N 9 30E
56 Aachen, Germany 50 47N 6 4E
81 Aakirkeby, Bornholm, Denmark 55 5N 14 51E
120 Aaiun, Span. Sahara .27 9N 13 12W
81 Aal, Denmark 55 39N 8 18E
81 Aalbæk, Denmark 57 37N 10 24E
81 Aalbæk B., Denmark .57 35N 10 40E
81 Aalborg, Denmark 57 3N 9 52E
81 Aalborg Amt, Jylland, Denmark 56 51N 9 30E
81 Aalborg B., Denmark 56 46N 10 40E
57 Aalen, Germany 48 49N 10 6E
81 Aalestrup, Denmark ...56 42N 9 30E
98 Aalma ech Chaab, Lebanon 33 7N 35 9E
54 Aalsmeer, Netherlands 52 17N 4 43E
81 Aalsö, Denmark 56 23N 10 52E
54 Aalst, Belgium 50 56N 4 2E
54 Aalst, Netherlands 50 57N 4 20E
54 Aalten, Netherlands ...51 56N 6 35E
82 Äänekoski, Finland ...62 38N 25 40E
57 Aarberg, Switzerland .47 3N 7 16E
57 Aargau, Cant., Switz. .47 26N 8 10E
81 Aarhus, Denmark 56 10N 10 12E
81 Aarhus Amt, Jylland, Denmark 56 10N 10 5E
81 Aars, Denmark 56 50N 9 30E
54 Aarschot, Belgium 50 59N 4 49E
45 Aasleagh, Ireland 53 37N 9 40W
81 Aastrup, Denmark 55 34N 8 49E
125 Aba, Nigeria 5 10N 7 19E
127 Aba, I., Sudan 13 30N 32 31E
76 Abacija–e–Oroshit, Alb. 41 52N 20 3E
100 Abadan, Iran 30 22N 48 20E
127 Abade, Ethiopia 9 22N 38 3E
101 Abadeh, Iran 31 8N 52 40E
62 Abadin, Spain 43 21N 7 29W
122 Abadla, Algeria 31 2N 2 45W
173 Abai, Paraguay 25 58S 55 54W
125 Abak, Nigeria 4 58N 7 50E
125 Abakaliki, Nigeria 6 22N 8 2E
91 Abakan, U.S.S.R. 53 40N 91 10E
126 Abal Nam, Si. Arabia 25 20N 38 37E
125 Abala, Niger 15 1N 3 20E
125 Abalemma, Niger 16 12N 7 50E
175 Aballetuba, Brazil 1 40S 51 15W
127 Abalti, Ethiopia 8 10N 37 30E
65 Abanilla, Spain 38 12N 1 3W
71 Abano Terme, Italy ...45 22N 11 46E

MAP
65 Abarán, Spain 38 12N 1 23W
101 Abarqu, Iran 31 10N 53 20E
98 Abasan, Egypt 31 19N 34 21E
127 Abasberes, Ethiopia ...11 33N 35 23E
114 Abashiri, Japan 44 0N 144 15E
144 Abau, Papua 10 1S 148 42E
59 Abaújszántó, Hungary 48 16N 21 12E
127 Abaya L., Ethiopa 6 30N 37 50E
71 Abbadia San Salvatore, Italy 42 53N 11 40E
127 Abbay R. (Blue Nile), Ethiopia 10 17N 35 22E
162 Abbaye, Pt., U.S.A. ...46 58N 88 4W
127 Abbe, L., Ethiopia 11 08N 41 47E
81 Abbetorp, Sweden 56 57N 16 8E
49 Abbeville, France 50 6N 1 49E
165 Abbeville, La., U.S.A. 30 0N 92 7W
163 Abbeville, S.C., U.S.A. 34 12N 82 21W
44 Abbey, Ireland 53 7N 8 25W
38 Abbey Town, Eng., U.K. 54 50N 3 18W
44 Abbeydorney, Ireland 52 21N 9 40W
44 Abbeyfeale, Ireland ...52 23N 9 20W
45 Abbeyleix, Ireland 52 55N 7 20W
45 Abbeyside, Ireland 52 5N 7 36W
70 Abbiategrasso, Italy ...45 23N 8 55E
145 Abbieglassie, Austral. 27 15S 147 28E
34 Abbots Bromley, Eng., U.K. 52 50N 1 52W
35 Abbots Langley, Eng., U.K. 51 43N 0 25W
36 Abbotsbury, Eng., U.K. 50 40N 2 36W
156 Abbotsford, B.C., Can. 49 0N 122 10W
161 Abbotsford, Que., Can. 45 25N 72 53W
164 Abbotsford, U.S.A. 44 55N 90 20W
102 Abbottabad, W. Pak. 34 10N 73 15E
99 Abd al Kuri I., Ind. Oc. 12 5N 52 20E
121 Abéché, Chad. 13 50N 20 35E
64 Abejar, Spain 41 48N 2 47W
127 Abekr, Sudan 12 45N 28 50E
122 Abêlessa, Algeria 22 58N 4 47E
124 Abengourou, Ivory C. 6 42N 3 27W
125 Abeokuta, Nigeria 7 3N 3 19E
131 Aber, Uganda 2 12N 32 25E
37 Aber–soch, Wales, U.K. 52 50N 4 31W

MAP
37 Aberayron Wales, U.K. 52 15N 4 16W
34 Abercarn, Mon., U.K. 51 39N 3 9W
43 Aberchirder, Scot., U.K. 57 34N 2 40W
145 Abercorn, Australia ...25 12S 151 5E
132 Abercorn, Zambia, *see* Mbala 8 46S 31 17E
37 Abercrave, Wales, U.K. 51 48N 3 42W
143 Abercrombie R., Austral. 34 0S 149 23E
37 Aberdare, Wales, U.K. 51 43N 3 27W
131 Aberdare Ra., Kenya . 0 15S 36 50E
37 Aberdaron, Wales, U.K. 52 48N 4 41W
157 Aberdeen, Canada 52 20N 106 8W
134 Aberdeen, S. Africa ...32 28S 24 2E
143 Aberdeen, Australia ...32 9S 150 56E
43 Aberdeen, Scot. U.K. 57 9N 2 6W
43 Aberdeen, co., Scot., U.K. 57 18N 2 30W
166 Aberdeen, Idaho, U.S.A. 43 0N 112 52W
163 Aberdeen, Miss., U.S.A. 33 45N 88 31W
164 Aberdeen, S.D., U.S.A. 45 30N 98 30W
166 Aberdeen, Wash., U.S.A. 47 0N 123 58W
134 Aberdeen Road, S. Afr. 32 43S 24 21E
41 Aberdour, Scot., U.K. 56 2N 3 18W
37 Aberdovey, Wales, U.K. 52 33N 4 3W
37 Aberdulais, Wales, U.K. 51 41N 3 46W
41 Aberfeldy, Scot., U.K. 56 37N 3 50W
37 Aberffraw, Wales, U.K. 53 11N 4 28W
40 Aberfoyle, Scot., U.K. 56 10N 4 23W
62 Abergaria–a–Velha, Port. 40 41N 8 32W
34 Abergavenny, Mon., U.K. 51 49N 3 1W
37 Abergele, Wales, U.K. 53 17N 3 35W
37 Abergwili, Wales, U.K. 51 52N 4 18W
37 Abergynolwyn, Wales, U.K. 52 39N 3 58W
37 Aberkenfig, Wales, U.K. 51 33N 3 36W

MAP
41 Aberlady, Scotland, U.K. 56 0N 2 51W
165 Abernathy, U.S.A. 33 49N 101 49W
41 Abernethy, Scot., U.K. 56 19N 3 18W
37 Aberporth, Wales, U.K. 52 8N 4 32W
34 Abersychan, Mon., U.K. 51 44N 3 3W
34 Abertillery, Mon., U.K. 51 44N 3 9W
37 Aberystwyth, Wales, U.K. 52 25N 4 6W
126 Abha, Saudi Arabia ...18 0N 42 34E
105 Abhayapuri, India 26 24N 90 38E
127 Abi Addi, Ethiopia 13 39N 39 3E
126 Abidiya, Sudan 18 18N 34 3E
124 Abidjan, Ivory Coast . 5 26N 3 58W
164 Abilene, Kans., U.S.A. 39 0N 97 16W
165 Abilene, Texas, U.S.A. 32 22N 99 40W
34 Abingdon, England, U.K. 51 40N 1 17W
164 Abingdon, Ill., U.S.A. 40 53N 90 23W
163 Abingdon, Va., U.S.A. 36 46N 81 56W
41 Abington, Scotland, U.K. 55 30N 3 42W
154 Abitibi L., Canada 48 40N 79 40W
89 Abkhaz A.S.S.R., U.S.S.R. 43 0N 41 0E
91 Abkit, U.S.S.R. 64 10N 157 10E
126 Abnûb, Egypt 27 18N 31 4E
125 Abocho, Nigeria 7 35N 6 56E
104 Abohar, India 30 10N 74 10E
124 Aboisso, Ivory Coast . 5 30N 3 5W
130 Abolo, Congo (Fr.) 0 10N 14 10E
125 Aboméy, Dahomey 7 10N 2 5E
51 Abondance, France ...46 18N 6 42E
128 Abong Mbang, Cam. . 4 0N 13 8E
125 Abonnema, Nigeria ... 4 41N 6 49E
59 Abony, Hungary 47 12N 20 3E
124 Aboso, Ghana 5 23N 1 57W
121 Abou Deia, Chad 11 20N 19 20E
43 Aboyne, Scotland, U.K. 57 4N 2 48W
100 Abqaiq, Saudi Arabia 26 0N 49 45E
135 Abrahamskraal, S. Afr. 28 52S 25 40E
63 Abrantes, Portugal 39 24N 8 7W
62 Abraveses, Portugal ...40 41N 7 55E
168 Abreojos Pta., Mexico 26 50N 113 40W
49 Abreschwiller, France 48 39N 7 6E

MAP
127 Abri, Kordofan Sudan 11 40N 30 21E
127 Abri, N. Prov., Sudan 20 50N 30 27E
175 Abrolhos Arch., Brazil 18 0S 38 30W
78 Abrud, Rumania 46 19N 23 5E
71 Abruzzi, Reg., Italy ...42 15N 14 0E
166 Absaroka Ra., U.S.A. 44 40N 110 0W
100 Abu al Khasib, Iraq ...30 25N 48 0E
100 Abu 'Ali I., Si. Arab. .27 20N 49 27E
99 Abu Arish, Si. Arab. .16 53N 42 48E
126 Abu Ballas (Pottery Hill), Egypt 24 26N 27 36E
127 Abu Deleiq, Sudan 15 57N 33 48E
101 Abu Dhabi, Tr. States 24 28N 54 36E
98 Abu Dis, Jordan 31 47N 35 16E
126 Adu Dis, Sudan 19 12N 33 38E
127 Abu Dom, Sudan 16 18N 32 25E
127 Abu Gabra, Sudan 11 2N 26 50E
127 Abu Gubeiha, Sudan .11 30N 31 15E
127 Abu Habl, W., Sudan 12 37N 31 0E
126 Abu Hamed, Sudan ...19 32N 33 13E
127 Abu Haraz, Blue Nile, Sudan 14 35N 34 30E
126 Abu Haraz, Northern Dist., Sudan 19 8N 32 18E
127 Abu Higar, Sudan 12 50N 33 59E
100 Abu Kamal, Syria 34 30N 41 0E
100 Abu Markha, Si. Arab. 25 4N 38 22E
126 Abu Qir, Egypt 31 18N 30 0E
126 Abu Qireiya, Egypt ...24 5N 35 28E
126 Abu Qurqâs, Egypt ...28 1N 30 44E
126 Abu Salama, Si. Arab. 27 10N 35 51E
127 Abu Satta, Hills, Sudan 6 0N 27 40E
126 Abu Tig, Egypt 27 4N 31 15E
127 Abu Tiga, Sudan 12 47N 34 12E
127 Abu Zabad, Sudan 12 25N 29 10E
127 Abu Zagholi, Sudan ...11 45N 34 29E
126 Abu Zenima, Egypt ...29 0N 33 15E
125 Abuja, Nigeria 9 16N 7 2E
114 Abukuma, R. Japan .37 30N 140 30E
174 Abunã, Brazil 9 40S 65 20W
174 Abunã R., Brazil 9 41S 65 20W
127 Abwong, Sudan 9 2N 32 14E
81 Åby, Sweden 58 40N 16 10E
134 Acacia, C. Prov., S. Afr. 32 16S 22 38E
168 Acambaro, Mexico 20 0N 100 40W
168 Acaponeta, Mexico 22 30N 105 20W
168 Acapulco de Juárez, Mexico 16 51N 99 56W

MAP
175 Acará, Brazil 2 11S 48 20W
168 Acatlan, Mexico 18 10N 98 3W
168 Acayucan, Mexico 17 59N 94 58W
70 Acceglio, Italy 44 28N 6 59E
162 Accomac, U.S.A. 37 43N 75 40W
125 Accra, Ghana 5 35N 0 6W
38 Accrington, Eng., U.K. 53 46N 2 22W
172 Acebal, Argentina 33 20S 60 50W
73 Acerenza, Italy 40 50N 15 58E
73 Acerra, Italy 40 57N 14 22E
63 Aceuchal, Spain 38 39N 6 30W
103 Achak Gomba, China 33 30N 96 25E
131 Achar, Uganda 2 57N 32 37E
43 Achavanich, Scot., U.K. 58 22N 3 25W
58 Achen See, L., Austria 47 26N 11 45E
58 Achenkirch, Austria 47 32N 11 45E
104 Acher, India 23 10N 72 32E
57 Achern, Germany 48 37N 8 5E
45 Achill, Ireland 53 56N 9 55W
45 Achill Hd., Ireland 53 59N 10 15W
45 Achill I., Ireland 53 58N 10 5W
45 Achill Sd., Ireland 53 53N 9 55W
45 Achillbeg I., Ireland 53 51N 9 58W
56 Achim, Germany 53 1N 9 2E
125 Achimota, Ghana 5 35N 0 15W
91 Achinsk, U.S.S.R. 56 20N 90 20E
42 Achnasheen, Scot., U.K. 57 35N 5 5W
42 Achnashellach, Scot., U.K. 57 28N 5 20W
127 Achol, Sudan 6 35N 31 32E
42 A'Chralaig, Mt., Scot., U.K. 57 11N 5 10W
73 Acireale, Italy 37 37N 15 9E
165 Ackerman, U.S.A. 33 20N 89 8W
144 Acland Mt., Queensland, Australia 24 50S 148 20E
169 Acklin's I., Bahamas 22 30N 74 0W
46 Aclare, Ireland 54 4N 8 54W
35 Acle, England, U.K. 52 38N 1 32E
156 Acme, Canada 51 33N 113 30W
172 Aconcagua Mt., Arg. 32 50S 70 0W
172 Aconcagua, prov., Chile 32 15S 70 30W
172 Aconquija, mt., Argentina 27 0S 66 0W
133 Acornhoek, S. Africa 24 31S 31 2E
71 Acquapendente, Italy 42 45N 11 50E
57 Acquarossa, Switz. 46 27N 8 58E
71 Acquasanta, Italy 42 46N 13 24E
73 Acquavivadelle Fonti, It. 40 53N 16 50E
70 Acqui, Italy 44 40N 8 28E
98 Acre, Israel 32 35N 35 4E
174 Acre R., Brazil 10 45S 68 25W
174 Acre, state, Brazil 9 0S 71 0W
73 Acri, Italy 39 29N 16 23E
59 Acs, Hungary 47 42N 18 0E
160 Actinolite, Canada 44 34N 77 20W
160 Acton, Canada 43 38N 80 3W
34 Acton Burnell, Eng., U.K. 52 37N 2 41W
99 Ad Dam, Saudi Arabia 20 33N 44 45E
100 Ad Dammam, Si. Arab. 26 20N 50 5E
100 Ad Dar al Hamra, Saudi Arabia 27 20N 37 45E
101 Ad Dawhah, Qatar 25 15N 51 35E
127 Ada, Ethiopia 8 48N 38 51E
125 Ada, Ghana 5 44N 0 40E
164 Ada, Minn., U.S.A. 47 20N 96 30W
165 Ada, Okla., U.S.A. 34 50N 96 45W
74 Ada, Yugoslavia 45 49N 20 9E
127 Adailo, Ethiopia 14 29N 40 50E
14 Adair C., Canada 71 50N 71 0W
62 Adajo R., Spain 41 15N 5 17W
80 Adalsliden, Sweden 63 27N 16 55E
101 Adam, Muscat & 'Oman 22 15N 57 28E
125 Adamaoua, Massif de L', Cameroon 7 20N 12 20E
70 Adamello Mt., Italy 46 10N 10 34E
143 Adaminaby, Austral. 36 0S 148 45E
127 Adamitullo, Ethiopia 7 53N 38 41E
161 Adams, Mass., U.S.A. 42 38N 73 8W
161 Adams, N.Y., U.S.A. 43 50N 76 3W
164 Adams, Wis., U.S.A. 43 59N 89 50W
156 Adams L., Canada 51 20N 119 40W
166 Adams Mt., U.S.A. 46 10N 121 28W
106 Adams Bridge, Ceylon 9 15N 79 40E
161 Adams Center, U.S.A. 43 51N 76 1W
106 Adam's Pk., Ceylon 6 55N 80 45E
63 Adamuz, Spain 38 02N 4 32W
100 Adana, Turkey 37 0N 35 16E
62 Adanero, Spain 40 56N 4 36W
100 Adapazari, Turkey 40 48N 30 25E
127 Adarama, Sudan 17 10N 34 52E
44 Adare, Ireland 52 34N 8 48W
15 Adare C., Antarctica 71 0S 171 0E
145 Adavale, Austral. 25 52S 144 32E
70 Adda R., Italy 45 25N 9 30E
127 Addagalla, Ethiopia 10 24N 42 15E
127 Addis Ababa (Addis Abeba), Ethiopia 9 2N 38 42E
127 Addis Alem, Ethiopia 9 0N 38 17E
160 Addison, N.Y., U.S.A. 42 9N 77 15W
161 Addison, Vt., U.S.A. 44 6N 73 18W
35 Addlestone, Eng., U.K. 51 22N 0 30W
135 Addo, C. Prov., S. Afr. 33 32S 25 44E
95 Addu Atoll, Ind. Oc. 0 30S 73 0E
125 Adebour, Niger 13 17N 11 50E
163 Adel, U.S.A. 31 10N 83 28W
135 Adelaide, S. Africa 32 42S 26 20E
145 Adelaide, S. Australia 34 55S 138 32E

MAP
15 Adelaide I., Antarc. 67 15S 68 30W
152 Adelaide Pen., Canada 67 60N 98 0W
15 Adélie Land, Antarc. 67 0S 140 0E
64 Ademuz, Spain 40 5N 1 13W
99 Aden, South Yemen 12 50N 45 0E
99 Aden, G. of, Asia 13 0N 50 0E
104 Adhoi, India 3 26N 70 32E
131 Adi, Congo 43 26N 30 48E
109 Adi I., Indon. 4 15S 133 30E
127 Adi Kaie, Ethiopia 14 51N 39 22E
127 Adi Kuala, Ethiopia 12 38N 38 48E
127 Adi Ugri, Ethiopia 14 58N 38 48E
138 Adieu, C., S. Australia 32 0S 132 10E
71 Adige, R., Italy 45 9N 11 25E
127 Adigrat, Ethiopia 14 20N 39 26E
106 Adilabad, India 19 33N 78 35E
166 Adin, U.S.A. 41 10N 121 0W
101 Adin Khel, Afghanistan 32 45N 68 5E
106 Adirampattinam, India 10 28N 79 20E
161 Adirondack Mts., U.S.A. 44 0N 74 15W
123 Adjim, Tunisia 33 47N 10 50E
125 Adjohon, Dahomey 6 41N 2 32E
78 Adjud, Rumania 46 07N 27 10E
155 Adlavik Is., Canada 55 2N 58 45W
89 Adler, U.S.S.R. 43 28N 39 52E
123 Admer, Algeria 20 21N 5 27E
123 Admer, Erg d', Algeria 24 0N 9 5E
15 Admiralty B., Falkland Is. Dependencies 62 0S 59 0W
138 Admiralty G., W. Austral. 14 20S 125 55E
157 Admiralty I., Alaska 57 40N 134 35W
144 Admiralty Is., Territory of New Guinea 2 5S 146 15E
166 Admiralty Inlet, U.S.A. 48 0N 122 40W
15 Admiralty Ra., Antarc. 72 0S 164 0E
125 Ado, Nigeria 6 36N 2 56E
125 Ado Ekiti, Nigeria 7 38N 5 12E
109 Adoea, Indon. 1 45S 129 50E
127 Adok, Sudan 8 10N 30 20E
127 Adola, Ethiopia 11 14N 41 44E
172 Adolfo Alsina, Arg. 37 10S 62 50W
109 Adonara I., Indonesia 8 15S 123 5E
106 Adoni, India 15 33N 77 18W
59 Adony, Hungary 47 06N 18 52E
50 Adour R., France 43 48N 0 50W
105 Adra, India 23 30N 86 42E
65 Adra, Spain 36 43N 3 3W
99 Adraj, Saudi Arabia 20 1N 51 0E
73 Adrano, Italy 37 40N 14 49E
122 Adrar, Algeria 27 51N 0 11W
125 Adrar des Iforas, Mali 19 40N 1 40E
121 Adré, Chad 13 40N 22 20E
123 Adri, Libya 27 32N 13 2E
71 Adria, Italy 45 4N 12 3E
162 Adrian, Mich., U.S.A. 41 55N 84 0W
165 Adrian, Tex., U.S.A. 35 19N 102 37W
66-67 Adriatic Sea, Europe 43 0N 16 0E
44 Adrigole, Ireland 51 44N 9 42W
131 Aduku, Uganda 2 03N 32 45E
106 Adur, India 9 8N 76 40E
127 Adwa, Ethiopia 14 15N 38 52E
100 Adwa, Saudi Arabia 27 15N 42 35E
39 Adwick le Street, Eng., U.K. 53 35N 1 12W
89 Adzhar A.S.S.R., U.S.S.R. 42 0N 42 0E
124 Adzopé, Ivory Coast 6 7N 3 49W
81 Æbelö I., Denmark 55 39N 10 10E
81 Æbeltoft, Denmark 56 12N 10 41E
81 Æbeltoft Vig. B., Den. 56 9N 10 35E
67 Ægean Is., Greece 38 0N 25 0E
67 Ægean Sea, Europe 37 0N 25 0E
79 Ænes, Norway 60 5N 6 8E
73 Æolian Is., Italy 38 40N 15 7E
81 Aerö I., Denmark 54 53N 10 20E
81 Ærösköbing, Denmark 54 53N 10 20E
77 Aëtós, Greece 37 15N 21 50E
123 Afafi, Massif d', Niger 22 11N 14 48E
77 Afándou, Greece 36 18N 28 12E
122 Afarag, Erg, Algeria 23 50N 2 47E
127 Afdera, Mt., Ethiopia 13 16N 41 5E
122 Affreville, *see* Khemis Miliania, Algeria 36 11N 2 14E
43 Affric, R., Scot., U.K. 57 16N 5 0W
101 Afghanistan, St., Asia 33 0N 65 0E
99 Afgoi, Somali Rep. 2 7N 44 59E
100 Afif, Saudi Arabia 23 53N 42 56E
125 Afikpo, Nigeria 5 53N 7 54E
122 Afisses, W., Algeria 28 30N 0 50E
122 Aflou, Algeria 34 1N 2 3E
73 Afragola, Italy 40 54N 14 15E
116 Africa, Cont. 10 0N 20 0E
135 Afrikaskop, S. Africa 28 12S 28 44E
161 Afton, U.S.A. 42 14N 75 31W
122 Aftout, Algeria 26 50N 3 45W
175 Afuá, Brazil 0 15S 50 10W
98 Afula, Israel 32 37N 35 17E
132 Afumba, Zambia 15 35S 24 54E
100 Afyon, Turkey 38 46N 30 33E
125 Agadés, Niger 16 58N 7 59E
122 Agadir, Morocco 30 28N 9 35W
122 Agadir Tissint, Morocco 29 57N 7 16W
114 Agano, R., Japan 37 50N 139 30E
104 Agar, India 23 40N 76 2E
127 Agaro, Ethiopia 7 50N 36 38E
103 Agartala, India 23 50N 91 23E
78 Agăş, Rumania 46 28N 26 15E
156 Agassiz, Canada 49 14N 121 52W
127 Agat, Ethiopia 15 38N 38 16E

MAP
133 Agatha, Trans., S. Afr. 23 56S 30 9E
125 Agbelouve, Togo 6 35N 1 14E
124 Agboville, Ivory Coast 5 55N 4 15W
89 Agdam, U.S.S.R. 40 0N 46 58E
50 Agde, France 43 19N 3 28E
122 Agdz, Morocco 30 47N 6 30W
50 Agen, France 44 12N 0 38E
81 Agersö, Denmark 55 12N 11 10E
81 Agger, Denmark 56 48N 8 16E
55 Agger, R., Germany 50 50N 7 20E
81 Aggersborg, Denmark 57 0N 9 16E
72 Aggius, Italy (Sardinia) 40 56N 9 4E
46 Aghalee, N. Ireland, U.K. 54 32N 6 17W
45 Aghavannagh, Ireland 52 55N 6 25W
44 Aghern, Ireland 52 5N 8 10W
102 Aghil Mts., China 36 0N 77 0E
102 Aghil Pass, China 36 15N 76 35E
113 Agincourt I., Taiwan 25 4N 122 2E
73 Agira, Italy 37 40N 14 30E
122 Aglagal, Djebel, Algeria 27 20N 2 0E
122 Aglou, Morocco 29 50N 9 50W
50 Agly R., France 42 46N 2 32E
142 Agnew, W. Australia 28 0S 120 30E
46 Agnews Hill, N. Ireland, U.K. 54 51N 5 55W
124 Agnibilékrou, Ivory C. 7 10N 3 11W
78 Agnita, Rumania 45 59N 24 40E
73 Agnone, Italy 41 49N 14 20E
125 Agofie, Ghana 8 27N 0 15E
70 Agogna R., Italy 45 8N 8 42E
125 Agogo, Ghana 6 50N 1 1W
127 Agogo, Sudan 7 50N 28 45E
48 Agon, France 49 02N 1 34W
80 Agön I., Sweden 61 34N 17 23E
127 Agordat, Ethiopia 15 30N 37 40E
71 Agordo, Italy 46 18N 12 2E
50 Agout R., France 43 40N 2 47E
104 Agra, India 27 17N 77 58E
64 Agramunt, Spain 41 48N 1 6E
64 Agreda, Spain 41 51N 1 55W
81 Agri, Denmark 56 14N 10 32E
74 Agri R., Italy 40 17N 16 15E
100 Agri Dagi, mt., Turkey 39 50N 44 15E
72 Agrigento, Italy 37 19N 13 33E
77 Agrinion, Greece 38 37N 21 27E
73 Agropoli, Italy 40 23N 14 59E
135 Agtertang, S. Africa 30 41S 25 18E
175 Agua Clara, Brazil 20 25S 52 45W
168 Agua Prieta, Mexico 31 20N 109 32W
174 Aguadas, Colombia 5 40N 75 38W
169 Aguadilla, Puerto Rico 18 27N 67 10W
155 Aguanish, Canada 50 14N 62 02W
172 Aguas Blancas, Chile 24 15S 69 55W
168 Aguascalientes, tn., & st., Mexico 22 0N 102 12W
63 Agudo, Spain 38 59N 4 52W
62 Agueda, Port. 40 34N 8 27W
62 Agueda R., Spain 40 45N 6 37W
122 Aguelt el Kadra, Maur. 25 3N 7 6W
122 Agueni N'Ikko, Morocco 32 29N 5 47W
123 Aguer Tai, Niger 20 0N 17 41E
123 Aguié, Niger 13 31N 7 46E
62 Aguilafuente, Spain 41 13N 4 7W
63 Aguilar, Sevilla, Spain 37 31N 4 40W
62 Aguilar de Campoo, Sp. 42 47N 4 15W
65 Aguilas, Spain 37 23N 1 35W
174 Aguja Pta., Peru 6 0S 81 0W
134 Agulhas, C., S. Africa 34 52S 20 0E
98 Agur, Israel 31 42N 34 55E
109 Agusan R., Phil. 9 20N 125 50E
89 Agvali, U.S.S.R. 42 36N 46 8E
123 Ahaggar, Mts., Algeria 23 0N 6 30E
125 Ahamansu, Ghana 7 38N 0 35E
100 Ahar, Iran 38 35N 47 0E
44 Ahascragh, Ireland 53 24N 8 20W
147 Ahaura, R., New Zealand 42 21S 171 34E
56 Ahaus, Germany 52 4N 7 1E
123 Ahelledjem, Algeria 26 37N 6 58E
146 Ahimanawa, Ra., N.Z. 39 5S 176 30E
146 Ahipara B., N.Z. 35 5S 173 5E
56 Ahlen, Germany 51 45N 7 52E
104 Ahmadabad (Ahmedabad), India 23 0N 72 40E
106 Ahmadnagar, (Ahmednagar), India 19 7N 74 46E
104 Ahmadpur, W. Pakistan 29 12N 71 10E
127 Ahmar Mts., Ethiopia 9 20N 41 15E
125 Ahoada, Nigeria 5 8N 6 36E
46 Ahoghill, N. Ireland, U.K. 54 52N 6 23W
56 Ahr R., Germany 50 25N 6 52W
55 Ahr-Gebirge, Germany 50 30N 6 48W
56 Ahrensbok, Germany 54 0N 10 34E
56 Ahrweiler, Germany 50 31N 7 3E
168 Ahuachapan, Salvador 13 54N 89 52W
147 Ahuriri R., N.Z. 44 27S 169 45E
81 Åhus, Sweden 55 57N 14 22E
100 Ahvaz, Iran 31 20N 48 40E
83 Ahvenanmaa Is., Fin. 60 15N 20 0E
101 Aibaq, Afghanistan 36 15N 68 5E
57 Aichach, Germany 48 28N 11 9E
114 Aichi, Pref., Japan 35 0N 137 15E
123 Aidabiyah, Libya 30 54N 20 4E
73 Aidone, Italy 37 26N 14 26E
73 Aiello Calabro, Italy 39 6N 16 12E
57 Aigle, Switzerland 46 18N 6 58E
49 Aignay le Duc, France 47 40N 4 43E

MAP
50 Aigre, France 45 54N 0 1E
173 Aigua, Uruguay 34 13S 54 46W
50 Aigueperse, France 46 3N 3 13E
51 Aigues Mortes, France 43 35N 4 12E
51 Aiguilles, France 44 47N 6 51E
50 Aigurande, France 46 27N 1 49E
112 Aihun, China 49 55N 127 30E
174 Aija, Peru 9 50S 77 45W
103 Aijal, India 23 40N 92 44E
163 Aiken, U.S.A. 33 34N 81 50W
49 Aillant, France 47 50N 3 21E
155 Aillik, Canada 55 11N 59 18W
49 Ailly-sur-Noye, France 49 45N 2 20E
40 Ailsa Craig, I., Scot., U.K. 55 15N 5 7W
91 Aim, U.S.S.R. 59 0N 133 55E
109 Aimere, Indonesia 8 45S 121 3E
172 Aimogasta, Argentina 28 33S 66 50W
175 Aimorés, Brazil 19 30S 41 10W
51 Ain, dept., France 46 5N 5 20E
51 Ain R., France 46 7N 5 22E
101 Ain Banaiyah, Si. Arab. 23 0N 51 0E
123 Ain Beida (Daoud), Algeria 35 50N 7 29E
122 Ain Ben Khelil, Algeria 33 15N 0 49W
122 Ain Ben Tili, Mauritania 25 59N 9 27W
126 Ain Dalla, Egypt 27 20N 27 23E
100 Ain Dar, Si. Arabia 25 55N 49 10E
122 Ain el Hadjan. Morocco 31 35N 9 37W
126 Ain el Mafki, Egypt 27 30N 28 15E
126 Ain Girba, Egypt 29 20N 25 14E
123 Ain Hadjel, Algeria 35 45N 3 56E
123 Ain Milla, Algeria 35 58N 6 35E
126 Ain Qeiqab, Egypt 29 42N 24 55E
123 Ain Rich, Algeria 34 38N 4 2E
122 Ain Sefra, Algeria 32 47N 0 37W
126 Ain Sheikh, Egypt 26 47N 27 45E
126 Ain Sukhna, Egypt 29 32N 32 20E
122 Ain Tédelès, Algeria 36 0N 0 21E
122 Ain Temouchent, Alg. 35 16N 1 4W
123 Ain Touta, Algeria 35 26N 5 59E
122 Ain Zora, Morocco 34 37N 3 27W
99 Ainabo, Somali Rep. 9 0N 46 25E
86 Ainaži, U.S.S.R. 57 50N 24 24E
121 Aine Galakka, Chad 18 10N 18 30E
77 Ainos Óros, mt., Greece 38 10N 20 35E
38 Ainsdale, England, U.K. 53 37N 3 2W
164 Ainsworth, U.S.A. 42 33N 99 52W
38 Aintree, England, U.K. 53 28N 2 56W
91 Aion, I., U.S.S.R. 69 50N 169 0E
125 Air (Azbine) dist., Niger 18 30N 8 0E
49 Airaines, France 49 58N 1 55E
43 Aird, The, dist., Scotland, U.K. 57 26N 4 30W
42 Aird Brenish, C., Scotland, U.K. 58 8N 7 8W
41 Airdrie, Scotland, U.K. 55 53N 3 57W
50 Aire, Landes, France 43 42N 0 16W
49 Aire, Pas de Calais, Fr. 50 37N 2 22E
64 Aire, Isla del, Spain 39 48N 4 16E
39 Aire, R., Eng., U.K. 53 42N 1 30W
49 Aire, R., France 49 18N 5 0E
48 Airvault, France 46 50N 0 10W
127 Aisalta, Ethiopia 11 33N 41 25E
127 Aiscia, Ethiopia 10 50N 42 23E
38 Aisgill, England, U.K. 54 23N 2 21W
49 Aisne, dépt., France 49 42N 3 40E
49 Aisne R., France 49 12N 4 47E
122 Ait Ami, Morocco 31 53N 5 16W
122 Ait Melloul, Morocco 30 25N 9 29W
144 Aitape, Terr. of N. Guinea 3 0S 142 25E
43 Aith, Scotland, U.K. 59 8N 2 38W
164 Aitkin, U.S.A. 46 40N 93 40W
77 Aitolia, *see* Akarnania Pref., Greece 38 45N 21 18E
77 Aitolikón, Greece 38 26N 21 21E
75 Aitos, Bulgaria 42 47N 27 16E
75 Aitosska Planina, Ra., Bulgaria 42 45N 27 30E
111 Aitush, China 39 54N 75 40E
78 Aiud, Rumania 46 19N 23 44E
51 Aix-en-Provence, Fr. 43 32N 5 27E
51 Aix-les-Bains, France 45 41N 5 53E
50 Aix les Thermes, Fr. 42 43N 1 51E
77 Aiyina & I., Greece 37 45N 23 26E
76 Aiyinion, Greece 40 28N 22 28E
77 Aiyion, Greece 38 15N 22 5E
48 Aizenay, France 46 44N 1 38W
86 Aizpute, U.S.S.R. 56 43N 21 40E
51 Ajaccio, Corsica, France 41 55N 8 40E
51 Ajaccio, G. de, France 41 52N 8 40E
142 Ajana, W. Australia 27 56S 114 35E
104 Ajanta Ra., India 20 28N 75 50E
160 Ajax, Canada 43 50N 79 1W
147 Ajax mt., N.Z. 42 35S 172 5E
166 Ajax, Mt., U.S.A. 45 27N 113 47W
71 Ajdouscina, Yugoslavia 45 54N 13 54E
98 'Ajlun, Jordan 32 18N 35 47E
101 Ajman, Tr. States 25 25N 55 30E
104 Ajmer, India 26 28N 74 37E
167 Ajo, U.S.A. 32 18N 112 54W
127 Ajok, Sudan 9 15N 28 28E
109 Aju Is., Indonesia 0 35N 131 5E
124 Ajua, Ghana 4 50N 1 55W
125 Akaba, Togo 8 10N 1 2E
122 Akabli, Algeria 26 49N 1 31E

MAP
127 Akaki, Ethiopia 8 55N 38 45E
127 Akala, Sudan 15 39N 36 13E
77 Akarnania & Aitolia, pref., Greece 38 45N 21 18E
147 Akaroa & Harb., N.Z. 43 49S 172 59E
126 Akasha, Sudan 21 10N 30 32E
114 Akashi, Japan 34 45N 135 0E
123 Akbou, Algeria 36 31N 4 31E
100 Akdag, mt., Turkey 36 30N 30 0E
125 Akegbe, Nigeria 6 17N 7 28E
109 Akelamo, Indonesia 1 35N 129 40E
79 Akershus Fylke, co., Norway 60 10N 11 15E
106 Akeru R., India 17 25N 80 0E
130 Aketi, Congo 2 38N 23 47E
77 Akhaïa, pref., Greece 38 5N 21 45E
89 Akhalkalaki, U.S.S.R. 41 27N 43 25E
89 Akhaltsikhe, U.S.S.R. 41 40N 43 0E
77 Akharnaí, Greece 38 5N 23 44E
77 Akhelóös, R., Greece 39 5N 21 25E
77 Akhendria, Greece 34 58N 25 16E
76 Akhéron, Greece 39 31N 20 29E
100 Akhisar, Turkey 38 56N 27 48E
77 Akhladhókambos, Gr. 37 31N 22 35E
126 Akhmîm, Egypt 26 31N 31 47E
75 Akhtopol, Bulgaria 42 6N 27 56E
89 Akhty, U.S.S.R. 41 30N 47 45E
86 Akhtyrka, U.S.S.R. 50 25N 35 0E
154 Akimiski I., Canada 52 50N 81 30W
88 Akimovka, U.S.S.R. 46 44N 35 0E
77 Akincilar, Turkey 37 57N 27 25E
144 Akinum, Terr. of New Guinea 6 15S 149 30E
114 Akita, Japan 39 45N 140 0E
114 Akita, pref., Japan 39 40N 140 30E
124 Akjoujt, Mauritania 19 45N 14 15W
122 Akka, Morocco 29 28N 8 9W
77 Akköy, Turkey 37 30N 27 18E
125 Aklampa, Dahomey 8 15N 2 10E
152 Aklavik, Canada 68 25N 135 0W
122 Aknoul, Morocco 34 47N 3 55W
125 Ako, Nigeria 10 19N 10 48E
128 Akoafim, Cameroon 2 20N 12 50E
127 Akobo R., Ethiopia 7 10N 34 25E
104 Akola, India 20 42N 77 2E
125 Akonolinga, Cameroon 3 50N 12 18E
125 Akosombo Dam, Ghana 6 20N 0 5E
104 Akot, India 21 10N 77 10E
127 Akot, Sudan 6 31N 30 9E
153 Akpatok I., Canada 60 30N 68 0W
79 Akrahamn, Norway 59 17W 5 13E
82 Akranes, Iceland 64 18N 21 53W
125 Akreïjit, Mauritania 18 19N 9 11W
77 Akrítas Venétiko Ákra, C., Greece 36 43N 21 54E
164 Akron, Colo., U.S.A. 40 13N 103 15W
160 Akron, Ohio, U.S.A. 41 7N 81 31W
76 Akrotiri Ákra, C., Gr. 40 26W 25 27W
102 Aksai Chih, Kashmir 35 30N 79 50E
100 Aksaray, Turkey 38 25N 34 2E
100 Aksehir, Turkey 38 18N 31 30E
91 Aksenovo Zilovskoye, U.S.S.R. 53 20N 117 40E
111 Aksu, China 41 4N 80 5E
127 Aksum, Ethiopia 14 5N 38 40E
76 Akti Mts., Greece 40 37N 24 6E
85 Aktyubinsk, U.S.S.R. 50 10N 57 3E
125 Aku, Nigeria 6 40N 7 18E
125 Akure, Nigeria 7 15N 5 5E
82 Akureyri, Iceland 65 37N 18 3W
114 Akuseki-shima, I., Jap. 29 26N 129 30E
89 Akusha, U.S.S.R. 42 18N 47 30E
103 Akyab, Burma 20 15N 92 45E
123 Al Abyar, Libya 32 9N 20 29E
100 Al Ahmadi, Kuwait 29 5N 48 10E
99 Al Ain, Saudi Arabia 19 35N 54 40E
100 Al Amadiyah, Iraq 37 5N 43 30E
100 Al Amarah, Iraq 31 55N 47 15E
100 Al Aqabah, Jordan 29 37N 35 0E
101 Al Ashkara, Mus. & 'O. 21 50N 59 30E
123 Al Aziziyeh, Libya 32 30N 13 1E
123 Al Barkat, Libya 24 56N 10 14E
100 Al Basrah (Basra), Iraq 30 30N 47 55E
121 Al Bayda (Beida), Libya 32 30N 21 40E
123 Al Bu'ayrat, Libya 31 24N 15 44E
100 Al Diwaniyah, Iraq 32 0N 45 0E
100 Al Fallujah, Iraq 33 20N 43 55E
100 Al Fâw (Fao), Iraq 30 0N 48 30E
100 Al Hadithan, Iraq 34 0N 42 23E
100 Al Hamad, Si. Arabia 31 30N 39 30E
100 Al Hamar, Si. Arabia 22 23N 46 6E
100 Al Hariq, Saudi Arabia 23 29N 46 27E
100 Al Hasakah, Syria 36 35N 40 45E
99 Al Hauta, S. Yemen 16 5N 48 20E
100 Al Hayy, Iraq 32 5N 46 5E
100 Al Hillah, Iraq 32 30N 44 25E
100 Al Hilwa, Saudi Arabia 23 24N 46 48E
100 Al Hina, Iraq 32 0N 44 25E
100 Al Hindiya, Iraq 32 30N 44 10E
122 Al Hoceima (Alhucemas), Morocco 35 8N 3 58W
123 Al Hufrah, Libya 25 32N 14 1E
123 Al Hufrah, Libya 29 5N 18 3E
100 Al Hufuf, Si. Arabia 25 25N 49 45E
123 Al Husayyat, Libya 30 24N 20 37E
98 Al Husn, Jordan 32 29N 35 6E
121 Al Irq, Libya 29 5N 24 0E
99 Al Ittihad, *see* Madinat al-Shaab, S. Yemen 12 50N 45 0E
100 Al Jalamid, Si. Arabia 31 20N 39 45E
100 Al Jahrah, Kuwait 29 25N 47 40E
121 Al Jarzirah, Libya 26 10N 22 45E

MAP
121 Al Jawf, Libya ....24 10N 23 24 E
100 Al Jawf, Saudi Arabia 29 55N 39 40 E
99 Al Jazir, Oman ....18 30N 56 31 E
100 Al Jubayl, Si. Arabia .27 0N 49 50 E
99 Al Juwara, Oman ......19 0N 57 13 E
101 Al Khabura, Mus. & Oman ....23 57N 57 5 E
98 Al Khalih, Jordan ....31 32N 35 6 E
123 Al Khums (Homs), Libya ....32 40N 14 17 E
100 Al Kut, Iraq ....32 30N 46 0 E
100 Al Kuwayt, Kuwait ...29 20N 48 0 E
100 Al Ladhiqiyah, Syria .35 30N 35 45 E
101 Al Manamah, Bahrain 26 10N 50 30 E
121 Al Marj (Barce), Libya ....32 25N 20 30 E
101 Al Matrah, Mus. & 'O. 23 37N 58 30 E
100 Al Mawsil, Iraq ....36 15N 43 5 E
100 Al Miqdadiyah, Iraq 34 0N 45 0 E
100 Al Mubarraz, Si. Arab. ....25 30N 49 40 E
101 Al Muharraq, Bahrain 26 15N 50 40 E
100 Al Musayyib, Iraq ....32 40N 44 25 E
100 Al Muwaylim, Si. Arab. ....27 40N 35 30 E
123 Al Qaddahiyah, Libya 31 15N 15 9 E
100 Al Qamishli, Turkey .37 10N 41 10 E
123 Al Qaryah ash Sharqiyah, Libya ...30 28N 13 40 E
123 Al Qasabat (Cussabat), Libya ...32 39N 14 1 E
100 Al Qatif, Saudi Arabia 26 35N 50 0 E
123 Al Qatrun, Libya ......24 56N 15 3 E
100 Al Qaysumah, Si. Arab. ....28 10N 46 20 E
126 Al Qunfidha, Si. Arabia ....19 3N 41 4 E
101 Al Quraiyat, Oman ...23 17N 58 53 E
100 Al Qurnah, Iraq ....31 1N 47 25 E
123 Al Ujaylat, Libya .....32 52N 12 16 E
100 Al Ula, Saudi Arabia ....26 35N 38 0 E
123 Al Uqaylah, Libya ....30 12N 19 10 E
100 Al Uqayr, Saudi Arabia ....25 40N 50 15 E
100 Al Uwayqiyah, Si. Arabia ....30 30N 42 10 E
100 Al Wajh, Si. Arabia ...26 10N 36 30 E
100 Al Wakrah, Qatar ....25 10N 51 40 E
100 Al Wari 'ah, Si. Arabia ....27 50N 47 30 E
123 Al Watiyah, Libya ....32 28N 11 57 E
70 Ala, Italy ....45 46N 11 0 E
80 Ala, Sweden ....61 13N 17 9 E
111 Ala Shan, mts., China 39 50N 103 30 E
163 Alabama R., U.S.A. ...31 30N 87 35w
163 Alabama, st., U.S.A. .31 0N 87 0w
77 Alacati, Turkey ....38 16N 26 23 E
62 Alaejos, Spain 41 18N 5 13w
127 Alafa, Ethiopia ....11 55N 36 55 E
70 Alagna Valsesia, Italy 45 51N 7 56 E
175 Alagôa Grande, Brazil 7 3s 35 35w
175 Alagôas, st., Brazil 9 40s 35 50w
175 Alagoinhas, Brazil 12 0s 38 20w
164 Alagón, Spain 41 46N 1 12w
62 Alagon R., Spain 39 50N 6 50w
108 Alahanpandjang, Indon. .... 1 10s 100 45 E
169 Alajuela, Costa Rica .10 2N 84 8w
84 Alakurtti, Finland ....67 0N 30 30 E
126 Alam Ajab, Mt., Egypt ....25 55N 27 14 E
63 Alameda, Spain 37 12N 4 39w
167 Alameda, N. Mex., U.S.A. 35 10N 106 43w
166 Alameda, S.D., U.S.A. 43 2N 112 30w
168 Alamitos, Sierra de los, Mexico 26 30N 1 8w
167 Alamo, U.S.A. 37 21N 115 10w
167 Alamogordo, U.S.A. ...32 59N 106 0w
168 Alamos, Mexico 27 0N 109 0w
167 Alamosa, U.S.A. 37 30N 106 0w
106 Aland, India ....17 36N 76 35 E
63 Alandroal, Portugal ...38 41N 7 24w
124 Alangouassou, Ivory C. 7 30N 4 34w
63 Alanis, Spain 38 3N 5 43w
100 Alanya, Turkey ....36 38N 32 0 E
90 Alapayevsk, U.S.S.R. 57 55N 62 0 E
62 Alar del Rey, Spain ...42 38N 4 20w
63 Alaraz, Spain 40 45N 5 17w
62 Alaraz, R., Spain 42 5N 3 56w
85 Alasehir, Turkey ....38 23N 28 30 E
152 Alaska, st., U.S.A. 65 0N 150 0w
152 Alaska, G. of, Pac. Oc. 58 0N 145 0w
156 Alaska Highway, Can. 60 0N 130 0w
152 Alaska Pen., Alaska ...56 0N 160 0w
152 Alaska Range, mts., Alaska 62 50N 151 0w
70 Alassio, Italy ....44 1N 8 10 E
72 Alatri, Italy ....41 44N 13 21 E
87 Alatyr, U.S.S.R. ....54 45N 46 35 E
87 Alatyr R., U.S.S.R.....54 45N 45 30 E
174 Alausi, Ecuador 2 0s 78 50w
64 Alava Prov., Spain 42 48N 2 28w
166 Alava C., U.S.A. 48 10N 124 40w
89 Alaverdi, U.S.S.R. ......41 2N 44 37 E
145 Alawoona, S. Australia ....34 45s 140 30 E
64 Alayor, Spain ....39 57N 4 8 E
89 Alazan R., U.S.S.R. ...41 25N 46 35 E
70 Alba, Italy ....44 41N 8 1 E
78 Alba, Reg., Rumania .46 10N 23 30 E
78 Alba–Iulia, Rumania .46 8N 23 39 E
78 Albac, Rumania ......46 28N 23 1 E
65 Albacete, Spain 39 0N 1 50w
65 Albacete, prov., Spain 38 50N 2 0w
143 Albacutya L., Austral. 35 45s 141 58 E
65 Albaida, Spain 38 51N 0 31w
64 Albalate de las Nogueras, Spain 40 22N 2 18w
64 Albalate del Arzobispo, Spain 41 6N 0 31w
76 Albania, Rep., Europe 41 0N 20 0 E
72 Albano Laziale, Italy .41 44N 12 40 E
163 Albany, Ga., U.S.A. ...31 40N 84 10w
164 Albany, Minn., U.S.A. 45 37N 94 38w
161 Albany, N.Y., U.S.A. .42 40N 73 47w
166 Albany, Oreg., U.S.A. 44 41N 123 0w
165 Albany, Tex., U.S.A. .32 45N 99 20w
142 Albany, W. Australia .35 1s 117 58 E
154 Albany R., Canada 51 30N 87 0w
172 Albardon, Argentina .31 20s 68 30w
64 Albarracin, Spain 40 25N 1 26w
144 Albatross B. Australia 12 45s 141 30 E
146 Albatross Pt., N.Z. ....38 7s 174 44 E
71 Albegna R., Italy ....42 40N 11 28 E
163 Albemarle, U.S.A. 35 27N 80 15w
163 Albemarle Sd., U.S.A. 36 0N 76 30w
70 Albenga, Italy ....44 3N 8 12 E
62 Alberche R., Spain 40 10N 4 30w
138 Alberga R., S. Australia ....26 50s 133 40 E
65 Alberique, Spain 39 7N 0 31w
156 Alberni, Canada 49 20N 124 50w
56 Albersdorf, Germany .54 8N 9 19 E
55 Albersloh, Germany ...51 52N 7 44 E
155 Albert Canada 45 51N 64 38w
49 Albert, France ....50 0N 2 38 E
143 Albert, N.S.W., Austral. ....32 45s 147 31 E
55 Albert Canal, Belgium ....50 54N 5 30 E
156 Albert Canyon, Canada ....51 0N 121 55 E
131 Albert L., Congo......... 1 30N 31 0 E
145 Albert L., S. Australia 35 30s 139 10 E
165 Albert L., U.S.A. 42 40N 120 8w
164 Albert Lea, U.S.A. 43 32N 93 20w
131 Albert Nile R., Uganda .... 3 16N 31 38 E
156 Alberta, prov., Canada 54 40N 115 0w
134 Albertinia, S. Africa ...34 11s 21 34 E
59 Albertirsa, Hungary ...47 14N 19 37 E
155 Alberton, Canada 46 50N 64 0w
145 Alberton, Australia ...38 36s 146 37 E
131 Albertville, see Kalemie, Congo .... 5 55s 29 9 E
51 Albertville, France ....45 40N 6 22 E
50 Albi, Tarn, France ....43 56N 2 9 E
164 Albia, U.S.A. 41 0N 92 50w
175 Albina, Surinam 5 37N 54 15w
70 Albino, Italy ....45 47N 9 48 E
166 Albion, Idaho, U.S.A. 42 21N 113 37w
162 Albion, Mich., U.S.A. .42 15N 84 45w
164 Albion, Neb., U.S.A. .41 47N 98 0w
160 Albion, Pa., U.S.A. ...41 53N 80 21w
55 Alblasserdam, Neth. ...51 52N 4 40 E
64 Albocácer, Spain ....40 21N 0 1 E
81 Alböke, Sweden ....56 57N 16 45 E
62 Alboran I., Spain 35 57N 3 0w
65 Alborea, Spain 39 17N 1 24w
65 Albox, Spain 37 23N 2 8w
156 Albreda, Canada 52 35N 119 10w
34 Albrighton, England, United Kingdom 52 38N 2 17w
63 Albufeira, Portugal ...37 5N 8 15w
57 Albula R., Switzerland ....46 28N 9 38 E
65 Albuñol, Spain 36 48N 3 11w
167 Albuquerque, U.S.A. .35 5N 106 47w
161 Alburg, U.S.A. 44 58N 73 19w
73 Alburno, Mte., Italy ...40 32N 15 20 E
63 Alburquerque, Spain .39 15N 7 1w
143 Albury, Australia ......36 0s 146 50 E
80 Alby, Sweden ....62 28N 15 29 E
63 Alcácer do Sal, Portugal 38 22N 8 33w
63 Alcacovas, Portugal ...38 23N 8 9w
64 Alcalá de Chivert, Sp. ....40 19N 0 13 E
63 Alcala de Guadaira, Sp. 37 20N 5 50w
64 Alcala de Henares, Sp. 40 28N 3 22w
63 Alcala de los Gazules, Spain 36 29N 5 43w
63 Alcalá la Real, Spain .37 27N 3 57w
72 Alcamo, Italy ....37 59N 12 55 E
64 Alcanadre, Spain 42 24N 2 7w
64 Alcanadre R., Spain ...41 43N 0 0
64 Alcanar, Spain ....40 33N 0 28 E
63 Alcanede, Portugal 39 25N 8 49w
62 Alcañices, Spain 41 41N 6 21w
64 Alcañiz, Spain 41 2N 0 8w
175 Alcântara, Brazil 2 20s 44 30w
63 Alcantara, Spain 39 41N 6 57w
65 Alcantarilla, Spain 37 59N 1 12w
65 Alcaracejos, Spain .....38 24N 4 58 E
65 Alcaraz, Spain 38 40N 2 29w
63 Alcaudete, Spain 37 35N 4 5w
65 Alcazar de San Juan, Sp. 39 24N 3 12w
34 Alcester, Eng., U.K. ...52 13N 1 52w
65 Alcira, Spain 39 9N 0 30w
163 Alcoa, U.S.A. 35 50N 84 0w
63 Alcobaça, Portugal 39 32N 9 0w
64 Alcobendas, Spain 40 32N 3 38w
135 Alcockspruit, S. Africa ....27 55s 30 1 E
64 Alcolea del Pinar, Spain 41 02N 2 28w
64 Alcora, Spain 40 5N 0 14w
63 Alcoutim, Portugal 37 25N 7 28w
166 Alcova, U.S.A. 42 37N 106 52w
65 Alcoy, Spain 38 43N 0 30w
64 Alcublas, Spain 39 48N 0 43w
64 Alcudia, Spain ....39 51N 3 9 E
64 Alcudia, Bahia de, Spain ....39 45N 3 14 E
11 Aldabra Is., Br. Indian Oc. Terr. .... 9 22s 46 28 E
91 Aldan, U.S.S.R. ....58 40N 125 30 E
91 Aldan R., U.S.S.R. ...62 30N 135 30 E
91 Aldanski Perevoz, U.S.S.R. ....62 5N 135 15 E
39 Aldborough, England, United Kingdom 54 6N 1 21w
34 Aldbourne, England, U.K. 51 28N 1 38w
39 Aldbrough, England, U.K. 53 50N 0 7w
35 Aldeburgh, England, U.K. ....52 9N 1 35 E
63 Aldeia Nova, Portugal 37 55N 7 24w
79 Alden I., Norway ......61 19N 4 45 E
166 Alder, U.S.A. 45 27N 112 3w
34 Alderbury, England, U.K. 51 4N 1 45w
38 Alderley Edge, Eng., U.K. 53 18N 2 15w
34 Aldermaston, Eng., U.K. 51 23N 1 9w
48 Alderney I., Chan. Is., United Kingdom 49 42N 2 12w
35 Aldershot, England, U.K. 51 15N 0 43w
156 Aldersyde, Canada 50 40N 113 53w
38 Aldingham, Eng., U.K. 54 8N 3 3w
164 Aledo, U.S.A. 41 10N 90 50w
173 Alegre, Brazil 20 50s 41 30w
173 Alegrete, Brazil 29 40s 56 0w
90 Aleisk, U.S.S.R. ....52 40N 83 0 E
137 Alejandro Selkirk I., S. Pacific 33 50s 80 15w
85 Aleksandriya, U.S.S.R. ....50 45N 26 22 E
88 Aleksandriya, U.S.S.R. ....48 42N 33 3 E
89 Aleksandriyskaya, U.S.S.R. ....43 59N 47 0 E
87 Aleksandrov, U.S.S.R. 56 28N 38 50 E
87 Aleksandrov Gay., U.S.S.R. ....50 15N 48 35 E
74 Aleksandrovac, Y.-slav ....44 28N 21 13 E
88 Aleksandrovka, U.S.S.R. ....48 55N 32 20 E
75 Aleksandrovo, Bulgaria ....43 14N 24 51 E
91 Aleksandrovsk, Sakhalin, U.S.S.R. .50 50N 142 20 E
91 Aleksandrovski Zavod, U.S.S.R. ....50 40N 117 50 E
90 Aleksandrovskoye, U.S.S.R. ....60 35N 77 50 E
60 Aleksandrów Kujawski, Poland ...52 53N 18 43 E
60 Aleksandrów Łódski, Poland ....51 49N 19 17 E
87 Alekseyevka, U.S.S.R. 50 43N 38 40 E
87 Aleksin, U.S.S.R. ....54 29N 36 57 E
74 Aleksinac, Yugoslavia 43 31N 21 42 E
172 Alemania, Argentina .25 40s 65 30w
79 Ålen, Norway ....62 49N 11 28 E
48 Alençon, France ....48 27N 0 4 E
158 Alenuihaha Chan., Hawaiian Is., U.S.A. 20 25N 156 0w
100 Aleppo, (Halab), Syria 36 10N 37 15 E
156 Alert B., Canada 50 30N 127 35w
51 Alès, France ....44 9N 4 5 E
78 Aleşd, Rumania ....47 3N 22 22 E
70 Alessandria, Italy ......44 54N 8 37 E
79 Ålesund, Norway ....62 28N 6 12 E
127 Alet, Sudan .... 8 14N 29 2 E
152 Aleutian Is., Pac. Oc. 52 0N 175 0w
164 Alexander, U.S.A. 47 51N 103 40w
152 Alexander Arch., Alaska, U.S.A. 57 0N 135 0w
134 Alexander B., S. Africa ....28 36s 16 33 E
163 Alexander City, U.S.A. 32 58N 85 57w
15 Alexander I., Antarc. .69 0s 70 0w
142 Alexander, Mt., W. Australia ....28 58s 120 16 E
147 Alexandra, N.Z. ....45 14s 169 25 E
143 Alexandra, Australia .37 8s 145 40 E
100 Alexandretta, see Iskenderun, Turkey 36 32N 36 10 E
156 Alexandria, B.C., Can 52 35N 122 20w
154 Alexandria, Ont., Can. 45 19N 74 38w
126 Alexandria, see El Iskandariya, Egypt 31 0N 30 0 E
78 Alexandria, Rumania .43 57N 25 24 E
40 Alexandria, Scotland, United Kingdom 55 59N 4 40w
135 Alexandria, S. Africa .33 38s 26 28 E
162 Alexandria, Ind., U.S.A. 40 18N 85 40w
165 Alexandria, La., U.S.A. 31 20N 92 30w
164 Alexandria, Minn., U.S.A. 45 50N 95 20w
164 Alexandria, S.D., U.S.A. 43 40N 97 45w
162 Alexandria, Va., U.S.A. 38 47N 77 1w
161 Alexandria B., U.S.A. 44 20N 75 52w
145 Alexandrina L., S. Australia ....35 30s 139 15 E
76 Alexandroúpolis, Gr. .40 50N 25 54 E
156 Alexis Creek, Canada .52 0N 123 20w
64 Alfambra, Spain 40 33N 1 5w
62 Alfandega da Fé, Port. 41 20N 6 59w
64 Alfaro, Spain 42 10N 1 50w
56 Alfeld, Germany ....52 0N 9 49 E
173 Alfenas, Brazil 21 40s 44 0w
77 Alfiós R., Greece ....37 36N 21 54 E
71 Alfonsine, Italy ....44 30N 12 1 E
39 Alford, England, U.K. 53 16N 0 10 E
43 Alford, Scot., U.K. 57 13N 2 42w
161 Alfred, Me., U.S.A. 43 28N 70 40w
160 Alfred, N.Y., U.S.A. .42 15N 77 45w
146 Alfredton, N.Z. ....40 41s 175 54 E
39 Alfreton, England, U.K. 53 6N 1 22w
35 Alfriston, England, U.K. ....50 48N 0 10 E
80 Alfta, Sweden ....61 19N 16 8 E
82 Alftanes, Iceland 64 29N 22 10w
127 Alga, Ethiopia ....12 15N 41 48 E
160 Alganac, U.S.A. 42 36N 82 34w
63 Algar, Spain 36 40N 5 39w
79 Ålgård, Norway ....58 45N 5 55 E
63 Algarinejo, Spain 37 19N 4 9w
172 Algarrobo del Aguila, Argentina 36 20s 72 50w
63 Algarve, reg., Portugal 37 15N 8 10w
63 Algeciras, Spain 36 9N 5 28w
65 Algemesi, Spain 39 11N 0 27w
122 Alger, Algeria ....36 42N 3 8 E
122 Algeria, st., Africa ....35 10N 3 11 E
72 Alghero, Italy ....40 34N 8 20 E
122 Algiers (Alger), Algeria ....36 42N 3 8 E
135 Algoa B., S. Africa ....33 50s 25 45 E
63 Algodanales, Spain 36 54N 5 24w
63 Algodor R., Spain 39 51N 3 48w
162 Algoma, Mich., U.S.A. 44 35N 87 27w
166 Algoma, Ore., U.S.A. .42 25N 121 54w
164 Algona, U.S.A. 43 1N 94 10w
154 Algonquin Park, Can. 45 35N 78 35w
65 Alhama de Almeria, Sp. 36 57N 2 34w
64 Alhama de Aragón, Sp. 41 18N 1 54w
63 Alhama de Granada, Sp. 37 0N 3 59w
65 Alhama de Murcia, Sp. 37 51N 1 25w
65 Alhambra, Spain 38 54N 3 4w
167 Alhambra, U.S.A. 34 0N 118 10w
63 Alhaurin el Grande, Sp. 36 39N 4 41w
122 Alhucemas, see Al Hoceima, Morocco .35 8N 3 58w
98 Ali Bayramly, U.S.S.R. ....39 43N 48 52 E
100 Ali al Gharbi, Iraq ....32 30N 46 45 E
127 Ali Sabiet, Fr. Terr. of the Afars & Issas ...11 10N 42 44 E
72 Alia, Italy ....37 47N 13 42 E
101 Aliabad, Iran ....28 10N 57 35 E
64 Aliaga, Spain 40 40N 0 42w
76 Aliákmon, R., Greece .40 10N 22 0 E
106 Alibag, India ....18 38N 72 56 E
127 Alibo, Ethiopia .... 9 52N 37 5 E
74 Alibunar, Yugoslavia .45 5N 20 57 E
65 Alicante, Spain 38 23N 0 30w
65 Alicante, Prov. Spain .38 30 0 37w
135 Alice, C. Prov., S. Africa ....32 48s 26 55 E
165 Alice, U.S.A. 27 47N 98 1w
144 Alice R., Australia ....23 50s 145 0 E
156 Alice Arm, Canada 55 29N 129 23w
138 Alice Springs, Australia ....23 36s 133 53 E
135 Alicedale, S. Africa ...33 15s 26 4 E
163 Aliceville, U.S.A. 33 9N 88 10w
73 Alicudi I., Italy ....38 33N 14 20 E
157 Alida, Canada 49 25N 101 55w
104 Aligarh, Raj., India ...25 55N 76 15 E
104 Aligarh, Ut. P., India 27 55N 78 10 E
100 Aligudarz, Iran ....33 25N 49 45 E
62 Al o, Portugal 41 16N 7 27w
130 Alima R., Congo (Fr.) 1 0s 15 20 E
73 Alimena, Italy ....37 42N 14 4 E
77 Alimnia I., Greece ....36 16N 27 43 E
103 Aling Kangri Mt., China ....32 48N 81 3 E
103 Aling Kangri Mts., China ....31 45N 84 45 E
81 Alingaabro, Denmark 56 50N 10 32 E
81 Alingsås, Sweden ......57 57N 12 36 E
105 Alipore, India ....22 32N 88 24 E
104 Alipur, Pakistan ....29 25N 70 55 E
105 Alipur Duar, India ....26 30N 89 35 E
160 Aliquippa, U.S.A. 40 38N 80 18w
62 Aliste R., Spain 41 48N 6 14w
86 Alitus, U.S.S.R. ....54 23N 24 0 E
77 Alivérion, Greece ......38 24N 24 2 E
135 Aliwal, N., S. Africa ...30 45s 26 45 E
63 Aljezur, Portugal 37 18N 8 49w
63 Aljustrel, Portugal 37 55N 8 10w
125 Alkamari, Niger ....13 27N 11 10 E
99 Alkhalaf, Oman ....20 30N 58 13 E
54 Alkmaar, Netherlands 52 37N 4 45 E
167 All American Canal, U.S.A. 32 45N 115 0w
39 All Saints, England, U.K. ....53 6N 0 16 E
125 Allada, Dahomey ...... 6 41N 2 9 E
104 Allah Dad, W. Pakistan ....25 38N 67 34 E
105 Allahabad, India ....25 25N 81 58 E
91 Allakh Yun, U.S.S.R. 60 50N 137 5 E
122 Allal–Tazi, Morocco ...34 30N 6 15w
50 Allanche, France ......45 14N 2 57 E
107 Allanmyo, Burma ......19 16N 95 17 E
135 Allanridge, S. Africa .27 45s 26 40 E
143 Allansford, Australia .38 26s 142 39 E
147 Allanton, New Zealand ....45 55s 170 15 E
89 Allanüekber Ra., Tur. 40 37N 42 27 E
154 Allanwater, Canada ...50 14N 90 10w
160 Allardale, Canada 44 23N 79 40w
62 Allariz, Spain 42 11N 7 50w
126 Allaqi, Wadi, Egypt ...22 15N 134 55 E
155 Allard Lake, Canada .50 40N 63 10w
162 Allegan, U.S.A. 42 32N 85 52w
160 Allegany, U.S.A. 41 30N 78 30w
162 Allegheny Mts., U.S.A. 38 0N 80 0w
160 Allegheny Res., U.S.A. 42 0N 78 55w
160 Allegheny R., U.S.A. .41 14N 79 50w
50 Allègre, France ....45 12N 3 41 E
45 Allen, Bog of, Ireland 53 15N 7 0w
46 Allen L., Ireland 54 30N 8 5w
38 Allen R., England, U.K. 54 53N 2 13w
98 Allenby (Hussein) Bridge, Jordan ......31 53N 35 33 E
38 Allendale, England, U.K. 54 55N 2 15w
168 Allende, Mexico 28 20N 100 50w
38 Allenheads, Eng., U.K. 54 49N 2 12w
161 Allentown, U.S.A. 40 36N 75 30w
58 Allentsteig, Austria ...48 41N 15 20 E
45 Allenwood, Ireland 53 16N 6 53w
106 Alleppey, India .... 9 30N 76 28 E
81 Allerød, Denmark ......55 54N 12 19 E
55 Alleur, Belgium ....50 39N 5 31 E
51 Allevard, France ....45 24N 6 5 E
164 Alliance, Neb., U.S.A. .41 14N 102 50w
160 Alliance, Ohio, U.S.A. 40 53N 81 7w
50 Allier, dépt., France ...46 25N 3 0 E
49 Allier R., France ....46 40N 3 10 E
144 Alligator Creek, Mackay, Australia .21 20s 149 12 E
144 Alligator Creek Townsville, Australia ....19 20s 146 55 E
44 Allihies, Ireland 51 39N 10 4w
81 Allingaabro, Denmark 56 28N 10 20 E
81 Allinge, Denmark ......55 17N 14 50 E
160 Alliston, Canada 44 15N 79 55w
41 Alloa, Scotland, U.K. 56 7N 3 49w
38 Allonby, England, U.K. 54 45N 3 27w
51 Allos, France ....44 15N 6 38 E
155 Alma, Canada 48 35N 71 40w
164 Alma, Kan. U.S.A. 39 1N 96 22w
162 Alma, Mich. U.S.A. ...43 25N 84 40w
164 Alma, Neb., U.S.A. 40 10N 99 25w
164 Alma, Wis., U.S.A. 44 19N 91 54w
90 Alma Ata, U.S.S.R. ...43 20N 76 50 E
63 Almada, Portugal 38 40N 9 9w
144 Almaden, Australia ...17 22s 144 40 E
63 Almadén, Spain 38 49N 4 52w
138 Almadeus, L., Australia ....24 45s 131 0 E
63 Almagro, Spain 38 50N 3 45w
166 Almanor, L., U.S.A. ...40 15N 121 11w
65 Almansa, Spain 38 51N 1 5w
62 Almanza, Spain 42 39N 5 3w
62 Almanzor, Pico de, mt., Spain 40 15N 5 18w
65 Almanzora R., Spain .37 22N 2 21w
78 Almas, Mţil, Mts., Rum. ....44 49N 22 12 E
64 Almazán, Spain 41 30N 2 30w
175 Almeirim, Brazil 1 10s 52 0w
63 Almeirim, Portugal ...39 12N 8 37w
54 Almelo, Netherlands .52 22N 6 42 E
64 Almenar, Spain 41 43N 2 12w
64 Almenara, Spain 39 46N 0 14w
63 Almendralejo, Spain ...38 41N 6 26w
65 Almeria, tn. & prov., Sp. 36 52N 2 32w
65 Almeria, G. de, Spain 36 41N 2 28w
81 Älmhult, Sweden ....56 32N 14 10 E
169 Almirante, Panama ... 9 10N 82 30w
172 Almirante Latorre, Chile 29 33s 71 15w
77 Almiropótamos, Greece ....38 16N 24 11 E
77 Almirós, Greece ....39 11N 22 45 E
63 Almodovar, Portugal .37 31N 8 3w
63 Almodovar del Campo, Spain 38 43N 4 10w
65 Almogia, Spain 36 50N 4 32w
63 Almonaster la Real, Sp. 37 52N 6 48w
41 Almond R., Scot., U.K. 56 27N 3 40w
36 Almondsbury, Eng., U.K. 51 33N 2 34w
160 Almont, U.S.A. 42 53N 83 2w
161 Almonte, Canada 45 15N 76 15w
63 Almonte, Spain 37 16N 6 31w
63 Almonte R., Spain 39 41N 6 12w
105 Almora, India ....29 38N 79 42 E
62 Almorox, Spain 40 14N 4 24w
63 Almuñécar, Spain 36 43N 3 41w
81 Almvik, Sweden ....57 49N 16 30 E
43 Alness, Scotland, U.K. 57 41N 4 15w
43 Alness R., Scotland, U.K. 57 45N 4 20w
122 Alnif, Morocco 31 10N 5 8w
39 Alnmouth, England, U.K. 55 24N 1 37w
80 Alnön I., Sweden ......62 26N 17 33 E
39 Alnwick, England, U.K. 55 25N 1 42w
157 Alonsa, Canada 50 50N 99 0w
109 Alor I., Indonesia ...... 8 10s 124 30 E
107 Alor Star, Malaysia ... 6 7N 100 22 E

MAP
63 Alora, Spain ...36 49N 4 46W
63 Alosno, Spain ...37 33N 7 7W
122 Alougoum, Morocco ...30 17N 6 56W
142 Aloysius Mt., W. Austral. ...26 0S 128 38E
62 Alpedrinha, Portugal .40 6N 7 27W
162 Alpena, U.S.A. ...45 6N 83 24W
51 Alpes-de-Haute-Provence, dépt., France ...44 12N 6 20E
51 Alpes-Maritimes, dépt., France ...43 55N 7 10E
144 Alpha, Australia ...23 45S 46 30E
36 Alphington, Eng., U.K. ...50 41N 3 32W
70 Alpi Apuan, mts., Italy ...44 7N 10 14E
58 Alpi Carniche, mts., Europe ...46 36N 13 0E
70 Alpi Lepontine, mts., It. ...46 22N 8 27E
70 Alpi Orobie, mts., Italy ...46 7N 10 0E
57 Alpi Pennine, mts., Switzerland ...46 4N 7 30E
57 Alpi Retiche, mts., Switzerland ...46 45N 10 0E
63 Alpiarço., Portugal ...39 15N 8 35W
167 Alpine, Ariz., U.S.A. ...33 57N 109 4W
165 Alpine, Tex., U.S.A. ...30 35N 103 35W
52 Alps, mts., Europe ...47 0N 8 0E
34 Alrewas, Eng., U.K. ...52 44N 1 44W
81 Alrö, Denmark ...55 51N 10 2E
81 Als, Denmark ...56 46N 10 18E
49 Alsace, Reg., France .48 15N 7 25E
38 Alsager, Eng., U.K. ...53 7N 2 20W
64 Alsasua, Spain ...42 54N 2 10W
55 Alsdorf, Germany ...50 53N 6 10E
81 Alseda, Sweden ...57 27N 15 20E
80 Alsen, Sweden ...63 26N 13 56E
56 Alsfeld, Germany ...50 44N 9 19E
59 Alsónémedi, Hungary 47 34N 19 15E
38 Alston, England, U.K. 54 48N 2 26W
172 Alta Gracia, Argentina ...31 40S 64 30W
156 Alta Lake, Canada ...50 10N 123 0W
82 Altaelv R., Norway ...69 0N 23 30E
174 Altagracia, Venezuela 10 45N 71 30W
111 Altai, China ...48 6N 87 2E
111 Altai Mts., Asia ...46 40N 92 45E
163 Altamaha R., U.S.A. .31 50N 82 0W
175 Altamira, Brazil ... 3 0S 52 50W
62 Altamira Cave, Spain .43 20N 4 5W
161 Altamont, U.S.A. ...42 43N 74 3W
73 Altamura, Italy ...40 50N 16 33E
112 Altanbulag, Mongolia .50 16N 106 30E
168 Altar, Mexico ...30 40N 111 50W
36 Altarnun, Eng., U.K. .50 35N 4 30W
168 Altata, Mexico ...24 30N 108 0W
162 Altavista, U.S.A. ...37 9N 79 22W
57 Altdorf, Switzerland .. 46 52N 8 36E
82 Alte Fjord, Norway ...70 10N 23 0E
65 Altea, Spain ...38 38N 0 2W
55 Altena, Germany ...51 18N 7 40E
56 Altenberg, Germany ...50 46N 13 47E
56 Altenbruch, Germany 53 48N 8 44E
56 Altenburg, Germany .50 59N 12 28E
56 Altenkirchen, Germany ...50 41N 7 38E
58 Altenmarkt, Austria ...47 43N 14 39E
63 Alter do Chao, Portugal ...39 12N 7 40W
49 Altkirch, France ...47 37N 7 15E
43 Altnaharra, Scot., U.K. ...58 17N 4 43W
175 Alto Araguaia, Brazil .17 15S 53 20W
132 Alto Chindio, Mozam.. 16 19S 35 25E
168 Alto Cuchumatanes, mt., Guatemala ...15 30N 91 10W
172 Alto del Inca, Chile ...24 10S 68 10W
129 Alto Molocue, Mozam. 15 50S 37 35E
173 Alto Parana R., Brazil ...25 0S 54 35W
173 Alto Uruguai, R., Brazil ...24 0S 53 30W
160 Alton, Canada ...43 54N 80 5W
35 Alton, England, U.K. 51 8N 0 59W
164 Alton, Ill., U.S.A. ...38 55N 90 5W
145 Alton Downs, S. Austral. ...26 12S 138 58E
143 Altona, Australia ...37 50S 145 40E
35 Altona, Germany ...53 32N 9 56E
161 Altoona, U.S.A. ...40 32N 78 24W
70 Altopascio, Italy ...43 50N 10 40E
38 Altrincham, Eng., U.K. ...53 25N 2 21W
57 Altstätten, Switzerland ...47 22N 9 33E
100 Altun Kopru, Iraq ...35 46N 44 10E
166 Alturas, U.S.A. ...41 36N 120 37W
165 Altus, U.S.A. ...34 30N 99 25W
111 Altyn Tagh, mts., China ...39 0N 90 0E
89 Alucra, Turkey ...40 22N 38 47E
86 Aluksene, U.S.S.R. ...57 24N 27 3E
99 Alula, Somali Rep. ...11 50N 50 45E
88 Alupka, U.S.S.R. ...44 23N 34 2E
88 Alushta, U.S.S.R. ...44 40N 34 25E
109 Alusi, Indonesia ... 7 35S 131 40E
64 Alustante, Spain ...40 36N 1 40W
41 Alva, Scotland, U.K. .56 9N 3 49W
165 Alva, U.S.A. ...36 50N 98 50W
62 Alvaiazere, Portugal .39 49N 8 23W
81 Älvängen, Sweden ...58 0N 12 7E
168 Alvarado, Mexico ...18 40N 95 50W
165 Alvarado, U.S.A. ...32 25N 97 15W
81 Alvastra, Sweden ...58 20N 14 44E
79 Alvdal, Norway ...62 12N 10 43E
172 Alvear, Argentina ...29 5S 57 40W
34 Alvechurch, Eng., U.K. ...52 22N 1 58W
63 Alverca, Portugal ...38 56N 9 1W
55 Alverskirchen, Ger. ...51 56N 7 48E
81 Alvesta, Sweden ...56 54N 14 35E
80 Älvho, Sweden ...61 30N 14 45E
43 Alvie, Scotland, U.K. 57 10N 3 50W
143 Alvie, Victoria, Austral. ...38 15N 143 30E
165 Alvin, U.S.A. ...29 23N 95 12W
160 Alvinston, Canada ...42 50N 81 53W
63 Alvito, Portugal ...38 15N 8 0W
80 Älvros, Sweden ...62 3N 14 40E
81 Älvsborg, Län, Sweden ...58 30N 12 30E
82 Älvsby, Sweden ...65 42N 20 52E
81 Älvsered, Sweden ...57 15N 12 52E
104 Alwar, India ...27 38N 76 34E
106 Alwaye, India ...10 8N 76 24E
139 Alyangula, Australia .13 55S 136 30E
89 Alyaty Pristan, U.S.S.R. ...39 58N 49 25E
41 Alyth, Scotland, U.K. 56 38N 3 15W
164 Alzada, U.S.A. ...45 3N 104 22W
70 Alzano Lombardo, Italy ...45 44N 9 43E
121 Am-Dam, Chad ...12 40N 20 35E
121 Am Djeress, Chad ...16 15N 22 50E
121 Am Guereda, Chad ...12 53N 21 14E
121 Am Timan, Chad ...11 0N 20 10E
135 Amabele, S. Africa ...32 40S 27 30E
138 Amadeus L., Australia 24 54S 131 0E
127 Amadi, Sudan ... 5 29N 30 25E
100 Amadia, Iraq ...37 6N 43 30E
153 Amadjuak, Canada ...64 0N 72 50W
153 Amadjuak L., Canada 65 0N 71 0W
63 Amadora, Portugal ...38 45N 9 13E
160 Amadore, U.S.A. ...43 12N 82 36E
114 Amagasaki, Japan ...34 42N 135 20E
81 Amager I., Denmark .55 37N 12 35W
125 Amagunze, Nigeria ... 6 20N 7 40W
109 Amahai, Indonesia ... 3 2S 128 15E
114 Amakusa I., Japan ...32 15N 130 10E
80 Åmal, Sweden ...59 2N 12 40E
106 Amalapuram, India ...16 35N 81 55E
73 Amalfi, Italy ...40 39N 14 34E
77 Amaliás, Greece ...37 47N 21 22E
104 Amalner, India ...21 5N 75 5E
113 Amami Gunto, Is., Jap. ...28 0N 129 0E
71 Amandola, Italy ...42 59N 13 21E
125 Amanfrom, Ghana ... 7 20N 0 25E
90 Amangeldy, U.S.S.R. .50 10N 65 10E
73 Amantea, Italy ...39 8N 16 3E
175 Amapá, Brazil ... 2 5N 50 50W
175 Amapá, Fed. Terr., Braz. ... 1 40N 52 0W
109 Amar, Indonesia ... 4 45S 131 40E
127 Amar Gedid, Sudan ...14 27N 25 13E
127 Amar Kokke, Ethiopia ... 5 15N 36 45E
100 Amara, Iraq ...31 57N 47 12E
127 Amara, Sudan ...10 25N 34 10E
175 Amarante, Brazil ... 6 15S 42 50W
62 Amarante, Portugal ...41 16N 8 5W
157 Amaranth, Canada ...50 36N 98 43W
104 Amaravati, India ...20 55N 77 45E
106 Amaravati, R., India .10 50N 77 42E
63 Amareleja, Portugal ...38 12N 7 13W
175 Amargosa, Brazil ...13 0S 39 50W
165 Amarillo, Tex., U.S.A. 35 14N 101 46W
71 Amaro, Mte., Italy ...42 5N 14 6E
105 Amarpur, Bihar, India ...25 5N 87 0E
103 Amarpur, Tripura, India ...23 30N 91 45E
100 Amasra, Turkey ...41 45N 32 30E
125 Amassama, Nigeria ... 5 1N 6 2E
100 Amasya, Turkey ...40 40N 35 50E
174 Amatari Brazil ... 3 0S 59 0W
135 Amatikulu, S. Africa .29 3S 31 33E
168 Amatitlán, Guatemala 14 29N 90 38W
71 Amatrice, Italy ...42 38N 13 16E
55 Amay, Belgium ...50 33N 5 19E
175 Amazon R., S. America ... 2 0S 53 30W
174 Amazonas, st., Brazil . 4 20S 64 0W
106 Ambad, India ...19 38N 75 50E
104 Ambala, India ...30 23N 76 56E
106 Ambalangoda, Ceylon 6 15N 80 5E
106 Ambalapuzha, India . 9 25N 76 25E
129 Ambalavao, Malagasy Rep. ...21 50S 46 56E
128 Amban, Cameroon ... 2 20N 11 15E
129 Ambanja, Malagasy Rep. ...13 40S 48 27E
91 Ambarchik, U.S.S.R. .69 40N 162 20E
106 Ambarnath, India ...19 12N 73 22E
106 Ambasamudram, India ... 8 43N 77 25E
174 Ambato, Ecuador ... 1 5S 78 42W
129 Ambatolampy, Malag. 20 39S 47 35E
129 Ambatondrazaka, Malagasy Rep. ...17 55S 48 28E
109 Ambelau I., Indonesia 3 50S 127 15E
109 Ambeno, Timor (Port) 9 20S 124 30E
57 Amberg, Germany ...49 25N 11 52E
168 Ambergris Cay, British Honduras ...18 0N 88 0W
51 Ambérieu, France ...45 57N 5 20E
147 Amberley, N.Z. ...43 9S 172 44E
50 Ambert, France ...45 33N 3 44E
124 Ambidédi, Mali ...14 35N 11 47W
105 Ambikapur, India ...23 15N 83 15E
126 Ambikol, Sudan ...21 20N 30 50E
129 Ambilobé, Malagasy Rep. ...13 10S 49 3E
81 Ambjörnarp, Sweden .57 26N 13 15E
39 Amble, England, U.K. 55 20N 1 36W
38 Ambleside, Eng., U.K. 54 26N 2 58W
55 Ambléve, Belgium ...50 21N 6 10E
55 Amblève R., Belgium 50 25N 5 45E
127 Ambo, Ethiopia ... 9 0N 37 48E
127 Ambo, Ethiopia ...12 20N 37 30E
174 Ambo, Peru ...10 5S 76 10W
109 Ambon, Indonesia ... 3 35S 128 20E
129 Ambositra Malagasy Rep. ...20 31S 47 25E
167 Amboy, Calif., U.S.A. 34 33N 115 51W
161 Amboy, N.J., U.S.A. .40 31N 74 18W
129 Ambre, C. de Mt., Malagasy Rep. ...12 40S 49 10E
160 Ambridge, U.S.A. ...40 36N 80 15W
130 Ambriz, Angola ... 7 48S 13 8E
130 Ambrizète, Angola ... 7 10S 12 52E
106 Ambur, India ...12 48N 78 43E
145 Amby, Australia ...26 30S 148 11E
90 Amderma, U.S.S.R. ...69 45N 61 30E
168 Ameca & R., Mexico .20 30N 104 0W
168 Amecameca, Mexico ...19 10N 98 57W
54 Ameland I., Netherlands ...53 27N 5 45E
71 Amelia, Italy ...42 34N 12 25E
50 Amelie, France ...42 29N 2 38E
122 Amellago, Morocco ...32 0N 4 57W
91 Amen, U.S.S.R. ...68 45N 180 0E
73 Amendolara, Italy ...39 58N 16 34E
55 America, Netherlands 51 27N 5 59E
166 American Falls, U.S.A. ...42 46N 112 56W
166 American Falls Res., U.S.A. ...43 0N 112 50W
15 American Highland, Antarctica ...73 0S 75 0E
173 Americana, Brazil ...27 10S 47 10W
163 Americus, U.S.A. ...32 0N 84 10W
55 Amern, Germany ...51 14N 6 14E
54 Amersfoort, Neth. ...52 9N 5 23E
133 Amersfoort, S. Africa .26 59S 29 53E
35 Amersham, Eng., U.K. ...51 40N 0 38W
142 Amery, W. Australia .31 10S 117 12E
122 Amerzgane, Morocco .31 4N 7 4W
164 Ames, U.S.A. ...42 0N 93 40W
34 Amesbury, Eng., U.K. 51 10N 1 46W
161 Amesbury, U.S.A. ...42 50N 70 52W
157 Amesdale, Canada ...50 2N 92 55W
154 Ameson, Canada ...49 50N 84 35W
77 Amfíklia, Greece ...38 38N 22 35E
77 Amfilokhía, Greece ...38 52N 21 9E
76 Amfípolis, Greece ...40 48N 23 52E
77 Amfissa, Greece ...38 32N 22 22E
91 Amga R., U.S.S.R. ...61 0N 132 0E
91 Amgu, U.S.S.R. ...45 45N 137 15E
103 Amherst, Burma ...16 2N 97 20E
155 Amherst, Canada ...45 48N 64 8W
161 Amherst, Mass., U.S.A. ...42 21N 72 30W
160 Amherst, Ohio, U.S.A. 41 23N 82 15W
165 Amherst, Tex., U.S.A. 34 0N 102 24W
161 Amherst I., Ont., Can. 44 8N 76 45W
71 Amiata Mte., Italy ...42 54N 11 40E
49 Amiens, France ...49 54N 2 16E
77 Amigdhalokefali, Gr. .35 23N 23 30E
76 Amindaion, Greece ...40 42N 21 42E
11 Amirante Is. Ind. Oc. 6 0S 53 0E
157 Amisk L., Canada ...54 35N 102 15W
106 Amismiz Morocco ...31 19N 8 6W
165 Amite, U.S.A. ...30 47N 90 31W
79 Åmli, Norway ...58 45N 8 32E
37 Amlwch, Wales, U.K. 53 24N 4 21W
127 Amm Adam, Sudan ...16 20N 36 1E
98 Amman, Jordan ...32 0N 35 52E
37 Ammanford, Wales, U.K. ...51 48N 4 0W
80 Ammeran R., Sweden 63 22N 15 45E
57 Ammersee, L., Ger. ...48 0N 11 7E
111 Amne Machin Shan, China ...34 25N 99 40E
98 Ammi'ad, Israel ...32 55N 35 32E
44 Amorbach, Germany .49 38N 9 15E
64 Amorebieta, Spain ...43 13N 2 44W
77 Amorgós & I., Greece 36 50N 25 57E
163 Amory, U.S.A. ...33 59N 88 30W
154 Amos, Canada ...48 35N 78 5W
79 Åmot, Norway ...59 35N 8 0E
79 Åmotsdal, Norway ...59 38N 8 23E
122 Amour, Djebel, Algeria ...33 42N 1 37E
113 Amoy, China ...24 25N 118 4E
129 Ampanihy, Malagasy Rep. ...24 40S 44 45E
125 Amper, Nigeria ... 9 25N 9 40E
123 Ampère, Algeria ...35 44N 5 45E
39 Ampleforth, Eng., U.K. ...54 13N 1 8W
64 Amposta, Spain ...40 43N 0 34E
35 Ampthill, England, U.K. ...52 3N 0 30W
98 Amqa, Israel ...32 59N 35 10E
155 Amqui, Canada ...48 28N 67 27W
104 Amraoti, India ...20 55N 77 45E
104 Amreli, India ...21 35N 71 17E
122 Amrenene el Kasba, Algeria ...22 10N 0 30E
104 Amritsar, India ...31 35N 74 57E
106 Amroha, India ...28 53N 78 30E
56 Amrum I., Germany .54 37N 8 21E
123 Amsel, Algeria ...22 47N 5 29E
53 Amsterdam, Netherlands ...52 23N 4 54E
133 Amsterdam, S. Africa 26 35S 30 45E
161 Amsterdam, U.S.A. ...42 58N 74 10W
11 Amsterdam I., Ind. Oc. ...37 30S 77 30E
58 Amstetten, Austria ...48 7N 14 51E
122 Amzeglouf, Algeria ...26 50N 0 1E
90 Amu Darya R., U.S.S.R. ...37 50N 65 0E
174 Amuay, Venezuela ...11 50N 70 10W
131 Amudat, Uganda ... 1 58N 34 58E
14 Amund Ringnes I., Can. ...78 0N 97 0W
152 Amundsen Gulf, Canada ...70 30N 123 0W
15 Amundsen Sea, Antarc. ...72 0S 115 0W
80 Amungen L., Sweden .61 10N 15 35E
108 Amuntai, Indonesia ... 2 28S 115 25E
91 Amur R., U.S.S.R. ...53 30N 122 30E
109 Amurang, Indonesia ... 1 5N 124 40E
147 Amuri Pass, N.Z. ...42 31S 172 11E
131 Amuria, Uganda ... 2 4N 33 38E
64 Amurrio, Spain ...43 3N 3 0W
62 Amusco, Spain ...42 10N 4 28W
77 Amvrakí kós Kólpos, G., Greece ...39 0N 27 55E
89 Anavrosievka, U.S.S.R. ...47 43N 38 30E
45 An Geata Mór, (Binghamstown), Ireland ...54 13N 10 0W
100 An Nafud, des., Arabia ...28 15N 41 0E
100 An Najaf, Iraq ...32 3N 44 15E
100 An Nasiriyah, Iraq ...31 0N 46 15E
107 An Nhon (Binh Dinh) S. Vietnam ...13 55N 109 7E
100 An Nu'ayriyah, Si. Arab. ...27 30N 48 30E
123 An Nawfaliyah, Libya 30 54N 17 58E
43 An Socach, Mt., Scotland, U.K. ...56 54N 3 52W
42 An Teallach, Mt., Scotland, U.K. ...57 49N 5 18W
46 An Uaimh, Ireland ...53 39N 6 40W
143 Ana Branch, R., Australia ...32 20S 143 0E
98 Anabta, Jordan ...32 19N 35 7E
79 Åna-Sira, Norway ...58 17N 6 25E
166 Anaconda, U.S.A. ...46 7N 113 0W
166 Anacortes, U.S.A. ...48 30N 122 40W
165 Anadarko, U.S.A. ...35 4N 98 15W
62 Anadia, Portugal ...40 26N 8 27W
91 Anadyr, U.S.S.R. ...64 35N 177 20E
91 Anadyr, G. of, U.S.S.R. ...64 0N 180 0E
91 Anadyr R., U.S.S.R. .66 50N 171 0E
77 Anáfi & I., Greece ...36 22N 25 48E
77 Anafopoulo I., Greece 36 17N 25 50E
72 Anagni, Italy ...41 44N 13 8E
168 Anáhuac, Mexico ...27 14N 100 9W
100 Anah, Iraq ...34 25N 42 0E
106 Anai Mudi, Mt., India 10 12N 77 20E
106 Anaimalai Hills, India 10 20N 76 40E
100 Anaiza, Saudi Arabia .26 4N 44 8E
144 Anakie, Australia ...23 32S 147 45E
89 Anaklia, U.S.S.R. ...42 22N 41 35E
129 Analalava, Malagasy Rep. ...14 35S 48 0E
125 Anam, Nigeria ... 6 19N 6 41E
104 Anambar R., W. Pak. 30 10N 68 50E
108 Anambas Is., Indonesia ... 3 20N 106 30E
164 Anamoose, U.S.A. ...47 55N 100 7W
164 Anamosa, U.S.A. ...42 7N 91 28W
100 Anamur, Turkey ...36 8N 32 58E
106 Anand, India ...22 32N 72 59E
105 Anandpur, India ...21 16N 86 13E
77 Anánes I., Greece ...36 33N 24 9E
106 Anantapur, India ...14 39N 77 42E
114 Anan, Japan ...33 54N 134 40E
102 Anantnag, Kashmir ...33 45N 75 10E
88 Ananyev, U.S.S.R. ...47 44N 29 57E
88 Anapa, U.S.S.R. ...44 55N 37 25E
175 Anápolis, Brazil ...16 15S 48 50W
101 Anar, Iran ...30 55N 55 13E
101 Anarak, Iran ...33 25N 53 40E
100 Anatolia, Reg., Asia ...38 0N 29 0E
166 Anatone, U.S.A. ...46 9N 117 4W
172 Añatuya, Argentina ...28 20S 62 50W
121 Anaye, Niger ...19 15N 12 50E
39 Ancaster, England, U.K. ...52 59N 0 32W
48 Ancenis, France ...47 21N 1 10W
152 Anchorage, Alaska, U.S.A. ...61 10N 149 50W
62 Ancião, Portugal ...39 56N 8 27W
174 Ancohuma Mt., Bolivia ...16 0S 68 50W
168 Ancon, Pan. Canal Zone ... 8 57N 79 33W
174 Ancon, Peru ...11 50S 77 10W
71 Ancona, Italy ...43 37N 13 30E
41 Ancrum, Scotland, U.K. ...55 31N 2 35W
132 Ancuaze, Mozambique 16 49S 34 31E
176 Ancud, Chile ...42 0S 73 50W
176 Ancud, G. of, Chile ...42 0S 73 0W
82 And Fd., Norway ...69 0N 16 30E
172 Andacolla, Argentina .37 10S 70 42W
172 Andacollo, Chile ...30 15S 71 10W
172 Andagala, Argentina .27 40S 66 30W
79 Andalsnes, Norway ...62 35N 7 43E
63 Andalusia, Reg., Spain ...37 35N 5 0W
163 Andalusia, U.S.A. ...31 51N 86 30W
107 Andaman Is., India ...12 30N 92 30E
107 Andaman Sea, Ind. Oc. ...13 0N 96 0E
107 Andaman Str., Andaman Islands, India ...12 15N 92 20E
129 Andara, S.W. Africa .18 2S 21 9E
49 Andelot, France ...46 51N 5 56E
82 Andenes, Norway ...69 18N 16 10E
54 Andenne, Belgium ...50 30N 5 5E
57 Andermatt, Switzerland ...46 38N 8 35E
56 Andernach, Germany .50 24N 7 25E
81 Anderslöv, Sweden ...55 28N 13 21E
143 Anderson, Australia ...38 3S 145 25E
166 Anderson, Calif., U.S.A. ...40 30N 122 19W
162 Anderson, Ind., U.S.A. ...40 5N 85 40W
165 Anderson, Mo., U.S.A. 36 43N 94 29W
163 Anderson, S.C., U.S.A. ...34 32N 82 40W
133 Anderson, Mt., S. Africa ...25 5S 30 42E
152 Anderson R., Canada .69 0N 127 0W
81 Anderstorp, Sweden ...57 19N 13 47E
170 Andes, Mts., S. America ...20 0S 68 0W
106 Andhra, L., India ...18 50N 73 32E
106 Andhra Pradesh, st., India ...15 0N 80 0E
77 Andikithira I., Greece 35 52N 23 15E
77 Andimilos I., Greece .36 47N 24 12E
77 Andiparos I., Greece .37 0N 25 3E
77 Andipaxoi I., Greece .39 9N 20 13E
77 Andipsara I., Greece .39 30N 25 29E
90 Andizhan, U.S.S.R. ...41 10N 72 0E
101 Andkhui, Afghanistan 36 52N 65 8E
143 Ando, N.S.W., Austral. ...36 43S 149 16E
106 Andol, India ...17 51N 78 4E
174 Andoas Nuevo, Ecuador ... 2 20S 76 50W
112 Andong, Korea ...36 40N 128 43E
64 Andorra, Rep., Europe ...42 30N 1 30E
64 Andorra La Vella, Andorra ...42 31N 1 32E
34 Andover, Eng., U.K. 51 13N 1 29W
160 Andover, N.Y., U.S.A. ...42 11N 77 48W
160 Andover, Ohio, U.S.A. 41 35N 80 35W
64 Andraitx, Mallorca, Sp. ...39 35N 2 25E
152 Andreanov Is., Alaska, U.S.A. ...51 0N 178 0W
86 Andreapol, U.S.S.R. ...56 40N 32 17E
38 Andreas, Isle of Man, United Kingdom ...54 23N 4 25W
163 Andrews, S.C., U.S.A. 33 29N 79 30W
165 Andrews, Tex., U.S.A. 32 18N 102 33W
73 Andria, Italy ...41 13N 16 17E
73 Andrian, Italy ...46 30N 11 13E
129 Andriba, Malagasy Rep. ...17 30S 46 58E
74 Andrijevica, Y.-slav. .42 45N 19 48E
77 Andritsaina, Greece ...37 29N 21 52E
129 Androka, Malagasy Rep. ...24 58S 44 2E
169 Andros I., Bahama Is. 24 30N 78 0W
77 Andros & I., Greece ...37 50N 24 50E
59 Andrychów, Poland ...49 51N 19 18E
63 Andujar, Spain ...38 3N 4 5W
130 Andulo, Angola ...11 25S 16 45E
81 Aneby, Sweden ...57 48N 14 49E
125 Anécho, Togo ... 6 12N 1 34E
169 Anegada I., Virgin Is. 18 45N 64 20W
176 Añelo, Argentina ...38 15S 68 40W
64 Aneto, Pico de, Mt., Sp. ...42 37N 0 40E
123 Anfeg, Algeria ...22 29N 5 58E
107 Ang Thong, Thailand .14 35N 100 31E
112 Angangki, China ...47 9N 123 48E
91 Angara R., U.S.S.R. .58 30N 97 0E
127 Angarab & R., Ethiopia ...13 11N 37 7E
91 Angarsk, U.S.S.R. ...52 30N 104 0E
142 Angas Ra., W. Australia ...23 0S 127 50E
145 Angaston, S. Australia 34 30S 139 8E
80 Ånge, Sweden ...62 31N 15 35E
80 Ängebo, Sweden ...61 58N 16 22E
168 Angel de la Guarda I., Mexico ...29 30N 113 30W
81 Angelholm, Sweden ...56 15N 12 58E
166 Angels Camp, U.S.A. .38 8N 120 30W
80 Ängelsberg, Sweden ...59 57N 15 58E
103 Angenong, China ...31 57N 94 10E
82 Angerman R., Sweden 64 0N 17 20E
80 Ångermanälven R., Sweden ...63 10N 17 10E
55 Angermund, Germany 51 22N 6 48E
56 Angermünde, Germany ...53 1N 14 0E
161 Angers, Canada ...45 31N 75 30W
48 Angers, France ...47 30N 0 35W
49 Angerville, France ...48 19N 2 0E
82 Angesan R., Sweden .66 50N 22 15E
71 Anghiari, Italy ...43 32N 12 3E
157 Angikuni L., Canada .62 10N 99 40W
36 Angle, Wales, U.K. ...51 40N 5 3W
147 Anglem Mt., N.Z. ...46 45S 167 53E
64 Anglés, Spain ...41 57N 2 38E
37 Anglesey I., Co., Wales, United Kingdom ...53 17N 4 20W
50 Anglet, France ...43 29N 1 31W
165 Angleton, U.S.A. ...29 12N 95 23W
49 Anglure, France ...48 35N 3 50E
14 Angmagssalik, Greenland ...65 40N 37 20W
35 Angmering, Eng., U.K. ...50 48N 0 28W
130 Ango, Congo ... 4 10N 26 5E
172 Angol, Chile ...37 56S 72 45W
162 Angola, Ind., U.S.A. .41 40N 85 0W
160 Angola, N.Y., U.S.A. .42 38N 79 2W
129 Angola, Col., Africa ...12 0S 18 0E
50 Angoulême, France ...45 39N 0 10E
50 Angoumois, Reg., Fr. .45 30N 0 25E
90 Angren, U.S.S.R. ...80 59N 69 3E
173 Angra dos Reis, Brazil 23 0S 44 10W
169 Anguilla I., Leeward Is.18 14N 63 5W

MAP
155 Anguille C., Canada ...47 54N 59 28W
127 Angur R., Ethiopia ... 9 30N 36 35E
43 Angus, Co., Scot., U.K. ...56 45N 2 55W
43 Angus, Braes of, Hills, Scotland, U.K. ...56 51N 3 0W
132 Angwa R., Rhodesia .16 15S 3 150E
55 Anhée, Belgium ...50 18N 4 53E
81 Anholt I., Denmark ...56 43N 11 35E
113 Anhwa, China ...28 18N 111 25E
113 Anhwei, Prov., China .31 50N 117 30E
113 Ani, China ...28 50N 115 29E
77 Ánidhros I.,Greece ...36 38N 25 43E
125 Anie, Togo ... 7 42N 1 8E
167 Animas, U.S.A. ...31 58N 108 58W
167 Animas Pk., U.S.A. ...31 33N 108 56W
81 Ånimskog, Sweden ...58 53N 12 35E
107 Anin, Burma ...15 36N 97 50E
104 Anjangaon, India ...21 10N 77 20E
104 Anjar India ...23 6N 70 10E
113 Anjeń, China ...26 46N 113 4E
109 Anjer-Lor Indonesia . 6 6S 105 56E
106 Anjidiv I., India ...14 40N 74 10E
48 Anjou, Reg., France ...47 20N 0 30W
129 Anjozorobe, Malagasy Rep. ...18 22S 47 52E
112 Anju, Korea ...39 32N 125 32E
125 Anka, Nigeria ...12 13N 5 58E
113 Ankang, China ...32 43N 109 27E
100 Ankara, Turkey ...40 0N 32 54E
81 Ankarsrum, Sweden ...57 41N 16 20E
129 Ankazobe, Malagasy Rep. ...18 20S 47 10E
113 Anki, China ...25 1N 118 4E
113 Anking, China ...30 34N 117 1E
56 Anklam, Germany ...53 50N 13 42E
104 Anklesvar, India ...21 38N 73 3E
127 Ankobar, Ethiopia ... 9 35N 39 40E
127 Ankwang, China ...45 23N 123 40E
113 Anlu, China ...31 23N 113 41E
80 Ånn, Sweden ...63 19N 12 34E
15 Ann C., Antarctica ...66 30S 50 30E
161 Ann C., U.S.A. ...42 39N 70 37W
80 Ånn L., Sweden ...63 15N 12 35E
162 Ann Arbor, U.S.A. ...42 17N 83 45W
165 Anna, U.S.A. ...37 28N 89 10W
87 Anna, U.S.S.R. ...51 38N 40 23E
123 Annaba (Bône) Algeria ...36 50N 7 55E
56 Annaberg, Germany ...50 34N 12 58E
46 Annagassan, Ireland .53 53N 6 20W
45 Annagh Hd., Ireland .54 15N 10 5W
46 Annalee R., Ireland ...54 3N 7 15W
143 Annalera Telegraph Office, Australia...41 16S 143 59E
46 Annalong, N. Ire., U.K. ...54 7N 5 55W
107 Annam, Reg. Vietnam ...16 30N 107 30E
107 Annam Cordillera, S.E. Asia ...17 0N 106 0E
41 Annan, Scotland, U.K. ...55 0N 3 17W
41 Annan R., Scot., U.K. 55 7N 3 25W
41 Annandale, Scot., U.K. ...55 10N 3 25W
155 Annapolis Royal, Can. 44 44N 65 32W
162 Annapolis, U.S.A. ...39 0N 76 30W
44 Annascaul, Ireland ...52 10N 10 3W
142 Annean, L., W. Australia ...26 54S 118 14E
81 Anneberg, Sweden ...57 33N 12 6E
51 Annecy, France ...45 55N 6 8E
51 Annecy, L d', France 45 52N 6 10E
51 Annemasse, France ...46 12N 6 16E
45 Annestown, Ireland ...52 8N 7 18W
39 Annfield Plain, Eng., United Kingdom ...54 52N 1 45W
142 Annie Peak, W. Australia ...33 53S 119 59E
111 Anning, China ...24 59N 102 6E
163 Anniston, U.S.A. ...33 45N 85 50W
117 Annobón Is., Sp. Guin. ... 1 35S 3 35E
51 Annonay, France ...45 15N 4 40E
51 Annot, France ...43 58N 6 38E
169 Annotto Bay, Jamaica ...18 17N 77 3W
143 Annuello, Australia ...34 53S 142 55E
161 Annville, U.S.A. ...40 18N 76 32W
133 Annysspruit, S. Africa 27 4S 30 32E
77 Ano Arkhánai, Greece 35 16N 25 11E
76 Áno Porróïa, Greece ...41 17N 23 2E
77 Ano Viánnos, Greece .35 2N 25 21E
164 Anoka U.S.A. ...45 10N 93 26W
113 Anping, Taiwan ...23 0N 120 6E
57 Ansbach, Germany ...49 17N 10 34E
127 Anseba R., Ethiopia .16 15N 37 45E
112 Anshan, China ...41 3N 122 58E
113 Anshun, China ...26 2N 105 57E
111 Ansi, China ...40 21N 96 10E
164 Ansley, U.S.A. ...41 19N 99 24W
64 Ansó, Spain ...42 51N 0 48W
165 Anson, U.S.A. ...32 20S 129 30E
138 Anson Bay, Australia 13 20S 129 30E
125 Ansongo, Mali ...15 25N 0 35E
161 Ansonia, U.S.A. ...41 21N 73 6W
154 Ansonville, Canada ...48 46N 80 43W
34 Anstey, England, U.K. ...52 41N 1 14W
41 Anstruther E. and W., Scotland, U.K. 56 14N 2 40W
109 Ansudu, Indonesia ... 2 11S 139 22E
112 Anta, China ...46 18N 125 34E
174 Anta, Peru ...13 15S 72 10W
176 Antabamba, Peru ...14 40S 73 0W
100 Antakya, Turkey ...36 14N 36 10E
129 Antalaha, Malagasy Rep. ...14 57S 50 20E
100 Antalya, Turkey ...36 52N 30 45E
100 Antalya Körfezi, B., Turkey ...36 15N 31 30E
129 Antananarivo, Malagasy Rep. ...18 55S 4 35E
15 Antarctica, cont. ...90 0S
15 Antarctic Pen., Antarc. ...67 0S 60 0W
132 Antelope, Rhodesia ...21 2S 28 31E
81 Anten, Sweden ...58 5N 12 22E
63 Antequera, Spain ...37 5N 4 33W
167 Antero Mt., U.S.A. ...38 45N 106 43W
76 Anthemoús, Greece ...40 31N 23 15E
165 Anthony, Kan., U.S.A. ...37 8N 98 2W
167 Anthony, N. Mex., U.S.A. ...32 1N 106 37W
122 Anti Atlas Mts. Mor., .30 30N 6 30W
51 Antibes, France ...43 34N 7 6E
51 Antibes C. d', France .43 31N 7 7E
155 Anticosti I., Canada ...49 20N 62 40W
48 Antifer, C. d', France .49 41N 0 10E
164 Antigo, U.S.A. ...45 8N 89 5W
155 Antigonish, Canada ...45 38N 61 58W
168 Antigua, Guatemala ...14 34N 90 41W
169 Antigua I., Leeward Is. ...17 0N 61 50W
176 Antilhue, Chile ...40 0S 73 15W
169 Antilla, Cuba ...20 40N 75 50W
167 Antimony, U.S.A. ...38 7N 112 0W
166 Antioch, U.S.A. ...38 1N 121 45W
174 Antioquia, Colombia . 6 40N 75 55W
136 Antipodes Is., Pac. Oc. ...49 45S 178 40E
1 Antisana, Vol., S. Amer. ... 0 30S 78 20W
134 Antjieskraal, S. Africa 33 0S 21 30E
164 Antler, U.S.A. ...48 58N 101 18W
165 Antlers, U.S.A. ...34 15N 95 35W
172 Antofagasta, Chile ...23 50S 70 30W
172 Antofallá, Mt., Arg. ...25 30S 68 5W
165 Anton, U.S.A. ...33 49N 102 5W
167 Anton Chico, U.S.A. .35 12N 105 5W
129 Antongil B. d', Malagasy Rep. ...15 30S 49 50E
173 Antonina, Brazil ...25 26S 48 42W
129 António Enes, Mozam. ...16 8S 40 0E
167 Antonito, U.S.A. ...37 4N 106 1W
89 Antonov, U.S.S.R. ...49 25N 51 42E
36 Antony, Eng., U.K. ...50 22N 4 13W
48 Antrain, France ...48 28N 1 30W
46 Antrim, N. Ireland, U.K. ...54 43N 6 13W
46 Antrim, Co., N. Ireland, United Kingdom ...54 58N 6 20W
46 Antrim, Mts. of, N. Ireland, U.K. ...54 57N 6 8W
71 Antrodoco, Italy ...42 25N 13 4E
87 Antropovo, U.S.S.R. .58 26N 42 51E
129 Antsalova, Malagasy Rep. ...18 40S 44 37E
129 Antsirabe, Malagasy Rep. ...19 55S 47 2E
129 Antsohihy, Malagasy Rep. ...14 50S 47 50E
1 Antuco, Vol., S. America ...37 22S 69 10W
112 Antung, China ...40 10N 124 18E
161 Antwerp, U.S.A. ...44 12N 75 36W
54 Antwerpen (Antwerp), Belgium ...51 13N 4 25E
54 Antwerpen, prov., Belg. ...51 15N 4 40E
104 Anupgarh, India ...29 10N 73 10E
106 Anuradhpura, Ceylon . 8 22N 80 28E
15 Anvers I., Antarctica .64 30S 63 40W
112 Anyang, China ...36 7N 114 26E
113 Anyi, China ...35 0N 110 44E
113 Anyuan, China ...24 59N 115 31E
113 Anyo, China ...30 4N 105 16E
174 Anza, Colombia ... 6 30N 75 55W
98 Anza, Jordan ...32 22N 35 12E
90 Anzhero-Sudzhensk, U.S.S.R. ...56 10N 83 40E
72 Anzio, Italy ...41 28N 12 37E
64 Aoiz, Spain ...42 46N 1 22W
114 Aomori, Japan ...40 45N 140 45E
114 Aomori, Pref., Japan .40 45N 140 40E
104 Aonla, India ...28 16N 79 11E
146 Aorangi Mts., N.Z. ...41 49S 175 22E
122 Aoreora, Morocco ...28 51N 10 53W
70 Aosta, Italy ...45 43N 7 20E
125 Aoudéras, Niger ...17 45N 8 20E
122 Aouinet Torkoz, Mor. 28 31N 9 46W
122 Aoukar, Mali ...23 50N 2 45W
122 Aoulef Arab, Algeria .26 55N 1 2E
122 Aoullouz, Morocco ...30 44N 8 1W
123 Aozi, Chad ...21 11N 18 34E
167 Apache, Ariz., U.S.A. 31 46N 109 6W
165 Apache, Okla., U.S.A. 34 53N 98 22W
163 Apalachee B., U.S.A. .30 0N 84 0W
163 Apalachicola, U.S.A. .29 40N 85 0W
125 Apapa, Nigeria ... 6 25N 3 25E
174 Apaporis R., Colombia ... 0 30S 70 30W
109 Aparri, Philippines ...18 15N 121 55E
78 Apateu, Rumania ...46 36N 21 47E
74 Apatin, Yugoslavia ...45 40N 19 0E
168 Apatzingán, Mexico ...19 0N 102 20W
54 Apeldoorn, Netherlands ...52 13N 5 57E
56 Apen, Germany ...53 12N 7 47E
108 Apenam, Indonesia ... 8 35S 116 13E
19 Apennines, Mts., Italy 44 20N 10 20E
1 Api, G., Vol., Indonesia ...10 0S 119 30E
136 Apia, W. Samoa ...13 50S 171 50W
146 Apiti, New Zealand ...39 58S 175 54E
168 Apizaco, Mexico ...19 26N 98 9W
174 Aplao, Peru ...16 0S 72 40W
109 Apo, Mt., Philippines . 6 53N 125 14E
56 Apolda, Germany ...51 1N 11 30E
77 Apollonía, Greece ...36 58N 24 43E
121 Apollonia, Libya ...32 52N 21 59E
174 Apolo, Bolivia ...14 30S 68 30W
164 Apostle Is., U.S.A. ...47 0N 90 30W
173 Apostoles, Argentina .28 0S 56 0W
88 Apostolovo, U.S.S.R. .47 39N 33 39E
174 Apoteri, Guyana ... 4 2N 58 32W
162 Appalachian Mts., U.S.A. ...38 0N 80 0W
163 Appalachicola, R., U.S.A. ...30 0N 85 0W
55 Appelhülsen, Germany ...51 53N 7 26E
73 Appenino, Mts., Italy 41 0N 15 0E
70 Appenino Ligure, Mts., Italy ...44 30N 9 0E
57 Appenzell, cant., Switz. ...47 20N 9 24E
71 Appiano, Trentino, It. 46 27N 11 17E
161 Apple Hill, Canada ...45 13N 74 46W
38 Appleby, England, U.K. ...54 35N 2 29W
42 Applecross, Scot., U.K. ...57 26N 5 50W
42 Applecross For., Scot., United Kingdom ...57 27N 5 40W
36 Appledore, Devon, Eng., United Kingdom ...51 3N 4 12W
35 Appledore, Kent, Eng., United Kingdom ...51 2N 0 47E
162 Appleton, U.S.A. ...44 17N 88 25W
175 Approuague, Fr. Guiana ... 4 20N 52 0W
87 Aprelevka, U.S.S.R. ...55 32N 36 58E
73 Apricena, Italy ...41 47N 15 25E
73 Aprigliano, Italy ...39 17N 16 19E
72 Aprilia, Italy ...41 38N 12 38E
89 Apsheronsk, U.S.S.R. 44 28N 39 42E
51 Apt, France ...43 53N 5 24E
173 Apucarana, Brazil ...23 55S 51 33W
174 Apure R., Venezuela . 8 0N 69 20W
174 Apurimac R., Peru ...12 10S 73 30W
78 Apuseni, Munţii, Mts., Rumania ...46 30N 22 45E
101 Aq Chah, Afghanistan 37 0N 66 5E
126 Aqaba, Jordan ...29 31N 35 0E
100 Aqaba, G. of, Red Sea 28 15N 33 20E
126 Aqiq, & G., Sudan ...18 5N 38 5E
100 'Aqra, Iraq ...36 46N 43 45E
98 'Aqraba, Jordan ...32 9N 35 20E
111 Aqsu, China ...41 10N 80 15E
175 Aquidauana, Brazil ...20 30S 55 50W
168 Aquiles Serdán, Mexico ...28 37N 105 54W
100 Ar Ramadi, Iraq ...33 25N 43 20E
100 Ar Rass, Saudi Arabia 25 50N 43 40E
100 Ar Rifai, Saudi Arabia ...31 50N 46 10E
100 Ar Riyad, Si. Arabia .24 40N 46 45E
100 Ar Rutbah, Iraq ...33 0N 40 15E
125 Araba, Nigeria ...13 7N 5 0E
88 Arabat Tongue, Pen., U.S.S.R. ...45 40N 35 0E
71 Arabba, Italy ...46 30N 11 51E
92 Arabia, Asia ...25 0N 45 0E
100 Arabian Emirates, Fed. of, Asia ...25 0N 52 30E
93 Arabian Sea, Indian Ocean ...16 0N 65 0E
126 Arabs Gulf, Egypt ...30 55N 29 0E
175 Aracajú, Brazil ...11 0S 37 0W
174 Aracataca, Colombia .10 38N 74 9W
175 Aracati, Brazil ... 4 30S 37 54W
173 Araçatuba, Brazil ...21 10S 50 30W
63 Aracena, Spain ...37 53N 6 38W
175 Aracruz, Brazil ...19 59S 40 12W
175 Araçuai, Brazil ...17 0S 42 0W
74 Arad, Rumania ...46 10N 21 20E
75 Arad, Reg., Rumania .46 15N 22 0E
121 Arada, Chad ...15 0N 20 20E
74 Aradul Nou, Rumania 46 8N 21 20E
109 Arafura Sea, E. Indies 10 0S 135 0E
89 Aragaz Mt., U.S.S.R. .40 30N 44 15E
64 Aragon, Reg., Spain ...41 25N 1 0W
64 Aragon R., Spain ...42 35N 0 50W
72 Aragona, Italy ...37 24N 13 36E
174 Aragua, Venezuela ... 9 35N 64 50W
175 Araguacema, Brazil ... 8 50S 49 20W
175 Araguaia R., Brazil ... 7 0S 49 15W
175 Araguari, Brazil ...18 40S 48 10W
175 Araguari, R., Brazil ... 1 0N 51 40W
122 Arak, Algeria ...25 20N 3 45E
103 Arakan Coast, Burma 19 0N 94 0E
103 Arakan Yoma, Mts., Burma ...20 0N 94 30E
77 Arákhova, Greece ...38 28N 22 35E
100 Araks, R., Iran ...39 10N 47 10E
85 Araks R., U.S.S.R. ...39 0N 47 0E
90 Aral Sea, U.S.S.R. ...44 30N 60 0E
90 Aralsk, U.S.S.R. ...46 50N 61 20E
143 Araluen, Australia ...35 36S 149 49E
78 Arama, Mţii de, mts., Rumania ...47 10N 22 30E
144 Aramac, Australia ...22 58S 145 14E
105 Arambagh, India ...22 53N 87 48E
46 Aran I., Ireland ...55 0N 8 30W
44 Aran Is., Ireland ...53 5N 9 42W
37 Aran Fawddwy, Mt., Wales, U.K. ...52 48N 3 40W
64 Aranda, de Duero, Spain ...41 39N 3 42W
74 Arandelovac, Y.-slav. 44 18N 20 37E
146 Aranga, New Zealand 35 44S 173 40E
62 Aranjuez, Spain ...40 1N 3 40W
129 Aranos, S. W. Africa .24 9S 19 7E
165 Aransas Pass, U.S.A. .28 0N 97 9W
107 Aranyaprathet, Thailand ...13 41N 102 30E
124 Araouane, Mali ...18 55N 3 30W
164 Arapahoe, U.S.A. ...40 22N 99 53W
147 Arapawa I., N.Z. ...41 13S 174 20E
100 Arapkir, Turkey ...39 5N 38 30E
173 Arapongas, Brazil ...23 29S 51 28W
146 Arapongas, N.Z. ...38 3S 175 37E
146 Arapuni, N.Z. ...38 3S 175 37E
100 Araq, Iran ...34 0N 49 40E
173 Ararangua, Brazil ...29 0S 49 30W
173 Araraquara, Brazil ...21 50S 48 0W
173 Araras, Brazil ... 5 15S 60 35W
143 Ararat, Australia ...37 16S 143 0E
100 Ararat, Mt., Turkey ...39 50N 44 15E
105 Araria, India ...26 9N 87 33E
79 Åras, Norway ...59 42N 10 31E
174 Arauca, Colombia ... 7 0N 70 40W
174 Arauca R., Venezuela 7 30N 69 0W
172 Arauco, Chile ...37 16S 73 25W
172 Arauco, prov., Chile ...37 40S 73 25W
147 Arawhata, N.Z. ...43 59S 168 38E
147 Arawhata R., N.Z. ...44 13S 168 40E
175 Araxa, Brazil ...19 45S 47 0W
174 Araya Pen., Venezuela ...10 40N 64 0W
127 Arba, Ethiopia ... 9 0N 40 20E
127 Arba Minch, Ethiopia 6 0N 37 30E
122 Arbaoua, Morocco ...34 58N 5 58W
72 Arbatax, Italy ...39 57N 9 42E
80 Arboga, Sweden ...59 28N 15 50E
49 Arbois, France ...46 55N 5 46E
133 Arbor, Trans. S. Africa ...26 4N 28 52E
127 Arbore, Ethiopia ... 5 3N 36 50E
157 Arborg, Canada ...51 0N 97 20W
80 Arbrå, Sweden ...61 58N 16 28E
41 Arbroath, Scotland, U.K. ...56 34N 2 35W
166 Arbuckle, U.S.A. ...39 3N 122 2W
72 Arbus, Italy ...39 30N 8 33E
88 Arbuzinka, U.S.S.R. .47 52N 31 25E
49 Arc, Haute Saône, Fr. 47 28N 5 34E
50 Arcachon, France ...44 40N 1 10W
50 Arcachon, Bassin d', Fr. ...44 42N 1 10W
160 Arcade, U.S.A. ...42 34N 78 25W
163 Arcadia, Fla., U.S.A. .27 20N 81 50W
165 Arcadia, La., U.S.A. .32 34N 92 53W
164 Arcadia, Neb., U.S.A. 41 29N 99 4W
160 Arcadia, Pa., U.S.A. .40 46N 78 54W
164 Arcadia, Wis., U.S.A. 44 13N 91 29W
166 Arcata, U.S.A. ...40 55N 124 4W
71 Arcevia, Italy ...43 29N 12 58E
74 Archar, Bulgaria ...43 50N 22 54E
161 Archbald, U.S.A. ...41 30N 75 31W
65 Archena, Spain ...38 9N 1 16W
144 Archer B., Australia ...13 20S 141 30E
131 Archers Post, Kenya . 0 35N 37 35E
63 Archidona, Spain ...37 6N 4 22W
43 Archiestown, Scot., U.K. ...57 28N 3 20W
72 Arci, Monte, Sardinia, Italy ...39 47N 8 44E
71 Arcidosso, Italy ...42 51N 11 30E
122 Arcila, *see* Asilah, Morocco ...35 29N 6 0W
49 Arcis-sur-Aube, France ...48 32N 4 10E
70 Arco, Italy ...45 55N 10 54E
166 Arco, U.S.A. ...43 45N 113 16W
157 Arcola, Canada ...49 40N 102 30W
64 Arcos, Spain ...36 45N 5 45W
62 Arcos de Valdevez, Port ...41 51N 8 25W
63 Arcos de los Frontera, Spain ...36 44N 5 47W
106 Arcot, India ...12 53N 79 20E
175 Arcoverde, Brazil ... 8 23S 37 0W
152 Arctic Red River, Can. ...67 15N 134 0W
14 Arctic Ocean ...78 0N 160 0W
75 Arda R., Bulgaria ...41 40N 25 40E
70 Arda R., Italy ...44 53N 9 52E
44 Ardagh, Limerick, Ire. 52 30N 9 5W
101 Ardakan, Iran ...30 20N 52 5E
79 Årdal, Rogaland, Nor. 59 9N 6 13E
79 Årdal, Sognfjordane, Norway ...61 15N 7 45E
63 Ardales, Spain ...36 53N 4 51W
46 Ardara, Ireland ...54 47N 8 25W
87 Ardatov, U.S.S.R. ...54 51N 46 15E
42 Ardavasar, Scot., U.K. ...57 3N 5 54E
46 Ardcath, Ireland ...53 36N 6 21W
42 Ardcharnich, Scot., U.K. ...57 52N 5 5W
42 Ardchyle, Scot., U.K. 56 26N 4 24W
51 Ardèche, dépt. France ...44 42N 4 16E
78 Arded, Rumania ...47 37N 22 52E
46 Ardee, Ireland ...53 51N 6 32W
160 Arden, Canada ...44 41N 76 59W
81 Arden, Denmark ...56 46N 9 53E
49 Ardennes, dépt., France ...49 35N 4 40E
54 Ardennes, Belgium ...49 30N 5 10E
49 Ardentes, France ...46 45N 1 50E
42 Ardentinny, Scot., U.K. ...56 3N 4 56E
101 Ardestan, Iran ...33 20N 52 25E
44 Ardfert, Ireland ...52 20N 9 49W
44 Ardfinnan, Ireland ...52 20N 7 53W
46 Ardglass, N. Ire. U.K. ...54 16N 5 38W
42 Ardgour, dist., Scot. U.K. ...56 45N 5 25W
44 Ardgroom, Ireland ...51 44N 9 53W
76 Árdhas, R. Greece ...41 36N 26 25E
42 Ardhasig, Scot., U.K. 57 55N 6 51W
76 Ardhéa, Greece ...40 58N 22 3E
63 Ardila R., Spain ...38 10N 7 20W
35 Ardingly, England, U.K. ...51 3N 0 3W
75 Ardino Bulgaria ...41 34N 25 9E
42 Ardivachar Pt., Scot., United Kingdom ...57 23N 7 25W
109 Ardjuno Mt., Indonesia ... 7 49S 112 39E
44 Ardkearagh, Ireland ...51 48N 10 11W
46 Ardkeen, N. Ire., U.K. ...54 27N 5 53W
143 Ardlethan, Australia .34 22S 146 53E
40 Ardlui, Scotland, U.K. ...56 19N 4 43W
45 Ardmore, Ireland ...51 58N 7 43W
144 Ardmore, Australia ...21 35S 139 20E
165 Ardmore, Okla., U.S.A. ...34 10N 97 5W
161 Ardmore Pa., U.S.A. .39 58N 75 18W
164 Ardmore, S.D., U.S.A. 43 0N 103 40W
45 Ardmore Hd., Ireland 51 58N 7 43W
40 Ardmore Pt., Scotland, United Kingdom ...55 40N 6 0W
44 Ardnacrusha, Ireland .52 43N 8 38W
42 Ardnamurchan, Pt. of, Scotland, U.K. 56 44N 6 14W
40 Ardnave Pt., Scot. U.K. ...55 54N 6 20W
143 Ardno, Australia ...37 49S 141 3E
73 Ardore, Marina, Italy 38 11N 16 10E
49 Ardres, France ...50 50N 2 0E
40 Ardrishaig, Scot., U.K. ...56 0N 5 27W
40 Ardrossan, Scot. U.K. ...55 39N 4 50W
89 Ardunac, Turkey ...41 8N 42 5E
43 Ardwell, Scotland U.K. ...57 20N 3 5W
80 Åre, Sweden ...63 22N 13 15E
169 'Arecibo, Puerto Rico 18 29N 66 42W
175 'Areia Branca, Brazil . 5 0S 37 0W
79 Aremark, Norway ...59 15N 11 41E
176 Arenales Mt., Chile ...47 5S 73 40W
62 Arenas, Spain ...40 17N 5 6W
62 Arenas de San Pedro Spain ...40 12N 5 5W
79 Arendal, Norway ...58 28N 8 46E
55 Arendonk, Belgium ...51 19N 5 5E
56 Arendsee, Germany ...52 52N 11 27E
37 Arenig Fach, Mt., Wales, United Kingdom ...52 55N 3 45E
37 Arenig Fawr, Mt., Wales, United Kingdom ...52 56N 3 45W
64 Arénys de Mar, Spain 41 35N 2 33E
70 Arenzano, Italy ...44 24N 8 40E
77 Areópolis, Greece ...36 40N 22 22E
174 Arequipa, Peru ...16 20S 71 30W
51 Arès, France ...44 47N 1 8W
62 Arevalo, Spain ...41 3N 4 43W
71 Arezzo, Italy ...43 28N 11 50E
64 Arga R., Spain ...42 30N 1 50W
76 Argalastí, Greece ...39 13N 23 13E
65 Argamasilla de Alba, Sp. ...39 8N 3 5W
64 Arganda, Spain ...40 19N 3 26W
62 Arganil, Portugal ...40 13N 8 3W
50 Argelès Gazost France ...43 0N 0 6W
50 Argelès-sur-Mer, Fr. .42 34N 3 1E
49 Argent, France ...47 33N 2 25E
156 Argenta, Canada ...50 20N 116 55W
71 Argenta, Italy ...44 37N 11 50E
48 Argentan, France ...48 45N 0 1W
71 Argentario, Mte., Italy ...42 23N 11 11E
50 Argentat, France ...45 6N 1 56E
70 Argentera, Italy ...44 23N 6 58E
49 Argenteuil, France ...48 57N 2 14E
155 Argentia, Canada ...47 18N 53 58W
72 Argentiera C. dell', Italy ...40 44N 8 8E
176 Argentina, Rep., South America ...35 0S 66 0W
176 Argentino L., Arg. ...50 10S 73 0W
50 Argenton, France ...46 36N 1 30E
48 Argenton, Chateau, Fr. ...47 3N 0 18W
78 Arges, Reg., Rumania 45 0N 24 55E
78 Arges R., Rumania ...44 30N 25 50E
126 Argo, Sudan ...19 28N 30 30E
77 Argolikós Kólpos, G., Greece ...37 20N 22 52E
77 Argolis, Pref., Greece .37 38N 22 50E
49 Argonne, Reg., France 49 0N 5 20E
77 Árgos, Greece ...37 40N 22 43E
76 Árgos Orestikón, Gr. .40 27N 21 26E
77 Argostólion, Greece ...38 12N 20 33E
64 Arguedas, Spain ...42 11N 1 36W
167 Arguello, Pt., U.S.A. .34 34N 120 40W
125 Argungu, Nigeria ...12 40N 4 31E
164 Argyle, U.S.A. ...48 23N 96 49W
40 Argyll, Co., Scot., U.K. ...56 18N 5 15W
40 Argyll, Dist., Scot., U.K. ...56 14N 5 10W
146 Aria, New Zealand ...38 33S 175 0E
114 Ariake-wan, Japan ...31 30N 131 10E
73 Ariano Irpino, Italy ...41 10N 15 4E
71 Ariano nel Polesine, It. ...44 56N 12 5E
125 Aribinda, Upper Volta 14 17N 0 52W
174 Arica, Chile ...18 32S 70 20W
174 Arica, Colombia ... 2 0S 71 50W
174 Arica, Peru ... 1 30S 75 30W
50 Ariège, Dépt., France 42 56N 1 30E

MAP
50 Ariège R., France ...43 15N 1 36E
78 Aries R., Rumania ...46 24N 23 20E
74 Arilje, Y.-slav. ...43 44N 20 7E
169 Arima, Trinidad ...10 38N 61 17W
40 Arinagour, Scot., U.K. ...56 38N 6 31W
174 Arinos R., Brazil ...11 15S 57 0W
168 Ario de Rosales, Mex. 19 12N 101 42W
174 Aripuana, Brazil ... 9 25S 60 30W
174 Aripuanã, R., Brazil . 7 30S 60 0W
174 Ariquemes, Brazil ... 9 55S 63 6W
42 Arisaig, Scot., U.K. ...56 55N 5 50W
42 Arisaig, dist., Scot., U.K. ...56 50N 5 40W
42 Arisaig, Sd. of, Scot., U.K. ...56 50N 5 50W
126 Arish, W. el, Egypt ...30 25N 34 52E
127 Arissa, Ethiopia ...11 10N 41 35E
156 Aristazabal I., Canada 52 40N 129 10W
167 Arivaca, U.S.A. ...31 37N 111 25W
106 Ariyalur, India ...11 8N 79 8E
64 Ariza, Spain ...41 19N 2 3W
172 Arizaro, Salina de, Arg. ...24 40S 67 50W
172 Arizona, Argentina ...35 45S 65 25W
167 Arizona, st., U.S.A. ...34 20N 111 30W
168 Arizpe, Mexico ...30 20N 110 11W
80 Årjäng, Sweden ...59 24N 12 9E
82 Arjeplog, Sweden ...66 3N 18 2E
174 Arjona, Colombia ...10 14N 75 22W
63 Arjona, Spain ...37 56N 4 4W
91 Arka, U.S.S.R. ...60 15N 142 0E
111 Arka Tagh, Mts., China ...36 30N 90 0E
87 Arkadak, U.S.S.R. ...51 58N 43 19E
165 Arkadelphia, U.S.A. ...34 5N 93 0W
77 Arkadhia, pref., Greece ...38 48N 21 30E
42 Arkaig, L., Scot., U.K. ...56 58N 5 10W
165 Arkansas, st., U.S.A. .35 0N 92 30W
165 Arkansas R., U.S.A. ...35 20N 93 30W
165 Arkansas City, U.S.A. 37 4N 97 3W
76 Arkathos R., Greece ...39 20N 21 4E
77 Arkhángelos, Greece ...36 13N 28 7E
84 Arkhangelsk, U.S.S.R. 64 40N 41 0E
87 Arkhangelskoye, U.S.S.R. ...51 32N 40 55E
127 Arkiko, Ethiopia ...15 33N 39 30E
38 Arkle R., England, U.K. ...54 25N 2 0W
45 Arklow, Ireland ...52 48N 6 10W
45 Arklow Hd., Ireland .52 46N 6 10W
81 Arlöv, Sweden ...55 40N 13 3E
77 Arkoi I., Greece ...37 24N 26 44E
56 Arkona, Germany ...54 41N 13 26E
106 Arkonam, India ...13 7N 79 43E
81 Arkösund, Sweden ...58 28N 16 55E
77 Arkhoúdhi I., Greece .38 33N 20 43E
50 Arlanc, France ...45 25N 3 42E
131 Arlanga Arba, Kenya 0 7N 40 28E
62 Arlanza R., Spain ...42 6N 4 0W
62 Arlanzón R., Spain ...42 12N 4 0W
166 Arlee, U.S.A. ...47 10N 114 4W
51 Arles, France ...43 41N 4 40E
45 Arless, Ireland ...52 53N 7 1W
135 Arlington, S. Africa ...28 1S 27 53E
166 Arlington, Ore, U.S.A. 45 48N 120 6W
164 Arlington, S.D., U.S.A. ...44 25N 97 4W
166 Arlington, Wash., U.S.A. ...48 11N 122 4W
54 Arlon, Belgium ...49 42N 5 49E
81 Arlöv, Sweden ...55 38N 13 5E
41 Armadale, Lothian, Scotland, U.K. ...55 54N 3 42W
42 Armadale, Skye, Scotland, U.K. ...57 25N 5 54W
142 Armadale, W. Australia ...32 12S 116 0E
155 Armagh, Canada ...46 41N 70 32W
46 Armagh, N. Ire., U.K. 54 22N 6 40W
46 Armagh, Co., N. Ire., U.K. ...54 16N 6 35W
50 Armagnac, dist., France ...43 44N 0 10E
49 Armancon R., France 47 51N 4 7E
89 Armavir, U.S.S.R. ...45 2N 41 7E
174 Armenia, Colombia ... 4 35N 75 45W
85 Armenia S.S.R., U.S.S.R. ...40 0N 41 0E
78 Armenis, Rumania ...45 13N 22 17E
49 Armentières, France ...50 40N 2 50E
145 Armidale, Australia ...30 36S 151 40E
164 Armour, U.S.A. ...43 20N 98 25W
46 Armoy, N. Ireland, U.K. ...55 8N 6 20W
154 Arms, Canada ...49 34N 86 3W
166 Armstead, U.S.A. ...45 0N 112 56W
156 Armstrong, B.C., Can. 50 25N 119 10W
154 Armstrong, Ont., Can. 50 20N 89 0W
165 Armstrong, U.S.A. ...26 59N 90 48W
106 Armur, India ...18 48N 78 16E
76 Arnaía, Greece ...40 30N 23 40E
49 Arnay-le Duc, France 47 10N 4 27E
64 Arnedillo, Spain ...42 13N 2 14W
64 Arnedo, Spain ...42 12N 2 5W
82 Arnes, Iceland ...66 2N 21 32W
79 Arnes, Norway ...60 07N 11 28E
165 Arnett, U.S.A. ...36 9N 99 44W
46 Arney R., N. Ire., U.K. ...54 17N 7 40W
54 Arnhem, Netherlands .51 58N 5 55E
138 Arnhem B., Australia 12 20S 136 10E
139 Arnhem C., Australia 12 18S 137 0E
138 Arnhem Ld. Australia ...13 10S 135 0E
106 Arni, India ...12 43N 79 19E
76 Árnissa, Greece ...40 47N 21 49E
134 Arniston, S. Africa ...34 30S 20 14E
70 Arno R., Italy ...43 44N 10 20E
39 Arnold, England, U.K. ...53 0N 1 8W
147 Arnold, N.Z. ...42 29S 171 25E
164 Arnold, Neb. U.S.A. .41 29N 100 10W
160 Arnold, Pa., U.S.A. ...40 36N 79 44W
58 Arnoldstein, Austria ...46 33N 13 43E
55 Arnoldsweiler, Germany ...50 49N 6 31E
157 Arnot, Canada ...55 46N 96 42W
82 Arnöy, I., Norway ...70 5N 20 30E
154 Arnprior, Canada ...45 23N 76 25W
56 Arnsberg, Germany ...51 25N 8 10E
38 Arnside, England, U.K. ...54 12N 2 49W
56 Arnstadt, Germany ...50 50N 10 56E
134 Aroab, S.W. Africa ...26 41S 19 39E
77 Aroánia Óri, Mt., Gr. 37 56E 22 12E
63 Aroche, Spain ...37 56N 6 57E
56 Arolsen, Germany ...51 23N 9 1E
70 Arona, Italy ...45 45N 8 32E
50 Arpajon, Cantal, Fr. .44 54N 2 28E
49 Arpajon, Seine et Oise, France ...48 37N 2 12E
72 Arpino, Italy ...41 40N 13 35E
44 Arra Mts., Ireland ...52 50N 8 22W
145 Arrabury, Australia ...26 45S 141 0E
105 Arrah, India ...25 35N 84 32E
168 Arraijan, Panama ... 8 56N 79 36W
63 Arraiolos, Portugal ...38 44N 7 59W
40 Arran I., Scotland, U.K. ...55 34N 5 12W
156 Arrandale, Canada ...54 57N 130 0W
49 Arras, France ...50 17N 2 46E
127 Arraua, Ethiopia ... 9 57N 41 58E
50 Arreau, France ...42 54N 0 22E
126 Arrecife, I., Canary Is. ...28 59N 13 40W
172 Arrecifes, Argentina ...34 6S 60 9W
48 Arrée, Mts. d', France 48 26N 3 55W
168 Arriaga, Mexico ...21 55N 101 23W
81 Arrild. Denmark ...55 8N 8 58E
142 Arrino, W. Australia .29 30S 115 40E
40 Arrochar, Scotland, U.K. ...56 12N 4 45W
48 Arromanches, France .49 20N 0 38W
63 Arronches, Portugal ...39 8N 7 16W
48 Arrou. France ...48 6N 1 8E
166 Arrow Rock Res., U.S.A. ...43 45N 115 50W
46 Arrow L., Ireland ...54 3N 8 20W
156 Arrowhead, Canada ...50 40N 117 55W
147 Arrowsmith, Mt., N.Z. 30 7N 141 38E
147 Arrowtown, N.Z. ...44 57S 16 50E
63 Arroyo de la Luz, Spain ...39 30N 6 38W
167 Arroyo Grande, U.S.A. ...35 9N 120 32W
48 Ars, Ile de Re, France 46 13N 1 30W
49 Ars-sur-Moselle, France ...49 5N 6 4E
157 Arsenault L., Canada .55 5N 108 50W
112 Arshan, China ...46 59N 120 0E
71 Arsiero, Italy ...45 49N 11 22E
106 Arsikere, India ...13 15N 76 15E
87 Arsk, U.S.S.R. ...56 10N 49 50E
80 Årskogen, Sweden ...62 8N 17 20E
80 Årsta, Sweden ...59 6N 18 12E
77 Arta, Greece ...39 8N 21 2E
64 Arta, Spain ...39 40N 3 20E
76 Arta, pref., Greece ...39 15N 26 0E
168 Arteaga, Mexico ...18 50N 102 20W
62 Arteijo, Spain ...43 19N 8 29W
91 Artem, U.S.S.R. ...43 5N 132 0E
89 Artem I., U.S.S.R. ...40 28N 50 20E
124 Artémou, Mauritania ...15 38N 12 16W
88 Artemovsk, U.S.S.R. .48 35N 37 55E
89 Artemovski, U.S.S.R. 54 45N 93 35E
49 Artenay, France ...48 5N 1 50E
56 Artern, Germany ...51 22N 11 18E
64 Artesa de Segre, Spain 41 54N 1 3E
132 Artesia, Botswana ...24 2S 26 19E
165 Artesia, U.S.A. ...32 55N 104 25W
165 Artesia Wells, U.S.A. .28 17N 99 18W
164 Artesian, U.S.A. ...44 2N 97 54W
50 Arthez, France ...43 29N 0 38W
124 Arthington, Liberia ... 6 35N 10 45W
147 Arthur's P., N.Z. ...42 54S 171 35E
45 Arthurstown, Ireland .52 15N 6 58W
172 Artigas, Uruguay ...30 20S 56 30W
89 Artik, U.S.S.R. ...40 38N 44 50E
49 Artois, reg., France ...50 20N 2 30E
77 Artotina, Greece ...38 42N 22 2E
112 Arts Bogd Uul, ra., Mongolia ...44 30N 102 30E
100 Artvin, Turkey ...41 14N 41 44E
109 Aru Is., Indonesia ... 6 0S 134 30E
131 Arua, Uganda ... 3 1N 30 58E
175 Aruana, Brazil ...15 0S 51 10W
131 Aruba, Kenya ... 3 25S 38 55E
169 Aruba I., Neth. W. Ind. ...12 30N 70 0W
50 Arudy, France ...43 7N 0 28W
143 Arumpo, Australia ...33 48S 142 55E
35 Arun R., England, U.K. ...50 48N 0 33W
105 Arun R., Nepal ...27 30N 87 15E
135 Arundel, S. Africa ...30 57S 25 2E
35 Arundel, England, U.K. ...50 52N 0 32W
106 Aruppukottai, India ... 9 31N 78 8E
131 Arusha, & dist., Tanzania ... 3 20S 36 40E
131 Arusha Chini, Tanz. ... 3 32S 37 20E
131 Arusha, prov., Tanz. . 4 0S 36 30E
127 Arusi, Prov., Ethiopia 7 45N 39 0E
130 Aruwimi R., Congo ... 1 30N 25 0E
46 Arva, Ireland ...53 57N 7 35W
166 Arvada, U.S.A. ...44 43N 106 6W
112 Arvayheer, Mongolia .46 15N 102 45E
51 Arve R., France ...45 56N 6 40E
104 Arvi, India ...20 59N 78 16E
155 Arvida, Canada ...48 16N 71 14W
82 Arvidsjaur, Sweden ...65 35N 19 10E
80 Arvika, Sweden ...59 42N 12 42E
76 Aryiradhes, Greece ...39 27N 19 58E
90 Arys, U.S.S.R. ...42 20N 68 30E
87 Arzamas, U.S.S.R. ...55 27N 43 55E
122 Arzew, Algeria ...35 50N 0 23W
89 Arzgir, U.S.S.R. ...45 18N 44 23E
71 Arzignano, Italy ...45 30N 11 20E
58 Aš, Czechoslovakia ...50 13N 12 12E
98 As Salt, Jordan ...32 2N 35 43E
100 As Samawah, Iraq ...31 15N 45 15E
101 As Sohar, Mus. & O. .24 20N 56 40E
100 As Sulamaniyah, Iraq 35 35N 45 30E
123 As Sultan, Libya ...31 4N 17 8E
101 As Suwaih, Mus. & O. 22 10N 59 33E
100 As Suwayda, Syria ...32 40N 36 30E
100 As Suwayrah, Iraq ...32 55N 45 0E
125 Asaba, Nigeria ... 6 12N 6 38E
100 Asadabad, Iran ...34 50N 48 10E
124 Asafo, Ghana ... 6 20N 2 40W
114 Asahigawa, Japan ...43 45N 142 30E
1 Asama, vol., Japan ...33 0N 140 0E
125 Asamankese, Ghana ... 5 50N 0 40W
174 Asangaro, Peru ...14 55S 70 10W
124 Asankrangwa, Ghana . 5 45N 2 30W
105 Asansol, India ...23 40N 87 1E
125 Asara, Nigeria ...13 30N 5 10E
80 Åsarna, Sweden ...62 40N 14 20E
155 Asbestos, Canada ...45 47N 71 58W
131 Asbestos Mts., S. Afr. 29 0S 23 0E
161 Asbury Park, U.S.A. .40 15N 74 1W
174 Ascención, Bolivia ...15 45S 63 0W
168 Ascension B. de la, Mex. ...20 20N 87 20W
17 Ascension I., Atlantic Oc. ... 8 0S 14 15W
135 Ascent, O.F.S., S. Afr. 27 12S 29 3E
57 Aschaffenburg, Ger. ...49 58N 9 8E
55 Ascheberg, Germany .51 47N 7 37E
56 Aschendorf, Germany 53 2N 7 22E
56 Aschersleben, Germany ...51 45N 11 28E
71 Asciano, Italy ...43 14N 11 32E
71 Ascoli Piceno, Italy ...42 51N 13 34E
73 Ascoli Satriano, Italy .41 11N 15 32E
174 Ascope, Peru ... 7 46S 79 8W
35 Ascot, England, U.K. 51 24N 0 41W
172 Ascotan, Chile ...21 45S 68 17W
127 Aseb, Ethiopia ...13 0N 42 40E
81 Åseda, Sweden ...57 10N 15 20E
122 Asedjrad, Algeria ...24 51N 1 29E
127 Aselle, Ethiopia ... 8 0N 39 0E
75 Asenovgrad, Bulgaria 42 1N 24 51E
79 Åseral, Norway ...58 37N 7 25E
49 Asfeld, France ...49 27N 4 5E
126 Asfûn el Matâ'na, Eg. 25 26N 32 30E
79 Åsgårdstrand, Norway 59 22N 10 27E
35 Ash, England, U.K. ...51 14N 0 43E
167 Ash Fork, U.S.A. ...35 14N 112 32W
165 Ash Grove, U.S.A. ...37 21N 93 36W
100 Ash Shamiyah, Iraq ...31 55N 44 35E
100 Ash Shatrah, Iraq ...31 30N 46 10E
125 Ashaira, Saudi Arabia 21 40N 40 40E
125 Ashanti, reg., Ghana . 7 30N 2 0W
39 Ashbourne, Eng., U.K. ...53 2N 1 44W
163 Ashburn, U.S.A. ...31 42N 83 40W
36 Ashburton, Eng., U.K. ...50 31N 3 45W
147 Ashburton & R., N.Z. 43 53S 171 48E
142 Ashburton, R., W. Australia ...22 5S 115 0E
142 Ashburton Downs, W. Australia ...23 30S 117 30E
34 Ashby-de-la-Zouch, England, U.K. ...52 45N 1 29W
34 Ashchurch, Eng., U.K. ...52 0N 2 7W
156 Ashcroft, Canada ...50 40N 121 20W
98 Ashdot Ya'aqov, Israel ...32 39N 35 35E
98 Ashdod Yam, Israel ...31 49N 34 35E
163 Asheboro, U.S.A. ...35 43N 79 46W
35 Ashdown Forest, England, U.K. ...51 4N 0 2E
165 Asherton, U.S.A. ...28 25N 99 43W
163 Asheville, U.S.A. ...35 39N 82 30W
154 Asheweig R., Canada .54 0N 88 0W
35 Ashford, England, U.K. ...51 8N 0 53E
145 Ashford, N.S.W., Austral. ...29 15S 151 3E
166 Ashford, U.S.A. ...46 45N 122 2W
35 Ashfordby, Eng., U.K. ...52 46N 0 58W
114 Ashikaga, Japan ...36 28N 139 29E
39 Ashington, Eng., U.K. 55 12N 1 35W
114 Ashizuri-saki, Japan .32 35N 132 50E
90 Ashkhabad, U.S.S.R. .38 0N 57 50E
165 Ashland, Kan., U.S.A. 37 13N 99 43W
162 Ashland, Ky., U.S.A. .38 25N 82 40W
155 Ashland, Me., U.S.A. .46 34N 68 26W
166 Ashland, Mont., U.S.A. ...45 41N 106 12W
164 Ashland, Neb., U.S.A. 41 5N 96 27W
160 Ashland, Ohio, U.S.A. 40 52N 82 20W
166 Ashland, Oreg., U.S.A. ...42 10N 122 38W
161 Ashland, Pa., U.S.A. .40 45N 76 22W
162 Ashland, Va., U.S.A. .37 46N 77 30W
164 Ashland, Wis., U.S.A. 46 40N 90 52W
164 Ashley, N.D., U.S.A. .46 3N 99 23W
161 Ashley, Pa., U.S.A. ...41 12N 75 55W
156 Ashmont, Canada ...54 7N 111 29W
126 Ashmûn, Egypt ...30 18N 30 55E
98 Ashquelon, Israel ...31 42N 34 55E
160 Ashtabula, U.S.A. ...41 52N 80 50W
106 Ashti, India ...18 50N 75 15E
134 Ashton, S. Africa ...33 0S 20 5E
166 Ashton, U.S.A. ...44 6N 111 30W
38 Ashton-u.-Lyne, England, U.K. ...53 30N 2 8W
155 Ashuanipi, L. Canada 52 30N 66 10W
113 Ashun, China ...25 10N 106 0E
146 Ashurst, New Zealand 40 16S 175 45E
35 Ashurstwood, Eng., U.K. ...51 6N 0 2E
36 Ashwater, England, U.K. ...50 43N 4 18W
36 Ashwick, England, U.K. ...51 13N 2 31W
92 Asia, cont. ...45 0N 75 0E
109 Asia Is., Indonesia ... 1 0N 131 13E
71 Asiago, Italy ...45 52N 11 30E
122 Asilah, Morocco ...35 29N 6 0W
72 Asinara, G. dell', Italy 41 0N 8 30E
72 Asinara I., Italy ...41 5N 8 15E
90 Asino, U.S.S.R. ...57 0N 86 0E
99 Asir, dist., Si. Arabia .18 40N 42 30E
99 Asir, Ras (C. Guardafui), Somali Rep. ...11 55N 51 0E
106 Aska, India ...19 37N 84 42E
44 Askeaton, Ireland ...52 37N 8 58W
79 Asker, Norway ...59 52N 10 26E
81 Askersund, Sweden ...58 58N 14 8E
79 Askim, Norway ...59 33N 11 10E
81 Åskloster, Sweden ...57 13N 12 11E
38 Askrigg, England, U.K. ...54 19N 2 6W
126 Asl, Egypt ...29 33N 32 44E
35 Aslackby, England, U.K. ...52 53N 0 23W
101 Asmar, Afghanistan ...35 10N 71 27E
127 Asmera (Asmara), Ethiopia ...15 19N 38 55E
81 Asnaes C., Denmark ...55 40N 10 53E
81 Åsnen, L., Sweden ...56 35N 15 34E
79 Åsnes, Norway ...60 37N 11 59E
122 Asni, Morocco ...31 17N 7 58W
114 Aso, vol., Japan ...33 0N 130 42E
71 Asola, Italy ...45 12N 10 25E
66 Asotin, U.S.A. ...46 14N 117 2W
38 Aspatria, England, U.K. ...54 45N 3 20W
65 Aspe, Spain ...38 20N 0 40W
167 Aspen, U.S.A. ...39 12N 106 56W
165 Aspermont, U.S.A. ...33 11N 100 15W
147 Aspiring Mt., N.Z. ...44 23S 168 46E
51 Aspres, France ...44 32N 5 44E
104 Aspur, India ...23 58N 74 7E
127 Assa, Ethiopia ...12 18N 41 15E
122 Assa, Morocco ...28 35N 9 6W
122 Assaka, Ifni ...29 7N 10 9W
127 Assale, L., Ethiopia ...14 0N 40 20E
103 Assam, st., India ...25 45N 92 30E
54 Asse, Belgium ...50 54N 4 6E
123 Assekrem, Algeria ...23 16N 5 49E
72 Assemini, Italy ...39 18N 9 0E
54 Assen, Netherlands ...53 0N 6 35E
81 Assens, Odense, Den. .56 40N 10 4E
81 Assens, Randers, Den. 55 16N 9 52E
55 Assesse, Belgium ...50 22N 5 2E
157 Assiniboia, Canada ...49 40N 106 0W
157 Assiniboine R., Canada ...49 45N 99 0W
154 Assinica L., Canada ...50 30N 75 20W
124 Assinie, Ivory Coast ... 5 9N 3 17W
173 Assis, Brazil ...22 40S 50 20W
71 Assisi, Italy ...43 4N 12 36E
77 Assos, Greece ...38 22N 20 33E
42 Assynt, dist., Scot., U.K. ...58 25N 5 10W
42 Assynt, L., Scot., U.K. ...58 10N 5 0W
77 Astakidha I., Greece .35 53N 26 50E
50 Astalfort, France ...44 4N 0 40E
100 Astara, Iran ...38 25N 48 52E
85 Astara, U.S.S.R. ...38 30N 48 50E
44 Astee, Ireland ...52 33N 9 36W
55 Asten, Netherlands ...51 24N 5 45E
70 Asti, Italy ...44 54N 8 11E
62 Astillero, Spain ...43 24N 3 49W
77 Astipalaia & I., Greece ...36 32N 26 22E
153 Aston C., Canada ...70 10N 67 40W
35 Aston Clinton, Eng., U.K. ...51 48N 0 44W
62 Astorga, Spain ...42 29N 6 8W
166 Astoria, U.S.A. ...46 16N 123 50W
81 Astorp, Sweden ...56 6N 12 55E
89 Astrakhan, U.S.S.R. .46 25N 48 5E
62 Astudillo, Spain ...42 12N 4 22W
62 Asturias, Reg., Spain .43 15N 6 0W
34 Astwood Bank, England, U.K. ...52 15N 1 55W
172 Asunción, Paraguay 25 21S 57 30W
81 Åsunden, Sweden ... 57 47N 13 18E
127 Asutri, Sudan ... 15 25N 35 45E
131 Aswa R., Uganda ... 2 30N 33 5E
126 Aswad, Rasal, Si. Arab. ...21 20N 39 0E
126 Aswân, Egypt ...24 4N 32 57E
126 Aswân Dam, Egypt ...24 10N 32 50E
126 Asyût, Egypt ...27 11N 31 4E
126 Asyûti, Wadi, Egypt .27 18N 31 20E
59 Aszód, Hungary ...47 39N 19 28E
100 At Tafilah, Jordan ...30 45N 35 30E
172 Atacama, dist., Arg. ...25 40S 67 40W
172 Atacama, prov., Chile 27 30S 70 0W
176 Atacama, Puna de, Arg. ...25 0S 67 30W
172 Atacama, Salar de, Chile ...24 0S 3 20W
176 Atacama Des., Chile ...24 0S 69 20W
123 Atakor, Mts., Algeria .23 27N 5 31E
125 Atakpamé, Togoland. 7 31N 1 13E
77 Atalándi, Greece ...38 39N 22 58E
174 Atalaya, Peru ...10 45S 73 50W
114 Atami, Japan ...35 0N 139 55E
120 Atar, Mauritania ...20 30N 13 5W
91 Atara, U.S.S.R. ...63 10N 129 10E
122 Ataram, Erg n-, Algeria ...23 57N 2 0E
63 Atarfe, Spain ...37 13N 3 40W
167 Atascadero, U.S.A. ...35 32N 120 44W
90 Atasu, U.S.S.R. ...48 30N 71 0E
109 Atauro I., Port. Timor ... 8 10S 125 30E
126 Atbara & R., Sudan ...17 50N 34 3E
90 Atbasar, U.S.S.R. ...51 50N 68 25E
165 Atchafalaya B., U.S.A. ...29 30N 91 20W
164 Atchison, U.S.A. ...39 40N 95 0W
125 Atebubu, Ghana ... 7 47N 1 0W
64 Ateca, Spain ...41 20N 1 49W
71 Aterno R., Italy ...42 18N 13 45E
71 Atessa, Italy ...42 5N 14 27E
54 Ath, Belgium ...50 38N 3 47E
100 Ath Thamami, Si. Arab. ...27 45N 35 30E
156 Athabasca, Canada ...54 45N 113 20W
157 Athabasca L., Canada 59 10N 109 30W
156 Athabasca R., Canada 55 50N 112 40W
45 Athboy, Ireland ...53 37N 6 55W
44 Athea, Ireland ...52 27N 9 18W
44 Athenry, Ireland ...53 18N 8 45W
161 Athens, Canada ...44 39N 75 55W
77 Athens, Greece ...37 58N 23 46E
163 Athens, Ala., U.S.A. .34 49N 86 58W
163 Athens, Ga., U.S.A. ...33 56N 83 24W
161 Athens, N.Y., U.S.A. .42 15N 73 48W
162 Athens, Ohio, U.S.A. .39 52N 82 6W
161 Athens, Pa., U.S.A. ...41 57N 76 36W
165 Athens, Tex., U.S.A. ..32 11N 95 48W
160 Atherly, Canada ...44 37N 79 20W
34 Atherstone, Eng., U.K. ...52 35N 1 32W
38 Atherton, Eng., U.K. .53 32N 2 30W
144 Atherton, Australia ...17 17S 145 30E
131 Athi River, Kenya ... 1 29S 36 58E
125 Athiéme, Dahomey ... 6 37N 1 40E
77 Athinai (Athens), Greece ...37 58N 23 46E
44 Athleague, Ireland ...53 34N 8 17W
98 Athlit (site), Israel ...32 42N 34 55E
44 Athlone, Ireland ...53 26N 7 57W
106 Athni, India ...16 44N 75 6E
147 Athol, New Zealand ...45 30S 168 35E
43 Atholl, Forest of, Scotland U.K. ...56 51N 1 0W
155 Atholville, Canada ...48 5N 67 5W
76 Athos, Mt., Greece ...40 9N 24 22E
45 Athy, Ireland ...53 0N 7 0W
127 'Ati, Sudan ...13 5N 29 02E
131 Atiak, Uganda ... 3 12N 32 2E
146 Atiamuri, N.Z. ...38 24S 176 5E
174 Aticó, Peru ... 6 14S 73 40W
64 Atienza, Spain ...41 12N 2 52W
154 Atikokan, Canada ...48 40N 91 40W
155 Atikonak L., Canada .53 45N 64 30W
1 Atitlan, Vol., Cent. Amer. ...14 38N 91 10W
108 Atjeh, Dist., Indon. ... 4 50N 96 0E
87 Atkarsk, U.S.S.R. ...51 55N 45 2E
164 Atkinson, U.S.A. ...42 53N 98 59W
163 Atlanta, Ga., U.S.A. .33 50N 84 24W
165 Atlanta, Tex., U.S.A. .33 7N 94 8W
164 Atlantic, U.S.A. ...41 25N 95 0W
162 Atlantic City, U.S.A. .39 25N 74 25W
16 Atlantic Ocean ... 0 0 20 0W
120 Atlas, Great, Mts., Afr. ...33 0N 5 0W
156 Atlin & L., Canada ...59 26N 133 53W
98 Atlit, Israel ...32 42N 34 56E
79 Atlöy I., Norway ...61 22N 5 00E
106 Atmakur, India ...14 37N 79 40E
163 Atmore, U.S.A. ...31 2N 87 30W
156 Atnarko, Canada ...52 25N 126 0W
174 Atocha, Bolivia ...21 0S 66 10W
165 Atoka, U.S.A. ...34 22N 96 10W
77 Átokos I., Greece ...38 28N 20 49E
168 Atotonilco, Mexico ...20 20N 98 40W
63 Atouguia, Portugal ...39 20N 9 20W
81 Ätrafors, Sweden ...57 02N 12 40E
101 Atrak R., Iran ...37 50N 57 0E
81 Ätran, Sweden ...57 07N 12 55E
104 Atrauli, India ...28 2N 78 20E
71 Atri, Italy ...42 35N 14 0E
163 Attalla, U.S.A. ...34 2N 86 5W
45 Attananna Ireland ...52 50N 7 19W
154 Attawapiskat & R., Can. ...53 0N 82 30W
154 Attawapiskat, L., Can. ...52 20N 88 0W
56 Attendorn, Germany .51 8N 7 54E
58 Attersee tn. & L., Aust. ...47 55N 13 31E
162 Attica, Ind., U.S.A. ...40 20N 87 15W
49 Attichy, France ...49 25N 3 03E
49 Attigny, France ...49 28N 4 35E
155 Attikamagen L., Can. 54 54N 66 25W
77 Attiki pref., Greece ...38 10N 23 40E
98 Attil, Jordan ...32 23N 35 4E
161 Attleboro, U.S.A. ...41 56N 71 18W
35 Attleborough, Eng., U.K. ...52 32N 1 1E
102 Attock, Pakistan ...33 52N 72 20E
107 Attopeu, Laos ...14 56N 106 50E
106 Attur, India ...11 35N 78 30E
44 Attymon, Ireland ...53 20N 8 37W
111 Atuntze, *see* Tehtsin, China ...28 45N 98 58E
174 Atures, Venezuela ... 5 30N 68 5W
81 Atvidaberg, Sweden ...58 13N 16 05E
167 Atwater, U.S.A. ...37 21N 120 37W
160 Atwood, Canada ...43 42N 81 2W

MAP
164 Atwood, U.S.A. 39 52N 101 3W
162 Au Sable R., U.S.A. ...44 39N 84 10W
51 Aubagne, France 43 17N 5 37E
109 Aubarede Pt. Phil. ...17 15N 122 20E
49 Aube, dépt., France ...48 15N 4 0E
51 Aubenas, France 44 37N 4 24E
49 Aubenton, France 49 50N 4 23E
49 Aubigny-sur-Nère, Fr. 47 30N 2 24E
50 Aubin, France 44 33N 2 15E
50 Aubrac, Mts. d', Fr. ...44 38N 2 58E
163 Auburn, Ala., U.S.A. .32 37N 85 30W
166 Auburn, Calif., U.S.A. 38 50N 121 10W
162 Auburn, Ind., U.S.A. .41 20N 85 0W
164 Auburn, Nebr., U.S.A. 40 25N 95 50W
161 Auburn, N.Y., U.S.A. 42 57N 76 39W
163 Auburndale, U.S.A. ...28 5N 81 45W
50 Aubusson, France 45 57N 2 11E
50 Auch, France 43 39N 0 36E
49 Auchel, France 50 30N 2 29E
43 Auchenblae, Scot., U.K. 56 54N 2 26W
41 Auchencairn, Scot., U.K. 54 51N 3 52W
125 Auchi, Nigeria 7 6N 6 13E
40 Auchinleck, Scot., U.K. 55 28N 4 18W
43 Auchness, Scot., U.K. 58 0N 4 36W
41 Auchterarder, Scot., U.K. 56 18N 3 43W
41 Auchtermuchty, Scotland, U.K. 56 18N 3 15W
142 Auchtertyre, Scot., U.K. 57 17N 5 35W
146 Auckland, N.Z. 36 52S 174 46E
146 Auckland, dist., N.Z. .37 0S 175 0E
136 Auckland Is., South Oc. 51 0S 166 0E
50 Aude, Dept, France ...43 8N 2 28E
50 Aude R., France 42 47N 2 9E
154 Auden, Canada 50 17N 87 54W
55 Auderghem, Belgium .50 49N 4 26E
48 Auderville, France 49 43N 1 57W
48 Audierne, France 48 1N 4 34W
49 Audincourt, France ...47 30N 6 50E
38 Audlem, England, U.K. 52 59N 2 31W
127 Audo Ra., Ethiopia ... 6 20N 41 50E
164 Audubon, U.S.A. 41 43N 94 56W
56 Aue, Germany 50 34N 12 43E
56 Auerbach, Germany ...50 30N 12 25E
48 Auffay, France 49 43N 1 07E
145 Augathella, Australia .26 2S 146 29E
46 Augher, N. Ire., U.K. 54 25N 7 10W
46 Aughnacloy, N. Ire., U.K. 54 25N 7 0W
44 Aughrim, Clare, Ireland 53 0N 8 57W
44 Aughrim, Galway, Ire. 53 18N 8 19W
45 Aughrim, Wicklow, Ire. 52 52N 6 20W
45 Aughrus More, Ireland 53 34N 10 10W
134 Augrabies Falls, S. Afr. 28 35S 20 20E
57 Augsburg, Germany ...48 22N 10 54E
73 Augusta, Italy 37 14N 15 12E
165 Augusta, Ark., U.S.A. 35 17N 91 25W
163 Augusta, Ga., U.S.A. .33 29N 81 59W
165 Augusta, Kan., U.S.A. 37 40N 97 0W
155 Augusta, Me., U.S.A. .44 20N 69 46E
166 Augusta, Mont., U.S.A. 47 30N 112 29W
164 Augusta, Wis., U.S.A. 44 41N 91 8W
142 Augusta, W. Australia 34 22S 115 10E
81 Augustenborg, Den. ...54 57N 9 52E
65 Augustine, U.S.A. 31 30N 94 37W
60 Augustów, Poland 53 51N 23 00E
142 Augustus, Mt., W. Australia 24 14S 116 48E
144 Augustus Downs, Australia 18 35S 139 55E
131 Augusto Cardosa, Mozambique 12 40S 34 50E
43 Auldearn, Scotland, U.K. 57 34N 3 50W
70 Aula, Italy 44 12N 9 57E
50 Aulnay, France 46 2N 0 22W
48 Aulne R., France 48 15N 3 35W
164 Ault, U.S.A. 40 40N 104 42W
48 Ault-Onival, France .50 5N 1 29E
42 Aultbea, Scotland, U.K. 57 50N 5 36W
50 Aulus, France 42 47N 1 17E
49 Aumale, France 49 45N 1 42E
50 Aumont, France 44 43N 3 17E
125 Auna, Nigeria 10 9N 4 42E
106 Aundh, India 17 33N 74 23E
50 Aunis, Reg., France ...46 0N 0 50W
109 Auponhia, Indonesia . 1 58S 125 27E
51 Aups, France 43 37N 6 15E
79 Aurahorten, Mt., Nor. 59 15N 6 53E
105 Auraiya, India 26 28N 79 33E
105 Aurangabad, Bihar, India 24 45N 84 18E
106 Aurangabad, Maharashtra, India 19 50N 75 23E
48 Auray, France 47 40N 3 0W
123 Aurès (Awras), Mts., Algeria 35 8N 6 30E
56 Aurich, Germany 53 28N 7 30E
79 Aurlandsvangen, Norway 60 55N 7 13E
50 Aurillac, France 44 55N 2 26E
71 Auronza, Italy 46 33N 12 27E
160 Aurora, Canada 44 0N 79 30W
134 Aurora, C. Prov., S. Afr. 32 40S 18 29E
164 Aurora, Colo., U.S.A. .39 44N 104 55W
162 Aurora, Ill., U.S.A. ...41 42N 88 20W
165 Aurora, Mo., U.S.A. ...36 58N 93 42W
160 Aurora, Ohio, U.S.A. .41 21N 81 20W
164 Aurora, Neb., U.S.A. .40 55N 98 0W
79 Aurskog, Norway 59 55N 11 27E
129 Aus, S.W. Africa 26 35S 16 12E
43 Auskerry I., Scot., U.K. 59 2N 2 35W
79 Austad, Norway 58 56N 7 32E
59 Austerlitz, *see* Slavkov, Cz. 49 10N 16 52E
79 Austervoll, Norway ...60 6N 5 15E
164 Austin, Minn., U.S.A. 43 37N 92 59W
166 Austin, Nev., U.S.A. .39 30N 117 1W
160 Austin, Pa., U.S.A. ...41 40N 78 7W
165 Austin, Tex., U.S.A. .30 20N 97 45W
142 Austin, W. Australia .27 40S 117 50E
142 Austin, L., W. Australia 27 40S 118 0E
139 Austral Downs, Austral. 20 32S 137 33E
137 Austral Is., *see* Tubai Is., Pacific Ocean ...25 0S 150 0E
139 Australia, cont. 23 0S 135 0E
143 Australian Alps, N.S.W., Australia ...36 30S 148 8E
143 Australian Cap. Terr., Australia 35 15S 149 8E
15 Australian Dependency, Antarctica 73 0S 90 0E
58 Austria, Rep., Europe 47 0N 14 0E
82 Austvågöy, I., Norway 68 20N 14 40E
50 Auterive, France 43 21N 1 29E
49 Authie R., France 50 15N 2 0E
168 Autlán, Mexico 19 40N 104 30W
49 Autun, France 46 58N 4 17E
55 Auvelais, Belgium 50 27N 4 38E
50 Auvergne Mts., France 45 0N 3 0E
50 Auvergne Reg., France 45 20N 3 0E
49 Auxerre, France 47 48N 3 32E
49 Auxi, France 50 13N 2 7E
49 Auxonne, France 47 10N 5 20E
50 Auzances, France 46 2N 2 30E
79 Alvaldsnes, Norway ...59 21N 5 20E
49 Avallon, France 47 30N 3 53E
155 Avalon Pen., Canada .47 0N 53 20W
165 Avalon Res., U.S.A. ...32 30N 104 30W
106 Avanigadda, India 16 0N 80 56E
173 Avare, Brazil 23 4S 48 58W
76 Ávas, Greece 40 57N 25 56E
100 Aveh, Iran 35 40N 49 15E
175 Aveiro, Brazil 3 10S 55 5W
62 Aveiro, tn. & dist., Port. 40 37N 8 38W
172 Avellaneda, Argentina 34 50S 58 10W
73 Avellino, Italy 40 54N 14 46E
55 Averbode, Belgium 51 2N 4 59E
79 Averöy I., Norway 63 0N 7 40E
73 Aversa, Italy 40 58N 14 11E
166 Avery, U.S.A. 47 22N 115 56W
174 Aves I., Venezuela 12 0N 67 40W
49 Avesnes, France 50 7N 3 55E
80 Avesta, Sweden 60 9N 16 8E
36 Aveton Gifford, England, U.K. 50 17N 3 51W
50 Aveyron, Dépt., France 44 22N 2 45E
71 Avezzano, Italy 42 2N 13 24E
77 Avgó, I., Greece 35 33N 25 37E
172 Aviá Terai, Argentina 26 45S 60 50W
71 Aviano, Italy 46 3N 12 35E
40 Avich, L., Scot., U.K. 56 17N 5 25W
43 Aviemore, Scot., U.K. 57 11N 3 50W
73 Avigliano, Basilicata, Italy 40 44N 15 41E
70 Avigliano, Piemonte, Italy 45 7N 7 13E
51 Avignon, France 43 57N 4 50E
62 Avila, Spain 40 39N 4 43W
62 Avila, Prov., Spain ...40 30N 5 0W
62 Aviles, Spain 43 35N 5 57W
77 Avionárion, Greece ...38 31N 24 8E
71 Aviso R., Italy 46 14N 11 18E
63 Aviz, Portugal 39 4N 7 53W
49 Avize, France 48 59N 4 0E
45 Avoca, Ireland 52 50N 6 10W
160 Avoca, U.S.A. 42 24N 77 25W
143 Avoca & R., Australia 35 50S 143 30E
43 Avoch, Scotland, U.K. 57 34N 4 10W
156 Avola, Canada 51 45N 119 30W
73 Avola, Italy 36 56N 15 7E
161 Avon, N.Y., U.S.A. ...43 0N 77 42W
164 Avon, S.D., U.S.A. ...43 0N 98 3W
34 Avon R., Hants., England, U.K. 50 57N 1 45W
34 Avon, R., Wilts., England, U.K. 51 22N 2 30W
34 Avon, R., Worcs., England, U.K. 52 8N 1 53W
43 Avon, R., Scotland, U.K. 57 9N 3 25W
142 Avon R., W. Australia 31 35S 116 0E
139 Avon Downs, Australia 19 58S 137 25E
160 Avon Lake, U.S.A. ...41 28N 82 3W
146 Avondale, New Zealand 36 54S 174 42E
132 Avondale, Rhodesia ...17 43S 30 58E
157 Avonlea, Canada 50 0N 105 0W
161 Avonmore, Canada 45 11N 74 57W
36 Avonmouth, Eng., U.K. 51 30N 2 42W
134 Avontuur, S. Africa ...33 43S 23 9E
48 Avranches, France 48 40N 1 20W
78 Avrig, Rumania 45 43N 24 21E
50 Avrillé, France 46 28N 1 28W
74 Avtovac, Y.-slav 43 9N 18 35E
127 Awag el Baqar, Sudan 10 10N 33 10E
101 Awali, Bahrain 26 0N 50 30E
146 Awanui, New Zealand 35 4S 173 17E
106 Arwarja R., India 18 0N 76 15E
98 Awarta, Jordan 32 10N 35 17E
147 Awarua Pt., N.Z. 44 15S 168 5E
127 Awash & R., Ethiopia 9 1N 40 10E
124 Awaso, Ghana 6 15N 2 22W
147 Awatere R., N.Z. 41 55S 173 35E
123 Awbari, Libya 26 46N 12 57E
40 Awe, L., Scotland, U.K. 56 15N 5 15W
127 Aweil, Sudan 8 42N 27 20E
125 Awgu, Nigeria 6 4N 7 24E
125 Awka, Nigeria 6 12N 7 5E
121 Awjilah, Libya 29 8N 21 7E
50 Axat, France 43 0N 2 14E
36 Axbridge, England, U.K. 51 17N 2 50W
36 Axe R., England, U.K. 51 17N 2 52W
38 Axe Edge, England, U.K. 53 14N 2 2W
14 Axel Heiberg I., Canada 80 0N 90 0W
81 Axelfors, Sweden 57 26N 13 7E
39 Axholme, Isle of, England, U.K. 53 30N 1 10E
124 Axim, Ghana 4 51N 2 15W
78 Axintele, Rumania 44 37N 26 47E
76 Axios R., Greece 40 57N 22 35E
80 Axmarsbruk, Sweden .61 3N 17 10E
36 Axminster, Eng., U.K. 50 47N 3 1W
36 Axmouth, Eng., U.K. 50 43N 3 2W
56 Axstedt, Germany 53 26N 8 43E
81 Axvall, Sweden 58 23N 13 34E
49 Ay, France 49 3N 4 0E
174 Ayabaca, Peru 4 40S 79 53W
114 Ayabe, Japan 35 20N 135 20E
172 Ayacucho, Argentina .37 5S 58 20W
174 Ayacucho, Peru 13 0S 74 0W
90 Ayaguz, U.S.S.R. 48 10N 80 0E
106 Ayakudi, India 10 57N 77 6E
124 Ayamé Dam, Ivory Coast 5 40N 3 25W
63 Ayamonte, Spain 37 12N 7 24W
91 Ayan, U.S.S.R. 56 30N 138 16E
88 Ayancik, Turkey 41 57N 34 18E
88 Ayas, Turkey 40 10N 32 14E
174 Ayaviri, Peru 14 50S 70 35W
100 Aydin, Turkey 37 52N 27 55E
77 Aydin, Prov., Turkey 37 45N 27 40E
107 Ayeritam, Malaysia ... 5 24N 100 15E
161 Ayers Cliff, Canada ...45 10N 72 3W
138 Ayers Rock, N. Terr., Australia 25 23S 131 5E
76 Ayía, Greece 39 43N 22 45E
77 Ayía Anna, Greece 38 52N 23 24E
77 Ayía Marina, Kasos, Gr. 35 27N 26 53E
77 Ayía Marina, Leros, Gr. 37 11N 26 48E
76 Ayía Paraskevi, Greece 39 14N 26 16E
77 Ayia Roumeli, Greece 35 14N 22 58E
77 Ayiássos, Greece 39 5N 26 23E
77 Áyios Andréas, Greece 37 21N 22 45E
77 Áyios Evstrátios, Gr. .39 34N 24 58E
76 Áyios Evstrátios I., Gr. 39 30N 25 0E
77 Áyios Ioánnis, Akra, C., Greece 35 20N 25 40E
77 Áyios Kiríkos, Greece .37 34N 26 17E
76 Áyios Matthaíos, Greece 39 30N 19 47E
77 Áyios Míron, Greece ...35 15N 25 1E
77 Áyios Nikoláos, Gr. ...35 11N 25 41E
77 Áyios Petros, Greece .38 38N 20 33E
77 Áyios Yeoryios I., Gr. 37 28N 23 57E
91 Aykhal, U.S.S.R. 66 0N 112 15E
77 Aykathonisi I., Greece 37 28N 27 0E
35 Aylesbury, Eng., U.K. 51 48N 0 49W
35 Aylesford, Eng., U.K. 51 18N 0 29E
160 Aylmer, Canada 42 48N 80 59W
152 Aylmer L., Canada 64 0N 109 0W
35 Aylsham, England, U.K. 52 48N 1 16E
100 Ayn Zalah, Iraq 36 45N 42 35E
123 Ayn Zaqqut, Libya 29 0N 19 30E
65 Ayna, Spain 38 34N 2 3W
34 Aynho, England, U.K. 51 59N 1 15W
172 Ayolas, Paraguay 27 10S 56 59W
127 Ayom, Sudan 7 49N 28 23E
65 Ayora, Spain 39 3N 1 3W
144 Ayr, Australia 19 35S 147 25E
40 Ayr, Scotland, U.K. ...55 28N 4 37W
40 Ayr, Co., Scotland, U.K. 55 25N 4 25W
40 Ayr, Heads of, Scotland, U.K. 55 25N 4 43W
40 Ayr R., Scotland, U.K. 55 29N 4 28W
38 Ayre, Pt. of, Isle of Man, U.K. 54 27N 4 21W
43 Ayre, Pt. of, Scot., U.K. 58 55N 2 43W
38 Aysgarth, England, U.K. 54 18N 2 0W
39 Ayton, England, U.K. 54 15N 0 29W
41 Ayton, Scotland, U.K. 55 51N 2 6W
144 Ayton, Australia 15 45S 145 25E
168 Ayutla, Mexico 16 58N 99 17W
107 Ayutthaya, Thailand .14 25N 100 30E
76 Ayvacik, Turkey 39 36N 26 23E
100 Ayvalik, Turkey 39 20N 26 46E
127 Az Daro, Ethiopia 14 20N 38 14E
98 Az Zahiriyan, Jordan 31 25N 34 58E
100 Az Zahran, Si. Arabia 26 10N 50 7E
123 Az Zawiyah, Libya ...32 52N 12 56E
123 Az Zintan, Libya 31 59N 12 9E
100 Az Zubayr, Iraq 30 20N 47 50E
123 Az Zuwaytinah, Libya 30 49N 20 3E
63 Azambuja, Portugal ...39 4N 8 51W
105 Azamgarh, India 26 35N 83 13E
125 Azare, Nigeria 11 55N 10 10E
48 Azay-le-Rideau, France 47 16N 0 30E
123 Azazga, Algeria 36 48N 4 30E
127 Azazo, Ethiopia 12 28N 37 15E
122 Azemmour, Morocco .33 14N 8 16W
85 Azerbaijan S.S.R., U.S.S.R. 40 20N 48 0E
123 Azetfoun (Port Gueydon), Algeria .36 51N 4 30E
122 Azilal, Morocco 32 0N 6 30W
105 Azimganj, India 24 14N 84 16E
63 Aznalcollar, Spain 37 32N 6 17W
174 Azogues, Ecuador 2 35S 78 0W
98 Azor, Israel 32 2N 34 48E
16 Azores Is., Atlantic Oc. 38 44N 29 0W
89 Azov, U.S.S.R. 47 3N 39 25E
88 Azov Sea, U.S.S.R. ...46 0N 36 30E
90 Azovy, U.S.S.R. 64 55N 64 35E
64 Azpeitia, Spain 43 12N 2 19W
122 Azrou, Morocco 33 28N 5 19W
167 Aztec, U.S.A. 36 54N 108 0W
169 Azua, Dom. Rep. 18 25N 70 44W
63 Azuaga, Spain 38 16N 5 39W
64 Azuara, Spain 41 15N 0 53W
64 Azuara R., Spain 41 12N 0 55W
65 Azuer R., Spain 38 50N 3 15W
169 Azuero Pen., Panama 7 30N 80 30W
172 Azul, Argentina 36 42S 59 43W
123 Azzaba, Algeria 36 48N 7 6E
71 Azzano Decimo, Italy 45 53N 12 46E

B

107 Ba Don, N. Vietnam .17 45N 106 26E
107 Ba, R., Vietnam 13 5N 109 0E
107 Ba Ngoi, S. Vietnam, *see* Cam Lam 5 0N 109 10E
109 Baa, Indonesia 10 50S 123 0E
62 Baamonde, Spain 43 7N 7 44W
54 Baarle Nassau, Belg. .51 27N 4 56E
54 Baarn, Netherlands ...52 12N 5 17E
99 Bab el Mandeb Str., Red Sea 12 35N 43 25E
75 Baba, Mt., Bulgaria ...42 44N 23 59E
76 Baba Burun, C., Turkey 39 29N 26 2E
89 Baba dag, mt., U.S.S.R. 41 0N 48 55E
78 Babadag, Rumania ...44 53N 28 44E
75 Babaeski, Turkey 41 26N 27 06E
174 Babahoyo, Ecuador ... 1 40S 79 30W
142 Babakin, W. Australia 32 11S 117 52E
125 Babana, Nigeria 10 31N 5 9E
123 Babar, Algeria 35 10N 7 6E
104 Babar, West Pakistan 31 7N 69 32E
109 Babar I., Indonesia ... 8 0S 129 30E
104 Babarkach, W. Pak. .29 45N 68 0E
87 Babayevo, U.S.S.R. ...59 24N 35 55E
166 Babb, U.S.A. 48 56N 113 27W
126 Babein, Gebel, Egypt 22 41N 25 2E
57 Babenhausen, Germany 49 57N 8 56E
78 Băbeni, Rumania 44 59N 24 11E
59 Babia Gora mt., Europe 49 38N 19 38E
127 Babile, Ethiopia 9 16N 42 11E
74 Babin Nos, mt., Bulg. 43 45N 22 20E
144 Babinda, Australia ...17 27S 146 0E
143 Babinda Hill, N.S.W., Australia 31 55S 146 28E
156 Babine L., Canada 54 40N 126 10W
109 Babo, Indonesia 2 30S 133 30E
59 Babocsa, Hungary 46 2N 17 21E
101 Babol, Iran 36 40N 52 50E
101 Babol Sar, Iran 36 45N 52 45E
123 Babor, Djebel, Algeria 36 30N 5 29E
128 Baboua, Cent. Afr. Rep. 5 49N 14 58E
74 Babuna R., Y.-slav ...41 27N 21 38E
125 Babura, Nigeria 12 51N 8 59E
87 Babushkin, U.S.S.R. .55 45N 37 40E
74 Babušnica, Y.-slav. ...43 7N 22 27E
113 Babuyan I., Philippines 19 0N 122 0E
100 Babylon, site of, Iraq 32 40N 44 30E
161 Babylon, U.S.A. 40 42N 73 20W
74 Bač, Yugoslavia 45 29N 19 17E
107 Bac Kan, Vietnam 22 5N 105 50E
107 Bac Lieu, Vietnam *see* Vinh Loi 9 20N 104 45E
107 Bac Ninh, Vietnam ...21 13N 106 4E
107 Bac Quang, Vietnam .22 30N 104 48E
175 Bacabal, Brazil 5 20S 56 45W
109 Bacarra, Philippines ...17 51N 117 0E
78 Bacau, Rumania 46 35N 26 55E
78 Bacau, Reg., Rumania 46 30N 26 50E
49 Baccarat, France 48 28N 6 42E
143 Bacchus Marsh, Austral. 37 28S 144 25E
78 Băcesti, Rumania 46 50N 27 11E
57 Bacharach, Germany .50 3N 7 46E
90 Bachelina, U.S.S.R. ...57 45N 67 20E
74 Bacina, Yugoslavia ...43 42N 21 23E
42 Back, Scotland, U.K. .58 17N 6 20W
152 Back R., Canada 65 10N 104 0W
74 Bačka Palanka, Y.-slav. 45 17N 19 27E
74 Bačka Topola, Y.-slav. 45 96N 19 37E
81 Bäckefors, Sweden 58 46N 12 13E
74 Bački Petrovac, Y.-slav. 45 29N 19 32E
57 Backnang, Germany .48 57N 9 26E
109 Baco, Mt., Philippines 13 0N 121 30E
109 Bacolod, Philippines .10 50N 123 0E
48 Bacqueville, France ...49 47N 1 0E
59 Bacs-Kiskun, Co., Hung. 46 43N 19 30E
59 Bacsalmas, Hungary .46 8N 19 17E
35 Bacton, England, U.K. 52 50N 1 29E
109 Bacuit, Philippines 11 20N 119 20E
127 Bacuma, Ethiopia 6 31N 36 1E
38 Bacup, England, U.K. 53 42N 2 12W
164 Bad R., U.S.A. 44 10N 100 50W
58 Bad Aussee, Austria ...47 43N 13 45E
160 Bad Axe, U.S.A. 43 48N 82 59W
56 Bad Bramstedt, Ger. .53 56N 9 53E
56 Bad Doberan, Germany 54 6N 11 55E
56 Bad Driburg, Germany 51 44N 9 0E
57 Bad Ems, Germany ...15 22N 7 44E
56 Bad Frankenhausen, Germany 51 21N 11 3E
56 Bad Godesburg, Ger. .50 41N 7 4E
58 Bad Hofgastein, Aus. .47 17N 13 6E
57 Bad Homburg, Ger. ...50 17N 8 33E
58 Bad Ischl, Austria 47 44N 13 38E
57 Bad Kissingen, Ger. ...50 11N 10 5E
57 Bad Kreuznach, Ger. .49 47N 7 47E
164 Bad Lands, U.S.A. 43 40N 102 10W
56 Bad Lauterberg, Ger. .51 38N 10 29E
56 Bad Lippspringe, Ger. 51 47N 8 46E
57 Bad Mergentheim, Ger. 49 29N 9 47E
55 Bad Nauenahr, Ger. ...50 33N 7 8E
57 Bad Nauheim, Germany 50 24N 8 45E
56 Bad Oeynhausen, Ger. 52 16N 8 45E
56 Bad Oldesloe, Germany 53 56N 10 17E
57 Bad Orb, Germany 50 16N 9 21E
56 Bad Pyrmont, Germany 51 59N 9 5E
56 Bad Salzuflen, Germany 52 8N 8 44E
56 Bad Segeberg, Germany 53 58N 10 16E
57 Bad Tölz, Germany ...47 43N 11 34E
57 Bad Wildungen, Ger. .51 7N 9 10E
56 Bad Zwischenahn, Ger. 53 15N 8 0E
106 Badagara, India 11 35N 75 40E
125 Badagri, Nigeria 6 25N 2 55E
174 Badajos, L., Brazil 3 15S 62 50W
63 Badajoz, Spain 38 50N 6 59W
63 Badajoz, Prov., Spain 38 40N 6 30W
101 Badakhshan, Prov., Afghanistan 36 30N 71 0E
127 Badalle, Ethiopia 8 31N 35 44E
64 Badalona, Spain 41 26N 2 15E
101 Badalzai, Afghanistan 29 50N 65 35E
100 Badanah, Saudi Arabia 30 58N 41 30E
108 Badas, Brunei 4 20N 114 37E
108 Badas Is., Indonesia . 0 45N 107 5E
102 Baddo R., W. Pakistan 28 15N 65 0E
59 Baden, Austria 48 1N 16 13E
160 Baden, Canada 43 24N 80 40W
57 Baden, Switzerland ...47 28N 8 18E
57 Baden-Württemberg, land, Germany 48 40N 9 0E
43 Badenoch, Dist., Scotland, U.K. 57 0N 4 0W
43 Badenscoth, Scot., U.K. 51 27N 2 30W
127 Badessa, Ethiopia 9 58N 40 52E
58 Badgastein, Austria ...47 7N 13 9E
155 Badger, Canada 49 0N 56 4W
100 Badia, Saudi Arabia ...22 0N 46 35E
104 Badin, W. Pakistan ...24 38N 68 54E
71 Badia Polesina, Italy 45 6N 11 30E
127 Badigeru, Swamp, Sudan 5 30W 32 10E
104 Badnera, India 20 48N 77 44E
105 Badrinath, India 30 45N 79 30E
99 Baduen, Somali Rep. . 7 15N 47 40E
106 Badulla, Ceylon 7 1N 81 7E
81 Bække, Denmark 55 35N 9 6E
63 Baena, Spain 37 37N 4 20W
174 Baetas, Brazil 6 5S 62 15W
63 Baeza, Spain 37 57N 3 25W
101 Bafa, Iran 31 40N 55 25E
77 Bafa Gölu, L. Turkey 37 30N 27 29E
124 Bafatá, Port Guinea ...12 8N 15 20E
14 Baffin Bay, Canada ...72 0N 65 0W
153 Baffin I., Canada 68 0N 77 0W
125 Bafia, Cameroon 4 40N 11 10E
125 Bafilo, Togo 9 22N 1 22E
124 Bafing, R., Guinea 11 40N 10 45W
124 Bafoulabe, Mali 13 50N 10 55W
101 Bafq, Iran 31 40N 55 20E
88 Bafra, Turkey 41 34N 35 54E
101 Baft, Iran 29 15N 56 38E
125 Bafut, Cameroon 6 6N 10 2E
131 Bafwasende, Congo ... 1 3N 27 5E
106 Bagalkot, India 16 10N 75 40E
131 Bagamoyo Tanzania ... 6 28S 38 55E
109 Baganga, Philippines . 7 36N 126 38E
108 Bagansiapiapi, Indon. 2 12N 100 50E
104 Bagasra, India 21 59N 71 77E
127 Bagawi, Sudan 12 20N 34 18E
173 Bage, Brazil 31 20S 54 15W
165 Baggs, U.S.A. 41 8N 107 46W
36 Baggy Pt., England, U.K. 51 11N 4 12W
100 Baghdad, Iraq 33 20N 44 30E

MAP
105 Bagherhat, E. Pakistan 22 40N 89 47E
72 Bagheria, Italy 38 5N 13 30E
101 Baghin, Iran 30 12N 56 45E
101 Baghlan, Afghanistan 36 12N 69 0E
45 Baginbun Hd., Ireland 52 10N 6 50W
164 Bagley, U.S.A. 47 30N 95 22W
71 Bagnacavallo, Italy ...44 25N 11 58E
73 Bagnara Calabra, Italy 38 16N 15 49E
50 Bagnères de Bigorre, Fr. 43 5N 0 9E
50 Bagnères de Luchon, Fr. 42 47N 0 38E
70 Bagni di Lucca, Italy 44 1N 10 37E
71 Bagno di Romagna, It. 43 50N 11 59E
71 Bagnoli di Sopra, Italy 45 11N 11 53E
48 Bagnoles, France 48 32N 0 25W
71 Bagnolo Mella, Italy .45 27N 10 14E
50 Bagnols-les Bains, Fr. 44 30N 3 40E
50 Bagnols-sur-Cèze, Fr. 44 10N 4 36E
71 Bagnoregio, Italy 42 38N 12 7E
70 Bagolino, Italy 45 49N 10 28E
155 Bagotville, Canada 48 22N 70 54W
111 Bagrash Gol., China ...42 0N 87 0E
74 Bagrdan, Yugoslavia .44 5N 21 11E
35 Bagshot, England, U.K. 51 22N 0 41W
109 Baguio, Philippines ...16 26N 120 34E
64 Bahabón de Esgueva, Spain 41 52N 3 43W
104 Bahadurgarh, India ...28 40N 76 57E
169 Bahama Is., W. Indies 24 40N 74 0W
126 Bahariya Oasis, Egypt 28 0N 28 50E
107 Bahau, Malaysia 2 48N 102 26E
104 Bahawalnagar, W. Pak. 30 0N 73 15E
104 Bahawalpur, W. Pak. 29 37N 71 40E
104 Bahawalpur, Prov., West Pakistan 29 5N 71 3E
105 Baheri, India 28 45N 79 34E
127 Baheta, Ethiopia 13 27N 42 10E
131 Bahi, Tanzania 5 58S 35 21E
175 Bahia, *see* Salvador, Brazil 13 0S 38 30W
175 Bahia, st., Brazil 12 0N 42 0E
169 Bahia, Islas de la, Hond. 16 45N 86 15W
172 Bahia Blanca, Arg. 38 35S 62 13W
174 Bahia de Caraquez, Ec. 0 40S 80 27W
176 Bahia Laura, Argentina 48 10S 66 30W
174 Bahia Negra, Paraguay 20 5S 58 5W
122 Bahmer, Algeria 27 32N 0 10W
59 Bahönye, Hungary 46 25N 17 28E
127 Bahr Dar, Ethiopia ...11 37N 37 10E
127 Bahr el Abiad, R., Sudan 9 30N 31 40E
127 Bahr el 'Arab, R. Sudan 9 50N 27 10E
127 Bahr el Azraq, R., Sudan 10 30N 35 0E
127 Bahr el Ghazal, R. Sudan 9 0N 30 0E
127 Bahr-el-Ghazal, Prov., Sudan 7 0N 28 0E
127 Bahr el Jebel, Sudan . 7 30N 30 30E
126 Bahr Yûsef, Egypt ...28 25N 30 35E
100 Bahra, Saudi Arabia .21 25N 39 32E
126 Bahra el Burullus, Eg. 31 28N 30 48E
126 Bahra el Manzala, Eg. 31 28N 32 01E
105 Bahraich, India 27 38N 81 50E
101 Bahrain I., Persian G. 26 0N 50 35E
101 Bahramabad, Iran 30 28N 56 2E
101 Bahu Kalat, Iran 25 50N 61 20E
107 Bai Bung Pt. (Mui Ca Mau), S. Vietnam ... 8 35N 104 42E
124 Bai, Mali 13 35N 3 28W
78 Baia-Mare, Rumania .47 40N 23 37E
63 Baia Setubal, Portugal 38 23N 9 0W
78 Baia-Sprie, Rumania .47 41N 23 43W
175 Baião, Brazil 2 50S 49 15W
121 Baibokoum, Cameroon 7 40N 14 45E
155 Baie Comeau, Canada 49 12N 68 10W
155 Baie de l'Abri, Canada 50 3N 67 0W
155 Baie de la Trinité, Can. 49 25N 67 20W
155 Baie Johan Beetz, Can. 50 18N 62 50W
155 Baie St. Paul, Canada 47 28N 70 32W
155 Baie Verte, Canada ...49 55N 56 12W
50 Baignes, France 45 28N 0 25W
49 Baigneux-les-Juifs, Fr. 47 31N 4 39E
100 Baiji, Iraq 35 0N 43 30E
91 Baikit, U.S.S.R. 61 50N 95 50E
90 Baikonur, U.S.S.R. ...47 48N 65 50E
106 Bailadila, Mt., India .18 43N 81 15E
39 Baildon, England, U.K. 53 52N 1 46W
45 Baile Atha Cliath, *see* Dublin, Ireland 53 20N 6 18W
127 Bailei, Ethiopia 6 44N 40 18E
63 Bailen, Spain 38 8N 3 48W
78 Băilesti, Rumania 44 01N 23 20E
135 Bailey, C. Prov., S. Afr. 31 45S 26 43E
106 Bailhongal, India 15 55N 74 53E
46 Baillieborough, Ireland 53 55N 7 0W
MAP
49 Bailleul, France 50 44N 2 41E
48 Bain de Bretagne, Fr. 47 50N 1 40W
38 Bainbridge, Eng., U.K. 54 18N 2 7W
163 Bainbridge, Ga., U.S.A. 30 53N 84 34W
161 Bainbridge, N.Y., U.S.A. 42 17N 75 29W
164 Bainville, U.S.A. 48 8N 104 10W
165 Baird, U.S.A. 32 25N 99 25W
152 Baird Mts., Alaska, U.S.A. 67 10N 160 15W
143 Bairnsdale, Australia .37 43S 147 35E
112 Baissoklyn, Mongolia .47 55N 102 20E
105 Baitadi, Nepal 29 35N 80 25E
126 Baiyuda, Sudan 17 35N 32 07E
59 Baja, Hungary 46 12N 18 59E
168 Baja Pta., Mexico 29 50N 116 0W
126 Bajah, Wadi, Si. Arab. 23 14N 39 20E
104 Bajana, India 23 7N 71 49E
74 Bajanovac, Y.-slav. ...42 28N 21 45E
145 Bajimba, N.S.W., Australia 29 22S 152 0E
74 Bajina Bašta, Y.-slav. 43 58N 19 35E
105 Bajitpur, E. Pak. 24 13N 91 0E
74 Bajmok, Y.-slav. 45 57N 19 24E
169 Bajo Boquete, Panama 8 49N 82 27W
125 Bajoga, Nigeria 10 57N 11 20E
144 Bajool, Australia 23 40S 150 35E
59 Bak, Hungary 46 43N 16 51E
121 Bakala, Cent. Afr. Rep. 6 15N 20 20E
71 Bakar, Yugoslavia 45 18N 14 32E
108 Bake, Indonesia 3 05S 100 20E
124 Bakel, Senegal 14 56N 12 20W
167 Baker, Calif., U.S.A. .35 16N 116 2W
164 Baker, Mont., U.S.A. .46 22N 104 12W
166 Baker, Nev., U.S.A. ...38 59N 114 7W
166 Baker, Oreg., U.S.A. ..44 50N 117 55W
136 Baker Is., Pacific Oc. . 0 10N 176 35E
152 Baker, L., Canada 64 0N 97 0W
152 Baker Lake, tn., Can. 64 20N 96 10W
166 Baker Mt., U.S.A. 48 50N 121 49W
154 Baker's Dozen Is., Can. 57 30N 79 0W
167 Bakersfield, Calif., U.S.A. 35 25N 119 0W
161 Bakersfield, Vt., U.S.A. 44 46N 72 48W
133 Bakerville, S. Africa ...26 00S 26 06E
39 Bakewell, Eng., U.K. .53 13N 1 40W
88 Bakhchisaray, U.S.S.R. 44 40N 33 45E
86 Bakhmach, U.S.S.R. .51 10N 32 45E
105 Bakhtapur, Nepal 27 44N 85 20E
127 Bakia, Cent. Afr. Rep. 5 18N 25 45E
100 Bakinskikh Komissarov, Azer, S.S.R, U.S.S.R. 39 20N 49 15E
101 Bakinskikh Komissarov, Turkman SSR, U.S.S.R. 39 20N 54 8E
75 Bakirköy, Turkey 40 59N 28 53E
79 Bakke, Norway 59 41N 6 21E
59 Bakony, R., Hungary 47 35N 17 54E
59 Bakony Hegyseg, Hung. 47 10N 17 30E
125 Bakori, Nigeria 11 34N 7 25E
121 Bakouma, Cent. Afr. Rep. 5 40N 22 56E
58 Bakov, Czechoslovakia 50 27N 14 55E
89 Baku, U.S.S.R. 40 25N 49 45E
130 Bakwanga, Congo, *see* Mbuji Mayi 3 51N 23 40E
160 Bala, Canada 45 2N 79 38W
98 Bal'a, Jordan 32 20N 35 6E
37 Bala, Wales, U.K. 52 54N 3 36W
37 Bala, L., Wales, U.K. 52 53N 3 38W
108 Bala Balakam Is. Indon. 7 5S 118 15E
108 Balabac I., Philippines 8 0N 117 0E
108 Balabac Str., E. Indies 7 53N 117 5E
100 Balabakk, Lebanon ...34 0N 36 10E
108 Balabalangen Is., Indonesia 2 20S 117 30E
78 Bălaciţa, Rumania 44 23N 23 05E
101 Balad Bani Bu 'Ali, Muscat & 'Oman 22 0N 59 20E
105 Balaghat, India 21 49N 80 12E
106 Balaghat Ra., Mts., India 18 50N 76 30E
64 Balaguér, Spain 41 50N 0 50E
130 Balaka, Congo 4 52S 19 57E
132 Balaka, Malawi 14 57S 34 55E
87 Balakhna, U.S.S.R. ...56 35N 43 40E
145 Balaklava, S. Australia 34 7S 138 22E
88 Balaklava, U.S.S.R. ...44 30N 33 30E
88 Balakleya, U.S.S.R. ...49 28N 36 55E
87 Balakovo, U.S.S.R. 52 4N 47 55E
87 Balanda, U.S.S.R. 51 30N 44 40E
105 Balangir, India 20 43N 8 35E
109 Balangnipa, Indonesia 5 15S 120 25E
104 Balapur, India 21 22N 76 45E
87 Balashikha, U.S.S.R. 55 43N 37 59E
87 Balashov, U.S.S.R. 51 30N 43 10E
104 Balasinor, India 22 57N 73 23E
105 Balasore, India 21 35N 87 3E
59 Balassagyarmat, Hung. 48 4N 19 15E
126 Balât, Egypt 25 36N 29 19E
132 Balate, Mozambique .22 50S 34 29E
59 Balaton L., Hungary .46 50N 17 40E
MAP
59 Balatonfured, Hungary 46 58N 17 54E
59 Balatonszentgyörgy, Hungary 46 41N 17 19E
65 Balazote, Spain 38 54N 2 09W
41 Balbeggie, Scot., U.K. 56 26N 3 19W
43 Balblair, Scotland, U.K. 57 39N 4 11W
168 Balboa, Pan. Can. Zone 9 0N 79 30W
168 Balboa Hill, Panama Canal Zone 9 6N 79 44W
46 Balbriggan, Ireland ...53 35N 6 10W
172 Balcarce, Argentina ...38 0S 58 10W
157 Balcarres, Canada 50 50N 103 35W
75 Balchik, Bulgaria 43 28N 28 11E
147 Balclutha, N.Z. 46 15S 169 45E
142 Bald Hill, W. Australia 24 40S 119 47E
165 Bald Knob, U.S.A. 35 20N 91 35W
39 Balderton, Eng., U.K. 53 3N 0 46W
36 Baldock, England, U.K. 51 59N 0 11W
45 Baldoyle, Ireland 53 24N 6 10W
162 Baldwin, Fla., U.S.A. 30 15N 82 10W
162 Baldwin, Mich., U.S.A. 43 54N 85 53W
161 Baldwinsville, U.S.A. .43 10N 76 19W
91 Baldzhikan, U.S.S.R. .49 20N 110 30E
71 Bale, Yugoslavia 45 4N 13 46E
64 Balearic Is., Spain 39 30N 3 0E
109 Balekambang, Indon. 7 13S 106 27E
55 Balen, Belgium 51 10N 5 10E
78 Bălenii, Rumania 44 50N 25 40E
109 Baler, Philippines 15 35N 121 40E
42 Baleshare I., Scotland 57 30N 7 21W
144 Balfe Creek, Australia 20 12S 145 57E
135 Balfour, C. Prov., S. Afr. 32 31S 26 40E
133 Balfour, S. Afr. 26 38S 28 35E
43 Balfour, Scotland, U.K. 59 2N 2 54W
142 Balfour Downs, W. Australia 22 45S 120 50E
98 Balfourya, Israel 32 38N 35 18E
40 Balfron, Scotland, U.K. 56 4N 4 20W
125 Bali, Cameroon 5 54N 10 0E
108 Bali I., Indonesia 8 20S 115 0E
109 Bali Str., Indonesia ... 8 30S 114 35E
59 Baligród, Poland 49 20N 22 17E
108 Balikpapan, Indonesia 1 10S 116 55E
100 Balikesir, Turkey 39 35N 27 58E
109 Balimbing, Philippines 5 10N 120 3E
107 Baling, Malaysia 5 41N 100 55E
74 Balint, Rumania 45 48N 21 54E
113 Balintang Chan., Phil. 19 50N 122 0E
113 Balintang Is., Phil. 19 55N 122 0E
43 Balintore, Scotland, U.K. 57 45N 3 55W
103 Balipara, India 26 50N 92 45E
175 Balisa, Brazil 16 0S 52 20W
161 Baliston Spa, U.S.A. .43 0N 73 52W
75 Balkan Mts., *see* Stara Planina, Europe 43 15N 23 0E
19 Balkan Pen., Europe .42 0N 22 0E
101 Balk, *see* Wazirabad, Afghanistan 36 44N 66 47E
90 Balkhash, U.S.S.R. ...46 50N 74 50E
90 Balkhash, L., U.S.S.R. 46 0N 74 50E
132 Balla Balla, Rhodesia 20 27S 29 3E
142 Balladonia, W. Austral. 32 20S 123 45E
46 Ballagan Pt., Ireland .54 0N 6 6W
46 Ballaghaderreen, Ire. .53 55N 8 35W
143 Ballan, Australia 38 50N 144 28E
40 Ballantrae, Scot., U.K. 55 6N 5 0W
143 Ballarat, Vic., Austral. 37 33S 143 50E
142 Ballard, L., W. Austral. 29 20S 120 10E
106 Ballarpur, India 19 50N 79 23E
38 Ballasalla, Isle of Man, United Kingdom 54 7N 4 36W
43 Ballater, Scotland, U.K. 57 2N 3 2W
38 Ballaugh, Isle of Man, United Kingdom 54 20N 4 32W
143 Balldale, Australia 36 20N 146 33E
168 Ballenas Channel, Mex. 29 10N 113 45W
15 Balleny Is., Antarctica 66 30S 163 0E
105 Ballia, India 25 46N 84 12E
142 Ballidu, W. Australia .30 33S 116 38E
45 Ballikmoyler, Ireland .52 54N 7 2W
46 Ballina, Mayo, Ireland 54 7N 9 10W
44 Ballina, Tipp., Ireland 52 49N 8 27W
145 Ballina, Australia 28 50S 153 31E
45 Ballinagar, Ireland 53 15N 7 21W
46 Ballinagh, Ireland 53 55N 7 25W
46 Ballinalack, Ireland ...53 38N 7 28W
46 Ballinalea, Ireland 53 0N 6 8W
46 Ballinalee, Ireland 53 46N 7 40W
46 Ballinamallard, N. Ire.54 30N 7 36W
46 Ballinameen, Ireland .53 54N 8 19W
46 Ballinamore, Ireland .54 3N 7 48W
44 Ballinamore Bridge, Ireland 53 30N 8 24W
44 Ballinascarty, Ireland 51 40N 8 52W
44 Ballinasloe, Ireland ..53 20N 8 12W
44 Ballincollig, Ireland ...51 52N 8 35W
44 Ballinderry, Ireland ...53 2N 8 13W
46 Ballinderry R., Northern Ireland, U.K. 54 40N 6 40W
MAP
46 Ballindine, Ireland 53 40N 8 57W
44 Ballineen, Ireland 51 43N 8 57W
81 Balling, Denmark 56 38N 8 51E
44 Ballingarry, Lim., Ire. 53 1N 8 3W
44 Ballingarry, Tipp., Ire. 52 29N 8 50W
45 Ballingarry, Tipp., Ire. 52 35N 7 32W
44 Ballingeary, Ireland ...51 51N 9 13W
165 Ballinger, U.S.A. 31 45N 99 58W
45 Ballinhassig, Ireland .51 48N 8 33W
46 Ballinlough, Ireland ...53 45N 8 39W
41 Ballinluig, Scot., U.K. 56 40N 3 40W
45 Ballinrobe, Ireland 53 36N 9 13W
44 Ballinskelligs, Ireland 51 50N 10 17W
44 Ballinskelligs B., Ire. .51 46N 10 11W
46 Ballintober, Ireland ...53 43N 8 25W
46 Ballintogher, Ireland .54 11N 8 21W
46 Ballintoy, Ireland 55 13N 6 20W
46 Ballintra, Ireland 54 35N 8 9W
46 Ballintubber, Ireland .53 43N 8 25W
45 Ballinunty, Ireland 52 36N 7 40W
45 Ballinure, Ireland 52 34N 7 46W
45 Ballivor, Ireland 53 32N 6 50W
85 Ballo Pt., Sierra Leone 8 55N 13 18W
40 Balloch, Scotland, U.K. 56 0N 4 35W
45 Ballon, Ireland 52 44N 6 47W
46 Ballybay, Ireland 54 8N 6 52W
46 Ballybofey, Ireland ...54 48N 7 47W
46 Ballybogy, N. Ire., U.K. 55 8N 6 33W
46 Ballyboley, N. Ire., U.K. 54 48N 5 57W
45 Ballybrittas, Ireland .53 7N 7 10W
45 Ballybroughal, Ireland 53 32N 6 17W
44 Ballybunion, Ireland .52 30N 9 40W
45 Ballycanew, Ireland ...52 37N 6 18W
45 Ballycarney, Ireland ..52 35N 6 44W
45 Ballycastle, Ireland ...54 17N 9 24W
46 Ballycastle, N. Ire., U.K. 55 12N 6 15W
46 Ballycastle B., Northern Ireland, U.K. 55 12N 6 15W
46 Ballyclare, Ireland 53 40N 8 0W
46 Ballyclare, N. Ire., U.K. 54 46N 6 0W
45 Ballyclerahan, Ireland 52 25N 7 48W
45 Ballyconneely, Ireland 53 27N 10 5W
44 Ballyconneely B., Ire. 53 23N 10 8W
46 Ballyconnell, Ireland .54 7N 7 35W
45 Ballycotton, Ireland ...51 50N 8 0W
44 Ballycotton B., Ireland 51 50N 7 55W
44 Ballycroneen B., Ire. .51 47N 8 5W
45 Ballycroy, Ireland 54 2N 9 49W
45 Ballycullane, Ireland .52 16N 6 50W
44 Ballydavid, Ireland ...53 12N 8 28W
44 Ballydavid Hd., Ireland 52 15N 10 20W
44 Ballydesmond, Ireland 52 11N 9 15W
44 Ballydonegan, Ireland 51 37N 10 12W
44 Ballydonegan B., Ire. 51 38N 10 6W
44 Ballyduff, Ireland 52 27N 9 40W
45 Ballyduff, Ireland 52 9N 8 2W
45 Ballyfin, Ireland 53 4N 7 27W
44 Ballyforan, Ireland 53 29N 8 18W
44 Ballygar, Ireland 53 33N 8 20W
45 Ballygarrett, Ireland .52 34N 6 15W
46 Ballygawley, N. Ire., U.K. 54 27N 7 2W
45 Ballyglass, Ireland 53 45N 9 9W
46 Ballyglass, Ireland 53 50N 8 38W
44 Ballyglunen Ho., Ire. .53 27N 8 51W
46 Ballygorman, Ireland .55 23N 7 20W
46 Ballygowan, N. Ire., U.K. 54 30N 5 48W
44 Ballyhahill, Ireland ...52 33N 9 13W
46 Ballyhaise, Ireland 54 3N 7 20W
46 Ballyhalbert, N. Ire., U.K. 54 30N 5 28W
45 Ballyhale, Ireland 52 28N 7 12W
46 Ballyhaunis, Ireland .53 47N 8 47W
44 Ballyhean, Ireland 53 44N 9 20W
44 Ballyheige B., Ireland 52 22N 9 56W
44 Ballyhooly, Ireland ...52 9N 8 23W
44 Ballyhoura Hills, Ire. .52 18N 8 33W
46 Ballyjamesduff, Ireland 53 52N 7 11W
44 Ballylanders, Ireland .52 25N 8 21W
45 Ballylaneen, Ireland ...52 10N 7 25W
44 Ballylongford, Ireland 52 34N 9 30W
45 Ballylooby, Ireland ...52 20N 7 59W
45 Ballylynan, Ireland ...52 57N 7 02W
45 Ballymacoda, Ireland 51 53N 7 56W
46 Ballymagorry, Northern Ireland, U.K. 54 52N 7 26W
45 Ballymahon, Ireland .53 35N 7 45W
46 Ballymartin, N. Ire.,U.K. 54 6N 5 57W
46 Ballymena, N. Ire., U.K. 54 53N 6 18W
46 Ballymoe, Ireland 53 41N 8 28W
46 Ballymoney, N. Ire., U.K. 55 5N 6 30W
45 Ballymore, Ireland 53 30N 7 40W
45 Ballymore Eustace, Ire. 53 8N 6 38W
46 Ballymote, Ireland 54 5N 8 30W
45 Ballymurphy, Ireland 52 33N 6 52W
45 Ballynabola, Ireland .52 21N 6 50W
44 Ballynacally, Ireland .52 42N 9 7W
45 Ballynacargy, Ireland 53 35N 7 32W
44 Ballynacorra, Ireland .51 53N 8 10W
45 Ballynagore, Ireland .53 24N 7 29W
MAP
44 Ballynahinch, Cas., Ire. 53 28N 9 52W
46 Ballynahinch, Northern Ireland, U.K. 54 24N 5 55W
44 Ballynahown, Ireland 53 21N 7 52W
45 Ballynakill Harb., Ire. 53 35N 10 3W
46 Ballynameen, Northern Ireland, U.K. 54 58N 6 41W
44 Ballynamona, Ireland 52 5N 8 39W
44 Ballynew, Ireland 53 13N 9 25W
46 Ballynure, N. Ire., U.K. 54 47N 5 59W
46 Ballyquintin, Pt., N. Ire., U.K. 54 20N 5 30W
45 Ballyragget, Ireland ...52 47N 7 20W
45 Ballyroan, Ireland 52 57N 7 20W
46 Ballyronan, N. Ire., U.K. 54 43N 6 32W
46 Ballyroney, N. Ire., U.K. 54 17N 6 8W
46 Ballysadare, Ireland ...54 12N 8 30W
46 Ballysadare B., Ireland 54 15N 8 38W
46 Ballyshannon, Ireland 54 30N 8 10W
44 Ballyvaughan ,Ireland 53 7N 9 10W
46 Ballyvoyh, N. Ire., U.K. 55 11N 6 11W
44 Ballyvourney, Ireland 51 57N 9 10W
46 Ballywalter, N. Ire., U.K. 54 33N 5 30W
45 Ballywilliam, Ireland .52 27N 6 52W
176 Balmaceda, Chile 46 0S 71 50W
41 Balmaclellan, Scot., U.K. 55 6N 4 5W
59 Balmazujváros, Hung. 47 37N 21 21E
43 Balmedie, Scot., U.K. 57 14N 2 4W
133 Balmoral, S. Africa ...25 51S 29 0E
143 Balmoral, Australia ...37 15S 141 48E
43 Balmoral Castle, Scotland, U.K. 57 3N 3 13W
43 Balmoral For., Scotland, U.K. 57 0N 3 15W
165 Balmorhea, U.S.A. 31 2N 103 41W
43 Balnapaling, Scot., U.K. 57 42N 4 2W
130 Balombo, Angola 12 21S 14 43E
130 Balombo, R., Angola .12 00S 13 45E
145 Balonne R., Queensland, Australia 28 47S 147 56E
132 Balovale, Zambia 13 30S 23 15E
143 Balpunga, Australia ...33 46S 141 45E
40 Balquhidder, Scot., U.K. 56 22N 4 22W
105 Balrampur, India 27 30N 82 20E
143 Balranald, Australia ...34 32S 143 34E
78 Bals, Rumania 44 22N 24 5E
160 Balsam L., Canada 44 35N 78 50W
175 Balsas R., Brazil 10 50S 47 30W
168 Balsas R., Mexico 18 30N 101 20W
80 Bålsta, Sweden 59 33N 17 32E
82 Balstad, Norway 68 2N 13 40E
78 Balta, Rumania 44 54N 22 38E
164 Balta, U.S.A. 48 12N 100 7W
89 Balta, U.S.S.R. 48 2N 29 45E
62 Baltands, Spain 41 56N 4 15E
42 Baltasound, Scot., U.K. 60 47N 0 53W
83 Baltic Sea, Europe 56 0N 20 0E
83 Baltiisk, U.S.S.R. 54 38N 19 55E
126 Baltim, Egypt 31 35N 31 10E
160 Baltimore, Canada 44 2N 78 10W
162 Baltimore, U.S.A. 39 18N 76 37W
45 Baltinglass, Ireland ...52 57N 6 42W
56 Baltrum I., Germany .53 43N 7 25E
101 Baluchistan, reg., Asia 27 30N 65 0E
105 Balurghat, India 25 15N 88 44E
40 Balvicar, Scotland, U.K. 56 17N 5 38W
101 Bam, Iran 29 7N 58 14E
103 Bam La Pass, China .29 25N 98 35E
125 Bama, Nigeria 11 33N 13 33E
124 Bamako, Mali 12 34N 7 55W
143 Bamawn, Australia 35 17S 144 39E
130 Bamba, Congo 5 42S 18 12E
125 Bamba, Mali 17 5N 1 0W
121 Bambari, Cent. Afr. Rep. 5 40N 20 35E
144 Bambaroo, Australia .18 57S 146 15E
57 Bamberg, Germany ...49 54N 10 53E
163 Bamberg, U.S.A. 33 19N 81 1W
144 Bamboo, Queensland, Australia 14 34S 143 20E
39 Bamburgh, Eng., U.K. 55 37N 1 43W
125 Bamenda, Cameroon . 5 57N 10 11E
156 Bamfield, Canada 48 45N 125 10W
102 Bamian, prov., Afghan. 35 0N 67 0E
125 Bamkin, Cameroon 6 3N 11 27E
34 Bampton, Eng., U.K. 51 44N 1 33W
101 Bampur, Iran 27 15N 60 21E
101 Bampur R., Iran 27 20N 59 30E
107 Ban Ban, Laos 19 40N 103 34E
107 Ban Bua Chum, Thai. 15 11N 101 12E
107 Ban Bua Yai, Thailand 15 40N 102 25E
107 Ban Houei Sai, Laos .20 20N 100 32E
107 Ban Kantang, Thailand 7 25N 99 35E
107 Ban Khe Bo, Vietnam 19 10N 104 39E
107 Ban Khun Yuam, Thai 18 50N 97 53E
107 Ban Mae Sariang, Thai. 17 45N 97 59E
107 Ban Me Thuot, S. Vietnam 2 40N 108 10E
107 Ban Nong Ping, Thai. 15 9N 100 11E

MAP
107 Ban Phai, Thailand ...16 6N 102 40E
107 Ban Takua Pa, Thai. . 8 55N 98 25E
107 Ban Thateng, Laos ...15 25N 106 27E
132 Bana, Malawi ...12 23S 34 2E
44 Banagher, Ireland ...53 12N 8 0W
131 Banagi, Tanzania ... 2 14S 34 52E
130 Banalia, Congo ... 1 32N 25 5E
107 Banam, Cambodia ...11 20N 105 17E
124 Banamba, Mali ...13 29N 7 22W
130 Banana, Congo ... 6 0S 12 20E
144 Banana, Australia ...24 32S 150 12E
175 Bananal I., Brazil ...11 30S 50 30W
105 Banaras, see Varanasi, India ...25 22N 83 8E
104 Banas R., Gujarat, India ...24 25N 72 30E
105 Banas R., Vindhya Pradesh, India ...24 15N 81 30E
126 Bânâs, Ras., Egypt ...23 57N 35 50E
46 Banbridge, N. Ire. U.K. ...54 21N 6 16W
34 Banbury, Eng., U.K. .52 4N 1 21W
43 Banchory, Scot., U.K. 57 3N 2 30W
154 Bancroft, Canada ...45 10N 77 50W
132 Bancroft, see Chililabombwe, Zambia ...12 18S 27 43E
105 Banda, India ...25 30N 80 26E
109 Banda Is., Indonesia . 4 37S 129 50E
168 Banda Punta, Mexico 31 47N 116 50W
109 Banda Sea, Indonesia ...6 0S 130 0E
108 Banda Atjeh, Indonesia ... 5 35N 95 20E
145 Banda Banda, Mt., N.S.W., Australia ...31 12S 152 12E
114 Bandaisan Mt., Japan 37 40N 140 15E
124 Bandama R., Ivory Coast ... 6 32N 5 30W
104 Bandanwara, India ...26 9N 74 38E
106 Bandar, see Masulipatnam, India ...16 12N 81 12E
101 Bandar Abbas, Iran ...27 15N 56 15E
101 Bandar-e Charak, Iran ...26 45N 54 20E
100 Bandar-e Deylam Iran ...30 5N 50 10E
101 Bandar-e Lengeh, Iran ...26 35N 54 58E
100 Bandar-e Ma'shur, Iran ...30 35N 49 10E
101 Bandar-e Nakhilu, Iran ...26 58N 53 30E
01 Bandar-e Rig, Iran ...29 30N 50 45E
101 Bandar-e Shah, Iran .37 0N 54 10E
100 Bandar-e-Shahpur, Iran ...30 30N 49 5E
100 Bandar-i-Pahlavi, Iran ...37 30N 49 30E
107 Bandar Maharani, see Muar, Malaya ... 2 3N 102 34E
107 Bandar Penggaram, see Batu Pahat, Malaya ... 1 50N 102 56E
132 Bandawe, Malawi ...11 58S 34 5E
62 Bande, Spain ...42 3N 7 58W
133 Bandelierkop, S. Africa ...23 21S 29 50E
172 Bandera, Argentina ...28 55S 62 20W
165 Bandera, U.S.A. ...29 45N 99 3W
168 Banderas B., Mexico .20 40N 105 30W
.101 Band-i-Turkistan, Ra., Afghanistan ...35 2N 64 0E
106 Bandia R., India ...19 30N 80 25E
124 Bandiagara, Mali ...14 12N 3 29W
100 Bandirma, Turkey ...40 20N 28 0E
109 Bandjar, Indonesia ... 7 24S 108 30E
108 Bandjarmasin, Indon. 3 20S 114 35E
109 Bandjarnegara, Indon. ... 7 24S 109 42E
44 Bandon, Ireland ...51 44N 8 45W
132 Bandua, Mozambique 20 5S 34 25E
132 Bandula, Mozambique 19 0S 33 7E
130 Bandundu (Banningville), Congo ... 3 15S 17 22E
109 Bandung, Indonesia ... 6 36S 107 48E
142 Bandya, W. Australia 27 40S 122 5E
78 Baneasa, Rumania ...45 56N 27 55E
65 Bañeres, Spain ...38 44N 0 38W
169 Banes, Cuba ...21 0N 75 42W
156 Banff, Alberta, Canada ...51 20N 115 40W
43 Banff, Scotland, U.K. 57 40N 2 32W
43 Banff. co., Scot., U.K. 57 23N 3 10W
124 Banfora, Upper Volta 10 40N 4 40W
107 Bang Hieng, R., Laos 16 24N 105 40E
107 Bang Lamung, Thailand ...12 58N 101 0E
107 Bang Saphan, Thailand ...11 14N 99 28E
125 Banga, Nigeria ...12 32N 6 42E
106 Bangalore, India ...12 59N 77 40E
145 Bangalow, Australia ...28 41S 153 30E
125 Bangangte, Cameroon 5 8N 10 32E
105 Bangaon, India ...23 0N 88 47E
130 Bangassou Central African Republic ... 4 55N 23 55E
109 Banggai, Indonesia ... 1 40S 123 30E
108 Banggi I., Sab., Malaysia ... 7 25S 117 20E
123 Banghâzi, Libya, see Benghazi
109 Bangil, Indonesia ... 7 36S 112 50E
127 Bangjang, Sudan ...11 23N 32 41E
109 Bangka, I. Cel., Indon. ... 1 50N 125 5E
108 Bangka I., Sumatra, Indonesia ... 2 0S 105 50E
108 Bangka Str., Indonesia ... 3 30N 105 30E
109 Bangkalan, Indonesia 7 2S 112 46E
108 Bangkinang, Indonesia ... 0 18N 100 5E
108 Bangko, Indonesia ... 2 5S 102 9E
107 Bangkok (Krung Thep), Thailand ...13 45N 100 35E
103 Bangladesh, st., Asia .24 0N 90 0E
46 Bangor, N. Ireland, UK 54 40N 5 40W
155 Bangor, Me., U.S.A. ...44 48N 68 42W
161 Bangor, Pa., U.S.A. ...40 51N 75 13W
37 Bangor, Wales, U.K. .53 13N 4 9W
109 Bangued, Philippines .17 40N 120 37E
130 Bangui, Cent. Afr. Rep. ... 4 23N 18 35E
132 Bangweulu L., Zambia ...11 0S 30 0E
132 Bangweulu Swamps, Zambia ...11 20S 30 15E
35 Banham, England, U.K. ...52 27N 1 3E
169 Bani, Dom. Rep. ...18 16N 70 22W
122 Bani, Djebel, Morocco 29 16N 8 0W
124 Bani, R., Mali ...12 40N 6 30W
98 Bani Na'im, Jordan ...31 31N 35 10E
98 Bani Suhaylah, Egypt 31 21N 34 19E
124 Bania, Ivory Coast ... 9 4N 3 6W
144 Baniara, Terr. of Papua ... 9 44S 149 54E
123 Banina, Libya ...32 0N 20 12E
100 Baniyas, Syria ...35 10N 36 0E
74 Banja Luka, Y.-slav. .44 49N 17 26E
108 Banjak Is., Indonesia 2 10N 97 10E
109 Banjumas, Indonesia . 7 32S 109 18E
109 Banjuwangi, Indonesia ... 8 13S 114 21E
41 Bankend, Scotland, U.K. ...55 2N 3 31W
81 Bankeryd, Sweden ...57 53N 14 6E
132 Banket, Rhodesia ...17 27S 30 19E
41 Bankfoot, Scot., U.K. 56 30N 3 31W
43 Bankhead, Scot., U.K. ...57 11N 2 10W
105 Bankipore, India ...25 35N 85 10E
156 Banks I., B.C., Canada ...53 20N 130 0W
14 Banks I., N.W. Terr., Canada ...73 30N 120 0W
144 Banks I., Australia ...10 10S 142 5E
147 Banks Peninsula, N.Z. 43 45S 173 15E
145 Banks Str., Australia .40 40S 148 10E
105 Bankura, India ...23 11N 87 18E
74 Bankya, Bulgaria ...42 43N 23 8E
46 Bann R., Down, Northern Ireland U.K. ...54 24N 6 23W
46 Bann R., Londonderry, N. Ire., U.K. ...55 2N 6 35W
48 Bannalec, France ...47 57N 3 42W
143 Bannerton, Victoria, Australia ...34 42S 142 47E
154 Banning, Canada ...48 44N 91 56W
167 Banning, U.S.A. ...33 58N 116 58W
130 Banningville, see Bandundu, Congo ... 3 15S 17 22E
160 Bannockburn, Canada 44 41N 77 31W
41 Bannockburn, Scot. U.K. ...56 5N 3 55W
132 Bannockburn, Rhodesia ...20 17S 29 48E
45 Bannow & B., Ireland 52 13N 6 48W
104 Bannu, W. Pakistan .33 0N 70 18E
64 Bañolas, Spain ...42 16N 2 44E
51 Banon, France ...44 2N 5 38E
63 Baños de la Encina, Sp. ...38 10N 3 46W
62 Banos de Molgas, Spain ...42 15N 7 40W
59 Banovce. Cz. ...48 44N 18 16E
59 Banská Bystrica, Cz. .48 46N 19 14E
59 Banská Štiavnica, Cz. 48 25N 18 55E
75 Bansko, Bulgaria ...41 52N 23 28E
104 Banswara, India ...23 32N 74 24E
125 Bantama, Ghana ... 7 48N 0 42W
44 Banteer, Ireland ...52 8N 8 53W
109 Banten, Indonesia ... 6 5S 106 8E
44 Bantry, Ireland ...51 40N 9 28W
44 Bantry, B., Ireland ...51 35N 9 50W
127 Bantu Liben, Ethiopia ... 8 32N 38 21E
109 Bantul, Indonesia ... 7 55S 110 19E
104 Bantva, India ...21 29N 70 12E
106 Bantval, India ...12 55N 75 0E
36 Banwell, England, U.K. ...51 19N 2 51W
75 Banya, Bulgaria ...42 33N 24 50W
130 Banyanga, Central African Republic ... 2 55N 16 14E
15 Banzare Coast, Antarc. ...66 30S 125 0E
130 Banzyville, Congo ... 4 15N 21 8E
104 Bap, India ...27 23N 72 18E
106 Bapatla, ,India ...15 55N 80 30E
49 Bapaume France ...50 7N 2 50E
198 Baqa, Israel ...32 25N 35 2E
100 Baqubah, Iraq ...33 45N 44 50E
72 Baquedano, Chile ...23 20S 69 52W
88 Bar, U.S.S.R. ...49 4N 27 40E
74 Bar, Yugoslavia ...42 8N 19 8E
43 Bar, The, Scot., U.K. 57 38N 3 47W
49 Bar-le-Duc, France ...48 47N 5 10E
49 Bar-sur-Aube, France 48 14N 4 40E
49 Bar-sur-Seine, France 48 7N 4 20E
155 Bar Harbor, U.S.A. ...44 15N 68 20W
78 Bâra, Rumania ...47 2N 27 3E
108 Barabai, Indonesia ... 2 32S 115 34E
90 Barabinsk, U.S.S.R. ...55 20N 78 20E
164 Baraboo, U.S.A. ...43 28N 89 46W
169 Baracoa, Cuba ...20 20N 74 30W
172 Baradero, Argentina .33 52S 59 29W
164 Baraga, U.S.A. ...46 49N 88 29W
169 Barahona, Dom. Rep. 18 13N 71 7W
64 Barahoma, Spain ...41 17N 2 39W
103 Barail Range, India ...25 15N 93 20E
126 Baraka R., Sudan ...17 30N 37 34E
103 Barakhola, India ...25 0N 92 45E
127 Barakit, Ethiopia ...14 38N 39 29E
105 Barakot, India ...21 33N 84 59E
145 Barakula, Australia ...26 30S 150 33E
144 Baralaba, Australia ...24 13S 149 50E
157 Baralzon, L., Canada .59 40N 97 45W
106 Baramati, India ...18 11N 74 33E
105 Baramba, India ...20 25N 85 23E
126 Barameiya, Sudan ...18 32N 36 38E
102 Baramula, Kashmir ...34 15N 74 20E
104 Baran, India ...25 9N 76 40E
157 Baranof I., Alaska, U.S.A. ...57 0N 135 10W
59 Baranya, Co., Hungary ...46 0N 18 15E
86 Baranovichi, U.S.S.R. 53 10N 26 0E
174 Barao de Melgaço, Braz. ...11 50S 60 45W
78 Baraolt, Rumania ...46 5N 25 34E
109 Barapasi, Indonesia ... 2 15S 137 5E
105 Barasat, India ...22 46N 88 31E
127 Barasoli, Ethiopia ...13 38N 42 0W
165 Barataria B., U.S.A. .29 15N 89 45W
104 Baraut, India ...29 13N 77 7E
173 Barbacena, Brazil ...21 15S 43 56W
174 Barbacoas, Colombia . 1 45N 78 0W
169 Barbados I., Wind. Is. 13 0N 59 30W
71 Barban, Yugoslavia ...45 0N 14 4E
64 Barbastró, Spain ...42 2N 0 5E
133 Barberspan, S. Africa 26 36S 25 32E
133 Barberton, S. Africa ...25 42S 31 2E
160 Barberton, U.S.A. ...41 0N 81 40E
63 Barbate, Spain ...36 13N 5 56W
105 Barbigha, India ...25 21N 85 47E
163 Barbourville, U.S.A. .36 57N 83 52W
169 Barbuda I., Leeward Is. ...17 30N 61 40W
78 Bârca, Rumania ...43 59N 23 36E
62 Barca d'Alva, Portugal ...41 0N 7 0W
144 Barcaldine, Australia 23 33S 145 13E
121 Barce, see Al Marj, Libya ...32 25N 20 40E
64 Barcelona, Spain ...41 21N 2 10E
174 Barcelona, Venezuela .10 10N 64 40W
64 Barcelona, Prov., Spain ...41 30N 2 0E
51 Barcelonette, France .44 23N 6 40E
174 Barcelos, Brazil ... 1 0S 63 0W
144 Barcoo R., Australia .24 33S 145 30E
59 Barcs, Hungary ...45 58N 17 28E
42 Bard, Hd., Scot., U.K. ...60 6N 1 5W
89 Barda, U.S.S.R. ...40 25N 47 10E
123 Bardai, Chad ...21 25N 17 0E
172 Bardas Blancas, Arg. .35 49S 69 45W
59 Bardejov, Cz. ...49 18N 21 15E
99 Bardera, Somali Rep. 2 20N 42 27E
70 Bardi, Italy ...44 38N 9 43E
21 Bardiyah, Libya ...31 45N 25 0E
39 Bardney, Eng., U.K. ...53 13N 0 19W
142 Bardoc, W. Australia .30 18S 121 12E
104 Bardoli, India ...21 12N 73 5E
37 Bardsey I., Wales, U.K. ...52 46N 4 47W
37 Bardsey Sound, Wales, United Kingdom ...52 47N 4 46W
62 Bardstown, U.S.A. ...37 50N 85 29W
105 Bareilly, India ...28 22N 79 27E
143 Barellan, Australia ...34 1S 146 30E
48 Barentin, France ...49 33N 0 58E
48 Barenton, France ...48 38N 0 50W
14 Barents Sea, Arctic Oc. ...73 0N 39 0E
127 Barentu, Ethiopia ...15 2N 37 35E
48 Barfleur, France ...49 40N 1 17W
34 Barford, England, U.K. ...52 15N 1 35W
70 Barga, Italy ...44 5N 10 30E
99 Bargal, Somali Rep. ...11 25N 51 0E
144 Bargara, Australia ...24 50S 152 25E
70 Barge, Italy ...44 43N 7 19E
127 Bargnop, Sudan ... 9 32N 28 25E
143 Bargo, N.S.W., Australia ...34 18S 150 35E
37 Bargoed, Wales, U.K. 51 42N 3 22W
56 Bargteheide, Germany 53 42N 10 13E
105 Barh, India ...25 29N 85 46E
105 Barhaj, India ...26 18N 83 44E
35 Barham, Eng., U.K. .51 12N 1 10E
143 Barham, Australia ...35 40S 144 10E
108 Barhau, Indonesia ... 5 20S 102 10E
105 Barhi, India ...24 15N 85 25E
104 Bari, India ...26 39N 77 39E
73 Bari, Italy ...41 6N 16 52E
104 Bari Doab, W. Pak. ...30 20N 73 0E
107 Baria, see Phuoc Le, S. Vietnam ...10 39N 107 19E
174 Barinas, Venezuela ... 8 36N 70 15W
152 Baring C., Canada ...70 0N 116 30W
131 Baringo & L., Kenya . 0 47N 36 16E
105 Baripada, India ...21 57N 86 45E
126 Bâris, Egypt ...24 42N 30 31E
105 Barisal, E. Pak. ...22 50N 90 32E
108 Barisan Mts., Indon. . 3 30S 102 15E
108 Barito R., Indonesia . 2 50S 114 50E
51 Barjac, Gard, France .44 20N 4 22E
51 Barjols, France ...43 34N 6 2E
123 Barjuj, W., Libya ...25 26N 12 12E
101 Barkah, Muscat & Oman ...23 40N 58 0E
35 Barking, England, U.K. ...51 31N 0 10E
126 Barkol, Wadi, Sudan .17 40N 32 0E
154 Bark L., Canada ...46 58N 82 25W
160 Bark L., Canada ...45 25N 77 40W
160 Barker, U.S.A. ...43 20N 78 35W
111 Barkha, Tibet, China .31 0N 81 10E
156 Barkley Sound, Canada ...48 50N 125 10W
135 Barkly Bridge, S. Afr. 33 37S 25 45E
144 Barkly Downs, Austral. ...20 30S 138 30E
135 Barkly East, S. Africa 30 58S 27 33E
138 Barkly Tableland, N. Terr., Australia ...19 50S 138 40E
133 Barkly W., S. Africa .28 32S 24 31E
111 Barkol, China ...43 37N 93 2E
165 Barksdale, U.S.A. ...29 47N 100 2W
39 Barlby, England, U.K. ...53 48N 1 3W
142 Barlee, L., W. Austral. ...29 15S 119 30E
142 Barlee, Mt., W. Austral. ...24 35S 128 10E
142 Barlee Ra., W. Austral. ...23 30S 116 0E
73 Barletta, Italy ...41 20N 16 17E
60 Barlinek, Poland ...53 0N 15 15E
81 Barlingbo, Sweden ...57 35N 18 27E
157 Barlow L., Canada ...61 50N 103 0W
39 Barmby Moor, Eng., U.K. ...53 55N 0 47W
143 Barmedman, Australia ...34 9S 147 21E
104 Barmer, India ...25 45N 71 20E
41 Barmoor Castle, Eng., U.K. ...55 55N 2 0W
37 Barmouth, Wales, U.K. ...52 44N 4 3W
56 Barmstedt, Germany .53 47N 9 46E
44 Barna, Ireland ...53 14N 9 10W
104 Barnagar, India ...23 7N 75 19E
38 Barnard Castle, England, United Kingdom ...54 33N 1 55W
143 Barnato, Australia ...31 38S 145 0E
90 Barnaul, U.S.S.R. ...53 20N 83 40E
15 Barne Inlet, Antarctica, ...80 15S 160 0E
143 Barnes, Australia ...36 2S 144 47W
163 Barnesville, U.S.A. ...33 6N 84 9W
35 Barnet, England, U.K. ...51 37N 0 15W
39 Barnetby England, U.K. ...53 35N 0 24W
54 Barneveld, Netherlands ...52 7N 5 36E
161 Barneveld, U.S.A. ...43 16N 75 14W
48 Barneville, France ...49 23N 1 46W
145 Barney, Mt., Queensland, Australia ...28 13S 152 32E
145 Barngo, Australia ...25 3S 147 20E
165 Barnhart, U.S.A. ...31 10N 101 8W
38 Barnoldswick, Eng., U.K. ...53 55N 2 11W
39 Barnsley, Eng., U.K. .53 33N 1 29W
36 Barnstaple, Eng., U.K. ...51 5N 4 3W
164 Barnsville, U.S.A. ...46 43N 96 28W
125 Baro, Nigeria ... 8 35N 6 18E
127 Baro R., Ethiopia ... 8 25N 33 40E
104 Baroda, Gurajat, India ...22 20N 73 10E
104 Baroda, Mad. P., India ...25 29N 76 35E
134 Baroe, S. Africa ...33 13S 24 32E
142 Barons Ra., W. Austral. ...23 30S 127 45E
132 Barotse, prov., Zambia ...15 0S 23 30E
105 Barpali, India ...21 11N 83 35E
105 Barpeta, India ...26 20N 91 10E
123 Barqin, Libya ...27 33N 13 34E
162 Barques, Pte. aux, U.S.A. ...44 5N 82 55W
63 Barquinha, Portugal .39 28N 8 25W
174 Barquisimeto, Ven. ... 9 58N 69 13W
172 Barquitos, Chile ...26 22S 71 10W
49 Barr, France ...48 25N 7 28E
40 Barr, Scotland, U.K. .55 13N 4 44W
175 Barra, Brazil ...11 0S 43 10W
124 Barra, Gambia ...13 21N 16 36W
42 Barra Hd., Scot., U.K. ...56 47N 7 40W
42 Barra, L., Scotland, U.K. ...57 0N 7 30W
42 Barra, Sd. of, Scot., U.K. ...57 4N 7 25W
175 Barra do Corda, Brazil ... 5 30S 45 10W
173 Barra do Pirai, Brazil 22 30S 43 50W
173 Barra Mansa, Brazil ...22 35S 44 12W
145 Barraba, Australia ...30 21S 150 35E
105 Barrackpur, India ...22 44N 88 30E
134 Barracouta, C., S. Afr. 34 26S 21 22E
73 Barrafranca, Italy ...37 22N 14 10E
174 Barranca, Peru ...10 45S 77 50W
174 Barranca, Peru ... 4 50S 76 50W
174 Barrancabermeja, Col. 7 0N 73 50W
174 Barrancas, Venezuela . 8 55N 62 5W
174 Barranco Branco, Braz. ...21 0S 57 50W
63 Barrancos, Portugal ...38 10N 7 1W
172 Barranqueras, Arg. ...27 30S 59 0W
174 Barranquilla, Colombia ...11 0N 74 50W
161 Barre, Vt., U.S.A. ...44 15N 72 30W
172 Barreal, Argentina ...31 33S 69 28W
175 Barreiras, Brazil ...12 0S 45 0W
175 Barreirinhas, Brazil ... 2 30S 42 50W
63 Barreiro, Portugal ...38 40N 9 6W
175 Barreiros, Brazil ... 8 50S 35 15W
51 Barrême, France ...43 57N 6 23E
17 Barren I., Andaman Is. ...12 17N 95 50E
129 Barren Is., Malagasy Rep. ...18 25S 43 40E
145 Barren Junc., Austral. 30 5S 149 0E
175 Barretos, Brazil ...20 30S 48 35W
156 Barrhead, Canada ...54 10N 114 30W
40 Barrhead, Scot., U.K. 55 48N 4 23W
40 Barrhill, Scotland, U.K. ...55 7N 4 46W
154 Barrie, Canada ...44 25N 79 45W
147 Barrier Ra., N.Z. ...44 5S 169 42E
144 Barrier Rf., Gt., Austral. ...19 0S 149 0E
162 Barrington, Ill., U.S.A. ...42 8N 88 5W
161 Barrington, R.I., U.S.A. ...41 43N 71 20W
157 Barrington L., Canada 56 55N 100 15W
143 Barrington Tops., mt., Australia ...32 6S 151 28E
145 Barringun, Australia .29 1S 145 41E
38 Barrow, England, U.K. ...54 8N 3 15W
138 Barrow Creek Telegraph Office, Australia ...21 18S 133 58E
138 Barrow I., W. Austral. ...20 45S 115 20E
14 Barrow & Pt., Alaska 71 28N 156 0W
142 Barrow Ra., W. Austral. ...26 0S 127 40E
45 Barrow, R., Ireland ...52 46N 7 0W
14 Barrow Strait, Canada 74 20N 95 0W
39 Barrow upon Humber, England, U.K. ...53 41N 0 22W
38 Barrowford, Eng., U.K. ...53 51N 2 14W
62 Barruecopardo, Spain 41 4N 6 40W
63 Barruelo, Spain ...42 54N 4 17W
37 Barry, Wales, U.K. ...51 23N 3 19W
37 Barry I., Wales, U.K. 51 23N 3 17W
134 Barrydale, S. Africa ...33 51S 20 44E
154 Barry's Bay, Canada .45 30N 77 40W
44 Barry's Pt., Ireland ...51 36N 8 40W
131 Barsaloi, Kenya ... 1 20N 36 52E
106 Barsi, India ...18 10N 75 50E
81 Barsö I., Denmark ...55 8N 9 32E
167 Barstow, Calif., U.S.A. ...34 58N 117 2W
175 Barstow, Tex., U.S.A. 31 30N 103 25W
174 Bartica, Guyana ... 6 25N 58 40W
144 Bartle Frère, Mt., Queensland, Austral. ...17 27S 145 50E
165 Bartlesville, U.S.A. ...36 50N 95 58W
165 Bartlett, U.S.A. ...30 46N 97 30W
156 Bartlett, L., Canada ...62 50N 118 20W
73 Bartolomeo in Galdo, Italy ...41 23N 15 2E
132 Bartolomeu Dias, Mozambique ...21 10S 35 8E
39 Barton, England, U.K. ...54 28N 1 38W
39 Barton-upon-Humber, England, U.K. ...53 41N 0 27W
60 Bartoszyce, Poland ...54 15N 20 55E
163 Bartow, U.S.A. ...27 53N 81 49W
112 Baruun Urt, Mongolia 46 46N 113 15E
109 Barung I., Indonesia . 8 23S 113 20E
56 Baruth, Germany ...52 3N 13 31E
42 Barvas Scotland, U.K. ...58 21N 6 31W
88 Barvenkovo, U.S.S.R. 48 57N 37 0E
104 Barwani, India ...22 2N 74 57E
34 Barwell, England, U.K. ...52 35N 1 22W
145 Barwon R., Australia .29 10S 148 47E
87 Barysh, U.S.S.R. ...49 2N 25 18E
78 Bârzava, Rumania ...46 7N 21 59E
49 Bas-Rhin, dept., Fr. .48 40N 7 30E
74 Bašaid, Yugoslavia ...45 38N 20 25E
101 Basa'idu, Iran ...26 35N 55 20E
130 Basankusu, Congo ... 1 5N 19 50E
78 Basarabi, Rumania ...44 10N 28 26E
172 Bascunan, Cabo, Chile 28 52S 71 35W
57 Basel (Basle), Switz. .47 35N 7 35E
57 Basel Cant., Switz. ...47 26N 7 45E
73 Basento R., Italy ...40 35N 16 10E
135 Bashee, C. Prov., S. Afr. ...31 55S 28 29E
135 Bashee R., S. Africa ...32 10S 28 45E
113 Bashi Channel, Phil. .21 15N 122 0E
84 Bashkir A.S.S.R., U.S.S.R. ...54 0N 57 0E
144 Basilaki, I., Terr. of Papua ...10 40S 150 53E
109 Basilan I., Philippines 6 35N 122 0E
109 Basilan Str., Philippines ...13 10S 122 0E
35 Basildon, England, U.K. ...51 34N 0 29E
73 Basilicata, Reg., Italy 40 30N 16 0E
166 Basin, U.S.A. ...44 22N 108 2W
34 Basing, England, U.K. ...51 16N 1 3W
34 Basingstoke, Eng., U.K. ...51 15N 1 5W
105 Basirhat, E. Pak. ...22 40N 88 54E
154 Baskatong Res., Can. .46 46N 75 50W
138 Baskerville C., W. Austral. ...17 10S 122 15E
106 Basmat, India ...19 15N 77 12E
104 Basoda, India ...23 52N 77 54E
130 Basoko, Congo ... 1 16N 23 40E

MAP
130 Basongo, Congo 4 15S 20 20E
100 Basra (Al Basrah), Iraq ...30 30N 47 50E
41 Bass Rock, Scot., U.K. ...56 5N 2 40W
145 Bass Strait, Australia 40 0S 146 0E
71 Bassano, del Grappa, Italy ...45 45N 11 45E
125 Bassari, Togo ... 9 19N 0 57E
124 Basse, Gambia ...13 13N 14 15W
169 Basse Terre, Guadeloupe I. W. I. ...16 0N 61 40W
103 Bassein, Burma ...16 45N 94 30E
106 Bassein, India ...19 26N 72 48E
38 Bassenthwaite, L., England, U.K. ...54 40N 3 14W
51 Basses-Alpes, dept., Fr. ...44 8N 6 10E
169 Basseterre, St. Christopher, W.I. ...17 17N 62 43W
164 Bassett, Neb., U.S.A. .42 37N 99 30W
163 Bassett, Va., U.S.A. ...36 48N 79 59W
104 Bassi, India ...30 44N 76 21E
49 Bassigny, Dist., France ...48 0N 5 10E
56 Bassum, Germany ...52 50N 8 42E
81 Båstad, Sweden ...56 28N 12 55E
101 Bastak, Iran ...27 15N 54 25E
106 Bastar, India ...19 25N 81 40E
105 Basti, India ...26 52N 82 55E
51 Bastia, Corsica, France ...42 40N 9 30E
71 Bastia Umbra, Italy .43 4N 12 34E
54 Bastogne, Belgium ...50 1N 5 43E
35 Baston, England, U.K. ...52 43N 0 19W
165 Bastrop, U.S.A. ...30 5N 97 22W
82 Bastutrask, Sweden ...64 47N 20 0E
135 Basutoland, Africa, *see* Lesotho ...29 0S 28 0E
98 Bat Yam, Israel ...32 2N 34 44E
128 Bata, Rio Muni ... 1 57N 9 50E
78 Bata, Rumania ...46 1N 22 4E
109 Bataan, pen., Philippines ...14 40N 120 25E
169 Batabanó, Cuba ...22 40N 82 20W
169 Batabanó, G. of, Cuba 22 30N 82 0W
109 Batac, Philippines ...18 5N 120 25E
63 Batalha, Portugal ...39 40N 8 50W
113 Batan I., Philippines .20 58N 122 05E
113 Batan Is., Philippines 20 25N 121 59E
111 Batang, *see* Paan, China ...30 0N 99 3E
109 Batang, Indonesia ... 6 55S 109 40E
121 Batangafo, Central African Republic ... 7 25N 18 20E
109 Batangas, Philippines 13 53N 121 9E
109 Batanta I., Indonesia 0 55S 130 40E
173 Batatais, Brazil ...20 54S 47 37W
160 Batavia, U.S.A. ...43 0N 78 10W
89 Bataysk, U.S.S.R. ...47 3N 39 45E
138 Batchelor, N. Terr., Australia ...13 4S 131 1E
143 Bateman's B., Australia ...35 40S 150 12E
163 Batesburg, U.S.A. ...33 54N 81 32W
165 Batesville, Ark., U.S.A. ...35 48N 91 40W
165 Batesville, Miss., U.S.A. ...34 17N 89 58W
165 Batesville, Tex., U.S.A. ...28 59N 99 38W
86 Batetski, U.S.S.R. ...58 47N 30 16E
36 Bath, England, U.K. .51 22N 2 22W
155 Bath, Maine, U.S.A. ...43 50N 69 49W
160 Bath, N.Y., U.S.A. ...42 20N 77 17W
34 Bathampton, Eng., U.K. ...51 23N 2 20W
36 Bathford, England, U.K. ...51 23N 2 18W
41 Bathgate, Scotland, U.K. ...55 54N 3 38W
143 Bathurst, Australia ...33 25S 149 31E
155 Bathurst, Canada ...47 37N 65 43W
124 Bathurst, Gambia ...13 28N 16 40W
135 Bathurst, S. Africa ...33 30S 26 55E
144 Bathurst B., Queensland, Australia ...14 16S 144 25E
14 Bathurst C., Canada .70 30N 128 30W
145 Bathurst Harb., Austral. ...43 15S 146 10E
138 Bathurst I., Australia 11 30S 130 10E
14 Bathurst I., Canada ...76 30N 130 10W
152 Bathurst Inlet & tn., N.W. Terr., Canada 67 15N 108 30W
143 Bathurst L., Australia 35 3S 149 44E
127 Batie, Ethiopia ...11 10N 40 00W
124 Batie, Upper Volta ... 9 53N 2 53W
109 Batjan Grp., Indonesia ... 0 35S 127 10E
109 Batjan I., Indonesia ... 0 50S 130 27E
39 Batley, England, U.K. ...53 43N 1 38W
133 Batlharo, S. Africa ...27 15S 23 22E
143 Batlow, Australia ...35 31S 148 15E
160 Batman, Turkey ...37 55N 41 5E
123 Batna, Algeria ...35 34N 6 15E
132 Batoka, Zambia ...16 45S 27 15E
165 Baton Rouge, U.S.A. .30 30N 91 5W
168 Batopilas, Mexico ...27 48N 107 54E
128 Batouri, Cameroon ... 4 30N 14 25E
82 Båtsfjord, Norway ...70 35N 29 45E
107 Battambang, Cambodia ...13 7N 103 12E
106 Batticaloa, Ceylon ... 7 43N 81 45E
55 Battice, Belgium ...50 39N 5 50E
73 Battipaglia, Italy ...40 38N 15 0E
98 Battir, Israel ...31 44N 35 8E
35 Battle, England, U.K. 50 55N 0 30E
144 Battle Camp, Queensland, Australia ...15 24S 144 50E
162 Battle Creek, U.S.A. .42 20N 85 10W
155 Battle Harbour, Canada ...52 13N 55 42W
164 Battle Lake, U.S.A. ...46 20N 95 43W
166 Battle Mountain, U.S.A. ...40 45N 117 0W
157 Battle R., Canada ...52 30N 111 30W
132 Battlefields, Rhodesia 18 37S 29 47E
157 Battleford, Canada ...52 45N 108 15W
59 Battonya, Hungary ...46 16N 21 03E
127 Batu, mt., Ethiopia ... 6 55N 39 45E
108 Batu Is., Indonesia ... 0 30S 98 25E
107 Batu Gajah, Malaysia 4 28N 101 3E
107 Batu Pahat, Malaysia 1 50N 102 56E
108 Batu Radja, Indonesia ... 4 11S 104 15E
109 Batulaki, Philippines . 5 40N 125 30E
89 Batumi, U.S.S.R. ...41 30N 41 30E
175 Baturite, Brazil ... 4 28S 38 45W
109 Baubau, Indonesia ... 5 25S 123 50E
125 Bauchi, Nigeria ...10 22N 9 48E
48 Baud, France ...47 52N 3 1W
164 Baudette, U.S.A. ...48 46N 94 35W
174 Baudo, Colombia ... 5 10N 77 20W
131 Baudouinville, Congo . 7 0S 29 48E
48 Baugé, France ...47 31N 0 8W
88 Baugh Fell, Eng., U.K. ...54 21N 2 28W
144 Bauhinia, Australia ...24 45S 149 20E
55 Baumberg, Germany .51 8N 6 53E
49 Baume les Dames, Fr. 47 22N 6 22E
72 Baunei, Italy ...40 2N 9 41E
173 Baurú, Brazil ...22 10S 49 0W
175 Baus, Brazil ...18 22S 52 47W
86 Bauska, U.S.S.R. ...56 25N 25 15E
56 Bautzen, Germany ...51 11N 14 25E
74 Bavanište, Yugoslavia 44 49N 20 53E
57 Bavaria, *see* Bayern, Germany ...49 7N 11 30E
80 Baven, L., Sweden ...59 3N 17 00E
134 Baviaanskloofberge Mts., South Africa .33 30S 24 0E
35 Bawdsey, England, U.K. ...52 1N 1 27E
107 Bawdwin Mines, Burma ...23 5N 97 50E
108 Bawean I., Indonesia . 5 46S 112 35E
125 Bawku, Ghana ...11 3N 0 19W
103 Bawlake, Burma ...19 0N 97 30E
39 Bawtry, England, U.K. ...53 25N 1 1W
163 Baxley, U.S.A. ...31 43N 82 23W
54 Baxtel, Netherlands ...51 36N 5 13E
165 Baxter Springs, U.S.A. ...37 3N 94 45W
123 Bay al Kabir, W., Libya ...30 15N 14 50E
155 Bay Bulls, Canada ...47 25N 52 50W
162 Bay City, Mich., U.S.A. ...43 35N 83 51W
166 Bay City, Ore., U.S.A. 45 45N 123 58W
165 Bay City, Tex., U.S.A. ...28 59N 95 55W
146 Bay of Islands, N.Z. .35 15S 174 6E
109 Bay, Laguna de, Phil. 14 15N 121 10E
165 Bay St. Louis, U.S.A. 30 18N 89 22W
161 Bay Shore, U.S.A. ...40 44N 73 15W
165 Bay Springs, U.S.A. ...31 58N 89 18W
146 Bay View, New Zealand ...39 25S 176 50E
169 Bayamo, Cuba ...20 20N 76 40W
169 Bayamón, Puerto Rico ...18 24N 66 10W
112 Bayan, Mongolia ...47 20N 107 55E
112 Bayan Agt, Mongolia .48 32N 101 16E
90 Bayan Aul, U.S.S.R. .50 45N 75 45E
111 Bayan Khara Shan, mts., China ...34 0N 98 0E
104 Bayana, India ...26 55N 77 18E
112 Bayandalay, Mongolia 43 30N 103 29E
112 Bayandelger, Mongolia ...47 45N 108 7E
111 Bayanhongor, Mongolia ...46 40N 100 20E
112 Bayan-Ovoo, Mongolia ...47 55N 112 0E
112 Bayantsogt, Mongolia 47 58N 105 1E
112 Bayan-Uul, Mongolia 49 6N 112 12E
112 Bayanzürh, Mongolia .47 48N 107 15E
164 Bayard, U.S.A. ...41 48N 103 17W
109 Baybay, Philippines ...10 40N 124 55E
42 Bayble, Scotland, U.K. ...58 12N 6 13W
100 Bayburt, Turkey ...40 15N 40 20E
57 Bayern, land, Germany ...49 7N 11 30E
48 Bayeux, France ...49 17N 0 42W
160 Bayfield, Canada ...43 34N 81 39W
164 Bayfield, U.S.A. ...46 50N 90 48W
112 Bayinhot, China ...38 58N 105 14E
100 Bayir, Jordan ...30 45N 36 55E
91 Baykal, L., U.S.S.R. .53 0N 108 0E
109 Bayombang, Phil. ...16 30N 121 10E
49 Bayon, France ...48 30N 6 20E
62 Bayona, Spain ...42 6N 8 52W
50 Bayonne, France ...43 30N 1 28W
161 Bayonne, U.S.A. ...40 40N 74 5W
174 Bayovar, Peru ... 5 50S 81 0W
106 Baypore, R., India ...11 10N 75 47E
57 Bayreuth, Germany ...49 56N 11 35E
57 Bayrischer Wald, Mts., Germany ...49 0N 13 0E
57 Bayrischzell, Germany 47 39N 12 1E
165 Baytown, U.S.A. ...29 42N 94 57W
65 Baza, Spain ...37 30N 2 47W
89 Bazar Dyuzi, U.S.S.R. ...41 12N 48 10E
87 Bazarny Karabulak, U.S.S.R. ...52 30N 46 20E
87 Bazarnyy Syzgan, U.S.S.R. ...53 45N 46 40E
89 Bazartobe, U.S.S.R. ...49 26N 51 45E
32 Bazaruto I., Mozam. .21 40S 35 28E
50 Bazas, France ...44 27N 0 13W
98 Bazuriye, Lebanon ...33 15N 35 16E
164 Beach, U.S.A. ...46 57N 104 0W
160 Beach City, U.S.A. ...40 38N 81 35W
107 Beachburg, Canada ...45 46N 76 50W
34 Beachley, England, U.K. ...51 37N 2 39W
145 Beachport, S. Australia ...37 29S 140 0E
35 Beachy Head, Eng., U.K. ...50 44N 0 16E
161 Beacon, U.S.A. ...41 32N 73 58W
142 Beacon, W. Australia .30 20S 117 55E
133 Beaconsfield, S. Africa 28 45S 24 46E
35 Beaconsfield, Eng., U.K. ...51 36N 0 39W
176 Beagle Chan., S. Amer. ...55 0S 68 30W
36 Beaminster, Eng., U.K. ...50 48N 2 44W
160 Beamsville, Canada ...43 12N 79 28W
14 Bear I. (Nor.), Arctic Oc. ...74 30N 19 0E
44 Bear I., Ireland ...51 38N 9 50W
160 Bear L., Canada ...45 28N 79 34W
166 Bear L., U.S.A. ...42 0N 111 20W
166 Bearcreek, U.S.A. ...45 11N 109 6W
154 Beardmore, Canada ...49 36N 87 59W
15 Beardmore Gl., Antarc. ...84 30S 170 0E
164 Beardstown, U.S.A. ...40 0N 90 25W
50 Béarn, Reg., France ...43 28N 0 36W
40 Bearsden, Scot., U.K. 55 55N 4 19W
154 Bearskin Lake, Canada ...53 58N 91 2W
166 Bearpaw Mt., U.S.A. .48 15N 109 55W
35 Bearsted, England, U.K. ...51 15N 0 35E
65 Beas de Segura, Spain 38 15N 2 53W
64 Beasain, Spain ...43 3N 2 11W
169 Beata C. & I., Dom. Rep. ...17 40N 71 30W
132 Beatrice, Rhodesia ...18 15S 30 55E
164 Beatrice, U.S.A. ...40 20N 96 40W
41 Beattock, Scotland, U.K. ...55 19N 3 27W
167 Beatty, U.S.A. ...36 58N 116 46W
51 Beaucaire, France ...43 48N 4 39E
49 Beauce, Plaines de, dist., France ...48 10N 2 0E
155 Beauceville, Canada ...46 13N 70 46W
145 Beaudesert, Australia 28 0S 152 48E
143 Beaufort, Australia ...37 25S 143 25E
163 Beaufort, N.C., U.S.A. 34 45N 76 40W
108 Beaufort, Sab., Malaysia ... 5 30N 115 40E
163 Beaufort, S.C., U.S.A. 32 25N 80 40W
14 Beaufort Sea, Arctic Oc. ...70 30N 146 0W
134 Beaufort-West, S. Africa ...32 18S 22 36E
49 Beaugency, France ...47 47N 1 38E
154 Beauharnois, Canada .45 20N 73 20W
51 Beaujeu, France ...46 10N 4 35E
51 Beaujolais, dist., France ...46 0N 4 25E
34 Beaulieu, England, U.K. ...50 49N 1 27W
50 Beaulieu, Loiret, France ...47 31N 2 49E
51 Beaulieu, Vendée, Fr. 46 41N 1 37W
156 Beaulieu, R., Canada 62 30N 113 0W
43 Beauly, Scotland, U.K. ...57 29N 4 27W
43 Beauly Firth, Scot., U.K. ...57 30N 4 20W
43 Beauly, R., Scot., U.K. ...57 26N 4 35W
37 Beaumaris, Wales, U.K. ...53 16N 4 7W
50 Beaumont, France ...44 45N 0 46E
147 Beaumont, N.Z. ...45 50S 169 33E
165 Beaumont, U.S.A. ...30 5N 94 8W
48 Beaumont-le-Roger, Fr. ...49 4N 0 47E
49 Beaumont-sur-Oise, Fr. ...49 9N 2 17E
49 Beaumetz-les-Loges, Fr. ...50 15N 2 40E
49 Beaune, Côte-d'Or, Fr. ...47 2N 4 50E
49 Beaune la Rolande, Loiret, France ...48 4N 2 25E
40 Beaupréau, France ...47 12N 1 0W
157 Beausejour, Canada ...50 5N 96 35E
133 Beauty, Trans., S. Afr. ...23 21S 27 52E
49 Beauvais, France ...49 25N 2 8E
157 Beauval, Canada ...55 9N 107 35W
50 Beauvoir, Deux Sèvres, France ...46 12N 0 30W
48 Beauvoir, Vendee, Fr. 46 55N 2 1W
165 Beaver Okla., U.S.A. .36 52N 100 31W
160 Beaver, Pa., U.S.A. ...40 40N 80 18W
167 Beaver, Utah, U.S.A. .38 20N 112 45W
157 Beaver R., Sask, Can. 54 20N 108 40W
164 Beaver City, U.S.A. ...40 13N 99 50W
164 Beaver Dam, U.S.A. .43 28N 88 50W
160 Beaver Falls, U.S.A. .40 44N 80 20W
157 Beaverhill L., Canada 54 5N 94 50W
156 Beaver Lodge, Canada 55 11N 119 29W
160 Beaverton, Canada ...44 26N 79 8W
104 Beawar, India ...26 3N 74 18E
173 Bebedouro, Brazil ...21 0S 48 25W
38 Bebington, Eng., U.K. ...53 23N 3 1W
56 Bebra, Germany ...50 59N 9 48E
35 Beccles, England ...52 27N 1 33E
78 Beceni, Rumania ...45 23N 26 48E
62 Becerrea, Spain ...42 51N 7 10W
122 Bechar, Algeria ...31 38N 2 18E
134 Bechuanaland, reg., South Africa ...26 30S 22 30E
129 Bechuanaland Prot., Africa, *see* Botswana ...23 0S 24 0E
58 Bechyne, Cz. ...49 17N 14 29E
38 Beckermet, Eng., U.K. ...54 26N 3 31W
41 Beckfoot, England, U.K. ...54 50N 3 25W
39 Beckingham, Eng., U.K. ...53 24N 0 49W
162 Beckley, U.S.A. ...37 50N 81 8W
48 Bécon, France ...47 30N 0 50W
59 Becva, R., Cz. ...49 31N 17 40E
39 Bedale, England, U.K. ...54 18N 1 35W
65 Bédar, Spain ...37 11N 1 59W
50 Bédarieux, France ...43 37N 3 10E
51 Bedarrides, France ...44 03N 4 54E
37 Beddgelert, Wales, U.K. ...53 2N 4 8W
56 Bederkesa, Germany .53 37N 8 50E
135 Bedford, S. Africa ...32 40S 26 10E
35 Bedford, England, U.K. ...52 8N 0 29W
35 Bedford, co., Eng. U.K. ...52 4N 0 28W
162 Bedford, Ind., U.S.A. 38 50N 86 30W
164 Bedford, Iowa, U.S.A. 40 40N 94 41W
160 Bedford, Ohio, U.S.A. 41 23N 81 32W
160 Bedford, Pa., U.S.A. .40 1N 78 30W
162 Bedford, Va., U.S.A. .37 25N 79 30W
35 Bedford Level, England, U.K. ...52 25N 0 5E
60 Bedków, Poland ...51 36N 19 44E
39 Bedlington, Eng., U.K. ...55 8N 1 35W
156 Bednesti, Canada ...53 50N 123 10W
71 Bednja, R., Yugoslavia ...46 12N 16 25E
87 Bednodemyanovsk, U.S.S.R. ...53 55N 43 15E
144 Bedourie, Queensland, Australia ...24 13S 139 22E
34 Bedwas, England, U.K. ...51 36N 3 10W
34 Bedworth, England, U.K. ...52 28N 1 29W
60 Bedzin, Poland ...50 19N 19 7E
42 Bee L., Scotland, U.K. ...57 22N 7 21W
142 Beebyn, W. Australia 27 0S 117 48E
143 Beech Forest, Australia ...38 37S 143 37E
162 Beech Grove, U.S.A. .39 40N 86 2W
143 Beechworth, Australia 36 20S 146 55E
157 Beechy, Canada ...50 53N 107 24W
39 Beeford, England, U.K. ...53 58N 0 18W
56 Beelitz, Germany ...52 14N 12 58E
143 Beemunnel, Australia 31 40S 147 51E
145 Beenleigh, Australia ...27 45S 153 0E
44 Beenoskee, Mt., Ireland ...52 13N 10 5W
36 Beer, England, U.K. .50 41N 3 5W
98 Beer Sheva, R., Israel 31 12N 34 40E
98 Beer Tuvya, Israel ...31 44N 34 42E
98 Beeri, Israel ...31 25N 34 30E
98 Beerotayim, Israel ...32 19N 34 59E
98 Beersheba, Israel ...31 15N 34 48E
55 Beerse, Belgium ...51 19N 4 51E
55 Beerze, R., Netherlands ...51 27N 5 13E
56 Beeskow, Germany ...52 9N 14 14E
133 Beestekraal, S. Africa 25 21S 27 32E
39 Beeston, England, U.K. ...52 55N 1 11W
56 Beetzendorf, Germany 52 42N 11 6E
165 Beeville, U.S.A. ...28 27N 97 44W
130 Befale, Congo ... 0 25N 20 45E
129 Befandriana, Malag. ...21 55S 44 0E
129 Befotaka, Malagasy Rep. ...14 30S 48 0E
46 Beg, L., N. Ire., U.K. 54 48N 6 28W
74 Bega Canal, Rumania 45 37N 20 46E
37 Begelly, Wales, U.K. .51 45N 4 44W
127 Begemdir & Simen Prov., Ethiopia ...13 55N 37 30E
79 Begna, R., Norway ...60 41N 9 42E
62 Begonte, Spain ...43 10N 7 40W
105 Begu-Sarai, India ...25 24N 86 9E
37 Beguildy, Wales, U.K. 52 25N 3 11W
121 Behagle, Chad, *see* Lai 9 25N 16 30E
129 Behara, Malagasy Rep. ...24 55S 46 20E
100 Behbehan, Iran ...30 30N 50 15E
104 Behror, India ...27 51N 76 20E
101 Behshahr, Iran ...36 45N 53 35E
121 Beida (Al Bayda), Libya ...32 30N 21 40E
39 Beighton, England, U.K. ...53 21N 1 21W
54 Beilen, Netherlands ...52 52N 6 27E
143 Beilpajah, Australia ...32 54S 143 52E
127 Beilul, Ethiopia ...13 2N 42 20E
132 Beira, Mozambique ...19 50S 34 52E
100 Beirut, Lebanon ...33 53N 35 31E
98 Beisan (Beit Shean) Isr. ...32 30N 35 30E
98 Beit Alfa, Israel ...32 31N 35 25E
98 Beit Aula, Jordan ...31 37N 35 2E
132 Beit Bridge, Zambia .14 58S 30 15E
98 Beit Dagon, Israel ...32 1N 34 49E
98 Beit Fajjar, Jordan ...31 38N 35 9E
98 Beit Furik, Jordan ...32 11N 35 20E
98 Beit Guvrin, Israel ...31 37N 34 54E
98 Beit Ha'emeq, Israel .32 58N 35 8E
98 Beit Hanum, Egypt ...31 32N 34 32E
98 Beit Hashitta, Israel .32 31N 35 27E
98 Beit Jala, Jordan ...31 43N 35 11E
98 Beit Jann, Israel ...32 57N 35 21E
98 Beit Lahiya, Egypt ...31 32N 34 30E
98 Beit Qeshet, Israel ...32 41N 35 21E
98 Beit Rima, Jordan ...32 2N 35 6E
98 Beit Sahur, Jordan ...31 42N 35 13E
98 Beit Shean, *see* Beisan, Israel ...32 30N 35 30E
98 Beit Ummar, Jordan .31 38N 35 7E
98 Beit 'Ur et Tahta, Jordan ...31 54N 35 5E
98 Beit Yosef, Israel ...32 34N 35 33E
98 Beita, Jordan ...32 9N 35 18E
98 Beitbridge, Rhodesia .22 12S 30 0E
40 Beith, Scotland, U.K. 55 45N 4 38W
98 Beitin, Jordan ...31 56N 35 14E
98 Beituniya, Jordan ...31 54N 35 10E
78 Beiuş, Rumania ...46 40N 22 21E
63 Beja, Portugal ...38 2N 7 53W
63 Beja, Dist., Portugal .37 55N 7 55W
123 Beja, Tunisia ...36 10N 9 0E
123 Bejaia, Algeria ...36 42N 5 2E
101 Bejestan, Iran ...34 30N 58 5E
109 Bekasi, Indonesia ... 6 20S 107 0E
59 Békés, & Co., Hungary ...46 47N 21 0E
59 Békéscsaba, Hungary 46 40N 21 10E
79 Bekkjarvik, Norway .60 1N 5 13E
107 Bekok, Malaysia ... 2 20N 103 7E
125 Bekwai, Ghana ... 6 30N 1 34W
105 Bela, India ...25 50N 82 0E
102 Bela, W. Pakistan ...26 12N 66 20E
74 Bela Crkva, Yugoslavia ...44 55N 21 27E
74 Bela Palanka, Y.-slav. ...43 13N 22 17E
130 Bela Vista, Angola ...12 33S 16 18E
172 Bela Vista, Brazil ...17 0S 49 0W
133 Bela Vista, Mozam. ...26 10S 32 44E
50 Belâbre, France ...46 34N 1 8E
127 Belaia, Mt., Ethiopia .11 25N 36 8E
63 Belalcazar, Spain ...38 35N 5 10W
74 Belanovica, Y.-slav. .44 15N 20 23E
130 Belas, Angola ... 8 55S 13 10E
108 Belawan Indonesia ... 3 33N 98 32E
84 Belaya, R., U.S.S.R. .54 45N 56 0E
89 Belaya Glina, U.S.S.R. ...46 5N 40 48E
89 Belaya Klitva, U.S.S.R. ...48 13N 40 50E
86 Belaya Tserkov, U.S.S.R. ...49 45N 30 10E
34 Belbroughton, England, United Kingdom ...52 23N 2 5W
78 Belceşti, Rumania ...47 19N 22 7E
60 Belchatów, Poland ...51 21N 19 22E
14 Belcher C., Alaska, U.S.A. ...75 0N 160 0W
154 Belcher Is., Canada ...56 20N 79 20W
64 Belchite, Spain ...41 18N 0 43W
46 Belcoo, N. Ire., U.K. .54 18N 7 52W
45 Belderg, Ireland ...54 18N 9 33W
81 Beldringe, Denmark ...55 28N 10 21E
84 Belebei, U.S.S.R. ...54 85N 54 5E
175 Belem (Pará), Brazil . 1 20S 48 30W
172 Belen, Argentina ...27 40S 67 5W
167 Belen, U.S.A. ...34 40N 106 50W
75 Belene, Bulgaria ...43 39N 25 10E
131 Belese Cogani, Somali Rep. ... 0 15N 41 39E
50 Belesta, France ...42 55N 1 56E
99 Belet Uen, Somali Rep. ... 4 30N 45 5E
87 Belev, U.S.S.R. ...53 50N 36 5E
147 Belfast, New Zealand .43 27S 172 39E
46 Belfast, N. Ire., U.K. .54 35N 5 56W
133 Belfast, Trans., S. Afr. ...25 42S 30 2E
155 Belfast, Maine, U.S.A. 44 30N 69 0W
160 Belfast, N.Y., U.S.A. .42 21N 78 9W
46 Belfast, L., N. Ire., U.K. ...54 40N 5 50W
55 Belfeld, Netherlands .51 18N 6 6E
155 Belfeoram, Canada ...47 32N 55 30W
164 Belfield, U.S.A. ...46 54N 103 11W
39 Belford, England, U.K. ...55 36N 1 50W
49 Belfort, France ...47 38N 6 50E
49 Belfort, dept., France 47 38N 6 52E
166 Belfry, U.S.A. ...45 10N 109 2W
106 Belgaum, India ...15 55N 74 35E
70 Belgioioso, Italy ...45 9N 9 21E
54 Belgium, King., Europe ...51 30N 5 0E
144 Belgooly, Ireland ...51 44N 8 30W
87 Belgorod, U.S.S.R. ...50 35N 36 35E
88 Belgorod Dnestrovskiy, U.S.S.R. ...46 11N 30 23E
166 Belgrade, U.S.A. ...45 50N 111 10W
74 Belgrade, Yugoslavia 44 50N 20 37E
147 Belgrove, New Zealand ...41 27S 172 59E
163 Belhaven, U.S.A. ...35 34N 76 35W
74 Beli Drim, R., Y.-slav. ...42 25N 20 34E
74 Beli Manastir, Y.-slav. ...45 45N 18 36E
74 Beli Timok, Y.-slav. .43 39N 22 14E
72 Belice R., Italy ...37 44N 12 58N
132 Belingwe, Rhodesia ...20 29S 29 57E

MAP
108 Belinju, Indonesia 1 35s 105 50e
108 Beliton, Is., Indonesia 3 10s 107 50e
78 Beliu, Rumania 46 30n 22 0e
168 Belize, Br. Honduras .17 25n 88 0w
74 Beljanica, Mt., Y.-slav. 44 08n 21 43e
155 Bell, Canada 53 50n 53 10e
155 Bell I., Canada 50 46n 55 35w
145 Bell Bay, Australia ...41 12s 146 50e
153 Bell Pen, Canada 64 0n 81 0w
41 Bell Rock, *see* Inchcape Rock, Scot., UK 56 26n 2 24w
172 Bell Ville, Argentina .32 40s 62 40w
156 Bella Bella, Canada ...52 10n 128 10w
156 Bella Coola, Canada ...52 25n 126 40w
172 Bella Union, Uruguay 30 15s 57 10w
172 Bella Vista, Argentina 28 33s 59 0w
124 Bella Yella, Liberia ... 7 24n 10 9w
46 Bellaghy, N. Ire., U.K. 54 50n 6 31w
70 Bellagio, Italy 45 59n 9 15e
160 Bellaire, Ohio, U.S.A. 40 1n 80 46w
46 Bellanagare, Ireland ...53 51n 8 23w
46 Bellananagh, Ireland .53 55n 7 25w
143 Bellarwi, Australia 34 15s 147 14e
106 Bellary, India 15 10n 76 56e
145 Bellata, Australia 29 53s 149 46e
164 Belle Fourche, U.S.A. 44 43n 103 52w
164 Belle Fourche R., U.S.A. 44 25n 105 0w
163 Belle Glade, U.S.A. ...26 43n 80 38w
48 Belle Ile, France 47 20n 3 10w
155 Belle Isle, Canada 51 57n 55 25w
48 Belle Isle en Terre, Fr. 48 33n 3 23w
155 Belle Isle, Str. of, Can. 51 30n 56 30w
164 Belle Plaine Minn., U.S.A. 44 35n 93 48w
164 Belle Plaine, Iowa, U.S.A. 41 51n 92 18w
51 Belledonne, Chaine de, France 45 11n 6 0e
155 Belledune, Canada 47 55n 65 50w
46 Belleek, N. Ire., U.K. 54 30n 8 6w
162 Bellefontaine, U.S.A. .40 20n 83 45w
160 Bellefonte, U.S.A. 40 56n 77 45w
51 Bellegarde, Ain, Fr. ...46 04n 3 49e
49 Bellegarde, Creuse, Fr. 45 59n 2 19e
49 Bellegarde, Loiret, Fr. 48 0n 2 26e
154 Belleville, Canada 44 15n 77 37w
51 Belleville, Rhône, Fr. .46 7n 4 45e
48 Belleville, Vendee, Fr. 46 48n 1 28w
164 Belleville, Ill., U.S.A. .38 30n 90 0w
164 Belleville, Kan., U.S.A. 39 51n 97 38w
161 Belleville, N.Y., U.S.A. 43 46n 76 10w
156 Bellevue, Canada 46 35n 84 10w
166 Bellevue, Idaho, U.S.A. 43 25n 144 23w
160 Bellevue, Ohio, U.S.A. 41 20n 82 48w
160 Bellevue, Pa., U.S.A. .40 29n 80 3w
51 Belley, France 45 46n 5 41e
53 Bellin (Payne Bay), Canada 60 0n 70 0w
145 Bellingen, Australia ...30 25s 152 50e
39 Bellingham, Eng., U.K. 55 09n 2 16w
166 Bellingham, U.S.A. 48 45n 122 27w
15 Bellinghausen Sea, S. Ocean, Antarctica ...66 0s 80 0w
57 Bellinzona, Switzerland 46 11n 9 1e
161 Bellows Falls, U.S.A. .43 10n 72 30w
104 Bellpat, W. Pakistan .29 0w 68 5e
64 Bellpuig, Spain 41 37n 1 1e
71 Belluno, Italy 46 8n 12 6e
134 Bellville, C. Prov., S. Afr. 33 53s 18 36e
160 Bellville, Ohio, U.S.A. 40 38n 82 32w
165 Bellville, Tex., U.S.A. 29 58n 96 18w
160 Bellwood, U.S.A. 40 36n 78 21w
161 Belmar, U.S.A. 40 10n 74 2w
63 Belmez, Spain 38 17n 5 17w
160 Belmont, Canada 42 54n 81 7w
134 Belmont, S. Africa 29 28s 24 22e
143 Belmont, Australia 33 4s 151 42e
160 Belmont, U.S.A. 42 14n 78 3w
175 Belmonte, Bahia, Brazil 16 0s 39 0w
62 Belmonte, Portugal ...40 21n 7 20w
64 Belmonte, Spain 39 34n 2 43w
168 Belmopan, Br. Hond. 17 12n 88 0w
45 Belmullet, Ireland 54 13n 9 58w
175 Belo Horizonte, Brazil 20 0s 44 0w
129 Belo Sur Tsiribihina, Malagasy Rep. 19 40s 44 30e
88 Belogorsk, U.S.S.R. ...45 3n 34 35e
91 Belogorsk, U.S.S.R. ...51 0n 128 20e
75 Belogradets, Bulgaria 43 22n 27 18e
74 Belogradtchik, Bulgaria 43 37n 22 40e
164 Beloit, Kan., U.S.A. ...39 32n 98 9w
164 Beloit, Wis., U.S.A. ...42 35n 89 0w
87 Belokholunitskiy, U.S.S.R. 58 55n 50 43e
84 Belomorsk, U.S.S.R. .64 35n 34 30e
103 Belonia, India 23 15n 91 30e
86 Belopolye, U.S.S.R. ...51 14n 34 20e
84 Beloretsk, U.S.S.R. ...54 0n 58 0e
90 Belovo, U.S.S.R. 54 30n 86 0e
84 Beloye L., U.S.S.R. ...60 10n 37 35e
89 Beloye Ozero, U.S.S.R. 45 15n 46 50e
84 Belozersk, U.S.S.R. ...60 0n 37 30e
73 Belpasso, Italy 37 37n 15 0e
39 Belper, England, U.K. 53 2n 1 29w
38 Belsay, England, U.K. 55 6n 1 53w
72 Belsito, Italy 37 50n 13 47e
145 Beltana, S. Australia .30 48s 138 25e
175 Belterra, Brazil 2 45s 55 0w
71 Beltinci, Yugoslavia ...46 37n 16 20e
35 Belton, England, U.K. 52 35n 1 39e
163 Belton, S.C., U.S.A. ...34 31n 82 39w
165 Belton, Tex., U.S.A. .31 4n 97 30w
45 Beltra, Mayo, Ireland 53 57n 9 24w
46 Beltra, Sligo, Ireland .54 12n 8 36w
45 Beltra L., Ireland 53 56n 9 28w
88 Beltsy, U.S.S.R. 47 48n 28 0e
46 Belturbet, Ireland 54 6n 7 28w
90 Belukha Mt., U.S.S.R. 49 50n 86 50e
108 Beluran, Sab., Malaysia 5 48n 117 35e
59 Beluša, Czechoslovakia 49 5n 18 27e
74 Belušic, Yugoslavia ...43 50n 21 10e
73 Belvedere Marittimo, It. 39 37n 15 52e
50 Belves, France 44 46n 1 0e
164 Belvidere, Ill., U.S.A. 42 15n 88 55w
161 Belvidere, N.J., U.S.A. 40 48n 75 5w
45 Belville, Ireland 54 40n 9 22w
63 Belvis de la Jara, Spain 39 45n 4 57w
29 Belvoir, Vale of, England, U.K. 52 54n 0 48w
90 Bely, I., U.S.S.R. 73 30n 71 0e
144 Belyando R., Australia 22 45s 146 37e
90 Belyj Jar, U.S.S.R., ...58 26n 84 30e
86 Belyy, U.S.S.R. 55 48n 32 51e
86 Belz, U.S.S.R. 50 23n 24 1e
56 Belzig, Germany 52 8n 12 36e
165 Belzoni, U.S.A. 33 12n 90 30w
132 Bembesi, & R., Rhod. 20 0s 28 58e
63 Bembezar, R., Spain .38 0n 5 20w
34 Bembridge, Eng., U.K. 50 41n 1 4w
164 Bemidji, U.S.A. 47 30n 94 50w
43 Ben a'Chaistell, Scot., U.K. 57 48n 4 44w
43 Ben a'Ghlo, Scot., U.K. 56 50n 3 40w
122 Ben Ahmed, Morocco .33 4n 7 9w
43 Ben Alder, Scot., U.K. 55 59n 4 30w
43 Ben Alligin, Scot., U.K. 57 35n 5 36w
43 Ben Avon, Scot., U.K. 57 6n 3 28w
40 Ben Bheigeir, Mt., Scot., U.K. 55 43n 6 6w
143 Ben Bullen, Australia 33 12s 150 2e
41 Ben Chonzine, Scot., U.K. 56 7n 4 0w
40 Ben Cruachan, Mt. Scot., U.K. 56 26n 5 8w
42 Ben Dearg, Scot., U.K. 57 47n 4 58w
43 Ben Dearg, Perth, Scot., U.K. 56 54n 3 49w
43 Ben Dhorain, Scotland, U.K.........58 7n 3 50w
40 Ben Dorian, Scot., U.K. 56 30n 4 42w
42 Ben Edra, Scot., U.K. 57 35n 6 15w
42 Ben Fhada, Scot., U.K. 57 13n 5 18w
123 Ben Gardane, Tunisia 33 11n 11 11e
122 Ben Guérir, Morocco .32 16n 7 56w
43 Ben Hee, Scotland, U.K. 58 16n 4 43w
43 Ben Hope, Mt., Scot., U.K. 58 24n 4 36w
43 Ben Klibreck, Scotland, U.K. 58 14n 4 25w
40 Ben Lawers, Mt., Scot., U.K. 56 33n 4 13w
40 Ben Lomond, Mt., Scot, U.K. 56 12n 4 39w
145 Ben Lomond, Mt., Tasmania, Australia 41 33s 147 40e
43 Ben Loyal, Scot., U.K. 58 25n 4 25w
40 Ben Lui, Mt., Scotland, U.K.........56 24n 4 50w
43 Ben Macdhui, Scot., U.K. 57 4n 3 40w
42 Ben Mhor, Skye, Scotland, U.K. 57 16n 7 21w
42 Ben Mhor, S. Uist, Scotland, U.K. 56 0n 6 40w
40 Ben More, Mull, Scot., U.K. 56 26n 6 2w
43 Ben More Assynt, Scotland, U.K. 58 7n 4 51w
147 Ben Nevis, Mt., New Zealand 45 15s 169 0e
42 Ben Nevis, Mt., Scotland, U.K. 56 48n 5 0w
147 Ben Ohau Ra., N.Z. ...44 1s 170 4e
43 Ben Sgeireach, Scot., U.K. 58 4n 4 39w
42 Ben Sgriol, Scot., U.K. 57 9n 5 34w
42 Ben Stack, Scot., U.K. 58 20n 4 58w
43 Ben Tharsiunn, Scotland, U.K. 57 47n 4 20w
40 Ben Venue, Scot., U.K. 56 13n 4 28w
40 Ben Vorlich, Mt., Perth, Scotland, U.K. 56 22n 4 15w
43 Ben Vrackie, Scot., U.K. 56 45n 3 43w
43 Ben Wyvis, Mt., Scot., U.K. 57 40n 4 35w
125 Bena, Nigeria 11 20n 5 50e
63 Benagalbón, Spain 36 45n 4 15w
145 Benageria, S. Australia 31 35s 140 25e
143 Benalla, Australia 36 30s 146 0e
143 Benambra, Mt., Austral. 36 31s 147 34e
63 Benameji, Spain 37 16n 4 33w
143 Benanee, Australia 34 26s 142 56e
105 Benares, *see* Varanasi, India 25 22n 83 8e
63 Benavente, Portugal .38 59n 8 49w
62 Benavente, Spain 42 2n 5 43w
62 Benavides, Spain 42 30n 5 54w
165 Benavides, U.S.A. 27 35n 98 28w
46 Benbane Hd., Northern Ireland, U.K. 55 15n 6 30w
44 Benbaun, Mt., Ireland 53 30n 9 50w
42 Benbecula, I., Scot., U.K. 57 26n 7 20w
145 Benbonyathe Hill, South Australia 30 25s 139 15e
46 Benbrack Mt., Ireland 54 8n 7 50w
46 Benburb, N. Ire. U.K. 54 25n 6 42w
142 Bencubbin, W. Austral. 30 45s 117 48e
166 Bend, U.S.A. 44 2n 121 15w
99 Bender Beila, Somali Rep. 9 30n 50 48e
99 Bender Cassim, Somali Rep. 11 12n 49 18e
142 Bendering, W. Austral. 32 20s 118 12e
88 Bendery, U.S.S.R. 46 50n 29 50e
143 Bendigo, Australia 36 40s 144 15e
124 Benena, Mali 13 9n 4 17w
40 Beneraird, Mt., Scotland, U.K. 55 4n 4 57w
58 Benešǒv, Cz. 49 46n 14 41e
49 Bénestroff, France 48 54n 6 45e
50 Benet, France 46 22n 0 35w
73 Benevento, Italy 41 7n 14 45e
49 Benfeld, France 48 22n 7 34e
132 Benga, Mozambique ...16 11s 33 40e
109 Bengawan Solo R., Indon. 7 5s 112 25e
123 Benghazi (Banghazi), Libya 32 11n 20 3e
108 Bengkalis, Indonesia . 1 30n 102 10e
108 Bengkulu, Indonesia . 3 50s 102 12e
157 Bengough, Canada 49 25n 105 10w
130 Benguela, Angola 12 37s 13 25e
130 Benguela, dist., Angola 12 45s 13 30e
132 Benguerua I., Mozam. 21 58s 35 28e
126 Benha, Egypt 30 26n 31 8e
131 Beni, Congo 0 30n 29 27e
174 Beni R., Bolivia 10 30s 96 0w
122 Beni Abbès, Algeria ...30 5n 2 5w
126 Beni Mazâr, Egypt 28 32n 30 44e
122 Beni Mellal, Morocco .32 21n 6 14w
122 Beni Ounif, Algeria ...32 0n 1 10w
122 Beni Saf, Algeria 35 17n 1 15w
126 Beni Suef, Egypt 29 5n 31 6e
64 Benicarló, Spain 40 23n 0 23e
65 Benidorm, Spain 38 33n 0 9w
65 Benidorm, Islote de, Sp. 38 31n 0 9w
125 Benin, Bight of, W. Africa 5 0n 3 0e
125 Benin City, Nigeria ... 6 20n 5 31e
65 Benisa, Spain 38 43n 0 03e
174 Benjamin Constant, Braz. 4 40s 70 15w
164 Benkelman, U.S.A. 40 7n 101 32w
144 Benlidi, Queensland, Australia 23 34s 145 38e
40 Bennane Hd., Scot., U.K. 55 10n 5 0w
147 Benmore Pk., N.Z. 44 25s 170 8e
55 Bennekom, Netherlands 52 0n 5 40e
156 Bennett, Canada 59 50n 135 0w
45 Bennettsbridge, Ireland 52 36n 7 12w
163 Bennettsville, U.S.A. .34 38n 79 39w
161 Bennington, U.S.A. ...42 52n 73 12w
130 Beno, Congo 3 41s 17 49e
108 Benoa, Indonesia 8 50s 115 20e
48 Bénodet, France 47 53n 4 7w
133 Benoni, Trans., S. Afr. 26 11s 28 18e
122 Benoud, Algeria 32 28n 0 10e
55 Bensberg, Germany ...50 57n 7 9e
57 Bensheim, Germany ...49 40n 8 38e
34 Benson, England, U.K. 51 37n 1 6w
167 Benson, U.S.A. 31 59n 110 19w
101 Bent, Iran 26 20n 59 25e
109 Benteng, Indonesia ... 6 10s 120 30e
144 Bentinck I., Australia 17 3s 139 35e
35 Bentley, Hants., England, U.K. 51 12n 0 52w
39 Bentley, Yorks, England, U.K. 53 33n 1 9w
165 Benton, Ark., U.S.A. .34 30n 92 35w
164 Benton, Ill., U.S.A. ...38 0n 88 55w
162 Benton Harbor, U.S.A. 42 10n 86 28w
107 Bentong, Malaysia 3 31n 101 55e
127 Bentiu, Sudan 9 10n 29 55e
125 Benue R., Nigeria 7 50n 6 30e
45 Benwee Hd., Ireland .54 20n 9 50w
45 Benwee Mt., Ireland .53 37n 9 33w
109 Beo, Indonesia 4 25n 126 50e
74 Beograd, *see* Belgrade, Y.-slav. 44 50n 20 37e
166 Beowawe, U.S.A. 40 45n 117 0w
114 Beppu, Japan 33 15n 131 30e
122 Ber Rechid, Morocco .33 18n 7 36w
46 Beragh, N. Ire., U.K. 54 34n 7 10w
76 Berati, Albania 40 43n 19 59e
126 Berber, Sudan 18 0n 34 0e
121 Berbera, Chad 10 33n 16 35e
99 Berbera, Somali Rep. .10 30n 45 2e
130 Berberati, Central African Rep. 4 15n 15 40e
65 Berbeira, Cabo, Spain 38 39n 1 24e
174 Berbice R., Guyana ... 5 20n 58 10w
70 Berceto, Italy 44 30n 10 0e
55 Berchem, Belgium 51 9n 4 25e
57 Berchtesgaden, Ger. ...47 37n 13 1e
49 Berck-sur-Mer, France 50 25n 1 36e
88 Berdichev, U.S.S.R. ...49 57n 28 30e
88 Berdyansk, U.S.S.R. .46 45n 36 50e
38 Bere Alston, England, United Kingdom 50 29n 4 11w
34 Bere Regis, England, United Kingdom 50 45n 2 13w
162 Berea, Kentucky, U.S.A. 37 35n 84 18w
160 Berea, Ohio, U.S.A. ...41 21n 81 50w
109 Berebere, Indonesia ... 2 25n 128 45e
99 Bereda, Somali Rep. .11 45n 51 0e
131 Bereku, Tanzania 4 27s 35 45e
124 Berekum, Ghana 7 29n 2 34w
126 Berenice, Egypt 24 2n 35 25e
157 Berens R., Canada 51 50n 93 30w
157 Berens River, Canada 52 25n 97 0w
86 Berestechko, U.S.S.R. 50 22n 25 5e
78 Beresti-Targ, Rumania 46 6n 27 50e
78 Beretau, R., Rumania 47 30n 22 7e
59 Berettyo, R., Hungary 47 32n 21 47e
59 Berettyóujfalu, Hung. 47 13n 21 33e
86 Bereza, U.S.S.R. 52 31n 24 51e
86 Berezan, U.S.S.R. 50 20n 31 30e
86 Berezhany, U.S.S.R. .49 26n 24 58e
86 Berezina R., U.S.S.R. 54 10n 28 10e
86 Berezna, U.S.S.R. 51 35n 30 46e
86 Berezniki, U.S.S.R. ...59 25n 56 5e
88 Berezovka, U.S.S.R. .47 25n 30 55e
90 Berezovo, U.S.S.R. 64 0n 65 0e
79 Berg, Norway 59 7n 11 18e
62 Berga, Spain 42 6n 1 48e
81 Berga, Kalmar, Sweden 57 14n 16 3e
81 Berga Kronoberg, Swed. 56 55n 14 0e
100 Bergama, Turkey 39 8n 27 15e
70 Bergamo, Italy 45 42n 9 40e
56 Bergedorf, Germany ...53 28n 10 12e
55 Bergeijk, Netherlands 51 19n 5 21e
56 Bergen, Germany 54 24n 13 26e
55 Bergen, Limburg, Neth. 52 40n 4 41e
54 Bergen, Noord Holland, Netherlands 52 40n 4 42e
79 Bergen, Norway 60 23n 5 27e
160 Bergen, U.S.A. 43 5n 77 56w
54 Bergen-op-Zoom, Neth. 51 30n 4 18e
50 Bergerac, France 44 51n 0 30e
56 Bergheim, Germany ...50 57n 6 38e
56 Bergisch Gladbach, Ger. 50 59n 7 9e
55 Bergischesland, Dist., Germany 51 0n 7 23e
55 Bergkamen, Germany 51 38n 7 38n
81 Bergkvara, Sweden 56 23n 16 5e
55 Bergneustadt Germany 51 3n 7 43e
55 Bergschenhoek, Neth. 51 59n 4 30e
80 Bergsjö, Sweden 61 59n 17 9e
122 Berguent, Morocco 33 55n 2 0w
49 Bergues, France 50 58n 2 24e
54 Bergum, Netherlands .53 13n 5 59e
80 Bergvik, Sweden 61 14n 16 49e
135 Bergville, Natal, S. Afr. 28 44s 29 26e
57 Bergzabern, Germany 49 6n 8 0e
108 Berhala Str., Indonesia 1 0s 104 15e
105 Berhampore, India 24 2n 88 27e
106 Berhampur, India 19 15n 84 54e
78 Berheci, R., Rumania 46 7n 27 19e
136 Bering Sea, Pac. Oc. .58 0n 167 0e
10 Bering Str., Alas., U.S.A. 66 0n 170 0w
142 Beringarra, W. Austral. 26 0s 116 55e
54 Beringen, Belgium 51 3n 5 14e
88 Berislav, U.S.S.R. 46 50n 33 30e
172 Berisso, Argentina 34 40s 58 0w
65 Berja, Spain 36 50n 2 56w
79 Berkåk, Norway 62 49n 10 2e
122 Berkane, Morocco 34 52n 2 28w
55 Berkel, Netherlands ...51 58n 4 28e
55 Berkel, R., Germany .51 57n 7 05e
34 Berkeley, England, U.K. 51 41n 2 28w
166 Berkeley, U.S.A. 38 0n 122 20w
35 Berkhamsted, Eng., U.K. 51 45n 0 33w
162 Berkley Springs, U.S.A. 39 38n 78 12w
15 Berkner I., Antarctica 79 30s 50 0w
75 Berkovitsa, Bulgaria .43 16n 23 8e
34 Berkshire, co., England, United Kingdom 51 30n 1 20w
29 Berkshire Downs, England, United Kingdom 51 30n 1 18w
63 Berlanga, Spain 38 17n 5 50w
56 Berleburg, Germany ...51 3n 8 22e
135 Berlin, C. Prov., S. Afr. 32 52s 27 33e
56 Berlin, Germany 52 32n 13 24e
162 Berlin, Md., U.S.A. ...38 19n 75 12w
161 Berlin, N.H., U.S.A. .44 29n 71 10w
172 Bermejo, R., Formosa, Argentina 26 30s 58 50w
172 Bermejo R., San Juan, Argentina 30 0s 68 0w
64 Bermeo, Spain 43 25n 2 47w
62 Bermillo de Sayago, Sp. 41 22n 6 8w
134 Bermolli, S. Africa 28 23s 22 52e
169 Bermuda, Atlantic Oc. 32 45n 65 0w
167 Bernalillo, U.S.A. 35 17n 106 37w
72 Bernam R., Malaysia . 3 47n 101 5e
57 Bern (Berne), Switz. .46 57n 7 28e
173 Bernado de Irigoyen, Argentina 26 15s 53 40w
73 Bernalda, Italy 40 24n 16 44e
107 Bernam R., Malaysia . 3 45n 101 5e
172 Bernasconi, Argentina 37 55s 63 44w
48 Bernay, Eure, France 49 5n 0 35e
58 Berndorf, Austria 47 59n 16 1e
57 Berner Alpen, Mts., Switzerland 46 27n 7 35e
42 Berneray, Gt. I., Scot., U.K. 58 14n 6 50w
42 Berneray I., Scot., U.K. 56 47n 7 40w
57 Bernese Oberland, Mts., Switz. 46 27n 7 35e
142 Bernier I., W. Austral. 24 50s 113 12e
129 Beroroha, Malagasy Rep. 21 40s 45 10e
125 Beroubouaye, Dahomey 10 34n 2 46e
58 Beroun Czechoslovakia 49 57n 14 5e
58 Berounka, R., Cz. 50 0n 13 47e
74 Berovo, Yugoslavia ...41 42n 22 51e
74 Berowra, Australia 33 35s 151 12e
123 Berrahal, Algeria 36 54n 7 33e
51 Berre, Etang de, France 43 27n 5 5e
145 Berri, S. Australia 34 14s 140 35e
43 Berriedale, Scot., U.K. 58 12n 3 30w
37 Berriew, Wales, U.K. .52 36n 3 12w
143 Berrigan, Australia 35 38s 145 49e
122 Berrouaghia, Algeria .36 10n 2 53e
143 Berry, Australia 34 46s 150 43e
36 Berry Head, Eng., U.K. 50 24s 3 29w
49 Berry, Reg., France ...47 0n 2 0e
165 Berryville, U.S.A. 36 23n 93 35w
56 Bersenbrück, Germany 52 33n 7 56e
43 Berst Ness, Scot., U.K. 59 16n 3 0w
164 Berthaund, U.S.A. 40 21n 105 5w
164 Berthold, U.S.A. 48 19n 101 45w
49 Bertincourt, France ...50 5n 2 58e
128 Bertoua, Cameroons ... 4 30n 13 45e
44 Bertraghboy, B., Ire. .53 22n 9 54w
164 Bertrand, U.S.A. 40 35n 99 38w
82 Berufjördur, Iceland .64 48n 14 25w
98 Berur Hayil, Israel 31 34n 34 38e
41 Berwick, co., Scot., U.K. 55 46n 2 30w
161 Berwick, Pa., U.S.A. .41 4n 76 17w
143 Berwick, Australia 38 2s 145 23e
39 Berwick-upon-Tweed, England, U.K. 55 47n 2 0w
37 Berwyn Mts., Wales, United Kingdom 52 54n 3 26w
74 Berzasca, Rumania ...44 39n 21 58e
59 Berzence, Hungary 46 12n 17 11e
129 Besalampy, Malagasy Republic 16 43s 44 29e
49 Besançon, France 47 15n 6 0e
108 Besar, Mt., Indonesia . 2 40s 116 0e
107 Beserah, Malaysia 3 50n 103 21e
86 Beshenkovichi, U.S.S.R. 55 2n 29 29e
74 Beška, Yugoslavia 45 8n 20 6e
74 Besna Kobila, Mt., Yugoslavia 42 31n 22 10e
77 Besparmak Dagi, Mt., Turkey 37 32n 27 30e
85 Bessarabia, region, U.S.S.R. 46 20n 29 0e
51 Bessèges, France 44 18n 4 8e
163 Bessemer, Ala., U.S.A. 33 25n 87 0w
164 Bessemer, Mich., U.S.A. 46 27n 90 0w
48 Bessin, Dist., France .49 21n 1 0w
81 Bested, Denmark 56 48n 8 24e
135 Besters, Natal, S. Afr. 28 26s 29 41e
122 Bet Tadjine, Djebel, Algeria 29 0n 3 30w
62 Betanzos, Spain 43 15n 8 12w
128 Bétaré-Oya, Cameroon 5 40n 14 5e
64 Bétera, Spain 39 35n 0 28w
133 Bethal, Trans., S. Afr. 26 27s 29 28e
134 Bethanien, S. W. Afr. 26 31s 17 8e
98 Bethany, *see* Eizariya, Jordan 31 47n 35 15e
135 Bethany, O.F.S., S. Afr. 29 34s 25 59e
164 Bethany, U.S.A. 40 18n 94 0w

MAP
161 Bethel, Conn., U.S.A. 41 22N 73 25W
160 Bethel, Pa., U.S.A. 40 20N 80 2W
161 Bethel, Vt., U.S.A. 43 50N 72 37W
37 Bethesda, Wales, U.K. 53 11N 4 3W
135 Bethelsdorp, S. Africa 33 50S 25 15E
98 Bethlehem, Jordan 31 43N 35 12E
135 Bethlehem, S. Africa .28 14S 28 18E
161 Bethlehem, Pa., U.S.A. 40 39N 75 24W
135 Bethulie, S. Africa 30 30S 25 59E
49 Béthune, France 50 30N 2 38E
48 Béthune R., France ...49 47N 1 20E
129 Betioky, Malagasy Republic 23 48S 44 20E
49 Beton Bazoches, Fr. ...48 42N 3 15E
107 Betong, Thailand 5 45N 101 5E
145 Betoota, Australia 25 40S 140 42E
78 Betoroaga, Rumania .44 8N 25 32E
130 Betou, Congo (Fr.) 3 0N 18 30E
129 Betroka, Malagasy Republic 23 16S 46 0E
98 Betset, Israel 33 4N 35 8E
155 Betsiamites, Canada ...48 56N 68 40W
129 Betsiboka R., Malagasy Republic .17 0S 47 0E
105 Bettiah, India 26 48N 84 33E
70 Bettola, Italy 44 46N 9 35E
37 Bettws Bledrws, Wales, United Kingdom 52 9N 4 2W
37 Bettws-y-Coed, Wales, United Kingdom 53 4N 3 49W
43 Bettyhill, Scot., U.K. 58 31N 4 12W
104 Betul, India 21 48N 77 59E
108 Betung, Indonesia 2 0S 103 10E
78 Beuca, Rumania 44 14N 24 56E
55 Beuel, Germany 50 44N 7 7E
51 Beuil, Alpes Maritimes, France .44 6N 7 0E
157 Beulah, Canada 50 16N 101 02W
164 Beulah, U.S.A. 47 18N 101 47W
143 Beulah, Australia 35 58S 142 29E
56 Bevensen, Germany ...53 5N 10 34E
55 Bévercé, Belgium 50 27N 6 03E
39 Beverley, England, U.K. 53 52N 0 26W
142 Beverley, W. Australia 32 9S 116 56E
156 Beverly, Canada 53 36N 113 21W
161 Beverly, Mass., U.S.A. 42 32N 70 50W
166 Beverly, Wash., U.S.A. 46 55N 119 59W
167 Beverly Hills, U.S.A. .34 4N 118 29W
55 Beverst, Belgium 50 53N 5 28E
54 Beverwijk, Netherlands 52 28N 4 38E
34 Bewdley, England, U.K. 52 23N 2 19W
57 Bex, Switzerland 46 15N 7 0E
35 Bexhill, England, U.K. 50 51N 0 29E
35 Bexley, England, U.K. 51 26N 0 10E
124 Beyin, Ghana 5 1N 2 41W
75 Beykoz, Turkey 41 8N 29 07E
124 Beyla, Guinea 8 30N 8 38W
50 Beynat, France 45 8N 1 44E
90 Beyneu, U.S.S.R. 45 10N 55 3E
100 Beypazari, Turkey ...40 10N 31 48E
100 Beysehir Golu, Turkey 37 40N 31 45E
74 Bezdan, Yugoslavia ...45 28N 18 57E
86 Bezhitsa, U.S.S.R. 53 25N 34 18E
50 Béziers, France 43 20N 3 12E
106 Bezwada, see Vijayawada, India .16 31N 80 39E
106 Bhadra, R., India 13 0N 76 0E
105 Bhadrakh, India 12 10N 86 30E
106 Bhadravati, India 13 49N 76 15E
105 Bhagalpur, India 25 10S 87 0E
105 Bhaisa, India 19 10N 77 58E
104 Bhakkar, W. Pak. 31 40N 71 5E
105 Bhakra Dam, India ...31 30N 76 45E
103 Bhamo, Burma 24 15N 97 15E
105 Bhamragarh, India 19 30N 80 40E
105 Bhandara, India 21 5N 79 42E
104 Bhanrer Ra., India 23 40N 79 45E
102 Bharat, see India, Asia 24 0N 78 0E
104 Bharatpur, India 27 15N 77 30E
106 Bhatghar L., India 73 48N 18 10E
104 Bhatinda, India 30 15N 74 57E
106 Bhatkal, India 14 2N 74 35E
105 Bhatpara, India 22 50N 88 25E
106 Bhattiprolu, India 16 7N 80 45E
104 Bhaun, West Pakistan 32 55N 72 40E
104 Bhaunagar, see Bhavnagar, India ...21 45N 72 10E
106 Bhavani, India 11 27N 77 43E
106 Bhavani, R., India 11 30N 77 15E
104 Bhavnagar, India 21 45N 72 10E
106 Bhawanipatna, India .19 55N 83 30E
104 Bhera, West Pakistan 32 29N 72 57E
104 Bhilsa, see Vidisha, India 23 28N 77 53E
104 Bhilwara, India 25 25N 74 38E
106 Bhima R., India 17 20N 76 30E
106 Bhimavaram, India ...16 30N 81 30E
104 Bhind, India 26 30N 78 46E
106 Bhiwandi, India 19 15N 73 0E
104 Bhiwani, India 28 50N 76 9E
106 Bhongir, India 17 30N 78 56E
104 Bhopal, India 23 20N 77 53E
106 Bhor, India 18 12N 73 53E
105 Bhubaneswar, India ...20 15N 85 50E
104 Bhuj, India 23 15N 69 49E
104 Bhusaval, India 21 1N 75 56E
105 Bhutan, st., Asia 27 25N 89 50E
125 Biafra, Bight of, Africa 3 30N 9 20E
109 Biak I., Indonesia 1 0S 136 0E
59 Biała, Poland 49 50N 19 8E
59 Biała, R., Poland 49 46N 20 53E
60 Biała Piska, Poland ...53 37N 22 5E
60 Biała Podlaska, Poland 52 4N 23 6E
50 Biatograd, Poland 54 2N 15 58E
60 Biały Bór, Poland 53 53N 16 51E
60 Białystok. tn., Poland 53 10N 23 10E
60 Białystok, Prov., Pol. 53 8N 23 10E
73 Biancavilla, Italy 37 39N 14 50E
130 Biano Plateau, see Manika Plateau, Congo 9 55S 26 24E
109 Biaro I., Indonesia 2 5N 125 26E
50 Biarritz, France 43 29N 1 33W
133 Bias B., China 22 30N 114 40E
57 Biasca, Switzerland ...46 22N 18 58E
126 Biba, Egypt 28 55N 31 0E
157 Bibby I., Canada 61 55N 93 0W
134 Bibby's Hoek, S. Africa 33 56S 22 57E
57 Biberach, Germany ...48 5N 9 49E
124 Bibiani, Ghana 6 30N 2 8W
106 Bibile, Ceylon 7 10N 81 25E
144 Biboohra, Australia ...16 35S 145 27E
34 Bibury, England, U.K. 51 46N 1 50W
155 Bic, Canada 48 20N 68 41W
76 Bicaj, Albania 42 0N 20 25E
78 Bicaz, Rumania 46 53N 26 5E
73 Biccari, Italy 41 23N 15 12E
34 Bicester, England, U.K. 51 53N 1 9W
127 Bichana, Ethiopia 10 28N 38 10E
162 Bicknell, Ind., U.S.A. 38 50N 87 20W
167 Bicknell, Utah, U.S.A. 38 16N 111 35W
78 Bicsad, Rumania 47 56N 23 28E
37 Bicton, England, U.K. 52 43N 2 47W
125 Bida, Nigeria 9 3N 5 58E
106 Bidar, India 17 55N 77 35E
155 Biddeford, Me., U.S.A. 43 30N 70 28W
35 Biddenden, Eng., U.K. 51 7N 0 40E
143 Biddon, Australia 31 30S 148 47E
98 Biddu, Jordan 31 50N 35 8E
38 Biddulph, England, U.K. 53 8N 2 11W
127 Biddwara, Ethiopia ... 5 11N 38 34E
98 Biddya, Jordan 32 7N 35 4E
36 Bideford Bay, Eng., U.K. 51 5N 4 20W
39 Bidford, England, U.K. 52 9N 1 53W
34 Bidford on Avon, England, United Kingdom 51 1N 4 12W
107 Bidor, Malaysia 4 6N 101 15E
130 Bié Plateau, Angola ...12 0S 16 0E
166 Bieber, U.S.A. 41 4N 121 6W
57 Biel, Switzerland 47 8N 7 14E
60 Bielawa, Poland 50 43N 16 37E
59 Biele Karpaty, Mts., Cz. 49 5N 18 0E
56 Bielefeld, Germany 52 2N 8 31E
57 Bieler See, Switzerland 47 6N 7 5E
70 Biella, Italy 45 33N 8 3E
60 Bielsk Podlaski, Poland 52 47N 23 12E
59 Bielsko, Poland 49 49N 19 1E
107 Biên Hoa, Vietnam 11 3N 106 53E
157 Bienfait, Canada 49 10N 102 50W
34 Bienne R., France 48 18N 0 10E
154 Bienville, Lac, Canada 55 10N 73 15W
64 Biescas, Spain 42 37N 0 20W
134 Biesiesfontein, S. Africa 30 57S 17 58E
134 Biesiespoort, S. Africa 31 43S 23 10E
57 Bietigheim, Germany .48 57N 9 8E
73 Biferno R., Italy 41 40N 14 38E
157 Big Beaver, Canada ...49 10N 105 10W
154 Big Beaver House, Can. 52 59N 89 50W
142 Big Bell, W. Australia 27 12S 117 45E
166 Big Belt Mts., U.S.A. .46 50N 111 30W
135 Big Bend, Swaziland .26 50S 32 2E
165 Big Bend Nat. Park, U.S.A. 29 15N 103 15W
165 Big Black, R., U.S.A. 32 35N 90 30W
164 Big Blue, R., U.S.A. .40 20N 96 40W
163 Big Cypress Swamp, U.S.A. 26 12N 81 10W
152 Big Delta, Alaska, U.S.A. 64 15N 145 0W
164 Big Falls, U.S.A. 48 11N 93 48W
166 Big Horn, U.S.A. 46 11N 107 25W
166 Big Horn Mts., see Bighorn Mts. U.S.A. 44 30N 107 30W
166 Big Horn R., U.S.A. .45 30N 108 10W
165 Big Lake, U.S.A. 31 12N 101 25W
161 Big Moose, U.S.A. 43 49N 74 58W
164 Big Muddy R., U.S.A. 48 25N 104 45W
167 Big Pine, U.S.A. 37 12N 118 23W
166 Big Piney, U.S.A. 42 32N 110 3W
157 Big Quill L., Canada .51 48N 105 40W
162 Big Rapids, U.S.A. 43 42N 85 27W
157 Big River, Canada 53 50N 107 0W
160 Big Run, U.S.A. 40 57N 78 55W
162 Big Sable Pt., U.S.A. .44 5N 86 30W
152 Big Salmon, Canada ...61 50N 136 0W
166 Big Sandy, U.S.A. 48 12N 110 9W
164 Big Sandy Cr., U.S.A. 38 52N 103 11W
164 Big Sioux R., U.S.A. 44 20N 96 53W
166 Big Snowy Mt., U.S.A. 46 50N 109 15W
165 Big Spring, U.S.A. 32 10N 101 25W
164 Big Springs, U.S.A. ...41 4N 102 3W
164 Big Stone City, U.S.A. 45 20N 96 30W
163 Big Stone Gap, U.S.A. 36 52N 82 45W
164 Big Stone L., U.S.A. .44 25N 96 35W
154 Big Trout L., Canada 53 40N 90 0W
36 Bigbury, England, U.K. 50 17N 3 52W
36 Bigbury B., Eng., U.K. 50 18N 3 58W
142 Bigerymunal, Mt., W. Australia 27 25S 120 40E
166 Bigfork, U.S.A. 48 3N 144 2W
157 Biggar, Canada 52 10N 108 0W
41 Biggar, Scotland, U.K. 55 38N 3 31W
145 Biggenden, Australia .25 31S 152 4E
35 Biggleswade, Eng., U.K. 52 6N 0 16W
166 Bighorn Mts., U.S.A. .44 30N 107 20W
57 Bignasco, Switzerland 46 21N 8 36E
124 Bignona, Senegal 12 52N 16 23W
50 Bigorre, dist., France .43 5N 0 2E
166 Bigtimber, U.S.A. 45 53N 110 0W
71 Bihač, Yugoslavia 44 49N 15 57E
105 Bihar, tn. & st., India 25 5N 85 40E
131 Biharamulo & dist., Tanzania 2 25S 31 25E
59 Biharkeresztes, Hung. 47 8N 21 44E
99 Bihen, Somali Rep. ... 8 42N 48 22E
78 Bihor, Munţii, Mts., Rumania 46 29N 22 47E
78 Bihor, Reg., Rum. 47 0N 22 10E
104 Bijaipur, Mad. P., India 26 2N 77 36E
106 Bijapur, Mad. P., India 18 50N 80 50E
106 Bijapur, Mysore, India 16 50N 75 55E
100 Bijar, Iran 35 52N 47 35E
74 Bijeljina, Yugoslavia .44 46N 19 17E
104 Bijnor, India 29 27N 78 11E
104 Bikaner, India 28 2N 73 18E
105 Bikapur, India 26 30N 82 7E
91 Bikin, U.S.S.R. 46 50N 134 20E
136 Bikini, atoll, Pac. Oc. 12 0N 167 30E
132 Bikita, Rhodesia 20 6S 31 41E
130 Bikoro, Congo 0 48S 18 15E
125 Bikoué Cameroon 5 55S 11 50E
104 Bilara, India 26 14N 73 53E
105 Bilaspur, Mad. P., India 22 2N 82 15E
104 Bilaspur, Punjab, India 31 19N 76 50E
107 Bilauktaung Ra., Thai. 13 30N 99 15E
64 Bilbao, Spain 43 16N 2 56W
78 Bilbor, Rumania 47 18N 25 30E
82 Bildudalur, Iceland 65 40N 23 40W
74 Biléća, Yugoslavia 42 53N 18 27E
100 Bilecik, Turkey 40 5N 30 5E
130 Bili R., Congo 4 5N 24 10E
91 Bilir, U.S.S.R. 65 40N 131 20E
76 Bilisht, Albania 40 37N 20 59E
164 Bill, U.S.A. 43 18N 105 18W
125 Billa, Nigeria 8 55N 12 15E
142 Billabalong, W. Austral. 27 20S 115 20E
143 Billabong Cr., Australia 35 12S 144 50E
55 Billerbeck, Germany .51 58N 7 20E
35 Billericay, Eng., U.K. 51 38N 0 25E
35 Billesdon, England, U.K. 52 38N 0 56W
132 Billiate. Malawi 15 2S 34 39E
143 Billimari, Australia ...33 20S 148 37E
39 Billingham, Eng., U.K. 54 36N 1 18W
39 Billinghay, Eng., U.K. 53 5N 6 17W
166 Billings, U.S.A. 45 43N 108 29W
80 Billingsfors, Sweden ...59 0N 12 14E
35 Billingshurst, Eng., U.K. 51 2N 0 28W
50 Billom, France 45 43N 3 20E
121 Bilma, Nigeria 18 50N 13 30E
74 Bilo Gora, Mts., Y.-slav. 45 53N 17 15E
144 Biloela, Australia 24 33S 150 40E
165 Biloxi, Miss., U.S.A. ...30 30N 89 0W
145 Bilpa Morea Claypan, Queens., Austral. 25 0S 140 0E
34 Bilston, England, U.K. 52 34N 2 5W
121 Biltine, Chad 14 40N 20 50E
144 Bilyana, Australia 18 5S 145 50E
109 Bima, Indonesia 8 22S 118 49E
125 Bimbéréké, Dahomey 10 11N 2 43E
126 Bimban, Egypt 24 24N 32 54E
125 Bimbila, Ghana 8 54N 0 5E
130 Bimbo, Central African Republic ... 4 15N 18 33E
122 Bin el Ouidane Barrage, Morocco ...32 10N 6 15W
104 Bina-Etawah, India ...24 13N 78 14E
74 Binaćka Morava, R., Yugoslavia 42 30N 19 35E
109 Binaja, Mt., Indonesia 3 20S 129 25E
109 Binalbagan, Philippines 10 15N 123 0E
143 Binalong, N.S.W., Australia 34 40S 148 39E
108 Binatang, Sar., Malaysia 2 10N 111 40E
144 Binbee, Australia 20 15S 147 48E
39 Binbrook, England, U.K. 53 26N 0 9W
54 Binche, Belgium 50 26N 4 10E
130 Binda, Congo 5 30S 13 15E
142 Bindi Bindi, W. Austral. 30 40S 116 28E
108 Bindjai, Indonesia 3 50N 98 30E
132 Bindura, Rhodesia 17 18S 31 18E
145 Bingara, Australia 29 40S 150 40E
145 Bingara, Australia 28 10S 144 37E
57 Bingen, Germany 49 57N 7 53E
124 Bingerville, Ivory Coast 5 18N 3 49W
39 Bingham, England, U.K. 52 57N 0 55W
155 Bingham, U.S.A. 45 5N 69 50W
166 Bingham Canyon, USA 40 31N 112 10W
161 Binghampton, U.S.A. 42 9N 75 54W
45 Binghamstown, see An Geata Mór, Ire. 54 13N 10 0W
38 Bingley, England, U.K. 53 51N 1 50W
100 Bingöl, Turkey 39 20N 41 0E
107 Binh Dinh, see An Nhon, Vietnam 13 55N 109 7E
107 Binh Son, Vietnam 15 20N 108 40E
143 Binnaway, Australia .31 28S 149 24E
109 Binongko I., Indonesia 5 55S 123 55E
101 Bint, Iran 26 22N 59 25E
98 Bint Jebeil, Lebanon .33 8N 34 25E
108 Bintan I., Indonesia ... 1 0N 104 0E
108 Bintuhan, Indonesia . 4 50S 103 25E
108 Bintulu, Sar., Malaysia 3 3N 113 8E
98 Binyamina, Israel 32 32N 34 56E
127 Binza, Sudan 5 25N 28 40E
172 Bio Bio, prov., Chile .37 35S 72 0W
127 Bio Culma, Ethiopia . 7 20N 42 15E
71 Biograd, Yugoslavia ...43 56N 15 29E
74 Biokovo Ra., Mts., Yugoslavia 43 23N 17 0E
122 Biougra, Morocco 30 15N 9 14W
98 Biq'at Beit Netofa, Isr. 32 49N 35 22E
106 Bir, India 19 0N 75 54E
126 Bir Abu Hashim, Egypt 23 42N 34 6E
126 Bir Abu Minqar, Egypt 26 33N 27 33E
126 Bir Adal Deib, Sudan 22 35N 36 10E
123 Bir al Malfa, Libya ...31 58N 15 18E
123 Bir Alapetite, Tunisia 30 46N 10 2E
126 Bir Asal, Egypt 25 55N 34 20E
121 Bir Autrun, Sudan 18 15N 26 40E
123 Bir Cheik Ali, Tunisia 33 4N 8 6E
123 Bir Dhu'fan, Libya ...31 59N 14 32E
126 Bir Diqnash, Egypt 31 3N 25 23E
122 Bir el Abbes, Algeria .26 7N 6 9W
123 Bir el Ater, Algeria ...34 46N 8 3E
126 Bir el Basur, Egypt ...29 51N 25 49E
126 Bir el Gellaz, Egypt ...30 50N 26 40E
126 Bir el Shaqqa, Egypt .30 54N 25 1E
126 Bir Fuad, Egypt 30 35N 26 28E
126 Bir Haimur, Egypt 22 45N 33 40E
122 Bir Jedid Chavent, Mor. 33 28N 7 58W
126 Bir Kanayis, Egypt 24 59N 33 15E
126 Bir Kerawein, Egypt .27 10N 28 25E
122 Bir Lemouissat, Maur 25 0N 10 32W
126 Bir Maql, Egypt 23 7N 33 40E
126 Bir Misaha, Egypt 22 13N 27 59E
123 Bir Mogrein, (Fort Trinquet), Mauritania 25 10N 11 25W
126 Bir Murr, Egypt 23 28N 30 10E
98 Bir Nabala, Jordan 31 52N 35 12E
126 Bir Nakheila, Egypt .24 1N 30 50E
126 Bir Qatrani, Egypt 30 55N 26 10E
126 Bir Ranga, Egypt 24 25N 35 15E
127 Bir Ras, Fr. Terr. of the Afars & Issas ...12 0N 44 0E
123 Bir Roumi, Algeria 33 45N 6 51E
126 Bir Sahara, Egypt 22 54N 28 40E
126 Bir Seiyâla, Egypt 25 10N 34 50E
122 Bir Semguine, Morocco 30 1N 5 39W
126 Bir Shalatein, Egypt .23 5N 35 25E
126 Bir Shebb, Egypt 22 25N 29 40E
126 Bir Shût, Egypt 23 50N 35 15E
126 Bir Terfawi, Egypt 22 57N 28 55E
126 Bir Umm Qubûr, Egypt 24 35N 34 2E
126 Bir Ungât, Egypt 22 8N 33 48E
126 Bir Za'farâna, Egypt .29 10N 32 40E
123 Bir Zamús, Libya 24 16N 15 6E
126 Bir Zeidûn, Egypt 25 45N 33 40E
98 Bir Zeit, Jordan 31 59N 35 11E
109 Bira, Indonesia 2 3S 132 2E
124 Biramfera, Guinea 11 40N 9 10W
121 Birao, Central African Republic 10 20N 22 40E
35 Birch, England 51 50N 0 54E
157 Birch Hills, Canada ...53 10N 105 10W
156 Birch Mts., Canada 58 0N 113 0W
35 Birchington, Eng., U.K. 51 22N 1 18E
143 Birchip, Australia 35 52S 143 0E
78 Birchis, Rumania 45 58N 22 0E
147 Birchwood, N.Z. 45 55S 167 53E
157 Bird, Canada 56 35N 94 5W
164 Bird City, U.S.A. 39 48N 101 33W
134 Bird I., C. Prov., S. Afr. 32 3S 18 17E
134 Birdfield, S. Africa 31 46S 18 35E
145 Birdhip, Victoria, Australia 35 52S 142 50E
34 Birdlip, England, U.K. 51 50N 2 7W
145 Birdsville, Australia ...25 51S 139 20E
138 Birdum, Australia 15 50S 133 0E
100 Birecik, Turkey 37 0N 38 0E
108 Bireuen, Indonesia 5 14N 96 39E
173 Birigui, Brazil 21 18S 50 16W
144 Birimgan, Australia ...22 41S 147 25E
125 Biriri, Nigeria 12 8N 11 45E
101 Birjand, Iran 32 57N 59 10E
126 Birk, Saudi Arabia 18 8N 41 30E
126 Birka (Ruins), Si.-Arab. 22 11N 40 38E
38 Birkdale, England, U.K. 53 38N 3 2W
38 Birkenhead, Eng., U.K. 53 24N 3 1W
146 Birkenhead, N.Z. 36 49S 174 46E
55 Birkesdorf, Germany .50 49N 6 27E
126 Birket Qârûn, Egypt .29 30N 30 40E
58 Birkfeld, Austria 47 21N 15 45E
78 Birlad, Rumania 46 15N 27 38E
34 Birmingham, Eng., U.K. 52 30N 1 55W
163 Birmingham, U.S.A. .33 31N 86 50W
125 Birni-Ngaoure, Nigeria 13 5N 2 51E
125 Birni n'Koni, Nigeria .13 55N 5 15E
125 Birnin Gwari, Nigeria 11 0N 6 45E
125 Birnin Kebbi, Nigeria 12 32N 4 12E
125 Birnin Kudu, Nigeria .11 30N 9 29E
125 Birnin Tudu, Nigeria .12 9N 5 24E
91 Birobidzhan, U.S.S.R. 48 50N 132 50E
98 Birqin, Jordan 32 23N 35 15E
44 Birr, Ireland 53 7N 7 55W
143 Birregurra, Australia .38 19S 143 51E
104 Birsilpur, India 28 11N 72 58E
84 Birsk, U.S.S.R. 55 25N 55 30E
78 Birtin, Rumania 46 59N 22 31E
157 Birtle, Canada 50 30N 101 5W
39 Birtley, Eng., U.K. 55 5N 2 12W
88 Biryuchiy, I., U.S.S.R. 46 10N 35 0E
86 Biržai, U.S.S.R. 56 11N 24 45E
109 Bisa, Indonesia 1 10S 127 40E
73 Bisaccio, Italy 41 0N 15 20E
72 Bisacquino, Italy 37 42N 13 13E
105 Bisalpur, India 28 14N 79 48E
167 Bisbee Ariz., U.S.A. .31 30N 110 0W
66 Biscay, B. of, Atlantic Ocean 45 0N 2 0W
163 Biscayne B., U.S.A. ...25 40N 80 12W
73 Bisceglie, Italy 41 14N 16 30E
58 Bischofshofen, Austria 47 26N 13 14E
56 Bischofswerda, Ger. ...51 8N 14 11E
49 Bischwiller, France ...48 47N 7 50E
15 Biscoe I., Antarctica .66 0S 67 0W
154 Biscotasing, Canada ..47 19N 82 8W
71 Biševo I., Yugoslavia .42 57N 16 3E
126 Bisha, Wadi, Si.-Arab. 20 30N 43 0E
130 Bishanga, Congo 4 31S 20 58E
167 Bishop, Calif., U.S.A. .37 20N 118 26W
165 Bishop, Tex., U.S.A. .27 35N 97 49W
39 Bishop Auckland, England, U.K. 54 40N 1 40W
34 Bishops Castle, England, U.K. 52 29N 3 0W
34 Bishop's Cleeve, England, U.K. 51 56N 2 3W
155 Bishop's Fall, Canada 49 2N 55 24W
34 Bishop's Frome, England, U.K. 52 8N 2 29W
36 Bishops Lydeard, England, U.K. 51 4N 3 12W
36 Bishop's Nympton, England, U.K. 50 58N 3 44W
35 Bishop's Stortford, England, U.K. 51 52N 0 11E
34 Bishop's Waltham, England, U.K. 50 57N 1 13W
36 Bishopsteignton, England, U.K. 50 32N 3 32W
34 Bishopstoke, Eng., U.K. 50 58N 1 19W
131 Bisina, L., Uganda 1 38N 33 56E
73 Bisignano, Italy 30 30N 16 17E
127 Biskia, Ethiopia 15 30N 37 31E
123 Biskra, Algeria 34 50N 5 52E
60 Biskupiec, Poland 53 53N 20 58E
109 Bislig, Philippines 8 15N 126 27E
56 Bismark, Germany 52 39N 11 31E
164 Bismarck, U.S.A. 46 49N 100 49W
144 Bismarck Arch., Territory of New Guinea 3 30S 148 30E
144 Bismarck Sea, Territory of New Guinea 4 10S 146 50E
131 Biso, Uganda 1 44N 31 26E
164 Bison, U.S.A. 45 34N 102 28W
80 Bispgården, Sweden ...63 2N 16 40E
124 Bissau, Port Guinea ...11 45N 15 45W
157 Bissett, Canada 46 14N 78 4W
124 Bissikrima, Guinea 10 50N 10 58W
78 Bistreţu, Rumania 43 54N 23 23E
71 Bistrica, see Ilirska Bistrica, Y.-slav. ...45 34N 14 14E
78 Bistrita, Rumania 47 9N 24 35E
78 Bistrita-Nôsăud, Reg., Rum. 47 10N 24 30E
78 Bistrita, R., Rumania 47 10N 24 30E
78 Bistriţei, Munţii, Mts., Rumania 47 15N 25 40E
105 Biswan, India 27 29N 81 2E
49 Bitche, France 49 3N 7 25E
100 Bitlis, Turkey 38 20N 42 3E
74 Bitola (Bitolj) 41 5N 21 21E
73 Bitonto, Italy 41 7N 16 40E
166 Bitter Creek, U.S.A. ...41 39N 108 36W
126 Bitter L., Gt., Egypt ..30 15N 32 40E
56 Bitterfeld, Germany ...51 36N 12 20E
134 Bitterfontein, S. Africa 31 0S 18 32E
166 Bitteroot, R., U.S.A. .46 30N 114 20W

MAP
166 Bitterroot Range, Mts., U.S.A. 46 0N 114 20W
72 Bitti, Italy 40 29N 9 20E
36 Bitton, England, U.K. 51 25N 2 27W
125 Bittou, Upper Volta ...11 17N 0 18W
156 Bitumount, Canada ...57 26N 112 40W
135 Bityi, C. Prov., S. Africa 31 48S 28 32E
125 Biu, Nigeria 10 40N 12 3E
78 Bivolari, Rumania 47 31N 27 27E
78 Bivolu, Mt., Rumania 47 16N 25 58E
114 Biwa-ko, lake, Japan 35 15N 135 45E
164 Biwabik, U.S.A. 47 33N 92 19W
90 Biysk, U.S.S.R. 52 40N 85 0E
165 Bizana, C. Prov., S. Afr. 30 50S 29 52E
123 Bizerte, Tunisia 37 15N 9 50E
81 Bjärka-Säby, Sweden 58 16N 15 44E
82 Bjarnanes, Iceland 64 20N 15 6W
74 Bjelasica Ra., Y.-slav. 42 50N 19 40E
74 Bjelašnica, Mt., Y.-slav. 43 11N 18 21E
74 Bjelo Polje, Y.-slav. .43 1N 19 45E
74 Bjelovar, Yugoslavia .45 56N 16 49E
81 Bjerringbro, Denmark 56 23N 9 39E
80 Björbo, Sweden 60 26N 14 45E
80 Björkhamre, Sweden .61 24N 16 25E
81 Björkhult, Sweden 57 50N 15 40E
80 Björneborg, Sweden ...59 13N 14 16E
81 Bjuv, Sweden 56 7N 12 56E
34 Blaby, England, U.K. 52 34N 1 10W
74 Blace, Yugoslavia 43 18N 21 17E
164 Black Butte, Mt., U.S.A. 46 23N 103 25W
38 Black Combe, mt., England, U.K. 54 16N 3 20W
156 Black Diamond, Can. .50 45N 114 22W
36 Black Down Hills, England, U.K. 50 57N 3 15W
41 Black Esk R., Scot., U.K. 55 14N 3 13W
38 Black Fell, Eng., U.K. 54 47N 2 33W
57 Black Forest, see Schwarzwald, Ger. .48 0N 8 0E
36 Black Hd., Eng., U.K. 50 1N 5 6W
44 Black Hd., Ireland 53 9N 9 18W
46 Black Hd., N. Ire., U.K. 54 56N 5 42W
164 Black Hills, U.S.A. 44 0N 103 50W
161 Black Island Sd., U.S.A. 41 17N 71 35W
43 Black Isle, dist., Scotland, U.K. 57 35N 4 10W
157 Black L., Sask., Can. .59 20N 105 30W
162 Black L., U.S.A. 45 28N 84 15W
37 Black Mt., see Mynydd du, Wales .51 45N 3 45W
7 Black Mts., Wales, U.K. 51 52N 3 50W
165 Black Mesa, Mt., U.S.A. 36 57N 102 55W
167 Black Range, Mts., U.S.A. 33 30N 107 55W
160 Black R., Ont., Canada 44 50N 79 5W
46 Black R., Ireland 53 54N 7 42W
165 Black R., U.S.A. 36 15N 90 45W
161 Black R., N.Y., U.S.A. 43 50N 75 30W
164 Black R. Fs., U.S.A. .44 18N 90 52W
67 Black Sea, Europe 43 30N 35 0E
143 Black Sugarloaf, Mt., N.S.W., Australia ...31 18S 151 35E
124 Black Volta R., W. Afr. 9 0N 2 40W
163 Black Warrior, R., U.S.A. 33 0N 87 45W
144 Blackall, Australia 24 26S 145 27E
147 Blackball, N.Z. 42 22S 171 26E
144 Blackbull, Australia ...18 0S 141 7E
38 Blackburn, Eng., U.K. 53 44N 2 30W
152 Blackburn, Mt., Alaska 61 5N 142 3W
145 Blackbutt, Australia .26 51S 152 6E
36 Blackdown Hills, Eng., U.K. 50 57N 3 15W
164 Blackduck, U.S.A. 47 43N 94 32W
166 Blackfoot, U.S.A. 43 13N 112 12W
166 Blackfoot, R., U.S.A. .47 0N 113 35W
41 Blackford, Scot., U.K. 56 15N 3 48W
143 Blackheath, Australia 33 39S 150 17E
36 Blackmoor Gate, England, U.K. 51 9N 3 55W
36 Blackmoor Vale, England, U.K. 50 54N 2 28W
38 Blackpool, Eng., U.K. 53 48N 3 3W
144 Blackridge, Australia .22 35S 147 35E
160 Blackriver, U.S.A. 44 46N 83 17W
45 Blackrock, Dublin, Ire. 53 18N 6 11W
155 Blacks Harbour, Can. 45 3N 66 49W
162 Blacksburg, U.S.A. 37 17N 80 23W
45 Blacksod B., Ireland .54 6N 10 0W
45 Blackstairs Mt., Ireland 52 33N 6 50W
162 Blackstone, U.S.A. 37 6N 78 0W
142 Blackstone Ra., W. Australia 26 0S 128 30E
143 Blacktown, Australia .33 48S 150 55E
155 Blackville, Canada 47 5N 65 58W
144 Blackwater, Australia 23 35S 149 0E
102 Blackwater, Canada ...53 20N 123 0W
145 Blackwater Cr., Austral. 25 40S 145 0E
35 Blackwater, R., England, U.K. 51 53N 0 37E
44 Blackwater, R., Cork, Ire. 52 5N 9 3W
46 Blackwater, R., Meath, Ireland 53 46N 7 0W
46 Blackwater, R., Northern Ireland, U.K. 54 25N 7 0W
40 Blackwater Res., Scotland, U.K. 56 42N 4 45W
165 Blackwell, U.S.A. 36 55N 97 20W
41 Blackwood, Scot., U.K. 55 40N 3 56W
134 Bladgrond, S. Africa .28 52S 19 57E
81 Blädinge, Sweden 56 52N 14 29E
37 Blaenau Ffestiniog, Wales, U.K. 53 0N 3 57W
34 Blaenavon, Eng., U.K. 51 46N 3 5W
74 Blagaj, Yugoslavia 43 16N 17 55E
36 Blagdon, England, U.K. 51 19N 2 42W
89 Blagodarnoye, U.S.S.R. 45 7N 43 37E
91 Blagoveshchensk, U.S.S.R. 50 20N 127 30E
74 Blagoyevgrad (Gorna Dzhumaya), Bulgaria 42 2N 23 5E
75 Blagoyevgrad, prov., Bulgaria 41 40N 23 30E
34 Blaina, England, U.K. 51 46N 3 10W
166 Blaine, Wash., U.S.A. 48 59N 122 43W
157 Blaine Lake, Canada .52 51N 106 52W
49 Blainville, France 48 33N 6 23E
164 Blair, U.S.A. 41 38N 96 10W
14 Blair Atholl, Australia 22 42S 147 31E
43 Blair Atholl, Scot., U.K. 56 46N 3 50W
41 Blairgowrie, Scot., U.K. 56 36N 3 20W
156 Blairmore, Canada 49 40N 114 25W
160 Blairs Mills, U.S.A. ...40 17N 77 45W
160 Blairsville, U.S.A. 40 27N 79 15W
78 Blaj, Rumania 46 10N 23 57E
164 Blake Pt., U.S.A. 48 12N 88 27W
163 Blakely, U.S.A. 31 22N 85 0W
34 Blakeney, Glos., England, U.K. 51 45N 2 29W
35 Blakeney, Norfolk, England, U.K. 52 57N 1 1E
49 Blâmont, France 48 35N 6 50E
120 Blanc C., Mauritania .20 50N 17 0W
123 Blanc, C., Tunisia 37 15N 9 56E
155 Blanc Sablon, Canada 51 24N 57 8W
176 Blanca Bay, Argentina 39 10S 61 30W
165 Blanchard, U.S.A. 35 8N 97 40W
145 Blanche L., S. Austral. 29 15S 139 40E
165 Blanco, U.S.A. 30 7N 98 30W
169 Blanco C., Costa Rica 9 34N 85 8W
174 Blanco C., Peru 4 10S 81 10W
65 Blanco C., Spain 39 21N 2 51E
166 Blanco C., U.S.A. 42 50N 124 40W
34 Blandford Forum, England, U.K. 50 52N 2 10W
167 Blanding, U.S.A. 37 35N 109 30W
64 Blanes, Spain 41 40N 2 48E
135 Blaney, C. Prov., S. Afr. 32 51S 27 30E
49 Blangy, France 49 14N 0 17E
58 Blanice, R., Cz. 49 10N 14 5E
54 Blankenberge, Belgium 51 20N 3 9E
56 Blankenburg, Germany 51 46N 10 56E
173 Blanquillo, Uruguay .32 53S 55 37W
59 Blansko, Cz. 49 22N 16 40E
132 Blantyre, Malawi 15 45S 35 0E
44 Blarney, Ireland 51 57N 8 35W
58 Blatna, Czechoslovakia 49 25N 13 52E
75 Blatnitsa, Racari, Bulg. 43 41N 28 32E
39 Blaydon, England, U.K. 54 56N 1 47W
50 Blaye, France 45 8N 0 40W
143 Blayney, N.S.W., Austral. 33 32S 149 14E
138 Blaze, Pt., Australia .12 56S 130 11E
59 Blazowa, Poland 49 53N 22 7E
36 Bleadon, England, U.K. 51 18N 2 57W
35 Blean, England, U.K. 51 18N 1 3E
38 Bleasdale Moors, England, U.K. 53 57N 2 40W
56 Bleckede, Germany ...53 18N 10 43E
71 Bled, Yugoslavia 46 27N 14 7E
90 Blednaya Mt., U.S.S.R. 65 50N 65 30E
58 Bleiburg, Austria 46 35N 14 49E
78 Blejești, Rumania 44 19N 25 27E
81 Blekinge Län, co., Swed. 56 15N 15 15E
160 Blenheim, Canada 42 21N 82 2W
147 Blenheim, New Zealand 41 38S 174 5E
133 Blesmanspos, S. Africa 27 42S 24 11E
34 Bletchingdon, England, United Kingdom 51 51N 1 16W
35 Bletchley, Eng., U.K. 51 59N 0 54W
122 Blida, Algeria 36 30N 2 49E
123 Blidet Amor, Algeria .32 59N 5 58E
80 Blidö I., Sweden 59 36N 18 54E
81 Blidsberg, Sweden 57 56N 13 25E
154 Blind River, Canada .46 15N 83 0W
76 Blinisht, Albania 41 52N 19 58E
34 Blisworth, Eng., U.K. 52 11N 0 56W
109 Blitar, Indonesia 8 5S 112 11E
125 Blitta, Togo 8 23N 1 6E
161 Block I., U.S.A. 41 13N 71 35W
34 Blockley, England, U.K. 52 1N 1 45W
135 Bloedrivier, Nat., S. Afr. 27 52S 30 38E
135 Bloemfontein, S. Africa 29 6S 26 14E
133 Bloemhof, Trans., S. Afr. 27 38S 25 32E
35 Blofield, England, U.K. 52 38N 1 25E
48 Blois, France 47 35N 1 20E
80 Blomskog, Sweden 59 19N 21 1E
46 Bloody Foreland, Ire. 55 10N 8 18W
164 Bloomer, U.S.A. 45 8N 91 30W
160 Bloomfield, Canada ...44 34N 77 39W
164 Bloomfield, Iowa, U.S.A. 40 44N 92 26W
164 Bloomfield, Neb., U.S.A. 42 38N 97 35W
167 Bloomfield, N. Mexico, U.S.A. 36 46N 107 59W
144 Bloomfield R. Mission, Queens., Austral. ...15 56S 145 22E
164 Bloomington, Ill., U.S.A. 40 25N 89 0W
162 Bloomington, Ind., U.S.A. 39 10N 86 30W
161 Bloomsburg, U.S.A. ...41 0N 76 30W
109 Blora, Indonesia 6 57S 111 25E
160 Blossburg, U.S.A. 41 40N 77 4W
133 Blouberg, Trans., S. Afr. 23 8S 29 0E
163 Blountstown, U.S.A. .30 28N 85 5W
34 Bloxham, England, U.K. 51 1N 1 22W
58 Bludenz, Austria 47 10N 9 50E
162 Blue I., U.S.A. 41 40N 87 40W
167 Blue Mesa Res., U.S.A. 38 30N 107 15W
169 Blue Mts., Jamaica ...18 0N 76 40W
143 Blue Mts., Australia ...33 40S 150 0E
166 Blue Lake, U.S.A. 40 52N 124 0W
166 Blue Mountains, U.S.A. 45 15N 119 0W
139 Blue Mud B., Australia 13 30S 136 0E
127 Blue Nile, prov., Sudan 12 30N 34 30E
127 Blue Nile R. (Bahr El Azrak), Sudan 10 30N 35 0E
163 Blue Ridge Mts., U.S.A. 36 30N 80 15W
46 Blue Stack Mts., Ireland 54 46N 8 5W
135 Bluecliff, S. Africa ...33 30S 25 28E
162 Bluefield, U.S.A. 37 18N 81 14W
169 Bluefields, Nicaragua .12 0N 83 50W
42 Bluemull Sd., Scot., U.K. 60 45N 1 0W
147 Blueskin B., N.Z. 45 44S 170 38E
144 Bluff, Australia 23 40S 149 0E
144 Bluff Downs, Australia 19 37S 145 30E
147 Bluff Harbour, N.Z. ...46 36S 168 21E
142 Bluff Pt., W. Australia 27 50S 114 5E
162 Bluffton, U.S.A. 40 43N 85 9W
173 Blumenau, Brazil 27 0S 49 0W
56 Blumenthal, Germany 53 5N 12 20E
35 Blundeston, Eng., U.K. 52 33N 1 42E
164 Blunt, U.S.A. 44 32N 100 0W
166 Bly, U.S.A. 42 23N 121 0W
80 Blyberg, Sweden 61 12N 14 11E
133 Blyde R., Trans., S. Afr. 24 30S 30 46E
160 Blyth, Canada 43 45N 81 25W
39 Blyth, Northumberland, England, U.K. 55 8N 1 32W
39 Blyth, Notts., England, United Kingdom 53 22N 1 2W
41 Blyth Bridge, Scot., U.K. 55 41N 3 22W
35 Blythburgh, Eng., U.K. 52 19N 1 36E
167 Blythe, U.S.A. 33 40N 114 33W
160 Blytheswood, Canada 42 8N 82 37W
39 Blyton, England, U.K. 53 25N 0 42W
133 Blyvooruitsig, S. Africa 26 20S 27 29E
98 Bnei Beraq, Israel 32 6N 34 29E
79 Bö, Norway 59 25N 9 3E
124 Bo, Sierra Leone 7 55N 11 50W
46 Boa I., N. Ire., U.K. .54 30N 7 50W
174 Boa Vista, Brazil 2 48N 60 30W
169 Boaco, Nicaragua 12 29N 85 35W
62 Boal, Spain 43 25N 6 49W
43 Boat of Garten, Scotland, U.K. 57 15N 3 45W
143 Bobadah, N.S.W., Australia 32 19S 146 41E
144 Bobawaba, Australia .19 46S 147 33E
106 Bobbili, India 18 35N 83 30E
70 Bobbio, Italy 44 57N 9 22E
154 Bobcaygeon, Canada .44 33N 78 35W
57 Böbingen, Germany ...48 15N 10 50E
124 Bobo-Dioulasso, Upper Volta 11 8N 4 13W
60 Bobolice, Poland 53 58N 16 37E
74 Boboshevo, Bulgaria .42 9N 23 0E
74 Bobov Dol, Bulgaria .42 20N 23 0E
60 Bobr R., Poland 51 50N 15 15E
88 Bobrinets, U.S.S.R. ...48 4N 32 5E
87 Bobrov, U.S.S.R. 51 5N 40 2E
86 Bobruysk, U.S.S.R. ...53 10N 29 15E
143 Bobundara, Australia 36 32S 148 59E
174 Boca do Acre, Brazil . 8 50S 66 27W
175 Bocaiuva, Brazil 17 10S 43 50W
124 Bocanda, Ivory Coast 7 5N 4 31W
121 Bocaranga, Central African Republic ... 7 0N 15 35E
169 Bocas del Toro, Panama 9 15N 82 20W
64 Boceguillas, Spain 41 20N 3 39W
174 Bochalema, Colombia 7 40N 72 30W
59 Bochnia, Poland 49 58N 29 27E
55 Bocholt, Belgium 51 10N 5 35E
56 Bocholt, Germany 51 50N 6 35E
58 Bochov, Czechoslovakia 50 9N 13 3E
56 Bochum, Germany 51 28N 7 12E
56 Bockenem, Germany .52 1N 10 8E
55 Bockum-Hövel, Ger. .51 43N 7 44E
127 Bocoggi, Ethiopia 7 40N 38 20E
55 Bocq, R., Belgium 50 20N 4 55E
74 Bosca Montană, Rumania 45 21N 21 47E
130 Boda, Central African Republic 4 19N 17 26E
81 Böda, Sweden 57 15N 17 12E
81 Bodafors, Sweden 57 31N 14 33E
91 Bodaibo, U.S.S.R. 57 50N 114 0E
143 Bodalla, Australia 36 4S 150 4E
43 Boddam, Scotland, U.K. 57 28N 1 46W
42 Boddam, Shetland Is., Scotland, U.K. 59 55N 1 16W
142 Boddington, W. Austral. 32 50S 116 30E
82 Bodedern, Wales, U.K. 53 18N 4 31W
82 Boden, Sweden 65 50N 21 42E
34 Bodenham, Eng., U.K. 52 9N 2 41W
56 Bodenteich, Germany 52 49N 10 41E
46 Boderg L., Ireland 53 52N 8 0W
106 Bodhan, India 18 40N 77 55E
35 Bodiam, England, U.K. 51 1N 0 33E
106 Bodinayakkanur, India 10 2N 77 10E
125 Bodinga, Nigeria 12 58N 5 10E
36 Bodinnick, Eng., U.K. 50 20N 4 37W
109 Bodjonegoro. Indonesia 7 11S 111 54E
36 Bodmin England, U.K. 50 28N 4 44W
36 Bodmin Moor, England, United Kingdom 50 33N 4 36W
82 Bodö, Norway 67 17N 14 27E
59 Bodrog R., Hungary .48 15N 21 35E
100 Bodrum, Turkey 37 5N 27 30E
59 Bodva, R., Hungary .48 19N 20 45E
44 Bodyke, Ireland 52 53N 8 38W
51 Boën, France 45 44N 4 0E
130 Boende, Congo 0 24S 21 12E
165 Boerne, U.S.A. 29 48N 98 41W
135 Boesmanskop, S. Africa 30 02S 27 07E
133 Boetsap, S. Africa 27 59S 24 30E
124 Boffa, Guinea 10 16N 14 3W
46 Bofin L., Ireland 53 51N 7 55W
80 Bofors, Sweden 59 19N 14 34E
107 Bogale, Burma 16 14N 95 26E
165 Bogalusa, U.S.A. 30 50N 89 55W
143 Bogan Gate, Australia 33 6S 147 44E
145 Bogan R., Australia ...32 23S 147 40E
143 Bogandyera Mt., Australia 35 45S 148 0E
143 Bogantungan, Austral. 23 41S 147 17E
165 Bogata, U.S.A. 33 26N 95 10W
74 Bogatić, Yugoslavia ...44 51N 19 30E
75 Bogdan, Mt., Bulgaria 42 37N 24 20E
129 Bogenfels, S. W. Africa 27 25S 15 25E
81 Bogense, Denmark 55 34N 10 5E
145 Boggabilla, Australia .28 36S 150 24E
145 Boggabri, Australia ...30 45S 150 0E
44 Boggeragh Mts., Ireland 52 2N 8 55W
124 Boghé, Mauritania 16 45N 14 10W
35 Bognor Regis, Eng., U.K. 50 47N 0 40W
81 Bogö, Denmark 54 56N 12 2E
109 Bogo, Philippines 10 54N 124 8E
86 Bogodukhov, U.S.S.R. 50 9N 35 33E
143 Bogong Mt., Australia 36 40S 147 15E
109 Bogor, Indonesia 6 36S 106 48E
125 Bogoro, Nigeria 9 37N 9 29E
87 Bogoroditsk, U.S.S.R. 53 47N 38 8E
87 Bogorodsk, U.S.S.R. .56 4N 43 30E
124 Bogoso, Ghana 5 38N 2 3W
174 Bogotá, Colombia 4 34N 74 0W
90 Bogotol, U.S.S.R. 56 15N 89 50E
87 Bogoyavlenskoye, U.S.S.R. 53 20N 40 10E
105 Bogra, East Pakistan .24 26N 89 22E
91 Boguchany, U.S.S.R. .58 40N 97 30E
89 Boguchar, U.S.S.R. ...49 55N 40 32E
88 Boguslav, U.S.S.R. 49 47N 30 53E
59 Boguszów, Poland 50 46N 16 15E
49 Bohain, France 49 59N 3 28E
58 Bohemia, Czechoslovakia 50 0N 14 0E
52 Bohemian Forest, Mts., Czechoslovakia 49 20N 13 0E
45 Boheraphuca, Ireland 53 1N 7 45W
71 Bohinjska Bistrica, Yugoslavia 46 17N 14 1E
57 Böhmer Wald, Mts., Germany 49 30N 12 40E
56 Bohmte, Germany 52 24N 8 20E
109 Bohol I., Philippines . 9 58N 124 20E
46 Bohola, Ireland 53 54N 9 4W
99 Bohotleh, Somali Rep. 8 20N 46 25E
125 Boi, Nigeria 9 35N 9 27E
173 Boi, Pta. de, Brazil ...23 55S 45 15W
73 Boiano, Italy 41 28N 14 29E
155 Boiestown, Canada 46 27N 66 26W
144 Boigu I., Terr. of Papua 9 15S 143 30E
74 Boinitsa, Bulgaria 43 58N 22 28E
42 Boisdale L., Scot., U.K. 57 9N 7 10W
166 Boise, U.S.A. 43 43N 116 9W
165 Boise City, U.S.A. 36 45N 102 30W
157 Boissevain, Canada ...49 15N 100 0W
71 Boite R., Italy 46 24N 12 13E
56 Boitzenburg, Germany 55 16N 13 36E
56 Boizenburg, Germany 53 22N 10 42E
120 Bojador C., Sp. Sahara 26 0N 14 30W
81 Bøjden, Denmark 55 6N 10 7E
101 Bojnurd, Iran 37 30N 57 20E
125 Boju, Nigeria 7 22N 7 55E
74 Boka, Yugoslavia 45 22N 20 52E
74 Boka Kotorska, C., Yugoslavia 42 23N 18 32E
130 Bokala, Congo 3 9S 17 4E
124 Bokala, Ivory Coast ... 8 31N 4 33W
124 Boké, Guinea 10 56N 14 17W
125 Bokkos, Nigeria 9 17N 9 1E
79 Boknafjord, Norway .59 12N 5 30E
121 Bokoro, Chad 12 25N 17 14E
121 Bokote, Congo 0 12S 21 8E
107 Bokpyin, Burma 11 18N 98 42E
133 Boksburg, Trans., S. Afr. 26 12S 28 14E
130 Bokungu, Congo 0 35S 22 50E
71 Bol, Yugoslavia 43 18N 16 38E
109 Bolaäng, Indonesia 0 56S 122 6E
143 Bolac, L., Australia ...37 43S 142 57E
124 Bolama, Port. Guinea 11 30N 15 30W
102 Bolan Pass, W. Pak. .29 50N 67 20E
168 Bolanos, R., Mexico ...22 0N 104 10W
48 Bolbec, France 49 30N 0 30E
78 Bolboşi, Rumania 44 44N 23 14E
90 Bolchereche, U.S.S.R. 56 4N 74 45E
78 Boldesti, Rumania 45 3N 26 2E
127 Bole, Ethiopia 6 36N 37 20E
124 Bole, Ghana 9 0N 2 28W
86 Bolekhov, U.S.S.R. ...49 0N 24 0E
78 Böleni, Rumania 45 48N 27 51E
60 Boleslawiec, Poland ...51 17N 15 37E
84 Bolgary ruins, U.S.S.R. 55 3N 48 50E
125 Bolgatanga, Ghana 10 44N 0 53W
88 Bolgrad, U.S.S.R. 45 40N 28 32E
127 Boli, Sudan 6 2N 28 48E
82 Boliden, Sweden 64 50N 20 20E
109 Bolinao C., Philippines 16 30N 119 55E
172 Bolivar, Argentina 36 2S 60 53W
174 Bolivar, Colombia 2 0N 77 0W
165 Bolivar, Mo., U.S.A. .37 38N 93 22W
165 Bolivar, Tenn., U.S.A. 35 14N 89 0W
174 Bolivia, Rep., S. Amer. 17 6S 64 0W
74 Boljevac, Yugoslavia .43 51N 21 58E
87 Bolkhov, U.S.S.R. 53 25N 36 0E
51 Bollène, France 44 18N 4 45E
38 Bollington, Eng., U.K. 53 18N 2 8W
80 Bollnäs Sweden 61 22N 16 28E
127 Bollo Selassie, Ethiopia 8 51N 39 27E
80 Bollstabruk, Sweden .62 59N 17 42E
63 Bollullos, Spain 37 19N 6 32W
81 Bolmen, Sweden 56 48N 13 43E
81 Bolmen L., Sweden ...56 57N 13 45E
130 Bolobo, Congo 2 6S 16 20E
71 Bologna, Italy 44 30N 11 20E
49 Bologne, France 48 10N 5 8E
86 Bologoye, U.S.S.R. 57 55N 34 0E
130 Bolomba, Congo 0 35N 19 0E
109 Bolong, Philippines ... 7 7N 122 16E
107 Bolovens Plateau, Laos 15 10N 106 30E
105 Bolpur India 23 40N 87 45E
71 Bolsena, Italy 42 40N 11 58E
71 Bolsena, L. di, Italy ...42 35N 11 55E
88 Bolshaya Belozeka, U.S.S.R. 47 23N 34 28E
87 B. Glushitsa, U.S.S.R. 52 24N 50 16E
88 B. Lepetrikha, U.S.S.R. 47 11N 33 57E
89 B. Martynovka, U.S.S.R. 47 12N 41 46E
88 B. Vradiyevka, U.S.S.R. 49 56N 30 38E
91 Bolshevik I., U.S.S.R. 78 30N 102 0E
91 Bolshoi I., U.S.S.R. ...73 30N 142 [illegible]
90 Bolshoi Altym U.S.S.R. 62 25N 66 50E
91 Bolshoi Mamyr, U.S.S.R. 56 20N 102 55E
88 Bolshoy Tokmak, see Tokmak, U.S.S.R. .47 16N 35 42E
86 Bol'soj T'uters I., U.S.S.R. 59 44N 26 57E
39 Bolsover, England, U.K. 53 14N 1 18W
54 Bolsward, Netherlands 53 3N 5 32E
36 Bolt Head, Eng., U.K. 50 13N 3 48W
36 Bolt Tail, Eng., U.K. .50 13N 3 55W
64 Boltana, Spain 42 28N 0 4E
57 Boltigen, Switzerland .46 38N 7 24E
160 Bolton, Canada 43 54N 79 51W

MAP
38 Bolton, England, U.K. ...53 35N 2 26W
38 Bolton Abbey, England, United Kingdom ...53 59N 1 53W
38 Bolton by Bowland, England, U.K. ...53 56N 2 21W
39 Bolton-in-Dearne, England, U.K. ...53 31N 1 19W
38 Bolton le Sands, England, U.K. ...54 7N 2 49W
100 Bolu, Turkey ...40 45N 31 35E
44 Bolus Hd., Ireland ...51 48N 10 20W
71 Bolzano, Italy ...46 30N 11 20E
175 Bom Despacho, Brazil 19 46S 45 15W
130 Bom Jesus, Angola ... 9 11S 13 34E
175 Bom Jesus da Lapa, Brazil ...13 10S 43 30W
130 Boma, Congo ... 5 50S 13 4E
143 Bomaderry, Australia 34 52S 150 37E
121 Bomba, G. of, Libya .32 20N 23 15E
143 Bombala, Australia ...36 56S 149 15E
63 Bombarral, Portugal .39 15N 9 9W
127 Bombash, Ethiopia ... 9 45N 34 40E
106 Bombay, India ...18 55N 72 50E
130 Bomboma, Congo ... 2 25N 18 55E
132 Bombwe, Zambia ...17 14S 25 21E
111 Bomda, China ...29 59N 96 25E
143 Bomera, Australia ...31 33S 149 49E
124 Bomi Hills, Liberia ... 7 1N 10 38E
79 Bömlo, Norway ...59 37N 5 13E
79 Bömlo I., Norway ...59 45N 5 10E
130 Bomongo, Congo ... 1 27N 18 21E
123 Bon C., Tunisia ...37 1N 11 2E
152 Bona Mt., Canada ...61 20N 140 0W
138 Bonaparte Archipelago, W. Australia ...15 0S 124 30E
169 Bonaire I., Neth. W. Ind. ...12 10N 68 15W
143 Bonang, Australia ...37 11S 148 41E
169 Bonanza, Nicaragua ...13 54N 84 35W
62 Boñar, Spain ...42 52N 5 19W
43 Bonarbridge, Scot., U.K. ...57 53N 4 20W
80 Bonäset, Sweden ...63 16N 18 45E
155 Bonaventure, Canada 48 5N 63 32W
155 Bonavista, Canada ...48 40N 53 5W
155 Bonavista B., Canada 48 58N 53 25W
41 Bonchester Bri., Scotland, U.K. ...55 23N 2 36W
71 Bondeno, Italy ...44 53N 11 22E
130 Bondo, Congo ... 3 55N 23 53E
124 Bondoukoro, Upper Volta ... 9 51N 4 25W
124 Bondoukou, Ivory C. . 8 2N 2 47W
109 Bondowoso, Indonesia 7 56S 113 49E
123 Bône, see Annaba, Algeria ...36 50N 7 55E
109 Bone, Gulf of, Indon. . 4 10S 120 50E
73 Bonefro, Italy ...41 42N 14 55E
55 Bönen Germany ...51 37N 7 44E
109 Bonerate, I., Indonesia ... 7 25S 121 5E
41 Bo'ness, Scotland, U.K. ...56 0N 3 38W
107 Bong Son, see Hoai Nhon, S. Vietnam ...14 28N 103 37E
130 Bongandanga, Congo . 1 24N 21 3E
127 Bonge, Ethiopia ... 6 5N 37 16E
130 Bongo, Serra do, Angola ...10 20S 15 30E
121 Bongor, Chad ...10 35N 15 20E
165 Bonham, U.S.A. ...33 30N 96 10W
51 Bonifacio, Corsica, Fr. 41 24N 9 10E
136 Bonin Is., Pacific Ocean ...27 0N 142 0E
56 Bonn, Germany ...50 43N 7 6E
50 Bonnat, France ...46 20N 1 53E
155 Bonne B., Canada ...40 31N 58 0W
155 Bonne Espérance, I., Canada ...51 24N 57 40W
165 Bonne Terre, U.S.A. .37 55N 90 38W
133 Bonnefoi, Trans., S. Afr. ...25 57S 30 11E
166 Bonners Ferry, U.S.A. 48 38N 116 21W
48 Bonnétable, France ...48 11N 0 25E
48 Bonneuil Matours, Fr. 46 41N 0 34E
51 Bonneville, France ...46 5N 6 24E
143 Bonnie Doon, Australia ...37 2S 145 53E
142 Bonnie Rock, Australia ...30 29S 118 22E
134 Bonnievale, S. Africa .33 55S 20 3E
49 Bonny, France ...47 34N 2 50E
125 Bonny, Nigeria ... 4 25N 7 13E
125 Bonny R., Nigeria ... 4 20N 7 14E
41 Bonnyrigg, Scot., U.K. ...55 52N 3 8W
157 Bonnyville, Canada ...54 20N 110 45W
109 Bonoi, Indonesia ... 1 45S 137 41E
72 Bonorva, Italy ...40 25N 8 47E
108 Bontang, Indonesia ... 0 10N 117 30E
109 Bonthain, Indonesia ... 5 34S 119 56E
124 Bonthe, Sierra Leone . 7 30N 12 33W
124 Bonyeri, Ghana ... 5 1N 2 46W
59 Bonyhád, Hungary ...46 18N 18 32E
142 Bonython Ra., Austral. ...23 40S 128 45E
142 Boogardie, W. Austral. ...28 0S 117 40E
165 Booker, U.S.A. ...36 29N 100 30W
142 Boolaloo, W. Australia ...22 30S 115 50E
143 Booligal, Australia ...33 58S 144 53E
142 Booloo Downs, W. Australia ...23 52S 119 33E
54 Boom, Belgium ...51 6N 4 20E
134 Boomrivier, S. Africa .29 33S 20 27E
145 Boonah, Australia ...28 0S 152 35E
164 Boone, Iowa, U.S.A. .42 5N 93 46W
163 Boone, N.C., U.S.A. ..36 14N 81 43W
165 Booneville, Ark., U.S.A. ...35 10N 93 54W
163 Booneville, Miss., U.S.A. ...34 39N 88 34W
144 Boongoondoo, Australia ...22 55S 145 55E
162 Boonville, Ind., U.S.A. ...38 3N 87 13W
164 Boonville, Mo., U.S.A. 38 57N 92 45W
161 Boonville, N.Y., U.S.A. ...43 31N 75 20W
145 Boorindal, Australia ...30 22S 146 11E
145 Booroodarra Downs, N.S.W., Australia ...31 10S 145 27E
143 Booroorban, Australia 34 53S 144 46E
143 Boorowa, Australia ...34 28S 148 44E
143 Boort, Australia ...36 7S 143 46E
38 Boot, England, U.K. .54 24N 3 18W
153 Boothia, Gulf of, Can. 70 0N 90 0W
152 Boothia Pen., Canada 70 30N 95 0W
38 Bootle, Cumb., England, United Kingdom ...54 17N 3 24W
38 Bootle, Lancs., England, United Kingdom ...53 28N 3 1W
128 Booué, Gabon ... 0 5S 11 55E
130 Bopako, Congo ... 1 57N 21 11E
145 Bopeechee Sta., South Australia ...29 35S 137 30E
85 Bopo, Nigeria ... 7 33N 7 50E
57 Boppard, Germany ...50 13N 7 36E
58 Bor, Czechoslovakia ...49 41N 12 45E
127 Bor, Sudan ... 6 10N 31 40E
74 Bor, Yugoslavia ...44 8N 22 7E
81 Bor, Sweden ...57 9N 14 7E
166 Borah, Mt., U.S.A. ...44 19N 113 46W
99 Boramo, Somali Rep. . 9 55N 43 7E
127 Borang, Sudan ... 4 50N 30 59E
81 Boras, Sweden ...57 42N 13 1E
101 Borazjan, Iran ...29 22N 51 10E
174 Borba, Brazil ... 4 12S 59 34W
63 Borba, Portugal ...38 50N 7 26W
89 Borçka, Turkey ...41 25N 40 41E
50 Bordeaux, France ...44 50N 0 36W
155 Borden, Canada ...46 18N 63 47W
142 Borden, W. Australia .34 3S 118 12E
14 Borden I., Canada ...78 30N 111 0W
133 Border, C. Prov., S. Afr. ...27 57S 24 50E
145 Bordertown, S. Austral. ...36 14S 140 58E
82 Bordeyri, Iceland ...65 12N 21 8W
70 Bordighera, Italy ...43 47N 7 40E
123 Bordj Djeneiene, Tunisia ...31 47N 10 3E
123 Bordj de Still, Algeria 34 5N 5 58E
123 Bordj el Hobra, Algeria ...32 9N 4 51E
122 Bordj Fly Ste Marie, Algeria ...27 19N 2 32W
123 Bordj-in-Eker, Algeria ...24 9N 5 3E
123 Bordj le Boeuf, Tunisia ...32 11N 10 2E
123 Bordj Nili, Algeria ...33 28N 3 2E
123 Bordj Sidi Toui, Tunisia ...32 41N 11 21E
122 Bordj Taguine, Algeria ...34 55N 2 19E
123 Bordj Zelfana, Algeria 32 27N 4 15E
35 Bordon Camp, Eng., U.K. ...51 6N 0 52W
35 Borehamwood, Eng., U.K. ...51 40N 0 15W
41 Boreland, Scotland, U.K. ...55 12N 3 16W
81 Borensberg, Sweden ...58 33N 15 15E
82 Borgarnes, Iceland ...64 33N 21 56W
54 Börger, Netherlands ...52 54N 7 33E
165 Borger, U.S.A. ...35 40N 101 20W
81 Borghamn, Sweden ...58 23N 14 43E
55 Borgharen, Netherlands ...50 53N 5 41E
81 Borgholm, Sweden ...56 54N 16 48E
73 Borgia, Italy ...38 50N 16 30E
43 Borgie R., Scot., U.K. 58 28N 4 20W
55 Borgloon, Belgium ...50 48N 5 21E
70 Borgo San Dalmazzo, It. ...44 19N 7 29E
71 Borgo San Lorenzo, It. ...43 57N 11 21E
70 Borgo Val di Taro, It. 44 29N 9 47E
71 Borgo Valsugano, Italy ...46 11N 11 59E
71 Borgocollefegato, Italy ...42 12N 13 14E
70 Borgomanero, Italy ...45 41N 8 28E
70 Borgonovo Val Tidone, Italy ...45 1N 9 28E
70 Borgosesia, Italy ...45 43N 8 9E
80 Borgvattnet, Sweden .63 25N 15 50E
79 Borhaug, Norway ...58 0N 6 33E
76 Boric, Albania ...42 8N 19 28E
91 Boris Vilkitski Strait, U.S.S.R. ...77 40N 105 0E
87 Borisoglebsk, U.S.S.R. 51 27N 42 5E
86 Borisov, U.S.S.R. ...54 17N 28 28E
87 Borisovo-Sudskoye, U.S.S.R. ...59 58N 35 57E
86 Borispol, U.S.S.R. ...50 21N 30 59E
174 Borja, Peru ... 4 20S 77 40W
64 Borja, Spain ...41 48N 1 34W
64 Borjas Blancas, Spain 41 31N 0 52E
56 Borken, Germany ...51 3N 9 21E
80 Borlänge, Sweden ...60 28N 14 33E
15 Borley C., Antarctica .66 15S 52 30E
70 Bormida, R., Italy ...44 35N 8 10E
70 Bormio, Italy ...46 28N 10 22E
56 Borna, Germany ...51 8N 12 31E
108 Borneo I., E. Indies ... 1 0N 115 0E
55 Bornheim, Germany ...50 46N 7 44E
81 Bornholm I., Denmark ...55 8N 14 55E
81 Bornholmsgattet, str., Europe ...54 30N 14 20E
63 Bornos, Spain ...36 48N 5 42W
125 Bornu Yassu, Nigeria 12 14N 12 25E
86 Borodino, U.S.S.R. ...55 31N 35 40E
124 Boromo, Upper Volta 11 45N 2 58W
109 Borongan, Philippines 11 31N 125 21E
144 Borooren, Australia ...24 13S 151 33E
127 Borotangba Mts., Central African Rep. ... 6 30N 25 0E
39 Boroughbridge, England, U.K. ...54 6N 1 23W
75 Borovan, Bulgaria ...43 27N 23 45E
86 Borovichi, U.S.S.R. ...58 25N 33 55E
87 Borovsk, U.S.S.R. ...55 12N 36 24E
81 Borrby, Sweden ...55 27N 14 10E
64 Borriol, Spain ...40 4N 0 4W
45 Borris, Ireland ...32 36N 6 57W
45 Borris-in-Ossory, Ire. 52 57N 7 40W
44 Borrisokane, Ireland .53 0N 8 8W
44 Borrisoleigh, Ireland .52 48N 7 58W
139 Borroloo, N. Terr., Australia ...16 4S 136 17E
38 Borrowdale, Eng. U.K. ...54 31N 3 10W
78 Borsa, Rumania ...47 41N 24 50E
104 Borsad, India ...22 24N 72 56E
82 Börselv, Norway ...70 20N 25 30E
50 Bort-les-Orgues, France ...45 24N 2 29E
37 Borth, Wales, U.K. ...52 29N 4 3W
100 Borujerd, Iran ...33 55N 48 50E
42 Borve, Scotland, U.K. 58 25N 6 28W
89 Borzhomi, U.S.S.R. ...41 48N 43 28E
86 Borzna, U.S.S.R. ...51 18N 32 26E
91 Borzya, U.S.S.R. ...50 24N 116 31E
72 Bosa, Italy ...40 17N 8 32E
74 Bosanska Brod, Y.-slav. ...45 10N 18 0E
71 Bos. Dubica, Y.-slav. 45 10N 16 50E
71 Bos. Grahovo, Y.-slav. ...44 12N 16 26E
71 Bos. Kostajnica, Y.-slav. ...45 11N 16 33E
71 Bos. Krupa, Y.-slav. .44 53N 16 10E
71 Bos. Petrovac, Y.-slav. ...44 35N 16 21E
74 Bos. Šamac, Y.-slav. .45 3N 18 29E
71 Bosanski Novi, Y.-slav. ...45 2N 16 22E
34 Bosbury, England, U.K. ...52 5N 2 27W
36 Boscastle, Eng., U.K. 50 42N 4 42W
73 Boscotrecase, Italy ...40 46N 14 28E
130 Boseki, Congo ... 2 30S 19 35E
35 Bosham, England, U.K. ...50 50N 0 51W
133 Boshoek, Trans., S. Afr. ...25 30S 27 9E
135 Boshof, O.F.S., S. Afr. 28 31S 25 13E
101 Boshruyeh, Iran ...33 50N 57 30E
74 Bosiljgrad, Yugoslavia 42 30N 22 27E
133 Boskop, Trans., S. Afr. ...26 32S 27 7E
59 Boskovice, Cz. ...49 29N 16 40E
133 Boskuil, Trans., S. Afr. ...27 23S 25 51E
114 Bosahanto, Pen., Japan ...35 20N 140 20E
74 Bosna R., Yugoslavia 44 50N 18 10E
74 Bosna i Hercegovina, rep., Yugoslavia ...44 0N 18 0E
109 Bosnek, Indonesia ... 1 5S 136 10E
130 Bosobolo, Congo ... 4 15N 19 50E
100 Bosporus, str., Turkey 41 10N 29 10E
121 Bossangoa, Central African Republic ... 6 35N 17 30E
121 Bossembelé, Central African Republic ... 5 25N 17 40E
165 Bossier City, U.S.A. ...32 28N 93 38W
138 Bossut C., W. Australia ...18 42S 121 35E
39 Boston, England, U.K. ...52 59N 0 2W
161 Boston, Mass., U.S.A. 42 20N 71 0W
156 Boston Bar, Canada ...49 52N 121 22W
74 Bosut, R., Yugoslavia 45 5N 19 2E
165 Boswell, Okla., U.S.A. 34 1N 95 30W
160 Boswell, Pa., U.S.A. ...40 9N 79 2W
104 Botad, India ...22 15N 71 40E
174 Botafago, Brazil ... 8 40S 69 40W
143 Botany B., Australia .34 2S 151 6E
75 Botevgrad, Bulgaria ...42 55N 23 47E
135 Bothaspas, S. Africa .27 33S 29 46E
135 Bothaville, S. Africa .27 23S 26 34E
41 Bothel, England, U.K. ...54 43N 3 16W
133 Bothithong, S. Africa .27 4S 23 50E
82 Bothnia, G. of, Eur. ...63 0N 21 0E
160 Bothwell, Canada ...42 37N 81 54W
99 Botiala, Somali Rep. .11 30N 49 58E
62 Boticas, Portugal ...41 41N 7 40W
132 Botletle R., Botswana 20 10S 24 10E
78 Botoşani, Rumania ...47 42N 26 41E
78 Botoşani, Reg., Rumania ...47 45N 26 50E
129 Botswana, state, Africa ...23 0S 24 0E
134 Botrivier, S. Africa ...34 14S 19 9E
134 Botterleegte, S. Africa 30 33S 21 20E
39 Bottesford, Eng., UK 52 57N 0 48W
164 Bottineau, U.S.A. ...48 49N 100 25W
56 Bottrop, Germany ...51 34N 6 59E
173 Botucatu, Brazil ...22 55S 48 30W
155 Botwood, Canada ...49 6N 55 23W
122 Bou Alam, Algeria ...33 50N 1 40E
122 Bou Ali, Algeria ...27 11N 0 4W
122 Bou Arfa, Morocco ...32 32N 1 58E
124 Bou Bjébéha, Mali ...18 25N 2 45W
122 Bou Garfa, Algeria ...27 4N 7 59W
123 Bou Grara, Tunisia ...33 33N 10 39E
122 Bou Guemma, Algeria 28 49N 0 30E
122 Bou Guern, Algeria ...33 55N 0 16W
122 Bou Iblane, Djebel, Mor. ...33 50N 4 0W
122 Bou Ismail, Algeria ...36 45N 2 51E
122 Bou Izakarn, Morocco 29 12N 6 46W
122 Bou Kahil, Djebel, Alg. ...34 22N 9 23E
123 Bou Saâda, Algeria ...35 11N 4 9E
124 Bouaké, Ivory Coast . 7 40N 5 2W
128 Bouar, Central African Republic ... 6 0N 15 40E
121 Bouca, Central African Republic ... 6 45N 18 25E
50 Boucau, France ...43 32N 1 29W
51 Bouches-du-Rhône, dépt., France ...43 37N 5 2E
122 Bouda, Algeria ...27 50N 0 27W
122 Boudenib, Morocco ...31 59N 3 31W
122 Boufarik, Algeria ...36 42N 2 58E
138 Bougainville C., W. Australia ...13 57S 126 4E
136 Bougainville I., Solomon Islands ... 6 0S 155 0E
123 Bougaroun, C., Algeria ...37 6N 6 30E
124 Bougouanou, Ivory C. 6 42N 4 15W
124 Bougouni, Mali ...11 30N 7 20W
54 Bouillon, Belgium ...49 44N 5 3E
123 Bouira, Algeria ...36 20N 3 59E
44 Bouladuff, Ireland ...52 42N 7 55W
142 Boulder, W. Australia 30 55S 121 28E
164 Boulder, Colo., U.S.A. 40 3N 105 10W
166 Boulder, Mont., U.S.A. ...46 14N 112 4W
167 Boulder City, U.S.A. .36 0N 114 58W
167 Boulder Dam, see Hoover Dam, U.S.A. ...36 0N 114 45W
154 Bouleau, Lac au, Can. 47 40N 77 35W
122 Boulhaut, Morocco ...33 30N 7 1W
144 Boulia, Australia ...22 52S 139 51E
48 Boulogne R., France .46 50N 1 25W
50 Boulogne sur Gesse, Fr. ...43 18N 0 38E
49 Boulogne-sur-Mer, Fr. ...50 42N 1 36E
125 Boultoum, Niger ...14 45N 10 25E
122 Boumaine, Morocco ...31 25N 6 0W
125 Boumba, Niger ...12 23N 2 52E
124 Bouna, Ivory Coast ... 9 10N 3 0W
124 Boundiali, Ivory Coast ... 9 30N 6 20W
166 Bountiful, U.S.A. ...40 57N 111 58W
136 Bounty I., Pac. Oc. ...46 0S 180 0E
91 Bour Khaya C., USSR ...71 50N 133 10E
50 Bourbon l'Archambault, France ...46 36N 3 4E
50 Bourbon Lancy, France ...46 37N 3 45E
50 Bourbonnais reg. Fr. .46 28N 3 0E
49 Bourbonne, France ...47 59N 5 45E
125 Bourem, Mali ...17 0N 0 24W
50 Bourg, Gironde, France ...45 3N 0 34W
51 Bourg Argental, France ...45 18N 4 32E
51 Bourg-de-Péage, France ...45 2N 5 3E
51 Bourg-en-Bresse, Fr. .46 13N 5 12E
51 Bourg St. Andéol, Fr. 44 23N 4 39E
51 Bourg St. Maurice, Fr. ...45 35N 6 46E
50 Bourganeuf, France ...45 57N 1 45E
49 Bourges, Cher., France ...47 5N 2 22E
161 Bourget, Canada ...45 25N 75 9W
51 Bourget, L. du, France ...45 44N 5 52E
48 Bourgneuf, France ...47 2N 1 58W
48 Bourgneuf, B. de, Fr. 47 3N 2 10W
49 Bourgogne, Reg. Fr. .47 0N 4 30E
51 Bourgoin, France ...45 36N 5 17E
145 Bourke, Australia ...30 8S 145 55E
154 Bourlamaque, Canada 48 5N 77 56W
35 Bourne, Linc., England, U.K. ...52 46N 0 22W
34 Bournemouth, England, U.K. ...50 43N 1 53W
50 Bourriot Bergonce, Fr. ...44 7N 0 14W
34 Bourton-on-the-Water, England, U.K. ...51 53N 1 45W
50 Boussac, France ...46 22N 2 13E
50 Boussens, France ...43 12N 1 2E
124 Boutilimit, Mauritania 17 45N 14 40W
70 Boves, Italy ...44 19N 7 33E
17 Bouvet I., S. Atlantic Ocean ...55 0S 3 30E
122 Bouznika, Morocco ...33 46N 7 6W
49 Bouzonville, France ...49 10N 6 30E
73 Bova Marina, Italy ...37 59N 15 56E
73 Bovalino Marina, Italy ...38 9N 16 10E
81 Bovallstrand, Sweden 58 31N 11 17E
71 Bovec, Yugoslavia ...46 20N 13 33E
70 Boves, Italy ...44 19N 7 29E
36 Bovey Tracey, England, U.K. ...50 36N 3 40W
54 Bovigny, Belgium ...50 12N 5 55E
166 Bovill, U.S.A. ...46 58N 116 27W
73 Bovino, Italy ...41 15N 15 20E
156 Bow Island, Canada ...49 50N 111 23W
156 Bow R., Canada ...51 10N 115 0W
164 Bowbells, U.S.A. ...48 47N 102 19W
164 Bowdle, U.S.A. ...45 30N 100 2W
142 Bowelling, W. Australia ...33 25S 116 30E
144 Bowen, Australia ...20 0S 148 16E
143 Bowen Mts., Australia 37 0S 148 0E
41 Bowes, England, U.K. 54 31N 1 59W
167 Bowie, Ariz., U.S.A. ...32 15N 109 30W
165 Bowie, Tex., U.S.A. ...33 33N 97 50W
135 Bowker's Park, S. Afr. ...31 50S 26 46E
38 Bowland, Forest of, England, U.K. ...54 0N 2 30W
162 Bowling Green, Ky., U.S.A. ...37 0N 86 25W
162 Bowling Green Ohio, U.S.A. ...41 22N 83 40W
164 Bowman, U.S.A. ...46 12N 103 21W
15 Bowman, I., Antarc. .65 0S 104 0E
145 Bowmans, S. Australia ...34 8S 138 10E
154 Bowmanville, Canada 43 55N 78 40W
40 Bowmore, Scot., U.K. 55 45N 6 18W
38 Bowness, Cumb., England, U.K. ...54 57N 3 13W
38 Bowness, Westmorland, England, U.K. ...54 22N 2 56W
156 Bowness Park, Canada ...50 55N 114 25W
143 Bowral, Australia ...34 26S 150 27E
143 Bowser Australia ...36 19S 146 23E
132 Bowwood, Zambia ...17 5S 26 20E
35 Box, England, U.K. ...51 24N 2 16W
35 Box Hill, England, U.K. ...51 16N 0 16W
166 Boxelder Creek, U.S.A. ...47 20N 108 30W
81 Boxholm, Sweden ...58 11N 15 4E
35 Boxley, England, U.K. ...51 17N 0 34E
55 Boxmeer, Netherlands 51 38N 5 56E
54 Boxtel, Netherlands ...51 36N 5 9E
88 Boyabat, Turkey ...41 28N 34 42E
142 Boyanup, W. Australia ...33 30S 115 40E
165 Boyce, U.S.A. ...31 25N 92 39W
154 Boyd L., Canada ...61 30N 103 20W
46 Boyle, Ireland ...53 58N 8 19W
162 Boyne City, U.S.A. ...45 12N 84 55W
163 Boynton Beach, U.S.A. ...26 31N 80 3W
142 Boyup Brook, W. Australia ...33 47S 116 40E
77 Bozburun, Turkey ...36 43N 28 8E
76 Bozcaada, tn. & I., Tur. ...39 49N 26 3E
35 Bozeat, England, U.K. ...52 14N 0 41W
166 Bozeman, U.S.A. ...45 40N 111 0W
60 Bozepole Wlk., Poland ...54 33N 17 56E
74 Boževac, Yugoslavia .44 32N 21 24E
50 Bozouls, France ...44 28N 2 43E
121 Bozoum, Central African Republic ... 6 25N 16 35E
78 Bozovici, Rumania ...44 56N 22 1E
70 Bra, Italy ...44 41N 7 50E
54 Brabant, Prov., Belg. 49 15N 5 20E
81 Brabrand, Denmark ...56 10N 10 9E
71 Brac I., Yugoslavia ...43 20N 16 40E
42 Bracadale, Scot., U.K. 57 22N 6 24W
42 Bracadale L., Scot., U.K. ...57 20N 6 30W
71 Bracciano, Italy ...42 6N 12 10E
154 Bracebridge, Canada .45 5N 79 20W
39 Bracebridge Heath, England, U.K. ...53 13N 0 32W
123 Brach, Libya ...27 31N 14 20E
49 Bracieux, France ...47 30N 1 30E
80 Bräcke, Sweden ...62 42N 15 32E
160 Brackenridge, U.S.A .40 38N 79 44W
165 Brackettville, U.S.A. .29 21N 100 20W
34 Brackley, England, U.K. ...52 3N 1 9W
35 Bracknell, Eng., U.K. 51 24N 0 45W
41 Braco, Scotland, U.K. 56 16N 3 55W
78 Brad, Rumania ...46 10N 22 50E
73 Bradano R., Italy ...40 41N 16 20E
38 Bradda Hd., Isle of Man, U.K. ...54 6N 4 46W
160 Braddock, U.S.A. ...40 24N 79 51W
163 Bradenton, U.S.A. ...27 25N 82 35W
160 Bradford, Canada ...44 8N 79 33W
38 Bradford, Eng., U.K. .53 47N 1 45W
160 Bradford, Pa., U.S.A. 41 58N 78 41W
161 Bradford, Vt., U.S.A. 43 59N 72 9W
34 Bradford-on-Avon, England, U.K. ...51 20N 21 5W
78 Brădiceni, Rumania ...45 3N 23 4E
34 Brading England, U.K. ...50 41N 1 9W
165 Bradley, Ark., U.S.A. 33 7N 93 39W
164 Bradley, S.D. U.S.A. .45 10N 97 40W
132 Bradley Institute, Rhodesia ...17 7S 31 25E
155 Bradore Bay, Canada 51 27N 57 18W
35 Bradwell-on-Sea, England, U.K. ...51 44N 0 55E
36 Bradworthy, Eng., U.K. ...50 54N 4 22W
165 Brady, U.S.A. ...31 8N 99 25W
42 Brae, Scotland, U.K. .60 23N 1 20W
81 Brædstrup, Denmark .55 58N 9 36E
145 Braemar, Australia ...25 35S 152 20E

BR INDEX BR

MAP
43 Braemar, Scot., U.K. .57 2N 3 20W
145 Braemar, S. Australia 33 12S 139 35E
43 Braemar, dist., Scotland, United Kingdom 57 2N 3 20W
43 Braemore, Scot., U.K. 58 16N 3 33W
43 Braeriach Mts., Scotland, U.K. 57 30N 3 44W
161 Braeside, Canada 45 25N 76 26W
62 Braga, Portugal 41 35N 8 32W
62 Braga, Dist., Portugal 41 30N 8 30W
172 Bragado, Argentina ...35 2S 60 27W
175 Bragança, Brazil 1 0S 47 2W
62 Bragança, Portugal ...41 48N 6 50W
62 Braganca, Dist. Port. 41 30N 6 45W
173 Bragança Paulisto, Braz. 22 55S 46 32W
105 Brahmanbaria, E. Pak. 23 50N 91 15E
105 Brahmani R., India ...21 0N 85 15E
103 Brahmaputra R., India....................26 30N 93 30E
37 Braich-y-pwll, Head, Wales, U.K. 52 47N 4 46W
143 Braidwood, Australia .35 27S 149 49E
78 Braila, Rumania 45 19N 27 59E
78 Brăila, Reg., Rum. 45 10N 27 35E
39 Brailsford, Eng., U.K. 52 58N 1 35W
55 Braine l'Alleud, Belg. 50 42N 4 23E
164 Brainerd, U.S.A. 46 20N 94 10W
35 Braintree, Eng., U.K. 51 53N 0 34E
161 Braintree, Mass., U.S.A. 42 11N 71 0W
55 Braives, Belgium 50 39N 5 7E
134 Brak, R., S. Africa 29 50S 23 10E
134 Brak R., Trans. S. Afr. 22 40S 29 30E
56 Brake, Germany 53 19N 8 30E
81 Bräkne-Hoby, Sweden 56 12N 15 8E
133 Brakpan, Trans., S. Afr. 26 13S 28 20E
134 Brakpoort, S. Africa .31 20S 23 22E
81 Brålanda, Sweden 58 33N 12 22E
156 Bralorne, Canada 50 50N 123 15W
35 Bramford, Eng., U.K. 52 5N 1 6E
81 Bramming, Denmark ..55 28N 8 42E
81 Bramön I., Sweden ...62 14N 17 40E
154 Brampton, Canada 43 45N 79 45W
38 Brampton, Cumb., England, U.K. 54 56N 2 43W
35 Brampton, Hunts., England, U.K. 52 19N 0 13W
56 Bramsche, Germany ...52 25N 7 58E
35 Bramshott, Eng., U.K. 51 5N 0 47W
144 Bramwell, Queensland, Australia 12 8S 142 37E
35 Brancaster, Eng., U.K. 52 58N 0 40E
174 Branco R., Brazil 1 30N 61 15W
55 Brand, Germany 52 1N 13 45E
81 Brande, Denmark 55 57N 9 7E
56 Brandenburg, Germany 52 24N 12 33E
40 Brander, Pass of, Scotland, U.K. 56 25N 5 10W
43 Branderburgh, Scotland, U.K. 57 43N 3 17W
135 Brandfort, S. Africa ...28 40S 26 30E
157 Brandon, Canada 49 50N 100 0W
39 Brandon, Durham, England, U.K. 54 46N 1 37W
35 Brandon, Suffolk, England, U.K. 52 27N 0 37E
161 Brandon, U.S.A. 43 48N 73 4W
44 Brandon B., Ireland ...52 17N 10 8W
44 Brandon, Mt., Kerry, Ireland 52 15N 10 15W
44 Brandon Pt., Ireland .52 18N 10 10W
133 Brandsiekfontein, S. Africa 27 50S 23 44E
79 Brandval, Norway 60 18N 12 2E
134 Brandvlei, S. Africa ...30 25S 20 30E
58 Brandýs, Czechoslovakia 50 10N 14 40E
161 Branford, U.S.A. 41 15N 72 48W
60 Braniewo, Poland 54 25N 19 50E
81 Brännarp, Sweden 56 46N 12 38E
145 Bransby, Australia 28 10S 142 0E
15 Bransfield Str. Falkland Is. Dependencies 63 0S 59 0W
165 Branson, Col., U.S.A. .37 4N 103 53W
165 Branson, Mo., U.S.A. .36 40N 93 18W
39 Branston, Eng., U.K. 53 13N 0 28W
154 Brantford, Canada 43 15N 80 15W
50 Brantôme, France 45 22N 0 39E
143 Branxholme, Australia 37 52S 141 49E
143 Branxton, N.S.W., Australia 32 38S 151 21E
70 Branzi, Italy 46 0N 9 46E
155 Bras d'or, L., Canada 46 3N 60 43W
174 Brasiléia, Brazil 10 9S 68 35W
175 Brasilia, fed. dist., Braz. 15 55S 47 40W
86 Braslav, U.S.S.R. 55 38N 27 0E
71 Braslovce, Yugoslavia 46 21N 15 3E
78 Brasov, Rumania 45 47N 25 39E
78 Brașov, Reg., Rum. ...45 50N 25 10E
125 Brass, Nigeria 4 35N 6 14E
125 Brass R., Nigeria 4 15N 6 13E
54 Brasschaat, Belgium .51 19N 4 27E
108 Brassey Ra., Malaysia 5 0N 117 15E
142 Brassey Ra., Western Australia 25 8S 122 15E
163 Brasstown Bald. Mt., U.S.A. 34 54N 83 45W
35 Brasted, Eng., U.K. ...51 16N 0 8E
75 Bratan, Mt., see Morozov, Bulgaria .42 30N 25 10E
57 Brateș, Rumania 46 55N 26 3E
59 Bratislava, Cz. 48 10N 17 7E
91 Bratsk, U.S.S.R. 56 10N 101 30E
81 Bratteborg, Sweden ...57 37N 14 4E
161 Brattleboro, U.S.A. ...42 53N 72 37W
36 Bratton Fleming, England, U.K. 51 7N 3 58W
79 Brattvaer, Norway 63 26N 7 49E
78 Brațul Chilia, R., Rum. 45 25N 29 20E
78 Brațul Sfântu Gheorghe R., Rumania 45 0N 29 20E
78 Bratul Sulina R., Rum. 45 10N 29 20E
74 Bratunac, Yugoslavia 44 13N 19 21E
58 Braunau, Austria 48 15N 13 3E
56 Braunschweig, Ger. ...52 17N 10 28E
36 Braunton, Eng., U.K. 51 6N 4 9W
99 Brava, Somali Rep. ... 1 20N 44 8E
81 Braviken, inlet, Swed. 58 43N 16 45E
168 Bravo del Norte, Rio, Mexico 30 30N 105 0W
167 Brawley, U.S.A. 32 58N 115 30W
49 Bray, dist., France 49 40N 1 40E
45 Bray & Hd., Ireland...53 12N 6 6W
44 Bray Hd., Ireland 51 52N 10 26W
49 Bray sur Seine, France 48 25N 3 14E
174 Brazil, rep., S. Amer. . 5 0N 20 0W
162 Brazil, U.S.A. 39 30N 87 8W
175 Brazilian Highlands, Brazil 18 0S 46 30W
172 Brazo Sur, R., Par.-Arg. 19 30S 64 35W
165 Brazos R., U.S.A. 30 30N 96 20W
130 Brazzaville, Congo (Fr.) 4 9S 15 12E
74 Brčko, Yugoslavia 44 54N 18 46E
144 Breadalbane, Australia 23 48S 139 33E
40 Breadalbane, dist., Scot., U.K. 56 30N 4 15W
142 Breaden, L., W. Australia 25 51S 125 28E
36 Breage, England, U.K. 50 6N 5 17W
146 Bream Bay, N.Z. 35 56S 174 35E
146 Bream Head, N.Z. 35 51S 174 36E
146 Bream Tail, N.Z. 36 3S 174 36E
34 Breamore, Eng., U.K. 50 58N 1 47W
172 Breas, Chile 25 29S 70 24W
109 Brebes, Indonesia 6 52S 109 3E
160 Brechin, Canada 44 33N 79 10W
43 Brechin, Scotland, U.K. 56 44N 2 40W
35 Brechland, reg., England, U.K. 52 30N 0 40E
43 Breck Ness, Scot., U.K. 58 57N 3 20W
166 Breckenridge, Colo., U.S.A. 39 30N 106 2W
164 Breckenridge, Minn., U.S.A. 46 20N 96 36W
165 Breckenridge, Tex., U.S.A. 32 48N 98 55W
55 Breckerfeld, Germany 51 16N 7 29E
37 Brecknock, Co., Wales, United Kingdom 51 58N 3 25W
59 Břeclav, Czechoslovakia 48 46N 16 53E
37 Brecon, Wales, U.K. ..51 57N 3 23W
37 Brecon Beacons, Mts., Wales, U.K. 51 53N 3 27W
54 Breda, Netherlands ...51 35N 4 45E
81 Bredaryd, Sweden 57 10N 13 22E
134 Bredasdorp, S. Africa 34 33S 20 2E
143 Bredbo, Australia 35 58S 149 10E
35 Brede, England, U.K. 50 56N 0 37E
34 Bredon Hill, Eng., U.K. 52 3N 2 2W
134 Breë R., C. Prov., S. Afr. 34 20S 20 45E
143 Breeza, Australia 31 16S 150 14E
74 Bregalnica, R., Y.-slav. 41 50N 22 20E
58 Bregenz, Austria 47 30N 9 45E
81 Bregning, Denmark ...56 8N 8 30E
48 Bréhal, France 48 53N 1 30W
48 Bréhat I., France 48 51N 3 0W
82 Breidi Fd., Iceland 65 15N 24 0W
51 Breil, France 43 56N 7 31E
57 Breisach, Germany 48 2N 7 37E
79 Brekke, Norway 61 1N 5 27E
79 Bremangerland, I., Nor. 61 50N 5 0E
79 Bremangerpollen, Norway 61 51N 5 0E
56 Bremen, Germany 53 4N 8 47E
56 Bremen, land, Germany 53 6N 8 46E
56 Bremerhaven, Germany 53 34N 8 35E
166 Bremerton, U.S.A. 47 30N 122 48W
56 Bremervörde, Germany 53 28N 9 10E
79 Bremnes, Norway 59 48N 5 11E
79 Bremsnes, Norway 63 6N 7 37E
36 Brendon Hills, England, U.K. 51 6N 3 25W
63 Brenes, Spain 37 32N 5 54W
165 Brenham, U.S.A. 30 5N 96 27W
58 Brenner Pass, Alps 47 0N 11 30E
70 Breno, Italy 45 57N 10 20E
154 Brent, Canada 46 0N 78 30W
35 Brent, England, U.K. 51 33N 0 18W
35 Brentwood, Eng., U.K.51 37N 0 19W
133 Brereton Park, S. Africa 26 55S 30 30E
73 Brescia, Italy 45 33N 10 13E
54 Breskens, Netherlands 51 23N 3 33E
60 Breslau, see Wroclaw, Pol. 51 5N 17 5E
49 Bresle R., France 49 58N 1 35E
49 Bresles, France 49 25N 2 13E
42 Bressay, Scotland, U.K. 60 10N 1 6W
42 Bressay I., Scot., U.K. 60 10N 1 5W
42 Bressay Sd., Scot., U.K. 60 8N 1 10W
49 Bresse Plaine de, dist., France 46 20N 5 10E
48 Bressuire, France 46 51N 0 30W
48 Brest, France 48 24N 4 31W
86 Brest, U.S.S.R. 52 10N 23 40E
48 Bretagne, reg., France 48 0N 3 0W
78 Bretçu, Rumania 46 7N 26 18E
48 Breteuil, Eure, France 48 5N 0 53E
49 Breteuil, Oise, France 49 38N 2 18E
165 Breton Sd., U.S.A. 29 40N 89 12W
57 Bretten, Germany 49 2N 8 43E
175 Breu Branco, Brazil ... 4 0S 49 30W
163 Brevard, U.S.A. 35 19N 82 42W
79 Brevik, Norway 59 6N 9 45E
145 Brewarrina, Australia 30 0S 146 51E
155 Brewer, U.S.A. 44 43N 68 50W
34 Brewood, Eng., U.K. .52 41N 2 10W
161 Brewster, N.Y., U.S.A. 41 23N 73 37W
166 Brewster, Wash., U.S.A. 48 10N 119 51W
14 Brewster C., Greenland 70 0N 25 0W
55 Breyell, Germany 51 17N 6 15E
133 Breyten, Trans., S. Afr. 26 16S 30 0E
87 Breytovo, U.S.S.R. ...58 18N 37 50E
163 Brewton, U.S.A. 31 9N 87 2W
122 Brezina, Algeria 33 4N 1 14E
58 Breznice, Cz. 49 32N 13 57E
74 Breznik, Bulgaria 42 44N 22 50E
59 Brezno, Czechoslovakia 48 50N 19 40E
121 Bria, Central Africa ... 6 30N 21 58E
51 Briançon, France 44 54N 6 39E
49 Briare, France 47 38N 2 45E
143 Bribbaree, Australia ...34 10S 147 51E
145 Bribie I., Australia 27 0S 152 58E
129 Brickaville, Malagasy Republic 18 49S 49 4E
49 Bricon, France 48 5N 5 0E
48 Bricquebec, France ...49 29N 1 39W
38 Bride, I. of M., U.K. .54 24N 4 23W
36 Bridestowe, Eng., U.K. 50 41N 4 7W
35 Bridge, England, U.K. 51 14N 1 8E
156 Bridge R., Canada 50 50N 122 40W
41 Bridge of Allan, Scotland, U.K. 56 9N 3 57W
43 Bridge of Don, Scotland, United Kingdom 57 10N 2 8W
41 Bridge of Earn, Scotland, U.K. 56 20N 3 25W
40 Bridge of Orchy, Scotland, U.K. 56 29N 4 48W
40 Bridge of Weir, Scotland, U.K. 55 51N 4 35W
161 Bridgehampton, U.S.A. 40 56N 72 19W
40 Bridgend, Scot., U.K. 55 46N 6 15W
37 Bridgend, Wales, U.K. 51 30N 3 35W
166 Bridgeport, Calif., U.S.A. 38 14N 119 15W
161 Bridgeport, Conn., U.S.A. 41 12N 73 12W
164 Bridgeport, Neb., U.S.A. 41 42N 103 10W
165 Bridgeport, Tex., U.S.A. 33 15N 97 45W
166 Bridger, U.S.A. 45 20N 108 58W
162 Bridgeton, U.S.A. 39 29N 75 10W
169 Bridgetown, Barbados 13 0N 59 30W
155 Bridgetown, Canada ...44 55N 65 12W
45 Bridgetown, Ireland ...52 13N 6 33W
142 Bridgetown, W. Australia 33 58S 116 7E
155 Bridgewater, Canada .44 25N 64 31W
161 Bridgewater, Mass., U.S.A. 41 59N 70 56W
164 Bridgewater, S.D., U.S.A. 43 34N 97 29W
143 Bridgewater, Australia 36 36S 143 59E
34 Bridgnorth, Eng., U.K. 52 33N 2 25W
161 Bridgton, U.S.A. 44 5N 70 41W
36 Bridgwater, Eng., U.K. 51 7N 3 0W
36 Bridgwater B., England, U.K. 51 15N 3 15W
39 Bridlington, Eng., U.K. 54 6N 0 11W
39 Bridlington B., England, U.K. 54 4N 0 10W
36 Bridport, Eng., U.K. .50 43N 2 45W
49 Brie, Comte Robert, Fr. 48 40N 2 35E
49 Brie, Plaine de, dist., Fr. 48 35N 3 10E
48 Briec, France 48 6N 4 0W
49 Brienne le Château, Fr. 48 24N 4 30E
49 Brienon, France 48 0N 3 35E
57 Brienz, Switzerland ...46 46N 8 2E
57 Brienzer See, Switz. ...46 44N 7 53E
38 Brierfield, Eng., U.K. 53 49N 2 15W
34 Brierley Hill, Eng., U.K. 52 29N 2 7W
49 Briey, France 49 14N 5 57E
124 Brifu, Gambia 13 30N 14 0E
57 Brig, Switzerland 46 18N 7 59E
39 Brigg, England, U.K. 53 33N 0 30W
164 Briggsdale, U.S.A. 40 40N 104 20W
166 Brigham City, U.S.A. 41 30N 112 1W
34 Brighstone, Eng., U.K. 50 38N 1 36W
143 Bright, Australia 36 42S 146 56E
35 Brightlingsea, England, U.K. 51 49N 1 1E
154 Brighton, Canada 44 3N 77 44W
35 Brighton, Eng., U.K. .50 50N 0 9W
145 Brighton, S. Australia 35 1S 138 30E
165 Brighton, Col., U.S.A. 39 59N 104 50W
100 Brighton, Mich., U.S.A. 42 33N 83 48W
160 Brighton, Pa., U.S.A. 40 42N 80 19W
147 Brightwater, N.Z. 41 22S 173 9E
48 Brignogan Plages, Fr. 48 40N 4 20W
51 Brignoles, France 43 25N 6 5E
35 Brigstock, Eng., U.K. 52 27N 0 38W
64 Brihuega, Spain 40 45N 2 52W
124 Brikama, Gambia 13 15N 16 45W
34 Brill, England, U.K. .51 49N 1 3W
156 Brilliant, Canada 49 19N 117 55W
160 Brilliant, U.S.A. 40 15N 80 39W
56 Brilon, Germany 51 23N 8 32E
37 Brimfield, Eng., U.K. 52 18N 2 42W
73 Brindisi, Italy 40 39N 17 55E
143 Bringagee, Australia .34 28S 145 44E
165 Brinkley, U.S.A. 34 55N 91 15W
34 Brinklow, Eng., U.K. 52 25N 1 22W
34 Brinkworth, Eng., U.K. 51 33N 1 59W
145 Brinkworth, S. Austral. 33 40S 138 20E
43 Brinyan, Scot., U.K. .59 8N 3 0W
155 Brion I., Canada 47 46N 61 26W
48 Brionne, France 49 11N 0 43E
50 Brioude, France 45 18N 3 23E
48 Briouze, France 48 42N 0 23W
145 Brisbane, Australia ...27 25S 152 54E
145 Brisbane R., Australia 27 0S 152 25E
36 Bristol, England, U.K. 51 26N 2 35W
161 Bristol, Conn., U.S.A. 41 44N 72 37W
161 Bristol, Mass., U.S.A. 41 40N 71 15W
161 Bristol, Pa., U.S.A. ...40 7N 74 52W
164 Bristol, S.D., U.S.A. .45 25N 97 43W
167 Bristol L., U.S.A. 34 23N 116 0W
36 Bristol Channel, England, U.K. 51 18N 3 30W
15 Bristol I., Falkland Is. Dependencies 58 45S 28 0W
35 Briston, England, U.K. 52 52N 1 4E
165 Bristow, U.S.A. 35 5N 96 28W
15 Br. Antarctic Territory, Antarctica 66 0S 45 0W
156 Br. Colombia, prov., Can. 55 0N 125 15W
174 Br. Guiana, see Guyana, S. Am. 5 0N 59 0W
168 Br. Honduras, col., Central America 17 0N 88 30W
11 British Indian Ocean Terr. 5 0S 70 0E
28 British Isles, Europe .55 0N 4 0W
37 Briton Ferry, Wales, United Kingdom 51 37N 3 50W
133 Brits, Trans., S. Africa 25 37S 27 48E
134 Britstown, S. Africa ...30 37S 23 30E
145 Britt, Canada 45 46N 80 35W
48 Brittany, reg., see Bretagne, France ...48 0N 3 0W
45 Brittas, Ireland 53 14N 6 29W
81 Brittatorp, Sweden 57 3N 14 58E
133 Britten, Trans., S. Afr. 27 42S 25 17E
164 Britton, S.D., U.S.A. .45 50N 97 47W
50 Brive, France 45 10N 1 32E
64 Briviesca, Spain 42 32N 3 19W
36 Brixham, Eng., U.K. .50 24N 3 31W
144 Brixton, Australia 23 32S 144 52E
35 Brixworth, Eng., U.K. 52 20N 0 54W
34 Brize Norton, Eng., U.K. 51 46N 1 35W
59 Brno, Czechoslovakia .49 10N 16 35E
80 Bro, Sweden 59 13N 13 2E
104 Broach, India 21 47N 73 0E
42 Broad B., Scot., U.K. 58 14N 6 16W
163 Broad R., U.S.A. 34 30N 81 26W
142 Broad Arrow, W. Australia 30 23S 121 15E
34 Broad Chalke, Eng., U.K. 51 2N 1 54W
36 Broad Clyst, Eng., U.K. 50 46N 3 27W
45 Broad Haven, Ireland 54 20N 9 55W
37 Broad Haven, Wales, United Kingdom 51 46N 5 6W
41 Broad Law, Mt., Scotland, U.K. 55 30N 3 22W
36 Broad Sd., Eng., U.K. 49 56N 6 19W
144 Broad Sd., Australia .22 0S 149 45E
44 Broadford, Clare, Ire. 52 48N 8 38W
44 Broadford, Limerick, Ireland 52 21N 8 59W
42 Broadford, Scot., U.K. 57 14N 5 55W
143 Broadford, Australia .37 14S 145 4E
36 Broadhembury, England. U.K. 50 49N 3 16W
142 Broadhurst Ra., W. Australia 22 30S 122 30E
35 Broadstairs, Eng., U.K. 51 21N 1 28E
164 Broadus, U.S.A. 45 28N 105 27W
34 Broadway, Eng., U.K. 52 2N 1 51W
45 Broadway, Ireland 52 13N 6 23W
36 Broadwindsor, England, U.K. 50 49N 2 49W
81 Broager, Denmark 54 52N 9 40E
81 Broaryd, Sweden 57 7N 12 55E
157 Brochet, Manitoba, Can. 57 55N 101 40W
154 Brochet, Quebec, Can. 47 12N 72 42W
157 Brochet, Lac, Canada 58 50N 101 30W
34 Brockenhurst, Eng., U.K. 50 49N 1 34W
56 Brocken, Mt., Germany 51 48N 10 40E
143 Brocklesby, Australia 35 48S 146 40E
142 Brockman Mt., Western Australia .22 25S 117 15E
160 Brockport, U.S.A. 43 12N 77 56W
161 Brockton, Mass., U.S.A. 42 8N 71 2W
160 Brockton, N.Y., U.S.A. 42 24N 79 27W
154 Brockville, Canada 44 37N 75 38W
164 Brockway, Mont., U.S.A. 47 18N 105 46W
160 Brockwayville, U.S.A. 41 14N 78 48W
34 Brockworth, Eng., U.K. 51 51N 2 9W
107 Brocton, U.S.A. 42 25N 79 26W
74 Brod, Yugoslavia 41 35N 21 17E
74 Brodarevo, Yugoslavia 43 14N 19 44E
153 Brodeur Pen., Canada 72 0N 88 0W
40 Brodick, Scotland, U.K. 55 34N 5 9W
60 Brodnica, Poland 53 15N 19 25E
86 Brody, U.S.S.R. 50 5N 25 10E
133 Broederspruit, S. Africa 26 49S 25 8E
166 Brogan, U.S.A. 44 14N 117 32W
48 Broglie, France 49 0N 0 30E
145 Broken B., Australia .33 30S 151 15E
164 Broken Bow, Neb., U.S.A. 41 25N 99 35W
165 Broken Bow, Okla., U.S.A. 34 2N 94 43W
143 Broken Hill, Australia 31 58S 141 29E
132 Broken Hill, see Kabwe, Zambia 14 27S 28 28E
81 Brokind, Sweden 58 11N 15 41E
55 Bröl R., Germany 50 53N 7 26E
38 Bromborough, Eng., U.K. 53 20N 3 0W
34 Bromfield, Eng., U.K. 52 24N 2 46W
34 Bromham, Eng., U.K. 51 23N 2 3W
157 Bromhead, Canada 49 18N 103 40W
35 Bromley, Eng. U.K. .51 20N 0 5E
81 Bromölla, Sweden 56 5N 14 25E
39 Brompton, Eng., U.K. 54 22N 1 25W
34 Bromsgrove, Eng., U.K. 52 20N 2 3E
34 Bromyard, Eng., U.K. 52 12N 2 30W
81 Brønderslev, Denmark 57 17N 9 55W
124 Brong Ahafo, Reg., Ghana 7 50N 2 0E
133 Bronkhorstspruit, Transvaal, S. Africa 25 46S 28 45E
82 Brønnöysund, Norway 65 27N 12 25E
87 Bronnitsy, U.S.S.R. ...55 27N 38 10E
30 Bronsa, Ireland 52 59N 7 54W
165 Bronte, U.S.A. 31 54N 100 18W
73 Bronte, Italy 37 48N 14 49E
46 Brookeborough, Northern Ireland U.K. 54 19N 7 23W
164 Brookfield, U.S.A. 39 50N 92 50W
165 Brookhaven, U.S.A. ...31 40N 90 25W
166 Brookings, Ore., U.S.A. 42 4N 124 10W
164 Brookings, S.D., U.S.A. 44 20N 96 45W
144 Brooklands, Australia 18 5S 144 0E
160 Brooklin, Canada 43 55N 78 55W
161 Brooklyn, N.Y., U.S.A. 40 45N 73 58W
156 Brookmere, Canada ...49 52N 120 53W
156 Brooks Canada 50 35N 111 55W
148 Brooks Ra., Alaska, ...68 40N 147 0W
163 Brooksville, U.S.A. 28 32N 82 21W
142 Brookton, W. Australia 32 22S 116 57E
162 Brookville, Ind., U.S.A. 39 25N 85 0W
160 Brookville, Pa., U.S.A. 41 10N 79 6W
145 Brooloo, Australia 26 30S 152 36E
42 Broom, L., Scot., U.K. 57 55N 5 15W
42 Broom L., Lit., Scotland, United Kingdom 57 52N 5 20W
138 Broome, W. Australia 18 0S 122 15E
142 Broomehill, W. Austral. 33 40S 117 36E
41 Broomhill, Eng., U.K. 55 19N 1 36W
48 Broons, France 48 20N 2 16W
43 Brora, Scotland, U.K. 58 0N 3 50W
43 Brora L., Scot., U.K. .58 3N 3 58W
43 Brora R., Scot., U.K. 58 4N 3 54W
81 Brösarp, Sweden 55 44N 14 8E
34 Broseley, Eng., U.K. .52 36N 2 30W
44 Brosna R., Lit., Ireland 53 8N 8 0W
78 Broșteni, Rumania 47 14N 25 43E

MAP
166 Brothers, U.S.A. 43 56N 120 39W
39 Brothertoft, Eng., U.K. 53 0N 0 5W
39 Brotton, Eng., U.K. ...54 34N 0 55W
79 Brøttum, Norway 61 2N 10 32E
38 Brough, Westermorland, England, U.K. 54 32N 2 19W
39 Brough, Yorks., England, United Kingdom 53 44N 0 35W
43 Brough Hd., Scot., U.K. 59 8N 3 20W
46 Broughshane, Northern Ireland, U.K. 54 54N 6 12W
144 Broughton, Australia .20 10s 146 20E
39 Broughton, Lincoln, England, U.K. 53 33N 0 36W
35 Broughton, Northampton, England, U.K. 52 22N 0 45W
39 Broughton, Yorkshire, England, U.K. 54 26N 1 8W
41 Broughton, Scot., U.K. 55 37N 3 25W
143 Broughton Is., Austral. 32 37s 152 20E
38 Broughton-in-Furnace, England, U.K. 54 17N 3 12W
41 Broughty Ferry, Scotland, U.K. 56 29N 2 50W
59 Broumov, Cz. 50 35N 16 20E
54 Brouwershaven, Neth. 51 45N 3 55E
81 Brovst, Denmark 57 6N 9 31E
164 Browerville, U.S.A. ...46 3N 94 50W
145 Brown Mt., S. Australia 32 30N 138 0E
36 Brown Willy, Mt., England, U.K. 50 35N 4 34W
165 Brownfield, U.S.A. 33 10N 102 15W
44 Browngrove, Ireland .53 33N 8 49W
34 Brownhills, Eng., U.K. 52 38N 1 57W
166 Browning, U.S.A. 48 35N 113 10W
157 Brownlee, Canada 50 43N 105 59W
146 Browns Bay, N.Z. 36 40s 174 40E
45 Browntown Hd., Ire. .52 8N 7 8W
166 Brownsville, Ore., U.S.A. 44 29N 123 0W
165 Brownsville, Tenn., U.S.A. 35 35N 89 15W
165 Brownsville, Tex., U.S.A. 25 56N 97 25W
165 Brownwood, U.S.A. ...31 45N 99 0W
165 Brownwood L., U.S.A. 31 51N 98 35W
41 Broxburn, Scot., U.K. 55 56N 3 23W
63 Brozas, Spain 39 37N 6 47W
107 Bruas, Malaysia 4 31N 100 46E
49 Bruay, France 50 29N 2 33E
147 Bruce B., N.Z. 43 35s 169 35E
142 Bruce Mt., W. Austral. 22 31s 118 6E
154 Bruce Mines, Canada .46 20N 83 45W
160 Bruce Pen., Canada ...45 0N 81 15W
142 Bruce Rock, W. Austral. 31 51s 118 2E
57 Bruchsal, Germany ...49 9N 8 39E
58 Bruck, Styria, Austria 47 24N 15 16E
59 Bruck, Lower Austria 48 1N 16 47E
57 Brückenau, Germany .50 17N 9 48E
36 Brue, R., England, U.K. 51 10N 2 50W
42 Bruernish Pt., Scotland, U.K. 57 0N 7 2 2W
44 Bruff, Ireland 52 29N 8 35W
54 Bruges, *see* Brugge, Belgium 51 13N 3 13E
57 Brugg, Switzerland ...47 29N 8 11E
54 Brugge, Belgium 51 13N 3 13E
54 Brühl, Germany 50 49N 6 51E
156 Brule, Canada 53 15N 117 58W
48 Brûlon, France 47 58N 0 15W
49 Brumath, France 48 43N 7 40E
79 Brumunddal, Norway 60 53N 10 56E
163 Brundidge, U.S.A. 31 43N 85 45W
166 Bruneau, U.S.A. 42 57N 115 55W
166 Bruneau, R., U.S.A. ...42 45N 115 50W
108 Brunei, tn., Brunei 4 52N 115 0E
108 Brunei, state, E. Indies 4 52N 115 0E
80 Brunflo, Sweden 63 4N 14 50E
80 Brunkeberg, Norway .59 25N 8 30E
80 Brunna, Sweden 59 54N 17 26E
57 Brunnen, Switzerland 46 59N 8 37E
147 Brunner, New Zealand 42 27s 171 20E
147 Brunner, L., N.Z. 42 27s 171 20E
80 Brunnsvik, Sweden ...60 14 15 8E
157 Bruno, Canada 52 20N 105 30W
80 Brunsberg, Sweden ...59 38N 12 52E
56 Brunsbüttelkoog, Ger. 53 52N 9 13E
55 Brunssum, Netherlands 50 57N 5 59E
56 Brunswick, *see* Braunschweig, Germany 52 17N 10 28E
163 Brunswick, Ga., U.S.A. 31 10N 81 30W
155 Brunswick, Me., U.S.A. 43 53N 69 50W
162 Brunswick, Md., U.S.A. 39 20N 77 38W
164 Brunswick, Mo., U.S.A. 39 26N 93 10W
160 Brunswick, Ohio, U.S.A. 41 15N 81 50W
138 Brunswick B., W. Australia 15 15s 124 50E
142 Brunswick Junc., W. Australia 33 15s 115 50E
176 Brunswick Pen., Chile 53 30s 71 30W
59 Bruntál, Cz. 50 0N 17 27E
41 Brunton Eng., U.K. .55 2N 2 6W
145 Bruny I., Australia ...43 20s 147 15E
44 Bruree, Ireland 52 25N 8 40W
74 Brusartsi, Bulgaria ...43 40N 23 5E
164 Brush, U.S.A. 40 17N 103 33W
161 Brushton, U.S.A. 44 50N 74 62W
57 Brusio, Switzerland ...46 14N 10 8E
173 Brusque, Brazil 27 5s 49 0W
54 Brussel (Bruxelles), Belg. 50 51N 4 21E
160 Brussels, Canada 43 45N 85 2W
36 Bruton, England, U.K. 51 6N 2 28W
79 Bruvik, Norway 60 29N 5 40E
54 Bruxelles (Brussel), Belgium 50 51N 4 21E
49 Bruyères, France 48 10N 6 40E
135 Bruyns Hill, S. Africa 29 29s 30 41E
75 Bryagovo, Bulgaria ...41 58N 25 8E
162 Bryan, Ohio, U.S.A. ...41 30N 84 30W
165 Bryan, Texas, U.S.A. .30 40N 96 27W
45 Bryan, Mt., S. Australia 33 30s 139 0E
86 Bryansk, U.S.S.R. 53 13N 34 25E
89 Bryanskoye, U.S.S.R. 44 9N 47 10E
64 Bryant, U.S.A. 44 39N 97 26W
60 Brydges, Canada 42 54N 81 28W
79 Bryggja, Norway 61 56N 5 27E
36 Bryher I., Eng., U.K. 49 57N 6 21W
37 Brymbo, Wales, U.K. 53 4N 3 5W
37 Brynamman, Wales, U.K. 51 49N 3 52W
79 Bryne, Norway 58 45N 5 36E
37 Bryn Mawr, Wales, U.K. 51 48N 3 10W
37 Bryncethin, Wales, U.K. 51 32N 3 34W
81 Bryrup, Denmark 56 2N 9 30E
163 Bryson City, U.S.A. ...35 28N 83 25W
74 Brza Palanka, Y.-slav. 44 28N 22 37E
74 Brzava, R., Yugoslavia 45 21N 20 45E
60 Brześć Kujawski, Poland 52 36N 18 55E
60 Brzeg, Poland 50 52N 17 30E
59 Brzesko, Poland 49 59N 20 34E
60 Brzeziny, Poland 51 49N 19 42E
59 Brzozów, Poland 49 41N 22 3E
123 Bu Athlah, Libya 30 1N 15 30E
83 Bu Nujaym, Libya 30 35N 15 40E
143 Buangor Mt., Australia 37 21s 143 11E
109 Buapinang, Indonesia 4 40s 121 30E
109 Buayan, Philippines ... 5 3N 125 28E
124 Buba, Port. Guinea ...11 40N 14 59W
100 Bubiyan I., Kuwait ...29 50N 48 15E
131 Bubu R., Tanzania 5 35s 35 27E
174 Bucaramanga, Col. 7 0N 73 0W
71 Bucchianico, Italy ...42 20N 14 10E
127 Buccurale, Ethiopia ... 4 32N 42 0E
78 Bucecea, Rumania 47 47N 26 28E
76 Bŭcha, R., Bulgaria ...41 53N 24 26E
86 Buchach, U.S.S.R. 49 5N 25 25E
143 Buchan, Australia 37 20s 148 12E
43 Buchan, dist., Scot., U.K. 57 32N 2 8W
43 Buchan Ness, Scotland, United Kingdom 57 29N 1 48W
157 Buchanan, Canada 51 40N 102 45W
124 Buchanan, Liberia 5 57N 10 2W
165 Buchanan, L., U.S.A. 30 50N 98 25W
155 Buchans, Canada 49 0N 57 2W
78 Bucharest, Rumania .44 27N 26 10E
56 Buchholz, Germany ...53 19N 9 51E
57 Buchloe, Germany 48 3N 10 45E
40 Buchlyvie, Scot., U.K. 56 7N 4 20W
43 Buck, The, mt., Scotland, U.K. 57 19N 3 0W
35 Buckden, Eng., U.K. .52 17N 0 16W
56 Buckeburg, Germany .52 16N 9 2E
167 Buckeye, U.S.A. 33 28N 112 40W
36 Buckfastleigh, England, U.K. 50 28N 3 47W
162 Buckhannon, U.S.A. .39 2N 80 10W
41 Buckhaven, Scot., U.K. 56 10N 3 2W
43 Buckie, Scotland, U.K. 57 40N 2 58W
154 Buckingham, Canada .45 37N 75 24W
35 Buckingham, Eng., U.K. 52 0N 0 59W
35 Buckingham, Co., England, U.K. 51 50N 0 55W
138 Buckingham B., N. Terr., Australia 12 10s 135 40E
106 Buckingham Can., India 14 0N 80 5E
36 Buckland, Eng., U.K. 50 51N 2 25W
36 Buckland Brewer, England, U.K. 50 56N 4 14W
166 Buckley, U.S.A. 47 10N 122 2W
37 Buckley, Wales, U.K. 53 10N 3 5W
165 Bucklin, U.S.A. 37 37N 99 40W
43 Bucksburn, Scot., U.K. 57 10N 2 10W
49 Bucquoy, France 50 9N 2 43E
155 Buctouche, Canada ...46 30N 64 45W
78 Bucuresti, Rumania ...44 27N 26 10E
162 Bucyrus, U.S.A. 40 48N 83 0W
47 Budacul, Munte, Mt., Rumania 47 5N 25 40E
59 Budafok, Hungary 47 26N 19 2E
103 Budalin, Burma 22 20N 95 10E
59 Budapest, Hungary ...47 29N 19 5E
104 Budaun, India 28 5N 79 10E
15 Budd Coast, Antarctica 67 0s 112 0E
41 Buddon Ness, Scotland, United Kingdom 56 29N 2 42W
72 Buddusò, Italy 40 35N 9 18E
36 Bude, England, U.K. .50 49N 4 33W
35 Bude Bay, Eng., U.K. 50 50N 4 40W
55 Buderiche, Germany .51 14N 6 39E
78 Budeşti, Rumania 44 13N 26 30E
105 Budge Budge, India ...22 30N 88 25E
64 Budia, Spain 40 38N 2 46W
82 Budir, Iceland 64 48N 23 21W
130 Budjala, Congo 2 50N 19 40E
36 Budleigh Salterton, England, U.K. 50 37N 3 19W
107 Budop, Vietnam 11 58N 106 50E
71 Budrio, Italy 44 31N 11 31E
74 Budva, Yugoslavia ...42 17N 18 50E
60 Budzyn, Poland 52 54N 16 59E
125 Buea, Cameroon 4 10N 9 9E
167 Buena Vista, Col., U.S.A. 38 56N 106 6W
162 Buena Vista, Va., U.S.A. 37 47N 79 23W
167 Buena Vista L., U.S.A. 35 15N 119 21W
172 Buenaventura, Chile .29 15s 69 40W
174 Buenaventura, Col. ... 4 0N 77 0W
172 Buenos Aires, Arg. 34 30s 58 20W
176 Buenos Aires L., Chile 46 35s 72 30W
157 Buffalo, Canada 50 49N 110 42W
165 Buffalo, Mo., U.S.A. ...37 40N 93 5W
160 Buffalo, N.Y., U.S.A. .42 55N 78 50W
165 Buffalo, Okla., U.S.A. 36 55N 99 42W
164 Buffalo, S.D., U.S.A. .45 39N 103 31W
166 Buffalo, Wyo., U.S.A. 44 25N 106 50W
156 Buffalo L., Canada 60 20N 115 30W
156 Buffalo Head Hills, Can. 58 0N 116 20W
157 Buffalo Narrows, Can. 55 52N 108 28W
134 Buffels, R., S. Africa 29 36s 17 15E
163 Buford, U.S.A. 34 5N 84 0W
53 Bug R., Poland 51 20N 23 40E
88 Bug R., U.S.S.R. 48 0N 31 0E
174 Buga, Colombia 4 0N 77 0W
131 Buganda, Prov., Uganda 0 0N 31 30E
131 Buganga, Uganda 0 25N 32 0E
50 Bugeat, France 45 36N 1 55E
38 Buglawton, Eng., U.K. 53 12N 2 11W
36 Bugle, England, U.K. 50 23N 4 46W
74 Bugojno, Yugoslavia .44 2N 17 25E
90 Bugrusian, U.S.S.R. ...53 42N 52 15E
108 Bugsuk I., Philippines 8 15N 117 15E
84 Bugulma, U.S.S.R. 54 38N 52 40E
125 Buguma, Nigeria 4 42N 6 55E
112 Bugun Shara Mts., Mongolia 48 30N 102 0E
131 Buguri, Uganda 0 35N 33 45E
78 Buhăeşti, Rumania ...46 47N 27 32E
166 Buhl, Idaho, U.S.A. ...42 35N 114 54W
164 Buhl, Minn., U.S.A. ...47 30N 92 46W
78 Buhuşi, Rumania 46 41N 26 45E
40 Buie L., Scot., U.K. ...56 20N 5 55W
37 Builth Wells, Wales, United Kingdom ...52 10N 3 26W
101 Buina Qara, Afghan. .36 20N 67 0E
87 Buinsk, U.S.S.R. 55 0N 48 18E
51 Buis les Baronnies, Fr. 44 17N 5 16E
62 Buitrago, Spain 41 0N 3 38W
63 Bujalance, Spain 37 54N 4 23W
64 Bujaraloz, Spain 41 29N 0 10W
71 Buje, Yugoslavia 45 24N 13 39E
101 Bujnurd, Iran 37 35N 57 15E
131 Bujumbura (Usumbura), Burundi 3 16s 29 18E
59 Bük, Hungary 47 22N 16 45E
91 Bukachacha, U.S.S.R. 52 55N 116 50E
130 Bukama, Congo 9 10s 25 50E
131 Bukandula, Uganda ... 0 13N 31 50E
76 Bukanik, Mt., Albania 41 0N 20 15E
131 Bukavu, Congo 2 20s 28 52E
131 Bukene, Tanzania 4 15s 32 48E
90 Bukhara, U.S.S.R. 39 50N 64 10E
131 Bukima, Tanzania 1 50s 33 25E
107 Bukit Mertajam, Malay. 5 22N 100 28E
108 Bukittinggi, Indonesia 0 20s 100 20E
106 Bukkapatnam, India .14 14N 77 46E
131 Bukoba, Tanzania 1 20s 31 49E
125 Bukuru, Nigeria 9 42N 8 48E
109 Bula, Indonesia 3 10s 130 20E
111 Bulak, China 45 2N 82 5E
109 Bulan, Philippines 12 45N 124 0E
104 Bulandshahr, India ...28 28N 77 58E
103 Bulantai, China 36 33N 92 18E
126 Bûlâq, Egypt 25 10N 30 38E
132 Bulawayo, Rhodesia .20 7s 28 32E
104 Buldana, India 20 30N 76 18E
34 Bulford, Eng., U.K. ...51 11N 1 45W
112 Bulgan, Mongolia 48 46N 103 28E
75 Bulgaria, rep., Europe 42 35N 25 30E
145 Bulgroo, Australia 25 47s 143 58E
99 Bulhar, Somali Rep. .10 25N 44 30E
109 Buli Bay, Indonesia ... 1 5N 128 25E
108 Buliluyan C., Phil. 8 20N 117 15E
91 Bulinski, U.S.S.R. 68 10N 123 5E
34 Bulkington, Eng., U.K. 52 29N 1 25W
91 Bulkur, U.S.S.R. 71 50N 126 30E
165 Bull Shoals L., U.S.A. 36 40N 93 5W
142 Bullabulling, Australia 31 0s 120 55E
55 Bullange, Belgium 50 24N 6 15E
63 Bullaque R., Spain 39 20N 4 13W
142 Bullara, W. Australia 22 30s 114 2E
142 Bullaring, W. Australia 32 28s 117 40E
65 Bullas, Spain 38 2N 1 40W
57 Bulle, Switzerland ...46 37N 7 3E
147 Buller Gorge, N.Z. 41 40s 172 10E
147 Buller R., N.Z. 41 45N 172 25E
142 Bullfinch, W. Australia 30 58s 119 3E
143 Bulli, Australia 34 15s 150 57E
144 Bullock Creek, Austral. 17 40s 144 30E
145 Bulloo R., Australia ...27 20s 144 40E
145 Bulloo Downs, Austral. 28 28s 143 0E
146 Bulls, New Zealand ...40 10s 175 24E
49 Bully-les-Mines, France 50 27N 2 44E
172 Bulnes, Chile 36 42s 72 19W
99 Bulo Burti, Somali Rep. 3 50N 45 33E
130 Bulongo, Congo 4 44s 21 30E
145 Buloo Downs, Australia 28 30s 144 10E
104 Bulsar, India 20 40N 72 58E
135 Bultfontein, S. Africa 28 18s 26 10E
109 Bulu Karakelong, Indon. 4 35N 126 50E
109 Buluan, Philippines ... 9 0N 125 30E
91 Bulun, U.S.S.R. 70 37N 127 30E
111 Bulun Tokchai, *see* Puluntohai, China .47 2N 87 29E
134 Bulwater, S. Africa ...32 29s 21 52E
39 Bulwell, England, U.K. 53 1N 1 12W
135 Bulwer, Natal, S. Afr. 29 46s 29 47E
130 Bumba, Congo 2 13N 22 30E
167 Bumble Bee, U.S.A. ...34 8N 112 18W
130 Bumbuli, Congo 3 25s 20 28E
125 Bumbum, Nigeria 14 10N 8 10E
103 Bumhpa Bum, Mt., Burma 26 40N 97 20E
132 Bumi, R., Rhodesia ...17 30s 28 30E
131 Buna, Kenya 2 58N 39 30E
144 Buna, Papua 8 31s 148 30E
100 Bunaiyin, Saudi Arabia 23 10N 51 8E
143 Bunaloo, Australia 35 47s 144 35E
44 Bunaw, Ireland 51 47N 9 50W
46 Bunbeg, Ireland 55 4N 8 18W
142 Bunbury, W. Australia 33 20s 115 35E
45 Bunclody, Ireland 52 40N 6 40W
46 Buncrana, Ireland 55 8N 7 28W
144 Bundaberg, Australia .24 54s 152 22E
56 Bünde, Germany 52 11N 8 33E
55 Bunde, Netherlands ...50 54N 5 44E
104 Bundi, India 25 30N 75 35E
46 Bundoran, Ireland 54 24N 8 17W
127 Bundukia, Sudan 5 14N 30 55E
143 Bundure, Australia 35 15s 146 2E
40 Bunessan, Scot., U.K. 56 18N 6 15W
35 Bungay, Eng. U.K. ...52 27N 1 26E
143 Bungendore, Australia 35 14s 149 30E
131 Bungoma, Kenya 0 34N 34 34E
114 Bungo-suido, chan., Japan 33 0N 132 15E
108 Bunguran (Natuna) Is., Indonesia 4 0N 108 0E
108 Bunguran N. Is., Indon. 4 45N 108 0E
108 Bunguran S. Is., Indon. 3 0N 109 55E
143 Bungwahl, Australia .32 25s 153 0E
131 Bunia, Congo 1 35N 30 20E
102 Bunji, Kashmir 35 45N 74 40E
108 Bunju I., Indonesia ... 3 35N 117 50E
167 Bunkerville, U.S.A. ...36 47N 114 6W
130 Bunkeya, Congo 10 22s 27 1E
165 Bunkie, U.S.A. 31 1N 92 12W
45 Bunmahon, Ireland ...52 8N 7 22W
46 Bunnanaddan, Ireland 54 3N 8 35W
163 Bunnell, U.S.A. 29 28N 81 12W
46 Bunnyconnellan, Ire. .54 7N 9 1W
146 Bunnythorpe, N.Z. 40 16s 175 39E
65 Buñol, Spain 39 25N 0 47W
35 Buntingford, Eng., U.K. 51 57N 0 1W
108 Buntok, Indonesia 1 40s 114 58E
125 Bununu, Nigeria 10 6N 9 25E
125 Bununu, Nigeria 9 51N 9 32E
35 Bunwell, Eng., U.K. .52 30N 1 9E
125 Bunza, Nigeria 12 8N 4 0E
109 Buol, Indonesia 1 15N 121 32E
14 Buor Khaya B., U.S.S.R. 73 0N 133 0E
126 Buqbuq, Egypt 31 29N 25 29E
99 Bur Acaba, Somali Rep. 3 12N 44 20E
100 Buraida, Saudi Arabia 26 20N 44 8E
101 Buraimi Oasis, Oman .24 15N 55 43E
99 Burao, Somali Rep. ... 9 32N 45 32E
165 Buras, U.S.A. 29 20N 89 33W
38 Burbage, Derby, England, U.K. 53 15N 1 55W
34 Burbage, Leics., England, U.K. 52 31N 1 20W
34 Burbage, Wilts., England, U.K. 51 21N 1 40W
167 Burbank, U.S.A. 34 9N 118 23W
145 Burcher, N.S.W., Australia 33 25s 147 10E
55 Burcht, Belgium 51 12N 4 21E
111 Burchun, China 48 0N 86 7E
100 Burdur, Turkey 37 45N 30 22E
105 Burdwan, India 23 16N 87 54E
35 Bure, R., Eng., U.K. .52 38N 1 38E
82 Bureå, Sweden 64 36N 21 15E
82 Burfell, Iceland 64 5N 20 56W
160 Burford, Canada 43 7N 80 27W
34 Burford, Eng., U.K. ...51 48N 1 38W
56 Burg Magdeburg, Ger. 52 16N 11 50E
56 Burg, Schleswig-Holstein, Germany 54 25N 11 10E
126 Burg el Arab, Egypt .30 54N 29 32E
126 Burg et Tuyur, Sudan 20 55N 27 56E
100 Burgan, Kuwait, Asia 29 0N 47 57E
75 Burgas, Bulgaria 42 33N 27 29E
75 Burgas, prov., Bulgaria 42 25N 27 0E
75 Burgaski Zaliv, B., Bulgaria 42 30N 27 39E
56 Burgdorf, Germany ...52 27N 10 0E
59 Burgdorf, Switzerland 47 3N 7 37E
59 Burgenland, prov., Austria 47 20N 16 20E
135 Burgersdorp, S. Africa 31 0s 26 20E
133 Burgersfort, S. Africa 24 38s 30 18E
134 Burgerville, S. Africa .30 44s 24 17E
35 Burgess Hill, Eng., U.K. 50 57N 0 7W
155 Burgeo, Canada 47 37N 57 38W
39 Burgh-le-Marsh, England, U.K. 53 10N 0 15E
34 Burghclere, Eng., U.K. 51 19N 1 20W
43 Burghead, Scot., U.K. 57 42N 3 30W
43 Burghead B., Scot., U.K. 57 40N 3 33W
72 Burgio, Italy 37 35N 13 18E
57 Burglengenfeld, Ger. .49 11N 12 2E
64 Burgo de Osma, Spain 41 35N 3 4E
62 Burgohondo, Spain 40 26N 4 47W
64 Burgos, Spain 42 21N 3 41W
62 Burgos, prov., Spain .42 21N 3 42W
56 Burgstädt, Germany .50 55N 12 49W
56 Burgsteinfurt, Ger. ...52 9N 7 23E
81 Burgsvik, Sweden 57 3N 18 19E
63 Burguillos del Cerro, Sp. 38 23N 6 35W
49 Burgundy (reg.), *see* Bourgogne, France .47 0N 4 30E
104 Burhanpur, India 21 18N 76 20E
48 Burhou Rocks, Channel Islands, U.K. 49 45N 2 15W
127 Buri Pen., Ethiopia ...15 25N 39 55E
109 Burias I., Philippines .13 5N 122 55E
131 Burigi, L., Tanzania ... 2 2s 31 22E
155 Burin, Canada 47 1N 55 14W
98 Burin, Jordan 32 11N 35 15E
107 Buriram, Thailand 15 0N 103 0E
127 Burji, Ethiopia 5 29N 37 51E
165 Burkburnett, U.S.A. .34 7N 98 35W
166 Burke, U.S.A. 47 31N 115 56W
144 Burke R., Australia ...22 35s 140 5E
144 Burketown, Australia 17 45s 139 33E
154 Burk's Falls, Canada .45 37N 79 10W
34 Burley, Hants, England, U.K. 50 49N 1 41W
39 Burley, Yorks., England, U.K. 53 55N 1 46W
166 Burley, U.S.A. 42 37N 113 55W
160 Burlington, Canada ...43 25N 79 45W
164 Burlington, Col., U.S.A. 39 21N 102 18W
164 Burlington, Iowa, U.S.A. 40 50N 91 5W
164 Burlington, Kan., U.S.A. 38 15N 95 47W
163 Burlington, N.C., U.S.A. 36 7N 79 27W
161 Burlington, N.J., U.S.A. 40 5N 74 50W
161 Burlington, Vt., U.S.A. 44 27N 73 14W
166 Burlington, Wash., U.S.A. 48 29N 122 19W
162 Burlington, Wis., U.S.A. 42 41N 88 18W
90 Burlyu-Tyube, U.S.S.R. 46 30N 79 10E
103 Burma, rep., Asia 21 0N 96 30E
113 Burma Road, Burma .25 53N 100 0E
142 Burnabbie, W. Australia 32 7s 125 37E
165 Burnet, U.S.A. 30 45N 98 11W
166 Burney, U.S.A. 40 56N 121 41W
46 Burnfoot, Ireland 55 4N 7 15W
142 Burngup, W. Australia 33 0s 118 35E
35 Burnham, Essex, England, U.K. 51 37N 0 50E
36 Burnham, Somerset, England, U.K. 51 14N 3 0W
160 Burnham, U.S.A. 40 37N 77 34W
35 Burnham Market, England, U.K. 52 57N 0 43E
145 Burnie, Australia 41 4s 145 56E
38 Burnley, England, U.K. 53 47N 2 15W
41 Burnmouth, Scot., U.K. 55 50N 2 4W
166 Burns, Ore., U.S.A. ...43 40N 119 4W
164 Burns, Wyo., U.S.A. .41 13N 104 18W
156 Burns L., Canada 54 20N 125 45W
142 Burnside, L., W. Australia 25 25s 123 0W
160 Burnt R., Canada 44 40N 78 42E
41 Burntisland, Scot., U.K. 56 4N 3 14W
157 Burntwood L., Canada 55 35N 99 40W
157 Burntwood R., Canada 55 45N 98 0W
98 Burqa, Jordan 32 18N 35 11E
145 Burra, S. Australia ...33 40s 138 55E

MAP
143 Burragorang, L., N.S.W., Australia ...33 52S 150 37E
42 Burravoe, Scot., U.K. 60 30N 1 3W
43 Burray I., Scot., U.K. 58 50N 2 54W
76 Burrel, Albania ...41 36N 20 1E
43 Burrelton, Scot., U.K. 56 30N 3 16W
44 Burren, Ireland ...53 9N 9 5W
143 Burrendong Res., N.S.W., Australia ...32 45S 149 10E
143 Burrewarra Pt., Austral. ...35 50S 150 15E
64 Burriana, Spain ...39 50N 0 4W
143 Burrinjuck Res., Australia ...34 50S 148 45E
168 Burro, Serranias del, Mts., Mexico ...29 0N 102 0W
40 Burrow Hd., Scot., U.K. ...54 40N 4 23W
37 Burry Port, Wales, U.K. ...51 41N 4 17W
100 Bursa, Turkey ...40 15N 29 5E
55 Burscheid, Germany .51 6N 7 8E
81 Burseryd, Sweden ...57 14N 12 57E
39 Burstwick, Eng., U.K. 53 43N 0 6W
143 Burta, Australia ...32 31S 141 5E
131 Burton B., Congo ... 4 14S 29 10E
154 Burton L., Canada ...54 45N 78 20W
39 Burton Agnes, England, United Kingdom ...54 4N 0 18W
36 Burton Bradstock, England, U.K. ...50 41N 2 43W
39 Burton Fleming, England, U.K. ...54 8N 0 20W
35 Burton Latimer, England, U.K. ...52 23N 0 41W
34 Burton-upon-Trent, England, U.K. ...52 48N 1 39W
46 Burtonport, Ireland ...54 59N 8 26W
143 Burtundy, Australia ...33 45S 142 15E
142 Burtville, W. Australia ...28 42S 122 33E
131 Buru, Kenya ... 1 5S 40 9E
109 Buru I., Indonesia ... 3 30S 126 30E
124 Burufu, Ghana ...10 25N 2 50W
100 Burujird, Iran ...33 58N 48 41E
131 Burundi, st., Africa ... 3 15S 30 0E
108 Burung, Indonesia ... 0 21N 108 25E
125 Burutu, Nigeria ... 5 20N 5 29E
35 Burwash, Eng., U.K. .50 59N 0 24E
35 Burwell, England, U.K. ...52 17N 0 20E
164 Burwell, U.S.A. ...41 49N 99 8W
38 Bury, England, U.K. .53 36N 2 19W
35 Bury St. Edmunds, England, U.K. ...52 15N 0 42E
91 Buryat A.S.S.R., U.S.S.R. ...53 0N 110 0E
60 Burzenin, Poland ...51 28N 18 47E
70 Busalla, Italy ...44 34N 8 58E
130 Busanga, Congo ... 5 53S 22 7E
132 Busango Swamp, Zam. ...14 15S 25 45E
100 Busayyah, Iraq ...30 0N 46 10E
156 Busby, Canada ...53 55N 114 0W
101 Bushehr, Iran ...28 55N 50 55E
167 Bushell, Canada ...59 35N 108 35W
35 Bushey, England, U.K. ...51 38N 0 20W
130 Bushimaie R., Congo . 7 30S 23 8E
101 Bushire (Bushehr), Iran ...28 55N 50 55E
134 Bushman Land, C. Prov., S. Afr. ...29 30S 19 30E
46 Bushmills N. Ire., U.K. ...55 14N 6 32W
164 Bushnell, Ill., U.S.A. .40 32N 90 30W
164 Bushnell, Neb., U.S.A. ...41 18N 103 50W
101 Bushrulyeh, Iran ...33 55N 57 25E
131 Busia, Uganda ... 0 25N 34 6E
131 Busia, dist., Kenya ... 0 25N 34 6E
124 Busie, Ghana ...10 29N 2 22W
60 Busko Zdroj, Poland ..50 28N 20 42E
74 Busovača, Yugoslavia 44 6N 17 53E
100 Busra, Syria ...32 30N 36 25E
125 Bussa, Nigeria ...10 11N 4 32E
49 Bussang, France ...47 50N 6 50E
142 Busselton, W. Australia ...33 42S 115 15E
54 Bussum, Netherlands .52 16N 5 10E
109 Busuanga I., Phil. ...12 10N 120 0E
130 Busu Djanoa, Congo . 1 50N 21 5E
56 Büsum, Germany ...54 7N 8 50E
130 Buta, Congo ... 2 50N 24 53E
131 Butare, Rwanda ... 2 31S 29 52E
40 Bute, co., Scot., U.K. 55 40N 5 10W
40 Bute I., Scot., U.K. .55 48N 5 2W
40 Bute, Kyles of, Scotland, U.K. ...55 55N 5 10W
40 Bute, Sd. of, Scot., U.K. ...55 43N 5 8W
131 Butemba, Uganda ... 1 9N 31 37E
131 Butembo, Congo ... 0 9N 29 18E
73 Butera, Italy ...37 10N 14 10E
131 Butere, Kenya ... 0 14N 34 31E
55 Bütgenbach, Belgium 50 26N 6 12E
135 Butha Buthe, Lesotho 28 45S 28 15E
131 Butiaba, Uganda ... 1 50N 31 20E
76 Butkóvou, Limni, Gr. 41 10N 23 2E
164 Butler, Mo., U.S.A. ...38 17N 94 18W
160 Butler, Pa., U.S.A. ...40 52N 79 52W
166 Butte, Mont., U.S.A. .46 0N 112 31W
164 Butte, Neb., U.S.A. ...42 56N 98 54W
142 Butterfield, Mt., Western Australia .24 45S 128 7E
41 Buttermere, Eng., U.K. ...54 32N 3 17W
107 Butterworth, Malaysia 5 24N 100 23E
135 Butterworth, S. Africa 32 20S 28 11E
44 Buttevant, Ireland ...52 14N 8 40E
55 Büttgen, Germany ...51 11N 6 36E
109 Butuan, Philippines ... 8 52N 125 36E
109 Butung I., Indonesia . 5 0S 122 45E
87 Buturlinovka, U.S.S.R. ...50 50N 40 35E
56 Butzbach, Germany ...50 24N 8 40E
105 Buxar, India ...25 34N 83 58E
133 Buxton, C. Prov., S. Afr. ...27 38S 24 42E
38 Buxton, Eng., U.K. ...53 16N 1 54W
49 Buxy, France ...46 44N 4 40E
87 Buy, U.S.S.R. ...58 30N 41 30E
91 Buyaga, U.S.S.R. ...59 50N 127 0E
76 Buyak Kemikli Burun, C., Turkey .40 20N 26 15E
89 Buynaksk, U.S.S.R. ...42 36N 47 42E
112 Buyr Nuur, L., Mongolia ...47 50N 117 35E
77 Buyuk, R., Turkey ...37 45N 27 40E
75 Büyük Çekmece, Tur. 41 2N 28 35E
48 Buzançais, France ...46 54N 1 25E
78 Buzău, Rumania ...45 10N 26 50E
78 Buzău, Reg., Rum. ...45 10N 26 50E
78 Buzău R., Rumania ...45 10N 27 20E
121 Buzaymah, Libya ...24 35N 22 0E
114 Buzen, Japan ...33 35N 131 5E
71 Buzet, Yugoslavia ...45 24N 13 58E
132 Buzi, R., Mozambique 19 52S 34 30E
74 Buziaş, Rumania ...45 38N 21 36E
84 Buzuluk, U.S.S.R. ...52 48N 52 12E
87 Buzuluk R., U.S.S.R. 50 50N 52 12E
161 Buzzards Bay, U.S.A. 41 45N 70 38W
132 Bwana Mkubwa, Zam. 13 8S 28 38E
132 Bwetweha, Malawi ...11 10S 34 10E
89 Bya, C., U.S.S.R. ...39 45N 49 28E
75 Byala, Bulgaria ...42 53N 27 55E
75 Byala, Bulgaria ...43 28N 25 44E
75 Byala Slatina, Bulgaria ...43 26N 23 55E
60 Bydgoszcz, Poland...53 10N 18 0E
60 Bydgoszcz, Prov., Pol. 53 16N 17 33E
86 Byelorussia, *see* White Russia, U.S.S.R. ...53 30N 27 0E
164 Byers, U.S.A. ...39 46N 104 13W
160 Byesville, U.S.A. ...39 56N 81 32W
34 Byfield, Eng., U.K. ...52 10N 1 15W
144 Byfield, Australia ...22 50S 150 40E
79 Bygland, Norway ...58 50N 7 50E
79 Byglandsfjord, Norway ...58 40N 7 50E
79 Byglandsfjord L., Nor. 58 44N 7 50E
165 Byhalia, U.S.A. ...34 53N 89 41W
86 Bykhov, U.S.S.R. ...53 31N 30 14E
89 Bykovo, U.S.S.R. ...49 50N 45 25E
79 Bykle, Norway ...59 21N 7 20E
167 Bylas, U.S.A. ...33 11N 110 9W
37 Bylchau, Wales, U.K. 53 9N 3 32W
81 Bylderup, Denmark ...54 58N 9 8E
153 Bylot I., Canada ...73 0N 78 0W
15 Byrd Land, Antarctica ...79 30S 125 0W
15 Byrd Sub-Glacial Basin, Antarctica ...82 0S 120 0W
145 Byrock, Australia ...30 40S 146 27E
155 Byron B., Canada ...54 42N 57 40W
145 Byron Bay, Australia 28 30S 153 30E
91 Byrrang Mts., U.S.S.R. ...75 0N 100 0E
81 Byrum, Denmark ...57 15N 11 1E
82 Byske, Sweden ...64 59N 21 17E
82 Byske R., Sweden ...65 20N 20 0E
60 Bystrzyca Ktodžka, Pol. ...50 19N 16 39E
91 Bysyttakh, U.S.S.R. .69 30N 124 10E
86 Byten, U.S.S.R. ...52 50N 25 27E
60 Bytom, Poland ...50 25N 19 0E
60 Bytów, Poland ...54 10N 17 30E
80 Byvalla, Sweden ...61 22N 16 27E
121 Bzéma, Libya ...24 50N 22 20E
59 Bzenec, Czechoslovakia ...48 58N 17 18E

C

107 Ca Mau, *see* Quan Long, Vietnam ... 9 7N 105 8E
107 Ca Mau, Mui, *see* Bai Bung, S. Vietnam ... 8 35N 104 42E
172 Caacupe, Paraguay ...25 23N 57 5W
175 Caatingas, reg., Brazil 7 0S 52 30W
173 Caazapa, Paraguay ...26 8S 56 19W
64 Caballeria, Cabo de, Sp. ...40 5N 4 5E
174 Caballo Cocha, Peru ... 4 0S 70 35W
62 Catanaquinta, Spain .43 39N 6 22W
109 Cabanatuan, Phil. ...15 30N 121 5E
64 Cabanes, Spain ...40 9N 0 2E
155 Cabano, Canada ...47 40N 68 56E
127 Cabbi, Ethiopia ... 5 32N 38 10E
175 Cabedeio, Brazil ... 7 0S 34 50W
65 Cabeza de Beuy, Mt., Spain ...38 38N 3 12W
63 Cabeza del Buey, Spain ...38 44N 5 13W
174 Cabezas, Bolivia ...18 45S 63 25W
172 Cabildo, Chile ...32 30S 71 5W
174 Cabimas, Venezuela ...10 30N 71 25W
128 Cabinda, Angola ... 5 40S 12 11E
128 Cabinda, Dist., Angola ... 5 0S 12 30E
166 Cabinet Mts., U.S.A. .48 0N 115 30W
130 Cabiri, Angola ... 8 55S 13 30E
142 Cables, W. Australia .27 55S 123 25E
176 Cabo Blanco, Arg. ...47 56S 65 47W
131 Cabo Delgado, Dist., Mozambique ...10 35S 40 35E
173 Cabo Frio, Brazil ...22 51S 42 3W
154 Cabonga, Res., Canada ...47 35N 76 40W
165 Cabool, U.S.A. ...37 10N 92 8W
145 Caboolture, Australia .27 5S 152 47E
168 Caborca (Heroica), Mex. ...30 40N 112 10W
160 Cabot Hd., Canada ...45 14N 81 18W
161 Cabot, Mt., U.S.A. ...44 30N 71 25W
155 Cabot Strait, Canada .47 15N 59 40W
63 Cabra, Spain ...37 30N 4 28W
65 Cabra del Sto. Cristo, Spain ...37 42N 3 16W
43 Cabrach, Scot., U.K. .57 20N 3 0W
143 Cabramurra, Australia 35 38S 148 25E
72 Cabras, Italy ...39 57N 8 30E
65 Cabrera I., Spain ...39 6N 2 59E
157 Cabri, Canada ...50 35N 108 25W
65 Cabriel, R., Spain ...39 20N 1 20W
175 Cabrobó, Brazil ... 8 30S 39 20W
174 Cabruta, Venezuela ... 7 50N 66 10W
130 Cabuto, Angola ... 9 50S 14 54E
109 Caburan, Philippines . 6 3N 125 45E
62 Cacabelos, Spain ...42 36N 6 44W
74 Čačak, Yugoslavia ...43 54N 20 20E
174 Caceres, Brazil ...16 5S 57 40W
63 Cáceres, Spain ...39 26N 6 23W
63 Cáceres, Prov., Spain .39 45N 6 0W
154 Cache B., Canada ...46 26N 80 1W
124 Cacheu, Port. Guinea .12 14N 16 8W
172 Cachi, Argentina ...25 5S 66 10W
175 Cachoeira, Brazil ...12 30S 39 0W
173 Cachoeira do Sul, Brazil ...30 3S 52 53W
173 Cachoeiro de Itapemirim, Brazil .20 51S 41 7W
63 Cachopo, Portugal ...37 20N 7 49W
129 Caconda, Angola ...13 48S 15 8E
130 Cacuaco, & Bay, Angola ... 8 47S 13 4E
130 Cacuso, Angola ... 9 26S 15 43E
45 Cadamstown, Ireland .53 7N 7 39W
145 Cadarga, Australia ...26 8S 150 58E
142 Cadaux, W. Australia 30 48S 117 15E
165 Caddo, U.S.A. ...34 8N 96 18W
59 Cadca, Czechoslovakia 49 26N 18 45E
37 Cader Idris, Mt., Wales, United Kingdom ...52 43N 3 56W
168 Cadereyta, Mexico ...25 40N 100 0W
154 Cadillac, Canada ...49 45N 108 0W
50 Cadillac, France ...44 38N 0 20W
162 Cadillac, U.S.A. ...44 16N 85 25W
109 Cadiz, Philippines ...11 30N 123 15E
63 Cadiz, Spain ...36 30N 6 20W
160 Cadiz, Ohio, U.S.A. ...40 13N 81 0W
63 Cadiz, G. de, Spain ...36 35N 6 20W
156 Cadomin, Canada ...52 59N 117 28W
50 Cadours, France ...43 44N 1 2E
48 Caen, France ...49 10N 0 22W
39 Caenby Corner, England, U.K. ...53 23N 0 32W
37 Caergwrle, Wales, U.K. ...53 6N 3 3W
37 Caerhun, Wales, U.K. 53 14N 3 50W
34 Caerleon, Eng., U.K. .51 36N 2 57W
37 Caernarvon, & Co., Wales, United Kingdom ...53 8N 4 17W
37 Caernarvon B., Wales, United Kingdom ...53 4N 4 40W
37 Caerphilly, Wales, U.K. ...51 34N 3 13W
37 Caersws, Wales, U.K. 52 32N 3 27W
34 Caerwent, Eng., U.K. 51 37N 2 47W
98 Caesarea, *see* Qeisari, Israel ...32 30N 34 53E
175 Caeté, Brazil ...20 0S 43 40W
175 Caetite, Brazil ...13 50S 42 50W
172 Cafayate, Argentina ...26 2S 66 0W
109 Cagayan de Oro, Phil. 8 30N 124 40E
109 Cagayan R., Philippines ...17 30N 121 42E
71 Cagli, Italy ...43 32N 12 38E
72 Cagliari, Italy ...39 15N 9 6E
72 Cagliari, G. di, Italy ...39 8N 9 10E
73 Cagnano Varano, Italy ...41 49N 15 47E
51 Cagnes-sur-Mer., France ...43 40N 7 9E
169 Caguas, Puerto Rico .18 14N 66 4W
44 Caha Mts., Ireland ...51 45N 9 40W
45 Caher I., Ireland ...53 44N 10 1W
44 Caherconlish, Ireland .52 36N 8 30W
44 Cahermore, Ireland ...51 35N 10 2W
44 Cahir, Ireland ...52 23N 7 56W
44 Cahirciveen, Ireland ...51 57N 10 13W
132 Cahora Bassa Rapids & Dam, Mozambique ...15 35S 32 55E
45 Cahore Pt., Ireland ...52 34N 6 11W
50 Cahors, France ...44 27N 1 27E
174 Cahuapanas, Peru ... 5 15S 77 0W
169 Caibarién, Cuba ...22 30N 79 30W
174 Caicara, Venezuela ... 7 50N 66 10W
175 Caicó, Brazil ... 6 20S 37 0W
169 Caicos Is., West Indies ...21 40N 71 40W
169 Caicos Passage, W. Ind. ...22 45N 72 45W
176 Caihaique, Chile ...45 30S 71 45W
160 Cainsville, Canada ...43 9N 80 15W
15 Caird Coast, Antarctica ...75 0S 25 0W
43 Cairn Gorm, Scot., U.K. ...57 7N 3 40W
41 Cairn Table, Scot., U.K. ...55 30N 4 0W
43 Cairn Toul, Scot., U.K. ...57 3N 3 44W
43 Cairngorm Mts., Scotland, U.K. ...57 6N 3 42W
40 Cairnryan, Scot., U.K. 54 59N 50 0W
144 Cairns, Australia ...16 55S 145 51E
126 Cairo, Egypt ...30 1N 31 14E
163 Cairo, Ga., U.S.A. ...30 52N 84 12W
165 Cairo, Missouri, U.S.A. ...37 0N 89 10W
70 Cairo Montenotte, Italy ...44 23N 8 16E
35 Caister-on-Sea, England, United Kingdom ...52 38N 1 43E
39 Caistor, England, U.K. ...53 29N 0 20W
43 Caithness, co., Scot., United Kingdom ...58 25N 3 25W
43 Caithness, Ord of, C., Scotland, U.K. ...58 35N 3 37W
129 Calundo, Angola ...15 50S 17 52E
172 Caiza, Bolivia ...21 50S 63 50W
174 Cajamarca, Peru ... 7 5S 78 28W
50 Cajarc, France ...44 29N 1 50E
175 Cajazeiras, Brazil ... 7 0S 38 30W
74 Čajetina, Yugoslavia .43 47N 19 42E
74 Čajnice, Yugoslavia ...43 34N 19 5E
89 Čakirgöl, Mt., Turkey 40 33N 39 40E
135 Cala, C. Prov., S. Africa ...31 30S 27 42E
63 Cala, Spain ...37 59N 6 21W
63 Cala, R., Spain ...37 50N 6 8W
125 Calabar, Nigeria ... 4 57N 8 20E
174 Calabozo, Venezuela ... 9 0N 67 20W
73 Calabria, Reg., Italy .39 4N 16 30E
64 Calaceite, Spain ...41 1N 0 11E
78 Calafat, Rumania ...43 58N 22 59E
176 Calafate, Argentina ...50 25S 72 25W
64 Calahorra, Spain ...42 18N 1 59W
49 Calais, France ...50 57N 1 56E
155 Calais, Maine, U.S.A. .45 5N 67 20W
172 Calalaste, Cord. de, Arg. ...25 0S 67 0W
174 Calama, Brazil ... 8 0S 62 50W
172 Calama, Chile ...22 30S 68 55W
174 Calamar, Colombia ...10 15N 74 55W
109 Calamian Group, Phil. 11 50N 119 55E
64 Calamocha, Spain ...40 50N 1 17W
174 Calanaque, Brazil ... 0 5S 64 0W
63 Calañas, Spain ...37 40N 6 53W
64 Calanda, Spain ...40 56N 0 15W
72 Calangianus, Italy ...40 56N 9 12E
109 Calapan, Philippines .13 25N 121 7E
78 Călărasi, Rumania ...44 14N 27 23E
65 Calasparra, Spain ...38 14N 1 41W
72 Calatafimi, Italy ...37 56N 12 50E
64 Calatayud, Spain ...41 20N 1 40W
109 Calauag, Philippines ...13 55N 122 15E
73 Calava, C., Italy ...38 11N 14 55E
109 Calavite Cape, Phil. ...13 0N 120 10E
113 Calayan, I., Philippines ...19 20N 121 30E
174 Calca, Peru ...13 10S 72 0W
70 Calchi, I., Ægean Sea 36 13N 27 37E
70 Calci, Italy ...43 44N 10 31E
105 Calcutta, India ...22 36N 88 24E
71 Caldaro, Italy ...46 23N 11 15E
63 Caldas da Rainha, Port. ...39 24N 9 8W
62 Caldas de Reyes, Spain ...42 36N 8 39W
38 Caldbeck, Eng., U.K. .54 45N 3 3W
38 Calder R., Eng., U.K. 53 44N 1 57W
38 Calder Bridge, England, United Kingdom ...54 27N 3 31W
172 Caldera, Chile ...27 5S 70 55W
38 Caldew R., Eng., U.K. ...54 47N 2 59W
100 Caldiran, Turkey ...39 7N 44 0E
166 Caldwell, Idaho, U.S.A. ...43 45N 116 42W
165 Caldwell, Kan., U.S.A. ...37 5N 97 37W
165 Caldwell, Texas, U.S.A. ...30 30N 96 42W
37 Caldy I., Wales, U.K. 51 38N 4 42W
134 Caledon, S. Africa ...34 14S 19 26E
46 Caledon, N. Ire., U.K. 54 22N 6 50W
139 Caledon B., Australia .12 45S 137 0E
135 Caledon, R., S. Africa 30 0S 26 46E
160 Caledonia, Canada ...43 7N 79 58W
160 Caledonia, U.S.A. ...42 57N 77 54W
42 Caledonian Can., Scotland U.K. ...57 27N 4 18W
64 Calella, Spain ...41 37N 2 40E
174 Caleta Buena, Chile ...19 55S 70 5W
167 Calexico, U.S.A. ...32 40N 115 33W
38 Calf of Man, Isle of Man, United Kingdom ...54 4N 4 48W
38 Calf, The, Eng., U.K. 54 23N 2 31W
156 Calgary Canada ...51 0N 114 10W
42 Calgary, Scotland, U.K. ...56 34N 6 17W
63 Calhoun, Ga., U.S.A. .34 30N 84 55W
174 Cali, Colombia ... 3 25N 76 35W
40 Caliach Pt., Scot., U.K. ...56 37N 6 20W
109 Calicoan, I., Philippines ...10 59N 125 50E
106 Calicut, (Kozhikode), India ...11 15N 75 43E
167 Caliente, U.S.A. ...37 43N 114 34W
164 California, Mo., U.S.A. ...38 37N 92 30W
160 California, Pa., U.S.A. 40 4N 79 55W
166 California, st., U.S.A. .37 25N 120 0W
168 California, G. of, Mex. 27 0N 111 0W
168 California, Lr., Mexico 27 0N 113 0W
172 Calilegua, Argentina ...23 45S 64 42W
78 Caliman Munţii, Mts., Rumania ...47 12N 25 0E
78 Călinesti, Rumania ...45 21N 24 18E
172 Calingasta, Argentina 31 15S 69 30W
167 Calipatria, U.S.A. ...33 8N 115 30W
166 Calistoga, U.S.A. ...38 36N 122 32W
73 Calitri, Italy ...40 54N 15 25E
134 Calitzdorp, S. Africa .33 30S 21 41E
145 Callabonna L., Austral ...29 40S 140 0E
48 Callac, France ...48 25N 3 27W
99 Callafo, Ethiopia ... 6 48N 43 47E
45 Callan, Ireland ...52 33N 7 25W
40 Callander, Scotland, United Kingdom ...56 15N 4 14W
42 Callanish, Scot., U.K. 58 12N 6 43W
174 Callao, Peru ...12 0S 77 0W
164 Callaway, U.S.A. ...41 20N 99 56W
144 Callide, Australia ...24 23S 150 33E
156 Calling L., Canada ...55 20N 113 20W
36 Callington, Eng., U.K. 50 30N 4 19W
144 Calliope, Australia ...24 0S 151 16E
65 Callosa de Ensarra., Sp. ...38 40N 0 8W
65 Callosa de Segura, Sp. 38 1N 0 53W
46 Callow, Ireland ...53 58N 9 2W
34 Calne, England, U.K. 51 26N 2 0W
78 Călnicu, Rumania ...44 54N 23 4E
73 Calore R., Italy ...41 8N 14 45E
145 Caloundra, Australia .26 45S 153 10E
65 Calpe, Spain ...38 39N 0 3E
34 Calshot, Eng., U.K. ...50 49N 1 18W
36 Calstock, Eng., U.K. .50 30N 4 13W
72 Caltabellotta, Italy ...37 36N 13 11E
73 Caltagirone, Italy ...37 13N 14 30E
72 Caltanissetta, Italy ...37 30N 14 3E
51 Caluire-et-Cuire, Fr. .45 49N 4 51E
130 Calulo, Angola ...10 1S 14 56E
70 Caluso, Italy ...45 18N 7 52E
48 Calvados, Dépt., Fr. ...49 5N 0 15W
165 Calvert, U.S.A. ...30 59N 96 50W
156 Calvert I., Canada ...51 30N 128 0W
142 Calvert Ra., W. Austral. ...24 0S 122 30E
134 Calvinia, S. Africa ...31 28S 19 45E
65 Calzada Almuradiel, Sp. ...38 32N 3 28W
63 Calzada de Calatrava, Spain ...38 42N 3 46W
88 Cam, C., Turkey ...40 37N 37 43E
35 Cam R., Eng., U.K. ...52 13N 0 9E
107 Cam Lam, (Ba Ngoi), S. Vietnam ... 5 0N 109 10E
107 Cam Ranh, S. Vietnam ...11 54N 109 12E
130 Camabatela, Angola ... 8 20S 15 26E
130 Camacupa, *see* Vila Gen. Machado, Angola ...11 58S 17 22E
169 Camagüey, Cuba ...21 20N 78 0W
70 Camaiore, Italy ...43 57N 10 18E
174 Camana, Peru ...16 30S 72 50W
48 Camaret, France ...48 16N 4 37W
172 Camargo, Bolivia ...20 38S 65 15E
51 Camargue Dist., Fr. ...43 20N 4 38E
62 Camariñas, Spain ...43 8N 9 12W
169 Camaron C., Honduras ...16 0N 85 0W
176 Camarones, Argentina 44 50S 66 0W
174 Camarones, Chile ...19 0S 69 58W
173 Camaquã, R., Brazil .30 50S 52 50W
166 Camas, U.S.A. ...45 43N 122 30W
166 Camas Valley, U.S.A. 43 0N 123 46W
62 Cambados, Spain ...42 31N 8 49W
143 Cambalong, Australia 37 35S 149 10E
173 Cambara, Brazil ...23 2S 53 5W
104 Cambay, India ...22 23N 72 33E
104 Cambay, G. of, India .20 45N 72 30E
173 Cambe, Brazil ...23 9S 51 19W
35 Camberley, Eng., U.K. ...51 20N 0 44W
65 Cambil, Spain ...37 40N 3 33W
39 Cambo, Eng., U.K. ...55 9N 1 57W
50 Cambo ,France ...43 22N 1 23W
107 Cambodia, st., *see* Khmer Rep. ...12 15N 105 0E
36 Camborne, Eng., U.K. 50 13N 5 18W
49 Cambral, France ...50 11N 3 14E
134 Cambria, S. Africa ...33 39S 24 31E
167 Cambria, U.S.A. ...35 36N 121 6W
37 Cambrian Mts., Wales, U.K. ...52 10N 3 52W
135 Cambridge, S. Africa .32 58S 27 55E
35 Cambridge, Eng., U.K. ...52 13N 0 8E
146 Cambridge, N.Z. ...37 54S 175 29E
166 Cambridge, Idaho, U.S.A. ...44 36N 116 52W
162 Cambridge, Mass., U.S.A. ...42 20N 71 8W
162 Cambridge, Md., U.S.A. ...38 33N 76 2W
164 Cambridge, Minn., U.S.A. ...45 34N 93 15W
164 Cambridge, Neb., U.S.A. ...40 20N 100 12W
161 Cambridge, N.Y., U.S.A. ...43 2N 73 22W
160 Cambridge, Ohio, U.S.A. ...40 1N 81 22W
35 Cambridge & Isle of Ely, co., Eng., U.K. 52 21N 0 5E
152 Cambridge Bay, Can. .69 10N 105 0W
138 Cambridge, Gulf, Western Australia .14 45S 128 0E
160 Cambridge Springs, U.S.A. ...41 47N 80 4W
64 Cambrils, Spain ...41 8N 1 3E
130 Cambulo, Angola ... 7 48S 21 11E
143 Camden, Australia ...34 5S 150 38E
35 Camden, Eng., U.K. .51 33N 0 10W
163 Camden, Ala., U.S.A. .31 59N 87 15W
165 Camden, Ark., U.S.A. 33 30N 92 50W

MAP
155 Camden, Me. U.S.A. .34 14N 69 6W
162 Camden, N.J., U.S.A. 39 57N 75 1W
163 Camden, S.C., U.S.A. .34 17N 80 34W
14 Camden, B. Alaska, U.S.A. 71 0N 145 0W
36 Camel R., Eng., U.K. 50 28N 4 49W
36 Camelford, Eng., U.K. 50 37N 4 41W
161 Camels Hump, U.S.A. 44 18N 72 55W
48 Camembert, France ...48 53N 0 10E
70 Cameri, Italy 45 30N 8 40E
71 Camerino, Italy 43 10N 13 4E
167 Cameron, Ariz., U.S.A. 35 55N 111 31W
165 Cameron, La., U.S.A. .29 50N 93 18W
164 Cameron, Mo., U.S.A. 39 42N 94 50W
165 Cameron, Tex., U.S.A. 30 53N 97 0W
154 Cameron Falls Canada 49 5N 88 20W
107 Cameron Highlands, Malaya, W. Malaysia 4 27N 101 22E
156 Cameron Hills, Canada 60 20N 118 0W
147 Cameron Mts., N.Z. ...46 1S 167 0E
128 Cameroon rep., Africa 3 30N 12 30E
125 Cameroon Mt., Cam. . 4 45N 8 55E
73 Camerota, Italy 40 2N 15 21E
125 Cameroun, R., Cam. ... 4 0N 9 35E
36 Camerton, Eng., U.K. 51 18N 2 27W
175 Cametá, Brazil 2 0S 49 30W
134 Camfer, C. Prov., S. Afr. 33 50S 22 27E
113 Camiguin, I., Phil. ...19 55N 122 0E
62 Caminha, Portugal ...41 50N 8 50W
166 Camino, U.S.A. 38 47N 120 40W
145 Camira Creek, Australia 29 15S 153 10E
160 Camlachie, Canada ...43 3N 82 9W
43 Cammachmore, Scotland, U.K. 57 2N 2 5W
160 Cammal, U.S.A. 41 24N 77 28W
175 Camocim, Brazil 2 55S 40 50W
70 Camogli, Italy 44 21N 9 9E
45 Camolin, Ireland 52 37N 6 26W
144 Camooweal, Australia 19 56S 138 7E
175 Camopi R., Fr. Guinea 2 30N 53 30W
164 Camp Crook, U.S.A. ...45 36N 103 59W
165 Camp Wood, U.S.A. ...29 47N 100 0W
172 Campagna, Italy 40 40N 15 5E
172 Campana, Argentine .34 10S 58 55W
176 Campana I., Chile 48 20S 75 10W
63 Campanario, Spain ...38 52N 5 36W
73 Campania, reg., Italy .40 50N 14 45E
136 Campbell I., S. Oc. 52 30S 169 0E
157 Campbell L., Canada .63 15N 106 25W
156 Campbell R., Canada 50 5N 125 20W
145 Campbell Town, Tas., Australia 41 52S 147 30E
160 Campbellford, Canada 44 17N 77 50W
162 Campbellsville, U.S.A. 37 23N 85 12W
156 Campbellton, Alta., Can. 53 32N 113 15W
155 Campbellton, N.B., Can. 47 57N 66 43W
143 Campbelltown, Austral. 34 5S 150 48E
43 Campbeltown, Scotland, United Kingdom 57 34N 4 2W
40 Campbeltown, Scotland, United Kingdom 55 25N 5 36W
168 Campeche, Mexico ...19 50N 90 32W
168 Campeche, G. of, Mex. 19 30N 93 0W
168 Campeche, st., Mexico 19 50N 90 32W
143 Camperdown, S. Africa 29 42S 30 33E
135 Camperdown, Australia 38 4S 143 12E
73 Campi Salentina, Italy 40 22N 180 2E
78 Campia Turzii, Rum. .46 34N 23 53E
70 Campiglia Marittima, Italy 43 3N 10 37E
64 Campillo de Altobucy, Spain 39 36N 1 49W
63 Campillo de Llerena, Spain 38 30N 5 50W
63 Campillos, Spain 37 4N 4 51W
175 Campina Grande, Brazil 7 20S 35 47W
173 Campinas, Brazil 22 50S 47 0W
55 Campine, Dist., Belg. .51 8N 5 20E
175 Campinho, Brazil 14 30S 39 10W
71 Campli, Italy 42 44N 13 40E
128 Campo, Cameroon 2 15N 9 58E
64 Campo, Spain 39 23N 3 7W
175 Campo Beló, Brazil ...21 0S 45 30W
65 Campo de Criptana, Sp. 39 25N 3 7W
175 Campo Formosa, Brazil 10 30S 40 20W
172 Campo Grande, Brazil 20 25S 54 40W
175 Campo Maior, Brazil . 4 50S 42 12W
63 Campo Maior, Portugal 38 59N 7 7W
71 Campo Tures, Italy ...46 53N 11 30E
174 Campoalegre, Colombia 2 48N 75 20W
73 Campobasso, Italy 41 34N 14 40E
72 Campobello di Licata, Italy 37 16N 13 55E
172 Campobello di Mazara, Italy 37 38N 12 45E
72 Campofelice, Italy 37 54N 13 53E
72 Camporeale, Italy 37 53N 13 3E
175 Campos, Brazil 21 50S 41 20W
175 Campos Belos, Brazil .13 10S 46 45W
65 Campos del Peurto, Sp. 39 26N 3 1E
173 Campos Novos, Brazil 27 21S 51 20W
64 Camprodón, Spain 42 19N 2 23E
40 Campsie Fells, Scotland, United Kingdom 56 2N 4 20W
78 Câmpurile, Rumania .46 5N 26 49E
156 Camrose, Canada 53 0N 112 50W
37 Camrose, Wales, U.K. 51 50N 5 2W
157 Camsell Portage, Can. 59 39N 109 12W
145 Camurra, Australia 29 21S 149 52E
107 Can Tho, S. Vietnam .10 2N 105 46E
132 Cana Cana, Mozam. ...15 55S 34 8E
161 Canaan, U.S.A. 42 1N 73 20W
152 Canada, st., N. Amer. 60 0N 100 0W
105 Canada Dam, India ...25 0N 87 30E
172 Canada de Gomez, Arg. 32 55S 61 30W
176 Cañada Honda, Arg. 32 0S 68 25W
165 Canadian, U.S.A. 35 56N 100 25W
165 Canadian R., U.S.A. .36 0N 98 45W
155 Canairiktok, R., Can. .54 30N 62 30W
76 Canakkale, Turkey 40 8N 26 30E
156 Canal Flats, Canada ...50 10N 115 55W
172 Canalejas, Argentina .35 15S 66 34W
172 Canals, Argentina 33 35S 62 40W
65 Canáls, Spain 38 58N 0 35W
160 Canandaigua, U.S.A. 42 55N 77 18W
168 Cananea, Mexico 31 0N 110 20W
169 Canarreos, Archipelago de los, Cuba 21 35N 81 40W
120 Canary Is. Atlantic Oc. 29 30N 17 0W
163 Canaveral, C., see Kennedy, C., U.S.A. 28 28N 80 31N
64 Cañaveras, Spain 40 27N 2 14W
175 Canavieiras, Brazil 15 45S 39 0W
143 Canbelego, Australia .31 32S 146 18E
143 Canberra, Cap. Terr., Australia 35 15S 149 8E
166 Canby, Calif., U.S.A. .41 26N 120 58W
164 Canby, Minn., U.S.A. .44 44N 96 15W
166 Canby, Oregon, U.S.A. 45 24N 122 45W
48 Cancale France 48 40N 1 50W
62 Candas, Spain 43 35N 5 45W
48 Candé, France 47 34N 1 0W
77 Candea, see Iraklion, Greece 35 20N 25 12E
73 Candela, Italy 41 8N 15 31E
173 Candelaria, Argentina 27 29S 55 44W
62 Candeleda, Spain 40 10N 5 14W
78 Cândeşti, Rumania 45 15N 26 42E
164 Cando, N.D., U.S.A. .48 30N 99 14W
15 Candlemas I., Falkland Is. Dependencies 57 5S 26 45E
135 Candover, Nat., S. Afr. 27 28N 31 57E
77 Canea, see Khania, Gr. 35 30N 24 4E
70 Canelli, Italy 44 44N 8 18E
173 Canelones, Uruguay 34 32S 56 10W
50 Canet Plage, France ...42 42N 3 3E
172 Cañete, Chile 37 50S 73 10W
174 Cañete, Peru 13 0S 76 30W
63 Canete de las Torres, Sp. 37 53N 4 19W
64 Canfranc, Spain 42 42N 0 31W
62 Cangas, Spain 43 23N 5 17W
62 Cangas de Narcea, Sp. 43 10N 6 32W
62 Cangas de Onis, Spain 43 21N 5 8W
175 Canguaretama, Brazil 6 20S 35 5W
173 Canguçu, Brazil 31 22S 52 43W
130 Cangumbe, Angola 11 57S 19 23E
130 Canhoca, Angola 9 10S 14 38E
123 Cani I., Tunisia 37 15N 10 8E
133 Canicado, Mozambique 24 2S 33 2E
72 Canicatti, Italy 37 21N 13 50E
73 Canicattini, Italy 37 1N 15 3E
156 Canim L., Canada 51 45N 120 50W
108 Canipaan, Philippines 8 33N 117 15E
43 Canisbay, Scot., U.K. 58 38N 3 6W
42 Canisp Mt., Scot., U.K. 58 8N 5 5W
160 Canisteo, U.S.A. 42 17N 77 37W
160 Canisteo R., U.S.A. ...42 15N 77 30W
65 Canjáyar, Spain 37 1N 2 44W
100 Cankiri, Turkey 40 40N 33 30E
131 Cankuzo, Burundi 3 10S 30 31E
156 Canmore, Canada 51 7N 115 18W
42 Canna I., Scot., U.K. .57 3N 6 33W
42 Canna, Sd. of, Scotland, United Kingdom 57 1N 6 30W
106 Cannamore, India 11 53N 75 27E
51 Cannes, France 43 32N 7 0E
43 Cannich, Scot., U.K. .57 20N 4 48W
138 Canning Basin, Austral. 19 50S 124 0E
142 Canning Hill, W. Austral. 28 44S 117 45E
105 Canning Town, India .22 23N 88 40E
160 Cannington, Canada ...44 20N 79 2W
36 Cannington, Eng., U.K. 51 8N 3 4W
34 Cannock, Eng., U.K. .52 42N 2 2W
29 Cannock Chase, hills, England, U.K. 52 43N 2 0W
164 Cannon Ball R., U.S.A. 46 20N 101 20W
43 Cannonbridge, Scotland, United Kingdom 57 33N 4 28W
164 Canon City, U.S.A. 39 30N 105 20W
143 Canonba, Australia 31 21S 147 22E
41 Canonbie, Scot., U.K. 55 4N 2 58W
40 Canonsburg, U.S.A. ...40 15N 80 11W
144 Canoona, Australia 23 7S 150 17E
157 Canora, Canada 51 40N 102 30W
73 Canosa di Puglia, Italy 41 13N 16 4E
143 Canowindra, Australia 33 35S 148 38E
123 Canrobert, Algeria 35 55N 7 6E
155 Canso, Canada 45 20N 61 0W
62 Cantabrian, Mts., Spain 43 0N 5 10W
50 Cantal, Dépt., France 45 4N 2 45E
62 Cantanhede, Portugal 40 20N 8 36W
64 Cantavieje, Spain 40 31N 0 25W
74 Čantavir, Yugoslavia .45 55N 19 46E
35 Canterbury, Eng., U.K. 51 17N 1 5E
147 Canterbury, dist., N.Z. 43 45S 171 19E
147 Canterbury Bight, N.Z. 44 16S 171 55E
147 Canterbury Plains, N.Z. 43 55S 171 22E
63 Cantillana, Spain 37 36N 5 50W
122 Cantin C., Morocco 32 37N 9 15W
136 Canton, Canton & Enderburg Is. 2 45S 171 40W
113 Canton (Kwangchow), China 23 10N 113 10E
163 Canton, Ga., U.S.A. ...34 13N 84 29W
164 Canton, Ill., U.S.A. ...40 32N 90 0W
161 Canton, Mass., U.S.A. 42 8N 71 8W
165 Canton, Miss., U.S.A. .32 40N 90 1W
164 Canton, Mo., U.S.A. ...40 10N 91 33W
161 Canton, N.Y., U.S.A. .44 32N 75 3W
160 Canton, Ohio U.S.A. .40 47N 81 22W
165 Canton, Okla. U.S.A. 36 5N 98 36W
164 Canton S.D., U.S.A. ..43 20N 96 35W
165 Canton L., U.S.A. 36 12N 98 40W
70 Cantu, Italy 45 44N 9 8E
174 Canudos, Brazil 7 13N 58 5W
174 Canutama, Brazil 6 30S 64 20W
167 Canulloit, U.S.A. 31 58N 106 36W
35 Canvey, England, U.K. 51 32N 0 35E
132 Canxixe, Mozambique 17 35S 34 19E
154 Canyon, Canada 47 25N 84 30W
165 Canyon, Texas, U.S.A. 35 0N 101 57W
166 Canyon, Wyo., U.S.A. 44 43N 110 36W
167 Canyonlands Nat. Park, U.S.A. 38 25N 109 30W
166 Canyonville. U.S.A. ...42 55N 123 14W
70 Canzo, Italy 45 54N 9 18E
40 Caolisport, Loch, Scotland, U.K. 55 22N 5 40W
71 Cáorle, Italy 45 36N 12 51E
155 Cap Chat, Canada 49 6N 66 40W
50 Cap Ferret, France 43 28N 1 15W
169 Cap Haitien, Haiti 19 40N 72 20W
73 Capa Stilo, Italy 38 25N 16 25E
73 Capáccio, Italy 40 26N 15 4E
70 Caparnoü, Italy 43 50N 10 33E
50 Capbreton, France 43 39N 1 26W
145 Cape Barren I., Austral. 40 25S 184 15E
155 Cape Breton I., Can. .46 0N 61 0W
162 Cape Charles, U.S.A. .37 15N 75 59W
125 Cape Coast, Ghana 5 5N 1 15W
162 Cape Cod B., U.S.A. .41 50N 70 18W
163 Cape Fear R., U.S.A. .34 30N 78 25W
165 Cape Girardeau, U.S.A. 37 20N 89 30W
145 Cape Jervis, S. Austral. 35 40S 138 5E
162 Cape May, U.S.A. 39 1N 74 53W
155 Cape Montague, Can. .46 5N 62 25W
124 Cape Palmas, Liberia . 4 25N 7 49W
138 Cape Preston, W Australia 20 51S 116 12E
134 Cape Province, prov., S. Afr. 32 0S 23 0E
134 Cape Town, S. Africa .33 55S 18 22E
16 Cape Verde Is., Atlantic Ocean 17 10N 25 20W
161 Cape Vincent, U.S.A. .44 9N 76 21W
144 C. York Pen., Australia 13 30S 142 30E
35 Capel, England, U.K. 51 8N 0 18W
37 Capel Curig, Wales, U.K. 53 6N 3 55W
175 Capela, Brazil 10 15S 37 0W
144 Capella, Australia 23 2S 148 1E
144 Capella, Mt., W. Irian, Indonesia 4 45S 140 50E
50 Capendu, France 43 11N 2 31E
98 Capernaum (site), Israel 32 54N 35 32E
175 Capim R., Brazil 3 0S 48 0W
167 Capitan, U.S.A. 33 40N 105 41W
73 Capizzi, Italy 37 50N 14 26E
74 Čapljina, Yugoslavia .43 35N 17 43E
73 Capo Vaticano, Italy .38 37N 15 50E
132 Capoche, R., Mozam. .15 0S 32 45E
130 Capolo, Angola 10 38S 14 0E
132 Caponda, Mozambique 15 55S 31 40E
44 Cappagh White, Ireland 52 35N 8 10W
44 Cappamore, Ireland ...52 38N 8 20W
44 Cappoquin, Ireland 52 9N 7 46W
70 Capraia I., Italy 43 2N 9 50E
71 Caprarola, Italy 42 21N 12 11E
154 Capreol, Canada 46 40N 80 50W
72 Caprera I., Italy 41 12N 9 28E
73 Capri I., Italy 40 34N 14 15E
142 Capricorn Ra., Austral. 23 20S 117 0E
70 Caprino Veronese, Italy 45 37N 10 47E
132 Caprivi Strip, S.W. Afr. 18 0S 23 0E
105 Captainganj, India 26 55N 83 45E
143 Captain's Flat, Austral. 35 35S 149 27E
50 Captieux, France 44 18N 0 16W
73 Capua, Italy 41 7N 14 5E
165 Capulin, U.S.A. 36 48N 103 59W
174 Caquetá R., Colombia 1 0N 75 30W
78 Caracal, Rumania 44 8N 24 22E
174 Caracas, Venezuela 10 30N 66 50W
175 Caracol Piaui, Brazil . 9 15S 43 45W
174 Caracol, Guaporé, Brazil 9 15S 64 20W
145 Caradoc, Australia 30 35S 143 5E
143 Caragabal, Australia .33 54S 147 50E
44 Caragh L., Ireland 52 3N 9 50W
44 Caragh R., Ireland 52 0N 9 52W
143 Caraghan Mt., Australia 31 20S 148 52E
70 Caraglio, Italy 44 25N 7 25E
173 Carangola, Brazil 20 50S 42 5W
142 Carani, W. Australia .30 57S 116 28E
78 Caransebeş, Rumania .45 28N 22 18E
73 Carapelle, R., Italy ...41 20N 15 35E
74 Caras-Severin, Reg., Rumania 45 0N 22 0E
74 Caraşova, Rumania ...45 11N 21 51E
169 Caratasca Lag., Hond. 15 30N 83 40W
48 Caratec, France 48 40N 3 55W
175 Caratinga, Brazil 19 50S 42 10W
155 Caratunk, U.S.A. 45 13N 69 55W
175 Carauari, Brazil 4 55S 66 57W
175 Caraúbas, Brazil 5 50S 37 25W
65 Caravaca, Spain 38 8N 1 52W
70 Caravaggio, Italy 45 30N 9 39E
174 Caravay, Cordillera de, Peru 14 0S 70 30W
175 Caravelas, Brazil 17 50S 39 20W
174 Caraveli, Peru 15 45S 73 25W
173 Carazinho, Brazil 28 0S 53 0W
62 Carballino, Spain 42 26N 8 5W
62 Carballo, Spain 43 13N 8 41W
157 Carberry, Canada 49 50N 99 25W
62 Carbia, Spain 42 48N 8 14W
156 Carbon, Canada 51 30N 113 20W
72 Carbonara, C., Italy ...39 8N 9 30E
166 Carbondale, Colo., U.S.A. 39 30N 107 10W
165 Carbondale, Ill., U.S.A. 37 45N 89 10W
161 Carbondale, Pa., U.S.A. 41 37N 75 30W
155 Carbonear, Canada 47 42N 53 13W
65 Carboneras, Spain 37 0N 1 53W
64 Carboneras de Guadazoán, Spain ...39 54N 1 50W
72 Carbonia, Italy 39 10N 8 30E
42 Carbost, Scot., U.K. ...57 19N 6 21W
45 Carbury, Ireland 53 22N 6 58W
63 Carcabuey, Spain 37 27N 4 17W
62 Carcagente, Spain 39 8N 0 28W
156 Carcajou, Canada 57 45N 117 0W
169 Carcasse, C., Haiti 18 30N 74 28W
50 Carcassonne, France ...43 13N 2 20E
65 Carche, Spain 38 26N 1 9W
156 Carcross, Canada 60 20N 134 40W
142 Cardabia, W. Australia 23 2S 113 55E
106 Cardamom Hills, India 9 30N 77 15E
107 Cardamom Mts., Cambodia 12 15N 103 5E
64 Cardanete, Spain 39 42N 1 41W
169 Cárdenas, Cuba 23 0N 81 30W
168 Cárdenas, Mexico 22 0N 99 41W
168 Cárdenas, Mexico 17 59N 93 21W
37 Cardiff, Wales, U.K. .51 28N 3 11W
37 Cardigan, & Co., Wales, U.K. 52 6N 4 41W
37 Cardigan B., Wales, United Kingdom 52 30N 4 30W
145 Cardillo Downs, Queens., Australia .26 39S 140 35E
161 Cardinal, Canada 44 48N 75 24W
133 Cardington, S. Africa .27 10S 23 30E
35 Cardington, Eng., U.K. 52 7N 0 23W
174 Cardón, Venezuela 12 10N 70 3W
64 Cardona, Spain 41 56N 1 40E
172 Cardona, Uruguay 33 53S 57 18W
64 Cardoner, R., Spain ...42 0N 1 33E
157 Cardross, Canada 49 50N 105 40W
156 Cardston, Canada 49 15N 113 20W
144 Cardwell, Australia ...18 14S 146 2E
78 Carei, Rumania 47 40N 22 29E
174 Carenero, Venezuela ...10 40N 66 5W
48 Carentan, France 49 19N 1 15W
166 Carey, Idaho, U.S.A. .43 19N 113 58W
162 Carey, Ohio, U.S.A. ...40 58N 83 22W
142 Carey, L., W. Australia 29 0S 122 15E
124 Careysburg, Liberia ... 6 34N 10 30W
11 Cargados Garajos, Is., Indian Ocean 17 0S 59 0E
51 Cargese, Corsica, France 42 7W 8 35E
48 Carhaix, France 48 18N 3 36W
169 Caribbean Sea, W. Ind. 15 0N 75 0W
156 Cariboo Mts., Canada .53 0N 121 0W
157 Caribou, Canada 55 30N 121 55W
155 Caribou, U.S.A. 46 55N 68 0W
154 Caribou I., Canada 47 23N 85 48W
155 Caribou L., Canada ...52 40N 90 40W
156 Caribou Mts., Canada 58 50N 115 40W
49 Carignan, France 49 38N 5 10E
70 Carignano, Italy 44 55N 7 40E
132 Carinde, Mozambique 15 41S 31 16E
64 Cariñena, Spain 41 20N 1 13W
175 Carinhanha, Brazil 14 15S 44 0W
72 Carini, Italy 38 9N 13 10E
42 Carinish, Scot., U.K. .57 31N 7 20W
72 Carinola, Italy 41 11N 13 58E
58 Carinthia, prov., see Karnten, Austria ...46 52N 13 30E
169 Caripito, Venezuela ...10 2N 63 0W
34 Carisbrooke, Eng., U.K. 50 42N 1 19W
174 Caritianas, Brazil 9 20S 63 0W
175 Carius, Brazil 6 35S 39 30W
38 Cark, England, U.K. .54 11N 0 59W
73 Carlentini, Sicily, Italy 37 15N 15 2E
154 Carleton Place, Canada 45 8N 76 11W
133 Carletonville, S. Africa 26 23S 27 22E
166 Carlin, U.S.A. 40 50N 116 5W
46 Carlingford, Ireland ...54 3N 6 10W
46 Carlingford L., Ireland 54 0N 6 5W
164 Carlinville, U.S.A. 39 20N 89 55W
38 Carlisle, Eng., U.K. ...54 54N 2 55W
160 Carlisle, U.S.A. 40 12N 77 10W
50 Carlitte, Pic, France ...42 35N 1 54E
72 Carloforte, Italy 39 10N 8 18E
41 Carlops, Scot., U.K. 55 47N 3 20W
172 Carlos Casares, Arg. ...35 53S 61 20W
172 Carlos Tejedor, Arg. ...35 25S 62 25W
45 Carlow, Ireland 52 50N 6 58W
45 Carlow, Co., Ireland ...52 43N 6 50W
42 Carloway, Scotland 58 17N 6 48W
167 Carlsbad, Calif., U.S.A. 33 11N 117 25W
165 Carlsbad, N. Mex., U.S.A. 32 20N 104 7W
39 Carlton, Eng., U.K. ...52 58N 1 6W
35 Carlton Colville, England, U.K. 52 27N 1 41E
39 Carlton Miniott, England, U.K. 54 13N 1 22W
35 Carlton Rode, England, United Kingdom 52 30N 1 6E
41 Carluke, Scotland, U.K. 55 44N 3 50W
157 Carlyle, Canada 49 40N 102 20W
164 Carlyle, U.S.A. 38 38N 89 23W
152 Carmacks, Canada 62 0N 136 0W
70 Carmagnola, Italy 44 50N 7 42E
157 Carman, Canada 49 30N 98 0W
156 Carmangay, Canada ...50 10N 113 10W
155 Carmanville, Canada .49 23N 54 19W
37 Carmarthen, Wales, United Kingdom 51 52N 4 20W
37 Carmarthen, Co., Wales, United Kingdom 53 40N 4 18W
37 Carmarthan B., Wales, U.K. 51 40N 4 30W
50 Carmaux, France 44 3N 2 10E
167 Carmel, Calif., U.S.A. 36 38N 121 55W
161 Carmel, N.Y. U.S.A. .41 25N 73 38W
37 Carmel Hd., Wales, U.K. 53 24N 4 34W
98 Carmel Mt., Israel 32 45N 35 3E
172 Carmelo, Uruguay 34 0S 58 10W
174 Carmen, Colombia 9 43N 75 6W
172 Carmen, Paraguay 27 13S 56 12W
168 Carmen I., Mexico 26 0N 111 20W
172 Carmen de Areco, Arg. 34 25S 59 48W
176 Carmen de Patagones, Argentina 40 50S 63 0W
62 Carmenes, Spain 42 58N 5 34W
172 Carmensa, Argentina .35 15S 67 40W
162 Carmi, U.S.A. 38 6N 88 10W
144 Carmila, Australia 21 53S 149 5E
63 Carmona, Spain 37 28N 5 42W
41 Carmyllie, Scot., U.K. 56 36N 2 41W
43 Carn Ban, Scot., U.K. 57 6N 4 15W
42 Carn Eige, Scot., U.K. 57 17N 5 9W
43 Carn Glas Chorie, Scotland, U.K. 57 20N 3 50W
43 Carn Mor, Scot., U.K. 57 14N 3 13W
43 Carn na Caim, Scotland, United Kingdom 56 54N 4 10W
43 Carn na Saobhaidh, Scotland, U.K. 57 12N 4 20W
44 Carna, Ireland 53 20N 9 50W
134 Carnarvon, S. Afr. 30 56S 22 8E
144 Carnarvon, Australia .25 0S 147 45E
142 Carnarvon, W. Austral. 24 51S 113 42E
145 Carnarvon Ra., Austral. 25 15S 148 30E
142 Carnarvon Ra., Austral. 25 0S 120 45E
106 Carnatic, Reg., India .12 0N 79 0E
63 Carnaxide, Portugal ...38 43N 9 14W
46 Carncastle, N. Ire., U.K. 54 55N 5 52W
46 Carndonagh, Ireland .55 15N 7 16W
157 Carnduff, Canada 49 10N 101 50W
37 Carnedd Llewelyn, Mt., Wales, U.K. 53 9N 3 58W
160 Carnegie, U.S.A. 40 24N 80 4W
142 Carnegie L., W. Austral. 26 5S 122 30E
45 Carnew, Ireland 52 43N 6 30W
46 Carney, Ireland 54 20N 8 30W
38 Carnforth, Eng., U.K. 54 8N 2 47W
46 Carnlough, N. Ire., U.K. 55 0N 6 0W
37 Carno, Wales, U.K. 52 34N 3 31W
138 Carnot B., W. Australia 17 20S 121 30E
41 Carnoustie, Scot., U.K. 56 30N 2 41W

MAP
45 Carnsore Pt., Ireland .52 10N 6 20W
41 Carnwath, Scot., U.K. 56 42N 3 38W
162 Caro, U.S.A. ...43 29N 83 27W
175 Carolina, Brazil ... 7 10S 47 30W
133 Carolina, Trans., S. Afr. ...26 5S 30 6E
137 Caroline I., Pac. Ocean ... 9 15S 150 3W
136 Caroline Is., Pac. Ocean ... 8 0N 150 0E
147 Caroline Pk., N.Z. ...45 57S 167 15E
156 Carolside, Canada ...51 20N 111 40W
134 Carolus, C. Prov., S. Afr. ...31 8S 24 53E
157 Caron, Canada ...50 30N 105 50W
174 Caroni R., Venezuela . 4 50N 62 20W
143 Caroona, Australia ...31 28S 150 5E
57 Carouge, Switzerland .46 11N 6 8E
73 Carovigno, Italy ...40 42N 17 40W
161 Carp, Canada ...45 20N 76 5E
59 Carpathians, mts., Eur. ...46 20N 26 0E
70 Carpendolo, Italy ...45 22N 10 25E
139 Carpentaria, G. of, N. Terr., Australia ...14 0S 139 0E
144 Carpentaria Downs, Queensland, Austral. ...18 44S 144 20E
51 Carpentras, France ...44 3N 5 2E
70 Carpi, Italy ...44 47N 10 52E
175 Carpina Grande, Brazil ... 7 50S 35 15W
73 Carpino, Italy ...41 50N 15 51E
167 Carpinteria, U.S.A. ...34 25N 119 37W
62 Carpio, Spain ...41 13N 5 7W
143 Carpolac, Vic., Austral. ...36 43S 141 18E
45 Carra L., Ireland ...53 41N 9 12W
163 Carrabelle, U.S.A. ...29 52N 84 40W
46 Carracastle, Ireland ...53 57N 8 42W
40 Carradale, Scot., U.K. 55 35N 5 30W
44 Carran Mt., Ireland ...51 51N 9 23W
70 Carrara, Italy ...44 5N 10 7E
64 Carrascosa de Campo, Spain ...40 2N 2 45W
174 Carrasquero, Venezuela ...10 55N 72 0W
143 Carrathool, Australia .34 22S 145 30E
44 Carrauntoohill Mt., Ire. ...52 0N 9 44W
145 Carraweena, S. Austral. ...29 10S 140 0E
43 Carrbridge, Scot., U.K. ...57 17N 3 50W
172 Carrera Pinto, Chile ...27 0S 170 0W
46 Carrick, Ireland ...54 40N 8 39W
40 Carrick, dist., Scotland, United Kingdom ...55 12N 4 38W
147 Carrick Ra., N.Z. ...45 15S 169 8E
46 Carrick-on-Shannon, Ire. ...53 57N 8 7W
45 Carrick-on-Suir, Ireland ...52 22N 7 30W
46 Carrickart, Ireland ...55 10N 7 47W
45 Carrickbeg, Ireland ...52 20N 7 25W
46 Carrickboy, Ireland ...53 36N 7 40W
46 Carrickfergus, Northern Ireland, U.K. ...54 43N 5 50W
46 Carrickmacross, Ire. ...54 0N 6 43W
145 Carrieton, S. Australia 32 27S 138 27E
44 Carrigaholt, Ireland ...52 37N 9 42W
44 Carrigahorig, Ireland .53 4N 8 10W
44 Carrigaline, Ireland ...51 49N 8 22W
44 Carrigallen, Ireland ...53 59N 7 40W
44 Carrigan Hd., Ireland 54 38N 8 40W
44 Carrignavar, Ireland .52 0N 8 29W
44 Carrigtwohill, Ireland 51 55N 8 15W
164 Carrington, U.S.A. ...47 30N 99 7W
62 Carrion, R., Spain ...42 42N 4 47W
62 Carrion de los Condes, Spain ...42 20N 4 37W
172 Carrizal Bajo, Chile ...28 5S 71 20W
172 Carrizalillo, Chile ...29 0S 71 30W
165 Carrizo Cr., U.S.A. ...36 30N 103 40W
165 Carrizo Springs, U.S.A. ...28 28N 99 50W
167 Carrizozo, U.S.A. ...33 40N 105 57W
164 Carroll, U.S.A. ...42 2N 94 55W
163 Carrollton, Ga., U.S.A. ...33 36N 85 5W
164 Carrollton, Ill., U.S.A. 39 20N 90 25W
162 Carrollton, Ky., U.S.A. ...38 40N 85 10W
164 Carrollton, Mo., U.S.A. ...39 19N 93 30W
160 Carrollton, Ohio, U.S.A. ...40 31N 81 9W
42 Carron L., Scot , U.K. 57 22N 5 35W
42 Carron R., Scot., U.K. 57 30N 5 30W
43 Carron R., Scot., U.K. 57 51N 4 40W
41 Carronbridge, Scotland, United Kingdom ...55 16N 3 46W
48 Carrouges, France ...48 34N 0 10W
46 Carrowkeel, Ireland ...55 7N 7 12W
45 Carrowmore L., Ireland ...54 12N 9 48W
46 Carryduff, N. Ire., U.K. ...54 32N 5 52W
100 Çarşamba, Turkey ...41 15N 36 45E
71 Carsoli, Italy ...42 7N 13 3E
164 Carson, U.S.A. ...46 27N 101 29W
166 Carson City, U.S.A. ...39 12N 119 52W
166 Carson L., U.S.A. ...39 50N 118 40W
162 Carsonville, U.S.A. ...43 25N 82 39W
40 Carsphairn, Scot., U.K. ...55 13N 4 15W
41 Carstairs, Scot., U.K. ..55 42N 3 41W
174 Cartagena, Colombia .10 25N 75 33W
65 Cartagena, Spain ...37 38N 0 59W
174 Cartago, Colombia ... 4 45N 75 55W
169 Cartago, Costa Rica ... 9 50N 84 0W
48 Cartaret, France ...49 23N 1 47W
63 Cartaxo, Portugal ...39 10N 8 47W
63 Cartaya, Spain ...37 16N 7 9W
163 Cartersville, U.S.A. ...34 11N 84 48W
146 Carterton, N.Z. ...41 2S 175 31E
165 Carthage, Ark., U.S.A. ...34 4N 92 32W
164 Carthage, Ill., U.S.A. .40 25N 91 10W
165 Carthage, Mo., U.S.A. 37 10N 94 20W
161 Carthage, N.Y., U.S.A. ...43 59N 75 37W
164 Carthage, S.D., U.S.A. 44 14N 97 38W
165 Carthage, Texas, U.S.A. ...32 8N 94 20W
38 Cartmel, England, U.K. ...54 13N 2 57W
155 Cartwright, Canada ...53 41N 56 58W
175 Caruaru, Brazil ... 8 15S 35 55W
174 Carupano, Venezuela .10 45N 63 15W
165 Caruthersville, U.S.A. 36 10N 89 40W
71 Carvarzere, Italy ...45 8N 12 7E
49 Carvin, France ...50 30N 2 57E
63 Carvoeira, Cabo Port. 39 21N 9 24W
174 Carvoeiro, Brazil ... 1 30S 61 59W
172 Casa Blanca, Chile ...33 20S 71 25W
63 Casa Branca, Portugal 38 29N 8 12W
167 Casa Grande, U.S.A. .32 53N 111 51W
175 Casa Nova, Brazil ... 9 10S 41 5W
122 Casablanca, Morocco ..33 43N 7 24W
73 Casacalenda, Italy ...41 45N 14 50E
71 Casalbordino, Italy ...42 10N 14 34E
73 Casal di Principe, Italy ...41 1N 14 8E
70 Casale Monferrato, Italy ...45 8N 8 28E
70 Casalmaggiore, Italy .44 59N 10 25E
70 Casalpusterlengo, Italy ...45 10N 9 40E
124 Casamance R., Senegal ...12 54N 15 0W
73 Casamássima, Italy ...40 58N 16 55E
73 Casarano, Italy ...40 0N 18 10E
63 Casares, Spain ...36 27N 5 16W
168 Casas Grandes, Mexico ...30 22N 108 0W
65 Casas Ibañez, Spain ...39 17N 1 20W
65 Casasimarro, Spain ...39 22N 2 3W
62 Casatejada, Spain ...39 54N 5 40W
62 Casavieja, Spain ...40 17N 4 46W
166 Cascade, Idaho, U.S.A. ...44 30N 116 2W
166 Cascade, Mont., U.S.A. ...47 16N 111 46W
166 Cascade Locks, U.S.A. 45 44N 121 5W
147 Cascade Pt., N.Z. ...44 1S 168 20E
166 Cascade Ra., U.S.A. ...44 0N 122 10W
63 Cascais, Portugal ...38 41N 9 25W
70 Cascina, Italy ...43 40N 10 32E
70 Caselle Tormese, Italy 45 12N 7 39E
73 Caserta, Italy ...41 5N 14 20E
44 Cashel, Ireland ...52 31N 7 53W
44 Cashla B., Ireland ...53 12N 9 37W
166 Cashmere, U.S.A. ...47 31N 120 30W
142 Cashmere Downs, W. Australia ...28 50S 119 30E
109 Casiguran, Philippines 16 15N 122 15E
172 Casilda, Argentina ...33 10S 61 10W
78 Casimcea, Rumania ...44 45N 28 23E
145 Casino, N.S.W., Austral. ...28 52S 153 3E
174 Casiquiare R., Ven. ... 2 45N 66 20W
58 Cáslav, Czechoslovakia ...49 54N 15 22E
174 Casma, Peru ... 9 30S 78 20W
71 Casola Valsenio, Italy 44 12N 11 40E
71 Casoli, Italy ...42 7N 14 18E
64 Caspe, Spain ...41 14N 0 1W
166 Casper, U.S.A. ...42 52N 106 27W
85 Caspian Sea, U.S.S.R. 43 0N 50 0E
48 Casquets, Rocks, Channel Islands, U.K. ...49 46N 2 15W
162 Cass City, U.S.A. ...43 34N 83 15W
164 Cass Lake, U.S.A. ...47 23N 94 38W
64 Cassá de la Selvá, Spain ...41 53N 2 52E
130 Cassai, Angola ...10 33S 21 59E
130 Cassai, R., Angola ...11 0S 21 30E
73 Cassanoallonio, Italy .39 47N 16 20E
49 Cassel, France ...50 48N 2 30E
161 Casselman, Canada ...45 18N 75 21W
164 Casselton, U.S.A. ...47 0N 97 15W
156 Cassiar Mts., Canada .59 30N 130 30W
143 Cassilis, N.S.W., Austral ...32 3S 149 58E
129 Cassinga, Angola ...15 5S 16 23E
156 Cassils, Canada ...50 29N 112 15W
72 Cassino, Italy ...41 30N 13 50E
175 Cassipore C., Brazil ... 3 50N 51 5W
51 Cassis, France ...43 14N 5 32E
165 Cassville, Mo., U.S.A. 36 45N 93 59W
70 Castagneto Carducci, It. ...43 9N 10 36E
70 Casteggio, Italy ...45 1N 9 8E
64 Castejón de Monegros, Spain ...41 37N 0 15W
73 Castel di Sangro, Italy 41 41N 14 5E
70 Castel San Giovanni, It. ...43 4N 9 25E
71 Castel San Pietro, Italy ...44 23N 11 30E
73 Castelbuono, Italy ...37 56N 14 4E
70 Casteldelfino, Italy ...44 35N 7 4E
70 Castelfiorentino, Italy 43 36N 10 58E
70 Castelfranco Emilia, It. ...44 37N 11 2E
71 Castelfranco Veneto, It. ...45 40N 11 56E
50 Casteljaloux, France .44 19N 0 6E
73 Castellabate, Italy ...40 18N 14 55E
72 Castellammare, G. di, It. ...35 5N 12 55E
72 Castellammare del Golfo, Italy ...38 2N 12 53E
73 Castellammare di Stábia, Italy ...40 47N 14 29E
70 Castellamonte, Italy ...45 23N 7 42E
73 Castellana Grotte, Italy ...40 53N 17 10E
51 Castellane, France ...43 50N 6 31E
73 Castellaneta, Italy ...40 40N 16 57E
65 Castellar de Santisteban, Spain .38 16N 3 8W
70 Castelleone, Italy ...45 19N 9 47E
172 Castelli, Argentina ...36 7S 57 47W
64 Castellón, Prov., Spain ...40 15N 0 5W
64 Castellon de Ampurias, Spain ...42 15N 3 4E
64 Castellón de la Plana, Spain ...39 58N 0 3W
64 Castellote, Spain ...40 48N 0 15W
64 Castelltersol, Spain ...41 45N 2 8E
73 Castelmauro, Italy ...41 50N 14 40E
50 Castelnau de Médoc, Fr. ...43 2N 0 48W
50 Castelnaudary, France 43 20N 1 58E
70 Castelnuevo ne Monti, Italy ...44 27N 10 26E
70 Castelnuovo di Val di Cécina, Italy ...43 12N 10 54E
62 Castelo Branco, Dist., Portugal...39 52N 7 45W
62 Castelo Branco, Port. .39 50N 7 31W
62 Castelo de Paiva, Port. ...41 2N 8 16W
63 Castelo de Vide, Port. 39 25N 7 27W
50 Castelsarrasin, France 44 2N 1 3E
72 Casteltermini, Italy ...37 32N 13 38E
72 Castelvetrano, Italy ...37 40N 12 46E
143 Casterton, Australia ...37 30S 141 30E
50 Castets, France ...43 52N 1 6W
71 Castiglione del Lago, It. ...43 7N 12 3E
70 Castiglione della Pescáia, Italy ...42 46N 10 53E
70 Castiglione della Stiviere, Italy ...45 23N 10 30E
71 Castiglione Fiorentino, Italy ...43 20N 11 55E
62 Castiblanco, Spain ...39 17N 5 5W
63 Castile, see New and Old Castile, Sp. ..40 15N 3 30W
50 Castillon, Ariège, France ...42 56N 1 1E
50 Castillon, Gironde, Fr. 44 51N 0 2W
50 Callonstinès, France ...44 39N 0 37E
173 Castillos, Uruguay ...34 12S 53 52W
35 Castle Acre, Eng., U.K. ...52 42N 0 42W
36 Castle Cary, Eng., U.K. ...51 5N 2 32W
166 Castle Dale, U.S.A. ...39 11N 111 1W
34 Castle Donington, England, U.K. ...52 50N 1 20W
41 Castle Douglas, Scotland, U.K. ...54 57N 3 57W
41 Castle Eden, Eng., U.K. ...54 45N 1 20W
169 Cas. Harbour, Bermuda ...32 17N 64 44W
164 Castle Rock, Colo., U.S.A. ...39 26N 104 50W
166 Castle Rock, Wash., U.S.A. ...46 20N 122 58W
45 Castlebar, Ireland ...53 52N 9 17W
42 Castlebay, Scot., U.K. 56 57N 7 30W
46 Castlebellingham, Ire. 53 53N 6 22W
44 Castleblakeney, Ireland ...53 26N 8 30W
46 Castleblayney, Ireland 54 7N 6 44W
45 Castlebridge, Ireland .52 23N 6 28W
146 Castlecliff, New Zealand ...39 54S 170 0E
45 Castlecomer, Ireland .52 49N 7 13W
44 Castleconnell, Ireland 52 44N 8 30W
46 Castledawson, Northern Ireland, U.K. ...54 47N 6 35W
46 Castlederg, N. Ire., U.K. ...54 43N 7 35W
45 Castledermot, Ireland 52 55N 6 50W
46 Castlefinn, Ireland ...54 47N 7 35W
39 Castleford, Eng., U.K. 53 43N 1 21W
156 Castlegar, Canada ...49 20N 117 40W
164 Castlegate, U.S.A. ...39 45N 110 57W
44 Castlegregory, Ireland 52 16N 10 0W
45 Castlehill, Ireland ...51 1N 9 49W
44 Castleisland, Ireland .52 14N 9 28W
44 Castlemaine, Ireland .52 10N 9 42W
143 Castlemaine, Australia 37 2S 144 12E
44 Castlemaine Harb., Ire. ...52 8N 9 50W
44 Castlemartyr, Ireland 51 54N 8 3W
46 Castlepollard, Ireland 53 40N 7 20W
46 Castlereagh, Ireland ...53 47N 8 30W
138 Castlereagh B., Austral ...12 10S 135 10E
143 Castlereagh R., Austral. ...30 30S 148 14E
39 Castleton, Eng., U.K. 54 27N 0 57W
161 Castleton, N.Y., U.S.A. ...42 33N 73 44W
38 Castletown, Isle of Man, United Kingdom ...54 4N 4 40W
45 Castletown, Laois, Ireland ...52 58N 7 31W
46 Castletown, Meath, Ire. ...53 47N 6 41W
43 Castletown, Scot., U.K. ...58 35N 3 22W
44 Castletown Bearhaven, Ireland 51 40N 9 54W
45 Castletown Geoghegan, Ireland 53 27N 7 30W
44 Castletownroche, Ire. .52 10N 8 28W
44 Castletownsend, Ire. ...51 31N 9 11W
144 Castlevale, Australia .24 30S 146 48E
46 Castlewellan, N. Ire., United Kingdom ...54 16N 5 57W
156 Castor, Canada ...52 15N 111 50W
161 Castoland, U.S.A. ...43 52N 75 31W
50 Castres, France ...43 37N 2 13E
169 Castries, St. Lucia, W.I. ...14 0N 60 50W
65 Castril, Spain ...37 48N 2 46W
173 Castro, Brazil ...24 45S 50 0W
176 Castro, Chile ...42 30S 73 50W
175 Castro Alves, Brazil ...12 46S 39 33W
63 Castro del Rio, Spain .37 41N 4 29W
63 Castro Marim, Portugal ...37 13N 7 26W
64 Castro Urdiales, Spain 43 23N 3 19W
63 Castro Verde, Portugal ...37 41N 8 4W
62 Castrojeriz, Spain ...42 17N 4 9W
62 Castropol, Spain ...43 32N 7 0W
51 Castrop-Rauxel, Ger. .51 34N 7 19E
73 Castrovillari, Italy ...39 49N 16 11E
165 Castroville, U.S.A. ...29 20N 98 53W
63 Castuera, Spain ...38 43N 5 37W
132 Casula, Mozambique .15 28S 33 40E
169 Cat I., Bahamas ...24 30N 75 30W
165 Cat I., U.S.A. ...30 15N 89 7W
154 Cat L., Canada ...51 40N 91 50W
59 Cata, Czechoslovakia .47 58N 18 38E
174 Catacaos, Peru ... 5 20S 80 45W
174 Catacocha, Ecuador ... 4 3S 79 40W
173 Cataguases, Brazil ...21 23S 42 39W
165 Catahoula L., U.S.A. .31 30N 92 5W
175 Catalão, Brazil ...18 5S 47 52W
100 Catalca, Turkey ...41 9N 28 28E
155 Catalina, Canada ...48 31N 53 4W
64 Catalonia, Prov., Spain ...41 40N 1 15E
172 Catamarca, Argentina 28 30S 65 50W
172 Catamarca, Prov., Arg. ...28 30S 65 50W
109 Catanduanes Is., Phil. 13 50N 124 20E
173 Catanduva, Brazil ...21 5S 48 58W
73 Catania, Sicily, Italy .37 31N 15 4E
73 Catania, G. di, Italy ...37 25N 15 8E
73 Catanzaro, Italy ...38 54N 16 38E
109 Catarman, Philippines 12 28N 124 1E
138 Catastrophe C., Austral. ...34 59S 136 0E
41 Catcleugh, Eng., U.K. 55 19N 2 22W
109 Cateel, Philippines ... 7 47N 126 24E
35 Caterham, Eng., U.K. 51 16N 0 4W
135 Cathcart, S. Africa ...32 18S 27 10E
143 Cathkin, Australia ...37 9S 145 6E
47 Catine, dist., France ...46 30N 0 15W
168 Cativá, Panama ... 9 21N 79 49W
166 Cathlamet, U.S.A. ...46 15N 123 29W
162 Catlettsburg, U.S.A. ...38 23N 82 38W
168 Catoche C., Mexico ...21 40N 87 0W
38 Caton, England, U.K. 54 5N 2 41W
65 Catral, Spain ...38 10N 0 47W
71 Catria, Mt., Italy ...43 28N 12 42E
174 Catrimani, Brazil ... 0 27N 61 41W
40 Catrine, Scot., U.K. ...55 30N 4 20W
35 Catsfield, Eng., U.K. .50 53N 0 28E
161 Catskill, U.S.A. ...42 14N 73 52W
161 Catskill Mts., U.S.A. .42 15N 74 15W
162 Cattaraugus, U.S.A. ...42 22N 78 52W
39 Catterick, Eng., U.K. 54 23N 1 38W
71 Cattólica, Emilia Romagna, Italy ...43 58N 12 43E
72 Cattólica Eraclea, Sicily, Italy ...37 27N 13 24E
38 Catton, England, U.K. ...54 56N 2 16W
127 Cattu, Ethiopia ... 8 38N 37 58E
130 Catumbela, Angola ...12 27S 13 31E
130 Catumbela, R., Angola ...12 30S 14 20E
132 Catur, Mozambique ...13 45S 35 30E
174 Cauca R., Colombia ... 7 30N 75 30W
89 Caucasus Ra., U.S.S.R. ...43 0N 44 0E
175 Caucia, Brazil ... 3 40S 38 55W
48 Caudebec, France ...49 30N 0 42E
65 Caudete, Spain ...38 42N 1 2W
49 Caudry, France ...50 7N 3 22E
41 Caulkerbush, Scot., U.K. ...54 54N 3 40W
48 Caulnes, France ...48 18N 2 10W
73 Caulónia, Italy ...38 23N 16 25E
130 Caúngula, Angola ... 8 15S 18 50E
172 Cauquenes, Chile ...36 0S 72 30W
132 Caura R., Venezuela ... 6 20N 64 30W
132 Cauresi, R., Mozam. ...17 40S 33 10E
155 Causapscal, Canada ...48 19N 67 12W
44 Causeway, Ireland ...52 25N 9 45W
50 Caussade, France ...44 10N 1 33E
50 Cauterets, France ...42 52N 0 8W
106 Cauvery R., India ...12 0N 77 45E
48 Caux, dist., France ...49 38N 0 35E
73 Cava dei Tirreni, Italy 40 42N 14 42E
62 Cavado, R., Portugal .41 37N 8 15W
51 Cavaillon, France ...43 50N 5 2E
51 Cavalaire, France ...43 10N 6 33E
71 Cavalese, Italy ...46 17N 11 29E
164 Cavalier, U.S.A. ...48 50N 97 39W
146 Cavalli Is., N.Z. ...35 0S 173 58E
51 Cavallo, I. de, France 41 22N 9 15E
124 Cavally R., Liberia ... 5 0N 7 40W
46 Cavan, Ireland ...54 0N 7 22W
46 Cavan, co., Ireland ...53 58N 7 10W
142 Cavanagh Ra., Austral. ...26 10S 122 50E
162 Cave City, U.S.A. ...37 13N 85 57W
143 Cavendish, Australia .37 31S 142 2E
154 Cavers, Canada ...48 55N 87 41W
175 Caviana I., Brazil ... 0 15N 50 0W
174 Cavianas, Bolivia ...12 40S 67 0W
70 Cavour, Italy ...44 47N 7 22E
74 Cavtat, Yugoslavia ...42 35N 18 13E
43 Cawdor, Scot., U.K. ...57 31N 3 56W
143 Cawndilla, L., Austral. ...32 30S 142 15E
105 Cawnpore, *see* Kanpur, India ...26 35N 80 20E
36 Cawsand, Eng., U.K. .50 20N 4 12W
35 Cawston, Eng., U.K. .52 47N 1 10E
173 Caxambú, Brazil ...22 0S 45 0W
175 Caxias, Maranhão, Braz. ... 5 0S 43 27W
173 Caxias do Sul, Brazil .29 10S 51 10W
122 Caxine, C., Algeria ...35 56N 0 27W
130 Caxito, Angola ... 8 30S 13 30E
130 Caxopa, Angola ...11 45S 20 57E
174 Cayambe, Ecuador ... 0 3N 78 22W
163 Cayce, U.S.A. ...33 59N 81 2W
175 Cayenne, Fr. Guinea . 5 0N 52 18W
49 Cayeux-sur-Mer., Fr. 50 10N 1 30E
50 Caylus, France ...44 15N 1 47E
169 Cayman Is., W. Indies 19 40N 79 50W
168 Cayo, Brit. Honduras 17 10N 89 0W
169 Cayo Romano, I., Cuba ...22 0N 73 30W
160 Cayuga, Canada ...42 59N 79 50W
161 Cayuga, U.S.A. ...42 54N 76 44W
161 Cayuga L., U.S.A. ...42 45N 76 45W
63 Cazalla, de la Sierra, Sp. ...37 56N 5 45W
78 Căzănești, Rumania ...44 36N 27 3E
50 Cazaux, Etang de, Fr. 44 30N 1 10E
50 Cazères, France ...43 13N 1 5E
71 Cazin, Yugoslavia ...44 57N 15 57E
71 Čazma, Yugoslavia ...45 45N 16 39E
130 Cazombo, Angola ...12 0S 22 48E
65 Cazorla, Spain ...37 55N 3 2W
62 Cea, R., Spain ...42 40N 5 5W
54 Ceadâr Lunga, U.S.S.R. ...46 2N 28 46E
46 Ceanannus Mor, Ireland ...53 42N 6 53W
175 Ceará, st., Brazil ... 5 0S 40 0W
175 Ceara Mirim, Brazil ... 5 38S 35 25W
172 Cebollar, Argentina ...29 10S 66 35W
62 Cebreros, Spain ...40 27N 4 28W
109 Cebu, Philippines ...10 30N 124 0E
109 Cebu, I., Philippines .10 23N 123 58E
72 Ceccano, Italy ...41 34N 13 18E
59 Cece, Hungary ...46 46N 18 39E
145 Cecil Plains, Australia 27 30S 151 11E
70 Cecina, Italy ...43 19N 10 33E
70 Cecina R., Italy ...43 19N 10 40E
62 Ceclavin, Spain ...39 50N 6 45W
167 Cedar City, U.S.A. ...37 41N 113 3W
165 Cedar Creek Res., U.S.A. ...32 15N 96 0W
164 Cedar Falls, U.S.A. ...42 39N 92 29W
163 Cedar Key, U.S.A. ...29 9N 83 5W
157 Cedar L., Canada ...53 30N 100 30W
164 Cedar Rapids, U.S.A. .42 0N 91 38W
164 Cedar R., U.S.A. ...41 50N 91 20W
162 Cedarburg, U.S.A. ...43 18N 87 55W
163 Cedartown, U.S.A. ...34 1N 85 15W
156 Cedarvale, Canada ...55 1N 128 22W
135 Cedarville, S. Africa ...30 23S 29 3E
166 Cedarville, U.S.A. ...41 37N 120 13W
62 Cedeira, Spain ...43 39N 8 2W
168 Cedral, Mexico ...23 50N 100 42W
72 Cedrino R., Italy ...40 8N 9 25E
175 Cedro, Brazil ... 6 34S 39 3W
168 Cedros, I. de, Mexico 28 10N 115 20W
138 Ceduna, S. Australia .32 7S 133 46E
156 Ceepeecee, Canada ...49 52N 126 42W
73 Cefalu, Italy ...38 3N 14 1E
62 Cega R., Spain ...41 17N 4 10W
59 Cegléd, Hungary ...47 11N 19 47E
73 Ceglie Messapico, Italy ...40 39N 17 31E
65 Cehegin, Spain ...38 6N 1 48W
78 Cehul Silvaniei, Rum. 47 24N 23 9E
78 Ceica, Rumania ...46 53N 22 10E
62 Ceira, R., Portugal ...40 15N 7 55W
123 Cekhira, Tunisia ...34 20N 10 5E
71 Celano, Italy ...42 6N 13 30E
62 Celanova, Spain ...42 9N 7 58W
45 Celbridge, Ireland ...53 20N 6 33W
109 Celebes I., *see* Sulawesi, Indonesia 2 0S 120 0E
109 Celebes Sea, Indonesia 3 0N 123 0E
127 Celga, Ethiopia ...12 38N 37 3E
74 Čelić, Yugoslavia ...44 43N 18 47E
162 Celina, U.S.A. ...40 32N 84 31W
71 Celje, Yugoslavia ...46 16N 15 18E
42 Cellar Hd., Scot., U.K. ...58 25N 6 10W
59 Celldömölk, Hungary .47 16N 17 10E
56 Celle, Germany ...52 37N 10 4E
62 Celorico da Beira, Port. ...40 38N 7 24W
37 Cemaes, Wales, U.K. .53 24N 4 27W
37 Cemaes Hd. Wales, United Kingdom ...52 7N 4 44W
165 Cement, U.S.A. ...34 56N 98 8W
37 Cemmaes Road, Wales, United Kingdom ...52 39N 3 41W
37 Cenarth, Wales, U.K. 52 3N 4 32W
51 Cenis, Col du Mt., Fr. 45 17N 7 0E

MAP
70 Ceno R., Italy 44 40N 9 52E
50 Cenon, France 44 50N 0 33W
70 Centallo, Italy 44 30N 7 35E
164 Center, N.D., U.S.A. .47 9N 101 17W
165 Center, Texas, U.S.A. 31 50N 94 10W
166 Centerfield, U.S.A. 39 9N 111 56W
163 Centerville, Ala., U.S.A. 32 55N 87 7W
164 Centerville, Iowa, U.S.A. 40 45N 92 57W
165 Centerville, Miss., U.S.A. 31 10N 91 3W
160 Centerville, Pa., U.S.A. 40 3N 79 59W
164 Centerville, S.D., U.S.A. 43 10N 96 58W
163 Centerville, Tenn., U.S.A. 35 46N 87 29W
165 Centerville, Tex., U.S.A. 31 15N 95 56W
71 Cento, san Giovanni, It. 44 43N 11 16E
168 Central America 10 0N 83 0W
162 Central City, Ky., U.S.A. 37 20N 87 7W
164 Central City, Neb., U.S.A. 41 8N 98 0W
131 Central I., L. Rudolf, Kenya 3 30N 36 0E
107 Central Highlands, S. Vietnam 13 20N 108 30E
161 Central Islip, U.S.A. .40 49N 73 13W
102 Central Makran Ra., West Pakistan 26 30N 64 15E
154 Central Patricia, Can. 51 20N 90 10W
29 Central Plain, Ireland 53 20N 8 0W
144 Central Ra., New Guinea 5 0S 143 0E
19 Central Russian Uplands, Europe 54 0N 36 0E
91 Central Siberian Plateau, U.S.S.R. 65 0N 105 0E
164 Centralia, Ill., U.S.A. .38 32N 89 5W
164 Centralia, Mo., U.S.A. 39 12N 92 6W
166 Centralia, Wash., U.S.A. 46 46N 122 59W
75 Centralni Rodopi, Range, Bulgaria 41 40N 24 45E
73 Centúripe, Italy 37 37N 14 41E
77 Cephalonia I., see Kefallinia, Greece ...38 28N 20 30E
74 Čepin, Yugoslavia 45 32N 18 34E
72 Ceprano, Italy 41 33N 13 30E
78 Ceptura, Rumania 45 1N 26 21E
109 Ceram I., Indonesia ... 3 10S 129 0E
109 Ceram Sea, Indonesia 2 30S 128 30E
50 Cerbère, France 42 26N 3 10E
51 Cerbicales, Iles, France 41 33N 9 22E
78 Cerbu, Rumania 44 46N 24 46E
63 Cercal, Portugal 37 48N 8 40W
73 Cercemaggiòre, Italy .41 27N 14 43E
62 Cerdela, Spain 42 33N 8 23W
71 Cerea, Italy 45 12N 11 13E
172 Ceres, Argentina 29 55S 61 55W
134 Ceres, C. Prov., S. Afr. 33 21S 19 18E
70 Ceres, Italy 45 19N 7 22E
41 Ceres, Scotland, U.K. 56 18N 2 57W
50 Céret, France 42 30N 2 42E
73 Cerignola, Italy 41 17N 15 53E
77 Cerigo I., see Kithira, Greece 36 9N 23 0E
50 Cérilly, France 46 37N 2 50E
49 Cerisiers, France 48 8N 3 30E
48 Cerizay, France 46 50N 0 40W
71 Cerknica, Yugoslavia .45 48N 14 21E
100 Çerkes, Turkey 40 40N 32 58E
74 Čermerno Ra., Y.-slav. 43 35N 20 25E
78 Cerna, Rumania 44 4N 28 17E
78 Cerna, R., Rumania ...44 45N 24 0E
78 Cernavodă, Rumania .44 22N 28 3E
49 Cernay, France 47 48N 7 10E
36 Cerne Abbas, Eng., U.K. 50 49N 2 29W
74 Černik, Yugoslavia 45 17N 17 22E
168 Cerralvo, I., Mexico ...24 20N 109 45E
73 Cerreto Sannita, Italy 41 17N 14 34E
37 Cerrig-y-druidion, Wales, U.K. 53 2N 3 34W
168 Cerritos, Mexico 22 20N 100 20W
167 Cerro, U.S.A. 36 47N 105 36W
174 Cerro Bolivar, Ven. ... 7 35N 62 45W
174 Cerro de Pasco Mt., Peru 10 45S 76 10W
70 Certaldo, Italy 43 32N 11 2E
73 Cervaro R., Italy 41 21N 15 30E
64 Cervera, Catalonia, Sp. 41 40N 1 16E
62 Cervera de Pisuerga, Sp. 42 51N 4 30W
64 Cervera del Rio Alhama, Spain 42 2N 1 58W
71 Cérvia, Italy 44 15N 12 20E
71 Cervignano del Friuli, Italy 45 49N 13 20E
73 Cervinara, Italy 41 2N 14 36E
51 Cervione, Corsica, Fr. 42 20N 9 29E
62 Cervo, Spain 43 40N 7 24W
73 Cesaro, Italy 37 50N 14 38E
71 Cesena, Italy 44 9N 12 14E
71 Cesenático, Italy 44 12N 12 22E
86 Cesis, U.S.S.R. 57 17N 25 28E
58 Česká Lipa, Cz. 50 43N 14 35E
59 Česka Třebova, Cz. 49 54N 16 27E
58 České Budějovice, Cz. 48 55N 14 25E
58 České Velenice, Cz. 48 45N 15 1E
58 Ceskomoravska Vrchovina Mts., Cz. 49 20N 15 45E
MAP
58 Český Brod, Cz. 50 4N 14 52E
58 Český Krumlov, Cz. ...48 43N 14 21E
59 Český Těšin, Cz. 49 45N 18 39E
77 Çeşme, Turkey 38 20N 26 23E
124 Cestos R., Liberia 5 30N 9 30W
143 Cessnock, Australia ...33 0S 151 15E
78 Cetatea, Rumania 44 7N 23 2E
71 Cetina, R., Y.-slavia .43 50N 16 30E
71 Cetingrad, Yugoslavia 45 8N 15 46E
74 Cetinje, Yugoslavia ...42 23N 18 59E
73 Cetraro, Italy 39 30N 15 56E
122 Ceuta, (Sebta), Morocco 35 52N 5 26W
70 Ceva, Italy 44 23N 8 0E
50 Cevennes, Mts., France 44 10N 3 50E
106 Ceylon, st., see Sri Lanka 7 30N 80 50E
55 Chaam, Netherlands ...51 30N 4 52E
51 Chabeuil, France 44 54N 5 1E
142 Chabjuwardoo B., Western Australia .23 0S 113 30E
51 Chablais, dist., France 46 20N 6 45E
49 Chablis, France 47 47N 3 48E
122 Chabounia, Algeria ...35 30N 2 45E
172 Chacabuco, Argentina 34 40S 60 27W
36 Chacewater, Eng., U.K. 50 15N 5 8W
174 Chachapoyas, Peru 6 15S 77 50W
107 Chachoengsao, Thailand 13 45N 101 12E
104 Chachro, W. Pakistan 25 5N 70 15E
172 Chaco, prov. Arg. 25 0S 61 0W
176 Chaco Austral, Arg. ...27 30S 61 40W
172 Chaco Boreal, reg., Par. 22 30S 60 10W
176 Chaco Central, Arg. ...24 0S 61 0W
121 Chad, L., Chad 13 30N 14 30W
121 Chad, Rep., Africa 12 30N 17 15E
164 Chadron, U.S.A. 42 50N 103 0W
132 Chadwa, Zambia 12 5S 32 35E
88 Chadyr Lunga, U.S.S.R. 46 3N 28 51E
101 Chagai Hills, Afghan. .29 30N 63 0E
36 Chagford, Eng., U.K. 50 40N 3 50W
49 Chagny, France 46 57N 4 45E
91 Chagoda, U.S.S.R. 58 45N 130 30E
86 Chagoda, U.S.S.R. 59 10N 35 25E
93 Chagos Arch. Br. Indian Ocean Terr. 6 0S 72 0E
168 Chagres R., Panama Canal Zone 9 5N 79 40W
169 Chaguaramas, Trinidad 10 46N 61 43W
101 Chah Bahar, Iran 25 20N 60 40E
101 Chahar Buriak, Afghan. 30 15N 62 0E
101 Chahbar, Iran 25 20N 60 40E
107 Chai-nat, Thailand 15 15N 100 25E
50 Chaillé les Marais, Fr. 46 25N 1 2W
104 Chaj Doab, W. Pak. ...32 0N 73 0E
172 Chajari, Argentina 30 42N 58 0W
132 Chakari, Rhodesia 18 5S 29 51E
131 Chake Chake, Tanzania 5 15S 39 45E
101 Chakhansur, Afghan. .31 10N 62 0E
104 Chaklashi, India 22 40N 72 52E
155 Chakonipau, L., Canada 56 10N 67 45W
105 Chakradharpur, India 22 45N 85 40E
104 Chakwal, W. Pak. 32 50N 72 45E
174 Chala, Peru 15 48S 74 20W
112 Chalainor, China 49 31N 117 30E
50 Chalais, France 45 16N 0 3E
106 Chalakudi, India 10 18N 76 20E
112 Chalantun, see Putehachi, China ...48 4N 122 45E
77 Chalcis, see Khalkis, Greece 38 27N 23 42E
34 Chale, England, U.K. 50 35N 1 19W
155 Chaleur, Baie de, Can. 47 55N 65 30W
35 Chalfont St. Peter, England, U.K. 51 36N 0 33W
174 Chalhuanca, Peru 14 15S 73 5W
113 Chaling, China 26 55N 113 30E
104 Chalisgaon, India 20 30N 75 10E
89 Chalkar, Kazakhstan, U.S.S.R. 50 35N 51 52E
89 Chalkar L., U.S.S.R. .50 40N 51 45E
55 Chalkidike, Prov. Gr. .40 28N 23 20E
147 Chalky Inlet, N.Z. 46 3S 166 31E
48 Challans, France 46 50N 2 0W
174 Challapata, Bolivia 19 0S 66 50W
49 Challerange, France ...49 18N 4 46E
166 Challis, U.S.A. 44 32N 114 25W
105 Chalna, E. Pakistan ..22 36N 89 35E
48 Chalonnes, France 47 20N 0 45W
49 Châlons-sur-Marne, Fr. 48 58N 4 20E
49 Châlons-sur-Saône, Fr. 46 48N 4 50E
135 Chalumna, S. Africa ...33 14S 27 30E
50 Chalus, France 45 39N 0 58E
57 Cham, Germany 49 12N 12 40E
167 Chama, U.S.A. 36 57N 106 37W
132 Chama, Zambia 11 5S 33 11E
102 Chaman, W. Pakistan 30 58N 66 25E
106 Chamarajanagar-Ramasamudram, India 11 52N 76 52E
64 Chamartin de la Rosa, Spain 40 28N 3 40W
104 Chamba, India 32 35N 76 10E
131 Chamba, Tanzania .. 11 37S 37 0E
104 Chambal, R., India ...26 0N 76 55E
164 Chamberlain, U.S.A. .43 50N 99 21W
167 Chambers, U.S.A. 35 13N 109 30W
162 Chambersburg, U.S.A. 39 53N 77 41W
51 Chambéry, France 45 34N 5 55E
132 Chambeshi, Zambia ...10 58S 31 5E
MAP
132 Chambeshi R., Zambia 10 20S 31 58E
123 Chambi, Djebel, Tunisia 35 12N 8 49E
132 Chambishi, Zambia ...12 39N 28 1E
161 Chambly, Canada 45 27N 73 17W
48 Chambois, France 48 48N 0 6E
155 Chambord, Canada 48 25N 72 6W
50 Chamboulive, France .45 26N 1 42E
144 Chambri L., New Guin. 4 15S 143 10E
111 Chamdo, China 31 21N 97 2E
103 Chamdo Area, China .31 1N 96 15E
132 Chametengo, Mozam. .17 1S 35 24E
172 Chamical, Argentina .30 22S 66 27W
51 Chamonix, France 45 55N 6 51E
105 Champa, India 22 2N 82 43E
156 Champagne, Canada ...60 49N 136 30W
49 Champagne, reg., Fr. .49 0N 4 40E
49 Champagnole, France 46 45N 5 55E
162 Champaign, Ill., U.S.A. 40 8N 88 14W
49 Champaubert, France 48 50N 3 45E
50 Champdeniers, France 46 29N 0 25W
50 Champeix, France 45 37N 3 8E
155 Champlain, Canada ...46 27N 72 24W
161 Champlain, L., U.S.A. 44 30N 73 20W
168 Champotón, Mexico ...19 20N 90 50W
63 Chamusca, Portugal ...39 21N 8 29W
172 Chañaral, Chile 26 15S 70 50W
104 Chanasma, India 23 44N 72 5E
63 Chanca, R., Portugal .37 49N 7 15W
172 Chanco, Chile 35 43S 72 35W
106 Chanda, India 19 57N 79 25E
104 Chandausi, India 28 27N 78 49E
65 Chandeleur Is., U.S.A. 29 45N 88 53W
165 Chandeleur Sd., U.S.A. 29 58N 88 40W
105 Chandernagore, India 22 52N 88 24E
104 Chandigarh, India 30 30N 76 58E
155 Chandler, Canada 48 18N 64 46W
167 Chandler, Ariz., U.S.A. 33 20N 111 56W
165 Chandler, Okla., U.S.A. 35 43N 97 20W
34 Chandler's Ford, England, U.K. 50 59N 1 23W
105 Chandpur, E. Pakistan 23 8N 90 42E
104 Chandpur, India 29 8N 78 19E
111 Chandmani, Mongolia 45 22N 98 2E
104 Chang, W. Pakistan ...26 59N 68 30E
106 Changanacheri, India . 9 25N 76 31E
132 Changane, R., Mozambique 23 30S 33 50E
132 Changara, Mozambique 16 50S 33 17E
112 Changchih, China 36 7N 113 0E
113 Changchow, China 31 45N 120 0E
112 Changchow, China 36 55N 118 3E
113 Changchow, China 24 32N 117 44E
112 Changchun, China 43 58N 125 9E
112 Changhai, China 39 12N 122 28E
113 Changhua, Taiwan 24 2N 120 30E
113 Changkiang (Shihlu), Hainan, China 19 25N 108 57E
113 Changkiang (Tsamkong), China .21 7N 110 21E
112 Changkwansai Mts., China 44 40N 129 0E
112 Changli, China 39 40N 119 19E
113 Changlo, China 24 0N 115 33E
113 Changning, China 26 25N 112 15E
112 Changpai, China 41 26N 128 0E
112 Changpai Shan Mts., China 42 0N 128 0E
112 Changping, China 40 15N 116 15E
113 Changping, China 25 30N 117 33E
112 Changpu, China 24 2N 117 31E
113 Changsha, China 28 5N 113 1E
113 Changshow, China 29 49N 107 10E
113 Changshu, China 31 33N 120 45E
113 Changtai, China 24 34N 117 50E
113 Changteh, China 29 12N 111 43E
113 Changting, China 25 46N 116 30E
112 Changtu, China 42 50N 124 0E
112 Changwu, China 42 21N 122 45E
111 Changyeh, China 39 0N 100 59E
112 Chanhwa, China 37 46N 117 44E
106 Channapatna, India ...12 40N 77 15E
48 Channel Is., U.K. 49 30N 2 40W
162 Channing, Mich., U.S.A. 46 9N 88 1W
165 Channing, Tex., U.S.A. 35 45N 102 20W
62 Chantada, Spain 42 36N 7 46W
107 Chanthaburi, Thailand 12 38N 102 12E
49 Chantilly, France 49 12N 2 38E
48 Chantonnay, France ...46 40N 1 3W
152 Chantrey Inlet, Canada 67 30N 96 0W
165 Chanute, U.S.A. 37 45N 95 25W
111 Chanyi, China 25 56N 104 1E
112 Chanyu, China 44 37N 122 39E
107 Chao Phraya, R., Thai. 15 0N 100 20E
107 Chao Phraya Lowlands, Thailand 15 30N 100 0E
113 Chaoan, China 23 45N 117 11E
113 Chaochow, China 23 45N 116 32E
113 Chaohwa, China 32 16N 105 41E
113 Chaoping, China 24 1N 110 59E
111 Chaotung, China 27 30N 103 40E
112 Chaoyan, China 37 23N 120 29E
112 Chaoyang, China 41 46N 120 16E
113 Chaoyang, China 23 10N 116 30E
90 Chap Kuduk, U.S.S.R. 48 45N 55 5E
168 Chapala L., Mexico ...20 10N 103 20W
MAP
89 Chapayevo, U.S.S.R. .50 25N 51 10E
87 Chapayevsk, U.S.S.R. 53 0N 49 40E
173 Chapeco, Brazil 27 14S 52 41W
163 Chapel Hill, U.S.A. ...35 53N 79 3W
38 Chapel-en-le-Frith, England, U.K. 53 19N 1 54W
154 Chapleau, Canada 47 45N 83 30W
88 Chaplino, U.S.S.R. 48 8N 36 15E
87 Chaplygin, U.S.S.R. ...53 15N 39 55E
105 Chapra, India 25 48N 84 50E
120 Char, Mauritania 21 40N 12 45W
172 Charadai, Argentina ...27 35S 60 0W
174 Charagua, Bolivia 19 45S 63 10W
101 Charak, Iran 26 46N 54 18E
174 Charambirá Pt., Col. . 4 20N 77 30W
174 Charaña, Bolivia 17 30S 69 35W
172 Charata, Argentina ...27 13S 61 14W
168 Charcas, Mexico 23 10N 101 20W
111 Charchan, China 38 4N 85 16E
111 Charchan, R., China ...39 0N 86 0E
15 Charcot I., Antarctica 70 0S 75 0W
157 Chard, Canada 55 55N 111 10W
36 Chard, England, U.K. 50 52N 2 59W
160 Chardon, Ohio, U.S.A. 41 34N 81 17W
90 Chardzhou, U.S.S.R. .39 0N 63 20E
50 Charente, dépt., France 45 50N 0 36W
50 Charente R., France ...45 41N 0 30W
50 Charente-Maritime, dépt., France 45 50N 0 35W
121 Chari R., Chad 10 55N 16 15E
101 Charikar, Afghanistan 35 0N 69 10E
35 Charing, Eng., U.K. ...51 12N 0 49E
164 Chariton R., U.S.A. ...40 10N 92 45W
105 Charkhari, India 25 24N 79 45E
104 Charkhi Dadri, India .28 37N 76 17E
111 Charkhlikh, China 39 16N 88 17E
34 Charlbury, Eng., U.K. 51 52N 1 29W
46 Charlemont, N. Ireland, United Kingdom 54 26N 6 40W
54 Charleroi, Belgium 50 24N 4 27E
160 Charleroi, U.S.A. 40 8N 79 54W
162 Charles, C., U.S.A. 37 10N 75 52W
164 Charles City, U.S.A. ...43 2N 92 41W
157 Charles L., Canada 59 45N 110 40W
162 Charles Town, U.S.A. 39 20N 77 50W
165 Charleston, Miss., U.S.A. 34 2N 90 3W
165 Charleston, Mo., U.S.A. 36 52N 89 20W
163 Charleston, W. Va., U.S.A. 38 24N 81 36W
163 Charlestone, S.C., U.S.A. 32 47N 79 56W
162 Charlestown, Ind., U.S.A. 38 29N 85 40W
161 Charleston L., Canada 44 34N 76 0W
163 Charleston Harb., U.S.A. 32 40N 80 0W
46 Charlestown, Ireland .53 58N 8 48W
135 Charlestown, S. Africa 27 26S 29 53E
162 Charlestown, Ind., U.S.A. 38 29N 85 40W
43 Charlestown of Aberlour, Scotland, U.K. 57 27N 3 13W
130 Charlesville, Congo 5 27S 20 59E
145 Charleville, Austral. ...26 24S 146 15E
49 Charleville, France 49 44N 4 40E
44 Charleville, see Rath Luirc, Ireland 52 21N 8 40W
162 Charlevoix, U.S.A. 45 19N 85 14W
51 Charlieu, France 46 10N 4 10E
162 Charlotte, Mich., U.S.A. 84 48N 42 36W
163 Charlotte, N.C., U.S.A. 35 16N 80 46W
169 Charlotte Amalie, Virgin Is. 18 22N 64 56W
163 Charlotte Harb., U.S.A. 26 45N 82 10W
138 Charlotte Waters, N. Terr., Australia 25 56N 134 54E
80 Charlottenberg, Sweden 59 54N 12 17E
162 Charlottesville, U.S.A. 38 1N 78 30W
155 Charlottetown, Canada 46 19N 63 3W
164 Charlton, U.S.A. 40 59N 93 20W
143 Charlton, Australia ...36 16S 143 24E
154 Charlton I., Canada ...52 0N 79 20W
34 Charlton Kings, England, U.K 51 52N 2 3W
35 Charlwood, Eng., U.K. 51 8N 0 12W
49 Charmes, France 48 22N 6 17E
36 Charminster, Eng., U.K. 50 43N 2 28W
36 Charmouth, Eng., U.K. 50 45N 2 54W
29 Charnwood Forest, England, U.K. 52 15N 1 18W
155 Charny, Canada 46 43N 71 15W
51 Charolles, France 46 27N 4 16E
49 Charost, France 47 0N 2 7E
122 Charouin, Algeria 29 11N 0 15W
132 Charre, Mozambique .17 19S 35 10E
122 Charrier, Algeria 35 1N 0 30E
50 Charroux, France 46 9N 0 25E
144 Charters Towers, Queens., Australia .20 5S 146 13E
35 Chartham, Eng., U.K. 51 14N 1 9E
48 Chartres, France 48 29N 1 30E
172 Chascomus, Argentina 35 30S 58 0W
132 Chasefu, Zambia 11 55N 32 58E
147 Chaslands Mistake, N.Z. 46 38S 169 22E
132 Chasonga, Zambia 15 14S 29 9E
104 Chata, India 27 42N 77 30E
MAP
75 Chatal Balkan, Ra., Bulgaria 42 50N 26 50E
49 Château Chinon, France 47 4N 3 56E
48 Château du Loir, France 47 40N 0 25E
48 Château Gontier, France 47 50N 0 42W
48 Château la Vallière, Fr. 47 30N 0 20E
49 Château Landon, France 48 8N 2 40E
49 Château Porcein, Fr. .49 31N 4 13E
48 Château Renault, Fr. .47 36N 0 56E
49 Château Salins, France 48 50N 6 30E
49 Château Thierry, Fr. .49 3N 3 20E
49 Châteaubourg, France 48 7N 1 25W
48 Châteaubriant, France 47 43N 1 23W
48 Châteaudun, France ...48 3N 1 20E
48 Châteaugiron, France .48 3N 1 30W
161 Châteauguay, Canada 45 24N 73 44W
48 Châteaulin, France ...48 11N 4 8W
50 Châteaumeillant, Fr. .46 35N 2 12E
48 Châteauneuf, France .48 35N 1 15E
48 Châteauneuf du Faou, France 48 11N 3 50W
50 Châteauneuf-sur-Charente, France 45 36N 0 3W
49 Châteauneuf-sur-Cher, France 46 52N 2 18E
49 Châteauneuf-sur-Loire, France 47 52N 2 13E
49 Chateaurenard, France 43 54N 4 53E
49 Chateauroux, France .46 50N 1 40E
50 Châtelaillon Plage, Fr. 46 5N 1 5W
50 Châtel-Guyon, France 45 55N 3 4E
48 Châtelaudren, France .48 33N 2 59W
48 Châtelierault, France .46 50N 0 30E
50 Châtelus Malvaleix, Fr. 46 18N 2 1E
156 Chatham, Alaska, U.S.A. 57 30N 135 0W
155 Chatham, N.B., Can. .47 2N 65 28W
154 Chatham, Ont., Can. .42 23N 82 15W
35 Chatham, Eng., U.K. .51 22N 0 32E
165 Chatham, La., U.S.A. 32 22N 92 26W
161 Chatham, N.Y., U.S.A. 42 21N 73 32W
136 Chatham Is., Pac. Oc. 44 0S 176 40W
157 Chatham Str., Alaska, U.S.A. 57 0N 134 40W
49 Châtillon, France 47 36N 2 44E
49 Châtillon, France 49 5N 3 43E
70 Chatillon, Italy 45 45N 7 40E
49 Châtillon Coligny, Fr. 47 50N 2 51E
49 Châtillon en Bazois, Fr. 47 3N 3 39E
51 Châtillon en Diois, Fr. 44 41N 5 29E
49 Châtillon-sur-Seine, Fr. 47 50N 4 33E
48 Châtillon-sur-Sèvre, Fr. 46 56N 0 45W
105 Chatmohar, E. Pak. ...24 15N 89 26E
105 Chatra, India 24 12N 84 56E
105 Chatrapur, India 19 22N 85 2E
161 Chats, L. des, Canada 45 30N 76 20W
160 Chatsworth, Canada ...44 27N 80 54W
163 Chattahoochee, U.S.A. 30 43N 84 51W
163 Chattanooga, U.S.A. .35 2N 85 17W
35 Chatteris, Eng., U.K. .52 27N 0 3E
41 Chatton, Eng., U.K. .55 34N 1 55W
50 Chaudes Aigues, France 44 51N 3 1E
122 Chauen (Chechaouen), Morocco 35 9N 5 15W
50 Chauffailes, France ...46 13N 4 20E
103 Chauk, Burma 21 0N 94 58E
103 Chaukan Pass, Burma 27 0N 97 15E
49 Chaulnes, France 49 48N 2 47E
49 Chaumont, France 48 7N 5 8E
161 Chaumont, U.S.A. 44 4N 76 9W
49 Chaumont-en-Vexin, Fr. 49 16N 1 53E
48 Chaumont-sur-Loire, Fr. 47 29N 1 11E
14 Chaun B., U.S.S.R. ...69 0N 170 0E
50 Chaunay, France 46 13N 0 9E
49 Chauny, France 49 37N 3 12E
48 Chausey Is., France ...48 52N 1 49W
49 Chaussin, France 46 59N 5 22E
160 Chautauqua, U.S.A. ...42 17N 79 30W
157 Chauvin, Canada 52 45N 110 10W
175 Chaves, Brazil 0 15S 49 55W
62 Chaves, Portugal 41 45N 7 32W
132 Chavuma, Zambia 13 10S 22 55E
131 Chaya, Tanzania 5 35S 34 5E
51 Chazelles, France 45 39N 4 22E
161 Chazy, U.S.A. 44 52N 73 28W
38 Cheadle, Ches., England, U.K. 52 23N 2 14W
38 Cheadle, Staffs., England, U.K. 52 59N 1 59W
38 Cheadle Hulme, England, U.K. 53 22N 2 12W
58 Cheb, Czechoslovakia .50 9N 12 20E
87 Cheboksary, U.S.S.R. 56 8N 47 30E
162 Cheboygan, U.S.A. ...45 38N 84 29W
87 Chebsara, U.S.S.R. ...59 10N 38 45E
122 Chech, Erg, Sahara ...25 0N 2 15W
89 Chechen I., U.S.S.R. .43 59N 47 40E
113 Checheng, China 34 4N 115 33E
89 Checheno-Ingush, A.S.S.R., U.S.S.R. .43 30N 45 29E
60 Checiny, Poland 50 46N 20 37E
165 Checotah, U.S.A. 35 31N 95 30W
155 Chedabucto B., Canada 45 25N 61 0W
127 Chedada, Ethiopia 5 30N 35 58E

MAP
36 Cheddar, England 51 16N 2 47W
38 Cheddleton, Eng., U.K. 53 5N 2 2W
103 Cheduba I. Burma ...18 45N 93 40E
145 Cheepie, Australia ...26 43S 144 59E
50 Chef-Boutonne, France 46 7N 0 4W
112 Chefoo, China 37 30N 121 21E
122 Chegga, Mauritania ...25 15N 5 40W
166 Chehalis, U.S.A. 46 44N 122 59W
113 Cheju, Korea 33 28N 126 30E
113 Cheju Do (Quelpart) I., Korea 33 29N 126 34E
87 Chekalin, U.S.S.R. 54 10N 36 10E
113 Chekiang, Prov., China 29 15N 120 0E
127 Chel R., see Kuru, Sudan 8 10N 26 50E
90 Cheleken, U.S.S.R. 39 26N 53 7E
157 Chelan, Canada 52 38N 103 22E
166 Chelan, U.S.A. 47 49N 120 0W
176 Chelforo, Argentina ...39 0S 66 40W
122 Cheliff, R., Algeria 36 0N 0 40E
90 Chelkar, U.S.S.R. 47 40N 59 32E
90 Chelkar Tengiz, L., U.S.S.R. 48 0N 62 30E
122 Chellala Dahrania, Alg. 33 2N 0 1E
49 Chelles, France 48 52N 2 33E
60 Chelm, Poland 51 8N 23 30E
34 Chelmarsh, Eng., U.K. 52 29N 2 25W
35 Chelmer, R., Eng., U.K. 51 45N 0 33E
60 Chelmno, Poland 53 20N 18 30E
35 Chelmsford, Eng., U.K. 51 44N 0 29E
60 Chelmza, Poland 53 10N 18 39E
161 Chelsea, Canada 45 30N 75 49W
165 Chelsea, Okla., U.S.A. 36 35N 95 25W
161 Chelsea, U.S.A. 43 59N 72 27W
143 Chelsea, Australia 38 5S 145 8E
34 Cheltenham, Eng., U.K. 51 53N 2 7W
64 Chelva, Spain 39 45N 1 0W
90 Chelyabinsk, U.S.S.R. 55 10N 61 35E
156 Chemainus, Canada ...48 54N 123 41W
132 Chemba, Mozambique 17 11S 34 53E
87 Chembar, U.S.S.R. 53 0N 43 25E
131 Chembe Ferry, Congo 11 40S 28 30E
48 Chemillé, France 47 14N 0 45W
56 Chemnitz, see Karl-Marx-Stadt, Germany 50 50N 12 55E
107 Chemor, Malaysia 4 44N 101 6E
166 Chemult, U.S.A. 43 14N 121 54W
161 Chemung, U.S.A. 42 2N 76 37W
91 Chen, Mt., U.S.S.R. ...65 10N 141 20E
104 Chenab R., W. Pak. ...30 40N 73 30E
122 Chenachane, W. Alg. .25 30N 3 30W
113 Chenan, China 33 16N 109 1E
161 Chenango Forks, U.S.A. 42 15N 75 51W
166 Cheney, U.S.A. 47 38N 117 34W
113 Chenfeng, China 25 30N 105 51E
113 Chengan, China 28 30N 107 30E
113 Chengcheng, China 35 6N 109 52E
113 Chengchow, China 34 47N 113 46E
113 Chengho, China 27 25N 118 46E
113 Chenghsien, China 29 30N 120 40E
111 Chengkiang, China 24 58N 102 59E
113 Chengku, China 33 13N 107 15E
113 Chengkung, China 27 8N 108 57E
113 Chengpu, China 26 12N 110 5E
112 Chengteh, China 41 0N 117 55E
112 Chengting, China 38 8N 114 37E
111 Chengtu, China 30 45N 104 0E
112 Chengyang, China 36 20N 120 16E
113 Chenhsien, China 25 45N 112 37E
113 Chenki, China 28 1N 110 2E
113 Chenning, China 25 57N 105 51E
112 Chentung, China 46 2N 123 1E
113 Chenyüan, China 27 0N 108 20E
112 Chenyuan, China 35 59N 107 2E
107 Cheo Reo, see Hau Bon, S. Vietnam 13 25N 108 28E
107 Cheom Ksan, Cambodia 14 25N 105 0E
75 Chepelare, Bulgaria ...41 44N 24 40E
174 Chepen, Peru 7 10S 79 15W
172 Chepes, Argentina 31 20S 66 35W
169 Chepo, Panama 9 10N 79 6W
34 Chepstow, Eng., U.K. 51 38N 2 40W
87 Cheptsa, R., U.S.S.R. 58 30N 51 0E
131 Cheptulil, Mt., Kenya 1 25N 35 35E
164 Chequamegon B., U.S.A. 46 40N 90 30W
49 Chér, Dépt., France ...47 10N 2 30E
49 Chér R., France 47 10N 2 10E
105 Cheran, India 25 45N 90 44E
70 Cherasco, Italy 44 39N 7 50E
55 Cheratte, Belgium 50 40N 5 41E
163 Cheraw, U.S.A. 34 42N 79 54W
48 Cherbourg, France 49 39N 1 40W
122 Cherchell, Algeria 36 35N 21 63E
87 Cherdakly, U.S.S.R. ...54 25N 48 50E
84 Cherdyn, U.S.S.R. 60 20N 56 20E
89 Cherek, R., U.S.S.R. .43 55N 43 35E
91 Cheremkhovo, U.S.S.R. 53 32N 102 40E
87 Cheremshan R., U.S.S.R. 54 30N 50 30E
90 Cherepanovo, U.S.S.R. 54 15N 83 30E
87 Cherepovets, U.S.S.R. 59 5N 37 55E
122 Chergui, Chott ech, Alg. 34 10N 0 25E
86 Cherikov, U.S.S.R. 53 32N 31 20E
75 Cherin, Mt., Bulgaria .42 35N 23 28E
34 Cheriton, Eng., U.K. .51 3N 1 9W
36 Cheriton Fitzpaine, England, U.K. 50 51N 3 38W
89 Cherkassy, U.S.S.R. ...49 30N 32 0E
89 Cherkessk, U.S.S.R. ...44 25N 42 10E
90 Cherlak, U.S.S.R. 54 15N 74 55E
86 Chernigov, U.S.S.R. ...51 28N 31 20E
91 Chernogorsk, U.S.S.R. 54 5N 91 10E
88 Chernomorskoye, U.S.S.R. 45 31N 32 46E
87 Chernovskoye, U.S.S.R. 58 48N 47 20E
88 Chernovtsy, U.S.S.R. .48 0N 26 0E
91 Chernoye, U.S.S.R. ...70 30N 89 10E
86 Chernyakhovsk, U.S.S.R. 54 29N 21 48E
91 Chernyshevskiy, U.S.S.R. 62 40N 112 30E
89 Chernyshkovskiy, U.S.S.R. 48 30N 42 28E
165 Cherokee, Okla., U.S.A. 36 45N 98 25W
164 Cherokee, Iowa, U.S.A. 42 40N 95 30W
165 Cherokees, L. of the, U.S.A. 36 50N 95 12W
176 Cherquenco, Chile 38 35S 72 0W
103 Cherrapunji, India 25 17N 91 47E
160 Cherry Creek, N.Y., U.S.A. 42 18N 79 6W
166 Cherry Creek, Nev., U.S.A. 39 56N 114 58W
143 Cherrypool, Australia .37 7S 142 13E
165 Cherryvale, U.S.A. 37 20N 95 33W
91 Cherskiy Ra., U.S.S.R. 65 0N 143 0E
89 Chertkovo, U.S.S.R. ...49 25N 40 19E
35 Chertsey, Eng., U.K. .51 23N 0 30W
86 Cherven, U.S.S.R. 53 45N 28 13E
75 Cherven Bryag, Bulg. 43 17N 24 7E
34 Cherwell, R., Eng., U.K. 51 56N 1 18W
162 Chesapeake, B., U.S.A. 38 0N 76 12W
84 Chesha B., U.S.S.R. ...67 20N 47 0E
35 Chesham, Eng., U.K. .51 42N 0 36W
36 Cheshire, Co., England, U.K. 53 14N 2 30W
29 Cheshire Plain, England, United Kingdom 53 8N 2 44W
35 Cheshunt, Eng., U.K. 51 42N 0 1W
36 Chesil Beach, Eng., U.K. 50 37N 2 33W
160 Chesley, Canada 44 17N 81 7W
65 Cheste, Spain 39 30N 0 41W
38 Chester, Eng., U.K. 53 12N 2 53W
166 Chester, Calif., U.S.A. 40 22N 121 22W
164 Chester, Ill., U.S.A. ...37 58N 89 50W
166 Chester, Mont., U.S.A. 48 31N 111 0W
161 Chester, N.Y., U.S.A. 41 22N 74 16W
162 Chester, Pa., U.S.A. ...39 54N 75 20W
163 Chester, S.C., U.S.A. .34 44N 81 13W
152 Chesterfield, Canada ...63 0N 91 0W
39 Chesterfield, Eng., U.K. 53 14N 1 26W
152 Chesterfield Inlet & tn., Canada 63 30N 91 0W
139 Chesterfield Is., Pac. Oc. 19 52S 158 15E
39 Chester-le-Street, England, U.K. 54 53N 1 34W
161 Chesterville, Canada ...45 7N 75 15W
155 Chesuncook L., U.S.A. 46 0N 69 10W
123 Chetaibi, Algeria 37 1N 7 20E
155 Cheticamp, Canada 46 37N 60 59W
168 Chetumal, Mexico 18 30N 88 20W
168 Chetumal B., Cent. Amer. 18 40N 88 10W
50 Chevanceaux, France .45 18N 0 14W
39 Cheviot, The, Mt., England, U.K. 55 28N 2 8W
41 Cheviot Hills, Eng. & Scot., U.K. 55 20N 2 30W
145 Cheviot Ra., Australia 25 20S 143 45E
127 Chew Bahir, L. (Stefanie) Ethiopia . 4 40N 30 50E
36 Chew Magna, Eng., U.K. 51 21N 2 37W
166 Chewelah, U.S.A. 48 25N 117 56W
165 Cheyenne, Okla., U.S.A. 35 40N 99 40W
164 Cheyenne, Wyo., U.S.A. 41 9N 104 49W
164 Cheyenne R., U.S.A. .44 50N 101 0W
164 Cheyenne Wells, U.S.A. 38 51N 102 23W
142 Cheyne Bay, W. Austral. 34 30S 118 45E
104 Chhabra, India 24 40N 76 54E
104 Chhatak, E. Pakistan 25 5N 91 37E
105 Chhatarpur, India 24 55N 79 43E
104 Chhindwara, India 22 2N 78 59E
107 Chhlong, Cambodia 12 11N 106 2E
131 Chiamboni, Ras., Somali Rep. 1 36S 41 36E
107 Chiang Mai, Thailand 18 55N 98 55E
168 Chiapas, st., Mexico ...17 0N 92 45W
73 Chiaramonte Gulfi, It. 37 1N 14 41E
71 Chiaravalle, Italy 38 41N 16 24E
73 Chiaravalle Centrale, It. 38 41N 16 25E
70 Chiari, Italy 45 31N 9 55E
70 Chiavari, Italy 44 20N 9 20E
70 Chiavenna, Italy 46 18N 9 23E
113 Chiayi, Taiwan 23 29N 120 25E
114 Chiba, Japan 35 30N 140 7E
132 Chibango, Angola 13 38S 21 55E
132 Chibi, Rhodesia 20 17S 30 30E
129 Chibia, Angola 15 10S 13 50E
154 Chibougamau, Canada 49 56N 74 24W
154 Chibougamau L., Can. 49 50N 74 20W
154 Chibougamau R., Can. 49 50N 75 40W
125 Chibuk, Nigeria 10 52N 12 50E
132 Chibwe, Zambia 14 12S 28 32E
106 Chicacole, see Srikakulam, India .18 14N 84 4E
162 Chicago, Ill., U.S.A. ...41 45N 87 40W
162 Chicago Heights, U.S.A. 41 29N 87 37W
162 Chicago North, U.S.A. 42 20N 87 50W
132 Chicale, Botswana 19 37S 22 27E
130 Chicapa, R., Angola ... 7 0S 20 35E
157 Chichagoof I., Alaska, U.S.A. 58 0N 136 0W
122 Chichaoua, Morocco ...31 44N 8 44W
35 Chichester, Eng., U.K. 50 50N 0 47W
114 Chichibu, Japan 36 5N 139 10E
112 Chichirin, China 50 35N 123 45E
112 Chichow, China 38 30N 115 25E
165 Chickasha, U.S.A. 35 0N 98 0W
42 Chicken Hd., Scot., U.K. 58 10N 6 15W
63 Chiclana de la Frontera, Spain 36 26N 6 9W
174 Chiclayo, Peru 6 42S 79 50W
166 Chico, U.S.A. 39 45N 121 54W
176 Chico R., Argentina ...44 0S 67 0W
176 Chico R., Argentina ...49 30S 69 30W
132 Chicoa, Mozambique .15 35S 32 20E
167 Chicoma Pk., U.S.A. .36 8N 106 40W
161 Chicopee, U.S.A. 42 6N 72 37W
155 Chicoutimi, Canada ...48 28N 71 5W
106 Chidambaram, India .11 20N 79 45E
35 Chiddingfold, Eng., U.K. 51 6N 0 37W
153 Chidley C., Canada 60 30N 64 15W
160 Chiefs Pt., Canada 44 42N 81 18W
57 Chiemsee, L., Germany 47 53N 12 27E
132 Chiengo, Angola 13 19S 21 59E
132 Chiengi, Zambia 8 38S 29 10E
112 Chienping, China 41 26N 119 37E
71 Chienti R., Italy 43 15N 13 30E
70 Chieri, Italy 45 0N 7 50E
70 Chiese, R., Italy 45 45N 10 35E
71 Chieti, Italy 42 22N 14 10E
155 Chignecto B., Canada 45 33N 64 50W
172 Chiguana, Bolivia 21 0S 67 50W
172 Chiguayante, Chile 36 52S 72 57W
112 Chihfeng, China 42 10N 118 56E
113 Chihing, China 25 2N 113 45E
113 Chihkiang, China 27 21N 109 45E
113 Chihkiang, China 30 25N 111 30E
113 Chihkin, China 26 30N 105 45E
112 Chihli, G. of (Po Hai), China 38 30N 119 0E
112 Chihsien (Weihwei), China 35 29N 114 1E
168 Chihuahua, Mexico 28 40N 106 3W
168 Chihuahua, st., Mexico 28 40N 106 3W
106 Chik Ballapur, India .13 25N 77 45E
104 Chikhli, India 20 20N 76 18E
106 Chikmagalur, India ...13 15N 75 45E
106 Chikodi, India 16 26N 74 38E
132 Chikolama, Zambia 15 19S 29 0E
132 Chikonde, Zambia 12 16S 31 38E
132 Chikote, Zambia 15 57S 26 46E
132 Chikwawa, Malawi 16 2S 34 50E
132 Chilanga, Zambia 15 33S 28 16E
168 Chilapa, Mexico 17 40N 99 20W
102 Chilas, Kashmir 35 25N 74 5E
145 Childers, Australia 25 15S 152 17E
165 Childress, U.S.A. 34 30N 100 50W
176 Chile, rep., S. Amer. ...35 0S 71 15W
172 Chilecito, Argentina ...29 0S 67 40W
174 Chilete, Peru 7 10S 78 50W
35 Chilham, Eng., U.K. .51 15N 0 59E
90 Chili, U.S.S.R. 44 10N 66 55E
132 Chililabombwe (Bancroft), Zambia .12 18S 27 43E
105 Chilka L., India 19 40N 85 25E
156 Chilko L., Canada 51 20N 124 10W
144 Chillagoe, Australia ...17 14S 144 33E
172 Chillan, Chile 36 40S 72 10W
1 Chillan, Vol., S. Amer. 36 37S 72 10W
164 Chillicothe, Ill., U.S.A. 40 55N 89 32W
164 Chillicothe, Mo., U.S.A. 39 45N 93 30W
162 Chillicothe, Ohio, U.S.A. 39 53N 82 58W
143 Chillingollah, Australia 35 16S 143 3E
156 Chilliwack, Canada 49 10N 122 0W
104 Chilo, India 27 12N 73 32E
132 Chiloane, I., Mozam. .20 40S 34 55E
176 Chiloé I., Chile 42 50S 73 45W
132 Chilonga, Zambia 12 2S 31 17E
168 Chilpancingo, Mexico .17 30N 99 40W
143 Chiltern, Australia 36 10S 146 36E
34 Chiltern Hills, Eng., U.K. 51 44N 0 42W
162 Chilton, U.S.A. 44 1N 88 12W
132 Chilubula, Zambia 10 14S 30 51E
132 Chilumba, Malawi 10 28S 34 12E
113 Chilung, Taiwan 25 3N 121 45E
132 Chilwa, L. (Shirwa), Malawi 15 15S 35 40E
132 Chimaco, Angola 15 14S 22 1E
166 Chimacum, U.S.A. 48 1N 122 53W
111 Chimai, China 34 0N 101 39E
54 Chimay, Belgium 50 3N 4 20E
174 Chimborazo Mt., Ec. . 1 20S 78 55W
174 Chimbote, Peru 9 0S 78 35W
90 Chimkent, U.S.S.R. ...42 40N 69 25E
132 Chimpembe, Zambia . 9 31S 29 33E
103 Chin Division, Burma 22 0N 93 0E
168 China, Mexico 25 40N 99 20W
111 China, rep., Asia 35 0N 100 0E
133 Chinamguamize, Mozam. 25 15S 32 30E
169 Chinandega, Nicaragua 12 30N 87 0W
165 Chinati Pk., U.S.A. ...30 0N 104 25W
174 Chincha Is., Peru 13 35S 76 20W
174 Chincha Alta, Peru 13 20S 76 0W
145 Chinchilla, Australia .26 45S 150 38E
65 Chinchilla, de Monte Aragón, Spain 38 53N 1 40W
64 Chinchón, Spain 40 9N 3 26W
112 Chinchow, China 41 10N 121 2E
162 Chincoteague, U.S.A. .37 58N 75 21W
129 Chinde, Mozambique .18 45S 36 30E
103 Chindwin R., Burma .22 30N 95 0E
111 Chinghai, Prov., China 36 0N 97 0E
106 Chingleput, India 12 42N 79 58E
132 Chingola, Zambia 12 31S 27 53E
132 Chingole, Malawi 13 4S 34 17E
112 Chingpo Resr., China .43 50N 128 50E
130 Chinguar, Angola 12 18S 16 45E
120 Chinguetti, Mauritania 20 25N 12 15W
132 Chingune, Mozambique 20 33S 35 0E
112 Chinhae, S. Korea 35 9N 128 58E
104 Chiniot, W. Pakistan .31 45N 73 0E
112 Chinju, S. Korea 35 12N 128 2E
113 Chinkiang, China 32 2N 119 29E
167 Chinle, U.S.A. 36 14N 109 38W
106 Chinnamanur, India ... 9 50N 77 16E
106 Chinnur, India 18 57N 79 43E
167 Chino Valley, U.S.A. .34 54N 112 28W
48 Chinon, France 47 10N 0 15E
157 Chinook, Canada 51 28N 110 59W
166 Chinook, U.S.A. 48 35N 109 19W
132 Chinsali, Zambia 10 30S 32 2E
105 Chinsura, India 22 53N 88 27E
106 Chintamani, India 13 26N 78 3E
132 Chinteche, Malawi 11 50S 34 5E
132 Chinunga, Mozambique 13 31S 35 55E
112 Chinwangtao, China ...40 0N 119 31E
112 Chinyuan, China 36 31N 112 15E
71 Chioggia, Italy 45 13N 12 15E
77 Chios I., see Khios, Greece 38 27N 26 9E
156 Chip Lake, Canada 53 35N 115 35W
132 Chipata (Ft. Jameson), Zambia .13 38S 32 28E
132 Chipera, Mozambique 15 22S 32 35E
132 Chipinga, Rhodesia ...20 13S 32 36E
63 Chipiona, Spain 36 44N 6 26W
163 Chipley, U.S.A. 30 45N 85 32W
106 Chiplun, India 17 31N 73 34E
155 Chipman, Canada 46 6N 65 53W
132 Chipoka, Malawi 13 57S 34 28E
74 Chiprovtsi, Bulgaria .43 24N 22 52E
160 Chippawa, Canada 43 5N 79 10W
34 Chippenham, Eng., U.K. 51 27N 2 7W
164 Chippewa Falls, U.S.A. 44 55N 91 22W
164 Chippewa R., U.S.A. .44 45N 91 55W
34 Chipping Campden, England, U.K. 52 4N 1 48W
34 Chipping Norton, England, U.K. 51 56N 1 32W
35 Chipping Ongar, England, U.K. 51 43N 0 15E
36 Chipping Sodbury, England, U.K. 51 31N 2 23W
174 Chiquian, Peru 10 10S 77 0W
168 Chiquimula, Guatemala 14 51N 89 37W
89 Chir R., U.S.S.R. 48 45N 42 10E
132 Chiradzulu, Malawi ...15 40S 35 11E
106 Chirala, India 15 50N 80 20E
132 Chiramba, Mozambique 16 55S 34 39E
101 Chiras, Afghanistan ...35 14N 65 40E
104 Chirawa, India 28 14N 75 42E
106 Chirayinkil, India 8 41N 76 49E
34 Chirbury, Eng., U.K. .52 35N 3 6W
90 Chirchik, U.S.S.R. 81 58N 69 15E
123 Chirfa (Ft. Pacot), Niger 20 55N 12 14E
132 Chiribira Falls, Rhod. 21 10S 32 19E
167 Chiricahua Pk., U.S.A. 31 53N 109 14W
169 Chiriqui, G. of, Panama 8 0N 82 10W
169 Chiriqui, Lag. de, Pan. 9 10N 82 0W
169 Chiriqui, vol., Panama 8 55N 82 35W
37 Chirk, Wales, U.K. 52 57N 3 4W
78 Chirnogi, Rumania 44 7N 26 32E
41 Chirnside, Scot., U.K. 55 47N 2 11W
132 Chiromo, Malawi 16 30S 35 7E
75 Chirpan, Bulgaria 42 10N 25 19E
132 Chirundu, Rhodesia ...16 0S 28 59E
132 Chisamba, Zambia 14 55S 28 20E
113 Chishan, Taiwan 22 44N 120 31E
132 Chisimba Falls, Zambia 10 12S 30 56E
74 Chişinău, Criş, Rumania 46 32N 21 37E
34 Chisledon, Eng., U.K. 51 30N 1 44W
70 Chisone R., Italy 45 0N 7 5E
165 Chisos Mts., U.S.A. ...29 20N 103 15W
104 Chistian Mandi, W. Pak. 29 50N 72 55E
87 Chistopol, U.S.S.R. 55 25N 50 38E
91 Chita, U.S.S.R. 52 0N 113 25E
129 Chitado, Angola 17 10S 14 8E
132 Chitambo, Zambia 12 50S 30 45E
132 Chitapa, Zambia 13 20S 25 50E
106 Chitapur, India 17 10N 76 50E
129 Chitembo, Angola 13 30S 16 50E
132 Chitipa, Malawi 9 41S 33 19E
132 Chitokoloki, Zambia ...13 43S 23 4E
104 Chitorgarh, India 24 52N 74 43E
106 Chitrakot, India 19 20N 81 40E
106 Chitradurga, India 14 15N 76 28E
102 Chitral, West Pakistan 35 50N 71 56E
106 Chitravati, R., India .14 30N 78 0E
169 Chitré, Panama 7 59N 80 27W
103 Chittagong, E. Pak. ...22 19N 91 55E
103 Chittagong, div., E. Pak. 24 5N 91 25E
106 Chittoor, India 13 15N 79 5E
106 Chittur, India 10 40N 76 45E
131 Chiulézi, R., Mozam. .12 50S 37 10N
130 Chiumbe, R., Congo ... 7 20S 21 30E
71 Chiusi, Italy 43 1N 11 58E
132 Chiuta, Mozambique .15 29S 33 20E
132 Chiuta, L., Mozam. ...14 30S 35 50E
132 Chiute, Mozambique .20 40S 33 10E
65 Chiva, Spain 39 27N 0 41W
70 Chivasso, Italy 45 10N 7 52E
172 Chivilcoy, Argentina .35 0S 60 0W
132 Chiwefwe, Zambia 13 37S 29 31E
84 Chkolov, U.S.S.R. 52 0N 55 5E
87 Chkolovsk, U.S.S.R. ...56 50N 43 10E
58 Chlumec, Cz. 50 9N 15 29E
60 Chmielnik, Poland 50 37N 20 43E
43 Chno Dearg, Mt., Scotland, U.K. 56 50N 4 38W
112 Choahsien, China 37 48N 114 46E
132 Chobe, R., Botswana .18 10S 24 10E
132 Chobe Swamp, Caprivi Strip, S.W. Africa 18 25S 24 15E
125 Chobol, Nigeria 11 53N 13 1E
60 Chocianów, Poland 51 25N 15 33E
106 Chodavaram, India 17 40N 82 50E
60 Chodzież, Poland 52 58N 17 0E
176 Choele Choele, Arg. ...39 11S 65 40W
112 Chohsien, China 39 30N 116 0E
49 Choisy, France 48 45N 2 24E
168 Choix, Mexico 26 40N 108 10W
60 Chojna, Poland 52 58N 14 25E
60 Chojnice, Poland 53 42N 17 40E
60 Chojnów, Poland 51 25N 15 58E
48 Cholet, France 47 4N 0 52W
38 Chollerton, Eng., U.K. 55 4N 2 7W
132 Cholo, Malawi 16 7S 35 5E
34 Cholsey, Eng., U.K. ...51 34N 1 10W
169 Choluteca and R., Hond. 13 20N 87 14W
132 Choma, Zambia 16 48S 26 59E
127 Chomen Swamp, Ethiopia 9 20N 37 10E
132 Chomo, Zambia 13 30S 32 10E
104 Chomu, India 27 15N 75 40E
58 Chomutov, Cz. 50 28N 13 23E
112 Chŏnan, S. Korea 36 56N 127 3E
107 Chonburi, Thailand ...13 21N 101 1E
174 Chone, Ecuador 0 40S 80 0W
112 Chongin, N. Korea 39 34N 125 25E
112 Chongjin, N. Korea 41 51N 129 58E
112 Chŏngju, S. Korea 35 50N 127 4E
176 Chonos Arch., Chile 45 0S 75 0W
104 Chopda, India 21 20N 75 15E
38 Chorley, Eng., U.K. ...53 39N 2 39W
123 Chormet el Melah, Libya 30 11N 16 29E
172 Chorolque, mt., Bolivia 20 59S 66 5W
60 Choroszcz, Poland 53 10N 22 59E
86 Chortkov, U.S.S.R. 49 2N 25 46E
105 Chorul Tso, Tibet, China 32 30N 82 30E
112 Chorwon, S. Korea 38 15N 127 10E
60 Chorzele, Poland 53 15N 21 2E
60 Chorzów, Poland 50 18N 19 0E
172 Chos Malal, Argentina 37 15S 70 5W
112 Chosan, N. Korea 40 57N 125 58E
114 Choshi, Japan 35 45N 140 45E
60 Choszczno, Poland 53 7N 15 25E
166 Choteau, U.S.A. 47 50N 112 10W
104 Chotila, India 22 30N 71 15E
113 Chow Hu, L., China ...31 35N 117 30E
167 Chowchilla, U.S.A. 37 11N 120 12W
113 Chowchin, China 34 5N 108 17E
113 Chowkow, China 33 42N 115 4E
112 Choybalsan, Mongolia 48 3N 114 28E
112 Choyr, Mongolia 46 24N 108 53E
34 Christchurch, Eng., U.K. 50 44N 1 47W
147 Christchurch, N.Z. 43 33S 172 47W
160 Christian I., Canada ...44 50N 80 39E
81 Christiansfeld, Denmark 55 21N 9 29E
81 Christiansö, I., Den. ...55 19N 15 12E
135 Christiana, S. Africa ...27 52S 25 8E
136 Christmas I., Ind. Oc. 10 0S 105 40E
137 Christmas I., Pac. Oc. 1 58N 157 27W
58 Chrudim, Cz. 49 58N 15 43E
59 Chrzanów, Poland 50 10N 19 21E
132 Chtimba, Malawi 10 35S 34 13E
90 Chu, U.S.S.R. 43 36N 73 42E
107 Chu, R., N. Vietnam ..19 50N 105 20E
156 Chu Chua, Canada 51 30N 120 10W
113 Chu Kiang China 22 15N 113 45E
113 Chuanchow, China 24 57N 118 31E
113 Chuanhsien, China 25 50N 111 12E
114 Chubu, Dist., Japan ...36 45N 137 0E
176 Chubut R., Argentina 43 0S 70 0W
112 Chucheng, China 36 0N 119 16E
113 Chuchow (Lishui), China 28 30N 119 50E
113 Chuchow, China 27 56N 113 3E
91 Chuchee or Chukot Sea, Arctic Ocean ...72 0N 168 0W
36 Chudleigh, Eng., U.K. 50 35N 3 36W

MAP
86 Chudovo, U.S.S.R. 59 10N 31 30E
86 Chudskoye L., U.S.S.R. 58 13N 27 30E
114 Chugoku, Dist., Japan 35 0N 133 0E
114 Chugoku-sammyaku, Ra., Japan 35 0N 133 0E
88 Chuguyev, U.S.S.R. ...49 55N 36 45E
164 Chugwater, U.S.A. 41 48N 104 47W
112 Chuho, see Shangchih, China 45 10N 127 59E
113 Chuhsien, China 30 51N 107 1E
112 Chuhsien, China 28 57N 118 58E
113 Chuhsien, China 35 31N 118 45E
131 Chuka, Kenya 0 23S 37 38E
107 Chukai, Malaysia 4 13N 103 25E
87 Chukhloma, U.S.S.R. .58 45N 42 40E
113 Chuki, China 29 30N 120 4E
113 Chuki, China 32 26N 110 0E
91 Chukot Ra., U.S.S.R. 68 0N 175 0E
167 Chula Vista, U.S.A. ...33 44N 117 8W
36 Chulmleigh, Eng., U.K. 50 55N 3 52W
174 Chulucanas, Peru 5 0S 80 0W
113 Chumatien, China 33 0N 114 4E
172 Chumbicha, Argentina 29 0S 66 10W
75 Chumerna, Mt., Bulg. 42 45N 25 55E
91 Chumikan, U.S.S.R. ...54 40N 135 10E
107 Chumphon, Thailand .10 35N 99 14E
132 Chumuare, Mozam. ...14 31S 31 50E
112 Chunchon, S. Korea ...37 58N 127 44E
113 Chungan, China 27 45N 118 0E
113 Chunghsien, China 30 17N 108 4E
112 Chungju, S. Korea 37 3N 127 57E
113 Chungking, China 29 30N 106 30E
113 Chungsiang, China 31 14N 112 42E
103 Chungtien, China 28 0N 99 30E
112 Chungwei, China 37 35N 105 10E
104 Chunian, W. Pak. 31 10N 74 0E
131 Chunya, Tanzania 8 30S 33 27E
131 Chunya, dist., Tanzania 7 48S 33 0E
174 Chuquibamba, Peru ...15 47N 72 44W
172 Chuquicamata, Chile .22 15S 69 0W
172 Chuquisaca, dept., Bol. 23 30S 63 30W
57 Chur, Switzerland 46 52N 9 32E
103 Churachandpur, India 24 20N 93 40E
46 Church Hill, Ireland ...55 0N 7 53W
156 Church House, Canada 50 20N 125 10W
34 Church Stretton, England, U.K. 52 32N 2 49W
34 Churchdown, Eng., U.K. 51 53N 2 9W
157 Churchill, Canada 58 45N 94 5W
157 Churchill L., Canada .56 0N 108 20W
156 Churchill Pk., Canada 58 10N 125 10W
155 Churchill Falls, Canada 53 32N 64 26W
157 Churchill R., Canada .57 5N 96 30W
155 Churchill, R., Canada 53 15N 63 0W
45 Churchtown, Ireland .52 12N 6 20W
36 Churston Ferrers, England, U.K. 50 23N 3 32W
104 Churu, India 28 20N 75 0E
113 Chusan I., China 30 0N 122 20E
113 Chushan, China 32 14N 110 30E
102 Chushul, Kashmir 33 40N 78 40E
84 Chusovoi, U.S.S.R. 58 15N 57 40E
113 Chuting, China 27 28N 113 1E
87 Chuvash, A.S.S.R., U.S.S.R. 55 30N 48 0E
112 Chwangho, China 39 45N 123 4E
74 Ciacovu, Rumania 45 35N 21 10E
162 Cicero, U.S.A. 41 48N 87 48W
64 Cidacos, R., Spain 42 15N 2 10W
88 Cide, Turkey 41 40N 32 50E
60 Ciechanów, Poland 52 52N 20 38E
169 Ciego de Avila, Cuba .21 50N 78 50W
174 Ciénaga Colombia 11 0N 74 10W
169 Cienfuegos, Cuba 22 10N 80 30W
60 Cieplice Śląskie Zdrój, Poland 50 50N 15 40E
50 Cierp, France 42 55N 0 40E
62 Cíes Islas, Spain 42 12N 8 55W
59 Cieszyn, Poland 49 45N 18 35E
65 Cieza, Spain 38 17N 1 23W
64 Cifuentes, Spain 40 47N 2 37W
107 Ciha Pa., N. Vietnam 22 20N 103 47E
89 Cildir, Turkey 41 10N 43 20E
37 Cilgerran, Wales, U.K. 52 4N 4 39W
100 Cilician Gates P., Tur. 37 20N 34 52E
100 Cilician Taurus Mt., Tur. 36 40N 34 0E
165 Cimarron, Kan., U.S.A. 37 50N 100 20W
165 Cimarron, N. Mex., U.S.A. 36 30N 104 52W
155 Cimarron R., U.S.A. .37 10N 102 10W
78 Cimpina, Rumania 45 10N 25 45E
78 Cimpulung, Rumania .45 17N 25 3E
78 Cimpulung, Rumania .47 32N 25 30E
78 Cimpulung Moldovenesc, Rumania 47 30N 25 32E
64 Cinca, R., Spain 42 20N 0 9E
74 Cincer, Mt., Y.-slav. .43 55N 17 5E
163 Cinch, R., U.S.A. 36 0N 84 15W
162 Cincinnati, Ohio, U.S.A. 39 10N 84 26W
34 Cinderford, Eng., U.K. 51 49N 2 30W
54 Ciney, Belgium 50 18N 5 5E
71 Cingoli, Italy 43 23N 13 10E
71 Cinigiano, Italy 42 53N 11 23E
51 Cinto, Mt., Corsica, Fr. 42 24N 8 54E
78 Cioranii, Rumania 44 45N 26 25E
71 Ciovo, I., Yugoslavia .43 30N 16 17E
164 Circle, U.S.A. 47 26N 105 35W
162 Circleville, Ohio, U.S.A. 39 35N 82 57W
167 Circleville, Utah, U.S.A. 38 12N 112 24W
34 Cirencester, Eng., U.K. 51 43N 1 59W
78 Cireşu, Rumania 44 47N 22 31E
49 Cirey, France 48 35N 6 57E
70 Ciriè, Italy 45 14N 7 35E
73 Ciro, Italy 39 23N 17 3E
165 Cisco, U.S.A. 32 25N 99 0W
78 Cislău, Rumania 45 14N 26 33E
59 Cisna, Poland 49 12N 22 20E
78 Cisnădie, Rumania 45 42N 24 9E
72 Cisterna di Latina, It. 41 35N 12 50E
73 Cisternino, Italy 40 45N 17 26E
168 Citaltepetl Mt., Mexico 19 0N 97 20W
131 Citega (Kitega), Burundi 3 30S 29 58E
134 Citrusdal, S. Africa 32 35S 19 0E
71 Citta della Pieve, Italy 42 57N 12 0E
71 Citta di Castello, Italy 43 27N 12 14E
71 Citta Sant' Angelo, It. 42 32N 14 5E
71 Cittadella, Italy 45 39N 11 48E
71 Cittaducale, Italy 42 24N 12 58E
73 Cittanova, Italy 38 22N 16 0E
78 Ciucas, Mt., Rumania 45 31N 25 56E
168 Ciudad Acuna, Mexico 29 20N 101 10W
168 Ciudad Altamirao, Mexico 18 20N 100 40W
174 Ciudad Bolivar, Ven. . 8 5N 63 30W
168 Ciudad Camargo, Mex. 27 41N 105 10W
168 Ciudad Delicias, see Delicias, Mexico 28 10N 105 30W
168 Ciudad de Valles, Mex. 22 0N 98 30W
168 Ciudad del Carmen, Mex. 18 20N 97 50W
169 Ciudad Guayana, Venezuela 8 20N 62 35W
168 Ciudad Guerrero, Mex. 28 33N 107 28W
168 Ciudad Guzmán, Mex. 19 40N 103 30W
168 Ciudad Juárez, Mexico 31 40N 106 28W
168 Ciudad Madero, Mexico 22 19N 97 50W
168 Ciudad Mante, Mexico 22 50N 99 0W
168 Ciudad Obregón, Mex. 27 28N 109 59W
63 Ciudad Real, Spain ...38 59N 3 55W
63 Ciudad Réal, Prov., Sp. 38 50N 4 0W
62 Ciudad Rodrigo, Spain 40 35N 6 32W
168 Ciudad Victoria, Mex. 23 41N 99 9W
64 Ciudadela, Spain 40 0N 3 50E
78 Ciulniţa, Rumania 44 26N 27 22E
88 Civa, C., Turkey 41 20N 36 40E
71 Cividale del Friuli, It. 46 6N 13 25E
71 Civita Castellana, Italy 42 18N 12 24E
71 Civitanova Marche, It. 43 18N 13 41E
71 Civitavecchia, Italy ...42 6N 11 46E
71 Civitella del Tronto, It. 42 48N 13 40E
50 Civray, France 46 10N 0 17E
100 Civril, Turkey 38 20N 29 55E
72 Cixerri, R., Sardinia, It. 39 45N 8 40E
100 Cizre, Turkey 37 19N 42 10E
46 Clabby, N. Ire. U.K. .54 24N 7 22W
40 Clach Leathed, Scotland, United Kingdom 56 36N 4 52W
42 Clachan, N. Uist., Scotland, U.K. 57 33N 7 20W
40 Clachan, Scot., U.K. .55 45N 5 35W
142 Clackline, W. Australia 31 40S 116 32E
41 Clackmannan, Scotland, United Kingdom 56 10N 3 44W
41 Clackmannan, co., Scotland, U.K. 56 10N 3 47W
35 Clacton-on-Sea, England, U.K. 51 47N 1 10E
40 Cladich, Scot., U K. ...56 21N 5 5W
156 Claire L., Canada 58 30N 112 0W
165 Clairemont, U.S.A. 33 9N 100 44W
160 Clairton, U.S.A. 40 18N 79 54W
51 Clairvaux, France 46 35N 5 45E
49 Clamecy, France 47 28N 3 30E
45 Clandalkin, Ireland ...52 40N 6 25W
45 Clane, Ireland 53 18N 6 40W
35 Clanfield, Eng., U.K. .50 56N 0 60W
165 Clanton, U.S.A. 32 48N 86 36W
134 Clanwilliam, S. Africa 32 11S 18 52E
45 Clara, Ireland 53 20N 7 38W
35 Clare, Eng., U.K. 52 5N 0 36E
45 Clare, co., Ireland 52 52N 8 55W
143 Clare, N.S.W., Austral. 33 20S 143 50E
46 Clare, N. Ireland, U.K. 54 25N 6 19W
162 Clare, U.S.A. 43 47N 84 45W
45 Clare I., Ireland 53 48N 10 0W
44 Clare R., Ireland 53 20N 9 0W
44 Clarecastle, Ireland ...52 50N 8 58W
44 Clareen, Ireland 53 4N 7 49W
44 Claregalway, Ireland 53 20N 8 57W
161 Claremont, U.S.A. 43 23N 72 20W
165 Claremore, U.S.A. 36 20N 95 20W
46 Claremorris, Ireland ...53 45N 9 0W
176 Clarence I., Chile 54 0S 72 0W
15 Clarence I., Antarctica 61 30S 53 50W
147 Clarence R., N.Z. 42 17S 173 15E
157 Clarence Str., Alaska, U.S.A. 55 40N 132 10W
165 Clarendon, Ark., U.S.A. 34 41N 91 20W
165 Clarendon, Tex., U.S.A. 34 58N 100 54W
135 Clarens, O.F.S., S. Afr. 28 30S 28 28E
155 Clarenville, Canada ...48 10N 54 1W
156 Claresholm, Canada ...50 0N 113 45W
15 Clarie Coast, Antarctica 67 0S 135 0E
44 Clarinbridge, Ireland .53 13N 8 55W
164 Clarinda, U.S.A. 40 45N 95 0W
164 Clarion, Ohio, U.S.A. 42 41N 93 46W
160 Clarion, Pa., U.S.A. ...41 12N 79 22W
160 Clarion, R., U.S.A. 41 19N 79 10W
164 Clark, U.S.A. 44 55N 97 45W
160 Clark Pt., Canada 44 4N 81 45W
166 Clark Fork, U.S.A. 48 9N 116 9W
166 Clark Fork, R., U.S.A. 48 0N 115 40W
163 Clark Res., U.S.A. 33 45N 82 20W
167 Clarkdale, U.S.A. 34 53N 112 3W
144 Clarke Ra., Australia .20 45S 148 20E
155 Clarke City, Canada ...50 12N 66 38W
143 Clarkefield, Australia .37 30S 44 40E
155 Clarkes Harbour, Can. 43 25N 65 38W
166 Clarks Fork, R., U.S.A. 45 0N 109 30W
161 Clarks Summit, U.S.A. 41 31N 75 44W
162 Clarksburg, U.S.A. 39 18N 80 21W
165 Clarksdale, U.S.A. 34 12N 90 33W
166 Clarkston, U.S.A. 46 28N 117 2W
165 Clarksville, Ark., U.S.A. 35 29N 93 27W
163 Clarksville, Tenn., U.S.A. 36 32N 87 20W
165 Clarksville, Tex., U.S.A. 33 37N 94 59W
44 Clashmore, Ireland 52 1N 7 51W
43 Clashmore, Scot., U.K. 57 33N 4 8W
166 Clatkanie, U.S.A. 46 9N 123 12W
165 Claude, U.S.A. 35 8N 101 22W
46 Claudy, N. Ire., U.K. .54 55N 7 10W
109 Claveria, Philippines .17 40N 121 30E
34 Claverley, Eng., U.K. 52 32N 2 19W
38 Clay Hd., Isle of Man, United Kingdom 54 13N 4 23W
164 Clay Centre, U.S.A. ...39 27N 97 9W
39 Clay Cross, Eng., U.K. 53 11N 1 26W
35 Claydon, Eng., U.K. .52 6N 1 7E
167 Claypool, U.S.A. 33 27N 110 55W
160 Claysville, U.S.A. 40 5N 80 25W
166 Clayton, Idaho, U.S.A. 44 12N 114 31W
165 Clayton, N. Mex., U.S.A. 36 30N 103 10W
166 Cle Elum, U.S.A. 47 15N 120 57W
44 Cleady, Ireland 51 53N 9 32W
44 Clear C., Ireland 51 26N 9 30W
44 Clear I., Ireland 51 26N 9 30W
166 Clear Lake, Calif., U.S.A. 39 5N 122 54W
164 Clear Lake, S.D., U.S.A. 44 48N 96 41W
166 Clear Lake, Wash, U.S.A. 48 27N 122 15W
166 Clear Lake Res., U.S.A. 41 55N 121 10W
160 Clearfield, Pa., U.S.A. 41 0N 78 27W
166 Clearfield, Utah, U.S.A. 41 10N 112 0W
166 Clearmont, U.S.A. 44 43N 106 29W
163 Clearwater, U.S.A. 27 58N 42 45W
154 Clearwater L., Canada 56 10N 75 0W
157 Clearwater Prov. Park, Canada 54 0N 101 0W
166 Clearwater Mts., U.S.A. 46 20N 115 30W
157 Clearwater R., Canada 56 40N 109 30W
156 Clearwater Station, Can. 51 38N 120 2W
43 Cleat, Scotland, U.K. .58 45N 2 56W
38 Cleator Moor, Eng., U.K. 54 30N 3 32W
165 Cleburne, U.S.A. 32 18N 97 25W
37 Cleddau R., Wales, U.K. 51 55N 4 44W
34 Clee Hills, Eng., U.K. 52 26N 2 35W
39 Cleethorpes, Eng., U.K. 53 33N 0 2W
34 Cleeve Cloud, Eng., U.K. 51 56N 2 0W
44 Cleggan, Ireland 53 33N 10 7W
51 Clelles, France 44 50N 5 38E
34 Clent, Eng., U.K. .52 25N 2 6W
34 Cleobury Mortimer, England, U.K. 52 23N 2 28W
15 Clerks Rks., Falkland Is. Dependencies 56 0S 36 30W
50 Clermont l'Hérault, Fr. 43 38N 3 26E
49 Clermont, Meuse, Fr. .49 5N 5 4E
49 Clermont, Oise, France 49 22N 2 24E
144 Clermont, Australia ...22 46S 147 38E
50 Clermont-Ferrand, Fr. 45 46N 3 4E
49 Clerval, France 47 25N 6 30E
49 Cléry, France 47 50N 1 46E
70 Cles, Italy 46 21N 11 4E
36 Clevedon, Eng., U.K. .51 26N 2 52W
145 Cleveland, Australia ...27 31S 153 3E
165 Cleveland, Miss., U.S.A. 33 43N 90 43W
160 Cleveland, Ohio, U.S.A. 41 28N 81 43W
165 Cleveland, Okla., U.S.A. 36 21N 96 33W
163 Cleveland, Tenn., U.S.A. 35 9N 84 52W
165 Cleveland, Tex., U.S.A. 30 18N 95 0W
144 Cleveland, C., Queensland, Australia 19 11S 147 1E
39 Cleveland, dist., England, U.K. 54 30N 1 12W
145 Cleveland, Mt., Austral. 41 25S 145 23E
160 Cleveland Heights, U.S.A. 41 32N 81 30W
39 Cleveland Hills, England, U.K. 54 25N 1 11W
173 Clevelandia, Brazil ...26 24S 52 23W
45 Clew Bay, Ireland 53 54N 9 50W
163 Clewiston, U.S.A. 26 44N 80 50W
35 Cley, England, U.K. .52 57N 1 3E
147 Clifden, Ireland 53 30N 10 2W
147 Clifden, New Zealand .46 1S 167 42E
44 Clifden B., Ireland 53 29N 10 5W
167 Cliff, U.S.A. 33 0N 108 44W
35 Cliffe, England, U.K. .51 27N 0 31E
46 Cliffony, Ireland 54 25N 8 28W
34 Clifford, England, U.K. 52 6N 3 6W
42 Clift Sound, Scot., U.K. 60 4N 1 17W
145 Clifton, Australia 27 59S 151 53E
167 Clifton, Ariz., U.S.A. .33 8N 109 23W
165 Clifton, Tex., U.S.A. .31 46N 97 35W
162 Clifton Forge, U.S.A. .37 49N 79 51W
157 Climax, Canada 49 10N 108 20W
167 Clint, U.S.A. 31 37N 106 11W
156 Clinton, B.C., Canada 51 0N 121 40W
160 Clinton, Ont., Canada 43 38N 81 33W
147 Clinton, New Zealand 46 12S 169 23E
165 Clinton, Ark., U.S.A. .35 37N 92 30W
164 Clinton, Ill., U.S.A. ...40 8N 89 0W
164 Clinton, Iowa, U.S.A. 41 50N 90 18W
162 Clinton, Ind., U.S.A. .39 40N 87 22W
161 Clinton, Mass., U.S.A. 42 26N 71 40W
164 Clinton, Mo., U.S.A. ...38 20N 93 40W
163 Clinton, N.C., U.S.A. .35 5N 78 15W
165 Clinton, Okla., U.S.A. 35 30N 99 0W
163 Clinton, S.C., U.S.A. .34 30N 81 54W
163 Clinton, Tenn., U.S.A. 36 6N 84 10W
144 Clinton C., Australia .22 30S 150 45E
152 Clinton Colden L., Can. 64 0N 107 0W
164 Clintonville, U.S.A. ...44 35N 88 46W
137 Clipperton I., Pac. Oc. 10 18N 109 13W
35 Clipston, Eng., U.K. .52 26N 0 58W
48 Clisson, France 47 5N 1 16W
38 Clitheroe, Eng., U.K. .53 52N 2 23W
146 Clive, New Zealand ...39 36S 176 58E
142 Cloates, Pt., Australia 22 29S 113 37E
135 Clocolan, S. Afr. 28 55S 27 34E
172 Clodomira, Argentina .27 35S 64 14W
45 Clogh, Ireland 52 51N 7 11W
46 Cloghan, Donegal, Ire. 54 50N 7 56W
44 Cloghan, Offaly, Ire. .53 13N 7 53W
45 Cloghan, W'meath, Ire. 53 33N 7 15W
44 Clogheen, Ireland 52 17N 8 0W
46 Clogher, Lough, Ire. ...53 47N 6 15W
46 Clogher, N. Ire., U.K. 54 25N 7 10W
46 Clogher Hd., Ireland .53 48N 6 15W
44 Cloghjordan ,Ireland .52 57N 8 2W
45 Cloghran, Ireland 53 26N 6 14W
44 Clonakilty, Ireland 51 37N 8 53W
44 Clonakilty B., Ireland 51 33N 8 50W
45 Clonard, Ireland 53 27N 7 2W
44 Clonbur, Ireland 53 32N 9 21W
144 Cloncurry, Australia ...20 40S 140 28E
44 Cloncurry, Ireland 53 26N 6 47W
45 Clondalkin, Ireland 53 20N 6 25W
45 Clonee, Ireland 53 25N 6 28W
46 Clones, Ireland 54 10N 7 13W
44 Clonkeen, Ireland 51 59N 9 20W
46 Clonmany, Ireland 55 16N 7 24W
45 Clonmel, Ireland 52 22N 7 42W
45 Clonmore, Ireland 52 49N 6 35W
45 Clonroche, Ireland 52 27N 6 42W
45 Clontarf, Ireland 53 22N 6 10W
46 Cloonakool, Ireland ...54 6N 8 47W
46 Cloone, Ireland 53 57N 7 47W
46 Cloontad, Ireland 53 41N 8 45W
56 Cloppenburg, Germany 52 50N 8 3E
164 Cloquet, U.S.A. 46 40N 92 30W
172 Clorinda, Argentina ...25 16S 57 45W
41 Closeburn, Scot., U.K. 55 13N 3 45W
166 Cloud Peak, mt., U.S.A. 44 30N 107 10W
167 Cloudcroft, U.S.A. 33 0N 105 48W
147 Cloudy B., N.Z. 41 25S 174 10E
46 Clough, N. Ire., U.K. .54 58N 6 16W
46 Clough, N. Ire., U.K. .54 18N 5 50W
39 Cloughton, Eng., U.K. 54 20N 0 27W
43 Clova, Scotland, U.K. 56 50N 3 4W
36 Clovelly, Eng., U.K. .51 0N 4 25W
166 Cloverdale, U.S.A. 38 49N 123 0W
167 Clovis, Calif., U.S.A. .36 54N 119 45W
165 Clovis, N. Mex., U.S.A. 34 20N 103 10W
39 Clowne, England, U.K. 53 18N 1 16W
44 Cloyne, Ireland 51 52N 8 7W
42 Cluanie L., Scot., U.K. 57 8N 5 6W
143 Club Terrace, Australia 37 30S 148 59E
42 Cluer, Scotland, U.K. 57 48N 6 48W
78 Cluj, Rumania 46 47N 23 38E
78 Cluj, Reg., Rumania .46 50N 23 40E
34 Clun, England, U.K. .52 26N 3 2W
34 Clun Forest, Eng., U.K. 52 27N 3 7W
34 Clunbury, Eng., U.K. 52 25N 2 55W
143 Clunes, Australia 37 20S 143 45E
51 Cluny, France 46 26N 4 38E
51 Cluses, France 46 5N 6 35E
70 Clusone, Italy 45 54N 9 58E
147 Clutha R., N.Z. 45 39S 169 25E
37 Clwyd, R., Wales, U.K. 53 12N 3 22W
37 Clwydian Ra., Wales, United Kingdom 53 10N 3 15W
37 Clydach Wales, U.K. 51 42N 3 54W
145 Clyde, Australia 28 48S 143 40E
147 Clyde, New Zealand ...45 12S 169 20E
160 Clyde, U.S.A. 43 8N 76 52W
40 Clyde, Firth of, Scotland, U.K. 55 20N 5 0W
40 Clyde, R., Scot., U.K. 55 46N 3 58W
40 Clydebank, Scot., U.K. 55 54N 4 25W
41 Clydesdale, Canada ...44 51N 78 3W
160 Clymer, U.S.A. 42 3N 79 39W
37 Clynnog-fawr, Wales, United Kingdom 53 2N 4 22W
62 Côa, R., Portugal 40 45N 7 0W
167 Coachella, U.S.A. 33 44N 116 13W
44 Coachford, Ireland 51 54N 8 48W
155 Coachman's Cove, Can. 50 6N 56 20W
46 Coagh, N. Ire. 54 50N 6 37W
165 Coahoma, U.S.A. 32 17N 101 20W
168 Coahuila, st., Mexico .27 0N 112 30W
147 Coal Creek Flat, N.Z. .45 27S 169 19E
147 Coal I., New Zealand .46 8S 166 40E
135 Coalbrook, S. Africa ...26 51S 27 53E
34 Coalbrookdale, England, United Kingdom 52 38N 2 30W
41 Coalburn, Scot., U.K. 55 35N 3 55W
168 Coalcomán, Mexico ...18 40N 103 10W
156 Coaldale, Canada 49 45N 112 35W
165 Coalgate, U.S.A. 34 35N 96 13W
167 Coalinga, U.S.A. 36 10N 120 21W
46 Coalisland, N. Ire., U.K. 54 33N 6 42W
156 Coalspur, Canada 53 15N 117 0W
34 Coalville, Eng., U.K. .52 43N 1 21W
166 Coalville, U.S.A. 40 58N 111 24W
174 Coari, Brazil 4 8S 63 7W
131 Coast, prov., Kenya ... 2 40S 39 45E
131 Coast, prov., Tanzania 7 0S 39 30E
156 Coast Mts., Canada ...52 0N 126 0W
166 Coast Range, N. Amer. 40 0N 124 0W
41 Coatbridge, Scot., U.K. 55 52N 4 2W
168 Coatepeque, Guatemala 14 46N 91 55W
162 Coatesville, U.S.A. 39 59N 75 30W
155 Coaticook, Canada 45 10N 71 46W
153 Coats I., Canada 62 30N 82 0W
15 Coats Land, Antarctica 77 0S 25 0W
168 Coatzacoalcos, Mexico 18 7N 94 35W
78 Cobadin, Rumania 44 5N 28 13E
154 Cobalt, Canada 47 25N 79 42W
168 Cobán, Guatemala 15 30N 90 21W
143 Cobar, Australia 31 27S 145 48E
143 Cobargo, Australia 36 20S 149 55E
143 Cobboras, Mt., Austral. 36 46S 148 10E
44 Cóbh, Ireland 51 50N 8 18W
145 Cobham, Australia 30 10S 142 0E
174 Cobija, Bolivia 11 0S 68 50W
161 Cobleskill, U.S.A. 42 40N 74 30W
160 Coboconk, Canada 44 40N 78 50W
154 Cobourg, Canada 44 0N 78 20W
138 Cobourg Pen., N. Terr., Australia 11 20S 132 15E
166 Cobre, U.S.A. 41 6N 114 25W
132 Cóbué, Mozambique ...12 0S 34 58E
57 Coburg, Germany 50 15N 10 58E
62 Coca, Spain 41 13N 4 32W
106 Cocanada, see Kakinada, India 16 55N 82 20E
65 Cocentaina, Spain 38 45N 0 27W
174 Cochabamba, Bolivia .17 15S 66 20W
57 Cochem, Germany 50 8N 7 7E
132 Cochemane, Mozam. ...17 0S 32 54E
173 Cochilha Grande de Albardao, Brazil ...28 30S 51 30W
106 Cochin, India 9 55N 76 22E
107 Cochin China, reg., South Vietnam 10 30N 106 0E
167 Cochise, U.S.A. 32 6N 109 58W
163 Cochran, U.S.A. 32 25N 83 23W
156 Cochrane, Alta., Can. .51 20N 114 30W
154 Cochrane, Ont., Canada 49 0N 81 0W
176 Cochrane L., Chile 47 10S 72 0W
138 Cockatoo I., W. Australia 16 6S 123 37E
143 Cockburn, N.S.W., Australia 32 5S 141 2E
143 Cockburn, S. Australia 32 5S 141 0E
176 Cockburn Chan., Chile 54 30S 72 0W
41 Cockburnspath, Scotland, U.K. 55 56N 2 23W
41 Cockenzie, Scot., U.K. 55 58N 2 59W
38 Cockerham, Eng., U.K. 53 58N 2 49W
38 Cockermouth, England, United Kingdom 54 40N 3 22W

MAP
35 Cockfield, Eng., U.K. ...52 8N 0 47E
142 Cocklebiddy, W. Australia ...32 0S 126 3E
107 Coco Chan., Andaman Is. India ...13 50N 93 25E
107 Coco Is., India ...14 0N 93 12E
169 Coco R. (Wanks), Central America ...14 10N 85 0W
168 Coco Solo, Panama Canal Zone ... 9 22N 79 53W
163 Cocoa, U.S.A. ...28 22N 80 40W
128 Cocobeach, Gabon ... 0 59N 9 34E
124 Cocoli, Rio, Port. Guin. ...12 0N 14 0W
122 Cocopara Ra., Austral. ...34 0S 146 4E
78 Cocora, Rumania ...44 45N 27 3E
137 Cocos I., Pacific Ocean ... 5 25N 87 55W
11 Cocos or Keeling Is., Indian Ocean ...12 12S 96 54E
162 Cod, C., Mass., U.S.A. 42 8N 70 10W
174 Codájas, Brazil ... 3 40S 62 0W
35 Coddenham, Eng., U.K. ...52 8N 1 8E
157 Coderre, Canada ...50 11N 106 31W
71 Codigoro, Italy ...44 50N 12 5E
175 Codó, Brazil ... 4 30S 43 55W
70 Codogno, Italy ...45 10N 9 42E
71 Codroipo, Italy ...45 57N 13 0E
78 Codru, Muntii, mts., Rumania ...46 30N 22 15E
44 Cods Hd., Ireland ...51 40N 10 7W
166 Cody, U.S.A. ...44 35N 109 0W
154 Coe Hill, Canada ...44 53N 77 44W
172 Coelemu, Chile ...36 30S 72 48W
144 Coen, Australia ...13 52S 143 12E
135 Coerney, S. Africa ...33 20S 25 30E
56 Coesfield, Germany ...51 56N 7 10E
166 Coeur d'Alene, U.S.A. 47 45N 116 51W
54 Coevorden, Netherlands ...52 40N 6 44E
165 Coffeyville, U.S.A. ...37 0N 95 40W
138 Coffin B. Pen., Austral. ...34 20S 135 10E
145 Coff's Harb., Australia 30 16S 153 5E
135 Cofimvaba, S. Africa .32 0S 27 35E
65 Cofrentes, Spain ...39 13N 1 5W
78 Cogealac, Rumania ...44 36N 28 36E
35 Coggeshall, Eng., U.K. ...51 53N 0 41E
72 Coghinas, R., Sardinia, Italy ...40 55N 8 48E
50 Cognac, France ...45 41N 0 20W
70 Cogne, Italy ...45 37N 7 21E
64 Cogolludo, Spain ...40 59N 3 10W
125 Cogon R., Guinea ...11 20N 14 32W
166 Cohagen, U.S.A. ...47 2N 106 45W
161 Cohoes, N.Y., U.S.A. .42 47N 73 42W
143 Cohuna, Australia ...35 45S 144 15E
169 Coiba I., Panama ... 7 30N 81 40W
176 Coig, R., Argentina ...51 0S 70 20W
42 Coigach, dist., Scotland, U.K. ...58 0N 5 10W
106 Coimbatore, India ...11 2N 76 59E
62 Coimbra, tn. & dist., Portugal ...40 15N 8 27W
63 Coin, Spain ...36 40N 4 48W
174 Cojimies, Ecuador ... 0 20N 80 0W
78 Cojocna, Rumania ...46 45N 23 50E
168 Cojutepequé, Salvador 13 41N 88 54W
74 Čoka, Yugoslavia ...45 57N 20 12E
166 Cokeville, U.S.A. ...42 4N 111 0W
70 Col di Tenda, France .44 7N 7 36E
106 Colaba Pt., India ...18 54N 72 47E
143 Colac, Australia ...38 10S 143 30E
106 Colachel, India ... 8 10N 77 15E
63 Colares, Portugal ...38 48N 9 30W
143 Colbinabbin, Australia 36 38S 144 48E
160 Colborne, Canada ...44 1N 77 52W
38 Colby, Is. of Man, U.K. ...54 6N 4 42W
164 Colby, U.S.A. ...39 27N 101 2W
172 Colchagua, prov., Chile ...34 30S 71 0W
35 Colchester, Eng., U.K. 51 54N 0 55E
135 Colchester, S. Africa ...33 41S 25 50E
38 Cold Fell, Eng., U.K. .54 54N 2 40W
41 Coldingham, Scot., U.K. ...55 53N 2 29W
41 Coldstream, Scot., U.K. ...55 39N 2 14W
160 Coldwater, Canada ...44 44N 79 40W
165 Coldwater, Kan., U.S.A. ...37 18N 99 24W
154 Coldwell, Canada ...48 45N 86 30W
145 Colebrook, Australia .42 32S 147 20E
161 Colebrook, U.S.A. ...44 54N 71 29W
36 Colebrooke, Eng., U.K. ...50 45N 3 44W
34 Coleford, Eng., U.K. .51 46N 2 38W
156 Coleman, Canada ...49 40N 114 30W
165 Coleman, U.S.A. ...31 52N 99 30W
100 Cölemerik, Turkey ...37 35N 43 45E
135 Colenso, S. Afr. ...28 44S 29 50E
46 Coleraine, N. Ire., U.K. ...55 8N 6 40E
143 Coleraine, Australia ...37 36S 141 40E
106 Coleroon, R., India ...11 0N 79 0E
135 Colesberg, S. Africa ...30 45S 25 5E
34 Coleshill, Eng., U.K. .52 30N 1 42W
165 Colfax, La., U.S.A. ...31 35N 92 39W
166 Colfax, Wash., U.S.A. 46 57N 117 28W
42 Colgrave Sd., Scot., U.K. ...60 35N 1 0W
176 Colhue Huapi L., Arg. 45 30S 69 0W
70 Colico, Italy ...46 8N 9 22E
143 Colignan, Australia ...34 35S 142 25E
51 Coligny, Ain, France .46 24N 5 21E
133 Coligny, S. Africa ...26 17S 26 18E
168 Colima, Mexico ...19 10N 103 40W
168 Colima, st., Mexico ...19 10N 103 40W
1 Colima, vol., Mexico ...19 30N 103 40W
172 Colina, Chile ...33 13S 70 45W
175 Colinas, Brazil ... 6 0S 44 10W
143 Colinton, Australia ...35 50S 149 10E
41 Colinton, Scot. U.K. ..55 54N 3 17W
40 Coll, I., Scot., U.K. ...56 40N 6 35W
174 Collahuasi, Chile ...21 5S 68 45W
167 Collbran, U.S.A. ...39 16N 107 58W
70 Colle Salvetti, Italy ...43 34N 10 27E
73 Colle Sannita, Italy ...41 22N 14 48E
71 Colle di Val d'Elsa. It. 43 24N 11 6E
132 Colleen Bawn, Rhod. .21 0S 29 12E
70 Collechio, Italy ...44 23N 10 10E
163 College Park, U.S.A. .33 42N 84 27W
155 Collette, Canada ...46 40N 65 30W
142 Collie, W. Australia ...33 25S 116 30E
138 Collier Bay, W. Austral. ...16 0S 124 0E
38 Collier Law Pk., England, U.K. ...54 47N 1 59W
41 Collin, Scotland, U.K. 55 4N 3 30W
70 Colline Metallifere, It. 43 10N 11 0E
34 Collingbourne, England, U.K. ...51 16N 1 39W
144 Collingwood, Australia 22 20S 142 31E
160 Collingwood, Canada .44 30N 80 20W
147 Collingwood, N.Z. ...40 42N 172 40E
144 Collingwood B., Papua ... 9 30S 149 30E
154 Collins, Canada ...50 20N 89 30W
144 Collinsville, Australia .20 30S 147 56E
172 Collipulli, Chile ...37 55S 72 30W
123 Collo, Algeria ...36 58N 6 37E
46 Collon, Ireland ...53 46N 6 29W
50 Collonges, France ...46 9N 5 52E
46 Collooney, Ireland ...54 11N 8 28W
49 Colmar, France ...48 5N 7 20E
51 Colmars, France ...44 11N 6 39E
62 Colmenar, Spain ...36 54N 4 20W
64 Colmenar de Oreja, Sp. ...40 6N 3 25W
62 Colmenar Viego, Spain ...40 39N 3 47W
40 Colmonel, Scot., U.K. 55 8N 4 55W
165 Colmor, U.S.A. ...36 18N 104 36W
38 Colne, England, U.K. 53 51N 2 11W
35 Colne, R., Essex, England, U.K. ...51 55N 0 50E
35 Colne, R., Herts., England, U.K. ...51 36N 0 30W
143 Colo, R., Australia ...33 20S 150 40E
71 Cologna Veneta, Italy 45 19N 11 21E
56 Cologne, see Köln, Ger.50 56N 9 58E
122 Colomb-Bechar, see Bechar, Algeria ...31 38N 2 18E
49 Colombey-les-Belles, Fr. ...48 32N 5 54E
49 Colombey les deux Églises, France ...48 20N 4 50E
174 Colombia, Rep., S. Amer. ... 3 45N 73 0W
106 Colombo, Ceylon ... 6 56N 79 58E
167 Colombus, U.S.A. ...31 54N 107 43W
164 Colome, U.S.A. ...43 20N 99 44W
172 Colón, Argentina ...32 12S 58 30W
169 Colón, Cuba ...22 42N 80 54W
168 Colón, Panama Rep. . 9 20N 80 0W
71 Colonella, Italy ...42 52N 13 50E
173 Colonia, Uruguay ...34 25S 57 50W
172 Colonia Dora, Arg. ...28 34S 62 59W
176 Colonia Las Heras, Arg. ...46 30S 69 0W
172 Colonia Santa Ara, Arg. ...27 25S 65 40W
176 Colonia Sarmiento, Arg. ...45 30S 68 15W
172 Colonia Suiza, Uruguay ...34 22S 57 10W
162 Colonial Hts., U.S.A. .37 20N 77 25W
74 Colonne, C., Italy ...39 2N 17 11E
157 Colonsay, Canada ...51 59N 105 52W
40 Colonsay I., Scot., U.K. ...56 4N 6 12W
158 Colorado, st., U.S.A. .37 40N 106 0W
167 Colorado Aqueduct, U.S.A. ...34 0N 115 20W
165 Colorado City, U.S.A. 32 25N 100 50W
158 Colorado Des., U.S.A. 34 20N 116 0W
168 Colorado I., Panama Canal Zone ... 9 12N 79 50W
167 Colorado Plat., U.S.A. 36 40N 110 30W
172 Colorado R., Arg. ...37 30S 69 0W
176 Colorado R., Arg. ...28 0S 67 20W
167 Colorado R., Ariz., U.S.A. ...33 30N 114 30W
167 Colorado R., Calif., U.S.A. ...34 0N 114 33W
165 Colorado R., Tex., U.S.A. ...29 40N 96 30W
164 Colorado Springs, U.S.A. ...38 55N 104 50W
70 Colorno, Italy ...44 55N 10 21E
43 Colpy, Scotland, U.K. ...57 23N 2 35W
35 Colsterworth, Eng., U.K. ...52 48N 0 37W
35 Coltishall, Eng., U.K. 52 44N 1 21E
161 Colton, N.Y., U.S.A. .44 34N 74 58W
166 Colton, Wash., U.S.A. 46 41N 117 6W
165 Columbia, La., U.S.A. 32 7N 92 5W
165 Columbia, Miss., U.S.A. ...31 16N 89 50W
164 Columbia, Mo., U.S.A. 38 58N 92 20W
161 Columbia, Pa., U.S.A. 40 2N 76 30W
163 Columbia, S.C., U.S.A. ...34 0N 81 0W
163 Columbia, Tenn., U.S.A. ...35 40N 87 0W
159 Columbia, District of, U.S.A. ...38 55N 77 0W
14 Columbia C., Canada .83 0N 70 0W
156 Columbia Mt., Canada 52 20N 117 30W
166 Columbia Plat., U.S.A. ...47 30N 118 30W
166 Columbia, R., N. Amer. ...45 49N 120 0W
162 Columbia City, U.S.A. 41 8N 85 30W
166 Columbia Falls, U.S.A. ...48 25N 114 16W
164 Columbia Hts., U.S.A. 45 5N 93 10W
160 Columbiana, U.S.A. ...40 53N 80 40W
130 Columbo, Angola ... 9 10S 13 28E
64 Columbretes Is., Spain 39 50N 0 50E
163 Columbus, Ga., U.S.A. 32 30N 84 58W
162 Columbus, Ind., U.S.A. ...39 14N 85 55W
165 Columbus, Kan., U.S.A. ...37 15N 94 30W
163 Columbus, Miss., U.S.A. ...33 30N 88 26W
166 Columbus, Mont., U.S.A. ...45 45N 109 14W
164 Columbus, Neb., U.S.A. ...41 30N 97 25W
164 Columbus, N.D., U.S.A. ...48 52N 102 48W
162 Columbus, Ohio, U.S.A. ...39 57N 83 1W
165 Columbus, Tex., U.S.A. ...29 42N 96 33W
164 Columbus, Wis., U.S.A. ...43 20N 89 2W
62 Colunga, Spain ...43 29N 5 16W
166 Colusa, U.S.A. ...39 15N 122 1W
166 Colville, U.S.A. ...48 39N 117 58W
146 Colville, C., N.Z. ...36 29S 175 21E
152 Colville R., Alas., U.S.A. ...69 10N 153 0W
41 Colwell, Eng., U.K. ...55 4N 2 4W
34 Colwich, Eng., U.K. ...52 48N 1 58W
37 Colwyn, Wales, U.K. .53 17N 3 43W
37 Colwyn Bay, Wales, United Kingdom ...53 17N 3 44W
36 Colyton, Eng., U.K. ...50 44N 3 4W
71 Comacchio, Italy ...44 41N 12 10E
132 Comácha, Mozam. ...17 45S 33 14E
176 Comallo, Argentina ...41 0S 70 5W
78 Comana, Rumania ...44 10N 26 10E
165 Comanche, Okla., U.S.A. ...34 27N 97 58W
165 Comanche, Tex., U.S.A. ...31 55N 98 35W
163 Combahee, R., U.S.A. 32 45N 80 50W
172 Combarbala, Chile ...31 10S 71 0W
36 Combe Martin, England, U.K. ...51 12N 4 2W
49 Combeaufontaine, Fr. 47 43N 5 45E
160 Comber, Canada ...42 15N 82 34W
46 Comber, N. Ire., U.K. 54 33N 5 45W
54 Comblain, Belgium ...50 29N 5 35E
49 Combles, France ...50 0N 2 50E
127 Combolcia, Ethiopia ...11 29N 39 42E
48 Combourg, France ...48 25N 1 46W
50 Combronde, France ...45 58N 3 5E
45 Comeragh Mts., Ireland ...52 17N 7 35W
144 Comet, Australia ...23 36S 148 38E
123 Comet Vale, W. Austral. ...29 55S 121 4E
132 Cometela, Mozam. ...21 51S 34 29E
70 Comilla, East Pakistan ...23 22N 91 18E
72 Comino, C., Sardinia, It. ...40 28N 9 47E
68 Comino (Kemmuna), I., Malta ...36 0N 14 22E
73 Comiso, Italy ...36 57N 14 35E
168 Comitán, Mexico ...16 18N 92 9W
50 Commentry, France ...46 20N 2 46E
163 Commerce, Ga., U.S.A. ...34 10N 83 25W
165 Commerce, Tex., U.S.A. ...33 15N 95 50W
49 Commercy, France ...48 46N 5 34E
153 Committee B., Canada 68 0N 87 0W
133 Commondale, S. Africa ...27 20S 30 56E
15 Commonwealth B., Ant. ...67 0S 144 0E
70 Como, Italy ...45 48N 9 5E
70 Como, L. of, Italy ...46 5N 9 17E
176 Comodoro Rivadavia, Argentina ...45 50S 67 40W
106 Comorin, C., India ... 8 3N 77 40E
74 Comorište, Rumania .45 10N 21 35E
11 Comoro Arch., Ind. Oc. ...10 0S 50 0E
156 Comox, Canada ...49 42N 125 0W
49 Compiègne, France ...49 24N 2 50E
70 Compiglia Marittima, Italy ...43 4N 10 37E
63 Comporta, Portugal ...38 22N 8 46W
41 Comrie, Scotland, U.K. ...56 22N 4 0W
34 Compton, Eng., U.K. .51 2N 1 19W
145 Compton Downs, Australia ...30 28S 146 30E
107 Con Son Is., S. Vietnam ... 8 45N 106 45E
124 Conakry, Guinea ... 9 29N 13 49W
145 Conara Junc., Austral. 41 48S 143 70E
168 Conatlán, Mexico ...24 30N 104 42W
48 Concarneau, France ...47 52N 3 56W
132 Conceiçao, Mozam. ...18 47S 36 7E
175 Conceiçao da Barra, Brazil ...18 50S 39 50W
175 Conceiçao do Araguaia, Brazil ... 8 0S 49 2W
172 Concepcion, Argentina 27 20S 65 35W
174 Concepción, Bolivia ...15 50S 61 40W
172 Concepción, Chile ...36 50S 73 0W
172 Concepcion, Paraguay 23 30S 57 20W
172 Concepcion, prov., Chile ...37 0S 72 30W
176 Concepción Chan., Chile ...50 50S 75 0W
174 Concepcion L., Bolivia 17 20S 61 10W
158 Concepcion, C., U.S.A. 34 30N 120 34W
168 Concepcion del Oro, Mexico ...24 40N 101 30W
172 Concepción del Urug., Argentina ...32 35S 58 20W
168 Concepcion, Punta, Mexico ...26 55N 111 50W
129 Conception B., South West Africa ...23 55S 14 22E
169 Conception I., Bahamas ...23 52N 75 9W
132 Concession, Rhodesia .17 27S 30 56E
165 Conchas Dam, U.S.A. 35 25N 104 10W
155 Conche, Canada ...50 48N 57 0W
148 Conches, France ...48 58N 0 58E
167 Concho, U.S.A. ...34 32N 109 43W
165 Concho R., U.S.A. ...31 30N 100 8W
168 Conchos R., Mexico ...29 20N 105 0W
172 Concon, Chile ...32 56S 71 33W
161 Concord, N.H., U.S.A. 43 5N 71 30W
163 Concord, N.C., U.S.A. 35 28N 80 35W
172 Concordia, Argentina .31 20S 58 2W
174 Concordia, Brazil ... 4 36S 66 36W
134 Concordia, S. Africa ...29 32S 17 55E
164 Concordia, U.S.A. ...39 35N 97 40W
50 Concots, France ...44 26N 1 40E
166 Concrete, U.S.A. ...48 35N 121 49W
145 Condamine, Australia 26 55S 150 3E
50 Condat, France ...45 21N 2 46E
49 Condé, Nord, France .50 26N 3 34E
164 Conde, U.S.A. ...45 13N 98 5W
48 Condé-sur-Noireau, Fr. ...48 51N 0 33W
175 Condeuba, Brazil ...15 0S 42 0W
143 Condobolin, Australia 33 4S 147 6E
50 Condom, France ...43 57N 0 22E
166 Condon, U.S.A. ...45 15N 120 8W
70 Condove, Italy ...45 8N 7 19E
34 Condover, Eng., U.K. 52 39N 2 46W
71 Conegliano, Italy ...45 53N 12 18E
65 Conejera I., Balearic Is., Spain ...39 11N 2 58E
160 Conemaugh R., USA .40 25N 79 0W
49 Conflans, France ...49 10N 5 52E
50 Confolens, France ...46 2N 0 40E
172 Confuso R., Paraguay 24 10S 59 0W
38 Congleton, Eng., U.K. 53 10N 2 12W
117 Congo Basin, Africa ... 0 10S 24 30E
130 Congo R., Congo ... 1 30N 23 0E
130 Congo, (Kinshasa) st., see Zaire... 3 0S 22 0E
130 Congo, Rep of, Afr. ... 1 0S 16 0E
36 Congresbury, Eng., U.K. ...51 20N 2 49W
167 Congress, U.S.A. ...34 11N 112 56W
115 Congucu, Brazil ...31 25S 52 30W
126 Conical Hill, Egypt ...23 22N 29 0E
44 Conigar Mt., Ireland .51 50N 9 20W
63 Conil, Spain ...36 17N 6 10W
39 Coningsby, Eng., UK .53 7N 0 9W
39 Conisbrough, Eng., U.K. ...53 29N 1 12W
154 Coniston, Canada ...46 32N 80 51W
38 Coniston, Eng., U.K. .54 22N 3 6W
38 Coniston Water, England, U.K. ...54 20N 3 5W
106 Conjeevaram, see Kancheepuram, India ...12 52N 79 45E
144 Conjuboy, Australia ...18 35S 144 45E
145 Conlea, Australia ...30 7S 144 35E
45 Conn, L., Ireland ...54 3N 9 15W
44 Conna, Ireland ...52 5N 8 8W
46 Connacht, prov., Ire. .53 23N 8 40W
37 Connah's Quay, Wales, United Kingdom ...53 13N 3 6W
160 Conneaut, U.S.A. ...41 55N 80 32W
161 Connecticut, R., U.S.A. ...42 15N 72 30W
161 Connecticut, st., U.S.A. ...41 40N 72 40W
40 Connel, Scot., U.K. ...56 27N 5 24W
166 Connell, U.S.A. ...46 45N 118 58W
40 Connel Park, Scot., U.K. ...55 22N 4 15W
44 Connemara, dist., Ire. 53 29N 9 45W
162 Connersville, U.S.A. ...39 40N 85 10W
160 Connolsville, U.S.A. ...40 5N 79 32W
44 Connonagh, Ireland ...51 35N 9 8W
144 Connors Ra., Queensland, Australia ...21 40S 149 10E
143 Conoble, N.S.W., Australia ...32 55S 144 42E
157 Conquest, Canada ...53 35N 107 0W
166 Conrad, U.S.A. ...48 11N 112 0W
165 Conroe, U.S.A. ...30 15N 95 28W
173 Conselheiro Lafaiete, Brazil ...20 40S 43 48W
38 Consett, England, U.K. ...54 52N 1 50W
161 Conshohocken, U.S.A. 40 5N 75 18W
174 Constancia dos Baetas, Brazil ... 6 5S 62 20W
78 Constanta, Rumania .44 14N 28 38E
78 Constanța, Reg., Rumania ...44 20N 28 30E
63 Constantina, Spain ...37 51N 5 40W
123 Constantine, Algeria ...36 25N 6 42E
172 Constitucion, Chile ...35 20S 72 30W
172 Constitucion. Uruguay 31 0S 58 10W
63 Consuegra, Spain ...39 28N 3 43W
157 Consul, Canada ...49 20N 109 30W
166 Contact, U.S.A. ...41 50N 114 56W
105 Contai, India ...21 54N 87 55E
174 Contamana, Peru ... 7 10S 74 55W
71 Contarina, Italy ...45 2N 12 13E
175 Contas R., Brazil ...13 55S 41 0W
133 Content, C. Prov., S. Afr. ...28 13S 24 48E
43 Contin, Scot., U.K. ...57 34N 4 35W
161 Contoocook, U.S.A. ...43 13N 71 45W
49 Contres, France ...47 24N 1 26E
49 Contrexéville, France .48 10N 5 53E
73 Conversano, Italy ...40 57N 17 8E
46 Convoy, Ireland ...54 52N 7 40W
144 Conway, Australia ...20 22S 148 42E
135 Conway, S. Africa ...31 43S 25 16E
37 Conway, Wales, U.K. 53 17N 3 50W
165 Conway, Ark., U.S.A. 35 5N 92 30W
161 Conway, N.H., U.S.A. 43 58N 71 8W
163 Conway, S.C., U.S.A. .33 49N 79 2W
37 Conway Bay, Wales, United Kingdom ...53 17N 3 57W
37 Conway, R., Wales, United Kingdom ...53 10N 3 50W
142 Coobina, W. Australia 23 22S 120 10E
105 Cooch Behar, India ...26 22N 89 29E
142 Cook, South Australia 30 42S 130 48E
164 Cook, U.S.A. ...47 49N 92 39W
176 Cook Bay, Chile ...55 10S 70 0W
137 Cook Is., Pacific Ocean ...22 0S 157 0W
147 Cook, Mount, N.Z. ...43 36S 170 9E
146 Cook Strait, N.Z. ...41 15S 174 29E
163 Cookeville, U.S.A. ...36 12N 85 30W
35 Cookham, Eng., U.K. 51 33N 0 42W
135 Cookhouse, S. Africa .32 44S 25 47E
161 Cookshire, Canada ...45 26N 71 38W
46 Cookstown, N. Ire., U.K. ...54 40N 6 43W
160 Cooksville, Canada ...43 36N 79 35W
144 Cooktown, Australia .15 30S 145 16E
145 Coolabah, Australia ...31 0S 146 15E
145 Cooladdi, Australia ...26 37S 145 23E
143 Coolah, N.S.W., Austral. ...31 48S 149 41E
143 Coolamon, Australia ...34 46S 147 8E
46 Coolaney, Ireland ...54 10N 8 36W
145 Coolangatta, Australia 28 11S 153 29E
46 Coole, Ireland ...53 42N 7 23W
142 Coolgardie, W. Austral. ...30 55S 121 8E
45 Coolgreany, Ireland ...52 46N 6 14W
167 Coolidge, U.S.A. ...33 1N 111 35W
167 Coolidge Dam, U.S.A. 33 10N 110 30W
46 Coolmore, Ireland ...54 33N 8 12W
143 Cooma, N.S.W., Austral. ...36 12S 149 8E
44 Coomacarrea Mts., Ire. ...51 59N 10 0W
143 Coonabarabran, Austral. ...31 14S 149 18E
145 Coonambie, Australia .30 56S 148 27E
142 Coonana, W. Australia ...31 0S 123 0E
106 Coondapoor, India ...13 42N 74 40E
145 Coongie, Australia ...27 9S 140 8E
145 Coongoola, Australia .27 43S 145 47E
106 Coonoor, India ...11 10N 76 45E
134 Cooper, C. Prov., S. Afr. ...34 12S 21 47E
165 Cooper, U.S.A. ...33 20N 95 40W
156 Cooper, Mt., Canada .50 10N 117 11W
138 Cooper Pedy, S. Australia ...29 1S 134 40E
163 Cooper, R., U.S.A. ...33 0N 79 55W
145 Cooper Cr., South Australia ...28 0S 139 0E
161 Cooperstown, U.S.A. .42 42N 74 57W
164 Cooperstown, U.S.A. .47 30N 98 14W
144 Coorabulka, Australia 23 41S 140 20E
143 Cooranbong, N.S.W., Australia ...33 2S 151 30W
145 Coorong, The, S. Austral ...35 50S 139 20E
142 Coorow, W. Australia 29 50S 115 59E
145 Cooroy, Australia ...26 22S 152 54E
166 Coos Bay, U.S.A. ...43 26N 124 7W
143 Cootamundra, Australia ...34 36S 148 1E
46 Cootehill, Ireland ...54 5N 7 5W
145 Cooyar, Australia ...26 59S 151 51E
144 Cooyeana, Australia ...44 25S 138 50E
168 Copainata, Mexico ...17 8N 93 11W
164 Cope, U.S.A. ...39 44N 102 50W
65 Cope, Cabo, Spain ...37 26N 1 28W
46 Copeland I. Ireland ...54 38N 5 33W
81 Copenhagen, see København, Denmark ...55 41N 12 34E
73 Copertino, Italy ...40 17N 18 2W
172 Copiapó, Chile ...27 15S 70 20E
43 Copinsay I., Scot., U.K. ...58 54N 2 40W
145 Copley, S. Australia ...30 31S 138 25E
71 Copparo, Italy ...44 52N 11 49E
152 Copper Center, Alaska, U.S.A. ...62 10N 145 25W
154 Copper Cliff, Canada .46 30N 81 4W
162 Copper Harbour, U.S.A. ...47 31N 87 55W
156 Copper Mountain, Can. ...49 20N 120 30W
132 Copper Queen, Rhod. .17 29S 29 18E
142 Copperfield, W. Australia ...29 1S 120 26E
152 Coppermine, Canada .68 0N 116 0W
152 Coppermine R., Canada ...66 30N 115 30W

MAP
112 Coptchil, China ...42 4N 112 50E
34 Copythorne, Eng., U.K. ...50 56N 1 34W
127 Coqe Mts., Ethiopia ...11 18N 37 15E
130 Coquilhatville, *see* Mbandaka, Congo ... 0 1N 18 18E
166 Coquille, U.S.A. ...43 15N 124 6W
172 Coquimbo, Chile ...30 0S 71 20W
78 Corabia, Rumania ...43 48N 24 30E
174 Coracora, Peru ...15 5S 73 45W
73 Coradi, Is., Italy ...40 27N 71 10E
136 Coral Sea, Pacific Ocean ...15 0S 150 0E
154 Coral Rapids, Canada 50 20N 81 40W
143 Corangamite, L., Vic., Australia ...38 0S 143 30E
160 Coraopolis, U.S.A. ...40 30N 80 10W
73 Corato, Italy ...41 12N 16 22E
49 Corbeil-Essonnes, Fr. 48 36N 2 25E
49 Corbie, France ...49 54N 2 30E
50 Corbières, Mts., France ...42 55N 2 35E
49 Corbigny, France ...47 16N 3 40E
162 Corbin, U.S.A. ...37 0N 84 3W
63 Corbones, R., Spain ...37 25N 5 35W
38 Corbridge, Eng., U.K. ...54 58N 2 0W
35 Corby, Lincs., England, United Kingdom ...52 49N 0 31W
35 Corby, Northants, England, U.K. ...52 29N 0 41W
65 Corcoles R., Spain ...39 12N 2 40W
167 Corcoran, U.S.A. ...36 6N 119 35W
1 Corcovado, Vol., Chile 43 10S 72 55W
62 Corcubión, Spain ...42 56N 9 12W
163 Cordele, U.S.A. ...31 55N 83 49W
165 Cordell, U.S.A. ...35 18N 99 0W
71 Cordenons, Italy ...45 59N 12 42E
50 Cordes, France ...44 5N 1 57E
174 Cordillera Central, Col. ... 6 0N 75 0W
169 Cord. Central, Costa Rica ...10 15N 84 0W
174 Cord. de Caravaya, Peru ...14 0S 70 30W
174 Cordillera Occidental, Col. ... 5 0N 76 30W
174 Cordillera Oriental, Col. ... 5 0N 74 0W
172 Córdoba, Argentina ...31 20S 64 10W
168 Cordoba, Durango, *see* Tiahualilo, Mexico .26 20N 103 20W
168 Córdoba, Vera Cruz, Mexico ...18 50N 97 0W
63 Cordoba, Spain ...37 50N 4 50W
172 Cordoba, Prov. Arg. ...31 22S 64 15W
63 Cordoba, Prov., Spain 38 5N 5 0W
172 Cordoba, Sierra de, Arg. ...31 10S 64 25W
109 Cordon, Philippines ...16 42N 121 32E
152 Cordova, Alaska, U.S.A. ...60 36N 145 45W
163 Cordova, U.S.A. ...33 45N 87 12W
64 Corella, Spain ...42 7N 1 48W
35 Corfe Castle, Eng., U.K. ...50 38N 2 3W
34 Corfe Mullen, Eng., U.K. ...50 45N 2 0W
144 Corfield, Australia ...21 40S 143 21E
76 Corfu., *see* Kerkira, Greece ...39 38N 19 50E
142 Corgo, Spain ...42 56N 7 25W
72 Cori, Italy ...41 39N 12 53E
62 Coria, Spain ...40 0N 6 33W
143 Coricudgy, Mt., Austral. ...32 51S 150 24E
73 Corigliano Calabro, It. 39 36N 16 31E
145 Corinna, Australia ...41 35S 145 10E
77 Corinth, *see* Korinthos, Greece ...37 56N 22 55E
163 Corinth, Miss., U.S.A. 34 54N 88 30W
161 Corinth, N.Y., U.S.A. 43 15N 73 50W
77 Corinth Canal, Greece 37 48N 23 0E
77 Corinth, G. of, *see* Korinthiakós Kólpos, Greece ...38 16N 22 30E
175 Corinto, Brazil ...18 20S 44 30W
169 Corinto, Nicaragua ...12 30N 87 10W
44 Cork, & Co., Ireland ...51 54N 8 30W
44 Cork Harbour, Ireland 51 46N 8 16W
48 Corlay, France ...48 20N 3 5W
72 Corleone, Italy ...37 48N 13 16E
73 Corleto Perticara, Italy ...40 23N 16 2E
75 Corlu, Turkey ...41 11N 27 49E
71 Cormons, Italy ...45 58N 13 29E
157 Cormorant, Canada ...54 5N 100 45W
169 Corn Is., Cent. Amer. .12 0N 83 0W
135 Cornelia, O.F.S., S. Afr. ...27 13S 28 52E
173 Cornélio Procópio, Braz. ...23 7S 50 40W
164 Cornell, U.S.A. ...45 10N 91 8W
155 Corner Brook, Canada 49 0N 58 0W
143 Corner Inlet, Australia ...38 40S 146 30E
41 Cornforth, Eng., U.K. 54 42N 1 28W
70 Corniglio, Italy ...44 29N 10 5E
165 Corning, Ark., U.S.A. 36 27N 90 34W
166 Corning, Calif. U.S.A. 39 56N 122 9W
164 Corning, Iowa, U.S.A. 40 57N 94 40W
160 Corning, N.Y., U.S.A 42 10N 77 3W
154 Cornwall, Canada ...45 5N 74 45W
36 Cornwall co., Eng. U.K. ...50 26N 4 40W
36 Cornwall, C., Eng., U.K. ...50 8N 5 42W
14 Cornwallis I., Canada .75 0N 95 0W
174 Coro, Venezuela ...11 30N 69 45W
MAP
175 Coroatá, Brazil ... 4 20S 44 0W
174 Corocoro, Bolivia ...17 15S 69 19W
44 Corofin, Ireland ...53 27N 8 50W
174 Coroico, Bolivia ...16 0S 67 50W
146 Coromandel, N.Z. ...36 45S 175 31E
106 Coromandel Coast, India ...12 30N 81 0E
146 Coromandel Pen., N.Z. ...37 0S 175 45E
146 Coromandel Ra., N.Z. 37 0S 175 40E
157 Coromorant, L., Canada ...54 20N 100 50W
167 Corona, Calif., U.S.A. 33 49N 117 36W
167 Corona, N. Mex., U.S.A. ...34 15N 105 32W
169 Coronada B., Costa Rica ... 9 0N 83 40W
167 Coronado, U.S.A. ...32 45N 117 9W
152 Coronation Gulf, Can. 68 0N 114 0W
156 Coronation I., Alaska, U.S.A. ...55 52N 134 20W
15 Coronation I., Antarc. 60 45S 46 0W
172 Coronda, Argentina ...31 58S 60 56W
172 Coronel, Chile ...37 0S 73 10W
172 Coronel Brandsen, Arg. ...35 48S 58 15W
176 Coronel Dorrego, Arg. 38 40S 61 10W
172 Coronel Oviedo, Par. .25 24S 56 30W
172 Coronel Pringles, Arg. 38 0S 61 30W
172 Coronel Suarez, Arg. .37 30S 62 0W
172 Coronel Vidal, Arg. ...37 28S 57 45W
175 Coronie, Surinam ... 5 55N 56 25W
76 Corovode, Albania ...40 31N 20 14E
143 Corowa, Australia ...35 58S 146 21E
168 Corozal, Brit. Hond. .18 30N 88 30W
168 Corozal, Pan. Can. Zone ... 8 59N 79 34W
42 Corpach, Scot., U.K. .56 50N 5 9W
51 Corps, France ...44 50N 5 56E
173 Corpus, Argentina ...27 10S 55 30W
165 Corpus Christi, U.S.A. 27 50N 97 28W
165 Corpus Christi L., U.S.A. ...28 5N 97 54W
174 Corque, Bolivia ...18 10S 67 50W
64 Corral de Almaguer, Sp. ...39 45N 3 10W
42 Corran, Scotland, U.K. ...56 44N 14W
142 Corrandibby Ra., W. Australia ...26 0S 115 20E
45 Corraun Pen., Ireland 53 58N 10 15W
70 Correggio, Italy ...44 46N 10 47E
132 Correntes, C. das, Mozambique ...24 6S 35 34E
50 Corrèze, dépt., France 45 20N 1 50E
44 Corrib, L., Ireland ...53 25N 9 10W
40 Corrie, Scotland, U.K. 55 39N 5 10W
172 Corrientes, Argentina .27 30S 58 45W
172 Corrientes, prov., Arg. 28 0S 57 0W
174 Corrientes, C., Colombia ... 5 30N 77 30W
169 Corrientes, C., Cuba ...21 43N 84 30W
174 Corrientes, R. Colombia ... 3 15S 75 58W
165 Corrigan, U.S.A. ...31 0N 94 48W
142 Corrigin, W. Australia ...32 18S 117 45E
39 Corringham, Eng., U.K. ...53 25N 0 42W
37 Corris, Wales, U.K. ...52 41N 3 49W
160 Corry, U.S.A. ...41 55N 79 39W
143 Corryong, Victoria, Australia ...36 12S 147 53E
40 Corryvrecken, G. of, Scotland, U.K. ...56 10N 5 44W
51 Corse, C., Corsica, Fr. 43 1N 9 25E
51 Corse, dept., France ...42 0N 9 0E
40 Corsewall Pt., Scotland, United Kingdom ...55 0N 5 10W
34 Corsham, Eng., U.K. .51 25N 2 11W
51 Corsica, I., Medit. Sea 42 0N 9 0E
165 Corsicana, U.S.A. ...32 5N 96 30W
34 Corsley, England, U.K. ...51 12N 14W
74 Corsnica, Mt., Y.-slav. ...43 36N 17 35E
41 Corsock, Scotland, U.K. ... 5 54N 3 56W
51 Corté, Corsica, France 42 19N 9 11E
63 Corte do Pinto, Port. .37 42N 7 29W
63 Cortegana, Spain ...37 52N 6 49W
167 Cortez, U.S.A. ...37 24N 108 35W
71 Cortina d'Ampezzo, It. ...46 32N 12 9E
161 Cortland, U.S.A. ...42 35N 76 11W
35 Corton, England, U.K. ...52 31N 1 46E
71 Cortona, Italy ...43 16N 12 0E
63 Coruche, Portugal ...38 57N 8 30W
100 Corum, Turkey ...40 30N 35 5E
175 Corumbá, Brazil ...16 0S 48 50W
174 Corumbá, Brazil ...19 0S 57 30W
175 Corumbá R., Brazil ...17 25S 48 30W
62 Coruña, prov., Spain .43 0N 8 37E
78 Corund, Rumania ...46 30N 25 13E
133 Corundum, S. Africa .24 2S 30 42E
62 Corunna, *see* La Coruna, Spain ...43 20N 8 25W
175 Coruripe, Brazil ...10 5S 36 10W
166 Corvallis, U.S.A. ...44 36N 123 15W
154 Corvette, L., Canada .53 25N 73 55W
37 Corwen, Wales, U.K. .52 59N 3 23W
164 Corydon, Iowa, U.S.A. ...40 42N 93 22W
168 Cosamaloapan, Mexico 18 23N 95 50W
34 Coseley, England, U.K. ...52 33N 2 6W
73 Cosenza, Italy ...39 17N 16 14E
78 Coşereni, Rumania ...44 38N 26 35E
MAP
34 Cosham, England, U.K. ...50 51N 1 3W
160 Coshocton, U.S.A. ...40 17N 81 51W
49 Cosne, France ...47 24N 2 54E
62 Cospeito, Spain ...43 12N 7 34W
172 Cosquin, Argentina ...31 15S 64 30W
70 Cossato, Italy ...45 34N 8 10E
48 Cossé le Vivien, France ...47 57N 0 54W
65 Costa Blanca, Reg., Sp. ...38 25N 0 10W
64 Costa Brava, Reg., Spain ...41 30N 3 0E
63 Costa del Sol, Reg., Sp. ...36 30N 4 30W
64 Costa Dorada, Spain .40 45N 1 15E
169 Costa Rica, Rep., Central America ...10 0N 84 0W
72 Costa Smeralda, Sardinia, Italy ...41 5N 9 35E
44 Costelloe, Ireland ...53 20N 9 33W
35 Costessey, Eng., U.K. 52 40N 1 11E
70 Costigliole d'Asti, Italy ...44 48N 8 11E
167 Costilla, U.S.A. ...37 0N 105 30W
78 Coştiui, Rumania ...47 53N 24 2E
56 Coswig, Germany ...51 52N 12 31E
109 Cotabato, Philippines . 7 8N 124 13E
172 Cotagaita, Bolivia ...20 45S 65 30W
51 Côte d'Azur, dist., Fr. 43 25N 6 50E
49 Côte d'Or, dépt., Fr. .47 30N 4 50E
49 Côte d'Or, ridge, Fr. .47 10N 4 50E
164 Coteau des Prairies, U.S.A. ...44 30N 97 0W
158 Coteau du Missouri, Plat. du, U.S.A. ...47 0N 101 0W
161 Coteau Sta., Canada ...45 17N 74 14W
48 Cotentin, dist., France 49 30N 1 30W
49 Côtes de Meuse, dist., France ...49 15N 5 22E
48 Côtes du Nord, dépt., France ...48 28N 2 50W
38 Cotherstone, Eng., U.K. ...54 34N 1 59W
74 Cotina, R., Yugoslavia ...43 36N 19 9E
125 Cotonou, Dahomey ... 6 20N 2 25E
174 Cotopaxi, vol., Ecuador ... 0 30S 78 30W
73 Cotronei, Italy ...39 9N 16 27E
35 Cotswold Hills, England, U.K. ...51 42N 2 10W
166 Cottage Grove, U.S.A. 43 48N 123 2W
56 Cottbus, Germany ...51 44N 14 20E
56 Cottbus, dist., E. Ger. 51 43N 13 30E
35 Cottenham, Eng., U.K. ...52 18N 0 8E
51 Cottiennes, Alpes, mts., France ...44 36N 6 40E
156 Cottonwood, Canada .53 5N 121 50E
167 Cottonwood, U.S.A. ...34 48N 112 1W
39 Cottingham, Eng., U.K. ...53 47N 0 25W
50 Coubre, Pte. de la, Fr. 45 42N 1 15W
49 Couches, France ...46 53N 4 30E
63 Couco, Portugal ...38 59N 8 17W
160 Coudersport, U.S.A. ...41 45N 78 1W
48 Couesnon, R., France 48 20N 1 15W
50 Couhé Vérac, France .46 18N 0 12E
49 Coulanges, Yonne, Fr. 47 30N 3 30E
50 Coulanges, Deux Sèvres, France ...46 58N 0 35W
166 Coulee City, U.S.A. ...47 44N 119 12W
15 Coulman I., Antarctica ...73 35S 170 0E
49 Coulommiers, France .48 50N 3 3E
155 Coulonge R., Canada .46 50N 77 20W
40 Coulpo, Scot., U.K. ...56 2N 4 55W
35 Coulsdon, Eng., U.K. .51 19N 0 7W
166 Council, U.S.A. ...44 45N 116 30W
164 Council Bluffs, U.S.A. 41 20N 95 50W
164 Council Grove, U.S.A. 38 41N 96 30W
41 Coupar Angus, Scotland, United Kingdom ...56 33N 3 17W
174 Courantyne R., S. Amer. ... 5 0N 57 45W
50 Courçon, France ...46 15N 0 50W
51 Cours, France ...46 7N 4 19E
48 Courseulles, France ...49 20N 0 29W
55 Court St. Etienne, Belg. ...50 38N 4 34E
156 Courtenay, Canada ...49 45N 125 0W
44 Courtmacsherry, Ireland ...51 38N 8 43W
44 Courtmacsherry B., Ire. ...51 37N 8 37W
45 Courtown, Ireland ...52 39N 6 14W
54 Courtrai, *see* Kortrijk, Belgium ...50 50N 3 17E
160 Courtright, Canada ...42 48N 82 55W
48 Courville, France ...48 28N 1 15E
165 Coushatta, U.S.A. ...32 3N 93 20W
48 Coutances, France ...49 3N 1 28W
48 Couterne, France ...48 30N 0 25W
55 Couthuin, Belgium ...50 32N 5 8E
50 Coutras, France ...45 3N 0 8W
132 Covane, Mozambique .21 25S 33 55E
64 Covarrubias Spain ...42 4N 3 31W
78 Covasna, Rumania ...45 50N 26 10E
78 Covasna, Reg., Rum. .46 0N 26 0E
43 Cove Bay, Scot., U.K. 57 5N 2 5W
34 Coventry, Eng., U.K. 52 25N 1 31W
157 Coventry L., Canada .61 15N 106 15W
38 Cover R., Eng., U.K. .54 14N 1 56W
36 Coverack, Eng., U.K. 50 2N 5 6W
62 Covilhã, Portugal ...40 17N 7 31W
163 Covington, Ga., USA .33 36N 83 50W
162 Covington, Ky., U.S.A. ...39 5N 84 30W
MAP
165 Covington, Okla., U.S.A. ...36 21N 97 36W
165 Covington, Tenn., U.S.A. ...35 34N 89 39W
40 Cowal, dist., Scot., U.K. ...56 5N 5 8W
144 Cowal Cr. Settlement Queens., Austral. ...10 30S 142 16E
143 Cowal L., Australia ...33 40S 147 25E
157 Cowan, Canada ...52 5N 100 45W
142 Cowan L., W. Australia ...31 45S 121 45E
143 Cowangie, Australia ...35 12S 141 26E
161 Cowansville, Canada .45 14N 72 46W
145 Cowarie, S. Australia .27 45S 138 15E
142 Cowarna, W. Australia ...30 55S 122 40E
37 Cowbridge, Wales, U.K. ...51 28N 3 28W
142 Cowcowing Lakes, W. Australia ...31 0S 117 30E
41 Cowdenbeath, Scot., U.K. ...56 7N 3 20W
145 Cowell, S. Australia ...33 38S 136 40E
34 Cowes, England, U.K. 50 45N 1 18W
35 Cowfold, England, U.K. ...50 58N 0 16W
34 Cowley, Eng., U.K. ...51 43N 1 12W
39 Cowpen, England, U.K. ...55 8N 1 34W
143 Cowra, N.S.W., Austral. ...33 49S 148 42E
175 Coxim, Brazil ...18 30S 54 55W
103 Cox's Bazar, E. Pakistan ...21 25N 92 3E
155 Cox's Cove, Canada ...49 7N 58 5W
40 Coylton, Scotland. U.K. ...55 26N 4 31W
168 Coyuca de Benítez, Mex. ...17 1N 100 8W
168 Coyuca de Catalan, Mex. ...18 58N 100 41W
164 Cozad, U.S.A. ...40 55N 99 57W
168 Cozumel, Isla de, Mex. ...20 30N 86 40W
45 Craanford, Ireland ...52 40N 6 23W
143 Craboon, Australia ...32 3S 149 30E
145 Cracow, Australia ...25 14S 150 24E
135 Cradock, S. Afr. ...32 8S 25 36E
160 Crafton, U.S.A. ...40 25N 80 4W
43 Craggie, Scot., U.K. ...57 25N 4 6W
157 Craig, Alaska, U.S.A. .55 30N 133 0W
166 Craig, U.S.A. ...40 32N 107 44W
43 Craigellachie, Scot., U.K. ...57 29N 3 9W
40 Craighouse, Scot., U.K. ...55 50N 5 58W
132 Craigmore, Rhodesia .20 28S 32 30E
40 Craignish, L., Scotland, United Kingdom ...56 11N 5 32W
43 Craigtown, Scot., U.K. ...58 30N 3 53W
41 Crail, Scotland, U.K. .56 16N 2 38W
57 Crailsheim, Germany .49 7N 10 5E
78 Craiova, Rumania ...44 21N 23 48E
39 Cramlington, Eng., U.K. ...55 5N 1 36W
144 Cramsie, Australia ...23 20S 144 15E
157 Cranberry Portage, Can. ...54 36N 101 22W
34 Cranborne, Eng., U.K. ...50 55N 1 55W
29 Cranborne Chase, England, U.K. ...50 56N 2 6W
145 Cranbrook, Australia .42 0S 148 5E
156 Cranbrook, Canada ...49 30N 115 55W
35 Cranbrook, Eng., U.K. ...51 6N 0 33E
142 Cranbrook, W. Austral. ...34 20S 117 35E
164 Crandon, U.S.A. ...45 32N 88 52W
166 Crane, Oregon, U.S.A. 43 21N 118 39W
165 Crane, Texas, U.S.A. .31 26N 102 27W
46 Cranfield Pt., Northern Ireland, U.K. ...54 1N 6 3W
35 Cranleigh, England, U.K. ...51 8N 0 29W
41 Cranshaws, Scot., U.K. ...55 51N 2 30W
161 Cranston, U.S.A. ...41 47N 71 27W
39 Cranwell, Lincs., England, U.K. ...53 4N 0 29W
48 Craon, France ...47 50N 0 58W
49 Craonne, France ...49 27N 3 42E
78 Crasna, Rumania ...46 32N 27 51E
78 Crasna, R., Rumania .47 44N 27 35E
166 Crater Lake, U.S.A. ...42 55N 122 3W
175 Crateus, Brazil ... 5 10S 40 50W
43 Crathie, Scot., U.K. ...57 3N 3 12W
73 Crati, R., Italy ...39 41N 16 30E
175 Crato, Brazil ... 7 10S 39 25W
63 Crato, Portugal ...39 16N 7 39W
51 Crau, dist., France ...43 32N 4 40E
44 Craughwell, Ireland ...53 15N 8 44W
34 Craven Arms, England, U.K. ...52 27N 2 49W
41 Crawford, Scot., U.K. 55 28N 3 40W
164 Crawford, U.S.A. ...42 40N 103 25W
162 Crawfordsville, U.S.A. 40 2N 86 51W
35 Crawley, England, U.K. ...51 7N 0 10W
73 Cray, Wales, U.K. ...51 55N 3 38W
166 Crazy Mts., U.S.A. ...46 14N 110 30W
49 Crécy, France ...48 50N 2 53E
49 Crécy-en-Ponthieu, Fr. ...50 15N 1 53E
49 Crécy-sur-Serre, France ...49 40N 3 32E
MAP
34 Credenhill, Eng., U.K. 52 6N 2 49W
160 Crediton, Canada ...43 19N 81 33W
36 Crediton, Eng., U.K. .50 47N 3 39W
142 Credo, W. Australia ...30 28S 120 45E
157 Cree L., Canada ...57 30N 107 0W
40 Cree, R., Scot., U.K. .55 3N 4 35W
167 Creede, U.S.A. ...37 56N 106 59W
44 Creegh, Ireland ...52 45N 9 25W
168 Creel, Mexico ...27 45N 107 38W
40 Creeside, Scot., U.K. .55 4N 4 41W
46 Creeslough, Ireland ...55 8N 7 55W
40 Creetown, Scotland, U.K. ...54 54N 4 23W
44 Creeves, Ireland ...52 33N 9 3W
46 Creggan, N. Ireland, U.K. ...54 39N 7 0W
45 Cregganbaun, Ireland 53 42N 9 48W
164 Creighton, U.S.A. ...42 30N 97 52W
49 Creil, France ...49 15N 2 34E
70 Crema, Italy ...45 21N 9 40E
70 Cremona, Italy ...45 8N 10 2E
74 Crepaja, Yugoslavia ...45 1N 20 38E
49 Crépy, France ...49 37N 3 32E
49 Crépy-en-Valois, France ...49 14N 2 54E
71 Cres, & I., Yugoslavia 44 58N 14 25E
164 Cresbard, U.S.A. ...45 13N 98 57W
165 Crescent, Okla., U.S.A. ...35 38N 97 36W
166 Crescent, Ore., U.S.A. 43 30N 121 37W
70 Crescentino, Italy ...45 11N 8 7E
71 Crespino, Italy ...44 59N 11 51E
154 Cressman, Canada ...47 40N 72 55W
143 Cressy, Australia ...38 10S 143 38E
51 Crest, France ...44 44N 5 2E
167 Crested Butte, U.S.A. 38 57N 107 0W
160 Crestline, U.S.A. ...40 46N 82 45W
156 Creston, Canada ...49 10N 116 40W
164 Creston, Iowa, U.S.A. 41 0N 94 20W
166 Creston, Wyo., U.S.A. 41 46N 107 50W
166 Creston, Wash., U.S.A. ...47 47N 118 36W
167 Crestone, U.S.A. ...35 2N 106 0W
163 Crestview, U.S.A. ...30 45N 86 35W
143 Creswick, Australia ...37 19S 143 50E
77 Crete, I., *see* Kriti, Greece ...35 15N 25 0E
164 Crete, U.S.A. ...40 38N 96 58W
77 Crete, Sea of, Greece .26 0N 25 0E
64 Créus, C., Spain ...42 20N 3 19E
50 Creuse, dépt., France .46 0N 2 0E
50 Creuse R., France ...46 55N 0 40E
56 Creuzburg, Germany .51 3N 10 15E
71 Crevalcore, Italy ...44 41N 11 10E
49 Crèvecoeur, France ...49 37N 2 5E
65 Crevillente, Spain ...38 12N 0 48W
38 Crewe, England, U.K. 53 6N 2 28W
36 Crewkerne, Eng., U.K. ...50 53N 2 48W
40 Crianlarich, Scot., U.K. ...56 24N 4 37W
143 Crib Point, Victoria, Australia ...38 15S 145 11E
37 Criccieth, Wales, U.K. 52 55N 4 15W
34 Crick, England, U.K. .52 22N 1 9W
37 Crickhowell, Wales, U.K. ...51 52N 3 8W
34 Cricklade, Eng., U.K. 51 38N 1 50W
41 Crieff, Scotland, U.K. 56 22N 3 50W
41 Criffell Mt., Scot., U.K. ...54 56N 3 38W
71 Crikvenica, Yugoslavia ...45 11N 14 40E
156 Crillon, Mt., Canada ...58 39N 137 14W
88 Crimea, Pen., U.S.S.R. ...45 0N 34 0E
56 Crimmitschau, Germany ...50 48N 12 23E
43 Crimond, Scot., U.K. .57 35N 1 53W
40 Crinan Canal, Scotland, U.K. ...56 4N 5 30W
44 Crinkill, Ireland ...53 5N 7 55E
78 Cristeşti, Rumania ...47 15N 26 33E
168 Cristobal, Pan. Can. Zone ... 9 10N 80 0W
74 Crişul Alb, R., Rum ...46 25N 21 40E
78 Crişul Negru, R., Rum ...46 38N 22 26E
78 Crişul Repede, R., Rum. ...47 20N 22 25E
56 Crivitz, Germany ...53 35N 11 39E
74 Crna Gora, Prov., Y.-slav. ...42 14N 21 28E
74 Crna Trava, Yugoslavia ...42 49N 22 19E
74 Crni Drim, R., Y.-slav. ...41 17N 20 40E
74 Crni Timok, R., Y.-slav. ...43 53N 22 0E
74 Crnoljeva Planina Ra., Yugoslavia ...42 20N 21 0E
71 Crnomelj, Yugoslavia .45 33N 15 10E
45 Croagh Patrick, mt., Ire. ...53 46N 9 40W
71 Croatia, prov., *see* Hrvatska, Y.-slav. 45 20N 16 0E
136 Crocker I., N. Terr., Australia ...11 12S 132 32E
103 Crocker Ra., Sabah, Malaysia ... 5 0N 116 30E
41 Crocketford, Scot., U.K. ...55 3N 3 40W
45 Crockets Town, Ireland ...54 8N 9 7W
165 Crockett, U.S.A. ...31 20N 95 30W
133 Crocodile R., S. Africa 24 30S 27 10E
50 Crocq, France ...45 52N 2 21E
46 Croghan, Ireland ...535 5N 8 13W
41 Croglin, England, U.K. ...54 50N 2 37W

MAP
46 Crohy Hd., Ireland 54 55N 8 28W
48 Croisic, Pte. du, Fr. .47 19N 2 31W
160 Croker C., Canada 44 57N 80 59W
46 Crolly, Ireland 55 2N 8 16W
42 Cromalt Hills, Scotland, United Kingdom 58 0N 5 2W
157 Cromarty, Canada 58 5N 94 10W
43 Cromarty, Scot., U.K. 57 40N 4 2W
43 Cromarty Firth, Scotland, U.K. 57 40N 4 15W
43 Cromdale, Hills of, Scotland, U.K. 57 20N 3 28W
35 Cromer, England, U.K. 52 56N 1 18E
42 Cromore, Scot., U.K. .58 6N 6 23W
147 Cromwell, N.Z. 45 3S 169 14E
49 Cronat, France 46 43N 3 40E
35 Crondall, Eng., U.K. .51 13N 0 51W
143 Cronulla, Australia 34 3S 151 8E
39 Crook, England, U.K. 54 43N 1 45W
169 Crooked I., Bahamas .22 50N 74 10W
166 Crooked R., U.S.A. 44 30N 121 0W
38 Crooklands, Eng., U.K. 54 16N 2 43W
164 Crookston, U.S.A. 47 50N 96 40W
164 Crookston, Neb., U.S.A. 42 56N 100 45W
44 Crookstown, Ireland ...51 50N 8 50W
162 Crooksville, U.S.A. 39 45N 82 8W
143 Crookwell, Australia ...34 28S 149 24E
44 Croom, Ireland 52 32N 8 43W
41 Crosby, Cumb., England, United Kingdom 54 45N 3 25W
38 Crosby, Lancs., England, United Kingdom 53 30N 3 2W
164 Crosby, Minn., U.S.A. 46 28N 93 57W
160 Crosby, Pa., U.S.A. ...41 45N 78 23W
38 Crosby Ravensworth, England, U.K. 54 34N 2 35W
165 Crosbyton, U.S.A. 33 37N 101 12W
129 Cross C., S.W. Africa .21 55S 13 57E
163 Cross City, U.S.A. 29 35N 83 5W
38 Cross Fell, Mt., Eng., U.K. 54 44N 2 29W
165 Cross Plains, U.S.A. ...32 8N 99 7W
125 Cross R., Nigeria 4 46N 8 20E
152 Cross Sound, Alaska, U.S.A. 58 20N 136 30W
46 Crossakiel, Ireland 53 43N 7 2W
42 Crossbost, Scot., U.K. 58 8N 6 27W
42 Crossdoney, Ireland 53 57N 7 27W
165 Crossett, U.S.A. 33 10N 91 57W
45 Crossfarnoge Pt., Ire. .52 10N 6 37W
156 Crossfield, Canada 51 25N 114 0W
46 Crossgar, Ireland 54 22N 5 46W
44 Crosshaven, Ireland 51 48N 8 19W
40 Crosshill, Scot., U.K. .55 19N 4 39W
147 Crossley, Mt., N.Z. 42 50S 172 5E
46 Crossmaglen, Northern Ireland, U.K. 54 5N 6 37W
45 Crossmolina, Ireland .54 6N 9 21W
161 Croton-on-Hudson, U.S.A. 41 19N 73 55W
73 Crotone, Italy 39 5N 17 6E
35 Crouch, R., Eng., U.K. 51 37N 0 40E
166 Crow Agency, U.S.A. .45 40N 107 30W
44 Crow Hd., Ireland 51 34N 10 9W
36 Crow Sound, Eng., U.K. 49 56N 6 16W
35 Crowborough, Eng., U.K. 51 3N 0 9E
143 Crowdy Hd., Australia 31 48S 152 44E
165 Crowell, U.S.A. 33 59N 99 45W
143 Crowes, Australia 38 43S 143 24E
35 Crowland, Eng., U.K. 52 41N 0 10W
39 Crowle, England, U.K. 53 36N 0 49W
165 Crowley, U.S.A. 30 15N 92 20W
42 Crowlin Is., Scot., U.K. 57 20N 5 50W
162 Crown Point, U.S.A. .41 24N 87 23W
145 Crow's Nest, Australia 27 14S 152 2E
156 Crowsnest P., Canada 49 40N 114 40W
36 Croyde, England, U.K. 51 7N 4 13W
144 Croydon, Australia 18 15S 142 14E
35 Croydon, Eng., U.K. .51 18N 0 5W
11 Crozet Is., Indian Ocean 46 27S 52 0E
48 Crozon, France 48 15N 4 30W
34 Crudgington, Eng., U.K. 52 46N 2 33W
46 Crumlin, N. Ire. U.K. 54 38N 6 12W
144 Crummer Peaks, Territory of Papua . 6 40S 144 0E
38 Crummock Water L., England, U.K. 54 33N 3 18W
44 Crusheen, Ireland 52 57N 8 52W
169 Cruz, C., Cuba 19 50N 77 50W
173 Cruz Alta, Brazil 28 40S 53 32W
172 Cruz del Eje, Argentina 30 45S 64 50W
173 Cruzeiro, Brazil 22 50S 45 0W
174 Cruzeiro do Sul, Brazil 7 35S 72 35W
74 Crvenka, Yugoslavia .45 45N 19 17E
37 Crymmych Arms, Wales, United Kingdom 51 59N 4 40W
164 Crystal City, Mo., USA 38 15N 90 23W
165 Crystal City, Tex., U.S.A. 28 40N 99 50W
162 Crystal Falls, U.S.A. .46 9N 88 11W
163 Crystal River, U.S.A. .28 54N 82 35W
165 Crystal Springs, U.S.A. 31 59N 90 25W
59 Csongrád, Hungary ...46 43N 20 12E
59 Csorna, Hungary 47 38N 17 18E
59 Csurgo, Hungary 46 16N 17 9E
100 Ctesiphon, Iraq 33 9N 44 35E
107 Cu Lao Hon, I., S. Vietnam 10 22N 109 12E
132 Cuácua, R., Mozam. ...18 0S 36 0E
129 Cuamba, *see* Nova Freixo, Mozam. 14 45S 36 22E
129 Cuando R., Angola 14 0S 19 30E
129 Cuangar, Angola 17 28S 14 40E
130 Cuango, R., Angola ... 9 45S 18 40E
130 Cuanza R., Angola 9 2S 13 30E
63 Cuba, Portugal 38 10N 7 54W
167 Cuba, N. Mex., U.S.A. 36 0N 107 0W
160 Cuba, N.Y., U.S.A. ...42 12N 78 18W
169 Cuba rep., W. Indies .22 0N 79 0W
142 Cuballing, W. Australia 32 50S 117 15E
129 Cubango, R., Africa ...16 15S 17 45E
132 Cubo, Mozambique 23 30S 33 51E
129 Cuchi, Angola 14 37S 17 10E
35 Cuckfield, Eng., U.K. 51 0N 0 8W
174 Cucuí, Brazil 1 10N 66 50W
174 Cúcuta, Colombia 7 54N 72 31W
162 Cudahy, U.S.A. 42 54N 87 50W
72 Cudalbi, Rumania 45 46N 27 41E
106 Cuddalore, India 11 46N 79 45E
106 Cuddapah, India 14 30N 78 47E
143 Cudgewa, Australia ...36 10S 147 42E
62 Cudillero, Spain 43 33N 6 9W
39 Cudworth, Eng., U.K. 53 35N 1 25W
142 Cue, W. Australia 27 20S 117 55E
62 Cuéllar, Spain 41 23N 4 21E
130 Cuemba, Angola 12 7S 18 10E
174 Cuenca, Ecuador 2 50S 79 9W
64 Cuenca, Spain 40 5N 2 10W
64 Cuenca, prov., Spain .40 0N 2 0W
168 Cuernavaca, Mexico ...18 50N 99 20W
165 Cuero, U.S.A. 29 5N 97 17W
51 Cuers, France 43 14N 6 5E
165 Cuervo, U.S.A. 35 5N 104 25W
65 Cuevas del Almanzora, Spain ...37 18N 1 58W
174 Cuevo, Bolivia 20 25N 63 30W
78 Cugir, Rumania 43 48N 23 25E
127 Cugno, Ethiopia 6 14N 42 31E
174 Cuhimbre, Colombia ... 0 10S 75 23W
175 Cuiaba, Brazil 15 30S 56 0W
175 Cuiaba R., Brazil 16 50S 56 30W
46 Cuilcagh, Mt., Ireland 54 12N 7 50W
42 Cuillin Hills, Scot., U.K. 57 14N 6 15W
42 Cuillin Sd., Scot., U.K. 57 4N 6 20W
130 Cuilo, R., Angola 8 45S 19 20E
129 Cuima, Angola 13 0S 15 45E
51 Cuiseaux, France 46 30N 5 22E
129 Cuito R., Angola 16 50S 19 30E
78 Cujmiru, Rumania 44 13N 22 57E
50 Culan, France 46 34N 2 20E
164 Culbertson, U.S.A. 48 9N 104 30W
143 Culcairn, Australia 35 41S 147 3E
46 Culdaff, Ireland 55 17N 7 10W
168 Culebra, Pan. Can. Zone 9 3N 79 40W
55 Culemborg, Netherlands 51 58N 5 14E
143 Culgoa, Australia 35 44S 143 6E
168 Culiacán, Mexico 24 50N 107 40W
109 Culion, I., Philippines 11 43N 120 10E
65 Cúllar de Baza, Spain 37 35N 2 34W
143 Cullarin Ra., Australia 34 50S 149 20E
46 Cullaville, N. Ire., U.K. 54 4N 6 40W
43 Cullen, Scotland, U.K. 57 45N 2 50W
144 Cullen Pt., Australia .11 50S 141 47E
65 Cullera, Spain 39 9N 0 17W
45 Cullin L., Ireland 53 58N 9 12W
133 Cullinan, Trans., S. Afr. 25 40S 28 31E
42 Cullivoe, Scot., U.K. .60 43N 1 0W
163 Cullman, U.S.A. 34 13N 86 50W
43 Culloden Moor, Scotland, U.K. 57 29N 4 7W
36 Cullompton, Eng., U.K. 50 52N 3 23W
46 Cullyhanna, N. Ireland, United Kingdom 54 8N 6 35W
36 Culm, R., Eng., U.K. .50 55N 3 14W
130 Culo, R., Angola 7 40S 15 45E
51 Culoz, France 45 47N 5 46E
162 Culpeper, U.S.A. 38 29N 77 59W
43 Culrain, Scotland, U.K. 57 55N 4 25W
41 Culross, Scotland, U.K. 56 4N 3 38W
43 Cults, Scotland, U.K. .57 8N 2 10W
175 Culuene, R., Brazil ...12 15S 53 10W
42 Culvain Mt., Scot., U.K. 56 55N 5 19W
147 Culverden, N.Z. 42 47S 172 49E
130 Cuma, Angola 12 51S 15 6E
77 Cumali, Turkey 36 42N 27 28E
174 Cumaná, Venezuela ...10 30N 64 5W
156 Cumberland, B.C, Can. 49 40N 125 0W
161 Cumberland, Que., Can. 45 30N 75 24W
162 Cumberland, Md., U.S.A. 39 40N 78 43W
164 Cumberland, Wis., U.S.A. 45 32N 92 3W
38 Cumberland, co., England, U.K. 54 44N 2 55W
144 Cumberland Is., Queens., Australia .20 45S 149 25E
163 Cumberland I., U.S.A. 30 52N 81 30W
153 Cumberland Pen., Can. 67 0N 65 0W
163 Cumberland Plat., U.S.A. 36 0N 84 30W
163 Cumberland R., U.S.A. 36 15N 87 0W
153 Cumberland Sd., Can. 65 30N 66 0W
41 Cumbernauld, Scotland, United Kingdom 55 57N 3 59W
145 Cumborah, Australia .29 40S 147 45E
40 Cumbrae Is., Scot., U.K. 55 46N 4 54W
63 Cumbres Mayores, Sp. 38 4N 6 39W
106 Cumbum, India 15 40N 79 10E
43 Cuminestown, Scotland, United Kingdom 57 32N 2 17W
56 Cummerower See, Ger. 53 47N 12 52E
41 Cummertrees, Scotland, United Kingdom 55 0N 3 20W
143 Cumnock, Australia ...32 59S 148 46E
40 Cumnock, Scot., U.K. 55 27N 4 18W
34 Cumnor, England, U.K. 51 44N 1 20W
175 Cumuruxatiba, Brazil 17 6S 39 13W
41 Cumwhinton, Eng., U.K. 54 51N 2 49W
175 Cunani, Brazil 3 0N 51 5W
142 Cunderdin, W. Australia 31 37S 117 12E
129 Cunene R., Angola 17 0S 15 0E
70 Cúneo, Italy 44 23N 7 31E
130 Cunhinga, R., Angola 11 10S 16 55E
65 Cunillera, I., Ibiza, Sp. 38 59N 1 13E
50 Cunlhat, France 45 38N 3 32E
145 Cunnamulla, Australia 28 2S 145 38E
70 Cuorgne, Italy 45 23N 7 39E
157 Cupar, Canada 51 0N 104 10W
41 Cupar, Scotland, U.K. 56 20N 3 0W
174 Cupica, Colombia 6 50N 77 30W
174 Cupica, B. of, Colombia 6 25N 77 30W
74 Cuprija, Yugoslavia ...34 57N 21 26E
169 Curaçao, I., Neth. W.I. 12 10N 69 0W
172 Curanilahue, Chile 37 29S 73 28W
174 Curaray, R., S. Amer. 1 30S 75 30W
172 Curepto, Chile 35 8S 72 1W
174 Curiapo, Venezuela 8 33N 61 5W
172 Curicó, Chile 34 55S 71 20W
172 Curico, prov., Chile ...34 50S 71 15W
173 Curitiba, Brazil 25 20S 49 10W
46 Curlew Mts., Ireland .54 0N 8 20W
143 Curlwaa, Australia 34 2S 141 59E
143 Currabubula, Australia 31 16S 150 44E
145 Curracunya, Australia 28 29S 144 9E
44 Curraglass, Ireland 52 5N 8 4W
175 Currais Novos, Brazil . 6 13S 36 30W
175 Curralinho, Brazil 1 35S 49 30W
44 Currane L., Ireland ...51 50N 10 8W
166 Currant, U.S.A. 38 51N 115 32W
145 Currawilla, Australia .25 10S 141 20E
165 Current R., U.S.A. 37 15N 91 10W
41 Currie, Scotland, U.K. 55 53N 3 17W
166 Currie, U.S.A. 40 16N 114 45W
163 Currituck Sd., U.S.A. .36 20N 75 50W
143 Currockbilly Mt., N.S.W., Australia ...35 25S 150 0E
36 Curry Rivel, Eng., U.K. 51 2N 2 52W
44 Curryglass, Ireland ...51 40N 9 50W
78 Curtea-de-Argeş Rum. 45 12N 24 42E
62 Curtis, Spain 43 7N 8 4W
164 Curtis, U.S.A. 40 41N 100 32W
144 Curtis, I., Australia ...23 40S 151 15E
175 Curuápanema, R., Brazil 7 0S 54 30W
175 Curuca, Brazil 0 35S 47 50W
173 Curuquaty, Paraguay 24 19S 55 49W
168 Curundu, Pan. Can. Zone 8 59N 79 38W
175 Cururupu, Brazil 1 50S 44 50W
172 Curuzu Cuatia, Arg. ...29 50S 58 5W
175 Curvelo, Brazil 18 45S 44 27W
143 Curyo, Vic., Australia 35 53S 142 54E
46 Cushendall, N. Ire., U.K. 55 5N 6 3W
46 Cushendun, N. Ire., U.K. 55 8N 6 3W
45 Cushina, Ireland 53 11N 7 10W
168 Cushuiriáchic, Mexico 28 10N 106 50W
123 Cussabat, Libya 32 39N 14 1E
50 Cusset, France 46 8N 3 28E
130 Cusso, Serra do, Angola 6 30S 15 0E
164 Custer, U.S.A. 43 45N 103 38W
166 Cut Bank, U.S.A. 48 40N 112 15W
130 Cutata, R., Angola 11 35S 16 20E
163 Cuthbert, U.S.A. 31 47N 84 47W
44 Cutra L., Ireland 53 2N 8 48W
73 Cutro, Italy 39 1N 16 58E
145 Cuttaburra R., Austral. 29 10S 145 0E
105 Cuttack, India 20 25N 85 57E
130 Cuva (Queve), R., Ang. 11 10S 14 30E
146 Cuvier I., N.Z. 36 27S 175 50E
56 Cuxhaven, Germany .53 51N 8 41E
160 Cuyahoga Falls, U.S.A. 41 8N 81 30W
160 Cuyahoga R., U.S.A. .41 20N 81 35W
109 Cuyo, Philippines 10 50N 121 5E
175 Cuyuni R., Guyana ... 7 0N 59 30W
174 Cuzco, Peru 13 32S 72 0W
174 Cuzco Mt., Bolivia 20 0S 66 50W
34 Cwmbran, Eng., U.K. 51 39N 3 0W
37 Cwrt, Wales, U.K. 52 35N 3 55W
77 Cyclades Is., *see* Kikladhes, Greece ...37 20N 24 30E
145 Cygnet, Tas., Australia 43 8S 147 1E
36 Cymmer, Wales, U.K. 51 37N 3 38W
162 Cynthiana, U.S.A. 38 23N 84 10W
37 Cynwyl Elfed, Wales, United Kingdom ...51 55N 4 22W
157 Cypress Hills, Canada 49 40N 109 30W
100 Cyprus I., E. Medit. Sea 35 0N 33 0E
121 Cyrenaica, prov., Libya 27 0N 20 0E
121 Cyrene, Lybya 32 39N 21 18E
60 Czaplinek, Poland 53 42N 16 58E
60 Czarne, Poland 53 42N 16 58E
60 Czarnków, Poland 52 55N 16 38E
59 Czechoslovakia, rep., Europe 49 0N 17 0E
60 Czeladz, Poland 50 16N 19 2E
60 Czersk, Poland 53 46N 17 58E
60 Czerwiensk, Poland ...52 1N 15 13E
60 Czestochowa, Poland .50 49N 19 7E
60 Czlopa, Poland 53 6N 16 6E
60 Człuchów, Poland 53 41N 17 22E

D

107 Da, R., N. Vietnam ...16 0N 107 0E
107 Da Lat, S. Vietnam ...12 3N 108 32E
107 Da-Nang, S. Vietnam 16 10N 108 7E
126 Dab'a, Ras el, Egypt .31 3N 28 31E
125 Dabai, Nigeria 11 25N 5 15E
124 Dabakala, Ivory Coast 8 15N 4 20W
124 Dabatou, Guinea 11 50N 9 20W
98 Dabburiya, Israel 32 42N 35 22E
104 Dabhoi, India 22 10N 73 20E
60 Dabie, Poland 53 27N 14 45E
124 Dabola, Guinea 10 50N 11 5W
124 Dabou, Ivory Coast ... 5 20N 4 23W
125 Dabou, Upper Volta .11 9N 1 51W
125 Daboya, Ghana 9 30N 1 20W
127 Dabra Berhan, Ethiopia 9 42N 39 15E
127 Dabra Sina, Ethiopia . 9 51N 39 45E
127 Dabra Tabor, Ethiopia 11 50N 37 58E
127 Dabra Zabit, Ethiopia 11 48N 38 30E
60 Dabrowa Gornicza, Pol. 50 15N 19 10E
59 Dabrowa Tarnowska, Poland 50 10N 21 0E
60 Dabrówno, Poland 53 27N 20 2E
127 Dabus, R., Ethiopia ...10 12N 35 0E
105 Dacca, E. Pakistan ...23 43N 90 26E
57 Dachau, Germany 48 16N 11 27E
88 Daday, Turkey 41 28N 33 35E
174 Dadanawa, Guyana ... 3 0N 59 30W
127 Daddeto, Fr. Terr. of the Afars & Issas ...12 24N 42 45E
163 Dade City, U.S.A. 28 20N 82 12W
122 Dades, R., Morocco ...31 0N 6 25W
125 Dadiya, Nigeria 9 35N 11 24E
104 Dadri, *see* Charkhi Dadri, India 28 37N 76 17E
104 Dadu, W. Pakistan ...26 45N 67 45E
78 Dǎeni, Rumania 44 51N 28 10E
41 Daer R., Scot., U.K. .55 23N 3 39W
109 Daet, Philippines 14 2N 122 55E
127 Dagaio, Ethiopia 6 8N 40 40E
124 Dagana, Senegal 16 30N 15 20W
126 Dagash, Sudan 19 19N 33 25E
89 Dagestan, A.S.S.R., U.S.S.R. 42 30N 47 0E
99 Daggah Bur, Ethiopia 8 11N 43 31E
147 Daggs Sd., N.Z. 45 23S 166 45E
126 Daghfeli, Sudan 19 18N 32 40E
127 Daghirie, Ethiopia 11 40N 41 50E
131 Dagoreti, Kenya 1 18S 36 4E
109 Dagupan, Philippines .16 3N 120 33E
160 Dagus Mines, U.S.A. .41 20N 78 36W
109 Dah, W. Irian, Indon. 7 25S 139 5E
126 Dahab, Egypt 28 30N 34 31E
127 Dahlak Arch, Ethiopia 15 40N 40 5E
127 Dahlak Kebir, I., Eth. 15 50N 40 10E
56 Dahlenburg, Germany 53 11N 10 43E
163 Dahlonega, U.S.A. 34 35N 83 59W
56 Dahme, Germany 51 51N 13 25E
125 Daho, Nigeria 10 28N 11 18E
125 Dahomey, rep., W. Afr. 8 0N 2 0E
122 Dahra, Massif de, Alg. 36 7N 1 21E
40 Dailly, Scotland, U.K. 55 16N 4 44W
65 Daimiel, Spain 39 5N 3 35W
45 Daingean, Ireland 53 18N 7 15W
144 Daintree, Australia 16 20S 145 20E
114 Daio-saki, C., Japan .34 15N 136 45E
112 Dairen, *see* Lü-ta, China 39 0N 121 31E
126 Dairût, Egypt 27 34N 30 43E
142 Dairy Creek, W. Austral. 25 12S 115 48E
105 Daitari, India 21 10N 85 46E
144 Dajarra, Australia 21 42S 139 30E
125 Dakala, Niger 14 27N 2 27E
124 Dakar, Senegal 14 34N 17 29W
126 Dakhla Oasis, Egypt .25 30N 28 50E
125 Dakingari, Nigeria 11 37N 4 1E
104 Dakor, India 22 45N 73 11E
164 Dakota City, U.S.A. ...42 27N 96 28W
74 Dakovica, Y.-slav. ...42 22N 20 26E
74 Dakovo, Yugoslavia ...45 19N 18 24E
124 Dakra, Senegal 15 22N 15 30W
107 Dalat, Vietnam 12 3N 108 32E
80 Dalälven, L., Sweden .61 27N 17 15E
112 Dalandzadgad, Mong. 43 37N 104 17E
102 Dalbandin, W. Pak. ...29 0N 64 23E
41 Dalbeattie, Scot., U.K. 54 55N 3 50W
81 Dalbosjön, L., Sweden 58 40N 12 45E
145 Dalby, Australia 27 10S 151 17E
81 Dalby, Sweden 55 42N 13 22E
80 Dalby, Sweden 60 37N 13 5E
79 Dale, Norway 61 22N 5 24E
79 Dale, Norway 61 27N 7 28E
37 Dale, Wales, U.K. 51 42N 5 11W
79 Dalen, Norway 59 27N 8 0E
126 Dalga, Egypt 27 39N 30 41E
142 Dalgaranger, mt., W. Australia 27 50E 117 5E
165 Dalhart, Texas, U.S.A. 36 0N 102 30W
155 Dalhousie, Canada 48 0N 66 26W
104 Dalhousie, India 32 38N 76 0E
65 Dalias, Spain 36 47N 2 53W
42 Daliburgh, Scot., U.K. 57 10N 7 23W
98 Daliyat el Karmel, Isr. 32 41N 35 3E
74 Dalj, Yugoslavia 45 28N 18 58E
41 Dalkeith, Scot., U.K. .55 54N 3 5W
45 Dalkey, Ireland 53 16N 6 7W
156 Dall I., Alaska, U.S.A. 54 59N 133 25W
145 Dallarnil, Australia ...25 19S 152 2E
43 Dallas, Scotland, U.K. 57 33N 3 32W
166 Dallas, Oregon, U.S.A. 45 0N 123 15W
165 Dallas, Texas, U.S.A. .32 50N 96 50W
127 Dallol, Ethiopia 14 14N 40 17E
40 Dalmally, Scot., U.K. 56 25N 5 0W
133 Dalmanutha, S. Africa 25 47S 30 9E
74 Dalmatia, dist., Y.-slav. 43 20N 17 0E
40 Dalmellington, Scotland, United Kingdom 55 20N 4 25W
124 Daloa, Ivory Coast 7 0N 6 30W
140 Dalry, Scotland, U.K. 55 44N 4 42W
40 Dalrymple, Scot., U.K. 55 24N 4 36W
81 Dalsjöfors, Sweden 57 46N 13 5E
81 Dalskog, Sweden 58 44N 12 18E
154 Dalton, Canada 60 10N 137 0W
41 Dalton, Scot., U.K. ...55 3N 3 22W
39 Dalton, Yorks., England, U.K. 54 28N 1 32W
135 Dalton, Natal, S. Africa 29 20S 30 40E
109 Dalton, Ga., U.S.A. ...34 45N 85 0W
161 Dalton, Mass., U.S.A. 42 28N 73 11W
164 Dalton, Neb., U.S.A. .41 27N 103 0W
105 Daltonganj, India 24 0N 84 4E
38 Dalton-in-Furness, England, U.K. 54 10N 3 11W
156 Dalton Post, Canada .66 42N 137 0W
113 Dalupuri, I., Philippines 19 2N 121 8E
82 Dalvik, Iceland 66 2N 18 20W
142 Dalwallinu, W. Australia 30 12S 116 33E
138 Daly R., Australia 14 0S 131 12E
138 Daly Waters, Australia 16 15S 133 24E
45 Dalystown, Ireland ...53 26N 7 23W
175 Dam, Surinam 4 45N 55 0W
126 Dama, Wadi, Sl. Arab. 27 12N 35 50E
104 Daman, India 20 25N 72 57E
109 Damar, I., Indonesia . 7 15S 128 30E
130 Damara, Central Africa 4 59N 18 45E
126 Damanhûr, Egypt 31 0N 30 30E
129 Damaraland, Dist., South-West Africa .21 0S 17 0E
100 Damascus, *see* Esh Sham, Syria 33 30N 36 18E
125 Damaturu, Nigeria 11 45N 11 55E
101 Damavand, Iran 35 45N 52 10E
130 Damba, Angola 6 44S 15 29E
127 Damba, Ethiopia 15 10N 38 47E
78 Dâmboviţa R., Rum. .44 40N 26 0E
78 Dâmbovnic, R., Rum. 44 28N 25 18E
34 Damerham, Eng., U.K. 50 57N 1 52W
101 Damghan, Iran 36 10N 54 17E
78 Damienesti, Rumania 46 44N 27 1E
126 Damietta, Egypt 31 24N 31 48E
98 Damiya, Jordan 32 6N 35 34E
101 Damin, Iran 27 30N 60 40E
98 Damiya, Jordan 32 8N 35 34E
55 Damm, Germany 51 43N 6 48E
100 Damman, Saudi Arabia 26 25N 50 2E
49 Dammarie, France 48 20N 1 30E
49 Dammartin, France ...49 3N 2 41E
56 Damme, Germany 52 32N 8 12E
105 Damodar, R., India ...23 17N 87 35E
105 Damoh, India 23 50N 79 28E
138 Dampier Arch, Western Australia .20 38S 116 32E
138 Dampier Downs, W. Australia 18 30S 123 15E
109 Dampier Str., Indon. . 0 40S 131 0E
144 Dampier Str., Territory of New Guinea 5 50S 148 0E
134 Damslaagte, S. Africa 32 50S 20 41E
48 Damville, France 48 51N 1 5E
49 Damvillers, France ...49 20N 5 21E
125 Dan Chadi, Nigeria ...12 47N 5 17E
125 Dan Dume, Nigeria ...11 28N 7 8E

MAP
125 Dan Gora, Nigeria 11 30N 8 7E
125 Dan Gulbi, Nigeria 11 40N 6 15E
125 Dan Sadau, Nigeria ...11 25N 6 20E
154 Dana, Lac, Canada 50 50N 76 50W
127 Danaba, Ethiopia 9 47N 39 10E
127 Darakil Depression,
Ethiopia 12 45N 41 0E
109 Danao, Philippines 10 40N 124 10E
127 Danbi, Ethiopia 8 5N 36 25E
161 Danbury, Conn.,
U.S.A. 41 23N 73 29W
167 Danby L., U.S.A. 34 17N 715 0W
142 Dandaragan,
Australia 30 40S 115 40E
130 Dande, R., Angola 8 28S 14 10E
105 Dandeldhura, Nepal ...29 20N 80 35E
143 Dandenong, Australia 37 52S 145 12E
155 Danforth, U.S.A. 45 39N 67 57W
127 Dangaz, Ethiopia 12 27N 37 43E
127 Dangela, Ethiopia 11 18N 36 56E
137 Danger Is., Pac. Oc. ...10 53S 165 49W
134 Danger Pt., S. Africa .34 40S 19 17E
107 Dangrek Range,
Thailand 14 40N 104 0E
166 Daniel, U.S.A. 42 56N 110 2W
155 Daniel's Harbour,
Can. 50 13N 57 35W
133 Danielskull, S. Africa .28 11S 23 33E
161 Danielson, U.S.A. 41 50N 71 52W
135 Danielsrus, S. Africa .28 1S 28 27E
87 Danilov, U.S.S.R. 58 16N 40 13E
74 Danilovgrad, Y.-slav. 42 38N 19 9E
87 Danilovka, U.S.S.R. ...50 25N 44 12E
125 Danja, Nigeria 11 29N 7 30E
125 Dankalwa, Nigeria 11 52N 12 12E
125 Dankama, Nigeria 13 20N 7 44E
135 Dankerpoort, S.
Africa 33 33S 25 32E
87 Dankov, U.S.S.R. 53 20N 39 5E
169 Danli, Honduras 14 4N 86 35W
161 Dannemora, U.S.A. ...44 41N 73 44W
56 Dannenberg, Germany 53 7N 11 4E
146 Dannevirke, N.Z. 40 12S 176 8E
135 Dannhauser, S. Africa 28 0S 30 3E
109 Dansalan, Philippines 8 2N 124 30E
160 Dansville, U.S.A. 42 32N 77 41W
105 Dantan, India 21 57N 87 20E
59 Danube, R., Europe ...45 0N 28 20W
161 Danvers, U.S.A. 42 34N 70 55E
162 Danville, Ill., U.S.A. .40 10N 87 40E
162 Danville, Ky., U.S.A. 37 40N 84 45E
163 Danville, Va., U.S.A. .36 40N 79 20E
60 Danzig, *see* Gdansk,
Pol. 54 22N 18 40E
109 Dao, Philippines 10 30N 122 6E
62 Dao, R., Portugal 40 28N 8 0W
104 Daosa, India 26 52N 76 20E
123 Daoud, *see* Ain Beida,
Algeria 35 50N 7 29E
48 Daoulas, France 48 22N 4 17W
125 Dapong, Togoland 10 55N 0 16E
143 Dapto, N.S.W.,
Australia 34 30S 150 47E
100 Dar al Hamra, Si.
Arab. 27 22N 37 43E
101 Darab, Iran 28 50N 54 30E
78 Darabani, Rumania ...48 10N 26 39E
123 Daraj, Libya 30 10N 10 28E
74 Daravica Ra.,
Y.-slav. 42 32N 20 8W
126 Daraw, Egypt 24 22N 32 51W
125 Darazo, Nigeria 11 1N 10 24W
102 Darband, W. Pakistan 34 30N 72 50E
105 Darbhanga, India 26 15N 86 3E
166 Darby, U.S.A. 46 2N 114 7W
156 D'Arcy, Canada 50 35N 122 30W
74 Darda, Yugoslavia 45 40N 18 41E
100 Dardanelles, Str., Tur. 40 0N 26 20E
165 Dardenelle, U.S.A. 35 12N 93 9W
35 Darent, R., Eng.,
U.K. 51 22N 0 12E
131 Dar-es-Salaam, Tanz. 6 50S 39 12E
143 Dareton, Australia 34 4S 142 3E
147 Darfield, N.Z. 43 29S 172 7E
70 Darfo, Italy 45 43N 10 11E
121 Darfur, prov., Sudan .12 35N 25 0E
102 Dargai, West
Pakistan 34 25N 71 45E
90 Dargan Ata, U.S.S.R. 40 40N 62 20E
146 Dargaville, N.Z. 35 57S 173 52E
143 Dargo & R., Australia 37 27S 147 15E
112 Darhan, Mongolia 49 27N 105 57E
127 Dari, Sudan 5 48N 30 26E
168 Darien, Pan. Can.
Zone 9 7N 79 46W
169 Darien, G. of,
Colombia 9 0N 77 0W
105 Darjeeling, India 27 3N 88 18E
155 Dark Cove, Canada ...49 54N 54 5W
142 Darkan, W. Australia 33 19S 116 37E
34 Darlaston, Eng., U.K. 52 35N 2 1W
134 Darling, C. Prov., S.
Afr. 33 24S 18 22E
139 Darling Downs,
Queens., Australia .28 30S 152 0E
142 Darling Ra., W.
Austral. 32 30S 116 0E
145 Darling R., Australia .31 0S 144 30E
39 Darlington, Eng.,
U.K. 54 33N 1 33W
163 Darlington S.C.,
U.S.A. 34 18N 79 50W
164 Darlington, Wis.,
U.S.A. 42 43N 90 7W
143 Darlington Point,
N.S.W., Australia ...34 34S 147 0E
60 Darlowo, Poland 54 25N 16 25E
78 Dărmănesti, Rumania 46 21N 26 33E
57 Darmstadt, Germany .49 51N 8 40E
48 Darnétal, France 49 25N 1 10E
MAP
49 Darney, France 48 5N 6 0E
143 Darnick, Australia 32 48S 143 38E
152 Darnley B., Canada ...69 30N 124 30W
15 Darnley, C.,
Antarctica 68 0S 69 0E
64 Daroca, Spain 41 9N 1 25W
144 Darr, Queensland,
Australia 24 34S 144 52E
44 Darragh, Ireland 54 48N 9 7W
147 Darran Mts., N.Z. 44 37S 167 59E
166 Darrington, U.S.A. 48 14N 121 37W
99 Darror R., Somali
Rep. 10 30N 50 0E
105 Darsana, E. Pakistan .23 35N 88 48E
106 Darsi, India 15 46N 79 44E
56 Darsser Ort, Germany 44 27N 12 30E
36 Dart, R., Eng., U.K. .50 34N 3 56W
147 Dart R., N.Z. 44 20S 168 20E
35 Dartford, Eng., U.K. .51 26N 0 15E
36 Dartington, Eng.,
U.K. 50 26N 3 42W
143 Dartmoor, Australia ...37 56N 141 19E
36 Dartmoor, Eng., U.K. 50 36N 4 0W
155 Dartmouth, Canada ...44 40N 63 30W
36 Dartmouth, Eng.,
U.K. 50 21N 3 35W
144 Dartmouth, Australia 23 30S 144 40E
39 Darton, England,
U.K. 53 36N 1 32W
64 Dartuch, C., Menorca,
Spain 39 55N 3 49E
144 Daru, Papua 8 53S 143 22E
124 Daru, Sierra Leone 8 0N 10 52W
40 Darvel, Scotland,
U.K. 55 37N 4 20W
109 Darvel Bay, Sabah,
Malaysia 4 50N 118 20E
38 Darwen, England,
U.K. 53 42N 2 29W
132 Darwendale, Rhodesia 17 41S 30 33E
104 Darwha, India 20 15N 77 45E
138 Darwin, Australia 12 20S 130 50E
132 Darwin, Mt.,
Rhodesia 16 45S 31 33E
101 Daryacheh-ye-Sistan,
L., Iran 31 0N 61 0E
104 Daryapur, India 20 55N 77 20E
127 Dase, Ethiopia 14 53N 37 15E
127 Dashato R., Ethiopia . 7 25N 42 40E
102 Dasht R., W.
Pakistan 25 40N 62 20E
101 Dasht-e-Kavir, Des.,
Iran 34 30N 55 0E
101 Dasht-e-Lut, Des.,
Iran 31 30N 58 0E
101 Dasht-i-Margo, Des.,
Afghanistan 30 40N 62 30E
112 Dashinchilen,
Mongolia 48 0N 105 59E
104 Daska, West Pakistan 32 20N 74 20E
133 Daspoort, Trans., S.
Afr. 25 42S 28 12E
125 Dassa-Zoumé,
Dahomey 7 46N 2 14E
134 Dassen I., S. Africa ...33 27S 18 3E
135 Dassiedeur, S. Africa .32 28S 25 45E
134 Dassiefontein, S.
Africa 31 35S 24 25E
77 Datça, Turkey 36 46N 27 40E
104 Datia, India 25 39N 78 27E
104 Dattapur, India 20 45N 78 15E
55 Datteln, Germany 51 39N 7 23E
55 Dattenberg, Germany 50 33N 7 18E
55 Dattenfeld, Germany .50 48N 7 34E
105 Daudkandi, E. Pak. ...23 40N 90 40E
86 Daugava, (Dvina,
W.), U.S.S.R. 57 0N 24 0E
86 Daugavpils, U.S.S.R. ...55 53N 26 32E
90 Daukara, U.S.S.R. 45 55N 59 30E
101 Daulat Yar, Afghan ...34 30N 65 45E
106 Daulatabad, India 19 57N 75 15E
157 Dauphin, Canada 51 15N 100 5W
163 Dauphin I., U.S.A. 30 16N 88 10W
157 Dauphin L., Canada ...51 20N 99 45W
51 Dauphiné, reg.,
France 45 15N 5 25E
126 Dauqa, Saudi Arabia .19 30N 41 0E
125 Daura, N. Reg., Nig. .13 2N 8 21E
125 Daura, N. Reg., Nig. .11 31N 11 24E
124 Davadi, Senegal 14 10N 16 3W
106 Davangere, India 14 25N 75 50E
109 Davao, Philippines 7 0N 125 40E
109 Davao, G. of, Phil. 6 30N 125 48E
101 Davar Panab, Iran 27 25N 62 15E
24 Dave, England, U.K. .52 55N 1 50W
133 Davel, Trans., S.
Africa 26 24S 29 40E
164 Davenport, Iowa,
U.S.A. 41 30N 90 40W
166 Davenport, Wash.,
U.S.A. 47 40N 118 5W
138 Davenport Ra., N.
Terr., Australia 20 28S 134 0E
34 Daventry, Eng., U.K. 52 16N 1 10W
169 David, Panama 8 30N 82 30W
164 David City, U.S.A. 41 18N 97 10W
86 David Gorodok,
U.S.S.R. 52 4N 27 8E
133 Daviesville, S. Africa .23 23S 30 0E
79 Davik, Norway 61 53N 5 33E
165 Davis, U.S.A. 38 39N 121 45W
167 Davis Dam, U.S.A. 35 20N 114 35W
155 Davis Inlet, Canada ...55 50N 60 45W
165 Davis Mts., U.S.A. 30 42N 104 15W
153 Davis Str., N.
America 66 30N 59 0W
57 Davos, Switzerland ...46 48N 9 49E
142 Davyhurst, W.
Austral. 30 2S 120 40E
127 Dawa R., Ethiopia 5 0N 39 5E
MAP
125 Dawaki, Nigeria 9 25N 9 33E
125 Dawaki, Nigeria 12 5N 8 23E
98 Dawayima, Israel 31 33N 34 55E
144 Dawes Ra., Australia .24 40S 150 40E
34 Dawley England,
U.K. 52 40N 2 29W
36 Dawlish, Eng., U.K. .50 34N 3 28W
103 Dawna Range, Burma 16 30N 98 30E
46 Dawros Hd., Ireland .54 48N 8 32W
52 Dawson, Canada 64 10N 139 30W
163 Dawson, Ga., U.S.A. .31 45N 84 28W
164 Dawson, N.D., U.S.A. 46 56N 99 45W
176 Dawson I., Chile 53 50S 70 50W
156 Dawson Creek,
Canada 55 45N 120 15W
132 Dawson's, Rhodesia ...17 0S 30 57E
150 Dax, France 43 43N 1 3W
143 Daylesford, Australia .37 21S 144 9E
126 Dayr al Balah, Egypt 31 26N 34 21E
100 Dayr az Zawr, Syria .35 20N 40 5E
156 Daysland, Canada 52 50N 112 20W
162 Dayton, Ohio, U.S.A. 39 45N 84 10W
160 Dayton, Pa., U.S.A. ...40 54N 79 18W
163 Dayton, Tenn., U.S.A. 35 30N 85 1W
166 Dayton, Wash.,
U.S.A. 46 20N 118 0W
163 Daytona Beach,
U.S.A. 29 14N 81 0W
166 Dayville, U.S.A. 44 33N 119 37W
134 De Aar, C. Prov., S.
Afr. 30 39S 24 0E
135 De Brug, O.F.S., S.
Afr. 29 8S 25 50E
134 De Doorns, S. Africa .33 26S 19 40E
163 De Funiak Springs,
U.S.A. 30 42N 86 10W
138 De Grey, W. Australia 20 30S 120 0E
164 De Kalb, Ill., U.S.A. .41 55N 88 45W
163 De Land, U.S.A. 29 1N 81 19W
165 De Leon, U.S.A. 32 9N 98 35W
91 De Long Is., U.S.S.R. 76 40N 149 20E
162 De Pere, U.S.A. 44 28N 88 1W
165 De Queen, U.S.A. 34 3N 94 24W
165 De Quincy, U.S.A. 30 30N 93 27W
165 De Ridder, U.S.A. 30 48N 93 15W
134 De Rust, S. Africa 33 29S 22 31E
164 De Smet, U.S.A. 44 25N 97 35W
162 De Tour Village,
U.S.A. 45 49N 83 56W
134 De Vlakte, S. Africa ...33 39S 23 37E
165 De Witt, U.S.A. 34 19N 91 20W
100 Dead Sea,
Jordan-Israel 31 30N 35 30E
39 Deadwater, Eng.,
U.K. 55 17N 2 37W
164 Deadwood, U.S.A. 44 25N 103 43W
142 Deakin, W. Australia .30 46S 129 0E
135 Deal, England, U.K. .51 13N 1 25E
135 Dealesville, S. Africa .28 41S 25 44E
34 Dean, Forest of,
England, U.K. 51 50N 2 35W
172 Dean Funes,
Argentina 30 20S 64 20W
143 Dean Marsh, Australia 38 25S 143 52E
160 Dearborn, U.S.A. 42 18N 83 15W
38 Dearham, Eng., U.K. 54 43N 3 28W
152 Dease Arm, Canada ...66 45N 120 6W
156 Dease L., Canada 58 40N 130 5W
167 Death Valley, U.S.A. .36 0N 116 40W
167 Death Valley Junc.,
U.S.A. 36 15N 116 30W
48 Deauville, France 49 23N 0 2E
125 Deba Habe, Nigeria ...10 14N 11 20E
88 Debaltsevo, U.S.S.R. .48 22N 38 26E
74 Debar, Yugoslavia 41 21N 20 37E
127 Debba, Ethiopia 14 20N 41 18E
157 Debden, Canada 53 30N 106 50W
122 Debdou, Morocco 33 59N 3 0W
132 Debeeti, Botswana 23 45S 26 32E
35 Debenham, Eng.,
U.K. 52 14N 1 10E
59 Debica, Poland 50 2N 21 25E
60 Deblin, Poland 51 34N 21 50E
124 Debo L., Mali 15 14N 3 57W
156 Debolt, Canada 55 12N 118 25W
142 Deborah, L., W.
Austral. 30 45S 119 0E
74 Debrc, Yugoslavia 44 38N 19 53E
127 Debre Markos,
Ethiopia 10 20N 37 40E
59 Debrecen, Hungary ...47 33N 21 42E
127 Decamere, Ethiopia 15 6N 39 0E
74 Decani, Yugoslavia ...42 30N 29 10E
163 Decatur, Ala., U.S.A. .34 35N 87 0W
163 Decatur, Ga., U.S.A. .33 47N 84 17W
164 Decatur, Ill., U.S.A. ...39 50N 89 0W
162 Decatur, Ind., U.S.A. 40 52N 85 28W
165 Decatur, Texas,
U.S.A. 33 15N 97 35W
50 Decazeville, France ...44 34N 2 15E
106 Deccan, Plat., India ...14 0N 77 0E
15 Deception I., Antarc. .63 0S 60 15W
58 Decin, Czechoslovakia 50 47N 14 12E
49 Decize, France 46 50N 3 28E
160 Deckerville, U.S.A. 43 33N 82 46W
73 Decollatura, Italy 39 2N 16 21E
164 Decorah, U.S.A. 43 20N 91 50W
78 Deda, Rumania 46 56N 24 50E
34 Deddington, Eng.,
U.K. 51 58N 1 19W
161 Dedham, U.S.A. 42 14N 71 10W
87 Dedilovo, U.S.S.R. 53 59N 37 50E
124 Dédougou, Upper
Volta 12 30N 3 35W
106 Deduru Oya, R.,
Ceylon 7 32N 81 45E
131 Dedza, Malawi 14 20S 34 20E
46 Dee R., Ireland 53 50N 6 40W
43 Dee, R., Scotland,
U.K. 57 4N 3 7W
MAP
37 Dee R., Wales 53 15N 3 7W
45 Deel R., Ireland 53 35N 7 9W
134 Deelfontein, S. Africa 30 90S 23 50E
44 Deelish, Ireland 51 41N 9 18W
35 Deeping St. Nicholas,
England, U.K. 52 44N 0 11W
134 Deepwalls, S. Africa ...33 51S 23 5E
145 Deepwater, Australia .29 25S 151 51E
157 Deer Lake, Ont., Can. 52 36N 94 20W
155 Deer Lake, Newf.,
Can. 49 11N 57 27W
166 Deer Lodge, U.S.A. ...46 25N 112 40W
166 Deer Park, U.S.A. 47 55N 117 21W
164 Deer River, U.S.A. 47 21N 93 44W
43 Deer Sound, Scot.,
U.K. 58 58N 2 50W
144 Deeral, Australia 17 20S 145 55E
43 Deerness, Scot., U.K. .58 57N 2 44W
104 Deesa, India 24 18N 72 10E
162 Defiance, U.S.A. 41 20N 84 20W
98 Deganiya, Israel 32 43N 35 34E
37 Deganwy, Wales,
U.K. 53 18N 3 49W
63 Degebe, R., Portugal .38 21N 7 37W
125 Degema, Nigeria 4 50N 6 48E
82 Degerfors, Sweden 64 16N 19 46E
81 Degersfor, Sweden 59 20N 14 28E
80 Degersiö, Sweden 63 13N 18 3E
57 Deggendorf, Germany 48 49N 12 59E
106 Degloor, India 18 34N 77 33E
101 Deh Bid, Iran 30 39N 53 11E
101 Deh Kheyr, Iran 28 45N 54 40E
123 Dehibat, Tunisia 32 0N 10 37E
106 Dehiwala, Ceylon 6 50N 79 51E
100 Dehkhvareqan, Iran ...37 50N 45 55E
104 Dehra Dun, India 30 20N 78 4E
105 Dehri, India 24 50N 84 15E
54 Deinze, Belgium 50 59N 3 53E
98 Deir Abu Sa'id,
Jordan 32 30N 38 42E
98 Deir Dibwan, Jordan .31 55N 35 15E
98 Deir el Ghusun,
Jordan 32 21N 35 4E
78 Dej, Rumania 47 10N 23 52E
80 Deje, Sweden 59 35N 13 29E
132 Dekar, Botswana 18 30S 23 10E
130 Dekese, Congo 3 24S 21 24E
167 Del Norte, U.S.A. 37 47N 106 27W
125 del Rey, Rio, Nigeria . 4 30N 8 48E
165 Del Rio, U.S.A. 29 15N 100 50W
36 Delabole, Eng., U.K. .50 37N 4 45W
133 Delagoa B.,
Mozambique 25 50S 32 45E
165 Delagua, U.S.A. 32 35N 104 40W
126 Delai, Sudan 17 21N 36 6E
167 Delano, U.S.A. 35 48N 119 13W
133 Delareyville, S. Africa 26 41S 25 26E
164 Delavan, Wis., U.S.A. 42 40N 89 2W
162 Delaware, U.S.A. 40 20N 83 0W
162 Delaware, st., U.S.A. .39 0N 75 40W
161 Delaware R., U.S.A. .41 50N 75 15W
74 Delčevo, Yugoslavia .41 58N 22 46E
43 Delchirach, Scot.,
U.K. 57 23N 3 20W
143 Delegate, Australia 37 3S 149 0E
57 Delémont,
Switzerland 47 22N 7 20E
54 Delft, Netherlands 52 1N 4 22E
106 Delft I., Ceylon 9 30N 79 40E
54 Delfzijl, Netherlands .53 20N 6 55E
131 Delgado, C., Mozam. .10 45S 40 40E
112 Delgerhet, Mongolia ...45 57N 110 28E
126 Delgo, Sudan 20 6N 30 40E
160 Delhi, Canada 42 54N 80 29W
104 Delhi, India 28 38N 77 17E
161 Delhi, U.S.A. 42 17N 74 56W
74 Deli Jovan Ra.,
Y.-slav. 44 13N 22 9E
168 Delicias, Mexico 28 10N 105 30W
56 Delitzsch, Germany ...51 32N 12 22E
167 Dell City, U.S.A. 31 58N 105 19W
164 Dell Rapids U.S.A. ...43 53N 96 44W
49 Dellé, France 47 30N 7 2E
123 Dellys, Algeria 36 50N 3 57E
161 Delmar, U.S.A. 42 37N 73 47W
133 Delmas, Trans., S.
Afr. 26 8S 28 43E
56 Delmenhorst,
Germany 53 3N 8 37E
175 Delmiro, Brazil 9 24S 38 6W
71 Delnice, Yugoslavia ...45 23N 14 50E
145 Deloraine, Australia ...41 30S 146 40E
157 Deloraine, Canada 49 15N 101 0W
155 Delorme, L., Canada .54 50N 69 30W
162 Delphi, U.S.A. 40 37N 86 40W
162 Delphos, U.S.A. 40 51N 84 17W
133 Delportshoop, S.
Africa 28 22S 24 20E
163 Delray Beach, U.S.A. 26 27N 80 4W
80 Delsbo, Sweden 61 47N 16 37E
167 Delta, Colo., U.S.A. ...38 44N 108 5W
166 Delta, Utah, U.S.A. ...39 21N 112 29W
145 Delungra, Australia ...29 40S 150 45E
45 Delvin, Ireland 53 37N 7 8W
76 Delvinákion, Greece ...39 57N 20 32E
76 Delvinë, Albania 39 59N 20 4E
109 Demak, Indonesia 6 50S 110 40E
130 Demba, Congo 5 28S 22 15E
127 Dembidolo, Ethiopia . 8 34N 34 50E
102 Demchok, Tibet,
China 32 40N 79 29E
54 Demer R., Belgium 51 0N 5 0E
154 Demerais, L., Canada 47 35N 77 0W
174 Demerara R., Guyana 7 0N 58 0W
86 Demidov, U.S.S.R. 55 10N 31 30E
167 Deming, U.S.A. 32 10N 107 50W
134 Demistkraal, S. Africa 33 25S 24 35E
56 Demmin, Germany 53 54N 13 2E
156 Demmit, Canada 55 20N 119 50W
122 Demnate, Morocco 31 50N 6 59W
MAP
70 Demonte, Italy 44 18N 7 18E
163 Demopolis, U.S.A. 32 30N 87 48W
108 Dempo, Mt.,
Indonesia 4 10S 103 15E
86 Demyansk, U.S.S.R. .57 30N 32 27E
54 Den Burg,
Netherlands 53 3N 4 47E
54 Den Helder, Neth. 52 57N 4 45E
54 Den Oever,
Netherlands 52 56N 5 2E
49 Denain, France 50 20N 3 22E
37 Denbigh, Wales, U.K. 53 12N 3 26W
37 Denbigh, co., Wales,
United Kingdom 53 8N 3 30W
39 Denby Dale, Eng.,
U.K. 53 35N 1 40W
103 Denchin, China 31 35N 95 15E
108 Dendang, Indonesia ... 3 7S 107 56E
54 Dendermonde,
Belgium 51 2N 4 5E
125 Denge, Nigeria 12 52N 5 21E
125 Dengi, Nigeria 9 25N 9 55E
142 Denham, W. Australia 25 56S 113 31E
142 Denham Sd., W.
Austral. 25 45S 113 15E
157 Denholm, Canada 52 40N 108 0W
65 Denia, Spain 38 49N 0 8E
143 Deniliquin, Australia .35 30S 144 58E
164 Denison, Iowa, U.S.A. 42 0N 95 18W
165 Denison, Texas,
U.S.A. 33 50N 96 40W
100 Denizli, Turkey 37 42N 29 2E
55 Denklingen, Germany 50 55N 7 39E
143 Denman, Australia 32 24S 150 42E
81 Denmark, king.,
Europe 55 30N 9 0E
142 Denmark, W.
Australia 34 59S 117 18E
16 Denmark Str.,
Atlantic 66 0N 30 0W
43 Dennis Hd., Scot.,
U.K. 59 23N 2 26W
160 Dennison, U.S.A. 40 21N 81 21W
147 Denniston, N.Z. 41 45S 171 49E
41 Denny, Scotland,
U.K. 56 1N 3 55W
108 Denpasar, Indonesia . 8 45S 115 5E
38 Dent, England, U.K. .54 17N 2 28W
74 Denta, Rumania 45 20N 21 15E
38 Denton, Lancs.,
England, U.K. 53 26N 2 10W
35 Denton, Sussex,
England, U.K. 50 48N 0 5E
166 Denton, Mont., U.S.A. 47 25N 109 56W
165 Denton, Texas, U.S.A. 33 12N 97 10W
144 D'Entrecasteaux Is.,
Papua 9 0S 151 0E
142 D'Entrecasteaux Pt.,
W. Australia 34 50S 115 57E
125 Denu, Ghana 6 4N 1 8E
164 Denver, U.S.A. 39 45N 105 0W
165 Denver City, U.S.A. ...32 58N 102 48W
104 Deoband, India 29 42N 77 43E
106 Deobhog, India 19 53N 82 44E
105 Deogarh, India 21 32N 84 45E
105 Deoghar, India 24 30N 86 59E
106 Deolali, India 19 50N 73 50E
104 Deoli, India 25 50N 75 50E
105 Deoria, India 26 31N 83 48E
102 Deosat, Mts., Kashmir 35 40N 75 0E
160 Depew, U.S.A. 42 55N 78 43W
161 Deposit, U.S.A. 42 5N 75 23W
160 Depot Harb., Canada .45 18N 80 5W
142 Depot Spring,
Austral. 27 55S 120 3E
98 Der'a, Syria 32 36N 36 7E
104 Dera Ghazi Khan,
Pak. 30 5N 70 43E
104 Dera Ismail Khan,
Pak. 31 50N 70 50E
89 Derbent, U.S.S.R. 42 5N 48 15E
39 Derby & Co.,
England, United
Kingdom 52 55N 1 28W
161 Derby, Conn., U.S.A. .41 20N 73 5W
160 Derby, N.Y., U.S.A. .42 40N 78 59W
138 Derby, W. Australia .17 18S 123 40E
133 Derdepoort, S. Africa .24 39S 26 25E
59 Derecske, Hungary ...47 20N 21 33E
44 Derg, L., Ireland 53 0N 8 20W
46 Derg, R., N. Ire.,
U.K 54 42N 7 38W
87 Dergachi, U.S.S.R. 50 3N 36 3E
103 Dergaon, India 26 45N 94 0E
143 Dergholm, Australia ...37 24S 141 14E
75 Dermantsi, Bulgaria ...43 8N 24 17E
121 Derna, Libya 32 40N 22 35E
165 Dernieres, Isles,
U.S.A. 29 0N 90 45W
46 Derravaragh, L., Ire. .53 38N 7 22W
132 Derre, Mozambique ...17 0S 36 10E
143 Derrinallum, Australia 37 57S 143 15E
143 Derriwong, Australia .33 6S 147 21E
45 Derry R., Ireland 52 43N 6 35W
44 Derrybrien, Ireland ...53 4N 8 38W
46 Derrygonnelly,
Northern Ireland,
U.K. 54 25N 7 50W
45 Derrygrogan, Ireland .53 19N 7 23W
46 Derrykeighan,
Northern Ireland,
U.K. 55 8N 6 30W
46 Derrylin, N. Ire.,
U.K. 54 12N 7 34W
44 Derrynasaggart Mts.,
Ire. 51 58N 9 15W
44 Derryrush, Ireland 53 23N 9 40W
46 Derryveagh Mts., Ire. 55 0N 8 40W
126 Derudub, Sudan 17 31N 36 7E
40 Dervaig, Scot., U.K. .56 35N 6 13W

MAP
48 Derval, France 47 40N 1 41W
77 Dervéni, Greece 38 8N 22 25E
157 Derwent, Canada 53 41N 111 0W
39 Derwent, R., Cumb., Eng., U.K. 54 42N 3 22W
39 Derwent, R., Derby, Eng., U.K. 53 26N 1 44W
38 Derwent R., Dur., England, U.K. 54 52N 2 5W
39 Derwent R., Yorks., England, U.K. 54 13N 0 35W
38 Derwent Water, L., England, U.K. 53 34N 3 9W
164 Des Moines, Iowa, U.S.A. 41 35N 93 37W
165 Des Moines, N. Mex., U.S.A. 36 50N 103 51W
164 Des Moines, R., U.S.A. 41 15N 93 0W
174 Desaguadero, R., Bolivia 17 30S 68 0W
172 Desaquadero, R., Arg. 33 28S 67 15W
35 Desborough Eng., U.K. 52 27N 0 50W
166 Deschuies, R., U.S.A. 45 30N 121 0W
127 Dese, Ethiopia 11 5N 39 40E
176 Deseado R., Argentina 40 0S 69 0W
70 Desenzano del Gardo, It. 45 28N 10 32E
167 Desert Center, U.S.A. 33 45N 115 27W
46 Desertmartin, Northern Ireland, U.K. 54 47N 6 40W
34 Desford, Eng., U.K. ...52 38N 1 19W
86 Desna, R., U.S.S.R. ...52 0N 33 15E
78 Desnătuiu, R., Rum. .44 15N 23 27E
176 Desolación, Chile 53 0S 74 0W
135 Despatch, S. Africa ...33 46S 25 30E
74 Despotovac, Y.-slav. .44 6N 21 30E
125 Dessa, Niger 14 44N 1 6E
56 Dessau, Germany 51 49N 12 15E
127 Dessye, *see* Dese, Ethiopia 11 5N 39 40E
145 D'Estrees B., S. Austral. 35 48S 137 45E
104 Desuri, India 25 18N 73 35E
49 Desvrès, France 50 40N 1 48E
74 Deta, Rumania 45 24N 21 13E
145 Detention River, Tas., Australia 40 55S 145 32E
74 Detinja, R., Y.-slav. .43 51N 19 45E
56 Detmold, Germany 51 55N 8 50E
162 Detour Pt., U.S.A. 45 37N 86 35W
160 Detroit, Mich., U.S.A. 42 20N 83 5W
165 Detroit Tex., U.S.A. .33 40N 95 10W
164 Detroit Lakes, U.S.A. 46 50N 95 50W
132 Dett, Rhodesia 18 32S 26 57E
54 Deurne, Belgium 51 12N 4 24E
54 Deurne, Netherlands .51 27N 5 49E
58 Deutschlandsberg, Aus. 46 49N 15 14E
48 Deux Sèvres, dept., Fr. 46 35N 0 20W
78 Deva, Rumania 45 53N 22 55E
106 Devakottai, India 9 55N 78 45E
106 Devaprayag, India 30 13N 78 35E
59 Dévaványa, Hungary 47 2N 20 59E
88 Deveci Mts., Turkey .40 0N 36 0E
59 Devecser, Hungary 47 6N 17 26E
54 Deventer, Netherlands 52 15N 6 10E
43 Deveron, R., Scot., U.K. 57 22N 3 0W
78 Devesel Rumania 44 28N 22 41E
106 Devgad, I., India 14 48N 74 5E
147 Devil R., Pk., N.Z. 40 56S 172 37E
106 Devil's Pt., Ceylon 9 26N 80 6E
37 Devils Bridge, Wales, United Kingdom 52 23N 3 50W
164 Devils Lake, U.S.A. ...48 5N 98 50W
44 Devilsbit Mt., Ireland 52 50N 7 58W
75 Devin, Bulgaria 41 44N 24 24E
34 Devizes, England, U.K. 51 21N 2 0W
76 Devoll, R., Albania ...40 57N 20 15E
156 Devon, Canada 53 24N 113 26W
14 Devon I., Canada 75 0N 86 0W
145 Devonport, Australia .41 12S 146 28E
36 Devonport, Eng., U.K. 50 23N 4 11W
146 Devonport, N.Z. 36 49S 174 49E
36 Devonshire, co., Eng., U.K. 50 50N 3 40W
104 Dewas, India 22 59N 76 3E
135 Dewetsdorp, S. Africa 29 33S 26 39E
104 Dewgad Baria, India .22 40N 73 55E
39 Dewsbury, Eng., U.K. 53 42N 1 38W
165 Dexter, Mo., U.S.A. ...36 50N 90 0W
165 Dexter, N. Mex., U.S.A. 33 15N 104 25W
101 Deyhuk, Iran 33 15N 104 25W
101 Deyyer, Iran 27 55N 51 55E
100 Dezful, Iran 32 20N 48 30E
100 Dezh Shanpur, Iran ...35 30N 46 25E
91 Dezhneva, C., U.S.S.R. 66 10N 169 3E
100 Dhaba, Saudi Arabia .27 25N 35 40E
77 Dháfni, Greece 37 48N 22 1E
126 Dhahaban, Si.-Arab. .21 58N 39 3E
98 Dhahiriya, *see* Az Zahirivan, Jordan ...31 25N 34 58E
100 Dhahran, Si.-Arabia .26 9N 50 10E
103 Dhama Dzong, Tibet, China 28 15N 91 15E
76 Dhamasi, Greece 39 43N 22 11E
104 Dhampur, India 29 19N 78 33E
105 Dhamtari, India 20 42N 81 35E
106 Dhanaora, India 20 17N 80 20E
105 Dhanbad, India 23 50N 86 30E
105 Dhankuta, Nepal 26 55N 87 20E
105 Dhanora, India 20 20N 80 22E
104 Dhar, India 22 35N 75 26E
104 Dharampur, Maharashtra, India 20 32N 73 17E
104 Dharampur, Mad. P., India 22 13N 75 18E
106 Dharapuram, India ...10 45N 77 34E
106 Dharmapuri, India 12 10N 78 10E
106 Dharmavaram, India .14 29N 77 44E
104 Dharmsala, (Dharamsala), India 32 16N 73 23E
106 Dharwar, India 15 29N 75 5E
105 Dhaulagiri Mt., Nepal 28 45N 83 45E
104 Dhebar, L., India 24 10N 74 0E
105 Dhenkanal, India 20 45N 85 35E
77 Dhenousa, I., Greece .37 8N 25 48E
77 Dhesfina, Greece 38 25N 22 31E
76 Dheskati, Greece 39 55N 21 49E
77 Dhespotiko, I., Greece 36 57N 24 58E
76 Dhidhimótikhon, Greece 41 22N 26 29E
77 Dhikti, Mt., Greece ...35 8N 25 29E
77 Dhilianata, Greece 38 15N 20 34E
77 Dhilos, I., Greece 37 23N 25 15E
77 Dhimitsana, Greece ...37 36N 22 3E
77 Dhírfis, Mt., Greece .38 40N 23 54E
77 Dhodhekanisos, Is. & Pref., Greece 36 35N 27 0E
99 Dhofar, reg., Muscat & Oman 17 0N 54 10E
76 Dholiana, Greece 39 54N 20 32E
77 Dhokós I., Greece 37 20N 23 20E
104 Dholka, India 22 44N 72 29E
77 Dhomokós, Greece 39 10N 22 18E
104 Dholpur, India 26 45N 77 59E
106 Dhond, India 18 26N 74 40E
104 Dhoraji, India 21 45N 70 37E
76 Dhoxáton, Greece 41 9N 24 16E
77 Dhragonisi, I., Greece 37 27N 25 29E
104 Dhrangadhra, India ...22 59N 71 31E
77 Dhriopis, Greece 37 35N 24 35E
104 Dhrol, India 22 40N 70 25E
101 Dhubaibah, Trucial States 23 25N 54 35E
105 Dhubri, India 26 2N 90 2E
99 Dhula, South Yemen .15 5N 48 5E
104 Dhulia, India 20 58N 74 50E
126 Dhurm, Saudi Arabia 20 18N 42 53E
107 Di Linh Plateau, S. Vietnam 11 30N 108 0E
77 Dia, I., Greece 35 26N 25 13E
175 Diable, I. du., Fr. Gui. 5 15N 52 45W
168 Diablo Heights, Panama Canal Zone 8 58N 79 34W
124 Diafarabé, Mali 14 17N 4 57W
124 Diala, Mali 13 59N 10 0W
124 Dialakono, Ivory Coast 8 16N 5 50W
124 Dialakoro, Mali. 12 18N 7 54W
124 Diallassagou Mali. 13 47N 3 41W
172 Diamante, Argentina .32 5S 60 40W
175 Diamantina, Brazil ...18 5S 43 40W
145 Diamantina R., Queens., Australia .24 0S 141 0E
175 Diamantino, Brazil 14 30S 56 30W
175 Diamond Harbour, India 22 11N 88 14E
139 Diamond Is., Australia 17 25S 151 5E
166 Diamond Mts., U.S.A. 40 0N 115 58W
166 Diamondville, U.S.A. .41 51N 110 30W
70 Diano Marina, Italy ...43 55N 8 3E
125 Diapaga, Upper Volta 12 5N 1 46E
125 Diapangou, Upper Volta 12 5N 0 10E
124 Diariaguila, Guinea ...10 35N 10 2W
101 Dibai (Dubai), Trucial States 25 15N 55 20E
130 Dibaya, Congo 6 30S 23 0E
130 Dibaya-Lubue, Congo 4 12S 19 54E
101 Dibba, Tr. States 25 45N 56 16E
34 Dibden, England, U.K. 50 53N 1 24W
100 Dibega, Iraq 35 50N 43 46E
134 Dibeng, C. Prov., S. Afr. 27 35S 22 54E
76 Dibër, Albania 41 38N 20 15E
103 Dibrugha, India 27 29N 94 58E
164 Dickinson, U.S.A. 46 50N 102 40W
163 Dickson, U.S.A. 36 5N 87 22W
161 Dickson City, U.S.A. .41 29N 75 40W
71 Dicomano, Italy 43 53S 11 30E
34 Didcot, England, U.K. 51 36N 1 14E
127 Didessa R., Ethiopia . 9 40N 35 50E
124 Didieni, Mali 14 5N 7 50W
156 Didsbury, Canada 51 35N 114 10W
104 Didwana, India 27 17N 74 25E
51 Die, France 44 47N 5 22E
134 Die Put, S. Africa 30 47S 23 59E
124 Diebougou, Upper Volta 11 0N 3 15W
11 Diego Garcia, I., Ind. Oc. 9 50S 75 0E
129 Diego Suarez, Malagasy Republic .12 25S 49 20E
54 Diekirch, Luxembourg 49 52N 6 10E
48 Dielette, France 49 33N 1 52W
124 Diema, Mali 14 32N 9 3W
107 Dien Bien Phu, N. Vietnam 21 20N 103 0E
55 Diepenbeek, Belgium .50 54N 5 25E
56 Diepholz, Germany ...52 37N 8 22E
48 Dieppe, France 49 54N 1 4E
54 Dieren, Netherlands ...52 3N 6 6E
165 Dierks, U.S.A. 34 9N 94 0W
54 Diest, Belgium 50 58N 5 4E
51 Dieulefit, France 44 32N 5 4E
49 Dieuze, France 48 30N 6 40E
131 Dif, Kenya 0 59N 40 57E
54 Differdange, Lux. 49 81N 5 54E
104 Dig, India 27 28N 77 20E
155 Digby, Canada 44 41N 65 50W
157 Digges, Canada 58 40N 94 0W
153 Digges Is., Canada 62 40N 77 50W
103 Dighinala, E. Pakistan 23 15N 92 5E
164 Dighton, U.S.A. 38 30N 100 26W
51 Digne, France 44 5N 6 12E
50 Digoin, France 46 29N 3 58E
109 Digos, Philippines 6 45N 125 20E
106 Digras, India 20 6N 77 45E
103 Dihang R., India 27 30N 96 30E
55 Dihle, R., Belgium 50 49N 4 37E
49 Dijon, France 47 20N 5 0E
127 Dikala, Sudan 4 45N 31 28E
127 Dikkil, Fr. Terr. of the Afars & Issas ...11 8N 42 20E
90 Dikson, U.S.S.R. 73 40N 80 5E
54 Diksmuide, Belgium ...51 3N 2 51E
125 Dikwa, Cameroon 12 4N 13 30E
100 Dilam, Saudi Arabia .23 55N 47 10E
109 Dili, Port, Timor 8 39S 125 34E
89 Dilizhan, U.S.S.R. 41 46N 44 57E
56 Dillenburg Germany .50 44N 8 17E
165 Dilley, U.S.A. 28 40N 99 12W
127 Dilling, Sudan 12 3N 29 35E
57 Dillingen, Germany ...49 22N 6 42E
157 Dillon, Canada 55 56N 108 54W
166 Dillon, Mont., U.S.A. .45 9N 112 36W
163 Dillon, S.C., U.S.A. ...34 26N 79 20W
130 Dilolo, Congo 10 28S 22 18E
145 Dilston, Australia 41 22S 147 10E
130 Dimbelenge, Congo 4 30S 23 0E
124 Dimbokro, Ivory Coast 6 45N 4 30W
143 Dimboola, Australia ...36 28S 142 0E
78 Dimbovita, Reg., Rumania 45 0N 25 25E
144 Dimbulah, Australia .17 2S 145 4E
91 Dimitri Laptev Str., U.S.S.R. 73 0N 140 0E
75 Dimitrov Dam, Bulgaria 42 35N 25 15E
75 Dimitrovgrad, Bulgaria 42 5N 25 35E
74 Dimitrovgrad, Y.-slav. 43 0N 22 48E
165 Dimmitt, U.S.A. 34 36N 102 16W
127 Dimo, Sudan 5 19N 29 10E
109 Dinagat I., Philippines 10 10N 125 40E
105 Dinajpur, E. Pak. 25 33N 88 43E
48 Dinan, France 48 28N 2 2W
54 Dinant, Belgium 50 16N 4 55E
105 Dinapore, India 25 38N 85 5E
100 Dinar, Turkey 38 5N 30 15E
48 Dinard, France 48 38N 2 6W
19 Dinaric Alps, Europe .44 0N 17 30E
37 Dinas Hd., Wales, U.K. 52 2N 4 56W
37 Dinas Mawddwy, Wales, United Kingdom 52 44N 3 41W
37 Dinas Powis, Wales, United Kingdom 51 25N 3 14W
127 Dincha, Ethiopia 6 15N 37 32E
127 Dinder R., Sudan 12 32N 35 0E
106 Dindi, R., India 16 24N 78 15E
106 Dindiulg, India 10 25N 78 0E
55 Dingden, Germany 51 46N 6 37E
56 Dingelstadt, Germany 51 19N 10 19E
44 Dingle, Ireland 52 9N 10 17W
134 Dingle, C. Prov., S. Afr. 27 48S 22 56E
44 Dingle B., Ire. 52 3N 10 20W
44 Dingle Harbour, Ire. .52 7N 10 12W
161 Dingmans Ferry, U.S.A. 41 13N 74 55W
144 Dingo, Australia 23 40S 149 27E
57 Dingolfing, Germany .48 38N 12 30E
126 Dinguiraye, Guinea ...11 30N 10 35W
43 Dingwall, Scot., U.K. 57 36N 4 26W
125 Dingyadi, Nigeria 13 0N 0 53E
166 Dinosaur National Monument, U.S.A. .40 30N 108 45W
55 Dinslaken, Germany .51 34N 6 41E
55 Dintel, R., Netherlands 4 25N 51 38E
55 Dinteloord, Netherlands 51 38N 4 22E
167 Dinuba, U.S.A. 36 37N 119 22W
81 Diö, Sweden 56 37N 14 15E
59 Diosgyör, Hungary 48 7N 20 43E
78 Diosig, Rumania 47 18N 22 2E
124 Diourbel, Senegal 14 39N 16 12W
104 Diplo, West Pakistan .24 25N 69 35E
109 Dipolog, Philippines ... 8 40N 123 30E
78 Dipsa, Rumania 46 58N 24 27E
147 Dipton, New Zealand .45 54S 168 22E
102 Dir, West Pakistan ...35 18N 71 59E
124 Dire, Mali 15 20N 3 25W
127 Dire Dawa, Ethiopia . 9 35N 41 45E
169 Diriamba, Nicaragua .11 51N 86 19W
129 Dirico, Angola 17 50S 20 42E
142 Dirk Hartog I., Western Australia .25 58S 113 1E
145 Dirranbandi, Austral. 28 33S 148 17E
127 Disa, Sudan 12 5N 34 15E
166 Disappointment C., U.S.A. 46 20N 124 0W
142 Disappointment L., Western Australia .23 20S 122 40E
143 Disaster B., Australia 37 15S 150 0E
145 Discovery B., Australia 38 10S 140 40E
57 Disentis, Switzerland .46 42N 8 50E
126 Dishna, Egypt 26 9N 32 32E
125 Disina, Nigeria 11 35N 9 50E
14 Disko B., Greenland ...60 0N 52 0W
14 Disko I., Greenland ...69 40N 54 0W
86 Disna, U.S.S.R. 55 32N 28 11E
86 Disna, R., U.S.S.R. 55 20N 27 30E
55 Dison, Belgium 50 37N 5 51E
35 Diss, England, U.K. ...52 23N 1 6E
38 Distington, Eng., U.K. 54 35N 3 33W
126 Disûq, Egypt 31 8N 30 35E
35 Ditchingham, Eng., U.K. 52 28N 1 26E
35 Ditchling & Beacon, Eng., U.K. 50 55N 0 7W
36 Dittisham, Eng., U.K. 50 22N 3 36W
34 Ditton Priors, Eng., U.K. 52 30N 2 33W
104 Diu I., India 20 45N 70 58E
154 Diver, Canada 46 44N 79 30W
48 Dives, France 49 18N 0 8W
48 Dives, R., France 48 55N 0 5W
106 Divi Pt., India 15 59N 81 9E
89 Divichi, U.S.S.R. 41 15N 48 57E
166 Divide, U.S.A. 45 48N 112 47W
142 Dividing Ra., Australia 27 45S 116 0E
132 Divinhe, Mozambique 20 38S 34 47E
175 Divinópolis, Brazil ...20 10S 45 0W
174 Diviso, Colombia 1 20N 78 5W
89 Divnoye, U.S.S.R. 45 55N 43 27E
124 Divo, Ivory Coast 5 48N 5 15W
101 Diwai Kol, Afghan. 34 20N 68 0E
166 Dixie, U.S.A. 45 37N 115 27W
164 Dixon, Ill. U.S.A. 41 50N 89 30W
166 Dixon, Mont., U.S.A. .47 19N 114 25W
167 Dixon, N. Mex., U.S.A. 36 15N 105 57W
157 Dixon Entrance, Alaska, U.S.A. 54 30N 132 0W
100 Diyarbakir, Turkey ...37 55N 40 18E
36 Dizzard Pt., Eng., U.K. 50 46N 4 38W
125 Djabotaoure, Togo 8 35N 0 58E
123 Djada, Massif du, Niger 21 29N 12 21E
123 Djado, Niger 21 4N 12 14E
109 Djailolo, Indonesia 1 10N 127 35E
109 Djajapura, Indonesia . 2 28S 140 38E
109 Djajawidjaja Mts., Indonesia 7 0S 139 0E
109 Djakarta, Indonesia ... 6 9S 106 49E
123 Djamaâ, Algeria 33 32N 5 59E
130 Djambala, Congo (Fr.) 2 20S 14 30E
108 Djambi, *see* Telanaipura, Indonesia 1 38S 103 30E
123 Djanet (Fort Charlet), Algeria 24 35N 9 32E
125 Djang, Cameroon 5 30N 10 5E
108 Djangeru, Indonesia ... 2 30S 116 40E
109 Djapara, Indonesia 6 30S 110 40E
109 Djatibarang, Indonesia 6 28S 108 18E
109 Djatinegara, Indonesia 6 13S 106 52E
123 Djebiniana, Tunisia ...35 1N 11 0E
123 Djedi, W., Algeria 34 1N 3 45E
122 Djelfa, Algeria 34 30N 3 20E
108 Djemadja, I., Indon. . 3 5N 105 45E
109 Djember, Indonesia ... 8 11S 113 41E
124 Djenne, Mali 14 0N 4 30W
123 Djenoun, Garet el, Alg. 25 4N 5 31E
123 Djerba, Tunisia 33 53N 10 57E
123 Djerba I., Tunisia 33 56N 11 0E
109 Djerik, Indonesia 4 3S 131 20E
123 Djerid, Chott, el, Tun. 33 50N 8 30E
125 Djibo, Upper Volta ...14 15N 1 35W
127 Djibouti, Fr. Terr. of the Afars & Issas ...11 30N 43 5E
123 Djidjelli, Algeria 36 52N 5 50E
107 Djirlange, S. Vietnam 11 44N 108 15E
123 Djofra Oasis, Libya ...28 59N 15 47E
130 Djolu, Congo 0 45N 22 5E
109 Djombang, Indonesia . 7 32S 112 12E
122 Djorf el Youdi, Mor. .32 14N 9 8W
108 Djorong, Indonesia 4 2S 114 55E
125 Djougou, Dahomey 9 40N 1 45E
128 Djoum, Cameroon 2 41N 12 35E
131 Djugu, Congo 1 55N 30 35E
80 Djursholm, Sweden ...59 25N 18 6E
81 Djursland, reg., Den. .56 27N 10 40E
86 Dmitriev-Lgovski, U.S.S.R. 52 10N 35 0E
87 Dmitrov, U.S.S.R. 56 25N 37 32E
86 Dmitrovsk Orlovskiy, U.S.S.R. 52 29N 35 10E
88 Dnepr R., U.S.S.R. 50 0N 31 0E
88 Dneprodzerzhinsk, U.S.S.R. 48 32N 34 30E
88 Dnepropetrovsk, U.S.S.R. 48 30N 35 0E
88 Dneprorudnoye, U.S.S.R. 47 21N 34 58E
88 Dnestr, R., U.S.S.R. .48 30N 26 30E
88 Dnestrovski, *see* Belgorod, U.S.S.R. .50 35N 36 35E
88 Dniester, *see* Dnestr, R., U.S.S.R. 48 30N 26 30E
86 Dno, U.S.S.R. 57 50N 29 58E
121 Doba, Chad. 8 40N 16 50E
71 Dobbiaco, Italy 46 44N 12 13E
144 Dobbyn, Australia 19 44S 139 59E
56 Döbeln, Germany 51 7N 13 10E
60 Dobiegniew, Poland ...52 59N 15 45E
176 Doblas, Argentina 37 5S 64 0W
109 Dobo, Indonesia 5 45S 134 15E
74 Doboj, Yugoslavia 44 46N 18 6E
60 Dobra, Poland 53 34N 15 20E
78 Dobra Rumania 45 54N 22 36E
60 Dobre Miasto, Poland 53 58N 20 26E
75 Dobrinishté, Bulgaria 41 49N 23 34E
58 Dobřis, Czechoslovakia 49 46N 14 10E
78 Dobriţa, Rumania 45 13N 23 10E
60 Dobrodzien, Poland ...50 45N 18 25E
78 Dobruja, reg., Rum. ...44 30N 28 30E
86 Dobrush, U.S.S.R. 52 28N 30 35E
127 Dobtong, Sudan 6 25N 31 40E
35 Docking, Eng., U.K. .52 55N 0 39E
80 Döda Fallet, Falls, Swed. 63 4N 16 35E
35 Doddington, Eng., U.K. 52 29N 0 3E
77 Dodecanese Is. & Pref., Greece 36 35N 27 0E
164 Dodge Center U.S.A. 44 1N 92 57W
165 Dodge City, U.S.A. ...37 42N 100 0W
164 Dodgeville, U.S.A. 42 55N 90 8W
36 Dodman Pt., Eng., U.K. 50 13N 4 49W
132 Dodo, Botswana 21 15N 25 25E
127 Dodo, Sudan 5 10N 29 57E
127 Dodolo, Ethiopia 6 59N 39 11E
131 Dodoma, Tanzania 6 8S 35 45E
131 Dodoma, dist., Tanzania 6 0S 36 0E
157 Dodsland, Canada 51 50N 108 45W
166 Dodson, U.S.A. 48 23N 108 4W
54 Doetinchem, Neth. 51 59N 6 18E
156 Dog L., Canada 51 10N 98 40W
156 Dog R., Canada 57 50N 94 40W
77 Doğanbey, Turkey 37 40N 27 10E
70 Dogliani, Italy 44 35N 7 55E
125 Dogondoutchi, Niger .13 38N 4 2E
125 Dogoraoua, Niger 14 0N 5 31E
104 Dogran, West Pakistan 31 48N 73 35E
104 Dóhad, India 22 50N 74 15E
103 Dohazari, E. Pakistan 22 10N 92 5E
154 Doheny, Canada 47 4N 72 35W
154 Doherty, Canada 46 58N 79 44W
109 Doi, I., Indonesia 2 21N 127 49E
107 Doi Luang, Mts., Thai. 18 20N 101 30E
100 Dokan Dam, Iraq 35 58N 44 40E
79 Dokka, Norway 60 49N 10 7E
79 Dokka, R., Norway ...61 7N 10 0E
54 Dokkum, Netherlands 53 20N 5 59E
104 Dokri, West Pakistan 27 25N 68 7E
48 Dol, France 48 34N 1 47W
164 Doland, U.S.A. 44 55N 98 5W
155 Dolbeau, Canada 48 25N 72 18W
49 Dôle, France 47 7N 5 31E
127 Doleib, R., Sudan 10 30N 33 15E
37 Dolgarrog Wales, U.K. 53 11N 3 50W
37 Dolgellau, Wales, U.K. 52 44N 3 53W
86 Dolginovo, U.S.S.R. ...54 39N 27 29E
43 Dolhalvaig, Scot., U.K. 58 27N 3 52W
72 Dolianovo, Italy 39 23N 9 11E
88 Dolinskaya, U.S.S.R. .48 16N 32 36E
130 Dolisie, Congo, (Fr.) ... 4 0S 13 10E
78 Dolj, Reg., Rum. 44 15N 23 35E
44 Dolla, Ireland 52 47N 8 12W
41 Dollar, Scotland 56 9N 3 41W
54 Dollart, Netherlands .53 20N 7 10E
75 Dolna Banya, Bulgaria 42 18N 23 44E
71 Dolo, Italy 45 25N 12 4E
71 Dolomites, Alps, Italy 46 30N 11 40E
172 Dolores, Argentina 36 20S 57 40W
167 Dolores, Colo., U.S.A. 37 30N 108 30W
165 Dolores, Tex., U.S.A. .27 40N 99 38W
165 Dolores, R., U.S.A. ...38 30N 108 55W
172 Dolores Uruguay 33 34S 58 15W
74 Dolovo, Yugoslavia ...44 55N 20 52E
176 Dolphin C., Falkland Is. 51 10S 59 0W
152 Dolphin and Union Str., Canada 69 30N 117 0W
41 Dolphinton, Scot., U.K. 55 42N 3 28W
36 Dolton, England, U.K. 50 53N 4 2W
37 Dolwyddelan, Wales, United Kingdom ...53 3N 3 53W
173 Dom Pedrito, Brazil ...31 0S 54 40W
125 Doma, Nigeria 8 25N 8 18E
132 Domasi, Malawi 15 22S 35 10E
58 Domazlice, Cz. 49 28N 13 0E
90 Dombarovka, U.S.S.R. 51 0N 59 10E
79 Dombås, Norway 62 6N 9 4E
49 Dombasle, France 49 8N 6 18E
129 Dombe Grande, Angola 12 56S 13 8E
51 Dombes, dist., France 46 3N 5 0E
59 Dombóvár, Hungary .46 21N 18 9E
59 Dombrad, Hungary ...48 13N 21 54E
54 Domburg, Netherlands 51 35N 3 30E
166 Dome Pk., U.S.A. 40 50N 106 40W
107 Domel, I., *see* Letsôk-aw-Kyun, Burma 11 30N 98 25E
147 Domett, New Zealand 42 53S 173 12E
172 Domeyko, Chile 29 0S 71 30W
48 Domfront, France 48 37N 0 40W
172 Dominador, Chile 24 21S 69 20W
169 Dominica I., Leeward Is. 15 20N 61 20W
169 Dominican Rep., W. Ind. 19 0N 70 30W
130 Domiongo, Congo 4 36S 21 15E
56 Dömitz, Germany 53 9N 11 13E
50 Domme, France 44 48N 1 12E
55 Dommel, R., Neth. 51 10N 5 30E
81 Dommerby, Denmark 56 33N 9 5E
78 Domniţa Elena, Rum. 43 50N 28 40E

MAP
99 Domo, Ethiopia 7 50N 47 10E
70 Domodossola, Italy ...46 6N 8 19E
49 Dompaire, France 48 14N 6 14E
50 Dompierre, France 46 31N 3 41E
124 Dompin, Ghana 5 10N 2 5W
49 Domrémy, France 48 26N 5 40E
80 Domsjö, Sweden 63 15N 18 45E
77 Domvraina, Greece 38 15N 22 59E
71 Domzale, Yugoslavia .46 9N 3 6E
39 Don R., England, U.K. 53 57N 1 0W
106 Don R., India 16 40N 75 55W
43 Don R., Scotland, U.K. 57 14N 2 15W
87 Don R., U.S.S.R. 49 35N 41 40E
63 Don Benito, Spain 38 53N 5 51W
65 Don Juan, R., Spain .38 50N 2 10W
168 Don Martin Res., Mex. 27 30N 100 50W
132 Dona Aña, Mozambique 17 25S 35 17E
45 Donabate, Ireland 53 30N 6 9W
45 Donadea, Ireland 53 20N 6 45W
46 Donaghadee, Northern Ireland, U.K. 54 38N 5 32W
45 Donaghmore, Ireland .52 54N 7 37W
46 Donaghmore, Northern Ireland, U.K. 54 33N 6 50W
143 Donald, Australia 36 25S 143 0E
156 Donalda, Canada 52 35N 112 34W
165 Donaldsonville, U.S.A. 30 2N 91 50W
163 Donalsonville, U.S.A. .31 3N 84 52W
45 Donard, Ireland 53 1N 6 37W
59 Donau (Danube) R., Austria 47 55N 17 20E
57 Donaueschingen, Ger. 47 57N 8 30E
58 Donawitz, Austria 47 22N 15 4E
39 Doncaster, Eng., U.K. 53 31N 1 9W
130 Dondo, Angola 9 45S 14 25E
109 Dondo B., Indonesia . 0 29N 120 45E
132 Dondo, Mozambique .19 33S 34 46E
106 Dondra Hd., Ceylon ... 5 55N 80 40E
46 Donegal, Ireland 54 39N 8 8W
46 Donegal, co., Ireland .54 53N 8 0W
46 Donegal B., Ireland ...54 30N 8 35W
46 Donegal Har., Ireland 54 35N 8 15W
44 Donegal Pt., Ireland .52 44N 9 38W
44 Doneraile, Ireland 52 13N 8 37W
87 Donets R., U.S.S.R. ...48 50N 38 45E
88 Donetsk, U.S.S.R. 48 0N 37 45E
125 Dong, Nigeria 9 20N 12 15E
107 Dong Hene, Laos 16 44N 105 14E
107 Dong Hoi, Vietnam ...17 18N 106 36E
125 Donga, Nigeria 7 45N 10 2E
142 Dongara, W. Australia 29 14S 114 57E
105 Dongargarh, India 21 10N 80 40E
131 Dongebesh, Tanzania . 6 0N 35 30E
55 Dongen, Netherlands .51 38N 4 56E
109 Donggala, & I., Indon. 0 30S 119 40E
126 Dongola, Sudan 19 9N 30 22E
130 Dongou, Congo, (Fr.) . 2 0N 18 5E
132 Dongwe R., Zambia ...14 10S 24 30E
34 Donhead, Eng., U.K. .51 1N 2 8W
172 Doñihue, Chile 34 12S 71 0N
39 Donington, Eng., U.K. 52 54N 0 12W
165 Doniphan, U.S.A. 36 40N 90 50W
71 Donja Stubica, Y.-slav. 45 59N 16 0E
74 Donji Dusnik, Y.-slav. 43 12N 22 5E
74 Donji Miholjac, Y.-slav. 45 45N 18 10E
74 Donji Milanovac, Yugoslavia 44 28N 22 6E
74 Donji Vakuf, Y.-slav. 44 8N 17 24E
165 Donna, U.S.A. 26 12N 98 2W
155 Donnaconna, Canada .46 41N 71 41W
146 Donnelly's Crossing, N.Z. 35 42S 173 38E
135 Donnybrook, S. Africa 29 57S 29 55E
142 Donnybrook, W. Austral. 33 34S 115 51E
160 Donora, U.S.A. 40 11N 79 50W
44 Donoughmore, Ireland 52 0N 8 42W
87 Donskoy, U.S.S.R. 53 55N 38 15W
71 Donya Lendava, Y.-slav. 46 35N 16 25E
51 Donzère, France 44 28N 4 43E
49 Donzy, France 47 20N 3 6E
45 Dooagh, Ireland 53 59N 10 7W
46 Doochary, Ireland 54 54N 8 10W
142 Doodlakine, W. Austral. 31 35S 117 28E
45 Dooega Hd., Ireland ..53 54N 10 3W
40 Doon L., Scot., U.K. .55 15N 4 22W
40 Doon R., Scot., U.K. .55 20N 4 28W
44 Doonbeg, Ireland 52 44N 9 31W
44 Doonbeg R., Ireland .52 42N 9 20W
98 Dor (Tantura), Israel .32 37N 34 55E
70 Dora Baltea R., Italy 45 42N 7 25E
138 Dora L., W. Australia 22 0S 123 0E
70 Dora Riparia R., Italy 45 7N 7 24E
127 Dorading, Sudan 8 30N 33 5E
81 Dörby, Sweden 56 20N 16 12E
34 Dorchester, Dorset, England, U.K. 50 42N 2 28W
34 Dorchester, Oxon., England, U.K. 51 38N 1 10W
153 Dorchester, C., Canada 65 40N 78 0W
50 Dordogne, dépt., Fr. .45 5N 0 40E
50 Dordogne R., France .44 50N 0 5E
35 Dordrecht, S. Africa ...31 20S 27 3E
54 Dordrecht, Netherlands 51 48N 4 39E
157 Dore L., Canada 54 45N 107 20W
50 Dore, Mt., France 45 32N 2 50E
50 Dore R., France 45 40N 3 35E
43 Dores, Scotland, U.K. 57 22N 4 20W
57 Dorfen, Germany 48 16N 12 10E
72 Dorgali, Italy 40 18N 9 35E
125 Dori, Upper Volta 14 3N 0 2W
134 Doring R., S. Africa ...32 30S 19 30E
134 Doringbos, S. Africa ...31 58S 19 12E
134 Doringdraai, S. Africa 32 48S 23 50E
154 Dorion, Canada 45 23N 74 3W
161 Dorion-Vaudreuil, Can. 45 25N 75 4W
35 Dorking, Eng., U.K. .51 14N 0 20W
124 Dormaa-Ahenkro, Ghana 7 15N 2 52W
55 Dormagen, Germany .51 8N 6 50E
127 Dormo, Ras, Ethiopia 13 14N 42 35E
71 Dornberg, Yugoslavia 45 45N 13 50E
58 Dornbirn, Austria 47 25N 9 45E
49 Dornes, France 46 48N 3 18E
42 Dornie, Scotland, U.K. 57 17N 5 30W
43 Dornoch, Scot., U.K. .57 52N 4 0W
43 Dornoch Firth, Scotland, U.K. 57 52N 4 0W
59 Dorog, Hungary 47 42N 18 45E
86 Dorogobuzh, U.S.S.R. 54 50N 33 10E
73 Dorohoi, Rumania 47 56N 26 30E
111 Döröö Nuur, L., Mongolia 48 0N 93 0E
142 Dorre I., W. Australia 25 13S 113 12E
145 Dorrigo, Australia 30 19S 152 38E
166 Dorris, U.S.A. 41 59N 121 58W
160 Dorset, Canada 45 14N 78 55W
160 Dorset, Ohio, U.S.A. .41 41N 80 42W
36 Dorset, co., Eng., U.K. 50 48N 2 25W
36 Dorset Heights, England, U.K. 50 51N 2 30W
56 Dorsten, Germany 51 40N 6 55E
34 Dorstone, Eng., U.K. .52 4N 3 0W
56 Dortmund, Germany .51 32N 7 28E
56 Dorum, Germany 53 40N 8 33E
127 Dorya R., Ethiopia ... 5 15N 41 30E
100 Dörtyol, Turkey 36 52N 36 12E
176 Dos Bahias, C., Arg. .44 58S 65 32W
167 Dos Cabezas, U.S.A. .32 1N 109 37W
63 Dos Hermanas, Spain 37 16N 5 55W
125 Dosara, Nigeria 12 20N 6 5E
101 Doshi, Afghanistan 35 35N 68 50E
125 Dosso, Niger 13 0N 3 13E
81 Döstrup, Denmark 56 41N 9 42E
156 Dot, Canada 50 12N 121 25W
163 Dothan, U.S.A. 31 10N 85 25W
49 Douai, Nord, France .50 21N 3 4E
125 Douala, Cameroon 4 0N 9 45E
48 Douarnenez, France ...48 6N 4 21W
145 Double I., Pt., Austral. 25 55S 153 30E
58 Doubravka R., Cz. 49 40N 15 30E
49 Doubs, dépt., France .47 10N 6 20E
49 Doubs R., France 47 8N 5 40E
142 Doubtful B., W. Austral. 34 15S 119 28E
147 Doubtful Sd., N.Z. 45 20S 166 49E
154 Doucet, Canada 48 15N 76 35W
48 Doudeville, France 49 43N 0 47E
48 Doué, France 47 11N 0 20W
124 Douentza, Mali 14 58N 2 48W
134 Douglas, C. Prov., S. Afr. 29 4S 23 46E
38 Douglas, I. of M., U.K. 54 9N 4 29W
41 Douglas, Scotland, U.K. 55 33N 3 50W
157 Douglas, Alaska, U.S.A. 58 23N 134 32W
167 Douglas, Ariz., U.S.A. 31 21N 109 30W
163 Douglas, Ga., U.S.A. .31 32N 82 52W
164 Douglas, Wyo., U.S.A. 42 45N 105 20W
166 Douglas, Mt., U.S.A. .45 11N 110 5W
155 Douglastown, Canada 48 46N 64 24W
163 Douglasville, U.S.A. ...33 46N 84 43W
122 Douirat, Morocco 33 2N 4 11W
77 Doukáton, Ákra, C., Gr. 38 34N 20 30E
49 Doulevant, France 48 22N 4 53E
49 Doullens, France 50 10N 2 20E
128 Doumé, Cameroon 4 15N 13 25E
124 Douna, Mali 12 40N 6 0W
43 Dounby, Scotland, U.K. 59 4N 3 13W
41 Doune, Scotland, U.K. 56 12N 4 3W
43 Dounreay, Scot., U.K. 58 40N 3 28W
176 Dourados, Brazil 22 9S 54 50W
49 Dourdan, France 48 30N 2 0E
62 Douro, R., Portugal ...41 1N 8 16W
123 Dourso, Niger 20 27N 16 1E
51 Douvaine, France 46 19N 6 16E
123 Douz, Tunisia 33 25N 9 0E
38 Dove R., England, U.K. 54 20N 0 55W
155 Dove Brook, Canada .53 40N 57 40W
167 Dove Creek, U.S.A. ...37 53N 108 59W
38 Dove Dale, Eng., U.K. 54 25N 0 55W
135 Dover, O.F.S. S. Africa 27 2S 27 46E
35 Dover, England, U.K. 51 7N 1 19E
162 Dover, Del., U.S.A. ...39 10N 75 31W
161 Dover, N.H., U.S.A. .43 5N 70 51W
161 Dover, N.J., U.S.A. ...40 53N 74 34W
160 Dover, Ohio, U.S.A. ...40 32N 81 30W
161 Dover Plains, U.S.A. .41 43N 73 43W
35 Dover, Strait of, England, U.K. 51 0N 1 30E
155 Dover-Foxcroft, U.S.A. 45 14N 69 14W
37 Dovey R., Wales, U.K. 52 32N 4 0W
79 Dovre fjell, Mts., Nor. 62 25N 9 30E
79 Dovre, Norway 62 0N 9 15E
132 Dow, L., Botswana ...21 15S 24 44E
132 Dowa, Malawi 13 38S 33 58E
162 Dowagiac, U.S.A. 42 0N 86 8W
101 Dowlatabad, Iran 28 20N 50 40E
46 Down, N. Ire., U.K. 54 20N 6 0W
166 Downey, U.S.A. 42 29N 112 3W
35 Downham Market, England, U.K. 52 36N 0 22E
46 Downhill, N. Ire., U.K. 55 10N 6 48W
166 Downieville, U.S.A. ...39 42N 120 56W
46 Downpatrick, Northern Ireland, U.K. 54 20N 5 43W
45 Downpatrick Hd., Ire. 54 20N 9 21W
145 Downs Div., Australia 27 10S 150 44E
34 Downton, England, U.K. 51 0N 1 44W
46 Dowra, Ireland 54 11N 8 2W
161 Doylestown, U.S.A. ...40 21N 75 10W
103 Doyung, China 33 40N 99 25E
122 Dra, Cap, Morocco 28 58N 11 0W
122 Dra, W., Morocco 28 50N 8 50W
54 Drachten, Netherlands 53 7N 6 5E
78 Draganestiolt, Rumania 44 9N 24 32E
78 Draganesti- Vlasca, Rumania 44 5N 25 33E
74 Dragas, Yugoslavia ...42 5N 20 35E
78 Drăgăsani, Rumania .44 39N 24 17E
74 Draginac, Yugoslavia .44 30N 19 25E
74 Dragocvet, Yugoslavia 44 0N 21 15E
169 Dragon's Mouth, Ven. 11 0N 61 50W
64 Dragonera, I., Spain .39 35N 2 19E
74 Dragovistica, (Berivol), Bulgaria .42 22N 22 39E
51 Draguignan, France ...43 30N 6 27E
166 Drain, U.S.A. 43 45N 123 17W
164 Drake, U.S.A. 47 56N 100 31W
15 Drake Pass., S. Oc. ...58 0S 68 0W
135 Drakensberg, Mts., S. Afr. 31 0S 25 0E
76 Drama, Greece 41 9N 24 10E
79 Drammen, Norway 59 42N 10 12E
78 Drănceni, Rumania ...46 49N 28 10E
45 Drangan, Ireland 52 32N 7 36W
79 Drangedal, Norway 59 5N 9 0E
78 Dranov, Ostrov, Rum. 44 55N 29 30E
46 Draperstown, Northern Ireland, U.K. 54 48N 6 47E
58 Drau R., Austria 47 46N 13 33E
74 Drava R., Yugoslavia 45 50N 18 0W
49 Draveil, France 48 41N 2 25E
71 Dravograd, Yugoslavia 46 36N 15 5E
60 Drawa, R., Poland 53 6N 15 56E
60 Drawno, Poland 53 13N 15 46E
60 Drawsko, Poland 53 35N 15 50E
156 Drayton Valley, Can. .53 25N 114 58W
40 Dreghorn, Scot., U.K. 55 36N 4 30W
81 Drejö, Denmark 54 58N 10 25E
74 Dren, Yugoslavia 43 8N 20 44E
46 Drenagh, N. Ire., U.K. 55 3N 6 55W
55 Drensteinfurt, Germany 51 48N 7 42E
54 Drenthe, prov., Neth. 52 52N 6 40E
160 Dresden, Canada 42 40N 82 15W
56 Dresden, Germany 51 2N 13 45E
55 Dreumel, Netherlands 51 51N 5 26E
135 Dreunberg, S. Africa .30 58S 26 20E
48 Dreux, France 48 44N 1 23E
135 Driefontein, S. Africa .28 22S 25 29E
39 Driffield, England, U.K. 54 0N 0 25W
154 Driftwood, Canada 49 8N 81 23E
160 Driftwood, U.S.A. 41 22N 78 9W
123 Drigana, Niger 20 51N 12 17E
166 Driggs, U.S.A. 43 50N 111 8W
44 Drimoleague, Ireland .51 40N 9 15W
76 Drin R., Albania 42 20N 20 0E
74 Drina R., Yugoslavia .44 30N 19 10E
78 Drincea, R., Rumania 44 20N 22 55E
76 Drin-i-zi, R., Albania 41 37N 20 28E
74 Drinjača, R., Y.-slav. 44 20N 19 0E
79 Driva, Norway 62 33N 9 38E
79 Driva, R., Norway 62 34N 9 33E
79 Drivstua, Norway 62 26N 9 40E
71 Drnis, Yugoslavia 43 51N 16 10E
60 Drobin, Poland 52 42N 19 58E
79 Dröbak, Norway 59 39N 10 48E
46 Drogheda, Ireland 53 45N 6 20W
86 Drogichin, U.S.S.R. ...52 15N 25 8E
86 Drogobych, U.S.S.R. .49 20N 23 30E
45 Droichead Nua, Ire. ...53 11N 6 50W
34 Droitwich, Eng., U.K. 52 16N 2 10W
55 Drolshagen, Germany 51 1N 7 46E
46 Dromahair, Ireland ...54 13N 8 18W
46 Dromara, N. Ire., U.K. 54 21N 6 1W
46 Dromard, Ireland 54 14N 8 40W
51 Drôme, dépt., France .44 38N 5 15E
51 Drome R., France 44 43N 5 5E
143 Dromedary, C., Austral. 36 17S 150 10E
46 Dromod, Ireland 53 52N 7 55W
143 Dromore, Australia ...32 25S 143 55E
46 Dromore, Down, Northern Ireland, U.K. 54 24N 6 10W
46 Dromore Tyrone, Northern Ireland, U.K. 54 31N 7 28W
46 Dromore West, Ireland 54 15N 8 50W
70 Dronero, Italy 44 29N 7 22E
144 Dronfield, Australia ...21 12S 140 3E
133 Dronfield, S. Africa ...28 38S 24 46E
39 Dronfield, Eng., U.K. 53 18N 1 29W
81 Dronninglund, Den. ...57 10N 10 19E
134 Drosdy, C. Prov., S. Afr. 33 13S 19 5E
58 Drosendorf, Austria ...48 52N 15 37E
143 Drouin, Australia 38 10S 145 53E
46 Drum, Ireland 54 6N 7 9W
46 Drumbeg, N. Ire., U.K. 54 33N 6 0W
42 Drumbeg, Scot., U.K. 58 15N 5 12W
160 Drumbo, Canada 43 16N 80 35W
46 Drumcard, N. Ire., U.K. 54 14N 7 42W
46 Drumcliffe, Ireland 54 20N 8 30W
44 Drumcolliher, Ireland 52 20N 8 53W
46 Drumcondra, Ireland .53 50N 6 40W
156 Drumheller, Canada ...51 25N 112 40W
40 Drumjohn, Scot., U.K. 55 14N 4 15W
46 Drumlish, Ireland 53 50N 7 47W
166 Drummond, U.S.A. ...46 46N 113 4W
144 Drummond Ra., Austral. 23 45S 147 10E
154 Drummondville, Can. .45 55N 72 25W
40 Drummore, Scot., U.K. 54 41N 4 53W
46 Drumquin, N. Ire., U.K. 54 38N 7 30W
165 Drumright, U.S.A. 35 59N 96 38W
46 Drumshanbo, Ireland .54 2N 8 4W
46 Drumsna, Ireland 53 57N 8 0W
55 Drunen, Netherlands .51 41N 5 8E
86 Druskieniki, U.S.S.R. 54 3N 23 58E
86 Drut R., U.S.S.R. 52 32N 30 0E
86 Druya, U.S.S.R. 55 45N 27 15E
71 Drvar, Yugoslavia 44 21N 16 2E
71 Drvenik, I., Y.-slav. .43 27N 16 3E
75 Dryanovo, Bulgaria ...42 59N 25 28E
157 Dryden, Canada 49 50N 92 50W
165 Dryden, U.S.A. 30 3N 102 3W
15 Drygalski I., Antarctica 66 0S 92 0E
37 Drygarn Fawr, Wales, United Kingdom 52 13N 3 39W
40 Drymen, Scotland, U.K. 56 4N 4 28W
143 Drysdale, Australia ...38 11S 144 32E
138 Drysdale, R., W. Austral. 15 0S 126 52E
125 Du, Ghana 10 26N 1 34W
160 Du Bois, U.S.A. 41 8N 78 46W
164 Du Quoin, U.S.A. 38 0N 89 10W
161 Duanesburg, U.S.A. ...42 45N 74 11W
144 Duaringa, Australia ...23 42S 149 42E
100 Duba, Saudi Arabia ...27 10N 35 40E
101 Dubai (Dibai), Trucial States 24 10N 55 20E
157 Dubawnt, L., Canada 63 0N 102 0W
143 Dubbo, N.S.W., Austral. 32 11S 148 35E
40 Dubh Artach, Scotland, United Kingdom 56 8N 6 40W
71 Dubica, Yugoslavia ...45 17N 16 48E
160 Dublin, Canada 43 32N 81 18W
45 Dublin, Ireland 53 20N 6 18W
163 Dublin, Ga., U.S.A. ...32 30N 83 0W
165 Dublin, Tex., U.S.A. .32 0N 98 20W
87 Dubna, U.S.S.R. 54 8N 36 52E
86 Dubno, U.S.S.R. 50 25N 25 45E
166 Dubois, U.S.A. 44 7N 112 9W
88 Dubossary, U.S.S.R. .47 15N 29 10E
89 Dubovka, U.S.S.R. 49 5N 44 50E
89 Dubovskoye, U.S.S.R. 47 28N 42 40E
105 Dubrajpur, India 23 48N 87 25E
124 Dubreka, Guinea 9 46N 13 31W
86 Dubrovitsa, U.S.S.R. .51 31N 26 35E
74 Dubrovnik, Yugoslavia 42 39N 18 6E
91 Dubrovskoye, U.S.S.R. 58 55N 111 0E
164 Dubuque, U.S.A. 42 30N 90 41W
166 Duchesne, U.S.A. 40 14N 110 22W
144 Duchess, Australia 21 20S 139 50E
132 Duchess Hill, Rhodesia 18 18S 30 11E
137 Ducie I., Pacific Ocean 24 47S 124 50W
157 Duck Lake, Canada ...52 50N 106 0W
157 Duck, Mt., Canada 51 27N 100 35W
157 Duck Mt. Prov. Park, Canada 51 45N 101 0W
35 Duddington, Eng., U.K. 52 36N 0 32W
38 Duddon R., Eng., U.K. 54 12N 3 15W
56 Duderstadt, Germany 51 30N 10 15E
91 Dudinka, U.S.S.R. 69 30N 86 0E
34 Dudley, England, U.K. 52 30N 2 5W
106 Dudna R., India 19 36N 76 20E
99 Dudo, Somali Rep. 9 20N 50 20E
62 Dueñas, Spain 41 52N 4 33W
81 Dueodde, C., Denmark 54 59N 15 6E
62 Duero, R., Spain 41 37N 4 25W
136 Duff Is., Pacific Ocean 9 0S 167 0E
55 Duffel, Belgium 51 6N 4 30E
39 Duffield, Eng., U.K. ...52 59N 1 30W
43 Dufftown, Scot., U.K. 57 26N 3 9W
71 Dugi Otok I., Y.-slav. 44 0N 15 0E
71 Dugo Selo, Yugoslavia 45 51N 16 18E
89 Duğur, Turkey 41 32N 42 43E
101 Duhak, Iran 33 20N 57 30E
56 Duisburg, Germany ...51 27N 6 42E
55 Duisdorf, Germany 50 42N 7 1E
55 Duiven, Netherlands .51 57N 6 1E
133 Duiwelskloof, S. Africa 23 42S 30 10E
127 Dukambia, Ethiopia .14 45N 37 30E
131 Dukana, Kenya 3 59N 37 20E
76 Dukat, Albania 40 16N 19 32E
157 Duke I., Alaska, U.S.A. 54 50N 131 20W
101 Dukhan, Qatar 25 25N 50 50E
86 Dukhovshchina, U.S.S.R. 55 15N 32 27E
38 Dukinfield, Eng., U.K. 53 29N 2 7W
59 Dukla, Poland 49 30N 21 35E
125 Duku, Nigeria 10 43N 10 43E
125 Duku, Nigeria 11 11N 4 55E
37 Dulas B., Wales, U.K. 52 22N 4 16W
109 Dulawan, Philippines . 7 5N 124 20E
169 Dulce, Gulf of, C. Rica 8 40N 83 20W
172 Dulce R., Argentina ...29 30S 63 0W
46 Duleek, Ireland 53 40N 6 24W
75 Dulgopol, Bulgaria 43 3N 27 22E
55 Dülken, Germany 51 15N 6 18E
55 Dulken, Germany 51 16N 6 20E
104 Dullewala, W. Pak. ...31 50N 71 25E
133 Dullstroom, S. Africa .25 24S 30 7E
56 Dülmen, Germany 51 49N 7 18E
43 Dulnain Bridge, Scotland, U.K. 57 19N 3 40W
75 Dulovo Acadanlar, Bulgaria 43 48N 27 9E
144 Dululu, Australia 23 48S 150 15E
164 Duluth, Minn., U.S.A. 46 48N 92 10W
36 Dulverton, Eng., U.K. 51 2N 3 33W
105 Dum Dum, India 22 39N 88 26E
103 Dum Duma, India 27 40N 95 40E
132 Duma, Botswana 18 48S 22 40E
109 Dumaguete, Philippines 9 17N 123 15E
108 Dumai, Indonesia 1 35N 101 20E
109 Dumaran I., Phil. 10 40N 119 55E
109 Dumaring, Indonesia . 1 46N 118 10E
165 Dumas, Ark., U.S.A. .33 52N 91 30W
165 Dumas, Okla., U.S.A. 35 50N 101 58W
79 Dumba I., Norway 61 43N 4 50E
40 Dumbarton, Scot., U.K. 55 58N 4 35W
142 Dumbleyung, Australia 33 17S 117 42E
78 Dumbraveni, Rumania 46 14N 24 34E
41 Dumfries, Co. Scot., U.K. 55 12N 3 30W
41 Dumfries, Scot., U.K. 55 4N 3 37W
105 Dumka, India 24 0N 87 22E
56 Dümmer See, Germany 52 20N 8 20E
154 Dumoine L., Canada .46 55N 77 55W
143 Dumosa, Vic., Australia 35 52S 143 6E
105 Dumraon, India 25 33N 84 8E
45 Dun Laoghaire, (Dunleary), Ireland 53 17N 6 9W
50 Dun le Palestel, Fr. ...46 18N 1 39E
49 Dun sur Auron, France 46 53N 2 33E
46 Dunaff Hd., Ireland ...55 18N 7 30W
59 Dunafoldvár, Hungary 46 50N 18 57E
59 Dunajec R., Poland ...50 12N 20 52E
59 Dunajska Streda, Cz. .48 0N 17 37E
46 Dunamanagh, Northern Ireland, U.K. 54 53N 7 20W
40 Dunans, Scot., U.K. ...56 30N 5 9W
46 Dunany Pt., Ireland .53 51N 6 15W
59 Dunapatai, Hungary .46 39N 19 4E
59 Dunaszekcso, Hungary 46 22N 18 45E
59 Dunaujvaros, Hungary 47 0N 18 57E
74 Dunav, R., Y.-slav. ...45 0N 20 21E
147 Dunback, New Zealand 42 23S 170 36E
144 Dunbar, Australia 16 0S 142 22E
41 Dunbar, Scot., U.K. ...56 0N 2 32W
40 Dunbarton, Co., Scotland, U.K. 56 4N 4 42W
43 Dunbeath, Scot., U.K. 58 15N 3 25W
41 Dunblane, Scot., U.K. 56 10N 3 58W
45 Dunboyne, Ireland 53 25N 6 30W
156 Duncan, Canada 48 45N 123 40W
167 Duncan, Ariz., U.S.A. 32 46N 109 6W
165 Duncan, Okla., U.S.A. 34 25N 98 0W
154 Duncan, L., Canada ...53 35N 77 55W
107 Duncan Pass., Ind. Oc. 11 0N 92 30E
160 Duncannon, U.S.A. ...40 23N 77 2W
43 Duncansby, Scot., U.K. 58 37N 3 3W
43 Duncansby Head, Scot., U.K. 58 39N 3 0W
34 Dunchurch, Eng., U.K. 52 21N 1 19W
45 Duncormick, Ireland .53 14N 6 40W
160 Dundalk, Canada 44 10N 80 24W
46 Dundalk, Ireland 53 55N 6 45W
46 Dundalk, B., Ireland .53 55N 6 15W
154 Dundas, Ont., Canada 43 17N 79 59W
157 Dundas I., Canada 54 30N 130 50W
138 Dundas Str., N. Terr., Australia 11 15S 131 35E

MAP
135 Dundee, Natal, S. Africa ...28 11S 30 15E
41 Dundee, Scotland, U.K. ...56 29N 3 0W
46 Dundonald, N. Ire., U.K. ...54 37N 5 50W
145 Dundoo, Australia ...27 40S 144 37E
41 Dundrennan, Scot., U.K. ...54 49N 3 56W
45 Dundrum, Ireland ...53 17N 6 15W
46 Dundrum, N. Ire., U.K. ...54 17N 5 50W
46 Dundrum B., Northern Ireland, U.K. ...54 12N 5 40W
104 Dundwara, India ...27 48N 79 9E
147 Dunedin, New Zealand ...45 50S 170 33E
134 Dunedin, S. Africa ...31 58S 22 27E
163 Dunedin, U.S.A. ...28 1N 82 45W
46 Dunfanaghy, Ireland .55 10N 7 59W
41 Dunfermline, Scot., U.K. ...56 5N 3 28W
160 Dungannon, Canada ...43 51N 81 35W
46 Dungannon, Northern Ireland, U.K. ...54 30N 6 47W
104 Dungarpur, India ...23 52N 73 45E
45 Dungarvan, Ireland ...52 6N 7 40W
45 Dungarvan Harb., Ire. ...52 5N 7 35W
111 Dungbure Range, Mts., Asia ...35 0N 90 0E
35 Dungeness, Pt., England, U.K. ...50 54N 0 59E
46 Dungiven, N. Ire., U.K. ...54 55N 6 56W
46 Dunglow, Ireland ...54 57N 8 20W
143 Dungog, Australia ...32 22S 151 40E
44 Dungourney, Ireland .51 58N 8 5W
131 Dungu, Congo ... 3 42N 28 32E
126 Dungunab, Sudan ...21 10N 37 9E
126 Dungunab, B., Sudan 21 5N 37 12E
106 Dunhinda Falls, Ceylon ... 7 5N 81 6E
144 Dunk I., Australia ...17 59S 146 14E
143 Dunkeld, Australia ...37 40S 142 22E
41 Dunkeld, Scot., U.K. .56 34N 3 36W
49 Dunkerque, France ...51 2N 2 20E
36 Dunkery Beacon, England, U.K. ...51 15N 3 37W
49 Dunkirk, see Dunkerque, France 51 2N 2 20E
160 Dunkirk, N.Y., U.S.A. 42 30N 79 18W
127 Dunkuj, Sudan ...11 15N 33 0E
127 Dunkur, Ethiopia ...11 58N 35 58E
37 Dyffryn Ceiriog, Wales, United Kingdom ...52 54N 3 17W
124 Dunkwa, Ghana ... 6 0N 1 47W
125 Dunkwa, Ghana ... 5 30N 1 0W
164 Dunlap, U.S.A. ...41 50N 95 30W
45 Dunlavin, Ireland ...53 3N 6 40W
46 Dunleer, Ireland ...53 50N 6 23W
44 Dunloe, Gap of, Ire. ...52 2N 9 40W
40 Dunlop, Scot., U.K. ...55 43N 4 32W
46 Dunloy, N. Ire., U.K. 55 1N 6 25W
44 Dunmanus B., Ireland 51 31N 9 50W
44 Dunmanway, Ireland .51 43N 9 8W
46 Dunmore, Ireland ...53 37N 8 44W
161 Dunmore, Pa., U.S.A. 41 27N 75 38W
45 Dunmore East, Ireland ...52 9N 7 0W
46 Dunmurry, N. Ire., U.K. ...54 33N 6 0W
163 Dunn, U.S.A. ...35 18N 78 36W
163 Dunnellon, U.S.A. ...29 4N 82 28W
43 Dunnet, Scot., U.K. ...58 37N 3 20W
43 Dunnet B., Scot., U.K. ...58 37N 3 23W
43 Dunnet Hd., Scot., U.K. ...58 38N 3 22W
41 Dunning, Scot., U.K. .56 18N 3 37W
164 Dunning, U.S.A. ...41 52N 100 4W
160 Dunnville, Canada ...42 57N 79 37W
143 Dunolly, Australia ...36 46S 143 44E
40 Dunoon, Scot., U.K. .55 57N 4 56W
126 Dunqul, Oasis, Egypt 23 40N 31 10E
41 Duns, Scotland, U.K. 55 47N 2 20W
41 Dunscore, Scot., U.K. 55 8N 3 48W
164 Dunseith, U.S.A. ...48 49N 100 2W
36 Dunsford, Eng., U.K. 50 41N 3 40W
45 Dunshaughlin, Ireland 53 31N 6 32W
166 Dunsmuir, U.S.A. ...41 0N 122 10W
35 Dunstable, Eng., U.K. 51 53N 0 31W
147 Dunstan Mts., N.Z. ...44 53S 169 35E
156 Dunster, Canada ...53 8N 119 50W
36 Dunster, England, U.K. ...51 11N 3 28W
34 Dunston, Eng., U.K. .52 46N 2 7W
43 Duntelchaig, L., Scotland, U.K. ...57 20N 4 18W
35 Dunton Green, England, U.K. ...51 17N 0 11E
147 Duntroon, New Zealand ...44 51S 170 40E
42 Dunvegan, Scot., U.K. ...57 26N 6 35W
42 Dunvegan Hd., Scotland, U.K. ...57 30N 6 42W
122 Dupleix, Algeria ...36 31N 1 50E
164 Dupree, U.S.A. ...45 4N 101 35W
166 Dupuyer, U.S.A. ...48 11N 112 31W
173 Duque de Caxias, Brazil ...22 45S 43 19W
160 Duquesne, Pa., U.S.A 40 22N 79 55W
98 Dura, Jordan ...31 31N 35 1E
174 Durán, Ecuador ... 2 0S 79 50W
51 Durance, R., France .44 30N 6 0E
162 Durand U.S.A. ...42 54N 83 58W
168 Durango, Mexico ...24 3N 104 39W
168 Durango, st., Mexico .25 0N 105 0W
64 Durango, Spain ...43 13N 2 40W
167 Durango, U.S.A. ...37 10N 107 50W
142 Duranillin, W. Austral. ...33 30S 116 45E
165 Durant, U.S.A. ...34 0N 96 25W
62 Duraton, R., Spain ...41 27N 4 0W
172 Durazno, Uruguay ...33 25S 56 38W
50 Durban, France ...43 0N 2 49W
135 Durban, S. Afr. ...29 49S 31 1E
63 Durcal, Spain ...37 0N 3 34W
74 Durdevác, Yugoslavia 46 2N 17 3E
56 Düren, Germany ...50 48N 6 30E
105 Durg, India ...21 15N 81 22E
105 Durgapur, India ...23 30N 87 9E
160 Durham, Canada ...44 10N 80 48W
39 Durham, Eng., U.K. .54 47N 1 34W
39 Durham, Co., Eng., U.K. ...54 42N 1 45W
163 Durham, U.S.A. ...36 0N 78 55W
145 Durham Downs, Queens., Australia .27 0S 141 49E
34 Durlstone Hd., England, U.K. ...50 35N 1 58W
74 Durmitor Mt., Y.-slav. ...43 18N 19 0E
43 Durness, Scot., U.K. .58 34N 4 45W
43 Durness, Kyle of, Scotland, U.K. ...58 35N 4 55W
144 Durrandella, Australia 24 3S 146 35E
76 Durrës, Albania ...41 19N 19 28E
145 Durrie, Australia ...25 40S 140 15E
34 Durrington, Eng., U.K. ...51 12N 1 47W
45 Durrow, Offaly, Ireland ...53 20N 7 31W
44 Durrus, Ireland ...51 37N 9 32W
44 Dursey Hd., Ireland ...51 34N 10 41W
44 Dursey I., Ireland ...51 36N 10 12W
34 Dursley, England, U.K. ...51 41N 2 21W
48 Durtal France ...47 40N 0 18W
147 D'Urville Island, N.Z. 40 50S 173 55E
161 Duryea, U.S.A. ...41 20N 75 45W
99 Dusa Mareb, Somali Rep. ... 5 40N 46 33E
90 Dushak, U.S.S.R. ...37 20N 60 10E
90 Dushanbe, U.S.S.R. ...38 40N 68 50E
126 Dùsh, Egypt ...24 35N 30 41E
89 Dusheti, U.S.S.R. ...42 0N 44 55E
56 Düsseldorf, Germany .51 15N 6 46E
60 Duszniki Zdrój, Poland ...51 26N 16 22E
152 Dutch Harb., Alaska, U.S.A. ...53 54N 166 35W
125 Dutsan Wai, Nigeria .10 50N 8 10E
160 Dutton, Canada ...42 40N 81 31W
80 Duved, Sweden ...63 24N 12 55E
74 Duvno, Yugoslavia ...43 42N 17 13E
100 Duwadami, Si. Arabia 24 35N 44 15E
75 Dve Mogili, Bulgaria .43 47N 25 55E
84 Dvina, W., U.S.S.R. .56 0N 24 0E
84 Dvina R. (N.), U.S.S.R. ...61 40N 45 30E
86 Dvinsk, see Daugavpils, U.S.S.R. ...55 33N 26 32E
71 Dvor, Yugoslavia ...45 4N 16 22E
59 Dvorce, Cz. ...49 50N 17 34E
58 Dvur Kralove, Cz., ...50 27N 15 50E
134 Dwaal, C. Prov., S. Afr. ...31 1S 24 46E
104 Dwarka, India ...22 18N 69 8E
133 Dwarsberge Mts., S. Afr. ...24 50S 26 25E
134 Dweka R., S. Africa ...32 45S 19 43E
142 Dwellingup, Australia 32 38S 115 58E
160 Dwight, Canada ...45 22N 79 0W
162 Dwight, U.S.A. ...41 5N 88 25W
135 Dwingfontein, S. Africa ...32 2S 25 50E
134 Dwyka, S. Africa ...32 59S 21 32E
87 Dyakovskoya, U.S.S.R. ...60 5N 41 12E
86 Dyatkov, U.S.S.R. ...53 40N 34 20E
144 Dyaul, I., New Guinea ... 3 0S 150 55E
43 Dyce, Scotland, U.K. .57 12N 2 11W
153 Dyer, C., Canada ...67 0N 61 0W
160 Dyer's B., Canada ...45 9N 81 24W
165 Dyersburg, U.S.A. ...36 2N 89 20W
59 Dyje R., Cz. ...48 50N 16 45E
144 Dyke Acland Bay, Papua ... 8 45S 148 45E
43 Dykehead, Scot., U.K. ...56 43N 3 0W
89 Dykh Tay, mt., U.S.S.R. ...43 5N 43 2E
35 Dymchurch, Eng., U.K. ...51 2N 1 0E
34 Dymock, Eng., U.K. .51 58N 2 27W
145 Dynevor Downs, Queensland, Austral. ...28 10S 144 20E
59 Dynów, Poland ...49 50N 22 11E
79 Dypvag, Norway ...79 40N 9 8E
82 Dyra Fd., Iceland ...65 50N 23 30W
79 Dyrnes, Norway ...63 25N 7 52E
41 Dysart, Scotland, U.K. ...56 8N 3 8W
80 Dysjön, Sweden ...62 38N 15 31E
134 Dysseldorp, S. Africa .33 31S 22 29E
75 Dyulgeri, Bulgaria ...42 18N 27 23E
89 Dzambeyty, U.S.S.R. 50 15N 52 30E
112 Dzamin Üüd, Mongolia ...43 52N 111 53E
89 Dzaudzhikau, see Ordzhonikidze, U.S.S.R. ...43 0N 44 35E
87 Dzerzhinsk, U.S.S.R. .56 15N 43 15E
90 Dzhailma, U.S.S.R. ...51 30N 61 50E
90 Dzhalal Abad, U.S.S.R. ...41 0N 73 0E
91 Dzhalinda, U.S.S.R. ...53 40N 124 0E
91 Dzhelinde, U.S.S.R. ...70 0N 114 20E
90 Dzhambul, U.S.S.R. ...43 10N 71 0E
88 Dzhankoi, U.S.S.R. ...45 40N 34 30E
89 Dzhanybek, U.S.S.R. .49 25N 46 50E
86 Dzerzhinsk, U.S.S.R. .53 48N 27 19E
90 Dzhetygara, U.S.S.R. 52 10N 61 0E
90 Dzhezkazgan, U.S.S.R. ...47 10N 67 40E
90 Dzhizak, U.S.S.R. ...40 20N 68 0E
91 Dzhugdzhur Ra., U.S.S.R. ...57 30N 138 0E
60 Dzialdowo, Poland ...53 15N 20 15E
60 Dziatoszyce, Poland ...50 22N 20 20E
60 Dziatoszyn, Poland ...51 6N 18 50E
60 Dzierzgon, Poland ...53 58N 19 20E
60 Dzierzoniow, Poland .50 45N 16 39E
123 Dzioua, Algeria ...33 14N 5 14E
111 Dzungaria, reg., China 44 10N 88 0E
112 Dzuunbulag, Mongolia 46 58N 115 30E
112 Dzuunmod, Mongolia .47 45N 106 58E

E

154 Eabamet, L., Canada .51 30N 88 0W
164 Eads, U.S.A. ...38 30N 102 46W
152 Eagle, Alaska, U.S.A. 64 44N 141 29W
166 Eagle, U.S.A. ...39 45N 106 55W
155 Eagle, L., U.S.A. ...46 10N 69 20W
166 Eagle L., Calif., U.S.A. ...40 35N 120 50W
155 Eagle L., Me., U.S.A. .46 23N 69 22W
164 Eagle Butt, U.S.A. ...45 1N 101 12W
164 Eagle Grove, U.S.A. ...42 37N 93 53W
165 Eagle Lake, U.S.A. ...29 35N 96 21W
167 Eagle Nest, U.S.A. ...36 33N 105 13W
165 Eagle Pass, U.S.A. ...28 45N 100 35W
164 Eagle River, U.S.A. ...45 55N 89 17W
143 Eaglehawk, Australia .36 43S 144 16E
145 Eaglehawk Neck, Tas., Australia ...43 0S 147 58E
41 Eaglesfield, Scot., U.K. ...55 3N 3 12W
40 Eaglesham, Scot., U.K. ...55 44N 4 18W
39 Eakring, Eng., U.K. .53 9N 0 59W
35 Ealing, Eng., U.K. 51 30N 0 19W
142 Earaheedy, W. Austral. ...25 30S 121 35E
38 Earby, England, U.K. 53 55N 2 8W
37 Eardisland, Eng., U.K. ...52 14N 2 50W
34 Eardisley, Eng., U.K. 52 8N 3 0W
157 Earl Grey, Canada ...50 57N 104 43W
34 Earl Shilton, Eng., UK. ...52 35N 1 20W
35 Earl Soham, Eng., U.K. ...52 14N 1 15E
165 Earle, U.S.A. ...35 18N 90 26W
167 Earlimart, U.S.A. ...35 57N 119 14W
35 Earls Barton, Eng., U.K. ...52 16N 0 44W
35 Earl's Colne, Eng., U.K. ...51 56N 0 43E
41 Earlsferry, Scot., U.K. ...56 11N 2 50W
41 Earlston, Scot., U.K. .55 39N 2 40W
41 Earn, R., Scot., U.K. .56 20N 3 40W
147 Earnslaw, Mt., N.Z. ...44 32S 168 27E
142 Earoo, W. Australia ...29 30S 118 10E
39 Earsdon, Eng., U.K. .55 4N 1 30W
165 Earth, U.S.A. ...34 18N 102 30W
35 Easebourne, Eng., U.K. ...51 0N 0 42W
39 Easington, Durham, England, U.K. ...54 50N 1 24W
39 Easington, Yorks., England, U.K. ...54 32N 0 50W
41 Easington Colliery, England, U.K. ...54 49N 1 19W
39 Easingwold, Eng., U.K. ...54 8N 1 11W
46 Easky, Ireland ...54 17N 8 58W
163 Easley, U.S.A. ...34 52N 82 35W
165 East, B., U.S.A. ...29 2N 89 16W
146 East C., New Zealand 37 42S 178 35E
142 East, Mt., W. Australia ...29 0S 122 30E
155 East P., Canada ...46 39N 61 24W
37 East Aberthaw, Wales, United Kingdom ...51 23N 3 23W
35 East Anglian Hts., England, U.K. ...52 10N 0 17E
155 East Angus, Canada ...45 30N 71 40W
160 East Aurora, U.S.A. ...42 46N 78 38W
35 East Barming, England, United Kingdom ...51 15N 0 29E
155 East Bathurst, Canada ...47 35N 65 40W
103 East Bengal, E. Pak. .23 0N 90 0E
36 East Bergholt, England, U.K. ...51 58N 1 2E
160 East Brady, U.S.A. ...40 59N 79 36W
36 East Brent, Eng., U.K. ...51 14N 2 55W
162 East Chicago, U.S.A. .41 40N 87 30W
113 East China Sea, Asia .30 5N 126 0E
156 East Coulee, Canada .51 23N 112 27W
34 East Cowes, Eng., U.K. ...50 45N 1 17W
35 East Dereham, England, United Kingdom ...52 40N 0 57E
176 East Falkland, Falk. Is. ...51 30S 58 30W
155 East Florenceville, Can. ...46 26N 67 36W
56 East Frisian Is., Ger. .53 45N 7 15E
164 East Grand Forks, U.S.A. ...47 55N 97 5W
161 East Greenwich, U.S.A. ...41 39N 71 27W
35 East Grinstead, Eng., U.K. ...51 8N 0 1W
35 East Harling, Eng., U.K. ...52 26N 0 55E
161 East Hartford, U.S.A. 41 45N 72 39W
166 East Helena, U.S.A. ...46 37N 111 58W
16 East Ilsley, Eng., U.K. ...51 33N 1 15W
108 East Indies, Asia ... 0 0 120 0E
162 East Jordan, U.S.A. ...45 10N 85 7W
39 East Kirby, Eng., U.K. ...53 5N 1 15W
162 East Lansing, U.S.A. .42 44N 84 37W
41 East Linton, Scot., U.K. ...56 0N 2 40W
160 East Liverpool, U.S.A. ...40 39N 80 35W
135 East London, S. Africa ...33 0S 27 55E
36 East Looe, Eng., U.K. 50 22N 4 28W
41 East Lothian, co., Scotland, U.K. ...56 0N 2 40W
143 East Lynne, Australia 35 10S 150 16E
155 East Main (Eastmain), Canada 52 20N 78 30W
39 East Markham, England, U.K. ...53 16N 0 53W
131 East Mengo, dist., Uganda ... 1 0N 32 25E
161 East Orange, U.S.A. .40 45N 74 15W
103 East Pakistan, st., see Bangladesh ...24 0N 90 0E
160 East Palestine, U.S.A. 40 50N 80 32W
156 East Pine, Canada ...55 48N 120 5W
163 East Point, U.S.A. ...33 40N 84 28W
161 East Providence, U.S.A. ...41 48N 71 22W
39 East Retford, Eng., U.K. ...53 19N 0 55W
39 East Riding, co. Yorks., England, U.K. ...53 55N 0 35W
164 East St. Louis, U.S.A. ...38 36N 90 10W
54 East Schelde R., Neth. ...51 38N 3 40E
91 E. Siberian Sea, U.S.S.R. ...73 0N 160 0E
161 E. Stroudsburg, U.S.A. ...41 1N 75 11W
162 East Tawas, U.S.A. ...44 17N 83 31W
145 East Toorale, Australia ...30 27S 145 28E
41 East Wemyss, Scotland, United Kingdom ...56 8N 3 5W
34 East Woodhay, England, U.K. ...51 21N 1 26W
146 Eastbourne, N.Z. ...41 19S 174 55E
35 Eastbourne, Eng., U.K. ...50 46N 0 18E
35 Eastchurch, Eng., U.K. ...51 23N 0 53E
157 Eastend, Canada ...49 32N 108 50W
137 Easter Islands, Chile, Pacific Ocean ...27 0S 109 0W
43 Easter Ross, dist., Scotland, U.K. ...57 50N 4 35W
106 Eastern Ghats, mts., India ...15 0N 80 0E
91 Eastern Sayan Mts., U.S.S.R. ...54 0N 96 0E
157 Easterville, Canada ...53 8N 99 40W
161 Easthampton, U.S.A. .42 15N 72 41W
165 Eastland, U.S.A. ...32 26N 98 45W
34 Eastleigh, Eng., U.K. 50 58N 1 21W
154 Eastmain (East Main), Canada ...52 20N 78 30W
154 Eastmain R., Canada .52 27N 72 26W
161 Eastman, Canada ...45 18N 72 19W
163 Eastman, U.S.A. ...32 13N 83 41W
34 Eastnor, Eng., U.K. ...52 2N 2 22W
36 Easton, Dorset, England, U.K. ...50 32N 2 27W
35 Easton, Northants, England, U.K. ...52 37N 0 31W
36 Easton, Somerset, England, U.K. ...51 28N 2 42W
162 Easton, Md., U.S.A. ...38 47N 76 7W
161 Easton, Pa., U.S.A. ...40 41N 75 15W
166 Easton, Wash., U.S.A. 47 14N 121 8W
135 Eastpoort, S. Africa ...32 38S 25 54E
155 Eastport, Me., U.S.A. 44 57N 67 0W
35 Eastry, England, U.K. ...51 15N 1 19E
154 Eastview, Canada ...45 27N 75 40W
39 Eastwood, Eng., U.K. 53 2N 1 17W
35 Eaton, England, U.K. ...52 52N 0 46W
164 Eaton, U.S.A. ...40 35N 104 42W
35 Eaton Socon, England, U.K. ...52 13N 0 18W
57 Eatonia, Canada ...51 20N 109 25W
163 Eatonton, U.S.A. ...33 22N 83 24W
163 Eau Claire, S.C., U.S.A. ...34 5N 81 2W
164 Eau Claire, Wis., U.S.A. ...44 46N 91 30W
50 Eauze, France ...43 53N 0 7E
42 Eaval, Mt., Scot., U.K. ...57 33N 7 12W
144 Ebagoola, Australia ...14 15S 143 12E
98 Ebal Mt., Jordan ...32 15N 35 15E
125 Eban, Nigeria ... 9 40N 4 50E
55 Ebbe Gebirge, Germany ...51 9N 7 50E
39 Ebberston, Eng., U.K. ...54 14N 0 35W
34 Ebbw Vale, Eng., U.K. ...51 47N 3 12W
123 Ebeggui, Algeria ...26 2N 6 0E
160 Ebensburg, U.S.A. ...40 29N 78 43W
58 Ebensee, Austria ...47 48N 13 46E
57 Eberbach, Germany ...49 27N 8 59E
56 Eberswalde, Germany 52 49N 13 50E
57 Ebingen, Germany ...43 13N 9 1E
130 Ebola R., Congo ... 3 35N 22 0E
73 Eboli, Italy ...40 39N 15 2E
125 Ebolowa, Cameroon ... 2 55N 11 10E
124 Ebrié, Lagune, Ivory C. ... 5 12N 4 40W
64 Ebro, R., Spain ...41 49N 1 5W
56 Ebstorf, Germany ...53 2N 10 23E
41 Ecclefechan, Scot., U.K. ...55 3N 3 18W
38 Eccles, England, U.K. 53 29N 2 20W
34 Eccleshall, Eng., U.K. 52 52N 2 14W
76 Eceabat, Turkey ...40 11N 26 21E
48 Eceuillé, France ...47 10N 1 19E
122 Ech Chebbi, Algeria ...26 41N 0 29E
135 Echaneni, Natal, S. Afr. ...27 33S 32 6E
89 Echmiadzin, U.S.S.R. 40 12N 44 19E
154 Echo Bay, Canada ...46 29N 84 4W
55 Echt, Netherlands ...51 7N 5 52E
43 Echt, Scotland, U.K. .57 8N 2 26W
54 Echternach, Lux. ...49 49N 6 3E
143 Echuca, Australia ...36 3S 144 46E
63 Ecija, Spain ...37 30N 5 10W
40 Eck L., Scot., U.K. ...56 5N 5 0W
55 Eckenhagen, Germany 50 59N 7 42E
56 Eckernförde, Germany ...54 26N 9 50E
39 Eckington, Eng., U.K. ...53 19N 1 21W
160 Ecorse, U.S.A. ...42 14N 83 10W
49 Ecos, France ...49 9N 1 35E
48 Ecouché, France ...48 42N 0 10W
174 Ecuador, Rep., S. Amer. ... 2 0S 78 0W
80 Ed, Sweden ...58 55N 11 55E
126 Ed Dabbura, Sudan ...17 40N 34 15E
126 Ed Damer, Sudan ...17 27N 34 0E
126 Ed Debba, Sudan ...18 0N 30 51E
127 Ed Deim, Sudan ...10 10N 28 20E
127 Ed Dueim, Sudan ...14 0N 32 10E
103 Ed Dzong, Tibet, China ...32 11N 90 12E
142 Edah, W. Australia ...28 12S 117 0E
54 Edam, Netherlands ...52 31N 5 3E
106 Edapally, India ...11 19N 78 3E
43 Eday, I., Orkney, Scotland, U.K. ...59 11N 2 47W
43 Eday Sd., Scot., U.K. 59 12N 2 45W
127 Edd, Ethiopia ...14 0N 41 30E
127 Eddaga Hamus, Ethiopia ...14 13N 39 35E
43 Edderton, Scot., U.K. 57 50N 4 10W
42 Eddrachillis B., Scotland, U.K. ...58 16N 5 10W
36 Eddystone, Eng., U.K. ...50 11N 4 16W
54 Ede, Netherlands ...52 4N 5 40E
125 Ede, Nigeria ... 7 45N 4 29E
80 Ede, Sweden ...62 10N 16 50E
125 Edea, Cameroon ... 3 51N 10 9E
157 Edehon L., Canada ...60 25N 97 5W
123 Edekel, Adrar, Algeria 23 56N 6 47E
38 Edel Land, W. Australia ...26 55S 114 0E
46 Eden, N. Ire., U.K. ...54 44N 5 47W
143 Eden, N.S.W., Austral. ...37 3S 149 55E
160 Eden, N.Y., U.S.A. ...42 39N 78 55W
165 Eden, Tex., U.S.A. ...31 16N 99 50W
166 Eden, Wyo., U.S.A. ...42 2N 109 27W
38 Eden, R., Eng., U.K. .54 32N 2 25W
35 Edenbridge, Eng., U.K. ...51 12N 0 4E
135 Edenburg, S. Africa ...29 43S 25 58E
133 Edenburg, Trans., S. Afr. ...26 1S 28 3E
147 Edendale, N.Z. ...46 19S 168 48E
45 Edenderry, Ireland ...53 21N 7 3W
143 Edenhope, Australia .37 4S 141 19E
163 Edenton, U.S.A. ...36 5N 76 36W
145 Edeowie, S. Australia 31 26S 138 23E
46 Ederny, N. Ire., U.K. 54 32N 7 40W
164 Edgar, U.S.A. ...40 25N 98 0W
161 Edgartown, U.S.A. ...41 22N 70 28W
34 Edge Hill, Eng., U.K. 52 7N 1 28W
14 Edge I., Spitsbergen .77 40N 23 0E
146 Edgecumbe, N.Z. ...37 59S 176 47E
163 Edgefield, U.S.A. ...33 43N 81 59W
164 Edgeley, U.S.A. ...46 27N 98 41W
164 Edgemont, U.S.A. ...43 15N 103 53W
160 Edgington, Canada ...45 24N 79 46W
76 Edhessa, Greece ...40 48N 22 5E
147 Edievale, N.Z. ...45 49S 169 22E
123 Edimpi, Chad ...21 4N 17 18E
124 Edina, Liberia ... 6 0N 10 19W
164 Edina, U.S.A. ...40 6N 92 10W
165 Edinburg, U.S.A. ...26 22N 98 10W
41 Edinburgh, Scot., U.K. ...55 57N 3 12W
54 Edingen, Belgium ...50 37N 4 2E
34 Edington, Eng., U.K. 51 17N 2 6W
75 Edirne, Turkey ...41 40N 26 45E
123 Edjeleh, Algeria ...28 25N 9 40E
161 Edmeston, U.S.A. ...42 42N 75 15W
165 Edmond, U.S.A. ...35 37N 97 30W
38 Edmondbyers, England, United Kingdom ...54 50N 1 59W

MAP
166 Edmonds, U.S.A. 47 47N 122 11w
144 Edmonton, Australia .16 55S 145 45E
156 Edmonton, Canada ...53 30N 113 30w
155 Edmundston, Canada 47 23N 68 20w
165 Edna, U.S.A. 29 0N 96 40w
156 Edna Bay, Alaska, U.S.A. 55 55N 133 40w
70 Edolo, Italy 46 10N 10 21E
100 Edremit, Turkey 39 40N 27 0E
80 Edsbyn, Sweden 61 22N 15 45E
15 Edsel Ford Ra., Antarc. 77 0S 143 0w
80 Edsele, Sweden 63 23N 116 30E
156 Edson, Canada 53 40N 16 28w
172 Eduardo Castex, Arg. 35 50S 64 25w
15 Edward VII Pen., Antarctica 80 0S 160 0w
131 Edward, L., Africa 0 25S 29 40E
143 Edward R., Australia 35 15S 144 28E
165 Edwards Plat., U.S.A. 30 30N 101 5w
161 Edwardsville, U.S.A. .41 15N 75 56w
43 Edzell, Scotland, U.K. 56 49N 2 40w
54 Eekloo, Belgium 51 11N 3 33E
134 Eendekuil, S. Africa ..32 41S 18 51E
135 Eensgevonden, S. Afr. 28 35S 26 36E
133 Eersbewoond, S. Africa 24 48S 28 25E
58 Eferding, Austria 48 18N 14 1E
123 Eferi, Algeria 24 30N 9 28E
162 Effingham, U.S.A. 39 8N 88 30w
125 Effiums, Nigeria 6 35N 8 0E
125 Efiduasi, Ghana 6 45N 1 25w
64 Ega, R., Spain 42 32N 1 58w
72 Egadi Is., Italy 37 55N 12 10E
154 Eganville, Canada 45 32N 77 5w
164 Egeland, U.S.A. 48 42N 99 6w
59 Eger, Hungary 47 53N 20 27E
59 Eger R., Hungary 47 43N 20 32E
142 Egerton, Mt., W. Austral. 24 42S 117 44E
157 Egg L., Canada 54 30N 73 0w
58 Eggenburg, Lr. Aus. .48 38N 15 50E
35 Egham, England, U.K. 51 25N 0 33w
55 Eghezee, Belgium 50 35N 4 55E
43 Egilsay I., Scot., U.K. 59 10N 2 56w
130 Egito, Angola 12 0S 13 50E
50 Egletons, France 45 24N 2 3E
146 Egmont, C., N.Z. 39 16S 173 45E
146 Egmont, Mt., N.Z. 39 17S 174 5E
127 Egogi Bad, Ethiopia .13 10N 41 30E
38 Egremont, Eng., U.K. 54 28N 3 33w
100 Egridir, Turkey 37 53N 30 50E
39 Egton, England, U.K. 54 27N 0 45w
81 Egtved, Denmark 55 38N 9 20E
174 Egua, Colombia 5 5N 68 0w
121 Eguel Timmi, Chad ...15 35N 16 25E
125 Egume, Nigeria 7 30N 7 14E
50 Eguzon, France 46 27N 1 33E
59 Egyek, Hungary 47 39N 20 52E
126 Egypt, U.A.R., Africa 28 0N 31 0E
125 Eha Amufu, Nigeria ... 6 30N 7 40E
38 Ehen R., Eng., U.K. 54 25N 3 31w
123 Ehi Sunni, Chad 20 47N 17 19E
123 Ehi Timmi, Chad 21 10N 16 19E
114 Ehime, pref., Japan ...33 30N 132 40E
57 Ehingen, Germany 48 16N 9 43E
58 Ehrwald, Austria 47 24N 10 56E
57 Eichstatt, Germany ...48 53N 11 12E
79 Eidanger, Norway 59 7N 9 43E
79 Eide, Norway 60 29N 6 45E
56 Eider R., Germany 54 15N 8 50E
79 Eidsberg, Norway 59 32N 11 12E
79 Eidsfoss, Norway 59 36N 10 2E
145 Eidsvold, Australia ...25 25S 151 12E
57 Eifel Mts., Germany ...50 10N 6 45E
132 Eiffel Flats, Rhodesia 18 20S 30 0E
79 Eigersund, Norway ...58 26N 5 59E
142 Eigg, I., Scot., U.K. ...56 54N 6 10w
42 Eigg, Sd. of, Scot., U.K. 56 52N 6 15w
138 Eighty Mile Beach, Western Australia .19 30S 120 40E
99 Eil, Somali Rep. 8 0N 49 50E
42 Eil, L., Scotland, U.K. 56 50N 5 15w
100 Eilat, Israel 29 30N 34 56E
143 Eildon, L., Australia .37 10S 146 0E
56 Eilenburg, Germany ...51 28N 12 38E
55 Eilendorf, Germany ...50 46N 6 10E
98 Ein Arik, Jordan 31 54N 35 8E
127 Ein el Luweiqa, Sudan 14 5N 33 50E
98 Ein Harod, Israel 32 33N 35 22E
98 Ein Kerem, Israel 31 47N 35 6E
144 Einasleigh, Australia .18 32S 144 5E
144 Einasleigh R., Austral. 17 33S 143 0E
56 Einbeck, Germany 51 48N 9 50E
54 Eindhoven, Netherlands 51 26N 5 30E
57 Einsiedeln, Switzerland 47 7N 8 46E
174 Eirunepé, Brazil 6 35S 70 0w
56 Eisenach, Germany ...50 58N 10 18E
56 Eisenberg, Germany ...50 59N 11 50E
58 Eisenerz, Austria 47 32N 15 54E
56 Eisenhuttenstadt, East Germany 52 9N 14 41E
58 Eisenkappel, Austria .46 29N 14 36E
59 Eisenstadt, Austria ...47 51N 16 31E
54 Eiserfeld, Germany ...50 50N 8 0E
57 Eisfeld, Germany 50 25N 10 54E
42 Eishort, L., Scot., U.K. 57 9N 6 0w
56 Eisleben, Germany 51 31N 11 31E
55 Eitorf, Germany 50 46N 7 28E
98 Eizariya (Bethany), Jordan 31 47N 35 15E
MAP
81 Ejby, Denmark 55 25N 9 56E
64 Ejea de los Caballeros, Spain 42 7N 1 9w
125 Ejura, Ghana 7 25N 1 25E
164 Ekalaka, U.S.A. 45 55N 104 30E
130 Ekéia, R., Cent. Africa 2 20N 16 10w
81 Ekeryd, Sweden 57 37N 14 6E
125 Eket, Nigeria 4 38N 7 56w
146 Eketahuna, N.Z. 40 38S 175 43E
76 Ekhinos, Greece 41 16N 25 1w
91 Ekimchan, U.S.S.R. ...53 0N 133 0w
132 Ekohlo, Malawi 12 2S 33 30E
80 Ekoln, I., Sweden 59 45N 17 40E
55 Eksel, Belgium 51 9N 5 24E
81 Eksjö, Sweden 57 37N 15 0w
154 Ekwan R., Canada 53 30N 84 0w
132 Ekwendeni, Mal. 11 29S 33 49E
120 El Aaiun, tn. & dist., Span. Sahara 27 0N 12 0w
172 El Abanico, Chile 37 25S 71 38E
122 El Abiodh, Algeria 32 56N 0 42E
122 El Ahmar, Morocco 31 59N 2 11E
122 El Aioun, Morocco 34 33N 2 30w
126 El 'Aiyât, Egypt 29 36N 31 15E
126 El 'Alamein, Egypt .30 48N 28 58E
63 El Arahal, Spain 37 15N 5 33w
126 El Araq, Egypt 28 40N 26 20E
122 El Arba, Algeria 36 28N 3 12E
122 El Arba du Rharb, Mor. 34 50N 5 59w
123 El Arfiane, Algeria 33 46N 5 59E
122 El Aricha, Algeria 34 9N 1 10w
126 El Arish, Egypt 31 8N 33 50E
123 El Arnaud, Algeria 36 7N 5 49E
123 El Arrouch, Algeria ...36 37N 6 53E
122 El Asnam, Algeria 36 30N 1 30E
168 El Azucar Reser., Mex.26 0N 99 5w
126 El Badâri, Egypt 27 4N 31 25E
126 El Bahrein, Egypt 28 30N 26 25E
126 El Bâllas, Egypt 26 2N 32 43E
126 El Balyana, Egypt 26 10N 32 3E
174 El Banco, Colombia ... 9 0N 74 0w
126 El Bageir, Sudan 18 40N 5 15w
62 El Barco de Avila, Sp. 40 21N 5 31w
62 El Barco de Waldeorras, Spain .42 23N 7 0w
126 El Baqa, Sudan 18 18N 33 52E
126 El Bawiti, Egypt 28 25N 28 45E
122 El Bayadh, Algeria ...33 40N 1 1E
122 El Biodh, Mauritania .26 0N 6 32w
96 El Bira, Jordan 31 55N 35 12E
65 El Bonillo, Spain 38 57N 2 35w
98 El Buqei'a, Jordan 32 15N 35 30E
167 El Cajon, U.S.A. 32 49N 117 0w
174 El Callao, Venezuela . 7 21N 61 49w
165 El Campo, U.S.A. 29 10N 96 20w
63 El Castillo, Spain 37 41N 6 19w
167 El Centro, U.S.A. 32 50N 115 40w
174 El Cerro, Bolivia 17 30S 61 40w
63 El Cerro, Spain 37 45N 6 57w
176 El Chorro, Argentina .23 5S 62 10w
63 El Coronil, Spain 37 5N 5 38w
176 El Cuy, Argentina 39 55S 68 25w
168 El Cuyo, Mexico 21 30N 87 40E
126 El Dab'a, Egypt 31 0N 28 27E
126 El Deir, Egypt 25 25N 32 20E
99 El Dere, Somali Rep. . 3 50N 47 8E
168 El Diaz, Mexico 20 40N 87 20w
123 El Djem, Tunisia 35 17N 10 54E
124 El Djouf, Mauritania .20 0N 11 30E
165 El Dorado, Ark., U.S.A. 33 10N 92 40w
165 El Dorado, Kan., U.S.A. 37 55N 96 56w
174 El Dorado, Venezuela 6 44N 61 38w
165 El Dorado Springs, U.S.A. 37 54N 93 59w
122 El Eglab, Algeria 26 20N 4 30w
174 El Encanto, Colombia 1 30S 73 15w
122 El Ethel, W., Algeria .28 31N 3 37w
126 El Faiyûm, Egypt 29 19N 30 50E
127 El Fasher, Sudan 13 33N 25 26E
126 El Fashn, Egypt 28 50N 30 54E
62 El Ferrol, Spain 43 29N 3 14w
127 El Fifi, Sudan 10 4N 25 0E
168 El Fuerte, Mexico 26 30N 108 40w
99 El Gal, Somali Rep. 10 58N 50 20E
127 El Gebir, Sudan 13 40N 29 40E
126 El Gedida, Egypt 25 40N 28 30E
121 El Geneina, Sudan 13 27N 22 45E
127 El Geteina, Sudan 14 50N 32 27E
127 El Gezira, Sudan 14 0N 33 0E
126 El Giza, Egypt 30 0N 31 10E
122 El Golea, Oasis, Alg. .30 30N 2 50E
174 El Guapo, Venezuela .10 20N 65 55w
127 El Hagiz, Sudan 15 15N 35 50E
126 El Haql, Saudi Arabia 29 15N 34 59E
122 El Hajeb, Morocco 33 37N 5 30w
123 El Hamma, Tunisia ...33 56N 9 58E
126 El Hammâm, Egypt .30 52N 29 25E
122 El Hank, Algeria 25 38N 5 29w
122 El Hank, Mauritania .24 37N 7 0w
122 El Harrach, Algeria ...36 45N 3 5E
127 El Hawata, Sudan 13 25N 34 42E
99 El Hur, Somali Rep. . 5 4N 48 12E
126 El Idisât, Egypt 25 30N 32 35E
122 El Jadida (Mazagan), Morocco 33 11N 8 17w
122 El Jorf Lasfar, Mor. ...33 5N 8 54w
126 El Kab, Sudan 19 27N 32 46E
123 El Kala, Algeria 36 50N 8 30E
127 El Kamlin, Sudan 15 3N 33 11E
123 El Kantara, Algeria 35 14N 5 45E
123 El Kantara, Tunisia ...33 45N 10 58E
126 El Karaba, Sudan 18 32N 33 41E
122 El Kelâa, Morocco 32 4N 7 27w
126 El Khandaq, Sudan ...18 30N 30 30E
126 El Khârga, oasis, Egypt 25 30N 30 33E
MAP
122 El Khemis Imouzer, Morocco 30 51N 9 26w
123 El Khroub, Algeria ...36 10N 6 55E
126 El Khureiba, Si. Arab. 28 3N 35 10E
123 El Kseur, Algeria 36 46N 4 49E
126 El Kuntilla, Egypt 30 1N 34 45E
100 El Ladhiqiya, Syria ...35 20N 35 30E
126 El Laqeita, Egypt 25 50N 33 15E
126 El Leiya, Sudan 16 15N 35 28E
126 El Maghra, Bir, Egypt 30 18N 28 54E
126 El Mahalla (el Kubra), Egypt 31 0N 31 0E
126 El Mahâriq, Egypt 25 35N 30 35E
122 El Mahiridja, Morocco 33 59N 3 7w
122 El Maiz, Algeria 28 19N 0 9w
126 El-Maks el-Bahari, Eg. 24 30N 30 40E
126 El Manshâh, Egypt ...26 26N 31 50E
122 El Mansour, Algeria ...27 47N 0 14w
126 El Mansura, Egypt 31 0N 31 19E
126 El Manzala, Egypt 31 10N 31 50E
126 El Marâgha, Egypt ...26 35N 31 10E
127 El Masid, Sudan 15 15N 33 0E
126 El Matariya, Egypt ...31 15N 32 0E
123 El Melfa, Libya 31 58N 15 18E
123 El Mengoub, Algeria .33 59N 4 48E
122 El Meraguen, Algeria .28 0N 0 7w
127 El Metemma, Sudan .16 50N 33 10E
122 El Milheas, Mauritania 25 27N 6 57w
123 El Milia, Algeria 36 51N 6 13E
126 El Minya, Egypt 28 7N 30 33E
64 El Molar, Spain 40 42N 3 45w
127 El Obeid, Sudan 13 8N 30 10E
168 El Oro, Mexico, see Sta. Maria del Oro .25 50N 105 20w
123 El Oued, Algeria 33 20N 6 58E
125 El Ouiz, Mali 19 28N 0 24E
122 El Ousseukr, Algeria .34 50N 1 37E
168 El Palmito Res., Mexico 25 40N 105 3w
62 El Pardo, Spain 40 31N 3 47w
167 El Paso, Tex., U.S.A. 31 50N 106 30w
64 El Pedernoso, Spain ...39 29N 2 45w
63 El Pedroso, Spain 37 51N 5 45w
64 El Pobo de Dueñas, Sp. 40 46N 1 39w
167 El Portal, U.S.A. 37 44N 119 49w
168 El Progreso, Honduras 15 26N 87 51w
65 El Provencio, Spain ...39 23N 2 35w
168 El Pueblito, Mexico ...29 3N 105 4w
126 El Qantara, Egypt 30 51N 32 20E
126 El Qasr, Egypt 25 44N 28 42E
127 El Qubba, Sudan 11 10N 27 5E
84 El Qurna, Egypt 25 45N 32 38E
126 El Quseima, Egypt 30 40N 34 15E
126 El Qusîya, Egypt 27 29N 30 44E
126 El Râshda, Egypt 25 36N 28 57E
126 El Reis, Egypt 27 50N 28 40E
165 El Reno, U.S.A. 35 30N 98 0w
122 El Rheauya, Mauritania 25 52N 6 30w
126 El Ridisîya, Egypt 24 56N 32 51E
63 El Ronquillo, Spain ...37 44N 6 10w
63 El Rubio, Spain 37 22N 5 0w
126 El Saff, Egypt 29 34N 31 16E
169 El Sauce, Nicaragua ...13 0N 86 40w
126 El Shallal, Egypt 24 0N 32 53E
126 El Thamad, Egypt 29 40N 34 28E
174 El Tigre, Venezuela ... 8 55N 64 15w
174 El Tocuyo, Venezuela 9 47N 69 48w
172 El Tofo, Chile 29 22S 71 18w
126 El Tûr, Egypt 28 14N 33 36E
176 El Turbio Mines, Arg. 51 30S 72 40w
64 El Vado, Spain 41 2N 3 18w
174 El Vigia, Venezuela ... 8 38N 71 39w
131 El Wak, Kenya 2 49N 40 56E
131 El Wak, Somali Rep. . 2 48N 40 55E
126 El Waqf, Egypt 25 45N 32 15E
126 El Wâsta, Egypt 29 19N 31 12E
127 El Weguet, Ethiopia . 5 28N 42 17E
172 El Zapallar, Argentina 26 29S 59 24w
127 Ela, Ethiopia 12 50N 42 20E
131 Ela, Kenya 1 20S 40 45E
77 Elafonisos I., Greece .36 29N 22 56E
143 Elaine, Vic., Australia 37 44S 144 2E
106 Elamanchili, see Yellamanchilli, India 17 26N 82 50E
37 Elan Village, Wales, United Kingdom 52 18N 3 34w
37 Elan R., Wales, U.K. 52 17N 3 40w
133 Elands R., S. Africa .24 15S 29 5E
133 Elands R., S. Africa ...25 10S 29 10E
134 Elandsberg, S. Africa .32 17S 21 0E
135 Elandsdrif, S. Africa .32 12S 25 57E
133 Elandshoek, S. Africa 25 30S 30 41E
135 Elandskop, S. Africa .29 43S 30 6E
135 Elandslaagte, S. Africa 28 25S 29 50E
134 Elandsvlei, S. Africa .32 19S 19 31E
77 Elassa, I., Greece 35 18N 26 21E
76 Elassón, Greece 39 53N 22 12E
109 Elat, Indonesia 5 40S 133 5E
77 Elátia, Greece 38 37N 22 46E
100 Elâziğ, Turkey 38 37N 39 22E
70 Elba I., Italy 42 48N 10 15E
163 Elba, U.S.A. 31 27N 86 4w
76 Elbasan, Albania 41 9N 20 9E
76 Elbasan-Berat, pref., Albania 40 58N 20 0E
56 Elbe R., Germany 53 25N 10 7E
67 Elbert, Mt., Colo., U.S.A. 39 12N 106 36w
162 Elberta, U.S.A. 44 35N 86 14w
163 Elberton, U.S.A. 34 7N 82 51w
48 Elbeuf, France 49 17N 1 2E
MAP
60 Elblag (Elbing), Poland 54 10N 19 25E
89 Elbrus, Mt., U.S.S.R. .43 30N 42 30E
54 Elburg, Netherlands ...52 26N 5 50E
101 Elburz Mts., Iran 36 0N 52 0E
65 Elche, Spain 38 15N 0 42w
65 Elche de la Sierra, Sp. 38 27N 2 3w
65 Elda, Spain 38 29N 0 47w
131 Eldama Ravine, Kenya 0 3N 35 43E
106 Eldon, Iowa, U.S.A. ...40 50N 92 12w
164 Eldon, Mo., U.S.A. 38 20N 92 38w
164 Eldora, U.S.A. 42 20N 93 5w
173 Eldorado, Argentina .26 28S 54 43w
106 Eldorado, Ont., Canada 44 40N 77 32w
157 Eldorado, Sask., Can. 59 35N 108 30w
168 Eldorado, Mexico 24 0N 107 30w
162 Eldorado, Ill., U.S.A. .37 50N 88 25w
165 Eldorado, Tex., U.S.A. 30 52N 100 35w
131 Eldoret, Kenya 0 30N 35 17E
160 Eldred, U.S.A. 41 57N 78 24w
165 Electra, U.S.A. 34 0N 99 0w
132 Elefantes, R., Mozam. 24 0S 32 15E
87 Elektrogorsk, U.S.S.R. 55 56N 38 50E
87 Elektrostal, U.S.S.R. ..55 41N 38 32E
125 Elele, Nigeria 5 5N 6 50E
75 Elena, Bulgaria 42 55N 25 53E
15 Elephant I., Antarc. .61 0S 55 0w
167 Elephant Butte Res., U.S.A. 33 45N 107 30w
106 Elephant Pass, Ceylon 9 35N 80 25E
75 Eleshnitsa, Bulgaria ...41 52N 23 36E
169 Eleuthera I., Bahamas 25 0N 76 20w
77 Elevsis, Greece 38 4N 23 26E
76 Elevtheroúpolis, Greece 40 52N 24 20E
80 Elgåhogna, mt., Norway 62 7N 12 7E
79 Elgepiggen, mt., Nor. 62 11N 11 22E
131 Elgeyo-Marakwet, dist., Kenya 1 0N 35 30E
155 Elgin, N.B., Canada ...45 48N 65 10w
161 Elgin, Ont., Canada ...44 37N 76 15w
43 Elgin, Scotland, U.K. 57 39N 3 20w
162 Elgin, Ill., U.S.A. 42 0N 88 20w
164 Elgin, Neb., U.S.A. ...41 58N 98 3w
167 Elgin, Nev., U.S.A. ...37 27N 114 36w
164 Elgin N.D., U.S.A. 46 24N 101 46w
166 Elgin, Ore., U.S.A. 45 37N 118 0w
165 Elgin, Texas, U.S.A. .30 21N 97 22w
131 Elgon, Mt., Africa 1 10N 34 30E
35 Elham, England, U.K. 51 9N 1 7E
109 Eliase, Indonesia 8 10S 130 55E
165 Elida, U.S.A. 33 56N 103 41w
157 Elie, Canada 49 48N 97 52w
41 Elie, Scotland, U.K. ...56 11N 2 50w
147 Elie de Beaumont, Mt., New Zealand ...43 30S 170 20E
77 Elikon, Mt., Greece ...38 18N 22 45E
75 Elin Pelin, Bulgaria ...42 40N 23 38E
130 Elingampangu, Congo 1 59S 24 2E
131 Elisabethville, see Lubumbashi, Congo 11 32S 27 38E
89 Elista, U.S.S.R. 46 25N 44 17E
127 Elit, Ethiopia 15 10N 37 0E
145 Eliza, L., S. Australia 37 25S 140 0E
161 Elizabeth, N.J., U.S.A. 40 37N 74 12w
163 Elizabeth City, U.S.A. 36 18N 76 16w
163 Elizabethton, U.S.A. .36 20N 82 13w
162 Elizabethtown, Ky., U.S.A. 37 40N 85 54w
161 Elizabethtown, N.Y., U.S.A. 44 13N 73 36w
161 Elizabethtown, Pa., U.S.A. 40 8N 76 36w
64 Elizondo, Spain 43 12N 1 30w
154 Elk L., Canada 47 40N 80 25w
164 Elk R., U.S.A. 45 17N 93 34w
165 Elk City, U.S.A. 35 25N 99 25w
157 Elk Point, Canada 54 10N 110 55w
166 Elk River, U.S.A. 46 50N 116 8w
162 Elkhart, Ind., U.S.A. .41 42N 85 55w
165 Elkhart, Kan., U.S.A. 37 3N 101 54w
157 Elkhorn, Canada 50 0N 101 11w
164 Elkhorn R., U.S.A. 42 0N 98 15w
89 Elkhotovo, U.S.S.R. ..43 19N 44 15E
75 Elkhovo, Bulgaria 42 10N 26 40E
163 Elkin, U.S.A. 36 17N 80 50w
162 Elkins, U.S.A. 38 53N 79 53w
156 Elko, Canada 49 20N 115 10w
166 Elko, U.S.A. 40 40N 115 50w
39 Elland, England, U.K. 53 41N 1 49w
14 Ellef Ringnes I., Can. 78 30N 102 2w
167 Ellen, mt., Utah, U.S.A. 38 4N 110 56w
38 Ellen R., Eng., U.K. .54 44N 3 24w
164 Ellendale, U.S.A. 46 3N 98 30w
166 Ellensburg, U.S.A. 47 0N 120 30w
161 Ellenville, U.S.A. 41 42N 74 23w
39 Eller Beck Bri., England, U.K. 54 23N 0 40w
143 Ellerslie, Vic., Australia 38 10S 142 44E
38 Ellesmere, Eng., U.K. 52 55N 2 53w
14 Ellesmere I., Canada .79 30N 80 0w
147 Ellesmere L., N.Z. 43 46S 172 27E
38 Ellesmere Port, England, United Kingdom 53 17N 2 55w
15 Ellesworth Land, Ant. 74 0S 85 0w
136 Ellice Is., Pacific Ocean 8 0S 176 0E
104 Ellichpur, India 21 22N 77 32E
MAP
41 Ellington, Eng., U.K. 55 14N 1 34w
164 Ellinwood, U.S.A. 38 27N 98 37w
135 Elliot, S. Afr. 31 22S 27 48E
154 Elliot Lake, Canada ...46 35N 82 35w
135 Elliotdale, S. Africa ...31 58S 28 43E
164 Ellis, U.S.A. 39 0N 99 39w
163 Ellisville, U.S.A. 31 38N 89 12w
43 Ellon, Scotland, U.K. 57 21N 2 5w
106 Ellore (Eluru), India .16 48N 81 8E
164 Ellsworth, Kan.,U.S.A. 38 47N 98 15w
57 Ellwangen, Germany .48 57N 10 9E
160 Ellwood City, U.S.A. .40 52N 80 19w
57 Elm, Switzerland 46 54N 9 10E
106 Elma, Iowa, U.S.A. ...43 12N 92 28w
166 Elma, Wash., U.S.A. .47 0N 123 30w
131 Elmenteita, Kenya 0 32S 36 14E
162 Elmhurst, U.S.A. 41 52N 87 58w
125 Elmina, Ghana 5 5N 1 21w
160 Elmira, Ont., Canada .43 38N 80 34w
155 Elmira, P.E.I., Canada 46 30N 61 59w
160 Elmira, N.Y., U.S.A. .42 8N 76 49w
143 Elmore, Vic., Australia 36 30S 144 37E
56 Elmshorn, Germany ...53 44N 9 40E
35 Elmswell, Eng., U.K. .52 14N 0 53E
160 Elmvale, Canada 44 35N 79 54w
160 Elmwood, Canada 44 14N 81 3w
160 Elora, Canada 43 43N 80 26w
167 Eloy, U.S.A. 32 46N 111 46w
49 Eloyes, France 48 6N 6 36E
46 Elphin, Ireland 53 50N 8 11w
42 Elphin, Scotland, U.K. 58 4N 5 3w
144 Elphinstone, Australia 21 30S 148 17E
157 Elrose, Canada 51 20N 108 0w
154 Elsas, Canada 48 32N 82 55w
81 Elsinore, see Helsingör, Denmark 56 2N 12 35E
167 Elsinore, Cal., U.S.A. .33 40N 117 15w
167 Elsinore, Utah, U.S.A. 38 40N 112 2w
55 Elst, Netherlands 51 55N 5 51E
56 Elsterwerda, Germany 51 27N 13 32E
35 Elstree, England, U.K. 51 38N 0 16w
143 Eltham, Vic., Australia 37 43S 145 12E
146 Eltham, N.Z. 39 26S 174 19E
89 Elton, U.S.S.R. 49 5N 46 52E
106 Eluru, see Ellore, India 16 48N 81 8E
63 Elvas, Portugal 38 50N 7 17w
48 Elven, France 47 44N 2 36w
79 Elverum, Norway 60 55N 11 34E
174 Elvira, Brazil 4 59S 72 51w
143 Elvire, mt., W. Austral. 29 14S 119 33E
70 Elvo, R., Italy 45 32N 8 14E
79 Elvran, Norway 63 27N 11 3E
162 Elwood, Ind., U.S.A. .40 20N 85 50w
164 Elwood, Neb., U.S.A. 40 38N 99 51w
35 Ely, England, U.K. ...52 24N 0 16E
164 Ely, Minn., U.S.A. 47 54N 91 52w
166 Ely, Nev., U.S.A. 39 10N 114 50w
35 Ely, I. of, Eng., U.K. 52 30N 0 5E
98 Elyashiv, Israel 32 23N 34 55E
160 Elyria, Ohio, U.S.A. ...41 22N 82 8w
80 Emådalen, Sweden 61 20N 14 45E
89 Emaiygi, R., U.S.S.R. 58 30N 26 30E
90 Emba, U.S.S.R. 48 50N 58 8E
62 Embalse de Almendra, Spain 41 09N 6 05w
172 Embarcación, Arg. 23 10S 64 0w
151 Embarras Portage, Can. 58 27N 111 29w
133 Embekelweni, Swazi .26 28S 31 25E
39 Embleton, Eng., U.K. 55 30N 1 38w
43 Embo, Scotland, U.K. 57 55N 4 0w
77 Embóna, Greece 36 13N 27 51E
51 Embrun, France 44 34N 6 30E
131 Embu, tn. & dist., Kenya 0 30S 37 30E
56 Emden, Germany 53 22N 7 12E
98 Emeq Hula, Israel 33 5N 35 8E
144 Emerald, Australia ...23 30S 148 11E
157 Emerson, Canada 49 0N 97 10w
167 Emery, Utah, U.S.A. .38 59N 111 17w
167 Emery Park, U.S.A. ...32 10N 110 59w
121 Emi Koussi, Mt., Chad 20 0N 18 55E
70 Emilia-Romagna, reg., Italy 44 33N 10 40E
70 Emilius, Mt., Italy 45 41N 7 23E
104 Eminabad, W. Pak. ...32 2N 74 8E
160 Emlenton, U.S.A. 41 11N 79 41w
56 Emlichheim, Germany 52 37N 6 51E
44 Emly, Ireland 52 28N 8 20w
81 Emmaboda, Sweden ...56 37N 15 30E
57 Emme R., Switzerland 47 0N 7 42E
54 Emmeloord, Neth. 52 44N 5 46E
54 Emmen, Netherlands .52 48N 6 57E
57 Emmendingen, Ger. ...48 7N 7 51E
57 Emmental, dist., Switz. 47 0N 7 35E
56 Emmerich, Germany .51 50N 6 12E
144 Emmet, Australia 24 45S 144 30E
164 Emmetsburg, U.S.A. ...43 3N 94 40w
166 Emmett, U.S.A. 43 51N 116 33w
59 Emöd, Hungary 47 57N 20 47E
75 Emona, Bulgaria 42 43N 27 53E
168 Empalme, Mexico 28 1N 110 49w
135 Empangeni, S. Afr. ...28 50S 31 48E
172 Empedrado, Argentina 28 0S 58 46w
70 Empoli, Italy 43 43N 10 57E
164 Emporia, Kans.,U.S.A. 38 25N 96 16w
163 Emporia, Va., U.S.A. .36 41N 77 32w
160 Emporium, U.S.A. 41 30N 78 17w
157 Empress, Canada 51 0N 110 0w

MAP
56 Ems R., Germany 52 37N 7 16E
160 Emsdale, Canada 45 30N 79 19W
56 Emsdetten, Germany .52 11N 7 31E
35 Emsworth, Eng., U.K. 50 51N 0 56W
143 Emu, Vic., Australia .36 45S 145 29E
144 Emu Park, Australia .23 13S 150 50E
142 Emu Ra., W. Australia 23 0S 122 0E
46 Emyvale, Ireland 54 20N 6 57W
127 En Nahud, Sudan 12 45N 28 25E
122 en Namous, W., Alg. .31 15N 0 10W
80 Enafors, Sweden 63 20N 12 10E
80 Enånger, Sweden 61 30N 17 9E
42 Enard B., Scot., U.K. 58 5N 5 20W
109 Encanto, Cape, Phil. .20 20N 121 40E
168 Encarnación, de Diaz, Mexico 21 30N 102 20W
173 Encarnación, Paraguay 27 15S 56 0W
124 Enchi, Ghana 5 53N 2 48W
165 Encinal, U.S.A. 28 3N 99 25W
167 Encino, U.S.A. 34 46N 106 16W
174 Encontrados, Ven. 9 3N 72 14W
145 Encounter B., S. Austral. 35 45S 138 45E
173 Encruzilhada, Serra, Brazil 30 30S 52 35W
127 Enda Sellase, Ethiopia 14 10N 38 15E
131 Endau, Kenya 1 16S 38 26E
107 Endau, Malaysia 2 40N 103 38E
107 Endau R., Malaysia ... 2 30N 103 30E
109 Ende, Indonesia 8 45S 121 30E
144 Endeavour Str., Austral. 10 45S 142 0E
127 Endeber, Ethiopia 8 7N 37 52E
81 Endelave I., Denmark 55 46N 10 18E
137 Enderbury I., Pac. Oc. 3 8S 171 5W
156 Enderby, Canada 50 35N 119 10W
34 Enderby, Eng., U.K. .52 35N 1 15W
15 Enderby Land, Antarc. 66 0S 53 0E
164 Enderlin, U.S.A. 46 45N 97 41W
161 Endicott, N.Y., U.S.A. 42 6N 76 2W
166 Endicott, Wash., U.S.A. 47 0N 117 45W
59 Endröd, Hungary 46 55N 20 47E
79 Enebakk, Norway 54 45N 11 8E
76 Enez, Turkey 40 45N 26 5E
123 Enfidaville, Tunisia ...36 6N 10 28E
35 Enfield, Eng., U.K. ...51 39N 0 4W
57 Engadin, Switzerland .46 30N 9 55E
169 Engaño C., Dom. Rep. 18 30N 68 20W
109 Engaño C., Philippines 18 35N 122 23E
135 Engcobo, S. Africa 31 39S 28 1E
98 Engeddi (site), Israel .31 28N 35 25E
57 Engelberg, Switzerland 46 48N 8 26E
87 Engels, U.S.S.R. 51 28N 46 6E
55 Engelskirchen, Germany 50 59N 7 15E
79 Enger, Norway 60 34N 10 21E
108 Enggano I., Indonesia 5 20S 102 40E
55 Engis, Belgium 50 35N 5 24E
108 Engkilili, Sar., Malaysia 1 3N 111 42E
33 England, Country, U.K. 53 0N 2 0W
165 England, U.S.A. 34 30N 91 58W
155 Englee, Canada 50 45N 56 5W
143 Englefield, Vic., Austral. 37 20S 141 40E
164 Englewood, Colo., U.S.A. 39 40N 105 0W
165 Englewood, Kan., U.S.A. 37 7N 99 59W
157 English R., Canada ...50 30N 93 50W
154 English River, Canada 49 20N 91 0W
105 English Bazar, India .24 58N 88 21E
48 English Chan., Europe 50 0N 2 0W
139 English Co. Is., Austral. 12 0S 137 0E
113 Engteng (Yungting), China 24 46N 116 45E
165 Enid, U.S.A. 36 26N 97 52W
76 Enipéus R., Greece 39 22N 22 17E
136 Eniwetok, Atoll, Pac. Oc. 11 30N 162 16E
127 Enjabara, Ethiopia ...11 10N 36 52E
122 Enjel, Morocco 33 12N 4 32W
125 Enji, Mauritania 15 50N 9 35W
132 Enkeldoorn, Rhodesia 19 2S 30 52E
54 Enkhuizen, Netherlands 52 42N 5 17E
80 Enköping, Sweden 59 37N 17 4E
73 Enna, Italy 37 34N 14 15E
157 Ennadai, Canada 61 10N 101 0W
157 Ennadai L., Canada ...61 0N 101 0W
45 Ennell L., Ireland 53 29N 7 25W
55 Ennepetal, Germany .51 18N 7 23E
38 Ennerdale Water, England, U.K. 54 32N 3 24W
145 Enngonia, Australia ...29 21S 145 50E
79 Enningdal, Norway ...58 59N 11 33E
44 Ennis, Ireland 52 51N 8 59W
166 Ennis, Mont., U.S.A. .45 27N 111 48W
165 Ennis, Texas, U.S.A. .32 15N 96 40W
45 Enniscorthy, Ireland .52 30N 6 35W
44 Enniskean, Ireland ...51 44N 8 56W
45 Enniskerry, Ireland ...53 12N 6 10W
46 Enniskillen, Northern Ireland, U.K. 54 20N 7 40W
44 Ennistimon, Ireland ...52 56N 9 18W
58 Enns, Austria 48 12N 14 28E
58 Enns, R., Austria 48 8N 14 27E
169 Enriquillo L., Dom. Rep. 18 20N 72 5W
54 Enschede, Netherlands 52 13N 6 53E
172 Ensenada, Argentina .34 55S 57 55W
168 Ensenada, Mexico 31 50N 116 50W
113 Enshih, China 30 18N 109 27E
49 Ensisheim, France 47 50N 7 20E
34 Enstone, Eng., U.K. .51 55N 1 25W
131 Entebbe, Uganda 0 4N 32 28E
166 Enterprise, Ore., U.S.A. 45 30N 117 11W
167 Enterprise, Utah, U.S.A. 37 37N 113 36W
156 Entrance, Canada 53 25N 117 50W
172 Entre Rios, Prov., Arg. 30 30S 58 30W
172 Entre Rios, Bolivia ...21 30S 64 25W
129 Entre Rios (Malemba), Mozam. 14 57S 37 20E
156 Entwistle, Canada ...53 30N 115 0W
125 Enugu, Nigeria 6 30N 7 30E
125 Enugu Ezike, Nigeria 7 0N 7 29E
166 Enumclaw, U.S.A. ...47 12N 122 0W
48 Envermeu, France ...49 53N 1 15E
130 Enyelle, Congo 2 49N 18 2E
70 Enza, R., Italy 44 33N 10 22E
73 Éolie o Lipari (Æolian Is.), Italy 38 30N 14 50E
144 Epa, Territory of Papua 8 28S 146 52E
76 Epanomi, Greece 40 25N 22 59E
54 Epe, Netherlands 52 21N 5 59E
125 Epe, Nigeria 6 36N 3 59E
130 Epena, Congo, (Fr.) ... 1 22N 17 32E
49 Epernay, France 49 3N 3 56E
49 Epernon, France 48 35N 1 40E
100 Ephesus, Turkey 38 0N 27 30E
166 Ephraim, U.S.A. 39 30N 111 37W
166 Ephrata, U.S.A. 47 28N 119 32W
64 Epila, Spain 41 36N 1 17W
49 Epinac, France 47 0N 4 28E
49 Epinal, France 48 19N 6 27E
76 Epirus, Prov., see Ipiros, Greece 39 30N 20 20E
78 Episcopia Bihor, Rum. 47 12N 21 55E
77 Epitálion, Greece 37 37N 21 30E
42 Eport L., Scot., U.K. .57 33N 7 10W
35 Epping, Eng., U.K. ...51 42N 0 8E
35 Epping Forest, England, United Kingdom 51 40N 0 5E
35 Epsom, England, U.K. 51 19N 0 16W
129 Epukiro, S. W. Africa 21 30S 19 0E
39 Epworth, England, U.K. 53 30N 0 50W
98 Eqron, Israel 31 52N 34 49E
130 Equateur, prov., Congo 1 0N 20 0E
127 Equatoria, prov., Sudan 5 0N 30 0E
48 Equeurdreville, France 49 40N 1 40W
127 Er Rahad, Sudan 12 45N 30 32E
122 Er Rif, Morocco 35 1N 4 1W
127 Er Roseires, Sudan ...11 55N 34 30E
98 Er Rumman, Jordan .32 9N 35 48E
104 Erandol, India 20 56N 75 20E
70 Erba, Italy 45 49N 9 12E
126 Erba, Sudan 19 5N 36 40E
91 Ercha, U.S.S.R. 69 45N 147 20E
100 Erciyaş dag, Mt., Tur. 38 30N 35 30E
112 Erdene, Mongolia 44 30N 111 10E
112 Erdenedalay, Mongolia 46 3N 105 1E
57 Erding, Germany 48 18N 11 55E
15 Erebus, Mt., Antarctica 77 35S 167 0E
173 Erechim, Brazil 27 35S 52 15W
100 Ereğli, Turkey 41 15N 31 30E
73 Erei, Monti, Italy 37 20N 14 20E
175 Erepecura R., Brazil . 0 30S 56 0W
62 Eresma, R., Spain ...41 13N 4 30W
77 Eressós, Greece 39 11N 25 57E
79 Erfjord, Norway 59 20N 6 15E
122 Erfoud, Morocco 31 30N 4 15W
55 Erft R., Germany 50 37N 6 43E
56 Erfurt, Germany 50 58N 11 2E
56 Erfurt Dist., E. Ger. .51 10N 10 30E
100 Ergani, Turkey 38 26N 39 49E
75 Ergene R., Turkey ...41 20N 27 0E
112 Erhlien, China 43 48N 111 59E
62 Eria, R., Spain 42 10N 6 8W
127 Eriba, Sudan 16 40N 36 10E
43 Eriboll, L., Scot., U.K. 58 28N 4 41W
72 Erice, Italy 38 4N 12 34E
43 Ericht, L., Scot., U.K. 56 50N 4 25W
160 Erie, Pa., U.S.A. 42 10N 80 7W
160 Erie Beach, Canada ...42 17N 82 1W
160 Erie Canal, U.S.A. 43 15N 78 0W
160 Erie, L., Can.–U.S.A. .42 30N 82 0W
154 Erieau, Canada 42 16N 81 57W
99 Erigavo, Somali Rep. .10 35N 47 35E
76 Erikoúsa, I., Greece ...39 55N 19 14E
157 Eriksdale, Canada 50 52N 98 7W
80 Eriksslund, Sweden ...62 34N 16 4E
77 Erimanthos, Mt., Gr. .37 57N 21 50E
114 Erimo-misaki, C., Japan 41 50N 143 15E
42 Eriskay I., Scot., U.K. 57 4N 7 18W
42 Eriskay, Sd. of, Scotland, U.K. 57 5N 7 20W
42 Erisort L., Scot., U.K. 58 5N 6 30W
156 Erith, Canada 53 25N 116 46W
77 Erithrai, Greece 38 13N 23 20E
127 Eritrea, prov. Ethiopia 14 0N 41 0E
62 Erjas, R., Portugal ...39 45N 6 52W
55 Erkelenz, Germany ...51 4N 6 19E
80 Erker, L., Sweden 59 51N 18 29E
55 Erkrath, Germany 51 13N 6 54E
57 Erlangen, Germany ...49 35N 11 0E
54 Ermelo, Netherlands .52 35N 5 35E
133 Ermelo, Trans., S. Afr. 26 31S 29 59E
100 Ermenek, Turkey 36 44N 33 0E
77 Ermióni, Greece 37 23N 23 15E
77 Ermoúpolis, see Siros, Greece 37 28N 24 57E
106 Ernakulam, India 9 59N 76 19E
46 Erne, Lough, Northern Ireland, U.K. 54 14N 7 30W
46 Erne, R., Ireland 54 30N 8 16W
48 Ernée, France 48 18N 0 56W
142 Ernest Giles Ra., W. Australia 27 0S 123 45E
106 Erode, India 11 24N 77 45E
145 Eromanga, Australia .26 40S 143 11E
48 Erquy, France 48 38N 2 29W
48 Erquy, Cap d', France 48 39N 2 29W
142 Errabiddy, W. Austral. 25 25S 117 5E
106 Erramala Hills, India 15 30N 78 15E
127 Errer, R., Ethiopia ...42 35N 8 40E
46 Errigal, Mt., Ireland .55 2N 8 8W
45 Erris Hd., Ireland 54 19N 10 0W
43 Errochty, L., Scot., U.K. 56 45N 4 10W
43 Errogie, Scot., U.K. ...57 16N 4 23W
41 Errol, Scotland, U.K. 56 24N 3 13W
76 Ersekë, Albania 40 22N 20 40E
164 Erskine, U.S.A. 47 37N 96 0W
57 Erstein, France 48 25N 7 38E
87 Ertil, U.S.S.R. 51 55N 40 50E
79 Ertvågöy, I., Norway 63 15N 8 25E
125 Eruwa, Nigeria 7 33N 3 26E
80 Ervalla, Sweden 59 28N 15 16E
49 Ervy, France 48 2N 3 55E
163 Erwin, U.S.A. 36 10N 82 28W
56 Erz Gebirge, Germany 50 25N 13 0E
100 Erzincan, Turkey 39 46N 39 30E
100 Erzurum, Turkey 39 57N 41 15E
123 Es Sider, Libya 30 50N 18 21E
125 Es Souk, Mali 18 48N 1 2E
127 Es Suki, Sudan 13 20N 34 58E
114 Esan-misaki, C., Japan 41 40N 141 10E
81 Esbjerg, Denmark 55 29N 8 29E
167 Escalante, U.S.A. 37 47N 111 37W
167 Escalante R., U.S.A. .37 45N 111 0W
168 Escalon, Mexico 26 40N 104 20W
62 Escalona, Spain 40 9N 4 29W
163 Escambia, R., U.S.A. .30 45N 87 15W
162 Escanaba, U.S.A. 45 44N 87 5W
55 Esch, Netherlands 51 37N 5 17E
54 Esch, Luxembourg 49 32N 6 0E
56 Eschede, Germany 52 44N 10 13E
56 Eschwege, Germany ...51 10N 10 3E
56 Eschweiler, Germany .50 49N 6 14E
62 Escobal, Panama 9 6N 80 1W
167 Escondido, U.S.A. 33 9N 117 4W
59 Escrick, England, U.K. 53 53N 1 3W
168 Escuinapa, Mexico 22 50N 105 50W
168 Escuintla, Guatemala 14 20N 90 48W
155 Escuminac, Canada 48 0N 67 0W
98 Esdraelon (Armageddon), Plain, Israel 32 37N 35 12E
125 Eseka, Cameroon 3 41N 10 44E
56 Esens, Germany 53 40N 7 35E
64 Esera, R., Spain 42 24N 0 22E
62 Esgueva, R., Spain ...41 46N 4 14W
100 Esh Sham (Damascus), Syria .33 30N 36 18E
98 Esh Shuma, Jordan ...32 32N 35 34E
42 Esha Ness, Scot., U.K. 60 30N 1 36W
135 Eshowe, Natal, S. Afr. 28 50S 31 30E
98 Eshtaol, Israel 31 47N 35 0E
124 Esiama, Ghana 4 48N 2 25W
71 Esino, R., Italy 43 28N 13 8E
38 Esk R., Cumb., England, U.K. 54 23N 3 21W
39 Esk, R., Yorks., England, U.K. 54 27N 0 48W
41 Esk, R., Scotland, U.K. 55 12N 3 10W
41 Eskdale, Scotland, U.K. 55 4N 3 10W
82 Eskifjördur, Iceland ...65 3N 13 55W
80 Eskilstuna, Sweden 59 22N 16 32E
157 Eskimo Pt., Canada ...61 10N 94 15W
100 Eskişehir, Turkey 39 50N 30 35E
62 Esla R., Spain 41 45N 5 50W
81 Eslöv, Sweden 55 50N 13 20E
172 Esmeralda, Paraguay .22 16S 62 33W
174 Esmeraldas, Ecuador . 1 0N 79 40W
55 Esneux, Belgium 50 32N 5 33E
79 Espa, Norway 60 35N 11 15E
50 Espalion, France 44 32N 2 47E
65 Espalmador, I., Spain 38 48N 1 26E
154 Espanola, Canada 46 15N 81 46W
65 Espardell, Isla del, Sp. 38 47N 1 25E
64 Esparraguera, Spain...41 33N 1 52E
90 Espe, U.S.S.R. 44 0N 74 5E
63 Espejo, Spain 37 40N 4 34W
142 Esperance, W. Austral. 33 45S 121 55E
142 Esperance B., Austral. 33 48S 121 55E
172 Esperanza, Argentina 31 29S 61 3W
79 Espevaer Lt. Ho., Nor. 59 36N 5 9E
63 Espichel C., Portugal .38 22N 9 16W
63 Espiel, Spain 38 11N 5 1W
174 Espinal, Colombia 4 9N 74 53W
62 Espinho, Portugal ...41 1N 8 38W
62 Espinosa de los Monteros, Spain 43 5N 3 34W
173 Espirito Santo, Brazil 20 23S 40 18W
168 Espiritu Santo, B. del, Mexico 19 15N 79 40W
168 Espiritu Santo, I., Mex. 24 30N 110 23W
64 Espluga de Francoli, Sp. 41 24N 1 7E
65 Espuña, mt., Spain ...37 51N 1 35W
176 Esquel, Argentina 42 40S 71 20W
152 Esquimalt, Canada 48 30N 123 23W
172 Esquina, Argentina ...30 0S 59 30W
122 Essaouira (Mogador), Morocco 31 32N 9 42W
54 Essen, Belgium 51 28N 4 28E
56 Essen, Germany 51 28N 6 59E
142 Essendon, Mt., Austral. 25 0S 120 30E
174 Essequibo R., Guyana 5 45N 58 50W
160 Essex, Canada 42 9N 82 50W
161 Essex, U.S.A. 44 17N 73 21W
35 Essex, co., Eng., U.K. 51 48N 0 30E
132 Essexvale, Rhodesia ..20 18S 29 0E
57 Esslingen, Germany ...48 43N 9 19E
49 Essonne, Dept., France 48 30N 2 20E
80 Essvik, Sweden 62 20N 17 24E
64 Estadilla, Spain 42 4N 0 16E
176 Estados I. de los, Arg. 54 40S 64 30W
50 Estagel, France 42 47N 2 40E
175 Estância, Brazil 11 15S 37 30W
133 Estancia, Trans., S. Afr. 26 17S 29 52E
167 Estancia, U.S.A. 34 50N 106 1W
62 Estarreja, Portugal ...40 45N 8 35W
50 Estats, P. d' Sp.–Fr. .42 40N 1 40E
135 Estcourt, Natal, S. Afr. 28 58S 29 53E
71 Este, Italy 45 12N 11 40E
62 Esteban, Spain 43 33N 6 5W
169 Esteli, Nicaragua 13 9N 86 22W
64 Estella, Spain 42 40N 2 0W
164 Estelline, S.D., U.S.A. 44 39N 96 52W
165 Estelline, Texas, U.S.A. 34 35N 100 27W
63 Estena, R., Spain 39 23N 4 44W
63 Estepa, Spain 37 17N 4 52W
63 Estepona, Spain 36 24N 5 7W
157 Esterhazy, Canada 50 37N 102 5W
49 Esternay, France 48 44N 3 33E
64 Esterri de Aneu, Spain 42 38N 1 5E
157 Estevan, Canada 49 10N 103 0W
164 Estherville, U.S.A. 43 25N 94 50W
49 Estissac, France 48 16N 3 48E
157 Eston, Canada 51 8N 108 40W
86 Estonia S.S.R., U.S.S.R. 58 30N 25 30E
63 Estoril, Portugal 38 42N 9 23W
65 Eshrelia, Mt., Spain ...38 25N 3 35W
63 Estremoz, Portugal ...38 51N 7 39W
59 Esztergom, Hungary .47 47N 18 44E
122 Et Tieta, Morocco 29 37N 9 15W
122 Et Tnine Riat, Morocco 32 3N 9 3W
98 Et Turra, Jordan 32 39N 35 39E
48 Etables, France 48 38N 2 51W
104 Etah, India 27 35N 78 40E
49 Etain, France 49 13N 5 38E
35 Étais, France 47 30N 3 20E
155 Etamamu, Canada 50 18N 59 59W
49 Étampes, France 48 26N 2 10E
49 Étang, France 46 52N 4 10E
49 Etaples, France 50 30N 1 39E
104 Etawah, India 26 48N 79 6E
163 Etawah, R., U.S.A. ...34 20N 84 15W
35 Etchingham, Eng., U.K. 51 0N 0 27E
125 Eteh, Nigeria 7 2N 7 28E
125 Etelia, Mali 19 10N 0 55E
142 Ethel Creek, W. Austral. 22 35S 120 15E
157 Ethelbert, Canada 51 32N 100 25W
99 Ethiopia, st., Africa ... 8 0N 40 0E
117 Ethiopian Highlands, Ethiopia 10 0N 37 0E
40 Etive, L., Scot., U.K. 56 30N 5 12W
73 Etna, Mt., Italy 37 45N 15 0E
79 Etne, Norway 59 40N 5 57E
131 Etoile, Congo 11 33S 27 30E
156 Etolin I., Alaska, U.S.A. 56 5N 132 20W
129 Etosha Pan, S.W. Afr. 18 40S 16 30E
35 Eton England, U.K. .51 29N 0 37W
130 Etoumbi, Congo, (Fr.) 0 2S 14 52E
163 Etowah, U.S.A. 35 20N 84 30W
48 Étretat, France 49 42N 0 12E
76 Etropole, Bulgaria 43 50N 24 0E
54 Ettelbrüch, Lux. 49 50N 6 5E
34 Ettington, Eng., U.K. 52 8N 1 38W
57 Ettlingen, Germany ...48 58N 8 25E
41 Ettrick Forest, Scotland, U.K. 55 30N 3 0W
41 Ettrick Pen, Scot., U.K. 55 20N 3 18W
41 Ettrick Water, Scotland, U.K. 55 31N 2 55W
168 Etzatlán, Mexico 20 48N 104 5W
48 Eu, France 50 3N 1 26E
143 Eubalong, Australia ...33 10S 146 55E
143 Euabalong W., Austral.33 7S 146 29E
77 Euboea, pref., see Evvoia, Greece 38 40N 23 40E
142 Eucla Motel, W. Australia 31 46S 128 50E
142 Eucla Basin, Australia 31 19S 126 9E
160 Euclid, U.S.A. 41 32N 81 31W
143 Eucumbene, L., Austral. 36 2S 148 40E
165 Eudora, U.S.A. 33 5N 91 17W
163 Eufaula, Ala., U.S.A. .31 55N 85 11W
165 Eufaula, L., U.S.A. ...35 15N 95 28W
165 Eufawla, Okla., U.S.A. 35 20N 95 33W
1 Euganean Hills, Italy 46 0N 13 0E
166 Eugene, U.S.A. 44 0N 123 8W
168 Eugenia, Punta, Mexico 27 50N 115 5W
143 Eugowra, Australia ...33 22S 148 24E
45 Eulo, Queens, Austral. 28 10S 145 0E
143 Eumungerie, Australia 31 56N 148 36E
165 Eunice, La., U.S.A. ...30 35N 92 28W
165 Eunice, N. Mex., U.S.A. 32 30N 103 10W
54 Eupen, Belgium 50 37N 6 3E
100 Euphrates (Firat), R., S.W. Asia 33 30N 43 0E
48 Eure, dépt., France ...49 6N 1 0E
48 Eure-et-Loire, dépt., Fr. 48 22N 1 30E
14 Eureka, Canada 80 0N 85 56W
166 Eureka, Calif., U.S.A. 40 50N 124 0W
165 Eureka, Kan., U.S.A. 37 50N 96 20W
166 Eureka Mont., U.S.A. 48 53N 115 6W
166 Eureka, Nev., U.S.A. .39 32N 116 2W
164 Eureka, S.D., U.S.A. .45 49N 99 38W
166 Eureka, Utah, U.S.A. 40 0N 112 0W
142 Eureka, Mt., W. Austral. 26 35S 121 35E
143 Euroa, Vic., Australia 36 38S 145 35E
62 Europa, Picos de, Mts., Spain 43 10N 5 0W
63 Europa Pt., Gibraltar 36 3N 5 21W
18 Europe, cont. 50 0N 10 0W
54 Europoort, Netherlands 51 57N 4 10E
114 Euse, Japan 34 40N 135 37E
56 Euskirchen, Germany 50 40N 6 45E
163 Eustis, U.S.A. 28 54N 81 36W
143 Euston, Australia 34 30S 142 46E
56 Eutin, Germany 54 7N 10 38E
57 Eutingen, Germany ...48 29N 8 45E
38 Euxton, England, U.K. 53 41N 2 42W
133 Evangelina, S. Africa .22 20S 29 5E
79 Evanger, Norway 60 39N 6 5E
164 Evans, U.S.A. 40 25N 104 43W
154 Evans L., Canada 50 50N 77 0W
161 Evans Mills, U.S.A. ...44 6N 75 48W
164 Evans P., U.S.A. 41 0N 105 35W
162 Evanston, Ill., U.S.A. 42 0N 87 40W
166 Evanston, Wy., U.S.A. 41 10N 111 0W
162 Evansville, Ind., U.S.A. 38 0N 87 35W
164 Evansville, Wis., U.S.A. 42 47N 89 18W
43 Evanton, Scot., U.K. .57 40N 4 20W
133 Evaton, Trans., S. Afr. 26 31S 27 54E
50 Evaux, France 46 12N 2 29E
74 Evdokiya, Bulgaria ...44 6N 22 57E
164 Eveleth, U.S.A. 47 35N 92 40W
98 Even Yahuda, Israel .32 16N 34 53E
79 Evenstad, Norway 61 26N 11 8E
138 Everard, L., S. Austral. 31 30S 135 0E
138 Everard Ras., S. Australia 27 5S 132 28E
36 Evercreech, Eng., U.K. 51 8N 2 30W
55 Evere, Belgium 50 52N 4 25E
105 Everest, Mt., Nepal ...28 5N 86 58E
160 Everett, Pa., U.S.A. ...40 2N 78 24W
166 Everett, Wash., U.S.A. 48 0N 122 10W
163 Everglades, Fla., U.S.A. 26 0N 80 30W
163 Evergreen, U.S.A. 31 28N 86 55W
81 Everöd, Sweden 55 33N 14 5E
166 Everson, U.S.A. 48 57N 122 22W
143 Everton, Vic., Austral. 36 25S 146 33E
34 Evesham, Eng., U.K. 52 6N 1 57W
48 Evian, France 46 24N 6 35E
77 Evinos, R., Greece ...38 27N 21 40E
51 Evisa, Corsica, France 42 15N 8 48E
79 Evje, Norway 58 36N 7 51E
63 Evora, tn. & dist., Port. 38 33N 7 57W
48 Evreux, France 49 0N 1 8E
77 Evritania, Nome, Gr. .39 5N 21 30E
48 Evron, France 48 23N 1 58W
76 Evros, pref., Greece ...41 10N 26 0E
77 Evrótas R., Greece ...36 50N 22 40E
77 Evvoia, pref., Greece .38 40N 23 40E
77 Evvoia (Euboea) I., Greece 38 30N 24 0E
131 Ewaso Ngiro, R., Kenya 1 10N 38 50E
42 Ewe, L., Scot., U.K.. 57 49N 5 38W
35 Ewell, England, U.K. 51 20N 0 15W
35 Ewhurst, Eng., U.K. .51 9N 0 25W
164 Ewing, U.S.A. 42 18N 98 22W
130 Ewo, Congo (Fr.) 0 48S 14 45E
174 Exaltacion, Bolivia ...13 10S 65 20W
143 Excelsior, Australia ...33 6S 149 59W
135 Excelsior, O.F.S., S. Africa 28 56S 27 6E
164 Excelsior Springs, U.S.A. 39 20N 94 10W
50 Excideuil, France 45 20N 1 4E
36 Exe R., England, U.K. 50 38N 3 27W

MAP
36 Exeter, England, U.K. 50 43N 3 31W
160 Exeter, Canada 43 20N 81 30W
167 Exeter, Cal., U.S.A. ...36 24N 119 8W
164 Exeter, Neb., U.S.A. .40 43N 97 30W
161 Exeter, N.H., U.S.A. .43 0N 70 58W
36 Exford, England U.K. 51 8N 3 39W
48 Exmes, France 48 45N 0 10E
36 Exminster, Eng., U.K. 50 40N 3 29W
36 Exmoor, Eng., U.K. .51 10N 3 55W
142 Exmouth, W. Australia 22 23S 114 7E
36 Exmouth, Eng., U.K. 51 10N 3 55W
142 Exmouth G., Australia 22 15S 114 15E
144 Expedition Range, Queens., Australia .24 30S 149 12E
35 Exton, England, U.K. 52 42N 0 38W
63 Extramadura, reg., Sp. 39 30N 6 5W
169 Exuma Sd., W. Indies 24 30N 76 20W
131 Eyasi, L., Tanzania ... 3 30S 35 0E
42 Eye Pen., Scot., U.K. 58 13N 6 10W
157 Eyeberry L., Canada 63 9N 104 40W
41 Eyemouth, Scot., U.K. 55 53N 2 5W
50 Eygurande, France ...45 40N 2 26E
88 Eyisen, Mt., Turkey ...41 0N 36 50E
82 Eyja Fd., Iceland 66 0N 18 15W
50 Eymet, France 44 40N 0 25E
50 Eymoutiers, France ...45 45N 1 45E
43 Eynhallow Sd., Scotland, U.K. 59 8N 3 7W
34 Eynsham, Eng., U.K. 51 47N 1 21W
82 Eyrarbakki, Iceland ...63 50N 21 1W
142 Eyre, W. Australia ...32 17S 126 25E
139 Eyre L., Australia ...28 30S 136 45E
147 Eyre Mts., New Zealand 45 25S 168 25E
138 Eyre Pen., S. Australia 33 30S 137 17E
44 Eyrecourt, Ireland 53 12N 8 8W
126 Ez Zeidab, Sudan 17 25N 33 55E
122 Ez Zergoun, W., Alg. .32 45N 2 25E
64 Ezcaray, Spain 42 19N 3 0W
76 Ezine, Turkey 39 48N 26 12E

F

81 Faaborg, Denmark 55 7N 10 15E
167 Fabens, U.S.A. 31 30N 106 8W
71 Fabriano, Italy 43 20N 12 52E
49 Fabrizia, Italy 38 29N 16 19E
78 Făcăeni, Rumania 44 32N 27 53E
174 Facatativa, Colombia . 4 49N 74 22W
50 Facture, France 44 39N 0 58W
121 Fada, Chad 17 13N 21 30E
125 Fada-n-Gourma, Upper Volta 12 10N 0 30E
59 Fadd, Hungary 46 28N 18 49E
91 Faddeyev I., U.S.S.R. 76 0N 150 0E
100 Fadhili, Saudi Arabia 26 55N 49 10E
126 Fadlab, Sudan 17 42N 13 58E
71 Faenza, Italy....44 17N 11 53E
125 Fafa, Mali 15 22N 0 48E
62 Fafe, Portugal 41 27N 8 11W
125 Fagam, Nigeria 11 1N 10 1E
78 Făgăras, Rumania 45 48N 24 58E
78 Făgăras, Munţii, Mts., Rumania 45 40N 24 40E
80 Fågelsjo, Sweden 61 50N 14 35E
81 Fagerhult, Sweden 57 8N 15 40E
79 Fagermes, Norway 61 0N 9 16E
80 Fagersta, Sweden 60 1N 15 46E
78 Făget, Rumania 45 52N 22 10E
78 Făget, Munţii, Mts., Rumania 45 50N 22 9E
81 Fåglavik, Sweden 58 6N 13 6E
176 Fagnano L., Chile 54 30S 68 0W
73 Fagnano Castello, Italy 39 31N 16 4E
49 Fagnières, France 48 58N 4 20E
101 Fahral, Iran 29 0N 59 0E
113 Fahsien, China 21 19N 110 33E
101 Fahūd, Mus. & 'O. ...22 18N 56 28E
100 Faid, Saudi Arabia ...27 1N 42 52E
144 Fair, C., Queensland, Australia 12 24S 143 16E
46 Fair Hd., N. Ire., U.K. 55 14N 6 10W
28 Fair Isle Scot., U.K. .59 30N 1 40W
167 Fairbank, U.S.A. 31 44N 110 12W
152 Fairbanks, Alaska, U.S.A. 64 59N 147 40W
37 Fairbourne, Wales, U.K. 52 42N 4 3W
164 Fairbury, U.S.A. 40 5N 97 5W
165 Fairfax, U.S.A. 36 37N 96 45W
143 Fairfield, Australia ...33 53S 150 57E
163 Fairfield, Ala., U.S.A. 33 30N 87 0W
166 Fairfield, Cal., U.S.A. 38 14N 122 1W
161 Fairfield, Conn., U.S.A. 41 8N 73 16W
166 Fairfield, Idaho, U.S.A. 43 27N 114 52W
162 Fairfield, Ill., U.S.A. .38 20N 88 20W
164 Fairfield, Iowa, U.S.A. 41 0N 91 58W
166 Fairfield, Mont., U.S.A. 47 40N 112 0W
165 Fairfield, Texas, U.S.A. 31 40N 96 0W
34 Fairford, Eng., U.K. .51 42N 1 48W
163 Fairhope, U.S.A. 30 35N 87 50W
147 Fairlie, New Zealand .44 5S 170 49E
40 Fairlie, Scotland, U.K. 55 44N 4 52W
35 Fairlight, Eng., U.K. .50 53N 0 40E
164 Fairmont, Minn., U.S.A. 43 37N 94 30W
162 Fairmont, W. Va., U.S.A. 39 29N 80 10W
156 Fairmont Hot Springs, Canada 50 20N 115 56W
167 Fairplay, U.S.A. 39 9N 107 0W
160 Fairport, N.Y., U.S.A. 43 8N 77 29W
160 Fairport, Ohio, U.S.A. 41 45N 81 17W
144 Fairview, Australia ...15 31S 144 17E
156 Fairview, Alta., Can. .56 5N 118 25W
164 Fairview, N. Dak., U.S.A. 47 49N 104 7W
165 Fairview, Okla., U.S.A. 36 19N 98 30W
166 Fairview, Utah, U.S.A. 39 50N 111 0W
152 Fairweather, Mt., Alaska, U.S.A. 58 55N 137 45W
164 Faith, U.S.A. 45 2N 102 4W
42 Faither, The, C., Scotland, U.K. 60 34N 1 30W
126 Faiyum, El, Egypt ...29 8N 30 40E
101 Faizabad, Afghanistan 37 7N 70 33E
105 Faizabad, India 26 45N 82 10E
104 Faizpur, India 21 14N 75 49E
169 Fajardo, P. Rico, W.I. 18 20N 65 39W
35 Fakenham, Eng., U.K. 52 50N 0 51E
109 Fakfak, Indonesia 3 0S 132 15E
175 Fakiya, Bulgaria 42 10N 27 4E
81 Fakse, Denmark 55 15N 12 8E
81 Fakse B., Denmark ...55 11N 12 15E
81 Fakse Ladeplads, Den. 55 16N 12 9E
112 Faku, China 42 50N 123 35E
48 Falaise, France 48 54N 0 12W
76 Falakrón Óros, Mts., Greece 41 15N 23 58E
103 Falam, Burma 23 0N 93 45E
46 Falcarragh, Ireland ...55 8N 8 8W
64 Falces, Spain 42 24N 1 48W
78 Fălciu, Rumania 46 17N 28 7E
122 Falcon, C., Algeria ...35 50N 0 50W
165 Falcon Dam, U.S.A. ...26 50N 99 20W
71 Falconara Marittima, It. 43 37N 13 23E
160 Falconer, U.S.A. 42 7N 79 13W
39 Faldingworth, Eng., U.K. 53 21N 0 22W
88 Faleshty, U.S.S.R. 47 32N 27 44E
165 Falfurrias, U.S.A. 27 8N 98 8W
156 Falher, Canada 55 50N 117 15W
56 Falkenberg, Canada ...45 9N 79 21W
56 Falkenberg, Germany 51 34N 13 13E
81 Falkenberg, Sweden ...56 56N 12 30E
56 Falkensee, Germany ...52 35N 13 6E
56 Falkenstein, Germany 50 27N 12 24E
41 Falkirk, Scot., U.K. ...56 0N 3 47W
41 Falkland, Scot., U.K. 56 15N 3 13W
176 Falkland Is., S. Atlantic 51 30S 59 0W
15 Falkland Is. Dep., S. Oc. 57 0S 40 0W
176 Falkland Sd., Falk. Is. 52 0S 60 0W
77 Falkonera I., Greece .36 50N 23 52E
81 Falköping, Sweden ...58 12N 13 33E
167 Fall Brook, U.S.A. ...33 25N 117 12W
161 Fall River, U.S.A. ...41 45N 71 5W
166 Fall River Mills, U.S.A. 41 1N 121 30W
45 Fallmore, Ireland 54 6N 10 5W
166 Fallon, Nev., U.S.A. .39 31N 118 51W
164 Fallon, Mont., U.S.A. 46 52N 105 8W
164 Falls City, Neb., U.S.A. 40 0N 95 40W
166 Falls City, Ore., U.S.A. 44 54N 123 29W
160 Falls Creek, U.S.A. ...41 8N 78 49W
169 Falmouth, Jamaica ...18 30N 77 40W
36 Falmouth, Eng., U.K. 50 9N 5 5W
162 Falmouth, Ky., U.S.A. 38 40N 84 20W
36 Falmouth B., Eng., U.K. 50 7N 5 3E
134 False B., C. Prov., S. Afr. 34 15S 18 40E
106 False Divi Pt., India .15 35N 80 50E
64 Falset, Spain 41 7N 0 50E
81 Falster I., Denmark ...54 49N 12 0E
81 Falsterbo, Sweden 55 23N 12 50E
78 Fălticeni, Rumania ...47 21N 26 20E
98 Faluja, Israel 31 48N 31 37E
80 Falun, Sweden 60 32N 15 39E
100 Famagusta, Cyprus ...35 8N 33 55E
127 Famaka, Sudan 11 24N 34 52E
172 Famatina, Cord., de, Argentina 29 5S 68 0W
76 Fan, R., Albania 41 56N 20 16E
124 Fana, Mali 13 0N 6 56W
79 Fana, Norway 60 15N 5 23E
46 Fanad Hd., Ireland ...55 17N 7 40W
76 Fanárion, Greece 39 50N 21 47E
113 Fancheng, China 31 2N 118 13E
129 Fandriana, Malagasy Republic 20 14S 47 21E
113 Fangcheng, China ...33 21N 113 2E
113 Fanghsien, China 32 0N 111 0E
112 Fankiatun, China 43 50N 125 6E
125 Fanna, Nigeria 11 39N 3 57E
42 Fannich, L., Scot., U.K. 57 40N 5 0W
144 Fanning, Australia ...19 56S 146 30E
137 Fanning I., Pac. Oc. . 3 51N 159 22W
156 Fanny Bay, Canada ...49 27N 124 58W
71 Fano, Italy 43 50N 13 0E
81 Fanö I., Denmark 55 25N 8 25E
156 Fanshaw, Alaska, U.S.A. 57 11N 133 30W
100 Fao (Al Fāw), Iraq ...30 0N 48 30E
104 Faqirwali, W. Pak. ...29 27N 73 0E
71 Fara in Sabina, Italy .42 13N 12 44E
16 Faraday Seamount Group, N. Atlantic Oc. 50 0N 27 0W
131 Faradje, Congo 3 50N 2 45E
129 Farafangana, Malagasy Republic .22 49S 47 50E
126 Farâfra Oasis, Egypt .27 15N 28 20E
101 Farah, Afghanistan ...32 20N 61 21E
126 Faraid, Gebel, Egypt .23 33N 35 19E
43 Faraid Hd., Scot., U.K. 58 35N 4 48W
124 Faramana, Upper Volta 11 56N 4 45W
124 Faranah, Guinea 10 3N 10 45W
99 Farasan Is., Red Sea .16 45N 41 55E
127 Farasan Kebir, I., Saudi Arabia 16 40N 42 0E
65 Fardes R., Spain 37 25N 3 10W
34 Fareham, Eng., U.K. .50 52N 1 11W
14 Farewell C., Greenland 59 40N 43 40W
147 Farewell, C., N.Z. 40 29S 172 43E
147 Farewell Spit, N.Z. 40 35S 173 0E
164 Fargo, N.D., U.S.A. ...47 0N 97 0W
98 Fari 'a R., Jordan ...32 12N 35 27E
164 Faribault, U.S.A. 44 15N 93 19W
104 Faridkot, India 30 44N 74 45E
105 Faridpur, E. Pakistan 23 36N 89 53E
105 Faridpur, India 18 14N 79 34E
80 Färila, Sweden 26 48N 15 55E
124 Farim, Port. Guinea ...21 27N 15 17W
101 Fariman, Iran 35 40N 60 0E
145 Farina, South Australia 30 3S 138 15E
34 Faringdon, Eng., U.K. 51 39N 1 34W
80 Faringe, Sweden 59 55N 18 7E
81 Färjestaden, Sweden .56 38N 16 25E
77 Farmakonisi, I., Greece 37 17N 27 8E
165 Farmerville, U.S.A. ...32 48N 92 23W
161 Farmington, N.H., U.S.A. 43 25N 71 7W
167 Farmington, N. Mex., U.S.A. 36 45N 108 28W
166 Farmington, Utah, U.S.A. 41 0N 111 58W
161 Farmington, R., U.S.A. 42 0N 73 5W
162 Farmville, U.S.A. 37 19N 78 22W
35 Farnborough, Eng., U.K. 51 17N 0 46W
41 Farne Is., Eng., U.K. 55 38N 1 37W
161 Farnham, Canada 45 20N 72 55W
35 Farnham, Eng., U.K. 51 13N 0 49W
156 Farnham Mt., Canada 50 25N 116 30W
39 Farnsfield, Eng., U.K. 53 7N 1 1W
38 Farnworth, Eng., U.K. 53 33N 2 33W
175 Faro, Brazil 2 0S 56 45W
63 Faro, tn. & dist., Port. 37 2N 7 55W
18 Faroe Is., N. Atl. Oc. .62 0N 7 0W
43 Farr, Scotland, U.K. .57 21N 4 13W
44 Farranfore, Ireland ...52 10N 9 32W
101 Farrashband, Iran ...28 57N 52 5E
160 Farrell, U.S.A. 41 13N 80 29W
145 Farrell Flat, S. Austral. 33 48S 138 48E
105 Farrukhabad, India ...27 30N 79 32E
76 Fársala, Greece 39 17N 22 23E
80 Farsö, Denmark 56 48N 9 20E
81 Farstrup, Denmark ...56 59N 9 28E
79 Farsund, Norway 58 3N 6 42E
125 Faru, Nigeria 12 48N 6 12E
81 Farum, Denmark 55 49N 12 27E
101 Farur I., Iran 26 20N 54 30E
165 Farwell, U.S.A. 34 25N 103 0W
101 Fasa, Iran 29 0N 53 32E
42 Fasag, Scot., U.K. 57 33N 5 32W
73 Fasano, Italy 40 50N 17 20E
127 Fashoda, Sudan 9 50N 32 2E
85 Faskari, Nigeria 11 42N 6 58E
40 Faslane, Scot., U.K. ...56 3N 4 49W
44 Fastnet Rock, Ireland 51 22N 9 37W
86 Fastov, U.S.S.R. 50 7N 29 57E
105 Fatehgarh, India 27 25N 79 35E
104 Fatehpur, Raj., India 28 0N 75 4E
105 Fatehpur Ut. P., India 27 8N 81 7E
113 Fati, China 23 10N 113 10E
124 Fatick, Senegal 14 19N 16 27W
63 Fátima, Portugal 39 37N 8 39W
113 Fatkeng, China 23 58N 113 29E
124 Fatoya, Guinea 11 37N 9 10W
113 Fatshan, China 23 0N 113 4E
49 Faucilles, Monts, France 48 5N 5 50E
41 Fauldhouse, Scot., U.K. 55 50N 3 44W
164 Faulkton, U.S.A. 45 4N 99 8W
49 Faurquemont, France 49 3N 6 36E
49 Fauquemberques, Fr. .50 36N 2 5E
142 Faure I., W. Australia 25 52S 113 50E
78 Făurel, Rumania 45 6N 27 19E
135 Fauresmith, S. Africa 29 44S 25 17E
82 Fauske, Norway 67 17N 1 25E
72 Favara, Italy 37 19N 13 39E
35 Faversham, Eng., U.K. 51 18N 0 54E
72 Favignana & I., Italy 37 56N 12 18E
51 Favone, France 41 47N 9 26E
154 Favourable Lake, Can. 52 40N 93 0W
34 Fawley, England, U.K. 50 49N 1 20W
154 Fawn R., Canada 54 20N 89 0W
82 Faxa Flói, Iceland 64 25N 23 0W
80 Faxälven. R., Sweden 63 20N 16 45E
121 Faya, see Largeau, Chad 17 58N 19 6E
51 Fayence, France 43 38N 6 42E
163 Fayette, Ala., U.S.A. .33 40N 87 50W
164 Fayette, Mo., U.S.A. .39 10N 92 40W
165 Fayetteville, Ark., U.S.A. 36 0N 94 5W
163 Fayetteville, N.C., U.S.A. 35 0N 78 0W
163 Fayetteville, Tenn., U.S.A. 35 0N 86 30W
64 Fayón, Spain 41 15N 0 20E
34 Fazeley, Eng., U.K. ...52 36N 1 42W
104 Fazilka, India 30 27N 74 2E
104 Fazilpur, W. Pakistan 29 18N 70 29E
120 F'Derik, Mauritania ...22 40N 12 45W
44 Feakle, Ireland 52 56N 8 41W
44 Feale R., Ireland 52 26N 9 28W
163 Fear, C., U.S.A. 33 45N 78 0W
43 Fearn, Scotland, U.K. 57 47N 4 0W
43 Fearnan, Scotland, U.K. 56 34N 4 6W
166 Feather R., U.S.A. ...39 30N 121 20W
146 Featherston, N.Z. 41 6S 175 20E
132 Featherstone, Rhodesia 18 42S 30 55E
143 Feathertop, Mt., Vic., Australia 36 53S 147 7E
48 Fécamp, France 49 45N 0 22E
44 Fecnagh, Ireland 52 9N 8 53W
122 Fedala, see Mohammeda, Morocco 33 44N 7 21W
44 Fedamore, Ire. 52 33N 8 36W
172 Federacion, Argentina 31 0S 57 55W
168 Federal District, Mexico 24 30N 99 10W
123 Fedjadj, Tunisia 33 54N 9 19E
79 Fedje, Norway 60 47N 4 45E
88 Fedorovka, U.S.S.R. .47 4N 35 18E
45 Feeagh L., Ireland 53 56N 9 35W
46 Feeny, N. Ire., U.K. .54 54N 7 0W
59 Fehergyarmat, Hungary....48 0N 22 30E
81 Fehmarn Baelt, str., Den. 54 35N 11 20E
56 Fehmarn I., Germany 54 26N 11 10E
113 Feihsien, China 35 12N 118 0E
146 Feilding, New Zealand 40 13S 175 35E
175 Feira, Brazil 12 20S 39 0W
132 Feira, Zambia 15 35S 30 16E
59 Fejér, co., Hungary ...47 9N 18 30E
81 Fejö I., Denmark 54 55N 11 30E
65 Felanitx, Spain 39 27N 3 7E
58 Feldbach, Austria 46 57N 15 52E
56 Feldberg, Germany ...53 20N 13 26E
57 Feldberg, mt., Germany 47 51N 7 58E
58 Feldkirch, Austria ...47 15N 9 37E
58 Feldkirchen, Austria .46 44N 14 6E
168 Felipe Carrillo Puerto, Mexico 19 38N 88 3W
123 Félix Faure, Algeria ...36 49N 3 37E
132 Felixburg, Rhodesia ...19 29S 30 51E
35 Felixstowe, Eng., U.K. 51 58N 1 22W
127 Felle, Ethiopia 16 40N 38 1E
50 Felletin, France 45 53N 2 11E
35 Felpham, Eng., U.K. .50 47N 0 38W
39 Felton, England, U.K. 55 18N 1 42W
71 Feltre, Italy 46 1N 11 55E
81 Femö I., Denmark 54 58N 11 53E
79 Femunden, L., Nor. ...62 5N 11 55E
46 Fenagh, Ireland 54 2N 7 50W
160 Fenelon Falls, Canada 44 31N 78 43W
129 Fénérive, Malagasy Rep. 17 22S 49 25E
76 Fengári, Mt., Greece .40 25N 25 32E
112 Fengchen, China 40 30N 113 0E
112 Fengcheng, China 40 28N 124 4E
112 Fengcheng, China 45 41N 128 54E
113 Fenghcheng, China 28 2N 115 46E
112 Fengcheng, China 36 40N 114 24E
113 Fenghsien, China 33 56N 106 41E
112 Fenghwa, China 29 37N 121 29E
113 Fengkieh (Kweichow), China 31 0N 109 33E
113 Fenglo, China 31 30N 112 29E
112 Fengman Dam, China 43 45N 126 35E
112 Fengning, China 41 10N 117 0E
113 Fengsiang, China 34 27N 107 30E
113 Fengsin, China 28 41N 115 11E
112 Fengtai, China 39 57N 116 21E
113 Fengtu, China 29 58N 107 59E
113 Fengy, China 23 48N 106 50E
113 Fengyuan, Taiwan ...24 10N 120 45E
144 Feni Is., Terr. of New Guinea 4 5S 153 25E
45 Fennagh, Ireland 52 42N 6 50W
164 Fennimore, U.S.A. ...42 58N 90 41W
105 Fenny East Pakistan 22 55N 91 32E
39 Fenny Bentley, England, U.K. 53 4N 1 43W
34 Fenny Compton, England, U.K. 52 9N 1 20W
35 Fenny Stratford, England, U.K. 51 59N 0 42W
51 Feno, C. de, Corsica, Fr. 41 58N 8 33E
35 Fens, The, Eng., U.K. 52 45N 0 2E
157 Fenton, Canada 53 0N 105 35W
162 Fenton, U.S.A. 42 47N 83 44W
40 Fenwick, Scot., U.K. .55 38N 4 25W
112 Fenyang, China 37 22N 111 31E
88 Feodosiya, U.S.S.R. ...45 2N 35 28E
123 Fer, C. de, Algeria ...37 3N 7 10E
44 Ferbane, Ireland 53 17N 7 50W
101 Ferdows, Iran 33 58N 58 2E
49 Fère Champenoise, Fr. 48 45N 4 0E
49 Fère en Tardenois, Fr. 49 10N 3 30E
72 Ferentino, Italy 41 42N 13 14E
99 Ferfer, Somali Rep. ... 5 18N 45 20E
90 Fergana, U.S.S.R. ...40 50N 71 50E
154 Fergus, Canada 43 43N 80 24W
44 Fergus R., Ireland ...52 45N 9 0W
164 Fergus Falls, U.S.A. ...46 25N 96 0W
154 Ferguson, Canada 47 50N 73 30W
144 Fergusson I., Papua ... 9 30S 150 40E
123 Feriana, Tunisia 34 59N 8 33E
74 Fericanci, Yugoslavia 45 32N 18 0E
123 Ferkane, Algeria 34 37N 7 26E
58 Ferlach, Austria 46 32N 14 18E
154 Ferland, Canada 50 19N 88 27W
124 Ferlo, Valeé du, Senegal 15 15N 14 15W
46 Fermanagh, co., N. Ireland, U.K. 54 21N 7 40W
71 Fermo, Italy 43 10N 13 42E
62 Fermoselle, Spain 41 19N 6 27W
44 Fermoy, Ireland 52 4N 8 18W
63 Fernan Núnez, Spain .37 40N 4 44W
172 Fernandez, Argentina 27 55S 63 50W
163 Fernandina, U.S.A. ...30 40N 81 30W
175 Fernando de Noronha, I., Brazil 4 0S 33 10W
115 Fernando Póo, I., Africa 3 30N 8 40E
166 Ferndale, Cal., U.S.A. 40 37N 124 12W
166 Ferndale, Wash., U.S.A. 48 51N 122 41W
43 Ferness, Scotland, U.K. 57 28N 3 44W
35 Fernhurst, Eng., U.K. 51 3N 0 43W
156 Fernie, B.C., Canada .49 30N 115 5W
42 Fernilea, Scot., U.K. .57 18N 6 24W
144 Fernlees, Australia ...23 55S 148 10E
166 Fernley, U.S.A. 39 42N 119 20W
106 Feroke, India 11 9N 75 46E
104 Ferozepore, India 30 55N 74 40E
76 Férrai, Greece 40 53N 26 10E
73 Ferrandina, Italy 40 30N 16 28E
71 Ferrara, Italy 44 50N 11 36E
72 Ferrato, C., Sardinia, It. 39 18N 9 39E
63 Ferreira do Alentejo, Portugal 38 4N 8 6W
174 Ferreñafe, Peru 6 35S 79 50W
49 Ferrette, France 47 30N 7 20E
165 Ferriday, U.S.A. 31 35N 91 33W
70 Ferriete, Italy 44 40N 9 30E
49 Ferrières, Loiret, France 48 5N 2 48E
62 Ferrol, Spain 43 29N 8 15W
166 Ferron, U.S.A. 39 3N 111 3W
39 Ferryhill, Eng., U.K. .54 42N 1 32W
164 Fertile, U.S.A. 47 37N 96 18W
59 Fertöszentmiklos, Hung. 47 35N 16 53E
122 Fès, Morocco 34 0N 5 0W
130 Feshi, Congo 6 0S 18 10E
164 Fessenden, U.S.A. ...47 42N 99 44W
79 Fet, Norway 59 57N 11 12E
78 Feteşti, Rumania 44 22N 27 51E
42 Fethaland, Pt., Scotland, U.K. 60 39N 1 20W
45 Fethard, Tipperary, Ire. 52 29N 7 42W
100 Fethiye, Turkey 36 36N 29 10E
42 Fetlar, I., Scot., U.K. 60 36N 0 52W
43 Fettercairn, Scot., U.K. 56 50N 2 33W
134 Fettluft-Nord, S.W. Afr. 27 34S 19 23E
51 Feurs, France 45 45N 4 13E
37 Ffestiniog, Wales, U.K. 52 58N 3 56W
37 Fforest Fawr, mt., Wales, U.K. 51 52N 3 35W
172 Fiambala, Argentina .27 45S 67 37W
129 Fianarantsoa, Malag. .21 20S 46 45E
121 Fianga, Cameroon 9 55N 15 20E
74 Fibiş, Rumania 45 57N 21 26E
155 Fichot, I., Canada ...51 12N 55 40W
57 Fichtel Geb., mts., Ger. 50 10N 12 0E
135 Ficksburg, S. Africa ...28 51S 27 53E
45 Fiddown, Ireland 52 20N 7 20W
70 Fidenza, Italy 44 51N 10 3E
125 Fiditi, Nigeria 7 45N 3 53E
142 Fields Finds, Australia 29 0S 117 10E
76 Fiéri, Albania 40 43N 19 33E
41 Fife, co., Scot., U.K. .56 13N 3 2W
41 Fife Ness, Scot., U.K. 56 17N 2 35W
127 Fifth Cataract, Sudan 18 15N 33 50E
50 Figeac, France 44 37N 2 2E
71 Figline Valdarno, Italy 43 37N 11 28E
132 Figtree, Rhodesia 20 22S 28 20E
62 Figueira da Foz, Port. 40 7N 8 54W
62 Figueira de Castelo Rodrigo, Portugal ...40 54N 6 58W
62 Figueiro dos Vinhos, Portugal 39 55N 8 16W
64 Figueras, Spain 42 18N 2 58E
122 Figuig, Morocco 32 5N 1 11W
136 Fiji Is., Pacific Ocean 17 20S 179 0E
125 Fika, Nigeria 11 5N 11 13E
132 Filabusi, Rhodesia ...20 30S 29 15E
73 Filadelfia, Italy 38 47N 16 17E
172 Filadelfia, Paraguay ...22 25S 60 0W
59 Filakovo, Cz. 48 17N 19 50E
35 Filby, England, U.K. .52 40N 1 39E
15 Filchner Ice Shelf, Antarctica 78 0S 60 0W

MAP
166 Filer, U.S.A. 42 30N 114 35W
39 Filey, England, U.K. .54 13N 0 18W
39 Filey B., Eng., U.K. .54 12N 0 15W
78 Filiaşi, Rumania 44 32N 23 31E
76 Filiátes, Greece 39 38N 20 16E
77 Filiatrá, Greece 37 9N 21 35E
73 Filicudi I., Italy 38 35N 14 33E
76 Filiouri, R., Greece 41 15N 25 40E
80 Filipstad, Sweden 59 42N 14 5E
57 Filisur, Switzerland ...46 41N 9 40E
157 Fillmore, Canada 49 50N 103 25W
167 Fillmore, Cal., U.S.A. 34 23N 118 58W
71 Filottrano, Italy 43 28N 13 20E
36 Filton, England, U.K. 51 29N 2 34E
88 Filyas, Turkey 41 34N 32 4E
100 Filyos, R., Turkey 41 35N 32 10E
130 Fimi, R., Congo 3 0S 17 15E
70 Finale Ligure, Italy ...44 10N 8 21E
71 Finale nell' Emilia, It. 44 50N 11 18E
65 Fiñana, Spain 37 10N 2 50W
161 Finch, Canada 45 10N 75 5W
35 Fincham, Eng., U.K. .52 38N 0 30E
43 Findhorn, R., Scot.,
U.K. 57 30N 3 45W
162 Findlay, U.S.A. 41 0N 83 41W
43 Findochty, Scot.,
U.K. 57 42N 2 53W
35 Findon, England,
U.K. 50 53N 0 24W
46 Finea, Ireland 53 46N 7 23W
35 Finedon, Eng., U.K. .52 20N 0 40W
157 Finger L., Canada 53 15N 93 35W
35 Fingest, Eng., U.K. ...51 35N 0 52W
45 Finglas, Ireland 53 22N 6 18W
132 Fingoé, Mozambique .15 12S 31 50E
100 Finike, Turkey 36 21N 30 10E
48 Finistére, dépt.,
France 48 20N 4 0W
62 Finisterre, Spain 42 54N 9 16W
62 Finisterre, Cabo,
Spain 42 50N 9 19W
84 Finland, rep., Europe 70 0N 27 0E
84 Finland, G. of,
Europe 60 0N 26 0E
143 Finley, N.S.W.,
Austral. 35 50S 145 40E
164 Finley, U.S.A. 47 35N 97 50W
46 Finn, R., Ire. 54 50N 7 55W
40 Finnart, Scot., U.K. ...56 7N 4 48W
81 Finnerödja, Sweden ...58 57N 14 24E
82 Finnmark, co.,
Norway 69 30N 25 0E
79 Finnöy, Norway 59 11N 5 46E
144 Finschhafen, N.E.
New Guinea 6 33S 147 48E
79 Finse, Norway 60 36N 7 30E
81 Finspang, Sweden 58 45N 15 43E
80 Finsta, Sweden 59 45N 18 34E
57 Finsteraarhorn Mt.,
Switzerland 46 31N 8 10E
56 Finsterwalde,
Germany 51 37N 13 42E
43 Finstown, Scot., U.K. 59 0N 3 8W
46 Fintona, N. Ire., U.K. 54 30N 7 20W
46 Fintown, Ireland 54 52N 8 8W
46 Finvoy, N. Ire., U.K. 55 0N 6 29W
42 Fionn L., Scot., U.K. .57 46N 5 30W
40 Fionnphort, Scot.,
U.K. 56 19N 6 23W
71 Fiora R., Italy 42 25N 11 35E
147 Fiordland National
Park, N.Z. 45 0S 167 50E
70 Fiorenzuola d'Arda,
It. 44 56N 9 54E
131 Fipa, Plat., Tanzania . 8 0S 31 10E
98 Fiq, Syria 32 46N 35 41E
100 Firat (Euphrates), R.,
Iraq & Turkey 33 30N 43 0E
154 Fire River, Canada 48 47N 83 36W
157 Firedrake L., Canada .61 25N 104 40W
71 Firenze (Florence),
Italy 43 47N 11 15E
124 Firkessédougou, Ivory
C. 9 35N 5 6W
172 Firmat, Argentine 33 29S 61 29W
51 Firminy, France 45 23N 4 18E
86 Firovo, U.S.S.R. 56 43N 33 37E
170 Firozabad, India 27 10N 78 25E
126 First Cataract, Egypt 24 1N 32 51E
101 Firuzabad, Iran 28 52N 52 35E
101 Firuzkuh, Iran 35 50N 52 40E
134 Fish R., S.W. Africa .27 40S 17 30E
143 Fish Creek, Australia .38 43S 146 7E
142 Fisher, S. Australia ...30 30S 131 0E
37 Fishguard, Wales,
U.K. 51 59N 4 59W
37 Fishguard B., Wales,
United Kingdom 52 2N 4 58W
157 Fishing L., Canada 52 10N 95 30W
124 Fishtown, Liberia 4 24N 7 45E
134 Fishwater, S. Africa ...31 41S 18 13E
79 Fiskum, Norway 59 42N 9 46E
49 Fismes, France 49 20N 3 40E
79 Fister, Norway 59 10N 6 5E
161 Fitchburg, U.S.A. 42 35N 71 47W
64 Fitero, Spain 42 4N 1 52W
42 Fitful Hd., Scot.,
U.K. 59 54N 1 20W
79 Fitjar, Norway 59 55N 5 20E
174 Fitzcarrald, Peru 11 58S 71 55W
163 Fitzgerald, U.S.A. 31 45N 83 10W
154 Fitzpatrick, Canada ...47 29N 72 46W
176 Fitz Roy, Argentina ...47 10S 67 0W
138 Fitzroy Crossing,
Western Australia .18 9S 125 38E
144 Fitzroy R., Australia .23 10S 150 10E
138 Fitzroy, R., W.
Austral. 17 30S 124 0E
160 Fitzwilliam I.,
Canada..................45 30N 81 45W
71 Fiume, see Rijeka,
Yugoslavia 45 20N 14 21E
73 Fiumefreddo Bruzio,
It. 39 14N 16 4E
44 Five Alley, Ireland 53 9N 7 51W
46 Fivemiletown,
Northern Ireland,
U.K. 54 23N 7 20W
132 Fiwila, Zambia 13 58S 29 33E
131 Fizi, Congo 4 17S 28 55E
79 Fjaere, Hordaland,
Nor. 59 53N 6 25E
79 Fjaere, Aust Agder,
Nor. 58 23N 8 36E
81 Fjellerup, Denmark ...56 29N 10 36E
81 Fjerreslev, Denmark .57 0N 9 12E
122 Fkih ben Salah, Mor. .32 45N 6 45W
79 Flå, Buskerud,
Norway 60 25N 9 26E
79 Flå, Sör Tröndelag,
Nor. 63 13N 10 18E
34 Fladbury, Eng., U.K. 52 7N 2 0W
164 Flagler, U.S.A. 39 20N 103 4W
135 Flagstaff, S. Africa 31 3S 29 31E
167 Flagstaff, U.S.A. 35 10N 111 40W
156 Flagstone, Canada 49 4N 115 10W
154 Flaherty. I., Canada .56 0N 79 55W
164 Flambeau R., U.S.A. .45 40N 90 50W
39 Flamborough, Eng.,
U.K. 54 7N 0 7W
39 Flamborough Hd.,
England, U.K. 54 8N 0 4W
166 Flaming Gorge Dam,
U.S.A. 40 50N 109 25W
166 Flaming Gorge L.,
U.S.A. 41 15N 109 30W
109 Flamingo B.,
Indonesia 5 30S 138 0E
54 Flandre Occid., prov.,
Belgium 51 0N 3 0E
54 Flandre Orientale,
prov., Belgium 51 0N 4 0E
54 Flandres, Plaines des,
Belg. 51 10N 3 15E
164 Flandreau, U.S.A. 44 5N 96 38W
28 Flannan Is., Scot.,
U.K. 58 9N 7 52W
81 Flåren L., Sweden 57 2N 14 5E
82 Flåsjön, L., Sweden ...64 11N 16 5E
165 Flat River, Mo.,
U.S.A. 37 50N 90 30W
166 Flathead L., U.S.A. ...47 50N 114 0W
166 Flattery, C., U.S.A. ...48 21N 124 31W
49 Flavy de Martel, Fr. .49 43N 3 12E
164 Flaxton, U.S.A. 48 52N 102 24W
35 Fleet, England, U.K. .51 16N 0 50W
43 Fleet L., Scot., U.K. .57 57N 4 2W
43 Fleet R., Scot., U.K. .57 43N 4 10W
38 Fleetwood, Eng.,
U.K. 53 55N 3 1W
79 Flekkefjord, Norway .58 22N 6 43E
160 Flemington, U.S.A. 41 7N 77 28W
80 Flen, Sweden 59 4N 16 39E
56 Flensburg, Germany .54 46N 9 28E
81 Flensburg, Fjord,
Den. 54 48N 9 45E
48 Flers, France 48 47N 0 33W
79 Flesberg, Norway 59 51N 9 22E
160 Flesherton, Canada ...44 15N 80 34W
44 Flesk, R., Ireland 52 3N 9 27W
35 Fletton, Eng., U.K. ...52 34N 0 13W
50 Fleurance, France 43 52N 0 40E
57 Fleurier, Switzerland .46 54N 6 35E
55 Fleurus, Belgium 50 29N 4 32E
80 Flickerbäcken,
Sweden 61 47N 12 34E
38 Flimby, Eng., U.K. ...54 42N 3 31W
157 Flin Flon, Canada 54 50N 102 0W
142 Flinders B., W.
Austral. 34 19S 115 9E
145 Flinders I., Australia .40 0S 148 0E
145 Flinders Ras., S.
Austral. 31 30S 138 30E
144 Flinders R., Australia 20 0S 141 35E
37 Flint, & Co., Wales,
United Kingdom ...53 14N 3 8W
162 Flint, Mich., U.S.A. ...43 0N 83 40W
137 Flint I., Pacific Ocean 10 5S 151 48W
163 Flint R., U.S.A. 31 20N 84 10W
145 Flinton, Australia 27 55S 149 32E
81 Fliseryd, Sweden 57 6N 16 15E
64 Flix, Spain 41 14N 0 32E
49 Flixecourt, France 50 0N 2 5E
35 Flitwick, England,
U.K. 51 59N 0 30W
80 Floda, Sweden 60 30N 14 53E
39 Flodden, England,
U.K. 55 37N 2 8W
164 Floodwood, U.S.A. 46 55N 92 55W
172 Flor de Chile, Chile 25 18S 69 57W
162 Flora, U.S.A. 38 40N 88 30W
79 Flora, N. Tröndelag,
Norway 63 27N 11 22E
79 Flora, Sogn &
Fjordane, Norway .61 36N 5 0E
50 Florac, France 44 20N 3 37E
163 Florala, U.S.A. 31 0N 86 20W
55 Floreffe, Belgium 50 26N 4 46E
71 Florence, see Firenze,
Italy 43 47N 11 15E
163 Florence, Ala., U.S.A. 34 50N 87 50W
167 Florence, Ariz.,
U.S.A. 33 0N 111 25W
164 Florence, Colo.,
U.S.A. 38 26N 105 0W
166 Florence, Ore., U.S.A. 44 0N 124 3W
163 Florence, S.C., U.S.A. 34 5N 79 50W
174 Florencia, Colombia ... 1 36N 75 36W
54 Florennes, Belgium ...50 15N 4 35E
54 Florenville, Belgium ...49 40N 5 19E
168 Flores, Guatemala 16 50N 89 40W
18 Flores I., Azores 39 26N 31 13W
156 Flores I., Canada 49 20N 126 10W
109 Flores I., Indonesia ... 8 35S 121 0E
108 Flores Sea, Indonesia . 6 30S 124 0E
165 Floresville, U.S.A. 29 10N 98 10W
175 Floriano, Brazil 6 50S 43 0W
173 Florianopolis, Brazil ...27 30S 48 30W
169 Florida, Cuba 21 32N 78 14W
173 Florida, Uruguay 34 7S 56 10W
163 Florida, st., U.S.A. 28 30N 82 0W
169 Florida B., U.S.A. 25 0N 81 20W
169 Florida Keys U.S.A. .25 0N 80 40W
169 Florida, Strait of,
U.S.A. 25 0N 80 0W
73 Florida, Italy 37 6N 15 9E
59 Floridsdorf, Austria ...48 15N 16 25E
76 Flórina, Greece 40 48N 21 26E
76 Flórina, pref., Greece .40 45N 21 20E
79 Florö, Norway 61 37N 5 6E
79 Flosta, Norway 58 32N 8 56E
80 Florningen, Sweden ...61 50N 12 16E
43 Flotta, I., Scot., U.K. 58 50N 3 8W
161 Flower Sta., Canada ...45 10N 76 42W
155 Flower's Cove,
Canada 51 14N 56 46W
165 Floydada, U.S.A. 33 58N 101 18W
109 Fluk, Indonesia 1 42S 127 38E
64 Flumen R., Spain 41 50N 0 25W
72 Flumendosa R., Italy 39 30N 9 25E
72 Fluminimaggiore,
Italy 39 25N 8 30E
54 Flushing, see
Vlissingen,
Netherlands 51 26N 3 34E
144 Fly R., Papua 7 50S 141 20E
157 Foam Lake, Canada ...51 40N 103 15W
74 Foča, Yugoslavia 43 31N 18 47E
43 Fochabers, Scot.,
U.K. 57 37N 3 7W
133 Fochville, Trans., S.
Afr. 26 29S 27 30E
78 Focsani, Rumania 45 41N 27 15E
144 Fofo Fofo, T. of
Papua 8 9S 147 6E
122 Foggaret el Arab, Alg. 27 3N 2 59E
122 Foggaret ez Zoua,
Alg. 27 20N 3 0E
73 Foggia, Italy 41 28N 15 31E
125 Foggo, Nigeria 11 21N 9 57E
71 Foglia R., Italy 43 50N 12 32E
155 Fogo I., Canada 49 40N 54 5W
58 Fohnsdorf, Austria 47 12N 14 40E
56 Föhr I., Germany 54 40N 8 30E
46 Foilclogh Mt., Ireland 51 53N 10 10W
43 Foinhaven Mt.,
Scotland, U.K. 58 25N 4 54W
50 Foix, France 42 58N 1 38E
50 Foix, reg., France 42 59N 1 35E
74 Fojnica, Yugoslavia ...43 59N 17 51E
77 Fokis, pref., Greece ...38 30N 22 15E
79 Fokstua, Norway 62 8N 9 16E
82 Folda, Norway 67 27N 15 35E
80 Foldan Fjord, Norway 64 43N 11 45E
79 Foldeak, Hungary 46 19N 20 30E
163 Foley, U.S.A. 30 25N 87 40W
154 Foleyet, Canada 48 15N 82 25W
79 Folgefonni, Norway ...60 23N 6 34E
71 Foligno, Italy 42 58N 12 40E
35 Folkestone, Eng.,
U.K. 51 5N 1 11E
163 Folkston, U.S.A. 30 55N 82 0W
165 Follett, U.S.A. 36 30N 100 12W
70 Follonica, Italy 42 55N 10 45E
166 Folsom, U.S.A. 38 41N 121 7W
157 Fond du lac, Canada .59 20N 107 10W
164 Fond du lac, U.S.A. ...43 46N 88 26W
157 Fond du lac R.,
Canada 58 55N 104 50W
161 Fonda, U.S.A. 42 57N 74 23W
122 Fondak, Morocco 35 34N 5 35W
72 Fondi, Italy 41 21N 13 25E
62 Fonfria, Spain 41 37N 6 9W
79 Fongen, Mt., Norway .63 11N 11 39E
62 Fonsagrada, Spain 43 8N 7 4W
168 Fonseca, G. of, C.
Amer. 13 10N 87 40W
49 Fontaine Française,
Fr. 47 32N 5 21E
49 Fontainebleau, France 48 24N 2 40E
174 Fonte Boa, Brazil 2 25S 66 0W
125 Fontem, Cameroon 5 32N 9 52E
50 Fontenay le Comte,
Fr. 46 28N 0 48W
155 Fontenelle, Canada 48 54N 64 33W
45 Fontstown, Ireland 53 2N 6 54W
59 Fonyod, Hungary 46 44N 17 33E
113 Foochow (Minhow)
China 26 2N 119 25E
113 Foping, China 33 47N 107 56E
70 Foppiano, Italy 46 21N 8 24E
81 Föra, Sweden 57 2N 16 52E
49 Forbach, France 49 10N 6 52E
143 Forbes, N.S.W.,
Austral. 33 22S 148 0E
46 Forbes L., Ireland 53 47N 7 53W
133 Forbes Reef,
Swaziland 26 10S 31 5E
105 Forbesganj, India 26 17N 87 18E
125 Forcados, Nigeria 5 26N 5 26E
125 Forcados R., Nigeria . 5 25N 5 20E
64 Forcall, R., Spain 40 40N 0 12W
51 Forcalquier, France ...43 58N 5 47E
57 Forchheim, Germany .49 42N 11 4E
45 Ford, Ireland 52 32N 6 15W
40 Ford, Scotland, U.K. .56 10N 5 27W
138 Ford, C., Australia 13 31N 129 55E
160 Ford City, U.S.A. 40 47N 79 31W
79 Förde, Norway 61 28N 5 45E
37 Forden, Eng., U.K. ...52 34N 3 8W
34 Fordham, Eng., U.K. 52 19N 0 23E
34 Fordingbridge,
England, U.K. 50 56N 1 48W
50 Fordongianus, Italy ...40 0N 8 50E
145 Fords Bridge,
Australia 29 41S 145 29E
43 Fordyce, Scot., U.K. .57 40N 2 45W
165 Fordyce, U.S.A. 33 50N 92 20W
124 Forécariah, Guinea 9 20N 13 10W
14 Forel Mt., Greenland .67 0N 36 0W
36 Foreland, The, C.,
England, U.K. 51 14N 3 48W
156 Foremost, Canada 49 26N 112 41W
73 Forenza, Italy 40 50N 15 50E
160 Forest, Canada 43 9N 82 0W
165 Forest, U.S.A. 32 21N 89 27W
165 Forest City, Ark.,
U.S.A. 35 0N 90 50W
164 Forest City, Iowa,
U.S.A. 43 12N 93 39W
163 Forest City, N.C.,
U.S.A. 35 23N 81 50W
161 Forest City, Pa.,
U.S.A. 41 39N 75 29W
166 Forest Gro., U.S.A. ...45 31N 123 4W
34 Forest of Dean,
England, U.K. 51 48N 2 35W
156 Forest Lawn, Canada .51 4N 114 0W
29 Forest Ridges,
England, U.K. 51 5N 0 15E
35 Forest Row, Eng.,
U.K. 51 6N 0 3E
156 Forestburg, Canada ...52 35N 112 1W
155 Forestville, Canada ...48 48N 69 20W
162 Forestville, U.S.A. 44 41N 87 29W
50 Forez, Mts. du,
France 45 40N 3 50E
43 Forfar, Scotland,
U.K. 56 40N 2 53W
49 Forges-les-Eaux,
France 49 37N 1 30E
154 Forget, Canada 49 40N 102 50W
46 Forkhill, N. Ire., U.K. 54 5N 6 25W
166 Forks, U.S.A. 47 56N 124 40W
71 Forli, Italy 44 14N 12 2E
164 Forman, U.S.A. 46 9N 97 43W
43 Formartine, dist.,
Scotland, U.K. 57 20N 2 15W
70 Formazza, Italy 46 23N 8 26E
38 Formby, Eng., U.K. .53 34N 3 4W
38 Formby Pt., Eng.,
U.K. 53 33N 3 7W
65 Formentera I., Spain .38 40N 1 30E
64 Formentor, C. de,
Balearic Is., Spain .39 58N 3 13E
72 Formia, Italy 41 15N 13 34E
70 Formigine, Italy 44 37N 10 51E
50 Formiguères, France .42 37N 2 5E
113 Formosa, see Taiwan,
I., Asia 23 30N 121 0E
172 Formosa, Argentina ...26 15S 58 10W
172 Formosa, prov., Arg. .26 5S 58 10W
131 Formosa Bay, Kenya . 2 40S 40 20E
113 Formosa Str., Asia 24 0N 119 10E
157 Formoso, Goiaz,
Brazil 15 25S 47 20W
81 Fornaes, C., Denmark 56 27N 10 58E
64 Fornells, Spain 40 4N 4 4E
62 Fornos de Algodres,
Portugal 40 38N 7 32W
70 Fornovo di Taro,
Italy 44 42N 10 7E
43 Forres, Scotland,
U.K. 57 37N 3 38W
143 Forrest, Vic.,
Australia 38 22S 143 40E
142 Forrest, W. Australia .30 50S 128 2E
142 Forrest Mt., W.
Austral. 22 55S 114 46E
80 Fors, Jämtland,
Sweden 63 0N 16 40E
80 Fors, Kopparberg,
Swed. 60 14N 16 20E
80 Forsa, Sweden 61 45N 16 59E
79 Forsand, Norway 58 56N 6 6E
144 Forsayth, Australia ...18 33S 143 34E
80 Forsbacka, Sweden 60 39N 16 54E
80 Forse, Sweden 63 8N 17 1E
81 Forserum, Sweden 57 42N 14 25E
80 Forshaga, Sweden 59 33N 13 29E
81 Forshem, Sweden 58 38N 13 30E
43 Forsinain, Scot., U.K. 58 25N 3 53W
43 Forsinard, Scot., U.K. 58 20N 3 53W
80 Forsmo, Sweden 63 15N 17 13E
83 Forssa, Finland 60 47N 23 35E
56 Forst, Germany 51 43N 14 37E
143 Forster, Australia 32 12S 152 31E
163 Forsyth, Ga., U.S.A. .33 4N 83 55W
166 Forsyth, Mont.,
U.S.A. 46 14N 106 37W
147 Forsyth I., N.Z. 40 58S 174 5E
154 Fort Albany, Canada .52 15N 18 35W
168 Fort Amador,
Panama Canal Zone 8 56N 79 32W
167 Fort Apache, U.S.A. .33 50N 110 0W
121 Fort Archambault,
Chad 9 5N 18 23E
156 Fort Assiniboine, Can. 54 20N 114 45W
43 Fort Augustus,
Scotland, U.K. 57 9N 4 40W
174 Fort Ayacucho, Par. .20 0S 59 50W
156 Fort Babine, Canada .55 22N 126 37W
131 Fort Banda, Uganda . 1 9N 32 35E
135 Fort Beaufort, S. Afr. 32 46S 26 40E
162 Fort Benton, U.S.A. .47 50N 110 40W
166 Fort Bragg, U.S.A. 39 28N 123 50W
121 Fort Bretonnet, Chad 10 34N 16 52E
166 Fort Bridger, U.S.A. .41 22N 110 20W
125 Fort Charlet, see
Djanet, Algeria 24 35N 9 32E
153 Fort Chima, Canada ...58 9N 68 12W
157 Fort Chipewyan, Can. 58 46N 111 9W
168 Fort Clayton, Panama
Canal Zone 9 0N 79 35W
164 Fort Collins, U.S.A. ...40 30N 105 4W
154 Fort Coulonge,
Canada 45 50N 76 45W
121 Fort Crampel, Central
African Republic ... 7 8N 19 81E
129 Fort Dauphin, Malag. 25 2S 47 0E
168 Fort Davis, Panama
Canal Zone 9 17N 79 56W
165 Fort Davis, U.S.A. 30 38N 103 53W
167 Fort Defiance, U.S.A. 35 47N 109 4W
169 Fort de France,
Martinique 14 36N 61 2W
128 Fort de Possel,
Central African
Republic 5 5N 19 10E
164 Fort Dodge, U.S.A. ...42 29N 94 10W
161 Fort Edward, U.S.A. .43 16N 73 35W
123 Fort Flatters, Alg., see
Zaouiet El Kahla ...27 10N 6 40E
121 Fort Foureau, Cam. ...12 0N 14 55E
157 Fort Frances, Canada 48 35N 93 25W
152 Fort Franklin, Canada 65 30N 123 45W
167 Fort Garland, U.S.A. .37 28N 105 30W
155 Fort George, Canada .53 40N 79 0W
154 Fort George R.,
Canada 53 50N 77 0W
152 Fort Good-Hope,
Can. 66 14N 128 40W
120 Fort Gouraud, see
F'Derik, Mauritania 22 40N 12 45W
156 Fort Grahame,
Canada 56 30N 124 35W
131 Fort Hall, see
Muranga, Kenya 1 0S 37 50E
167 Fort Hancock, U.S.A. 31 19N 105 56W
103 Fort Hertz (Putao),
Burma 27 28N 97 30E
154 Fort Hope, Canada ...51 30N 88 10W
167 Fort Hauchuca,
U.S.A. 31 32N 110 30W
132 Fort Jameson, see
Chipata, Zambia 13 38S 32 38E
132 Fort Jonston,
Malawi 14 25S 35 16E
155 Fort Kent, U.S.A. 47 12N 68 30W
166 Fort Klamath, U.S.A. 42 45N 122 0W
123 Fort Lallemand,
Algeria 31 13N 6 17E
121 Fort Lamy, Chad 12 4N 15 8E
123 Fort Laperrine, see
Tamanrasset,
Algeria 22 56N 5 30E
164 Fort Laramie, U.S.A. .42 15N 104 30W
163 Fort Lauderdale,
U.S.A. 26 10N 80 5W
156 Fort Liard, Canada ...60 20N 123 30W
169 Fort Liberté, Haiti ...19 42N 71 51W
164 Fort Lupton, U.S.A. .40 8N 104 48W
156 Fort Macleod, Alta.,
Canada 49 45N 113 30W
156 Fort Mackay, Canada 57 12N 111 41W
155 Fort McKenzie,
Canada 56 50N 69 0W
122 Fort MacMahon,
Algeria 29 51N 1 45E
152 Fort McPherson,
Canada 67 30N 134 55W
164 Fort Madison, U.S.A. .40 39N 91 20E
163 Fort Meade, U.S.A. ...27 45N 81 45W
122 Fort Miribel, Algeria .29 31N 2 55E
164 Fort Morgan, U.S.A. .40 10N 103 50W
123 Fort Motylinski,
Algeria 22 47N 5 59E
163 Fort Myers, U.S.A. ...26 30N 82 0W
156 Fort Nelson, Canada .58 50N 122 30W
156 Fort Nelson R.,
Canada 59 20N 123 30W
152 Fort Norman, Canada 64 57N 125 30W
123 Fort Pacot (Chirfa),
Niger 20 55N 12 14E
163 Fort Payne, U.S.A. ...34 25N 85 44W
166 Fort Peck, U.S.A. 47 1N 105 30W
166 Fort Peck Dam,
U.S.A. 48 0N 106 20W
166 Fort Peck Res.,
U.S.A. 47 40N 107 0W
164 Fort Pierce, U.S.A. ...27 29N 80 19W
164 Fort Pierre, U.S.A. ...44 25N 100 25W
122 Fort Pierre Bordes,
Algeria 20 0N 2 55E
161 Fort Plain, U.S.A. ...42 56N 74 39W
131 Fort Portal, Uganda . 0 40N 30 20E
156 Fort Providence, Can. 61 20N 117 30W
157 Fort Qu'Appelle, Can. 50 45N 103 50W
168 Fort Randolph,
Panama Canal Zone 9 23N 79 53W
157 Fort Reliance, Canada 62 40N 109 0W
156 Fort Resolution,
Canada 61 10N 114 40W
132 Fort Rixon, Rhodesia 20 2S 29 17E
132 Fort Rosebery, see
Mansa, Zambia 11 10S 28 50E
130 Fort Rousset, Congo
(Fr.) 0 35S 16 5E
154 Fort Rupert (Rupert
House), Canada 51 30N 78 40W
123 Fort Saint, Tunisia 30 13N 9 31E
156 Fort St. James,
Canada 54 30N 124 10W
156 Fort St. John, Canada 56 15N 120 50W
104 Fort Sandeman, W.
Pak. 31 20 69 25E
156 Ft. Saskatchewan
Can. 53 40N 113 15W
165 Fort Scott, U.S.A. 38 0N 94 40W
152 Fort Selkirk, Canada .62 43N 137 22W

MAP
154 Fort Severn, Canada .56 0N 87 40W
168 Fort Sherman, Panama Canal Zone 9 22N 79 56W
89 Fort Shevchenko, U.S.S.R. ...44 30N 50 10W
121 Fort Sibut, Central African Republic ... 5 52N 19 10W
156 Fort Simpson, Canada 61 45N 121 30W
156 Fort Smith, Canada ...60 1N 112 4W
165 Fort Smith, U.S.A. 35 25N 94 25W
167 Fort Stanton, U.S.A. .33 33N 105 36W
165 Fort Stockton, U.S.A. 30 48N 103 2W
165 Fort Sumner, U.S.A. .34 24N 104 8W
167 Fort Thomas, U.S.A. .33 2N 109 59W
120 Fort Trinquet, *see* Bir Mogrein, Maur. ...25 10N 11 25W
163 Fort Valley, U.S.A. ...32 33N 83 52W
156 Fort Vermillion, Canada ...58 20N 116 0W
132 Fort Victoria, Rhodesia ...20 8S 30 55E
163 Ft. Walton Beach, U.S.A. ...30 25N 86 40W
162 Fort Wayne, U.S.A. ...41 5N 85 10W
154 Fort William, Canada 48 20N 89 10W
42 Fort William, Scot., U.K. ...56 48N 5 8W
165 Fort Worth, U.S.A. ...32 45N 97 25W
164 Fort Yates, U.S.A. 46 8N 100 38W
152 Fort Yukon, Alaska, U.S.A. ...66 35N 145 12W
175 Fortaleza (Ceará), Brazil ... 3 35S 38 35W
174 Forte Coimbra, Brazil 19 55S 57 48W
129 Forte Rocadas, Angola ...16 38S 15 22E
155 Forteau, Canada ...51 28N 57 1W
138 Fortescue, W. Austral. ...21 4S 116 4E
138 Fortescue R., Australia ...21 20S 116 45E
41 Forth, Scotland, U.K. 55 45N 3 42W
41 Forth Bridge, Scot., U.K. ...56 0N 3 24W
41 Forth, Firth of, Scotland, U.K. ...56 5N 2 55W
40 Forth R., Scot., U.K. 56 9N 4 18W
122 Forthassa Rharbia, Alg. ...32 52N 1 11W
174 Fortin Corrales, Par. .22 21S 60 35W
174 Fortin Guachalla, Par. 22 22S 62 23W
174 Fortin Siracuas, Par. .21 3S 61 46W
172 Fortin Teniente Montania, Paraguay 22 1S 59 45W
71 Fortore R., Italy ...41 40N 15 0E
43 Fortrie, Scot., U.K. ...57 30N 2 32W
43 Fortrose, Scot., U.K. .57 35N 4 10W
147 Fortrose, New Zealand ...46 38S 168 45E
65 Fortuna Spain ...38 11N 1 7W
133 Fortuna, Trans., S. Afr. ...26 33S 28 33E
166 Fortuna, Cal., U.S.A. .48 38N 124 8W
164 Fortuna, N.D., U.S.A. 48 55N 103 48W
155 Fortune Bay, Canada 47 30N 55 22W
152 Forty Mile, Canada ...64 20N 140 30W
174 Fos do Jordão, Brazil 9 30S 72 14W
112 Foshan, China ...48 32N 130 38E
71 Fossacesia, Italy ...42 15N 14 30E
70 Fossano, Italy ...44 39N 7 40E
166 Fossil, U.S.A. ...45 0N 120 9W
144 Fossilbrook, Australia 17 47S 144 29E
71 Fossombrone, Italy ...43 41N 12 49E
164 Fosston, U.S.A. ...47 33N 95 39W
143 Foster, Vic., Australia 38 40S 146 15E
161 Foster, Canada ...45 20N 72 30W
162 Fostoria, Ohio, U.S.A. 41 8N 83 25W
41 Fothergill, Eng., U.K. 54 43N 3 30W
35 Fotheringhay, Eng., U.K. ...52 32N 0 28W
48 Fougères, France ...48 21N 1 14W
106 Foul Pt., Ceylon ... 8 35N 81 25E
28 Foula, I., Scot., U.K. .60 10N 2 5W
45 Foulksmills, Ireland ...52 18N 6 46W
35 Foulness I., Eng., U.K. ...51 36N 0 55E
35 Foulness Pt., Eng., U.K. ...51 36N 0 59E
35 Foulsham, Eng., U.K. 52 48N 1 1E
122 Foum el Alba, Mali ...20 45N 3 0W
122 Foum el Kreneg, Alg. 29 0N 0 58W
123 Foum Tatahouine, Tun. ...32 57N 10 29E
122 Foum Zguid, Morocco 30 2N 6 59W
125 Foumban, Cameroon . 5 45N 10 50E
124 Foundiougne, Senegal 14 5N 16 32W
164 Fountain, Colo., U.S.A. ...38 42N 104 40W
166 Fountain, Utah, U.S.A. ...39 41N 111 50W
41 Fountainhall, Scot., U.K. ...55 45N 2 55W
39 Fountains Abbey, England, U.K. ...54 8N 1 35W
49 Fourchambault, France ...47 0N 3 3E
155 Fourchu, Canada ...45 43N 60 17W
135 Fourlesburg, S. Africa 28 38S 28 14E
49 Fourmies, France ...50 1N 4 2E
77 Fournás, Greece ...39 3N 21 52E
77 Fournoi, & I., Greece .37 36N 26 32E
49 Fours, France ...46 50N 3 42E
124 Fouta Djalon, Guinea 11 20N 12 10W
169 Foux, Cap- à Haiti ...19 43N 73 27W
34 Fovant, England, U.K. ...51 4N 2 0W
147 Foveaux Str., N.Z. ...46 42S 168 10E
36 Fowey, England, U.K. ...50 20N 4 39W
36 Fowey R., Eng., U.K. 50 20N 4 39W
167 Fowler, Cal., U.S.A. ...36 41N 119 47W
164 Fowler, Colo., U.S.A. .38 10N 104 0W
165 Fowler, Kan., U.S.A. .37 28N 100 7W
138 Fowlers Bay, S. Austral. ...32 0S 132 29E
165 Fowlerton, U.S.A. ...28 26N 98 50W
113 Fowliang, China ...27 8N 117 12E
113 Fowling, China ...29 39N 107 29E
37 Fownhope, Eng., U.K. ...52 0N 2 37W
113 Fowning, China ...33 47N 119 57E
173 Fowping, China ...38 40N 114 20E
113 Fowyang (Yingchow) China ...33 0N 116 0E
157 Fox Valley, Canada ...50 30N 109 25W
38 Foxdale, I. of M., U.K. ...54 12N 4 38W
153 Foxe Basin, Canada ...68 30N 77 0W
153 Foxe Channel, Canada 66 0N 80 0W
153 Foxe Pen., Canada ...65 0N 76 0W
80 Foxen, L., Sweden ...59 25N 11 55E
46 Foxford, Ireland ...54 0N 9 7W
166 Foxpark, U.S.A. ...41 4N 106 6W
146 Foxton, New Zealand 40 29S 175 18E
43 Foyers, Scotland, U.K. ...57 15N 4 30W
46 Foyle, Lough, Northern Ireland, U.K. ...55 6N 7 8W
46 Foyle R., N. Ire., U.K. ...54 58N 7 22W
44 Foynes, Ireland ...52 37N 9 5W
62 Foz, Spain ...43 33N 7 20W
174 Foz do Gregório, Brazil ... 6 47S 71 0W
173 Foz do Iguacu, Brazil 25 30S 54 30W
161 Frackville, U.S.A. ...40 46N 76 15W
36 Fraddon, Eng., U.K. .50 22N 4 55W
64 Fraga, Spain ...41 32N 0 21E
161 Framingham, U.S.A. .42 18N 71 26W
35 Framlingham, Eng., U.K. ...52 14N 1 20E
130 Fran Joseph Falls, Congo ... 7 34S 17 14E
175 Franca, Brazil ...20 25S 47 30W
71 Francavilla al Mare, It. ...42 25N 14 16E
73 Francavilla Fontana, It. ...40 32N 17 35E
47 France, rep., Europe .47 0N 3 0E
156 Frances L., Canada ...61 30N 129 20W
138 Frances Creek, N. Terr., Australia ...13 40S 131 40E
130 Franceville, Congo ... 1 40S 13 32E
49 Franche Comté, prov., France ...46 30N 5 50E
155 Francis Harbour, Can. 52 34N 55 44W
122 Francis–Garnier, Algeria ...36 30N 1 30E
168 Francisco I. Madero, Mexico ...25 48N 103 18W
132 Francistown, Botswana ...21 7S 27 33E
73 Francofonte, Italy ...37 13N 14 50E
156 Francois L., Canada ...54 0N 125 30W
166 Francs Peak, Mt., U.S.A. ...43 50N 109 5W
54 Franeker, Netherlands 53 12N 5 33E
57 Fränk Saale, R., Ger. .50 7N 9 49E
127 Frankado, Fr. Terr. of the Afars & Issas ...12 30N 43 12E
57 Franken Wald, Mts., Germany ...50 20N 11 36E
56 Frankenberg, Germany ...51 3N 8 47E
57 Frankenthal, Germany ...49 32N 8 21E
135 Frankfort, O.F.S., S. Afr. ...27 16S 28 30E
162 Frankfort, Ind., U.S.A. ...40 20N 86 33W
164 Frankfort, Kan., U.S.A. ...39 42N 96 26W
162 Frankfort, Ky., U.S.A. ...38 12N 85 44W
162 Frankfort, Mich., U.S.A. ...44 38N 86 14W
56 Frankfurt, dist., E. Ger. ...52 30N 14 0E
57 Frankfurt-am-Main, Germany ...50 7N 8 40E
56 Frankfurt-am-Oder, Germany ...52 20N 14 31E
57 Fränkische Jura, Mts., Germany ...49 23N 11 30E
153 Franklin, terr., Canada ...71 0N 99 0W
135 Franklin, S. Africa ...30 18S 29 30E
163 Franklin, Ky., U.S.A. 36 40N 86 30W
165 Franklin, La., U.S.A. .29 45N 91 30W
161 Franklin, Mass., U.S.A. ...42 4N 71 23W
164 Franklin, Neb., U.S.A. ...40 9N 98 55W
161 Franklin, N.H., U.S.A. ...43 28N 71 39W
161 Franklin, N.J., U.S.A. 41 9N 74 38W
160 Franklin, Pa., U.S.A. .41 22N 79 45W
163 Franklin Tenn., U.S.A. ...35 54N 86 53W
163 Franklin, Va., U.S.A. .36 40N 76 58W
162 Franklin, W. Va., U.S.A. ...38 38N 79 21W
14 Franklin B., Canada .70 0N 126 0W
15 Franklin I., Antarctica ...76 10S 168 30E
166 Franklin, L., U.S.A. ...40 20N 115 26W
152 Franklin Mts., Canada 66 0N 125 0W
147 Franklin Mt., N.Z. ...44 55S 167 45E
152 Franklin Str., Canada 72 0N 96 0W
166 Franklin D. Roosevelt L., U.S.A. ...48 30N 118 16W
165 Franklinton, U.S.A. ...30 53N 90 10W
160 Franklinville, U.S.A. .42 21N 78 28W
147 Franklyn Mts., N.Z. ...42 4S 172 42E
143 Frankston, Australia .38 8S 145 8E
146 Frankton Junc., N.Z. .37 47S 175 16E
134 Franschhoek, S. Africa ...33 56S 19 4E
80 Fransta, Sweden ...62 30N 16 16E
35 Frant, England, U.K. 51 5N 0 17E
154 Franz, Canada ...48 25N 84 30W
14 Franz Josef Fd., Green ...73 20N 22 0E
90 Franz Josef Land, U.S.S.R. ...76 0N 62 0E
56 Franzburg, Germany .54 9N 12 52E
72 Frascati, Italy ...41 48N 12 41E
156 Fraser L., Canada ...54 0N 124 50W
142 Fraser, Mt., W. Austral. ...25 35S 118 20E
145 Fraser or Great Sandy I., Queens., Australia ...25 15S 153 0E
156 Fraser R., Canada ...53 30N 120 40W
134 Fraserburg, S. Afr. ...31 55S 21 30E
43 Fraserburgh, Scot., U.K. ...57 41N 2 0W
154 Fraserdale, Canada ...49 55N 81 30W
146 Frasertown, N.Z. ...38 58S 177 28E
76 Frasher, Albania ...40 23N 20 26E
49 Frasne, France ...46 50N 6 10E
154 Frater, Canada ...47 20N 84 25W
57 Frauenfeld, Switzerland ...47 34N 8 54E
172 Fray Bentos, Uruguay 33 10S 58 15W
62 Frechilla, Spain ...42 8N 4 50W
81 Fredericia, Denmark .55 34N 9 43E
162 Frederick, Md., U.S.A. ...39 25N 77 23W
165 Frederick, Okla., U.S.A. ...34 22N 99 0W
164 Frederick, S.D., U.S.A. ...45 55N 98 29W
157 Frederick Sd., Alaska 57 10N 134 0W
162 Fredericksburg, Va., U.S.A. ...38 16N 77 29W
165 Fredericksburg, Tex., U.S.A. ...30 17N 98 55W
165 Frederickstown, U.S.A. ...37 35N 90 15W
155 Fredericton, Canada ...45 57N 66 40W
155 Fredericton Junc., Can. ...45 41N 66 40W
80 Frederiksberg, Sweden 60 12N 14 25E
81 Frederiksborg Amt, Den. ...55 50N 12 10E
14 Frederikshaab, Green. 62 0N 49 30W
81 Frederikshavn, Den. .57 28N 10 31E
81 Frederikssund, Den. ...55 50N 12 3E
133 Frederikstad, S. Africa ...26 29S 27 9E
81 Frederiksværk, Den. .56 0N 12 4E
174 Fredonia, Colombia ... 6 0N 75 45W
167 Fredonia, Ariz., U.S.A. ...36 59N 112 36W
165 Fredonia, Kan., U.S.A. ...37 34N 95 50W
160 Fredonia, N.Y., U.S.A. ...42 26N 79 20W
79 Fredrikstad, Norway .59 12N 10 59E
161 Freehold, U.S.A. ...40 15N 74 18W
161 Freeland, U.S.A. ...41 3N 75 48W
164 Freeman, U.S.A. ...43 25N 97 20W
155 Freeport, Canada ...44 15N 66 20W
164 Freeport, Ill., U.S.A. .42 18N 89 40W
165 Freeport, Tex., U.S.A. 28 55N 95 22W
124 Freetown, Sierra Leone ... 8 30N 13 10W
43 Freevater Forest, Scotland, U.K. ...57 51N 4 45W
63 Fregenal de la Sierra, Spain ...38 10N 6 39W
72 Fregene, Italy ...41 50N 12 12E
48 Fréhel C., France ...48 40N 2 20W
56 Freiberg, Germany ...50 55N 13 20E
57 Freiburg, Baden, Ger. 48 0N 7 52E
56 Freiburg, Saxony, Ger. ...53 49N 9 17E
56 Freienwalde, Germany 52 46N 14 2E
176 Freire, Chile ...39 0S 72 50W
172 Freirina, Chile ...28 30S 70 27W
57 Freising, Germany ...48 24N 11 47E
58 Freistadt, Austria ...48 30N 14 30E
56 Freital, Germany ...51 0N 13 40E
51 Fréjus, France ...43 25N 6 44E
142 Fremantle, W. Austral. ...32 1S 115 47E
162 Fremont, Mich., U.S.A. ...43 29N 85 59W
164 Fremont, Neb., U.S.A. ...41 30N 96 30W
162 Fremont, Ohio, U.S.A. ...41 20N 83 5W
166 Fremont, L., U.S.A. ...43 0N 109 50W
167 Fremont R., U.S.A. ...38 15N 110 20W
160 French Cr., R., U.S.A. .41 30N 80 2W
175 Fr. Guiana, col., S. Amer. ... 4 0N 53 0W
143 French I., Australia ...28 24S 145 25E
127 French Terr. of the Afars & Issas, Afr. .11 30N 42 15E
166 Frenchglen, U.S.A. ...42 56N 119 0W
157 Frenchman Butte, Can. ...53 36N 109 36W
166 Frenchman, R., Canada ...49 25N 108 20W
164 Frenchman Cr., U.S.A. ...40 34N 101 35W
46 Frenchpark, Ireland ...53 53N 8 25W
122 Frenda, Algeria ...35 2N 1 1E
135 Frere, Natal, S. Africa 28 52S 29 47E
175 Fresco, R., Brazil ... 7 15S 51 30W
15 Freshfield, C. Antarc. .68 25S 151 10E
45 Freshford, Ireland ...52 45N 7 25W
34 Freshwater, Eng., U.K. ...50 42N 1 31W
168 Fresnillo, Mexico ...23 10N 103 0W
167 Fresno, Calif., U.S.A. .36 47N 119 50W
166 Fresno Res., U.S.A. ...48 47N 110 0W
62 Fresno Alhandiga, Sp. 40 42N 5 37W
43 Freswick, Scot., U.K. 58 35N 3 5W
41 Freuchie, Scot., U.K. .56 14N 3 8W
57 Freudenstadt, Germany ...48 27N 8 25E
49 Frévent, France ...50 15N 2 17E
142 Freycinet, C., Western Australia ...34 9S 115 0E
145 Freycinet Pen., Austral. ...42 10S 148 25E
172 Frias, Argentina ...28 40S 65 5W
57 Fribourg, Switzerland 46 49N 7 9E
57 Fribourg, Can., Switz. 45 40N 7 0E
81 Fridafors, Sweden ...56 25N 14 41E
39 Fridaythorpe, Eng., U.K. ...54 2N 0 40W
57 Friedberg, Bavaria, Ger. ...48 21N 10 59E
57 Friedberg, Hesse, Ger. 50 19N 8 45E
57 Friedland, Germany ...53 40N 13 33E
57 Friedrichshafen, Ger. .47 39N 9 29E
56 Friedrichskoog, Ger. ...54 1N 8 52E
56 Friedrichsort, Germany ...54 24N 10 11E
56 Friedrichstad, Germany ...54 23N 9 6E
136 Friendly (Tonga) Is. ...19 50S 174 30W
58 Friesach, Austria ...46 57N 14 24E
56 Friesack, Germany ...52 43N 12 35E
54 Friesland, Prov., Neth. ...53 5N 5 50E
56 Friesoythe, Germany .53 1N 7 51E
154 Frigate, L., Canada ...53 15N 74 45W
168 Frijoles, Panama Canal Zone ... 9 11N 79 48W
81 Frillesås, Sweden ...57 20N 12 12E
35 Frimley, Eng., U.K. ...51 18N 0 43W
81 Frinnaryd, Sweden ...57 55N 14 50E
35 Frinton–on–Sea, England, U.K. ...51 50N 1 16E
165 Frio, R., U.S.A. ...29 40N 99 40W
41 Friockheim, Scot., U.K. ...56 39N 2 40W
165 Friona, U.S.A. ...34 40N 102 42W
40 Frisa, Loch, Scot., U.K. ...56 34N 6 5W
54 Frisian Is., Neth., Ger. ...53 30N 6 0E
81 Fristad, Sweden ...57 48N 12 59E
165 Fritch, U.S.A. ...35 40N 101 35W
81 Fritsla, Sweden ...57 35N 12 47E
56 Fritzlar, Germany ...51 8N 9 19E
71 Friuli–Venezia Guilia, Reg., Italy ...46 0N 13 0E
38 Frizington, Eng., U.K. ...54 33N 3 30W
153 Frobisher B., Canada .63 0N 67 0W
157 Frobisher, L., Canada 56 30N 108 0W
153 Frobisher Sd., Canada 62 30N 66 0W
38 Frodsham, Eng., U.K. 53 17N 2 45W
164 Froid, U.S.A. ...48 20N 104 29W
89 Frolovo, U.S.S.R. ...49 45N 43 30E
166 Fromberg, U.S.A. ...45 19N 108 58W
36 Frome, England, U.K. 51 16N 2 17W
145 Frome, L., S. Australia ...30 45S 139 45E
36 Frome R., Dorset, England, U.K. ...50 44N 2 35W
145 Frome Downs, Austral. ...31 12S 139 48W
48 Fromentine, France ...46 53N 2 9W
62 Fromista, Spain ...42 16N 4 25W
166 Front Range, U.S.A. .40 0N 105 10W
162 Front Royal, U.S.A. .38 55N 78 10W
63 Fronteira, Portugal ...39 3N 7 39W
168 Frontera, Mexico ...18 30N 92 40W
50 Frontignan, France ...43 27N 3 45E
72 Frosinone, Italy ...41 38N 13 20E
73 Frosolone, Italy ...41 34N 14 27E
162 Frostburg, U.S.A. ...39 43N 78 57W
82 Frostisen, Mt., Norway ...68 17N 17 5E
49 Frouard, France ...48 47N 6 8E
80 Frövi, Sweden ...59 28N 15 24E
44 Frower Pt., Ireland ...51 40N 8 30W
82 Fröya I., Norway ...63 45N 8 45E
49 Fruges, France ...50 30N 2 8E
78 Frumoasa, Rumania .46 28N 25 48E
90 Frunze, U.S.S.R. ...42 40N 74 50E
74 Fruška Gora, Mts., Yugoslavia ...45 7N 19 30E
175 Frutal, Brazil ...20 0S 49 0W
57 Frutigen, Switzerland 46 35N 7 38E
59 Frydek–Mistek Cz. ...49 40N 18 20E
58 Frýdlant, Cz. ...50 56N 15 9E
59 Frydlant, Cz. ...49 35N 18 20E
59 Fryvaldov, *see* Jesenik, Mts., Cz. ...50 0N 17 8E
77 Fthiotis, pref., Greece 38 50N 22 25E
80 Fu, Sweden ...60 57N 14 44E
70 Fucecchio, Italy ...43 44N 10 51E
112 Fuchin, China ...47 10N 132 0E
112 Fuchow, China ...39 45N 121 45E
113 Fuchow, China ...27 50N 116 14E
113 Fuchung, China ...24 25N 110 16E
50 Fucino L., Italy ...42 0N 13 30E
1 Fuego, Vol., Guat. ...14 40N 91 10W
63 Fuencaliente, Spain ...38 25N 4 18W
63 Fuengirola, Spain ...36 32N 4 41W
65 Fuente–Alamo, Spain 38 44N 1 24W
63 Fuente de Cantos, Sp. 38 15N 6 18W
63 Fuente del Maestre, Sp. ...38 31N 6 28W
63 Fuente el Fresno, Spain ...39 14N 3 46W
63 Fuente Ovejuna, Spain ...38 15N 5 25W
63 Fuentes de Andalusia, Spain ...37 28N 5 20W
64 Fuentes de Ebro, Spain ...41 31N 0 38W
63 Fuentes de Leon, Spain ...38 5N 6 32W
62 Fuentes de Onoro, Sp. 40 33N 6 52W
62 Fuentesauco, Spain ...41 15N 5 30W
168 Fuerte R., Mexico ...26 0N 109 0W
172 Fuerte Olimpo, Par. ...21 0S 58 0W
120 Fuerteventura I., Canary Is. ...28 30N 14 0W
46 Fuertey, Ireland ...53 37N 8 16W
174 Fuerto Olimpo, Paraguay ...21 6S 58 0W
113 Fuga, I., Philippines .19 55N 121 10E
101 Fujaira, Trucial States ...25 7N 56 18E
114 Fuji San, Mt., Japan .35 20N 138 30E
114 Fujinomiya, Japan ...35 20N 138 40E
113 Fukien, Prov., China .25 55N 117 40E
113 Fukow, China ...34 11N 114 36E
114 Fukuchiyama, Japan .35 25N 135 9E
114 Fukui, Japan ...36 0N 136 10E
114 Fukui, Pref., Japan ...36 0N 136 12E
114 Fukuoka, Japan ...33 30N 130 30E
114 Fukuoka, Pref., Japan 33 30N 131 0E
114 Fukuyama, (Honshu), Japan ...34 35N 133 20E
56 Fulda, Germany ...50 32N 9 41E
167 Fullerton, U.S.A. ...33 52N 117 58W
164 Fullerton, U.S.A. ...41 25N 98 0W
59 Fulopszállás, Hungary 46 49N 19 16E
164 Fulton, Mo., U.S.A. ...38 50N 91 55W
161 Fulton, N.Y., U.S.A. .43 20N 76 22W
80 Fuluälven, R., Sweden ...61 35N 13 0E
80 Fulufjallet, Mt., Sweden ...61 32N 12 40E
38 Fulwood, Eng., U.K. .53 47N 2 41W
49 Fumay, France ...50 0N 4 40E
125 Fumbusi, Ghana ...10 25N 1 20W
50 Fumel, France ...44 30N 0 58E
114 Funabashi, Japan ...35 45N 140 0E
136 Funafuti, I., Pac. Oc. 8 30S 179 0E
120 Funchal, Madeira, Port. ...32 45N 16 55W
174 Fundación, Colombia .10 31N 74 11W
62 Fundão, Portugal ...40 8N 7 30W
132 Fundu, Zambia ...14 58S 30 14E
155 Fundy, B. of, Canada 45 0N 66 0W
113 Fungchun, China ...23 27N 111 30E
132 Fungulwe, Zambia ...13 28S 27 10E
113 Funing, China ...23 45N 105 30E
113 Funiu Shan, Mts., China ...33 40N 112 30E
124 Funsi, Ghana ...10 21N 1 54W
125 Funtua, Nigeria ...11 35N 7 25E
81 Fur I., Denmark ...56 53N 9 2E
132 Furancungo, Mozam. .14 51S 33 39E
87 Furmanov, U.S.S.R. .57 25N 41 3E
89 Furmanovo, U.S.S.R. 49 42N 49 25E
145 Furneaux Group, Tas., Australia ...40 10S 147 50E
38 Furness, dist., England, United Kingdom ...54 14N 3 8W
56 Fürstenau, Germany .52 32N 7 40E
50 Fürstenfeld, Austria ...47 3N 16 3E
57 Fürstenfeldbruck, Ger. ...48 10N 11 15E
56 Fürstenwalde, Ger. ...52 20N 14 3E
57 Fürth, Germany ...49 29N 11 0E
57 Fürth i. Wald, Ger. ...49 19N 12 51E
57 Furtwangen, Germany 48 3N 8 14E
80 Furudal, Sweden ...61 10N 15 11E
80 Furusund, Sweden ...59 38N 18 58E
153 Fury and Hecla Str., Canada ...69 40N 81 0W
79 Fusa, Norway ...60 12N 5 38E
174 Fusagasuga, Colombia 4 30N 74 30W
114 Fuse, Japan ...34 40N 135 37E
73 Fuscaldo, Italy ...39 25N 16 1E
112 Fushan, China ...37 30N 121 5E
112 Fushun, China ...42 0N 123 59E
112 Fusin, China ...42 12N 121 33E
57 Füssen, Germany ...47 34N 10 42E
113 Fusui, China ...22 35N 107 58E
113 Futing, China ...27 15N 120 10E
113 Futsing, China ...25 46N 119 29E
125 Futuk, Nigeria ... 9 45N 10 56E
136 Futuna I., Pac. Oc. ...14 25S 178 20E
126 Fuwa, Egypt ...31 12N 30 33E
113 Fuyang, R., China ...38 14N 116 5E
112 Fuyu, China ...45 5N 124 50E
112 Fuyuan, China ...48 9N 134 3E
59 Fuzesgyarmat, Hung. 47 6N 21 14E
132 Fwaka, Zambia ...12 5S 29 25E
81 Fyn, I. Denmark ...55 18N 10 20E
40 Fyne, L., Scot., U.K. .56 0N 5 20W
81 Fynshav, Denmark ...54 59N 9 59E
79 Fyresvatn, L., Norway ...59 7N 8 15E
43 Fyvie, Scotland, U.K. 57 26N 2 24W

G

125 Gaanda, Nigeria ...10 10N 12 27E
127 Gaba, Ethiopia ... 6 20N 35 7E
88 Gaba Tula, Kenya ... 0 20N 38 35E
99 Gabah, C., Somali Rep. ... 8 0N 50 0W
125 Gabarin, Nigeria ...11 8N 10 27E

MAP
130 Gabela, Angola ... 11 0s 14 37E
133 Gaberone, Botswana . 24 37s 25 57E
123 Gagès, Tunisia ... 33 53N 10 2E
123 Gabes, G. of Tunisia . 34 0N 10 30E
126 Gabgaba, W., Egypt . 22 10N 33 5E
60 Gabin, Poland ... 52 23N 19 41E
143 Gabo I., Vic.,
Australia ... 37 33s 149 57E
128 Gabon, Rep., Africa ... 0 10s 10 0E
99 Gabredarre, Ethiopia . 6 45N 44 17E
161 Gabriels, U.S.A. ... 44 26N 74 12W
75 Gabrovo, Bulgaria ... 42 52N 25 27E
48 Gacé, France ... 48 49N 0 20E
101 Gach Saran, Iran ... 30 15N 50 45E
74 Gacko, Yugoslavia ... 43 10N 18 33E
125 Gada, Nigeria ... 13 38N 5 36E
106 Gadag, India ... 15 30N 75 45E
127 Gadamai, Sudan ... 17 11N 36 10E
104 Gadap, Pakistan ... 25 5N 67 28E
104 Gadarwara, India ... 22 50N 78 50E
82 Gäddede, Sweden ... 64 30N 14 15E
56 Gadebusch, Germany . 53 41N 11 6E
127 Gadein, Sudan ... 8 10N 28 45E
104 Gadhada, India ... 22 0N 71 35E
163 Gadsden, Ala., U.S.A. 34 1N 86 0W
167 Gadsden, Ariz.,
U.S.A. ... 32 35N 114 47W
106 Gadwal, India ... 16 10N 77 50E
37 Gaerwen, Wales, U.K. 53 13N 4 17W
78 Gaesti, Rumania ... 44 48N 25 19E
72 Gaeta, Italy ... 41 12N 13 35E
72 Gaeta, G. of, Italy ... 41 0N 13 25E
163 Gaffney, U.S.A. ... 35 10N 81 31W
123 Gafsa, Tunisia ... 34 24N 8 51E
86 Gagarin (Gzhatsk),
U.S.S.R. ... 55 30N 35 0E
155 Gagetown, Canada ... 45 46N 66 29W
87 Gagino, U.S.S.R. ... 55 15N 45 10E
73 Gagliano del Capo, It. 39 50N 18 23E
124 Gagnoa, Ivory Coast . 6 4N 5 55W
155 Gagnon, Canada ... 51 50N 68 5W
157 Gagnon, L., Canada ... 61 55N 110 40W
129 Gago Coutinho,
Angola ... 14 18s 21 18E
89 Gagra, U.S.S.R. ... 43 20N 40 10E
50 Gah, France ... 43 12N 0 27W
131 Gahini, Rwanda ... 1 50s 30 30E
55 Gahlen, Germany ... 51 40N 6 52E
105 Gahmar, India ... 25 27N 83 55E
105 Gaibandha, E. Pak. ... 25 20N 89 36E
77 Gaidhouronisi, I., Gr. . 34 53N 25 41E
165 Gail, U.S.A. ... 32 48N 101 25W
58 Gail, R., Austria ... 46 37N 13 15E
50 Gaillac, France ... 43 54N 1 54E
48 Gaillon, Eure, France 49 10N 1 20E
160 Gaines, U.S.A. ... 41 45N 77 35W
163 Gainesville, Fla.,
U.S.A. ... 29 38N 82 20W
163 Gainesville, Ga.,
U.S.A. ... 34 17N 83 47W
165 Gainesville, Mo.,
U.S.A. ... 36 35N 92 26W
165 Gainesville, Tex.,
U.S.A. ... 33 40N 97 10W
39 Gainford, Eng., U.K. . 54 34N 1 44W
39 Gainsborough,
England, United
Kingdom ... 53 23N 0 46W
138 Gairdner L., S.
Austral. ... 31 30s 136 0E
132 Gairezi, R., Rhodesia . 17 25s 32 55E
42 Gairloch, Scot.,
U.K. ... 57 43N 5 40W
42 Gairloch L., Scot.,
U.K. ... 57 43N 5 45W
42 Gairlochy, Scot., U.K. 56 55N 5 0W
43 Gairsay, I., Scot.,
U.K. ... 59 4N 2 59W
74 Gaj, Yugoslavia ... 45 28N 17 3E
125 Gajale, Nigeria ... 11 25N 8 10E
125 Gajiram, Nigeria ... 12 29N 13 9E
106 Gal Oya Res., Ceylon . 8 5N 80 55E
105 Galachipa, E.
Pakistan ... 22 8N 90 26E
99 Galadi, Ethiopia ... 6 59N 46 30E
125 Galadi, Nigeria ... 13 5N 6 20E
131 Galana R., Kenya ... 3 0s 39 10E
129 Galangue, Angola ... 13 48s 16 3E
59 Galanta,
Czechoslovakia ... 48 11N 17 45E
137 Galapagos Is., Pac.
Oc. ... 0 0 89 0W
107 Galas R., Malaya ... 4 55N 101 57E
41 Galashiels, Scot., U.K. 55 37N 2 50W
77 Galatas, Greece ... 37 30N 23 26E
146 Galatea, New Zealand 38 24s 176 45E
78 Galati, Rumania ... 45 27N 28 2E
78 Galati, Reg., Rumania 45 40N 27 40E
73 Galatina, Italy ... 40 10N 18 10E
73 Galatone, Italy ... 40 8N 18 3E
163 Galax, U.S.A. ... 36 42N 80 57W
77 Galaxidhion, Greece ... 38 22N 22 23E
44 Galbally, Ireland ... 52 24N 8 17W
144 Galbraith, Australia ... 16 25s 141 30E
175 Galcanhar C., Brazil ... 5 10s 35 15W
79 Galdhopiggen, Mt.,
Nor. ... 61 45N 8 40E
109 Galela, Indonesia ... 1 50N 127 55E
142 Galena, W. Australia . 27 48s 114 42E
65 Galera, Spain ... 37 45N 2 33W
164 Galesburg, U.S.A. ... 40 57N 90 23W
160 Galeton, U.S.A. ... 41 43N 77 40W
44 Galey R., Ireland ... 52 30N 9 23W
38 Galgate, Eng., U.K. ... 53 59N 2 47W
87 Galich, R.S.F.S.R.,
U.S.S.R. ... 58 23N 42 18E
86 Galich, Uk., U.S.S.R. . 49 10N 24 40E
75 Galiche, Bulgaria ... 43 34N 23 50E
62 Galicia, reg., Spain ... 42 43N 8 0W
98 Galilee, dist., Israel . 32 53N 35 18E
160 Galion, U.S.A. ... 40 43N 82 48W
123 Galite Is., Tunisia ... 37 30N 8 59E
167 Galivro Mts., U.S.A. . 32 40N 110 30W
42 Gallan Hd., Scot.,
U.K. ... 58 14N 7 0W
70 Gallarte, Italy ... 45 40N 8 48E
163 Gallatin, U.S.A. ... 36 24N 86 27W
106 Galle, Ceylon ... 6 5N 80 10E
47 Gallego R., Spain ... 42 23N 0 30W
176 Gallegos R.,
Argentina ... 51 50s 71 0W
44 Galley Hd., Ireland ... 51 32N 8 56W
70 Galliate, Italy ... 45 27N 8 44E
73 Gallipoli, Italy ... 40 8N 18 0E
76 Gallipoli, see Gelibolu,
Turkey ... 40 28N 26 43E
162 Gallipolis, U.S.A. ... 38 50N 82 10W
160 Gallitzin, U.S.A. ... 40 28N 78 32W
82 Gällivare, Sweden ... 67 7N 20 32E
80 Gällö, Sweden ... 62 56N 15 15E
72 Gallo, C. di, Italy ... 38 13N 13 19E
64 Gallocanta, Laguna
de, Spain ... 40 58N 1 30W
156 Galloway, Canada ... 53 30N 116 50W
40 Galloway, dist.,
Scotland, U.K. ... 55 0N 4 25W
40 Galloway, Mull of,
Scotland, U.K. ... 54 38N 4 50W
167 Gallup, U.S.A. ... 35 30N 108 54W
64 Gallur, Spain ... 41 52N 1 19W
131 Galma Galla, Kenya . 1 11s 40 49E
98 Gal-on, Israel ... 31 38N 34 51E
131 Galole, Kenya ... 1 30s 40 3E
143 Galong, Australia ... 34 37s 148 34E
40 Galston, Scot., U.K. ... 55 36N 4 22W
154 Galt, Ontario, Canada 43 21N 80 19W
80 Galstrom, Sweden ... 62 10N 17 30E
58 Galtür, Austria ... 46 58N 10 11E
44 Galty Mts., Ireland ... 52 22N 8 10W
44 Galtymore, Mt.,
Ireland ... 52 22N 8 12W
131 Galula, Tanzania ... 8 40s 33 0E
109 Galumpang, Indonesia 2 32s 119 32E
164 Galva, U.S.A. ... 41 10N 90 0W
64 Galve de Sorbe, Spain 41 13N 3 10W
165 Galveston, Tex.,
U.S.A. ... 29 15N 94 48W
165 Galveston B., U.S.A. . 29 30N 94 50W
172 Galvez, Argentina ... 32 0s 61 20W
63 Galvez, Spain ... 39 42N 4 16W
44 Galway, Ireland ... 53 16N 9 4W
44 Galway B., Ireland ... 53 10N 9 20W
44 Galway, Co., Ireland . 53 16N 9 3W
75 Galyamo Konare,
Bulg. ... 42 16N 24 33E
127 Gamarri, L., Ethiopia 11 32N 41 40E
125 Gamawa, Nigeria ... 12 10N 10 31E
125 Gambaga, Ghana ... 10 30N 0 28W
104 Gambat, West
Pakistan ... 27 17N 68 26E
130 Gambe, Angola ... 10 22s 16 58E
127 Gambela, Ethiopia ... 8 14N 34 38E
167 Gamerco, U.S.A. ... 35 33N 108 56W
124 Gambia, state, W.
Afr. ... 13 25N 16 0W
125 Gambia, R., W.
Africa ... 13 20N 15 45W
168 Gamboa, Panama
Canal Zone ... 9 8N 79 42W
104 Gamboli, West
Pakistan ... 29 53N 68 24E
130 Gamboma, Congo,
(Fr.) ... 1 55s 16 0E
144 Gamboola, Australia . 16 29s 143 43E
175 Gameleira, Brazil ... 7 50s 50 0W
81 Gamleby, Sweden ... 57 54N 16 20W
35 Gamlingay, Eng.,
U.K. ... 52 9N 0 11W
109 Gamsungi, Indonesia . 0 20N 128 50E
135 Gamtoos, S. Africa ... 33 52s 24 55E
134 Gamtoos R., S. Africa 33 45s 24 30E
82 Gamvik, Norway ... 71 0N 28 15E
95 Gan (Addu Atoll),
Indian Ocean ... 0 10s 71 10E
98 Gan Shemuel, Israel ... 32 28N 34 56E
98 Gan Yavne, Israel ... 31 48N 34 42E
167 Ganado Ariz., U.S.A. . 35 46N 109 41W
165 Ganado, Tex., U.S.A. . 29 4N 96 31W
127 Ganale R., Ethiopia ... 6 0N 39 30E
154 Gananoque, Canada ... 44 20N 76 10W
101 Ganaveh, Iran ... 29 35N 50 35E
105 Gandak, R., India ... 27 0N 84 8E
104 Gandava, W.
Pakistan ... 28 32N 67 32E
155 Gander, Canada ... 49 1N 54 33W
155 Gander L., Canada ... 48 58N 54 45W
132 Ganderowe Fs., Rhod. 17 20s 29 10E
64 Gandesa, Spain ... 41 3N 0 26E
125 Gandi, Nigeria ... 12 55N 5 49E
65 Gandia, Spain ... 38 58N 0 9W
70 Gandino, Italy ... 45 50N 9 52E
125 Gandole, Nigeria ... 8 28N 11 35E
109 Ganedidalem, Indon. . 0 48s 128 14E
126 Ganetti, Sudan ... 18 0N 31 10E
105 Ganga (Ganges) R.,
India ... 25 0N 88 0E
104 Ganganagar, India ... 29 56N 73 56E
104 Gangapur, India ... 26 32N 76 37E
125 Gangara, Niger ... 14 35N 8 40E
106 Gangavati, India ... 15 30N 76 36E
103 Gangaw, Burma ... 22 5N 94 15E
50 Ganges, France ... 43 56N 3 42E
105 Ganges (Ganga) R.,
India ... 25 0N 88 0E
105 Ganges, Mouth of the,
India ... 21 30N 90 0E
78 Gangiova, Rumania ... 43 54N 23 50E
104 Gangoh, India ... 29 46N 77 18E
105 Gangtok, India ... 27 20N 88 40E
130 Gangwa, Congo ... 3 30s 20 54E
104 Ganj, India ... 27 45N 78 47E
50 Gannat, France ... 46 7N 3 11E
166 Gannett Pk., U.S.A. ... 43 15N 109 47W
164 Gannvalley, U.S.A. ... 44 3N 98 57W
134 Gansbaai, C. Prov.,
South Africa ... 34 36s 19 22E
59 Ganserndorf, Austria 48 20N 16 43E
124 Ganta (Gompa),
Liberia ... 7 15N 8 59W
138 Gantheaume B.,
Western Australia . 27 40s 114 10E
86 Gantsevichi, U.S.S.R. 52 42N 26 30E
89 Ganyushkino,
U.S.S.R. ... 46 35N 49 20E
127 Ganzi, Sudan ... 4 30N 31 15E
125 Gao, Mali ... 16 15N 0 5W
125 Gao, dist., Mali ... 18 0N 1 0E
107 Gao Bang, N.
Vietnam ... 22 37N 106 18E
124 Gaoua, Upper Volta ... 10 20N 3 8W
124 Gaoual, Guinea ... 11 45N 13 25W
51 Gap, France ... 44 33N 6 5E
46 Gara, L., Ireland ... 53 57N 8 26W
169 Garachine, Panama ... 8 0N 78 12W
175 Garanhuns, Brazil ... 8 50s 36 30W
165 Garber, U.S.A. ... 36 30N 97 36W
166 Garberville, U.S.A. ... 40 11N 123 50W
35 Garboldisham, Eng.,
U.K. ... 52 24N 1 4W
78 Gârbovi, Rumania ... 44 47N 26 47E
51 Gard, dépt., France ... 44 2N 4 10E
70 Garda Lake, Italy ... 45 40N 10 40E
127 Gardala, Ethiopia ... 5 40N 37 25E
51 Gardanne, France ... 43 27N 5 27E
56 Gardelegen, Germany 52 32N 11 21E
165 Garden City, Kan.,
U.S.A. ... 38 0N 100 45W
165 Garden City, Tex.,
U.S.A. ... 31 52N 101 28W
43 Gardenstown, Scot.,
U.K. ... 57 40N 2 20W
101 Gardez, Afghanistan . 33 31N 68 59E
77 Gardhiki, Greece ... 38 50N 21 55E
121 Gardian, Chad ... 15 45N 19 40E
154 Gardiner, Canada ... 49 19N 81 2W
166 Gardiner, Mont.,
U.S.A. ... 45 3N 110 53W
165 Gardiner, New
Mexico, U.S.A. ... 36 55N 104 29W
161 Gardiners I., U.S.A. ... 41 4N 72 5W
161 Gardner, U.S.A. ... 42 35N 72 0W
166 Gardnerville, U.S.A. ... 38 59N 119 47W
40 Gare, L., Scot., U.K. . 56 1N 4 50W
40 Garelochhead,
Scotland, United
Kingdom ... 56 7N 4 50W
74 Garešnica, Y.-slav. ... 45 36N 16 56E
70 Garessio, Italy ... 44 12N 8 1E
166 Garfield, Utah, U.S.A. 40 45N 112 15W
166 Garfield, Wash.,
U.S.A. ... 47 3N 117 8W
39 Garforth, Eng., U.K. . 53 48N 1 22W
77 Gargaliánoi, Greece ... 37 4N 21 38E
50 Gargans, Mt., France . 45 37N 1 39E
154 Gargantua C., Canada 47 35N 85 0W
38 Gargrave, Eng., U.K. 53 58N 2 7W
104 Garshankar, India ... 31 13N 76 11E
166 Garibaldi, Canada ... 49 56N 123 15W
134 Garies, C. Prov., S.
Afr. ... 30 32s 17 59E
72 Garigliano R., Italy ... 41 13N 13 44E
131 Garissa, Kenya ... 0 25s 39 40E
125 Garkida, Nigeria ... 10 27N 12 36E
125 Garko, Nigeria ... 11 45N 8 53E
166 Garland, U.S.A. ... 41 47N 112 10W
70 Garlasco, Italy ... 45 11N 8 55E
40 Garliestown, Scot.,
U.K. ... 54 47N 4 22W
90 Garm, U.S.S.R. ... 39 0N 70 20E
57 Garmisch-Parten-
kirchen, Germany ... 47 30N 11 5E
43 Garmouth, Scot.,
U.K. ... 57 40N 3 8W
101 Garmsar, Iran ... 35 20N 52 25E
164 Garner, U.S.A. ... 43 4N 93 37W
164 Garnett, U.S.A. ... 38 18N 95 12W
105 Garo Hills, India ... 25 30N 90 30E
99 Garoe, Somali Rep. ... 8 35N 48 40E
145 Garoke, Vic.,
Australia ... 36 45s 141 30E
50 Garonne R., France ... 44 45N 0 32W
125 Garoua (Garwa), Cam. 9 19N 13 21E
124 Garraway, Liberia ... 4 35N 8 0W
50 Garrigues, dist., Fr. ... 43 40N 3 30E
46 Garrison, Ireland ... 54 25N 8 5W
166 Garrison, Mont.,
U.S.A. ... 46 37N 112 56W
164 Garrison, N.D.,
U.S.A. ... 31 50N 94 28W
165 Garrison, Tex., U.S.A. 47 39N 101 27W
164 Garrison Res., U.S.A. 47 30N 102 0W
46 Garron Pt., Northern
Ireland, U.K. ... 55 3N 6 0W
63 Garrovillas, Spain ... 39 40N 6 33W
65 Garrucha, Spain ... 37 11N 1 49W
152 Garry L., Canada ... 65 40N 101 20W
42 Garry L., Scot., U.K. . 57 5N 4 52W
43 Garry R., Scot., U.K. 56 47N 4 0W
38 Garsdale Head,
England, U.K. ... 54 20N 2 20W
131 Garsen, Kenya ... 2 20s 40 5E
154 Garson, Canada ... 50 5N 96 50W
38 Garstang, Eng., U.K. . 53 53N 2 47W
38 Garston, Eng., U.K. ... 53 21N 2 55W
50 Gartempe R., France . 46 13N 0 54E
127 Gartok, Sudan ... 5 35N 31 20E
111 Gartok, Tibet, China . 31 59N 80 30E
56 Gartz, Rostock, Ger. . 54 17N 13 21E
125 Garu, Ghana ... 10 55N 0 20W
125 Garu, Nigeria ... 13 35N 5 25E
175 Garupa, Brazil ... 1 25s 51 35W
109 Garut, Indonesia ... 7 14s 107 53E
46 Garvagh, N. Ire.,
U.K. ... 55 0N 6 41W
46 Garvaghey, Northern
Ireland, U.K. ... 54 30N 7 7W
63 Garváo, Portugal ... 37 42N 8 21W
40 Garvellachs, Is.,
Scotland, U.K. ... 56 14N 5 48W
147 Garvie Mts., N.Z. ... 45 27s 169 59E
105 Garwa, India ... 24 11N 83 47E
60 Garwolin, Poland ... 51 55N 21 38E
162 Gary, Ind., U.S.A. ... 41 35N 87 20W
174 Garzón, Colombia ... 2 10N 75 40W
50 Gascogne, reg., Fr. ... 43 45N 0 20E
90 Gasan Kuli, U.S.S.R. . 37 40N 54 20E
142 Gascoyne, Mt.,
Western Australia . 24 50s 116 35E
142 Gascoyne R., W.,
Austral. ... 24 15s 114 15E
142 Gascoyne Junc. Teleg.
Off., W. Austral. ... 25 2s 115 17E
64 Gascuena, Spain ... 40 18N 2 31W
127 Gash R., Ethiopia ... 15 0N 37 15E
125 Gashaka, Nigeria ... 7 20N 11 29E
111 Gashiun Nor, L.,
China ... 42 20N 100 40E
125 Gashua, Nigeria ... 12 54N 11 0E
144 Gasmata, Terr. of
New Guinea ... 6 15s 150 30E
155 Gaspé, Canada ... 48 52N 64 30W
155 Gaspé, C., Canada ... 48 48N 64 7W
155 Gaspé Pass., Canada . 49 10N 64 0W
155 Gaspé Pen., Canada ... 48 45N 65 40W
155 Gaspesian Prov. Park,
Can. ... 49 0N 66 45W
162 Gassaway, U.S.A. ... 38 42N 80 43W
70 Gassino, Tormese,
Italy ... 45 8N 7 50E
125 Gassol, Nigeria ... 8 34N 10 25E
163 Gastonia, U.S.A. ... 35 17N 81 10W
77 Gastoúni, Greece ... 37 51N 21 15E
76 Gastoúri, Greece ... 39 34N 19 54E
176 Gastre, Argentina ... 42 10s 69 15W
65 Gata, C. de, Spain ... 36 41N 2 13W
74 Gataia, Rumania ... 45 26N 21 30E
86 Gatchina, U.S.S.R. ... 59 35N 30 0E
40 Gatehouse of Fleet,
Scotland, U.K. ... 54 53N 4 10W
39 Gateshead, Eng.,
U.K. ... 54 57N 1 37W
165 Gatesville, U.S.A. ... 31 29N 97 45W
132 Gaths, Rhodesia ... 26 2s 30 32E
172 Gatico, Chile ... 22 29s 70 15W
49 Gatinais, dist., France 48 5N 2 40E
161 Gatineau, Canada ... 45 28N 75 40W
154 Gatineau R., Canada . 46 20N 76 0W
38 Gatley, Eng., U.K. ... 53 25N 2 15W
133 Ga-Tihose, S. Africa . 25 50s 23 16E
132 Gatooma, Rhodesia ... 18 20s 29 52E
70 Gattinara, Italy ... 45 37N 8 22E
168 Gatun, Pan. Can.
Zone ... 9 16N 79 55W
168 Gatun Dam, Pan.
Can. ... 9 16N 79 55W
168 Gatun, L., Panama ... 9 7N 79 56W
168 Gatun Locks, Pan.
Can. ... 9 16N 79 55W
63 Gaucin, Spain ... 36 31N 5 19W
157 Gauer L., Canada ... 57 10N 97 30W
105 Gauhati, India ... 26 5N 91 55E
86 Gauja R., U.S.S.R. ... 57 10N 24 45E
79 Gaula R., Norway ... 62 57N 11 0E
15 Gaussberg, Mt.,
Antarc. ... 66 45s 89 0E
79 Gausta, Mt., Norway . 59 50N 8 37E
64 Gavà, Spain ... 41 18N 2 0E
50 Gavarnie, France ... 42 44N 0 0E
101 Gavater, Iran ... 25 10N 61 23E
77 Gavdhopoúla, I.,
Greece ... 34 56N 24 0E
77 Gavdhos, I., Greece .. 34 50N 24 5E
63 Gaviao, Portugal ... 39 28N 7 50W
80 Gävle, Sweden ... 60 41N 17 13E
80 Gävleborg Län,
Sweden ... 61 35N 16 0E
70 Gavorrano, Italy ... 42 55N 10 55E
48 Gavray, France ... 49 55N 1 20W
77 Gavrion, Greece ... 37 54N 24 44E
80 Gavunda, Sweden ... 60 46N 14 15E
104 Gawilgarh Hills, India 21 15N 76 45E
145 Gawler, S. Australia ... 34 30s 138 42E
138 Gawler Ranges, South
Australia ... 32 30s 135 45E
38 Gawthwaite, Eng.,
U.K. ... 54 16N 3 6W
125 Gaya, Niger ... 11 58N 3 28E
105 Gaya, Bihar, India ... 24 47N 85 4E
125 Gaya, Nigeria ... 11 57N 9 0E
162 Gaylord, U.S.A. ... 45 1N 84 35W
145 Gayndah, Australia ... 25 35s 151 39E
88 Gaysin, U.S.S.R. ... 48 57N 28 25E
35 Gayton, Eng., U.K. ... 52 45N 0 35E
88 Gayvoron, U.S.S.R. ... 48 22N 29 45E
35 Gaywood, Eng., U.K. 52 46N 0 26E
98 Gaza, Egypt ... 31 30N 34 28E
132 Gaza, dist.,
Mozambique ... 23 0s 33 0E
98 Gaza Strip, Egypt ... 31 29N 34 25E
125 Gazafa, Niger ... 13 30N 9 45E
144 Gazelle Pen., New
Guin. ... 4 30s 152 0E
131 Gazi, Kenya ... 4 25s 39 30E
100 Gaziantep, Turkey ... 37 6N 37 23E
124 Gbanga, Liberia ... 7 19N 9 13W
125 Gbekebo, Nigeria ... 6 26N 4 48E
125 Gboko, Nigeria ... 7 17N 9 4E
125 Gbongan, Nigeria ... 7 28N 4 20E
124 Gbanhui, Ivory Coast 8 18N 3 2W
60 Gdansk (Danzig), Pol. 54 22N 18 40E
86 Gdov, U.S.S.R. ... 58 40N 27 55E
60 Gdynia, Poland ... 54 35N 18 33E
45 Geashill, Ireland ... 53 14N 7 20W
109 Gebe, I., Indonesia ... 0 5N 129 25E
126 Gebeit Mine, Sudan ... 21 3N 36 29E
127 Gecoa, Ethiopia ... 7 30N 35 18E
127 Gedame, Ethiopia ... 8 58N 34 35E
127 Gedaref, Sudan ... 14 2N 35 28E
98 Gedera, Israel ... 31 49N 34 46E
35 Gedney, Eng., U.K. ... 52 47N 0 5W
127 Gedo, Ethiopia ... 9 2N 37 25E
50 Gèdre, France ... 42 47N 0 2E
81 Gedser, Denmark ... 54 35N 11 55E
81 Gedser Odde, C., Den. 54 30N 12 5E
55 Geel, Belgium ... 51 10N 4 59E
143 Geelong, Vic.,
Australia ... 38 2s 144 20E
109 Geelvink B.,
Indonesia ... 3 0s 135 20E
142 Geelvink Chan.,
Austral. ... 28 30s 114 0E
54 Geeraardsbergen,
Belg. ... 50 45N 3 53E
56 Geestenseth, Germany 53 31N 8 51E
56 Geesthacht, Germany 53 25N 10 20E
55 Geffen, Netherlands ... 51 44N 5 28E
101 Geh, Iran ... 26 10N 60 0E
98 Geia, Israel ... 31 38N 34 37E
125 Geidam, Nigeria ... 12 57N 11 57E
56 Geilenkirchen,
Germany ... 50 58N 6 8E
127 Geili, Sudan ... 16 1N 32 37E
79 Geilo, Norway ... 60 32N 8 14E
59 Geinica,
Czechoslovakia ... 48 51N 20 55E
57 Geisingen, Germany ... 47 55N 8 37E
57 Geisingen, Germany ... 48 36N 9 51E
131 Geita, Tanzania ... 2 48s 32 12E
127 Gel River, & R.,
Sudan ... 7 5N 29 10E
73 Gela, Golfo di, Italy ... 37 0N 14 8E
54 Gelderland,
Netherlands ... 52 5N 6 10E
54 Geldermalsen, Nether. 51 52N 5 17E
56 Geldern, Germany ... 51 32N 6 18E
54 Geldrop, Netherlands . 51 25N 5 32E
54 Geleen, Netherlands ... 50 57N 5 49E
124 Gelehun, Sierra Leone 8 10N 10 30W
88 Gelendzhik, U.S.S.R. . 44 33N 38 17E
76 Gelibolu, Turkey ... 40 28N 26 43E
57 Gelnhausen, Germany 50 12N 9 12E
56 Gelsenkirchen, Ger. ... 51 30N 7 5E
56 Gelting, Germany ... 54 43N 9 53E
133 Geluk, C. Prov., S.
Afr. ... 27 1s 24 18E
135 Geluksburg, Nat., S.
Africa ... 28 30s 29 33E
107 Gemas, Malaysia ... 2 37N 102 36E
54 Gembloux, Belgium ... 50 34N 4 43E
143 Gembrook, Vic.,
Austral ... 37 58s 145 37E
55 Gemen, Germany ... 51 52N 6 52E
130 Gemena, Congo ... 3 20N 19 40E
100 Gemerek, Turkey ... 39 15N 36 10E
55 Gemert, Netherlands . 51 33N 5 41E
100 Gemlik, Turkey ... 40 28N 29 13E
55 Gemmenich, Belgium . 50 45N 6 0E
71 Gemona del Friuli,
Italy ... 46 16N 13 7E
126 Gemsa, Egypt ... 27 39N 33 35E
127 Gemu-Gofa, Prov.,
Ethiopia ... 5 40N 36 40E
57 Gemünden, Germany . 50 3N 9 43E
50 Gençay, France ... 46 23N 0 23E
54 Gendringen, Neth. ... 51 52N 6 21E
126 Geneina, Gebel, Egypt 29 2N 33 55E
172 General Acha, Arg. ... 37 20s 64 38W
172 Gen. Alvear, B. A.,
Arg. ... 36 0s 60 0W
172 Gen. Alvear, Mend.,
Arg. ... 35 0s 67 40W
172 General Artigas, Par. . 26 52s 56 16W
172 General Belgrano,
Arg. ... 36 0s 58 30W
172 General Cabrera, Arg. 32 53s 63 58W
175 General Carneiro,
Brazil ... 15 45s 52 40W
172 General Guido, Arg. ... 36 40s 57 50W
172 General Gutierrez,
Arg. ... 32 55s 68 55W
172 Gen. Juan Madariaga,
Argentina ... 37 0s 57 0W
172 General La Madrid,
Arg. ... 37 30s 61 10W
109 General MacArthur,
Phil. ... 11 18N 125 28E
172 General Paz,
Argentina ... 27 45s 57 36W
176 General Paz L., Chile . 44 0s 72 0W
172 General Pico,
Argentina ... 35 45s 63 50W
172 General Pinedo, Arg. . 27 15s 61 30W
172 General Pinto, Arg. ... 34 45s 61 50W
176 General Roca, Arg. ... 30 0s 67 40W
75 General Toshevo,
Bulg. ... 43 42N 28 6E
172 General Viamonte,
Arg. ... 35 1s 61 3W
172 General Villegas, Arg. 35 0s 63 0W
166 Genesee, Idaho,
U.S.A. ... 46 31N 116 59W
160 Genesee, Mich.,
U.S.A. ... 43 7N 83 38W
160 Genesee, Pa., U.S.A. . 42 0N 77 54W
160 Genesee, R., U.S.A. ... 41 35N 78 0W
164 Geneseo, Ill., U.S.A. ... 41 25N 90 10W
164 Geneseo, Kan., U.S.A. 38 32N 98 8W
160 Geneseo, N.Y., U.S.A. 42 49N 77 49W
57 Geneva (Genève),
Switz. ... 46 12N 6 9E

MAP
39 Geneva, L., of (Lac Leman), Switzerland ......46 26N 6 30 E
163 Geneva, Ala., U.S.A. .31 2N 85 52w
164 Geneva, Neb., U.S.A. .40 35N 97 35w
160 Geneva, N.Y., U.S.A. 42 53N 77 0w
160 Geneva, Ohio, U.S.A. .41 49N 80 58w
162 Geneva, L., U.S.A. ...42 38N 88 30w
57 Genève (Geneva), Switz. ......46 12N 6 9 E
88 Genichesk, U.S.S.R. ..46 12N 34 50 E
63 Genil, R., Spain 37 12N 3 50w
51 Genissiat Dam, France ......46 1N 5 48 E
54 Genk, Belgium ......50 58N 5 32 E
49 Genlis, France ......47 15N 5 12 E
54 Gennep, Netherlands ...51 41N 5 59 E
48 Gennes, France 47 20N 0 17w
70 Genoa (Genova), Italy 44 24N 8 57 E
164 Genoa, Neb., U.S.A. ..41 31N 97 44w
161 Genoa, N.Y., U.S.A. ...42 40N 76 32w
143 Genoa & Australia 37 28 s 149 33 E
70 Genova (Genoa), Italy 44 24N 8 56 E
70 Genova, Golfo di, Italy ......44 0N 9 0 E
54 Gent, Belgium ......51 2N 3 37 E
109 Genteng, Indonesia .. 7 25 s 106 23 E
56 Genthin, Germany ....52 24N 12 10 E
133 Genyesa, C. Prov., S. Afr. ......26 36 s 24 15 E
142 Geographe B., Western Australia .33 30 s 115 15 E
142 Geographe Chan., Western Australia .24 30 s 113 0 E
89 Geokchay, U.S.S.R. ...40 42N 47 43 E
155 George, Canada 46 12N 62 32w
134 George, C. Prov., S. Afr. ......33 58 s 22 29 E
143 George, L., Australia .35 10 s 149 25 E
131 George, L., Uganda .. 0 5N 30 10 E
163 George, L., Fla., U.S.A. 29 15N 81 35w
161 George, L., N.Y., U.S.A. 43 30N 73 30w
142 George, L., W. Australia ......22 45 s 123 40 E
142 George, Mt., W. Australia ....25 17 s 119 0 E
153 George, see Port Nouveau, Que., Can. 58 30N 65 50w
15 George V Coast, Antarc. ......67 0 s 148 0 E
145 George Town, Australia ......41 5 s 148 55 E
165 George West, U.S.A. .28 18N 98 5w
144 Georgetown, Australia 18 17N 143 33 E
154 Georgetown, Ont., Can. 43 40N 80 0w
155 Georgetown, P.E.I., Can. 46 13N 62 24w
124 Georgetown, Gambia .13 30N 14 47w
174 Georgetown, Guyana . 6 50N 58 12w
107 Georgetown, Malaysia 5 25N 100 19 E
166 Georgetown, Colo., U.S.A. 39 46N 105 49w
162 Georgetown, Ohio, U.S.A. 38 50N 83 50w
163 Georgetown, S.C., U.S.A. 33 22N 79 15w
165 Georgetown, Tex., U.S.A. 30 45N 58 10w
89 Georgia, S.S.R., U.S.S.R. ......41 0N 45 0 E
162 Georgia, st., U.S.A. ...32 0N 82 0w
154 Georgian B., Canada .45 15N 81 0w
89 Georgievsk, U.S.S.R. .44 12N 43 28 E
139 Georgina R., Australia 20 15 s 138 0 E
56 Gera, Germany ......50 53N 12 5 E
56 Gera, dist., E. Germany ......50 45N 11 30 E
147 Geraldine, New Zealand ......44 5 s 171 15 E
166 Geraldine, U.S.A. 47 45N 109 15w
154 Geraldton, Canada ...49 44N 86 59w
142 Geraldton, W. Australia ......28 48 s 114 32 E
49 Gerardmer, France ...48 3N 6 50 E
152 Gerdine, Mt., Alas., U.S.A. 61 32N 152 30w
88 Gerede, Turkey ......40 45N 32 10 E
65 Gérgal, Spain 37 7N 2 31w
99 Geriban, Somali Rep. . 7 10N 48 55 E
164 Gering, U.S.A. 41 51N 103 40w
98 Gerizim Mt., Jordan ..32 13N 35 15 E
166 Gerlach, U.S.A. 40 43N 119 27w
59 Gerlachovka, Mt., Cz. 49 11N 20 7 E
81 Gerlev, Denmark ......56 36N 10 9 E
99 Gerlogubi, Ethiopia . 6 53N 45 3 E
74 German Planina, Ra., Yugoslavia ......42 33N 22 0 E
156 Germansen Landing, Canada 55 43N 124 40w
56 Germany, East, st., Eur. ......52 0N 12 0 E
56 Germany, West, st., Eur. ......52 0N 9 0 E
57 Germersheim, Germany ......49 13N 8 0 E
133 Germiston, S. Africa .26 15 s 28 10 E
57 Gernsheim, Germany .49 44N 8 29 E
57 Gerolstein, Germany .50 12N 6 24 E
64 Gerona, Spain ......41 58N 2 46 E
64 Gerona, prov., Spain .42 11N 2 30 E
36 Gerrans B., Eng., U.K. 50 12N 4 57w
35 Gerrards Cross, England, U.K. ...51 35N 0 32w
1 Gerrild, Denmark ....56 30N 10 50 E
50 Gers, dépt. France ....43 35N 0 38 E

106 Gersoppa Falls, India 14 12N 74 46 E
132 Gerufa, Botswana ......19 8 s 26 0 E
100 Gerze, Turkey ......41 45N 35 10 E
56 Geseke, Germany .....51 38N 8 29 E
109 Geser, Indonesia ...... 3 50N 130 35 E
70 Gesso, R., Italy ......44 21N 7 20 E
55 Gesves, Belgium ......50 24N 5 4 E
62 Getafe, Spain 40 18N 3 44w
155 Gethsemani, Canada .50 17N 60 28w
55 Gette R., Belgium ....50 52N 5 8 E
162 Gettysburg, Pa., U.S.A. 39 47N 77 18w
164 Gettysburg, S.D., U.S.A. 45 3N 99 56w
15 Getz Ice Shelf, Antarc. ......75 0 s 130 0w
54 Geul R., Netherlands .50 46N 5 56 E
50 Gevaudan, dist., Fr. ...44 40N 3 40 E
55 Gevelsberg, Germany .51 21N 7 7 E
74 Gevgelija, Yugoslavia 41 9N 22 30 E
55 Gex, France ......46 21N 6 3 E
76 Geyikli, Turkey ......39 50N 26 12 E
133 Geysdorp Trans., S. Africa ......26 31 s 25 17 E
166 Geyser, U.S.A. 47 17N 110 30w
88 Geyve, Turkey ......40 32N 30 18 E
98 Gezer (site), Israel ...31 51N 34 51 E
105 Ghaghara, R., India ...26 0N 84 20 E
100 Ghail, Saudi Arabia ..21 40N 46 20 E
127 Ghalla, Wadi el, Sudan ......12 0N 28 58 E
125 Ghana, state, W. Afr. 6 0N 1 0w
102 Ghandhi Dam, India .24 30N 75 35 E
105 Ghansor, India ......22 39N 80 1 E
132 Ghanzi, & dist., Botswana ......21 50 s 21 45 E
126 Ghard Abu Muharik, Egypt ......26 50N 30 0 E
122 Ghardaïa, Algeria ...32 31N 3 37 E
123 Gharyan, Libya ......32 10N 13 0 E
126 Gharib, G., Egypt ...28 6N 32 54 E
123 Ghât, Libya ......24 59N 10 19 E
100 Ghat Ghat, Si. Arabia 26 0N 45 5 E
105 Ghatal, India ......22 40N 87 46 E
105 Ghatampur, India ...26 8N 80 13 E
106 Ghatprabha, R. India 16 15N 75 20 E
121 Ghazal Bahr el, Chad 15 0N 17 0 E
122 Ghazaouet, Algeria ...35 8N 1 50w
104 Ghaziabad, India .....28 42N 77 35 E
105 Ghazipur, India ......25 38N 83 35 E
101 Ghazni, Afghanistan .33 30N 68 17 E
102 Ghazni, prov., Afghan. ......33 0N 68 0 E
98 Ghazzah, see Gaza, Egypt ......31 30N 34 28 E
70 Ghedi, Italy ......45 24N 10 16 E
78 Ghelari, Rumania ...45 42N 22 45 E
99 Ghelinsor. Somali Rep. ...... 6 35N 46 55 E
54 Ghent (Gent), Belg. ..51 4N 3 43 E
78 Gheorghe Gheorghiu-Dej, Rumania ......46 17N 26 47 E
78 Gheorgheni, Rumania 46 43N 25 41 E
78 Ghergani, Rumania ..44 37N 25 37 E
122 Gheris, W., Morocco ..31 30N 4 30w
78 Gherla, Rumania ......47 0N 23 57 E
123 Ghesendor, Chad ....21 41N 18 14 E
72 Ghilarza, Italy ......40 8N 8 50 E
78 Ghimpati, Rumania ..44 12N 25 47 E
73 Ghisonaccia, France ..42 1N 9 26 E
129 Ghivemba, Angola ...15 48 s 14 8 E
106 Ghod, R., India ......18 40N 74 15 E
102 Ghorat, prov., Afghan. ......34 0N 64 20 E
154 Ghost River, Canada .51 25N 83 20w
126 Ghot Ogrein, Egypt ..31 20N 26 0 E
104 Ghotaru, India ......27 20N 70 1 E
104 Ghotki, Pakistan ....28 5N 69 30 E
123 Ghudamis, Libya ....30 11N 9 29 E
105 Ghughri, India ......22 39N 80 41 E
106 Ghugus, India ......20 0N 79 0 E
104 Ghulam Mohammad Barrage, W. Pak. ..25 30N 67 0 E
101 Ghurian, Afghanistan 34 17N 61 25 E
107 Gia Lai, see Pleiku, S. Vietnam ......14 3N 108 0 E
107 Gia Nghia, S. Vietnam ......12 0N 107 42 E
103 Giamda Dzong, China 30 3N 93 2 E
70 Giannutri I., Italy ....42 16N 11 5 E
58 Giant Mts., see Krkonose, Cz. ...50 50N 16 10 E
135 Giant's Castle, Mt., Nat., South Africa .29 20 s 29 30 E
46 Giant's Causeway, Northern Ireland, U.K. 55 15N 6 30w
121 Giarabub, see Jaghbub, Libya .29 42N 24 38 E
73 Giarre, Italy ......37 44N 15 10 E
70 Giaveno, Italy ......45 3N 7 20 E
169 Gibara, Cuba 21 0N 76 20w
164 Gibbon, U.S.A. 40 49N 98 45w
72 Gibellina, Italy ......37 48N 13 0 E
129 Gibeon, S.W. Africa ..25 7 s 17 45 E
63 Gibraleon, Spain 37 23N 6 58w
63 Gibraltar, Europe 36 7N 5 22w
39 Gibraltar Pt., England, United Kingdom ......53 6N 0 20 E
63 Gibraltar, Str. of, Mediterranean Sea .35 55N 5 40w
142 Gibson Des., W. Austral. ......24 0 s 126 0 E
156 Gibsons, Canada 49 24N 123 32w
14 Gida, G., U.S.S.R. ...72 30N 77 0 E
106 Giddalur, India ......15 20N 78 57 E
165 Giddings, U.S.A. 30 11N 96 58w
49 Gien, France ......47 40N 2 36 E
56 Giessen, Germany ....50 34N 8 40 E

126 Gifatin, Geziret, Egypt ......27 10N 33 50 E
41 Gifford, Scot., U.K. ...55 54N 2 45w
56 Gifhorn, Germany ....52 29N 10 32 E
114 Gifu, Japan ......35 30N 136 45 E
114 Gifu, pref., Japan ....36 0N 137 0 E
115 Gigane, Nigeria ......13 3N 5 15 E
89 Gigant, U.S.S.R. ......46 28N 41 30 E
168 Giganta, Sa. de la, Mex. 25 30N 111 30w
75 Gigen, Bulgaria ......43 40N 24 28 E
38 Giggleswick, Eng., U.K. 54 5N 2 19w
40 Gigha, I., Scot., U.K. 55 42N 5 45w
70 Giglio, I., Italy ......42 20N 10 52 E
50 Gignac, France ......43 39N 3 32 E
64 Giguela, R., Spain ...39 47N 3 0w
62 Gijón, Spain 43 32N 5 42w
167 Gila Bend, U.S.A. 33 0N 112 46w
167 Gila Bend Mts., U.S.A. 33 15N 113 0w
167 Gila R., U.S.A. 33 5N 108 40w
78 Gilău, Rumania 46 45N 23 23w
144 Gilau, Terr. of N. Guin. ...... 5 38 s 149 3 E
125 Gilbedi, Nigeria ......13 40N 5 45 E
156 Gilbert Mt., Canada ..50 50N 124 15w
136 Gilbert and Ellice Is., Pacific Ocean ... 1 0 s 176 0 E
157 Gilbert Plains, Canada 51 9N 100 28w
144 Gilbert River Post Office, Australia ...18 9 s 142 50 E
144 Gilberton, Australia ..19 16 s 143 35 E
98 Gilboa, Israel ......32 31N 35 25 E
126 Gilf Kebir Plat., Egypt ......23 0N 26 0 E
46 Gilford, N. Ire., U.K. .54 23N 6 20w
156 Gilford I., Canada 50 40N 126 30w
142 Gilgai, W. Australia ..31 15 s 120 5 E
143 Gilgandra, Australia ..31 38 s 148 35 E
131 Gilgil, Kenya ...... 0 30N 36 20 E
102 Gilgit, Kashmir ......35 50N 74 15 E
145 Giligulgul. Australia ..26 26 s 150 0 E
74 Gilijeva Planina, Ra., Yugoslavia ......43 9N 20 0 E
46 Gill L., Ireland 54 15N 8 25w
157 Gillam Canada 56 20N 94 40w
81 Gilleleje, Denmark ...56 8N 12 19 E
147 Gillespie Pt., N.Z. ...43 24 s 169 49 E
164 Gillette, U.S.A. 44 20N 105 38w
144 Gilliat, Queens., Austral. ......20 40 s 141 28 E
34 Gillingham, Dorset, England, U.K. 51 2N 2 15w
35 Gillingham, Kent, England, U.K. ....51 23N 0 34 E
55 Gilly, Belgium ......50 25N 4 30 E
165 Gilmer, U.S.A. 32 44N 94 55w
143 Gilmore, Australia ...35 14 s 148 12 E
154 Gilmour, Canada 44 48N 77 37w
78 Gilort, R., Rumania ..44 38N 23 32 E
167 Gilroy, U.S.A. 37 10N 121 37w
82 Gilsbakki, Iceland 64 44N 21 3w
38 Gilsland, Eng., U.K. ..55 0N 2 34w
80 Gilmåfors, Sweden ...62 40N 16 25 E
127 Gimbi, Ethiopia ...... 9 3N 35 42 E
55 Gimborn, Germany ...51 4N 7 28 E
73 Gimigliano, Italy ....38 55N 16 32 E
157 Gimli, Canada 50 40N 97 10w
127 Gimmi, Ethiopia ...... 9 0N 37 20 E
80 Gimo, Sweden ......60 11N 18 12 E
50 Gimont, France ......43 38N 0 52 E
98 Gimzo, Israel ......31 56N 34 56 E
106 Gin Ganga, R., Ceylon 6 0N 80 7 E
145 Gin Gin, Australia ...25 0 s 152 0 E
126 Gināh, Egypt ......25 21N 30 30 E
144 Gindie, Australia ....23 45 s 148 10 E
127 Giner, Ethiopia ...... 7 12N 40 40 E
142 Gingin, W. Australia ..32 23 s 115 37 E
135 Gingindlovu, S. Africa 29 0 s 31 36 E
55 Ginneken, Netherlands ......51 34N 4 47 E
73 Ginosa, Italy ......40 35N 16 45 E
62 Ginzo de Limia, Spain 42 3N 7 47w
161 Gioia Táuro, Italy ...38 26N 15 53 E
73 Gioia del Colle, Italy .40 49N 16 55 E
73 Gioia, G. of, Italy ....38 30N 15 50 E
73 Gioiosa, Ionica, Italy .38 20N 16 19 E
77 Giona, Mt., Greece ...38 38N 22 14 E
51 Giovi, P. dei, Italy ...44 30N 8 55 E
73 Giovinazzo, Italy .....41 10N 16 40 E
143 Gippsland, Australia .37 45 s 147 15 E
104 Gir Hills, India ......21 0N 71 0 E
104 Girab, India ......26 2N 70 38 E
100 Giresun, Turkey ......40 45N 38 30 E
126 Girga, Egypt ......26 17N 31 55 E
40 Glen Coe, Scot., United Kingdom ...56 40N 5 0w
143 Girgarre, Vic., Austral. ......36 18 s 145 0 E
130 Giri, R., Congo ...... 3 57N 19 0 E
105 Giridih, India ......24 10N 86 21 E
73 Girifalco, Italy ......38 49N 16 25 E
143 Girilambone, Australia ......31 16 s 146 57 E
125 Giro, Nigeria ......11 7N 4 42 E
101 Girishk, Afghanistan .31 47N 64 24 E
49 Giromagny, France ...47 44N 6 50 E
50 Gironde, dépt., France 44 45N 0 30w
50 Gironde, R., France ..45 30N 1 0w
64 Gironella, Spain ......42 2N 1 53 E

144 Giru, Queens., Austral. ......19 30 s 147 5 E
40 Girvan, Ayr, Scot., U.K. 55 15N 4 50w
40 Girvan R., Scot., U.K. 55 18N 4 30w
146 Gisborne, New Zealand ......38 39 s 178 5 E
146 Gisborne, dist., N.Z. .38 30 s 177 40 E
131 Gisenyi, Rwanda ..... 1 41 s 29 30 E
79 Giske, Norway ......62 30N 6 3 E
81 Gislaved, Sweden ....57 19N 13 30 E
49 Gisors, France ......49 15N 1 40 E
73 Giugliano in Camp., Italy ......40 55N 14 12 E
71 Giulianova, Italy ....42 45N 13 58 E
78 Giurgiu, Rumania ...43 52N 25 57 E
98 Give't Brenner, Is. ...31 52N 34 47 E
49 Give, Denmark ......55 51N 9 13 E
49 Givet, France ......50 8N 4 49 E
51 Givors, France ......45 35N 4 45 E
49 Givry, France ......46 41N 4 46 E
126 Giza (El Giza), Egypt 30 1N 31 11 E
91 Gizhiga, U.S.S.R. .....62 0N 150 27 E
91 Gizhiga, U.S.S.R. .61 0N 158 0 E
60 Gizycko, Poland ......54 2N 21 48 E
73 Gizzeria, Italy ......38 57N 16 10 E
79 Gjerpen, Norway ....59 15N 9 33 E
79 Gjerstad, Norway ....58 54N 9 0 E
76 Gji-i-Vlores, G. Alb. ..40 29N 19 27 E
76 Gjirokastër, Albania ..40 7N 20 16 E
79 Gjovdal, Norway ....58 52N 8 19 E
79 Gjøvik, Norway ......60 47N 10 43 E
155 Glace Bay, Canada ...46 11N 59 58w
156 Glacier B., Alas., U.S.A. 58 30N 136 10w
166 Glacier National Park, U.S.A. 48 40N 114 0w
166 Glacier Peak Mt., U.S.A. 48 3N 121 0w
55 Gladbeck, Germany ..51 34N 6 59 E
165 Gladewater, U.S.A. ...32 30N 94 58w
157 Gladstone, U.S.A. 45 52N 87 1w
157 Gladstone, Canada ...50 20N 99 0w
144 Gladstone, Australia .23 52 s 151 16 E
162 Gladwin, U.S.A. 43 59N 84 29w
80 Glafsfiorden, L., Sweden ......59 30N 12 45 E
82 Glama Jökull Mt., Ice. 65 48N 22 58w
79 Glama, R., Norway ...60 30N 12 8 E
82 Glamfjord, Norway ..66 45N 14 0 E
41 Glamis, Scot., U.K. ...56 37N 3 0w
71 Glamoc, Yugoslavia ..44 3N 16 51 E
37 Glamorgan, co., Wales, United Kingdom 51 37N 3 35w
29 Glamorgan, Vale of, Wales, U.K. 50 45N 3 15w
109 Glan, Philippines .... 5 45N 125 20 E
81 Glan, L., Sweden .....58 37N 16 0 E
37 Glanaman, Wales, U.K. 51 49N 3 54w
44 Glanaruddery Mts., Ire. 51 33N 9 27w
44 Glandore, Ireland 51 33N 9 7w
44 Glandore Harb., Ireland 51 33N 9 8w
39 Glanton, Eng., U.K. ..55 25N 1 54w
44 Glanworth, Ireland ...52 10N 8 25w
57 Glarus, Switzerland ..47 3N 9 4 E
43 Glas Maol, Scot., United Kingdom ...56 52N 3 20w
164 Glasco, Kan., U.S.A. .39 25N 97 50w
40 Glasco, N.Y., U.S.A. .42 3N 73 57w
40 Glasgow, Scot., U.K. .55 52N 4 14w
162 Glasgow, Ky., U.S.A. .37 2N 85 55w
166 Glasgow, Mont., U.S.A. 48 12N 106 35w
45 Glasnevin, Ireland ...53 22N 6 18w
45 Glasslough, Ireland ..54 20N 6 53w
44 Glasson, Ireland 53 29N 7 52w
36 Glastonbury, Eng., U.K. 51 5N 2 42w
161 Glastonbury, U.S.A. ..41 42N 72 36w
56 Glauchau, Germany ..50 50N 12 33 E
89 Glazov, U.S.S.R. ......58 0N 52 30 E
156 Gleichen, Canada 50 50N 113 0w
56 Gleidorf, Austria ....47 6N 15 44 E
135 Glen, O.F.S., S. Africa 28 56 s 26 20 E
161 Glen, U.S.A. 44 7N 71 10w
42 Glen B., Ireland 54 43N 8 45w
42 Glen Affric, Scot., U.K. 57 15N 5 0w
146 Glen Afton, N. Zealand ......37 46 s 175 4 E
41 Glen Almond, Scot., U.K. 56 28N 3 50w
167 Glen Canyon Dam, U.S.A. 37 0N 111 25w
167 Glen Canyon Nat. Recreation Area, U.S.A. 37 30N 111 0w
40 Glen Coe, Scot., United Kingdom ...56 40N 5 0w
161 Glen Cove, U.S.A. 40 51N 73 37w
43 Glen Esk, Scot., United Kingdom ...56 53N 2 50w
40 Glen Etive, Scot., U.K. 56 37N 5 0w
42 Glen Florrie, W. Austral. ......22 55 s 115 59 E
42 Glen Garry, Inv., Scotland, U.K. ...57 3N 5 7w
43 Glen Garry, Per., Scotland, U.K. ...56 47N 4 5w
134 Glen Harry, S. Africa 32 7N 24 43 E

38 Glen Helen, I. of M., U.K. 54 14N 4 35w
145 Glen Innes, Australia .29 40 s 151 39 E
40 Glen Lyon, Scot., U.K. 56 35N 4 20w
161 Glen Lyon, U.S.A. 41 10N 76 7w
146 Glen Massey, N.Z. ...37 38 s 175 2 E
43 Glen Mor, Scot., U.K. 57 12N 4 30 E
40 Glen Orchy, Scot., U.K. 56 27N 4 52w
43 Glen Orrin, Scot., U.K. 57 30N 4 45w
43 Glen Shee, Scot., U.K. 56 45N 3 25w
42 Glen Shiel, Scot., U.K. 57 8N 5 20w
43 Glen Spean, Scot., U.K. 56 53N 4 40w
143 Glen Thompson, Vic., Australia ......37 38 s 142 35 E
164 Glen Ullin, U.S.A. ...46 48N 101 46w
46 Glenade, Ireland 54 22N 8 17w
143 Glenaladale, Australia .36 30 s 143 48 E
45 Glenamoy, Ireland ...54 14N 9 40w
48 Glénans, Is. de, France 47 42N 4 0w
46 Glenarm, N. Ire., U.K. 54 58N 5 58w
45 Glenart Castle, Ireland 52 48N 6 12w
147 Glenavy, New Zealand ......44 54 s 171 7 E
46 Glenavy, N. Ire., U.K. 54 36N 6 12w
40 Glenbarr, Scot., U.K. .55 34N 5 40w
44 Glenbeigh, Ireland ...52 3N 9 57w
160 Glencoe, Canada 42 45N 81 46w
135 Glencoe, Natal, S. Afr. ......28 11 s 30 11 E
145 Glencoe, S. Australia .37 43 s 140 31 E
164 Glencoe, U.S.A. 44 45N 94 10w
46 Glencolumbkille, Ire. .54 43N 8 41w
135 Glenconnor, S. Africa 33 22 s 25 12 E
154 Glendale, Canada 46 24N 84 2w
132 Glendale, Rhodesia ...17 22 s 31 5 E
167 Glendale, Ariz., U.S.A. 33 40N 112 8w
167 Glendale, Calif., U.S.A. 34 7N 118 18w
166 Glendale, Ore., U.S.A. 42 44N 123 29w
164 Glendive, U.S.A. 47 7N 104 40w
164 Glendo, U.S.A. 42 30N 105 0w
41 Gleneagles, Scot., U.K. 56 16N 3 44w
45 Glenealy, Ireland 52 59N 6 10w
44 Gleneely, Ireland 52 14N 7 8w
40 Glenelg, Scot., U.K. ..57 13N 5 37w
145 Glenelg, S. Australia .34 58 s 138 30 E
143 Glenelg, R., Australia 37 10 s 141 30 E
42 Glenfinnan, Scot., U.K. 56 52N 5 28w
46 Glengad Hd., Ireland .55 19N 7 11w
44 Glengariff, Ireland ...51 45N 9 33w
46 Glengormley, Northern Ireland U.K. 54 41N 5 57w
147 Glenham, New Zealand ......46 26 s 168 52 E
147 Glenhope, New Zealand ......41 40 s 172 39 E
45 Glenisland, Ireland ...53 54N 9 24w
40 Glenkens, The, Scotland, United Kingdom 55 10N 4 15w
44 Glenluce, Scot., U.K. .54 53N 4 50w
147 Glenmary, Mt., N.Z. .44 0 s 169 55 E
38 Glenmaye, I. of M., U.K. 54 11N 4 42w
165 Glenmora, U.S.A. 31 1N 92 34w
144 Glenmorgan, Australia 27 15 s 149 30 E
44 Glennagevlagh, Ireland 53 36N 9 41w
46 Glennamaddy, Ireland 53 37N 8 33w
143 Glennie's Creek, N.S.W., Australia ...32 30 s 151 8 E
166 Glenn's Ferry, U.S.A. 43 0N 115 15w
46 Glenoe, N. Ire., U.K. .54 47N 5 50w
145 Glenorchy, Australia .42 49 s 147 18 E
143 Glenorchy, Australia .36 55 s 142 41 E
144 Glenore, Australia ...17 50 s 141 12 E
144 Glenormiston, Austral. ......22 55 s 138 50 E
145 Glenreagh, Australia .30 2 s 153 1 E
166 Glenrock, U.S.A. 42 50N 105 55w
41 Glenrothes, Scot., U.K. 56 12N 3 11w
138 Glenroy, W. Australia 17 16 s 126 14 E
161 Glens Falls, U.S.A. ...43 20N 73 40w
135 Glenside, Nat., S. Afr. 29 25 s 30 47 E
45 Glenties, Ireland 54 48N 8 18w
162 Glenville, U.S.A. 38 56N 80 50w
156 Glenwood, Alta., Can. 49 21N 113 24w
155 Glenwood, Newf., Can. 49 0N 54 47w
165 Glenwood Ark., U.S.A. 34 20N 93 30w
164 Glenwood, Iowa, U.S.A. 41 7N 95 41w
164 Glenwood, Minn., U.S.A. 45 38N 95 21w
166 Glenwood Sprs., U.S.A. 39 39N 107 15w
44 Glin, Ireland 52 34N 9 17w
71 Glina, Yugoslavia ....45 20N 16 6 E
60 Glinojeck, Poland ....52 49N 20 21 E
44 Glinsk, Ireland 53 23N 9 49w
79 Glittertind, mt., Nor. .61 40N 8 32 E
60 Gliwice (Gleiwitz), Pol. ......50 22N 18 41 E
167 Globe, Ariz., U.S.A. ..33 25N 110 53w

MAP
58 Glödnitz, Austria 46 53N 14 7E
58 Gloggnitz, Austria 47 41N 15 56E
60 Glogów, Poland 51 37N 16 5E
129 Glorieuses, Is., Ind. Oc. 11 30S 47 20E
40 Gloslunde, Denmark .54 46N 11 11E
38 Glossop, Eng., U.K. ...53 27N 1 56W
143 Gloucester, Australia .32 0S 151 59E
34 Gloucester, Eng., U.K. 51 52N 2 15W
161 Gloucester, Mass.,U.S.A. 42 38N 70 39W
144 Gloucester, I., Austral. 20 0S 148 30E
34 Gloucestershire, co., England, U.K. 51 45N 2 10W
161 Gloversville, N.Y., U.S.A. 43 5N 74 18W
155 Glovertown, Canada ...48 40N 54 03W
60 Glówno, Poland 51 59N 19 42E
59 Gloubczyce, Poland 50 13N 17 52E
89 Gluboki, U.S.S.R. 48 35N 40 25E
86 Glubokoye, U.S.S.R. .55 10N 27 45E
60 Glucholazy, Poland 50 19N 15 24E
56 Glücksburg, Germany 54 48N 9 34E
56 Glückstadt, Germany .53 46N 9 28E
86 Glukhov, U.S.S.R. 51 40N 33 50E
86 Glussk, U.S.S.R. 52 53N 28 41E
37 Glyn-ceiriog, Wales, United Kingdom 52 56N 3 12W
37 Glyncorrwg, Wales, United Kingdom 51 40N 3 39W
81 Glyngöre, Denmark ...56 46N 8 52E
37 Glyn Neath, Wales, United Kingdom 51 45N 3 37W
45 Glynn, Ireland 52 29N 6 55W
58 Gmünd, Kärnten, Aust. 46 54N 13 31E
58 Gmünd, Niederös-terreich, Pol. 48 47N 15 1E
58 Gmunden, Austria 47 55N 13 48E
80 Gnarp, Sweden 62 3N 17 16E
80 Gnesta, Sweden 59 3N 17 17E
60 Gniew, Poland 53 50N 18 50E
60 Gniezo, Pol. 52 33N 17 39E
56 Gnoien, Germany 53 58N 12 41E
127 Gnopp, Sweden 8 47N 29 50E
34 Gnosall, England, U.K. 52 48N 2 15W
81 Gnosjö, Sweden 57 22N 13 43E
142 Gnowangerup, Western Australia .33 58S 117 59E
107 Gô-Công, S. Vietnam .10 12N 107 0E
106 Goa, India 15 33N 73 59E
134 Goageb, S.W. Africa .26 49S 17 15E
134 Goageb R., S.W. Africa 27 45S 17 20E
143 Goalen Hd., Australia 36 33S 150 4E
105 Goalpura, India 26 11N 90 40E
105 Goalundo, E. Pakistan 23 50N 89 47E
124 Goaso, Ghana 6 48N 2 30W
40 Goat Fell, mt., Scotland, United Kingdom 55 37N 5 11W
127 Goba, Ethiopia 7 1N 39 59E
133 Goba, Mozambique 26 15S 32 13E
129 Gobabis, S. W. Africa 22 16S 19 0E
111 Gobi, or Shamo, des., Asia 44 0N 111 0E
106 Gobichettipalayam, India 11 31N 77 21E
127 Gobo, Sudan 5 40N 30 10E
56 Goch, Germany 51 40N 6 9E
129 Gochas, S.W. Africa ...24 59S 19 25E
35 Godalming, Eng., U.K. 51 12N 0 37W
106 Godavari Point, India 17 0N 82 20E
106 Godavari R., India 19 5N 79 0E
155 Godbout, Canada 49 20N 67 38W
105 Godda, India 24 50N 87 20E
123 Goddua, Libya 26 26N 14 19E
81 Godegård, Sweden 58 43N 15 8E
154 Goderich, Canada 43 45N 81 41W
48 Goderville, France 49 38N 0 22E
14 Godhavn, Greenland .69 22N 53 30W
104 Godhra, India 22 49N 73 40E
35 Godmanchester 52 19N 0 11W
172 Godoy Cruz, Argentina 32 56S 68 52W
36 Godrevy Pt., Eng., U.K. 50 15N 5 24W
154 Gods L., Canada 54 40N 94 10W
154 Gods R., Canada 55 30N 93 30W
34 Godshill, I. of W., England, U.K. 50 38N 1 13W
35 Godstone, England, United Kingdom 51 15N 0 3W
14 Godthaab, Greenland .64 15N 51 0W
102 Godwin Austen (K2), mt., Asia 36 0N 77 0E
154 Goeland, L., Canada .49 50N 76 40W
54 Goeree I., Netherlands 51 50N 4 0E
54 Goes, Netherlands 51 30N 3 55E
154 Gogama, Canada 47 35N 81 35W
144 Gogango, Queensland, Australia 23 40S 150 2E
164 Gogebic, L., U.S.A. ...46 30N 89 34W
104 Gogha, India 21 32N 72 9E
103 Gogra, R., *see* Ghaghara, R. 26 0N 84 20E
127 Gogrial, Sudan 8 30N 28 0E
175 Goiania, Brazil 16 35S 49 20W
175 Goias, Brazil 15 55S 50 10W
175 Goias, st., Brazil 12 10S 48 0W
40 Goil L., Scotland, U.K. 56 8N 4 52W
55 Goirle, Netherlands ...51 31N 5 4E
62 Gois, Port, Portugal ...40 10N 8 6W
58 Goisern, Austria 47 38N 13 38E

MAP
127 Gojam, prov., Ethiopia 10 55N 36 30E
127 Gojeb, R., Ethiopia ... 7 12N 36 40E
104 Gojra, Pakistan 31 10N 72 40E
88 Gök, R., Turkey 41 40N 34 30E
106 Gokak, India 16 11N 74 52E
105 Gokarannath, India ...27 57N 80 39E
106 Gokarn, India 14 33N 74 17E
103 Gokteik, Burma 22 26N 97 0E
104 Gokurt, West Pakistan 29 47N 67 26E
132 Gokwe, Rhodesia 18 2S 28 47E
81 Göl, Denmark 57 7N 9 40E
143 Gol Gol, Australia 34 12S 142 14E
105 Gola, India 28 3N 80 32E
46 Gola I., Ireland 55 4N 8 20W
105 Golakganj, India 26 8N 89 52E
14 Golchikha, U.S.S.R. ...71 45N 84 0E
166 Golconda, Nev., U.S.A. 40 58N 117 32W
166 Gold Beach, U.S.A. ...42 25N 124 25W
145 Gold Coast, Queensland, Australia 28 0S 153 25E
125 Gold Coast, reg., W. Afr. 4 0N 1 40W
166 Gold Hill, U.S.A. 42 28N 123 2W
156 Gold River, B.C., Canada 49 40N 126 10E
56 Goldberg, Germany ...53 34N 12 6E
156 Golden, Canada 51 20N 117 0W
44 Golden, Ireland 52 30N 8 0W
164 Golden, U.S.A. 39 42N 105 30W
147 Golden Bay, N.Z. 40 40S 172 50E
166 Golden Gate, U.S.A. .37 54N 122 30W
160 Golden Lake, Canada .45 34N 77 14W
157 Golden Prairie, Canada 50 13N 109 37W
106 Golden Rock, India ...10 45N 78 48E
44 Golden Vale. Ireland .52 33N 8 17W
166 Goldendale, U.S.A. 45 53N 120 48W
167 Goldfield, U.S.A. 37 45N 117 13W
157 Goldpines, Canada 50 45N 93 05W
163 Goldsboro, U.S.A. 35 24N 77 59W
163 Goldsmith, U.S.A. 32 0N 102 40W
165 Goldthwaite, U.S.A. ...31 25N 98 32W
44 Goleen, Ireland 51 30N 9 43W
63 Golegã, Portugal 39 24N 8 29W
133 Golela, Trans., S. Afr. 27 22S 31 55E
60 Goleniów, Poland 53 35N 14 50E
64 Golfe de Gascoigne, Fr. 44 0N 2 0W
169 Golfito, Costa Rica 8 41N 83 5W
72 Golfo Aranci, Italy 41 0N 9 38E
165 Goliad, U.S.A. 28 40N 97 22W
74 Golija, mt., Yugoslavia 43 22N 20 15E
74 Golija, ra., Yugoslavia 43 5N 18 45E
75 Golitsa, Bulgaria 42 55N 27 33E
111 Golmo, China 36 30N 95 10E
51 Golo R., France 42 24N 9 10E
88 Golovanesvsk, U.S.S.R. 48 25N 30 30E
88 Gölpazari, Turkey 40 17N 30 17E
43 Golspie, Scot., U.K. ...57 58N 3 58W
60 Golub Dobrzyn, Poland 53 7N 19 2E
74 Golubac, Yugoslavia .44 38N 21 38E
75 Golyama Kamchiya, R., Bulgaria 43 2N 27 18E
131 Goma, Congo 1 37S 29 10E
131 Goma, Rwanda 2 11S 29 18E
132 Gomare, Botswana 19 25S 22 8E
105 Gomati R., India 26 30N 81 50E
125 Gombe, Nigeria 10 19N 11 2E
131 Gombe R., Tanzania . 4 30S 32 50E
125 Gombi, Nigeria 10 12N 12 45E
86 Gomel, U.S.S.R. 52 28N 31 0E
120 Gomera Is., Canary Is. 28 10N 17 5W
40 Gometra I., Scot., U.K. 56 30N 6 18W
168 Gomez Palacio, Mexico 25 40N 104 40W
56 Gommern, Germany...52 54N 11 47E
109 Gomogomo, Indonesia 6 25S 134 53E
101 Gonabad, Iran 34 15N 58 45E
169 Gonaives, Haiti 19 20N 72 50W
169 Gonaives, Gulf of, Haiti 19 29N 72 42W
59 Gönc, Hungary 48 28N 21 14E
105 Gonda, India 27 9N 81 58E
101 Gondab-e Kavus, Iran 37 20N 55 25E
104 Gondal, India 21 58N 70 52E
127 Gonder, Ethiopia 12 23N 37 30E
105 Gondia, India 21 30N 80 10E
132 Gondola, Mozambique 19 4S 33 37E
62 Gondomar, Portugal .41 10N 8 35W
63 Gondomar, Spain 42 7N 8 45W
127 Gondor, Mt. Ethiopia 9 55N 36 28E
49 Gondrecourt, France .48 30N 5 30E
125 Gongola R., Nigeria ...10 30N 10 22E
60 Goniadz, Poland 53 30N 22 44E
125 Goniri, Nigeria 11 30N 12 15E
131 Gonja, Tanzania 4 15S 38 0E
72 Gonnesa, Italy 39 17N 8 27E
76 Gonnos, Greece 39 52N 22 29E
72 Gonnosfanadiga, Italy 39 30N 8 39E
114 Gono R., Japan 35 0N 132 40E
132 Gonye Falls, Zambia .16 38S 23 38E
167 Gonzales, Calif., U.S.A. 36 35N 121 30W
165 Gonzales, Tex., U.S.A. 29 30N 97 30W
172 Gonzalez Chaves, Argentina 38 02S 60 05W
143 Goobang Cr., Australia 33 20S 147 50E
134 Good Hope, S. Africa .31 51S 21 55E

MAP
134 Good Hope, C. of, S. Afr. 34 24S 18 30E
144 Goodenough I., Papua 9 15S 150 20E
154 Gooderham, Canada ...44 54N 78 21W
157 Goodeve, Canada 51 10N 103 10W
134 Goodhouse, S. Africa .28 57S 18 13E
166 Gooding, U.S.A. 43 0N 114 50W
164 Goodland, U.S.A. 39 22N 101 44W
165 Goodnight, U.S.A. 35 4N 101 13W
34 Goodrich, Eng., U.K. .51 52N 2 38W
157 Goodsoil, Canada 54 24N 109 12W
117 Goodsprings, U.S.A. ...35 51N 115 30W
37 Goodwick, Wales, U.K. 52 0N 5 0W
35 Goodwood, Eng., U.K. 50 53N 0 44W
39 Goole, England, U.K. 53 42N 0 52W
143 Goolgowi, Australia ...33 58S 154 39E
143 Goolma, Australia 32 18S 149 10E
145 Goolwa, S. Australia .35 30S 138 47E
142 Goomalling, W. Austral. 31 15S 116 42E
145 Goombalie, Australia .29 59S 145 26E
132 Goonda, Mozambique 19 48S 33 57E
145 Goondiwindi, Australia 28 30S 150 21E
143 Goonumbla, Australia 32 59S 148 11E
54 Goor, Netherlands 52 13N 6 33E
145 Gooray, Australia 28 25S 150 2E
155 Goose Bay, Canada ...53 15N 60 20W
166 Goose L., U.S.A. 42 0N 120 30W
144 Goothinga, Australia .17 36S 140 50E
106 Gooty, India 15 7N 77 41E
105 Gopalganj, E. Pak. 23 1N 89 55E
105 Gopalganj, India 26 28N 84 30E
57 Göppingen, Germany .48 42N 9 40E
65 Gor, Spain 37 23N 2 58W
125 Gora, Niger 13 55N 6 30E
60 Góra, Poland 51 40N 16 31E
89 Goragorski, U.S.S.R. .43 30N 45 10E
105 Gorakhpur, India 26 47N 83 32E
43 Gorazde, Yugoslavia .43 41N 18 59E
87 Gorbatov, U.S.S.R. 56 12N 43 2E
169 Gorda Punta, Nicaragua 14 10N 83 10W
145 Gordon, S. Australia .32 7S 138 20E
41 Gordon, Scot., U.K. 55 41N 2 32W
164 Gordon, U.S.A. 42 49N 102 6W
138 Gordon Downs, W. Australia 18 48S 128 40E
142 Gordon River, W. Australia 34 10S 117 15E
134 Gordonia, dist., S. Afr. 28 13S 21 10E
144 Gordonvale, Australia 17 5S 145 50E
121 Gore, Chad 7 59N 16 49E
127 Gore, Ethiopia 8 12N 35 32E
147 Gore, New Zealand 46 5S 168 58E
156 Gore B., Canada 45 57N 82 20W
41 Gorebridge, Scot., U.K.55 51N 3 2W
45 Goresbridge, Ireland .52 38N 7 0W
34 Gorey, Chan. Is., U.K. 49 11N 2 0W
45 Gorey, Ireland 52 41N 6 18W
101 Gorgan, Iran 36 55N 54 30E
144 Gorge, The, ra., Austral. 18 27S 145 30E
174 Gorgona I., Colombia . 3 0N 78 10W
70 Gorgona I., Italy 43 27N 9 52E
127 Gorgora, Ethiopia 12 15N 37 17E
161 Gorham Mt., U.S.A. ...43 42N 70 37W
161 Gorham, N.H., U.S.A. 44 23N 71 10W
89 Gori, U.S.S.R. 42 0N 44 7E
54 Gorinchem, Netherlands 51 50N 4 50E
34 Goring, Oxon., Eng., U.K. 51 31N 1 8W
35 Goring, Sussex, England, U.K. 50 49N 0 26W
71 Gorizia, Italy 45 56N 13 37E
78 Gorj, Reg., Rumania .45 0N 23 25E
60 Gorka, Poland 51 39N 16 58E
87 Gorki, U.S.S.R. 56 20N 44 0E
87 Gorki, U.S.S.R. 54 12N 31 5E
87 Gorkiy, Res., U.S.S.R. 57 2N 43 4E
35 Gorleston, Eng., U.K. 52 35N 1 44E
81 Gorley, Denmark 55 30N 11 15E
59 Gorlice, Poland 49 35N 21 11E
60 Görlitz, Germany 51 10N 14 59E
87 Gorlovka U.S.S.R. 48 25N 37 58E
165 Gorman, U.S.A. 32 15N 98 43W
75 Gorna Oryakhovitsa, Bulgaria 43 7N 25 40E
71 Gorna Radgona, Y.-slav. 46 40N 16 2E
74 Gornja Tuzla, Y.-slav. 44 35N 18 46E
71 Gornji Grad, Y.-slav. 46 20N 14 52E
74 Gornji Milanovac, Y.-slav. 44 00N 20 29E
74 Gornji, Milan., Y.-slav. 74 44N 20 29E
74 Gornji Vafuk, Y.-slav. 43 57N 17 34E
75 Gorno Ablanovo, Bulg. 43 37N 25 43E
90 Gorno Filinskoye, USSR 60 5N 70 0E
87 Gornyy, U.S.S.R. 51 50N 48 30E
88 Gorodenka, U.S.S.R. .48 41N 25 29E
87 Gorodets, U.S.S.R. 56 38N 43 28E
87 Gorodische, U.S.S.R. .53 13N 45 40E
86 Gorodnitsa, U.S.S.R. .50 46N 27 26E
86 Gorodnya, U.S.S.R. ...51 55N 31 33E
86 Gorodok, U.S.S.R. 49 46N 23 32E
86 Gorodok, U.S.S.R. 55 30N 30 3E
144 Goroka, New Guinea . 5 50S 145 30E
143 Goroke, Victoria, Australia 36 43S 141 29E
86 Gorokhov, U.S.S.R. ...50 15N 24 45E

MAP
87 Gorokhovets, U.S.S.R. 56 13N 42 39E
132 Goromonzi, Rhodesia .17 52S 31 22E
109 Gorong I., Indonesia . 4 5S 131 15E
132 Gorongose R., Mozam. 20 40S 34 30E
109 Gorontalo, Indonesia . 0 35N 123 13E
125 Goronyo, Nigeria 13 29N 5 39E
48 Gorron, France 48 25N 0 50W
44 Gort, Ireland 53 4N 8 50W
46 Gortin, N. Ire., U.K. .54 43N 7 13W
105 Gorumahisani, India .22 20N 86 24E
44 Gorumna I., Ireland ...53 15N 9 44W
43 Görzke, Germany 52 10N 12 24E
60 Gorzkowice, Poland ...51 13N 19 36E
60 Gorzów Slaski, Poland 51 3N 18 22E
60 Gorzów Wielkopolski, Poland 52 43N 15 15E
35 Gosberton, Eng., U.K. 52 52N 0 10W
143 Gosford, Australia 33 23N 151 18E
38 Gosforth, Cumb., England, U.K. 54 24N 3 27W
162 Goshen, Ind., U.S.A. .41 36N 85 46W
161 Goshen, N.Y., U.S.A. .41 23N 74 21W
133 Goshen, dist., S. Africa 25 50S 25 0E
131 Goshi, R., Kenya 3 21S 39 40E
56 Goslar, Germany 51 55N 10 23E
71 Gospic, Yugoslavia 44 35N 15 23E
34 Gosport, Eng., U.K. ...50 48N 1 8W
79 Gossa, I., Norway 62 52N 6 50E
55 Gosselies, Belgium 50 28N 4 24E
74 Gostivar, Yugoslavia .41 48N 20 57E
60 Gostyn, Poland 51 50N 17 3E
60 Gostynin, Poland 52 26N 19 29E
81 Göta, Sweden 58 6N 12 10E
81 Göta R. Canal, Sweden 58 45N 14 15E
81 Gota älv, R., Sweden .57 45N 12 0E
81 Göteborg, Sweden 57 43N 11 59E
81 Götene, Sweden 58 33N 13 30E
56 Gotha, Germany 50 56N 10 42E
81 Gothenburg, *see* Göteborg, Sweden ...57 43N 11 59E
164 Gothernburg, U.S.A. ...40 58N 100 8W
83 Gotland I., Sweden ...57 15N 18 30E
114 Goto-retto, Is., Japan 32 55N 129 5E
75 Gotse Delchev (Nevrokop), Bulgaria 41 43N 23 46E
83 Gotska Sandon I., Swed. 58 24N 19 15E
56 Gottingen, Germany .51 31N 9 55E
59 Gottwaldov (Zlin), Cz. 49 14N 17 40E
54 Gouda, Netherlands ...52 1N 4 42E
35 Goudhurst, Eng., U.K. 51 7N 0 28E
124 Goudiri, Senegal 14 15N 12 45E
17 Gough I., S. Atl., Oc. .40 10S 4 45W
154 Gouin Res., Canada ...48 35N 74 40W
122 Goula Touila, Mali 21 50N 1 57E
143 Goulburn, Australia ...32 22S 149 31E
138 Goulburn Is., Australia 11 40S 133 20E
143 Goulburn R., Australia 36 30S 145 20E
142 Gould, mt., Australia .25 46S 117 18E
122 Goulimine, Morocco ...28 50N 10 0W
122 Goulmina, Morocco 31 37N 4 54W
76 Gouménissa, Greece ...40 56N 22 37E
123 Goumeur, Chad 20 40N 18 30E
124 Goundam, Mali 16 25N 3 45W
77 Goúra, Greece 37 56N 22 20E
122 Gourara, des., Algeria 29 0N 0 30E
122 Gouraya, Algeria 36 31N 1 56E
50 Gourdon, France 44 44N 1 23E
43 Gourdon, Scot., U.K. .56 50N 2 15W
125 Gouré, Niger 14 0N 10 10E
134 Gourits R., S. Africa .34 15S 21 45E
125 Gourma-Rarous, Mali 16 55N 2 5W
121 Gouro, Chad 19 30N 19 30E
40 Gourock, Scot., U.K. .55 58N 4 49W
143 Gourock Ra., Australia 36 0S 149 25E
122 Gourrama, Morocco ...32 36N 3 59W
125 Gourselik, Chad 13 40N 10 40E
161 Gouverneur, U.S.A. ...44 18N 75 30W
50 Gouzon, France 46 12N 2 14E
157 Govan, Canada 51 20N 105 0W
139 Gove, N. Terr., Australia 12 25S 136 55E
88 Goverla, U.S.S.R. 49 9N 24 30E
175 Gov. Valadares, Brazil 18 15S 41 57W
160 Gowanda, U.S.A. 42 29N 78 58W
37 Gower, pen., Wales, United Kingdom 51 35N 4 10W
37 Gowerton, Wales, U.K. 51 38N 4 2W
46 Gowna, L., Ireland 53 52N 7 35W
45 Gowran, Ireland 52 38N 7 5W
172 Goya, Argentina 29 10S 59 10W
145 Goyder's Lagoon, S. Australia 27 3S 139 58E
174 Goyllarisquiga, Peru .10 19S 76 31W
121 Goz Beida, Chad 12 20N 21 30E
127 Goz Regeb, Sudan 16 3N 35 33E
68 Gozo (Ghaudex), I., Malta 36 0N 14 13E
134 Graaff-Reinet, S. Africa 32 13S 32 13E
134 Graafwater, S. Africa .32 10S 18 35E
81 Graasten, Denmark ...54 57N 9 34E
122 Grab, Chebka bou, Mor. 32 58N 2 56W
134 Grabouw, S. Africa 34 10S 18 58E
56 Grabow, Germany 53 17N 11 31E
60 Grabów, Poland 51 31N 18 7E
71 Gracac, Yugoslavia 44 18N 15 57E
74 Gracanica, Yugoslavia 44 43N 18 18E
49 Graçay, France 47 10N 1 50E
166 Grace, U.S.A. 42 38N 111 46W
164 Graceville, U.S.A. 45 36N 96 23W

MAP
169 Gracias à Dios, C., Central America 15 0N 83 20W
74 Gradačac, Yugoslavia 44 52N 18 26E
74 Gradeska Planina, ra., Yugoslavia 41 30N 22 15E
75 Gradets, Bulgaria 42 46N 26 30E
75 Gradnitsa, Bulgaria ...42 57N 24 58E
71 Grado, Italy 45 40N 13 20E
62 Grado, Spain 43 23N 6 4W
145 Gradule, Australia 28 32S 149 15E
165 Grady, U.S.A. 34 52N 103 15E
78 Graeca, Balta, L., Rum. 44 5N 26 10E
43 Graemsay I., Scot., U.K. 58 56N 3 17W
145 Grafton, Australia 29 35S 152 0E
164 Grafton, U.S.A. 48 30N 97 25W
73 Gragnano, Italy 40 42N 14 30E
143 Graham, Australia 34 2S 148 33E
154 Graham, Canada 49 20N 90 30W
163 Graham, N.C., U.S.A. 36 5N 79 22W
165 Graham, Tex., U.S.A. 33 7N 98 38W
156 Graham I., Canada 53 40N 132 30W
90 Graham Bell, I., U.S.S.R. 80 5N 70 0E
15 Graham Land, Antarc. 65 0S 64 0W
167 Graham Mt., U.S.A. ...32 46N 109 58W
157 Grahamdale, Canada .51 30N 98 34W
135 Grahamstown, S. Africa 33 19S 26 31E
74 Grahovo, Yugoslavia .42 40N 18 4E
123 Graiba, Tunisia 34 37N 10 11E
51 Graie, Alpi, mts., Fr. .45 25N 7 0E
45 Graigue, Ireland 52 51N 6 56W
45 Graiguenamanagh, Ire. 52 32N 6 58W
124 Grain Coast, reg., W. Afr. 4 20N 10 0W
39 Grainthorpe, Eng., U.K. 53 27N 0 5E
86 Graivoron, U.S.S.R. ...50 29N 35 39E
175 Grajaú, Brazil 5 50S 46 30W
60 Grajewo, Poland 53 39N 22 30E
74 Gramada, Bulgaria 43 49N 22 39E
50 Gramat, France 44 48N 1 43E
42 Gramisaale, Scot., U.K. 57 29N 7 18W
76 Grammos, Oros, mts., Gr. 40 25N 20 50E
73 Grammichele, Italy ...37 12N 14 37E
143 Grampians, Mts., Vic., Australia 37 0S 142 20E
43 Grampian Highlands, Scotland, U.K. 56 50N 4 0W
76 Gramsh, Albania 40 52N 20 12E
79 Gran, Norway...........60 23N 10 31E
120 Gran Canaria, Can. Is. 27 55N 15 35W
112 Gran Chaco, reg., S. Amer. 25 0S 61 0W
70 Gran Paradiso, mt, It. 49 33N 7 17E
71 Gran Sassa d'Italia It. 42 25N 13 30E
169 Granada, Nicaragua...11 58N 86 0W
65 Granada, Spain 37 10N 3 35W
164 Granada, U.S.A. 38 5N 102 13W
46 Granard, Ireland 53 47N 7 30W
80 Granbo, Sweden 61 16N 16 33E
165 Granbury, U.S.A. 32 28N 97 48W
154 Granby, Canada 45 25N 72 45W
162 Grand I., Mich., U.S.A. 46 30N 86 40W
155 Grand L., N.B., Canada 45 57N 66 7W
155 Grand L., Newf., Can. 48 45N 57 45W
165 Grand L., U.S.A. 29 55N 92 45W
164 Grand R., Mo., U.S.A. 39 45N 93 20W
169 Grand Bahama I., Bahama Islands 26 40N 78 30W
155 Grand Bank, Canada .47 6N 55 48W
124 Grand Bassa, Liberia . 6 0N 10 2W
124 Grand Bassam, Ivory C. 5 10N 3 49W
169 Grand Bourg, Marie-Galante, Leeward Is. 15 53N 61 19W
113 Grand Canal, China ...35 0N 117 0E
44 Grand Canal, Ireland .53 15N 8 10W
167 Grand Canyon National Park, U.S.A. 36 15N 112 20W
169 Grand Cayman, I., W.I. 19 20N 81 20W
124 Grand Cess, Liberia ... 4 40N 8 12W
166 Grand Coulee, U.S.A. .47 48N 119 1W
166 Gr. Coulee Dam, U.S.A. 48 0N 118 50W
122 Grand Erg Occi., Alg. 30 20N 1 0E
123 Grand Erg Oriental, Alg. 30 0N 6 30E
163 Grand Cays, Bahama Is. 27 10N 78 20W
155 Grand Falls, N.B., Can. 47 2N 67 46W
156 Grand Forks, Canada .49 0N 118 30W
164 Grand Forks, U.S.A. .48 0N 97 3W
162 Grand Haven, U.S.A. 43 3N 86 13W
164 Grand Island, U.S.A. .40 59N 98 25W
165 Grand Isle, U.S.A. 29 15N 89 58W
167 Grand Junction, U.S.A. 39 0N 108 30W
166 Grand Lake, U.S.A. ...40 20N 105 54W
154 Grand Lac, Vic., Canada 47 35N 77 35W
124 Gr. Lahou, Ivory Coast 5 10N 5 0W
166 Grand Lake, U.S.A. ...40 20N 105 54W
48 Grand Lieu, Lac de, Fr. 47 6N 1 40W

MAP
155 Grand Manan I., Can. 44 45N 66 52W
164 Grand Marais, Canada 47 45N 90 25W
162 Grand Marais, U.S.A. 46 39N 85 59W
154 Grand Mère, Canada .46 36N 72 40W
125 Grand Popo, Togo 6 15N 1 44E
164 Grand R., U.S.A. 45 45N 101 30W
157 Grand Rapids, Canada 53 12N 99 19W
162 Gr. Rapids, Mich., USA 42 57N 85 40W
164 Gr. Rapids, Minn., U.S.A. 47 19N 93 29W
166 Grand Teton, U.S.A. .43 45N 110 57W
155 Grand Vallée, Canada 49 14N 65 8W
166 Grand Valley, U.S.A. .39 30N 108 2W
157 Grand View, Canada .51 11N 100 51W
62 Grandas de Salime, Sp. 43 13N 6 53W
176 Grande B., Argentina 50 30S 68 20W
155 Grande Baie, Canada .48 19N 70 52W
168 Grande de Santiago, Rio, Mexico 21 20N 105 50W
174 Grande R., Bolivia 18 35S 63 0W
175 Grande R., Baia, Brazil 11 30S 44 30W
175 Grande R., Brazil 20 0S 50 0W
65 Grande, R., Spain 39 6N 0 48W
165 Grande, Rio, U.S.A. ...29 20N 100 40W
156 Grande Cache, Alta., Canada 53 35N 119 27W
155 Grande-Entrée, Canada 47 30N 61 40W
156 Grande Prairie, Canada 55 15N 118 50W
155 Grande Rivière, Canada 48 26N 64 30W
155 Gr. Bergeronnes, Can. 48 16N 69 35W
165 Grandfalls, U.S.A. 31 21N 102 51W
55 Grand-Halleux, Belgium 50 20N 5 55E
55 Grandhan, Belgium ...50 20N 5 25E
63 Grandola, Portugal ...38 12N 8 35W
49 Grandpré, France 49 20N 4 50E
166 Grandview, U.S.A. 46 13N 119 58W
49 Grandvilliers, France .49 40N 1 57E
172 Graneros, Chile 34 5S 70 45W
44 Graney L., Ireland 53 0N 8 40W
46 Grange, Ireland 54 24N 8 32W
46 Grange-over-Sands, England, U.K. 54 12N 2 55W
41 Grangemouth, Scot., U.K. 56 1N 3 43W
166 Granger, U.S.A. 46 25N 120 5W
80 Grängesberg, Sweden .60 6N 15 1E
39 Grangetown, Eng., U.K. 54 36N 1 7W
166 Grangeville, U.S.A. ...45 57N 116 4W
164 Granite City, U.S.A. .38 45N 90 3W
164 Granite Falls, U.S.A. .44 45N 95 35W
166 Granite Pk., Mt., U.S.A. 45 8N 109 52W
124 Granite Peak, W. Australia 25 40S 121 20E
147 Granity, New Zealand 41 39S 171 51E
175 Granja, Brazil 3 17S 40 50W
62 Granja de Moreruela, Spain 41 48N 5 44W
63 Granja de Torrehermosa, Spain 38 19N 5 35W
81 Granna, Sweden 58 0N 14 33E
64 Granollers, Spain 41 39N 2 18E
56 Gransee, Germany 53 0N 13 10E
154 Grant, Canada 50 6N 86 18W
164 Grant, U.S.A. 40 53N 101 42W
164 Grant City, U.S.A. 40 30N 94 25W
166 Grant Mt., U.S.A. 38 39N 118 52W
167 Grant Range Mts., U.S.A. 38 30N 115 30W
39 Grantham, Eng., U.K. 52 55N 0 39W
43 Grantown-on-Spey, Scotland, U.K. 57 19N 3 36W
167 Grants, U.S.A. 35 14N 107 57W
166 Grant's Pass, U.S.A. .42 30N 123 22W
164 Grantsburg, U.S.A. ...45 46N 92 44W
41 Grantshouse, Scot., U.K. 55 53N 2 17W
166 Grantsville, U.S.A. 40 35N 112 32W
48 Granville, France 48 50N 1 35W
46 Granville, N. Ire., U.K. 54 30N 6 47W
162 Granville, N.Y., U.S.A. 43 24N 73 16W
164 Granville, N.D., U.S.A. 48 18N 100 48W
157 Granville L., Canada .56 20N 100 35W
65 Grao de Gandia, Spain 39 0N 0 27W
175 Grão Mogul, Brazil 16 25S 42 35W
165 Grapeland, U.S.A. 31 30N 95 25W
152 Gras, L. de, Canada ...65 0N 110 30W
133 Graskop, Trans., S. Afr. 24 56S 30 49E
80 Gräsmark, Sweden 59 58N 12 44E
38 Grasmere, Eng., U.K. 54 28N 3 2W
38 Grasmere, L., Eng., U.K. 54 28N 3 2W
80 Gräsö, I., Sweden 60 28N 18 35E
134 Graspan, C. Prov., S. Afr. 29 19S 24 27E
166 Grass Range, U.S.A. .47 0N 109 0W
157 Grass R. Prov. Park, Man., Canada 54 35N 101 0W
166 Grass Valley, Calif., U.S.A. 39 18N 121 0W
166 Grass Valley, Ore., U.S.A. 45 28N 120 48W
73 Grassano, Italy 40 38N 16 17E
51 Grasse, France 43 38N 6 56E

MAP
38 Grassington, Eng., U.K. 54 5N 2 0W
155 Grate's Cove, Canada .48 8N 53 0W
57 Graubünden (Grisons), cant., Switzerland ...46 45N 9 30E
50 Graulhet, France 43 45N 1 58E
64 Graus, Spain 42 11N 0 20E
50 Grave, Pte. de, France 45 34N 1 4W
157 Gravelbourg, Canada .49 50N 105 35W
49 Gravelines, France 51 0N 2 10E
133 Gravelotte, S. Africa .23 56S 30 35E
160 Gravenhurst, Canada .44 52N 79 20W
81 Graversfors, Sweden ...58 42N 16 8E
35 Gravesend, Eng., U.K. 51 25N 0 22E
145 Gravesend, Australia .29 35S 150 20E
73 Gravina di Puglia, Italy 40 48N 16 25E
42 Gravir, Scotland, U.K. 58 2N 6 25W
169 Gravois, Pointe- à Haiti 16 15N 73 45W
51 Gravone R., Corsica, Fr. 42 3N 8 54E
81 Grävsnäs, Sweden 58 5N 12 29E
49 Gray, France 47 27N 5 35E
166 Gray Peak, Mt., U.S.A. 39 41N 105 55W
162 Grayling, U.S.A. 44 40N 84 42W
38 Grayrigg, Eng., U.K. .54 22N 2 40W
166 Grays Harbor, U.S.A. 46 55N 124 8W
166 Grays L., U.S.A. 43 8N 111 30W
35 Grays Thurrock, England, U.K. 51 28N 0 23E
157 Grayson, Canada 50 45N 102 40W
86 Grayvoron, U.S.S.R. .50 29N 35 39E
58 Graz, Austria 47 4N 15 27E
63 Grazalema, Spain 36 46N 5 23W
74 Grdelica, Yugoslavia .42 55N 22 3E
166 Great Basin, U.S.A. ...40 30N 116 20W
166 Great Falls, U.S.A. 47 32N 111 12W
44 Great I., Ireland 51 52N 8 15W
169 Great Abaco I., Bahamas 26 15N 77 10W
39 Great Ayton, Eng., U.K. 54 29N 1 8W
145 Gt Austral Basin, Artesian Basin, Austral 26 0S 140 0E
138 Great Australian Bight, South Australia 33 30S 130 0E
35 Great Baddow, England, United Kingdom 51 43N 0 31E
146 Great Barrier I., N.Z. 37 12S 175 25E
144 Gt. Barrier Rf., Austral. 19 0S 149 0E
161 Great Barrington, U.S.A. 42 11N 73 22W
158 Great Basin, U.S.A. ...40 0N 116 30W
152 Great Bear L., Canada 65 0N 120 0W
152 Great Bear R., Canada 65 0N 124 0W
81 Great Belt, Denmark .55 20N 11 0E
172 Great Bena, U.S.A. ...41 57N 75 45W
164 Great Bend, U.S.A. ...38 25N 98 55W
134 Great Berg, R., S. Afr. 32 50S 18 20E
35 Great Bentley, England, U.K. 51 51N 1 5E
142 Great Bernera, I., Scotland, U.K. 58 15N 6 50W
126 Great Bitter Lake, Eg. 30 15N 32 40E
44 Great Blasket, I., Ire. 52 5N 10 30W
18 Great Britain, Europe 54 0N 2 15W
156 Great Central, Canada 49 20N 125 10W
35 Great Chesterford, England, U.K. 52 4N 0 11E
38 Great Clifton, Eng., U.K. 54 39N 3 29W
107 Gt. Coco I., Burma ...14 10N 93 25E
122 Gt. Desert (Sahara), Afr. 23 0N 9 0E
144 Great Divide, Australia 23 0S 146 0E
35 Great Dunmow, England, U.K. 51 52N 0 22E
169 Great Exuma I., Bahama Is. 23 30N 75 50W
135 Great Fish Pt., S. Africa 33 30S 27 10E
134 Great Fish R., S. Africa 31 30S 20 16E
135 Great Fish R., S. Africa 33 28S 27 5E
39 Great Gonerby, England, U.K. 52 56N 0 40W
127 Great Hanish I., Ethiopia 13 40N 43 0E
169 Gt. Inagua I., Bahamas 21 0N 73 20W
104 Gt. Indian Des., India 27 40N 72 0E
155 Great Jarvis, Canada .47 39N 57 12W
134 Gt. Karas Mts., S.W. Africa 27 10S 18 45E
134 Gt. Karoo, reg., S. Africa 32 30S 23 0E
135 Great Kei, R., S. Africa 32 15S 27 45E
112 Gt. Khingan Mts., China 48 0N 121 0E
157 Great Lakes, Canada .44 0N 82 0W
34 Great Malvern, England, U.K. 52 7N 2 19W
35 Great Massingham, England, U.K. 52 47N 0 41E

MAP
35 Great Missenden, England, U.K. 51 42N 0 42W
134 Great Namaqualand, South-West Africa .26 0S 18 0E
37 Great Orme's Hd., Wales, U.K. 53 20N 3 52W
35 Great Ouse, R., England, U.K. 52 20N 0 8E
148 Great Plains, N. Amer. 45 0N 100 0W
131 Great Ruaha R., Tanz. 7 30S 35 0E
57 Gt. St. Bernard P., Switz. 45 50N 7 10E
165 Great Salt Plains Res., U.S.A. 36 40N 98 15W
166 Great Salt Lake, U.S.A. 41 0N 112 30W
166 Great Salt Lake Desert, U.S.A. 40 20N 113 50W
138 Great Sandy Desert, W. Australia 21 0S 124 0E
145 Great Sandy I., see Fraser I., Austral. .25 15S 153 0E
109 Gt. Sangihe, I., Indon. 3 45N 125 30E
59 Gt. Schutt I., Cz. 48 5N 17 20E
38 Great Shunner Fell, England, U.K. 54 22N 2 16W
124 Great Scarcies R., Sierra Leone 9 30N 12 40W
44 Great Skellig I., Ire. ...51 47N 10 32W
156 Great Slave, L. Canada 61 30N 114 20W
35 Great Stour, R., Kent, England, U.K. 51 15N 0 57E
45 Gt. Sugar Loaf, Mt., Ire. 53 10N 6 10W
36 Great Torrington, England, U.K. 50 57N 4 9W
133 Great Usutu R., Swazi 26 45S 31 45E
142 Gt. Victoria Des., W. Austral. 29 30S 126 30E
112 Great Wall, China 38 30N 109 30E
35 Gt. Waltham, Eng., U.K. 51 47N 0 29E
154 Great Whale R., Can. 55 20N 75 30W
38 Gt. Whernside, Mt., England, U.K. 54 9N 1 59W
34 Great Wyrley, England, United Kingdom 52 40N 2 1W
35 Great Yarmouth, England, U.K. 52 40N 1 45E
35 Great Yeldham, England, U.K. 52 1N 0 33E
169 Greater Antilles, W. Ind. 17 40N 74 0W
35 Greater London, England, U.K. 51 31N 0 6W
108 Greater Sunda Is., Indonesia 2 30S 110 0E
41 Greatham, Eng., U.K. 54 38N 1 14W
81 Grebbestad, Sweden ...58 42N 11 15E
72 Greco, Mt., Italy 41 48N 14 0E
76 Greece, State, Europe 40 0N 23 0E
133 Greefdale, S. Africa ...27 50S 24 43E
164 Greeley, Colo., U.S.A. 40 30N 104 40W
164 Greeley, Neb., U.S.A. 41 36N 98 32W
162 Green Bay, U.S.A. 44 30N 88 0W
162 Green B., U.S.A. 45 0N 87 30W
143 Green C., Australia ...37 13S 150 1E
163 Green Cove Springs, U.S.A. 29 59N 81 40W
147 Green I., New Zealand 45 54S 170 27E
144 Green I., New Guinea 4 30S 154 30E
162 Green R., Ky., U.S.A. 37 15N 86 30W
167 Green R., Utah, U.S.A. 39 0N 110 6W
166 Green R., Wyo., U.S.A. 41 44N 109 28W
166 Green R., Wyo., U.S.A. 43 2N 110 2W
39 Green Hammerton, England, U.K. 54 2N 1 17W
160 Greenbush, Mich., U.S.A. 44 35N 83 19W
164 Greenbush, Minn., U.S.A. 48 46N 96 10W
46 Greencastle, Ireland ...55 12N 7 0W
46 Greencastle, Northern Ireland, U.K. 54 2N 6 5W
162 Greencastle, U.S.A. ...39 40N 86 48W
161 Greene, N.Y., U.S.A. .42 20N 75 45W
163 Greenville, U.S.A. 36 13N 82 51W
163 Greenfield, Ind., U.S.A. 39 47N 85 51W
164 Greenfield, Iowa, U.S.A. 41 18N 94 28W
161 Greenfield, Mass., U.S.A. 42 38N 72 38W
165 Greenfield, Miss., U.S.A. 37 28N 93 50W
161 Greenfield Park, Can. .45 26N 73 28W
41 Greenhead, Eng., U.K. 54 58N 2 31W
154 Greening, Canada 48 10N 74 55W
46 Greenisland, Ireland ...54 42N 5 50W
14 Greenland, N. Amer. .66 0N 45 0W
14 Greenland Sea, Arctic Ocean 73 0N 10 0W
135 Greenlands, S. Africa .27 9S 27 43E
41 Greenlaw, Scot., U.K. 55 42N 2 28W
40 Greenock, Scot., U.K. 55 57N 4 46W
46 Greenore, Ireland 54 2N 6 8W
45 Greenore Pt., Ireland .52 15N 6 20W
161 Greenport, U.S.A. 41 5N 72 23W

MAP
143 Greens Creek, Australia 36 57S 143 0E
163 Greensboro, Ga., U.S.A. 33 34N 83 12W
163 Greensboro, N.C., U.S.A. 36 7N 79 46W
162 Greensburg, Ind., U.S.A. 39 20N 85 30W
165 Greensburg, Kan., U.S.A. 37 38N 99 20W
160 Greensburg, Pa., U.S.A. 40 18N 79 31W
42 Greenstone Pt., Scotland, U.K. 57 55N 5 38W
135 Greenvale, Natal, S. Afr. 29 59S 50 0W
124 Greenville, Liberia 5 7N 9 6W
163 Greenville, Ala., U.S.A. 31 50N 86 37E
166 Greenville, Calif., U.S.A. 40 15N 121 0W
164 Greenville, Ill., U.S.A. 38 53N 89 22W
155 Greenville, Me., U.S.A. 45 30N 69 32W
162 Greenville, Mich., U.S.A. 43 12N 85 14W
165 Greenville, Miss., U.S.A. 33 25N 91 0W
163 Greenville, N.C., U.S.A. 35 37N 77 26W
162 Greenville, Ohio, U.S.A. 40 5N 84 38W
160 Greenville, Pa., U.S.A. 41 23N 80 22W
163 Greenville, S.C., U.S.A. 34 54N 82 24W
165 Greenville, Tex., U.S.A. 33 5N 96 5W
37 Greenway, Wales, U.K. 51 56N 4 49W
35 Greenwich, Eng., U.K. 51 28N 0 0
161 Greenwich, N.Y., U.S.A. 43 2N 73 36W
160 Greenwich, Ohio, U.S.A. 41 1N 82 32W
156 Greenwood, Canada ...49 10N 118 40W
165 Greenwood, Miss., U.S.A. 33 30N 90 4W
163 Greenwood, S.C., U.S.A. 34 13N 82 13W
55 Grefrath, Germany 51 20N 6 21E
164 Gregory, U.S.A. 43 14N 99 20W
144 Gregory, R., Australia 18 58S 139 0E
144 Gregory Downs, Austral. 18 35S 138 45E
138 Gregory L., Western Australia 20 10S 127 30E
144 Gregory Ra., Australia 19 0S 143 10E
42 Greian Hd., Scot., U.K. 57 1N 7 30W
56 Greiffenberg, Germany 53 6N 13 57E
56 Greifswald, Germany .54 6N 13 23E
56 Greifswalder Bodden, Germany 54 12N 13 35E
56 Greifswalder Oie. I., Ger. 54 15N 13 55E
58 Grein, Austria 48 14N 14 51E
58 Greiner Wald, Mts., Austria 48 30N 15 0E
56 Greiz, Germany 50 39N 12 12E
84 Gremikha, U.S.S.R. ...67 50N 39 40E
81 Grenaa, Denmark 56 26N 10 51E
165 Grenada, U.S.A. 33 45N 89 50W
169 Grenada I., West Indies 12 10N 61 40W
169 Grenadines, West Indies 12 40N 61 20W
81 Grenen (Skaw) C., Den. 57 46N 10 34E
157 Grenfell, Australia 33 52S 148 8E
157 Grenfell, Canada 50 30N 102 50W
51 Grenoble, France 45 12N 5 42E
164 Grenora, U.S.A. 48 38N 103 54W
143 Grénville, Vic., Austral. 37 57S 143 40E
51 Gréoux, France 43 46N 5 52E
166 Gresham, U.S.A. 45 36N 122 31W
109 Gresik, Indonesia 9 13S 112 38E
55 Gressenich, Germany .50 46N 6 17E
70 Gressoney St. Jean, It. 45 49N 7 47E
38 Greta R., Cumb., England, U.K. 54 36N 3 5W
165 Gretna, U.S.A. 30 0N 90 2W
41 Gretna, Scot., U.K. 54 59N 3 4W
41 Gretna Green, Scotland, United Kingdom 55 0N 3 3W
35 Gretton, Eng., U.K. ...52 33N 0 40W
56 Greven, Germany 52 7N 7 36E
76 Grevená, tn., & prov., Greece 40 4N 21 25E
55 Grevenbicht, Neth. 51 2N 5 47E
56 Grevenbroich, Germany 51 6N 6 32E
54 Grevenmacher, Lux. .49 40N 6 28E
56 Grevesmuhlen, Ger. ...53 51N 11 10E
81 Grevie, Sweden 56 22N 12 46E
81 Grevinge, Denmark 55 48N 11 34E
145 Grey Range, Australia 27 0S 143 30E
147 Grey R., N.Z. 42 17N 171 35E
46 Greyabbey, N. Ire., U.K. 54 32N 5 35W
166 Greybull, U.S.A. 44 30N 108 3W
133 Greylingstad, S. Africa 26 44S 28 45E
147 Greymouth, N.Z. 42 29S 171 13E

MAP
45 Greystones, Ireland ...53 9N 6 4W
134 Greyton, S. Africa 34 5S 19 35E
135 Greytown, Natal, S. Afr. 29 1S 30 36E
146 Greytown, N.Z. 41 5S 175 29E
76 Griba, Mts., Albania .40 17N 19 45E
87 Gribanovskiy, U.S.S.R. 51 28N 41 50E
36 Gribbin Head, England, United Kingdom 50 18N 4 41W
166 Gridley, U.S.A. 39 27N 121 47W
134 Griekwastad, S. Africa 28 49S 23 15E
163 Griffin, U.S.A. 33 17N 84 14W
143 Griffith, Australia 34 14S 145 46E
157 Griffith Mine, Canada 50 47N 93 25W
168 Grijalva, R., Mexico ...16 20N 92 20W
107 Grik, Malaysia 5 23N 101 10E
80 Grillby, Sweden 59 38N 17 10E
86 Grimailov, U.S.S.R. ...49 20N 26 5E
121 Grimari, Central African Republic ... 5 43N 20 0E
81 Grimeton, Sweden 57 6N 12 25E
42 Griminish Pt., Scot., U.K. 57 40N 7 30W
56 Grimma, Germany 51 14N 12 44E
56 Grimmen, Germany ...54 6N 13 2E
42 Grimsay I., Scot., U.K. 57 29N 7 12W
160 Grimsby, Canada 43 12N 79 33W
39 Grimsby, Eng., U.K. .53 35N 0 5W
156 Grimshaw, Canada 56 10N 117 40W
79 Grimstad, Norway 58 22N 8 35E
57 Grindelwald, Switz. ...46 38N 8 2E
81 Grindsted, Denmark .55 46N 8 55E
155 Grindstone Island, Can. 47 25N 62 0W
78 Grindşul, Mt., Rumania 46 40N 26 7E
164 Grinnell, U.S.A. 41 45N 92 50W
62 Grinon, Spain 40 13N 3 51W
79 Grip, Norway 63 16N 7 37E
133 Griqualand E., dist., C. Prov., S. Afr. 30 30S 29 0E
134 Griqualand W., dist., C. Prov., S. Afr. 28 40S 23 30E
155 Griquet, Canada 51 30N 55 35W
49 Griz Nez, C., France .50 50N 1 35E
38 Grizebeck, Eng., U.K. 54 16N 3 10W
50 Grisolles, France 43 49N 1 19E
57 Grisons, Can., Switz. .46 40N 9 30E
80 Grisslehamn, Sweden 60 5N 18 57E
43 Gritley, Scot., U.K. ...58 56N 2 45W
71 Grmeč Planina, Y.-slav. 44 43N 16 16E
155 Groais I., Canada 50 55N 55 35W
55 Grobbendonk, Belgium 51 12N 4 44E
133 Groblersdal, S. Africa 25 15S 29 25E
134 Groblershoop, S. Africa 28 55S 20 59E
58 Grobming, Austria 47 27N 13 54E
74 Grocka, Yugoslavia 44 40N 20 42E
86 Grodek, Poland 52 46N 23 38E
60 Grodkow, Poland 50 43N 17 40E
86 Grodno, U.S.S.R. 53 42N 23 52E
60 Grodzisk Mazowiecki, Poland 52 7N 20 37E
60 Grodzisk Wlkp., Poland 52 15N 16 22E
86 Grodzyanka, U.S.S.R. 53 31N 28 42E
135 Groenheuwels, S. Africa 33 15S 26 2E
55 Groesbeek, Netherlands 51 47N 5 58E
165 Groesbeck, U.S.A. 31 32N 96 34W
48 Groix, France 47 38N 3 29W
48 Groix, I. de, France ...47 38N 3 28W
60 Grójec, Poland 51 50N 20 58E
56 Gronau, Germany 52 13N 7 2E
82 Grong, Norway 64 25N 12 8E
54 Groningen, Netherlands 53 15N 6 35E
54 Groningen, prov., Neth. 53 16N 6 40E
81 Gronskåra, Sweden 57 5N 15 43E
165 Groom, U.S.A. 35 12N 100 59W
46 Groomsport, Northern Ireland, U.K. 54 41N 5 37W
134 Groot R., S. Africa 33 10S 23 35E
134 Groot-Brakrivier, S. Afr. 34 2S 22 18E
133 Groot Letaba R., S. Afr. 23 40S 30 45E
133 Groot Marico, S. Africa 25 34S 26 27E
133 Groot Marico, R., S. Afr. 24 30S 26 26E
133 Gr. Shingwedzi R., Trans., South Africa 23 10S 31 0E
133 Groot Spelonke, S. Afr. 23 30S 30 0E
135 Groot Winterhoekberge, Mts., S. Afr. 33 35S 25 0E
134 Grootdrink, S. Africa .28 31S 21 44E
139 Groote Eylandt, N. Terr., Australia 14 0S 136 50E
129 Grootfontein, S.W. Africa 19 31S 18 6E
134 Grootrivierdrif, S. Afr. 33 25S 24 40E
133 Grootvlei, Trans., S. Afr. 26 44S 28 32E
134 Grootvloer, S. Africa .30 0S 20 40E
65 Grosa, Punta, Spain ...39 6N 1 36E
70 Grosio, Italy 46 18N 10 17E
51 Grosne, R., France 46 30N 4 40E
58 Gross Glockner, Mt., Austria 47 5N 12 40E

MAP
56 Gross Ottersleben, Ger. 52 5N 11 33E
55 Gross Reken, Germany 51 50N 7 3E
175 Grossa Pta., Brazil 1 20N 50 0W
56 Grossenbrode, Germany 54 21N 11 4E
56 Grossenhain, Germany 51 17N 13 32E
70 Grosseto, Italy 42 45N 11 7E
58 Grossgerungs, Austria 48 34N 14 57E
155 Grosswater B., Canada 54 20N 57 10W
161 Groton, Conn., U.S.A. 41 22N 75 5W
73 Grottaglie, Italy 40 32N 17 25E
73 Grottaminarda, Italy .41 5N 15 4E
122 Grou, R., Morocco 33 49N 6 30W
48 Grouin, Pointe du, France 48 43N 1 51W
154 Groundhog, R., Canada 48 45N 82 20W
166 Grouse Creek, U.S.A. .41 51N 113 57W
160 Grove City, U.S.A. 41 10N 80 5W
80 Grovelsjön, Sweden ...62 6N 12 16E
161 Groveton, N.H., U.S.A. 44 34N 71 30W
165 Groveton, Tex., U.S.A. 31 5N 95 4W
71 Groznjan, Yugoslavia 45 22N 13 43E
89 Groznyy, U.S.S.R. 43 20N 45 45E
55 Grubbenvorst, Neth. .51 25N 6 9E
74 Grubišno Palje, Y.-slav. 45 44N 17 12E
60 Grudusk, Poland 53 3N 20 38E
60 Grudziadz, Poland 53 30N 18 47E
42 Gruinard B., Scot., U.K. 57 56N 5 35W
50 Gruissan, France 43 8N 3 7E
73 Grumo Appula, Italy .41 2N 16 43E
80 Grums, Sweden 59 22N 13 5E
134 Grunău, S.W. Africa .27 45S 18 26E
56 Grunberg, Germany ...50 37N 8 55E
82 Grundarf, Iceland 64 55N 23 12W
164 Grundy Center, U.S.A. 42 22N 92 45W
79 Grungedal, Norway ...59 44N 7 37E
42 Gruting Voe, Scot., U.K. 60 12N 1 32W
165 Gruver, U.S.A. 36 19N 101 20W
57 Gruyères, Switzerland 46 35N 7 4E
74 Gruza, Yugoslavia 44 5N 20 46E
87 Gryazi, U.S.S.R. 52 30N 39 58E
87 Gryazovets, U.S.S.R. .58 50N 40 20E
59 Grybów, Poland 49 36N 20 55E
80 Gryckbo, Sweden 60 40N 15 35E
60 Gryfice, Poland 53 55N 15 13E
60 Gryfino, Poland 53 16N 14 29E
81 Grytgöl, Sweden 58 49N 15 33E
80 Grythyttan, Sweden ...59 41N 14 32E
15 Grytviken, S. Georgia 53 50S 37 10W
57 Gstaad, Switzerland ...46 28N 7 18E
169 Guacanayabo, G. of, Cuba 20 40N 77 20W
168 Guadalajara, Mexico .20 40N 103 20W
64 Guadalajara, Spain 40 37N 3 12W
64 Guadalajara, prov., Sp. 40 47N 3 0W
63 Guadalcanal, Spain 38 5N 5 52W
136 Guadalcanal, I., Pac. Oc. 10 0S 160 0E
65 Guadalén R., Spain ...38 30N 3 7W
72 Guadales, Argentina ...34 30S 67 55W
63 Guadalete R., Spain ...36 45N 5 47W
63 Guadalhorce, R., Spain 36 50N 4 42W
65 Guadalimar, R., Spain 38 10N 2 53W
65 Guadalmena, R., Spain 38 31N 2 50W
63 Guadalmez R., Spain .38 33N 4 42W
64 Guadalope, R., Spain .41 0N 0 13W
63 Guadalquivir R., Spain 38 0N 4 0W
63 Guadalupe, Spain 39 27N 5 17W
167 Guadalupe, U.S.A. 34 59N 120 33W
168 Guadalupe Bravos, Mex. 31 20N 106 10W
137 Guadalupe I., Pac. Oc. 21 20N 118 50W
167 Guadalupe Pk., U.S.A. 31 50N 105 30W
165 Guadalupe R., U.S.A. 29 25N 97 30W
169 Guadeloupe I., Fr. W.I. 16 20N 61 40W
169 Guadeloupe Passage, Leeward Is. 16 50N 68 15E
63 Guadiamar, R., Spain 37 9N 6 20W
63 Guadiana R., Spain ...37 9N 6 20W
65 Guadiana Menor, R., Sp. 37 45N 3 7W
63 Guadiaro, R., Spain ...36 39N 5 17W
63 Guadiato, R., Spain ...37 55N 4 53W
64 Guadiela, R., Spain ...40 30N 2 23W
63 Guadix, Spain 37 18N 3 11W
176 Guafo, G. of, Chile 43 35S 74 0W
173 Guaira, Brazil 24 5S 54 10W
176 Guaitecas Is., Chile ...44 0S 74 30W
174 Guajará-Mirim, Brazil 10 50S 65 20W
174 Guajaratuba, Brazil ... 5 0S 63 0W
174 Guajira Pen., Colombia 12 0N 72 0W
174 Gualaquiza, Ecuador . 3 30S 78 30W
71 Gualdo Tadino, Italy .43 14N 12 46E
172 Gualeguay, Argentina 33 10S 59 20W
172 Gualeguaychu, Arg. ...33 3S 58 31W
136 Guam I., Pacific Ocean 13 27N 144 45E
172 Guamini, Argentina ...37 1S 62 28W
168 Guamuchil, Mexico 25 25N 108 3W
169 Guanabacoa, Cuba 23 8N 82 18W
173 Guanabara, St., Brazil 23 0S 43 25W
169 Guanacaste, Costa Rica 10 40N 85 30W
169 Guanacaste, Cordillera del, Costa Rica 10 40N 85 4W
168 Guanacevi, Mexico 25 40N 106 0W
169 Guanajay, Cuba 22 56N 82 42W
168 Guanajuato, Mexico ...21 0N 101 20W
168 Guanajuato, st., Mexico 20 40N 101 20W
174 Guanare, Venezuela ... 9 0N 69 50W
172 Guandacol, Argentina 29 30S 68 40W
169 Guane, Cuba 22 10N 84 0W
169 Guantanamo, Cuba ...20 10N 75 20W
169 Guápiles, Costa Rica .10 10N 83 46W
173 Guaporé Brazil 12 0S 64 0W
173 Guaporé R., Brazil 13 0S 63 0W
174 Guaqui, Bolivia 16 41S 68 54W
173 Guarapuava, Brazil ...25 20S 51 30W
173 Guaratinguetá, Brazil 22 49S 45 9W
173 Guaratuba, Brazil 25 53S 48 38W
41 Guard Bridge, Scotland, United Kingdom 56 21N 2 52W
62 Guarda, tn. & dist., Port. 40 32N 7 20W
99 Guardafui, C, Somali Rep, see Asir, Ras .11 55N 51 10E
65 Guardamar de Suguva, Spain 38 5N 0 39W
73 Guardavalle, Italy ...38 31N 16 30E
71 Guardiagrele, Italy ...42 11N 14 11E
62 Guardo, Spain 42 47N 4 50W
63 Guarena, Spain 38 51N 6 6W
62 Guarena, R., Spain ...41 25N 5 25W
173 Guaruja, Brazil 24 2S 46 25W
173 Guarulhos, Brazil 23 25S 46 35W
173 Guarus, Brazil 21 30S 41 20W
174 Guasdualito, Venezuela 7 15N 70 44W
174 Guasipati, Venezuela . 7 28N 61 54W
70 Guastalla, Italy 44 55N 10 40E
168 Guatemala, rep., Central America 15 40N 90 30W
168 Guatemala, Guatemala 14 40N 90 30W
174 Guaviare R., Colombia 3 30N 71 0W
173 Guaxupé, Brazil 21 10S 47 5W
174 Guayaquil, Ecuador ... 2 15S 79 52W
174 Guayaquil, G. of, Ecuador 3 10S 81 0W
169 Guayama, Puerto Rico 18 5N 66 7W
172 Guaymallen, Argentina 32 50S 68 45W
168 Guaymas, Mexico 27 50N 111 0W
130 Guba, Congo 10 38S 26 27E
127 Guba, Ethiopia 12 50N 39 18E
143 Gubbata, Australia ...33 37S 146 30E
71 Gubbio, Italy 43 20N 12 34E
60 Gubin, Poland 51 58N 14 45E
125 Gubio, Nigeria 12 30N 12 42E
74 Guča, Yugoslavia 43 46N 20 15E
107 Guchil, Malaysia 5 35N 102 10E
112 Guchin-Us, Mongolia .45 28N 102 10E
106 Gudalur, India 11 30N 76 29E
89 Gudata, U.S.S.R. 43 7N 40 32E
161 Guddy Barrage, W. Pak. 28 30N 69 50E
81 Gudenaå R., Denmark 56 23N 9 45E
89 Gudermes, U.S.S.R. ...43 24N 46 20E
81 Gudheim, Sweden 55 12N 14 58E
106 Gudivada, India 16 30N 81 15E
106 Gudiyatam, India 12 57N 78 55E
80 Gudmundra, Sweden .62 56N 17 47E
106 Gudur, India 14 12N 79 55E
49 Guebwiller, France 47 55N 7 12E
62 Guecho, Spain 43 21N 2 59W
124 Guekedou, Guinea 8 40N 10 5W
123 Guelma, Algeria 36 25N 7 29E
154 Guelph, Canada 43 35N 80 20W
122 Guelt es Stel, Algeria .35 12N 3 1E
123 Guémar, Algeria 33 30N 6 57E
48 Guémené-sur-Scorff, Fr. 48 4N 3 13W
38 Guéméné Penfao, Fr. .47 38N 1 50W
172 Güemes, Argentina 24 50S 65 0W
125 Guéné, Dahomey 11 44N 3 16E
48 Guer, France 47 54N 2 8W
48 Guérande, France 47 20N 2 26W
122 Guercif, Morocco 34 11N 3 15W
50 Guéret, France 46 11N 1 51E
49 Guérigny, France 47 6N 3 10E
64 Guernica, Spain 43 19N 2 40W
164 Guernsey, U.S.A. 42 19N 104 45W
48 Guernsey I., Chan. Is., U.K. 49 30N 2 35W
122 Guerrara, Algeria 28 5N 0 8W
123 Guerrara, Algeria 32 51N 4 35E
168 Guerrero, st., Mexico .17 30N 100 0W
122 Guerzim Algeria 29 45N 1 47W
35 Guestling Green, England, U.K. 50 53N 0 40E
122 Guettara, Algeria 29 40N 8 3W
51 Gueugnon, France 45 36N 4 3E
165 Gueydan, U.S.A. 30 3N 92 30W
123 Guezendi, see Ghesendor, Chad 21 41N 18 14E
71 Guglionesi, Italy 51 55N 14 54E
101 Guhra, Iran 27 36N 56 8E
175 Guiana Highlands, S. America 5 0N 60 0W
134 Guibes, S.W. Africa ...26 41S 16 49E
125 Guider, Cameroon 9 55N 13 59E
125 Guidimouni, Niger 13 42N 9 31E
124 Guiglo, Ivory Coast ... 6 45N 7 30W
133 Guija, Mozambique ...34 35S 33 15E
62 Guijo de Coria, Spain .40 6N 6 28W
35 Guildford, Eng., U.K. 51 14N 0 34W
155 Guilford, Me., U.S.A. .45 12N 69 25W
161 Guilford, Conn., U.S.A. 41 15N 72 40W
51 Guillaymes, France ...44 5N 6 52E
51 Guillestre, France 44 39N 6 40E
37 Guilsfield, Wales, U.K. 52 42N 3 9W
48 Guilvinec, France 47 48N 4 17E
175 Guimaraes, Brazil 2 9S 44 35W
62 Guimarãis, Portugal ...41 28N 8 24W
109 Guimaras I., Philippines 10 30N 122 30E
117 Guinea, Reg., Africa . 9 0N 5 0E
125 Guinea, Gulf of, W. Afr. 3 0N 2 30E
124 Guinea, Port, W. Africa 12 0N 15 0W
124 Guinea, Rep., W. Africa 10 20N 10 0W
169 Guines, Cuba 22 50N 82 0W
48 Guingamp, France 48 34N 3 10W
48 Guipavas, France 48 26N 4 29W
64 Guipuzcoa, prov., Sp. 43 12N 2 15W
122 Guir, R., Algeria 31 29N 2 58W
169 Güiria, Venezuela 10 32N 62 18W
39 Guisborough, Eng., U.K. 54 32N 1 2W
49 Guiscard, France 49 40N 3 0E
49 Guise, France 49 52N 3 35E
62 Guitiriz, Spain 43 11N 7 50W
55 Guitrode, Belgium 51 5N 5 36E
109 Guivan, Philippines ...11 5N 125 55E
104 Gujarat, St. India 23 20N 71 0E
104 Gujranwala, Pakistan 32 10N 74 12E
104 Gujrat, Pakistan 32 40N 74 2E
107 Gukhothae, Thailand .17 2N 99 50E
89 Gukovo, U.S.S.R. 48 1N 39 58E
125 Gulak, Nigeria 10 50N 13 30E
143 Gular, N.S.W., Austral. 31 19N 148 27E
101 Gulbahar, Afghanistan 35 5N 69 10E
106 Gulbargā, India 17 20N 76 50E
81 Guldborg Sd., Denmark 54 39N 11 50E
106 Guledgud, India 16 3N 75 48E
165 Gulfport, U.S.A. 30 28N 89 3W
143 Gulgong, Australia 32 20S 149 30E
104 Gulistan, W. Pakistan 30 36N 66 35E
157 Gull Lake, Canada 50 10N 108 55W
41 Gullane, Scot., U.K. ...56 2N 2 50W
81 Gullringen, Sweden ...57 48N 15 44E
77 Güllük, Turkey 37 12N 27 36E
125 Gulma, Nigeria 12 40N 4 23E
127 Gulnam, Sudan 6 55N 29 30E
100 Gulpaigan, Iran 33 26N 50 20E
55 Gulpen, Netherlands .50 49N 5 53E
76 Gülpinar, Turkey 39 32N 26 10E
90 Gulshat, U.S.S.R. 46 45N 74 25E
79 Gulsvik, Norway 60 24N 9 38E
131 Gulu, Uganda 2 48N 32 17E
131 Gulwe, Tanzania 6 30S 36 25E
143 Gum Lake, Australia .32 42S 143 9E
111 Guma, China 38 0N 78 20E
104 Gumal, R., W. Pak. ...32 5N 70 5E
104 Gumbaz, W. Pakistan 30 2N 69 0E
131 Gumbiro, Tanzania ...10 1S 35 20E
125 Gumel, Nigeria 12 39N 9 22E
64 Gumiel de Hizán, Spain 41 46N 3 41W
144 Gumlu, Queensland, Australia 19 53S 147 41E
114 Gumma, Pref., Japan 36 30N 138 20E
56 Gummersbach, Ger. ...51 2N 7 32E
125 Gummi, Nigeria 12 4N 5 9E
135 Gumtree, O.F.S., S. Afr. 28 50S 27 44E
100 Gümüsane, Turkey 40 30N 39 30E
88 Gümüşhaciköy, Turkey 40 50N 35 18E
109 Gumzai, Indonesia 5 28S 134 42E
104 Guna, India 24 40N 77 19E
127 Guna Mt., Ethiopia ...11 50N 37 40E
101 Gunabad, Iran 34 22N 58 40E
143 Gunbar, Australia 34 3S 145 24E
143 Gunbower, Australia .35 59S 144 24E
143 Gundagai, Australia ...35 3S 148 6E
109 Gundih, Indonesia 7 10S 110 56E
106 Gundlakamma, R., India 15 30N 80 15E
143 Gunebang, Australia .33 5S 146 38E
143 Gungal, Australia 32 17S 150 32E
127 Gungi, Ethiopia 10 20N 38 3E
130 Gungu, Congo 5 43S 19 20E
125 Gungura, Nigeria 10 40N 10 20E
145 Gunnedah, Australia .30 59S 150 15E
36 Gunnislake, Eng., U.K. 50 32N 4 12W
167 Gunnison, Colo., U.S.A. 38 32N 106 56W
166 Gunnison, Utah, U.S.A. 39 11N 111 48W
167 Gunnison, R., U.S.A. .38 50N 108 30W
107 Gunong Tahan, Mt., Malaysia 4 45N 102 25E
106 Guntakal, India 15 11N 77 27E
163 Guntersville, U.S.A. ...34 18N 86 16W
106 Guntur, India 16 23N 80 30E
108 Gunung Sitoli, Indon. 1 15N 97 30E
109 Gunungapi I., Indonesia 6 45S 126 30E
106 Gunupur, India 19 5N 83 50E
157 Gunworth, Canada 51 20N 108 10W
57 Gunzenhausen, Ger. ...49 6N 10 45E
102 Gupis, Kashmir 36 15N 73 20E
104 Gura, India 25 12N 71 39E
78 Gura Humorului, Rum. 47 35N 25 53E
78 Gura Teghii, Rumania 45 30N 26 25E
127 Gurage. Mt., Ethiopia 8 20N 38 20E
100 Gurchan Iran 34 55N 49 25E
104 Gurdaspur, India 32 5N 75 25E
165 Gurdon, U.S.A. 33 55N 93 10W
101 Gurgan, Iran 36 51N 54 25E
104 Gurgaon, India 28 33N 77 10E
78 Gurghiu, Munţii, Mts., Rumania 46 41N 25 15E
70 Guria, reg., Italy 44 30N 9 0E
169 Guri Dam, Venezuela . 7 50N 63 0W
58 Gurk, R., Austria 46 48N 14 20E
105 Gurkha, Nepal 28 5N 84 40E
105 Guria Mandhata, Mt., Tibet, Chinese Rep. 30 30N 81 10E
145 Gurley, Australia 29 45S 149 48E
36 Gurnard's Head, England, U.K. 50 12N 5 37W
144 Gurrumbah, Queensland, Australia 17 30S 144 55E
107 Gurun, Malaysia 5 49N 100 27E
100 Gürün, Turkey 38 41N 37 22E
175 Gurupá & I., Brazil ... 1 20S 51 45W
175 Gurupi R., Brazil 3 20S 47 20W
112 Gurvandzagal, Mong. .48 44N 114 51E
89 Guryev, U.S.S.R. 47 5N 52 0E
55 Gurzenich, Germany .50 47N 6 28E
125 Gusau, Nigeria 12 18N 6 31E
86 Gusev, U.S.S.R. 54 35N 22 20E
125 Gushiago, Ghana 9 55N 0 15W
74 Gusinje, Yugoslavia ...42 35N 19 50E
112 Gusinoczersk, U.S.S.R. 51 16N 106 27E
87 Gus-Khrsutainyy, U.S.S.R. 55 42N 40 35E
72 Guspini, Sardinia, Italy 39 32N 8 38E
80 Gusselby, Sweden 59 38N 15 14E
59 Güssing, Austria 47 3N 16 20E
71 Gustanj, Yugoslavia ...46 36N 14 49E
156 Gustavus, Alaska, U.S.A. 58 25N 135 58W
167 Gustine, U.S.A. 37 21N 121 0W
56 Güstrow, Germany 53 47N 12 12E
81 Gusum, Sweden 58 16N 16 30E
132 Guta, Rhodesia 19 35S 31 10E
56 Gütersloh, Germany ...51 54N 8 25E
142 Gutha, W. Australia .28 58S 115 55E
144 Guthalungra, Australia 19 52S 147 50E
143 Guthega Dam, Austral 36 20S 148 27E
165 Guthrie, U.S.A. 35 55N 97 30W
164 Guttenberg, U.S.A. ...42 46N 91 10W
174 Guyana, St., S. Amer. 5 0N 59 0W
50 Guyenne, Reg., France 44 30N 0 40E
165 Guyman, U.S.A. 36 45N 101 30W
145 Guyra, N.S.W., Austral. 30 15S 151 40E
103 Gwa, Burma 17 30N 94 40E
132 Gwaai, Rhodesia 19 15S 27 45E
132 Gwaai R., Rhodesia ...19 15S 27 40E
145 Gwabegar, Australia .30 31S 149 0E
125 Gwadabawa, Nigeria .13 20N 5 15E
102 Gwadar, W. Pakistan 25 10N 62 18E
125 Gwagwada, Nigeria ...10 15N 7 15E
37 Gwalchmai, Wales, U.K. 53 16N 4 23W
142 Gwalia, W. Australia .28 58S 121 30E
104 Gwalior, India 26 12N 78 10E
125 Gwanara, Nigeria 18 55N 3 10E
132 Gwanda, Rhodesia 20 55S 29 0E
125 Gwandu, Nigeria 12 30N 4 41E
131 Gwao, Tanzania 5 10S 34 45E
125 Gwaram Nigeria 11 15N 9 51E
125 Gwarzo, Nigeria 12 20N 8 55E
125 Gwasero, Nigeria 9 30N 8 30E
101 Gwatar, Iran 25 10N 61 22E
37 Gwaun-Cae-Gurwen, Wales, U.K. 51 46N 3 51W
46 Gweebarra B., Ireland 54 52N 8 21W
46 Gweedore, Ireland 55 4N 8 15W
36 Gweek, England, U.K. 50 6N 5 12W
132 Gwelo, Rhodesia 19 28S 29 45E
132 Gwelo, R., Rhodesia .18 50S 29 0E
132 Gwembe, Zambia 16 30S 27 40E
36 Gwennap, Eng., U.K. 50 12N 5 9W
125 Gwi, Nigeria 9 0N 7 10E
162 Gwinn, U.S.A. 46 15N 87 29W
125 Gwio Kura, Nigeria ...12 40N 11 2E
124 Gwolu, Ghana 10 58N 1 59W
125 Gwoza, Nigeria 11 12N 13 40E
37 Gwyddelwern, Wales, United Kingdom 53 2N 3 23W
105 Gya Pass, Tibet, China 28 45N 84 45E
103 Gyangtse, Tibet, China 28 50N 89 33E
90 Gyda Pen., U.S.S.R. .70 0N 78 0E
79 Gyland, Norway 58 24N 6 45E
145 Gympie, Australia 26 11S 152 38E
114 Gyoda, Japan 36 10N 139 30E
59 Gyoma, Hungary 46 56N 20 58E
59 Gyöngyös, Hungary ...47 48N 20 15E
59 Györ, Hungary 47 41N 17 40E
59 Gyor-Sopron, co., Hung. 47 40N 17 20E
157 Gypsumville, Canada .51 45N 98 40W
80 Gyttorp, Sweden 59 31N 14 58E
59 Gyula, Hungary 46 38N 21 17E
86 Gzhatsk, see Gagarin, U.S.S.R. 55 30N 35 0E

H

107 Ha Giang, N. Vietnam 22 46N 104 56E
107 Ha Nam, see Phu-Ly, N. Vietnam 20 35N 105 50E
42 Haa, The, Scot., U.K. 60 20N 1 0E
57 Haag, Germany 48 11N 12 12E
135 Haaks, O.F.S., S. Africa 27 58S 28 26E
55 Haan, Germany 51 11N 7 1E
82 Haapamäki, Finland .62 18N 24 28E
86 Haapsalu, U.S.S.R. ...58 56N 23 30E
81 Haarby, Denmark 55 13N 10 8E
55 Haard, dist., Germany 51 42N 7 10E
134 Haarlem, S. Africa 33 43S 23 20E
54 Haarlem, Netherlands 52 23N 4 39E
147 Haast, New Zealand .43 51S 169 1E
147 Haast P., New Zealand 44 6S 169 21E
147 Haast R., New Zealand 43 58S 169 25E
102 Hab Nadi Chauki, Pak. 25 0N 66 50E
102 Hab R., W. Pak. 25 15N 67 8E
100 Haba, Saudi Arabia ...27 10N 47 0E
156 Habay, Canada 55 43N 124 40W
105 Habiganj, E. Pakistan 24 24N 91 30E
81 Hablingbo, Sweden ...57 8N 18 16E
81 Habo, Sweden 57 55N 14 6E
55 Haccourt, Belgium 50 44N 5 40E
56 Hachenburg, Germany 50 40N 7 49E
114 Hachijo Shima, I., Jap. 30 0N 139 45E
114 Hachioji, Japan 33 3N 139 55E
114 Hachinohe, Japan 40 30N 141 29E
145 Hack, Mt., S. Australia 30 45S 138 55E
45 Hackestown, Ireland .52 52N 6 35W
156 Hackett, Canada 52 9N 112 28W
35 Hackney, Eng., U.K. .51 33N 0 2W
38 Hackthorpe, Eng., U.K. 54 37N 2 42W
104 Hadali, West Pakistan 32 16N 72 11E
127 Hadama, Ethiopia 8 45N 39 15E
101 Hadd, Ras al, Oman .22 35N 59 50E
35 Haddenham, Eng., U.K. 51 46N 0 56W
41 Haddington, Scot., U.K. 55 57N 2 48W
125 Hadeija, Nigeria 12 30N 9 59E
125 Hadeija R., Nigeria ...12 20N 9 30W
98 Hadera, Israel 32 27N 34 55E
81 Haderslev, Denmark .55 17N 9 30E
81 Haderslev, Amt, co., Den. 55 18N 9 15E
126 Hadhra, Saudi Arabia 20 10N 41 5E
99 Hadhramaut, reg., South Yemen 15 30N 49 30E
123 Hadjeb el Aioun, Tunisia 35 21N 9 32E
35 Hadleigh, Eng., U.K. .52 3N 0 58E
34 Hadley, Eng., U.K. ...52 42N 2 28W
35 Hadlow, Eng., U.K. ...51 12N 0 20E
38 Hadrian's Wall, England, U.K. 55 0N 2 30E
81 Hadsten, Denmark 56 19N 10 3E
81 Hadsund, Denmark 56 44N 10 8E
112 Haeju, North Korea ...38 12N 125 41E
133 Haenertsburg, S. Africa 23 53S 29 58E
100 Hafar al Batin, Si. Arab. 28 25N 46 50E
104 Hafizabad, W. Pakistan 32 5N 73 40E
103 Haflong, India 25 10N 93 5E
82 Hafnarfjördhur, Iceland 64 3N 21 55W
100 Haft-Gel, Iran 31 30N 49 32E
121 Hagar Banga, Sudan .10 40N 22 45E
106 Hagari R., India 14 0N 76 45E
56 Hagen, Germany 51 21N 7 29E
56 Hagenow, Germany 53 25N 11 10E
165 Hagerman, U.S.A. 33 5N 104 22W
162 Hagerstown, U.S.A. ...39 39N 77 46W
50 Hagetmau, France 43 39N 0 37W
80 Hagfors, Sweden 60 3N 13 45E
80 Häggenas, Sweden 63 24N 14 55E
82 Hagi, Iceland 65 28N 23 25W
114 Hagi, Japan 34 30N 131 30E
76 Hagion Evstratios I., Greece 39 30N 25 0E
76 Hagion Oros Pen., Greece 40 37N 24 6E
44 Hags Hd., Ireland 52 57N 9 30W
54 Hague, The, see 's Gravenhage, Neth. .52 7N 4 17E
49 Haguenau, France 48 49N 7 47E
134 Haib, S.W. Africa 28 30S 18 20E
112 Haicheng, China 40 56N 122 51E
98 Haifa, Israel 32 46N 35 0E
142 Haig, W. Australia 30 55S 126 10E
56 Haiger, Germany 50 44N 8 12E
113 Haikow, Hainan, China 20 0N 110 20E
100 Hail, Saudi Arabia ...27 28N 42 2E
112 Hailar China 49 12N 119 37E
112 Hailar Ho, R. China .49 30N 118 30E
166 Hailey, U.S.A. 43 30N 114 15W
154 Haileybury, Canada ...47 30N 79 38W
112 Hailin, China 44 32N 129 24E
35 Hailsham, Eng., U.K. 50 52N 0 17E
112 Hailun, China 47 24N 127 0E
112 Hailung, China 42 46N 125 57E
82 Hailuoto (Karlö), Fin. 65 0N 24 50E
113 Haimen, China 31 48N 121 8E
113 Hainan, I., China 19 0N 110 0E
54 Hainaut, prov., Belgium 50 30N 4 0E
59 Hainburg, Austria ...48 9N 16 56E
157 Haines, Alaska, U.S.A. 59 20N 135 36W
166 Haines, U.S.A. 44 51N 117 59W
163 Haines City, U.S.A. ...28 6N 81 35W
58 Hainfeld, Austria 48 3N 15 48E

MAP
113 Haining, China 30 16N 120 47E
39 Hainton, Eng., U.K. .53 21N 0 13W
107 Haiphong, N. Vietnam 20 55N 105 42E
113 Haitan Tao Is., China 25 30N 119 45E
169 Haiti, Rep., Hispaniola 19 0N 72 30W
126 Haiya Junc., Sudan ...18 20N 36 40E
112 Haiyang, China 36 45N 121 15E
113 Haiyen, China 30 28N 120 57E
112 Haiyuan, China 36 32N 105 31E
109 Haja, Indonesia 3 19S 129 37E
59 Hajdu-Bihar, co., Hung. 47 30N 21 30E
59 Hajdubözörmény, Hungary 47 40N 21 30E
59 Hajdúdurog, Hungary 47 48N 21 30E
59 Hajdúhadház, Hungary 47 40N 21 40E
59 Hajdúnánás, Hungary 47 50N 21 26E
59 Hajdúsamson, Hungary 47 37N 21 42E
59 Hajdúszobaszlo, Hung. 47 27N 21 22E
102 Haji Langar, Kashmir 35 50N 79 20E
105 Hajipur, India 25 45N 85 20E
101 Hajr, dist., Oman 24 0N 56 34E
130 Hakansson Mts., Congo 8 40S 25 45E
81 Håkantorp, Sweden ...58 18N 12 55E
147 Hakataramea, N.Z. ...44 30S 170 30E
147 Hakataramea R., N.Z. 44 35S 170 40E
114 Hakodate, Japan 41 45N 140 44E
100 Halab, see Aleppo, Syria 36 10N 37 15E
100 Halabjah, Iraq 35 10N 45 58E
126 Halaib, Sudan 22 5N 36 30E
126 Halbe, Saudi Arabia .19 40N 42 15E
56 Halberstadt, Germany 51 53N 11 2E
36 Halberton, Eng., U.K. 50 55N 3 24W
146 Halcombe, N.Z. 40 8S 175 30E
79 Halden, Norway 59 7N 11 30E
56 Haldens-leben, Ger. ...52 17N 11 30E
105 Haldwani, India 29 25N 79 30E
38 Hale, England, U.K. .53 24N 2 21W
142 Hale, Mt., W. Australia 26 0S 117 16E
135 Halesowen, S. Africa .32 13S 25 41E
34 Halesowen, Eng., U.K. 52 27N 2 2W
35 Halesworth, Eng., U.K. 52 21N 1 30E
163 Haleyville, U.S.A. 34 15N 87 40W
124 Half Assini, Ghana 5 1N 2 50W
147 Halfmoon B., N.Z. ...46 50S 168 5E
166 Halfway, U.S.A. 44 56N 117 8W
98 Halhul, Jordan 31 35N 35 7E
126 Hali, Saudi Arabia 18 40N 41 15E
154 Haliburton, Canada ...45 3N 78 30W
59 Halicz Mts., Cz. 49 5N 22 38E
144 Halifax, Queensland, Australia 18 32S 146 22E
155 Halifax, Canada 44 38N 63 35W
38 Halifax, Eng., U.K. ...53 43N 1 51W
144 Halifax B., Australia .18 50S 147 0E
101 Halil, R., Iran 27 40N 58 30E
43 Halkirk, Scot., U.K. .58 30N 3 30W
58 Hall, Austria 47 17N 11 30E
14 Hall Land, Greenland 82 0N 55 0W
81 Hallabro, Sweden 56 22N 15 7E
80 Halland, Sweden 57 0N 12 30E
18 Hallands Lan, Sweden 57 0N 12 37E
81 Hallands Vaderö, Swed. 56 25N 12 34E
81 Hallandsaåen, Hill, Sweden 56 22N 13 2E
54 Halle, Belgium 50 44N 4 13W
56 Halle, Saxony-Anhalt, Germany 51 29N 12 0E
56 Halle, N. Rhine-Westphalia, Ger. 52 4N 8 20E
56 Halle, dist., E. Ger. ...51 28N 11 58E
80 Halléfors, Orebro, Swed. 59 46N 14 30E
81 Hallefors, Kalmar, Sweden 57 35N 15 45E
58 Hallein, Austria 47 40N 13 5E
81 Hallekis, Sweden 58 38N 13 27E
145 Hallett, S. Australia ...33 25S 138 55E
165 Hallettsville, U.S.A. ...29 28N 96 57W
81 Hallevadsholm, Sweden 58 37N 11 33E
164 Halliday, U.S.A. 47 20N 102 25W
106 Hallia, R., India 16 55N 79 10E
79 Hallingdalselv, R., Nor. 60 34N 9 12E
79 Hallingskeid, Norway 60 40N 7 17E
82 Hallnas, Sweden 64 18N 19 40E
34 Hallow, Eng., U.K. ...52 14N 2 15W
138 Hall's Creek, Australia 18 20S 128 0E
80 Hallsberg, Sweden 59 5N 15 7E
80 Hallstahammar, Swed. 59 38N 16 15E
58 Hallstatt, Austria 47 33N 13 38E
80 Hallstavik, Sweden ...60 5N 19 20E
161 Hallstead, U.S.A. 41 56N 75 45W
36 Hallsworthy, Eng., U.K. 50 38N 4 34W
109 Halmahera I., Indon. . 0 40N 128 0E
78 Halmeu, Rumania 47 57N 23 2E
81 Halmstad, Sweden 56 37N 12 56E
123 Halq el Oued (La Goulette), Tunisia ...36 53N 10 10E
81 Hals, Denmark 56 59N 10 20E
79 Halsa, Norway 63 3N 8 14E
79 Halsa Fjord, Norway .63 3N 8 9E
81 Hälsingborg, Sweden .56 3N 12 42E
164 Halstad, U.S.A. 47 21N 96 41W
35 Halstead, England, U.K. 51 57N 0 39E
79 Haltdälen, Norway ...62 53N 11 15E
56 Haltern, Germany 51 44N 7 10E
38 Haltwhistle, Eng., U.K. 54 58N 2 27W
55 Halver, Germany 51 11N 7 30E
49 Ham, France 49 44N 3 3E
127 Hamad, Sudan 15 20N 33 32E
114 Hamada, Japan 34 50N 132 10E
100 Hamadan, Iran 34 52N 48 32E
126 Hamadh, Saudi Arabia 24 55N 39 3E
122 Hamadia, Algeria 35 28N 1 57E
100 Hamah, Syria 35 5N 36 40E
124 Hamale, Ghana 10 56N 2 45W
114 Hamamatsu, Japan ...34 45N 137 45E
78 Hamangia, Rumania .44 42N 28 48E
79 Hamar, Norway 60 48N 11 7E
82 Hamaröy, Norway 68 8N 15 47E
126 Hamata, Gebel, Egypt 24 17N 35 0E
34 Hambledon, Eng., U.K. 50 56N 1 6W
39 Hambleton Hills, England, U.K. 54 17N 1 12W
56 Hamburg, Germany ...53 32N 9 59E
135 Hamburg, S. Africa ...33 16S 27 29E
165 Hamburg, Ark., U.S.A. 33 15N 91 47W
164 Hamburg, Iowa, U.S.A. 40 37N 95 38W
160 Hamburg, N.Y., U.S.A. 42 44N 78 50W
161 Hamburg, Pa., U.S.A. 40 33N 76 0W
56 Hamburg, land, Ger. .53 30N 10 0E
83 Hämeenlinna, Finland 61 3N 24 26E
142 Hamelin Pool, Austral. 26 22S 114 20E
56 Hameln, Germany 52 7N 9 24E
161 Hamer, U.S.A. 42 38N 76 11W
112 Hamhung, N. Korea .40 0N 127 30E
138 Hammersley Ra., Western Australia .22 0S 117 45E
138 Hamersley Home Sta., W. Australia .22 17S 117 42E
111 Hami, China 42 54N 93 28E
122 Hamidouch, Morocco .32 0N 9 28W
143 Hamilton, Vic., Austral. 37 37S 142 0E
169 Hamilton, Bermuda ...32 15N 64 45W
154 Hamilton, Canada 43 20N 79 50W
146 Hamilton, New Zealand 37 47S 175 19E
141 Hamilton, Scot., U.K. 55 47N 4 2W
164 Hamilton, Mo., U.S.A. 39 45N 93 59W
166 Hamilton, Mont., U.S.A. 46 20N 114 6W
161 Hamilton, N.Y., U.S.A. 42 49N 75 31W
162 Hamilton, Ohio, U.S.A. 39 20N 84 35W
165 Hamilton, Tex., U.S.A. 31 40N 98 5W
155 Hamilton Inlet, Canada 54 20N 57 30W
144 Hamilton, R., Australia 22 55S 140 25E
138 Hamilton, R., S. Australia 26 40S 134 20E
144 Hamilton Hotel, Australia 22 45S 140 40E
157 Hamiota, Canada 50 11N 100 38W
163 Hamlet, U.S.A. 34 56N 79 40W
145 Hamley Bridge, South Australia 34 17S 138 35E
160 Hamlin, N.Y., U.S.A. 43 17N 77 55W
165 Hamlin, Tex., U.S.A. .32 58N 100 8W
56 Hamm, Germany 51 40N 7 58E
124 Hammamet, Tunisia .36 28N 10 49E
123 Hammamet, Gulf of, Tunisia 36 10N 10 48E
133 Hammanskraal, S. Afr. 25 28N 28 16E
80 Hammarö, I., Sweden 59 20N 13 30E
86 Hammarstrand, Sweden 63 7N 16 20E
55 Hamme Mille, Belgium 50 47N 4 43E
81 Hammel, Denmark 56 16N 9 50E
57 Hammelburg, Germany 50 7N 9 54E
162 Hammonton, U.S.A. .39 40N 74 47W
81 Hammeren, C., Den. .55 18N 14 47E
82 Hammerfest, Norway 70 33N 23 50E
142 Hammersley Ra., W. Australia 22 30S 118 30E
35 Hammersmith, England, U.K. 51 30N 0 15W
55 Hamminkeln, Germany 51 43N 6 36E
161 Hammond, Ont., Can. 45 26N 75 15W
162 Hammond, Ind., U.S.A. 41 40N 87 30W
165 Hammond, La., U.S.A. 30 32N 90 30W
42 Hamnavoe, Zetland, Scotland, U.K. 60 25N 1 5W
81 Hamneda, Sweden 56 41N 13 53E
147 Hampden, N.Z. 45 18S 170 50E
34 Hampshire, Co., England, U.K. 51 3N 1 20W
29 Hampshire Downs, England, U.K. 51 10N 1 10W
165 Hampton, Ark., U.S.A. 33 35N 92 29W
164 Hampton, Iowa, U.S.A. 42 42N 93 12W
161 Hampton, N.H., U.S.A. 42 56N 70 48W
163 Hampton, S.C., U.S.A. 32 52N 81 21W
162 Hampton, Va., U.S.A. 37 4N 76 8W
138 Hampton Harbour, W. Australia 20 30S 116 30E
34 Hampton in Arden, England, U.K. 52 26N 1 42W
142 Hampton Tableland, W. Australia 32 0N 127 0E
100 Hamra, Saudi Arabia . 24 2N 38 55E
80 Hamrånge, Sweden ...60 59N 17 5E
127 Hamrat esh Sheikh, Sudan 14 45N 27 55E
79 Hamre, Norway 60 33N 5 20E
101 Hamun-e-Helmand, L., Iran 31 15N 61 15E
102 Hamun-i-Mashkel, Pak. 28 30N 63 0E
102 Hamun-i-Lora, Pak. .29 38N 64 58E
113 Han Klang R., China .31 40N 112 20E
126 Hanak, Saudi Arabia .25 32N 37 0E
57 Hanau, Germany 50 8N 8 56E
112 Hanbogd, Mongolia ...43 8N 107 21E
112 Hancheng, China 35 14N 110 22E
113 Hanchung (Nancheng), China .33 10N 107 2E
113 Hanchwang, China 34 40N 117 25E
164 Hancock, Mich., U.S.A. 47 10N 88 35W
164 Hancock, Minn., U.S.A. 45 26N 95 46W
161 Hancock, Pa., U.S.A. .41 57N 75 19W
114 Handa, Japan 34 53N 137 0E
99 Handa, Somali Rep. ...10 37N 51 2E
42 Handa I., Scot., U.K. 58 23N 5 10W
80 Handen, Sweden 59 12N 18 12E
131 Handeni, Tanzania 5 25S 38 2E
159 Handlova, Cz. 48 45N 18 35E
112 Handshur, China 48 29N 118 2E
126 Handub, Sudan 19 15N 37 25E
156 Haney, Canada 49 12N 122 40W
167 Hanford, U.S.A. 36 25N 119 45W
111 Hangayn Nuruu, Mt., Mongolia 48 0N 99 0E
113 Hangchow, China 30 12N 120 1E
113 Hangchow Wan, China 30 30N 121 30E
113 Hangchwang, China ...34 34N 117 27E
81 Hånger, Sweden 57 6N 13 58E
134 Hangklip, C., S. Africa 34 26S 18 48E
112 Hanh, Mongolia 51 32N 100 35E
99 Hanish I., Red Sea ...13 45N 42 46E
98 Hanita, Israel 33 5N 35 10E
164 Hankinson, U.S.A. 46 9N 96 58W
83 Hanko, (Hangö), Finland 59 50N 23 2E
113 Hankow, China 30 32N 114 20E
167 Hanksville, U.S.A. 38 19N 110 45W
112 Hanku, China 39 16N 117 50E
147 Hanmer, New Zealand 42 32S 172 50E
138 Hann, Mt., W. Austral 15 50S 125 50E
56 Hann-Munden, Ger. ...51 25N 9 42E
156 Hanna, Canada 51 40N 112 0W
164 Hannaford, U.S.A. 47 23N 98 18W
164 Hannah, U.S.A. 49 0N 98 56W
154 Hannah B., Canada 51 20N 80 0W
143 Hannahs Bridge, N.S.W., Australia ...31 55S 149 41E
164 Hannibal, U.S.A. 39 42N 91 22W
126 Hannik, Sudan 18 12N 32 20E
35 Hanningfield Water, England, U.K. 51 40N 0 30E
56 Hannover, Germany .52 23N 9 43E
81 Hanö, I., Sweden 56 2N 14 50E
81 Hanöbukten B., Sweden 55 35N 14 30E
107 Hanoi, N. Vietnam 21 5N 150 40E
160 Hanover, Canada 44 9N 81 2W
134 Hanover, S. Africa 31 4S 24 29E
161 Hanover, N.H., U.S.A. 43 43N 72 17W
160 Hanover, Ohio, U.S.A. 40 5N 82 17W
162 Hanover, Pa., U.S.A. .39 46N 76 59W
56 Hanover, see Hannover, Ger. 52 23N 9 43E
176 Hanover I., Chile 51 0S 74 50W
134 Hanover Road, S. Afr. 30 58S 24 33E
81 Hansholm, Denmark .57 8N 8 38E
104 Hansi, India 29 10N 75 57E
80 Hansjö, Sweden 61 10N 14 40E
81 Hansted, Denmark 57 8N 8 36E
112 Hantan, China 36 42N 114 30E
112 Hanuy Gol, R., Mongolia 48 20N 101 30E
143 Hanwood, Australia ...34 26S 146 3E
113 Hanyang, China 30 30N 114 19E
113 Hanyint, China 32 56N 108 50E
82 Haparanda, Sweden ...65 52N 24 8E
165 Happy, U.S.A. 34 47N 101 50W
166 Happy Camp, U.S.A. .41 52N 123 30W
155 Happy Valley, Canada 155 53N 60 10W
104 Hapur, India 28 45N 77 45E
100 Haql, Saudi Arabia 29 10N 35 0E
109 Har, Indonesia 5 16S 133 14E
112 Har-Ayrag, Mongolia 45 50N 109 30E
98 Har Meiron, Israel 32 59N 35 24E
98 Har Tuv, Israel 31 46N 35 5E
111 Har Us Nuur, L., Mongolia 48 0N 92 0E
112 Haraa Gol, R., Mongolia 49 0N 106 0E
112 Hara Narinula, (Lang Shan), China 41 30N 107 0E
99 Haradera, Somali Rep. 4 33N 47 38E
100 Haradh, Saudi Arabia 24 15N 49 0E
82 Harads, Sweden 66 3N 21 10E
79 Haramsöy, I., Norway 62 39N 6 12E
100 Haran, Turkey 36 48N 39 0E
121 Haraze, Chad 14 20N 19 12E
112 Harbin, China 45 46N 126 51E
81 Harboöre, Denmark ...56 38N 8 12E
162 Harbor Beach, U.S.A. 43 50N 82 38W
155 Harbour Breton, Can. 47 29N 55 50W
155 Harbour Deep, Canada 50 25N 56 30W
162 Harbor Springs, U.S.A. 45 28N 85 0W
155 Harbour Grace, Canada 47 40N 53 22W
56 Harburg, Germany 53 27N 9 58E
144 Harcourt, Australia ...24 17S 149 55E
104 Harda, India 22 27N 77 5E
79 Hardanger Fd., Norway 60 15N 6 0E
79 Hardangerjökulen, Mt., Norway 60 30N 7 0E
79 Hardangervidda, Nor. 60 20N 7 20E
54 Hardenberg, Neth. 52 34N 6 37E
166 Hardin, U.S.A. 45 50N 107 35W
135 Harding, Natal, S. Afr. 30 22S 29 55E
55 Hardinxveld, Neth. ...51 49N 4 53E
156 Hardisty, Canada 52 40N 111 25W
166 Hardman, U.S.A. 45 12N 119 49W
105 Hardoi, India 27 26N 80 15E
104 Hardwar, India 29 58N 78 16E
161 Hardwick, U.S.A. 44 30N 72 20W
165 Hardy, Ark., U.S.A. ...36 20N 91 30W
176 Hardy Pen., Chile 55 30S 68 20W
56 Haren, Germany 52 47N 7 18E
127 Harer, Ethiopia 9 20N 42 8E
127 Harer, prov., Ethiopia 7 12N 42 0E
48 Harfleur, France 49 30N 0 10E
99 Hargeisa, Somali Rep. 9 30N 44 2E
78 Härghita Mții, Mts., Rumania 46 25N 25 35E
78 Harghita, Reg., Rum. 46 30N 25 30E
80 Hargshamn, Sweden .60 12N 18 30E
108 Hari R., Indonesia 1 10S 101 50E
101 Hari R., Afghanistan .34 20N 64 30E
122 Haricha, Hamada el, Mali 22 40N 3 15W
106 Harihar, India 14 32N 75 44E
66 Harim, J. al, 'Oman 26 0N 56 10E
35 Haringey, Eng., U.K. 51 35N 0 7W
106 Haripad, India 9 14N 76 28E
101 Harirud, R., Iran 35 0N 61 0E
80 Härjechågna, Mt., Sweden 61 43N 12 10E
126 Harkat, Saudi Arabia 20 25N 39 40E
164 Harlan, Iowa, U.S.A. .41 37N 95 20W
163 Harlan, Tenn., U.S.A. 36 58N 83 20W
78 Hârlău, Rumania 47 23N 27 0E
37 Harlech, Wales, U.K. 52 52N 4 7W
166 Harlem, U.S.A. 48 29N 108 39W
35 Harleston, Eng., U.K. 52 25N 1 18E
54 Harlingen, Netherlands 53 11N 5 25E
165 Harlingen, U.S.A. 26 30N 97 50W
35 Harlow, Eng., U.K. 51 47N 0 9E
166 Harlowton, U.S.A. 46 30N 109 54W
80 Harmånger, Sweden ...61 55N 17 20E
166 Harney Basin, U.S.A. 43 30N 119 0W
166 Harney L., U.S.A. 43 0N 119 0W
164 Harney Pk., U.S.A. 43 52N 103 33W
80 Härnön, I., Sweden 62 38N 18 0E
57 Härnösand, Sweden ...62 38N 18 5E
64 Haro, Spain 42 35N 2 55W
42 Haroldswick, Scot., U.K. 60 48N 0 50W
155 Harp L., Canada 55 10N 61 40W
106 Harpenhalli, India 14 47N 76 2E
35 Harpenden, Eng., U.K. 51 48N 0 20W
124 Harper, Liberia 4 25N 7 43E
81 Harplinge, Sweden 56 45N 12 45E
42 Harport L., Scot., U.K. 57 20N 6 20W
100 Harput, Turkey 38 48N 39 15E
104 Harrand, W. Pakistan 29 28N 70 3E
126 Harrat al Uwairidh, Saudi Arabia 26 50N 38 0E
126 Harrat Khaibar, Mts., Saudi Arabia 25 45N 40 0E
126 Harrat Kishib, Si. Arab. 22 30N 40 15E
126 Harrat Nawasif, Saudi Arabia 21 30N 42 0E
43 Harray, L. of, Scotland, United Kingdom 59 0N 3 15W
154 Harricanaw R., Canada 50 30N 79 10W
35 Harrietsham, Eng., U.K. 51 15N 0 41E
163 Harriman, U.S.A. 36 0N 84 35W
38 Harrington, Eng., U.K. 54 37N 3 55W
155 Harrington Harb., Can. 50 31N 59 30W
42 Harris, dist., Scot., U.K. 57 50N 6 55W
138 Harris L., S. Australia 31 10S 135 10E
147 Harris Mts., N.Z. 44 49S 168 49E
42 Harris, Sd. of, Scotland, United Kingdom 57 44N 7 6W
133 Harrisburg, S. Africa .27 8S 26 25E
165 Harrisburg, Ill., U.S.A. 37 42N 88 30W
164 Harrisburg, Neb., U.S.A. 41 36N 103 46W
166 Harrisburg, Ore., U.S.A. 44 25N 123 10W
160 Harrisburg, Pa., USA 40 18N 76 52W
135 Harrismith, S. Africa .28 15S 29 8E
165 Harrison, Ark., U.S.A. 36 10N 93 4W
166 Harrison, Idaho, U.S.A. 47 30N 116 51W
164 Harrison, Neb., U.S.A. 42 42N 103 52W
14 Harrison B., Alas., U.S.A. 70 25N 151 0W
162 Harrisonburg, U.S.A. .38 28N 78 52W
164 Harrisonville, U.S.A. .38 45N 93 45W
154 Harriston, Canada 43 57N 80 53W
160 Harrisville, Mich., U.S.A. 44 40N 83 19W
39 Harrogate, Eng., U.K. 53 59N 1 32W
160 Harrow, Canada 42 2N 82 53W
35 Harrow, Eng., U.K. ...51 35N 0 15W
56 Harsefeld, Germany ...53 26N 9 31E
78 Hârşova, Rumania 44 40N 27 59E
82 Harsprånget, Sweden .66 26N 19 40E
82 Harstad, Norway 68 48N 16 30E
162 Hart, U.S.A. 43 42N 86 21W
41 Hart Fell, Mt., Scotland, U.K. 55 24N 3 25W
133 Hartbess, Trans., S. Afr. 25 30S 28 44E
134 Hartbees R., S. Africa 29 8N 20 48E
133 Hartbeesfontein, S. Afr. 26 42S 26 26E
134 Hartbeeskuil, S. Africa 32 55S 23 35E
58 Hartberg, Austria 47 17N 15 58E
79 Harteigen, Mt., Norway 60 11N 7 5E
35 Hartest, Eng., U.K. ...52 7N 0 41E
135 Hartfontein, S. Africa 31 42S 26 19E
161 Hartford, Conn., U.S.A. 41 47N 72 41W
162 Hartford, Ky., U.S.A. 37 26N 86 50W
164 Hartford, S.D., U.S.A. 43 40N 96 58W
164 Hartford, Wis., U.S.A. 43 18N 88 25W
162 Hartford City, U.S.A. 40 22N 85 20W
41 Harthill, Scot.,U.K. ...55 52N 3 45W
38 Hartington, Eng., U.K. 53 8N 1 49W
155 Hartland, Canada 46 20N 67 32W
36 Hartland, Eng., U.K. 50 59N 4 29W
36 Hartland Pt., Eng., U.K. 51 2N 4 32W
34 Hartlebury, Eng., U.K. 52 20N 2 13W
41 Hartley, Eng., U.K. ...55 1N 1 27W
132 Hartley, Rhodesia 18 10S 30 7E
156 Hartley Bay, Canada .46 4N 80 45W
157 Hartney, Canada 49 30N 100 35W
34 Hartpury, Eng., U.K. 51 55N 2 18W
133 Harts R., S. Africa 27 15S 25 12E
163 Hartselle, U.S.A. 34 25N 86 55W
165 Hartshorne, U.S.A. 34 51N 95 30W
163 Hartsville, U.S.A. 34 23N 80 2W
133 Hartswater, S. Africa .27 46S 24 49E
163 Hartwell, U.S.A. 34 21N 82 52W
104 Harunabad, W. Pak. .29 35N 73 2E
106 Harur, India 12 3N 78 29E
167 Harvard, Mt., U.S.A. .39 0N 106 5W
162 Harvey, Ill., U.S.A. ...41 40N 87 40W
164 Harvey, N.D., U.S.A. 47 40N 99 58W
142 Harvey, W. Australia 33 4S 115 48E
34 Harwell, Eng., U.K. ...51 40N 1 17W
35 Harwich, Eng., U.K. .51 56N 1 18E
160 Harwood, Canada 44 7N 78 11W
104 Haryana, St., India ...29 0N 76 10E
56 Harz Mts., Germany .51 40N 10 40E
55 Harzé, Belgium 50 27N 5 40E
56 Harzgerode, Germany 51 38N 11 8E
100 Hasa reg., Si. Arabia .26 0N 49 0E
100 Hasa Oasis, Si. Arabia 25 20N 00 00E
127 Hasaheisa, Sudan 14 25N 33 20E
104 Hasanpur, India 28 51N 78 9E
56 Haselünne, Germany .52 40N 7 30E
80 Håsjö, Sweden 63 2N 16 20E
165 Haskell, Kan., U.S.A. 35 51N 95 40W
165 Haskell, Tex., U.S.A. .33 10N 99 45W
42 Haskier Is., Scotland .57 42N 7 40W
57 Haslach, Germany 48 16N 8 7E
81 Hasle, Denmark 55 11N 14 44E
35 Haslemere, Eng., U.K. 51 5N 0 41W
81 Haslev, Denmark 55 18N 11 57E
38 Haslingden, Eng., U.K. 53 43N 2 20W
50 Hasparren, France 43 24N 1 18W
100 Hassan, India 13 0N 76 5E
42 Hasselfelde, Germany 51 41N 10 51E
54 Hasselt, Belgium 50 56N 5 21E
122 Hassene, Ad., Algeria 21 0N 4 0E
57 Hassfurt, Germany 50 2N 10 30E
123 Hassi Berekrem, Alg. .33 45N 5 16E
123 Hassi Douala, Algeria 33 4N 5 38E
123 Hassi el Biod, Algeria 28 30N 6 0E
123 Hassi el Rhenami, Alg. 31 57N 5 58E
122 Hassi Inifel, Algeria ...29 50N 3 41E
122 Hassi Marroket, Algeria 30 10N 3 0E
123 Hassi Messaoud, Alg. .31 15N 6 35E
122 Hassi Zerzour, Morocco 30 51N 3 56W
81 Hässleby, Sweden 57 37N 15 30E
81 Hässleholmen, Sweden 56 9N 13 45E
43 Hastigrow, Scot., U.K. 58 32N 3 15W
160 Hastings, Canada 44 18N 77 56W
35 Hastings, Eng., U.K. .50 51N 0 36E
146 Hastings, New Zealand 39 39S 176 52E
162 Hastings, Mich., U.S.A. 42 40N 85 20E
164 Hastings, Minn., U.S.A. 44 41N 92 51W

MAP
164 Hastings, Neb., U.S.A. 40 34N 98 22W
160 Hastings, Pa., U.S.A. .40 40N 78 45W
145 Hastings Ra., Australia 31 15S 152 14E
81 Hästveda, Sweden 56 16N 13 55E
107 Hat Nhao, Laos 14 46N 106 32E
112 Hatanbulag, Mongolia 43 8N 109 14E
167 Hatch, U.S.A. 32 45N 107 8W
138 Hatches Cr., N. Terr., Australia 20 56S 135 12E
78 Hateg, Rumania 45 36N 22 55E
78 Hateg, Mţii, Mts., Rumania 45 25N 23 0E
35 Hatfield, Eng., U.K. .51 46N 0 11W
143 Hatfield, Post Office, Australia 33 54N 143 49E
35 Hatfield Broad Oak, England, U.K. 51 48N 0 16E
111 Hatgal, Mongolia 50 40N 100 0E
35 Hatherleigh, Eng., U.K. 50 49N 4 4W
39 Hathersage, Eng. U.K. 53 20N 1 39W
104 Hathras, India 27 36N 78 6E
143 Hattah, Vic., Australia 34 48N 142 17E
163 Hatteras, C., U.S.A. ...35 10N 75 30W
165 Hattiesburg, U.S.A. ...31 20N 89 20W
55 Hattingen, Germany .51 24N 7 10E
135 Hattingspruit, S. Africa 28 9S 30 11E
157 Hatton, Sask., Canada 50 2N 109 50W
43 Hatton, Scot., U.K. ...57 24N 1 57W
59 Hatvan, Hungary 47 40N 19 45E
107 Hau Bon (Cheo Reo), S. Vietnam 13 25N 108 28E
168 Hauchinango, Mexico 20 12N 97 45W
79 Haug, Norway 60 10N 10 15E
79 Haugastöl, Norway ...60 30N 7 50E
79 Haugesund, Norway .59 23N 5 13E
41 Haugh of Urr, Scotland, U.K. 55 0N 3 51W
35 Haughley, Eng., U.K. 52 13N 0 59E
146 Haughangaroa Ra., N.Z. 38 42S 175 40E
79 Haukelisæter, Norway 59 51N 7 9E
82 Haukipuda, Finland ...65 12N 25 20E
99 Haura, South Yemen .13 50N 47 35E
164 Hauraki Gulf., N.Z. ...36 35S 175 5E
147 Hauroko L., N.Z. 45 59S 167 21E
58 Hausruck, Mt., Austria 48 6N 13 30E
49 Haut-Rhin, dépt., France 48 0N 7 15E
100 Hauta Oasis, Sl. Arab. 23 40N 47 0E
50 Haute-Garonne, dépt., France 43 28N 1 30E
50 Haute-Loire, dépt., Fr. 45 5N 3 50E
49 Haute-Marne, dépt., Fr. 48 10N 5 20E
49 Haute-Saône, dépt., Fr. 47 45N 6 10E
51 Haute-Savoie, dépt., France 46 0N 6 20E
50 Haute-Vienne, dépt., Fr. 45 50N 1 10E
155 Hauterive Canada ...49 10N 68 25W
55 Hautes Fagnes, dist., Belgium 50 34N 6 6E
50 Hautes-Pyrénées, dépt., France 43 0N 0 10E
49 Hauts-de-Seine, dépt., France 48 52N 2 15E
51 Hauteville, France 45 59N 5 35E
49 Hautmont, France 50 15N 3 55E
39 Hauxley, England, U.K. 55 21N 1 35W
169 Havana, Cuba 23 8N 82 22W
164 Havana, U.S.A. 40 19N 90 3W
35 Havant, England, U.K. 50 51N 0 59W
78 Havarna, Rumania ...48 4N 26 43E
167 Havasu, L., U.S.A. 34 37N 114 30W
81 Havdham, Sweden 57 7N 18 20E
84 Havelange, Belgium ...50 23N 5 15E
154 Havelock, N.B., Can. .46 2N 65 24W
155 Havelock, Ont., Canada 44 26N 77 53W
147 Havelock, New Zealand 41 17S 173 48E
146 Havelock N., N.Z. 39 42S 176 53E
107 Havelock I., Andaman I. 11 55N 93 2E
37 Haverfordwest, Wales, United Kingdom 51 48N 4 59W
35 Haverhill, England, U.K. 52 6N 0 27E
161 Haverhill, Mass., U.S.A. 42 50N 71 2W
106 Haveri, India 14 53N 75 24E
38 Haverigg, Eng., U.K. 54 12N 3 16W
35 Havering, Eng., U.K. 51 33N 0 20E
161 Haverstraw, U.S.A. ...41 12N 73 58W
81 Håverud, Sweden 58 50N 12 28E
55 Havixbeck, Germany .51 59N 7 26E
49 Havlíčkův Brod, Cz. .49 36N 15 38E
81 Havneby, Denmark ...55 5N 8 34E
166 Havre, U.S.A. 48 40N 109 34W
155 Havre-Aubert, Canada 47 12N 62 0W
155 Havre St. Pierre, Can. 50 18N 63 33W
100 Havza, Turkey 41 0N 35 35E
163 Haw, R., U.S.A. 37 43N 80 52W
137 Hawaii I., Hawaii, U.S.A. 20 0N 155 0W
137 Hawaiian I., Pac. Oc. 20 30N 156 0W
157 Hawarden, Canada 51 25N 106 30W
37 Hawarden, Wales, U.K. 53 11N 3 2W
164 Hawarden, U.S.A. 43 2N 96 28W
147 Hawea Flat, N.Z. 44 40S 169 19E
147 Hawea L., N.Z. 44 28S 169 19E
147 Hawera, New Zealand 39 35S 174 19E
146 Hawera, New Zealand 39 35S 174 19E
38 Hawes, England, U.K. 54 18N 2 12W
38 Hawes Water, L., England, U.K. 54 32N 2 48W
41 Hawick, Scotland, U.K. 55 25N 2 48W
36 Hawkchurch, Eng., U.K. 50 47N 2 56W
147 Hawkdun Ra., N.Z. ...44 53S 170 5E
146 Hawke B., N.Z. 39 25N 177 20E
146 Hawke Bay, N.Z. 39 45S 176 35E
154 Hawke Junc., Canada 48 05N 84 35W
145 Hawker, S. Australia .31 59S 138 22E
155 Hawke's Harbour, Can. 53 2N 55 50W
154 Hawkesbury, Canada .45 35N 74 40W
36 Hawkesbury Upton, Eng., U.K. 51 34N 2 19W
160 Hawkestone, Canada .44 31N 79 27W
35 Hawkhurst, Eng., U.K. 51 2N 0 31E
163 Hawkinsville, U.S.A. .32 17N 83 30W
38 Hawkshead, Eng., U.K. 54 23N 3 0W
145 Hawkwood, Australia 25 45S 150 50E
164 Hawley, U.S.A. 46 58N 98 20W
38 Haworth, Eng., U.K. .53 50N 1 57W
127 Hawsen, Ethiopia 13 58N 39 28E
134 Hawston, S. Africa 34 26S 19 4E
166 Hawthorne, U.S.A. 38 37N 118 47W
164 Haxtun, U.S.A. 40 40N 102 39W
143 Hay, N.S.W., Austral. 34 30S 144 51E
37 Hay, Wales, U.K. 52 4N 3 9W
156 Hay Lakes, Canada ...53 12N 113 2W
139 Hay R., Australia 24 0S 137 30E
156 Hay River, Canada ...60 50N 115 50W
164 Hay Springs, U.S.A. .42 40N 102 38W
49 Hayange, France 49 20N 6 2E
39 Hayburn Wyke, England, U.K. 54 22N 0 28W
167 Hayden, Ariz., U.S.A. 33 2N 110 54W
166 Hayden, Wyo., U.S.A. 40 30N 107 22W
144 Haydon, Australia 18 0S 141 30E
38 Haydon Bridge, England, U.K. 54 58N 2 15W
14 Hayes Pen., Greenland 75 30N 65 0W
157 Hayes R., Canada 56 0N 93 20W
164 Hayes, U.S.A. 44 22N 101 1W
36 Hayle, England, U.K. 50 12N 5 25W
100 Hayman, Turkey 39 30N 32 35E
165 Haynesville, U.S.A. ...33 0N 93 7W
164 Hays, U.S.A. 38 55N 99 25W
154 Haysport, Canada 54 12N 130 10W
38 Hayton, Eng., U.K. ...54 55N 2 45W
164 Hayward, U.S.A. 46 2N 91 30W
35 Hayward's Heath, England, U.K. 51 0N 0 5W
162 Hazard, U.S.A. 37 18N 83 10W
105 Hazaribagh, India 23 58N 85 26E
105 Hazaribagh Rd., India 24 12N 85 57E
49 Hazebrouck, France ...50 42N 2 31E
156 Hazelton, Canada 55 20N 127 42W
164 Hazelton, N.D., U.S.A. 46 30N 100 15W
161 Hazelton, Pa., U.S.A. 40 58N 76 0W
164 Hazen, N.D., U.S.A. .47 22N 101 45W
166 Hazen, Nev., U.S.A. .39 37N 119 2W
163 Hazelhurst, U.S.A. 31 50N 82 35W
98 Hazor (site), Israel ...33 2N 35 2E
101 Hazrat Imam, Afghan. 37 15N 68 50E
35 Heacham, Eng., U.K. 52 55N 0 30E
35 Headcorn, Eng., U.K. 51 10N 0 39E
44 Headford, Galway, Ire. 53 28N 9 6W
34 Headington, Eng., U.K. 51 46N 1 13W
132 Headlands, Rhodesia .18 15S 32 2E
166 Healdsburg, U.S.A. ...38 33N 122 51W
165 Healdton, U.S.A. 34 16N 97 31W
143 Healesville, Australia .37 35S 145 30E
39 Heanor, Eng., U.K. ...53 1N 1 20W
132 Heany Junc., Rhodesia 20 3S 28 43E
11 Heard I., Southern Oc. 53 0S 74 0E
165 Hearne, U.S.A. 30 54N 96 35W
154 Hearst, Canada 49 40N 83 41W
164 Heart, R., U.S.A. 46 40N 101 30W
155 Heart's Content, Can. 47 54N 53 27W
147 Heath Mts., N.Z. 45 39S 167 9E
157 Heath Pt., Canada 49 8N 61 40W
143 Heathcote, Australia .36 58S 144 43E
35 Heathfield, Eng., U.K. 50 58N 0 18E
42 Heaval Mt., Scot., U.K. 56 58N 7 30W
165 Heavener, U.S.A. 34 54N 94 36W
165 Hebbronville, U.S.A. .27 20N 98 40W
39 Hebburn, Eng., U.K. .54 59N 1 30W
38 Hebden Bridge, England, U.K. 53 45N 2 0W
165 Heber Springs, U.S.A. 35 29N 91 39W
166 Hebgen, L., U.S.A. 44 50N 111 15W
42 Hebrides, Inner Is., Scotland, U.K. 57 20N 6 40W
42 Hebrides, Outer Is., Scotland, U.K. 57 50N 7 25W
153 Hebron, Canada 58 10N 62 50W
98 Hebron (Al Khalil), Jordan 31 32N 35 6E
164 Hebron, N.D., U.S.A. 46 56N 102 2W
164 Hebron, Neb., U.S.A. 40 15N 97 33W
80 Heby, Sweden 59 56N 16 53E
156 Hecate Str., Canada ...53 10N 130 30W
57 Hechingen, Germany .48 20N 8 58E
55 Hechtel, Belgium 51 8N 5 22E
39 Heckington, Eng., U.K. 52 59N 0 17W
164 Hecla, U.S.A. 45 56N 98 8W
157 Hecla I., Canada 51 10N 96 50W
42 Hecla Mt., Scot., U.K. 57 18N 7 15W
146 Hector Mt., N.Z. 40 56S 175 18E
79 Heddal, Norway 59 36N 9 9E
39 Heddon, Eng., U.K. ...55 0N 1 47W
48 Hedé, France 48 18N 1 49W
80 Hede, Sweden 62 23N 13 43E
80 Hedemora, Sweden ...60 18N 15 58E
147 Hedgehope, N.Z. 46 12S 168 34E
165 Hedley, U.S.A. 34 53N 100 39W
79 Hedmark, Fylke, Nor. 61 45N 11 0E
34 Hednesford, Eng., U.K. 52 43N 2 0W
39 Hedon, Eng., U.K. 53 44N 0 11W
79 Hedrum, Norway 59 7N 10 5E
54 Heemstede, Netherlands 52 19N 4 37E
54 Heerde, Netherlands .52 24N 6 2E
54 Heerenveen, Neth. 52 57N 5 55E
133 Heerenveen, S. Africa 26 6S 30 26E
55 Heerenwerve, Germany 51 35N 7 43E
54 Heerlen, Netherlands .50 55N 6 0E
55 Heeze, Netherlands ...51 23N 5 35E
59 Hegyalja, Mts., Hun. .48 25N 21 25E
56 Heide, Germany 54 10N 9 7E
57 Heidelberg, Germany .49 23N 8 41E
134 Heidelberg, C. Prov., S. Africa 34 6S 20 59E
133 Heidelberg, Rans., S. Africa 26 30S 28 23E
57 Heidenheim, Germany 48 40N 10 10E
43 Heilam, Scot., U.K. ...58 31N 4 40W
135 Heilbron, O.F.S., S.Afr. 27 16S 27 59E
57 Heilbronn, Germany .49 8N 9 13E
58 Heiligenblut, Austria .47 2N 12 51E
56 Heiligenhafen, Germany 54 21N 10 58E
55 Heiligenhaus, Germany 51 21N 6 58E
56 Heiligenstadt, Germany 51 22N 10 9E
112 Heilungkiang, prov., China 47 30N 129 0E
79 Heim, Norway 63 26N 9 5E
55 Heimersheim, Germany 50 33N 7 11E
83 Heinola, Finland 61 13N 26 10E
157 Heinsburg, Canada ...53 50N 110 30W
107 Heinze Is., Burma 14 25N 97 45E
79 Heistad, Norway 59 35N 9 40E
55 Heist-op-den-Berg, Belg. 51 5N 4 44E
100 Hejaz, reg., Sl. Arabia 26 0N 37 30E
100 Hekimhan, Turkey 38 50N 38 0E
82 Hekla, vol., Iceland ...63 56N 19 35W
66 Hel, Poland 54 38N 18 50E
80 Helagsfjället, Mt., Swed. 62 54N 12 25E
55 Helchteren, Belgium .51 4N 5 22E
63 Helechosa, Spain 39 22N 4 53W
165 Helena, Ark., U.S.A. .34 30N 90 35W
166 Helena, Mont., U.S.A. 46 40N 112 0W
143 Helensburgh, Australia 34 11S 151 1E
40 Helensburgh, Scot., U.K. 56 0N 4 44W
146 Helensville, N.Z. 36 41S 174 29E
98 Helets, Israel 31 36N 34 39E
81 Helgasjön, L., Sweden 57 0N 14 54E
82 Helgeland, dist., Nor. 66 20N 13 30E
79 Helgeroa, Norway 59 0N 9 45E
56 Helgoland, I., Germany 54 10N 7 51E
80 Helgum, Sweden 63 25N 16 50E
126 Heliopolis, Egypt 30 6N 31 17E
81 Hellebaek, Denmark .56 4N 12 32E
79 Helleland, Norway 58 33N 6 7E
55 Hellendoorn, Neth. ...52 24N 6 27E
54 Hellevoetsluis, Neth. .51 50N 4 8E
42 Helli Ness, Scot., U.K. 60 3N 1 10W
15 Hellick Kenyon Plateau, Antarctica 82 0S 110 0W
38 Hellifield, Eng., U.K. .54 0N 2 13W
65 Hellin, Spain 38 31N 1 40W
130 Hell's Gate, see Hinde Rapids, Congo 5 25S 27 3E
81 Hellum, Denmark 57 16N 10 10E
129 Hellville, Malagasy Rep. 13 20S 48 12E
101 Helmand, R., Afghan. 34 0N 67 0E
134 Helmeringhausen, South West Africa .25 53S 16 50E
54 Helmond, Netherlands 51 29N 5 41E
43 Helmsdale & R., Scot., U.K. 58 7N 3 40W
39 Helmsley, Eng., U.K. 54 15N 1 2W
56 Helmstedt, Germany .52 16N 11 0E
81 Helnaes, Denmark 55 9N 10 0E
166 Helper, U.S.A. 39 44N 110 56W
39 Helperby, Eng., U.K. 54 8N 1 20W
135 Helpmekaar, S. Africa 28 29S 30 29E
38 Helsby, Eng., U.K. ...53 16N 2 47W
81 Helsinge, Denmark ...56 2N 12 12E
83 Helsingfors, see Helsinki, Finland ...60 15N 25 3E
81 Helsingör, Denmark ...56 2N 12 35E
83 Helsinki, Finland 60 15N 25 3E
36 Helston, Eng., U.K. ...50 7N 5 17W
38 Helvellyn, Eng., U.K. 54 31N 3 1W
135 Helvetia, O.F.S., S. Afr. 29 51S 26 32E
45 Helvick Hd., Ireland .52 3N 7 33W
126 Helwân, Egypt 29 50N 31 20E
79 Hem, Norway 59 26N 10 0E
106 Hemavati R., India ...12 50N 67 0E
130 Hembe, Congo 1 50N 22 35E
35 Hemel Hempstead, England, U.K. 51 45N 0 28W
55 Hemer, Germany 51 23N 7 44E
167 Hemet, U.S.A. 33 45N 116 59W
55 Hemiksen, Belgium ...51 9N 4 20E
164 Hemingford, U.S.A. ...42 21N 103 4W
165 Hemphill, U.S.A. 31 21N 93 49W
165 Hempstead, U.S.A. 30 5N 96 5W
81 Hemse, Sweden 57 15N 18 20E
80 Hemsö I., Sweden 62 43N 18 5E
39 Hemsworth, Eng., U.K. 53 37N 1 21W
36 Hemyock, Eng., U.K. 50 55N 1 13W
146 Hen & Chicken Is., N.Z. 35 58S 174 45E
64 Henares R., Spain 40 55N 3 0W
50 Hendaye, France 43 23N 1 47W
172 Henderson, Argentina 36 18S 61 43W
42 Henderson, Scot., U.K. 57 42N 5 47W
162 Henderson, Ky., U.S.A. 37 50N 87 38W
163 Henderson, N.C., U.S.A. 36 18N 78 23W
167 Henderson, Nev., U.S.A. 36 2N 115 0W
163 Henderson, Pa., U.S.A. 35 25N 88 40W
165 Henderson, Tex., U.S.A. 32 5N 94 49W
163 Hendersonville, U.S.A. 35 21N 82 28W
145 Hendon, Australia 28 5S 151 50E
78 Hendorf, Rumania 46 4N 24 5E
55 Hendrik Ido Ambacht, Netherlands 51 51N 4 38E
133 Hendrina, Trans., S. Afr. 26 11S 29 45E
35 Henfield, Eng., U.K. .50 56N 0 17W
54 Hengelo, Netherlands 52 15N 6 48E
113 Henghsien, China 22 36N 109 16E
36 Hengoed, Wales, U.K. 51 39N 3 14W
112 Hengshan, China 38 0N 109 2E
113 Hengshan, China 27 10N 112 45E
112 Hengtaohotze, China .44 55N 129 3E
113 Hengyang, China 26 57N 112 28E
49 Henin Lietard, France 50 25N 2 58E
35 Henley, Eng., U.K. 51 32N 0 53W
34 Henley-in-Arden, England, U.K. 52 18N 1 47W
37 Henllan, Wales, U.K. 53 13N 3 29W
162 Henlopen C., U.S.A. ...38 48N 75 5W
35 Henlow, Eng., U.K. ...51 2N 0 18W
80 Hennan, L., Sweden ...62 3N 15 55E
81 Henne, Denmark 55 44N 8 11E
48 Hennebont, France ...47 49N 3 19W
55 Hennef, Germany 50 47N 7 17E
135 Hennenman, S. Africa 27 59S 27 1E
165 Hennessy, U.S.A. 36 8N 97 53W
56 Hennigsdorf, Germany 52 38N 13 13E
157 Henribourg, Canada ...53 25N 105 38W
49 Henrichemont, France 47 20N 2 30W
165 Henrietta, U.S.A. 33 50N 98 15W
154 Henrietta Maria C., Can. 55 10N 82 30W
164 Henry, U.S.A. 41 5N 89 20W
165 Henryetta, U.S.A. 35 2N 96 0W
160 Hensall, Canada 43 27N 81 32W
36 Henstridge, Eng., U.K. 50 59N 2 24W
112 Hentiyn Nuruu, Mt., Mongolia 48 30N 108 30E
143 Henty, N.S.W., Austral. 35 30N 147 0E
103 Henzada, Burma 17 38N 95 35E
55 Heppen, Belgium 51 7N 5 14E
55 Heppenbach, Belgium 50 22N 6 13E
166 Heppner, U.S.A. 45 27N 119 34W
160 Hepworth, Canada 44 40N 81 10W
79 Herad, Norway 58 8N 6 47E
101 Herat, Afghanistan ...34 20N 62 7E
50 Hérault, dépt., France 43 34N 3 15E
50 Hérault R., France 43 45N 3 32E
55 Herbede, Germany 51 25N 7 15E
157 Herbert, Canada 50 30N 107 10W
144 Herbert Downs, Queens., Australia .23 0S 139 11E
144 Herberton, Australia .17 28S 145 25E
134 Herbertsdale, S. Africa 34 0S 21 45E
44 Herbertstown, Ireland 52 32N 8 29W
48 Herbignac, France 47 27N 2 18W
56 Herborn, Germany 50 40N 8 19E
60 Herby, Poland 50 45N 18 50E
74 Hercegnovi, Y.-slav. .42 30N 18 33E
74 Hercegovina, prov., Yugoslavia 43 20N 18 0E
55 Herchen, Germany 50 47N 7 30E
55 Herdecke, Germany ...51 23N 7 41E
79 Herdla, Norway 60 34N 4 56E
34 Hereford & co., Eng., U.K. 52 4N 2 42W
165 Hereford, U.S.A. 34 50N 102 28W
79 Herefoss, Norway 58 32N 8 23E
146 Herekino, New Zealand 35 18S 173 11E
55 Herent, Belgium 50 54N 4 40E
54 Herentals, Belgium ...51 12N 4 51E
81 Herfölge, Denmark ...55 26N 12 9E
56 Herford, Germany 52 7N 8 40E
49 Hericourt, France 47 32N 6 55E
56 Heringsdorf, Germany 53 56N 14 10E
164 Herington, U.S.A. 38 43N 97 0W
57 Herisau, Switzerland .47 22N 9 17E
50 Hérisson, France 46 32N 2 42E
55 Herk R., Belgium 50 56N 5 12E
55 Herkenbosch, Neth. ...51 9N 6 4E
161 Herkimer, U.S.A. 43 0N 74 59W
48 Herm I., Chan. Is., United Kingdom 49 30N 2 28W
42 Herma Ness, Scot., U.K. 60 50N 0 54W
58 Hermagor, Austria 46 38N 13 23E
164 Herman, U.S.A. 45 51N 96 8W
164 Hermann, U.S.A. 38 40N 91 25W
56 Hermannsburg, Ger. .52 49N 10 6E
134 Hermanus, S. Africa .34 27S 19 12E
133 Hermanusdorings, Transvaal, S. Africa 24 10S 27 50E
50 Herment, France 45 45N 2 24E
34 Hermes, France 49 20N 2 15E
143 Hermidale, Australia .31 30S 146 42E
166 Hermiston, U.S.A. 45 50N 119 16W
147 Hermitage, N.Z. 43 44S 170 5E
155 Hermitage B., Canada 47 33N 56 10W
176 Hermite Is., Chile 55 50S 68 0W
100 Hermon, Mt., Syria ...33 20N 36 0E
168 Hermosillo, Mexico ...29 10N 111 0W
59 Hernad R., Hungary .48 20N 21 15E
173 Hernandarias, Paraguay 25 20S 54 40W
172 Hernando, Argentina .32 28S 64 50W
165 Hernando, U.S.A. 34 50N 89 59W
56 Herne, Germany 51 33N 7 12E
35 Herne Bay, Eng., U.K. 51 22N 1 8E
142 Herne Hill, W. Austral. 31 45S 116 5E
81 Herning, Denmark 56 8N 9 0E
154 Heron Bay, Canada ...48 40N 85 25W
79 Heröy, Norway 62 18N 5 45E
164 Herreid, U.S.A. 45 53N 100 5W
63 Herrera, Spain 39 12N 5 3W
63 Herrera de Alcantara, Spain 39 39N 7 25W
62 Herrera de Pisuerga, Sp. 42 35N 4 20W
63 Herrera del Duque, Sp. 39 10N 5 3W
145 Herrick, Tas., Austral. 41 5S 147 55E
165 Herrin, U.S.A. 37 50N 89 0W
55 Herringen, Germany .51 41N 7 49E
81 Herrljunga, Sweden ...58 5N 13 5E
57 Hersbruck, Germany .49 30N 11 25E
14 Herschel I., Canada ...69 0N 135 0W
56 Hersfeld, Germany......50 52N 9 42E
135 Hershel, C. Prov., S. Afr. 30 37S 27 10E
35 Herstmonceux, England, U.K. 50 53N 0 21E
79 Hersvik, Norway 61 10N 4 53E
55 Herten, Germany 51 36N 7 9E
35 Hertford, Eng., U.K. .51 47N 0 4W
35 Hertford, co., Eng., U.K. 51 51N 0 5W
54 's Hertogenbosch, Neth. 51 42N 5 18E
135 Hertzogville, S. Africa 28 9S 25 30E
62 Hervas, Spain 40 16N 5 52W
55 Herve, Belgium 50 38N 5 48E
137 Hervey Is., Pac. O. ...19 30S 159 0W
154 Hervey Junc., Canada 46 50N 72 29W
56 Herzberg, Lr. Sax., Ger. 51 38N 10 20E
56 Herzberg, Cottbus, Ger. 51 40N 13 13E
98 Herzliya, Israel 32 10N 34 50E
58 Herzogenburg, Austria 48 17N 15 41E
55 Herzogenrath, Germany 50 51N 6 6E
49 Hesdin, France 50 21N 2 0E
56 Hesel, Germany 53 18N 7 36E
79 Heskestad, Norway ...58 28N 6 22E
160 Hespeler, Canada 43 28N 80 19W
56 Hessen, land, Germany 50 57N 9 20E
39 Hessle, Eng., U.K. 53 44N 0 28E
55 Heteren, Netherlands .51 58N 5 46E
35 Hethersett, Eng., U.K. 52 35N 1 10E
164 Hettinger, U.S.A. 46 8N 102 38W
39 Hetton-le-Hole, England, U.K. 54 49N 1 26W
56 Hettstedt, Germany ...51 39N 11 30E
134 Heuningneskloof C. Prov., S. Africa .29 13S 24 32E
135 Heuningspruit, S. Afr. 27 26S 27 28E
55 Heusden, Belgium 51 2N 5 17E
48 Hève, C. de la, France 49 30N 0 5E
55 Heverlee, Belgium 50 52N 4 42E
59 Heves, Co., Hungary .47 50N 20 0E
98 Hevron, R., Isr.-Jord. 31 28N 34 52E
38 Hexham, Eng., U.K. .54 58N 2 7W
35 Heybridge, Eng., U.K. 51 44N 0 42E
143 Heyfield, Vic., Austral. 37 59S 146 47E
38 Heysham, Eng., U.K. 54 5N 2 53W
34 Heytesbury, Eng., U.K. 51 11N 2 7W
38 Heywood, Eng., U.K. 53 36N 2 13W
143 Heywood, Vic., Austral. 38 8S 141 37E
164 Hiawatha, Kan., U.S.A. 39 55N 95 33W
166 Hiawatha, Utah, U.S.A. 39 37N 111 1W
164 Hibbing, U.S.A. 47 30N 93 0W
165 Hickman, U.S.A. 36 35N 89 8W

MAP
163 Hickory, U.S.A. 35 46N 81 17W
146 Hicks Bay, N.Z. 37 34S 178 21E
161 Hicksville, U.S.A. 40 46N 73 30W
78 Hida, Rumania 47 10N 23 19E
168 Hidalgo, st., Mexico ...20 30N 99 10W
168 Hidalgo del Parral, Mex. 26 10N 104 50W
56 Hiddensee I., Germany 54 30N 13 6E
58 Hieflau, Austria 47 36N 14 46E
64 Hiendelaencina, Spain 41 5N 3 0W
120 Hierro I., Can. I., Sp. 27 57N 17 56W
113 Hifung, China 22 59N 115 17E
165 Higgins, U.S.A. 36 9N 100 1W
142 Higginsville, W. Austral. 31 42S 121 38E
163 Higgs I. L., U.S.A. 36 20N 78 30W
155 High I., Canada 56 40N 61 10W
120 High Atlas, Mts., N. Afr. 32 30N 5 0W
38 High Bentham, England, U.K. 54 8N 2 31W
38 High Borrow Bri., England, U.K. 54 26N 2 43W
38 High Ercall, Eng., U.K. 52 46N 2 37W
41 High Hesket, Eng., U.K. 54 47N 2 49W
165 High Island, U.S.A. ...29 32N 94 22W
38 High Pike, Mt., England, U.K. 54 43N 3 4W
163 High Point, U.S.A. 35 57N 79 58W
156 High Prairie, Canada .55 30N 116 30W
156 High River, Canada ...50 30N 113 50W
163 High Springs, U.S.A. .29 50N 82 40W
36 High Willhays, hill, England, U.K. 50 41N 3 59W
35 High Wycombe, England, U.K. 51 37N 0 45W
35 Higham Ferrers, England, U.K. 52 18N 0 36W
147 Highbank, New Zealand 47 34S 171 45E
36 Highbridge, Eng., U.K. 51 13N 2 59W
147 Highbank, New Zealand 47 34S 171 45E
34 Highclere, Eng. U.K. 51 20N 1 22W
135 Highflats, Natal, S. Afr. 30 16S 30 13E
162 Highland Pk., Ill., U.S.A. 42 10N 87 50W
160 Highland Pk., Mich., U.S.A. 42 25N 83 6W
135 Highlands, S. Africa ...33 21S 26 22E
34 Highley, Eng., U.K. ...52 25N 2 23W
164 Highmore, U.S.A. 44 35N 99 26W
41 Hightae, Scot., U.K. .55 5N 3 27W
34 Highworth, Eng., U.K. 51 38N 1 42W
167 Higley, U.S.A. 33 27N 111 46W
86 Hiiumaa I., U.S.S.R. .58 50N 22 45E
64 Hijar, Spain 41 10N 0 27W
167 Hiko, U.S.A. 37 30N 115 13W
114 Hikone, Japan 35 15N 136 10E
146 Hikurangi, New Zealand 37 54S 178 5E
146 Hikurangi, Mt., N.Z. .37 55S 178 4E
57 Hildburghhausen, Ger. 50 24N 10 43E
55 Hilden, Germany 51 10N 6 56E
56 Hildesheim, Germany 52 9N 9 55E
35 Hilgay, England, U.K. 52 34N 0 23E
166 Hill City, Idaho, U.S.A. 43 20N 115 2W
164 Hill City, Kan., U.S.A. 39 25N 99 51W
164 Hill City, Minn., U.S.A. 46 57N 93 35W
164 Hill City, S.D., U.S.A. 43 58N 103 35W
157 Hill Island L., Canada 60 30N 109 50W
100 Hilla, Iraq 32 30N 44 27E
100 Hilla, Saudi Arabia ...23 35N 46 50E
81 Hillared, Sweden 57 37N 13 10E
81 Hilleröd, Denmark 55 56N 12 19E
81 Hillerstorp, Sweden ...57 20N 13 52E
55 Hillesheim, Germany .50 17N 6 39E
35 Hillingdon, Eng., U.K. 51 33N 0 29W
162 Hillman, U.S.A. 45 5N 83 52W
157 Hillmond, Canada 53 26N 109 41W
164 Hillsboro, Kan., U.S.A. 38 28N 97 10W
167 Hillsboro, N. Mex., U.S.A. 33 0N 107 35W
164 Hillsboro, N.D., U.S.A. 47 23N 97 9W
161 Hillsboro, N.H., U.S.A. 43 8N 71 56W
166 Hillsboro, Oreg., U.S.A. 45 31N 123 0W
165 Hillsboro, Tex., U.S.A. 32 0N 97 10W
46 Hillsborough, N. Ireland, U.K. 54 28N 6 6W
162 Hillsdale, Mich., U.S.A. 41 55N 84 40W
161 Hillsdale, N.Y., U.S.A. 42 11N 73 30W
154 Hillsport, Canada 49 27N 85 34W
143 Hillston, Australia 33 30S 145 31E
42 Hillswick, Scot., U.K. 60 29N 1 28W
46 Hilltown, N. Ire., U.K. 54 12N 6 8W
132 Hillwood, Zambia 11 10S 24 15E
158 Hilo, Hawaii, U.S.A. .19 44N 155 5W
109 Hilonghilong, Mt., Phil. 9 10N 125 45E
38 Hilpsford Pt., Eng., U.K. 54 4N 3 12W
160 Hilton, U.S.A. 43 16N 77 48W
43 Hilton of Cadboll, Scotland, U.K. 57 46N 3 53W
54 Hilversum, Neth. 52 14N 5 10E
104 Himachal Pradesh, st., India 31 30N 77 0E
103 Himalaya Range, Asia 29 0N 84 0E
76 Himare, Albania 40 8N 19 43E
114 Himeji, Japan 34 50N 134 40E
114 Himi, Japan 36 50N 137 0E
81 Himmerland, reg., Den. 56 50N 9 38E
131 Himo, Tanzania 3 26S 37 34E
100 Hims, see Homs, Syria 34 40N 36 45E
108 Hinako Is., Indonesia 0 50N 97 20E
144 Hinchinbrook I., Queens., Australia .18 20S 146 15E
34 Hinckley, Eng., U.K. .52 33N 1 21W
166 Hinckley, U.S.A. 39 18N 112 41W
81 Hindas, Sweden 57 42N 12 29E
104 Hindaun, India 26 44N 77 5E
130 Hinde Rapids (Hells Gate), Congo 5 25S 27 3E
39 Hinderwell, Eng., U.K. 54 32N 0 45W
35 Hindhead, Eng., U.K. 51 6N 0 42W
131 Hindi Somali Rep. 2 15N 42 0E
38 Hindley, Eng., U.K. .53 32N 2 35W
143 Hindmarsh L., Austral. 35 50S 141 55E
105 Hindol, India 20 40N 85 10E
147 Hinds, New Zealand .43 59S 171 36E
81 Hindsholm Pen., Den. 55 32N 10 38E
104 Hindu Bagh, W. Pak. 30 56N 67 57E
101 Hindu Kush, Mts., Asia 36 0N 71 0E
106 Hindupur, India 13 49N 77 32E
156 Hines Creek, Canada .56 20N 118 40W
113 Hingan, China 25 39N 110 43E
104 Hinganghat, India 20 30N 78 59E
112 Hingchen, China 40 21N 120 10E
35 Hingham, Eng., U.K. 52 35N 0 59E
166 Hingham, U.S.A. 48 40N 110 29W
113 Hingi, China 25 4N 105 2E
113 Hingkwo, China 26 15N 115 13E
113 Hingning, China 24 2N 115 55E
102 Hingol, R., W. Pak. ...25 30N 65 30E
106 Hingoli, India 19 41N 77 15E
34 Hinkley Pt., Eng., U.K. 50 59N 3 32W
14 Hinlopen Strait, Spitsbergen 79 30N 19 0E
125 Hinna, Nigeria 10 25N 11 28E
82 Hinnöy I., Norway 68 40N 16 28E
114 Hino, C., Japan 35 28N 132 45E
63 Hinoiosa del Duque, Spain 38 30N 5 17W
166 Hinsdale, U.S.A. 48 26N 107 2W
34 Hinstock, Eng., U.K. .52 50N 2 28W
57 Hinterrhein R., Switz. 46 40N 9 25E
156 Hinton, Canada 53 26N 117 28W
163 Hinton, U.S.A. 37 40N 80 51W
54 Hippolitushoe, Neth. .52 56N 45 9E
105 Hirakud, India 21 32N 83 51E
105 Hirakud Dam, India .21 32N 83 45E
123 Hirhafok, Algeria 23 49N 5 45E
114 Hiratsuka, Japan 35 40N 139 36E
114 Hirosaki, Japan 40 35N 140 25E
114 Hiroshima, Japan 34 30N 132 30E
81 Hirsholmene, I., Den. 57 30N 10 36E
49 Hirson, France 49 55N 4 4E
81 Hirtshals, Denmark ...57 36N 9 55E
37 Hirwaun, Wales, U.K. 51 43N 3 30W
79 Hisöy, Norway 58 26N 8 44E
169 Hispaniola I., W. Ind. 19 0N 71 0W
104 Hissar, India 29 12N 75 45E
80 Hissmofors, Sweden ...63 20N 14 28E
35 Histon, Eng., U.K. 52 15N 0 5E
114 Hitachi, Japan 36 40N 140 35E
114 Hita, Japan 33 42N 130 52E
35 Hitchin, Eng., U.K. ...51 57N 0 16W
114 Hitoyoshi, Japan 32 13N 130 45E
82 Hitra I., Norway 63 30N 8 45E
56 Hitzacker, Germany ...53 9N 11 1E
112 Hiungyao, China 40 10N 122 9E
157 Hjalmar L., Canada ...61 35N 109 15W
80 Hjalmare Kanal, Swed. 59 20N 15 59E
80 Hjälmaren L., Sweden 59 18N 15 40E
79 Hjartdal, Norway 59 37N 8 41E
81 Hjärtsäter, Sweden 58 35N 12 3E
81 Hjelm, Denmark 54 56N 12 15E
79 Hjerkinn, Norway 62 13N 9 33E
81 Hjerpsted, Denmark .55 2N 8 39E
81 Hjo, Sweden 58 22N 4 10E
81 Hjörring, Denmark 57 29N 9 59E
81 Hjörring Amt., co., Den. 57 19N 10 0E
81 Hjorted, Sweden 57 43N 16 13E
81 Hjortkvarn, Sweden ...58 54N 15 26E
135 Hlabisa, Natal, S. Afr. 28 8S 31 52E
133 Hlatikulu, Swaziland .26 59S 31 22E
58 Hlinsko, Czechoslovakia 49 45N 15 54E
135 Hlobane, Natal, S. Afr. 27 42S 13 0E
59 Hlohovec, Cz. 48 26N 17 49E
135 Hluhluwe, Natal, S. Afr. 28 5S 32 20E
125 Ho, Ghana 6 37N 0 27E
107 Hoa Binh, Vietnam ...20 52N 105 21E
107 Hoa Da (Phan Ri), S. Vietnam 11 16N 108 40E
156 Hoadley, Canada 52 45N 114 30W
107 Hoai Nhon (Bon Son), S. Vietnam 14 28N 103 37E
153 Hoare B., Canada 65 30N 62 30W
145 Hobart, Tas., Australia 42 50S 147 21E
165 Hobart, Okla., U.S.A. 35 0N 99 5W
165 Hobbs, U.S.A. 32 40N 103 3W
135 Hobhouse, S. Africa ...29 30S 27 10E
81 Hobjærg, Denmark 56 19N 9 32E
54 Hoboken, Belgium 51 11N 4 21E
161 Hoboken, U.S.A. 40 45N 74 4W
81 Hobro, Denmark 56 39N 9 46E
81 Hoburg C., Sweden ...56 54N 18 8E
165 Hochatown, U.S.A. ...34 11N 94 39W
55 Hochdahl, Germany ...51 13N 6 57E
113 Hochih, China 24 43N 107 43E
57 Höchst, Germany 50 6N 8 33E
113 Hochwan, China 30 0N 106 15E
57 Hockenheim, Germany 49 18N 8 33E
81 Hodde, Denmark 55 42N 8 39E
38 Hodder R., Eng., U.K. 53 57N 2 27W
35 Hoddesdon, Eng., U.K. 51 45N 0 1W
99 Hodeida, Yemen 14 50N 43 0E
157 Hodgson, Canada 51 20N 97 40W
59 Hódmezovásárhely, Hungary 46 28N 20 22E
123 Hodna, Chott el, Algeria 35 30N 5 0E
59 Hodonin, Cz. 48 50N 17 0E
81 Hodsager, Denmark ...56 19N 8 51E
48 Hoédic I., France 47 21N 2 52W
55 Hoellaart, Belgium 50 46N 4 28E
54 Hoek van Holland, Netherlands 52 0N 4 7E
55 Hoensbroek, Neth. 50 55N 5 55E
112 Hoeryong, Korea 42 30N 129 58E
55 Hoeven, Netherlands .51 35N 4 35E
57 Hof, Germany 50 18N 11 55E
82 Hof, Iceland 64 33N 14 30W
113 Hofei, China 31 45N 116 36E
113 Hofeng, China 29 55N 110 5E
41 Hoff, England, U.K. .54 34N 2 31W
56 Hofgeismar, Germany 51 29N 9 23E
135 Hofmeyr, S. Africa 31 39S 25 50E
80 Hofors, Sweden 60 35N 16 15E
82 Hofsos, Iceland 65 53N 19 18W
114 Hofu, Japan 34 0N 130 30E
100 Hofuf, Saudi Arabia ...25 20N 49 40E
79 Hög–Gia, Mt., Norway 62 23N 10 7E
81 Högnanäs, Sweden 56 13N 12 34E
165 Hogansville, U.S.A. 33 14N 84 50W
166 Hogeland, U.S.A. 48 50N 108 29W
80 Högen, Sweden 61 47N 14 11E
106 Hogenaki Falls, India 12 6N 77 50E
80 Högfors, Örebro, Swed. 59 58N 15 3E
80 Högfors, Västmanlands, Sweden 60 2N 16 3E
123 Hoggar Mts., Algeria .23 0N 6 30E
35 Hog's Back, hill, England, U.K. 51 13N 0 40W
44 Hogs Hd., Ireland 51 46N 10 13W
81 Högsäter, Sweden 58 38N 12 5E
81 Högsby, Sweden 57 10N 16 3E
80 Högsjö, Sweden 59 4N 15 44E
39 Hogsthorpe, Eng., U.K. 53 13N 0 19E
55 Höhe Eifel, Mts., Ger. 50 20N 6 57E
57 Höhe Rhön, Mts., Ger. 50 24N 9 58E
58 Höhe Tauern, Mts., Austria 47 11N 12 40E
59 Hohenau, Austria 48 36N 16 55E
58 Hohenems, Austria ...47 22N 9 42E
55 Hohenlimburg, Ger. ...51 21N 7 35E
56 Hohenstein Ernstthal, Germany 50 48N 12 43E
163 Hohenwald, U.S.A. ...35 35N 87 30W
56 Hohenwestedt, Ger. ...54 6N 9 40E
125 Hohoe, Ghana 7 8N 0 32E
112 Hohpi, China 35 59N 114 13E
113 Hohsien, China 24 14N 111 31E
107 Hoi An, S. Vietnam ...15 52N 108 19E
107 Hoi Xuan, N. Vietnam 20 25N 105 9E
113 Hoinong (Luichow), China 20 55N 110 3E
113 Hoiping, China 22 30N 112 12E
164 Hoisington, U.S.A. 38 33N 98 50W
81 Hojer, Denmark 54 55N 8 43E
81 Hok, Sweden 57 35N 14 16E
112 Hokang, China 47 36N 130 28E
81 Hökensås, reg., Sweden 58 6N 14 2E
81 Hökerum, Sweden 57 51N 13 20E
146 Hoklanga Harb., N.Z. 35 31S 173 22E
113 Hokiang, China 28 50N 105 50E
112 Hokien, China 38 30N 116 2E
147 Hokitika, New Zealand 42 42S 171 0E
114 Hokkaido, I., dist. & pref., Japan 43 30N 143 0E
79 Hokksund, Norway ...59 44N 9 51E
107 Hokow, China 22 39N 103 57E
112 Hokowchen, China 40 16N 111 4E
127 Hol Hol., Fr. Terr. of the Afars & Issas ...11 20N 42 50E
81 Holbaek, Denmark 55 42N 11 40E
35 Holbeach, Eng., U.K. 52 48N 0 1E
35 Holbeach Marsh, England, U.K. 52 52N 0 5E
43 Holborn Hd., Scotland, U.K. 58 37N 3 30W
143 Holbrook, Australia ...35 42S 147 18E
167 Holbrook, U.S.A. 35 0N 110 0W
156 Holden, Canada 53 13N 112 11W
166 Holden Fillmore, U.S.A..................... 39 0N 112 26W
165 Holdenville, U.S.A. ...35 5N 96 25W
39 Holderness, Eng., U.K. 53 45N 0 5W
164 Holdrege, U.S.A. 40 25N 99 30W
79 Hole, Norway 60 6N 10 12E
106 Hole–Narsipur, India .12 48N 76 16E
59 Holešov, Czechoslovakia 49 20N 17 35E
135 Holfontein, S. Africa .27 52S 27 5E
169 Holguín, Cuba 20 50N 76 20W
59 Holic, Czechoslovakia 48 49N 17 10E
35 Holkham, Eng., U.K. 52 57N 0 48E
127 Holla, Mt., Ethiopia ... 7 5N 36 35E
58 Hollabrunn, Austria ...48 34N 16 5E
129 Hollams Bird I. South-West Africa .24 40S 14 30E
35 Holland, dist., England, United Kingdom 52 50N 0 10W
162 Holland, U.S.A. 42 47N 86 0W
160 Holland Landing, Can. 44 7N 79 30W
109 Hollandia, see Djajapura, Indonesia 2 28N 140 38E
35 Holland–on–Sea, England, U.K. 51 48N 1 12E
43 Hollandstown, Scotland, U.K. 59 22N 2 25W
79 Höllen, Norway 58 6N 7 49E
142 Holleton, W. Australia 31 55S 119 0E
160 Hollidaysburg, U.S.A. 40 26N 78 25W
165 Hollis, U.S.A. 34 45N 99 55W
167 Hollister, Calif., U.S.A. 37 55N 121 30W
160 Hollister, Idaho, U.S.A. 42 21N 114 36W
164 Holly, Kan., U.S.A. ...38 7N 102 7W
163 Holly Hill, U.S.A. 29 15N 81 3W
165 Holly Springs, U.S.A. 34 45N 89 25W
46 Hollymount, Ireland .53 40N 9 7W
45 Hollywood, Ireland ...53 6N 6 35W
158 Hollywood, Calif., U.S.A. 34 0N 118 10W
163 Hollywood, Fla., U.S.A. 26 0N 80 9W
80 Holm, Sweden 62 40N 16 40E
82 Holmavik, Iceland 65 42N 21 40W
133 Holmdene, S. Africa ...26 48S 29 3E
39 Holme, E. Riding, Yorks., England, U.K. 53 50N 0 48W
38 Holme, W. Riding, Yorks., England, U.K. 53 34N 1 50W
79 Holmedal, Fjordane, Norway 61 22N 5 11E
79 Holmedal, Hordaland, Norway 59 46N 5 50E
79 Holmegil, Norway 59 10N 11 44E
35 Holmes Chapel, England, U.K. 53 13N 2 21W
79 Holmestrand, Norway 59 31N 10 14E
39 Holmfirth, Eng., U.K. 53 34N 1 48W
79 Holmsbu, Norway 59 32N 10 40E
80 Holmsjön, L., Sweden 62 26N 15 20E
80 Holmsjön, L., Sweden 62 42N 16 30E
81 Holmsland Klit, Den. 56 0N 8 9E
82 Holmsund, Sweden 63 41N 20 20E
35 Holmwood, Eng., U.K. 51 12N 0 19W
36 Holne, England, U.K. 50 30N 3 50W
80 Hölö, Sweden 59 3N 17 36E
78 Holod, Rumania 46 49N 22 8E
98 Holon, Israel 32 2N 34 47E
79 Holsen, Norway 61 25N 6 8E
81 Holstebro, Denmark .56 22N 8 33E
153 Holsteinborg, Green. .67 0N 53 20W
36 Holsworthy, Eng., U.K. 50 48N 4 21W
35 Holt, Eng., U.K. 52 55N 1 4E
38 Holte, Wales, U.K. 53 4N 2 52W
81 Holte, Denmark 55 50N 12 29E
155 Holton Harbour, Can. 54 31N 57 12W
39 Holton Le Clay, England, U.K. 53 29N 0 3W
167 Holtville, U.S.A. 32 50N 115 27W
79 Holum, Norway 58 6N 7 32E
54 Holwerd, Netherlands 53 23N 55 5E
41 Holy I., Eng., U.K. 55 42N 1 48W
40 Holy I., Scot., U.K. ...55 31N 5 4W
37 Holy I., Wales, U.K. .53 17N 4 37W
37 Holyhead & B., Wales, U.K. 53 18N 4 38W
161 Holyoke, Mass., U.S.A. 42 14N 72 37W
164 Holyoke, Neb., U.S.A. 40 39N 102 18W
155 Holyrood, Canada 47 27N 53 8W
37 Holywell, Wales, U.K. 53 16N 3 14W
46 Holywood, N. Ire., U.K. 54 38N 5 50W
56 Holzminden, Germany 51 49N 9 31E
131 Homa Bay, Kenya 0 36S 34 22E
103 Homalin, Burma 24 55N 95 0E
56 Homberg, Hesse, Ger. 51 2N 9 20E
55 Homberg, Germany ...51 27N 6 41E
125 Hombori, Mali 15 20N 1 38E
55 Hombourg, Belgium ...50 43N 5 55E
57 Homburg, Saar, Ger. .49 19N 7 21E
153 Home B., Canada 68 40N 67 10W
144 Home Hill, Australia .19 43S 147 25E
166 Homedale, U.S.A. 43 42N 116 59W
152 Homer, Alaska, U.S.A. 59 40N 151 35W
165 Homer, La., U.S.A. ...32 50N 93 4W
163 Homestead, Fla., U.S.A. 25 29N 80 27W
160 Homestead, Id., U.S.A. 45 3N 116 58W
144 Homestead, Australia 20 20S 145 40E
165 Hominy, U.S.A. 36 26N 96 24W
106 Homnabad, India 17 45N 77 5E
132 Homoine, Mozambique 23 55S 35 8E
78 Homorod, Rumania ...46 5N 25 15E
123 Homs (Al Khums), Libya 32 40N 14 17E
100 Homs (Hims), Syria ...34 40N 36 45E
107 Hon Chong, S. Vietnam 10 16N 104 38E
113 Honan, prov., China ..33 50N 113 15E
174 Honda, Colombia 5 12N 74 45W
134 Hondeklipbaal, S. Afr. 30 19S 17 17E
165 Hondo, U.S.A. 29 22N 99 6W
169 Honduras, rep., Central America 14 40N 86 30W
168 Honduras, G. of, Central America 16 50N 87 0W
79 Hönefoss, Norway 60 10N 10 12E
161 Honesdale, U.S.A. 41 34N 75 17W
166 Honey L., U.S.A. 40 13N 120 14W
34 Honeybourne, Eng., U.K. 52 6N 1 49W
48 Honfleur, France 49 25N 0 10E
81 Höng, Denmark 55 30N 11 14E
107 Hongha (Red), R., N. Vietnam 22 0N 104 0E
113 Hongkong, Brit. Crown Col., China ...22 11N 114 14E
55 Höngen, Germany 50 52N 6 13E
113 Honghai B., China 22 45N 115 15E
112 Hongor, Mongolia 45 56N 112 50E
136 Honiara, Solomon Is. . 9 30S 160 0E
36 Honiton, Eng., U.K. .50 48N 3 11W
126 Honkorâb, Ras, Egypt 24 35N 35 10E
38 Honley, Eng., U.K. ...53 36N 1 48W
56 Honnef, Germany 50 39N 7 13E
55 Hönningen, Germany .50 32N 7 19E
137 Honolulu, Hawaii, U.S.A. 21 19N 157 52W
114 Honshu I., Japan 36 0N 138 0E
64 Hontoria del Pinar, Sp. 41 50N 3 10W
35 Hoo, Eng., U.K. 51 25N 0 33E
166 Hood Mt.,U.S.A. 45 15N 122 0W
166 Hood River, U.S.A. ...45 45N 121 37W
166 Hoodsport, U.S.A. 47 30N 123 7W
56 Hooge I., Germany 54 31N 8 36E
54 Hoogeveen, Neth. 52 44N 6 30E
54 Hoogezand Neth. 53 11N 6 45E
105 Hooghly R., India 21 59N 88 10E
35 Hook, England, U.K. 51 17N 0 55W
45 Hook Hd., Ireland 52 8N 6 57W
144 Hook I., Australia 20 4S 149 0E
165 Hooker, U.S.A. 36 55N 101 10W
157 Hoonah, Alaska, U.S.A. 58 15N 135 30W
162 Hoopeston, U.S.A. 40 30N 87 40W
135 Hoopstad, S. Africa ...27 50S 25 55E
81 Höör, Sweden 55 55N 13 33E
54 Hoorn, Netherlands ...52 38N 5 4E
161 Hoosick Falls, U.S.A. 42 54N 73 21W
167 Hoover Dam, U.S.A. .36 0N 114 45W
160 Hooversville, U.S.A. .40 8N 78 57W
161 Hop Bottom, U.S.A. .41 41N 75 47W
89 Hopa, Turkey 41 28N 41 30E
161 Hopbottom, U.S.A. ...41 42N 75 46W
165 Hope, Ark., U.S.A. 33 40N 93 30W
156 Hope, Canada 49 25N 121 25E
43 Hope L., Scot., U.K. .58 24N 4 38W
164 Hope, N.D., U.S.A. ...47 21N 97 42W
37 Hope, Wales, U.K. 53 7N 3 2W
15 Hope Bay, Ant. 65 0S 55 0W
152 Hope Pt., Alaska, U.S.A. 68 20N 166 40W
163 Hope Town, Bahama Is. 26 30N 76 30W
155 Hopedale, Canada 55 27N 60 22W
134 Hopefield, S. Africa ...33 3S 18 22E
112 Hopei, prov., China ...39 25N 116 45E
168 Hopelchén, Mexico ...19 46N 89 50W
43 Hopeman, Scot., U.K. 57 42N 3 26W
79 Hopen, Norway 63 27N 8 2E
143 Hopetoun, Australia .35 48S 142 25E
142 Hopetoun, W. Austral. 33 54S 120 6E
134 Hopetown, S. Africa .29 34S 24 3E
113 Hoping, China 24 31N 115 2E
164 Hopkins, U.S.A. 40 31N 94 45W
142 Hopkins, L., W. Austral. 24 15S 128 35E
143 Hopkins, R., Australia 37 55S 142 40E
163 Hopkinsville, U.S.A. .36 52N 87 26W
166 Hopland, U.S.A. 39 0N 123 0W
113 Hoppo, China 21 32N 109 6E
81 Hoptrup, Denmark 55 14N 9 28E
166 Hoquiam, U.S.A. 47 0N 123 55W
58 Horazdovice, Cz. 49 19N 13 42E
81 Hörby, Sweden 55 50N 13 44E
64 Horcajo de Santiago, Sp. 39 50N 3 1W
79 Hordaland Fylke, Nor. 60 25N 6 45E
55 Horde, Germany 51 29N 7 30E
138 Hordern Hills, N. Terr., Australia 20 40S 130 20E
99 Hordio, Somali Rep. .10 36N 51 8E
41 Hordon, Eng., U.K. ...54 46N 1 17W
78 Horezu, Rumania 45 6N 24 0E
57 Horgen, Switzerland .47 15N 8 35E
74 Horgos, Yugoslavia ...46 10N 20 0E
58 Horice, Czechoslovakia 50 21N 15 39E
35 Horley, England, U.K. 51 10N 0 10W
15 Horlick Mts., Ant. 84 0S 102 0W
101 Hormoz, Iran 27 35N 55 0E

MAP
101 Hormuz I., Iran 27 8N 56 28E
101 Hormuz Str., Persian G. 26 30N 56 30E
58 Horn, Austria 48 39N 15 40E
176 Horn, C., Chile 55 50S 67 30W
46 Horn Head, Ireland ...55 13N 8 0W
163 Horn, I., U.S.A. 30 17N 88 40W
156 Horn Mts., Canada ...62 0N 119 0W
82 Horna Fd., Iceland ...64 18N 15 15W
63 Hornachuelos, Spain .37 50N 5 14W
82 Hornavan L., Sweden 66 7N 17 0E
81 Hornbæk, Denmark ...56 5N 12 26E
165 Hornbeck, U.S.A. 31 22N 93 20W
166 Hornbrook, U.S.A. 41 58N 122 37W
56 Hornburg, Germany ...52 2N 10 36E
147 Hornby, New Zealand 43 33S 172 33E
39 Hornby, Yorks, England, U.K. 54 20N 1 40W
39 Horncastle, Eng., U.K. 53 13N 0 8W
80 Horndal, Sweden 60 18N 16 23E
34 Horndean, Eng., U.K. 50 56N 1 5W
160 Hornell, U.S.A. 42 23N 77 41W
79 Hornindal, Norway ...61 58N 6 35E
34 Horningsham, Eng., U.K. 51 11N 2 16W
79 Hornnes, Norway 58 34N 7 45E
49 Hornoy, France 49 50N 1 54E
154 Horne Payne, Canada 49 14N 84 48W
80 Hornsberg, Jamtland, Sweden 63 14N 14 40E
80 Hornsberg, Kronobergs, Sweden 56 37N 13 47E
143 Hornsby, Australia 33 42S 151 2E
39 Hornsea, Eng., U.K. .53 55N 0 10W
80 Hornslandet Pen., Swed. 61 35N 17 37E
81 Hornslet, Denmark ...56 18N 10 19E
56 Hörnum, Germany 54 44N 8 18E
114 Horoshiri Dake Mt., Japan 42 40N 142 40E
58 Horovice, Cz. 49 48N 13 53E
172 Horqueta, Paraguay .23 15S 56 55W
81 Horred, Sweden 57 22N 12 25E
164 Horse Cr., U.S.A. 41 33N 104 45W
156 Horse Is., Canada 50 15N 55 50W
143 Horse Lake, Australia 32 4S 142 5E
45 Horseleap, Ireland 53 25N 7 34W
81 Horsens, Denmark 55 52N 9 51E
81 Horsens Fd., Denmark 55 51N 10 6E
142 Horseshoe, W. Austral. 25 27S 118 31E
167 Horseshoe Dam, U.S.A. 33 45N 111 35W
39 Horsforth, Eng., U.K. 53 50N 1 39W
35 Horsham, Eng., U.K. 51 4N 0 20W
35 Horsham St. Faith, England, U.K. 52 41N 1 15E
143 Horsham, Vic., Austral. 36 44S 142 13E
58 Horsovsky Tyn, Cz. ...49 31N 12 58E
35 Horsted Keynes, England, U.K. 51 2N 0 1W
79 Horten, Norway 59 25N 10 32E
111 Hotien (Khotan), China 37 6N 79 59E
59 Hortobágy, R., Hung. 47 30N 21 6E
164 Horton, U.S.A. 39 42N 95 30W
38 Horton-in-Ribblesdale, England, U.K. 54 9N 2 19W
152 Horton R., Canada 68 47N 124 0W
81 Hörviken, Sweden 56 2N 14 44E
38 Horwich, Eng., U.K. .53 37N 2 33W
154 Horwood, L., Canada .48 01N 82 55W
127 Hosa'enna, Ethiopia . 7 30N 37 47E
106 Hosdurga, India 13 46N 76 17E
108 Hose, Mts., Malaysia . 2 5N 4 6E
104 Hoshangabad, India ...22 45N 77 45E
104 Hoshiarpur, India 31 30N 75 58E
166 Hosmer, U.S.A. 45 36N 99 29W
106 Hospet, India 15 15N 76 20E
44 Hospital, Ireland 52 30N 8 28W
64 Hospitalet, Spain 41 21N 2 6E
176 Hoste I., Chile 55 0S 69 0W
50 Hostens, France 44 30N 0 40W
81 Hostrup, Ribe, Den. .55 34N 8 22E
45 Hostwick, Scot., U.K. .60 0N 1 15W
107 Hot, Thailand 18 8N 98 29E
166 Hot Creek Ra., U.S.A. 39 0N 116 0W
165 Hot Springs, Ark, U.S.A. 34 30N 93 0W
164 Hot Springs, S.D., U.S.A. 43 25N 103 30W
82 Hotagen, L., Sweden .63 50N 14 30E
167 Hotchkiss, U.S.A. 38 55N 107 47W
82 Hoting, Sweden 64 8N 16 15E
134 Hottentotskloof, S. Afr. 33 14S 19 36E
48 Houat I., France 47 24N 2 58W
167 Houck, U.S.A. 35 15N 109 15W
49 Houdan, France 48 48N 1 35E
54 Houffalize, Belgium ...50 8N 5 48E
164 Houghton, Mich., U.S.A. 47 9N 88 39W
162 Houghton L., U.S.A. .44 20N 84 40W
39 Houghton-le-Spring, England, U.K. 54 51N 1 28W
146 Houhora, New Zealand 34 49S 173 9E
155 Houlton, U.S.A. 46 5N 68 0W
165 Houma, U.S.A. 29 35N 90 50W
134 Houmoed, S.'Africa ...29 21S 19 30E
124 Houndé, Upper Volta 11 34N 3 31W
35 Hounslow, Eng., U.K. 51 29N 0 20W
42 Hourn L., Scot., U.K. 57 7N 5 35W
156 Houston, Canada 54 25N 126 30W
165 Houston, Mo., U.S.A. 37 20N 92 0W
165 Houston, Tex., U.S.A. 29 50N 95 20W
MAP
133 Houtbosdorp, S. Africa 23 48S 29 58E
134 Houtkraal, S. Africa .30 23S 24 5E
81 Hova, Sweden 58 53N 14 14E
79 Hövag, Norway 58 10N 8 15E
111 Hovd (Jargalant), Mongolia 48 2N 91 37E
79 Hovden, Norway 59 33N 7 22E
35 Hove, England, U.K. .50 50N 0 10W
35 Hoveton, Eng., U.K. .52 45N 1 23E
79 Hovin, Norway 59 51N 9 0E
39 Hovingham, Eng., U.K. 54 10N 0 59W
81 Hovmantorp, Sweden 56 47N 15 7E
112 Hövsgöl Nuur, Mong. 51 0N 100 30E
80 Hovsta, Sweden 59 22N 15 15E
127 Howakil I., Ethiopia .15 10N 40 16E
127 Howar, W., (Shau) Sud. 17 0N 25 30E
145 Howard, Australia 25 16S 152 32E
165 Howard, Kan., U.S.A. 37 30N 96 16W
160 Howard, Penn., U.S.A. 41 0N 77 40W
164 Howard, S.D., U.S.A. 44 2N 97 30W
142 Howatharra, W. Austral. 28 29S 114 33E
39 Howden, Eng., U.K. .53 45N 0 52W
166 Howe, U.S.A. 43 48N 113 0W
143 Howe C., Australia 37 30S 150 0E
162 Howell, U.S.A. 42 38N 84 0W
161 Howick, Canada 45 10N 73 53W
135 Howick, Natal, S. Afr. 29 28S 30 14E
146 Howick, New Zealand 36 54S 174 48E
144 Howick Group, Austral. 14 20S 145 30E
155 Howley, Canada 49 12N 57 2W
42 Howmore, Scot., U.K. 57 18N 7 23W
105 Howrah, India 22 37N 88 27E
45 Howth, Ireland 53 23N 6 3W
45 Howth Hd., Ireland ...53 21N 6 0W
35 Hoxne, England, U.K. 52 22N 1 11E
56 Höxter, Germany 51 45N 9 26E
43 Hoy I., Scot., U.K. ...58 50N 3 15W
43 Hoy Sd., Scot., U.K. .58 57N 3 20W
56 Hoya, Germany 52 47N 9 10E
79 Höyanger, Norway 61 25N 6 50E
79 Höydalsmo, Norway .59 30N 8 15E
56 Hoyerswerda, Germany 51 26N 14 14E
38 Hoylake, England, U.K. 53 24N 3 11W
79 Höyland, Norway 58 50N 5 43E
62 Hoyos, Spain 40 9N 6 45W
103 Hpungan Pass, Burma 27 30N 96 55E
58 Hrádec Králové, Cz. .50 15N 15 50E
59 Hrádek, Czechoslovakia 48 46N 16 16E
59 Hranice, Czechoslovakia 49 34N 17 45E
59 Hron, R., Czechoslovakia 48 0N 18 4E
60 Hrubieszów, Poland ...50 49N 23 51E
59 Hrubý Nizky, Mts., Cz. 50 7N 17 10E
71 Hrvatska (Croatia), prov., Yugoslavia ...45 20N 16 0E
113 Hsaichwan Shan, Is., China 21 34N 112 30E
113 Hsaio Shan, Mts., China 34 0N 111 30E
103 Hsenwi, Burma 23 22N 97 55E
113 Hsinchow, China 19 37N 109 17E
113 Hsinchu, Taiwan 24 55N 121 0E
113 Hsinying, Taiwan 23 16N 120 15E
113 Hsüchang, China 34 2N 114 0E
107 Hua Hin, Thailand 12 18N 99 51E
172 Huachipato, Chile 36 45S 73 09W
174 Huacho, Peru 11 10S 77 35W
174 Huachon, Peru 10 35S 76 0W
174 Huacrachuco, Peru 8 35S 76 50W
113 Huain, China 36 26N 119 12E
174 Huaitara, Peru 13 36S 75 10W
168 Huajuapam, Mexico ...17 50N 98 0W
113 Hualien, Taiwan 24 0N 121 30E
174 Huallaga R., Peru 7 30S 76 10W
167 Hualpai Pk, Mt., U.S.A. 35 8N 113 58W
130 Huambo, dist., Angola 12 30S 16 0E
174 Huancabamba, Peru . 5 10S 79 15W
174 Huancane, Peru 15 10S 69 50W
174 Huancapi, Peru 13 25S 74 0W
174 Huancavelica, Peru ...12 50S 75 5W
174 Huancayo, Peru 12 5S 75 0W
174 Huanchaca, Bolivia ...20 15S 66 40W
174 Huanchaca, Bolivia ...14 50S 61 10W
113 Huanglui, China 18 30N 108 46E
113 Huangnipo, China 27 40N 105 10E
174 Huánuco, Peru 9 55S 76 15W
174 Huaras, Peru 9 30S 77 32W
174 Huari, Bolivia 19 0S 66 50W
174 Huarmey, Peru 10 5S 78 5W
174 Huascaran Mt., Peru . 9 0S 77 30W
172 Huasco, Chile 28 24S 71 15W
168 Huatabampo, Mexico .26 50N 109 50W
168 Huautla, Mexico 18 20N 96 50W
168 Huay Namota, Mex. .21 56N 104 30W
174 Huaylas, Peru 8 52S 77 53W
174 Huayllay, Peru 11 03S 76 21W
165 Hubbard, U.S.A. 31 50N 96 50W
106 Hubli, India 15 22N 75 15E
113 Huchow, China 30 57N 120 1E
168 Huchuetenango, Guat. 15 25N 91 30W
55 Hückelhoven-Ratheim, Germany 51 5N 6 14W
55 Hückeswagen, Germany 51 9N 7 20E
39 Hucknall, Eng., U.K. 53 3N 1 12W
MAP
127 Hudat, Ethiopia 5 20N 39 12E
39 Huddersfield, Eng., U.K. 53 38N 1 49W
126 Hudi, Sudan 17 43N 34 28E
80 Hudiksvall, Sweden ...61 43N 17 10E
157 Hudson, Canada 50 6N 92 09W
161 Hudson, Mass., U.S.A. 42 23N 71 35W
162 Hudson, Mich., U.S.A. 41 50N 84 20W
161 Hudson, N.Y., U.S.A. 42 15N 73 46W
164 Hudson, Wis., U.S.A. 44 57N 92 45W
166 Hudson, Wyo., U.S.A. 42 54N 108 37W
153 Hudson Bay, Canada .60 0N 86 0W
157 Hudson Bay, tn., Can. 52 51N 102 23W
161 Hudson Falls, U.S.A. .43 18N 73 34W
156 Hudson Hope, Canada 56 0N 121 54W
161 Hudson R., U.S.A. 41 35N 74 0W
152 Hudson Str., Canada .62 0N 70 0W
107 Hué, S. Vietnam 16 30N 107 35E
62 Huebra, R., Spain 40 54N 6 28E
78 Huedin, Rumania 46 52N 23 2E
48 Huelgoat, France 48 22N 3 46W
63 Huelma, Spain 37 39N 3 28W
63 Huelva, Spain 37 18N 6 57W
63 Huelva, R., Spain 37 46N 6 15W
172 Huentelauquen, Chile 31 38S 71 33W
65 Huércal Overa, Spain 37 23N 2 3W
172 Huerta, Sa., de la, Arg. 31 10S 67 30W
64 Huerva, R., Spain 41 13N 1 15W
64 Huesca, Spain 42 8N 0 25W
64 Huesca, prov., Spain .42 20N 0 1E
65 Huescar, Spain 37 44N 2 35W
168 Huetamo, Mexico 18 36N 100 54W
64 Huete, Spain 40 10N 2 43W
36 Hugh Town, Eng., U.K. 49 55N 6 19W
144 Hughenden, Australia 20 52S 144 10E
142 Hughes, S. Australia .30 40S 129 30E
164 Hugo, Colo., U.S.A. ...39 12N 103 27W
165 Hugo, Okla., U.S.A. ...34 0N 95 30W
165 Hugoton, U.S.A. 37 18N 101 22W
113 Huhehot, China 40 52N 111 36E
146 Huiarau Ra., N.Z. 38 45S 176 55E
168 Huichapan, Mexico ...20 24N 99 40W
174 Huila Mt., Colombia . 3 0N 76 0W
113 Huiling Shan Is., China 21 35N 111 57E
112 Huinan, China 42 40N 126 5E
172 Huinca Renanco, Arg. 34 51S 64 22W
112 Huinung, China 39 0N 106 45E
146 Huiroa, New Zealand .39 15S 174 30E
100 Huiya, Saudi Arabia .24 40N 49 15E
103 Hukawng Val., Burma 26 30N 96 30E
113 Hukow, China 29 38N 116 25E
127 Hukuma, Sudan 14 55N 36 2E
127 Hula, Ethiopia 6 33N 38 30E
100 Hulaifa, Saudi Arabia 25 58N 41 0E
112 Hulan, China 46 0N 126 44E
111 Huld, Mongolia 45 24N 105 29E
98 Hulda, Israel 31 50N 34 51E
112 Hulin, China 45 45N 133 0E
154 Hull, Quebec, Canada 45 20N 75 40W
39 Hull, England, U.K. .53 45N 0 20W
39 Hull R., Eng., U.K. ...53 55N 0 23W
34 Hullavington, Eng., U.K. 51 31N 2 9W
55 Hullern, Germany 51 45N 7 17E
38 Hulme End, Eng., U.K. 53 8N 1 51W
55 Hüls, Germany 51 22N 6 28E
54 Hulst, Netherlands ...51 17N 4 2E
81 Hultsfred, Sweden 57 30N 15 50E
112 Huma, China 51 44N 126 42E
172 Humahuaca, Argentina 23 10S 65 25W
174 Humaitá, Brazil 7 35S 62 40W
172 Humaita, Paraguay ...27 02S 58 31W
134 Humansdorp, S. Africa 34 2S 24 46E
39 Humber, R., Eng., U.K. 53 42N 0 20W
160 Humberstone, Canada 42 53N 79 16W
165 Humble, U.S.A. 29 59N 95 10W
157 Humboldt, Canada 52 15N 105 9W
164 Humboldt, Iowa, U.S.A. 42 42N 94 15W
163 Humboldt, Tenn., U.S.A. 35 50N 88 55W
14 Humboldt Gl., Green .79 30N 63 0W
166 Humboldt, R., U.S.A. 40 55N 116 0W
147 Humbolt Mts., N.Z. ...44 30S 168 15E
143 Hume L., Vic., Austral. 36 0S 147 0E
59 Humenné, Cz. 48 55N 21 50E
167 Humphreys Pk, Mt., U.S.A. 35 24N 111 38W
58 Humpolec, Cz. 49 31N 15 20E
38 Humshaugh, Eng., U.K. 55 3N 2 8W
143 Humula, Australia 35 30S 147 46E
23 Hun, Libya 29 2N 16 0E
82 Huna Floi, Iceland 65 50N 21 0W
113 Hunan, prov., China .27 30N 111 30E
112 Hunchun, China 42 49N 130 31E
81 Hundested, Denmark .55 58N 11 52E
37 Hundred House, Wales, United Kingdom 52 11N 3 17W
80 Hundshögen, Mt., Swed. 62 57N 13 46E
78 Hunedoara, Rumania 45 40N 22 50E
78 Hunedoara, Reg.,Rum. 45 45N 23 00E
56 Hünfeld, Germany 50 40N 9 47E
113 Hung Ho, R., China ...33 20N 115 0E
59 Hungary, rep., Europe 47 20N 19 20E
19 Hungary, Plain of, Eur. 47 0N 20 0E
MAP
34 Hungerford, Eng., U.K. 51 25N 1 30W
145 Hungerford, Queensland, Australia 28 58S 144 24E
113 Hunghu (Sinti), China 29 49N 113 30E
113 Hungkiang, China 27 0N 109 49E
112 Hungnam, N. Korea .39 59N 127 40E
113 Hungshui Ho, China .24 20N 107 10E
112 Hungting, China 36 11N 111 41E
113 Hungtze Hu, China ...33 20N 118 35E
124 Huni Valley, Ghana ... 5 33N 1 56W
39 Hunmanby, Eng., U.K. 54 12N 0 19W
134 Huns Mts., S.W. Africa 27 58S 17 5E
57 Hunsrück Mts., Ger. .50 0N 7 30E
35 Hunstanton, Eng., U.K. 52 57N 0 30E
106 Hunsur, India 12 16N 76 16E
56 Hunte R., Germany ...52 47N 8 28E
147 Hunter, New Zealand 44 36S 171 2E
164 Hunter, N.D., U.S.A. .47 12N 97 17W
161 Hunter, N.Y., U.S.A. .42 13N 74 13W
156 Hunter I., Canada 51 55N 128 0W
145 Hunter Is., Australia .40 30S 144 46E
147 Hunter Mts., N.Z. 45 43S 167 25E
143 Hunter R., New Zealand 44 15S 169 29E
147 Hunter R., New Zealand 44 15S 169 29E
143 Hunter Ra., Australia 32 45S 150 15E
147 Hunter Hill, The, N.Z. 44 26S 170 46E
40 Hunterston, Scot., U.K. 55 43N 4 55W
132 Hunter's Road, Rhodesia 19 9S 29 49E
145 Hunterton, Australia .26 12S 148 30E
146 Hunterville, N.Z. 39 56S 175 35E
162 Huntingburg, U.S.A. .38 20N 86 58W
154 Huntingdon, Canada .45 10N 74 10W
35 Huntingdon, Eng., U.K. 52 20N 0 11W
161 Huntingdon, N.Y., U.S.A. 40 52N 73 25W
160 Huntingdon, Pa., U.S.A. 40 28N 78 1W
155 Huntingdon I., Canada 53 48N 56 45W
39 Huntington, Eng., U.K. 54 0N 1 4W
35 Huntingdonshire & Peterborough, Co., U.K. 52 23N 0 10W
166 Huntington, Id., USA 44 22N 117 21W
162 Huntington, Ind., U.S.A. 40 52N 85 30W
166 Huntington, Ut., USA 39 24N 111 1W
162 Huntington W. Va., U.S.A. 38 20N 82 30W
167 Huntington Beach, U.S.A. 34 40N 118 0W
167 Huntington Park, U.S.A. 34 58N 118 15W
146 Huntly, New Zealand 37 34S 175 11E
43 Huntly, Scot., U.K. ...57 27N 2 48W
154 Huntsville, Canada 45 20N 79 14W
163 Huntsville, Ala., U.S.A. 34 45N 86 35W
165 Huntsville, Tex., U.S.A. 30 50N 95 35W
132 Hunyani Dams. Rhod. 18 0S 31 10E
132 Hunyani R. & Dam, Rhodesia 18 0S 31 10E
144 Huon Gulf, N.E.E. Guin. 7 0S 147 30E
145 Huonville, Australia ...43 0S 147 5E
113 Hupei, prov., China ...31 5N 113 5E
59 Hurbanovo, Cz. 47 51N 18 11E
160 Hurd C., Canada 45 15N 81 40W
78 Hurezani, Rumania ...44 49N 23 40E
126 Hurghada, Egypt 27 15N 33 50E
167 Hurley, N. Mex., U.S.A. 32 45N 108 7W
164 Hurley, Wis., U.S.A. .46 26N 90 10W
40 Hurlford, Scot., U.K. .55 35N 4 29W
43 Hurliness, Scot., U.K. 58 47N 3 15W
160 Huron, Ohio, U.S.A. .41 22N 82 34W
164 Huron, S.D., U.S.A. ...44 30N 98 20W
160 Huron, L., Can.-U.S.A. 45 0N 83 0W
167 Hurricane, U.S.A. 37 10N 113 12W
34 Hursley, Eng., U.K. ...51 1N 1 23W
34 Hurstbourne Tarrant, England, U.K. 51 17N 1 27W
143 Hurstbridge, Australia 37 40S 145 10E
35 Hurstpierpoint, England, U.K. 50 56N 0 11W
55 Hürth, Germany 50 52N 6 51E
79 Hurum, Buskend, Nor. 59 36N 10 23E
79 Hurum, Opp., Nor. ...61 9N 8 46E
147 Hurunui R., N.Z. 42 48S 172 25E
81 Hurup, Tisted, Den. ...56 46N 8 25E
81 Husaby, Sweden 58 35N 13 25E
82 Husavik, Iceland 66 3N 17 13W
35 Husband's Bosworth, England, U.K. 52 27N 1 3W
78 Husi, Rumania 46 41N 28 7E
42 Husinish Pt., Scot., U.K. 57 59N 7 6W
81 Huskvarna, Sweden ...57 47N 14 15E
98 Husn, Jordan 32 29N 35 52E
79 Husöy, Norway 61 3N 4 44E
98 Hussein (Allenby) Br., Jordan 31 53N 35 33E
59 Hustopece, Cz. 48 57N 16 43E
56 Husum, Germany 54 27N 9 3E
MAP
80 Husum, Sweden 63 21N 19 12E
112 Hutag Mongolia 49 25N 102 34E
167 Hutch Mt., U.S.A. 34 55N 111 26W
134 Hutchinson, S. Africa 31 30S 23 9E
165 Hutchinson, Kan., U.S.A. 38 3N 97 59W
164 Hutchinson, Minn, U.S.A. 44 50N 94 22W
112 Huto Ho, R., China ...38 30N 113 45E
58 Huttenberg, Austria ...46 56N 14 33E
54 Hüttental, Germany .50 53N 8 1E
165 Huttig, U.S.A. 33 5N 92 10W
142 Hutton Ra., W. Austral. 24 45S 124 30E
98 Huwwara, Jordan 32 9N 35 15E
54 Huy, Belgium 50 31N 5 15E
38 Huyton, England, U.K. 53 25N 2 52W
79 Hvaler, Norway 59 4N 10 59E
71 Hvar, Yugoslavia 43 10N 16 45E
71 Hvar, I., Yugoslavia .43 11N 16 28E
71 Hvarski Kanal, Y.-slav. 43 15N 16 35E
79 Hvitsten, Norway 59 35N 10 42E
112 Hwachwan, China 47 1N 130 50E
113 Hwahsien, China 34 26N 109 45E
113 Hwai Ho, China 32 20N 114 30E
113 Hwainan, China 32 44N 117 1E
113 Hwaiyang, China 33 50N 115 2E
112 Hwan Ho, China 37 10N 117 30E
112 Hwang Ho., R., China 37 15N 117 40E
113 Hwangan, China 31 30N 114 40E
113 Hwangshih, China 30 27N 115 0E
113 Hwangyen, China 28 34N 121 12E
112 Hwanjen, China 41 24N 125 26E
112 Hwateh, China 41 58N 113 58E
112 Hwatien, China 43 0N 126 52E
113 Hwelan, China 25 2N 118 56E
113 Hweichang, China 25 33N 115 41E
112 Hweihsien, China 35 30N 113 46E
113 Hweilai, China 23 0N 116 15E
112 Hweining, China 35 45N 105 0E
111 Hweitseh, China 26 32N 103 6E
112 Hwohsien, China 36 30N 111 42E
113 Hwokiu, China 32 23N 116 15E
164 Hyannis, U.S.A. 42 3N 101 45W
162 Hyattsville, U.S.A. 38 59N 76 55W
80 Hybo, Sweden 61 49N 16 15E
156 Hydaburg, Alaska, U.S.A. 55 15N 132 45W
38 Hyde, England, U.K. 53 26N 2 6W
147 Hyde, New Zealand ...45 18S 170 16E
142 Hyden, W. Australia .32 24S 118 46E
106 Hyderabad, India 17 10N 78 29E
104 Hyderabad, W. Pak. .25 23N 68 36E
104 Hyderabad, div., Pak. 25 3N 68 24E
51 Hyères, France 43 8N 6 9E
51 Hyères Is., d', France 43 0N 6 28E
156 Hyland R., Canada 60 30N 128 20W
145 Hyland Post, Canada .57 40N 128 10W
79 Hylestad, Norway 59 6N 7 29E
79 Hyllested, Denmark ...56 17N 10 46E
81 Hyltebruk, Sweden ...56 59N 13 15E
166 Hyndman Pk., U.S.A. 44 4N 114 0W
42 Hynish, Scotland, U.K. 56 27N 6 54W
40 Hynish B., Scot., UK 56 29N 6 40W
114 Hyogo, Pref., Japan ...35 15N 135 0E
166 Hyrum, U.S.A. 41 35N 111 56W
166 Hysham, U.S.A. 46 21N 107 11W
35 Hythe, Kent, Eng., U.K. 51 4N 1 5E
83 Hyvinkää, Finland 60 38N 25 0E

I

122 I-n-Tabedog, Mali 19 51N 1 1E
122 Iabès, Erg., Algeria ...27 30N 2 2W
174 Iaco, R., Brazil 10 25S 70 30W
78 Ialomița, Reg., Rumania 44 20N 27 30E
44 Iar Connacht, dist., Ire. 53 20N 9 20W
78 Iara, Rumania 46 31N 23 35E
78 Iași (Jassy), Rumania 47 10N 27 40E
78 Iași, Reg., Rumania ...47 10N 27 30E
153 Iaucdjouac, (Port Harrison), Canada .58 25N 78 15W
174 Iauarete, Colombia 0 30N 69 5W
109 Iba, Philippines 15 22N 120 0E
125 Ibadan, Nigeria 7 22N 3 58E
174 Ibagué, Colombia 4 27N 73 14W
76 Iballe, Albania 42 12N 20 0E
78 Ibanești, Rumania 46 45N 24 50E
74 Ibar, R., Yugoslavia .43 15N 20 40E
114 Ibaraki, Pref., Japan .36 10N 140 10E
174 Ibarra, Ecuador 0 21N 78 7W
127 Ibba, Sudan 4 49N 29 2E
127 Ibba, R., Sudan 53 0N 28 55E
56 Ibbenbüren, Germany 52 16N 7 41E
18 Iberian Peninsula, Eur. 40 0N 5 0W
154 Iberville, Canada 5 19N 73 17W
154 Iberville, Lac d', Can. 55 40N 73 30W
125 Ibi, Nigeria 8 15N 9 50E
175 Ibiá, Brazil 19 30S 46 30W
172 Ibicuy, Argentina 33 55S 59 10W
175 Ibiraçu, Brazil 19 50S 40 30W
65 Ibiza (Iviza) I., Spain 39 0N 1 30E
131 Ibo, Mozambique 12 22S 40 30E
109 Ibonma, Indonesia 3 22S 133 31E
175 Ibotirama, Brazil 12 13S 43 12W
76 Ibriktepe, Turkey 41 2N 26 33E
126 Ibshawâi, Egypt 29 21N 30 40E
34 Ibstock, Eng., U.K. ...52 42N 1 23W
109 Ibu, Indonesia 1 35N 127 25E
56 Iburg, Germany 52 10N 8 3E
132 Ibwe Munyama, Zam. 16 5S 28 31E
174 Icá, Peru 14 0S 75 30W
174 Iça R., Brazil 2 55S 69 0W

MAP
174 Içana, Brazil ... 0 21N 67 19W
174 Icana, R., Brazil ... 1 25N 67 55W
82 Iceland, I., Atlantic Oc. ... 65 0N 19 0W
91 Icha, U.S.S.R. ... 55 30N 156 0E
113 Ichang, China ... 30 48N 111 29E
106 Inchapuram, India ... 19 10N 84 40E
55 Ichendorf, Germany ... 50 56N 6 41E
114 Ichiharan, Japan ... 35 45N 39 42E
114 Ichikawa, Japan ... 35 45N 139 50E
174 Ichilo, R., Bolivia ... 16 30S 64 45W
114 Ichinomiya, Japan ... 35 20N 136 50E
86 Ichnya, U.S.S.R. ... 50 50N 32 20E
122 Icht, Morocco ... 29 6N 8 54W
113 Ichun, China ... 27 51N 114 12E
112 Ichun, China ... 35 24N 109 9E
112 Ichun, China ... 47 42N 129 8E
113 Ichung, China ... 25 30N 112 29E
112 Ichwan, China ... 36 9N 109 58E
14 Icy C., Alaska, U.S.A. 70 25N 162 0W
157 Icy Str., Alaska, U.S.A. ... 58 20N 135 30W
164 Ida Grove, U.S.A. ... 42 20N 95 25W
142 Ida Valley, W. Australia ... 28 42S 120 29E
165 Idabel, U.S.A. ... 33 53N 94 50W
125 Idah, Nigeria ... 6 10N 6 40E
166 Idaho, st., U.S.A. ... 44 10N 114 0W
166 Idaho City, U.S.A. ... 43 50N 115 52W
166 Idaho Falls, U.S.A. ... 43 30N 112 10W
166 Idaho Springs, U.S.A. 39 49N 105 30W
62 Idanha-a-Nova, Port. 39 50N 7 15W
57 Idar Oberstein, Ger. ... 49 43N 7 19E
125 Idanre, Nigeria ... 7 8N 5 5E
121 'Idd el Ghanam, Sudan ... 11 30N 24 25E
99 Iddan, Somali Rep. ... 6 10N 49 5E
123 Idehan, des., Libya ... 27 10N 11 30E
123 Idehan Marzuq, Libya 24 50N 13 51E
123 Idelès, Algeria ... 23 58N 5 53E
109 Idenburg R., Indon. ... 3 0S 138 5E
126 Idfu, Egypt ... 25 0N 32 49E
77 Idhi Oros, Mt., Cyprus ... 35 15N 24 45E
77 Idhra, & I., Greece ... 37 20N 23 28E
108 Idi, Indonesia ... 4 55N 97 45E
130 Idiofa, Congo ... 4 55S 19 42E
80 Idkerberget, Sweden .60 22N 15 15E
39 Idle, England, U.K. ... 53 50N 1 45W
34 Idmiston, Eng., U.K. .51 8N 1 43W
98 Idna, Jordan ... 31 34N 34 58E
71 Idrija, Yugoslavia ... 46 0N 14 5E
86 Idritsa, U.S.S.R. ... 56 25N 28 57E
57 Idstein, Germany ... 50 13N 8 17E
35 Idsworth, Eng., U.K. .50 56N 0 56W
135 Idutywa, S. Africa ... 32 8S 28 18E
54 Ieper (Ypres), Belgium ... 50 51N 2 53E
77 Ierápetra, Greece ... 35 0N 25 44E
76 Ierissós, Greece ... 40 22N 23 52E
76 Ierissóu Kólpos, G., Gr. ... 40 27N 23 57E
72 Ierzu, Italy ... 39 48N 9 32E
71 Iesi, Italy ... 43 32N 13 12E
65 Ifach, Punta, Spain ... 38 38N 0 5E
129 Ifanadiana, Malagasy Republic ... 21 29S 47 39E
125 Ife, Nigeria ... 7 30N 4 31E
125 Iférouane, Niger ... 19 5N 8 35E
125 Ifon, Nigeria ... 6 58N 5 40E
175 Igarapava, Brazil ... 20 0S 48 0W
175 Igarape Acu, Brazil ... 1 4S 47 33W
91 Igarka, U.S.S.R. ... 67 30N 87 20E
106 Igatpuri, India ... 19 40N 73 35E
125 Igbetti, Nigeria ... 8 44N 4 8E
125 Igbo-Ora, Nigeria ... 7 10N 3 15E
125 Igboho, Nigeria ... 8 40N 3 50E
80 Iggesund, Sweden ... 61 39N 17 10E
122 Igherm, Morocco ... 30 7N 8 18W
122 Ighil, Djebel, Morocco 31 37N 6 31W
122 Ighil Izane, Algeria ... 35 44N 0 49E
122 Iglene, Algeria ... 22 57N 4 58E
72 Iglesias, Italy ... 39 19N 8 27E
122 Igli, Algeria ... 30 25N 2 12W
122 Igma, Algeria ... 29 9N 6 11W
126 'Igma, Gebel el, Egypt ... 28 55N 34 0E
87 Igoshevo, U.S.S.R. ... 59 25N 42 35E
76 Igoumenítsa, Greece ... 39 32N 20 18E
154 Ignace, Canada ... 49 30N 91 40W
173 Iguaçu, R., Brazil ... 25 30S 53 10W
168 Iguala, Mexico ... 18 20N 99 40W
64 Igualada, Spain ... 41 37N 1 37E
173 Iguape R., Brazil ... 24 40S 48 0W
173 Iguatú, Brazil ... 6 20S 39 25W
128 Iguéla, Gabon ... 2 0S 9 16E
125 Igumale, Nigeria ... 6 47N 7 55E
125 Ihiala, Nigeria ... 5 40N 6 55E
113 Ihing, China ... 31 21N 119 51E
129 Ihosy, Malagasy Rep. 22 24S 46 8E
112 Ihsien, China ... 41 45N 121 3E
113 Ihwang, China ... 27 30N 116 2E
14 Iida, Japan ... 35 35N 138 0E
182 Iisalmi, Finland ... 63 38N 27 10E
112 Iizuka, Japan ... 33 38N 130 42E
125 Ijebu-Igbo, Nigeria ... 6 56N 4 1E
125 Ijebu-Ode, Nigeria ... 6 47N 3 52E
55 IJssel, R., Netherlands ... 51 54N 4 38E
54 IJsselmeer, Netherlands ... 52 45N 5 20E
54 IJmuiden, Netherlands ... 52 28N 4 35E
47 Ikamatua, New Zealand ... 42 15S 171 41E
77 Ikaria, I., Greece ... 37 35N 26 10E
125 Ikare, Nigeria ... 7 18N 5 40E
81 Ikast, Denmark ... 56 8N 9 10E
125 Ikeja, Nigeria ... 6 28N 3 45E
130 Ikela, Congc ... 1 0S 23 35E
125 Ikerre, Nigeria ... 7 25N 5 19E
78 Ikhtiman, Bulg. ... 42 23N 23 55E
114 Iki, I., Japan ... 33 45N 129 42E
131 Ikimba L., Tanzania . 1 30S 31 20E
125 Ikire, Nigeria ... 7 10N 4 15E
125 Ikirun, Nigeria ... 7 54N 4 40E
125 Ikole, Nigeria ... 7 40N 5 37E
125 Ikom, Nigeria ... 6 0N 8 42E
125 Ikot Ekpene, Nigeria . 5 12N 7 40E
125 Ila, Nigeria ... 8 0N 4 51E
105 Ilam, Nepal ... 26 58N 87 58E
112 Ilan, China ... 46 14N 129 33E
54 Ilaomita, R., Rumania ... 44 47N 27 0E
125 Ilaro Agege, Nigeria ... 6 53N 3 3E
106 Ilayangudi, India ... 9 34N 78 37E
144 Ilbilbie, Australia ... 21 45S 149 20E
36 Ilchester, Eng., U.K. .51 0N 2 41W
157 Ile a la Crosse, L., Can. ... 55 30N 108 0W
48 Ile Bouchard, L', Fr. .47 7N 0 26E
49 Ile de France, Prov., Fr. ... 49 0N 2 20E
130 Ilebo, Congo ... 4 17S 20 47E
84 Ilek, R., U.S.S.R. ... 51 0N 51 10E
44 Ilen R., Ireland ... 51 38N 9 19W
125 Ilero, Nigeria ... 8 0N 3 20E
125 Ilesha, Nigeria ... 7 37N 4 40E
125 Ilesha, Nigeria ... 8 57N 3 28E
78 Ilfov, Reg., Rumania .44 10N 26 10E
144 Ilfracombe, Australia .23 30S 144 30E
36 Ilfracombe, Eng., U.K. ... 51 13N 4 8W
63 Ilha Berlenga, Port. ... 39 25N 9 30W
62 Ilhavo, Portugal ... 40 33N 8 43W
175 Ilhéus, Brazil ... 15 0S 39 10W
90 Ili, U.S.S.R. ... 44 10N 77 20E
78 Ilia, Rumania ... 45 57N 22 40E
77 Ilia, Pref., Greece ... 37 45N 21 35E
90 Ilich, U.S.S.R. ... 41 0N 68 10E
172 Ilico, Chile ... 34 50S 72 20W
164 Iliff, U.S.A. ... 40 50N 103 3W
77 Iliki, L., Greece ... 38 24N 23 15E
76 Iliodhrómia, I., Greece ... 39 12N 23 50E
161 Ilion, N.Y., U.S.A. ... 43 0N 75 3W
71 Ilirska Bistrica, Y.-slav. ... 45 34N 14 14E
106 Ilkal, India ... 15 57N 76 8E
39 Ilkeston, Eng., U.K. .52 59N 1 19W
112 Ilkhuri Shan, Mts., China ... 51 30N 124 0E
38 Ilkley, England, U.K. 53 56N 1 49W
109 Illana B., Philippines . 7 40N 124 0E
172 Illapel, Chile ... 32 0S 71 10W
98 'Illar, Jordan ... 32 23N 35 7E
48 Ille-et-Vilaine, dépt., Fr. ... 48 10N 1 30W
57 Iller, R., Germany ... 47 53N 10 10E
62 Illescas, Spain ... 40 8N 3 51W
99 Illig, Somali Rep. ... 7 47N 49 45E
174 Illimani Mt., Bolivia ... 16 30S 67 50W
159 Illinois, st. & R., U.S.A. ... 40 15N 89 30W
123 Illizi, Algeria ... 26 31N 8 32E
63 Illora, Spain ... 37 17N 3 53W
135 Illovo Beach, S. Africa ... 30 7S 30 51E
86 Ilmen L., U.S.S.R. ... 58 15N 31 10E
56 Ilmenau, Germany ... 50 41N 10 55E
36 Ilminster, Eng., U.K. 50 55N 2 56W
174 Ilo, Peru ... 17 40S 71 20W
125 Ilobu, Nigeria ... 7 45N 4 25E
109 Iloilo, Philippines ... 10 45N 122 33E
74 Ilok, Yugoslavia ... 45 15N 19 20E
125 Ilora, Nigeria ... 7 45N 3 50E
125 Ilorin, Nigeria ... 8 30N 4 35E
87 Ilovatka, U.S.S.R. ... 50 30N 46 50E
87 Ilovinskaya, U.S.S.R. 49 15N 44 2E
89 Ilovlya, R., U.S.S.R. .49 38N 44 20E
127 Ilubabor, prov., Ethiopia ... 7 25N 35 0E
86 Ilukste, U.S.S.R. ... 55 55N 26 20E
78 Ilva Mică, Rumania ... 47 17N 24 40E
109 Ilwaki, Indonesia ... 7 55S 126 30E
88 Ilyichevsk, U.S.S.R. ... 46 10N 30 35E
114 Imabari, Japan ... 34 4N 133 0E
122 Imadahane, Morocco .32 8N 7 0W
91 Iman, U.S.S.R. ... 45 50N 133 40E
84 Imandra L., U.S.S.R. 67 45N 33 0E
114 Imari, Japan ... 33 15N 129 52E
126 Imasa, Sudan ... 18 0N 36 12E
76 Imathía, Pref., Greece 40 30N 22 15E
126 Imbaba, Egypt ... 30 5N 31 12E
166 Imbler, U.S.A. ... 45 31N 118 0W
76 Imbros & I., see Imroz, Turkey ... 40 10N 26 0E
174 Imeri, Serra, Ven. ... 0 50N 65 25W
168 Infernillo Dam, Mexico ... 18 9N 102 9E
127 Imi (Hinna), Ethiopia 6 35N 42 30E
122 Imi n'Tanout, Morocco ... 31 15N 8 54W
112 Imienpo, China ... 45 0N 128 16E
89 Imishly, U.S.S.R. ... 39 49N 48 4E
122 Imiteg, Morocco ... 29 43N 8 10W
166 Imlay, U.S.A. ... 40 45N 118 9W
160 Imlay City, U.S.A. ... 43 0N 83 2W
135 Immigrant, S. Africa .29 5S 25 36E
39 Immingham, Eng., U.K. ... 53 37N 0 12W
163 Immokalee, U.S.A. ... 26 25N 81 20W
71 Imola, Italy ... 44 20N 11 42E
71 Imotski, Yugoslavia ... 43 27N 17 21E
123 Imoudait, W., Algeria 28 37N 9 30E
135 Impendle, Natal, S. Afr. ... 29 37S 29 55E
175 Imperatriz, Brazil ... 15 30S 47 20W
70 Imperia, Italy ... 43 52N 8 0E
157 Imperial, Canada ... 51 21N 105 28W
167 Imperial, Calif., U.S.A. ... 32 52N 115 34W
64 Imperial, Neb., U.S.A. 40 38N 101 39W
67 Imperial Dam, U.S.A. .32 50N 114 30W
130 Impfondo, Congo (Fr.) 1 40N 18 0E
103 Imphal, India ... 24 15N 94 0E
76 Imroz & I., Turkey ... 40 10N 26 0E
58 Imst, Austria ... 47 15N 10 44E
109 Imuruan B., Philippines ... 10 40N 119 10E
135 Imvani, C. Prov., S. Afr. ... 32 1S 27 3E
98 'Imwas, Jordan ... 31 51N 34 59E
123 In-Azaoua, Niger ... 20 45N 7 31E
122 In Belbel, Algeria ... 27 55N 1 12E
122 In Echaie, Mali ... 20 10N 2 5W
122 In Rhar, Algeria ... 27 10N 1 59E
114 Ina, Japan ... 35 50N 138 0E
44 Inagh, Ireland ... 52 53N 9 11W
147 Inangahua Junc., N.Z. ... 41 52S 171 59E
174 Inapari, Peru ... 11 0S 69 40W
82 Inari, Finland ... 68 54N 27 5E
82 Inari L., Finland ... 69 0N 28 0E
114 Inawashiro-ko, L., Japan ... 37 28N 140 2E
64 Inca, Spain ... 39 43N 2 54E
172 Inca de Oro, Chile ... 26 43S 70 0W
172 Incaguasi, Chile ... 29 12S 71 5W
38 Ince, England, U.K. .53 32N 2 38W
44 Inch, Tipperary, Ireland ... 52 42N 8 8W
44 Inch Br., Ireland ... 52 49N 9 6W
42 Inchard, Loch, Scot., U.K. ... 58 28N 5 2W
41 Inchcape Rock, Scotland, U.K. ... 56 26N 2 24W
44 Inchigeelagh, Ireland .51 50N 9 8W
41 Inchkeith, I., Scot., U.K. ... 56 2N 3 8W
41 Inchnadamph, Scotland, U.K. ... 58 9N 5 0W
112 Inchon, S. Korea ... 37 32N 126 45E
41 Inchture, Scot., U.K. .56 26N 3 8W
62 Incio, Spain ... 42 39N 7 21W
133 Incomtai R., Mozam. .25 15S 32 35E
51 Incudine, l', Mte., Fr. 41 50N 9 12E
40 Indaal L., Scot., U.K. 55 44N 6 20W
80 Indalsälven, L., Swed. 63 15N 15 15E
80 Indalsälven, R., Swed. 62 36N 17 0E
103 Indaw, Burma ... 24 15N 96 5E
55 Inde R., Germany ... 50 43N 6 11E
167 Independence, Calif., U.S.A. ... 36 51N 118 7W
164 Independence, Iowa, U.S.A. ... 42 27N 91 52W
165 Independence, Kan., U.S.A. ... 37 10N 95 50W
164 Independence, Mo., U.S.A. ... 39 3N 94 25W
166 Independence, Ore., U.S.A. ... 44 53N 123 6W
14 Independence B., Green. ... 82 30N 25 0W
166 Independence Mts., U.S.A. ... 41 30N 116 2W
78 Independența, Rum. .45 25N 27 42E
108 Inderapura, Indonesia 2 5S 101 2E
89 Inderborskiy, U.S.S.R. ... 48 30N 51 42E
102 India (Bharat), rep., Asia ... 23 0N 77 30E
167 India, U.S.A. ... 33 46N 116 15W
157 Indian Head, Canada .50 30N 103 35W
155 Indian House L., Can. 56 30N 64 30W
11 Indian Ocean ... 5 0S 75 0E
160 Indiana, U.S.A. ... 40 38N 79 9W
162 Indiana, st., U.S.A. ... 40 0N 86 0W
162 Indianapolis, U.S.A. ... 39 42N 86 10W
164 Indianola, Iowa, U.S.A. ... 41 20N 93 38W
165 Indianola, Miss., U.S.A. ... 33 27N 90 40W
84 Indiga, U.S.S.R. ... 67 50N 48 50E
91 Indigirka R., U.S.S.R. 69 0N 147 0E
74 Indija, Yugoslavia ... 45 6N 20 7E
108 Indonesia, rep., Asia . 5 0S 115 0E
106 Indore, India ... 22 42N 75 53E
109 Indramaju, tn. & C., Indonesia ... 6 21S 108 20E
106 Indravati R., India ... 19 0N 81 15E
49 Indre, dépt., France ... 47 12N 1 39E
48 Indre R., France ... 47 2N 1 8E
48 Indre-et-Loire, dépt, Fr. ... 47 12N 0 40E
79 Indre Söndeled, Norway ... 58 46N 9 5E
104 Indus, R., W. Pakistan ... 28 40N 70 10E
135 Indwe, C. Prov., S. Afr. ... 31 27S 27 22E
100 Inebolu, Turkey ... 41 55N 33 40E
74 Ineu, Rumania ... 46 26N 21 51E
65 Infantes, Spain ... 38 43N 3 1W
62 Infiesto, Spain ... 43 21N 5 21W
125 In-Gall, Mali ... 16 51N 7 1E
35 Ingatestone, Eng., U.K. ... 51 40N 0 23W
143 Ingebyra, Australia ... 36 39S 148 31E
130 Ingende, Congo ... 0 12S 18 57E
160 Ingersoll, Canada ... 43 4N 80 55W
81 Ingesvang, Denmark .56 10N 9 20E
144 Ingham, Australia ... 18 43S 146 10E
38 Ingleborough, mt., England, U.K. ... 54 11N 2 23W
14 Inglefield G., Greenland ... 77 0N 67 0W
143 Inglega, Australia ... 31 20S 147 50E
38 Ingleton, England, U.K. ... 54 9N 2 29W
143 Inglewood, Australia .36 29S 143 53E
145 Inglewood, Australia .28 25S 151 8E
146 Inglewood, New Zealand ... 39 9S 174 14E
167 Inglewood, U.S.A. ... 33 58N 118 27W
135 Ingogo, Natal, S. Africa ... 27 32S 29 56W
57 Ingolstadt, Germany .48 45N 11 26W
166 Ingomar, U.S.A. ... 46 43N 107 37E
155 Ingonish, Canada ... 46 42N 60 18E
88 Ingul R., U.S.S.R. ... 47 30N 32 15E
88 Ingulets, R., U.S.S.R. 47 20N 33 20E
89 Inguri, R., U.S.S.R. ... 42 58N 42 17E
135 Ingwavuma, S. Africa 27 8S 32 2E
132 Ingwe, Zambia ... 13 0S 26 13E
133 Inhaca I., Mozambique ... 26 1S 32 57E
132 Inhacro, Mozambique 16 45S 24 10E
132 Inhambane, Mozambique ... 23 54S 35 30E
132 Inhambane, dist., Mozambique ... 22 30S 34 20E
132 Inhaminga, Mozam. ... 18 26S 35 0E
129 Inharrime & R., Mozambique ... 24 30S 35 0E
65 Iniesta, Spain ... 39 27N 1 45W
113 Ining, Kwangsi-Chuang A.R., China ... 25 8N 109 57E
111 Ining (Kuldja), Sinkiang-Uigur, China ... 43 57N 81 20E
174 Inirida R., Colombia . 3 0N 69 0W
46 Inisbrush, N. Ire., U.K. ... 54 52N 6 32W
44 Inishannon, Ireland ... 51 46N 8 40W
44 Inishark, Ireland ... 53 36N 10 17W
45 Inishark I., Ireland ... 53 38N 10 17W
46 Inishbofin I., Ireland .55 10N 8 10W
45 Inishbofin I., Ireland .53 35N 10 12W
44 Inisheer, Ireland ... 53 3N 9 32W
46 Inishfree B., Ireland .55 4N 8 20W
45 Inishkea Is., Ireland .54 8N 10 10W
44 Inishmaan I., Ireland 53 5N 9 35W
44 Inishmore, I., Ireland 53 8N 9 45W
46 Inishmurray I., Ireland ... 54 26N 8 40W
46 Inishowen Hd., Ire. ... 55 14N 6 56W
46 Inishowen, Pen., Ire. .55 14N 7 15W
44 Inishtooskert I., Ireland ... 52 10N 10 35W
40 Inishtrahull I., Ireland ... 54 26N 7 12W
45 Inishturk I., Ireland .53 42N 10 8W
44 Inishvickillane, Ireland ... 52 3N 10 37W
45 Inistioge, Ireland ... 52 30N 7 5W
145 Injune, Australia ... 25 46S 148 32E
34 Inkberrow, Eng., U.K. ... 52 13N 1 59W
127 Inkinni, Ethiopia ... 8 55N 37 37E
130 Inkisi, R., Congo ... 5 20S 15 10E
156 Inklin, Tn. and R., Can. ... 58 50N 132 30W
166 Inkom, U.S.A. ... 42 51N 112 7W
107 Inle Lake, Burma ... 20 30N 96 58E
145 Innamincka, S. Austral. ... 27 44S 140 46E
40 Innellan, Scot., U.K. .55 54N 4 58W
103 Inle L., Burma ... 20 30N 96 50E
42 Inner Hebrides, Is., Scotland, U.K. ... 58 0N 7 0W
42 Inner Sound, Skye, Scotland, U.K. ... 57 30N 5 55W
112 Inner Mongolia, Auto. Reg., China ... 44 50N 117 40E
160 Innerkip, Canada ... 43 12N 80 41W
41 Innerleithen, Scot., U.K. ... 55 37N 3 4W
154 Innetalling I., Canada 55 50N 79 5W
45 Innfield, Ireland ... 53 25N 6 50W
46 Inniscrone, Ireland ... 54 13N 69 0W
144 Innisfail, Australia ... 17 33S 146 5E
156 Innisfail, Canada ... 52 0N 114 0W
46 Inniskeen, Ireland ... 54 0N 6 35W
58 Innsbruck, Austria ... 47 16N 11 23E
130 Inongo, Congo ... 1 55S 18 30E
60 Inowroclaw, Poland ... 52 50N 18 20E
174 Inquisivi, Bolivia ... 16 50S 66 45W
122 In Salah, Algeria ... 27 10N 2 32E
43 Insch, Scot., U.K. ... 57 20N 2 39W
103 Insein, Burma ... 16 46N 96 18E
78 Insurăței, Rumania ... 44 50N 27 40E
172 Intendente Alvear, Arg. ... 35 12S 63 32W
164 Interior, U.S.A. ... 43 46N 101 59W
57 Interlaken, Switzerland ... 46 41N 7 50E
164 International Fs., U.S.A. ... 48 30N 93 25W
107 Interview I., Andaman Islands, India ... 12 55N 92 42E
107 Inthanon, mt., Thailand ... 18 35N 98 29E
172 Intiyaco, Argentina ... 28 50S 60 0W
176 Inutil B., Chile ... 53 30S 70 15W
46 Inver, & B., Ireland ... 54 40N 8 16W
43 Inverallochy, Scot., U.K. ... 57 40N 1 56W
44 Inveran, Ireland ... 53 14N 9 28W
43 Inveran, Scot., U.K. .57 58N 4 26W
40 Inveraray, Scot., U.K. ... 56 13N 5 5W
43 Inverbervie, Scot., U.K. ... 56 50N 2 17W
147 Invercargill, N.Z. ... 46 24S 168 24E
145 Inverell, Australia ... 29 48S 151 36E
43 Invergarry, Scot., U.K. ... 57 5N 4 48W
43 Invergordon, Scot., U.K. ... 57 41N 4 10W
41 Invergowrie, Scot., U.K. ... 56 29N 3 5W
42 Inverie, Scot., U.K. ... 57 2N 5 40W
41 Inverkeilor, Scot., U.K. ... 56 38N 2 33W
41 Inverkeithing, Scot., U.K. ... 56 2N 3 24W
156 Invermere, Canada ... 50 51N 116 9W
43 Invermoriston, Scotland, U.K. ... 57 13N 4 38W
155 Inverness, Canada ... 46 15N 61 19W
43 Inverness, & Co., Scotland, U.K. ... 57 29N 4 12W
163 Inverness, U.S.A. ... 28 50N 82 20W
42 Invershiel, Scot., U.K. 57 13N 5 25W
43 Inverurie, Scot., U.K. 57 15N 2 21W
138 Investigator Group, South Australia ... 34 45S 134 20E
145 Investigator Str., South Australia ... 35 30S 137 0E
160 Invona, U.S.A. ... 40 46N 78 35W
132 Inyanga, Rhodesia ... 18 12S 32 40E
132 Inyangani, Mts., Rhod. ... 18 20S 32 20E
132 Inyantue, Rhodesia ... 18 30S 26 40E
132 Inyati, Rhodesia ... 19 40S 28 40E
132 Inyazura, Rhodesia ... 18 40S 31 40E
167 Inyo Range, mts., U.S.A. ... 37 0N 118 0W
167 Inyokern, U.S.A. ... 35 37N 117 54W
87 Inza, U.S.S.R. ... 53 55N 46 25E
87 Inzhavino, U.S.S.R. ... 52 22N 42 23E
76 Ioánnina (Janinà), Gr. 39 39N 20 57E
165 Iola, U.S.A. ... 38 0N 95 20W
78 Ion Corvin, Rumania .44 7N 27 50E
40 Iona I., Scot., U.K. ... 56 20N 6 25W
166 Ione, Calif., U.S.A. ... 38 20N 121 0W
166 Ione, Wash., U.S.A. ... 48 44N 117 29W
130 Iongo, Angola ... 9 15S 17 32E
162 Ionia, U.S.A. ... 42 59N 85 7W
77 Ionian Is., Greece ... 38 40N 20 0E
67 Ionian Sea, Europe ... 37 30N 17 30E
77 Iónioi Nisoi Is., Greece ... 38 40N 20 8E
89 Iori, R., U.S.S.R. ... 41 12N 46 10E
77 Ios Is., Greece ... 36 41N 25 20E
164 Iowa, st., U.S.A. ... 42 18N 93 30W
164 Iowa City, U.S.A. ... 41 40N 91 35W
164 Iowa Falls, U.S.A. ... 42 30N 93 15W
131 Ipala, Tanzania ... 4 30S 33 5E
175 Ipameri, Brazil ... 17 44S 48 9W
77 Ipáti, Greece ... 38 52N 22 14E
89 Ipatovo, U.S.S.R. ... 45 45N 42 50E
59 Ipel, R., Europe ... 48 10N 19 35E
174 Ipiales, Colombia ... 1 0N 77 45W
111 Ipin, China ... 28 58N 104 45E
76 Ipiros, pref., Greece ... 39 30N 20 30E
174 Ipixuna, Brazil ... 7 10S 72 20W
107 Ipoh, Malaysia ... 4 36N 101 4E
121 Ippy, Cent. Afr. Rep. 6 5N 21 7E
76 Ipsala, Turkey ... 40 55N 26 23E
76 Ipsárion Óros, mts., Gr. ... 40 40N 24 40E
145 Ipswich, Australia ... 27 38S 152 37E
35 Ipswich, Eng., U.K. ... 52 4N 1 9E
161 Ipswich, N.H., U.S.A. 42 40N 70 50W
164 Ipswich, S.D., U.S.A. .45 28N 99 20W
175 Ipu, Brazil ... 4 23S 40 44W
108 Ipuh, Indonesia ... 2 58S 101 8E
132 Ipusukilo, Zambia ... 10 22S 30 0E
86 Iput R., U.S.S.R. ... 53 0N 32 10E
174 Iquique, Chile ... 20 19S 70 5W
174 Iquitos, Peru ... 3 45S 73 10W
175 Iracoubo, French Guiana ... 5 30N 53 10W
77 Irákila, I., Greece ... 36 50N 25 28E
77 Iráklion, Greece ... 35 20N 25 12E
77 Iráklion, pref., Greece 35 10N 25 10E
173 Irala, Paraguay ... 25 55S 54 35W
123 Iraouene, mt., Algeria 27 5N 5 20E
101 Iran, (Persia), King., Asia ... 33 0N 53 0E
108 Iran Ra., Sar., Malaysia ... 2 20N 114 50E
106 Iranamadu Tank, L., Cey. ... 9 23N 80 29E
101 Iranshahr, Iran ... 27 75N 60 40E
168 Irapuato, Mexico ... 20 40N 101 40W
100 Iraq, Rep., Asia ... 33 0N 44 0E
122 Irarrar, W., Mali ... 20 10N 1 30E
173 Irati, Brazil ... 25 25S 50 38W
1 Irazu Vol., Costa Rica 10 10N 84 20W
98 Irbid, Jordan ... 32 35N 35 48E
100 Irbil, Iraq ... 36 15N 44 5E
35 Irchester, Eng., U.K. .52 17N 0 40W
130 Irebu, Congo ... 0 40S 17 55E
38 Ireby, England, U.K. 54 45N 3 12W
64 Iregua, R., Spain ... 42 22N 2 24E
33 Ireland, rep., Europe .53 0N 8 0W
45 Ireland's Eye, Ireland 53 25N 6 4W
125 Irele, Nigeria ... 7 40N 5 40E
112 Iren L., China ... 43 50N 111 50E
128 Irena, Chad ... 8 30N 19 0E
133 Irene, Trans., S. Africa ... 25 51S 28 13E
112 Irentala Steppe, China 43 45N 112 15E
91 Iret, U.S.S.R. ... 60 10N 154 5E
87 Irgiz Gt., R., U.S.S.R. 52 10N 49 10E
123 Irharharene, Algeria ... 27 37N 7 30E
123 Irharrhar W. Algeria 27 30N 6 0E
112 Iri, S. Korea ... 35 59N 127 0E
124 Irié, Guinea ... 8 15N 9 10W
131 Iringa, & dist., Tanzania ... 7 48S 35 43E
106 Irinjalakuda, India ... 10 21N 76 14E
113 Iriomote, I., Japan ... 24 25N 123 58E
175 Iriri, R., Brazil ... 4 20S 54 0W
29 Irish Sea, British Isles 54 0N 145 12E

MAP
145 Irish Town, Australia 40 55s 5 0w
91 Irkutsk, U.S.S.R. ...52 10n 104 20e
38 Irlam, Eng., U.K. ...53 26n 2 27w
46 Iron, L., Ireland ...53 37n 7 34w
145 Iron Baron, S. Austral. ...33 3s 137 11e
78 Iron Gate, Rumania ...44 42n 22 30e
145 Iron Knob, S. Austral. ...32 46s 137 8e
162 Iron Mountain, U.S.A. 45 49n 88 4w
164 Iron River, U.S.A. ...46 6n 88 40w
34 Ironbridge, Eng., U.K. ...52 38n 2 29w
160 Irondale, Canada ...44 51n 78 30w
144 Ironhurst, Australia ...18 0s 143 35e
165 Ironton, Mo., U.S.A. .37 40n 90 40w
162 Ironton, Ohio, U.S.A. 38 35n 82 40w
164 Ironwood, U.S.A. ...46 30n 90 10w
154 Iroquois Falls, Canada 48 40n 80 40w
86 Irpen, U.S.S.R. ...50 30n 30 8e
103 Irrawaddy R., Burma 19 30n 95 15e
112 Irshih, China ...47 8n 119 57e
73 Irsina, Italy ...40 45n 16 15e
38 Irt R., England, U.K. 54 24n 3 25w
38 Irthing R., Eng., U.K. ...55 3n 2 32w
38 Irthington, Eng., U.K. ...54 58n 2 48w
35 Irthlingborough, England, U.K. ...52 20n 0 37w
90 Irtysh R., U.S.S.R. ...53 36n 75 30e
131 Irumu, Congo ... 1 32n 29 53e
64 Irun, Spain ...43 20n 1 52w
64 Irurzun, Spain ...42 55n 1 50w
40 Irvine & R., Scotland, U.K. ...55 37n 4 40w
162 Irvine, U.S.A. ...37 42n 83 58w
46 Irvinstown, N. Ire., U.K. ...54 28n 7 38w
143 Irymple, Vic., Australia ...34 14s 142 8e
125 Isa, Nigeria ...13 14n 6 24e
82 Isa Fd., Iceland ...66 10n 23 0w
164 Isabel, U.S.A. ...45 27n 101 22w
169 Isabella, Cord, mts., Nic. ...13 30n 85 25w
82 Isafjördhur, Iceland ...66 10n 23 15w
104 Isagarh, India ...24 48n 77 51e
130 Isaka, Congo ... 2 30s 18 54e
131 Isaka, Tanzania ... 3 56s 32 59e
135 Isandhlwana, S. Africa ...28 20s 30 40e
130 Isangi, Congo ... 0 52n 24 10e
71 Isarco, Italy ...46 40n 11 35e
77 Isari, Greece ...37 22n 22 0e
49 Isbergues, France ...50 36n 2 24e
72 Ischia I., Italy ...40 45n 13 51e
81 Isefjord, Denmark ...55 53n 11 50e
70 Iseo, Italy ...45 40n 10 3e
71 Isère, dept., France ...45 15n 5 40e
50 Isère R., France ...45 15n 5 30e
56 Iserlohn, Germany ...51 22n 7 40e
73 Isernia, Italy ...41 35n 14 12e
114 Ise-wan, B., Japan ...34 45n 136 45e
125 Iseyin, Nigeria ... 8 0n 3 36e
99 Isha Baidoa, Somali Rep. ... 3 8n 43 30e
112 Ishan, China ...24 18n 108 35e
125 Ishara, Nigeria ... 6 40n 3 40e
113 Ishigaki, I., Japan ...24 26n 124 10e
114 Ishikari-wan (Otaru-wan), Japan 43 20n 141 20e
114 Ishikawa, Japan ...35 30n 138 30e
90 Ishim, & R., U.S.S.R. 56 10n 69 18e
114 Ishinomaki, Japan ...38 32n 141 20e
101 Ishkashim, Afghanistan ...36 30n 71 40e
102 Ishkuman, Kashmir ...36 40n 73 50e
76 Ishm, Albania ...41 33n 19 34e
162 Ishpeming, U.S.A. ...46 30n 87 40w
125 Ishua, Nigeria ... 7 15n 5 50e
112 Ishui, China ...35 50n 118 32e
88 Işik, mt., Turkey ...40 40n 32 35e
50 Isili, Italy ...39 45n 9 6e
131 Isiolo, Kenya ... 0 24n 37 33e
131 Isiro (Paulis), Congo . 2 53n 27 58e
144 Isisford, Australia ...24 15s 144 21e
91 Isitskoye, U.S.S.R. ...61 0n 125 0e
75 Iskăr, R., Bulgaria ...43 35n 24 20e
100 Iskenderun, Turkey ...36 32n 36 10e
88 Iskilip, Turkey ...40 50n 34 20e
43 Isla R., Scot., U.K. ...56 44n 3 20w
64 Isla Cristina, Spain ...37 13n 7 17w
104 Islamkot, W. Pakistan ...24 42n 70 13e
106 Islampur, India ...17 2n 72 9e
154 Island Falls, Canada .49 35n 81 20w
155 Island Falls, U.S.A. ...46 0n 68 25w
157 Island L., Canada ...53 40n 94 30w
161 Island Pond, U.S.A. ...44 50n 71 50w
155 Islands, B. of, Canada 49 11n 58 15w
146 Islands, B. of, N.Z. ...35 20s 174 20e
40 Islay, I. & Sd., Scotland, U.K. ...55 46n 6 10w
155 Isle aux Morts, Canada ...47 35n 59 0w
39 Isle of Axholme, England, U.K. ...53 30n 0 50w
34 Isle of Purbeck, England, U.K. ...50 38n 2 0w
40 Isle of Whithorn, Scotland, U.K. ...54 42n 4 22w
42 Isle Ornsay, Scot., U.K. ...57 9n 5 50w
164 Isle Royale, U.S.A. ...48 0n 88 50w
35 Isleham, Eng., U.K. ...52 21n 0 24e
167 Isleta, U.S.A. ...34 58n 106 46w
34 Islip, Oxford, England, United Kingdom ...51 49n 1 12w
126 Ismailia, Egypt ...30 37n 32 18e
164 Ismay, U.S.A. ...46 33n 104 44w
126 Isna, Egypt ...25 17n 32 30e
132 Isoka, Zambia ...10 4s 32 42e
72 Isola del Liri, Italy ...41 39n 13 32e
70 Isola della Scala, Italy 45 16n 11 0e
73 Isola di Capo Rizzuto, Italy ...38 56n 17 5e
100 Isparta, Turkey ...37 47n 30 30e
75 Isperikh, Bulgaria ...43 43n 26 50e
73 Ispica, Sicily, Italy ...36 47n 14 53e
89 Ispir, Turkey ...40 40n 40 50e
98 Israel, st., Asia ...32 0n 34 50e
142 Isseka, W. Australia .28 22s 114 35e
55 Issel R., Germany ...51 48n 6 25e
124 Issia, Ivory Coast ... 6 33n 6 33w
50 Issoire, France ...45 32n 3 15e
49 Issoudun, France ...46 57n 2 0e
55 Issum, Germany ...51 32n 6 25e
49 Is-sur-Tille, France ...47 30n 5 10e
90 Issyk-Kul, L., U.S.S.R. ...42 30n 77 30e
100 Istanbul, Turkey ...41 0n 29 0e
77 Istiaia, Greece ...38 57n 23 10e
74 Istok, Yugoslavia ...42 45n 20 24e
163 Istokpoga, L., U.S.A. .27 22n 81 14w
87 Istra, U.S.S.R. ...55 55n 36 50e
71 Istra, dist., Yugoslavia ...45 10n 14 0e
75 Istranca Dağlari, mts., Turkey ...41 48n 27 30e
51 Istres, France ...43 31n 4 59e
175 Itabaiana, Brazil ... 7 18s 35 19w
175 Itaberaba, Brazil ...12 25s 40 30w
175 Itabira, Brazil ...19 29s 43 23w
175 Itabuna, Brazil ...14 55s 39 25w
175 Itaeté, Brazil ...13 0s 41 5w
175 Itaituba, Brazil ... 4 10s 55 50w
173 Itajaí, Brazil ...27 0s 48 45w
173 Itajuba, Brazil ...22 24s 45 30w
99 Itala, Somali Rep. ... 2 58n 46 27e
68 Italy, rep., Europe ...42 0n 13 0e
175 Itambe, mt., Brazil ...18 30s 43 15w
173 Itanhaem, Brazil ...24 9s 46 47w
175 Itapecurú, Brazil ... 3 20s 44 15w
173 Itaperuna, Brazil ...21 10s 42 0w
173 Itapetininga, Brazil ...23 36s 48 7w
173 Itapeva, Brazil ...23 59s 48 59w
175 Itapicurú R., Baia, Braz. ...10 50s 38 40w
175 Itapicuru R., Maranha, Brazil ... 5 40s 44 30w
175 Itapura, Brazil ...20 30s 51 30w
173 Itaquari, Brazil ...20 12s 40 25w
174 Itaquatiana, Brazil ... 2 58s 58 30w
176 Itaqui, Brazil ...29 0s 56 30w
173 Itarare, Brazil ...24 6s 49 23w
104 Itarsi, India ...22 36n 77 51e
175 Itatiaia, mt., Brazil ...22 20s 44 5w
174 Itatuba, Brazil ... 5 40s 63 20w
175 Itaunas, Brazil ...18 30s 39 50w
113 Itbayat I., Philippines 21 45n 121 50e
34 Itchen R., Eng., U.K. 50 57n 1 20w
77 Itéa, Greece ...38 25n 22 25e
77 Ithaca, see Itháki, Greece ...38 25n 20 43e
161 Ithaca, U.S.A. ...42 25n 76 30w
77 Itháki & I., Greece ...38 25n 20 43e
37 Ithan R., Wales, U.K. 52 16n 3 23w
114 Ito, Japan ...34 58n 139 5e
174 Itonamas R., Bolivia ...13 0s 64 25w
126 Itsa, Egypt ...29 15n 30 40e
72 Ittiri, Italy ...40 38n 8 32e
173 Itu, Brazil ...23 20s 47 15w
125 Itu, Nigeria ... 5 10n 7 58e
175 Ituaçu, Brazil ...13 50s 41 30w
112 Ituliho, China ...50 40n 121 30e
175 Ituiutaba, Brazil ...19 0s 49 25w
175 Itumbiara, Brazil ...18 20s 49 10w
112 Itung, China ...43 25n 125 21e
172 Iturbe, Argentina ...23 0s 65 25w
130 Ituri R., Congo ... 1 45n 26 45e
91 Iturup I., Kurils, U.S.S.R. ...45 0n 148 0e
172 Ituvuro, R., Argentina ...22 40s 63 50w
56 Itzehoe, Germany ...53 56n 9 31e
122 Itzer, Morocco ...32 55n 5 2w
75 Ivailovgrad, Bulgaria .41 32n 26 8e
82 Ivalo, & R., Finland .68 38n 27 35e
76 Ivanaj, Albania ...42 17n 19 25e
78 Ivăneşti, Rumania ...46 45n 24 50e
74 Ivangrad, Yugoslavia 42 51n 19 50e
143 Ivanhoe, Australia ...32 56s 144 20e
157 Ivanhoe L., Canada ...60 25n 106 30w
71 Ivanicgrad, Yugoslavia ...45 41n 16 25e
74 Ivanjica, Yugoslavia .43 35n 20 12e
71 Ivanjscie mt., Y.-slav. ...46 12n 16 13e
86 Ivano-Frankovsk, (Stanislav), U.S.S.R. ...49 0n 24 40e
87 Ivanovo, R.S.F.S.R., U.S.S.R. ...57 5n 41 0e
86 Ivanovo, White Russia, U.S.S.R. ...52 7n 25 29e
35 Ivinghoe, Eng., U.K. .51 50n 0 38w
173 Ivinheima, R., Brazil .21 48s 54 15w
65 Iviza, see Ibiza, Spain 39 0n 1 30e
124 Ivory Coast Rep., Afr. 7 30n 5 0e
81 Ivösjön, L., Sweden ...56 8n 14 25e
70 Ivrea, Italy ...45 30n 7 52e
153 Ivugivik, (N.D. d'Ivugivic), Canada 62 18n 77 50w
36 Ivybridge, Eng., U.K. 50 24n 3 56w
108 Iwahig, Philippines ... 8 35n 117 32e
114 Iwakuni, Japan ...34 15n 132 8e
114 Iwata, Japan ...34 49n 137 59e
114 Iwate, pref., Japan ...39 30n 141 30e
125 Iwo, Nigeria ... 7 39n 4 9e
174 Ixiamas, Bolivia ...13 50s 68 5w
135 Ixopo, Natal, South Africa ...30 11s 30 5e
168 Ixtepec, Mexico ...16 40n 95 10w
168 Ixtlán del Juarez, Mexico ...17 23n 96 28w
168 Ixtlán del Rio, Mexico 21 5n 104 28w
35 Ixworth, Eng., U.K. .52 18n 0 50e
113 Iyang, China ...34 10n 112 32e
168 Izabal L., Guatemala .15 30n 89 10w
168 Izamal, Mexico ...20 56n 89 1w
89 Izberbash, U.S.S.R. ...42 35n 47 45e
78 Izbiceni, Rumania ...43 45n 24 40e
54 Izegem, Belgium ...50 55n 3 12e
75 Izgrev, Bulgaria ...43 36n 26 58e
84 Izhevsk, U.S.S.R. ...56 50n 53 0e
88 Izmail, U.S.S.R. ...45 22n 28 46e
85 Izmir (Smyrna), Turkey ...38 25n 27 8e
100 Izmit, Turkey ...40 45n 29 50e
63 Iznajar, Spain ...37 15n 4 19w
65 Iznalloz, Spain ...37 24n 3 30w
71 Izola, Yugoslavia ...45 32n 13 39e
114 Izumisano, Japan ...34 40n 135 43e
114 Izumo, Japan ...35 20n 132 55e
86 Izyaslav, U.S.S.R. ...50 5n 25 50e
88 Izyum, U.S.S.R. ...49 12n 37 28e

J

98 Jaba', Jordan ...32 20n 35 13e
100 Jabal al Jalas, ra., Saudi Arabia ...27 30n 36 30e
99 Jabal at Tuwaiq, Saudi Arabia ...25 30n 46 0e
100 Jabal Shamar, Si. Arab. ...27 40n 41 0e
98 Jabaliya, Egypt ...31 32n 34 27e
63 Jabalón R., Spain ...38 45n 3 35w
105 Jabalpur, India ...23 9n 79 58e
100 Jablah, Syria ...35 20n 36 0e
71 Jablanac, Yugoslavia .44 42n 14 56e
58 Jablonec, Cz. ...50 43n 15 10e
59 Jablonica, Cz. ...48 37n 17 26e
60 Jablonowo, Poland ...53 23n 19 10e
173 Jaboticabal, Brazil ...21 15s 48 17w
100 Jabrin, Saudi Arabia .23 7n 48 52e
74 Jabukovac, Yugoslavia ...44 22n 22 21e
174 Jaburú, Brazil ... 4 0s 66 25w
64 Jaca, Spain ...42 35n 0 33w
173 Jacarei, Brazil ...23 20s 46 0w
173 Jacarezinho, Brazil ...23 5s 50 0w
172 Jachal, Argentina ...30 5s 69 0w
58 Jáchymov, Cz. ...50 22n 12 55e
155 Jack Lane B., Canada 55 45n 60 35w
154 Jackfish, Canada ...48 45n 87 0w
155 Jackman, U.S.A. ...45 35n 70 17w
165 Jacksboro, Tex., U.S.A. ...33 14n 98 15w
145 Jackson, Australia ...26 40s 149 30e
163 Jackson, Ala., U.S.A. .31 32n 87 53w
163 Jackson, Calif., U.S.A. 37 25n 89 42w
166 Jackson, Ill., U.S.A. ...38 25n 120 47w
162 Jackson, Ky., U.S.A. .37 35n 83 22w
162 Jackson, Mich., U.S.A. ...42 18n 84 25w
164 Jackson, Minn., U.S.A. ...43 35n 95 30w
165 Jackson, Miss., U.S.A. 32 20n 90 10w
162 Jackson, Ohio, U.S.A. 39 0n 82 40w
163 Jackson, Tenn., U.S.A. ...35 40n 88 50w
166 Jackson, Wyo., U.S.A. ...43 30n 110 49w
156 Jackson Bay., tn., Can. ...50 32n 125 57w
147 Jackson B., N.Z. ...43 58s 168 42e
147 Jackson Hd., N.Z. ...40 59s 174 20e
166 Jackson, L., U.S.A. ...43 55n 110 40w
147 Jacksons, New Zealand 42 46n 171 32e
163 Jacksonville, Ala., U.S.A. ...33 49n 85 45w
163 Jacksonville, Fla., U.S.A. ...30 15n 81 38w
164 Jacksonville, Ill., U.S.A. ...39 42n 90 15w
163 Jacksonville, N.C., U.S.A. ...34 50n 77 29w
166 Jacksonville, Ore., U.S.A. ...42 13n 122 56w
165 Jacksonville, Tex., U.S.A. ...31 58n 95 12w
163 Jacksonville Beach, U.S.A. ...30 19n 81 26w
169 Jacmel, Haiti ...18 20n 72 40w
167 Jacob Lake, U.S.A. ...36 45n 112 12w
104 Jacobabad, W. Pak. ...28 20n 68 29e
78 Jacobeni, Rumania ...47 25n 25 20e
175 Jacobina, Brazil ...11 0s 40 30w
134 Jacobsdal, S. Africa ...29 10s 24 47e
98 Jacob's Well, Jordan .32 13n 35 13e
155 Jacques Cartier, Mt., Canada ...48 57n 66 0w
155 Jacques Cartier Pass, Canada ...49 50n 62 30w
124 Jacqueville, Ivory Coast ... 5 12n 4 25w
175 Jacuipe R., Brazil ...11 30s 39 45w
56 Jade, Germany ...53 22n 8 14e
56 Jadebusen, B., Ger. ...53 30n 8 15e
130 Jadotville, see Liskasi, Congo ...10 55s 26 48e
74 Jadovnik, Ra., Y.-slav. ...43 20n 19 45e
64 Jadraque, Spain ...40 55n 2 55w
123 Jadu, Libya ...32 0n 12 0e
174 Jaen, Peru ... 5 25s 78 40w
63 Jaen, & prov., Spain .37 44n 3 43w
122 Jafène, Sahara ...20 35n 5 30w
98 Jaffa, see Tel-Aviv-Jaffa, Israel ...32 4n 34 48e
145 Jaffa C., S. Australia .36 49s 139 38e
106 Jaffna, Ceylon ... 9 45n 80 2e
104 Jagadhri, India ...30 10n 77 20e
105 Jagadishpur, India ...25 30n 84 21e
106 Jagdalpur, India ...19 3n 82 6e
135 Jagersfontein, S. Africa ...29 44s 25 27e
104 Jagraon, India ...30 50n 75 25e
121 Jaghbub, Libya ...29 42n 24 38e
57 Jagst, R., Germany ...49 13n 10 0e
106 Jagtial, India ...18 50n 79 0e
173 Jaguarao, Brazil ...32 30s 53 30w
173 Jaguariaiva, Brazil ...24 10s 49 50w
175 Jaguaribe, R., Brazil . 6 0s 38 35w
169 Jaguey, Cuba ...22 35n 81 7w
104 Jahangirabad, India ...28 19n 78 4e
101 Jahrom, Iran ...28 30n 53 31e
105 Jainti, India ...26 45n 89 40e
104 Jaipur, India ...26 54n 72 52e
101 Jajarm, Iran ...37 5n 56 20e
74 Jajce, Yugoslavia ...44 19n 17 17e
125 Jajere, Nigeria ...11 58n 10 25e
105 Jajpur, India ...20 53n 86 22e
74 Jakupica, Ra., Y.-slav. ...41 45n 21 22e
165 Jal, U.S.A. ...32 8n 103 8w
101 Jala, Iran ...27 30n 62 40e
101 Jalalabad, Afghanistan ...34 30n 70 29e
105 Jalalabad, India ...26 41n 79 42e
104 Jalalpur Jattan, W. Pak. ...32 38n 74 19e
168 Jalapa, Guatemala ...14 45n 89 59w
168 Jalapa, Mexico ...19 30n 96 50w
105 Jalaun, India ...26 8n 79 25e
105 Jaleswar, Nepal ...26 38n 85 48e
104 Jalgaon, Maharashtra, India ...21 0n 75 42e
104 Jalgaon, Mad. P., India ...21 2n 76 31e
125 Jalingo, Nigeria ... 8 55n 11 25e
168 Jalisco, st., Mexico ...20 0n 104 0w
62 Jallas, R., Spain ...42 57n 9 0w
143 Jallumba, Vic., Austral. ...36 55n 141 57e
106 Jalna, India ...19 48n 75 57e
64 Jalón R., Spain ...41 20n 1 40w
168 Jalpa, Mexico ...21 38n 102 58w
105 Jalpaiguri, India ...26 32n 88 46e
101 Jalq, Iran ...27 35n 62 33e
136 Jaluit I., Pacific Ocean ... 6 0n 169 30e
125 Jamaari, Nigeria ...11 44n 9 53e
169 Jamaica, I., W. Indies ...18 10n 77 30w
105 Jamalpur, E. Pakistan ...24 52n 90 2e
105 Jamalpur, India ...25 18n 86 28e
105 Jamalpurganj, India .23 2n 88 1e
175 Jamanxim, R., Brazil 6 30s 55 50w
109 Jambe, Indonesia ... 1 15s 132 10e
55 Jambes, Belgium ...50 27n 4 52e
104 Jambusar, India ...22 3n 72 51e
109 Jamdena I., Indonesia 7 45s 131 20e
132 James, Malawi ... 9 32s 33 10e
154 James B., Canada ...53 30n 80 30w
147 James Pk., N.Z. ...45 15s 169 0e
164 James R., S.D., U.S.A. ...44 50n 98 0w
138 James Ras., Australia 24 10s 132 0e
15 James Ross I., Br. Antarctic Terr. ...66 58s 50 49w
135 Jamestown, S. Africa .31 6s 26 45e
145 Jamestown, S. Australia ...33 10s 138 32e
162 Jamestown, Ky., U.S.A. ...37 0n 85 5w
164 Jamestown, N.D., USA ...47 0n 98 30w
160 Jamestown, N.Y., USA ...42 5n 79 18w
160 Jamestown, Penn., U.S.A. ...41 22n 80 27w
163 Jamestown, Tenn., U.S.A. ...36 25n 85 0w
106 Jamkhandi, India ...16 30n 75 15e
98 Jamma'in, Jordan ...32 8n 35 12e
106 Jammalamadugu, India ...14 51n 78 25e
81 Jammerbugt, B., Den. 57 10n 9 10e
135 Jammerdrif, S. Africa 29 43s 27 0e
104 Jammu, Jammu & Kashmir ...32 46n 75 57e
104 Jamnagar, India ...22 30n 70 0e
104 Jamner, India ...20 45n 75 45e
104 Jampur, W. Pakistan 29 39n 70 32e
102 Jamrud, W. Pakistan 34 2n 71 24e
105 Jamshedpur, India ...22 44n 86 20e
105 Jamtara, India ...23 59n 86 41e
80 Jamtlands Län, Sweden ...62 40n 14 30e
174 Jamundá R., Brazil ... 1 25s 58 0w
134 Jan Forieskraal, S. Afr. ...33 35s 21 48e
14 Jan Mayen Is. (Norway), Arctic Ocean ...71 0n 11 0w
102 Jand, West Pakistan .33 30n 72 0e
100 Jandaq, Iran ...34 3n 54 22e
104 Jandola, West Pakistan ...32 20n 70 9e
145 Jandowae, Australia .26 45s 151 7e
63 Jandula, R., Spain ...38 25n 3 55w
146 Jane Pk., N.Z. ...45 15s 168 20e
164 Janesville, Wis., U.S.A. ...42 39n 89 1w
125 Janga, Ghana ...10 5n 1 0w
132 Jangamo, Mozambique ...24 7s 35 23e
106 Jangaon, India ...17 44n 79 5e
125 Jangero, Nigeria ...13 2n 6 25e
101 Jani Khel, Afghanistan ...32 45n 68 25e
74 Janja, Yugoslavia ...44 40n 19 17e
74 Janjevo, Yugoslavia ...42 35n 21 19e
74 Janjina, Yugoslavia ...42 58n 17 25e
59 Janoshalma, Hungary 46 18n 19 21e
59 Janosháza, Hungary .47 8n 17 12e
60 Janów, Poland ...50 43n 22 30e
46 Janów, U.S.S.R. ...52 10n 25 24e
60 Janów Podlaski, Poland ...52 11n 23 11e
60 Janowiec, Poland ...52 45n 17 30e
134 Jansenville, S. Africa .32 57s 24 39e
175 Januária, Brazil ...15 25s 44 25w
49 Janville, France ...48 10n 1 50e
48 Janzé, France ...47 55n 1 28w
112 Jaoho, China ...47 12n 134 15e
104 Jaora, India ...23 40n 75 10e
114 Japan, st., Asia ...36 0n 136 0e
114 Japan, Sea of, Asia ...40 0n 135 0e
136 Japan Trench, Pac. Oc. ...28 0n 145 0e
109 Japen I., Indonesia ... 1 50s 136 0e
109 Japen Str., Indonesia . 1 20s 136 0e
174 Jaque, Panama ... 7 27n 78 15w
63 Jaraicejo, Spain ...39 40n 5 49e
62 Jaraiz, Spain ...40 4n 5 45w
64 Jarama, R., Spain ...40 50n 3 20w
167 Jarales, U.S.A. ...34 44n 106 51w
62 Jarandilla, Spain ...40 8n 5 39w
104 Jaranwala, W. Pak. ...31 15n 73 20e
98 Jarash, Jordan ...32 17n 35 54e
80 Järbo, Sweden ...60 42n 16 38e
166 Jarbridge, U.S.A. ...41 56n 115 27w
169 Jardines de la Reina Is., Cuba ...20 50n 78 50w
111 Jargalant (Kobdo), Mongolia ...48 0n 91 43e
112 Jargalant, Mongolia ...47 2n 115 1e
49 Jargeau, France ...47 50n 2 7e
56 Jarmen, Germany ...53 56n 13 20e
80 Järna, Kopp, Sweden 60 33n 14 26e
80 Järna, Stockholm, Sweden ...59 7n 17 35e
50 Jarnac, France ...45 40n 0 11w
60 Jarocin, Poland ...51 59n 17 29e
58 Jaroměr, Cz. ...50 22n 15 52e
59 Jaroslavl, Poland ...50 2n 22 42e
81 Järpås, Sweden ...58 23n 12 57e
80 Järpen, Sweden ...63 20n 13 40e
142 Jarrahdale, W. Austral. ...32 24s 116 5e
39 Jarrow, Eng., U.K. ...54 58n 1 28w
127 Jarso, Ethiopia ... 5 15n 37 30e
80 Järved, Sweden ...63 16n 18 43e
160 Jarvis, Canada ...42 56n 80 6w
137 Jarvis I., Pacific Ocean ... 0 15s 159 55w
39 Jarvornik, Cz. ...50 23n 17 2e
105 Jarwa, India ...27 45n 82 30e
74 Jaša Tomic, Y.-slavia 45 26n 20 50e
107 Jasin, W. Malaysia ... 2 20n 102 26e
101 Jask, Iran ...25 38n 57 45e
59 Jaslo, Poland ...49 45n 21 30e
156 Jasper, Alb., Canada .52 55n 118 0w
161 Jasper, Ont., Canada .44 52n 75 57w
163 Jasper, Ala., U.S.A. ...33 48n 87 16w
166 Jasper, Ark., U.S.A. ...36 0n 93 10w
163 Jasper, Fla., U.S.A. ...30 31n 82 58w
165 Jasper, La., U.S.A. ...30 59n 93 58w
164 Jasper, S.D., U.S.A. ...43 52n 96 22w
156 Jasper Place, Canada .53 33n 113 25w
71 Jastrebarsko, Y.-slavia ...45 41n 15 39e
60 Jastrowie, Poland ...53 26n 16 49e
59 Jászapáti, Hungary ...47 32n 20 10e
59 Jászárokszállás, Hung. ...47 39n 20 1e
59 Jászbereny, Hungary .47 30n 19 55e
59 Jászkiser, Hungary ...47 27n 20 20e
59 Jaszladany, Hungary ...47 23n 20 18e
175 Jatai, Brazil ...17 50s 51 45w
104 Jati, West Pakistan ...24 27n 68 19e
65 Játiva, Spain ...39 0n 0 32w
175 Jatoba, Brazil ... 4 35s 49 33w
98 Jatt, Israel ...32 24n 35 2e
173 Jau, Brazil ...22 10s 48 30w
99 Jau al Milah, Yemen .15 15n 45 40e
174 Jauja, Peru ...11 45s 75 30w
105 Jaunpur, India ...25 46n 82 44e
108 Java Sea, Indonesia ... 4 35s 107 15e
109 Java I., Indonesia ... 7 0s 110 0e
106 Javadi Hills, India ...12 40n 78 40e
65 Jávea, Spain ...38 48n 0 10e
111 Javhlant, see Ulyasutay, Mongolia ...47 42n 13 10e
106 Javla, India ...17 18n 75 9e
74 Javor, Mt., Y.-slavia ...43 37n 20 3e
48 Javron, France ...48 25n 0 25w
60 Jawor, Poland ...51 4n 16 11e
59 Jaworzno, Poland ...50 13n 19 22e
165 Jay, U.S.A. ...36 28n 94 46w
157 Jaydot, Canada ...49 15n 110 15w
165 Jayton, U.S.A. ...33 17n 100 35w
167 Jean, U.S.A. ...35 47n 115 20w
165 Jeanerette, U.S.A. ...29 52n 91 38w
160 Jeannette, U.S.A. ...40 20n 79 36w
169 Jean-Rabel, Haiti ...20 0n 73 30w
122 Jebba (Puerto Capaz), Morocco ...35 11n 4 43w
125 Jebba, Nigeria ... 9 9n 4 48e
74 Jebel, Rumania ...40 35n 21 15e
127 Jebel Aulia, Sudan ...15 10n 32 31e

MAP

126 Jebel et Tubeiq, Jordan 29 30N 37 30E
127 Jebel Qerri, Sudan 16 16N 32 50E
89 Jebel Yusha, Mt., Israel 32 4N 35 41E
41 Jedburgh, Scot., U.K. 55 28N 2 33W
60 Jedrzejów, Poland 50 35N 20 15E
56 Jeetze, R., Germany .52 58N 11 6E
164 Jefferson, Iowa, U.S.A. 42 3N 94 25W
160 Jefferson, Ohio, U.S.A. 41 40N 80 46W
165 Jefferson, Tex., U.S.A. 32 45N 94 23W
164 Jefferson, Wis., U.S.A. 43 0N 88 49W
166 Jefferson, Mt., Calif., U.S.A. 38 51N 117 0W
166 Jefferson, Mt., Ore., U.S.A. 44 45N 121 50W
163 Jefferson City, U.S.A. 36 8N 83 30W
162 Jeffersonville, Ind., U.S.A. 38 20N 85 42W
134 Jeffreys Bay, S. Africa 34 6S 24 53E
125 Jega, Nigeria 12 15N 4 23E
99 Jejega, Ethiopia 9 20N 42 50E
86 Jekabpils, U.S.S.R. ...56 29N 25 57E
55 Jeker, R., Belgium 50 46N 5 32E
60 Jelenia Gora, Poland .50 50N 15 45E
86 Jelgava, U.S.S.R. 56 41N 22 49E
74 Jelica, Ra., Y.-slavia .43 50N 20 17E
127 Jelli, Sudan 5 25N 31 45E
154 Jellicoe, Canada 49 40N 87 30W
59 Jelšava, Czechoslovakia 48 37N 20 15E
108 Jembongan, I., E. Malaysia 6 45N 117 20E
55 Jemeppe, Belgium 50 37N 5 30E
58 Jemnice, Cz. 49 1N 15 34E
56 Jena, Germany 50 56N 11 33E
165 Jena, U.S.A. 31 41N 92 7W
113 Jenhwai, China 28 5N 106 10E
98 Jenin, Jordan 32 28N 35 18E
162 Jenkins, U.S.A. 37 13N 82 41W
165 Jennings, U.S.A. 30 10N 92 45W
81 Jenny, Sweden 57 47N 16 35E
143 Jeparit, Vic., Australia 36 8S 142 1E
175 Jequié, Brazil 13 55S 40 5W
175 Jequitinhonho, & R., Brazil 16 30S 41 0W
122 Jerada, Morocco 34 16N 2 4W
107 Jerantut, W. Malaysia 3 56N 102 22E
169 Jerémie, Haiti 18 40N 74 10W
168 Jérez de Garcia Salinas, Mexico 22 39N 103 0W
63 Jerez de la Frontera, Sp. 36 41N 6 7W
63 Jerez de los Caballeros, Spain ...38 20N 6 45W
168 Jerez, Punta, Mexico .22 58N 97 40W
144 Jericho, Australia 23 38S 146 6E
98 Jericho, Jordan 31 52N 35 27E
133 Jericho, Trans., S. Africa 25 18S 27 46E
56 Jerichow, Germany ...52 30N 12 2E
143 Jerilderie, Australia ...35 20S 145 41E
161 Jermyn, U.S.A. 41 31N 75 31W
167 Jerome, U.S.A. 34 50N 112 0W
48 Jersey I., Chan. Is., U.K. 49 13N 2 7W
161 Jersey City, U.S.A. ...40 41N 74 8W
160 Jersey Shore, U.S.A. .41 17N 77 18W
164 Jerseyville, U.S.A. ...39 5N 90 20W
98 Jerusalem, Israel and Jordan 31 47N 35 10E
143 Jervis B., Austral. Comm. Terr. 35 8S 150 46E
71 Jesenice, Czechoslovakia 50 6N 13 28E
59 Jesenik (Frývaldov), Cz. 50 15N 17 11E
59 Jesenik, Mts., Cz. 50 0N 17 8E
59 Jesenske, Cz. 48 20N 20 10E
108 Jesselton, see Kota Kinabalu, Malaysia 6 0N 116 12E
79 Jessheim, Norway 60 7N 11 6E
56 Jessnitz, Germany 51 42N 12 19E
105 Jessore, E. Pakistan ...23 10N 89 10E
163 Jesup, U.S.A. 31 30N 82 0W
172 Jesus Maria, Argentina 30 59S 64 5W
165 Jetmore, U.S.A. 38 10N 99 57W
104 Jetpur, India 21 45N 70 10E
79 Jevnaker, Norway 60 15N 10 26E
160 Jewett, Ohio, U.S.A. .40 22N 81 2W
165 Jewett, Tex., U.S.A. .31 20N 96 8W
161 Jewett City, U.S.A. ...41 36N 72 0W
106 Jeypore, India 18 50N 82 38E
104 Jhajjar, India 28 37N 76 14E
102 Jhal Jhao, W. Pakistan 26 20N 65 35E
104 Jhalawar, India 24 35N 76 10E
104 Jhang Maghiana, W. Pakistan 31 15N 72 15E
104 Jhansi, India 25 30N 78 36E
105 Jharia, India 23 45N 86 18E
105 Jharsugra, India 21 52N 84 6E
172 Jhiaty, Paraguay 25 45S 56 35W
104 Jhelum, West Pakistan 33 0N 73 45E
104 Jhelum R., W. Pak. ...31 50N 72 10E
104 Jhunjhunu, India 28 10N 75 20E
105 Jiachan, Tibet, China 31 46N 81 12E
127 Jibalan Nūbah (Nuba Mts.), Sudan 12 0N 31 0E
125 Jibiya, Nigeria 13 5N 7 12E
78 Jibou, Rumania 47 15N 23 17E
58 Jičín, Czechoslovakia .50 25N 15 20E
103 Jida, India 29 2N 94 58E
127 Jidda, Ethiopia 9 52N 35 5E
99 Jidda, Saudi Arabia ...21 29N 39 16E
98 Jifna, Jordan 31 58N 35 13E
142 Jiggalong Mission, W. Australia 23 28S 120 45E
113 Jihchao, China 35 18N 119 28E
58 Jihlava, Czechoslovakia 49 28N 15 35E
58 Jihocesky, reg., Cz. ...49 8N 14 35E
59 Jihomoravsky, reg., Cz. 49 5N 16 30E
65 Jijona, Spain 38 34N 0 30W
125 Jikamshi, Nigeria 12 12N 7 45E
127 Jilbabo Plain, Ethiopia 4 20N 40 0E
64 Jiloca, R., Spain 41 0N 1 20W
58 Jilové, Czechoslovakia 49 52N 14 29E
127 Jima, Ethiopia 7 40N 36 55E
74 Jimbolia, Rumania 45 47N 20 57E
63 Jimena de la Frontera, Spain 36 27N 5 24W
168 Jimenez, Mexico 27 10N 105 0W
104 Jind, India 29 19N 76 16E
143 Jindabyne, Australia .36 25S 148 35E
58 Jindrichuv Hradec, Cz. 49 10N 15 2E
131 Jinja, Uganda 0 25N 33 12E
124 Jinjini, Ghana 7 20N 3 42W
101 Jinnah Barrage, W. Pakistan 32 58N 71 33E
112 Jinné, China 51 32N 121 25E
169 Jinotega, Nicaragua ...13 6N 85 59W
169 Jinotepe, Nicaragua ...11 50N 86 10W
174 Jiparaná (Machado), R., Brazil 8 45S 62 20W
174 Jipijapa, Ecuador 1 0S 80 40W
168 Jiquilpan, Mexico 19 57N 102 42W
100 Jisresh Shughur, Syria 35 49N 36 18E
142 Jitarning, W. Australia 32 48S 117 57E
107 Jitra, W. Malaysia 6 16N 110 25E
78 Jiu, R., Rumania 44 50N 23 20E
58 Jizera, R., Cz. 50 21N 14 48E
126 Jizl Wadi, Saudi Arabia 26 30N 38 0E
173 Joaçaba, Brazil 27 5S 51 31W
132 João, Mozambique 19 40S 34 30E
173 João Dias, Pta. de, Braz. 26 5S 48 40W
175 João Pessoa, Brazil ... 7 10S 35 0W
172 Joaquin V. González, Argentina 25 10S 64 0W
173 Joatinga, Cabo, Brazil 23 20S 44 30W
48 Jobourg, Nez de, Fr. .49 41N 1 57W
65 Jódar, Spain 37 50N 3 21W
104 Jodhpur, India 26 23N 73 2E
84 Joensuu, Finland 62 37N 29 49E
49 Joeuf, France 49 12N 6 1E
132 Jofane, Mozambique .21 15S 34 18E
155 Joggins, Canada 45 42N 64 27W
109 Jogjakarta, Indonesia 7 49S 110 22E
133 Johannesburg, S. Afr. 26 10S 28 8E
80 Johannisnäs, Sweden .62 45N 16 15E
81 Johansfors, Sweden ...56 50N 12 58E
166 John Days R., U.S.A. 45 0N 120 0W
43 John o' Groats, Scotland, U.K. 58 39N 3 3W
43 Johnshaven, Scot., U.K. 56 48N 2 20W
165 Johnson, U.S.A. 37 35N 101 48W
161 Johnson Cy., N.Y., U.S.A. 42 9N 67 0W
163 Johnson Cy., Tenn., U.S.A. 36 18N 82 21W
165 Johnson Cy., Tex., U.S.A. 30 15N 98 24W
142 Johnson Ra., Australia 29 40S 119 15E
160 Johnsonburg, U.S.A. .41 30N 78 40W
156 Johnsons Crossing, Can. 60 33N 133 27W
146 Johnsonville, N.Z. ...41 11S 174 41E
37 Johnston, Wales, U.K. 51 45N 5 5W
132 Johnston Fs., Zambia .10 31S 28 45E
137 Johnston I., Pac. Oc. .17 10N 169 8E
142 Johnston Ls., Australia 32 20S 120 45E
40 Johnstone, Scot., U.K. 55 50N 4 31W
45 Johnstown, Kilkenny, Ireland 52 46N 7 34W
161 Johnstown, N.Y., U.S.A. 43 1N 74 20W
160 Johnstown, Pa., U.S.A. 40 19N 78 53W
40 Johnstown Bridge, Ireland 53 23N 6 53W
107 Johore, st., W. Malaysia 2 5N 103 20E
107 Johore R., W. Malaysia 1 45N 103 47E
107 Johore Bahru, W. Malaysia 1 28N 103 46E
49 Joigny, France 48 0N 3 20E
173 Joinville, Brazil 26 15S 48 55W
49 Joinville, France 48 27N 5 10E
15 Joinville I., Antarctica 63 15N 55 30W
82 Jokkmokk, Sweden ...66 35N 19 58E
82 Jökulsa R., Iceland ...65 30N 16 15W
162 Joliet, Ill., U.S.A. 41 30N 88 0W
154 Joliette, Canada 46 3N 73 24W
109 Jolo I., Philippines 6 0N 121 0E
109 Jome I., Indonesia 1 16S 127 30E
81 Jönaker, Sweden 58 44N 16 43E
86 Jonava, U.S.S.R. 55 8N 24 12E
154 Jones C., Canada 54 33N 79 35W
14 Jones Sd., Canada 76 0N 85 0W
165 Jonesboro, Ark., U.S.A. 35 50N 90 45W
165 Jonesboro, Ill., U.S.A. 37 26N 89 18W
165 Jonesboro, La., U.S.A. 32 15N 92 41W
155 Jonesport, U.S.A. 44 32N 67 38W
86 Joniskis, U.S.S.R. 56 13N 23 35E
81 Jönköping, Sweden ...57 45N 14 15E
155 Jonquière, Canada 48 27N 71 14W
81 Jonsberg, Sweden 58 30N 16 48E
81 Jonserod, Sweden 57 47N 12 17E
50 Jonzac, France 45 27N 0 28W
165 Joplin, Mo., U.S.A. ...37 0N 94 25W
109 Jordan, Philippines ...10 41N 122 38E
166 Jordan, U.S.A. 47 25N 106 58W
100 Jordan, king., Asia ...31 0N 36 0E
98 Jordan R., Jordan-Israel 32 10N 35 32E
166 Jordan Valley, U.S.A. 43 0N 117 2W
103 Jorhat, India 26 45N 94 20E
82 Jörn, Sweden 65 5N 20 12E
79 Jörpeland, Norway 59 3N 6 1E
125 Jos, Nigeria 9 53N 8 51E
74 Jošanička Banja, Y.-slav. 43 24N 20 47E
173 José Batlle y Ordoñez, Uruguay .33 20S 55 10W
78 Joseni, Rumania 47 42N 25 29E
166 Joseph, U.S.A. 45 27N 117 13W
155 Joseph, Lac, Canada .52 40N 65 40W
160 Joseph L., Canada 45 15N 79 50W
138 Joseph Bonaparte G., Australia 14 0S 129 0E
167 Joseph City, U.S.A. ...35 0N 110 16W
48 Josselin, France 47 57N 2 33W
79 Jostedal, Norway 61 35N 7 15E
79 Jostedalsbre, Mt., Nor. 61 45N 7 0E
79 Jotunheimen, Mts., Nor. 61 30N 9 0E
134 Joubertina, S. Africa .33 48S 23 48E
133 Joubertskroon, S. Africa 23 49S 29 58E
100 Jounieh, Lebanon 33 59N 35 30E
165 Jourdanton, U.S.A. ...28 54N 98 32W
156 Joussard, Canada 55 22N 115 50W
169 Jovellanos, Cuba 22 40N 81 10W
132 Joverega, Botswana ...19 12S 24 20E
44 Joyce's Country, dist., Ireland 53 32N 9 30W
51 Joyeuse, France 44 29N 4 16E
135 Jozini Dam, S. Africa 27 27S 32 7E
168 Juan Aldama, Mex. ...24 20N 103 23W
167 Juan Bautista, U.S.A. 36 55N 121 33W
166 Juan de Fuca Str., U.S.A. 48 15N 124 0W
137 Juan Fernandez, Arch de, Pacific Ocean ...33 50S 80 0W
172 Juan Lacaze, Uruguay 34 26S 57 25W
172 Juarez, Argentina 37 40S 59 43W
168 Juárez, Sierra, Mexico 32 0N 116 0W
175 Juazeiro, Brazil 9 30S 40 30W
175 Juazeiro do Norte, Braz. 7 10S 39 18W
127 Juba, Sudan 4 57N 31 35E
117 Juba R., Africa 1 30N 42 35E
100 Jubaila, Saudi Arabia 24 55N 46 25E
126 Jubal, Str. of, Egypt .27 30N 34 0E
105 Jubbulpore, see Jabalpur, India 23 9N 79 58E
56 Jübek, Germany 54 31N 9 24E
89 Jubga, U.S.S.R. 44 19N 38 48E
142 Jubilee L., W. Austral. 29 0S 126 50E
120 Juby C., Morocco 28 0N 12 59W
64 Júcar R., Spain 40 8N 2 13W
55 Juchen, Germany 51 7N 6 31E
168 Juchitán, Mexico 16 27N 95 5W
98 Judaea, dist., Israel ...31 35N 34 57E
58 Judenburg, Austria ...47 12N 14 38E
161 Judith Pt., U.S.A. 41 20N 71 30W
166 Judith, R., U.S.A. 47 30N 109 30W
166 Judith Gap, U.S.A. ...46 48N 109 46W
113 Juian, China 27 57N 120 29E
169 Juigalpa, Nicaragua ...12 6N 85 26W
50 Juillac, France 45 20N 1 19E
56 Juist I., Germany 53 40N 7 0E
173 Juiz de Fora, Brazil ...21 43S 43 19W
172 Jujuy, Argentina 24 10S 65 25W
172 Jujuy, Prov., Arg. 23 20S 65 40W
113 Jukao, China 31 10N 120 32E
164 Julesberg, U.S.A. 41 0N 102 20W
174 Juli, Peru 16 10S 69 25W
144 Julia Creek, Australia 20 40S 141 55E
174 Juliaca, Peru 15 25S 70 10W
167 Julian, U.S.A. 33 4N 116 38W
71 Julian Alps, Y.-slav. .46 15N 14 1E
55 Juliana Canal, Neth. .51 6N 5 52E
14 Julianehaab, Greenland 60 40N 45 40W
46 Julianstown, Ireland .53 40N 6 16W
56 Jülich, Germany 50 55N 6 21E
39 Julier P., Switzerland 46 28N 9 32E
70 Julijske Alpe, Y.-slav. 46 15N 14 1E
104 Jullundur, India 31 20N 75 40E
132 Jumbo, Rhodesia 17 30S 30 58E
169 Jumento Cays, W. Ind. 23 40N 75 40E
54 Jumet, Belgium 50 27N 4 25E
65 Jumilla, Spain 38 28N 1 19W
105 Jumla, Nepal 29 15N 82 13E
104 Jumna R., see Yamuna, India 27 0N 78 30E
104 Junagadh, India 21 30N 70 30E
113 Junan, China 33 0N 114 23E
165 Junction, Tex., U.S.A. 30 29N 99 48W
167 Junction, Utah, U.S.A. 38 10N 112 15W
164 Junction Cy, Kan, USA 39 4N 96 55W
166 Junction Cy., Ore., U.S.A. 44 20N 123 12W
144 Jundah, Australia 24 46S 143 2E
173 Jundial, Brazil 23 10S 47 0W
157 Juneau, Alaska, U.S.A. 58 26N 134 30W
147 Junee, N.S.W., Australia 34 49S 147 32W
57 Jungfrau, Mt., Switz. .46 32N 7 58E
104 Jungshahi, W. Pakistan 24 52N 67 44E
160 Juniata, R., U.S.A. ...40 30N 77 40W
172 Junin, Argentina 34 33S 60 57W
174 Junin, L., Peru 11 2S 76 7W
176 Junin de los Andes, Arg. 39 45S 71 0W
55 Jünkerath, Germany .50 20N 6 36E
112 Junkuren, R., Mongolia 47 40N 113 0E
106 Junnar, India 19 12N 73 58E
166 Juntura, U.S.A. 43 44N 119 4W
127 Jur R., Sudan 8 45N 29 0E
49 Jura, dépt., France ...46 47N 5 45E
40 Jura I., Scot., U.K. ...56 0N 5 50W
49 Jura Mts., Fr.-Switz. .46 35N 6 5E
40 Jura, Paps of, mts., Scotland, U.K. 55 55N 6 0W
40 Jura, Sd. of, Scot., U.K. 55 57N 5 45W
174 Jurado, Colombia 7 7N 77 46W
38 Jurby Hd., Isle of Man, United Kingdom 54 23N 4 31W
78 Jurifofca, Rumania ...44 46N 28 52W
175 Juruti, Brazil 2 10S 56 0W
101 Jurm, Afghanistan 36 50N 70 45E
174 Juruá R., Brazil 5 20S 67 40W
174 Juruena, Brazil 13 0S 58 10W
174 Juruena, R., Brazil ...10 30S 58 20W
173 Jurumirim Dam, Brazil 26 55N 49 20W
49 Jussey, France 47 50N 5 55E
172 Justo Daract, Argentina 33 52S 65 12W
56 Jüterbog, Germany ...51 59N 13 6E
169 Juticalpa, Honduras ..14 40N 85 50W
18 Jutland, pen., Europe 56 0N 8 0E
48 Juvigny, Orne, France 48 33N 0 30W
49 Juvisy, France 48 43N 2 23E
101 Juwain, Afghanistan .31 45N 61 30E
49 Juzennecourt, France 48 10N 5 0E
103 Jye-kundo, China 33 0N 96 50E
82 Jylhama, Finland 64 34N 26 40E
81 Jylland (Jutland), Den. 56 25N 9 30E
82 Jyväskylä, Finland ...62 12N 25 47E

K

102 K2, Mt., Kashmir 36 0N 77 0E
131 Kaabong, Uganda 3 33N 34 6E
135 Kaalspruit, S. Africa .29 15S 26 10E
134 Kaap Plateau, S. Afr. 28 30S 24 0E
133 Kaapmuiden, S. Africa 25 32S 31 22E
109 Kabaena I., Indonesia 5 15S 122 0E
124 Kabala, Sierra Leone . 9 38N 11 37W
131 Kabale, Uganda 1 15S 30 0E
130 Kabalo, Congo 6 0S 27 0E
131 Kabambare, Congo 4 41S 27 39E
108 Kabandjahe, Indonesia 8 2N 98 27E
132 Kabanga, Zambia 17 30S 26 55E
130 Kabango, Congo 8 35S 28 30E
124 Kabara, Mali 16 40N 2 50W
88 Kabardinka, U.S.S.R. 44 40N 37 57E
89 Kabardino-Balkar, A.S.S.R., U.S.S.R. .43 30N 43 30E
109 Kabasalon, Philippines 7 49N 122 34E
125 Kabba, Nigeria 7 57N 6 3E
127 Kabele, Ethiopia 12 52N 40 40E
125 Kabi, Niger 13 30N 12 35E
130 Kabinda, Congo 6 3S 24 28E
126 Kabna, Sudan 19 6N 32 40E
132 Kabompo, Zambia 13 35S 24 10E
132 Kabompo & R., Zambia 13 30S 24 14E
130 Kabondo, Congo 8 58S 25 40E
130 Kabongo, Congo 7 22S 25 33E
125 Kabou, Togo 9 28N 0 55E
144 Kabra, Australia 23 25S 150 25E
130 Kabubu, Congo 9 42S 24 40E
101 Kabud Gonbad, Iran .37 5N 59 45E
125 Kabuiri, Nigeria 11 30N 13 40E
101 Kabul, Afghanistan ...34 28N 69 18E
102 Kabul, prov., Afghan. 34 0N 68 30E
132 Kabulwebulwe, Zambia 14 48S 26 2E
132 Kabunda, Congo 12 27S 29 21E
130 Kabundi, Congo 10 15S 27 14E
109 Kaburuang, Indonesia 3 50N 126 30E
134 Kabus, S.W. Africa ...26 20S 18 12E
127 Kabushiya, Sudan 16 54N 33 41E
108 Kabuwe, Indonesia 5 25S 102 14E
132 Kabuyu, Zambia 17 30S 26 0E
130 Kabwanga, Congo 7 2S 22 36E
132 Kabwe (Broken Hill), Zambia 14 30S 28 29E
74 Kačanik, Yugoslavia .42 13N 21 12E
86 Kachanovo, U.S.S.R. .57 25N 27 38E
132 Kachebere, Zambia ...13 56S 32 50E
103 Kachin, st., Burma 26 0N 97 0E
132 Kachindu, Zambia 17 45S 27 15E
131 Kachira, Lake, Uganda 0 40S 31 0E
90 Kachiry, U.S.S.R. 53 10N 75 50E
89 Kaçkar, Turkey 40 45N 41 30E
107 Kadan Kyun (King I.), Burma 12 30N 98 20E
59 Kadarkut, Hungary ...46 13N 17 39E
106 Kadayanallur, India . 9 3N 77 22E
125 Kaddi, Nigeria 13 40N 5 40E
125 Kade, Ghana 6 7N 0 56W
130 Kadei R., Cent. Africa 4 0N 15 0E
104 Kadi, India 23 18N 72 23E
145 Kadina, South Australia 34 0S 137 43E
106 Kadiri, India 14 12N 78 13E
89 Kadiyevka, U.S.S.R. .48 35N 38 30E
164 Kadoka, U.S.A. 43 50N 101 31W
87 Kadom, U.S.S.R. 54 37N 42 24E
125 Kaduna, Nigeria 10 30N 7 21E
125 Kaduna, R., Nigeria .10 5N 8 10E
125 Kaele, Cameroon 10 15N 14 15E
146 Kaeo, New Zealand ...35 6S 173 49E
112 Kaesong, N. Korea ...38 1N 126 46E
100 Kaf, Saudi Arabia ...31 25N 37 20E
130 Kafakumba, Congo ... 9 38S 23 46E
85 Kafan, U.S.S.R. 39 18N 46 15E
125 Kafanchan, Nigeria ... 9 40N 8 20E
125 Kafareti, Nigeria 10 25N 11 12E
135 Kaffir River, S. Africa 29 27S 26 8E
135 Kaffraria, dist., S. Afr. 33 0S 27 30E
124 Kaffrine, Senegal 14 8N 15 36W
121 Kafia Kingi, Sudan ... 9 20N 24 25E
132 Kafinda, Zambia 12 32S 30 20E
77 Kafirevs, Akra, C., Gr. 38 9N 24 8E
101 Kafiristan, dist, Afghan. 35 0N 70 30E
78 Kafr Ana, Israel 32 2N 34 48E
98 Kafr 'Ein, Jordan 32 3N 35 7E
126 Kafr el Dauwar, Egypt 31 8N 30 8E
98 Kafr Kama, Israel ...32 44N 35 26E
98 Kafr Kanna, Israel ...32 45N 35 20E
98 Kafr Malik, Jordan ...32 0N 35 18E
98 Kafr Manda, Israel ...32 49N 35 15E
98 Kafr Quaddum, Jordan 32 14N 35 7E
98 Kafr Ra'i, Jordan 32 23N 35 9E
98 Kafr Sir, Lebanon 33 19N 35 23E
98 Kafr Yasif, Israel 32 58N 35 10E
131 Kafu R., Uganda 1 15N 31 15E
132 Kafue, Zambia 15 46S 28 9E
132 Kafue, R., Zambia ...15 30S 26 0E
132 Kafue Gorge, & Dam., Zambia 16 0S 28 0E
132 Kafulwe, Zambia 9 0S 29 1E
130 Kafumba, Congo 5 19S 19 0E
132 Kafuta, Zambia 14 5S 23 45E
90 Kagan, U.S.S.R. 39 50N 64 45E
131 Kagera R., Tanzania . 1 15S 31 20E
114 Kagoshima, Japan 31 36N 130 40E
114 Kagoshima-wan., B., Japan 31 0N 130 40E
88 Kagul, U.S.S.R. 45 50N 28 15E
131 Kagulu, Uganda 1 13N 33 18E
108 Kahajan R., Indonesia 2 10S 114 0E
131 Kahama, Tanzania 4 8S 32 30E
131 Kahe, Tanzania 3 30S 37 25E
130 Kahemba, Congo 7 18S 18 55E
147 Kaherekoau, Mts., N.Z. 45 45S 167 15E
101 Kahnuj, Iran 27 55N 57 40E
164 Kahoka, U.S.A. 40 25N 91 42W
158 Kahoolawe, I., Hawaii, U.S.A. 20 33N 156 35W
147 Kahvrangi, Pt., N.Z. .40 50S 172 10E
109 Kai Is., Indonesia 5 55S 132 45W
125 Kaiama, Nigeria 9 36N 4 1E
147 Kaiapoi, N.Z. 43 24S 172 40E
113 Kaifeng, China 34 49N 114 30E
113 Kaihwa, China 29 0N 118 21E
146 Kaikohe, N.Z. 35 25S 173 49E
147 Kaikoura, & Pen., N.Z. 42 25S 173 43E
147 Kaikoura Ra., N.Z. ...41 59S 173 41E
124 Kailahun, Sierra Leone 8 18N 10 39W
105 Kailas Range, Tibet, China 31 0N 82 0E
113 Kailu, China 43 25N 120 36E
109 Kaimana, New Guinea 3 30S 133 45E
146 Kaimanawa Mts., N.Z. 39 15S 175 56E
147 Kaimata, N.Z. 42 34S 171 28E
105 Kaimganj, India 27 33N 79 24E
105 Kaimur Hill, India ...24 30N 82 0E
146 Kaingaroa Forest, N.Z. 38 30S 176 30E
125 Kainji Res., Nigeria ...10 1N 4 40E
146 Kaipara Harb., N.Z. .36 25S 174 14E
112 Kaiping, China 40 28N 122 10E
155 Kaipokok B., Canada 55 10N 59 20W
104 Kairana, India 29 33N 77 15E
144 Kairiru, I., Terr. of, New Guinea 3 20S 143 20E
109 Kaironi, Indonesia ... 0 47S 133 40E
123 Kairouan, Tunisia 35 45N 10 5E
144 Kairuku, Terr. of Papua 8 57S 146 35E
57 Kaiserslautern, Ger. ...49 30N 7 43E
146 Kaitaia, New Zealand 35 8S 173 17E
147 Kaitangata, N.Z. 46 17S 169 51E
104 Kaithal, India 29 48N 76 26E
112 Kaitung, China 44 58N 123 2E
112 Kaiyüan, China 42 40N 124 30E
82 Kajaani, Finland 64 17N 27 46E
144 Kajabbi, Australia ...20 0S 140 1E
108 Kajan R., Indonesia . 2 40N 116 40E
107 Kajang, W. Malaysia . 2 59N 101 48E
109 Kajeli, Indonesia 3 20S 127 10E
131 Kajiado, Kenya 1 53S 36 48E

MAP
127 Kajo Kaji, Sudan 3 58N 31 40E
109 Kajoa I., Indonesia ... 0 1N 127 28E
108 Kajuagung, Indonesia 32 8S 104 46E
127 Kaka, Sudan 10 38N 32 10E
154 Kakabeka Falls, Can. 48 24N 89 37W
134 Kakamas, S. Africa ...28 45S 20 33E
131 Kakamega & dist., Kenya 0 20N 34 46E
74 Kakanj, Yugoslavia ...44 9N 18 7E
147 Kakanui Mts., N.Z. ...45 10S 170 30E
147 Kakapotahi, N.Z. 43 0S 170 45E
157 Kake, Alaska, U.S.A. .57 0N 134 0W
114 Kakegawa, Japan 34 45N 138 1E
89 Kakhib, U.S.S.R. 42 28N 46 34E
88 Kakhovka, Res., U.S.S.R. 47 5N 34 16E
129 Kakia, Botswana 24 48S 23 22E
106 Kakinada, (Cocanada), India ...16 50N 82 11E
127 Kakkisi, Ethiopia 9 40N 37 57E
132 Kakoaka, Botswana ...18 35S 24 15E
131 Kakuma, Kenya 3 45N 34 50E
130 Kakuni, Congo 10 59S 24 45E
125 Kala, Cameroon 12 2N 14 40E
106 Kala Oya., Ceylon 8 15N 80 0E
123 Kalaa-Kebira, Tunisia 35 59N 10 32E
104 Kalabagh, W. Pakistan 33 0N 71 28E
76 Kalabaka, Greece 39 42N 21 39E
132 Kalabo, Zambia 14 58S 22 33E
87 Kalach, U.S.S.R. 50 22N 41 0E
103 Kaladan R., Burma ...21 30N 92 45E
160 Kaladar, Canada 44 37N 77 5W
133 Kalahari, Desert, Africa 24 0S 22 0E
106 Kalahasti, India 13 45N 79 44E
91 Kalakan, U.S.S.R. 55 15N 116 45E
131 Kalama, Congo 2 52S 28 35E
165 Kalama, U.S.A. 46 0N 122 55W
77 Kalamata, Greece 37 3N 22 10E
162 Kalamazoo, & R., U.S.A. 42 20N 85 35W
76 Kalamaria, Greece 40 33N 22 55E
106 Kalamb, India 18 3N 74 48E
131 Kalambo Falls, Tanz. 8 37S 31 35E
77 Kálamos, Greece 38 37N 20 59E
77 Kalamos, I., Greece ...38 37N 20 55E
77 Kalamoti, Greece 38 15N 26 4E
142 Kalamunda, W. Austral. 32 0S 116 0E
142 Kalannie, W. Australia 30 12S 117 17E
109 Kalao, I., Indonesia ... 7 21S 121 0E
109 Kalaotoa I., Indonesia 7 20S 121 50E
80 Kälarne, Sweden 62 59N 16 8E
59 Kalarovo, Cz. 47 54N 18 0E
107 Kalasin, Thailand 16 26N 103 30E
102 Kalat, West Pakistan 29 8N 66 31E
101 Kalat-i-Ghilzai, Afghan 32 15N 66 58E
77 Kalathos (Calato), Ródhos, Greece 36 9N 28 8E
89 Kalaus, R., U.S.S.R. .45 40N 43 30E
77 Kalávryita, Greece ...38 3N 22 8E
124 Kalba, Ghana 9 30N 2 42W
134 Kalbaskraal, S. Africa 33 36S 18 39E
55 Kaldenkirchen, Ger. ...51 19N 6 11E
79 Kaldhovd, Norway 60 5N 8 20E
88 Kalecik, Turkey 40 4N 33 26E
103 Kalegauk I., Burma ...15 33N 97 35E
131 Kalehe, Congo 2 6S 28 50E
131 Kalemera, Tanzania ... 2 20S 33 37E
130 Kalemie, Congo 5 55S 29N 9E
103 Kalewa, Burma 23 15N 94 20E
112 Kalgan, China 40 52N 114 45E
142 Kalgoorlie, W. Austral. 30 40S 121 22E
108 Kalianda, Indonesia ... 5 50S 105 45E
109 Kalibo, Philippines 11 40N 122 30E
130 Kalima, Congo 2 33S 26 32E
108 Kalimantan, prov., Indon. 0 1S 115 0E
77 Kalimnos I., Greece ...37 0N 27 0E
105 Kalimpong, India 27 4N 88 35E
106 Kalinadi R., India 14 50N 74 20E
87 Kalinin, U.S.S.R. 56 55N 35 55E
91 Kalinina, U.S.S.R. 60 0N 108 15E
86 Kaliningrad, U.S.S.R. 54 42N 20 32E
89 Kalinino, U.S.S.R. 45 12N 38 59E
86 Kalinkovichi, U.S.S.R. 52 12N 29 20E
132 Kalinku, Zambia 11 12S 33 12E
74 Kalinovik, Yugoslavia 43 31N 18 29E
75 Kalipetrovo (Stančevo), Bulg. ...44 5N 27 14E
131 Kaliro, Uganda 0 56N 33 30E
76 Kalirrakhi, Greece 40 40N 24 35E
166 Kalispell, U.S.A. 46 10N 114 22W
60 Kalisz, Poland 53 17N 15 55E
60 Kalisz Pom, Poland ...51 45N 18 8E
131 Kaliua, Tanzania 5 5S 31 48E
106 Kaliveli Tank, L., India 12 5N 79 50E
80 Kalix, Sweden 65 53N 23 12E
82 Kalix R., Sweden 67 0N 22 0E
104 Kalka, India 30 56N 76 57E
55 Kalkar, Germany 51 45N 6 15E
162 Kalkaska, U.S.A. 0 44N 85 9W
133 Kalkbank, S. Africa ...23 35S 29 22E
135 Kalkfontein Dam, South Africa 29 30S 24 15E
135 Kalkpan, O.F.S., S. Afr. 28 15S 25 38E
129 Kalkrand, S.W. Africa 21 15S 17 35E
55 Kall, Germany 50 33N 6 33E
80 Kall L., Sweden 63 35N 13 10E
106 Kallakurichi, India 11 44N 79 1E
81 Kållandsö, I., Sweden 58 40N 13 5E
81 Källby, Sweden 58 30N 13 8E
93 Kallia, Jordan 31 46N 35 30E
77 Kallonis, Kolpos, G. of, Greece 39 10N 26 10E
106 Kallidaikurichi, India 8 38N 77 31E
81 Kallinge, Sweden 56 15N 15 18E
77 Kallithéa, Greece 37 5N 23 41E
76 Kallmet, Albania 41 51N 19 41E
81 Källtorp, Sweden 58 23N 13 20E
125 Kalmalo, Nigeria 13 40N 5 20E
81 Kalmar, Sweden 56 39N 16 22E
81 Kalmar Län, co., Swed. 57 25N 16 30E
81 Kalmar Sund, Sweden 56 50N 16 45E
55 Kalmthout, Belgium .51 23N 4 29E
89 Kalmyk A.S.S.R., U.S.S.R. 46 5N 46 1E
85 Kalmykovo, U.S.S.R. 49 0N 51 35E
105 Kalna, India 23 13N 88 25E
144 Kalo, Terr. of Papua .10 0S 147 42E
59 Kalocsa, Hungary 46 32N 19 0E
75 Kalofer, Bulgaria 42 37N 24 59E
104 Kalol, India 23 15N 72 33E
104 Kalol, India 22 37N 73 31E
77 Kalolimnos, I., Greece 37 4N 27 8E
132 Kalomo, Zambia 17 0S 26 30E
77 Kaloneròn, Greece 37 20N 21 38E
132 Kalonga, Zambia 15 12S 22 59E
132 Kalonje, Zambia 12 8S 31 15E
131 Kalossia, Kenya 1 37N 35 55E
105 Kalpi, India 26 8N 79 47E
106 Kalrayan Hills, India 11 45N 78 40E
106 Kalsubai, Mt., India .17 35N 73 45E
125 Kaltungo, Nigeria 9 48N 11 19E
104 Kalu, West Pakistan .25 5N 67 39E
87 Kaluga, U.S.S.R. 54 35N 36 10E
81 Kalundborg, Denmark 55 41N 11 5E
132 Kalungswisi R., Zambia 9 30S 29 30E
86 Kalush, U.S.S.R. 42 9N 24 12E
106 Kalutara, Ceylon 6 35N 80 0E
132 Kalwa, Zambia 13 10S 30 22E
104 Kalyan, India 20 30N 74 3E
106 Kalyani, India 17 53N 76 59E
87 Kalyazin, U.S.S.R. 57 15N 37 45E
107 Kam Keut, Laos 18 20N 104 48E
84 Kama R., U.S.S.R. ...60 0N 53 0E
125 Kamaguenam, Niger .13 36N 10 30E
114 Kamaishi, Japan 39 20N 142 0E
104 Kamalia, W. Pakistan 30 44N 72 42E
132 Kamapanda, Zambia .12 5S 24 0E
99 Kamaran I., Red Sea .15 28N 42 35E
132 Kamativi, Rhodesia ...18 15S 0 27E
125 Kamba, Nigeria 11 50N 3 45E
132 Kambalda, W. Australia 31 10S 121 37E
106 Kambam, India 9 45N 77 16E
104 Kambar, W. Pakistan 27 37N 68 1E
124 Kambia, Sierra Leone 9 3N 12 53W
132 Kambole, Zambia 8 47S 30 48E
130 Kambove, Congo 10 51S 26 33E
91 Kamchatka, Pen., U.S.S.R. 57 0N 160 0E
144 Kamde, Indonesia 8 0S 140 58E
133 Kameel, C. Prov., S. Afr. 26 38S 24 58E
55 Kamen, Germany 51 36N 7 39E
90 Kamen, U.S.S.R. 53 50N 81 30E
86 Kamen Kashirskiy, U.S.S.R. 51 39N 24 56E
132 Kamena, Tanzania 3 5S 32 20E
74 Kamenica, Yugoslavia 44 25N 19 40E
58 Kamenice, Cz. 49 18N 15 2E
71 Kamenjak, Rt., Yugoslavia 44 47N 13 55E
84 Kamenka, U.S.S.R. ...65 58N 44 0E
87 Kamenka, U.S.S.R. ...50 47N 39 20E
88 Kamenka, U.S.S.R. ...48 0N 30 20E
86 Kamenka Bugskaya, U.S.S.R. 50 8N 24 16E
88 Kamenka Dneprovskaya, U.S.S.R. 47 29N 34 14E
90 Kamensk, U.S.S.R. ...56 25N 62 45E
89 Kamensk, Shakhtinskiy, U.S.S.R. 48 23N 40 20E
87 Kamenskiy, U.S.S.R. .50 48N 45 25E
91 Kamenskoye, U.S.S.R. 62 45N 165 30E
75 Kamenyak, Bulgaria ..43 24N 26 57E
111 Kamet, Mt., Tibet, China 31 3N 79 25E
56 Kamenz, Germany ...51 17N 14 7E
40 Kames, Scot., U.K. ...55 44N 5 15W
113 Kami, C., China 20 14N 109 50E
166 Kamiah, U.S.A. 46 12N 116 2W
60 Kamien, Poland 53 57N 14 43E
60 Kamien, Poland 53 32N 17 32E
60 Kamiensk, Poland 51 12N 19 29E
60 Kamienna Gora, Poland 50 48N 16 2E
134 Kamieskroon, S. Africa 30 18S 18 6E
77 Kamilonisi, I., Greece 35 50N 26 15E
157 Kamilukuak, L., Can. 62 40N 100 0W
130 Kamina, Congo 8 45S 25 0E
157 Kaminak L., Canada .62 0N 95 0W
156 Kamloops, Canada 50 40N 120 20W
147 Kamo, New Zealand .35 42S 174 20E
104 Kamoke, West Pakistan 32 4N 74 4E
58 Kamp R., Austria 48 35N 15 26E
55 Kamp-Lintfort, Ger. .51 31N 6 32E
108 Kampa, Indonesia 1 42S 105 24E
131 Kampala, Uganda 0 20N 32 30E
107 Kampar, W. Malaysia 4 18N 101 9E
108 Kampar R., Indonesia 0 30N 102 0E
54 Kampen, Netherlands 52 33N 5 53E
132 Kampoka R., Zambia 14 0S 30 0E
107 Kampot, Cambodia ...10 36N 104 10E
104 Kamptee, India 21 9N 79 19E
124 Kampti, Upper Volta 10 7N 3 25W
109 Kamrau Bay, Indon. . 3 30S 133 45E
157 Kamsack, Canada 51 35N 101 50W
87 Kamskoye Ustye, U.S.S.R. 55 10N 49 20E
131 Kamuli, Uganda 0 57N 33 3E
87 Kamyshin, U.S.S.R. ...50 10N 45 30E
89 Kamyzyak, U.S.S.R. .46 4N 48 10E
154 Kanaaupscow, Canada 54 0N 76 40W
167 Kanab, U.S.A. 37 3N 112 29W
167 Kanab Creek, U.S.A. .37 0N 112 40W
114 Kanagawa, pref., Japan 35 20N 139 20E
106 Kanakapura, India 12 33N 77 28E
76 Kanalia, Greece 39 30N 22 53E
112 Kananchen, China 45 45N 121 55E
130 Kananga, Congo........ 5 55S 22 18E
167 Kanarraville, U.S.A. .37 34N 113 12W
76 Kanastraion, Akra. C., Greece 39 54N 23 40E
87 Kanash, U.S.S.R. 55 48N 47 32E
162 Kanawha R., U.S.A. .39 40N 82 0W
126 Kanayis, Ras el, Egypt 31 30N 28 5E
114 Kanazawa, Japan 36 30N 136 38E
107 Kanchanaburi, Thailand 14 8N 99 31E
105 Kanchenjunga, mt. Nep. 27 50N 88 10E
106 Kanchipuram (Conjeeveram), India 12 52N 79 45E
113 Kanchow, China 25 58N 114 55E
112 Kanchuan, China 36 29N 109 24E
59 Kanczuga, Poland 49 58N 22 25E
130 Kanda Kanda, Congo 6 52S 23 48E
85 Kandagach, U.S.S.R. . 49 20N 57 15E
101 Kandahar, Afghan. 31 32N 65 30E
84 Kandalaksha, U.S.S.R. 67 9N 32 30E
130 Kandale, Congo 6 8S 19 10E
108 Kandangan, Indonesia 2 50S 115 20E
77 Kandanos, Crete, Greece 35 19N 23 44E
77 Kandhila, Greece 37 46N 22 22E
104 Kandhkot, W. Pakistan 28 16N 69 8E
104 Kandhla, India 29 18N 77 19E
124 Kandi, Dahomey 11 7N 2 55E
105 Kandi, India 23 58N 88 5E
100 Kandira, Turkey 41 5N 30 10E
104 Kandla, India 23 0N 70 10E
143 Kandos, Australia 32 45S 149 58E
102 Kandrach, Pakistan ...25 30N 65 30E
106 Kandukur, India 15 12N 79 57E
106 Kandy, Ceylon 7 18N 80 43E
160 Kane, U.S.A. 41 39N 78 53W
14 Kane B., Canada 79 0N 70 0W
113 Kanen, China 18 46N 108 33E
89 Kaneyskaya, U.S.S.R. 46 3N 39 3E
71 Kanfanar, Yugoslavia 45 7N 13 50E
101 Kang, Afghanistan 30 55N 61 55E
107 Kangar, W. Malaysia . 6 27N 100 12E
143 Kangaroo Flat, Austral. 36 45S 144 20E
145 Kangaroo I., S. Austral. 35 45S 137 0E
144 Kangaroo Mts., Austral. 23 25S 142 0E
100 Kangavar, Iran 34 40N 48 0E
108 Kangean Is., Indonesia 6 55S 115 23E
14 Kangerdlugssuak, Greenland 68 15N 30 30W
131 Kangetet, Kenya 1 57N 36 4E
112 Kanggye, N. Korea ...41 0N 126 35E
128 Kango, Gabon 0 11N 10 5E
130 Kangoya, Congo 9 57S 22 49E
113 Kangshan, Taiwan 22 43N 120 14E
103 Kangto, Mt., India 27 50N 92 35E
106 Kanhangad, India 12 21N 74 58E
106 Kanheri, India 19 13N 72 50E
103 Kani, China 29 25N 95 25E
155 Kaniapiskau L., Can. .53 52N 69 20W
155 Kaniapiskau R., Can. 55 15N 68 40E
84 Kanin Nos, C., U.S.S.R. 68 45N 43 20E
84 Kanin Pen., U.S.S.R. .68 0N 45 0E
76 Kanino, Albania 40 23N 19 30E
146 Kaniva, Vic., Australia 36 22S 141 18E
74 Kanjiza, Yugoslavia ...46 3N 20 4E
162 Kankakee, Ill., U.S.A. 41 6N 87 50W
162 Kankakee R., U.S.A. .41 13N 87 0W
124 Kankan, Guinea 10 30N 9 15W
163 Kannapolis, U.S.A. ...35 32N 80 37W
105 Kannauj, India 27 3N 79 26E
125 Kano, Nigeria 12 2N 8 30E
132 Kanona, Zambia 13 0S 30 37E
108 Kanowit, Sar., Malaysia 2 14N 112 20E
142 Kanowna, W. Australia 30 32S 121 31E
114 Kanoya, Japan 31 25N 130 50E
131 Kapedo, Kenya 1 6N 36 5E
131 Kapenguria, Kenya 1 4N 35 7E
103 Kanpetlet, Burma 21 10N 93 59E
105 Kanpur, India 26 35N 80 20E
132 Kansanshi, Zambia ...12 0S 26 22E
164 Kansas, st., U.S.A. 38 40N 98 0W
164 Kansas Cy, Kans, U.S.A. 39 0N 94 40W
164 Kansas Cy, Mo, U.S.A. 39 3N 94 30W
164 Kansas R., U.S.A. 39 15N 96 20W
130 Kansenia, Congo 10 20S 26 0E
91 Kansk, U.S.S.R. 56 20N 95 37E
112 Kansu, prov., China ...35 30N 104 30E
125 Kantche, Niger 13 31N 8 30E
89 Kantemirovka, U.S.S.R. 49 43N 39 55E
114 Kanto, dist., Japan ...36 25N 140 30E
111 Kantse, China 31 30N 100 29E
114 Kanuma, Japan 36 44N 139 42E
134 Kanus, S.W. Africa ...27 50 18 39E
131 Kanyada, Kenya 0 37S 34 30E
133 Kanye, Botswana 25 0S 25 28E
132 Kanyenda, Malawi 12 30S 34 3E
132 Kanyu, Botswana 20 7S 24 37E
113 Kanyu, China 34 56N 119 8E
130 Kanzenze, Congo 10 30S 25 12E
113 Kaoan, China 28 20N 115 17E
113 Kaohsiun, Taiwan 22 35N 120 16E
129 Kaoko Otavi, S.W. Afr. 18 12S 13 45E
124 Kaolack, Senegal 14 5N 16 8W
112 Kaomi, China 36 25N 119 45E
112 Kaoping, China 35 57N 113 0E
113 Kaoyu, China 32 46N 119 32E
104 Kapadvanj, India 23 5N 73 0E
132 Kapalala Ferry, Zam. 12 24S 29 20E
130 Kapanga, Congo 8 30S 22 40E
89 Kapanovka, U.S.S.R. 47 28N 46 50E
132 Kapata, Zambia 14 16S 26 15E
132 Kapatu, Zambia 9 43S 30 42E
55 Kapelle, Germany 51 44N 7 35E
55 Kapellen, Belgium 51 19N 4 25E
55 Kapellen, Germany ...51 34N 6 21E
77 Kapello, Akra, C., Gr. 36 9N 23 3E
58 Kapfenberg, Austria .47 26N 15 18E
132 Kaphambale, Malawi .12 3S 33 57E
154 Kapiskau, Canada 52 50N 82 1W
154 Kapiskau R., Canada .52 20N 83 40W
108 Kapit, Sar., E. Malaysia 2 0N 113 5E
146 Kapiti I., N.Z. 40 50S 174 56E
58 Kaplice, Czechoslovakia 48 42N 14 30E
127 Kapoeta, Sudan 4 50N 33 35E
58 Kapolnasnyek, Hung. 47 16N 18 42E
130 Kapombo, Congo 10 39S 23 30E
147 Kaponga, N.Z. 39 29S 174 9E
59 Kapos R., Hungary ...46 30N 18 20E
59 Kaposvár, Hungary ...46 25N 17 47E
109 Kapotjol, Indonesia ... 2 0S 130 9E
56 Kappeln, Germany 54 37N 9 56E
71 Kaprije, I., Y.-slavia .43 42N 15 43E
131 Kapsabet, Kenya 0 14N 35 5E
86 Kapsukas, see Mariyampole, U.S.S.R. 54 33N 23 19E
108 Kapuas R., Indonesia 0 20N 111 40E
108 Kapuas Hulu Ra., Sar., E. Malaysia ... 1 30N 113 30E
132 Kapuka, Zambia 10 30S 32 55E
145 Kapunda, S. Australia 34 20S 138 56E
104 Kapurthala, India 31 23N 75 25E
154 Kapuskasing, Canada 49 25N 82 30W
154 Kapuskasing R., Can. 49 0N 82 50W
89 Kapustin Yar, U.S.S.R. 48 37N 45 40E
145 Kaputar, Mt., Austral. 30 15S 150 10E
131 Kaputir, Kenya 2 5N 35 28E
59 Kapuvár, Hungary 47 36N 17 1E
127 Kar Kur Hills, Sudan 12 30N 26 15E
77 Kara, Turkey 38 29N 26 19E
90 Kara, U.S.S.R. 69 10N 65 25E
77 Kara, I., Turkey 36 58N 27 30E
85 Kara-Bogaz-Gol, USSR. 41 0N 53 30E
77 Kara Burun, C., Turkey 38 41N 26 28E
90 Kara Kalpak, A.S.S.R., U.S.S.R. .43 0N 60 0E
90 Kara Kum, U.S.S.R. .39 30N 60 0E
111 Kara Nor, mt., China 38 45N 98 0E
90 Kara Sea, U.S.S.R. ...75 0N 70 0E
126 Kara, Wadi, Si. Arab. 20 40N 42 0E
88 Karabuk, Turkey 41 10N 32 30E
76 Karaburun, Albania ...40 25N 19 20E
90 Karabutak, U.S.S.R. .50 0N 60 45E
89 Karachala, U.S.S.R. ...39 45N 48 53E
87 Karachev, U.S.S.R. 53 10N 35 5E
89 Karacheyevsk, U.S.S.R. 43 50N 42 0E
143 Karachi, Australia 36 58S 148 45E
104 Karachi, Pakistan 24 53N 67 0E
106 Karad, India 17 15N 74 10E
88 Karadeniz Bogazi (Bosporus), Turkey 41 10N 29 5E
125 Karaga, Ghana 9 58N 0 28W
90 Karagajly, U.S.S.R. ...49 26N 76 0E
90 Karaganda, U.S.S.R. .49 50N 73 0E
91 Karaginski I., U.S.S.R. 58 45N 164 0E
124 Karagoroula, Mali 12 25N 4 50W
106 Karaikal, India 10 59N 79 50E
106 Karaikkudi, India 10 0N 78 45E
106 Karaitivu, I., Ceylon . 9 45N 79 52E
100 Karaj, Iran 35 4N 51 0E
76 Karajë, Albania 41 11N 19 33E
98 Karak, Jordan 31 14N 35 40E
90 Karakas, U.S.S.R. 48 20N 83 30E
109 Karakitang, I., Indon. 3 14N 125 28E
112 Karakorum, Mongolia 47 30N 102 20E
102 Karakoram Ra. & Pass, Kashmir 35 20N 78 0E
91 Karalon, U.S.S.R. 57 5N 115 50E
75 Karalsen, Bulgaria ...43 22N 25 21E
111 Karamai, China 45 57N 84 30E
100 Karaman, Turkey 37 14N 33 13E
108 Karambu, Indonesia . 3 53S 116 6E
147 Karamea, New Zealand 41 14S 172 6E
147 Karamea Bight, N.Z. .41 22S 171 40E
147 Karamea R., N.Z. 41 13S 172 25E
132 Karamechen, Botswana 21 36S 27 40E
104 Karamsad, India 22 35N 72 50E
109 Karanganjar, Indonesia 7 38S 109 37E
104 Karanja, India 20 29N 77 31E
146 Karapoir, New Zealand 37 53S 175 32E
88 Karaşar, Turkey 40 21N 31 55E
134 Karasburg, S.W. Africa 28 0S 18 44E
90 Karasino, U.S.S.R. 66 50N 86 50E
82 Karasjok, Norway 69 27N 25 30E
90 Karasuk, U.S.S.R. 53 44N 78 2E
90 Karatau, U.S.S.R. 43 10N 70 28E
106 Karativu, I., Ceylon .. 8 22N 79 52E
98 Karatiya, Israel 31 39N 34 43E
114 Karatsu, Japan 33 30N 130 0E
104 Karauli, India 26 30N 77 4E
90 Karauzyak, U.S.S.R. .43 30N 59 30E
76 Karavasta, Albania ...40 53N 19 28E
77 Karavi, I., Greece 36 45N 23 35E
58 Karawanken Mts., Eur. 46 30N 14 40E
100 Karbala, Iraq 32 47N 44 3E
80 Karböle, Sweden 61 59N 15 22E
59 Karcag, Hungary 47 19N 21 1E
81 Kärda, Sweden 57 10N 13 49E
77 Kardhamila, Greece ...38 35N 26 5E
76 Kardhitsa, Greece 39 23N 21 54E
86 Kardla, U.S.S.R. 58 50N 22 40E
135 Karee, O.F.S., S. Africa 28 50S 26 22E
134 Kareeberge, mts., C. Prov., S. Afr. 30 50S 22 0E
134 Kareedouw, S. Africa 33 58S 24 16E
134 Kareekloof, S. Africa .29 50S 23 30E
126 Kareima, Sudan 18 30N 31 49E
107 Karen, Andaman Is. .12 49N 92 53E
100 Karganrud, Iran 37 55N 49 0E
90 Kargat, U.S.S.R. 55 10N 80 15E
88 Kargi, Turkey 41 11N 34 30E
102 Kargil, Kashmir 34 32N 76 12E
122 Karia, Morocco 34 15N 5 17W
77 Karial, Greece 40 14N 24 19E
132 Kariba, & Dam, Rhodesia 16 28S 28 36E
132 Kariba, L., Rhodesia .16 40S 28 25E
132 Kariba Gorge, Zambia 16 30S 28 35E
129 Karibib, S.W. Africa .21 0S 15 56E
134 Kariega R., S. Africa .32 45S 23 35E
106 Karikal, India 10 59N 79 50E
100 Karikkale, Turkey 39 55N 33 30E
108 Karimata I., Indonesia 1 40S 109 0E
108 Karimata Str., Indon. 2 0S 108 20E
106 Karimnagar, India 18 26N 79 10E
108 Karimundjawals, Indon. 5 50S 110 30E
99 Karin, Somali Rep. ...10 50N 45 52E
77 Karistos, Greece 38 1N 24 29E
114 Kariya, Japan 34 58N 137 1E
132 Kariyangwe, Rhodesia 18 0S 27 29E
106 Karkal, India 13 15N 74 56E
144 Karkar I., New Guinea 4 40S 146 0E
88 Karkinitskiy, Gulf of, U.S.S.R. 45 36N 32 35E
98 Karkur, Israel 32 29N 34 57E
126 Karkur Tohl, Egypt ...22 5N 25 5E
86 Karl Libknekht, U.S.S.R. 51 40N 35 45E
56 Karl-Marx-Stadt, Ger. 50 50N 12 55E
76 Kárla, L., Greece 39 35N 22 45E
60 Karlino, Poland 54 3N 15 53E
71 Karlobag, Y.-slavia ...44 32N 15 5E
71 Karlovac, Y.-slavia ...45 31N 15 36E
88 Karlovka, U.S.S.R. 49 29N 35 8E
58 Karlovy Vary, Cz. 50 13N 12 51E
81 Karlsborg, Sweden 58 33N 14 33E
81 Karlshamn, Sweden ...56 13N 14 56E
81 Karlskoga, Sweden 59 22N 14 33E
81 Karlskrona, Sweden ...56 12N 15 42E
57 Karlsruhe, Germany .49 3N 8 23E
80 Karlstad, Sweden 59 24N 13 35E
164 Karlstad, U.S.A. 48 38N 96 30W
79 Karmöy I., Norway ...59 15N 5 10E
104 Karnal, India 29 42N 77 2E
105 Karnali R., Nepal 29 0N 82 0E
107 Karnaphuli Res., E. Pakistan 22 40N 92 20E
165 Karnes City, U.S.A. ...28 53N 97 53W
124 Karni, Ghana 10 45N 2 40W
75 Karnobat, Bulgaria ...42 40N 27 0E
58 Karnten (Carinthia) prov., Austria 46 52N 13 30E
124 Karo, Upper Volta ...12 16N 2 22W
132 Karoi, Rhodesia 16 48S 29 45E
132 Karonga, Malawi 9 57S 33 55E
145 Karoonda, S. Australia 35 1S 139 59E
77 Karos, Is., Greece 36 54N 25 40E
76 Karousådhes, Greece .39 47N 19 45E
81 Karpalund, Sweden ...56 4N 14 5E
77 Karpathos I., Greece .35 37N 27 10E
84 Karpogory, U.S.S.R. .63 59N 44 27E
81 Karrebaek, Denmark .55 12N 11 39E
100 Kars, Turkey 40 40N 43 5E
90 Karsakpay, U.S.S.R. .47 55N 66 40E
89 Karsha, U.S.S.R. 49 45N 51 35E
90 Karshi, U.S.S.R. 39 0N 65 55E
87 Karsun, U.S.S.R. 54 14N 46 57E
76 Kartal Oros, mts., Gr. 41 15N 25 13E
104 Kartapur, India 31 27N 75 32E
90 Kartaly, U.S.S.R. 53 10N 60 50E
160 Karthaus, U.S.A. 41 8N 78 9W
60 Kartuzy, Poland 54 22N 18 10E
109 Karufa, Indonesia 3 50S 133 20E
144 Karumba, Australia ...17 31S 140 50E
131 Karumo, Tanzania 2 25S 32 50E

MAP
131 Karungu, Kenya 0 50S 34 10E
81 Karup, Denmark 56 19N 9 10E
106 Karur, India 10 59N 78 2E
59 Karvina, Cz. 49 53N 18 25E
105 Karwi, India 25 12N 80 57E
107 Kas Kong, Cambodia .11 27N 102 12E
132 Kasabi, Zambia 14 52S 23 55E
132 Kasache, Malawi 13 25S 34 20E
130 Kasai, R., Congo & Angola 8 20S 22 0E
130 Kasai Oriental, Prov., Congo 5 0S 24 0E
130 Kasai Occidental, Prov., Congo 6 30S 22 30E
130 Kasaji, Congo 10 25S 23 27E
132 Kasama, Zambia 10 16S 31 9E
131 Kasanga, Tanzania 8 30S 31 10E
130 Kasangulu, Congo 4 15S 15 15E
106 Kasaragod, India 12 30N 74 58E
157 Kasba L., Canada 60 20N 102 10W
122 Kasba Tadla, Morocco 32 47N 6 10W
81 Kåseberga, Sweden ...55 24N 14 8E
130 Kaseke, Congo 2 22S 30 47E
132 Kasempa, Zambia 13 30S 25 44E
130 Kasenye, Congo 1 25N 30 27E
131 Kasese, Uganda 0 13N 30 3E
132 Kasewa, Zambia 14 28S 28 53E
104 Kasganj, India 27 48N 78 42E
154 Kashabowie, Canada .48 40N 90 26W
101 Kashan, Iran 34 5N 51 30E
111 Kashgar, China 39 46N 75 52E
130 Kashimbo, Congo 11 12S 26 19E
87 Kashin, U.S.S.R. 57 32N 37 22E
113 Kashing, China 30 45N 120 41E
104 Kashipur, India 29 15N 79 0E
106 Kashipur, India 19 16N 83 3E
87 Kashira, U.S.S.R. 54 45N 38 10E
132 Kashitu, Zambia 13 37S 28 38E
101 Kashmar, Iran 35 16N 58 26E
102 Kashmir, st., Asia 32 44N 74 54E
104 Kashmor, W. Pak. 28 28N 69 32E
87 Kashpirovka, U.S.S.R. 53 0N 48 30E
103 Kashum Tso L. Tibet, China 34 45N 86 0E
87 Kasimov, U.S.S.R. 54 55N 41 20E
132 Kasinka, Botswana ...18 13S 24 22E
132 Kasisi Plains, Zambia 13 5S 22 25E
164 Kaskaskia R., U.S.A. .38 40N 89 12W
82 Kaskinen (Kaskö), Finland 62 22N 21 13E
156 Kaslo, Canada 49 55N 117 0W
130 Kasongo, Congo 4 30S 26 33E
130 Kasongo Lunda, Congo 6 35S 17 0E
77 Kasos, I., Greece 35 20N 26 55E
77 Kasos Strait, Greece .35 30N 26 30E
89 Kaspi, U.S.S.R. 41 54N 44 17E
89 Kaspiyskiy, U.S.S.R. .45 22N 47 23E
89 Kaspiysk, U.S.S.R. ...42 45N 47 40E
107 Kas Rong I., Cambodia 10 45N 103 15E
127 Kassab ed Doleib, Sud. 13 30N 33 35E
126 Kassaba, Egypt 22 40N 29 55E
127 Kassala, Sudan 15 23N 36 26E
76 Kassándra Pen., Greece 40 0N 23 30E
56 Kassel, Germany 51 19N 9 32E
126 Kassinger, Sudan 18 46N 31 51E
76 Kassiopi, Corfu I., Gr. 39 48N 19 55E
109 Kassue, Indonesia 6 58S 139 21E
100 Kastamonu, Turkey ...41 25N 33 43E
71 Kastav, Y.-slavia 45 22N 14 20E
77 Kastelli, Crete, Greece 35 29N 23 38E
77 Kastellion, Crete, Gr. .35 12N 25 20E
77 Kastellou, Akra, C., Gr. 35 30N 27 15E
81 Kastlösa, Sweden 56 26N 16 25E
77 Kastóri, Greece 37 10N 22 17E
76 Kastoria, Greece 40 30N 21 19E
76 Kastorias, L., Greece .40 30N 21 20E
87 Kastornoye, U.S.S.R. 51 55N 38 2E
77 Kastos, I., Greece 38 35N 20 55E
76 Kástron, Greece 39 53N 25 8E
77 Kastrosikia, Greece ...39 6N 20 36E
131 Kasulu & dist., Tanz. 4 37S 30 5E
89 Kasumkent, U.S.S.R. 41 47N 48 15E
132 Kasungu, Malawi 13 0S 33 29E
132 Kasupi, Malawi 15 12S 35 15E
104 Kasur, West Pakistan 31 5N 74 25E
102 Kataghan prov., Afghan. 36 0N 69 0E
130 Katako Kombe, Congo 3 25S 24 20E
77 Katakolon, Greece 37 38N 21 19E
109 Kataloka, Indonesia ... 3 54S 131 27E
127 Katama, Ethiopia 9 35N 38 36E
143 Katamatite, Australia 36 6S 145 41E
130 Katanda, Congo 8 0S 24 32E
131 Katanda, Congo 0 55S 29 21E
128 Katanga, Prov., Congo 8 0S 25 0E
91 Katangli, U.S.S.R. 51 42N 143 14E
127 Katanich, Sudan 6 0N 33 40E
142 Katanning, W. Austral. 33 40S 117 33E
77 Katastari, Greece 37 50N 20 45E
131 Katavi Swamps, Tanz. 6 50S 31 10E
76 Katerini, Greece 40 18N 22 37E
156 Kate's Needle, Mt., Can. 56 55N 132 10W
46 Katesbridge, Ireland .54 18N 6 8W
103 Katha, Burma 24 10N 96 30E
126 Katherina, Gebel, mt., Sinai, Egypt 28 30N 33 57E
138 Katherine, Australia .14 27S 132 20E
124 Kati, Mali 12 41N 8 4W
146 Katikati, New Zealand 37 32S 175 57E
108 Katiet, Indonesia 2 21S 99 44E
105 Katihar, India 25 34N 87 36E
132 Katima Mulilo Rapids, Zambia 17 28S 24 13E
132 Katimbira, Malawi 12 40S 34 0E
108 Katingan R., Indonesia 1 30S 113 0E
124 Katiola, Ivory Coast . 8 10N 5 10W
74 Katlanovo, Y.-slavia .41 52N 21 40E
1 Katmai, vol., Alas., U.S.A. 58 20N 154 59W
105 Katmandu, Nepal 27 45N 85 12E
77 Kato Akhaia, Greece .38 8N 21 33E
76 Kato Stazros, Greece .40 39N 23 43E
104 Katol, India 21 17N 78 38E
132 Katombora, Zambia ...18 0S 25 30E
131 Katonga R., Uganda . 0 15N 31 50E
143 Katoomba, N.S.W., Australia 33 30S 150 0E
60 Katowice, Poland 50 17N 19 5E
40 Katrine L., Scot.,U.K. 56 15N 4 30W
80 Katrineholm, Sweden 59 3N 16 12E
125 Katsina, Nigeria 7 10N 9 20E
125 Katsina Ala, R., Nigeria 6 52N 9 40E
114 Katsuura, Japan 35 15N 140 20E
101 Kattawaz, Afghanistan 32 48N 68 23E
81 Kattegat, Denmark 56 50N 11 20E
131 Katungu, Kenya 2 55S 40 3E
105 Katwa, India 23 30N 89 25E
54 Katwijk-aan-Zee, Neth. 52 12N 4 24E
60 Katy, Poland 51 2N 16 45E
91 Katyiyktakh, U.S.S.R. 68 50N 134 5E
98 Kaufakha, Israel 31 29N 34 40E
57 Kaufbeuren, Germany 47 42N 10 37E
165 Kaufman, U.S.A. 32 35N 96 20W
162 Kaukauna, U.S.A. 44 20N 88 13W
132 Kaumpi, Zambia 14 50S 24 15E
86 Kaunas, U.S.S.R. 54 54N 23 54E
125 Kaura Namoda, Nigeria 12 37N 6 33E
107 Kau Tao, I., Thailand 10 6N 99 48E
158 Kauai, I. &Chan., Hawaii, U.S.A. 21 50N 158 40E
82 Kautokeino, Norway .69 0N 23 15E
74 Kavadarci, Y.-slavia .41 26N 22 3E
106 Kavali, India 14 55N 80 1E
76 Kavála, Greece 40 57N 24 28E
76 Kavalla, Kolpos G., Gr. 40 50N 21 25E
75 Kavarna, Bulgaria 43 26N 28 22E
130 Kavava, Congo 8 52S 22 18E
144 Kavieng, New Guinea 2 30S 150 48E
132 Kavimba, Botswana .18 5S 24 38E
131 Kavirondo Gulf, Kenya 0 20S 34 15E
81 Kävlinge, Sweden 55 47N 13 9E
35 Kavousi, Crete, Greece 35 7N 25 51E
131 Kavu, R., Tanzania ... 7 30S 31 45E
175 Kaw (Caux), Fr. Guiana 4 30N 52 15W
127 Kawa, Sudan 13 42N 32 34E
160 Kawagama L., Canada 45 18N 78 45W
114 Kawagoye, Japan 36 0N 139 30E
114 Kawaguchi, Japan 35 52N 138 45E
146 Kawakawa, N.Z. 35 23S 174 6E
132 Kawambwa, Zambia . 9 48S 29 3E
114 Kawana, Japan 35 5N 135 27E
147 Kawarau, New Zealand 45 3S 169 0E
105 Kawardha, India 22 0N 81 17E
114 Kawasaki, Japan 35 35N 138 42E
146 Kawau I., New Zealand 36 25S 174 52E
154 Kawene, Canada 48 45N 91 15W
146 Kawerau, New Zealand 38 7S 176 42E
146 Kawhia Harbour, N.Z. 38 5S 174 51E
113 Kawnro, China 22 48N 99 8E
107 Kawthaung, (Victoria Point), Burma 10 5N 98 36E
107 Kawthoolei, div., Burma 18 0N 97 30E
125 Kaya, Upper Volta ...13 25N 1 10W
103 Kayah, st., Burma 19 15N 97 15E
89 Kayakent, U.S.S.R. ...42 45N 47 52E
132 Kayambi, Zambia 9 28S 31 59E
106 Kayangulam, India 9 10N 76 33E
166 Kaycee, U.S.A. 43 45N 106 46W
130 Kayenda, Congo 10 48S 23 6E
167 Kayenta, U.S.A. 36 46N 110 15W
124 Kayes, Mali 14 25N 11 30W
124 Kayima, Sierra Leone 8 54N 11 15W
130 Kayombo, Congo 9 31S 26 10E
125 Kayoro, Ghana 11 0N 1 28W
145 Kayrunnera, Australia 30 40S 142 30E
89 Kaysatskoye, U.S.S.R. 49 47N 46 49E
100 Kayseri, Turkey 38 45N 35 30E
166 Kaysville, U.S.A. 41 2N 111 58W
91 Kazache, U.S.S.R. 70 52N 135 58E
89 Kazakhstan, U.S.S.R. 49 0N 50 0E
87 Kazan & R., U.S.S.R. 55 48N 49 3E
75 Kazanluk, Bulgaria ...42 38N 25 35E
89 Kazanskaya, U.S.S.R. 49 50N 40 30E
88 Kazatin, U.S.S.R. 49 45N 28 50E
132 Kazembe, Zambia 12 10S 32 30E
101 Kazerun, Iran 29 38N 51 40E
89 Kazi Magomed, U.S.S.R. 40 3N 49 0E
130 Kaziza, Congo 10 40S 23 52E
89 Kaztalovka, U.S.S.R. 49 47N 48 43E
130 Kazumba, Congo 6 25S 22 5E
132 Kazumba, Zambia 13 55S 26 40E
100 Kazvin, Iran 36 15N 50 0E
90 Kazym R., U.S.S.R. .63 40N 68 30E
60 Kcynia, Poland 53 0N 17 30E
124 Ké, Mali 13 58N 5 18W
36 Kea, England, U.K. ...50 13N 5 4W
77 Kea & I., Greece 37 35N 24 22E
46 Keady, N. Ire., U.K. .54 15N 6 42W
40 Keal, Loch na, Scotland, United Kingdom 56 30N 6 5W
44 Kealkill, Ireland 51 45N 9 20W
167 Keams Canyon, U.S.A. 35 53N 110 9W
164 Kearney, U.S.A. 40 45N 99 3W
135 Kearsney, Natal, S. Afr. 29 15S 31 16E
100 Keban, Turkey 38 50N 38 50E
123 Kebili, Tunisia 33 47N 9 0E
121 Kebkabiya, Sudan 13 50N 24 0E
82 Kebnekaise, mt., Swed. 67 55N 18 35E
109 Kebumen, Indonesia . 7 42S 109 40E
59 Kecel, Hungary 46 31N 19 16E
59 Kecskemet, Hungary .46 57N 19 35E
131 Keckorak, Kenya 1 35S 35 13E
107 Kedah, st., W. Malaysia 5 50N 100 40E
86 Kedainiai, U.S.S.R. ...55 15N 23 57E
155 Kedgwick, Canada 47 40N 67 20W
109 Kediri, Indonesia 7 51S 112 1E
124 Kedougou, Senegal 12 35N 12 10W
156 Keefers, Canada 50 0N 121 40W
45 Keel, Ireland 53 59N 10 2W
136 Keeling Is., *see* Cocos Is. 12 12S 96 54E
113 Keelung. Taiwan 25 3N 121 45E
44 Keenagh, Ireland 53 36N 7 50W
161 Keene, U.S.A. 42 57N 72 17W
44 Keeper, hill, Ireland .52 46N 8 17W
55 Keerbergen, Belgium .51 1N 4 38E
38 Keele, England, U.K. 53 0N 2 17W
144 Keer-Weer, C., Queensland, Australia 14 0S 141 32E
161 Keeseville, U.S.A. 44 29N 73 30W
134 Keetmanshoop, South-West Africa .26 35S 18 8E
157 Keewatin, terr., Can. .63 20N 94 40W
164 Keewatin, U.S.A. 47 23N 93 0W
127 Kefa, Prov., Ethiopia 6 55N 36 30E
77 Kefallinia, I., Greece .38 28N 20 30E
109 Kefannanu, Indonesia 9 28S 124 38E
98 Kefar Ata, Israel 32 48N 35 7E
98 Kefar Etsyon, Jordan 31 39N 35 7E
98 Kefar Hasidim, Israel 32 47N 35 5E
98 Kefar Hittim B., Israel 32 48N 35 27E
98 Kefar Sava, Israel 32 11N 34 54E
98 Kefar Szold, Israel 33 11N 35 34E
98 Kefar Vitkin, Israel ...32 22N 34 53E
98 Kefar Yehezqel, Israel 32 34N 35 22E
98 Kefar Yona, Israel 32 20N 34 54E
98 Kefar Zekariya, Israel 31 43N 34 57E
125 Keffi, Nigeria 8 55N 7 43E
82 Keflavik. Iceland 64 2N 22 35W
156 Keg River, Canada 57 45N 117 50W
106 Kegalla, Ceylon 7 15N 80 21E
155 Kegashka, Canada 50 14N 61 18W
34 Kegworth, Eng., U.K. 52 50N 1 17W
57 Kehl, Germany 48 34N 7 50E
135 Kei Mouth, S. Africa .32 41S 28 23E
135 Kei Road, S. Africa ...32 43S 27 31E
38 Keighley, Eng., U.K. .53 52N 1 54W
44 Keimaneigh, P. of, Ire. 51 49N 9 17W
134 Keimoes, S. Africa 28 41S 21 0E
135 Keiskammahoek, Cape Province, S. Africa 32 40S 27 10E
43 Keiss, Scotland, U.K. 58 33N 3 6W
43 Keith, Scotland, U.K. 57 33N 2 58W
145 Keith, S. Australia 36 0S 140 20E
152 Keith Arm, Canada ...65 30N 122 0W
104 Kekri, India 26 0N 75 10E
127 Kelamet, Ethiopia 16 0N 38 20E
106 Kelani Ganga, R., Cey. 6 58N 79 50E
107 Kelantan R., Malaysia 5 35N 102 8E
107 Kelantan, st., W. Malay. 5 10N 102 0E
38 Keld, England, U.K. .54 24N 2 11W
123 Kelibia, Tunisia 36 50N 11 3E
43 Kellas, Scot., U.K. 57 33N 32 9W
125 Kellé, Niger 14 18N 10 10E
55 Kellen, Germany 51 49N 6 10E
166 Keller, U.S.A. 48 2N 118 44W
142 Kellerberrin, W. Austral. 31 36S 117 38E
14 Kellett C., Canada 72 0N 125 40W
161 Kelleys I., U.S.A. 41 35N 82 42W
166 Kellogg, U.S.A. 47 30N 116 5W
82 Kelloselkö, Finland 66 50N 29 0E
45 Kells, Kerry, Ireland .52 0N 10 7W
46 Kells, Kilkenny, Ire. .52 33N 7 18W
46 Kells (Ceanannus Mor), Meath, Ireland 53 42N 6 53W
86 Kelmentsy, U.S.S.R. .48 30N 26 50E
156 Kelowna, Canada 49 50N 119 25W
37 Kelsall, Eng., U.K. 53 14N 2 44W
35 Kelsale, Eng., U.K. ...52 15N 1 30E
156 Kelsey Bay, Canada ...50 25N 126 0W
135 Kelso, Natal, S. Africa 30 22S 30 43E
147 Kelso, New Zealand ...45 54S 169 15E
41 Kelso, Scot., U.K. 55 36N 2 27W
166 Kelso, U.S.A. 46 10N 122 57W
35 Kelvedon, U.K. 51 50N 0 43E
157 Kelvington, Canada ...52 20N 103 30W
124 Ke-Macina, Mali 14 5N 5 20W
84 Kem, U.S.S.R. 65 0N 34 38E
84 Kem R., U.S.S.R. 64 45N 32 20E
122 Kem-Kem, Morocco .30 40N 4 30W
109 Kema, Indonesia 1 22N 125 8E
100 Kemah, Turkey 39 32N 39 5E
156 Kemano, Canada 53 35N 128 0W
130 Kembé, Cen. Afr. Rep. 4 27N 21 58E
34 Kemble, Eng., U.K. ...51 40N 2 1W
127 Kembolcha, Ethiopia .11 29N 39 42E
88 Kemenets-Podolskiy, U.S.S.R. 48 40N 26 30E
90 Kemerovo, U.S.S.R. ...55 20N 85 50E
82 Kemi Finland 65 48N 24 43E
82 Kemi R., Finland 67 30N 28 30E
82 Kemijärvi, Finland ...66 42N 27 30E
166 Kemmerer, U.S.A. 41 52N 110 30W
43 Kemnay, Scotland, U.K. 57 14N 2 28W
15 Kemp Coast, Antarc. .69 0S 55 0E
165 Kemp L., U.S.A. 33 45N 99 15W
55 Kempen, Germany 51 22N 6 22E
55 Kempenich, Germany 50 27N 7 5E
145 Kempsey, Australia ...31 1S 152 50E
34 Kempsey, Eng., U.K. 52 8N 2 11W
35 Kempston, Eng., U.K. 52 7N 0 30W
154 Kempt, L., Canada ...47 25N 74 30W
57 Kempten, Germany ...47 42N 10 18E
154 Kemptville, Ont., Can. 45 0N 75 38W
41 Ken L., Scot., U.K. 55 0N 4 0W
122 Kenadsa, Algeria 31 48N 2 26W
130 Kenboma, Cameroon . 0 48N 13 43E
38 Kendal, Eng., U.K. ...54 19N 2 44W
109 Kendal, Indonesia 6 56S 110 14E
143 Kendall, Australia 31 35S 152 44E
162 Kendallville, U.S.A. ...41 25N 85 15W
109 Kendari, Indonesia 3 50S 122 30E
108 Kendawangan, Indon. 2 32S 110 17E
125 Kende, Nigeria 11 30N 4 12E
142 Kendenup, W. Austral. 34 22S 117 1E
105 Kendrapara, India 20 35N 86 30E
134 Kendrew, S. Africa ...32 30S 24 30E
166 Kendrick, U.S.A. 46 43N 116 41W
124 Kenema, Sierra Leone 7 48N 11 4W
130 Kenge, Congo 4 50S 16 55E
131 Kengeja, Tanzania 5 26S 39 45E
107 Keng Tawng, Burma .20 46N 98 20E
103 Keng Tung, Burma ...21 0N 99 30E
134 Kenhardt, S. Africa ...29 19S 21 12E
112 Kenho, China 50 43N 121 30E
133 Kenilworth, S. Africa .28 42S 24 47E
34 Kenilworth, Eng., U.K. 52 22N 1 35W
124 Keninkoumou, Maur. .15 17N 12 18W
122 Kenitra, (Mina Hassan Tani), Morocco 34 15N 6 40W
44 Kenmare, & R., Ire. ...51 52N 9 35W
164 Kenmare, U.S.A. 48 40N 102 4W
143 Kenmore, Australia ...34 44S 149 45E
41 Kenmore, Scot., U.K. 56 35N 4 0W
160 Kennaway, Canada 45 9N 78 11W
164 Kennebec, U.S.A. 43 56N 99 54W
132 Kennedy, Rhodesia ...18 52S 27 10E
163 Kennedy, C., U.S.A. .28 28N 80 31W
142 Kennedy Ra., Austral. 24 45S 115 10E
142 Kenneth Ra., Australia 23 40S 117 0E
165 Kennett, U.S.A. 36 7N 90 0W
166 Kennewick, U.S.A. 46 11N 119 2W
35 Kenninghall, Eng., U.K. 52 26N 1 0E
152 Keno Hill, Yukon, Canada 63 57N 135 25W
154 Kenogami, R., Canada 50 20N 85 20W
157 Kenora, Canada 49 50N 94 35W
162 Kenosha, Wis., U.S.A. 42 33N 87 48W
165 Kensington, Canada ...46 28N 63 34W
164 Kensington, U.S.A. ...39 48N 99 2W
144 Kensington Downs, Queens., Australia .22 31S 144 10E
160 Kent, Ohio, U.S.A. 41 8N 81 20W
166 Kent, Ore., U.S.A. 45 11N 120 45W
165 Kent, Tex., U.S.A. 31 5N 104 12W
35 Kent, Co., Eng., U.K. 51 12N 0 40E
152 Kent Pen., Canada 68 30N 107 0W
135 Kentani, S. Africa 32 30S 28 22E
142 Kentdale, W. Australia 35 0S 117 0E
36 Kentisbeare, Eng., U.K. 50 51N 3 18W
162 Kentland, U.S.A. 40 45N 87 25W
36 Kenton. Eng., U.K. ...50 37N 3 28W
162 Kenton, U.S.A. 40 40N 83 35W
162 Kentucky, st., U.S.A. 37 20N 85 0W
162 Kentucky Dam, U.S.A. 37 2N 88 15W
163 Kentucky L., U.S.A. .36 0N 88 0W
162 Kentucky R., U.S.A. .38 30N 85 0W
155 Kentville, Canada 45 6N 64 29W
165 Kentwood, U.S.A. 31 0N 90 30W
131 Kenya, state, Africa ... 2 20N 38 0E
131 Kenya, Mt., Kenya 0 10S 37 18E
164 Keokuk, U.S.A. 40 25N 91 30W
76 Kep-i-Gjuhezes, C., Alb. 40 28N 19 15E
76 Kep-i-Lagit, Albania 41 10N 19 28E
76 Kep-i-Palit, Albania .41 25N 19 21E
76 Kep-i-Rodonit, Albania 41 32N 19 30E
147 Kepler Mts., N.Z. 45 25S 167 20E
60 Kepno. Poland 51 18N 17 58E
100 Kepsut, Turkey 39 40N 28 15E
109 Kepulauan, R., Indon. 5 30S 139 0E
106 Kerala, st., India 11 0N 76 15E
143 Kerang, Vic., Australia 35 40S 143 55E
77 Keratéa, Greece 37 48N 23 58E
101 Keray, Iran 26 15N 57 30E
88 Kerch, U.S.S.R. 45 20N 36 20E
88 Kerch, Str. of, U.S.S.R. 45 10N 36 30E
125 Kerchoual, Mali 17 20N 0 20E
98 Kerem Maharel, Israel 32 39N 34 59E
144 Kerema, Papua 7 50S 145 50E
127 Keren, Ethiopia 15 45N 38 28E
124 Kerewan, Gambia 13 35N 16 10W
11 Kerguelen I., Ind. Oc. 48 30S 69 40E
77 Keri, Greece 37 40N 20 49E
127 Keri Kera, Sudan 12 21N 32 37E
147 Kerikeri, New Zealand 35 12S 173 59E
108 Kerintji, mt., Indon. . 2 5S 101 0E
123 Kerkenah Is., Tunisia 34 48N 11 1E
90 Kerki, U.S.S.R. 37 44N 65 9E
76 Kérkira, Greece 39 38N 19 50E
54 Kerkrade, Netherlands 50 53N 6 4E
126 Kerma, Sudan 19 33N 30 32E
136 Kermadec Is., Pacific Ocean 31 8S 175 16W
101 Kerman, Iran 30 15N 57 1E
100 Kermanshah, Iran 34 23N 47 0E
77 Kerme Korfezi, G., Tur. 36 55N 27 50E
75 Kermen, Bulgaria 42 30N 26 16E
165 Kermit, U.S.A. 31 56N 103 3W
55 Kermt, Belgium 50 57N 5 15E
167 Kern, R., U.S.A. 35 40N 118 45W
55 Kerpen, Germany 50 52N 6 40E
146 Kerr, Pt., N. Zealand 34 25S 173 5E
40 Kerrera I., Scot., U.K. 56 24N 5 32W
157 Kerrobert, Canada 52 0N 109 11W
165 Kerrville, U.S.A. 30 1N 99 8W
37 Kerry, Wales, U.K. ...52 28N 3 16W
44 Kerry. Co., Ireland ...52 7N 9 35W
44 Kerry Hd., Ireland 52 26N 9 56W
29 Kerry, mts. of, Ireland 51 55N 9 55W
80 Kerstinbo, Sweden 60 16N 16 58E
122 Kert, R., Morocco 35 3N 3 11W
81 Kerteminde, Denmark 55 28N 10 39E
109 Kertosono, Indonesia . 7 38S 112 9E
127 Keru, Ethiopia 15 40N 37 5E
112 Kerulen R., Mongolia 48 0N 114 0E
122 Kerzaz, Algeria 29 30N 1 37W
154 Kesagami L. & R., Can. 50 30N 80 10W
76 Kesan, Turkey 41 49N 26 38E
46 Kesh, Northern Ireland 54 31N 7 43W
82 Keski Suomen Prov., Finland 62 45N 25 15E
55 Kessel, Belgium 51 8N 4 38E
55 Kessel-Lo, Belgium ...50 53N 4 43E
35 Kessingland, Eng., U.K. 52 25N 1 41E
135 Kestell, O.F.S., S. Afr. 28 17S 28 42E
84 Kestenga, U.S.S.R. ...66 0N 31 50E
39 Kesteven, dist., England, U.K. 53 2N 0 25W
38 Keswick, Eng., U.K. .54 35N 3 9W
59 Keszthely, Hungary ...46 50N 17 15E
125 Keta, Ghana 5 49N 1 0E
108 Ketapang. Indonesia . 1 55S 110 0E
157 Ketchikan, Alas., U.S.A. 55 25N 131 40W
166 Ketchum, U.S.A. 43 50N 114 27W
125 Kete Krachi, Ghana ... 7 55N 0 1W
104 Keti Bandar, W. Pak. 24 8N 67 27E
104 Ketri, India 28 1N 75 50E
60 Ketrzyn, Poland 54 7N 21 22E
35 Kettering, Eng., U.K. 52 24N 0 44W
42 Kettla, Ness, Scot., U.K. 60 3N 1 20W
166 Kettle Falls, U.S.A. ...48 41N 118 2W
39 Kettle Ness, Eng., U.K. 54 32N 0 41W
38 Kettlewell, Eng., U.K. 54 8N 2 2W
55 Kettwig, Germany 51 22N 6 53E
59 Kety, Poland 49 51N 19 16E
55 Kevelaer, Germany ...51 35N 6 15E
166 Kevin, U.S.A. 48 51N 112 0W
164 Kewanee, Ill., U.S.A. 41 18N 90 0W
162 Kewaunee, U.S.A. 44 27N 87 30W
162 Keweenaw B., U.S.A. 47 0N 88 0W
162 Keweenaw Pen., U.S.A. 47 30N 88 0W
162 Keweenaw Pt., U.S.A. 47 26N 87 40W
39 Kexby, Eng., U.K. 53 21N 0 41W
154 Key Harbour, Canada 45 50N 80 45W
46 Key., L., Ireland 54 0N 8 15W
169 Key West, U.S.A. 24 40N 82 0W
39 Keyingham, Eng., U.K. 53 42N 0 7W
35 Keymer, Eng., U.K. .50 55N 0 5W
36 Keynsham, Eng., U.K. 51 25N 2 30W
132 Keynshamburg, Rhod. 19 15S 29 40E
161 Keyport, U.S.A. 40 26N 74 12W
162 Keyser, U.S.A. 39 26N 79 0W
164 Keystone, S.D., U.S.A. 43 54N 103 27W
162 Keystone, W. Va., U.S.A. 37 30N 81 30W
34 Keyworth, Eng., U.K. 52 52N 1 8W
91 Kezhma, U.S.S.R. 59 15N 100 57E

MAP
59 Kežmarok, Cz. 49 10N 20 28E
90 Khabarovo, U.S.S.R. .69 30N 60 30E
91 Khabarovsk, U.S.S.R. 48 20N 135 0E
89 Khachmas, U.S.S.R. .41 31N 48 42E
104 Khachraud, India 23 25N 75 20E
127 Khadari, W. el, R., Sud. 10 35N 26 16E
104 Khadro, W. Pakistan .26 11N 68 50E
89 Khadyzhensk, U.S.S.R. 44 26N 39 32E
105 Khagaria, India 25 18N 86 32E
100 Khaibar, Saudi Arabia 25 38N 39 28E
126 Khaibor Oasis, Si. Arab. 25 49N 39 16E
104 Khair, India 27 57N 77 46E
105 Khairabad, India 27 33N 80 47E
105 Khairagarh, India 21 27N 81 2E
104 Khairpur, W. Pakistan 29 34N 72 17E
104 Khairpur, W. Pakistan 27 32N 68 49E
104 Khairpur, Prov., Pak. 23 30N 69 8E
123 Khalij Surat (Gulf of Sidra), Libya 31 40N 18 30E
126 Khalig el Tina, B., Eg. 31 20N 32 42E
105 Khalilabad, India 26 48N 83 5E
76 Khalki, Greece 39 36N 22 30E
77 Khalki, I., Greece 36 15N 27 35E
76 Khalkidhiki, pref. Gr. 40 25N 23 20E
76 Khalkis, Greece 38 27N 23 42E
90 Khalmer-Sede, U.S.S.R. 67 30N 78 30E
90 Khalmen Yu, U.S.S.R.67 58N 65 1E
87 Khalturin, U.S.S.R. ...58 40N 48 50E
105 Khamaria, India 23 10N 80 52E
132 Khama's Country, dist., Bots. 21 45S 26 30E
103 Khamba Dzong, Tibet, China 28 25N 88 30W
104 Khambhalia, India 22 14N 69 41E
104 Khamgaon, India 20 42N 76 37E
106 Khammam, India 17 11N 80 6E
111 Khan Tengri, mt. China 42 25N 80 10E
98 Khan Yunus, Egypt .31 21N 34 18E
101 Khanabad, Afghanistan 36 45N 69 5E
100 Khanaqin, Iraq 34 23N 45 25E
77 Khandrá, Greece 35 3N 26 8E
104 Khandwa, India 21 49N 76 22E
104 Khanewal, W. Pakistan 30 20N 71 55E
123 Khanga Sidi Nadji, Alg. 34 50N 6 50E
77 Khania, Greece 35 30N 24 4E
77 Khanion Kolpos, G., Gr. 35 33N 23 55E
91 Khanka, L., U.S.S.R. 45 0N 132 30E
104 Khanna, India 30 42N 76 16E
104 Khanpur, W. Pak. 28 42N 70 35E
90 Khanty-Mansiisk, U.S.S.R. 61 0N 69 0E
105 Kharagpur, India 22 20N 87 25E
126 Kharaij, Saudi Arabia 21 25N 41 0E
102 Kharan Kalat, W. Pak. 28 34N 65 21E
101 Kharanaq, Iran 32 20N 54 45E
106 Kharda, India 18 40N 75 40E
100 Kharfa, Saudi Arabia 22 0N 46 35E
100 Kharg I., Iran 29 15N 50 28E
126 Kharit, Wadi el, R., Eg. 24 5N 34 10E
126 Kharga Oasis, Egypt .25 0N 30 0E
104 Khargone, India 21 45N 75 40E
88 Kharkov, U.S.S.R. 49 58N 36 20E
75 Kharmanli, Bulgaria .41 55N 25 55E
87 Kharovsk, U.S.S.R. ...59 56N 40 13E
100 Kharsaniya, Si. Arabia 27 10N 49 10E
127 Khartoum, Sudan 15 31N 32 35E
127 Khartoum, N., Sudan 15 40N 32 31E
101 Khasab, Oman 26 14N 56 15E
89 Khasavyurt, U.S.S.R. 43 30N 46 40E
132 Khasebake, Botswana 20 42S 24 29E
101 Khash, Iran 28 15N 61 5E
127 Khashm el Girba, Sudan 14 59N 35 58E
105 Khasi Hills, India 25 30N 91 30E
75 Khaskovo, Bulgaria ...41 56N 25 30E
91 Khatanga, U.S.S.R. ...72 0N 102 20E
14 Khatanga B., U.S.S.R. 66 0N 112 0E
104 Khatauli, India 29 17N 77 43E
91 Khatyn, U.S.S.R. 62 10N 175 0E
126 Khawa, Saudi Arabia 29 45N 40 25E
106 Khed, India 18 51N 73 56E
106 Khed, India 17 43N 73 27E
104 Khekra, India 28 52N 77 20E
122 Khemis Miliana, (Affreville), Algeria .36 11N 2 14E
122 Khemisset, Morocco ...33 50N 6 1W
107 Khemmarat, Thailand 16 10N 105 15E
123 Khenchela, Algeria 35 28N 7 11E
122 Khenifra, Morocco 32 58N 5 46W
123 Kherrata, Algeria 36 27N 5 13E
88 Kherson, U.S.S.R. 46 35N 32 35E
77 Khersonisos Akrotiri, Pen., Crete, Gr. 35 30N 24 10E
103 Khetinsiring, China ...32 54N 92 50E
77 Khiliomodhion, Greece 37 48N 22 51E
91 Khilok, U.S.S.R. 51 30N 110 45E
87 Khimki, U.S.S.R. 55 50N 37 20E
77 Khíos, & I., Greece ...38 27N 26 9E
75 Khisar, Bulgaria 42 30N 24 44E
90 Khiva, U.S.S.R. 41 30N 60 18E
100 Khiyav, Iran 38 30N 47 45E
122 Khlaouia, Mauritania .25 50N 6 32W
MAP
107 Khlong R., Thailand .15 30N 98 50E
88 Khmelnitsky, U.S.S.R. 49 23N 27 0E
107 Khmer Rep., st., Asia.12 15N 105 0E
100 Khoi, Iran 38 40N 45 0E
86 Khoiniki, U.S.S.R. 51 54N 29 55E
102 Khojak P., Afghan. ...30 55N 66 30E
87 Khokhol, U.S.S.R. 51 35N 38 50E
86 Kholm, U.S.S.R. 57 10N 31 15E
91 Kholmsk, Sakhalin, U.S.S.R. 35 5N 139 48E
100 Khomayn, Iran 33 40N 50 7E
132 Khomo, Botswana 21 7S 24 35E
132 Khomodimo, Bots. 22 46S 23 52E
107 Khon Kaen, Thailand 16 30N 102 47E
107 Khong, Cambodia 13 55N 105 56E
107 Khong R., Laos 15 0N 106 50E
107 Khong R., Thailand ...17 45N 104 20E
107 Khonh Hung (Soc Trang), South Vietnam 9 37N 105 50E
91 Khonu, U.S.S.R. 66 30N 143 25E
87 Khoper R., U.S.S.R. .52 0N 43 20E
127 Khor el 'Atash, Sudan 13 20N 34 15E
77 Khóra, Greece 37 3N 21 42E
77 Khora Sfákion, Greece 35 15N 24 9E
107 Khorat Plat., Thailand 15 30N 102 50E
122 Khorb el Ethel, Algeria 28 44N 6 11W
90 Khorog, U.S.S.R. 37 40N 71 55E
88 Khorol, U.S.S.R. 49 48N 33 15E
100 Khorramabad, Iran ...33 30N 48 25E
100 Khorramshahr, Iran ...30 29N 48 15E
111 Khotan, *see* Hotien, China 37 6N 79 59E
88 Khotin, U.S.S.R. 48 31N 26 27E
122 Khouribga, Morocco ...32 58N 6 50W
103 Khowal, India 24 5N 91 40E
89 Khrami, R., U.S.S.R. 41 30N 44 30E
87 Khrenovoye, U.S.S.R. 51 4N 40 6E
77 Khristiana I., Greece .36 14N 25 13E
77 Khtapodhia I., Greece 37 24N 25 34E
100 Khufaifiya, Si. Arabia 24 50N 44 35E
107 Khukhan, Thailand ...15 7N 104 15E
105 Khulna, E. Pakistan .22 45N 89 34E
89 Khulo, U.S.S.R. 41 33N 42 19E
89 Khunzakh, U.S.S.R. ..42 35N 46 42E
101 Khur, Iran 32 55N 58 18E
104 Khurai, India 24 3N 78 23E
100 Khurais, Saudi Arabia 24 55N 48 5E
101 Khurasan, prov., Iran 34 0N 57 0E
104 Khurja, India 28 15N 77 58E
100 Khurma, Saudi Arabia 21 58N 42 3E
104 Khushab, Pakistan 32 20N 72 20E
102 Khuzdar, W. Pakistan 27 52N 66 30E
87 Khvalynsk, U.S.S.R. .52 30N 48 2E
87 Khvatovka, U.S.S.R. .52 24N 46 32E
101 Khvor, Iran 33 45N 55 0E
101 Khvormuj, Iran 28 40N 51 30E
101 Khvoy, Iran 38 35N 45 0E
86 Khvoynaya, U.S.S.R. 58 49N 34 28E
101 Khwaja Muhammad, ra., Afghanistan 36 0N 70 0E
101 Khyber Pass, Afghan. 34 10N 71 8E
106 Kiadho, R., India 19 50N 76 55E
112 Kiahsien, China 38 10N 110 8E
143 Kiama, N.S.W., Austral. 34 40S 150 50E
109 Kiamba, Philippines . 6 0N 124 40E
131 Kiambu & dist., Kenya 1 8S 36 50E
112 Kiamusze, China 46 45N 130 30E
113 Kian, China 27 1N 114 58E
143 Kiandra, Australia 35 53S 148 31E
113 Kianghwa, China 25 26N 111 29E
113 Kiangling, China 30 28N 113 16E
113 Kiangpen, China 29 40N 106 30E
113 Kiangshan, China 28 51N 118 38E
113 Kiangsi, prov., China .27 20N 115 40E
113 Kiangsu, prov., China 33 0N 119 50E
113 Kiangyin, China 31 51N 120 0E
113 Kiangyu, China 31 41N 104 26E
112 Kiaochow Wan., China 36 10N 120 15E
112 Kiaohsien, China 36 20N 120 0E
113 Kiawang, China 34 23N 117 28E
81 Kibæk, Denmark 56 2N 8 50E
131 Kibali R., Congo 3 30N 29 14E
130 Kibamba, Congo 4 56S 26 35E
131 Kibanga Port, Uganda 0 10S 32 58E
128 Kibangou, Congo (Fr.) 3 18S 12 22E
131 Kibara, Tanzania 2 8S 33 30E
131 Kibara Mts., Congo ... 8 25S 27 10E
131 Kibi, Congo 6 15S 29 5E
131 Kiboga, Uganda 0 59N 31 30E
130 Kibombo, Congo 3 57S 25 53E
131 Kibondo, Tanzania 3 35S 30 54E
131 Kibuye, Burundi 3 39S 29 59E
131 Kibwezi, Kenya 2 27S 37 57E
35 Kibworth Beauchamp, England, U.K. 52 33N 0 59W
74 Kičevo, Yugoslavia ...41 34N 20 59E
91 Kichiga, U.S.S.R. 59 50N 163 5E
113 Kichow, China 30 0N 115 30E
143 Kickabil, Australia 31 50S 148 30E
156 Kicking Horse Pass, Canada 51 27N 116 25W
125 Kidal, Mali 17 50N 1 22E
34 Kidderminster, England, U.K. 52 24N 2 13W
131 Kidete, Tanzania 6 25S 37 17E
34 Kidlington, Eng., U.K. 51 49N 1 18W
38 Kidsgrove, Eng., U.K. 53 6N 2 15W
144 Kidston, Australia 18 52S 144 8E
MAP
38 Kidstones, Eng., U.K. 54 15N 2 2W
131 Kidugalle, Tanzania ... 6 49S 38 15E
37 Kidwelly, Wales, U.K. 51 44N 4 20W
56 Kiel, Germany 54 16N 10 8E
55 Kiel Canal, Germany .54 15N 9 40E
60 Kielce, & Prov., Poland 50 58N 20 42E
39 Kielder, Eng., U.K. ...55 14N 2 35W
56 Kieler Bucht, Germany 54 30N 10 30E
103 Kienchwan, China 26 30N 99 45E
131 Kienge, Congo 10 30S 27 30E
113 Kienhinghsien, China .26 50N 116 50E
113 Kienhsien, China 34 30N 108 16E
113 Kienko, China 31 50N 105 30E
113 Kienning, China 27 4N 118 21E
113 Kienow, China 27 0N 118 16E
111 Kienshui, China 23 57N 102 45E
113 Kiensi, China 26 58N 106 0E
113 Kienteh, China 29 30N 119 28E
113 Kienyang, Fukien, China 27 30N 118 0E
113 Kienyang, Hunan, China 27 10N 109 50E
113 Kienyang, China 30 27N 104 30E
55 Kierspe, Germany 51 9N 7 36E
86 Kiev, (Kiyev), U.S.S.R. 50 30N 30 28E
134 Kiewietskuil, S. Africa 32 31S 23 30E
124 Kiffa, Mauritania 16 50N 11 15W
77 Kifisia, Greece 38 4N 23 49E
77 Kifissós Voiotikós, R., Greece 38 30N 23 0E
100 Kifri, Iraq 34 45N 45 0E
131 Kigali, Rwanda 1 57S 30 4E
131 Kigarama, Tanz. 1 1S 31 50E
131 Kigoma, & dist. Tanz. 5 30S 30 0E
131 Kigoma, reg., Tanz. ... 4 50S 30 30E
131 Kigwa, Tanzania 5 10S 33 15E
145 Kihee, Australia 27 30S 142 25E
146 Kihikhi, New Zealand 38 2S 175 22E
112 Kihsien, China 36 20N 110 35E
114 Kii Chan., Japan 33 40N 135 0E
131 Kijabe, Kenya 0 56S 36 33E
113 Kikiang, China 28 58N 106 44E
74 Kikinda, Yugoslavia .45 50N 20 30E
77 Kikládhes, Is., Greece 37 20N 24 30E
130 Kikole, Congo 9 24S 26 0E
130 Kikongo, Congo 4 12S 17 13E
144 Kikori & R., Papua . 7 13S 144 15E
130 Kikwit, Congo 5 5S 18 45E
80 Kil, Sweden 59 30N 13 20E
80 Kilafors, Sweden 61 14N 16 36E
106 Kilakarai, India 9 12N 78 47E
158 Kilauea Crater, Hawaii, U.S.A. 19 24N 155 17W
44 Kilbaha, Ireland 52 35N 9 51W
45 Kilbeggan, Ireland 53 22N 7 30W
44 Kilbeheny, Ireland 52 18N 8 13W
44 Kilbennan, Ireland 53 33N 8 54W
40 Kilbirnie, Scot., U.K. 55 46N 4 42W
40 Kilbrannan Sd., Scotland, U.K. 55 40N 5 23W
45 Kilbride, Ireland 52 56N 6 5W
45 Kilbrien, Ireland 52 12N 7 40W
45 Kilbrittain, Ireland 51 40N 8 42W
42 Kilchoan, Scot., U.K. 56 42N 6 8W
112 Kilchu, N. Korea 41 0N 129 20E
45 Kilcock, Ireland 53 24N 6 40W
44 Kilcoe, Ireland 51 33N 9 26W
44 Kilconly, Ireland 53 35N 8 59W
44 Kilconnell, Ireland 53 20N 8 25W
46 Kilcoo, N. Ireland 54 14N 6 1W
45 Kilcormac, Ireland 53 11N 7 44W
145 Kilcoy, Queensland, Australia 26 59S 152 30E
44 Kilcrohane, Ireland ...51 35N 9 44W
45 Kilcullen, Ireland 53 8N 6 45W
46 Kilcurry, Ireland 54 3N 6 26W
45 Kildare, Ireland 53 10N 6 50W
45 Kildare, co., Ireland ...53 10N 6 50W
45 Kildavin, Ireland 52 41N 6 42W
44 Kildemo, Ireland 52 37N 8 50W
40 Kildonan, Scot., U.K. 58 10N 3 50W
44 Kildorrery, Ireland 52 15N 8 25W
131 Kilembe, Uganda 0 15N 30 3E
44 K'lfernora, Ireland 53 0N 9 13W
40 Kilfinan, Scot., U.K. ..55 57N 5 19W
44 Kilfinnane, Ireland 52 21N 8 30W
44 Kilgarvan, Ireland 51 54N 9 28W
165 Kilgore, U.S.A. 32 22N 94 40W
131 Kilgoris, Kenya 1 0S 34 53E
39 Kilham, Eng., U.K. ...54 4N 0 22W
102 Kilian Qurghan, China 36 52N 78 3E
131 Kilifi & dist., Kenya... 3 40S 39 48E
131 Kilimfedha, Tanzania 2 18S 34 59E
131 Kilimanjaro, mt., Tanz. 3 7S 37 20E
131 Kilimatinde, Tanzania 5 55S 34 58E
88 Kilinç, mt , Turkey ...40 30N 38 21E
131 Kilindini, *see* Mombasa & Kilindini, Ken. 4 4S 39 40E
131 Kilindoni, Mafia I., Tanz. 7 59S 39 38E
100 Kilis, Turkey 36 50N 37 10E
88 Kiliya, U.S.S.R. 45 28N 29 16E
45 Kilkea, Ireland 52 57N 6 55W
44 Kilkee, Ireland 52 41N 9 40W
46 Kilkeel, N. Ire., U.K. 54 4N 6 0W
44 Kilkelly, Ireland 53 53N 8 50W
45 Kilkenny, Ireland 52 40N 7 17W
45 Kilkenny, co., Ireland 52 35N 7 15W
44 Kilkerrin, Ireland 53 32N 8 36W
36 Kilkhampton, England, United Kingdom 50 53N 4 30W
44 Kilkieran B., Ireland .53 18N 9 45W
MAP
76 Kilkis & pref., Greece 40 58N 22 57E
44 Kilkishen, Ireland 52 49N 8 45W
46 Kilknock, Ireland 53 42N 8 53W
45 Kill, Waterford, Ireland 52 11N 7 20W
45 Killadoon, Ireland 53 44N 9 53W
44 Killadysert, Ireland ...52 40N 9 7W
46 Killala & B., Ireland .54 13N 9 12W
44 Killaloe, Ireland 52 48N 8 28W
160 Killaloe Sta., Canada .45 34N 77 25W
45 Killane, Ireland 53 20N 7 6W
45 Killare, Ireland 53 28N 7 34W
145 Killarney, Australia ...28 19S 152 14E
154 Killarney, Man., Can. 49 10N 99 40W
157 Killarney, Ont., Can. .45 55N 81 30W
44 Killarney, Ireland 52 2N 9 30W
45 Killary Harb., Ireland 53 38N 9 52W
46 Killashee, Ireland 53 40N 7 52W
45 Killavally, Ireland 53 22N 7 23W
44 Killavullen, Ireland ...52 8N 8 32W
160 Killbuck, U.S.A. 40 29N 81 58W
40 Killchianaig, Scot., U.K. 56 2N 5 48W
157 Killdeer Canada 49 6N 106 22W
164 Killdeer, U.S.A. 47 26N 102 48W
44 Killeagh, Ireland 51 56N 8 0W
40 Killean, Scot., U.K. ...55 38N 5 40W
165 Killeen, U.S.A. 31 7N 97 45W
44 Killeenleigh, Ireland .51 58N 8 49W
45 Killeigh, Ireland 53 14N 7 27W
45 Killenagh, Ireland 52 36N 6 16W
45 Killenaule Ireland 52 35N 7 40W
46 Killeshandra, Ireland .54 0N 7 32W
45 Killianspick, Ireland .52 21N 7 18W
43 Killiecrankie P., Scotland, U.K. 56 44N 3 46W
44 Killimor, Ireland 53 10N 8 17W
40 Killin, Scotland, U.K. 56 28N 4 20W
45 Killiney, Ireland 53 15N 6 8W
79 Killingdal, Norway 62 47N 11 26E
39 Killinghall, Eng., U.K. 54 1N 1 33W
77 Killini, Greece 37 55N 21 8E
77 Killini, mt., Greece 37 54N 22 25E
45 Killinick, Ireland 52 15N 6 29W
44 Killorglin, Ireland 52 6N 9 48W
46 Killough, N. Ire., U.K. 54 16N 5 40W
44 Killtullagh, Ireland 53 17N 8 37W
45 Killucan, Ireland 53 30N 7 10W
44 Killybegs, Ireland 54 38N 8 26W
46 Killyleagh, N. Ire., U.K. 54 24N 5 40W
40 Kilmacolm, Scot., U.K. 55 54N 4 39W
45 Kilmacthomas, Ireland 52 13N 7 27W
45 Kilmaganny, Ireland .52 26N 7 20W
44 Kilmaine, Ireland 53 33N 9 10W
44 Kilmaley, Ireland 52 50N 9 11W
44 Kilmallock, Ireland ...52 22N 8 35W
42 Kilmaluag Scot., U.K. 57 40N 6 18W
45 Kilmanagh, Ireland ...52 38N 7 28W
143 Kilmany, Vic., Austral. 38 8S 146 55E
40 Kilmany, Scot., U.K. .56 26N 3 0W
40 Kilmarnock, Scot., U.K. 55 36N 4 30W
40 Kilmartin, Scot., U.K. 56 8N 5 29W
40 Kilmaurs, Scot., U.K. 55 37N 4 33W
45 Kilmeaden, Ireland ...52 15N 7 15W
44 Kilmeedy, Ireland 52 25N 8 55W
40 Kilmelford, Scot., U.K. 56 16N 5 30W
87 Kilmez, R., U.S.S.R. .56 58N 51 10E
44 Kilmichael, Ireland ...51 49N 9 4W
44 Kilmihill, Ireland 52 44N 9 18W
45 Kilmore, Ireland 52 12N 6 35W
45 Kilmore Quay, Ireland 52 10N 6 36W
43 Kilmuir, Scot., U.K. .57 44N 4 7W
44 Kilmurry, Ireland 52 47N 9 30W
44 Kilmurvy, Ireland 53 9N 9 46W
46 Kilnaleck, Ireland 53 52N 7 21W
40 Kilninver, Scot., U.K. 56 20N 5 30W
131 Kilombero R., Tanz. . 8 12S 37 4E
131 Kilosa, Tanzania 6 48S 37 0E
44 Kilpatrick, Ireland 51 46N 8 42W
46 Kilrea, N. Ire. U.K. ...54 58N 6 34W
41 Kilrenny, Scot., U.K. 56 15N 2 40W
44 Kilronan, Ireland 53 8N 9 40W
44 Kilrush, Ireland 52 39N 9 30W
34 Kilsby, Eng., U.K. 52 20N 1 11W
45 Kilsheelan, Ireland 52 23N 7 37W
80 Kilsmo, Sweden 59 6N 15 35E
45 Kiltealy, Ireland 52 34N 6 45W
45 Kiltegan, Ireland 52 55N 6 35W
44 Kiltoom, Ireland 53 30N 8 0W
131 Kilwa, dist., Tanzania 9 0S 39 0E
131 Kilwa Kisiwani, Tanz 8 58S 39 32E
131 Kilwa Kivinje, Tanz. . 8 45S 39 25E
131 Kilwa Masoko, Tanz. . 8 55S 39 30E
40 Kilwinning, Scot., U.K. 55 40N 4 41W
44 Kilworth, mts., Ire....52 10N 8 15W
165 Kim, U.S.A. 37 18N 103 20W
131 Kimamba, Tanzania . 6 45S 37 10E
138 Kimba, S. Australia ...33 8S 136 23E
164 Kimball, Neb., U.S.A. 41 17N 103 20W
164 Kimball, S.D., U.S.A. 43 47N 98 57W
130 Kimbanda, Congo 4 10S 17 56E
144 Kimbe B., Terr. of New Guinea 5 3S 150 45E
156 Kimberley, Canada ...49 40N 116 10W
133 Kimberley, S. Africa .28 43S 24 46E
138 Kimberley, dist., Western Australia .16 20S 127 0E
166 Kimberly, U.S.A. 42 33N 114 25W
MAP
35 Kimbolton, Eng., U.K. 52 17N 0 23W
112 Kimchaek, N. Korea .40 40N 129 10E
112 Kimchon, S. Korea ...36 11N 128 4E
77 Kimi, Greece 38 38N 24 6E
77 Kimolos, & I., Greece 36 48N 24 37E
124 Kimparana, Mali 12 48N 5 0W
87 Kimry, U.S.S.R. 56 55N 37 15E
156 Kimsquit, Canada 52 45N 127 5W
81 Kimstad, Sweden 58 35N 15 58E
108 Kinabalu, mt., Sabah, E. Malaysia 6 0N 116 0E
77 Kinaros, I., Greece ...36 59N 26 15E
45 Kinawley, N. Ire., U.K. 54 14N 7 40W
43 Kinbrace, Scot., U.K. 58 16N 3 56W
157 Kincaid, Canada 49 40N 107 0W
154 Kincardine, Canada ...44 10N 81 40W
43 Kincardine, Scot., U.K. 56 4N 3 43W
41 Kincardine, Scot., U.K. 57 52N 4 20W
112 Kinchwan, China 42 28N 126 6E
43 Kincraig, Scot., U.K. .57 8N 3 57W
130 Kinda, Kasai, Congo . 4 48S 21 50E
130 Kinda, Katanga, Congo 9 20S 25 5E
157 Kindersley, Canada ...51 30N 109 10W
124 Kindia, Guinea 10 0N 12 52W
130 Kindu-Port Empain, Congo 2 55S 25 50E
87 Kinel, U.S.S.R. 53 15N 50 40E
87 Kineshma, U.S.S.R. ...57 30N 42 5E
35 Kineton, Eng., U.K. .52 10N 1 30W
14 King Christian IX Land, Greenland 68 0N 35 0W
14 King Christian X Land, Greenland 73 0N 26 0W
167 King City, U.S.A. 36 11N 121 8W
14 King Frederick VI Land, Greenland 63 0N 43 0W
14 King Frederick VIII Land, Greenland 77 30N 25 0W
176 K. George B., Falk. Is. 51 30S 60 30W
15 King George I., Antarctica 60 0S 60 0W
153 King George Is., Can. 53 40N 80 30W
107 King I., *see* Kadan Kyun, Burma 12 30N 98 20E
145 King I., Tas., Australia 39 40S 144 0E
138 King Leopold Range, Western Australia .17 20S 124 20E
14 King Oscar Fd., Green. 73 0N 23 0W
138 King Sd., W. Australia 16 50S 123 20E
152 King William I., Can. 69 0N 98 0W
135 King William's Town, C. Prov., S. Africa .32 51S 27 22E
40 Kingairloch, dist., Scotland, U.K. 56 37N 5 30W
145 Kingaroy, Australia ...26 32S 151 51E
40 Kingarth, Scot., U.K. 55 45N 5 2W
165 Kingfisher, U.S.A. 35 50N 97 55W
41 Kinghorn, Scot., U.K. 56 4N 3 10W
86 Kingisepp, U.S.S.R. ...59 25N 28 40E
86 Kingisepp (Kuressaare), U.S.S.R. 58 15N 22 15E
113 Kingkiang Res., China 30 10N 112 10E
111 Kingku, China 23 49N 100 30E
167 Kingman, Ariz., U.S.A. 35 12N 114 2W
165 Kingman, Kan., U.S.A. 37 41N 96 9W
113 Kingmen, China 31 10N 112 15E
113 Kingning, China 27 55N 119 30E
112 Kingpeng, China 43 10N 117 25E
14 Kings B., Spitzbergen 78 0N 15 0E
167 Kings R., U.S.A. 36 57N 119 0W
167 Kings Canyon National Park, U.S.A. 37 0N 118 45W
35 King's Lynn, England, United Kingdom 52 45N 0 25E
163 Kings Mt., U.S.A 35 13N 81 20W
166 King's Peak, mt., U.S.A. 40 46N 110 27W
163 Kingsport, U.S.A. 36 33N 82 36W
34 King's Sutton, England, United Kingdom 52 1N 1 16W
34 King's Worthy, England, U.K. 51 6N 1 18W
41 Kingsbarns, Scot., U.K. 56 18N 2 40W
36 Kingsbridge, Eng., U.K. 50 17N 3 46W
167 Kingsburg, U.S.A. 36 35N 119 36W
34 Kingsbury, Eng., U.K. 52 33N 1 41W
145 Kingscote, S. Australia 35 33S 137 31E
46 Kingscourt, Ireland ...53 55N 6 48W
36 Kingskerswell, England, United Kingdom 50 30N 3 34W
34 Kingsland, Eng., U.K. 52 15N 2 49W
135 Kingsley, Natal, S. Afr. 27 55S 30 33E
164 Kingsley, U.S.A. 42 37N 95 58W
164 Kingsley Dam, U.S.A. 41 20N 101 40W
36 Kingsteignton, England, United Kingdom 50 32N 3 35W
154 Kingston, Canada 44 20N 76 30W
34 Kingston, Eng., U.K. 51 23N 0 20W

MAP
169 Kingston, Jamaica 18 0N 76 50W
147 Kingston, N.Z. 45 20S 168 43E
161 Kingston, N.Y., U.S.A. 41 55N 74 0W
161 Kingston, Pa., U.S.A. 41 19N 75 58W
161 Kingston, R.I., U.S.A. 41 29N 71 30W
35 Kingston-upon-Thames, England, U.K. 51 23N 0 20W
145 Kingston South East, S. Australia 36 51S 139 55E
169 Kingstown, St. Vincent 13 10N 61 10W
163 Kingstree, U.S.A. 33 40N 79 48W
154 Kingsville, Canada 42 3N 82 45W
165 Kingsville, U.S.A. 27 30N 97 53W
36 Kingswear, Eng., U.K. 50 21N 3 33W
36 Kingswood, Eng., U.K. 51 26N 2 31W
133 Kingswood, S. Africa .27 29S 25 46E
112 Kingtai, China 37 4N 103 59E
113 Kingtehchen (Fowliang), China ...29 8N 117 21E
34 Kington, Eng., U.K. .52 12N 3 2W
103 Kingtung, China 24 30N 100 50E
113 Kingtzekwan, China ...33 25N 111 10E
43 Kingussie, Scot., U.K. 57 4N 4 2W
112 Kingyang, China 36 6N 107 49E
112 Kinhsien, China 39 4N 121 48E
113 Kinhwa, China 29 5N 119 32E
131 Kiniama, Congo 11 29S 28 25E
130 Kinkala, Congo (Fr.) . 4 18S 14 49E
160 Kinkardine, Canada ...44 12N 81 36W
114 Kinki, Dist., Japan ...33 30N 136 0E
146 Kinleith, New Zealand 38 20S 175 56E
42 Kinloch, Scot., U.K. .57 0N 6 18W
43 Kinloch, Sutherland, Scotland, U.K. 58 17N 4 50W
40 Kinloch Rannoch, Scotland, U.K. 56 41N 4 12W
42 Kinlochbervie, Scotland, United Kingdom 58 28N 5 5W
42 Kinlochewe, Scot., U.K. 57 37N 5 20W
42 Kinlochiel, Scot., U.K. 56 52N 5 20W
40 Kinlochleven, Scot., U.K. 56 42N 4 59W
43 Kinloss, Scot., U.K. ...57 38N 3 37W
46 Kinlough, Ireland 54 27N 8 16W
113 Kinmen (Quemoy) Is., China 24 25N 118 24E
160 Kinmount, Canada 44 45N 78 40W
79 Kinn, Norway 61 37N 4 46E
81 Kinna, Sweden 57 32N 12 42E
43 Kinnaird's Hd., Scotland, U.K. 57 40N 2 0W
81 Kinnared, Sweden 57 2N 13 7E
45 Kinnegad, Ireland 53 28N 7 8W
98 Kinneret, Israel 32 44N 35 34E
81 Kinneviken, B., Sweden 58 38N 18 20E
45 Kinnity, Ireland 53 6N 7 44W
127 Kinoni, Cent. Afr. Rep. 5 40N 26 10E
131 Kinoni, Uganda 0 41S 30 28E
157 Kinosota, Canada 50 52N 98 57W
107 Kinping, China 22 56N 103 15E
41 Kinross & co., Scotland, U.K. 56 13N 3 25W
133 Kinross, Trans., S. Afr. 26 22S 29 3E
44 Kinsale & Harb., Ire. .51 42N 8 31W
44 Kinsale Old Hd., Ire. .51 37N 8 32W
79 Kinsarvik, Norway 60 24N 6 44E
130 Kinshasa (Leopoldville), Congo 4 20S 15 15E
113 Kinsiang, China 35 4N 116 25E
165 Kinsley, U.S.A. 37 57N 99 30W
163 Kinston, U.S.A. 35 18N 77 35W
125 Kintampo, Ghana 8 5N 1 41W
42 Kintaravay, Scot., U.K. 58 4N 6 42W
131 Kintinku, Tanzania ... 6 0S 35 20E
43 Kintore, Scot., U.K. .57 14N 2 20W
142 Kintore Ra., W. Australia 23 15S 128 47E
40 Kintyre, pen., Scot., U.K. 55 30N 5 35W
40 Kintyre, Mull of, Scotland, U.K. 55 17N 5 4W
156 Kinuso, Canada 55 25N 115 25W
44 Kinvara, Ireland 53 8N 8 57W
131 Kinyangiri, Tanzania . 4 35S 34 37E
130 Kinzia, Congo 3 36S 18 26E
160 Kinzua, U.S.A. 41 52N 78 58W
160 Kinzua Dam, U.S.A. .41 53N 79 0W
130 Kiobo, Congo 5 40S 13 17E
77 Kioni, Greece 38 27N 20 41E
131 Kioru, Kenya 0 3S 38 18E
113 Kioshan, China 32 50N 114 0E
154 Kiosk, Canada 46 6N 78 53W
165 Kiowa, Kan., U.S.A. .37 3N 98 30W
165 Kiowa, Okla., U.S.A. .34 45N 95 50W
77 Kiparissia, Greece 37 15N 21 40E
77 Kiparissiakos Kolpos, G., Greece 37 25N 21 25E
154 Kipawa Res. Prov. Park, Canada 47 0N 78 30W
154 Kipawa L., Canada ...46 50N 79 0W
131 Kipengere Ra., Tanz. . 9 12S 34 15E
131 Kipili, Tanzania 7 28S 30 32E
132 Kipilingu, Congo 13 14S 29 0E
131 Kipini, Kenya 2 30S 40 32E
40 Kippen, Scot., U.K. ...56 8N 4 12W
45 Kippure, mt., Ireland 53 11N 6 23W
132 Kipusha, Congo 12 55S 29 35E
104 Kiratpur, India 29 32N 78 12E
38 Kirby, England, U.K. 53 29N 2 55W
39 Kirby Moorside, England, U.K. 54 16N 0 55W
56 Kirchhain, Germany .50 49N 8 54E
57 Kirchheim Bolanden, Germany 49 40N 8 0E
55 Kirchhellen, Germany 51 36N 6 54E
59 Kirchschlag, Austria .47 30N 16 19E
46 Kircubbin, N. Ire., U.K. 54 30N 5 33W
91 Kirensk, U.S.S.R. 57 50N 107 55E
90 Kirgizia SSR, USSR. .42 0N 75 0E
130 Kiri, Congo 1 29S 19 25E
134 Kiries West, S.W. Afr. 26 30S 19 0E
146 Kirikopuni, N.Z. 35 50S 174 1E
87 Kirillov, U.S.S.R. 59 51N 38 14E
112 Kirin, China 43 58N 126 31E
112 Kirin, prov., China 43 45N 125 20E
106 Kirindi Oya, R., Ceylon 6 15N 81 20E
144 Kiriwina Is., see Trobriand Is. 8 40S 151 0E
144 Kirk River, Australia 20 0S 146 38E
41 Kirkbean, Scot., U.K. 54 56N 3 35W
38 Kirkbride, Eng., U.K. 54 54N 3 13W
39 Kirkburton, Eng., U.K. 53 36N 1 42W
39 Kirkby-in-Ashfield, England, U.K. 53 6N 1 15W
38 Kirkby Lonsdale, England, U.K. 54 13N 2 36W
39 Kirkby Malzeard, England, U.K. 54 10N 1 38W
38 Kirkby Stephen, England, U.K. 54 27N 2 23W
38 Kirkby Thore, England, United Kingdom 54 38N 2 34W
41 Kirkcaldy, Scot., U.K. 56 7N 3 10W
40 Kirkcolm, Scot., U.K. 54 59N 5 4W
41 Kirkconnel, Scot., U.K. 55 23N 4 0W
40 Kirkcowan, Scot., U.K. 54 53N 4 38W
41 Kirkcudbright, Scotland, United Kingdom 54 50N 4 3W
81 Kirkeby, Denmark 55 7N 8 33E
106 Kirkee, India 18 34N 73 56E
80 Kirkenaer, Norway ...60 27N 12 6E
82 Kirkenes, Norway 69 40N 30 5E
38 Kirkham, Lancs, England, U.K. 53 47N 2 52W
40 Kirkinner, Scot., U.K. 54 59N 4 28W
41 Kirkintilloch, Scot., U.K. 55 57N 4 10W
167 Kirkland, Ariz., U.S.A. 34 29N 112 46W
166 Kirkland, Wash., U.S.A. 47 40N 122 10W
154 Kirkland Lake, Canada 48 15N 80 0W
75 Kirklareli, Turkey 41 44N 27 15E
41 Kirkliston, Scot., U.K. 55 55N 3 27W
147 Kirkliston Ra., N.Z. ...44 25S 170 34E
38 Kirkmichael, Isle of Man, U.K. 54 17N 4 35W
43 Kirkmichael, Scot., U.K. 56 43N 3 31W
38 Kirkoswald, Eng., U.K. 54 46N 2 41W
40 Kirkoswold, Scot., U.K. 55 19N 4 48W
38 Kirkstone P., Eng., U.K. 54 29N 2 55W
164 Kirksville, U.S.A. 40 8N 92 35W
100 Kirkuk, Iraq 35 30N 44 21E
43 Kirkwall, Scot., U.K. .58 59N 2 59W
39 Kirkwhelpington, England, U.K. 55 9N 2 0W
135 Kirkwood, S. Africa ...33 22S 25 15E
106 Kirlampudi, India 17 12N 82 12E
57 Kirn, Germany 49 46N 7 29E
86 Kirov, U.S.S.R. 58 35N 49 40E
87 Kirov, U.S.S.R. 54 3N 34 12E
89 Kirovabad, U.S.S.R. .40 45N 46 10E
89 Kirovakan, U.S.S.R. .41 0N 44 0E
88 Kirovograd, U.S.S.R. .48 35N 32 20E
84 Kirovsk, U.S.S.R. 67 48N 33 50E
89 Kirovski, U.S.S.R. 45 51N 48 11E
157 Kirriemuir, Canada ...51 56N 110 20W
43 Kirriemuir, Scot., U.K. 56 41N 3 0W
87 Kirsanov, U.S.S.R. 52 35N 42 40E
100 Kirşehir, Turkey 39 14N 34 5E
133 Kirstonia, S. Africa ...25 30S 23 45E
125 Kirtachi, Niger 12 52N 2 30E
102 Kirthar Range, W. Pak. 27 0N 67 0E
35 Kirtley, England, U.K. 52 11N 0 29E
34 Kirtlington, Eng., U.K. 51 54N 1 9W
39 Kirton, England, U.K. 52 56N 0 3W
39 Kirton-in-Lindsey, England, U.K. 53 29N 0 35W
82 Kiruna, Sweden 67 50N 20 20E
130 Kirundu, Congo 0 50S 25 35E
142 Kirup, W. Australia ...33 40S 115 50E
109 Kiruru, Indonesia 3 55S 134 55E
87 Kiryu, U.S.S.R. 55 5N 46 45E
114 Kiryu, Japan 36 25N 139 20E
87 Kirzhach, U.S.S.R. 56 12N 38 50E
81 Kisa, Sweden 57 58N 15 37E
131 Kisaga, Tanzania 4 30S 34 23E
77 Kisamou, Kolpos G., Greece 35 30N 23 38E
131 Kisangani (Stanleyville), Congo 0 35N 25 15E
109 Kisar I., Indonesia 8 5S 127 10E
108 Kisaran, Indonesia 2 47N 99 29E
114 Kisaratzu, Japan 35 25N 139 59E
131 Kisarawe, Tanzania ... 6 53S 39 0E
59 Kisbér, Hungary 47 30N 18 0E
90 Kiselevski, U.S.S.R. ...54 5N 86 6E
105 Kishanganj, India 26 3N 88 14E
104 Kishangarh, India 27 50N 70 30E
125 Kishi, Nigeria 9 1N 3 45E
88 Kishinoi, U.S.S.R. 47 1N 28 50E
114 Kishiwada, Japan 34 50N 135 25E
44 Kishkeam, Ireland 52 15N 9 12W
98 Kishon, Israel 32 33N 35 12E
105 Kishorganj, E. Pak. ...24 26N 90 40E
42 Kishorn L., Scot., U.K. 57 22N 5 40W
113 Kishow, China 28 16N 109 47E
102 Kishtwar, Kashmir ...33 20N 75 48E
112 Kisi, China 45 21N 131 0E
131 Kisii, & dist., Kenya ... 0 40S 34 45E
131 Kisiju, Tanzania 7 23S 39 19E
89 Kisir, Mt., Turkey 41 0N 43 5E
152 Kiska I., Alaska, U.S.A. 52 0N 177 30E
59 Kiskomárom, Hungary 46 33N 17 10E
59 Kiskőrös, Hungary 46 37N 19 20E
59 Kiskundorozsma, Hung. 46 16N 20 5E
59 Kiskunfelegyháza, Hungary 46 42N 19 53E
59 Kiskunhalas, Hungary 46 28N 19 37E
59 Kiskunmajsa, Hungary 46 30N 19 48E
89 Kislovodsk, U.S.S.R. .43 50N 42 45E
115 Kismayu, Somali Rep. 0 20S 42 30E
114 Kiso R., Japan 35 20N 137 0E
59 Kispest, Hungary 47 27N 19 9E
124 Kissidougou, Guinea . 9 5N 10 0W
163 Kissimmee, U.S.A. 28 18N 81 22W
163 Kissimmee R., U.S.A. 27 20N 81 0W
71 Kistanje, Yugoslavia .43 58N 15 55E
59 Kisterenye, Hungary .48 3N 19 50E
59 Kisújszállas, Hungary 47 12N 20 50E
131 Kisumu, Kenya 0 3S 34 45E
131 Kisumu Londiani, dist., Kenya 0 2S 35 20E
59 Kisvárda, Hungary ...48 14N 22 4E
131 Kiswani, Tanzania 4 5S 37 57E
164 Kit Carson, U.S.A. 38 48N 102 45W
124 Kita, Mali 13 5N 9 25W
111 Kitai, China 44 0N 89 27E
114 Kitaibaraki, Japan 36 50N 140 45E
114 Kitakami R., Japan ...39 30N 141 15E
114 Kitakyushu, Japan 33 50N 130 50E
131 Kitale, Kenya 1 0N 35 12E
132 Kitambala, Congo 12 30S 29 10E
131 Kitangiri, L., Tanzania 4 5S 34 20E
154 Kitchener, Canada 43 30N 80 30W
142 Kitchener, W. Austral. 30 55S 124 8E
154 Kitchigami, R., Canada 50 35N 78 5W
113 Kitchioh, China 22 57N 116 2E
131 Kitega, see Citega, Burundi 3 30S 29 58E
131 Kitgum Matadi, Uganda 3 17N 32 52E
77 Kithira, & I., Greece .36 9N 23 0E
77 Kithnos, & I., Greece .37 26N 24 27E
156 Kitimat, Canada 53 55N 129 0W
127 Kitiyab, Sudan 17 13N 33 35E
130 Kitombe, Congo 5 22S 18 57E
76 Kitros, Greece 40 22N 22 34E
160 Kittanning, U.S.A. 40 49N 79 30W
161 Kittatinny Mts., U.S.A. 41 0N 75 0W
161 Kittery, U.S.A. 43 7N 70 42W
82 Kittilä, Finland 67 38N 25 0E
131 Kitui, Kenya 1 17S 38 0E
131 Kitui, dist., Kenya 1 30S 38 25E
132 Kitwe, Zambia 12 54S 28 7E
113 Kityang, China 23 30N 116 29E
58 Kitzbühel, Austria 47 27N 12 24E
57 Kitzingen, Germany ...49 44N 10 9E
111 Kiuchuan, China 39 51N 98 30E
113 Kiukiang, China 29 37N 116 2E
113 Kiungchow, China 19 57N 110 17E
113 Kiungchow Strait, China 20 40N 110 0E
82 Kivalo, Mts., Finland 66 18N 26 0E
104 Kivarli, India 24 33N 72 46E
77 Kivotós, Greece 40 13N 21 26E
131 Kivu L., Congo 1 48S 29 0E
131 Kiyuanshan, China 28 6N 117 46E
113 Kiyang, China 26 36N 111 42E
84 Kizel, U.S.S.R. 59 0N 57 0E
88 Kizil R., Turkey 40 30N 34 15E
88 Kizilcahaman, Turkey 40 30N 32 30E
89 Kizil-Irmak R., Tur. .39 15N 36 0E
90 Kizil Kiya, U.S.S.R. .40 20N 72 35E
131 Kizimkazi, Tanzania . 6 28S 39 30E
89 Kizlyar, U.S.S.R. 43 51N 46 40E
81 Kjellerup, Denmark ...56 17N 9 20E
134 Klaarstroom, S. Africa 33 16S 22 30E
108 Klabat B., Indonesia . 1 30S 105 40E
74 Kladanj, Yugoslavia .44 14N 18 42E
74 Kladnica, Yugoslavia .43 23N 20 2E
58 Kladno, Czechoslovakia 50 10N 14 7E
74 Kladovo, Yugoslavia .44 36N 22 33E
58 Klagenfurt, Austria ...46 38N 14 20E
86 Klaipeda, U.S.S.R. 55 43N 21 10E
81 Klågerup, Sweden 55 36N 13 17E
81 Klågshamn, Sweden ...55 32N 12 53E
81 Klagstorp, Sweden 55 22N 13 23E
81 Klakring, Denmark ...55 42N 9 59E
166 Klamath Falls, U.S.A. 42 20N 121 50W
166 Klamath Mts., U.S.A. 41 20N 123 0W
166 Klamath R., U.S.A. ...41 40N 123 30W
109 Klamono, Indonesia ... 1 10S 131 30E
107 Klang, W. Malaysia ... 3 1N 101 33E
71 Klanjec, Yugoslavia ...46 3N 15 45E
80 Klarälven R., Sweden 60 32N 13 15E
109 Klaten, Indonesia 7 43S 110 36E
58 Klatovy, Cz. 49 23N 13 18E
157 Klawak, Alaska, U.S.A 55 35N 133 0W
134 Klawer, C. Prov., S. Afr. 31 44S 18 36E
75 Klebarovo, Bulg. 43 36N 26 14E
60 Kleczew, Poland 52 22N 18 9E
156 Kleena Kleene, Can. .52 0N 124 50W
166 Klein, U.S.A. 46 26N 108 31W
134 Klein-Karas, S.W. Afr. 27 33S 18 7E
133 Klein Letaba R., S. Afr. 23 20S 30 40E
133 Kleinood, Trans., S. Afr. 24 40S 28 25E
55 Kleinoosterwijk, Neth. 51 53N 5 4E
134 Kleinpoort, S. Africa .33 19S 24 51E
71 Klekovaca, Mt., Y.-slav. 44 25N 16 32E
156 Klemtu, Canada 52 35N 128 55W
59 Klenovec, Cz. 48 36N 19 54E
74 Klenovec, Yugoslavia 31 32N 20 49E
79 Klepp Norway 59 48N 5 36E
133 Klerksdorp, S. Africa .26 51S 26 38E
86 Kletnya, U.S.S.R. 53 30N 33 2E
86 Kletsk, U.S.S.R. 53 5N 26 45E
89 Kletskaya, U.S.S.R. ...49 20N 43 0E
56 Kleve, Germany 51 46N 6 10E
166 Klickitat, U.S.A. 45 50N 12 10W
86 Klimovichi, U.S.S.R. .53 36N 32 0E
87 Klin, U.S.S.R. 56 28N 36 48E
81 Klinte, Denmark 55 35N 10 12E
81 Klintehamn, Sweden .57 22N 18 14E
87 Klintsy, U.S.S.R. 52 50N 32 10E
134 Klipbakke, S. Africa .28 50S 21 21E
134 Klipbank, S. Africa ...32 27S 22 28E
134 Klipdale, S. Africa 34 17S 19 58E
133 Klipdam, S. Africa 28 18S 24 40E
134 Klipdam, S.W. Africa 27 15S 19 59E
134 Klipfontein, S. Africa 29 18S 23 50E
134 Klipheuwel, S. Africa .33 43S 18 37E
134 Klipkrans, S. Africa ...32 46S 22 55E
135 Klippan, O.F.S., S. Afr. 27 45S 26 27E
81 Klippan, Sweden 56 8N 13 10E
134 Klipplaar, S. Africa ...33 0S 24 22E
75 Klisura, Bulgaria 42 40N 24 28E
81 Klitmöller, Denmark...57 3N 8 30E
71 Kljuc, Yugoslavia 44 32N 16 48E
60 Klobuck, Poland 50 55N 19 5E
60 Klodawa, Poland 53 16N 18 52E
60 Klodzko, Poland 50 28N 16 38E
152 Klondike, dist., Canada 64 0N 139 40W
76 Klos, Albania 41 28N 26 10E
59 Klosterneuburg, Austria 48 18N 16 19E
57 Klosters, Switzerland .46 52N 9 52E
80 Kloten, Sweden 59 54N 15 19E
56 Klötze, Germany 52 38N 11 9E
125 Klouto,Togoland 6 57N 0 44E
81 Klovborg, Denmark ...55 56N 9 30E
80 Klövsjöfj, Mt., Sweden 62 36N 13 57E
152 Kluane, L., Canada ...61 25N 138 50W
107 Kluang, W. Malaysia . 1 59N 103 20E
60 Kluczbork, Poland 50 58N 18 12E
55 Kluppelberg, Germany 51 7N 7 30E
91 Klyuchevsk, Mt., U.S.S.R. 55 50N 160 30E
86 Kmelnitski, U.S.S.R. .49 23N 27 0E
135 Knapdaar, S. Africa ...30 43S 26 9E
40 Knapdale, dist., Scotland, U.K. 55 55N 5 30W
39 Knaresborough, England, U.K. 54 1N 1 29W
35 Knebworth, England, U.K. 51 52N 0 11W
123 Kneiss Is., Tunisia 34 19N 10 16E
75 Knezha, Bulgaria 43 30N 23 56E
74 Knić, Yugoslavia 43 53N 20 45E
34 Knighton, Wales, U.K. 52 21N 3 2W
166 Knight's Landing, U.S.A. 38 50N 121 49W
71 Knin, Yugoslavia 44 1N 16 17E
58 Knittelfeld, Austria ...47 13N 14 51E
74 Knjaževac, Yugoslavia 43 35N 22 18E
46 Knock, Ireland 53 48N 8 55W
45 Knockananna, Ireland 52 52N 6 34W
44 Knockannis Mt., Ire. .52 58N 8 42W
44 Knockhoy Mt., Ire. ...51 49N 9 27W
46 Knocklayd Mt., Northern Ireland, U.K. 55 10N 6 15W
44 Knocklofty, Ireland ...52 20N 7 49W
45 Knockmahon, Ireland 52 8N 7 21W
44 Knockmealdown Mts., Ireland 52 16N 8 0W
44 Knocknaskagh Mt. Ire. 52 7N 8 25W
54 Knokke, Belgium 51 20N 3 17E
38 Knott End, Eng., U.K. 53 55N 3 0W
39 Knottingley, Eng., U.K. 53 42N 1 15W
34 Knowle, England, U.K. 52 42N 1 43W
143 Knowsley, Vic., Austral. 36 50S 144 35E
162 Knox, U.S.A. 41 18N 86 36W
165 Knox City, U.S.A. 33 26N 99 38W
15 Knox Coast, Antarctica 66 30S 108 0E
164 Knoxville, Iowa, U.S.A. 41 20N 93 5W
163 Knoxville, Pa., U.S.A. 41 57N 77 26W
163 Knoxville, Tenn., U.S.A. 35 58N 83 57W
42 Knoydart, dist., Scot., U.K. 57 3N 5 33W
38 Knutsford, Eng., U.K. 53 18N 2 22W
79 Knutshö Mt., Norway 62 20N 9 42E
134 Knysna, C. Prov., S. Afr. 34 2S 23 2E
60 Knyszyn, Poland 53 20N 22 56E
107 Ko Chang I., Thailand 12 0N 102 20E
107 Ko Phangan I., Thai . 9 45N 100 10E
107 Ko Phra Thong, Thai. 9 6N 98 15E
107 Ko Samui I., Thailand 9 30N 100 0E
153 Koartac (Notre Dame de Koartac), Canada 61 5N 69 36E
109 Koba, Aru I., Indon. . 6 37S 134 37E
108 Koba, Bangka I., Indon. 2 26S 106 14E
71 Kobarid, Yugoslavia .46 15N 13 30E
114 Kobayashi, Japan 31 56N 130 59E
114 Kobe, Japan 34 45N 135 10E
88 Kobelyaki, U.S.S.R. ...49 11N 34 9E
81 København, Denmark 55 41N 12 34E
57 Koblenz, Germany 50 21N 7 36E
131 Koboko, Uganda 3 23N 31 0E
86 Kobrin, U.S.S.R. 52 15N 24 22E
109 Kobroor I., Indonesia 6 10S 134 30E
89 Kobuleti, U.S.S.R. 41 55N 41 45E
87 Kobylkino, U.S.S.R. .54 8N 43 46E
86 Kobylnik, U.S.S.R. 54 58N 26 39E
74 Kočane, Yugoslavia ...41 53N 22 27E
74 Kočani, Yugoslavia ...41 55N 22 25E
77 Kocarli, Turkey 37 45N 27 43E
74 Koceljevo, Yugoslavia 44 28N 19 50E
71 Kočevje, Yugoslavia .45 39N 14 50E
105 Kochas, India 25 15N 83 56E
114 Kochi, Japan 33 30N 133 35E
106 Kodaikanal, India 10 13N 77 32E
106 Koddiyat Bay, Ceylon 8 33N 81 15E
152 Kodiak I., Alaska, U.S.A. 57 30N 152 45W
107 Kodiang, W. Malaysia 6 21N 100 18E
104 Kodinar, India 20 46N 70 46E
89 Kodori, R., U.S.S.R. .43 0N 41 40E
134 Koedoesberge Mts., C. Prov., S. Africa .32 40S 20 12E
134 Koedoeskloot, S. Africa 32 23S 23 28E
134 Koegas, C. Prov., S. Afr. 29 16S 22 20E
133 Koekemoer, S. Africa .26 48S 26 50E
134 Koekenapp, S. Africa .31 30S 18 18E
129 Koes, S.W. Africa 26 0S 19 15E
143 Koetong, Vic., Austral. 36 10S 147 30E
135 Koffiefontein, S. Africa29 22S 24 58E
58 Köflach, Austria 47 4N 15 4E
125 Koforidua, Ghana 6 3N 0 17W
114 Kofu, Japan 35 40N 138 30E
145 Kogan, Australia 27 2S 150 40E
81 Köge, & B., Denmark 55 27N 12 10E
125 Kogin Baba, Nigeria . 7 55N 11 35E
100 Kogizman, Turkey 40 5N 43 10E
101 Koh-i-Bab, Mts., Afghanistan 34 30N 67 0E
107 Koh Kong, I., Cambodia 11 20N 103 0E
102 Kohat, West Pakistan 33 40N 71 29E
103 Kohima, India 25 35N 94 10E
15 Kohler Ra., Antarctica 77 0N 110 0W
55 Kohlscheid, Germany 50 50N 6 6E
86 Kohtla-Järve, U.S.S.R. 59 20N 27 20E
146 Kohukohu, N.Z. 36 31S 173 38E
59 Kojetin, Czechoslovakia 49 21N 17 20E
142 Kojonup, W. Australia 33 48S 117 10E
126 Koka, Sudan 20 5N 30 35E
90 Kokand, U.S.S.R. 41 0N 71 10E
59 Kokava, Czechoslovakia 48 35N 19 50E
90 Kokchetav, U.S.S.R. .53 20N 69 10E
87 Kokhma, U.S.S.R. 56 55N 41 18E
111 Kokiu, China 23 30N 103 0E
82 Kokkola (Gamlakarleby), Finland 63 50N 23 8E
125 Koko, Nigeria 11 28N 4 29E
125 Koko, Nigeria 6 5N 5 28E
103 Koko Shili, Mts., China 35 20N 91 0E
144 Kokoda, Papua 9 0S 148 0E
162 Kokomo, Ind., U.S.A. 40 30N 86 6W
111 Koko-Nor, L., China .37 0N 100 0E
144 Kokopo, New Guinea . 4 23S 152 15E
91 Kokora, U.S.S.R. 71 35N 144 50E
153 Koksoak, R., Canada .54 5N 64 10W
135 Kokstad, S. Africa 30 32S 29 29E
107 Ko Kut, I., Thailand .11 40N 102 32E
84 Kola, U.S.S.R. 68 45N 33 8E
84 Kola B., U.S.S.R. 69 23N 34 0E
109 Kola, I., Indonesia 5 35S 134 30E
84 Kola Pen., U.S.S.R. ...67 30N 38 0E

MAP
109 Kolagede, Indonesia ... 7 54S 110 26E
124 Kolahun, Liberia ... 8 15N 10 4W
109 Kolaka, Indonesia ... 4 3S 121 46E
112 Kolan, China ...38 58N 111 28E
106 Kolar, India ...13 12N 78 15E
106 Kolar Gold Fields, India ...12 58N 78 16E
75 Kolarovgrad, see Sumen, Bulgaria ...43 27N 26 42E
59 Kolarovo, Cz. ...47 56N 18 0E
74 Kolašin, Yugoslavia ...42 50N 19 31E
80 Kolbäck, Sweden ...59 36N 16 16E
81 Kolby, Denmark ...55 49N 10 33E
87 Kolchugino, U.S.S.R. .56 25N 39 6E
124 Kolda, Senegal ...12 55N 14 50W
14 Koldewey I., Greenland ...77 0N 18 0W
81 Kolding, Denmark ...55 30N 9 29E
130 Kole, Congo ... 3 16S 22 42E
122 Koléa, Algeria ...36 44N 2 50E
109 Kolepom I., Indonesia 8 0S 138 30E
80 Kölfors, Sweden ...62 9N 16 30E
84 Kolguyev I., U.S.S.R. 69 20N 48 30E
106 Kolhapur, India ...16 43N 74 15E
58 Kolin, Czechoslovakia 50 2N 15 9E
81 Kolind,, Denmark ...56 21N 10 34E
56 Kölleda, Germany ...51 11N 11 14E
106 Kollegal, India ...12 9N 77 9E
106 Kolleru L., India ...16 40N 81 10E
56 Köln, (Cologne), Ger .50 56N 9 58E
60 Kolo, Poland ...52 14N 18 40E
60 Kolobrzeg, Poland ...54 10N 15 35E
87 Kologriv, U.S.S.R. ...58 48N 44 25E
124 Kolokani, Mali ...13 35N 7 45W
87 Kolomna, U.S.S.R. ...55 8N 38 45E
88 Kolomyya, U.S.S.R. ..48 31N 25 2E
109 Kolonodale, Indonesia 2 3S 121 25E
103 Kolosib, India ...24 15N 92 45E
90 Kolpashevo, U.S.S.R. 58 20N 83 5E
86 Kolpino, U.S.S.R. ...59 44N 30 39E
87 Kolpny, U.S.S.R. ...52 12N 37 10E
74 Kolubara, R., Y-slav. 44 35N 20 15E
60 Koluszki, Poland ...51 45N 19 46E
130 Kolwezi, Congo ...10 40S 25 25E
87 Kolyberovo, U.S.S.R. 55 15N 38 40E
91 Kolyma R., U.S.S.R. .64 40N 153 0E
91 Kolyma Ra., U.S.S.R. 63 0N 157 0E
126 Kom Ombo, Egypt ...24 25N 32 52E
127 Koma, Ethiopia ... 8 29N 36 53E
134 Komaggas, S. Africa .29 50S 17 26E
91 Komandorskiye, Is., U.S.S.R. ...55 0N 167 0E
59 Komárno, Cz. ...47 49N 18 5E
59 Komarom, Hungary ...47 49N 18 7E
86 Komarovo, U.S.S.R. .58 38N 33 40E
133 Komati, R., Swaz. ...25 48S 31 50E
133 Komatipoort, S. Afr. .25 25S 31 57E
130 Komba, Congo ... 2 50N 24 2E
77 Komboti, Greece ...39 6N 21 5E
71 Komen, Yugoslavia ...45 49N 13 45E
125 Komenda, Ghana ... 5 4N 1 28W
135 Komga, C. Prov., S. Afr. ...32 37S 27 56E
84 Komi, A.S.S.R., U.S.S.R. ...64 0N 55 0E
71 Komiza, Yugoslavia ...43 3N 16 11E
59 Komló, Hungary ...46 15N 18 16E
135 Kommadagga, S. Africa ...33 8S 25 56E
106 Kommamur Canal, India ...16 0N 80 25E
135 Kommissiepoort, S. Afr. ...29 15S 27 20E
89 Kommunarsk, U.S.S.R. ...48 30N 38 45E
79 Komnes, Norway ...59 30N 9 53E
109 Komodo, Indonesia ... 8 37S 119 20E
130 Komono, Congo (Fr.) . 3 15S 13 20E
60 Komorze, Poland ...62 8N 17 38E
76 Komotini, Greece ...41 9N 25 26E
107 Kompong Cham, Cambodia ...11 54N 105 30E
107 Kompong Chhnang, Cambodia ...12 20N 104 35E
107 Kompong Som, Cambodia ...11 3N 103 41E
107 Kompong Speu, Cambodia ...11 26N 104 32E
107 Kompong Thom, Cambod. ...12 35N 104 51E
88 Komrat, U.S.S.R. ...46 18N 28 40E
91 Komsomolets I., U.S.S.R. ...80 30N 95 0E
91 Komsomolsk, U.S.S.R. ...50 30N 137 0E
87 Komsomolskiy, U.S.S.R. ...53 30N 49 40E
125 Kona, Nigeria ... 8 58N 11 15E
103 Konam Dzong, China 29 5N 93 0E
165 Konawa, U.S.A. ...34 59N 96 46W
106 Kondagaon, India ...19 35N 81 35E
131 Konde, Zan., Tanzania ... 4 57S 39 45E
76 Kondiá, Greece ...39 52N 25 10E
142 Kondinin, W. Australia ...32 34S 118 8E
131 Kondoa, Tanzania ... 4 0S 36 0E
91 Kondarshevo, U.S.S.R. ...57 30N 98 30E
125 Konduga, Nigeria ...11 35N 13 26E
124 Kong, Ivory Coast ... 8 54N 4 36W
81 Konga, Sweden ...56 28N 15 10E
81 Kongeaa R., Denmark 55 24N 8 45E
112 Kongju, Korea ...36 30N 127 0E
103 Konglu, Burma ...27 13N 97 57E
113 Kongmoon, China ...22 35N 113 1E
130 Kongo Central, Prov., Congo ... 5 0S 16 0E
130 Kongolo, Katanga, Congo ... 5 22S 27 0E
79 Kongsberg, Norway ...59 37N 9 38E
79 Kongsvinger, Norway 60 12N 12 2E
79 Kongsvoll, Norway ...62 20N 9 36E
131 Kongwa, Tanzania ... 6 11S 36 26E
130 Koni & Mts., Congo ...10 40S 27 11E
60 Koniecpol, Poland ...50 46N 19 40E
86 Königsberg, see Kaliningrad, U.S.S.R. ...54 42N 20 32E
56 Königslutter, Germany ...52 14N 10 50E
55 Königswinter, Germany ...50 41N 7 12E
56 Königswusterhausen, Germany ...52 19N 13 38E
60 Konin, Poland ...52 12N 18 15E
133 Koning, C. Prov., S. Afr. ...27 38S 23 30E
76 Konispol, Albania ...39 42N 20 10E
76 Kónitsa, Greece ...40 5N 20 48E
71 Konjice, Yugoslavia ...43 42N 18 0E
125 Konkoure, R., Guinea 10 30N 13 40W
56 Könnern, Germany ...51 40N 11 45E
106 Konnur, India ...16 14N 74 49E
124 Kono, dist., S. Leone . 8 30N 11 5W
88 Konoğlu. Mt.,Turkey .40 35N 31 50E
125 Konongo, Ghana ... 6 40N 1 15W
84 Konosha, U.S.S.R. ...61 0N 40 5E
86 Konotop, U.S.S.R. ...51 12N 33 7E
88 Konskaya, R., U.S.S.R. ...47 30N 35 0E
60 Końskie, Poland ...51 15N 20 23E
79 Konsmo, Norway ...58 17N 7 22E
134 Konstabel, S. Africa ...33 13S 20 15E
88 Konstantinovka, U.S.S.R. ...48 32N 37 39E
87 Konstantinovski, U.S.S.R. ...57 45N 39 35E
89 Konstantinovski, U.S.S.R. ...47 33N 41 10E
60 Konstantynów Lódzki, Poland ...51 45N 19 20E
57 Konstanz, Germany ...47 39N 9 10E
125 Kontagora, Nigera ...10 23N 5 27E
55 Kontich, Belgium ...51 8N 4 26E
107 Kontum, S. Vietnam ..14 24N 108 0E
100 Konya, Turkey ...37 52N 32 35E
57 Konz Karthaus, Ger. .49 41N 6 36E
131 Konza, Kenya ... 1 45S 37 0E
143 Koo-wee-rup, Austral. ...38 13S 145 28E
142 Kookynie, W. Austral. ...29 17S 121 22E
138 Koolan I., W. Australia ...16 0S 123 45E
142 Kooline, W. Australia 22 57S 116 20E
143 Kooloonong, Austral. .34 48S 143 10E
142 Koolyanobbing, W. Australia ...30 48S 119 36E
135 Koonap, C. Prov., S. Afr. ...32 59S 26 37E
143 Koondrook, Austral. .35 33S 144 8E
133 Koopmanfontein, S. Africa ...28 14S 24 1E
142 Koorakee, Australia ...34 27S 142 56E
143 Koorawatha, Australia ...34 2S 148 33E
142 Koorda, W. Australia 30 48S 117 35E
166 Kooskia, U.S.A. ...46 9N 115 59W
157 Kootastak, Canada ...51 26N 97 26W
166 Kootenai, R., U.S.A. .48 30N 115 30W
157 Kootenay L., Canada .49 30N 117 0W
134 Kootjieskolk, S. Africa ...31 15S 20 21E
74 Kopaonik Ra., Y.-slav. ...43 10N 21 0E
106 Kopargaon, India ...19 51N 74 28E
82 Kopavogur, Iceland ...64 10N 21 50W
71 Koper, Yugoslavia ...45 31N 13 44E
79 Kopervik, Norway ...59 17N 5 20E
90 Kopeysk, U.S.S.R. ...54 55N 61 31E
80 Köping, Sweden ...59 31N 16 3E
71 Kopiste, I., Yugoslavia ...42 48N 16 42E
76 Kopliku, Albania ...42 15N 19 25E
80 Köomanholmen, Sweden ...63 10N 18 35E
81 Köpmannebro. Sweden ...58 45N 12 30E
106 Koppal, India ...15 23N 76 5E
79 Koppang, Norway ...61 34N 11 3E
80 Kopparbergs Län, Sweden ...61 20N 14 15E
101 Koppeh Dagh, Mts., Asia ...38 0N 58 0E
79 Koppera, Norway ...63 24N 11 52E
135 Koppies, O.F.S., S. Afr. ...27 13S 27 33E
80 Koppom, Sweden ...59 43N 12 10E
71 Koprivnica, Yugoslavia ...46 12N 16 45E
86 Kopychintsy, U.S.S.R. ...49 7N 25 58E
39 Korakiana, Greece ...39 42N 19 45E
74 Korab Mt., Yugoslavia ...41 44N 20 40E
106 Koraput, India ...18 50N 82 40E
107 Korat, see Nakhon Ratchasima, Thailand ...14 59N 102 12E
105 Korba, India ...22 20N 82 45E
56 Korbach, Germany ...51 17N 8 50E
75 Korçe, & pref., Albania ...40 37N 20 50E
71 Korčula & I., Y.-slav. ...42 57N 16 55E
71 Korculanski Kanal, Yugoslavia ...43 3N 16 40E
127 Kordofan, prov., Sudan ...13 0N 29 0E
112 Korea Bay, Yellow Sea ...39 0N 124 0E
112 Korea Strait, Korea–Japan ...34 0N 129 30E
106 Koregaon, India ...17 40N 74 10E
86 Korenevo, U.S.S.R. ...51 27N 34 55E
86 Korets, U.S.S.R. ...50 40N 27 5E
126 Korgus, Sudan ...19 16N 33 48E
124 Korhogo, Ivory Coas 9 29N 5 28W
145 Koridina, Australia ...29 42S 143 25E
109 Korim, Indonesia ... 0 58S 136 10E
134 Koringplaas, S. Africa 32 45S 20 50E
77 Korinthia, pref., Greece ...37 50N 22 35E
77 Korinthiakós Kolpos, G., Greece ...38 16N 22 30E
77 Korinthos, Greece ...37 56N 22 55E
124 Korioumé, Mali ...16 35N 3 0W
114 Kōriyama, Japan ...37 25N 140 20E
111 Korla, China ...41 45N 86 4E
59 Körmend, Hungary ...47 5N 16 35E
71 Kornat I., Yugoslavia 43 50N 15 20E
88 Korneshty, U.S.S.R. .47 21N 28 1E
59 Korneuburg. Austria .48 20N 16 20E
81 Korning, Denmark ...56 30N 9 44E
79 Kornsjö, Norway ...58 55N 11 40E
79 Kornstad, Norway ...62 57N 7 29E
124 Koro, Ivory Coast ... 8 32N 7 30W
124 Koro, Mali ...14 1N 2 58W
87 Korocha, U.S.S.R. ...50 55N 37 30E
131 Korogwe, Tanzania ... 5 5S 38 25E
143 Koroit, Vic., Australia 38 18S 142 24E
109 Koronadal, Phil. ... 6 12N 125 14E
77 Koroni, Greece ...36 48N 21 57E
76 Koronia, L., Greece ...40 47N 23 37E
77 Koronis, Greece ...37 12N 25 35E
60 Koronowo, Poland ...53 19N 17 55E
59 Körös, R., Hungary ...46 45N 20 20E
59 Koröstarcsa, Hungary 46 53N 21 3E
86 Korosten, U.S.S.R. ...50 57N 28 25E
87 Korotoyak, U.S.S.R. .51 1N 39 2E
91 Korsakov, U.S.S.R. ...46 30N 142 42E
79 Korshavn, Norway ...58 2N 7 0E
81 Korsör, Denmark ...55 20N 11 9E
60 Korsze, Poland ...54 11N 21 9E
126 Korti, Sudan ...18 0N 31 40E
54 Kortrijk, Belgium ...50 50N 3 17E
143 Korumburra, Australia ...38 26S 145 50E
104 Korwai, India ...24 7N 78 5E
91 Koryak Ra., U.S.S.R. 61 0N 171 0E
77 Kos, & I., Greece ...36 52N 27 19E
88 Kosa, R., Turkey ...41 0N 30 20E
87 Kosaya Gora, U.S.S.R. ...54 10N 37 30E
85 Koschagye, U.S.S.R. .46 40N 54 0E
60 Koscian, Poland ...52 5N 16 40E
60 Koscierzyna, Poland .54 8N 17 59E
165 Kosciusko, U.S.A. ...33 3N 89 34W
152 Kosciusko, I., Alas., U.S.A. ...56 0N 133 40W
143 Kosciusko Mt., Austral. ...36 27S 148 16E
59 Kösely, R., Hungary .47 25N 21 30E
106 Kosgi, India ...16 58N 77 43E
126 Kosha, Sudan ...20 50N 30 30E
104 Kosi, India ...27 48N 77 29E
135 Kosi, L., S. Africa ...27 0S 32 50E
59 Košice, Czechoslovakia ...48 42N 21 15E
74 Kosjerić, Yugoslavia .44 0N 19 55E
84 Koslan, U.S.S.R. ...63 28N 48 52E
112 Kosong, N. Korea ...38 50N 128 25E
74 Kosovo Auton. Prov., Y.-slav. ...42 30N 21 0E
74 Kosovska-Mitrovica, Yugoslavia ...42 54N 20 52E
127 Kossa, Ethiopia ... 7 50N 36 50E
71 Kostajnica, Yugoslavia ...45 17N 16 30E
71 Kostanjevica, Y.-slav. 45 51N 15 27E
59 Kostelec, Cz. ...50 14N 16 35E
133 Koster Trans., S. Afr. 25 52S 26 54E
127 Kosti, Sudan ...13 8N 32 43E
74 Kostolac, Yugoslavia .44 43N 21 15E
86 Kostopol, U.S.S.R. ...50 32N 26 34E
87 Kostroma, U.S.S.R. ...57 50N 41 0E
87 Kostroma, Res., U.S.S.R. ...57 52N 40 49E
60 Kostrzyń, Poland ...52 24N 17 14E
86 Kostyukovichi, U.S.S.R. ...53 10N 32 4E
60 Koszalin, Poland ...54 12N 16 8E
59 Köszeg, Hungary ...47 23N 16 33E
104 Kot Adu, W. Pakistan ...30 30N 71 0E
104 Kot Moman, W. Pak. 32 13N 73 0E
104 Kota, India ...25 14N 75 49E
107 Kota Bharu, Malaysia 6 7N 102 14E
108 Kota Kinabalu (Jesselton), E. Malaysia ... 6 0N 116 12E
132 Kota-Kota, see Nkhota Kota, Malawi ...12 55S 34 15E
107 Kota Tinggi, Malaysia 1 44N 103 53E
108 Kotaagung, Indonesia 5 38S 104 29E
108 Kotabaru, Indonesia . 3 20S 116 20E
108 Kotabumi, Indonesia . 4 49S 104 46E
108 Kotagadang, Indonesia ... 0 3N 100 29E
109 Kotamobagu, Indonesia ... 0 57N 124 31E
108 Kotawaringin, Indon. 2 28S 111 27E
75 Kotel, Bulgaria ...42 52N 26 26E
87 Kotelnich, U.S.S.R. ...58 20N 48 10E
89 Kotelnikovo, U.S.S.R. 47 45N 43 15E
91 Kotelny, I., U.S.S.R. .75 10N 139 0E
106 Kothagudam, India ...17 30N 80 40E
106 Kothapet, India ...19 21N 79 28E
56 Köthen, Germany ...51 44N 11 59E
105 Kothi, India ...24 45N 80 40E
131 Kotido, Uganda ... 3 0N 34 2E
104 Kotiro, W. Pakistan .26 17N 67 13E
83 Kotka, Finland ...60 30N 26 28E
84 Kotlas, U.S.S.R. ...61 15N 47 0E
75 Kotlenska, Planina, Range, Bulgaria ...42 56N 26 30E
102 Kotli, Kashmir ...33 30N 73 55E
125 Kotonkoro, Nigeria ...11 3N 5 58E
74 Kotor, Yugoslavia ...42 25N 18 47E
74 Kotor Varoš, Y.-slav. 44 38N 17 22E
71 Kotoriba, Yugoslavia .46 37N 16 48E
88 Kotovsk, U.S.S.R. ...47 55N 29 35E
104 Kotputli, India ...27 43N 76 12E
106 Kotri, R., India ...19 45N 80 35E
106 Kotri, West Pakistan .25 22N 68 22E
77 Kotronas, Greece ...36 38N 22 29E
58 Kötschach, Austria ...46 41N 13 1E
106 Kottayam, India ... 9 35N 76 33E
106 Kottur, India ...10 34N 76 56E
91 Kotui, R., U.S.S.R. ...70 30N 103 0E
152 Kotzebue Sd., Alas., U.S.A. ...66 30N 164 0W
121 Kouango, Cent. Afr. Rep. ... 5 0N 20 10E
123 Koubba Sidi Moussa, Algeria ...32 55N 7 27E
124 Koudougou, Upper Volta ...12 10N 2 20W
77 Koufonisi I., Crete, Gr. ...34 56N 26 8E
77 Koufonisia I., Greece .36 57N 25 35E
121 Kouga, Central Africa 9 55N 21 0E
134 Kouga Mts., S. Africa 33 40S 23 55E
134 Kouga R., S. Africa ...33 48S 24 20E
128 Kouilou R., Congo, (Fr.) ... 4 10S 12 5E
128 Kouki, Cent. Afr. Rep. ... 7 22N 17 3E
128 Koula Moutou, Gabon 1 15S 12 25E
107 Koulen, Cambodia ...13 50N 104 40E
124 Koulikoro, Mali ...12 40N 7 50W
144 Koumala, Australia ...21 38S 149 15E
124 Koumankoun, Mali ...11 58N 6 6W
124 Koumbia, Guinea ...11 54N 13 40W
124 Koumbia, Upper Volta ...11 10N 3 50W
124 Koumboum, Guinea ...10 25N 13 0W
121 Koumra, Chad ... 8 50N 17 35E
90 Kounradski, U.S.S.R. 47 20N 75 0E
165 Kountze, U.S.A. ...30 20N 94 22W
124 Kouroussa, Guinea ...10 45N 9 45W
124 Koutiala, Mali ...12 25N 5 35W
83 Kouvola, Finland ...60 53N 26 43E
86 Kovel, U.S.S.R. ...51 10N 25 0E
153 Kovik, Canada ...61 40N 77 40W
106 Kovilpatti, India ... 9 10N 77 50E
74 Kovin, Yugoslavia ...44 44N 20 59E
87 Kovrov,U.S.S.R. ...56 25N 41 25E
106 Kovur, India ...17 3N 81 39E
106 Kovur, India ...14 30N 80 1E
60 Kowa I., Poland ...52 32N 19 7E
154 Kowkash, Canada ...50 20N 87 20W
113 Kowloon, Hong Kong 22 20N 114 15E
112 Kowpangtze, China ...41 24N 121 56E
108 Koyan Range, Sarawak. Malaysia . 3 15N 114 30E
113 Koylu, China ...23 2N 112 28E
152 Koyukuk R., Alas., USA ...65 45N 156 30W
88 Koyulhisar, Turkey ...40 20N 37 52E
100 Kozan, Turkey ...37 35N 35 50E
76 Kozáni, tn. & prov., Greece ...40 19N 21 47E
71 Kozara, Mts., Y.-slavia ...45 0N 17 0E
71 Kozarac, Yugoslavia .44 58N 16 48E
86 Kozelsk, U.S.S.R. ...53 39N 35 59E
106 Kozhikode, see Calicut, India ...11 15N 75 43E
84 Kozhva, U.S.S.R. ...65 10N 57 0E
71 Kozje, Yugoslavia ...46 5N 15 35E
60 Kozle, Poland ...50 20N 18 8E
75 Kozloduĭ, Bulgaria ...43 45N 23 42E
75 Kozlovets, Bulgaria ...43 30N 25 20E
60 Kožmin, Poland ...51 48N 17 27E
125 Kpabia, Ghana ... 9 10N 0 20W
125 Kpandae, Ghana ... 8 30N 0 2W
125 Kpandu, Ghana ... 7 2N 0 18E
107 Kra, Isthmus of, Thai. ...10 15N 99 30E
107 Kra Buri, Thailand ...10 22N 98 46E
134 Kraankuil, S. Africa ...29 52S 24 10E
109 Kragen, Indonesia ... 6 43S 111 38E
79 Kragerö, Norway ...58 56N 9 30E
74 Kragujevac, Y.-slavia 44 2N 20 56E
108 Krakatau, Indonesia . 6 10S 105 20E
134 Krakeelrivier, S. Africa ...33 46S 23 44E
59 Kraków & prov., Pol. 50 4N 19 57E
109 Kraksaan, Indonesia . 7 43S 113 23E
81 Kråksmåla, Sweden ...57 2N 15 20E
79 Kråkstad, Norway ...59 40N 10 50E
59 Králiky, Czechoslovakia ...50 6N 16 45E
74 Kraljevo, Yugoslavia .43 44N 20 41E
58 Kralovice, Cz. ...49 59N 13 29E
59 Kralovsky Chimec, Cz. ...48 27N 22 0E
58 Kralupy, Czechoslovakia ...50 13N 14 20E
88 Kramatorsk, U.S.S.R. 48 50N 37 30E
167 Kramer, U.S.A. ...35 0N 117 38W
80 Kramfors, Sweden ...62 55N 17 48E
122 Kramis, C., Algeria ...36 26N 0 45E
80 Krangede, Sweden ...63 9N 16 10E
76 Kraniá, Greece ...39 53N 21 18E
77 Kranidhion, Greece ...37 20N 23 10E
71 Kranj, Yugoslavia ...46 16N 14 22E
71 Kranjska Gora, Y.-slav. ...46 29N 13 48E
135 Kranskop, Natal, S. Afr. ...28 57S 30 57E
71 Krapina, Yugoslavia .46 10N 15 52E
71 Krapina, R., Yugoslavia ...46 0N 15 65E
60 Krapkowice, Poland ...50 29N 17 55E
87 Krapivna, U.S.S.R. ...53 58N 37 10E
112 Kraskino, U.S.S.R. ...42 45N 130 58E
86 Krāslāva, U.S.S.R. ...55 52N 27 12E
58 Kraslice, Czechoslovakia ...50 19N 12 31E
87 Krasnaya Gorbatka, U.S.S.R. ...55 52N 41 45E
89 Kras, Polyana, U.S.S.R. ...43 40N 40 25E
60 Krasnik, Poland ...50 55N 22 5E
89 Krasnoarmeysk, U.S.S.R. ...48 30N 44 25E
87 Krasnoarmeysk, U.S.S.R. ...50 32N 45 50E
88 Krasnoarmeiskoye, U.S.S.R. ...48 18N 37 11E
89 Krasnodar, U.S.S.R. .45 5N 38 50E
89 Krasnodonetskaya, U.S.S.R. ...48 5N 40 50E
87 Krasnogorskiy, U.S.S.R. ...56 10N 48 28E
88 Krasnog Dardeiskoye, U.S.S.R. ...45 32N 34 16E
88 Krasnograd, U.S.S.R. 49 27N 35 27E
89 Krasnogvardeyskoye, U.S.S.R. ...45 52N 41 33E
84 Krasnokamsk, U.S.S.R. ...58 0N 56 0E
90 Krasnoselkupsk, U.S.S.R. ...65 20N 82 10E
86 Krasnokutsk, U.S.S.R. ...50 10N 34 50E
89 Krasnoslobodsk, U.S.S.R. ...48 42N 44 33E
87 Krasnoslobodsk, U.S.S.R. ...54 30N 43 45E
90 Krasnoturinsk, U.S.S.R. ...59 39N 60 1E
84 Krasnoufimsk, U.S.S.R. ...56 30N 57 37E
90 Krasnouralsk, U.S.S.R. ...58 0N 60 0E
85 Krasnovodsk, U.S.S.R. ...40 0N 52 52E
91 Krasnoyarsk, U.S.S.R. ...56 8N 93 0E
89 Krasnoye, U.S.S.R. ...46 16N 45 0E
87 Krasnoye, R.S.F.S.R., U.S.S.R. ...59 15N 47 40E
86 Krasnoye, Ukr., U.S.S.R. ...49 56N 24 42E
88 Krasny Liman, U.S.S.R. ...48 58N 37 50E
89 Krasny Sulin, U.S.S.R. ...47 52N 40 8E
60 Krasnystaw, Poland ...50 57N 23 5E
87 Krasnyy Kholm, U.S.S.R. ...58 10N 37 10E
87 Krasnyy Kut, U.S.S.R. ...50 50N 47 0E
87 Krasnyy Yar, U.S.S.R. ...50 42N 44 45E
89 Krasnyy Yar, U.S.S.R. ...46 43N 48 23E
87 Krasnyy Yar, U.S.S.R. ...53 30N 50 30E
59 Kraszna, R., Hungary 48 0N 22 20E
107 Kratie, Cambodia ...12 32N 106 10E
74 Kratovo, Yugoslavia .42 6N 22 10E
109 Krawang, Indonesia ... 6 19N 107 18E
56 Krefeld, Germany ...51 20N 6 22E
88 Kremenchug, U.S.S.R. ...49 5N 33 25E
86 Kremenets, U.S.S.R. .50 8N 25 43E
74 Kremenica, Y.-slavia 40 55N 21 25E
56 Kremmen, Germany .52 45N 13 1E
166 Kremmling, U.S.A. ...40 10N 106 30W
59 Kremnica, Cz. ...48 45N 18 50E
58 Krems, Austria ...48 25N 15 36E
58 Kremsmünster, Austria ...48 3N 14 8E
91 Krestovski, U.S.S.R. .71 50N 101 30E
86 Kretinga, U.S.S.R. ...55 53N 21 15E
122 Krettamia, Algeria ...28 47N 3 27W
86 Krettsy, U.S.S.R. ...58 15N 32 30E
123 Kriba, Tunisia ...35 0N 10 58E
125 Kribi, Cameroon ... 2 57N 9 56E
86 Krichev, U.S.S.R. ...53 45N 31 50E
71 Krim, Mt., Y.-slavia .45 53N 14 30E
77 Krionéri, Greece ...38 20N 21 35E
106 Krishna R., India ...16 30N 77 0E
106 Krishnagiri, India ...12 32N 78 16E
105 Krishnanagar, India ...23 24N 88 33E
106 Krishnaraja Sagara, L., India ...12 20N 76 30E
81 Kristianopel, Sweden .56 12N 16 0E
79 Kristiansand, Norway 58 5N 7 50E
81 Kristianstad, Sweden .56 5N 14 7E
79 Kristiansund, Norway 63 10N 7 45E
82 Kristiinankaupunki, Fin. ...62 18N 21 25E
82 Kristineberg, Sweden .63 5N 18 40E
80 Kristinehamn, Sweden 59 18N 14 13E
82 Kristinestad, Finland .62 18N 21 25E
77 Kriti, I., Greece ...35 15N 25 0E
77 Kritsá, Crete, Greece .35 10N 25 41E
74 Kriva, R., Y.-slavia ...42 12N 22 18E
74 Kriva Palanka, Y.-slav. ...42 11N 22 19E
74 Krivaja R., Y.-slavia 44 15N 18 22E
74 Krivelj, Yugoslavia ...44 8N 22 5E

MAP
88 Krivoi Rog, U.S.S.R. .47 51N 33 20E
71 Križevci, Yugoslavia .46 3N 16 32E
71 Krk, & I., Yugoslavia 45 5N 14 56E
71 Krka, R., Yugoslavia .45 50N 15 30E
58 Krkonose, Czechoslovakia 50 50N 15 30E
59 Krnov, Czechoslovakia 50 5N 17 40E
60 Krobia, Poland 51 47N 16 59E
58 Kročehlavy, Cz. 50 8N 14 9E
107 Kroeng Krai,, Thailand 14 55N 98 30E
60 Krokawo, Poland 54 47N 18 9E
77 Krokeai, Greece 36 53N 22 32E
79 Kroken, Norway 58 57N 9 8E
79 Kroken, Sweden 59 2N 11 23E
133 Krokodilpoort, S. Africa 25 30S 31 11E
80 Krokom, Sweden 63 20N 14 30E
86 Krolevets, U.S.S.R. ...51 35N 33 20E
59 Kroměříž, Cz. 49 18N 17 21E
59 Krompachy, Cz. 48 54N 20 52E
134 Kromrivier, S. Africa .32 0S 23 0E
86 Kromy, U.S.S.R. 52 40N 35 40E
81 Kronobergs Län, Swed. 56 45N 14 30E
86 Kronshtadt & I., U.S.S.R. 60 5N 29 35E
135 Kroonstad, S. Africa .27 43S 27 19E
56 Kröpelin, Germany ...54 4N 11 48E
89 Kropotkin, U.S.S.R. .58 50N 115 10E
56 Kropp, Germany 54 24N 9 32E
60 Krósniewice, Poland .52 15N 19 11E
59 Krosno, Poland 49 35N 21 56E
60 Krosno Odrz., Poland 52 3N 15 7E
60 Krotoszyn, Poland 51 42N 17 23E
76 Krrabe Mt., Albania ...41 13N 19 59E
71 Krsko, Y.-slavia 45 57N 15 30E
74 Krstača, Mt., Y.-slavia 42 57N 20 8E
133 Kruger Nat. Pk., S. Afr. 24 0S 31 40E
135 Krugers, O.F.S., S. Afr. 29 57S 25 51E
133 Krugersdorp, S. Africa 26 5S 27 46E
133 Krugerspos, S. Africa .24 55S 30 31E
108 Krui, Indonesia 5 10S 104 0E
134 Kruidfontein, S. Africa 32 48S 21 59E
76 Kruje, Albania 41 32N 19 46E
86 Krulevshchina, U.S.S.R. 55 5N 27 45E
76 Krume, Albania 42 37N 20 28E
75 Krumovgrad, Bulg. ...41 29N 25 38E
107 Krung Thep, Thailand 13 45N 100 35E
74 Krupanj, Yugoslavia .44 25N 19 22E
59 Krupina, Cz. 48 22N 19 5E
59 Krupinica R., Cz. 48 15N 19 5E
74 Kruševac, Yugoslavia 43 35N 21 28E
74 Krušovo, Yugoslavia .41 23N 21 19E
156 Kruzof I., Alas., U.S.A. 57 10N 135 40W
80 Krylbo, Sweden 60 7N 16 15E
88 Krymskaya, U.S.S.R. 44 57N 37 50E
59 Krynica, Poland 49 25N 20 57E
60 Krynki, Poland 53 17N 23 43E
60 Krzepice, Poland 50 58N 18 50E
60 Krzywin, Poland 51 58N 16 50E
60 Krzyz, Poland 52 52N 16 0E
122 Ksabi, Algeria 29 8N 0 58W
122 Ksabi, Morocco 32 51N 4 13W
122 Ksar Chellala, Algeria 35 14N 2 27E
122 Ksar el Boukhari 35 5N 2 52E
122 Ksar el Kebir, Morocco 35 0N 6 0W
122 Ksar és Souk, Morocco 31 58N 4 28W
123 Ksar Rhilane, Tunisia 33 0N 9 39E
122 Ksiba, Morocco 32 46N 6 0W
122 Ksour, Mts. des, Algeria 32 45N 0 30W
108 Kuala, Indonesia 2 46N 105 47E
107 Kuala Belait, Brunei . 4 45N 114 25E
107 Kuala Dungun, Malay. 4 46N 103 25E
107 Kuala Kangsar, Malay. 4 49N 100 57E
107 Kuala Krai, Malaysia 5 32N 102 12E
107 Kuala Kubu Bahru, Malaya, W. Malaysia 3 35N 101 38E
107 Kuala Lipis, Malaysia 4 22N 102 5E
107 Kuala Lumpur, Malay. 3 9N 101 41E
107 Kuala Pilah, Malaysia 2 45N 102 14E
107 Kuala Sedili, Malaysia 1 57N 104 8E
107 Kuala Selangor, Malay. 3 20N 101 15E
107 Kuala Trengganu, W. Malaysia 5 20N 103 8E
108 Kualakapuas, Indonesia 2 55S 114 20E
108 Kualakurun, Indonesia 1 10S 113 50E
108 Kualapembuang, Indon. 3 14S 112 38E
109 Kuandang, Indonesia . 0 56N 123 1E
107 Kuantan, Malaysia 3 49N 103 20E
127 Kuaram, Ethiopia 12 25N 39 30E
127 Kub Kub, Ethiopia ...16 20N 38 25E
89 Kuba, U.S.S.R. 41 21N 48 32E
102 Kubak, Iran 27 10N 63 10E
88 Kuban R., U.S.S.R. ...45 5N 38 0E
87 Kubena L., U.S.S.R. .59 40N 39 25E
89 Kuberle, U.S.S.R. 47 0N 42 20E
75 Kubrat, Bulgaria 43 49N 26 31E
74 Kučevo, Yugoslavia ...44 30N 21 40E
111 Kucha, China 41 50N 82 30E
104 Kuchaman, India 27 13N 74 47E
113 Kuchen, China 33 29N 117 27E
57 Kuchenspitze, Mt., Aust. 47 3N 10 14E
108 Kuching, Sar., Malaysia 1 33N 110 25E
76 Kucove, see Qytet Stalin, Albania 40 47N 19 57E
76 Kücük Kuyu, Turkey 39 35N 26 27E
106 Kudalier R., India 18 20N 78 40E
108 Kudat, Sabah, Malay. 7 0N 116 42E
143 Kudgee, Australia 32 43S 141 38E
106 Kudremukh, Mt., India 13 15N 75 20E
132 Kudumalapshwe, Bots. 23 52S 24 57E
109 Kudus, Indonesia 6 48S 110 51E
121 Kufra Oasis, Libya 24 17N 23 15E
98 Kufrinja, Jordan 32 20N 35 41E
58 Kufstein, Austria 47 35N 12 11E
154 Kugong, I., Canada ...56 25N 80 0W
101 Kuhak, Iran 27 12N 63 10E
101 Kuh-e-Hazaran, Mt., Iran 29 35N 57 20E
101 Kuh-e-Jebel Barez, ra., Iran 29 0N 58 0E
101 Kuh-e-Alijuq, Iran ...31 30N 51 41E
101 Kuh-e-Sorkh, ra., Iran 35 30N 58 45E
101 Kuh-e-Taftan, Mt., Iran 28 40N 61 0E
101 Kuhha-ye-Bashakerd, Ra., Iran 26 45N 59 0E
100 Kuhha-ye Sabalan, Mt., Iran 38 15N 47 45E
58 Kuhnsdorf, Austria ...46 37N 14 38E
101 Kuhpayeh, Iran 32 44N 52 20E
129 Kuiseb R., S.W. Africa 23 40S 15 30E
84 Kuito Lakes, U.S.S.R. 64 40N 31 0E
157 Kuiu I., Alaska, U.S.A. 56 40N 134 10W
74 Kukavica, Mt., Y.-slav. 42 48N 21 57E
125 Kukawa, Nigeria 12 58N 13 27E
142 Kukerin, W. Australia 33 13S 118 0E
76 Kukës, Albania 42 5N 20 20E
76 Kukës, region, Albania 42 25N 20 15E
127 Kukko, Ethiopia 8 26N 41 35E
87 Kukmar, U.S.S.R. 56 15N 50 45E
87 Kukvidze, U.S.S.R. ...50 40N 43 15E
74 Kula, Bulgaria 43 52N 22 36E
74 Kula, Yugoslavia 45 37N 19 32E
107 Kulai, Malaysia 1 44N 103 35E
89 Kulaly, I., U.S.S.R. ...45 0N 50 0E
106 Kulasekharapattanam, India 8 20N 78 0E
86 Kuldiga, U.S.S.R. 56 58N 21 59E
111 Kuldja, see Ining, China 44 0N 81 0E
127 Kuldu, Sudan 12 50N 28 30E
87 Kulebaki, U.S.S.R. 55 22N 42 25E
71 Kulenvakuf, Yugoslavia 44 35N 16 2E
89 Kuli, U.S.S.R 42 2N 46 12E
142 Kulin, W. Australia ...32 40S 118 2E
142 Kulja, W. Australia ...30 35S 117 31E
164 Kulm, U.S.A. 46 22N 98 58W
90 Kulsary, U.S.S.R. 46 59N 54 1E
89 Kultay, U.S.S.R. 45 5N 51 40E
105 Kulti, India 23 43N 86 50E
112 Kulu, China 37 12N 115 2E
144 Kulumadau, Papua ... 9 15S 152 50E
90 Kulunda, U.S.S.R 52 45N 79 15E
112 Kulunkai, China 42 46N 121 55E
143 Kulwin, Vic., Australia 35 0S 142 42E
90 Kulyab, U.S.S.R. 37 55N 69 50E
111 Kum Darya, R., China 41 0N 89 0E
90 Kum Tekei, U.S.S.R. .43 10N 79 30E
89 Kuma, R., U.S.S.R. ...44 55N 45 57E
125 Kumaganum, Nigeria 13 8N 10 38E
108 Kumai, Indonesia 2 52S 111 45E
114 Kumamoto, Japan 32 45N 130 45E
74 Kumanovo, Yugoslavia 42 9N 21 42E
147 Kumara, New Zealand 42 37S 171 12E
142 Kumari, W. Australia 32 45S 121 30E
124 Kumasi, Ghana 6 41N 1 38W
125 Kumba, Cameroon 4 36N 9 24E
106 Kumbakonam, India .10 58N 79 25E
145 Kumbarilla, Australia 27 15S 150 55E
125 Kumbo, Cameroon 6 15N 10 36E
106 Kumbukkan Oya, R., Ceylon 6 35N 81 40E
113 Kume, I., Japan 26 8N 126 45E
87 Kumeny, U.S.S.R. 58 10N 49 47E
131 Kumi, Uganda 1 30N 33 58E
76 Kumkale, Turkey 40 30N 26 13E
80 Kumla, Sweden 59 8N 15 10E
125 Kumo, Nigeria 10 1N 11 12E
106 Kumta, India 14 29N 74 32E
89 Kumtorkala, U.S.S.R. 43 2N 46 50E
89 Kumylzhenskaya, U.S.S.R. 49 51N 42 38E
59 Kunágota, Hungary ...46 26N 21 3E
143 Kunama, Australia ...35 35S 148 4E
91 Kunashiri, Kunile Is. .44 0N 146 0E
104 Kunch, India 26 0N 79 10E
86 Kunda, U.S.S.R. 59 30N 26 34E
104 Kundla, India 21 21N 71 25E
101 Kunduz, Afghanistan .36 50N 68 50E
145 Kungala, Australia 29 58S 153 7E
82 Kungälv, Sweden 57 54N 12 0E
113 Kungan, China 30 0N 112 2E
112 Kungchuling, China ...43 31N 124 58E
111 Kungho, China 36 28N 100 45E
90 Kungrad, U.S.S.R. 43 6N 58 54E
81 Kungsbacka, Sweden .57 30N 12 7E
84 Kungur, U.S.S.R. 57 20N 56 40E
144 Kungurri, Australia ...21 3S 148 46E
113 Kungyifow, China 22 24N 112 41E
59 Kunhegyes, Hungary .47 22N 20 36E
113 Kunhsien, China 32 30N 111 17E
103 Kunlong, Burma 23 20N 98 50E
103 Kunlun, Mts., China .36 0N 82 0E
111 Kunlun Shan, Mts., Asia 36 0N 86 30E
59 Kunmadaras, Hungary 47 28N 20 45E
111 Kunming, China 25 11N 102 37E
106 Kunnamkulam, India 10 38N 76 7E
112 Kunsan, S. Korea 35 59N 126 45E
113 Kunshan, China 31 16N 121 0E
59 Kunszentmárton, Hung. 46 50N 20 20E
87 Kuntsevo, U.S.S.R. 55 48N 37 25E
138 Kununurra, W. Austral. 15 40S 128 39E
144 Kunwararo, Australia 22 55S 150 7E
82 Kuopio & prov., Fin. .62 53N 27 35E
71 Kupa R., Yugoslavia .45 30N 15 10E
109 Kupang, Indonesia 10 19S 123 39E
112 Kupehkow, China 40 45N 117 15E
152 Kupreanof I., Alaska, U.S.A. 56 50N 133 30W
74 Kupres, Yugoslavia ...44 1N 17 15E
88 Kupyansk, U.S.S.R. ...49 45N 37 35E
88 Kupyansk-Uzlovoi, U.S.S.R. 49 52N 37 34E
89 Kura R., U.S.S.R. 41 20N 46 15E
132 Kurametsi, Botswana 23 25S 27 5E
144 Kuranda, Queensland, Australia 16 48S 145 35E
114 Kurayoshi, Japan 35 26N 133 50E
144 Kuranda, Australia ...16 45S 145 37E
106 Kurandvad, India 16 45N 74 39E
114 Kurashiki, Japan 34 40N 133 50E
100 Kurdistan, dist., Asia 37 30N 42 0E
106 Kurduvadi, India 18 8N 75 29E
75 Kurdzhali, Bulgaria ...41 38N 25 21E
86 Kuressaare, see Kingisepp, U.S.S.R. 58 15N 22 15E
90 Kurgaldzhino, U.S.S.R. 50 35N 70 20E
90 Kurgan, U.S.S.R. 55 30N 65 0E
91 Kurgan, U.S.S.R. 64 5N 172 50W
89 Kurgannaya, U.S.S.R. 44 50N 40 40E
99 Kuria Muria Is., Arabia 17 30N 55 58E
106 Kurichchi, India 11 36N 77 35E
144 Kuridala, Australia ...21 16S 140 29E
91 Kuril Is., U.S.S.R. 45 0N 150 0E
136 Kuril Trench, Pac. Oc. 44 0N 153 0E
55 Kuringen, Belgium 50 56N 5 18E
123 Kurkurah, Libya 31 30N 20 1E
126 Kurkur Oasis, Egypt .23 50N 32 0E
106 Kurla, India 19 5N 72 52E
134 Kurland, S. Africa 33 55S 23 30E
87 Kurlovski, U.S.S.R. ...55 25N 40 40E
127 Kurma, Sudan 13 55N 24 40E
127 Kurmuk, Sudan 10 33N 34 21E
142 Kurnalpi, W. Australia 30 29S 122 16E
143 Kurnell, Australia 34 2S 151 12E
106 Kurnool, India 15 45N 78 0E
87 Kurovskoye, U.S.S.R. 55 35N 38 55E
147 Kurow, New Zealand .44 4S 170 29E
143 Kurrajong, Australia .33 33S 150 42E
142 Kurrajong, W. Austral. 28 39S 120 59E
143 Kurri Kurri, Australia 32 50S 151 28E
105 Kurseong, India 26 56N 88 18E
86 Kuršhenai, U.S.S.R. ...56 1N 23 3E
87 Kursk, U.S.S.R. 51 42N 36 11E
74 Kursumlija, Yugoslavia 43 9N 21 19E
74 Kuršumlijska Banja, Yugoslavia 43 3N 21 11E
100 Kurtalon, Turkey 37 55N 41 40E
127 Kuru (Chel) R., Sudan 8 10N 26 50E
133 Kuruman, S. Africa ...27 28S 23 28E
133 Kuruman Hills, S. Afr. 27 30S 23 10E
133 Kuruman R., S. Africa 27 5S 21 30E
114 Kurume, Japan 33 15N 130 30E
106 Kurunegala, Ceylon ... 7 30N 80 18E
91 Kurya, U.S.S.R. 61 15N 108 10E
77 Kuşadasi, Turkey 37 52N 27 15E
77 Kuşadasi Körfezi, G., Turkey 37 56N 27 0E
113 Kusagaki, Ryukyu Is. 30 54N 129 28E
156 Kusawa L., Canada ...60 25N 136 20W
57 Kusel, Germany 49 31N 7 25E
112 Kushan, China 39 58N 123 30E
89 Kushchevskaya, U.S.S.R. 46 33N 39 35E
90 Kushevat, U.S.S.R. ...65 10N 65 30E
113 Kushih, China 32 12N 115 43E
114 Kushiro, Japan 43 0N 144 30E
101 Kushk, Afghanistan ...34 55N 62 30E
90 Kushka, U.S.S.R. 35 20N 62 18E
105 Kushtia, E. Pakistan .23 55N 89 5E
89 Kushum, R., U.S.S.R. 50 40N 50 20E
152 Kuskokwim Bay, Alaska, U.S.A. 59 50N 162 56W
14 Kuskokwim, R., Alaska, U.S.A. 61 48N 157 0W
90 Kustanai, U.S.S.R. 53 20N 63 45E
89 Kutaisi, U.S.S.R. 42 19N 42 40E
108 Kutaradja, see Banda Atjeh, Indonesia 5 35N 95 20E
108 Kutatjane, Indonesia . 3 45N 97 50E
104 Kutch, G. of, India ...22 50N 69 1E
104 Kutch, Rann of, India 24 0N 70 0E
71 Kutina, Yugoslavia ...45 29N 16 48E
104 Kutiyana, India 21 36N 70 2E
74 Kutjevo, Yugoslavia .45 23N 17 55E
89 Kutkashen, U.S.S.R. .40 58N 47 47E
58 Kutná Hora, Cz. 49 57N 15 16E
60 Kutno, Poland 52 15N 19 23E
144 Kuttabul, Australia ...21 5S 148 48E
130 Kutu, Congo 2 40S 18 11E
130 Kutu Moke, Congo 2 45S 17 25E
127 Kutum, Sudan 14 20N 24 10E
59 Kúty, Czechoslovakia 48 40N 17 3E
86 Kuvshinovo, U.S.S.R. 57 2N 34 3E
100 Kuwait (Al Kuwayt) .29 30N 47 30E
100 Kuwait, st., Arabia ...29 30N 47 30E
112 Kuyang, China 41 8N 110 1E
87 Kuybyshev, U.S.S.R. .53 10N 50 15E
88 Kuybyshevo, U.S.S.R. 47 25N 36 40E
87 Kuybyshev Res., U.S.S.R. 55 2N 49 30E
112 Kuyüan, China 35 50N 106 20E
113 Kuyung, China 32 0N 119 8E
106 Kuzhithura, India 8 18N 77 11E
74 Kuzmin, Yugoslavia .45 2N 19 25E
87 Kuznetsk, U.S.S.R. ...53 12N 46 40E
84 Kuzomen, U.S.S.R. ...66 22N 36 50E
82 Kvaenangen, Norway 69 55N 21 15E
82 Kvalsund, Norway 70 30N 24 10E
79 Kvam, Norway 61 40N 9 44E
79 Kvamsöy, Norway 61 7N 6 25E
82 Kvarken, Is., Finland 63 30N 21 0E
71 Kvarner G., Yugoslavia 44 50N 14 10E
71 Kvarneric, Yugoslavia 44 43N 14 37E
80 Kvarnsveden, Sweden 60 32N 15 25E
80 Kvarntorp, Sweden ...59 8N 15 17E
79 Kvås, Norway 58 16N 7 14E
79 Kvernes, Norway 63 1N 7 44E
81 Kvillsfors, Sweden 57 24N 15 29E
79 Kvina, R., Norway 58 43N 6 52E
79 Kvinesdal, Norway 58 18N 6 59E
79 Kviteseid, Norway 59 25N 8 28E
133 Kwaggablad, S. Africa 27 29S 24 13E
135 Kwaggashoek, S. Africa 28 30S 25 52E
175 Kwakoegron, Surinam 5 25N 55 25W
131 Kwale, Kenya 4 15S 39 31E
131 Kwale, dist., Kenya ... 4 15S 39 10E
130 Kwamouth, Congo 3 9S 16 20E
129 Kwando, R., Angola & Zam. 16 48S 22 45E
113 Kwangan, China 30 35N 106 40E
113 Kwangchow, see Canton, China 23 10N 113 10E
113 Kwangchow, Wan., China 21 0N 111 0E
112 Kwangju, S. Korea ...35 10N 126 45E
111 Kwangnan, China 24 10N 105 0E
112 Kwangnung, S. Korea 37 45N 128 59E
130 Kwango, prov., Congo.................... 6 40S 17 40E
112 Kwangping, China 36 40N 114 41E
113 Kwangshui, China 31 45N 114 0E
113 Kwangsi-Chuang, auto. reg., China 23 30N 108 55E
113 Kwangtseh, China 27 30N 117 25E
113 Kwangtsi, China 30 2N 115 46E
113 Kwangtung, prov. China 23 35N 114 0E
113 Kwangyuan, China 32 30N 105 49E
111 Kwanhsien, China 30 59N 103 40E
112 Kwantien, China 40 45N 124 45E
111 Kwantung, China 25 12N 101 37E
112 Kwantung Pen., China 39 0N 121 0E
113 Kwanyun, China 34 28N 119 29E
109 Kwatisore, Indonesia . 3 7S 139 59E
113 Kweichih, China 30 40N 117 30E
113 Kweichow, see Fengkieh, China 31 0N 109 33E
113 Kweichow, prov., China 26 40N 107 0E
113 Kweihsien, China 22 59N 109 44E
113 Kweihwa, see Mingki, China 26 10N 117 14E
113 Kweiki, China 28 10N 117 8E
113 Kweilin, China 25 16N 110 15E
113 Kweiping, China 23 12N 110 0E
113 Kweishun, see Tsingsing, China 38 1N 114 4E
113 Kweitung, China 26 0N 113 35E
113 Kweiyang, China 26 30N 106 35E
113 Kweiyang, China 25 50N 112 25E
130 Kwenge R., Congo 6 30S 18 30E
60 Kwidzyń, Poland 54 5N 18 58E
130 Kwilu, R., Congo 4 5S 18 10E
142 Kwinana, W. Australia 32 15S 115 47E
113 Kwo, R., China 23 20N 116 50E
113 Kwohwa, China 23 10N 107 0E
113 Kwoyang, China 33 35N 116 15E
121 Kyabe, Chad 9 30N 19 0E
143 Kyabram, Vic., Austral. 36 19S 145 4E
107 Kyaikto, Burma 17 20N 97 3E
91 Kyakhta, U.S.S.R. 50 30N 106 25E
103 Kyangin, Burma 18 20N 95 20E
111 Kyargas Nuur, Mongolia 49 0N 93 0E
103 Kyaring Nor. L., China 34 40N 97 20E
103 Kyaring Tso, L., Tibet, China 31 5N 88 25E
103 Kyaukpadaung, Burma 20 52N 95 8E
103 Kyaukpyu, Burma 19 28N 93 30E
103 Kyaukse, Burma 21 36N 96 10E
131 Kyegegwa, Uganda ... 0 30N 31 0E
103 Kyeikdon, Burma 16 3N 98 25E
131 Kyenjojo, Uganda 0 40N 30 37E
40 Kyle, dist., Scot., U.K. 55 32N 4 25W
42 Kyle of Lochalsh, Scotland, U.K. 57 17N 5 43W
57 Kyllburg, Germany ...50 2N 6 34E
143 Kyneton, Vic., Austral. 37 10S 144 29E
114 Kyoga-saki, C., Japan 35 45N 135 15E
131 Kyoga, L., Uganda ... 1 35N 33 0E
145 Kyogle, Australia 28 40S 153 0E
112 Kyongju, S. Korea 35 59N 129 26E
103 Kyongpyaw, Burma ...17 12N 95 10E
131 Kyotera, Uganda 0 35S 31 33E
114 Kyoto, Japan 35 0N 135 45E
114 Kyoto, pref., Japan ...35 15N 135 30E
100 Kyrenia, Cyprus 35 20N 33 20E
56 Kyritz, Germany 52 57N 12 25E
80 Kyrkebyn, Sweden 59 18N 13 3E
79 Kyrping, Norway 59 45N 6 5E
91 Kystatym, U.S.S.R. ...67 20N 123 10E
91 Kytalyktakh, U.S.S.R. 65 30N 123 40E
91 Kyulyunken, U.S.S.R. 64 10N 137 5E
103 Kyunhla, Burma 23 25N 95 15E
156 Kyuquot, Canada 50 3N 127 25W
156 Kyuquot Sd., Canada 50 0N 127 25W
89 Kyurdamir, U.S.S.R. .40 25N 48 3E
114 Kyushu, I. & dist., Japan 32 30N 131 0E
114 Kyushu-sammyaku, ra., Japan 32 45N 131 40E
74 Kyustendil, Bulgaria .42 25N 22 41E
143 Kywong, Australia 34 58S 146 44E
91 Kyzyl, U.S.S.R. 51 50N 94 30E
90 Kyzyl Kum, U.S.S.R. 42 0N 65 0E
90 Kyzyl Rabot, U.S.S.R. 37 45N 74 55E
90 Kzyl-Orda, U.S.S.R. .44 50N 65 10E

L

63 La Albuera, Spain 38 45N 6 49W
63 La Algaba, Spain 37 27N 6 1W
64 La Almarcha, Spain ...39 41N 2 24W
64 La Almuria de Doña Godina, Spain 41 29N 1 23W
176 La Argentino, Arg. 50 20S 71 50W
174 La Asuncion, Ven. 11 2N 63 53W
64 La Baña, Punta de, Sp. 40 33N 0 40E
172 La Banda, Argentina .27 45S 64 10W
62 La Bañeza, Spain 42 17N 5 43W
166 La Barca, Mexico 20 20N 102 40W
166 La Barge, U.S.A. 41 12N 110 4W
49 La Bassée, France 50 31N 2 49E
50 La Bastide, Ardeche, Fr. 44 35N 3 55E
48 La Baule, France 47 18N 2 23W
163 La Belle, U.S.A. 26 45N 81 22W
64 La Bisbal, Spain 41 58N 3 2E
168 La Boca, Pan. Can. Zone 9 0N 79 30W
172 La Calera, Chile 32 50S 71 10W
62 La Cañiza, Spain 42 13N 8 16W
49 La Capelle, France 49 59N 3 50E
172 La Carlota, Argentina 33 30S 63 20W
63 La Carolina, Spain 38 17N 3 38W
169 La Ceiba, Honduras ...15 40N 86 50W
174 La Ceiba, Venezuela ... 9 30N 71 0W
174 La Ceja, Colombia 6 2N 75 20W
50 La Chaise Dieu, France 45 20N 3 40E
48 La Chaize le Vicomte, France 46 40N 1 18W
49 La Chapelle d'Angillon, France .47 21N 2 25E
48 La Chapelle Glain, Fr. 47 38N 1 11W
49 La Charité, France 47 10N 3 0E
48 La Chartre, France 47 42N 0 34E
48 La Châtaignerie, France 46 38N 0 45W
50 La Châtre, France 46 35N 1 59E
57 La Chaux de Fonds, Switzerland 47 7N 6 50E
174 La Chorrera, Colombia 0 44S 73 1W
168 La Chorrera, Panama 8 50N 79 50W
51 La Ciotat, France 43 12N 5 36E
51 La Clayette, France ...46 17N 4 19E
172 La Cocha, Argentina .27 50S 65 40W
125 La Concepción, Fernando Póo 3 28N 84 0E
168 La Concordia, Mexico 16 8N 92 38W
166 La Conner, U.S.A. 48 22N 122 27W
62 La Coruña (Corunna), Spain 43 20N 8 25W
51 La Côte St. André, Fr. 45 24N 5 15E
50 La Courtine, France ...45 43N 2 16E
50 La Crèche, France 46 23N 0 19W
164 La Crosse, Kan., U.S.A. 38 33N 99 20W
164 La Crosse, Wis., U.S.A. 43 48N 91 13W
168 La Cruz, Sinaloa, Mexico 23 55N 106 54W
174 La Dorado, Colombia . 5 30N 74 40W
172 La Esperanza, Argentina 24 9S 64 52W
174 La Esperanza, Bolivia 14 20S 62 0W
62 La Estrada, Spain 42 43N 8 27W
161 La Fargeville, U.S.A. .44 12N 75 58W
162 La Fayette, U.S.A. 40 22N 86 52W
49 La Fère, France 49 40N 3 20E
49 La Ferté, France 48 57N 3 6E
48 La Ferté Bernard, Fr. 48 10N 0 40E
48 La Ferté Mace, France 48 35N 0 21W
49 La Ferté St. Aubin, Fr. 47 42N 1 57E

LA INDEX LA

MAP
48 La Ferté Vidame, Fr. 48 37N 0 53E
48 La Flèche, France 47 42N 0 5W
163 La Folette, U.S.A. 36 23N 84 9W
62 La Fregeneda, Spain .40 58N 6 54W
62 La Fuente de San Esteban, Spain 40 49N 6 15W
65 La Gineta, Spain 39 8N 2 1W
123 La Goulette, *see* Halq el Oued, Tunisia 36 53N 10 10E
51 La Grand Comb, Fr. .44 13N 4 2E
166 La Grande, U.S.A. 45 15N 118 0W
163 La Grange, Ga., U.S.A. 33 4N 85 0W
162 La Grange, Ky., U.S.A. 38 20N 85 20W
165 La Grange, Tex., U.S.A. 29 54N 96 52W
138 La Grange, W. Austral 18 45S 121 43E
172 La Guaira, Venezuela 10 36N 66 56W
172 La Guardia, Chile 27 43S 69 32W
62 La Guardia, Spain 41 56N 8 52W
62 La Gudina, Spain 42 4N 7 8W
48 La Guerche, France ...47 57N 1 16W
49 La Guerche-sur l'Aubois, France 46 58N 2 56E
164 La Harpe, U.S.A. 40 30N 91 0W
48 La Haye Descartes, Fr. 46 58N 0 42E
48 La Haye du Puits, Fr. 49 17N 1 33W
172 La Higuera, Chile 29 33S 71 15E
62 La Horra, Spain 41 44N 3 53W
55 La Hulpe, Belgium 50 43N 4 30E
167 La Jara, U.S.A. 37 16N 106 0W
64 La Junquera, Spain ...42 25N 2 53E
165 La Junta, U.S.A. 38 0N 103 30W
172 La Ligua, Chile 32 30S 71 16W
63 La Linea, Spain 36 15N 5 23W
157 La Loche L., Canada .56 40N 109 30W
54 La Louvière, Belgium 50 27N 4 10E
49 La Machine, France ...46 54N 3 27E
72 La Maddalena, Italy .41 13N 9 25E
155 La Malbaie, Canada ...47 40N 70 10W
65 La Mancha, reg., Sp. .39 10N 2 54W
152 La Martre, L. & R., Can. 63 0N 118 0W
174 La Merced, Peru 11 0S 75 20W
167 La Mesa, Calif., U.S.A. 32 48N 117 5W
167 La Mesa, N. Mex., U.S.A. 32 6N 106 48W
64 La Mola, Cabo de, Sp. 39 53N 4 19E
48 La Mothe Archard, Fr. 46 37N 1 39W
51 La Motte, France 44 20N 6 3E
51 La Motte Chalançon, Fr. 44 30N 5 21E
164 La Moure, U.S.A. 46 27N 98 17W
64 La Muela, Spain 41 36N 1 7W
51 La Mure, France 44 55N 5 48E
65 La Nao, Cabo de, Spain 38 44N 0 14E
172 La Negra, Chile 23 46S 70 18W
50 La Pacaudière, France 46 10N 3 50E
169 La Palma, Panama ... 8 15N 78 0W
63 La Palma, Spain 37 21N 6 38W
172 La Paloma, Chile 30 35S 71 0W
172 La Pampa, prov., Arg. 38 0S 66 0W
174 La Paragua, Venezuela 6 50N 63 20W
172 La Paz, Entre Rios, Arg. 30 50S 59 45W
172 La Paz, San Luis, Arg. 33 30S 67 20W
174 La Paz, Bolivia 16 20S 68 10W
168 La Paz, Honduras 14 20N 87 47W
168 La Paz, Mexico 24 10N 110 20W
174 La Paz, Venezuela 10 43N 72 1W
168 La Paz B., Mexico 24 20N 110 40W
93 La Perouse Str., Japan 45 40N 142 0E
168 La Piedad, Mexico 20 20N 102 1W
166 La Pine, U.S.A. 40 53N 80 45W
164 La Plant, U.S.A. 45 11N 100 40W
172 La Plata, Argentina ...35 0S 57 55W
172 La Plata, Rio de, S. Amer. 35 0S 56 40W
64 La Pobla de Lillet, Sp. 42 16N 1 59E
62 La Pola de Gordon, Sp. 42 51N 5 41W
162 La Porte, U.S.A. 41 40N 86 40W
64 La Puebla, Spain 39 50N 4 25W
63 La Puebla de los Infantes, Spain 37 47N 5 24W
62 La Puebla de Montalban, Spain ...39 52N 4 22W
65 La Puerta, Spain 38 22N 2 45W
172 La Quiaca, Argentina 22 5S 65 35W
63 La Rambla, Spain 37 37N 4 45W
154 La Reine, Canada 48 50N 79 30W
50 La Réole, France 44 35N 0 1W
172 La Rioja, Argentina ...29 20S 67 0W
172 La Rioja, prov., Arg. .29 30S 67 0W
62 La Robla, Spain 42 50N 5 41W
51 La Roche, France 46 4N 6 19E
48 La Roche Bernard, Fr. 47 32N 2 18W
50 La Roche Canillac, Fr. 45 12N 1 57E
48 La Roche sur Yon, Fr. 46 40N 1 25W
50 La Rochefoucauld, Fr. 45 44N 0 24E
50 La Rochelle, France ...46 10N 1 9W
65 La Roda, Spain 39 13N 2 15W
169 La Romana, Dom. Rep. 18 27N 68 57W
157 La Ronge L., Canada .55 10N 105 0W

MAP
65 La Sagra Mt., Spain ...38 0N 2 35W
164 La Salle, U.S.A. 41 20N 89 5W
154 La Sarre, Canada 48 45N 79 15W
155 La Scie, Canada 49 58N 55 36W
172 La Serena, Chile 29 55S 71 10W
51 La Seyne-sur-Mer, Fr. 43 7N 5 52E
73 La Sila Mts., Italy 39 15N 16 35E
123 La Skhirra, *see* Cekhira, Tunisia 34 20N 10 5E
65 La Solana, Spain 38 59N 3 14W
50 La Souterraine, France 46 15N 1 30E
70 La Spezia, Italy 44 8N 9 50E
48 La Suze, France 47 54N 0 2E
174 La Tugua, Colombia . 0 3N 74 40W
50 La Teste, France 44 34N 1 9W
51 La Tour du Pin, France 45 34N 5 27E
50 La Tranche, France ...46 20N 1 26W
50 La Tremblade, France 45 46N 1 8W
154 La Tuque, Canada 47 30N 72 50W
176 La Unión, Chile 40 10S 73 0W
168 La Unión, Salvador ...13 20N 87 50W
65 La Unión, Spain 37 38N 0 53W
174 La Urbana, Venezuela 7 8N 66 56W
172 La Valdivia, Chile 34 43S 72 5W
62 La Vecilla, Spain 42 51N 5 27W
169 La Vega, Dom. Rep. .19 20N 70 30W
174 La Vela, Venezuela ...11 30N 69 30W
174 La Victoria, Venezuela 10 14N 67 20W
51 La Voulte, France 44 49N 4 48E
63 La Zarza, Spain 37 42N 6 51W
59 Laa, Austria 48 43N 16 23E
56 Laage, Germany 53 55N 12 21E
143 Laanecoorie Res., Vic., Australia 36 52S 143 50E
56 Laasphe, Germany 50 56N 8 23E
89 Laba R., U.S.S.R. 45 0N 40 30E
109 Labala, Indonesia 8 35S 123 32E
44 Laban, Ireland 53 8N 8 50W
44 Labasheeda, Ireland ...52 37N 9 15W
50 Labastide Mura , Fr. .44 39N 1 33E
125 Labbezenga, Mali 15 2N 0 48E
123 Labdah, (Leptis Magna), Libya 32 40N 14 12E
124 Labé, Guinea 11 24N 12 16W
58 Labe R., Czechoslovakia 50 3N 15 20E
59 Laberec, R., Cz. 21 57N 49 7E
156 Laberge, L., Canada ...61 15N 135 0W
122 L'Arba, Algeria 36 40N 3 9E
71 Labin, Yugoslavia 45 5N 14 8E
89 Labinsk, U.S.S.R. 44 40N 40 48W
107 Labis, W. Malaysia ... 2 22N 103 2E
109 Laboa, Indonesia 8 6S 122 50E
56 Laboe, Germany 54 25N 10 13E
142 Labouchere, Mt., W. Australia 25 12S 118 15E
50 Labouheyre, France ...44 13N 0 55W
172 Laboulaye, Argentina 34 10S 63 30W
153 Labrador, Canada 53 20N 61 0W
155 Labrador City, Canada 52 42N 67 0W
174 Lábrea, Brazil 7 15S 64 51W
50 Labrède, France 44 41S 0 32W
108 Labuan I., E. Malaysia 5 15N 115 38W
109 Labuha, Indonesia 0 30S 127 30E
109 Labuhan, Indonesia ... 6 26S 105 50E
109 Labuhanbadjo, Indon. 8 28S 120 1E
108 Labuk B., E. Malaysia 6 10N 117 50E
84 Labytnangi, U.S.S.R. 66 29N 66 40E
155 Lac Bouchette, Canada 48 16N 72 11W
164 Lac du Flambeau, U.S.A. 46 1N 89 51W
155 Lac Edouard, Canada 47 40N 72 16W
156 Lac la Biche, Canada .54 45N 111 50W
157 Lac la Ronge, Canada 55 5N 105 20W
57 Lac Leman, Switz. 46 30N 6 30E
157 Lac Seul, Canada 50 28N 92 0W
50 Lacanau, Étang de, Fr. 44 58N 1 7W
50 Lacanau Médoc, France 44 59N 1 5W
63 Lacara, R., Spain 39 7N 6 25W
50 Lacauna, Mts. de, Fr. 43 43N 2 50E
50 Lacaune, France 43 43N 2 40E
93 Laccadive Is., Ind. Oc. 10 0N 72 30E
39 Laceby, Eng., U.K. ...52 32N 0 10W
138 Lacepede Is., W. Austral. 16 55S 122 0E
132 Lacerdónia, Mozam. ...18 3S 35 35E
154 Lachine, Canada 45 30N 73 40W
98 Lachish (site), Israel .31 34N 34 51E
143 Lachlan R., Australia 34 0S 144 45E
104 Lachmangarh, India .27 50N 75 4E
154 Lachute, Canada 45 39N 74 21E
46 Lackagh Hills, Ireland 54 14N 8 0W
160 Lackawanna, U.S.A. .42 49N 78 50W
34 Lacock, England, U.K. 51 24N 2 8W
161 Lacolle, Canada 45 6N 73 24W
156 Lacombe, Canada 52 30N 113 50W
161 Lacona, U.S.A. 43 37N 76 5W
161 Laconia, U.S.A. 43 32N 71 30W
50 Lacq, France 43 25N 0 35W
166 Lacrosse, Wash., U.S.A. 46 51N 117 58W
102 Ladakh Ra., Kashmir 34 0N 78 0E
43 Ladder Hills, Scot., U.K. 57 15N 3 15W
42 Ladhar Bheinn, Scotland, U.K. 57 5N 5 37W
77 Ladhon, R., Greece ...37 40N 21 50E

MAP
88 Lâdik, Turkey 40 57N 35 58E
134 Ladismith, S. Africa ...33 28S 21 15E
101 Ladiz, Iran 28 55N 61 15E
104 Ladnun, India 27 38N 74 25E
36 Ladock, Eng., U.K. ...50 19N 4 58W
84 Ladoga, L., U.S.S.R. .61 15N 30 30E
49 Ladon, France 48 0N 2 30E
132 Lady Babbie, Rhodesia 18 30S 29 20E
154 Lady Beatrix L., Can. 5 20N 76 50W
135 Lady Frere, S. Africa .31 44S 27 1E
135 Lady Grey, S. Africa .30 43S 27 13E
41 Ladybank, Scot., U.K. 56 16N 3 8W
135 Ladybrand, S. Africa .29 9S 27 29E
45 Lady's I. Lake, Ireland 52 12N 6 23W
156 Ladysmith, Canada ...49 0N 124 0W
135 Ladysmith, Nat., S. Afr. 28 32S 29 46E
164 Ladysmith, U.S.A. 45 27N 91 4W
144 Lae, Terr. of N. Guin. 6 48S 146 53E
108 Laehobang, Indonesia 2 32N 96 1E
81 Laesö I., Denmark 57 15N 10 53E
81 Laeso Rende str., Den. 57 15N 10 50E
163 Lafayette, Ga., U.S.A. 34 44N 85 15W
164 Lafayette, Colo., U.S.A. 40 0N 105 2W
165 Lafayette, La., U.S.A. 30 18N 92 0W
163 Lafayette, Tenn., U.S.A. 36 35N 86 0W
161 Lafayette, Mt., U.S.A. 44 9N 71 37W
154 Laferte, Canada 48 37N 78 48W
45 Laffan's Bridge, Ireland 52 36N 7 45W
125 Lafia, Nigeria 8 30N 8 34E
125 Lafiagi, Nigeria 8 52N 5 20E
157 Laflèche, Canada 49 45N 106 40W
127 Lafon, Sudan 5 5N 32 29E
154 Laforest, Canada 47 4N 81 12W
80 Laforsen, falls, Sweden 61 56N 15 35E
46 Lagan R., N Ire., U.K. 54 35N 5 55W
81 Lagan R., Sweden 56 30N 13 30E
173 Lagarto, Serra do, Brazil 23 0S 57 15W
56 Lage, Germany 52 0N 8 47E
62 Lage, Spain 43 13N 9 0W
79 Lagen, R., Norway 61 29N 10 2E
56 Lägerdorf, Germany ...53 53N 9 35E
40 Laggan, Banff, Scotland, U.K. 57 24N 3 6W
43 Laggan, Inverness, Scotland, U.K. 57 3N 4 48W
40 Laggan B., Scot., U.K. 55 40N 6 20W
43 Laggan L., Scot., U.K. 56 57N 4 30W
46 Laggan R., Ireland ...53 56N 6 40W
122 Laghouat, Algeria 33 50N 2 59E
46 Laghy, Ireland 54 37N 8 7W
89 Lagich, U.S.S.R. 40 50N 48 20E
51 Lagnieu, France 45 55N 5 20E
49 Lagny, France 48 52N 2 40E
73 Lago, Italy 39 9N 16 8E
176 Lago Buenos Aires, Arg. 46 20S 70 50W
63 Lagôa, Portugal 37 8N 8 27W
62 Lagoaça, Portugal ...41 11N 6 44W
89 Lagodekhi, U.S.S.R. .41 50N 46 22E
73 Lagonegro, Italy 40 8N 15 45E
109 Lagonoy Gulf, Phil. ...13 50N 123 50E
176 Lagos, Chile 39 55S 72 55W
125 Lagos, Nigeria 6 25N 3 27E
63 Lagos, Portugal 37 5N 8 41W
168 Lagos de Moreno, Mex. 21 21N 101 55W
64 Laguardia, Spain 42 33N 2 35W
50 Laguépie, France 44 8N 1 57E
173 Laguna, Brazil 28 30S 48 50W
167 Laguna, U.S.A. 35 3N 107 28W
62 Laguna Antela, Spain 47 7N 7 40W
167 Laguna Beach, U.S.A. 33 31N 117 52W
167 Laguna Dam, U.S.A. .32 55N 114 30W
63 Laguna de Janda, Spain 36 15N 5 45W
172 Laguna Limpia, Arg. .26 32S 59 45W
108 Laguna Madre, U.S.A. 27 0N 97 20W
172 Laguna Olmos, Arg. ...33 25S 63 19W
71 Laguna Veneta, Italy 45 23N 12 25E
172 Lagunas, Chile 21 0S 69 45W
172 Lagunas, Peru 5 10S 75 35W
174 Lagunillas, Venezuela 10 8N 71 16W
112 Laha, China 48 9N 124 30E
109 Lahad Datu, Malaysia 5 0N 118 30E
46 Lahardaun, Ireland ...54 2N 9 20W
105 Laharpur, India 27 43N 80 56E
108 Lahat, Indonesia 3 45S 103 30E
108 Lahewa, Indonesia 1 22N 97 12E
101 Lahijan, Iran 37 10N 50 6E
56 Lahn R., Germany 50 52N 8 35E
81 Laholm, Sweden 56 30N 13 2E
81 Laholmsbukten B., Sweden 56 35N 12 45E
166 Lahontan Res., U.S.A. 39 28N 118 58W
104 Lahore, W. Pakistan .31 32N 74 22E
104 Lahore, St., Pakistan .31 55N 74 5E
57 Lahr, Germany 48 20N 7 52E
83 Lahti, Finland 60 59N 25 45E
121 Lai (Béhagle), Chad ... 9 25N 16 30E
107 Lai Chau N. Vietnam 22 5N 103 3E
112 Laichow Wan, China .37 30N 119 30E
145 Laidley, Australia 27 39S 152 20E
40 Laidon L., Scot., U.K. 56 40N 4 40W
113 Laifeng, China 29 30N 109 30E
48 Laigle, France 48 46N 0 38E

MAP
49 Laignes, France 47 50N 4 20E
50 L'Aiguillon, France ...46 20N 1 16W
100 Laila, Saudi Arabia ...22 10N 46 40E
174 Laillahue Mt., Peru ...17 0S 69 30W
135 Laings Nek P., S. Africa 27 28S 29 53E
134 Laingsburg, S. Africa .33 9S 20 52E
113 Laipin, China 23 45N 109 10E
43 Lairg, Scotland, U.K. 58 1N 4 24W
108 Lais, Indonesia 3 35S 102 0E
112 Laiyang, China 37 0N 120 50E
173 Lajes, Brazil 27 48S 50 20W
74 Lajkovac, Yugoslavia 44 27N 20 14E
59 Lajosmizse, Hungary .47 3N 19 32E
104 Lakaband, W. Pakistan 31 2N 69 15E
164 Lake Andes, U.S.A. ...43 10N 98 32W
162 Lake Anse, U.S.A. 46 42N 88 25W
165 Lake Arthur, U.S.A. .30 8N 92 40W
143 Lake Boga, Australia .35 26S 143 38E
143 Lake Cargelligo, N.S.W., Australia ...33 15S 146 22E
165 Lake Charles U.S.A. .31 10N 93 10W
167 Lake City, Colo, U.S.A. 38 3N 107 27W
163 Lake City, Fla., U.S.A. 30 10N 82 40W
164 Lake City, Iowa, U.S.A. 42 12N 94 42W
162 Lake City, Mich., U.S.A. 44 20N 85 10W
164 Lake City, Minn., U.S.A. 44 28N 92 21W
160 Lake City, Pa., U.S.A. 42 2N 80 20W
163 Lake City, S.C., U.S.A. 33 51N 79 44W
147 Lake Coleridge, N.Z. .43 17S 171 30E
29 Lake District, England, United Kingdom 54 45N 3 15W
161 Lake George, U.S.A. .43 25N 73 36W
142 Lake Grace, W. Austral. 33 20S 118 30E
142 Lake King, W. Austral. 33 5S 119 45E
156 Lake Louise, Canada .51 30N 116 10W
142 Lake Mason, W. Austral. 27 30S 119 30E
167 Lake Mead Nat. Rec. Area, U.S.A. 36 20N 114 30W
164 Lake Mills, U.S.A. 43 23N 93 33W
144 Lake Nash, Australia 20 57S 138 0E
159 Lake of the Woods, Can. 49 0N 95 0W
165 Lake Providence, U.S.A. 32 49N 91 12W
154 Lake River, Canada ...54 30N 82 30W
154 Lake Superior Prov. Park, Can. 47 45N 85 0W
147 Lake Tekapo, N.Z. 43 55S 170 30E
154 Lake Traverse, Can. ...45 56N 78 4W
143 Lake Tyers, Australia 37 52S 148 5E
142 Lake Varley, W. Austral. 32 48S 119 40E
143 Lake Victoria Res., N.S.W., Australia ...34 0S 141 17E
165 Lake Village, U.S.A. .33 20N 91 19W
163 Lake Walès, U.S.A. ...27 55N 81 32W
163 Lake Worth, U.S.A. ...26 36N 80 3W
154 Lakefield, Canada 44 25N 78 16W
163 Lakeland, Fla., U.S.A. 28 0N 82 0W
35 Lakenheath, Eng. U.K. 52 25N 0 30E
160 Lakeport, Mich., U.S.A. 43 7N 82 30W
166 Lakeport, Calif., U.S.A. 39 1N 122 56W
143 Lakes Entrance, Vic., Australia 37 50S 148 0E
167 Lakeside, Ariz., U.S.A. 34 12N 109 59W
164 Lakeside, Neb., U.S.A. 42 5N 102 24W
162 Lakeview, N.Y., U.S.A. 42 43N 78 57W
166 Lakeview, Ore., U.S.A. 42 15N 120 22W
163 Lakewood, N.J., U.S.A. 40 5N 74 13W
160 Lakewood, Ohio, U.S.A. 41 28N 81 50W
77 Lakhaniá, Rhodes, Gr. 35 58N 27 54E
77 Lakhi, Crete, Greece .35 24N 23 27E
105 Lakhimpur, India 27 14N 94 7E
104 Lakhpat, India 23 48N 68 47E
165 Lakin, U.S.A. 37 58N 101 18W
102 Lakki, W. Pakistan ...32 38N 70 50E
77 Lakonia, pref., Greece 36 55N 22 30E
77 Lakonikós Kólpos, G., Greece 36 40N 22 40E
109 Lakor I., Indonesia ... 8 15S 128 17E
124 Lakota, Ivory Coast ... 5 50N 5 30W
164 Lakota, U.S.A. 48 0N 98 22W
82 Lakse Fd., Norway 70 40N 27 0E
82 Lakselv, Norway 69 56N 25 0E
105 Lakshmi Kantapur, India 22 5N 88 20E
103 Lala Ghat, India 24 30N 92 40E
104 Lala Musa, W. Pakistan 32 40N 73 57E
132 Lalapanzi, Rhodesia ...19 20S 30 15E
143 Lalbert, Vic., Australia 35 38S 143 20E
105 Lalganj, India 25 52N 85 13E
127 Lalibala, Ethiopia 12 8N 39 10E
112 Lalin, China 45 14N 126 52E
62 Lalin, Spain 42 40N 8 5W
50 Lalinde, France 44 50N 0 44E
105 Lalitapur, Nepal 27 42N 85 12E

MAP
104 Lalitpur, India 24 42N 78 28E
125 Lama Kara Togo 9 30N 1 15E
127 Lama Shillindi, Ethiopia 4 50N 42 6E
103 Lamaing, Burma 15 25N 97 53E
164 Lamar, Colo., U.S.A. .38 9N 102 35W
165 Lamar, Mo., U.S.A. ...37 30N 94 20W
174 Lamas, Peru 6 28S 76 31W
112 Lamatientze, China ...46 46N 124 46E
43 Lamb Hd., Scot., U.K. 59 5N 2 34W
58 Lambach, Austria 48 6N 13 51E
48 Lamballe, France 48 29N 2 31W
128 Lambaréné, Gabon 0 20S 10 12E
45 Lambay I., Ireland ...53 30N 6 0W
174 Lambayeque, Peru 6 45S 79 55W
35 Lamberhurst, Eng., U.K. 51 5N 0 21E
164 Lambert, U.S.A. 47 44N 104 39W
134 Lambert's Bay, S. Afr. 32 5S 18 17E
14 Lamberts Land, Green. 78 0N 30 0W
57 Lambesc, France 43 39N 5 16E
123 Lambèse, Algeria 35 29N 6 11E
35 Lambeth, Eng., U.K. .51 27N 0 7W
107 Lambi Kyun, (Sullivan I.), Burma 10 50N 98 20E
77 Lámbia, Greece 37 52N 21 53E
38 Lambley, Eng., U.K. .54 56N 2 30W
34 Lambourn, Eng., U.K. 51 31N 1 31W
70 Lambro R., Italy 45 18N 9 20E
44 Lambs Hd., Ireland ...51 44N 10 10W
124 Lambusie, Ghana 10 50N 2 48E
125 Lame, Nigeria 10 27N 9 12E
166 Lame Deer, U.S.A. 45 45N 106 40W
62 Lamego, Portugal 41 5N 7 52W
155 Lameque, Canada 47 45N 64 38W
145 Lameroo, S. Australia 35 19S 140 33E
165 Lamesa, U.S.A. 32 45N 101 57W
81 Lamhult, Sweden 57 12N 14 36E
77 Lamia, Greece 38 55N 22 41E
1 Lamington, Mt., Papua 7 0S 156 0E
109 Lamitan, Philippines . 6 40N 122 10E
40 Lamlash, Scot., U.K. .55 32N 5 8W
133 Lammerkop, S. Africa 25 38S 29 26E
41 Lammermuir, Scotland, United Kingdom 55 50N 2 25W
41 Lammermuir Hs., Scotland, U.K. 55 50N 2 40W
55 Lammersdorf, Germany 50 38N 6 17E
166 Lamoille, U.S.A. 40 47N 115 31W
109 Lamon Bay, Phil. 14 30N 122 20E
156 Lamont, Canada 53 40N 112 50W
174 Lampa, Peru 15 10S 70 30W
107 Lampang, Thailand ...18 40N 98 53E
165 Lampasas, U.S.A. 31 5N 98 10W
168 Lampazos, Mexico 27 2N 100 32N
48 Lampaul, France 48 28N 5 7W
168 Lampazos, Mexico 27 0N 100 30W
68 Lampedusa I., Medit. 35 36N 12 40E
123 Lampeone, I., Medit. .35 33N 12 20E
37 Lampeter, Wales, U.K. 52 6N 4 6W
157 Lampman, Canada 49 25N 102 50W
58 Lamprechtshausen, Austria 48 0N 12 58E
131 Lamu, Kenya 2 10S 40 55E
131 Lamu, dist. Kenya ... 2 25S 40 54E
131 Lamu I., Kenya 2 17S 40 54E
167 Lamy, U.S.A. 35 30N 105 58W
158 Lanai I., Hawaii, U.S.A. 20 50N 156 55W
109 Lanao, L., Philippines 7 50N 124 50E
161 Lanark, Canada 44 59N 76 21W
41 Lanark, Scot., U.K. ...55 40N 3 48W
41 Lanark, co., Scot., U.K. 55 37N 3 50W
38 Lancashire, co., Eng., U.K. 53 40N 2 30W
29 Lancashire Plain, England, U.K. 53 30N 2 45W
155 Lancaster, N.B., Can. 45 17N 66 10W
161 Lancaster, Ont., Can. .45 10N 74 30W
38 Lancaster, Eng., U.K. 54 3N 2 48W
167 Lancaster, Calif., U.S.A. 34 47N 118 8W
162 Lancaster, Ky., U.S.A. 37 40N 84 40W
161 Lancaster, N.H., U.S.A. 44 27N 71 33W
160 Lancaster, N.Y., U.S.A. 42 53N 78 43W
161 Lancaster, Pa., U.S.A. 40 4N 76 19W
163 Lancaster, S.C., U.S.A. 34 45N 80 47W
164 Lancaster, Wis., U.S.A. 42 48N 90 43W
14 Lancaster Sd., Canada 74 0N 84 0W
143 Lancefield Vic., Austral. 37 18S 144 45E
39 Lanchester, Eng. U.K. 54 50N 1 44W
112 Lanchow, China 36 4N 103 44E
71 Lanciano, Italy 42 15N 14 22E
35 Lancing, Eng., U.K. .50 49N 0 19W
59 Lancut, Poland 50 10N 22 20E
128 Lândana, Cabinda, Ang. 5 11S 12 5E
57 Landau, Germany 49 12N 8 7E
58 Landeck, Austria 47 9N 10 34E
55 Landen, Belgium 50 45N 5 3E
166 Lander, U.S.A. 42 4950N 1 08W
48 Landerneau, France ...48 28N 4 17W
81 Landeryd, Sweden 57 7N 13 15E
50 Landes, dépt., France 43 57N 0 48W

MAP
64 Landete, Spain 39 56N 1 25W
102 Landi Kotal, W. Pak. 34 7N 71 6E
48 Landivisiau, France ...48 31N 4 6W
36 Landkey, Eng., U.K. .51 2N 4 0W
142 Landor, W. Australia .25 10S 117 0E
57 Landquart,
Switzerland 46 58N 9 32E
49 Landrecies, France 50 7N 3 40E
14 Land's End, Canada .76 10N 123 0W
36 Land's End, Eng.,
U.K. 50 4N 5 43W
57 Landsberg, Germany .48 3N 10 52E
81 Landsbro, Sweden 57 24N 14 56E
56 Landshut, W. Ger. 48 31N 12 10E
81 Landskröna, Sweden .56 55N 12 57E
81 Landvetter, Sweden ...57 41N 12 17E
81 Lane, Sweden 58 25N 12 3E
161 Lanesboro, U.S.A. 41 57N 75 34W
46 Lanesborough, Ireland 53 40N 8 0W
163 Lanett, U.S.A. 33 0N 85 15W
113 Lanfeng, China 34 50N 114 58E
82 Lang, Jökull, Mts.,
Ice. 64 40N 20 30W
112 Lang Shan (Hara
Narinula), China 41 30N 107 0E
81 Langaa, Viborg, Den. 56 23N 9 51E
76 Lángadhás, Greece 40 46N 23 2E
77 Langádhia, Greece 37 43N 22 1E
80 Langan R., Sweden ...61 30N 14 30E
127 Langana, L., Ethiopia 7 35N 38 45E
42 Langavat L., Scot.,
U.K. 58 4N 6 48W
113 Langchung (Paoning),
China 31 30N 106 0E
164 Langdon, U.S.A. 48 47N 98 24W
55 Langdorp, Belgium ...50 59N 4 52E
50 Langeac, France 45 7N 3 29E
126 Langeb, R., Sudan 17 28N 36 50E
134 Langeberge, Mts., S.
Africa 33 55S 21 20E
134 Langeberge, mts., S.
Africa 28 15S 22 33E
134 Langeberge, mts., S.
Afr. 30 40S 18 45E
81 Langeland I.,
Denmark 54 56N 10 48E
81 Langeland Bælt, Den. 54 55N 10 56E
57 Langen, Germany 53 36N 8 36E
55 Langenberg, Germany 49 14N 9 50E
58 Langeness, I.,
Germany 54 34N 8 35E
55 Langenfeld, Germany 51 7N 6 57E
58 Langenlois, Austria ...48 29N 15 40E
56 Langensalza,
Germany 51 6N 10 40E
56 Langeoog I. Germany 53 44N 7 33E
81 Langeskov, Denmark .55 22N 10 35E
79 Langesund, Norway ...59 0N 9 42E
112 Langfeng, China 48 4N 121 10E
81 Långhem, Sweden 57 36N 13 14E
70 Langhirano, Italy 44 39N 10 16E
41 Langholm, Scot.,
U.K. 55 9N 2 59W
107 Langkawi I., Malaysia 6 20N 99 45E
134 Langklip, S. Africa 28 12S 20 20E
108 Langkon, Sab,
Malaysia 6 38N 116 49E
135 Langkrans, Nat., S.
Afr. 27 50S 31 1E
154 Langlade, Canada 48 14N 76 10W
166 Langlois, U.S.A. 42 54N 124 26W
57 Langnau, Switzerland 46 56N 7 47E
38 Langness, I. of M.,
U.K. 54 3N 4 37W
50 Langogne, France 44 43N 3 50E
50 Langon, France 44 33N 0 16W
82 Langöy I., Norway 68 45N 15 10E
36 Langport, Eng., U.K. 51 2N 2 51W
49 Langres, France 47 52N 5 20E
49 Langres Plateau, Fr. .47 45N 5 20E
108 Langsa, Indonesia 4 30N 97 57E
55 Langschede, Germany 51 20N 7 42E
80 Långsele, Sweden 63 11N 17 5E
80 Langshyttan, Sweden 60 28N 16 5E
107 Langson, N. Vietnam .21 52N 106 42E
38 Langstrothdale Chase,
England, U.K. 54 14N 2 13W
35 Langtoft, Eng., U.K. .52 42N 0 19W
36 Langtree, Eng., U.K. .50 55N 4 11W
165 Langtry, U.S.A. 29 50N 101 33W
50 Languedoc, prov., Fr. 43 58N 3 22E
55 Lanklaar, Belgium 51 1N 5 44E
80 Lanna, Sweden 59 16N 14 56E
50 Lannemezan, France .43 8N 0 23E
144 Lannercost, Australia 18 35S 146 0E
48 Lannilis, France 48 35N 4 32W
48 Lannion, France 48 46N 3 29W
154 L'Annonciation, Can. .46 25N 74 55W
161 Lansdale, U.S.A. 40 14N 75 18W
143 Lansdowne, Australia 31 48S 152 30E
161 Lansdowne, Canada ...44 25N 76 1W
154 Lansdowne House,
Can. 52 5N 88 0W
155 L'Anse au Loup,
Canada 51 32N 56 50W
161 Lansford, U.S.A. 40 48N 75 55W
162 Lansing, Mich.,
U.S.A. 42 47N 84 32W
51 Lanslebourg, France .45 17N 6 52E
103 Lantsien, China 32 4N 96 6E
109 Lantuna, Indonesia ... 8 19S 124 8E
172 Lanus, Argentina 34 44S 58 27W
72 Lanusei, Italy 39 53N 9 31E
120 Lanzarote I., Canary
Is. 29 0N 13 40W
70 Lanzo Torinese, Italy 45 16N 7 29E
107 Lao Cai, N. Vietnam .22 40N 104 0E
73 Lao, R., Italy 39 45N 15 45E
109 Laoag, Philippines 18 7N 120 34E
109 Laoang, Philippines ...12 32N 125 8E

MAP
45 Laois, co., Ireland 53 0N 7 20W
49 Laon, France 49 33N 3 35E
162 Laona, U.S.A. 45 32N 88 41W
107 Laos, st., Asia 17 45N 105 0E
173 Lapa, Brazil 25 46S 49 44W
50 Lapalisse, France 46 15N 3 44E
109 Laparan Cap, I., Phil. 6 0N 120 0E
162 Lapeer, U.S.A. 43 3N 83 20W
36 Lapford, Eng., U.K. .50 52N 3 49W
82 Lapland, reg., see
Lappland, Eur. 68 7N 24 0E
161 Laporte, U.S.A. 41 27N 76 30W
74 Lapovo, Yugoslavia ...44 10N 21 2E
82 Lappi, dist., Finland .64 33N 25 10E
82 Lappland, reg.,
Europe 68 7N 24 0E
161 Laprairie, Canada 45 25N 73 30W
172 Laprida, Argentina 37 34S 60 45W
91 Laptev Sea, U.S.S.R. .76 0N 125 0E
166 Lapush, U.S.A. 47 56N 124 33W
78 Lăpusu, R., Rumania 47 25N 23 40E
71 L'Aquila, Italy 42 21N 13 24E
101 Lar, Iran 27 40N 54 14E
124 Larabanga, Ghana 9 16N 1 56W
122 Larache, Morocco 35 10N 6 5W
45 Laragh, Ireland 53 0N 6 20W
51 Laragne, France 44 18N 5 49E
164 Laramie, U.S.A. 41 15N 105 29W
164 Laramie, mts., U.S.A. 42 0N 105 30W
173 Laranjeiras do Sul,
Braz. 25 23S 52 23W
109 Larantuka, Indonesia 8 5S 122 55E
109 Larap, Philippines 14 15N 122 47E
109 Larat, I., Indonesia ... 4 50S 131 40E
109 Larat, I., Indonesia ... 7 0S 132 0E
41 Larbert, Scot., U.K. ...56 2N 3 50W
51 L'Arbresle, France 45 50N 4 26E
83 Larbro, Sweden 57 47N 18 50E
153 Larch, R., Canada 57 30N 71 0W
79 Lardal, Norway 59 20N 8 25E
154 Larder Lake, Canada .48 5N 79 40W
77 Lardhos, Akra,
Ródhos, Greece 36 4N 28 10E
131 Lare, Kenya 0 20N 37 56E
64 Laredo, Spain 43 26N 3 28W
165 Laredo, U.S.A. 27 34N 99 29W
121 Largeau (Faya), Chad 17 58N 19 6E
49 Largentière, France ...44 34N 4 18E
40 Largs, Scotland, U.K. 55 48N 4 51W
70 Lari, Italy ....43•34N 10 35E
109 Lariang, Indonesia 1 35S 119 25E
164 Larimore, U.S.A. 47 55N 97 35W
73 Larino, Italy 41 48N 14 54E
76 Larisa, Greece 39 38N 22 28E
76 Lárisa, pref., Greece ...39 39N 22 24E
104 Larkana, W. Pakistan 27 32N 68 2E
41 Larkhall, Scot., U.K. ..55 44N 4 0W
79 Larkollen, Norway 59 20N 10 41E
100 Larnaca, Cyprus 35 0N 33 35E
46 Larne, N. Ireland,
U.K. 54 52N 5 50W
46 Larne L., Ire.,
U.K. 54 52N 5 50W
164 Larned, U.S.A. 38 15N 99 10W
40 Laroch, Scot., U.K. ...56 40N 5 9W
50 Laroquebrou, France .44 58N 2 12E
138 Larrimah, N. Terr.,
Australia 15 35S 133 12E
15 Larsen Ice Shelf,
Antarc. 67 0S 62 0W
125 Larteh, Ghana 5 50N 0 5W
130 Laru, Congo 2 54N 24 25E
79 Larvik, Norway 59 5N 10 5E
90 Laryak, U.S.S.R. 61 15N 80 0E
50 Larzac, Causse du
mts., France 44 0N 3 17E
165 Las Animas, U.S.A. ...38 8N 103 18W
99 Las Anod, Somali
Rep. 8 26N 47 19E
65 Las Blancos, Spain 37 38N 0 49W
172 Las Brenas, Arg. 27 5S 61 7W
63 Las Cabezas de San
Juan, Spain 37 0N 5 58W
168 Las Cascadas,
Panama Canal Zone 9 5N 79 41W
172 Las Catitas, Argentina 33 10S 68 0W
167 Las Cruces, U.S.A. 32 25N 106 50W
168 Las Delicias, Panama 9 27N 79 35W
99 Las Dureh, Somali
Rep. 10 10N 46 0E
172 Las Flores, Argentina 36 0S 59 0W
65 Las Huertas, Cabo de,
Spain 38 22N 0 24W
99 Las Khoreh, Somali
Rep. 11 4N 48 20E
176 Las Laias, Argentina .38 30S 70 25W
172 Las Lomitas, Arg. 24 35S 60 50W
63 Las Marismas, Spain .37 5N 6 20W
63 Las Navas de la
Concepcion, Spain .37 56N 5 30W
172 Las Palmas,
Argentina 27 8S 58 45W
120 Las Palmas, Canary
Is. 28 10N 15 28W
176 Las Plumas,
Argentina 43 40S 67 15W
172 Las Ramadas, Chile ...31 0S 70 30W
172 Las Rosas, Argentina .32 30S 61 40W
169 Las Tablas, Panama . 7 49N 80 14W
172 Las Varillas,
Argentina 32 0S 62 50W
167 Las Vegas, N.M.,
U.S.A. 35 35N 105 10W
167 Las Vegas, Nev.,
U.S.A. 36 10N 115 5W
173 Lascano Uruguay 33 35S 54 18W
50 Lascaux, France 45 5N 1 10E
157 Lashburn, Canada 53 10N 10 40W
103 Lashio, Burma 23 0N 98 0E
104 Lashkar, India 26 10N 78 10E

MAP
60 Lasin, Poland 53 30N 19 2E
39 Laskill, Eng., U.K. 54 19N 1 6W
71 Lasko, Yugoslavia 46 10N 15 16E
48 Lassay, France 48 27N 0 30W
166 Lassen, Pk., U.S.A. ...40 20N 121 0W
130 Lassonga, Angola 7 58S 22 45E
41 Lasswade, Scot., U.K. 55 53N 3 8W
130 Lastoursville,
Cameroon 0 52S 12 48E
71 Lastovo, & I.,
Y.-slavia 42 46N 16 55E
71 Lastovski Kanal,
Y.-slav. 42 50N 17 0E
174 Latacunga, Ecuador ... 0 50S 78 35W
100 Latakia, see Al
Ladhiqiya, Syria 35 30N 35 45E
154 Latchford, Canada 47 20N 79 50W
73 Laterza, Italy 40 38N 16 47E
142 Latham, W. Australia 29 44S 116 20E
56 Lathen, Germany 52 51N 7 21E
43 Latheron, Scot., U.K. 58 17N 3 20W
73 Latiano, Italy 40 33N 17 43E
72 Latina, Italy 41 26N 12 53E
112 Lating, China 39 23N 118 55E
71 Latisana, Italy 45 47N 13 1E
71 Latium, Italy 42 0N 12 30E
59 Latorica, R., Cz. 48 31N 22 0E
145 Latrobe, Tas.,
Austral. 41 14S 146 30E
143 Latrobe, Vic.,
Australia 38 8S 146 44E
160 Latrobe, U.S.A. 40 19N 79 21W
145 Latrobe, Mt.,
Victoria, Australia .39 0S 146 23E
73 Latronico, Italy 40 5N 16 0E
98 Latrun, Jordan 31 50N 34 58E
106 Latur, India 18 25N 76 40E
86 Latvia S.S.R.,
U.S.S.R. 56 45N 24 30E
79 Laudal Norway 58 15N 7 30E
41 Lauder, Scot., U.K. ...55 43N 2 45W
41 Lauderdale, Scot.,
U.K. 55 43N 2 44W
56 Lauenburg Germany .53 23N 10 33E
37 Laugharne, Wales,
U.K. 51 45N 4 28W
65 Laujar, Spain 37 0N 2 54W
145 Launceston, Australia 41 24S 147 8E
36 Launceston, Eng.,
U.K. 50 38N 4 21W
44 Laune R., Ireland 52 5N 9 40W
107 Launglon Kok Is..
(S. Moscos Is.)
Burma 13 50N 97 54E
57 Laupheim, Germany .48 13N 9 53E
144 Laura Australia 15 32S 144 32E
44 Lauragh, Ireland 51 46N 9 46W
73 Laureana di Borrello,
It. 38 28N 16 5E
165 Laurel, Miss., U.S.A. .31 50N 89 0W
166 Laurel, Mont., U.S.A. 45 46N 108 49W
43 Laurencekirk, Scot.,
U.K. 56 50N 2 30W
44 Laurencetown,
Ireland 53 14N 8 11W
163 Laurens, U.S.A. 34 32N 82 2W
155 Laurentian Plat., Can. 51 30N 65 0W
73 Lauria, Italy 40 3N 15 50E
15 Laurie I., Antarctica .60 0S 46 0W
157 Laurie L., Canada ...56 35N 101 50W
41 Laurieston, Scot.,
U.K. 54 57N 4 2W
163 Laurinburg, U.S.A. ...34 50N 79 25W
162 Laurium, U.S.A. 47 31N 88 36W
57 Lausanne, Switzerland 46 32N 6 38E
108 Laut I., Indonesia 3 40S 116 10E
56 Lauterbach, Germany 50 39N 9 23E
57 Lauterecken, Ger. 49 38N 7 35E
155 Lauzon, Que., Canada 46 48N 71 4W
166 Lava Hot Springs,
U.S.A. 42 38N 112 1W
62 Lavadores, Spain 42 14N 8 41W
70 Lavagna, Italy 44 18N 9 22E
48 Laval, France 48 4N 0 48W
172 Lavalle, Argentina 32 45S 68 30W
76 Lávara, Greece 41 19N 26 22E
50 Lavardac, France 44 12N 0 20E
50 Lavaur, France 43 42N 1 49E
50 Lavaveix, France 46 5N 2 8E
50 Lavelanet, France 42 57N 1 51E
73 Lavello, Italy 41 4N 15 47E
35 Lavendon, Eng., U.K. 52 11N 0 39W
35 Lavenham, Eng.,
U.K. 52 7N 0 48E
154 Laverendrye Prov.
Park, Canada 46 15N 17 15W
165 Laverne, U.S.A. 36 43N 99 58W
142 Laverton, W.
Australia 28 44S 122 29E
98 Lavi Israel 32 47N 35 25E
79 Lavik, Norway 61 6N 5 30E
57 Lavin, Switzerland 46 47N 10 8E
77 Lávkos, Greece 39 9N 23 14E
62 Lavos, Portugal 40 6N 8 49W
173 Lavras, Minas Gerais,
Brazil 21 20S 45 0W
63 Lavre, Portugal 38 46N 8 22W
77 Lávrion, Greece 37 40N 24 4E
133 Lavumisa, Swaziland .27 20S 31 55E
108 Lawas, Sar., Malaysia 4 57N 115 23E
109 Lawele, Indonesia 5 16S 123 3E
43 Lawers, Eng., U.K. ...56 31N 4 9W
144 Lawn Hill, Australia .18 36S 138 33E
103 Lawng Pit, ra.,
Burma 26 45N 98 35E
124 Lawra, Ghana 10 39N 2 51W
147 Lawrence, New
Zealand 45 55S 169 41E
164 Lawrence, Kan.,
U.S.A. 39 0N 95 10W

MAP
161 Lawrence, Mass.,
U.S.A. 42 40N 71 9W
162 Lawrenceburg,
Indiana, U.S.A. 39 5N 84 50W
163 Lawrenceburg, Tenn.,
U.S.A. 35 12N 87 19W
163 Lawrenceville, Ga.,
U.S.A. 33 55N 83 59W
165 Lawton, U.S.A. 34 33N 98 25W
109 Lawu Mt., Indonesia . 7 40S 111 13E
80 Laxa, Sweden 59 0N 14 37E
38 Laxey, I. of Man,
U.K. 54 15N 4 23W
35 Laxfield, Eng., U.K. .52 18N 1 23E
42 Laxford L., Scot.,
U.K. 58 25N 5 10W
106 Laxmeshwar, India ...15 9N 75 28E
137 Laysan I., Pacific
Ocean 25 30N 167 0W
166 Laytonville, U.S.A. ...39 44N 123 29W
46 Laytown, Ireland 53 40N 6 15W
74 Lazarevac, Yugoslavia 44 23N 20 17E
71 Lazio (Latium), reg.,
It. 42 0N 12 30E
38 Lazonby, Eng., U.K. .54 45N 2 42W
50 Le Bacarès, France ...42 47N 3 3E
51 Le Beausset, France ...43 10N 5 46E
50 Le Blanc, France 46 37N 1 3E
50 Le Bleymard, France .44 30N 3 42E
48 Le Bourgneuf, France 48 10N 0 59W
50 Le Bouscat, France ...44 53N 0 32W
155 Le Bouthillier,
Canada 47 47N 64 55W
50 Le Bugue, France 44 55N 0 56E
50 Le Canourgue, France 44 26N 3 13E
49 Le Cateau, France 50 6N 3 30E
51 Le
Chambon-Feugerolles,
France 45 24N 4 18E
50 Le Château, France ...45 52N 1 12W
50 Le Châtelet, Cher, Fr. 46 40N 2 20E
49 Le Châtelet, Seine et
Marne, France 48 30N 2 47E
49 Le Chesne, France 49 30N 4 45E
51 Le Cheylard, France .44 55N 4 25E
48 Le Conquet, France ...48 21N 4 46W
49 Le Creusot, France ...46 50N 4 24E
48 Le Croisic, France ...47 18N 2 30W
50 Le Donjon, France 46 22N 3 48E
50 Le Dorat, France 46 14N 1 5E
169 Le François,
Martinique 14 38N 60 57W
48 Le Grand Fougeray,
Fr. 47 44N 1 43W
48 Le Grand Pressigny,
Fr. 46 55N 0 48E
48 Le Havre, France 49 30N 0 5E
123 Le Kef, Tunisia 36 12N 8 47E
122 Le Kreider, Algeria ...34 6N 0 2E
123 Le Kroul, Algeria
see El Karoub
48 Le Lion d'Angers,
Fr. 47 38N 0 42W
57 Le Locle, Switzerland 47 3N 6 44E
48 Le Louroux
Beconnais, France .47 30N 0 55W
51 Le Luc, France 43 23N 6 21E
72 Le Madonie, Mts.,
Sicily, Italy 37 50N 13 50E
48 Le Mans, France 48 0N 0 10E
130 Le Marinel Congo 10 25S 25 17E
164 Le Mars, U.S.A. 43 0N 96 0W
155 Le Mayne, L., Canada 57 5N 68 30W
48 Le Merlerault, France 48 41N 0 16E
50 Le Monastier, France .44 57N 4 0E
51 Le Monêtier les Bains,
France 44 58N 6 30E
50 Le Mont-Dore,
France 45 35N 2 50E
169 Le Moule, Guadeloupe 16 20N 61 22W
51 Le Muy, France 43 28N 6 34E
48 Le Palais, France 47 21N 3 10W
50 Le Perthus, France ...42 30N 2 53E
48 Le Petit-Quevilly, Fr. 49 26N 1 0E
50 Le Puy, France 45 3N 3 52E
134 Le Roux, S. Africa 33 30S 22 29E
165 Le Roy U.S.A. 38 8N 95 35W
50 Le Rozier, France 44 13N 3 12E
164 Le Sueur, U.S.A. 44 25N 93 52W
50 Le Teich, France 44 38N 0 59W
51 Le Teil, France 44 34N 4 41E
48 Le Teilleul, France 48 31N 0 52W
49 Le Thillot, France 47 52N 6 55E
49 Le Touquet, France ...50 30N 1 36E
48 Le Tréport, France 50 3N 1 20E
49 Le Valdahon, France .47 8N 6 20E
49 Le Verdon, France 45 32N 1 5W
50 Le Vigan, France 43 59N 3 24E
164 Lead, U.S.A. 44 20N 103 40W
39 Leadenham, Eng.,
U.K. 53 13N 0 33W
157 Leader, Canada 50 50N 109 30W
41 Leadgate, Eng., U.K. 54 52N 1 48W
41 Leadhills, Scot., U.K. 55 25N 3 47W
143 Leadville, Australia ...32 1N 149 38E
167 Leadville, U.S.A. 39 17N 106 23W
153 Leaf R., Canada 58 15N 71 0W
165 Leaf R., U.S.A. 31 45N 89 20W
165 Leakey, U.S.A. 29 45N 99 45W
163 Leaksville, U.S.A. 36 30N 79 49W
42 Lealt, Scot., U.K. 57 35N 6 10W
132 Lealui, Zambia 15 10S 23 2E
156 Leamington, Canada .42 10N 82 30W
146 Leamington, N.Z. 37 55S 175 29E
34 Leamington, Eng.,
U.K. 52 18N 1 32W
166 Leamington, U.S.A. ...39 37N 112 17W
173 Leandro, N. Alem,
Arg. 27 34S 55 15W
44 Leane L., Ireland 52 2N 9 32W

MAP
78 Leaoto, mt., Rumania 45 20N 25 20E
44 Leap, Ireland 51 34N 9 11W
142 Learmonth, W.
Austral. 22 40S 114 10E
157 Leask, Canada 53 5N 106 45W
35 Leatherhead, Eng.,
U.K. 51 18N 0 20W
164 Leavenworth, Mo.,
USA 39 25N 95 0W
166 Leavenworth, Wash.,
U.S.A. 47 44N 120 37W
60 Leba, Poland 54 45N 17 32E
109 Lebak, Philippines 6 32N 124 5E
74 Lebane, Yugoslavia ...42 56N 21 44E
100 Lebanon, St., Asia 34 0N 36 0E
162 Lebanon, Ind.,
U.S.A. 40 3N 86 55W
164 Lebanon, Kans.,
U.S.A. 39 50N 98 35W
162 Lebanon, Ky., U.S.A. 37 35N 85 15W
165 Lebanon, Mo., U.S.A. 37 40N 92 40W
161 Lebanon, N.H.,
U.S.A. 43 38N 72 15W
166 Lebanon, Ore., U.S.A. 44 31N 122 57W
161 Lebanon, Pa., U.S.A. .40 20N 76 28W
163 Lebanon, Tenn.,
U.S.A. 36 15N 86 20W
167 Lebec, U.S.A. 34 36N 118 59W
86 Lebedin, U.S.S.R. 50 35N 34 30E
87 Lebedyan, U.S.S.R. ...53 0N 39 10E
82 Lebesby, Norway 70 28N 27 3E
133 Lebombo Mts., S. Afr. 24 30S 32 0E
60 Lebork, Poland 54 33N 17 46E
63 Lebrija, Spain 36 53N 6 5W
172 Lebu, Chile 37 40S 73 47W
73 Lecce, Italy 40 20N 18 10E
70 Lecco, Italy 45 50N 9 27E
70 Lecco, L. di., Italy 45 51N 9 22E
64 Lécera, Spain 41 13N 0 43W
58 Lech, Austria 47 13N 10 9E
58 Lech, R., Austria 47 19N 10 27E
55 Lechenich, Germany .50 48N 6 42E
34 Lechlade, Eng., U.K. .51 42N 1 40W
58 Lechtaler Alpen, Mts.,
Austria 47 15N 10 30E
50 Lectoure, France 43 56N 0 38E
60 Leczyca, Poland 52 5N 19 15E
34 Ledbury, Eng., U.K. .52 3N 2 25W
58 Ledec, Czechoslovakia 49 41N 15 18E
172 Ledesma, Argentina ...23 50S 64 50W
62 Ledesma, Spain 41 6N 5 59W
156 Leduc, Canada 53 20N 113 30W
60 Ledyczek, Poland 53 33N 16 59E
34 Lee, England, U.K. ...50 47N 1 11W
161 Lee, Mass., U.S.A. 42 17N 73 18W
166 Lee Nev., U.S.A. 40 35N 115 36W
44 Lee R., Ireland 51 51N 9 2W
164 Leech L., U.S.A. 47 15N 94 23W
165 Leedey, U.S.A. 35 53N 99 24W
39 Leeds, Yorks, Eng,
U.K. 53 48N 1 34W
163 Leeds, U.S.A. 33 32N 86 30W
38 Leek, England, U.K. .53 7N 2 2W
45 Leenaun, Ireland ... .53 35N 9 41W
134 Leendertsplaas, S.
Afr. 31 42S 21 0E
56 Leer, Germany 53 13N 7 29E
55 Leerdam, Netherlands 51 54N 5 6E
163 Leesburg, Fla., U.S.A. 28 47N 81 52W
147 Leeston, New Zealand 43 45N 172 19E
165 Leesville, U.S.A. 31 12N 93 15W
143 Leeton, N.S.W.,
Austral. 34 23S 146 23E
160 Leetonia, U.S.A. 40 53N 80 45W
134 Leeu-Gamka, S.
Africa 32 43S 21 59E
54 Leeuwarden, Neth. 53 15N 5 48E
133 Leeudoringstad, S.
Afr. 27 15S 26 10E
133 Leeupoort, S. Africa ..24 57S 27 46E
133 Leeuspruit, S. Africa .26 47S 28 31E
142 Leeuwin, C., W.
Austral. 34 20S 115 9E
169 Leeward Is., W.
Indies 16 30N 63 30W
42 Leezen, Germany 53 51N 10 14E
130 Lefini R., Congo, (Fr.) 2 55S 15 30E
75 Lefka, Bulgaria 41 52N 26 15E
165 Lefors, U.S.A. 35 30N 100 50W
142 Lefroy L., W.
Australia 31 21S 121 40E
156 Legal, Canada 53 55N 113 45W
109 Legaspi, Philippines ...13 10N 123 46E
70 Leghorn, see Livorno,
Italy 43 32N 10 18E
132 Legion, Rhodesia 21 25S 28 30E
60 Legionowo, Poland 52 25N 20 50E
70 Legnago Italy 45 10N 11 19E
70 Legnano, Italy 45 35N 8 55E
60 Legnica, Poland 51 12N 16 10E
46 Legioniel, N. Ire.,
U.K. 54 38N 6 0W
71 Legrad, Yugoslavia ...46 17N 16 51E
145 Legume, NSW.,
Austral 28 20S 152 12E
102 Leh, Kashmir 34 15N 77 35E
166 Lehi, U.S.A. 40 20N 112 0W
161 Lehighton, U.S.A. 40 50N 75 44W
44 Lehinch, Ireland 52 56N 9 21E
78 Lehliu, Rumania 44 29N 26 20E
56 Lehrte, Germany 52 22N 9 58E
132 Lehututu, Botswana .23 54S 21 55E
104 Leiah, West Pakistan 30 58N 70 58E
58 Leibnitz, Austria 46 47N 15 34E
34 Leicester, Eng., U.K. .52 39N 1 9W
34 Leicester, Co.,
England, United
Kingdom 52 40N 1 10W
144 Leichhardt Ra.,
Austral. 20 46S 147 40E

MAP
144 Leichhardt, R., Austral. 17 50S 139 49E
55 Leichlingen, Germany 51 7N 7 1E
54 Leiden, Netherlands 52 9N 4 30E
54 Leie R., Belgium 50 55N 3 25E
35 Leigh, Essex, Eng., U.K. 51 32N 0 40E
34 Leigh, Worcester, England, U.K. 52 10N 2 21W
143 Leigh, R., Vic., Austral. 37 50S 144 0E
145 Leigh Creek, S. Austral. 30 28S 138 24E
45 Leighlinbridge, Ireland 52 45N 7 2W
35 Leighton Buzzard, England, U.K. 51 55N 0 39W
45 Leinster, prov., Ire. 53 0N 7 10W
45 Leinster, Mt., Ireland 52 38N 6 47W
34 Leintwardine, Eng. U.K. 52 22N 2 51W
134 Leipoldtville, S. Africa 32 14S 18 30E
56 Leipzig, Germany 51 20N 12 23E
56 Leipzig, dist., E. Ger. 51 20N 12 30E
63 Leiria tn., & dist. Portugal 39 46N 8 53W
113 Leishan, China 25 55N 108 15E
142 Leisler, Mt., S. Austral. 23 23S 129 30E
35 Leiston, Eng., U.K. 52 13N 1 35E
35 Leith Hill, Eng., U.K. 51 10N 0 23W
59 Leitha, R. Aust.-Hung. 47 57N 17 5E
41 Leitholm, Scot., U.K. 55 42N 2 16W
46 Leitrim, Ireland 54 0N 8 5W
46 Leitrim, co., Ire. 54 8N 8 0W
113 Leiyang, China 26 30N 112 38E
64 Leiza, Spain 43 5N 1 55W
76 Lekáni, Greece 41 10N 24 35E
130 Leketi Mts., Congo, (Fr.) 2 25S 14 0E
77 Lekhainá, Greece 37 57N 21 16E
67 Leknice, Poland 51 34N 14 45E
165 Leland, Miss., U.S.A. 33 25N 90 52W
60 Lelången L., Sweden 59 13N 12 0E
176 Leleque, Argentina 42 15S 71 0W
54 Lelystad, Netherlands 52 30N 5 25E
125 Lema, Nigeria 12 58N 4 13E
109 Lemery, Philippines 13 58N 120 56E
56 Lemgo, Germany 52 2N 8 52E
166 Lemhi Ra., U.S.A 44 30N 113 30W
164 Lemmon, U.S.A. 45 59N 102 10W
167 Lemmon Mt., U.S.A. 32 30N 110 48W
167 Lemoore, U.S.A. 36 23N 119 54W
50 Lempdes, France 45 22N 3 17E
81 Lemvig, Denmark 56 33N 8 20E
91 Lena, R., Siberia, U.S.S.R. 64 30N 127 0E
46 Lenadoon Pt., Ireland 54 19N 9 3W
48 Lencloitre, France 46 50N 0 20E
40 Lendalfoot, Scot., U.K. 55 12N 4 55W
71 Lendinara, Italy 45 4N 11 37E
55 Lendringsen, Germany 51 26N 7 50E
46 Lene L., Ireland 53 40N 7 12W
56 Lengerich, Germany 52 12N 7 50E
107 Lenggong, W. Malaysia 5 5N 100 57E
59 Lengyeltóti, Hungary 46 40N 17 40E
35 Lenham, Eng., U.K. 51 14N 0 44E
81 Lenhovda, Sweden 57 0N 15 20E
127 Lenia, Ethiopia 4 10N 37 25E
89 Lenin, U.S.S.R. 48 20N 40 56E
90 Leninabad, U.S.S.R. 40 10N 69 40E
89 Leninakan, U.S.S.R. 41 0N 42 50E
86 Leningrad, U.S.S.R. 59 55N 30 20E
90 Leninogorsk, U.S.S.R. 50 20N 83 30E
89 Leninsk, U.S.S.R. 56 38N 46 10E
90 Leninsk-Kuznetskiy, U.S.S.R. 55 10N 86 10E
87 Leninskaya, U.S.S.R. 56 7N 44 29E
87 Leninskoye, U.S.S.R. 58 23N 47 3E
57 Lenk, Switzerland 46 27N 7 28E
85 Lenkoran, U.S.S.R. 39 45N 48 50E
109 Lenmaloe, W. Irian. Indonesia 1 58S 130 0E
40 Lennoxtown, Scot., U.K. 55 58N 4 14W
161 Lennoxville, Canada 45 23N 71 53W
70 Leno, Italy 45 24N 10 14E
163 Lenoir, U.S.A. 35 55N 81 36W
163 Lenoir City, U.S.A. 35 40N 84 20W
164 Lenora, U.S.A. 39 39N 100 1W
161 Lenox, Mass., U.S.A. 42 20N 73 18W
49 Lens, France 50 26N 2 50E
91 Lensk (Mukhtuya), U.S.S.R. 60 48N 114 55E
88 Lenskoye U.S.S.R. 45 3N 34 1E
73 Lentini, Italy 37 18N 15 0E
56 Lenzen, Germany 53 6N 11 26E
124 Léo, Upper Volta 11 3N 2 2W
58 Leoben, Styria, Austria 47 22N 15 5E
164 Leola, U.S.A. 45 47N 98 58W
34 Leominster, Eng., U.K. 52 15N 2 43W
161 Leominster, U.S.A. 42 30N 71 44W
50 Léon, France 43 53N 1 18W
168 Leon Mexico 21 7N 101 30W
169 León, Nicaragua 12 20N 86 51W
62 Leon, Spain 42 38N 5 34W
62 Leon, prov., Spain 41 40N 5 55W
164 Leon, U.S.A. 40 40N 93 40W
142 Leonara, W. Australia 28 47S 121 15E
162 Leonardtown, U.S.A. 38 19N 76 39W
58 Leonfelden, Austria 48 31N 14 18E
73 Leonforte, Italy 37 39N 14 22E
143 Leongatha, Australia 38 30S 145 58E

MAP
77 Leonidhion, Greece 37 9N 22 52E
130 Leopold II, L., Congo 2 0S 18 0E
173 Leopoldina, Brazil 21 28S 42 40W
54 Leopoldsburg, Belgium 51 7N 5 13E
130 Léopoldville, see Kinshasa, Congo 4 20S 15 15E
164 Leoti, U.S.A. 38 31N 101 19W
157 Leoville, Canada 53 39N 107 33W
63 Lepe, Spain 37 15N 7 12W
86 Lepel, U.S.S.R. 54 50N 28 40E
132 Lephepe, Botswana 23 22S 25 50E
91 Lepikha, U.S.S.R. 64 45N 125 55E
70 Lepontine Alps, Italy 46 22N 8 27E
59 Lepsény, Hungary 47 0N 18 15E
64 Lequeitio, Spain 43 20N 2 32W
80 Lerbäck, Sweden 58 56N 15 2E
72 Lercara Friddi, Sic., It. 37 42N 13 36E
125 Lere, Nigeria 10 22N 8 31E
135 Leribe, Lesotho 28 51S 28 3E
70 Lerici, Italy 44 4N 9 48E
64 Lerida, Spain 41 37N 0 39E
64 Lérida, prov., Spain 42 6N 1 0E
62 Lerma, Spain 42 0N 4 37W
77 Léros, I., Greece 37 10N 26 50E
49 Lérouville, France 48 50N 5 30E
42 Lerwick, Shet. I., Scotland U.K. 60 10N 1 10W
78 Les, Rumania 46 58N 21 50E
51 Les Abrets, France 45 32N 5 35E
48 Les Andelys, France 49 15N 1 25E
51 Les Baux, France 43 45N 4 51E
169 Les Cayes, Haiti 18 15N 73 46W
51 Les Echelles, France 45 27N 5 45E
48 Les Essarts, France 46 47N 1 12W
155 Les Etroits, Canada 47 24N 68 54W
48 Les Herbiers, France 46 52N 1 0W
50 Les Landes, dist., Fr. 44 20N 1 0W
48 Les Ponts de Cé, France 47 25N 0 30W
50 Les Sables d'Olonne Fr. 46 30N 1 45W
51 Les Saintes Maries, Fr. 43 27N 4 25E
168 Les Tres Marías Is., Mex. 12 20N 106 30W
51 Les Vans, France 44 26N 4 9E
77 Lesbos, I., see Lésvos, Greece 39 0N 26 20E
41 Lesbury, Eng., U.K. 55 25N 1 37W
71 Lesina, L. di, Italy 41 45N 15 25E
79 Lesja, Norway 62 7N 8 51E
79 Lesjaverk Norway 62 12N 8 34E
59 Lesko, Poland 49 30N 22 23E
15 Leskov, I., Falkland Is. Dependencies 56 0S 28 0W
74 Leskovac, Y.-slavia 43 0N 21 58E
76 Leskovic, Albania 40 10N 20 34E
41 Leslie, Fife, Scot., U.K. 56 12N 3 12W
133 Leslie, S. Africa 26 16S 28 55E
165 Leslie, U.S.A. 35 50N 92 35W
41 Lesmahagow, Scot., U.K. 55 38N 3 55W
48 Lesneven, France 48 35N 4 20W
84 Lesnoi, U.S.S.R. 66 50N 34 20E
86 Lesnoye, U.S.S.R. 58 15N 35 31E
135 Lesotho, st., Africa 29 40S 28 0E
91 Lesozavodsk, U.S.S.R. 45 30N 133 20E
50 Lesparre-Medoc, France 45 18N 0 57W
48 Lessay, France 49 14N 1 30W
54 Lesse R., Belgium 50 10N 5 0E
169 Lesser Antilles, W. Ind. 12 30N 61 0W
156 Lesser Slave L., Can. 55 30N 115 10W
108 Lesser Sunda Is., prov., Indonesia 7 30S 117 0E
54 Lessines, Belgium 50 42N 3 50E
157 Lestock, Canada 51 25N 104 0W
132 Lesuma, Botswana 17 58S 25 12E
77 Lésvos, I., Greece 39 0N 26 20E
40 Leswalt, Scot., U.K. 54 56N 5 6W
60 Leszno, Poland 51 50N 16 30E
133 Letaba R., S. Africa 23 42S 31 25E
35 Letchworth, Eng., U.K. 51 58N 0 13W
78 Letea, Ostrov, L., Rum. 45 18N 29 20E
143 Lethbridge, Australia 37 58S 144 6E
156 Lethbridge, Canada 49 45N 112 45W
109 Leti Indonesia 8 10S 127 40E
109 Leti Is., Indonesia 8 10S 128 0E
132 Letiahau, R., Botswana 21 40S 23 30E
174 Leticia, Colombia 4 0S 70 0W
134 Letjiesbos S. Africa 32 31S 22 16E
55 Letmathe, Germany 51 22N 7 36E
103 Letpadan, Burma 17 45N 96 0E
103 Letpan, Burma 19 28N 93 52E
107 Letsök-aw-Kyun (Domel I.), Burma 11 30N 98 25E
143 Lette, N.S.W., Austral. 34 3S 143 4E
46 Letterbreen, N. Ireland, United Kingdom 54 18N 7 43W
44 Letterfrack, Ireland 53 33N 9 58W
46 Letterkenny, Ireland 54 57N 7 42W
46 Lettermacaward, Ire. 54 51N 8 18W
44 Lettermore I., Ireland 53 18N 9 40W
44 Lettermullan, Ireland 53 15N 9 44W
37 Letterston, Wales, UK 51 56N 5 0W
43 Lettoch, Scot., U.K. 57 22N 3 30W
78 Leu, Rumania 44 10N 24 0E
50 Leucate, France 42 56N 3 3E
41 Leuchars, Scot., U.K. 56 23N 2 53W
57 Leuk, Switzerland 46 19N 7 37E

MAP
108 Leuser, Mt., Indonesia 4 0N 96 51E
55 Leutesdorf, Germany 50 27N 7 24E
57 Leutkirch, Germany 47 49N 10 1E
54 Leuven (Louvain), Belg. 50 52N 4 42E
54 Leuze, Belgium 50 36N 3 37E
87 Lev Tolstoy, U.S.S.R. 53 13N 39 29E
77 Levadhia, Greece 38 27N 22 54E
166 Levan, U.S.A. 39 37N 111 32W
76 Levan-Samari, Albania 40 40N 19 28E
82 Levanger, Norway 63 43N 11 12E
70 Levanto, Italy 44 10N 9 37E
72 Levanzo I., Italy 38 0N 12 19E
165 Levelland, U.S.A. 33 38N 102 17W
39 Leven, England, U.K. 53 54N 0 18W
41 Leven, Scotland, U.K. 56 12N 3 0W
40 Leven, L., Scot., U.K. 56 12N 3 22W
75 Leven, prov., Bulgaria 43 20N 24 45E
39 Leven R., Yorks., England, U.K. 54 27N 1 15W
51 Levens, France 43 50N 7 12E
138 Levêque C., W. Austral. 16 20S 123 0E
73 Leverano, Italy 40 16N 18 0E
42 Leverburgh, Scot. U.K. 57 46N 7 0W
56 Leverkusen, Germany 51 2N 6 59E
49 Levet, France 46 56N 2 22E
59 Levice, Czechoslovakia 48 13N 18 35E
15 Levick, Mt., Antarctica 75 0S 164 0E
71 Levico, Italy 46 0N 11 18E
49 Levier, France 46 58N 6 8E
146 Levin, New Zealand 40 37S 175 18E
155 Levis, Canada 46 48N 71 9W
77 Levitha, I., Greece 37 0N 26 28E
161 Levittown, U.S.A. 40 10N 74 51W
77 Lévka, Mt., Crete, Gr. 35 18N 24 3E
77 Levkás, Greece 38 48N 20 43E
77 Levkás I., Greece 38 40N 20 43E
76 Levkimmi, Greece 39 25N 20 3E
59 Levoca, Czechoslovakia 48 59N 20 35E
49 Levroux, France 47 0N 1 38E
75 Levski, Bulgaria 43 21N 25 10E
75 Levskigrad, Bulgaria 42 38N 24 47E
164 Lewellen, U.S.A. 41 22N 102 5W
35 Lewes, England, U.K. 50 53N 0 2E
162 Lewes, U.S.A. 38 45N 75 8W
152 Lewes, L., Canada 60 30N 134 20W
60 Lewin Brzeski, Poland 50 45N 17 37E
42 Lewis, Butt of, Scotland, U.K. 58 30N 6 12W
42 Lewis, dist., Scot., U.K. 58 10N 6 40W
166 Lewis R., U.S.A. 48 0N 113 15W
160 Lewisburg, Pa., U.S.A. 40 57N 76 57W
163 Lewisburg, Tenn., U.S.A. 35 29N 86 46W
35 Lewisham, Eng., U.K. 51 27N 0 1E
155 Lewisporte, Canada 49 15N 55 3W
43 Lewiston, Scot., U.K. 57 19N 4 30W
166 Lewiston, Idaho, U.S.A. 45 58N 117 0W
166 Lewiston, Utah, U.S.A. 42 0N 111 56W
166 Lewistown, Mont, U.S.A. 47 0N 109 25W
160 Lewistown, Pa., U.S.A. 40 37N 77 33W
164 Lexington, Ill., U.S.A. 40 37N 88 47W
162 Lexington, Ky., U.S.A. 38 6N 84 30W
165 Lexington, Miss., U.S.A. 33 8N 90 2W
164 Lexington, Mo., U.S.A. 39 7N 93 55W
164 Lexington, Neb., U.S.A. 40 48N 99 45W
163 Lexington, N.C., U.S.A. 35 50N 80 13W
160 Lexington, Ohio, U.S.A. 40 39N 82 35W
166 Lexington, Ore., U.S.A. 45 29N 119 46W
163 Lexington, Tenn., U.S.A. 35 38N 88 25W
38 Leyburn, Eng., U.K. 54 19N 1 50W
133 Leysdorp, Trans., S. Afr. 23 59S 30 30E
38 Leyland, Eng., U.K. 53 41N 2 42W
35 Leysdown on Sea, Eng., U.K. 51 23N 0 57E
109 Leyte I., Philippines 11 0N 125 0E
50 Lezay, France 46 17N 0 0
76 Lezhe, Albania 41 47N 19 42E
50 Lézignan Corbières, Fr. 43 13N 2 43E
50 Lezoux, France 45 49N 3 21E
86 Lgov, U.S.S.R. 51 42N 35 10E
103 Lhariguo, China 30 29N 93 4E
43 Lhanbryde, Scot., U.K. 57 38N 3 12W
111 Lhasa, Tibet, China 29 50N 91 3E
111 Lhatse Dzong, Tibet, China 29 10N 87 45E
108 Lhokseumawe Indon. 5 20N 97 10E
50 L'Hospitalet, France 44 23N 1 26E
103 Lhuntse Dzong Tibet, China 28 25N 92 20E
82 Li, & R., Finland 65 20N 25 20E
77 Liádhoi, I., Greece 36 50N 26 11E
132 Liandambia, Zambia 13 10S 22 25E
109 Liang Liang, Philippines 5 58N 121 30E
109 Lianga, Philippines 8 50N 126 0E

MAP
108 Liangpran, Mt., Indon. 1 0N 115 0E
112 Liangsiang, China 39 55N 116 15E
113 Liangtang, China 33 59N 106 21E
112 Liao Ho, R., China 42 20N 123 20E
112 Liaochung, China 41 35N 122 45E
112 Liaoning, prov., China 41 40N 122 30E
112 Liaotung, dist., China 40 0N 122 30E
112 Liaotung, Wan, China 40 0N 120 45E
112 Liaotung Pen., China 40 10N 123 0E
112 Liaoyang, China 41 15N 123 10E
112 Liaoyuan, China 42 59N 125 8E
76 Liaphadhes, Corfu, Gr. 39 42N 19 40E
156 Liard R., Canada 61 20N 122 30W
166 Libby, U.S.A. 48 20N 115 40W
130 Libenge, Congo 3 40N 18 55E
165 Liberal, Kan., U.S.A. 37 4N 101 0W
165 Liberal, Mo., U.S.A. 37 35N 94 30W
174 Liberdade, Brazil 7 15S 71 50W
58 Liberec, Czechoslovakia 50 47N 15 7E
169 Liberia, Costa Rica 10 40N 85 30W
124 Liberia, st., West Africa 6 30N 9 30W
164 Liberty, Mo., U.S.A. 39 15N 94 24W
161 Liberty, N.Y., U.S.A. 41 48N 74 45W
165 Liberty, Tex., U.S.A. 30 5N 94 50W
135 Libode, C. Prov. S. Afr. 31 31S 29 2E
76 Libohovë, Albania 40 3N 20 10E
50 Libourne, France 44 55N 0 15W
54 Libramont, Belgium 49 55N 5 23E
76 Librazhd, Albania 41 12N 20 22E
128 Libreville, Gabon 0 25N 9 26E
121 Libya, King., N. Africa 28 30N 17 30E
75 Libyakhovo, Bulgaria 41 29N 23 50E
116 Libyan Des., N. Africa 27 35N 25 0E
126 Libyan Plat., Egypt 30 40N 26 30E
172 Licanten, Chile 34 55S 72 0W
72 Licata, Italy 37 6N 13 55E
34 Lichfield, Eng., U.K. 52 40N 1 50W
133 Lichtenburg, S. Africa 26 8S 26 8E
57 Lichtenfels, Germany 50 7N 11 4E
167 Lida, U.S.A. 37 30N 117 30W
86 Lida, U.S.S.R. 53 53N 25 15E
81 Lidhult, Sweden 56 49N 13 35E
80 Lidingo, Sweden 59 22N 18 10E
81 Lidköping, Sweden 58 31N 13 14E
81 Lidnäs, Sweden 57 4N 14 37E
71 Lido, Italy 45 25N 12 23E
60 Lidzbark, Poland 53 15N 19 49E
60 Lidzbark Warminski, Poland 54 7N 20 34E
56 Liebenwalde, Germany 52 51N 13 23E
55 Lieberhausen, Germany 51 4N 7 40E
56 Lieberose, Germany 51 59N 14 18E
74 Liebling, Rumania 45 36N 21 20E
57 Liechtenstein, Principality, Europe 47 8N 9 35E
54 Liége, Belgium 50 38N 5 35E
54 Liége, prov., Belgium 50 32N 5 35E
60 Liegnitz, see Legnica, Poland 51 12N 16 10E
113 Lienhua, China 26 58N 113 59E
112 Lienshankwan, China 41 0N 123 59E
113 Lienyang, China 26 11N 119 30E
113 Lienyunkang, China 34 45N 119 30E
58 Lienz, Austria 46 50N 12 46E
86 Liepaya Latvia, U.S.S.R. 56 30N 21 0E
54 Lier, Belgium 51 7N 4 34E
112 Lieshankwan, China 40 56N 124 51E
78 Liesti, Rumania 45 38N 27 34E
49 Liévin, France 50 24N 2 47E
154 Lievre, R., Canada 45 40N 75 40W
58 Liezen, Austria 47 34N 14 15E
45 Liffey R., Ireland 53 21N 6 20W
46 Lifford, Ireland 54 50N 7 30W
48 Liffré, Ille et Vilaine, Fr. 48 12N 1 30W
79 Lifjell, Mt., Norway 59 32N 8 48W
130 Ligasa, Congo 0 44N 23 49E
145 Lightning Ridge, N.S.W., Australia 29 22S 148 0E
71 Lignano, Italy 45 42N 13 8E
49 Ligny en Barrois, Fr. 48 41N 5 20E
49 Ligny le Châtel, France 47 54N 3 45E
77 Ligourion, Greece 37 37N 23 2E
70 Ligurian Sea, Italy 43 20N 9 0E
144 Lihir Group, Terr. of New Guin. 3 0S 152 35E
158 Lihue, Kauai, Hawaii, U.S.A. 21 59N 159 24W
113 Lihsien, China 34 10N 105 0E
103 Lihwa, China 30 4N 100 18E
130 Likasi (Jadotville), Congo 10 55S 26 48E
130 Likati, Congo 3 20N 24 0E
130 Likati, R., Congo 3 2N 23 56E
86 Likhoslavl, U.S.S.R. 57 12N 35 30E
89 Likhovski, U.S.S.R. 48 10N 40 10E
111 Likiang, China 26 50N 100 15E
132 Likoma I., Malawi 12 3S 34 45E
130 Likouala, R., Congo 0 15S 16 40W
130 Likouala aux herbes, R., Congo, (Fr.) 0 40N 17 12E
132 Likumburu, Tanzania 9 43S 35 8E
112 Likunpu, China 36 31N 106 12E
113 Liling, China 27 47N 113 30E
49 Lille, France 50 38N 3 3E
81 Lille Baelt (Little Belt), str., Denmark 55 30N 9 45E
48 Lillebonne, France 49 30N 0 32E

MAP
79 Lillehammer, Norway 61 8N 10 30E
49 Lillers, France 50 35N 2 28E
79 Lillesand, Norway 58 12N 8 23E
34 Lilleshall, Eng., U.K. 52 45N 2 22W
79 Lilleström, Norway 59 58N 11 5E
80 Lillhamra, Sweden 61 39N 14 45E
133 Lilliput, Trans., S. Afr. 22 30S 29 55E
64 Lillo, Spain 39 45N 3 20W
132 Lilongwe, Malawi 14 0S 33 48E
109 Liloy, Philippines 8 4N 122 39E
143 Lilydale, Vic., Austral. 37 43S 145 29E
74 Lim R., Yugoslavia 43 0N 19 40E
109 Lima, Indonesia 3 37S 128 4E
174 Lima, Peru 12 0S 77 0W
80 Lima, Sweden 60 55N 13 20E
166 Lima, Mont., U.S.A. 44 41N 112 38W
162 Lima, Ohio, U.S.A. 40 42N 84 5W
143 Lima, Vic., Australia 36 44S 146 10E
62 Lima R., Portugal 41 50N 8 18W
172 Limache Chile 33 0S 71 10W
59 Limanowa, Poland 49 42N 20 22E
100 Limassol, Cyprus 34 42N 33 1E
46 Limavady, N. Ire., U.K. 55 3N 6 58W
176 Limay R., Argentina 39 40S 69 45W
172 Limay Mahuida, Arg. 37 10S 66 45W
108 Limbang, Brunei 4 42N 115 6E
72 Limbara Monti, Italy 40 50N 9 0E
104 Limbdi, India 22 34N 71 51E
132 Limbe, Malawi 15 55S 35 2E
54 Limbourg, prov., Belg. 51 2N 5 25E
145 Limbri, N.S.W., Austral 31 3S 151 5E
57 Limburg, Germany 50 22N 8 4E
54 Limburg, prov., Neth. 51 20N 5 55E
81 Lime, Denmark 56 36N 8 43E
80 Limedsforsen, Sweden 60 52N 13 25E
173 Limeira, Brazil 22 35S 47 28W
76 Limenária, Greece 40 38N 24 32E
44 Limerick, Ireland 52 40N 8 38W
44 Limerick, co., Ireland 52 30N 8 50W
44 Limerick Junction, Ire. 52 30N 8 12W
160 Limestone, U.S.A. 42 2N 78 39W
81 Limfjorden, str., Den. 56 52N 9 0E
62 Limia, R., Spain 41 55N 8 8W
113 Limko, China 20 57N 109 43E
81 Limmared, Sweden 57 34N 13 20E
138 Limmen Bight, Austral. 14 40S 135 35E
77 Limni, Greece 38 43N 23 18E
76 Limni Voiviis, L., Gr. 39 35N 22 45E
175 Limoeiro do Norte, Brazil 5 5S 38 0W
161 Limoges, Canada 45 20N 75 16W
50 Limoges, France 45 50N 1 15E
76 Limnos, I., Greece 39 50N 25 5E
169 Limón, Costa Rica 10 0N 83 2W
168 Limon, Panama 9 20N 79 45W
164 Limon, U.S.A. 39 18N 103 38W
168 Limon B., Pan. Can. Zone 9 22N 79 56W
70 Limone, Piedmont, Italy 44 12N 7 32E
50 Limousin, reg., France 46 0N 1 0E
50 Limousin, Plateau de, Fr. 46 0N 1 0E
50 Limoux, France 43 4N 2 12E
133 Limpopo Dam, Mozambique 24 22S 32 55E
133 Limpopo R., Mozam. 23 15S 32 5E
35 Limpsfield, Eng., U.K. 51 15N 0 1E
131 Limuru, Kenya 1 2S 36 35E
76 Lin, Albania 41 4N 20 38E
172 Linares, Chile 35 50S 71 40W
168 Linares, Mexico 24 50N 99 40W
65 Linares, Spain 38 10N 3 40W
172 Linares, prov., Chile 36 0S 71 0W
72 Linas Mte., Italy 39 25N 8 38E
113 Lincheng, China 35 0N 117 20E
112 Lincheng, China 37 20N 114 30E
41 Lincluden, Scot.,U.K. 55 5N 3 40W
172 Lincoln, Argentina 34 55N 61 30W
39 Lincoln, & co., Eng., U.K. 53 14N 0 32W
147 Lincoln, New Zealand 43 38S 172 30E
164 Lincoln, Ill., U.S.A. 40 10N 89 20W
164 Lincoln, Kans., U.S.A. 39 6N 98 9W
155 Lincoln, Maine, U.S.A. 45 27N 68 29W
164 Lincoln, Neb., U.S.A. 40 50N 96 42W
167 Lincoln, N. Mex., U.S.A. 33 30N 105 26W
29 Lincoln Heath, England, United Kingdom 53 15N 0 25W
39 Lincoln Heights, England, United Kingdom 53 10N 0 32W
14 Lincoln Sea, Arc. Oc. 84 0N 55 0W
39 Lincoln Wolds, England, U.K. 53 20N 0 5W
163 Lincolnton, U.S.A. 35 30N 81 15W
144 Lind, Queens., Austral. 18 58S 144 30E
166 Lind, U.S.A. 47 0N 118 33W
38 Lindale, England, U.K. 54 14N 2 54W
81 Lindås, Sweden 56 38N 15 35E
79 Lindås, Norway 60 44N 5 10E
57 Lindau, Bavaria, Ger. 47 33N 9 41E
165 Linden, U.S.A. 33 0N 94 20W
81 Linderöd, Sweden 55 56N 13 47E
81 Linderödsåsen, Sweden 55 40N 13 55E

MAP

80 Lindesberg, Sweden ...59 36N 15 15E
79 Lindesnes C., Norway 57 58N 7 3E
35 Lindfield, England, U.K. ...51 2N 0 5W
131 Lindi, Tanzania ...10 0S 39 35E
131 Lindi & dist., Tanzania ... 9 58S 39 38E
130 Lindi, R., Congo ... 1 25N 25 50E
55 Lindlar, Germany ...51 2N 7 22E
135 Lindley, S. Africa ...27 52S 27 56E
62 Lindoso Portugal ...41 52N 8 11W
56 Lindow, Germany ...52 58N 12 58E
154 Lindsay, Canada ...44 22N 78 43W
167 Lindsay, California U.S.A. ...36 14N 119 6W
165 Lindsay, Okla., U.S.A. ...34 51N 97 37W
164 Lindsborg, U.S.A. ...38 35N 97 40W
39 Lindsey, dist., Eng., U.K. ...53 26N 0 20W
112 Linfen, China ...36 0N 111 30E
103 Lingakok, Tibet, China ...29 55N 87 38E
109 Lingayen, Philippines 16 8N 120 20E
109 Lingayen G., Phil. ...16 20N 120 10E
56 Lingen, Germany ...52 32N 7 21E
35 Lingfield, Eng., U.K. .51 11N 0 1W
108 Lingga Arch., Indon. . 0 10S 104 30E
80 Linghed, Sweden ...60 48N 15 55E
112 Linghsien, China ...37 20N 116 30E
164 Lingle, U.S.A. ...42 10N 104 18W
113 Lingling, China ...26 14N 111 30E
113 Linglo, China ...24 20N 105 25E
113 Lingshan, China ...22 11N 109 6E
112 Lingshih, China ...36 59N 111 43E
113 Lingshui, China ...18 27N 110 0E
113 Lingtai, China ...34 58N 107 30E
124 Linguéré, Senegal ...15 25N 15 5W
107 Linh Cam, Vietnam ...18 31N 105 31E
113 Linhai, China ...28 50N 121 8E
112 Linho, China ...40 56N 107 48E
112 Linhsien, China ...38 10N 111 10E
112 Lini, China ...35 2N 118 10E
113 Linkao, Hainan, China ...19 58N 109 35E
112 Linkian, China ...41 57N 126 59E
112 Linkiang, China ...46 2N 133 56E
36 Linkinhorne, Eng., U.K. ...50 31N 4 22W
81 Linköping, Sweden ...58 28N 15 36E
112 Linkow, China ...45 16N 130 18E
41 Linlithgow, Scot., U.K. ...55 58N 3 38W
166 Linn, Mt., U.S.A. ...40 0N 123 0W
37 Linney Hd., Wales, U.K. ...51 37N 5 4W
40 Linnhe, L., Scot., U.K. ...56 36N 5 25W
123 Linosa, I., Medit. Sea 35 51N 12 50E
113 Linping, China ...24 25N 114 32E
173 Lins, Brazil ...21 40S 49 44W
112 Linsi, China ...43 30N 118 5E
111 Linsia, China ...35 50N 103 0E
35 Linslade, England, U.K. ...51 55N 0 40W
111 Lintan, China ...34 59N 103 49E
112 Lintao, China ...35 16N 103 38E
57 Linth R., Switzerland 46 54N 9 0E
57 Linthal, Switzerland .46 54N 9 0E
112 Lintien, China ...46 8N 124 58E
155 Linton, Canada ...47 15N 72 16W
35 Linton, Cambs., Eng., U.K. ...52 6N 0 19E
162 Linton, Ind., U.S.A. ...39 0N 87 10W
164 Linton, N. Dak., U.S.A. ...46 21N 100 12W
112 Lintsing, China ...36 50N 115 45E
112 Lintung, China ...43 59N 119 8E
145 Linville, Australia ...26 50S 152 11E
160 Linwood, Canada ...43 35N 80 43W
113 Linwu, China ...25 25N 112 10E
50 Linxe, France ...43 56N 1 13W
132 Linyanti, R., *see* Chobe, R., Afr. ...18 10S 24 10E
112 Linyi, China ...37 10N 116 50E
58 Linz, Austria ...48 18N 14 18E
56 Linz, Germany ...50 33N 7 18E
73 Lioni, Italy ...40 52N 15 10E
50 Lion, G. of, France ...43 0N 4 0W
132 Lion's Den, Rhodesia .17 15S 30 5E
160 Lion's Head, Canada .44 58N 81 15W
135 Lions River, Nat., S. Afr. ...29 27S 30 8E
113 Lioyang, China ...33 30N 106 0E
86 Liozno U.S.S.R. ...55 0N 30 50E
132 Lipali, Mozambique ...15 50S 35 50E
73 Lipari, Italy ...38 26N 14 58E
73 Lipari Is., Italy ...38 40N 15 0E
87 Lipetsk, U.S.S.R. ...52 45N 39 35E
78 Lipia, Rumania ...45 7N 26 43E
60 Lipiany, Poland ...53 2N 14 58E
113 Liping, China ...26 12N 109 0E
88 Lipkany, U.S.S.R. ...48 14N 26 25E
74 Lipljan, Yugoslavia ...42 31N 21 7E
59 Lipnik, Czechoslovakia ...49 32N 17 36E
60 Lipno, Poland ...52 49N 19 15E
113 Lipo, China ...25 33N 107 45E
74 Lipova, Rumania ...46 8N 21 42E
88 Lipovets, U.S.S.R. ...49 12N 29 1E
52 Lippe, dist., Germany 51 58N 9 0E
56 Lippstadt, Germany ...51 40N 8 19E
165 Lipscomb, U.S.A. ...36 16N 110 18W
77 Lipsói, I., Greece ...37 19N 26 50E
59 Liptovsky Svaty Mikulaš, Cz. ...49 6N 19 35E
143 Liptrap C., Vic., Austral. ...38 50S 145 55E
76 Liqen-i-Maliqit, L., Alb. ...40 45N 20 45E
131 Lira, Uganda ... 2 17N 32 57E
174 Lircay, Peru ...13 0S 74 45W
72 Liri R., Italy ...41 25N 13 45E
64 Liria, Spain ...39 37N 0 35W
135 Lisala, Congo ... 2 12N 21 38E
46 Lisbellaw, N. Ire., U.K. ...54 20N 7 32W
63 Lisboa, dist., Portugal 39 0N 9 12W
63 Lisbon, Portugal ...38 42N 9 10W
164 Lisbon, N. Dak., U.S.A. ...46 30N 97 46W
161 Lisbon, N.H., U.S.A. .44 13N 71 52W
160 Lisbon, Ohio, U.S.A. .40 45N 80 42W
46 Lisburn, N. Ire., U.K. 54 30N 6 9W
14 Lisburn, C., Alas, U.S.A. ...68 50N 166 0W
44 Liscannor, & B., Ireland ...52 57N 9 24W
44 Liscarroll, Ireland ...52 15N 8 44W
72 Liscia, R., Sardinia. It. ...41 5N 9 17E
155 Liscomb, Canada ...45 2N 62 0W
44 Lisdoonvarna, Ireland 53 2N 9 18W
45 Lisduff, Ireland ...52 52N 7 43W
113 Lishui, China ...28 20N 119 48E
136 Lisianski I., Pac. Oc. .25 30N 174 0W
89 Lischansk, U.S.S.R. ...48 55N 38 30E
48 Lisieux, France ...49 10N 0 12E
36 Liskeard, England, U.K. ...50 27N 4 29W
87 Liski, U.S.S.R. ...51 3N 39 20E
50 L'Isle, Tarn, France ...43 52N 1 49E
51 L'Isle, Vaucluse, France ...43 55N 5 3E
49 L'Isle Adam, France .49 6N 2 5E
50 L'Isle Jourdain, Fr. ...43 37N 1 5E
49 L'Isle sur le Doubs, Fr. ...47 28N 6 33E
155 L'Islet, Canada ...47 4N 70 23W
44 Lismore, Ireland ...52 8N 7 58W
145 Lismore, Australia ...28 44S 153 21E
40 Lismore I., Scot., U.K. ...56 30N 5 30W
46 Lisnacree, N. Ire., U.K. ...54 4N 6 5W
46 Lisnaskea, N. Ire., U.K. ...54 15N 7 27W
35 Liss, England, U.K. ...51 3N 0 53W
44 Lissatinning Bri., Ire. 51 55N 10 1W
44 Lisselton, Ireland ...52 30N 9 34W
44 Lissycasey, Ireland ...52 44N 9 12W
79 Lista, Norway ...58 7N 6 39E
56 List, Germany ...55 1N 8 26E
15 Lister, Mt., Antarctica 78 0S 162 0E
55 Lister Res., Germany .55 51S 7 18E
145 Liston, N.S.W., Austral. ...28 35S 152 0E
154 Listowel, Canada ...44 44N 80 58W
44 Listowel, Ireland ...52 27N 9 30W
145 Listowel Dns., Austral. ...25 10S 145 12E
50 Lit-et-Mixe, France ...44 2N 1 15W
113 Litang, China ...23 6N 109 2E
109 Litang, Sab., Malaysia 5 27N 118 31E
35 Litcham, England, U.K. ...52 43N 0 49E
161 Litchfield, Conn., U.S.A. ...41 44N 73 12W
164 Litchfield, Ill., U.S.A. ...39 10N 89 40W
164 Litchfield, Minn., U.S.A. ...45 5N 95 0W
78 Liteni, Rumania ...47 32N 26 32E
126 Lith, Saudi Arabia ...20 9N 40 15E
38 Litherland, Eng., U.K. ...53 29N 3 0W
143 Lithgow, N.S.W., Austral. ...33 25S 150 8E
77 Líthinon, Ákra, Crete, Greece ...34 55N 24 44E
86 Lithuania S.S.R., U.S.S.R. ...55 30N 24 0E
71 Litija, Yugoslavia ...46 3N 14 50E
76 Litókhoron, Greece ...40 8N 22 34E
58 Litoměrice, Cz. ...50 33N 14 10E
58 Litomysl, Cz. ...49 52N 16 20E
58 Litschau, Austria ...48 58N 15 4E
163 Little Abaco I., W. Ind. ...26 50N 77 30W
99 Little Aden, S. Arabia 12 41N 45 6E
15 Little America, Antarc. ...79 0N 160 0W
107 Little Andaman I., India ...10 40N 92 15E
146 Little Barrier I., N.Z. 36 12S 175 8E
80 Little Belt, Denmark .55 8N 9 55E
166 Little Belt Mts., U.S.A. ...46 50N 111 0W
164 Little Blue R., U.S.A. 40 18N 97 45W
134 Little Bushman Land, S. Africa ...29 10S 18 10E
107 Little Coco I., Andaman Islands, India ...14 0N 93 15E
167 Little Colorado, R., U.S.A. ...36 0N 111 31W
154 Little Current, Canada ...45 55N 82 0W
154 Little Current R., Can. ...50 40N 86 0W
164 Little Falls, Minn., U.S.A. ...45 58N 94 19W
161 Little Falls, N.Y., U.S.A. ...43 3N 74 50W
157 Lit. Grand Rapids, Can. ...52 0N 95 29W
166 Lit. Humboldt, R., U.S.A. ...41 20N 117 27W
169 Lit. Inagua I., Bahamas ...21 40N 73 50W
134 Little Karoo, S. Africa ...33 45S 21 30E
112 Little Khingan Mts., China ...49 0N 127 0E
167 Little Lake, U.S.A. ...35 58N 117 58W
108 Little Laut Is., Indon. 4 45S 115 40E
154 Little Longlac, Canada ...49 42N 86 58W
164 Little Marais, U.S.A. .47 24N 91 8W
155 Little Mecatiná I., Can. ...50 30N 59 25W
42 Little Minch, Scotland 57 35N 6 45W
155 Lit. Miquelon I., N. Amer. ...46 45N 56 25W
164 Lit. Missouri R., U.S.A.46 40N 103 50W
134 Little Namaqualand, C. Prov., S. Afr. ...29 0S 17 9E
37 Little Ormes Hd., Wales, United Kingdom ...53 19N 3 47W
108 Lit. Paternoster Is., Indonesia ... 2 30S 117 20E
104 Little Rann of Kutch, India ...23 25N 71 25E
165 Little Red R., U.S.A. 35 40N 92 15W
147 Little River, N.Z. ...43 45S 172 49E
165 Little Rock, U.S.A. ...34 41N 92 10W
131 Little Ruaha R., Tanz. ... 7 50S 35 30E
162 Little Sable Pt., U.S.A. ...43 40N 86 32W
129 Little Scarcies R., Sierra Leone ... 9 30N 12 25W
164 Little Sioux R., U.S.A. ...42 20N 95 55W
166 Little Snake. R., U.S.A. ...40 45N 108 15W
160 Little Valley, U.S.A. .42 15N 78 48W
162 Little Wabash, R., U.S.A. ...38 40N 88 20W
35 Little Walsingham, England, U.K. ...52 53N 0 51E
154 Little Whale R., Can. 55 50N 75 0W
38 Littleborough, Eng., U.K. ...53 38N 2 8W
165 Littlefield, U.S.A. ...33 57N 102 17W
164 Littlefork, U.S.A. ...48 24N 93 35W
35 Littlehampton, England, U.K. ...50 48N 0 32W
43 Littlemill, Scot., U.K. 57 31N 3 49W
35 Littleport Eng., U.K. 52 27N 0 18E
35 Littlestone-on-Sea, England, U.K. ...50 59N 0 59E
161 Littleton, U.S.A. ...44 19N 71 47W
45 Littletown, Ireland ...52 39N 7 44W
132 Litunde, Mozambique 13 19S 35 48E
113 Liuan, China ...31 50N 116 35E
113 Liucheng. China ...24 5N 109 3E
113 Liuchow, China ...24 10N 109 10E
131 Liuli, Tanzania ...11 3S 34 38E
112 Liupan Shan, China ...35 40N 106 10E
113 Liupa, China ...33 40N 107 0E
132 Liuwa Plain, Zambia .14 20S 22 30E
78 Livada, Rumania ...47 52N 23 5E
76 Livadherón. Greece ...40 2N 21 57E
48 Livarot, France ...49 0N 0 9E
163 Live Oak, U.S.A. ...30 17N 83 0W
165 Livermore, Mt., U.S.A. ...30 45N 104 8W
155 Liverpool, N.S. Can. ..44 5N 64 41W
143 Liverpool, Australia ...33 55S 150 52E
38 Liverpool, Eng., United Kingdom ...53 25N 3 0W
14 Liverpool Bay, Canada ...70 0N 128 0W
145 Liverpool Plains, N.S.W., Australia ...31 15S 150 0E
143 Liverpool Ra., Australia ...31 42S 150 10E
168 Livingston, Guatemala ...15 50N 88 50W
51 Livingston, Scot., U.K. ...55 52N 3 33W
166 Livingston, U.S.A. ...45 40N 110 40W
165 Livingstone, U.S.A. ...30 44N 94 54W
130 Livingstone Falls, Congo ... 5 25S 13 35E
15 Livingstone I., Antarc. ...63 0S 60 15W
132 Livingstone Memorial, Zambia ...12 20S 30 18E
147 Livingstone Mts., N.Z. 45 15S 168 9E
131 Livingstone Mts., Tanz. ... 9 40S 34 20E
132 Livingstonia, Malawi .10 38S 34 5E
74 Livno, Yugoslavia ...43 50N 17 0E
87 Livny, U.S.S.R. ...52 30N 37 30E
70 Livorno Italy ...43 32N 10 18E
173 Livramento, Brazil ...30 55S 55 30W
51 Livron, France ...44 46N 4 51E
44 Lixnaw, Ireland ...52 24N 9 37W
77 Lixóurion, Greece ...38 14N 20 24E
36 Lizard, England, U.K. 49 58N 5 10W
44 Lizard I., Australia ...14 42S 145 30E
36 Lizard Pt., Eng., U.K. ...49 57N 5 11W
36 Lizard Town. Eng., U.K. ...49 58N 5 12W
73 Lizzano, Italy ...40 23N 17 25E
74 Lješnica, Yugoslavia .44 39N 19 20E
74 Ljig, Yugoslavia ...44 13N 20 18E
71 Ljubija, Yugoslavia ...44 55N 16 35E
74 Ljubinje, Yugoslavia .42 58N 18 5E
71 Ljubliana, Yugoslavia 46 4N 14 33E
71 Ljubno, Yugoslavia ...46 25N 14 46E
74 Ljuboten, Mt., Yugoslavia ...42 12N 21 8E
74 Ljubovija, Yugoslavia 44 11N 19 22E
74 Ljubuški, Yugoslavia .43 12N 17 34E
81 Ljung, Sweden ...58 1N 13 3E
80 Ljungan R., Sweden .62 40N 13 30E
80 Ljungaverk, Sweden .62 30N 16 5E
81 Ljungby, Sweden ...56 49N 13 55E
80 Ljungris. Sweden ...62 56N 12 44E
80 Ljusdal, Sweden ...61 46N 16 3E
81 Ljusfors, Sweden ...58 36N 15 52E
80 Ljusnan R. Sweden ...62 10N 14 0E
80 Ljusne, Sweden ...61 15N 17 14E
71 Ljutomer Yugoslavia 46 31N 16 11E
37 Lladogo, England, U.K. ...51 43N 2 42W
64 Llagostera, Spain ...41 50N 2 54E
37 Llanaber, Wales, U.K. 52 45N 4 5W
37 Llanaelhaiarn, Wales, U.K. ...52 59N 4 24W
37 Llanafan-fawr, Wales, U.K. ...52 12N 3 29W
37 Llanarmon, Wales, U.K. ...53 6N 3 13W
37 Llanarmon Dyffryn Ceiriog, Wales, U.K. ...52 53N 3 15W
37 Llanarth, Wales, U.K. 52 12N 4 19W
37 Llanarthney, Wales, U.K. ...51 51N 4 9W
37 Llanbedr, Wales, U.K. ...52 40N 4 7W
37 Llanbedrog, Wales, U.K. ...52 52N 4 29W
37 Llanberis, Wales, U.K. ...53 7N 4 7W
37 Llanbister, Wales, U.K. ...52 22N 3 19W
43 Llanbryd, Scot., U.K. 57 38N 3 12W
37 Llanbrynmair, Wales, United Kingdom ...52 36N 3 19W
37 Llandaff, Wales, U.K. 51 29N 3 13W
37 Llanddewi-Brefi, Wales, United Kingdom ...52 11N 3 57W
37 Llandilo, Wales, U.K. 51 54N 4 0W
37 Llandovery, Wales, U.K. ...51 59N 3 49W
37 Llandrillo, Wales, U.K. ...52 56N 3 27W
37 Llandrindod Wells. Wales, U.K. ...52 15N 3 23W
37 Llandudno, Wales, U.K. ...53 19N 3 51W
37 Llandygwydd, Wales, United Kingdom ...52 3N 4 33W
37 Llandyrnog, Wales, U.K. ...53 10N 3 19W
37 Llandyssilio, Wales, United Kingdom ...51 51N 4 45W
37 Llandyssul Wales, U.K. ...52 3N 4 20W
37 Llanelltyd, Wales, U.K. ...52 45N 3 54W
37 Llanelli (Llanelly), Wales, U.K. ...51 41N 4 11W
37 Llanenddwyn, Wales, United Kingdom ...52 48N 4 7W
37 Llanerchymedd, Wales, United Kingdom ...53 20N 4 22W
62 Llanes Spain ...43 25N 4 50W
37 Llanfaelog, Wales, U.K. ...53 13N 4 29W
37 Llanfair-ar-y-bryn, Wales, U.K. ...52 4N 3 43W
37 Llanfair Caereinion, Wales, U.K. ...52 39N 3 20W
37 Llanfair Talhaiarn, Wales, U.K. ...53 13N 3 37W
37 Llanfairfechan, Wales, United Kingdom ...53 15N 3 58W
37 Llanfechell, Wales, U.K. ...52 23N 4 25W
37 Llanfyllin, Wales, U.K. ...52 47N 3 17W
37 Llangadog, Wales, U.K. ...51 56N 3 53W
37 Llangammarch, Wales, United Kingdom ...52 7N 3 33W
37 Llangefni, Wales, U.K. ...53 15N 4 20W
37 Llangelynin, Wales, U.K. ...52 39N 4 7W
37 Llangennech, Wales, United Kingdom ...51 41N 4 10W
37 Llangerniew, Wales, United Kingdom ...53 12N 3 41W
37 Llangollen, Wales, U.K. ...52 58N 3 10W
37 Llangranog, Wales, U.K. ...52 11N 4 29W
37 Llangurig. Wales, U.K. ...52 25N 3 36W
37 Llangynog, Wales, U.K. ...52 50N 3 24W
37 Llanharan, Wales, U.K. ...51 32N 3 28W
37 Llanidloes, Wales, U.K. ...52 28N 3 31W
37 Llanilar, Wales, U.K. 52 22N 4 2W
37 Llannor, Wales. U.K. 52 55N 4 25W
37 Llanllyfni, Wales, U.K. ...53 2N 4 18W
165 Llano R., U.S.A. ...30 50N 99 0W
158 Llano Estacado (Staked Plains), U.S.A. ...34 0N 103 0W
37 Llanon, Wales, U.K. .52 17N 4 9W
174 Llanos, reg., S. America ... 3 25N 71 35W
37 Llanpumpsaint, Wales, United Kingdom ...51 56N 4 19W
37 Llanrhaiadr-ym Mochnant, Wales, U.K. ...52 50N 3 19W
37 Llanrhidian, Wales, U.K. ...51 36N 4 11W
37 Llanrhystyd, Wales, United Kingdom ...52 19N 4 9W
37 Llanrian, Wales, U.K. 51 56N 5 10W
37 Llanrwst. Wales U.K. 53 8N 3 49W
37 Llansannan, Wales, United Kingdom ...53 10N 3 35W
37 Llansawel, Wales, U.K. ...52 0N 4 1W
34 Llanstephan, Wales, United Kingdom ...51 46N 4 24W
37 Llanthony, Eng., U.K. ...51 57N 3 2W
37 Llantrisant, Wales, U.K. ...51 33N 32 2W
37 Llantwit-Major, Wales, United Kingdom ...51 24N 3 29W
37 Llanuwchllyn, Wales, United Kingdom ...52 52N 3 41W
37 Llanvihangel Crucorney, Wales, U.K. ...51 53N 2 58W
37 Llanwenog, Wales U.K. ...52 6N 4 11W
37 Llanwrda, Wales, U.K. ...51 58N 3 52W
37 Llanwrtyd Wells, Wales. United Kingdom ...52 6N 3 39W
37 Llanybyther, Wales, United Kingdom ...52 4N 4 10W
37 Llanymynech, Eng. U.K. ...52 48N 3 6W
37 Llanystymdwy, Wales, United Kingdom ...52 56N 4 17W
112 Llaoyang, China ...41 14N 123 6E
37 Llechryd, Wales, U.K. 52 5N 4 37W
63 Llerena, Spain ...38 17N 6 0W
37 Llethr Mt., Wales, U.K. ...52 47N 3 58W
37 Lleyn Peninsula, Wales, United Kingdom ...52 55N 4 35W
64 Lloret de Mar, Spain .41 41N 2 53E
105 Lloyd Barrage, W. Pak. ...27 46N 68 50E
64 Lluchmayor, Majorca, Spain ...39 29N 2 53E
144 Lloyd B., Australia ...12 45S 143 27E
157 Lloydminster, Canada 53 20N 110 0W
172 Llullaillaco Mt., Chile 24 30S 68 30W
37 Llwyngwril, Wales, U.K. ...52 41N 4 6W
37 Llyswen, Wales, U.K. 52 2N 3 18W
113 Lo Ho, R., Honan, China ...34 15N 111 10E
112 Lo Ho., R., Shensi, China ...36 0N 109 25E
167 Loa, U.S.A. ...38 18N 111 46W
172 Loa R., Chile ...21 30S 70 0W
130 Loange R., Congo ... 5 30S 20 10E
130 Loango, Congo ... 2 0S 28 55E
41 Loanhead, Scot., U.K. 55 53N 3 10W
70 Loano, Italy ...44 8N 8 14E
40 Loans, Scotland, U.K. 55 33N 4 39W
133 Lobatsi, Botswana ...25 12S 25 40E
130 Lobaye R. Central African Republic ... 4 30N 17 0E
55 Lobberich, Germany .51 19N 6 21E
56 Lobenstein, Germany .50 25N 11 39E
172 Loberia, Argentina ...38 10S 58 40W
60 Lobez, Poland ...53 38N 15 39E
130 Lobito, Angola ...12 18S 13 35E
174 Lobitos, Peru ... 4 20S 81 10W
80 Lobonäs Sweden ...61 33N 15 20E
172 Lobos, Argentina ...35 2S 59 0W
170 Lobos Is., Peru ... 6 35S 80 45W
155 Lobstick L., Canada ...54 0N 65 12W
107 Loc Binh, Vietnam ...21 46N 106 54E
107 Loc Ninh, Vietnam ...11 50N 106 34E
57 Locarno, Switzerland .46 10N 8 47E
42 Loch B., Scotland, U.K. ...57 30N 6 35W
42 Lochaber, dist., Scot. U.K. ...56 55N 5 0W
42 Lochailort, Scot., U.K. ...56 53N 5 40W
40 Lochaline, Scot., U.K. 56 32N 5 47W
40 Lochans, Scot., U.K. .54 52N 5 1W
42 Lochboisdale, Scotland, U.K. ...57 10N 7 20W
40 Lochbuie, Scot., U.K. 56 21N 5 52W
42 Lochcarron, Scot., U.K. ...57 25N 5 30W
40 Lochdonhead, Scotland, United Kingdom ...56 27N 5 40W
40 Lochearnhead, Scot., United Kingdom ...56 24N 4 19W
54 Lochem, Netherlands .52 9N 6 26E
48 Loches, France ...47 7N 1 0E
41 Lochgelly, Scot. U.K. 56 7N 3 18W
40 Lochgilphead, Scot., U.K. ...56 2N 5 37W
40 Lochgoilhead, Scot., U.K. ...56 10N 4 54W
42 Lochinver, Scot., U.K. ...58 9N 5 15W
43 Lochlaggan Hotel, Scotland, U.K. ...56 59N 4 25W
41 Lochmaben, Scot., U.K. ...55 8N 3 27W
42 Lochmaddy, Scot., U.K. ...57 36N 7 10W

MAP
144 Lochnagar, Queensland, Australia ...24 34S 144 52E
43 Lochnagar, Mt., Scot., U.K. ...56 57N 3 14W
40 Lochranza, Scot., U.K. ...55 42N 5 18W
112 Lochwan, China ...35 59N 109 30E
40 Lochwinnoch, Scotland, United Kingdom ...55 47N 4 39W
42 Lochy, R., Scot., U.K. ...56 52N 5 3W
43 Lochy, L., Scot., U.K. 56 58N 4 55W
160 Lock Haven, U.S.A. ...41 7N 77 31W
155 Lockeport, Canada ...43 47N 65 4W
41 Lockerbie, Scot., U.K. 55 7N 3 21W
143 Lockhart, Australia ...35 14S 146 40E
165 Lockhart, U.S.A. ...29 55N 97 40W
160 Lockport, U.S.A. ...43 12N 78 42W
48 Locminé, France ...47 54N 2 51W
73 Locri, Italy ...38 14N 16 14E
48 Locronan, France ...48 7N 4 15W
48 Loctudy, France ...47 50N 4 12W
79 Lodalskåpa, Mt., Nor. 61 47N 7 13E
35 Loddon, England, U.K. ...52 32N 1 29E
50 Lodève, France ...43 44N 3 19E
166 Lodge Grass, U.S.A. ...45 21N 107 27W
164 Lodgepole, U.S.A. ...41 12N 102 40W
164 Lodgepole Cr., U.S.A. 41 20N 104 30W
104 Lodhran, West Pakistan ...29 32N 71 30E
70 Lodi, Italy ...45 19N 9 30E
166 Lodi, U.S.A. ...38 12N 121 16W
130 Lodja, Congo ... 3 30S 23 23E
109 Lodji, Indonesia ... 1 38S 127 28E
64 Lodosa, Spain ...42 25N 2 4W
81 Lödöse, Sweden ...58 5N 12 10E
131 Lodwar, Kenya ... 3 10N 35 40E
60 Łódź, Poland ...51 45N 19 27E
107 Loei, Thailand ...17 29N 101 35E
134 Loeriesfontein, S. Africa ...30 56S 19 26E
58 Lofer, Austria ...47 35N 12 41E
82 Lofoten Is., Norway ...68 20N 14 0E
80 Lofsån R., Sweden ...62 5N 13 0E
80 Lofsdalen, Sweden ...62 10N 13 20E
81 Loftahammar, Sweden 57 54N 16 50E
38 Lofthouse, Eng., U.K. 54 10N 1 50W
39 Loftus, England, U.K. 54 33N 0 52W
142 Lofty Ra., W. Austral. ...24 15S 119 30E
132 Lofu R., Zambia ... 9 15S 30 30E
133 Logageng, S. Africa ...25 58S 24 41E
164 Logan, Kan., U.S.A. .39 23N 99 35W
162 Logan, Ohio, U.S.A. ...39 35N 82 22W
166 Logan, Utah, U.S.A. .41 45N 111 50W
162 Logan, W. Va., U.S.A. ...31 51N 81 59W
152 Logan Mt., Canada ...60 40N 140 0W
162 Logansport, Ind., U.S.A. ...40 40N 86 20W
165 Logansport, La., U.S.A. ...31 58N 93 58W
80 Lögdö, Sweden ...62 34N 17 25E
127 Logo, Sudan ... 5 20N 30 18E
127 Logo Dergo, Sudan ... 6 10N 29 18E
64 Logrono, Spain ...42 28N 2 32W
64 Logrono, prov., Spain 42 28N 2 27W
63 Logrosan, Spain ...39 20N 5 32W
81 Løgstør, Denmark ...56 58N 9 14E
105 Lohardaga, India ...23 27N 84 45E
134 Lohatlha, S. Africa ...28 1S 23 2E
99 Loheia, Yemen ...15 45N 42 40E
83 Lohja, Finland ...60 12N 24 0E
113 Loho, China ...33 42N 114 9E
57 Lohr, Germany ...50 0N 9 35E
131 Loigorien, Kenya ... 1 15S 34 55E
103 Loikaw, Burma ...19 40N 97 17E
83 Loimaa, Finland ...60 50N 23 5E
49 Loire-et-Cher, dépt., Fr. ...47 40N 1 20E
51 Loire, dépt., France ...45 40N 4 5E
48 Loire R., France ...47 25N 0 20W
48 Loire Atlantiqué, dépt., France ...47 25N 1 40W
49 Loiret, dépt., France .47 58N 2 10E
56 Loitz, Germany ...53 58N 13 8E
131 Loiyangalani, Kenya . 2 47N 36 43E
174 Loja, Ecuador ... 3 59S 79 16W
63 Loja, Spain ...37 10N 4 10W
130 Loje R., Angola ... 7 20S 14 30E
130 Loka, Congo ... 0 12N 18 2E
127 Loka, Sudan ... 4 13N 31 0E
130 Lokandu, Congo ... 2 30S 25 45E
79 Lokén, Norway ...59 50N 11 25E
54 Lokeren, Belgium ...51 6N 3 59E
86 Lokhvitsa, U.S.S.R. ...50 25N 33 18E
131 Lokichar, Kenya ... 2 23N 35 40E
131 Lokichoko, Kenya ... 4 19N 34 13E
113 Lokchong, China ...25 15N 113 0E
131 Lokitaung, Kenya ... 4 12N 35 48E
82 Loka Res., Finland .68 0N 27 50E
81 Løkken, Denmark ...57 22N 9 41E
79 Løkken, Norway ...63 8N 9 45E
86 Loknya, U.S.S.R. ...56 49N 30 4E
127 Lokobo, Sudan ... 4 20N 30 30E
125 Lokoja, Nigeria ... 7 47N 6 45E
130 Lokolama, Congo ... 2 35S 19 50E
130 Lokolo R., Congo ... 1 30S 20 0E
113 Loktung, China ...18 41N 109 5E
127 Lokuti, Sudan ... 4 21N 33 15E
131 Lokwakangolo, Kenya 3 32N 35 54E
113 Lokwei, China ...19 12N 110 30E
127 Lol, Sudan ... 5 28N 29 36E
127 Lol R., Sudan ... 9 0N 28 10E
124 Lola, Guinea ... 7 52N 8 29W
127 Lolibai Mts., Sudan ... 3 50N 33 50E
127 Lolimi, Sudan ... 4 35N 34 0E
MAP
81 Lolland, I., Denmark .54 45N 11 30E
56 Lollar, Germany ...50 39N 8 43E
166 Lolo U.S.A. ...46 50N 114 8W
125 Lolodorf, Cameroon ... 3 16N 10 49E
108 Lolowau, Indonesia ... 0 50N 97 33E
103 Lolungchung, China ...30 43N 96 7E
131 Lolwa, Congo ... 1 28N 29 30E
75 Lom, Bulgaria ...43 48N 23 20E
74 Lom, R., Bulgaria ...43 45N 23 7E
166 Loma, U.S.A. ...47 59N 110 29W
130 Lomami, R., Congo ... 1 0S 24 40E
174 Lomas, Peru ...15 25S 74 55W
172 Lomas de Zomora, Arg. ...34 45S 58 25W
166 Lombard, U.S.A. ...46 7N 111 28W
70 Lombardia, reg., Italy 45 35N 9 45E
44 Lombardstown, Ireland ...52 7N 8 48W
70 Lombardy, reg., Italy 45 35N 9 45E
130 Lombe, Angola ... 9 27S 16 13E
50 Lombez, France ...43 29N 0 55E
130 Lombia, Congo ... 0 15S 15 58E
109 Lomblen I., Indonesia 8 30S 123 32E
108 Lombok I., Indonesia 8 35S 116 20E
125 Lomé, Togoland ... 6 9N 1 20E
130 Lomela, Congo ... 2 5S 23 52E
130 Lomela R., Congo ... 1 30S 22 50E
70 Lomello, Italy ...45 11N 8 46E
165 Lometa, U.S.A. ...31 15N 98 25W
128 Lomie, Cameroon ... 3 13N 13 38E
127 Loming, Sudan ... 4 27N 33 40W
81 Lomma, Sweden ...55 43N 13 6E
55 Lommel, Belgium ...51 14N 5 19E
156 Lomond, Canada ...50 24N 112 36W
40 Lomond, L., Scot., U.K. ...56 8N 4 38W
145 Lomond, Mt., Australia ...30 0S 151 45E
86 Lomonosov, U.S.S.R. ..55 37N 32 22E
86 Lomonsovo, U.S.S.R. ..55 35N 32 25E
190 Lompobatang, Mt., Indon. ... 5 24S 119 56E
167 Lompoc, U.S.A. ...34 41N 120 32W
79 Lomseggi, Mt., Norway ...61 50N 8 20E
79 Lomshurrungen, Mt., Norway ...61 57N 8 27E
60 Lomza, Poland ...53 10N 22 2E
106 Lonavla, India ...18 46N 73 29E
176 Loncoche, Chile ...39 20S 72 50W
106 Londa, India ...15 30N 74 30E
39 Londesborough, England, United Kingdom ...53 53N 0 40W
131 Londiani, Kenya ... 0 10S 35 33E
48 Londinières, France ...49 50N 1 25E
154 London, Canada ...43 0N 81 15W
35 London, England, U.K. ...51 30N 0 5W
162 London, Ky., U.S.A. .37 11N 84 5W
162 London, Ohio, U.S.A. 39 54N 83 28W
35 London & co., Eng., U.K. ...51 30N 0 5W
46 Londonderry, & co., N. Ireland, U.K. ...55 0N 7 20W
138 Londonderry C., W. Australia ...13 50S 127 15E
176 Londonderry I., Chile 55 0S 71 0W
39 Londonthorpe, England, United Kingdom ...52 57N 0 35W
173 Londrina, Brazil ...23 0S 51 10W
167 Lone Pine, U.S.A. ...36 35N 118 2W
132 Lonely, Rhodesia ...19 30S 28 49E
167 Long Beach, Calif., U.S.A. ...33 46N 118 12W
161 Long Beach, N.Y., U.S.A. ...40 35N 73 40W
166 Long Beach, Wash., U.S.A. ...46 20N 124 1W
39 Long Bennington, England, U.K. ...52 59N 0 45W
161 Long Branch, U.S.A. .40 19N 74 0W
34 Long Buckby, England, United Kingdom ...52 18N 1 5W
35 Long Clawson, England, U.K. ...52 51N 0 56W
34 Long Compton, England, U.K. ...51 59N 1 35W
35 Long Crendon, England, United Kingdom ...51 47N 1 0W
39 Long Eaton, Eng., U.K. ...52 54N 1 16W
144 Long I., Australia ...22 8S 149 53E
169 Long I., Bahamas ...23 20N 75 10W
154 Long I., Canada ...44 23N 66 19W
44 Long I., Ireland ...51 30N 9 35W
144 Long I., New Guinea . 5 25S 147 0E
161 Long I., N.Y., U.S.A. 40 50N 73 20W
161 Long I. Sd., U.S.A. ...41 10N 73 0W
154 Long L., Ont., Canada 49 30N 86 50W
40 Long, L., Dunbarton, Scotland, U.K. ...56 4N 4 50W
42 Long, L., Ross and Cromarty, Scot., U.K. ...57 17N 5 30W
161 Long L., N.Y., U.S.A. 43 57N 74 25W
37 Long Mt., Wales, U.K. ...52 38N 3 7W
34 Long Itchington, England, U.K. ...52 16N 1 24W
38 Long Marton, Eng. UK. ...54 38N 2 31W
35 Long Melford, Eng., U.K. ...52 5N 0 44E
34 Long Mynd, The, hill, Eng., U.K. ...52 35N 2 50W
164 Long Pine, U.S.A. ...43 33N 99 50W
MAP
144 Long Pocket, Australia ...18 30S 146 0E
38 Long Preston, Eng., U.K. ...54 0N 2 16W
160 Long Pt. Ont., Canada ...42 35N 80 10W
147 Long Pt., N.Z. ...46 34S 169 36E
160 Long Pt. Bay, Canada 42 40N 80 20W
155 Long Ra., Canada ...49 30N 57 30W
14 Long Str., U.S.S.R. ...70 0N 175 0E
35 Long Stratton, England, U.K. ...52 30N 1 13E
35 Long Sutton, Eng. UK. ...57 47N 0 9E
107 Long Xuyen, S. Vietnam ...10 19N 105 28E
77 Longá, Greece ...36 53N 21 55E
42 Longa I., Scot., U.K. .57 45N 5 50W
130 Longa, R., Angola ...10 15S 14 0E
71 Longarone, Italy ...46 15N 12 18E
39 Longbenton, Eng., U.K. ...55 2N 1 35W
146 Longburn, N.Z. ...40 23S 175 35E
103 Longdam, China ...28 12N 98 16E
49 Longeau, France ...47 47N 5 20E
15 Longford, Tas., Austral. ...41 32S 147 3E
34 Longford, Eng., U.K. 51 53N 2 14W
46 Longford, Ireland ...53 43N 7 50W
46 Longford, co., Ireland 53 42N 7 45W
41 Longforgan, Scot., U.K. ...56 28N 3 8W
41 Longframlington, England, U.K. ...55 18N 1 47W
135 Long Hope, S. Africa .32 47S 25 49E
39 Longhorsley, Eng., U.K. ...55 15N 1 46W
39 Longhoughton, England, U.K. ...55 26N 1 38W
131 Longido, Tanzania ... 2 43S 36 35E
108 Longiram, Indonesia . 0 5S 115 45E
154 Longlac, Canada ...49 45N 86 25W
103 Longling, China ...24 42N 98 58E
164 Longmont, U.S.A. ...40 10N 105 4W
108 Longnawan, Indonesia 21 50N 114 55E
38 Longnor, England, U.K. ...53 11N 1 52W
132 Longo, Zambia ...17 35S 27 15E
73 Longobucco, Italy ...39 27N 16 37E
121 Longone, R., Cameroon ...10 0N 15 40E
144 Longreach, Australia .23 28S 144 14E
38 Longridge, Eng., U.K. ...53 50N 2 37W
166 Long's Peak, U.S.A. ...40 20N 105 50W
36 Longships, Eng., U.K. 50 5N 5 45W
43 Longside, Scot., U.K. 57 30N 1 57W
144 Longton, Australia ...21 0S 145 55E
38 Longton, Lancs., England, U.K. ...53 43N 2 48W
38 Longton, Stafford, England, U.K. ...53 0N 2 8W
38 Longtown, Cumb., England, U.K. ...55 1N 2 59W
48 Longué, France ...47 22N 0 8W
48 Longueau, France ...49 52N 2 22E
161 Longueuil, Canada ...45 32N 73 28W
49 Longuyon, France ...49 27N 5 35E
156 Longview, Canada ...50 32N 114 10W
165 Longview, Tex., U.S.A. ...32 30N 94 45W
166 Longview, Wash., U.S.A. ...46 9N 122 58W
49 Longwy, France ...49 30N 5 45E
71 Lonigo, Italy ...45 23N 11 22E
113 Loning, China ...34 28N 111 42E
56 Löningen, Germany ...54 43N 7 44E
71 Lonja, R., Yugoslavia 45 30N 16 40E
105 Lonkor Tso, Tibet, China ...32 40N 83 15E
165 Lonoke, U.S.A. ...34 48N 91 57W
50 Lonouaille, France ...46 30N 1 35E
49 Lons-le-Saunier, France ...46 40N 5 31E
82 Lönsdal, Norway ...66 46N 15 26E
81 Lönstrup, Denmark ...57 29N 9 47E
36 Looe, E. & W., England, U.K. ...50 21N 4 26W
109 Looc, Philippines ...12 20N 112 5E
154 Lookout C., Canada ...55 20N 84 30W
163 Lookout C., U.S.A. ...34 30N 76 30W
157 Loomis, Canada ...49 15N 108 45W
157 Loon L., Canada ...44 50N 77 15W
142 Loongana, W. Australia ...30 52S 127 5E
55 Loop-op-Zand, Neth. 51 38N 5 5E
44 Loop Hd., Ireland ...52 34N 9 55W
124 Loos Is., Guinea ... 9 30N 13 50E
111 Lop Nor, China ...40 20N 90 10E
74 Lopare, Yugoslavia ...44 39N 18 46E
89 Lopatin, U.S.S.R. ...43 50N 47 35E
127 Lopaye, Sudan ... 6 37N 33 40E
112 Lopei, China ...47 40N 131 12E
63 Lopera, Spain ...37 56N 4 14W
128 Lopez C., Gabon ... 0 47S 8 40E
127 Lopodi. Sudan ... 5 5N 33 15E
130 Lopori R., Congo ... 1 35N 22 0E
82 Lopphavet I., Norway ...70 12N 22 30E
63 Lora del Rio, Spain ...37 39N 5 33W
101 Lora Rud, R., Afghan. ...32 0N 67 15E
160 Lorain, U.S.A. ...41 20N 82 5W
104 Loralai, West Pakistan ...30 29N 68 30E
65 Lorca, Spain ...37 41N 1 42W
136 Lord Howe I., Pac. Oc. ...31 33S 159 6E
167 Lordsburg, U.S.A. ...32 15N 108 45W
173 Lorena, Brazil ...23 5S 45 10W
MAP
144 Lorengau, New Guinea ... 2 10S 147 23E
109 Lorentz, R., Indonesia 5 20S 138 0E
175 Loreto, Brazil ... 7 5S 45 30W
71 Loreto, Italy ...43 26N 13 36E
17 Loreto Aprutina, Italy ...42 24N 13 59E
51 Lorgues, France ...43 28N 6 22E
131 Lorian Swamp, Kenya 1 20N 40 0E
48 Lorient, France ...47 45N 3 23W
143 Lorne, Vic., Australia 38 33S 143 59E
40 Lorne, dist., Scot., U.K. ...56 26N 5 10W
40 Lorne, Firth of, Scotland, U.K. ...56 20N 5 40W
57 Lörrach, Germany ...47 36N 7 38E
49 Lorraine, dist., France 49 0N 6 0E
154 Lorrainville, Canada .47 21N 79 23W
124 Los Is., Guinea ... 9 30N 13 50W
167 Los Alamos, U.S.A. ...35 57N 106 17W
172 Los Andes, Chile ...32 50S 70 40W
172 Los Angeles, Chile ...37 28S 72 23W
167 Los Angeles, U.S.A. ...34 0N 118 10W
167 Los Angeles Aqueduct, U.S.A. ...35 0N 118 20W
63 Los Barrios, Spain ...36 11N 5 30W
167 Los Banos, U.S.A. ...37 8N 120 56W
172 Los Blancos, Argentina ...23 45S 62 30W
167 Los Gatos, U.S.A. ...37 15N 121 59W
168 Los Lamentos, Mexico 30 36N 105 50W
172 Los Loras, Chile ...27 54S 70 6W
167 Los Lunas, U.S.A. ...34 55N 106 47W
168 Los Mochis, Mexico ...25 45N 109 5W
167 Los Olivos, U.S.A. ...34 43N 120 7W
65 Los Muertos, Punta de, Spain ...36 57N 1 54W
63 Los Palacios y Villafranca, Spain ...37 10N 5 55W
63 Los Santos de Maimona, Spain ...38 27N 6 22W
172 Los Sauces, Chile ...38 0S 72 50W
174 Los Testigos Is., Ven. 11 23N 63 6W
172 Los Vilos, Chile ...32 0S 71 30W
63 Los Yebeñes, Spain ...39 36N 3 55W
132 Losefe, Mozambique ...13 59S 34 48E
113 Loshing, China ...24 45N 108 58E
91 Loshkalakh, U.S.S.R. 62 45N 147 20E
71 Lošinj I, Yugoslavia .44 55N 14 45E
43 Lossiemouth, Scot., U.K. ...57 43N 3 17W
36 Lostwithiel, Eng., U.K. ...50 24N 4 41W
144 Losuia, Terr. of Papua ... 8 25S 146 3E
50 Lot, dépt., France ...44 39N 1 40E
50 Lot R., France ...44 27N 0 38E
172 Lota, Chile ...37 5S 73 10W
127 Lotagipi Swamp, Sudan ... 4 55N 35 0E
50 Lot-et-Garonne, dépt., France ...44 22N 0 30E
79 Løten, Norway ...60 51N 11 21E
133 Lothair, Trans., S. Afr. ...26 26S 30 27E
41 Lothian, Co., Scot. U.K. ...55 55N 3 35W
49 Lothiers, France ...46 42N 1 33E
133 Lothlakane, S. Africa .26 5S 25 38E
132 Lothlekane, Botswana 21 25S 25 35E
43 Lothmore, Scot., U.K. 58 4N 3 45W
112 Loting, Hopei, China .39 28N 119 0E
113 Loting, Kwangtung, China ...22 50N 111 25E
57 Lötschberg Tun, Switz. ...46 25N 7 53E
128 Loto, Congo ...28 50S 22 28E
80 Lottefors, Sweden ...61 25N 16 27E
133 Loubad, Trans., S. Afr. ...24 33S 28 13E
48 Loudéac, France ...48 11N 2 47W
130 Loudima, Congo (Fr.) 4 6S 13 5E
163 Loudon, U.S.A. ...35 41N 84 22W
160 Loudonville, U.S.A. ...40 40N 82 15W
48 Loudun, France ...47 0N 0 5E
48 Loue R., France ...47 4N 6 10E
124 Louga, Senegal ...15 45N 16 5W
34 Loughborough, Eng., U.K. ...52 46N 1 11W
46 Loughbrickland, N. Ireland, U.K. ...54 19N 6 19W
46 Loughglynn, Ireland .53 50N 8 35W
44 Loughmore, Ireland ...52 45N 7 50W
37 Loughor, Wales, U.K. 51 39N 4 5W
44 Loughrea, Ire. ...53 11N 8 33W
46 Loughros More, B., Ire. ...54 48N 8 30W
51 Louhans, France ...46 38N 5 12E
122 Louis Gentil, Morocco 32 16N 8 31W
133 Louis Trichardt, S. Afr. ...23 0S 29 55E
162 Louisa, U.S.A. ...38 5N 82 40W
155 Louisbourg, Canada ...45 55N 60 0W
44 Louisburgh, Ireland ...53 46N 9 49W
156 Louise I., Canada ...52 55N 131 40W
154 Louiseville, Canada ...46 20N 73 0W
144 Louisiade Arch., Papua ...10 50S 152 30E
164 Louisiana, Mo., U.S.A. ...39 25N 91 0W
165 Louisiana st., U.S.A. .30 50N 92 0W
162 Louisville, Ky., U.S.A. ...38 15N 85 45W
165 Louisville, Miss., U.S.A. ...33 7N 89 3W
130 Loukolela, Congo, (Fr.) ... 1 4S 17 10E
50 Loulay, France ...46 3N 0 30W
63 Loule, Portugal ...37 9N 8 0W
157 Lount L., Canada ...50 10N 94 20W
MAP
58 Louny, Czechoslovakia ...50 20N 13 48E
164 Loup City, U.S.A. ...41 19N 98 57W
50 Lourdes, France ...43 6N 0 3W
133 Lourenço Marques, Mozambique ...25 58S 32 32E
63 Loures, Portugal ...38 50N 9 9W
63 Lourinhã, Portugal ...39 14N 9 17W
62 Lousã, Portugal ...40 7N 8 14W
145 Louth, N.S.W., Austral. ...30 30S 145 8E
39 Louth, England, U.K. 53 23N 0 0W
46 Louth, Ireland ...53 47N 6 33W
46 Louth, co., Ireland ...53 55N 6 30W
77 Loutrá Aidhipsoú, Gr. 38 54N 23 2E
77 Loutráki, Greece ...38 0N 22 57E
55 Louveigne, Belgium ...50 32N 5 42E
48 Louviers, France ...49 12N 1 10E
135 Louwsburg, Nat., S. Afr. ...27 33S 31 21E
132 Louzha, Zambia ...13 0S 25 25E
86 Lovat R., U.S.S.R. ...56 30N 31 20E
164 Loveland, U.S.A. ...40 27N 105 4W
166 Lovell, U.S.A. ...44 51N 108 20W
166 Lovelock, U.S.A. ...40 17N 118 25W
55 Lövenich, Germany ...50 56N 6 46E
70 Lovere, Italy ...45 50N 10 4E
75 Lovets, Bulgaria ...43 8N 24 42E
83 Loviisa (Lovisa), Finland ...60 31N 26 20E
165 Loving, U.S.A. ...32 17N 104 4W
165 Lovington, U.S.A. ...33 0N 103 20W
62 Lovios, Spain ...41 55N 8 4W
58 Lovosice, Cz. ...50 30N 14 2E
71 Lovran, Yugoslavia ...45 18N 14 15E
74 Lovrin, Rumania ...45 58N 20 48E
80 Lovstaviken, B., Swed. ...60 35N 18 45E
130 Lovua, R., Congo ... 7 2S 20 20E
145 Low Rocky Pt., Austral. ...42 50S 145 30E
131 Lowa, Congo ... 1 25S 27 47E
131 Lowa R., Congo ... 1 15S 27 40E
161 Lowell, Mass., U.S.A. .42 38N 71 19W
166 Lower L., U.S.A. ...41 17N 120 3W
135 Lower Adamson, C. Prov., S. Africa ...31 3S 26 16E
156 Lower Arrow L., Can. 49 40N 118 5W
58 Lower Austria, prov., Austria ...48 25N 15 40E
35 Lower Beeding, England, U.K. ...51 2N 0 15W
135 Lr. Blinkwater, S. Afr. ...32 40S 26 35E
168 Lr. California, st., Mex. ...28 0N 112 30W
134 Lr. Dikgatlon, S. Africa ... 27 6S 22 56E
146 Lower Hutt, N.Z. ...41 10S 174 55E
166 Lower Lake, U.S.A. ...38 56N 122 36W
155 Lower Neguac, Canada ...47 20N 65 10W
135 Lower Pitseng, S. Afr. 30 45S 28 21E
156 Lower Post, Canada ...60 0N 128 40W
155 Lower Sackville, Canada ...45 45N 63 43W
56 Lower Saxony (Nieder Sachsen), land., Ger. 52 45N 9 0E
154 Lower Seal, L., Canada ...56 30N 74 23W
91 Lower Tunguska R., U.S.S.R. ...64 20N 93 0E
144 Lower Woolgar, Queens., Australia .19 47S 143 27E
38 Lowes Water L., England, U.K. ...54 35N 3 23W
35 Lowestoft, Eng., U.K. 52 29N 1 44E
38 Lowgill, England, U.K. ...54 24N 2 36W
39 Lowick, England, U.K. ...55 38N 1 57W
60 Lowicz, Poland ...52 6N 19 55E
41 Lowther Hills, Scotland, U.K. ...55 20N 3 40W
161 Lowville, U.S.A. ...43 48N 75 30W
134 Loxton, C. Prov., S. Afr. ...31 30S 22 22E
42 Loy R., Scotland, U.K. ...56 54N 5 10W
43 Loyal L., Scot., U.K. 58 24N 4 20W
136 Loyalty Is., Pac. Oc. .21 0S 167 30E
113 Loyang, China ...34 40N 112 28E
86 Loyev, U.S.S.R. ...57 7N 30 58E
131 Loyoro, Uganda ... 3 22N 34 14E
113 Loyuan, China ...26 25N 119 33E
113 Loyung, China ...24 25N 109 25E
71 Loz, Yugoslavia ...45 43N 14 14E
50 Lozère, dépt., France .44 28N 3 34E
74 Loznica, Yugoslavia ..44 32N 19 14E
88 Lozovaya, U.S.S.R. ...49 0N 36 27E
112 Lü-ta (Dairen-P. Arthur), China ...39 0N 121 31E
132 Luabo, Mozambique ...18 30S 36 10E
130 Luacono, Angola ...11 15S 21 37E
130 Lualaba, R., Congo ... 5 45S 26 50E
131 Luama, R., Congo ... 4 33S 27 40E
132 Luamata, Zambia ...11 55S 24 25E
132 Luambe, Zambia ...12 30S 32 15E
132 Luampa, Zambia ...15 4S 24 20E
109 Luan, Philippines ... 6 10N 124 25E
107 Luan Chau, N. Vietnam ...21 38N 103 24E
130 Luanda, Angola ... 8 58S 13 9E
130 Luanda, dist., Angola 8 35S 13 15E
107 Luang Prabang, Laos 19 45N 102 10E
132 Luanginga, R., Zambia ...14 40S 22 35E
132 Luangwa, R., Zambia 14 25S 30 25E
132 Luangwa R., Bri. Mozam ...15 0S 30 15E

MAP
132 Luangwa Val., Zambia 13 30s 31 30e
132 Luanshya, Zambia 13 3s 28 28e
132 Luapula, prov. & R., Zambia 11 0s 29 0e
132 Luapula, R. Congo & Zambia 12 0s 28 50e
62 Luarca, Spain 43 32n 6 32w
130 Luashi, Congo 10 50s 23 36e
130 Lubamiti, Congo 2 28s 17 47e
60 Luban, Poland 51 5n 15 15e
86 Lubana L., U.S.S.R. .56 45n 27 0e
109 Lubang Is., Philippines 13 50n 120 12e
60 Lubartow, Poland 51 28n 22 42e
60 Lubawa, Poland 53 30n 19 48e
98 Lubban, Jordan 32 9n 35 14e
56 Lübben, Germany 51 56n 13 54e
56 Lübbenau, Germany .51 49n 13 59e
165 Lubbock, U.S.A. 33 40n 102 0w
56 Lübeck, Germany 53 52n 10 41e
56 Lübecker Bucht, Ger. 54 3n 11 0e
130 Lubefu, & R., Congo . 4 47s 24 27e
131 Lubero, *see* Luofo, Congo 0 1s 29 15e
60 Lubien, Poland 52 23n 19 9e
60 Lübin, Poland 51 24n 16 11e
60 Lublin, Poland 51 12n 22 38e
60 Lublin, prov., Poland 51 5n 22 30e
60 Lubliniec, Poland 50 43n 18 45e
86 Lubny, U.S.S.R. 50 3n 32 58e
108 Lubok Antu, Malaysia 1 14n 112 4e
59 Lubotin, Cz. 49 17n 20 53e
60 Lubsko, Poland 51 45n 14 57e
56 Lübtheen, Germany ...53 18n 11 4e
109 Lubuagan, Philippines 17 21n 121 19e
108 Lubuanbatu, Indonesia 2 33n 100 14e
130 Lubudi, Congo 6 50s 21 20e
130 Lubudi R., Congo 9 30s 25 0e
108 Lubuk Linggau, Indon. 3 15s 102 55e
108 Lubuk Sikaping, Indon. 0 10n 100 15e
131 Lubumbashi (Elizabethville), Congo 11 32s 27 28e
130 Lubutu, Congo 0 45s 26 30e
51 Luc en Diois, France .44 36n 5 28e
130 Lucala, Angola 9 13s 15 18e
130 Lucala, R., Angola 9 5s 15 50e
160 Lucan, Canada 43 13n 81 25w
45 Lucan, Ireland 53 21n 6 27w
73 Lucania, reg., Italy ...40 30n 16 0e
152 Lucania, Mt., Alas., U.S.A. 60 48n 141 25w
70 Lucca, Italy 43 50n 10 30e
40 Luce Bay, Scot., U.K. 54 45n 4 48w
163 Lucedale, U.S.A. 30 55n 88 34w
109 Lucena, Philippines ...13 55n 121 25e
63 Lucena, Spain 37 27n 4 31w
64 Lucena del Cid, Spain 40 9n 0 17w
59 Lučenec, Cz. 48 18n 19 42e
73 Lucera, Italy 41 30n 15 20e
57 Lucerne, *see* Luzern, Switz. 47 3n 8 18e
65 Luchena, R., Spain ...37 50n 2 0w
131 Lucheringo, R., Mozam. 12 0s 36 5e
111 Luchow, China 29 2n 105 10e
113 Luchow, China 28 57n 105 26e
56 Lüchow, Germany 52 58n 11 8e
129 Lucira, Angola 14 0s 12 35e
132 Lucite, R., Mozambique 20 0s 33 10e
56 Luckau, Germany 51 50n 13 43e
56 Luckenwalde, Germany 52 5n 13 11e
39 Lucker, England, U.K. 55 34n 1 46w
134 Luckhoff, O.F.S., S. Afr. 29 42s 24 49e
105 Lucknow, India 26 50n 81 0e
50 Luçon, France 46 28n 1 10w
75 Luda Kamchiya, R., Bulgaria 42 50n 27 0e
71 Ludbreg, Yugoslavia .46 15n 16 38e
56 Ludenscheid, Germany 51 13n 7 37e
129 Lüderitz, S.W. Africa 26 41s 15 8e
34 Ludgershall, Eng., U.K. 51 15n 1 38w
36 Ludgvan, Eng., U.K. .50 9n 5 30w
104 Ludhiana, India 30 57n 75 56e
56 Lüdinghausen, Ger. ...51 46n 7 28e
162 Ludington, U.S.A. 43 58n 86 27w
34 Ludlow, Eng., U.K. ...52 23n 2 42w
167 Ludlow, Calif., U.S.A. 34 43n 116 10w
161 Ludlow, Vt., U.S.A. ...43 25n 72 40w
81 Ludnö, Denmark 56 38n 9 9e
78 Ludus, Rumania 46 29n 24 5e
80 Ludvika, Sweden 60 8n 15 14e
57 Ludwigsburg, Germany 48 53n 9 11e
57 Ludwigshafen, Ger. ...49 27n 8 27e
56 Ludwigslust, Germany 53 19n 11 28e
86 Ludza, U.S.S.R. 56 32n 27 43e
130 Luebo, Congo 5 21s 21 17e
130 Lueki, Congo 3 20s 25 48e
130 Luena, Congo 9 28s 25 43e
132 Luena, Zambia 10 40s 30 25e
132 Luena Flats, Zambia .14 40s 23 30e
130 Luena R., Angola 12 0s 21 0e
132 Luena R., Zambia......14 25s 24 0e
42 Luerbost, Scot., U.K 58 9n 6 29w
132 Luezé, Zambia 17 15s 26 18e
130 Lufira R., Congo 9 30s 27 0e
165 Lufkin, U.S.A. 31 25n 94 40w
132 Lufubu, R., *see* Lofu R., Zambia 9 15s 30 30e
130 Lufupa, Congo 10 32s 24 50e
86 Luga, U.S.S.R. 58 40n 29 55e
86 Luga, R., U.S.S.R. 59 5n 28 30e
57 Lugano, Switzerland .46 0n 8 57e
57 Lugano, L. di, Switz. .46 0n 9 0e
89 Lugansk, *see* Voroshilovgrad, U.S.S.R.....48 38n 39 15e
131 Lugard's Falls, Kenya 3 6s 38 41e
131 Lugenda, R., Mozam. 12 35s 36 50e
99 Lugh Ganana, Somali Rep. 3 48n 42 40e
45 Lugnaquilla Mt., Ire. .52 48n 6 28w
80 Lugnvik, Sweden 62 55n 18 20e
71 Lugo, Italy 44 25n 11 53e
62 Lugo, Spain 43 2n 7 35w
62 Lugo, prov., Spain 43 0n 7 30w
74 Lugoj, Rumania 45 42n 21 57e
62 Lugones, Spain 43 26n 5 50w
90 Lugovoi, U.S.S.R. 43 0n 72 20e
131 Lugufu, R., Tanzania 5 40s 30 15e
34 Lugwardine, Eng., U.K. 52 4n 2 38w
56 Luhe, R., Germany 53 7n 10 0e
130 Luia, R., Congo 8 20s 21 40e
132 Luia, R., Mozambique 16 25s 32 30e
129 Luiana, R., Angola ...17 25s 22 30w
43 Luichart L., Scot., U.K. 57 36n 4 43w
113 Luichow, *see* Hoihong, China 20 55n 110 3e
113 Luichow Pen., China ..20 30n 110 0e
132 Luido, Mozambique ...21 30n 34 40e
130 Luilaka, R., Congo 2 0s 21 0e
130 Luilu, R., Congo 6 50s 23 37e
40 Luing I Scot., U.K. .56 15n 5 40w
70 Luino, Italy 46 0n 8 42e
113 Luipa, China 33 43n 107 2e
175 Luis Correia, Brazil ... 3 0s 41 35w
130 Luisa, Congo 7 40s 22 30e
130 Luishia, Congo 11 20s 27 0e
15 Luitpold Coast, Antarc. 78 0s 30 0w
172 Lujan, Argentina 34 45s 59 5w
132 Lukala, Zambia 15 35s 28 40e
130 Lukala, Congo 5 30s 14 25e
113 Lukang, Taiwan 24 0n 120 19e
130 Lukanga, Congo 1 35s 18 10e
132 Lukanga Swamp, Zam. 14 30s 27 40e
142 Luke, Mt., W. Austral. 27 10s 116 50e
130 Lukenie R., Congo 3 0s 18 50e
105 Lukhisaral, India 27 11n 86 5e
113 Luki, China 28 10n 109 58e
130 Lukolela, Congo 1 10s 17 12e
132 Lukosi, Rhodesia 18 30s 26 30e
76 Lukovë, Albania 40 0n 19 56e
75 Lukovit, Bulgaria 43 13n 24 11e
87 Lukoyanov, U.S.S.R. .55 2n 44 20e
131 Lukuga R., Congo 5 50s 28 30e
132 Lukulu, Zambia 14 35s 23 25e
132 Lukulu R., Zambia ...10 30s 31 0e
131 Lukushashi R.,Zam. ...14 0s 30 3e
82 Luleå, Sweden 65 35n 22 10e
75 Lüleburgaz, Turkey ...41 23n 27 28e
172 Lules, Argentina 26 54s 65 18w
165 Luling, U.S.A. 29 45n 97 40w
130 Lulonga R., Congo 1 0n 19 0e
15 Lützov-Holm B., Antarc. 69 0s 44 0e
130 Lulua R., Congo 6 30s 22 50e
130 Luluabourg, *see* Kananga, Congo 5 55s 22 18e
112 Lulung, China 39 40n 118 40e
109 Lumadjang, Indonesia 8 8s 113 16e
129 Lumai, Angola 13 20s 21 25e
130 Lumbala, Angola 12 36s 22 30e
130 Lumbala, R., Angola .12 55s 21 50e
165 Lumberton, Miss., USA 31 4n 89 28w
163 Lumberton, N.C., U.S.A. 34 37n 78 59w
167 Lumberton, N. Mex., U.S.A. 36 58n 106 57w
49 Lumbres, France 50 40n 2 5e
131 Lumbwa, Kenya 0 12s 35 28e
156 Lumby, Canada 50 10n 118 50w
127 Lumeyen, Sudan 5 5s 33 28e
43 Lumphanan, Scot., U.K. 57 8n 2 41w
143 Lumsden, N.Z. 45 44s 168 27e
43 Lumsden, Scot., U.K. 57 16n 2 51w
107 Lumut, Malaysia 4 13n 100 37e
108 Lumut, Tg., Indon. ... 3 50s 105 58e
112 Lun, Mongolia 47 55n 105 1e
41 Lunan B., Scot., U.K. 56 40n 2 25w
104 Lunavada, India 23 8n 73 37e
78 Lunca, Rumania 47 22n 25 1e
79 Lund, Norway 58 27n 6 30e
81 Lund, Sweden 55 41n 13 12e
166 Lund, U.S.A. 38 53n 115 0w
132 Lundazi, Zambia 12 20s 33 7e
79 Lunde, Norway 59 17n 9 5e
79 Lunder, Norway 60 16n 9 55e
81 Lunderskov, Denmark 55 29n 9 19e
132 Lundi R., Rhodesia ...21 15s 31 25e
41 Lundin Links, Scotland, United Kingdom 56 13n 2 57w
108 Lundu, Sar., Malaysia 1 44n 109 57e
36 Lundy, I., Eng., U.K. 51 10n 4 41w
38 Lune, R., Eng., U.K. .54 0n 2 51w
56 Lüneberg, Germany 53 15n 10 23e
56 Luneburger Heide, dist., Germany 53 0n 10 0e
51 Lunel, France 43 39n 4 9e
56 Lünen, Germany 51 36n 7 31e
155 Lunenburg, Canada ...44 22n 64 18w
49 Lunéville, France 48 36n 6 30e
132 Lunga, R., Zambia 13 0s 26 33e
113 Lungan, China 23 5n 107 32e
113 Lungchuan, China 24 1n 116 8e
82 Lungholt, Iceland 63 35n 18 10e
113 Lunghsien, China 34 47n 107 0e
112 Lunghwa, China 41 15n 117 51e
124 Lungi Airport, S. Leone 8 40n 16 47e
112 Lungkiang, China 47 22n 123 4e
112 Lungkow, China 37 40n 120 25e
103 Lungleh, India 22 55n 92 45e
113 Lungmoon, China 23 50n 114 18e
113 Lungshan, China 29 26n 109 31e
113 Lungsheng, China 25 41n 109 59e
113 Lungsi, China 35 0n 104 35e
112 Lungtai, China 37 58n 117 0e
112 Lungteh, China 35 30n 106 5e
113 Lungtsin, China 22 20n 106 52e
132 Lungwebunga, R., Zam. 13 40s 22 25e
113 Lungyan, China 25 6n 117 2e
104 Luni, India 26 0n 73 6e
104 Luni R., India 25 40n 72 20e
166 Luning, U.S.A. 38 30n 118 14w
86 Luninets, U.S.S.R. 52 15n 27 0e
87 Lunino, U.S.S.R. 53 35n 45 6e
42 Lunna Ness, Scot., U.K. 60 27n 1 4w
79 Lunner, Norway 60 19n 10 35e
132 Lunsemfwa Falls, Zam. 14 30s 29 6e
132 Lunsenfwa R., Zambia 14 50s 30 10e
130 Lunuango, Angola 6 30s 12 35e
131 Luofu (Lubero) Congo 0 1s 29 15e
130 Luozi, Congo 4 54s 14 0e
78 Lupeni, Rumania 45 21n 23 13e
132 Lupumaula, Zambia ...15 5s 26 40e
132 Lupundu, Zambia 14 18s 26 45e
172 Luque, Paraguay 25 19s 57 25w
63 Luque, Spain 37 35n 4 16w
162 Luray, U.S.A. 38 39n 78 26w
49 Lure, France 47 40n 6 30e
42 Lurgainn L., Scot., U.K. 58 1n 5 15w
46 Lurgan, N. Ire., U.K. 54 28n 6 20w
129 Lurio R., Mozambique 14 0s 38 30e
100 Luristan, Iran 33 20n 47 0e
132 Lusaka, Zambia 15 28s 28 16e
130 Lusambo, Congo 4 58s 23 28e
157 Luseland, Canada 52 4n 109 26w
113 Lushan, China 26 33n 107 58e
113 Lushan, China 33 45n 113 10e
76 Lushnje, Albania 40 55n 19 41e
131 Lushoto, & dist., Tanz. 4 47s 38 20e
50 Lusignan, France 46 26n 0 8e
49 Lusigny, France 48 16n 4 15e
135 Lusikisiki, S. Africa ...31 21s 29 36e
45 Lusk, Ireland 53 32n 6 10w
164 Lusk, U.S.A. 42 47n 104 27w
40 Luss, Scotland, U.K. .56 6n 4 40w
50 Lussac les Châteaux, Fr. 46 42n 0 44e
55 Lustin, Belgium 50 23n 4 54e
132 Luswishi R., Zambia .13 30s 27 17e
133 Luthle, Botswana 24 8s 23 48e
132 Lutoba, Zambia 13 9s 24 58e
35 Luton, England, U.K. 51 53n 0 24w
108 Lutong, Sar., Malaysia 0 29s 114 1e
130 Lutshima, R. Congo . 7 0s 18 40e
86 Lutsk, U.S.S.R. 50 50n 25 15e
34 Lutterworth, Eng., U.K. 52 28n 1 12w
134 Luttig, C. Prov., S. Afr. 32 37s 22 10e
164 Luverne, U.S.A. 43 35n 96 12w
130 Luvua, Congo 8 48s 25 17e
130 Luvua R., Congo 6 50s 27 30e
133 Luvuvhu, R., S. Africa 22 40s 30 55e
131 Luwegu R., Tanzania 9 30s 36 20e
132 Luwingu, Mt., Zambia 10 15s 30 2e
109 Luwuk, Indonesia 10 0s 122 40e
54 Luxembourg, Luxem. 49 37n 6 9e
54 Luxembourg, duchy, Europe 50 0n 6 0e
54 Luxembourg, prov, Belg. 49 58n 5 30e
49 Luxeuil les Bains, Fr. 47 49n 6 24e
126 Luxor Egypt 25 41n 32 38e
36 Luxulyan, Eng., U.K. 50 23n 4 44w
50 Luz, France 42 53n 0 1e
57 Luzern (Lucerne), Switz. 47 3n 8 18e
57 Luzern, cant., Switz. .47 2n 7 55e
175 Luziania, Brazil 16 20s 48 0w
52 Luzické Hory (Lusatian Mts.), Cz. 50 40n 15 0e
109 Luzon I., Philippines .16 30n 121 30e
49 Luzy, Nièvre, France .46 47n 3 58e
73 Luzzi, Italy 39 28n 16 17e
86 Lvov, U.S.S.R. 49 40n 24 0e
112 Lwanhsien, China 39 45n 118 45e
60 Lwowek, Poland 52 28n 16 10e
60 Lwowek, Poland 51 7n 15 38e
91 Lyakhov Is., U.S.S.R. 73 40n 141 0e
86 Lyakhovichi, U.S.S.R. 53 2n 26 32e
89 Lyaki, U.S.S.R. 40 34n 47 22e
146 Lyall Mt., N.Z. 45 16s 167 32e
104 Lyallpur, W. Pakistan 31 30n 73 5e
131 Lyantonde, Uganda ... 0 24s 31 7e
75 Lyaskovets, Bulgaria .43 6n 25 44e
43 Lybster, Scot., U.K. .58 18n 3 16w
56 Lychen, Germany 53 13n 13 20e
81 Lyckeby, Sweden 56 12n 15 37e
82 Lycksele, Sweden 64 38n 18 40e
35 Lydd, Eng., U.K. 50 57n 0 56e
98 Lydda, *see* Lod, Israel 31 57n 34 54e
133 Lydenburg, S. Africa .25 10s 30 29e
36 Lydford, Eng., U.K. .50 38n 4 7w
34 Lydham, Eng., U.K. .52 31n 2 59w
144 Lyndhurst, Queensland, Australia 18 56s 144 30e
34 Lydney, Eng., U.K. ...51 43n 2 32w
147 Lyell, New Zealand ...41 48s 172 4e
147 Lyell Range, N.Z. 41 38s 172 20e
81 Lygnern, L., Sweden .57 30n 12 15e
79 Lygra, Norway 60 42n 5 6e
79 Lykling, Norway 59 42n 5 12e
166 Lyman, U.S.A. 41 24n 110 15w
36 Lyme Bay, Eng., U.K. 50 36n 2 55w
36 Lyme Regis, Eng., U.K. 50 44n 2 57w
35 Lyminge, Eng., U.K. .51 7n 1 6e
34 Lymington, Eng., U.K. 50 46n 1 32w
38 Lymm, Eng., U.K. 53 23n 2 30w
35 Lympne, Eng., U.K. .51 4n 1 2e
161 Lyn, Canada 44 36n 75 47w
162 Lynchburg, U.S.A. 37 23n 79 10w
160 Lynden, Canada 43 14n 80 10w
166 Lynden, U.S.A. 48 56n 122 32w
81 Lynderup, Denmark .56 34n 9 19e
143 Lyndhurst, Australia .33 41s 149 2e
34 Lyndhurst, Eng., U.K. 50 53n 1 33w
145 Lyndhurst, S. Australia 30 15s 138 18e
160 Lyndonville, N.Y., U.S.A. 43 19n 78 25w
161 Lyndonville, Vt., U.S.A. 44 32n 72 1w
38 Lyne, R., Eng., U.K. .55 2n 2 48w
34 Lyneham, Eng., U.K. 51 30n 1 57w
79 Lyngdal, Agder, Nor. .58 8n 7 7e
79 Lyngdal, Buskerud, Nor. 59 54n 9 32e
81 Lyngs, Denmark 56 40n 8 28e
36 Lynmouth, Eng., U.K. 51 14n 3 50w
161 Lynn, Mass., U.S.A. ...42 28n 70 57w
157 Lynn Canal, Alas., U.S.A. 58 50n 135 20w
157 Lynn L., Canada 56 30n 101 40w
36 Lynton, Eng., U.K. ...51 14n 3 50w
86 Lyntupy, U.S.S.R. 55 4n 26 23e
157 Lynx L., Canada 62 30n 106 25w
81 Lyö, Denmark 55 3n 10 9e
51 Lyonnais, prov., Fr. ...45 45n 4 15e
51 Lyons, France 45 46n 4 50e
164 Lyons, Colo., U.S.A. .40 17n 105 15w
163 Lyons, Ga., U.S.A. 32 10n 82 15w
164 Lyons, Kans., U.S.A. .38 24n 98 13w
160 Lyons, N.Y., U.S.A. ...43 3n 77 0w
142 Lyons, R., W. Australia 24 0s 116 0e
81 Lyrestad, Sweden 58 48n 14 4e
58 Lysá, Czechoslovakia .50 11n 14 51e
81 Lysekil, Sweden 58 15n 11 28e
87 Lyskovo, U.S.S.R. 56 0n 45 3e
80 Lysvik, Sweden 60 1n 13 9e
34 Lytchett Minster, England, U.K. 50 44n 2 3w
38 Lytham St. Anne's, England, U.K. 53 45n 2 58w
39 Lythe, Eng., U.K. 54 30n 0 40w
165 Lytle, U.S.A. 29 14n 98 46w
147 Lyttelton, New Zealand 43 35s 172 44e
156 Lytton, Canada 50 13n 121 31w
86 Lyuban, U.S.S.R. 59 16n 31 18e
87 Lyubertsy, U.S.S.R. ...55 27n 37 54e
87 Lyubim, U.S.S.R. 58 20n 40 50e
86 Lyubom, U.S.S.R. 51 10n 24 2e
88 Lyubotin, U.S.S.R. 50 0n 36 4e
86 Lyubytino, U.S.S.R. .58 50n 33 16e
75 Lyuta, Bulgaria 43 32n 23 22e

M

111 Ma Chu R., China 34 0n 99 20e
81 Maabjærg, Denmark .56 24n 8 33e
98 Ma'ad, Jordan 32 37n 35 36e
44 Maam Cross, Ireland .53 28n 9 32w
100 Ma'an, Jordan 30 12n 35 44e
113 Maanshan, China 31 46n 118 41e
83 Maarianhamina, (Marienhamn), Fin. 60 5n 19 55e
81 Maarslet, Denmark 56 4n 10 10e
46 Maas, Ireland 54 49n 8 21w
54 Maas R., Netherlands 51 48n 5 30e
54 Maaseik, Belgium 51 6n 5 45e
108 Maasin, Philippines ...10 5n 124 55e
54 Maassluis, Neth. 51 56n 4 16e
54 Maastricht, Netherlands 50 50n 5 40e
121 Maatin-es-Sarra, Libya 21 45n 22 0e
132 Mababe Depression, Botswana 18 50s 23 58e
39 Mablethorpe, Eng., U.K. 53 21n 0 14e
132 Mabote, Mozambique .22 3s 34 9e
125 Mabrouk, Mali 19 29n 1 15w
166 Mabton, U.S.A. 46 13n 120 1w
133 Mabula, Trans., S. Afr. 24 45s 28 1e
130 Mabwe, Congo 8 40s 26 30e
172 Macachin, Argentina .37 10s 63 43w
173 Macae, Brazil 22 20s 41 55w
161 McAdoo, U.S.A. 40 54n 76 0w
165 McAlester, U.S.A. 34 57n 95 40w
142 McLeod, L., W. Aust. 24 9s 113 47e
63 Mação, Portugal 39 35n 7 59w
113 Macão, Port. terr., China 22 16n 113 35e
175 Macapa, Brazil 0 5n 51 10w
138 McArthur R., Australia 16 45s 136 0e
175 Macau, Brazil 5 0s 36 40w
156 McBride, Canada 53 20n 120 10w
165 McCamey, U.S.A. 31 8n 102 15w
166 McCammon, U.S.A. ...42 41n 112 11w
38 Macclesfield, Eng., U.K. 53 16n 2 9w
157 McClintock, Canada ...57 45n 94 15w
152 McClintock Chan., Can. 71 0n 103 0w
166 McCloud, U.S.A. 41 14n 122 5w
109 McCluer Gulf, Indon. . 2 20s 133 0w
160 McClure, U.S.A. 40 42n 77 20e
14 M'Clure Str., Canada .74 0n 120 0w
164 McClusky, U.S.A. 47 30n 100 31w
165 McComb, U.S.A. 31 20n 90 30w
156 McConnell Creek, Can. 56 53n 126 30w
164 McCrook, U.S.A. 40 15n 100 35w
156 McCulloch, Canada 49 45n 119 15w
156 McDame, Canada 59 44n 128 59w
166 McDermitt, U.S.A. 42 0n 117 45w
11 McDonald I. (Australia), Indian Ocean 54 0s 73 0e
142 Macdonald L., Austral. 23 30s 129 0e
138 Macdonnell Ranges, N. Terr., Australia .23 40s 133 0e
152 Macdougall L., Canada 66 20n 98 30w
154 MacDowell L., Canada 52 15n 92 45w
43 Macduff, Scot., U.K. .57 40n 2 30w
154 Mace, Canada 48 55n 80 0w
62 Maceda, Spain 42 16n 7 39w
62 Macedo de Cavaleiros, Portugal 41 31n 6 57w
74 Macedonia, prov., Greece 40 39n 22 0e
175 Maceió, Brazil 9 40s 35 41w
63 Maceira, Portugal 39 41n 8 55w
124 Macenta, Guinea 8 35n 9 20w
71 Macerata, Italy 43 19n 13 28e
46 Macfin, N. Ire., U.K. 55 5n 6 37w
165 McGehee, U.S.A. 33 40n 91 25w
166 McGill, U.S.A. 39 27n 114 50w
44 Macgillycuddy's Reeks, Mts., Ireland 52 2n 9 45w
157 Macgregor, Canada 49 57n 98 48w
164 McGregor, Iowa, U.S.A. 42 58n 91 15w
164 McGregor, Minn., U.S.A. 46 37n 93 17w
145 McGregor Ra., Queensland, Australia 27 0s 142 45e
102 Mach, West Pakistan .29 50n 67 20e
134 Machache Mts., Lesotho 29 20s 28 0e
174 Machachi, Ecuador 0 30s 78 15w
174 Machado, R., *see* Jiparaná, Brazil 8 45s 62 20w
133 Machadodorp, S. Africa 25 40s 30 14e
172 Machagai, Argentina .26 56s 60 2w
131 Machakos, & dist., Kenya 1 30s 37 15e
174 Machala, Ecuador 3 10s 79 50w
132 Machanga, Mozambique 20 59s 35 0e
127 Machar Marshes, Sudan 9 28n 33 21e
40 Machars, The, dist., Scotland, U.K. 54 46n 4 30w
133 Machava, Mozambique 25 54s 32 28e
48 Machecoul, France 47 0n 1 49w
132 Macheke, Rhodesia 18 8s 31 50e
55 Machelen, Belgium 50 55n 4 26e
113 Macheng, China 31 5n 114 55e
91 Machevna, U.S.S.R. ...61 20n 172 20e
63 Machezo, Mt., Spain ...39 21n 4 20w
155 Machias, Maine, U.S.A. 44 40n 67 34w
64 Machichaco, Cabo, Sp. 43 28n 2 47w
132 Machili R., Zambia ...17 15s 25 0e
174 Machiques, Venezuela 10 4n 72 34w
40 Machrihanish, Scotland, United Kingdom 55 25n 5 42w
174 Machupicchu, Peru 13 8s 72 30w
37 Machynlleth, Wales, United Kingdom 52 36n 3 51w
144 McIlwraith Ra., Queens., Australia .13 50s 143 20e
78 Măcin, Rumania 45 16n 28 8e
124 Macina, dist., Mali 14 40n 4 50w
124 Macina, Canal de, Mali 13 50n 5 40w
164 McIntosh, U.S.A. 45 57n 101 20w
145 Macintyre, R., Austral. 28 50s 151 0e
144 Mackay, Australia 21 36s 148 39e
166 Mackay, U.S.A. 43 58n 113 37w
142 Mackay L., W. Austral. 22 40s 128 35e
142 McKay Ra., W. Austral. 23 0s 122 30e
160 McKees Rock, U.S.A. 40 27n 80 3w
160 McKeesport, U.S.A. ...40 21n 79 50w
163 McKenzie, U.S.A. 36 10n 88 31w
152 Mackenzie, R., Canada 67 0n 130 30w
166 McKenzie R., U.S.A. ..44 2n 122 30w
14 Mackenzie Bay, Canada 69 0n 137 30w
174 Mackenzie City, Guy. . 6 0n 58 10w
152 Mackenzie Mts., Canada 64 0n 128 0w

MA INDEX MA

MAP
147 Mackenzie Plains, N.Z. ...44 10s 170 25w
153 Mackenzie, Terr., Can. 61 30N 144 30w
147 McKerrow L., N.Z. ...44 25s 168 5E
162 Mackinaw City, U.S.A. ...45 45N 84 41w
148 McKinley Mt., Alaska, U.S.A. ...63 10N 151 30w
14 McKinley Sea, Arc. Oc. ...84 0N 10 0w
165 McKinney, U.S.A. ...33 10N 96 40w
131 Mackinnon Road, Kenya ... 3 40s 39 0E
142 Mackintosh Ra., Western Australia .27 39s 125 32E
167 McKittrick, U.S.A. ...35 18N 119 39w
80 Mackmyra, Sweden ...60 40N 17 3E
145 Macksville, Australia .30 40s 152 56E
164 McLaughlin, U.S.A. ...45 50N 100 50w
145 Maclean, N.S.W, Austral. ...29 26s 153 16E
165 McLean, U.S.A. ...35 15N 100 35w
164 McLeansboro, U.S.A. .38 5N 88 30w
135 Maclear, C. Prov. S. Africa ...31 2s 28 23
156 McLennan, Canada ...55 42N 116 50w
156 McLeod, Alta., *see* Ft. Macleod, Can. ...49 45N 113 30w
156 MacLeod, B. Canada .62 45N 110 0w
156 MacLeod Lake, Canada ...54 58N 123 0w
166 McLoughlin, Mt., U.S.A. ...42 30N 122 30w
132 Macloutsi, Botswana .22 0s 28 27E
132 Macloutsi R., Botswana ...22 0s 28 30E
132 Macloutsie Siding, Bots. ...21 35s 27 20E
166 McLure, Canada ...50 55N 120 20w
160 McMechen, U.S.A. ...39 57N 80 44w
166 McMillan L., U.S.A. ...32 40N 104 20w
166 McMinnville, Ore., U.S.A. ...45 16N 123 11w
163 McMinnville, Tenn., U.S.A. ...35 43N 85 45w
157 McMorran, Canada ...51 19N 108 42w
15 McMurdo Sd., Antarc. 77 0s 170 0E
156 McMurray, Canada ...56 45N 111 27w
167 McNary, U.S.A. ...34 4N 109 53w
46 Macnean L., Ireland ...54 19N 7 52w
164 Macomb, U.S.A. ...40 25N 90 40w
72 Macomer, Sardinia, It. 40 16N 8 48E
51 Mâcon, France ...46 19N 4 50E
163 Macon, Ga., U.S.A. ...32 50N 83 37w
165 Macon, Miss., U.S.A. .33 7N 88 31w
164 Macon, Mo., U.S.A. ...39 40N 92 26w
130 Macondo, Angola ...12 37s 23 46E
46 Macosquink, N. Ire., U.K. ...55 5N 6 43w
132 Macossa, Mozambique 17 52s 33 56E
164 McPherson, U.S.A. ...38 25N 97 40w
145 Macquarie Harb., Tas., Australia ...42 18s 145 25E
136 Macquarie I., S. Ocean ...55 0N 160 0E
143 Macquarie R., Australia ...31 0s 147 31E
15 MacRobertson Coast, Antarctica ...68 30s 63 0E
44 Macroom, Ireland ...51 54N 8 57w
46 McSwyne's B. Ireland...54 37N 8 25w
160 Mac Tier, Canada ...45 9N 79 46w
70 Macugnaga, Italy ...45 57N 7 58E
132 Macuirima, Mozambique ...19 14s 35 5E
132 Macuiza, Mozambique 8 7s 34 29E
139 Macumba R., S. Austral. ...27 11s 136 0E
125 Madagali, Nigeria ...10 56N 13 33E
129 Madagascar, I., Africa 20 0s 47 0E
123 Madama, Niger ...22 0N 14 0E
155 Madame I., Canada ...45 30N 60 58w
106 Madanapalle, India ...13 33N 78 34E
144 Madang, N.E. New Guin. ... 5 0s 145 46E
125 Madaoua, Niger ...14 5N 6 27E
125 Madara, Nigeria ...11 45N 10 35E
78 Mădăras, Rumania ...46 37N 24 24E
105 Madaripur, E. Pakistan ...23 2N 90 15E
103 Madauk, Burma ...17 56N 96 52E
160 Madawaska, Canada ...45 30N 77 55w
160 Madawaska, R., Canada ...45 20N 77 30w
103 Madaya, Burma ...22 20N 96 10E
127 Madbar, Sudan ... 6 17N 30 45E
72 Maddalena I., Italy ...41 15N 9 23E
73 Maddaloni, Italy ...41 4N 14 23E
168 Madden Dam, Panama Canal Zone 9 13N 79 37w
168 Madden Lake, Panama Canal Zone 9 20N 79 37w
42 Maddy, L., Scot., U.K. ...57 36N 7 8w
127 Madebele, Ethiopia ...12 30N 41 10E
120 Madeira Is., Atlan. Oc. ...32 50N 17 0w
174 Madeira R., Brazil ... 5 30s 61 20w
34 Madeley, Salop, England, U.K. ...52 38N 2 28w
38 Madeley, Staffs, England, U.K. ...52 59N 2 20w
132 Madenda, Malawi ...13 42s 35 1w
167 Madera, U.S.A. ...37 0N 120 1w
106 Madha, India ...18 0N 75 55E
105 Madhubani, India ...26 21N 86 7E
105 Madhupur, India ...24 18N 86 37E
104-5 Madhya Pradesh, st., India ...21 50N 81 0E
131 Madi Opei, Uganda ... 3 47N 33 5E
133 Madibogo, S. Africa ...26 25s 25 10E
165 Madill, U.S.A. ...34 5N 96 49w
130 Madimba, Congo ... 5 0s 15 0E
132 Madinare, Botswana .22 0s 27 40E
99 Madinat al-Shaab, S. Yemen ...12 50N 45 0E
130 Madingou, Congo, (Fr.) ... 4 10s 13 33E
163 Madison, Florida U.S.A. ...30 29N 83 26w
162 Madison, Idaho U.S.A. ...38 42N 85 20w
164 Madison, Neb., U.S.A. 41 53N 97 25w
160 Madison, Ohio, U.S.A. 41 45N 81 4w
164 Madison, S.D., U.S.A. 44 0N 97 8w
164 Madison, Wis., U.S.A. 43 5N 89 25w
164 Madison City, U.S.A. .43 5N 93 10w
166 Madison Junc., U.S.A. 44 42N 110 56w
166 Madison R., U.S.A. ...45 0N 111 48w
162 Madisonville, U.S.A. .37 42N 87 30w
132 Madista, Botswana ...21 15s 25 6E
109 Madiun, Indonesia ... 7 38s 111 32E
109 Madjalengka, Indonesia ... 6 55s 108 14E
109 Madjene, Indonesia ... 3 27s 118 57E
34 Madley, Eng., U.K. ...52 3N 2 51w
131 Mado Gashi, Kenya ... 0 47N 39 12E
127 Madol, Sudan ... 9 3N 27 45E
132 Madona, Zambia ...10 48s 28 33E
100 Madraga, Saudi Arabia ...21 42N 40 9E
106 Madras, India ...13 8N 80 19E
106 Madras, st., see Tamil Nadu, India ...11 0N 77 0E
166 Madras, U.S.A. ...44 40N 121 10w
165 Madre L., U.S.A. ...26 30N 90 20w
176 Madre de Dios I. Chile ...50 20N 75 10w
174 Madre de Dios R., Bol. ...11 30s 67 30w
168 Madre del Sur, Sierra, Mexico ...17 30N 100 0w
168 Madre, Laguna, Mexico ...25 0N 97 30w
168 Madre Occidental, Sierra, Mexico ...27 0N 107 0w
168 Madre Oriental, Sierra, Mexico ...25 0N 100 0w
168 Madre, Sierra, Mexico 16 0N 93 0w
109 Madre, Sierra, Phil. ...17 0N 122 0E
104 Madri, India ...24 16N 73 32E
62 Madrid, Spain ...40 25N 3 45w
62 Madrid, prov., Spain .40 30N 3 45w
63 Madridejos, Spain ...39 28N 3 33w
63 Madroñera, Spain ...39 26N 5 42w
127 Madu, Sudan ...14 37N 26 4E
109 Madura I., Indonesia . 7 0s 113 20E
109 Madura Str., Indonesia ... 7 30s 113 20E
142 Madura Motel, W. Australia ...31 55s 127 0E
106 Madurai, India ... 9 55N 78 10E
106 Madurantakam, India 12 30N 79 50E
106 Maduru Oya R., Ceylon ... 7 40N 81 7E
89 Madzhalis, U.S.S.R. ...42 9N 47 47E
107 Mae Hong Son, Thai. .19 16N 98 8E
107 Mae Sot, Thailand ...16 43N 98 34E
79 Mael, Norway ...59 55N 8 50E
64 Maella, Spain ...41 8N 0 7E
37 Maentwrog, Wales, U.K. ...52 57N 4 0w
78 Maerus, Rumania ...45 53N 25 31E
37 Maesteg, Wales, U.K. 51 36N 3 40w
169 Maestra, Sierra, Cuba 20 15N 77 0w
123 Mafan, Libya ...25 56N 14 56E
127 Mafaza, Sudan ...13 38N 34 30E
157 Mafeking, Canada ...52 40N 101 10w
133 Mafeking, S. Africa ...25 50s 25 38E
124 Maféré, Ivory Coast ... 5 30N 3 2w
133 Mafeteng, Lesotho ...29 51s 27 15E
143 Maffra, Vic., Australia 37 53s 146 58E
131 Mafia I., Tanzania ... 7 45s 39 50E
173 Mafra, Brazil ...26 10s 50 0w
63 Mafra, Portugal ...38 55N 9 20w
98 Mafraq, Jordan ...32 17N 36 14E
175 Mafrense, Brazil ... 8 10s 41 10w
132 Mafungabusi Plateau, Rhodesia ...18 30s 29 8E
91 Magadan, U.S.S.R. ...59 30N 151 0E
131 Magadi & L., Kenya . 1 54s 36 19E
133 Magaliesberg Mts., South Africa ...25 45s 27 30E
133 Magaliesburg, S.Afr. ...26 1s 27 32E
169 Magangue, Colombia . 9 14N 74 45w
174 Magdalena, Bolivia ...13 13s 63 57w
125 Magaria, Niger ...13 4N 9 5E
124 Magburaka, Sierra Leone ... 8 47N 12 0w
98 Magdal, (Migdal), Israel ...32 51N 35 30E
155 Magdalen Is., Canada 47 30N 61 40w
174 Magdalena, Bolivia ...13 13s 63 57w
167 Magdalena, U.S.A. ...34 10N 107 20w
168 Magdalena B., Mexico 24 30N 112 10w
176 Magdalena I., Chile ...44 40s 73 0w
108 Magdalena I., Mexico .24 40N 112 15w
108 Magdalena, Mt., Sabah, Malaysia ... 4 45N 117 30E
174 Magdalena, R., Col. ... 8 30N 74 0w
168 Magdalena & R., Mex. 30 50N 112 0w
56 Magdeburg, Germany 52 8N 11 36E
56 Magdeburg, dist., E. Germany ...52 20N 11 40E
172 Magdelena, Argentina 35 5s 57 30w
168 Magdelena, Llano de la, Mexico ...25 0N 111 30w
98 Magdiel, Israel ...32 10N 34 54E
127 Magdub, Sudan ...13 42N 25 5E
165 Magee, U.S.A. ...31 53N 89 45w
165 Magee, I., N.Ire. U.K. 54 48N 5 44w
109 Magelang, Indonesia . 7 29s 110 13E
176 Magellan's Str., Chile .52 30s 75 0w
70 Magenta, Italy ...45 28N 8 53E
57 Maggia R., Switzerland ...46 18N 8 36E
70 Maggiorasca, Mt., Italy ...44 33N 9 29E
70 Maggiore, L., Italy ...46 0N 8 35E
124 Maghama, Mauritania 15 32N 12 57w
98 Maghar, Israel ...32 54N 35 24E
46 Maghera, N. Ire. U.K. 54 51N 6 40w
46 Magherafelt, N. Ireland, U.K ...54 44N 6 37w
38 Maghull, Eng., U.K. .53 31N 2 56w
122 Maghnia, Algeria ...34 50N 1 50w
46 Magilligan, N. Ire., U.K. ...55 10N 6 53w
46 Magilligan Pt., Northern Ireland, U.K. ...55 10N 6 58w
71 Magione, Italy ...43 10N 12 12E
74 Maglaj, Yugoslavia ...44 33N 18 7E
71 Magliano in Toscana, It. ...42 36N 11 18E
73 Maglie, Italy ...40 8N 18 17E
126 Magna, Saudi Arabia .28 25N 34 46E
50 Magnac-Laval, France ...46 13N 1 11E
14 Magnetic Pole, 1965 (North), Canada ...75 0N 101 0w
15 Magnetic Pole, 1965, (South), Antarctica 66 30s 139 30E
76 Magnisia pref., Greece ...39 24N 22 46E
84 Magnitogorsk, U.S.S.R. ...53 20N 59 0E
165 Magnolia, Ark., U.S.A. ...33 18N 93 12w
165 Magnolia, Miss., U.S.A. ...31 8N 90 28w
79 Magnor, Norway ...59 56N 12 15E
49 Magny, France ...49 9N 1 45E
155 Magog, Canada ...45 18N 72 9w
131 Magoro, Uganda ... 1 45N 34 12E
132 Magoye, Zambia ...16 1s 27 30E
156 Magpie L., Canada ...51 0N 64 40w
156 Magrath, Canada ...49 25N 112 50w
65 Magro, R., Spain ...39 20N 0 45w
127 Magrur R., Sudan ...16 5N 26 30E
175 Maguarinho, C., Brazil 0 15s 48 30w
133 Magude, Mozambique 25 2s 32 40E
132 Magüe, Mozambique .15 45s 31 42E
46 Maguire's Bri., Northern Ireland, U.K. ...54 18N 7 28w
157 Maguse L., Canada ...61 35N 95 20w
157 Maguse R., Canada ...61 20N 94 25w
103 Magwe, Burma ...20 10N 95 0E
100 Mahabad, Iran ...36 50N 45 45E
105 Mahabharat Range, Mts., Nepal ...28 30N 82 0E
129 Mahabo. Malag. Rep. 20 23s 44 40E
106 Mahad, India ...18 6N 73 29E
104 Mahadeo Hills. India .22 20N 78 30E
162 Mahadeopur, India ...18 48N 80 0E
131 Mahagi, Congo ... 2 20N 31 0E
129 Mahajamba, B. de, Malagasy Republic .15 24s 47 5E
104 Mahajan, India ...28 48N 73 56E
131 Mahaji Port, Congo ... 2 9N 31 14E
108 Mahakam, R., Indonesia ... 1 0N 114 40E
133 Mahalapye, Botswana 23 1s 26 51E
126 Mahalla el Kubra, El, Egypt ...31 10N 31 0E
101 Mahallat, Iran ...33 55N 50 30E
133 Mahamba, Swaziland .27 7s 31 10E
44 Mahanagh, Ireland ...53 31N 8 42w
105 Mahanadi R., India ...20 33N 85 0E
129 Mahanoro, Malagasy Republic ...19 59s 48 48E
161 Mahanoy City, U.S.A. 40 48N 76 10w
102 Maharashtra, St., India ...19 30N 75 30E
123 Maharès, Tunisia ...34 32N 10 29E
131 Mahari Mts., Tanzania 6 20s 30 0E
132 Mahave, Mozambique 21 4s 34 47E
106 Mahaweli Ganga, R., Cey. ... 8 0N 81 10E
106 Mahboobabad, India .17 42N 80 2E
106 Mahbubnagar, India .16 45N 77 59E
100 Mahd Dhahab, Si. Arab. ...25 55N 45 30E
123 Mahdia, Tunisia ...35 28N 11 0E
106 Mahe, India ...11 42N 75 34E
106 Mahendra Giri, Mt., India ... 8 20N 77 30E
131 Mahenge, Tanzania ... 8 45s 36 35E
147 Maheno, New Zealand 45 10s 170 50E
146 Mahia Pen., N.Z. ...39 9s 177 55E
135 Mahlabatini, S. Africa 28 14s 31 30E
127 Mahmiya, Sudan ...17 5N 33 50E
104 Mahmud Kot, W. Pak. ...30 16N 71 0E
78 Mahmudia, Rumania .45 5N 29 5E
164 Mahnomen, U.S.A. ...47 22N 95 57w
105 Mahoba, India ...25 15N 79 55E
64 Mahon, Spain ...39 50N 4 18E
155 Mahone Bay, Canada .44 30N 64 20w
131 Mahunda, Mozambique ...11 41s 39 30E
125 Mahuta, Nigeria ...11 32N 4 58E
104 Mahuva, India ...25 7N 71 46E
127 Mai Chio, Ethiopia ...12 50N 39 42E
49 Maiche, France ...47 16N 6 48E
175 Maicuru R., Brazil ... 1 0s 54 30w
73 Maida, Italy ...38 51N 16 21E
34 Maiden Bradley, England, U.K. ...51 9N 2 18w
36 Maiden Newton, England, U.K. ...50 46N 2 35w
35 Maidenhead, Eng., U.K. ...51 31N 0 42w
127 Maidi, Yemen ...16 20N 42 45E
157 Maidstone, Canada ...53 5N 109 20w
35 Maidstone, Eng., U.K. 51 16N 0 31E
125 Maiduguri, Nigeria ...12 0N 13 20E
49 Maignelay, France ...49 32N 2 30E
127 Maigudo, Mt., Ethiopia ... 7 30N 37 8E
105 Maijdi (Noakhali), E. Pakistan ...22 48N 91 10E
105 Maikala Ra.. India ...22 0N 81 0E
130 Maiko R., Congo ... 0 20s 26 20E
49 Mailly le Camp, France ...48 41N 4 12E
104 Mailsi, West Pakistan 29 48N 72 15E
101 Maimana, Afghanistan 35 53N 64 38E
57 Main R., Germany ...50 13N 11 0E
46 Main R., N. Ire., U.K. 54 49N 6 20w
145 Main Barrier Ra., N.S.W. Australia ...31 10s 141 20E
160 Main Chan., Canada ...45 22N 81 45w
144 Main Coast Ra., Queensland, Australia ...16 22s 145 10E
57 Mainburg, Germany ...48 37N 11 49E
106 Maindargi, India ...17 33N 74 21E
48 Maine, reg., France ...48 0N 0 10E
155 Maine, st., U.S.A. ...45 20N 69 0w
44 Maine R., Ireland ...52 10N 9 40w
48 Maine-et-Loire, dépt., France ...47 31N 0 30w
103 Maingkwan, Burma ...26 15N 96 45E
109 Mainit, L., Philippines 9 10N 125 30E
43 Mainland, I., Orkneys 59 0N 3 10w
42 Mainland, I., Shetlands, Scotland, U.K. ...60 15N 1 22w
104 Mainpuri, India ...27 18N 79 4E
49 Maintenon, France ...48 35N 1 35E
129 Maintirano, Malagasy Republic ...18 3s 44 5E
57 Mainz, Germany ...50 0N 8 17E
1 Maipo, vol., Argentina 34 10s 69 55w
172 Maipú, Argentina ...37 0s 58 0w
70 Maira R., Italy ...44 29N 7 15E
103 Mairabari, India ...26 30N 92 30E
169 Maisi C., Cuba ...20 10N 74 10w
49 Maisse, France ...48 24N 2 21E
143 Maitland, Australia ...32 44s 151 36E
145 Maitland, S. Australia 34 23s 137 40E
160 Maitland R., Canada .43 45N 81 33w
125 Maiyema, Nigeria ...12 5N 4 25E
133 Maizefield, S. Africa ...26 28s 29 31E
114 Maizuru, Japan ...35 25N 135 22E
82 Majavatn, Norway ...65 10N 13 20E
98 Majd el Kurum, Israel ...32 56N 35 15E
76 Mai'-e-Tomorrit, Mt., Albania ...40 42N 20 11E
74 Majevica Planina, Mts., Yugoslavia ...44 45N 18 50E
127 Maji, Ethiopia ... 6 20N 35 30E
100 Majma'a, Saudi Arabia ...25 57N 45 22E
64 Majorca (Mallorca) I., Balearic Is. ...39 30N 3 0E
109 Maju I., Indonesia ... 1 30N 126 30E
135 Majuba Hill, S. Africa 27 28s 29 52E
129 Majunga, Malagasy Rep ...15 40s 46 25E
124 Maka-Koulibentane, Mauritania ...13 40N 14 13w
132 Makaha, Rhodesia ...17 17s 32 35E
125 Makak, Cameroon ... 3 35N 11 0E
132 Makalamabedi, Bots. .20 19s 23 51E
154 Makamik, Canada ...48 45N 79 0w
131 Makania, Tanzania ... 4 21s 37 49E
147 Makarewa, N.Z. ...46 20s 168 21E
132 Makarikari Saltpan, Botswana ...20 40s 25 45E
91 Makarovo, U.S.S.R. ...57 40N 107 45E
74 Makarska, Yugoslavia 43 20N 17 2E
84 Makaryev, U.S.S.R. ...57 52N 43 50E
109 Makasar, Indonesia ... 5 10s 119 20E
109 Makasar Str. of, Indon. ... 1 0s 118 20E
90 Makat, U.S.S.R. ...47 39N 53 19E
130 Makaw, Congo ... 3 29s 18 22E
76 Makedhonia, Greece ...40 39N 22 0E
74 Makedonija, prov., Y.-slavia ...41 53N 21 40E
158 Makena, Hawaii, U.S.A. ...20 39N 156 27w
124 Makeni, Sierra Leone . 8 55N 12 5w
36 Maker, England, U.K. 50 20N 4 10w
131 Makere, Tanzania ... 4 17s 30 32E
88 Makeyevka, U.S.S.R .48 0N 38 0E
133 Makgobistad, S. Africa ...25 45s 25 12E
89 Makhachkala, U.S.S.R. ...43 0N 47 15E
89 Makharadze, U.S.S.R. 41 55N 42 2E
75 Makhlata, Bulgaria ...43 26N 24 17E
109 Makian I., Indonesia . 0 12N 127 20E
136 Makin, I., Pacific Ocean ... 3 30N 174 0E
131 Makindu, Kenya ... 2 7s 37 40E
155 Makkovik, Canada ...55 0N 59 10w
91 Maklakovo, U.S.S.R. .58 16N 92 29E
59 Makó, Hungary ...46 14N 20 33E
130 Makokou, Gabon ... 0 40N 12 50E
133 Makokskraal, S. Africa ...26 18s 26 36E
132 Makoli, Zambia ...17 28s 26 5E
131 Makoro, Congo ... 3 10N 29 59E
130 Makoua, Congo ... 0 5s 15 50E
59 Makow Podhal, Poland ...49 43N 19 45E
77 Makra I., Greece ...36 15N 25 54E
101 Makran, dist., Iran & West Pakistan ...26 15N 61 30E
102 Makran Coast Range Mts., West Pakistan 25 40N 64 0E
104 Makrana, India ...27 2N 74 46E
76 Mákri, Greece ...40 52N 25 40E
90 Maksimoyarskoye, U.S.S.R. ...58 50N 86 50E
123 Maktar, Tunisia ...35 56N 9 12E
100 Maku, Iran ...39 15N 44 31E
132 Makumbe, Botswana .20 15s 24 26E
130 Makumbi, Congo ... 5 50s 20 44E
114 Makurazaki, Japan ...31 15N 130 20E
125 Makurdi, Nigeria ... 7 43N 8 28E
133 Makwassie, S. Africa .27 17s 26 0E
132 Makwiro, Rhodesia ...17 58s 30 28E
44 Mal B., Ireland ...52 50N 9 30w
71 Mala Kapela, mts., Y.-slavia ...44 45N 15 30E
109 Malabang, Philippines 7 43N 124 3E
106 Malabar Coast, India .11 0N 75 0E
107 Malacca, W. Malaysia 2 15N 102 15E
107 Malacca, st., Malaya, Malaysia ... 3 0N 101 0E
108 Malacca, Str. of, Indon. ... 3 0N 101 0E
59 Malacky, Cz. ...48 27N 17 0E
166 Malad City, U.S.A. ...41 10N 112 20E
18 Maladetta Mt., Europe ...42 40N 0 30E
127 Malafaburi, Ethiopia .10 37N 40 30E
63 Malaga, Spain ...36 43N 4 23w
165 Malaga, U.S.A. ...32 12N 104 2w
63 Malaga, prov., Spain .36 38N 4 58w
131 Malagarasi, Tanzania . 5 5s 30 50E
131 Malagarasi R., Tanzania ... 5 2s 31 2E
129 Malagasy Rep., Africa 19 0s 46 0E
63 Malagón, Spain ...39 11N 3 52w
63 Malagón R., Spain ...37 40N 7 20w
45 Malahide, Ireland ...53 26N 6 10w
102 Malakand, W. Pakistan ...34 40N 71 55E
127 Malakal, Sudan ... 9 33N 31 50E
165 Malakoff, U.S.A. ...32 10N 95 55w
156 Malakwa, Canada ...50 55N 118 50w
91 Malamyzh, U.S.S.R. ...50 0N 136 50E
109 Malang, Indonesia ... 7 59s 112 35E
130 Malange, Angola ... 9 30s 16 20E
130 Malanje, dist., Angola 9 50s 17 22E
80 Malaren, L. Sweden .59 30N 17 10E
172 Malargue, Argentina .35 40s 69 30w
154 Malartic, Canada ...48 9N 78 9w
100 Malatya, Turkey ...38 25N 38 20E
132 Malawi, st., E. Africa .13 0s 34 0E
132 Malawi, L. (Lago Niassa), Africa ...12 30s 34 30E
107 Malaya, S.E. Asia ... 4 0N 102 0E
86 Malaya Vishera, U.S.S.R. ...58 55N 32 25E
109 Malaybalay, Philippines ... 8 5N 125 15E
100 Malayer, Iran ...28 22N 56 38E
108 Malaysia, Fed., S.E. Asia ... 5 0N 110 0E
100 Malazgirt, Turkey ...39 10N 42 33E
144 Malbon, Australia ...21 5s 140 17E
60 Malbork, Poland ...54 3N 19 10E
127 Malca Dube, Ethiopia 6 40N 41 52E
56 Malchin, Germany ...53 43N 12 44E
56 Malchow, Germany ...53 29N 12 25E
142 Malcolm, W. Australia 28 51s 121 25E
54 Maldegem, Belgium ...51 14N 3 26E
161 Malden, Mass., U.S.A. 42 26N 71 5w
165 Malden, Mo., U.S.A. ...36 35N 90 0w
137 Malden I., Pacific Ocean ... 4 3N 155 1w
93 Maldive Is., Ind. Oc. . 2 0N 73 0E
143 Maldon, Vic., Australia ...37 0s 144 6E
35 Maldon, England, U.K. ...51 43N 0 41E
173 Maldonado, Uruguay .35 0s 55 0w
168 Maldonado, Punta, Mex. ...16 19N 98 35w
70 Malé, Italy ...46 20N 10 55E
76 Mal'-e-Cikës, Mt., Alb. ...40 14N 19 33E
59 Malé Karpaty, Mts., Cz. ...48 30N 17 20E
77 Maléa Akrá, Mt., Gr. .36 58N 23 7E
104 Malegaon, India ...20 30N 74 30E
127 Malek, Sudan ... 6 2N 11 38E
130 Malela, Congo ... 4 22s 26 8E
131 Malemba, Congo ... 6 5s 29 4E
132 Malenge, Zambia ...10 4s 26 42E
81 Mâlerâs, Sweden ...56 54N 15 34E
104 Malerkotla, India ...30 32N 75 58E
77 Máles, Crete, Greece ...35 6N 25 35E
49 Malesherbes, France ...48 15N 2 20E
74 Maleske Planina, Ra., Y.-slav. Bulg. ...41 38N 23 7E
48 Malestroit, France ...47 49N 2 25w
73 Malfa, Italy ...38 35N 14 50E
89 Malgobek, U.S.S.R. ...43 30N 44 52E
80 Malgomaj L., Sweden .64 40N 16 30E
125 Malgorou, Niger ...12 10N 3 38E
64 Malgrat, Spain ...41 39N 2 46E
38 Malham Tarn, Eng. UK. ...54 6N 2 11w
166 Malheur L., U.S.A. ...43 19N 118 42w
166 Malheur R., U.S.A. ...43 55N 117 55w
124 Mali, Guinea ...12 10N 12 20w
125 Mali, Rep., Africa ...15 0N 10 0w
103 Mali R., Burma ...26 20N 97 40E
74 Mali Canal, Y.-slavia .45 36N 19 24E

MAP
76 Mal-i-Gjalicës, mt., Alb. 42 2N 20 25E
71 Mali Kvarner, Yugoslavia 44 50N 14 10E
107 Mali Kyun (Tavoy I.), Burma 13 0N 98 20E
98 Malih, R., Jordan 32 20N 35 29E
109 Malik, Indonesia 0 39S 123 16E
109 Malili, Indonesia 2 42S 121 23E
81 Målilla, Sweden 57 25N 15 48E
131 Malimba Mts., Congo . 7 30S 29 30E
46 Malin, Ireland 55 18N 7 16W
86 Malin, U.S.S.R. 50 46N 29 15E
46 Malin Hd., Ireland 55 18N 7 16W
46 Malin Pen., Ireland 55 20N 7 17W
108 Malinau, Indonesia 3 35N 116 30E
131 Malindi, Kenya 3 12S 40 5E
55 Malines, see Mechelen, Belgium 51 2N 4 29E
109 Maling, Mt., Indonesia 1 0N 121 0E
109 Malingping, Indonesia 6 45S 106 2E
109 Malita, Philippines 6 19N 125 39E
131 Malka Mari, Kenya ... 4 16N 40 46E
104 Malkapur, India 20 53N 76 17E
106 Malkapur, India 16 57N 74 0W
60 Malkinia, Poland 52 42N 21 58E
75 Malko Turnovo, Bulg. 41 59N 27 31E
143 Mallacoota, Australia .37 40S 149 40E
143 Mallacoota Inlet, Vic., Australia 37 40S 149 40E
98 Mallaha, Israel 33 6N 35 35E
42 Mallaig, Scotland, U.K. 57 0N 5 50W
105 Mallawan, India 27 4N 80 12E
126 Mallawi, Egypt 27 44N 30 44E
143 Mallee, dist., Australia 35 10S 142 20E
70 Malles Venosta, Italy .46 42N 10 32E
77 Mallia, Crete, Greece .35 17N 25 27E
64 Mallorca (Majorca), I., Balearic Is. 39 30N 3 0E
161 Mallorytown, Canada .44 29N 75 53W
44 Mallow, Ire. 52 8N 8 40W
37 Malltraeth B., Wales, United Kingdom 53 7N 4 30W
37 Mallwyd, Wales, U.K. 52 43N 3 41W
81 Malmbäck, Sweden 57 34N 14 28E
82 Malmberget, Sweden .67 11N 20 40E
54 Malmédy, Belgium 50 25N 6 2E
34 Malmesbury, Eng., U.K. 51 35N 2 5W
134 Malmesbury, S. Africa 33 28S 18 41E
81 Malmö, Sweden 55 33N 13 8E
81 Malmöhus Län, Sweden 55 45N 13 25E
81 Malmslätt, Sweden 58 27N 15 33E
87 Malmyzh Mozhga, U.S.S.R. 56 35N 50 30E
78 Malnaş, Rumania 46 2N 25 49E
75 Malo Konare, Bulgaria 42 12N 24 24E
87 Maloarkhangelsk, U.S.S.R. 52 28N 36 30E
109 Malolos, Philippines ...14 50N 21 2E
132 Malombe L., Malawi .14 40S 35 15E
75 Mal omir, Bulgaria 42 16N 26 30E
161 Malone, U.S.A. 44 50N 74 19W
130 Malonga, Congo.........10 25S 23 5E
130 Malonga Funga, Congo 11 5S 25 30E
55 Malonné, Belgium 50 27N 4 48E
75 Malorad, Bulgaria 43 28N 23 41E
86 Malorita, U.S.S.R. 51 41N 24 3E
135 Maloti Mts., Lesotho .29 10S 28 20E
87 Maloyaroslovets, U.S.S.R. 55 2N 36 20E
63 Malpartida, Spain 39 26N 6 30W
38 Malpas, England, U.K. 53 3N 2 47W
174 Malpelo I., Colombia . 4 3N 80 35W
62 Malpica, Spain 43 19N 8 50W
106 Malprabha, R., India .15 40N 74 50E
132 Malsambo, Mozambique 23 25S 32 30E
81 Målsryd, Sweden 57 40N 13 4E
68 Malta, st., Medit. 35 50N 14 30E
166 Malta, Mont., U.S.A. .48 20N 107 55W
166 Malta, Idaho, U.S.A. .42 15N 113 50W
72 Malta Channel, Medit. 36 40N 14 0E
129 Maltahohe, S.W. Africa.......24 45S 17 2E
39 Maltby, England, U.K.53 25N 1 12W
147 Malte Brun Mt., N.Z. .43 38S 170 22E
160 Malton, Canada 43 41N 79 38W
39 Malton, England, U.K. 54 9N 0 48W
130 Maluku, Congo 4 2S 15 40E
109 Maluku (Moluccas) Is. & prov., Indonesia . 3 0S 128 0E
125 Malumfashi, Nigeria ...11 48N 7 39E
80 Malung, Sweden 60 38N 13 50E
106 Malvalli, India 12 28N 77 8E
106 Malvan, India 16 2N 73 30E
165 Malvern, Ark., U.S.A. 34 22N 92 50W
160 Malvern, Ohio, U.S.A. 40 31N 81 12W
29 Malvern Hills, Eng., U.K. 52 0N 2 19W
34 Malvern Wells, England, U.K. 52 4N 2 19W
133 Malverniă, Mozambique 22 6S 31 42E
79 Malvik, Norway 63 25N 10 40E
133 Mamabule, Botswana .23 32S 26 32E
87 Mamadysh, U.S.S.R. .55 44N 51 23E
78 Mamaia, Rumania 44 18N 28 37E
146 Mamaku, New Zealand 38 5S 176 8E
175 Mamanguape, Brazil . 6 50S 35 4W
109 Mamasa, Indonesia 2 55S 119 20E
130 Mamba, Congo 9 35S 27 2E
131 Mambasa, Congo 1 22N 29 3E

MAP
109 Mamberamo R., Indon. 2 0S 137 50E
131 Mambirima, Congo 11 25S 27 33E
131 Mambrui, Kenya 3 5S 40 5E
48 Mamers, France 48 21N 0 22E
125 Mamfe, Cameroon 5 50N 9 15E
132 Mamilis, S.W.Africa ...18 2S 24 0E
154 Mammamattawa, Can. 50 25N 84 23W
73 Mammola, Italy 38 23N 16 13E
167 Mammoth, U.S.A. 32 46N 110 43W
113 Mamoi, China 26 0N 119 25E
124 Mamou, Guinea 10 15N 12 0W
108 Mampawah, Indonesia 0 30N 109 5E
125 Mampong, Ghana 7 6N 1 26W
109 Mamudju, Indonesia . 2 50S 118 50E
38 Man, Calf of, I. of M., U.K. 54 3N 4 51W
124 Man, Ivory Coast 7 30N 7 40W
38 Man, I. of, U.K. 54 15N 4 30W
106 Man R., India 17 20N 75 0E
103 Man Na, Burma 23 27N 97 19E
175 Mana, Fr. Guiana 5 45N 53 55W
108 Mana, Indonesia 4 25S 102 55E
127 Mana R., Ethiopia 5 20N 40 41E
106 Manaar, Gulf of, Asia 8 30N 79 0E
174 Manacapuru, Brazil ... 3 10S 60 50W
64 Manacor, Spain 39 32N 3 12E
109 Manado, Indonesia 1 40N 124 45E
169 Managua, Nicaragua .12 0N 86 20W
169 Managua L., Nicaragua 12 20N 86 30W
146 Manaia, New Zealand 39 33S 174 8E
129 Manakara, Malagasy Republic 22 8S 48 1E
147 Manakau Mt., N.Z. 42 15S 173 42E
144 Manam I., Terr. of New Guinea 4 5S 145 5E
101 Manamah, Bahrain I. 26 11N 50 35E
129 Mananara, Malagasy Republic 16 10S 49 30E
129 Mananjary, Malagasy Republic 21 13S 48 20E
129 Manantenina, Malag. .24 17S 47 19E
147 Manapouri, N.Z. 45 34S 167 39E
147 Manapouri, L., N.Z. ...45 32S 167 32E
106 Manar, R., India 18 50N 77 20E
111 Manasarowar L., Tibet, China 30 45N 81 20E
101 Manasir, Si. Arabia ...24 30N 51 10E
161 Manasquan, U.S.A. ...40 7N 74 3W
111 Manass, China 44 20N 86 21E
167 Manassa, U.S.A. 37 12N 105 58W
174 Manáus, Brazil 3 0S 60 0W
146 Manawatu, R., N.Z. ...40 28S 175 12E
109 Manay, Philippines 7 17N 126 33E
39 Manby, England, U.K. 53 22N 0 6E
162 Mancelona, U.S.A. 44 54N 85 5W
63 Mancha Real, Spain ...37 48N 3 39W
48 Manche, Dépt., France 49 10N 1 20W
174 Manchester, Bolivia ...11 10N 68 10W
38 Manchester, Eng., U.K. 53 30N 2 15W
161 Manchester, Conn, U.S.A. 41 47N 72 30W
163 Manchester, Ga., U.S.A. 32 53N 84 32W
164 Manchester, Iowa, U.S.A. 42 28N 91 27W
162 Manchester, Ky., U.S.A. 37 10N 83 45W
161 Manchester, N.H. U.S.A. 42 58N 71 29W
160 Manchester, N.Y. U.S.A. 42 56N 77 16W
161 Manchester Depot, U.S.A. 43 10N 73 5W
112 Manchouli, China 49 46N 117 24E
71 Manciano, Italy 42 35N 11 30E
127 Mancifa, Ethiopia 6 53N 41 50E
101 Mand R., Iran 28 20N 52 30E
131 Manda, Southern, Tanzania 10 30S 34 40E
131 Manda, Southern Highlands, Tanzania 7 51S 32 29E
129 Mandabé, Malagasy Republic 21 0S 44 55E
79 Mandal, Norway 58 2N 7 25E
103 Mandalay, Burma 22 0N 96 10E
109 Mandala Pk., Indonesia 4 30S 141 0E
112 Mandalgovi, Mongolia 45 47N 106 15E
100 Mandali, Iraq 33 52N 45 28E
77 Mandalya Korfezi, G., Turkey 37 15N 27 20E
164 Mandan, U.S.A. 46 50N 101 0W
106 Mandapeta, India 16 47N 81 56E
109 Mandar, Gulf of, Indon. 3 35S 119 4E
113 Mandarin B., China ...21 0N 110 20E
72 Mandas, Italy 39 40N 9 8E
104 Mandasor (Mandsaur), India 24 3N 75 8E
108 Mandawai (Katingan) R., Indon. 1 30S 113 0E
132 Mandeka, S.W. Africa 17 55S 23 42E
55 Manderfeld, Belgium .50 20N 6 20E
104 Mandi, India 31 39N 76 58E
132 Mandi, Zambia 14 30S 23 45E
132 Mandie, Mozambique .16 28S 33 31E
109 Mandih, Philippines ... 8 10N 123 5E
132 Mandimba, Mozambique 14 20S 35 40E
109 Mandioli, Indonesia ... 0 40S 127 20E
132 Mandjane, Mozambique 15 8S 33 15E
105 Mandla, India 22 39N 80 30E
81 Mandö I., Denmark ...55 18N 8 33E
77 Mandoúdhion, Greece 38 48N 23 29E

MAP
78 Mandra Mt., see Paringul-Mare, Rum. 45 20N 23 37E
77 Mandráki, Greece 36 36N 27 11E
129 Mandritsara, Malagasy Republic .15 50S 48 49E
104 Mandsaur (Mandasor), India 24 3N 75 8E
142 Mandurah, W. Australia 32 36S 115 48E
73 Manduria, Italy 40 25N 17 38E
104 Mandvi, India 22 51N 69 22E
106 Mandya, India 12 30N 77 0E
104 Mandzai, W. Pakistan 30 55N 67 6E
79 Måne, R., Norway 59 53N 8 15E
35 Manea, England, U.K. 52 29N 0 10E
106 Maner R., India 18 30N 79 40E
144 Maneroo, Australia 23 40S 143 52E
126 Manfalut, Egypt 27 20N 30 52E
143 Manfred, N.S.W., Austral. 33 19S 143 45E
73 Manfredonia, Italy 41 40N 15 55E
73 Manfredonia, G. of Italy 41 30N 16 10E
146 Mangahao, N.Z. 40 26S 175 48E
130 Mangal, Congo 4 2S 19 33E
146 Mangakino, N.Z. 38 25S 175 48E
106 Mangalagiri, India 16 26N 80 36E
78 Mangalia, Rumania ...43 50N 28 35E
106 Mangalore, India 12 55N 74 47E
62 Manganeses, Spain 41 45N 5 43W
133 Manganore, S. Africa .28 10S 23 15E
106 Mangaon, India 18 15N 73 20E
109 Mangawitu, Indonesia 4 8S 133 32E
79 Manger, Norway 60 38N 5 3W
44 Mangerton Mt., Ireland 51 58N 9 30W
108 Manggar, Indonesia ... 2 50S 108 10E
103 Mangin Range, Mts., Burma 24 15N 95 45E
105 Mangla Dam, W. Pak. 33 32N 73 50E
104 Manglaur, India 29 44N 77 49E
109 Mangole I., Indonesia 1 50S 125 55E
146 Mangonui, N.Z. 35 1S 173 32E
143 Mangoplah, Australia .35 25S 147 17E
132 Mangorre, Mozambique 24 0S 33 48E
36 Mangotsfield, Eng., UK 51 29N 2 29W
62 Mangualde, Portugal .40 38N 7 48W
121 Mangueigne, Chad 10 40N 21 5E
173 Mangueira, Lagoa da, Braz. 33 0S 52 50W
123 Manguéni, Plateau de, Chad 22 47N 12 56E
165 Mangum, U.S.A. 34 50N 99 30W
130 Mangungu, Congo 5 16S 19 36E
111 Mangyai, China 38 6N 91 37E
89 Mangyshlak B., U.S.S.R. 44 35N 51 0E
90 Mangyshlak Pen., U.S.S.R. 43 40N 52 30E
164 Manhattan, Kan., U.S.A. 39 10N 96 40W
166 Manhattan, Nev., U.S.A. 38 40N 117 3W
130 Manhongo, Angola 12 10S 18 38E
176 Manhuacu, Brazil 20 20S 42 10W
103 Mani, Tibet, China 34 52N 87 11E
71 Maniago, Italy 46 11N 12 40E
132 Manica e Sofala, dist., Mozambique 19 0S 33 45E
132 Manicaland, dist., Rhodesia 19 0S 32 30E
174 Manicoré, Brazil 6 0S 61 10W
155 Manicouagan L., Can. 51 25N 68 15W
155 Manicouagan R., Can. 50 30N 68 30W
100 Manifah, Si. Arabia ...27 30N 49 0E
137 Manihiki I., Pac. Oc. .10 24S 161 1W
130 Manika (Biano) Plateau, Congo 10 0S 25 55E
109 Manila, Philippines 14 40N 121 3E
166 Manila, U.S.A. 41 0N 109 44W
109 Manila B., Philippines 14 0N 120 0E
143 Manildra, Australia ...33 11S 148 41E
145 Manilla, N.S.W., Australia 30 45S 150 43E
103 Manipur R., Burma 23 45N 93 40E
103 Manipur, st., India 24 30N 94 0E
100 Manisa, Turkey 38 38N 27 30E
162 Manistee, U.S.A. 44 15N 86 20W
162 Manistee, R., U.S.A. ..44 20N 85 50W
162 Manistique, U.S.A. 45 59N 86 18W
157 Manitoba, prov., Can. 55 30N 97 0W
157 Manitoba L., Canada .50 40N 98 30W
157 Manitou, Canada 49 20N 98 40W
162 Manitou Is., U.S.A. ...45 8N 86 0W
157 Manitou L., Ont., Can. 49 15N 93 0W
155 Manitou L., Que., Can. 50 55N 65 17W
154 Manitoulin I., Canada 45 40N 82 30W
154 Manitowaning, Canada 45 46N 81 49W
162 Manitowoc, U.S.A. 44 8N 87 40W
174 Manizales, Colombia ... 5 5N 75 32W
129 Manja, Malagasy Rep. 21 26S 44 20E
129 Manjacaze, Mozam. ...24 45S 34 0E
106 Manjeri, India 11 7N 76 11E
104 Manjhand, W. Pakistan 25 50N 68 10E
100 Manjil, Iran 36 46N 49 30E
142 Manjimup, W. Austral. 34 15S 116 6E
106 Manjra R., India 18 20N 77 20E
133 Mankaiana, Swaziland 26 38S 31 6E
164 Mankato, Kan., U.S.A. 39 49N 98 11W
164 Mankato, Minn., U.S.A. 44 8N 93 59W

MAP
124 Mankono, Ivory Coast 8 10N 6 10W
157 Mankota, Canada 49 25N 107 5W
132 Mankoya, Zambia 14 58S 24 57E
64 Manlleú, Spain 42 2N 2 17E
143 Manly, N.S.W., Austral. 43 36S 151 14E
104 Manmad, India 20 18N 74 28E
106 Mannar, Ceylon 9 1N 79 54E
106 Mannar Island, Ceylon 9 5N 79 45E
106 Mannar (Manaar) G. of, Asia 8 30N 79 0E
106 Mannargudi, India 10 45N 79 32E
57 Mannheim, Germany .49 28N 8 29E
156 Manning, Canada 56 53N 117 39W
163 Manning, U.S.A. 33 40N 80 9W
162 Mannington, U.S.A. ...39 35N 80 25W
35 Manningtree Eng., U.K. 51 56N 1 3E
72 Mannu C. Sardinia, It. 40 2N 8 24E
72 Mannu, R., Italy 39 35N 8 56E
145 Mannum, S. Australia 34 57S 139 12E
124 Mano, Sierra Leone ... 8 3N 12 12W
109 Manokwari, Indonesia 0 54N 134 0E
77 Manolás, Greece 38 4N 21 21E
129 Manombo, Malag. 22 57S 43 28E
131 Manono, Congo 7 15S 27 20E
37 Manorbier, Wales, U.K. 51 38N 4 48W
46 Manorhamilton, Ireland 54 19N 8 11W
51 Manosque, France 43 49N 5 47E
155 Manouane L., Canada 50 45N 70 45W
64 Manresa, Spain 41 48N 1 50E
104 Mansa, Gujarat, India 23 27N 72 45E
104 Mansa, Punjab, India 30 0N 75 27E
132 Mansa (Ft. Rosebery), Zambia 11 13S 28 55E
153 Mansel I., Canada 62 0N 80 0W
143 Mansfield, Vic., Austral. 37 0S 146 0E
39 Mansfield, Eng., U.K. 53 8N 1 12W
165 Mansfield, La., U.S.A. 32 2N 93 40W
161 Mansfield, Mass., U.S.A. ....42 ?N 71 12W
160 Mansfield, Ohio, U.S.A. 40 45N 82 30W
160 Mansfield, Pa., U.S.A. 41 48N 77 4W
166 Mansfield, Wash., U.S.A. 47 51N 119 44W
39 Mansfield Woodhouse, England, U.K. 53 11N 1 11W
72 Mansilla de las Mulas, Spain 42 30N 5 25W
50 Mansle, France 45 52N 0 9E
175 Manso R., Brazil 14 0S 52 0W
124 Mansôa, Port. Guinea 12 0N 15 20W
156 Manson Cr., Canada ...55 37N 124 25W
123 Mansoura, Algeria 36 1N 4 31E
174 Manta, Ecuador 1 0S 80 40W
108 Mantalingajan, Mt., Philippines 8 55N 117 45E
131 Mantare, Tanzania 2 42S 33 13E
167 Manteca, U.S.A. 37 50N 121 12W
163 Manteo, U.S.A. 35 55N 75 41W
49 Mantes-la-Jolie, France 49 0N 1 41E
48 Manthelan, France 47 9N 0 47E
166 Manti, U.S.A. 39 23N 111 32W
173 Mantiqueira, Serra da, Brazil 22 0S 44 0W
35 Manton, England, U.K. 52 37N 0 41W
162 Manton, U.S.A. 44 23N 85 25W
81 Mantorp, Sweden 58 21N 15 20E
70 Mantova, Italy 45 10N 10 47E
82 Mänttä, Finland 62 0N 24 40E
70 Mantua (Mantova), It. 45 9N 10 48E
52 Mantua, region, Italy .45 9N 10 48E
160 Mantua, U.S.A. 41 15N 81 14W
87 Manturova, U.S.S.R. .58 10N 44 30E
57 Mäntyharju, Finland .61 24N 26 58E
174 Manu, Peru 12 10S 71 0W
46 Manualla, Ireland 53 51N 9 12W
109 Manucan, Philippines . 8 14N 123 3E
109 Manui I., Indonesia ... 3 35S 123 5E
146 Manukau, New Zealand37 1S 174 55E
146 Manukau Harbour, N.Z. 37 3S 174 45E
145 Manumbar, Australia .26 25S 152 10E
146 Manunui, New Zealand 38 54S 175 21E
144 Manus I., Terr. of New Guinea 2 10S 147 0E
106 Manvi, India 15 57N 76 59E
164 Manville, U.S.A. 42 48N 104 36W
106 Manwath, India 19 19N 76 32E
165 Many, U.S.A. 31 36N 93 28W
144 Many Peaks, Australia 24 32S 151 25E
132 Manyane, Botswana ...23 21S 21 42E
131 Manyani, Kenya 3 4S 38 30E
131 Manyara L. Tanzania 3 40S 35 50E
89 Manych R., U.S.S.R. .47 0N 41 15E
89 Manych-Gudilo, L., U.S.S.R. 46 24N 42 38E
131 Manyonga R., Tanzania 4 0S 34 0E
131 Manyoni & dist., Tanzania 5 45S 34 55E
127 Manza, Cent. Afr. Rep. 5 25N 27 12E
104 Manzai, W. Pakistan .32 20N 70 15E
65 Manzanares, Spain 39 0N 3 22W
169 Manzanillo, Pta., Pan. 9 30N 79 40W
169 Manzanillo, Cuba 20 20N 77 10W
168 Manzanillo, Mexico 19 0N 104 20W
167 Manzano Mts., U.S.A. 34 30N 106 45W
133 Manzini, Swaziland ...26 30S 31 25E

MAP
121 Mao, Chad 14 4N 15 19E
108 Maoke Mts., Indonesia 3 40S 137 30E
45 Maone, Ireland 52 57N 6 49W
125 Maouri, Dallol, Niger .14 20N 4 5E
133 Mapai, Mozambique. .22 51S 32 0E
132 Mapanza, Zambia 16 15S 26 56E
133 Mapela, Trans., S. Afr. 23 55S 28 40E
168 Mapimi, Mexico 25 50N 103 31W
166 Mapleton, Ore., U.S.A. 44 4N 123 58W
164 Maplewood, U.S.A. 38 33N 90 18W
144 Maprik, N.E. N. Guin. 3 40S 143 5E
106 Mapuca, India 15 36N 73 46E
174 Mapuera R., Brazil 0 30S 58 25W
135 Mapumulo, Nat., S. Afr. 29 11S 31 2E
133 Maputo R., Africa 26 35S 32 30E
127 Maqdala, Ethiopia 11 24N 39 10E
100 Maqna, Saudi Arabia .28 25N 34 50E
130 Maquela do Zombo Ang. 6 0S 15 15E
176 Manquinchao, Arg. 41 15S 68 50W
164 Maquoketa, U.S.A. 42 4N 90 40W
172 Mar Chiquita, L., Arg. 30 40S 62 50W
172 Mar del Plata, Arg. ...38 0S 57 30W
65 Mar Menor L., Spain .37 40N 0 45W
109 Mara, Indonesia 4 41S 120 24E
133 Mara, Trans., S. Afr. ...23 0S 29 37E
174 Mara, Venezuela 10 53N 71 53W
174 Maraâ, Brazil 1 43S 65 25W
175 Marabá, Brazil 5 20S 49 5W
133 Marabastad, S. Africa 23 57N 29 22E
175 Maracá I., Amapa, Braz. 2 10N 50 30W
174 Maraca I., Rio Branco, Brazil 3 30N 61 40W
174 Maracaibo, Venezuela 10 40N 71 37W
174 Maracaibo, L. Ven. 9 20N 71 30W
174 Maracay, Venezuela ...10 20N 67 35W
123 Maradah, Libya 29 4N 19 4E
125 Maradi, Niger 13 35N 8 10E
125 Maradun, Nigeria 12 35N 6 18E
100 Maragheh, Iran 37 30N 46 12E
175 Marajo I., Brazil 1 0S 49 30W
174 Marakanata, Guyana . 3 57N 59 22W
131 Maralal, Kenya 1 0N 36 38E
138 Maralinga, S. Australia 29 10S 131 15E
145 Marama, S. Australia 35 10S 140 15E
132 Maramba, Zambia 17 50N 25 50E
145 Marampa, Sierra Leone 8 45N 10 28W
78 Maramures, Reg. Rum. 47 39N 24 0E
167 Marana, U.S.A. 32 30N 111 9W
64 Maranchón, Spain 41 6N 2 15W
100 Marand, Iran 38 30N 45 45E
132 Marandellas, Rhodesia 18 5S 31 42E
175 Maranguape, Brazil ... 3 55S 38 50W
175 Maranhão, st., Brazil . 5 0S 46 0W
71 Marano, L. di, Italy ...45 42N 13 13E
145 Maranoa R., Australia 27 10S 148 5E
174 Marañon, R., Peru 4 50S 75 35W
1 Marapi, vol., Indonesia 1 0S 130 0E
131 Mararui, Kenya 1 58S 41 20E
100 Maras, Turkey 37 37N 36 53E
78 Mărăşeşti, Rumania ...45 52N 27 5E
73 Maratea, Italy 39 59N 15 43E
63 Marateca, Portugal 38 34N 8 40W
77 Marathokambos, Gr. .37 43N 26 42E
154 Marathon, Canada 48 44N 86 23W
77 Marathon, Greece 38 11N 23 58E
144 Marathon, Australia ...20 51S 143 32E
161 Marathon, N.Y., U.S.A. 42 25N 76 3W
165 Marathon, Tex., U.S.A. 30 15N 103 15W
109 Maratua I. Indonesia 2 10N 118 35E
127 Maraua, Ethiopia 7 40N 36 54E
36 Marazion, England U.K. 50 8N 5 29W
99 Marbat, Muscat & Oman 17 0N 54 45E
55 Marbeck, Germany 51 48N 6 53E
63 Marbella, Spain 36 30N 4 57W
138 Marble Bar, W. Austral. 21 9S 119 44E
165 Marble Falls, U.S.A. .30 30N 98 15W
133 Marble Hall, S. Africa 24 59S 29 21E
161 Marblehead, U.S.A. ...42 29N 70 51W
56 Marburg, Germany 50 49N 8 44E
80 Marby, Sweden 63 7N 14 18E
59 Marcal R., Hungary ...47 21N 17 15E
59 Marcali, Hungary 46 35N 17 25E
70 Marcaria, Italy 45 7N 10 34E
35 March, England, U.K. 52 33N 0 5E
130 Marchal, Congo 5 17S 14 59E
122 Marchand, see Rommani, Morocco 33 20N 6 40W
134 Marchand, S. Africa ...28 40S 20 27E
50 Marché, reg., France .46 0N 1 20E
71 Marche, reg., Italy 43 22N 13 10E
49 Marche-en-Famenne, Belgium 50 14N 5 19E
63 Marchena, Spain 37 18N 5 23W
55 Marchienne au Pont, Belgium 50 25N 4 22E
172 Marchigue, Chile 34 21S 71 45W
55 Marchin, Belgium 50 28N 5 14E
70 Marciana Marina, Italy 42 44N 10 12E
73 Marcianise, Italy 41 3N 14 16E
51 Marcigny, France 46 17N 4 2E
50 Marcillac Vallon, Fr. .44 29N 2 27E
50 Marcillat, France 46 12N 2 38E
49 Marck, France 50 57N 1 57E
49 Marckolsheim, France 48 10N 7 30E
172 Marcos Juarez, Arg. ...32 42S 62 5W

MAP
136 Marcus I., Pac. Oc. ...24 0N 153 45E
161 Marcy Mt., U.S.A. 44 7N 73 55W
34 Marden Here., Eng., United Kingdom 52 7N 2 42W
100 Mardin, Turkey 37 20N 40 36E
42 Maree L., Scot., U.K. 57 40N 5 30W
144 Mareeba, Australia 16 59S 145 28E
133 Mareetsane, S. Africa .26 9S 25 25E
39 Mareham le Fen, England, U.K. 53 7N 0 3W
74 Marek (Stanke Dimitrov), Bulg. 42 27N 23 9E
124 Marena, Mali 14 0N 7 30W
71 Marenberg, Yugoslavia 46 38N 15 13E
164 Marengo, U.S.A. 41 42N 92 5W
50 Marennes, France 45 49N 1 5W
131 Marenyi, Kenya 4 22S 39 8E
72 Marettimo I., Sicily, It. 37 58N 12 5E
50 Mareuil, Vendee, Fr. .46 32N 1 11W
165 Marfa, U.S.A. 30 15N 104 0W
39 Marfleet, England, U.K. 53 45N 0 15W
127 Margable, Ethiopia 12 54N 42 38E
37 Margam, Wales, U.K. 51 33N 3 45W
88 Marganets, U.S.S.R. ...47 40N 34 40E
106 Margao, India 14 12N 73 58E
155 Margaree Harbour, Can. 46 26N 61 8W
138 Margaret R., W. Austral. 18 0S 126 30E
156 Margaret Bay, Canada 51 20N 127 20W
142 Margaret River, W. Australia 33 57S 115 7E
168 Margarita, Panama Canal Zone 9 20N 79 55W
174 Margarita I., Ven. 11 0N 64 0W
76 Margaritíon, Greece ...39 22N 20 26E
35 Margate, England, U.K. 51 23N 1 24E
135 Margate, Natal, S. Afr. 30 50S 30 20E
90 Margelan, U.S.S.R. 81 5N 72 1E
50 Margeride, Mts. de la, France 44 43N 3 38E
73 Margherita di Savola, It. 41 25N 16 5E
78 Marghita, Rumania ...47 22N 22 22E
63 Margueira, Portugal ...38 41N 9 9W
156 Marguerite, Canada ...52 30N 122 15W
122 Marhoum, Algeria 34 27N 0 11W
87 Mari, A.S.S.R., U.S.S.R. 56 30N 48 0E
145 Maria I., Tas., Austral. 42 35S 148 0E
172 Maria Elena, Chile 22 18S 69 40W
172 Maria Grande, Arg. ...31 45S 59 55W
146 Maria van Dieman, C., New Zealand 34 29S 172 40E
81 Mariager, Denmark 56 40N 10 0E
81 Mariager Fd., Denmark 56 42N 10 19E
131 Mariakani, Kenya 3 50S 39 27E
136 Mariana Is., Pac. Oc. .17 0N 145 0E
136 Mariana Trench, Pacific Ocean 13 0N 145 0W
169 Marianao, Cuba 23 8N 82 24W
165 Marianna, Ark., U.S.A. 34 48N 90 48W
163 Marianna, Fla., U.S.A. 30 45N 85 15W
58 Mariánské Lazně, Cz. .49 57N 12 41E
81 Mariannelund, Sweden 57 36N 15 55E
166 Marias, R., U.S.A. 48 26N 111 40W
134 Mariasdal, S. Africa ...31 17S 19 30E
169 Mariato, Punta, Pan. . 7 12N 80 52W
58 Mariazell, Austria 47 47N 15 19E
99 Marib, Yemen 15 25N 45 20E
81 Maribo, Denmark 54 48N 11 30E
81 Maribo Amt., co., Den. 54 58N 11 30E
71 Maribor, Yugoslavia ...46 36N 15 40E
167 Maricopa Ariz., U.S.A. 33 5N 112 2W
167 Maricopa, Calif., U.S.A. 35 7N 119 27W
127 Maridi, Sudan 5 10N 29 25E
127 Maridi R., Sudan 5 25N 29 21E
169 Marie Galante I., W. Ind. 16 0N 61 20W
153 Mariecourt (Wakeham Bay), Canada 61 30N 72 0W
80 Mariefred, Sweden 59 15N 17 12E
83 Mariehamn, (Maarianhamina), Finland 60 12N 19 53E
54 Mariembourg, Belgium 50 6N 4 31E
54 Marienberg, Neth. 52 30N 6 35E
56 Marienberg, Germany 50 40N 13 10E
144 Marienberg, Terr. of New Guinea 3 54S 144 10E
129 Mariental, S.W. Africa 24 35S 18 0E
160 Marienville, U.S.A. 41 27N 79 8W
81 Mariestad, Sweden 58 42N 13 55E
163 Marietta, Ga., U.S.A. .34 0N 84 30W
162 Marietta, Ohio, U.S.A. 39 27N 81 27W
161 Marieville, Canada 45 24N 73 11W
90 Mariinsk, U.S.S.R. 56 10N 87 20E
87 Mariinskiy Posad, U.S.S.R. 59 9N 47 20E
73 Marilia, Brazil 22 0S 50 0W
62 Marin, Spain 42 23N 8 42W
173 Marina di Ciro, Italy .39 22N 17 8E
144 Marina Plains, Queensland, Australia 14 37S 143 57E
109 Marinduque, Phil. 13 20N 122 35E
162 Marine City, U.S.A. ...42 45N 82 29W
72 Marineo, Italy 37 57N 13 23E
167 Marinette, Ariz., U.S.A. 33 41N 112 16W
162 Marinette, Wis., U.S.A. 45 4N 87 40W
173 Maringa, Brazil 23 35S 51 50W
130 Maringa R., Congo 0 30N 21 0E
62 Marinha, Grande, Port. 39 45N 8 56W
87 Marino, Italy 41 47N 12 40E
163 Marion, Ala., U.S.A. .32 33N 87 20W
165 Marion, Ill., U.S.A. ...37 45N 88 55W
162 Marion, Ind., U.S.A. .40 35N 85 40W
164 Marion, Iowa, U.S.A. .42 2N 91 36W
164 Marion, Kan., U.S.A. .38 25N 97 2W
162 Marion, Mich., U.S.A. 44 7N 85 8W
163 Marion, N.C., U.S.A. .35 42N 82 0W
162 Marion, Ohio, U.S.A. .40 38N 83 8W
163 Marion, S.C., U.S.A. ...34 11N 79 22W
163 Marion, Va., U.S.A. ...36 51N 81 29W
163 Marion L., U.S.A. 33 30N 80 15W
167 Mariposa, U.S.A. 37 31N 119 59W
172 Mariscal Estigarribia, Paraguay 22 3S 60 40W
51 Maritime Alps, France 44 10N 7 10E
75 Maritsa, Bulgaria 42 1N 25 50E
75 Maritsa R., Bulgaria .42 15N 24 0E
77 Maritsa, Greece 36 22N 28 10E
86 Mariyampole, U.S.S.R. 54 33N 23 19E
101 Marjan, Afghanistan .32 5N 68 20E
40 Mark, Scotland, U.K. 55 2N 5 1W
55 Mark R., Netherlands 51 38N 4 40E
106 Markapur, India 15 44N 79 19E
81 Markaryd, Sweden 56 28N 13 40E
160 Markdale, Canada 44 19N 80 38W
165 Marked Tree, U.S.A. .35 35N 90 24W
56 Markelsdorfer Huk, Ger. 54 33N 11 0E
54 Marken, Netherlands .52 26N 5 6E
34 Market Bosworth, England, U.K. 52 37N 1 24W
35 Market Deeping, England, U.K. 52 40N 0 20W
38 Market Drayton, England, U.K. 52 55N 2 30W
35 Market Harborough, England, U.K. 52 29N 0 55W
34 Market Lavington, England, U.K. 51 17N 1 59W
39 Market Rasen, England, U.K. 53 24N 0 20W
39 Market Weighton, England, U.K. 53 52N 0 40W
46 Markethill, N. Ire., U.K. 54 18N 6 31W
34 Markfield, Eng., U.K. 52 42N 1 18W
160 Markham, Canada 43 54N 79 16W
14 Markham I., Greenland 84 0N 0 45W
157 Markham L., Canada .62 30N 102 35W
15 Markham Mts., Antarc. 83 0S 164 0E
41 Markinch, Scot., U.K. 56 12N 3 9W
77 Markoupoulon, Greece 37 53N 23 57E
74 Markovac, Yugoslavia 44 14N 21 7E
87 Marks, U.S.S.R. 51 45N 46 50E
35 Marks Tey, Eng., U.K. 51 53N 0 48E
165 Marksville, U.S.A. 31 10N 92 2W
57 Markt Schwaben, Ger. 48 14N 11 49E
57 Marktredwitz, Germany 50 1N 12 2E
55 Marl, Germany 51 39N 7 4E
161 Marlboro, U.S.A. 42 19N 71 33W
144 Marlborough, Australia 22 46S 149 52E
34 Marlborough, Eng., U.K. 51 26N 1 44W
174 Marlborough Guyana 7 31N 58 38W
127 Marlborough, dist., N.Z. 41 45S 173 33E
34 Marlborough Downs, England, U.K. 51 25N 1 55W
49 Marle, France 49 43N 3 47E
165 Marlin, U.S.A. 31 25N 96 50W
143 Marlo, Vic., Australia 37 40S 148 34E
35 Marlow, England, U.K. 51 34N 0 47W
56 Marlow, Germany 54 8N 12 34E
165 Marlow, U.S.A. 34 40N 97 58W
106 Marmagao, India 15 25N 73 56E
55 Marmagen, Germany .50 28N 6 36E
50 Marmande, France 44 30N 0 10E
123 Marmar, Chad 20 2N 16 28E
69 Marmara I., Turkey ...40 35N 27 38E
100 Marmara Denizi (Sea of Marmara), Turkey 40 45N 28 15E
100 Marmaris, Turkey 36 50N 28 14E
164 Marmarth, U.S.A. 46 21N 103 52W
154 Marmion L., Canada .48 55N 91 30W
142 Marmion Mt., W. Austral. 29 16S 119 50E
71 Marmolada, Mte., Italy 46 25N 11 55E
63 Marmolejo, Spain 38 3N 4 13W
154 Marmora, Canada 44 28N 77 41W
49 Marnay, France 47 20N 5 48E
56 Marne, Germany 53 57N 9 1E
49 Marne, dépt., France .49 0N 4 10E
49 Marne R., France 48 53N 4 25E
36 Marnhull, Eng., U.K. .50 58N 2 20W
143 Marnoo, Vic., Australia 36 40S 142 54E
129 Maroantsetra, Malagasy Republic .15 26S 49 44E
175 Maroni, R., Fr. Guiana 4 0N 52 0W
76 Maronia, Greece 40 53N 25 24E
145 Maroochydore, Austral. 26 35S 153 10W
143 Maroona, Vic., Austral. 37 27S 142 54E
59 Maros R., Hungary ...46 25N 20 20E
71 Marostica, Italy 45 44N 11 40E
125 Maroua, Cameroon 10 40N 14 20E
129 Marovoay, Malagasy Republic 16 6S 46 39E
38 Marple, England, U.K. 53 23N 2 5W
135 Marquard, S. Africa ...28 40S 27 28E
137 Marquesas Is., Pac. Oc. 9 30S 140 0W
162 Marquette, U.S.A. 46 30N 87 21W
49 Marquise, France 50 50N 1 40E
145 Marra, N.S.W., Austral. 31 12S 144 10E
127 Marra Hills, Sudan 7 20N 27 35E
71 Marradi, Italy 44 5N 11 37E
122 Marrakech, Morocco ...31 40N 8 0W
143 Marrar, N.S.W., Austral. 34 50S 147 23E
100 Marrat, Si. Arabia......25 0N 45 35E
145 Marree, S. Australia ...29 39S 138 1E
132 Marrimane, Mozam. ...22 58S 33 34E
132 Marromeu, Mozam. ...18 40S 36 25E
129 Marrupa, Mozambique 13 8S 37 30E
127 Marsa Fatma, Ethiopia 14 57N 40 17E
131 Marsabit, Kenya 2 18N 38 0E
121 Marsa Susa (Apollonia), Libya .32 52N 21 59E
72 Marsala, Italy 37 48N 12 25E
78 Mârşani, Rumania 44 1N 23 59E
68 Marsaxlokk (Medport), Malta ...35 47N 14 32E
71 Marsciano, Italy 42 54N 12 20E
143 Marsden, N.S.W., Australia 33 47N 147 32E
50 Marseillan, France 43 23N 3 31E
51 Marseilles, France 43 18N 5 23E
135 Marseilles, S. Africa ...29 8S 27 20E
165 Marsh I., U.S.A. 29 35N 91 50W
124 Marshall, Liberia 6 8N 10 22W
165 Marshall, Ark., U.S.A. 35 58N 92 40W
162 Marshall, Mich., U.S.A. 42 17N 84 59W
164 Marshall, Minn., U.S.A. 44 25N 95 45W
164 Marshall, Mo., U.S.A. 39 8N 93 15W
165 Marshall, Tex., U.S.A. 32 29N 94 20W
136 Marshall Is., Pac. Oc. 9 0N 171 0E
164 Marshalltown, U.S.A. .42 0N 93 0W
132 Marshbrook, Rhodesia 13 33S 31 9E
165 Marshfield, Mo., U.S.A. 37 20N 92 58W
164 Marshfield, Wis., U.S.A. 44 42N 90 10W
73 Marsico, Nuovo, Italy 40 26N 15 43E
39 Marske by the sea, England, U.K. 54 35N 1 0W
80 Märsta, Sweden 59 37N 17 52E
81 Marstal, Denmark 54 51N 10 30E
39 Marston Moor, Eng. UK 53 58N 1 17W
81 Marstrand, Sweden 57 53N 11 35E
165 Mart, U.S.A. 31 34N 96 51W
71 Marta R., Italy 42 18N 11 47E
103 Martaban, Burma 16 30N 97 35E
103 Martaban, G. of, Burma 15 40N 96 30E
73 Martano, Italy 40 14N 18 18E
108 Martapura, Indonesia 3 22S 114 56E
125 Marte, Nigeria 12 23N 13 46E
44 Martel, France 44 57N 1 35E
54 Martelange, Belgium .49 49N 5 43E
35 Martham, Eng., U.K. 52 42N 1 38E
161 Martha's Vineyard, U.S.A. 41 25N 70 35W
48 Martigne Ferchaud, France 47 50N 1 20W
57 Martigny, Switzerland 46 6N 7 3E
51 Martigues, France 43 24N 5 4E
122 Martil, Morocco 35 36N 5 15W
164 Martin, S.D., U.S.A. .43 11N 101 45W
165 Martin, Tenn., U.S.A. 36 23N 88 51W
163 Martin, L., U.S.A. 32 45N 85 50W
64 Martin R., Spain 41 2N 0 43W
73 Martina Franca, Italy 40 42N 17 20E
146 Martinborough, N.Z. .41 14S 175 29E
169 Martinique, I., W.I. ...14 40N 61 0W
169 Martinique Pass, W.I. 15 15N 61 0W
77 Martinon, Greece 38 35N 23 15E
161 Martins Ferry, U.S.A. 40 5N 80 46W
58 Martinsberg, Austria .48 22N 15 9E
160 Martinsburg, Pa., U.S.A. 40 18N 78 21W
162 Martinsburg, W. Va., U.S.A. 39 30N 77 57W
162 Martinsville, Ind., U.S.A. 39 29N 86 23W
163 Martinsville, Va., U.S.A. 36 41N 79 52W
36 Martock England, U.K. 50 58N 2 47W
146 Marton, New Zealand 40 4S 175 23E
64 Martorell, Spain 41 28N 1 56E
63 Mártos, Spain 37 44N 3 58W
89 Martuni, U.S.S.R. 40 9N 45 10E
125 Maru, Nigeria 12 22N 6 22E
108 Marudi, Sar., Malaysia 4 10N 114 25E
101 Maruf, Afghanistan ...31 30N 67 0E
114 Marugame, Japan 34 15N 133 55E
73 Maruggio, Italy 40 20N 17 33E
143 Marulan, N.S.W., Australia 34 43S 150 3E
132 Marunga, Zambia 14 20S 23 11E
131 Marungu Mt., Congo . 7 30S 30 0E
50 Marvejols, France 44 33N 3 19E
167 Marvine Mt., U.S.A. ...38 44N 111 40W
104 Marwar, India 25 43N 73 45E
90 Mary, U.S.S.R. 37 40N 61 50E
145 Mary R., Australia 26 10S 152 28E
144 Mary Kathleen, Queens., Australia .20 35S 139 48E
145 Maryborough, Austral. 25 31S 152 37E
143 Maryborough, Austral. 37 0S 143 44E
45 Maryborough, *see* Port Laoise, Ireland 53 2N 7 20W
134 Marydale, S. Africa ...29 23S 22 5E
87 Maryets, U.S.S.R. 56 17N 49 47E
157 Maryfield, Canada 49 50N 101 35W
43 Marykirk, Scotland, U.K. 56 47N 2 30W
162 Maryland, st., U.S.A. .39 10N 76 40W
132 Maryland Jc., Rhodesia 12 45S 30 31E
38 Maryport England, U.K. 54 43N 3 30W
155 Mary's Harbour, Can. 52 18N 55 51W
155 Marystown, Canada ...47 10N 55 10W
167 Marysvale, U.S.A. 38 25N 112 17W
156 Marysville, Canada 49 35N 116 0W
166 Marsville, Calif., U.S.A. 39 14N 121 40W
164 Marysville, Kan., U.S.A. 39 50N 96 38W
160 Marysville, Mich., U.S.A. 42 55N 82 29W
162 Marysville, Ohio. USA 40 15N 83 20W
36 Marytavy, Eng., U.K. 50 34N 4 6W
145 Maryvale, Australia ...28 4S 152 12E
163 Maryville, U.S.A. 35 50N 84 0W
43 Marywell, Scot., U.K. 56 35N 2 31W
123 Marzuq (Mourzouk), Libya 25 53N 14 10E
98 Masada (site), Israel ...31 20N 35 19E
132 Masafa, Zambia 13 50S 27 30E
131 Masai Steppe, Tanzania 4 30S 36 30E
131 Masaka, Uganda 0 21S 31 45E
125 Masakali, Nigeria 13 2N 12 32E
108 Masalima I., Indonesia 4 50S 116 50E
109 Masamba, Indonesia . 2 30S 120 15E
112 Masan, S. Korea 35 15N 128 30E
65 Masanasa, Spain 39 25N 0 25W
131 Masanga, Congo 6 17S 29 22E
132 Masango, Rhodesia 15 40S 29 54E
131 Masasi, Tanzania 10 45S 38 52E
131 Masasi, dist., Tanzania 11 5S 38 40E
169 Masaya, Nicaragua 12 0N 86 7W
125 Masba, Nigeria 10 35N 13 1E
109 Masbate & I., Phil....12 20N 123 30E
122 Mascara, Algeria 35 26N 0 6E
168 Mascota, Mexico 20 30N 104 50W
132 Maseme, Botswana 18 46S 25 3E
135 Maseru, Lesotho 29 18S 27 30E
132 Mashaba, Rhodesia ...20 2S 30 29E
100 Mashabih I., Si. Arabia 25 35N 36 30E
39 Masham, Eng., U.K. .54 15N 1 40W
101 Mashhad, (Meshed), Iran 36 20N 59 35E
125 Mashi, Nigeria 13 0N 7 54E
114 Mashike, Japan 43 31N 141 30E
102 Mashki Chah, W. Pak. 29 5N 62 30E
154 Mashkode, Canada 47 2N 84 7W
132 Mashonaland, North, dist., Rhodesia 16 30S 30 0E
132 Mashonaland, South, dist., Rhodesia 18 0S 31 30E
89 Mashtagi, U.S.S.R. 40 35N 50 0E
82 Masi, Norway 69 26N 23 50E
130 Masi Manimba, Congo 4 40S 18 5E
131 Masindi, Uganda 1 40N 31 43E
131 Masindi Port, Uganda 1 43N 32 2E
99 Masirah I., Muscat & Oman 20 25N 58 50E
174 Masisea, Peru 8 35S 74 15W
131 Masisi, Congo 1 23S 28 49E
133 Masitonto, R., Africa .24 48S 32 10E
100 Masjed Solyman, Iran 31 55N 49 25E
45 Mask, L., Ireland 53 36N 9 24W
106 Maski, India 15 56N 76 46E
75 Maslen Nos, C., Bulg. 42 18N 27 48E
71 Maslinica, Yugoslavia 43 24N 16 13E
129 Masoala, C., Malagasy Republic 15 59S 50 13E
164 Mason, S.D., U.S.A. ...45 12N 103 27W
165 Mason, Tex., U.S.A. ...30 45N 99 15W
147 Mason B., N.Z. 46 55S 167 45E
166 Mason City, Wash., U.S.A. 48 0N 119 0W
101 Masqat (Muscat), Muscat and Oman 23 37N 58 35E
70 Massa, Tuscany, Italy 44 2N 10 7E
122 Massa, R., Morocco ...30 0N 9 30W
70 Massa Marittima, Italy 43 3N 10 52E
161 Massachusetts, st., U.S.A. 42 25N 72 0W
162 Massachusetts B., U.S.A. 42 30N 70 0W
98 Massade, Syria 33 12N 35 45E
73 Massafra, Italy 40 35N 17 8E
121 Massakori, Chad 13 0N 15 49E
132 Massamba, Mozambique 15 34S 33 35E
132 Massangena, Mozam. .21 34S 33 0E
132 Massara, Mozambique 20S 34 5E
70 Massarosa, Italy 43 53N 10 17E
50 Massat, France 42 53N 1 21E
127 Massawa, *see* Mesewa, Ethiopia..............15 35N 39 25E
127 Massawa Channel, Ethiopia 15 30N 40 0E
161 Massena, U.S.A. 44 52N 74 55W
121 Massenya, Chad 11 30N 16 25E
156 Masset, Canada 54 0N 132 0W
50 Massiac, France 45 15N 3 11E
50 Massif Central Mts., Fr. 45 30N 2 21E
160 Masillon, U.S.A. 40 47N 81 30W
132 Massinga, Mozambique 25 15S 35 22E
132 Massingir, Mozam. ...23 46S 32 4E
80 Masslingen, Sweden ...62 42N 12 48E
144 Massman, Australia ...16 25S 145 25E
132 Massocha, Mozam. 22 42S 32 12E
161 Masson, Canada 45 31N 75 26W
15 Masson I., Antarctica 66 10S 93 20E
126 Mastaba, Saudi Arabia 20 52N 39 30E
146 Masterton, New Zealand 40 56S 175 39E
77 Mastikho, Akra, C., Gr. 38 10N 26 2E
102 Mastuj, W. Pakistan .36 20N 72 36E
70 Mastung, W. Pakistan 29 50N 66 42E
126 Mastura, Saudi Arabia 23 7N 38 52E
114 Masuda, Japan 34 45N 132 0E
106 Masulipatnam, (Bandar), India 16 12N 81 12E
83 Masurian Lakes, Poland 53 30N 21 30E
131 Maswa, dist., Tanz. 3 10S 34 15E
76 Mat R., Albania 41 40N 20 0E
132 Matabele Plain, Zambia 16 15S 22 30E
132 Matabeleland, dist., Rhodesia 20 0S 28 0E
109 Mataboor, Indonesia . 1 41S 138 3E
63 Matachel R., Spain ...38 32N 6 0W
154 Matachewan, Canada .47 50N 80 55W
112 Matad, Mongolia 47 11N 115 27E
130 Matadi, Congo 5 52S 13 31E
157 Matador, Canada 50 49N 107 56W
169 Matagalpa, Nicaragua 13 10N 85 40W
154 Matagami, Canada 49 45N 77 34W
154 Matagami, L., Canada 49 50N 77 40W
165 Matagorda, U.S.A. 28 43N 96 0W
165 Matagorda, B., U.S.A. 28 30N 96 15W
165 Matagorda I., U.S.A. .28 10N 96 40W
108 Matak I., Indonesia ... 3 18N 106 16E
143 Matakana, Australia ...33 1S 145 57E
146 Matakana, I., N.Z. 37 32S 176 5E
132 Matala, Zambia 15 8S 27 12E
131 Matalamma, Kenya ... 2 8N 38 11E
106 Matale, Ceylon 7 30N 80 44E
124 Matam, Senegal 15 34N 13 17W
146 Matamata, N.Z. 37 48S 175 47E
168 Matamoros, Coahuila, Mexico 25 45N 103 1W
168 Matamoros, Puebla, Mexico 18 2N 98 17W
168 Matamoros, Tamaulipas, Mexico 25 50N 97 30W
109 Matana L., Indonesia . 2 30S 121 25E
131 Matandu R., Tanzania 8 35S 39 40E
155 Matane, Canada 48 50N 67 33W
152 Matanuska, Alaska, U.S.A. 61 38N 149 0W
169 Matanzas, Cuba 23 0N 81 40W
132 Matapa, Botswana 23 16S 24 34E
77 Matapan, C., Greece ...36 22N 22 27E
155 Matapedia, Canada 48 0N 66 59W
106 Matara, Ceylon 5 58N 80 30E
108 Mataram, Indonesia ... 8 41S 116 10E
138 Mataranka, N. Terr., Australia 14 55S 133 4E
174 Matarani, Peru 16 50S 72 10W
122 Matarka, Morocco 33 14N 2 39W
64 Mataro, Spain 41 32N 2 29E
64 Matarraña R., Spain .40 55N 0 8E
74 Mataruška Bania Yugoslavia 43 40N 20 45E
146 Matata, New Zealand 37 54S 176 48E
135 Matatiele, S. Africa ...30 20S 28 49E
147 Mataura, New Zealand 46 11S 168 51E
147 Mataura R., N.Z. 45 49S 168 44E
168 Matehuala, Mexico 23 40N 100 50W
132 Mateke Hs., Rhodesia 21 48S 31 0E
71 Matelica, Italy 43 15N 13 0E
132 Matema, Mozambique 15 42S 33 26E
73 Matera, Italy 40 40N 16 37E
132 Matereca. Mozambique 18 26S 33 24E
59 Mátészalka, Hungary .47 58N 22 20E
132 Matetsi, Rhodesia 18 12S 26 0E
123 Mateur, Tunisia 37 0N 9 48E
89 Mateyev, Kurgan, U.S.S.R. 47 35N 38 47E
80 Matfors, Sweden 62 21N 17 10E
50 Matha, France 45 52N 0 20W
157 Matheson I., Canada .51 45N 96 56W
147 Mathias Pass, N.Z. 43 7S 171 6E
168 Matias Romero, Mexico 16 53N 95 2W
165 Mathis, U.S.A. 28 4N 97 48W
143 Mathoura, Australia ...35 50S 144 55E
37 Mathry, Wales, U.K. .51 56N 5 6W
104 Mathura, India 27 30N 77 48E
109 Mati, Philippines 6 55N 126 15E
109 Matjan Is., Indonesia . 6 30S 121 10E
134 Matjiesfontein, S. Afr. 33 12S 20 32E
133 Matlabas, Trans., S. Afr. 24 12S 27 28E
133 Matlapin R., S. Africa 25 48S 24 20E
39 Matlock, Eng., U.K. .53 8N 1 32W
123 Matmata, Tunisia 33 30N 9 59E
127 Matna, Sudan 13 49N 35 10E
130 Mato, Congo 8 1S 24 56E

MAP
175 Mato Grosso, st., Brazil 14 0s 55 0w
175 Mato Grosso, Plat. of, Brazil 15 0s 54 0w
90 Matochkin Shar, U.S.S.R. 73 10N 56 40E
133 Matola, Mozambique .26 0s 32 29E
132 Matopo Hills, Rhod. .20 36s 28 20E
132 Matopos, Rhodesia 20 20s 28 29E
62 Matosinhos, Portugal .41 11N 8 42w
51 Matour, France 46 19N 4 29E
134 Matroosberg, S. Africa 31 28s 19 50E
126 Matrûh, Egypt 31 19N 27 9E
103 Matsang R., Tibet, China 29 25N 88 0E
134 Matsap, C. Prov., S. Afr. 28 38s 22 47E
125 Matsena, Nigeria 13 5N 10 5E
89 Matsesta, U.S.S.R. 43 34N 39 44E
114 Matsue, Japan 35 25N 133 10E
114 Matsumoto, Japan 36 15N 138 0E
114 Matsuyama, Japan 33 45N 132 45E
114 Matsuzaka, Japan 34 35N 136 25E
106 Mattancheri, India 9 50N 76 15E
154 Mattawa, Canada 46 20N 78 45w
155 Mattawamkeag, U.S.A. 45 30N 68 30w
57 Matterhorn, Mt., Switz. 45 58N 7 39E
59 Mattersburg, Austria .47 44N 16 24E
174 Matthews Ridge, Guyana 7 37N 60 10w
154 Mattice, Canada 49 40N 83 20w
161 Mattituck, U.S.A. 40 58N 72 32w
80 Mattmar, Sweden 63 18N 13 54E
162 Mattoon, U.S.A. 39 30N 88 20w
108 Matua, Indonesia 2 58s 110 52E
174 Matucana, Peru 11 55s 76 15w
101 Matun, Afghanistan ...33 22N 69 58E
174 Maturín, Venezuela ... 9 45N 63 11w
90 Matylka, U.S.S.R. 63 55N 82 0E
131 Mau Escarpment, Ken. 0 40s 36 2E
104 Mau-Ranipur, India .25 16N 79 8E
154 Mauagami R., Canada 49 30N 82 0w
49 Maubeuge, France 50 17N 3 57E
50 Maubourguet, France .43 29N 0 1w
129 Mauch Berg. Mt., S. Afr. 25 13s 30 30E
40 Mauchline, Scot., U.K. 55 31N 4 23w
43 Maud, Scotland, U.K. 57 30N 2 8w
143 Maude, N.S.W., Austral. 34 29s 144 18E
15 Maudheim, Antarctica 71 5s 11 0w
132 Mauele, Mozambique .24 18s 34 2E
174 Maués, Brazil 3 20s 57 45w
38 Maughold, I. of M., U.K. 54 18N 4 17w
38 Maughold Hd., Isle of Man, U.K. 54 18N 4 17w
158 Maui I., Hawaii, U.S.A. 20 45N 156 20E
103 Maukmai, Burma 20 14N 97 44E
172 Maule, prov., Chile 36 5s 72 30w
50 Mauléon, Licharre, Fr. 43 14N 0 54w
44 Maum, Ireland 53 31N 9 35w
162 Maumee, U.S.A. 41 35N 83 40w
162 Maumee R., U.S.A. ...41 15N 85 0w
109 Maumere, Indonesia ... 8 38s 122 13E
44 Maumturk Mts., Ireland 53 32N 9 42w
132 Maun, Botswana 20 0s 23 26E
158 Mauna Loa, Mt., Hawaii, U.S.A. 19 50N 155 28w
105 Maunath Bhanjan, India 25 56N 83 33E
146 Maungaturoto, N.Z. ...36 6s 174 23E
107 Maungmagan Is., Burma 41 0s 97 48E
131 Maungu, Kenya 3 32s 38 42E
166 Maupin, U.S.A. 45 12N 121 9w
108 Mauradjulai, Indonesia 0 6s 114 4E
48 Maure de Bretagne, Fr. 47 53N 2 0w
165 Maurepas L., U.S.A. .30 18N 90 35w
51 Maures, Mts., France .43 15N 6 15E
50 Mauriac, France 45 13N 2 19E
138 Maurice L., S. Austral. 29 30s 131 0E
146 Mauriceville, N.Z. 40 45s 175 35E
51 Maurienne, dist., Fr. .45 15N 6 20E
55 Maurik, Netherlands .51 58N 5 27E
120 Mauritania, Rep., Afr. 20 50N 10 0w
11 Mauritius, Indian Ocean 20 0s 57 0E
50 Maurs, France 44 43N 2 12E
164 Mauston, U.S.A. 43 48N 90 5w
58 Mauterndorf, Austria .47 9N 13 40E
50 Mauvezin, France 43 44N 0 53E
50 Mauzé, France 46 12N 0 41w
106 Mavelikara, India 9 14N 76 32E
129 Mavinga, Angola 15 50s 20 10E
132 Mavita, Mozambique .19 33s 33 10E
104 Mavli, India 24 45N 73 55E
98 Mavqui'im, Israel 31 38N 34 32E
76 Mavrovë, Albania 40 26N 19 32E
132 Mavuradona Mts., Rhod. 16 30s 31 30E
130 Mawa, Congo 2 45N 26 33E
104 Mawana, India 29 6N 77 58E
104 Mawand, West Pakistan 29 33N 68 38E
157 Mawer, Canada 50 46N 106 22w
36 Mawgan, Eng., U.K. .50 4N 5 10w
103 Mawk Mai, Burma 20 14N 97 50E
15 Mawson Base, Antarc. 67 30N 65 0E
164 Max, U.S.A. 47 50N 101 20w
168 Maxcanú, Mexico 20 40N 90 10w
132 Maxixe, Mozambique .23 54s 35 17E
161 Maxville, Canada 45 18N 74 50w
41 Maxwellheugh, Scotland, U.K. 55 35N 2 23w
144 Maxwelton, Australia .15 45s 142 30E
146 Maxwelltown, N.Z. 39 51s 174 49E
41 Maxwelltown, Scot., U.K. 55 4N 3 38w
41 May, I. of, Scot., U.K. 56 11N 2 32w
144 May Downs, Australia 22 25s 148 35E
169 May Pen, Jamaica 17 58N 77 15w
64 Maya, Spain 43 12N 1 29w
168 Maya Mts., Brit. Hond. 16 30N 89 0w
91 Maya R., U.S.S.R. 58 20N 135 0E
169 Mayaguana Island, Bahamas 21 30N 72 44w
169 Mayagüez, Puerto Rico 18 12N 67 9w
64 Mayals, Spain 41 22N 0 30E
130 Mayama, Congo, (Fr.) 3 50s 14 52E
142 Mayanup, W. Australia 33 58s 116 25E
169 Mayarí, Cuba 20 40N 75 39w
106 Mayavaram, *see* Mayuram, India 11 3N 79 42E
166 Maybell, U.S.A. 40 30N 108 4w
40 Maybole, Scot., U.K. .55 21N 4 41w
145 Maydena, Tas., Austral. 42 40s 146 30E
76 Maydos, Turkey 40 13N 26 20E
114 Mayebashi, Japan 36 30N 139 0E
57 Mayen, Germany 50 18N 7 10E
48 Mayenne, France 48 20N 0 38w
48 Mayenne, dépt., Fr. ...48 10N 0 40w
167 Mayer, U.S.A. 34 28N 112 17w
156 Mayerthorpe, Canada .53 57N 115 15w
39 Mayfield, Staffs, England, U.K. 53 1N 1 47w
35 Mayfield, Sussex, England, U.K. 51 1N 0 17E
163 Mayfield, U.S.A. 36 45N 88 40w
167 Mayhill, U.S.A. 32 58N 105 30w
89 Maykop, U.S.S.R. 44 35N 40 25E
142 Maynard Hills, Austral. 28 44s 119 45E
154 Maynooth, Canada 45 14N 77 56w
45 Maynooth, Ireland 53 22N 6 38w
46 Mayo Bridge, Northern Ireland, U.K. 54 11N 6 13w
46 Mayo, co., Ire. 53 47N 9 7w
125 Mayo Daga, Nigeria ... 6 59N 11 25E
152 Mayo, Canada 63 38N 135 57w
146 Mayor I., N.Z. 37 16s 176 17E
162 Maysville, U.S.A. 38 43N 84 16w
106 Mayuram (Mayavaram), India 11 3N 79 42E
164 Mayville, N.D., U.S.A. 47 30N 97 23w
160 Mayville, N.Y., U.S.A. 42 14N 79 31w
62 Mayorga, Spain 42 10N 5 16w
132 Mazabuka, Zambia 15 52s 27 44E
122 Mazagan, *see* El Jadida, Morocco 33 11N 8 17w
175 Mazagão, Brazil 0 20s 51 50w
156 Mazama, Canada 49 43N 120 8w
50 Mazamet, France 43 30N 2 20E
172 Mazán, Argentina 28 40s 66 30w
174 Mazán, Peru 3 15s 73 0w
122 Mazar, W., Algeria 32 25N 1 18E
72 Mazara del Vallo, Italy 37 40N 12 34E
101 Mazar-i-Sharif, Afghan. 36 41N 67 0E
176 Mazarredo, Argentina 47 10s 66 50w
65 Mazarrón, Spain 37 38N 1 19w
65 Mazarrón, Golfo de, Sp. 37 27N 1 19w
174 Mazaruni R., Guyana 6 15N 60 0w
168 Mazatenango, Guatemala 14 35N 91 30w
168 Mažatlan, Mexico 23 10N 106 30w
171 Mazhan, Iran 32 30N 59 0E
186 Mazheikyai, U.S.S.R. .56 20N 22 20E
101 Mazinan, Iran 36 25N 56 48E
132 Mazoe, Mozambique ...16 42s 33 7E
132 Mazoe, Rhodesia 17 28s 30 58E
132 Mazoe R., Mozambique 16 45s 32 30E
127 Mazrub, Sudan 14 0N 29 20E
73 Mazzarino, Italy 37 19N 14 12E
131 Mbaba, Somali Rep. ... 1 30s 41 40E
133 M'babane, Swaziland .26 18s 31 6E
124 M'Bagne, Mauritania .16 6N 14 47w
124 Mbahiakro, Ivory Coast 7 33N 4 19w
130 Mbaiki, Cent. Afr. Rep. 3 53N 18 1E
132 Mbala (Abercorn), Zam. 25 12s 151 5E
131 Mbale, Uganda 1 8N 34 12E
125 Mbalmayo, Cameroon 3 33N 11 33E
131 Mbamba Bay, Tanz. .11 13s 34 49E
130 Mbandaka, (Coquilhatville), Congo 0 1s 18 18E
125 Mbanga, Cameroon 4 30N 9 33E
131 Mbaragani, Tanz. 3 22s 33 55E
131 Mbarara, Uganda 0 35s 30 25E
131 Mbate, Tanzania 8 55s 39 10E
131 Mbemkuru R., Tanz. . 9 25s 39 50E
131 Mbereshi, Zambia 9 45s 28 45E
125 Mberubu, Nigeria 6 10N 7 38E
131 Mbeya, Tanzania 8 54s 33 29E
131 Mbeya, reg., Tanzania 8 15s 33 30E
127 Mbia, Sudan 6 15N 29 18E
132 Mbimbi, Zambia 13 25s 23 2E
132 Mbinga & dist., Tanz. 10 50s 35 0E
131 Mbirira, Tanzania 4 20s 30 12E
131 Mbirizi, Uganda 0 24s 31 28E
127 Mbiti, Sudan 5 42N 28 3E
130 Mboi, Congo 6 54s 2 0E
130 M'Bouoma, Congo 0 55s 15 6E
124 Mbour, Senegal 14 22N 16 54w
124 M'Bout, Mauritania ...16 1N 12 38w
131 Mbozi, Tanzania 9 0s 32 58E
131 Mbulu, Tanzania 3 45s 35 30E
130 Mbuji-Mayi, Congo ... 6 9s 23 40E
172 Mburucuyá, Argentina 28 1s 58 14w
122 Mcherrah, reg., Algeria 27 0N 4 30w
123 M'Chiguig, Tunisia 30 59N 10 9E
131 Mchungu, Tanzania ... 7 50s 39 20E
122 Mdennah, reg., Maur. .24 37N 6 0w
68 Mdina, Malta 35 51N 14 25E
167 Mead L., U.S.A. 36 10N 114 10w
154 Meade, Canada 49 26N 83 51w
165 Meade, U.S.A. 37 18N 100 25w
142 Meadow, W. Australia 26 35s 114 40E
157 Meadow Lake, Canada 54 10N 108 10w
157 Meadow Lake Prov. Park, Canada 54 25N 109 0w
160 Meadville, U.S.A. 41 39N 80 9w
160 Meaford, Canada 44 40N 80 36w
62 Mealhada, Portugal ...40 22N 8 27w
38 Mealsgate, Eng., U.K. 54 46N 3 14w
155 Mealy Mts., Canada ...53 30N 59 0w
156 Meander River, Canada 59 3N 117 30w
166 Meare's, C., U.S.A. 45 37N 124 0w
43 Mearns, Howe of the, Scotland, U.K. 56 52N 2 26w
46 Meath, Co., Ireland ...53 32N 6 40w
157 Meath Park, Canada .53 27N 105 22w
50 Meaulne, France 40 36N 2 36E
49 Meaux, France 48 58N 2 50E
132 Mecanhelas, Mozam. .15 12s 35 54E
126 Mecca, Saudi Arabia .21 30N 39 54E
167 Mecca, U.S.A. 33 37N 116 3w
160 Mechanicsburg, U.S.A. 40 12N 77 0w
161 Mechanicville, U.S.A. .42 54N 73 41w
123 Mechehed Salah, Tunisia 32 16N 11 4E
54 Mechelen, Belgium 51 2N 4 29E
122 Méchéria, Algeria 33 35N 0 18w
56 Mechernich, Germany 50 35N 6 39E
89 Mechetinskaya, U.S.S.R. 46 45N 40 32E
122 Mechra-bel-Ksiri, Mor. 34 38N 5 58w
76 Mecidiye, Turkey 40 38N 26 32E
88 Mecitözü, Turkey 40 32N 35 25E
56 Mecklenburg B., Ger. .54 20N 11 40E
129 Meconta, Mozambique 14 59s 39 50E
62 Meda, Portugal 40 57N 7 18w
138 Meda R., W. Australia 17 20s 124 30E
122 Medaguine, Algeria 33 41N 3 26E
106 Medak, India 18 1N 78 15E
108 Medan, Indonesia 3 40N 98 38w
176 Medanosa, Pta., Arg. .48 0s 66 0E
106 Medawachchiya, Ceylon 8 30N 80 30E
122 Medea, Algeria 36 12N 2 50E
74 Mededa, Yugoslavia ...43 44N 19 15E
174 Medellín, Colombia 6 15N 75 35w
54 Medemblik, Netherlands 52 46N 5 8E
123 Medenine, Tunisia 33 20N 10 29E
127 Meder, Ethiopia 14 42N 40 44E
166 Medford, Ore., U.S.A. 42 20N 122 52w
164 Medford, Wis., U.S.A. 45 9N 90 21w
78 Medgidia, Rumania ...44 15N 28 19E
127 Medi, Sudan 5 4N 30 42E
172 Media Agua, Argentina 31 58s 68 25w
172 Media Luna, Argentina 34 45s 66 44w
78 Medias, Rumania 46 9N 24 22E
166 Medical Lake, U.S.A. .47 41N 117 42w
71 Medicina, Italy 44 29N 11 38E
166 Medicine Bow, U.S.A. 41 56N 106 11w
157 Medicine Hat, Canada 50 0N 110 45w
164 Medicine Lake, U.S.A. 48 30N 104 30w
165 Medicine Lodge, U.S.A. 37 20N 98 37w
100 Medina, Saudi Arabia 24 35N 39 52E
160 Medina, Ohio, U.S.A. .41 9N 81 50w
164 Medina N.D., U.S.A. .46 57N 99 20w
160 Medina, N.Y., U.S.A. .43 15N 78 27w
165 Medina L., U.S.A. 29 35N 98 58w
165 Medina R., U.S.A. 29 10N 98 20w
62 Medina del Campo, Sp. 41 18N 4 55w
62 Medina de Rioseco, Sp. 41 53N 5 3w
63 Medina-Sidonia, Spain 36 28N 5 57w
64 Medinaceli, Spain 41 12N 2 30w
66 Mediterranean Sea 35 0N 15 0E
123 Medjerda, R., Tunisia 36 35N 8 30E
75 Medkovets, Bulgaria .43 37N 23 10E
50 Médoc, dist., France ...45 10N 0 56w
157 Medstead, Canada 53 19N 108 5w
34 Medstead, Eng., U.K. 51 7N 1 4w
71 Medulin, Yugoslavia .44 49N 13 55E
74 Medveda, Yugoslavia .42 50N 21 32E
87 Medveditsa R., U.S.S.R. 50 30N 44 0E
87 Medvedok, U.S.S.R. ...57 20N 50 1E
91 Medvezhi Is., U.S.S.R. 71 0N 161 0E
84 Medvezhyegorsk, U.S.S.R. 63 0N 34 25E
35 Medway R., Eng., U.K. 51 12N 0 23E
87 Medyn, U.S.S.R. 54 59N 35 56E
59 Medzev, Czechoslovakia 48 43N 20 55E
59 Medzilaborce, Cz. 49 17N 21 52E
142 Meeberrie, W. Australia 26 57s 116 0E
142 Meekatharra, W. Austral. 26 32s 118 29E
166 Meeker, U.S.A. 40 1N 107 58w
155 Meelpaeg L., Canada .48 18N 56 35w
56 Meerane, Germany 50 51N 12 30E
55 Meerhout, Belgium 51 7N 5 4E
104 Meerut, India 29 1N 77 50E
166 Meeteetsa, U.S.A. 44 10N 108 56w
127 Mega, Ethiopia 3 57N 38 30E
77 Megalo Khorió, Greece 36 27N 27 24E
77 Megalo Petali, I., Gr. .38 0N 24 15E
77 Megalópolis, Greece ...37 25N 22 7E
77 Meganísi, I., Greece ...38 39N 20 48E
155 Mégantic, Canada 45 36N 70 56w
77 Megara, Greece 37 58N 23 22E
77 Megdhova, R., Greece 39 10N 21 45E
51 Mégève, France 45 51N 6 37E
127 Meghezez, Mt., Ethiopia 9 18N 39 26E
105 Meghna, R., E. Pak. .23 45N 90 40E
98 Megiddo, Israel 32 36N 35 11E
98 Megiddo, Site, Israel .32 35N 35 11E
78 Mehadia, Rumania 44 56N 22 23E
55 Mehargne R., Belgium 50 36N 4 58E
122 Mehaiguene, W., Alg. .33 0N 2 45E
78 Mehedinti, Reg., Rum. 44 40N 22 50E
126 Meheisa, Sudan 19 38N 32 57E
105 Mehndawal, India 26 58N 83 5E
104 Mehsana, India 23 39N 72 26E
49 Méhun Sur Yèvre, Fr. 47 10N 2 13E
131 Meia Meia, Tanzania . 5 50s 35 48E
37 Meidrim, Wales, U.K. 51 51N 4 3w
43 Meig, R., Scot., U.K. .57 33N 4 50w
46 Meigh, N. Ireland, U.K. 54 8N 6 22w
112 Meihokow, China 42 37N 125 46E
113 Meihsien, China 24 20N 116 0E
103 Meiktila, Burma 21 0N 96 0E
55 Meinerzhagen, Germany 51 6N 7 38E
56 Meiningen, Germany .50 32N 10 25E
57 Meiringen, Switzerland 46 43N 8 12E
113 Meishan Dam, China .31 58N 115 59E
56 Meissen, Germany 51 10N 13 29E
113 Meitan, China 27 45N 107 45E
98 Meithalun, Jordan ...32 21N 35 16E
128 Meiyganga, Cameroon 6 20N 14 10E
50 Méjean, Causse, Mts., France 44 15N 3 30E
172 Mejillones, Chile 23 10s 70 30w
142 Meka, W. Australia ...27 25s 116 48E
125 Mekkaw, Nigeria 7 26N 2 55E
107 Meklong, *see* Samut Songkhram, Thailand 13 24N 100 1E
122 Meknès, Morocco 33 57N 5 39w
95 Mekong R., Asia 18 0N 104 15E
109 Mekongga, Mt., Indon. 3 50s 121 30E
106 Melagiri Hills, India ...12 20N 77 30E
122 Melah, Sebkra el, Alg. 29 20N 1 30w
108 Melalan, Sab., Malaysia 5 10N 116 5E
77 Mélambes, Crete, Greece 35 8N 24 40E
136 Melanesia, arch., Pacific Ocean 4 0s 155 0E
106 Melapalaiyam, India . 8 39N 77 44E
82 Melbo, Norway 68 31N 14 50E
42 Melbost, Scot., U.K. .58 14N 6 20w
35 Melbourn, Eng., U.K. 52 5N 0 1E
143 Melbourne, Vic., Austral. 37 40s 145 0E
34 Melbourne, Eng., UK 52 50N 1 25w
163 Melbourne, Fla., U.S.A. 28 13N 80 14w
70 Melcésine, Italy 45 46N 10 48E
168 Melchor Múzquiz, Mexico 27 50N 101 40w
168 Melchor Ocampo (San Pedro Ocampo), Mex. 24 52N 101 40w
71 Meldola, Italy 44 7N 12 3E
56 Meldorf, Germany 54 5N 9 5E
70 Melegnano, Italy 45 21N 9 20E
87 Melekess, U.S.S.R. 54 25N 49 33E
74 Melenci, Yugoslavia ...45 32N 20 20E
87 Melenki, U.S.S.R. 55 20N 41 37E
88 Melet, R., Turkey 41 0N 39 49E
121 Melfi, Chad. 11 0N 17 59E
73 Melfi, Italy 41 0N 15 40E
157 Melfort, Canada 52 50N 105 40w
40 Melfort, Loch, Scotland, United Kingdom 56 13N 5 33w
132 Melfort, Rhodesia 18 0s 31 25E
175 Melgaço, Brazil 1 45s 50 50w
62 Melgaço, Portugal 42 7N 8 15w
62 Melgar de Fernamental, Spain 42 27N 4 17w
79 Melhus, Norway 63 17N 10 18E
77 Meligalá, Greece 37 15N 21 59E
122 Melilla, Sp. Morocco ...35 21N 2 57w
48 Melilot, Israel 31 22N 34 37E
172 Melipilla, Chile 33 42s 71 15w
77 Mélissa Óros, Mt., Gr. 37 32N 26 4E
157 Melita, Canada 49 15N 101 5w
73 Melito di Porto Salvo, It. 37 55N 15 47E
88 Melitopol, U.S.S.R. ...46 50N 35 22E
58 Melk, Austria 48 13N 15 20E
34 Melksham, Eng., U.K. 51 22N 2 9w
80 Mellan Fryken L., Swed. 59 43N 13 22E
82 Mellansel, Sweden 63 25N 18 10E
50 Melle, France 46 14N 0 10w
56 Melle, Germany 52 12N 8 20E
123 Mellégue, R., Tunisia .36 15N 8 30E
164 Mellen, U.S.A. 46 19N 90 36w
81 Mellerud, Sweden 58 41N 12 28E
164 Mellette, U.S.A. 45 11N 98 29w
62 Mellid, Spain 42 55N 8 1w
133 Melliodora, S. Africa .26 45s 26 6E
127 Mellit, Sudan 14 15N 25 40E
42 Mellon Charles, Scotland, U.K. 57 52N 5 37w
41 Melmerby, Eng., U.K. 54 44N 2 35w
135 Melmoth, Natal, S. Afr. 28 33s 31 28E
43 Melness, Scot., U.K. ...58 32N 4 27w
58 Melnik, Czechoslovakia 50 22N 14 23E
173 Melo, Uruguay 32 20s 54 10w
89 Melovoye, U.S.S.R. ...49 25N 40 5E
123 Melrhir, Chott, Algeria 34 25N 6 24E
143 Melrose, N.S.W., Australia 32 42s 147 1E
41 Melrose, Scot., U.K. ...55 35N 2 44w
165 Melrose, U.S.A. 34 27N 103 33w
142 Melrose, W. Australia 27 50s 121 15E
39 Melsonby, Eng., U.K. 54 28N 1 41w
82 Melstadhur, Iceland ...65 18N 20 50w
166 Melstone, U.S.A. 46 45N 108 0w
56 Melsungen, Germany .51 8N 9 34E
35 Melton, England, U.K. 52 7N 1 20E
35 Melton Constable, England, U.K. 52 52N 1 1E
35 Melton Mowbray, England, U.K. 52 46N 0 52w
49 Meluni, France 48 32N 2 39E
106 Melur, India 10 2N 78 23E
127 Melut, Sudan 10 30N 32 20E
42 Melvaig, Scot., U.K. .57 48N 5 49w
43 Melvich, Scot., U.K. .58 33N 3 55w
157 Melville, Canada 51 0N 102 50w
139 Melville B., Australia .12 0s 136 45E
138 Melville I., Australia .11 30s 131 0E
14 Melville I., Canada ...75 30N 111 0w
155 Melville L., Canada ...53 45N 59 40w
153 Melville Pen., Canada 68 0N 84 0w
46 Melvin L., Ireland 54 26N 8 10w
59 Mélykut, Hungary 46 11N 19 25E
129 Memba, Mozambique .14 11s 40 30E
109 Memboro, Indonesia ... 9 30s 119 30E
65 Membrilla, Spain 38 59N 3 21w
135 Memel, O.F.S., S. Africa 27 38s 29 36E
86 Memel, *see* Klaipeda, U.S.S.R. 55 43N 21 10E
57 Memmingen, Germany 47 59N 10 12E
165 Memphis, Tenn., U.S.A. 35 7N 90 0w
165 Memphis, Tex., U.S.A. 34 45N 100 30w
161 Memphremagog L., U.S.A. 45 8N 72 17w
165 Mena, U.S.A. 34 40N 94 15w
37 Menai Bridge, Wales, United Kingdom 53 14N 4 11w
37 Menai Strait, Wales, United Kingdom 53 7N 4 20w
125 Menaka, Niger 15 59N 2 18E
165 Menard, U.S.A. 30 57N 99 58w
162 Menasha, U.S.A. 44 13N 88 27w
108 Menate, Indonesia 0 12s 112 47E
113 Mencheng, China 33 27N 116 45E
50 Mende, France 44 31N 3 30E
127 Mendebo Mts., Ethiopia 7 0N 39 22E
55 Menden, Germany 51 26N 7 48E
100 Menderes R., Turkey .37 52N 28 45E
127 Mendi, Ethiopia 9 47N 35 4E
36 Mendip Hills, Eng., U.K. 51 17N 2 40w
35 Mendlesham, Eng., U.K. 52 15N 1 4E
166 Mendocino, U.S.A. 39 26N 123 50w
105 Mendong Gampa, Tibet, China 31 16N 85 11E
143 Mendooran, N.S.W., Australia 32 0s 149 22E
167 Mendota, Calif., U.S.A. 36 46N 120 24w
164 Mendota, Ill., U.S.A. .41 35N 89 5w
172 Mendoza, Argentina ...32 50s 68 52w
172 Mendoza, prov., Arg. .33 0s 69 0w
108 Mendung, Indonesia ... 0 38N 103 8E
174 Mene de Mauroa, Venezuela 10 45N 70 50w
54 Menen (Menin), Belgium 50 47N 3 7E
123 Ménerville, Algeria ...36 45N 3 30E
72 Menfi, Italy 37 36N 12 57E
107 Meng Wang, China 22 18N 100 31E
71 Mengěs, Yugoslavia ...46 24N 14 35E
108 Menggala, Indonesia . 4 20s 105 15E
63 Mengibar, Spain 37 58N 3 48w
107 Mengla, China 21 25N 101 30E
122 Mengoub, Algeria 29 49N 5 26w
122 Mengoub, Morocco 32 10N 2 27w
103 Meng-pan, China 23 5N 100 19E
113 Mengshan, China 24 2N 110 32E
107 Meng-so, China 22 33N 99 31E
111 Mengtsz, China 23 20N 103 20E
103 Meng-wang, China 22 17N 100 32E
112 Mengyin, China 35 40N 117 55E
36 Menheniot, Eng., U.K. 50 26N 4 24w
155 Menihek L., Canada ...54 0N 67 0w
54 Menin, Belgium 50 47N 3 7E

MAP
143 Menindee & L., Australia 32 20N 142 25E
103 Menkong, China 28 38N 98 24E
162 Menominee, U.S.A. 45 9N 87 39W
162 Menominee, R., U.S.A. 45 30N 87 50W
164 Menomonie, U.S.A. ...44 50N 91 54W
64 Menorca, Balearic Is., Spain 40 0N 4 0E
122 Menouarar, Algeria ...31 11N 2 9W
108 Mentawai Is., Indonesia 2 0S 99 0E
35 Mentmore, Eng., U.K. 51 52N 0 40W
51 Menton, France 43 50N 7 29E
160 Mentor, U.S.A. 41 40N 81 21W
123 Menzel Temime, Tunisia 36 50N 11 0E
123 Menzel-Bourguiba, Tunisia 39 9N 9 49E
142 Menzies, W. Australia 29 40S 120 58E
98 Me'ona (Tarshiha), Isr. 33 1N 35 15E
132 Mepaco, Mozambique .15 57S 30 48E
54 Meppel, Netherlands .52 52N 6 12E
56 Meppen, Germany 52 41N 7 20E
64 Mequinenza, Spain 41 22N 0 17E
165 Mer Rouge, U.S.A. 32 47N 91 48W
77 Merabellou, Kolpos, Gr. 35 10N 25 50E
108 Merah, Indonesia 0 53N 116 54E
109 Merak, Indonesia 5 55S 106 1E
71 Merano, Italy 46 40N 11 10E
1 Merapi, vol., Indonesia 8 5N 110 0E
70 Merate, Italy 45 42N 9 23E
109 Merauke, Indonesia ... 8 29S 140 24E
109 Merbabu Mt., Indonesia 7 30S 110 40E
143 Merbein, Vic., Australia 34 10S 142 2E
99 Merca, Somali Rep. ... 1 48N 44 50E
64 Mercadal, Spain 39 59N 4 5E
106 Mercara, India 12 30N 75 45E
71 Mercato Saraceno, Italy 43 57N 12 11E
167 Merced, U.S.A. 37 25N 120 30W
172 Mercedes, Buenos Aires, Argentina 34 40S 59 30W
172 Mercedes, Corrientes, Argentina 29 10S 58 5W
172 Mercedes, San Luis, Arg. 33 5S 65 21W
172 Mercedes, Uruguay 33 12S 58 0W
172 Merceditas, Chile 28 20S 70 35W
146 Mercer, New Zealand .37 16S 175 5E
160 Mercer, U.S.A. 41 14N 80 13W
57 Merching, Germany ...48 15N 11 0E
146 Mercury Is., N.Z. 36 40S 175 45E
153 Mercy C., Canada 65 0N 62 30W
48 Merdrignac, France ...48 11N 2 27W
34 Mere, Wilts., Eng., U.K. 51 5N 2 16W
176 Meredith C., Falk. Is. 52 15S 60 40W
165 Meredith, L., U.S.A. .35 30N 101 35W
88 Merefa, U.S.S.R. 49 56N 36 2W
121 Méréke, Cent. Afr. Rep. 7 35N 23 0E
49 Méréville, France 48 20N 2 5E
89 Mergenevskiy, U.S.S.R. 49 59N 51 15E
107 Mergui, Burma 12 30N 98 35E
107 Mergui Arch, Burma .11 30N 97 30E
168 Merida, Mexico 20 50N 89 40W
63 Merida, Spain 38 55N 6 25W
174 Mérida, Venezuela 8 36N 71 8W
169 Merida, Cord. de, Venezuela 9 0N 71 0W
34 Meriden, England, UK 52 27N 1 36W
161 Meriden, U.S.A. 41 33N 72 47W
166 Meridian, Idaho, U.S.A. 43 41N 116 25W
163 Meridian, Miss., U.S.A. 32 20N 88 42W
165 Meridian, Tex., U.S.A. 31 55N 97 37W
122 Meridj, Morocco 32 52N 3 29W
122 Méridja, Algeria 31 46N 2 52W
143 Merimula, N.S.W., Australia 36 54S 149 54E
143 Meringur, Vic., Austral. 34 20S 141 19E
143 Merino, Vic., Australia 37 44S 141 35E
37 Merioneth, co., Wales, United Kingdom 52 49N 3 55W
175 Meriruma, Brazil 1 15N 54 50W
165 Merkel, U.S.A. 32 30N 100 0W
54 Merksem, Belgium 51 16N 4 25E
55 Merkstein, Germany ...50 52N 6 7E
81 Mern, Denmark 55 3N 12 3E
126 Merowe, Sudan 18 29N 31 46E
142 Merredin, W. Australia 31 28S 118 18E
40 Merrick, Mt., Scot., U.K. 55 8N 4 30W
161 Merrickville, Canada .44 54N 75 51W
166 Merrill, Oregon, U.S.A. 42 2N 121 37W
164 Merrill, Wis., U.S.A. .45 11N 89 41W
160 Merriton, Canada 43 12N 79 13W
156 Merritt, Canada 50 10N 120 45W
143 Merriwa, Australia 32 6S 150 22E
143 Merriwagga, Australia 33 47S 145 43E
142 Merroe, W. Australia .27 53S 117 50E
154 Merry I., Canada 55 57N 77 40W
143 Merrygoen, Australia .31 51S 149 12E
165 Merryville, U.S.A. 30 47N 93 31W
54 Mersch, Luxembourg .49 44N 6 7E
41 Merse, dist., Scot., U.K. 55 40N 2 30W
35 Mersea I., Eng., U.K. 51 48N 0 55E
56 Merseburg, Germany .51 20N 12 0E
38 Mersey, R., Eng., U.K. 53 20N 2 56W
100 Mersin, Turkey 36 51N 34 36E
107 Mersing, W. Malaysia 2 25N 103 50E
104 Merta, India 26 39N 74 4E
37 Merthyr Tydfil, Wales, United Kingdom 51 45N 3 23W
143 Mertoa, Vic., Australia 36 33S 142 29E
63 Mertola, Portugal 37 40N 7 40E
35 Merton, England, U.K. 51 25N 0 13W
165 Mertzon, U.S.A. 31 17N 100 48W
49 Méru, France 49 13N 2 8E
131 Meru & dist., Kenya . 0 3N 37 40E
131 Meru Mt., Tanzania ... 3 15S 36 46E
49 Merville, France 50 38N 2 38E
134 Merweville, S. Africa .32 37S 21 31E
49 Méry, France 48 30N 3 52E
88 Merzifon, Turkey 41 53N 35 32E
57 Merzig, Germany 49 26N 6 37E
123 Merzouga, Erg Tin, Alg. 24 0N 11 4E
167 Mesa, U.S.A. 33 20N 111 56W
123 Mesach Mellet, Libya .24 30N 11 30E
73 Mesagne, Italy 40 34N 17 48E
77 Mesaras, Kolpos, Crete, Greece 35 6N 24 47E
56 Meschede, Germany ...51 20N 8 17E
127 Mesewa, Ethiopia 15 35N 39 25E
154 Mesgouez, L., Canada 51 20N 75 0W
86 Meshchovsk, U.S.S.R. 54 22N 35 17E
101 Meshed, see Mashhad, Iran 36 20N 59 35E
161 Meshoppen, U.S.A. 41 36N 76 3W
162 Mesick, U.S.A. 44 24N 85 42W
167 Mesilla, U.S.A. 32 20N 107 0W
48 Meslay du Maine, Fr. .47 58N 0 33W
57 Mesocco, Switzerland .46 23N 9 12E
77 Mesolóngion, Greece ...38 27N 21 28E
100 Mesopotamia, dist., Asia 33 30N 44 0E
73 Mesoraca, Italy 39 5N 16 47E
77 Mésou Volímais, Greece 37 53N 27 35E
48 Messac, France 47 49N 1 50W
122 Messad, Algeria 34 8N 3 30E
125 Méssaména, Cameroon 3 48N 12 49E
135 Messelfontein, S. Africa 28 1S 30 55E
73 Messina, Italy 38 10N 15 32E
133 Messina, Trans. S. Afr. 22 20S 30 12E
73 Messina, Str. of, Italy 38 5N 15 35E
77 Messíni, Greece 37 4N 22 1E
77 Messinía, pref., Greece 37 10N 22 0E
77 Messiniakós, Kólpos, G., Greece 36 45N 22 5E
77 Mesta, Akra, C., Greece 38 16N 25 53E
75 Mesta R., Bulgaria ...41 30N 24 0E
122 Mestasa, Morocco 35 7N 4 21W
58 Meśto Teplá, Cz. 49 59N 12 52E
71 Mestre, Italy 45 30N 12 13E
58 Městys Zelezná Ruda, Czechoslovakia 49 8N 13 15E
174 Meta R., Ven. & Col. . 6 20N 68 5W
154 Metagama, Canada 47 0N 81 55W
127 Metahara, Ethiopia ... 8 58N 39 57E
166 Metaline Falls, U.S.A. 48 54N 117 28W
172 Metán, Argentina 25 30S 65 0W
71 Metauro R., Italy 43 45N 12 59E
156 Metchosin, Canada 48 15N 123 37W
127 Metemma, Ethiopia ...12 56N 36 13E
77 Methana Pen., Greece 37 35N 23 23E
39 Metheringham, England, U.K. 53 9N 0 22W
41 Methil, Scot., U.K. 56 10N 3 1W
43 Methlick, Scot., U.K. .57 26N 2 13W
77 Methóni, Greece 36 49N 21 42E
161 Methuen, U.S.A. 42 43N 71 10W
147 Methven, N.Z. 43 38S 171 40E
41 Methven, Scot., U.K. .56 25N 3 35W
142 Methwin, Mt., Australia 25 3S 120 45E
35 Methwold, Eng., U.K. 52 30N 0 33E
129 Metil, Mozambique 16 24S 39 0E
74 Metković, Yugoslavia 43 6N 17 39E
157 Metlakatla, Alas., U.S.A. 55 10N 131 33W
123 Metlaoui, Tunisia 34 24N 8 24E
71 Metlika, Yugoslavia ...45 40N 15 20E
132 Metolola, Mozambique 16 36S 35 44E
132 Metove, Mozambique .20 9S 33 1E
145 Metowra, Australia 25 3S 146 15E
165 Metropolis, U.S.A. 37 10N 88 47W
76 Métsovon, Greece 39 48N 21 12E
55 Mettet, Belgium 50 19N 4 41E
55 Mettmann, Germany .51 15N 6 49E
106 Mettuppalaiyam, India 11 18N 76 59E
106 Mettur, India 11 48N 77 47E
105 Mettur Dam, India 11 45N 77 45E
98 Metulla, Israel 33 17N 35 34E
49 Metz, France 49 8N 6 10E
108 Meulaboh, Indonesia . 4 11N 96 3E
49 Meulan, France 49 0N 1 52E
49 Meung, France 47 50N 1 40E
108 Meureudu, Indonesia . 5 19N 96 10E
49 Meurthe, R., France ...48 24N 6 30E
49 Meurthe-et-Moselle, dépt., France 48 52N 6 0E
49 Meuse, dépt., France .49 8N 5 25E
54 Meuse R., Europe 50 32N 5 20E
56 Meuselwitz, Germany .51 3N 12 18E
36 Mevagissey, Eng., U.K. 50 16N 4 48W
36 Mevagissey Bay, England, U.K. 50 15N 4 40W
43 Mey, Scotland, U.K. .58 38N 3 12W
39 Mexborough, Eng., U.K. 53 29N 1 18W
165 Mexia, U.S.A. 31 38N 96 32W
175 Mexiana I., Brazil 0 0N 49 30W
168 Mexicali, Mexico 32 40N 115 30W
168 Mexico, rep., America 20 0N 100 0W
161 Mexico, Me., U.S.A. ...44 35N 70 30W
164 Mexico, Mo., U.S.A. ...39 10N 91 55W
149 Mexico, G. of, America 25 0N 90 0W
168 Mexico City, Mexico ...19 20N 99 10W
100 Meyadin, Syria 35 0N 40 30E
56 Meyenburg, Germany 53 19N 12 15E
133 Meyerton, Trans., S. Afr. 26 31S 28 1E
50 Meymac, France 45 32N 2 10E
51 Meyrarguès, France ...43 38N 5 32E
55 Meyrode, Belgium 50 20N 6 11E
50 Meyrueis, France 44 12N 3 27E
50 Meyssac, France 45 3N 1 40E
50 Mèze, France 43 27N 3 36E
84 Mezen, U.S.S.R. 65 50N 44 20E
86 Mezha, R., U.S.S.R. ...55 50N 31 45E
48 Mezidon, France 49 5N 0 1W
49 Mezières, Ardennes, Fr. 49 45N 4 42E
51 Mézilhac, France 44 49N 4 21E
50 Mezin, France 44 4N 0 16E
59 Mezöberny, Hungary 46 49N 21 3E
59 Mezofalva, Hungary ...46 55N 18 49E
59 Mezöhegyes, Hungary 46 19N 20 49E
59 Mezökovacshaza, Hung. 46 25N 20 57E
59 Mezökövesd, Hungary 47 49N 20 35E
50 Mezos, France 44 5N 1 10W
59 Mezötúr, Hungary ...47 0N 20 41E
70 Mezzolombando, Italy 46 13N 11 5E
135 Mfolozi R., Nat., S. Afr. 28 28S 32 4E
86 Mglin, U.S.S.R. 53 2N 32 50E
132 Mhlaba Hills, Rhodesia 18 30S 30 30E
135 Mhlume, Swaziland ...26 15S 32 6E
104 Mhow, India 22 33N 75 50E
168 Miahuatlán, Mexico ...16 21N 96 36W
63 Miajadas, Spain 39 9N 5 54W
104 Mialar, India 26 15N 70 20E
144 Miallo, Queens., Austral. 16 28S 145 22E
132 Miami, Rhodesia 16 40S 29 49E
167 Miami, Ariz., U.S.A. .33 25N 111 0W
163 Miami, Fla., U.S.A. ...25 52N 80 15W
165 Miami, Tex., U.S.A. ...35 44N 100 38W
162 Miami R., U.S.A. 39 20N 84 40W
163 Miami Beach, U.S.A. .25 49N 80 6W
162 Miamisburg, U.S.A. ...39 40N 84 11W
100 Miandow Ab, Iran 37 0N 46 5E
100 Mianeh, Iran 37 30N 47 40E
104 Mianwali, W. Pakistan 32 38N 71 28E
112 Miao Tao, China 38 10N 120 50E
113 Miaoli, Taiwan 24 33N 120 42E
129 Miarinarivo, Malagasy Republic 18 50S 46 58E
90 Miass, U.S.S.R. 54 59N 60 6E
60 Miastko, Poland 54 0N 16 58E
133 Mica, Trans., S. Africa 24 9S 30 46E
78 Micăsasa, Rumania ...46 7N 24 7E
174 Micay, Colombia 3 0N 77 40E
59 Michalovce, Cz. 48 44N 21 54E
112 Micheh, China 37 58N 110 1E
34 Micheldever, Eng., U.K. 51 9N 1 17W
57 Michelstadt, Germany 49 40N 9 0E
159 Michigan, st., U.S.A. .44 40N 85 40W
162 Michigan, L., U.S.A. .44 0N 87 0W
162 Michigan City, Indiana, U.S.A. 41 42N 86 56W
155 Michikamau L., Canada 54 0N 64 0W
154 Michipicoten Harb., Can. 47 55N 84 55W
154 Michipicoten I., Canada 47 40N 85 50W
168 Michoacan, st., Mexico 19 0N 102 0W
75 Michurin, Bulgaria ...42 9N 27 51E
87 Michurinsk, U.S.S.R. .52 58N 40 27E
38 Mickle Fell, Eng., UK 54 38N 2 16W
39 Mickleover, Eng., UK 52 55N 1 32W
34 Mickleton, Eng., U.K. 52 5N 1 45W
38 Mickleton, Yorks., England, U.K. 54 36N 2 3W
144 Miclere, Australia 22 30S 147 30E
130 Miconje, Angola 4 26S 12 48E
136 Micronesia, arch., Pacific Ocean 17 0N 160 0E
41 Mid Calder, Scot., U.K. 55 53N 3 23W
42 Mid Yell, Scot., U.K. .60 36N 1 5W
108 Midai I., Indonesia ... 3 0N 107 42E
157 Midale, Canada 49 25N 103 20W
166 Midas, U.S.A. 41 14N 116 56W
80 Middagsfjället, mt., Sweden 63 48N 12 18E
54 Middelburg, Neth. 51 30N 3 36E
135 Middelburg, Cape Prov., S. Africa 31 30S 25 0E
133 Middelburg, Trans., S. Africa 25 49N 29 28E
81 Middelfart, Denmark .55 30N 9 43E
134 Middelpos, S. Africa ...31 55S 20 13E
133 Middelwit, S. Africa ...24 48S 27 8E
166 Middle Alkali L., U.S.A. 41 30N 120 3W
107 Middle Andaman I., India 12 30N 92 30E
155 Middle Brook, Canada 48 40N 54 20W
36 Middle Zoy, Eng., U.K. 51 5N 2 54W
161 Middleboro, U.S.A. 41 56N 70 52W
161 Middleburg, N.Y., U.S.A. 42 36N 74 19W
160 Middleburg, Pa., U.S.A. 40 46N 77 5W
161 Middlebury, U.S.A. ...44 0N 73 9W
135 Middledrif, S. Africa .32 48S 27 0E
38 Middleham, Eng., U.K. 54 17N 1 49W
147 Middlemarch, N.Z. 45 30S 170 9E
36 Middlemarsh, Eng., U.K. 50 51N 2 29W
162 Middleport, Ohio, U.S.A. 39 0N 82 5W
165 Middlesboro, U.S.A. .36 40N 83 40W
39 Middlesbrough, Eng., U.K. 54 34N 1 13W
161 Middlesex, U.S.A. 40 36N 74 30W
155 Middleton, Canada 44 57N 65 4W
35 Middleton, Norfolk, Eng., U.K. 52 43N 0 29E
38 Middleton, Westmorland, England, U.K. 54 17N 2 34W
135 Middleton, S. Africa ...32 56S 25 50E
34 Middleton Cheney, England, U.K. 52 4N 1 17W
38 Middleton-in-Teesdale, England, U.K. 54 38N 2 5W
39 Middleton in the Wolds, England, U.K. 53 56N 0 35W
46 Middletown, N. Ire., U.K. 54 18N 6 50W
161 Middletown, Conn., U.S.A. 41 37N 72 40W
162 Middletown, Del., U.S.A. 39 30N 84 21W
161 Middletown, N.Y., U.S.A. 41 28N 74 28W
161 Middletown, Pa., U.S.A. 40 12N 76 44W
38 Middlewich, Eng., U.K. 53 12N 2 28W
122 Midelt, Morocco 32 46N 4 44W
35 Midhurst, Eng., U.K. .50 59N 0 44W
146 Midhurst, New Zealand 39 17S 174 18E
50 Midi, Canal du, France 43 50N 1 15E
135 Mid-Illova, Nat., S. Afr. 29 59S 30 25E
154 Midland, Ont., Canada 44 45N 79 50W
162 Midland, Mich., U.S.A. 43 37N 84 17W
160 Midland, Pa., U.S.A. .40 39N 80 27W
165 Midland, Tex., U.S.A. 32 0N 102 3W
132 Midlands, dist., Rhod. 19 40S 29 0E
142 Midland Junc., Austral. 31 50S 115 58E
44 Midleton, Ireland 51 52N 8 12W
144 Midlothian, Australia 17 10S 141 12E
165 Midlothian, U.S.A. 32 30N 97 0W
41 Midlothian, Co., Scotland, U.K. 55 45N 3 15W
105 Midnapore, India 22 25N 87 21E
81 Midskog, Sweden 58 56N 14 5E
36 Midsomer Norton, England, U.K. 51 17N 2 29W
166 Midvale, U.S.A. 40 39N 111 58W
136 Midway Is., Pac. Oc. .28 13N 177 22W
166 Midwest, U.S.A. 43 27N 106 11W
74 Midžor, Mt., Bulgaria 43 24N 22 40E
114 Mie, pref., Japan 34 20N 136 20E
60 Miechów, Poland 50 21N 20 5E
60 Miedzychod, Poland ...52 35N 15 53E
60 Międzvrzec, Podlaski, Poland 51 58N 22 45E
60 Międzyrzecz, Poland .52 26N 15 35E
60 Miejska Górka, Poland 51 39N 16 58E
50 Miélan, France 43 27N 0 19E
144 Mielelek, New Guinea 6 1S 148 58E
113 Mienchih, China 34 47N 111 49E
113 Mienhsien, China 33 15N 105 33E
113 Mienyang, China 30 10N 113 20E
113 Mienyang, China 31 18N 104 26E
78 Miercurea Ciuc, Rum. 46 21N 25 48E
62 Mieres, Spain 43 18N 5 48W
60 Mieszkowice, Poland .52 47N 14 30E
156 Miette, Canada 53 0N 117 51W
160 Mifflintown, U.S.A. ...40 34N 77 24W
76 Mifoli, Albania 40 36N 19 27E
98 Migdal, Israel 32 51N 35 30E
98 Migdal Afea, Israel ...32 5N 34 58E
71 Migliarino, Italy 44 54N 11 56E
114 Mihara, Japan 34 24N 133 5E
168 Miguel Alemán Res., Mexico 18 15N 96 40W
175 Miguel Alves, Brazil ... 4 11S 42 55W
64 Mijares R., Spain 40 15N 0 50W
63 Mijas, Spain 36 36N 4 40W
125 Mijilu, Nigeria 10 22N 13 19E
131 Mikese, Tanzania 6 48S 37 55E
89 Mikha Tskhakaya, U.S.S.R. 42 15N 42 7E
87 Mikhailov, U.S.S.R. ...54 20N 39 0E
75 Mikhailovgrad, Bulgaria 43 27N 23 16E
88 Mikhailovka, Ukraine, U.S.S.R. 47 16N 35 27E
89 Mikhaylovka, Azerbaijan, U.S.S.R. 41 31N 48 25E
87 Mikhaylovka, R.S.F.S.R., U.S.S.R. 50 3N 43 5E
87 Mikhnevo, U.S.S.R. ...55 4N 37 59E
77 Mikínai, Greece 37 43N 22 46E
131 Mikindani, Tanzania .10 15S 40 2E
83 Mikkeli, Finland 61 43N 27 25E
127 Mikniya, Sudan 17 0N 33 45E
59 Mikotow, Poland 50 10N 18 50E
77 Mikonos, I., Greece ...37 30N 25 25E
130 Mikope, Congo 4 58S 20 43E
76 Mikrón Dherion, Gr. .41 19N 26 6E
59 Mikulov, Cz. 48 48N 16 39E
84 Mikun, U.S.S.R. 62 20N 50 0E
114 Mikura Shima I., Japan 33 40N 139 40E
164 Milaca, U.S.A. 45 45N 93 40W
174 Milagio, Ecuador 2 0S 79 30W
172 Milagro, Argentina 30 59S 65 59W
70 Milan, see Milano, Italy 45 28N 9 10E
164 Milan, Mo., U.S.A. 40 10N 93 5W
163 Milan, Tenn., U.S.A. .35 55N 88 45W
145 Milang, S. Austral. 35 20S 138 55E
132 Milange, Mozambique 16 3S 35 45E
70 Milano, Italy 45 28N 9 10E
100 Milas, Turkey 37 20N 27 50E
73 Milazzo, Italy 38 13N 15 13E
164 Milbank, U.S.A. 45 17N 96 38W
36 Milborne Port, Eng., U.K. 50 58N 2 28W
157 Milden, Canada 51 29N 107 32W
35 Mildenhall, Eng., U.K. 52 20N 0 30E
160 Mildmay, Canada 44 3N 81 9W
143 Mildura, Vic., Austral. 34 8S 142 7E
76 Miléai, Greece 39 20N 23 9E
145 Miles, Queens., Austral. 26 37S 150 10E
131 Milepa, Mozambique . 1 50S 36 25E
165 Miles, U.S.A. 31 39N 100 11W
164 Miles City, U.S.A. 46 30N 105 50W
73 Mileto, Italy 38 37N 16 3E
73 Miletto, Mte., Italy ...41 26N 14 25E
142 Mileura, W. Australia 26 25S 117 15E
58 Milevsko, Cz. 49 27N 14 21E
44 Milford, Ireland 52 20N 8 52W
161 Milford, Conn., U.S.A. 41 13N 73 4W
162 Milford, Del., U.S.A. .38 52N 75 27W
161 Milford, Mass., U.S.A. 42 8N 71 30W
161 Milford, Pa., U.S.A. ...41 20N 74 47W
167 Milford, Utah, U.S.A. 38 20N 113 0W
37 Milford Haven, Wales, United Kingdom 51 43N 5 2W
34 Milford on Sea, England, U.K. 50 44N 1 36W
147 Milford Sd., N.Z. 44 34S 167 47E
142 Milgun, W. Australia .25 6S 118 20E
121 Milh, Ras el, Libya ...32 0N 24 55E
60 Milicz, Poland 51 31N 17 19E
122 Miliana, Algeria 36 12N 2 15E
122 Miliana, Algeria 27 20N 2 32E
142 Miling, W. Australia .30 30S 116 17E
73 Militello, Italy 37 16N 14 46E
156 Milk River, Canada ...49 10N 111 30W
166 Milk, R., U.S.A. 48 40N 107 15W
127 Milk, W. el., R., Sudan 16 30N 29 0E
15 Mill, I., Antarctica ...66 0S 101 30E
166 Mill City, U.S.A. 44 45N 122 28W
144 Millaa Millaa, Austral. 17 30S 145 32E
50 Millau, France 44 8N 3 4E
160 Millbridge, Canada ...44 43N 77 35W
160 Millbrook, Canada 44 10N 78 23W
36 Millbrook, Eng., U.K. 50 19N 4 12W
164 Mille Lacs, L., U.S.A. 46 10N 93 30W
154 Mille Lacs, L. de, Can. 48 45N 90 35W
163 Milledgeville, U.S.A. .33 7N 83 15W
163 Millen, U.S.A. 32 50N 81 57W
134 Miller, C. Prov., S. Afr. 33 5S 23 57E
164 Miller, U.S.A. 44 35N 98 59W
89 Millerovo, U.S.S.R. ...48 57N 40 28E
147 Miller's Flat, N.Z. 45 39S 169 23E
160 Millersburg, Ohio, U.S.A. 40 32N 81 52W
160 Millersburg, Pa., U.S.A. 40 32N 76 58W
147 Millerton, N.Z. 41 39N 171 54E
161 Millerton, U.S.A. 41 57N 73 32W
155 Millertown Junc., Can. 48 49N 56 28W
40 Milleur Pt., Scot., U.K. 55 2N 5 5W
50 Millevaches, Plat. de, Fr. 45 45N 2 0E
145 Millicent, S. Australia 37 34S 140 21E
55 Millingen, Germany ...51 50N 6 24E
155 Millinocket, U.S.A. 45 45N 68 45W
46 Millisle, N. Ireland ...54 38N 5 33W
145 Millmerran, Australia .27 53S 151 16E
38 Millom, England, U.K. 54 13N 3 16W
40 Millport, Scotland, U.K. 55 45N 4 55W
156 Mills L., Canada 61 30N 118 20W
160 Millsboro, U.S.A. 40 0N 80 0W
44 Millstreet, Ireland 52 4N 9 5W
143 Millthorpe, Australia .33 27S 148 14E
46 Milltown, Galway, Ire. 53 37N 8 54W
44 Milltown, Kerry, Ire. .52 9N 9 42W
44 Milltown Malbay, Ireland 52 51N 9 25W
162 Millville, U.S.A. 39 22N 74 0W
165 Millwood Res., U.S.A. 33 45N 94 0W
49 Milly, France 48 24N 2 20E
71 Milna, Yugoslavia 43 20N 16 28E
41 Milnathort, Scot., U.K. 56 14N 3 25W

MAP
153 Milne Inlet, Canada ...72 30N 80 0W
40 Milngavie, Scot., U.K. 55 57N 4 20W
164 Milnor, U.S.A. 46 19N 97 29W
38 Milnthorpe, Eng., U.K. 54 14N 2 47W
77 Milos & I., Greece 36 44N 24 25E
74 Miloševo, Yugoslavia .45 42N 20 20E
42 Milovaig, Scot., U.K. .57 27N 6 45W
57 Miltenberg, Germany .49 41N 9 13E
143 Milton, N.S.W., Australia 35 20S 150 27E
34 Milton, Hants., Eng., U.K. 50 45N 1 40W
35 Milton, Northants, England, U.K. 52 12N 0 55W
147 Milton, New Zealand .46 7S 169 59E
40 Milton, Scotland, U.K. 55 18N 4 50W
163 Milton, Fla., U.S.A. ...30 38N 87 0W
160 Milton, Pa., U.S.A. 41 0N 76 53W
36 Milton Abbot, Eng., U.K. 50 35N 4 16W
166 Milton–Freewater, U.S.A. 45 57N 118 24W
35 Milton Keynes, Eng., U.K. 52 3N 0 42W
160 Milton West, Canada .43 33N 79 53W
160 Milverton, Canada 43 35N 80 43W
36 Milverton, Eng., U.K. 51 2N 3 15W
162 Milwaukee, U.S.A. 43 9N 87 58W
166 Milwaukie, U.S.A. 45 33N 122 39W
124 Mim, Ghana 6 57N 2 33W
109 Mimika, Indonesia 4 42S 136 24E
50 Mimizan, France 44 12N 1 13W
58 Mimoň, Czechoslovakia 50 38N 14 43E
135 Mimosa, C. Prov., S. Afr. 33 20S 25 50E
166 Mina, U.S.A. 38 21N 118 9W
172 Mina Pirquitas, Arg. .22 40S 66 40W
100 Mina Saud, Arabia 28 45N 48 20E
101 Minab, Iran 27 10N 57 1E
157 Minaki, Ont., Canada .50 0N 94 40W
114 Minamata, Japan 32 10N 130 30E
173 Minas, Uruguay 34 20S 55 15W
155 Minas Basin, Canada .45 20N 64 12W
174 Minas–Cue, Paraguay 22 4S 59 40W
63 Minas de Rio Tinto, Sp. 37 41N 6 37W
63 Minas de San Quintin, Spain 38 49N 4 23W
175 Minas Gerais, st., Brazil 18 50S 46 0W
168 Minas, Sierra de las, Guatemala 15 9N 89 31W
168 Minatitlán, Mexico 17 58N 94 35W
103 Minbu, Burma 20 10N 95 0E
42 Minch, The, Scot., U.K. 58 10N 5 50W
143 Mincha, Vic., Australia 36 1S 144 6E
34 Minchinhampton, England, U.K. 51 42N 2 10W
70 Mincio R., Italy 45 8N 10 55E
109 Mindanao, I., Phil. 8 0N 125 0E
109 Mindanao Sea, Phil. ... 8 50N 123 0E
109 Mindanao Trench, Pac. Oc. 8 0N 128 0E
57 Mindelheim, Germany 48 4N 10 30E
160 Minden, Canada 44 56N 78 44W
56 Minden, Germany 52 18N 8 54E
165 Minden, U.S.A. 32 40N 93 20W
109 Mindoro, I., Philippines 13 0N 121 0E
109 Mindoro Strait, Phil. .12 30N 119 30E
130 Mindouli, Congo (Fr.) 4 12S 14 28E
45 Mine Hd., Ireland 52 0N 7 37W
36 Minehead, Eng., U.K. 51 12N 3 29W
165 Mineola, U.S.A. 32 40N 95 30W
37 Minera, Wales, U.K. .53 3N 3 7W
165 Mineral Wells, U.S.A. 32 50N 98 5W
89 Mineralnyye Vody, U.S.S.R. 44 18N 43 15E
161 Minersville, Pa., U.S.A. 40 40N 76 17W
167 Minersville, Utah, U.S.A. 38 14N 112 58W
160 Minerva, U.S.A. 40 43N 81 8W
73 Minervino Murge, Italy 41 6N 16 4E
163 Minette, U.S.A. 30 54N 87 43W
161 Minetto, U.S.A. 43 24N 76 28W
155 Mingan, Canada 50 20N 64 0W
112 Mingan, see Pangkiang, China ...43 4N 112 30E
42 Mingary, Scotland, U.K. 56 42N 6 5W
89 Mingechaur Res., U.S.S.R. 40 56N 47 20E
143 Mingela, Australia 19 42S 146 42E
142 Mingenew, W. Austral. 29 12S 115 21E
103 Mingin, Burma 22 50N 94 30E
42 Minginish, Dist., Scotland, U.K. 57 14N 6 15W
113 Mingki (Kweihwa), China 26 10N 117 14E
64 Minglanilla, Spain 39 34N 1 38W
62 Mingorria, Spain 40 42N 4 40N
131 Mingoyo, Tanzania 10 9S 39 29E
42 Mingulay I., Scot., U.K. 56 50N 7 40W
113 Minhow, see Foochow, China 26 2N 119 12E
111 Minhsien, China 34 31N 104 0E
74 Minićevo, Yugoslavia .43 42N 22 18E
166 Minidoka, U.S.A. 42 47N 113 34W
142 Minigwal L., W. Austral. 29 31S 123 14E
142 Minilya, W. Australia 23 55S 114 0E
142 Minilya R., W. Austral. 23 45S 114 0E
113 Minkiang, China 32 30N 114 10E
125 Minna, Nigeria 9 37N 6 30E
164 Minneapolis, Kan., U.S.A. 39 11N 97 40W
164 Minneapolis, Minn., U.S.A. 44 58N 93 20W
157 Minnedesa, Canada ...50 20N 99 50W
164 Minnesota, st., U.S.A. 46 40N 94 0W
79 Minnesund, Norway ...60 23N 11 14E
40 Minnigaff, Scot., U.K. 54 58N 4 30W
62 Miño R., Spain 41 58N 8 40W
64 Minorca I., see Menorca 40 0N 4 0E
164 Minot, U.S.A. 48 10N 101 15W
48 Minquiers, les, Rks., Chan. Is., U.K. 48 58N 2 8W
56 Minsen, Germany 53 43N 7 58E
86 Minsk, U.S.S.R. 53 52N 27 30E
60 Minsk Mazowiecki, Pol. 52 10N 21 33E
35 Minster, Thanet, England, U.K. 51 20N 1 20E
35 Minster–on–Sea, Sheppey, Eng., U.K. 51 25N 0 50E
34 Minsterley, Eng., U.K. 52 38N 2 56W
43 Mintlaw, Scotland, U.K. 57 32N 1 59W
113 Mintsing, China 26 8N 118 57E
166 Minturn, U.S.A. 39 45N 106 25W
72 Minturno, Italy 41 15N 13 43E
126 Minuf, Egypt 30 26N 30 52E
91 Minusinsk, U.S.S.R. ...53 50N 91 20E
103 Minutang, India 28 15N 96 30E
111 Minya Konka, Mt., China 29 50N 101 50E
143 Minyip, Vic., Australia 36 29S 142 36E
74 Mionica, Yugoslavia ...44 14N 20 6E
109 Mios Num I., Indon. . 1 30S 135 10E
155 Miquelon, I., Terr. of M. & St. Pierre 47 8N 56 24W
89 Mir–Bashir, U.S.S.R. .40 11N 46 58E
71 Mira, Italy 45 26N 12 9E
62 Mira, Portugal 40 26N 8 44W
63 Mira R., Portugal 37 30N 8 30W
73 Mirabella Eclano, Italy 41 3N 14 59E
168 Miraflores Locks, Panama Canal Zone 8 59N 79 36W
106 Miraj, India 16 50N 74 45E
132 Mirama, Mozambique 23 50S 35 35E
172 Miramar, Argentina ...38 15S 57 50W
51 Miramas, France 43 33N 4 59E
50 Mirambeau, France 45 23N 0 35W
155 Miramichi B., Canada 47 15N 65 0W
50 Miramont, France 44 37N 0 21E
175 Miranda, Brazil 20 10S 56 15W
131 Miranda, Mozambique 12 30S 35 23E
64 Miranda de Ebro, Spain 42 41N 2 57W
62 Miranda, do Duow, Port. 41 32N 6 20W
50 Mirande, France.........43 32N 0 24E
62 Mirandela, Portugal ...41 32N 98 59W
165 Mirando City, U.S.A. .27 28N 98 59W
70 Mirandola, Italy 44 53N 11 2E
132 Mirango, Malawi 13 32S 34 58E
144 Mirani, Queensland, Australia 21 12S 148 59E
71 Mirano, Italy 45 29N 12 6E
174 Mirapinima, Brazil 2 10S 61 9W
143 Mirboo, Vic., Australia 38 15S 146 7E
126 Mirear I., Egypt 23 15N 35 41E
49 Mirebeau, Cote d'Or, Fr. 47 25N 5 20E
48 Mirebeau, Vienne, Fr. 46 49N 0 10E
49 Mirecourt, France 48 20N 6 10E
101 Mirfa, Trucial Oman .24 0N 53 24E
39 Mirfield, England, U.K. 53 40N 1 40W
86 Mirgorod, U.S.S.R. 49 58N 33 50E
108 Miri, Sarawak, Malaysia 4 18N 114 0E
144 Mirim Vale, Australia 24 20S 151 39E
173 Mirim, Lagoa, Brazil .32 40S 52 58W
15 Mirny, Antarctica 66 0S 95 0E
91 Mirnyy, U.S.S.R. 62 33N 113 53E
104 Mirpur Bibiwari, Pak. 28 33N 67 44E
104 Mirpur Khas, W. Pak. 25 30N 69 0E
104 Mirpur Sakro, W. Pak. 24 33N 67 41E
143 Mirrool, N.S.W., Austral. 34 24S 147 5E
156 Mirror, Canada 52 30N 113 0W
132 Miruro, Mozambique .15 21S 30 28E
131 Mirwani, Kenya 1 10S 38 1E
112 Miryang, S. Korea 35 34N 128 42E
89 Mirzaani, U.S.S.R. 41 24N 46 5E
105 Mirzapur, India 25 10N 82 45E
155 Miscou I., Canada 47 57N 64 31W
100 Mish'ab Ra'as al, Saudi Arabia 28 15N 48 43E
112 Mishan, China 45 31N 132 2E
162 Mishawaka, U.S.A. 41 40N 86 8W
126 Mishbih, Gebel, Egypt 22 48N 34 38E
114 Mishima, Japan 35 10N 138 52E
98 Mishmar Aiyalon, Isr. 31 52N 34 57E
98 Mishmar Ha'emeq, Isr. 32 37N 35 7E
98 Mishmar Hanegev, Isr. 31 32N 34 48E
98 Mishmar Hayarden, Isr. 33 0N 35 56E
72 Misilmeri, Italy 38 2N 13 25E
144 Misima I., Papua 10 40S 152 50E
173 Misiones, terr., Arg. ...27 0S 55 0W
101 Miskin, Muscat & Oman 23 44N 56 52E
169 Miskito Cays, Nicaragua 14 26N 82 50W
59 Miskolc, Hungary 48 7N 20 50E
109 Misool I., Indonesia ... 2 0S 130 0E
123 Misratah (Misurata), Liberia 32 18N 15 3E
154 Missanabie, Canada ...48 20N 84 6W
154 Missinaibi L., Canada 48 14N 83 15W
154 Missinaibi R., Canada 50 30N 82 40W
122 Misserghin, Algeria 35 44N 0 49W
156 Mission City, Canada .49 10N 122 15W
164 Mission, S.D., U.S.A. .43 21N 100 36W
165 Mission, Tex., U.S.A. .26 15N 98 30W
154 Missisa L., Canada 52 20N 85 7W
165 Mississippi, st., U.S.A. 33 0N 90 0W
161 Mississippi L., Canada 45 5N 76 12W
165 Mississippi, R., U.S.A. 35 30N 90 0W
165 Mississippi Sd., U.S.A. 30 25N 89 0W
166 Missoula, U.S.A. 47 0N 114 0W
122 Missour, Morocco 33 0N 3 59W
164 Missouri, st., U.S.A. ...38 25N 92 30W
164 Missouri, R., U.S.A. ...40 20N 95 40W
166 Missouri R., Lit., U.S.A. 46 0N 111 35W
164 Missouri Valley, U.S.A. 41 30N 95 50W
157 Mistake B., Canada ...62 8N 93 0W
154 Mistassini L., Canada . 51 0N 73 40W
155 Mistastin L., Canada .55 58N 63 40W
59 Mistelbach, Austria ...48 34N 16 34E
73 Misterbianco, Italy 37 32N 15 0E
36 Misterton, Som., England, U.K. 50 51N 2 46W
39 Misterton, Lincoln, England, U.K. 53 27N 0 49W
1 Misti Vol., Peru 16 10S 71 10W
73 Mistretta, Italy 37 56N 14 20E
126 Mit Ghamr, Egypt 30 42N 31 12E
127 Mitatib, Sudan 15 59N 36 12E
37 Mitchel Troy, Eng., U.K. 51 46N 2 45W
34 Mitcheldean, Eng., U.K. 51 51N 2 29W
145 Mitchell, Australia 26 29S 147 58E
160 Mitchell, Canada 43 29N 81 21W
162 Mitchell, Ind., U.S.A. 38 42N 86 25W
164 Mitchell, Neb., U.S.A. 41 58N 103 45W
166 Mitchell, Ore., U.S.A. 44 31N 120 8W
164 Mitchell, S.D., U.S.A. 43 40N 98 0W
163 Mitchell Mt., U.S.A. ...35 40N 82 20W
143 Mitchell R., Australia 37 20S 147 0E
44 Mitchelstown, Ireland 52 16N 8 18W
104 Mitha Tiwana, W. Pak. 32 13N 72 6E
76 Mithimna, Greece 39 20N 26 12E
143 Mitiamo, Vic., Austral. 36 19S 144 14E
77 Mitilini, Greece 39 6N 26 35E
76 Mitilini I., see Lésvos I., Greece 39 0N 26 20E
77 Mitilinoi, Greece 37 42N 26 56E
114 Mito, Japan 36 20N 140 30E
146 Mitre Pk., Mt., N.Z. ...44 35S 167 45E
129 Mitsinjo, Malagasy Republic 16 1S 45 52E
143 Mitta Mitta, & R., Victoria, Australia .36 45S 147 36E
143 Mittagong, Australia .34 28S 150 29E
56 Mittelland Kanal, Ger. 52 23N 7 45E
56 Mittenwalde, Germany 52 16N 13 33E
56 Mittweida, Germany .50 59N 13 0E
143 Mittyack, Vic., Austral. 35 8S 142 36E
174 Mitu, Colombia 1 8N 70 3W
130 Mitumba Range, Congo 10 0S 26 20E
131 Mitwaba, Congo 8 32N 27 17E
131 Mityana, Uganda 0 23N 32 2E
128 Mitzick, Gabon 0 45N 11 40E
89 Mius R., U.S.S.R. 47 30N 39 0E
114 Miyagi, préf., Japan ...38 15N 140 45E
126 Miyâh, W. el, Egypt .25 10N 33 30E
114 Miyake–jima, I., Japan 34 0N 139 30E
114 Miyako, Japan 39 40N 141 75E
113 Miyako Retto, Is., Japan 24 47N 125 20E
114 Miyakonojo, Japan 31 32N 131 5E
114 Miyazu, Japan 35 35N 135 10E
114 Miyazaki, Japan 32 0N 131 30E
112 Miyun, China 40 25N 116 50E
109 Mizamis, see Ozamiz, Philippines 8 15N 123 50E
123 Mizdah, Libya 31 30N 13 0E
144 Mitzen Hd., Cork, Ire. 51 27N 9 50W
45 Mizen Hd., Wick., Ire. 52 52N 6 4W
78 Mizil, Rumania 44 59N 26 29E
135 Mjanyana, S. Africa ...31 4S 28 9E
81 Mjoback, Sweden 57 28N 12 53E
81 Mjolby, Sweden 58 20N 15 10E
79 Mjomna, Norway 60 55N 4 55E
81 Mjörn, L., Sweden 57 55N 12 25E
79 Mjösa, L., Norway 60 45N 11 0E
122 Mkam Sidi Cheikh, Alg. 34 2N 1 15E
135 Mkemani, S. Africa ...30 40S 29 2E
131 Mkokotoni, Zan., Tanz. 5 55S 39 15E
131 Mkomazi, Tanzania 4 40S 38 7E
135 Mkomanzi R., S. Africa 30 13S 30 57E
131 Mkonumbi, Kenya 2 22S 40 44E
132 Mkushi, Zambia 14 20S 29 20E
132 Mkushi River, Zambia 13 38S 29 40E
135 Mkuze R., Natal, S. Afr. 27 45S 32 30E
131 Mkwaja, Tanzania 5 45S 38 50E
131 Mkwaya, Tanzania 6 17S 35 40E
131 Mlala Hills, Tanzania . 7 0S 31 3E
58 Mlada Boleslav, Cz. ...50 27N 14 53E
74 Mladenovac, Y.–slav. .44 28N 20 44E
131 Mlala Hills, Tanzania . 6 50S 31 40E
132 Mlanje, Malawi 16 2S 35 33E
74 Mlava R., Yugoslavia 44 35N 21 18E
60 Mtawa, Poland 53 9N 20 25E
71 Mlinista, Yugoslavia .44 15N 16 50E
74 Mljet, I., Yugoslavia .42 43N 17 30E
60 Mlynary, Poland 54 12N 19 46E
134 Mmamagodi, S. Africa.........................28 4S 22 57E
125 Mme, Cameroon 6 18N 10 14E
132 Mneni, Rhodesia 20 38S 30 2E
80 Mo, Sweden 63 34N 18 30E
82 Mo i Rana, Norway ...66 15N 14 7E
109 Moa, I., Indonesia 8 0S 128 0E
124 Moa R., Sierra Leone . 7 0N 11 40W
167 Moab, U.S.A. 38 40N 109 35W
145 Moalla Park, Austral. 29 42S 143 3E
143 Moama, N.S.W., Australia 36 3S 144 45E
133 Moamba, Mozambique 25 34S 32 16E
62 Moaña, Spain 42 18N 8 43W
167 Moapa, U.S.A. 36 45N 114 43W
45 Moate, Ireland 53 25N 7 43W
130 Mobaye Cent. Afr. Rep. 4 25N 21 5E
164 Moberley, U.S.A. 39 25N 92 25W
154 Mobert, Ont., Canada 48 41N 85 40W
163 Mobile, U.S.A. 30 41N 88 3W
163 Mobile B., U.S.A. 30 30N 88 0W
163 Mobile, Pt., U.S.A. 30 15N 88 0W
81 Möborg, Denmark 56 24N 8 21E
164 Mobridge, U.S.A. 45 40N 100 28W
130 Mocaba, Sierra de, Ang. 7 0S 15 0E
130 Mocabe Kasari, Congo 9 58S 26 12E
132 Mocapa, Mozambique 17 59S 36 9E
132 Mochiara Grove, Bots. 20 43S 21 50E
133 Mochudi, Botswana ...24 27S 26 7E
131 Macimboa da Praia, Mozam. 11 25S 40 20E
131 Moçimboa do Ruvuma, Mozam. ...11 20S 39 18E
78 Mociu, Rumania 46 46N 24 3E
81 Mockeln L., Sweden ...56 40N 14 15E
166 Moclips, U.S.A. 47 29N 124 10W
174 Mocoa, Colombia 1 15N 76 45W
173 Mococa, Brazil 21 28S 47 0W
168 Mocorito, Mexico 25 20N 108 0W
129 Mocuba, Mozambique 16 54S 37 25E
51 Modane, France 45 12N 6 40E
104 Modasa, India 23 30N 73 21E
36 Modbury, England, U.K. 50 21N 3 53W
135 Modder R., S. Africa .28 50S 24 50E
134 Modderivier, S. Africa 29 2S 24 38E
135 Modderpoort, S. Africa 29 3S 27 29E
70 Modena, Italy 44 39N 10 55E
167 Modena, U.S.A. 37 55N 113 56W
167 Modesto, U.S.A. 37 43N 121 0W
73 Modica, Italy 36 52N 14 45E
71 Modigliana, Italy 44 9N 11 48E
109 Modjokerto, Indonesia 7 29S 112 25E
60 Modlin, Poland 52 24N 20 41E
60 Mödling, Austria 48 5N 16 17E
127 Modo, Sudan 5 31N 30 33E
59 Modra, Czechoslovakia 48 19N 17 20E
123 Modra, Chad 20 41N 17 51E
44 Modreeny, Ireland 52 57N 8 6W
74 Modriča, Yugoslavia .44 57N 18 17E
143 Moe, Vic., Australia ...38 12S 146 19E
107 Moei R., Thailand 17 25N 98 10E
37 Moelfre, Wales, U.K. .53 21N 4 15W
175 Moengo, Surinam 5 45N 54 20W
55 Moers, Germany 51 27N 6 38E
41 Moffat, Scot., U.K. 55 20N 3 27W
104 Moga, India 30 48N 75 8E
99 Mogadishu (Mogadiscio), Somali Rep. 2 2N 45 25E
122 Mogador, see Essaouira, Morocco 31 32N 9 42W
62 Mogadouro, Portugal .41 22N 6 47W
133 Mogalakwena R., S. Afr. 23 0S 28 40E
114 Mogami R., Japan 38 45N 140 0E
103 Mogaung, Burma 25 20N 97 0E
81 Mögeltönder, Denmark 54 57N 8 48E
65 Mogente, Spain 38 52N 0 43W
123 Moggar, Algeria 33 14N 6 2E
127 Mogho, Ethiopia 4 54N 40 16E
173 Mogi das Cruzes, Brazil 23 45S 46 20W
173 Mogi Mirim, Brazil 22 20S 47 0W
60 Mogielnica, Poland 51 42N 20 41E
86 Mogilev, U.S.S.R. 53 55N 30 18E
88 Mogilev Podolskiy, U.S.S.R. 48 20N 27 40E
143 Mogilla, N.S.W., Austral. 36 41S 149 38E
60 Mogilno, Poland 52 39N 17 55E
129 Mogincual, Mozambique 15 35S 40 25E
71 Mogliano Veneto, Italy 45 33N 12 15E
91 Mogocha, U.S.S.R. 53 40N 119 50E
132 Mogogelo, R., Bots. ...19 35S 24 0E
109 Mogoi, Indonesia 1 55S 133 10E
103 Mogôk, Burma 23 0N 96 40E
167 Mogollon, U.S.A. 33 25N 108 55W
167 Mogollon Mesa Mts., U.S.A. 43 40N 111 0W
63 Moguer, Spain 37 15N 6 52W
142 Mogumber, W. Austral. 31 2S 116 7E
135 Moguntia, Natal, S. Afr. 30 45S 30 9E
59 Mohács, Hungary 45 58N 18 41E
146 Mohaka R., N.Z. 39 13S 176 39E
135 Mohaleshoek, Lesotho 30 7S 27 26E
164 Mohall, U.S.A. 48 46N 101 30W
122 Mohammadia, Algeria 35 33N 0 3E
101 Mohammadabad, Iran 37 30N 59 5E
122 Mohammedia, Morocco 33 44N 7 21W
167 Mohave (Mojave) Desert, U.S.A. 35 0N 117 30W
167 Mohawk, U.S.A. 32 45N 113 50W
81 Moheda, Sweden 57 1N 14 35E
129 Mohembo, Botswana .18 15S 21 43E
44 Moher, Cliffs of, Ireland 52 58N 9 30W
46 Mohill, Ireland 53 57N 7 52W
56 Möhne R., Germany ...51 29N 8 10E
81 Moholm, Sweden 58 37N 14 5E
112 Moho, China 53 15N 122 27E
49 Mohon, France 48 2N 2 31W
131 Mohoro, Tanzania 8 6S 39 8E
127 Moia, Sudan 5 3N 28 2E
42 Moidart, L., Scot., U.K. 56 47N 5 52W
106 Moinabad, India 17 44N 77 16E
78 Moineşti, Rumania 46 28N 26 21E
90 Mointy, U.S.S.R. 47 40N 73 45E
46 Moira, N. Ire., U.K. ...54 28N 6 16W
77 Moirais, Crete, Greece 35 4N 24 56E
51 Moirans, Isère, France 45 20N 5 33E
51 Moirans, Jura, France 46 26N 5 43E
86 Moisakula, U.S.S.R. ...58 3N 24 38E
155 Moisie, Canada 50 7N 66 1W
50 Moissac, France 44 7N 1 5E
38 Moita, Corsica, France 42 17N 9 27E
63 Moita, Portugal 38 38N 8 58W
65 Mojácar, Spain 37 6N 1 55W
62 Mojados, Spain 41 26N 4 40W
167 Mojave, U.S.A. 35 8N 118 8W
167 Mojave Desert, U.S.A. 35 0N 117 30W
127 Mojjio, Ethiopia 8 35N 39 5E
108 Mojo I., Indonesia 8 10S 117 40E
146 Mokai, New Zealand .38 32S 175 56E
105 Mokameh, India 25 24N 85 55E
146 Mokau, New Zealand .38 42S 174 39E
146 Mokay R., New Zealand 38 35S 174 55E
99 Mokha, Yemen 13 18N 43 15E
77 Mokhós, Greece 35 16N 25 27E
135 Mokhotlong, Les. 29 22S 29 2E
147 Mokihinui, N.Z. 41 33S 171 58E
109 Mokmer, Indonesia 1 8S 136 1E
123 Moknine, Tunisia 35 35N 10 58E
103 Mokokchung, India ...26 15N 94 30E
113 Mokpo, S. Korea 34 50N 126 30E
74 Mokra Gora, Ra., Yugoslavia 42 50N 20 30E
75 Mokren, Bulgaria 52 45N 26 39E
71 Mokronog, Yugoslavia 45 57N 15 9E
87 Moksha R., U.S.S.R. .54 45N 43 40E
87 Mokshan, U.S.S.R. 52 25N 44 35E
124 Mokta Spera, Mauritania 16 38N 9 6W
130 Mokwangu Falls, Congo 3 55N 23 0E
54 Mol, Belgium 51 11N 5 5E
73 Mola di Bari, Italy 41 3N 17 5E
79 Moland, Norway 59 11N 8 6E
77 Moláoi, Greece 36 49N 22 56E
71 Molat, I., Yugoslavia .44 15N 14 50E
90 Molchanovo, U.S.S.R. 57 40N 83 50E
37 Mold, Wales, U.K. 53 10N 3 10W
59 Moldava nad Bodvou, Czechoslovakia 48 38N 21 0E
78 Moldavia, reg., Rum. .46 30N 27 0E
88 Moldavia, S.S.R., U.S.S.R. 47 0N 28 0E
79 Molde, Norway 62 46N 7 12E
74 Moldova Nouă, Rum. 44 45N 21 41E
75 Moldoveanu, Mt., Rumania 45 36N 24 45E
55 Molen Beersel, Belgium 51 14N 5 44E
133 Molepolole, Botswana 24 28S 25 28E
127 Molepso, Ethiopia 16 3N 38 17E
147 Molesworth, N.Z. 42 5S 173 16E
73 Molfetta Italy 41 12N 16 35E
64 Molina de Aragón, Sp. 40 46N 1 52W
164 Moline, Ill., U.S.A. 41 30N 90 30W
71 Molinella, Italy 44 38N 11 40E
172 Molinos, Argentina 25 28S 66 15W
131 Moliro, Congo 8 12S 30 30E
71 Molise, Reg., Italy 41 45N 14 30E
73 Moliterno, Italy 40 14N 15 50E
81 Mölle, Sweden 56 17N 12 31E
62 Molledo, Spain 43 8N 4 6W
174 Mollendo, Peru 17 0S 72 0W
64 Mollerusa, Spain 41 37N 0 54E
63 Mollina, Spain 37 8N 4 38W
56 Mölln, Germany 53 37N 10 41E
81 Mollösund, Sweden 58 4N 11 30E
81 Molltorp, Sweden 58 30N 14 26E
81 Molndal, Sweden 57 40N 12 3E
88 Molochnaya R., U.S.S.R. 47 0N 35 30E
86 Molodechno, U.S.S.R. 54 20N 26 50E
158 Molokai I., Hawaii, U.S.A. 21 8N 157 0W
87 Moloma, R., U.S.S.R. 59 0N 48 15E
143 Molong, N.S.W., Austral. 33 5S 148 54E
129 Molopo R., Botswana 25 40S 24 30E

MAP
134 Molopo R., South Africa 28 25S 20 20E
77 Mólos, Greece 38 47N 22 37E
91 Molotov C., U.S.S.R. ..81 10N 95 0E
49 Molsheim, France 48 33N 7 29E
135 Molteno, C. Prov., S. Afr. 31 22S 26 22E
109 Molu I., Indonesia 6 45S 131 40E
109 Molucca Sea, Indonesia 4 0S 124 0E
109 Moluccas (Malaku) Is. Prov., Indon. 1 0S 127 0E
130 Molumbu, Congo 0 47N 17 56E
132 Molusi, Botswana 20 21S 24 29E
86 Molvotitsy, U.S.S.R. .57 21N 32 24E
129 Moma, Mozambique ...16 47S 39 4E
131 Mombasa & Kilindini, Kenya 4 2S 39 43E
131 Mombo, Tanzania 4 57S 38 20E
130 Momboyo R., Congo . 0 40S 20 20E
62 Mombuey, Spain 42 3N 6 20W
75 Momchilgrad, Bulgaria 41 33N 25 23E
174 Mompós, Colombia 9 14N 74 26W
81 Mön, Sweden 58 56N 11 47E
81 Mön I., Denmark 54 57N 12 15E
103 Mon R., Burma 20 25N 94 30E
169 Mona I., Puerto Rico .18 5N 67 54W
169 Mona Passage, W. Ind. 18 0N 67 40W
130 Mona Quimbundo, Ang. 9 54S 19 57E
42 Monach Is., Scot., U.K. 57 32N 7 40W
42 Monach, Sd. of, Scotland, U.K. 57 34N 7 26W
50 Monaco, Principality, Europe 43 36N 7 23E
43 Monadhliath Mts., Scotland, U.K. 57 10N 4 4W
46 Monaghan, Ireland 54 15N 6 58W
46 Monaghan, Co., Ireland 54 10N 7 0W
165 Monahans, U.S.A. 31 35N 102 50W
132 Monaka Bantu, Zambia 15 56S 25 19E
42 Monar For., Scot., U.K. 57 27N 5 10W
42 Monar L., Scot., U.K. 57 26N 5 8W
156 Monarch Mt., Canada 51 55N 125 57W
143 Monaro Ra., Australia 36 20S 149 0E
46 Monasterboice, Ireland 53 46N 6 22W
45 Monasterevan, Ireland 53 10N 7 5W
123 Monastir, Tunisia 35 50N 10 49E
86 Monastyriska, U.S.S.R. 49 8N 25 14E
45 Monavullagh Mts., Ire. 52 14N 7 35W
64 Moncada, Spain 39 30N 0 24W
70 Moncalieri, Italy 45 0N 7 40E
70 Moncalvo, Italy 45 3N 8 15E
62 Monção, Portugal 42 4N 8 27W
163 Moncarapacho, Port. .37 5N 7 46W
64 Moncayo, Mt., Spain .41 48N 1 50W
56 Monchen-gladbach, Ger. 51 12N 6 23E
63 Monchique, Portugal .37 19N 8 38W
168 Monclova, Mexico 26 50N 101 30W
48 Moncontour, France ...48 22N 2 38W
48 Moncoutant, France ...46 43N 0 36W
155 Moncton, Canada 46 7N 64 51W
62 Mondego R., Portugal 40 28N 8 0W
62 Mondego, Cabo, Port. 40 11N 8 54W
109 Mondoedo, Indonesia . 3 21S 122 9E
71 Mondolfo, Italy 43 45N 13 8E
62 Mondonedo, Spain 43 25N 7 23E
70 Mondovi, Italy 44 23N 7 56E
164 Mondovi, U.S.A. 44 37N 91 40W
51 Mondragon, France ...44 13N 4 44E
72 Mondragone, Italy 41 8N 13 52E
77 Monemvasia, Greece ...36 41N 23 3E
160 Monessen, Pa., U.S.A. 40 9N 79 50W
63 Monesterio, Spain 38 6N 6 15W
51 Monestier de Clermont, France ...44 55N 5 38E
154 Monet, Canada 48 10N 75 40W
165 Monett, U.S.A. 36 55N 93 56W
44 Moneygall, Ireland 52 54N 7 59W
46 Moneymore, N. Ire., U.K. 54 42N 6 40W
71 Monfalcone, Italy 45 49N 13 32E
50 Monflanquin, France .44 32N 0 47E
63 Monforte, Portugal 39 6N 7 25W
62 Monforte, Spain 42 31N 7 33W
107 Mong Cai, N. Vietnam 21 27N 107 54E
103 Möng Hsu, Burma ...21 54N 98 30E
103 Möng Kung, Burma ...21 35N 97 35E
107 Mong Lang, Burma ...20 29N 97 52E
103 Möng Nai, Burma 20 32N 97 55E
103 Möng Pai, Burma 19 40N 97 15E
103 Mong Pawk, Burma ...22 4N 99 16E
103 Mong Ton, Burma 20 25N 98 45E
103 Mong Wa, Burma 21 26N 100 27E
103 Mong Yai, Burma 22 28N 98 3E
130 Mongala R., Congo 2 20N 20 30E
127 Mongalla, Sudan 5 8N 31 55E
130 Monganga, Congo 2 17S 25 51E
105 Mongar Dzong, Bhutan 27 15N 91 20E
142 Monger L., W. Austral. 29 0S 117 15E
105 Monghyr, India 25 23N 86 30E
105 Mongla, E. Pakistan .22 8N 89 35E
121 Mongo, Chad 12 14N 18 43E
111 Mongolia, rep., Asia ..47 0N 103 0E
112 Mongolia, Inner, Autonomous Reg., China 44 15N 117 0E
125 Mongonu, Nigeria 12 40N 13 32E
128 Mongororo, Chad 12 22N 22 26E
107 Mongpang, China 23 5N 100 25E
132 Mongu, Zambia 15 16S 23 12E
41 Moniaive, Scot., U.K. 55 11N 3 55W
41 Monifieth, Scot., U.K. 56 30N 2 48W
124 Monimpébougou, Mali 14 11N 5 28W
50 Monistrol, France 45 17N 4 11E
44 Monivea, Ireland 53 22N 8 42W
157 Monk, Canada 47 7N 69 59W
132 Monkey Bay, Malawi .14 7S 35 1E
144 Monkira, Australia 24 46S 140 30E
130 Monkoto, Congo 1 38S 20 35E
160 Monkton, Canada 43 37N 81 5W
40 Monkton, Scot., U.K. 55 30N 4 37W
34 Monmouth, Eng., U.K. 51 48N 2 43W
164 Monmouth, U.S.A. 40 50N 90 40W
34 Monmouth, co., U.K. .51 34N 3 5W
34 Monnow R., Eng., U.K. 51 54N 2 48W
167 Mono, L., U.S.A. 38 0N 119 0W
169 Mono, Punta del, Nic. 12 0N 83 30W
160 Monongahela, U.S.A. .40 12N 79 56W
73 Monopoli, Italy 40 57N 17 18E
59 Monor, Hungary 47 21N 19 27E
65 Monovar, Spain 38 28N 0 53W
147 Monowai, & L., N.Z. .45 53S 167 25E
64 Monreal del Campo, Sp. 40 47N 1 20W
72 Monreale Italy 38 6N 13 16E
165 Monroe, La., U.S.A. ...32 32N 92 4W
162 Monroe, Mich., U.S.A. 41 55N 83 26W
161 Monroe, N.Y., U.S.A. 41 19N 74 11W
163 Monroe, N.C., U.S.A. .35 2N 80 37W
167 Monroe, Utah, U.S.A. 38 45N 111 39W
164 Monroe, Wis., U.S.A. .42 38N 89 40W
164 Monroe City, U.S.A. ...39 40N 91 40W
163 Monroeville, U.S.A. ...31 33N 87 15W
124 Monrovia, Liberia 6 18N 10 47W
167 Monrovia, U.S.A. 34 7N 118 1W
54 Mons, Belgium 50 27N 3 58E
81 Möns Klint, C. Den. .54 57N 12 33E
63 Monsaraz, Portugal ...38 28N 7 22W
109 Monse, Indonesia 4 0S 123 10E
50 Monségur, France 44 38N 0 4E
71 Monselice, Italy 45 13N 11 45E
81 Mönsted, Denmark 56 27N 9 11E
81 Monsterås, Sweden 57 3N 16 33E
135 Mont-aux-Sources, Mt., S. Africa 28 44S 28 52E
51 Mont Blanc, Mt., France and Italy ...45 48N 6 50E
51 Mont Cenis (Frejus) Tunnel, France 45 15N 6 30E
50 Mont de Marsan, Fr. .43 54N 0 31W
49 Mont d'Or, Tunnel, Fr. 46 45N 6 18E
155 Mont Joli, Canada 48 37N 68 10W
154 Mont Laurier, Canada 46 35N 75 30W
155 Mont Luis, France ...42 31N 2 6E
48 Mont St. Michel France 48 40N 1 30W
154 Mont Tremblant Prov. Park, Canada 46 30N 74 30W
56 Montabaur, Germany .50 26N 7 49E
37 Montagnac, France 43 29N 3 28E
71 Montagnana, Italy 45 13N 11 29E
15 Montagu I., Falk. Is. Dependencies 58 30S 26 15W
134 Montagu, S. Africa ...33 45S 20 8E
166 Montague, Calif., U.S.A. 41 47N 122 30W
161 Montague, Mass., U.S.A. 42 31N 72 33W
143 Montague I., Australia 36 16S 150 13E
168 Montague I., Mexico .31 40N 144 46W
142 Montague Ra., Austral. 27 15S 119 45E
48 Montaigu, France 46 59N 1 18W
63 Montalbán, Spain 40 50N 0 45W
73 Montalbano di Elicona, Italy 38 1N 15 0E
73 Montalbano Lonico, It. 40 17N 16 33E
64 Montalbo, Spain 39 53N 2 42W
71 Montalcino, Italy 43 4N 11 30E
62 Montalegre, Portugal .41 49N 7 47W
73 Montalto di Castro, Italy 42 20N 11 36E
73 Montalto Uffugo, Italy 39 25N 16 9E
62 Montamarta, Spain ...41 39N 5 49W
174 Montana, dist., Peru . 6 0S 73 0W
158 Montana, st., U.S.A. .47 0N 110 0W
62 Montanas de Léon, Sp. 42 30N 6 20W
63 Montanchez, Spain 39 15N 6 8W
50 Montargis, France 48 0N 2 43E
50 Montauban, France 44 0N 1 21E
161 Montauk, U.S.A. 41 3N 71 57W
49 Montbard, France 47 38N 4 20E
49 Montbéliard, France ...47 31N 6 48E
64 Montblanch, Spain 41 23N 1 4E
51 Montbrison, France ...45 36N 4 3E
103 Montcalm, L., Tibet, China 34 40N 89 0E
50 Montcalm, Pic de, Fr. 42 40N 1 30E
49 Montceau-les-Mines, Fr. 46 40N 4 23E
161 Montclair, U.S.A. 40 53N 74 49W
49 Montcornet, France ...49 40N 4 0E
50 Montcuq, France 44 21N 1 13E
49 Montdidier, France ...49 38N 2 35E
172 Monte, Argentina 35 23S 58 50W
175 Monte Alegre, Brazil . 2 0S 54 0W
138 Monte Bello Is., W. Australia 20 30S 115 45E
51 Monte Carlo, Monaco .43 46N 7 23E
172 Monte Caseros, Arg. ...30 10S 57 50W
71 Monte Coman, Arg. ...34 40S 68 0W
172 Monte Lindo R., Par. 25 30S 58 40W
172 Monte Quemado, Arg. 25 53S 62 41W
62 Monte Redondo, Port. 39 53N 8 50W
72 Monte San Guiliano, It. 38 3N 12 33E
71 Monte San Savino, It. 43 20N 11 42E
73 Monte Sant Angelo, It. 41 42N 15 59E
72 Monte Santo C. di, It. 40 5N 9 42E
167 Monte Visto, U.S.A. ...37 40N 106 8W
173 Monteagudo, Argentina 27 14S 54 8W
65 Montealegre, Spain ...38 48N 1 17W
154 Montebello, Canada ...45 40N 74 55W
71 Montebelluna, Italy ...45 47N 12 3E
48 Montebourg, France ...49 30N 1 20W
71 Montecastrilli, Italy ...42 40N 12 30E
70 Montecatini Terme, It. 43 55N 10 48E
174 Montecristi, Ecuador 1 0S 80 40W
70 Montecristo I., Italy 42 20N 10 20E
71 Montefalco, Italy 42 53N 12 38E
71 Montefiascone, Italy ...42 31N 12 2E
63 Montefrio, Spain 37 20N 3 39W
55 Montegnée, Belgium ...50 38N 5 31E
169 Montego B., Jamaica .18 30N 78 0W
71 Montegranaro, Italy ..43 13N 13 38E
65 Montejicar, Spain 37 33N 3 30W
51 Montélimar, France ...44 33N 4 45E
73 Montella, Italy 40 50N 15 0E
63 Montellano, Spain 36 59N 5 36W
164 Montello, U.S.A. 43 49N 89 21W
70 Montelupo Florentino, Italy 43 44N 11 2E
63 Montemór-o-Novo, Port. 38 40N 8 12W
62 Montemor o Velho, Portugal 40 11N 8 40W
168 Montemorelos, Mexico 25 11N 99 42W
50 Montendre, France 45 16N 0 26W
173 Montenegro, Brazil 29 39S 51 29W
74 Montenegro, fed., (Crna Gora) unit, Y.-slav. 42 40N 19 20E
71 Montenero di Bisaccia, Italy 42 0N 14 47E
129 Montepuez, Mozam. ...13 8S 38 59E
71 Montepulciano Italy .43 5N 11 46E
71 Montereale, Italy 42 31N 13 13E
49 Montereau, France 48 22N 2 57E
167 Monterey, Calif., U.S.A. 36 35N 121 57W
174 Monteria, Colombia ... 8 46N 75 53W
172 Monteros, Argentina .27 11S 65 30W
71 Monterotondo, Italy ...42 3N 12 36E
168 Monterrey, Mexico 25 40N 100 30W
175 Montes Claros, Brazil .16 30S 43 50W
63 Montes de Toledo, Sp. 39 35N 4 30W
166 Montesano, U.S.A. 47 0N 123 39W
73 Montesarchio, Italy ...41 5N 14 37E
73 Montescaglioso, Italy .40 34N 16 40E
71 Montesilvano, Italy ...42 30N 14 8E
71 Montevarchi, Italy 43 30N 11 32E
173 Montevideo, Uruguay 34 50S 56 11W
164 Montezuma, U.S.A. ...41 32N 92 35W
51 Montfaucon, Haute-Loire, France 45 11N 4 20E
49 Montfaucon, Meuse, Fr. 49 16N 5 8E
49 Montfort l'Amaury, Fr. 48 47N 1 49E
48 Montfort-sur-Meu, Fr. 48 8N 1 58W
51 Montgenèvre, France .44 56N 6 42E
37 Montgomery, & Co., Wales, U.K. 52 34N 3 9W
163 Montgomery, Ala., U.S.A. 32 20N 86 20W
162 Montgomery, W. Va., U.S.A. 38 9N 81 21W
104 Montgomery, see Sahiwal, W. Pak. ...30 45N 73 8E
50 Montguyon, France ...45 12N 0 12W
157 Monthey, Switzerland 46 15N 6 56E
72 Monti del Gennargentu, Sardinia, Italy 40 0N 9 15E
73 Monti Iblei, Sicily, Italy 37 15N 14 45E
73 Monti Nebrodi, Sicily, It. 37 48N 14 20E
73 Monti Peloritani, Sic., It. 38 2N 15 15E
70 Monticelli d'Ongina, It. 45 3N 9 56E
165 Monticello, Ark., U.S.A. 33 40N 91 48W
163 Monticello, Fla., U.S.A. 30 35N 83 50W
162 Monticello, Ind. U.S.A. 40 40N 86 45W
164 Monticello, Iowa, U.S.A. 42 18N 91 18W
163 Monticello, Ky., U.S.A. 36 52N 84 50W
164 Monticello, Minn., U.S.A. 45 17N 93 52W
165 Monticello, Miss., U.S.A. 31 35N 90 8W
161 Monticello, N.Y., U.S.A. 41 37N 74 42W
167 Monticello, Utah, U.S.A. 37 55N 109 27W
70 Montichiari, Italy 45 28N 10 29E
49 Montieri, France 48 30N 4 45E
50 Montignac, France 45 4N 1 10E
55 Montignies-sur-Sambre, Belgium 50 24N 4 29E
49 Montigny les Metz, Fr. 49 7N 6 10E
49 Montigny sur Aube, Fr. 47 57N 4 45E
63 Montijo, Spain 38 52N 6 39W
63 Montilla, Spain 37 36N 4 40W
164 Montivideo, U.S.A. 44 55N 95 40W
49 Montlhery, France 48 39N 2 15E
50 Montluçon, France 46 22N 2 36E
155 Montmagny, Canada .46 58N 70 34W
59 Montmarault, France .46 20N 2 57E
157 Montmartre, Canada .50 20N 103 15W
49 Montmédy, France 49 30N 5 20E
51 Montmelian, France ...45 30N 6 4E
49 Montmirail, France ...48 51N 3 30E
50 Montmoreau, France .45 23N 0 7E
155 Montmorency, Canada 46 53N 71 11W
50 Montmorillon, France 46 26N 0 50E
49 Montmort, France 48 55N 3 49E
144 Monto, Queens., Austral. 24 52S 151 12E
71 Montorio al Vomano, It. 42 35N 13 38E
63 Montoro, Spain 38 1N 4 27W
160 Montour Falls, U.S.A. 42 20N 76 51W
166 Montpelier, Id., U.S.A. 42 15N 111 29W
162 Montpelier, Ohio, U.S.A. 41 34N 84 40W
161 Montpelier, Vt., U.S.A. 44 15N 72 38W
50 Montpellier, France ...43 37N 3 52E
50 Montpézat de Quercy, France 44 15N 1 30E
50 Montpon, France 45 2N 0 11E
50 Montréal, Aude, France 43 13N 2 8E
154 Montreal, Canada 45 31N 73 34W
157 Montreal L., Canada .54 20N 105 45W
50 Montredon Labessonnié, France 43 45N 2 18E
50 Montréjeau, France ...43 6N 0 35E
48 Montrésor, France 47 10N 1 10E
49 Montreuil, France 50 27N 1 45E
48 Montreuil Bellay, Fr. .47 8N 0 9W
57 Montreux, Switzerland 46 26N 6 55E
48 Montrevault, France .47 17N 1 2W
51 Montrevel, France 46 21N 5 8E
48 Montrichard, France .47 20N 1 10E
43 Montrose, Scot., U.K. 56 43N 2 28W
167 Montrose, Col., U.S.A. 38 30N 107 52W
161 Montrose, Pa., U.S.A. 41 50N 75 55W
155 Monts, Pte des, Canada 49 27N 67 12W
50 Montsalvy, France 44 41N 2 30E
49 Montsauche, France ...47 13N 4 0E
169 Montserrat I., W.I. ...16 40N 62 10W
62 Montuenga, Spain 41 3N 4 38W
64 Montuiri, Spain 39 34N 2 59E
55 Montzen, Belgium 50 42N 5 58E
43 Monymusk, Scot., U.K. 57 13N 2 32W
103 Mönywa, Burma 22 7N 95 11E
70 Monza, Italy 45 35N 9 15E
132 Monze, Zambia 16 17S 27 29E
102 Monze, C., W. Pakistan 24 47N 66 37E
64 Monzón, Spain 41 52N 0 10E
133 Mooifontein, S. Africa 26 52S 29 53E
134 Mooipan, S. Africa 28 51S 22 53E
135 Mooirivier, Nat., S. Afr. 29 13S 29 50E
133 Mooketsi, Trans., S. Afr. 23 40S 30 9E
145 Moolawatana, S. Austral. 29 55S 139 45E
142 Mooligbeenee, Australia 31 15S 116 5E
133 Moolman, Trans., S. Afr. 27 10S 30 53E
142 Mooloogool, W. Austral. 26 2S 119 5E
154 Moonbeam, Canada ...49 20N 82 10W
45 Mooncoin, Ireland 52 18N 7 17W
143 Moondarra, Australia .38 2S 146 30E
145 Moonie, R., Australia .29 0S 148 30E
145 Moonie, Queens., Austral. 27 37S 150 17E
145 Moonta, S. Australia .34 6S 137 32E
142 Moora, W. Australia .30 37S 115 58E
145 Mooraberree, Australia 25 13S 140 54E
142 Moorarie, W. Australia 24 55S 117 30E
164 Moorcroft, U.S.A. 44 17N 104 58W
133 Moorddrif, S. Africa ...24 15S 28 59E
55 Moordrecht, Neth. 51 59N 4 40E
142 Moore, L., W. Australia 29 30S 117 30E
142 Moore River, W. Austral. 31 7S 115 42E
162 Moorefield, U.S.A. 39 5N 78 59W
161 Moores Res., U.S.A. ...44 45N 71 50W
163 Mooresville, U.S.A. 35 36N 80 45W
41 Moorfoot Hills, Scotland, U.K. 55 44N 3 8W
164 Moorhead, U.S.A. 47 0N 97 0W
143 Moorland, Australia ...31 46S 152 38E
143 Mooroopna, Australia 36 25S 145 22E
134 Moorreesburg, S. Afr. .33 6S 18 38E
57 Moosburg, Germany ...48 28N 11 57E
154 Moose Factory, Canada 52 20N 80 40W
157 Moose Jaw, Canada ...50 30N 105 30W
164 Moose Lake, U.S.A. ...46 27N 92 48W
154 Moose R., Canada 51 20N 81 15W
154 Moose River, tn., Can. 51 10N 81 47W
155 Moosehead L., U.S.A. 45 40N 69 40W
157 Moosomin, Canada 50 9N 101 40W
154 Moosonee, Canada 51 25N 80 51W
161 Moosup, U.S.A. 41 44N 71 52W
131 Mooti, Somali Rep. ... 0 34N 41 37E
132 Mopeia, Mozambique .17 30S 35 40E
127 Mopoi, Central Africa 5 6N 26 54E
145 Moppin, N.S.W., Austral. 29 12S 146 45E
124 Mopti, Mali 14 30N 4 0W
127 Moqatta, Sudan 14 38N 35 50E
174 Moquegua, Peru 17 15S 70 46W
59 Mór, Hungary 47 25N 18 12E
63 Mora, Portugal 38 55N 8 10W
80 Mora, Sweden 61 2N 14 38E
164 Mora, Minn., U.S.A. ...45 52N 93 19W
167 Mora, N. Mex., U.S.A. 35 58N 105 21W
64 Mora de Ebro, Spain .41 6N 0 38E
64 Mora la Nueva, Spain 41 7N 0 39E
64 Mora de Rubielos, Spain 40 15N 0 45W
74 Morača R., Y.-slavia .42 40N 19 20E
104 Moradabad, India 28 50N 78 50E
129 Morafenoie, Malagasy Rep. 17 50S 44 53E
60 Morag, Poland 53 55N 19 56E
65 Moral de Calatrava, Sp. 38 51N 3 33W
129 Moramanga, Malag. Rep. 18 56S 48 12E
62 Moraleja, Spain 40 6N 6 43W
165 Moran, Kan., U.S.A. .37 53N 94 35W
166 Moran, Wyo., U.S.A. .43 53N 110 37W
73 Morano, Calabro, Italy 39 51N 16 8E
169 Morant Pt., Jamaica .17 55N 76 12W
42 Morar, Scot., U.K. 56 58N 5 49W
42 Morar L., Scot., U.K. 56 57N 5 40W
65 Moratalla, Spain 38 14N 1 49W
106 Moratuwa, Ceylon 6 45N 79 55E
59 Morava R., Cz. 49 50N 16 50E
59 Moravia, hist. prov., Cz. 49 7N 15 57E
134 Moravia, C. Prov., S. Afr. 32 56S 18 38E
164 Moravia, Iowa, U.S.A. 40 50N 92 50W
19 Moravian Heights, Czechoslovakia 49 30N 15 40E
74 Moravica R., Y.-slavia 43 40N 20 8E
59 Moravice R., Cz. 49 50N 17 43E
59 Moravská Trebová, Cz. 49 45N 16 40E
58 Moravske Budejovice, Czechoslovakia 49 4N 15 49E
142 Morawa, W. Australia 29 13S 116 0E
174 Morawhanna, Guyana 8 30N 59 40W
43 Moray, co., Scot., U.K. 57 32N 3 25W
57 Morbach, Germany 49 48N 7 7E
70 Morbegno, Italy 46 8N 9 34E
48 Morbihan, dépt., Fr. .47 55N 3 0W
50 Morcenx, France 44 0N 0 55W
48 Mordelles, France 48 5N 1 52W
157 Morden, Canada 49 15N 98 10W
143 Mordialloc, Australia .38 1S 145 6E
87 Mordovian S.S.R., U.S.S.R. 54 20N 44 30E
87 Mordovo, U.S.S.R. 52 13N 40 50E
43 More, Glen, Scot., U.K. 57 18N 4 30W
43 More L., Scotland, United Kingdom 58 18N 4 52W
77 Morea, Greece 37 45N 22 10E
164 Moreau R., U.S.A. ...45 15N 102 45W
36 Morebath, Eng., U.K. 51 1N 3 28W
41 Morebattle, Scot., U.K. 55 30N 2 20W
38 Morecambe, Eng., U.K. 54 5N 2 52W
145 Moree, N.S.W., Austral. 29 28S 149 48E
162 Morehead, U.S.A. 38 12N 83 22W
163 Morehead City, U.S.A. 34 46N 76 44W
168 Morelia, Mexico 19 40N 101 11W
144 Morella, Queensland, Australia 23 0S 143 47E
64 Morella Spain 40 35N 0 2E
168 Morelos, st., Mexico ...18 40N 99 10W
167 Morenci, U.S.A. 33 7N 109 20W
78 Moreni, Rumania 44 59N 25 36E
174 Moreno, Colombia 5 53N 71 54W
173 Mores, I., Bahama Is. 26 15N 77 35W
156 Moresby I., Canada ...52 30N 131 40W
51 Morestel, France 45 40N 5 28E
49 Moret, France 48 22N 2 48E
144 Moreton Telegraph Office, Australia ...12 22S 142 30E
145 Moreton, I., Australia 27 10S 153 10E
36 Moretonhampstead, England, U.K. 50 39N 3 45W
34 Moreton-in-Marsh, England, U.K. 51 59N 1 42W
49 Moreuil, France 49 46N 2 30E
51 Morez, France 46 31N 6 2E
145 Morgan, S. Australia .34 0S 139 35E
166 Morgan, U.S.A. 41 3N 111 44W
165 Morgan City, U.S.A. .29 40N 91 15W
162 Morganfield, U.S.A. ...37 40N 87 55W
163 Morganton, U.S.A. ...35 46N 81 48W
162 Morgantown, U.S.A. ..39 39N 75 58W
163 Morganville, Australia 25 10S 152 0E
48 Morgat, France 48 15N 4 32E
133 Morgenzon, S. Africa .26 45S 29 36E
57 Morges, Switzerland ...46 31N 6 29E
49 Mörhange, France 48 55N 6 38E
70 Mori, Italy 45 51N 10 59E
167 Moriarty, U.S.A. 35 3N 106 2W
156 Morice L., Canada 53 50N 127 40W
135 Morija, Lesotho 29 34S 27 31E
125 Moriki, Nigeria 12 52N 6 30E
156 Morinville, Canada 53 49N 113 41W

MAP
114 Morioka, Japan 39 45N 141 8E
43 Moriston, Glen, Scot., U.K. 57 10N 5 0W
43 Moriston, R., Scot., U.K. 57 10N 5 0W
143 Morkalla, Vic., Austral. 34 18S 141 4E
50 Morlaas, France 43 21N 0 18W
40 Morlaix, France 48 36N 3 52W
39 Morley, England, U.K.53 45N 1 36W
73 Mormanno, Italy 39 53N 15 59E
49 Mormant, France 48 37N 2 52E
145 Morney, Australia 25 22S 141 23E
143 Mornington, Australia 38 15S 145 5E
46 Mornington, Ireland ...53 42N 6 17W
144 Mornington I., Austral. 16 30S 139 30E
176 Mornington I., Chile ...49 50S 75 30W
77 Mórnos R., Greece 38 30N 22 0E
127 Moro, Sudan 10 50N 30 9E
109 Moro G., Philippines . 7 0N 123 0E
144 Morobe, Terr. of New Guinea 7 49S 147 38E
122 Morocco, King., N. Afr. 32 0N 5 50W
174 Morococha, Peru 11 40S 76 5W
131 Morogoro, Tanzania ... 6 50S 37 40E
131 Morogoro, reg., Tanz. . 8 0S 37 20E
131 Morogoro, prov., Tanz. 7 30S 37 30E
109 Moroimu, Indonesia ... 6 35S 139 45E
133 Morokweng, S. Africa 26 12S 23 45E
168 Moroleón, Mexico 20 8N 101 32W
129 Morombé, Malagasy Rep. 21 45S 43 22E
172 Moron, Argentina 34 40S 58 40W
169 Morón, Cuba 22 0N 78 30W
64 Morón de Almazán, Sp. 41 29N 2 27W
63 Morón de la Frontera, Spain 37 6N 5 28W
174 Morona, Ecuador 2 40S 77 35W
129 Morondava, Malagasy Rep. 20 17S 44 17E
109 Morotai I., Indonesia 2 10N 128 30E
131 Moroto, Uganda 2 28N 34 42E
75 Morozov (Bratan), Mt., Bulgaria 42 30N 25 10E
89 Morozovsk, U.S.S.R. .48 25N 41 50E
143 Morpeth, N.S.W, Austral. 32 44S 151 39E
39 Morpeth, Eng., U.K. .55 11N 1 41W
165 Morrilton, U.S.A. 35 10N 92 45W
175 Morrinhos, Brazil 17 45S 49 10W
146 Morrinsville, N.Z. 37 40S 175 32E
157 Morris, Canada 49 25N 97 30W
162 Morris, Ill., U.S.A. ...41 20N 88 20W
164 Morris, Minn., U.S.A. 45 33N 95 56W
154 Morrisburg, Canada ...44 55N 75 7W
164 Morrison, U.S.A. 41 47N 90 0W
167 Morristown, Ariz., U.S.A. 33 54N 112 45W
161 Morristown, N.J., U.S.A. 40 48N 74 30W
164 Morristown, S.D., U.S.A. 45 57N 101 44W
163 Morristown, Tenn., U.S.A. 36 18N 83 20W
167 Morro Bay, U.S.A. 35 27N 120 54W
172 Morro, Pta., Chile 27 6S 71 0W
174 Morrosquillo, Gulf of, Colombia 9 35N 75 40W
81 Morrum, Sweden 56 11N 14 42E
132 Morrumbala, Mozam. .17 18S 35 39E
81 Mors, I., Denmark 56 47N 8 40E
55 Morsbach, Germany ...50 52N 7 41E
87 Morshank, U.S.S.R. ...53 28N 41 50E
80 Mörsil, Sweden 63 19N 13 40E
50 Mortagne, Charente Maritime, France ...45 28N 0 49W
48 Mortagne, Orne, France 48 30N 0 32E
48 Mortagne, Vendée, Fr. 46 59N 0 57W
49 Mortagne, R., France .48 30N 6 30E
48 Mortain, France 48 40N 0 57W
70 Mortara, Italy 45 15N 8 43E
36 Morte Bay, Eng., UK 51 10N 4 13W
36 Morte Pt., Eng., U.K. 51 13N 4 14W
49 Morteau, France 47 3N 6 35E
36 Mortehoe, Eng., U.K. 51 12N 4 12W
172 Morteros, Argentina ...30 50S 62 0W
135 Mortimer, S. Africa ...32 19S 25 43E
34 Mortimer's Cross, England, U.K. 52 17N 2 50W
143 Mortlake, Vic., Austral. 38 5S 142 50E
165 Morton, Tex., U.S.A. .33 39N 102 49W
166 Morton, Wash., U.S.A. 46 42N 122 11W
35 Morton Fen, Eng., U.K. 52 45N 0 23W
42 Moruisg Mt., Scot., U.K. 57 30N 5 10W
143 Morundah, Australia .34 57S 146 19E
143 Moruya, N.S.W., Austral. 35 58N 150 3E
49 Morvan, Mts., du, France 47 5N 4 0E
145 Morven, Queensland, Australia 26 22S 147 5E
147 Morven, N.Z. 44 50S 171 6E
40 Morven, dist., Scotland, U.K. 56 38N 5 44W
43 Morven, Mt., Aberdeen, Scotland, U.K. 57 8N 3 1W
43 Morven, Mt., Caithness, Scotland, U.K. 58 15N 3 40W
MAP
40 Morvern, dist., Scot., U.K. 56 38N 5 44W
104 Morvi, India 22 25N 72 5E
43 Morwell, Vic., Australia 38 10S 146 22E
36 Morwenstow, Eng., U.K. 50 53N 4 32W
86 Mosalsk, U.S.S.R. 54 30N 34 55E
57 Mosbach, Germany 49 21N 9 9E
71 Moscenice, Y.-slavia .45 17N 14 16E
71 Mosciano Sant' Angelo, Italy 42 42N 13 52E
166 Moscow, U.S.A. 46 45N 116 59W
87 Moscow, U.S.S.R. 55 45N 37 35E
133 Moseberg, S. Africa ...28 30S 24 9E
57 Mosel R., Germany ...49 48N 6 45E
49 Moselle, dépt., France 48 59N 6 35E
49 Moselle R., France ...48 30N 6 10E
166 Moses Lake, U.S.A. ...47 16N 119 17W
147 Mosgiel, N.Z. 45 53S 170 21E
131 Moshi, & dist., Tanzania 3 22S 37 18E
60 Mosina, Poland 52 15N 16 50E
82 Mosjöen, Norway 65 52N 13 20E
82 Moskenesoy, I., Norway 67 38N 13 0E
82 Moskenstraumen, Nor. 67 45N 13 0E
87 Moskva, R., U.S.S.R. .55 42N 36 0E
71 Moslavacka Gora, Yugoslavia 45 40N 16 37E
59 Mosonmagyaróvár, Hungary 47 52N 17 18E
59 Mosonszentjános, Hung. 47 47N 17 11E
74 Mosorin, Yugoslavia ...45 19N 20 4E
88 Mospina, U.S.S.R. ...47 52N 38 6E
174 Mosquera, Colombia ... 2 35N 78 30W
165 Mosquero, U.S.A. 35 48N 103 57W
64 Mosqueruela, Spain ...40 21N 0 27W
169 Mosquitos, G. of, Pan. 9 15N 81 10W
79 Moss, Norway 59 27N 10 40E
143 Moss Vale, Australia .34 32S 150 25E
129 Mossâmedes, Angola .15 7S 12 11E
157 Mossbank, Canada 50 0N 106 0W
147 Mossburn, N.Z. 45 41S 168 15E
134 Mosselbaai, S. Africa .34 11S 22 8E
143 Mossgiel, N.S.W., Austral. 33 15S 144 30E
38 Mossley, Eng., U.K. ...53 31N 2 1W
175 Mossoró, Brazil 5 10S 37 15W
79 Mösstrand, Norway ...59 52N 7 44E
129 Mossuril, Mozambique 14 57S 40 42E
58 Most, Czechoslovakia .50 31N 13 38E
72 Mostaganem, Algeria .35 51N 0 7E
74 Mostar, Yugoslavia ...43 22N 17 50E
173 Mostardas, Brazil 31 2S 50 51W
79 Moster, Norway 59 43N 5 22E
79 Mosteröy, Norway 59 5N 5 37E
75 Mostiska, U.S.S.R. ...49 48N 23 4E
46 Mostrim, Ireland 53 42N 7 38W
86 Mosty, U.S.S.R. 53 27N 24 38E
37 Mostyn, Eng., U.K. ...53 18N 3 14W
100 Mosul (Al Mawsil), Iraq 36 20N 43 5E
113 Mosun, China 23 35N 109 30E
79 Mösvatn, L., Norway .59 53N 8 0E
64 Mota del Cuervo, Spain 39 30N 2 52W
62 Mota del Marques, Sp. 41 38N 5 11W
174 Motacucito, Bolivia ...17 32S 61 32W
81 Motala, Sweden 58 32N 15 1E
174 Motatan, Venezuela ... 9 25N 70 40W
78 Motaţei, Rumania ...44 7N 23 13E
34 Motcombe, Eng., U.K. 51 1N 2 12W
41 Motherwell, Scot., U.K. 55 48N 4 0W
105 Motihari, India 26 37N 85 1E
64 Motilla del Palancar, Spain 39 34N 1 55W
135 Motkop, C. Prov., S. Afr. 30 52S 27 16E
71 Motnik, Yugoslavia ...46 14N 14 54E
168 Motozintla de Mendoza, Mexico ...15 21N 92 14W
71 Motovun, Yugoslavia .45 20N 13 50E
65 Motril, Spain 36 44N 3 37W
78 Motru R., Rumania ...44 44N 22 59E
98 Motsa, Israel 31 48N 35 8E
164 Mott, U.S.A. 46 25N 102 14W
34 Mottisfont, Eng., U.K. 51 22N 1 32W
73 Mottola, Italy 40 38N 17 0E
147 Motueka, N.Z. 41 7S 173 1E
168 Motul, Mexico 21 0N 89 20W
76 Moúdhros, Greece 39 50N 25 18E
124 Moudjeria, Mauritania 17 50N 12 15W
57 Moudon, Switzerland .46 40N 6 49E
128 Moulna, Gabo 1 50S 11 0E
128 Mouila, Gobon 1 50S 11 0E
128 Mouka, Cent. Afr. Rep. 7 20N 21 45E
143 Moulamein, Australia .35 3S 144 1E
143 Moulamein Cr., Austral. 35 6S 144 3E
50 Moulins, France 46 35N 3 19E
103 Moulmein, Burma 16 30N 97 40E
122 Moulouya W., Morocco 34 45N 2 51W
35 Moulton, Eng., U.K. .52 46N 0 4W
165 Moulton, U.S.A. 29 35N 97 8W
163 Moultrie, U.S.A. 31 11N 83 47W
163 Moultrie, L., U.S.A. ...33 25N 80 10W
164 Mound City, Mo., U.S.A. 40 2N 95 25W
164 Mound City, S.D., U.S.A. 45 46N 100 3W
77 Moúnda, Akra, C., Gr. 38 5N 27 45E
121 Moundou, Chad 8 40N 16 10E
160 Moundsville, U.S.A. ...39 53N 80 43W
MAP
163 Mount Airy, U.S.A. ...36 31N 80 37W
160 Mount Albert, Canada 44 10N 79 20W
135 Mount Alida, S. Africa 29 9S 30 18E
166 Mount Angel, U.S.A. .45 4N 122 46W
135 Mount Arthur, S. Africa 31 40S 27 10E
142 Mount Augustus, W. Australia 24 10S 116 55E
135 Mount Ayliff, S. Africa 30 48S 29 22E
44 Mount Bellew, Bri., Ire. 53 28N 8 31W
145 Mt. Barker, S. Austral. 35 5S 138 52E
142 Mt. Barker, W. Austral. 34 38S 117 40E
144 Mount Buckley, Austral. 20 6S 148 0E
162 Mt. Carmel, Ill., U.S.A. 38 20N 87 48W
161 Mt. Carmel, Pa., U.S.A. 40 46N 76 25W
160 Mount Clemens, U.S.A. 42 35N 82 50W
144 Mount Coolon, Austral. 21 25S 147 25E
132 Mount Darwin, Rhod. 16 47S 31 38E
155 Mount Desert I., U.S.A. 44 25N 68 25W
163 Mount Dora, U.S.A. ...28 49N 81 32W
144 Mount Douglas, Austral. 21 35S 146 50E
138 Mount Enid, W. Australia 21 42S 116 26E
143 Mount Evelyn, Austral. 37 45S 145 29W
135 Mt. Fletcher, S. Africa 30 40S 28 31E
154 Mount Forest, Canada 43 59N 80 43W
144 Mount Fox, Australia 18 45S 145 45E
135 Mount Frere, S. Africa 30 51S 29 0E
145 Mt. Gambier, S. Austral. 37 38S 140 44E
144 Mount Garnet, Austral. 17 37S 145 6E
138 Mount Goldsworthy, West Australia 20 25S 119 39E
162 Mount Hope, U.S.A. .37 52N 81 9W
164 Mount Horeb, U.S.A. .43 0N 89 42W
143 Mount Hotham, Austral. 37 2S 146 52E
144 Mount Isa, Australia .20 42S 139 26E
143 Mount Jagungal, N.S.W., Australia ...36 12S 148 28W
161 Mount Joy, U.S.A. 40 6N 76 30W
142 Mount Keith, Australia 27 15S 120 30E
102 Mount Lavinia, Ceylon 6 50N 79 50E
142 Mt. Magnet, W. Austral. 28 2S 117 47E
146 Mt. Maunganui, N.Z. .37 40S 176 14E
144 Mount Molloy, Austral. 16 32S 145 20E
142 Mount Monger, W. Australia 31 0S 122 0E
144 Mount Morgan, Austral. 23 40S 150 25E
160 Mt. Morris, Mich., U.S.A. 43 8N 83 42W
160 Mt. Morris, N.Y., U.S.A. 42 43N 77 50W
144 Mt. Mulligan, Australia 16 45S 144 47E
142 Mount Narryer, W. Australia 26 30S 115 55E
142 Mount Newman, W. Australia 23 16S 119 33E
142 Mount Nicholas, W. Australia 22 54S 120 27E
144 Mount Oxide, Australia 19 30S 139 29E
145 Mount Perry, Australia 25 13S 151 42E
142 Mount Phillips, W. Australia 24 25S 116 15E
164 Mt. Pleasant. Iowa, U.S.A. 41 0N 91 35W
162 Mt. Pleasant, Mich, U.S.A. 43 38N 84 46W
160 Mt. Pleasant, Pa, U.S.A. 40 9N 79 31W
163 Mt. Pleasant, S.C., U.S.A. 32 45N 79 48W
163 Mt. Pleasant, Tenn, U.S.A. 35 31N 87 11W
165 Mt. Pleasant, Tex, U.S.A. 33 5N 95 0W
166 Mt. Pleasant, Ut, U.S.A. 39 40N 111 29W
161 Mount Pocono, U.S.A. 41 8N 75 21W
166 Mt. Ranier Nat. Park, U.S.A. 46 50N 121 20W
156 Mount Robson, Canada 52 56N 119 15W
142 Mount Sandiman, W. Australia 24 25S 115 30E
166 Mount Shasta, U.S.A. 41 20N 122 18W
132 Mount Silinda Rhod. .20 26S 32 38E
143 Mt. Singleton, Australia 32 30S 151 3E
147 Mount Somers, New Zealand 43 45S 171 27E
162 Mt. Sterling, Ill., U.S.A. 40 0N 90 40W
162 Mt. Sterling, Ky,U.S.A.38 0N 84 0W
144 Mt. Surprise, Australia 18 10S 144 17E
44 Mount Talbot, Ireland 53 31N 8 18W
MAP
142 Mount Tom Price, W. Australia 22 50S 117 40E
160 Mount Union, U.S.A. .40 22N 77 51W
164 Mt. Vernon, Ind., U.S.A. 38 17N 88 57W
161 Mt. Vernon, N.Y., U.S.A. 40 57N 73 49W
162 Mt. Vernon, Ohio, U.S.A. 40 20N 82 30W
166 Mt. Vernon, Wash, U.S.A. 48 27N 122 18W
142 Mount Whaleback, W. Australia 24 38S 113 33E
37 Mountain Ash, Wales, United Kingdom 51 42N 3 22W
166 Mountain Cy. Nev., U.S.A. 41 54N 116 0W
163 Mountain Cy. Tenn, U.S.A. 36 30N 81 50W
165 Mountain Grove, U.S.A. 37 5N 92 20W
165 Mountain Home, Ark., U.S.A. 36 20N 92 25W
166 Mountain Home, Idaho, U.S.A. 43 11N 115 45W
164 Mountain Iron, U.S.A. 47 30N 92 87W
156 Mountain Park., Canada 52 50N 117 15W
165 Mountain View, Ark., U.S.A. 35 52N 92 10W
167 Mountain View, Calif., U.S.A. 37 26N 122 5W
167 Mountainair, U.S.A. ...34 35N 106 15W
46 Mountcharles, Ireland 54 37N 8 12W
46 Mountfield, N. Ireland, United Kingdom 54 34N 7 10W
45 Mountmellick, Ireland 53 7N 7 20W
46 Mountnorris, N. Ireland, United Kingdom 54 15N 6 29W
45 Mountrath, Ireland ...53 0N 7 30W
36 Mounts Bay, Eng., U.K. 50 3N 5 27W
174 Moura, Brazil 1 25S 61 45W
63 Moura, Portugal 38 7N 7 30W
144 Moura, Queens., Austral. 24 35S 149 58E
63 Mourão, Portugal 38 22N 7 22W
124 Mourdhia, Mali 14 35N 7 25W
125 Mouri, Ghana 5 6N 1 14W
144 Mourilyan, Australia .17 35S 146 10E
49 Mourmelon le Grand, Fr. 49 30N 4 31E
46 Mourne Mts., N. Ire., U.K. 54 10N 6 0W
46 Mourne R., N. Ireland, U.K. 54 45N 7 25W
142 Mouroubra, W. Australia 29 42S 117 52E
42 Mousa I., Scot., U.K. .60 0N 1 10W
54 Mouscron, Belgium ...50 45N 3 12E
36 Mousehole, Eng., U.K. 50 5N 5 32W
121 Moussoro, Chad 13 50N 16 35E
49 Mouthe, France 46 44N 6 12E
57 Moutier, Switzerland .47 16N 7 21E
51 Moutiers, France 45 29N 6 31E
49 Mouy, France 49 18N 2 20E
122 Mouydir, Algeria 25 20N 4 15E
76 Mouzáki, Greece 39 25N 21 37E
46 Moville, Ireland 55 11N 7 3W
113 Mowming, China 21 50N 110 32E
112 Mowping, China 37 25N 121 34E
130 Moxico, dist., Angola .11 55S 20 8E
46 Moy, N. Ire., U.K. 54 27N 6 40W
43 Moy, Inverness, Scotland, U.K. 57 22N 4 3W
46 Moy R., Ireland 54 5N 8 50W
142 Moyagee W. Australia 27 48S 117 48E
127 Moyale, Kenya 3 30N 39 0E
124 Moyamba, Sierra Leone 8 15N 12 30W
44 Moyasta, Ireland 52 40N 9 31W
44 Moycullen, Ireland 53 20N 9 10W
156 Moyie, Canada 49 17N 115 50W
46 Moylett, Ireland 53 57N 7 7W
44 Moylough (Newtown Bellew), Ireland ...53 30N 8 34W
46 Moynalty, Ireland 53 48N 6 52W
45 Moyne, Tipp., Ireland 52 45N 7 43W
131 Moyo, Uganda 3 38N 31 43E
174 Moyobamba, Peru 6 0S 77 0W
45 Moyvalley, Ireland 53 26N 6 55W
129 Mozambique, tn., Mozambique 15 3S 40 42E
129 Mozambique, Port. Overseas terr., Afr. 19 0S 35 0E
89 Mozdok, U.S.S.R. 43 45N 44 48E
87 Mozhaisk, U.S.S.R. ...55 30N 36 2E
71 Mozirje, Yugoslavia ...46 22N 14 58E
86 Mozyr, U.S.S.R. 52 0N 29 15E
131 Mpanda & dist., Tanzania 6 23S 31 40E
132 Mpangwe, Zambia 14 8S 32 10E
130 Mpata, Congo 5 5S 19 20E
135 Mpemvana, Nat., S. Afr. 27 31S 30 44E
124 Mpesoba, Mali 12 31N 5 39W
132 Mphoengs, Rhodesia .21 10S 27 51E
131 Mpigi, Uganda 0 14N 32 19E
132 Mpika, Zambia 11 51S 31 25E
132 Mporokoso, Zambia ... 9 25S 30 5E
125 Mpraeso, Ghana 6 50N 0 50W
132 Mpulungu, Zambia 8 51S 31 5E
131 Mpwapwa, Tanzania . 6 30S 36 30E
135 Mqanduli, S. Africa ...31 48S 28 47E
60 Mragowo, Poland 53 57N 21 18E
123 M'Raier, Algeria 33 55N 5 58E
74 Mramor, Yugoslavia ...43 20N 21 45E
MAP
132 Mrewa, Rhodesia 17 35S 31 45E
122 Mrimina, Morocco 29 50N 7 9W
74 Mrkonjić Grad, Y.-slav. 44 26N 17 4E
71 Mrkopalje, Yugoslavia 45 21N 14 52E
131 Msagali, Tanzania 6 28S 36 22E
123 Msaken, Tunisia 35 49N 10 33E
131 M'Salu, R., Mozam. ...12 25S 39 15E
132 Msambansovu, Mt., Rhodesia 15 50S 30 3E
123 M'sila, Algeria 35 46N 4 30E
132 Msoro, Zambia 13 35S 31 50E
86 Msta R., U.S.S.R. 58 30N 33 30E
86 Mstislavl, U.S.S.R. 54 0N 31 50E
60 Mszczonów Poland ...51 58N 20 33E
131 Mtama, Tanzania 10 17S 39 21E
132 Mtilikwe R., Rhodesia 21 0S 31 12E
131 Mtito Andei, Kenya ... 2 41S 38 12E
132 Mtoko, Rhodesia 17 25S 32 28E
131 Mtowa Mbu, Tanzania 3 21S 35 51E
87 Mtsensk, U.S.S.R. ...53 25N 36 30E
89 Mtskheta, U.S.S.R. ...41 52N 44 45E
135 Mtubatuba, Nat., S. Afr. 28 23S 32 12E
131 Mtwara, Tanzania....10 25S 40 0E
131 Mtwara & dist., Tanzania 10 20S 40 20E
131 Mtwara, reg., Tanzania 9 40S 38 30E
42 Mu Ness, Scot. U.K. .60 41N 0 50W
107 Mu R., Burma 23 0N 95 20E
175 Muaná, Brazil 1 25S 49 15W
107 Muang Chiang Rai, Thailand 19 52N 99 50E
107 Muang Kalasin, Thai. *see* Kalasin 16 26N 103 30E
107 Muang Lampang, Thai. *see* Lampang .18 16N 99 32E
107 Muang Lamphun, Thai. 18 40N 98 53E
107 Muang Nan, Thailand 18 52N 100 42E
107 Muang Phetchabun, Thai. *see* Phetahbun 16 22N 101 12E
107 Muang Phichit, Thai. .16 29N 100 21E
107 Muang Sakon Nakhon, Thai. *see* Sakon Nakhan. 17 10N 104E
107 Muang Ubon, Thai. *see* Ubon Ratchathani 15 15N 104 50E
107 Muang Yasothon, Thai. 15 50N 104 10E
107 Muar, W. Malaysia 2 3N 102 34E
107 Muar, R., W. Malaysia 2 15N 102 48E
108 Muarabungo, Indonesia 1 40S 101 10E
108 Muaraenim, Indonesia 3 40S 103 50E
108 Muarakaman, Indon. . 0 2S 116 45E
108 Musrasipongi, Indon. . 0 27N 4 54E
108 Muaratembesi, Indon. 1 42S 103 2E
108 Muaratewe, Indonesia 0 50S 115 0E
108 Muaratungkal, Indon. 0 56S 103 19E
100 Mubairik, Saudi Arabia 23 22N 39 8E
105 Mubarakpur, India 26 12N 83 24E
55 Much, Germany 50 55N 7 25E
37 Much Dewchurch, England, U.K. 51 58N 2 45W
34 Much Marcle, Eng., U.K. 51 59N 2 27W
34 Much Wenlock, England, U.K. 52 36N 2 34W
43 Muchalls, Scot., U.K. .57 2N 2 10W
56 Müchein, Germany ...51 18N 11 49E
132 Muchinga Mts., Zambia 11 30S 31 30E
87 Muchkapskiy, U.S.S.R. 51 52N 42 28E
42 Muck, I., Scot., U.K. 56 50N 6 15W
145 Muckadilla, Australia .26 32S 148 36E
42 Muckle Roe I., Scotland, U.K. 60 22N 1 22W
44 Muckross Abbey, Ire. .52 1N 9 30W
46 Muckross Hd., Ireland 54 37N 8 35W
175 Mucuri, Brazil 18 0S 40 0W
166 Mud L., U.S.A. 40 15N 120 15W
100 Mudanya, Turkey 40 25N 28 50E
167 Muddy R., U.S.A. 38 30N 110 55W
143 Mudgee, N.S.W., Austral. 32 32S 149 31E
100 Mudhnib, Saudi Arabia 25 50N 44 18E
131 Mueda, Mozambique .11 36S 39 28E
46 Muff, Ireland 55 4N 7 16W
132 Mufulira, Zambia 12 32S 28 15E
131 Mufumbio Range, Ugan. 1 25S 29 30E
62 Mugardos, Spain 43 27N 8 15W
63 Muge, Portugal 39 3N 8 40W
63 Muge R., Portugal 39 15N 8 18W
71 Muggia, Italy 45 36N 13 47E
62 Mugia, Spain 43 3N 9 17W
131 Mugila Mts., Congo ... 7 0S 28 50E
100 Mugla, Turkey 37 15N 28 28E
77 Mugla, Prov., Turkey 37 8N 27 45E
75 Múglizh, Bulgaria 42 37N 25 32E
105 Mugu, Nepal 29 45N 82 30E
126 Muhammad Qol, Sudan 20 53N 37 9E
126 Muhammad Râs, Egypt 27 50N 34 0E
105 Muhammadabad, India 26 4N 83 25E
98 Muharraqa, *see* Sa'ad, Israel 31 28N 34 33E
131 Muhesi R., Tanzania . 6 40S 35 5E
131 Muheza, Tanzania 5 9S 38 48E
57 Mühldorf, Germany ...48 14N 12 23E
56 Mühlhausen, Germany 51 12N 10 29E

MAP
15 Muhlig-Hofmann Mts., Antarctica 72 30S 5 0E
131 Muhutwe, Tanzania ... 1 35S 31 45E
107 Mui Ca Mau, *see* Bai Bung, S. Vietnam ... 8 35N 104 42E
45 Muine Bheag, Ireland 52 42N 6 59W
62 Muinos, Spain 41 58N 7 59W
43 Muir of Ord, Scot., U.K. 57 30N 4 35W
41 Muirdrum, Scot., U.K. 56 31N 2 40W
41 Muirhead, Scot., U.K. 55 54N 4 5W
41 Muirkirk, Scot., U.K. .55 31N 4 6W
42 Muirnag Mt., Scot., U.K. 58 21N 6 20W
127 Muja, Ethiopia 12 2N 39 30E
98 Mujeidil, Israel 32 41N 35 14E
86 Mukachevo, U.S.S.R. .48 27N 22 45E
108 Mukah, Sar., Malaysia 2 55N 112 5E
99 Mukalla, South Yemen 14 33N 49 2E
132 Mukasa, Caprivi Strip, S. W. Africa 17 51S 24 31E
126 Mukawwa I., Egypt ...23 55N 35 53E
112 Mukden (Shenyang), China 41 35N 123 30E
99 Mukeiras, Yemen 13 59N 45 52E
38 Muker, England, U.K. 54 23N 2 10W
99 Mukha, Yemen 13 18N 43 15E
87 Mukhtolovo, U.S.S.R. 55 29N 43 15E
91 Mukhtuya, U.S.S.R. *see* Lensk
142 Mukinbudin, W. Austral. 30 55S 118 5E
132 Mukinge, Zambia 13 33S 25 46E
108 Mukomuko, Indonesia 2 20S 101 10E
104 Muktsar, India 30 30N 74 30E
101 Mukur, Afghanistan ...32 50N 67 50E
132 Mukwela, Zambia 17 0S 26 40E
65 Mula, Spain 38 3N 1 33W
106 Mula R., India 19 16N 74 20E
109 Mulanay, Philippines .13 30N 122 30E
132 Mulanda, Angola 14 58S 22 0E
132 Mulandi, Zambia 13 6S 24 31E
130 Mulange, Congo 3 40S 27 10E
169 Mulatas, Arch. de las, Panama 6 51N 78 31W
172 Mulchen, Chile 37 45S 72 20W
56 Mulde R., Germany ...50 55N 12 42E
164 Mule Creek, U.S.A. 43 19N 104 8W
131 Muleba, Tanzania 1 50S 31 37E
165 Muleshoe, U.S.A. 34 17N 102 42W
155 Mulgrave, Canada 45 38N 61 31W
144 Mulgrave I., Australia 10 5S 142 0E
65 Mulhacen Mt., Spain .37 4N 3 20W
56 Mulheim, Germany 51 26N 6 53W
49 Mulhouse, France 47 44N 7 20E
103 Muli, China 28 21N 100 40E
132 Mulipa, Mozambique .14 45S 31 48E
40 Mull I., Scotland, U.K. 56 27N 6 0W
40 Mull, Ross of, dist., Scotland, U.K. 56 20N 6 15W
40 Mull, Sound of, Scotland, U.K. 56 30N 5 50W
43 Mull Head, Orkney, Scotland, U.K. 59 23N 2 53W
46 Mullagh, Cavan, Ireland 53 49N 6 58W
44 Mullagh, Galaway, Ire. 53 13N 8 25W
44 Mullaghareirk Mts., Ire. 52 20N 9 10W
106 Mullaittvu, Ceylon 9 15N 80 55E
42 Mullardoch L., Scotland, U.K. 57 20N 5 0W
164 Mullen, U.S.A. 42 5N 101 0W
143 Mullengudgery, N.S.W., Australia ...31 43S 147 29E
162 Mullens, U.S.A. 37 34N 81 22W
108 Muller Ra., Mts., Indon. 0 30N 113 30E
144 Muller Ra., North East New Guinea ... 5 30S 143 0E
45 Mullet Pen., Ireland ...54 10N 10 2W
142 Mullewa, W. Australia 28 29S 115 30E
56 Mülheim, Germany 47 48N 7 37E
165 Mullin, U.S.A. 31 33N 98 38W
45 Mullinahone, Ireland .52 30N 7 31W
45 Mullinavat, Ireland ...52 23N 7 10W
45 Mullingar, Ireland 53 31N 7 20W
163 Mullins, U.S.A. 34 12N 79 15W
143 Mullion Creek, Australia 33 9S 149 7E
36 Mullion, England, U.K. 50 1N 5 15W
81 Mullsjö, Sweden 57 56N 13 55E
145 Mullumbimby, Australia 28 30S 153 30E
132 Mulobezi, Zambia 16 45S 25 7E
45 Mulrany, Ireland 53 54N 9 47W
46 Mulroy B., Ireland 55 15N 7 45W
106 Mulshi L., India 18 30N 73 20E
104 Multai, India 21 39N 78 15E
104 Multan, West Pakistan 30 15N 71 30E
104 Multan, st., Pakistan .30 29N 72 29E
80 Multrå, Sweden 63 10N 17 19E
131 Mulumbe Mts., Congo 8 40S 27 30E
130 Mulundu, Congo 6 42S 20 57E
132 Mulungushi Dam, Zam. 14 48S 28 48E
165 Mulvane, U.S.A. 37 30N 97 15W
126 Mulwad, Sudan 18 45N 30 39E
143 Mulwala, N.S.W., Austral. 35 59S 146 0E
107 Mum R., Thailand 15 17N 103 0E
37 Mumbles, Wales, U.K. 51 34N 4 0W
37 Mumbles Hd., Wales, United Kingdom 51 33N 4 0W

MAP
132 Mumbotula Falls, Zam. 12 19S 29 38E
132 Mumbwa, Zambia 15 0S 27 2E
132 Mumpanda, Zambia ...14 18S 25 14E
89 Mumra, U.S.S.R. 45 45N 47 41E
109 Muna I., Indonesia 5 0S 122 30E
57 Munchberg, Germany 50 11N 11 48E
56 Muncheberg, Germany 52 30N 14 9E
57 München (Munich), Germany 48 8N 11 33E
162 Muncie, U.S.A. 40 10N 85 20W
106 Mundakayam, India ... 9 30N 76 32E
132 Mundandamu, Zambia 9 27N 76 50E
156 Mundare, Canada 53 35N 112 30W
165 Munday, U.S.A. 33 26N 99 39W
56 Münden, Germany 51 25N 9 42E
35 Mundesley, Eng., U.K. 52 53N 1 24E
65 Mundo R., Spain 38 30N 2 15W
175 Mundo Novo, Brazil ...11 50S 40 29W
104 Mundra, India 22 54N 69 26E
132 Mundrabilla, W. Australia 31 52S 127 51E
132 Munene, Angola 14 26S 21 48E
65 Munera, Spain 39 2N 2 29W
106 Muneru R., India 16 45N 80 3E
144 Mungana, Australia ...17 8S 144 27E
104 Mungaoli, India 24 24N 78 7E
132 Mungari, Mozambique 17 12S 33 42E
132 Mungau, Angola 13 55S 21 54E
131 Mungbere, Congo 2 36N 28 28E
145 Mungindi, Australia ...28 58S 149 1E
130 Munhango R., Angola 11 30S 19 30E
57 Munich, Germany 48 8N 11 35E
162 Munising, U.S.A. 46 25N 86 39W
126 Munjiye, Saudi Arabia 18 47N 41 20W
81 Munka-Ljungby, Swed. 56 17N 13 8E
81 Munkedal, Sweden 58 28N 11 31E
80 Munkfors, Sweden 59 50N 13 38E
176 Muñoz, Pen., Chile 52 30S 75 3E
145 Munro, Australia 25 30S 142 45E
157 Munroe L., Canada 59 0N 98 40W
49 Münster, France 48 2N 7 8E
56 Münster, Lr. Sax., Germany 52 59N 10 5E
56 Munster, North Rhine-Westphalia, Germany 51 58N 7 37E
44 Munster, prov., Ire. ...52 20N 8 40W
56 Munstereifel, Germany 50 33N 6 46E
142 Muntadgin, W. Austral. 31 48S 118 30E
78 Muntelui Mare, Mt., Rumania 46 30N 23 12E
108 Muntok, Indonesia 2 5S 105 10E
107 Muong La, Laos 20 52N 102 5E
107 Muong Ngoi, Laos 20 41N 102 39E
107 Muon Pak Beng, Laos 19 51N 101 4E
107 Muong Sing, Laos 21 12N 101 12E
107 Muong Soui, Laos 19 32N 102 47E
82 Muonio & R., Finland 67 57N 23 40E
146 Muotohora, N.Z. 38 18S 177 40E
129 Mupa, Angola 16 5S 15 50E
101 Muqab, Trucial Oman 23 0N 53 0E
127 Muqaddam, Wadi, Sud. 17 0N 32 0E
48 Mur de Bretagne, Fr. .48 12N 3 0W
58 Mûr, R., Austria 47 7N 13 55E
71 Mura, R., Yugoslavia .46 37N 16 9E
176 Murallon Mt., Chile ...49 55S 73 30W
131 Muranga (Ft. Hall), Kenya 0 45S 37 9E
87 Murashi, U.S.S.R. 59 30N 49 0E
50 Murat, Cantal, France 45 7N 2 53E
58 Murau, Austria 47 6N 14 10E
72 Muravera, Italy 39 25N 9 35E
62 Murca, Portugal 41 24N 7 28W
143 Murchison, Australia .36 39S 145 14E
147 Murchison, N.Z. 41 49S 172 21E
142 Murchison Downs, W. Australia 26 45S 118 55E
131 Muchison Falls, Ugan. 2 15N 31 38E
142 Murchison House, W. Australia 27 39S 114 14E
147 Murchison Mts., N.Z. .45 13S 167 23E
142 Murchison R., Australia 27 30S 115 0E
138 Murchison Ra., N. Terr., Australia 20 0S 134 10E
132 Murchison Rapids, Malawi 15 55S 34 35E
65 Murcia, Spain 38 2N 1 10W
65 Murcia, prov., Spain .37 50N 1 30W
65 Murcia, reg., Spain 38 35N 1 50W
164 Murdo, U.S.A. 43 56N 100 43W
78 Mures, Reg., Rumania 46 30N 24 30E
78 Mures R., Rumania ...46 0N 22 0E
50 Muret, France 43 30N 1 20E
163 Murfreesboro, U.S.A. .35 50N 86 21W
78 Murgeni, Rumania 46 12N 28 1E
145 Murgon, Australia 26 15S 151 54E
142 Murgoo, W. Australia 27 24S 116 28E
173 Muriaé, Brazil 21 8S 42 23W
62 Murias, de Paredes, Spain 42 52N 6 19W
132 Muriel Mine, Rhodesia 17 14S 30 40E
109 Muris, Indonesia 2 23S 140 5E
56 Muritz See, L., Ger. ...53 25N 12 40E
109 Murjo Mt., Indonesia . 6 36S 110 53E
131 Murka, Kenya 3 27S 37 58E
84 Murmansk, U.S.S.R. .68 57N 33 10E
57 Murnau, Germany 47 40N 11 11E
51 Muro, Corsica, France 42 34N 8 54E
64 Muro, Mallorca, Spain 39 45N 3 3E
51 Muro, C. di Corsica, Fr. 41 44N 8 37E
73 Muro Lucano, Italy ...40 45N 15 30E

MAP
87 Murom, U.S.S.R. 55 35N 42 3E
114 Muroran, Japan 42 25N 141 0E
62 Muros, Spain 42 45N 9 5W
62 Muros y de Noya, Ria de, Spain 42 45N 9 0W
114 Muroto-saki, C., Japan 33 15N 134 10E
166 Murphy, U.S.A. 43 11N 116 33W
165 Murphysboro, U.S.A. .37 50N 89 20W
126 Murrat, Sudan 18 51N 29 33E
163 Murray, Ky., U.S.A. .36 40N 88 20W
166 Murray, Utah, U.S.A. 40 41N 111 58W
145 Murray Br., S. Austral. 35 6S 139 14E
155 Murray Harb., Canada 46 0N 62 28W
163 Murray, L., U.S.A. 34 8N 81 30W
145 Murray R., Australia .35 50S 147 40E
134 Murraysburg, S. Africa 31 58S 23 47E
143 Murrayville, Australia 35 20S 140 16E
102 Murree, W. Pakistan...33 56N 73 28E
57 Mürren, Switzerland ...46 33N 7 45E
142 Murrin Murrin, Austral. 28 50S 121 45E
143 Murringo, Australia ...34 16S 148 32E
44 Murrough, Ireland 53 7N 9 18W
143 Murrumbidgee R., N.S.W., Australia ...34 30S 145 30E
143 Murrumburrah, N.S.W., Australia ...34 30S 148 15E
143 Murrurundi, Australia 31 42S 150 51E
126 Murshid, Sudan 21 40N 31 10E
105 Murshidabad, India ...24 11N 88 19E
71 Murska Sobota, Y.-slavia 46 39N 16 12E
104 Murtazapur, India 20 40N 77 25E
143 Murtoa, Vic., Australia 36 29S 142 29E
41 Murton, Eng., U.K. ...54 51N 1 22W
62 Murtosa, Portugal 40 44N 8 40W
127 Muru, Sudan 6 36N 29 16E
131 Murungu, Tanzania ... 4 12S 31 10E
146 Murupara, New Zealand 38 30S 178 40E
105 Murwara, India 23 46N 80 28E
145 Murwillumbah, Austral. 28 18S 153 27E
58 Mürz, R., Austria 47 30N 15 25E
58 Mürzzuschlag, Austria 47 36N 15 41E
100 Mus, Turkey 38 45N 41 30E
126 Musa, Gebel (Sinai Mt.), Egypt 28 32N 33 59E
102 Musa Qala (Musa Kala), Afghanistan .32 20N 64 50E
104 Musaffargarh, Pakistan 30 10N 71 10E
126 Musairik, Wadi, Saudi Arabia 19 30N 43 10E
104 Musakhel, W. Pakistan 30 29N 69 52E
108 Musala I., Indonesia . 1 41N 98 28E
75 Musalla Mt., Bulgaria 42 13N 23 37E
112 Musan, S. Korea 42 12N 129 12E
130 Musangu, Congo 10 28S 23 55E
131 Musasa, Tanzania 3 25S 31 30E
101 Muscat (Masqat), Muscat & 'Oman ...23 37N 58 36E
99 Muscat & 'Oman, *see* Oman 23 0N 58 0E
164 Muscatine, U.S.A. 41 25N 91 5W
62 Musel, Spain 43 34N 5 42W
132 Musetula, Zambia 14 28S 24 1E
138 Musgrave, Ra., Austral. 26 0S 132 0E
132 Mushandike Dam, Rhodesia 20 10S 30 40E
130 Mushie, Congo 2 56S 17 4E
132 Mushima, Zambia 14 6S 25 1E
125 Mushin, Nigeria 6 32N 3 21E
131 Mushoshi, Congo 11 56S 27 43E
106 Musi R., India 17 10N 79 25E
108 Musi, R., Indonesia ... 2 55S 103 40E
162 Muskegon, U.S.A. 43 15N 86 17W
162 Muskegon, R., U.S.A. 43 25N 86 0W
162 Muskegon Hts., U.S.A. 43 12N 86 17W
80 Muskö I., Sweden 59 5N 18 25E
165 Muskogee, U.S.A. 35 50N 95 25W
126 Musmar, Sudan 18 6N 35 40E
132 Musofu, Zambia 13 30S 29 0E
130 Musokantanda, Congo 10 56S 25 7E
132 Musola, Zambia 12 55S 30 22E
131 Musoma, Tanzania 1 30S 33 48E
155 Musquaro, L., Canada 50 42N 61 15W
155 Musquodoboit Harbour, Canada ...44 50N 63 9W
41 Musselburgh, Scot., U.K. 55 57N 3 3W
130 Mussende, Angola 10 35S 16 2E
166 Musselshell, R., U.S.A. 46 30N 108 15W
50 Mussidan, France 45 2N 0 22E
72 Mussomeli, Italy 37 35N 13 43E
104 Mussoorie, India 30 27N 78 6E
81 Mustadfors, Sweden ...58 57N 12 19E
100 Mustafa Kemalpasa, Turkey 40 3N 28 25E
100 Mustajidda, Si. Arabia 26 30N 41 50E
105 Mustang, Nepal 29 10N 83 55E
123 Mustapha, C., Tunisia 36 55N 11 3E
176 Musters L., Argentina 45 20S 69 25W
145 Muswelbrook, Austral. 32 16S 150 56E
59 Muszyna, Poland 49 22N 20 55E
126 Mût, Egypt 25 28N 28 58E
100 Mut, Turkey 36 40N 33 28E
129 Mutanda, Angola 16 15S 14 15E
132 Mutanda, Mozambique 21 0S 33 34E
132 Mutanda, Zambia 12 15S 26 13E

MAP
112 Mutankiang, China 44 35N 129 30E
41 Muthill, Scot., U.K. ...56 20N 3 50W
130 Mutshatsha, Congo ...10 35S 24 20E
144 Muttaburra, Australia 22 38S 144 29E
155 Mutton Bay, Canada .50 50N 59 2W
44 Mutton I., Ireland 52 50N 9 31W
106 Muvatupusha, India ... 9 53N 76 35E
100 Muwaih, Saudi Arabia 22 35N 41 32E
130 Muxima, Angola 9 25S 13 52E
131 Muyinga, Burundi 2 48S 30 21E
132 Muyombe, Zambia 10 31S 33 31E
102 Muzaffarabad, Kashmir 34 25N 73 30E
104 Muzaffargarh, W. Pak. 30 5N 71 14E
104 Muzaffarnagar, India .29 26N 77 40E
105 Muzaffarpur, India 26 7N 85 32E
98 Muzeiri'a, Israel 32 3N 34 53E
90 Muzhi, U.S.S.R. 65 25N 64 40E
48 Muzillac, France 47 35N 2 30W
132 Muzoka, Zambia 16 37S 27 20E
157 Muzon C., Alaska, U.S.A. 54 40N 132 40W
111 Muztagh Mt., China ...36 30N 87 22E
127 Mvolo, Sudan 6 10N 29 53E
131 Mwadui, Tanzania 3 35S 33 40E
132 Mwamba Falls, Zambia 16 36S 23 16E
130 Mwanza, Congo 7 55S 26 43E
130 Mwanza, Congo 5 29S 17 43E
132 Mwanza, Malawi 15 34S 34 32E
132 Mwanza, Zambia 16 57S 24 27E
131 Mwanza, Tanzania 2 30S 32 58E
131 Mwanza, prov. Tanz. . 2 40S 32 30E
131 Mwaya, Tanzania 9 32S 33 55E
45 Mweelrea, Mt., Ireland 53 37N 9 48W
130 Mweka, Congo 4 50S 21 40E
130 Mwendjila, Congo 7 14S 18 47E
130 Mwenga, Congo 3 1S 28 21E
132 Mwengwa Zambia 15 15S 26 7E
130 Mwepo, Congo 11 50S 26 13E
132 Mweru Swamp, Congo 9 0S 29 0E
132 Mweru Swamp, Zam. . 9 0S 29 0E
132 Mweza Range, Rhod. .21 0S 30 0E
132 Mwgambwa, Zambia .15 27S 26 31E
131 Mwimbi, Tanzania 8 38S 31 39E
132 Mwinilunga & Mt., Zambia 11 43S 24 25E
131 Mwirasandu, Uganda . 0 56S 30 22E
107 My Tho, S. Vietnam .10 29N 106 23E
122 Mya, W., Algeria 28 47N 2 58E
130 Myadhi, Cameroon 1 16N 13 10E
143 Myall L., & R., Austral. 32 30S 152 25E
103 Myanaung, Burma 18 25N 95 10E
103 Myaungmya, Burma ..16 30N 95 0E
43 Mybster, Scot., U.K. .58 27N 3 24W
37 Myddfai, Wales, U.K. 51 59N 3 47W
37 Myddle, Eng., U.K. ...52 49N 2 47W
132 Myera, Malawi 14 48S 35 14E
161 Myerstown, U.S.A. 40 22N 76 18W
107 Myingyan, Burma 21 30N 95 30E
103 Myitkyina, Burma 25 30N 97 26E
59 Myjava, Cz. 48 41N 17 37E
105 Mymensingh, *see* Nasirabad, E. Pak. .24 42N 90 30E
164 Myndmere, U.S.A. 46 23N 97 7W
134 Mynfontein, S. Africa 30 55S 23 57E
37 Mynydd Bach, Mt., Wales, U.K. 52 16N 4 6W
29 Mynydd Du, (Black Mt.), Wales, U.K. ...51 45N 3 45W
37 Mynydd Epynt, Mt., Wales, U.K. 52 4N 3 30W
37 Mynydd Prescelly, Mt., Wales, U.K. ...51 57N 4 48W
107 Myogi, Burma 21 24N 96 28E
79 Myrdal, Norway 60 43N 7 10E
163 Myrtle Beach, U.S.A. .33 43N 78 50W
166 Myrtle Creek, U.S.A. .43 0N 123 19W
166 Myrtle Point, U.S.A. .43 0N 124 4W
143 Myrtleford, Australia .36 34S 146 44E
79 Mysen, Norway 59 37N 11 20E
59 Myslenice, Poland 49 51N 19 57E
59 Myslibórz, Poland 52 55N 14 50E
59 Mystowice, Poland 50 15N 19 12E
106 Mysore, India 12 17N 76 41E
106 Mysore, st., India 13 15N 77 0E
161 Mystic, Conn., U.S.A. 41 21N 71 58W
59 Myszkow, Poland 50 45N 19 22E
87 Mystishchi, U.S.S.R. .57 50N 37 50E
166 Myton, U.S.A. 40 10N 110 2W
58 Mze R., Czechoslovakia 49 47N 12 50E
131 Mzenga, Tanzania 6 58S 38 43E
131 Mziha, Tanzania 5 56S 37 46E
132 Mzimba, Malawi 11 48S 33 33E
135 Mzimkulu, S. Africa ...30 18S 29 58E
135 Mzimkulu R., S. Afr. .30 40S 30 15E
135 Mzimvubu R., S. Afr. 31 30S 29 30E
132 Mzuzu, Malawi 11 30S 33 55E

N

127 Na'am, Sudan 9 42N 28 27E
98 Na'an, Israel 31 53N 34 52E
83 Naantali, Finland 60 27N 21 57E
45 Naas, Kildare, Ireland 53 12N 6 40W
134 Nababeep, S. Africa ...29 36S 17 46E
105 Nabadwip, India 23 34N 88 20E
109 Nabas, Philippines 11 47N 122 6E
142 Nabberu, L., Australia 25 30S 120 30E
131 Naberera, Tanzania ... 1 25N 32 17E
123 Nabeul, Tunisia 36 30N 10 51E
104 Nabha, India 30 26N 76 14E
98 Nabi Rubin, Israel 31 56N 34 44E
109 Nabire, Indonesia 3 15S 136 27E
104 Nabisar, W. Pakistan 25 8N 69 40E

MAP
131 Nabiswera, Uganda ... 1 27N 32 15E
98 Nablus, Jordan 32 14N 35 15E
133 Naboomspruit, S. Africa 24 32S 28 40E
126 Nabq, Egypt 28 5N 29 23E
129 Nacala, Mozambique .14 32S 40 34E
166 Naches, U.S.A. 46 48N 120 49W
113 Nachi, China 28 50N 105 25E
131 Nachingwea, Tanzania 10 49S 38 49E
131 Nachingwea, dist., Tanz. 9 20S 38 0E
104 Nachna, India 27 34N 71 41E
59 Nachod, Czechoslovakia 50 25N 16 8E
172 Nacimiento, Chile 37 36S 72 43W
80 Nacka, Sweden 59 17N 18 12E
145 Nackara, S. Australia 32 48S 139 12E
80 Näckten, L., Sweden .62 50N 14 45E
167 Naco, U.S.A. 31 24N 109 58W
165 Nacogdoches, U.S.A. .31 33N 95 30W
168 Nacozari, Mexico 30 30N 109 50W
126 Nadi, Sudan 18 40N 33 41E
104 Nadiad, India 22 41N 72 56E
74 Nadlac, Rumania 46 10N 20 50E
122 Nador, Morocco 35 14N 2 58W
101 Nadushan, Iran 32 2N 53 35E
86 Nadvornaya, U.S.S.R. 48 40N 24 35E
90 Nadym, U.S.S.R. 63 35N 72 42E
90 Nadym R., U.S.S.R. .65 30N 73 0E
79 Nærbö, Norway 58 40N 5 39E
81 Naestved, Denmark ...55 13N 11 44E
125 Nafada, Nigeria 11 8N 11 20E
39 Nafferton, Eng., U.K. 54 1N 0 24W
100 Naft-i-Shah, Iran 34 0N 45 30E
100 Nafud Dahi, des., Saudi Arabia 22 0N 45 0E
123 Nafusah, Gebel, Libya 32 12N 12 30E
126 Nag 'Hamâdi, Egypt .26 2N 32 18E
113 Naga, Ryukyu Is. 26 34N 127 43E
109 Naga, Philippines 13 38N 123 15E
122 Naga, Kreb en, Sahara 24 12N 6 0W
154 Nagagami R., Canada 49 40N 84 40W
104 Nagai Parker, W. Pak. 24 28N 70 46E
127 Nagalle, Ethiopia 5 20N 39 30E
143 Nagambie, Vic., Austral. 36 47S 145 10E
114 Nagano, Japan 36 40N 138 10E
114 Nagano, pref., Japan .36 15N 138 0E
114 Nagaoka, Japan..........37 30N 138 50E
106 Nagappattinam, India 10 46N 79 51E
106 Nagari Hills, India 15 30N 79 45E
114 Nagasaki, Japan 32 47N 129 50E
114 Nagasaki, Pref., Japan 32 50N 129 40E
114 Nagashima, Japan 34 15N 136 15E
104 Nagaur, India 27 15N 73 45E
105 Nagbhir, India 20 34N 79 42E
103 Nagchu Dzong, Tibet, China 31 22N 91 54E
106 Nagercoil, India 8 12N 77 33E
44 Nages Mts., Ireland ...52 8N 8 28W
104 Nagina, India 29 30N 78 30E
101 Nagineh, Iran 34 20N 57 15E
102 Nagir Mt., Kashmir ...36 10N 74 30E
144 Nagoorin, Australia ...24 17S 151 15E
87 Nagorskoye, U.S.S.R. 59 18N 50 48E
131 Nagorum, Kenya 4 1N 34 33E
114 Nagoya, Japan 35 10N 136 50E
104 Nagpur, India 21 8N 79 10E
103 Nagrong, Tibet 32 46N 84 16E
59 Nagyatád, Hungary ...46 14N 17 22E
59 Nagyecsed, Hungary .47 53N 22 24E
59 Nagykanizsa, Hung. ...46 28N 17 0E
59 Nagykörös, Hungary .47 2N 19 48E
59 Nagyléta, Hungary ...47 23N 21 55E
113 Naha, Okinawa 26 12N 127 40E
98 Nahalal, Israel 32 41N 35 12E
156 Nahanni Butte, Canada 61 5N 123 30W
98 Naharayim, Israel 32 28N 35 33E
98 Nahariya, Israel 33 1N 35 5E
100 Nahavand, Iran 34 10N 48 30E
57 Nahe, R., Germany ...49 48N 7 33E
98 Nahf, Israel 32 56N 35 18E
126 Nahiya, Wadi, Egypt 27 37N 32 0E
126 Nahud, Saudi Arabia .18 12N 41 40E
157 Naicam, Canada 52 30N 104 30W
57 Naila, Germany 50 19N 11 43E
36 Nailsea, Eng., U.K. ...51 25N 2 44W
34 Nailsworth, Eng., U.K. 51 41N 2 12W
155 Nain, Canada 56 34N 61 40W
101 Na'in, Iran 32 54N 53 0E
105 Naini Tal, India 29 23N 79 30E
109 Naira I., Indonesia 4 28S 130 0E
43 Nairn, Scotland, U.K. 57 35N 3 54W
43 Nairn, co., Scot., U.K. 57 28N 3 52W
43 Nairn R., Scot., U.K. 57 32N 3 58W
131 Nairobi, Kenya 1 17S 36 48E
84 Naistenyarvi, U.S.S.R. 62 25N 32 27E
131 Naivasha, & dist., Kenya 0 40S 36 30E
131 Naivasha L., Kenya ... 0 42S 36 20E
50 Najac France 44 14N 1 58E
101 Najafabad, Iran 32 40N 51 15E
64 Najera, Spain 42 26N 2 48W
64 Najerilla, R., Spain ...42 15N 2 45W
104 Najibabad, India 29 40N 78 20E
112 Najin, N. Korea 42 12N 130 15E
131 Nakalagba, Congo 2 50N 27 58E
114 Nakamura, Japan 33 0N 133 0E
114 Nakano Shima, I., Jap. 29 50N 130 0E
127 Nakfa, Ethiopia 16 40N 38 25E
85 Nakhichevan, U.S.S.R. 39 14N 45 24E
126 Nakhl, Egypt 29 55N 33 43E

MAP
100 Nakhl Mubarak, Saudi Arabia 24 10N 38 10E
91 Nakhodka, U.S.S.R. 43 10N 132 45E
107 Nakhon Phanom, Thai. 17 23N 104 43E
107 Nakhon Ratchasima, Thailand 14 59N 102 12E
107 Nakhon Si Thammarat, Thailand 8 29N 100 0E
107 Nakhon Sawan, Thai. 15 35N 100 10E
154 Nakina, Ont., Canada 50 10N 86 40W
60 Nakto, Poland 53 9N 17 38E
104 Nakodar, India 31 8N 75 31E
164 Nakomis, U.S.A. 39 19N 89 19W
132 Nakonde, Zambia 9 8S 32 47E
134 Nakop, S.W. Africa 28 5S 19 57E
81 Nakskov, Denmark 54 50N 11 8E
104 Nakur, India 30 2N 77 32E
131 Nakuru, & dist., Kenya 0 15S 36 5E
156 Nakusp, Canada 50 20N 117 45W
102 Nal R., W. Pakistan 27 0N 65 50E
112 Nalayh, Mongolia 47 43N 107 22E
132 Nalázi, Mozambique 24 3S 33 20E
89 Nalchik, U.S.S.R. 43 30N 43 33E
80 Nalden, Sweden 63 21N 14 20E
89 Näldsjön L., Sweden 63 25N 14 20E
125 Nalerigu, Ghana 10 35N 0 25W
106 Nalgonda, India 17 6N 79 15E
105 Nalharti, India 24 17N 87 52E
55 Nalinnes, Belgium 50 19N 4 27E
106 Nallamala Hills, India 15 30N 78 50E
62 Nalon R., Spain 43 35N 6 10W
123 Nälüt, Libya 31 54N 11 0E
107 Nam Dinh, N. Vietnam 20 25N 106 5E
107 Nam Phong, Thailand 16 42N 102 52E
107 Nam Tha, Laos 20 58N 101 30E
111 Nam Tso, Tibet, China 30 40N 90 30E
113 Nama, China 23 45N 108 1E
129 Namacurra, Mozam. 17 30S 36 50E
106 Namakkal, India 11 13N 78 13E
113 Naman, China 25 0N 118 30E
112 Naman, N. Korea 41 48N 129 52E
90 Namangan, U.S.S.R. 41 30N 71 30E
129 Namapa, Mozambique 13 43S 39 50E
134 Namaqualand, S. Africa 30 0S 18 0E
131 Namasagali, Uganda 1 2N 33 0E
144 Namatanai, Terr. of New Guinea 4 35S 152 30E
124 Nambala, Mali 14 1N 5 58W
109 Namber, Indonesia 1 2S 134 57E
145 Nambour, Australia 26 38S 152 49E
145 Nambucca Heads, N.S.W., Australia 30 40S 152 48E
111 Namcha Barwa, Mt., China 29 30N 95 10E
105 Namche Bazar, Nepal 27 51N 86 47E
55 Namêche, Belgium 50 28N 5 0E
55 Namedy, Germany 50 27N 7 21E
108 Nameh, Indonesia 2 42N 116 32E
59 Náměšt nad Oslavou, Czechoslovakia 49 12N 16 10E
59 Namestovo, Cz. 49 24N 19 25E
129 Namib Des., S.W. Afr. 22 30S 15 0W
105 Namja Pass, Nepal 30 0N 82 25E
109 Namlea, Indonesia 3 10S 127 5E
113 Namoa I., China 23 30N 117 0E
145 Namoi, R., Australia 30 16S 149 15E
166 Nampa, U.S.A. 43 40N 116 40W
112 Nampo, N. Korea 38 52N 125 28E
129 Nampula, Mozambique 15 6S 39 7E
109 Namrole, Indonesia 3 46S 126 46E
82 Namsen R., Norway 64 40N 13 0E
82 Namsos, Norway 64 28N 11 35E
103 Namtu, Burma 23 5N 97 28E
156 Namu, Canada 51 45N 127 50W
54 Namur, Belgium 50 27N 4 52E
54 Namur, prov., Belgium 50 17N 5 0E
129 Namutoni, S.W. Africa 18 49S 16 55E
132 Namwala, Zambia 15 44S 26 30E
60 Namyslow, Poland 51 6N 17 42E
113 Namyung, China 25 15N 114 5E
43 Nan Clar L., Scot., U.K. 58 18N 4 5W
111 Nan shan, Mt., China 38 0N 98 0E
78 Nana, Rumania 44 17N 26 34E
156 Nanaimo, B.C., Canada 49 10N 124 0W
145 Nanango, Australia 26 40S 152 0E
114 Nanao, Japan 37 0N 137 0E
175 Nanaque, Brazil 17 48S 40 20W
113 Nanchang, Hupei, China 31 50N 111 50E
113 Nanchang, Kiangsi, China 28 34N 115 48E
113 Nancheng, Kiangsi, China 27 30N 116 28E
113 Nancheng, see Hanchung, China 33 10N 107 2E
113 Nanchung China 30 47N 105 59E
113 Nanchwan, China 29 10N 107 15E
49 Nancy, France 48 42N 6 12E
105 Nanda Devi, Mt., India 30 30N 80 30E
106 Nander, India 19 10N 77 20E
131 Nandi, Dist., Kenya 0 15N 35 0E
106 Nandikotkur, India 15 52N 78 18E
104 Nandura, India 20 52N 76 25E
104 Nandurbar, India 21 20N 74 15E
106 Nandyal, India 15 30N 78 30E
142 Nanga, W. Australia 26 7S 113 45E
125 Nanga Eboko, Cam. 4 40N 12 26E
102 Nanga Parbat, Mt., Kashmir 35 10N 74 35E
131 Nangeya Mts., Uganda 3 30N 33 30E
113 Nangfeng, China 27 10N 116 20E
49 Nangis, France 48 33N 3 0E
125 Nangodi, Ghana 10 58N 0 42W
124 Nangola, Mali 12 41N 6 35W
132 Nangoma, Zambia 15 30S 23 0E
102 Nangrahar, prov., Afghan. 34 20N 70 0E
109 Nangtud, Mt., Phil. 11 21N 122 16E
106 Nanjangud, India 12 6N 76 43E
132 Nanjeko, Zambia 5 31S 23 30E
104 Nankana Sahib, W. Pak. 31 27N 73 38E
113 Nankang, China 25 42N 114 35E
113 Nankiang, China 32 20N 106 50E
113 Nankiang, China 32 52N 106 17E
113 Nanking, China 32 10N 118 50E
142 Nannine, W. Australia 26 51S 118 18E
113 Nanning, China 22 50S 108 5E
142 Nannup, W. Australia 33 59S 115 48E
105 Nanpara, India 27 52N 81 33E
112 Nanpi, China 38 0N 116 40E
113 Nanping, China 26 45N 118 5E
113 Nanping, China 33 20N 103 56E
114 Nanpo Is., Japan 33 0N 140 15E
113 Nanpu, China 31 17N 105 59E
14 Nansen Sd., Canada 81 0N 91 0W
131 Nansio, Tanzania 2 3S 33 4E
50 Nant, France 44 1N 3 18E
113 Nantan, China 25 12N 107 40E
48 Nantes, France 47 12N 1 33W
49 Nanteuil le Haudouin, France 49 9N 2 48E
50 Nantiat, France 46 1N 1 11E
161 Nanticoke, Pa., U.S.A. 41 12N 76 1W
156 Nanton, Canada 50 20N 113 50W
113 Nantou, Taiwan 23 57N 120 35E
51 Nantua, France 46 10N 5 35E
162 Nantucket I., U.S.A. 41 16N 70 0W
162 Nantucket Sd., U.S.A. 41 30N 70 15W
131 Nantuege, Mozambique 11 55S 38 4E
113 Nantung, China 32 0N 120 50E
38 Nantwich, Eng., U.K. 53 5N 2 31W
113 Nanyang, China 33 4N 112 55E
113 Nanyuan, China 39 45N 116 30E
88 Nanyuki, Kenya 0 2N 37 4E
132 Nanzhila, Zambia 16 4S 26 6E
155 Naococane L., Canada 52 50N 70 45W
114 Naoetsu, Japan 37 12N 138 10E
105 Naogaon, E. Pakistan 24 52N 88 52E
76 Naousa, Greece 40 42N 22 9E
109 Napabalana, Indonesia 4 42S 127 43E
154 Napanee, Canada 44 15N 77 0W
161 Napanoch, U.S.A. 41 44N 74 2W
146 Napier, New Zealand 39 30S 176 56E
134 Napier, C. Prov., S. Afr. 34 30S 19 54E
73 Naples (Napoli), Italy 40 50N 14 5E
163 Naples, Fla., U.S.A. 26 10N 81 45W
160 Naples, N.Y., U.S.A. 42 35N 77 25W
73 Naples, Gulf of, Italy 44 40N 14 10E
174 Napo R., Peru 3 5S 73 0W
164 Napoleon, N. Dak., U.S.A. 46 32N 99 49W
162 Napoleon, Ohio, U.S.A. 41 24N 84 7W
73 Napoli, Italy 40 50N 14 5E
73 Napoli, G. di, Italy 40 40N 14 10E
38 Nappa, Eng., U.K. 53 58N 2 14W
145 Nappa Merrie, Queensland, Australia 27 7N 141 7E
126 Naqâda, Egypt 25 53N 32 42E
98 Naqura, Lebanon 33 7N 35 8E
124 Nara, Mali 15 25N 7 20W
114 Nara, Japan 34 40N 135 49E
114 Nara, pref., Japan 34 30N 136 0E
104 Nara Canal, W. Pak. 26 0N 69 20E
165 Nara Visa, U.S.A. 35 39N 103 10W
145 Naracoorte, S. Austral. 36 50S 140 44E
143 Naradhan, Australia 33 34S 146 17E
106 Narasapur, India 16 26N 81 50E
106 Narasaropet, India 16 14N 80 4E
107 Narathiwat, Thailand 6 40N 101 55E
105 Narayanganj, E. Pak. 23 31N 90 33E
106 Narayanpet, India 16 45N 77 30E
37 Narberth, Wales, U.K. 51 48N 4 45W
50 Narbonne, France 43 11N 3 0E
34 Narborough, Eng., U.K. 52 34N 1 12W
62 Narcea, R., Spain 43 15N 6 30W
73 Nardo, Italy 40 10N 18 0E
142 Narembeen, W. Austral. 32 7S 118 17E
148 Nares Str., N. America 81 0N 65 0W
142 Naretha, W. Australia 31 0S 124 45E
104 Nari, R., W. Pakistan 29 10N 67 50E
174 Naricual, Venezuela 10 0N 64 25W
134 Nariep, C. Prov., S. Afr. 30 45S 17 42E
101 Narin, Afghanistan 36 5N 69 0E
129 Narinda, B. de, Malag. 14 55S 47 30E
104 Narmad, R., India 22 40N 77 30E
104 Narnaul, India 28 5N 76 11E
71 Narni, Italy 42 30N 12 30E
124 Naro, Ghana 10 22N 2 27W
72 Naro, Italy 37 18N 13 48E
87 Naro Fominsk, U.S.S.R. 55 23N 36 32E
84 Narodnaya, Mt., U.S.S.R. 65 5N 60 0E
131 Narok & dist., Kenya 1 20S 33 30E
62 Naron, Spain 43 32N 8 9W
143 Narooma, N.S.W., Austral. 36 14S 150 4E
104 Narowal, W. Pakistan 32 6N 74 52E
145 Narrabri, N.S.W., Austral. 30 19S 149 46E
145 Narran R., Australia 29 20S 147 30E
143 Narrandera, Australia 34 42S 146 31E
143 Narriah, N.S.W., Austral. 33 56S 146 43E
142 Narrogin, W. Australia 32 58S 117 14E
143 Narromine, Australia 32 12S 148 12E
42 Narrows, str., Scot., U.K. 57 20N 6 5W
106 Narsampet, India 17 57N 79 58E
104 Narsinghpur, India 22 54N 79 14E
134 Narubis, S.W. Africa 26 50S 18 56E
86 Narva, U.S.S.R. 59 10N 28 5E
86 Narva R., U.S.S.R. 59 10N 27 50E
82 Narvik, Norway 68 28N 17 35E
104 Narwana, India 29 39N 76 6E
84 Naryan-Mar, U.S.S.R. 68 0N 53 0E
145 Naryilco, Queensland, Australia 28 37S 141 53E
90 Narym, U.S.S.R. 59 0N 81 58E
90 Narymskoye, U.S.S.R. 49 10N 84 15E
90 Naryn, U.S.S.R. 41 30N 76 10E
125 Nasarawa, Nigeria 8 32N 7 41E
78 Năsăud, Rumania 47 19N 24 29E
80 Näsbruk, Sweden 60 12N 16 28E
113 Nase, Japan 28 20N 129 29E
35 Naseby, Eng., U.K. 52 24N 0 59W
147 Naseby, New Zealand 45 1S 170 10E
80 Näsfj, Mt., Sweden 61 23N 12 56E
37 Nash Pt., Wales, U.K. 51 24N 3 34W
161 Nashua, N.H., U.S.A. 42 50N 71 25W
164 Nashua, Iowa, U.S.A. 42 55N 92 34W
166 Nashua, Mont., U.S.A. 48 10N 106 25W
165 Nashville, Ark., U.S.A. 33 56N 93 50W
163 Nashville, Ga., U.S.A. 31 13N 83 15W
163 Nashville, Tenn., U.S.A. 36 12N 86 46W
74 Našice, Yugoslavia 45 32N 18 4E
104 Nasik, India 20 2N 73 50E
105 Nasirabad, (Mymensingh), E. Pak. 24 42N 90 30E
104 Nasirabad, India 26 15N 74 45E
104 Nasirabad, W. Pakistan 28 25N 68 25E
73 Naso, Italy 38 8N 14 46E
130 Nasondoye, Congo 10 22S 25 3E
101 Nasratabad, Iran 29 55N 59 53E
169 Nassau Bahamas 25 0N 77 30W
161 Nassau, U.S.A. 42 30N 73 34W
176 Nassau G., Chile 55 20S 68 0W
126 Nasser, L., Egypt 23 0N 32 30E
81 Nässjö, Sweden 57 38N 14 45E
154 Nastopoka Is., Canada 57 0N 77 0W
81 Näsum, Sweden 56 10N 14 29E
80 Näsviken, Sweden 61 46N 16 52E
113 Nata, Hainan, China 19 37N 109 17E
100 Nata, Saudi Arabia 27 15N 48 35E
132 Nata R., Rhodesia 19 55S 27 8E
174 Natagaima, Colombia 3 37N 75 6W
174 Natal, Amaz., Brazil 6 55N 60 25W
175 Natal, Brazil 5 50S 35 10W
108 Natal, Indonesia 0 35N 99 0E
135 Natal, prov., S. Africa 28 30S 30 30E
74 Natalinci, Yugoslavia 44 15N 20 49E
74 Natanya, Israel 32 20N 34 51E
101 Natanz, Iran 33 30N 51 55E
155 Natashquan, Canada 50 14N 61 46W
155 Natashquan Pt., Can. 50 8N 61 40W
155 Natashquan R., Canada 51 48N 62 0W
165 Natchez, U.S.A. 31 35N 91 25W
165 Natchitoches, U.S.A. 31 47N 93 4W
145 Nathalia, Vic., Australia 36 1S 145 7E
104 Nathdwara, India 24 55N 73 50E
161 Natick, U.S.A. 42 16N 71 19W
101 Natih, Muscat & Oman 22 25N 56 30E
143 Natimuk, Vic., Austral. 36 35S 141 59E
167 National City, U.S.A. 32 45N 117 7W
157 National Mills, Canada 52 52N 101 40W
125 Natitingou, Dahomey 10 20N 1 26E
175 Natividade, Brazil 11 30S 47 57W
107 Natkyizin, Burma 14 57N 97 59E
164 Natoma U.S.A. 39 14N 99 0W
55 Natoye, Belgium 50 19N 5 4E
80 Nätra, Sweden 63 8N 18 31E
131 Natron L., Tanzania 2 20S 36 0E
160 Natrona, U.S.A. 40 39N 79 43W
126 Natrûn, W. el., Egypt 30 25N 30 0E
108 Natuna Is., Indon. 4 0N 108 0E
161 Natural Bridge, U.S.A. 44 5N 75 30W
145 Naturaliste C., Australia 40 50S 148 15E
138 Naturaliste, C., W. Austral. 33 32S 115 0E
138 Naturaliste Channel, Western Australia 25 20S 113 0E
50 Naucelle, France 44 13N 2 20E
58 Nauders, Austria 46 54N 10 30E
56 Nauen, Germany 52 36N 12 52E
161 Naugatuck, U.S.A. 41 28N 73 4W
86 Naujoji Vilnia, U.S.S.R. 54 48N 25 27E
56 Naumburg, Germany 51 10N 11 48E
136 Nauru I., Pacific Ocean 0 25N 166 0E
174 Nauta. Peru 4 20S 73 35W
168 Nautla, Mexico 20 20N 96 50W
62 Nava del Rey, Spain 41 22N 5 6W
62 Navahermosa, Spain 39 41N 4 28W
62 Navalcarnero, Spain 40 17N 4 5W
62 Navalmoral de la Mata, Spain 39 52N 5 16W
63 Navalvillar de Pela, Sp. 39 9N 5 24W
46 Navan, see An Uaimh, Ire. 53 39N 6 40W
176 Navarino I., Chile 55 0S 67 30W
64 Navarra, reg., Spain 42 40N 1 40W
160 Navarre, U.S.A. 40 43N 81 31W
50 Navarre, reg., France 43 15N 1 20E
50 Navarreux, France 43 20N 0 47W
62 Navas del Marques, Sp. 40 38N 4 22W
165 Navasota, U.S.A. 30 20N 96 5W
169 Navassa I. (U.S.), W.I. 18 30N 75 0W
70 Nave, Italy 45 35N 10 17E
39 Navenby Eng. U.K. 53 7N 0 32W
43 Naver L., Scot., U.K. 58 18N 4 20W
43 Naver R., Scot., U.K. 58 24N 4 10W
62 Navia, Spain 43 24N 6 42W
62 Navia R., Spain 43 15N 6 50W
62 Navia de Suarna, Spain 42 58N 6 59W
86 Navlya, U.S.S.R. 52 53N 34 15E
168 Navojoa, Mexico 27 0N 109 30W
84 Navolok, U.S.S.R. 62 33N 39 57E
77 Návpaktos Greece 38 23N 21 42E
77 Návplion, Greece 37 33N 22 50E
125 Navrongo, Ghana 10 57N 0 58W
104 Navsari, India 20 57N 72 59E
104 Nawa Kot, W. Pak. 28 21N 71 24E
105 Nawabganj, India 28 32N 79 40E
105 Nawabganj, India 26 56N 81 14E
105 Nawabganj, E. Pak. 24 35N 88 18E
104 Nawabshah, W. Pak. 26 15N 68 25E
105 Nawada, India 24 50N 85 25E
105 Nawakot, Nepal 28 0N 85 10E
104 Nawalgarh, India 27 50N 75 15E
105 Nawapara, India 20 52N 82 33E
126 Nawi, Sudan 18 32N 13 50E
77 Náxos, Greece 37 8N 25 25E
77 Náxos I., Greece 37 5N 25 30E
50 Nay, France 43 10N 0 18W
101 Nay Band, Iran 27 20N 52 40E
91 Nayakhan, U.S.S.R. 62 10N 159 0E
168 Nayarit, st., Mexico 22 0N 105 0W
124 Nayes, Senegal 14 28N 12 12W
99 Nayfah, Saudi Arabia 19 59N 50 46E
175 Nazaré, Brazil 13 0S 39 0W
175 Nazaré-da-Mata, Brazil 7 40S 35 10W
63 Nazaré, Portugal 39 36N 9 4W
98 Nazareth, Israel 32 42N 35 17E
168 Nazas, Mexico 25 10N 104 0W
168 Nazas, R., Mexico 25 20N 104 4W
35 Naze, The, Eng., U.K. 51 43N 1 18E
103 Nazir Hat, E. Pak. 22 35N 91 55E
156 Nazko, Canada 52 50N 123 25W
132 Nchacoongo, Mozam. 24 20S 35 9E
132 Nchanga, Zambia 12 30S 27 49E
132 Nchelenge, Zambia 9 20S 28 50E
132 Ncheu, Malawi 14 50S 34 37E
132 Nchinji, Malawi 13 50S 32 58E
124 Nchira, Ghana 12 54N 2 0W
132 Ndabala, Zambia 13 25S 29 53E
131 Ndala, Tanzania 4 45S 33 23E
121 Ndélé, Cent. Afr. Rep. 8 25N 20 36E
76 Ndërfanë, Albania 41 47N 19 49E
132 Ndevu, Zambia 14 36S 33 30E
128 N'Djolé, Gabon 0 10S 10 45E
132 Ndola, Zambia 13 0S 28 34E
131 Ndoto Mts., Kenya 2 0N 37 0E
131 Nduguti, Tanzania 4 18S 34 41E
79 Nea R., Norway 63 15N 11 20E
77 Nea Epidhavros, Greece 37 40N 33 7E
76 Néa Filippiás, Greece 39 12N 20 53W
76 Néa Kallikrátia, Greece 40 21N 23 1E
76 Néa Vissi, Greece 41 34N 26 33E
46 Neagh, Lough, Northern Ireland, U.K. 54 35N 6 25W
166 Neah Bay, U.S.A. 48 19N 124 29W
142 Neale L., S. Australia 24 15S 130 0E
138 Neales R., S. Australia 28 0S 136 0E
78 Neamç, Reg., Rumania 47 0N 26 20E
77 Neápolis, Crete, Greece 35 15N 25 36E
76 Neápolis, Kozan, Greece 40 20N 21 24E
77 Neápolis, Lakonia, Gr. 36 27N 23 8E
136 Near Is., Alustian Is., U.S.A. 53 0N 172 0
37 Neath, Wales, U.K. 51 39N 3 49W
37 Neath R., Wales, U.K. 51 46N 3 35W
133 Nebo, Trans., S. Africa 24 52S 29 54E
86 Nebolchiy, U.S.S.R. 59 12N 32 58E
164 Nebraska, st., U.S.A. 41 30N 100 0W
164 Nebraska City, U.S.A. 40 40N 95 52W
164 Necedah, U.S.A. 44 2N 90 7W
156 Nechako R., Canada 53 30N 125 0W
165 Neches R., U.S.A. 31 80N 94 20W
174 Nechi, Colombia 8 5N 74 50W
57 Neckar R., Germany 48 43N 9 15E
172 Necochea, Argentina 38 30S 58 50W
71 Nedelisce, Yugoslavia 46 23N 16 22E
55 Neder Rijn, R., Neth. 51 57N 5 35E
79 Nederlandsöy I. Nor. 62 20N 5 35E
77 Nedha R., Greece 37 25N 21 45E
122 Nédroma, Algeria 35 1N 1 45W
79 Nedstrand, Norway 59 21N 5 49E
35 Needham Market, England, U.K. 52 9N 1 2E
142 Needilup, W. Australia 33 55S 118 45E
167 Needles, U.S.A. 34 50N 114 35W
146 Needles, Pt., N.Z. 36 3S 175 25E
34 Needles, The, Eng., U.K. 50 39N 1 35W
104 Neemuch (Nimach), India 24 30N 74 50E
162 Neenah, U.S.A. 44 10N 88 30W
157 Neepawa, Canada 50 20N 99 30W
55 Neerpelt, Belgium 51 13N 5 26E
123 Nefta, Tunisia 33 53N 7 58E
89 Neftegorsk, U.S.S.R. 44 25N 39 45E
85 Neftyannye Kamni, U.S.S.R. 40 20N 50 55E
106 Negapatam, see Nagappattiñam, India 10 46N 79 38E
162 Negaunee, U.S.A. 46 30N 87 36W
98 Negba, Israel 31 40N 34 41E
107 Negeri Sembilan, st., Malaya, Malaysia 2 50N 102 10E
78 Negoiul, Mt., Rumania 45 48N 24 32E
106 Negombo, Ceylon 7 12N 79 50E
74 Negotin, Macedonia, Yugoslavia 41 29N 22 9E
74 Negotin, Serbia, Y.-slav. 44 16N 22 37E
109 Negra Pt., Philippines 18 40N 120 50E
103 Negrais C. Burma 16 0N 94 30E
62 Negreira, Spain 42 54N 8 45W
78 Negreşti, Rumania 46 50N 27 30E
174 Negrillos, Bolivia 18 45S 68 45W
123 Negrine, Algeria 34 30N 7 30E
174 Negritos, Peru 4 55S 81 5W
122 Negro C., Morocco 35 40N 5 11W
176 Negro R., Argentina 40 0S 64 0W
174 Negro R., Brazil 0 25S 64 0W
173 Negro R., Uruguay 32 30S 55 30W
109 Negros I., Philippines 10 0N 123 0E
78 Negru Vodă, Rumania 43 47N 28 21E
101 Nehbandan, Iran 31 35N 60 5E
56 Neheim, Germany 51 27N 7 58E
78 Nehoiaşu, Rumania 45 24N 26 20E
157 Neidpath, Canada 50 12N 107 20W
166 Neihart, U.S.A. 47 0N 110 52W
113 Neikiang, China 29 35N 105 10E
143 Neilrex, N.S.W., Austral. 31 38S 149 25E
143 Neila Gaari Post Office, N.S.W., Australia 32 1S 142 48E
40 Neilston, Scotland, U.K. 55 47N 4 27W
166 Neilton, U.S.A. 47 24N 123 59W
62 Neira de Jusa, Spain 42 53N 7 14W
113 Neisiang, China 33 10N 112 0E
56 Neisse R., Pol.-Ger. 51 0N 15 0E
174 Neiva, Colombia 2 56N 75 18W
157 Nejanilini, L., Canada 59 30N 97 30W
100 Nejd, prov., Si. Arabia 26 30N 42 0E
127 Nejo, Ethiopia 9 30N 35 28E
127 Nekemte, Ethiopia 9 4N 36 30E
126 Nekheb, Egypt 25 10N 33 0E
88 Nekhvoroshcha, U.S.S.R. 49 7N 34 43E
81 Neksö, Denmark 55 4N 15 8E
62 Nelas, Portugal 40 32N 7 52W
79 Nelaug, Norway 58 39N 8 40E
144 Nelia, Queens., Austral. 20 39S 142 12E
164 Neligh, U.S.A. 42 11N 98 2W
91 Nelkan, U.S.S.R. 57 50N 136 15E
106 Nellikuppam, India 11 46N 79 43E
106 Nellore, India 14 27N 79 59E
91 Nelma U.S.S.R. 47 30N 139 0E
143 Nelson, Vic., Australia 38 3S 141 2E
156 Nelson, B.C., Canada 49 30N 117 20W
38 Nelson, England, U.K. 53 50N 2 14W
147 Nelson, New Zealand 41 18S 173 16E
167 Nelson, Ariz., U.S.A. 35 35N 113 24W
167 Nelson, Nev., U.S.A. 35 46N 114 55W
143 Nelson Bay, N.S.W., Australia 32 43S 152 9E
147 Nelson, dist., N.Z. 42 11S 172 15E
143 Nelson, C., Vic., Austral. 38 14S 141 33E
157 Nelson R., Canada 55 30N 96 50W
156 Nelson Forks, Canada 59 30N 124 0W
156 Nelson House, Canada 55 50N 99 0W
176 Nelson Strait, Chile 51 30S 75 0W
134 Nelspoort, S. Africa 32 8S 22 59E
133 Nelspruit, Trans., S. Afr. 25 29S 30 59E
135 Nelsrus, Natal, S. Africa 29 45S 30 22E
124 Néma, Mauritania 16 40N 7 15W
86 Neman (Nemunas) R., U.S.S.R. 53 30N 25 10E
77 Neméa, Greece 37 49N 22 40E
154 Nemegos, Canada 47 40N 83 15W
77 Nëmerckë, Mts., Alb. 40 15N 20 15E
78 Nemira, Mt., Rumania 46 17N 26 19E
154 Nemiscam, Canada 49 30N 111 15W
49 Nemours, France 48 16N 2 40E
91 Nemui, U.S.S.R. 55 40N 135 55E
114 Nemuro, Japan 43 20N 145 35E
114 Nemuro-kaikyō, Str., Japan 43 30N 145 30E
44 Nenagh, Ireland 52 52N 8 11W

MAP
35 Nene R., England, U.K. 52 38N 0 7E
132 Neno, Malawi 15 25S 34 40E
109 Nenusa I., Indonesia . 4 45N 127 1E
165 Neodesha, U.S.A. 37 30N 95 37W
76 Néon Petrítsi, Greece .41 16N 23 15E
165 Neosho, U.S.A. 36 56N 94 28W
165 Neosho R., U.S.A. 35 59N 95 10W
105 Nepal, king., Asia 28 0N 84 30E
105 Nepalganj, Nepal 28 0N 81 40E
166 Nephi, U.S.A. 39 43N 111 52W
45 Nephin, Mt., Ireland 54 1N 9 21W
45 Nephin Beg, Mt., Ire. 54 2N 9 40W
45 Nephin Beg Ra., Ire. .54 0N 9 40W
58 Nepomuk, Cz. 49 29N 13 35E
161 Neptune City, U.S.A. .40 13N 74 4W
74 Nera R., Rumania 44 52N 21 45E
50 Nérac, France 44 9N 0 20E
91 Nerchinsk, U.S.S.R. 52 0N 116 39E
91 Nerchinski Zavod, U.S.S.R. 51 10N 119 30E
78 Nereju, Rumania 45 43N 26 43E
155 Neret L., Canada 54 40N 71 0W
74 Neretva R., Yugoslavia 43 30N 17 50E
74 Neretvanski, Chan., Yugoslavia 43 7N 17 10E
63 Nerja, Spain 36 43N 3 55W
87 Neri R., U.S.S.R. 56 30N 40 30E
77 Nerokoúru, Crete, Gr. 35 29N 24 3E
65 Nerpio, Spain 38 11N 2 16W
63 Nerva, Spain 37 42N 6 30W
82 Nes, Iceland 65 53N 17 16W
98 Nes Tsiyona, Israel ...31 56N 34 48W
75 Nesebur, Bulgaria 42 41N 27 46E
79 Nesbyen, Norway 60 34N 9 6E
79 Nesflaten, Norway 59 38N 6 48E
79 Nesland, Norway 59 31N 7 59E
79 Neslandsvatn, Norway 58 57N 9 10E
49 Nesle, France 49 45N 2 53E
79 Nesodden, Norway 59 48N 10 40E
42 Ness, dist., Scot., U.K. 58 27N 6 20W
43 Ness, Loch, Scot., U.K. 57 15N 4 30W
82 Nesseby, Norway 70 9N 28 56E
38 Neston, England, U.K. 53 17N 3 3W
76 Nestórion Oros, Mt., Gr. 40 24N 20 55E
76 Néstos R., Greece 41 20N 24 35E
79 Nesttun, Norway 60 17N 5 24E
86 Nesvizh, U.S.S.R. 53 14N 26 38E
54 Nethe R., Belgium 51 5N 4 55E
36 Nether Stowey, England, U.K. 51 10N 3 10W
36 Netherbury, Eng., U.K. 50 46N 2 45W
143 Netherby, Vic., Austral. 36 8S 141 40E
144 Netherdale, Australia .21 10S 148 33E
54 Netherlands, king., Eur. 52 0N 5 30E
175 Netherlands Guiana, Col., S. Amer. 4 0N 56 0W
43 Nethy Bridge, Scotland, United Kingdom 57 15N 3 40W
34 Netley, England, U.K. 50 53N 1 21W
34 Netley Marsh, Eng., U.K. 50 55N 1 32W
73 Neto R., Italy 39 10N 16 58E
105 Netrakona, E. Pakistan 24 53N 90 47E
49 Nettancourt, France .48 51N 4 57E
55 Nette R., Germany 50 21N 7 21E
153 Nettilling L., Canada .66 30N 71 0W
35 Nettlebed, Eng., U.K. 51 34N 0 54W
39 Nettleham, Eng., U.K. 53 15N 0 28W
72 Nettuno, Italy 41 29N 12 40E
57 Neu Ulm, Germany 48 23N 10 2E
56 Neubrandenburg, Ger. 55 33N 13 17E
56 Neubukow, Germany .54 1N 11 40E
57 Neuburg, Germany 48 43N 11 11E
57 Neuchâtel, & Cant., Switz. 47 0N 6 55E
57 Neuchâtel, Lac de, Switz. 4 53N 6 50E
58 Neudau, Austria 47 11N 16 6E
56 Neuenhaus, Germany .52 30N 6 55E
49 Neuf Brisach, France .48 0N 7 30E
54 Neufchâteau, Belgium 49 50N 5 25E
49 Neufchâteau, France .48 21N 5 40E
49 Neufchâtel, France 49 43N 1 30E
49 Neufchâtel sur Aisne, France 49 26N 4 0E
56 Neuhaus, Lr. Sax., Ger. 53 16N 10 54E
49 Neuilly St. Front, Fr. 49 10N 3 15E
57 Neu-Isenburg, Germany 50 3N 8 42E
57 Neukalen, Germany 53 49N 12 48E
57 Neumarkt, Germany .49 16N 11 28E
56 Neumünster, Germany 54 4N 9 58E
49 Neung-sur-Beuvron, Fr. 47 30N 1 50E
58 Neunkirchen, Austria .47 43N 16 4E
57 Neunkirchen, Germany 49 23N 7 6E
176 Neuquén, Argentina ...38 0S 68 0E
176 Neuquén, prov., Arg. .38 0S 69 50W
56 Neuruppin, Germany .52 56N 12 48E
165 Neuse R., U.S.A. 35 5N 77 40W
59 Neusiedl, Austria 47 57N 16 50E
59 Neusiedler See, L., Aust. 47 50N 16 47E
56 Neuss, Germany 51 12N 6 39E
50 Neussargues, France .45 9N 2 59E
57 Neustadt, Bavaria, Ger. 49 42N 12 10E
57 Neustadt, Bav., Ger. .48 48N 11 47E
57 Neustadt, Bav., Ger. .50 23N 11 0E
57 Neustadt, Bav., Ger. .49 34N 10 37E
56 Neustadt, Hesse, Ger. 50 51N 9 9E
56 Neustadt, Lr. Sax., Ger. 52 30N 9 30E
56 Neustadt, Potsdam, Ger. 52 50N 12 27E
57 Neustadt, Rhld-Pal, Ger. 49 21N 8 10E
57 Neustadt, S.-Holst., Ger. 54 6N 10 49E
56 Neustadt, Sera, E. Ger. 50 45N 11 43E
56 Neustrelitz, Germany .53 22N 13 4E
50 Neuvic, Corrèze, France 45 23N 2 16E
49 Neuville aux Bois, Fr. 48 4N 2 3E
50 Neuvy St. Sépulchure, France 46 35N 1 48E
49 Neuvy-sur-Barangeon, France 47 20N 2 15E
56 Neuwerk I., Germany 53 55N 8 30E
56 Neuwied, Germany 50 26N 7 29E
80 Neva, Sweden 60 13N 14 9E
84 Neva, R., U.S.S.R. 59 50N 30 30E
165 Nevada, U.S.A. 37 20N 94 40W
166 Nevada, st., U.S.A. ...39 20N 117 0W
166 Nevada City, U.S.A. .39 20N 121 0W
172 Nevado, Mt., Argentina 35 30S 68 20W
168 Nevado de Colima, Mt., Mexico 19 35N 103 45W
98 Nevalat, Israel 31 59N 34 57E
91 Nevanka, U.S.S.R. 56 45N 98 55E
106 Nevasa, India 19 34N 75 0E
86 Nevel, U.S.S.R 56 0N 29 55E
91 Nevelski Mt., U.S.S.R. 50 0N 143 30E
37 Nevern, Wales, U.K. .52 2N 4 49W
49 Nevers, France 47 0N 3 9E
143 Nevertire, N.S.W., Australia 31 50S 147 44E
55 Neviges, Germany 51 18N 7 5E
157 Neville, Canada 49 58N 107 39W
37 Nevin, Wales, U.K. ...52 57N 4 30W
89 Nevinnomyssk, U.S.S.R. 44 40N 42 0E
169 Nevis I., Leeward Is. .17 0N 62 30W
42 Nevis, L., Scot., U.K. 57 0N 5 43W
79 Nevlunghamn, Norway 58 58N 9 53E
142 Nevoria, W. Australia 31 25S 119 25E
75 Nevrokop, Bulgaria ...41 43N 23 46E
100 Nevsehir, Turkey 38 33N 34 40E
41 New Abbey, Scot., U.K. 54 59N 3 38W
43 New Aberdour, Scot., U.K. 57 39N 2 12W
125 New Adawso, Ghana . 6 50N 0 37E
162 New Albany, Ind., U.S.A. 38 20N 85 50W
165 New Albany, Miss., U.S.A. 34 30N 89 0W
161 New Albany, Pa., U.S.A. 41 35N 76 28W
34 New Alresford, England, U.K. 51 6N 1 44W
174 New Amsterdam, Guy. 6 15N 57 30W
161 New Bedford, U.S.A. .41 40N 70 52W
161 New Bern, U.S.A. 35 8N 77 3W
160 New Bethlehem, U.S.A. 41 0N 79 22W
45 New Birmingham, Ire. 52 36N 7 38W
160 New Bloomfield, U.S.A. 40 24N 77 12W
165 New Boston, U.S.A. ...33 27N 94 21W
165 New Braunfels, U.S.A. 29 43N 98 9W
38 New Brighton, England, U.K. 53 27N 3 2W
147 New Brighton, N.Z. ...43 29S 172 43E
161 New Britain, U.S.A. ...41 41N 72 47W
144 New Britain I., Territory of New Guinea 6 0S 151 0E
161 New Brunswick, U.S.A. 40 30N 74 28W
155 New Brunswick, prov. Canada 46 50N 66 30W
46 New Buildings, Northern Ireland, U.K. 54 57N 7 21W
15 New Byrd, Antarctica 80 0S 120 0W
136 New Caledonia I. & Fr. Col., Pac. Oc. ...21 0S 165 0E
63 New Castile, Spain 39 45N 3 20W
162 New Castle, Ind., U.S.A. 39 55N 85 23W
160 New Castle, Pa., U.S.A. 41 0N 80 20W
44 New Chapel Cross, Ire. 51 51N 10 12W
161 New City, U.S.A. 41 8N 74 0W
168 New Cristobal, Panama Canal Zone 9 25N 79 40W
160 New Cumberland, U.S.A. 40 30N 80 36W
40 New Cumnock, Scot. U.K. 55 24N 4 13W
43 New Deer, Scot., U.K. 57 30N 2 10W
133 New Denmark, S. Africa 26 41S 20 18E
156 New Denver, Canada .50 0N 117 25W
145 New England Ra., N.S.W., Australia ...29 30S 152 0E
135 New England, S. Africa 30 50S 27 30E
164 New England, U.S.A. 46 36N 102 47W
34 New Forest, Eng., U.K. 50 53N 1 40W
41 New Galloway, Scot. U.K. 55 4N 4 10W
155 New Glasgow, Canada 45 35N 62 36W
136 New Guinea I., Australasia 4 0S 136 0E
144 N. Guin., Terr. of, Austral. Trust Terr. 4 0S 146 0E
160 New Hamburg, Canada 43 24N 80 43W
161 New Hampshire, st., U.S.A. 43 40N 71 40W
164 New Hampton, U.S.A. 43 2N 92 20W
135 New Hanover, S. Africa 29 22S 30 31E
144 New Hanover I., New Guinea 2 30S 150 15E
161 New Haven, Conn., U.S.A. 41 20N 72 54W
160 New Haven, Mich., U.S.A. 42 44N 82 46W
156 New Hazelton, Canada 55 20N 127 30W
136 New Hebrides Is., Pacific Ocean 15 0S 168 0E
34 New Heyford, Eng. U.K. 51 54N 1 17W
39 New Holland, Eng. U.K. 53 42N 0 22W
35 New Hunstanton, England, U.K. 52 57N 0 30E
165 New Iberia, U.S.A. 30 2N 91 54W
45 New Inn, Ireland 53 5N 7 10W
144 New Ireland I., Terr. of New Guinea 3 0S 151 30E
161 New Jersey, st., U.S.A. 39 50N 74 10W
160 New Kensington, U.S.A. 40 36N 79 43W
162 New Lexington, U.S.A. 39 40N 82 15W
154 New Liskeard, Canada 47 31N 79 41W
161 New London, Conn., U.S.A. 41 23N 72 8W
164 New London, Minn., U.S.A. 45 17N 94 55W
160 New London, Ohio, U.S.A. 41 4N 82 25W
164 New London, Wis., U.S.A. 44 23N 88 43W
40 New Luce, Scot., U.K. 54 57N 4 50W
165 New Madrid, U.S.A. ...36 40N 89 30W
161 New Market, U.S.A. ...43 4N 70 57W
166 New Meadows, U.S.A. 45 0N 116 10W
158 New Mexico, st., U.S.A. 34 30N 106 0W
161 New Milford, Conn., U.S.A. 41 35N 73 25W
161 New Milford, Pa., U.S.A. 41 50N 75 45W
38 New Mills, Eng., U.K. 53 22N 2 0W
142 New Norcia, W. Australia 30 57S 116 13E
145 New Norfolk, Australia 42 45S 147 0E
145 New Norfolk, Tasmania, Australia 42 46S 142 3W
165 New Orleans, U.S.A. .30 0N 90 5W
160 New Philadelphia, U.S.A. 40 29N 81 25W
43 New Pitsligo, Scot U.K. 57 35N 2 11W
146 New Plymouth, N.Z. .39 4S 174 5E
169 New Providence I., Bahamas 25 0N 77 30W
37 New Quay, Wales, U.K. 52 13N 4 21W
37 New Radnor, Wales, U.K. 52 15N 3 10W
164 New Richmond, U.S.A. 45 6N 92 34W
165 New Roads, U.S.A. ...30 43N 91 30W
161 New Rochelle, U.S.A. 40 55N 73 46W
164 New Rockford, U.S.A. 47 44N 99 7W
35 New Romney, Eng., U.K. 50 59N 0 57E
45 New Ross, Ireland 52 24N 6 58W
39 New Rossington, England, U.K. 53 30N 1 4W
164 New Salem, U.S.A. 46 51N 101 25W
41 New Scone, Scot., U.K. 56 25N 3 25W
34 New Shefford, Eng. U.K. 51 28N 1 26W
91 New Siberia I., U.S.S.R. 75 0N 150 0E
91 New Siberian Is. U.S.S.R. 75 0N 140 0E
163 New Smyrna Beach, U.S.A. 29 0N 80 50W
144 New South Wales, st., Australia 33 0S 146 0E
142 New Springs, W. Austral. 25 0S 120 0E
125 New Tamale, Ghana . 9 10N 1 10W
37 New Tredegar, Wales, United Kingdom ...51 43N 3 15W
164 New Ulm, U.S.A. 44 15N 94 30W
155 New Waterford, Canada 46 13N 60 4W
156 New Westminster, Can. 49 10N 122 52W
161 New York, st., U.S.A. 42 40N 76 0W
161 New York City, U.S.A. 40 45N 74 0W
146 New Zealand, st. 40 0N 176 0W
131 Newala, Tanzania 10 58S 39 10E
131 Newala, dist., Tanzania 11 0S 39 30E
39 Newark, England, U.K. 53 6N 0 48W
162 Newark, Del., U.S.A. .39 42N 75 45W
161 Newark, N.J., U.S.A. .40 41N 74 12W
160 Newark, N.Y., U.S.A. 43 2N 77 10W
160 Newark, Ohio, U.S.A. 40 5N 82 30W
162 Newaygo, U.S.A. 43 23N 85 50W
166 Newberg, U.S.A. 45 22N 123 0W
162 Newberry, Mich., U.S.A. 46 20N 85 32W
163 Newberry, S.C., U.S.A. 34 17N 81 36W
41 Newbigging, Scot., U.K. 55 42N 3 33W
39 Newbiggin-by-the-Sea, England, U.K. 55 12N 1 31W
46 Newbliss, Ireland 54 10N 7 8W
37 Newborough, Wales, U.K. 53 10N 4 22W
44 Newbridge, Ireland ...52 33N 9 0W
45 Newbridge, Ireland ...53 11N 6 50W
37 Newbridge-on-Wye, Wales, U.K. 52 13N 3 27W
156 Newbrook, Canada ...54 24N 112 57W
43 Newburgh, Aberdeen, Scotland, U.K. 57 19N 2 0W
41 Newburgh, Fife, Scotland, U.K. 56 21N 3 15W
161 Newburgh, U.S.A. 41 30N 74 1W
39 Newburn, Eng., U.K. 54 57N 1 45W
34 Newbury, Eng., U.K. 51 24N 1 19W
161 Newbury, U.S.A. 44 7N 72 6W
161 Newburyport, U.S.A. .42 48N 70 50W
38 Newby Bridge, Eng. U.K. 54 16N 2 59W
43 Newbyth, Scot., U.K. 57 35N 2 17W
143 Newcastle, Australia .32 52S 151 49E
155 Newcastle, N.B., Can. 47 1N 65 38W
160 Newcastle, Ont., Can. 43 54N 78 34W
45 Newcastle, Ireland ...53 5N 6 4W
44 Newcastle, Ireland ...52 16N 7 50E
135 Newcastle, S. Africa ...27 45S 29 58E
46 Newcastle, N. Ire., U.K. 54 13N 5 54W
161 Newcastle, Me., U.S.A. 43 4N 70 41W
164 Newcastle, Wyo., U.S.A. 43 50N 104 12W
144 Newcastle B., Australia 10 45S 142 30E
37 Newcastle Emlyn, Wales, U.K. 52 2N 4 29W
38 Newcastle-under-Lyme, Eng., U.K. 53 2N 2 15W
39 Newcastle-upon-Tyne, England, U.K. 54 59N 1 37W
138 Newcastle Waters, N. Terr., Australia 17 30S 133 28E
41 Newcastleton, Scot. UK 55 10N 2 50W
37 Newchurch, Wales, U.K. 52 9N 3 10W
142 Newdegate, W. Austral. 33 17N 118 58E
164 Newell, U.S.A. 44 48N 103 25W
34 Newent, England U.K. 51 56N 2 24W
155 Newfoundland, prov., Canada 48 28N 56 0W
155 Newfoundland I., Can. 48 30N 56 0W
43 Newhall, Scotland, U.K. 57 40N 4 11W
35 Newham, England, U.K. 51 31N 0 2E
35 Newhaven, Eng.,U.K. 50 47N 0 4E
35 Newington, S. Kent, England, U.K. 51 5N 1 8E
35 Newington, N. Kent, England, U.K. 51 21N 0 40E
133 Newington, S. Africa .24 46S 31 21E
44 Newinn, Ireland 52 28N 7 54W
165 Newkirk, U.S.A. 36 52N 97 3W
36 Newlyn, England, U.K. 50 6N 5 33W
36 Newlyn East, Eng., U.K. 50 22N 5 3W
160 Newmarket, Canada ...44 5N 79 30W
35 Newmarket, Eng., U.K. 52 15N 0 23E
44 Newmarket, Ireland ...52 13N 9 0W
42 Newmarket, Scot., U.K. 58 14N 6 24W
161 Newmarket, U.S.A. ...43 4N 70 57W
44 Newmarket-on-Fergus, Ireland 52 46N 8 54W
43 Newmill, Scotland, U.K. 57 34N 2 58W
46 Newmills, Ireland 54 56N 7 49W
40 Newmilns, Scot., U.K. 55 36N 4 20W
163 Newnan, U.S.A. 33 22N 84 48W
143 Newnes, N.S.W., Austral. 33 10S 150 10E
34 Newnham, Eng., U.K. 51 48, 2 27W
143 Newport, N.S.W., Austral. 33 40S 151 20E
45 Newport, Mayo, Ire. 53 54N 9 34W
44 Newport, Tipp., Ire. ...52 43N 8 25W
34 Newport, I. of W., England, U.K. 50 43N 1 18W
34 Newport, Mon., England, U.K. 51 34N 2 59W
37 Newport, Pembs., Wales, U.K. 52 1N 4 51W
34 Newport, Salop, England, U.K. 52 47N 2 22W
41 Newport, Scot., U.K. .56 27N 2 56W
165 Newport, Ark., U.S.A. 35 38N 91 15W
162 Newport, Ky., U.S.A. 39 5N 84 23W
161 Newport, N.H., U.S.A. 43 23N 72 8W
166 Newport, Ore., U.S.A. 44 41N 124 2W
160 Newport, Pa., U.S.A. .40 28N 77 8W
161 Newport, R.I., U.S.A. 41 30N 71 19W
163 Newport, Tenn., U.S.A. 35 39N 83 12W
161 Newport, Vt., U.S.A. .44 57N 72 17W
166 Newport, Wash., U.S.A. 48 11N 117 2W
45 Newport B., Ireland ...53 52N 9 38W
44 Newport R., Ireland .52 43N 8 24W
167 Newport Beach, U.S.A. 33 40N 117 58W
162 Newport News, U.S.A. 37 2N 76 54W
35 Newport Pagnell, England, U.K. 52 5N 0 42W
36 Newquay, Eng., U.K. 50 24N 5 6W
46 Newry, N. Ire., U.K. .54 10N 6 20W
36 Newton, England, U.K. 50 49N 2 25W
164 Newton, Iowa, U.S.A. 41 40N 93 3W
165 Newton, Kan., U.S.A. 38 2N 97 30W
162 Newton, Mass., U.S.A. 42 21N 71 10W
165 Newton, Miss., U.S.A. 38 2N 97 25W
61 Newton, N.J., U.S.A. 41 3N 74 46W
163 Newton, N.C., U.S.A. 35 42N 81 10W
165 Newton, Texas, U.S.A. 30 54N 93 42W
36 Newton Abbot, England, U.K. 50 32N 3 37W
41 Newton Arlosh, England, U.K. 54 53N 3 15W
39 Newton-Aycliffe, England, U.K. 54 36N 1 33W
145 Newton Boyd, Australia 29 45S 152 0E
36 Newton Ferrers, England, U.K. 50 19N 4 3W
38 Newton le Willows, England, U.K. 53 28N 3 27W
36 Newton St. Cyres, England, U.K. 50 46N 3 35W
40 Newton Stewart, Scotland, U.K. 54 57N 4 30W
41 Newtongrange, Scot. U.K. 55 52N 3 4W
43 Newtonmore, Scot. U.K, ...57 4N 4 7W
143 Newtown, Australia ...37 38S 143 40E
44 Newtown, Ireland 52 20N 8 47W
41 Newtown, Scot, U.K. .55 34N 2 38W
37 Newtown, Wales, U.K. 52 31N 3 19W
44 Newtown, Bellew, Ire. 53 30N 8 34W
46 Newtown Crommelinh, N. Ireland, U.K. 54 59N 6 13W
46 Newtown Cunningham, Ireland 55 0N 7 32W
46 Newtown Forbes, Ire. 53 46N 7 50W
46 Newtown Gore, Ireland 54 3N 7 41W
46 Newtown Hamilton, N. Ireland, U.K. ...54 12N 6 35W
46 Newtownabbey, Ireland 54 40N 5 55W
46 Newtownards, Northern Ireland, U.K. 54 37N 5 40W
46 Newtownbutler, N. Ireland, U.K. 54 12N 7 22W
45 Newtownmountkennedy, Ireland 53 5N 6 7W
44 Newtownsandes, Ire. .52 30N 9 23W
46 Newtownstewart, N. Ireland, U.K. 54 43N 7 22W
160 Newville, U.S.A. 40 10N 77 24W
56 Nexon, France 45 41N 1 10E
87 Neya, U.S.S.R. 58 21N 43 49E
37 Neyland, Wales, U.K. 51 43N 4 58W
101 Neyriz, Iran 29 15N 54 55E
101 Neyshabur, Iran 36 10N 58 20E
106 Neyyattinkara, India . 8 26N 77 5E
86 Nezhin, U.S.S.R. 51 5N 31 55E
166 Nezperce, U.S.A. 46 13N 116 15W
108 Ngabang, Indonesia ... 0 30N 109 55E
130 N'Gabe, Congo (Fr.) ... 3 20S 16 10E
135 Ngagane, Natal, S. Afr. 27 50S 30 0E
125 Ngambé, Cameroon ... 5 48N 11 29E
132 Ngami, L. (Former), Botswana 20 30S 22 46E
132 Ngamo, Rhodesia 19 3S 27 25E
109 Ngandjuk, Indonesia . 7 32S 111 55E
128 Ngaoundere, Cameroon 7 15N 13 35E
147 Ngapara, N.Z. 44 57S 170 46E
132 Ngara Malawi 10 12S 34 0E
131 Ngara & dist., Tanzania 2 29S 30 40E
146 Ngaruawahia, N.Z. 37 42S 175 11E
146 Ngatapa, N.Z. 38 32S 177 45E
146 Ngauruhoe, Mt., N.Z. 39 13S 175 45E
109 Ngawi, Indonesia 7 24S 111 26E
131 Ngerengere, Tanzania 6 47S 38 10E
125 Ngetera, Nigeria 12 40S 12 46E
107 Ngha Lo, N. Vietnam 21 33N 104 28E
132 Ngoma, Malawi 13 8S 33 45E
132 Ngomahura, Rhodesia 20 33S 30 57E
131 Ngomba, Tanzania 8 20S 32 53E

MAP
131 Ngomeni, Ras, Kenya 3 0s 40 20E
131 Ngong, Kenya 1 25s 36 39E
127 Ngop, Sudan 6 17N 30 9E
131 Ngora, Uganda 1 27N 33 46E
111 Ngoring Nor, L., China 34 50N 98 0E
124 Ngorkou, Mali 15 40N 3 41W
131 Ngorongoro & crater, Tanz. 3 11s 35 32E
132 Ngosa, Zambia 12 20s 27 26E
135 Ngqeleni, S. Africa 31 40s 29 3E
131 Ngudu, Tanzania 2 58s 33 25E
127 Ngungu, Sudan 6 15N 28 16E
121 N'Guigrai, Niger 14 20N 13 20E
132 N'Guo, Mozambique 12 23s 34 35E
125 Nguru, Nigeria 12 56N 10 29E
131 Nguru Mts., Tanzania 6 0s 37 30E
132 Ngusi, Malawi 14 3s 34 54E
130 Ngwele Falls, Congo 5 6s 25 56E
133 Ngwenya, Swaziland 26 5s 31 7E
107 Nha Trang, S. Vietnam 12 16N 109 10E
132 Nhachengue, Mozam. 22 50s 35 11E
132 Nhacoongo, Mozam. 24 18s 35 14E
132 Nhamuai, Mozam. 15 4s 30 50E
132 Nhangutazi L., Mozam. 24 0s 34 29E
132 Nhanvoo L., Mozam. 22 0s 35 7E
143 Nhill, Vic., Australia 36 18s 141 40E
135 Nhlangano, Swaziland 27 5s 31 2E
124 Niafounké, Mali 16 0N 4 5W
162 Niagara, Mich., U.S.A. 45 45N 88 0W
154 Niagara Falls, N. Amer. 43 5N 79 5W
160 Niagara Falls, Ont., Can. 43 7N 79 5W
160 Niagara Falls, U.S.A. 43 5N 79 0W
160 Niagara-on-the-Lake, Canada 43 15N 79 4W
108 Niah, Sar., Malaysia 3 58s 113 46E
125 Niamey, Niger 13 27N 2 6E
124 Nianforando, Guinea 9 37N 10 36W
80 Nianfors, Sweden 61 36N 16 46E
131 Niangara Congo 3 50N 27 50E
130 Niari R., Congo (Fr.) 4 0s 14 10E
108 Nias I., Indonesia 1 0N 97 40E
132 Niassa, dist., Mozam. 13 30s 36 0E
132 Niassa, Lago, Mozam. 12 30s 34 30E
70 Nibbiano, Italy 44 54N 9 20E
81 Nibe, Denmark 56 59N 9 38E
107 Nibong Tebal, Malaysia 5 10N 100 29E
169 Nicaragua, rep., Central America 11 40N 85 30W
169 Nicaragua L., Central America 12 50N 85 30W
73 Nicastro, Italy 39 0N 16 18E
51 Nice, France 43 42N 7 14E
163 Niceville, U.S.A. 30 30N 86 30W
114 Nichinan, Japan 31 28N 131 26E
169 Nicholas, Chan., W. Ind. 23 30N 80 30W
162 Nicholasville, U.S.A. 37 54N 84 31W
161 Nichols, U.S.A. 42 1N 76 22W
154 Nicholson, Canada 47 58N 83 47W
161 Nicholson, U.S.A. 41 37N 75 47W
142 Nicholson Ra., Austral. 27 12s 116 40E
93 Nicobar Is., Indian Ocean 9 0N 93 0E
156 Nicola, Canada 50 8N 120 40W
154 Nicolet, Canada 46 17N 72 35W
100 Nicosia, Cyprus 35 10N 33 25E
73 Nicosia, Italy 37 45N 14 22E
73 Nicotera, Italy 38 33N 15 57E
169 Nicoya, G. of, Costa Rica 10 0N 85 0W
169 Nicoya Peninsula, Costa Rica 9 45N 85 40W
39 Nidd, R., England, U.K. 54 1N 1 32W
56 Nidda, Germany 50 24N 9 2E
57 Nidda R., Germany 50 25N 9 2E
39 Nidderdale, Eng., U.K. 54 5N 1 46W
60 Nidzica, Poland 53 25N 20 28E
56 Niebüll, Germany 54 45N 8 49E
55 Nieder Krüchten, Ger. 51 12N 6 12E
58 Nieder Österreich, prov., Aust. 48 25N 15 40E
55 Nieder Zissen, Germany 50 27N 7 13E
55 Niederau, Germany 50 46N 6 30E
56 Niederaula, Germany 50 48N 9 37E
49 Niederbronn, France 48 57N 7 39E
102 Niedere Tauern, Mts., Austria 47 18N 14 0E
134 Niederkshoop, S. Africa 29 20s 22 50E
56 Niedermarsberg, Ger. 51 28N 8 52E
56 Niedersachsen, (Lower Saxony), Germany 52 45N 9 0E
55 Niel, Belgium 51 7N 4 20E
134 Nielersdrif, S. Africa 28 46s 21 0E
124 Niellé, Ivory Coast 10 5N 5 38W
131 Niemba, Congo 5 58s 28 24E
143 Niemur, N.S.W., Austral. 35 17s 144 9E
56 Nienburg, Germany 52 38N 9 15E
112 Nientzeshan, China 47 38N 122 58E
59 Niepolomice, Poland 50 3N 20 13E
55 Niers R., Germany 51 35N 6 13E
56 Niesky, Germany 51 18N 14 48E
60 Nieszawa, Poland 52 52N 18 42E
55 Nieukerk, Germany 51 27N 6 22E
134 Nieu-Bethesda, S. Afr. 31 51s 24 34E
175 Nieuw Nickerie, Surinam 6 0N 57 10W
55 Nieuwenhagen, Netherlands 50 55N 6 3E
134 Nieuwoudtville, S. Afr. 31 22s 19 6E
54 Nieuwpoort, Belgium 51 8N 2 45E
55 Nievenheim, Germany 51 8N 6 43E
62 Nieves, Spain 42 7N 7 26W
49 Nièvre, dépt., France 47 10N 3 40E
133 Nigel, S. Africa 26 27s 28 25E
125 Niger, rep., W. Africa 13 30N 10 0E
125 Niger Delta, Nigeria 4 0N 5 30W
125 Niger R., West Africa 10 0N 4 40E
125 Nigeria, Federation of, West Africa 8 30N 8 0E
43 Nigg B., Scotland, U.K. 57 41N 4 5W
147 Nightcaps, New Zealand 45 57s 168 14E
76 Nigrita, Greece 40 56N 23 29E
104 Nihtaur, India 29 27N 78 23E
114 Nii-jima, I., Japan 34 20N 139 15E
114 Niigata, Japan 37 58N 139 0E
114 Niigata, pref., Japan 37 15N 138 45E
114 Niihama, Japan 33 55N 133 10E
158 Niihau, I., Hawaii, U.S.A. 21 55N 160 10W
65 Nijar, Spain 36 53N 2 15W
54 Nijkerk, Netherlands 52 13N 5 30E
55 Nijlen, Belgium 51 10N 4 40E
54 Nijmegen, Netherlands 51 50N 5 52E
125 Nike, Nigeria 6 26N 7 29E
82 Nikel, U.S.S.R. 69 30N 30 5E
109 Nikiniki, Indonesia 9 40s 124 30E
76 Nikitas, Greece 40 17N 23 34E
86 Nikitinka, U.S.S.R. 55 28N 33 20E
125 Nikki, Dahomey 9 58N 3 21E
114 Nikko, Japan 36 45N 139 35E
74 Nikola Pass, Bulgaria 43 25N 22 38E
88 Nikolayev, U.S.S.R. 46 58N 32 7E
91 Nikolayevsk, U.S.S.R. 53 40N 140 50E
87 Nikolayevskiy, U.S.S.R. 50 10N 45 35E
87 Nikolsk, U.S.S.R. 59 30N 45 28E
91 Nikolskoye, U.S.S.R. 47 50N 131 5E
75 Nikopol, Bulgaria 43 43N 24 54E
88 Nikopol, U.S.S.R. 47 35N 34 25E
88 Niksar, Turkey 40 31N 37 2E
101 Nikshah, Iran 26 15N 60 10E
74 Nikšić, Yugoslavia 42 50N 18 57E
167 Niland, U.S.A. 33 16N 115 30W
126 Nile R., Africa 27 30N 30 30E
126 Nile Delta, Egypt 31 40N 31 0E
160 Niles, Ohio, U.S.A. 41 8N 80 40W
106 Nilgiri Hills, India 11 30N 76 30E
173 Nilopolis, Brazil 22 45s 43 35W
104 Nimach, India 24 30N 74 50E
104 Nimar, India 21 49N 76 22E
104 Nimbahera, India 24 37N 74 45E
51 Nîmes, France 43 50N 4 23E
76 Nimfaíon, Akra C., Gr. 40 5N 24 20E
138 Nimingarra, W. Australia 20 31s 119 55E
143 Nimmitabel, Australia 36 29s 149 15E
127 Nimule, Sudan 3 32N 32 3E
71 Nin, Yugoslavia 44 16N 15 12E
156 Ninemile, Alaska, U.S.A. 56 0N 130 7W
45 Ninemilehouse, Ireland 52 28N 7 29W
146 Ninety Mile Beach, N.I., New Zealand 34 45s 173 0E
143 Ninety Mile Beach, The, Vic., Austral. 38 30s 147 10E
100 Nineveh, site, Iraq 36 25N 43 10E
35 Ninfield, England, U.K. 50 53N 0 26E
112 Ningan, China 44 16N 129 30E
112 Ninghsien, China 35 35N 107 58E
112 Ninghwa, China 32 58N 119 59E
113 Ningming, China 22 10N 107 10E
113 Ningpo, China 29 50N 121 30E
113 Ningshen, China 33 11N 108 45E
112 Ningsia Hui, Auto. Reg., China 37 20N 106 0E
113 Ningteh, China 26 45N 120 0E
103 Ningtsin China 29 44N 98 28E
112 Ningtsin, China 37 40N 115 0E
113 Ningtu, China 26 25N 115 45E
112 Ningwu, China 39 2N 112 15E
107 Ninh Binh, N. Vietnam 20 15N 105 55E
113 Ninkiang, China 32 50N 106 20E
54 Ninove, Belgium 50 51N 4 2E
173 Nioaque, Brazil 21 5s 55 50W
164 Niobrara, U.S.A. 42 48N 97 59W
164 Niobrara, R., U.S.A. 42 30N 103 0W
124 Nioro, Mali 15 30N 9 30W
124 Nioro du Rip, Senegal 13 40N 15 50W
50 Niort, France 46 19N 0 29W
125 Niou, Upper Volta 12 42N 2 1W
144 Nipan, Queens., Austral. 24 45s 150 0E
106 Nipani, India 16 20N 74 25E
157 Nipawin, Canada 53 20N 104 0W
154 Nipigon, Canada 49 0N 88 17W
154 Nipigon L., Ont., Can. 49 40N 88 30W
154 Nipissing L., Canada 46 20N 79 40W
167 Nipomo, U.S.A. 35 4N 120 29W
126 Niqrib, Gebel, Egypt 22 52N 34 57E
175 Niquelândia, Brazil 14 33s 48 23W
106 Nira, R., India 18 5N 74 25E
98 Nirim, Israel 31 14N 34 21E
106 Nirmal, India 19 3N 78 20E
105 Nirmali, India 26 20N 86 35E
74 Nis, Yugoslavia 43 19N 21 58E
63 Nisa, Portugal 39 30N 7 41W
60 Nisa, R., Poland 51 20N 15 0E
99 Nisab, South Yemen 14 25N 46 29E
74 Nišava, R., Yugoslavia 43 20N 22 10E
73 Niscemi, Sicily, Italy 37 8N 14 21E
114 Nishinomiya, Japan 34 45N 135 20E
77 Nisiros, I., Greece 36 35N 27 12E
60 Nisko, Poland 50 35N 22 7E
80 Nissafors, Sweden 57 24N 13 34E
144 Nissan I., Terr. of New Guinea 4 30s 154 10E
81 Nissan R., Sweden 57 15N 13 30E
79 Nissedal, Norway 59 10N 8 30E
79 Nisser L., Norway 59 7N 8 28E
81 Nissum Fd., Denmark 56 23N 8 11E
55 Nister R., Germany 50 42N 7 46E
155 Nitchequon, Canada 53 10N 70 58W
173 Niteroi, Brazil 22 52s 43 0W
41 Nith R., Scot., U.K. 55 20N 3 5W
41 Nithsdale, Scot., U.K. 55 14N 3 50W
109 Nitibe, Indonesia 9 30s 123 58E
34 Niton, England U.K. 50 35N 1 14W
59 Nitra, Czechoslovakia 48 19N 18 4E
59 Nitra R., Cz. 48 30N 18 7E
136 Niue I. (Savage I.), Pacific Ocean 19 2s 169 54W
108 Niut Mt., Indonesia 0 55N 109 30E
54 Nivelles, Belgium 50 35N 4 20E
49 Nivernais, prov., Fr. 47 0N 3 40E
166 Nixon, Nev., U.S.A. 39 54N 119 22W
165 Nixon, Tex., U.S.A. 29 17N 97 45W
106 Nizam Sagar L., India 18 10N 77 58E
106 Nizamabad, India 18 45N 78 7E
103 Nizamghat, India 28 20N 95 45E
91 Nizhne Angarsk, U.S.S.R. 56 0N 109 30E
91 Nizhne Kamenka, U.S.S.R. 52 20N 136 30E
91 Nizhne, Kolymsk, U.S.S.R. 68 40N 160 55E
88 Nizhnegorskiy, U.S.S.R. 45 27N 34 38E
91 Nizhneudinsk U.S.S.R. 55 0N 99 20E
89 Nizhniy Baskunchak, U.S.S.R. 48 16N 46 52E
87 Nizhni Novgorod, U.S.S.R. 56 20N 44 0E
87 Nizhniy Lamov, U.S.S.R. 53 34N 43 38E
90 Nizhniy Tagil, U.S.S.R. 57 45N 60 0E
59 Nizké Tatry, Mts., Cz. 48 55N 20 0E
70 Nizza Monferrato, Italy 44 46N 8 22E
132 Njakwa, Malawi 11 1s 33 56E
74 Njegoš, Mt., Yugoslavia 42 55N 18 45E
131 Njombe, Tanzania 9 0s 34 35E
131 Njombe, dist., Tanzania 9 20s 34 49E
131 Njombe R., Tanzania 7 15s 34 30E
80 Njupeskärs, Sweden 61 40N 12 31E
80 Njurunda, Sweden 62 17N 17 20E
132 Nkala, Zambia 15 55s 26 0E
125 Nkambe, Cameroon 6 35N 10 40E
132 Nkana, Zambia 13 0s 28 8E
135 Nkandla, Natal, S. Afr. 28 38s 31 8E
125 Nkawkaw, Ghana 6 36N 0 49W
132 Nkeyema, Zambia 14 58s 25 35E
132 Nkhata Bay, Malawi 11 33s 34 16E
132 Nkhota Kota, Malawi 12 55s 34 15E
125 Nkongsamba, Cam. 4 55N 9 55E
132 Nkunka, Zambia 14 57s 25 58E
135 Nkwalini, Natal, S. Afr. 28 45s 31 33E
124 Nkwanta, Ghana 6 10N 2 10W
103 Nmai Pit, R., Burma 25 30N 98 0E
125 Nnewi, Nigeria 6 0N 6 59E
174 Noanamó, Colombia 4 42N 76 56W
14 Noatak, R., Alaska, U.S.A. 68 0N 161 0W
46 Nobber, Ireland 53 49N 6 45W
160 Nobel, Canada 45 25N 80 4W
114 Nobeoka, Japan 32 36N 131 41E
64 Noblejas, Spain 39 58N 3 26W
134 Noblesfontein, S. Africa 31 46s 23 8E
162 Noblesville, U.S.A. 40 1N 85 59W
70 Noce R., Italy 46 22N 11 0E
73 Nocera Inferiore, Italy 40 45N 14 37E
73 Nocera Terinese, Italy 39 2N 16 9E
71 Nocera Umbra, Italy 43 8N 12 47E
73 Noci, Italy 40 47N 17 7E
145 Nockatunga, Queens., Australia 27 46s 142 36E
165 Nocona, U.S.A. 33 48N 97 45W
78 Nocrich, Rumania 45 55N 24 26E
91 Noda, U.S.S.R. 47 30N 142 5E
165 Noel, U.S.A. 36 36N 94 29W
168 Nogales (Heroica), Mex. 31 36N 94 29W
167 Nogales, Ariz., U.S.A. 31 33N 110 59W
114 Nogata, Japan 33 48N 130 54E
49 Nogent-en-Bassigny, Fr. 48 0N 5 20E
48 Nogent le Rotrou, Fr. 48 20N 0 50E
49 Nogent-sur-Seine, Fr. 48 30N 3 30E
142 Noggerup, W. Australia 33 32s 116 5E
87 Noginsk, U.S.S.R. 55 50N 38 25E
91 Noginsk, Sib., U.S.S.R. 64 30N 90 50E
172 Nogoya, Argentina 32 24s 59 50W
59 Nógrád, Co., Hungary 48 0N 19 30E
62 Nogueira de Ramuin, Spain 42 21N 7 43W
64 Noguera Pallaresa, R., Spain 42 15N 1 0E
64 Noguera Ribagorzana, R., Spain 42 15N 0 45E
104 Nohar, India 29 11N 74 49E
107 Noi R., Thailand 14 50N 100 15E
48 Noires Mts., France 48 11N 3 40W
50 Noirétable, France 45 48N 3 46E
48 Noirmoutier, France 47 0N 2 15W
48 Noirmoutier, I. de, Fr. 46 58N 2 10W
102 Nok Kundi, W. Pak. 28 50N 62 45E
91 Nokhtuisk, U.S.S.R. 60 0N 117 45E
83 Nokia, Finland 61 30N 23 20E
157 Nokomis, Canada 51 35N 105 0W
81 Nol, Sweden 57 56N 12 8E
130 Nola, Cent. Afr. Rep. 3 35N 16 10E
73 Nola, Italy 40 54N 14 29E
49 Nolay, France 46 58N 4 35E
80 Nolby, Sweden 62 17N 17 26E
70 Noli, C. di, Italy 44 12N 8 26E
87 Nolinsk, U.S.S.R. 57 28N 49 57E
130 Noma, Angola 9 30s 20 42E
143 Nombinnie, Australia 32 56s 145 53E
14 Nome, Alaska, U.S.A. 64 30N 165 30W
48 Nonancourt, France 48 47N 1 11E
48 Nonant le Pin, France 48 42N 0 12E
144 Nonda, Australia 20 40s 142 28E
107 Nong Khae, Thailand 14 29N 100 53E
107 Nong Khai, Thailand 17 50N 102 46E
135 Nongoma, Natal, S. Afr. 27 53s 31 42E
168 Nonoava, Mexico 27 22N 106 38W
77 Nonólithos, Greece 36 8N 27 46E
50 Nontron, France 45 31N 0 40E
143 Noojee, Vic., Australia 37 57s 146 1E
164 Noonan, U.S.A. 48 51N 102 59W
145 Noondoo, Australia 28 35s 148 30E
54 Noord Beveland I., Neth. 51 45N 3 50E
54 Noordost Polder, Neth. 52 45N 5 45E
156 Nootka I., Canada 49 40N 126 50W
130 Noqui, Angola 5 55s 13 30E
80 Nora, Sweden 59 32N 15 7E
127 Nora I., Ethipia 16 6N 40 4E
143 Norah Head, N.S.W., Australia 33 15s 151 35E
154 Noranda, Canada 48 20N 79 0E
80 Norberg, Sweden 60 4N 16 1E
82 Norbotten, prov., Swed. 66 58N 20 0E
71 Norcia, Italy 42 50N 13 5E
49 Nord, dépt., France 50 15N 3 30E
79 Nord Fd., Norway 61 55N 5 10E
79 Nordagutu, Norway 59 29N 9 20E
81 Nordborg, Denmark 55 5N 9 43E
81 Nordby, Fano I., Den. 55 27N 8 24E
81 Nordby, Samsö I., Den. 55 58N 10 32E
79 Norddal, Norway 62 15N 7 12E
79 Norddalsfjord, Norway 61 39N 5 25E
56 Norddeich, Germany 53 37N 7 10E
156 Nordegg, Canada 52 29N 116 5W
35 Nordelph, Eng., U.K. 52 34N 0 18E
56 Norden, Germany 53 35N 7 12E
56 Nordenham, Germany 53 29N 8 28E
79 Norderhov, Norway 60 7N 10 17E
56 Norderney, Germany 53 42N 7 9E
56 Norderney I., Germany 53 42N 7 15E
79 Nordfjord, Norway 61 49N 5 40E
56 Nordhausen, Germany 51 29N 10 47E
56 Nordhorn, Germany 52 27N 7 4E
19 Nordkapp (North Cape), Norway 71 15N 25 40E
19 Nordkinn, Norway 71 3N 28 0E
82 Nordland, co., Norway 67 0N 15 0E
57 Nördlingen, Germany 48 50N 10 30E
79 Nordmöre, dist., Nor. 62 56N 7 27E
56 Nordostsee Kanal, Ger. 54 5N 9 15E
79 Nordöyane I., Norway 62 45N 6 30E
56 Nordrdhein-Westfalen, land, Germany 51 45N 7 30E
56 Nordstrand I., Germany 54 27N 8 50E
91 Nordvik, U.S.S.R. 73 40N 110 57E
79 Nore, Norway 60 10N 8 56E
79 Norefjell, Mt., Norway 60 19N 9 24E
80 Noresund, Norway 60 11N 9 33E
35 Norfolk, co., Eng., U.K. 52 39N 1 0E
164 Norfolk, Nebr., U.S.A. 42 3N 97 25W
161 Norfolk, N.Y., U.S.A. 44 47N 75 1W
162 Norfolk, Va., U.S.A. 36 52N 76 15W
35 Norfolk Broads, England, U.K. 52 30N 1 15E
136 Norfolk I., Pac. Oc. 28 58s 168 3E
165 Norfork Res., U.S.A. 36 25N 92 0W
39 Norham, Eng., U.K. 55 44N 2 9W
91 Norilsk, U.S.S.R. 69 20N 88 0E
145 Norley, Queens., Austral. 27 45s 143 48E
164 Normal, U.S.A. 40 30N 89 0W
165 Norman, U.S.A. 35 12N 97 30W
144 Norman R., Australia 19 15s 142 10E
152 Norman Wells, Canada 65 40N 126 45W
146 Normanby, N.Z. 39 32s 174 18E
144 Normanby I., Papua 9 55s 151 0E
48 Normandie, Collines de, Mts., France 48 55N 0 45W
154 Normandin, Canada 48 49N 72 31W
48 Normandy, reg., Fr. 49 0N 0 0
142 Normanhurst, Mt., Western Australia 25 13s 122 30E
144 Normanton, Australia 17 40s 141 10E
39 Normanton, Eng., U.K. 53 41N 1 26W
142 Nornalup, W. Australia 34 57s 116 40E
176 Norquinco, Argentina 41 51s 70 55W
80 Norr Ulvön I., Sweden 63 5N 18 40E
81 Norrahammar, Sweden 57 49N 14 5E
81 Nörre Aaby, Denmark 55 27N 9 52E
81 Nörre Nebel, Denmark 55 47N 8 17E
81 Nörresundby Denmark 57 5N 9 52E
166 Norris, U.S.A. 45 40N 111 48W
161 Norristown, U.S.A. 40 9N 75 15W
81 Norrköping, Sweden 58 37N 16 17E
80 Norrtalje, Sweden 59 44N 18 46E
142 Norseman, W. Australia 32 8s 121 43E
81 Norsesund, Sweden 57 52N 12 30E
81 Norsholm, Sweden 58 31N 15 59E
79 Norsjö I., Sweden 64 53N 19 30E
91 Norsk, U.S.S.R. 52 30N 130 0E
15 North C., Antarctica 71 0N 166 0E
155 North C., Canada 47 2N 60 20W
19 North Cape, Norway 71 15N 25 40E
14 North C., Spitsbergen 80 40N 20 0E
131 North I., L. Rudolf, Kenya 4 5N 36 5E
146 North I., New Zealand 38 0s 175 0E
161 North Adams, U.S.A. 42 42N 73 6W
148 North America, Continent 40 0N 70 0W
107 North Andaman I., India 13 15N 92 40E
16 North Atlantic Ocean 30 0N 50 0W
42 North Ballachulish, Scotland, U.K. 56 42N 5 9W
157 North Battleford, Can. 52 50N 108 10W
154 North Bay, Ont., Can. 46 20N 79 30W
154 North Belcher Is., Can. 56 30N 79 0W
156 North Bend, Canada 49 50N 121 35W
166 North Bend, Ore., U.S.A. 43 28N 124 7W
160 North Bend, Pa., U.S.A. 41 20N 77 42W
41 North Berwick, Scotland, U.K. 56 4N 2 44W
161 North Berwick, U.S.A. 43 18N 70 43W
147 North Br. Ashburton R., New Zealand 43 30s 171 30E
165 North Canadian R., U.S.A. 36 48N 103 0W
154 North Caribou L., Can. 52 50E 90 50W
163 N. Carolina, st., U.S.A. 35 30N 80 0W
39 North Cave, Eng., U.K. 53 47N 0 40W
34 North Cerney, Eng., U.K. 51 46N 1 58W
14 North Channel, Br. Is. 55 0N 5 30W
154 North Channel, North America 46 0N 83 0W
162 North Chicago, U.S.A. 42 19N 87 50W
39 North Collingham, England, U.K. 53 8N 0 46W
164 North Dakota, st. U.S.A. 47 30N 100 0W
142 North Dandalup, W. Australia 32 30s 116 2E
29 N. Dorset Downs, England, U.K. 50 50N 2 30W
35 North Downs, England, U.K. 51 17N 0 30W
160 North East, U.S.A. 42 17N 79 50W
103 North East Frontier Agency, Assam, India 28 0N 95 0E
14 N.E. Land, Spitsbergen 80 0N 24 0E
144 N.E. New Guinea, Terr. of N. Guin. 5 30s 144 30E
43 North Esk, R., Scotland, U.K. 56 54N 2 45W
19 North European Plain 55 0N 25 0E
35 N. Foreland, Pt., England, U.K. 51 22N 1 28E
56 North Frisian Is., Ger. 54 50N 8 20E
42 N. Harris, dist., Scotland, U.K. 58 0N 6 55W
36 North Hill, Eng., U.K. 50 33N 4 26W
131 North Horr, Kenya 3 20N 37 8E
39 North Hykeham, England, U.K. 53 10N 0 35W
156 North Kamloops, Can. 50 40N 120 25W
43 North Kessock, Scotland, U.K. 57 30N 4 15W
160 North Kingsville, U.S.A. 41 53N 80 42W
157 North Knife L., Canada 58 0N 97 0W
105 North Koel R., India 23 50N 84 5E
112 North Korea, rep., Asia 40 0N 127 0E
103 N. Lakhimpur, India 27 15N 94 10E
167 N. Las Vegas, U.S.A. 36 15N 115 6W
147 North Mavora L., N.Z. 45 13s 168 11E
36 North Molton, England, United Kingdom 51 3N 3 48W

MAP
89 North Ossetian A.S.S.R., U.S.S.R. .43 30N 44 30E
167 North Palisade, U.S.A. 37 6N 118 32W
36 North Petherton, England, U.K. 51 6N 3 1W
164 North Platte, U.S.A. .41 10N 100 50W
166 North Platte R., U.S.A. 42 50N 106 50W
155 North Pt., P.E.I., Canada 47 5N 64 0W
14 North Pole, Arctic Reg. 90 0N 0 0E
166 North Powder, U.S.A. 45 2N 117 59W
41 North Queensferry Scotland, U.K. 56 1N 3 22W
39 North Riding, co., Yorks, Eng., U.K. .54 22N 1 30W
42 North Roe, dist., Scotland, U.K. 60 40N 1 22W
43 North Ronaldsay, Scotland, U.K. 59 20N 2 30W
44 North Sea, N.W. Eur. 56 0N 4 0E
39 North Shields, England, United Kingdom 55 1N 1 25W
39 North Somercotes, England, U.K. 53 28N 0 9E
44 North Sound, Ireland 53 10N 9 48W
43 North Sound, The, Scotland, U.K. 59 18N 2 45W
77 North Sporádes, Is., Gr. 39 0N 24 10E
39 North Sunderland England, U.K. 55 35N 1 40W
155 North Sydney Canada 46 12N 60 21W
146 N. Taranaki Bt., N.Z. 38 45S 174 20E
36 North Tawton, England, United Kingdom 50 48N 3 55W
42 North Thoresby, England, U.K. 53 27N 0 3W
34 North Tidworth, England, U.K. 51 14N 1 40W
42 North Tolsta, Scot., U.K. 58 21N 6 13W
160 N. Tonawanda, U.S.A. 43 5N 78 50W
161 North Troy, U.S.A. ...44 59N 72 24W
167 N. Truchas Pk., U.S.A. 36 0N 105 30W
154 North Twin I., Canada 53 20N 80 0W
42 North Uist I., Scotland, U.K. 57 40N 7 15W
156 North Vancouver, Can. 49 25N 123 20W
156 North Vermilion, Can. 58 25N 116 0W
162 North Vernon, U.S.A. 39 0N 85 35W
107 North Vietnam, st., Asia 22 0N 105 0E
169 North Vil'age, Bermuda 32 15N 64 45W
35 North Walsham, England, U.K. 52 49N 1 22E
142 N.W. Basin, W.Austral. 25 45S 115 0E
138 North West C., W. Australia 21 45S 114 9E
155 North West River, Can. 53 30N 60 10W
152 Northwest Terr., Can. 65 0N 100 0W
39 North York Moors, England, U.K. 54 25N 0 50W
36 Northallerton, Eng., U.K. 54 20N 1 26W
36 Northam, Eng., U.K. 51 2N 4 13W
133 Northam, Trans., S. Afr. 24 55S 27 15E
142 Northam, W. Australia 31 35S 116 42W
35 Northampton, Eng., U.K. 52 14N 0 54W
161 Northampton, Mass., U.S.A. 42 22N 72 39W
161 Northampton, Pa., U.S.A. 40 38N 75 24W
142 Northampton, W. Australia 28 21S 114 33E
35 Northampton, co., England, U.K. 52 16N 0 55W
144 Northampton Downs, Queensland, Austral. 24 35S 145 48E
161 Northbridge, U.S.A. ...42 12N 71 40W
142 Northcliffe, W. Austral. 34 38S 116 0E
169 Northeast Providence Channel, W. Indies 26 0N 76 0W
56 Northeim, Germany ...51 42N 10 0E
56 Northern Circars, India 17 30N 82 30E
46 Northern Ireland, U.K. 54 45N 7 0W
154 Northern Lights L., Can. 49 15N 90 45W
138 Northern Territory, Australia 16 0S 133 0E
164 Northfield, Minn. U.S.A. 44 37N 93 10W
35 Northfleet, Eng., U.K. 51 26N 0 20E
35 Northiam, Eng., U.K. 50 59N 0 39E
34 Northleach, Eng., U.K. 51 49N 1 50W
164 Northome, U.S.A. 47 53N 94 15W
37 Northop, Wales, U.K. 53 13N 3 8W
163 Northport, Ala., U.S.A. 33 15N 87 35W
162 Northport, Mich., U.S.A. 45 8N 85 39W
166 Northport, Wash., U.S.A. 48 57N 117 56W
35 Northrepps, Eng., U.K. 52 53N 1 20E
39 Northumberland, co. England, U.K. 55 12N 2 0W
144 Northumberland Is., Queens., Austral. ...21 45S 150 20E
155 Northumberland Str., Canada 46 20N 64 0W
169 N.W. Providence Chan., W. Indies 26 0N 78 0W
38 Northwich, Eng., U.K. 53 16N 2 30W
35 Northwold, Eng., U.K. 52 33N 0 37E
164 Northwood, Iowa, U.S.A. 43 27N 93 12W
164 Northwood, N.D., U.S.A. 47 44N 97 30W
35 Norton, England, U.K. 52 15N 0 52E
34 Norton, Worcs., Eng. U.K. 52 10N 2 10W
39 Norton, Yorks., England, U.K. 54 9N 0 48W
132 Norton, Rhodesia 17 52S 30 40E
164 Norton, Kans., U.S.A. 39 50N 100 0W
36 Norton Fitzwarren, England, U.K. 51 1N 3 10W
152 Norton Sd., Alas., U.S.A. 64 0N 165 0W
56 Nortorf, Germany 54 14N 10 47E
135 Norvalspont, S. Africa 30 38S 25 27E
161 Norwalk, Conn., U.S.A. 41 9N 73 25W
160 Norwalk, Ohio, U.S.A. 41 13N 82 38W
82 Norway, King., Eur. .67 0N 11 0E
162 Norway, U.S.A. 45 46N 87 57W
157 Norway House, Canada 53 55N 98 50W
15 Norwegian Dependency, Antarctica 66 0S 15 0E
16 Norwegian Sea, North Atlantic Ocean 66 0N 1 0E
160 Norwich, Canada 43 1N 80 39W
35 Norwich, Eng., U.K. .52 38N 1 17E
161 Norwich, Conn., U.S.A. 41 33N 72 5W
161 Norwich, N.Y., U.S.A. 42 32N 75 30W
160 Norwood, Canada 44 25N 77 59W
161 Norwood Mass., U.S.A. 42 10N 71 10W
75 Nos Emine, C., Bulgaria 42 40N 27 56E
75 Nos Kaliakra, C., Bulg. 43 21N 28 30E
81 Nosaby, Sweden 56 4N 14 6E
114 Noshiro R., Japan 40 15N 140 15E
90 Nosok, U.S.S.R. 70 10N 82 20E
86 Nosovka, U.S.S.R. 50 50N 31 30E
101 Norsratabad, Iran 29 55N 60 0E
43 Noss Hd., Scot., U.K. 58 29N 3 4W
42 Noss, I. of, Scot., U.K. 60 8N 1 1W
81 Nossebro, Sweden 58 12N 12 9E
129 Nossi-bé, I., Malagasy Rep. 13 25S 48 15E
129 Nossi Mitsiou, I., Malag. 12 55S 48 20E
134 Nossob, R., Africa 25 15S 20 30E
129 Nosy Varika, Malag. .20 35S 48 32E
124 Nota, Mali 15 20N 4 38W
157 Notigi Dam, Canada .56 35N 99 0W
156 Notikewin, Canada 56 55N 117 50W
77 Notios Evvoikós Kólpos, G., Greece .38 20N 24 0E
113 Notituchow, China 24 25N 107 20E
73 Noto, Italy 36 52N 15 4E
73 Noto, G. di, Sicily, Italy 36 50N 15 10E
79 Notodden, Norway 59 35N 9 14E
114 Noto-hanto, pen., Japan 37 0N 137 0E
155 Notre Dame, Canada .46 18N 64 46W
155 Notre Dame B., Canada 49 45N 55 30W
153 Notre Dame de Koartac, Canada 60 55N 69 40W
153 Notre Dame d'Ivugivic, Canada .62 20N 78 0W
160 Nottawasaga, B. Can. 44 40N 80 25W
155 Nottaway R., Canada 50 50N 78 20W
79 Nötteröy, Norway 59 15N 10 25E
39 Nottingham, Eng., U.K. 52 57N 1 10W
39 Nottingham, co., England, U.K. 53 10N 1 0W
135 Nottingham Rd., S. Afr. 29 22S 30 0E
162 Nottoway R., U.S.A. .37 0N 77 45W
55 Nottuln, Germany 51 57N 7 21E
133 Notwani R., Botswana 24 14S 26 20E
120 Nouadhibou, Mauritania 21 0N 17 0W
124 Nouakchott, Mauritania 18 20N 15 50W
136 Noumea, New Caledonia 22 17S 166 30E
43 Noup Hd., Scot., U.K. 59 20N 3 2W
135 Noupoort, S. Africa ...31 10S 24 57E
154 Nouveau Comptoir (Paint Hills), Can. .53 2N 78 55W
49 Nouzonville, France ...49 48N 4 44E
59 Nová Baňa, Cz. 48 28N 18 39E
58 Nova Byštrice, Cz. 49 2N 15 8E
130 Nova Chaves, Angola .10 50S 21 15E
175 Nova Cruz, Brazil 6 40S 35 25W
129 Nova Freixo, Mozambique 14 45S 36 22E
173 Nova Friburgo, Brazil 22 10S 42 30W
130 Nova Gaia, Angola 10 10S 17 35E
74 Nova Gradiška, Y.-slav. 45 17N 17 28E
175 Nova Granada, Brazil 20 30S 49 20W
173 Nova Iguaçu, Brazil ...22 45S 43 28W
117 Nova Iorque, Brazil ... 7 0S 44 5W
124 Nova Lamego, Portuguese Guinea .12 19N 14 11W
175 Nova Lima, Brazil 20 5S 44 0W
130 Nova Lisboa, Angola .12 42S 15 54E
132 Nova Lusitânia, Mozam. 19 50S 34 34E
132 Nova Mambone, Mozambique 21 0S 35 3E
71 Nova Mesto, Y.-slavia 45 47N 15 12E
58 Nova Paka, Cz. 50 29N 15 30E
60 Nova Ruda, Poland 50 36N 16 28E
109 Nova Sagres, Portuguese Timor ... 8 25S 127 15E
155 Nova Scotia, prov., Canada 45 10N 63 0W
130 Nova Sintra, Angola .12 9S 17 14E
132 Nova Sofala, Mozam. .20 7S 34 48E
175 Nova Venécia, Brazil .18 50S 40 30W
74 Nova Varos, Yugoslavia 43 29N 19 48E
75 Nova Zagora, Bulgaria 42 32N 25 59E
78 Novaci, Rumania 45 10N 23 42E
74 Novaci, Yugoslavia ...41 5N 21 29E
175 Novalorque, Brazil 6 48S 44 0W
70 Novara, Italy 45 27N 8 36E
84 Novaya Ladoga, U.S.S.R. 60 7N 32 16E
90 Novaya Lyalya, U.S.S.R. 58 50N 60 35E
90 Novaya Zemlya Is., U.S.S.R. 75 0N 56 0E
59 Nové Mésto, Cz. 49 33N 16 7E
65 Novelda, Spain 38 24N 0 45W
70 Novellara, Italy 44 50N 10 43E
71 Noventa, Vicentina, It. 45 18N 11 30E
86 Novgorod, U.S.S.R. ...58 30N 31 25E
86 Novgorod Severskiy, U.S.S.R. 52 2N 33 10E
86 Novgorod Volynski, U.S.S.R. 50 38N 27 47E
74 Novi Becej., Y.-slavia 45 36N 20 10E
71 Novi Grad, Y.-slavia .45 19N 13 33E
74 Novi Knezeua, Y.-slav. 46 4N 20 8E
70 Novi Ligure, Italy 45 45N 8 47E
75 Novi-Pazar, Bulgaria 43 25N 27 15E
74 Novi Pazar, Yugoslavia 43 12N 20 28E
74 Novi Sad, Yugoslavia 45 18N 19 52E
71 Novi Vinod, Y.-slavia 45 10N 14 48E
71 Novigrad, Yugoslavia 44 10N 15 32E
90 Novoataysk, U.S.S.R. 53 30N 84 0E
89 Novo Aleksandrovskaya, U.S.S.R. 45 29N 41 17E
87 Novo-Annenskiy, U.S.S.R. 50 32N 42 39E
173 Novo Hamburgo, Braz. 29 37S 51 7W
173 Novo Horizonte, Brazil 21 25S 49 10W
109 Novo Luso, Port Timor 4 3S 126 6E
130 Novo Redondo, Angola 11 10S 13 48E
74 Novo Selo, Bulgaria ...44 11N 22 47E
88 Novo Ukrainka, U.S.S.R. 46 25N 31 30E
87 Novo-Zavidovskiy, U.S.S.R. 56 32N 36 29E
86 Novobelitsa, U.S.S.R. 52 27N 31 2E
89 Novobogatinskoye, U.S.S.R. 47 26N 51 17E
89 Novocherkassk, U.S.S.R. 47 27N 40 5E
87 Novodevichye, U.S.S.R. 53 37N 48 58E
88 Novogeorgiyevsk, U.S.S.R. 49 4N 33 1E
86 Novograd Volynskiy, U.S.S.R. 50 40N 27 35E
86 Novogrudok, U.S.S.R. 53 40N 25 50E
90 Novokazalinsk, U.S.S.R. 45 40N 61 40E
87 Novokhopersk, U.S.S.R. 51 5N 41 50E
90 Novokuznetsk, U.S.S.R. 54 0N 87 10E
88 Novomirgorod, U.S.S.R. 48 57N 31 33E
88 Novomoskovsk, Ukraine, U.S.S.R. ...48 33N 35 17E
87 Novomoskovsk R.F.S.R., U.S.S.R. .54 5N 38 15E
89 Novorossiysk, U.S.S.R. 44 43N 37 52E
86 Novorzhev, U.S.S.R. .57 3N 29 25E
88 Novoselitsa, U.S.S.R. .48 14N 26 15E
89 Novoshakhtinsk, U.S.S.R. 47 39N 39 58E
90 Novosibirsk, U.S.S.R. 55 0N 83 5E
87 Novosil, U.S.S.R. 52 58N 36 58E
86 Novosokolniki, U.S.S.R. 56 33N 28 42E
84 Novotroitsk, U.S.S.R. 51 10N 58 15E
87 Novouzensk, U.S.S.R. 50 32N 48 17E
86 Novozybkov, U.S.S.R. 52 30N 32 0E
74 Novska, Yugoslavia ...45 19N 17 0E
88 Novy Bug, U.S.S.R. ...47 34N 34 29E
58 Novy Bydzov, Cz. 50 14N 15 29E
60 Novy Dwór, Poland ...52 26N 20 44E
59 Novy Jičin, Cz. 49 35N 18 0E
90 Novy Port, U.S.S.R. .67 40N 72 30E
87 Novyy Oskol, U.S.S.R. 50 44N 37 55E
101 Now Shahr, Iran 36 40N 51 40E
143 Nowa Nowa, Australia 37 44S 148 3E
60 Nowa Sól, Poland 51 48N 15 44E
60 Nowe, Poland 53 41N 18 44E
60 Nowe Miasto, Lódź, Pol. 51 38N 20 34E
60 Nowe Miasto, Lubowskie, Poland .53 27N 19 33E
60 Nowe Warpno, Poland 53 42N 14 18E
44 Nowen Hill, Ireland ...51 42N 9 15W
143 Nowendoc, Australia .31 32S 151 44E
103 Nowgong, India 26 20N 92 50E
143 Nowingi, Vic., Australia 34 33S 142 15E
60 Nowogard, Poland 53 41N 15 10E
60 Nowogród, Poland 53 14N 21 53E
143 Nowra, N.S.W., Austral. 34 53S 150 35E
102 Nowshera, W. Pakistan 34 0N 71 55E
142 Nowthanna Mt., W. Australia 27 0S 118 40E
60 Nowy Dwór, Bialystok, Poland ...53 40N 23 0E
60 Nowy Dwór Warszawa, Poland .52 27N 20 44E
60 Nowy Korczyn, Poland 50 19N 20 48E
59 Nowy Sacz, Poland ...49 40N 20 41E
60 Nowy Staw, Poland ...54 13N 19 2E
59 Nowy Targ, Poland ...49 30N 20 2E
60 Nowy Tomysl, Poland 52 19N 16 10E
161 Noxen, U.S.A. 41 25N 76 4E
166 Noxon, U.S.A. 48 0N 115 54W
62 Noya, Spain....42 48N 8 53W
48 Noyant, France 47 30N 0 6E
49 Noyers, France 47 40N 4 0E
157 Noyes, I., Alaska, U.S.A. 55 30N 133 40W
49 Noyon, France 49 34N 3 0E
135 Nqamakwe, S. Africa .32 13S 27 59E
135 Nqutu, Natal, S. Africa 28 13S 30 41E
129 Nriquinha, Angola 16 0S 21 25E
132 Nsanje, Malawi 16 55S 35 12E
125 Nsawam, Ghana 5 50N 0 24W
132 Nsomba, Zambia 10 45S 29 59E
125 Nsukka, Nigeria 7 0N 7 50E
135 Nsuze, Natal, S. Africa 28 32S 31 0E
132 Nuala, Zambia 13 22S 28 9E
132 Nuanetsi, Rhodesia ...21 15S 30 48E
132 Nuanetsi R., Rhodesia 21 10S 31 20E
125 Nuatja, Togo 7 0N 1 10E
127 Nuba Mts., Sudan 12 0N 31 0E
126 Nubian Desert, Sudan 21 30N 33 30E
109 Nuboai, Indonesia 2 10S 136 30E
174 Nudo Ausangate Mt., Peru 13 45S 71 10W
174 Nudo de Vilcanota, Peru 14 30S 70 0W
101 Nudushan, Iran 32 2N 53 20E
174 Nudo Coropuna, Mt., Peru 15 30S 72 30W
165 Nueces R., U.S.A. ...28 18N 98 39W
175 Nueltin L., Canada ...60 0N 100 0W
169 Nueva Gerona, I. de Pinos, Cuba 21 53N 82 49W
176 Nueva Imperial, Chile 38 45S 72 58W
172 Nueva Palmira, Urug. 33 52S 58 20W
168 Nueva Rosita, Mexico 28 0N 101 20W
168 Nuala San Salvador, Salvador 13 40N 89 25W
172 Nuéve de Julio, Arg. .35 30S 61 0W
169 Nuevitas, Cuba 21 30N 77 20W
176 Nuevo G., Argentina .43 0S 64 30W
168 Nuevo Laredo, Mexico 27 30N 99 40W
168 Nuevo Leon, st., Mex. 25 0N 100 0W
174 Nuevo Rocafuerte, Ecuador 0 55S 76 50W
147 Nugget Pt., N.Z. 46 27S 169 50E
126 Nugrus Gebel, Egypt 24 58N 39 34E
146 Nuhaka, New Zealand 39 3S 177 45E
109 Nuhurowa, I., Indon. . 5 30S 132 45E
109 Nuhutjuk, I., Indon. . 5 30S 133 5E
49 Nuits, France 47 10N 4 56E
49 Nuits St. George, Fr. .47 10N 4 56E
89 Nukha, U.S.S.R. 41 10N 47 5E
90 Nukus, U.S.S.R. 42 20N 59 40E
64 Nules, Spain 39 51N 0 9W
143 Nulla Nulla, Australia 33 47S 141 28E
138 Nullagine, W. Australia 21 53S 120 6E
142 Nullarbor, S. Australia 31 28S 130 55E
138 Nullarbor Plains, Austral. 31 20S 128 0E
125 Numan, Nigeria 9 29N 12 3E
55 Numansdorp, Neth. ...51 43N 4 26E
127 Numatinna R., Sudan 6 38N 27 15E
114 Numazu, Japan 35 7N 138 51E
55 Numbrecht, Germany 50 54N 7 32E
109 Numfoor, I., Indonesia 1 0S 134 50E
143 Numurkah, Australia .36 0S 145 26E
123 Nuna, W., Libya 29 37N 15 14E
155 Nunaksaluk, I., Canada 55 40N 60 12W
34 Nuneaton, Eng., U.K. 52 32N 1 29W
112 Nungan, China 44 29N 125 38E
142 Nungarin, W. Australia 31 21S 118 41E
131 Nungwe, Tanzania 2 48S 32 2E
152 Nunivak I., Alas., U.S.A. 60 0N 166 0W
112 Nunkiang, China 49 11N 125 12E
36 Nunney, Eng., U.K. ...51 13N 2 20W
54 Nunspeet, Netherlands 52 21N 5 45E
72 Nuoro, Italy 40 20N 9 20E
123 Nuqayy, Jabal, Libya 23 11N 19 30E
143 Nurcoung, Vic., Austral. 36 45S 141 42E
70 Nure, R., Italy 44 40N 9 32E
142 Nurina, W. Australia .30 55S 126 23E
145 Nuriootpa S., Australia 34 27S 139 0E
87 Nurlat, U.S.S.R. 54 29N 50 45E
57 Nürnberg (Nuremburg), Germany 49 26N 11 5E
72 Nurri, Sardinia, Italy .39 43N 9 13E
106 Nurzvid, India 16 47N 80 53E
109 Nusa Kambangan C., Indonesia 7 47S 109 0E
108 Nusa Tenggara, prov., Indon. 7 30S 117 0E
102 Nushki, W. Pakistan .29 35N 65 65E
153 Nutak, Canada 57 30N 61 59W
126 Nuwaiba, Egypt 28 58N 34 40E
105 Nuwakot, Nepal 28 10N 83 55E
106 Nuwara Eliya, Ceylon 6 58N 80 55E
133 Nuwe Smitsdorp, S. Afr. 24 8S 29 20E
134 Nuwerus, S. Africa 31 8S 18 24E
134 Nuweveldberge Mts., C. Prov., S. Africa .32 10S 21 45E
134 Nuy, C. Prov., S. Africa 33 41S 19 34E
138 Nuyts Arch., S. Australia 32 12S 133 20E
79 Ny Hellesund, Norway 58 3N 7 47E
124 Nyaake (Webo), Liberia 4 52N 7 37W
142 Nyabing, W. Australia 33 30S 118 7E
161 Nyack, U.S.A. 41 5N 73 57W
80 Nyadal, Sweden 62 48N 17 59E
90 Nyagyn, U.S.S.R. 62 8N 63 36E
143 Nyah, Vic., Australia .35 12S 143 25E
143 Nyah West, Victoria, Australia 35 11S 143 21E
131 Nyahua, Tanzania 5 25S 33 23E
131 Nyakanazi, Tanzania . 3 2S 31 10E
125 Nyakrom, Ghana 5 40N 0 50W
127 Nyala, Sudan 12 2N 24 58E
135 Nyaliza, Natal, S. Africa 27 34S 31 32E
132 Nyamandhlovu, Rhod. 19 55S 28 16E
131 Nyambiti, Tanzania ... 2 48S 33 27E
132 Nyangwena, Zambia .15 18S 28 45E
132 Nyanje, Zambia 14 25S 31 46E
125 Nyankpala, Ghana 9 21N 0 58W
131 Nyanza, Rwanda 2 20S 29 42E
131 Nyanza Reg., Kenya . 0 10S 34 15E
132 Nyasa L., E. Africa 12 0S 34 30E
107 Nyaunglebin, Burma .17 52N 96 42E
130 Nyavikungu, Congo ...11 26S 25 56E
132 Nyazwidzi R., Rhod. .19 35S 32 0E
81 Nyborg, Denmark 55 20N 10 49E
81 Nybro, Sweden 56 44N 15 55E
43 Nybster, Scot., U.K. .58 34N 3 6W
90 Nyda, U.S.S.R. 66 40N 73 10E
111 Nyenchen, mts., Tibet, China 30 0N 87 0E
103 Nyenchen Tanglha Ra., China 30 30N 95 0E
132 Nyengo Swamp, Zam. 14 45S 23 0E
131 Nyeri, & dist., Kenya 0 23S 36 56E
127 Nyerol, Sudan 8 41N 32 1E
80 Nyhem, Sweden 62 54N 15 40E
127 Nyiel, Sudan 6 9N 31 4E
132 Nyika Plat., Malawi ...10 30S 36 0E
132 Nyimba, Zambia 14 33S 30 49E
124 Nyinahin, Ghana 6 43N 2 3W
59 Nyirbátor, Hungary ...47 49N 22 9E
59 Nyiregyháza, Hungary 48 0N 21 47E
131 Nyiru Mt., Kenya 2 11N 36 49E
79 Nykirke, Norway 59 53N 9 50E
81 Nyköbing, Holbæk, Denmark 55 57N 11 44E
81 Nyköbing, Maribo, Den. 54 46N 11 52E
81 Nyköbing, Tisted, Den. 56 49N 8 50E
81 Nyköping, Sweden 58 45N 17 0E
80 Nykroppa, Sweden 59 37N 14 18E
80 Nykvarn, Sweden 59 11N 17 25E
133 Nyl Vlei R., S. Africa 24 15S 29 0E
80 Nyland, Sweden 62 59N 17 43E
133 Nylstroom, S. Africa .24 42S 28 22E
58 Nymburk, Cz. 50 10N 15 1E
81 Nymindegab, Denmark 55 50N 8 12E
80 Nynäshamn, Sweden .58 58N 18 0E
143 Nyngan, N.S.W., Australia 31 30S 147 8E
57 Nyon, Switzerland 46 23N 6 14E
51 Nyons, France 44 22N 5 10E
143 Nyora, Vic., Australia 38 20S 145 41E
81 Nyord, Denmark 55 4N 12 28E
60 Nysa, Poland 50 40N 17 22E
166 Nyssa, U.S.A. 43 56N 117 2W
81 Nysted, Denmark 54 40N 11 44E
131 Nzega, & dist., Tanzania 4 10S 33 12E

124 Nzérékoré, Guinea 7 49N 8 48W
130 N'zilo Dam, Congo 10 30S 25 45E
130 N'zilo Falls, Congo 10 18S 25 27E
131 Nzima, Tanzania 3 8S 32 30E
131 Nzubuka, Tanzania 4 45S 32 50E

O

114 O Shima, I., Japan 34 45N 139 25E
40 Oa, Mull of, Scot., U.K. 55 35N 6 20W
40 Oa, The Pen., Scot., U.K. 55 36N 6 17W
34 Oadby, Eng., U.K. 52 37N 1 7W
164 Oacoma, U.S.A. 43 50N 99 26W
164 Oahe, U.S.A. 44 33N 100 29W
164 Oahe Dam, U.S.A. 44 28N 100 25W
164 Oahe Res, U.S.A. 45 30N 100 15W
137 Oahu I., Hawaii, U.S.A. 21 30N 158 0W
166 Oak Creek, U.S.A. 40 15N 106 59W
166 Oak Harb., U.S.A. 48 20N 122 38W
157 Oak Lake, Canada 49 45N 100 45W
162 Oak Park, U.S.A. 41 55N 87 45W
163 Oak Ridge, Ten., U.S.A. 36 1N 84 5W
145 Oakbank, S. Australia 33 0S 140 20E
167 Oakdale, Calif., U.S.A. 37 49N 120 56W
165 Oakdale, La., U.S.A. .30 50N 92 38W
34 Oakengates, Eng., U.K. 52 42N 2 29W
164 Oakes, U.S.A. 46 14N 98 4W
166 Oakesdale, U.S.A. 47 11N 117 9W
145 Oakey, Queens., Austral. 27 25S 151 43E
35 Oakham, Eng., U.K. .52 40N 0 43W
162 Oakhill, U.S.A. 38 0N 81 7W
166 Oakland, Calif., U.S.A. 37 50N 122 18W
162 Oakland City, U.S.A. .38 20N 87 20W
143 Oaklands, N.S.W., Australia 35 34S 146 10E
143 Oakleigh, Vic., Austral. 37 54S 145 6E
166 Oakley, U.S.A. 42 14N 113 55W
166 Oakridge, U.S.A. 43 47N 122 31W
165 Oakwood, U.S.A. 31 35N 95 47W
147 Oamaru, New Zealand 45 5S 170 59E
78 Oancea, Rumania 45 4N 28 7E
15 Oates Coast, Antarctica 69 0S 160 0E
134 Oatlands, S. Africa 32 48S 24 18E
167 Oatman, U.S.A. 35 1N 114 19W
168 Oaxaca, Mexico 17 2N 96 40W
168 Oaxaca, st., Mexico ...17 0N 97 0W
90 Ob, G. of, U.S.S.R. ...70 0N 73 0E
90 Ob, R., U.S.S.R. 62 40N 66 0E
154 Oba, Canada 49 4N 84 7W
125 Obala, Cameroon 4 9N 11 32E
147 Oban, New Zealand ...46 55S 168 10E
40 Oban, Scotland, U.K. 56 25N 5 30W
154 Obatogamau L., Can. .49 34N 74 26W
99 Obbia, Somali Rep. ... 5 25N 48 30E
134 Obbogora, S. Africa ...27 19S 20 4E
156 Obed, Canada 53 30N 117 10W
101 Obeh, Afghanistan ...34 28N 63 10E
58 Ober Österreich (Upper Austria) prov., Aust.48 17N 13 45E
55 Oberpleis, Germany ...50 43N 7 17E
173 Obera, Argentina 27 21S 55 2W
57 Oberammergau, Ger. .47 35N 11 3E
58 Oberdrauburg, Austria 46 44N 12 58E
56 Oberhausen, Germany 51 28N 6 50E
57 Oberkirch, Germany .48 31N 8 5E
164 Oberlin, Kan., U.S.A. 39 52N 100 31W
165 Oberlin, La., U.S.A. ...30 42N 92 42W
160 Oberlin, Ohio, U.S.A. .41 15N 82 10W
49 Obernai, France 48 28N 7 30E
57 Oberndorf, Germany .48 17N 8 35E
143 Oberon, N.S.W., Austral. 33 43S 149 52E
57 Oberpfalzer, Wald, Mts., Germany 49 30N 12 25E
57 Oberstdorf, Germany .47 25N 10 16E
109 Obi Latu, I., Indonesia 1 20S 127 20E
125 Obiaruku, Nigeria 5 51N 6 9E
175 Obidos, Brazil 1 50S 55 30W
63 Obidos, Portugal 39 19N 9 10W
114 Obihiro, Japan 42 55N 143 10E
89 Obilnoye, U.S.S.R. 47 32N 44 30E
56 Öbisfelde, Germany ...52 27N 10 57E
50 Objat, France 45 16N 1 24E
91 Obluche, U.S.S.R. 49 10N 130 50E
127 Obo, Cent. Afr. Rep. . 5 20N 26 32E
127 Obock, Fr. Terr. of the Afars & Issas ...12 0N 43 20E
60 Oborniki, Poland 52 39N 16 59E
127 Obot, Ethiopia 4 32N 37 13E
125 Obout, Cameroon 3 28N 11 47E
87 Oboyan, U.S.S.R. 51 20N 36 28E
84 Obozerskaya, U.S.S.R. 63 20N 40 15E
74 Obrenovac, Yugoslavia 44 40N 20 11E
44 O'Briensbridge, Ireland 52 46N 8 30W
71 Obrovac, Yugoslavia .44 11N 15 41E
19 Obshchi Syrt, U.S.S.R. 52 0N 53 0E
125 Obuasi, Ghana 6 17N 1 40W
125 Obubra, Nigeria 6 8N 8 20E
163 Ocala, U.S.A. 29 11N 82 5W
168 Ocampo, Mexico 28 9N 108 8W
174 Ocaña, Colombia 8 15N 73 20W
64 Ocaña, Spain 39 55N 3 30W
164 Ocanomowoc, U.S.A. .43 7N 88 30W
165 Ocate, U.S.A. 36 12N 104 59W
162 Ocean City, N.J., U.S.A. 39 18N 74 34W
156 Ocean Falls, Canada .52 25N 127 40W
136 Ocean I., Pacific Ocean 0 45S 169 50E
166 Ocean Park, U.S.A. ...46 30N 124 2W
166 Oceanlake, U.S.A. 45 0N 124 0W
161 Oceanport, U.S.A. 40 20N 74 3W
167 Oceanside, U.S.A. 33 13N 117 26W
64 Ochagavia, Spain 42 55N 1 5W
88 Ochakov, U.S.S.R. 46 35N 31 30E
89 Ochamchire, U.S.S.R. 42 46N 41 32E
41 Ochil Hills, Scot., U.K. 56 14N 3 40W
40 Ochiltree, Scot., U.K. 55 26N 4 23W
57 Ochsenfurt, Germany .49 38N 10 3E
163 Ocilla, U.S.A. 31 35N 83 12W
80 Ockelbo, Sweden 60 51N 16 40E
163 Ocmulgee R., U.S.A. .32 0N 83 19W
74 Ocna-de-Fier, Rum. .45 21N 21 47E
78 Ocna Mure Sului, Rum. 46 23N 23 49E
78 Ocna-Sibiului, Rum. .45 52N 24 2E
78 Ocnele Mari, Rumania 45 8N 24 18E
163 Oconee R., U.S.A. 32 30N 82 55W
162 Oconto, U.S.A. 44 52N 87 53W
162 Oconto Falls, U.S.A. .44 52N 88 10W
169 Ocotal, Honduras 13 41N 86 41W
168 Ocotlán, Mexico 20 21N 102 42W
62 Ocreza, R. ,Portugal .39 50N 7 35W
59 Ócsa, Hungary 47 17N 19 15E
167 Octave, U.S.A. 34 10N 112 43W
48 Octeville, France 49 38N 1 40W
91 October Revolution I., U.S.S.R. 79 30N 97 0E
174 Ocumare del Tuy, Ven. 10 7N 66 46W
109 Ocussi, Port Timor 9 20S 124 30E
125 Oda, Ghana 5 50N 1 5W
82 Odadahraun, dist., Ice. 65 5N 17 0W
81 Ödåkra, Sweden 56 9N 12 37E
114 Odawara, Japan 35 20N 139 6E
81 Odby, Denmark 56 37N 8 31E
79 Odda, Norway 60 3N 6 35E
81 Odder, Denmark 55 58N 10 10E
82 Oddeyri, Iceland 64 50N 18 5W
127 Oddobo, Ethiopia 12 21N 42 6E
81 Ödeborg, Sweden 58 33N 12 0E
63 Odemirã, Portugal 37 35N 8 40W
100 Odemis, Turkey 38 15N 28 0E
135 Odendaalsrus, S. Afr. .27 48S 26 43E
81 Odense Amt, co., Denmark 55 22N 10 20E
56 Odenwald, Mt., W. Ger. 49 18N 9 0E
56 Oder R., Germany 53 0N 14 12E
71 Oderzo, Italy 45 47N 12 29E
81 Odessa, Ont., Canada .44 16N 76 42W
165 Odessa, Tex., U.S.A. .31 51N 102 23W
166 Odessa, Wash., U.S.A. 47 25N 118 35W
88 Odessa, U.S.S.R. 46 30N 30 45E
63 Odiel R., Spain 37 30N 6 55W
124 Odienné, Ivory Coast . 9 30N 7 34W
34 Odiham, Eng., U.K. ...51 16N 0 56W
125 Odoben, Ghana 5 38N 0 56E
78 Odobești, Rumania ...45 43N 27 4E
165 O'Donnell, U.S.A. 33 0N 101 48W
78 Odorhei, Rumania 46 21N 25 21E
87 Odóyevo, U.S.S.R. ...53 48N 36 6E
59 Odra, R., Cz. 49 43N 17 47E
60 Odra, R., Poland 52 40N 14 28E
62 Odra, R., Spain 42 30N 4 15W
81 Ödum, Denmark 56 18N 10 8E
74 Odžaci, Yugoslavia 45 30N 19 17E
74 Odžak, Yugoslavia 45 3N 18 18E
132 Odzi, Rhodesia 19 0S 32 20E
55 Oedt, Germany 51 19N 6 23E
55 Oeflelt, Netherlands ...51 42N 5 56E
175 Oeiras, Brazil 7 0S 42 5W
63 Oeiras, Portugal 38 41N 9 18W
164 Oelrichs, U.S.A. 43 11N 103 14W
56 Oelsnitz, Germany 50 24N 12 11E
164 Oelwein, U.S.A. 42 39N 91 55W
55 Oer-Erkenschwick, Ger. 51 40N 7 15E
73 Ofanto R., Italy 41 8N 15 50E
125 Offa, Nigeria 8 13N 4 42E
45 Offaly, co., Ire. 53 15N 7 30W
57 Offenbach, Germany .50 6N 8 46E
57 Offenburg, Germany .48 27N 7 56E
80 Offerdal, Sweden 63 28N 14 3E
71 Offida, Italy 42 56N 13 40E
48 Offranville, France 49 52N 1 0E
77 Ofidhoúsa, I., Greece .36 33N 26 8E
82 Ofot Fd., Norway 68 27N 17 0E
154 Ogahalla, Canada 50 6N 85 51W
114 Ogaki, Japan 35 25N 136 35E
162 Ogallala, U.S.A. 41 12N 101 40W
125 Ogbomosho, Nigeria ... 8 1N 3 29E
34 Ogbourne, Eng., U.K. 51 27N 1 43W
164 Ogden, Iowa, U.S.A. .42 3N 94 0W
166 Ogden, Utah, U.S.A. .41 13N 112 1W
161 Ogdensburg, N.Y., U.S.A. 44 40N 75 27W
163 Ogeechee R., U.S.A. ...32 30N 81 32W
133 Ogies, Trans., S. Africa 26 2S 29 4E
70 Oglio R., Italy 45 15N 10 15E
144 Ogmore, Australia 22 37S 149 35E
37 Ogmore R., Wales, U.K. 51 29N 3 37W
37 Ogmore Vale, Wales, U.K. 51 35N 3 32W
79 Ogna, Norway 58 34N 5 44E
49 Ognon R., France 47 43N 6 32E
125 Ogoja, Nigeria 6 38N 8 39E
154 Ogoki, Canada 51 35N 86 0W
154 Ogoki Res., Canada ...50 45N 88 15W
128 Ogooué, R., Gabon 1 0S 10 0E
75 Ogosta. R., Bulgaria .43 35N 23 35E
134 Ograbies, S. Africa ...29 17S 17 7E
74 Ogražden, Ra., Y.-slav. 41 30N 22 50E
126 Ogrein, Sudan 17 55N 34 50E
71 Ogulin, Yugoslavia ...45 16N 15 16E
125 Oguta, Nigeria 5 44N 6 44E
125 Ogwashi-Uku, Nigeria 6 15N 6 30E
125 Ogwe, Nigeria 5 0N 7 14E
147 Ohai, New Zealand 44 55S 168 0E
147 Ohau, L., New Zealand 44 15S 169 53E
146 Ohaupo, New Zealand 37 56S 175 20E
54 Ohey, Belgium 50 26N 5 8E
172 O'Higgins, prov., Chile 34 15S 71 1W
162 Ohio, st., U.S.A. 40 20N 83 0W
162 Ohio R., U.S.A. 38 0N 86 0W
146 Ohiwa Harbour, N.Z. .37 59S 177 10E
58 Ohre R., Czechoslovakia 50 10N 12 30E
74 Ohrid, Yugoslavia 41 8N 20 52E
133 Ohrigstad, S. Africa ...24 41S 30 36E
57 Öhringen, Germany ...49 11N 9 31E
146 Ohura, New Zealand .38 51S 174 59E
160 Oil City, U.S.A. 41 26N 79 40W
45 Oilgate, Ireland 52 25N 6 30W
91 Oimyakon, U.S.S.R. ...63 25N 143 10E
77 Oinousa, I., Greece ...38 33N 26 14E
90 Oirot Tura, U.S.S.R. .51 50N 86 5E
49 Oise, dépt., France 49 28N 2 30E
49 Oise R., France 49 53N 3 50E
55 Oisterwijk, Netherlands 51 35N 5 12E
114 Oita, Japan 33 15N 131 36E
114 Oita, pref., Japan 33 0N 131 30E
167 Ojai, U.S.A. 34 28N 119 16W
172 Ojo der Aqua, Argentina 29 30S 63 44W
168 Ojocaliente, Mexico ...30 25N 106 30W
176 Ojos del Salado, Argentina 27 0S 68 40W
87 Oka R., U.S.S.R. 54 50N 38 0E
129 Okahandja, S.W. Africa 22 0S 16 59E
146 Okahukura, N.Z. 38 48N 175 14E
146 Okaihau, N.Z. 35 19S 173 36E
146 Okakune, N.Z. 39 26S 175 24E
156 Okanagan L., Canada 50 0N 119 30W
166 Okanogan, U.S.A. 48 24N 119 24W
166 Okanogan R., U.S.A. .48 40N 119 24W
59 Okany, Hungary 46 52N 21 21E
104 Okara, West Pakistan 30 50N 73 25E
147 Okarito, New Zealand 43 15S 170 9E
146 Okato, New Zealand .39 12S 173 53E
129 Okavango R., Angola 17 40S 19 30E
132 Okavangos Swamp, Bots. 19 30S 23 0E
114 Okaya, Japan 36 0N 138 10E
114 Okayama, Japan 34 40N 133 54E
114 Okayama, pref., Japan 35 0N 133 50E
114 Okazaki, Japan 34 36N 137 0E
125 Oke-Iho, Nigeria 8 1N 3 18E
163 Okeechobee, U.S.A. ...27 16N 80 46W
163 Okeechobee L., U.S.A. 27 0N 80 50W
163 Okefenokee Swamp, U.S.A. 30 50N 82 15W
36 Okehampton, Eng., U.K. 50 44N 4 1W
125 Okene, Nigeria 7 32N 6 11E
56 Oker R., Germany 52 7N 10 34E
91 Okha, U.S.S.R. 53 40N 143 0E
77 Ókhi Óros, Mts., Greece 38 5N 24 25E
91 Okhotsk, U.S.S.R. 59 20N 143 10E
91 Okhotsk, Sea of, Asia 55 0N 145 0E
114 Oki-gunto, Japan 36 15N 133 15E
118 Oki no Erabu, Is., Ryukyu Is. 27 15N 128 45E
134 Okiep, C. Prov., S. Afr. 29 39S 17 53E
125 Okigwi, Nigeria 5 52N 7 20E
125 Okija, Nigeria 5 54N 6 55E
113 Okinawa I., Ryukyu Is.26 40N 128 0E
113 Okinawa Gunto, Is., Ryukyu Is. 26 0N 127 30E
125 Okitipupa, Nigeria 6 31N 4 50E
165 Oklahoma, st., U.S.A. 35 20N 97 30W
165 Oklahoma City, U.S.A. 35 25N 97 30W
165 Okmulgee, U.S.A. 35 38N 96 0W
88 Oknitsa, U.S.S.R. 48 25N 27 20E
131 Okolo, Uganda 2 37N 31 8E
130 Okondja, Gabon 0 35S 13 45E
125 Okrika, Nigeria 4 47N 7 4E
81 Oksby, Denmark 55 33N 8 8E
113 Oku, Japan 26 35N 127 50E
86 Okulovka, U.S.S.R. ...58 19N 33 16E
147 Okuru, New Zealand .43 55S 168 55E
114 Okushiri I., Japan 42 15N 139 30E
125 Okuta, Nigeria 9 14N 3 12E
132 Okwa, R., Botswana .22 25S 22 30E
125 Okwoga, Nigeria 7 3N 7 42E
165 Ola, U.S.A. 35 2N 93 10W
82 Olafsvik, Iceland 64 53N 23 43W
167 Olancha, U.S.A. 36 15N 118 1W
169 Olanchito, Honduras .15 30N 86 30W
81 Öland I., Sweden 56 45N 16 50E
50 Olargues, France 43 34N 2 53E
164 Olathe, U.S.A. 38 50N 94 50W
172 Olavarria, Argentina .36 55S 60 20W
172 Olazcoaga, Argentina .35 15S 60 39W
60 Olawa, Poland 50 57N 17 20E
72 Olbia, Sardinia, Italy .40 55N 9 30E
72 Olbia, G. di, Sard., It. 40 55N 9 35E
169 Old Bahama Chan., W.I. 22 10N 77 30W
62 Old Castile, reg., Spain 41 55N 4 0W
46 Old Castle, Ireland 53 46N 7 10W
144 Old Cork, Australia ...22 57S 142 0E
152 Old Crow, Canada 67 30N 140 5E
43 Old Deer, Scot., U.K. 57 30N 2 3W
126 Old Dongola, Sudan ...18 11N 30 44E
154 Old Factory, Canada .52 36N 78 43W
161 Old Forge, N.Y., U.S.A. 43 43N 74 58W
161 Old Forge, Pa., U.S.A. 41 20N 75 46W
40 Old Kilpatrick, Scotland, U.K. 55 56N 4 34W
39 Old Leake, Eng., U.K. 53 2N 0 6E
45 Old Leighlin, Ireland .52 46N 7 2W
37 Old Radnor, Wales, U.K. 52 14N 3 7W
127 Old Sennar, Sudan 13 39N 33 33E
132 Old Serenje, Zambia .13 7S 30 45E
131 Old Shinyanga, Tanz. 3 33S 33 27E
161 Old Speckle, Mt., U.S.A. 44 35N 70 57W
132 Old Tati, Botswana ...21 22S 27 46E
155 Old Town, U.S.A. 45 0N 68 50W
157 Old Wives L., Canada 50 5N 105 55W
34 Oldbury, England, U.K. 52 30N 2 0W
56 Oldenburg, Lower Saxony, Germany ...53 10N 8 10E
56 Oldenburg, S.-Holst, Germany 54 16N 10 53E
54 Oldenzaal, Netherlands 52 19N 6 53E
38 Oldham, Eng., U.K. ...53 33N 2 8W
43 Oldmeldrum, Scot. UK 57 20N 2 19W
156 Olds, Canada 51 50N 114 10W
160 Olean, N.Y., U.S.A. ...42 8N 78 25W
70 Oleggio, Italy 45 36N 8 38E
62 Oleiros, Portugal 39 56N 7 56W
91 Olekma R., U.S.S.R. .58 0N 121 30E
91 Olekminsk, U.S.S.R. .60 40N 120 30E
91 Olenek, U.S.S.R. 68 20N 112 30E
91 Olenek, R., U.S.S.R. .71 0N 123 50E
86 Olenino, U.S.S.R. 56 15N 33 20E
50 Oleron, Î. d', France .45 55N 1 15W
60 Olesnica, Poland 51 13N 17 22E
60 Olesno, Poland 50 51N 18 26E
86 Olevsk, U.S.S.R. 51 18N 27 39E
138 Olga, Mt., Australia ...25 20S 130 40E
91 Olga, U.S.S.R. 43 50N 135 0E
14 Olga Strait, Spitsbergen 79 0N 21 0E
81 Ølgod, Denmark 55 50N 8 37E
43 Olgrinmole, Scot., U.K. 58 29N 3 33W
63 Olhao, Portugal 37 3N 7 48W
71 Olib & I., Yugoslavia .44 23N 14 44E
72 Oliena, Italy 40 18N 9 22E
64 Oliete, Spain 41 1N 0 41W
133 Olifants R., S. Africa .24 5S 31 20E
134 Olifants R., S. Africa .31 40S 18 27E
133 Olifantsfontein, S. Afr. 25 58S 28 14E
134 Olifantshoek, S. Africa 27 57S 22 42E
134 Olifantsvlei, S. Africa 30 10S 21 30E
77 Ólimbos, Greece......35 46N 27 11E
76 Olimbos, Oros, Mt., Gr. 40 6N 22 23E
65 Olite, Spain 42 29N 1 40W
172 Oliva, Argentina 32 0S 63 38W
65 Oliva, Spain 38 58N 0 15W
63 Oliva de la Frontera, Sp. 38 17N 6 54W
64 Olivares, Spain 39 46N 2 20W
175 Oliveira, Brazil 20 50S 44 50W
62 Oliveira de Azemeis, Portugal 40 49N 8 29W
63 Olivenza, Spain 38 41N 7 9W
156 Oliver, Canada 49 20N 119 30W
147 Olivine Ra., N.Z. 44 15S 168 30E
89 Olkhovka, U.S.S.R. ...49 48N 44 32E
60 Olkusz, Poland 50 18N 19 33E
82 Ollafsvellir, Iceland ...64 0N 20 33W
172 Ollague, Chile 21 15S 68 10W
44 Ollatrim R., Ireland ...52 53N 8 5W
39 Ollerton, England, U.K. 53 12N 1 1W
172 Ollita, Cord. de, Chile 31 0S 70 45W
131 Oloitokitok, Kenya 2 56S 37 30E
62 Olmedo, Spain 41 20N 4 43W
35 Olney, England, U.K. 52 9N 0 42W
162 Olney, Ill., U.S.A. 38 40N 88 0W
165 Olney, Tex., U.S.A. ...33 25N 98 45W
125 Oloma, Cameroon 3 29N 11 19E
59 Olomouc, Cz. 49 38N 17 12E
84 Olonets, U.S.S.R. 61 10N 33 0E
109 Olongapo, Philippines 14 50N 120 18E
50 Oloron, France 43 11N 0 38W
64 Olot, Spain 42 11N 2 30E
74 Olovo, Yugoslavia 44 8N 18 35E
81 Olovström, Sweden ...56 16N 14 30E
91 Olovyannaya, U.S.S.R. 50 50N 115 10E
56 Olpe, Germany 51 2N 7 50E
88 Olshanka, U.S.S.R. ...48 16N 30 58E
81 Ölst, Denmark 56 23N 10 6E
40 Olstrup, Denmark 56 7N 8 24E
60 Olsztyn, Poland 53 48N 20 29E
60 Olsztynek, Poland 53 34N 20 19E
78 Olt, Reg., Rumania ...44 25N 24 25E
78 Olt R., Rumania 43 50N 24 40E
57 Olten, Switzerland ...47 21N 7 53E
78 Oltenita, Rumania 44 7N 26 42E
165 Olton, U.S.A. 34 16N 102 7W
100 Oltu, Turkey 40 35N 41 50E
64 Olvega, Spain 41 47N 2 0W
63 Olvera, Spain 36 55N 5 18W
77 Olympia, plain, Greece 37 39N 21 39E
166 Olympia, U.S.A. 47 0N 122 58W
166 Olympic Mts., U.S.A. .48 0N 124 0W
76 Olympos Mt., Greece .40 6N 22 23E
166 Olympic Nat. Park, U.S.A. 47 35N 123 30W
166 Olympus Mt., U.S.A. .47 52N 123 40W
161 Olyphant, U.S.A. 41 27N 75 36W
114 Omachi, Japan 36 30N 137 50E
46 Omagh, N. Ire. U.K.. 54 36N 7 20W
164 Omaha, U.S.A. 41 15N 96 0W
166 Omak, U.S.A. 48 25N 119 24W
99 Oman, sultanate, Arabia 23 0N 58 0E
101 Oman, G. of, S.W. Asia 24 30N 58 30E
146 Omapere, N.Z. 35 37S 173 25E
129 Omaruru, S.W. Africa 21 26S 16 0E
174 Omate, Peru 16 45S 71 0W
109 Ombai Strait, Indonesia 8 30S 124 50E
34 Ombersley, Eng., U.K. 52 17N 2 12W
79 Ombo I., Norway 59 18N 6 0E
128 Omboue, Gabon 1 35S 9 15E
70 Ombrone R., Italy 42 48N 11 15E
132 Omdraai, Botswana ...20 5S 21 56E
134 Omdraaisvlei, S. Africa 30 8S 23 8E
125 Omdurman, Sudan 15 40N 32 28E
70 Omegna, Italy 45 52N 8 23E
169 Ometepe I., Nicaragua 11 32N 85 35W
168 Ometepec, Mexico 16 39N 98 23W
98 Omets, Israel 32 22N 35 0E
71 Omiš, Yugoslavia 43 28N 16 40E
71 Omisalj, Yugoslavia ...45 13N 14 32E
81 Omme R., Denmark ...55 56N 8 40E
127 Omo R., Ethiopia 6 25N 36 10E
75 Omortag, Bulgaria 43 8N 26 26E
90 Omsk, U.S.S.R. 55 0N 73 38E
112 Omu, China 43 48N 128 10E
75 Omul, mt., Rumania 45 27N 25 29E
14 Omulyak B., U.S.S.R. 72 30N 146 0E
114 Omura, Japan 33 8N 130 0E
129 Omuramba, S.W. Africa 20 0S 17 50E
114 Omuta, Japan 33 0N 130 26E
87 Omutninsk, U.S.S.R. .58 45N 52 4E
64 Oña, Spain 42 43N 3 25W
164 Onaga, U.S.A. 39 32N 96 12W
164 Onalaska, U.S.A. 43 53N 91 14W
164 Onamia, U.S.A. 46 4N 93 38W
109 Onan, Indonesia 3 2S 118 55E
162 Onancock, U.S.A. 37 42N 75 49W
154 Onaping L., Canada ...47 3N 81 30W
79 Onarheim, Norway 59 57N 5 39E
64 Oñate, Spain 43 3N 2 25W
168 Onavas, Mexico 28 28N 109 30W
164 Onawa, U.S.A. 42 2N 96 2W
162 Onaway, U.S.A. 45 21N 84 11W
64 Onda, Spain 39 55N 0 17W
129 Ondangua, S.W. Africa17 57S 16 4E
112 Ondarhaan, Mongolia .47 22N 110 31E
64 Ondárroa, Spain 43 19N 2 25W
59 Ondava R., Czechoslovakia 48 50N 21 40E
134 Onderstedorings S. Afr. 30 11S 20 35E
125 Ondo, Nigeria 7 4N 4 47E
84 Onega, U.S.S.R. 64 0N 38 10E
84 Onega, G. of, U.S.S.R. 64 30N 37 0E
84 Onega, L., U.S.S.R. ...62 0N 35 30E
84 Onega R., U.S.S.R. ...63 0N 39 0E
146 Onehunga, N.Z. 36 55N 174 50E
161 Oneida, N.Y., U.S.A. .43 5N 75 40W
161 Oneida L., U.S.A. 43 12N 76 0W
164 O'Neill, U.S.A. 42 30N 98 38W
91 Onekotan, I., Kuril Is. 40 59N 114 0E
163 Oneonta, Ala., U.S.A. 33 58N 86 29W
161 Oneonta, N.Y., U.S.A. 42 26N 75 5W
146 Onerahi, New Zealand 35 45S 174 22E
143 One Tree, Australia ...34 13S 144 42E
146 Ongarue, N.Z. 38 42S 175 19E
134 Ongeluksfontein, C. Prov., S. Afr. 32 31S 21 29E
142 Ongerup, W. Australia 33 49S 118 33E
112 Ongiyn Gol. Mongolia 45 56N 103 0E
130 Ongoka. Congo 1 20S 26 0E
106 Ongole, India 15 33N 80 2E
89 Oni, U.S.S.R. 42 33N 43 26E
164 Onida, U.S.A. 44 42N 100 5W
129 Onilahy, R., Malagasy Rep. 23 30S 44 0E
125 Onitsha, Nigeria 6 6N 6 42E
123 Onnour, Chad 19 45N 18 3E
114 Onoda, Japan 34 2N 131 10E
62 Ons, Islas de, Spain ...42 23N 8 55W
81 Onsala, Sweden 57 26N 12 0E
134 Onseepkans, S. Afr. ...28 46S 19 14E
138 Onslow, W. Australia .21 40S 115 0E
163 Onslow B., U.S.A. 34 10N 77 0W
79 Onsöy, Norway 59 15N 10 51E
54 Onstwedde, Netherlands 52 2N 7 4E
114 Ontake Mt., Japan 35 50N 137 15E
62 Ontaneda, Spain 43 12N 3 57W
154 Ontario, Prov., Canada 52 0N 88 10W
167 Ontario, Calif., U.S.A. 34 2N 117 40W
166 Ontario, Ore., U.S.A. .44 1N 117 1W
160 Ontario L., Can.-U.S.A. 43 40N 78 0W
65 Onteniente, Spain 38 50N 0 35W
164 Ontonagon, U.S.A. 46 58N 89 12W
138 Oodnadatta, S. Austral. 27 33S 135 30E

MAP
14 Ooglaamie, Alas., U.S.A. 72 1N 157 0W
138 Ooldea, S. Australia ...30 27S 131 50E
144 Oo'indi, Australia 20 40S 141 1E
54 Oostende, Belgium 51 15N 2 50E
54 Oosterhout, Neth. 51 38N 4 51E
106 Ootacamund, India ...11 30N 76 44E
133 Ootsi, Botswana 25 2S 25 45E
75 Opaka, Bulgaria 43 28N 26 10E
130 Opala, Congo 1 11S 24 45E
91 Opala, U.S.S.R. 52 15N 156 15E
60 Opalenica, Poland 52 18N 16 24E
75 Opan, Bulgaria 42 13N 25 41E
106 Opanake, Ceylon 6 35N 80 40E
146 Opapa, New Zealand .39 47S 176 42E
154 Opasatika, Canada 49 30N 82 50W
71 Opatija, Yugoslavia ...45 21N 14 17E
60 Opatów, Poland 50 50N 21 27E
59 Opava, Czechoslovakia 49 57N 17 58E
165 Opelousas, U.S.A. 30 35N 92 0W
154 Opemisca L., Canada .50 0N 75 0W
147 Open Bay Is., N.Z. 43 51S 168 51E
55 Opglabbeek, Belgium .51 3N 5 35E
55 Opgrimbie, Belgium ...50 57N 5 41E
166 Opheim, U.S.A. 48 52N 106 30W
43 Ophir, Scotland, U.K 58 56N 3 11W
142 Ophthalmia Ra., Western Australia .23 15S 119 30E
125 Opi, Nigeria 6 36N 7 28E
154 Opinaca L., Canada ...52 32N 76 31W
154 Opinaca R., Canada ...52 40N 77 10W
155 Opiskotish, L., Canada 53 0N 67 51W
55 Opladen, Germany 51 4N 7 2E
55 Oploo, Netherlands ...51 37N 5 52E
125 Opobo Town, Nigeria . 4 35N 7 34E
86 Opochka, U.S.S.R. 56 42N 28 45E
60 Opoczno, Poland 51 22N 20 18E
60 Opole, Poland 50 42N 17 58E
60 Opole, prov., Poland .50 40N 17 56E
62 Oporto (Porto), Port. .41 8N 8 40W
146 Opotiki, New Zealand 38 1S 177 19E
163 Opp, U.S.A. 31 19N 86 13W
79 Oppegard, Norway 59 48N 10 44E
57 Oppenheim, Germany 49 50N 8 22E
73 Oppido Mamertina, It. 38 16N 15 59E
79 Oppland Fylke, co., Norway 61 15N 9 30E
79 Opstad, Norway 60 17N 11 43E
146 Opua, New Zealand ...35 19S 174 9E
146 Opunake, New Zealand 39 26S 173 52E
74 Opuzen, Yugoslavia ...43 1N 17 34E
98 Or Yehuda, Israel 32 2N 34 50E
71 Ora, Italy 46 20N 11 19E
142 Ora Banda, W. Austral. 30 20S 121 0E
167 Oracle, U.S.A. 32 45N 110 46W
78 Oradea, Rumania 47 2N 21 58E
82 Oraefa Jökull Mt., Ice. 64 2N 16 35W
74 Orahovac, Yugoslavia 42 24N 20 40E
74 Orahovica, Yugoslavia 45 35N 17 52E
105 Orai, India 25 58N 79 30E
51 Oraison, France 43 55N 5 55E
122 Oran (Ouahran), Algeria 35 37N 0 39W
172 Oran, Argentina 23 10S 64 20W
43 Oran, Ireland 53 40N 8 20W
51 Orange, France 44 8N 4 47E
143 Orange, N.S.W., Australia 33 15S 149 7E
161 Orange, Mass., U.S.A. 42 35N 72 15W
165 Orange, Tex., U.S.A. .30 0N 93 40W
162 Orange, Va., U.S.A. ...38 17N 78 5W
175 Orange C., Brazil 4 20N 51 30W
129 Orange Free State, prov., South Africa 28 30S 27 0E
129 Orange, R., South Africa 28 30S 18 0E
165 Orange Grove, U.S.A. 27 57N 97 57W
163 Orangeburg, U.S.A. ...33 27N 80 53W
129 Orangemouth, S.W. Afr. 23 38S 16 24E
144 Orangerie B., Papua .10 30S 149 30E
154 Orangeville, Canada ...43 55N 80 5W
56 Oranienburg, Germany 52 45N 13 15E
133 Oranjefontein, S. Afr. 23 28S 27 42E
134 Oranjerivier, S. Africa 29 40S 24 12E
135 Oranjeville, S. Africa .27 0S 28 15E
44 Oranmore, Ireland 53 16N 8 57W
109 Oras, Philippines 12 9N 125 22E
74 Orašje, Yugoslavia 45 1N 18 42E
78 Orăştie, Rumania 45 50N 23 10E
59 Orava R., Cz. 49 24N 19 20E
74 Oravita, Rumania 45 6N 21 43E
50 Orb R., France 43 28N 3 5E
70 Orba R., Italy 44 45N 8 40E
81 Orbæk, Denmark 55 17N 10 39E
123 Orbata, Djebel, Tunisia 34 25N 9 21E
57 Orbe, Switzerland 46 43N 6 32E
48 Orbec, France 49 1N 0 23E
71 Orbetello, Italy 42 26N 11 11E
62 Orbigo R., Spain 42 40N 5 45W
43 Orbliston Junc., Scotland, U.K. 57 36N 3 10W
143 Orbost, Vic., Australia 37 40S 148 29E
80 Örbyhus, Sweden 60 15N 17 43E
65 Orce, Spain 37 44N 2 28W
65 Orce, R., Spain 37 45N 2 30W
49 Orchies, France 50 28N 3 14E
43 Orchy, Bridge of, Scotland, U.K. 56 30N 4 46W
40 Orchy, Glen, Scot., U.K. 56 27N 4 52W
70 Orco R., Italy 45 20N 7 45E
138 Ord, Mt., W. Australia 17 20S 125 34E
138 Ord, R., W. Australia 16 20S 128 37E
43 Ord of Caithness, Scotland, U.K. 58 8N 3 35W
62 Ordenes, Spain 43 5N 8 29W
167 Orderville, U.S.A. 37 18N 112 43W
43 Ordhead, Scotland, U.K. 57 10N 2 31W
43 Ordie, Scotland, U.K. 57 6N 2 54W
81 Ording, Denmark 56 43N 8 45E
112 Ordos, Des., China 39 25N 108 45E
100 Ordu, Turkey 40 55N 37 53E
64 Orduña, Spain 42 58N 2 58W
65 Orduña, mt., Spain ...37 20N 3 30W
164 Ordway, U.S.A. 38 15N 103 42W
89 Ordzhonikidze, R.S.F.S.R., U.S.S.R. 43 0N 44 35E
88 Ordzhonikidze, Ukraine S.S.R., U.S.S.R. 47 32N 34 3E
80 Ore, Sweden 61 8N 15 14E
56 Ore Mts., Czechoslovakia 50 25N 13 0E
74 Orebic, Yugoslavia 43 0N 17 11E
80 Örebro, Sweden 59 20N 15 18E
80 Örebro Län, co., Swed. 59 27N 15 0E
164 Oregon, U.S.A. 42 1N 89 20W
166 Oregon, st., U.S.A. 44 0N 120 0W
166 Oregon City, U.S.A. ...45 28N 122 35W
80 Öregrund, Sweden 60 21N 18 30E
80 Öregrundsgrepen, Sd., Sweden 60 30N 18 15E
88 Orekhov, U.S.S.R. 47 30N 35 32E
87 Orekhovo, Zuyevo, U.S.S.R. 55 50N 38 55E
87 Orel, U.S.S.R. 52 57N 36 3E
88 Orel R., U.S.S.R. 49 5N 35 25E
174 Orellana, Peru 6 50S 75 10W
63 Orellana la Vieja, Sp. .39 1N 5 32W
166 Orem, U.S.A. 40 27N 111 45W
77 Ören, Turkey 37 3N 27 57E
62 Orense, Spain 42 19N 7 55W
62 Orense, prov., Spain ..42 15N 7 30W
147 Orepuki, New Zealand 46 19S 167 46E
76 Orestiás, Greece 41 30N 26 33E
81 Öresund, str., Europe 55 45N 12 45E
147 Oreti R., New Zealand 45 39S 168 14E
35 Orford, England, U.K. 52 6N 1 31E
35 Orford Ness, Eng., U.K. 52 6N 1 31E
64 Orgaña, Spain 42 13N 1 20E
63 Orgaz, Spain 39 39N 3 53W
51 Orgon, France 43 47N 5 3E
111 Orhon Gol, Mongolia .49 30N 106 0E
73 Oria, Italy 40 30N 17 38E
145 Orient, Queens., Austral. 28 7S 143 3E
154 Orient Bay, Canada ...49 20N 88 10W
49 Origny, France 49 50N 3 30E
65 Orihuela, Spain 38 7N 0 55W
64 Orihuela del Tremedal, Spain 40 33N 1 39W
160 Orillia, Canada.........44 40N 79 24W
174 Orinoco, Delta of, Ven. 8 30N 61 0W
174 Orinoco, R., Venezuela 5 45N 67 40W
157 Orion, Canada 49 28N 110 49W
103 Orissa, st., India 21 0N 85 0E
72 Oristano, Italy 39 54N 8 35E
72 Oristano, Golfo di, Italy 39 50N 8 22E
168 Orizaba, Mexico 18 50N 97 10W
75 Orizare, Bulgaria 42 44N 27 39E
79 Orje, Norway 59 28N 11 36E
74 Orjen, Mt., Yugoslavia 42 35N 18 34E
65 Orjiva, Spain 36 53N 3 24W
79 Orkanger, Norway 63 16N 9 57E
79 Orkdal, Norway 63 18N 9 49E
81 Örkelljunga, Sweden .56 17N 13 20E
81 Örken, L., Sweden 57 11N 15 0E
59 Orkery, Hungary 47 9N 19 26E
79 Orkla, Norway 63 0N 9 45E
133 Orkney, Trans. S. Afr. 26 42S 26 40E
43 Orkney, co., Scot., U.K. 59 0N 3 0W
166 Orland, U.S.A. 39 46N 120 10W
163 Orlando, U.S.A. 28 30N 81 25W
73 Orlando C'd', Italy 38 10N 14 43E
49 Orléanais, prov., Fr. ...48 0N 2 0E
49 Orleans, France 47 54N 1 52E
161 Orleans, U.S.A. 44 49N 72 10W
162 Orléans, I. d', Canada 46 54N 70 58W
58 Orlice, R., Cz. 50 15N 16 30E
59 Orlicke Hory, mts., Cz. 50 15N 16 30E
59 Orlov, Czechoslovakia 49 17N 20 51E
87 Orlov Gay, U.S.S.R. .51 4N 48 19E
74 Orlovat, Yugoslavia ...45 14N 20 33E
102 Ormara, West Pakistan 25 16N 64 33E
70 Ormea, Italy 44 9N 7 54E
35 Ormesby St. Margaret, Norfolk, U.K. 52 39N 1 42E
76 Ormilia, Greece 40 16N 23 33E
109 Ormoc, Philippines 11 2N 124 35E
146 Ormond, New Zealand 38 33S 177 56E
163 Ormond, U.S.A. 29 13N 81 5W
146 Ormondville, N.Z. 40 5S 176 19E
71 Ormoz, Yugoslavia 46 25N 16 10E
38 Ormskirk, England, U.K. 53 35N 2 53W
161 Ormstown, Canada 45 9N 74 0W
49 Ornans, France 47 7N 6 10E
48 Orne, dépt., France ...48 40N 0 0E
60 Orneta, Poland 54 8N 20 9E
81 Örnhöj, Denmark 56 12N 8 34E
80 Ornö, I., Sweden 59 2N 18 30E
80 Ornsköldvik, Sweden .63 17N 18 50E
168 Oro, R., Mexico 26 8N 105 58W
174 Orocué, Colombia 4 48N 71 20W
125 Orodo, Nigeria 5 34N 7 4E
167 Orogrande, U.S.A. 32 20N 106 4W
62 Orol, Spain 43 34N 7 39W
155 Oromocto, Canada 45 54N 66 37W
98 Oron, Israel 30 55N 35 1E
125 Oron, Nigeria 4 48N 8 14E
160 Orono, Canada 44 0N 78 35W
40 Oronsay I., Scot., U.K. 56 0N 6 14W
40 Oronsay, Pass of, Scotland, U.K. 56 0N 6 10W
62 Oropesa, Toledo, Spain 39 57N 5 10W
109 Oroquieta, Philippines 8 32N 123 44E
175 Oros, Brazil 6 15S 39 0W
72 Orosei, G. di, Italy 40 15N 9 40E
59 Orosháza, Hungary ...46 32N 20 42E
166 Orrville, U.S.A. 48 58N 119 30W
166 Oroville, U.S.A. 39 40N 121 30W
147 Orowia, New Zealand 46 1S 167 50E
174 Oroya, Peru 11 35S 75 52W
81 Orrefors, Sweden 56 48N 15 45E
160 Orrville, U.S.A. 40 50N 81 46W
80 Orsa, Sweden 61 7N 14 40E
73 Orsara di Puglia, Italy 41 17N 15 16E
80 Orsasjön, L., Sweden .61 7N 14 37E
86 Orsha, U.S.S.R. 54 30N 30 25E
80 Orsjön, L., Sweden 61 37N 16 22E
84 Orsk, U.S.S.R. 51 20N 58 34E
81 Örslev, Odense, Den. .55 24N 9 55E
81 Örslev, Soro, Denmark 55 22N 11 56E
71 Orsogna, Italy 42 13N 14 17E
78 Orsova, Rumania 44 41N 22 25E
81 Örsted, Randers, Den. 56 31N 10 21E
70 Orta, L. d', Italy 45 48N 8 21E
73 Orta Nova, Italy 41 20N 15 40E
71 Orte, Italy 42 28N 12 23E
82 Ortegal C., Spain 43 43N 7 52W
50 Orthez, France 43 29N 0 48W
62 Ortigueira, Spain 43 40N 7 50W
70 Ortles, mt., Italy 46 31N 10 33E
174 Orton R., Bolivia 10 50S 67 0W
38 Orton Tebay, Eng., UK 54 28N 2 35W
71 Ortona, Italy 42 21N 14 24E
81 Orum, Hjörring, Den. 57 12N 10 7E
72 Orune, Sardinia, Italy 40 25N 9 20E
174 Oruro, Bolivia 18 0S 67 19W
81 Orust I., Sweden 58 12N 11 35E
71 Orvieto, Italy 42 43N 12 8E
160 Orwell, U.S.A. 41 32N 80 52W
35 Orwell, R., Eng., U.K. 52 2N 1 12E
75 Oryakhovo, Bulgaria .43 40N 23 57E
70 Orzinuovi, Italy 45 24N 9 55E
60 Orzysz, Poland 53 50N 21 58E
79 Os, Norway 60 9N 5 30E
84 Osa, U.S.S.R. 57 9N 55 57E
169 Osa, Pen., Costa Rica 8 0N 84 0W
164 Osage, Iowa, U.S.A. ...43 15N 92 50W
164 Osage, Wyo., U.S.A. .43 59N 104 25W
164 Osage R., U.S.A. 38 15N 92 30W
164 Osage City, U.S.A. 38 43N 95 51W
114 Osaka, tn. & Pref., Jap. 34 40N 135 30E
71 Osar, Yugoslavia 44 43N 14 27E
164 Osawatomie, U.S.A. ...38 30N 94 55W
164 Osborne, U.S.A. 39 30N 98 45W
81 Ösby, Sweden 55 15N 9 38E
165 Osceola, Ark., U.S.A. .35 40N 90 0W
164 Osceola, Iowa, U.S.A. 41 0N 93 20W
56 Oschatz, Germany 51 17N 13 8E
56 Oschersleben, Germany 52 2N 11 13E
72 Oschiri, Italy 40 43N 9 7E
160 Oscoda, U.S.A. 44 26N 83 20W
74 Osečina, Yugoslavia ...44 23N 19 34E
91 Osenovka, U.S.S.R. ...70 40N 120 50E
154 Oshawa, Canada 43 50N 78 45W
129 Oshikango, Angola 17 9S 16 10E
162 Oshkosh, Neb., U.S.A. 41 27N 102 20W
162 Oshkosh, Wis., U.S.A. 44 3N 88 35W
86 Oshmyany, U.S.S.R. .54 26N 25 58E
125 Oshogbo, Nigeria 7 48N 4 37E
78 Osica, Rumania 44 14N 24 20E
74 Osijek, Yugoslavia 45 34N 18 41E
72 Osilo, Italy 40 45N 8 41E
71 Osimo, Italy 43 30N 13 30E
91 Osinino, U.S.S.R. 70 55N 148 50E
90 Osinniki, U.S.S.R. 53 58N 87 58E
86 Osintorf, U.S.S.R. 54 34N 30 31E
86 Osipovichi, U.S.S.R. .53 25N 28 33E
164 Oskaloosa, U.S.A. 41 18N 92 40W
81 Oskarshamn, Sweden .57 15N 16 25E
154 Oskelaneo, Canada 48 5N 75 15W
87 Oskol R., U.S.S.R. 50 20N 38 0E
79 Oslo, Norway 59 53N 10 52E
109 Oslob, Philippines 9 34N 133 22E
79 Oslofjord, Norway 58 30N 10 0E
106 Osmanabad, India 18 5N 76 10E
88 Osmancik, Turkey 40 45N 34 47E
100 Osmaniye, Turkey 37 5N 36 10E
80 Ösmo, Sweden 58 58N 17 55E
39 Osmotherley, Eng., UK 54 22N 1 18W
56 Osnabrück, Germany .52 16N 8 2E
59 Osoblaha, Cz. 50 17N 17 44E
57 Osogna, Switzerland ...46 18N 9 0E
173 Osorio, Brazil 29 53S 50 17W
176 Osorno, Chile 40 25S 73 0W
176 Osorno, vol., Chile 41 0N 72 30W
156 Osoyoos, Canada 49 0N 119 30W
54 Oss, Netherlands 51 46N 5 32E
145 Ossa, Mt., Tas., Austral. 41 80S 146 0E
76 Óssa, mt., Greece 39 47N 22 42E
65 Ossa de Montiel, Spain 38 58N 2 45W
163 Ossabaw I., U.S.A. 31 45N 81 8W
39 Ossett, England, U.K. 53 40N 1 35W
161 Ossining, U.S.A. 41 9N 73 50W
161 Ossipee, U.S.A. 43 41N 71 9W
155 Ossokmanuan L., Can. 53 25N 65 0W
86 Ostashkov, U.S.S.R. .57 4N 33 2E
56 Oste R., Germany 53 30N 9 12E
54 Ostend (Oostende), Belg. 51 14N 2 55E
86 Oster, U.S.S.R. 50 57N 30 46E
55 Osterath, Germany 51 16N 6 37E
56 Osterburg, Germany .52 47N 11 44E
80 Österby, Sweden 60 13N 17 55E
81 Österbymo, Sweden ...57 49N 15 15E
80 Osterdalälven, R., Swed. 61 30N 13 45E
56 Osterholz-Scharmbeck, Germany 53 14N 8 48E
81 Österild, Denmark 57 3N 8 50E
81 Österkorsberga, Sweden 57 17N 15 5E
79 Österöy, Norway 60 32N 5 28E
80 Osterskar, Sweden 59 28N 18 19E
80 Östersund, Sweden 63 10N 14 45E
57 Ostfold Fylke, co., Nor. 59 25N 11 25E
56 Ost Friesland, dist., Ger. 53 27N 7 30E
72 Ostia Lido (Lido di Roma), Italy 41 43N 12 17E
71 Ostiglia, Italy 45 4N 11 9E
59 Ostrava, Czechoslovakia 49 51N 18 18E
60 Ostróda, Poland 53 42N 19 58E
86 Ostrog, U.S.S.R. 50 20N 26 30E
87 Ostrogozhsk, U.S.S.R. 50 55N 39 7E
60 Ostrołeka, Poland 53 4N 21 38E
75 Ostrov, Bulgaria 43 40N 24 9E
78 Ostrov, Rumania 44 6N 27 24E
86 Ostrov, U.S.S.R. 57 25N 28 20E
60 Ostrów, Poland 51 36N 17 44E
60 Ostrów Mazowiecka, Pol. 52 50N 21 51E
60 Ostrowiec, Poland 50 55N 21 22E
74 Ostrožac, Yugoslavia .43 43N 17 49E
60 Ostrzeszów, Poland ...51 25N 17 52E
79 Östsinni, Norway 60 53N 10 3E
73 Ostuni, Italy 40 44N 17 34E
75 Osum, R., Albania 40 40N 20 10E
114 Osumi-gunto, Is., Japan 30 30N 130 45E
114 Osumi-kaikyo Channel, Japan 30 55N 131 0E
75 Osum, R., Bulgaria ...43 35N 25 0E
63 Osuna, Spain 37 14N 5 8W
38 Oswaldtwistle, Eng. UK 53 44N 2 27W
161 Oswego, N.Y., U.S.A. 43 29N 76 30W
34 Oswestry, Eng., U.K. 52 52N 3 3W
59 Oświęcim, Poland 50 2N 19 11E
147 Otago Harb., N.Z. 45 47S 170 42E
147 Otago Pen., N.Z. 45 48S 170 45E
146 Otahuhu, N.Z. 36 56S 174 51E
114 Otake, Japan 34 27N 132 25E
146 Otaki, New Zealand ...40 45S 175 10E
130 Otala, Congo 0 55S 25 10E
146 Otane, New Zealand .39 54S 176 39E
114 Otaru-wan, Japan 43 20N 141 20E
147 Otautau, New Zealand 46 9S 168 1E
58 Otava, R., Cz. 49 16N 13 32E
174 Otavalo, Ecuador 0 20N 78 20W
129 Otavi, S.W. Africa 19 40S 17 24E
74 Otelec, Rumania 45 36N 20 50E
62 Otero de Rey, Spain .43 6N 7 36W
55 Othée, Belgium 50 43N 5 28E
166 Othello, U.S.A. 46 53N 119 8W
76 Othonoi, I., Greece 39 52N 19 22E
77 Othris, Oros, mt., Gr. 39 4N 22 42E
147 Otira, New Zealand ...42 49S 171 35E
147 Otira Gorge, N.Z. 42 53S 171 33E
164 Otis, U.S.A. 40 12N 102 58W
129 Otjiwarongo, S.W. Afr. 20 30S 16 33E
39 Otley, England, U.K. 53 54N 1 41W
79 Otnes, Norway 61 45N 11 9E
71 Otočac, Yugoslavia ...44 53N 15 12E
146 Otorohanga, N.Z. 38 12S 175 14E
91 Otpor, U.S.S.R. 49 40N 117 10E
79 Otra, R., Norway 59 17N 7 30E
73 Otranto, Italy 40 9N 18 28E
73 Otranto, C.d', Italy ...40 7N 18 30E
73 Otranto, Str. of, Adriatic Sea 40 15N 18 40E
114 Otsu, Japan 42 35N 143 40E
79 Otta, Norway 61 46N 9 32E
79 Otta, R., Norway 61 55N 8 10E
106 Ottapalam, India 10 46N 76 23E
154 Ottawa, Canada 45 27N 75 42W
162 Ottawa, Ill., U.S.A. ...41 20N 88 55W
164 Ottawa, Kans., U.S.A. 38 40N 95 10W
153 Ottawa Is., Canada 59 50N 80 0W
154 Ottawa R., Canada 47 45N 78 35W
80 Ottebol, Sweden 59 42N 12 28E
125 Ottélé, Cameroon 3 38N 11 19E
81 Ottenby, Sweden 56 15N 16 30E
40 Ottter Ferry, Scot., U.K. 56 1N 5 20W
36 Otter R., Eng., U.K. .50 47N 3 12W
157 Otter Rapids, Canada 55 45N 104 46W
39 Otterburn, Eng., U.K. 55 14N 2 12W
56 Otterndorf, Germany .53 47N 8 52E
79 Otteröy, I., Norway ...62 45N 6 50E
58 Ottersheim, Austria ...48 21N 14 12E
43 Otters Wick, B., Scotland, U.K. 59 17N 2 32W
81 Otterup, Denmark 55 30N 10 22E
160 Otterville, Canada 42 57N 80 36W
36 Ottery St. Mary, England, U.K. 50 45N 3 16W
132 Otto Beit Bridge, Rhod. 15 59S 28 56E
133 Ottosdal, Trans. S. Afr. 26 46S 25 59E
133 Ottoshoop, S. Africa .25 45S 26 58E
80 Ottsjo, Sweden 63 13N 13 5E
164 Ottumwa, U.S.A. 41 0N 92 25W
125 Otu, Nigeria 8 14N 3 22E
125 Otukpa (Al Owuho), Nig. 7 9N 7 41E
125 Oturkpo, Nigeria 7 10N 8 15E
176 Otway B., Chile 53 30S 74 0W
60 Otwock, Poland 52 5N 21 20E
58 Ötz. tn. & R., Austria 47 13N 10 53E
58 Ötztaler Alpen, mts., Austria 46 58N 11 0E
125 Ouacha, Niger 13 26N 9 11E
165 Ouachita Mts., U.S.A. 34 50N 94 30W
165 Ouachita R., U.S.A. ...33 0N 92 15W
120 Ouadane, Mauritania .20 50N 11 40W
121 Ouadda, Cent. Afr. Rep. 8 15N 22 20E
125 Ouagadougou, Upper Volta 12 25N 1 30W
124 Ouahigouya, Upper Volta 13 40N 2 25W
122 Ouahila, Algeria 27 50N 5 0W
122 Ouahran, see Oran, Algeria 35 37N 0 39W
125 Oualata, Mauritania ...17 20N 6 55W
122 Oualidia, Morocco 32 49N 8 57W
122 Ouallene, Algeria 24 41N 1 11E
121 Ouanda Djalé, Central African Republic ... 8 55N 22 53E
130 Ouango, Cent. Afr. Rep. 4 19N 22 30E
123 Ouargla, Algeria 31 59N 5 25E
122 Ouarkziz, Djebel, Alg. 28 50N 8 0W
122 Ouarzazate, Morocco .31 0N 6 45W
124 Ouasso, Upper Volta .11 4N 2 47W
130 Oubangi, R., Cent. Afr. 5 0N 20 0E
134 Ouberg, C. Prov., S. Afr. 32 7S 24 26E
49 Ouche, R., France 47 11N 5 10E
55 Oud-Beijerland, Neth. 51 50N 4 25E
54 Ouddorp, Netherlands 51 50N 35 7E
54 Oude Rijn, R., Neth. .52 9N 4 45E
54 Oudenaerde, Belgium .50 50N 3 37E
55 Oudenbosch, Neth. 51 35N 4 32E
48 Oudon, France 47 22N 1 19W
48 Oudon, R., France 47 47N 1 2W
123 Oudref, Tunisia 33 59N 10 0E
134 Oudtshoorn, S. Africa 33 35S 22 14E
122 Oued Aissa, Algeria ...29 40N 0 1W
122 Oued Sbita, Algeria ...25 50N 5 2W
122 Oued Zem, Morocco ...32 57N 6 37W
124 Ouéllé, Ivory Coast .. 7 26N 4 1W
48 Ouessant, I. d', France 48 28N 5 6W
128 Ouesso, Congo (Fr.) ... 1 37N 16 5E
122 Ouezzane, Morocco 34 51N 5 42W
55 Ouffet, Belgium 50 26N 5 28E
46 Oughter L., Ireland ...54 2N 7 30W
44 Oughterard, Ireland ...53 26N 9 20W
125 Ouidah, Dahomey 6 25N 2 0E
154 Ouimet, Canada 48 43N 88 35W
48 Ouistreham, France ...49 17N 0 18W
120 Oujeft, Mauritania 20 2N 13 0W
82 Oulainen, Finland 64 17N 24 50E
123 Ouled Djellal, Algeria 34 28N 5 2E
122 Ouled Nail, Mts. des., Algeria 34 46N 3 30E
122 Oulmès, Morocco 33 17N 6 0W
35 Oulton, England, U.K. 52 29N 1 40E
35 Oulton Broad, England, U.K. 52 28N 1 43E
82 Oulu, Finland 64 58N 25 40E
82 Oulu L., Finland 64 25N 27 30E
82 Oulu, R., Finland 64 50N 26 20E
122 Oum el Ksil, Algeria ...29 4N 6 59W
122 Oum er Rbia, Morocco 32 30N 6 30W
124 Oume, Ivory Coast 5 21N 5 27W
82 Ounas R., Finland 67 30N 25 0E
35 Oundle, England, U.K. 52 28N 0 28W
125 Ounlivou, Togo 7 20N 1 34E
124 Ouossou, Ivory Coast . 6 16N 4 59W
134 Ouplaas, C. Prov., S. Afr. 32 15S 23 48E
54 Our, R., Luxembourg 49 55N 6 5E
167 Ouray, U.S.A. 38 3N 107 48W
175 Ouricuri, Brazil 7 50S 40 5W
173 Ourinhos, Brazil 23 0S 49 54W
63 Ourique, Portugal 37 38N 8 16W
173 Ouro Fino, Brazil 22 16S 46 25W
173 Ouro Preto, Brazil 20 20S 43 30W
130 Ourombi, Congo 0 4S 17 9E
54 Ourthe R., Belgium ...50 3N 5 35E
114 Ou-sammyaku, ra., Jap. 39 20N 140 35E
43 Ousdale, Scotland, U.K. 58 10N 3 34W
145 Ouse, Tas., Australia .42 25S 146 42E
35 Ouse, R., Sussex, England, U.K. 50 58N 0 3E
39 Ouse, R., Yorks., England, U.K. 54 3N 0 7E
35 Ouse, Great R., England, U.K. 52 21N 0 7E
35 Ouse, Little R., England, U.K. 52 25N 0 45E

MAP
50 Oust, France 42 52N 1 13E
48 Oust R., France 48 8N 2 49W
42 Out Skerries, Is., Scotland, U.K. 60 25N 0 50W
155 Outardes, R., Canada 50 0N 69 4W
42 Outer Hebrides, Is., Scotland, U.K. 57 30N 7 40W
155 Outer I., Canada 51 10N 58 35W
62 Outes, Spain 42 52N 8 55W
129 Outjo, S.W. Africa 20 5S 16 7E
157 Outlook, Canada 51 30N 107 0W
164 Outlook, U.S.A. 48 53N 104 46W
49 Outreau, France 50 40N 1 36E
143 Outtrim, Vic., Australia 38 32S 145 45E
35 Outwell, England, U.K. 52 36N 0 14E
143 Ouyen, Vic., Australia 35 1S 142 22E
70 Ovada, Italy 44 39N 8 40E
172 Ovalle, Chile 30 33S 71 18W
87 Ovamboland, dist., South West Africa 17 20S 16 30E
80 Ovansjo, Sweden 60 38N 16 40E
62 Ovar, Portugal 40 51N 8 40E
128 Ovem, Gabon 1 42N 11 43E
143 Ovens, R., Vic., Austral. 36 30S 146 30E
54 Over Flakkee, I., Neth. 51 45N 4 5E
34 Over Wallop, Eng., U.K. 51 9N 1 35W
80 Overath, Germany 50 56N 7 17E
43 Overbister, Scot., U.K. 59 16N 2 33W
55 Overijse, Belgium 50 46N 4 32E
54 Overijssl, prov., Neth. 52 25N 6 35E
82 Overkalix, Sweden 66 19N 22 50E
54 Overpelt, Belgium 51 12N 5 20E
35 Overstrand, Eng., U.K. 52 55N 1 20W
37 Overton, Flint., Wales, U.K. 52 58N 2 56W
34 Overton, Hants., Eng., U.K. 51 14N 1 16W
167 Overton, U.S.A. 36 32N 114 31W
81 Öerum, Sweden 57 58N 16 20E
164 Ovid, U.S.A. 41 0N 102 17W
88 Ovidiopol, U.S.S.R. 46 15N 30 30E
62 Oviedo, Spain 43 25N 5 50W
62 Oviedo, prov. Spain 43 20N 6 0W
80 Oviken, Sweden 62 58N 14 23E
80 Oviksfjällen, mts., Swed. 63 0N 13 45E
125 Ovoro, Nigeria 5 26N 7 16E
80 Övre Fryken, L., Swed. 60 7N 13 50E
79 Övre Sirdal, Norway 58 48N 6 43E
86 Ovruch, U.S.S.R. 51 25N 28 45E
147 Owaka, New Zealand 46 27S 169 40E
114 Owase, Japan 34 7N 136 5E
164 Owatonna, U.S.A. 44 3N 93 17W
161 Owego, U.S.A. 42 6N 76 17W
45 Owel, L., Ireland 53 34N 7 24W
131 Owen Falls, Uganda 0 30N 33 5E
147 Owen Mt., N.Z. 41 35S 152 33E
160 Owen Sound, Canada 44 35N 80 55W
144 Owen Stanley Range, Territory of Papua 8 30S 147 0E
45 Oweniny R., Ireland 54 13N 9 32W
46 Owenkillew R., Northern Ireland, U.K. 54 44N 7 15W
167 Owens L., U.S.A. 36 30N 118 0W
162 Owensboro, U.S.A. 37 40N 87 5W
164 Owensville, U.S.A. 38 20N 91 30W
125 Owerri, Nigeria 5 29N 7 0E
146 Owhango, N.Z. 31 51S 175 20E
125 Owo, Nigeria 7 18N 5 30E
162 Owosso, U.S.A. 43 0N 84 10W
39 Owston Ferry, England, U.K. 53 28N 0 47W
166 Owyhee, U.S.A. 42 0N 116 3W
166 Owyhee Res., U.S.A. 43 30N 117 30W
166 Owyhee R., U.S.A. 43 10N 117 37W
46 Ox Mts., Ireland 54 6N 9 0W
80 Oxberg, Sweden 61 7N 14 10E
81 Oxelösund, Sweden 58 43N 17 15E
34 Oxford, & co., Eng., U.K. 51 45N 1 15W
147 Oxford, New Zealand 43 18S 172 11E
165 Oxford, Miss., U.S.A. 34 22N 89 30W
163 Oxford, N.C., U.S.A. 36 19N 78 36W
162 Oxford, Ohio, U.S.A. 39 30N 84 40W
157 Oxford L., Canada 54 50N 96 0W
167 Oxnard, U.S.A. 34 10N 119 14W
77 Oxia, I., Greece 38 17N 21 6E
77 Oxilithos, Greece 38 35N 24 7E
143 Oxley, NSW, Australia 34 12S 144 6E
144 Oxley Creek, Australia 20 22S 144 45E
143 Oxleys Pk., Australia 31 51S 50 22E
135 Oxton, C. Prov., S. Afr. 32 14S 26 41E
108 Oya, Sarawak, Malaysia 2 55N 111 55E
79 Öyeren, L., Norway 59 50N 11 15E
79 Oyestad, Norway 58 28N 8 42E
82 Oyjord, Norway 68 29N 17 33E
43 Oykel Bridge, Scot., U.K. 57 58N 4 45W
43 Oykell R., Scot., U.K. 58 2N 4 52W
125 Oyo, Nigeria 7 46N 3 56E
51 Oyonnax, France 46 16N 5 40E
143 Oyster B., Tas., Austral. 42 15S 148 5E
161 Oyster B., U.S.A. 40 52N 73 32W
79 Öystese, Norway 60 22N 6 9E
109 Ozamis (Mizamis), Phil. 8 15N 123 50E
163 Ozark, Ala., U.S.A. 31 29N 85 39W
165 Ozark, Ark., U.S.A. 35 30N 93 50W
165 Ozark, Mo., U.S.A. 37 0N 93 15W
165 Ozark Plateau, U.S.A. 37 20N 91 40W
164 Ozarks, L. of, U.S.A. 38 10N 93 0W
59 Ozd, Hungary 48 14N 20 15E
86 Ozerhinsk, U.S.S.R. 53 40N 27 7E
87 Ozery, U.S.S.R. 54 52N 38 28E
72 Ozieri, Italy 40 35N 9 0E
165 Ozona, U.S.A. 30 43N 101 11W
60 Ozorkow, Poland 51 57N 19 16E
74 Ozren, Mt., Y.-slavia 43 55N 18 29E
168 Ozuluama, Mexico 21 40N 97 50W
78 Ozun, Rumania 45 47N 25 50E

P

124 Pa, Upper Volta 11 33N 3 19W
107 Pa Sak, R., Thailand 15 30N 101 0E
103 Pa-an, Burma 16 45N 97 40E
111 Paan (Batang), China 30 0N 99 3E
57 Paar, R., Germany 48 42N 11 27E
134 Paarl, C. Prov., S. Afr. 33 45S 18 56E
102 Pab Hills, W. Pakistan 26 30N 66 45E
42 Pabbay I., Scot., U.K. 57 46N 7 12W
42 Pabbay, Sd. of, Scot., U.K. 57 45N 7 4W
60 Pabianice, Poland 51 40N 19 20E
105 Pabna, East Pakistan 24 1N 89 18E
86 Pabrade, U.S.S.R. 55 0N 25 56E
134 Pacaltsdorp, S. Africa 34 0S 22 28E
174 Pacaraima Mts., Guyana 6 1N 6 0E
174 Pacasmayo, Peru 7 20S 79 35W
72 Paceco, Italy 37 59N 12 32E
104 Pachhar, India 24 40N 77 42E
73 Pachino, Italy 36 43N 15 4E
104 Pachora, India 20 38N 75 29E
168 Pachuca, Mexico 20 10N 98 40W
113 Pachung, China 31 58N 106 40E
167 Pacific Grove, U.S.A. 37 36N 121 58W
137 Pacific Ocean 10 0N 140 0W
156 Pacoh, Canada 53 0N 132 30W
58 Pacov, Czechoslovakia 49 27N 15 0E
59 Pacsa, Hungary 46 44N 17 2E
48 Pacy, France 49 2N 1 22E
109 Padalarang, Indonesia 7 50S 107 30E
108 Padang, Indonesia 1 0S 100 20E
108 Padang Pandjang, Indonesia 0 30S 100 20E
108 Padang I., Indonesia 1 0S 100 10E
108 Padang-Sidimpuan, Indonesia 1 30N 99 15E
81 Padborg, Denmark 54 49N 9 21E
172 Paddock, Natal, S. Afr. 30 45S 30 16E
35 Paddock Wood, England, U.K. 51 13N 0 24E
157 Paddockwood, Canada 53 30N 105 30W
109 Padeaido Is., Indonesia 1 5S 138 0E
56 Paderborn, Germany 51 42N 8 44E
78 Padesul, mt., Rumania 45 40N 22 22E
38 Padiham, Eng., U.K. 53 48N 2 20W
78 Padina, Rumania 44 50N 27 8E
157 Padlei, Canada 62 10N 97 5W
106 Padmanabhapuram, India 8 16N 77 17E
71 Padova (Padua), Italy 45 24N 11 52E
104 Padra, India 22 15N 73 7E
165 Padre I., U.S.A. 27 0N 97 20W
105 Padrauna, India 26 54N 34 1E
62 Padrón, Spain 42 41N 8 39W
135 Padrone C., S. Africa 33 46S 26 30E
36 Padstow, Eng., U.K. 50 33N 4 57W
36 Padstow Bay, Eng., U.K. 50 35N 4 58W
71 Padua (Padova), Italy 45 24N 11 52E
162 Paducah, Ky., U.S.A. 37 0N 88 40W
165 Paducah, Tex., U.S.A. 34 3N 100 16W
73 Padula, Italy 40 20N 15 40E
106 Padwa, India 18 27N 82 37E
146 Paekakariki, N.Z. 40 59S 174 58E
146 Paegaroa, N.Z. 37 49S 176 29E
146 Paeroa, New Zealand 37 23S 175 41E
70 Paesana, Italy 44 40N 7 18E
132 Pafuri, Mozambique 22 27S 31 22E
71 Pag, Yugoslavia 44 27N 15 5E
71 Pag I., Yugoslavia 44 50N 15 0E
125 Paga, Ghana 11 1N 1 8W
108 Pagai, S., I., Indonesia 3 0S 100 15E
108 Pagai, N. I., Indonesia 2 35S 100 0E
108 Pagain I., Indonesia 3 0S 100 15E
109 Pagadian, Philippines 7 55N 123 30E
109 Pagaralam, Indonesia 4 0S 103 17E
76 Pagastikós Kólpos, G., Greece 39 15N 23 12E
108 Pagatan, Indonesia 3 33S 115 59E
164 Page, U.S.A. 47 11N 97 37W
71 Paglieta, Italy 42 10N 14 30E
127 Pagnau, Ethiopia 8 15N 34 7E
49 Pagny-sur-Moselle, Fr. 48 59N 6 2E
167 Pagosa Springs, U.S.A. 37 16N 107 4W
154 Pagwa River, Canada 50 2N 85 14W
158 Pahala, Hawaii, U.S.A. 20 25N 156 0W
107 Pahang, st., Malaya, Malaysia 3 30N 103 9E
107 Pahang R., Malaysia 3 30N 103 9E
146 Pahiatua, N.Z. 40 27S 175 50E
163 Pahokee, U.S.A. 26 50N 80 30E
167 Pahrump, U.S.A. 36 15N 116 0W
112 Pahsien, China 39 10N 116 20E
42 Paible, Scotland, U.K. 57 35N 7 30W
112 Paicheng, China 45 50N 122 53E
86 Paide, U.S.S.R. 58 57N 25 31E
36 Paignton, Eng., U.K. 50 26N 3 33W
83 Päijanne, L., Finland 61 30N 25 30E
107 Pailin, Cambodia 12 46N 102 36E
48 Paimbœuf, France 47 17N 2 0W
48 Paimpol, France 48 48N 3 4W
108 Painan, Indonesia 1 15S 100 40E
160 Painesville, U.S.A. 41 42N 81 18W
37 Painscastle, Wales, U.K. 52 7N 3 13W
34 Painswick, Eng., U.K. 51 47N 2 11W
167 Painted Desert, U.S.A. 36 40N 112 0W
162 Paintsville, U.S.A. 37 50N 82 50W
160 Paisley, Canada 44 20N 81 28W
40 Paisley, Scotland, U.K. 55 51N 4 27W
166 Paisley, U.S.A. 42 43N 120 40W
174 Paita, Peru 5 5S 81 0W
62 Paiva R., Portugal 40 50N 7 55W
112 Paiyin, China 36 45N 104 4E
103 Paiyu, China 31 12N 98 45E
112 Paiyu Shan, mts., China 37 20N 108 0E
112 Paiyunopo, China 42 10N 109 28E
108 Pajakumbuh, Indonesia 0 20S 100 35E
62 Pajares, Spain 39 57N 1 48W
82 Pajala, Sweden 67 13N 23 30E
107 Pak Lay, Laos 18 15N 101 27E
107 Pak Phanang, Thail. 8 21N 100 12E
107 Pak Sane, Laos 18 25N 103 36E
106 Pakala, India 13 29N 79 8E
108 Pakanbaru, Indonesia 0 30N 101 15E
132 Pakemba, Zambia 13 3S 29 58E
143 Pakenham, Australia 38 6S 145 30E
161 Pakenham, Canada 45 18N 76 18W
113 Pakhoi, China 21 30N 109 10E
134 Pakhuis, S. Africa 32 8S 19 0E
103 Pakistan, East *see* Bangladesh 24 0N 90 0E
102 Pakistan, st., Asia 30 0N 70 0E
103 Pakokku, Burma 21 30N 95 0E
113 Pakonghow, China 23 50N 113 0E
104 Pakpattan, W. Pak. 30 25N 71 16E
74 Pakrac, Yugoslavia 45 27N 17 12E
59 Paks, Hungary 46 38N 18 55E
107 Pakse, Laos 15 5N 105 52E
102 Paktya, prov., Afghan. 33 0N 69 15E
131 Pakwach, Uganda 2 28N 31 27E
102 Pal, China 33 45N 79 33E
121 Pala, Chad 9 25N 15 5E
133 Pala Camp, Botswana 23 45S 26 50E
165 Palacios, U.S.A. 28 44N 96 12W
64 Palafrugell, Spain 41 55N 3 10E
73 Palagiano, Italy 40 35N 17 0E
73 Palagonia, Italy 37 20N 14 43E
77 Palaiokastron, Greece 35 12N 26 18E
77 Palaiokhora, Greece 35 16N 23 39E
77 Palairos, Greece 38 45N 20 51E
106 Palakol, India 16 31N 81 46E
90 Palakhino, U.S.S.R. 67 45N 86 5E
133 Palala R., S. Africa 23 45S 28 15E
76 Palamás, Greece 39 26N 22 4E
64 Palamos, Spain 41 50N 3 10E
104 Palampur, India 32 10N 76 30E
91 Palana, U.S.S.R. 59 10N 160 10E
109 Palanan, Philippines 17 12N 122 33E
104 Palanpur, India 24 10N 72 25E
133 Palapye Rd., Botswana 22 30S 27 7E
106 Palar, R., India 12 27N 80 13E
76 Palase, Albania 40 11N 19 33E
163 Palatka, U.S.A. 29 40N 81 40W
136 Palau Is., Pac. Ocean 7 30N 134 30E
109 Palauig, Philippines 15 26N 120 0E
107 Palauk, Burma 13 10N 98 40E
107 Palaw, Burma 13 0N 98 50E
108 Palawan, I., Philippines 10 0N 119 0E
106 Palayankottai, India 8 45N 77 45E
73 Palazzo San Gervasio, It. 40 53N 15 58E
51 Palazzo, Pte., Corse, Fr. 42 28N 8 30E
73 Palazzolo Acreida, Italy 37 4N 14 43E
143 Palchewoflock, Austral. 35 20S 142 15E
86 Paldisk, U.S.S.R. 59 23N 24 9E
74 Pale, Yugoslavia 43 50N 18 38E
134 Paleisheuwel, S. Africa 32 27S 18 40E
109 Paleleh, Indonesia 1 10N 121 50E
108 Palembang, Indonesia 3 0S 104 50E
176 Palena, Chile 43 40S 73 0W
62 Palencia, Spain 42 1N 4 34W
62 Palencia, prov., Spain 42 31N 4 33W
72 Palermo, Italy 38 8N 13 20E
166 Palermo, U.S.A. 39 30N 121 37W
98 Palestine, *see* Israel & Jordan 32 0N 35 0E
98 Palestine Potash Co. (North), Jordan 31 48N 35 31E
165 Palestine, U.S.A. 31 42N 95 35W
72 Palestrina, Italy 41 50N 12 52E
103 Paletwa, Burma 21 30N 92 50E
106 Palghat, India 10 46N 76 42E
35 Palgrave, Eng., U.K. 52 22N 1 7E
142 Palgrave, Mt., Austral. 23 13S 116 1E
104 Pali, India 25 50N 73 20E
125 Palime, Togo 6 57N 0 37E
73 Palinuro C., Italy 40 1N 15 14E
112 Palinyuchi (Tapanshang), China 43 40N 118 20E
164 Palisade, U.S.A. 40 35N 101 10W
104 Palitana, India 21 32N 71 49E
168 Palizada, Mexico 18 18N 92 8W
73 Palizza, Italy 37 58N 15 59E
106 Palk Bay, India-Ceylon 9 30N 79 30E
106 Palkonda, India 18 36N 83 48E
106 Palkonda Ra., India 13 50N 79 20E
106 Palk Strait, India-Cey. 10 0N 80 0E
133 Palla Rd., Botswana 23 29S 26 37E
70 Pallanza, Italy 45 50N 8 55E
44 Pallasgreen, Ireland 52 35N 8 22W
44 Pallaskenry, Ireland 52 39N 8 53W
87 Pallasovka, U.S.S.R. 50 4N 47 0E
106 Palleru, R., India 17 30N 79 40E
131 Pallisa, Uganda 1 12N 33 43E
146 Palliser Bay, N.Z. 41 26S 175 5E
146 Palliser, C., N.Z. 41 37S 175 14E
104 Pallu, India 28 59N 74 14E
163 Palm Beach, U.S.A. 26 46N 80 0W
144 Palm I., Australia 18 45S 146 35E
167 Palm Springs, U.S.A. 33 51N 116 35W
64 Palma, Balearic Is., Sp. 39 33N 2 39E
131 Palma, Mozambique 10 46S 40 29E
63 Palma del Rio, Spain 37 43N 5 17W
72 Palma di Montechiaro, Sicily, Italy 37 12N 13 46E
120 Palma I., Can. Is., Spain 28 45N 17 50W
174 Palma Sola, Venezula 10 40N 58 35W
169 Palma Soriano, Cuba 20 15N 76 0W
71 Palmanova, Italy 45 54N 13 18E
175 Palmares, Brazil 8 35S 35 30W
72 Palmarola I., Italy 40 57N 12 50E
173 Palmas, Brazil 26 29S 52 0W
124 Palmas, C., Liberia 4 27N 7 46W
72 Palmas, G. of, Italy 39 0N 8 30E
167 Palmdale, U.S.A. 34 36N 118 7W
175 Palmeira dos Indios, Brazil 9 25S 36 30W
130 Palmeirinhas, Ponta das, Angola 9 2S 12 57E
63 Palmela, Portugal 38 32N 8 57W
161 Palmer, Mass., U.S.A. 42 9N 72 21W
15 Palmer Arch, Antarc. 64 15S 65 0W
164 Palmer Lake, U.S.A. 39 10N 104 52W
138 Palmer R., Australia 24 30S 133 0E
144 Palmer R., Australia 15 46S 143 30E
15 Palmer Pen., Antarc. 73 0S 60 0W
160 Palmerston, Canada 43 50N 80 40W
147 Palmerston, N.Z. 45 29S 170 43E
146 Palmerston N., N.Z. 40 21S 175 39E
161 Palmerton, U.S.A. 40 47N 75 36W
163 Palmetto, U.S.A. 27 33N 82 33W
73 Palmi, Italy 38 21N 15 51E
172 Palmira, Argentina 32 59S 68 25W
174 Palmira, Colombia 3 32N 76 16W
160 Palms, U.S.A. 43 37N 82 47W
100 Palmyra, Syria 34 30N 37 55E
164 Palmyra, Mo., U.S.A. 39 45N 91 30W
160 Palmyra, N.Y., U.S.A. 34 5N 77 18W
137 Palmyra Is., Pac. Oc. 5 52N 162 5W
106 Palni, India 10 30N 77 30E
106 Palni Hills, India 10 14N 77 33E
167 Palo Alto, U.S.A. 37 25N 122 8W
73 Palo del Colle, Italy 41 4N 16 43E
71 Palombara, Sabina, It. 42 4N 12 45E
109 Palopo, Indonesia 3 0S 120 16E
127 Paloich, Sudan 10 32N 32 30E
65 Palos, Cabo, Spain 37 38N 0 40W
166 Palouse, U.S.A. 46 59N 117 5W
144 Palparara, Australia 24 47S 141 22E
80 Pålsboda, Sweden 29 3N 15 22E
100 Palu, Turkey 38 45N 40 0E
109 Palu, Indonesia 1 0S 119 59E
109 Paluan, Philippines 13 35N 120 29E
104 Palwal, India 28 8N 77 19E
125 Pama, Upper Volta 11 19N 0 44E
143 Pamamaroo, L., Austral. 32 17S 142 28E
109 Pamanukan, Indonesia 6 16S 107 49E
106 Pamban I., Ceylon 9 24N 79 35E
109 Pamekasan, Indonesia 7 10S 113 29E
109 Pameungpeuk, Indon. 7 38S 107 44E
112 Pamiencheng, China 43 16N 124 4E
50 Pamiers, France 43 7N 1 39E
90 Pamirs, Ra., U.S.S.R. 37 40N 73 0E
163 Pamlico R., U.S.A. 35 25N 76 40W
163 Pamlico Sd., U.S.A. 35 20N 76 0W
165 Pampa, U.S.A. 35 35N 100 58W
172 Pampa de las Salinas, Reg., Argentina 32 1S 66 58W
109 Pampanua, Indonesia 4 22S 120 14E
70 Pamparato, Italy 44 16N 7 54E
114 Pampas, Peru 12 20S 74 50W
176 Pampas, Pls., Arg. 34 0S 64 0W
174 Pamplona, Colombia 7 23N 72 39W
64 Pamplona, Spain 42 48N 1 38W
154 Pampoenpoort, S. Afr. 31 3S 22 40E
133 Pan, Transvaal, S. Afr. 25 44S 29 41E
164 Pana, U.S.A. 39 25N 89 0W
167 Panaca, U.S.A. 37 51N 114 50W
75 Panagyurishte, Bulgaria 42 49N 24 15E
109 Panaitan I., Indonesia 6 35S 105 10E
169 Panama, Pan. Rep. 9 0N 79 25W
168 Panama Canal, Central America 9 10N 79 56W
168 Panama Canal Zone, Central America 9 10N 79 56W
163 Panama City, U.S.A. 30 10N 85 41W
167 Panamint Mts., U.S.A. 36 15N 117 20W
174 Panão, Peru 9 55S 75 55W
73 Panarea I., Italy 38 38N 15 3E
70 Panaro R., Italy 44 48N 11 5E
109 Panarukan, Indonesia 7 40S 113 52E
109 Panay, G., Philippines 0 11N 122 30E
109 Panay I., Philippines 11 0N 122 30E
133 Panbuit, Trans., S. Afr. 26 45S 30 27E
167 Pancake Ra., mts., U.S.A. 38 30N 116 0W
74 Pančevo, Yugoslavia 44 52N 20 41E
78 Panciu, Rumania 45 54N 27 8E
74 Pancota, Rumania 46 20N 21 45E
109 Pandan, Philippines 11 45N 122 10E
109 Pandegelang, Indonesia 6 25S 106 0E
106 Pandharpur, India 17 41N 75 20E
104 Pandhurna, India 21 36N 78 35E
64 Pandilla, Spain 41 32N 3 43W
173 Pando, Uruguay 34 30S 56 0W
86 Panevezys, U.S.S.R. 55 42N 24 25E
90 Panfilov, U.S.S.R. 44 30N 80 0E
87 Panfilovo, U.S.S.R. 50 25N 42 46E
103 Pang-Long Burma 23 11N 98 45E
103 Pang-Yang, China 22 7N 98 48E
109 Pangalengan, Indon. 7 9S 107 30E
76 Pangalon Öros mts., Gr. 40 50N 24 0E
131 Pangani & dist., Tanzania 5 25S 38 58E
131 Pagani R., Tanzania 4 40S 37 50E
34 Pangbourne, Eng., U.K. 51 28N 1 5W
107 Panghai, Burma 23 0N 97 25E
130 Pangi, Congo 3 10S 26 35E
108 Pangkalanberandan, Indonesia 4 1N 98 20E
108 Pangkalansusu, Indon. 4 2N 98 42E
112 Pangkiang (Mingan), China 43 4N 112 30E
107 Pangkor I., Malaysia 4 16N 100 30E
133 Pangola R., S. Africa 23 40S 27 43E
109 Pangrango Mt., Indon. 6 46S 107 1E
167 Panguitch, U.S.A. 37 52N 112 30W
109 Pangutaran Group, Phil. 6 18N 120 34E
165 Panhandle, U.S.A. 35 23N 101 23W
104 Pani Mines, India 22 29N 73 50E
104 Panipat, India 29 25N 77 2E
143 Panitya, Vic., Australia 35 15S 141 0E
104 Panjal Range, India 32 30N 76 50E
102 Panjgur, West Pakistan 27 0N 64 5E
106 Panjim, India 15 25N 73 50E
101 Panjinad Barrage, W. Pakistan 29 22N 71 15E
109 Pankadjene, Indonesia 4 46S 119 34E
108 Pankal Pinang, Indon. 2 0S 106 0E
125 Pankshin, Nigeria 9 25N 9 25E
105 Panna, India 24 40N 80 15E
105 Panna Hills, India 24 40N 81 15E
106 Pannuru, India 16 5N 80 34E
106 Panruti, India 11 46N 79 35E
112 Panshan, China 41 15N 122 0E
112 Panshih, China 42 59N 126 0E
167 Pantano, U.S.A. 32 0N 110 32W
62 Pantano del Ebro, Spain 43 0N 4 0W
109 Pantar I., Indonesia 8 28S 124 10E
72 Pantelleria & I., Italy 36 52N 12 0E
109 Pantjo, Indonesia 8 42S 118 40E
62 Panton, Spain 42 31N 7 37W
109 Pantukan, Philippines 7 17N 125 58E
130 Panu, Congo 35 0S 19 10E
106 Panvel, India 18 58N 73 6E
168 Panuco, Mexico 22 0N 98 25W
125 Panyam, Nigeria 9 27N 9 8E
112 Paochang, China 41 46N 115 30E
112 Paocheng, China 33 12N 107 0E
113 Paokang, China 31 57N 111 21E
113 Paoki, China 34 25N 107 15E
113 Paoko, China 34 22N 107 12E
73 Páola, Italy 39 21N 16 2E
164 Paola, U.S.A. 38 36N 94 50W
167 Paonia, U.S.A. 38 56N 107 37W
103 Paoshan, China 25 13N 99 17E
112 Paoteh, China 39 0N 110 45E
112 Paoting, China 38 50N 115 30E
112 Paotow, China 40 45N 110 0E
112 Paotsing, China 28 35N 109 35E
121 Paoua, Cent. Afr. Rep. 7 25N 16 30E
113 Paoying, China 33 10N 119 20E
59 Pápa, Hungary 47 22N 17 30E
43 Papa Sd., Scot., U.K. 59 20N 2 56W
42 Papa, Sd. of, Scot., U.K. 60 19N 1 40W
42 Papa Stour I., Scotland, U.K. 60 20N 1 40W
43 Papa Stronsay I., Scotland, U.K. 59 10N 2 37W
43 Papa Westray I., Scotland, U.K. 59 20N 2 55W
106 Papagni R., India 14 0N 78 30E
175 Papai, Surinam 2 28N 56 21W
168 Papagayo R., Brazil 12 30S 58 10W
169 Papagayo Gulf, Costa Rica 10 4N 85 50W
146 Papakura, New Zealand 37 4S 174 59E
168 Papalantla de Olarte, Mexico 20 30N 97 21W
168 Papaloapan, R., Mexico 18 2N 96 51W

MAP
168 Papantla, Mexico 20 27N 97 19w
108 Papar, Sab., Malaysia 5 45N 116 0 E
146 Paparoa, New
Zealand ....36 6 s 174 16 E
147 Paparoa Range, N.Z. .42 5 s 171 35 E
77 Pápas, Ákra C.,
Greece ....38 13N 21 6 E
56 Papenburg, Germany .53 7N 7 25 E
172 Paposo, Chile ....25 0 s 70 30w
44 Paps, The, mts., Ire. .52 0N 9 15w
144 Papua, Gulf of, Papua 9 0 s 144 50 E
144 Papua, Terr. of,
Austral. N. Guin. .. 8 0 s 145 0 E
71 Papuca, Yugoslavia ...44 22N 15 30 E
172 Papudo, Chile ....32 29 s 71 27w
74 Papuk, mts.,
Yugoslavia ......45 30N 17 30 E
103 Papun, Burma ....18 0N 97 30 E
175 Pará, st., Brazil .... 3 20 s 52 0w
175 Pará R., Brazil .... 0 40 s 48 30w
73 Parabita, Italy ....40 3N 18 8 E
175 Paracatú, Brazil ....17 10 s 46 50w
108 Paracel Is., Asia ......16 49N 111 2 E
145 Parachilna, S.
Australia ....31 10 s 138 21 E
102 Parachinar, W. Pak. .34 0N 70 5 E
74 Paracin, Yugoslavia ..43 54N 21 27 E
63 Paradas, Spain 37 18N 5 29w
105 Paradeep, India ....20 15N 86 35 E
62 Parádhista, Spain 42 44N 7 37w
166 Paradise, U.S.A. 47 27N 114 54w
166 Paradise Valley,
U.S.A. 41 30N 117 28w
109 Parado, Indonesia ... 8 42 s 118 30 E
60 Paradyz, Poland ......51 19N 20 2 E
165 Paragould, U.S.A. 36 5N 90 30w
173 Paraguaçu Paulista,
Brazil ....22 22 s 50 35w
174 Paraguai, R., Brazil ..16 0 s 57 52w
172 Paraguari, Paraguay .25 36 s 57 0w
176 Paraguay, rep., S.
America ....23 0 s 57 0w
172 Paraguay R.,
Paraguay ....24 30 s 58 20w
175 Paraíba, st., Brazil .. 7 0 s 37 0w
175 Paraíba, R., Brazil ... 7 0 s 35 0w
83 Parainen, Finland ....60 21N 22 11 E
86 Parakhino Paddubye,
U.S.S.R. ....58 46N 33 10 E
125 Parakou, Dahomey ... 9 25N 2 40 E
77 Paralion-Astrous Gr. .37 25N 22 45 E
106 Paramagudi, India ... 9 31N 78 35 E
175 Paramaribo, Surinam . 5 50N 55 10w
76 Paramithia, Greece ...39 30N 20 35 E
91 Paramushir, I., Kuril
Is. ....40 24N 156 0 E
172 Paraná, Argentina ....32 0 s 60 30w
175 Paraná, Brazil ....12 30 s 47 40w
173 Paraná, st., Brazil ...24 30 s 51 0w
175 Paraná, R., Brazil ....22 25 s 53 1w
173 Paranaguá, Brazil ....25 30 s 48 30w
175 Paranaíba, Brazil .....18 0 s 49 12w
175 Paranam, Surinam ... 5 45N 55 10w
173 Paranapiacaba. Serra,
Brazil ....24 31 s 48 35w
109 Parang, Jolo, Phil. .. 6 0N 121 2 E
109 Parang, Mindanao,
Phil. .... 7 30N 124 16 E
175 Paraopeba, Brazil ....19 0 s 44 10w
147 Paraparaumu, N.Z. ..40 57 s 175 5 E
77 Parapola, I., Greece ..36 55N 23 27 E
77 Parasa 	Sport, Ákra, C.,
Gr. ....35 55N 27 15 E
175 Paratinga, Brazil .....12 40 s 43 10w
145 Paratoo, S. Australia .32 38 s 139 15 E
145 Parattah, Tas.,
Austral. ....42 22 s 147 23 E
51 Paray le Monial, Fr. ..46 27N 4 7 E
104 Parbati R., India .....24 0N 77 10 E
106 Parbhani, India ....19 8N 76 52 E
56 Parchim, Germany ....53 25N 11 50 E
60 Parczew, Poland ......51 9N 22 52 E
98 Pardes Hanna, Israel .32 28N 34 57 E
62 Pardilla, Spain 41 33N 3 43w
175 Pardo R., Mato
Grosso, Brazil .....21 0 s 53 25w
175 Pardo R., Sao Paulo,
Brazil ....20 45 s 48 0w
58 Pardubice, Cz. ....50 3N 15 45 E
131 Pare Mts., Tanzania .. 4 0 s 37 5 E
109 Pare, Indonesia .... 7 43 s 112 12 E
174 Parecis, Brazil ....14 8 s 57 10w
62 Paredes-de-Nava,
Spain 42 9N 4 42w
91 Paren, U.S.S.R. ......62 45N 163 0 E
146 Parengarenga
Harbour, N.Z. ...34 31 s 173 0 E
154 Parent, Canada ....47 55N 74 35 w
154 Parent, Lac., Canada .48 31N 77 1 w
50 Parentis en Born, Fr. .44 21N 1 / w
109 Parepare, Indonesia .. 4 0 s 119 40 E
86 Parfino, U.S.S.R. ....57 59N 31 34 E
161 Parham, Canada ......44 40N 76 40 w
169 Paria, G. of,
Venezuela 10 20N 62 0w
175 Paria Pen., Venezuela 10 40N 62 30w
109 Parigi, Celebes, Indon. 0 50 s 120 5 E
174 Pariaguan, Venezuela 8 52N 64 34w
174 Pariaguán, Venezuela 8 51N 64 43w
108 Pariaman, Indonesia . 0 47 s 100 11 E
174 Parika, Guyana 6 50N 58 20w
174 Parinari, Peru .... 4 35 s 74 25w
174 Pariñas, Pta.,
Ecuador .... 4 45 s 81 22w
78 Parincea, Rumania ....46 27N 27 ;0 E
78 Paríngul-Mare, mt.,
Rumania ....45 20N 23 37 E
175 Parintins, Brazil ...... 2 40 s 56 50w
154 Paris, Canada 43 20N 80 25w

49 Paris, France ....48 50N 2 20 E
166 Paris, Idaho, U.S.A. ..42 13N 111 30w
162 Paris, Ky., U.S.A. 38 12N 84 12w
163 Paris, Tenn., U.S.A. ..36 20N 88 20w
165 Paris, Tex., U.S.A. ...33 40N 95 30w
161 Parish, U.S.A. 43 24N 76 9w
109 Pariti, Indonesia ...... 9 55 s 123 30w
42 Park, dist., Scot.,
U.K. 58 2N 6 33w
166 Park City, U.S.A. 40 42N 111 35w
164 Park Falls, U.S.A. ....45 58N 90 27 E
160 Park Head, Canada ...44 36N 81 10w
166 Park Range, U.S.A. ...40 0N 106 30w
164 Park Rapids, U.S.A. ..46 56N 95 0w
164 Park River, U.S.A. ...48 25N 97 17w
167 Park View, U.S.A. 36 45N 106 37w
82 Parkano, Finland .....62 5N 23 0 E
167 Parker, Ariz., U.S.A. .34 8N 114 16w
164 Parker, S.D., U.S.A. .43 25N 97 7w
167 Parker Dam, U.S.A. ..34 13N 114 5w
162 Parkersburg, U.S.A. ..39 18N 81 31w
157 Parkerview (Sask.),
Can. 51 28N 103 18w
143 Parkes, N.S.W.,
Austral. ....33 9 s 148 11 E
44 Parknasilla, Ireland ..51 49N 9 50w
164 Parkston, U.S.A. 43 25N 98 0w
156 Parksville (B.C.), Can. 49 20N 124 21w
106 Parlakimedi, India ...18 45N 84 5 E
70 Parma, Italy ....44 50N 10 20 E
166 Parma, Idaho, U.S.A. .43 49N 116 59w
160 Parma, Ohio, U.S.A. .41 25N 81 42w
70 Parma R., Italy ....44 27N 10 3 E
175 Parnaguá, Brazil ......10 10 s 44 10w
175 Parnaíba, Piauí,
Brazil .... 3 0 s 41 40w
175 Parnaíba, São Paulo,
Brazil ....19 34 s 51 14w
175 Parnaíba R., Brazil .. 3 35 s 43 0w
77 Parnassós Mt., Greece 38 32N 22 41 E
147 Parnassus, New
Zealand ....42 43 s 173 23 E
77 Párnis Mt., Greece ...38 14N 23 45 E
77 Parnon Oros, mts.,
Gr. ....37 15N 22 45 E
86 Parnu, U.S.S.R. ......58 12N 24 33 E
104 Parola, India ....20 47N 75 7 E
145 Paroo Chan.,
Australia ....30 50 s 143 35 E
145 Paroo R., Australia ..30 0 s 144 5 E
101 Paropamisus Range,
Afghanistan ......34 45N 63 0 E
77 Páros, Greece ....37 5N 25 9 E
77 Páros I., Greece ......37 5N 25 12 E
167 Parowan, U.S.A. 37 54N 112 56w
36 Parracombe, Eng.,
U.K. 51 11N 3 55w
172 Parral, Chile ....36 10 s 72 0w
143 Parramatta, Australia 33 48 s 151 1 E
168 Parras, Mexico 25 30N 102 20w
57 Parrentruy,
Switzerland ......47 28N 7 7 E
163 Parris I., U.S.A. 32 20N 80 30w
155 Parrsboro, Canada ...45 30N 64 10w
157 Parry, Canada 49 47N 104 41w
14 Parry Is., Canada 77 0N 110 0w
160 Parry Sound, Canada .45 20N 80 0w
164 Parshall, U.S.A. 47 56N 102 11w
165 Parsons, U.S.A. 37 20N 95 10w
106 Partabpur, India .....20 0N 80 42 E
72 Partanna, Italy ....37 43N 12 51 E
104 Partapgarh, India ....24 2N 74 40 E
48 Parthenay, France 46 38N 0 16w
81 Partille, Sweden ......57 48N 12 18 E
72 Partinico, Italy ....38 3N 13 6 E
39 Partney, Eng., U.K. ..53 12N 0 7 E
38 Parton, Eng., U.K. ...54 34N 3 35w
45 Partry Mts., Ireland ..53 40N 9 28w
106 Partur, India ....19 40N 76 14 E
175 Paru R., Brazil .... 0 20 s 53 30w
106 Parur, India ....10 13N 76 14 E
174 Paruro, Peru ....13 45 s 71 50w
106 Parvatipuram, India .18 50N 83 25 E
77 Parwan, prov.,
Afghan. ....35 0N 69 0 E
81 Påryd, Sweden ....56 34N 15 49 E
135 Parys, O.F.S.S Africa 26 52 s 27 29 E
37 Parys, Mt., Wales,
UK 53 23N 4 18w
49 Pas-de-Calais, dépt.,
Fr. ....50 30N 2 30 E
167 Pasadena, Calif.,
U.S.A. 34 5N 118 0w
165 Pasadena, Tex.,
U.S.A. 29 45N 95 14w
174 Pasaje, Ecuador ...... 3 10 s 79 40w
109 Pasay City,
Philippines ......14 20N 120 55 E
165 Pascagoula, U.S.A. ...30 30N 88 30w
165 Pascagoula R., U.S.A. 30 40N 88 35w
78 Pașcani, Rumania ....47 14N 26 45 E
166 Pasco, U.S.A. 46 10N 119 0w
142 Pascoe, Mt., W.
Australia ....27 25 s 120 40 E
56 Pasewalk, Germany ...53 30N 14 0 E
86 Pasha, R., U.S.S.R. ...60 20N 33 0 E
107 Pasir Mas., Malaysia . 6 2N 102 8 E
107 Pasir Puteh, Malaysia 5 50N 102 24 E
109 Pasirian, Indonesia .. 8 13 s 113 8 E
71 Pasman I.,
Yugoslavia ......43 58N 15 20 E
102 Pasni, West Pakistan .25 15N 63 27 E
176 Paso de los Indios,
Arg. ....43 55 s 69 0w
172 Paso de los Libres,
Arg. ....29 44 s 57 10w
172 Paso de los Toros,
Urug. ....32 36 s 56 37w
167 Paso Robles, U.S.A. ..35 40N 120 45w
155 Paspebiac, Canada ...48 3N 65 17w

104 Pasrur, West Pakistan 32 16N 74 43 E
45 Passage East, Ireland 52 15N 7 0w
44 Passage West, Ireland 51 52N 8 20w
161 Passaic, U.S.A. 40 50N 74 8w
57 Passau, Germany .....48 34N 13 27 E
73 Passero, C., Italy .....36 42N 15 8 E
70 Passo del Tonale,
Italy ....46 15N 10 34 E
173 Passo Fundo, Brazil ...28 10 s 52 30w
175 Passos, Brazil ....20 45 s 46 29w
56 Passow, Germany .....53 13N 14 3 E
174 Pastaza R., Peru ..... 2 45 s 76 50w
174 Pasto, Colombia 1 13N 77 17w
64 Pastrana, Spain 40 27N 2 53w
78 Pasul Buzău, Pass,
Rumania ....45 35N 26 12 E
78 Pasul Prislop, Pass,
Rumania ....47 37N 25 15 E
109 Pasuruan, Indonesia . 7 40 s 112 53 E
60 Pasym, Poland ....53 48N 20 49 E
59 Pásztó, Hungary .....47 52N 19 43 E
176 Patagonia, reg., S.
Arg. ....45 0 s 69 0w
167 Patagonia, U.S.A. 31 35N 110 45w
106 Patan, India ....17 22N 73 48 E
104 Patan, India ....23 54N 72 14 E
112 Pataokiang, China ....41 58N 126 30 E
104 Pataudi, India ....28 18N 76 48 E
49 Patay, France ....48 2N 1 40 E
35 Patcham, Eng., U.K. .50 52N 0 9w
161 Patchogue, U.S.A. 40 46N 73 1w
147 Patea, New Zealand ..39 45 s 174 30 E
125 Pategi, Nigeria .... 8 50N 5 45 E
37 Pateley Bridge,
England, U.K. 54 5N 1 45w
134 Patensie, S. Africa ...33 46 s 24 49 E
73 Paterno, Italy ....37 34N 14 53 E
134 Paternoster, S. Africa 32 48 s 17 52 E
108 Paternoster Is., see
Balabalangan ... 2 20 s 117 30 E
166 Pateros, U.S.A. 48 4N 119 58w
143 Paterson, N.S.W.,
Austral. ....32 37 s 151 39 E
161 Paterson, N.J., U.S.A. 40 55N 74 10w
147 Paterson Inlet, N.Z. ..46 56 s 168 12 E
104 Pathankot, India .....32 18N 75 45 E
166 Pathfinder Res.,
U.S.A. 42 0N 107 0w
109 Páti, Indonesia .... 6 45 s 111 3 E
124 Patiala, India ....30 23N 76 26 E
124 Patim-Kouta, Senegal 12 45N 13 45w
109 Pätjitan, Indonesia ... 8 12 s 111 8 E
103 Patkai Bum, Mts.,
India ....27 0N 95 30 E
77 Patmos & I., Ægean
Sea ....37 21N 26 36 E
40 Patna, Scotland, U.K. 55 21N 4 30w
105 Patna, Bihar, India ...25 35N 85 18 E
131 Patonga, Uganda ..... 2 45N 33 15 E
175 Patos de Minas, Brazil 18 25 s 46 30w
175 Patos, Para, Brazil .. 3 20 s 49 20w
173 Patos, Lagôa dos,
Brazil ....31 20 s 51 0 E
172 Patquia, Argentina ...30 0 s 66 55w
77 Pátrai, Greece ....38 14N 21 47 E
77 Patraikós, Kólpos, G.,
Greece ....38 17N 21 30 E
82 Patreks Fd., Iceland .65 35N 24 8w
14 Patrick, I. of M.,
U.K. 54 13N 4 41w
39 Patrington, Eng.,
U.K. 53 41N 0 1w
175 Patrocinio, Brazil .....19 0 s 47 0w
131 Patta & I., Kenya .... 2 10 s 41 2 E
72 Pattada, Italy ....40 35N 9 7 E
106 Pattanapuram, India . 9 6N 76 33 E
107 Pattani, Thailand ....6 48N 101 15 E
38 Patten, U.S.A. 45 59N 68 28w
38 Patterdale, Eng.,
U.K. 54 33N 2 55w
135 Patterson, S. Africa ..33 24 s 24 2 E
167 Patterson, Calif.,
U.S.A. 37 30N 121 9w
165 Patterson, La., U.S.A. 29 44N 91 20w
104 Patti, India ....31 17N 74 54 E
73 Patti Castroreale,
Italy ....38 8N 14 57 E
104 Pattoki, West
Pakistan ....31 5N 73 52 E
160 Patton, U.S.A. 40 38N 78 40w
105 Patuakhali, E.
Pakistan ....22 20N 90 25 E
169 Patuca, Punta, Hond. 15 49N 84 14w
169 Patuca R., Honduras .15 20N 84 40w
106 Pattukkotta, India ...10 25N 79 20 E
113 Patung, China ....31 5N 110 30 E
146 Patutahi, N.Z. ....38 38 s 177 55 E
168 Pátzcuaro, Mexico 19 30N 101 40w
50 Pau, France 43 19N 0 25w
50 Pauillac, France 45 11N 0 46w
175 Pauini R., Brazil ...... 7 40 s 68 10 E
103 Pauk, Burma ....21 55N 94 30 E
155 Paul I., Canada 56 30N 61 20w
135 Paul Roux, OFS, S.
Afr. ....28 18 s 27 59 E
176 Pedro Luro,
Argentina ....39 25 s 62 50w
131 Paulis, see Isiro,
Congo .... 2 53N 27 58 E
175 Paulistana, Brazil .... 8 0 s 41 15w
36 Paulton, Eng., U.K. ..51 18N 2 29w
105 Pauni, India ....20 48N 79 40 E
38 Pavelets, U.S.S.R. ....53 49N 39 14 E
70 Pavia, Italy ....45 10N 9 10 E
75 Pavlikeni, Bulgaria ...43 14N 25 20 E

90 Pavlodar, U.S.S.R. ...52 33N 77 0 E
88 Pavlograd, U.S.S.R. ..48 30N 25 52 E
87 Pavlovo, Gorki, USSR 55 58N 43 5 E
91 Pavlovo, Yakut
A.S.S.R., U.S.S.R. .63 5N 115 25 E
87 Pavlovsk, Voronezh,
U.S.S.R. ....50 26N 40 5 E
89 Pavlovskaya,
U.S.S.R. ....46 17N 39 47 E
87 Pavlovskiy Posad,
U.S.S.R. ....55 37N 38 42 E
70 Pavullo nel Frignano,
It. ....44 20N 10 50 E
165 Pawhuska, U.S.A. 36 40N 96 25w
161 Pawling, U.S.A. 41 35N 73 37w
165 Pawnee, U.S.A. 36 24N 96 50w
161 Pawnee City, U.S.A. ..40 8N 96 10w
161 Pawtucket, U.S.A. 41 51N 71 22w
77 Paximádhia, Is., Crete 35 0N 24 35 E
77 Paxoí, I., Greece .....39 14N 20 12 E
162 Paxton, Ill., U.S.A. ...40 25N 88 0w
165 Paxton, Neb., U.S.A. .41 12N 101 27w
107 Paya Bakri, Malaysia 2 3N 102 44 E
112 Payen, China ....45 57N 127 58 E
57 Payerne, Switzerland .46 49N 6 56 E
164 Payette, U.S.A. 44 0N 117 0w
63 Paymogo, Spain 37 44N 7 21w
153 Payne L., Canada 59 30N 74 30w
153 Payne R., Canada 60 0N 70 0w
142 Paynes Find, W.
Austral. ....29 15 s 117 30 E
124 Paynesville, Liberia . 6 20N 10 45w
164 Paynesville, U.S.A. ..45 21N 94 44w
172 Paysandu, Uruguay ..32 19 s 58 8w
167 Payson, Ariz., U.S.A. .34 17N 111 15w
167 Payson, Utah, U.S.A. 40 8N 111 41w
174 Paz del Rio, Colombia 6 10N 72 35w
102 Pazar, Turkey ....41 10N 40 50 E
75 Pazardzhik, Bulgaria .42 12N 24 20 E
71 Pazin, Yugoslavia ....45 14N 13 56 E
74 Pčinja, R.,
Yugoslavia ......42 0N 21 45 E
166 Pe Ell, Winlock,
U.S.A. 46 30N 122 59w
161 Peabody, U.S.A. 42 31N 70 56w
156 Peace River, Canada .56 15N 117 18w
156 Peace R., Canada 59 30N 111 30w
167 Peach Springs, U.S.A. 35 36N 113 30w
35 Peacehaven, Eng.,
U.K. ....50 47N 0 1 E
37 Peachdale, S. Africa ..26 30 s 24 42 E
144 Peak Downs,
Australia ....22 55 s 148 0 E
143 Peak Hill, N.S.W.,
Austral. ....32 39 s 148 11 E
142 Peak Hill, W.
Australia ....25 35 s 118 43 E
144 Peak Range, Australia 22 50 s 148 20 E
38 Peak, The, mt.,
England, U.K. 53 24N 1 53w
145 Peake, S. Australia ...35 25 s 140 0 E
167 Peale Mt., U.S.A. 38 25N 109 12w
167 Pearce, U.S.A. 31 57N 109 56w
106 Pearl Banks, Ceylon .. 8 45N 79 45 E
165 Pearl, R., U.S.A. 31 50N 90 0w
165 Pearsall, U.S.A. 28 55N 99 8w
156 Pearse I., Canada .....54 9N 130 4 E
135 Pearston, S. Africa ...33 33 s 25 7 E
14 Peary Ld., Greenland 83 0N 35 0w
166 Pease R., U.S.A. 34 18N 100 15w
35 Peasenhall, Eng.,
U.K. ....52 17N 1 24 E
129 Pebane, Mozambique 17 10 s 38 8 E
174 Pebas, Peru .... 3 10 s 71 55w
70 Peccioli, Italy ....43 32N 10 43 E
84 Pechea, Rumania .....45 36N 27 49 E
88 Pechenezhin, U.S.S.R. 48 30N 24 48 E
84 Pechenga, U.S.S.R. ..69 30N 31 25 E
84 Pechora R., U.S.S.R. .68 40N 54 0 E
84 Pechora G., U.S.S.R. .62 30N 56 30 E
74 Pecica, Rumania .....46 10N 21 3 E
74 Pecora C., Italy ......39 28N 8 23 E
74 Pečka, Yugoslavia ....44 18N 19 33 E
165 Pecos, U.S.A. 31 25N 103 35w
165 Pecos R., U.S.A. 31 22N 102 30w
59 Pécs, Hungary ....46 5N 18 15 E
106 Peddapalli, India .....18 40N 79 24 E
106 Peddapuram, India ...17 6N 82 5 E
106 Peddavagu R., India 16 33N 79 8 E
135 Peddie, C. Prov., S.
Afr. ....33 10 s 27 9 E
124 Pedembu, Sierra
Leone 8 7N 10 48w
108 Pedjantan I., Indon. . 0 5 s 106 15 E
175 Pedra Azul, Brazil ...16 2 s 41 17w
175 Pedreiras, Brazil ..... 4 32 s 44 40w
175 Pedro Afonso, Brazil . 9 0 s 48 10w
172 Pedro de Valdivia,
Chile ....22 33 s 69 38w
130 Pedro do Feitico,
Ang. .... 5 58 s 12 45 E
173 Pedro Juan Caballero,
Paraguay ....22 30 s 55 40w
168 Pedro Miguel Locks,
Panama Canal Zone 9 1N 79 36w
65 Pedro Muñoz, Spain ..39 25N 2 56w
62 Pedrógão Grande,
Port. 39 55N 8 0w
144 Peebinga, S. Australia 34 52 s 140 57 E
41 Peebles, Scotland,
U.K. 55 40N 3 12w
41 Peebles, co., Scot.,
U.K. 55 37N 3 4w
161 Peekshill, U.S.A. 41 18N 73 57w
38 Peel, I. of Man, U.K. .54 14N 4 40w
41 Peel Fell, mt., Eng.,
U.K. 55 17N 2 35w

152 Peel, R., Canada 67 0N 135 0w
56 Peene R., Germany ...53 52N 13 35 E
145 Peera Peera Poolanna
L. South Australia .26 30 s 138 0 E
147 Pegasus Bay, N.Z. ....43 20 s 173 10 E
58 Peggau, Austria ......47 12N 15 21 E
65 Pego, Spain 38 51N 0 8w
41 Peggwood, Eng., U.K. 55 12N 1 38w
103 Pegu, Burma ....17 20N 96 29 E
103 Pegu Yoma Mts.,
Burma ....19 0N 96 0 E
35 Pegwell Bay, Eng.,
U.K. ....51 18N 1 22 E
112 Pehan, China ....48 17N 120 31 E
71 Pehcevo, Yugoslavia .41 41N 23 3 E
113 Pehpei, China ....29 44N 106 29 E
112 Pehtaiho, China ......39 50N 119 30 E
172 Pehuajo, Argentina ...36 0 s 62 0w
172 Peine, Chile ....23 45 s 68 08w
56 Peine, Germany ....52 19N 10 12 E
57 Peissenberg, Germany 47 48N 11 4 E
56 Peitz, Germany ....51 50N 14 23 E
175 Peixe, Brazil ....12 0 s 48 40w
77 Pek, R., Yugoslavia ..44 58N 21 55 E
109 Pekalongan, Indonesia 6 53 s 109 40 E
107 Pekan, W. Malaysia .. 3 30N 103 25 E
164 Pekin, China 40 35N 89 40w
112 Peking (Peiping),
China ....39 50N 116 20 E
109 Pelabuhanratu,
Indon. .... 7 0 s 106 32 E
76 Pélagos, I., Greece ...39 17N 24 4 E
71 Pelagruza Is.,
Y.-slavia ....42 24N 16 15 E
108 Pelaihari, Indonesia . 3 55 s 114 45 E
78 Peleaga, mt.,
Rumania ....45 22N 22 55 E
154 Pelee I., Canada 41 40N 82 40w
169 Pelée Mt., Martinique
I. 14 40N 61 0w
109 Peleng I., Indonesia . 1 20 s 123 30 E
163 Pelham, U.S.A. 31 5N 84 6w
58 Pelhrimov, Cz. ....49 25N 15 12 E
156 Pelican, Chichagof I.,
Alaska, U.S.A. ...58 12N 136 28w
157 Pelican Narrows, Can. 55 12N 102 55w
156 Pelican Portage, Can. 55 51N 113 0w
157 Pelican Rapids,
Canada 52 38N 100 42w
169 Peligre Dam, Haiti ...19 1N 71 58w
55 Pelkum, Germany ....51 19N 7 44 E
134 Pella, C. Prov. S. Afr.29 1 s 19 6 E
164 Pella, U.S.A. 41 20N 93 0w
76 Pélla, pref., Greece ..40 52N 22 0 E
73 Péllaro, Italy ....38 1N 15 40 E
56 Pellworm I., Germany 54 30N 8 40 E
152 Pelly L., Canada 66 0N 102 0w
152 Pelly, R., Canada 62 15N 133 30w
77 Peloponnesos, Greece .37 10N 22 0 E
73 Peloro, C., Italy ......38 15N 15 40 E
147 Pelorus Sound, N.Z. ..40 59 s 173 59 E
173 Pelotas, Brazil ....31 42 s 52 23w
51 Pelvoux, Massif de,
Fr. ....44 52N 6 20 E
109 Pemalang, Indonesia . 6 53 s 109 23 E
108 Pematang I.,
Indonesia .... 2 50N 96 55 E
108 Pematang Siantar,
Indonesia .... 2 57N 99 5 E
132 Pemba, Zambia ....16 30 s 27 28 E
131 Pemba Channel, Tanz. 5 0 s 39 37 E
131 Pemba, I., Tanz. ..... 5 0 s 39 45 E
156 Pemberton, Canada ..50 25N 122 50w
142 Pemberton, W.
Austral. ....34 30 s 116 0 E
162 Pembine, U.S.A. 45 38N 87 59w
37 Pembrey, Wales, U.K. 51 42N 4 17w
34 Pembridge, Eng.,
U.K. 52 13N 2 54w
154 Pembroke, Canada ...45 50N 77 15w
37 Pembroke, Wales,
U.K. 51 41N 4 57w
163 Pembroke, U.S.A. 32 5N 81 32w
37 Pembroke, co., Wales,
United Kingdom ..51 40N 5 0w
37 Pembroke Dock,
Wales, U.K. 51 41N 4 57w
35 Pembury, Eng., U.K. 51 8N 0 20 E
161 Pen Argyl, U.S.A. ....40 52N 75 17 E
64 Peña Roya, mt.,
Spain 40 24N 0 40w
62 Peñafiel, Portugal ...41 12N 8 17w
64 Peñafiel, Spain 41 35N 4 7w
37 Penally, Wales, U.K. .51 39N 4 44w
62 Penamacor, Portugal .40 10N 7 10w
107 Penang I., W.
Malaysia .... 5 25N 100 15 E
173 Penápolis, Brazil .....21 30 s 50 0w
62 Peñaranda de
Bracamonte, Spain .40 53N 5 13w
36 Penare Hd., Eng.,
U.K. 50 12N 4 55w
143 Penarie, N.S.W.,
Austral. ....34 30 s 143 35 E
63 Penarroya
Puebonuevo, Spain .38 19N 5 16w
37 Penarth, Wales, U.K. 51 26N 3 11w
62 Peñas. C. de, Spain ..43 42N 5 52w
176 Peñas, G. of, Chile ..47 0 s 75 0w
172 Penco, Chile ....36 45 s 73 0w
37 Pencoed, Wales, U.K. 51 31N 3 30w
166 Pend Oreille, L.,
U.S.A. 48 0N 116 30w
166 Pend Oreille R.,
U.S.A. 48 30N 117 8w
76 Pendálofon, Greece ..40 14N 21 12 E
77 Pendelikón, Mt., Gr. .38 5N 23 53 E
37 Pendine, Wales, U.K. 51 44N 4 33w
38 Pendle Hill, Eng.,
U.K. 53 53N 2 18w

MAP

166 Pendleton, U.S.A. 45 35N 118 50W
175 Penedo, Brazil 10 15S 36 40W
154 Penetanguishene, Can. 44 50N 79 55W
113 Pengan, China 31 0N 106 18E
113 Pengchia Yu (Agincourt) Is., Taiwan 25 4N 122 2E
113 Penghu (Pescadores) Is., Taiwan 23 30N 119 30E
112 Penglai (Tengchowfu), China 37 50N 120 50E
113 Pengpu, China 33 0N 117 25E
113 Pengshui, China 29 20N 108 15E
145 Penguin, Tas. Austral. 41 8S 146 6E
132 Penhalonga, Rhodesia 18 52S 32 40E
63 Peniche, Portugal 39 19N 9 22W
41 Penicuik, Scot., U.K. ..55 50N 3 14W
108 Penida I., Indonesia ... 8 45S 115 30E
64 Peñiscola, Spain 40 22N 0 24E
39 Penistone, Eng., U.K. 53 31N 1 38W
112 Penki, China 41 20N 132 50E
34 Penkridge, Eng., U.K. 52 44N 2 8W
37 Penmachno, Wales, UK 53 2N 3 47W
37 Penmaenmawr, Wales, United Kingdom 53 16N 3 55W
48 Penmarch, France 47 49N 4 21W
48 Penmarch, Pte. de, Fr. 47 48N 4 22W
160 Penn Yan, U.S.A. 42 39N 77 7W
71 Pennabilli, Italy 43 50N 12 17E
71 Penne, Italy 42 28N 13 56E
106 Penner R., India 14 50N 78 20E
38 Pennines, Mts., Eng., U.K. 54 50N 2 20W
125 Pennington R., Nigeria 4 45N 5 20E
71 Pennino, Mte., Italy ...43 6N 12 54E
162 Pennsylvania st., U.S.A. 40 50N 78 0W
156 Penny, Canada 53 58N 121 1W
86 Peno, U.S.S.R. 57 2N 32 33E
145 Penola, South Australia 37 12S 140 51E
169 Penomoné, Panama ... 8 37N 80 25W
138 Penong, South Australia 31 59S 133 5E
41 Penpont, Scotland, U.K. 55 14N 3 49W
137 Penrhyn Is., Pac. Oc. 9 0S 150 30W
38 Penrith, England, U.K. 54 40N 2 45W
143 Penrith, N.S.W., Austral. 33 43S 150 38E
36 Penryn, England, U.K. 50 10N 5 7W
163 Pensacola, U.S.A. 30 30N 87 10W
15 Pensacola Mts., Antarc. 84 0S 40 0W
35 Penshurst, Eng., U.K. 51 10N 0 12E
143 Penshurst, Vic., Austral. 37 49S 142 20W
156 Penticton, Canada 49 30N 119 30W
35 Pentire Pt., Eng., U.K. 50 35N 4 57W
144 Pentland, Australia ...20 32S 145 25E
43 Pentland Firth, Scot., U.K. 58 43N 3 10W
41 Pentland Hills, Scotland, U.K. 55 48N 3 25W
43 Pentland Skerries, Scotland, U.K. 58 41N 2 53W
37 Pentraeth, Wales, U.K. 53 17N 4 13W
37 Pentre Foelas, Wales, United Kingdom 53 2N 3 41W
106 Penukonda, India 14 5N 77 38E
37 Penybont, Wales, U.K. 52 17N 3 18W
37 Pen-y-Ghent, mt., England, U.K. 54 10N 2 15W
37 Pen-y-groes, Caernarvon, Wales, U.K. 53 3N 4 18W
37 Pen-y-groes, Carmarthen, Wales, U.K. 51 48N 4 3W
87 Penza, U.S.S.R. 53 15N 45 5E
36 Penzance, Eng., U.K. 50 7N 5 32W
57 Penzberg, Germany ...47 46N 11 23E
91 Penzhina G., U.S.S.R. 61 30N 163 0E
56 Penzlin, Germany 53 32N 13 6E
167 Peoria, Ariz., U.S.A. .33 40N 112 15W
164 Peoria, Ill., U.S.A. 40 40N 89 40W
55 Pepinster, Belgium 50 34N 5 47E
166 Pepperwood, U.S.A. ...40 23N 124 0W
76 Peqin, Albania 41 4N 19 44E
98 Pequ'in, Israel 32 58N 35 20E
175 Pequiri R., Matto Grosso, Brazil 17 35S 56 0W
173 Pequiri R., Parana, Braz. 24 0S 53 30W
107 Perak, st., W. Malaysia 5 0N 101 0E
107 Perak R., W. Malaysia 5 10N 101 4E
77 Perakhôra, Greece 38 2N 22 56E
64 Perales de Alfambra, Sp. 40 38N 1 0W
62 Perales del Puerto, Sp. 40 10N 6 40W
64 Peralta, Spain 42 21N 1 49W
77 Pérama, Crete, Greece 34 55N 24 22E
74 Perast, Yugoslavia 42 31N 18 47E
48 Perche, reg., France ...48 31N 1 1E
48 Perche, Collines de la, Fr. 42 30N 2 5E
48 Percy, France 48 55N 1 11W
144 Percy Is., Australia ...21 39S 150 16E
144 Percyville, Australia 19 2S 143 45E
135 Perdeberg, OFS, S. Afr. 28 53S 25 3E
133 Perdekop, Trans., S. Afr. 27 13S 29 38E
143 Perekerton, Australia .34 53S 143 49E
174 Pereira, Colombia 4 49N 75 43W
75 Perelik, mt., Bulgaria 44 37N 24 32E
142 Perenjori, W. Australia 29 25S 116 43E
86 Pereslavl-Zelesskiy, U.S.S.R. 56 45N 38 58E
86 Pereyaslav-Khmeinitskiy, U.S.S.R. 50 3N 31 28E
58 Perg, Austria 48 15N 14 38E
172 Pergamino, Argentina 33 52S 60 30W
71 Pergine Valsugano, It. 46 4N 11 15E
71 Pergola, Italy 43 35N 12 50E
164 Perham, U.S.A. 46 36N 95 36W
34 Perham Down Camp, England, U.K. 51 14N 1 38W
107 Perhentian Besar Is., W. Malaysia 5 54N 102 42E
74 Periam, Rumania 46 2N 20 59E
155 Peribonca, L., Canada 50 1N 71 0W
172 Perico, Argentina 24 20S 65 5W
168 Pericos, Mexico 25 3N 107 42W
48 Périers, France 49 11N 1 25W
109 Perigi, Indonesia 7 41S 10 27E
50 Périgord, reg., France 45 0N 0 40E
50 Périgueux, France 45 10N 0 42E
99 Perim, I., Red Sea 12 39N 43 25E
77 Peristéra, I., Greece ...39 15N 23 58E
106 Periyakulam, India ...10 5N 77 30E
106 Periyar, L., India 9 25N 77 10E
106 Periyar, R., India 10 15N 78 10E
71 Perković, Yugoslavia .43 41N 16 10E
108 Perlak, Indonesia 4 48N 97 45E
169 Perlas, Arch. de las, Pan. 8 41N 79 7W
169 Perlas, Punta de, Nic. 11 30N 83 30W
56 Perleberg, Germany ...53 5N 11 50E
87 Perlevka, U.S.S.R. 51 56N 38 57E
74 Perlez, Yugoslavia 45 11N 20 22E
107 Perlis, st., W. Malaysia 6 30N 100 15E
84 Perm (Molotov), U.S.S.R. 58 0N 57 10E
76 Permet, Albania 40 15N 20 21E
175 Pernambuco, see Recife, Brazil 8 0S 35 0W
175 Pernambuco, st., Braz. 8 30S 38 0W
142 Peron, C., W. Austral. 25 30S 113 30E
142 Peron Pen., W. Austral. 26 0S 113 10E
49 Péronne, France 49 55N 2 57E
70 Perosa Argentina, Italy 44 57N 7 11E
87 Perovo, U.S.S.R. 55 45N 37 35E
156 Perow, Canada 54 35N 126 10W
50 Perpignan, France 42 42N 2 53E
36 Perranporth, Eng., U.K. 50 21N 5 9W
36 Perranzabuloe, Eng., U.K. 50 18N 5 7W
48 Perros-Guirec, France 48 49N 3 28W
163 Perry, Fla., U.S.A. 30 9N 83 10W
163 Perry, Ga., U.S.A. 32 25N 83 41W
164 Perry, Iowa, U.S.A. ...41 48N 94 5W
165 Perry, Maine, U.S.A. .44 59N 67 20W
160 Perry, N.Y., U.S.A. ...42 44N 77 59W
165 Perry, Okla., U.S.A. ...36 20N 97 20W
165 Perryton, U.S.A. 36 28N 100 48W
80 Persberg, Sweden 59 47N 14 15E
101 Persepolis (ruin), Iran 29 55N 52 50E
34 Pershore, England, U.K. 52 7N 2 4W
101 Persia, see Iran 35 0N 50 0E
101 Persian Gulf, Asia 27 0N 50 0E
81 Perstorp, Sweden 56 10N 13 25E
154 Perth, N.B., Canada .46 43N 67 42W
162 Perth, Ontario, Canada 44 55N 76 20W
41 Perth, Scotland, U.K. 56 24N 3 27W
142 Perth, W. Australia ...31 57S 115 52E
41 Perth, co., Scot., U.K. 56 30N 4 0W
161 Perth U.S.A. 40 33N 74 36W
51 Pertuis, France 43 42N 5 30E
50 Pertuis Breton, France 46 17N 1 25W
50 Pertuis d'Antioche, Fr. 46 6N 1 20W
164 Peru, Ill., U.S.A. 41 18N 89 12W
162 Peru, Ind., U.S.A. 40 42N 86 0W
174 Peru, rep., S. America 8 0S 75 0W
71 Perugia, Italy 43 6N 12 24E
71 Perušic, Yugoslavia ...44 40N 15 22E
88 Pervomaysk, U.S.S.R. 48 5N 30 55E
90 Pervouralsk, U.S.S.R. 56 55N 60 0E
71 Pesaro, Italy 43 55N 12 53E
113 Pescadores, see Penghu Is., Taiwan 22 30N 119 30E
71 Pescara, Italy 42 28N 14 13E
89 Peschanokopskoye, U.S.S.R. 46 14N 41 4E
87 Peski, U.S.S.R. 51 14N 42 12E
70 Pescia, Italy 43 54N 10 40E
71 Pescina, Italy 42 0N 13 39E
102 Peshawar, W. Pakistan 34 2N 71 37E
76 Peshkopi, Albania 41 41N 20 25E
75 Peshtera, Bulgaria 42 2N 24 18E
162 Peshtigo, U.S.A. 45 4N 87 46W
87 Peskovka, U.S.S.R. 59 9N 52 28E
62 Pêso da Régua, Port. .41 10N 7 47W
175 Pesqueira, Brazil 8 20S 36 46W
133 Pessene, Mozambique 23 40S 32 20E
59 Pest, co., Hungary 47 29N 19 5E
86 Pestovo, U.S.S.R. 58 33N 35 18E
87 Pestravka, U.S.S.R. 52 28N 49 57E
77 Péta, Greece 39 10N 21 2E
98 Petah Tiqva, Israel ...32 6N 34 53E
77 Petalidhion, Greece ...36 57N 21 55E
107 Petaling Jaya, Malaya, Malaysia ... 3 4N 101 42E
166 Petaluma, U.S.A. 38 13N 122 45W
54 Petange, Luxembourg 49 33N 5 55E
168 Petatlán, Mexico 17 31N 101 16W
132 Petauke, Zambia 14 14S 31 12E
154 Petawawa, Canada 45 54N 77 17W
14 Peter Is., U.S.S.R. 76 15N 118 30E
15 Peter 1st I., S. Oc. 69 0S 91 0W
157 Peter Pond L., Canada 56 0N 109 0W
154 Peterbell, Canada 48 36N 83 21W
161 Peterboro, U.S.A. 42 55N 71 59W
160 Peterborough, Canada 44 20N 78 20W
35 Peterborough, Eng., U.K. 52 35N 0 14W
145 Peterborough, Austral. 33 0S 138 45E
34 Peterchurch, Eng., U.K. 52 3N 2 57W
43 Peterculter, Scot., U.K. 57 5N 2 18W
43 Peterhead, Scot., U.K. 57 30N 1 49W
39 Peterlee, England, U.K. 54 45N 1 18W
135 Petersburg, S. Africa .32 17S 24 58E
157 Petersburg, Alas., U.S.A. 56 50N 133 0W
162 Petersburg, Ind., U.S.A. 38 30N 87 15W
162 Petersburg, Va., U.S.A. 37 17N 77 26W
162 Petersburg, W. Va., U.S.A. 38 59N 79 10W
34 Petersfield, Eng., U.K. 51 0N 0 56W
44 Peterswell, Ireland 53 7N 8 46W
144 Petford, Queens., Australia 17 20S 144 50E
73 Petilia Policastro, It. .39 7N 16 48E
163 Petit Bois I., U.S.A. ..30 16N 88 25W
155 Petit Cap, Canada 48 58N 63 58W
169 Petit Goâve, Haiti 18 27N 72 51W
155 Petitcodiac, Canada ...45 57N 65 11W
155 Petite Saguenay, Can. 47 59N 70 1W
155 Petitsikapau L., Can. .54 50N 66 30W
104 Petlad, India 22 30N 72 45E
168 Peto, Mexico 20 10N 89 0W
146 Petone, New Zealand .41 13S 174 53E
162 Petoskey, U.S.A. 45 21N 84 55W
98 Petra (site), Jordan ...30 20N 35 22E
64 Petra, Spain 39 37N 3 6E
73 Petralia, Italy 37 49N 14 4E
65 Petrel, Spain 38 30N 0 46W
75 Petrich, Bulgaria 41 25N 23 12E
71 Petrijanec, Yugoslavia 46 23N 16 17E
86 Petrikov, U.S.S.R. 52 11N 28 29E
78 Petrila, Rumania 45 29N 23 29E
71 Petrinja, Yugoslavia .45 28N 16 18E
175 Petrolandia, Brazil 9 0S 38 20W
154 Petrolia, Canada 42 54N 82 9W
175 Petrolina, Brazil 9 10S 40 40W
91 Petropavlovsk-Kamchatskiy, U.S.S.R. 53 16N 159 0E
90 Petropavlovsk, U.S.S.R. 55 0N 69 0E
89 Petropavlovskiy, USSR 48 27N 46 7E
173 Petrópolis, Brazil 22 33S 43 9W
78 Petroşani, Rumania ...45 28N 23 20E
71 Petrova Gora, Y.-slav. 45 15N 15 45E
74 Petrovac, Yugoslavia .42 13N 18 57E
74 Petrovaradin, Y.-slav. 45 16N 19 55E
91 Petrovsk, Chita, U.S.S.R. 51 26N 108 30E
87 Petrovsk, Saratov, U.S.S.R. 52 22N 45 19E
89 Petrovskoye, U.S.S.R. 45 25N 42 58E
84 Petrozavodsk, U.S.S.R. 61 41N 34 20E
135 Petrus Steyn, S. Africa 27 38S 28 8E
135 Petrusburg, S. Africa .29 4S 25 26E
134 Petrusville, S. Africa .30 5S 24 41E
46 Pettigo, Ireland 54 32N 7 49W
35 Petworth, Eng., U.K. 50 59N 0 37W
91 Pevek, U.S.S.R. 69 15N 171 0E
35 Pevensey, Eng., U.K. 50 49N 0 20E
70 Peveragno, Italy 44 20N 7 37E
34 Pewsey, England, U.K. 51 20N 1 46W
34 Pewsey Vale of, England, U.K. 51 20N 1 46W
50 Peyrehorade, France .43 34N 1 7W
51 Peyruis, France 44 1N 5 56E
50 Pézénas, France 43 28N 3 24E
59 Pezinok, Czechoslovakia 48 17N 17 17E
57 Pfaffenhofen, Germany 48 31N 11 31E
55 Pfalzdorf, Germany ...51 42N 6 9E
57 Pfarrkirchen, Germany 48 25N 12 57E
57 Pforzheim, Germany .48 53N 8 43E
57 Pfungstadt, Germany 49 47N 8 36E
104 Phalodi, India 27 12N 72 24E
49 Phalsbourg, France ...48 46N 7 15E
107 Phan Rang, S., Vietnam 11 40N 109 9E
107 Phan Thiet, S., Vietnam 11 1N 108 9E
107 Phangnga, Thailand ... 8 28N 98 30E
105 Pharenda India 27 5N 83 17E
111 Pharo Dzong, Tibet, China 27 45N 89 14E
107 Phatthalung, Thailand 7 39N 100 6E
160 Phelps, N.Y., U.S.A. .42 57N 77 5W
164 Phelps, Wis., U.S.A. .46 2N 89 2W
163 Phenix City, U.S.A. ...32 30N 85 0W
107 Phet Buri, Thailand ...13 1N 99 55E
107 Phetchabun, Thailand 16 25N 101 8E
107 Phetchabun Ra., Thailand 16 20N 100 55E
107 Phichai, Thailand 17 22N 100 10E
134 Philadelphia, S. Africa 33 40S 18 34E
165 Philadelphia, Miss., USA 32 47N 89 5W
161 Philadelphia, N.Y., USA 44 9N 75 40W
162 Philadelphia, Pa., USA 40 0N 75 10W
164 Philip, U.S.A. 44 4N 101 42W
123 Philippe Thomas, Tun., ...34 21N 8 28E
123 Philippeville, see Skikda 36 50N 6 58E
54 Philippeville, Belgium 50 12N 4 33E
144 Philippi L., Queensland, Australia 24 20S 138 55E
109 Philippines, Rep. & Is., Asia 12 0N 123 0E
135 Philippolis, OFS, S. Afr. 30 15S 25 16E
75 Philippopolis, see Plovdiv, Bulgaria ...42 8N 24 44E
166 Philipsburg, Mont., U.S.A. 46 20N 113 21W
160 Philipsburg, Pa., U.S.A. 40 53N 78 10W
134 Philipstown, S Africa .30 28S 24 30E
143 Phillip I., Vic., Austral. 38 20S 145 15E
165 Phillips, Texas, U.S.A. 35 48N 101 17W
164 Phillips, Wis., U.S.A. .45 41N 90 22W
161 Phillipsburg, Penn., U.S.A. 40 43N 75 12W
164 Phillipsburg, Kan., U.S.A. 39 48N 99 20W
145 Phillott, Queensland, Australia 27 53S 145 50E
161 Philmont, U.S.A. 42 14N 73 37W
166 Philomath, U.S.A. 44 28N 123 21W
107 Phitsanulok, Thailand 16 50N 100 12E
1 Phlegraean Field, Italy 40 47N 14 10E
107 Phnom Penh, Cambodia 11 33N 104 55E
107 Phnom Thibeng, Meanchey, Cambodia 13 50N 104 56E
107 Phnom Thiberg Meanchey, Cambodia13 50N 104 56E
167 Phoenix, Ariz., U.S.A. 33 30N 112 10W
161 Phoenix, N.Y., U.S.A. 43 13N 76 18W
137 Phœnix Is., Pac. Oc. . 3 30S 172 0W
161 Phoenixville, U.S.A. ...40 12N 75 29W
107 Phong Saly, Laos 21 42N 102 9E
103 Phongdo, Tibet, China 30 14N 91 14E
107 Phrae, Thailand 18 7N 100 9E
107 Phrao, Thailand 19 23N 99 15E
107 Phu Doan, Vietnam ...21 40N 105 10E
107 Phu Loi Mt., Laos 20 14N 103 14E
107 Phu Ly (Ha Nam), N. Vietnam 20 35N 105 50E
107 Phu Qui, Vietnam 19 20N 105 20E
107 Phu Quoc I., Cambodia 10 15N 104 0E
107 Phuket, Thailand 8 0N 98 28E
104 Phulera (Phalera), India 26 52N 75 16E
107 Phuoc Le (Baria), S. Vietnam 10 39N 107 19E
78 Pia, Rumania 45 30N 23 4E
144 Piabla, Queens., Austral. 25 12S 152 45E
70 Piacenza, Italy 45 2N 9 42E
70 Piadena, Italy 45 8N 10 22E
145 Pian Cr., N.S.W., Austral. 30 0S 149 0E
71 Pianella, Italy 42 24N 14 5E
143 Piangil, Vic., Australia 43 25S 35 5E
71 Pianoro, Italy 44 20N 11 20E
71 Pianosa I., Italy 42 12N 15 44E
70 Pianosa I., Italy 42 36N 10 4E
157 Piapot, Canada 49 59N 109 8W
63 Pias, Portugal 38 1N 7 29W
78 Piatra, Rum. 43 51N 25 9E
78 Piatra Neamţ, Rum. .46 56N 26 21E
175 Piaui, st., Brazil 7 20S 42 30W
71 Piave R., Italy 45 50N 13 9E
73 Piazza Armerina, Italy 37 21N 14 20E
127 Pibor, Sudan 6 52N 33 0E
127 Pibor Post, Sudan 6 47N 33 3E
174 Pica, Chile 20 35S 69 25W
49 Picard, Plaine de. dist., France 50 0N 2 0E
49 Picardie, Reg., France 50 0N 2 15E
165 Picayune, U.S.A. 30 40N 89 40W
132 Piccadilly, Zambia 14 0S 29 30E
73 Picerno, Italy 40 40N 15 37E
172 Pichanel, Argentina ...23 15S 64 10W
113 Pichieh, China 27 25N 105 0E
172 Pichilemu, Chile 34 22S 72 9W
174 Pichinchal, vol., Ec. ... 0 10S 78 30W
154 Pickerel L., Canada ...48 40N 91 25W
39 Pickering, Eng., U.K. 54 15N 0 46W
39 Pickering, Vale of, England, U.K. 54 0N 0 45W
154 Pickle Crow, Canada .51 30N 90 0W
18 Pico I., Azores 38 28N 28 20W
176 Pico Truncado, Arg. ...46 40S 68 10W
49 Picquigny, France 49 56N 2 10E
143 Picton, N.S.W., Austral. 34 12S 150 34E
154 Picton, Canada 44 1N 77 9W
147 Picton, New Zealand .41 18S 174 3E
155 Pictou, Canada 45 41N 62 42W
156 Picture Butte, Canada 49 55N 112 45W
176 Picún-Leufú, Arg. 39 30S 69 5W
35 Pidley, England, U.K. 52 33N 0 4W
106 Pidurutalagala, mt., Cey. 7 10N 80 50E
70 Piedicavallo, Italy 45 41N 7 57E
163 Piedmont, U.S.A. 33 55N 85 39W
163 Piedmont Plat., U.S.A. 34 0N 81 30W
73 Piedmonte d'Alife, Italy 41 22N 14 22E
64 Piedra, R., Spain 41 10N 1 45W
63 Piedrabuena, Spain ...39 0N 4 10W
62 Piedrahita, Spain 40 28N 5 23W
174 Piedras R., Peru 11 40S 70 50W
167 Piedras Blancas Pt., U.S.A. 35 45N 121 18W
168 Piedras Negras, Mexico 28 35N 100 35W
82 Pieksämäki, Finland .62 26N 27 12E
84 Pielinen, L., Finland .63 20N 30 15E
70 Piemonte (Piedmont), reg., Italy 45 0N 7 30E
51 Piena, Corsica, France 42 15N 8 34E
133 Pienaars R., S. Africa 25 10S 28 0E
133 Pienaarsrivier, S. Africa 25 16S 28 16E
166 Pierce, U.S.A. 46 46N 115 53W
161 Piercefield, U.S.A. 44 13N 74 35W
76 Pieria, pref., Greece ...40 13N 22 25E
43 Pierowall, Scot., U.K. 59 20N 3 0W
49 Pierre, France 46 54N 5 13E
164 Pierre, U.S.A. 44 23N 100 20W
49 Pierrefonds, France ...49 20N 3 0E
49 Pierrefontaine, France 47 14N 6 32E
50 Pierrefort, France 44 55N 2 50E
51 Pierrelatte, France 44 23N 4 43E
133 Piesanghoek, S. Africa 22 59S 30 8W
59 Pieštany, Cz. 48 35N 17 50E
59 Piesting, R., Austria .48 0N 16 19E
133 Piet Retief, S. Africa .27 1S 30 50E
82 Pietarsaari (Jacobstad), Finland 63 41N 22 40E
135 Pietermaritzburg, Natal, South Africa 29 35S 30 25E
133 Pietersburg, S. Africa 23 54S 29 25E
73 Pietraperzia, Italy 37 26N 14 8E
70 Pietrasanta, Italy 43 57N 10 12E
78 Pietrosul Mt., Rumania 47 35N 24 43E
78 Pietrosul, mt., Rum. .47 12N 25 8E
71 Pieve di Cadore, Italy 46 25N 12 22E
70 Pieve di Teco, Italy ...44 3N 7 54E
70 Pievepelago, Italy 44 12N 10 35E
77 Pigádhia, Greece 35 30N 27 12E
76 Pigadhítsa, Greece 39 59N 21 23E
106 Pigeon I., India 14 2N 74 20E
154 Pigeon R., Canada 48 1N 89 42W
165 Piggott, U.S.A. 36 20N 90 10W
133 Pigg's Peak, Swaziland 25 58S 31 15E
70 Pigna, Italy 43 57N 7 40E
172 Pigue, Argentina 37 36S 62 25W
105 Pihani, India 27 36N 80 15E
164 Pikes Peak, U.S.A. 38 50N 105 10W
134 Piketberg, S. Africa ...32 54S 18 42E
162 Pikeville, U.S.A. 37 30N 82 30W
157 Pikwitonei, Canada ...55 35N 97 11W
60 Pila, Poland 53 10N 16 48E
65 Pila, mt., Spain 38 16N 1 11W
76 Pilaía, Greece 40 32N 22 59E
76 Pilanë, Albania 41 42N 19 40E
133 Pilanesberg, S. Africa 25 14S 27 4E
104 Pilani, India 28 22N 75 33E
175 Pilar, Brazil 14 30S 49 45W
172 Pilar, Paraguay 26 50S 58 10W
109 Pilas, I., Philippines ... 6 45N 121 28E
138 Pilbara, W. Australia .21 14S 118 19E
172 Pilcomayo R., Par. 19 30S 64 35W
133 Pilgrim's Rest, S. Africa 24 53S 30 46E
77 Pili, Greece 36 50N 27 15E
105 Pilibhit, India 28 40N 79 50E
76 Pílion, Mt., Greece 39 27N 23 7E
59 Pilis, Hungary 47 17N 19 35E
59 Pilisvörösvár, Hung. .47 38N 18 56E
104 Pilkhawa, India 28 43N 77 42E
38 Pilling, England, U.K. 53 55N 2 54W
44 Pilltown, Ireland 51 59N 7 49W
77 Pilos, Greece 36 55N 21 42E
157 Pilot Mound, Canada .49 15N 99 0W
165 Pilot Point, U.S.A. 33 26N 97 0W
166 Pilot Rock, U.S.A. 45 30N 118 58W
58 Pilsen, see Plzeň, Czech. 49 45N 13 22E
71 Pilštanj, Yugoslavia ...56 8N 15 39E
36 Pilton, England, U.K. 51 0N 2 35W
45 Piltown, Kilkenny, Ire. 52 22N 7 18W
45 Piltown, Waterford, Ire. 51 59N 7 49W
59 Pilzno, Poland 50 0N 21 16E
145 Pimba, South Australia 31 18S 136 46E
174 Pimenta Bueno, Brazil 11 35S 61 10W
174 Pimenten, Peru 6 57S 79 50W
64 Pina, Spain 41 29N 0 33W
169 Pinar del Rio, Cuba ...22 26N 83 40W
152 Pinawa, Canada 50 15N 95 50W

MAP
155 Pince C., Canada 46 38N 53 45W
156 Pincher Creek, Canada 49 30N 113 35W
164 Pinckneyville, U.S.A. .38 5N 89 20W
104 Pind Dadan Khan, West Pakistan 32 55N 73 47E
142 Pindar West Australia 28 22S 115 45E
125 Pindiga Nigeria 9 58N 10 53E
76 Pindus Mts., (Pindhos Óros). Greece 40 0N 21 0E
167 Pine. U.S.A. 34 27N 111 30W
165 Pine Bluff, Ark. U.S.A. 34 10N 92 0W
164 Pine City, U.S.A. 45 46N 93 0W
138 Pine Creek, Australia .13 51S 131 52E
157 Pine Falls, Canada 50 51N 96 11W
144 Pine Hill, Australia ...23 42S 147 0E
156 Pine Point, tn., Canada 60 50N 114 40W
156 Pine Point. Canada ...61 0N 114 26W
164 Pine Ridge, U.S.A. 42 2N 102 35W
157 Pine River, Canada ...51 45N 100 30W
164 Pine River, U.S.A. 46 40N 94 20W
167 Pinedale, U.S.A. 34 23N 110 16W
167 Pinetop, U.S.A. 34 10N 109 57W
58 Pinega, U.S.S.R. 64 45N 43 40E
84 Pinega R., U.S.S.R. 64 20N 43 0E
70 Pinerolo, Italy 44 47N 7 21E
71 Pineto. Italy 42 36N 14 4E
135 Pinetown, Nat., S. Afr. 29 48S 30 54E
164 Pinetree, U.S.A. 43 42N 105 52W
163 Pineville, Ky., U.S.A. 36 42N 83 42W
165 Pineville La., U.S.A. .31 22N 92 30W
157 Pinewood, Canada 48 45N 94 10W
157 Piney, Canada 49 5N 96 10W
49 Piney, France 48 22N 4 21E
107 Ping R., Thailand 16 40N 99 30E
142 Pingaring, W. Australia 32 40S 118 32E
142 Pingelly W. Australia 32 29S 116 59E
113 Pinghuo, China 24 14N 117 2E
113 Pingkiang, China 28 45N 113 30E
112 Pingliang, China 35 20N 106 40E
113 Pinglo, China 24 30N 110 45E
112 Pinglo, China 38 58N 106 30E
113 Pingnam, China 23 30N 110 15E
142 Pingrup W. Australia 33 25S 118 25E
113 Pingsiang China 22 2N 106 55E
113 Pingsiang China 27 43N 113 50E
112 Pinting China 37 45N 113 34E
113 Pingtung, Taiwan 22 36N 120 30E
113 Pingwu, China 32 27N 104 25E
113 Pingyang, China 27 45N 120 25E
112 Pingyao, China 37 12N 112 0E
173 Pinhal, Brazil 22 10S 46 46W
62 Pinhel, Portugal 40 18N 7 0W
36 Pinhoe, England, U.K. 50 44N 3 29W
113 Pinhsien, China 35 10N 108 10E
108 Pini I., Indonesia 0 10N 98 40E
77 Pinios, R., Ilia Greece 37 38N 21 20E
76 Pinios R., Trikkala, Gr. 39 55N 22 10E
142 Pinjarra, W. Australia 32 37S 115 52E
59 Pinkafeld, Austria 47 22N 16 9E
142 Pinnacles, W. Australia 28 12S 120 26E
145 Pinnaroo, S. Australia 35 13S 140 56E
168 Pinos, Mexico 22 20N 101 40W
169 Pinos, I. de, Cuba 21 40N 82 40W
167 Pinos Pt., U.S.A. 36 50N 121 57W
63 Pinos Puente, Spain ...37 15N 3 45W
109 Pinrang Indonesia 3 46S 119 34E
86 Pinsk U.S.S.R. 52 10N 26 8E
174 Pintados, Chile 20 35S 69 40W
40 Pinwherry, Scot., U.K. 55 9N 4 50W
113 Pinyang China 23 12N 108 35E
84 Pinyug, U.S.S.R. 60 5N 48 0E
70 Pinzolo, Italy 46 9N 10 45E
167 Pioche U.S.A. 38 0N 114 35W
70 Piombino, Italy 42 54N 10 30E
91 Pioner, I.. U.S.S.R. ...79 50N 92 0E
174 Piorini L., Brazil 3 15S 62 35W
60 Piotrków Trybunalsk, Poland 51 23N 19 43E
71 Piove di Sacco, Italy .45 18N 12 1E
101 Pip, Iran 26 45N 60 10E
104 Pipar, India 26 25N 73 31E
104 Pipariya, India 22 45N 78 23E
76 Pipéri I., Greece 39 20N 24 19E
164 Pipestone, U.S.A. 44 0N 96 20W
146 Pipiriki, New Zealand 38 28S 175 5E
155 Pipmuacan, L., Canada 49 40N 70 25W
48 Pipriac, France 47 49N 1 58W
162 Piqua, U.S.A. 40 10N 84 10W
173 Piracicaba, Brazil 22 45S 47 30W
175 Piracuruca, Brazil 3 50S 41 50W
77 Piraievs (Piræus), Gr. 37 57N 23 42E
77 Piraievs, prov., Greece 37 0N 23 30E
73 Piraino, Italy 38 10N 14 52E
176 Pirámide Mt., Chile ...49 0S 73 30W
71 Piran (Pirano), Y.-slav. 45 31N 13 33E
172 Piranė Argentina 25 25S 59 30W
175 Piranhas R., Brazil 6 10S 37 10W
175 Pirapora, Brazil 17 20S 45 0W
86 Piratyin, U.S.S.R. 50 15N 32 25E
35 Pirbright, England, U.K. 51 17N 0 40W
75 Pirdop. Bulgaria 42 40N 24 10E
175 Pirenopolis, Brazil 15 50N 49 0W
105 Pirganj, E. Pakistan .25 51S 88 24E
77 Pirgos, Messinta, Gr. .36 50N 22 16E
77 Pirgos, Ilia, Greece 37 40N 21 27E
75 Pirgovo Bulgaria 43 44N 25 43E
48 Piriac France 47 23N 2 31W
172 Piribebuy, Paraguay .25 26S 57 2W
75 Pirin Planina, Ra., Bulg. 41 40N 23 30E
175 Piripiri, Brazil 4 15S 41 46W
57 Pirmasens, Germany .49 12N 7 30E
56 Pirna, Germany 50 57N 13 57E
105 Pirojpur, E. Pakistan 22 35N 90 1E
74 Pirot, Yugoslavia 43 9N 22 39E
89 Pirsagat, R., U.S.S.R. 40 15N 48 45E
167 Pirtleville. U.S.A. 31 25N 109 35W
77 Piryí, Greece 38 13N 25 59E
70 Pisa, Italy 43 43N 10 23E
147 Pisa Ra., N.Z. 44 52S 169 12E
174 Pisagua, Chile 19 40S 70 15W
71 Pisarovina, Yugoslavia 45 35N 15 50E
73 Pisciotta, Italy 40 7N 15 12E
174 Pisco. Peru 13 50S 76 5W
78 Piscu, Rumania 45 30N 27 43E
58 Pisek, Czechoslovakia 49 19N 14 10E
109 Pising, Indonesia 5 8S 121 53E
50 Pissos, France 44 19N 0 49W
73 Pisticci, Italy 40 24N 16 33E
70 Pistoia, Italy 43 57N 10 53E
62 Pisuerga, R., Spain ...42 10N 4 15W
60 Pisz, Poland 53 38N 21 49E
143 Pitarpunga, L., Austral. 34 24S 143 30E
137 Pitcairn I. Pac. Oc. 25 5S 130 5W
82 Pite, R., Sweden 65 22N 21 15W
82 Pitea, Sweden 65 55N 21 25E
78 Piteşti Rumania 44 52N 24 54E
106 Pithapuram, India 17 10N 82 15E
142 Pithara, W. Australia 30 20S 116 35E
76 Pithion, Greece 41 24N 26 40E
49 Pithiviers, France 48 10N 2 13E
71 Pitigliano, Italy 42 38N 11 40E
41 Pitlochry, Scot., U.K. 56 43N 3 43W
135 Pitseng, Lesotho 28 58S 28 16E
156 Pitt I., Canada 53 30N 129 50W
41 Pittenweem, Scot., U.K 56 13N 2 43W
166 Pittsburg, Calif., U.S.A. 38 1N 121 50W
165 Pittsburg, Kan., U.S.A. 37 21N 94 43W
165 Pittsburg, Tex., U.S.A. 32 59N 94 58W
160 Pittsburgh, U.S.A. 40 25N 79 55W
164 Pittsfield, Ill., U.S.A. .39 35N 90 46W
161 Pittsfield, Mass., U.S.A. 42 28N 73 17W
161 Pittsfield, N.H., U.S.A. 43 17N 71 18W
161 Pittston, U.S.A. 41 19N 75 50W
145 Pittsworth, Australia .27 41S 151 37E
174 Piura, Peru 5 5S 80 45W
74 Piva, R., Yugoslavia .43 15N 18 50E
59 Piwniczna, Poland 49 27N 20 42E
77 Pixariá Óros, mt., Gr. 38 42N 23 39E
76 Piyai, Greece 39 17N 21 25E
113 Piyang, China 32 50N 113 30E
57 Piz Bernina, Mt., Switz 46 23N 9 45E
73 Pizzo, Italy 38 44N 16 10E
155 Placentia, Canada 47 20N 54 0W
155 Placentia B., Canada .47 0N 54 40W
166 Placerville, U.S.A. 38 47N 120 51W
169 Placetas, Cuba 22 15N 79 44W
74 Plačkovica, Ra., Y.-slav. 41 45N 22 30E
40 Pladda, I., Scot., U.K. 55 25N 5 7W
55 Plaidt, Germany 50 25N 7 23E
165 Plain Dealing, U.S.A. 32 56N 93 41W
161 Plainfield, U.S.A. 40 37N 74 28W
165 Plains, Kan., U.S.A. .37 20N 100 35W
166 Plains, Mont., U.S.A. .47 27N 114 57W
165 Plains, Tex., U.S.A. ...33 11N 102 50W
164 Plainview, Neb., U.S.A. 42 25N 97 48W
165 Plainview, Tex., U.S.A. 34 10N 101 40W
164 Plainville, U.S.A. 39 18N 99 19W
162 Plainwell, U.S.A. 42 28N 85 40W
50 Plaisance, France 43 36N 0 3E
76 Pláka, Greece 36 45N 24 26E
108 Plampang, Indonesia . 8 48S 117 46E
172 Plan Esmeralda, Chile 25 56S 70 43W
58 Planá, Czechoslovakia 49 50N 12 44E
175 Planaltina, Brazil 15 30S 47 45W
48 Plancoët, France 48 32N 2 13W
123 Plane I., Tunisia 37 10N 10 15E
71 Planina, Yugoslavia ...45 47N 14 19E
71 Planina, Yugoslavia ...40 10N 15 12E
74 Planište, Yugoslavia .45 16N 21 10E
56 Planitz, Germany 49 23N 13 28E
164 Plankinton, U.S.A. 43 45N 98 27W
165 Plano, U.S.A. 33 0N 96 45W
163 Plant City, U.S.A. 28 0N 82 15W
165 Plaquemine, U.S.A. ...30 20N 91 15W
62 Plasencia, Spain 40 3N 6 8W
71 Plaški, Yugoslavia 45 4N 15 22E
79 Plassen, Norway 61 6N 12 38E
155 Plaster Rock, Canada 46 53N 67 22W
133 Plaston, Trans., S. Afr. 25 24S 31 2E
72 Platani R., Italy 37 28N 13 23E
176 Plate, R., est., South America 35 30S 56 0W
15 Plateau. Antarctica ...70 55S 40 0E
164 Plateau du Coteau du Missouri, U.S.A. 47 9N 101 5W
76 Plati, Ákra, C., Greece 40 27N 24 0E
133 Platrand, Trans., S. Afr. 27 8S 29 29E
164 Platte, U.S.A. 43 28N 98 50W
164 Platte R., U.S.A. 41 0N 98 0W
164 Platteville, U.S.A. 40 18N 104 47W
57 Plattling, Germany ...48 46N 12 53E
161 Plattsburgh, U.S.A. ...44 41N 73 30W
164 Plattsmouth, U.S.A. .41 0N 96 0W
56 Plau, Germany 53 27N 12 16E
56 Plauen, Germany 50 29N 12 9E
74 Plav, Yugoslavia 42 38N 19 57E
74 Plavnica, Yugoslavia .42 10N 19 20E
87 Plavsk, U.S.S.R. 53 40N 37 9E
63 Playa de Castilla, dist., Spain 41 25N 0 12W
157 Playgreen L., Canada 53 20N 98 0W
147 Pleasant Pt., N.Z. 44 16S 171 9E
164 Pleasant Bay, Canada 46 51N 60 43W
164 Pleasant Hill, U.S.A. .38 48N 94 14W
143 Pleasant Hills, Austral. 35 28S 146 50E
165 Pleasanton, U.S.A. 29 0N 98 30W
162 Pleasantville, U.S.A. .39 25N 74 30W
50 Pléaux, France 45 8N 2 13E
107 Pleiku (Gia Lai), South Vietnam 14 3N 108 0E
48 Plélan le Grand, Fr. ...48 0N 2 7W
49 Pléneuf, France 48 37N 2 32W
78 Plenita, Rumania 44 14N 23 10E
146 Plenty, Bay of, N.Z. .37 45S 177 0E
164 Plentywood, U.S.A. ...48 45N 104 35W
84 Plesetsk, U.S.S.R. 62 40N 40 10E
155 Plessisville, Canada ...46 14N 71 46W
48 Plestin les Grèves. Fr. 48 40N 3 39W
60 Pleszew, Poland 51 53N 17 47E
74 Pleternica, Yugoslavia 45 17N 17 48E
155 Pletipi L., Canada 51 45N 70 12W
134 Plettenbergbaai, S. Afr. 34 2S 23 22E
75 Pleven, Bulgaria 43 26N 24 37E
74 Plevlja, Yugoslavia ...43 21N 19 21E
74 Pločе, Y-slav. 43 2N 17 27E
60 Plock, Poland 52 32N 19 40E
71 Plocken P., Italy 46 37N 12 57E
42 Plockton, Scot., U.K. 57 20N 5 40W
48 Ploërmel, France 47 55N 2 26W
78 Ploeşti, Rumania 44 57N 26 5E
77 Plomárion, Greece 38 58N 26 24E
50 Plomb du Cantal, Fr. .45 2N 2 48E
49 Plombières, France 47 59N 6 27E
71 Plomin, Yugoslavia ...45 8N 14 10E
56 Plön, Germany 54 8N 10 22E
56 Plöner See, L., Germany 53 9N 15 5E
60 Płońsk, Poland 52 37N 20 21E
60 Ploty, Poland 53 48N 15 18E
48 Plouay, France 47 55N 3 21W
48 Ploudalmézeau France 48 34N 4 41W
48 Plougasnou, France ...48 42N 3 49W
48 Plouha, France 48 41N 2 57W
75 Plovdiv, Bulgaria 42 8N 24 44E
161 Plum I., U.S.A. 41 10N 72 12W
46 Plumbridge, N. Ire., U.K. 54 46N 7 15W
166 Plummer, U.S.A. 47 21N 116 59W
132 Plumtree, Rhodesia ...20 27S 27 55E
86 Plunge, U.S.S.R. 55 53N 21 51E
48 Pluvigner, France 47 46N 3 1W
36 Plymouth Eng., U.K. 50 23N 4 9W
162 Plymouth, Ind., U.S.A. 41 20N 86 19W
161 Plymouth, Mass., U.S.A. 41 58N 70 40W
163 Plymouth, N.C., U.S.A. 35 54N 76 55W
161 Plymouth, N.H., U.S.A. 43 44N 71 41W
161 Plymouth, Pa., U.S.A. 41 17N 76 0W
162 Plymouth, Wis., U.S.A. 43 42N 87 58W
36 Plympton, Eng., U.K. 50 24N 4 2W
36 Plymstock, Eng., U.K. 50 22N 4 6W
37 Plynlimon, mt., Wales, U.K. 52 29N 3 47W
86 Plyussa, U.S.S.R. 47 40N 29 0E
86 Plyussa R., U.S.S.R. .58 40N 28 30E
58 Plzeň, Czechoslovakia 49 45N 13 22E
133 Pniel, C. Prov., S. Afr. 28 32S 24 28E
60 Pniewy, Poland 52 31N 16 16E
107 Pnom Penh, Cambodia 11 33N 104 55E
125 Po, Upper Volta 11 14N 1 5W
71 Po, Mouths of the, It. 44 58N 12 28E
70 Po. R., Italy 45 0N 10 45E
112 Po Hai, China 38 30N 119 0E
125 Pobé, Dahomey 7 0N 2 38E
90 Pobeda Pk., U.S.S.R. 40 45N 79 58E
90 Pobedino, U.S.S.R. ...49 51N 142 49E
60 Pobiedziska, Poland ...52 29N 17 19E
64 Pobla de Segur, Spain 42 15N 0 58E
62 Pobladura de Valle, Sp. 42 6N 5 44W
164 Pocahontas, Iowa, U.S.A. 42 41N 94 42W
165 Pocahontas Va., U.S.A. 37 18N 81 20W
166 Pocatello, U.S.A. 42 50N 112 25W
58 Počátky, Cz. 49 15N 15 14E
86 Pochep, U.S.S.R. 52 58N 33 15E
87 Pochinki, U.S.S.R. 54 41N 44 59E
86 Pochinok, U.S.S.R. 54 28N 32 29E
58 Pöchlarn, Austria 48 12N 15 12E
168 Pochutla, Mexico 15 50N 96 31W
39 Pocklington, Eng., U.K. 53 56N 0 48W
162 Pocomoke City, U.S.A. 38 4N 75 32W
173 Pocos de Caldas, Brazil 21 50S 46 45W
58 Podebrady, Cz. 50 9N 15 8E
50 Podensac, France 44 40N 0 22W
74 Podgorac, Yugoslavia 45 28N 18 13E
91 Podkamennaya, Tunguska, U.S.S.R. 61 50N 90 26E
71 Podlapac, Yugoslavia 44 45N 15 47E
58 Podmokly, Cz. 50 48N 14 10E
78 Podoleni, Rumania 46 46N 26 39E
59 Podolinec, Czechoslovakia 49 16N 20 31E
87 Podolsk, U.S.S.R. 55 30N 37 30E
124 Podor, Senegal 16 40N 14 50W
74 Podravska Slatina, Y.-slav. 45 42N 17 45E
71 Podsreda, Yugoslavia 45 42N 17 41E
78 Podu Turcului, Rum. .46 11N 27 25E
74 Podujevo, Yugoslavia 42 54N 21 10E
56 Poel, I., Germany 54 0N 11 25E
134 Pofadder, S. Africa 29 10S 19 22E
154 Pogamasing, Canada .46 55N 81 50W
73 Poggiardo, Italy 40 3N 18 21E
71 Poggibonsi, Italy 43 27N 11 8E
78 Pogoanele, Rumania .44 55N 27 0E
76 Pogradec. Albania 40 57N 20 48E
112 Pogranichnyy, U.S.S.R. 44 21N 131 23E
109 Poh, Indonesia 0 46S 122 51E
112 Pohang, S. Korea 36 8N 129 23E
59 Pohorela, Cz. 48 50N 20 2E
59 Pohorelice, Cz. 48 59N 16 31E
71 Pohorje, Mts., Y.-slavia 46 30N 15 7E
113 Pohsien, China 33 56N 115 59E
78 Poiana Mare, Rumania 43 57N 23 5E
78 Poiana Ruscal, Muntii, Mts., Rumania 45 45N 22 25E
142 Point Cloates, Austral. 22 40S 113 45E
154 Point Edward, Canada 43 10N 82 30W
169 Point Fortin, Trinidad 10 9N 61 46W
106 Point Pedro, Ceylon ... 9 50N 80 15E
162 Point Pleasant, U.S.A. 38 50N 82 7W
165 Point Rock, U.S.A. 31 30N 99 56W
165 Pointe-a-la Hache, U.S.A. 29 35N 89 55W
128 Pte. Noire, Congo (Fr.) 4 48S 12 0E
169 Pte. à Pitre, Guadeloupe 16 10N 61 30W
70 Poirino, Italy 44 55N 7 50E
142 Poisonbush Ra., W. Australia 22 30S 121 30E
49 Poissy, France 48 55N 2 0E
48 Poitiers, France 46 35N 0 20W
50 Poitou Plaines du, Fr. 46 30N 0 1W
49 Poix, France 49 47N 2 0E
49 Poix-Terron, France .49 38N 4 38E
167 Pojoaque, U.S.A. 35 55N 106 0W
145 Pokataroo, Australia .29 30S 148 34E
130 Poko, Congo 3 7N 26 52E
127 Poko, Sudan 5 41N 31 55E
112 Pokotu, China 48 47N 122 7E
113 Pokpak, China 22 20N 109 45E
133 Pokwani, S. Africa 27 46S 24 48E
62 Pol, Spain 43 9N 7 20W
86 Pola, R., U.S.S.R. 57 30N 32 0E
62 Pola de Allande, Spain 43 16N 6 37W
62 Pola de Lena, Spain ...43 10N 5 49W
62 Pola de Siero, Spain ...43 24N 5 39W
62 Pola de Someido, Spain 43 5N 6 15W
167 Polacca, U.S.A. 35 52N 110 25W
60 Poland, St., Europe ...52 0N 20 0E
101 Polan, Iran 25 30N 1 10E
60 Polanów, Poland 54 7N 16 41E
55 Polch, Germany 50 16N 7 19E
172 Polcura, Chile 37 10S 71 50W
60 Polcyn Zdrój, Poland .53 47N 16 5E
36 Polden Hills, Eng., U.K. 51 7N 2 50W
35 Polegate, Eng., U.K. .50 49N 0 15E
86 Polessk, U.S.S.R. 54 50N 21 8E
35 Polesworth, Eng., U.K. 52 37N 1 37W
109 Polewali, Indonesia ... 3 21S 119 31E
109 Polewali, Indonesia ... 4 8S 119 43E
59 Polgar, Hungary 47 54N 21 6E
112 Poli, China 43 43N 130 28E
128 Poli, Cameroon 8 34N 12 54E
77 Poliaigos, I., Greece ...36 45N 24 38E
176 Policarpo, Argentina .54 45S 65 50W
73 Policastro, G. of, Italy 39 55N 15 35E
59 Polička, Czechoslovakia 49 43N 16 15E
73 Polignanoa Mare, Italy 41 0N 17 12E
49 Poligny, Jura, France 46 50N 5 42E
77 Palikhnitas, Greece ...39 4N 26 10E
109 Polillo I., Philippines .14 56N 122 0E
100 Polis, Cyprus 35 3N 32 30E
73 Polistena, Italy 38 25N 16 4E
76 Políyiros, Greece 40 23N 23 25E
160 Polk, U.S.A. 41 22N 79 57W
73 Polla, Italy 40 31N 15 27E
106 Pollachi, India 10 35N 77 0E
45 Pollaphouca Res., Ire. 53 8N 6 37W
64 Pollensa, Spain 39 54N 3 2E
64 Pollensa, B. de, Spain 39 55N 3 5E
73 Pollica, Italy 40 13N 15 3E
73 Pollino, Mte., Italy 39 54N 16 13E
164 Pollock, U.S.A. 45 58N 100 18W
46 Pollremon, Ireland 53 40N 8 38W
86 Polna, U.S.S.R. 58 31N 28 0E
90 Polnovat, U.S.S.R. 63 50N 66 5E
164 Polo, U.S.A. 42 0N 89 38W
88 Pologi, U.S.S.R. 47 29N 36 15E
86 Polonnoye, U.S.S.R. .50 6N 27 30E
86 Polotsk, U.S.S.R. 55 30N 28 50E
36 Polperro, Eng., U.K. .50 19N 4 31W
36 Polruan, Eng., U.K. ...50 17N 4 36W
166 Polson, U.S.A. 47 45N 114 12W
55 Polsum, Germany 50 38N 7 3E
88 Poltava, U.S.S.R. 49 35N 34 35E
106 Polur, India 12 32N 79 11E
84 Polyarney, U.S.S.R. ...69 8N 33 20E
137 Polynesia, reg., Pac. Oc. 10 0S 162 0W
70 Pomarance, Italy 43 18N 10 51E
73 Pomarico, Italy 40 31N 16 33E
175 Pombal, Brazil 6 55S 37 50W
62 Pombal, Portugal 39 55N 8 40W
77 Pómbia, Crete, Greece 35 0N 24 51E
162 Pomeroy, Ohio, U.S.A. 39 0N 82 0W
166 Pomeroy, Wash., U.S.A. 46 30N 117 33W
167 Pomona U.S.A. 34 2N 117 49W
75 Pomorie, Bulgaria 42 26N 27 41E
163 Pompano, U.S.A. 26 12N 80 6W
173 Pompeia, Brazil 22 4S 50 16W
73 Pompeii, site of Italy 40 45N 14 30E
166 Pompeys Pillar, U.S.A. 46 0N 108 0W
136 Ponape I., Pac. Oc. ... 6 55N 158 10E
154 Ponask, L., Canada ...54 0N 92 30W
164 Ponca, U.S.A. 42 38N 96 41W
165 Ponca City, U.S.A. 36 40N 97 5W
169 Ponce, Puerto Rico ...18 1N 66 37W
165 Ponchatoula, U.S.A. .30 27N 90 25W
51 Poncin, France 46 6N 5 25E
14 Pond Inlet, Canada ...72 30N 75 0W
106 Pondicherry, India 11 59N 79 50E
135 Pondoland, dist., S. Afr. 31 10S 29 30W
155 Ponds, I. of, Canada .53 27N 55 52W
62 Ponferrada, Spain 42 32N 6 35W
125 Pong Tamale, Ghana . 9 40N 0 46W
135 Pongala R., Nat., S. Afr. 27 15S 32 13E
146 Pongaroa, N.Z. 40 33S 176 15E
127 Pongo R., Sudan 8 0N 27 20E
60 Poniec, Poland 51 48N 16 50E
106 Ponnalyar, R., India .11 50N 79 45E
106 Ponnani & R., India .10 45N 75 59E
106 Ponneri, India 13 20N 80 15E
103 Ponnyadaung Range, mts., Burma 22 0N 94 10E
84 Ponoi, U.S.S.R. 67 0N 41 0E
84 Ponoi R., U.S.S.R. 67 10N 39 0E
156 Ponoka, Canada 52 35N 113 40W
109 Ponorogo, Indonesia . 7 52S 111 29E
50 Pons. France 45 35N 0 34W
64 Pons, Spain 41 55N 1 12E
63 Ponsul, R., Portugal .39 54N 8 45E
38 Pont R., Eng., U.K. .55 3N 1 55W
49 Pont-à-Mousson, France 48 54N 6 1E
48 Pont Audemer, France 49 21N 0 30E
48 Pont Aven, France 47 51N 3 47W
70 Pont Canavese, Italy .45 24N 7 33E
48 Pont Château, France 47 26N 2 8W
49 Pont de Roide, France 47 23N 6 45E
50 Pont de Salars, France 44 18N 2 44E
51 Pont de Vaux, France 46 26N 4 56E
51 Pont de Veyle, France 46 17N 4 53E
48 Pont l'Abbé, France ...47 52N 4 15W
155 Pont Lafrance, Canada 47 40N 64 58W
51 Pont St. Esprit, France 44 16N 4 40E
49 Pont-sur-Yonne, France 48 18N 3 10E
173 Ponta Grossa, Brazil .25 0S 50 10W
173 Ponta Pora, Brazil 22 20S 55 35W
50 Pontacq, France 43 11N 0 8W
49 Pontailler, France 47 18N 5 24E
37 Pontardawe, Wales, United Kingdom 51 43N 3 51W
37 Pontardulais, Wales, United Kingdom 51 42N 4 3W
49 Pontarlier, France 46 54N 6 20E
71 Pontassieve, Italy 43 47N 11 25E
48 Pontaubault, France .48 40N 1 20W
50 Pontaumur, France 45 52N 2 40E
165 Pontchartrain, L., U.S.A. 30 12N 90 0W
62 Ponte de Lima, Portugal 41 43N 8 39W
63 Ponte de Sor, Portugal 39 17N 7 57W
70 Ponte dell 'Olio, Italy 44 52N 9 39E
70 Ponte di Legno, Italy 46 15N 10 30E
132 Ponte do Pungüe, Mozambique 19 30S 34 33E
51 Ponte Leccia, Corse, Fr. 42 28N 9 13E
71 Ponte nell' Alpi, Italy 46 10N 12 18E
173 Ponte Nova, Brazil ...20 25S 42 54W
70 Ponte San Martino, It. 45 36N 7 47E
70 Ponte San Pietro, Italy 45 42N 9 35E
71 Pontebba, Italy 46 30N 13 17E
72 Pontecorvo, Italy 41 28N 13 40E
70 Pontedera, Italy 43 40N 10 37E
39 Pontefract, Eng., U.K. 53 42N 1 19W
157 Ponteix, Canada 49 46N 107 29W
39 Ponteland, Eng., U.K. 53 3N 1 45W
73 Pontelandolio, Italy ...41 17N 14 41E
62 Pontevedra, Spain 42 26N 8 40W
62 Pontevedra, prov., Sp. 42 25N 8 39W
70 Pontevico, Italy 45 16N 10 6E

MAP
164 Pontiac, Ill., U.S.A. ...40 50N 88 40W
162 Pontiac, Mich., U.S.A. 42 40N 83 20W
107 Pontian Kechil, Malay 1 29N 103 23E
108 Pontianak, Indonesia . 0 3S 109 15E
72 Pontine Is., Italy 40 55N 13 0E
100 Pontine Mts., Turkey .41 30N 35 0E
72 Pontinia, Italy 41 25N 13 2E
48 Pontivy, France 48 5N 3 0W
49 Pontoise, France 49 3N 2 5E
48 Pontorson, France 48 34N 1 30W
70 Pontremoli, Italy 44 22N 9 52E
37 Pontrhydfendigaid,
Wales, U.K. 52 17N 3 50W
48 Pontrieux, France 48 42N 3 10W
34 Pontrilas, Eng., U.K. .51 56N 2 53W
160 Pontypool, Canada 44 6N 78 36W
34 Pontypool, Mon.,
U.K. 51 42N 3 1W
37 Pontypridd, Wales,
U.K. 51 36N 3 21W
72 Ponza I., Italy 40 55N 12 57E
34 Poole, England, U.K. 50 42N 2 2W
34 Poole Harb., Eng., 4
U.K. 50 1N 2 0W
42 Poolewe, Scot., U.K. .57 45N 5 38W
38 Pooley Bridge,
England, United
Kingdom 54 37N 2 49W
106 Poona, India 18 29N 73 57E
106 Poonamallee, India ...13 3N 80 10E
143 Pooncarie, Australia ...33 22S 142 31E
74 Poopó L., Bolivia 18 30S 67 35W
146 Poor Knights Is., New
Zealand 35 29S 174 43E
134 Poortjie, S. Africa 30 13S 22 44E
155 Poortugaal, Neth. 51 52N 4 23E
107 Popak, China 22 15N 109 56E
142 Popanyinning,
Austral. 32 40S 117 2E
174 Popayán, Colombia ... 2 27N 76 36W
54 Poperinge, Belgium ...50 51N 2 42E
143 Popio, L., N.S.W.,
Austral. 33 10S 141 52E
164 Poplar, U.S.A. 48 3N 105 9W
165 Poplar Bluff, U.S.A. ...36 45N 90 22W
165 Poplarville, U.S.A. 30 55N 89 30W
168 Popocatepetl, vol.,
Mex. 19 10N 98 40W
130 Popokabaka, Congo ... 5 49S 16 40E
175 Popakai, Surinam 3 20N 55 30W
143 Popilta, N.S.W.,
Austral. 32 12S 141 46E
71 Popoli, Italy 42 12N 13 50E
71 Popovača, Yugoslavia 45 30N 16 41E
75 Popovo, Bulgaria 43 21N 26 18E
55 Poppel, Belgium 51 27N 5 2E
59 Poprád,
Czechoslovakia 49 3N 20 18E
59 Poprád, R., Cz. 49 15N 20 30E
146 Porangahau, N.Z. 40 17S 176 37E
104 Porbandar, India 21 44N 69 43E
156 Porcher I., Canada 53 50N 130 30W
63 Porcuna
Torredonjimeno,
Spain 37 52N 4 11W
152 Porcupine, R., Alaska,
U.S.A. 67 0N 143 0W
71 Pordenone, Italy 45 58N 12 40E
75 Pordim, Bulgaria 43 23N 24 51E
71 Porec, Yugoslavia 45 14N 13 36E
87 Poretskoye, U.S.S.R. .55 9N 46 21E
83 Pori, Finland 61 27N 21 50E
77 Pori, I., Greece 37 31N 23 29E
146 Porirua, New Zealand 41 8S 174 52E
82 Porjus, Sweden 66 57N 19 50E
83 Porkkala, (Ekenas),
Finland 60 15N 24 30E
70 Porlezza, Italy 46 2N 9 8E
36 Porlock, Eng., U.K. ...51 13N 3 36W
36 Porlock B., Eng.,
U.K. 51 14N 3 37W
40 Porlock Hill, Eng.,
U.K. 51 12N 3 40W
62 Porma, R., Spain 42 45N 5 21W
48 Pornic, France 47 7N 2 5W
91 Poronaisk, U.S.S.R. ...49 20N 143 0E
77 Póros & I., Greece 37 30N 23 30E
59 Poroszló, Hungary 47 39N 20 40E
131 Poroto Mts., Tanzania 9 0S 33 30E
142 Porraburdoo,
Australia 23 15S 117 28E
64 Porreras, Spain 39 29N 3 2E
82 Porsangen, Norway ...70 30N 25 35E
79 Porsgrunn, Norway ...59 10N 9 40E
49 Port, France 47 43N 6 4E
145 Pt. Adelaide, S.
Austral. 34 46S 138 30E
156 Port Alberni, B.C.,
Can. 49 15N 124 50E
143 Port Albert, Australia 38 42S 146 42W
104 Pt. Albert Victor,
India 21 0N 71 30E
155 Port Alfred, Canada ...48 18N 70 53W
135 Port Alfred, S. Africa 33 36S 26 55E
156 Port Alice, Canada 50 25N 127 25W
160 Port Allegany, U.S.A. 41 49N 78 17W
165 Port Allen, U.S.A. 30 30N 91 15W
144 Port Alma, Australia .23 38S 150 53E
166 Port Angeles, U.S.A. .48 0N 123 30W
169 Port Antonio,
Jamaica 18 10N 76 30W
165 Port Aransas, U.S.A. .27 49N 97 4W
145 Port Arthur, Australia 43 7S 147 50E
112 Port Arthur, China 38 50N 121 15E
165 Port Arthur, U.S.A. ...30 0N 94 0W
40 Port Askaig, Scot.,
U.K. 55 51N 6 8W
155 Port au Port B.,
Canada 48 40N 58 50W
169 Port au Prince, Haiti .18 40N 72 20W
MAP
145 Pt. Augusta, S.
Austral. 32 30S 137 45E
145 Pt. Augusta, W.
Austral. 32 30S 137 50E
160 Port Austin, U.S.A. ...44 3N 82 59W
155 Port aux Basques,
Can. 47 32N 59 8W
146 Port Awanui, N.Z. 37 50S 178 29E
40 Port Bannatyne,
Scotland, U.K. 55 51N 5 4W
134 Port Beaufort, S.
Africa 34 23S 20 51E
131 Port Bell, Uganda 0 18N 32 35E
129 Port Bergé Vaovao,
Malagasy Rep. 15 33S 47 40E
107 Port Blair, Andaman
Is. 11 40N 92 30E
155 Port Blandford,
Canada 48 30N 53 50W
165 Port Bolivar, U.S.A. .29 20N 94 40W
64 Port Bou, Spain 42 25N 3 9E
124 Port Bouet, Ivory C. . 5 16N 4 57W
139 Port Bradshaw,
Austral. 12 30S 137 0E
154 Port Burwell, Canada 42 40N 80 48W
105 Port Canning, India ...22 17N 88 48E
38 Port Carlisle, Eng.,
U.K. 54 56N 3 12W
155 Port Cartier, Canada .50 10N 66 50W
147 Port Chalmers, N.Z. ...45 49S 170 38E
40 Port Charlotte,
Scotland, U.K. 55 44N 6 22W
161 Port Chester, U.S.A. .41 0N 73 41W
136 Port Clements I., Can. 53 40N 132 10W
144 Port Clinton,
Australia 22 30S 150 46E
162 Port Clinton, U.S.A. .41 30N 83 0W
154 Port Colborne,
Canada 42 50N 79 10W
156 Port Coquitlam, Can. .49 20N 122 45W
160 Port Credit, Canada ...43 34N 79 35W
160 Port Dalhousie,
Canada 43 13N 79 17W
176 Port Darwin, Falk. Is. 51 50S 59 0W
145 Port Davey, Australia 43 16S 145 55E
169 Port de Paix, Haiti ...19 50N 72 50W
107 Port Dickson,
Malaysia 2 30N 101 49E
37 Port Dinorwic, Wales,
United Kingdom 53 11N 4 12W
144 Port Douglas,
Australia 16 30S 145 30E
160 Port Dover, Canada ...42 45N 80 10W
135 Port Durnford, S.
Africa 28 53S 31 53E
135 Port Edward, S.
Africa 31 2S 30 13E
160 Port Elgin, Canada ...44 25N 81 25W
135 Port Elizabeth, S.
Afr. 33 58S 25 40E
40 Port Ellen, Scot.,
U.K. 55 38N 6 10W
145 Port Elliott, S.
Austral. 35 32S 138 41E
38 Port Erin, I. of M.,
U.K. 54 5N 4 45W
43 Port Erroll, Scot.,
U.K. 57 25N 1 50W
120 Port Etienne, see Nouadhibou
Mauritania 21 0N 17 0W
143 Port Fairy, Australia .38 13S 142 14E
146 Port Fitzroy, N.Z. 36 8S 175 20E
130 Port Francqui, see
Ilebo, Congo 4 17S 20 47E
128 Port Gentil, Gabon 0 47S 8 40E
165 Port Gibson, U.S.A. ...31 57N 91 0W
40 Port Glasgow, Scot.,
U.K. 55 57N 4 40W
125 Port Harcourt,
Nigeria 4 40N 7 10E
156 Port Hardy, Canada .50 41N 127 30W
153 Port Harrison,
Canada 58 25N 78 15W
155 Port Hawkesbury,
Can. 45 36N 61 22W
138 Port Hedland,
Austral. 20 25S 118 35E
161 Port Henry, U.S.A. ...44 0N 73 30W
155 Port Hood, Canada ...46 0N 61 32W
154 Port Hope, Canada ...44 0N 78 20W
162 Port Huron, U.S.A. ...43 0N 82 28W
36 Port Isaac, Eng.,
U.K. 50 35N 4 50W
36 Port Isaac B., Eng.,
UK 50 36N 4 50W
165 Port Isabel, U.S.A. 26 12N 97 9W
143 Port Jackson,
Australia 33 53S 151 12E
161 Port Jefferson, U.S.A. 40 58N 73 5W
161 Port Jervis, U.S.A. 41 22N 74 42W
48 Port Joinville, France 46 45N 2 23W
89 Port Katon, U.S.S.R. 46 27N 38 56E
174 Port Kaituma,
Guyana 8 3N 59 58W
143 Port Kembla,
Australia 34 29S 150 56E
45 Port Laois, Ire. 53 2N 7 20W
165 Port Lavaca, U.S.A. .28 38N 96 38W
138 Port Lincoln, S.
Austral. 34 42S 135 52E
40 Port Logan, Scot.,
U.K. 54 42N 4 57W
124 Port Loko, Sierra
Leone 8 48N 12 46W
48 Port Louis, France 47 42N 3 22W
147 Port Lyttelton, N.Z. .43 37N 172 50E
145 Pt. Macquarie,
Austral. 31 25S 152 54E
155 Port Maitland, N.S.,
Canada 44 0N 66 2W
MAP
160 Port Maitland, Ont.,
Canada 42 53N 79 35W
156 Port Mellon, Canada .49 32N 123 31W
155 Port Menier, Canada .49 51N 64 15W
144 Port Moresby, Papua . 9 24S 147 8E
155 Port Mouton, Canada 43 58N 64 50W
144 Port Musgrave,
Austral. 11 55S 141 50E
48 Port Navalo, France .47 34N 2 54W
157 Port Nelson, Canada .57 5N 92 56W
146 Port Nicholson, N.Z. .41 20S 174 52E
134 Port Nolloth, S.
Africa 29 17S 16 52E
153 Port Nouveau-Quebec
(George R.), Canada 58 30N 65 50W
165 Port O'Connor,
U.S.A. 28 26N 96 24W
169 Port of Spain,
Trinidad 10 40N 61 20W
166 Port Orchard, U.S.A. .47 31N 122 47W
166 Port Oxford, U.S.A. ...42 45N 124 28W
138 Port Patterson,
Austral. 12 40S 130 30E
147 Port Pegasus, N.Z. 47 12S 167 41E
160 Port Perry, Canada ...44 6N 78 56W
143 Port Phillip B.,
Austral. 38 0S 145 0E
145 Port Pirie, S.
Australia 33 10S 137 58E
161 Port Pleasant, U.S.A. 40 5N 74 4W
152 Port Radium, Canada 66 10N 117 40W
156 Port Renfrew, Canada 48 30N 124 20W
160 Port Rowan, Canada .42 40N 80 30W
160 Port Ryerse, Canada .42 47N 80 15W
126 Port Safâga, Egypt ...26 43N 33 57E
126 Port Said, Egypt 31 16N 32 18E
163 Port St. Joe, U.S.A. ...29 49N 85 20W
135 Port St. Johns, S.
Africa 31 38S 29 33E
51 Port St. Louis, France 43 23N 4 50E
38 Port St. Mary, I. of
M., U.K. 54 5N 4 45W
155 Port St. Servain, Can. 51 21N 58 0W
160 Port Sanilac, U.S.A. ...43 26N 82 33W
155 Port Saunders,
Canada 50 40N 57 18W
160 Port Severn, Canada .44 47N 79 43W
135 Port Shepstone, S.
Afr. 30 44S 30 28E
156 Port Simpson, Canada 54 30N 130 20W
138 Port Site Three, W.
Australia 19 55S 120 33E
154 Port Stanley, Canada .42 40N 81 10W
143 Port Stephens,
Austral. 32 38S 152 12E
126 Port Sudan, Sudan 19 32N 37 9E
38 Port Sunlight, Eng.,
U.K. 53 22N 3 0W
107 Pt. Swettenham,
Malaya 3 0N 101 23E
37 Port Talbot, Wales,
U.K. 51 35N 3 48W
126 Port Taufiq. Egypt ...29 54N 32 32E
166 Port Townsend,
U.S.A. 48 0N 122 50W
50 Port Vendres, France .42 32N 3 8E
162 Port Washington,
U.S.A. 43 25N 87 52W
107 Port Weld, Malaysia . 4 50N 100 38E
40 Port William, Scot.,
U.K. 54 46N 4 35W
174 Portachuelo, Bolivia .17 10S 63 20W
45 Portacloy, Ireland 54 20N 9 48W
46 Portadown
(Craigavon), N. Ire.,
U.K. 54 27N 6 26W
46 Portaferry, N. Ire.,
U.K. 54 23N 5 32W
155 Portage, Canada 46 40N 64 5W
164 Portage, U.S.A. 43 31N 89 25W
157 Portage la Prairie,
Can. 49 58N 98 18W
156 Portage Mt. Dam,
Canada 56 0N 122 0W
165 Portageville, U.S.A. ...36 25N 89 40W
63 Portalegre, tn. &
prov., Portugal 39 19N 7 25W
165 Portales, U.S.A. 34 12N 103 25W
45 Portarlington, Ireland 53 10N 7 10W
63 Portel, Portugal 38 19N 7 41W
134 Porterville, S. Africa .33 0S 18 57E
167 Porterville, U.S.A. 36 5N 119 0W
36 Portesham, Eng.,
U.K. 50 40N 2 33W
37 Porteynon, Wales,
U.K. 51 33N 4 13W
46 Portglenone, N. Ire.,
U.K. 54 53N 6 30W
43 Portgordon, Scot.,
U.K. 57 40N 3 1W
37 Porth Neigwl, Wales,
United Kingdom 52 48N 4 35W
37 Porthcawl, Wales,
U.K. 51 28N 3 42W
166 Porthill, U.S.A. 49 0N 116 30W
36 Porthleven, Eng.,
U.K. 50 5N 5 19W
34 Portishead, Eng.,
U.K. 51 29N 2 46W
43 Portknockie, Scot.,
U.K. 57 40N 2 52W
143 Portland, N.S.W.,
Austral. 33 13S 149 59E
161 Portland, Canada 44 42N 76 11W
161 Portland, Conn.,
U.S.A. 41 34N 72 39W
155 Portland, Me., U.S.A. 43 40N 70 15W
162 Portland, Mich.,
U.S.A. 42 52N 84 58W
146 Portland I., N.Z. 39 20S 177 51E
MAP
166 Portland, Oreg.,
U.S.A. 45 35N 122 40W
143 Portland B. &,
Australia 38 15S 141 45E
36 Portland Bill, Eng.,
U.K. 50 31N 2 27W
36 Portland, I. of,
England, U.K. 50 32N 2 25W
153 Portland Prom., Can. .59 0N 78 0W
45 Portlaw, Ireland 52 18N 7 20W
43 Portlethen, Scot.,
U.K. 57 4N 2 7W
37 Portmadoc, Wales,
U.K. 52 51N 4 8W
44 Portmagee, Ireland ...51 53N 10 22W
43 Portmahomack,
Scotland, U.K. 57 50N 3 50W
45 Portmarnock, Ireland 53 25N 6 10W
40 Portnacroish, Scot.,
U.K. 56 34N 5 24W
42 Portnaguiran, Scot.,
U.K. 58 15N 6 10W
40 Portnahaven, Scot.,
U.K. 55 40N 6 30W
155 Portneuf, Canada 46 43N 71 55W
62 Porto, Portugal 41 8N 8 40W
51 Porto G., Corsica, Fr. 42 17N 8 34E
62 Porto, dist., Portugal .41 8N 8 20W
133 Porto Agricola de
Umbeluzi, Mozam. .26 6S 32 24E
173 Porto Alegre, Rio
Grande do Sul,
Braz. 30 5S 51 3W
175 Porto Alegre, Mato
Grosso, Brazil 21 40S 53 30W
129 Port Alexandre,
Angola 15 55S 11 55E
130 Porto Amboim,
Angola 10 50S 13 50E
129 Porto Amelia, Mozam. 12 58S 40 30E
70 Porto Argentera, Italy 44 15N 7 27E
175 Porto Artur, Brazil ...13 0S 54 40W
72 Porto Botte, Italy 39 3N 8 33E
71 Porto Civitanova,
Italy 43 19N 13 44E
175 Porto de Moz, Brazil . 1 41S 52 22W
72 Porto Empedocle,
Sicily 37 18N 13 30E
174 Porto Esperança,
Brazil 19 37S 57 29W
175 Porto Franco, Brazil . 9 45S 47 0W
71 Porto Garibaldi, Italy 44 41N 12 14E
76 Pórto Lágo, Greece ...41 1N 25 6E
70 Porto Longone, Italy .42 46N 10 24E
173 Porto Mendes, Brazil .24 30S 54 15W
174 Porto Murtinho,
Brazil 21 45S 57 55W
175 Porto Nacional, Brazil 10 40S 48 30W
125 Porto Novo, Dahomey 6 23N 2 42E
106 Porto Novo, India 11 30N 79 38E
71 Porto Recanati, Italy 43 26N 13 40E
130 Porto Rico, Angola ... 6 10S 12 30E
71 Porto San Giorgio,
Italy 43 11N 13 49E
76 Porto San Stefano, It. 42 26N 11 6E
120 Porto Santo I.,
Madeira 33 45N 16 25W
175 Porto Seguro, Brazil .16 20S 39 0W
71 Porto Tolle, Italy 44 57N 12 20E
72 Porto Torres, Italy 40 50N 8 23E
173 Porto União, Brazil ...26 10S 51 10W
174 Porto Valter, Brazil ... 8 5S 72 40W
174 Portobelo, Panama 9 35N 79 42W
70 Portoferraio, Italy 42 50N 10 20E
71 Portogruaro, Italy 45 47N 12 50E
166 Portola, U.S.A. 39 49N 120 28W
71 Portomaggiore, Italy .44 41N 11 47E
34 Porton Camp, Eng.,
U.K. 51 8N 1 42W
72 Portoscuso, Italy 39 12N 8 22E
70 Portovenere, Italy 44 2N 9 50E
174 Portoviejo, Ecuador ... 1 0S 80 20W
40 Portpatrick, Scot.,
U.K. 54 50N 5 7W
42 Portree, Scot., U.K. ...57 25N 6 11W
44 Portroe, Ireland 52 53N 8 20W
46 Portrush, N. Ire.,
U.K. 55 13N 6 40W
48 Portsall, France 48 37N 4 45W
46 Portsalon, Ireland 55 12N 7 37W
36 Portscatho, Eng.,
U.K. 50 11N 4 59W
43 Portskerra, Scot.,
U.K. 58 35N 3 55W
35 Portslade, Eng., U.K. 50 50N 0 11W
161 Portsmouth, Canada .44 14N 76 34W
34 Portsmouth, Eng.,
U.K. 50 48N 1 6W
161 Portsmouth, N.H.,
U.S.A. 43 5N 70 45W
162 Portsmouth, Ohio,
U.S.A. 38 45N 83 0W
161 Portsmouth, R.I.,
U.S.A. 41 35N 71 44W
162 Portsmouth, Va.,
U.S.A. 36 50N 76 20W
43 Portsoy, Scot., U.K. .57 41N 2 41W
46 Portstewart, N. Ire.,
United Kingdom 55 12N 6 43W
82 Porttipahta Res.,
Finland 68 5N 26 40E
62 Portugal, st., Europe .40 0N 7 0W
64 Portugalete, Spain 43 19N 3 4W
174 Portuguesa R., Ven. ... 9 0N 68 20W
124 Portuguese Guinea,
terr., West Africa ...12 0N 15 0W
109 Portuguese Timor,
E.I. 8 0S 126 30E
44 Portumna, Ireland 53 5N 8 12W
160 Portville, U.S.A. 42 3N 78 21W
MAP
176 Porvenir, Chile 53 10S 70 30W
83 Porvoo (Borga),
Finland 60 27N 25 50E
55 Porz, Germany 50 43N 7 4E
63 Porzuna, Spain 39 9N 4 9W
72 Posada R., Italy 40 40N 9 35E
63 Posadas, Spain 37 47N 5 11W
173 Posados. Argentina ...27 30S 56 0W
57 Poschiavo,
Switzerland 46 19N 10 4E
113 Poseh, China 23 50N 106 0E
76 Posidhion, Akra, C.,
Gr. 39 57N 23 20E
60 Poslek, Poland 54 3N 19 41E
109 Poso & L., Indonesia . 1 20S 120 55E
175 Posse, Brazil 14 4S 46 18W
15 Possession I.,
Antarctica 72 4S 172 0E
56 Possneck, Germany ...50 42N 11 34E
165 Post, U.S.A. 33 13N 101 21W
166 Post Falls, U.S.A. 47 50N 116 59W
86 Postavy, U.S.S.R. 55 4N 26 58E
36 Postbridge, Eng.,
U.K. 50 36N 3 54W
154 Poste de la Baleine,
Canada 55 20N 77 40E
122 Poste Maurice Cortier
(Bidon 5), Algeria ...22 14N 1 2E
55 Posterholt,
Netherlands 51 8N 6 1E
109 Postiljon I., Indonesia 6 30S 118 50E
134 Postmasburg, S. Afr. .28 18S 23 5E
71 Postojna, Yugoslavia .45 46N 14 12E
77 Potamós, Greece 39 38N 19 53E
133 Potchefstroom, S. Afr. 26 41S 27 7E
78 Potcoava, Rumania ...44 30N 24 39E
165 Poteau, U.S.A. 35 5N 94 37W
165 Poteet, U.S.A. 29 4N 98 35W
78 Potelu, Balta L.,
Rum. 43 44N 24 20E
73 Potenza, Italy 40 40N 15 50E
71 Potenza Picena, Italy 43 22N 13 37E
147 Poteriteri, L., N.Z. 46 5S 167 10E
62 Potes, Spain 43 15N 4 42W
134 Potfontein, S. Africa .30 12S 24 8E
133 Potgietersrus, S.
Africa 24 10S 29 3E
89 Poti, U.S.S.R. 42 10N 41 38E
125 Potiskum, Nigeria 11 39N 11 2E
78 Potlogi, Rumania 44 34N 25 34E
162 Potomac R., U.S.A. ...39 40N 78 25W
174 Potosi, Bolivia 19 38S 65 50W
172 Potosi, dept., Bolivia .20 31S 67 0W
112 Potow, China 38 8N 116 31E
172 Potrerillos, Chile 26 20S 69 30W
172 Potros, Cerro del, mt.,
Chile 28 32S 69 0W
56 Potsdam, Germany ...52 23N 13 4E
56 Potsdam, dist., E.
Ger. 52 40N 13 30E
161 Potsdam, U.S.A. 44 40N 74 59W
164 Potter, U.S.A. 41 15N 103 20W
35 Potter Heigham,
England, U.K. 52 44N 1 33E
34 Potterne, Eng., U.K. .51 19N 2 0W
35 Potters Bar, Eng.,
U.K. 51 42N 0 11W
35 Potterspury, Eng.,
U.K. 52 5N 0 52W
126 Pottery Hill, see Abu
Ballas, Egypt 24 26N 27 36E
161 Pottstown, Pa.,
U.S.A. 40 17N 75 40W
161 Pottsville, U.S.A. 40 39N 76 12W
48 Pouancé, France 47 44N 1 10W
156 Pouce Coupé, Canada 55 40N 120 10W
161 Poughkeepsie, U.S.A. .41 40N 73 57W
49 Pouilly, Nièvre,
France 47 18N 2 57E
48 Pouldu, le, France 47 41N 3 36W
107 Poulo Condore Is.,
South Vietnam 8 45N 106 45E
166 Poulsbo, U.S.A. 47 45N 122 45W
38 Poulton le Fylde,
England, U.K. 53 51N 2 59W
36 Poundstock, Eng.,
U.K. 50 44N 4 34W
134 Poupan, C. Prov., S.
Afr. 30 2S 24 10E
175 Pouso Alegre, Mato
Grosso, Brazil 11 55S 57 0W
173 Pouso Alegre, Minas
Gerais, Brazil 22 14S 45 57W
50 Pouzages, France 46 40N 0 50W
84 Povenets, U.S.S.R. 62 50N 34 50E
146 Poverty Bay, N.Z. 38 43S 178 2E
62 Povoa de Lanhosa,
Port. 41 33N 8 15W
62 Povóa de Varzim
Port. 41 25N 8 46W
87 Povorino, U.S.S.R. 51 12N 42 28E
154 Powassan, Canada 46 5N 79 25W
164 Powder R., U.S.A. 46 15N 105 5W
166 Powder R., U.S.A. 44 0N 106 15W
166 Powell, Wyo., U.S.A. .44 45N 108 45W
156 Powell River, Can. 49 48N 125 20W
138 Powell's Creek,
Austral. 18 6S 133 46E
162 Powers, Mich., U.S.A. 45 40N 87 32W
166 Powers, Ore., U.S.A. .42 53N 124 2W
164 Powers Lake, U.S.A. .48 37N 102 38W
34 Powick, Eng., U.K. ...52 9N 2 15W
29 Powis, Vale of, Wales,
United Kingdom 52 40N 3 10W
113 Poyang L., China 29 10N 116 10E
46 Poyntzpass, N.
Ireland, United
Kingdom 54 17N 6 22W
58 Poysdorf, Austria 48 40N 16 37E
64 Poza de la Sal, Spain .42 35N 3 31W

MAP
168 Poza Rica, Mexico 20 33N 97 27W
74 Pozarevac, Yugoslavia 44 35N 21 18E
74 Pozega, Yugoslavia ...45 21N 17 41E
60 Poznan, Poland 52 25N 17 0E
160 Poznan, prov., Poland 52 30N 18 0E
74 Pozo Almonte, Chile .20 10S 69 50W
63 Pozoblanco, Spain 38 23N 4 51W
173 Pozzallo, Italy 36 44N 15 40E
125 Pra R., Ghana 5 30N 1 38W
60 Prabuty, Poland 53 47N 19 15E
74 Prača, Yugoslavia 43 47N 18 43E
58 Prachatice, Cz. 49 1N 14 0E
107 Prachin Buri, Thailand 14 0N 101 25E
107 Prachuap Khiri Khan, Thailand 11 44N 99 46E
50 Pradelles, France 44 46N 3 52E
50 Prades, France 42 38N 2 23E
175 Prado, Brazil 17 20S 39 20W
63 Prado del Rey, Spain .36 48N 5 33W
81 Præstö, Denmark 55 8N 12 2E
81 Præstö Amt., co., Denmark 51 15N 12 2E
71 Pragersko, Yugoslavia 46 27N 15 42E
58 Prague, (Praha), Cz. ...50 5N 14 22E
50 Prahecq, France 46 19N 0 26W
106 Prahita, R., India 19 0N 79 55E
78 Prahova, Reg., Rum. .45 00N 26 00E
78 Prahova R., Rum. 44 50N 25 50E
74 Prahovo, Yugoslavia ..44 18N 22 39E
78 Praid, Rumania 46 32N 25 10E
74 Prainha, Amazona, Braz. 7 10S 60 30W
75 Prainha, Para, Brazil . 1 45S 53 30W
144 Prairie, Australia 20 50S 144 35E
165 Prairie R., U.S.A. 34 45N 101 15W
166 Prairie City, U.S.A. ...45 27N 118 44W
164 Prairie du Chien, U.S.A. 43 1N 91 9W
108 Praja, Indonesia 8 39S 116 27E
76 Pramanda, Greece 39 32N 21 8E
125 Prang, Ghana 8 1N 0 56W
108 Prapat, Indonesia 2 41N 98 58E
175 Prappia, Brazil 10 15S 37 1W
60 Praszka, Poland 51 32N 18 31E
175 Prata, Minas Gerais, Brazil 19 25S 49 0W
175 Prata, Pará, Brazil 1 10S 47 35W
72 Pratica di Mare, Italy 41 40N 12 26E
70 Prato, Tuscany, Italy 43 53N 11 5E
71 Pratola Poligna, Italy 42 7N 13 51E
71 Pratovecchio, Italy ...43 44N 11 43E
50 Prats de Mollo, France 42 25N 2 27E
165 Pratt, U.S.A. 37 40N 98 45W
163 Prattville, U.S.A. 32 30N 86 28W
106 Pravara, R., India 19 30N 74 28E
87 Pravdinsk, U.S.S.R. ...56 29N 43 28E
62 Pravia, Spain 43 30N 6 12W
36 Prawle Pt., Eng., U.K. 50 13N 3 41W
109 Pre Pare, Indonesia ... 3 59S 119 45E
70 Pré St. Didier, Italy ...45 45N 7 0E
172 Precordillera, Argentina 30 0S 69 1W
71 Predappio, Italy 44 7N 11 58E
71 Predazzo, Italy 46 19N 11 37E
74 Predejane, Yugoslavia 42 51N 22 9E
157 Preeceville, Canada ...52 0N 102 50W
48 Pré-en-Pail, France ...48 28N 0 12W
38 Prees, Eng., U.K. 52 54N 2 40W
38 Preesall, Eng., U.K. ...53 55N 2 58W
48 Préfailles, France 47 9N 2 11W
71 Pregrada, Yugoslavia .46 11N 15 45E
71 Preko, Yugoslavia 44 7N 15 14E
71 Prelog, Yugoslavia 46 18N 16 32E
143 Premer, N.S.W., Austral. 31 29S 149 56E
165 Premont, U.S.A. 27 19N 91 8W
71 Premuda I., Yugoslavia 44 20N 14 36E
74 Prenj, mt., Y.-slavia .43 33N 17 53E
164 Prentice, U.S.A. 45 31N 90 19W
56 Prenzlau, Germany ...53 19N 13 51E
74 Prepansko Jezero, L., Yugoslavia 40 45N 21 0E
103 Preparis I., India 14 55N 93 45E
107 Preparis North Channel, Andaman Islands 15 12N 93 40E
107 Preparis South Channel, Andaman Islands 14 36N 93 40E
59 Přerov, Czechoslovakia 49 28N 17 27E
38 Prescot, Eng., U.K. ...53 27N 2 49W
154 Prescott, Canada 44 45N 75 30W
167 Prescott, Ariz., U.S.A. 34 35N 112 30W
165 Prescott, Ark., U.S.A. 33 49N 93 22
147 Preservation Inlet, N.Z. 46 8S 166 35E
74 Preševo, Yugoslavia ...42 19N 21 39E
164 Presho, U.S.A. 43 56N 100 4W
34 Preshute, Eng., U.K. .51 24N 1 45W
73 Presicce, Italy 39 53N 18 13E
172 Presidencia de la Plaza, Argentina 27 0S 60 0W
172 Presidencia Roque Saenz Pena, Argentina 26 45S 60 30W
174 Pres. Hermes, Brazil .11 0S 61 55W
175 Pres. Murtinho, Brazil 15 45S 54 0W
173 Pres. Prudente, Brazil 22 5S 51 25W
173 Presidente Venceslau, Brazil 21 52S 51 51W
165 Presidio, U.S.A. 29 30N 104 20W
75 Preslav, Bulgaria 43 10N 26 52E
75 Prespa, Mt., Bulgaria .41 44N 25 0E
155 Presque Isle, Me., U.S.A. 46 40N 68 0W
MAP
37 Prestatyn, Wales, U.K. 53 20N 3 24W
34 Prestbury, Eng., U.K. 51 54N 2 2W
124 Prestea, Ghana 5 22N 2 7W
37 Presteigne, Wales, U.K. 52 17N 3 0W
58 Prestice, Czechoslovakia 49 34N 13 20E
160 Preston, Canada 43 25N 80 20W
34 Preston, Dorset, England, U.K. 50 38N 2 26W
38 Preston, Lancs., England, U.K. 53 46N 2 42W
39 Preston, Yorks., England, U.K. 53 45N 0 10W
41 Preston, Scot., U.K. ...55 48N 2 18W
166 Preston, Idaho, U.S.A. 42 0N 112 0W
164 Preston, Minn., U.S.A. 43 39N 92 3W
166 Preston, Nev., U.S.A. 38 59N 115 2W
41 Prestonpans, Scot., U.K. 55 58N 3 0W
38 Prestwich, Eng., U.K. 53 32N 2 18W
40 Prestwick, Scot., U.K. 55 30N 4 38W
133 Pretoria, Trans., S. Afr. 25 44S 28 12E
133 Pretoria North, S. Afr. 25 38S 28 11E
134 Pretoriusvlei, S. Africa 28 30S 22 59E
77 Préveza, Greece 38 57N 20 47E
107 Prey Veng, Cambodia 11 35N 105 29E
88 Priazovskoye, U.S.S.R. 46 22N 35 28E
14 Pribilof Is., Bering Sea 56 0N 170 0W
74 Priboj, Yugoslavia 43 35N 19 32E
58 Pribram, Cz. 49 41N 14 2E
166 Price, U.S.A. 39 40N 110 48W
89 Prichalnaya, U.S.S.R. 48 57N 44 33E
64 Priego, Spain 40 38N 2 21W
63 Priego de Cordoba, Sp. 37 27N 4 12W
86 Priekule, U.S.S.R. 57 27N 21 45E
134 Prieska, C. Prov., S. Afr. 29 40S 22 42E
166 Priest L., U.S.A. 48 30N 116 55W
166 Priest River, U.S.A. ...48 11N 117 0W
59 Prievidza, Cz. 48 46N 18 36E
71 Prijedor, Yugoslavia .44 58N 16 41E
74 Prijepolje, Yugoslavia 43 27N 19 40E
74 Prilep, Yugoslavia 41 21N 21 37E
86 Priluki, U.S.S.R. 50 30N 32 15E
75 Primorsko, Bulgaria ...42 15N 27 44E
88 Primorsko-Akhtarsk, U.S.S.R. 46 2N 38 10E
157 Primrose L., Canada .54 55N 109 40W
157 Prince Albert, Canada 53 15N 105 50W
152 Prince Albert Pen., Can. 72 0N 116 0W
134 Prince Albert Road, C. Prov., S. Africa .32 55S 21 40E
14 Prince Alfred C., Can. 74 0N 124 0W
134 Pr. Alfred Hamlet, C. Prov., S. Afr. 33 20S 19 20E
153 Prince Charles I., Can. 68 0N 76 0W
11 Prince Edward Is., Indian Oc. 45 15S 39 0E
155 Prince Edward I., prov., Canada 44 2N 77 20W
156 Prince George, Canada 53 50N 122 50W
15 Prince Harald Coast, Antarctica 70 0S 35 1E
157 Prince of Wales I., Alas., U.S.A. 53 30N 131 30W
152 Prince of Wales I., Can. 73 0N 99 0W
144 Pr. of Wales, I. Austral. 10 35S 142 0E
15 Prince Olav. Coast, Ant. 69 0S 42 0E
14 Prince Patrick I., Can. 77 0N 120 0W
14 Pr. Regent Inlet, Can. 73 0N 90 0W
156 Prince Rupert, Canada 54 20N 130 20W
55 Princenhage, Neth. 51 9N 4 45E
35 Princes Risborough, England, U.K. 51 43N 0 50W
144 Princess Charlotte B. Queens., Australia .14 15S 144 0E
15 Princess Martha Coast, Antarctica ...73 30S 10 0W
15 Princess Ragnhild Coast, Antarctica ...70 0S 30 0E
156 Princess Royal I., Can. 53 0N 128 40W
156 Princeton, B.C., Can. .49 27N 120 30W
162 Princeton, Ill., U.S.A. 41 25N 89 25W
162 Princeton, Ind., U.S.A. 38 20N 87 35W
162 Princeton Ky., U.S.A. 37 6N 87 55W
164 Princeton, Mo., U.S.A. 40 23N 93 35W
161 Princeton, N.J., U.S.A. 40 18N 74 40W
162 Princeton, W. Va., U.S.A. 37 21N 81 8W
36 Princetown, Eng., U.K. 50 33N 4 0W
174 Principe da Beira, Brazil 12 20S 64 30W
166 Prineville, U.S.A. 44 17N 120 57W
134 Prins Albert, S. Africa 33 12S 22 2E
62 Prior, C., Spain 43 34N 8 17W
135 Priors, O.F.S., S. Africa 30 27S 25 36E
MAP
86 Pripet Marshes, U.S.S.R. 52 30N 28 30E
86 Pripyat (Pripet) R., U.S.S.R. 51 30N 30 0E
74 Priština, Yugoslavia ...42 40N 21 13E
163 Pritchard, U.S.A. 30 47N 88 5W
56 Pritzwalk, Germany ...53 10N 12 11E
51 Privas, France 44 45N 4 37E
72 Priverno, Italy 41 29N 13 10E
87 Privolzhskiy, U.S.S.R. 51 25N 46 3E
87 Privolzhye, U.S.S.R. .52 52N 48 33E
89 Priyutnoye, U.S.S.R. .47 12N 43 30E
74 Prizren, Yugoslavia ...42 13N 20 45E
72 Prizzi, Italy 37 44N 13 24E
74 Prnjavor, Yugoslavia .44 52N 17 43E
109 Probolinggo, Indonesia 7 46S 113 13E
36 Probus, Eng., U.K. ...50 17N 4 55W
72 Procida I., Italy 40 46N 14 0E
106 Proddatur, India 14 45N 78 30E
63 Proenca-a-Nova, Port. 37 45N 7 54W
168 Progreso, Yucatan, Mex. 21 20N 89 40W
89 Prokhladnyy, U.S.S.R. 43 50N 44 2E
76 Prokletije, mts., Alb. .42 30N 19 45E
90 Prokopyevsk, U.S.S.R. 54 0N 87 3E
74 Prokuplje, Yugoslavia 43 16N 21 36E
89 Proletarskaya, U.S.S.R. 46 42N 41 50E
103 Prome, Burma 18 45N 95 30E
51 Propriano, Corsica, Fr. 41 41N 8 52E
144 Proserpine, Australia .20 21S 148 36E
166 Prosser, U.S.A. 46 11N 119 52W
59 Prostejov, Cz. 49 30N 17 9E
145 Proston, Australia 26 14S 151 32E
59 Proszowice, Poland ...50 13N 20 16E
165 Protection, U.S.A. 37 16N 99 30W
134 Protem, C. Prov., S. Afr. 34 15S 20 4E
77 Próti, I., Greece 37 5N 21 32E
75 Provadija, Bulgaria ...43 12N 27 30E
51 Provence, prov., Fr. ...43 40N 5 46E
162 Providence, Ky., U.S.A. 37 25N 87 46W
161 Providence, R.I., U.S.A. 41 41N 71 15W
154 Providence Bay, Can. 45 41N 82 15W
127 Providence C., N.Z. ...45 59S 166 29E
167 Providence Mts., U.S.A. 35 0N 115 30W
169 Providencia I., Col. 13 25N 81 26W
107 Prov. Wellesley, Malaya, Malaysia ... 5 15N 100 20E
162 Provincetown, U.S.A. 42 5N 70 11W
49 Provins, France 48 33N 3 15E
166 Provo, U.S.A. 40 16N 111 37W
157 Provost, Canada 52 25N 110 20W
74 Prozor, Yugoslavia 43 50N 17 34E
135 Prudhoe, S. Africa 33 24S 27 6E
38 Prudhoe, Eng., U.K. .54 57N 1 52W
144 Prudhoe I., Queensland, Australia 21 23S 149 45E
14 Prudhoe Land, Green. 78 1N 65 0W
60 Prudnik, Poland 50 20N 17 38E
57 Prum, Germany 50 14N 6 22E
60 Pruszcz, Poland 54 17N 19 40E
60 Pruszków, Poland 52 9N 20 49E
78 Prut, R., Rumania 46 3N 28 10E
71 Prvic, I., Yugoslavia .44 55N 14 47E
15 Prydz B., Antarctica .69 0S 74 0E
165 Pryor, U.S.A. 36 17N 95 20W
60 Przasnysz, Poland 53 2N 20 45E
60 Przedbórz, Poland 51 6N 19 53E
59 Przemyś, Poland 49 50N 22 45E
59 Przeworsk, Poland 50 6N 22 32E
60 Przewóz, Poland 51 28N 14 57E
90 Przhevalsk, U.S.S.R. .42 30N 78 20E
77 Psakhná, Greece 38 34N 23 35E
77 Psarà I., Greece 38 37N 25 38E
176 Psathoura, I., Greece .39 30N 24 12E
88 Psel R., U.S.S.R. 49 25N 33 50E
77 Pserimos, I., Greece ...36 56N 27 12E
86 Pskov, U.S.S.R. 57 50N 28 25E
74 Psunj, Mt., Yugoslavia 45 25N 17 19E
59 Pszczyna, Poland 49 59N 18 58E
77 Pteleón, Greece 39 3N 22 57E
86 Ptich R., U.S.S.R. 52 30N 28 45E
76 Ptolemaïs, Greece 40 30N 21 43E
71 Ptuj, Yugoslavia 46 28N 15 50E
71 Ptujska Gora, Y.-slav. 46 23N 15 47E
72 Puan, Argentina 37 30S 63 0W
113 Puan, China 25 45N 105 2E
155 Pubnico, Canada 43 47N 65 50W
174 Pucallpa, Peru 8 25S 74 30W
113 Pucheng, China 28 0N 118 30E
78 Pucheni, Rumania 45 12N 25 17E
113 Puchi, China 29 42N 113 54E
71 Pucisce, Yugoslavia ...43 22N 16 43E
60 Puck, Poland 54 45N 18 23E
36 Puddletown, Eng., U.K. 50 45N 2 21W
133 Pudimoe, S. Africa 27 26S 24 44E
39 Pudsey, Eng., U.K. 53 47N 1 40W
106 Pudukkottai, India 10 28N 78 47E
168 Puebla, Mexico 19 0N 98 10W
168 Puebla, st., Mexico ...18 30N 98 0W
63 Puebla de Alcocer, Sp. 38 59N 5 14W
65 Puebla de Don Fadrique, Spain 37 58N 2 25W
63 Puebla de Don Rodrigo, Spain 39 5N 4 37W
62 Puebla de Sanabria, Sp. 42 4N 6 38W
MAP
62 Puebla de Trives, Spain 42 20N 7 10W
62 Puebla del Caramiñal, Sp. 42 37N 8 56W
63 Puebla de la Cazalla, Sp. 37 14N 5 18W
164 Pueblo, Colo., U.S.A. 38 20N 104 40W
167 Pueblo Bonito, U.S.A. 36 4N 107 57W
172 Pueblo Bovril, Arg. ...31 20S 59 26W
63 Pueblo de Guzman, Sp. 37 37N 7 15W
172 Pueblo Hundido, Chile 26 20S 69 30W
172 Puelches, Argentina ...38 5S 66 0W
172 Puelen, Argentina 37 32S 67 38W
172 Puemo, Chile 34 21S 71 19W
172 Puente Alto, Chile 33 32S 70 35W
62 Puente del Arzobispo, Sp. 39 48N 5 10W
63 Puente Genil, Spain ...37 22N 4 47W
62 Puentearas, Spain 42 10N 8 28W
62 Puentedeume, Spain .43 24N 8 10W
167 Puerco R., U.S.A. 35 10N 109 45W
111 Puerh, China 23 11N 100 56E
176 Puerredón L., Argentina 47 20S 72 0W
169 Puerto Armuelles, Pan. 8 20N 83 10W
174 Puerto Asis, Colombia 0 30N 76 30W
176 Puerto Aysen, Chile ...45 10S 73 0W
168 Puerto Barrios, Guat. 15 40N 88 40W
113 Puerto Belgrano, Arg. 38 50S 62 0W
172 Puerto Bermejo, Arg. 26 55S 58 34W
174 Puerto Bermudez, Peru 10 20S 75 0W
174 Puerto Berrio, Colombia 6 30N 74 30W
174 Puerto Bolivar, Ec. ... 3 10S 79 55W
174 Puerto Cabello, Ven. .10 28N 68 1W
169 Puerto Cabezas, Nic. .14 0N 83 30W
122 Puerto Capaz, *see* Jebba, Morocco 35 11N 4 43W
174 Puerto Carreño, Col. . 6 12N 67 22W
172 Puerto Casado, Par. ...22 19S 57 56W
169 Puerto Castilla, Hond. 16 0N 86 0W
174 Puerto Chicama, Peru 7 45S 79 20W
176 Pueto Coig, Argentina..............50 54S 69 15W
174 Puerto Colombia, Col. 10 59N 74 58W
174 Puerto Córdoba, Col. . 1 15S 69 50W
169 Puerto Cortés, C. Rica 8 20N 82 20W
168 Puerto Cortes, Hond. .15 51N 88 0W
120 Puerto de Cabras, Canary Is. 28 40N 13 30W
174 Puerto Grether, Bolivia 17 0S 64 40W
174 Puerto de Hierro, Ven. 10 32N 61 58W
168 Puerto de Morelos, Mex. 20 49N 86 52W
63 Pto. de Sta. Maria, Sp. 36 35N 6 15W
176 Puerto Deseado, Arg. .47 45S 66 0W
174 Puerto Eten, Peru 7 0S 79 50W
174 Puerto Heath, Bolivia 12 25S 68 45W
168 Puerto Juárez, Mexico 21 11N 86 49W
174 Puerto Leguizamo, Col. 0 12S 74 46W
168 Puerto Libertad, Mex. 29 55N 112 41W
176 Puerto Lobos, Argentina 42 0S 65 3W
65 Puerto Lumbreras, Sp. 37 34N 1 48W
176 Puerto Madryn, Arg. .42 48S 65 4W
174 Puerto Maldonado, Peru 12 30S 69 10W
65 Puerto Mazarrón, Spain 37 34N 1 15W
176 Pto. Natales, Chile 51 45S 72 25W
169 Puerto Padre, Cuba ...21 13N 76 35W
174 Puerto Páez, Venezuela 6 13N 67 28W
172 Puerto Pilcomayo, Par. 25 19S 57 52W
172 Puerto Pinasco, Par. .22 30S 57 50W
176 Puerto Piramides, Arg. 42 35S 64 20W
174 Puerto Piritu, Ven. 10 5N 65 0W
169 Pto. Plata, Dom. Rep. 19 40N 70 45E
104 Puerto Princesa, Phil. 9 55N 118 50W
169 Pto. Quepas, C. Rica . 9 29N 84 6W
174 Puerto Quijarro, Bol. .17 49S 57 45W
63 Puerto Real, Spain 36 33N 6 12W
169 Puerto Rico, W. Indies 18 15N 66 45W
16 Puerto Rico Trough, North Atlantic Ocean 20 0N 63 0W
172 Puerto Sastre, Par. 22 25S 57 55W
174 Puerto Suarez, Bolivia 18 58S 57 52W
168 Puerto Vallarta, Mexico 20 26N 105 15W
174 Puerto Villamizar, Col. 8 25N 72 30W
174 Puerto Wilches, Col. . 7 21N 73 54W
63 Puertollano, Spain 38 43N 4 7W
62 Puertomarin, Spain ...42 48N 7 37W
78 Puesti, Rumania 46 25N 27 33E
44 Puffin I., Ireland 51 50N 10 25W
37 Puffin I., Wales, U.K. 53 19N 4 1W
87 Pugachev, U.S.S.R. 52 0N 48 55E
131 Puge, Tanzania 4 45S 33 11E
166 Puget Sd., U.S.A. 47 15N 123 30W
51 Puget Théniers, France 43 58N 6 53E
73 Puglia (Apulia), reg., It. 41 6N 16 0E
131 Pugu, Tanzania 6 55S 39 4E
146 Puha, New Zealand ...38 30S 177 50E
MAP
64 Puig Mayor, Mt., Spain 39 49N 2 47E
64 Puigcerda, Spain 42 24N 1 50E
49 Puisaye, Collines de, Fr. 47 34N 3 28E
49 Puiseaux, France 48 11N 2 30E
147 Pukaki L., N.Z. 44 5S 170 1E
157 Pukatawagan, Canada 55 45N 101 20W
76 Pukë, Albania 42 2N 19 53E
146 Pukearuhe, N.Z. 38 55S 174 31E
146 Pukekohe, N.Z. 37 12S 174 55E
147 Puketeraki Ra., N.Z. .42 58S 172 13E
147 Pukeuri, New Zealand 45 4S 171 2E
113 Pukow, China 32 15N 118 45E
72 Pula, Italy 39 0N 9 0E
71 Pula (Pola), Y.-slavia 44 54N 13 57E
76 Pulaj, Albania 41 53N 19 40E
112 Pulantien, China 39 25N 122 0E
161 Pulaski, N.Y., U.S.A. 43 32N 76 9W
163 Pulaski, Tenn., U.S.A. 35 10N 87 0W
162 Pulaski, Va., U.S.A. ...37 4N 80 49W
60 Pulawy, Poland 51 23N 21 59E
35 Pulborough, Eng., U.K. 50 58N 0 30W
104 Pulgaon, India 20 44N 78 21E
106 Pulicat L., India 13 40N 80 15E
106 Puliyangudi, India 9 11N 77 24E
125 Pulmakong, Ghana 11 2N 0 2E
166 Pullman, U.S.A. 46 49N 117 10W
109 Pulog, Mt., Philippines 16 40N 120 50E
108 Puloraja, Indonesia ... 4 55N 95 24E
60 Pultusk, Poland 52 43N 21 6E
111 Puluntohai (Bulun Tokhai), China 47 2N 87 29E
37 Pumlumon Fawr, mt., Wales, U.K. 52 29N 3 47W
37 Pumpsaint, Wales, U.K. 52 3N 3 58W
174 Puna, Bolivia 19 45S 65 28W
174 Puna I., Ecuador 2 55S 80 5W
172 Puna de Atacama, Arg. 25 0S 67 0W
105 Punakha, Bhutan 27 42N 89 52E
106 Punalur, India 9 0N 76 56E
104 Punasar, India 27 6N 73 6E
174 Punata, Bolivia 17 25S 65 50W
102 Punch, Kashmir 33 48N 74 4E
133 Punda Milia, S. Africa 22 40S 31 5E
132 Pungüè R., Mozam. ...19 0S 34 0E
104 Punjab, st., India 31 0N 76 0E
174 Puno, Peru 15 55S 70 3W
176 Punta Arenas, Chile ...53 0S 71 0W
172 Punta de Diaz, Chile .28 0S 70 45W
172 Punta de Lobos, Chile 20 58S 70 19W
62 Pta. de la Candelaria, Sp. 43 45N 8 0W
62 Punta de la Estaca, Sp. 43 48N 7 39W
176 Punta del Lago Viedma, Tn., Argentina 49 45S 72 0W
62 Punta del Oliva, Spain 43 37N 5 28W
73 Punta dell' Alice, Italy 39 23N 17 10E
72 Punta dello Scorno, It. 41 7N 8 23E
168 Punta Gorda, Br. Hond. 16 10N 88 45W
169 Punta Gorda, Nicaragua 14 20N 83 14W
163 Punta Gorda, U.S.A. .26 55N 82 0W
73 Punta Licosa, Italy 40 15N 14 53E
63 Punta Marroqui, Spain 36 0N 5 37W
63 Punta Mona, Spain 36 43N 3 45W
169 Punta Patuca, Hond. .15 54N 84 15W
125 Punta de Santiago, Fernando Po 3 12N 8 40W
72 Punta Serpeddi, Italy 39 19N 9 28E
169 Puntarenas, Costa Rica 10 0N 84 50W
62 Puntes de Garcia Rodriguez, Spain ...43 27N 7 50W
169 Punto Fijo, Venezuela 11 42N 70 13W
160 Punxsutawney, U.S.A. 40 56N 79 0W
113 Punyü, China 22 58N 113 16E
174 Puquio, Peru 14 45S 74 10W
174 Puquios, Chile 18 0S 69 50W
90 Pur R., U.S.S.R. 65 30N 77 40E
174 Purace, Vol., Colombia 2 21N 76 23W
74 Puračič, Yugoslavia ...44 33N 18 28E
34 Purbeck, Isle of, England, U.K. 50 40N 2 5W
165 Purcell, U.S.A. 35 0N 97 25W
65 Purchena Tetica, Spain 37 21N 2 21W
144 Purdy Is., Terr. of New Guinea 3 0S 146 0E
35 Purfleet, England, U.K. 51 29N 0 15E
105 Puri, India 19 50N 85 58E
34 Purley, England, U.K. 51 29N 1 4W
106 Purli, India 18 50N 76 35E
54 Purmerend, Neth. 52 30N 4 58E
106 Purna, R., India 19 55N 76 20E
105 Purnea, India 25 45N 87 31E
107 Pursat, Cambodia 12 34N 103 50E
108 Puruktjau, Indonesia . 0 35S 114 35E
105 Purulia, India 23 17N 86 33E
174 Purús, R., Brazil 5 25S 64 0W
75 Pürvomai, Bulgaria ...42 8N 25 17E
109 Purwakarta, Indonesia 6 35S 107 29E
109 Purwodadi, Java, Indon. 7 7S 110 55E

MAP
109 Purwodadi, Java, Indon. ... 7 51S 110 0E
109 Purworedjo, Indonesia 7 43S 110 2E
106 Pus, R., India ...19 50N 77 45E
106 Pusad, India ...19 56N 77 36E
112 Pusan, S. Korea ...35 5N 129 0E
91 Pushchino, U.S.S.R. ...54 20N 158 10E
86 Pushkin, U.S.S.R. ...59 45N 30 25E
87 Pushkino, U.S.S.R. ...51 16N 47 9E
154 Puskitamika L., Canada ...49 20N 76 30W
59 Püspokladany, Hung. 47 19N 21 6E
86 Pustoshka, U.S.S.R. ...56 11N 29 30E
157 Putahow L., Canada .59 52N 101 28W
103 Putao, Burma ...27 28N 97 30E
56 Putbus, Germany ...54 19N 13 29E
112 Putehachi (Chalantun), China .48 4N 122 45E
78 Puteni, Rumania ...45 49N 27 42E
113 Putien, China ...25 28N 119 0E
73 Putignano, Italy ...40 50N 17 5E
56 Putlitz, Germany ...53 15N 12 3E
78 Putna, Rumania ...47 50N 25 33E
78 Putna, R., Rumania .45 42N 27 26E
161 Putnam, U.S.A. ...41 55N 71 55W
59 Putnok, Hungary ...48 18N 20 26E
146 Putorino, N.Z. ...39 4S 177 9E
134 Putsonderwater S. Afr. ...29 9S 21 51E
106 Puttalam Lagoon, Cey. ... 8 15N 79 45E
54 Putten, Netherlands ...52 16N 53 37E
56 Puttgarden, Germany 54 28N 11 15E
106 Puttur, India ...12 46N 75 12E
174 Putumayo R., Col. ... 1 30S 70 0W
108 Putussibau, Mt., Indon. ... 0 45N 113 50E
146 Pututahi, N.Z. ...38 39S 77 53E
50 Puy-de-Dôme, dépt., Fr. ...45 47N 3 0E
50 Puy-de-Dôme, Mts., Fr. ...45 46N 2 57E
50 Puy de Sancy, Mt., Fr. ...45 32N 2 41E
50 Puy l'Evêque, France 44 31N 1 9E
50 Puy Guillaume, Fr. ...45 57N 3 28E
166 Puyallup, U.S.A. ...47 10N 122 22W
112 Puyang, China ...35 45N 115 22E
50 Puylaurens, France ...43 35N 2 0E
50 Puyôo, France ...43 33N 0 56W
125 Pwalagu, Ghana ...10 38N 0 50W
131 Pweto, Congo ... 8 25S 28 51E
37 Pwllheli, Wales, U.K. 52 54N 4 26W
84 Pya L., U.S.S.R. ...66 8N 31 22E
87 Pyana, R., U.S.S.R. ...55 30N 45 0E
103 Pyapon, Burma ...16 5N 95 50E
91 Pyasina R., U.S.S.R. .72 30N 90 30E
89 Pyatigorsk, U.S.S.R. .44 2N 43 0E
88 Pyatikhatki, U.S.S.R. 48 28N 33 38E
103 Pyinmana, Burma ...19 45N 96 20E
37 Pyle, Wales, U.K. ...51 31N 3 41W
112 Pyongyang, N. Korea 39 0N 125 30E
165 Pyote, U.S.A. ...31 34N 103 5W
133 Pyramid, Trans., S. Afr. ...25 32S 28 15E
143 Pyramid Hill, Victoria, Australia .36 2S 144 6E
126 Pyramids, Egypt ...29 58N 31 9E
166 Pyramid L., U.S.A. ...40 0N 119 30W
50 Pyrénées, Mts., Europe ...42 45N 0 18E
50 Pyrénées Atlantiques, dépt., France...43 16N 0 46W
50 Pyrénées Orientales, dépt., France ...42 35N 2 26E
46 Pyrzyce, Poland ...53 10N 14 55E
87 Pyshchug, U.S.S.R. ...58 57N 45 27E
86 Pytalovo, U.S.S.R. ...57 5N 27 55E
132 Python, Rhodesia ...17 56S 29 10E
79 Pytteggja, Mt., Norway ...62 13N 7 45E
103 Pyu, Burma ...18 30N 96 35E
60 Pyzdry, Poland ...52 11N 17 42E

Q
126 Qaar Zeitun, Egypt ...29 10N 25 48E
98 Qabalan, Jordan ...32 8N 35 17E
101 Qadam, Afghanistan .32 55N 66 45E
100 Qadhimah, Si. Arabia 22 20N 39 13E
104 Qadian, India ...31 51N 74 19E
100 Qal'at al Akhdhar, Saudi Arabia ...28 0N 37 10E
100 Qal at Salih, Iraq ...31 40N 47 18E
126 Qal'at Saura, Si. Arab. ...26 10N 38 40E
126 Qal at Shajwa, Si. Arab. ...25 2N 38 57E
104 Qala-i-Jadid (Spin Baldak), Afghanistan ...31 1N 66 25E
101 Qala-i-Kirta, Afghan. 32 15N 63 0E
101 Qala Nau, Afghan. ...35 0N 63 5E
101 Qala Punja, Afghan. .37 0N 72 40E
98 Qalqiliya, Israel ...32 12N 34 58E
126 Qalyûb, Egypt ...30 12N 31 11E
98 Qam, Jordan ...32 36N 35 43E
135 Qamata, C. Prov., S. Afr. ...31 58S 27 30E
104 Qamruddin Karez, Pak. ...31 45N 68 20E
99 Qamr Bay, S. Vietnam ...16 20N 52 30E
98 Qana, Lebanon ...33 12N 35 17E
126 Qara, Egypt ...29 38N 26 30E
126 Qara, Saudi Arabia ...29 55N 40 3E
100 Qarachuk, Syria ...37 0N 42 2E
127 Qardud, Sudan ...10 20N 29 56E
127 Qarrasa, Sudan ...14 38N 32 5E
127 Qarsa, Ethiopia ... 9 28N 41 48E
123 Qasr al Hajj, Libya ...32 2N 12 8E
123 Qaşr Bū Hādi, Libya .31 1N 16 45E
101 Qasr-e-Qand, Iran ...26 15N 60 45E
126 Qast Farafra, Egypt .27 0N 28 1E
98 Qastina, Israel ...31 44N 34 45E
101 Qatar, st., S.W. Asia .25 30N 51 15E
126 Qattara, Egypt ...30 12N 27 3E
126 Qattara Depression, Eg. ...29 30N 27 30E
101 Qayen, Iran ...33 40N 59 10E
100 Qazvin, Iran ...36 15N 50 0E
98 Qeisari, (Caesarea), Isr. ...32 30N 34 53E
126 Qena, Egypt ...26 10N 32 43E
126 Qena, Wadi, Egypt ...26 57N 32 50E
76 Qendrevica Mt., Albania ...40 20N 19 48E
101 Qeshm, Iran ...26 55N 56 10E
101 Qeshm, I., Iran ...26 50N 56 0E
102 Qila Safed, W. Pak. ...29 0N 61 30E
104 Qila Saifulla, W. Pak. 30 45N 68 17E
98 Qiryat 'Anavim, Israel ...31 49N 35 7E
98 Qiryat Bialik, Irael ...32 50N 35 5E
98 Qir. Haiyim, Israel ...32 49N 35 4E
98 Qiryat Shemona Israel ...33 13N 35 35E
98 Qiryat Yam, Israel ...32 51N 35 4E
123 Qirzah, W., Libya ...30 31N 14 6E
98 Qishon R., Israel ...32 42N 35 7E
127 Qizan, Saudi Arabia ...16 57N 42 34E
101 Qolleh-ye-Damavand, Mt., Iran ...36 0N 52 0E
101 Qom, Iran ...34 40N 51 0E
127 Quabbo, Ethiopia ...12 2N 39 56E
56 Quackenbrück, Ger. ...52 40N 7 59E
35 Quadring, England, U.K. ...52 53N 0 9W
35 Quainton, Eng., U.K. 51 51N 0 53W
142 Quairading, W. Austral. ...32 0S 117 21E
161 Quakerstown, U.S.A. .40 27N 75 20W
142 Qualeup, W. Australia 33 48S 116 48E
143 Quambatook, Australia ...35 49S 143 34E
145 Quambone, Australia .30 57S 147 53E
107 Quan Long, S. Vietnam ... 9 7N 105 8E
165 Quanan, U.S.A. ...34 20N 99 45W
143 Quandialla, N.S.W., Australia ...34 1S 147 47E
107 Quang Nam, S. Vietnam ...15 55N 108 15E
107 Quang Ngai, S. Vietnam ...15 13N 108 58E
107 Quang Yen, N. Vietnam ...21 3N 106 52E
36 Quantock Hills, The, England, U.K. ...51 8N 3 10W
172 Quarai, Brazil ...30 15S 56 20W
49 Quarré les Tombes, Fr. ...47 21N 4 0E
72 Quartu Sant' Elena It. ...39 15N 9 10E
167 Quartzsite, U.S.A. ...33 44N 114 16W
34 Quatford, Eng., U.K. .52 31N 2 23W
156 Quatsino, Canada ...50 30N 127 40W
156 Quatsino Sd., Canada 50 42N 127 58W
98 Qubab, see Mishmar Aiyalon, Israel ...31 52N 34 57E
98 Qubatiya, Jordan ...32 25N 35 17E
101 Quchan, Iran ...37 10N 58 27E
132 Que Que, Rhodesia ...18 58S 29 48E
143 Queanbeyan, Australia ...35 17S 149 14E
155 Quebec, Canada ...46 52N 71 13W
155 Quebec, prov., Canada 50 0N 70 0W
56 Quedlinburg, Germany ...51 47N 11 9E
176 Qn. Adelaide Arch, Chile ...52 20S 74 0W
15 Queen Alexandra Ra., Antarctica ...85 0S 170 0E
156 Queen Bess Mt., Can. .51 13N 124 35W
156 Queen Charlotte, Can. 53 28N 132 2W
156 Qn. Charlotte Is., Can. ...53 10N 132 0W
147 Qn. Charlotte Sd., N.Z. ...41 10S 174 15E
156 Qn. Charlotte Str., Can. ...51 0N 128 0W
10 Qn. Elizabeth Is., Can. ...75 0N 95 0W
15 Qn. Mary Coast, Antarc. ...70 0S 95 0E
152 Queen Maud G., Can. .68 15N 102 0W
15 Queen Maud Land, Ant. ...75 0S 10 0E
35 Queenborough, Eng. U.K. ...51 24N 0 46E
138 Queen's Chan., Austral. ...15 0S 129 30E
38 Queensbury, Eng., U.K. ...53 46N 1 50W
143 Queenscliff, Australia .38 8S 144 37E
38 Queensferry, Eng., U.K. ...53 13N 3 2W
41 Queensferry, Scot., U.K. ...56 0N 3 25W
144 Queensland, st., Austral. ...15 0S 142 0E
174 Queenstown, Guyana . 7 20N 58 30W
147 Queenstown, N.Z. ...45 1S 168 40E
135 Queenstown, S. Africa 31 52S 26 52E
145 Queenstown, Australia 42 4S 145 35E
176 Queilen, Chile ...42 50S 74 0W
175 Queimadas, Brazil ...11 0S 39 16W
135 Quela, Angola ... 9 10S 16 56E
129 Quelimane, Mozam. ...17 53S 36 58E
176 Quellón, Chile ...43 0S 73 50W
113 Quelpart, I., see Cheju Do, S. Korea ...33 29N 126 34E
167 Quemado, N. Mex., U.S.A. ...34 17N 108 28W
165 Quemado, Tex., U.S.A. ...28 58N 100 35W
113 Quemoy Is., see Kinmen Is., China .24 25N 118 24E
172 Quemu-Quemu, Arg. .36 3S 63 36W
42 Quendale, B. of, Scotland, U.K. ...59 53N 1 20W
172 Quequen, Argentina ...38 30S 58 30W
168 Queretaro, Mexico ...20 40N 100 23W
168 Queretaro, st., Mexico 20 30N 100 30W
56 Querfurt, Germany ...51 22N 11 33E
65 Quesada, Spain ...37 51N 3 4W
156 Quesnel, Canada ...53 5N 122 30W
156 Quesnel L., Canada ...52 30N 121 20W
167 Questa, U.S.A. ...36 45N 105 35W
48 Questembert, France .47 40N 2 28W
154 Quetico, Canada ...48 45N 90 55W
154 Quetico Prov. Park, Canada ...48 15N 91 45W
102 Quetta, Pakistan ...30 15N 66 55E
130 Queve R., see Cuva, Angola ...11 10S 14 30E
168 Quezaltenango, Guat. 14 40N 91 30W
109 Quezon City, Phil. ...14 50N 121 0E
107 Qui Nhon, S. Vietnam 13 40N 109 13E
130 Quibaxi, Angola ... 8 24S 14 27E
174 Quibdo, Colombia ... 5 42N 76 40W
48 Quiberon, France ...47 29N 3 9W
56 Quickborn, Germany .53 42N 9 52E
156 Quiet L., Canada ...61 0N 132 40W
172 Quiindy, Paraguay ...25 58S 57 14W
176 Quilan, C., Chile ...43 15S 74 30W
174 Quilca, Peru ...16 50S 72 29W
129 Quilengues, Angola ...14 12S 14 12E
172 Quilimari, Chile ...32 5S 70 30W
172 Quilino, Argentina ...30 14S 64 29W
174 Quillabamba, Peru ...12 50S 72 50W
172 Quillagua, Chile ...21 40S 69 40W
172 Quillaicillo, Chile ...31 17S 71 40W
50 Quillan, France ...42 53N 2 10E
48 Quillebeuf, France ...49 28N 0 30E
172 Quillota, Chile ...32 54S 71 16W
172 Quillmes, Argentina ...34 50S 58 0W
106 Quilon, India ... 8 50N 76 38E
145 Quilpie, Australia ...26 35S 144 11E
172 Quilpue, Chile ...33 5S 71 33W
44 Quilty, Ireland ...52 50N 9 27W
130 Quimbundo, Angola ... 8 4S 14 57E
172 Quimili, Argentina ...27 40S 62 30W
48 Quimper, France ...48 0N 4 9W
48 Quimperlé, France ...47 53N 3 33W
44 Quin, Ireland ...52 50N 8 52W
42 Quinag, Scotland, U.K. ...58 13N 5 5W
166 Quincy, Calif., U.S.A. 39 56N 121 0W
163 Quincy, Fla., U.S.A. .30 34N 84 34W
164 Quincy, Ill., U.S.A. ...39 55N 91 20W
61 Quincy, Mass., U.S.A. 42 14N 71 0W
166 Quincy, Wash., U.S.A. ...47 22N 119 56W
129 Quinga, Mozambique .15 49S 40 15E
49 Quingey, France ...47 7N 5 52E
63 Quintana de la Serena, Spain ...38 45N 5 40W
168 Quintana Roo, st., Mex. ...19 0N 88 0W
64 Quintanar de la Orden, Spain ...39 36N 3 5W
64 Quintanar de la Sierra Spain ...41 57N 2 55W
65 Quintanar del Rey, Sp. ...39 21N 1 56W
172 Quintero, Chile ...32 45S 71 30W
48 Quintin, France ...48 26N 2 56W
64 Quinto, Spain ...41 25N 0 32W
145 Quinyambie, S. Austral. ...30 15S 141 0E
65 Quipar R., Spain ...37 58N 2 3W
172 Quirihue, Chile ...36 15S 72 35W
143 Quirindi, N.S.W., Austral. ...31 28S 150 40E
130 Quirimbo, Angola ...10 42S 14 14E
62 Quiroga, Spain ...42 28N 7 18W
155 Quirpon I., Canada ...51 32N 55 28W
51 Quissac, France ...43 55N 4 0E
131 Quissanga, Mozam. ...12 24S 40 28E
131 Quiterajo, Mozambique ...11 55S 40 30E
172 Quitilipi, Argentina ...26 50S 60 13W
163 Quitman, Ga., U.S.A. 30 49N 83 35W
163 Quitman, Miss., U.S.A. ...32 2N 88 42W
165 Quitman, Tex., U.S.A. 32 48N 95 25W
174 Quito, Ecuador ... 0 15S 78 35W
175 Quixadá, Brazil ... 4 55S 39 0W
126 Qul'an, Is., Egypt ...24 22N 35 31E
135 Qumbu, C. Prov., S. Afr. ...31 9S 28 53E
98 Qumran, Jordan ...31 43N 35 27E
98 Quneitra, Syria ...33 7N 35 48E
145 Quondong, S., Australia ...33 4S 140 20E
42 Quoich L., Scotland, U.K. ...57 4N 5 20W
147 Quoin Pt., N.Z. ...46 19S 170 11E
134 Quoin Pt., S. Africa ...34 46S 19 37E
145 Quorn, S. Australia ...32 25S 138 0E
154 Quorn, Canada ...49 25N 90 55W
34 Quorndon, Eng., U.K. 52 45N 1 10W
127 Qurein, Sudan ...13 30N 34 50E
126 Qus, Egypt ...25 55N 32 50E
126 Quseir, Egypt ...26 7N 34 16E
98 Qusra, Jordan ...32 5N 35 20E
135 Quthing, Lesotho ...30 25S 27 36E
76 Qytet Stalin (Kucove), Albania .40 47N 19 57E

R
81 Råå, Sweden ...56 0N 12 45E
59 Raab, R., Hungary ...47 20N 17 10E
82 Raahe, Finland ...64 40N 24 35E
55 Raamsdonksveer, Neth. ...51 43N 4 52E
98 Ra'anana, Israel ...32 12N 34 52E
40 Raarup, Denmark ...55 46N 9 56E
42 Raasay I., Scot., U.K. 57 25N 6 4W
42 Raasay, Sd. of, Scot., U.K. ...57 30N 6 8W
71 Rab & I., Yugoslavia .44 45N 14 45E
109 Raba, Indonesia ... 8 36S 118 55E
62 Rabaçal R., Portugal .41 41N 7 15W
125 Rabah, Nigeria ...13 5N 5 30E
131 Rabai, Kenya ... 3 50S 39 31E
50 Rabastens, Hautes Pyrénées, France ...43 25N 0 10E
50 Rabastens, Tarn, Fr. .43 50N 1 43E
68 Rabat, Malta ...35 53N 14 25E
122 Rabat, Morocco ...33 28N 6 48W
144 Rabaul, Terr. of, New Guinea ... 4 24S 152 18E
81 Rabbalshede, Sweden 58 40N 11 27E
157 Rabbit L., Canada ...47 0N 79 38W
100 Rabigh, Saudi Arabia 22 50N 39 5E
59 Rabka, Poland ...49 37N 19 59E
74 Rača, Yugoslavia ...44 14N 21 0E
73 Racale, Italy ...39 57N 18 6E
72 Racalmuto, Italy ...37 25N 13 41E
72 Racconigi, Italy ...44 47N 7 41E
174 Răcăşdia, Rumania ...44 59N 21 36E
155 Race C., Canada ...46 40N 53 18W
107 Rach Gia, S. Vietnam 10 5N 105 5E
60 Raciaz, Poland ...52 46N 20 10E
59 Racibórz (Ratibor), Pol.50 7N 18 18E
162 Racine, U.S.A. ...42 41N 87 51W
35 Rackheath, Eng., U.K. ...52 41N 1 22E
74 Radan Mt., Yugoslavia ...42 59N 21 29E
78 Rădăuţi, Rumania ...47 50N 25 59E
58 Radbuza R., Cz. ...49 35N 13 5E
38 Radcliffe, Lancs., England, U.K. ...53 35N 2 19W
39 Radcliffe, Notts., England, U.K. ...52 57N 1 3W
79 Råde, Norway ...59 21N 10 53E
56 Radeburg, Germany ...51 6N 13 45E
71 Radece, Yugoslavia ...46 5N 15 14E
86 Radekhov, U.S.S.R. ...50 25N 24 32E
55 Radevormwald, Ger. .51 12N 7 22E
162 Radford, U.S.A. ...37 8N 80 32W
60 Radgiejów, Poland ...52 40N 18 30E
104 Radhanpur, India ...23 50N 71 38E
74 Radika R., Yugoslavia ...41 38N 20 37E
157 Radisson, Canada ...52 30N 107 20W
145 Radium Hill, S. Austral. ...32 30S 140 42E
156 Radium Hot Springs, Canada ...50 48N 116 12W
109 Radja Ampat, Arch., Indonesia ... 0 30S 129 40E
108 Radja Pt., Indonesia . 3 40N 96 25E
34 Radley, England, U.K. ...51 42N 1 14W
74 Radna, Rumania ...46 7N 21 41E
75 Radnevo, Bulgaria ...42 17N 25 58E
58 Radnice, Czechoslovakia ...49 51N 13 35E
37 Radnor, co., Wales, United Kingdom ...52 20N 3 20W
37 Radnor Forest, Wales, United Kingdom ...52 17N 3 10W
57 Radolfzell, Germany .47 45N 8 58E
60 Radom, Poland ...51 23N 21 12E
74 Radomir, Bulgaria ...42 37N 23 4E
60 Radomsko, Poland ...51 5N 19 28E
86 Radomyshl, U.S.S.R. .50 30N 29 12E
59 Radomysl Wielki, Pol. 50 14N 21 15E
60 Radoszyce, Poland ...51 4N 20 15E
74 Radoviš, Yugoslavia .41 38N 22 28E
71 Radovljica, Yugoslavia ...46 22N 14 12E
79 Radöy I., Norway ...60 40N 4 55E
56 Radstadt, Austria ...47 24N 13 28E
36 Radstock, Eng., U.K. 51 17N 2 25W
78 Răducaneni, Rumania 46 58N 27 54E
74 Radusa, Yugoslavia ...42 7N 21 15E
86 Radviliškis, U.S.S.R. .55 49N 23 33E
157 Radville, Canada ...49 30N 104 15W
36 Radyr, Wales, U.K. ...51 32N 3 16W
60 Radzanów, Poland ...52 56N 20 8E
156 Rae, Canada ...62 45N 115 50W
105 Rae Bareli, India ...26 18N 81 20E
153 Rae Isthmus, Canada 66 40N 87 30W
142 Raeside, L., W. Austral. ...29 20S 122 0E
146 Raetihi, New Zealand 39 25S 175 17E
172 Rafaela, Argentina ...31 10S 61 30W
126 Rafah, Egypt ...31 18N 34 14E
130 Rafai, Cent. Afr. Rep. 4 59N 23 58E
72 Raffadali, Italy ...37 23N 13 29E
100 Rafha, Si. Arabia ...29 35N 43 35E
98 Rafid, Syria ...32 57N 35 52E
101 Rafsanjan, Iran ...30 30N 56 5E
127 Ragag, Sudan ...10 59N 24 40E
142 Ragged Mt., W. Australia ...33 27S 123 25E
144 Raglan, Australia ...23 48S 150 45E
34 Raglan, England, U.K. ...51 46N 2 51W
146 Raglan & Harb., N.Z. 37 55S 174 55E
155 Ragueneau, Canada ...49 11N 68 18W
80 Ragunda, Sweden ...63 6N 16 23E
73 Ragusa, Italy ...36 56N 14 42E
109 Raha, Indonesia ... 8 20S 118 40E
121 Rahad el Berdi, Sudan ...11 20N 23 40E
127 Rahad R., Sudan ...12 40N 35 30E
56 Rahden, Germany ...52 26N 8 36E
127 Raheita, Ethiopia ...12 46N 43 4E
104 Rahimyar Khan, Pak. 28 30N 70 25E
146 Rahotu, New Zealand 39 20S 173 49E
106 Raichur, India ...16 10N 77 20E
105 Raiganj, India ...25 37N 88 10E
105 Raigarh, India ...21 56N 83 25E
106 Raigarh, India ...19 51N 82 6E
100 Rails, Saudi Arabia ...23 33N 38 43E
145 Railton, Tas., Austral. 41 25S 146 28E
143 Rainbow, Vic., Austral. ...35 55S 142 0E
35 Rainham, Eng., U.K. 51 22N 0 36E
166 Rainier, U.S.A. ...46 4N 123 0W
166 Rainier, Mt., U.S.A. ...46 50N 121 50W
39 Rainworth, Eng., U.K. ...53 8N 1 6W
157 Rainy L., Canada ...48 30N 92 30W
157 Rainy River, Canada .48 50N 94 30W
105 Raipur, India ...21 17N 81 45E
154 Raith, Canada ...48 50N 90 0W
76 Raja, Albania ...42 16N 20 1E
109 Rajahmundry, India .17 1N 81 48E
82 Rajajooseppi, Finland 68 8N 28 29E
108 Rajang, Sar., Malaysia ... 2 30N 113 30E
106 Rajapalaiyarm, India 9 25N 77 35E
104 Rajasthan, st., India .26 45N 73 30E
104 Rajasthan Canal, India ...30 31N 71 0E
105 Rajbari, East Pakistan ...23 47N 89 41E
104 Rajgarh, Mad. P., India ...24 2N 76 45E
104 Rajgarh, Raj., India .28 40N 75 25E
71 Rajhenburg, Y.-slavia 46 1N 15 29E
104 Rajkot, India ...22 15N 70 56E
105 Rajmahal Hills India 24 30N 87 30E
105 Rajnandgaon, India ...21 5N 81 5E
104 Rajpipla, India ...21 50N 73 30E
104 Rajpura, India ...30 32N 76 32E
105 Rajshahi, East Pakistan ...24 22N 88 39E
147 Rakaia, New Zealand 43 45S 172 1E
147 Rakaia R., N.Z. ...43 26S 171 47E
102 Rakaposhi, Kashmir .36 10N 74 0E
105 Rakas L., Tibet, China ...30 40N 81 10E
126 Rakha, Saudi Arabia .18 25N 41 30E
104 Rakhni, West Pakistan ...30 4N 69 56E
75 Rakitovo, Bulgaria ...41 59N 24 5E
79 Rakkestad, Norway ...59 25N 11 24E
59 Rákospalota, Hungary ...47 30N 19 5E
71 Rakovica, Yugoslavia 44 59N 15 38E
58 Rakovnik, Cz. ...50 6N 13 42E
74 Rakovo, Bulgaria ...42 4N 22 42E
154 Raleigh, Canada ...49 30N 92 5W
163 Raleigh, N.C., U.S.A. .35 46N 78 38W
163 Raleigh B., U.S.A. ...34 50N 76 15W
74 Ralja, Yugoslavia ...44 33N 20 34E
165 Ralls, U.S.A. ...33 40N 101 20W
98 Rama, Israel ...32 56N 35 21E
73 Ramacca, Italy ...37 24N 14 40E
106 Ramachandrapuram, India ...16 50N 82 4E
100 Ramadi, Iraq ...33 28N 43 15E
64 Ramales de la Victoria, Spain ...43 15N 3 28W
98 Ramallah, Jordan ...31 55N 35 10E
106 Ramanathapuram, India ... 9 25N 78 55E
106 Ramas C., India ...15 5N 73 55E
98 Ramat Gan, Israel ...32 4N 34 48E
98 Ramatayim, Israel ...32 9N 34 54E
133 Ramatlhabama, Bots. 25 37S 25 33E
49 Rambervillers, France 48 20N 6 38E
109 Rambipudji, Indonesia ... 8 12S 113 37E
49 Rambouillet, France .48 40N 1 48E
106 Ramdurg, India ...15 58N 75 22E
36 Rame Head, Eng., U.K. ...50 19N 4 14W
105 Ramechhap, Nepal ...27 25N 86 10E
109 Ramelau Mt., Port. Tim. ... 8 55S 126 22E
87 Ramenskoye, U.S.S.R. ...55 32N 38 15E
55 Ramet, Belgium ...50 35N 5 27E
105 Ramgarh Bihar, India 23 40N 85 35E
104 Ramgarh, India ...27 30N 70 36E
104 Ramagarh, India ...27 16N 75 14E
100 Ramhormoz, Iran ...31 15N 49 35E
98 Ramla, Israel ...31 55N 34 52E
123 Ramlat Zaltan, Libya 28 30N 19 30E
127 Ramlu Mt., Ethiopia .13 32N 41 40E
80 Ramme, Denmark ...56 30N 8 11E
98 Rammun, Jordan ...31 55N 35 17E
78 Ramna R., Rumania .45 36N 27 3E
42 Ramna Stacks, Is., Scotland, U.K. ...60 40N 1 20W
106 Ramnad, see Ramanathapuram, India ... 9 25N 78 55E
80 Ramnäs, Sweden ...59 46N 16 12E
78 Râmnicu-Sărat, Rum. ...45 26N 27 3E
78 Râmnicu Vâlcea, Rum. ...45 9N 24 21E
87 Ramon, U.S.S.R. ...52 8N 39 21E
167 Ramona, U.S.A. ...33 1N 116 56W
46 Ramor L., Ireland ...53 50N 7 5W
154 Ramore, Canada ...48 30N 80 25W
168 Ramos Arizpe, Mexico 23 35N 100 59W
132 Ramotsaodi, Botswana ...19 48S 22 15E
133 Ramoutsa, Botswana .24 50S 25 52E
38 Rampside, Eng., U.K. 54 6N 3 10W

RA INDEX RH

MAP
104 Rampur, H.P., India .31 26N 77 43E
104 Rampur, M.P., India .23 25N 73 53E
105 Rampur, Orissa, India 21 48N 83 58E
104 Rampur, U.P., India .28 50N 79 5E
105 Rampurhat, India 24 10N 87 50E
104 Rampura, India 24 30N 75 27E
103 Ramree, I., Burma 19 0N 94 0E
154 Ramsey, Canada 47 25N 82 20W
38 Ramsbottom, Eng., UK 53 36N 2 20W
34 Ramsbury, Eng., U.K. 51 26N 1 37W
55 Ramsel, Belgium 51 2N 4 50E
82 Ramsele, Sweden 63 31N 16 31E
35 Ramsey, Essex, England, U.K. 51 55N 1 12E
35 Ramsey, Hunts., England, U.K. 52 27N 0 6W
38 Ramsey, I. of M., U.K. 54 20N 4 21W
38 Ramsey B. I. of M., U.K. 54 19N 4 23W
37 Ramsey I., Wales, U.K. 51 52N 5 21W
58 Ramsey, L., Canada ...47 15N 82 20W
35 Ramsgate, Eng., U.K. 51 20N 1 25E
80 Rämshyttan, Sweden .60 17N 15 15E
80 Ramsjö, Sweden 62 11N 15 45E
98 Ramtha, Jordan 32 34N 36 0E
131 Ramu, Kenya 3 56N 41 13E
80 Ramvik, Sweden 62 49N 17 54E
105 Ranaghat, India 23 15N 88 35E
104 Ranahu, West Pakistan 25 55N 69 45E
172 Rancagua, Chile 34 10S 70 50W
48 Rance R., France 48 34N 1 59W
166 Ranchester, U.S.A. 44 57N 107 12W
105 Ranchi, India 23 19N 85 27E
78 Rancu, Rumania 44 32N 24 15E
143 Rand, N.S.W., Austral. 35 33S 146 32E
133 Rand, Trans., S. Africa 26 0S 27 0E
46 Randalstown, N. Ireland, U.K. 54 45N 6 20W
50 Randan, France 46 2N 3 21E
73 Randazzo, Italy 37 53N 14 56E
81 Randböl, Denmark 55 43N 9 17E
81 Randers, Denmark 56 29N 10 1E
81 Randers Amt, co., Den. 56 25N 10 25E
81 Randers Fd., Denmark 56 37N 10 20E
133 Randfontein, S. Africa 26 8S 27 45E
160 Randolph, N.Y., U.S.A. 42 10N 78 59W
166 Randolph, Utah, U.S.A. 41 43N 111 10W
161 Randolph, Vt., U.S.A. 43 55N 72 39W
167 Randsburg, U.S.A. 35 26N 117 44W
79 Randsfjord L., Norway 60 29N 10 25E
82 Rane R., Sweden 66 15N 21 30E
82 Råneå, Sweden 65 53N 22 30E
147 Ranfurly, New Zealand 45 7S 170 6E
146 Rangataua, N.Z. 39 26S 175 28E
146 Rangaunu B., N.Z. 34 51S 173 15E
81 Rångedala, Sweden ...57 47N 13 5E
166 Rangely, Colo., U.S.A. 40 3N 108 53W
161 Rangeley, Me., U.S.A. 44 58N 70 33W
165 Ranger, U.S.A. 32 30N 98 42W
103 Rangia, India 26 15N 91 20E
147 Rangiora, N.Z. 43 19S 172 36E
146 Rangitaiki & R., N.Z. 38 25S 176 48E
147 Rangitata & R., N.Z. .43 45S 171 15E
146 Rangitikei R., N.Z.....40 17S 175 15E
146 Rangitoto Range, N.Z. 38 25S 175 35E
109 Rangkasbitung, Indon. 6 22S 106 16E
103 Rangoon, Burma 16 45N 96 20E
103 Rangoon R., Burma ...16 28N 96 40E
105 Rangpur, E. Pakistan 25 42N 89 22E
131 Rangwe, Kenya 0 38S 34 35E
106 Ranibennur, India 14 35N 75 30E
105 Raniganj, India 23 40N 87 15E
106 Ranipet, India 12 56N 79 23E
165 Rankin, U.S.A. 31 16N 101 56W
143 Rankin's Springs, N.S.W., Austral. 33 49S 146 14E
144 Rannes, Australia 24 6S 150 11E
40 Rannoch, dist., Scotland, U.K. 56 41N 4 20W
40 Rannoch L., Scot., U.K. 56 41N 4 20W
40 Rannoch Moor, Scotland, U.K. 56 38N 4 48W
40 Rannoch Sta., Scot., UK 56 40N 4 32W
129 Ranohira, Malagasy Republic 22 29S 45 24E
107 Ranong, Thailand 9 56N 98 40E
108 Rantau, Indonesia 4 15N 98 5E
108 Rantau Prapat, Indon. 2 15N 99 50E
109 Rantemario Mt., Indon. 3 15S 119 57E
98 Rantis, Jordan 32 4N 35 3E
162 Rantoul, U.S.A. 40 18N 88 10W
81 Ranum, Denmark 56 54N 9 14E
126 Ranya Wadi, Si. Arab. 21 0N 42 22E
122 Raoui, Erg er, Algeria 29 0N 2 0W
137 Rapa Iti, I., Pac. Oc. .27 35S 144 20W
70 Rapallo, Italy 44 21N 9 12E
109 Rapang, Indonesia 3 45S 119 55E
101 Rapch, Iran 25 40N 59 15E
172 Rapel, Chile 33 57S 71 55W
46 Raphoe, Ireland 54 52N 7 36W
164 Rapid City, U.S.A. 44 0N 103 0W
162 Rapid River, U.S.A. .45 55N 87 0W
154 Rapides des Joachims, Canada 46 13N 77 43W
86 Rapla, U.S.S.R. 58 88N 24 52E
43 Rapness, Scotland, U.K. 59 15N 2 51W
100 Raqqa, Syria 36 0N 38 55E
46 Rareagh, Ireland 53 37N 8 37W
137 Rarotonga I., Pac. Oc. 21 30S 160 0W
123 Ras Ajdir, Libya 33 4N 11 44E
101 Ras al Hadd, Muscat & Oman 22 30N 59 50E
101 Ras al Khaima, Trucial States 25 50N 56 5E
100 Ra's at Tannurah, Saudi Arabia 26 40N 50 10E
127 Ras Dashen, Mt., Ethiopia 13 8N 37 45E
122 Ras el Ma, Algeria 34 26N 0 50W
123 Ras el Oued, Algeria .35 57N 5 3E
98 Ras en Naqura, Israel 33 5N 35 5E
100 Ras Fartak, Si. Arabia 28 0N 34 30E
126 Ras Gharib, Egypt 28 6N 33 18E
99 Ras Hafun C., Somali Republic 10 29N 51 20E
123 Ras Kaboudia, Tunisia 35 10N 11 3E
126 Ras Mallap, Egypt 29 18N 32 50E
101 Ras Masandam, Trucial Oman 26 30N 56 30E
176 Rasa, Punta, Argentina 40 50S 62 15W
101 Ras Rakan, Qatar 26 10N 51 20E
80 Råsboda, Sweden 60 8N 16 58E
86 Raseiniai, U.S.S.R. 55 25N 23 5E
127 Rashad, Sudan 11 55N 31 0E
126 Rashid, *see* Rosetta, Egypt 31 21N 30 22E
100 Rasht, Iran 37 20N 49 40E
106 Rasipuram, India 11 30N 78 25E
74 Raška, Yugoslavia 43 19N 20 39E
78 Râsnov, Rumania 45 35N 25 27E
175 Raso C., Brazil 1 50N 50 0W
142 Rason, L., W. Austral. 28 45S 124 25E
78 Raşova, Rumania 44 15N 27 55E
75 Rasovo, Bulgaria 43 42N 23 17E
105 Rasra, India 25 50N 83 50E
87 Rasskazovo, U.S.S.R. 52 35N 41 50E
57 Rastatt, Germany 48 50N 8 12E
78 Rastu, Rumania 43 53N 23 16E
152 Rat Is., Aleutian Is., U.S.A. 52 0N 177 30W
107 Rat Buri, Thailand ...13 30N 99 54E
156 Rat R., Canada 56 0N 99 30W
80 Rätan, Sweden 62 27N 14 33E
104 Ratangarh, India 28 5N 74 35E
105 Rath, India 25 36N 79 37E
44 Rath Luirc (Charleville), Ire. ...52 21N 8 40W
45 Rathangan, Ireland ...53 13N 7 0W
45 Rathconrah, Ireland .53 30N 7 32W
45 Rathcoole, Ireland 53 17N 6 29W
44 Rathcormack, Ireland 52 5N 8 19W
45 Rathdowney, Ireland .52 52N 7 36W
45 Rathdrum, Ireland 52 57N 6 13W
166 Rathdrum, U.S.A. 47 50N 116 58W
43 Rathen, Scot., U.K. ...57 38N 1 58W
56 Rathenow, Germany .52 38N 12 23E
46 Rathfriland, N. Ire., UK 54 12N 6 12W
44 Rathkeale, Ireland 52 32N 8 57W
46 Rathkenny, Ireland ...53 45N 6 39W
46 Rathlin I., N. Ire., U.K. 55 18N 6 14W
46 Rathlin O'Birne I., Ire. 54 50N 8 50W
46 Rathmelton, Ireland .55 3N 7 35W
45 Rathmolyon, Ireland .53 30N 6 49W
44 Rathmore, Cork, Ire. .51 30N 9 21W
44 Rathmore, Kerry, Ire. 52 5N 9 12W
45 Rathmore, Kildare, Ire. 53 13N 6 35W
46 Rathmullen, Ireland .55 6N 7 32W
45 Rathnure, Ireland 52 30N 6 47W
45 Rathvilly, Ireland 52 54N 6 42W
55 Ratingen, Germany ...51 18N 6 51E
104 Ratlam, India 23 20N 75 0E
106 Ratnagiri, India 16 57N 73 18E
106 Ratnapura, Ceylon 6 40N 80 20E
45 Ratoath, Ireland 53 30N 6 27W
165 Raton, U.S.A. 37 0N 104 30W
58 Ratten, Austria 47 28N 15 44E
41 Rattray, Scotland, U.K. 56 36N 3 20W
43 Rattray Hd., Scot. UK 57 38N 1 50W
80 Rättvik, Sweden 60 52N 15 12E
56 Ratzeburg, Germany .53 41N 10 46E
107 Raub, Malaysia 3 47N 101 52E
172 Rauch, Argentina 36 45S 59 5W
82 Raufarhöfn, Iceland ...66 30N 15 49W
79 Raufoss, Norway 60 44N 10 37E
146 Raukumara Ra., N.Z. 38 5S 177 55E
79 Rauland, Norway 59 43N 8 0E
83 Rauma, Finland 61 10N 21 30E
79 Rauma R., Norway ...62 16N 8 15E
79 Raundal, Norway 60 40N 6 37E
109 Raung Mt., Indonesia 8 8S 114 4E
105 Raurkela, India 22 14N 84 50E
86 Rava Russkaya, U.S.S.R. 50 15N 23 42E
72 Ravanusa, Italy 37 16N 13 58E
101 Ravar, Iran 31 20N 56 51E
55 Ravels, Belgium 51 22N 5 0E
161 Ravena, U.S.A. 42 28N 73 49W
38 Ravenglass, Eng., U.K. 54 21N 3 25W
71 Ravenna, Italy 44 28N 12 15E
164 Ravenna, Neb., U.S.A. 41 3N 98 58W
160 Ravenna, Ohio, U.S.A. 41 11N 81 15W
57 Ravensburg, Germany 47 48N 9 38E
144 Ravenshoe, Australia .17 43S 145 33E
55 Ravenstein, Neth. 51 47N 5 39E
38 Ravenstonedale, England, U.K. 54 26N 2 26W
144 Ravenswood, Australia 20 5S 146 55E
162 Ravenswood, U.S.A. .38 58N 81 47W
174 Raventasón, Peru 6 10S 81 0W
104 Ravi R., W. Pakistan 31 0N 73 0E
71 Ravna Gora, Y.-slavia 45 24N 14 50E
74 Ravna Reka, Y.-slavia 43 59N 21 35E
81 Ravnstrup, Denmark .56 27N 9 17E
60 Rawa Mazowiecka, Pol. 51 46N 20 12E
102 Rawalpindi, W. Pak. .33 38N 73 8E
100 Rawanduz, Iraq 36 40N 44 30E
107 Rawang, Malaysia 3 20N 101 35E
154 Rawdon, Canada 46 3N 73 40W
146 Rawene, New Zealand 35 25S 173 32E
60 Rawicz, Poland 51 36N 16 52E
142 Rawlinna, W. Austral. 30 58S 125 28E
166 Rawlins, U.S.A. 41 50N 107 20W
39 Rawmarsh, Eng., U.K. 53 27N 1 20W
176 Rawson, Argentina 43 15S 65 0W
38 Rawtenstall, Eng., U.K. 53 42N 2 18W
125 Rawuya, Nigeria 12 10N 6 50E
165 Ray, N. Mex., U.S.A. 35 57N 104 8W
164 Ray, N.D., U.S.A. 48 21N 103 6W
155 Ray, C., Canada 47 33N 59 15W
106 Rayachoti, India 14 4N 78 50E
106 Rayadrug, India 14 40N 76 50E
106 Rayagada, India 19 15N 83 20E
101 Rayin, Iran 29 40N 57 22E
35 Rayleigh, Eng., U.K. .51 36N 0 38E
156 Raymond, Canada 49 30N 112 35W
166 Raymond, U.S.A. 46 45N 123 48W
165 Raymondville, U.S.A. 26 30N 97 50W
165 Rayne, U.S.A. 30 16N 92 16W
107 Rayong, Thailand 12 40N 101 20E
133 Rayton, Trans., S. Afr. 25 45S 28 32E
165 Rayville, U.S.A. 32 30N 91 45W
48 Raz, Pte. du, France .48 2N 4 47W
74 Ražana, Yugoslavia ...44 6N 19 55E
74 Ražanj, Yugoslavia ...43 40N 21 31E
75 Razdelna, Bulgaria 43 13N 27 41E
78 Răzelm L., Rumania .44 50N 29 0E
75 Razgrad, Bulgaria 43 33N 26 34E
75 Razlog, Bulgaria 41 53N 23 28E
104 Razmak, W. Pakistan 32 45N 69 50E
106 Razole, India 16 56N 81 48E
156 Razor Back Mt., Can. 51 32N 125 0W
50 Ré, Île de, France 46 12N 1 30W
44 Rea, L., Ireland 53 10N 8 32W
35 Reading, Eng., U.K. .51 27N 0 57W
161 Reading, U.S.A. 40 20N 75 53W
134 Read's Drift, S. Africa 29 12S 23 22E
172 Realico, Argentina 35 0S 64 15W
50 Réalmont, France 43 48N 2 10E
107 Réam, Cambodia 10 34N 103 39E
43 Reay, Scotland, U.K. 58 33N 3 48W
49 Rebais, France 48 50N 3 10E
142 Rebecca L., W. Austral. 30 0S 122 30E
109 Rebi, Indonesia 5 30S 134 7E
121 Rebiana, Libya 24 12N 22 10E
114 Rebun, I., Japan 44 40N 142 45E
71 Recanati, Italy 43 24N 13 32E
74 Recas, Rumania 45 46N 21 30E
44 Recess, Ireland 53 29N 9 4W
142 Recherche, Arch. of the, W. Austral. 34 0S 124 30E
86 Rechitsa, U.S.S.R. 52 13N 30 15E
175 Recife, Brazil 8 0S 35 0W
135 Recife C., S. Africa 34 2S 25 44E
56 Recklinghausen, Ger. .51 36N 7 10E
172 Reconquista, Argentina 29 10S 59 45W
172 Recreo, Argentina 29 25S 65 10W
35 Reculver, Eng., U.K. .51 22N 1 12E
46 Red B., N. Ire., U.K. 55 4N 6 2W
164 Red L., U.S.A. 48 0N 95 0W
164 Red R., Minn., U.S.A. 48 10N 97 0W
165 Red, R., Tex., U.S.A. 33 57N 95 30W
161 Red Bank, U.S.A. 40 21N 74 4W
166 Red Bluff, U.S.A. 40 11N 122 11W
165 Red Bluff L., U.S.A. .31 59N 103 58W
164 Red Cloud, U.S.A. 40 8N 98 33W
156 Red Deer, Canada 52 20N 113 50W
157 Red Deer L., Canada .52 55N 101 30W
41 Red Dial, Eng., U.K. .54 48N 3 9W
143 Red Hill S., Australia 38 25S 145 2E
155 Red Indian L., Canada 48 35N 57 0W
157 Red Lake, Canada 51 1N 94 1W
164 Red Lake Falls, U.S.A. 47 54N 96 30W
166 Red Lodge, U.S.A. 45 10N 109 10W
164 Red Oak, U.S.A. 41 0N 95 10W
164 Red Rock, L., U.S.A. 41 30N 93 15W
99 Red Sea, Africa–Asia .25 0N 36 0E
37 Red Wharf Bay, Wales, U.K.............53 18N 4 10W
164 Red Wing, U.S.A. 44 32N 92 35W
60 Reda, Poland 54 40N 18 19E
107 Redang I., Malaysia ... 5 46N 103 2E
35 Redbridge, Eng., U.K. 51 35N 0 7E
39 Redcar, Eng., U.K. ...54 37N 1 4W
157 Redcliff, Canada 50 10N 110 50W
145 Redcliffe, Australia ...27 12S 153 0E
142 Redcliffe, Mt., Austral. 28 30S 121 30E
145 Redcliffs, Vic., Australia 34 16S 142 10E
135 Reddersburg, S. Africa 29 41S 26 10E
166 Redding, U.S.A. 40 30N 122 25W
34 Redditch, Eng., U.K. 52 18N 1 57W
143 Redesdale Australia .37 2S 144 31E
164 Redfield, U.S.A. 45 0N 98 30W
35 Redhill, Eng., U.K. ...51 14N 0 10W
43 Redland, Scot., U.K. .59 6N 3 4W
167 Redlands, U.S.A. 34 0N 117 0W
34 Redlynch, Eng., U.K. 50 59N 1 42W
39 Redmile, Eng., U.K. .52 54N 0 48W
166 Redmond, U.S.A. 44 19N 121 11W
48 Redon, France 47 40N 2 6W
62 Redondela, Spain 42 15N 8 38W
63 Redondo, Portugal 38 39N 7 37W
167 Redondo Beach, U.S.A. 33 52N 118 26W
145 Redpa, Tas., Australia 40 48S 144 49E
36 Redruth, Eng., U.K. .50 14N 5 14E
157 Redvers, Canada 49 35N 101 40W
156 Redwater, Canada 53 55N 113 0W
161 Redwood, U.S.A. 44 18N 75 48W
167 Redwood City, U.S.A. 37 30N 122 15W
164 Redwood Falls, U.S.A. 44 30N 95 2W
44 Ree, Lough, Ireland ...53 35N 8 0W
162 Reed City, U.S.A. 43 52N 85 30W
164 Reeder, U.S.A. 47 7N 102 52W
35 Reedham, Eng., U.K. 52 34N 1 33E
167 Reedley, U.S.A. 34 40N 119 27W
164 Reedsburg, U.S.A. 43 34N 90 5W
166 Reedsport, U.S.A. 43 45N 124 4W
147 Reefton, N.Z. 42 6S 171 51E
35 Reepham, Eng., U.K. 52 46N 1 6E
55 Rees, Germany 51 46N 6 21E
72 Ref Lo Valdes, Chile .33 47S 70 9W
79 Refsnes, Norway 61 9N 7 14E
181 Reftele, Sweden 57 11N 13 35E
165 Refugio, U.S.A. 28 18N 97 17W
60 Rega R., Poland 53 52N 15 16E
73 Regalbuto, Italy 37 40N 14 38E
98 Regavim, Israel 32 32N 35 2E
57 Regen, Germany 48 58N 13 9E
57 Regensburg, Germany 49 1N 12 7E
73 Reggio di Calabria, It. 38 7N 15 38E
70 Reggio nell' Emilia, It. 44 2N 10 38E
78 Reghin, Rumania 46 46N 24 41E
157 Regina, Canada 50 30N 104 35W
133 Regina, Trans., S. Africa 27 2S 26 30E
101 Registan, dist., Afghan. 30 15N 65 0E
173 Registro, Brazil 24 29S 47 49W
173 Registro do Araguaia, Brazil 15 40S 52 0W
63 Reguengos de Monsaraz, Portugal 38 25N 7 32W
105 Rehar, India 23 36N 82 52E
129 Rehoboth, S.W. Africa 17 55S 15 5E
129 Rehoboth, S.W. Africa 23 15S 17 4E
98 Rehovot, Israel 31 54N 34 48E
121 Rei Bouba, Cameroon 8 40N 14 15E
56 Reichenbach, Germany 50 36N 12 19E
142 Reid, Western Australia 28 40S 30 45E
144 Reid River, Australia 19 40S 146 48E
163 Reidsville, U.S.A. 36 21N 79 40W
35 Reigate, Eng., U.K. ...51 14N 0 11W
55 Reijen, Netherlands ...51 35N 4 55E
64 Reillo, Spain 39 54N 1 53W
49 Reims, France 49 15N 4 0E
98 Reina, Israel 32 43N 35 18E
164 Reinbeck, U.S.A. 42 18N 92 40W
157 Reindeer I., Canada ...52 30N 98 0W
157 Reindeer L., Canada .57 20N 102 20W
62 Reinosa, Spain 43 2N 4 15W
127 Reira, Sudan 15 25N 34 50E
43 Reiss, Scotland, U.K. 58 29N 3 7W
135 Reitz, O.F.S., S. Africa 27 48S 28 29E
71 Reka R., Yugoslavia .45 40N 14 0E
74 Rekovac, Yugoslavia .43 51N 21 3E
55 Remagen, Germany ...50 35N 7 12E
174 Remanso, Amaz., Braz. 7 35S 65 45W
175 Remanso, Baia, Brazil 9 30S 42 20W
145 Remarkable Mt., S. Australia 32 52S 138 0E
109 Rembang, Indonesia . 6 42S 111 21E
122 Remchi, Algeria 35 2N 0 18E
101 Remeshk, Iran 26 55N 58 50E
78 Remetea, Rumania ...46 45N 29 29E
54 Remich, Luxembourg 49 32N 6 22E
49 Remiremont, France .48 0N 6 36E
89 Remontnoye, U.S.S.R. 47 44N 43 37E
51 Remoulins, France 43 55N 4 35E
56 Remscheid, Germany .51 11N 7 12E
79 Rena, Norway 61 8N 11 20E
79 Rena, R., Norway 61 10N 11 18E
132 Renco, Rhodesia 20 35S 30 19E
73 Rende, Italy 39 19N 16 11E
77 Rendina, Greece 39 4N 21 58E
56 Rendsburg, Germany .54 18N 9 41E
91 Rene, U.S.S.R. 66 2N 178 1W
154 Renfrew Canada 45 30N 76 40W
40 Renfrew & co., Scotland, U.K. 55 52N 4 24W
108 Rengat, Indonesia 0 30S 102 45E
172 Rengo, Chile 34 24S 70 50W
88 Reni, U.S.S.R. 45 28N 28 15E
106 Renigunta, India 13 38N 79 30E
42 Renish Pt., Scot., U.K. 57 44N 6 59W
54 Renkum, Netherlands 51 58N 5 43E
145 Renmark, S. Australia 34 5S 140 46E
156 Rennel Sd., Canada ...53 32N 133 28W
138 Renner Springs Teleg. Off., N. Terr., Austral. 18 20S 133 47E
48 Rennes, France 48 7N 1 41W
79 Rennesöy, Norway 59 06N 5 43E
143 Rennie, N.S.W., Australia 35 49S 146 8E
166 Reno, U.S.A. 39 30N 119 50W
71 Reno, R., Italy 44 45N 11 40E
134 Renoster, R., S. Africa 31 22S 20 30E
160 Renovo, U.S.A. 41 20N 77 47W
162 Rensselaer, Ind., U.S.A. 41 0N 87 10W
161 Rensselaer, N.Y., U.S A. 42 38N 73 41W
64 Reneteria, Spain 43 19N 1 54W
166 Renton, U.S.A. 47 30N 122 9W
147 Renwicktown, N.Z. ...41 30S 173 51E
124 Réo, Upper Volta 12 28N 2 35E
105 Reotipur, India 25 33N 83 45E
106 Repalle, India 16 2N 80 45E
59 Repcelak, Hungary ...47 24N 17 1E
34 Repton, Eng., U.K. ...52 50N 1 32W
162 Republic, Mich., U.S.A. 46 25N 87 59W
166 Republic, Wash., U.S.A. 48 38N 118 42W
164 Republican R., U.S.A. 40 0N 98 30W
164 Republican City, U.S.A. 40 9N 99 20W
15 Repulse B., Antarctica 64 30S 99 30E
127 Reqqe, Ethiopia 10 50N 39 53E
65 Requena, Spain 39 30N 1 4W
174 Requena, Peru 5 5S 73 52W
80 Resele, Sweden 63 22N 17 10E
74 Resen, Yugoslavia 41 5N 21 0E
167 Reserve, U.S.A. 33 50N 108 54W
100 Resht, Iran 37 20N 49 40E
172 Resistencia, Argentina 27 30S 59 0W
74 Reşiţa, Rumania 45 18N 21 53E
60 Resko, Poland 53 47N 15 25E
153 Resolution I., Canada 61 30N 65 0W
147 Resolution I., N.Z. 45 40S 166 40E
37 Resolven, Wales, U.K. 51 43N 3 42W
133 Ressano Garcia, Mozam. 25 25S 32 0E
41 Reston, Scot., U.K. ...55 51N 2 11W
168 Retalhuleu. Guatemala 14 33N 91 46W
78 Reteag, Rumania 47 10N 24 0E
130 Retenue, Lac de, Congo 11 0S 27 0E
49 Rethel, France 49 30N 4 20E
56 Rethem, Germany 52 47N 9 25E
77 Rethimnon Greece 35 23N 24 28E
48 Retiers, France 47 55N 1 25W
172 Retiro, Chile 35 59S 71 47W
62 Retortillo, Spain 40 48N 6 21W
59 Retsag, Hungary 47 58N 19 10E
11 Réunion I., Indian Oc. 22 0S 56 0E
64 Réus, Spain 41 10N 1 5E
57 Reutlingen, Germany .48 28N 9 13E
58 Reutte, Austria 47 29N 10 42E
50 Revel, France 43 28N 2 0E
105 Revelganj, India 25 50N 84 40E
156 Revelstoke, Canada ...51 0N 118 0W
49 Revigny, France 48 50N 5 0E
137 Revilla Gigedo Is., Pacific Ocean 18 40N 112 0W
157 Revillagigedo I., Alaska, U.S.A. 55 50N 131 20W
49 Revin, France 49 55N 4 39E
132 Revuè R., Mozambique 19 30S 33 35E
105 Rewa, India 24 33N 81 25E
104 Rewari, India 28 15N 76 40E
166 Rexburg, U.S.A. 43 45N 111 50W
166 Rexford, U.S.A. 48 56N 115 8W
82 Reydarfjord, Iceland .64 51N 13 45W
82 Reykjahlid, Iceland ...65 40N 16 49W
82 Reykjanæs C., Iceland 63 48N 22 40W
82 Reykjavik, Iceland 64 10N 22 0W
138 Reynolds Ra., Austral. 22 30S 133 0E
160 Reynoldsville, U.S.A. .41 5N 78 58W
168 Reynosa, Mexico 26 5N 98 18W
100 Reza'iyeh, Iran 37 40N 45 0E
100 Rezā'iyeh (Urmia), L., Iran 37 30N 45 30E
86 Rèzekne, U.S.S.R. 56 30N 27 17E
75 Rezovo, Bulgaria 42 0N 28 0E
75 Rgatina, Yugoslavia .44 1N 22 18E
37 Rhaeadr Ogwen, Wales, U.K. 53 8N 4 0W
37 Rhayader, Wales, U.K. 52 19N 3 30W
55 Rhede, West Germany 51 51N 6 37E
54 Rheden, Netherlands .52 0N 6 3E
37 Rheidol, R., Wales, UK 52 25N 5 37W
157 Rhein, Canada 51 25N 102 15W
56 Rhein R., Germany ...51 42N 6 20E
56 Rheinbach, Germany .50 38N 6 54E
55 Rheinberg, Germany .51 33N 6 33E
56 Rheine, Germany 52 17N 7 25E
57 Rheinland Pfalz, land, Germany 50 50N 7 0E

MAP
56 Rheinsberg, Germany 53 6N 12 52E
56 Rheydt, Germany 51 10N 6 24E
123 Rhilane, Tunisia 35 2N 8 14E
49 Rhinau, France 48 19N 7 43E
56 Rhine R. (Rhein), Ger. 51 48N 6 18E
164 Rhinelander, U.S.A. ...45 38N 89 29W
131 Rhino Camp, Uganda 3 0N 31 22E
40 Rhins, The, dist., Scotland, U.K. 54 50N 5 0W
55 Rhisnes, Belgium 50 31N 4 48E
37 Rhiw, Wales, U.K. 52 49N 4 37W
70 Rho, Italy 45 31N 9 2E
161 Rhode Island, st., U.S.A. 41 38N 71 37W
135 Rhodes, C. Prov., S. Afr. 30 47S 27 59E
77 Rhodes, I., see Ródhos, Greece 36 15N 28 10E
132 Rhodes' Tomb, Rhod. 20 30S 28 30E
132 Rhodesia, st., Africa .20 0S 30 0E
75 Rhodope Mts., Bulg. .41 40N 24 20E
37 Rhondda, Wales, U.K. 51 39N 3 30W
51 Rhône, dépt., France .45 54N 4 35E
51 Rhône R., France 43 28N 4 42E
37 Rhos-on-Sea, Wales, United Kingdom 53 18N 3 46W
37 Rhosllanerchrugog, Wales, U.K. 53 3N 3 4W
37 Rhossilli, Wales, U.K. 51 34N 4 18W
42 Rhu Coigach, C., Scotland, U.K. 58 6N 5 27W
37 Rhuddlan, Wales, U.K. 53 17N 3 28W
42 Rhum I., Scot., U.K. .57 0N 6 20W
37 Rhyl, Wales, U.K. 53 19N 3 29W
37 Rhymney, Wales, U.K. 51 45N 3 17W
43 Rhynie, Scotland, UK 57 20N 2 50W
175 Riachão, Brazil 7 20S 46 45W
62 Riaño. Spain 42 59N 5 0W
51 Rians, France 43 37N 5 44E
64 Riansares R., Spain ...40 0N 3 0W
102 Riasi, Kashmir 33 10N 74 50E
108 Riau Arch., Indonesia 0 30N 104 20E
108 Riau, Prov., Indon. ... 0 0N 102 35E
62 Riaza, Spain 41 18N 3 30W
62 Riaza R., Spain 41 16N 3 29W
64 Riba de Saelices, Spain 40 55N 2 18E
62 Ribadéo, Spain 43 35N 7 5W
62 Ribadesella, Spain 43 30N 5 7W
64 Ribas. Spain 42 19N 2 15E
38 Ribble, R., Eng., U.K. 54 13N 2 20W
81 Ribe, Denmark 55 19N 8 44E
81 Ribe Amt., Denmark .55 34N 8 30E
49 Ribeauville, France ...48 10N 7 20E
49 Ribécourt, France 49 30N 2 55E
173 Ribeira, Brazil 24 40S 48 0W
62 Ribeira, Spain 42 36N 8 58W
173 Ribeirão Preto, Brazil 21 10S 47 50W
49 Ribémont, France 49 47N 3 27E
72 Ribera, Italy 37 30N 13 13E
50 Ribérac, France 45 15N 0 20E
174 Riberalta, Bolivia 11 0S 66 0W
71 Ribnica, Yugoslavia ...45 45N 14 45E
58 Ričany, Czechoslovakia 50 0N 14 40E
39 Riccall, Eng., U.K. ...53 50N 1 4W
147 Riccarton, New Zealand 43 32S 172 37E
41 Riccarton Junc., Scotland, U.K. 55 16N 2 43W
73 Riccia, Italy 41 30N 14 50E
71 Riccione, Italy 44 0N 12 39E
160 Rice L., Canada 44 10N 78 10W
164 Rice Lake, U.S.A. 45 30N 91 42W
122 Rich, Morocco 32 24N 4 22W
165 Rich Hill, U.S.A. 38 5N 94 22W
135 Richards B., Nat., S. Afr. 28 48S 32 6E
17 Richards Deep, Pac. Oc. 25 0S 73 0W
147 Richardson Mts., N.Z. 44 49S 168 34E
164 Richardton, U.S.A. ...46 56N 102 22W
48 Richelieu, France 47 0N 0 20E
164 Richey, U.S.A. 47 42N 105 5W
166 Richfield, Idaho, U.S.A. 43 2N 114 5W
167 Richfield, Utah, U.S.A. 38 50N 112 0W
161 Richford, U.S.A. 45 0N 72 40W
155 Richibucto, Canada ...46 42N 64 54W
163 Richland, Ga., U.S.A. 32 7N 84 40W
166 Richland, Ore., U.S.A. 44 49N 117 9W
166 Richland, Wash., U.S.A. 46 15N 119 15W
164 Richland Center, U.S.A. 43 21N 90 22W
162 Richlands, U.S.A. 37 7N 81 49W
35 Richmond, Surrey, England, U.K. 51 28N 0 18W
39 Richmond, Yorks, England, U.K. 54 24N 1 43W
134 Richmond, S. Africa .31 23S 23 56E
135 Richmond, Nat., S. Africa 29 51S 30 18E
143 Richmond, Australia .33 35S 150 42E
147 Richmond, N.Z. 41 21S 173 12E
144 Richmond, Australia .20 43S 143 8E
166 Richmond, Calif., U.S.A. 38 0N 122 30W
162 Richmond, Ind., U.S.A. 39 50N 84 50W
162 Richmond, Ky., U.S.A. 37 40N 84 20W
160 Richmond, Mich., U.S.A. 42 47N 82 45W
164 Richmond, Mo., U.S.A. 39 15N 93 58W
161 Richmond, N.Y., U.S.A. 40 35N 74 6W
165 Richmond, Tex., U.S.A. 29 32N 95 42W
162 Richmond, Va., U.S.A. 37 33N 77 27W
147 Richmond, Mt., N.Z. .41 32S 173 22E
147 Richmond Ra., N.Z. .41 32S 173 22E
154 Richmond Gulf, Canada 56 20N 75 50W
163 Richton, U.S.A. 31 23N 88 58W
162 Richwood, U.S.A. 38 17N 80 32W
35 Rickmansworth, England, U.K. 51 38N 0 28W
64 Ricla, Spain 41 31N 1 24W
80 Riddarhyttan, Sweden 59 55N 15 40E
55 Ridderkerk, Neth. 51 52N 4 35E
157 Ridgedale, Canada 53 0N 104 10W
163 Ridgeland, U.S.A. 32 30N 80 58W
144 Ridgelands, Australia 23 16S 150 17E
154 Ridgetown, Canada ...42 26N 81 52W
160 Ridgway, U.S.A. 41 25N 78 43W
142 Ridley Mt., W. Austral. 33 12S 122 7E
135 Riebeek E., S. Africa .33 13S 26 12E
56 Riebnitz, Germany 54 14N 12 24E
58 Ried, Upper, Austria .48 14N 13 30E
71 Rienza R., Italy 46 49N 11 47E
56 Riesa, Germany 51 19N 13 19E
73 Riesi, Italy 37 16N 14 4E
135 Riet, R., O.F.S., S. Afr. 29 20S 25 0E
134 Rietbron, S. Africa 32 50S 23 8E
134 Rietfontein, S. Africa .26 44S 20 1E
71 Rieti, Italy 42 23N 12 50E
135 Rietkull, O.F.S., S. Afr. 27 34S 29 1E
134 Rietpoel, S. Africa 34 15S 19 47E
50 Rieupeyroux, France .44 19N 2 12E
39 Rievaulx, Eng., UK ...54 16N 1 7W
51 Riez, France 43 49N 6 6E
166 Rifle, U.S.A. 39 40N 107 50W
121 Rig Rig, Chad 14 13N 14 25E
86 Riga, G. of, U.S.S.R. .57 40N 23 45E
161 Rigaud, Canada 45 28N 74 20W
166 Rigby, U.S.A. 43 41N 111 58W
166 Riggins, U.S.A. 45 29N 116 26W
50 Rignac, France 44 25N 2 16E
144 Rigo, Terr. of Papua . 9 41S 147 31E
155 Rigolet, Canada 54 10N 58 23W
83 Riihimaki, Finland 60 45N 24 45E
15 Riiser-Larsen Pen., Ant. 68 0S 35 0E
114 Riishiri I., Japan 45 10N 140 17E
125 Rijau, Nigeria 11 8N 5 17E
74 Rijeka Crnojevica, Yugoslavia 42 24N 19 1E
71 Rijeka (Fiume), Y.-slav. 45 20N 14 21E
55 Rijkevorsel, Belgium .51 21N 4 46E
54 Rijn R., Netherlands .52 5N 4 50E
55 Rijsbergen, Netherlands 51 31N 4 41E
54 Rijssen, Netherlands .52 19N 6 30E
54 Rijswijk, Netherlands 52 4N 4 22E
127 Rikita, Sudan 5 5N 28 29E
75 Rila, Bulgaria 42 7N 23 7E
74 Rila Planina, ra., Bulg. 42 10N 23 30E
39 Rillington, Eng., U.K. 54 10N 0 41W
49 Rilly, France 49 11N 4 3E
103 Rima, China 28 35N 97 5E
125 Rima R., Nigeria 13 15N 5 15E
59 Rimavská Sobota, Cz. 48 22N 20 2E
156 Rimbey, Canada 52 35N 114 15W
80 Rimbo, Sweden 59 44N 18 21E
81 Rimforsa, Sweden 58 10N 15 40E
125 Rimi, Nigeria 12 58N 7 43E
71 Rimini, Italy 44 3N 12 33E
155 Rimouski, Canada 48 27N 68 30W
73 Rindjani Mt., Indon. . 8 20S 116 30E
81 Ringarum, Sweden 58 21N 16 26E
81 Ringe, Denmark 55 15N 10 28E
41 Ringford, Scot., U.K. 54 55N 4 3W
125 Ringim, Nigeria 12 13N 9 10E
81 Ringköbing, Denmark 56 5N 8 15E
81 Ringkobing Amt., Denmark 56 15N 8 30E
166 Ringling, U.S.A. 46 16N 110 56W
35 Ringmer, Eng., U.K. .50 53N 0 5E
79 Ringsaker, Norway ...60 54N 10 45E
46 Ringsend, N. Ire., UK 55 2N 6 45W
81 Ringsjön L., Sweden .55 55N 13 30E
81 Ringsted, Denmark ...55 25N 11 46E
82 Ringvassöy, Norway .69 53N 19 25E
45 Ringville, Ireland 52 3N 7 37W
34 Ringwood, Eng., U.K. 50 50N 1 48W
1 Rinihue, vol., S. Amer. 40 1S 68 58W
77 Rinía I., Greece 37 23N 25 13E
56 Rinteln, Germany 52 11N 9 3E
109 Rintja I., Indonesia ... 8 45S 119 35E
65 Rio, Punta del, Spain 36 49N 2 24W
174 Rio Arica, Peru 1 35S 75 30W
174 Rio Branco, Brazil 9 55S 67 55W
174 Rio Branco, Brazil 9 59S 67 49W
173 Rio Branco, Uruguay 32 40S 53 40W
173 Rio Claro, Brazil 22 19S 47 35W
169 Rio Claro, Trinidad ...10 20N 61 25W
176 Rio Colorado, Argentina 39 0S 64 0W
172 Rio Cuarto, Argentina 33 10S 64 25W
165 Rio Grande City, U.S.A. 26 30N 91 55W
132 Rio das Pedras, Mozam. 23 8S 35 28W
173 Rio de Janeiro, Brazil 23 0S 43 12W
173 Rio de Janeiro, st., Braz. 22 50S 43 0W
125 Rio del Rey, Cameroon 4 42N 8 37E
173 Rio do Sul, Brazil 27 95S 49 37W
176 Rio Gallegos, Arg. 51 35S 69 15W
176 Rio Grande, Argentina 53 50S 67 45W
173 Rio Grande, Brazil 32 0S 52 20W
173 Rio Grande, st., Brazil 29 0S 53 0W
167 Rio Grande R., U.S.A. 37 47N 106 15W
165 Rio Grande City, U.S.A. 26 30N 91 55W
158 Rio Grand del Norte, R., North America .20 0N 97 0W
176 Rio Hondo, Argentina 27 30S 64 55W
175 Rio Largo, Brazil 9 28S 35 50W
63 Rio Major, Portugal ...39 19N 8 57W
70 Rio Marina, Italy 42 48N 10 25E
174 Rio Mulatos, Bolivia .19 40S 66 50W
128 Rio Muni, Sp. col., Afr. 1 30N 10 0E
172 Rio Negro, Argentina 40 0S 65 51W
173 Rio Negro, Brazil 26 0S 50 0W
175 Rio Pardo, Mato Grosso, Brazil 20 30S 53 50W
175 Rio Pardo, Minas Gerais, Brazil 15 55S 42 30W
173 Rio Pardo, Rio Grande do Sul, Brazil 30 0S 52 30W
172 Rio Seco, Argentina ...30 0S 63 43W
172 Rio Segundo, Arg. 31 40S 63 59W
172 Rio Tercero, Argentina 32 15S 64 8W
62 Rio Tinto, Portugal ...41 11N 8 34W
175 Rio Verde, Brazil 17 50S 51 0W
168 Rio Verde, Mexico 21 56N 99 59W
166 Rio Vista, U.S.A. 38 11N 121 44W
174 Riobamba, Ecuador ... 1 50S 78 45W
174 Riohacha, Colombia ...11 33N 72 55W
50 Riom, France 45 54N 3 7E
50 Riom-és-Montagnes, Fr. 45 17N 2 39E
73 Rionero in Vulture, It. 40 55N 15 40E
62 Rios, Spain 41 58N 7 16W
174 Riosucio, Colombia 5 30N 75 40W
174 Riosucio, Colombia 7 27N 77 7W
70 Riparia, Dora-, R., It. 45 7N 7 24E
174 Ripartimento, Brazil . 2 10N 62 25W
71 Ripatransone, Italy ...43 0N 13 45E
160 Ripley, Canada 44 4N 81 32W
39 Ripley, Derby, Eng., UK 53 3N 1 24W
39 Ripley, Yorks, Eng., UK 54 3N 1 34W
160 Ripley, N.Y., U.S.A. .42 16N 79 44W
165 Ripley, Tenn., U.S.A. 35 43N 89 34W
64 Ripoll, Spain 42 15N 2 13E
39 Ripon, England, U.K. 54 8N 1 31W
162 Ripon, U.S.A. 43 51N 88 50W
73 Riposto, Italy 37 44N 15 12E
74 Risan, Yugoslavia 42 32N 18 42E
34 Risca, England, U.K. 51 36N 3 6W
50 Riscle, France 43 39N 0 5W
132 Riscom, Rhodesia 19 1S 29 46E
98 Rishon le Zion, Israel 31 58N 34 48E
98 Rishpon Israel 32 12N 34 49E
38 Rishton Eng., U.K. 53 46N 2 26W
79 Riska, Norway 58 56N 5 52E
48 Risle R., France 48 55N 0 41E
165 Rison, U.S.A. 33 57N 92 11W
79 Risör, Norway 58 43N 9 10E
133 Rita, Trans., S. Africa 23 42S 29 34E
107 Ritchie's Archipelago, Andaman Islands ...12 5N 94 0E
125 Riti, Nigeria 7 57N 9 41E
160 Rittman, U.S.A. 40 57N 81 48W
166 Ritzville, U.S.A. 47 10N 118 21W
109 Riung, Indonesia 8 22S 121 7E
70 Riva, Italy 45 53N 10 50E
48 Riva Bella Ouistreham, France 49 17N 0 18W
172 Rivadavia, Buenos Aires, Argentina 35 29S 62 59W
172 Rivadavia, Mendoza, Argentina 33 13S 68 30W
172 Rivadavia, Salta, Arg. 24 5S 63 0W
172 Rivadavia, Chile 29 50S 70 35W
62 Rivadavia, Spain 42 17N 8 8W
70 Rivarolo Canavese, It. 45 20N 7 42E
169 Rivas, Nicaragua 11 30N 85 50W
51 Rive-de-Gier, France 45 32N 4 37E
124 River Cess, Liberia 5 30N 9 25W
160 River Rouge, U.S.A. .42 16N 83 9W
173 Rivera, Uruguay 31 0S 55 50W
45 Riverchapel, Ireland .52 38N 6 14W
161 Riverhead, U.S.A. 40 53N 72 40W
157 Riverhurst, Canada ...50 55N 106 50W
142 Riverina, W. Australia 29 45S 120 40E
156 Rivers Inlet, Canada .51 40N 127 20W
147 Riversdale, N.Z. 45 45S 168 45E
134 Riversdale, S. Africa .34 7S 21 15E
160 Riverside, Canada 42 17N 82 59W
135 Riverside, Nat., S. Afr. 30 6S 29 46E
167 Riverside, Calif., U.S.A. 34 0N 117 15W
166 Riverside, Wyo., U.S.A. 41 12N 106 57W
144 Riversleigh, Australia 19 5S 138 48E
157 Riverton, Canada 51 5N 97 0W
147 Riverton, New Zealand 46 21S 168 0E
133 Riverton, S. Africa ...28 30S 24 45E
166 Riverton, U.S.A. 43 1N 108 27W
50 Rivesaltes, France 42 47N 2 50E
70 Riviera, Italy & France 44 0N 8 30E
68 Riviera di Levante, It. 44 23N 9 15E
68 Riviera di Ponente, It. 43 50N 7 58E
155 Rivière à Pierre, Canada 46 57N 72 12W
155 Rivière Bleue, Canada 47 26N 69 2W
155 Rivière du Loup, Can. 47 50N 69 30W
155 Riviere Pontecote, Can. 49 57N 67 1W
70 Rivoli, Italy 45 3N 7 31E
145 Rivoli B., S. Australia 37 25S 140 0E
147 Riwaka, New Zealand 41 5S 172 59E
100 Riyadh (Ar Riyad.), Saudi Arabia 24 41N 46 42E
100 Rize, Turkey 41 0N 40 30E
73 Rizzuto, C., Italy 38 54N 17 5E
79 Rjukan, Norway 59 54N 8 33E
79 Roa, Norway 60 17N 10 37E
62 Roa, Spain 41 41N 3 56W
34 Road Weedon, England, U.K. 52 14N 1 6W
35 Roade, England, UK .52 10N 0 53W
41 Roadhead, Eng., U.K. 55 4N 2 44W
42 Roag, E. & W. L., Scotland, U.K. 58 10N 6 55W
132 Roan Antelope, Zam. .13 2S 28 19E
51 Roanne, France 46 3N 4 4E
163 Roanoke, Ala., U.S.A. 33 9N 85 23W
162 Roanoke, Va., U.S.A. 37 19N 79 55W
163 Roanoke I., U.S.A. 35 55N 75 40W
163 Roanoke R., U.S.A. ...36 15N 77 20W
163 Roanoke Rapids, U.S.A. 36 36N 77 42W
44 Roaringwater B., Ire. 51 30N 9 30W
145 Robbins I., Australia .40 42S 145 0E
143 Robe, Mt., Australia .31 40S 141 20E
56 Röbel, East Germany 53 24N 12 37E
165 Robert Lee U.S.A. 31 55N 100 26W
142 Robert Pt., W. Austral. 32 34S 115 40E
41 Roberton, Scot., U.K. 55 24N 2 53W
166 Roberts, U.S.A. 43 44N 112 8W
124 Robertsfield, Liberia . 6 10N 10 28E
102 Robertsganj, India 24 44N 83 12E
143 Robertson, Australia .34 37S 150 36E
134 Robertson, S. Africa .33 46S 19 50E
15 Robertson I., Antarc. 68 0S 75 0W
142 Robertson Ra., Western Australia .23 15S 121 0E
124 Robertsport, Liberia . 6 45N 11 26W
45 Robertstown, Ireland .53 16N 6 50W
55 Robertville, Belgium . 5 28N 6 8E
154 Roberval, Canada 48 32N 72 15W
14 Robeson Chan., Canada 82 0N 60 0W
39 Robin Hood's B., England, U.K. 54 26N 0 31W
154 Robinson, Canada 50 20N 91 20W
137 Robinson Crusoe I., Pac. Oc. 33 50S 78 30W
143 Robinvale, Australia .34 40S 142 45E
157 Roblin Canada 51 21N 101 25W
174 Roboré, Bolivia 18 10S 59 45W
156 Robson Mt., Canada .53 10N 119 10W
165 Robstown, U.S.A. 27 47N 97 40W
63 Roca, C. da, Portugal 38 40N 9 31W
174 Rocafuerte, Peru 0 55S 75 10W
175 Rocas I., Brazil 4 0S 34 1W
73 Rocca d'Aspide, Italy 40 27N 15 10E
71 Rocca San Casciano, It. 44 3N 11 30E
71 Roccalbegna, Italy 42 47N 11 30E
71 Roccastrada, Italy 43 0N 11 10E
73 Roccella, Ionica, Italy 37 57N 15 0E
38 Rocester, Eng., U.K. .52 56N 1 50W
173 Rocha, Uruguay 34 30S 54 25W
38 Rochdale, Eng., U.K. 53 36N 2 10W
36 Roche, England, U.K. 50 24N 4 50W
50 Rochechouart, France 45 50N 0 49E
55 Rochefort, Belgium 50 9N 5 12E
50 Rochefort, France 45 56N 0 57W
48 Rochefort en Terre, Fr. 47 42N 2 22W
164 Rochelle, U.S.A. 41 55N 89 5W
156 Rocher River, Canada 61 12N 114 0W
44 Roches Pt., Ireland ...51 48N 8 15W
48 Rocheserviere, France 46 57N 1 30W
143 Rochester, Vic., Austral. 36 22S 144 41E
35 Rochester, Kent, England, U.K. 51 22N 0 30E
39 Rochester, Northum., England, U.K. 55 16N 2 16W
162 Rochester, Ind., U.S.A. 41 5N 86 15W
164 Rochester, Minn., U.S.A. 44 1N 92 28W
161 Rochester, N.H., U.S.A. 43 19N 70 57W
160 Rochester, N.Y., U.S.A. 43 10N 77 40W
160 Rochester, Pa., U.S.A. 40 41N 80 17W
35 Rochford, Eng., U.K. 51 36N 0 42E
45 Rochfortbridge, Ire. ...53 25N 7 19W
63 Rociana, Spain 37 19N 6 35W
78 Rociu, Rumania 44 43N 25 2E
163 Rock Hill, U.S.A. 34 55N 81 2W
163 Rock Island, U.S.A. ...41 30N 90 35W
164 Rock Lake, U.S.A. 48 50N 99 13W
164 Rock Rapids, U.S.A. .43 25N 96 10W
166 Rock River, U.S.A. ...41 49N 106 0W
167 Rock Sprs., Ariz., U.S.A. 34 2N 112 11W
166 Rock Sprs., Mont., U.S.A. 46 55N 106 11W
165 Rock Sprs., Tex., U.S.A. 30 2N 100 11W
166 Rock Sprs., Wyo., U.S.A. 41 40N 109 10W
164 Rock Valley, U.S.A. ...43 10N 96 17W
18 Rockall I., North Atlantic Ocean 57 37N 13 42W
38 Rockcliffe, Eng., U.K. 54 58N 3 0W
46 Rockcorry, Ireland 54 7N 7 0W
165 Rockdale U.S.A. 30 40N 97 0W
15 Rockefeller Plat., Ant. 84 0S 130 0W
164 Rockford, U.S.A. 42 20N 89 0W
144 Rockhampton, Austral. 23 22S 150 32E
44 Rockhill, Ireland 52 25N 8 44W
35 Rockingham, Eng., U.K. 52 32N 0 43W
142 Rockingham, W. Austral. 32 15S 115 38E
144 Rockingham B., Queens., Australia .18 5S 146 10E
35 Rockingham For., England, U.K. 52 28N 0 42W
161 Rockland, Canada 45 30N 75 19W
166 Rockland, Idaho, U.S.A. 42 37N 112 57W
155 Rockland, Me., U.S.A. 44 0N 69 0W
164 Rockland, Mich., U.S.A. 46 40N 89 10W
163 Rockmart, U.S.A. 34 1N 85 2W
44 Rockmills, Ireland 52 13N 8 25W
164 Rockport, Mo., U.S.A. 40 26N 95 30W
165 Rockport, Tex., U.S.A. 28 2N 97 3W
174 Rockstone, Guyana ... 6 0N 58 30W
161 Rockville, Conn., U.S.A. 41 51N 72 27W
162 Rockville, Md., U.S.A. 39 7N 77 10W
165 Rockwall, U.S.A. 32 55N 96 30W
143 Rockwell, Australia ...32 3S 141 32E
164 Rockwell City, U.S.A. 42 20N 94 35W
163 Rockwood, U.S.A. 35 52N 84 40W
164 Rocky Ford, U.S.A. ...38 7N 103 45W
142 Rocky Gully, W. Austral. 34 30S 117 0E
163 Rocky Mount, U.S.A. 35 55N 77 48W
152 Rocky Mts., N. Amer. 48 0N 113 0W
142 Rocky Pt., W. Austral. 33 30S 123 57E
156 Rockyford, Canada ...51 20N 113 10W
49 Rocroi, France 49 55N 4 30E
102 Rod, W. Pakistan 28 10N 63 5E
79 Rodberg, Norway 60 17N 8 56E
81 Rödby, Denmark 54 41N 11 23E
81 Rödbyhavn, Denmark 54 39N 11 22E
155 Roddickton (Newf.), Canada 50 51N 56 8W
81 Rödding, Denmark 55 23N 9 3E
81 Rödekro, Denmark 55 4N 9 20E
79 Rödenes, Norway 59 35N 11 34E
56 Rodenkirchen, Ger. ...53 24N 8 26E
50 Rodez, France 44 21N 2 33E
76 Rodholivos, Greece 40 55N 24 0E
77 Ródhos (Rhodes) & I., Greece 36 15N 28 10E
35 Roding R., Eng., U.K. 51 43N 0 16E
81 Rödjenäs, Sweden 57 33N 14 50E
78 Rodna, Rumania 47 25N 24 50E
160 Rodney, Canada 42 34N 81 43W
87 Rodniki, U.S.S.R. 57 7N 41 37E
11 Rodriguez, I., Ind. Oc. 20 0S 65 0E
46 Roe, R. N. Ire., U.K. 55 0N 6 56W
161 Roebling, U.S.A. 40 7N 74 45W
138 Roebourne, W. Austral. 20 44S 117 9E
138 Roebuck B., W. Austral. 18 5S 122 20E
54 Roermond, Netherlands 51 12N 6 0E
153 Roes Welcome Sd., Can. 65 0N 87 0W
54 Roeselare, Belgium 50 57N 3 7E
86 Rogachev, U.S.S.R. 53 8N 30 5E
74 Rogačica, Yugoslavia 44 4N 19 40E
174 Rogagua L., Bolivia ...14 0S 66 50W
38 Rogans Seat, Mt., England, U.K. 54 25N 2 10W
71 Rogaska Slatina, Yugoslavia 46 15N 15 42E
35 Rogate, Eng., U.K. ...51 0N 0 51W
71 Rogatec, Yugoslavia .46 15N 21 46E
86 Rogatin, U.S.S.R. 29 24N 24 36E
165 Rogers, U.S.A. 36 20N 94 0W
162 Rogers City, U.S.A. 45 25N 83 49W
166 Rogerson, U.S.A. 42 10N 114 40W
163 Rogersville, U.S.A. 36 27N 83 1W
155 Roggan River, Canada 54 24N 78 5W
134 Roggeveldberge, Mts., C. Prov., S. Afr. 32 10S 20 10E
73 Roggiano Gravina, Italy 39 37N 16 9E
51 Rogliano, Corsica, Fr. 42 57N 9 30E
73 Rogliano, Italy 39 11N 16 20E
82 Rognan, Norway 67 7N 15 25E
174 Rogoaguado L., Bolivia 13 0S 65 30W
60 Rogowo, Poland 52 43N 17 38E
60 Rogozno, Poland 52 45N 16 59E
166 Rogue, R., U.S.A. 42 30N 124 0W
48 Rohan, France 48 4N 2 45W
49 Rohrbach, France 49 3N 7 15E
104 Rohri, W. Pakistan ...27 45N 68 51E
104 Rohri Canal, W. Pak. 26 15N 68 27E
104 Rohtak, India 28 55N 76 43E
107 Roi Et, Thailand 15 56N 103 40E
42 Rois Bheinn, Scot., UK 56 50N 5 40W

MAP
49 Roisel, France 49 58N 3 6E
172 Rojas, Argentina 34 10s 60 45w
108 Rokan R., Indonesia . 1 30N 100 50E
86 Rokiskis, U.S.S.R. 55 55N 25 35E
87 Rokitnoye, U.S.S.R. .50 57N 35 56E
58 Rokycany, Cz. 49 43N 13 35E
173 Rolandia, Brazil 23 5s 52 0w
79 Röldal, Norway 59 47N 6 50E
164 Rolette, U.S.A. 48 42N 99 50w
81 Rolfstorp, Sweden 57 11N 12 27E
165 Rolla, Missouri, U.S.A. 38 0N 91 42w
165 Rolla, Kansas, U.S.A. 37 10N 101 40w
164 Rolla, N. Dak., U.S.A. 48 50N 99 36w
79 Rollag, Norway 60 1N 9 18E
147 Rolleston, New Zealand 43 35s 172 24E
144 Rollingstone, Australia 19 0s 146 15E
127 Rom, Sudan 9 54N 32 16E
145 Roma, Queens., Austral. 26 32s 148 49E
83 Roma, Gotland, Sweden 57 32N 18 28E
75 Roman, Bulgaria 43 8N 23 54E
78 Roman, Rumania 46 57N 26 55E
170 Romang I., Indonesia 7 30s 127 20E
126 Romāni, Egypt 30 59N 32 38E
74 Romanija Mts., Y.-slav. 43 50N 18 45E
169 Romano, Cayo, Cuba .22 0N 77 30w
70 Romano di Lombardia, Italy ...45 32N 9 45E
70 Romans, France 45 3N 5 3E
57 Romanshorn, Switz. ...47 33N 9 22E
72 Rome, Italy 41 54N 12 30E
163 Rome, Ga., U.S.A. 34 20N 85 0w
161 Rome, N.Y., U.S.A. 43 14N 75 29w
81 Romeleåsen, reg., Swed. 55 30N 13 30E
51 Romenây, France 46 30N 5 1E
155 Romeo, Canada 47 28N 57 4w
79 Romerike, Norway 60 11N 11 15E
49 Romilly, Aube, France 48 31N 3 44E
122 Rommani, Morocco ...33 20N 6 40w
55 Rommerskirchen, Ger. 51 2N 6 42E
160 Romney, Canada 42 9N 82 23w
162 Romney, U.S.A. 39 21N 78 45w
35 Romney Marsh, England, U.K. 51 0N 1 0E
86 Romny, U.S.S.R. 50 48N 33 28E
81 Römö I., Denmark 55 10N 8 30E
86 Romodan, U.S.S.R. ...50 0N 33 15E
87 Romodanovo, U.S.S.R. 54 26N 45 23E
57 Romont, Switzerland .46 42N 6 54E
49 Romorantin, France ...47 20N 1 44E
79 Romsdal, Norway 62 39N 7 45E
79 Romsdal R., Norway .62 25N 8 0E
55 Romsée Belgium 50 37N 5 40E
34 Romsey, Eng., U.K. .51 0N 1 29w
131 Rona, Congo 2 22N 30 42E
42 Rona I., Scot., U.K. .57 33N 6 0w
166 Ronan, U.S.A. 47 30N 114 11w
142 Ronas Hill, Scot., U.K. 60 33N 1 25w
42 Ronay I., Scot., U.K. 57 30N 7 10w
162 Ronceverte, U.S.A. ...37 45N 80 28w
72 Ronciglione, Italy 42 18N 12 12E
71 Ronco R., Italy 44 26N 12 15E
63 Ronda, Spain 36 46N 5 12w
79 Rondane, Plat., Nor. .61 66N 9 57E
60 Rondeau Park, Canada 42 10N 81 55w
174 Rondônia st., Brazil ...11 0s 63 0w
75 Rondorf, W. Germany 50 52N 6 58E
146 Rongotea, N.Z. 40 19s 175 25E
81 Rönne, Denmark 55 6N 14 44E
15 Ronne Land, Antarctica 83 0s 70 0w
81 Ronneby, Sweden 56 14N 15 20E
54 Ronse, Belgium 50 45N 3 35E
133 Roodebank, S. Africa .26 33s 29 0E
133 Roodepoort–Maraisburg, Trans., S. Afr. 26 8s 27 52E
167 Roof Butte, U.S.A. ...36 29N 109 5w
133 Rooiberg, Trans., S. Afr. 24 45s 27 44E
135 Rooihoogte S, Africa .31 47s 24 53E
133 Rooikraal, S. Africa ...25 19s 29 35E
135 Rooiwal, O.F.S., S. Africa 27 16s 27 31E
104 Roorkee, India 29 52N 77 59E
164 Roosevelt, Minn., U.S.A. 48 51N 95 2w
166 Roosevelt, Utah, U.S.A. 40 19N 110 1w
15 Roosevelt I., Antarctica 79 0s 161 0w
156 Roosevelt Mt., Canada 58 20N 125 20w
167 Roosevelt Res., U.S.A. 33 46N 111 0w
54 Roosendaal, Neth. 51 32N 4 29E
46 Roosky, Ireland 53 50N 7 55w
133 Roossenekal, S. Africa 25 11s 29 58E
138 Roper R., Australia ...14 30s 134 20E
165 Ropesville, U.S.A. 33 25N 102 10w
172 Roque Perez, Arg. 35 25s 59 24w
50 Roquefort, France 44 2N 0 20w
50 Roquefort sur Soulzon, France 43 58N 2 59E
51 Roquemaure, France ..44 3N 4 48E
64 Roquetas, Spain 40 50N 0 30E
51 Roquevaire France ...43 20N 5 36E
174 Roraima Mt., S. Amer. 5 10N 60 40w
174 Roraima, st., Brazil ... 2 0N 61 30w
157 Rorketon, Canada 51 24N 99 35w
79 Röros, Norway 62 33N 11 18E
57 Rorschach, Switz. 47 28N 9 30E
82 Rorvik, Norway 64 54N 11 15E
166 Rosa, U.S.A. 38 15N 122 16w
132 Rosa, Zambia 9 33s 31 15E
123 Rosa, C., Algeria 37 0N 8 16E
51 Rosa, Monte, Alps, Switzerland–Italy ...45 57N 7 53E
62 Rosal, Spain 41 57N 8 51w
63 Rosal de la Frontera, Sp. 37 59N 7 13w
166 Rosalia, U.S.A. 47 26N 117 25w
51 Rosans, France 44 24N 5 29E
172 Rosario, Argentina 33 0s 60 50w
175 Rosario, Maran., Brazil 3 0s 44 15w
176 Rosario, Rio Grande do Sul, Brazil 30 15s 55 0w
168 Rosario, Durango, Mex. 26 30N 105 35w
168 Rosario, Lower California, Mexico ...30 0N 116 0s
168 Rosario, Sinaloa, Mex. 23 0N 106 0w
172 Rosario, Uruguay 34 20s 57 20w
172 Rosario de Lerma, Arg. 24 59s 65 35w
172 Rosario de la Frontera, Argentina 25 50s 65 0w
173 Rosario do Sul, Brazil 30 15s 54 55w
172 Rosario Tala, Argentina 32 20s 59 10w
73 Rosarno, Italy 38 29N 15 59E
64 Rosas, Spain 42 19N 3 10E
55 Rosbach, Germany 50 48N 7 38E
147 Rosburgh, New Zealand 45 33s 169 19E
48 Roscoff, France 48 44N 4 0w
46 Roscommon, & Co., Ire. 53 38N 8 11w
162 Roscommon, U.S.A. ...44 27N 84 35w
44 Roscrea, Ire. 52 58N 7 50w
43 Rose Ness, Scot., U.K. 58 52N 2 50w
155 Rose Blanche, Canada...................47 38N 58 45w
156 Rose Harbour, Canada 52 15N 131 10w
157 Rose Valley, Canada .52 19N 103 49w
169 Roseau, Dominica, W.I. 15 20N 61 30w
164 Roseau, U.S.A. 48 56N 96 0w
166 Rosebud, Mont., U.S.A. 46 15N 106 19w
165 Rosebud, Texas, U.S.A. 31 5N 97 0w
143 Rosebud, Vic., Australia 38 21s 144 54E
166 Roseburg, U.S.A. 43 10N 123 10w
144 Rosedale, Australia ...24 38s 151 53E
143 Rosedale, Vic., Austral. 38 11s 146 48E
165 Rosedale, U.S.A. 33 51N 91 0w
39 Rosedale Abbey, England, U.K. 54 22N 0 51w
44 Rosegreen, Ireland 52 28N 7 51w
43 Rosehall, Scotland, U.K. 57 59N 4 36w
43 Rosehearty, Scot., U.K. 57 42N 2 8w
43 Rosemarkie, Scot., U.K. 57 35N 4 8w
45 Rosenallis, Ireland 53 10N 7 25w
40 Roseneath, Scotland, U.K. 56 0N 4 47w
165 Rosenberg, U.S.A. 29 30N 95 48w
49 Rosendaël, France 51 3N 2 24E
57 Rosenheim, Germany .47 51N 12 9E
71 Roseto degli Abruzzi, It. 42 40N 14 2E
157 Rosetown, Canada 51 35N 108 3w
126 Rosetta, Egypt 31 21N 30 22E
166 Roseville, U.S.A. 38 46N 121 41w
145 Rosewood, Australia 27 39s 152 36E
98 Rosh Pinna, Israel 32 58N 35 32E
98 Rosh Ze'ira, Israel 31 14N 35 15E
81 Roshage C., Denmark 57 7N 8 35E
49 Rosiéres, France 48 36N 6 20E
70 Rosignano Marittimo, It. 43 23N 10 28E
174 Rosignol, Guyana 6 15N 57 30w
78 Rosiorfi–de–Vede, Rum. 44 9N 25 0E
75 Rositsa, Bulgaria 43 57N 27 57E
75 Rositsa R., Bulgaria ..43 10N 25 30E
46 Roskeeragh Pt., Ire. ...54 22N 8 40w
42 Roskhill, Scotland, U.K. 57 24N 6 31w
81 Roskilde, Denmark ...55 38N 12 3E
81 Roskilde Fd., Denmark 55 50N 12 2E
146 Roskill, Mt., N.Z. 36 55s 174 45E
86 Roslavi, U.S.S.R. 53 57N 32 55E
143 Roslyn, N.S.W., Austral. 34 31s 149 46E
63 Rosmaninhal, Portugal 39 44N 7 5w
135 Rosmead, S. Africa ...31 29s 25 8E
81 Rösnaes C., Denmark 55 49N 11 0E
73 Rosolini, Italy 36 49N 14 58E
48 Rosporden, France 47 57N 3 50w
55 Rösrath, West Germany 50 54N 7 11E
34 Ross, Eng., U.K. 51 55N 2 34w
147 Ross, New Zealand 42 53s 170 49E
42 Ross and Cromarty, co., Scotland, U.K. .57 43N 4 50w
15 Ross I., Antarctica 77 30s 168 0E
15 Ross Dependency, Ant. 70 0s 170 5w
15 Ross Ice Shelf, Antarc. 80 0s 180 0w
166 Ross L., U.S.A. 48 50N 121 0w
144 Ross River, Australia 19 20s 146 37E
15 Ross Sea, Antarctica .74 0s 178 0E
38 Rossall Pt., Eng., U.K. 53 55N 3 2w
46 Rossan Pt., Ireland ...54 42N 8 47w
73 Rossano Calabro, Italy 39 36N 16 39E
44 Rosscahill, Ireland 53 23N 9 15w
44 Rosscarbery, Ireland .51 39N 9 1w
44 Rosscarbery B., Ireland 51 32N 9 0w
160 Rosseau, Canada 45 26N 79 39w
144 Rossel I., Terr. of Papua 11 30s 154 30E
46 Rosses B., Ireland 55 2N 8 30w
46 Rosses, The, Ireland .55 2N 8 20w
46 Rosses Point, Ireland .54 17N 8 34w
154 Rossignol, Lac, Canada 52 43N 74 0w
155 Rossignol, L., Canada 44 12N 65 0w
129 Rössing, S.W. Africa .22 30s 14 50E
156 Rossland, Canada 49 6N 117 50w
45 Rosslare, Ireland 52 17N 6 23w
56 Rosslau, Germany 51 52N 12 15E
46 Rosslea, Nre., I., U.K. 54 15N 7 11w
124 Rosso, Mauritania 16 40N 15 45w
87 Rossosh, U.S.S.R. 50 15N 39 20E
154 Rossport, Canada 48 50N 87 30w
144 Rossville, Australia ...15 48s 145 15E
157 Rosthern, Canada 52 40N 106 20w
56 Rostock, East Germany 54 4N 12 9E
87 Rostov, U.S.S.R. 57 14N 39 15E
89 Rostov–on–Don, U.S.S.R. 47 15N 39 45E
48 Rostrenen, France 48 14N 3 21w
46 Rostrevor, N. Ire., U.K. 54 7N 6 12w
82 Rösvatn L., Norway .65 45N 14 0E
165 Roswell, U.S.A. 33 26N 104 32w
41 Rosyth, Scotland, U.K. 56 2N 3 26w
63 Rota, Spain 36 37N 6 20w
80 Rotälven R., Sweden .61 30N 14 10E
165 Rotan, U.S.A. 32 52N 100 30w
56 Rotenburg, Germany 53 6N 9 24E
39 Rothbury, Eng., U.K. 55 19N 1 55w
57 Rothenburg ob der Tauber, Germany ...49 21N 10 11E
35 Rother R., Eng., U.K. 50 59N 0 40w
39 Rotherham, Eng. U.K. 53 26N 1 21w
43 Rothes Scotland U.K. 57 31N 3 12w
155 Rothesay, Canada 45 23N 66 0w
40 Rothesay, Scot., U.K. 55 50N 5 3w
43 Rothienorman, Scotland, U.K. 57 24N 2 28w
142 Rothsay, W. Australia 29 15s 116 50E
35 Rothwell, Northants, England, U.K. 52 25N 0 48w
39 Rothwell, Yorks., England, U.K. 53 46N 1 29w
109 Roti I., Indonesia 10 50s 123 0E
143 Roto, N.S.W., Austral. 33 0s 145 30E
146 Roto Aira L., N.Z. 39 3s 175 55E
146 Rotoehu L., N.Z. 38 1s 176 32E
146 Rotoiti L., N.Z. 41 51s 172 49E
146 Rotoma L., N.Z. 38 2s 176 35E
73 Rotondella, Italy 40 10N 16 30E
146 Rotoroa Lake, N.Z. 41 55s 172 39E
146 Rotorua, New Zealand 38 9s 176 16E
43 Rottal, Scotland 56 48N 3 1w
57 Rottenburg, Germany 48 28N 8 56E
58 Rottenmann, Austria .47 31N 14 22E
54 Rotterdam, Netherlands 51 55N 4 30E
35 Rottingdean, Eng., U.K. 50 48N 0 3w
142 Rottnest I., W. Austral. 32 0s 115 27E
54 Rotumeroog I., Neth. 53 33N 6 33E
57 Rottweil, Germany 48 9N 8 38E
136 Rotuma, I., Pac. Oc. .12 25s 177 5E
49 Roubaix, France 50 40N 3 10E
58 Roudnice, Cz. 50 25N 14 15E
48 Rouen, France 49 27N 1 4E
51 Rouergue, dist., France 44 20N 2 20E
44 Rough Pt., Ireland 52 19N 10 0w
147 Rough Ridge, N.Z. 45 10s 169 55E
50 Rouillac, France 45 47N 0 4w
157 Rouleau, Canada 50 10N 104 50w
166 Round Knob, Mt., U.S.A. 40 14N 78 4w
145 Round Mt., Australia .30 30s 152 7E
166 Round Mountain, U.S.A. 38 46N 117 3w
44 Roundstone, Ireland .53 24N 9 55w
166 Roundup, U.S.A. 46 25N 108 35w
45 Roundwood, Ireland .53 4N 6 14w
105 Rourkela, India, *see* Raurkela 22 14N 84 50E
43 Rousay, I., Scot., U.K. 59 10N 3 2w
161 Rouses Point, U.S.A. .44 58N 73 22w
46 Rousky, N. Ire., U.K. 54 44N 7 10E
51 Rousse, L'Ile, Corse, Fr. 42 37N 8 57E
51 Roussillon, Isère, Fr. .45 24N 4 49E
135 Rouxville, O.F.S., S. Afr. 30 11s 26 50E
154 Rouyn, Canada 48 20N 79 0w
82 Rovaniemi, Finland ...66 29N 25 52E
70 Rovato, Italy 45 34N 10 0E
89 Rovenki, U.S.S.R. 48 5N 39 27E
70 Rovereto, Italy 45 53N 11 3E
71 Rovigo, Italy 45 4N 11 48E
78 Rovinari, Rumania 46 56N 23 10E
71 Rovinj, Yugoslavia 45 18N 13 40E
86 Rovno, U.S.S.R. 50 40N 26 10E
87 Rovnoye, U.S.S.R. 50 52N 46 3E
41 Rowanburn, Scot., U.K. 55 5N 2 54w
143 Rowes, N.S.W., Australia 36 59s 149 12E
167 Rowood, U.S.A. 32 18N 112 54w
38 Rowrah, England, U.K. 54 34N 3 26w
109 Roxas, Philippines.....11 36N 122 49E
163 Roxboro, U.S.A. 36 24N 78 59w
144 Roxborough Downs, Queensland. Austral. 22 20s 138 45E
147 Roxburgh, New Zealand 45 33s 169 19E
41 Roxburgh & Co., Scotland, U.K. 55 34N 2 30w
81 Roxen L., Sweden 58 30N 15 40E
166 Roy, U.S.A. 47 17N 109 0w
142 Roy Hill, W. Australia 22 30s 120 0E
45 Royal Canal, Ireland .53 29N 7 0w
162 Royal Oak, U.S.A. 42 30N 83 5w
50 Royan, France 45 37N 1 2w
43 Roybridge, Scot., U.K. 56 53N 4 50w
49 Roye, France 47 40N 6 31E
79 Röyken, Norway 59 45N 10 30E
35 Royston, Eng., U.K. .52 3N 0 1w
38 Royton, Eng, U.K. 53 34N 2 7w
74 Rožaje, Yugoslavia ...42 50N 20 15E
86 Rozdol, U.S.S.R. 49 30N 24 1E
59 Rožnava, Cz. 48 37N 20 35E
49 Rozoy, France 48 40N 2 56E
49 Rozoy sur Serre, Fr. .49 40N 4 8E
60 Rozwadów, Poland 50 37N 22 2E
74 Rtanj Mt., Yugoslavia 43 45N 21 50w
87 Rtishchevo, U.S.S.R. .52 35N 43 50E
62 Rúa, Spain 42 24N 7 6w
37 Ruabon, Wales, U.K. 53 0N 3 3w
146 Ruahine Ra., N.Z. 39 55s 176 2E
146 Ruamahanga R., N.Z. 41 24s 175 8E
131 Ruanda, Tanzania 10 33s 34 54E
146 Ruapehu, New Zealand 39 17s 175 35E
147 Ruapuke I., N.Z. 46 46s 168 31E
146 Ruatorea, New Zealand 37 55s 178 20E
123 Ruaus, W., Libya 30 14N 15 0E
146 Ruawai, New Zealand 36 15s 173 59E
99 Rub 'al Khali, Si. Arab. 21 0N 51 0E
133 Rubbervale, S. Africa 23 51s 30 40E
131 Rubeho, Mts., Tanzania 6 50s 36 25E
34 Rubery, England, U.K. 52 24N 1 59w
88 Rubezhnoye, U.S.S.R. 49 6N 38 25E
42 Rubha Ardvule C., Scotland, U.K. 57 17N 7 32w
42 Rubha Hunish, C., Scotland, U.K. 57 42N 6 20w
130 Rubi, Congo 2 43N 25 21E
71 Rubicone R., Italy 44 0N 12 20E
174 Rubio, Venezuela 7 43N 72 22w
131 Rubona, Uganda 0 29N 30 9E
90 Rubtsovsk, U.S.S.R. .51 30N 80 50E
166 Ruby L., U.S.A. 40 10N 115 28w
166 Ruby, Mts., U.S.A. 40 30N 115 30w
144 Rubyvale, Australia ...23 25s 147 45E
88 Rucava, U.S.S.R. 56 9N 20 32E
60 Ruciane, Poland 53 40N 21 32E
79 Rud, Norway 60 1N 10 1E
81 Ruda, Sweden 57 6N 16 10E
81 Ruda Ślaska, Poland .50 16N 18 50E
101 Rudbar, Afghanistan .30 0N 62 30E
56 Ruden I., E. Germany 54 13N 13 47E
35 Rudgwick, Eng., U.K. 51 7N 0 54w
40 Rudh a'Mhail, C., Scotland, U.K. 55 55N 6 25w
42 Rudh an Dunain, C., Scotland, U.K. 57 10N 6 20w
42 Rudha–nan–Clach, C., Scotland, U.K. 57 18N 6 30w
81 Rudköbing, Denmark 54 56N 10 41E
60 Rudna, Poland 51 30N 16 17E
84 Rudnichny, U.S.S.R. .59 40N 52 20E
75 Rudnik, Bulgaria 42 36N 27 30E
74 Rudnik & Mt., Y.-slav. 44 7N 20 35E
86 Rudnya, U.S.S.R. 54 55N 31 13E
74 Rudo, Yugoslavia 43 41N 19 23E
111 Rudok, China 33 30N 79 40E
131 Rudolf L., Kenya 4 10N 36 10E
56 Rudolstadt, Germany 50 44N 11 20E
39 Rudston, Eng., U.K. .54 6N 0 19w
162 Rudyard, U.S.A. 46 14N 84 35E
49 Rue, France 50 15N 1 40E
132 Ruenya R., Rhodesia .17 0s 33 10E
127 Rufa'a, Sudan 14 44N 33 32E
50 Ruffec Charente, Fr. .46 2N 0 12w
38 Rufford, England, U.K. 53 38N 2 50w
127 Rufi, Sudan 5 58N 30 18E
131 Rufiji R., Tanzania ... 7 50s 38 15E
172 Rufino, Argentina 34 20s 62 50w
124 Rufisque, Senegal 14 40N 17 15w
132 Rufunsa, Zambia 15 4s 29 34E
34 Rugby, England, U.K. 52 23N 1 16w
164 Rugby, U.S.A. 48 21N 100 0w
34 Rugeley, Eng., U.K....52 47N 1 56w
56 Rügen I., Germany ...54 22N 13 25E
131 Rugezi, Tanzania 2 6s 33 18E
48 Rugles, France 48 50N 0 40E
98 Ruhama, Israel 31 31N 34 43E
56 Ruhla, Germany 50 53N 10 21E
56 Ruhland, Germany 51 27N 13 52E
56 Ruhr, R., Germany ...51 25N 7 15E
131 Ruhuhu, R., Tanzania 10 15s 34 55E
165 Ruidosa, U.S.A. 29 59N 104 39w
167 Ruidoso, U.S.A. 33 19N 105 39w
74 Ruj Mt., Bulgaria 42 52N 22 42E
74 Rujen Mt., Yugoslavia 42 9N 22 30E
104 Ruk, West Pakistan ...27 50N 68 42E
130 Ruki, R., Congo 0 10s 18 40E
132 Rukori, Rhodesia 16 48s 32 42E
131 Rukungiri, Uganda ... 0 53s 29 58E
131 Rukwa L., Tanzania . 7 50s 32 10E
138 Rum Jungle, Australia 13 1s 131 0E
74 Ruma, Yugoslavia 45 8N 19 50E
100 Rumah, Saudi Arabia 25 35N 47 10E
67 Rumania, st., Europe 46 0N 25 0E
127 Rumbek, Sudan 6 54N 29 37E
58 Rumburk, Cz. 50 57N 14 32E
161 Rumford, U.S.A. 44 30N 70 30w
51 Rumilly, France 45 53N 5 56E
37 Rumney, Eng. U.K. .51 32N 3 7w
131 Rumonge, Burundi ... 3 59s 29 26E
132 Rumpi, Malawi 10 59s 33 54E
156 Rumsey, Canada 51 51N 112 48w
55 Rumst, Belgium 51 5N 4 25E
144 Rumula, Australia 16 28s 145 20E
131 Rumuruti, Kenya 0 17N 36 32E
46 Runabay Hd., Northern Ireland, U.K. 55 10N 6 2w
147 Runanga, N.Z. 42 25s 171 15E
38 Runcorn, England, U.K. 53 20N 2 44w
55 Runderoth, W. Germany 50 59N 7 28E
131 Rungwa, Tanzania 6 55s 33 32E
131 Rungwa, R., Tanzania 7 15s 33 10E
132 Rungwe, Rhodesia 21 0s 31 20E
131 Rungwe & Mt., Tanz. 9 11s 33 32E
125 Runka, Nigeria 12 28N 7 20E
80 Runn L., Sweden 60 35N 15 49E
142 Runton Ra., W. Austral. 23 35s 123 15E
103 Rupā, India 27 15N 92 30E
143 Rupanyup, Australia .36 39s 14 39E
104 Rupar, India 31 2N 76 38E
108 Rupat, I., Indonesia . 1 45N 101 40E
154 Rupert House, *see* Fort Rupert, Canada 51 30N 78 40w
154 Rupert R., Canada 51 20N 77 30w
55 Ruppichteroth, Ger. ...50 51N 7 28E
105 Rupsa, India 21 44N 87 20E
175 Rupununi R., Guyana 3 30N 59 30w
55 Rur, R., Germany 50 54N 6 24E
55 Rur Reservoir, Ger. ...50 39N 6 24E
174 Rurrenabaque, Bolivia 14 30s 67 32w
64 Rus R., Spain 39 30N 2 30w
132 Rusambo, Rhodesia ...16 30s 32 4E
132 Rusape, Rhodesia 18 35s 32 8E
75 Ruse (Ruschuk), Bulg. 43 48N 25 59E
78 Ruşetu, Rumania 44 57N 27 14E
45 Rush, Ireland 53 31N 6 7w
35 Rushden, Eng., U.K. ..52 17N 0 37w
164 Rushford, U.S.A. 43 48N 91 46w
162 Rushville, Ill., U.S.A. 40 6N 90 35w
162 Rushville, Ind., U.S.A. 39 38N 85 22w
164 Rushville, Neb., U.S.A. 42 43N 102 35w
143 Rushworth, Australia 36 32s 145 1E
81 Rusken L., Sweden ...57 57N 14 17E
39 Ruskington, Eng., U.K. 53 5N 0 23w
133 Rusplaas, Trans., S Afr. 24 28s 30 32E
175 Russas, Brazil 4 56s 38 2w
157 Russell, Man., Canada....................50 50N 101 20w
161 Russell, Ont., Canada 45 16N 75 21w
146 Russell, New Zealand 35 16s 174 10E
164 Russell, U.S.A. 38 56N 98 55w
105 Russellkonda, India ...19 57N 84 42E
165 Russellville, Ark., U.S.A. 35 15N 93 0w
163 Russellville, Ky., U.S.A. 36 50N 86 50w
163 Russellville, Ala., U.S.A. 34 30N 87 44w
71 Russi, Italy 44 21N 12 1E
91 Russian S.F.S.R. 62 0N 105 0E
14 Russkoye Ustie, U.S.S.R. 71 0N 149 0E
59 Rust, Austria 47 49N 16 42E
89 Rustavi, U.S.S.R. 41 45N 44 30E
133 Rustenburg, S. Africa 25 41s 27 14E
135 Rustig, O.F.S., S. Africa 27 22s 27 9E
165 Ruston, U.S.A. 32 30N 92 40w
100 Rutba, Iraq 33 4N 40 15E
63 Rute, Spain 37 19N 4 29w
109 Ruteng, Indonesia 8 26s 120 30E
160 Ruth, Mich., U.S.A. ...43 42N 82 45w
166 Ruth, Nev., U.S.A. 39 15N 115 1w
143 Rutherglen, Australia 36 5s 146 29E
40 Rutherglen, Scot., U.K. 55 50N 4 11w
37 Ruthin, Wales, U.K. .53 7N 3 20w
43 Ruthven, Scot., U.K. .57 4N 4 2w
41 Ruthwell, Scot., U.K. 55 0N 3 24w
73 Rutigliano, Italy 41 1N 17 0E

MAP
35 Rutland, co., Eng., U.K. ...52 38N 0 40W
161 Rutland, U.S.A. ...43 38N 73 0W
107 Rutland I., Andaman Is. ...11 25N 92 40E
157 Rutledge L., Canada .16 58N 110 58W
131 Rutshuru, Congo ... 1 13S 29 25E
54 Ruurlo, Netherlands .52 5N 6 24E
73 Ruvo di Puglia, Italy 41 7N 16 27E
131 Ruvu, Tanzania ... 6 49S 38 43E
131 Ruvuma, prov., Tanz. 11 0S 36 30E
131 Ruvuma, R., Tanzania ...11 30S 36 10E
100 Ruwaidha, Si. Arabia 23 40N 44 40E
100 Ruwandiz, Iraq ...36 40N 44 32E
131 Ruwenzori Mts., Africa ... 0 30N 29 55E
132 Ruya R., Rhodesia ...17 0S 31 0E
87 Ruzayevka, U.S.S.R. .54 10N 45 0E
75 Rŭzhevo Konare, Bulg. ...42 23N 24 46E
131 Ruzizi, R., Congo ... 2 55S 29 10E
59 Ružomberok, Cz. ...49 3N 19 17E
86 Rylsk, U.S.S.R. ...51 30N 34 51E
131 Rwanda, st., Africa ... 2 0S 30 0E
81 Ryaberg, Sweden ...56 47N 13 15E
75 Ryakhovo, Bulgaria ...44 0N 26 18E
40 Ryan, L., Scot., U.K. 55 0N 5 2W
87 Ryazan, U.S.S.R. ...54 50N 39 40E
87 Ryazhsk, U.S.S.R. ...53 45N 40 3E
90 Rybache, U.S.S.R. ...46 40N 81 20E
84 Rybachi Pen., U.S.S.R. ...69 43N 32 0E
87 Rybinsk (Shcherbakov), U.S.S.R. ...58 5N 38 50E
87 Rybinsk Res., U.S.S.R. ...58 30N 38 0E
59 Rybnik, Poland ...50 6N 18 32E
88 Rybnitsa, U.S.S.R. ...47 45N 29 0E
60 Rychwal, Poland ...52 4N 18 10E
81 Ryd, Sweden ...56 27N 14 42E
38 Rydal, England, U.K. 54 28N 2 59W
34 Ryde, England, U.K. .50 44N 1 9W
81 Rydö, Sweden ...56 58N 13 10E
81 Rydsnäs, Sweden ...56 47N 15 12E
81 Rye, Denmark ...56 5N 9 45E
35 Rye & B., Eng., U.K. 50 57N 0 46E
166 Rye Patch Res., U.S.A. ...40 45N 118 20W
166 Ryegate, U.S.A. ...46 21N 109 27W
39 Ryehope, Eng., U.K. .54 52N 1 21W
143 Rylstone, N.S.W., Austral. ...32 46S 149 58E
59 Rymanów, Poland ...49 35N 21 51E
81 Ryningsnäs, Sweden .87 17N 15 58E
60 Rypin, Poland ...53 3N 19 32E
39 Ryton, Durham, England, U.K. ...54 58N 1 44W
34 Ryton, Warwick, England, U.K. ...52 23N 1 25W
113 Ryukyu Is., Asia ...26 0N 127 0E
60 Rzepin, Poland ...52 20N 14 49E
59 Rzeszów, Poland ...50 5N 21 58E
86 Rzhev, U.S.S.R. ...56 20N 34 20E

S

107 Sa Dec, S. Vietnam ...10 20N 105 46E
98 Sa'ad (Muharraga), Isr. ...31 28N 34 33E
101 Sa'ādatābād, Iran ...30 10N 53 5E
135 Saaibult, O.F.S., S. Afr. ...28 31S 27 30E
56 Saale R., Germany ...51 25N 11 56E
56 Saaler Boden, G., Ger. 55 17N 12 25E
56 Saalfeld, Germany ...50 39N 11 21E
56 Saalfelden, Austria ...47 26N 12 51E
57 Saane R., Switzerland 46 23N 7 18E
57 Saanen, Switzerland ...46 29N 7 15E
57 Saar, land, Germany .49 20N 0 75E
49 Saar (Sarre) R., Ger .49 20N 6 45E
57 Saarbrücken, Germany ...49 15N 6 58E
57 Saarburg, Germany ...49 36N 6 32E
86 Saaremaa, U.S.S.R. ...58 30N 22 30E
57 Saarlouis, Germany ...49 19N 6 45E
176 Saavedra, Chile ...38 50S 73 20W
169 Saba I., Leeward Is. .17 30N 63 10W
74 Sabac, Yugoslavia ...44 48N 19 42E
64 Sabadell, Spain ...41 28N 2 7E
108 Sabah, terr., Malaysia 6 0N 117 0E
107 Sabak, Malaysia ... 3 46N 100 58E
131 Sabaki, R., Kenya ... 3 9S 40 8E
169 Sabana, Dom. Rep. ...19 7N 69 40W
174 Sabanalarga, Colombia ...10 38N 74 55W
108 Saband, I., Indonesia . 5 50N 95 15E
175 Sabará Brazil ...19 55S 43 55W
109 Sabarania, Indonesia . 2 5S 138 18E
106 Sabari R., India ...18 0N 81 25E
98 Sabastya, Jordan ...32 17N 35 12E
161 Sabattis, U.S.A. ...44 6N 74 40W
72 Sabaudia, Italy ...41 17N 13 2E
127 Sabderat, Ethiopia ...15 26N 36 42E
123 Sabhah, Libya ...27 9N 14 29E
123 Sabhah Oasis, Libya .27 15N 14 6E
132 Sabi, R., Rhodesia ...18 50S 31 40E
133 Sabie, Trans., S. Africa ...25 4S 30 48E
168 Sabinal, Mexico ...30 50N 107 25W
165 Sabinal, U.S.A. ...29 20N 99 27W
168 Sabinas, Mexico ...27 50N 101 10W
168 Sabinas Hidalgo, Mex. 26 40N 100 10W
165 Sabine, U.S.A. ...29 42N 93 54W
165 Sabine, R., U.S.A. ...31 30N 93 35W
68 Sabine, Monti, Italy ...42 15N 12 50E
59 Sabinov, Czechoslovakia ...49 6N 21 5E
89 Sabirabad, U.S.S.R. ...40 0N 48 30E
123 Sabkhat Tawurgha, Lib. ...31 48N 15 30E
109 Sablayan, Philippines 12 5N 120 50E
48 Sable, France ...47 50N 0 21W
133 Sable, Trans., S. Africa ...25 3S 30 49E
155 Sable C., Canada ...43 29N 65 38W
159 Sable, C., U.S.A. ...25 5N 81 0W
155 Sable I., Canada ...44 0N 60 0W
62 Sabor R., Portugal ...41 16N 7 10W
124 Sabou, Upper Volta ...12 1N 2 28W
123 Sabratha (Sabrata), Libya ...32 47N 12 29E
15 Sabrina Coast, Antarc. ...67 0S 120 0E
113 Sabtang I., Philippines ...20 15N 121 30E
62 Sabugal, Portugal ...40 20N 7 5W
101 Sabzevār, Iran ...36 15N 57 40E
101 Sabzvāran, Iran ...28 45N 57 50E
164 Sac City, U.S.A. ...42 26N 95 0W
64 Sacedón, Spain ...40 29N 2 41W
154 Sachigo, L., Canada ...53 50N 92 12W
89 Sachkhere, U.S.S.R. ...42 25N 43 28E
71 Sacile, Italy ...45 58N 16 7E
161 Sackett's Harbor, U.S.A. ...43 56N 72 38W
57 Säckingen, W. Germany ...47 34N 7 56E
162 Saco, Me., U.S.A. ...43 30N 70 27W
166 Saco, Mont., U.S.A. ...48 28N 107 19W
43 Sacquoy Hd., Scot., U.K. ...59 12N 3 5W
166 Sacramento, U.S.A. ...38 39N 121 30E
167 Sacramento Mts., U.S.A. ...32 30N 105 30W
166 Sacramento, R., U.S.A. ...39 30N 122 0W
65 Sacratif, Cabo, Spain .36 42N 3 28W
39 Sacriston, Eng., U.K. 54 49N 1 38W
78 Săcueni, Rumania ...47 20N 22 5E
62 Sada, Spain ...43 22N 8 15W
64 Sadaba, Spain ... 2 19N 1 12W
131 Sa'dani, Tanzania ... 5 58S 38 35E
107 Sadao, Thailand ... 6 38N 100 26E
106 Sadasivpet, India ...17 38N 77 50E
40 Saddall, Scotland, U.K. ...55 31N 5 30W
45 Saddle, Hd., Ireland .54 0N 10 10W
42 Saddle, The, Scot., U.K. ...57 10N 5 27W
125 Sade, Nigeria ...11 22N 10 45E
132 Sadiba, Botswana ...18 53S 23 1E
114 Sado, I., Japan ...38 15N 138 30E
63 Sado R., Portugal ...38 10N 8 22W
103 Sadon, Burma ...25 28N 98 0E
89 Sadon, U.S.S.R. ...42 52N 43 58E
104 Sadri, India ...24 28N 74 30E
81 Sæby, Denmark ...57 21N 10 30E
160 Saegerstown, U.S.A. ...80 10N 41 42W
64 Saelices, Spain ...39 55N 2 49W
126 Safāga I., Egypt ...26 42N 34 0E
126 Safaha, Saudi Arabia .26 25N 39 0E
100 Sataniy, Saudi Arabia 28 5N 48 42E
59 Šafárikovo Cz. ...48 25N 20 20E
101 Safed Koh, Mts., Afghan. ...34 15N 64 0E
80 Saffle, Sweden ...59 8N 12 55E
167 Safford, U.S.A. ...32 54N 109 52W
35 Saffron Walden, England, U.K. ...52 2N 0 15E
98 Safi, Jordan ...31 2N 35 28E
122 Safi, Morocco ...32 25N 9 9W
48 Safiah, Israel ...31 27N 34 46E
86 Safonovo, U.S.S.R. ...65 40N 47 50E
98 Safranbolu, Turkey ...41 15N 32 34E
161 Sag Harbour, U.S.A. .40 59N 72 17W
109 Saga, Indonesia ... 2 40S 132 55E
114 Saga, Japan ...33 15N 130 20E
103 Sagaing, Burma ...22 0N 96 0E
124 Sagala, Mali ...14 9N 6 38W
104 Sagar, India ...23 50N 78 50E
106 Sagara, India ...14 14N 75 6E
80 Sågen, Sweden ...60 17N 14 10E
37 Sageston, Wales, U.K. 51 41N 4 48W
162 Saginaw, U.S.A. ...43 26N 83 55W
111 Sagil, Mongolia ...50 15N 91 15E
153 Saglout (Sugluk), Canada ...62 30N 74 15W
51 Sagone, Corsica, France ...42 7N 8 42E
51 Sagone G., Corsica, Fr. ...42 4N 8 40E
63 Sagres, Portugal ...37 0N 8 58W
169 Sagua la Grande, Cuba ...22 50N 80 10W
167 Saguache, U.S.A. ...38 10N 106 4W
155 Saguenay R., Canada .48 22N 70 30W
64 Sagunto, Spain ...39 42N 0 18W
79 Sagvåg, Norway ...59 46N 5 25E
126 Sahaba, Sudan ...18 57N 30 25E
62 Sahágun, Spain ...42 18N 5 2W
98 Saham, Jordan ...32 42N 35 46E
120 Sahara Desert, Africa 23 0N 5 0W
122 Saharien, Atlas, Mts., Algeria ...34 9N 3 29E
104 Saharanpur, India ...29 58N 77 33E
104 Sahaswan, India ...28 5N 78 45E
124 Sahel, Canal du, Mali .14 20N 6 0W
105 Sahibganj, India ...25 12N 87 55E
98 Sahl Arraba, Jordan .37 26N 35 12E
104 Sahiwal, W.Pakistan .30 45N 73 8E
168 Sahuaripa, Mexico ...29 30N 109 0W
167 Sahuarita, U.S.A. ...31 58N 110 59W
168 Sahuayo, Mexico ...20 4N 102 43W
59 Sahy, Czechoslovakia .48 4N 18 55E
121 Sa'id Bundas, Sudan . 8 24N 24 48E
101 Sa'īdābād, Iran ...29 30N 55 45E
122 Saida, Algeria ...34 50N 0 11E
106 Saidapet, India ...13 0N 80 15E
102 Saidu, Pakistan ...34 50N 72 15E
101 Saighan, Afghanistan ...35 10N 67 55E
50 Saignes, France ...45 20N 2 31E
99 Saihut, S. Yemen ...15 12N 51 10E
107 Saigon, S. Vietnam ...10 58N 106 40E
101 Saih-al-Malih, Muscat & Oman ...23 37N 58 31E
114 Saijo, Japan ...34 0N 133 5E
114 Saiki, Japan ...32 35N 131 50E
103 Saikhoa Ghat, Iran ...27 50N 95 40E
51 Saillans, France ...44 42N 5 12E
109 Sailolof, Indonesia ... 1 7S 130 46E
84 Saimaa L., Finland ...61 33N 29 35E
41 St. Abbs, Scot., U.K. .55 54N 2 7W
41 St. Abbs' Head, Scotland, U.K. ...55 55N 2 10W
58 St. Aegyd, Austria ...47 52N 15 33E
50 St. Affrique, France ...43 58N 2 52E
36 St. Agnes, Eng., U.K. 50 18N 5 13W
36 St. Agnes Hd., England, U.K. ...50 19N 5 14W
36 St. Agnes I., Eng., U.K. ...49 53N 6 20W
51 St. Agrève, France ...45 1N 4 23E
48 St. Aignan, France ...47 16N 1 21E
155 St. Albans, Canada ...47 51N 55 50W
144 St. Albans, Australia .24 43S 139 56E
35 St. Albans, Eng., U.K. ...51 44N 0 19W
161 St. Albans, Vt., U.S.A. ...44 49N 73 7W
162 St. Albans, W. Va., U.S.A. ...38 21N 81 50W
34 St. Albans Head, England, U.K. ...50 34N 2 3W
156 St. Albert, Canada ...53 37N 113 40W
49 St. Amand, France ...50 25N 3 6E
50 St. Amand Montrond, France ...46 3N 2 30E
49 St. Amarin, France ...47 53N 7 3E
51 St. Amour, France ...46 27N 5 20E
58 St. Andra, Austria ...46 46N 14 50E
48 St. André de l'Eure, Fr. ...48 54N 1 16E
50 St. André de Cubzac, Fr. ...44 59N 0 29W
51 St. André les Alpes, Fr. ...43 58N 6 30E
129 St. André, C. Malag. .16 10S 44 27E
155 St. Andrews, Canada .47 45N 59 15W
147 St. Andrews, N.Z. ...44 33S 171 10E
41 St. Andrews, Scot., U.K. ...56 20N 2 48W
161 St. Anicet, Canada ...45 9N 74 23W
155 St. Ann B., Canada ...46 22N 60 25W
48 St. Anne, Chan. Is., U.K. ...49 43N 2 11W
38 St. Anne's, Eng., U.K. ...53 45N 3 2W
41 St. Ann's, Scot., U.K. 55 14N 3 28W
37 St. Anns Hd., Wales, United Kingdom ...51 41N 5 11W
166 St. Anthony, U.S.A. ...44 0N 111 49W
50 St. Antonin, France ...44 10N 1 45E
143 St. Arnaud, Australia 36 32S 143 16E
147 St. Arnaud Ra., N.Z. .42 1S 172 53E
155 St. Arthur, Canada ...47 32N 67 28W
37 St. Asaph, Wales, U.K. ...53 15N 3 27W
48 St. Aubin du Cormier, France ... 8 15N 41 24W
155 St. Augustin, Canada .51 19N 58 48W
163 St. Augustine, U.S.A. 29 52N 81 20W
49 St. Avold, France ...49 7N 6 40E
74 St. Bar, Yugoslavia ...42 7N 19 13E
169 St. Barthelémy I., W.I. ...17 50N 62 50W
147 St. Bathans, N.Z. ...44 53S 170 0E
147 St. Bathan's Mt., N.Z. ...44 45S 169 45E
38 St. Bees, Eng., U.K. .54 29N 3 36W
50 St. Benoit du Sault, Fr. ...46 27N 1 22E
51 St. Bernard, Col du Pt., France ...45 40N 7 0E
57 St. Blasien, Germany .47 47N 8 7E
36 St. Blazey, Eng., U.K. ...50 22N 4 48W
157 St. Boniface, Canada .49 50N 97 10W
51 St. Bonnet, France ...44 40N 6 5E
41 St. Boswells, Scot., U.K. ...55 34N 2 39W
48 St. Brévin, France ...47 14N 2 10W
34 St. Briavels, Eng., U.K. ...51 44N 2 39W
48 St. Brice en Coglès, France ...48 25N 1 21W
155 St. Bride's, Canada ...46 56N 54 10W
48 St. Brieuc, France ...48 31N 2 48W
36 St. Budeaux, Eng., U.K. ...50 23N 4 10W
36 St. Buryan, Eng., U.K. ...50 4N 5 34W
48 St. Cast, France ...48 39N 2 16W
154 St. Catharines, Canada ...43 10N 79 15W
163 St. Catherines I., U.S.A. ...31 35N 81 10W
34 St. Catherine's Pt. England, U.K. ...50 34N 1 18W
50 St. Céré, France ...44 52N 1 53E
57 St. Cergue, Switzerland ...46 27N 6 10E
50 St. Cernin, France ...45 5N 2 25E
51 St. Chamond, France .45 31N 4 32E
162 St. Charles, Ill., U.S.A. ...41 55N 88 21W
164 St. Charles, Mo., U.S.A. ...38 46N 90 30W
50 St. Chely d'Apcher, Fr. ...44 48N 3 16E
50 St. Chinian, France ...43 26N 2 56E
169 St. Christopher (St. Kitts), Leeward Is. .17 20N 62 40W
50 St. Ciers, France ...45 16N 0 38W
160 St. Clair, Mich, U.S.A. 42 47N 82 27W
161 St. Clair, Pa., U.S.A. .40 42N 76 12W
160 St. Clair, L., Canada .42 30N 82 45W
160 St. Clair R., N. Amer. 42 40N 82 20W
160 St. Clairsville, U.S.A. .40 5N 80 53W
50 St. Claud, France ...45 54N 0 27E
51 St. Claude, France ...46 24N 5 52E
37 St. Clears, Wales, U.K. ...51 48N 4 30W
163 St. Cloud, Fla., U.S.A. 28 15N 81 15W
164 St. Cloud, Minn., U.S.A. ...45 30N 94 11W
155 St. Coeur de Marie, Can. ...48 39N 71 43W
36 St. Columb Major, England, U.K. ...50 26N 4 56W
43 St. Combs, Scot., U.K. ...57 40N 1 55W
169 St. Croix I., Virgin Is. 17 45N 64 45W
164 St. Croix R., U.S.A. ...45 20N 92 50W
164 St. Croix Falls, U.S.A. 45 18N 92 22W
50 St. Cyprien France ...42 37N 3 0E
43 St. Cyrus, Scot., U.K. 56 47N 2 25W
70 St. Damiano d'Asti, It. ...44 51N 8 4E
37 St. David's Head, Wales, U.K. ...51 54N 5 16W
48 St. Denis d'Orques, Fr. ...48 2N 0 20W
49 St. Denis, Seine, France ...48 57N 2 20E
49 St. Dié, France ...48 18N 6 56E
49 St. Dizier, France ...48 40N 5 0E
37 St. Dogmaels, Wales, United Kingdom ...52 6N 4 42W
36 St. Dominick, Eng., U.K. ...50 28N 4 15W
37 St. Donats, Wales, U.K. ...51 23N 3 32W
152 St. Elias, Mt., Alas., U.S.A. ...60 20N 141 59W
152 St. Elias Mts., Canada 60 0N 138 0W
50 St. Eloy, France ...46 10N 2 51E
36 St. Endellion Eng., U.K. ...50 33N 4 49W
36 St. Enoder, Eng., U.K. ...50 22N 4 57W
36 St. Erth, England, U.K. ...50 10N 5 26W
51 St. Étienne, Loire, Fr. 45 27N 4 22E
51 St. Étienne de Tinée, Fr. ...44 15N 6 57E
161 St. Eugene, Canada ...45 30N 74 28W
169 St. Eustatius I., Leeward Islands ...17 20N 63 0W
154 St. Félicien, Canada ...48 40N 72 25W
43 St. Fergus, Scot., U.K. ...57 33N 1 50W
41 St. Fillans, Scot., U.K ...56 25N 4 7W
44 St. Finian's B., Ireland ...51 50N 10 22W
155 St. Fintan's, Canada .48 10N 58 50W
51 St. Florent, Corsica, Fr. ...42 40N 9 20E
49 St. Florent sur Cher, Fr. ...47 0N 2 1E
49 St. Forentin, France .48 0N 3 42E
50 St. Flour, France ...45 3N 3 7E
51 St. Fons, France ...45 43N 4 52E
164 St. Francis, U.S.A. ...39 48N 101 47W
134 St. Francis C., S. Africa ...34 14S 24 49E
135 St. Francis B., S. Africa ...34 12S 24 55E
161 St. Francis L., Canada 45 10N 74 20W
165 St. Francis R., U.S.A. 32 25N 90 36W
48 St. Fulgent, France ...46 50N 1 10W
154 St. Gabriel de Brandon, Canada ...46 17N 73 24W
57 St. Gallen, Switzerland ...47 25N 9 22E
50 St. Gaudens, France ...43 7N 0 44E
48 St. Gaultier, France ...46 37N 1 24E
51 St. Gengoux le National, France ...46 40N 4 39E
50 St. Geniez d'Olt, France ...44 28N 2 58E
145 St. George, Australia .28 1S 148 41E
169 St. George, Bermuda .32 24N 64 42W
155 St. George, Canada ...45 11N 66 57W
163 St. George, S.C., U.S.A. ...33 13N 80 37W
167 St. George, Utah, U.S.A. ...37 10N 113 35W
144 St. George, Queens., Austral. ...28 2S 148 35E
155 St. George C., Canada 48 30N 59 16W
163 St. George, C., U.S.A. 29 36N 85 2W
143 St. George Hd., N.S.W., Australia ...35 11S 150 45E
157 St. George West, Can. 50 33N 96 7W
155 St. George's, Canada .48 26N 58 31W
155 St. Georges, Canada ...46 8N 70 40W
154 St. Georges, Canada ...46 42N 72 35W
54 St. Georges, Belgium .50 37N 4 20E
175 St. Georges, Fr. Gui. . 4 0N 52 0W
169 St. George's, Grenada 12 5N 61 43W
29 St. George's Channel, U.K. ...52 0N 6 0W
55 St. Gérard, Belgium ...50 21N 4 44E
49 St. Germain, France ...48 53N 2 5E
50 St. Germain de Calberte France ...44 14N 3 50E
50 St. Germain des Fossés, France ...46 12N 3 21E
49 St. Germain-du-Plain, France ...46 45N 5 0E
51 St. Germain-Laval, Fr. ...45 49N 4 2E
50 St. Germain-Lembron, France ...45 27N 3 13E
36 St. Germans, Eng., U.K. ...50 24N 4 19W
51 St. Gervais, Haute Savoie, France ...45 53N 6 42E
50 St. Gervais, Puy de Dôme, France ...46 4N 2 50E
48 St. Gildas, Pte. de, Fr. ...47 8N 2 13W
51 St. Gilles, Gard, France ...43 41N 4 26E
48 St. Gilles, Vendée, Fr. 46 42N 1 56W
50 St. Girons, Ariège, Fr. 42 58N 1 7E
80 St. Gla, L., Sweden ...59 35N 12 30E
57 St. Gotthard P., Switz. ...46 33N 8 33E
37 St. Gowans Hd., Wales, U.K. ...51 35N 4 56W
37 St. Harmon, Wales, U.K. ...52 21N 3 29W
81 St. Heddinge, Denmark ...55 9N 12 26E
17 St. Helena I., Atl. Oc. 15 55S 5 44W
66 St. Helena, U.S.A. ...38 29N 122 30W
134 St. Helena B., S. Africa ...32 40S 18 10E
34 St. Helens, I.o.W., England, U.K. ...50 42N 1 7W
38 St. Helens, Lancs., England, U.K. ...53 28N 2 43W
166 St. Helens, U.S.A. ...45 55N 122 50W
48 St. Helier, Jersey, U.K. ...49 11N 2 6W
48 St. Hilaire, France ...48 35N 1 7W
49 St. Hippolyte, Doubs, France ...47 20N 6 50E
50 St. Hippolyte du Fort, France ...43 58N 3 52E
49 St. Honoré, France ...46 54N 3 50E
54 St. Hubert, Belgium .50 2N 5 23E
55 St. Hubert, W. Ger. ...51 23N 6 26E
154 St. Hyacinthe, Canada ...45 40N 72 58W
162 St. Ignace, U.S.A. ...45 53N 84 43W
154 St. Ignace I., Canada .48 45N 88 0W
166 St. Ignatius, U.S.A. ...47 25N 114 2W
57 St. Imier, Switzerland 47 9N 6 58E
57 St. Ingbert, Germany 49 16N 7 6E
36 St. Issey, Eng., U.K. .50 30N 4 55W
36 St. Ives, Cornwall, England, U.K. ...50 13N 5 29W
35 St. Ives, Hunts., England, U.K. ...52 20N 0 5W
36 St. Ives Bay, Eng., U.K. ...50 15N 5 27W
48 St. James, France ...48 30N 1 20W
164 St. James, U.S.A. ...43 57N 94 40W
156 St. James C., Canada .51 55N 131 0W
154 St. Jean, Canada ...45 20N 73 50W
157 St. Jean Baptiste, Can. ...49 15N 97 20W
128 St. Jean, C., Rio Muni ... 1 5N 9 20E
50 St. Jean de Luz, France ...43 24N 1 39W
51 St. Jean de Maurienne, France .45 17N 6 20E
48 St. Jean de Monts, Fr. 46 47N 2 3W
50 St. Jean du Gard, Fr. 44 7N 3 52E
51 St. Jean-en-Royans, Fr. ...45 1N 5 18E
155 St. Jean-Port-Joli, Can. ...47 15N 70 13W
155 St. Jérome, L. St. John, Quebec, Can. 48 26N 71 53W
154 St. Jerome, Terrebonne, Quebec, Canada ...45 45N 74 0W
58 St. Johann, Austria ...47 22N 13 12E
155 St. John, Canada ...45 20N 66 8W
165 St. John, Kan., U.S.A. ...37 59N 98 45W
164 St. John, N.D., U.S.A. ...48 58N 99 40W
155 St. John L., Canada ...48 40N 72 0W
155 St. John R., Canada .46 30N 67 40W
155 St. John's, Canada ...47 35N 52 40W
38 St. Johns, I. of M., U.K. ...54 13N 4 38W
167 St. Johns, Ariz., U.S.A. ...34 31N 109 26W
162 St. Johns, Mich., U.S.A. ...43 0N 84 38W
162 St. John's I. (Zeberged, Geziret) Egypt ...23 40N 36 12E
46 St. John's Pt., Ireland 54 35N 8 26W
46 St. Johns Pt., N. Ire., U.K. ...54 14N 5 40W
163 St. Johns, R., U.S.A. .30 20N 81 30W
38 St. Johns Chapel, England, U.K. ...54 44N 2 10W
161 St. Johnsbury, U.S.A. 44 25N 72 1W
46 St. Johnstown, Ireland ...54 56N 7 29W
161 St. Johnsville, U.S.A. 43 0N 74 43W
55 St. Joris Winge, Belg. 50 54N 4 52E
165 St. Joseph, La., U.S.A. ...31 55N 91 15W
162 St. Joseph's, Mich., U.S.A. ...42 5N 86 30W
164 St. Joseph, Mo., U.S.A. ...39 40N 94 50W

MAP
154 St. Joseph I., Canada 46 12N 83 58W
154 St. Joseph L., Canada 51 10N 90 50W
162 St. Joseph R., U.S.A. 42 0N 85 30W
154 St. Jovite, Canada 46 8N 74 38W
51 St. Julien, Chapteuil, Fr. 45 3N 4 4E
51 St. Julien, Haute Savoie, France 46 8N 6 5E
49 St. Julien du Sault, Fr. 48 1N 3 17E
50 St. Junien, France 45 53N 0 52E
36 St. Just, England, U.K. 50 7N 5 41W
50 St. Just en Chevalet, Fr. 45 55N 3 50E
49 St. Just en Chaussée, Fr. 49 30N 2 27E
50 St. Justin, France 43 59N 0 14W
81 St. Karlsö, I., Sweden 57 17N 17 58E
36 St. Keverne, Eng., U.K. 50 3N 5 5W
36 St. Kew, England, U.K. 50 34N 4 48W
147 St. Kilda, New Zealand 45 53S 170 31E
28 St. Kilda, I., Scot., U.K. 57 40N 8 50W
161 St. Kitts (St. Christopher) Leeward Is. 17 20N 62 40W
157 St. Laurent, Canada ...50 25N 97 58W
51 St. Laurent, Jura, Fr. 46 35N 5 56E
51 St. Laurent du Pont, France 45 24N 5 42E
155 St. Lawrence, Gulf of, & R., Canada 48 25N 62 0W
155 St. Lawrence, Canada 46 54N 55 23W
144 St. Lawrence, Australia 22 16S 149 31E
152 St. Lawrence I., Alaska, U.S.A. 63 0N 170 0W
155 St. Leonard, Canada .47 12N 67 58W
50 St. Léonard de Noblat, France 45 50N 1 30E
35 St. Leonards, Eng., U.K. 50 51N 0 34E
36 St. Levan, Eng., U.K. 50 3N 5 36W
154 St. Lin, Canada 45 44N 73 46W
48 St. Lô, France 49 8N 1 6W
124 St. Louis, Senegal 16 8N 16 27W
162 St. Louis, Mich., U.S.A. 43 27N 84 38W
164 St. Louis, Mo., U.S.A. 38 40N 90 20W
164 St. Louis R., U.S.A. ...47 15N 92 45W
49 St. Loup sur Semouse, France 47 53N 6 16E
169 St. Lucia I., Wind. Is. 14 0N 60 50W
135 St. Lucia Lake, S. Afr. 28 5S 32 30E
169 St. Maarten I., Leew. Is. 18 0N 63 5W
36 St. Mabyn, Eng., U.K. 50 30N 4 45W
42 St. Magnus B., Scot. U.K. 60 25N 1 35W
50 St. Maixent, France ...46 25N 0 12W
48 St. Malo, France 48 40N 2 0W
48 St. Malo, G. de France 48 50N 2 30W
169 St. Marc, Haiti 19 10N 72 50W
51 St. Marcellin, France .45 10N 5 20E
48 St. Marcouf Is., France 49 30N 1 10W
35 St. Margaret's-at-Cliffe, England, U.K. 51 10N 1 23E
43 St. Margarets Hope, Scotland, U.K. 58 49N 2 58W
166 St. Maries, U.S.A. 47 17N 116 34W
135 St. Marks, S. Africa ...32 0S 27 26E
49 St. Martin, France 50 42N 1 38E
169 St. Martin I., Leeward Is. 18 0N 63 0W
157 St. Martin L., Canada 51 40N 98 30W
51 St. Martin Yésubie, Fr. 44 4N 7 15E
155 St. Martins, Canada ...45 22N 65 38W
36 St. Martin's I., England, United Kingdom 49 58N 6 16W
165 St. Martinsville, U.S.A. 30 10N 91 50W
50 St. Martory, France ...43 10N 0 55E
155 St. Mary B., Canada .46 50N 53 50W
124 St. Mary C., Gambia .13 24N 13 10E
106 St. Mary Is., India 13 20N 74 35E
34 St. Mary Bourne, England, U.K. 51 16N 1 24W
145 St. Mary's, Australia .41 32S 148 11E
160 St. Mary's, Ont., Canada 43 20N 81 10W
155 St. Mary's, Newf., Canada 46 56N 53 34W
43 St. Marys, Scot., U.K. 58 53N 2 55W
162 St. Mary's, Ohio, U.S.A. 40 33N 84 20W
160 St. Mary's, Pa., U.S.A. 41 30N 78 33W
155 St. Mary's Bay, Canada 46 56N 53 45W
155 St. Mary's, C., Canada 46 50N 54 12W
36 St. Mary's I., Scilly Is., U.K. 49 55N 6 18W
36 St. Mary's Sd., England, United Kingdom 49 53N 6 19W
48 St. Mathieu, Pt. de, Fr. 48 20N 4 48W
107 St. Matthew's I., Burma, see Zadetkyi Kyon 10 0N 98 25E
49 St. Maur, France 48 49N 2 30E
154 St. Maurice R., Canada 47 20N 72 50W
36 St. Mawes, Eng., U.K. 50 10N 5 1W
50 St. Médard de Guizières, France ...45 1N 0 3W
48 St. Méen, France 48 10N 2 11W
36 St. Merryn, Eng., U.K. 50 31N 4 58W
14 St. Michael, Alas., U.S.A. 63 30N 162 10W
167 St. Michaels, U.S.A. ...35 45N 109 5W
36 St. Michael's Mt., England, U.K. 50 7N 5 30W
51 St. Michel, Savoie, Fr. 45 15N 6 29E
49 St. Mihiel, France 48 54N 5 30E
36 St. Minver, Eng., U.K. 50 34N 4 52W
41 St. Monans, Scot., U.K. 56 13N 2 46W
57 St. Moritz, Switzerland 46 30N 9 50E
48 St. Nazaire, France ...47 18N 2 11W
35 St. Neots, Eng., U.K. 52 14N 0 16W
49 St. Nicholas, France ...48 38N 6 18E
54 St. Niklaas, Belgium .51 10N 4 9E
42 St. Ninians, I., Scot., U.K. 59 59N 1 20W
160 St. Ola Sta., Canada .44 50N 77 38W
81 St. Olaf, Sweden 55 40N 14 12E
49 St. Omer, France 50 45N 2 13E
35 St. Osyth, Eng., U.K. 51 47N 1 4E
49 St. Ouen, France 48 50N 2 20E
155 St. Pacome, Canada ...47 24N 69 58W
50 St. Palais, France 45 40N 1 8W
155 St. Pamphile, Canada 46 58N 69 48W
50 St. Pardoux, France ...45 29N 0 44E
155 St. Pascal, Canada 47 32N 69 48W
44 St. Patrickswell, Ireland 52 36N 8 43W
157 St. Paul, Canada 51 34N 57 47W
164 St. Paul, Minn., U.S.A. 44 54N 93 5W
164 St. Paul, Neb., U.S.A. 41 15N 98 30W
16 St. Paul, I., Atlantic Oc. 0 50N 31 40W
155 St. Paul, I., Canada ...47 12N 60 9W
11 St. Paul, I., Ind. Oc. .30 40S 77 34E
50 St. Paul de Fenouillet, France 42 50N 2 28E
155 St. Paul's B., Canada .49 48N 57 58W
51 St. Péray, France 44 57N 4 52E
48 St. Père en Retz, Fr. .47 12N 2 1W
45 St. Peter, Styria, Austria 47 11N 14 12E
164 St. Peter, U.S.A 44 15N 93 57W
48 St. Peter Port, Channel Is., U.K. ...49 27N 2 31W
155 St. Peters, N.S., Can. .45 40N 60 53W
155 St. Peters, P.E.I., Can. 46 20N 62 25W
163 St. Petersburg, U.S.A. 27 45N 82 40W
48 St. Philbert, France ...47 2N 1 39W
50 St. Pierre, France 45 57N 1 17W
48 St. Pierre Eglise, Fr. .49 40N 1 25W
48 St. Pierre en Port, Fr. 49 48N 0 30E
48 St. Pierre sur Dives, Fr. 49 2N 0 1W
155 St. Pierre & Miquelon, I., N. Amer. 46 49N 56 15W
49 St. Pol, France 50 21N 2 20E
48 St. Pol de Leon, France 48 42N 4 0W
49 St. Pol sur Mer, France 51 1N 2 15E
58 St. Pölten, Austria 48 12N 15 38E
50 St. Pons, France 43 30N 2 45E
49 St. Poucain sur Sioule, France 46 20N 3 16E
49 St. Quentin, Aisne, Fr. 49 55N 3 20E
34 St. Quentin, Somme, Fr. 50 17N 1 35E
51 St. Rambert d'Albon, Fr. 45 17N 1 35E
51 St. Raphael, France ...43 25N 6 47E
166 St. Regis, Mont., U.S.A. 47 20N 115 3W
161 St. Regis, N.Y., U.S.A. 44 39N 74 34W
51 St. Remy, France 43 48N 4 51E
48 St. Renan, France 48 26N 4 39W
48 St. Saens, France 49 42N 1 20E
49 St. Sauveur, Yonne, Fr. 47 37N 3 10E
48 St. Sauveur le Vicomte, Manche, France 49 22N 1 30W
50 St. Savin, Vienne, Fr. 46 34N 0 50E
50 St. Savinien, France ...45 53N 0 42W
129 St. Sebastien, C., Malag. 12 26S 48 44E
49 St. Seine L'Abbaye, Fr. 47 28N 4 48E
50 St. Sernin, France 43 54N 2 35E
48 St. Servan, France 48 39N 2 0W
48 St. Sever Calvados, Fr. 48 50N 1 4W
155 St. Simeon, Canada ...47 51N 69 54W
155 St. Stephen, Canada ...45 16N 67 17W
36 St. Stephen, Eng., U.K. 50 20N 4 52W
50 St. Sulpice la Pte., Fr. 43 47N 1 41E
50 St. Sulpice Laurière, Fr. 46 3N 1 28E
36 St. Teath, Eng., U.K. 50 34N 4 45W
48 St. Thégonnec, France 48 32N 3 58W
154 St. Thomas, Canada ...42 45N 81 10W
154 St. Tite, Canada 46 45N 72 40W
54 St. Trond, Belgium 50 48N 5 10E
51 St. Tropez, France 43 17N 6 38E
54 St. (Sint-) Truiden (St. Trond), Belgium 50 48N 5 12E
37 St. Tudwal's Is., Wales, United Kingdom 52 48N 4 28W
36 St. Tudy, Eng., U.K. .50 33N 4 45W
48 St. Vaast la Hougue, Fr. 49 36N 1 17W
58 St. Valentin, Austria .48 11N 14 33E
49 St. Valéry, France 50 10N 1 38E
48 St. Valery en Caux, Fr. 49 50N 0 42E
51 St. Vallier, Drôme, Fr. 45 11N 4 50E
51 St. Vallier, Var, France 43 41N 6 51E
48 St. Varent, France 46 53N 0 14W
58 St. Veit, Austria 46 54N 14 22E
16 St. Vincent, C. Verde Is. 18 0N 26 1W
129 St. Vincent C., Malag. 21 58S 43 20E
63 St. Vincent, C. Port. .37 0N 9 0W
122 St. Vincent G., Austral. 35 0S 138 0E
169 St. Vincent I., Wind. Is. 13 10N 61 10W
50 St. Vincent de Tyrosse, France 43 39N 1 18W
57 St. Wendel, Germany 49 27N 7 9E
58 St. Wolfgang, Austria 47 43N 13 27E
50 St. Yrieix, France 45 30N 1 12E
48 Ste. Adresse, France .49 31N 0 5E
155 Ste. Anne de Beaupré, Canada 47 2N 70 58W
155 Ste. Anne de Portneuf, Canada ...48 38N 69 8W
49 Ste. Benoite, France .49 47N 3 30E
155 Ste. Cecile, Canada 47 56N 64 34W
50 Ste. Foy la Grande, Fr. 44 50N 0 14E
164 Ste. Genevieve, U.S.A. 37 59N 90 2W
155 Ste. Germaine, Canada 46 24N 70 24W
50 Ste. Hermine, France .46 34N 1 3W
50 Ste. Livrade, France .44 24N 0 36E
169 Ste. Marie, Martinique 14 48N 61 1W
129 Ste. Marie, C., Malag. 25 36S 45 8E
129 Ste. Marie I., Malag. .16 50S 49 55E
49 Ste. Marie aux-Mines, France 48 15N 7 10E
155 Ste. Marie de la Madaleine, Canada .46 26N 71 0W
48 Ste. Maure, France 47 7N 0 38E
51 Ste. Maxine, France ...43 18N 6 40E
49 Ste. Menehould, France 49 7N 4 52E
48 Ste. Mère, France 49 25N 1 20W
169 Ste. Rose, Guadaloupe 16 20N 61 45W
157 Ste. Rose du lac, Can. 51 10N 99 30W
172 Ste. Teresa, Argentina 33 33S 60 54W
50 Saintes, France 45 45N 0 40W
46 Saintfield, N. Ire., UK 54 28N 5 50W
50 Saintonge, prov., Fr. .45 40N 0 50W
103 Sairang, India 23 50N 92 45E
174 Sajama Mt., Bolivia ...18 0S 68 55W
74 Sajan, Yugoslavia 45 50N 20 58E
59 Sajószentpéter, Hung. 48 12N 20 44E
131 Saka, Kenya 0 11S 39 30E
102 Saka Kalat, W. Pak. .27 20N 64 7E
114 Sakai, Japan 34 30N 135 30E
114 Sakai Shimane, Japan 35 30N 133 25E
114 Sakaimachi,Japan 35 30N 133 15E
114 Saikaide, Japan 34 32N 133 50E
100 Sakaka, Saudi Arabia 30 0N 40 8E
154 Sakami, L., Canada ...53 10N 77 0W
132 Sakania, Congo 12 43S 28 30E
144 Sakar, I., Terr. of New Guinea 5 30S 148 0E
88 Sakarya R., Turkey ...40 5N 31 0E
113 Sakashima Gunto Is., Japan 24 30N 124 0E
114 Sakata, Japan 38 55N 139 56E
125 Sakete, Dahomey 6 40N 2 32E
91 Sakhalin I., U.S.S.R. .51 0N 143 0E
105 Sakhi Gopal, India 19 58N 85 50E
98 Sakhnin, Israel 32 52N 35 12E
87 Saki, U.S.S.R. 45 16N 33 34E
86 Sakiai, U.S.S.R. 54 59N 23 0E
107 Sakon Nakhon, Thailand 17 0N 104 0E
104 Sakrand, W. Pakistan 26 10N 68 15E
105 Sakri, India 21 2N 74 40E
134 Sakrivier, S. Africa 30 54S 20 28E
81 Sakskøbing, Denmark 54 49N 11 36E
83 Säkylä, Finland 61 4N 22 20E
89 Sal R., U.S.S.R. 47 25N 42 20E
59 Sal'a, Czechoslovakia .48 10N 17 50E
80 Sala, Sweden 59 58N 16 35E
73 Sala Consilina, Italy ...40 23N 15 35E
172 Saladas, Argentina 28 15S 58 40W
172 Saladillo, Argentina ...35 40S 59 55W
172 Salado, Chile 26 16S 70 10W
172 Salado R., Santa Fé, Argentina 27 0S 63 40W
172 Salado R., Buenos Aires, Argentina 35 40S 58 10W
125 Salaga, Ghana 8 31N 0 31W
78 Sălaj, Reg., Rum. 47 10N 23 15E
109 Salajar I., Indonesia . 6 15S 120 30E
124 Salala, Liberia 6 42N 10 7W
126 Salala, Sudan 21 17N 36 16E
99 Salālah, Muscat & Oman 16 56N 53 59E
98 Salama, Israel 32 3N 34 48E
172 Salamanca, Chile 32 0S 71 25W
62 Salamanca, Spain 40 57N 5 40W
160 Salamanca, U.S.A. 42 10N 78 42W
144 Salamaua, Terr. of New Guinea 7 10S 147 0E
77 Salamis, Greece 37 56N 23 30E
176 Salar de Atacama, Chile 23 30S 68 25W
174 Salar de Uyuni, Bolivia 20 30S 67 45W
78 Sălard, Rumania 47 12N 22 3E
62 Salas, Spain 43 25N 6 15W
64 Salas de los Infantes, Sp. 42 2N 3 17W
112 Salatu, Mongolia 44 25N 107 58E
174 Salaverry, Peru 8 15S 79 0W
137 Sala-y-Gomez I., Pacific Ocean 26 28S 105 28W
64 Salazar, R., Spain 42 45N 1 8W
49 Salbris, France 47 25N 2 3E
78 Salcia, Rumania 43 56N 24 55E
36 Salcombe, Eng., U.K. 50 14N 3 47W
36 Salcombe Regis, England, U.K. 50 41N 3 11W
62 Saldaña, Spain 42 32N 4 48W
134 Saldanha & B., S. Afr. 33 0S 17 58E
134 Saldanha Bay, S. Africa 33 6S 18 0E
86 Saldus, U.S.S.R. 56 45N 22 37E
38 Sale, England, U.K. ...53 26N 2 19W
122 Salé, Morocco 33 29N 6 47W
143 Sale, Victoria, Austral. 38 7S 147 0E
125 Salea-koira, Mali 16 54N 0 46W
109 Salebabu, Indonesia ... 3 45N 125 55E
101 Sālehābād, Iran 35 40N 61 2E
90 Salekhard, U.S.S.R. ...66 30N 66 25E
106 Salem, India 11 40N 78 11E
162 Salem, Ind., U.S.A. ...38 38N 86 0W
161 Salem, Mass., U.S.A. .42 29N 70 53W
165 Salem, Mo., U.S.A. 37 40N 91 30W
162 Salem, N.J., U.S.A. ...39 34N 75 29W
160 Salem, Ohio, U.S.A. ...40 52N 80 50W
166 Salem, Oreg., U.S.A. .45 0N 123 0W
162 Salem, Va., U.S.A. 37 19N 80 8W
108 Salembu I., Indonesia 5 35S 114 30E
72 Salemi, Italy 37 49N 12 47E
40 Salen, Scotland, U.K. 56 42N 5 48W
51 Salernes, France 43 34N 6 15E
73 Salerno, Campania, It. 40 40N 14 44E
73 Salerno, G. di, Italy ...40 35N 14 45E
98 Salfit, Jordan 32 5N 35 11E
38 Salford, England, U.K. 53 30N 2 17W
34 Salford Priors, Eng., U.K. 52 10N 1 52W
88 Salgir, R., U.S.S.R. ...45 30N 34 30E
59 Salgótarjan, Hungary 48 5N 19 47E
122 Sali, Algeria 26 58N 0 1W
50 Saliès, France 43 29N 0 56W
132 Salima, Malawi 13 47S 34 28E
164 Salina, Kan., U.S.A. .38 50N 97 40W
73 Salina I., Italy 38 35N 14 50E
168 Salina Cruz, Mexico ...16 10N 95 10W
176 Salina Grande, Arg. ...42 50S 64 0W
175 Salinas, Brazil 16 20S 42 10W
174 Salinas, Ecuador 2 10S 80 50W
169 Salinas B., Nicaragua 11 4N 85 45W
65 Salinas, Cabo de, Spain 39 16N 3 4E
167 Salinas R., U.S.A. 36 10N 121 10W
168 Salinas (de Hidalgo), Mexico 22 30N 101 40W
172 Salinas Grandes, Arg. 29 30S 65 0W
164 Saline, R., U.S.A. 39 10N 99 5W
175 Salinópolis, Brazil 0 40S 47 20W
49 Salins, France 46 58N 5 52E
63 Salir, Portugal 37 14N 8 2W
132 Salisbury, Rhodesia ...17 50S 31 2E
34 Salisbury, Eng., U.K. 51 4N 1 48W
145 Salisbury, S. Australia 34 45S 138 35E
162 Salisbury, Md., U.S.A. 38 20N 75 38W
163 Salisbury, N.C., U.S.A. 35 42N 80 29W
34 Salisbury Plain, England, U.K. 51 13N 2 0W
78 Saliste, Rumania 45 45N 23 56E
125 Salka, Nigeria 10 20N 4 58E
64 Sallent, Spain 41 49N 1 54E
50 Salles, Curan, France .44 11N 2 47E
81 Salling, dist., Denmark 56 40N 9 0E
165 Sallisaw, U.S.A. 35 26N 94 45W
126 Sallom Junc., Sudan .19 23N 37 6E
64 Salmerón, Spain 40 33N 2 29W
156 Salmo, Canada 49 10N 117 20W
166 Salmon, U.S.A. 45 12N 113 56W
166 Salmon R., U.S.A. 46 0N 116 30W
156 Salmon Arm, Canada .50 40N 119 15W
166 Salmon Falls, U.S.A. .42 55N 114 59W
142 Salmon Gums, Austral. 32 45S 121 30E
166 Salmon River Mts., U.S.A. 45 0N 114 30W
83 Salo, Finland 60 22N 23 3E
70 Salo, Italy 45 37N 10 32E
167 Salome, U.S.A. 33 51N 113 37W
51 Salon, France 43 39N 5 6E
130 Salonga R., Congo 0 50S 21 20E
76 Salonica, see Thessaloniki, Greece 40 38N 22 58E
78 Salonta, Rumania 46 49N 21 42E
64 Salou, Spain 41 5N 1 8E
64 Salou, Cabo, Spain 41 3N 1 10E
172 Salsacate, Argentina .31 20S 65 5W
80 Salsåker, Sweden 62 59N 18 20E
50 Salses, France 42 50N 2 55E
102 Salsette I., India 19 5N 72 50E
89 Salsk, U.S.S.R. 46 28N 41 30E
73 Salso R., Sicily, Italy .37 6N 13 55E
70 Salsomaggiore, Italy .44 48N 9 59E
98 Salt, Jordan 32 2N 35 43E
82 Salt Fd., Norway 67 15N 14 5E
167 Salt R., U.S.A. 33 50N 110 25W
104 Salt Ra., W. Pakistan 32 30N 72 25E
145 Salt Creek Telegraph Office, S. Australia .36 0S 139 35E
165 Salt Fork R., U.S.A. .37 25N 98 40W
166 Salt Lake City, U.S.A. 40 45N 111 58W
172 Salta, Argentina 24 48S 65 30W
36 Saltash, England, U.K. 50 25N 4 13W
39 Saltburn by Sea, England, U.K. 54 35N 0 58W
40 Saltcoats, Scot., U.K. 55 38N 4 47W
45 Saltee Is., Ireland 52 7N 6 37W
39 Saltergate, Eng., U.K. 54 20N 0 40W
39 Saltfleet, Eng., U.K. .53 25N 0 11E
39 Saltfleetby, Eng., U.K. 53 23N 0 10E
44 Salthill, Ireland 53 15N 9 6W
81 Saltholm I., Denmark 55 38N 12 43E
168 Saltillo, Mexico 25 30N 100 57W
172 Salto, Argentina 34 20S 60 15W
172 Salto, Uruguay 31 20S 57 59W
172 Salto Augusto, Brazil . 8 30S 58 0W
167 Salton Sea, U.S.A. 33 20N 116 0W
125 Saltpond, Ghana 5 15N 1 3W
80 Saltsjöbaden, Sweden 59 15N 18 20E
156 Saltspring, Canada 48 54N 123 37W
35 Saltwood, Eng., U.K. 51 4N 1 5E
163 Salula, R., U.S.A. 34 12N 81 45W
126 Salûm, Egypt 31 31N 25 9E
106 Salur, India 18 27N 83 18E
70 Saluzzo, Italy 44 39N 7 29E
175 Salvador (Bahia), Brazil 13 0S 38 30W
157 Salvador, Canada 52 20N 109 25W
168 Salvador, rep., Central America 13 50N 89 0W
165 Salvador L., U.S.A. ...29 46N 90 16W
63 Salvaterra de Magos, Portugal 39 1N 8 47W
62 Salvora, Isla, Spain ...42 30N 8 58E
101 Salwa, Qatar 24 45N 50 55E
103 Salween R., Burma ...20 0N 98 0E
111 Salween R., China 30 0N 97 30E
58 Salza, R., Austria 47 43N 15 0E
58 Salzach, R., Austria ...47 15N 12 25E
58 Salzburg, Austria 47 48N 13 2E
56 Salzgitter, Germany ...52 2N 10 22E
56 Salzwedel, Germany ...52 50N 11 11E
104 Sam Neua, Laos 20 29N 104 0E
107 Sam Ngao, Thailand .17 18N 99 0W
165 Sam Rayburn Res., U.S.A. 31 15N 94 0W
90 Sama, U.S.S.R. 60 10N 60 25E
62 Sama de Langreo, Spain 43 18N 5 40W
109 Samak, Indonesia 4 40S 122 46E
109 Samales Group, Phil. 6 0N 122 20E
105 Samalkot, India 17 3N 82 13E
126 Samâlût, Egypt 28 20N 30 42E
104 Samana, India 30 10N 76 13E
174 Samanco, Peru 9 10S 78 30W
130 Samangwa, Congo 4 23S 24 10E
109 Samar, I., Philippines 12 0N 125 0E
88 Samara R., U.S.S.R. .52 30N 53 0E
144 Samarai, Terr. of Papua 10 32S 150 35E
98 Samaria (Site), Jordan 32 15N 35 13E
108 Samarinda, Indonesia 0 28S 117 16E
90 Samarkand, U.S.S.R. .39 40N 67 0E
100 Samarra, Iraq 34 16N 43 55E
105 Samastipur, India 25 50N 85 50E
130 Samba, Congo 0 13N 21 25E
73 Sambaise, Italy 38 58N 16 16E
105 Sambalpur, India 21 28N 83 58E
108 Sambas, Indonesia 1 20N 109 20E
129 Sambava, Malagasy Rep. 14 16S 50 10E
132 Sambawizi, Rhodesia .18 24S 26 13E
104 Sambhal, India 28 35N 78 37E
104 Sambhar, India 26 52N 11 16E
70 Sambonifacio, Italy ...45 24N 11 16E
86 Sambor, U.S.S.R. 49 30N 23 10E
172 Samborombon, Bahia, Argentina 36 5S 57 20W
54 Sambre R., Belg.-Fr. .50 2N 4 15E
72 Sambuca, Sicily, Italy 37 39N 13 6E
112 Samchŏk, S. Korea 37 30N 129 0E
49 Samer, France 50 38N 1 44E
77 Sami, Greece 38 15N 20 39E
126 Samna, Saudi Arabia .25 12N 37 17E
79 Samnager, Norway 60 23N 5 39E
123 Samnu, Libya 27 15N 14 55E
172 Samo Alto, Chile 30 22S 71 0W
136 Samoa Is., Pac. Oc. ...14 0S 171 0W
71 Samobor, Yugoslavia .45 47N 15 44E
51 Samoens, France 46 5N 6 45E
124 Samorogouan, Upper Volta 11 21N 4 57W
62 Samos, Spain 42 44N 7 20W
74 Samos, Yugoslavia 45 13N 20 49E
77 Samos I., Greece 37 45N 26 50E
108 Samosir Balige, Indon. 2 20N 98 50E
76 Samothráki & I. Greece 40 28N 25 38E
124 Sampa, Ghana 8 0N 2 36W
172 Sampacho, Argentina .33 20S 64 50W
109 Sampang, Indonesia ... 7 11S 113 13E
64 Samper de Calanda, Sp. 41 11N 04 2W
36 Sampford Courtenay, England, U.K. 50 47N 3 58W
108 Sampit, Indonesia 2 20S 113 0E
100 Samra, Saudi Arabia .25 35N 41 0E
124 Samreboi, Ghana 5 34N 7 28E
125 Samri, Nigeria 11 50N 6 44E
113 Samshui, China 23 7N 112 58E
81 Samsö I., Denmark ...55 50N 10 35E
81 Samsö Belt, Denmark 55 50N 10 55E

MAP
100 Samsun, Turkey 41 15N 36 15E
77 Samsun Daği Mt., Tur. 37 45N 27 10E
89 Samtredia, U.S.S.R. 42 7N 42 24E
98 Samu', Jordan 31 24N 35 4E
89 Samur, R., U.S.S.R. 41 30N 48 0E
130 Samusole, Congo 10 2S 24 3E
107 Samut Prakan (Paknam), Thailand 13 32N 100 40E
107 Samut Sakhon, Thai. .13 31N 100 20E
107 Samut Songkhram (Mekong), Thailand 13 24N 100 1E
104 Samwari, W. Pakistan 28 5N 66 46E
124 San, Mali 13 15N 4 45W
59 San R., Poland 50 25N 22 20E
62 San Adrian, G. de, Sp. 43 21N 8 50W
109 San Agustin, C., Phil. 6 20N 126 13E
137 San Ambrosio I., Pac. Oc. 26 35S 79 30W
166 San Andreas, U.S.A. .38 17N 120 39W
169 San Andrés I., Col. 12 42N 81 46W
166 San Andres Mts., U.S.A. 33 0N 106 45W
168 San Andrés Tuxtla, Mex. 18 30N 95 20W
115 San Angelo, U.S.A. ...31 30N 100 30W
172 San Antonio, Chile 23 35S 69 10W
172 San Antonio, Chile 33 40S 71 40W
167 S. Antonio, N. Mex., U.S.A. 33 58N 106 57W
165 S. Antonio, Tex., U.S.A. 29 30N 98 30W
172 San Antonio C., Arg. .36 15S 56 40W
169 San Antonio, C., Cuba 21 50N 84 57W
65 S. Antonio, C. de., Sp. 38 48N 0 12E
165 San Antonio R., U.S.A. 28 30N 97 14W
65 San Antonio Abad, Sp. 38 59N 1 19E
169 San Antonio de los Banos, Cuba 22 54N 82 31W
176 San Antonio Oeste, Arg. 40 40S 65 0W
70 San Benedetto, Italy .45 2N 10 57E
71 San Benedetto del Tronto, Italy 42 57N 13 52E
165 San Benito, U.S.A. 26 5N 97 32W
167 San Bernardino, U.S.A. 34 7N 117 18W
172 San Bernardo, Chile ...33 40S 70 50W
174 San Bernardo I. de, Col. 9 45N 75 50W
168 San Blas, Sinaloa, Mex. 26 10N 108 40W
163 San Blas, C., U.S.A. ...29 40N 85 25W
169 San Blas, Cord. de Pan. 9 15N 78 30W
174 San Borja, Bolivia 15 0S 67 12W
168 San Buenaventura, Mex. 27 4N 101 32W
172 San Carlos, Argentina 33 50S 69 0W
112 San Carlos, Chile 36 25S 72 0W
125 S. Carlos, Fernando Poo 3 29N 8 33E
168 San Carlos, Mexico 29 0N 101 10W
169 San Carlos, Nicaragua 11 12N 84 50W
109 San Carlos, Philippines 10 33N 123 23E
173 San Carlos, Uruguay .34 46S 54 58W
167 San Carlos, U.S.A. 33 24N 110 27W
174 San Carlos, Venezuela 1 55N 67 4W
174 San Carlos, Venezuela 9 40N 68 36W
167 San Carlos L., U.S.A. .33 20N 110 10W
176 San Carlos de Bariloche, Argentina 41 10S 71 25W
64 San Carlos de la Rapita, Spain 40 37N 0 35E
72 San Cataldo, Italy 37 30N 13 58E
64 San Celoni, Spain 41 42N 2 30E
172 San Clemente, Chile ...35 30S 71 39W
65 San Clemente, Spain .39 24N 2 25W
167 San Clemente, U.S.A. 33 29N 117 45W
167 San Clemente I., U.S.A. 33 0N 118 30W
71 San Constanzo, Italy .43 46N 13 5E
172 San Cristobal, Argentina 30 20S 61 10W
168 San Cristóbal de las Casas, Mexico 16 50N 92 33W
174 San Cristobal, Ven. ... 7 46N 72 14W
71 S. Daniel del Friule, It. 46 10N 13 0E
73 San Demetrio Corone, It. 39 34N 16 22E
167 San Diego, Calif., U.S.A. 32 50N 117 10W
165 San Diego, Tex., U.S.A. 27 47N 98 15W
176 San Diego C. Arg. 54 40S 65 10W
174 San Diego de Cabrutica, Venezuela 8 30N 64 50W
71 San Dona di Piave, It. 45 38N 12 34E
71 San Elpidio a Mare, It. 43 16N 13 41E
64 San Esteban de Gormaz, Spain 41 34N 3 13W
172 San Fabián de Alico, Chile 36 30S 71 40W
70 San Felice sul Panaro, Italy 44 51N 11 9E
172 San Felipe, Chile 32 43S 70 50W
174 San Felipe, Venezuela 10 20N 68 45W
64 San Feliu du Guixols, Sp. 41 45N 3 1E
64 San Feliu de Llobregat, Spain 41 23N 2 2E
172 San Felix, Chile 28 58S 70 30W
174 San Felix, Venezuela . 8 20N 62 35W
137 San Felix I. Pac. Oc. 26 30S 80 0W
172 San Fernando, Arg. ...34 24S 58 34W
172 San Fernando, Chile ...34 30S 71 0W
168 San Fernando, Mexico 30 0N 115 10W
109 San Fernando, Phil. ...15 5N 120 37E
109 San Fernando, Phil. ...16 40N 120 23E
63 San Fernando, Spain .36 22N 6 17W
169 San Fernando, Trinidad 10 20N 61 30W
167 San Fernando, U.S.A. 34 15N 118 29W
74 San Fernando, Ven. ... 8 0N 67 30W
168 San Fernando, R., Mex. 25 0N 99 0W
174 San Fernando de Atabapo, Venezuela 4 3N 67 42W
73 San Fernando di Puglia, Italy 41 18N 16 5E
172 San Francisco, Arg. ...31 30S 62 5W
172 San Francisco, Arg. ...32 45S 66 10W
167 San Francisco, U.S.A. 37 35N 122 30W
174 San Francisco, C., Ec. 0 50N 80 0W
167 San Francisco, R., U.S.A. 33 30N 109 0W
169 San Francisco de Marcoris, Dom. Rep. 19 19N 70 15W
168 San Francisco del Oro, Mexico 26 52N 105 50W
65 S. Francisco Javier, Sp. 38 40N 1 25E
165 San Francisville, U.S.A. 30 48N 91 22W
73 San Fratello Italy 38 1N 14 33E
72 S. Gavino Monreale, It. 39 33N 8 47E
174 San Gil, Colombia 6 33N 73 8W
70 San Gimignano, Italy 43 28N 11 3E
71 San Giorgio di Nogaro, Italy 45 50N 13 13E
73 San Giorgio Ionico, It. 40 27N 17 23E
70 San Giovanni Bianco, It 45 52N 9 40E
73 San Giovanni in Fiore, Italy 39 16N 16 42E
71 San Giovanni, in Persiceto, Italy 44 39N 11 12E
73 San Giovanni Rotondo, Italy 41 41N 15 42E
71 S. Giovanni Valdarno, It. 43 32N 11 30E
70 San Giuliano Terme, It. 43 45N 10 26E
72 San Guiseppe Iato, It. 37 37N 13 11E
173 San Ignacio, Argentina 27 15S 55 32W
174 San Ignacio, Bolivia ...16 20S 60 55W
109 San Ildefonso C., Phil. 16 0N 122 10E
172 San Javier, Argentina 30 30S 60 10W
174 San Javier, Bolivia ...16 18S 62 30W
172 San Javier, Chile 35 40S 71 45W
65 San Javier, Spain 37 49N 0 50W
167 San Joaquin R., U.S.A. 37 0N 120 0W
168 San Jorge B., Mexico .31 20N 113 20W
176 San Jorge, G. of, Arg. 46 0S 66 0W
64 San Jorge, G. de, Spain 40 50N 0 55W
174 San Jose, Bolivia 17 45S 60 50W
174 San Jose del Guaviare, Colombia 2 40N 72 0W
169 San Jose, Costa Rica .10 0N 84 2W
168 San José, Guatemala .14 0N 90 50W
109 San José, Philippines .15 45N 120 55E
109 San José, Philippines .10 50N 122 5E
65 San José, Spain 38 55N 1 18E
167 San Jose, Calif., U.S.A. 37 20N 122 0W
165 San Jose, N. Mex., U.S.A. 35 26N 105 30W
172 San José de Feliciano, Argentina 30 26S 58 46W
172 San José de Mayo, Urug. 34 27S 56 27W
174 San José de Ocuné, Col. 4 15N 70 20W
168 San José del Cabo, Mex. 23 0N 109 50W
176 San José G., Argentina 42 0S 64 0W
168 San José I., Mexico ...25 0N 110 50W
167 San Jose R., U.S.A. ...35 15N 108 10W
172 San Juan, Argentina ..31 30S 68 30W
174 San Juan, Bolivia 18 0S 60 0W
169 San Juan, Dom. Rep. 18 49N 71 12W
168 San Juan, Mexico 23 50N 106 20W
168 S. Juan, Coahuila, Mex. 29 34N 101 53W
168 San Juan, Jalisco, Mex. 21 20N 102 50W
168 S. Juan, Queretaro, Mex. 20 25N 100 0W
109 San Juan, Philippines 8 35N 126 20E
169 San Juan, Puerto Rico, W.I. 18 28N 66 37W
167 San Juan Mts., U.S.A. 38 30N 108 30W
172 San Juan, prov., Arg. 31 0S 69 0W
169 San Juan R., Nicaragua 11 0N 84 30W
167 San Juan R., U.S.A. .37 20N 110 20W
167 S. Juan Capistrano, U.S.A. 33 29N 117 46W
65 San Juan Bautista, Sp. 39 5N 1 31E
172 San Juan Bautista, Par. 26 37S 57 6W
174 San Juan de los Morros, Venezuela . 9 55N 67 21W
169 San Juan del Norte Bay, Nicaragua 11 30N 83 40W
63 S. Juan del Puerto, Sp. 37 20N 6 50W
169 San Juan del Sur, Nic. 11 20N 86 0W
176 San Julian, Argentina 49 15S 68 0W
172 San Justo, Argentina .30 55S 60 30W
168 S. Lazaro, Sa. de, Mex. 23 25N 110 0W
167 San Leandro, U.S.A. .37 40N 122 6W
64 San Leonardo, Spain .41 51N 3 5W
172 San Lorenzo, Argentina 32 45S 60 45W
64 San Lorenza de la Parilla, Spain 39 51N 2 22W
174 San Lorenzo, Ecuador 1 15N 78 50W
174 San Lorenzo I., Peru .12 20S 77 35W
176 San Lorenzo, Mt., Arg. 47 40S 72 20W
64 San Lorenzo de Morunys, Spain 42 8N 1 35E
174 San Lucas, Bolivia 20 5S 65 0W
168 San Lucas C., Mexico .22 50N 110 0W
73 San Lucido, Italy 39 18N 16 3E
172 San Luis, Argentina ...33 20S 66 20W
167 San Luis, U.S.A. 37 14N 105 26W
167 San Luis Obispo, U.S.A. 35 21N 120 38W
168 San Luis Potosi, Mex. 22 10N 101 0W
168 San Luis de la Paz, Mex. 21 19N 100 32W
168 San Luis Rio Colorado, Mexico ...32 29N 114 48W
73 S. Marco Argentano, It. 39 34N 16 8E
73 S. Marco dei Cavoti, It. 41 20N 14 50E
73 San Marco in Lamis, It. 41 43N 15 38E
168 San Marcos, Guatemala 14 59N 91 52W
165 San Marcos, U.S.A. ...29 53N 98 0W
71 San Marino, San Marino 43 56N 12 25E
71 San Marino, rep. Italy 43 56N 12 25E
172 San Martin, Argentina 33 5S 68 28W
176 San Martin, Argentina 44 0S 70 20W
174 San Martin, Bolivia ...14 50S 61 45W
176 San Martin L., Arg. ...48 50S 72 50W
62 San Martin de Valdeiglesias, Spain 40 21N 4 24W
168 San Martin Tuxtla Vulcan, Mexico 18 29N 95 14W
70 San Martino de Calvi, It. 45 57N 9 41E
64 San Mateo, Spain 40 28N 0 10E
167 San Mateo, U.S.A. 37 32N 122 25W
174 San Matias, Bolivia ...16 25S 58 20W
176 San Matias, G. of Arg. 41 30S 64 0W
174 San Miguel, R., Bolivia 16 0S 62 45W
168 San Miguel, Salvador .13 30N 88 12W
65 San Miguel, Spain 39 3N 1 26E
65 S. Miguel de Salinas, Sp. 37 59N 0 47W
70 San Miniato, Italy 43 40N 10 50E
109 San Narciso, Phil. 15 2N 120 3E
172 San Nicolas, Argentina 33 17S 60 10W
158 San Nicolas I., U.S.A. 33 16N 119 30W
172 San Pablo, Bolivia 21 43S 66 38W
73 S. Paolo di Civitate, It. 41 44N 15 16E
172 San Pedro, Argentina 33 43S 59 45W
172 San Pedro, Argentina 24 12S 64 55W
172 San Pedro, Chile 21 58S 68 30W
169 San Pedro, Dom. Rep. 18 30N 69 18W
124 San Pedro, Ivory Coast 4 50N 6 33W
172 San Pedro, Paraguay .24 0S 57 0W
168 San Pedro R., Mexico 28 20N 106 10W
167 San Pedro, R., U.S.A. 32 45N 110 35W
172 San Pedro de Atacama, Chile 22 55S 68 15W
174 San Pedro de Lloc, Peru 7 15S 79 28W
168 San Pedro de las Colonias, Mexico 25 50N 102 59W
176 San Pedro del Parana, Paraguay 26 43S 56 13W
168 San Pedro Martir, Sierra, Mexico 31 0N 115 30W
168 San Pedro Mixtepec, Mexico 16 2N 97 0W
168 S. Pedro Ocampo, Mex. 24 52N 101 40W
65 S. Pedro del Pinatar, Sp. 37 50N 0 50W
168 San Pedro Sula, Hond. 15 30N 88 0W
72 San Pietro I., Italy ...39 9N 8 17E
73 San Pietro Vernotico, It. 40 28N 18 0E
109 San Quintin, Philippines 16 1N 120 56E
172 San Rafael, Argentina 34 40S 68 30W
174 San Rafael, Colombia 6 2N 69 45W
166 S. Rafael, Calif., U.S.A. 38 0N 122 40W
167 S. Rafael, N. Mex., U.S.A. 35 6N 107 58W
70 San Remo, Italy 43 48N 7 47E
172 San Roque, Argentina 28 15S 58 45W
63 San Roque, Spain 36 17N 5 21W
172 San Rosendo, Chile ...37 10S 72 50W
165 San Saba, U.S.A. 31 12N 98 45W
168 San Salvador, Salvador 13 40N 89 20W
169 San Salvador (Watlings) I., Bahamas 24 0N 74 40W
176 San Sebastian, Arg. ...53 10S 68 30W
64 San Sebastian, Spain .43 17N 1 58W
71 San Serverino, Italy ...43 13N 13 10E
71 San Severo, Italy 41 41N 15 23E
167 San Simon, U.S.A. 32 14N 109 16W
71 S. Stefano di Cadore, It. 46 34N 12 33E
176 San Valentin Mt., Chile 46 30S 73 30W
63 San Vicente de Alcantara, Spain 39 22N 7 8W
62 San Vicente de la Barquera, Spain 43 30N 4 29W
70 San Vicenzo, Italy 43 9N 10 32E
73 San Vito, dei Normanni, Italy 40 40N 17 40E
71 San Vito, al Tagliamento, Italy .45 55N 12 50E
72 San Vito C., Italy 38 11N 12 41E
71 San Vito Chietino, Italy 42 19N 14 27E
165 San Ygnacio, U.S.A. .27 6N 92 24W
167 San Ysidro, U.S.A. 32 33N 117 5W
99 San'a, Yemen 15 27N 44 12E
71 Sana R., Yugoslavia .44 40N 16 43E
124 Sanaba, Upper Volta .12 25N 3 47W
126 Sanâfir, I., Si. Arab. ...27 49N 34 37E
109 Sanana, Indonesia 2 5S 125 50E
104 Sanand, India 22 59N 72 25E
100 Sanandaj. Iran 35 25N 47 7E
74 Sânandrei, Rumania .45 52N 21 13E
104 Sanawad, India........22 11N 76 5E
107 Sanbor, Cambodia 12 46N 106 0E
49 Sancergues, France 47 10N 2 54E
49 Sancerre, France 47 20N 2 50E
104 Sanchor, India 24 52N 71 49E
109 Sanco, Pt., Philippines 8 15N 126 24E
49 Sancoins, France 46 51N 2 56E
169 Sancti Spiritus, Cuba .21 52N 79 33W
135 Sand R., O.F.S., S. Afr. 28 5S 26 30E
133 Sand R., Trans., S. Afr. 22 25S 30 5E
154 Sand Lake, Canada ...47 46N 84 31W
165 Sand Springs, U.S.A. .36 12N 96 5W
40 Sanda I., Scot., U.K. .55 17N 5 35W
126 Sandah, Saudi Arabia 20 35N 39 32E
108 Sandakan, Malaysia ... 5 53N 118 10E
107 Sandan, Cambodia 12 46N 106 0E
75 Sandanski, Bulgaria ...41 35N 23 16E
124 Sandare, Mali 14 40N 10 15W
42 Sanday I., Inner Hebrides, Scot., UK 57 2N 6 30W
43 Sanday I., Orkneys, Scotland, U.K. 59 15N 2 30W
38 Sandbach, Eng., U.K. 53 9N 2 23W
133 Sandbult, Trans., S. Afr. 23 42S 27 19E
134 Sanddrif, S. Africa 28 52S 24 2E
79 Sande, Möre og Romsdal, Norway ...62 15N 5 27E
79 Sande, Sogn og Fjordane, Norway .61 20N 5 48E
79 Sandefjord, Norway 59 10N 10 15E
79 Sandeid, Norway 59 33N 5 52E
167 Sanders, U.S.A. 35 12N 109 25W
165 Sanderson, U.S.A. 30 5N 102 30W
82 Sandfell, Iceland 63 57N 16 48W
134 Sandfontein, S.W. Afr.28 44S 18 30E
133 Sandfontein, S. Africa 23 45S 29 5E
145 Sandgate, Australia ...27 19S 152 53E
35 Sandgate, Eng., U.K. 51 5N 1 9E
81 Sandhammaren, C., Sweden 55 23N 14 14E
40 Sandhead, Scot., U.K. 54 48N 4 58W
35 Sandhurst, Eng., U.K. 51 21N 0 48W
174 Sandia, Peru 14 10S 69 30W
100 Sandikli, Turkey 38 30N 30 20E
142 Sandiman, mt., Western Australia .24 21S 115 20E
79 Sandnes, Norway 58 50N 5 45E
42 Sandness, Scot., U.K. 60 18N 1 38W
130 Sandoa, Congo 9 48S 23 0E
60 Sandomierz, Poland ...50 40N 21 43E
103 Sandoway, Burma 18 20N 94 30E
34 Sandown, I. of Wight, England, U.K. 50 39N 1 9W
166 Sandpoint, U.S.A. 48 20N 116 40W
42 Sandray I., Scot., U.K. 56 53N 7 30W
35 Sandringham, Eng., U.K. 52 50N 0 30E
133 Sandrivierspoort, Trans., S. Africa 24 25S 28 7E
80 Sandslån, Sweden 62 2N 17 49E
133 Sandspruit, S. Africa .27 18S 29 48E
142 Sandstone, W. Austral. 28 0S 119 15E
160 Sandusky, Mich., U.S.A. 43 26N 82 50W
160 Sandusky, Ohio, U.S.A. 41 25N 82 40W
81 Sandvig, Denmark 55 18N 14 48E
80 Sandvig, Sweden 55 32N 14 47E
79 Sandvika, Norway 59 54N 10 29E
80 Sandviken, Sweden ...60 38N 16 58E
35 Sandwich, Eng., U.K. 51 16N 1 21E
155 Sandwich B., Canada .53 40N 57 15W
15 Sandwich Is., South Falkland Islands ...57 0S 27 0W
103 Sandwip Channel, Pak. 22 35N 91 35E
35 Sandy, England, U.K. 53 8N 0 18W
142 Sandy Bight, W. Austral. 33 50S 123 20E
144 Sandy C., Australia ...24 41S 153 8E
102 Sandy Desert, W. Pak. 28 0N 65 0E
154 Sandy L., Canada 52 10N 94 30W
154 Sandy Lake, Canada .53 0N 93 0W
166 Sandy Cr., R., U.S.A. 42 20N 109 30W
143 Sandy Hollow, Austral. 32 36S 150 15E
161 Sandy Hook, U.S.A. .40 22N 74 0W
134 Sandykop, S. Africa ...32 18S 22 14E
163 Sanford, Fla., U.S.A. .28 45N 81 20W
161 Sanford, Me., U.S.A. .43 28N 70 47W
163 Sanford, N.C., U.S.A. 35 30N 79 10W
152 Sanford Mt., Alas., U.S.A. 62 30N 143 0W
107 Sang Ke, R., Cambodia 12 50N 103 4E
132 Sanga, Mozam. 12 22S 35 21E
130 Sanga R., Congo (Fr.) 1 0N 16 30E
132 Sangame, Mozambique 17 40S 34 59E
106 Sangamner, India 19 30N 74 15E
108 Sangasanga, Indonesia 0 29S 117 13E
91 Sangatolon, U.S.S.R. .61 50N 149 40E
113 Sangchih, China 29 25N 109 30E
109 Sangeang, I., Indonesia 8 12S 119 6E
167 Sanger, U.S.A. 36 47N 119 35W
56 Sangerhausen, Germany 51 28N 11 18E
108 Sanggau, Indonesia ... 0 5N 110 30E
109 Sangihe Is., Indonesia 3 0N 126 0E
108 Sangkapura, Indonesia 5 52S 112 40E
108 Sangkulirang, Indonesia 1 0N 118 0E
106 Sangli, India 16 55N 74 33E
125 Sangmelina, Cameroon 2 57N 12 1E
65 Sangonera R., Spain .37 39N 2 0W
165 Sangre de Cristo Mts., U.S.A. 37 0N 105 0W
169 Sangre Grande, Trinidad 10 35N 61 8W
71 Sangro R., Italy 42 10N 14 30E
111 Sangsang, Tibet, China 29 30N 86 0E
156 Sangudo, Canada 53 50N 115 0W
64 Sangüesa, Spain 42 37N 1 17W
51 Sanguinaires, Iles, Corsica, France 41 51N 8 31E
176 Sañicó, Argentina 40 15S 70 30W
164 Sanish, U.S.A. 48 0N 102 30W
131 Sanje, Uganda 0 49S 31 30E
106 Sankaranayinarkovil, India 9 10N 77 35E
106 Sankeshwar, India 16 23N 74 23E
113 Sankiang, China 25 39N 109 30E
128 Sankuru, R., Congo ... 3 45S 21 10E
63 Sanlúcar la Mayor, Sp. 37 26N 6 18W
63 Sanlucar de Barrameda, Spain ...36 43N 6 23W
72 Sanluri, Italy 39 35N 8 55E
78 Sanmártin, Rumania .46 19N 25 58E
113 Sanmen Gorge, China 35 0N 111 30E
113 Sanmen Wan, China .29 10N 121 45E
113 Sanmenhsia, China 34 46N 111 30E
135 Sannaspos, OFS, S. Afr. 29 6S 26 34E
73 Sannicandro Garganico, Italy 41 50N 15 34E
74 Sânnicolaul-Maré, Rum. 46 5N 20 39E
79 Sannidal, Norway 58 55N 9 15E
133 Sannieshof, S. Africa .26 30S 25 47E
124 Sanniquellie, Liberia . 7 19N 8 38W
59 Sanok, Poland 49 35N 22 10E
145 Sanpah, N.S.W., Austral. 30 32S 141 12E
41 Sanquhar, Scot., U.K. 55 21N 3 56W
124 Sansanding Dam, Mali 13 37N 6 0W
125 Sansanné-Mango, Togo 10 20N 0 30E
71 Sansepolcro, Italy 43 34N 12 8E
71 Sanski Most, Yugoslavia 44 46N 16 40E
73 Sant' Agata de Goti, It. 41 6N 14 30E
73 Sant' Agata di Militello, Italy 38 2N 14 40E
174 Santa Ana, Bolivia 13 50S 65 40W
174 Santa Ana, Ecuador ... 1 10S 80 20W
168 Santa Ana, Mexico 30 31N 111 8W
168 Santa Ana, Salvador .14 0N 89 40W
167 Santa Ana, U.S.A. 33 48N 117 55W
70 Sant' Angelo Lodigiano, Italy 45 14N 9 25E
72 Sant' Antioco, Italy ...39 2N 8 30E
72 Sant' Antioco, I., Italy 39 2N 8 30E
71 Sant' Arcangelo di Romagna, Italy 44 4N 12 26E
172 Santa Barbara, Chile .37 40S 72 0W
174 Santa Barbara, Brazil 16 0S 59 0W
168 Santa Barbara, Mexico 26 48N 105 50W
64 Santa Barbara, Spain 40 42N 0 29E
65 Santa Barbara, mt., Sp. 37 23N 2 50W
167 Santa Barbara, U.S.A. 34 25N 119 40W
167 Santa Barbara Is., U.S.A. 33 31N 119 0W
167 Santa Catalina, G. of, U.S.A. 33 0N 118 0W
167 Santa Catalina, I., U.S.A. 33 20N 118 30W
173 Santa Catarina, st., Brazil 27 25S 48 30W
173 Santa Catarina, I., Braz. 27 30S 48 40W
73 Santa Caterina, Italy .37 37N 14 1E
169 Santa Clara, Cuba ...22 20N 80 0W

MAP
167 Santa Clara, Calif., U.S.A. 37 21N 122 0W
167 Santa Clara, Utah, U.S.A. 37 10N 113 38W
173 Santa Clara de Olimar, Uruguay ...32 50S 54 54W
174 Santa Clotilde, Peru ... 2 25S 73 45W
64 Santa Coloma de Farnes, Spain 41 50N 2 39E
62 Santa Comba, Spain ...43 2N 8 49W
73 Sta. Croce Camerina, It. 36 50N 14 30E
176 Santa Cruz, Argentina 50 0S 68 50W
174 Santa Cruz, Bolivia ...17 43S 63 10W
172 Santa Cruz, Chile 34 38S 71 27W
169 Santa Cruz, Costa Rica 10 15N 85 41W
120 Santa Cruz, Canary Is. 28 29N 16 26W
109 Santa Cruz, Philippines 14 20N 121 30E
167 Santa Cruz, Calif., U.S.A. 36 55N 122 10W
167 Sta. Cruz, N. Mexico, U.S.A. 35 59N 106 1W
136 Santa Cruz I., Pac. Oc. 10 30S 166 0E
158 Santa Cruz I., U.S.A. .34 0N 119 45W
176 Santa Cruz R., Arg. ...50 10S 70 0W
65 Sta. Cruz de Mudela, Sp. 38 39N 3 28W
62 Santa Cruz del Retamar, Spain 40 8N 4 14W
169 Santa Cruz del Retamar, Spain 40 8N 4 14W
169 Santa Cruz del Sur, Cuba 20 50N 78 0W
173 Santa Cruz do Rio Pardo, Brazil 22 54S 49 37W
173 Santa Cruz do Sul, Braz. 29 42S 52 25W
172 Santa Elena, Argentina 30 58S 59 47W
169 Santa Elena, Costa Rica 10 54N 85 56W
174 Santa Elena, Ecuador 2 16S 80 52W
50 Santa Enimie, France 44 24N 3 26E
73 Santa Eufemia, G. of, It. 38 50N 16 10E
65 Santa Eulalia, Spain .40 34N 1 20W
172 Santa Fé, Argentina ...31 35S 60 41W
63 Santa Fé, Spain 37 11N 3 43W
167 Santa Fé, U.S.A. 35 40N 106 0W
172 Santa Fé, prov., Arg. .31 50S 60 55W
175 Santa Filomena, Brazil 9 0S 45 50W
73 Santa Groce di Magliano, Italy 41 43N 14 59E
176 Santa Inés I. Chile 54 0S 73 0W
63 Santa Inés, Mt., Spain 38 32N 5 37W
172 Santa Isabel, Argentina 36 10S 67 0W
174 Santa Isabel, Brazil ...13 45S 60 30W
173 Santa Isabel, Brazil ...13 45S 56 30W
125 Sta. Isabel, Fernando Poo 3 45N 8 50E
125 Santa Isabel Pk., Fernando Poo 4 43N 8 49E
172 Santa Lucia, Argentina 28 58S 59 5W
172 Santa Lucia, Argentina 31 30S 68 45W
65 Santa Lucia, Spain 37 35N 0 58W
167 Santa Lucia Range, Mts., U.S.A. 36 0N 121 30W
172 Santa Margarita, Arg. 38 18S 61 35W
168 Santa Margarita, Mex. 24 30N 112 0W
70 Santa Margherita, Ligure, Italy 44 20N 9 11E
172 Santa Maria, Argentina 26 40S 66 0W
173 Santa Maria, Brazil ...29 40S 53 40W
73 Santa Maria, Italy ...41 3N 14 29E
168 Santa Maria, Mexico .27 40N 114 40W
174 Santa Maria, Peru ... 2 35S 74 50W
167 Santa Maria, U.S.A. ...34 58N 120 29W
132 Santa Maria, Zambia .11 5S 29 58E
64 Sta Maria, Majorca, Sp. 39 39N 2 45E
168 Santa Maria, B., Mex. 25 10N 108 40W
63 Santa Maria, Cabo de, Portugal 36 39N 7 53W
175 Santa Maria da Vitória, Brazil 13 30S 44 20W
63 Santa Maria de Nieva, Spain 37 28N 2 0W
168 Sta. Maria del Oro, Mexico 25 30N 105 20W
73 Santa Maria di Leuca, C., Italy 39 48N 18 20E
174 Santa Marta, Colombia 11 15N 74 13W
62 Sta. Marta, Ria de, Sp. 43 44N 7 45W
63 Santa Marta, Spain ...38 37N 6 39W
173 Santa Marta Grande, C., Brazil 28 43S 48 50W
167 Santa Monica, U.S.A. 34 0N 118 30W
166 Santa Napa, U.S.A. ...38 28N 122 45W
63 Santa Olalla, Spain ...37 54N 6 14W
62 Santa Olalla, Spain ...40 2N 4 25W
73 Sant' Onofrio, Italy ...38 42N 16 10E
167 Santa Paula, U.S.A. ...34 20N 119 2W
65 Santa Pola, Spain 38 13N 0 35W
167 Santa Rita, U.S.A. 32 50N 108 0W
172 Santa Rosa, Argentina 31 8S 63 20W
172 Santa Rosa, La Pampa, Argentina .36 40S 64 30W
MAP
172 Santa Rosa, Sanhuis, Argentina 32 30S 65 10W
174 Santa Rosa, Bolivia ...10 25S 67 20W
168 Santa Rosa Honduras......14 40N 89 0W
166 Sta. Rosa, Calif., U.S.A. 38 20N 122 50W
165 Santa Rosa, N. Mexico, U.S.A. 34 58N 104 40W
167 Sta. Rosa I., Calif., U.S.A. 34 0N 120 15W
163 Sta. Rosa I., Fla., U.S.A. 30 23N 87 0W
166 Santa Rosa Mts., U.S.A. 41 45N 117 30W
168 Santa Rosalia, Mexico 27 20N 112 30W
71 Santa Sofia, Italy 43 57N 11 55E
168 Santa Tecla, *see* Nueva San Salvador 13 40N 89 25W
71 Sta. Teresa, di Riva, It. 37 58N 15 21E
72 Sta. Teresa Gallura, It. 41 14N 9 12E
173 Sta. Vitória do Palmar, Brazil 33 32S 53 25W
72 Santadi, Italy 39 5N 8 42E
62 Santander, Spain 43 27N 3 51W
168 Santander Jimenez, Mex. 24 11N 98 29W
65 Santanyi, Spain 39 20N 3 5E
166 Santaquin, U.S.A. 40 0N 111 51W
175 Santarém, Brazil 2 25S 54 42W
63 Santarém, tn. & dist., Portugal 39 12N 8 42W
73 Santeramo in Colle, It. 40 48N 16 45E
71 Santerno R., Italy 44 10N 11 38E
70 Santhia, Italy 45 20N 8 10E
173 Santiago, Brazil 29 11S 54 52W
172 Santiago, Chile 33 24S 70 50W
169 Santiago, Dom. Rep. .19 30N 70 40W
169 Santiago, Panama 8 0N 81 0W
174 Santiago de Cao, Peru 8 0S 79 10W
62 Santiago de Compostela, Spain .42 52N 8 37W
169 Santiago de Cuba, Cuba 20 0N 75 49W
172 Santiago del Estero, Argentina 27 50S 64 20W
163 Santiago do Cacem, Portugal 38 1N 8 42W
168 Santiago Ixcuintla, Mex. 21 50N 105 11W
168 Santiago Papasquiaro, Mexico 25 0N 105 20W
62 Santillana del Mar, Sp. 43 24N 4 6W
105 Santipur, India 23 17N 88 25E
65 Santisteban del Puerto, Spain 38 17N 3 15W
175 Santo Amaro, Baia, Brazil 12 30S 38 50W
173 Santo Andre, Brazil ...23 39S 46 29W
173 Santo Angelo, Brazil .28 15S 54 15W
174 Santo Antonio, Amazonas, Brazil ... 3 0S 67 50W
174 Santo Antonio, Guaporé, Brazil 12 30S 63 40W
175 Santo Antonio, Mato Grosso, Brazil 15 50S 56 0W
174 Santo Corazón, Bolivia 18 0S 58 45W
169 Santo Domingo, Dominican Republic 18 30N 70 0W
169 Santo Domingo, Nic. .12 14N 84 59W
64 Santo Domingo de la Calzada, Spain 42 26N 2 27W
73 Santo Stefano di Camastro, Italy 38 1N 14 22E
71 Santo Stino di Livenza, Italy 45 45N 12 40E
174 Santo Tomas, Peru 14 34S 72 30W
173 Santo Tomé, Argentina 28 40S 56 5W
62 Santoña, Spain 43 29N 3 20W
173 Santos, Brazil 24 0S 46 20W
173 Santos Dumont, Brazil 22 55S 43 10W
113 Santu, China 25 59N 113 3E
113 Santuaho, China 26 36N 119 42E
98 Sanur, Jordan 32 22N 35 15E
113 Sanyuan, China 34 30N 108 59E
173 São Anastacio, Brazil .22 0S 51 40W
63 São Bartolomeu de Messines, Portugal .37 15N 8 17W
173 São Bernardo do Campo, Brazil 23 45S 46 34W
173 São Borja, Brazil 28 45S 56 0W
63 São Braz d'Alportel, Portugal 37 8N 7 58W
173 São Carlos, Brazil 22 0S 47 50W
175 São Cristovao, Brazil .11 0S 37 15W
175 São Domingos, Brazil 13 25S 46 10W
124 São Domingos, Port. Guin. 12 22N 16 8W
175 São Francisco, Minas Gerais, Brazil 16 0S 44 50W
173 São Francisco, Santa Catarina, Brazil 26 15S 48 36W
175 São Francisco R., Braz. 9 0S 39 0W
173 São Gabriel, Brazil 30 10S 54 30W
173 São Goncalo, Brazil ...22 48S 43 5W
175 São João, Pará, Brazil 5 20S 48 50W
173 São João de Boa Vista, São Paulo, Brazil 22 0S 46 52W
162 São João da Pesqueira, Portugal 41 8N 7 24W
MAP
173 São João del Rei, Braz. 21 8S 44 15W
175 São João do Piaui, Braz. 8 10S 42 15W
173 São João Nepomuceno, Brazil 21 33S 43 4W
173 São Jose do Rio Pardo, Brazil 21 55S 46 49W
173 São Jose do Rio Preto, Brazil 20 50S 49 20W
173 São Jose dos Campos, Brazil 23 7S 45 52W
173 São Leopoldo, Brazil .29 50S 51 10W
175 São Lourenco, Brazil .16 30S 55 0W
175 São Lourenço R., Brazil 16 40S 56 0W
175 São Luis (Maranhão), Brazil 2 39S 44 15W
173 São Luiz Gonzaga, Braz. 28 25S 55 0W
175 São Marcos B., Brazil 2 0S 44 0W
62 São Martinho, Portugal 39 30N 9 8W
175 São Mateus, Brazil 18 50S 39 50W
18 São Miguel I., Azores .37 47N 25 30W
173 São Paulo, Brazil 23 40S 46 50W
173 São Paulo, st., Brazil .22 0S 49 0W
174 São Paulo de Olivenca, Brazil 3 30S 69 0W
62 São Pedro do Sul, Port. 40 46N 8 4W
174 São Romão, Brazil 5 53S 67 50W
175 São Roque C., Brazil . 5 30S 35 10W
173 São Sebastião do Paraiso, Brazil 20 54S 46 59W
63 São Teotonio, Portugal 37 30N 8 42W
173 São Tome C., Brazil ...22 0S 41 10W
117 São Tomé I., G. of Guin. 0 10N 7 0E
173 São Vicente, Brazil 23 57S 46 23W
63 São Vicente, Cabo de, Portugal 37 1N 8 59W
49 Saône R., France 46 25N 4 50E
49 Saône-et-Loire, dépt., France 46 25N 4 50E
122 Saoura, W., Algeria ...29 55N 1 50W
76 Sapai, Greece 41 2N 25 43E
172 Sapaleri Cerro Mt., South America 22 50S 67 10W
109 Saparua I., Indonesia 3 33S 128 40E
125 Sapele, Nigeria 5 50N 5 40E
163 Sapelo I., U.S.A. 31 28N 81 15W
77 Sapientza I., Greece ...36 33N 21 43E
130 Sapindji, Congo 9 39S 23 12E
174 Saposoa, Peru 6 55S 76 30W
87 Sapozhok, U.S.S.R. ...53 59N 40 51E
166 Sapphire Mts., U.S.A. 46 30N 113 55W
114 Sapporo, Japan 43 0N 141 15E
73 Sapri, Italy 40 5N 15 37E
109 Sapudi, I., Indonesia . 7 2S 114 17E
165 Sapulpa, U.S.A. 36 0N 96 40W
127 Saqota, Ethiopia 12 40N 39 1E
100 Saqqez, Iran 36 15N 46 20E
74 Sar Planina Mts., Yugoslavia 42 10N 21 0E
101 Sar-i-Pul, Afghanistan 36 10N 66 0E
124 Sara, Upper Volta 11 40N 4 53W
100 Sarab, Iran 38 0N 47 30E
64 Saragossa, Spain 41 39N 0 53W
174 Saraquro, Ecuador 3 35S 79 16W
78 Sarai, Rumania 44 43N 28 10E
105 Saraipalli, India 21 20N 82 59E
74 Sarajevo, Yugoslavia .43 52N 18 26E
108 Saran, Mt., Indonesia 0 30S 111 25E
161 Saranac Lake, U.S.A. 44 20N 74 10W
131 Saranda, Tanzania 5 45S 34 59E
76 Sarandí, Albania 39 59N 19 55E
173 Sarandí, Uruguay 33 20S 55 50W
173 Sarandí del Yi, Urug. 33 18S 55 38W
109 Sarangani Bay, Phil. . 5 50N 125 2E
109 Sarangani Is., Phil. ... 5 50N 125 10E
87 Saransk, U.S.S.R. 54 10N 45 10E
84 Sarapul, U.S.S.R. 56 35N 53 40E
163 Sarasota, U.S.A. 27 10N 82 30W
166 Saratoga, Wyo., U.S.A. 41 30N 106 56W
161 Saratoga Springs, U.S.A. 43 5N 73 47W
87 Saratov, U.S.S.R. 51 30N 46 2E
87 Saratov Res., U.S.S.R. 51 15N 46 15E
107 Saravane, Laos 15 42N 106 3E
108 Sarawak, ter., Malay. . 2 0S 113 0E
101 Sarbaz, Iran 26 38N 61 19E
101 Sarbisheh, Iran 32 30N 59 40E
59 Sárbogárd, Hungary .46 55N 18 40E
70 Sarca, R., Italy 46 5N 10 45E
104 Sardarshahr, India 28 30N 74 29E
72 Sardegna, reg., Italy .39 57N 9 0E
104 Sardhana, India 29 9N 77 39E
123 Sardalas, Libya 25 50N 10 54E
72 Sardinia I., Italy 40 0N 9 0E
127 Sardo, Ethiopia 11 56N 41 14E
82 Sarektjakko, Mt., Swed. 67 29N 17 40E
74 Šarengrad, Yugoslavia 45 14N 19 16E
124 Saréyamou, Mali 16 25N 3 10W
164 Sargent, U.S.A. 41 42N 99 24W
103 Sargodha, W. Pakistan 32 10N 72 40E
16 Sargasso Sea, Atlan. Oc. 27 0N 72 0W
90 Sargumei, U.S.S.R. ...45 20N 74 45E
101 Sari, Iran 36 30N 53 11E
77 Saria I., Greece 35 54N 27 17E
98 Sarida R., Jordan 32 4N 35 3E
100 Sarikamis, Turkey 40 22N 42 35E
108 Sarikei, Sar., Malaysia 2 8N 111 22E
MAP
144 Sarina, Queens, Austral. 21 22S 149 13E
64 Sarinena, Spain 41 47N 0 10W
123 Sarir Tibasti, Libya ...22 50N 18 30E
165 Sarita, U.S.A. 27 14N 90 49W
112 Sariwon, N. Korea 38 37N 125 56E
75 Sariyer, Turkey 41 10N 29 3E
48 Sark I., Channel Is., U.K. 49 25N 2 20W
127 Sarka, Ethiopia 8 10N 36 52E
50 Sarlat, France 44 54N 1 13E
164 Sarles, U.S.A. 48 58N 98 57W
78 Sărmaşu, Rumania 46 45N 25 13E
109 Sarmi, Indonesia 1 49S 138 38E
80 Särna, Sweden 61 41N 12 58E
71 Sarnano, Italy 43 2N 13 17E
57 Sarnen, Switzerland ...46 53N 8 13E
154 Sarnia, Ont., Canada .43 0N 82 30W
73 Sarno, Italy 40 48N 14 35E
86 Sarny, U.S.S.R. 51 17N 26 40E
81 Särö, Sweden 57 31N 11 55E
77 Saronikós Kolpos, G., Greece 37 45N 23 45E
76 Saros Korfezi, G., Turkey 40 30N 26 15E
59 Sarospatak, Hungary .48 18N 21 33E
74 Sarosul Romanesc, Rum. 45 34N 21 43E
79 Sarpsborg, Norway 59 16N 11 12E
49 Sarralbe, France 49 0N 7 2E
64 Sarracin, Spain 42 15N 3 45W
49 Sarre, R., France 48 49N 7 0E
49 Sarrebourg, France 48 43N 7 3E
49 Sarre-Union, France .48 55N 7 4E
49 Sarreguemines, France 49 6N 7 4E
62 Sarria, Spain 42 41N 7 29W
64 Sarrion, Spain 40 9N 0 49W
124 Sarro, Mali 13 40N 5 5W
122 Sarro, Djebel, Morocco 31 6N 5 30W
56 Sarstedt, Germany 52 13N 9 50E
51 Sartène, Corsica, Fr. .41 38N 9 0E
48 Sarthe, dépt., France .47 58N 0 10E
48 Sarthe R., France 48 8N 0 10E
48 Sartilly, France 48 45N 1 28W
90 Sartynya, U.S.S.R. ...63 30N 62 50E
126 Sarum, Saudi Arabia .21 11N 39 10E
101 Sarur, Muscat & Oman 23 17N 58 4E
59 Sarvar, Hungary 47 15N 16 56E
101 Sarveston, Iran 29 20N 53 10E
80 Sarvfjallet, Mt., Sweden 62 42N 13 30E
59 Sárviz, R., Hungary ...46 40N 18 40E
90 Sary Shagan, U.S.S.R. 46 12N 73 48E
90 Sary Tash, U.S.S.R. ...39 45N 73 40E
88 Sarych C., U.S.S.R. ...44 25N 33 25E
78 Sarzana, Italy 44 7N 9 57E
48 Sarzeau, France 47 31N 2 48W
98 Sasa, Israel 33 2N 35 23E
105 Sasaram, India 24 57N 84 5E
74 Sasca Montana, Rum. 44 41N 21 45E
114 Sasebo, Japan 33 15N 129 50E
102 Saser Mt., Kashmir ...34 50N 77 50E
157 Saskatchewan, prov., Canada 54 40N 106 0W
157 Saskatchewan R., Can. 53 40N 103 30W
157 Saskatoon, Canada 52 10N 106 45W
99 Sasabani, Ethiopia 7 59N 44 43E
135 Sasolburg, OFS, S. Afr. 26 46S 27 49E
87 Sasovo, U.S.S.R. 54 25N 41 55E
124 Sassandra, Ivory Coast 5 0N 6 8W
72 Sassari, Italy 40 45N 8 33E
56 Sassnitz, Germany 54 29N 13 39E
71 Sasso Marconi, Italy 44 22N 11 12E
71 Sassocorvaro, Italy 43 47N 12 30E
71 Sassoferrato, Italy 43 26N 12 51E
124 Sasstown, Liberia 4 45N 8 27W
70 Sassuolo, Italy 44 31N 10 47E
64 Sastago, Spain 41 19N 0 21W
131 Sasumua Dam, Kenya 0 54S 36 46E
78 Sasyk, Ozero, L., U.S.S.R. 45 45N 30 0E
124 Satadougou, Mali 12 40N 11 25W
165 Satanta, U.S.A. 37 30N 101 0W
106 Satara, India 17 44N 73 58E
80 Säter, Sweden 60 22N 15 50E
163 Satilla, R., U.S.A. 31 15N 81 50W
105 Satkhira, E. Pakistan 22 43N 89 8E
104 Satmala Hills, India ...20 15N 74 40E
105 Satna, India 24 35N 80 50E
71 Sator, Mt., Yugoslavia 44 11N 16 43E
59 Sátoraljaujhely, Hung. 48 25N 21 41E
104 Satpura Ra., India 21 40N 75 0E
56 Satrup, Germany 54 39N 9 38E
106 Sattenpalle, India 16 25N 80 6E
78 Satu-Mare, Rumania .47 46N 22 55E
78 Satu-Mare, Reg., Rum. 47 45N 23 0E
108 Satui, Indonesia 3 50S 115 20E
174 Saturnina, R., Brazil .12 15S 58 10W
107 Satun, Thailand 6 43N 100 2E
172 Sauce, Argentina 30 5S 58 46W
79 Sauda, Norway 59 38N 6 28E
82 Saudarkrokur, Iceland 65 45N 19 40W
99 Saudi Arabia Kingdom, Asia 26 0N 44 0E
56 Sauerland, Mts., Ger. .51 0N 8 0E
160 Saugeen R., Canada ...44 20N 81 15W
161 Saugerties, U.S.A. 42 4N 73 58W
50 Saugues, France 44 58N 3 32E
79 Sauherad, Norway 59 25N 9 15E
122 Sauid el Amia, Maur .25 57N 6 8W
50 Saujon, France 45 41N 0 55W
164 Sauk Center, U.S.A. ...45 42N 94 56W
164 Sauk Rapids, U.S.A. .45 35N 94 10W
MAP
57 Saulgau, Germany 48 4N 9 32E
49 Saulieu, France 47 17N 4 14E
51 Sault, Vaucluse, France 44 6N 5 24E
154 Sault Ste. Marie, Can. 46 30N 84 20W
162 Sault Ste. Marie, U.S.A. 46 27N 84 22W
109 Saumlaki, Indonesia ... 7 55S 131 20E
48 Saumur, France 47 15N 0 5W
156 Saunders, Canada 52 58N 115 40W
147 Saunders C., N.Z. 45 53S 170 45E
15 Saunders I., Falkland Is. Dependencies 57 30S 27 30W
37 Saundersfoot, Wales, United Kingdom ...51 43N 4 42W
82 Saurbær, Iceland 64 24N 21 35W
132 Saûte, Mozambique ...23 23S 32 55E
50 Sauveterre, B., France 43 25N 0 57W
50 Sauzé Vaussais, France 46 8N 0 7E
73 Sava, Italy 40 28N 17 32E
71 Sava R., Yugoslavia .44 40N 19 50E
164 Savage, U.S.A. 47 43N 104 20W
125 Savalou, Dahomey 7 57N 2 4E
144 Savanah Downs, Queens., Australia .19 30S 141 30E
132 Savane, Mozambique .19 37S 35 8E
164 Savanna, U.S.A. 42 5N 90 10W
169 Savanna la Mar, Jam. 18 10N 78 10W
163 Savannah, Ga., U.S.A. 32 4N 81 4W
164 Savannah, Mo., U.S.A. 39 55N 94 46W
163 Savannah Tenn., U.S.A. 35 12N 88 18W
163 Savannah R., U.S.A. .33 0N 81 30W
107 Savannakhet, Laos 16 30N 104 49E
154 Savant Lake, Canada .50 20N 90 40W
106 Savantvadi, India 15 55N 73 54E
106 Savanur, India 14 59N 75 28E
104 Savda, India 21 9N 75 56E
125 Savé, Dahomey 8 2N 2 17E
132 Save R., Mozambique 21 16S 34 0E
100 Saveh, Iran 35 2N 50 20E
87 Savelovo, U.S.S.R. 56 51N 37 20E
125 Savelugu, Ghana 9 38N 0 54W
48 Savenay, France 47 20N 1 55W
50 Saverdun, France 43 14N 1 34E
34 Savernake, Eng., U.K. 51 22N 1 40W
49 Saverne, France 48 44N 7 20E
70 Savigliano, Italy 44 39N 7 40E
50 Savigny sur Braye, Fr. 47 53N 0 49E
62 Savinao, Spain 42 35N 7 38W
71 Savio R., Italy 43 58N 12 10E
74 Savnik, Yugoslavia ...42 59N 19 10E
51 Savoie (Savoy), dépt., Fr. 45 26N 6 35E
70 Savona, Italy 44 19N 8 29E
84 Savonlinna, Finland ...61 55N 28 55E
81 Savsjö, Sweden 57 23N 14 43E
81 Sävsjoström, Sweden .57 1N 15 25E
108 Sawah Lunto, Indon . 0 52S 100 52E
109 Sawai, Indonesia 3 0S 129 5E
104 Sawai Madhopur, India 26 0N 76 25E
114 Sawara, Japan 35 55N 140 30E
167 Sawatch Mts., U.S.A. .38 30N 106 30W
35 Sawbridgeworth England, U.K. 51 49N 0 10E
123 Sawda, Jabal as., Libya 28 51N 15 12E
108 Sawe, Indonesia 1 28N 97 24E
46 Sawel Mt., N. Ire., U.K. 54 48N 7 5W
123 Sawfajjin, W., Libya .31 46N 14 30E
132 Sawmills, Rhodesia ...19 30S 28 2E
35 Sawston, Eng., U.K. .52 7N 0 11E
35 Sawtry, Eng., U.K. ...52 26N 0 17W
109 Sawu I., Indonesia 10 35S 121 50E
109 Sawu Sea, E. Indies ... 9 30S 121 50E
161 Sawyerville, Canada ...45 19N 71 35W
39 Saxilby, Eng., U.K. ...53 16N 0 40W
35 Saxlingham Nethergate, England, U.K. 52 33N 1 16E
35 Saxmundham Eng., UK 52 13N 1 29E
160 Saxton, U.S.A. 40 12N 79 18W
125 Say, Niger 13 8N 2 22E
125 Saya, Nigeria 9 30N 3 18E
155 Sayabec, Quebec, Can. 48 35N 67 41W
174 Sayar, Peru 11 0S 77 25W
89 Sayasan, U.S.S.R. 42 56N 46 15E
100 Sayda, Lebanon 33 35N 35 25E
143 Sayer's Lake, Australia 32 40S 143 30E
112 Saynshand, Mongolia .44 50N 110 20E
165 Sayre, Okla., U.S.A. 35 20N 99 40W
161 Sayre, Pa., U.S.A. 42 0N 76 30W
168 Sayula, Mexico 19 50N 103 40W
161 Sayville, U.S.A. 40 45N 73 7W
76 Sazan, I., Albania 40 30N 19 20E
58 Sázava R., Cz. 49 50N 15 0E
102 Sazin, Kashmir 35 35N 73 30E
75 Sazlika, R., Bulgaria .42 15N 25 50E
123 Sbeitla, Tunisia 35 12N 9 7E
48 Scaër, France 48 2N 3 42W
38 Scafell Pikes., Eng., U.K. 54 27N 3 14W
40 Scalasaig, Scot., U.K. 56 4N 6 10W
39 Scalby, England, U.K. 54 18N 0 26W
73 Scalea, Italy 39 49N 15 47E
42 Scalloway, Scot., U.K. 60 9N 1 16W
42 Scalpay I., Inner Hebrides, Scot., U.K. 57 18N 6 0W

MAP
42 Scalpay I., Outer Hebrides, Scot., U.K. ...57 51N 6 40W
156 Scandia, Canada ...50 20N 112 0W
70 Scandiano, Italy ...44 36N 10 40E
19 Scandinavia, pen., Eur. ...64 0N 12 0E
71 Scansano, Italy ...42 40N 11 20E
43 Scapa Flow, Scot., U.K. ...58 52N 3 0W
39 Scapwick, Eng., U.K. 33 8N 0 22W
40 Scarba I., Scot., U.K. 56 10N 5 42W
39 Scarborough, Eng., U.K. ...54 17N 0 24W
169 Scarborough, Tobago .11 11N 60 42W
147 Scargill, New Zealand 42 56S 172 58E
44 Scariff, Ireland ...52 55N 8 32W
44 Scariff I., Ireland ...51 43N 10 15W
40 Scarinish, Scot., U.K. 56 30N 6 48W
42 Scarp I., Scot.,U.K. ...58 1N 7 8W
49 Scarpe, R., France ...50 22N 3 0E
44 Scattery I., Ireland ...52 37N 9 30W
42 Scavaig, L., Scot., U.K. ...57 8N 6 10W
71 Scedro, I., Yugoslavia 43 6N 16 43E
164 Scenic, U.S.A. ...43 49N 102 32W
56 Schaal See, Germany .53 40N 10 57E
55 Schaesberg, Netherlands ...50 54N 6 0E
57 Schaffhausen, Switz. .47 42N 8 36E
54 Schagen, Netherlands 52 49N 4 48E
55 Schaijk, Netherlands .51 44N 5 38E
58 Schärding, Austria ...48 27N 13 27E
56 Scharhörn I., Germany ...53 58N 8 24E
58 Scharnitz, Austria ...47 23N 11 15E
56 Scheessel, Germany ...53 10N 9 33E
155 Schefferville, Canada .54 50N 66 40W
58 Scheibbs, Austria ...48 1N 15 9E
54 Schelde, R., Belgium .51 10N 4 20E
161 Schenectady, U.S.A. .42 50N 73 58W
56 Scherfede, Germany ...51 32N 9 2E
43 Schichallion Mt., Scotland, U.K. ...56 40N 4 5W
54 Schiedam, Netherlands ...51 55N 4 25E
54 Schiermonnikoog I., Netherlands ...53 30N 6 15E
57 Schifferstadt, Germany ...49 22N 8 23E
55 Schijndel, Netherlands 51 37N 5 27E
49 Schiltigheim, France .48 35N 7 45E
71 Schio, Italy ...45 42N 11 21E
49 Schirmeck, France ...48 29N 7 12E
58 Schladming, Austria ...47 23N 13 41E
56 Schlei R., Germany ...54 45N 9 52E
56 Schleiden, Germany ...50 32N 6 26E
56 Schleswig, Germany ...54 32N 9 34E
56 Schleswig-Holstein, land, Germany ...54 10N 9 40E
57 Schlüchtern, Germany 50 20N 9 32E
56 Schmalkalden, Germany ...50 43N 10 28E
55 Schmidtheim, W. Ger. 50 25N 6 34E
133 Schmidtsdrif, S. Africa ...28 41S 24 2E
56 Schmolln, Germany ...50 54N 12 22E
56 Schneeberg, Germany 50 35N 12 39E
58 Schneeberg, Mt., Aust. ...47 53N 15 55E
164 Schofield, Wis., U.S.A. ...44 54N 89 39W
56 Schönberg, Rostock, Ger. ...53 50N 10 55E
56 Schönberg, Schleswig-Holstein, Germany ...54 23N 10 20E
56 Schönebeck, Germany 52 2N 11 42E
56 Schöningen, Germany 52 8N 10 57E
135 Schoombee, S. Africa .31 28S 25 30E
55 Schoonhoven, Neth. ...51 57N 4 51E
144 Schouten Is., Indonesia ... 1 0S 136 0E
54 Schouwen I., Neth. ...51 43N 3 45E
57 Schramberg, Germany 48 12N 8 24E
58 Schrankogl, Mt., Aust. 47 3N 11 7E
154 Schreiber, Canada ...48 45N 87 20W
58 Schruns, Austria ...47 5N 9 56E
55 Schulen, Belgium ...50 57N 5 10E
58 Schuls, Switzerland ...46 48N 10 18E
154 Schumacher, Canada .48 30N 81 16W
166 Schurz, U.S.A. ...38 59N 118 57W
164 Schuyler, U.S.A. ...41 30N 97 3W
161 Schuylkill Haven, USA ...40 37N 76 11W
57 Schwabach, Germany 49 19N 11 3E
57 Schwabisch Gmund, West Germany ...48 49N 9 48E
57 Schwabisch Hau, West Germany ...49 7N 9 45E
57 Schwabischer Jura, Mts., West Germany ...48 30N 9 30E
108 Schwaner Ra., Indon. 1 0S 112 30E
112 Schwangcheng, China 45 27N 126 27E
112 Schwangyashan, China ...46 35N 131 15E
58 Schwarza, R., Austria 50 30N 11 30E
56 Schwarzenberg, Ger. .50 31N 12 49E
57 Schwarzwald, Germany ...48 0N 8 0E
58 Schwaz, Austria...47 20N 11 44E
56 Schwedt, Germany ...53 4N 14 18E
57 Schweinfurt, Germany 50 3N 10 12E
133 Schweizer Reneke, Transvaal, S. Africa 27 11S 25 18E
55 Schweim, W. Ger. ...51 17N 7 17E
57 Schwenningen, Ger. ...48 3N 8 32E
56 Schwerin, Germany ...53 37N 11 22E
56 Schweriner See Ger. .53 45N 11 26E
55 Schwerte, Germany ...51 26N 7 33E
57 Schwetzingen, Germany ...49 22N 8 35E
57 Schwyz, Switzerland .47 2N 8 39E
72 Sciacca, Italy ...37 30N 13 3E
73 Scicli, Italy ...36 48N 14 41E
131 Scidlei, Somali Rep. ... 1 8S 41 52E
99 Scillave, Ethiopia ... 6 22N 44 32E
36 Scilly, Isles of, Eng., U.K. ...49 55N 6 15W
60 Scinawa, Poland ...51 25N 16 26E
162 Scioto R., U.S.A. ...39 0N 83 0W
164 Scobey, U.S.A. ...48 47N 105 30W
143 Scone, N.S.W., Austral. ...32 0S 150 52E
73 Scordia, Italy ...37 19N 14 50E
42 Score Hd., Scot., U.K. 60 12N 1 5W
14 Scoresby Sund, Green. 70 30N 22 0W
166 Scotia, Calif., U.S.A. .40 36N 124 4W
15 Scotia Sea, Antarctica 56 5S 56 0W
33 Scotland, Country, United Kingdom ...57 0N 4 0W
164 Scotland, U.S.A. ...43 10N 97 45W
163 Scotland Neck., U.S.A. ...36 6N 77 24W
15 Scott, Antarctica ...77 0S 165 0E
15 Scott, C., Antarctica .71 30S 168 0E
15 Scott, I., Antarctica ...67 0S 179 0E
153 Scott Inlet, Canada ...71 0N 71 30W
157 Scott, L., Canada ...60 0N 106 0W
164 Scott City, U.S.A. ...38 30N 100 52W
135 Scottburgh, Nat., S. Afr. ...30 15S 30 47E
164 Scottsbluff, U.S.A. ...41 55N 103 35W
163 Scottsboro, U.S.A. ...34 40N 86 0W
162 Scottsburg, U.S.A. ...38 40N 85 46W
160 Scottdale, U.S.A. ...40 8N 79 35W
163 Scottsville, Ky., U.S.A. ...36 48N 86 10W
160 Scottsville, N.Y., U.S.A. ...43 2N 77 47W
144 Scottville, Australia ...20 35S 147 40E
162 Scottville, U.S.A. ...43 57N 86 18W
42 Scourie, Scot., U.K. ...58 20N 5 10W
42 Scousburgh, Scot., U.K. ...59 58N 1 20W
46 Scrabby, Ireland ...53 53N 7 32W
43 Scrabster, Scot., U.K. 58 36N 3 31W
46 Scramoge, Ireland ...53 46N 8 4W
161 Scranton, Pa., U.S.A. 41 22N 75 41W
44 Screeb, Lough, Ireland ...53 24N 9 34W
48 Screggan, Ireland ...53 15N 7 32W
41 Scremerston, Eng., U.K. ...55 44N 1 59W
40 Scridain, L., Scot., U.K. ...56 23N 6 7W
160 Scugog L., Canada ...44 8N 78 53W
39 Scunthorpe, Eng., U.K. ...53 35N 0 38W
99 Scusciuban, Somali Rep. ...10 28 50 5E
160 Sea Breeze, U.S.A. ...43 12N 77 32W
143 Sea Lake, Vic., Austral. ...35 28S 142 55E
143 Seaford, Vic., Australia ...38 10S 145 11E
35 Seaford, Eng., U.K. ...50 46N 0 8E
162 Seaford, U.S.A. ...38 37N 75 36W
154 Seaforth, Canada ...43 35N 81 25W
42 Seaforth L., Scot., U.K. ...57 52N 6 36W
165 Seagraves, U.S.A. ...32 56N 102 30W
39 Seaham, Eng., U.K. ...54 51N 1 20W
134 Seal C., C. Prov., S. Afr. ...34 7S 23 25E
157 Seal R., Canada ...58 50N 97 30W
155 Seal Cove, Newf., Can. ...49 57N 56 22W
42 Sealga, L. na, Scot., U.K. ...57 50N 5 18W
165 Sealy, U.S.A. ...29 46N 96 9W
39 Seamer, England, U.K. ...54 14N 0 27W
167 Searchlight, U.S.A. ...35 31N 111 57W
165 Searcy, U.S.A. ...35 15N 91 45W
167 Searles, L., U.S.A. ...35 47N 117 17W
38 Seascale, England, U.K. ...54 24N 3 29W
166 Seaside, U.S.A. ...45 59N 124 0W
143 Seaspray, Vic., Austral. ...38 25S 147 15E
36 Seaton, England, U.K. ...50 42N 3 3W
39 Seaton Delaval, England, U.K. ...55 5N 1 33W
166 Seattle, U.S.A. ...47 41N 122 15W
144 Seaview Ra., Australia ...19 0S 146 10E
147 Seaward Kaikouras, Mts., New Zealand .42 10S 173 44E
168 Sebastian Vizcaino B., Mexico ...28 0N 114 30W
166 Sebastopol, U.S.A. ...38 16N 122 56W
122 Sebdou, Algeria ...34 47N 1 12W
78 Sebeş, Rumania ...45 56N 23 40E
162 Sebewaing, U.S.A. ...43 45N 83 27W
86 Sebezh, U.S.S.R. ...56 14N 28 22E
122 Sebgag, R., Algeria ...34 30N 2 0E
124 Sebi, Mali ...15 50N 4 12W
88 Sebin Karahisar, Tur. 40 22N 38 28E
132 Sebina, Botswana ...20 55S 27 17E
78 Sebiş, Rumania ...46 23N 22 13E
122 Sebou R., Morocco ...34 30N 5 0W
122 Sebkra Azzel Mati, Alg. ...26 10N 0 43E
122 Sebkra Mekerghene, Alg. ...26 21N 1 30E
163 Sebring, Fla., U.S.A. .27 36N 81 47W
160 Sebring, Ohio, U.S.A. 40 55N 81 2W
160 Sebringville, Canada .43 25N 81 4W
122 Sebta, see Ceuta, Morocco ...35 52N 5 26W
108 Sebuku I., Indonesia . 3 30S 116 25E
74 Sečanj, Yugoslavia ...45 25N 20 47E
70 Secchia R., Italy ...44 30N 10 40E
156 Sechelt, Canada ...49 25N 123 42W
55 Sechtem, W. Germany 50 46N 6 58E
49 Seclin, France ...50 33N 3 2E
174 Sechura B., Peru ... 5 40S 81 0W
174 Sechura Des., Peru ... 6 0S 80 30W
48 Secondigny, France ...46 37N 0 26W
59 Sečovce, Cz. ...48 42N 21 40E
147 Secretary I., N.Z. ...45 15S 166 56E
106 Secunderabad, India .17 28N 78 30E
63 Seda, R., Portugal ...39 6N 7 53W
164 Sedalia, Mo., U.S.A. ...38 40N 93 18W
49 Sedan, France ...49 43N 4 57E
145 Sedan, South Australia ...34 35S 139 29E
165 Sedan, U.S.A. ...37 10N 96 11W
56 Sedano, Spain ...42 43N 3 49W
38 Sedbergh, Eng., U.K. 54 20N 2 31W
147 Seddon, New Zealand 41 40S 174 7E
147 Seddonville, N.Z. ...41 33S 172 1E
98 Sede Ya'aqov, Israel .32 43N 35 7E
39 Sedgefield, Eng., U.K. 54 40N 1 27W
156 Sedgewick, Canada ...52 48N 111 41W
124 Sedhiou, Senegal ...12 50N 15 30W
71 Sedico, Italy ...46 8N 12 6E
58 Sedicany, Cz. ...49 40N 14 25E
157 Sedley, Canada ...50 10N 104 0W
98 Sedom, Israel ...31 5N 35 20E
90 Sedov Pk., U.S.S.R. ...73 20N 55 10E
123 Sedrata, Algeria ...36 7N 7 31E
166 Sedro Woolley, U.S.A. 48 30N 122 15W
86 Seduva, U.S.S.R. ...55 45N 23 45E
58 Seefeld, Germany ...51 53N 13 17E
56 Seehausen, Germany .52 52N 11 43E
134 Seeheim, S.W. Africa .26 32S 17 52E
134 Seekoegat, S. Africa ...33 0S 22 31E
56 Seelaw, Germany ...52 32N 14 22E
34 Seend, England, U.K. 51 20N 2 2W
48 Sees, France ...48 38N 0 10E
56 Seesen, Germany ...51 53N 10 10E
124 Sefadu, Sierra Leone . 8 35N 10 58W
122 Sefrou, Morocco ...33 52N 4 52W
147 Sefton, N.Z. ...43 15S 172 41E
147 Sefton Mt., N.Z. ...43 40S 170 5E
124 Sefwi Bekwai, Ghana . 6 10N 2 25W
84 Seg, L., U.S.S.R. ...63 0N 33 10E
107 Segamat, Malaysia ... 2 30N 102 50E
132 Segara, Botswana ...20 10S 25 18E
78 Segarcea, Rumania ...44 6N 23 43E
124 Segbwema, Sierra Leone ... 8 0N 11 0W
109 Sege, Indonesia ... 2 10S 132 5E
122 Seggueur, W., Algeria 32 25N 2 0E
127 Segid I., Saudi Arabia 16 55N 42 0E
50 Segonzac, France ...45 36N 0 14W
62 Segorbe, Spain ...39 50N 0 30W
124 Segou, Mali ...13 30N 6 10W
62 Segovia, Spain ...40 57N 4 10W
48 Segré, France ...47 40N 0 52W
124 Séguéla, Ivory Coast . 7 55N 6 40W
165 Seguin, U.S.A. ...29 35N 97 58W
165 Segundo, U.S.A. ...37 12N 104 50W
65 Segura R., Spain ...38 9N 0 40W
104 Sehore, India ...23 10N 77 5E
104 Sehwan, W. Pakistan .26 28N 67 53E
78 Seica Mare, Rumania .46 1N 24 7E
40 Seil, I., Scotland, U.K. ...56 17N 5 37W
82 Seiland, Norway ...70 18N 23 10E
165 Seiling, U.S.A. ...36 10N 99 5W
51 Seille, R., France ...46 35N 5 0E
55 Seilles, Belgium ...50 30N 5 6E
91 Seimchan, U.S.S.R. ...62 40N 152 30E
82 Seinäjoki, Finland ...62 47N 22 58E
49 Seine, dépt., France ...49 0N 3 0E
48 Seine, R., France ...49 28N 0 15E
49 Seine-et-Marne, dépt., France ...48 45N 3 0E
48 Seine-Maritime, dépt., France ...49 40N 1 0E
49 Seine-St. Denis, dépt., France ...48 55N 2 28E
78 Seini, Rumania ...47 44N 23 21E
101 Seistan, dist., Iran ...30 50N 61 0E
165 Seiyala, Egypt ...22 57N 32 41E
174 Sejal, Colombia ... 2 45N 68 0W
81 Sejerö B., Denmark ...55 54N 11 28E
81 Sejerö I., Denmark ...55 53N 11 9E
108 Sekaju, Indonesia ... 2 58S 103 58E
135 Sekake's, Lesotho ...29 58S 28 27E
113 Sekibi Sho, Is., Japan 25 45N 124 35E
122 Sekkane, Erg in, Mali 20 30N 1 30W
166 Sekiu, U.S.A. ...48 30N 124 29W
124 Sekondi, Ghana ... 5 2N 1 48W
133 Sekuma, Botswana ...24 30S 23 57E
166 Selah, U.S.A. ...46 44N 120 30W
107 Selama, Malaysia ... 5 12N 100 42E
107 Selangor, st., Malaya, Malaysia ... 3 20N 101 30E
72 Selargius, Sardinia, Italy ...39 14N 9 14E
109 Selaru I., Indonesia ... 8 18S 131 0E
108 Seletan, Tg., C., Indon. ... 4 10S 114 40E
133 Selati R., Trans., S. Afr. ...24 0S 31 7E
57 Selb, Germany ...50 9N 12 9E
35 Selbourne, Eng., U.K. 51 5N 0 55W
39 Selby, England, U.K. 53 47N 1 5W
164 Selby, U.S.A. ...45 34N 99 55W
71 Selce, Yugoslavia ...43 20N 16 50E
164 Selden, U.S.A. ...39 24N 100 39W
73 Sele, R., Italy ...40 27N 15 0E
111 Selenga R., Mongolia .49 20N 101 0E
130 Selenge, Congo ... 1 58S 18 11E
112 Selenge, Mongolia ...49 35N 104 4E
112 Selenge Mörön, R., Mongolia ...49 25N 103 45E
76 Selenicë, Albania ...40 33N 19 39E
56 Selenter See, Germany 54 19N 10 26E
49 Selestat, France ...48 15N 7 27E
80 Selet, Sweden ...63 15N 15 45E
78 Seletin, Rumania ...47 50N 25 12E
74 Selevac, Yugoslavia ...44 44N 20 52E
164 Selfridge, U.S.A. ...46 3N 100 57W
124 Selibaby, Mauritania .15 20N 12 15W
86 Seliger L., U.S.S.R. ...57 15N 33 0E
167 Seligman, U.S.A. ...35 17N 112 56W
89 Selim, Turkey ...40 15N 42 58E
126 Selima O., Sudan ...21 28N 29 31E
132 Selinda Spillway, Bots. ...18 35S 23 10E
77 Selinoûs, Greece ...37 35N 21 37E
105 Selipuk Gompa Tibet 31 23N 82 49E
86 Selizharovo, U.S.S.R. .57 1N 33 17E
79 Selje, Norway ...62 3N 5 22E
79 Seljord, Norway ...59 30N 8 40E
157 Selkirk, Canada ...50 10N 97 20W
41 Selkirk, & co. Scotland., U.K. ...55 33N 2 50W
156 Selkirk Mts., Canada .51 0N 117 10W
49 Selles sur Cher, France ...47 16N 1 33E
49 Sellières, France ...46 50N 5 32E
35 Sellindge, Eng., U.K. .51 6N 1 0E
167 Sells, U.S.A. ...31 57N 111 57W
59 Sellye, Hungary ...45 52N 17 51E
163 Selma, Ala., U.S.A. ...32 30N 87 0W
167 Selma, Calif., U.S.A. .36 39N 119 39W
163 Selma, N.C., U.S.A. ...35 32N 78 15W
163 Selmer, Tenn., U.S.A. 35 9N 88 36W
76 Selo Mt., Greece ...41 10N 126 0E
49 Selongey, France ...47 36N 5 10E
133 Selons River, S. Africa ...25 37S 29 38E
109 Selpele Indonesia ... 0 1S 130 5E
35 Selsey, England, U.K. 50 44N 0 47W
35 Selsey Bill, Eng., U.K. ...50 44N 0 47W
49 Seltz, France ...48 54N 8 7E
109 Selu, I. Indonesia ... 7 26S 130 55E
132 Selukwe, Rhodesia ...19 40S 30 0E
48 Selune R., France ...48 35N 1 15W
172 Selva, Argentina ...29 50S 62 0W
64 Selva, Spain ...41 13N 1 8E
174 Selvas, reg., Brazil ... 6 30S 67 0W
144 Selwyn, Australia ...21 30S 140 29E
157 Selwyn L., Canada ...60 0N 104 30W
144 Selwyn Ra. Australia 21 10S 140 0E
76 Seman, R., Albania ...40 45N 19 50E
109 Semarang, Indonesia . 7 0S 110 26E
131 Sembabule, Uganda ... 0 3S 31 29E
127 Semeih, Sudan ...12 43N 30 53E
87 Semenov, U.S.S.R. ...56 43N 44 30E
88 Semenovka, U.S.S.R. .49 37N 33 2E
109 Semeru Mt., Indonesia 8 4S 113 3E
87 Semiluki, U.S.S.R. ...51 41N 39 10E
166 Seminoe Res., U.S.A. .42 0N 107 0W
165 Seminole, Okla., U.S.A. ...35 15N 96 45W
165 Seminole, Tex., U.S.A. ...32 41N 102 38W
90 Semiozerny, U.S.S.R. .52 35N 64 0E
90 Semipalatinsk, U.S.S.R. ...50 30N 80 10E
109 Semirara Is., Phil. ...12 0N 121 20E
108 Semitau, Indonesia ... 0 29N 111 57E
90 Semiyarsk, U.S.S.R. ...50 55N 78 30E
131 Semliki R., Uganda ... 1 0N 30 0E
58 Semmering Pass., Aust. ...43 41N 15 45E
101 Semnan, Iran ...35 55N 53 25E
54 Semois R., Belgium ...49 47N 5 13E
109 Semporna, Malaysia ... 4 30N 118 33E
49 Semur en Auxois, Fr. .47 30N 4 20E
107 Sen, R. Cambodia ...13 45N 105 12E
174 Sena Madureira, Brazil ... 9 5S 68 45W
175 Senador Pompeu, Brazil ... 5 40S 39 20W
107 Senai, Malaysia ... 1 38N 103 38E
108 Senaja, Sabah, Malaysia ... 6 49S 117 2E
132 Senane, Mozambique .22 46S 34 1E
132 Senanga, Zambia ...16 2S 23 14E
165 Senatobia, U.S.A. ...34 38N 89 57W
127 Senafa, Ethiopia ... 9 11N 39 3E
114 Sendai, Kagoshima, Jap. ...31 50N 130 20E
114 Sendai, Miyagi, Japan 38 15N 141 0E
106 Sendamangalam, India ...11 17N 78 17E
56 Sendenhorst, Germany ...51 50N 7 49E
104 Sendurjana, India ...21 32N 78 24E
59 Senec, Czechoslovakia 48 12N 17 23E
166 Seneca, Ore., U.S.A. ...44 10N 119 2W
163 Seneca, S.C., U.S.A. ...34 43N 82 59W
160 Seneca L., U.S.A. ...42 40N 76 58W
160 Seneca Falls, U.S.A ...42 55N 76 50W
124 Senegal, Rep. of W.Afr. ...14 30N 14 30W
124 Senegal R., W. Africa 16 30N 15 30W
135 Senekal, O.F.S., S. Afr. ...28 18S 27 36E
56 Senftenberg, Germany 51 30N 13 51E
87 Sengiley, U.S.S.R. ...53 58N 48 54E
175 Senhor-do-Bonfim, Braz. ...10 30S 40 10W
59 Senica Czechoslovakia ...48 41N 17 25E
71 Senigallia, Italy ...43 42N 13 12E
71 Senio, R., Italy ...44 18N 11 47E
71 Senj. Yugoslavia ...45 0N 14 58E
82 Senja I., Norway ...69 15N 17 30E
113 Senkaku Gunto, Is., Jap. ...25 50N 123 30E
49 Senlis, France ...49 13N 2 35E
107 Senmonorom, Cambodia ...12 50N 107 15E
127 Sennar, Sudan ...13 30N 33 35E
127 Sennar Dam, Sudan ...13 31N 33 38E
36 Sennen, England, U.K. ...50 4N 5 42W
154 Senneterre, Canada ...48 25N 77 15W
86 Senno, U.S.S.R. ...54 45N 29 58E
72 Sennori, Italy ...40 49N 8 36E
37 Senny Bridge, Wales, United Kingdom ...51 57N 3 35W
48 Senonches, France ...48 34N 1 2E
72 Senorbi, Italy ...39 33N 9 8E
105 Seorinayan, India ...21 45N 82 34E
71 Senozece, Yugoslavia .45 43N 14 3E
49 Sens, France ...48 11N 3 15E
74 Senta, Yugoslavia ...45 55N 20 3E
50 Sentein, France ...42 53N 0 58E
130 Sentery, Congo ... 5 17S 25 42E
167 Sentinel, U.S.A. ...32 56N 113 13W
107 Sentinel, I., North, Andamen Is. ...11 35N 92 15E
107 Sentinel, I., South, Andaman Is. ...11 1N 92 16E
109 Sentolo, Indonesia ... 7 55S 110 13E
125 Senya Beraku, Ghana 5 28N 0 31W
64 Séo de Urgel, Spain ...42 22N 1 23E
104 Seohara, India ...29 15N 78 33E
105 Seoni, India ...22 5N 79 30E
112 Seoul, South Korea ...37 31N 127 6E
155 Separation Point, Can. ...53 40N 57 16W
144 Sepik R., Terr. of New Guinea ... 4 5S 143 0E
60 Sepolno, Poland ...53 26N 17 30E
60 Sepolno, Poland ...52 26N 18 29E
107 Sepone, Laos ...16 45N 106 13E
132 Sepopa, Botswana ...18 49S 22 12E
155 Sept Îles, Canada ...50 13N 66 22W
144 Septimus, Australia ...21 20S 148 35E
62 Sepulveda, Spain ...41 18N 3 45W
62 Sequeros, Spain ...40 31N 6 2W
166 Sequim, U.S.A. ...48 3N 123 9W
167 Sequoia Nat. Park, U.S.A. ...36 20N 118 30W
89 Serafimovich, U.S.S.R. ...49 30N 42 50E
54 Seraing, Belgium ...50 35N 5 32E
105 Serampore, India ...22 44N 88 30E
109 Serang, Indonesia ... 6 8S 106 10E
108 Serasan, I., Indonesia 2 29N 109 4E
70 Seravezza, Italy ...43 59N 10 13E
74 Serbia, see Srbija, Y.-slav. ...43 30N 21 0E
78 Sercaia, Rumania ...45 49N 25 9E
127 Serdo, Ethiopia ...11 56N 41 14E
87 Serdobsk, U.S.S.R. ...52 28N 44 10E
86 Seredka, U.S.S.R. ...58 12N 28 3E
70 Seregno, Italy ...45 40N 9 12E
107 Seremban, Malaysia ... 2 43N 101 53E
131 Serengeti Plain, Tanz. 2 40S 35 0E
132 Serenje, Zambia ...13 14S 30 15E
99 Serenli, Somali Rep. ... 2 28N 42 8E
87 Sergach, U.S.S.R. ...55 30N 45 30E
64 Serge, R., Spain ...42 5N 1 21E
87 Sergievsk, U.S.S.R. ...54 0N 51 10E
175 Sergipe, st., Brazil ...10 30S 37 20W
108 Seria, Brunei ... 4 37N 114 30E
108 Serian Sar., Malaysia 1 0N 110 40E
70 Seriate, Italy ...45 42N 9 43E
108 Seribu Arch., Indonesia ... 5 40S 106 42E
49 Sérifontaine, France ...49 20N 1 45E
77 Serifos, I., Greece ...37 9N 24 30E
50 Sérignan, France ...43 17N 3 17E
100 Serik, Turkey ...36 55N 31 10E
49 Sermaize les Bains, Fr. ...48 47N 4 54E
109 Sermata I., Indonesia 8 15S 128 50E
71 Sermide, Italy ...45 0N 11 17E
124 Sero, Mali ...14 42N 10 59W
65 Seron, Spain ...37 20N 2 29W
64 Seros, Spain ...41 27N 0 24E
90 Serov, U.S.S.R. ...59 40N 60 20E
133 Serowe, Botswana ...22 25S 26 43E
129 Serpa Pinto, Angola ...14 48S 17 52E
63 Serpa,Portugal ...37 57N 7 38E
72 Serpentara, Sard., Italy ...39 8N 9 38E
142 Serpentine, W. Austral. ...32 30S 116 30E
142 Serpentine L., S. Austral. ...28 30S 129 10E
169 Serpent's Mouth, Ven. 10 0N 61 30W
65 Serpis, R., Spain ...38 45N 0 21W
87 Serpukhov, U.S.S.R. .54 55N 37 28E
175 Serra Acarai, Brazil ... 1 50N 57 50W
129 Sá da Bandeira, Ang. .14 50S 13 40E
174 Sa. da Desordem, Brazil ... 4 0S 46 30W
62 Serra da Estrela, Port. ...40 10N 7 45W
132 Sa da Gorongosa, Mozam. ...18 30S 34 20E
170 Sa da Mantiqueira, Braz. ...22 30S 45 0W
175 Sa. da Tabatinga, Braz. ...10 30S 44 0W
173 Serra dàs Ararás, Brazil ...25 0S 53 10W
175 Serra de Baturite, Braz. ... 4 25S 39 0W
173 Serra de Fartura, Brazil ...26 15S 52 40W
175 Serra do Araripe, Brazil ... 7 20S 39 40W

MAP
175 Sa. do Cachimbo, Braz. 9 30s 55 0w
175 Serra do Chifre, Brazil 17 0s 41 0w
173 Serra do Espigao, Braz. 26 35s 50 30w
175 Sa. do Espinhaco, Braz. 17 0s 43 30w
173 Serra do Espinilho, Braz. 28 30s 55 0w
175 Serra do Estrondo, Braz. 7 20s 48 0w
174 Serra do Norte Brazil 11 30s 59 0w
176 Serra do Mar, Brazil .25 30s 49 0w
175 Serra do Periperi, Braz. 14 50s 40 30w
175 Serra do Piaui, Brazil 9 30s 43 30w
175 Serra do Roncador, Braz. 12 30s 52 30w
175 Serra do Sincorá, Brazil 13 30s 41 0w
175 Serra do Tombador, Baia, Brazil 12 0s 41 30w
174 Serra do Tombador, Mato Grosso, Brazil 12 30s 58 30w
175 Serra do Valentim, Braz. 6 0s 43 20w
175 Serra dos Aimorés, Braz. 17 50s 40 30w
174 Serra dos Apiacás, Braz. 9 50s 57 0w
175 Serra dos Carajas, Braz. 6 0s 51 30w
175 Serra dos Javaés, Brazil 8 25s 48 30w
174 Serra dos Parecis, Braz. 13 0s 60 0w
175 Sa. dos Penitentes, Braz. 8 0s 46 25w
173 Serra dos Tapes, Brazil 31 25s 52 45w
175 Serra Formosa, Brazil 12 0s 55 0w
175 Serra Geral, Brazil 26 25s 50 0w
175 Sa. Geral de Goias, Braz. 12 0s 46 0w
175 Sa. Grande, Piaui, Braz. 4 30s 41 20w
175 Serra Negra, Brazil 6 0s 46 20w
174 Serra Parima, Brazil . 3 0N 64 30w
73 Serra San Bruno, Italy 38 35N 16 20E
174 Serra Tapirapeco, Ven. 1 10N 65 0w
175 Serra Tumucumuque, Brazil 2 0N 55 0w
73 Serra Capriola, Italy .41 47N 15 12E
76 Sérrai, Greece 41 5N 23 37E
62 Serradilla, Spain 39 50N 6 9w
72 Serramanna, Sard., It. 39 26N 8 56E
64 Serrania de Cuenca, Sp. 40 10N 1 50w
123 Serrat, C., Tunisia 37 14N 9 10E
51 Serres, France 44 26N 5 43E
172 Serrezuela, Argentina .30 40s 65 20w
175 Serrinha, Brazil 11 30s 39 0w
73 Sersale, Italy 39 1N 16 44E
175 Sertânia, Brazil 8 0s 37 20w
175 Sertao, Desert, Brazil 10 0s 40 20w
109 Serui, Indonesia 1 45s 136 10E
132 Serule, Botswana 21 57s 27 11E
76 Sérvia, Greece 40 9N 21 58E
143 Serviceton, Vic., Austral. 36 25s 141 55E
108 Sesajap Lama, Indon. 3 32N 117 11E
131 Sese Is., Uganda 0 30s 32 30E
109 Sesepe, Indonesia 1 30s 127 59E
129 Sesfontein, S. Africa 19 7s 13 39E
132 Sesheke, Zambia 17 29s 24 13E
70 Sesia R., Italy 45 35N 8 23E
63 Sesimbra, Portugal 38 28N 9 20w
72 Sessa, Aurunca, Italy .41 14N 13 55E
112 Sessy, China 42 40N 110 30E
64 Sestao, Spain 43 18N 3 0w
70 Sesto S. Giovanni, Italy 45 32N 9 14E
70 Sestri Levante, Italy .44 17N 9 22E
70 Sestrieres, Italy 44 58N 6 56E
71 Sestrunj, I., Y.-slavia 44 10N 15 0E
72 Sestu, Sardinia, Italy .39 18N 9 6E
50 Sète, France 43 25N 3 42E
175 Sete Lagôas, Brazil 19 20s 44 16w
123 Setif, Algeria 36 9N 5 26E
133 Setlagole, S. Africa 26 15s 25 8E
133 Setlagole, R., S. Africa 26 0s 25 0E
114 Setonaikai (Inland Sea), Japan 34 10N 133 10E
122 Settat, Morocco 33 0N 7 40w
128 Setté Cama, Gabon 2 32s 9 57E
70 Settimo Tor, Italy 45 9N 7 46E
38 Settle, England, U.K. 54 5N 2 18w
163 Settlement Pt., Bahamas 26 40N 79 0w
133 Settlers, Trans., S. Afr. 24 55s 28 36E
70 Setto Calende, Italy 45 44N 8 37E
63 Setubal, tn. & dist., Port. 38 30N 8 58w
154 Seul L., Canada 50 25N 92 30w
108 Seulimeum, Indonesia 5 27N 95 15E
89 Sevan L., U.S.S.R. 40 20N 45 28E
88 Sevastopol, U.S.S.R. .44 35N 33 30E
44 Seven Heads, Ireland .51 35N 8 43w
44 Seven Hogs, Is., Ireland 52 20N 10 0w
37 Seven Sisters, Wales, United Kingdom 51 46N 3 43w
35 Sevenoaks, Eng., U.K. 51 16N 0 11E
135 Sevenoaks, Nat., S. Afr. 29 12N 39 36E
50 Sévérac le Chateau, Fr. 44 20N 3 5E
36 Severn Beach, Eng., U.K. 51 34N 2 39w
154 Severn R., Canada 44 52N 79 30w
34 Severn R., Eng., U.K. 52 35N 2 38w
34 Severn Stoke, Eng., U.K. 52 5N 2 13w
91 Severnaya Zemlya Is., U.S.S.R. 79 0N 100 0E
84 Severodvinsk, U.S.S.R. 64 27N 39 58E
176 Sewell, Chile 34 10s 70 45w
59 Severomoravsky, reg., Czechoslovakia 49 38N 17 40E
167 Sevier, U.S.A. 38 39N 112 11w
166 Sevier L., U.S.A. 39 0N 113 20w
167 Sevier, R., U.S.A. 39 10N 2 50w
63 Sevilla, Spain 37 23N 6 0w
63 Seville, region, Spain .37 0N 6 0w
71 Sevnica, Yugoslavia 46 2N 15 19E
86 Sevsk, U.S.S.R. 52 10N 34 30E
10 Seward, Alaska, U.S.A. 60 0N 149 40w
152 Seward Pen., Alaska, U.S.A. 65 0N 164 0w
11 Seychelles Is., Indian Ocean 5 0s 56 0E
109 Sewer, Indonesia 5 46s 134 40E
160 Sewickley, U.S.A. 40 33N 80 12w
82 Seydhisfjördur, Iceland 65 12N 13 52w
86 Seym R., U.S.S.R. 51 45N 35 0E
143 Seymour, Vic., Austral. 36 58s 145 10E
135 Seymour, S. Africa 32 32s 26 50E
161 Seymour, Conn., U.S.A. 41 23N 73 5w
162 Seymour, Ind., U.S.A. 39 0N 85 50w
165 Seymour, Tex., U.S.A. 33 35N 99 18w
162 Seymour, Wis., U.S.A. 44 30N 88 20w
51 Seyne, France 44 21N 6 22E
71 Sežana, Yugoslavia 45 43N 13 41E
49 Sézanne, France 48 40N 3 40E
72 Sezze, Italy 41 30N 13 3E
74 Sfanta Ano, Rumania 46 20N 21 30E
78 Sfântu Gheorghe, Rum. 45 52N 25 48E
123 Sfax, Tunisia 34 49N 10 48E
55 's Gravendeel, Neth. .51 48N 4 37E
54 's Gravenhage, Neth. .52 7N 4 17E
42 Sgurr Ban, Scot., U.K. 57 43N 5 29w
42 Sgurr Mor, Scot., U.K. 57 42N 5 0w
42 Sgurr na Ciche, Scot., U.K. 47 0N 5 29w
42 Sgurr na Lapaich, Scotland, U.K. 57 23N 5 5w
103 Shaba Gamba, Tibet, China 32 8N 88 55E
132 Shabani, Rhodesia 20 17s 30 2E
75 Shabla, Bulgaria 43 31N 28 32E
155 Shabogama L., Canada 48 40N 77 0w
131 Shabunda, Congo 2 40s 27 16E
112 Shacheng, China 40 18N 115 27E
15 Shackleton, Antarctica 78 30s 36 1w
15 Shackleton Inlet, Ant. 83 0s 160 0E
126 Shaddad, Saudi Arabia 21 25N 40 2E
126 Shadwan I., Egypt 27 30N 34 0E
125 Shaffa, Nigeria 10 30N 12 6E
34 Shaftesbury, Eng., U.K. 51 0N 2 12w
167 Shafter, U.S.A. 35 32N 119 14w
147 Shag Pt., N.Z. 45 29s 170 52E
125 Shagamu, Nigeria 6 51N 3 39E
104 Shah Bunder, W. Pak. 24 13N 67 50E
106 Shahabad, And. P., India 17 10N 78 11E
104 Shahabad, Raj., India 25 15N 77 11E
104 Shahabad, Punjab, India 30 10N 76 55E
105 Shahabad, Uttar Pradesh, India 27 36N 79 56E
100 Shahabad, Iran 34 10N 46 30E
101 Shahabad, Iran 37 40N 56 50E
104 Shahada, India 21 33N 74 30E
106 Shahapur, India 15 50N 74 34E
101 Shahdad, Iran 30 30N 57 40E
104 Shahdapur, W. Pak. .25 55N 68 35E
104 Shahdadkot, W. Pak. 27 50N 67 55E
105 Shahganj, India 26 3N 82 44E
121 Shahhat (Cyrene), Libya 32 40N 21 35E
101 Shahi, Iran 36 30N 52 55E
105 Shahjahanpur, India .27 54N 79 57E
113 Shaho, China 28 29N 113 2E
106 Shahpur, Mysore, India 16 40N 76 48E
104 Shahpur, M. Pr., India 22 12N 77 58E
104 Shahpur, W. Pakistan 28 46N 68 27E
100 Shahpur, Iran 38 12N 44 45E
105 Shahpura, India 23 10N 80 45E
101 Shahr Kord, Iran 32 15N 50 55E
101 Shahr-e Babak, Iran .30 10N 55 20E
100 Shahraban, Iraq 34 0N 45 0E
101 Shahreza, Iran 32 0N 51 55E
104 Shahrig, Pakistan 30 15N 67 40E
101 Shahriza, Iran 32 0N 51 50E
101 Shahrud, Iran 36 30N 55 0E
101 Shahrukh, Iran 33 50N 60 10E
101 Shahsavar, Iran 36 45N 51 12E
113 Shahsien, China 26 25N 117 50E
101 Shaikhabad, Afghan. .34 0N 68 45E
104 Shajapur, India 23 20N 76 15E
104 Shakargarh, W. Pak. .32 17N 75 43E
132 Shakawe, Botswana 18 28s 21 49E
89 Shakhty, U.S.S.R. 47 40N 40 10E
87 Shakhunya, U.S.S.R. .57 40N 47 0E
125 Shaki, Nigeria 8 41N 3 21E
164 Shakopee, U.S.A. 44 45N 93 30w
127 Shala Lake, Ethiopia . 7 30N 38 30E
36 Shaldon, Eng., U.K. .50 32N 3 31w
160 Shallow Lake, Canada 44 37N 81 6w
113 Shalu, Taiwan 24 24N 120 26E
101 Sham J. ash, 'Oman 23 10N 57 5E
125 Shama, Ghana 5 1N 1 42w
132 Shamaoma, Zambia 15 6s 27 29E
127 Shambe, Sudan 7 2N 30 46E
127 Shambo, Ethiopia 9 32N 37 3E
105 Shamgong Dzong, Bhu 27 19N 90 35E
101 Shamil, Iran 27 30N 56 55E
104 Shamil, India 29 32N 77 18E
111 Shamo (Gobi), des., Asia 44 0N 111 0E
127 Shamo, L., Ethiopia 5 45N 37 30E
161 Shamokin, Pa., U.S.A. 40 47N 76 33w
165 Shamrock, U.S.A. 35 15N 100 15w
132 Shamva, Rhodesia 17 20s 31 32E
103 Shan State, Burma 21 30N 98 30E
44 Shanagolden, Ireland .52 35N 9 6w
127 Shanan, R., Ethiopia . 8 0N 40 20E
112 Shanchengtze, China .42 29N 125 30E
125 Shanga, Nigeria 9 1N 5 2E
130 Shangalowe, Congo 10 50s 26 30E
132 Shangani, & R., Rhod. 18 45s 28 0E
113 Shangcheng, China 31 50N 115 27E
112 Shangchih, (Chuho), China 45 10N 127 59E
113 Shangchwan Shan, Is., China 21 35N 112 45E
113 Shanghai, China 31 15N 121 30E
113 Shanghsien, China 33 30N 109 58E
113 Shangjao, China 28 25N 117 50E
113 Shangkao, China 28 10N 114 44E
113 Shangkiu, China 34 28N 115 42E
112 Shangpancheng, China 40 52N 118 4E
113 Shangsze, China 22 0N 107 45E
113 Shangyu, China 25 59N 114 29E
112 Shanh, Mongolia 47 5N 102 55E
125 Shani, Nigeria 10 14N 12 2E
166 Shaniko, U.S.A. 45 0N 120 15w
34 Shanklin, I. of W., Eng., U.K. 50 39N 1 9w
146 Shannon, N.Z. 40 33s 175 25E
44 Shannon Airport, Ire. 52 42N 85 7w
44 Shannon Bridge, Ireland 53 17N 8 2w
14 Shannon I., Greenland 75 0N 18 0w
44 Shannon R., Ireland .53 10N 8 10w
112 Shansi, prov., China 38 20N 112 0E
91 Shantar I., U.S.S.R. 55 9N 137 40E
112 Shantung Pen. 37 0N 120 0E
112 Shantung, prov., China 36 0N 117 30E
113 Shanyang, China 33 39N 110 2E
113 Shaohing, China 30 0N 120 32E
113 Shaowu, China 27 25N 117 30E
113 Shaoyang, China 27 2N 111 25E
38 Shap, England, U.K. .54 32N 2 40w
43 Shapinsay I., Scot., U.K. 59 2N 2 50w
100 Shaqra, Saudi Arabia .25 15N 45 16E
127 Sharafa (Ogr), Sudan .11 59N 27 7E
106 Sharavati, R., India 14 32N 74 0E
161 Sharbot Lake, Canada 44 47N 76 41w
101 Sharhjui, Afghanistan 32 30N 67 22E
100 Shari, Saudi Arabia 27 20N 43 45E
112 Sharin Gol, Mongolia .49 12N 106 27E
101 Sharjah, Trucial States 25 23N 55 26E
142 Shark B., W. Australia 25 15s 133 20E
126 Sharm el Sheikh, Egypt 27 53N 34 15E
160 Sharon, Pa., U.S.A. 41 18N 80 30w
98 Sharon, Plain of, Israel 32 12N 34 49E
154 Sharpe, L., Canada 54 10N 93 21w
34 Sharpness, Eng., U.K. 51 43N 2 28w
160 Sharpsburg, U.S.A. 40 30N 79 56w
160 Sharpsville, U.S.A. 41 16N 80 28w
87 Sharya, U.S.S.R. 54 12N 45 40E
127 Shasha, Ethiopia 6 29N 35 59E
132 Shashi, R., Rhod. & Botswana 21 40s 28 40E
132 Shashi R., Rhodesia 21 37s 28 30E
113 Shasi, China 30 16N 112 20E
166 Shasta, Mt., U.S.A. 41 45N 122 0w
166 Shasta Res., U.S.A. 40 50N 122 15w
87 Shatsk, U.S.S.R. 54 0N 41 45E
100 Shatt al Arab, R., Iraq 30 0N 48 31E
165 Shattuck, U.S.A. 36 17N 99 55w
89 Shaumyani, U.S.S.R. .41 13N 44 45E
157 Shaunavon, Canada 49 35N 108 40w
144 Shaw I., Australia 20 30s 149 10E
138 Shaw R., W. Australia 20 30s 119 15E
111 Shawan, China 44 45N 85 29E
160 Shawanaga, Canada 45 31N 80 14w
162 Shawano, U.S.A. 44 45N 88 38w
42 Shawbost, Scot., U.K. 58 20N 6 40w
34 Shawbury, Eng., U.K. 52 48N 2 40w
154 Shawinigan Falls, Can. 46 35N 72 50w
165 Shawnee, Okla., U.S.A. 35 15N 97 0w
103 Shaziz, Tibet, China 33 10N 82 43E
87 Shchigri, U.S.S.R. 51 55N 36 58E
87 Shchurovo, U.S.S.R. .55 0N 38 51E
36 Shabbear, Eng., U.K. 50 52N 4 12w
87 Shebekino, U.S.S.R. 50 28N 37 0E
99 Shebelle R., Somali Rep. 2 0N 44 0E
162 Sheboygan, Wis., U.S.A. 43 46N 87 45w
98 Shechem, site, Jordan 32 13N 35 21E
155 Shediac, Canada 46 14N 64 32w
45 Sheefry Hills, Ireland 53 40N 9 40w
46 Sheelin Lough, Ireland 53 48N 7 20w
46 Sheep Haven, Ireland 55 12N 7 55w
133 Sheepmoor, S. Africa .26 42s 30 13E
44 Sheeps Hd., Ireland 51 32N 9 50w
35 Sheerness, Eng., U.K. 51 26N 0 47E
155 Sheet Harbour, Canada 44 56N 62 31w
98 Shefar'am, Israel 32 48N 35 10E
98 Shefeiya, Israel 32 35N 34 58E
39 Sheffield, Eng., U.K. .53 23N 1 28w
147 Sheffield, New Zealand 41 22s 146 21E
163 Sheffield, Ala., U.S.A. 34 45N 87 42w
161 Sheffield, Mass., U.S.A. 42 6N 73 23w
160 Sheffield, Pa., U.S.A. .41 42N 79 3w
165 Sheffield, Tex. U.S.A. 30 42N 101 49w
35 Shefford, England, U.K. 52 2N 0 20w
104 Shegaon, India 20 48N 76 59E
44 Shehy Mts., Ireland 51 47N 9 15w
105 Sheikhpura, India 25 9N 85 53E
105 Shekar Dzong, Tibet, China 28 45N 87 0E
104 Shekhupura, W. Pak. 31 42N 73 58E
113 Shekichen, China 33 10N 113 0E
113 Shekki, China 22 30N 113 15E
113 Sheklung, China 23 5N 113 55E
87 Sheksna R., U.S.S.R. .59 30N 38 30E
154 Shelburne, Ont., Canada 44 4N 80 15w
155 Shelburne, N.S., Canada 43 47N 65 20w
161 Shelburne, U.S.A. 44 23N 73 15w
144 Shelburne B., Australia 11 50s 143 0E
161 Shelburne Falls, U.S.A. 42 36N 72 45w
162 Shelby, Mich., U.S.A. 43 34N 86 27w
166 Shelby Mont., U.S.A. 48 30N 111 59w
163 Shelby, N.C., U.S.A. .35 18N 81 34w
160 Shelby, Ohio, U.S.A. .40 52N 82 40w
164 Shelbyville, Ill., U.S.A. 39 25N 88 45w
162 Shelbyville, Ind., U.S.A. 39 30N 85 42w
163 Shelbyville, Tenn., U.S.A. 35 30N 86 25w
135 Sheldon, C. Prov. S. Afr. 32 59s 25 55E
164 Sheldon, U.S.A. 43 6N 95 51w
155 Sheldrake, Canada 50 20N 64 51w
91 Shelekhov G., U.S.S.R. 59 30N 157 0E
157 Shell Lake, Canada 53 19N 107 6w
42 Shell L., Scot., U.K. .58 0N 6 28w
142 Shell Lakes, W. Australia 29 20s 127 30E
143 Shellharbour, Australia 34 31s 150 51E
86 Shelon R., U.S.S.R. 58 10N 30 30E
155 Shelter Bay, Canada .50 30N 67 20w
161 Shelton, Conn., U.S.A. 41 18N 73 7w
166 Shelton, Wash., U.S.A. 47 15N 123 6w
89 Shemakha, U.S.S.R. 40 50N 48 28E
164 Shenandoah, Iowa, U.S.A. 40 50N 95 25w
161 Shenandoah, Pa., U.S.A. 40 49N 76 13w
162 Shenandoah, Va., U.S.A. 38 30N 78 38w
162 Shenandoah R., U.S.A. 38 30N 78 38w
112 Shenchih, China 39 12N 112 2E
106 Shencottah, India 8 59N 77 18E
125 Shendam, Nigeria 9 10N 9 30E
127 Shendi, Sudan 16 46N 33 33E
104 Shendurni, India 20 39N 75 36E
35 Shenfield, Eng., U.K. 51 39N 0 21E
76 Shengjergj, Albania 41 22N 20 10E
76 Shengjergj, Albania 42 18N 19 57E
76 Shengjin, Albania 41 50N 19 35E
112 Shensi prov., China 35 45N 109 30E
142 Shenton, Mt., W. Australia 27 57s 123 22E
111 Shentsa, Tibet, China 30 56N 88 25E
112 Shenyang (Mukden), China 41 35N 123 30E
86 Shepetovka, U.S.S.R. 50 10N 27 0E
98 Shephelah, dist., Israel 31 30N 34 43E
143 Shepparton, Australia 36 18s 145 25E
35 Sheppey, I. of, Eng., U.K. 51 23N 0 50E
161 Sheppton, U.S.A. 40 52N 76 10w
34 Shepshed, Eng., U.K. 52 47N 1 18w
36 Shepton Mallet, Eng. U.K. 51 11N 2 31w
127 Sherada, Ethiopia 7 25N 36 30E
36 Sherborne, Eng., U.K. 50 56N 2 31w
135 Sherborne, S. Africa 31 18s 25 0E
124 Sherbro I., Sierra Leone 7 30N 12 40w
155 Sherbrooke, Canada 45 24N 71 57w
39 Sherburn, Durham, England, U.K. 54 46N 28 1w
39 Sherburn, East Yorks., England, U.K. 54 12N 0 32w
39 Sherburn, West Yorks., England, U.K. 53 47N 1 15w
46 Shercock, Ireland 54 0N 6 54w
123 Sherda, Chad 20 7N 16 46E
35 Shere, England. U.K. 51 13N 0 28w
126 Shereik, Sudan 18 52N 33 40E
34 Sherfield English, England, U.K. 51 1N 1 35w
165 Sheridan, Ark., U.S.A. 34 20N 92 25w
164 Sheridan, Col., U.S.A. 39 44N 105 3w
166 Sheridan, Wyo., U.S.A. 44 50N 107 0w
39 Sheriff Hutton, England, U.K. 54 5N 1 0w
41 Sheriff Muir, Scot., U.K. 56 12N 3 53w
35 Sheringham, Eng., U.K. 52 56N 1 11E
44 Sherkin I., Ireland 51 38N 9 25w
104 Sherkot, India 29 22N 78 35E
165 Sherman, Tex., U.S.A. 33 40N 96 35w
105 Sherpur, India 25 1N 90 3E
157 Sherridon, Canada 55 10N 101 5w
34 Sherston, England, U.K. 51 35N 2 13w
55 s'Hertogenbosch, Neth. 51 42N 5 17E
164 Sherwood, N.D., U.S.A. 48 59N 101 36w
165 Sherwood, Tex., U.S.A. 31 18N 100 45w
39 Sherwood For., Eng., U.K. 53 5N 1 5w
156 Sheslay, Canada 58 25N 131 45w
28 Shetland Is., Scot., U.K. 60 30N 1 30w
106 Shevaroy Hills, India. 11 58N 78 12E
85 Shevchenko, U.S.S.R. 44 25N 51 20E
127 Shewa, prov., Ethiopia 9 33N 38 10E
164 Sheyenne, U.S.A. 47 52N 99 8w
164 Sheyenne, R., U.S.A. .47 40N 98 15w
42 Shiant Is., Scotland 57 54N 6 20w
42 Shiant, Sd. of, Scot., U.K. 57 54N 6 30w
99 Shibam, South Yemen 16 0N 48 36E
102 Shiberghan, prov., Afghanistan 35 45N 66 0E
126 Shibin El Kôm, Egypt 30 31N 30 55E
114 Shibushi, Japan 31 25N 131 0E
42 Shiel, L., Scot., U.K. .56 48N 5 32w
34 Shifnal, England, U.K. 52 40N 2 23w
114 Shiga, pref., Japan 35 20N 136 0E
121 Shigaib, Sudan 15 5N 23 35E
111 Shigatse, Tibet, China 29 10N 89 0E
113 Shihchüan, China 33 5N 108 30E
112 Shihkiachwang, China 38 0N 114 32E
112 Shihkwaikow, China 40 59N 110 4E
113 Shihlu, China 19 15N 109 0E
113 Shihpu, China 29 12N 121 58E
113 Shihtao, China 36 55N 122 25E
112 Shihtsien, China 27 28N 108 3E
112 Shihwei, China 51 28N 119 59E
76 Shijak, Albania 41 21N 19 33E
104 Shikarpur, India 28 17N 78 7E
104 Shikarpur, W. Pakistan 27 57N 68 39E
104 Shikohabad, India 27 6N 78 38E
104 Shikoku I., and dist., Japan 33 30N 133 30E
39 Shilbottle, Eng., U.K. 55 23N 1 42w
39 Shildon, England, U.K. 54 37N 1 39w
91 Shilka, U.S.S.R. 52 0N 115 55E
45 Shillelagh, Ireland 52 46N 6 32w
34 Shillingstone, Eng., U.K. 50 54N 2 15w
103 Shillong, India 25 30N 92 0E
98 Shiloh (Site), Jordan .32 4N 35 10E
87 Shilovo, U.S.S.R. 54 25N 41 8E
114 Shimabara, Japan 32 48N 130 20E
114 Shimada, Japan 34 49N 138 19E
114 Shimane, pref., Japan 35 0N 132 30E
114 Shimano R., Japan 36 50N 138 30E
91 Shimanovski, U.S.S.R. 52 15N 127 30E
114 Shimizu, Japan 35 0N 138 30E
114 Shimodate, Japan 36 20N 139 55E
106 Shimoga, India 13 57N 75 32E
131 Shimoni, Kenya 4 38s 39 20E
114 Shimonoseki, Japan 33 58N 131 0E
90 Shimpek, U.S.S.R. 44 50N 74 10E
106 Shimsha, R., India 13 15N 76 54E
86 Shimsk, U.S.S.R. 58 15N 30 50E
43 Shin L., Scot., U.K. 58 7N 4 30w
43 Shin R., Scot., U.K. 58 0N 4 26w
101 Shin Dand, Afghanistan 33 12N 62 8E
114 Shingu, Japan 33 40N 135 55E
112 Shinankow, China 48 40N 121 32E
125 Shinkafe, Nigeria 13 8N 6 29E
112 Shinkiachwang, China 38 0N 114 31E
130 Shinkolobwe, Congo 11 10s 26 30E
44 Shinrone, Ireland 53 0N 7 58w
131 Shinyanga, Tanzania . 3 35s 33 20E
131 Shinyanga, dist., Tanz. 3 45s 33 27E
114 Shiono-misaki, C., Jap. 33 25N 135 45E
165 Ship I., U.S.A. 30 16N 88 55w
35 Shipbourne, Eng., U.K. 51 13N 0 19E
35 Shipdham, Eng., U.K. 52 38N 0 53E
38 Shipley, England. U.K. 53 50N 1 47w
155 Shippegan, Canada 47 45N 64 45w
160 Shippensburg, U.S.A. .40 4N 77 32w

MAP
167 Shiprock, U.S.A. 36 51N 108 45W
34 Shipston-on-Stour, England, U.K. 52 4N 1 38W
34 Shipton-under-Wychwood, Eng., U.K. ...51 51N 1 35W
101 Shir Kūh mt., Iran ...31 45N 53 30E
131 Shirati, Tanzania 1 10S 34 0E
101 Shiraz, Iran 29 42N 52 30E
132 Shire Highlands, Malawi 15 34S 35 0E
132 Shiré R., Malawi 16 30S 35 0E
39 Shirebrook, Eng., U.K. 53 13N 1 11W
87 Shiringushi, U.S.S.R. .42 54N 53 56W
114 Shiriya-misaki, C., Jap. 41 25N 141 30E
106 Shirol, India 16 47N 74 41E
104 Shirpur, India 21 21N 74 57E
101 Shirvan, Iran 37 30N 57 50E
132 Shirwa L., (Chilwa), Malawi 15 55S 35 40E
113 Shiukwah, China 24 58N 113 3E
106 Shivali, (Sirkall) India 11 15N 79 41E
104 Shivpuri, India 25 18N 77 42E
98 Shivta, (site), Israel ...30 53N 34 40E
132 Shiwele Ferry, Zambia 11 25S 28 31E
126 Shiyata, Egypt 29 25N 25 7E
114 Shizuoka, Japan 35 0N 138 30E
114 Shizuoka, pref., Japan 35 15N 138 40E
86 Shklov, U.S.S.R. 54 10N 30 15E
76 Shkodër & Pref., Alb. 42 6N 19 20E
76 Shkumbin R., Albania 41 5N 19 50E
91 Shmidt I., U.S.S.R. ...81 0N 91 0E
127 Shoa Ghimirra, (Wota), Ethiopia ... 7 4N 35 51E
157 Shoal Lake, Canada ...50 30N 100 35W
143 Shoalhaven R., Austral. 34 55S 150 5E
144 Shoalwater B., Austral. 22 15S 150 20E
35 Shoeburyness, Eng., U.K. 51 31N 0 49E
127 Shogali, Ethiopia 10 40N 35 27E
112 Shohsien, China 39 30N 112 25E
106 Sholapur, India 17 43N 75 56E
98 Shomera, Israel 33 4N 35 17E
42 Shona I., Scotland, United Kingdom 56 48N 5 50W
167 Shongopovi, U.S.A. ...35 49N 110 37W
106 Shoranur, India 10 46N 76 19E
106 Shorapur, India 16 31N 76 48E
35 Shoreham-by-Sea, England, U.K. 50 50N 0 17W
166 Shoshone, U.S.A. 43 0N 114 27W
166 Shoshone L., U.S.A. ...44 0N 111 0W
166 Shoshone Mts., U.S.A. 39 30N 117 30W
166 Shoshoni, U.S.A. 43 13N 108 5W
86 Shostka, U.S.S.R. 51 57N 33 32E
41 Shotts, Scotland, U.K. 55 49N 3 45W
167 Show Low, U.S.A. 34 16N 110 0W
112 Showyang, China 38 0N 113 4E
88 Shpola, U.S.S.R. 49 1N 31 30E
165 Shreveport, U.S.A. 32 30N 93 50W
34 Shrewsbury, Eng., U.K. 52 42N 2 45W
34 Shrewton, Eng., U.K. 51 11N 1 55W
106 Shrivardhan, India 18 10N 73 3E
34 Shrivenham, Eng., U.K. 51 36N 1 39W
34 Shropshire, co., England, U.K. 52 36N 2 45W
44 Shrule, Ireland 53 32N 9 7W
113 Shucheng, China 31 25N 117 2E
103 Shugden Gomba, China 29 35N 96 55E
113 Shuikiahu, China 32 14N 117 4E
104 Shujalpur, India 23 43N 76 40E
112 Shulan, China 44 18N 126 50E
152 Shumagin Is., Alas., U.S.A. 55 0N 159 0W
123 Shumayakh, Libya 31 24N 14 0E
87 Shumerlya, U.S.S.R. ..55 30N 46 10E
90 Shumikha, U.S.S.R. ...55 15N 63 30E
113 Shunan, China 29 37N 119 0E
113 Shunchang, China 26 52N 117 58E
89 Shungay, U.S.S.R. 48 30N 46 45E
103 Shunning, China 24 35N 99 50E
113 Shuntak, China 22 54N 113 8E
99 Shuqra, S. Yemen 13 22N 45 34E
101 Shur, R., Iran 28 30N 55 0E
101 Shusf, Iran 31 50N 60 5E
100 Shushtar, Iran 32 5N 48 50E
133 Shushong, Botswana .22 59S 26 30E
100 Shushtar, Iran 32 0N 48 50E
98 Shuweika, Jordan 32 20N 35 1E
87 Shuya, U.S.S.R. 56 50N 41 28E
113 Shuyang, China 34 16N 119 1E
112 Shwangliao, China 43 39N 123 40E
103 Shwebo, Burma 22 30N 95 45E
103 Shwegu, Burma 24 15N 96 50E
103 Shweli R., Burma 23 45N 96 45E
102 Shyok, Kashmir 34 15N 78 5E
102 Shyok R., Kashmir 34 30N 78 15E
107 Si, R., Thailand 15 40N 104 20E
107 Si Racha, Thailand ...13 20N 101 10E
100 Siah, Saudi Arabia 22 0N 47 0E
112 Siachengtze, China 44 35N 130 37E
102 Siahan Range, mts., West Pakistan 27 30N 64 40E
112 Siahoyen, China 42 30N 120 30E
108 Saki Sri Inderapura, Indonesia 0 51N 102 0E
111 Siakwan, China 25 45N 100 10E
157 Silcox, Canada 57 14N 94 0W
104 Sialkot, West Pakistan 32 32N 74 30E
107 Siam, G. of, Asia 11 30N 101 0E
113 Sian, China 34 2N 109 0E
113 Siang K., R., China ...27 10N 112 45E
113 Siangcheng, China 33 16N 115 2E
113 Siangfan, China 32 15N 112 2E
112 Siangning, China 36 0N 110 50E
113 Siangsiang, China 27 50N 112 30E
113 Siangtan, China 28 0N 112 55E
113 Siangyang, China 32 18N 111 0E
113 Siangyin, China 28 45N 113 0E
108 Siantan, I., Indonesia 3 14N 106 5E
112 Siaohaotze, China 46 52N 124 22E
113 Siapu, China 26 53N 120 0E
101 Siareh, Iran 28 5N 60 20E
109 Siargao I., Philippines 10 0N 126 3E
109 Siasi, Philippines 5 34N 120 50E
76 Siátista, Greece 40 15N 21 33E
109 Siau I., Indonesia 2 50N 125 25E
86 Siauliai, U.S.S.R. 55 56N 23 15E
89 Siazan, U.S.S.R. 41 3N 48 7E
126 Sibâi, Gebel el, Egypt 25 45N 34 10E
133 Sibasá, Trans., S. Africa 22 53S 30 25E
157 Sibbald, Canada 51 24N 110 10W
71 Sibenik, Yugoslavia ...43 48N 15 54E
94 Siberia, reg., N. Asia .60 0N 100 0E
108 Siberut I.. Indonesia . 1 30S 99 0E
104 Sibi, West Pakistan ...29 30N 67 48E
130 Sibiti, Cong. (Fr.) 3 38S 3 19E
78 Sibiu, Rumania 45 45N 24 9E
78 Sibiu, Reg., Rum. 45 45N 24 10E
35 Sible Hedingham, England, U.K. 51 58N 0 37E
164 Sibley, Iowa, U.S.A. .43 21N 95 43W
165 Sibley, La., U.S.A. 32 34N 93 16W
108 Sibolga, Indonesia 1 50N 98 45E
103 Sibsagar, India 27 0N 94 36E
39 Sibsey, England, U.K. 53 3N 0 1E
108 Sibu, Sar., Malaysia ... 2 20N 111 57E
109 Sibuguey B., Phil. 7 50N 122 45E
109 Sibuko, Philippines ... 7 20N 122 10E
108 Sibuko, B., Malaysia . 4 0N 118 10E
109 Sibutu I., Philippines . 4 45N 119 30E
109 Sibutu Passage, E. Ind. 4 50N 120 0E
109 Sibuyan, I., Philippines 12 25N 122 40E
174 Sicasica, Bolivia 17 20S 67 45W
156 Sicamous, Canada 50 49N 119 0W
109 Sicapoo, Philippines ...18 9N 121 34E
111 Sichang, China 28 0N 102 10E
113 Sichwan, China 33 6N 111 30E
73 Sicilia, reg., Italy 37 30N 14 30E
72 Sicilian Channel, Italy 37 25N 12 30E
72 Sicily, I., Italy 37 30N 14 0E
174 Sicuani, Peru 14 10S 71 10W
72 Siculiana, Italy 37 20N 13 23E
133 Sicunusa, Swaziland ...26 44S 30 58E
71 Sid, Yugoslavia 45 6N 19 16E
127 Sidamo, prov., Ethiopia 5 0N 37 50E
125 Sidaouet, Niger 18 34N 8 3E
124 Sidaradougou, Upper Volta 10 42N 4 12W
36 Sidbury, Eng., U.K. 50 43N 3 12W
106 Siddipet, India 18 0N 79 0E
80 Sidensjo, Sweden 63 20N 18 20E
73 Siderno Marina, Italy 38 16N 16 17E
77 Sidheros, Akra, C., Gr. 35 19N 26 19E
76 Sidhirokastron, Greece 37 20N 21 46E
104 Sidhpur, India 23 56N 71 25E
126 Sidi Abd el Rahmân, Egypt 30 55N 28 41E
122 Sidi Abdallah, Morocco 34 8N 9 29E
126 Sidi Barrani, Egypt ...31 32N 25 58E
122 Sidi Bel Abbès, Algeria 35 13N 0 10W
123 Sidi Bouzid, Tunisia ...35 0N 9 29E
126 Sidi Haneish, Egypt ...31 10N 27 35E
122 Sidi Ifni, Morocco 29 29N 10 3W
122 Sidi Kacem, Morocco .34 11N 5 40W
123 Sidi Miftâh, Libya 31 8N 16 58E
122 Sidi Moktar, Morocco .31 45N 8 59W
126 Sidi Omar, Egypt 31 24N 24 57E
122 Sidi Slimane, Algeria .30 57N 1 0W
122 Sidi Smain, Morocco .32 51N 8 29W
123 Sidi Yahhyâ, Libya ...30 55N 16 30E
122 Sidi Zlaa, Morocco 31 31N 9 32W
41 Sidlaw Hills, Scot., U.K. 56 32N 3 10W
35 Sidlesham, Eng., U.K. 50 46N 0 46W
36 Sidmouth, Eng., UK .50 40N 3 13W
164 Sidney, Mont., U.S.A. 47 51N 104 7W
161 Sidney, N.Y., U.S.A. .42 18N 75 20W
162 Sidney, Ohio, U.S.A. .40 18N 84 6W
109 Sidoardjo, Indonesia . 7 30S 112 46E
100 Sidon, (Saida), Lebanon 33 38N 35 28E
67 Sidra, G. of, (Khalij Surt), Libya 31 40N 18 30E
60 Siedlce, Poland 52 10N 22 20E
56 Siegburg, Germany 50 48N 7 12E
56 Siegen, Germany 50 52N 8 2E
55 Sieglar, Germany 50 48N 7 16E
107 Siem Reap, Cambodia 13 20N 103 52E
71 Siena, Italy 43 20N 11 20E
113 Sienfeng, China 29 45N 109 10E
113 Sienyang, China 34 20N 108 48E
59 Sieniawa, Poland 50 11N 22 38E
60 Sieradz, Poland 51 37N 18 41E
49 Sierck, France 49 26N 6 20E
60 Sierpc, Poland 52 55N 19 43E
64 Sierra Alta, Spain 40 31N 1 30W
62 Sierra Avilá, Spain 40 37N 5 8W
63 Sierra Bermeja, Spain 36 45N 5 11W
167 Sierra Blanca, U.S.A. .31 11N 105 17W
167 Sierra Blanca, mt., U.S.A. 33 20N 105 54W
166 Sierra City, U.S.A. 39 42N 120 42W
176 Sierra Colorado, Arg. .40 35S 67 50W
65 Sierra de Alcaraz, Spain 38 40N 2 20W
64 Sierra de Alcubierre, Sp. 41 45N 0 22W
65 Sierra de Almenara, Sp. 37 34N 1 32W
172 Sierra de Ambato, Arg. 28 25N 66 10W
63 Sierra de Aracena, Spain 37 55N 6 50W
62 Sierra de Avila, Spain 40 40N 5 0W
174 Sierra de Baudo, Col. . 6 0N 77 0W
64 Sierra de Cantabria, Sp. 42 40N 2 30W
64 Sierra de Cebollera, Sp. 42 0N 2 30W
65 Sierra de Gador, Spain 36 57N 2 45W
62 Sierra de Gata, Spain .40 20N 6 20W
62 Sierra de Gredos, Spain 40 20N 5 0W
63 Sa. de Guadalupe, Spain 39 28N 5 30W
62 Sa. de Guadarrama, Sp. 41 0N 4 0W
64 Sierra de Guara, Spain 42 19N 0 15W
62 Sierra de Meira, Spain 43 15N 7 15W
64 Sierra de Montsant, Sp. 41 17N 0 1E
62 Sa. de Peñade Francia, Sp. 40 32N 6 10W
174 Sierra de Perija, Col. . 9 30N 73 3W
162 Sa. de Picos Ancares, Spain 42 51N 6 52W
64 Sierra de San Just, Sp. 40 45N 0 41W
172 Sierra de San Luis, Arg. 37 25N 66 10W
63 Sierra de San Pedro, Sp. 39 18N 6 40W
65 Sierra de Segura, Spain 38 5N 2 45W
172 Sierra de Velasco, Arg. 29 20N 67 10W
63 Sierra de Yeguas, Spain 37 7N 4 52W
62 Sierra del Eje, Spain .42 24N 6 56W
64 Sierra del Montsech, Sp. 42 0N 0 45E
63 Sierra de la Alcudia, Sp. 38 34N 4 30W
62 Sierra de la Culebra, Sp. 41 55N 6 20W
64 Sa. de la Demanda, Sp. 42 15N 3 0W
64 Sierra de la Peña, Sp. 42 32N 0 45W
65 Sa. de los Filabres, Sp. 37 12N 2 20W
63 Sierra de los Santos, Sp. 38 7N 5 12W
172 Sierra Gorda, Chile 23 0S 69 15W
124 Sierra Leone, st., W. Afr. 9 0N 12 0W
63 Sierra Madrona, Spain 38 27N 4 16W
168 Sierra Majada, Mexico 27 19N 103 42W
63 Sierra Martés, Spain ...39 20N 1 0W
63 Sierra Morena, Spain .38 20N 4 0W
63 Sierra Nevada, Spain .37 3N 3 15W
166 Sierra Nevada, mts., U.S.A. 39 0N 120 30W
174 Sierra Nevada de Santa Marta, Colombia 10 55N 73 50W
174 Sierra Pacaraima, Ven. 4 0N 63 0W
57 Sierre, Switzerland 46 17N 7 31E
77 Sifnos I., Greece 37 0N 24 45E
122 Sig, Algeria 27 10N 2 32E
109 Sigaboy, Philippines ... 6 39N 126 10E
79 Sigdal, Norway 60 4N 9 38E
50 Sigean, France 43 2N 2 58E
78 Sighet, Rumania 47 57N 23 52E
78 Sighisoara, Rumania .46 12N 24 50E
108 Sigli, Indonesia 5 25N 96 0E
82 Siglufjördhur, Iceland 66 12N 18 55W
109 Sigma, Philippines 11 29N 122 40E
57 Sigmaringen, Germany 48 5N 9 13E
89 Signakhi, U.S.S.R. 40 52N 45 57E
15 Signy I., Antarctica ...60 45S 46 30W
49 Signy l'Abbaye, France 49 40N 4 25E
174 Sigsig, Ecuador 3 0S 78 50W
80 Sigtuna, Sweden 59 36N 17 44E
64 Sigüenza, Spain 41 3N 2 40W
124 Siguiri, Guinea 11 31N 9 10W
86 Sigulda, U.S.S.R. 57 10N 24 55E
167 Sigurd, U.S.A. 38 57N 112 0W
107 Sihanoukville, *see* Kompong Som
113 Siho, China 34 0N 105 0E
113 Sihsien, China 29 55N 118 23E
113 Sihsien, China 36 45N 111 0E
98 Si'ir, Jordan 31 35N 35 9E
100 Siirt, Turkey 37 57N 41 55E
132 Sijarira, Ra., Rhodesia 17 36S 27 45E
132 Sikalongo, Zambia 16 54S 27 12E
104 Sikandarabad, India .28 30N 77 39E
104 Sikandra Rao, India ..27 43N 78 24E
104 Sikar, India 27 39N 75 10E
108 Sikariman, Indonesia . 2 33S 99 59E
124 Sikasso, Mali 11 7N 5 35W
165 Sikeston, U.S.A. 36 52N 89 35W
91 Sikhote Alin Ra., U.S.S.R. 46 0N 136 0E
76 Sikia, Greece 39 49N 22 3E
77 Sikinos I., Greece 36 40N 25 8E
77 Sikionia, Greece 38 0N 22 44E
105 Sikkim, st., India 27 50N 88 50E
59 Siklos, Hungary 45 50N 18 19E
124 Sikoro, Sudan 12 19N 7 8W
113 Siku, China 33 48N 104 18E
62 Sil R., Spain 42 23N 7 30W
108 Silagui, Indonesia 1 10S 98 46E
70 Silandro, Italy .... .46 38N 10 48E
98 Silat edh Dhahr, Jordan 32 19N 35 11E
71 Silba, & I., Yugoslavia 44 24N 14 41E
100 Silchar, India 24 45N 93 0E
163 Siler City, U.S.A. 35 44N 79 30W
106 Sileru, R., India 18 0N 82 0E
122 Silet, Algeria 22 44N 4 37E
105 Silgarhi Doti, Nepal ...29 15N 82 0E
103 Silghat, India 26 35N 93 0E
100 Silifke, Turkey 36 22N 33 58E
105 Siliguri, India 26 45N 88 25E
113 Silin, China 24 10N 105 36E
112 Silinhot, China 43 16N 116 0E
72 Siliqua, Italy 39 20N 8 49E
75 Silistra, Bulgaria 44 6N 27 19E
80 Siljan L., Sweden 60 55N 14 45E
81 Silkeborg, Denmark ...56 10N 9 32E
174 Sillajhuay, Mt., Chile .19 40S 68 40W
48 Sille le Guillaume, Fr. 48 10N 0 8W
38 Silloth, Eng., U.K. 54 53N 3 25W
165 Siloam Springs, U.S.A. 36 15N 94 31W
165 Silsbee, U.S.A. 30 20N 94 8W
38 Silsden, Eng., U.K. ...53 55N 1 55W
86 Silute, U.S.S.R. 55 21N 21 33E
130 Silva Porto, Angola ...12 22S 16 55E
130 Silva Porto Gare, Angola 12 20S 16 59E
166 Silver Cr. R., U.S.A. .43 30N 119 30W
168 Silver City, Panama Canal Zone 9 21N 79 53W
166 Silver City, Calif., U.S.A. 36 19N 119 44W
167 Silver City, New Mexico, U.S.A. 32 50N 108 18W
160 Silver Creek, U.S.A. ...42 33N 79 9W
166 Silver Lake, U.S.A. ...43 9N 121 4W
134 Silver Streams, S. Africa 28 20S 23 33E
80 Silverhojden, Sweden .60 2N 15 0E
44 Silvermine, Mts., Ireland 52 47N 8 15W
44 Silvermines, Ireland ...52 48N 8 15W
34 Silverstone, Eng., U.K. 52 5N 1 3W
143 Silverton, N.S.W., Australia 31 52S 141 10E
36 Silverton, Eng., U.K. .50 49N 3 29W
167 Silverton, Colo., U.S.A. 37 51N 107 45W
165 Silverton, Tex., U.S.A. 34 30N 101 16W
135 Silvervale, S. Africa ...32 57S 27 56E
63 Silves, Portugal 37 11N 8 26W
166 Silvies, R., U.S.A. 43 57N 119 5W
57 Silvretta, mt., Switz. .46 50N 10 5E
126 Silwa Bahari, Egypt .24 45N 32 55E
98 Silwan, Jordan 31 59N 35 15E
104 Silwani, India 23 18N 78 27E
133 Silwerkrans, S. Africa 25 26S 26 41E
58 Silz, Austria 47 16N 10 56E
122 Sim, C., Morocco 31 26N 9 51W
108 Simalubek, Indonesia . 1 36S 98 40E
108 Simanggang, Malaysia 1 10N 111 45E
154 Simard, Lac, Canada .47 40N 78 40W
101 Simarun, Iran 31 16N 51 40E
131 Simba, Kenya 2 11S 37 35E
57 Simbach, Germany 48 16N 13 3E
131 Simbo, Tanzania 4 51S 29 41E
154 Simcoe, Canada 42 50N 80 20W
91 Simenga, U S.S.R. 62 50N 107 55E
108 Simeulue I., Indonesia 2 45N 95 45E
88 Simferopol, U.S.S.R. .44 55N 34 3E
77 Simi & I., Greece 36 35N 27 50E
105 Simikot, Nepal 30 0N 81 50E
104 Simla, India 31 2N 77 15E
78 Simleul-Silvaniei, Rum. 47 17N 22 50E
56 Simmern, Germany 49 59N 7 32E
157 Simmie, Canada 49 56N 108 6W
82 Simo, L. & R., Finland 66 0N 27 0E
36 Simonsbath, Eng., U.K. 51 7N 3 45W
134 Simonstown, S. Afr. ...34 14S 18 26E
59 Simontornya, Hungary 46 45N 18 33E
132 Simoya, Zambia 13 52S 23 11E
108 Simpang, Indonesia ... 1 0S 110 43E
107 Simpagn, Malaysia 4 50N 100 40E
57 Simplon P., Switzerland 46 15N 8 0E
57 Simplon Tunnel, Switz. 46 15N 8 7E
139 Simpson Des., Austral. 25 0S 137 0E
81 Simrishamn, Sweden .55 33N 14 22E
108 Simunjan, Sar., Malay. 3 30S 110 49E
91 Simushir, I., Kuril Is. 46 50N 152 30E
106 Sina, R., India 18 25N 75 28E
108 Sinabang, Indonesia ... 2 30N 46 30E
126 Sinai, Mt., (Musa, Gebel), Egypt 28 32N 33 59E
126 Sinai, Pen. of, Egypt .29 0N 34 0E
78 Sinaia, Rumania 45 21N 25 38E
168 Sinaloa, Mexico 25 50N 108 20W
168 Sinaloa, st., Mexico 25 0N 107 30W
71 Sinalunga, Italy 43 12N 11 43E
123 Sinawan, Libya 31 0N 10 30E
132 Sinazong we, Zambia .17 15S 27 25E
174 Sincelejo, Colombia ... 9 18N 75 24W
113 Sincheng, China 34 25N 113 56E
113 Sincheng, China 24 1N 108 35E
113 Sinchengtu, China 23 55N 108 30E
166 Sinclair, U.S.A. 41 47N 107 35W
156 Sinclair Mills, Canada 54 5N 121 40E
43 Sinclairs B., Scot., U.K. 58 30N 3 0W
104 Sind Sagar Doab, Pak. 32 0N 71 30E
81 Sindal, Denmark 57 28N 10 10E
109 Sindangbarang, Indon. 7 27S 107 9E
132 Sinde, Zambia 17 28S 25 51E
109 Sindjai, Indonesia 5 0S 120 20E
88 Sinelnikovo, U.S.S.R. 48 25N 35 30E
63 Sines, Portugal 37 56N 8 51W
63 Sines, Cabo de, Portugal 37 58N 8 53W
64 Sineu, Spain 39 39N 3 0E
113 Sinfeng, China 25 28N 114 40E
113 Sinfeng, China 26 59N 106 55E
124 Sinfra, Ivory Coast 6 35N 5 56W
127 Singa, Sudan 13 10N 33 57E
106 Singanallurt, India 11 2N 77 1E
109 Singaparna, Indonesia 7 23S 108 4E
107 Singapore, st., Asia ... 1 17N 103 51E
107 Singapore, Straits of, Asia 1 10N 103 40E
108 Singaradja, Indonesia 8 15S 115 10E
57 Singen, Germany 47 45N 8 50E
131 Singida & dist., Tanzania 4 49S 34 48E
76 Singitikos, Kólpos, G., Greece 40 6N 24 0E
103 Singkaling Hkamti, Burma 26 0N 95 45E
108 Singkawang, Indonesia 1 0N 109 5E
108 Singkep I., Indonesia . 0 30S 104 20E
35 Singleton, Eng., U.K. 50 55N 0 45W
142 Singleton, Mt., Austral. 29 27S 117 15E
80 Singö, I., Sweden 60 14N 18 55E
104 Singoli, India 25 0N 75 16E
112 Singtai, China 37 2N 114 30E
113 Singtze, China 29 30N 116 4E
113 Singyang, China 32 10N 114 0E
113 Sinhailien, China 34 31N 119 0E
112 Sinhsien, China 38 25N 112 45E
113 Sinhwa, China 27 36N 111 6E
76 Siniatsikon, Mt., Gr. .40 25N 21 35E
111 Sining, China 36 35N 101 50E
72 Siniscola, Italy 40 35N 9 40E
71 Sinj, Yugoslavia 43 42N 16 39E
74 Sinjajevina, Ra., Y.-slav. 42 57N 19 22E
98 Sinjil, Jordan 32 3N 35 15E
113 Sinkan, China 27 45N 115 30E
126 Sinkat, Sudan 18 55N 36 49E
112 Sinkiang, China 35 35N 111 25E
111 Sinkiang-Uigur, Auto. Reg., China 42 0N 85 0E
112 Sinkin, China 39 30N 122 29E
112 Sinlo, China 38 25N 114 50E
112 Sinmak, North Korea 38 34N 126 15E
112 Sinmin, China 42 0N 122 50E
72 Sinnai Sardinia, Italy 39 18N 9 13E
106 Sinnar, India 19 48N 74 0E
73 Sinni R., Italy 40 6N 16 15E
126 Sinnûris, Egypt 29 26N 30 31E
78 Sinoe L., Rumania 44 35N 28 50E
132 Sinoia, Rhodesia 17 20S 30 8E
100 Sinop, Turkey 42 1N 35 11E
88 Sinop, C., Turkey 42 1N 35 2E
112 Sinpin, China 41 50N 125 0E
113 Sinsiang, China 35 15N 113 55E
112 Sinsien, China 38 30N 113 0E
113 Sintai, China 30 59N 105 0E
108 Sintang, Indonesia 0 5N 111 35E
113 Sinti, (Hunghu), China 29 49N 113 30E
165 Sinton, U.S.A. 28 1N 97 30W
63 Sintra, Portugal 38 47N 9 25W
112 Sinuiju, North Korea .39 59N 124 30E
113 Sinyang, China 32 6N 114 2E
88 Sinyukha, R., U.S.S.R. 48 31N 30 31E
55 Sinzig, Germany 50 31N 7 14E
59 Siofok, Hungary 46 54N 18 4E
57 Sion, Switzerland 46 14N 7 20E
46 Sion Mills, Ireland 54 47N 7 29W
164 Sioux City, U.S.A. 42 32N 96 25W
164 Sioux Falls, U.S.A. 43 35N 96 40W
154 Sioux Lookout, Canada 50 10N 91 50W
113 Sipa, China 33 34N 118 59E
169 Siparia, Trinidad 10 15N 61 30W
108 Sipera, I., Indonesia ... 2 18S 99 40E
113 Siping, China 33 25N 114 10E
135 Sipofu, Natal, S. Africa 30 27S 30 25E
132 Sipolilo, Rhodesia 16 37S 30 42E
144 Sipul, Terr. of N. Guin. 5 50S 148 28E
169 Siqia R., Nicaragua ...12 30N 84 30W
109 Siquijor, Philippines ... 9 12N 123 45E
139 Sir Edward Pellew Group, Australia 15 40S 137 10E
142 Sir Samuel Mt., W. Australia 27 45S 120 40E
142 Sir Thomas, Mt., W. Australia 27 10S 129 45E
156 Sir Wilfred Laurier, Mt., Canada 52 48N 119 49W
106 Sira, India 13 41N 76 49E
79 Sira, R., Norway 58 43N 6 40E
73 Siracusa, Italy 37 4N 15 17E
105 Sirajganj, E. Pakistan 24 25N 89 47E
144 Sirake, Terr. of Papua 9 1S 141 2E
78 Siret, Rumania 47 55N 26 5E
78 Siret R., Rumania 47 58N 26 5E

MAP
74 Siria, Rumania 46 16N 21 38E
106 Sirkali (Shivali), India 11 15N 79 41E
77 Sirna I., Greece 36 22N 26 42E
45 Sirnitz, Austria 46 49N 14 4E
104 Sirohi, India 24 52N 72 53E
74 Siroki Brijeg, Y.-slavia 43 21N 17 36E
104 Sironj, India 24 5N 77 45E
77 Siros, & I., Greece 37 28N 24 57E
104 Sirsa, India 29 33N 75 4E
106 Sirsi, India 14 40N 74 49E
63 Siruela, Spain 38 58N 5 3W
71 Sisak, Yugoslavia 45 30N 16 21E
107 Sisaket, Thailand 15 8N 104 23E
65 Sisante, Spain 39 25N 2 12W
62 Sisargas, Islas, Spain 43 21N 8 50W
134 Sishen, C. Prov., S. Afr. 27 55S 22 59E
113 Sisiang, China 33 2N 107 48E
157 Sisipuk L., Canada 55 40N 102 0W
107 Sisophon, Cambodia 13 31N 102 59E
164 Sisseton, U.S.A. 45 43N 97 3W
49 Sissonne, France 49 34N 3 51E
51 Sisteron, France 44 12N 5 57E
166 Sisters, U.S.A. 44 21N 121 32W
105 Sitamarhi, India 26 37N 85 30E
105 Sitapur, India 27 38N 80 45E
64 Sitges, Spain 41 17N 1 47E
76 Sithoniá, pen., Greece 40 0N 23 45N
77 Sitia, Crete, Greece 35 13N 26 6E
156 Sitka, Alaska, U.S.A. 57 9N 134 58W
126 Sitra, Egypt 28 40N 26 53E
103 Sittang R., Burma 18 20N 96 45E
54 Sittard, Netherlands 51 0N 5 52E
56 Sittensen, Germany 53 17N 9 32E
35 Sittingbourne, Eng., U.K. 51 20N 0 43E
109 Situbondo, Indonesia 7 45S 114 0E
113 Siuwu, China 35 10N 113 30E
112 Siuyen, China 40 20N 123 15E
106 Sivaganga, India 9 50N 78 28E
106 Sivagiri, India 9 16N 77 26E
106 Sivakasi, India 9 24N 77 47E
101 Sivand, Iran 30 5N 52 55E
100 Sivas, Turkey 39 43N 36 58E
100 Siverek, Turkey 37 50N 39 25E
100 Sivrihisar, Turkey 39 30N 31 35E
126 Siwa & Oasis, Egypt 29 10N 25 30E
105 Siwalik Range, Nepal 28 0N 83 0E
105 Siwan, India 26 13N 84 27E
44 Sixmilebridge, Ireland 52 45N 8 46W
46 Sixmile Cross, Northern Ireland, U.K. 54 34N 7 7W
104 Siyana, India 28 37N 78 6E
35 Sizewell, Eng., U.K. 52 13N 1 38E
81 Sjaelland I., Denmark 55 30N 11 30E
81 Sjaellands Odde, peninsula, Denmark 56 0N 11 15E
80 Själevad, Sweden 63 19N 18 40E
74 Sjarinska Banja, Y.-slav. 42 45N 21 38E
74 Sjenica, Yugoslavia 43 16N 20 0E
79 Sjernaröy, Norway 59 15N 5 50E
79 Sjoa, Norway 61 41N 9 40E
81 Sjöbo, Sweden 55 37N 13 45E
81 Sjöholt, Norway 62 27N 6 52E
82 Sjönstå, Norway 67 10N 16 3E
81 Sjösa, Sweden 58 47N 17 9E
82 Sjövegan, Norway 68 45N 17 58E
88 Skadovsk, U.S.S.R. 46 17N 32 52E
81 Skælskör, Denmark 55 16N 11 18E
81 Skærbaek, Denmark 55 9N 8 45E
82 Skaga Fd., Iceland 65 50N 19 30W
81 Skagen, Denmark 57 45N 10 35E
81 Skagerrak, Den.-Nor. 57 50N 9 0E
80 Skagern, L., Sweden 59 0N 14 20E
79 Skaget, Mt., Norway 61 17N 9 13E
157 Skagway, Alas., U.S.A. 59 30N 135 20W
88 Skala Podolskaya, U.S.S.R. 48 50N 26 15E
86 Skalat, U.S.S.R. 49 23N 25 55E
60 Skalbmierz, Poland 50 20N 20 25E
81 Skalderviken, B., Swed. 56 22N 12 30E
59 Skalicd, Czechoslovakia 48 50N 17 15E
81 Skallingen, pen., Den. 55 32N 8 13E
81 Skals, Denmark 56 34N 9 22E
81 Skanderborg, Denmark 56 2N 9 55E
81 Skanderborg, co., Den. 56 0N 9 30E
79 Skånevik, Norway 59 43N 5 58E
81 Skanninge, Sweden 58 24N 15 5E
81 Skanör, Sweden 55 24N 12 50E
77 Skantzoura. I., Greece 39 5N 24 6E
81 Skara, Sweden 58 25N 13 30E
81 Skaraborgs, Co., Swed. 58 20N 13 30E
81 Skarblacka, Sweden 58 36N 15 50E
79 Skardhö, Mt., Norway 62 30N 8 47E
102 Skardu, Kashmir 35 20N 75 35E
81 Skaresta, Sweden 58 26N 16 22E
81 Skarild, Denmark 55 58N 8 52E
60 Skarszewy, Poland 54 4N 18 25E
79 Skarvane, Mt., Norway 63 18N 11 27E
60 Skarzysko Kamienna, Poland 51 7N 20 52E
43 Skateraw, Scot., U.K. 57 1N 2 9W
79 Skåtöy, Norway 50 50N 9 30E
80 Skattungbyn, Sweden 61 10N 14 56E
81 Skaw (Grenen), C., Den. 57 46N 10 34E
42 Skaw Taing, Scot., U.K. 60 23N 0 57W
80 Skebo, Sweden 59 58N 18 37E
80 Skebokvarn, Sweden 59 7N 16 45E
80 Skee, Sweden 58 55N 11 18E
156 Skeena Mts. Canada 56 40N 128 0W
156 Skeena R., Canada 54 20N 129 20W
82 Skeggjastadir, Iceland 66 3N 14 50W
39 Skegness, Eng., U.K. 53 9N 0 20E
174 Skeldon, Guyana 6 0N 57 20W
82 Skellefteå, Sweden 64 45N 20 59E
82 Skelleftestrand, Sweden 64 45N 21 15E
38 Skelmersdale, Eng., U.K. 53 34N 2 49W
40 Skelmorlie, Scot., U.K. 55 52N 4 53W
41 Skelton, Cumb., England, U.K. 54 42N 2 50W
39 Skelton, Yorks., England, U.K. 54 33N 0 59W
74 Skender Vakuf, Y.-slav. 44 29N 17 22E
81 Skene, Sweden 57 30N 12 35E
134 Skerpioendrif, S. Africa 31 5S 21 33E
45 Skerries, Ireland 53 35N 6 7W
46 Skerries, Rks., Northern Ireland, U.K. 55 14N 6 40W
77 Skhiza I., Greece 36 41N 20 40E
77 Skhoinoúsa, I., Greece 36 53N 25 31E
79 Ski, Norway 59 43N 10 52E
77 Skiathos I., Greece 39 12N 23 30E
44 Skibbereen, Ireland 51 33N 9 16W
38 Skiddaw, Mt., Eng., U.K. 54 39N 3 9W
56 Skidegate, Inlet, Canada 53 20N 132 0W
79 Skien, Norway 59 12N 9 35E
60 Skierniewice, Poland 51 58N 20 19E
123 Skikda, (Philippeville), Algeria 36 50N 6 58E
80 Skillvngmark, Sweden 59 48N 120 1E
81 Skillingaryd, Sweden 57 27N 14 5E
81 Skillinge, Sweden 55 30N 14 16E
77 Skinári, Akrá, C., Gr. 37 56N 20 40E
40 Skipness, Scot., U.K. 55 46N 5 20W
39 Skipsea, Eng., U.K. 53 58N 0 13W
143 Skipton, Vic., Australia 37 39S 143 21E
38 Skipton, Eng., U.K. 53 57N 2 1W
81 Skirild, Denmark 55 58N 8 53E
77 Skiropoúla. I., Greece 38 50N 24 21E
77 Skiros, & I., Greece 38 55N 24 34E
81 Skivarp, Sweden 55 25N 13 32E
81 Skive, Denmark 56 33N 9 2E
79 Skjak, Norway 61 52N 8 22E
82 Skjalfandi, Fd., Iceland 66 5N 17 30W
79 Skjeberg, Norway 59 12N 11 12E
81 Skjern, Denmark 55 57N 8 30E
79 Skjönne, Norway 60 16N 9 1E
59 Skoczów, Poland 49 49N 18 45E
79 Skodje, Norway 62 30N 6 43E
71 Skofja Loka, Y.-slavia 46 9N 14 19E
79 Skoger, Norway 59 42N 10 16E
80 Skoghall, Sweden 59 20N 13 30E
81 Skoghult, Sweden 56 59N 15 55E
37 Skokholm, I., Wales, United Kingdom 51 42N 5 16W
60 Skoki, Poland 52 40N 17 11E
86 Skole, U.S.S.R. 49 3N 23 30E
37 Skomer, I., Wales, U.K. 51 44N 5 19W
80 Skonsberg, Sweden 62 25N 17 21E
133 Skoonoord, S. Africa 26 0S 29 45E
77 Skópelos & I., Greece 39 9N 23 47E
87 Skopin, U.S.S.R. 53 55N 39 32E
74 Skopje, Yugoslavia 42 1N 21 32E
80 Skorped. Sweden 63 23N 17 55E
60 Skórcz, Poland 43 47N 18 30E
79 Scotfoss, Norway 59 15N 9 14E
86 Skoudas, U.S.S.R. 56 21N 21 45E
81 Skövde, Sweden 58 24N 13 52E
155 Skowhegan, U.S.A. 44 49N 69 40W
157 Skowman, Canada 51 58N 99 35W
71 Skradin, Yugoslavia 43 52N 15 53E
81 Skreanas, Sweden 56 52N 12 35E
79 Skudeneshavn, Norway 59 10N 5 10E
133 Skukuza, Trans., S. Afr. 24 52S 31 35E
81 Skromberga, Sweden 55 59N 9 14E
44 Skull, Ireland 51 32N 9 40W
81 Skultorp, Sweden 58 24N 13 45E
88 Skulyany, U.S.S.R. 47 19N 27 39E
164 Skunk R., U.S.A. 41 10N 91 45W
81 Skurup, Sweden 55 28N 13 30E
80 Skutskar, Sweden 60 37N 17 34E
88 Skvira, U.S.S.R. 49 44N 29 32E
60 Skwierzyna, Poland 52 46N 15 30E
42 Skye, I., Scot., U.K. 57 15N 6 10W
166 Skykomish U.S.A. 47 43N 121 16W
77 Skyros (Skiros), I., Gr. 38 52N 24 37E
135 Slabberts, OFS, S. Afr. 28 23S 28 13E
81 Slagelse, Denmark 55 23N 11 19E
38 Slaidburn, Eng. U.K. 53 57N 2 28W
38 Slaley, England, U.K. 54 55N 2 4W
108 Slamet, Mt., Indonesia 7 16S 109 8E
143 Slammannon, Australia 32 1S 143 41E
46 Slane, Ireland 53 42N 6 32W
45 Slaney R., Ireland 52 52N 6 45W
81 Slangerup, Denmark 55 50N 12 11E
134 Slangfontein, S. Africa 31 40S 22 27E
78 Slănic, Rumania 45 14N 25 58E
74 Slankamen, Yugoslavia 45 8N 20 15E
74 Slano, Yugoslavia 42 48N 17 53E
86 Slantsy, U.S.S.R. 59 7N 28 5E
58 Slany, Czechoslovakia 50 13N 14 6E
113 Slaokan, China 30 57N 114 2E
81 Slatbaken, Inlet, Swed. 58 28N 16 30E
154 Slate Is., Canada 48 40N 87 0W
78 Slatina, Rumania 44 28N 24 22E
165 Slaton, U.S.A. 33 27N 101 38W
125 Slave Coast, W. Africa 6 0N 2 30E
156 Slave Lake, Canada 55 25N 114 50W
156 Slave Pt., Canada 61 15N 116 0W
156 Slave R., Canada 60 40N 112 50W
90 Slavgorod, U.S.S.R. 53 10N 78 50E
74 Slavinja, Yugoslavia 43 14N 22 50E
59 Slavkov (Austerlitz), Cz. 49 10N 16 52E
86 Slavnoye, U.S.S.R. 29 15E 54 24N
74 Slavonski, Požega, Yugoslavia 45 20N 17 40E
74 Slavonski Brod, Y.-slav. 45 11N 18 0E
86 Slavuta, U.S.S.R. 50 15N 27 2E
88 Slavyansk, U.S.S.R. 45 15N 38 11E
88 Slavyanskaya, U.S.S.R. 48 55N 37 30E
60 Slawno, Poland 54 20N 16 41E
60 Slawoborze, Poland 53 55N 15 42E
44 Slea Hd., Ireland 52 7N 10 30W
39 Sleaford Eng., U.K. 53 0N 0 22W
42 Sleat, Pt. of, Scot., U.K. 57 1N 6 0W
42 Sleat, Sd. of, Scot., U.K. 57 5N 5 47W
39 Sledmere, Eng., U.K. 54 4N 0 35W
153 Sleeper, Is., Canada 56 50N 80 30W
153 Sleepers, The, Canada 58 30N 81 0W
164 Sleepy Eye, U.S.A. 44 15N 94 45W
109 Sleman, Indonesia 7 40S 110 20E
79 Slemmestad, Norway 59 47N 10 30E
60 Ślesiń, Poland 52 22N 18 14E
81 Sletterhage, C., Den. 56 7N 10 31E
165 Slidell, U.S.A. 30 20N 89 48W
54 Sliedrecht, Netherlands 51 50N 4 45E
44 Slieve Anierin, Ireland 54 5N 7 58W
44 Slieve Aughty, Ireland 53 4N 8 30W
46 Slieve Beagh, Ireland 54 20N 7 12W
44 Slieve Bernagh, Ireland 52 50N 8 30W
45 Slieve Bloom, Ireland 53 4N 7 40W
44 Slieve Callan, Ireland 52 51N 9 16W
45 Slieve Car, Ireland 54 5N 9 38W
44 Slieve Carran, Ireland 53 6N 9 0W
46 Slieve Donard, Northern Ireland, U.K. 54 10N 5 57W
29 Slieve Elva, Ireland 53 5N 9 16W
44 Slieve Felim, Ireland 52 40N 8 20W
46 Slieve Gallion, Northern Ireland U.K. 54 45N 6 45W
46 Slieve Gamph, Ireland 54 6N 9 0W
46 Slieve Gullion, Northern Ireland, U.K. 54 8N 6 26W
46 Slieve League, Ireland 54 40N 8 42W
44 Slieve Mish, Ireland 52 12N 9 50W
44 Slieve Miskish, Ireland 51 40N 10 10W
45 Slieve More, Ireland 54 1N 10 3W
46 Slieve Snaght, Ireland 54 59N 8 7W
46 Slieve Tooey, Ireland 54 46N 8 39W
45 Slievenamon Mt., Ire. 52 25N 7 37W
46 Sligo, Ireland 54 17N 8 28W
46 Sligo, Ire. 54 17N 8 28W
46 Sligo, co., Ireland 54 10N 8 35W
46 Sligo B., Ire. 54 20N 8 40W
107 Slim R., Malasia 3 50N 101 29E
42 Slioch, mt., Scot., U.K. 57 40N 5 20W
83 Slite, Sweden 57 42N 18 45E
75 Sliven, Bulgaria 42 42N 26 19E
74 Slivnitsa, Bulgaria 42 50N 23 0E
71 Sljeme, Mt., Y.-slavia 45 57N 15 58E
161 Sloansville, U.S.A. 42 45N 74 22W
87 Slobodskoy, U.S.S.R. 58 40N 50 6E
78 Slobozia, Bucarest, Rum. 44 34N 27 23E
78 Slobozia, Pitesti, Rum. 44 30N 25 14E
81 Slöinge, Sweden 56 54N 12 40E
86 Slonim, U.S.S.R. 53 4N 25 19E
35 Slough, England, U.K. 51 30N 0 35W
59 Slovakia, historic prov., Czechoslovakia 48 30N 19 0E
71 Slovenija (Slovenia) prov., Yugoslavia 45 58N 14 30E
71 Slovenska Bistrica, Yugoslavia 46 24N 15 35E
59 Slovenske Krusnohorie, Cz. 48 45N 20 0E
86 Sluch R., U.S.S.R. 51 10N 26 20E
54 Sluis, Netherlands 51 18N 3 23E
71 Slunj, Yugoslavia 45 6N 15 33E
60 Slupca, Poland 52 15N 17 52E
60 Slupsk, Poland 54 30N 17 3E
44 Slyne Hd., Ireland 53 25N 10 10W
91 Slyudyanka, U.S.S.R. 51 40N 103 30E
81 Smaalandsfarvandet, Sea, Denmark 55 10N 11 20E
81 Smål-Taberg, Sweden 57 42N 14 5E
81 Smålandsstenar, Swed. 57 9N 13 24E
122 Smara, Spanish Sahara 26 48N 11 31W
71 Smarje, Yugoslavia 46 15N 15 34E
81 Smedberg, Sweden 58 35N 12 0E
74 Smederevo, Yugoslavia 44 40N 20 57E
81 Smedstorp, Sweden 55 38N 13 58E
88 Smela, U.S.S.R. 49 30N 32 0E
44 Smerwick Harb., Ire. 52 12N 10 23W
160 Smethport, U.S.A. 41 50N 78 28W
34 Smethwick, Eng., U.K. 52 29N 1 58W
75 Smilyan, Bulgaria 41 29N 24 46E
156 Smith, Canada 55 10N 114 0W
156 Smith Arm, Canada 66 30N 123 0W
164 Smith Center U.S.A. 39 50N 98 50W
14 Smith Sound, Canada 78 0N 75 0W
46 Smithborough, Ireland 54 13N 7 8W
156 Smithers, Canada 54 45N 127 10W
41 Smithfield, Eng., U.K. 54 59N 2 51W
135 Smithfield, S. Afr. 30 13S 26 32E
163 Smithfield, N.C., U.S.A. 35 31N 78 16W
166 Smithfield, Utah, U.S.A. 41 50N 111 56W
154 Smith's Falls, Canada 44 55N 76 0W
145 Smithton, N.S.W., Austral. 31 0S 152 48E
145 Smithton, Tas., Austral. 40 53S 145 6E
160 Smithville, Canada 43 7N 79 32W
165 Smithville, U.S.A. 30 2N 97 12W
154 Smoky Falls, Canada 50 10N 82 10W
164 Smoky Hill, R., U.S.A. 38 45N 98 0W
156 Smoky Lake, Canada 54 10N 112 30W
79 Smöla I., Norway 63 23N 8 3E
86 Smolensk, U.S.S.R. 54 45N 32 0E
76 Smólikas Mt., Greece 40 9N 20 58E
59 Smolnik, Czechoslovakia 48 43N 20 44E
75 Smolyan, Bulgaria 41 36N 24 38E
154 Smooth Rock Falls, Can. 49 17N 81 37W
86 Smorgon, U.S.S.R. 54 28N 26 24E
78 Smulti, Rumania 45 57N 27 44E
75 Smyadovo, Bulgaria 43 2N 27 1E
100 Smyrna (Izmir), Turkey 38 25N 27 8E
38 Snaefell, Isle of Man, United Kingdom 54 18N 4 26W
82 Snaefells Jökull, Iceland 64 45N 23 25W
39 Snainton, England, U.K. 54 14N 0 33W
39 Snaith, England. U.K. 53 42N 1 1W
143 Snake I., Vic., Australia 38 47S 146 33E
166 Snake R., U.S.A. 46 31N 118 50W
166 Snake Ra., Mts., U.S.A. 39 0N 114 30W
166 Snake River Plain, U.S.A. 43 13N 113 0W
42 Snap, The, Scot., U.K. 60 35N 0 50W
35 Snape, Suffolk, England. United Kingdom 52 11N 1 29E
79 Snarum, Norway 60 1N 9 54E
82 Snåsa, Norway 64 15N 12 23E
80 Snasahögarna, Mt., Sweden 63 10N 12 15E
81 Snedsted, Denmark 56 55N 8 32E
54 Sneek, Netherlands 53 2N 5 40E
44 Sneem, Ireland 51 50N 9 55W
81 Snejbjærg, Denmark 56 8N 8 44E
35 Snettisham, Eng., U.K. 52 52N 0 30E
58 Snĕzka, Mt. (Schneekoppe), Cz. & Pol. 50 41N 14 55E
71 Snežnik, Mt., Y.-slavia 45 36N 14 35E
88 Snigirevka, U.S.S.R. 47 2N 32 35E
59 Snina, Czechoslovakia 49 0N 22 9E
42 Snizort L., Scot., U.K. 57 33N 6 28W
79 Snöhetta, Mt., Norway 62 19N 9 16E
166 Snohomish, U.S.A. 47 53N 122 0W
82 Snoksdalur, Iceland 64 58N 21 44W
79 Snönuten, Mt., Norway 59 31N 6 50E
162 Snow Hill, U.S.A. 38 10N 75 21W
157 Snowbird L., Canada 60 45N 103 0W
37 Snowdon, Mt., Wales, United Kingdom 53 4N 4 8W
157 Snowdrift, & R., Canada 62 10N 110 0W
167 Snowflake, U.S.A. 34 30N 110 4W
156 Snowshoe, Canada 53 43N 121 0W
166 Snowville, U.S.A. 41 59N 112 47W
143 Snowy Mts., Australia 36 15S 148 20E
143 Snowy R., N.S.W., Austral. 36 13S 148 30E
88 Snyatyn, U.S.S.R. 48 28N 25 33E
165 Snyder. Okla., U.S.A. 34 4N 99 0W
165 Snyder, Tex., U.S.A. 32 45N 100 57W
147 Soaker, Mt., N.Z. 45 23S 167 15E
129 Soalala, Malagasy Rep. 16 6S 45 20E
166 Soap Lake, U.S.A. 47 29N 119 31W
42 Soay I., Scot., U.K. 57 9N 6 13W
42 Soay Sd., Scot., U.K. 57 10N 6 15W
127 Sobat R., Sudan 8 32N 32 40E
62 Sobĕslav, Cz. 49 16N 14 45E
104 Sobhapur, India 22 47N 78 17E
131 Sobik, Kenya 0 45S 35 10E
87 Sobinka, U.S.S.R. 56 0N 40 0E
60 Sobótka, Poland 50 54N 16 44E
175 Sobrado, Brazil 5 35S 53 0W
62 Sobrado, Spain 43 2N 8 2W
75 Sobral, Brazil 3 50S 40 30W
62 Sobreira Formosa, Port. 39 46N 7 51W
107 Soc Trang, see Khonh Hung, S. Vietnam 9 37N 105 50E
71 Soča, R., Yugoslavia 46 20N 13 40E
78 Socariciu, Rumania 44 15N 27 35E
60 Sochaczew, Poland 52 15N 20 13E
111 Soche (Yarkand), China 38 24N 77 20E
89 Sochi, U.S.S.R. 43 35N 39 40E
137 Society Is., Pac. Oc. 17 0S 151 0W
172 Socompa, vol., Chile 24 27S 68 18W
174 Socorro, Colombia 6 29N 73 16W
161 Socorro, U.S.A. 34 3N 106 58W
99 Socotra I. Ind. Oc. 12 30N 54 0E
65 Socuéllamos, Spain 39 16N 2 47W
156 Soda Creek, Canada 52 25N 122 10W
167 Soda L., U.S.A. 35 7N 116 2W
102 Soda Plains, Kashmir 35 30N 79 0E
116 Soda Springs, U.S.A. 42 4N 111 40W
82 Sodankyla, Finland 67 29N 26 40E
127 Soddu, Ethiopia 7 0N 37 57E
80 Söderfjärden, Sweden 62 3N 17 25E
80 Söderfors, Sweden 60 23N 17 25E
81 Söderhamn, Sweden 61 18N 17 10E
81 Söderköping, Sweden 58 31N 16 35E
80 Södermanlands Län, Sweden 59 10N 16 30E
80 Södertälje, Sweden 59 12N 17 50E
134 Sodium, C. Prov., S. Afr. 30 15S 15 45E
81 Södra Vi, Sweden 57 45N 15 45E
71 Sodrazica, Yugoslavia 45 45N 14 39E
160 Sodus, U.S.A. 43 13N 77 5W
160 Sodus Pt., U.S.A. 43 15N 77 0W
133 Soekmekaar, S. Africa 23 30S 29 55E
56 Soest, Germany 51 34N 8 7E
54 Soest, Netherlands 52 9N 5 19E
76 Sofadhes, Greece 39 28N 22 4E
132 Sofala. Botswana 23 4S 27 25E
124 Sofara, Mali 13 59N 4 9W
75 Sofia, Bulgaria 42 45N 23 20E
129 Sofia R., Malagasy Rep. 15 25S 48 40E
88 Sofievka, U.S.S.R. 47 58N 34 14E
77 Sofikon, Greece 37 47N 23 3E
75 Sofiya (Sofia), Bulgaria 42 45N 23 20E
109 Sogad, Philippines 10 30N 125 0E
125 Sogakofe, Ghana 6 2N 0 39E
174 Sogamoso, Colombia 5 43N 72 56W
56 Sögel, Germany 52 50N 7 32E
79 Sogn & Fjordane Fylker, co., Norway 61 40N 6 0E
79 Sogndal, Norway 58 20N 6 15E
79 Sognefjord, Norway 61 10N 6 0E
126 Sohâg, Egypt 26 27N 31 43E
35 Soham. England, U.K. 52 20N 0 20E
54 Soignies, Belgium 50 35N 4 5E
127 Soira, Mt., Ethiopia 14 45N 39 30E
49 Soissons. France 49 25N 3 19E
59 Soitava, R., Cz. 49 30N 16 37E
104 Sojat, India 25 55N 73 38E
87 Sok R., U.S.S.R. 53 30N 50 30E
86 Sokal, U.S.S.R. 50 31N 24 15E
77 Söke, Turkey 37 48N 27 28E
130 Sokele, Congo 9 45S 24 40E
76 Sökhós, Greece 40 48N 23 22E
101 Sokhta Chinar, Afghan. 35 5N 67 35E
79 Sokna, Norway 60 16N 9 50E
79 Soknedal, Norway 62 57N 10 13E
74 Soko Banja, Y.-slavia 43 40N 21 51E
125 Sokode, Togo 9 0N 1 11E
87 Sokol, U.S.S.R. 59 30N 40 5E
60 Sokolka, Poland 53 25N 23 30E
58 Sokolov, Czechoslovakia 50 12N 12 40E
59 Sokolow Matopolski, Poland 50 12N 22 7E
60 Sokolow Podlaski, Pol. 52 25N 22 15E
125 Sokoto, Nigeria 13 2N 5 16E
125 Sokoto R., Nigeria 13 30N 6 10E
84 Sol Iletsk, U.S.S.R. 51 20N 54 50E
131 Solai, Kenya 0 25N 36 12E
79 Sola, Norway 58 53N 5 36E
79 Sola. R., Poland 49 38N 19 8E
131 Solai, Kenya 0 2N 36 12E
109 Solano, Philippines 16 25N 121 15E
62 Solares, Spain 43 23N 3 43W
81 Solberga, Sweden 57 45N 14 43E
81 Solbjærg, Aarlborg, Den. 56 50N 10 8E
78 Solca, Rumania 47 40N 25 50E
174 Soledad, Colombia 10 55N 74 46W
167 Soledad, U.S.A. 36 27N 121 16W
174 Soledad, Venezuela 8 10N 63 34W
34 Solent, The, Eng., U.K. 50 45N 1 25W
51 Solenzara, Corsica, Fr. 41 53N 9 23E
131 Solesia, Tanzania 8 48S 31 58E
49 Solesmes, France 50 10N 3 30E
79 Solfonn, Mt., Norway 60 2N 6 57E
87 Soligalich, U.S.S.R. 59 5N 42 10E
34 Solihull, Eng., U.K. 52 26N 1 47W
84 Solikamsk, U.S.S.R. 59 38N 56 50E
123 Soliman, Tunisia 36 48N 10 30E
174 Solimões R., Brazil 2 15S 66 30W
56 Solingen, Germany 51 10N 7 4E
42 Sollas, Scotland, U.K. 57 39N 7 20W
81 Sollebrunn, Sweden 58 10N 12 34E
80 Sollentuna, Sweden 59 26N 17 56E
80 Sollefteå, Sweden 63 12N 17 20E
64 Soller, Spain 39 43N 2 45E
80 Sollerön, Sweden 62 54N 14 38E
80 Solna, Sweden 59 22N 18 1E

MAP
87 Solnechnogorsk, U.S.S.R. 56 10N 36 57E
79 Sölnkletten, Mt., Norway 61 55N 10 18E
49 Sologne, dist., France 47 40N 2 0E
108 Solok, Indonesia 0 55S 100 40E
168 Sololá, Guatemala 14 49N 91 10W
131 Sololo, Kenya 3 33N 38 39E
136 Solomon Is., Pac. Oc. 8 0S 160 0E
164 Solomon, N. Fork, R., U.S.A. 39 45N 99 0W
164 Solomon, S. Fork, R., U.S.A. 39 25N 99 12W
98 Solomon's Pools, Site, Jordan 31 42N 35 7E
164 Solon Springs, U.S.A. 46 19N 91 47W
109 Solor, I., Indonesia 8 27S 123 0E
87 Solotcha, U.S.S.R. 54 27N 39 59E
57 Solothurn, Switzerland 47 13N 7 32E
57 Solothurn, can., Switz. 47 18N 7 40E
64 Solsona, Spain 42 0N 1 31E
59 Solt, Hungary 46 45N 19 1E
71 Solta, I., Yugoslavia .43 24N 16 15E
101 Soltanabad, Iran 36 29N 58 5E
100 Soltaniyeh, Iran 36 20N 48 55E
56 Soltau, Germany 52 59N 9 50E
86 Soltsy, U.S.S.R. 58 10N 30 10E
112 Solun, China 46 40N 120 40E
79 Solund, Norway 61 5N 4 50E
79 Solund I., Norway 61 7N 4 50E
74 Solunska Gl., Mt., Yugoslavia 41 44N 21 31E
37 Solva, Wales, U.K. 51 52N 5 12W
161 Solvay, U.S.A. 43 5N 76 17W
81 Sölvesborg, Sweden 56 5N 14 35E
38 Solway Firth, Irish Sea 54 45N 3 30W
132 Solwesi, Zambia 12 20S 26 21E
132 Somabula, Rhodesia ...19 40S 29 38E
99 Somali Rep., E. Africa 7 0N 47 0E
127 Somaliland, Fr *see* Fr Terr Afars & Issas .12 0N 43 0E
105 Sombe Dzong, Bhutan 27 13N 89 8E
49 Sombernon. France ...47 20N 4 40E
74 Sombor, Yugoslavia ...45 46N 19 17E
160 Sombra, Canada 42 43N 82 28W
168 Sombrerete, Mexico ...23 40N 103 40W
169 Sombrero I., Leeward Is. 18 30N 63 30W
35 Somerby, Eng., U.K. .52 42N 0 49W
166 Somers, U.S.A. 48 4N 114 18W
144 Somerset, Australia ...10 45S 142 25E
169 Somerset, & I., Bermuda 32 20N 64 55W
167 Somerset, Colo., U.S.A. 38 55N 107 30W
162 Somerset, Ky., U.S.A. 37 5N 84 40W
161 Somerset, Mass., U.S.A. 41 45N 71 10W
160 Somerset, Pa., U.S.A. 40 1N 79 4E
36 Somerset, co., England, United Kingdom 51 9N 3 0W
135 Somerset East, S. Afr. 32 42S 25 35E
134 Somerset West, S. Afr. 34 8S 18 50E
152 Somerset, Is., Canada 73 30N 93 0W
35 Somersham, Eng., U.K. 52 24N 0 1W
161 Somersworth, U.S.A. .43 15N 70 51W
34 Somerton, Oxon, England, U.K. 51 58N 1 14W
167 Somerton, U.S.A. 32 41N 114 47W
161 Somerville, N.J., U.S.A. 40 34N 74 36W
78 Somes, R., Rumania .47 15N 23 45E
78 Somesu, Mic, R., Rum. 47 0N 23 51E
78 Somesul Mare, R., Rum. 47 18N 24 30E
135 Somkele, Natal, S. Afr. 28 18S 32 10E
70 Somma Lombardo, It. 45 41N 8 42E
73 Somma Vesuviana, It. 40 52N 14 23E
73 Sommatino (Sicily), It. 37 20N 14 0E
48 Somme, B. de la, France 5 22N 1 30E
49 Somme, dépt., France 40 0N 2 15E
49 Somme R., France 50 12N 1 30E
81 Sommen, Sweden 58 12N 15 0E
81 Sommen L., Sweden ...58 0N 15 15E
49 Somme-py, France 49 15N 4 31E
56 Sömmerda, Germany .51 10N 11 8E
81 Sommersted, Denmark 55 19N 9 18E
49 Sommesous, France ...48 44N 4 12E
51 Sommières, Gard, Fr. .43 47N 4 6E
59 Somogy, co., Hungary 46 19N 17 30E
59 Somogyszob, Hungary 46 18N 17 20E
35 Sompting, Eng., U.K. 50 51N 0 20W
79 Son, Norway 59 32N 10 42E
62 Son, Spain 42 43N 8 58W
105 Son, R., India 24 51N 81 40E
107 Son La., N. Vietnam .21 20N 103 50E
105 Sonamukhi, India 23 18N 87 27E
70 Soncino, Italy 45 24N 9 52E
70 Sondalo, Italy 46 20N 10 20E
81 Sönder Hornum, Den. 56 32N 9 38E
81 Sönder Nissum, Den. 56 19N 8 11E
81 Sönder Omme, Den. ...55 50N 8 54E
81 Sönderborg, Denmark 54 55N 9 49E
81 Sönderho, Denmark ...55 21N 8 28E
56 Sonderhausen, Germany 51 22N 10 50E
79 Sondre Höland, Nor. .59 44N 11 30E
79 Sondre Land, Norway 60 44N 10 21E
153 Söndre Stromfjord, Greenland 66 30N 50 52W
70 Sondrio, Italy 46 10N 9 53E
132 Sone, Mozambique 17 23S 34 55E
104 Sonepat, India 29 0N 77 5E
105 Sonepur, India 20 55N 83 50E
107 Song Cau, S. Vietnam 13 20N 109 18E
79 Songa, R., Norway 59 57N 7 30E
131 Songea, Tanzania 10 40S 35 40E
131 Songea, dist., Tanzania 10 42S 35 35E
49 Songeons, France 49 32N 1 50E
112 Songjin, Korea 40 30N 129 10E
107 Songkhla, Thailand ... 7 13N 100 37E
130 Songololo, Congo 5 40S 14 5E
130 Songwe, Congo 3 20S 26 16E
132 Songwe, Malawi 9 44S 33 58E
87 Sonkovo, U.S.S.R. 57 50N 37 5E
102 Sonmiani, Pakistan ...25 25N 66 40E
75 Sonneberg, Germany .50 22N 11 11E
35 Sonning, Eng., U.K. .51 28N 0 53W
72 Sonnino, Italy 41 25N 13 13E
167 Sonora, Calif., U.S.A. .37 59N 120 27W
165 Sonora, Texas, U.S.A. 30 33N 100 37W
166 Sonora P., U.S.A. 38 17N 119 35W
168 Sonora, st., Mexico 28 0N 111 0W
135 Sonskyn, C. Prov. S. Afr. 30 47S 26 28E
168 Sonsonate, Salvador ...13 45N 89 45W
57 Sonthofen, Germany .47 31N 10 16E
162 Soo Junction, U.S.A. .46 20N 85 14W
113 Soochow, China 31 18N 120 41E
109 Sopi, Indonesia 2 40N 128 28E
127 Sopo R., Sudan 8 40N 26 30E
60 Sopot, Poland 54 27N 18 31E
74 Sopot, Yugoslavia 44 29N 20 30E
57 Sopron, Hungary 47 41N 16 37E
155 Sop's Arm, Canada 49 46N 56 56W
63 Sor, R., Portugal 39 7N 9 52E
79 Sör-Fron, Norway 61 35N 9 59E
15 Sor Rondane, Mts., Ant. 72 0S 25 0E
82 Sör Tröndelag Fylke, Co., Norway 63 0N 11 0E
72 Sora, Italy 41 45N 13 36E
105 Sorada, India 19 32N 84 45E
104 Sorah, West Pakistan 27 13N 68 56E
80 Söraker, Sweden 62 30N 17 32E
70 Sorano, Italy 42 40N 11 42E
174 Sorata, Bolivia 15 50S 68 50W
65 Sorbas, Spain 37 6N 2 7W
40 Sorbie, Scot., U.K. 54 46N 4 26W
43 Sordale, Scot., U.K. 58 33N 3 26W
48 Sordeval, France 48 44N 0 55W
154 Sorel, Canada 46 0N 73 10W
70 Soresina, Italy 45 17N 9 51E
82 Sörfold, Norway 67 5N 14 20E
51 Sorgues, France 44 1N 4 53E
64 Soria, Spain 41 43N 2 32W
64 Soria, prov., Spain 41 46N 2 28W
172 Soriano, Uruguay 33 25S 58 21W
42 Sorisdale, Scotland U.K. 56 40N 6 28W
40 Sorn, Scotland, U.K. .55 31N 4 18W
81 Sorö, Denmark 55 26N 11 32E
124 Soro, Guinea 10 9N 9 48W
81 Sorö, Co., Denmark ...55 24N 11 40E
173 Sorocaba, Brazil 23 31S 47 35W
88 Soroki, U.S.S.R. 48 8N 28 12E
59 Soroksár, Hungary 47 24N 19 9E
104 Soron, India 27 55N 78 45E
109 Sorong, Indonesia 0 55S 131 15E
131 Soroti, Uganda 1 43N 33 35E
82 Soröya, I., Norway 70 35N 22 45E
82 Soröy Sd., Norway 70 25N 23 0E
79 Söröyane, I., Norway .62 25N 5 32E
63 Sorraia, R., Portugal .38 55N 8 35W
73 Sorrento, Italy 40 38N 14 23E
82 Sorsele, Sweden 65 31N 17 30E
72 Sorso, Italy 40 50N 8 34E
109 Sorsogon, Philippines .13 0N 124 0E
43 Sortat, Scot., U.K. 58 32N 3 12W
73 Sortino Italy 37 9N 15 1E
64 Sos, Spain 42 30N 1 13W
81 Sosdala, Sweden 56 2N 13 41E
154 Soseumica, L., Canada 50 15N 77 30W
87 Sosna R., U.S.S.R. 52 30N 38 0E
60 Sosnowiec, Poland 50 20N 19 10E
51 Sospel, France 43 52N 7 27E
71 Šoštanj, Yugoslavia ...46 23N 15 4E
168 Soto la Marina, R., Mex. 23 40N 97 40W
62 Soto y Amio, Spain ...42 46N 5 53W
79 Sotra I., Norway 60 15N 5 0E
48 Sotteville, France 49 24N 1 5E
130 Souanke, Congo (Fr.) . 2 10N 14 10E
124 Soufi, Mauritania 15 13N 12 17W
76 Souflion, Greece 41 12N 26 18E
1 Soufriere, la, vol., Guadeloupe I. 16 20N 61 40W
1 Soufriere, vol., St. Vincent 13 10N 61 10W
50 Souillac, France 44 53N 1 29E
123 Souk Ahras, Algeria ...36 23N 8 0E
122 Souk el Arba du Rharb, Morocco 34 50N 5 59W
123 Souk-el-Khemis, Tunisia 36 45N 9 2E
50 Soulac, France 45 30N 1 4W
49 Soultz, France 48 57N 7 52E
77 Sounion, Akra, C., Gr. 37 37N 24 1E
123 Sour el Ghozlane, Alg. 36 10N 3 45E
175 Soure, Brazil 0 35S 48 30W
62 Soure, Portugal 40 4N 8 38W
155 Souris, Canada 49 40N 100 20W
164 Souris R., U.S.A. 48 35N 101 29W
77 Soúrpi, Greece 39 6N 22 54E
122 Sous, R., Morocco 30 31N 9 27W
175 Sousa, Brazil 7 0S 38 10W
175 Sousel, Brazil 2 38S 52 29W
63 Sousel, Portugal 38 57N 7 40W
123 Sousse, Tunisia 35 50N 10 33E
50 Soustons, France 43 45N 1 19W
147 South I., New Zealand 43 0S 170 0E
155 South Pt., Canada 49 6N 62 11W
44 South Sound, Ireland .53 2N 9 28W
129 South Africa, Rep. of Afr. 30 0S 25 0E
170 South America, cont. .10 0S 60 0W
138 South Australia, st., Australia 32 0S 139 0E
167 South Baldy, Mt. U.S.A. 34 6N 107 27W
39 South Bank, Eng., U.K. 54 35N 1 11W
162 South Bend, Indiana, U.S.A. 41 38N 86 20W
166 South Bend, Wash., U.S.A. 46 44N 123 52W
35 South Benfleet, Eng., U.K. 51 33N 0 34E
161 South Berwick, U.S.A. 43 15N 70 47W
163 South Boston, U.S.A. 36 42N 78 58W
155 South Branch, U.S.A. 44 30N 83 55W
147 South Br. Ashburton R., New Zealand 43 30S 171 15E
36 South Brent, Eng., U.K. 50 26N 3 50W
163 South Carolina, st., U.S.A. 33 45N 81 0W
39 South Cave, Eng., U.K. 53 46N 0 37W
162 South Charleston, U.S.A. 38 20N 81 40W
113 South China Sea, Asia 20 0N 115 0E
164 South Dakota, st., U.S.A. 45 0N 100 0W
42 South Dell, Scot. U.K. 58 28N 6 20W
35 South Downs, Eng., U.K. 50 53N 0 10W
142 South East Is., Austral. 34 17S 123 30E
39 South Elkington, England, U.K. 53 22N 0 5W
35 South Foreland, Eng., U.K. 51 7N 1 23E
166 South Fork, R., U.S.A. 47 54N 113 15W
168 South Gamboa, Panama Canal Zone 9 4N 79 40W
15 South Georgia, Falk. Is. Dep., Antarctica 54 30S 37 0W
42 South Harris, district, Scotland, U.K. 56 51N 3 10W
162 South Haven, U.S.A. .42 22N 86 20W
35 South Hayling, Eng., U.K. 50 47N 0 56W
157 South Henik, L., Can. 61 30N 98 0W
131 South Horr, Kenya ... 2 12N 36 56E
147 South Invercargill, N.Z. 46 26N 168 23E
39 South Kirby,Eng., UK 53 35N 1 25W
13 South Island, L., Rudolf, Kenya 2 40N 36 35E
112 South Korea, st., Asia 36 0N 128 0E
131 South Mafia Channel, Tanzania 9 10S 39 35E
15 South Magnetic Pole (1965) 66 30S 139 30E
162 South Milwaukee, U.S.A. 42 50N 87 52W
36 South Molton, Eng., UK 51 1N 3 50W
42 South Morar, district, Scotland, U.K. 56 57N 5 40W
42 South Nesting B., Scot. 60 18N 1 5W
15 South Orkney Is., Falk. Is. Dep. 63 0S 45 0W
131 South Pare Mts., Tanz. 4 5S 37 52E
166 South Pass, U.S.A. 42 20N 108 58W
36 South Petherton, England, U.K. 50 57N 2 49W
36 South Petherwin, England, U.K. 50 35N 4 22W
163 South Pittsburg, U.S.A. 35 3N 85 44W
163 South Pines, U.S.A. ...35 10N 79 25W
164 South Platte R., U.S.A. 40 50N 102 45W
15 South Pole 90 0S 0 0E
154 South Porcupine, Can. 48 30N 81 12W
3 South Ronaldsay I., Scotland, U.K. 58 46N 2 58W
154 South River, Canada .45 52N 79 21W
17 S. Sandwich Is., Falk. Is. Dep., Antarc. 57 0S 27 0W
17 South Sandwich Trench, Southern Oc. 55 0S 25 0W
157 South Saskatchewan R., Canada 51 0N 109 0W
15 South Shetland Is., Ant. 62 0S 59 0W
39 South Shields, Eng., U.K. 54 59N 1 26W
164 South Sioux City, U.S.A. 42 30N 96 30W
146 South Taranaki Bight, New Zealand 39 40S 174 5E
36 South Tawton, Eng. U.K. 50 44N 3 55W
154 South Twin I., Canada 53 0N 79 50W
38 South Tyne R., England, U.K. 54 46N 2 25W
42 South Uist, I., Scot., U.K. 57 10N 7 10W
80 South Ulvön, I., Swed. 63 0N 18 45E
107 South Vietnam, st., Asia 14 0N 108 40E
43 South Walls I., Scot., U.K. 58 45N 3 7W
147 South West Cape, N.Z. 47 16S 167 31E
129 South West Africa, mandate, South Africa 22 0S 18 9E
113 South-West Islands, Jap. 29 0N 129 0E
99 South Yemen, st., Asia 15 0N 48 0E
34 Southam, Eng., U.K. .52 16N 1 24W
154 Southampton, Canada 44 30N 81 25W
34 Southampton, Eng., U.K. 50 54N 1 23W
161 Southampton, U.S.A. .40 54N 72 22W
153 Southampton I., Can. 64 30N 84 0W
34 Southampton Water, England, U.K. 50 52N 1 21W
147 Southbridge, N.Z. 43 48S 172 16E
161 Southbridge, U.S.A. ...42 4N 72 2W
157 Southend, Canada 56 28N 103 14W
40 Southend, Scot., U.K. 55 18N 5 38W
35 Southend-on-Sea, England, U.K. 51 32N 0 43E
147 Southern Alps, N.Z. ...43 41S 170 11E
142 Southern Cross, Austral. 31 12S 119 15E
142 Southern Hill, Austral. 32 15S 122 40E
157 Southern Indian Lake, Canada 57 0N 99 0W
15 Southern Ocean 62 0S 160 0W
41 Southern Uplands, Scotland, U.K. 55 30N 4 0W
41 Southerness, Scot., U.K. 54 50N 3 40W
35 Southery, England, U.K. 52 32N 0 23E
135 Southeyville, S. Africa 31 46S 20 29E
161 Southington, U.S.A. ...41 37N 72 53W
147 Southland, N.Z. 45 51S 168 13E
35 Southminster, Eng., U.K. 51 40N 0 51E
161 Southold, U.S.A. 41 4N 72 26W
145 Southport, Australia .28 0S 153 25E
38 Southport, Eng., U.K. 53 38N 3 1W
163 Southport, U.S.A. 33 55N 78 0W
35 Southrepps, Eng., U.K. 52 53N 1 20E
34 Southsea, England, U.K. 50 48N 1 5W
35 Southwark, Eng. U.K. 51 29N 0 5W
35 Southwick, Eng., U.K. 50 50N 0 14W
35 Southwold, Eng., U.K. 52 19N 1 41E
133 Soutpansberge, Mts., Trans., S. Afr. 22 55S 29 30E
50 Souvigny, France 46 33N 3 10E
78 Sovata, Rumania 46 35N 25 3E
86 Sovetsk, Lithuania, U.S.S.R. 55 6N 21 50E
87 Sovetsk, R.S.F.S.R., U.S.S.R. 57 38N 48 53E
91 Sovetskaya Gavan, U.S.S.R. 48 50N 140 0E
71 Soviclile, Italy 43 16N 11 12E
74 Sovra, Yugoslavia 42 44N 17 34E
39 Sowerby, England, U.K. 54 13N 1 19W
114 Soya, pref., Japan 45 30N 142 30E
114 Soya-misaki, C., Japan 45 30N 142 0E
86 Sozh R., U.S.S.R. 53 50N 31 50E
75 Sozopol, Bulgaria 42 23N 27 42E
48 Spa, Belgium 50 29N 5 53E
61 Spain, rep., Europe ...40 0N 5 0W
35 Spalding, England, U.K. 52 47N 0 9W
164 Spalding, U.S.A. 41 45N 98 27W
81 Spandet, Denmark 55 15N 8 54E
80 Spånga, Sweden 59 23N 17 55E
81 Spångenäs, Sweden ...57 36N 16 7E
79 Spangereid, Norway ...58 3N 7 9E
160 Spangler, U.S.A. 40 39N 78 48W
155 Spaniard's Bay, Canada 47 38N 53 20W
154 Spanish, Canada 46 12N 82 20W
166 Spanish Fork, U.S.A. .40 10N 111 37W
44 Spanish Pt. Ireland ...52 51N 9 27W
120 Spanish Sahara, Sp. Prov., Africa 25 0N 13 0W
169 Spanish Town, Jamaica 18 0N 77 20W
36 Sparkford, Eng., U.K. 51 2N 2 33W
166 Sparks, U.S.A. 39 30N 119 45W
77 Sparta, Greece 37 5N 22 25E
163 Sparta, Ga., U.S.A. ...33 18N 82 59W
164 Sparta, Wis., U.S.A. .43 55N 91 10W
160 Spartanburg, Pa., U.S.A. 41 48N 79 43W
163 Spartanburg, S.C., U.S.A. 35 0N 82 0W
122 Spartel C., Morocco ...35 53N 5 56W
77 Spárti (Sparta), Greece 37 5N 22 25E
73 Spartivento C., Italy .37 56N 16 4E
72 Spartivento C., Sard., It. 38 52N 8 50E
87 Spas-Klepiki, U.S.S.R. 54 34N 40 2E
91 Spassk Dalni, U.S.S.R. 44 40N 132 40E
87 Spassk-Ryazanskiy, U.S.S.R. 54 30N 40 25E
77 Spátha Akra C., Greece 35 42N 23 43E
43 Spean Bridge, Scot. U.K. 56 53N 4 55W
164 Spearfish, U.S.A. 44 32N 103 52W
165 Spearman, U.S.A. 36 15N 101 10W
143 Speed, Vic., Australia 35 21S 142 27E
131 Speke Gulf, L. Victoria, Tanzania . 2 20S 32 50E
134 Spektakel, S. Africa ...29 40S 17 33E
40 Spelve L., Scot., U.K. 56 22N 5 45W
152 Spenard, Alaska, U.S.A. 61 0N 149 50W
156 Spences Bridge, Canada 50 25N 121 20W
166 Spencer. Idaho, U.S.A. 44 18N 112 8W
164 Spencer, Iowa, U.S.A. 43 5N 95 3W
164 Spencer, Neb., U.S.A. 42 52N 98 43W
161 Spencer, N.Y., U.S.A. 42 14N 76 13W
162 Spencer, W. Va., U.S.A. 38 47N 81 24W
145 Spencer, C., S. Austral. 35 20S 136 45E
139 Spencer G., S. Austral. 34 30S 137 0E
161 Spencerville, Canada .44 51N 75 34W
39 Spennymoor, Eng., U.K. 54 43N 1 35W
147 Spenser Mts., N.Z. 42 15S 172 45E
77 Sperkhios, R., Greece .38 57N 22 3E
46 Sperrin Mts., N. Ire., U.K. 54 50N 7 0W
57 Spessart, Germany 50 0N 9 20E
77 Spetsai, Greece 37 16N 23 9E
77 Spétsai Is., Greece 37 15N 23 10E
43 Spey Bay, Scotland, U.K. 57 39N 3 4W
43 Spey, R., Scotland, U.K. 57 26N 4 30W
43 Spey, Strath, Scot., U.K. 57 15N 3 40W
57 Speyer, Germany 49 19N 8 26E
57 Speyer, R., Germany .49 18N 7 52E
70 Spezia (La Spezia), Italy 44 7N 9 49E
73 Spezzano Albanese, It. 39 41N 16 19E
44 Spiddal, Ireland 53 14N 9 19W
56 Spiekeroog, I., Germany 53 45N 7 42E
71 Spielfeld, Austria 46 43N 15 38E
57 Spiez, Switzerland 46 40N 7 40E
77 Spili, Crete, Greece 35 13N 24 31E
71 Spilimbergo, Italy 46 7N 12 53E
156 Spillimacheen, Canada 51 6N 117 0W
39 Spilsby, England, U.K. 53 10N 0 6E
101 Spin Baldak, Afghan. 31 3N 66 16E
73 Spinazzola, Italy 40 58N 16 5E
49 Spincourt, France 49 20N 5 39E
79 Spind, Norway 58 6N 6 53E
78 Spineni, Rumania 44 43N 24 37E
164 Spirit Lake, U.S.A. ...47 56N 116 56W
156 Spirit River, Canada .55 45N 119 0W
157 Spiritwood, Canada ...53 24N 107 33W
59 Spisská Nová Ves, Cz. 48 58N 20 34E
59 Spisské Podhradie, Cz. 49 0N 20 48E
43 Spitalburn, Scot., U.K. 56 57N 2 33W
35 Spithead, England, U.K. 50 43N 0 56W
58 Spittal, Austria 46 48N 13 31E
41 Spittal, England, U.K. 55 46N 1 59W
14 Spitzbergen (Svalbard), Norway 78 0N 17 0E
71 Split, Yugoslavia 43 31N 16 26E
157 Split L., Canada 56 15N 96 0W
71 Splitski Kan, Y.-slavia 43 31N 16 20E
57 Splügen Pass, Switz. .46 30N 9 20E
165 Spofford, U.S.A. 29 10N 100 27W
39 Spofforth, Eng., U.K. 53 57N 1 28W
166 Spokane, Wash., U.S.A. 47 45N 117 25W
79 Sponvika, Norway 59 7N 11 15E
164 Spooner, U.S.A. 45 49N 91 51W
90 Spory Navolok C., U.S.S.R. 75 50N 68 40E
154 Spragge, Canada 46 15N 82 40W
166 Sprague, U.S.A. 47 25N 117 59W
166 Sprague River, U.S.A. 42 49N 121 31W
108 Spratly, I. S. China Sea 8 20N 112 0E
166 Spray, U.S.A. 44 56N 119 46W
56 Spree R., Germany 52 23N 13 52E
55 Spremberg, Germany .51 33N 14 21E
167 Spring Mts., U.S.A. ...36 20N 115 43W
166 Spring City, U.S.A. ...39 31N 111 28W
164 Spring Valley, Minn., U.S.A. 43 40N 92 30W
161 Spring Valley, N.Y., U.S.A. 41 7N 74 4W
134 Springbok, S. Africa ...29 42S 17 54E
147 Springburn, N.Z. 43 40S 171 32E
155 Springdale, Canada ...49 30N 56 6W
165 Springdale, Ark., U.S.A. 36 10N 94 5W
166 Springdale, Wash., U.S.A. 48 1N 117 50W
56 Springe, Germany 52 12N 9 35E
167 Springerville, U.S.A. .34 10N 109 16W
160 Springfield, Canada ...42 52N 80 57W

MAP
147 Springfield, N.Z. 43 19S 171 56E
165 Springfield, Colo., U.S.A. 37 26N 102 40W
164 Springfield, Ill., U.S.A. 39 58N 89 40W
161 Springfield, Mass., U.S.A. 42 8N 72 37W
165 Springfield, Mo., U.S.A. 37 15N 93 20W
162 Springfield, Ohio, U.S.A. 39 50N 83 48W
166 Springfield, Ore., U.S.A. 44 2N 123 0W
163 Springfield, Tenn., U.S.A. 36 35N 86 55W
161 Springfield, Vt., U.S.A. 43 20N 72 30W
135 Springfontein, S. Africa 30 15S 25 40E
155 Springhill, Canada 45 40N 64 4W
156 Springhouse, Canada .51 56N 122 7W
143 Springhurst, Australia 36 12S 146 24E
135 Springmount, S. Africa 33 40S 26 2E
133 Springs, Trans., S. Afr. 26 13S 28 25E
144 Springsure, Australia .24 8S 148 6E
161 Springvale, U.S.A. 43 28N 70 48W
160 Springville, N.Y., U.S.A. 42 31N 78 41W
166 Springville, Utah, U.S.A. 40 14N 111 35W
157 Springwater, Canada .51 58N 108 23W
39 Sproatley, Eng., U.K. 53 46N 0 9W
160 Spruce-Creek, U.S.A. .40 36N 78 9W
55 Sprundel, Netherlands 51 32N 4 35E
132 Spungabera, Mozam. .20 28S 32 47E
165 Spur, U.S.A. 33 28N 100 50W
39 Spurn Hd., Eng., U.K. 53 34N 0 8W
74 Spuz, Yugoslavia 42 32N 19 10E
156 Spuzzum, Canada 49 37N 121 23W
79 Spydeberg, Norway ...59 37N 11 4E
134 Spyfontein, S. Africa .28 55S 24 42E
156 Squamish, Canada 49 45N 123 10W
155 Square Islands, Canada 52 47N 55 47W
73 Squillace, G. of, Italy 38 43N 16 35E
73 Squinzano, Italy 40 27N 18 1E
142 Squires, Mt., W. Austral. 26 14S 127 46E
109 Sragen, Indonesia 7 28S 110 59E
74 Srbac, Yugoslavia 45 7N 17 30E
74 Srbija, Prov., Y.-slavia 43 30N 21 0E
74 Srbobran, Yugoslavia 45 32N 19 48E
107 Sre Umbell, Cambodia 11 8N 103 46E
74 Srebrnica, Yugoslavia 44 10N 19 18E
75 Sredets, Bulgaria 42 20N 27 10E
91 Sredinnyy Ra., U.S.S.R. 57 0N 160 0E
71 Sredisce, Yugoslavia .46 24N 16 17E
75 Sredna Gora Mts., Bulg. 42 40N 25 0E
91 Sredne Kolymsk, U.S.S.R. 67 20N 154 40E
91 Sredne Tambovskoye, U.S.S.R. 50 55N 137 45E
91 Sredne Vilyuisk, U.S.S.R. 63 50N 123 5E
60 Srem, Poland 52 6N 17 2E
91 Sretensk, U.S.S.R. 52 10N 117 40E
106 Sri Lanka, st., Asia ... 7 30N 80 50E
106 Sriharikota, I., India .13 40N 81 30E
106 Srikakulam, India 18 14N 84 4E
102 Srinagar, Kashmir 34 12N 74 50E
105 Sripur, East Pakistan 24 14N 90 30E
106 Srirangam, India 10 54N 78 42E
106 Srirangapatnam, India 12 26N 76 43E
106 Srivilliputtur, India ... 9 31N 77 40E
60 Sroda, Poland 52 15N 17 19E
60 Sroda Slaska, Poland .51 10N 16 35E
74 Srpska Crnja, Y.-slav. 45 38N 20 44E
74 Srpska Itabej, Y.-slav. 45 35N 20 44E
56 Staber Huk, Germany 54 23N 11 18E
44 Stack's Mts., Ireland .52 20N 9 34W
82 Stadarholskirkja, Ice. 65 23N 21 58E
56 Stade, Germany 53 35N 9 31E
58 Stadil, Denmark 56 12N 8 12E
80 Städjan, Mt., Sweden .61 56N 12 30E
80 Stadsforsen, Falls, Swed. 63 0N 16 45E
79 Stadlandet, Norway ...62 10N 5 5E
56 Stadthagen, Germany 52 20N 9 14E
56 Stadtlohn, Germany ...51 59N 6 52E
56 Stadtroda, E. Ger.......50 51N 11 44E
82 Stadur, Iceland 63 49N 22 30W
40 Staffa, I., Scot., U.K. 56 26N 6 21W
34 Stafford, England, U.K. 52 49N 2 9W
34 Stafford, co., Eng., U.K. 52 53N 2 10W
165 Stafford, U.S.A. 38 0N 98 35
161 Stafford Springs, U.S.A. 41 58N 72 20W
72 Stagnone, I., Italy 37 50N 12 28E
39 Staindrop, Eng., U.K. 54 35N 1 49W
35 Staines, England, U.K. 51 26N 0 30W
39 Stainforth, Eng., U.K. 53 37N 0 59W
38 Stainmore For., England, U.K. 54 29N 2 5W
39 Stainton, England, U.K. 53 17N 0 23W
58 Stainz, Austria 46 53N 15 17E
39 Staithes, England, U.K. 54 33N 0 47W
81 Stakkroge, Denmark .55 53N 8 51E
74 Stalac, Yugoslavia 43 43N 21 28E
36 Stalbridge, Eng., U.K. 50 57N 2 22W
35 Stalham, England, U.K. 52 46N 1 31E
156 Stalin Mt., Canada 58 10N 124 45W
89 Stalingrad, see Volgograd 48 40N 44 25E
87 Stalinogorsk, see Novomoskovsk, U.S.S.R. 54 5N 38 15E
39 Stallingborough, England, U.K. 53 36N 0 11W
38 Stalybridge, Eng., U.K. 53 29N 2 2W
144 Stamford, Australia ...21 15S 143 46E
161 Stamford, Conn., U.S.A. 41 5N 73 30W
35 Stamford, Eng., U.K. 52 39N 0 29W
165 Stamford, Tex., U.S.A. 32 58N 99 50W
39 Stamford Bridge, England, U.K. 53 59N 0 53W
38 Stamfordham, Eng. UK 55 3N 1 53W
165 Stamps, U.S.A. 33 22N 93 30W
164 Stanberry, U.S.A. 40 12N 94 32W
133 Standerton, S. Africa .26 55S 29 13E
38 Standish, Eng., U.K. .53 35N 2 39W
162 Standish, U.S.A. 43 58N 83 57W
35 Standon, England, U.K. 51 53N 0 2E
134 Stanford, S. Africa 34 29S 19 28E
166 Stanford, U.S.A. 47 11N 110 10W
79 Stange, Norway 60 40N 11 5E
135 Stanger, Natal, S. Africa 29 18S 31 21E
38 Stanhope, Eng., U.K. 54 45N 2 0W
59 Stanišic, Yugoslavia ...45 53N 19 12E
86 Stanislav, see Ivano-Frankovsk, U.S.S.R. 49 0N 24 40E
74 Stanke Dimitrov, Bulg. 42 27N 23 9E
145 Stanley, Tas., Australia 40 46S 145 19E
155 Stanley, N.B., Canada 46 20N 66 50W
157 Stanley, Sask., Canada 55 20N 104 40W
39 Stanley England, U.K. 54 53N 1 42W
176 Stanley, Falkland Is. .51 40S 58 0W
41 Stanley, Scotland, U.K. 56 29N 3 28W
166 Stanley, Idaho, U.S.A. 44 10N 114 59W
164 Stanley, N.D., U.S.A. 48 20N 102 23W
160 Stanley, N.Y., U.S.A..42 48N 77 6W
164 Stanley, Wis., U.S.A. .44 57N 91 0W
130 Stanley Falls, Congo . 0 12N 25 25E
130 Stanley Pool, Congo ... 4 10S 15 30E
106 Stanley Res., India ...11 50N 77 40E
130 Stanleyville, see Kisangani, Congo ... 0 41N 52 11E
168 Stann Creek, Br. Hond. 17 0N 88 20W
39 Stannington, Eng., U.K. 55 7N 1 41W
91 Stanovoy Ra., U.S.S.R. 55 0N 130 0E
35 Stansted, England, U.K. 51 54N 0 13E
145 Stanthorpe, Australia 28 36S 151 59E
152 Stanton, Canada 69 45N 128 52W
165 Stanton, Tex., U.S.A. 32 8N 101 45W
39 Stapleford, Eng., U.K. 52 56N 1 16W
35 Staplehurst, Eng., U.K. 51 9N 0 35E
164 Stapleton, U.S.A. 41 30N 100 31W
157 Star City, Canada 52 55N 104 20W
89 Stara Minskaya, U.S.S.R. 46 33N 39 0E
74 Stara Moravica, Y.-slav. 45 50N 19 30E
74 Stara Pazova, Y.-slavia 45 0N 20 10E
75 Stara Planina (Balkan Mts.), Bulgaria 43 15N 23 0E
75 Stara Zagora, Bulgaria 42 26N 25 39E
60 Starachowice-Wierzbnik, Poland .51 3N 21 2E
86 Staraya Russa, U.S.S.R. 57 58N 31 10E
137 Starbuck I., Pac. Oc. . 5 37S 155 55W
56 Stargard, Germany 53 29N 13 19E
60 Stargard, Poland 53 20N 15 0E
74 Stari Bečej, Y.-slavia 45 36N 20 3E
71 Stari Trg., Y.-slavia .45 29N 15 7E
86 Staritsa, U.S.S.R. 56 33N 35 0E
163 Starke, U.S.A. 30 0N 82 10W
165 Starkville, Colo., U.S.A. 37 10N 104 31W
163 Starkville, Miss., U.S.A. 33 26N 88 48W
57 Starnberg, Germany ...48 0N 11 20E
57 Starnberger See, Ger. .48 0N 11 0E
89 Staro- Minskaya, U.S.S.R. 39 0N 46 33E
89 Starobelsk, U.S.S.R. .49 27N 39 0E
86 Starodub, U.S.S.R. 52 30N 32 50E
60 Starogard, Poland 53 55N 18 30E
36 Start Bay, Eng., U.K. 50 15N 3 35W
36 Start Pt., Eng., U.K. .50 13N 3 38W
43 Start Pt., Scot., U.K. 59 17N 2 25W
91 Stary Kheidzhan, U.S.S.R. 60 0N 144 50E
59 Stary Sacz, Poland 49 33N 30 26E
89 Staryy Biryuzyak, U.S.S.R. 44 46N 46 50E
86 Staryy Chartoriysk, U.S.S.R. 51 15N 25 47E
87 Staryy Oskol, U.S.S.R. 51 12N 37 55E
56 Stassfurt, Germany 51 51N 11 34E
160 State College, U.S.A. .40 47N 77 49W
176 Staten I. (I. de los Estados), Argentina 54 40S 64 0W
161 Staten I., U.S.A. 40 35N 74 10W
163 Statesboro, U.S.A. 32 26N 81 46W
163 Statesville, U.S.A. 35 48N 80 51W
79 Stathelle, Norway 59 3N 9 36E
34 Staunton, Eng., U.K. 51 58N 2 19W
164 Staunton, Ill., U.S.A. .39 0N 89 49W
162 Staunton, Va., U.S.A. 38 7N 79 4W
79 Stavanger, Norway ...58 57N 5 40E
39 Staveley, Derby, England, U.K. 53 16N 1 20W
38 Staveley, Westmorland, England, U.K. 54 24N 2 49W
54 Stavelot, Belgium 50 23N 5 55E
56 Stavenhagen, Germany 53 41N 12 54E
79 Stavern, Norway 59 0N 10 1E
79 Stavfjord, Norway 61 30N 5 0E
54 Stavoren, Netherlands 52 53N 5 21E
80 Stavre, Sweden 62 51N 15 25E
89 Stavropol, U.S.S.R. ...45 5N 42 0E
76 Stavroúpolis, Greece .41 12N 24 45E
81 Stavsjö, Sweden 48 42N 16 30E
143 Stawell, Vic., Australia 36 58S 142 47E
60 Stawiszyn, Poland 51 56N 18 4E
43 Staxigoe, Scot., U.K. .58 28N 3 2W
160 Stayner, Canada 44 25N 80 5W
166 Steamboat Springs, U.S.A. 40 30N 106 58W
60 Stebark, Poland 53 30N 20 10E
165 Steele, U.S.A. 46 56N 99 52W
133 Steelpoort, S. Africa ...24 41S 30 14E
133 Steelpoort R., S. Africa 24 50S 29 59E
160 Steelton, U.S.A. 40 17N 76 50W
55 Steenbergen, Neth. 51 35N 4 19E
134 Steenkampspoort, C. Prov., S. Afr. 32 6S 21 45E
49 Steenvorde, France 50 48N 2 33E
157 Steep Rock, Man., Can. 51 30N 98 40W
154 Steep Rock Lake, Can. 48 50N 91 38W
78 Stefaneşti, Rumania ...47 44N 27 15E
127 Stefanie Lake, see Chew Bahir, Ethiopia 4 40N 30 50E
81 Stege, Denmark 55 0N 12 18E
135 Stegi, Swaziland 26 32S 31 58E
135 Steidrif, O.F.S., S. Africa 27 48S 28 42E
74 Steierdorf Anina, Rum. 45 6N 21 51E
57 Steiger Wald, Mts., West Germany 49 45N 10 30E
42 Stein, Scotland, U.K. .57 30N 6 35W
157 Steinbach, Canada 49 32N 96 40W
175 Steinen, R., Brazil 12 0S 54 20W
54 Steinfort, Luxembourg 49 39N 5 55E
56 Steinheim, Germany .51 50N 9 6E
79 Steinkjer, Norway 63 59N 11 46E
134 Steinkopf, S. Africa ...29 15S 17 48E
133 Stella, C. Prov., S. Afr. 26 38S 24 48E
133 Stella Land, S. Africa 26 45S 24 50E
134 Stellenbosch, S. Africa 33 58S 18 50E
55 Stembert, Belgium 50 36N 5 54E
79 Stemshaug, Norway ...63 19N 8 44E
56 Stendal, Germany 52 36N 11 50E
41 Stenhousemuir, Scot. U.K. 56 2N 3 46W
81 Stenmagle, Denmark .55 49N 11 39E
43 Stenness, L., of, Scot. U.K. 59 0N 3 15W
82 Stensele, Sweden 65 3N 17 20E
81 Stenstorp, Sweden 58 17N 13 45E
81 Stenungsund, Sweden 58 6N 11 46E
89 Stepanakert, U.S.S.R. 40 0N 46 25E
164 Stephan, U.S.A. 48 30N 96 53W
147 Stephen I., N.Z. 40 40S 174 1E
143 Stephens Creek, Austral. 31 50S 141 30E
155 Stephenville, Canada .48 31N 58 30W
165 Stephenville, U.S.A. ...32 12N 98 12W
60 Stepnica, Poland 53 38N 14 36E
89 Stepnoi, see Elista, U.S.S.R. 46 25N 44 17E
77 Stereá Ellas, region, Gr. 38 55N 22 0E
134 Sterkaar, S. Africa 31 4S 23 43E
135 Sterkstroom, S. Africa 31 32S 26 32E
133 Sterkwater, S. Africa .24 0S 28 47E
14 Sterlego, C., U.S.S.R. .80 30N 90 0E
164 Sterling, Colo., U.S.A. 40 40N 103 15W
164 Sterling, Ill., U.S.A. ...41 45N 89 45W
164 Sterling, Kan., U.S.A. 38 17N 98 13W
165 Sterling City, U.S.A. .31 50N 100 59W
160 Sterling Run, U.S.A. .41 25N 78 12W
84 Sterlitamak, U.S.S.R. 53 40N 56 0E
56 Sternberg, Germany ...53 42N 11 48E
59 Šternberk, Cz. 49 45N 17 15E
60 Stettin, see Szczecin, Poland 53 27N 14 27E
56 Stettiner Haff, Germany 53 50N 14 25E
156 Stettler, Canada 52 25N 112 40W
160 Steubenville, U.S.A. ...40 21N 80 39W
135 Steumekaar, S. Africa 29 30S 25 30E
35 Stevenage, Eng., U.K. 51 54N 0 11W
164 Stevens Port, U.S.A. .44 32N 89 34W
138 Stevenson R., Australia 46 15S 134 10E
40 Stevenston, Scotland, U.K 55 38N 4 45W
81 Stevns Klint C., Den. 55 17N 12 28E
176 Stewart I., Chile 54 50S 71 30W
147 Stewart I., N.Z. 46 58S 167 54E
152 Stewart River, Can. ...63 25N 139 30W
40 Stewarton, Scot., U.K. 55 40N 4 30W
46 Stewartstown, N. Ireland, U.K. 54 35N 6 40W
155 Stewiacke, Canada 45 9N 63 22W
35 Steyning, Eng., U.K. .50 54N 0 19W
135 Steynsburg, S. Africa .31 15S 25 49E
133 Steynsdorp, S. Africa .26 7S 30 58E
135 Steynsrus, OFS, S. Afr. 27 58S 27 33E
58 Steyr, Austria 48 3N 14 25E
58 Steyr, R., Austria 48 57N 14 15E
134 Steytlerville, S. Africa 33 17S 24 19E
71 Stia, Italy 43 48N 11 41E
58 Stiermark (Styria), prov., Austria 47 26N 15 0E
165 Stigler, U.S.A. 35 19N 95 6W
73 Stigliano, Italy 40 24N 16 13E
81 Stigsnæs, Denmark 55 13N 11 18E
81 Stigtomta, Sweden 58 47N 16 48E
152 Stikine Mts., Canada .59 30N 129 30W
156 Stikine R., Canada 58 0N 131 0W
133 Stilfontein, S. Africa .26 50S 26 50E
77 Stilis, Greece 38 55N 22 37E
134 Stillbaai, S. Africa 34 22S 21 27E
39 Stillington, Eng., U.K. 54 7N 1 5W
164 Stillwater, Minn., U.S.A. 45 3N 92 47W
161 Stillwater, N.Y., U.S.A. 42 55N 73 41W
165 Stillwater, Okla., U.S.A. 36 5N 97 3W
166 Stillwater Mts., U.S.A. 39 45N 118 6W
165 Stilwell, U.S.A. 35 52N 94 36W
77 Stimfalias, L., Greece .37 51N 22 27E
154 Stimson, Canada 48 58N 80 30W
40 Stinchar R., Scot., U.K. 55 10N 4 50W
74 Stip, Yugoslavia 41 42N 22 10E
34 Stiperstones Mt., England, U.K. 52 36N 2 57W
77 Stira, Greece 38 9N 24 14E
49 Stiring Wendel, France 49 12N 6 57E
144 Stirling, Australia 17 12S 141 35E
156 Stirling, Alta., Canada 49 30N 112 30W
147 Stirling, New Zealand 46 14S 169 49E
41 Stirling, Scotland, U.K. 56 17N 3 57W
40 Stirling, co., Scot., U.K. 56 3N 4 10W
142 Stirling Ra., W. Austral. 34 0S 118 0E
161 Stittsville, Canada 45 15N 75 58W
81 Stjärneborg, Sweden .57 53N 14 45E
80 Stjarnsfors, Sweden ...60 2N 13 45E
79 Stjördalshalsen, Nor. .63 29N 10 51E
41 Stobo, Scotland, U.K. 55 38N 3 18W
44 Stockach, Germany 47 51N 9 0E
81 Stockaryd, Sweden 57 40N 14 36E
34 Stockbridge, Eng., U.K. 51 7N 1 30W
59 Stockerau, Austria 48 24N 16 12E
166 Stockett, U.S.A. 47 23N 111 7W
80 Stockholm, Sweden ...59 17N 18 3E
80 Stockholm, co., Sweden 59 40N 18 45E
143 Stockinbingal, Austral. 34 30S 147 53E
38 Stockport, Eng., U.K. 53 25N 2 11W
39 Stocksbridge, Eng., U.K. 53 30N 1 36W
143 Stockton, N.S.W., Australia 32 56S 151 47E
166 Stockton, Calif., U.S.A. 38 0N 121 20W
164 Stockton, Kan., U.S.A. 39 30N 99 20W
165 Stockton, Mo., U.S.A. 37 40N 93 48W
39 Stockton-on-Tees, England, U.K. 54 34N 1 20W
80 Stockvik, Sweden 62 17N 17 23E
80 Stöde, Sweden 62 28N 16 35E
42 Stoer, Scotland, U.K. 58 12N 5 20W
42 Stoer, Pt. of, Scot., UK 58 16N 5 23W
133 Stoffberg, S. Africa 25 27S 29 49E
74 Stogovo, Ra., Y.-slavia 41 31N 20 38E
34 Stoke, Eng., U.K. 51 26N 0 41E
147 Stoke, New Zealand ...43 19S 172 29E
35 Stoke Ferry, Eng., U.K. 52 34N 0 31E
36 Stoke Fleming, England, U.K. 50 19N 3 36W
35 Stoke Mandeville, Eng., ,U.K. 51 46N 0 47W
38 Stoke-on-Trent, England, U.K. 53 1N 2 11W
34 Stoke Prior, Eng., U.K. 52 18N 2 5W
36 Stokenham, Eng., U.K. 50 15N 3 40W
154 Stokes Bay, Canada ...45 0N 81 22W
39 Stokesley, Eng., U.K. 54 27N 1 12W
79 Stokke, Norway 59 18N 10 26E
79 Stokken, Norway 58 31N 8 53E
74 Stolac, Yugoslavia 43 8N 17 59E
56 Stolberg, E. Germany 51 33N 11 0E
56 Stolberg, W. Germany 51 40N 6 15E
87 Stolbovaya, U.S.S.R. .55 10N 37 32E
91 Stolbovoye, U.S.S.R. .64 50N 153 50E
86 Stolin, U.S.S.R. 51 53N 26 50E
78 Stolnici, Rumania 44 31N 24 48E
134 Stolzenfels, S.W. Africa 28 29S 19 40E
74 Ston, Yugoslavia 42 51N 17 43E
35 Stone, Bucks., Eng., U.K. 51 48N 0 52W
38 Stone, Stafford, England, U.K. 52 55N 2 10W
154 Stonecliffe, Canada ...46 13N 77 56W
43 Stonehaven, Scot., U.K. 56 58N 2 11W
34 Stonehouse, Eng., U.K. 51 45N 2 18W
41 Stonehouse, Scot., U.K. 55 42N 4 0W
157 Stonewall, Canada 50 10N 96 50W
79 Stongfjord, Norway ...61 28N 14 0E
35 Stonham Aspall, England, U.K. 52 11N 1 7E
160 Stony L., Canada 44 35N 78 15W
157 Stony Rapids, Canada 59 15N 105 55W
35 Stony Stratford, England, U.K. 52 4N 0 51W
91 Stony Tunguska R., U.S.S.R. 60 30N 98 0E
60 Stopnica, Poland 50 27N 20 57E
79 Stor Elvdal, Norway .61 30N 11 46E
57 Stora Borge Fjell, Mt., Norway 65 12N 14 0E
82 Stora Lulevatten, Swed. 67 20N 19 0E
82 Storavan, L., Sweden .65 45N 18 10E
79 Stord Leirvik, I., Nor. 59 48N 5 27E
81 Store Baelt, Str., Den. 55 28N 11 0E
143 Store Creek, Australia 32 54S 149 6E
79 Stören, Norway 63 0N 10 20E
79 Storfjord, Norway 62 25N 6 20E
79 Storfjorden, Norway .62 7N 6 43E
145 Storm B., Tas., Austral. 43 10S 147 30E
164 Storm Lake, U.S.A. ...42 35N 95 5W
135 Stormberg, S. Africa .31 16S 26 17E
135 Stormberge, Mts., C. Prov., S. Africa 31 26S 26 32E
42 Stornoway, Scot., U.K. 58 12N 6 23W
88 Storozhinets, U.S.S.R. 48 14S 25 45E
42 Storr, The, Mt., Scotland, U.K. 57 30N 6 12W
80 Storsjö, Sweden 62 49N 13 5E
79 Storsjö, L., Norway ...60 20N 11 40E
79 Storsjö, L., Norway ...61 30N 11 14E
80 Storsjön, L., Gävleborg, Sweden .60 35N 16 45E
80 Storsjön, L., Jämtland, Sweden .62 50N 13 8E
80 Storsjön, L., Jämtland, Sweden .63 15N 14 22E
82 Storuman, L., Sweden 65 5N 17 10E
80 Storvätteshagna, Mt., Sweden 62 6N 12 30E
80 Storvik, Sweden 60 35N 16 33E
35 Stotfold, England, U.K. 52 2N 0 13W
157 Stoughton, Canada 49 40N 103 0W
34 Stour R., Dorset, England, U.K. 50 48N 2 7W
34 Stour R., Kent, Eng., U.K. 51 15N 0 57E
35 Stour, R., Suffolk, England, U.K. 52 7N 0 28E
34 Stour R., Worcs., England, U.K. 52 25N 2 13W
34 Stourbridge, Eng., U.K. 52 28N 2 8W
34 Stourport, Eng., U.K. 52 21N 2 18W
157 Stout, L., Canada 52 0N 94 40W
41 Stow, Scotland, U.K. .55 41N 2 50W
35 Stow Bardolph, England, U.K. 52 38N 0 24E
35 Stowmarket, Eng., U.K. 52 11N 1 0E
34 Stow-on-the-Wold, England, U.K. 51 55N 1 42W
35 Stowupland, Eng., U.K. 52 12N 1 3E
46 Strabane, N. Ire., U.K. 54 50N 7 28W
43 Strachan, Scot., U.K. 57 1N 2 31W
44 Strachur, Scot., U.K. .56 10N 5 5W
74 Stracin, Yugoslavia ...42 13N 22 2E
44 Stradbally, Kerry, Ire. 52 15N 10 4W
46 Stradbally, Laoighis, Ireland 53 2N 7 10W
45 Stradbally, Waterford, Ireland .52 7N 7 28W
35 Stradbroke, Eng., U.K. 52 19N 1 16E
45 Strade, Ireland 53 56N 9 8W
70 Stradella, Italy 45 4N 9 20E
46 Stradone, Ireland 54 0N 7 12W
55 Straelen, Germany 51 27N 6 16E
145 Strahan, Tas., Australia 42 8S 145 24E
58 Strakonice, Cz. 49 15N 13 53E
75 Straldzha, Bulgaria ...42 35N 26 40E
56 Stralsund, Germany ...54 17N 13 5E
134 Strand, C. Prov., S. Afr. 34 9S 18 48E
79 Strand, Hedmark, Nor. 61 18N 11 15E
79 Strand, Rogaland, Nor. 59 3N 5 56E
79 Stranda, Norway 62 19N 6 58E
81 Strandby, Denmark ...56 47N 9 13E
79 Strandebarm, Norway 60 17N 6 0E

MAP
46 Strandhill, Ireland 54 16N 8 34W
79 Strandlvkja, Norway .60 30N 11 15E
79 Strandvik, Norway 60 9N 5 41E
46 Strangford, N. Ire., U.K. 54 23N 5 34W
46 Strangford, L., Northern Ireland, U.K. 54 30N 5 37W
80 Strängnäs, Sweden 59 23N 17 8E
46 Stranorlar, Ireland 54 58N 7 47W
40 Stranraer, Scot., U.K. 54 54N 5 0W
157 Strasbourg, Canada ...51 10N 104 55W
49 Strasbourg, France 48 35N 7 42E
56 Strasburg, Germany ...53 30N 13 44E
164 Strasburg, N.D., U.S.A. 46 12N 101 9W
34 Stratfieldsaye, Eng., U.K. 51 21N 1 0W
143 Stratford, Vic., Austral. 37 59S 147 5E
154 Stratford, Canada 43 23N 81 0W
146 Stratford, New Zealand 39 20S 174 19E
167 Stratford, Calif., U.S.A. 36 10N 119 55W
161 Stratford, Conn., U.S.A. 41 13N 73 8W
165 Stratford, Tex., U.S.A. 36 20N 102 3W
34 Stratford on Avon, Eng., U.K. 52 12N 1 42W
35 Stratford St. Mary, England, U.K. 51 58N 0 59E
43 Strath Avon, Scot., U.K. 57 19N 3 23W
43 Strath Dearn, Scot. U.K. 57 20N 4 0W
41 Strath Earn, Scot., U.K. 56 20N 3 50W
43 Strath Halladale, Scotland, U.K. 58 30N 3 51W
43 Strath Naver, Scot., U.K. 58 24N 4 12W
145 Strathalbyn, Australia 35 13S 138 53E
41 Strathaven, Scot., U.K. 55 40N 4 4W
43 Strathbogie, Dist., Scotland, U.K. 57 25N 2 45W
43 Strathdon, Scot., U.K. 57 12N 3 4W
41 Stratmiglo Scot., U.K. 56 16N 3 15W
144 Strathmore, Australia 17 50S 142 35E
156 Strathmore, Canada ...51 5N 113 25W
43 Strathmore, dist., Scot., U.K. 58 23N 4 40W
43 Strathpeffer, Scot., U.K. 57 35N 4 32W
154 Strathroy, Canada 42 58N 81 38W
43 Strathy, Scotland, U.K. 58 30N 4 0W
43 Strathy Pt., Scot., U.K. 58 35N 4 0W
40 Strathyre, Scot., U.K. 56 14N 4 20W
36 Stratton, England, U.K. 50 49N 4 31W
164 Stratton, Calif., U.S.A. 39 20N 102 36W
34 Stratton St. Margaret, England, U.K. 51 35N 1 45W
57 Straubing, Germany ...48 53N 12 35E
79 Straumsnes, Norway ...63 4N 8 2E
166 Strawberry Res., U.S.A. 40 0N 111 0W
165 Strawn, U.S.A. 32 36N 98 30W
59 Strážnice, Cz. 48 54N 17 19E
138 Streaky B., S. Austral. 32 51S 134 18E
143 Streatham, Vic., Austral. 37 43S 143 5E
34 Streatley, Eng., U.K. .51 31N 1 9W
164 Streator, U.S.A. 41 9N 88 52W
58 Stredocesky, reg., Cz. .49 55N 14 30E
59 Stredoslovensky, reg., Cz. 48 30N 19 15E
36 Street, England, U.K. 51 7N 2 43W
160 Streetsville, Canada ...43 36N 79 43W
78 Strehaia, Rumania 44 37N 23 10E
91 Strelka, U.S.S.R. 58 5N 93 10E
38 Stretford, Eng., U.K. .53 27N 2 19W
38 Stretton, Eng., U.K. .53 21N 2 34W
143 Strezlecki, Vic., Austral. 38 16S 145 50E
58 Stříbro, Czechoslovakia 49 44N 13 0E
43 Strichen, Scot., U.K. .57 35N 2 5W
144 Strickland R., Papua . 7 0S 141 45E
76 Strimón R., Greece 41 0N 23 30E
76 Strimonikós Kólpos, G., Greece 40 33N 24 0E
40 Striven L., Scot., U.K. 55 58N 5 9W
77 Strofadhes, I., Greece 37 15N 21 0E
46 Strokestown, Ireland .53 47N 8 6W
79 Strom, Norway 60 17N 11 44E
80 Ström, Sweden 61 52N 17 20E
43 Stroma, I. of, Scot., UK 58 40N 3 8W
80 Strombacka, Sweden .61 58N 16 44E
73 Stromboli I., Italy 38 48N 15 12E
42 Stromeferry, Scot., U.K. 57 20N 5 33W
42 Stromemore, Scot., UK 57 22N 5 33W
43 Stromness, Scot., U.K. 58 58N 3 18W
80 Stromsberg, Sweden ...60 28N 17 44E
81 Stromsnasbruk, Sweden 56 35N 13 45E
82 Ströms Vattudal L., Sweden 64 0N 15 30E

MAP
164 Stromsburg, U.S.A. ...41 10N 97 38W
80 Stromstad, Sweden 58 55N 11 15E
82 Stromsund, Sweden ..63 51N 15 35E
40 Stronachlachar, Scotland, U.K. 56 15N 4 35W
73 Strongoli, Italy 39 16N 17 2E
43 Stronsay Firth, Scotland, U.K. 59 4N 2 50W
43 Stronsay I., Scot., U.K. 59 8N 2 38W
42 Strontian, Scot., U.K. 56 42N 5 32W
35 Strood, England, U.K. 51 23N 0 30E
46 Stroove, Ireland 55 13N 6 57W
59 Stropkov, Cz. 49 13N 21 39E
143 Stroud, N.S.W., Austral. 32 25S 152 9E
34 Stroud, England, U.K. 51 44N 2 12W
143 Stroud Road, Australia 32 21S 151 48E
161 Stroudsburg, U.S.A. ...40 59N 75 15W
81 Struer, Denmark 56 30N 8 35E
74 Struga, Yugoslavia 41 13N 20 44E
86 Strugi Krasnye, U.S.S.R. 58 21N 28 51E
74 Struma R., Bulgaria .41 50N 23 18E
37 Strumble Hd., Wales, United Kingdom 52 3N 5 6W
74 Strumica, Yugoslavia .41 28N 22 41E
74 Strumica, R., Y.-slavia 41 26N 27 46E
79 Strusshamn, Norway .60 24N 5 10E
160 Struthers, U.S.A. 41 6N 80 38W
43 Struy, Scotland, U.K. 57 25N 4 40W
75 Stryama, Bulgaria 42 16N 24 54E
134 Strydenburg, S. Africa 29 58S 23 40E
134 Strydomsvlei, S. Africa 33 9S 23 1E
86 Stryi, U.S.S.R. 49 16N 23 48E
60 Stryków, Poland 51 55N 19 33E
60 Strzegom, Poland 50 58N 16 20E
60 Strzelce Krajenskie, Pol. 52 52N 15 33E
60 Strzelin, Poland 50 46N 17 2E
60 Strzelno, Poland 52 35N 18 9E
59 Strzyżów, Poland 49 52N 21 47E
36 Stuart Bay, Eng., U.K. 50 16N 3 35W
163 Stuart, Fla., U.S.A. ...27 11N 80 12W
164 Stuart, Neb., U.S.A. .42 39N 99 8W
156 Stuart L., Canada 54 40N 124 40W
147 Stuart Mts., N.Z. 45 2S 167 39E
143 Stuart Town, Australia 32 47S 149 10E
138 Stuart's Ra., Australia 29 10S 135 0E
81 Stubbekøbing, Denmark 54 53N 12 2E
58 Stuben, Austria 46 58N 10 31E
147 Studholme Junc., N.Z. 44 42S 171 9E
34 Studland, Eng., U.K. .50 39N 1 58W
34 Studley, Eng., U.K. ...52 16N 1 54W
80 Stugsund, Sweden 61 16N 17 18E
80 Stugun, Sweden 63 10N 15 40E
157 Stull, L., Canada 54 26N 92 20W
107 Stung-Treng, Cambodia 13 26N 106 0E
87 Stupino, U.S.S.R. 54 57N 38 2E
157 Sturgeon B., Canada .52 0N 98 0W
154 Sturgeon Falls, Canada 46 25N 79 57W
160 Sturgeon L., Ont., Can. 44 30N 78 45W
162 Sturgeon Bay, U.S.A. 44 52N 87 20W
162 Sturgis, Mich., U.S.A. 41 50N 85 25W
164 Sturgis, S.D., U.S.A. .44 25N 103 30W
81 Sturkö, I., Sweden 56 5N 15 42E
34 Sturminster Marshall, England, U.K. 50 48N 2 4W
36 Sturminster Newton, England, U.K. 50 56N 2 18W
59 Stúrovo, Czechoslovakia 47 48N 18 41E
138 Sturt Cr., W. Australia 19 0S 128 15E
39 Sturton, Eng., U.K. ...53 22N 0 49W
135 Stutterheim, S. Africa 32 33S 27 28E
57 Stuttgart, Germany ...48 46N 9 10E
165 Stuttgart, U.S.A. 34 30N 91 33W
161 Stuyvesant, U.S.A. 42 23N 73 45W
82 Stykkisholmur, Iceland 65 2N 22 40W
86 Styr R., U.S.S.R. 51 4N 25 20E
58 Styria, *see* Stiermark, Austria 47 26N 15 0E
126 Suakin, Sudan 19 0N 37 20E
113 Suancheng, China 30 58N 118 57E
113 Süanen, China 30 0N 109 30E
113 Suanhan, China 31 17N 107 46E
112 Suanhwa, China 40 35N 115 0E
113 Suao, Taiwan 24 32N 121 42E
107 Suay Rieng, Cambodia 11 9N 105 45E
109 Subang, Indonesia 7 30S 107 45E
108 Subi, I., Indonesia ... 2 58N 108 50E
71 Subiaco, Italy 41 56N 13 5E
74 Subotica, Yugoslavia .46 6N 19 29E
157 Success, Canada 50 28N 108 6W
78 Suceava, Rumania 47 38N 26 16E
78 Suceava, Reg., Rum. 47 40N 25 50E
78 Suceava, R., Rumania 47 38N 26 16E
59 Sucha, Poland 49 44N 19 35E
168 Suchitoto, Salvador ...13 56N 89 0W
113 Süchow, China 34 10N 117 20E
60 Suchowola, Poland ...53 33N 23 3E
55 Süchteln, Germany 51 18N 6 20E
174 Sucre, Bolivia 19 0S 65 15W
174 Sucunduri, R., Brazil . 6 20N 58 35W

MAP
71 Sucuraj, Yugoslavia ...43 10N 17 8E
87 Suda R., U.S.S.R. 59 40N 36 30E
88 Sudak, U.S.S.R. 44 51N 34 57E
121 Sudan, st., E. Africa .15 0N 30 0E
117 Sudan, The, reg., Africa 11 0N 9 0E
165 Sudan, U.S.A. 34 8N 102 26W
87 Suday, U.S.S.R. 59 0N 43 15E
154 Sudbury, Canada 46 30N 81 0W
34 Sudbury, Derby, England, U.K. 52 53N 1 43W
35 Sudbury, Suffolk, England, U.K. 52 2N 0 44E
127 Sudd, The, swamp, Sudan 8 20N 29 30E
56 Suerbrarup, W. Ger. .54 38N 9 47E
56 Suderlugum, W. Ger. .54 50N 8 46E
59 Sudetes (Sudery), Mts., Pol & Cz. 50 20N 16 45E
108 Sudirman Mts., Indonesia 4 30N 137 0E
78 Suditi, Rumania 44 35N 27 38E
55 Südlohn, West Germany 51 56N 6 51E
87 Sudogda, U.S.S.R. 55 55N 40 50E
126 Sudr, Egypt 29 40N 32 42E
86 Sudzha, U.S.S.R. 51 14N 34 25E
65 Sueca, Spain 39 12N 0 21W
126 Suez (El Suweis), Egypt 29 58N 32 31E
126 Suez Canal, Egypt 31 0N 32 20E
126 Suez, G. of, Egypt 28 40N 33 0E
98 Suf, Jordan 32 19N 35 49E
100 Sufaina, Saudi Arabia 23 6N 40 44E
162 Suffolk, U.S.A. 36 47N 76 33W
35 Suffolk, co., Eng., UK 52 16N 1 0E
35 Suffolk, East, co., England, U.K. 52 16N 1 10E
35 Suffolk, West, co., England, U.K. 52 16N 0 45E
111 Sufu, China 39 44N 75 53E
101 Sufuk Wells, Trucial States 23 50N 51 50E
78 Sugag, Rumania 45 47N 23 37E
164 Sugar City, U.S.A. 38 18N 103 38W
44 Sugarloaf Mt., Ireland 51 42N 9 38W
143 Sugarloaf Pt., Australia 32 22S 152 30E
153 Sugluk, Canada, *see* Saglout 62 10N 75 40W
131 Suguti, Tanzania 1 45S 33 40E
78 Suhaia, Balta, L., Rum. 43 45N 25 15E
112 Suhbaatar, Mongolia .50 15N 105 4E
56 Suhl, Germany 50 35N 10 40E
56 Suhl, dist., E. Germany 50 37N 10 43E
125 Suhum, Ghana 6 5N 0 27W
112 Suichung, China 40 45N 120 46E
112 Suifenho, China 44 30N 131 2E
113 Suihsien China 31 58N 113 20E
113 Suhsien, China 33 28N 117 54E
112 Suihwa, China 46 40N 126 57E
113 Suiknai, China 21 17N 110 19E
113 Suining, China 26 11N 109 5E
172 Suipacha, Argentina ...34 46S 59 44W
113 Suiping, China 33 15N 114 6E
49 Suippes, France 49 8N 4 30E
112 Suiteh, China 37 35N 110 5E
104 Sujangarh, India 27 42N 47 31E
74 Sujica, Yugoslavia 43 52N 17 11E
109 Sukabumi, Indonesia . 6 56S 106 57E
108 Sukadana, Indonesia . 1 10S 110 0E
109 Sukarnapura, *see* Djajapura, Indonesia 2 28N 140 38E
109 Sukarno Pk., Indonesia 3 57S 137 17E
86 Sukhinichi, U.S.S.R. .54 8N 35 10E
84 Sukhona R., U.S.S.R. 60 30N 45 0E
89 Sukhumi, U.S.S.R. 43 0N 41 0E
10 Sukkertoppen, Green. 65 40N 53 0W
104 Sukkur, & Barrage, West Pakistan 27 50N 68 46E
106 Sukma, India 18 24N 81 37E
74 Sukovo, Yugoslavia ...43 4N 22 37E
109 Sula Is., Indonesia 1 45S 125 0E
86 Sula, R., U.S.S.R. 50 0N 33 0E
28 Sula Sgeir, I., Scot., U.K. 58 35N 6 5W
104 Sulaiman Ra., W. Pak. 30 30N 69 50E
104 Sulaimanke Headworks, Pakistan 30 27N 73 55E
100 Sulaimaniya, Iraq 35 35N 45 29E
89 Sulak, R., U.S.S.R. ...43 20N 47 20E
98 Sulam Tsor, Israel 33 4N 35 6E
109 Sulawesi I., Prov., Indon. 2 0S 120 0E
38 Sulby, Isle of Man, U.K. 54 18N 4 29W
60 Sulechów, Poland 52 5N 15 40E
60 Sulecin, Poland 52 26N 15 10E
60 Sulejów, Poland 51 26N 19 53E
124 Sulima, Sierra Leone . 6 58N 11 32W
78 Sulina, Rumania 45 10N 29 40E
56 Sulingen, Germany 52 41N 8 47E
78 Suliţa, Rumania 47 39N 20 59E
82 Sulitjelma, Norway ...61 7N 16 8E
82 Sulitjelma, Mt., Sweden 67 17N 17 28E
174 Sullana, Peru 5 0S 80 45W
164 Sullivan, Ill., U.S.A. .39 40N 88 40W
162 Sullivan, Ind., U.S.A. 39 5N 87 26W
164 Sullivan, Mo., U.S.A. .38 10N 91 10W
156 Sullivan Bay, Canada 50 55N 126 50W
107 Sullivan I., Burma, *see* Lambi Kyun 10 50N 98 20E
42 Sullom Voe, Scot., U.K. 60 30N 1 20W

MAP
49 Sully, Loire, France ...47 45N 2 20E
71 Sulmona, Italy 42 3N 13 55E
165 Sulphur, La., U.S.A. .30 20N 93 22W
165 Sulphur, Okla., U.S.A. 34 35N 97 0W
156 Sulphur Pt., Canada .60 50N 114 50W
165 Sulphur Springs, U.S.A. 33 5N 95 30W
165 Sulphur Springs, Cr., U.S.A. 32 50N 102 8W
154 Sultan, Canada 47 36N 82 47W
131 Sultan Hamud, Kenya 2 1S 37 30E
105 Sultanpur, India 26 18N 82 10E
109 Sulu Arch, Philippines 6 0N 121 0E
109 Sulu Sea, E. Indies 8 0N 120 0E
1 Sulu, Vol., Philippines 6 0N 121 10E
127 Sululta, Ethiopia 9 10N 38 43E
123 Suluq, Libya 31 44N 20 14E
55 Sülz, R., W. Germany 48 21N 8 38E
57 Sulzbach, Germany ...49 30N 11 46E
57 Sulzbach-Rosenburg, West Germany 49 30N 11 46E
109 Sumalata, Indonesia . 1 0N 122 37E
172 Sumampa, Argentina .29 25S 63 29W
108 Sumatra I., Indonesia 0 40N 100 20E
166 Sumatra, U.S.A. 46 45N 107 37W
109 Sumba I., Indonesia ... 9 45S 119 35E
109 Sumba, Str., Indonesia 9 0S 118 40E
108 Sumbawa, Indonesia . 8 26S 117 30E
109 Sumbawa I., Indonesia 8 34S 117 17E
109 Sumbing Mt., Indonesia 7 19S 110 3E
132 Sumba, Zambia 8 35S 30 25E
112 Sümber, Mongolia 46 40N 108 50E
42 Sumburgh Hd., Scotland, U.K. 59 52N 1 17W
109 Sumedang, Indonesia . 6 49S 107 56E
59 Sümeg, Hungary 46 59N 17 20E
75 Sumen (Kolarovgrad), Bulgaria 43 27N 26 42E
109 Sumenep, Indonesia ... 7 3S 113 51E
89 Sumgait, U.S.S.R. 40 34N 49 10E
42 Summer Is., Scot., U.K. 58 0N 5 27W
166 Summer L., U.S.A. ...42 50N 120 50W
45 Summerhill, Ireland ...53 30N 6 44W
155 Summerside, Canada .46 29N 63 41W
163 Summerville, Ga., U.S.A. 34 30N 85 20W
163 Summerville, S.C., U.S.A. 33 2N 80 11W
154 Summit, Canada 47 50N 72 20W
156 Summit L., Canada ...54 20N 122 40W
167 Summit Pk., Mt., U.S.A. 37 20N 106 48W
147 Sumner, New Zealand 43 35S 172 48E
164 Sumner, U.S.A 42 49N 92 7W
147 Sumner L., N.Z. 42 42S 172 15E
59 Sumperk, Cz. 49 59N 17 0E
163 Sumter, U.S.A. 33 55N 80 10W
86 Sumy, U.S.S.R. 50 57N 34 50E
42 Sunart, dist., Scot., U.K. 56 40N 5 40W
40 Sunart, L., Scot., U.K. 56 42N 5 35W
166 Sunburst, U.S.A. 48 56N 111 59W
161 Sunbury, U.S.A. 40 50N 76 46W
143 Sunbury, Vic., Australia 37 30S 144 40E
172 Sunchales, Argentina .30 58S 61 35W
172 Suncho Corral, Arg. ...27 55S 63 14W
112 Sunchon, South Korea 34 52N 127 31E
161 Suncook, U.S.A. 43 8N 71 27W
79 Sund, Norway 60 13N 5 10E
108 Sunda Str., Indonesia 6 20S 105 30E
164 Sundance, U.S.A. 44 27N 104 27W
105 Sundarbans, The, India and Pakistan 22 0N 89 0E
124 Sunday Town, Liberia 5 6N 7 40W
134 Sundays R., S. Africa 32 10S 24 40E
135 Sundays R., S. Africa 28 42S 30 30E
81 Sundby, Denmark 56 53N 8 40E
80 Sundbyberg, Sweden .59 22N 17 58E
160 Sunderland, Canada ...44 16N 79 3W
39 Sunderland, Eng., U.K. 54 54N 1 22W
161 Sunderland, U.S.A. ...42 27N 72 36W
156 Sundre, Canada 51 49N 114 46W
154 Sundridge, Canada ...45 45N 79 25W
35 Sundridge, Eng., U.K. 51 15N 0 10E
81 Sunds, Denmark 56 13N 9 1E
80 Sundsjö, Sweden 63 0N 15 10E
80 Sundsvall, Sweden ...62 23N 17 25E
108 Sungaianjar, Indonesia 2 53S 116 14E
108 Sungaigerung, Indon. . 4 58S 105 7E
108 Sungaigerung, Indon. . 2 57S 104 50E
108 Sungaipakning, Indon. 1 19N 102 0E
108 Sungaipenuh, Indonesia 2 1S 101 20E
108 Sungaitiram, Indonesia 0 45S 117 8E
112 Sungari, R., China ...47 0N 130 50E
112 Sungari, Res., China .43 0N 127 0E
107 Sungei Lembing, Malay 2 53N 103 4E
107 Sungei Patani, Malaysia 5 38N 100 29E
107 Sungei Siput, Malaysia 4 51N 101 6E
109 Sungguminasa, Indon. 5 17S 119 30E
113 Sunghsien, China 34 10N 112 10E
127 Sungikai, Sudan 12 20N 29 51E
113 Sungkiang, China 31 0N 121 20E
111 Sungpan, China 32 50N 103 20E
113 Sungtao, China 28 10N 109 0E
113 Sungtze, China 30 25N 111 50E

MAP
130 Sungu, Congo 6 48S 20 13E
132 Sungüé, Mozambique .21 18S 32 28E
88 Sungurlu, Turkey 40 12N 34 21E
113 Sungyang, China 28 16N 119 29E
71 Sunja, Yugoslavia 45 21N 16 35E
39 Sunk Island, Eng., U.K. 53 38N 0 7W
80 Sunnåsbruk, Sweden .61 10N 7 12E
79 Sundalsöra, Norway ...62 40N 8 36E
80 Sunne, Jämtland, Sweden 63 7N 14 30E
80 Sunne, Värmland, Swed. 59 52N 13 12E
79 Sunnfjord, dist., Nor. .16 26N 5 32E
79 Sunnhordland, dist., Nor. 59 50N 5 30E
35 Sunninghill, Eng., U.K. 51 25N 0 40W
79 Sunnmöre Dist., Nor. 62 15N 6 30E
166 Sunnyside, Utah, U.S.A. 39 40N 110 24W
166 Sunnyside, Wash., U.S.A. 46 24N 120 2W
165 Sunray, U.S.A. 36 1N 101 47W
143 Sunshine, Vic., Australia 37 48S 144 52E
125 Sunson, Ghana 9 35N 0 2W
91 Suntar, U.S.S.R. 62 15N 117 30E
124 Sunyani, Ghana 7 21N 2 22W
82 Suolahti, Finland 62 38N 25 59E
82 Suonenjoki, Finland ...62 37N 27 20E
167 Supai, U.S.A. 36 1N 112 44W
105 Supaul, India 26 10N 86 40E
167 Superior, Ariz., U.S.A.33 19N 111 9W
166 Superior, Mont., U.S.A. 47 15N 114 57W
164 Superior, Neb., U.S.A. 40 3N 98 2W
164 Superior, Wis., U.S.A. 46 45N 92 0W
159 Superior, L., Canada–U.S.A. 47 40N 87 0W
71 Supetar, Yugoslavia ...43 25N 16 32E
107 Suphan Buri, Thailand 14 30N 100 10E
60 Suprasl, Poland 53 13N 23 19E
113 Supu, China 27 57N 110 15E
123 Suq al Jumah, Libya .32 58N 13 12E
100 Sur, Lebanon 33 19N 35 16E
167 Sur, Pt., U.S.A. 36 12N 121 55W
87 Sura R., U.S.S.R. 55 30N 46 20E
109 Surabaja, Indonesia ... 7 17S 112 45E
80 Surahammar, Sweden 59 42N 23 19E
78 Suraia, Rumania 45 40N 27 25E
109 Surakarta, Indonesia . 7 35S 110 48E
89 Surakhany, U.S.S.R. .40 13N 50 1E
106 Surandai, India 8 58N 77 26E
59 Šurany, Czechoslovakia 48 6N 18 10E
104 Surat India 21 12N 72 55E
145 Surat, Queens., Austral. 27 10S 149 6E
107 Surat Thani, Thailand 9 3N 99 28E
104 Suratgarh, India 29 18N 73 55E
86 Surazh, U.S.S.R. 53 5N 32 27E
135 Surbiton, S. Africa ...32 22S 27 14E
78 Surduc, Rumania 47 15N 23 25E
78 Surduc Pass, Rumania 45 21N 23 23E
74 Surdulica, Yugoslavia 42 41N 22 11E
54 Sûre R., Luxembourg 49 5N 5 50E
104 Surendranagar, India .22 45N 71 40E
156 Surf Inlet Canada 53 8N 128 50W
50 Surgères, France 46 7N 0 47W
90 Surgut, U.S.S.R. 61 20N 73 28E
105 Suri, India 23 50N 87 34E
78 Surian, Mt., Rumania 45 33N 23 31E
106 Suriapet, India 17 10N 79 40E
98 Surif, Jordan 31 40N 35 4E
107 Surin, Thailand 14 50N 103 34E
175 Surinam (Netherlands Guiana), S. America 4 0N 56 15W
175 Suriname R., Guyana 4 30N 55 30W
89 Sürmene, Turkey 41 0N 40 1E
89 Surovikino, U.S.S.R. .48 32N 42 55E
35 Surrey, co., England, U.K. 51 16N 0 30W
57 Sursee, Switzerland ...47 11N 8 6E
123 Surt, Libya 31 11N 16 46E
123 Surt Desert, Libya 30 0N 17 50E
82 Surtsey I., Iceland 63 27N 20 15W
114 Suruga-wan, B., Japan 34 45N 138 30E
108 Surulangun, Indonesia 2 30S 102 30E
109 Surup, Philippines 6 27N 126 17E
101 Surur, Muscat & Oman 23 20N 58 10E
70 Susa, Italy 45 8N 7 3E
81 Susaa, R., Denmark ...55 20N 11 42E
71 Sušac, I., Yugoslavia .42 46N 16 30E
71 Susak, I., Yugoslavia .44 30N 14 28E
100 Susangerd, Iran 31 35N 48 20E
91 Susanino, U.S.S.R. 52 50N 140 14E
166 Susanville, U.S.A. 40 28N 120 40W
58 Susice, Czechoslovakia 49 17N 13 30E
161 Susquehanna, R., U.S.A. 41 50N 76 20W
161 Susquehanna Depot, U.S.A. 41 55N 75 36W
172 Susques, Argentina 23 35S 66 25W
155 Sussex, Canada 45 45N 65 37W
161 Sussex, U.S.A. 41 12N 74 38W
35 Sussex, co., Eng., U.K. 50 55N 0 20W
35 Sussex, E., co., England, U.K. 51 0N 0 0E
35 Sussex, W., co., England, U.K. 51 0N 0 30W
91 Susuman, U.S.S.R. 62 47N 148 10E
60 Susz, Poland 53 44N 19 20E
78 Suţeşti, Rumania 45 13N 27 27E
157 Sutherland, Canada ...52 15N 106 40W

MAP
134 Sutherland, S. Afr. 32 33s 20 40E
164 Sutherland, U.S.A. 41 12N 101 11w
43 Sutherland, co., Scot., U.K. 58 10N 4 30w
135 Sutherland Mt., S. Afr. 29 55s 29 11E
139 Sutherland Pt., Queensland, Australia 28 15s 153 35E
142 Sutherland, Ra., Western Australia .25 42s 125 21E
166 Sutherlin, U.S.A. 43 28N 123 16w
71 Sutivan, Yugoslavia ...43 23N 16 30E
104 Sutlej, R., India 29 50N 72 20E
104 Sutlej, R., W. Pakistan 30 0N 73 0E
39 Sutterton, Eng., U.K. 52 54N 0 8w
161 Sutton, Canada 45 8N 72 36w
35 Sutton, Eng., U.K. 51 22N 0 13w
147 Sutton, New Zealand .45 34s 170 8E
164 Sutton, U.S.A. 40 40N 97 50w
35 Sutton Bridge, England, U.K. 52 46N 0 12E
34 Sutton Coldfield, England, U.K. 52 33N 1 50w
34 Sutton Courtenay, Eng., U.K. 51 39N 1 16w
39 Sutton-in-Ashfield, Eng., U.K. 53 8N 1 16w
39 Sutton-on-Sea, England, United Kingdom 53 18N 0 18E
34 Sutton Scotney, Eng., U.K. 51 9N 1 20w
135 Suurberge Mts., Cape Province, S. Africa .33 15s 25 30E
134 Suurbraak, S. Africa .34 0s 20 39E
135 Suurveld, OFS, S. Afr. 27 53s 29 10E
136 Suva, Fiji Islands 17 40s 178 8E
74 Suva Gora, Yugoslavia 41 45N 21 3E
74 Suva Planina, Y.-slavia 43 10N 22 5E
74 Suva Reka, Yugoslavia 42 21N 20 50E
137 Suvarov Is., Pac. Oc. .13 15s 163 30w
137 Suvorovo, Bulgaria ...43 20N 27 35E
74 Suvo Rudiste, Mt., Yugoslavia 43 17N 20 49E
60 Suwalki, Poland 54 8N 22 59E
163 Suwannee, R., U.S.A. 30 0N 83 0w
113 Suwen, China 20 27N 110 2E
112 Süwon, S. Korea 37 25N 126 55E
113 Suyung, China 28 12N 105 10E
87 Suzdal, U.S.S.R. 56 29N 40 26E
114 Suzuka, Japan 34 55N 136 36E
70 Suzzara, Italy 45 0N 10 45E
14 Svalbard, *see* Spitzbergen 78 0N 17 0E
81 Svalöv, Sweden 55 57N 13 8E
80 Svana, Sweden 59 46N 15 23E
82 Svanvik, Norway 68 44N 30 0E
79 Svarstad, Norway 59 27N 9 56E
153 Svartenhuk, Pen., Green. 71 30N 52 30w
82 Svartisen, Mt., Norway 66 40N 14 16E
80 Svartvik, Sweden 62 19N 17 24E
88 Svatovo, U.S.S.R. 49 35N 38 5E
81 Svedala, Sweden 55 30N 13 15E
80 Sveg, Sweden 62 2N 14 27E
79 Sveio, Norway 59 33N 5 23E
79 Svelvik, Norway 59 37N 10 24E
81 Svendborg, Denmark .55 14N 10 35E
81 Svendborg, co., Den. .55 11N 10 25E
79 Svene, Norway 59 45N 9 31E
81 Svenljunga, Sweden ...57 31N 13 8E
81 Svensbro, Sweden 58 15N 13 52E
80 Svenstavik, Sweden ...62 45N 14 31E
81 Svenstrup, Denmark .56 58N 9 50E
90 Sverdlovsk, U.S.S.R. .56 50N 60 30E
14 Sverdrup Is., Canada .79 0N 97 0w
71 Svetac, I., Yugoslavia 43 3N 15 43E
71 Sveti Ivan Zelina, Yugoslavia 45 57N 16 16E
71 Sveti Jurij, Yugoslavia 46 14N 15 24E
71 Sveti Lenart, Y.-slavia 46 36N 15 48E
74 Sveti Nikole, Y.-slavia 41 51N 21 56E
71 Sveti Trojica, Y.-slavia 46 37N 15 33E
74 Svetozarevo, Y.-slavia 44 0N 21 15E
59 Svidnik, Czechoslovakia 49 20N 21 37E
71 Svilaja Pl., Yugoslavia 43 49N 16 31E
74 Svilajnac, Yugoslavia 44 15N 21 11E
75 Svilengrad, Bulgaria .41 49N 26 12E
81 Svinö, Denmark 55 6N 11 44E
84 Svir, R., U.S.S.R. 61 2N 34 50E
86 Svisloch, U.S.S.R. 53 26N 24 2E
75 Svishov, Bulgaria 43 36N 25 23E
59 Svitavy, Czechoslovakia 49 47N 16 28E
91 Svobodny, U.S.S.R. ...51 20N 128 0E
87 Svolvær, Norway 68 15N 14 40E
59 Svratka R., Cz. 49 27N 16 12E
74 Svrljig, Yugoslavia 43 25N 22 6E
57 Swabian Alps, Germany 48 30N 9 30E
34 Swadlincote, Eng., U.K. 52 47N 1 34w
35 Swaffham, Eng., U.K. 52 38N 0 42E
144 Swain Reefs, Australia 21 45s 152 20w
163 Swainsboro, U.S.A. ...32 38N 82 22w

MAP
129 Swakopmund, S. Afr. .22 37s 14 30E
39 Swale R., Eng., U.K. .54 18N 1 30w
35 Swallowfield, Eng., U.K. 51 23N 0 56w
169 Swan Islands, W. Ind. 17 22N 83 57w
157 Swan L., Canada 52 30N 100 50w
143 Swan Hill, Vic., Austral. 35 15s 143 31E
157 Swan River, Canada .52 10N 101 25w
34 Swanage, Eng., U.K. .50 36N 1 59w
46 Swanlinbar, Ireland ...54 11N 7 42w
143 Swansea, N.S.W., Austral. 33 3s 151 35E
37 Swansea, Wales, U.K. 51 37N 3 57w
37 Swansea Bay, Wales, United Kingdom 51 34N 3 55w
135 Swartberg, S. Africa ...30 15s 29 23E
135 Swartberge, Mts., S. Afr. 33 20s 22 0E
133 Swartbooistad, S. Afr. 25 14s 28 10E
134 Swartmodder, S. Africa 34 0s 20 39E
133 Swartruggens, S. Africa 25 39s 26 42E
135 Swart-Umfolozi, S. Afr. 27 52s 31 15E
60 Swarzedz, Poland 52 25N 17 4E
154 Swastika, Canada 48 7N 80 6w
102 Swat, dist., W. Pak. ...35 0N 72 20E
113 Swatow, China 23 25N 116 40E
46 Swatragh, N. Ire., U.K. 54 55N 6 40w
133 Swaziland, Prot., Africa 26 30s 31 30E
82 Sweden, king., Eur. ...67 0N 15 0E
125 Swedru, Ghana 5 32N 0 41w
166 Sweet Home, U.S.A. .44 26N 122 38w
165 Sweetwater, U.S.A. ...32 30N 100 28w
166 Sweetwater R., U.S.A. 42 31N 107 30w
134 Swellendam, S. Africa 34 1s 20 26E
60 Swidnica, Poland 50 50N 16 30E
60 Swidwin, Poland 53 47N 15 49E
60 Swiebodzice, Poland ...50 51N 16 20E
60 Swiebodzin, Poland ...52 15N 15 37E
60 Swiecie, Poland 53 25N 18 30E
60 Swietokrzyskie, Gory, Mts., Poland 51 0N 20 30E
157 Swift Current, Canada 50 20N 107 45w
46 Swilly L., Ireland 55 12N 7 35w
46 Swilly, R., Ireland 54 56N 7 50w
36 Swimbridge, Eng., U.K. 51 3N 3 59w
135 Swinburne, S. Africa .28 20s 29 14E
156 Swindle, I., Canada ...52 30N 128 35w
34 Swindon, Eng., U.K. .51 33N 1 47w
39 Swineshead, Eng., U.K. 57 57N 0 9w
46 Swinford, Ireland 53 57N 8 57w
60 Swinoujscie, Poland ...53 54N 14 16E
38 Swinton, Lancs., England, U.K. 53 31N 2 21w
39 Swinton, Yorks., England, U.K. 53 28N 1 20w
41 Swinton, Scot., U.K. .55 43N 2 10E
55 Swist R., Germany 50 44N 6 4w
56 Switzerland, rep., Eur. 46 30N 8 50E
43 Swona, I., Orkney, Scotland, U.K. 58 30N 3 3w
45 Swords, Ireland 53 27N 6 15w
86 Syasstroy, U.S.S.R. ...60 5N 32 15E
44 Sybil Pt., Ireland 52 12N 10 28w
133 Sybrandskraal, S. Afr. 25 29s 28 37E
86 Sychevka, U.S.S.R. ...55 45N 34 10E
60 Syców Poland 51 19N 17 40E
143 Sydney, N.S.W., Austral. 33 53s 151 10E
155 Sydney, Canada 46 7N 60 7w
164 Sydney, U.S.A. 41 12N 103 0w
155 Sydney Mines, Canada 46 18N 60 15w
14 Sydpröven, Greenland 60 30N 45 20w
135 Syfergat, S. Africa 31 25s 26 25E
133 Syferkuil, S. Africa 26 29s 26 29E
56 Syke, Germany 52 55N 8 50E
84 Syktyvkar, U.S.S.R. .61 45N 50 40E
163 Sylacauga, U.S.A. 33 10N 86 15w
80 Sylarna, Mt. Sweden .63 2N 12 20E
103 Sylhet, East Pakistan 24 43N 91 55E
56 Sylt I., Germany 54 50N 8 20E
156 Sylvan Lake, Canada .52 20N 114 10w
163 Sylvania, U.S.A. 32 45N 81 37w
163 Sylvester, U.S.A. 31 31N 83 50w
90 Sym, U.S.S.R. 60 20N 87 50E
41 Symington, Scot., U.K. 55 35N 3 36w
34 Symonds Yat, Eng., U.K. 51 50N 2 38w
90 Syr Darya R., U.S.S.R. 45 0N 65 0E
165 Syracuse, Kan., U.S.A. 38 0N 101 40w
161 Syracuse, N.Y., U.S.A. 43 4N 76 11w
100 Syria, Rep., Asia 35 0N 38 0E
107 Syriam, Burma 16 44N 96 19E
100 Syrian Des., S.W. Asia 31 30N 40 0E
34 Syston, England, U.K. 52 42N 1 5w
91 Syuldyukar, U.S.S.R. 63 25N 113 40E
75 Syutkya, Mt. Bulgaria 41 50N 24 16E
87 Syzran, U.S.S.R. 53 12N 48 30E
59 Szabolcs-Szatmar, Co., Hungary 48 2N 21 45E
60 Szamocin, Poland 53 2N 17 7E
60 Szamotuly, Poland 52 35N 16 34E
59 Szaraz, R., Hungary .46 28N 20 44E
59 Szărvas, Hungary 46 50N 20 38E
59 Szczara R., U.S.S.R. .53 15N 25 10E
60 Szczebrzeszyn, Poland 50 42N 22 59E

MAP
60 Szczecin (Stettin), Pol. 53 27N 14 27E
60 Szcecin, Prov., Poland 53 25N 14 32E
60 Szczecinek, Poland 53 43N 16 41E
60 Szczekocimy, Poland .50 38N 19 48E
60 Szczuczyn, Poland 53 36N 22 19E
60 Szczytno, Poland 53 33N 21 0E
113 Szechwan, prov., China 30 10N 106 0E
59 Szécsény, Hungary 48 7N 19 30E
59 Szeged, Hungary 46 16N 20 10E
59 Szeghhalom, Hungary 47 1N 21 10E
59 Székesfehérvár, Hung. 47 15N 13 25E
59 Szekszárd, Hungary ...46 22N 18 42E
111 Szemao, China 22 50N 101 0E
113 Szenan, China 27 50N 108 25E
59 Szendró, Hungary 48 24N 20 41E
113 Szengen, China 23 20N 108 5E
113 Szengen, China 24 50N 108 0E
59 Szentendre, Hungary .47 39N 19 4E
59 Szentes, Hungary 46 39N 20 21E
59 Szentgotthárd, Hung. 46 58N 16 19E
59 Szentlörinc, Hungary .46 3N 18 1E
112 Szeping, China 43 10N 124 18E
59 Szerencs, Hungary 48 10N 21 12E
113 Szeshui, China 34 50N 113 20E
113 Szewui, China 23 30N 112 35E
59 Szigetvár, Hungary ...46 3N 17 46E
59 Szob, Hungary 47 48N 18 53E
59 Szolnok, Hungary 47 10N 20 15E
59 Szolnok, co., Hungary 47 15N 20 30E
59 Szombathely, Hungary 47 14N 16 38E
60 Szprotawa, Poland 51 33N 15 35E
60 Sztum, Poland 53 55N 19 1E
60 Sztutowo, Poland 54 20N 19 15E
60 Szydlowiec, Poland ...51 15N 20 51E
60 Szypliszki, Poland 54 17N 23 2E

T

1 Taal, Vol., Philippines 14 2N 121 33E
81 Taarbæk, Denmark ...55 47N 12 34E
81 Taars, Denmark 57 25N 10 15E
81 Taasing I., Denmark .55 0N 10 35E
100 Taba, Saudi Arabia ...26 55N 42 30E
109 Tabaco, Philippines ...13 14N 123 43E
135 Tabankulu, S. Africa .30 58s 29 20E
144 Tabar Is., Terr. of, New Guinea 3 0s 152 20E
65 Tabarca, Isla de, Spain 38 17N 0 30w
123 Tabarka, Tunisia 36 55N 8 55E
65 Tabarra, Spain 38 37N 1 44E
101 Tabas, Iran 32 48N 60 12E
101 Tabas, Iran 33 35N 56 55E
169 Tabasara, Snía de, Pan. 8 35N 81 40w
168 Tabasco, st., Mexico ...17 45N 93 30w
174 Tabatinga, Brazil 4 11s 69 58w
122 Tabelbala, Kahal de, Algeria 28 47N 2 0w
122 Tabelkaza, Algeria 29 50N 0 55E
122 Taberbourt, Morocco .30 49N 8 13w
65 Tabernas, Spain 37 4N 2 26w
65 Tabernas de Valldigna, Spain 39 5N 0 13w
98 Tabigha (site), Israel .32 53N 35 33E
109 Tablas I., Philippines .12 20N 122 10E
155 Table B., Canada 53 40N 56 15w
134 Table B., S Africa 33 35s 18 25E
134 Table Mt., S. Africa ...34 0s 18 22E
144 Table Top Mt., Austral. 23 30s 147 0E
58 Tábor, Czechoslovakia 49 25N 14 39E
98 Tabor (site), Israel 32 42N 35 24E
131 Tabora, Tanzania 5 2s 32 57E
131 Tabora, dist., Tanzania 5 25s 32 30E
131 Tabora, prov., Tanzania 6 20s 32 30E
124 Tabou, Ivory Coast . 4 30N 7 20w
100 Tabriz, Iran 38 7N 46 20E
100 Tabuk, Saudi Arabia .28 30N 36 25E
64 Tabuenca, Spain 41 42N 1 32w
80 Täby, Sweden 59 29N 18 4E
113 Tachin Shah, Mts., China 26 0N 116 15E
112 Tachintala, China 45 13N 121 37E
174 Táchira, Venezuela 8 7N 72 21w
58 Tachov, Czechoslovakia 49 47N 12 39E
113 Tachu, China 30 50N 107 20E
73 Tacina R., Italy 39 5N 16 51E
109 Tacloban, Philippines 11 1N 125 0E
174 Tacna, Peru 18 0s 70 20w
166 Tacoma, Wash., U.S.A. 47 15N 122 30w
174 Tacora Vol., Peru 17 40s 70 0w
173 Tacuarembo, Uruguay 31 45s 56 0w
39 Tadcaster, Eng., U.K. 53 53N 1 16w
122 Taddert, Morocco 31 28N 7 22w
122 Tademait, Plateau du, Algeria 28 30N 2 30E
122 Tadjemout, Algeria ...33 54N 2 30E
122 Tadjerouna, Algeria ...33 31N 2 3E
122 Tadjmout, Algeria 25 37N 3 48E
127 Tadjoura, T.F.A.I. 11 50N 44 55E
127 Tadjoura, G. of, T.F.A.I. 11 50N 45 0E
34 Tadley, Eng., U.K. ...51 21N 1 8w
147 Tadmor, New Zealand 41 27s 172 45E
100 Tadmor, Syria 34 30N 37 55E
155 Tadoussac, Canada 48 11N 69 42w
90 Tadzhikistan S.S.R., U.S.S.R. 35 30N 70 0E
112 Taegu, South Korea ...35 50N 128 25E
112 Taejon, South Korea .35 30N 127 22E
31 Taf, R., Wales 51 45N 4 25w
64 Tafalla, Spain 42 30N 1 41w

MAP
127 Tafar, Sudan 6 52N 28 15E
98 Tafas, Syria 32 44N 36 5E
123 Tafassasset W., Algeria 23 0N 9 11E
135 Tafelberg, S. Africa ...31 36s 25 14E
109 Tafermaar, Indonesia . 6 47s 134 10E
122 Tafelney, C., Morocco 31 3N 9 51w
109 Tafermaar, Indonesia . 6 47s 134 10E
122 Tafersit, Morocco 35 0N 3 30w
37 Taff, R., Wales 51 35N 3 12w
172 Tafi Viejo, Argentina .26 43s 65 17w
122 Tafnidilt, Morocco 28 47N 10 58w
122 Tafraout, Morocco 29 50N 8 58w
122 Tafraout, Morocco 29 50N 8 58w
109 Taft, Philippines 11 57N 125 30E
167 Taft, Ala., U.S.A. 35 10N 119 28w
165 Taft, Tex., U.S.A. 27 58N 97 23w
105 Taga Dzong, Bhutan .27 5N 90 0E
89 Taganrog, U.S.S.R. ...47 12N 38 50E
89 Taganrog G., U.S.S.R. 47 0N 38 30E
124 Tagant, Mauritania ...18 20N 11 0w
109 Tagbilaran, Philippines 9 42N 124 3E
70 Taggia, Italy 43 52N 7 50E
122 Taghbalt, Morocco 30 48N 5 10w
45 Taghmon, Ireland 52 19N 6 40w
123 Taghrifat, Libya 29 5N 17 26E
122 Taghzout, Morocco 33 30N 4 49w
156 Tagish L., Canada 60 15N 134 30w
71 Tagliacozzo, Italy 42 4N 13 13E
71 Tagliamento R., Italy 45 38N 13 5E
71 Taglio di Po, Italy 45 0N 12 12E
65 Tagomago, Isla de, Sp. 39 2N 1 39E
173 Taguaritinga, Brazil ...21 35s 48 35w
175 Taguatinga, Brazil 12 26s 45 40w
144 Tagula I., Papua 11 40s 153 15E
109 Tagum (Hijo), Phil. ... 7 33N 125 53E
61 Tagus (Tajo, Tejo), R., Spain-Portugal .39 44N 5 50w
108 Tahahbala I., Indon. . 0 30s 98 30E
147 Tahakopa, New Zealand 46 30s 169 23E
122 Tahala, Morocco 34 0N 4 28w
123 Tahat Mt., Algeria 23 18N 5 21E
111 Tahcheng, China 46 50N 83 1E
112 Taheiho, China 50 10N 127 20E
101 Tahiri, Iran 27 31N 52 22E
137 Tahiti I., Pacific Ocean 17 45s 149 30w
165 Tahoka, U.S.A. 33 12N 101 45w
166 Tahoe, Nev., U.S.A. ...39 12N 119 54w
166 Tahoe, L., U.S.A. 39 6N 120 0w
146 Tahora, New Zealand 39 2s 174 49E
125 Tahoua, Niger 14 57N 5 16E
113 Tahsien, China 31 12N 108 13E
126 Tahta, Egypt 26 44N 31 32E
109 Tahulandang I., Indon. 2 27N 125 23E
109 Tahuna, Indonesia 3 45N 125 30E
124 Tai, Ivory Coast 5 55N 7 30w
113 Tai, Hu, L., China 31 10N 120 0E
112 Taian, China 36 20N 117 0E
113 Taichow, China 32 30N 119 50E
113 Taichow Wan., China 28 55N 121 10E
113 Taichung, Taiwan 24 10N 120 35E
147 Taieri R., N.Z. 45 30s 170 18E
99 Taif, Saudi Arabia 21 5N 40 27E
123 Taiga Madema, Libya 23 46N 15 25E
112 Taihan Shan, China ...36 0N 114 0E
146 Taihape, New Zealand 39 41s 175 48E
113 Taiho, China 26 50N 114 54E
112 Taihsien, China 39 9N 112 58E
113 Taihu, China 30 30N 116 25E
113 Taikang, China 34 3N 115 0E
113 Taikiang, China 26 45N 108 44E
107 Taikkyi, Burma 17 20N 96 0E
112 Taiku, China 37 46N 112 28E
113 Taikung, China 26 50N 108 40E
112 Tailagein Shara, Mts., Mongolia 44 10N 106 0E
112 Tailai, China 46 28N 123 18E
145 Tailem Bend, Australia 35 12s 139 29E
57 Tailfingen, Germany .48 15N 9 1E
43 Tain, Scotland, U.K. .57 49N 4 4w
113 Tainan, Taiwan 23 0N 120 15E
77 Tainaron, Akra, C., Gr. 36 22N 22 27E
113 Taining, China 27 0N 117 15E
113 Taipei, Taiwan 25 2N 121 30E
107 Taiping, Malaysia 4 50N 100 43E
113 Taishan, China 27 29N 119 34E
91 Taishet, U.S.S.R. 55 58N 97 25E
131 Taita Hills, Kenya 3 25s 38 15E
176 Taitao Pen., Chile 46 30s 75 0w
113 Taitung, Taiwan 22 43N 121 4E
113 Taiwan (Formosa), I., Asia 23 30N 121 0E
101 Taiwara, Afghanistan 33 30N 64 24E
77 Taiyetos Óros, Mts., Gr. 37 0N 22 23E
98 Taiyiba, Israel 32 36N 35 27E
98 Taiyiba, Jordan 31 55N 35 17E
112 Taiyüan, China 38 0N 112 30E
108 Tajan, Indonesia 0 6s 110 2E
123 Tajarhi, Libya 24 15N 14 46E
168 Tajicaringa, Mexico ...23 15N 104 44w
63 Tajo (Tagus) R., Spain 40 35N 1 52w
168 Tajumulco, Volcan de, Mexico 15 20N 91 50w
123 Tajura, Libya 32 51N 13 27E
107 Tak, Thailand 17 0N 99 10E
114 Takada, Japan 37 7N 138 15E
147 Takaka, New Zealand 40 51N 172 50E
114 Takamatsu, Japan 34 20N 134 5E
114 Takaoka, Japan 36 40N 137 0E
146 Takapau, New Zealand 40 2s 176 21E

MAP
144 Takapuna, New Zealand 36 47s 174 47E
114 Takásaki, Japan 36 20N 139 0E
114 Takatsuki, Japan 34 40N 135 37E
131 Takaungu, Kenya 3 38s 39 52E
114 Takayama, Japan 36 10N 137 5E
114 Takefu, Japan 35 50N 136 10E
35 Takeley, Eng., U.K. ...51 52N 0 16E
107 Takeo, Cambodia 11 3N 104 50E
81 Takern L., Sweden 58 22N 14 45E
100 Takestan, Iran 36 0N 49 50E
113 Takhing, China 23 10N 111 45E
108 Takingeun, Indonesia 4 45N 96 50E
127 Takkazye R., Ethiopia 13 50N 37 50E
156 Takla Landing, Canada 55 20N 125 50w
111 Takla Makan, des., China 39 40N 85 0E
124 Takoradi, Ghana 4 58N 1 55w
156 Taku, Canada 59 31N 133 59w
112 Taku, China 38 55N 117 35E
125 Takum, Nigeria 7 18N 9 36E
130 Takundi, Congo 4 43s 16 33E
112 Takushan, China 39 55N 123 30E
91 Tala, U.S.S.R. 72 40N 113 30E
122 Talaat n' Yakoub, Mor. 31 0N 8 2w
112 Talachi, China 36 45N 105 0E
172 Talagante, Chile 33 40s 70 50E
112 Talai, China 45 30N 124 20w
122 Talaint, Morocco 29 37N 9 45w
125 Talak, reg., Niger 18 0N 5 0E
169 Talamanca, Cordillera de, Cent. Amer. 9 20N 83 20w
135 Talaneni, Nat., S. Africa 28 33s 31 3E
108 Talangbetutu, Indon. . 2 50s 104 35E
174 Talara, Peru 4 30s 81 10E
144 Talasea, Terr. of New Guinea 5 14s 150 5E
125 Talata Mafara, Nigeria 12 38N 6 4E
109 Talaud Is., Indonesia . 4 30N 127 10E
62 Talavera de la Reina, Spain 39 55N 4 46w
142 Talawana, W. Australia 23 12s 121 10E
109 Talayan, Philippines . 6 52N 124 24E
138 Talbot C., W. Austral. 13 56s 125 49E
143 Talbragar R., Australia 32 11s 148 39E
172 Talca, Chile 35 20s 71 46w
172 Talca, prov., Chile 35 20s 71 46w
172 Talcahuano, Chile 36 40s 73 10w
87 Taldom, U.S.S.R. 56 45N 37 29E
90 Taldy Kurgan, U.S.S.R. 45 10N 78 45E
102 Taleqan, prov., Afghan. 36 40N 69 30E
98 Talfit, Jordan 32 5N 35 17E
37 Talgarth, Wales, U.K. 51 59N 3 15w
126 Talguharai, Sudan 18 19N 35 56E
113 Tali, China 34 48N 109 48E
111 Tali, Yunnan, China .25 50N 100 0E
127 Tali Post, Sudan 5 55N 30 44E
109 Taliabu I., Indonesia . 1 45s 125 0E
111 Taliang Shan, Mts., China 28 0N 103 0E
109 Taliban, Philippines ...10 4N 124 17E
165 Talihina, U.S.A. 34 45N 95 1w
106 Talikoti, India 16 29N 76 17E
107 Taling Sung, Thailand 15 5N 99 11E
100 Talish, Mts., Iran 39 0N 48 30E
108 Taliwang, Indonesia ... 8 50s 116 55E
152 Tapkeetna, Alaska, U.S.A. 62 20N 150 10w
126 Talla, Egypt 28 5N 30 43E
42 Talladale, Scot., U.K. 57 41N 5 20w
163 Talladega, U.S.A. 33 28N 86 2w
163 Tallahassee, U.S.A. ...30 25N 84 15w
143 Tallangatta, Australia 36 10s 147 14E
143 Tallarook, Vic., Austral. 37 5s 145 6E
80 Tallasen, Sweden 61 52N 16 15E
80 Tällberg, Sweden 60 51N 15 2E
142 Tallering Peak, W. Australia 28 6s 115 37E
86 Tallinn (Reval), U.S.S.R. 59 29N 24 58E
44 Tallow, Ireland 52 6N 8 0w
44 Tallowbridge, Ireland 52 6N 8 1w
165 Tallulah, U.S.A. 32 25N 91 12w
98 Talluza, Jordan 32 17N 35 18E
78 Talmaciu, Rumania ...45 38N 24 19E
157 Talmage, Canada 49 46N 103 40w
143 Talmalmo, Australia .35 51s 148 58E
50 Talmont, France 46 27N 1 37w
88 Talnoye, U.S.S.R. 48 57N 30 35E
104 Taloda, India 21 34N 74 19E
127 Talodi, Sudan 10 35N 30 22E
87 Talovaya, U.S.S.R. ...51 13N 40 38E
37 Talsarnau, Wales, UK 52 54N 4 4w
122 Talsint, Morocco 32 41N 3 29w
172 Taltal, Chile 25 23s 70 40w
108 Talu, Indonesia 0 12N 99 50E
145 Talwood, Australia 28 27s 149 20E
143 Talyawalka Cr., N.S.W., Austral. 32 20s 143 0E
37 Talybont, Brecon, Wales, United Kingdom 51 52N 3 18w
37 Tal-y-llyn, Wales, U.K. 52 40N 3 44w
37 Tal-y-sarn, Wales, U.K. 53 3N 4 12w
164 Tama, U.S.A. 41 56N 92 37w
108 Tama Abu Ra., Malay. 3 10N 115 0E
142 Tamala, W. Australia 26 35s 113 40E

MAP

125 Tamale, Ghana 9 22N 0 50W
88 Taman, U.S.S.R. 45 14N 36 41E
122 Tamanar, Morocco 31 1N 9 46W
114 Tamano, Japan 34 35N 133 59E
122 Tamanrasser, W., Alg. 22 0N 2 0E
123 Tamanrasset (Fort Laperrine), Algeria .22 56N 5 30E
161 Tamaqua, U.S.A. 40 46N 75 58W
36 Tamar, R., Eng., U.K. 50 33N 4 15W
64 Tamarite de Litera, Sp. 41 52N 0 25E
59 Tamási, Hungary 46 40N 18 18E
125 Tamaské, Niger 14 55N 5 55E
129 Tamatave, Malagasy Republic 18 10S 49 25E
168 Tamaulipas, st., Mex. 24 0N 99 0W
168 Tamaulipas, Sierra de, Mexico 23 30N 98 20W
168 Tamazula, Mexico 24 55N 106 58W
124 Tambacounda, Senegal 13 55N 13 45W
127 Tambai, Ethiopia 16 32N 37 13E
132 Tambara, Mozambique 16 45S 34 10E
108 Tambelan Is., Indon. . 1 0N 107 30E
142 Tambellup, W. Austral. 34 4S 117 37E
144 Tambo, Australia 24 54S 146 14E
174 Tambo de Mora, Peru 13 30S 76 20W
108 Tambora Mt., Indon. . 8 12S 118 5E
87 Tambov, U.S.S.R. 52 45N 41 20E
62 Tambre R., Spain 42 55N 8 30W
109 Tambuku, Mt., Indon. 7 8S 113 40E
127 Tambura, Sudan 5 40N 27 25E
124 Tamchakett, Mauritania 17 25N 10 40W
34 Tame R., Eng., U.K. .52 43N 1 45W
62 Tamega R., Portugal .41 12N 8 5W
122 Tamegroute, Morocco 30 12N 5 49W
176 Tamel Aike, Argentina 48 10S 71 0W
123 Tamelelt, Algeria 26 30N 6 14E
122 Tamelelt, Morocco 31 51N 7 21W
103 Tamenglong, India 25 0N 93 35E
36 Tamerton Foliot, England, U.K. 50 25N 4 10W
123 Tamerza, Tunisia 34 23N 7 58E
125 Tamgak, Mts., Niger .19 12N 8 35E
168 Tamiahua, Laguna de, Mexico 21 30N 97 30W
106 Tamil Nadu, st., India 11 0N 77 0E
55 Tamines, Belgium 50 27N 4 27E
112 Taming, China 36 20N 115 10E
57 Tamins, Switzerland .46 50N 9 24E
105 Tamiuk, India 22 18N 87 58E
83 Tammisaari, Finland .60 0N 23 29E
98 Tammun', Jordan 32 18N 35 23E
80 Tämnaren L., Sweden 60 10N 17 25E
163 Tampa, U.S.A. 27 57N 82 30W
163 Tampa B., U.S.A. 27 40N 82 40W
83 Tampere, Finland 61 30N 23 50E
168 Tampico, Mexico 22 20N 97 50W
107 Tampin, Malaysia 2 28N 102 13E
122 Tamri, Morocco 30 49N 9 50W
99 Tamridah, Socotra I. .12 35N 54 2E
112 Tamsagbulag, Mong. .47 15N 117 5E
122 Tamsagout, Mali 24 5N 6 35W
86 Tamsalu, U.S.S.R. 59 11N 26 8E
174 Tamshiyacu, Peru 4 0S 73 0W
113 Tamsui, Taiwan 25 10N 121 28E
58 Tamsweg, Austria 47 7N 13 49E
103 Tamu, Burma 24 13N 94 12E
63 Tamuja R., Spain 39 33N 6 8W
145 Tamworth, Australia .31 0S 150 58E
34 Tamworth, Eng., U.K. 52 38N 1 2W
113 Tan Kiang, R., China 33 25N 111 0E
82 Tana, Norway 70 23N 28 13E
82 Tana Fd., Norway 70 35N 28 30E
127 Tana, L., Ethiopia 13 5N 37 30E
131 Tana R., Kenya 0 50S 39 45E
56 Tana R., Norway 69 50N 26 0E
152 Tanacross, Alas., USA 63 40N 143 30W
73 Tangaro R., Italy 40 35N 15 25E
109 Tanahdjampea I., Indon. 7 10S 120 35E
108 Tanahgrogot, Indon. . 1 55S 116 15E
108 Tanahmasa I., Indon. 0 5S 98 29E
109 Tanahmerah, Indon.... 6 0S 140 7E
138 Tanami Des., N. Terr., Australia 23 15S 132 20E
152 Tanana, Alaska, U.S.A. 65 10N 152 15W
152 Tanana R., Alas., U.S.A. 64 25N 145 30W
129 Tananarive, Malag. ...18 55S 47 31E
79 Tananger, Norway 58 57N 5 37E
122 Tanant, Morocco 31 54N 6 56W
70 Tanaro R., Italy 44 9N 7 50E
72 Tanaunella, Italy 40 42N 9 45E
145 Tanbar, Australia 25 55S 142 0E
48 Tancarville, France ...46 50N 0 55W
113 Tanchai, China 25 58N 107 49E
112 Tanchon, North Korea 40 30N 129 0E
113 Tanchow, China 19 33N 109 22E
105 Tanda, India 28 57N 78 56E
105 Tanda, India 26 33N 82 35E
109 Tandag, Philippines ... 9 4N 126 9E
131 Tandala, Tanzania 9 25S 34 15E
78 Tăndarei, Rumania ...44 39N 27 40E
172 Tandil, Argentina 37 15S 59 6W
122 Tandjara, W., Alg. 23 24N 3 15E
108 Tandjung, Indonesia . 2 10S 115 25E
108 Tandjung Balai, Indon. 2 55N 99 44E
108 Tandjung Redeb, Indon. 2 12N 117 35E
108 Tandjung Selor, Indon. 2 55N 117 25E
108 Tandjungbatu, Indon. 2 23N 118 3E
108 Tandjungenim, Indon. 3 51S 103 35E
108 Tandjungkarang, Indon. 5 20S 105 10E
108 Tandjungpandan, Indon. 2 43S 107 38E
108 Tandjungpinang, Indon. 1 5N 104 30E
109 Tandjungpriok, Indon. 6 8S 106 55E
108 Tandjungpura, Indon. 3 59N 98 21E
104 Tandlianwald, W. Pak. 31 3N 73 9E
104 Tando Adam, W. Pak. 25 45N 68 40E
143 Tandou I., Australia .32 40S 142 0E
46 Tandragee, N. Ire., U.K. 54 22N 6 23W
80 Tandsbyn, Sweden 63 0N 14 35W
106 Tandur, India 19 11N 79 30E
146 Taneatua, New Zealand 38 4S 177 1E
114 Tanega-shima, I., Japan 30 30N 131 0E
107 Tanen Range, Thailand 19 40N 99 0E
122 Tanezrouft, Algeria ...23 9N 0 11E
44 Tang, Ireland 53 31N 7 49W
103 Tang Pass, Tibet, China 32 59N 92 17E
131 Tanga, & dist., Tanzania 5 5S 39 2E
130 Tanga, reg., Tanzania 5 20S 38 0E
144 Tanga Is., N. Guin. ... 3 45S 148 17E
105 Tangail, East Pakistan 24 15N 90 0E
131 Tanganyika, L., E. Afr. 6 40S 30 0E
132 Tangata, Mozambique 17 13S 34 17E
109 Tangerang, Indonesia 6 12S 106 39E
56 Tangerhütte, Germany 52 26N 11 50E
56 Tangermünde, Germany 52 32N 11 57E
113 Tanghing, China 21 30N 108 2E
111 Tanghla Range, Mts., Asia 33 10N 90 0E
113 Tangho, China 32 47N 113 2E
122 Tangier (Tanger), Mor. 35 50N 5 49W
107 Tangkak, Malaysia 2 18N 102 34E
112 Tangku, China 39 0N 117 40E
103 Tangla Ra., Tibet, China 33 0N 90 0E
144 Tangorin, Australia ...21 45S 144 9E
103 Tangra Tso, L., Tibet, China 31 25N 85 30E
113 Tangshan, Anhwei, China 34 23N 116 34E
112 Tangshan, Hopei, China 39 40N 118 10E
113 Tangtu, China 31 37N 118 39E
125 Tanguiéta, Dahomey .10 40N 1 21E
131 Tangulbwe, Kenya 0 45N 35 25E
113 Tangyang, China 30 50N 111 45E
113 Tanhsien (Nata), China 19 30N 109 17E
109 Tanimbar Is., Indon. . 7 30S 131 30E
113 Taning, see Wuki, China 31 27N 109 46E
109 Tanjay, Philippines ... 9 30N 123 5E
106 Tanjore, see Thanjavur10 48N 79 12E
104 Tank, West Pakistan .32 14N 70 25E
80 Tänndalen, Sweden ...62 33N 12 18E
154 Tannin, Canada 49 40N 91 0W
81 Tannis B., Denmark .57 40N 10 10E
111 Tannu Ola Mts., Asia .51 0N 94 0E
124 Tano R., Ghana 6 0N 2 30W
123 Tanoumrout, Algeria .23 2N 5 31E
125 Tanout, Niger 14 50N 8 55E
126 Tanta, Egypt 30 45N 30 57E
122 Tantan, Morocco 28 29N 11 1W
168 Tantoyuca, Mexico ...21 21N 98 10W
98 Tantura, see Dor, Israel 32 37N 34 55E
106 Tanuku, India 16 45N 81 44E
58 Tanum, Sweden 58 42N 11 20E
145 Tanunda, S. Australia 34 30S 139 0E
106 Tanur, India 11 1N 75 46E
50 Tanus, France 44 8N 2 19E
34 Tanworth, Eng., U.K. 52 20N 1 50W
131 Tanzania, state, E. Afr. 6 40S 34 0E
113 Taohsien, China 25 37N 111 24E
112 Taokow, China 35 30N 114 30E
112 Taonan, China 45 30N 122 20E
73 Taormina, Italy 37 52N 15 16E
167 Taos, U.S.A. 36 28N 105 35W
122 Taoudenni, Mali 22 40N 3 55W
122 Taoudrart, Adrar, Alg. 24 25N 2 24E
122 Taounate, Morocco 34 32N 4 41W
122 Taourirt, Algeria 26 37N 0 8E
122 Taourirt, Morocco 34 20N 2 47W
122 Taouz, Morocco 31 2N 4 0W
113 Taoyuan, China 29 8N 111 15E
113 Taoyuan, Taiwan 25 0N 121 4E
86 Tapa, U.S.S.R. 59 15N 26 0E
113 Tapa Shan, Mts., China 31 45N 109 30E
107 Tapah, Malaysia 4 12N 101 15E
175 Tapajós R., Brazil 4 30S 56 10W
108 Tapaktuan, Indonesia 3 30N 97 10E
112 Tapanshang, China 43 40N 118 20E
147 Tapanui, New Zealand 45 56S 169 18E
174 Tapauá, Brazil 5 40S 64 20W
174 Tapauá R., Brazil...... 6 0S 65 40W
62 Tapia, Spain 43 34N 6 56W
59 Tapiószele, Hungary .47 45N 19 55E
59 Tapolca, Hungary 46 53N 17 29E
162 Tappahannock, U.S.A. 37 56N 76 50W
124 Tappita, Liberia 6 36N 8 52W
124 Tappo, Ghana 10 10N 2 35E
103 Tapsing, China 30 22N 96 25E
104 Tapti R., India 21 25N 75 0E
109 Tapul Group, Is., Phil. 5 35N 121 3E
174 Tapuruquara, Brazil . 0 23S 65 1W
173 Taquara, Brazil 29 36N 50 46W
175 Taquari R., Brazil 18 10S 56 0W
145 Tara, Queens., Austral. 27 17S 150 31E
160 Tara, Canada 44 28N 81 9W
132 Tara, Zambia 16 58S 26 45E
90 Tara, U.S.S.R. 56 55N 74 30E
132 Tara, Zambia 16 58S 26 45E
74 Tara R., Yugoslavia ...43 10N 19 20E
100 Tarabulus, Lebanon ...34 31N 33 52E
123 Tarabulus, Libya see Tripoli 32 49N 13 7E
146 Taradale, New Zealand 39 33S 176 53E
143 Tarago, N.S.W., Austral. 35 6S 149 39E
108 Tarakan, Indonesia ... 3 20N 117 35E
143 Taralga, N.S.W., Austral. 34 26S 149 52E
147 Taramakau R., N.Z. .42 43S 171 51E
143 Tarana, N.S.W., Austral. 33 31S 149 52E
104 Taranagar, India 28 43N 75 9E
146 Taranaki, dist., N.Z. .39 5S 174 51E
64 Tarancón, Spain 40 1N 3 1W
104 Taranga, India 23 56N 72 43E
104 Taranga Hill, India ...24 0N 72 40E
42 Taransay I., Scot., U.K. 57 54N 7 0W
42 Taransay, Sd. of, Scotland, U.K. 57 52N 7 0W
73 Taranto, Italy 40 30N 17 11E
73 Taranto G. di, Italy ...40 0N 17 15E
174 Tarapaca, Colombia ... 2 56S 69 46W
172 Tarapaca, prov., Chile 20 45S 69 30W
51 Tarare, France 45 54N 4 26E
146 Tararua Range, N.Z. .40 45S 175 25E
50 Tarascon, Ariège, Fr. .42 50N 1 37E
51 Tarascon, Bouches-du-Rhone, France 43 48N 4 39E
88 Tarashcha, U.S.S.R. ...49 30N 30 31E
123 Tarat, Algeria 26 4N 9 7E
174 Tarauacá, Brazil 8 6S 70 48W
174 Tarauaca R., Brazil ... 7 30S 70 30W
51 Taravo R., Corsica, Fr. 41 48N 8 52E
109 Tarawasi, Indonesia ... 2 19S 139 32E
146 Tarawera, N.Z. 39 2S 176 36E
146 Tarawera Lake, N.Z. .38 13S 176 27E
146 Tarawera Mt., N.Z. ...38 14S 176 32E
64 Tarazona, Spain 41 55N 1 43W
65 Tarazona de la Mancha, Spain 39 16N 1 55W
111 Tarbagatai Mts., Mong. 48 30N 99 0E
131 Tarbaj, Kenya 2 13N 40 7E
43 Tarbat Ness, Scot., U.K. 57 52S 3 48W
44 Tarbert, Ireland 52 34N 9 22W
40 Tarbert, Argyll, Scotland, U.K. 55 55N 5 25W
42 Tarbert, Harris, Scotland, U.K. 57 54N 6 49W
42 Tarbert L. E., Harris, Scotland, U.K. 57 50N 6 45W
40 Tarbert L. W., Argyll, Scotland, U.K. 55 58N 5 30W
42 Tarbert L. W., Harris, Scotland, U.K. 57 55N 6 56W
50 Tarbes, France 43 15N 0 3E
40 Tarbet, Dunbarton, Scotland, U.K. 56 13N 4 44W
42 Tarbet, Inverness, Scotland, U.K. 56 58N 5 38W
40 Tarbolton, Scot., U.K. 55 30N 4 30W
163 Tarboro, U.S.A. 35 55N 77 3W
123 Tarbu, Libya 26 0N 15 5E
78 Tarcau, Munţii, Mts., Rumania 46 39N 26 7E
71 Tarcento, Italy 46 12N 13 12E
138 Tarcoola, S. Australia 30 44S 134 36E
145 Tarcoon, N.S.W., Austral. 30 15S 146 35E
122 Tarda, Morocco 31 40N 4 37W
50 Tardets, France 43 7N 0 53W
111 Tardin, China 37 16N 92 30E
143 Taree, N.S.W., Austral. 31 50S 152 30E
127 Tareina, Ethiopia 10 48N 40 36E
51 Tarentaise, dist., Fr. .45 30N 6 35E
126 Tarf Shaqq al Abd, Saudi Arabia 26 50N 36 6E
126 Tarfa, Waldi el, Egypt 28 16N 31 15E
122 Tarfaya, Morocco 27 55N 12 55W
50 Targon, France 44 44N 0 16W
78 Târgu-Frumos, Rum. 47 12N 27 2E
78 Târgu Neamt, Rum. .47 12N 26 25E
78 Târgu Ocna, Rumania 46 16N 26 39E
78 Târgu Săcuesc, Rum. .46 0N 26 10E
122 Targuist, Morocco 34 59N 4 14W
122 Tarhit, Algeria 30 58N 2 0W
123 Tarhunch, Libya 37 27N 13 43E
126 Tarib, Wadi, Si. Arabia 18 30N 43 23E
63 Tarifa, Spain 36 1N 5 36W
172 Tarija, Bolivia 21 30S 64 40W
172 Tarija, dept., Bolivia .21 30S 63 30W
111 Tarim R., China 40 40N 85 20E
131 Tarime, Tanzania 1 17S 34 24E
109 Taritoe R., Indon. 3 0S 138 5E
135 Tarkastad, S. Africa ...32 0S 26 16E
88 Tarkhankut C., U.S.S.R. 45 25N 32 30E
90 Tarko Sale, U.S.S.R. .64 55N 77 50E
124 Tarkwa, Ghana 5 20N 2 0W
109 Tarlac, Philippines 15 30N 120 25E
43 Tarland, Scot., U.K. .57 8N 2 51W
38 Tarleton, Eng., U.K. .53 41N 2 50W
81 Tarm, Denmark 55 56N 8 31E
174 Tarma, Peru 11 25S 75 45W
50 Tarn, dépt., France ...43 9N 2 8E
50 Tarn R., France 43 57N 2 25E
50 Tarn-et-Garonne, dépt., France 44 8N 1 20E
82 Tärna, Sweden 65 45N 15 10E
59 Tarna R., Hungary ...48 0N 20 5E
78 Târnava Mare R., Rum. 46 15N 24 30E
78 Târnava Mica R., Rum. 46 17N 24 30E
81 Tarnby, Denmark 55 37N 12 36E
78 Tânova, Rumania 45 23N 22 1E
59 Tarnów, Poland 50 3N 21 0E
60 Tarnowskie Góry, Pol. 50 27N 18 54E
70 Taro R., Italy 44 37N 9 58E
145 Tarong, Australia 26 48S 151 45E
145 Taroom, Australia 25 36S 149 48E
122 Taroudannt, Morocco .30 30N 8 52W
56 Tarp, Germany 54 40N 9 25E
163 Tarpon Springs, U.S.A. 28 8N 82 42W
38 Tarporley, Eng., U.K. 53 10N 2 42W
71 Tarquinia, Italy 42 15N 11 45E
98 Tarqumiya, Jordan ...31 35N 35 1E
64 Tarragona, Spain 41 5N 1 17E
64 Tarragona, prov., Spain 41 0N 1 0E
145 Tarraleah, Tas., Austral. 42 9S 146 14E
64 Tarrasa, Spain 41 26N 2 1E
64 Tárrega, Spain 41 39N 1 9E
131 Tarri Marshen, Somali Rep. 0 45N 41 28E
161 Tarrytown, U.S.A. 41 5N 73 52W
98 Tarshiha, see Me'ona, Israel 33 1N 35 15E
123 Tarso Emissi, Chad ...21 27N 18 36E
123 Tarso Tieroko, Chad .20 46N 17 58E
123 Tarso Toon, Chad 21 2N 17 39E
123 Tarso Tourari, Mt., Chad 21 37N 17 16E
100 Tarsus, Turkey 36 58N 34 55E
172 Tartagal, Argentina ...22 30S 63 50W
91 Tartary Str., U.S.S.R. 54 0N 141 0E
143 Tartna Point, Australia 32 54S 142 24E
86 Tartu, U.S.S.R. 58 25N 26 58E
100 Tartus, Syria 34 55N 35 55E
87 Tarussa, U.S.S.R. 54 44N 37 10E
107 Tarutao, Ko, I., Thailand 6 33N 99 40E
108 Tarutung, Indonesia . 2 0N 99 0E
43 Tarves, Scot., U.K. ...57 22N 2 13W
71 Tarvisio, Italy 46 31N 13 35E
123 Tarz Ulli, Algeria 25 46N 9 44E
123 Tasawah, Libya 26 0N 13 37E
154 Taschereau, Canada ...48 40N 78 40W
156 Taseko Mt., Canada ...51 12N 123 7W
106 Tasgaon, India 17 2N 74 39E
127 Ta'shan, Saudi Arabia 16 31N 42 33E
90 Tashauz, U.S.S.R. 42 0N 59 20E
105 Tashi Chho Dzong, Bhutan 27 31N 89 45E
111 Tashigong, Tibet, China 33 0N 79 30E
112 Tashihkao, China 40 47N 122 29E
90 Tashkent, U.S.S.R. ...41 20N 69 10E
90 Tashkumyr, U.S.S.R. .41 40N 72 10E
111 Tashkurgan, China 37 51N 74 57E
101 Tashkurghan, Afghan. 36 45N 67 40E
113 Tasi Ho, R., China 28 20N 119 40E
109 Tasikmalaja, Indonesia 7 18S 108 12E
113 Tasin (Yangli), China .22 57N 107 15E
82 Tasjön L., Sweden 64 15N 15 45E
98 Taşköpru, Turkey 41 30N 34 15E
147 Tasman Bay, N.Z. 40 59S 173 25E
147 Tasman Mount, N.Z. .43 34S 170 12E
147 Tasman Mts., N.Z. 41 3S 172 25E
139 Tasman Pen., Australia 43 10S 147 52E
147 Tasman R., N.Z. 45 52S 170 9E
136 Tasman Sea, Pac. Oc. 42 30S 168 0E
145 Tasmania, I. st., Australia 49 0S 146 30E
78 Tăşnad, Rumania 47 30N 22 33E
123 Tassil n-Ajjer, Algeria 25 47N 8 1E
123 Tassili-Oua-Ahaggar, Algeria 20 41N 5 30E
122 Tassil Tin-Rerhoh, Alg. 20 5N 3 55E
59 Tata, Hungary 47 37N 18 19E
122 Tata, Morocco 29 46N 7 50W
59 Tatabánya, Hungary .47 32N 18 25E
87 Tatar A.S.S.R., U.S.S.R. 55 30N 51 30E
90 Tatarsk, U.S.S.R. 55 20N 75 50E
114 Tateyama, Japan 35 0N 139 50E
156 Tathlina L., Canada ...60 30N 117 30W
113 Tatien, China 25 45N 118 0E
113 Tating, China 27 0N 105 35E
157 Tatinnai L., Canada ...60 50N 97 50W
156 Tatlayoka Lake, Can. 51 35N 124 24W
157 Tatnam C., Canada ...57 20N 91 0W
143 Tatong, Vic., Australia 36 43S 146 9E
53 Tatra Mts., Cz. 49 20N 20 0E
111 Tatsaitan, China 37 55N 95 0E
113 Tatsu, China 29 40N 105 45E
104 Tatta, West Pakistan 24 42N 67 55E
38 Tattenhall, Eng., U.K. 53 7N 2 47W
173 Tatui, Brazil 23 25S 48 0W
165 Tatum, U.S.A. 33 16N 103 16W
113 Tatung, Anhwei, China 30 50N 117 45E
112 Tatung, Shansi, China 40 10N 113 10E
112 Tatungkow, China 39 55N 124 10E
143 Tatura, Vic., Australia 36 29S 145 16E
100 Tatvan, Turkey 37 28N 42 27E
174 Tauapecacu, Brazil 2 35S 61 0W
173 Taubate, Brazil 23 5S 45 30W
57 Tauberbischofsheim, Germany 49 37N 9 40E
56 Taucha, Germany 51 22N 12 31E
58 Tauern Tunnel, Austria 47 0N 13 12E
127 Taufikia, Sudan 9 24N 31 37E
146 Taumarunui, N.Z. 38 53S 175 15E
174 Taumaturgo, Brazil ... 9 0S 73 50W
133 Taung, C. Prov., S. Afr. 27 33S 24 47E
103 Taungdwingyi, Burma 20 1N 95 40E
103 Taunggyi, Burma 20 50N 97 0E
103 Taungup, Burma 18 48N 94 20E
103 Taungup Pass, Burma 18 20N 93 40E
105 Taunsa Barrage, West Pakistan (inset) ...31 0N 71 0E
36 Taunton, Eng., U.K. .51 1N 3 7W
29 Taunton, Vale of, England, U.K. 51 3N 3 10W
57 Taunus Mt., W. Ger. .50 15N 8 20E
146 Taupo, New Zealand .38 41S 176 7E
146 Taupo L., New Zealand 38 46S 175 55E
100 Tauq, Iraq 35 12N 44 29E
146 Tauranga, New Zealand 37 35S 176 11E
146 Tauranga Harb., N.Z. 37 30S 176 5E
86 Taurage, U.S.S.R. 55 14N 22 28E
154 Taureau, Lac, Canada 46 50N 73 40W
73 Taurianova, Italy 38 22N 16 1E
100 Taurus Mts., Turkey .37 0N 35 0E
64 Táuste, Spain 41 58N 1 18W
89 Tauz, U.S.S.R. 41 0N 45 40E
157 Tavani, Canada 62 10N 93 30W
100 Tavas, Turkey 37 35N 29 8E
90 Tavda, U.S.S.R. 58 7N 65 8E
90 Tavda R., U.S.S.R. ...59 30N 63 0E
49 Taverny, France 49 2N 2 13E
131 Taveta, Tanzania 3 31N 37 37E
55 Tavier, Belgium 50 30N 5 28E
51 Tavignano R., Corsica, France 42 14N 9 20E
63 Tavira, Portugal 37 8N 7 40W
160 Tavistock, Canada 43 21N 80 53W
36 Tavistock, Eng., U.K. 50 33N 4 9W
72 Tavolara I., Italy 40 55N 9 40E
62 Tavora R., Portugal ...41 0N 7 30W
103 Tavoy, Burma 14 7N 98 18E
107 Tavoy I. (Mali Kyun), Burma 13 0N 98 20E
36 Taw R., Eng., U.K. ...50 58N 3 58W
103 Tawang, India 27 37N 91 50E
162 Tawas City, U.S.A. ...44 16N 83 31W
108 Tawau, E. Malaysia ... 4 12N 117 58E
46 Tawnyinah, Ireland ...53 55N 8 45W
123 Taworgha, Libya 32 1N 15 2E
113 Tawu, Taiwan 22 30N 120 50E
41 Tay, Firth of, Scot., U.K. 56 25N 3 8W
41 Tay L., Scot., U.K. ...56 30N 4 10W
142 Tay, L., W. Australia 32 55S 120 48E
41 Tay R., Scot., U.K. ...56 37N 3 58W
41 Tay Bridge, Scot., U.K. 56 28N 3 0W
107 Tay Ninh, S. Vietnam 11 20N 106 5E
174 Tayabamba, Peru 8 15S 77 10W
113 Tayen, China 30 4N 115 0E
161 Taylor, Pa., U.S.A. ...41 23N 75 43W
165 Taylor, Tex., U.S.A. .30 30N 97 30W
147 Taylor, Mt., N.Z. 43 30S 171 20E
167 Taylor Mt., U.S.A. 35 16N 107 50W
164 Taylorville, U.S.A. 39 32N 89 20W
100 Tayma, Saudi Arabia .27 35N 38 45E
91 Taymyr L., U.S.S.R. .74 50N 102 0E
91 Taymyr Pen., U.S.S.R. 75 0N 100 0E
40 Taynuilt, Scot., U.K. .56 25N 5 15W
41 Tayport, Scot., U.K. .56 27N 2 52W
109 Taytay, Philippines ...10 45N 119 30E
113 Tayu, China 25 38N 114 9E
111 Tayulehsze, China 29 15N 98 1E
113 Tayung, China 29 8N 110 30E
90 Taz R., U.S.S.R. 65 40N 82 0E
122 Taza, Morocco 34 10N 4 0W
122 Tazenakht, Morocco ...30 46N 7 3W
157 Tazin L., Canada 59 40N 109 0W
122 Tazoult, Morocco 30 30N 7 49W
89 Tbilisi (Tiflis), U.S.S.R. 41 50N 44 50E
121 Tchad (Chad), rep., Afr. 12 30N 17 15E
125 Tchaourou, Dahomey 8 58N 2 40E
128 Tchibanga, Gabon 2 45S 11 12E
113 Tchpao (Tienpao), China 23 25N 106 47E
60 Tczew, Poland 54 8N 18 50E
147 Te Anau L., N.Z. 45 15S 167 45E
146 Te Araroa, N.Z. 37 39S 178 25E
146 Te Aroha, N.Z. 37 32S 175 44E
146 Te Awamutu, N.Z. 38 1S 175 20E
146 Te Kaha, New Zealand 37 44S 177 44E
146 Te Karaka, N.Z. 38 26S 177 53E

MAP
146 Te Kauwhata, N.Z. ...37 25S 175 9E
147 Te Kinga, New Zealand 42 35S 171 31E
146 Te Kopuru, N.Z. 36 2S 173 56E
146 Te Kuiti, New Zealand 38 20S 175 11E
146 Te Puke, New Zealand 37 46S 176 22E
147 Te Waewae B., N.Z. .46 13S 167 33E
78 Teaca, Rumania 46 55N 24 30E
165 Teague, U.S.A. 31 40N 96 20W
42 Teangue, Scotland, U.K. 57 7N 5 52W
73 Teano, Italy 41 15N 14 1E
142 Teano Ra., W. Austral. 24 20S 118 0E
168 Teapa, Mexico 17 35N 92 56W
63 Teba, Spain 36 59N 4 55W
127 Tebbe, Ethiopia 9 6N 37 8E
89 Teberda, U.S.S.R. 43 30N 43 54E
123 Tébessa, Algeria 35 28N 8 9E
108 Tebing Tinggi, Indon. 3 38S 102 1E
123 Tébourba, Tunisia 36 35N 9 2E
123 Téboursouk, Tunisia .36 29N 9 10E
126 Tebuk, Saudi Arabia .28 28N 36 30E
89 Tebulos Mt., U.S.S.R. 42 36N 45 25E
1 Tecapa, Vol. Central America 13 30N 86 0W
124 Techiman, Ghana 7 35N 1 58W
168 Tecuala, Mexico 22 24N 105 30W
78 Tecuci, Rumania 45 51N 27 27E
162 Tecumseh, U.S.A. 42 1N 83 59W
46 Tedavnet, Ireland 54 19N 7 2W
39 Tees B., Eng., U.K. ...54 37N 1 10W
38 Tees, R., Eng., U.K. .54 36N 1 58W
41 Teesdale, Eng., U.K. .54 37N 2 10W
39 Teesside, Eng., U.K. .54 37N 1 13W
160 Teeswater, Canada 44 0N 81 16W
109 Teeth, The, Mt., Phil. 9 27N 118 25E
174 Tefé, Brazil 3 25S 64 50W
109 Tegal, Indonesia 6 52S 109 8E
54 Tegelen, Netherlands .51 20N 6 9E
73 Tegiano, Italy 40 24N 15 32E
105 Teghra, India 25 30N 85 34E
125 Tegina, Nigeria 10 5N 6 11E
169 Tegucigalpa, Hond. ...14 10N 87 0W
167 Tehachapi, U.S.A. 35 11N 118 29W
167 Tehachapi Mts., U.S.A. 35 0N 118 40W
126 Tehamiyam, Sudan ...18 20N 36 45E
126 Tehilla, Sudan 17 42N 36 6E
124 Tehini, Ivory Coast ... 9 39N 3 32W
112 Tehping, China 37 26N 117 0E
101 Tehran, Iran 35 44N 51 30E
111 Tehtsin (Atuntze), China 28 45N 98 58E
168 Tehuacan, Mexico 18 20N 97 30W
168 Tehuantepec, Mexico .16 10N 95 19W
168 Tehuantepec, Isthmus of, Mexico 17 0N 94 30W
37 Teifi R., Wales, U.K. .52 4N 4 14W
36 Teign R., Eng., U.K. .50 41N 3 52W
36 Teignmouth, Eng., U.K. 50 33N 3 30W
87 Teikovo, U.S.S.R. 56 55N 40 30E
86 Teishyai, U.S.S.R. 55 59N 22 14E
131 Teita, dist., Kenya 3 45S 38 0E
78 Teius, Rumania 46 12N 23 40E
124 Teixeira Pinto (Canchunga), Port. Guin. 12 10N 13 55E
63 Tejo (Tagus), R., Port. 39 15N 8 35W
164 Tekamah, U.S.A. 41 48N 96 14W
147 Tekapo, L., N.Z. 43 53S 170 33E
147 Tekapo R., N.Z. 44 15S 170 23E
168 Tekax, Mexico 20 20N 89 30W
90 Tekeli, U.S.S.R. 44 50N 79 0E
78 Tekija, Yugoslavia 44 42N 22 26E
100 Tekirdag, Turkey 40 58N 27 30E
106 Tekkali, India 18 43N 84 24E
166 Tekoa, U.S.A. 47 19N 117 4W
98 Tel Adashim, Israel ...32 39N 35 17E
98 Tel Aviv–Jaffa, Israel 32 4N 34 48E
98 Tel Hanan, Israel 32 47N 35 3E
98 Tel Malhata, Israel 31 13N 35 2E
98 Tel Mond, Israel 32 15N 34 56E
169 Tela, Honduras 15 40N 87 28W
122 Télagh, Algeria 34 51N 0 32W
108 Telanaipura, Indonesia 1 38S 103 30E
89 Telavi, U.S.S.R. 42 0N 45 30E
78 Telciu, Rumania 47 25N 24 24E
78 Telega, Rumania 45 17N 25 45E
156 Telegraph Cr., Canada 58 0N 131 10W
86 Telekhany, U.S.S.R. .52 30N 25 46E
79 Telemark Fylke, Co., Norway 59 30N 8 30E
62 Teleño, Spain 42 23N 6 22W
78 Teleorman R., Rum. .44 15N 25 20E
78 Teleorman, Reg., Rum. 44 0N 25 10E
174 Teles Pires (São Manuel), R., Brazil . 8 40S 57 0W
167 Telescope Peak, Mt., U.S.A. 36 6N 117 7W
34 Telford, England 52 42N 2 29W
58 Telfs, Austria 47 19N 11 4E
56 Telgte, Germany 51 59N 7 46E
145 Telichie, S. Australia .31 45S 139 59E
124 Télimélé, Guinea 10 54N 13 2W
112 Telisze, China 39 50N 112 0E
156 Telkwa, Canada 54 41N 126 56W
98 Tell, Jordan 32 12N 35 12E
98 Tell Asur Mt., Jordan 31 59N 35 17E
162 Tell City, U.S.A. 38 0N 86 44W
14 Teller, Alaska, U.S.A. 65 12N 166 24W
106 Tellicherry, India 11 45N 75 30E
167 Telluride, U.S.A. 37 58N 107 54W
122 Telmesti, Morocco 31 48N 9 11W
107 Telok Anson, Malaysia 4 0N 101 10E
107 Telom R., Malaysia ... 4 20N 101 46E
122 Telouet M'Goun, Mor. 31 26N 7 4W
84 Telpos Iz., Mt., USSR 63 35N 57 30E
176 Telsen, Argentina 42 30S 66 50W
56 Teltow, Germany 52 24N 13 15E
108 Teluk Betung, Indon. 5 29S 105 17E
108 Telukbutun, Indonesia 4 5N 108 7E
108 Telukdalem, Indonesia 0 45N 97 50E
125 Tema, Ghana 5 41N 0 0E
154 Temagami L., Canada 47 0N 80 10W
109 Temanggung, Indonesia 7 18S 110 10E
168 Temax, Mexico 21 10N 88 50W
130 Temba, Angola 10 33S 15 45E
107 Tembeling R., Malaysia 4 20N 102 23E
90 Temirtau, U.S.S.R. ...50 5N 72 56E
64 Tembleque, Spain 39 41N 3 30W
135 Tembuland, dist., C. Prov., S. Afr. 31 35S 28 0E
167 Temecula, U.S.A. 33 26N 117 6W
34 Teme R., Eng., U.K. .52 23N 3 5W
107 Temerloh, Malaysia ... 3 27N 102 25E
90 Temir Tau, U.S.S.R. .53 10N 87 20E
154 Témiskaming, Canada 46 44N 79 5W
145 Temma, Tas., Australia 41 17S 144 50E
87 Temnikov, U.S.S.R. ...54 40N 43 11E
72 Temo R., Italy 40 20N 8 30E
143 Temora, N.S.W., Austral. 34 30S 147 30E
168 Temosachic, Mexico ...28 58N 107 50W
108 Tempaka, Indonesia ... 4 53S 114 50E
135 Tempe, O.F.S., S. Africa 29 1S 26 13E
167 Tempe, U.S.A. 33 26N 111 59W
108 Tempino, Indonesia ... 1 55S 103 23E
72 Tempio, Pausania, Italy 40 53N 9 6E
165 Temple, U.S.A. 31 5N 97 28W
144 Temple B., Australia .12 15S 143 3E
41 Temple Sowerby, England, U.K. 54 38N 2 33W
44 Templemore, Ireland .52 48N 7 50W
44 Templenoe, Ireland 51 52N 9 40W
144 Templeton, Australia .18 30S 142 30E
37 Templeton, Wales, U.K. 51 46N 4 45W
144 Templeton R., Austral. 21 0S 138 40E
56 Templin, Germany 53 8N 13 31E
46 Tempo, N. Ire., U.K. .54 23N 7 28W
88 Temryuk, U.S.S.R. 45 15N 37 11E
74 Temska R., Y.–slavia 43 17N 22 33E
176 Temuco, Chile 38 50S 72 50W
147 Temuka, N.Z. 44 14S 171 17E
168 Tenabo, Mexico 20 2N 90 12W
156 Tenakee Springs, Alaska, U.S.A. 57 50N 135 25W
106 Tenali, India 16 15N 80 35E
168 Tenango, Mexico 19 0N 99 40W
168 Tenancingo, Mexico ...18 98N 99 33W
107 Tenasserim, Burma 12 6N 99 3E
107 Tenasserim, st., Burma 14 0N 98 30E
51 Tenay, France 45 55N 5 30E
34 Tenbury, Eng., U.K. .52 18N 2 35W
37 Tenby, Wales, U.K. ...51 40N 4 42W
112 Tenchow, China 37 26N 116 20E
51 Tenda, France 44 5N 7 34E
51 Tenda, Col de, France 44 9N 7 32E
127 Tendelti, Sudan 13 1N 31 55E
123 Tendjedi, Adrar, Alg. .23 41N 7 32E
122 Tendrara, Morocco 33 3N 1 58W
126 Teneida, Egypt 25 30N 29 19E
123 Ténéré, Sahara 23 2N 16 0E
120 Tenerife, I., Canary Is. 28 20N 16 40W
122 Ténès, Algeria 36 31N 1 14E
113 T'eng Ch'ung, China .25 9N 98 22E
107 Teng R., Burma 20 30N 98 10E
112 Tengchowfu, *see* Penglai, China 37 50N 120 50E
111 Tengchung, China 24 58N 98 30E
107 Tenggoi I., Malaysia . 4 48N 103 39E
113 Tenghsien, China 35 10N 117 10E
90 Tengiz L., U.S.S.R. ...50 30N 69 0E
113 Tengko, China 32 30N 98 0E
112 Tengkow, China 39 45N 106 40E
113 Tengyün, China 23 20N 111 0E
113 Tenille, U.S.A. 32 58N 82 50W
142 Tenindewa, W. Austral. 28 30S 115 20E
106 Tenkasi, India 8 55N 77 20E
130 Tenke, Congo 11 22S 26 40E
125 Tenkodogo, Upper Volta 12 0N 0 10W
71 Tenna R., Italy 43 12N 13 43E
138 Tennant Creek, Austral 19 30S 134 0E
159 Tenessee, st., U.S.A. .36 0N 86 30W
163 Tennessee R., U.S.A. .34 30N 86 20W
108 Tenom, Malaysia 5 4N 115 38E
168 Tenosique, Mexico 17 30N 91 24W
114 Tenryu R., Japan 35 30N 137 45E
122 Tensift R., Morocco ...31 50N 8 30W
35 Tenterden, Eng., U.K. 51 4N 0 42E
145 Tenterfield, Australia .29 0S 152 0E
175 Teófilo–Otoni, Brazil .17 50S 41 30W
124 Tepa, Ghana 6 57N 20 3W
64 Ter R., Spain 42 0N 2 30E
54 Ter Apel, Netherlands 52 53N 7 5E
125 Tera, Niger 14 0N 0 57E
71 Teramo, Italy 42 40N 13 40E
143 Terang, Vic., Australia 38 3S 142 59E
146 Terawhiti, C., N.Z. 41 16S 174 38E
123 Terazit Massif de, Niger 20 2N 8 30E
100 Tercan, Turkey 39 50N 40 30E
18 Terceira I., Azores 38 43N 24 13W
106 Terdal, India 16 33N 75 9E
86 Tereboviya, U.S.S.R. .49 18N 25 44E
78 Teregova, Rumania ...45 10N 22 16E
87 Tereshka R., U.S.S.R. 52 0N 46 36E
175 Teresina, Brazil 5 2S 42 45W
63 Terges R., Portugal ...37 49N 7 41W
49 Tergnier, France 49 40N 3 17E
122 Terhazza, Mali 23 45N 4 59W
55 Terheijden, Neth. 51 38N 4 45E
122 Terkezi, Chad 18 27N 21 40E
73 Terlizzi, Italy 41 8N 16 32E
172 Termas de Chillan, Chile 36 50S 71 31W
88 Terme, Turkey 41 11N 37 0E
90 Termez, U.S.S.R. 37 0N 67 15E
49 Termini Imerese, Italy 37 59N 13 51E
168 Términos, Laguna de, Mexico 18 35N 91 30W
71 Termoli, Italy 42 0N 15 0E
46 Termon, Ireland 55 3N 7 50W
46 Termonfeckin, Ireland 53 47N 6 15W
109 Ternate, Indonesia 0 45N 127 25E
54 Terneuzen, Netherlands 51 20N 3 50E
71 Terni, Italy 42 34N 12 38E
58 Ternitz, Austria 47 43N 16 2E
86 Ternopol, U.S.S.R. 49 30N 25 40E
145 Terowie, S. Australia .38 10S 138 50E
15 Terra Nova B., Antarc. 74 50S 164 40E
156 Terrace, Canada 54 30N 128 35W
72 Terracina, Italy 41 17N 13 12E
72 Terralba, Italy 39 42N 8 38E
71 Terranuova, Italy 43 38N 11 35E
72 Terrasini Favarotta, It. 38 10N 13 4E
50 Terrasson, France 45 7N 1 19E
49 Territoire de Belfort, dept., France 47 40N 6 55E
162 Terre Haute, U.S.A. ...46 30N 75 13W
155 Terrebonne B., U.S.A. 29 15N 90 28W
122 Terrecht, Mali 20 10N 0 10W
165 Terrell, U.S.A. 32 44N 96 19W
164 Terry, U.S.A. 46 47N 105 20W
44 Terryglass, Ireland 53 3N 8 14W
54 Terschelling I., Neth. .53 25N 5 20E
89 Terter R., U.S.S.R. 40 5N 46 15E
64 Teruel, Spain 40 22N 1 8W
64 Teruel, prov., Spain ...40 48N 1 0E
75 Tervel, Bulgaria 43 45N 27 28E
82 Tervola, Finland 66 6N 24 59E
132 Tesachirire, Mozam. ...15 25S 33 15E
74 Tešanj, Yugoslavia 44 38N 17 59E
87 Tesha R., U.S.S.R. 55 32N 43 0E
114 Teshio R., Japan 44 45N 142 0E
74 Tešica, Yugoslavia 43 27N 21 45E
74 Teslic, Yugoslavia 44 37N 17 54E
156 Teslin, Canada 60 20N 132 45W
156 Teslin L., Canada 60 13N 132 50W
111 Tess R., Mongolia 50 40N 93 20E
125 Tessaoua, Niger 13 47N 7 56E
55 Tessenderlo, Belgium .51 4N 5 5E
127 Tessenei, Ethiopia 15 5N 36 42E
157 Tessier, Canada 51 48N 107 26W
56 Tessin, Germany 54 2N 12 28E
34 Test, R., Eng., U.K. .51 7N 1 30W
73 Testa del Gargano, It. 41 50N 16 10E
55 Testelt, Belgium 51 1N 4 57E
59 Tet, Hungary 47 30N 17 33E
34 Tetbury, Eng., U.K. .51 37N 2 9W
132 Tete, Mozambique 16 13S 33 33E
132 Tete, dist., Mozam. 15 15S 32 40E
86 Teterev R., U.S.S.R. .50 30N 29 30E
56 Teterow, Germany 53 45N 12 34E
75 Teteven, Bulgaria 42 58N 24 17E
88 Tetiev, U.S.S.R. 49 22N 29 38E
39 Tetney, England, U.K. 53 30N 0 1W
166 Teton R., U.S.A. 47 58N 111 0W
74 Tetovo, Yugoslavia ...42 1N 21 2E
34 Tettenhall, Eng., U.K. 52 35N 2 7W
122 Tetuan, Morocco 35 30N 5 25W
91 Tetyukhe, U.S.S.R. ...44 45N 135 40E
172 Teuco R., Argentina .25 30S 60 25W
72 Teulada, Italy 38 59N 8 47E
157 Teulon, Canada 50 30N 97 20W
71 Tevere (Tiber) R., It. .42 30N 12 20E
135 Teviot, C. Prov., S. Afr. 31 42S 25 35E
41 Teviot R., Scot., U.K. 55 21N 2 51W
41 Teviotdale, Scot., U.K. 55 25N 2 50W
41 Teviothead, Scot., U.K. 55 19N 2 55W
145 Tewantin, Australia ...26 27S 153 3E
34 Tewkesbury, Eng., U.K. 51 59N 2 8W
156 Texada I., Canada 49 38N 64 45W
165 Texarkana, Ark., U.S.A. 33 25N 94 0W
165 Texarkana, Tex., U.S.A. 33 25N 94 0W
145 Texas, Queens., Austral. 28 49S 151 15E
165 Texas, st., U.S.A. 31 40N 98 30W
165 Texas City, U.S.A. 27 20N 95 20W
54 Texel I., Netherlands .53 5N 4 50E
165 Texhoma, U.S.A. 36 32N 101 47W
165 Texoma L., U.S.A. 34 0N 96 38W
165 Texline U.S.A. 36 26N 103 0W
87 Teykovo, U.S.S.R. 56 55N 40 30E
35 Teynham, Eng., U.K. 51 19N 0 50E
98 Teyr Zebna, Lebanon 33 14N 35 23E
87 Teza R., U.S.S.R. 56 41N 41 45E
168 Teziutlán, Mexico 19 50N 97 30W
103 Tezpur, India 26 40N 92 45E
107 Tha Nun, Thailand ... 8 12N 98 17E
135 Thaba Chitja, S. Africa 30 20S 28 26E
135 Thaba Nchu, S. Africa 29 10S 26 52E
135 Thaba Putsoa Mt., Les. 29 48S 27 54E
135 Thaba Putsoa Ra., Les. 29 45S 28 0E
135 Thabana Ntlenyana, Mt., Lesotho 29 30S 29 9E
133 Thabazimbi, S. Africa 24 40S 26 4E
133 Thabina, Trans., S. Afr. 23 57S 30 16E
107 Thai Nguyen, N. Vietnam 21 35N 105 46E
107 Thailand (Siam), king., Asia 16 0N 101 0E
107 Thakhek, Laos 17 25N 104 45E
102 Thal Desert, W. Pak. .31 0N 71 30E
102 Thal, West Pakistan .33 28N 70 33E
123 Thala, Tunisia 35 45N 8 43E
103 Thala Pass, Burma 28 25N 97 23E
145 Thallon, Australia 28 30S 148 57E
57 Thalwil, Switzerland .47 17N 8 35E
35 Thame, Eng., U.K. ...51 44N 0 58W
35 Thame, R., Eng., U.K. 51 52N 0 47W
160 Thames, Canada 42 35N 82 1W
146 Thames, New Zealand 37 7S 175 34E
146 Thames, Firth of, N.Z. 37 0S 175 25E
160 Thames R., Canada ...42 25N 82 15W
35 Thames, R., Eng., U.K. 51 24N 0 24W
146 Thames R., N.Z. 37 32S 175 45E
35 Thames, R., Eng., U.K. 51 24N 0 24W
161 Thames, R., U.S.A. ...41 25N 72 9W
160 Thamesford, Canada .43 5N 81 0W
123 Thamit, W., Libya 30 51N 16 14E
106 Thana, India 19 12N 72 59E
104 Thanesar, India 30 1N 76 52E
35 Thanet, I. of, Eng., U.K. 51 21N 1 20E
107 Thang Binh, S. Vietnam 15 50N 108 20E
144 Thangool, Queensland, Australia 24 29S 150 35E
107 Thanh Hoa, N. Vietnam 19 35N 105 40E
106 Thanjavur (Tanjore), India 10 48N 79 12E
49 Thann, France 47 48N 7 5E
49 Thaon, France 48 15N 6 25E
104 Thar (Great Indian) Desert, India 28 25N 72 0E
104 Tharad, India 24 30N 71 30E
145 Thargomindah, Austral. 27 58S 143 46E
103 Tharrawaddy, Burma 17 30N 96 0E
100 Tharthar Depression, Iraq 34 0N 43 0E
76 Thasopoúla I., Greece 40 49N 24 45E
76 Thasos, Greece 40 50N 24 50E
76 Thásos I., Greece 40 40N 24 40E
34 Thatcham, Eng., U.K. 51 24N 1 17W
167 Thatcher, Ariz., U.S.A. 32 54N 109 46W
167 Thatcher, Colo., U.S.A. 32 54N 109 46W
103 Thatòn, Burma 17 0N 97 39E
103 Thaungdut, Burma ...24 30N 94 40E
35 Thaxted, England, U.K. 51 57N 0 20E
165 Thayer, U.S.A. 36 34N 91 34W
103 Thayetmyo, Burma ...19 20N 95 18E
103 Thazi, Burma 21 0N 96 5E
38 The Calf, Mt., Eng., U.K. 54 23N 2 30W
166 The Dalles, U.S.A. 45 40N 121 11W
145 The Diamantina, Swamp, S. Australia 26 45S 139 30E
45 The Downs, Ireland ...53 30N 7 15W
143 The Entrance, N.S.W., Australia ...33 21S 151 30E
134 The Fisheries, S. Africa 34 21S 21 51E
169 The Flatts, Bermuda .32 19N 64 45W
143 The Grampians, Mts., Victoria, Australia .37 0S 142 30E
138 The Granites, N. Terr., Australia 20 35S 130 21E
143 The Great Divide, Australia 35 0S 149 17E
54 The Hague (s'Gravenhage), Neth. 52 7N 7 14E
169 The Lake, Great Inagua Island, Bahamas 21 5N 73 34W
46 The Loup, N Ire., U.K. 54 42N 6 32W
36 The Manacles, England, U.K. 50 3N 5 0W
157 The Pas, Canada 53 45N 101 15W
36 The Quantocks, hills, England, U.K. 51 8N 3 10W
132 The Range, Rhodesia .19 2S 31 2E
143 The Rock, Australia ...35 15S 147 2E
145 The Round Mountain, N.S.W., Australia ...30 1S 151 47E
37 The Skerries, Anglesey, Wales, U.K. 53 24N 4 36W
36 The Sound, England, United Kingdom 50 21N 4 9W
147 The Thumbs, Mts., N.Z. 43 35S 170 40E
143 The Vale, N.S.W., Austral. 33 34S 143 49E
134 The Willows, S. Africa 31 32S 24 39E
34 Theale, Eng., U.K. 51 26N 1 5W
126 Thebes, Egypt 25 40N 32 35E
160 Thedford, Canada 43 10N 81 50W
164 Thedford, U.S.A. 41 59N 100 31W
145 Theebine, Australia ...26 0S 152 30E
157 Thekulthili L., Canada 61 3N 110 0W
157 Thelon R., Canada 62 35N 104 3W
48 Thénezay, France 46 44N 0 2W
50 Thenon, France 45 9N 1 3E
145 Theodore, Australia ...24 55S 150 3E
174 Theodore Roosevelt River, Brazil 9 30S 60 30W
49 Therain R., France 49 30N 2 0E
161 Theresa, U.S.A. 44 13N 75 50W
76 Thermaïkós Kólpos, G., Greece 40 15N 22 45E
77 Thermopilai P., Greece 38 48N 22 45E
166 Thermopolis, U.S.A. ...43 14N 108 10W
76 Thesprotia, pref., Gr. .39 27N 20 22E
76 Thessalia (Thessaly), Div., Greece 39 30N 22 0E
154 Thessalon, Canada 46 20N 83 30W
76 Thessaloniki (Salonika), Greece ...40 38N 23 0E
76 Thessaloníki, pref., Gr. 40 45N 23 0E
35 Thetford, Eng., U.K. .52 25N 0 44E
155 Thetford Mines, Canada 46 8N 71 18W
135 Theunissen, S. Africa .28 26S 26 43E
55 Theux, Belgium 50 32N 5 49E
76 Thiámis R., Greece 39 34N 20 28E
48 Thiberville, France 49 9N 0 29E
157 Thicket Portage, Can. 55 25N 97 45W
165 Thief River Falls, U.S.A. 48 15N 96 10W
166 Thielsen Mt., U.S.A. .43 10N 122 0W
71 Thiene, Italy 45 42N 11 29E
49 Thierache, dist., France 49 51N 3 45E
50 Thiers, France 45 52N 3 33E
124 Thiès, Senegal 14 50N 16 51W
127 Thiet, Sudan 7 37N 28 49E
131 Thika & dist., Kenya . 1 1S 37 5E
105 Thimphu (Tashi Chho Dzong), Bhutan 27 31N 89 45E
82 Thingvallavatn L., Ice. 64 10N 21 10W
127 Thio, Ethiopia 14 41N 40 57E
49 Thionville, France 49 20N 6 10E
77 Thíra & I., Greece 36 23N 25 27E
77 Thirasía I., Greece 36 26N 25 21E
143 Thirlmere, Australia ...34 11S 150 35E
39 Thirsk, England, U.K. 54 15N 1 20W
77 Thívai, Greece 38 19N 23 19E
50 Thiviers, France 45 25N 0 54E
51 Thizy, France 46 2N 4 18E
82 Thjorsa R., Iceland ...64 25N 19 0W
51 Thoissey, France 46 12N 4 48E
162 Thomas, W. Va., U.S.A. 39 10N 79 30W
165 Thomas, Okla., U.S.A. 35 48N 98 48W
135 Thomas River, S. Africa 32 28S 27 19E
44 Thomas Street, Ireland 53 27N 8 15W
45 Thomastown, Ireland .52 32N 7 10W
163 Thomasville, Ala., U.S.A. 31 55N 87 42W
163 Thomasville, Fla., U.S.A. 30 50N 84 0W
163 Thomasville, N.C., U.S.A. 35 5N 80 4W
157 Thompson, Canada 55 50N 97 34W
156 Thompson R., Canada 50 30N 121 14W
157 Thompson Landing, Canada 62 45N 111 7W
144 Thompson R., Austral. 24 30S 142 50E
164 Thompson R., U.S.A. 40 25N 93 43W
166 Thompson Falls, U.S.A. 47 37N 115 26W
167 Thompsons, U.S.A. ...39 0N 109 50W
161 Thompsonville, U.S.A. 42 0N 72 37W
131 Thomson's Falls, Kenya 0 2N 36 27E
107 Thonburi, Thailand ...13 50N 100 36E
51 Thônes, France 45 54N 6 18E
107 Thongwa, Burma 16 45N 96 33E
51 Thonon-les-Bains, Fr. 46 22N 6 29E
89 Thorez, U.S.S.R. 48 4N 38 34E
82 Thorlakshöfn, Iceland 63 52N 21 20W
39 Thornaby on Tees, England, U.K. 54 36N 1 19W
144 Thornborough, Austral. 16 54S 145 2E
160 Thornbury, Canada ...44 34N 80 28W
36 Thornbury, Glos., England, U.K. 51 36N 2 31W
147 Thornbury, N.Z. 46 17S 168 9E
35 Thorndon, Eng., U.K. 5216N 1 8E
39 Thorne, England, U.K. 53 36N 0 56W
15 Thorne Glacier, Antarc. 87 30N 150 0E
35 Thorney, England, U.K. 52 37N 0 8W
39 Thornham, Eng., U.K. 52 59N 0 35E
41 Thornhill, Scot., U.K. 55 15N 3 46W
41 Thornthwaite, Eng. U.K. 54 36N 3 13W

MAP
38 Thornton Cleveleys, England, U.K. 53 52N 3 1W
39 Thornton Dale, Eng. U.K. 54 14N 0 41W
160 Thorold, Canada 43 8N 79 13W
35 Thorpe, England, U.K. 52 38N 1 20E
143 Thorpedale, Australia 38 19S 146 13E
35 Thorpe le Soken, England, U.K. 51 50N 1 11E
82 Thorshöfn, Iceland 66 18N 15 15W
49 Thouarce, France 47 17N 0 30W
131 Thowa R., Kenya 1 35S 39 8E
76 Thrace (Thráki), div., Greece 41 10N 26 0E
76 Thraki, Greece 41 9N 25 30E
76 Thrakikón Pelagos, Gr. 40 30N 25 0E
35 Thrapston, Eng., U.K. 52 24N 0 32W
35 Three Bridges, Eng., U.K. 51 7N 0 9W
166 Three Forks, U.S.A. ...45 5N 111 40W
156 Three Hills, Canada ...51 43N 113 15W
144 Three Hummock I., Tasmania, Austral. .40 30S 144 59E
146 Three Kings Is., N.Z. .34 10S 172 10E
164 Three Lakes, U.S.A. ...45 41N 89 10W
107 Three Pagodas P., Thai, ...15 16N 98 23E
124 Three Points, C., Ghana 4 42N 2 6W
165 Three Rivers, U.S.A. .28 30N 98 10W
142 Three Rivers, Western Australia 25 10S 119 5E
166 Three Sisters, Mt., U.S.A. 44 10N 121 52W
38 Threlkeld, Eng., U.K. 54 37N 3 2W
38 Threshfield, Eng., U.K. 54 5N 2 2W
161 Throop, U.S.A. 41 24N 75 39W
142 Throssell, L., Australia 27 31S 121 45E
138 Throssell Ra., Western Australia .22 0S 121 45E
43 Thrumster, Scotland, U.K. 58 24N 3 8W
51 Thueyts, France 44 41N 4 9E
143 Thuddungra, Australia 34 8S 148 8E
54 Thuin, Belgium 50 20N 4 17E
14 Thule, Greenland 76 0N 68 0W
57 Thun, Switzerland 46 45N 7 38E
142 Thundelarra, Western Australia 28 48S 117 0E
160 Thunder B., U.S.A. ...45 0N 83 20W
154 Thunder Bay, Canada 48 25N 89 10W
156 Thunder River, Can. .52 13N 119 20W
47 Thuner See, L., Switz. 46 42N 7 42E
142 Thundulda, W. Austral. 32 15S 126 3E
107 Thung Song, Thailand 8 10N 99 40E
105 Thunkar, Bhutan 27 55N 91 0E
57 Thur R., Switzerland .47 32N 9 10E
57 Thurgau, can., Switz. .47 34N 9 10E
56 Thüringer Wald, Mts., Germany 50 35N 11 0E
35 Thurlby, England, U.K. 52 45N 0 21W
44 Thurles, Ireland 52 40N 7 53W
145 Thurloo Downs, N.S.W., Australia ...29 15S 143 30E
34 Thurmaston, Eng., U.K. 52 40N 1 8W
35 Thurrock, Eng., U.K. 51 28N 0 22E
38 Thursby, Eng., U.K. .54 40N 3 3W
144 Thursday, I., Australia 10 30S 142 3E
154 Thurso Canada 45 36N 75 15W
43 Thurso, Scotland, U.K. 58 34N 3 31W
43 Thurso R., Scot., U.K. 58 3N 3 30W
160 Thurston, U.S.A. 39 50N 82 33W
15 Thurston I., Antarctica 72 0S 100 0W
48 Thury-Harcourt, Fr. .49 0N 0 30W
130 Thysville, Congo 5 12S 14 53E
145 Tia, N.S.W., Australia 31 15S 151 40E
168 Tiahualilo, Mexico 26 20N 103 30W
124 Tiankoura, Upper Volta 10 47N 3 17W
122 Tiaret (Tagdent), Algeria 35 28N 1 21E
124 Tiassale, Ivory Coast . 5 58N 4 57W
133 Tibanefontein, S. Africa 23 43S 29 3E
127 Tibari, Sudan 5 2N 31 48E
125 Tibati, Cameroon 6 22N 12 30E
72 Tiber R., Italy 42 30N 12 20E
166 Tiber Res., U.S.A. 48 20N 111 15W
98 Tiberias, Israel 32 47N 35 32E
98 Tiberias, Lake, Israel .32 49N 35 36E
166 Tiber Res., U.S.A. 48 20N 111 15W
123 Tibesti, dist, and Mts., Chad 21 0N 17 30E
103 Tibet, st., Asia 32 30N 86 0E
78 Tibles Mt., Rumania .47 32N 24 15E
78 Tibles, Mții, Mts., Rum. 47 41N 24 6E
98 Tibnine, Lebanon 33 12N 35 24E
145 Tibooburra, N.S.W., Australia 29 26S 142 1E
81 Tibro, Sweden 58 28N 14 10E
168 Tiburon I., Mexico 29 0N 112 30W
35 Ticehurst, Eng., U.K. 51 2N 0 23E
124 Tichit, Mauritania 18 35N 9 20W
57 Ticino, can., Switz. 46 20N 8 45E
70 Ticino R., Italy 45 23N 8 47E
57 Ticino R., Switzerland 46 20N 8 56E
39 Tickhill, England, U.K. 53 25N 1 8W
161 Ticonderoga, U.S.A. ...43 50N 73 28W
168 Ticul, Mexico 20 20N 89 50W
81 Tidaholm, Sweden 58 12N 13 55E
103 Tiddim, Burma 23 20N 93 45E
122 Toderidjaouine, Adrar, Algeria 23 0N 2 15E
39 Tideswell, Eng., U.K. 53 17N 1 46W
122 Tidikelt, Algeria 26 58N 1 30E
109 Tidore, Indonesia 0 40N 127 25E
124 Tiébissou, Ivory Coast 7 9N 5 18W
167 Tieera Amarilla, U.S.A. 36 42N 106 35W
124 Tiego, Upper Volta ...12 6N 2 38E
112 Tiehling, China 42 25N 123 51E
54 Tiel, Netherlands 51 54N 5 5E
54 Tielt, Belgium 51 0N 3 20E
101 Tien Shan, Mts., Asia 42 0N 80 0E
112 Tienchen, China 40 32N 114 0E
54 Tienen, Belgium 50 48N 4 57E
113 Tienho, China 24 58N 108 35E
77 Tienkianghsien, China 30 25N 107 30E
113 Tieno China 25 3N 107 3E
113 Tienpao, China 23 25N 106 47E
113 Tienshui, China 34 30N 105 34E
112 Tientsin, China 39 10N 117 0E
113 Tientu, China 18 12N 109 33E
113 Tientung, China 23 47N 107 2E
135 Tierfontein, S. Africa .28 1S 26 20E
80 Tierp, Sweden 60 20N 17 30E
172 Tierra Amarilla, Chile 27 28S 70 18W
176 Tierra del Fuego, I., South America 54 0S 69 0W
62 Tietar, R., Spain 39 55N 5 50W
162 Tiffin, U.S.A. 41 8N 83 10W
122 Tiflet, Morocco 33 51N 6 11W
98 Tifrah, Israel 31 19N 34 42E
163 Tifton, U.S.A. 31 28N 83 32W
109 Tifu, Indonesia 3 39S 126 18E
122 Tighmart, Morocco . ..31 21N 4 3W
40 Tighnabruaich, Scot. U.K. 55 55N 5 13W
155 Tignish, Canada 46 58N 63 57W
172 Tigre, Argentina 34 27S 58 40W
127 Tigre, prov., Ethiopia 13 35N 39 15E
174 Tigre R., Colombia 3 30S 74 58W
100 Tigris, R., Iraq 37 0N 42 30E
103 Tigu, Tibet, China 29 48N 91 38E
123 Tiguentourine, Algeria 28 8N 8 58E
125 Tiguila, Mali 14 44N 1 50W
78 Tigveni, Rumania 45 10N 24 31E
103 Tigyaing, Burma 23 45N 96 10E
126 Tih, Gebel el, Egypt .29 32N 33 26E
123 Tihodaine, Dunes de, Algeria 25 15N 7 15E
111 Tihua, China 43 40N 87 50E
71 Tijesno, Yugoslavia ...44 45N 15 41E
109 Tijiamis, Indonesia 7 16S 108 29E
109 Tijibadok, Indonesia . 6 53S 106 47E
123 Tijl, Libya 30 0N 11 18E
168 Tijuana, Mexico 32 30N 117 10W
167 Tikal, site, Guatemala 17 2N 89 35W
104 Tikamgarh, India 24 44N 78 57E
144 Tikan, New Guinea ... 5 58S 149 2E
113 Tikang, China 31 7N 118 2E
125 Tikau, Nigeria 11 40N 11 7E
89 Tikhoretsk, U.S.S.R. .45 56N 40 5E
86 Tikhvin, U.S.S.R. 59 35N 33 30E
122 Tikkadouine, Adrar, Alg. 24 28N 1 30E
125 Tiko, Cameroon 4 4N 9 20E
100 Tikrit, Iraq 34 35N 43 37E
91 Tiksi, U.S.S.R. 71 50N 129 0E
172 Tilama, Chile 32 0S 71 14W
109 Tilamuta, Indonesia ... 0 40N 122 15E
54 Tilburg, Netherlands .51 31N 5 6E
54 Tilbury, Canada 42 17N 84 23W
35 Tilbury, England, U.K. 51 27N 0 24E
172 Tilcara, Argentina 23 30S 65 23W
164 Tilden, U.S.A. 42 3N 97 45W
125 Tilemsi, Vallee du, Mali 17 42N 0 15E
55 Tilff, Belgium 50 34N 5 35E
105 Tilhar, India 28 0N 79 45E
122 Tilia, W., Algeria 27 32N 0 55E
91 Tilichiki, U.S.S.R. 61 0N 166 5E
88 Tiligui R., U.S.S.R. ...47 35N 30 30E
122 Tililane, Algeria 27 49N 0 6W
77 Tilissos, Greece 38 15N 25 0E
166 Tillamook, U.S.A. 45 29N 123 55E
80 Tillberga, Sweden 59 42N 16 39E
156 Tilley, Canada 50 28N 111 38W
41 Tillicoultry, Scot., U.K. 56 9N 3 44W
160 Tillsonburg, Canada ...42 53N 80 55W
55 Tilly, Belgium 50 33N 4 33E
35 Tilmanstone, Eng., U.K. 51 13N 1 18E
77 Tilos I., Greece 36 27N 27 27E
145 Tilpa, N.S.W., Austral. 30 58S 144 30E
122 Tilrhemt, Algeria 33 6N 3 28E
43 Tilt R., Scotland, U.K. 56 50N 3 50W
161 Tilton, U.S.A. 43 25N 71 36W
45 Timahoe, Laois, Ire. ...52 59N 7 12W
84 Timan Ridge, Mts., U.S.S.R. 65 58N 50 5E
147 Timaru, New Zealand 44 23S 171 14E
89 Timashevskaya, U.S.S.R. 45 35N 39 0E
131 Timau, Kenya 0 4N 37 15E
77 Timbakion, Greece 35 4N 24 45E
124 Timbédra, Mauritania 16 17N 8 16W
164 Timber L., U.S.A. 45 29N 101 0W
143 Timbilica, Australia ...37 22S 149 42E
143 Timboon, Vic., Austral. 38 31S 143 0E
124 Timbuktu, see Tombouctou, Mali .16 50N 3 0W
122 Timdjaouine, Algeria .21 47N 4 30E
76 Timfi Óros, Mt., Greece 39 59N 20 45E
77 Timfristós Mt., Greece 38 57N 21 50E
122 Timhadit, Morocco 33 23N 5 17W
122 Timidert, Morocco 30 45N 6 8W
122 Timimoun, Algeria 29 14N 0 16E
122 Timimoun, Sebkra de Algeria 28 50N 0 46E
74 Timis, Reg., Rum. 45 40N 21 15E
78 Timiş R., Rumania ...45 30N 21 0E
74 Timişoara, Rumania .45 43N 21 15E
154 Timmis, Canada 48 28N 81 25W
74 Timok R., Yugoslavia 44 10N 22 40E
44 Timoleague, Ireland ...51 40N 8 51W
45 Timolin, Ireland 52 59N 6 49W
175 Timon, Brazil 5 8S 42 52W
109 Timor I., East Indies . 9 0S 125 0E
138 Timor Sea, Indian Oc. 10 0S 127 0E
123 Tin Alkoum, Algeria .24 30N 10 17E
135 Tina R., S. Africa 31 5S 28 55E
109 Tinaca Pt., Philippines 5 30N 125 25E
109 Tinambacan, Phil. 12 5N 124 32E
145 Tinapagee, Australia .29 25S 144 15E
144 Tinaroo Falls, Austral. 17 5S 145 4E
78 Tinca, Rumania 46 46N 21 58E
48 Tinchebray, France ...48 47N 0 45W
106 Tindivanam, India 12 15N 79 35E
122 Tindouf, Algeria 27 50N 8 4W
105 Tindzhe Dzong, Tibet, China 28 20N 88 8E
122 Tinejdad, Morocco 31 31N 4 58W
122 Ti-n-Emensan, Algeria 22 59N 4 45E
62 Tineo, Spain 43 21N 6 27W
122 Tinerhir, Morocco 31 47N 5 30W
122 Tinfouchi, Algeria 28 58N 5 54W
122 Ti-n-Geloulet, Algeria 25 58N 4 2E
34 Tingewick, Eng., U.K. 51 59N 1 4W
113 Tinghai, China 30 0N 122 10E
112 Tinghsien, China.......38 30N 115 0E
81 Tinglev, Denmark 54 57N 9 13E
113 Tingnan, China 24 45N 114 50E
174 Tingo Maria, Peru 9 10S 76 0W
112 Tingpien, China 37 30N 107 50E
112 Tingsi, China 35 50N 104 17E
81 Tingsryd, Sweden 56 31N 15 0E
81 Tingvalla, Sweden 58 47N 12 2E
45 Tinhely, Ireland 53 15N 6 27W
125 Tinié, Upper Volta 14 17N 1 30W
172 Tinnia, Argentina 27 0S 62 45W
122 Tinioulig, Sebkra, Mauritania 22 30N 6 45W
122 Tinjoub, Algeria 29 45N 5 40W
142 Tinkurrin, W. Australia 33 0S 117 38E
106 Tinnevelly, India 8 45N 77 45E
79 Tinnoset, Norway 59 45N 9 3E
79 Tinnsjö L., Norway ...59 55N 8 54E
172 Tinogasta, Argentina .28 0S 67 40W
77 Tinos & I., Greece 37 33N 25 8E
65 Tinoso, C., Spain 37 32N 1 6W
113 Tinpak, China 21 40N 111 15E
36 Tintagel, Eng., U.K. .50 40N 4 45W
36 Tintagel Hd., Eng., U.K. 50 40N 4 46W
123 Ti-n-Tarabine, W., Alg. 21 37N 7 11E
34 Tintern, England, U.K. 51 42N 2 41W
45 Tintern, Ireland 52 14N 6 50W
145 Tintinara, S. Australia 35 48S 140 2E
63 Tinto R., Spain 37 30N 5 33W
146 Tinui, New Zealand ...40 52S 176 5E
147 Tinwald, New Zealand 43 55S 171 43E
160 Tioga, co., U.S.A. 41 54N 77 9W
107 Tioman, I., Malaysia . 2 50N 104 10E
154 Tionaga, Canada 48 0N 82 0W
70 Tione di Trento, Italy 46 3N 10 44E
160 Tionesta, U.S.A. 41 29N 79 28W
127 Tior, Sudan 6 26N 31 11E
122 Tioulilin, Algeria 27 1N 0 2W
103 Tipongpani, India 27 20N 95 55E
44 Tipperary, Ireland 52 28N 8 10W
44 Tipperary, co., Ireland 52 37N 7 55W
167 Tipton, Calif., U.S.A. .36 3N 119 0W
34 Tipton, England, U.K. 52 32N 2 4W
162 Tipton, Ind., U.S.A. ...40 17N 86 30W
164 Tipton, Iowa, U.S.A. .41 45N 91 12W
165 Tiptonville, U.S.A. 36 22N 89 30W
35 Tiptree, Eng., U.K. ...51 48N 0 46E
106 Tiptur, India 13 15N 76 26E
98 Tira, Israel 32 14N 34 56E
101 Tiran, Iran 32 45N 51 0E
126 Tiran I., Saudi Arabia 27 56N 34 35E
76 Tiranë, Albania 41 18N 19 49E
76 Tiranë-Durrës, pref., Albania 41 35N 20 0E
70 Tirano, Italy 46 13N 10 11E
134 Tiras Plateau, S.W. Afr. 26 17S 17 15E
88 Tiraspol, U.S.S.R. 46 55N 29 35E
98 Tirat Carmel, Israel ...32 46N 34 58E
98 Tirat Tsevi, Israel 32 26N 35 31E
98 Tirat Yehuda, Israel .32 1N 34 56E
122 Tiratimine, Algeria 25 56N 3 37E
100 Tire, Turkey 38 5N 27 50E
100 Tirebolu, Turkey 40 58N 38 45E
40 Tiree, I., Scot., U.K. .56 31N 6 49W
40 Tiree, Passage of, Scotland, U.K. 56 30N 6 30W
78 Tirgovişte, Rumania .44 55N 25 27E
78 Tirgu-Jiu, Rumania ...45 5N 23 19E
78 Tirgu Mures, Rumania 46 31N 24 38E
102 Tirich Mir Mt., W. Pak. 36 15N 71 35E
73 Tiriola, Italy 38 57N 16 32E
106 Tirna R., India 18 5N 76 30E
78 Tirnaveni, Rumania ...46 19N 24 13E
76 Tirnavos, Greece 39 45N 22 18E
58 Tirol, prov., Austria ...47 3N 10 43E
57 Tirschenreuth, Germany 49 51N 12 20E
72 Tirso, L., Italy 40 8N 8 56E
72 Tirso R., Italy 40 33N 9 12E
81 Tirstrup, Denmark 56 18N 10 42E
146 Tirua, New Zealand ...38 25S 174 40E
106 Tiruchendur, India 8 30N 78 11E
106 Tiruchengodu, India .11 23N 77 56E
106 Tiruchchirappalli (Trichinopoly), India 10 45N 78 45E
106 Tirumangalam, India . 9 49N 77 58E
106 Tirunelveli (Tinnevelly), India . 8 45N 77 45E
106 Tirupati, India 13 45N 79 30E
106 Tiruppattur, India 12 30N 78 30E
106 Tiruppur, India 11 12N 77 22E
106 Tiruturaipundi, India 10 32N 79 41E
106 Tiruvadaimarudur, India 11 2N 79 27E
106 Tiruvallar, India 13 9N 79 57E
106 Tiruvannamalai, India 12 10N 79 12E
106 Tiruvarur (Negapatam), India 10 46N 79 38E
106 Tiruvatipuram, India .12 39N 79 33E
106 Tiruvottiyur, India ...13 10N 80 22E
74 Tisa, R., Yugoslavia .45 30N 20 20E
34 Tisbury, England, U.K. 51 4N 2 4W
157 Tisdale, Canada 52 50N 104 0W
122 Tiseirhatène, Mares de, Mauritania 22 51N 9 30W
165 Tishomingo, U.S.A. ...34 14N 96 38W
80 Tisjön L., Sweden 60 56N 13 0E
80 Tisnaren L., Sweden .58 58N 15 46E
59 Tišnov, Czechoslovakia 49 21N 16 25E
59 Tisovec, Czechoslovakia 48 41N 19 56E
122 Tissemsilt, Algeria 35 35N 1 50E
81 Tissö L., Denmark 55 35N 11 18E
105 Tista, R., India 27 33N 88 30E
81 Tisted, Denmark 56 58N 8 40E
81 Tisted, Amt., co., Den. 57 0N 8 30E
59 Tisza R., Hungary 47 38N 20 44E
59 Tiszafüred, Hungary .47 38N 20 50E
59 Tiszalök, Hungary 48 0N 21 10E
123 Tit, Algeria 23 0N 5 10E
122 Tit, Algeria 27 0N 1 37E
64 Titaguas, Spain 39 53N 1 6W
146 Titahi, B., New Zealand 41 7S 174 50E
127 Titai Damer, Ethiopia 16 43N 37 25E
34 Titchfield, Eng., U.K. 50 51N 1 13W
74 Titel, Yugoslavia 45 29N 20 18E
174 Titicaca, L., Bolivia-Peru 15 30S 69 30W
125 Titiwa, Nigeria 12 14N 12 53E
105 Titilagarh, India 20 15N 83 5E
74 Titograd, Yugoslavia .42 30N 19 19E
74 Titov-Veles, Y.-slavia 41 46N 21 47E
71 Titova Korenica, Y.-slav. 44 45N 15 41E
74 Titovo Uzice, Y.-slavia 43 55N 19 50E
130 Titule, Congo 3 15N 25 31E
160 Titusville, U.S.A. 41 35N 79 39W
42 Tiumpan Hd., Scot., U.K. 58 15N 6 10W
124 Tivaouane, Senegal 14 56N 16 45W
74 Tivat, Yugoslavia 42 28N 18 43E
81 Tiveden, reg., Sweden 58 50N 14 35E
36 Tiverton, Eng., U.K. .50 54N 3 30W
71 Tivoli, Italy 41 58N 12 45E
101 Tiwi, Muscat & Oman 22 45N 59 12E
123 Tizi Ouzan, Algeria ...36 48N 4 2E
168 Tizimin, Mexico 21 0N 88 1W
122 Tiznit, Morocco 29 48N 9 45W
109 Tjabanbungin, Indon. 6 1S 107 2E
109 Tjalang, Indonesia 4 30N 95 43E
108 Tjangkuang, Tg., (Java Head), Indonesia 7 0S 105 0E
109 Tjareme Mt., Indonesia 6 55S 108 27E
82 Tjeggelvas L., Sweden 66 30N 18 0E
109 Tjepu Indonesia 7 12S 111 31E
109 Tjiandjur, Indonesia . 6 51S 107 7E
109 Tjibatu, Indonesia 7 8S 107 59E
109 Tjidulang, Indonesia . 7 42S 108 27E
109 Tjikadjang, Indonesia 7 25S 107 48E
109 Tjikampek, Indonesia 6 23S 107 28E
109 Tjilatjap, Indonesia ... 7 43S 109 0E
109 Tjimahi, Indonesia 6 53S 107 33E
109 Tjipatuda, Indonesia . 7 42S 108 2E
109 Tjirebon, Indonesia ... 6 45S 108 32E
79 Tjöllong, Norway 59 6N 10 3E
132 Tjolojo, Rhodesia 15 48S 27 43E
79 Tjöme, Norway 59 8N 10 26E
81 Tjörn I., Sweden 58 0N 11 35E
81 Tjuls, Sweden 57 30N 18 15E
108 Tjurup, Indonesia 4 26S 103 12E
89 Tkibuli, U.S.S.R. 42 26N 43 0E
168 Tlaxcala, Mexico 19 20N 98 14W
168 Tlaxcala, st., Mexico .19 30N 98 20W
168 Tlaxiaco, Mexico 17 10N 97 40W
122 Tlemcen, Algeria 34 52N 1 15W
122 Tleta di Sidi Bouguedra, Morocco 32 16N 8 58W
133 Tlhakgameng, S. Africa 26 11S 24 18E
132 Tlhapin, Botswana 23 19S 21 47E
86 Tlumach, U.S.S.R. ...48 46N 25 0E
60 Tluszcz, Poland 52 25N 21 25E
89 Tlyarata, U.S.S.R. 42 9N 46 26E
123 Tmassah, Libya 26 19N 15 51E
123 Tmisan, Libya 27 23N 13 30E
172 Toay, Argentina 36 50S 64 30W
114 Toba, Japan 34 30N 136 45E
108 Toba L., Indonesia 2 40N 98 50E
104 Toba Kakar Hills, West Pakistan 31 30N 69 0E
104 Toba Tek Singh, West Pakistan 30 55N 72 25E
169 Tobago I., W. Indies .11 10N 60 30W
109 Tobelo, Indonesia 1 25N 127 56E
46 Tobercurry, Ireland ...54 3N 8 43W
46 Tobermore, N. Ire., U.K. 54 49 6 43W
144 Tobermorey, Australia 22 12S 138 0E
160 Tobermory, Canada ...45 12N 81 40W
40 Tobermory, Scot., U.K. 56 37N 6 4W
157 Tobin L., Canada 53 35N 103 30W
108 Toboali, Indonesia 3 0S 106 25E
109 Toboli, Indonesia 0 38S 120 12E
70 Tobolsk, U.S.S.R. 58 0N 68 10E
121 Tobruk, Libya 32 7N 23 55E
161 Tobyhanna, U.S.A. ...41 10N 75 15W
175 Tocantinópolis, Brazil 6 20S 47 25W
175 Tocantins R., Brazil ...14 30S 49 0W
163 Tocca, U.S.A. 34 6N 83 17W
70 Toce R., Italy 46 5N 8 29E
114 Tochigi, Japan 36 25N 139 45E
114 Tochigi, pref., Japan .36 45N 139 45E
63 Tocina, Spain 37 37N 5 44W
172 Toco, Chile 22 0S 69 40W
172 Tocopilla, Chile 22 5S 70 10W
172 Tocorpuri Mt., Bolivia 22 0S 67 10W
143 Tocumwal, Australia .35 45S 145 31E
35 Toddington, Eng., U.K. 51 57N 0 31W
109 Todeli, Indonesia 1 38S 124 34E
131 Todenyang, Kenya 4 35N 35 56E
71 Todi, Italy 42 47N 12 24E
109 Todjo, Indonesia 1 20S 121 15E
38 Todmorden, Eng., U.K. 53 43N 2 7W
175 Todos B., Brazil 13 5S 38 45W
168 Todos Santos, Mexico 23 30N 110 20W
168 Todos Santos B., Mex. 31 50N 116 50W
57 Todtnau, Germany 47 50N 7 56E
44 Toe Hd., Ireland 51 29N 9 13W
42 Toe Hd., Scot., U.K. .57 50N 7 10W
135 Toekoms, S. Africa ...33 9S 25 6E
147 Toetoes B., N.Z. 46 42S 168 41E
156 Tofield, Canada 53 25N 112 50W
80 Töfsingdalems National Park, Sweden 62 15N 12 44E
81 Tofta, Sweden 57 11N 12 20E
81 Toftlund, Denmark 55 11N 9 2E
114 Togara Strait, Japan .30 0N 130 0E
124 Togba, Mauritania 17 26N 10 25W
111 Toghral Ombo, Tibet, China 35 10N 81 40E
109 Togian Is., Indonesia . 0 20S 121 50E
89 Togliatti, U.S.S.R. 53 37N 49 18E
125 Togo, rep., West Africa 6 15N 1 35E
114 Tohoku, dist., Japan .38 40N 142 0E
127 Toinya, Sudan 6 17N 29 46E
112 Toirim, Mongolia 46 0N 106 50E
146 Tokaanu, N.Z. 38 58S 175 46E
59 Tokaj, Hungary 48 8N 21 27E
109 Tokala, mt., Indonesia 1 30S 121 40E
114 Tokamachi, Japan 37 8N 138 43E
147 Tokanui, New Zealand 46 34S 168 56E
113 Tokara Is., Japan 29 0N 129 0E
147 Tokarahi, New Zealand 44 56S 170 39E
100 Tokat, Turkey 40 22N 36 35E
136 Tokelau Is., Pac. Oc. . 9 0S 172 0W
88 Tokmak, U.S.S.R. 47 16N 35 42E
90 Tokmak, U.S.S.R. 42 55N 75 45E
146 Tokomaru B., N.Z. 38 7S 178 15E
125 Tokombere, Nigeria ...11 18N 3 30E
107 Tokong, Malaysia 5 27N 100 23E
146 Tokoroa, New Zealand 38 20S 175 50E
112 Tokoto, China 40 18N 111 0E
113 Toku no Shima, Is., Jap. 27 50N 129 2E
127 Tokule, Ethiopia 14 54N 38 26E
114 Tokushima, Japan 34 0N 134 45E
114 Tokushima, pref., Japan 35 50N 134 30E
114 Tokuyama, Japan 34 5N 131 25E
114 Tokyo, Japan 35 45N 139 45E
114 Tokyo, pref., Japan ...35 40N 139 30E
146 Tolaga Bay, N.Z. 38 21S 178 20E
75 Tolbukhin, Bulgaria ...43 37N 27 49E
62 Toledo, Spain 39 50N 4 2W
63 Toledo, prov., Spain ...39 40N 4 0W
162 Toledo, Ohio, U.S.A. .41 37N 83 33W
166 Toledo, Ore., U.S.A. ...44 40N 123 59W
166 Toledo, Wash., U.S.A. 42 29N 122 58W
71 Tolentino, Italy 43 12N 13 17E
156 Tolfino, Canada 49 6N 125 54W
123 Tolga, Algeria 34 46N 5 22E
79 Tolga, Norway 62 26N 11 1E
174 Tolima, mt., Colombia 4 40N 75 19W
109 Tolitoli, Indonesia 1 5N 120 50E
81 Tollarp, Sweden 55 55N 14 10E
35 Tollesbury, Eng., U.K. 51 46N 0 51E
167 Tolleson, U.S.A. 33 29N 112 10W

MAP
86 Tolmachevo, U.S.S.R. 58 56N 29 57E
71 Tolmezzo, Italy 46 23N 13 0E
71 Tolmin, Yugoslavia ...46 11N 13 45E
59 Tolna, Hungary 46 25N 18 48E
59 Tolna, co., Hungary ...46 30N 18 30E
81 Tolne, Denmark 57 28N 10 20E
109 Tolo, G. of, Indonesia 2 20s 122 10E
144 Tolokiwa I., Terr. of New Guinea 5 30s 147 30E
125 Tolon, Ghana 9 26N 1 3W
64 Tolosa, Spain 43 8N 2 5W
63 Tolox, Spain 36 41N 4 54W
42 Tolsta Hd , Scot., U.K. 58 20N 6 10W
168 Toluca, Mexico 19 20N 99 50W
112 Tolun, China 42 22N 116 30E
133 Tom Burke, S. Africa 23 5s 28 4E
164 Tomahawk, U.S.A. 45 28N 89 40W
63 Tomar, Portugal 39 36N 8 25W
76 Tómaros Mt., Greece .39 29N 20 48E
60 Tomaszów Lubelski, Poland 50 29N 23 23E
60 Tomaszów Mazowiecki Poland 51 30N 19 57E
43 Tomatin, Scot., U.K. .57 20N 4 0W
127 Tombe, Sudan 5 53N 31 40E
163 Tombigbee R., U.S.A. 32 0N 88 6W
124 Tombouctou (Timbuktu), Mali ...16 50N 3 0W
167 Tombstone, U.S.A. 31 40N 110 4W
42 Tomdoun, Scot., U.K. 57 4N 5 2W
172 Tome, Chile 36 36s 73 6W
81 Tomelilla, Sweden 55 33N 13 54E
65 Tomelloso, Spain 39 10N 3 2W
143 Tomerong, Australia .34 58s 150 30E
143 Tomingley West, N.S.W., Australia ...32 34s 148 12E
109 Tomini, Indonesia 0 30N 120 30E
109 Tomini, G. of, Indonesia 0 10s 122 0E
62 Tomiño, Spain 41 59N 8 46W
43 Tomintoul, Scot., U.K. 57 15N 3 22W
142 Tomkinson Ranges, Western Australia .26 0s 128 0E
91 Tommot, U.S.S.R. 58 50N 126 20E
43 Tomnavoulin, Scot. UK 57 19N 3 18W
143 Tomorong, Australia .35 0s 151 9E
161 Toms River, U.S.A. ...39 59N 74 12W
90 Tomsk, U.S.S.R. 56 30N 85 12E
81 Tomtabacken, Hill, Sweden 57 25N 14 30E
168 Tonalá, Mexico 16 8N 93 41W
167 Tonalea, U.S.A. 36 17N 110 58W
174 Tonantins, Brazil 2 45s 67 45W
166 Tonasket, U.S.A. 48 45N 119 30W
166 Tonawanda, U.S.A. ...43 0N 78 54W
35 Tonbridge, Eng., U.K. 51 12N 0 18E
109 Tondano, Indonesia ... 1 35N 124 54E
62 Tondela, Portugal 40 31N 8 5W
81 Tönder, Denmark 54 58N 8 50E
81 Tönder Amt., co., Den. 55 8N 8 50E
106 Tondi, India 9 45N 79 4E
70 Tondo, Mte., Italy 44 19N 9 50E
36 Tone R., England, U.K. 50 59N 3 15W
114 Tone R., Japan 36 15N 139 30E
34 Tong, England, U.K. .52 39N 2 18W
136 Tonga Is. (Friendly Is.), Pacific Ocean .20 0s 173 0W
136 Tonga Trench Pac. Oc. 18 0s 175 0W
135 Tongaat, Natal S. Af. 29 33s 31 9E
137 Tongareva I, Pac. Oc. 9 0s 158 0W
146 Tongariro, mt., N.Z. .39 7s 175 50E
54 Tongeren, Belgium 50 47N 5 28E
107 Tongking, prov., North Vietnam 21 30N 105 0E
107 Tongking, G. of, Asia .20 0N 108 0E
172 Tongoy, Chile 30 25s 71 40W
55 Tongrinne, Belgium ...50 32N 4 36E
43 Tongue, Scotland, U.K. 58 29N 4 25W
43 Tongue, Kyle of, Scotland, U.K. 58 30N 4 30W
166 Tongue R., U.S.A. 48 30N 106 30W
55 Tonisberg, Germany ...51 26N 6 31E
127 Tonj, Sudan 7 20N 28 44E
104 Tonk, India 26 6N 75 54E
165 Tonkawa, U.S.A. 36 44N 67 22W
107 Tonlé Sap (Great Lake), Cambodia ...13 0N 104 0E
50 Tonnay Charente, Fr. 45 56N 0 55W
50 Tonneins, France 44 42N 0 20E
49 Tonnerre, France 47 50N 4 0E
56 Tönning, Germany 54 18N 8 57E
167 Tonopah, U.S.A. 38 4N 117 12W
79 Tönsberg, Norway 59 19N 11 3E
79 Tonstad, Norway 58 40N 6 45E
67 Tonto Basin, U.S.A. ...33 58N 111 15W
36 Tonyrefail, Wales, U.K. 51 35N 3 26W
166 Tooele, U.S.A. 40 30N 112 20W
44 Toombeola, Ireland ...53 26N 9 52W
44 Toomevara, Ireland ...52 50N 8 2W
145 Toompine, Australia .27 15s 144 19E
143 Toongi, N.S.W., Austral. 32 28s 148 30E
144 Toonpan, Australia ...19 28s 146 48E
44 Toormore, Ireland 51 31N 9 41W
145 Toowong, Australia ...27 30s 152 58E
145 Toowoomba, Australia 27 32s 151 56E
84 Top L., U.S.S.R. 65 35N 32 0E
78 Topal, Rumania 44 31N 28 3E
164 Topeka, U.S.A. 39 3N 95 40W
90 Topki, U.S.S.R. 55 25N 85 20E
59 Topla R., Cz. 49 0N 21 36E
156 Topley, Canada 54 32N 126 5W
74 Toplica R., Yugoslavia 43 15N 21 30E
78 Toplita, Rumania 46 55N 25 27E
72 Topocalma, Pta., Chile 34 10s 72 2W
167 Topock, U.S.A. 34 46N 114 29W
74 Topola, Yugoslavia ...44 17N 20 32E
59 Topolčany, Cz. 48 35N 18 12E
89 Topoli, U.S.S.R. 47 59N 51 45E
75 Topolnitsa R., Bulg. .42 21N 24 0E
168 Topolobampo, Mexico 25 40N 109 10W
75 Topolovgrad, Bulgaria 42 5N 26 20E
74 Topolvătul Mare, Rum. 45 46N 21 41E
166 Toppenish, U.S.A. 46 27N 120 16W
36 Topsham, Eng., U.K. 50 40N 3 27W
71 Topusko, Yugoslavia .45 18N 15 59E
36 Tor Bay, Eng., U.K. .50 26N 3 31W
43 Tor Ness, Scot., U.K. 58 47N 3 18W
64 Tora, Spain 41 49N 1 25E
127 Tora Kit, Sudan 11 2N 32 30E
174 Torata, Peru 17 3s 70 1W
101 Torbat-e Heydariyeh, Iran 35 15N 59 12E
101 Torbat-e Jam, Iran ...35 8N 60 35E
155 Torbay, Canada 47 40N 52 42W
36 Torbay, England, U.K. 50 26N 3 31W
143 Torbreck Mt., Austral. 37 10s 145 57E
86 Torchin, U.S.S.R. 50 45N 25 0E
79 Tördal, Norway 59 10N 8 45E
62 Tordesillas, Spain 41 30N 5 0W
62 Tordoya, Spain 43 6N 8 36W
82 Töre, Sweden 65 55N 22 40E
81 Töreboda, Sweden 58 41N 14 7E
56 Torgau, Germany 51 32N 13 0E
54 Torhout, Belgium 51 5N 3 7E
127 Tori, Ethiopia 7 53N 33 35E
48 Torigni, France 49 2N 0 59W
64 Torija, Spain 40 44N 3 2W
168 Torin, Mexico 27 33N 110 5W
62 Toriñana, C., Spain ...43 3N 9 17W
70 Torino (Turin), Italy .45 4N 7 40E
127 Torit, Sudan 4 20N 32 55E
86 Torkovichi, U.S.S.R. .58 51N 30 30E
74 Tormac, Rumania 45 30N 21 30E
155 Tormentine, Canada ..46 6N 63 46W
62 Tormes R., Spain 41 7N 6 0W
156 Tornado Mt., Canada .49 55N 114 40W
81 Tornby, Denmark 57 32N 9 56E
82 Torne R., Sweden 67 30N 21 30E
82 Torneo, Finland 65 57N 24 12E
43 Torness, Scotland, U.K. 57 18N 4 22W
82 Torneträsk, Sweden ...68 14N 19 40E
82 Tornio, Finland 65 57N 24 12E
172 Tornquist, Argentina .38 0s 62 15W
62 Toro, Spain 41 35N 5 24W
81 Torö I., Sweden 58 48N 17 57E
168 Toro, Pta., Panama Canal Zone 9 22N 79 57W
172 Toro, Cerro del Mt., Chile 29 0s 69 50W
59 Törökszentmiklós, Hungary 47 11N 20 27E
76 Toronaíos Kólpos, G., Greece 40 5N 23 30E
143 Toronto, N.S.W., Austral. 33 0s 151 30E
154 Toronto, Canada 43 39N 79 20W
160 Toronto, U.S.A. 40 27N 80 36W
168 Toronto L., Mexico ...27 40N 105 30W
86 Toropets, U.S.S.R. 56 30N 31 40E
131 Tororo, Uganda 0 45N 34 12E
43 Torphins, Scot., U.K. 57 7N 2 37E
36 Torpoint, Eng., U.K. .50 23N 4 12W
80 Torpshammar, Sweden 62 29N 16 25E
143 Torquay, Vic., Australia 38 20s 144 19E
36 Torquay, Eng., U.K. .50 27N 3 31W
62 Torquemada, Spain ...42 2N 4 19W
63 Torralba de Calatrava, Spain 39 1N 3 44W
40 Torran Rocks, Scot. UK 56 14N 6 24W
63 Torrão, Portugal 38 16N 8 11W
72 Torre Annunziata, Italy 40 45N 14 26E
62 Torre de Moncorve, Port. 41 12N 7 8W
73 Torre del Greco, Italy 40 47N 14 22E
63 Torre del Mar, Spain .36 44N 4 6W
70 Torre Pellice, Italy 44 49N 7 13E
64 Torreblanca, Spain 40 14N 0 12E
63 Torrecampo, Spain 38 29N 4 41W
64 Torrecilla en Cameros, Spain 42 15N 2 38W
62 Torrejoncillo, Spain ...39 54N 6 28W
64 Torrelaguna, Spain 40 50N 3 38W
62 Torrelavega, Spain 43 20N 4 5W
73 Torremaggiore, Italy .41 42N 15 17E
63 Torremolinos, Spain ...36 38N 4 30W
144 Torrens Creek, Austral. 20 48s 145 3E
145 Torrens, L., S. Austral. 31 0s 137 45E
65 Torrente, Spain 39 27N 0 28W
65 Torrenueva, Spain 38 38N 3 22W
168 Torreón, Mexico 25 33N 103 25W
65 Torreperogil, Spain ...38 2N 3 17W
62 Torres, Spain 41 6N 5 0W
63 Törres Novas, Portugal 39 27N 8 33W
144 Torres Strait, Australia 10 20s 142 0E
63 Torres Vedras, Portugal 39 5N 9 15W
65 Torrevieja, Spain 37 59N 0 42W
167 Torrey, U.S.A. 38 12N 111 30W
36 Torridge R., Eng., U.K. 50 57N 4 10W
42 Torridon, Scot., U.K. .57 33N 5 34W
42 Torridon, L., Scot., U.K. 57 35N 5 50W
42 Torridon L., Up., Scotland, U.K. 57 32N 5 38W
62 Torrijos, Spain 39 59N 4 18W
81 Törring, Denmark 55 52N 9 29E
161 Torrington, Conn., U.S.A. 41 50N 73 9W
164 Torrington, Wyo., U.S.A. 42 5N 104 8W
43 Torroboll, Scot., U.K. 58 0N 4 23W
64 Torroella de Montgri, Spain 42 2N 3 8E
143 Torrowangee, Australia 31 22s 141 30E
63 Torrox, Spain 36 46N 3 57W
81 Torsås, Sweden 56 24N 16 0E
80 Torsby, Sweden 60 7N 13 0E
80 Torshälla, Sweden 59 25N 16 28E
81 Torsö I., Sweden 58 44N 13 40E
41 Torthorwald, Scot., U.K. 55 7N 3 30W
169 Tortola, I., Virgin Is. .18 19N 65 0W
62 Tortoles de Esgueva, Sp. 41 49N 4 2W
70 Tortona, Italy 44 53N 8 54E
71 Tortoreto, Italy 42 50N 13 55E
73 Tortorici, Italy 38 2N 14 48E
64 Tortosa, Spain 40 49N 0 31E
64 Tortosa C., Spain 40 41N 0 52E
62 Tortosendo, Portugal .40 15N 7 31W
169 Tortue, I., de la, Haiti 20 5N 72 57W
174 Tortuga I., Venezuela 7 8N 67 2W
101 Torud, Iran 35 25N 55 5E
111 Torugart Pass. Asia ...40 30N 74 50E
60 Toruń, Poland 53 0N 18 39E
81 Torup, Sweden 56 57N 13 5E
79 Torvastad, Norway 59 23N 5 15E
38 Torver, England, U.K. 54 20N 3 7W
46 Tory I., Ireland 55 17N 8 12W
160 Tory Hill, Canada 44 56N 78 18W
59 Torysa R., Cz. 48 50N 21 15E
86 Torzhok, U.S.S.R. 57 5N 34 55E
114 Tosa-wan, B., Japan .33 15N 133 30E
42 Toscaig, Scotland, U.K. 57 23N 5 49W
70-71 Toscana (Tuscany), reg., Italy 43 30N 11 5E
86 Tosno, U.S.S.R. 59 30N 30 58E
64 Tossa, Spain 41 43N 2 56E
172 Tostado, Argentina ...29 15s 61 50W
56 Tostedt, Germany 53 17N 9 42E
60 Toszek, Poland 50 27N 18 32E
79 Totak L., Norway 59 40N 8 0E
65 Totana, Spain 37 45N 1 30W
79 Toten, Norway 60 37N 10 37E
132 Toteng, Botswana 20 22s 22 58E
59 Tókomlós, Hungary ...46 24N 20 45E
34 Totland, Eng, U.K. ...50 41N 1 32W
84 Totma, U.S.S.R. 60 0N 42 40E
36 Totnes, England, U.K. 50 26N 3 41W
168 Totonicapán, Guat. ...14 50N 91 20W
143 Tottenham, Australia 32 15s 147 15E
160 Tottenham, Canada ...44 2N 79 48W
34 Totton, England, U.K. 50 55N 1 29W
114 Tottori, Japan 35 30N 134 15E
114 Tottori, Pref., Japan .35 30N 134 12E
122 Touat, Algeria 27 30N 0 30E
124 Touba, Ivory Coast ... 8 15N 7 40W
122 Toubkal, Djebel, Mor. 31 0N 8 0W
49 Toucy, France 47 44N 3 15E
124 Tougan, Upper Volta .13 11N 2 58W
123 Touggourt, Algeria 33 10N 6 0E
124 Tougué, Guinea 11 25N 11 50W
123 Toukmatine, Algeria .24 49N 7 11E
49 Toul, France 48 40N 5 53E
51 Toulon, France 43 10N 5 55E
50 Toulouse, France 43 37N 1 28E
124 Toumodi, Ivory Coast 6 32N 5 4W
122 Tounassine, Hamada, Algeria 28 48N 5 0W
103 Toungoo, Burma 19 0N 96 30E
48 Touques R., France ...49 0N 0 8E
48 Touraine, reg., France 47 20N 0 30E
49 Tourcoing, France 50 42N 3 10E
125 Tourcoingbam, Upper Volta 13 23N 1 33W
54 Tournai, Belgium 50 35N 3 25E
48 Tournan, France 48 44N 2 44E
50 Tournay, France 43 13N 0 13E
51 Tournon, Ardèche, Fr. 45 5N 4 50E
48 Tournon, Vienne, Fr. .46 45N 0 57E
51 Tournus, France 46 35N 4 54E
48 Tours, France 47 22N 0 40E
123 Touside, Pic, Chad 21 1N 16 18E
134 Touwsrivier, S. Africa 33 20s 20 0E
87 Tovarkovskiy, U.S.S.R. 53 40N 38 5E
79 Tovdal, Norway 58 47N 8 15E
79 Tovdalselv, R., Nor. .58 20N 8 16E
143 Towamba, Australia ...37 6s 149 55E
161 Towanda, U.S.A. 41 46N 76 30W
35 Towcester, Eng., U.K. 52 7N 0 56W
164 Tower, U.S.A. 47 49N 92 17W
164 Towner, U.S.A. 48 25N 100 26W
166 Townsend, U.S.A. 46 25N 111 32W
143 Townsend Mt., Austral. 36 25s 148 16E
144 Townshend, I., Austral. 22 16s 150 31E
144 Townsville, Australia .19 15s 146 45E
143 Towong, Vic., Australia 36 8s 147 59E
113 Towshan, China 22 5N 112 50E
162 Towson, U.S.A. 39 26N 76 34W
109 Towuti L., Indonesia . 2 40s 121 30E
37 Towy R., Wales, U.K. 51 54N 4 0W
37 Towyn, Wales, U.K. .52 37N 4 8W
165 Toyah, U.S.A. 31 20N 103 48W
165 Toyahvale, U.S.A. 30 58N 103 45W
114 Toyama, Japan 36 40N 137 15E
114 Toyama, pref., Japan 36 45N 137 30E
114 Toyama-wan, B., Japan 37 0N 137 30E
114 Toyohashi, Japan 34 45N 137 25E
114 Toyokawa, Japan 34 48N 137 27E
114 Toyonaka, Japan 34 50N 135 35E
114 Toyooka, Japan 35 35N 135 55E
114 Toyooka, Japan 34 50N 138 15E
123 Tozeur, Tunisia 33 54N 8 4E
62 Trabancos R., Spain .41 0N 5 3E
100 Trabzon, Turkey 41 0N 39 45E
155 Tracadie, Canada 47 30N 64 55W
167 Tracey, Calif., U.S.A. .37 46N 121 27W
164 Tracy, Minn., U.S.A. .44 12N 95 3W
70 Tradate, Italy 45 43N 8 54E
111 Tradom, Tibet, China 30 0N 83 59E
61 Trafalgar, C., Spain ...36 10N 6 2W
143 Tragalgar, Vic., Austral. 38 14s 146 12E
123 Traghan, Libya 26 0N 14 30E
143 Tragowel, Vic., Austral. 35 51s 143 59E
78 Trăian, Rumania 45 9N 27 42E
156 Trail, Canada 49 5N 117 40W
44 Tralee, Ireland 52 16N 9 42W
44 Tralee B., Ireland 52 17N 9 55W
45 Tramore, Ireland 52 10N 7 10W
45 Tramore B., Ireland ...52 9N 7 10W
81 Tranås, Sweden 58 3N 14 59E
62 Trancoso, Portugal 40 49N 7 21W
81 Tranebjærg, Denmark 55 51N 10 36E
81 Tranemo, Sweden 57 30N 13 20E
41 Tranent, Scotland, U.K. 55 57N 2 58W
107 Trang, Thailand 7 33N 99 38E
109 Trangan I., Indonesia 6 40s 134 20E
143 Trangie, N.S.W., Austral. 32 4s 148 0E
80 Trångsviken, Sweden .63 19N 14 0E
107 Tranninh Plat., Laos .19 30N 103 10E
106 Tranquebar, India 11 1N 79 54E
73 Trani, Italy 41 17N 16 24E
173 Tranqueras, Uruguay .31 8s 56 0W
131 Trans Nzoia, dist., Kenya 1 0N 35 0E
157 Transcona, Canada 49 50N 97 0W
172 Transito, Chile 28 54s 70 16W
135 Transkei, Bantu Area, S. Afr. 32 15s 28 15E
81 Träslöv, Sweden 57 8N 12 21E
80 Transtrand, Sweden ...61 6N 13 20E
133 Transvaal, province, S. Africa 25 0s 29 0E
78 Transylvania, reg. Rum. 46 19N 25 0E
78 Transylvanian Alps, Rumania 45 30N 25 0E
72 Trápani, Italy 38 1N 12 30E
166 Trappe Peak, Mt., U.S.A. 45 56N 114 29W
143 Traralgon, Vic., Austral. 38 6s 146 31E
81 Traryd, Sweden 56 35N 13 45E
124 Trarza, dist., Mauritania 17 30N 15 0W
71 Trasacco, Italy 41 58N 13 30E
78 Trascău, Mţii, mts., Rumania 46 14N 23 14E
71 Trasimeno L., Italy ...43 10N 12 5E
107 Trat, Thailand 12 14N 102 33E
58 Traun, Austria 48 14N 14 15E
57 Traunsee, L., Austria .47 48N 13 45E
57 Traunstein, Germany .47 52N 12 40E
81 Trävad, Sweden 58 15N 13 5E
56 Travemünde, Ger. 53 58N 10 52E
147 Travers, Mt., N.Z. 42 1s 172 45E
162 Traverse City, U.S.A. 44 45N 85 39W
15 Traverse I., Falk. Is. Dep. 48 0s 28 0E
74 Travnik, Yugoslavia .44 17N 17 39E
46 Trawbreaga B., Ireland 55 20N 7 20W
46 Trawenagh B., Ireland 54 53N 8 20W
37 Trawsfynydd, Wales, United Kingdom 52 55N 3 55W
142 Trayning, W. Australia 31 8s 117 42E
157 Traynor, Canada 52 20N 108 32W
62 Trazo, Spain 43 0N 8 30W
71 Trbovlje, Yugoslavia .46 12N 15 5E
70 Trebbia R., Italy 44 52N 9 30E
56 Trebel R., Germany ...54 0N 12 50E
74 Trebinje, Yugoslavia .42 44N 18 22E
73 Trebisacce, Italy 39 52N 16 32E
74 Trebišnica R., Y.-slav. 42 47N 18 8E
59 Trebišov, Cz. 48 38N 21 41E
74 Trebizat, Yugoslavia .43 15N 17 30E
58 Třeboň, Czechoslovakia 48 59N 14 48E
63 Trebujena, Spain 36 52N 6 11W
70 Trecate, Italy 45 29N 8 42E
34 Tredegar, England, U.K. 51 47N 3 16W
37 Trefeglwys, Wales, U.K. 52 31N 3 31W
37 Trefriw, Wales, U.K. .53 9N 3 50W
37 Tregaron, Wales, U.K. 52 14N 3 56W
48 Tregastel Plage, France 48 49N 3 30W
71 Tregnago, Italy 45 31N 11 10E
139 Tregosse Is., Australia 17 40s 150 50E
48 Tréguier, France 48 47N 3 16W
37 Tregynon, Wales, U.K. 52 32N 3 19W
37 Treharris, Wales, U.K. 51 40N 3 17W
157 Treherne, Canada 49 39N 98 41W
71 Treia, Italy 43 20N 13 20E
43 Treig L., Scot., U.K. .56 48N 4 42W
50 Treignac, France 45 32N 1 48E
173 Treinta-y-Tres, Uruguay 33 10s 54 50W
57 Treis, Germany 50 9N 7 19E
132 Trelawney, Rhodesia .17 30s 30 27E
81 Trelde Næs, C., Den. .55 38N 9 53E
37 Trelech, Wales, U.K. .51 56N 4 28W
176 Trelew, Argentina 43 10s 65 20W
81 Trelleborg, Sweden 55 20N 13 5E
49 Trélon, France 50 5N 4 6E
37 Tremadoc, Wales, U.K. 52 57N 4 9W
37 Tremadoc, Bay, Wales, U.K. 52 51N 4 18W
165 Trementina, U.S.A. ...35 27N 105 30W
71 Tremiti I., Italy 42 8N 15 30E
166 Tremonton, U.S.A. 41 45N 112 10W
64 Tremp, Spain 42 10N 0 52E
162 Trenary, U.S.A. 46 12N 86 59W
59 Trenčin, Czechoslovakia 48 52N 18 4E
109 Trenggalek, Indonesia 8 5s 111 44E
107 Trengganu, st., Malaya 4 55N 103 0E
172 Trenque Lauquen, Arg. 36 0s 62 45W
39 Trent, R., Eng., U.K. 53 33N 0 44W
38 Trentham, Eng., U.K. 52 59N 2 12W
70-71 Trentino-Alto Adige, reg., Italy 46 5N 11 0E
70 Trento, Italy 46 5N 11 8E
154 Trenton, Canada 44 10N 77 40W
164 Trenton, Mo., U.S.A. .40 5N 93 37W
164 Trenton, Neb., U.S.A. 40 14N 101 4W
161 Trenton N.J., U.S.A. .40 15N 74 41W
165 Trenton, Tenn., U.S.A. 35 58N 88 57W
155 Trepassey, Canada 46 43N 53 25W
56 Treptow, Germany 53 42N 13 15E
73 Trepuzzi, Italy 40 26N 18 4E
172 Tres Arroyos, Argentina 38 20s 60 20W
173 Tres Coraçoes, Brazil .21 30s 45 30W
174 Tres Esquinas, Col. ... 9 43N 75 5W
122 Tres Forcas, C., Mor. .35 26N 3 0W
175 Três Lagâos, Brazil ...20 50s 51 50W
172 Tres Lomas, Argentina 36 30s 62 50W
176 Tres Montes C., Chile .47 0s 75 35W
173 Tres Pontas, Brazil ...21 23s 45 29W
172 Tres Puentes, Chile ...27 50s 70 15W
176 Tres Puntas C., Arg. .47 0s 66 0W
173 Tres Rios, Brazil 22 20s 43 30W
36 Tresco I., Eng., U.K. .49 57N 6 20W
40 Treshnish Is., Scot., U.K. 56 30N 6 25W
74 Treska R., Yugoslavia 41 45N 21 11E
74 Treskavika Planina, Ra., Yugoslavia 43 40N 18 20E
64 Trespaderne, Spain 42 47N 3 24W
37 Tretower, Wales, U.K. 51 53N 3 11W
51 Trets, France 43 27N 5 41E
57 Treuchtlingen, Ger. ...48 58N 10 55E
37 Treuddyn, Wales,
37 Treuddyn, Wales, U.K. 53 7N 3 8W
56 Treuenbrietzen, Ger. .52 6N 12 51E
70 Treviglio, Italy 45 31N 9 35E
71 Treviso, Italy 45 40N 12 15E
36 Trevose Hd., Eng., U.K. 50 33N 5 3W
51 Trévoux, France 45 57N 4 47E
56 Treysa, West Germany 50 55N 9 11E
74 Trgovište, Yugoslavia 42 20N 22 10E
145 Triabunna, Australia .42 28s 148 0E
123 Triaga, Tunisia 30 0N 10 28E
77 Trianda, Greece 36 25N 28 10E
107 Triang, Malaysia 3 13N 102 27E
132 Triangle, Rhodesia 21 0s 31 26E
49 Triaucourt, France 48 59N 5 2E
56 Tribsees, Germany 54 4N 12 46E
164 Tribune, U.S.A. 38 30N 101 45W
73 Tricarico, Italy 40 37N 16 9E
73 Tricase, Italy 39 56N 18 20E
133 Trichard, Trans., S. Afr. 26 28s 29 13E
106 Trichinopoly, see Tiruchchirappalli, India 10 45N 78 45E
106 Trichinopoly, India ...10 30N 76 18E
106 Trichur, India 10 30N 76 18E
143 Trida, N.S.W., Austral. 33 2s 144 57E
57 Trier, Germany 49 45N 6 37E
71 Trieste, Italy 45 39N 13 45E
71 Trieste, G. di, Trieste .45 37N 13 40E
73 Triggiano, Italy 41 4N 16 58E
71 Triglav Mt., Y.-slavia 46 30N 13 45E
71 Trigno R., Italy 41 55N 14 37E
63 Trigueros, Spain 37 24N 6 50W
77 Trikeri, Greece 39 6N 23 5E
77 Trikhonis, Limni, L., Gr. 38 34N 21 30E
76 Trikkala, Greece 39 34N 21 47E
76 Trikkala, pref., Greece 39 41N 21 30E
109 Trikora Pk., Indonesia 4 11s 138 0E
71 Trilj, Yugoslavia 43 38N 16 42E

MAP
64 Trillo, Spain 40 42N 2 35W
45 Trim, Ireland 53 34N 6 48W
41 Trimdon, England, U.K. 54 43N 1 23W
35 Trimley, England, U.K. 51 59N 1 19E
106 Trincomalee, Ceylon ... 8 38N 81 15E
174 Trinidad, Bolivia 14 54S 64 50W
169 Trinidad, Cuba 21 40N 80 0W
165 Trinidad, U.S.A. 37 15N 104 30W
172 Trinidad, Uruguay 33 30S 56 50W
176 Trinidad I., Argentina 39 10S 62 0W
17 Trinidad I., Southern Atlantic Ocean 20 20S 29 50W
169 Trinidad & Tobago, st., West Indies 10 30N 61 20W
73 Trinitapoli, Italy 41 22N 16 5E
155 Trinity, Canada 48 22N 53 29W
165 Trinity, U.S.A. 30 50N 95 20W
155 Trinity B., Canada 48 20N 53 10W
165 Trinity Mts., U.S.A. ...40 20N 118 50W
165 Trinity R., Calif., U.S.A. 30 30N 95 0W
70 Trino, Italy 45 10N 8 18E
163 Trion, U.S.A. 34 35N 85 18W
73 Trionto C., Italy 39 38N 16 47E
70 Triora, Italy 44 0N 7 46E
123 Tripoli (Tarabulus), Libya 32 49N 13 7E
77 Tripolis, Greece 37 31N 22 25E
103 Tripura, st., India 24 0N 92 0E
164 Tripp, U.S.A. 43 16N 97 58W
56 Trischen I., W. Ger. ...54 3N 8 32E
17 Tristan da Cunha I., Atlantic Ocean 37 6S 12 20W
175 Triumpho, Brazil 7 0S 50 50W
106 Trivandrum, India 8 31N 77 0E
73 Trivento, Italy 41 48N 14 31E
59 Trnava, Czechoslovakia 48 23N 17 35E
144 Trobriand, Terr. of Papua 8 40S 15 10E
156 Trochu, Canada 51 50N 113 20W
154 Trodely I., Canada 52 20N 79 20W
71 Trogir, Yugoslavia 43 32N 16 15E
71 Troglav, Mt., Y.-slavia 43 56N 16 36E
79 Trögstad, Norway 59 37N 11 16E
73 Tróia, Italy 41 22N 15 19E
154 Troilus, L., Canada ...50 50N 74 35W
73 Troina, Italy 37 47N 14 34E
155 Trois Pistoles, Canada 48 5N 69 10W
154 Trois Rivières, Canada 46 25N 72 40W
90 Troitsk, U.S.S.R. 54 10N 61 35E
84 Troitsko-Pechorsk, U.S.S.R. 62 40N 56 10E
81 Trollhättan, Sweden ...58 17N 12 20E
79 Trollheimen Mts., Nor. 62 46N 9 1E
79 Tromöy, Norway 58 28N 8 53E
82 Troms, co., Norway ...69 19N 19 0E
135 Trompsburg, S. Afr. ...30 2S 25 05E
82 Tromsö, Norway 69 40N 19 0E
176 Tronador, Mt., Arg. ...41 53S 71 0W
82 Tröndelag, N., co., Nor. 65 0N 12 0E
82 Tröndelag, S., co., Nor. 62 0N 10 0E
79 Trondheim, Norway ...63 25N 10 25E
82 Trondheim Fd., Nor. .63 40N 10 45E
81 Trönninge, Sweden 56 38N 12 59E
80 Trönö, Sweden 61 22N 16 54E
71 Tronto R., Italy 42 50N 13 46E
100 Troodos Mt., Cyprus .34 58N 32 55E
40 Troon, Scotland, U.K. 55 33N 4 40W
73 Tropea, Italy 38 40N 15 53E
167 Tropic, U.S.A. 37 44N 112 4W
74 Tropojë, Albania 42 23N 20 10E
40 Trossachs, The, dist., Scotland, U.K. 56 14N 4 24W
46 Trostan Mt., N. Ireland, U.K. 55 4N 6 10W
57 Trostberg, Germany ...48 2N 12 33E
42 Trotternish, dist., Scotland, U.K. 57 32N 6 15W
165 Troup, U.S.A. 32 10N 95 3W
43 Troup Hd., Scot., U.K. 57 41N 2 18W
156 Trout L., N.W. Terr., Canada 60 40N 121 40W
157 Trout L., Ont., Canada 51 20N 93 15W
48 Trouville, France 49 21N 0 54E
34 Trowbridge, Eng., U.K. 51 18N 2 12W
100 Troy, site, Turkey 39 55N 26 20E
163 Troy, Alabama, U.S.A. 31 50N 85 58W
164 Troy, Kan., U.S.A. 39 47N 95 2W
164 Troy, Mo., U.S.A. 38 56N 90 59W
166 Troy, Montana, U.S.A. 48 30N 115 58W
161 Troy, N.Y., U.S.A. 42 45N 73 39W
162 Troy, Ohio, U.S.A. 40 0N 84 10W
160 Troy, Pa., U.S.A. 41 46N 76 48W
75 Troyan, Bulgaria 42 57N 24 43E
49 Troyes, France 48 19N 4 3E
74 Trpanj, Yugoslavia ...43 1N 17 15E
59 Trstena, Czechoslovakia 49 21N 19 37E
74 Trstenik, Yugoslavia .43 36N 21 0E
86 Trubchevsk, U.S.S.R. 52 33N 33 47E
101 Trucial States, Asia 24 0N 54 30E
166 Truckee, U.S.A. 39 29N 120 12W
169 Trujillo, Honduras 16 0N 86 0W
174 Trujillo, Peru 8 0S 79 0W
63 Trujillo, Spain 39 28N 5 55W
165 Trujillo, U.S.A. 35 34N 104 44W
174 Trujillo, Venezuela 9 22N 70 26W
136 Truk Is., U.S. Pac. Is. Trust Terr. 7 25N 151 46E
36 Trull, England, United Kingdom 50 58N 3 8W
165 Trumann, U.S.A. 35 42N 90 32W
167 Trumbull, Mt., U.S.A. 36 25N 113 32W
35 Trumpington, Eng., U.K. 52 11N 0 6E
48 Trun, France 48 50N 0 2E
143 Trundle, N.S.W., Austral. 32 52S 147 35E
155 Truro, Canada 45 21N 63 14E
36 Truro, England, U.K. 50 17N 5 2W
46 Truskmore, mt., Ire. .54 23N 8 20W
142 Truslove, W. Australia 33 20S 121 45E
81 Trustrup, Denmark ...56 20N 10 46E
167 Truth or Consequences, U.S.A. 33 9N 107 16W
58 Trutnov, Cz. 50 37N 15 54E
50 Truyère R., France ...44 56N 3 8E
37 Trwyn Cilan, Wales, United Kingdom 52 47N 4 31W
163 Tryon, U.S.A. 35 15N 82 16W
160 Tryonville, U.S.A. 41 42N 79 48W
60 Trzciel, Poland 52 23N 15 50E
60 Trzeblatów, Poland ...54 3N 15 18E
59 Trzebinia, Poland 50 11N 19 30E
60 Trzebiez, Poland 53 38N 14 31E
60 Trzebnica, Poland 51 20N 17 1E
60 Trzemeszno, Poland ...52 33N 17 48E
71 Tržič, Yugoslavia 46 22N 14 18E
129 Tsabong, Botswana ...26 2S 22 29E
98 Tsafriya, Israel 31 59N 34 51E
112 Tsagaan-Üür, Mongolia 50 27N 101 35E
111 Tsaidam, swamp, China 37 0N 95 0E
76 Tsamandás, Greece 39 46N 20 21E
113 Tsamkong (Chankiang), China .21 7N 110 21E
103 Tsana Dzong, Tibet, China 28 0N 91 55E
132 Tsane, Botswana 24 5S 21 54E
103 Tsanga, China 30 43N 100 32E
112 Tsanghsien, China 38 24N 116 57E
111 Tsangpo R., Tibet, China 29 40N 89 0E
113 Tsaochwang, China ...35 11N 115 28E
113 Tsaohsien, China 34 50N 115 45E
129 Tsaratanana, Malg. ...16 47S 47 39E
111 Tsaring Nor, L., China 35 0N 97 0E
76 Tsaritsáni, Greece 39 53N 15 14E
131 Tsavo, Kenya 3 0S 38 28E
88 Tsebrikovo, U.S.S.R. .47 9N 30 10E
98 Tseelim, Israel 31 13N 34 32E
98 Tsefa, Israel 31 3N 35 14E
90 Tselinograd, U.S.S.R. 51 10N 71 30E
86 Tsementny, U.S.S.R. .53 30N 34 10E
113 Tsenkung, China 27 3N 108 40E
132 Tsessebe, Botswana ...20 43S 27 32E
112 Tsetserling, Mongolia .47 29N 101 10E
111 Tsetserleg, Mongolia ...47 36N 101 32E
130 Tshela, Congo 5 4S 13 0E
130 Tshikapa, Congo 6 17S 21 0E
131 Tshinsenda, Congo 12 15S 28 0E
130 Tshitadi, Congo 6 46S 21 43E
130 Tshofa, Congo 5 8S 25 8E
129 Tshombe, Malagasy Rep. 25 18S 45 29E
132 Tshongola, Congo 12 14S 29 47E
130 Tshuapa, dist., Congo 0 5S 21 5E
130 Tshuapa R., Congo 0 33S 21 56E
129 Tshwane, Botswana ...22 24S 22 1E
112 Tsian, China 41 12N 126 5E
113 Tsiaotse, China 35 11N 113 37E
89 Tsimlyansk, U.S.S.R. 47 45N 42 0E
89 Tsimlyansk Res., U.S.S.R. 48 0N 43 0E
112 Tsimo, China 36 25N 120 29E
159 Tsin, Ling Shan, mts., China 34 0N 107 30E
113 Tsinan, China 34 50N 105 40E
112 Tsinan, China 36 41N 116 59E
112 Tsincheng, China 35 30N 113 0E
76 Tsinga, mt., Greece ...41 23N 24 44E
113 Tsinghai, China 38 56N 116 52E
111 Tsinghai, reg., China .35 10N 96 0E
113 Tsinghsien, China 26 30N 109 30E
113 Tsingkiang, China 27 50N 114 38E
113 Tsingkiang, China 33 30N 119 2E
113 Tsingliu, China 26 0N 116 50E
113 Tsinglo, China 38 40N 112 0E
113 Tsingning, China 35 25N 105 50E
113 Tsingshih, China 29 43N 112 13E
113 Tsingsi (Kweishun), China 23 6N 106 25E
112 Tsingsi, China 38 1N 114 4E
112 Tsingtao, China 36 0N 120 25E
112 Tsingtung Res., China 37 34N 105 40E
112 Tsingyuan, China 37 43N 104 35E
113 Tsingyün, China 23 45N 112 55E
112 Tsining, China 35 30N 116 35E
112 Tsining, China 40 59N 112 59E
113 Tsingyang, China 35 2N 112 59E
98 Tsippori, Israel 32 64N 35 16E
135 Tsitsa Bridge, S. Africa 31 12S 28 27E
112 Tsitsihar, China 47 20N 124 0E
134 Tsitsikammaberge, mts, C. Prov., S. Afr. 33 50S 23 40E
87 Tsivilsk, U.S.S.R. 55 50N 47 25E
129 Tsivory, Malagasy Rep. 24 4S 46 5E
89 Tskhinvali, U.S.S.R. .42 14N 44 1E
132 Tsodilo Hill, Botswana 18 49S 21 43E
135 Tsoelike, Lesotho 29 53N 28 47E
135 Tsolo, C. Prov., S. Afr. 31 18S 28 46E
135 Tsomo, C. Prov., S.Afr. 32 2S 27 51E
87 Tsna R., U.S.S.R. 54 0N 41 57E
103 Tsona Dzong, Tibet, China 28 0N 91 55E
112 Tsowhsien, China 35 29N 117 0E
114 Tsu, Japan 34 45N 136 25E
114 Tsuchiura, Japan 36 12N 140 15E
114 Tsugaru Str., Japan ...41 30N 140 30E
112 Tsuiluan, China 47 58N 28 27E
129 Tsumeb, S.W. Africa .19 9S 17 44E
129 Tsumis, S.W. Africa ...23 39S 17 29E
113 Tsungfa, China 23 35N 113 35E
113 Tsungming Tao, China 31 40N 121 40E
112 Tsungsin, China 35 2N 107 0E
113 Tsungtso, China 22 26N 107 34E
113 Tsunyi, China 27 40N 107 0E
114 Tsuruga, Japan 35 35N 136 0E
114 Tsushima I., Japan ...34 20N 129 20E
114 Tsushima Str., Jpan ...34 20N 130 0E
114 Tsuyama, Japan 35 0N 134 0E
88 Tsvetkovo, U.S.S.R. .49 15N 31 33E
107 Tu, R., Burma 22 50N 97 15E
63 Tua R., Portugal 41 19N 7 15W
147 Tuai, New Zealand 38 47S 177 15E
146 Tuakau, New Zealand 37 16S 174 59E
109 Tual, Indonesia 5 30S 132 50E
44 Tuam, Ireland 53 30N 8 50W
147 Tuamarina, N.Z. 41 25S 173 59E
44 Tuamgraney, Ireland .52 54N 8 32W
137 Tuamotu Arch., Pac. Oc. 17 0S 144 0W
113 Tuan, China 23 59N 108 3E
109 Tuao, Philippines 17 47S 121 30E
89 Tuapse, U.S.S.R. 44 5N 39 10E
147 Tuatapere, N.Z. 48 7S 167 43E
40 Tuath Loch, Scot., U.K. 56 2N 6 15W
167 Tuba City, U.S.A. 36 8N 111 12W
167 Tubac, U.S.A. 31 45N 111 2W
136 Tubai Is. (Austral Is.), Pac. Oc. 25 0S 150 0W
108 Tuban, Indonesia 6 57S 112 4E
173 Tubarão, Brazil 28 30S 49 0W
98 Tubas, Jordan 32 20N 35 22E
108 Tubau, Sar., Malaysia 3 11N 113 45E
56 Tübingen, Germany ...48 31N 9 4E
126 Tubja, W., Si.-Arabia 25 27N 38 55E
121 Tubruq (Tobruk), Libya 32 7N 23 55E
174 Tucabaca, Bolivia 18 30S 58 55W
174 Tucacas, Venezuela ...10 48N 68 19W
113 Tuchang, China 25 19N 116 15E
60 Tuchola, Poland 53 33N 17 52E
59 Tuchów, Poland 49 54N 21 1E
142 Tuckanarra, W. Austral. 27 8S 118 1E
169 Tucker's Town, Bermuda 32 19N 64 43W
167 Tucson, U.S.A. 32 14N 110 59W
172 Tucumán, Argentina .26 50S 65 20W
172 Tucumán, prov., Arg. 26 48S 66 2W
165 Tucumcari, U.S.A. 35 12N 103 45W
174 Tucupita, Venezuela . 9 14N 62 3W
64 Tudela, Spain 42 4N 1 39W
62 Tudela de Duero, Spain 41 37N 4 39W
155 Tudor, Lac, Canada ...55 50N 65 0W
78 Tudora, Rumania 47 31N 26 45E
37 Tudweiliog, Wales, U.K. 52 54N 4 37W
62 Tuella R., Portugal ...41 50N 7 10W
145 Tuen, Queens., Austral. 28 33S 145 37E
144 Tufi, Terr. of Papua ... 9 3S 149 16E
135 Tugela, Natal, S. Africa 29 9S 31 29E
135 Tugela R., Natal, S. Afr. 28 44S 31 0E
109 Tuguegarao, Philippines 17 35N 121 42E
91 Tugur, U.S.S.R. 53 50N 136 45E
113 Tuhshan, China 25 40N 107 30E
133 Tuinplaas, S. Africa ...24 52S 28 48E
109 Tukangbesi Is., Indon. 6 0S 124 0E
154 Tukarak I., Canada ...56 15N 78 10W
124 Tukobo, Ghana 5 1N 2 47W
123 Tukrah, Libya 32 30N 20 37E
127 Tuku, mt., Ethiopia ... 9 10N 36 43E
86 Tukums, U.S.S.R. 57 2N 23 3E
131 Tukuyu, Tanzania 9 17S 33 35E
168 Tula Hidalgo, Mexico 20 0N 99 20W
168 Tula, Tamaulipas, Mex. 23 0N 99 40W
125 Tula, Nigeria 9 51N 11 27E
87 Tula, U.S.S.R. 54 13N 37 32E
101 Tulak, Afghanistan ...33 55N 63 40E
111 Tulan, China 37 24N 98 1E
167 Tulare, U.S.A. 36 15N 119 26W
167 Tulare Lake, U.S.A. ...36 0N 119 53W
167 Tularosa, U.S.A. 33 4N 106 1W
134 Tulbagh, S. Africa 33 16S 19 6E
174 Tulcan, Ecuador 0 48N 77 43W
78 Tulcea, Rumania 45 13N 28 46E
78 Tulcea, Reg., Rum. 45 0N 28 50E
88 Tulchin, U.S.S.R. 48 41N 28 55E
129 Tuléar, Malagasy Rep. 23 21S 43 40E
157 Tulemalu L., Canada .62 50N 100 0W
78 Tulghes, Rumania 4 58N 25 45E
109 Tuli, Indonesia 1 24S 122 26E
132 Tuli, Rhodesia 21 58S 29 13E
132 Tuli R., Rhodesia 21 30S 29 0E
98 Tulkarm, Jordan 32 19N 35 10E
44 Tulla, Ireland 52 53N 8 45W
165 Tulla, U.S.A. 34 35N 101 44W
40 Tulla L., Scot., U.K. .56 33N 4 47W
46 Tullaghoge, N. Ire., U.K. 54 36N 6 43W
163 Tullahoma, U.S.A. 35 23N 86 12W
45 Tullaghought, Ireland 52 25N 7 22W
143 Tullamore, Australia .32 39S 147 36E
45 Tullamore, Ireland 53 17N 7 30W
45 Tullaroan, Ireland 52 40N 7 27W
50 Tulle, France 45 16N 1 47E
143 Tullibigeal, Australia .34 19S 146 20E
51 Tullins, France 45 18N 5 29E
58 Tulln, Austria 48 20N 16 4E
45 Tullow, Ireland 52 48N 6 45W
127 Tullus, Sudan 11 7N 24 40E
46 Tully, Ireland 53 44N 8 9W
144 Tully, Queens., Austral. 17 30S 141 0E
44 Tully Cross, Ireland ...53 35N 9 59W
121 Tulmaythah, Libya ...32 40N 20 55E
144 Tulmur, Australia 22 40S 142 20E
78 Tulnici, Rumania 45 51N 26 38E
75 Tulovo, Bulgaria 42 33N 25 32E
165 Tulsa, U.S.A. 36 10N 96 0W
156 Tulsequah, Canada 58 39N 133 35W
46 Tulsk, Ireland 53 47N 8 15W
127 Tulu Milki, Ethiopia . 9 55N 38 14E
127 Tulu Welel, Mt., Ethiopia 8 56N 35 30E
174 Tuluá, Colombia 4 6N 76 11W
91 Tulun, U.S.S.R. 54 40N 100 10E
109 Tulungagung, Indon. . 8 5S 111 54E
109 Tum, Indonesia 3 28S 130 21E
87 Tuma, U.S.S.R. 55 10N 40 30E
169 Tuma R., Nicaragua . 13 18N 84 50W
174 Tumaco, Colombia 1 50N 78 45W
174 Tumatumari, Guyana 5 20N 58 55W
80 Tumba, Sweden 59 12N 17 48E
130 Tumba L., Congo 0 50S 18 0E
143 Tumbarumba, Australia 35 44S 148 0E
174 Tumbes, Peru 3 30S 80 20W
130 Tumbwe, Congo 11 25S 27 15E
138 Tumby B., S. Australia 34 21S 136 8E
112 Tumen, China 42 46N 129 59E
112 Tumen Ra., N. Korea 41 45N 129 15E
112 Tumen R., China 42 30N 130 0E
174 Tumeremo, Venezuela 7 18N 61 30W
106 Tumkur, India 13 18N 77 12E
81 Tumleberg, Sweden ...58 16N 12 52E
41 Tummel L., Scot., U.K. 56 43N 3 55W
41 Tummel R., Scot., U.K. 56 42N 4 5W
123 Tummo, Libya 22 45N 14 8E
123 Tummo Dhoba, mts., Niger 22 30N 14 31E
102 Tump, West Pakistan 26 7N 62 16E
107 Tumpat, Malaysia 6 11N 102 10E
105 Tumsar, India 21 26N 79 45E
124 Tumu, Ghana 10 56N 1 56E
143 Tumut, N.S.W., Austral. 35 16S 148 13E
166 Tumwater, U.S.A. 47 0N 122 58W
169 Tunas de Zaca, Cuba .21 39N 79 34W
145 Tunbridge, Tas., Australia 42 5S 147 28E
135 Tunbridge Wells, England, U.K. 51 7N 0 16E
143 Tuncurry, Australia 32 9S 152 29E
132 Tunduma, Tanzania ... 9 20S 32 48E
131 Tunduru, Tanzania ...11 0S 37 25E
75 Tundzha R., Bulgaria 42 0N 26 35E
79 Tune, Norway 59 16N 11 2E
113 Tung-Shan I., China .23 40N 117 25E
106 Tunga R., India 13 42N 75 20E
103 Tunga Pass, India 29 0N 94 14E
106 Tungabhadra Dam, India 15 21N 76 23E
106 Tungabhadra R., India 15 30N 77 0E
113 Tungcheng, China 31 0N 117 3E
112 Tungchow, China 39 58N 116 50E
113 Tungchuan, China 35 4N 109 2E
112 Tungfanghsien, (Paso), China 18 50N 108 33E
112 Tunghsien, China 39 50N 116 45E
112 Tunghwa, China 41 46N 126 0E
113 Tungien, China 27 45N 109 3E
113 Tungjen, China 27 40N 109 10E
113 Tungkang, Taiwan 22 18N 120 29E
112 Tungkiang, Heilungkiang, China 47 40N 132 30E
113 Tungkiang, Szechwan, China 31 55N 107 30E
112 Tungkingcheng, China 44 5N 129 15E
113 Tungkun, China 23 0N 113 45E
112 Tungkwan, China 37 50N 116 35E
113 Tungkwan, China 34 40N 110 10E
169 Tungla, Nicaragua 13 24N 84 15W
113 Tunglan, China 24 30N 107 0E
112 Tungliao, China 43 42N 122 11E
113 Tungliu, China 30 13N 117 1E
113 Tunglu, China 29 50N 119 35E
112 Tungping, China 35 50N 116 20E
103 Tungpu, China 31 42N 98 19E
113 Tungshan, China 29 36N 144 28E
113 Tungshan, Is., China .23 40N 117 31E
112 Tungsheng, China 39 57N 110 0E
166 Tungsten, U.S.A. 40 50N 118 10W
113 Tungtai, China 32 55N 120 15E
113 Tungtao, China 26 15N 109 25E
113 Tungtze, China 27 59N 106 56E
91 Tunguska, Lower, R., U.S.S.R. 64 0N 95 0E
91 Tunguska, Stony, R., U.S.S.R. 61 0N 98 0E
113 Tungyang, China 29 12N 120 12E
112 Tunhwa, China 43 27N 128 16E
111 Tunhwang, China 40 5N 94 46E
106 Tuni, India 17 22N 82 43E
165 Tunica, U.S.A. 34 43N 90 23W
123 Tunis, Tunisia 36 50N 10 11E
123 Tunis, Gulf of, Tunisia 37 0N 10 30E
123 Tunisia, Rep., Africa .33 30N 9 10E
174 Tunja, Colombia 5 40N 73 25W
161 Tunkhannock, U.S.A. 41 32N 75 56W
113 Tunki, China 29 44N 118 4E
112 Tunsiu, China 36 15N 112 45E
82 Tunnsjöen, L., Norway 64 45N 13 25E
81 Tunö I., Denmark 55 58N 10 27E
35 Tunstall, England, U.K. 52 7N 1 28E
155 Tunungayualuk I., Can. 56 0N 61 0W
172 Tunuyan, Argentina ...33 55S 69 0W
167 Tuolumne, U.S.A. 37 59N 120 16W
173 Tupa, Brazil 21 57S 50 28W
163 Tupelo, U.S.A. 34 15N 88 42W
174 Tupinambaranas I., Brazil 3 0S 58 0W
172 Tupiza, Bolivia 21 30S 65 40W
161 Tupper L., U.S.A. 44 18N 74 30W
172 Tupungato, mt., Arg. .33 15S 69 50W
174 Tuquerres, Colombia . 1 5N 77 37W
98 Tur, Jordan 31 47N 35 14E
106 Tura, India 25 30N 90 16E
91 Tura, U.S.S.R. 64 20N 99 30E
126 Turaba, W., Si. Arabia 21 15N 41 32E
106 Turaiyur, India 11 9N 78 38E
146 Turakina, N.Z. 40 3S 175 16E
146 Turakirae, Hd., N.Z. .41 26S 174 56E
89 Turali C., U.S.S.R. 42 51N 47 32E
101 Turan, Iran 35 45N 56 50E
90 Turanain Pl., U.S.S.R. 45 0N 63 0E
100 Turayf, Saudi Arabia .31 45N 38 30E
59 Turbacz, mt., Poland .49 35N 20 13E
102 Turbat, W. Pakistan .26 0N 63 0E
74 Turbe, Yugoslavia 44 15N 17 35E
174 Turbo, Colombia 8 6N 76 43W
59 Turciansky Svaty Martin, Cz. 49 6N 18 48E
78 Turda, Rumania 46 35N 23 48E
80 Tureberg, Sweden 59 30N 17 58E
62 Turegano, Spain 41 9N 4 1W
60 Turek, Poland 52 3N 18 30E
111 Turfan China 43 4N 89 24E
111 Turfan Depression, China 43 0N 88 0E
75 Turgovishte, Bulgaria 43 17N 26 38E
100 Turgutlu, Turkey 38 30N 27 48E
132 Turgwe R., Rhodesia .20 17S 31 46E
88 Turhal, Turkey 40 24N 36 19E
175 Turi Pta., Brazil 1 25S 44 50W
64 Turia R., Spain 39 43N 1 0W
175 Turiaçu, Brazil 1 40S 45 28W
175 Turiaçu R., Brazil 3 0S 46 0W
69 Turiec R., Cz. 48 52N 18 30E
70 Turin (Torino), Italy .45 3N 7 40E
156 Turin Taber, Canada .49 47N 112 24W
86 Turka, U.S.S.R. 49 10N 23 0E
90 Turkestan, U.S.S.R. ...43 10N 68 10E
59 Turkeve, Hungary 47 6N 20 44E
87 Turkey, rep., Asia & Europe 39 0N 36 0E
87 Turki, U.S.S.R. 52 0N 43 15E
90 Turkmenistan (Turkmen S.S.R.), U.S.S.R. 39 0N 59 0E
169 Turks Is., West Indies 21 20N 71 20W
169 Turks Island Passage, West Indies 21 30N 71 20W
83 Turku (Abo), Finland 60 27N 22 14E
83 Turku-Pori, prov., Fin. 60 27N 22 15E
167 Turlock, U.S.A. 37 30N 120 55W
131 Turkwel, R., Kenya ... 3 0N 35 25E
157 Turnberry, Canada 53 25N 101 45W
40 Turnberry, Scotland, U.K. 55 19N 4 50W
169 Turneffe Is., Br. Hond. 17 20N 87 50W
166 Turner, U.S.A. 48 52N 108 25W
156 Turner Valley, Canada 50 40N 114 30W
161 Turners Falls, U.S.A. 42 36N 72 34W
54 Turnhout, Belgium 51 19N 4 57E
55 Türnich, Germany 50 52N 6 42E
58 Turnitz, Austria 47 55N 15 29E
157 Turnor L., Canada 56 35N 108 50W
58 Turnov, Czechoslovakia 50 34N 15 10E
75 Tŭrnovo, Bulgaria 43 5N 25 41E
75 Tŭrnovo, Prov., Bulg. 43 4N 25 39E
78 Turnu Măgurele, Rum. 43 46N 24 56E
78 Turnu Roşu Pass, Rum. 45 33N 24 17E
78 Turnu-Severin, Rum. 44 39N 22 41E
81 Turö, Denmark 55 2N 10 40E
165 Turon, U.S.A. 37 48N 98 27W
1 Turrialba, Vol., Central America 10 2N 83 45W
87 Tursha, U.S.S.R. 56 50N 47 45E
73 Tursi, Italy 40 15N 16 27E
144 Turtle Hd. I., Austral. 10 50S 142 37E
164 Turtle L., N.D., U.S.A. 47 30N 100 55W
164 Turtle L., Wis., U.S.A. 45 22N 92 10W
157 Turtleford, Canada ...53 30N 108 50W
146 Turua, New Zealand .37 14S 175 35E

MAP
100 Turūbah, Saudi Arabia 28 20N 43 15E
91 Turukhansk, U.S.S.R. 65 50N 87 50E
58 Turya, U.S.S.R. 62 50N 50 15E
59 Turzovka, Cz. 49 25N 18 41E
163 Tuscaloosa, U.S.A. 33 13N 87 31W
70 Tuscan Arch, Italy 42 30N 10 30E
71 Tuscania, Italy 42 25N 11 53E
70-71 Tuscany (Toscana), reg., Italy 43 28N 11 15E
162 Tuscola, Ill., U.S.A. ...39 48N 88 15W
165 Tuscola, Tex., U.S.A. .32 15N 99 48W
163 Tuscumbia, Ala., U.S.A. 34 42N 87 42W
112 Tushikow, China 41 25N 115 55E
87 Tushino, U.S.S.R. 55 44N 37 29E
163 Tuskegee, U.S.A. 32 24N 85 39W
79 Tustna I., Norway 63 10N 8 10E
60 Tuszyn, Poland 51 36N 19 33E
81 Tutaryd, Sweden 56 54N 13 59E
87 Tutayev, U.S.S.R. 57 55N 39 30E
34 Tutbury, England, U.K. 52 52N 1 41W
106 Tutikorin, India 8 50N 78 12E
74 Tutin, Yugoslavia 43 0N 20 20E
175 Tutoia, Brazil 2 45S 42 20W
147 Tutoko Mt., N.Z. 44 35S 168 1E
108 Tutong, Brunei 4 47N 114 34E
78 Tutova R., Rumania .46 20N 27 30E
75 Tutrakan, Bulgaria ...44 2N 26 40E
57 Tuttlingen, Germany .47 59N 8 50E
137 Tutila I., U.S. Samoa 14 20S 170 5W
1 Tutupaca, Vol., S. Amer. 17 0S 70 28W
112 Tuul Gol, R., Mongolia 48 30N 104 25E
91 Tuva A.S.S.R., U.S.S.R. 51 30N 95 0E
169 Tuxford, England, U.K. 53 14N 0 52W
168 Tuxpan, Mexico 20 50N 97 30W
168 Tuxtla Gutierrez, Mex. 16 50N 93 10W
62 Tuy, Spain 42 3N 8 39W
107 Tuy Hoa, S. Vietnam 13 5N 109 17E
107 Tuyen Hoa, S. Vietnam 17 55N 106 3E
113 Tuyun, China 26 5N 107 20E
100 Tuz Gölü, L., Turkey .38 45N 33 30E
100 Tuz Khurmatli, Iraq .34 52N 44 41E
100 Tuz Khurmātu, Iraq .34 50N 44 45E
74 Tuzla, Yugoslavia 44 34N 18 41E
89 Tuzlov, R., U.S.S.R. .47 28N 39 45E
88 Tuzly, U.S.S.R. 45 50N 30 5E
81 Tvååker, Sweden 57 4N 12 25E
81 Tværsted, Denmark ...57 36N 10 12E
75 Tvarditsa, Bulgaria ...42 42N 25 53E
81 Tvarskog, Sweden 56 34N 16 0E
81 Tved, Denmark 56 12N 10 25E
79 Tvedestrand, Norway 58 38N 8 58E
79 Tvelt, Norway 60 30N 7 11E
79 Tveitsund, Norway 59 2N 8 31E
43 Twatt, Scotland, U.K. 59 6N 3 15W
133 Twee Buffels, S. Afr. 26 9S 26 30E
160 Tweed, Canada 44 30N 77 20W
41 Tweed, R., Scot., U.K. 55 42N 2 10W
39 Tweedmouth, Eng., U.K. 55 46N 2 1W
41 Tweedshaws, Scot., U.K. 55 26N 3 29W
156 Tweedsmuir Prov., Park, Canada 53 10N 126 20W
135 Tweeling, O.F.S., S. Africa 27 38S 28 30E
134 Tweevulpoort, S. Africa 30 1S 24 50E
167 Twentynine Palms, U.S.A. 34 10N 116 4W
155 Twillingate, Canada ...49 42N 54 45W
166 Twin Bridges, U.S.A. .45 33N 112 23W
166 Twin Falls, U.S.A. ...42 30N 114 30W
126 Twin Hills, Egypt 24 52N 26 42E
45 Two Mile Borris, Ire. .52 41N 7 43W
166 Twin Peaks, mt. U.S.A. 44 40N 114 25W
164 Twin Valley, U.S.A. ...47 18N 96 15W
166 Twisp, U.S.A. 48 21N 120 5W
55 Twistenden, Germany 51 34N 6 13E
56 Twistringen, Germany 52 48N 8 38E
164 Two Harbors, U.S.A. .47 6N 91 30W
162 Two Rivers, U.S.A. 44 10N 87 31W
147 Two Thumb R., N.Z. .43 45S 170 44E
144 Two Tree, Australia ...18 25S 140 3E
143 Twofold B., Australia 37 8S 149 59E
127 Twong, Sudan 5 18N 28 29E
35 Twyford, Berks., England, U.K. 51 29N 0 51W
34 Twyford, Hants., England, U.K. 51 1N 1 19W
81 Ty, reg., Denmark 56 27N 8 32E
81 Tyborön, Denmark 56 42N 8 12E
35 Tydd St. Mary, England, U.K. 52 45N 0 9E
60 Tykocin, Poland 53 13N 22 46E
38 Tyldesley, Eng., U.K. 53 31N 2 29W
165 Tyler, U.S.A. 32 20N 95 15W
164 Tyler, Minn., U.S.A. .44 18N 96 15W
79 Tylldal, Norway 62 7N 10 45E
81 Tylösand, Sweden 56 33N 12 40E
58 Tyn nad Vltavou, Cz. 49 13N 14 26E
74 Tynagh, Ireland 53 10N 8 22W
147 Tyndall Mt., N.Z. 43 15S 170 55E
40 Tyndrum, Scot., U.K. 56 26N 4 41W
38 Tyne R., Eng., U.K. .54 58N 1 56W
41 Tyne R., Scot., U.K. .55 58N 2 45W
39 Tynemouth, Eng., U.K. 55 1N 1 27W
39 Tyneside, Eng., U.K. 55 0N 1 27W
79 Tynset, Norway 62 17N 10 47E
MAP
98 Tyre, see Sur, Lebanon 33 19N 35 16E
143 Tyrell L. & Cr., Austral. 35 22S 143 0E
143 Tyrendarra, Australia 38 12S 141 50E
79 Tyrifjorden L., Nor. ...60 2N 10 3E
81 Tyringe, Sweden 56 9N 13 35E
79 Tyristrand, Norway ...60 5N 10 5E
112 Tyrma, U.S.S.R. 50 0N 132 2E
89 Tyrny Auz, U.S.S.R. .43 21N 42 45E
58 Tyrol (Tirol), prov., Austria 46 50N 11 20E
46 Tyrone co., N. Ire., U.K. 54 40N 7 15W
160 Tyrone, Pa., U.S.A. ...40 39N 78 10W
66 Tyrrhenian Sea, Europe 40 0N 12 30E
82 Tys Fd., Norway 68 5N 16 28E
79 Tysnesöy I., Norway .60 1N 5 30E
79 Tyssedal, Norway 60 7N 6 35E
81 Tystberga, Sweden 58 51N 17 15E
86 Tysmenitsa, U.S.S.R. .48 58N 24 50E
90 Tyumen, U.S.S.R. 57 0N 65 18E
79 Tyvoll, Norway 62 43N 11 21E
36 Tywardreath, Eng., U.K. 50 21N 4 40W
37 Tywi, R., Wales, U.K. 52 2N 3 53W
133 Tzaneen, Trans., S. Afr. 23 47S 30 9E
113 Tzechung, China 29 47N 104 50E
112 Tzehsien, China 36 25N 114 24E
113 Tzeki, China 27 40N 117 5E
113 Tzekung, China 29 25N 104 30E
113 Tzekwei, China 31 0N 110 46E
112 Tzepo, China 36 28N 117 58E
77 Tzermiadhes Neapolis, Greece 35 11N 25 29E
113 Tzetung, China 31 31N 105 1E
113 Tzeyang, China 32 47N 108 58E
112 Tzeyang, China 35 44N 116 51E
76 Tzoumerka Mt., Greece 39 30N 21 26E
103 Tzuchien, China 27 43N 98 34E

U

122 Uad Ernt, W. Spanish Sahara 26 30N 9 30W
42 Uamh, L., nan, Scot. U.K. 56 50N 5 45W
133 Uanetsi R., Mozambique 24 35S 32 29E
99 Uarsciek, Somali Rep. 2 28N 45 55E
131 Uasin-Gishu, dist., Ken. 0 42N 35 0E
98 Uassem, Syria 32 59N 36 2E
174 Uatumá R., Brazil 1 30S 59 25W
174 Uaupés, Brazil 0 8S 67 5W
174 Uaupés, R., Brazil 0 2N 67 16W
74 Ub, Yugoslavia 44 28N 20 6E
173 Uba, Brazil 21 0S 43 0W
55 Ubach-Palenberg, Ger. 50 55N 6 9E
173 Ubatuba, Brazil 23 27S 45 6W
104 Ubauro, West Pakistan 28 15N 69 45E
114 Ube, Japan 34 6N 131 20E
65 Ubeda, Spain 38 3N 3 23W
175 Uberaba, Brazil 19 50S 48 0W
175 Uberlandia, Brazil 19 0S 48 20W
125 Ubiaja, Nigeria 6 41N 6 22E
135 Ubombo, Natal, S. Afr. 27 31S 32 4E
107 Ubon Ratchathani, Thailand 15 15N 10 50E
86 Ubort R., U.S.S.R. 51 45N 28 30E
63 Ubrique, Spain 36 41N 5 27W
130 Ubundi, Congo 0 22S 25 30E
174 Ucayali, R., Peru 6 0S 75 0W
157 Uchi Lake, Canada 51 10N 92 40W
90 Uchinya, U.S.S.R. 60 5N 65 15E
116 Uchiura, B., Japan 42 25N 140 40E
56 Uchte, Germany 52 29N 8 52E
56 Uckerath, W. Germany 50 44N 7 22E
35 Uckfield, England, U.K. 50 58N 0 6E
156 Ucluelet, Canada 48 57N 125 32W
78 Ucuris, Rumania 46 41N 21 58E
104 Udaipur, India 24 36N 73 44E
105 Udaipur Garhi, Nepal 27 0N 86 35E
106 Udamalpet, India 10 35N 77 15E
71 Udbina, Yugoslavia ...44 31N 15 47E
81 Udby, Randers, Den. .56 36N 10 20E
80 Uddeholm, Sweden 60 1N 13 38E
81 Uddevalla, Sweden 58 21N 11 55E
41 Uddingston, Scot., U.K. 55 50N 4 3W
82 Uddjaur, L., Sweden .65 55N 17 50E
55 Uden, Netherlands 51 40N 5 37E
106 Udgir, India 18 25N 77 5E
104 Udhampur, Jammu, Kashmir 33 0N 75 5E
125 Udi, Nigeria 6 23N 7 21E
71 Udine, Italy 46 5N 13 10E
71 Udine, region, Italy ...46 3N 13 13E
106 Udipi, India 13 25N 74 42E
87 Udmurt, A.S.S.R., U.S.S.R. 57 30N 52 30E
107 Udon Thani, Thailand 17 29N 102 46E
125 Udubo, Nigeria 11 52N 10 35E
131 Udzungwa Range, Tanz. 11 15S 35 10E
114 Ueda, Japan 36 30N 138 10E
14 Uedineniya I., U.S.S.R. 78 0N 85 0E
42 Uerdingen, Germany .51 21N 6 38E
130 Uele, R., Congo 3 50N 22 40E
91 Uelen, U.S.S.R. 66 10N 170 0W
56 Uelzen, Germany 53 0N 10 33E
84 Ufa, U.S.S.R. 54 45N 55 55E
MAP
84 Ufa R., U.S.S.R. 56 30N 58 10E
36 Uffculme, Eng., U.K. .50 45N 3 19W
35 Ufford, England, U.K. 52 6N 1 22E
131 Ufipa, dist., Tanzania 8 0S 30 50E
129 Ugab R., S.W. Africa 20 55S 14 30E
131 Ugalla R., Tanzania ... 6 0S 32 0E
134 Ugamas, S.W. Africa .28 0S 19 41E
131 Uganda, state, E. Africa 2 0N 32 0E
36 Ugborough, Eng., U.K. 50 22N 3 53W
73 Ugento, Italy 39 55N 18 10E
125 Ugep, Nigeria 5 53N 8 2E
135 Ugie, C. Prov., S. Africa 31 10S 28 13E
65 Ugijar, Spain 36 58N 3 7W
51 Ugine, France 45 45N 6 25E
126 Ugla, Saudi Rabia 25 40N 37 42E
91 Uglegorsk, U.S.S.R. ...49 10N 142 5E
87 Uglich, U.S.S.R. 57 33N 38 13E
71 Ugljane, Yugoslavia ...43 35N 16 46E
86 Ugra R., U.S.S.R. 54 45N 35 30E
75 Ugŭrchin, Bulgaria 43 6N 24 26E
59 Uh, R., Czechoslovakia 48 40N 22 0E
59 Uherské Hradiste, Cz. 49 4N 17 30E
59 Uhersky Brod, Cz. 49 1N 17 40E
160 Uhrichsville, U.S.A. ...40 23N 81 22W
42 Uig, Lewis, Scot., U.K. 58 13N 7 1W
42 Uig, Skye, Scot., U.K. 57 35N 6 20W
130 Uige, dist., Angola 7 0S 15 30E
112 Uiju, North Korea 40 15N 124 35E
166 Uinta Mts., U.S.A. 40 45N 110 30W
42 Uist, N. & S., Is., Scotland, U.K. 57 35N 7 15W
135 Uitenhage, S. Africa ...33 40S 25 28E
54 Uithuizen, Netherlands 53 24N 6 41E
134 Uitkoms, S. Africa ...32 44S 24 37E
122 Ujda (Oujda), Morocco 34 45N 2 0W
59 Ujfehértó, Hungary ...47 49N 21 41E
104 Ujhani, India 28 0N 79 6E
131 Ujiji, Tanzania 4 50S 29 45E
104 Ujjain, India 23 9N 75 43E
59 Ujpest, Hungary 47 33N 19 6E
59 Ujszász, Hungary 47 19N 20 7E
91 Uka, U.S.S.R. 57 50N 162 0E
131 Ukara I., Tanzania 1 44S 33 0E
125 Ukehe, Nigeria 6 40N 7 24E
131 Ukerewe Is., Tanzania 2 0S 33 0E
87 Ukholovo, U.S.S.R. ...54 57N 39 58E
103 Ukhrul, India 25 10N 94 25E
84 Ukhta, U.S.S.R. 63 55N 54 0E
166 Ukiah, U.S.A. 39 10N 123 9W
86 Ukmerge, U.S.S.R. 55 15N 24 45E
85 Ukraine S.S.R., U.S.S.R. 48 0N 35 0E
131 Ukuti, Uganda 3 38N 33 31E
112 Ulaan Nuur, Mongolia 44 30N 103 40E
112 Ulaangom, Mongolia .50 0N 92 10E
112 Ulan-Bator (Ulaanbaatar), Mongolia 48 0N 107 0E
91 Ulan Ude, U.S.S.R. ...52 0N 107 30E
131 Ulanga, dist, Tanzania 8 40S 36 50E
112 Ulanhot, China 46 5N 122 1E
131 Ulaya, Tanzania...... . 7 3S 36 55E
43 Ulbster, Scot., U.K. ...58 21N 3 9W
39 Ulceby Cross, Eng., U.K. 53 14N 0 6E
74 Ulcinj, Yugoslavia 41 58N 19 10E
112 Uldz Gol, R., Mongolia 49 30N 114 0E
79 Ulefoss, Norway 59 17N 9 16E
81 Ulfborg, Denmark 56 19N 8 20E
106 Ulhasnagar, India 19 15N 73 10E
130 Ulindi R., Congo 2 30S 27 0E
74 Uljma, Yugoslavia 45 2N 21 10E
62 Ulla, R., Spain 42 45N 8 30W
143 Ulladulla, N.S.W., Austral. 35 21S 150 29E
80 Ullånger, Sweden 62 58N 18 16E
42 Ullapool, Scot., U.K. .57 54N 5 10W
81 Ullared, Sweden 57 8N 12 42E
63 Ulldecona, Spain 40 36N 0 20E
38 Ullswater, L., Eg., U.K. 54 35N 2 52W
112 Ullung Do, S. Korea .37 30N 130 30E
80 Ullvättern, L., Sweden 59 30N 14 21E
57 Ulm, Germany 48 23N 10 0E
143 Ulmarra, N.S.W., Austral. 29 31S 153 6E
78 Ulmeni, Rumania 45 4N 46 40E
78 Ulmu, Rumania 44 16N 27 0E
81 Ulricehamn, Sweden .57 46N 13 26E
79 Ulsberg, Norway 62 45N 10 3E
79 Ulstein, Norway 62 21N 5 53E
46 Ulster, Prov., N. Ire., U.K. 54 45N 6 30W
46 Ulster Canal, Ireland .54 15N 7 0W
75 Ulstrem, Bulgaria 42 1N 26 27E
143 Ultima, Vic., Australia 35 22S 143 18E
105 Ulubaria, India 22 31N 88 4E
103 Ulugh Muztagh, mt., China 36 40N 87 30E
131 Uluguru Mts., Tanzania 7 15S 37 30E
40 Ulva I., Scotland, U.K. 56 30N 6 12W
38 Ulverston, Eng., U.K. 54 13N 3 7W
145 Ulverstone, Australia .41 11S 146 11E
79 Ulvik, Norway 60 35N 6 54E
81 Ulvo, Sweden 56 40N 14 37E
87 Ulyanovsk, U.S.S.R. .54 25N 48 25E
MAP
111 Ulyasutay, (Javhlant), Mongolia 47 56N 97 28E
165 Ulysses, U.S.A. 37 39N 101 25W
70 Ulzio, Italy 45 2N 6 49E
98 Umm Qeis, Jordan 32 40N 35 41E
71 Umag, Yugoslavia 45 26N 13 31E
174 Umala, Bolivia 17 25S 68 5W
88 Uman, U.S.S.R. 48 40N 30 12E
14 Umanak, Greenland ...70 40N 52 0W
10 Umanak Fd., Greenland 70 40N 52 0W
106 Umarkhed, India 19 37N 77 38E
104 Umarkot, W. Pakistan 25 15N 69 40E
166 Umatilla, U.S.A. 45 58N 119 17W
133 Umbabat R., S. Africa 24 25S 31 30E
71 Umbertide, Italy 43 18N 12 20E
135 Umbogintwini, S. Africa 30 0S 30 58E
144 Umboi I., Terr. of New Guinea 5 59S 148 0E
147 Umbrella Mts., New Zealand 45 35S 169 5E
71 Umbria, reg., Italy 42 53N 12 30E
82 Ume, R., Sweden 64 45N 18 30E
82 Umeå, Sweden 63 45N 20 20E
109 Umera, Indonesia 0 12S 129 30E
132 Umfuli R., Rhodesia .17 50S 29 40E
132 Umgusa, Rhodesia 19 29S 27 52E
132 Umgwasema, Rhodesia 15 55S 29 10E
135 Umhlali, Natal, S. Afr. 29 29S 31 15E
74 Umka, Yugoslavia 44 40N 20 19E
135 Umkomaas, S. Africa .30 13S 30 48E
101 Umm al Qaiwain, Trucial States 25 30N 55 35E
127 Umm Arda, Sudan 15 17N 32 31E
101 Umm az Zamul, Muscat & 'Oman ...22 35N 55 18E
127 Umm Bel, Sudan 13 35N 28 0E
127 Umm Digulgulaya, Sud. 10 28N 24 58E
127 Umm Dubban, Sudan 15 23N 32 52E
123 Umm al Aranib, Libya 26 10N 14 54E
98 Umm el Fahm, Israel 32 31N 35 9E
127 Umm Hagar, Sudan ...14 20N 36 39E
127 Umm Koweika, Sudan 13 10N 32 16E
100 Umm Lajj, Saudi Arabia 25 0N 37 23E
126 Umm Merwa, Sudan .18 4N 32 30E
127 Umm Qurein, Sudan .16 3N 28 49E
127 Umm Ruwaba, Sudan 12 50N 31 10E
101 Umm Said, Qatar 25 0N 51 40E
127 Umm Sidr, Sudan 14 29N 25 10E
126 Umm Zehetir Peak, Eg. 28 58N 32 19E
125 Ummadau, Nigeria 12 40N 7 18E
56 Ummanz I., Germany 54 29N 13 9E
132 Umniati, R., Rhodesia 18 0S 29 0E
152 Umnak I., Aleutian Is., U.S.A. 53 0N 168 0W
107 Umpang, Thailand 16 3N 98 54E
166 Umpqua R., U.S.A. ...43 30N 123 30W
104 Umrer, India 20 51N 79 18E
104 Umreth, India 22 41N 73 4E
132 Umtali, Rhodesia 18 58S 32 38E
135 Umtamvuna, R., S. Africa 31 5S 30 9E
135 Umtata, C. Prov., S. Afr. 31 36S 28 49E
135 Umtwalume S. Africa 30 30S 30 38E
125 Umuahia-Ibeku, Nigeria 5 33N 7 29E
132 Umvukwe Ra., Rhodesia 16 45S 30 45E
132 Umvuma, Rhodesia 19 16S 30 30E
135 Umzimvuba, R., S. Africa 31 30S 29 30E
132 Umzingwane R., Rhod. 21 30S 29 30E
135 Umzinto, Natal, S. Africa 30 15S 30 45E
135 Umzumbe, Nat., S. Afr. 30 37S 30 32E
104 Una, India 20 46N 71 8E
147 Una, Mt., New Zealand 42 13S 172 36E
71 Una R., Yugoslavia ...44 50N 16 15E
71 Unac, R., Yugoslavia .44 42N 16 15E
161 Unadilla, U.S.A. 42 20N 75 17W
91 Unagaidaya, U.S.S.R. 59 10N 142 0E
152 Unalanaska I., Alas., U.S.A. 54 0N 164 30W
64 Uncastillo, Spain 42 21N 1 8W
174 Uncia, Bolivia 18 25S 66 40W
129 Uncocua, Angola 16 30S 13 40E
167 Uncompahgre Pk., Mt., U.S.A. 38 5N 107 32W
81 Unden L., Sweden 58 50N 14 30E
135 Underberg, Nat., S. Afr. 29 48S 29 32E
143 Underbool, Vic., Austral. 35 10S 141 51E
80 Undersaker, Sweden ...63 19N 13 21E
80 Undersvik, Sweden 61 36N 16 20E
79 Undredal, Norway 60 57N 7 6E
86 Unecha, U.S.S.R. 52 50N 32 37E
143 Ungarie, N.S.W., Austral. 33 38S 146 56E
153 Ungava Bay, Canada .59 30N 67 0W
148 Ungava Pen., Canada 60 0N 75 0W
88 Ungeny, U.S.S.R. 47 11N 27 51E
112 Unggi, North Korea ...42 16N 130 28E
127 Ungwatiri, Sudan 16 52N 36 10E
87 Uni, U.S.S.R. 56 44N 51 47E
MAP
175 União, Ceara, Brazil ... 4 50S 37 50W
173 União da Vitoria, Brazil 26 5S 51 0W
60 Uniejów, Poland 51 59N 18 46E
71 Unije, I., Yugoslavia .44 40N 14 15E
152 Unimak I., Alas., U.S.A. 54 30N 164 30W
152 Unimak Pass., Alas. U.S.A. 53 30N 165 15W
164 Union, Mo., U.S.A. ...38 25N 91 0W
161 Union, N.J., U.S.A. ...40 47N 74 3W
163 Union, S.C., U.S.A. ...34 49N 81 39W
161 Union City, N.J., U.S.A. 40 47N 74 5W
162 Union City, Ohio, U.S.A. 40 11N 84 49W
160 Union City, Pa., U.S.A. 41 53N 79 50W
165 Union City, Tenn., USA 36 25N 89 0W
163 Union Gap, U.S.A. 46 38N 120 29W
167 Union, Mt., U.S.A. 34 34N 112 21W
90-91 Union of Soviet Socialist Republics .47 0N 100 0E
163 Union Springs, U.S.A. 32 9N 85 44W
134 Uniondale, S. Africa ...33 39S 23 7E
134 Uniondale Road, Cape Province, S. Africa 33 39S 23 7E
162 Uniontown, Pa., U.S.A. 39 54N 79 45W
115 United Arab Republic, (Egypt) ...27 5N 30 0E
33 United Kingdom of Gt. Brit. & N. Ire. .55 0N 3 0W
158-159 United States of America, republic ...37 0N 96 0W
157 Unity, Canada 52 30N 109 5W
104 Unjha, India 23 46N 72 24E
55 Unna, Germany 51 32N 7 40E
105 Unnao, India 26 35N 80 30E
157 Uno, Canada 50 17N 101 3W
46 Unshin R., Ireland 54 8N 8 26W
42 Unst, I., Scot., U.K. .60 50N 0 55W
56 Unstrut R., Germany 51 16N 11 29E
57 Unter Walden, cant., Switzerland 46 50N 8 15E
36 Uny Lelant, Eng., U.K. 50 11N 5 27W
88 Unye, Turkey 41 5N 37 15E
87 Unzha, U.S.S.R. 57 40N 44 8E
87 Unzha R., U.S.S.R. ...58 0N 43 40E
59 Upa, R., Czechoslovakia 50 45N 16 15E
127 Upal, Sudan 6 56N 34 12E
174 Upata, Venezuela 8 1N 62 24W
34 Upavon, Eng., U.K. 51 17N 1 49W
130 Upenba L., Congo 8 40S 26 20E
14 Upernavik, Greenland 72 45N 56 0W
134 Upington, S. Africa ...28 25S 21 15E
104 Upleta, India 21 46N 70 16E
156 Upper Arrow L., Can. 50 30N 117 50W
58 Upper Austria, prov., Austria 48 15N 14 10E
37 Upper Chapel, Wales, United Kingdom ...52 3N 3 26W
46 Upper L. Erne, N. Ire. 54 14N 7 22W
146 Upper Hutt, N.Z. 41 8S 175 5E
131 Upper Juba, reg., Somali Rep. 3 0N 41 10E
166 Upper Klamath L., U.S.A. 42 16N 121 55W
166 Upper Lake, Calif., U.S.A. 39 10N 122 55W
166 Upper Lake (Alkali), U.S.A. 41 47N 120 0W
155 Upper Musquodobolt, Canada 45 10N 62 58W
127 Upper Nile, prov., Sud. 8 50N 29 55E
162 Upper Sandusky, U.S.A. 40 50N 83 17W
91 Upper Taymyr R., U.S.S.R. 73 40N 96 0E
124-125 Upper Volta, st., Africa 12 0N 0 30W
44 Upperchurch, Ireland 52 43N 8 2W
81 Upphärad, Sweden 58 9N 12 19E
35 Uppingham, Eng., U.K. 52 36N 0 43W
80 Uppsala, Sweden 59 53N 17 42E
80 Uppsala Lan, co., Swed. 60 0N 17 30E
38 Upton, England, U.K. 53 14N 2 52W
164 Upton, U.S.A. 44 8N 104 35W
34 Upton-on-Severn, England, U.K. 52 4N 2 12W
36 Upwey, England, U.K. 50 40N 2 29W
100 Ur, Iraq 30 55N 46 25E
174 Uracará, Brazil 2 20S 57 50W
57 Urach, Germany 48 29N 9 25E
143 Ural, Mt., N.S.W., Austral. 33 21S 146 12E
84 Ural Mts., U.S.S.R. 60 0N 59 0E
89 Ural, R., U.S.S.R. 49 0N 52 0W
145 Uralla, N.S.W., Austral. 30 37S 151 29E
84 Uralsk, U.S.S.R. 51 20N 51 20E
131 Urambo, Tanzania 5 4S 32 47E
143 Urana & L., Australia 35 15S 146 21E
157 Uranium City, Canada 59 28N 108 40W
143 Uranquinty, Australia 35 6S 147 12E
106 Uravakonda, India 14 57N 77 12E
114 Urawa, Japan 35 50N 139 40E
162 Urbana, Ill., U.S.A. ...40 7N 88 12W
162 Urbana, Ohio, U.S.A. 40 9N 83 44W
71 Urbania, Italy 43 40N 12 31E
64 Urbel, R., Spain 42 30N 3 49W
71 Urbino, Italy 43 43N 12 38E

MAP
174 Urcos, Peru ....13 30 s 71 30w
63 Urda, Spain 39 25N 3 43w
89 Urda, U.S.S.R. ....48 52N 47 23 E
172 Urdinarrain, Argentina ....32 37 s 58 52w
50 Urdos, France 42 51N 0 35w
90 Urdzhar, U.S.S.R. ....47 5N 81 38 E
132 Urema, Mozambique .18 59 s 34 33 E
87 Uren, U.S.S.R. ....57 35N 45 55 E
168 Ures, Mexico 29 30N 110 30w
100 Urfa, Turkey ....37 12N 38 50 E
58 Urfahr, Austria ....48 19N 14 17 E
55 Urft Res., Germany ...50 12N 6 27 E
90 Urgench, U.S.S.R. ....41 40N 60 30 E
101 Urgun, Afghanistan ...32 55N 69 12 E
57 Uri, cant., Switzerland ....46 43N 8 35 E
174 Uribia, Colombia 11 43N 72 16w
98 Urim, Israel ....31 18N 34 32 E
54 Urk, Netherlands ......52 39N 5 36 E
100 Urla, Turkey ....38 20N 26 55 E
78 Urlati, Rumania ....44 59N 26 15 E
100 Urmia (Rezā'iyeh), Iran....................37 40N 45 0 E
100 Urmia, L., Iran, see Rezā'iyeh, L. ....37 30N 45 30 E
38 Urmston, Eng., U.K. .53 28N 2 22w
74 Uroševac, Yugoslavia 42 23N 21 10 E
81 Urshutt, Sweden ......56 31N 14 50 E
127 Urso, Ethiopia .... 9 35N 41 33 E
175 Uruaca, Brazil ....14 35 s 49 16w
168 Uruapan, Mexico 19 30N 102 0w
174 Urubamba, Peru ....13 5 s 72 10w
174 Urubamba R., Peru ...11 0 s 73 0w
175 Urucui, Brazil .... 7 20 s 44 28w
172 Uruguaiana, Brazil ....29 50 s 57 0w
172-173 Uruguay, rep., South America ....32 30 s 55 30w
173 Uruguay R., S. Amer. 28 0 s 56 0w
111 Urumchi (Tihua), China ....43 40N 87 50 E
108 Urung, Indonesia ...... 2 31N 95 52 E
111 Urungu R., China ......46 30N 88 50 E
91 Urup, I., Kiril Is., U.S.S.R. ....43 0N 151 0 E
89 Urup, R., U.S.S.R. ....44 19N 41 30 E
102 Uruzgan, prov., Afghan. ....33 30N 66 0 E
109 Urville, C. d', Indonesia .... 1 35 s 137 50 E
87 Uryupinsk, U.S.S.R. .50 45N 42 3 E
87 Urzhum, U.S.S.R. ....57 10N 49 56 E
78 Urziceni, Rumania ....44 46N 26 42 E
84 Usa R., U.S.S.R. ......66 20N 56 0 E
100 Uşak, Turkey ....38 43N 29 28 E
129 Usakos, S.W. Africa ...22 0 s 15 31 E
131 Usambara Mts., Tanz. 4 50 s 38 20 E
74 Ušce, Yugoslavia .....43 43N 20 39 E
56 Usedom, Germany ....53 50N 13 55 E
131 Useko, Tanzania .... 5 8 s 32 24 E
126 Usfan, Saudi Arabia ...21 58N 39 27 E
14 Ushakova I., U.S.S.R. 82 0N 80 0 E
48 Ushant (Ile d'Ouessant), I., Fr. .48 25N 5 5w
131 Ushashi, Tanzania .... 1 59 s 33 57 E
127 Ushat, Sudan .... 7 59N 29 28 E
131 Ushetu, Tanzania ...... 4 10 s 32 18 E
176 Ushuaia, Argentina ...54 50 s 68 23w
34 Usk, England, U.K. ...51 42N 2 53w
37 Usk R., Wales, U.K. .51 37N 2 56w
79 Uskedal, Norway ......59 56N 5 53 E
100 Üsküdar, Turkey ......41 0N 29 5 E
56 Uslar, Germany ....51 39N 9 39 E
87 Usman, U.S.S.R. ......52 5N 39 48 E
91 Usole Sibirskoye, U.S.S.R. ....52 40N 103 40 E
125 Usoro, Nigeria .... 5 33N 6 11 E
172 Uspallata Pass, Arg. .32 30 s 69 28w
90 Uspenski, U.S.S.R. ...48 50N 72 55 E
50 Ussel, France ....45 32N 2 18 E
91 Ussuriysk, U.S.S.R. ...43 40N 131 50 E
58 Ust, Czechoslovakia ...50 41N 14 2 E
91 Ust Aldan, U.S.S.R. ...63 50N 129 15 E
91 Ust Amginskoye, U.S.S.R. ....62 30N 134 50 E
91 Ust Bolsheretsk, U.S.S.R. ....52 40N 156 30 E
87 Ust Buzulukskaya, U.S.S.R. ....50 8N 42 11 E
89 Ust Doneckij, U.S.S.R. ....47 35N 40 55 E
91 Ust Ilga, U.S.S.R. ....55 5N 104 55 E
91 Ust Ilimpeya, U.S.S.R. ....63 20N 105 0 E
90 Ust Ishim, U.S.S.R. ...57 45N 71 10 E
91 Ust Kamchatsk, U.S.S.R. ....56 10N 162 0 E
90 Ust Kamenogorsk, U.S.S.R. ....50 0N 82 20 E
91 Ust Karengi, U.S.S.R. 54 40N 116 45 E
91 Ust Khairyuzovo, U.S.S.R. ....57 15N 156 55 E
91 Ust Kut, U.S.S.R. ....56 50N 105 10 E
89 Ust Labinsk, U.S.S.R. 45 15N 39 50 E
86 Ust Luga, U.S.S.R. ...59 35N 28 26 E
91 Ust Maya, U.S.S.R. ...60 30N 134 20 E
91 Ust Mil, U.S.S.R. ......59 50N 133 0 E
91 Ust Nera, U.S.S.R. ....64 35N 193 15 E
91 Ust Olenek, U.S.S.R. .73 0N 120 10 E
90 Ust Port, U.S.S.R. ....70 0N 84 10 E
91 Ust Tigil, U.S.S.R. ....58 0N 158 10 E
84 Ust Tsilma, U.S.S.R. .65 25N 52 0 E
91 Ust Tungir, U.S.S.R. .55 25N 120 15 E
90 Ust Urt Plat., U.S.S.R. ....44 0N 55 0 E
84 Ust Usa, U.S.S.R. ....66 0N 56 30 E
90 Ust Vorkuta, U.S.S.R. 67 7N 63 35 E
79 Ustaoset, Norway ......60 30N 8 2 E
87 Uste, U.S.S.R. ....59 35N 39 40 E
59 Usti na Orlici, Cz. ......49 58N 16 38 E

MAP
58 Usti (nad Laben) Cz. .50 41N 14 3 E
72 Ustica I., Italy ....38 42N 13 10 E
59 Ustrzyki Dolne, Poland ....49 27N 22 40 E
60 Ustka, Poland ....54 35N 16 55 E
91 Ustye, U.S.S.R. ....55 30N 97 30 E
87 Ustyuzhna, U.S.S.R. .58 50N 36 32 E
114 Usuki, Japan ....33 5N 131 40 E
168 Usulután, Salvador ...13 25N 88 28w
168 Usumacinta, R., Mex. 17 0N 91 0w
166 Utah, st., U.S.A. 39 30N 111 30w
166 Utah, L., U.S.A. 40 10N 111 58w
165 Ute, Cr., U.S.A. 36 5N 103 45w
86 Utena, U.S.S.R. ....55 27N 25 40 E
56 Ütersen, Germany ....53 40N 9 40 E
107 Uthai Thani, Thailand 15 22N 100 3 E
100 Uthmaniyah, Si. Arab. ....25 5N 49 6 E
174 Utiariti, Brazil ....13 0 s 58 10w
161 Utica, N.Y., U.S.A. ...43 5N 75 18w
160 Utica, Ohio, U.S.A. ...40 13N 82 26w
64 Utiel, Spain 39 37N 1 11w
157 Utik L., Canada 55 20N 96 5w
156 Utikuma L., Canada .55 50N 115 30w
80 Utö, I., Sweden ....58 56N 18 20 E
136 Utrecht, Natal, S. Afr. ....27 38 s 30 20 E
54 Utrecht, Netherlands .52 3N 5 8 E
54 Utrecht, prov., Neth. .52 6N 5 7 E
63 Utrera, Spain 37 12N 5 48w
114 Utsunomiya, Japan ...36 30N 139 50 E
104-105 Uttar Pradesh, st., India ....27 0N 80 0 E
107 Uttaradit, Thailand ...17 36N 100 5 E
80 Uttersberg, Sweden ...59 45N 15 39 E
81 Uttersley, Denmark ...54 56N 11 11 E
160 Utterson, Canada 45 13N 79 20w
38 Uttoxeter, Eng., U.K. 52 53N 1 50w
56 Utze, Germany ....52 28N 10 11 E
83 Uudenmaa, prov., Fin. ....60 25N 23 0 E
112 Uuldza, Mongolia ......49 8N 112 10 E
82 Uusikaarlepyy, Finland ....63 33N 22 35 E
83 Uusikaupunki (Nykarleby), Finland ....60 47N 21 28 E
74 Uvac, R., Yugoslavia .43 35N 19 40 E
165 Uvalde, U.S.A. 29 15N 99 48w
84 Uvaly Hills, U.S.S.R. 60 5N 51 15 E
87 Uvarovo, U.S.S.R. ....51 59N 42 14 E
90 Uvat, U.S.S.R. ....59 5N 68 50 E
131 Uvinza, Tanzania ...... 5 5 s 30 24 E
131 Uvira, Congo .... 3 22 s 29 3 E
58 Uvlova R., Cz. ....49 34N 13 20 E
111 Uvs Nuur, Mongolia ...50 20N 92 30 E
100 Uwainhid, Saudi Arabia ....24 50N 46 0 E
114 Uwajima, Japan ....33 10N 132 35 E
160 Uxbridge, Canada 44 10N 79 9w
168 Uxmal, site, Mexico ...20 22N 89 46w
42 Uyeasound, Scot., U.K. 60 42N 0 55w
125 Uyo, Nigeria .... 5 1N 7 53 E
100 Uyun, Saudi Arabia ...26 30N 43 50 E
174 Uyuni, Bolivia ....20 35 s 66 55w
174 Uyuni Salar de, Bolivia ....20 10 s 68 0w
90 Uzbekistan (Uzbek S.S.R.), U.S.S.R. ...40 5N 65 0 E
89 Uzen, Gt., R., U.S.S.R. ....50 0N 49 30 E
89 Uzen, Lit., R., U.S.S.R. ....50 0N 48 30 E
50 Uzerche, France ....45 25N 1 35 E
51 Uzes, France ....44 1N 4 26 E
86 Uzh R., U.S.S.R. ....51 15N 29 45 E
86 Uzhgorod, U.S.S.R. ...48 36N 22 18 E
87 Uzlovaya, U.S.S.R. ...54 0N 38 5 E
75 Uzunköprü, Turkey ...41 16N 26 43 E

V
135 Vaal, R., South Africa 27 40 s 25 30 E
134 Vaalkoppiesfontein, C. Prov., S. Africa ......31 55 s 21 0 E
55 Vaals, Netherlands ....50 46N 6 1 E
133 Vaalwater, S. Africa ...24 15 s 28 8 E
82 Vaasa (Vasa), Finland 63 10N 21 35 E
82 Vaasa, prov., Finland 63 6N 23 0 E
50 Vabre, France ....43 42N 2 24 E
59 Vác, Hungary ....47 49N 19 10 E
173 Vacaria, Brazil ....28 31 s 50 52w
166 Vacaville, U.S.A. 38 21N 122 0w
169 Vache, I.-à, Haiti 18 2N 73 35w
80 Väddö I., Sweden ......59 55N 19 0 E
81 Väderum, Sweden ......57 32N 16 11 E
104 Vadnagar, India ....23 47N 72 40 E
70 Vado Ligure, Italy ....44 16N 8 26 E
82 Vadsö, Norway ....70 3N 29 50 E
81 Vadstena, Sweden ......58 28N 14 58 E
57 Vaduz, Liechtenstein .47 8N 9 31 E
82 Vaeröy, I., Norway ...67 40N 12 40 E
79 Vaeröy, I., Norway ...61 17N 4 45 E
81 Vaggeryd, Sweden .....57 30N 14 10 E
80 Vagnhärad, Sweden ...58 57N 17 33 E
62 Vagos, Portugal 40 33N 8 42w
79 Vågsöy, I., Norway ...62 0N 5 0 E
59 Váh, R., Czechoslovakia ......49 10N 18 20 E
15 Vaihsel B., Antarctica 75 0 s 35 0w
90 Vaigach, U.S.S.R. ......70 10N 59 0 E
90 Vaigach I., U.S.S.R. .70 0N 60 0 E
106 Vaigai, R., India .... 9 47N 78 23 E
48 Vaiges, France 48 2N 0 30w
57 Vaihingen, Germany .48 44N 8 58 E
106 Vaijapur, India ....19 58N 74 45 E
106 Vaikam, India .... 9 45N 76 25 E
42 Vaila I., Scotland, U.K. 60 12N 1 34w

MAP
49 Vailly Aisne, France .49 25N 3 30 E
106 Vaippar, R., India .... 9 0N 78 25 E
104 Vajpur, India ....21 24N 73 45 E
75 Vakarel, Bulgaria ......42 35N 23 40 E
79 Vaksdal, Norway ....60 29N 5 45 E
59 Vál, Hungary ....47 22N 18 40 E
49 Val-de-Marne, dept., France ....48 45N 2 28 E
49 Val-d'Oise, dept., Fr. 49 5N 2 0 E
154 Val d'Or, Canada 48 7N 77 47w
157 Val Marie, Canada 49 15N 107 45w
62 Valadares, Portugal ...41 5N 8 38w
57 Valais, can., Switz. ....46 8N 7 40 E
74 Valandovo, Yugoslavia ....41 19N 22 34 E
59 Valasske, Meziriči, Cz. 49 29N 17 59 E
77 Valáxa, I., Greece ......38 50N 24 29 E
74 Vâlcani, Rumania ......46 0N 20 26 E
176 Valcheta, Argentina ...40 40 s 66 20w
71 Valdagno, Italy ....45 38N 11 18 E
86 Valday, U.S.S.R. ....57 58N 31 9 E
63 Valdeazogues, R., Sp. 38 45N 4 55w
81 Valdermarsvik, Sweden ....58 14N 16 40 E
65 Valdepeñas Ciudad Real, Spain 38 43N 3 25w
63 Valdepenas, Jaen, Sp. 31 33N 3 47w
62 Valderaduey, R., Spain 42 30N 5 0w
64 Valderrobres, Spain ...40 53N 0 9 E
176 Valdes Pen., Argentina ....42 30 s 63 45w
152 Valdez, Alaska, U.S.A. 61 14N 146 10w
133 Valdezia, Trans., S. Afr. ....23 5 s 30 14 E
176 Valdivia, Chile ....39 50 s 73 14w
71 Valdobbiadene, Italy .45 53N 12 0 E
163 Valdosta, U.S.A. 30 50N 83 48w
62 Valdoviño, Spain 43 36N 8 8w
79 Valdres, Norway ....61 0N 91 3 E
166 Vale, U.S.A. 44 0N 117 15w
89 Vale, U.S.S.R. ....41 30N 42 58 E
78 Valea lui Mihai, Rum. 47 32N 22 11 E
173 Valença, Baia, Brazil .13 20 s 39 15w
175 Valença, Piaui, Brazil 6 20 s 41 50w
62 Valença, Portugal 42 1N 8 34w
51 Valence, Drôme, France ....44 57N 4 54 E
50 Valence d'Agen, France ....44 8N 0 54 E
65 Valencia, Spain 39 27N 0 23w
65 Valencia, prov., Spain 39 20N 0 40w
65 Valencia, reg., Spain .39 25N 0 45w
174 Valencia, Venezuela ...10 11N 68 0w
65 Valencia, G. of, Spain 39 30N 0 20 E
61 Valencia, Albuferra, de, L., Spain ....39 20N 0 27 E
63 Valencia de Alcantara, Spain 39 25N 7 14w
62 Valencia de Don Juan, Spain 42 17N 5 31w
63 Valencia des Ventoso, Spain 38 15N 6 29w
49 Valenciennes, France .50 20N 3 34 E
78 Văleni, Rumania ......44 15N 24 45 E
51 Valensole, France ......43 50N 5 59 E
44 Valentia Harb., Ire. ...51 56N 10 17w
44 Valentia I., Ire. 51 54N 10 22w
164 Valentine, Neb., U.S.A. 42 50N 100 35w
165 Valentine, U.S.A. 30 36N 104 28w
70 Valenza, Italy ....45 2N 8 39 E
79 Våler, Norway ....60 48N 11 38 E
174 Valera, Venezuela 9 19N 70 37w
73 Valguarnera, Caropepe, Italy ......37 30N 14 22 E
166 Valier, U.S.A. 48 15N 112 9w
51 Valinco, G., France ....41 40N 8 52 E
74 Valjevo, Yugoslavia ...44 18N 19 53 E
55 Valkenburg, Neth. .....50 52N 5 50 E
54 Valkenswaard, Neth. .51 21N 5 29 E
64 Vall de Uxo, Spain 40 49N 0 15w
80 Valla, Sweden ....59 2N 16 20 E
62 Valladolid, & prov., Sp. 41 38N 4 43w
168 Valladolid, Mexico 20 30N 88 20w
73 Vallata, Italy ....41 3N 15 16 E
78 Valldalssæter, Norway 59 56N 6 57 E
79 Valle, Norway ....59 13N 7 33 E
70 Valle d'Aosta, reg., It. 45 45N 7 22 E
62 Valle de Cabuérniga, Sp. 43 14N 4 18w
174 Valle de la Pascua, Ven. 9 13N 66 0w
168 Valle de Santiago, Mex. 20 25N 101 15w
168 Valle Hermoso, Mexico ....25 35N 102 25 E
62 Vallecas, Spain 40 23N 3 41w
166 Vallejo, U.S.A. 38 12N 122 15w
172 Vallenar, Chile ....28 30 s 70 50w
50 Valleraugue, France ...44 6N 3 39 E
48 Vallet, France 47 10N 1 15w
68 Valletta, Malta ....35 54N 14 30 E
37 Valley, Wales, U.K. ...53 17N 4 31w
164 Valley City, U.S.A. ...46 57N 98 0w
166 Valley Falls, U.S.A. ...42 33N 120 8w
165 Valley Okolona, U.S.A. 34 0N 88 45w
154 Valleyfield, Canada ...45 15N 74 8w
156 Valleyview, Canada ...55 5N 117 25w
71 Valli di Comacchio, It. ....44 40N 12 15 E
73 Vallo della Lucania, It. ....40 14N 15 16 E
51 Vallon, France ....44 25N 4 23 E
57 Vallorbe, Switzerland .46 42N 6 20 E
64 Valls, Spain ....41 18N 1 15 E
80 Vallsta, Sweden ....61 30N 16 25 E

MAP
64 Valmaseda, Spain 43 11N 3 12w
86 Valmiera, U.S.S.R. ....57 37N 25 38 E
48 Valmont, France ....49 45N 0 30 E
72 Valmontone, Italy .....41 48N 12 55 E
49 Valmy, France ....49 5N 4 45 E
64 Valnera, Mte., Spain .43 9N 3 40w
48 Valognes, France 49 30N 1 28w
76 Valona (Vlórë), Albania ....40 32N 19 28 E
62 Valongo, Portugal 40 37N 8 27w
62 Valpacos, Portugal 41 36N 7 17w
172 Valparaiso, Chile ......33 2 s 71 40w
172 Valparaiso, prov., Chile ....33 2 s 71 40w
168 Valparaiso, Mexico ...22 50N 103 32w
162 Valparaiso, U.S.A. 41 27N 87 2w
74 Valpovo, Yugoslavia .45 39N 18 25 E
51 Valréas, France ....44 24N 5 0 E
57 Vals, Switzerland ......46 39N 10 11 E
57 Vals les Bains, France 44 42N 4 24 E
80 Valskog, Sweden ....59 27N 16 1 E
76 Válta, Greece ....40 3N 23 25 E
70 Valtellina, Italy ....46 9N 10 2 E
87 Vuluyiki, U.S.S.R. ....50 10N 38 5 E
63 Valverde del Camino, Spain 37 35N 6 47w
62 Valverde del Fresno, Sp. 40 15N 6 51w
78 Vama, Rumania ....47 34N 25 42 E
81 Vamdrup, Denmark ...55 26N 9 10 E
83 Vammala, Finland ....61 20N 22 55 E
77 Vámos, Greece ....35 24N 24 13 E
106 Vamsadhara, R., India ....18 22N 84 15 E
100 Van, Turkey ....38 30N 43 20 E
165 Van Alstyne, U.S.A. .33 25N 96 36 E
165 Van Buren, Ark., U.S.A. 35 28N 94 18w
163 Van Buren, Me., U.S.A. 47 10N 68 1w
165 Van Buren, Mo., U.S.A. 37 0N 91 0w
144 Van Diemen C., Austral. ....16 30 s 139 46 E
138 Van Diemen G., Austral. ....12 0 s 132 0 E
100 Van Gölü L., Turkey .38 30N 43 0 E
167 Van Horn, U.S.A. 31 3N 104 55w
135 Van Reenen P., S. Afr. ....28 22 s 29 27 E
164 Van Tassell, U.S.A. ...42 40N 104 3w
106 Van Tivu, I., India ... 8 51N 78 15 E
162 Van Wert, U.S.A. 40 52N 84 31w
156 Vancouver, Canada ...49 20N 123 10w
166 Vancouver, U.S.A. 45 44N 122 41w
156 Vancouver I., Canada 49 50N 126 30w
164 Vandalia, Ill., U.S.A. .38 57N 89 4w
164 Vandalia, Mo., U.S.A. 39 18N 91 30w
81 Vandborg, Denmark .56 32N 8 10 E
106 Vandeloos Bay, Ceylon .... 8 0N 81 45 E
133 Vanderbijlpark, S. Afr. ....26 42 s 27 54 E
160 Vandergrift, U.S.A. ...40 36N 79 33w
156 Vanderhoof, Canada ...54 0N 124 0w
139 Vanderlin I., Australia ....15 59 s 138 1 E
132 Vanduzi, R., Mozam. .18 0 s 33 26 E
144 Vandyke, Australia ...24 8 s 142 45 E
133 Vandyksdrif, S. Africa 26 6 s 29 19 E
81 Vänern L., Sweden ....58 47N 13 50 E
81 Vanersborg, Sweden ...58 26N 12 27 E
107 Vang Vieng, Laos .....18 58N 102 32 E
131 Vanga, Kenya .... 4 35 s 39 12 E
129 Vangaindrano, Malag. 23 21 s 47 36 E
157 Vanguard, Canada 49 55N 107 20w
144 Vanimo, North East New Guinea .... 2 50 s 141 25 E
106 Vanivilasa Sagara, L., India ....13 45N 76 30 E
106 Vaniyambadi, India ...12 46N 78 44 E
154 Vankleek Hill, Canada 45 32N 74 40w
82 Vännäs, Sweden ....63 58N 19 48 E
48 Vannes, Morbihan, Fr. 47 40N 2 47w
82 Vannöy, I., Norway ...70 6N 19 50 E
134 Vanrhynsdorp, S. Afr. 31 36 s 18 44 E
135 Vanstadensrus, S. Africa ....29 59 s 27 2 E
80 Vansbro, Sweden ....60 32N 14 15 E
79 Vanse, Norway ....58 6N 6 41 E
104 Vanthli, India ....21 28N 70 25 E
136 Vanua Levu, Fiji Is., Pacific Ocean ....15 45 s 179 10 E
134 Vanwyksdorp, S. Africa ....33 42 s 21 28 E
134 Vanwyksvlei, S. Africa ....30 18 s 21 49 E
79 Vanylven, Norway ....62 5N 5 33 E
88 Vapnyarka, U.S.S.R. .48 32N 28 45 E
51 Var, dépt., France ....43 27N 6 18 E
81 Vara, Sweden ....58 16N 12 55 E
106 Varada, R., India ......14 46N 75 15 E
48 Varades, France 47 25N 1 1w
70 Varaita R., Italy ....44 35N 7 15 E
79 Varaldsöy, I., Norway 60 6N 5 59 E
70 Varallo, Italy ....45 50N 8 13 E
105 Varanasi (Benares), India ....25 22N 83 8 E
82 Varanger Fd., Norway 69 50N 31 0 E
71 Varazdin, Yugoslavia .46 20N 16 20 E
70 Varazze, Italy ....44 21N 8 36 E
81 Varberg, Sweden ....57 17N 12 20 E
74 Vardar R., Yugoslavia 41 25N 22 20 E
81 Varde, Denmark ....55 38N 8 29 E
81 Varde R., Denmark ....55 43N 8 40 E
56 Varel, Germany ....53 23N 8 9 E
86 Varena, U.S.S.R. ....54 12N 24 30 E
81 Vărendseke, Sweden ...57 4N 15 0 E
50 Varennes sur Allier, Fr. ....49 12N 5 0 E

MAP
74 Vares, Yugoslavia ......44 12N 18 23 E
70 Varese, Italy ....45 49N 8 50 E
70 Varese Ligure, Italy ...44 22N 9 33 E
81 Vargårdå, Sweden ......58 5N 12 30 E
173 Varginha, Brazil ....21 33 s 45 25w
81 Vargön, Sweden ....58 22N 12 20 E
79 Varhaug, Norway ....58 37N 5 41 E
172 Varillas, Chile ....24 0 s 70 10w
81 Väring, Sweden ....58 30N 14 0 E
80 Värmdö, I., Sweden ...59 18N 18 45 E
80 Värmeln, L., Sweden .59 30N 13 0 E
80 Värmlands, Län, co., Sweden ....59 45N 13 0 E
80 Varmlandssaby, Swed. 59 7N 14 48 E
75 Varna, Bulgaria ....43 13N 27 56 E
106 Varna, R., India ....17 13N 73 50 E
81 Värnamo, Sweden ......57 10N 14 3 E
58 Varnsdorf, Cz. ....49 56N 14 38 E
81 Väröbacka, Sweden ...51 16N 12 15 E
81 Varpelev, Denmark ...55 22N 12 17 E
161 Vars, Canada 45 22N 75 22w
81 Värsjö, Sweden ....56 23N 13 27 E
79 Varteig, Norway ....59 23N 11 12 E
100 Varto, Turkey ....39 10N 41 28 E
81 Vartofta, Sweden ......58 6N 13 40 E
45 Vartry Res., Ireland .53 3N 6 12w
74 Varvarin, Yugoslavia .43 43N 21 20 E
101 Varzaneh. Iran ....32 25N 52 40 E
70 Varzi, Italy ....44 50N 9 12 E
70 Varzo, Italy ....46 12N 8 15 E
49 Varzy, France ....47 22N 3 20 E
59 Vasárosnamény, Hung. 48 9N 22 19 E
81 Väsby, Sweden ....56 13N 12 37 E
63 Vascao, R., Portugal .37 44N 8 15w
78 Vaşcău, Rumania ......46 28N 22 30 E
64 Vascongadas, reg., Sp. 42 50N 2 45w
80 Väse, Sweden ....59 23N 13 49 E
101 Vasht, Iran ....28 20N 61 6 E
75 Vasil Levski, Bulgaria 43 23N 25 26 E
86 Vasilevichi, U.S.S.R. .52 15N 29 50 E
91 Vasilevka, U.S.S.R. ...58 0N 125 10 E
77 Vasilikón, Greece ......38 25N 23 40 E
86 Vasilkov, U.S.S.R. .....50 7N 30 28 E
78 Vaslui, Rumania ....46 38N 27 42 E
78 Vaslui, Reg., Rum. ....46 30N 27 50 E
80 Väsman, L., Sweden .60 9N 15 0 E
157 Vassar, Canada 49 10N 95 55w
162 Vassar, U.S.A. 43 23N 83 33w
80 Vast Silen, L., Sweden 59 15N 12 15 E
80 Västerås, Sweden ....59 37N 16 38 E
82 Västerbotten, co., Sweden ....64 58N 18 0 E
80 Västerdalälven R., Sweden ....60 30N 14 0 E
82 Vasternorrlands, prov., Sweden ....63 30N 16 45 E
80 Västernorrland, co., Sweden ....63 145N 18 0 E
81 Västervik, Sweden ....57 43N 16 43 E
80 Västmanland, co., Swed. ....89 5N 16 20 E
71 Vasto, Italy ....42 8N 14 40 E
59 Vasvár, Hungary ......47 3N 16 47 E
49 Vatan, France ....47 4N 1 50 E
42 Vaternish Pt., Scot., U.K. 57 36N 6 40w
42 Vatersay I., Scot., U.K. 56 55N 7 32w
77 Vathí, Greece ....37 46N 27 1 E
77 Váthia, Greece ....36 29N 22 29 E
71 Vatican City, Italy ....41 54N 12 27 E
74 Vatin, Yugoslavia ......45 12N 21 20 E
82 Vatna Jökull Mts., Iceland 64 30N 16 30w
79 Vatnås, Norway ....59 57N 9 33 E
79 Vatne, Norway ....62 33N 6 38 E
129 Vatomandry, Malag. .19 20 s 48 59 E
78 Vatra-Dornei, Rum. .47 22N 25 22 E
79 Vats, Norway ....59 29N 5 45 E
81 Vättern L., Sweden ....58 25N 14 30 E
51 Vaucluse, dépt., France ....44 3N 5 10 E
49 Vaucouleurs, France .48 37N 5 40 E
57 Vaud, can., Switzerland ....46 35N 6 30 E
167 Vaughan, N. Mex., U.S.A. 34 37N 105 12w
166 Vaughn, U.S.A. 47 37N 111 36w
156 Vauxhall, Canada 50 5N 112 9w
49 Vavincourt, France ...48 49N 5 12 E
80 Vaxholm, Sweden ......59 25N 18 25 E
81 Växjö, Sweden ....56 52N 14 50 E
175 Vaza Barris, R., Brazil ....10 0 s 37 30w
46 Veagh L., Ireland 55 2N 8 0w
54 Vechte, R., Netherlands ....52 31N 6 25 E
59 Vecsés, Hungary ....47 26N 19 19 E
106 Vedaraniam, India ....10 25N 79 50 E
81 Vedbæk, Denmark .....55 50N 12 33 E
81 Veddige, Sweden ....57 17N 12 20 E
78 Vedea R., Rumania ....44 0N 25 20 E
172 Vedia, Argentina ....34 30 s 61 31w
65 Vedra, Isla del, Spain 38 52N 1 12 E
55 Vedrin, Belgium ....50 30N 4 52 E
54 Veendam, Netherlands ....53 5N 6 52 E
54 Veenendaal, Neth. .....52 2N 5 34 E
82 Vefsna, R., Norway ....65 51N 13 10 E
165 Vega, U.S.A. 35 18N 102 26w
82 Vega Fd. & I., Norway ....65 37N 12 0 E
62 Vegadeo, Spain 43 27N 7 4w
56 Vegesack, Germany ....53 10N 8 38 E
81 Veggerby, Denmark ....56 54N 9 39 E
79 Veggli, Norway ....60 2N 9 11 E
54 Veghel, Netherlands ...51 37N 5 32 E
76 Vegorritis, Limni, L., Greece ....40 45N 21 45 E
156 Vegreville, Canada 53 30N 112 5w

MAP
79 Vegusdal, Norway 58 36N 8 10E
71 Veii, Italy 42 0N 12 24E
176 Veinte y Cinco de Mayo, Argentina 35 20S 60 5W
176 Veinte y Cinco de Mayo, Argentina ...38 0S 67 40W
81 Vejen, Denmark 55 30N 9 9E
63 Vejer de la Frontera, Spain 36 15N 5 59W
81 Vejle, Denmark 55 47N 9 30E
81 Vejle, Amt. co., Den. .55 2N 11 22E
81 Vejle Fjord, Denmark 55 40N 9 45E
81 Vejlo, Denmark 55 10N 11 45E
71 Vela Luka, Yugoslavia 42 59N 16 44E
106 Velanai I., Ceylon 9 45N 79 45E
167 Velarde, U.S.A. 36 11N 106 1W
165 Velasco, U.S.A. 29 0N 95 20W
50 Velay, Mts. du, France 45 0N 3 40E
55 Velbert, Germany 51 20N 7 0E
134 Velddrif, S. Africa 32 42S 18 11E
71 Velebit Planina, Y.-slav. 44 50N 15 20E
71 Velebitski Kanal, Yugoslavia 44 45N 14 55E
75 Veleka, R., Bulgaria .42 4N 27 30E
71 Velenje, Yugoslavia ...46 23N 15 8E
76 Velestinon, Greece 39 23N 22 45E
174 Velez, Colombia 6 2N 73 43W
74 Velež, mt., Yugoslavia 43 19N 18 2E
63 Velez Blanco, Spain ...37 41N 2 5W
63 Velez Malaga, Spain ...36 48N 4 5W
65 Velez Rubio, Spain 37 41N 2 5W
175 Velhas R., Brazil 17 45S 44 30W
74 Velika, Yugoslavia 45 27N 17 40E
71 Velika Goricá Y.-slavia 45 44N 16 5E
74 Velika Gradište, Y.-slav. 44 46N 21 30E
74 Velika Jastrebad, Ra., Yugoslavia 43 25N 21 30E
74 Velika Kapela, Y.-slav. 45 10N 15 5E
71 Velika Kladusa, Y.-slav. 45 11N 15 48E
74 Velika Morava, R., Yugoslavia 44 30N 21 9E
74 Velika Plana, Y.-slavia 44 20N 21 1E
86 Velikaya R., U.S.S.R. 56 40N 28 40E
59 Veliké Kapusany, Cz. 48 34N 22 5E
71 Velike Lasce, Y.-slavia 45 49N 14 45E
74 Veliki Bačka Canal, Yugoslavia 45 45N 19 15E
84 Veliki Ustyug, U.S.S.R. 60 47N 46 20E
86 Velikiye Luki, U.S.S.R. 56 25N 30 32E
75 Veliko Tarnovo (Tŭrnovo), Bulgaria 43 5N 25 41E
106 Velikonda Range, India 14 45N 79 10E
87 Velikoye, L., U.S.S.R. 55 15N 40 0E
75 Velingrad, Bulgaria ...42 4N 23 58E
71 Velino Mt., Italy 42 10N 13 20E
86 Velizh, U.S.S.R. 55 30N 31 11E
59 Velké Karlovice, Cz. .49 20N 18 17E
58 Velke Meziřici, Cz. 49 21N 16 1E
59 Velky Ostrov Zitny, Cz. 48 5N 17 20E
44 Vellberg, Germany 49 5N 9 59E
106 Vellar, R. India 11 30N 79 36E
72 Velletri, Italy 41 43N 12 43E
81 Velling, Denmark 56 2N 8 20E
81 Vellinge, Sweden 55 29N 13 0E
56 Vellir, Iceland 65 55N 18 28W
106 Vellore, India 12 57N 79 10E
54 Velsen, Netherlands ...52 27N 4 40E
84 Velsk, U.S.S.R. 61 10N 42 5E
56 Velten, Germany 52 40N 13 11E
164 Velva, U.S.A. 48 6N 100 56W
76 Velvendós, Greece 40 15N 22 6E
81 Vem, Denmark 56 21N 8 21E
106 Vembanad Lake, India 9 36N 76 15E
79 Veme, Norway 60 14N 10 7E
81 Ven, I., Sweden 55 55N 12 45E
81 Vena, Sweden 57 31N 16 0E
168 Venado, Mexico 22 50N 101 10W
172 Venado Tuerto, Arg. .33 50S 62 0W
73 Venafro, Italy 41 28N 14 3E
49 Venarey les Laumes, Fr. 47 32N 4 26E
70 Venaria, Italy 45 12N 7 39E
74 Venčane, Yugoslavia .44 24N 20 28E
51 Vence, France 43 43N 7 6E
63 Vendas Novas, Portugal 38 39N 8 27W
48 Vendée, Collines de, hills, France 46 35N 0 45W
50 Vendée, dépt., France 46 40N 1 20W
48 Vendée, dist., France .46 50N 1 35W
48 Vendée R., France 46 30N 0 45W
49 Vendeuvre, France 48 14N 4 27E
48 Vendôme, France 47 47N 1 3E
64 Vendrell, Spain 41 10N 1 30E
81 Vendsyssel, reg., Den. 57 22N 10 15E
71 Veneta, Laguna, Italy 45 19N 12 13E
71 Veneto, reg., Italy 45 30N 12 0E
87 Venev, U.S.S.R. 54 27N 38 8E
71 Venezia (Venice), Italy 45 27N 12 20E
71 Venezia, Golfo di, Italy 45 20N 13 0E
174 Venezuela, rep., S. Amer. 8 0N 65 0W
174 Venezuela, G. of. Ven. 11 30N 71 0W
106 Venguria, India 15 53N 73 45E
106 Vengurla Rocks, India 15 50N 73 22E
71 Venice, see Venezia, Italy 45 27N 12 20E
51 Vénissieux, France 45 43N 4 53E
80 Venjansjön, L., Sweden 60 58N 14 2E
106 Venkatagiri, India 14 0N 79 35E
106 Venkatapuram, India 18 20N 80 30E
54 Venlo, Netherlands 51 22N 6 11E
79 Vennesla, Norway 58 15N 8 0E
81 Venö, Is., Denmark ...56 33N 8 38E
54 Venraij, Netherlands .51 31N 6 0E
63 Venta de Cardena, Sp. 38 16N 4 20W
62 Venta de San Rafael, Spain 40 42N 4 12W
168 Ventana, Punta de la, Mexico 24 4N 109 48W
135 Ventersburg, S. Africa 28 7S 27 9E
133 Ventersdorp, S. Africa 26 17S 26 48E
133 Venterskroon, S. Africa 26 59S 27 16E
135 Venterstad, S. Africa .30 47S 25 48E
70 Ventimiglia, Italy 43 50N 7 39E
34 Ventnor, Eng., U.K. .50 35N 1 12W
72 Ventotene I., Italy 40 48N 13 25E
44 Ventry, Ireland 52 8N 10 21W
86 Ventspils, U.S.S.R. 57 25N 21 32E
174 Ventuari R., Venezuela 5 20N 66 0W
167 Ventura, U.S.A. 34 16N 119 25W
79 Veöy, & Is., Norway .62 45N 7 30E
172 Vera, Argentina 29 30S 60 20W
65 Vera, Spain 37 15N 1 15W
168 Vera Cruz, Mexico 19 10N 96 10W
168 Vera Cruz, st., Mexico 19 0N 96 15W
104 Veraval, India 20 53N 70 27E
73 Verbicaro, Italy 39 46N 15 54E
70 Vercelli, Italy 45 19N 8 25E
86 Verchnedvinsk, U.S.S.R. 55 45N 27 58E
176 Verde R., Argentina ...41 55S 66 0W
168 Verde, R., Mexico 21 10N 102 50W
76 Verdhikoúsa, Greece .39 47N 21 59E
56 Verden, Germany 52 56N 9 15E
164 Verdigre, U.S.A. 42 38N 98 0W
49 Verdun, Meuse, France 49 12N 5 24E
49 Verdun sur le Doubs, Saône et Loire, Fr. .46 54N 5 0E
133 Verdwaalvlakte, Cape Province, S. Africa .26 42S 24 41E
133 Vereeniging, S. Africa 26 38S 27 57E
64 Vergara, Spain 43 9N 2 28W
70 Vergato, Italy 44 18N 11 8E
161 Vergennes, U.S.A. 44 9N 73 15W
50 Vergt, France 45 2N 0 43E
62 Verin, Spain 41 57N 7 27W
62 Verina, Spain 43 32N 5 43W
135 Verkeerdevlei, S. Africa 28 48S 26 48E
89 Verkhneye, U.S.S.R. .48 50N 38 30E
91 Verkhne Kolymsk, U.S.S.R. 65 50N 150 30E
89 Verkhniy Baskunchak, U.S.S.R. 48 5N 46 50E
87 Verkhovye, U.S.S.R. .52 55N 37 15E
91 Verkhoyansk, U.S.S.R. 67 50N 133 50E
91 Verkhoyansk Ra., U.S.S.R. 66 0N 129 0E
157 Verlo, Canada 50 25N 108 35W
79 Verma, Norway 62 21N 8 3E
133 Vermaas, Trans., S. Afr. 26 30S 25 59E
49 Vermenton, France 47 40N 3 42E
157 Vermilion, Canada 53 20N 110 50W
157 Vermilion Bay, Canada 49 50N 93 20W
165 Vermilion, B., U.S.A. .29 45N 91 55W
164 Vermillion, U.S.A. 42 50N 96 56W
161 Vermont, St., U.S.A. .43 40N 72 50W
166 Vernal, U.S.A. 40 28N 109 35W
154 Verner, Canada 46 25N 80 8W
49 Verneuil, France 48 45N 0 56E
134 Verneukpan L., S. Afr. 30 0S 21 0E
156 Vernon, Canada 50 20N 119 15W
48 Vernon, France 49 5N 1 30E
165 Vernon, U.S.A. 34 0N 99 15W
163 Vero Beach, U.S.A. ...27 39N 80 23W
76 Véroia, Greece 40 34N 22 18E
70 Verolanuova, Italy 45 20N 10 5E
72 Veroli, Italy 41 43N 13 24E
70 Verona, Italy 45 27N 11 0E
91 Veropol, U.S.S.R. 66 0N 168 0E
49 Versailles, France 48 48N 2 8E
124 Vert C., Senegal 14 45N 17 30W
48 Vertou, France 47 10N 1 28W
49 Vertus, France 48 54N 4 0E
135 Verulam, Nat., S. Afr. 29 38S 31 2E
54 Verviers, Belgium 50 37N 5 52E
49 Vervins, France 49 50N 3 53E
157 Verwood, Canada 49 30N 105 40W
34 Verwood, England, U.K. 50 53N 1 53W
36 Veryan, England, U.K. 50 13N 4 56W
36 Veryan Bay, Eng., U.K. 50 12N 4 51W
71 Verzej, Yugoslavia 46 34N 16 13E
55 Vesdre, R., Belgium ...50 36N 6 0E
58 Veseli n. Luž, Cz. 49 12N 14 45E
75 Vesellya, Bulgaria 42 18N 27 38E
89 Veselyy Res., U.S.S.R. 47 0N 41 0E
89 Veshenskaya, U.S.S.R. 49 35N 41 44E
49 Vesle R., France 49 17N 3 50E
49 Vesoul, France 60 40N 6 11E
81 Vessigebro, Sweden ...56 58N 12 40E
82 Vest-Agder Fylke, Co., Norway 58 30N 7 0E
79 Vest Fjorden, Norway 68 0N 15 0E
79 Vestby, Norway 59 37N 10 45E
81 Vester Hassing, Den. .57 4N 10 8E
82 Vesterålen Is., Norway 69 0N 15 0E
79 Vestmarka, Norway ...59 56N 12 0E
79 Vestfold Fylke, Co., Norway 59 15N 10 0E
82 Vestmannaeyjar, Ice. .63 27N 20 15W
79 Vestnes, Norway 62 39N 7 5E
70 Vestone, Italy 45 43N 10 25E
82 Vestvågøy, Norway ...68 18N 15 20E
82 Vestvågøy I., Norway 68 15N 13 50E
73 Vesuvius Mt., Italy ...40 50N 14 22E
59 Veszprem, Hungary ...47 8N 17 57E
59 Veszprem, Co., Hung. 47 5N 17 55E
59 Vesztö, Hungary 46 55N 21 16E
135 Vet R., O.F.S., S. Afr. 27 50S 25 55E
135 Vetrivier, O.F.S., S. Afr. 28 29S 26 40E
106 Vetapalam, India 15 47N 80 18E
81 Vetlanda, Sweden 57 24N 15 3E
87 Vetluga, U.S.S.R. 57 53N 45 45E
87 Vetluzhskiy, U.S.S.R. 57 17N 45 12E
75 Vetovo, Bulgaria 43 42N 26 16E
71 Vetralla, Italy 42 20N 12 2E
75 Vetren, Bulgaria 42 15N 24 3E
55 Vettelschoss, Germany 50 38N 7 20E
71 Vettore, Mte., Italy ...44 38N 7 5E
54 Veurne, Belgium 51 5N 2 40E
57 Vevey, Switzerland ...46 28N 6 51E
76 Vévi, Greece 40 47N 21 38E
100 Veys, Iran 31 30N 49 0E
49 Vézelise, France 48 30N 6 5E
75 Vezhen Mt., Bulgaria .42 50N 24 20E
174 Viacha, Bolivia 16 30S 68 5W
70 Viadana, Italy 44 55N 10 30E
176 Viana, Brazil 3 0S 44 40W
64 Viana, Spain 42 31N 2 22W
62 Viana del Bollo, Spain 42 10N 7 10W
63 Viana do Castelo, Port. 41 41N 8 50W
55 Vianen, Netherlands .51 59N 5 5E
62 Vianna do Castelo, dist., Portugal 41 50N 8 30W
175 Vianopolis, Brazil 16 40S 48 35W
62 Viar, R., Spain 37 45N 5 54W
70 Viareggio, Italy 43 52N 10 13E
157 Vibank, Canada 50 25N 104 0W
62 Vibey, R., Spain 42 21N 7 15E
73 Vibo Valentia, Italy ...38 40N 16 5E
81 Viborg, Denmark 56 27N 9 23E
81 Viborg, Amt, Co., Den. 56 30N 9 20E
50 Vic Fézensac, France .43 47N 0 19E
45 Vicarstown, Ireland ...53 5N 7 7W
50 Vic-en-Bigorre, France 43 24N 0 3E
71 Vicenza, Italy 45 32N 11 31E
64 Vich, Spain 41 58N 2 19E
87 Vichuga, U.S.S.R. 57 25N 41 55E
50 Vichy, France 46 9N 3 26E
38 Vickerstown, Eng., U.K. 54 8N 3 17W
162 Vicksburg, Mich., U.S.A. 42 10N 85 30W
165 Vicksburg, Miss., U.S.A. 32 22N 90 56W
71 Vico L., di, Italy 42 20N 12 10E
173 Vicosa, Min. Ger., Brazil 20 45S 42 53W
175 Vicosa, Pernambuco, Brazil 9 28S 36 25W
50 Vic-sur-Cère, France .44 59N 2 38E
49 Vic-sur-Seille, France 48 45N 6 33E
164 Victor, Col., U.S.A. ...38 43N 105 7W
160 Victor, N.Y., U.S.A. .42 58N 77 24W
145 Victor Harb., S. Austral. 35 30S 138 37E
172 Victoria, Argentina ...32 40S 60 10W
144 Victoria, Queens., Austral. 21 16S 149 3E
125 Victoria, Cameroon ... 4 1N 9 10E
156 Victoria, Canada 48 30N 123 25W
176 Victoria, Chile 38 22S 72 29W
113 Victoria, Hong Kong .22 25N 114 15E
108 Victoria, Sab., Malaysia 5 20N 115 20E
165 Victoria, Tex., U.S.A. 28 50N 97 0W
164 Victoria, Va., U.S.A. .38 52N 99 8W
132 Victoria, dist., Rhod. .21 0S 31 30E
143 Victoria, st., Australia 37 0S 144 0E
153 Victoria, I., N.W.T., Canada 71 0N 11 0W
131 Victoria, L., E. Africa 1 0S 33 0E
143 Victoria, L., Australia 38 0S 147 35E
103 Victoria, Mt., Burma .21 15N 93 55E
144 Victoria, Mt., Territory of New Guinea 8 40S 147 20E
156 Victoria Pk., Canada .50 10N 126 0W
147 Victoria Ra., N.Z. 42 12S 172 7E
138 Victoria R., Australia 15 30S 131 0E
157 Victoria Beach, Canada 50 45N 96 32W
169 Victoria de las Tunas, Cuba 20 58N 76 59W
132 Victoria Falls, Rhodesia 17 58S 25 45E
154 Victoria Harb., Canada 44 45N 79 45W
15 Victoria Ld., Antarctica 75 0S 160 0E
131 Victoria Nile R., Uganda 2 25N 31 50E
138 Victoria R. Downs, N. Terr., Austral. 16 30S 131 20E
134 Victoria West, S. Africa 31 25S 23 4E
155 Victoriaville, Canada .46 4N 71 56W
172 Victorica, Argentina ...36 20S 65 30W
172 Vicuña, Chile 30 0S 70 50W
172 Vicuna Mackenna, Arg. 33 53S 64 25W
163 Vidalia, U.S.A. 32 13N 82 25W
51 Vidauban, France 43 25N 6 27E
79 Videlv, R., Norway ...58 50N 8 32E
63 Vidigueira, Portugal ...38 12N 7 48W
62 Vidio, Cabo, Spain 43 35N 6 14W
104 Vidisha (Bhilsa), India 23 28N 77 53E
81 Vidöstern, L., Sweden 57 1N 14 0E
78 Vidra, Rumania 45 56N 26 55E
74 Viduša, Ra., Y.-slavia 42 55N 18 21E
86 Vidzy, U.S.S.R. 54 40N 26 37E
176 Viedma, Argentina 40 50S 63 0W
176 Viedma L., Argentina 49 30S 72 30W
62 Vieira, Portugal 41 38N 8 8W
64 Viella, Spain 42 43N 0 44E
107 Vien Pou Kha, Laos .20 45N 101 5E
56 Vienenburg, W. Ger. .51 57N 10 35E
59 Vienna (Wien), Austria 48 12N 16 22E
165 Vienna, U.S.A. 37 29N 88 54W
51 Vienne, France 45 31N 4 53E
50 Vienne, dépt., France 46 30N 0 30E
48 Vienne R., France 47 5N 0 30E
107 Vientiane, Laos 18 7N 102 35E
135 Vierfontein, S. Africa .27 3S 26 46E
55 Vierlingsbeek, Neth. ...51 36N 6 1E
56 Viersen, Germany 51 15N 6 23E
135 Viertien Strome, S. Afr. 28 9S 24 48E
57 Vierwaldstätter See, Switzerland 47 0N 8 30E
49 Vierzon, France 47 13N 2 5E
50 Vieux Boucau, France 43 48N 1 23W
51 Vif, France 45 5N 5 41E
120 Vigan, Philippines 17 35N 120 28E
70 Vigevano, Italy 45 18N 8 50E
175 Vigia, Brazil 0 50S 48 5W
49 Vignacourt, France ...50 1N 2 15E
50 Vignemale, Pic du, Fr. 42 47N 0 10W
49 Vigneulles, France 48 59N 5 40E
70 Vignola, Italy 44 29N 11 0E
62 Vigo, Spain 42 12N 8 41W
62 Vigo, Ria de, Spain ...42 15N 8 45W
142 Vigors, Mt., W. Austral. 22 29S 118 15E
81 Vigsö B., Denmark 57 8N 8 47E
48 Vihiers, France 47 10N 0 30W
106 Vijayadurg, India 16 30N 73 25E
106 Vijayawada (Bezwada), India ...16 31N 80 39E
76 Vijosë R., Albania 40 35N 19 30E
79 Vikedal, Norway 59 30N 5 55E
81 Viken, L., Sweden 58 40N 14 30E
79 Vikesund, Norway 59 58N 9 58E
156 Viking, Canada 53 7N 111 50W
106 Vikramasingapuram, India 8 40N 76 47E
80 Viksjö, Sweden 62 45N 17 30E
90 Vikulovo, U.S.S.R. 56 50N 70 40E
129 Vila Arriaga, Angola .14 35S 13 30E
174 Vila Bittencourt, Brazil 1 20S 69 20W
132 Vila Cabral, Mozam. .13 13S 35 11E
132 Vila Caldas Xavier, Mozambique 14 26S 33 0E
132 Vila Coutinho, Mozam. 14 37S 34 19E
129 Vila da Maganja, Mozambique 17 18S 37 30E
129 Vila da Ponte, Angola 14 35S 16 40E
129 Vila de Aljustrel, Ang. 13 30S 19 45E
129 Vila da Ponte, Angola 14 35S 16 40E
129 Vila de João Belo, Mozambique 25 2S 33 34E
109 Vila de Liquica, Portuguese Timor ... 8 40S 125 20E
132 Vila de Manica, Mozam. 18 58S 32 59E
63 Vila de Rei, Portugal .39 41N 8 9W
132 Nila de Sena, Mozam. 17 25S 35 0E
63 Vila do Bispo, Portugal 37 5N 8 53W
62 Vila do Conde, Portugal 41 21N 8 45W
174 Vila Feijó, Brazil 8 30S 70 30W
132 Vila Fontes, Mozam. .17 51S 35 24E
63 Vila Franca de Xira, Portugal 38 57N 8 59W
132 Vila Gamito, Mozam. .14 12S 33 0E
130 Vila General Machado (Camacupa), Angola 11 58S 17 22E
132 Vila Gomes da Costa, Mozambique 24 20S 33 37E
132 Vila Gouveia, Mozam. 18 3S 33 11E
130 Vila Henrique de Carvalho, Angola ... 9 40S 20 12E
133 Vila Luisa, Mozam. ...25 45S 32 35E
130 Vila Luso, Angola 11 53S 19 55E
132 Vila Machado, Mozam. 19 15S 34 14E
130 Vila Mariano Machado, Angola ...13 3S 14 35E
132 Vila Mouzinho, Mozam. 14 48S 34 25E
174 Vila Murtinho, Brazil .10 20S 65 20W
62 Vila Nova de Fozcôa, Port. 41 5N 7 9W
63 Vila Nova de Ourem, Portugal 39 40N 8 35W
62 Vila Novo de Gaia, Port. 41 4N 8 40W
130 Vila Novo de Seles, Ang. 11 35S 14 22E
129 Vila Paiva Couceiro, Angola 14 37S 14 40E
132 Vila Paiva de Andrada, Mozam. ...18 37S 34 2E
129 Vila Pereira d'Eça, Angola 16 48S 15 50E
132 Vila Pery, Mozambique 19 4S 33 29E
62 Vila Pouca de Aguiar, Portugal 41 30N 7 38W
62 Vila Real, Portugal ...41 17N 7 48W
63 Vila Real de Santo Antonio, Portugal ...37 10N 7 28W
130 Vila Robert Williams, Angola 12 46S 15 30E
130 Vila Salazar, Angola . 9 12S 14 48E
109 Vila Salazar, Port. Timor 5 25S 123 50E
130 Vila Teixeira da Silva, Angola 12 10S 15 50E
130 Vila Teixeira de Sousa, Angola 10 40S 22 12E
132 Vila Vasco da Gama, Mozambique 14 54S 32 14E
130 Vila Verissimo, Sarmento, Angola ... 8 15S 20 50E
63 Vila Viçosa, Portugal .38 45N 7 27W
174 Vila Vila, Bolivia 18 0S 65 40W
62 Vilaboa, Spain 42 21N 8 39W
48 Vilaine R., France 47 35N 2 10W
132 Vilanculos, Mozam. 22 1S 35 17E
62 Vilar Formosa, Portugal 40 38N 6 45W
62 Vilareal, dist., Portugal 41 36N 7 35W
78 Vilceo, Reg., Rum. 45 5N 24 5E
86 Vileyka, U.S.S.R. 54 30N 27 0E
82 Vilhelmina, Sweden ...64 35N 16 50E
174 Vilhena, Brazil 12 30S 60 0W
91 Viliga, U.S.S.R. 60 2N 156 56E
86 Viliya R., U.S.S.R. 54 57N 24 35E
86 Viljandi, U.S.S.R 58 28N 25 30E
135 Viljoenskroon, S. Africa 27 12S 27 0E
172 Villa Abecia, Bolivia .21 0S 68 18W
168 Villa Ahumada, Mexico 30 30N 106 40W
172 Villa Ana, Argentina .28 28S 59 40W
172 Villa Angela, Argentina 27 34S 60 45W
174 Villa Bella, Bolivia 10 25S 65 30W
120 Villa Bens (Tarfaya) Morocco 27 55N 12 55W
172 Villa Burruyacu, Arg. 26 30S 64 40W
172 Villa Canas, Argentina 34 0S 61 35W
172 Villa Cisneros, Spanish Sahara 23 50N 15 53W
120 Villa Cisneros, dist., Span. Sahara 25 0N 13 30W
172 Villa Colon, Argentina 31 38S 68 20W
172 Villa Constitucion, Arg. 33 15S 60 20W
172 Villa Crespo, Argentina 32 0S 60 20W
169 Villa de Cura, Ven. 10 2N 67 29W
172 Villa de Rosario, Par. 24 30S 57 35W
172 Villa Dolores, Argentina 31 58S 65 15W
172 Villa Franca, Paraguay 26 14S 58 20W
172 Villa Guillermina, Arg. 28 15S 59 29W
172 Villa Hayes, Paraguay 25 0S 57 20W
172 Villa Iris, Argentina ...38 12S 63 12W
169 Villa Julia Molina, Dominican Republic 19 5N 69 45W
168 Villa Madero, Mexico .24 28N 104 10W
172 Villa Maria, Argentina 32 20S 63 10W
70 Villa Minozzo, Italy ...44 21N 10 30E
172 Villa Mentes, Bolivia .21 10S 63 30W
172 Villa San Agustin, Arg. 30 35S 67 30W
172 Villa San Martin, Arg. 28 9S 64 9W
73 Villa San Giovanni, It. 38 13N 15 38E
172 Villa Santina, Italy 46 25N 12 55E
62 Villablino, Spain 42 57N 6 19W
99 Villabruzzi, Somali Rep. 3 3N 45 18E
64 Villacañas, Spain 39 38N 3 20W
64 Villacarlos, Spain 39 53N 4 17E
64 Villacarriedo, Spain ...43 14N 3 48W
65 Villacarrillo, Spain 38 7N 3 3W
62 Villacastin, Spain 40 46N 4 25W
58 Villach, Austria 46 37N 13 51E
72 Villaciaro, Italy 39 27N 8 45E
62 Villada, Spain 42 15N 4 59W
62 Villadiego, Spain 42 31N 4 1W
70 Villadossola, Italy 46 4N 8 16E
64 Villafeliche, Spain 41 10N 1 30W
64 Villafranca, Spain 42 17N 1 46W
65 Villafranca de los Caballeros, Spain ...39 26N 3 21W
63 Villafranca de los Barros, Spain 38 35N 6 18W
62 Villafranca del Bierzo, Spain 42 38N 6 50W
64 Villafranca del Cid, Sp. 40 26N 0 16W
64 Villafranca del Panadés, Spain 41 21N 1 40E
70 Villafranca di Verona, Italy 45 20N 10 51E
62 Villagarcia, Spain 42 34N 8 46W
172 Villaguay, Argentina .32 0S 58 45W
63 Villaharta, Spain 38 9N 4 54W

MAP
65 Villahermosa, Spain ...38 46N 2 52W
168 Villahermosa, Mexico .17 45N 92 50W
48 Villaines la Juhel, Fr. 48 21N 0 20W
65 Villajoyosa, Spain 38 30N 0 12W
62 Villalba, Spain 40 36N 3 59W
62 Villalba de Guardo, Sp. 42 42N 4 49W
62 Villalon de Campos, Sp. 42 5N 5 4W
62 Villalpando, Spain 41 51N 5 25W
62 Villaluenga, Spain 40 2N 3 54W
62 Villamañan, Spain 42 19N 5 35W
62 Villamartin, Spain 36 52N 5 38W
64 Villamayor, Spain 41 42N 0 43W
50 Villamblard, France ...45 2N 0 32E
72 Villanova Monteleone, Italy 40 30N 8 28E
167 Villanueva, U.S.A. 35 16N 105 31W
65 Villanueva de Castellón, Spain 39 5N 0 31W
63 Villanueva de Córdoba, Spain 38 20N 4 38W
65 Villanueva de la Fuente, Spain 38 42N 2 42W
63 Villanueva de la Serena, Spain 38 59N 5 50W
62 Villanueva de la Sierra, Spain 40 12N 6 24W
63 Villanueva de los Castillejos, Spain ...37 30N 7 15W
65 Villanueva del Arzobispo, Spain 38 10N 3 0W
63 Villanueva del Duque, Spain 38 20N 4 38W
63 Villanueva del Fresno, Spain 38 23N 7 10W
64 Villanueva y Geltru, Sp. 41 13N 1 40E
62 Villaodrid, Spain 43 20N 7 11W
72 Villaputzu, Italy 39 28N 9 33E
64 Villar del Arzobispo, Sp. 39 44N 0 50W
63 Villar del Rey, Spain .39 7N 6 50W
64 Villarcayo, Spain 42 56N 3 34W
62 Villarino de los Aires, Sp. 41 18N 6 23W
73 Villarosa, Italy 37 36N 14 9E
62 Villarramiel, Spain 42 2N 4 55W
64 Villarreal, Spain 39 55N 0 3W
176 Villarrica, Chile 39 15S 72 30W
172 Villarrica, Paraguay ...25 40S 56 30W
1 Villarrica, Vol., S. Amer. 39 0S 70 0W
65 Villarrobledo, Spain ...39 18N 2 36W
64 Villarroya de la Sierra, Spain 41 27N 1 46W
65 Villarrubia de los Ojos, Spain 39 14N 3 36W
51 Villars, Ain, France ...46 0N 5 2E
65 Villarta de San Juan, Spain 39 15N 3 25W
64 Villasayas, Spain 41 24N 2 39W
62 Villaseco de los Gamitos, Spain 41 2N 6 7W
64 Villastar, Spain 40 17N 1 9W
64 Villatobas, Spain 39 54N 3 20W
72 Villavicencio, Argentina 32 28S 69 0W
174 Villavicencio, Colombia 4 9N 73 37W
62 Villaviciosa, Spain 43 32N 5 27W
172 Villazon, Bolivia 22 0S 65 35W
49 Ville de Paris, dépt., France 48 50N 2 20E
154 Ville Marie, Canada ...47 20N 79 30W
165 Ville Platte, U.S.A. ...30 45N 92 17W
48 Villedieu, France 48 50N 1 12W
50 Villefort, France 44 28N 3 56E
49 Villefranche, France ...47 19N 1 46E
50 Villéfranche de Lauragais, France ...43 25N 1 44E
50 Villefranche de Rouergue, France ...44 21N 2 2E
50 Villefranche du Périgord, France 44 38N 1 5E
51 Villefranche-sur-Saône, France 45 59N 4 43E
64 Villel, Spain 40 14N 1 12W
49 Villemaur, France 48 14N 3 40E
50 Villemur, France 43 52N 1 31E
65 Villena, Spain 38 39N 0 52W
49 Villenauxe, France 48 36N 3 30E
50 Villeneuve, France 48 42N 2 25E
70 Villeneuve, Italy 45 40N 7 10E
49 Villeneuve l'Archeveque, France 48 14N 3 32E
51 Villeneuve les Avignon, France 43 57N 4 49E
50 Villeneuve sur Allier, Fr. 46 40N 3 13E
50 Villeneuve-sur-Lot, Fr. 44 24N 0 42E
50 Villeréal, France 44 38N 0 45E
48 Villers Bocage, France 49 3N 0 40W
49 Villers Bretonneux, Fr. 49 50N 2 30E
49 Villers Cotterets, France 49 15N 3 4E
48 Villers-sur-Mer, France 49 21N 0 2W
49 Villersexel, France 47 33N 6 26E
55 Villers-le-Bouillet, Belg. 50 34N 5 15E
81 Villerslev, Denmark ...56 49N 8 29E
49 Villerupt, France 49 28N 5 55E
51 Villeurbanne, France .45 46N 4 55E
48 Villerville, France 49 26N 0 5E
172 Villeta, Paraguay 25 31S 57 28W
MAP
135 Villers, O.F.S., S. Africa 27 2S 28 36E
134 Villiersdorp, S. Africa 34 0S 19 16E
57 Villingen, Germany ...48 3N 8 29E
164 Villisca, U.S.A. 40 55N 94 59W
106 Villupuram, India 11 59N 79 31E
86 Vilnyus (Vilna, Wilno), U.S.S.R. 54 38N 25 25E
58 Vils, Austria 47 33N 10 37E
57 Vilsbiburg, Germany .48 27N 12 23E
81 Vilslev, Denmark 55 24N 8 42E
74 Vilusi, Yugoslavia 42 44N 18 34E
54 Vilvoorde, Belgium ...50 56N 4 26E
91 Vilyuy R., U.S.S.R. ...63 58N 125 0E
91 Vilyuysk, U.S.S.R. 63 40N 121 20E
70 Vimercate, Italy 45 38N 9 25E
62 Vimiosa, Portugal 41 35N 6 13W
81 Vimmerby, Sweden ...57 40N 15 55E
80 Vimo, Sweden 60 50N 14 20E
48 Vimoutiers, France ...48 57N 0 10E
58 Vimperk, Cz. 49 3N 13 46E
172 Viña del Mar, Chile ...33 0S 71 30W
64 Vinaroz, Spain 40 30N 0 27E
162 Vincennes, U.S.A. 38 42N 87 29W
172 Vinchina, Argentina ...28 45S 68 15W
82 Vindel R., Sweden 64 50N 19 0E
81 Vinderup, Denmark ...56 29N 8 45E
104 Vindhya Ra., India ...22 50N 77 0E
162 Vineland, U.S.A. 39 30N 75 0W
74 Vinga, Rumania 46 0N 21 14E
79 Vinges, Norway 61 7N 10 58E
107 Vinh, North Vietnam .18 45N 105 38E
107 Vinh Loi, S. Vietnam . 9 20N 104 45E
62 Vinhais, Portugal 41 50N 7 0W
132 Vinho, Mozambique ...16 13S 32 25E
71 Vinica, Yugoslavia 41 53N 22 30E
71 Vinica, Yugoslavia 45 28N 15 16E
165 Vinita, U.S.A. 36 40N 95 12W
74 Vinkovci, Yugoslavia .45 19N 18 48E
88 Vinnitsa, U.S.S.R. 49 15N 28 30E
79 Vinstra, Norway 61 37N 9 44E
164 Vinton, Iowa, U.S.A. .42 8N 92 1W
165 Vinton, La., U.S.A. 30 13N 93 35W
78 Vinţul de Jos, Rum. .46 0N 23 30E
56 Viöl, Germany 54 32N 9 12E
143 Violet Town, Australia 36 19S 145 37E
71 Vipava, Yugoslavia ...45 51N 13 38E
71 Vipiteno, Italy 46 55N 11 25E
109 Viqueque, Port. Timor 8 42S 126 30E
71 Vir, I., Yugoslavia 44 17N 15 3E
109 Virac, Philippines 13 30N 124 20E
106 Virajpet, India 12 15N 75 50E
104 Viramgam, India 23 5N 72 0E
106 Virarajendrapet (Virajpet), India 12 10N 75 50E
106 Viravanallur, India 8 40N 79 30E
157 Virden, Canada 49 50N 101 0W
48 Vire, France 48 50N 0 53W
169 Virgin Gorda, I., Virgin Islands, W.I. 18 45N 64 26W
169 Virgin Is., W. Indies .18 40N 64 30W
167 Virgin R., U.S.A. 36 50N 114 10W
46 Virginia, Ireland 53 50N 7 5W
135 Virginia, O.F.S., S. Afr. 28 8S 26 55E
164 Virginia, U.S.A. 47 30N 92 32W
162 Virginia, st., U.S.A. ...37 45N 78 0W
162 Virginia Beach, U.S.A. 36 54N 75 58W
166 Virginia City, Mont., U.S.A. 45 25N 111 58W
166 Virginia City, Nev., U.S.A. 39 25N 119 48W
176 Virgins C., Argentina .52 10S 68 30W
154 Virginiatown, Canada 48 9N 79 36W
51 Virieu le Grand, Fr. ...45 51N 5 39E
74 Virje, Yugoslavia 46 4N 16 59E
164 Viroqua, U.S.A. 43 33N 90 57W
74 Virovitica, Yugoslavia 45 51N 17 21E
74 Virpaza R., Yugoslavia 42 14N 19 6E
81 Virserum, Sweden 57 20N 15 30E
54 Virton, Belgium 49 35N 5 32E
86 Virtsu, U.S.S.R. 58 32N 23 33E
106 Virudhunagar, India . 9 30N 78 0E
71 Vis, & I., Yugoslavia .43 0N 16 10E
71 Vis Kanal, Yugoslavia 43 4N 16 5E
167 Visalia, U.S.A. 36 25N 119 18W
109 Visayan Sea, Phil. 11 30N 123 30E
81 Visby, Sweden 57 37N 18 25E
14 Viscount Melville Sd., Canada 78 0N 108 0W
54 Visé, Belgium 50 44N 5 41E
74 Višegrad, Yugoslavia .43 47N 19 17E
175 Viseu, Brazil 1 10S 46 20W
62 Viseu, tn. & dist., Portugal 40 40N 7 55W
78 Vişeu, Rumania 47 45N 24 25E
106 Vishakhapatnam, India 17 45N 83 20E
105 Vishnupur, India 23 8N 87 20E
15 Visikoi I., Falkland Is. Dependencies 56 30S 26 40E
81 Visingsö I., Sweden ...58 2N 14 15E
81 Viskafors, Sweden 57 37N 12 50E
81 Vislanda, Sweden 56 46N 14 30E
60 Vislinskil Zaliv (Zalew Wislany), Poland ...54 20N 19 50E
104 Visnagar, India 23 45N 72 32E
71 Visnja Gora, Y.-slavia 45 58N 14 45E
70 Viso, Mte., Italy 44 38N 7 5E
65 Viso del Marques, Sp. 38 32N 3 34W
74 Visoko, Yugoslavia 43 58N 18 10E
57 Visp, Switzerland 46 17N 7 52E
135 Visrivier, S. Africa 31 51S 25 25E
56 Visselhövede, Germany 52 59N 9 36E
174 Vista Alegre, Brazil ... 1 50N 61 5W
MAP
76 Vistonis, Limni, L., Gr. 41 0N 25 7E
60 Vistula (Wisla) R., Pol. 52 30N 19 40E
75 Vit, R., Bulgaria 43 30N 24 30E
71 Vitanje, Yugoslavia ...46 40N 15 18E
86 Vitebsk, U.S.S.R. 55 10N 30 15E
71 Viterbo, Italy 42 25N 12 8E
144 Vitiaz Str., Territory of New Guinea 5 46S 147 0E
36 Viti Levu, Fiji Is., Pacific Ocean 17 30S 177 30E
62 Vitigudino, Spain 41 1N 6 35W
91 Vitim, U.S.S.R. 59 45N 112 25E
91 Vitim R., U.S.S.R. 58 40N 112 50E
77 Vitina, Greece 37 40N 22 10E
74 Vitina, Yugoslavia 43 17N 17 29E
175 Vitória, Espiritu Santo, Brazil 20 20S 40 22W
64 Vitoria, Spain 42 50N 2 41W
175 Vitoria da Conquista, Brazil 15 0S 42 0W
175 Vitória de Santo Antao, Brazil 8 10S 35 20W
132 Vitorinho, Mozambique 17 9S 35 50E
74 Vitorog, Mt., Y.-slavia 44 7N 17 2E
48 Vitré, France 48 8N 1 12W
49 Vitry-le-Francois, Fr. 48 43N 4 33E
76 Vitsi, Mt., Vernow, Gr. 40 40N 21 25E
82 Vittangi, Sweden 67 41N 21 40E
49 Vitteaux, France 47 24N 4 30E
160 Vittoria, Canada 42 48N 81 21W
73 Vittoria, Italy 36 58N 14 30E
71 Vittorio Veneto, Italy 45 59N 12 18E
55 Vivegnis, Belgium 50 42N 5 39E
64 Viver, Spain 39 55N 0 36W
62 Vivero, Spain 43 39N 7 38W
51 Viviers, France 44 30N 4 40E
50 Vivonne, France 46 36N 0 15E
80 Vivsta-Nas, Sweden ...62 30N 17 40E
168 Vizcaino, Sierra, Mex. 27 30N 114 0W
168 Vizcaino Desert, Mex. 27 40N 113 50W
64 Vizcaya, Prov., Spain 43 15N 2 45W
106 Vizianagaram, India .18 6N 83 10E
51 Vizille, France 45 5N 5 46E
71 Vizinada, Yugoslavia .45 20N 13 46E
78 Viziru, Rumania 45 0N 27 43E
59 Vizovice, Cz. 49 12N 17 56E
73 Vizzini, Italy 37 9N 14 43E
54 Vlaardingen, Neth. 51 55N 4 19E
78 Vladesa Mt., Rumania 46 47N 22 50E
74 Vladicin, Han, Y.-slav. 42 42N 22 1E
87 Vladimir, U.S.S.R. 56 8N 40 20E
86 Vladimir Volynskiy, U.S.S.R. 50 50N 24 18E
74 Vladimirci, Yugoslavia 44 36N 19 45E
74 Vladimirovac, Y.-slav. 45 1N 20 53E
89 Vladimirovka, U.S.S.R. 48 27N 46 5E
89 Vladimirovka, U.S.S.R. 44 37N 44 41E
88 Vladislavovka, U.S.S.R. 45 15N 35 15E
88 Vladivostok, U.S.S.R. 43 10N 131 53E
134 Vlaklaagte, S. Africa .32 42S 23 39E
134 Vlakteplaas, S. Africa 33 28S 22 43E
142 Vlaming Head, W. Australia 21 48S 114 5E
74 Vlasenica, Yugoslavia 44 11N 18 59E
74 Vlašic, Mt., Yugoslavia 44 19N 17 37E
58 Vlasim, Czechoslovakia 49 40N 14 53E
74 Vlasinsko Jezero, L., Yugoslavia 42 44N 22 37E
74 Vlasotinci, Yugoslavia 42 59N 22 7E
133 Vleesfontein, S. Africa 24 47S 26 18E
134 Vleifontein, S. Africa .33 6S 21 4E
54 Vlieland I., Neth. 53 30N 4 55E
55 Vlijmen, Netherlands .51 42N 5 14E
54 Vlissingen (Flushing), Netherlands 51 26N 3 34E
76 Vlore (Valona), Albania 40 32N 19 28E
76 Vlorë, pref., Albania .40 12N 20 0E
58 Vltava R., Cz. 49 35N 14 10E
70 Vobarno, Italy 45 38N 10 30E
74 Vočin, Yugoslavia 45 37N 17 33E
71 Vodice, Yugoslavia 43 47N 15 47E
58 Vodňany, Cz. 49 9N 14 11E
71 Vodnjan, Yugoslavia .44 59N 13 52E
42 Voe, Shetland Is., Scotland, U.K. 60 21N 1 15W
135 Voël R., C. Prov., S. Afr. 32 45S 25 10E
125 Voga, Togo 6 23N 1 30E
109 Vogelkop, Indonesia ... 1 25S 133 0E
70 Voghera, Italy 44 59N 9 1E
129 Vohémar, Malagasy Rep. 13 25S 50 0E
129 Vohipeno, Malagasy Rep. 22 21S 47 51E
131 Voi, Kenya 3 29S 38 32E
131 Voi R., Kenya 3 30S 39 40E
49 Void, France 48 40N 5 36E
40 Voil L., Scotland, U.K. 56 20N 4 25W
78 Voineşti, Rumania 47 5N 27 27E
78 Voineşti, Rumania 45 5N 25 14E
77 Voiotia, pref., Greece .38 20N 23 0E
51 Voiron, France 45 22N 5 35E
155 Voiseys B., Canada ...56 15N 61 0W
58 Voitsberg, Austria 47 3N 15 9E
MAP
76 Voiviis Limni, L., Gr. 39 30N 22 45E
81 Vojens, Denmark 55 16N 9 18E
81 Vojmsjon, L., Sweden 64 55N 16 40E
71 Vojnic, Yugoslavia 45 19N 15 43E
74 Vojnik, Yugoslavia 42 59N 19 0E
74 Vojvodina, Autonomous Prov., Yugoslavia 45 20N 20 0E
87 Vokhma, U.S.S.R. 59 0N 46 45E
87 Vokhma, R., U.S.S.R. 59 0N 46 44E
87 Vokhtoga, U.S.S.R. ...58 46N 41 8E
158 Volary, Cz. 48 54N 13 52E
164 Volborg, U.S.A. 45 50N 105 44W
36 Volcano Is., Pac. Oc. .26 0N 145 0E
87 Volchansk, U.S.S.R. ...50 17N 36 58E
88 Volchya, R., U.S.S.R. 48 0N 37 0E
79 Volda, Norway 62 9N 6 5E
87 Volga, U.S.S.R. 57 58N 38 16E
87 Volga, R., U.S.S.R. ...52 20N 48 0E
85 Volga Heights, U.S.S.R. 51 0N 46 0E
87 Volga Res., U.S.S.R. .56 40N 36 30E
89 Volgodonsk, U.S.S.R. 47 33N 42 5E
89 Volgograd, U.S.S.R. ...48 40N 44 25E
77 Volissós, Greece 38 29N 25 54E
58 Völkermarkt, Austria .46 39N 14 39E
86 Volkhov, U.S.S.R. 59 55N 32 15E
86 Volkhov R., U.S.S.R. 59 30N 32 0E
57 Volklingen, Germany .49 15N 6 50E
86 Volkovysk, U.S.S.R. .53 9N 24 30E
133 Volksrust, S. Africa ...27 24S 29 53E
54 Vollenhove, Neth. 52 40N 5 58E
88 Volnovakha, U.S.S.R. 47 35N 37 30E
143 Volo, N.S.W., Australia 31 37S 143 0E
91 Volochayevka, U.S.S.R. 48 40N 134 30E
87 Volodary, U.S.S.R. 56 12N 43 15E
87 Vologda, U.S.S.R. 59 25N 40 0E
87 Volokolamsk, U.S.S.R. 56 5N 36 0E
87 Volokonovka, U.S.S.R. 50 33N 37 58E
88 Volontirovka, U.S.S.R. 46 28N 29 28E
76 Vólos, Greece 39 24N 22 59E
86 Volosovo, U.S.S.R. 59 27N 29 32E
86 Volozhin, U.S.S.R. 54 3N 26 30E
87 Volsk, U.S.S.R. 52 5N 47 28E
134 Volstruisleegte, S. Afr. 33 0S 23 29E
81 Volstrup, Denmark ...57 19N 10 27E
125 Volta, L., Ghana 7 30N 0 15E
25 Volta, R., Ghana 8 0N 0 10W
173 Volta Redonda, Brazil 22 31S 44 5W
70 Volterra, Italy 43 24N 10 50E
70 Voltri, Italy 44 25N 8 43E
73 Volturara, Appula, It. 41 30N 15 2E
73 Volturno R., Italy 41 18N 14 20E
122 Volubilis, Morocco 34 2N 5 33W
76 Vólvi, L., Greece 40 40N 23 34E
87 Volzhsk, U.S.S.R. 55 57N 48 23E
89 Volzhskiy, U.S.S.R. ...48 56N 44 46E
77 Vónitsa, Greece 38 53N 20 58E
134 Voor Bay, S. Africa ...34 9S 22 5E
54 Voorburg, Netherlands 52 5N 4 24E
82 Vopna Fd., Iceland 65 45N 14 45W
58 Vorarlberg, prov., Aust. 47 20N 10 0E
76 Vóras Óros, Mts., Gr. .40 57N 21 45E
81 Vorbasse, Denmark ...55 39N 9 6E
81 Vordingborg, Denmark 55 0N 11 54E
77 Voríai Sporádhes, Is., Greece 39 15N 23 30E
77 Vórios Evvoïkós Kólpos, G., Greece .38 45N 23 15E
84 Vorkuta, U.S.S.R. 67 48N 64 20E
79 Vorma, R., Norway ...60 15N 11 15E
87 Vorona R., U.S.S.R. .52 0N 42 20E
87 Voronezh, U.S.S.R. ...51 40N 39 10E
87 Voronezh R., U.S.S.R. 52 30N 39 30E
86 Voronezh, Ukraine, U.S.S.R. 51 47N 33 28E
89 Vorontsovo Aleksandrovskoye, see Zelenokumsk, U.S.S.R. 44 30N 44 1E
89 Voroshilovgrad, U.S.S.R. 48 38N 39 15E
89 Voroshilovsk (Alchevsk), U.S.S.R. 48 3N 38 40E
91 Vorovskoye, U.S.S.R. 54 30N 155 50E
55 Vorselaar, Belgium 51 12N 4 46E
88 Vorskla, R., U.S.S.R. .49 30N 34 31E
81 Vorupör, Denmark 56 58N 8 22E
134 Vosburg, S. Africa 30 33S 22 52E
49 Vosges, dépt., France .48 12N 6 20E
49 Vosges, Mts., France .48 20N 7 10E
76 Voskopojë, Albania ...40 40N 20 33E
87 Voskresensk, U.S.S.R. 55 27N 38 31E
87 Voskresenskoye, U.S.S.R. 56 51N 45 30E
79 Voss, Norway 60 38N 6 26E
137 Vostok I., Pacific Ocean 10 5S 152 23W
58 Votice, Cz. 49 38N 14 39E
84 Votkinsk, U.S.S.R. 57 0N 53 55E
62 Vouga R., Portugal ...40 46N 8 10W
76 Vounása, Mt., Greece .39 58N 21 46E
76 Voúrinos, Mt., Greece 40 11N 21 40E
77 Vouxa, Ákra, C., Greece 35 37N 20 32E
62 Vouzela, Portugal 40 43N 8 7W
49 Vouziers, France 49 22N 4 40E
48 Voves, France 48 15N 1 38E
80 Voxna R., Sweden 61 20N 15 25E
Greece 35 37N 20 32E
43 Voy, Scotland, U.K. .59 1N 3 16W
MAP
84 Vozhe, L., U.S.S.R. ...60 45N 39 0E
87 Vozhgaly, U.S.S.R. ...58 24N 50 1E
88 Voznesensk, U.S.S.R. .47 35N 31 15E
84 Vosnesenye, U.S.S.R. .61 0N 35 45E
59 Vrâble, Czechoslovakia 48 15N 18 16E
74 Vrácevšnica, Y.-slavia 44 2N 20 34E
79 Vrådal, Norway 59 20N 8 25E
77 Vrakhnéika, Greece ...38 10N 21 40E
78 Vrancea, Reg., Rumania 45 50N 27 0E
78 Vrancei, Munti, Mts., Rumania 46 0N 26 30E
74 Vranje, Yugoslavia 42 34N 21 54E
80 Vrangtjärn, Sweden ...62 14N 16 37E
74 Vranica, Mt., Y.-slavia 43 59N 18 0E
74 Vranjska Banja, Y.-slav. 42 34N 22 1E
59 Vranov, Czechoslovakia 48 53N 21 40E
71 Vransko, Yugoslavia .46 17N 14 58E
75 Vratsa, Bulgaria 43 13N 23 30E
75 Vratsa, prov., Bulgaria 43 30N 23 30E
74 Vrbas, Yugoslavia 45 0N 17 27E
74 Vrbas R., Yugoslavia .44 30N 17 10E
71 Vrbnik, Yugoslavia ...45 4N 14 32E
71 Vrboviec, Yugoslavia 45 53N 16 28E
71 Vrbovsko, Yugoslavia 45 24N 15 5E
58 Vrchlabí, Cz. 49 38N 15 37E
135 Vrede, O.F.S., S. Africa 27 24S 29 6E
135 Vredefort, O.F.S., S. Afr. 27 0S 26 58E
134 Vredenburg, S. Africa 32 51S 18 0E
134 Vredendal, S. Africa ...31 41S 18 35E
81 Vrena, Sweden 58 54N 16 45E
74 Vrgorac, Yugoslavia ...43 12N 17 20E
71 Vrhnika, Yugoslavia .45 58N 14 15E
106 Vriddhachalam, India 11 30N 79 10E
124 Vridi, & Canal, Ivory Coast 5 15N 4 3W
104 Vrindaban, India 27 37N 77 40E
71 Vrnograc, Yugoslavia 43 12N 17 20E
77 Vrondádhes, Greece ...38 25N 26 7E
74 Vrpolje, Yugoslavia ...43 42N 16 1E
74 Vršac, Yugoslavia 45 8N 21 18E
74 Vrsački Canal, Y.-slav. 45 15N 21 0E
133 Vryburg, S. Africa 26 55S 24 45E
135 Vryheid, Natal, S. Afr. 27 54S 30 47E
59 Vsetin, Cz. 49 20N 18 0E
74 Vučitrn, Yugoslavia ...42 49N 20 59E
54 Vught, Netherlands ...51 38N 5 20E
74 Vuka, R., Yugoslavia 45 28N 18 30E
74 Vukovar, Yugoslavia .45 21N 18 59E
156 Vulcan, Canada 50 25N 113 15W
78 Vulcan, Rumania 45 23N 23 17E
162 Vulcan, U.S.A. 45 46N 87 51W
73 Vulcano I., Italy 38 25N 14 58E
75 Vŭlchedrŭm, Bulgaria 43 42N 23 16E
71 Vulci, Italy 42 23N 11 37E
88 Vulkaneshty, U.S.S.R. 45 35N 28 30E
132 Vunduzi, R., Mozam. .18 0S 33 45E
107 Vung Tau, S. Vietnam 10 28N 107 10E
75 Vŭrbitsa, Bulgaria 42 59N 26 40E
78 Vutcani, Rumania 46 26N 27 59E
106 Vuyyuru, India 16 28N 80 50E
104 Vyara, India 21 8N 73 28E
87 Vyatka R., U.S.S.R. .56 30N 51 0E
87 Vyatskiye Polyany, U.S.S.R. 56 5N 51 0E
86 Vyazma, U.S.S.R. 55 10N 34 15E
87 Vyasniki, U.S.S.R. 56 10N 42 10E
84 Vyborg, U.S.S.R. 60 43N 28 47E
84 Vychegda R., U.S.S.R. 61 50N 52 30E
59 Vychodni Beskydy, Mts., Europe 49 30N 22 0E
58 Vychodocesky, reg., Cz. 50 20N 15 45E
59 Vychodoslovensky, reg., Czechoslovakia 48 50N 21 0E
84 Vyg, L., U.S.S.R. 63 30N 34 0E
87 Vyksa, U.S.S.R. 55 27N 42 4E
106 Vypin, I., India 10 10N 76 15E
37 Vyrnwy, L., Wales, U.K. 52 48N 3 30W
37 Vyrnwy R., Wales, U.K. 52 43N 3 22W
86 Vyshniy Volochek, U.S.S.R. 57 30N 34 30E
59 Vyškov, Czechoslovakia 49 17N 17 0E
59 Vysoké, Myto, Cz. 49 58N 16 23E
59 Vysoké Tatry, Mts., Europe 49 30N 20 0E
87 Vysokovsk, U.S.S.R. .56 22N 36 30E
86 Vysotsk, U.S.S.R. 51 43N 36 32E
58 Vyšši Brod, Cz. 48 36N 14 20E
84 Vytegra, U.S.S.R. 61 15N 36 40E

W

124 Wa, Ghana 10 7N 2 25W
54 Waal, R., Netherlands 51 54N 5 35E
55 Waalwijk, Netherlands 51 42N 5 4E
155 Wabana, Canada 47 40N 53 0W
127 Wabara, Ethiopia 6 29N 40 33E
156 Wabasca, Canada 55 57N 113 45W
162 Wabash, U.S.A. 40 48N 85 46W
162 Wabash R., U.S.A. ...39 10N 87 30W
162 Wabeno, U.S.A. 45 25N 88 40W
127 Wabi, R., Ethiopia 7 35N 40 5E
127 Wabi Gestro, R., Ethiopia 6 0N 41 35E
127 Wabi Shaballe, R., Ethiopia 8 0N 40 45E
157 Wabigoon, L., Canada 49 44N 92 34W

MAP
157 Wabowden, Canada ...54 55N 98 35W
60 Wabrzezno, Poland ...53 16N 18 57E
154 Wabuk Pt., Canada ...55 30N 85 30W
155 Wabush City, Canada 52 40N 67 0W
166 Wabuska, U.S.A. 39 16N 119 13W
165 Waco, Texas, U.S.A. .31 33N 97 5W
154 Waconichi, L., Canada 50 0N 74 0W
100 Wad ar Rimsa, Si. Arab. 26 5N 41 30E
127 Wad Ban Naqa, Sudan 16 32N 33 9E
127 Wad Banda, Sudan ...13 10N 27 50E
127 Wad el Haddad, Sudan 13 50N 33 30E
127 Wad en Nau, Sudan ...14 10N 33 34E
127 Wad Hamid, Sudan ...16 20N 32 45E
127 Wad Medani, Sudan ...14 28N 33 30E
145 Waddamana, Australia 41 59S 146 34E
123 Wadden, Libya 29 9N 16 45E
123 Wadden, Jabal, Libya 29 0N 16 15E
142 Wadderin Hill, Austral. 32 0S 118 25E
34 Waddesdon, Eng., U.K. 51 50N 0 54W
39 Waddingham, Eng., U.K. 53 28N 0 31W
39 Waddington, Eng., U.K. 53 10N 0 31W
161 Waddington, U.S.A. ...44 51N 75 12W
156 Waddington Mt., Can. 51 10N 125 20W
36 Wadebridge, Eng., U.K. 50 31N 4 51W
157 Wadena, Canada 52 0N 103 50W
164 Wadena, U.S.A. 46 25N 95 2W
57 Wädenswil, Switzerland 47 14N 8 30E
163 Wadesboro, U.S.A. 35 2N 80 2W
156 Wadhams, Canada 51 30N 127 30W
35 Wadhurst, Eng., U.K. 51 3N 0 21E
125 Wadi, Nigeria 13 5N 11 40E
123 Wadi ash Shaki, Libya 27 30N 15 0E
123 Wadi Bani Walid, Libya 31 49N 14 0E
126 Wadi Germal I., Egypt 24 35N 35 10E
126 Wadi Halfa, Sudan ...21 53N 31 19E
99 Wadi Masila, S. Arabia 16 30N 49 0E
100 Wadi Sabha, Si. Arab. 23 50N 48 30E
60 Wadlew, Poland 51 31N 19 23E
59 Wadowice, Poland 49 52N 19 30E
166 Wadsworth, U.S.A. ...39 44N 119 22W
37 Waenfawr, Wales, U.K. 53 7N 4 10W
100 Wafra, Saudi Arabia .28 33N 48 3E
54 Wageningen, Neth. ...51 58N 5 40E
153 Wager B., Canada 65 50N 88 0W
153 Wager Bay, tn. Can. .66 0N 91 0W
143 Wagga Wagga, Austral. 35 7S 147 24E
125 Wagin, Nigeria 12 42N 7 10E
125 Wagin, W. Australia .33 17S 117 25E
165 Wagon Mound, U.S.A. 36 10N 105 0W
165 Wagoner, U.S.A. 36 0N 95 20W
60 Wagrowiec, Poland ...52 48N 17 19E
143 Wahgunyah, Australia 35 57S 146 25E
109 Wahai, Indonesia 2 48S 129 35E
55 Wahn, Germany 50 52N 70 6E
164 Wahoo, U.S.A. 41 15N 96 35W
164 Wahpeton, U.S.A 46 20N 96 35W
106 Wai, India 17 56N 73 57E
147 Waiai R., New Zealand 45 36S 167 45E
158 Waianae, Oahu I. Hawaii, U.S.A. 21 25N 158 8W
147 Waiau, New Zealand .42 39S 173 5E
106 Waiawe Ganga, R., Cey. 6 15N 81 0E
109 Waibeem, Indonesia ... 0 30S 132 50E
57 Waiblingen, Germany 48 49N 9 20E
58 Waidhofen, Lr., Austria 48 49N 15 17E
58 Waidhofen, Lr. Austria 47 57N 14 46E
109 Waigeo I., Indonesia . 0 20S 130 40E
147 Waiha Downs, N.Z. ...44 48S 170 55E
147 Waihao R., N.Z. 44 46S 171 10E
146 Waiheke Islands, N.Z. 36 48S 175 6E
146 Waihi, New Zealand .37 23S 175 52E
147 Waihola, New Zealand 46 1S 170 8E
147 Waihola L., N.Z. 45 59S 170 8E
109 Waikabubak, Indonesia 9 45S 119 25E
147 Waikaka, N.Z. 45 55S 169 1E
146 Waikare Lake, N.Z. ...37 26S 175 13E
146 Waikaremoana, N.Z. .38 42S 177 12E
146 Waikaremoana L., N.Z. 38 49S 177 9E
147 Waikari, New Zealand 42 58S 172 41E
146 Waikato R., N.Z. 37 32S 174 45E
145 Waikerie, S. Australia 34 9S 140 0E
146 Waikiekie, N.Z. 35 57S 174 16E
146 Waikokopu, N.Z. 39 3S 177 52E
146 Waikokopu Harb., N.Z. 39 4S 177 53E
147 Waikouaiti, N.Z. 45 36S 170 41E
147 Waikaoiti, Downs, N.Z. 45 36S 170 41E
147 Waimakahiri R., N.Z. 43 17S 171 59E
147 Waimangaroa, N.Z. ...41 43S 171 46E
158 Waimanola, Oahu I., Hawaii, U.S.A. 21 19N 157 43W
147 Waimarie, N.Z. 41 35S 171 58E
147 Waimate, N.Z. 44 33S 171 3E
158 Waimea, Kauai I., Hawaii, U.S.A. 21 57N 159 39W
147 Waimea Plain, N.Z. ...45 55S 168 35E
55 Waimes, Belgium 50 25N 6 7E
39 Wainfleet, Eng., U.K. 53 7N 0 16E
105 Wainganga R., India .21 0N 79 45E
09 Waingapu, Indonesia . 9 35S 120 11E
146 Wainuiomata, N.Z. ...41 17S 174 56E
157 Wainwright, Canada .52 50N 110 50W
146 Waiotapu, N.Z. 38 21S 176 25E
146 Waiouru, N.Z. 39 28S 175 41E
147 Waipahi, N.Z. 46 6S 169 15E
147 Waipapa Pt., N.Z. 46 40S 168 51E
147 Waipara, N.Z. 43 3S 172 46E
146 Waipawa, N.Z. 39 56S 176 38E
146 Waipiro, New Zealand 38 2S 176 22E
147 Waipori, New Zealand 45 50S 169 52E
146 Waipu, New Zealand .35 59S 174 29E
146 Waipukurau, N.Z. 40 1S 176 33E
146 Wairakei, N.Z. 38 37S 176 6E
146 Wairarapa L, N.Z. 41 14S 175 15E
147 Wairau River, N.Z. ...41 38S 173 15E
146 Wairo, New Zealand .45 59S 168 3E
146 Wairoa, New Zealand 39 3S 177 25E
146 Wairoa R., N.Z. 35 53S 177 32E
147 Waitaki Plains, N.Z. .44 22S 170 0E
147 Waitaki R., N.Z. 44 23S 169 55E
146 Waitara, New Zealand 38 59S 174 15E
146 Waitoa, New Zealand 37 37S 175 35E
146 Waitotara, N.Z. 39 49S 174 44E
166 Waitsburg, U.S.A. 46 15N 118 10W
146 Waiuku, New Zealand 37 15S 174 45E
113 Waiyeung, China 23 12N 114 32E
109 Wajabula Rau, Indon. 2 29N 128 17E
114 Wajima, Japan 37 30N 137 0E
131 Wajir, Kenya 1 42N 40 20E
131 Wajir, dist., Kenya ... 1 42N 40 20E
147 Wakaia, New Zealand 45 44S 168 51E
114 Wakamatsu, Fukuota, Japan 33 50N 130 45E
114 Wakasa-wan, B., Japan 35 45N 135 30E
147 Wakatipu, L., N.Z. ...45 5S 168 33E
114 Wakayama, Japan 34 15N 135 15E
114 Wakayama, pref., Jap. 33 50N 135 30E
163 Wake Forest, U.S A. .35 58N 78 30W
136 Wake I., Pacific Ocean 19 18N 166 36E
39 Wakefield, Eng., U.K. 53 41N 1 31W
147 Wakefield, N.Z. 41 24S 173 5E
161 Wakefield, Mass., U.S.A. 42 30N 71 3W
164 Wakefield, Mich., U.S.A. 46 28N 89 53W
107 Wakema, Burma 16 40N 95 18E
101 Wakhan, dist. Afghan. 37 0N 73 0E
114 Wakkanai, Japan 45 28N 141 35E
133 Wakkerstroom, S. Afr. 27 24S 30 10E
154 Wako, Canada 49 50N 91 22W
143 Wakool & R., Australia 35 25S 144 15E
109 Wakre, Indonesia 0 30S 131 5E
155 Wakuach L., Canada .55 20N 67 10W
78 Walachia, dist., Rum. 44 40N 25 0E
132 Walamba, Zambia 13 30S 28 42E
35 Walberswick, Eng., U.K. 52 18N 1 39E
60 Walbrzych, Poland 50 45N 16 18E
34 Walbury Hill, Eng., U.K. 51 22N 1 28W
145 Walcha, Australia 30 55S 151 31E
54 Walcheren I., Neth. ...51 30N 3 35E
166 Walcott, U.S.A. 41 50N 106 55W
60 Walcz, Poland 53 17N 16 27E
57 Wald, Switzerland 47 17N 8 56E
56 Waldbröl, Germany ...50 52N 7 36E
56 Waldeck, Germany 51 12N 9 4E
161 Walden, U.S.A. 41 32N 74 13W
166 Walden, U.S.A. 40 47N 106 20W
166 Waldport, U.S.A. 44 30N 124 2W
157 Waldron, Canada 50 53N 102 35W
35 Waldron, Eng., U.K. ..50 56N 0 13E
165 Waldron, U.S.A. 34 52N 94 4W
57 Waldsee, Germany 47 56N 9 46E
57 Waldshut, Germany ...47 37N 8 12E
127 Waldya, Ethiopia 11 50N 39 34E
142 Walebing, W. Australia 30 40S 116 15E
124 Walembele, Ghana 10 30N 1 14W
37 Wales, country, U.K. 52 30N 3 30W
125 Walewale, Ghana 10 21N 0 50W
145 Walgett, N.S.W., Austral. 30 0S 148 5E
143 Walhalla, Vic., Austral. 37 50S 146 25E
55 Walheim, Germany ...50 43N 6 10E
127 Waliso, Ethiopia 8 33N 38 1E
142 Walkaway, W. Austral. 28 59S 114 48E
167 Walker, U.S.A. 34 30N 112 21W
164 Walker, U.S.A. 47 4N 94 35W
155 Walker L., Canada 50 20N 67 11W
166 Walker L., U.S.A. 38 56N 118 46W
144 Walkerston, Australia 21 11S 149 8E
160 Walkerton, Canada ...44 10N 81 10W
164 Wall, U.S.A. 44 0N 102 14W
166 Walla Walla, U.S.A. .46 3N 118 25W
144 Wallabadah, Australia 17 57S 142 15E
160 Wallace, Canada 45 12N 78 9W
164 Wallace, Neb., U.S.A. 40 51N 101 12W
163 Wallace, N.C., U.S.A. 34 50N 77 59W
166 Wallace, Idaho, U.S.A. 47 30N 116 0W
154 Wallaceburg, Canada .42 40N 82 30W
147 Wallacetown, N.Z. 46 21S 168 19E
19 Wallachia, reg., Europe 44 35N 25 0E
145 Wallal, Queensland, Australia 26 32S 146 7E
145 Wallangarra, Australia 28 56S 151 58E
145 Wallaroo, S. Australia 33 55S 137 33E
38 Wallasey, Eng., U.K. 53 26S 3 2W
57 Walldurn, Germany ...49 34N 9 23E
57 Wallensee, L., Switz. .47 7N 9 15E
143 Wallerawang, Australia 33 25S 150 4E
34 Wallingford, Eng., U.K. 51 36N 1 7W
161 Wallingford, U.S.A. ...43 27N 72 58W
136 Wallis Arch., Pac. Oc. 13 20S 176 20E
143 Wallis, L., Australia ...32 15S 152 28E
166 Wallowa, U.S.A. 45 40N 117 35W
166 Wallowa, Mts., U.S.A. 45 20N 117 30W
42 Walls, Scotland, U.K. 60 14N 1 32W
39 Wallsend, England, U.K. 54 59N 1 30W
135 Wallsend, Nat., S. Afr. 28 12S 30 10E
143 Wallsend, Australia ...32 55S 151 40E
166 Wallula, U.S.A. 46 3N 118 59W
145 Wallumbilla, Australia 26 33S 149 9E
35 Walmer, England, U.K. 51 12N 1 23E
157 Walmsley, L., Canada 63 25N 109 0W
38 Walney, Isle of, England, U.K. 54 5N 3 15W
165 Walnut Ridge, U.S.A. 36 7N 90 58W
143 Walpeup, Vic., Austral. 35 10S 142 2E
35 Walpole, England, U.K. 52 44N 0 13E
34 Walsall, England, U.K. 52 36N 1 59W
165 Walsenburg, U.S.A. ...37 42N 104 45W
144 Walsh, Queens., Austral 16 40S 144 0E
165 Walsh, U.S.A. 37 28N 102 15W
35 Walsoken, Eng., U.K. 52 41N 0 12E
55 Walsum, Germany 51 32N 6 41E
106 Waltair, India 17 44N 83 23E
56 Walsrode, Germany ...52 51N 9 37E
163 Walterboro, U.S.A. ...32 53N 80 40W
165 Walters, U.S.A. 34 25N 98 20W
56 Waltershausen, Ger. ...50 53N 10 33E
154 Waltham, Canada 45 57N 76 57W
39 Waltham, Eng., U.K. 53 32N 0 6W
161 Waltham, U.S.A. 42 22N 71 12W
35 Waltham Abbey, England, U.K. 51 40N 0 1E
35 Waltham Forest, England, U.K. 51 37N 0 2E
35 Waltham on the Wolds, England, U.K. 52 49N 0 48W
166 Waltman, U.S.A. 43 8N 107 15W
36 Walton, Somerset, England, U.K. 51 27N 2 50W
161 Walton, U.S.A. 42 12N 75 9W
38 Walton-le-Dale, England, U.K. 53 45N 2 41W
35 Walton-on-the-Naze, England, U.K. 51 52N 1 17E
55 Waltrop, Germany 51 36N 7 24E
129 Walvis Bay, S. Africa 23 0S 14 28E
17 Walvis Ridge, South Atlantic Ocean 30 0S 3 0E
99 Walwal, Ethiopia 7 5N 45 25E
131 Wamala L., Uganda ... 0 20N 31 50E
131 Wamba, Congo 2 10N 27 57E
131 Wamba, Kenya 0 58N 37 19E
125 Wamba, Nigeria 8 58N 8 34E
130 Wamba R., Congo 7 0S 17 50E
143 Wamberra, Australia .33 52S 142 21E
164 Wamego, U.S.A. 39 14N 96 22W
131 Wami R., Tanzania ... 6 10S 38 30E
103 Wampo, Tibet, China 31 30N 86 38E
161 Wampsville, U.S.A. ...43 4N 75 42W
109 Wamsasi, Indonesia ... 3 27S 126 7E
112 Wan Ta Shan, Mts., China 46 20N 132 20E
104 Wana, West Pakistan 32 20N 69 32E
147 Wanaka L., N.Z. 44 33S 169 7E
113 Wanan, China 26 25N 114 50E
109 Wanapiri, Indonesia ... 4 30S 135 50E
154 Wanapitei, Canada 46 30N 80 45W
154 Wanapitei L., Canada 46 45N 80 40W
145 Wanbi, S. Australia ...34 46S 140 21E
34 Wanborough, Eng., U.K. 51 33N 1 40W
112 Wanchuan, China 40 53N 114 32E
132 Wanderer, Rhodesia ...19 36S 30 1E
106 Wandiwash, India 12 30N 79 30E
127 Wando, Ethiopia 6 40N 38 27E
145 Wandoan, Australia ...26 5S 149 55E
35 Wandsworth, Eng., U.K. 51 28N 0 15W
127 Wang Kai (Ghabet el Arab), Sudan 9 3N 29 23E
107 Wang Saphung, Thailand 17 29N 101 33E
109 Wangal, Indonesia 6 8S 134 9E
143 Wanganella, Australia 35 6S 144 49E
146 Wanganui, N.Z. 39 35S 175 3E
146 Wanganui R., N.I., New Zealand 39 25S 175 4E
147 Wanganui R., S.I., New Zealand 43 3S 170 26E
143 Wangaratta, Australia 36 20S 146 7E
112 Wangching, China 43 15N 129 37E
56 Wangerooge I., Ger. ...53 47N 7 52E
109 Wangiwangi I., Indonesia 5 22S 123 37E
113 Wangkiang, China 30 6N 116 45E
112 Wangtu, China 38 42N 115 4E
113 Wanhsien, China 30 50N 108 30E
112 Wanhsien, China 36 45N 107 24E
104 Wankaner, India 22 42N 71 0E
132 Wankie & dist., Rhod. 18 18S 26 30E
55 Wankum, Germany ...51 23N 6 18E
157 Wanless, Canada 54 11N 101 21W
55 Wanne-Eickel, Germany 51 31N 7 8E
113 Wanning, China 18 45N 110 28E
143 Wannon, R., Australia 37 40S 141 53E
147 Wanstead, N.Z. 40 8S 176 30E
34 Wantage, Eng., U.K. .51 35N 1 25W
113 Wantsai, China 28 1N 114 5E
113 Wanyuan, China 32 3N 108 16E
123 Wanzarik, Libya 27 31N 13 30E
55 Wanze, Belgium 50 32N 5 13E
162 Wapakoneta, U.S.A. .40 35N 84 10W
166 Wapato, U.S.A. 46 30N 120 25W
154 Wapikopa L., Canada 42 50N 88 10W
154 Wapiti R., Canada 55 5N 119 0W
161 Wappingers Fs., U.S.A. 41 35N 73 56W
164 Wapsipinicon R., U.S.A. 42 10N 91 30W
99 Warandab, Ethiopia . 7 20N 44 2E
143 Waranga Res., Austral. 36 38S 145 4E
106 Warangal, India 17 58N 79 45E
145 Waratah Tas., Austral. 41 30S 145 30E
143 Waratah B., Australia 38 45S 146 8E
35 Warboys, Eng., U.K. .52 25N 0 5W
56 Warburg, Germany ...51 29N 9 10E
143 Warburton, Australia 37 41S 145 42E
142 Warburton Ra., Austral. 25 55S 126 28E
139 Warburton R., Austral. 27 30S 138 30E
45 Ward, Ireland 53 25N 6 19W
147 Ward, New Zealand ...41 49S 174 11E
156 Ward Cove, Alas., U.S.A. 55 25N 132 10W
99 Wardair, Ethiopia 6 58N 45 1E
135 Warden, O.F.S., S. Afr. 27 50S 29 0E
104 Wardha, India 20 45N 78 39E
34 Wardington, Eng., U.K. 52 8N 1 17W
38 Wardle, Eng., U.K. ...53 7N 2 35W
156 Wardlow, Canada 50 56N 111 31W
38 Wards Stone, mt., England, U.K. 54 2N 2 39W
156 Ware, Canada 57 26N 125 41W
35 Ware, England, U.K. .51 48N 0 2W
161 Ware, U.S.A. 42 16N 72 15W
34 Wareham, Eng., U.K. 50 41N 2 8W
161 Wareham, U.S.A. 41 45N 70 44W
55 Waremme, Belgium ...50 43N 5 15E
56 Waren, Germany 53 30N 12 41E
56 Warendorf, Germany .51 57N 8 0E
145 Warialda, Australia ...29 29S 150 33E
109 Wariap, Indonesia 1 30S 134 5E
39 Wark, England, U.K. 55 5N 2 14W
109 Warkopi, Indonesia ... 1 12S 134 9E
39 Warkworth, Eng., U.K. 55 22N 1 38W
146 Warkworth, N.Z. 36 24S 174 41E
34 Warley, Eng., U.K. ...52 29N 2 0W
167 Warm Springs, U.S.A. 38 16N 116 32W
166 Warm Springs, U.S.A. 46 11N 112 56W
157 Warman, Canada 52 25N 106 30W
134 Warmbad, S.W. Africa 28 25S 18 42E
133 Warmbad, S. Africa ...24 51S 28 19E
49 Warmeriville, France .49 20N 4 13E
34 Warminster, Eng., U.K. 51 12N 2 11W
143 Warncoort, Australia .38 30S 143 45E
56 Warnemünde, Germany 54 9N 12 5E
166 Warner Range, Mts., U.S.A. 41 30S 120 20W
163 Warner Robins, U.S.A. 32 41N 83 36W
56 Warnow R., Germany 54 0N 12 9E
106 Warora, India 20 14N 79 1E
143 Warracknabeal, Austral. 36 9S 142 26E
143 Warragul, Vic., Austral. 38 1S 145 57E
127 Warrayelu, Ethiopia .10 40N 39 28E
145 Warrego R., Australia 26 30S 146 0E
143 Warren, N.S.W., Austral. 31 42S 147 51E
165 Warren, Ark., U.S.A. .33 35N 92 3W
160 Warren, Ohio, U.S.A. 41 18N 80 52W
160 Warren, Pa., U.S.A. ...41 52N 79 10W
161 Warren, R.I., U.S.A. .41 43N 71 19W
46 Warrenpoint, Northern Ireland, U.K. 54 7N 6 15W
157 Warrens Landing, Can. 53 40N 98 0W
164 Warrensburg, Mo., U.S.A. 38 45N 93 45W
133 Warrenton, S. Africa .28 9S 24 47E
166 Warrenton, U.S.A. 46 11N 123 59W
125 Warri, Nigeria 5 30N 5 41E
142 Warriedar, W. Australia 29 8S 117 9E
133 Warrenton, S. Africa .28 9S 24 47E
38 Warrington, Eng., U.K. 53 25N 2 38W
147 Warrington, N.Z. 45 43S 170 35E
163 Warrington, U.S.A. ...30 22N 87 16W
143 Warrnambool, Australia 38 12S 142 31E
144 Warnambool Downs, Queens., Australia .22 50S 142 45E
142 Waroona, W. Australia 32 50S 115 58E
145 Warrenville, Australia 25 48S 147 22E
142 Warrie, W. Australia .22 12S 119 40E
164 Warroad, U.S.A. 49 0N 95 20W
60 Warsaw (Warszawa), Poland 52 13N 21 0E
162 Warsaw, Ind., U.S.A. 41 14N 85 50W
160 Warsaw, N.Y., U.S.A. 42 46N 78 10W
160 Warsaw, Ohio, U.S.A. 40 20N 82 0W
60 Warszawa, Poland 52 13N 21 0E
60 Warszawa, prov., Pol. 52 35N 21 0E
39 Warsop, Eng., U.K. ...53 13N 1 9W
56 Warstein, Germany 51 26N 8 20E
60 Warta R., Poland 52 40N 16 10E
109 Waru, Indonesia 3 30S 130 36E
104 Warud, India 21 30N 78 16E
145 Warwick, Australia ...28 10S 152 1E
34 Warwick, Eng., U.K. .52 17N 1 36W
34 Warwick, co., Eng., U.K. 52 20N 1 30W
161 Warwick, U.S.A. 41 43N 71 25W
156 Wasa, Canada 49 45N 115 50W
160 Wasaga Beach, Canada 44 31N 80 0W
166 Wasatch, Mt., Ra., U.S.A. 40 30N 111 15W
135 Wasbank, Nat., S. Afr. 28 15S 30 9E
43 Wasbister, Scot., U.K. 59 11N 3 2W
167 Wasco, U.S.A. 35 37N 119 16W
166 Wasco, U.S.A. 45 45N 120 46W
164 Waseca, U.S.A. 44 3N 93 31W
39 Wash, The, Eng., U.K. 52 58N 0 20W
160 Washago, Canada 44 46N 79 21W
164 Washburn, N.D., U.S.A. 47 23N 101 0W
164 Washburn, Wis., U.S.A. 46 38N 90 55W
36 Washford, Eng., U.K. 51 9N 3 22W
39 Washington, Eng., U.K. 54 55N 1 30W
162 Washington, D.C., U.S.A. 38 52N 77 0W
163 Washington, Ga., U.S.A. 33 45N 82 45W
162 Washington, Ind., U.S.A. 38 40N 87 8W
164 Washington, Iowa, U.S.A. 41 20N 91 45W
164 Washington, Miss., U.S.A. 38 35N 91 20W
163 Washington, N.C., U.S.A. 35 35N 77 1W
161 Washington, N.J., U.S.A. 40 45N 74 59W
162 Washington, Ohio, U.S.A. 39 34N 83 26W
160 Washington, Pa., U.S.A. 40 10N 80 20W
167 Washington, Utah, U.S.A. 37 10N 113 30W
166 Washington, st., U.S.A. 47 45N 120 30W
37 Washington I., Pac. Oc. 4 43N 160 25W
162 Washington I., U.S.A. 45 24N 86 54W
161 Washington Mt., U.S.A. 44 15N 71 18W
162 Washington Court House, U.S.A. 39 34N 83 26W
109 Wasian, Indonesia 1 47S 133 19E
60 Wasilkow, Poland 53 12N 23 13E
157 Waskaiowaka, L., Can. 56 35N 96 40W
126 Wasm, Saudi Arabia .18 2N 41 32E
54 Wassenaar, Netherlands 52 8N 4 24E
57 Wasserburg, Germany 48 4N 12 15E
49 Wassy, France 48 30N 4 58E
38 Wast Water, L., England, U.K. 54 26N 3 18W
154 Waswanipi L., Canada 49 35N 76 40W
109 Watampone, Indonesia 4 29S 120 25E
147 Wataroa, N.Z. 43 18S 170 24E
147 Wataroa R., N.Z. 43 7S 170 16E
109 Watawaha, I., Indon. 6 30S 122 20E
36 Watchet, Eng., U.K. .51 10N 3 20W
165 Water Valley, U.S.A. .34 9N 89 38W
35 Waterbeach, Eng., U.K. 52 16N 0 11E
129 Waterberg, S.W. Africa 20 30S 17 18E
133 Waterberge, Mts., S. Afr. 24 14S 28 0E
161 Waterbury, Conn., U.S.A. 41 32N 73 0W
161 Waterbury, Vt., U.S.A. 44 22N 72 44W
157 Waterbury, L., Canada 58 16N 105 0W
160 Waterdown, Canada ...43 21N 79 53W
160 Waterford, Canada 42 58N 80 20W
45 Waterford, Ireland 52 16N 7 8W
135 Waterford, S. Africa .33 6S 25 0E
45 Waterford, co., Ireland 51 10N 7 40W
45 Waterford Harb., Ire. 52 10N 6 58W
36 Watergate Bay, England, U.K. 50 26N 5 4W
44 Watergrasshill, Ireland 52 1N 8 20W
157 Waterhen L., Canada .52 10N 99 40W
54 Waterloo, Belgium 50 43N 4 25E
161 Waterloo, Que., Canada 45 22N 72 32W
154 Waterloo, Ont., Canada 43 30N 80 32W

MAP
38 Waterloo, Eng., U.K 53 29N 3 2W
124 Waterloo, Sierra Leone ... 8 26N 13 8W
164 Waterloo, Ill., U.S.A. .38 22N 90 6W
164 Waterloo, Iowa, U.S.A. ...42 27N 92 20W
160 Waterloo, N.Y., U.S.A. ...42 54N 76 53W
42 Waternish, Scot., U.K. ...57 32N 6 35W
160 Waterpoint, U.S.A. ...43 19N 78 15W
133 Waterpoort, S. Africa 22 53S 29 38E
164 Watermeet, U.S.A. ...46 15N 89 12W
161 Watertown, Conn., U.S.A. ...41 36N 73 7W
164 Watertown, S.D. U.S.A. ...44 57N 97 5W
161 Watertown, N.Y., U.S.A. ...43 58N 75 57W
164 Watertown, Wis., U.S.A. ...43 15N 88 45W
133 Waterval-Boven, Africa ...25 40S 30 18E
161 Waterville, Canada ...45 17N 71 53W
44 Waterville, Ireland ...51 49N 10 10W
155 Waterville, Me., U.S.A. ...44 35N 69 40W
161 Waterville, N.Y., U.S.A. ...42 56N 75 23W
160 Waterville, Pa., U.S.A. ...41 19N 77 21W
166 Waterville, Wash., U.S.A. ...47 45N 120 1W
161 Watervliet, U.S.A. ...42 46N 73 43W
109 Wates, Indonesia ... 7 53S 110 6E
160 Watford, Canada ...42 58N 81 52W
35 Watford, England, U.K. ...51 38N 0 23W
164 Watford City, U.S.A. .47 50N 103 23W
39 Wath, England, U.K. 53 29N 1 20W
142 Watheroo, W. Australia ...30 15S 116 0W
160 Watkins Glen, U.S.A. 42 25N 76 55W
35 Watlington, Norfolk, England, U.K. ...52 40N 0 24E
35 Watlington, Oxford, England, U.K. ...51 38N 1 0W
165 Watonga, U.S.A. ...35 51N 98 24W
157 Watrous, Canada ...51 40N 105 25W
165 Watrous, U.S.A. ...35 50N 104 55W
131 Watsa, Congo ... 3 4N 29 30E
162 Watseka, U.S.A. ...40 45N 87 45W
157 Watson, Canada ...52 10N 104 30W
138 Watson, S. Australia .30 19S 131 41E
156 Watson Lake, Canada 60 12N 129 0W
167 Watsonville, U.S.A. ...37 58N 121 49W
43 Watten, Scotland, U.K. ...58 29N 3 20W
55 Wattenscheid, Germany ...51 28N 7 7E
143 Wattle Hill, Australia 38 42S 143 17E
35 Watton, England, U.K. ...52 35N 0 50E
57 Wattwil, Switzerland .47 18N 9 6E
109 Watubela Is., Indon. 4 28S 131 54E
127 Wau, Sudan ... 7 45N 28 1E
144 Wau, N.E. New Guinea ... 7 25S 146 42E
160 Waubamik, Canada ...45 29N 80 3W
164 Waubay, U.S.A. ...45 42N 97 17W
143 Waubra, Vic., Australia ...37 21S 143 39E
163 Wauchula, U.S.A. ...27 35N 81 50W
157 Waugh, Canada ...49 40N 95 20W
162 Waukegan, U.S.A. ...42 22N 87 54W
162 Waukesha, U.S.A. ...43 0N 88 15W
164 Waukon, U.S.A. ...43 14N 91 33W
164 Wauneta, U.S.A. ...40 27N 101 25W
164 Waupaca, U.S.A. ...44 22N 89 8W
164 Waupun, U.S.A. ...43 38N 88 44W
165 Waurika, U.S.A. ...34 12N 98 0W
164 Wausau, Wis., U.S.A. 44 57N 89 40W
164 Wautoma, U.S.A. ...44 3N 89 20W
162 Wauwatosa, U.S.A. ...43 6N 87 59W
138 Wave Hill, Australia .17 32N 131 0E
35 Waveney R., Eng., U.K. ...52 24N 1 20E
38 Waver R., Eng., U.K. 54 50N 3 15W
146 Waverley, N.Z. ...39 46S 174 37E
135 Waverley, S. Africa ...31 58S 26 28E
164 Waverly, Iowa, U.S.A. ...42 40N 92 30W
161 Waverly, N.Y., U.S.A. ...42 0N 76 33W
54 Wavre, Belgium ...50 43N 4 38E
123 Waw an Namus, Libya ...24 24N 18 11E
125 Wawa, Nigeria ... 9 54N 4 27E
126 Wawa, Sudan ...20 30N 30 22E
157 Wawanesa, Canada ...49 30N 99 40W
165 Waxahachie, U.S.A. ...32 22N 96 53W
57 Waxweiler, Germany .50 6N 6 22E
142 Way, L., W. Australia 26 45S 120 16E
143 Way Way, N.S.W., Australia ...33 30S 151 18E
145 Wayatinah, Australia 42 15S 146 15E
163 Waycross, U.S.A. ...31 12N 82 25W
127 Wayi, Sudan ... 5 8N 30 10E
164 Wayne, Mich., U.S.A. 42 16N 97 0W
162 Wayne, W. Va., U.S.A. ...38 15N 82 27W
163 Waynesboro, Miss., U.S.A. ...31 40N 88 39W
162 Waynesboro, Pa., U.S.A. ...39 46N 77 32W
162 Waynesboro, Va., U.S.A. ...38 4N 78 57W
162 Waynesburg, U.S.A. .39 54N 80 12W
163 Waynesville, N.C., U.S.A. ...35 31N 83 0W
MAP
165 Waynoka, U.S.A. ...36 38N 98 53W
123 Wazin, Libya ...31 58N 10 51E
101 Wazirabad, Afghanistan ...36 44N 66 47E
104 Wazirabad, W. Pakistan ...32 30N 74 8E
35 Weald, The, Eng., U.K. ...51 7N 0 9E
39 Wear R., Eng., U.K. .54 44N 1 58W
41 Weardale, Eng., U.K. 54 44N 2 5W
38 Wearhead, Eng., U.K. 54 45N 2 14W
165 Weatherford, Okla., U.S.A. ...35 30N 98 45W
165 Weatherford, Tex., U.S.A. ...32 45N 97 48W
38 Weaver R., Eng., U.K. ...53 17N 2 35W
38 Weaverham, Eng., U.K. ...53 15N 2 30W
165 Webb City, U.S.A. ...37 9N 94 30W
146 Weber, New Zealand .40 24S 176 20E
161 Webster, Mass., U.S.A. ...42 4N 71 54W
160 Webster, N.Y., U.S.A. 43 11N 77 27W
164 Webster, S.D., U.S.A. 45 24N 97 33W
164 Webster, Wis., U.S.A. 45 53N 92 25W
164 Webster City, U.S.A. .42 30N 93 50W
164 Webster Green, U.S.A. ...38 38N 90 20W
162 Webster Springs, U.S.A. ...38 30N 80 25W
109 Weda & B., Indonesia 0 30N 127 50E
176 Weddell I., Falk. Is. .51 50S 61 0W
15 Weddell Sea, Antarctica ...72 30S 40 0W
143 Wedderburn, Australia ...36 20S 143 33E
36 Wedmore, Eng., U.K. 51 14N 2 50W
34 Wednesbury, Eng., U.K. ...52 33N 2 1W
34 Wednesfield, Eng., U.K. ...52 36N 2 3W
132 Wedza, Rhodesia ...18 40S 31 33E
143 Wee Elwah, Australia 32 56S 145 20E
145 Wee Waa, Australia ...30 11S 149 26E
166 Weed, U.S.A. ...41 29N 122 22W
161 Weedsport, U.S.A. ...43 3N 76 35W
160 Weedville, U.S.A. ...41 17N 78 28W
145 Weemelah, Australia .39 0S 149 15E
135 Weenen, Natal, S. Afr. ...28 48S 30 7E
56 Weener, Germany ...53 10N 7 23E
54 Weert, Netherlands ...51 15N 5 43E
143 Weetallba, Australia .32 37S 149 41E
55 Weeze, Germany ...51 37N 6 12E
55 Wegberg, Germany ...51 9N 6 16E
60 Wegliniec, Poland ...51 18N 15 10E
60 Wegorzewo, Poland ...54 13N 21 43E
60 Węgrów, Poland ...52 24N 22 0E
108 Weh, Indonesia ... 6 3N 95 56E
112 Wei Ho, R., China ...35 45N 114 30E
113 Weichow Tao, Is., China ...21 0N 109 1E
56 Weida, Thuringia, Ger. ...50 47N 12 3E
57 Weiden, Germany ...49 40N 12 10E
112 Weifang, China ...36 52N 119 7E
112 Weihai, China ...37 30N 122 10E
56 Weilburg, Germany ...50 28N 8 17E
57 Weilheim, Bavaria, Ger. ...47 50N 11 9E
56 Weimar, Germany ...51 0N 11 20E
113 Weinan, China ...34 25N 109 26E
59 Weiner Neustadt, Aust. ...47 50N 16 15E
57 Weingarten, Germany 47 49N 9 39E
57 Weinheim Germany .49 33N 8 40E
144 Weipa, Queens., Austral. ...12 24S 142 0E
157 Weir River, Canada ...57 0N 94 10W
160 Weirton, U.S.A. ...40 22N 80 35W
166 Weiser, U.S.A. ...44 10N 117 0W
103 Wei-si, China ...27 18N 99 18E
57 Weissenburg, Germany ...49 2N 10 58E
56 Weissenfels, Germany 51 11N 11 58E
56 Weisswasser, Germany ...51 30N 14 36E
58 Weitra, Austria ...48 41N 14 54E
112 Weiyüan, Kansu, China ...35 10N 104 20E
113 Weiyuan, Szechwan, China ...29 35N 104 30E
58 Weiz, Austria ...47 13N 15 39E
60 Wejherowo, Poland ...54 35N 18 12E
157 Wekusko, Canada ...54 45N 99 45W
157 Wekusko L., Canada .54 40N 99 50W
157 Welby, Canada ...50 33N 101 29W
162 Welch, U.S.A. ...37 29N 81 36W
144 Welcome, Australia ...15 20S 144 40E
41 Weldon, England, U.K. ...55 16N 1 46W
127 Welega, prov., Ethiopia ... 9 25N 34 20E
34 Welford, Berks., Eng., U.K. ...51 28N 1 24W
34 Welford, Northampton, England, U.K. ...52 26N 1 5W
135 Welgelee, OFS, S. Afr. 28 12S 26 50E
55 Welkenraedt, Belgium 50 39N 5 58W
135 Welkom O.F.S. S. Afr. ...28 0S 26 50E
154 Welland, Canada ...43 0N 79 10W
35 Welland, R., Eng., U.K. ...52 43N 0 10W
55 Wellen, Belgium ...50 50N 5 21E
144 Wellesley Is., Australia ...17 20S 139 30E
54 Wellin, Belgium ...50 5N 5 6E
MAP
35 Wellingborough, England, U.K. ...52 18N 0 41W
143 Wellington, Australia .32 30S 149 0E
154 Wellington, Canada ...43 57N 77 20W
34 Wellington, Salop, England, U.K. ...52 42N 2 31W
34 Wellington, Somerset, England, U.K. ...50 58N 3 13W
146 Wellington, N.Z. ...41 19S 174 46E
134 Wellington, S. Africa .33 38S 18 57E
145 Wellington, S. Austral. ...35 16S 139 21E
164 Wellington, Col., U.S.A. ...40 43N 105 0W
165 Wellington, Kan., U.S.A. ...37 15N 97 25W
166 Wellington, Nev. U.S.A. ...38 47N 119 28W
160 Wellington, Ohio U.S.A. ...41 9N 82 12W
165 Wellington, Okla., U.S.A. ...34 55N 100 13W
146 Wellington, dist., N.Z. 40 8S 175 36E
176 Wellington I., Chile ...49 30S 75 0W
143 Wellington L., Austral. ...38 5S 147 22E
146 Wellington, Mt., N.Z. 36 55S 174 52E
45 Wellington Bridge Ire. ...52 15N 6 45W
36 Wellow, England, U.K. ...51 20N 2 22W
35 Wells, Norfolk, Eng., U.K. ...52 57N 0 51E
36 Wells, Somerset, England, U.K. ...51 12N 2 39W
161 Wells, Me., U.S.A. ...43 18N 70 35W
164 Wells, Minn., U.S.A. .43 44N 93 45W
166 Wells, Nev., U.S.A. ...41 8N 115 0W
156 Wells Gray Prov. Park, Canada ...52 30N 120 0W
142 Wells L., W. Australia 26 44S 123 15E
161 Wells River, U.S.A. ...44 9N 72 4W
160 Wellsboro, U.S.A. ...41 46N 77 20W
160 Wellsburg, U.S.A. ...40 15N 80 36W
146 Wellsford, N.Z. ...36 16S 174 32E
164 Wellsville, Mo., U.S.A. ...39 4N 91 30W
160 Wellsville, N.Y., U.S.A. ...42 9N 77 53W
160 Wellsville, Ohio, U.S.A. ...40 36N 80 40W
166 Wellsville, Utah, U.S.A. ...41 35N 111 59W
167 Wellton, U.S.A. ...32 46N 114 6W
127 Welmal, R., Ethiopia . 6 0N 40 20E
35 Welney, England, U.K. ...52 31N 0 15E
127 Welo, prov., Ethiopia 11 50N 39 48E
58 Wels, Austria ...48 9N 14 1E
143 Welshpool, Vic., Austral. ...38 42S 146 26E
37 Welshpool, Wales U.K. ...52 40N 3 9W
39 Welton England, U.K. ...53 19N 0 29W
157 Welwyn, Canada ...50 20N 101 30W
35 Welwyn, England, U.K. ...51 49N 0 11W
35 Welwyn Garden City, Eng., U.K. ...51 49N 0 11W
34 Wem, England, U.K. .52 52N 2 45W
131 Wembere, R., Tanzania ... 4 45S 34 0E
36 Wembury, Eng., U.K. 50 19N 4 6W
40 Wemyss Bay, Scot., U.K. ...55 52N 4 54W
166 Wenatchee, U.S.A. ...47 30N 120 17W
113 Wenchang, China ...19 45N 110 50E
124 Wenchi, Ghana ... 7 46N 2 8W
113 Wenchow, China ...28 0N 120 35E
166 Wendell, U.S.A. ...42 50N 114 51W
35 Wendover, Eng., U.K. 51 46N 0 45W
166 Wendover, U.S.A. ...40 49N 114 1W
112 Wengniu, China ...43 2N 118 54E
112 Wengteng, China ...37 15N 122 10E
144 Wenlock R., Australia 12 15S 142 0E
34 Wenlock Edge, hills, England, U.K. ...52 30N 2 43W
109 Wenoet, Indonesia ... 3 11S 133 19E
112 Wensi, China ...35 25N 111 7E
113 Wensiang, China ...34 35N 110 40E
38 Wensleydale, Eng., UK ...54 18N 2 0W
111 Wensu, China ...41 6N 80 3E
149 Wentworth, Australia 34 2S 141 54E
34 Weobley, England, U.K. ...52 9N 2 52W
166 Weott, U.S.A. ...40 19N 123 56W
135 Wepener, O.F.S., S. Afr. ...29 42S 27 3E
56 Werder, Germany ...52 23N 12 56E
56 Werdohl, Germany ...51 15N 7 47E
109 Weri, Indonesia ... 3 10S 132 30E
55 Wermelskirchen, Ger. 51 8N 7 11E
56 Werne, Germany ...51 38N 7 38E
56 Wernigerode, Germany ...51 49N 0 45E
143 Werribee, Vic., Austral. ...37 54S 144 40E
143 Werrimull, Vic., Austral. ...34 22S 143 30E
36 Werrington, Eng., U.K. ...50 31N 4 22W
143 Werris Creek, Australia ...31 18S 150 38E
109 Wersar, Indonesia ... 1 30S 131 55E
57 Wertheim, Germany .49 44N 9 32E
127 Wesca Weca, Ethiopia 5 51N 35 37E
55 Weseke, Germany ...51 5N 6 51E
56 Wesel, Germany ...51 39N 6 34E
MAP
55 Wesemaal, Belgium ...50 57N 4 45E
56 Weser R., Germany ...53 33N 8 30E
109 Wesiri, Indonesia ... 7 30S 126 30E
155 Wesleyville, Canada ...49 8N 53 36W
160 Wesleyville, U.S.A. ...42 9N 80 1W
139 Wessel Is., Australia .11 10S 136 45E
56 Wesselburen, Germany ...54 11N 8 53E
55 Wesseling, Germany ...50 50N 6 58E
135 Wesselsbron, S Africa 27 50S 25 23E
135 Wesselsnek, Nat. S. Afr. ...28 22S 30 5E
164 Wessington, U.S.A. ...44 30N 98 40W
164 Wessington Springs, U.S.A. ...44 10N 98 35W
165 West U.S.A. ...31 50N 97 5W
155 West B., Canada ...45 53N 82 8W
165 West, B., U.S.A. ...29 5N 89 27W
39 West Auckland, England, U.K. ...54 38N 1 42W
162 West Bend. U.S.A. ...43 25N 88 10W
105 West Bengal, prov., India ...25 0N 90 0E
59 West Beskids (Západné Beskydy), Cz. ...49 30N 19 20E
162 West Branch, U.S.A. .44 16N 84 13W
39 West Bridgford, England, U.K. ...52 56N 1 8W
34 West Bromwich, England, U.K. ...52 32N 2 1W
42 West Burra, I., Scot. U.K. ...60 5N 1 21W
41 West Calder, Scot., U.K. ...55 51N 3 34W
161 West Chazy, U.S.A. ...44 49N 73 28W
162 West Chester, U.S.A. .39 58N 75 36W
36 West Coker, Eng., U.K. ...50 55N 2 40W
165 West Columbia, U.S.A. ...29 10N 95 38W
164 West Des Moines, U.S.A. ...41 30N 93 45W
176 West Falkland Island, Falkland Islands ...51 30S 60 0W
164 West Frankfort, U.S.A. ...37 56N 89 0W
54 West Frisian Is., Neth. ...53 30N 5 30E
35 West Grinstead, England, U.K. ...50 58N 0 19W
34 West Haddon, England, United Kingdom ...52 21N 1 5W
147 West Harbour, N.Z. ...45 51S 170 33E
161 West Hartford, U.S.A. ...41 45N 72 45W
39 West Hartlepool, England, U.K. ...54 42N 1 11W
161 West Haven, U.S.A. .41 18N 72 57W
165 West Helena, U.S.A. .34 30N 90 40W
164 West Indies, arch., Atlantic Ocean ...15 0N 70 0W
109 West Irian, prov., Indon. ... 3 0S 137 0E
109 West Java, prov., Indonesia ... 6 35S 106 42E
40 West Kilbride, Scot. UK ...55 41N 4 50W
38 West Kirby, Eng., UK ...53 22N 3 11W
131 West Lake Prov., Tanzania ... 2 5S 31 20E
34 West Lavingtor, England, U.K. ...51 16N 1 59W
41 West Linton, Scot. UK ...55 45N 3 24W
36 West Looe, Eng., U.K. ...50 21N 4 29W
160 West Lorne, Canada .42 37N 81 41W
35 West Lulworth, England, U.K. ...50 37N 2 14W
132 West Lunga, R., Zam. 12 35S 24 45E
35 West Malling, Eng., U.K. ...51 16N 0 25E
165 West Memphis, U.S.A. ...35 5N 90 3W
131 West Mengo, dist., Uganda ... 0 15N 32 15E
34 West Meon, Eng., U.K. ...51 2N 1 3W
35 West Mersea, Eng., U.K. ...51 46N 0 55E
165 West Monroe, U.S.A. .32 32N 92 7W
160 West Newton, U.S.A. 40 14N 79 46W
132 West Nicholson, Rhod. ...21 2S 29 20E
102 West Pakistan, Asia ...27 0N 67 0W
163 West Palm Beach, U.S.A. ...26 44N 80 3W
107 West Paris, U.S.A. ...44 18N 70 30W
34 West Parley, Eng., U.K. ...50 46N 1 52W
161 West Pittston, U.S.A. 41 19N 75 49W
165 West Plains, U.S.A. ...36 45N 91 50W
155 West Point, Canada ...49 55N 64 30W
169 West Point, Jamaica .18 14N 78 30W
163 West Point, Ga., U.S.A. ...32 54N 85 10W
163 West Point, Miss., U.S.A. ...33 36N 88 38W
162 West Point Va. U.S.A. ...37 35N 76 47W
164 West Point, U.S.A. ...41 50N 96 43W
39 West Rasen, Eng., U.K. ...53 23N 0 23W
39 West Riding, co., England, U.K. ...53 50N 1 30W
54 West Schelde R., Neth. ...51 23N 3 50E
MAP
90 West Siberian Plain, U.S.S.R. ...62 0N 75 0E
14 West Spitsbergen, Spitsbergen ...79 0N 15 0E
54 West Terschelling, Neth. ...53 22N 5 13E
163 West Virginia, st., U.S.A. ...39 0N 18 0W
35 West Wittering, England, U.K. ...50 44N 0 53W
143 West Wyalong, Austral. ...33 56S 147 10E
166 West Yellowstone, U.S.A. ...44 47N 111 4W
156 Westbank, Canada ...49 50N 119 25W
35 Westbourne Eng., U.K. ...50 53N 0 55W
162 Westbrook, U.S.A. ...43 40N 70 22W
165 Westbrook, U.S.A. ...32 25N 101 0W
34 Westbury, Salop, England, U.K. ...52 40N 2 57W
34 Westbury, Wilts., England U.K. ...51 16N 2 11W
145 Westbury, Tas., Austral. ...41 30S 146 51E
145 Westbury, Tas., Austral. ...41 30S 146 51E
34 Westbury-on-Severn, England, U.K. ...51 49N 2 24W
143 Westby, N.S.W., Australia ...35 30S 147 24E
164 Westby, Mont., U.S.A. ...48 52N 104 3W
42 Wester Ross, dist., Scotland, U.K. ...57 37N 5 0W
35 Westerham, Eng., U.K. ...51 16N 0 5E
55 Westerholt, Germany .51 36N 7 6E
56 Westerland, Germany 54 51N 8 20E
138 Western Australia, st., Comm. of Australia 25 0S 118 0E
155 Western Bay, Canada 46 50N 52 30W
126 Western Desert, Egypt ...27 40N 26 30E
56 Western Germany, st., Europe ...50 0N 8 0E
106 Western Ghats Mts., India ...15 30N 74 30E
136 Western Samoa, state, Pacific Ocean ...14 0S 172 0W
91 Western Sayan, mts., U.S.S.R. ...52 30N 94 0E
162 Westernport, U.S.A. .30 30N 79 5W
56 Westerstede, Germany 51 15N 7 55E
56 Westerwald Mts., Ger. 50 39N 8 0E
35 Westfield, Eng., U.K. 50 53N 0 30E
161 Westfield, Mass., U.S.A. ...42 9N 72 49W
160 Westfield, N.Y., U.S.A. ...42 20N 79 38W
160 Westfield, Pa., U.S.A. 41 54N 77 32W
164 Westhope, U.S.A. ...48 55N 101 0W
38 Westhoughton, England, U.K. ...53 34N 2 30W
147 Westland, dist., N.Z. .43 33S 169 59E
147 Westland Bight, N.Z. 42 55S 170 5E
135 Westleigh, O.F.S., S. Afr. ...27 31S 27 21E
156 Westlock, Canada ...54 20N 113 55W
45 Westmeath, co., Ire. .53 30N 7 30W
142 Westmine, W. Australia ...29 2S 116 8E
162 Westminster, Md., USA ...39 34S 77 1W
38 Westmorland, co., Eng., U.K. ...54 28N 2 40W
167 Westmorland, U.S.A. .33 2N 115 42W
34 Weston, England, U.K. ...52 51N 2 2W
108 Weston, Sab., Malaysia ... 5 10N 115 35E
166 Weston, U.S.A. ...45 50N 118 30W
162 Weston, W. Va., U.S.A. ...39 3N 80 29W
154 Weston I., Canada ...52 30N 79 50W
36 Weston-super-Mare, England, U.K. ...51 20N 2 59W
161 Westport, Canada ...44 38N 76 28W
45 Westport, Ireland ...53 44N 9 31W
147 Westport, N.Z. ...41 46S 171 37E
166 Westport, Wash., U.S.A. ...46 48N 124 4W
45 Westport B., Ireland .53 48N 9 38W
43 Westray Firth, Scotland, United Kingdom ...59 15N 3 0W
43 Westray I., Scot., U.K. ...59 18N 3 0W
154 Westree, Canada ...47 26N 81 34W
41 Westruther, Scot., U.K. ...55 45N 2 34W
156 Westview, Canada ...49 50N 124 31W
162 Westville, U.S.A. ...40 3N 87 36W
165 Westville, U.S.A. ...36 0N 94 33W
36 Westward Ho!, England, U.K. ...51 2N 4 16W
166 Westwood, U.S.A. ...40 26N 121 0W
109 Wetar, I., Indonesia ... 7 30S 126 30E
156 Wetaskiwin, Canada .52 55N 113 24W
131 Wete, Zan. Tanzania . 5 3S 39 43E
39 Wetherby, Eng., U.K. 53 56N 1 23W
55 Wetten, Germany ...51 35N 6 17E
55 Wetter, Germany ...51 23N 7 23E
54 Wetteren, Belgium ...51 0N 3 53E
143 Wetupoa, Australia ...35 16S 143 46E
39 Wetwang, Eng., U.K. 54 2N 0 35W
56 Wetzlar, Germany ...50 33N 8 30E
144 Wewak, N.E. N. Guinea ... 3 29S 143 28E
165 Wewaka, U.S.A. ...35 10N 96 35W

MAP
45 Wexford, Ireland 52 20N 6 28W
45 Wexford, co., Ire. 52 20N 6 25W
45 Wexford Harb., Ireland 52 20N 6 25W
35 Wey R., England, U.K. 51 19N 0 29W
35 Weybourne, Eng., U.K. 52 57N 1 9E
35 Weybridge, Eng., U.K. 51 22N 0 28W
157 Weyburn, Canada 49 40N 103 50W
58 Weyer, Austria 47 51N 14 40E
154 Weymont, Canada 47 50N 73 50W
155 Weymouth, Canada ...44 30N 66 1W
36 Weymouth, Eng., U.K. 50 36N 2 28W
161 Weymouth, U.S.A. 42 13N 70 53W
146 Whakamaru, N.Z. 38 23S 175 63E
146 Whakatane, N.Z. 37 57S 177 1E
42 Whale Firth, Scot., UK 60 40N 1 10W
153 Whale, R., Canada 57 40N 67 0W
15 Whales, B. of Antarc. 78 0S 165 0W
38 Whaley Bridge, England, U.K. 53 20N 2 0W
38 Whalley, Eng., U.K. .53 49N 2 25W
42 Whalsay I., Scot., U.K. 60 22N 1 0W
41 Whalton, England, U.K. 55 7N 1 46W
113 Whampoa, China 23 5N 113 20E
146 Whangamomona, N.Z. 39 8S 174 44E
146 Whangarei, N.Z. 35 43S 174 21E
146 Whangaroa, N.Z. 35 4S 173 46E
146 Whangaroa Hrb., N.Z. 35 4S 173 46E
146 Whangumata, N.Z. ...37 12S 175 53E
35 Whaplode, Eng., U.K. 52 42N 0 3W
147 Wharanui, N.Z. 41 55S 174 6E
38 Wharfedale, Eng., U.K. 54 7N 2 4W
161 Wharton, N.J., U.S.A. 40 53N 74 36W
160 Wharton, Pa., U.S.A. 41 31N 78 1W
165 Wharton, Tex., U.S.A. 29 20N 96 6W
40 Whauphill, Scot., U.K. 54 48N 4 31W
145 Whayjonta, Australia 29 40S 142 35E
164 Wheatland, U.S.A. 42 4N 105 58W
160 Wheatley, Canada 42 7N 82 29W
160 Wheaton, U.S.A. 45 50N 96 29W
164 Wheeler, Ore., U.S.A. 45 45N 123 57W
165 Wheeler, Tex., U.S.A. 35 29N 100 15W
166 Wheeler Peak, Mt. U.S.A. 38 57N 114 15W
160 Wheeling, U.S.A. 40 2N 80 41W
38 Whernside, Mt., England, U.K. 54 14N 2 24W
38 Whernside, Gt., Mt., England, U.K. 54 10N 1 59W
38 Whichham, Eng., U.K. 54 14N 3 22W
138 Whidbey Is., S. Austral. 34 30S 135 3E
44 Whiddy, I., Ireland 51 41N 9 30W
36 Whimple, Eng., U.K. .50 46N 3 21W
35 Whipsnade, Eng., U.K. 51 51N 0 32W
156 Whiskey Gap, Canada 49 0N 113 3W
157 Whiskey Jack, L., Canada 58 25N 101 55W
35 Whissendine, Eng., U.K. 52 43N 0 46W
163 Whistler, U.S.A. 30 50N 88 10W
38 Whiston, England, U.K. 53 25N 2 45W
41 Whitburn, Scot., U.K. 55 52N 3 41W
160 Whitby, Canada 43 50N 78 50W
39 Whitby, England, U.K. 54 29N 0 37W
36 Whitchurch, Devon, England, U.K. 50 31N 4 7W
34 Whitchurch, Hants., England, U.K. 51 14N 1 20W
34 Whitchurch, Here., England, U.K. 51 51N 2 41W
38 Whitchurch, Salop, England, U.K. 52 58N 2 42W
37 Whitchurch, Wales, U.K. 51 32N 3 15W
147 Whitcombe, Mt. & P., New Zealand 43 12S 171 0E
155 White B., Canada 50 0N 56 35W
146 White I., N.Z. 37 30S 177 13E
161 White L., Canada 45 17N 76 35W
165 White L., U.S.A. 29 45N 92 30W
167 White Mts., U.S.A. 37 30N 118 6W
53 White Mts., Cz. 49 0N 17 50E
161 White Mts., U.S.A. 44 15N 71 15W
165 White R., Ark., U.S.A. 36 28N 93 55W
166 White R., Colo., U.S.A. 40 8N 108 52W
162 White R., Ind., U.S.A. 39 25N 86 30W
164 White R., S.D., U.S.A. 43 10N 102 52W
84 White Sea, U.S.S.R. ...66 0N 38 0E
166 White Bird, U.S.A. 45 46N 116 21W
43 White Bridge, Scot. U.K. 57 11N 4 32W
164 White City, U.S.A. 38 50N 96 45W
145 White Cliffs, Australia 30 50S 143 10E
147 White Cliffs, N.Z. 43 26S 171 55E
41 White Coomb Mt., Scotland, U.K. 55 25N 3 20W
165 White Deer, U.S.A. 35 30N 101 8W
41 White Esk, R., Scotland, U.K. 55 14N 3 11W
164 White Hall, U.S.A. 39 25N 90 27W
161 White Haven, U.S.A. .41 3N 75 47W
34 White Horse Hill, Eng., U.K. 57 35N 1 35W
29 Whitehorse, Vale of, Eng., U.K. 51 37N 1 30W
127 White Nile R. (Bahr el Abiad), Sudan 9 30N 31 40E
127 White Nile Dam, Sudan 15 24N 32 30E
154 White Otter L., Canada 49 5N 91 55W
156 White Pass, Canada ...59 40W 135 3W
161 White Plains, U.S.A. .41 2N 73 44W
154 White River, Canada .48 35N 85 20W
164 White River, U.S.A. .43 48N 100 5W
161 White River Junc., U.S.A. 43 38N 72 20W
86 White Russia (Byelorussia), S.S.R., U.S.S.R. 53 30N 27 0E
166 White Sulphur Springs, Mont., U.S.A. 46 35N 111 0W
162 White Sulphur Springs, W. Va., U.S.A. 37 50N 80 16W
125 White Volta R., (Volta Blanche), Up. Volta & Ghana 10 0N 1 0W
142 White Well, S. Austral. 31 25S 131 3E
41 Whiteadder Water, R., Scotland, U.K. .55 47N 2 20W
43 Witchyburn, Scot., U.K. 57 36N 2 36W
156 Whitecourt, Canada ...54 10N 115 45W
165 Whiteface, U.S.A. 33 35N 102 40W
161 Whitefield, U.S.A. 44 23N 71 37W
166 Whitefish, U.S.A. 48 25N 114 22W
157 Whitefish L., Canada .62 35N 107 20W
162 Whitefish Pt., U.S.A. .46 45N 85 0W
44 Whitegate, Clare, Ire. 52 58N 8 24W
44 Whitegate, Cork, Ire. .51 49N 8 15W
155 Whitegull, L., Canada 55 30N 64 40W
45 Whitehall, Ireland 52 42N 7 2W
43 Whitehall, Scot., U.K. 59 9N 2 36W
162 Whitehall, Mich., U.S.A. 43 21N 86 20W
166 Whitehall, Mont., U.S.A. 45 52N 112 4W
161 Whitehall, N.Y., U.S.A. 43 32N 73 28W
164 Whitehall, Wis., U.S.A. 44 20N 91 19W
38 Whitehaven, Eng., U.K. 54 33N 3 35W
46 Whitehead, N. Ire., U.K. 54 45N 5 42W
156 Whitehorse, Canada ...60 45N 135 10W
41 Whitekirk, Scot., U.K. 56 2N 2 36W
144 Whiteman Ra., Territory of New Guinea 5 54S 149 56E
157 Whitemouth, Canada .50 0N 96 10W
43 Whiten Hd., Scot., U.K. 58 34N 4 35W
124 White Plains, Liberia . 6 28N 10 40W
156 Whitesail, L., Canada 53 35N 127 45W
36 Whitesand, B., England, United Kingdom 50 18N 4 20W
161 Whitesboro, New York, U.S.A. 43 8N 75 20W
165 Whitesboro, Tex., U.S.A. 33 40N 96 58W
164 Whitetail, U.S.A. 48 54N 105 15W
163 Whiteville, U.S.A. 34 20N 78 40W
162 Whitewater, U.S.A. ...42 50N 88 45W
167 Whitewater Baldy, Mt., U.S.A. 33 20N 108 44W
154 Whitewater L., Canada 50 50N 89 10W
144 Whitewood, Australia 21 28S 143 30E
157 Whitewood, Canada ...50 20N 102 20W
143 Whitfield, Vic., Austral. 36 42S 146 24E
40 Whithorn, Scot., U.K. 54 55N 4 25W
146 Whitianga, N.Z. 36 47S 175 41E
37 Whitland, Wales, U.K. 51 49N 4 38W
39 Whitley Bay, Eng., U.K. 55 4N 1 28W
161 Whitman, U.S.A. 42 4N 70 55W
163 Whitmire, U.S.A. 34 33N 81 40W
160 Whitney, Canada 45 31N 78 14W
167 Whitney, Mt., U.S.A. 36 35N 118 14W
161 Whitney Pt., U.S.A. .42 19N 75 59W
35 Whitstable, Eng., U.K. 51 21N 1 2E
144 Whitsunday I., Austral. 20 15S 149 4E
152 Whittier, Alaska, U.S.A. 60 46N 148 45W
39 Whittington, Derby, England, U.K. 53 17N 1 26W
34 Whittington, Salop, England, U.K. 52 53N 3 0W
155 Whittle, C., Canada ...50 11N 60 8W
143 Whittlesea, Australia .37 27S 145 9E
135 Whittlesea, S. Africa .32 11S 26 50E
35 Whittlesey, Eng., U.K. 52 34N 0 8W
35 Whittlesford, Eng., U.K. 52 6N 0 9E
39 Whitton, Eng., U.K. .53 42N 0 39W
143 Whitton, N.S.W., Austral. 34 30S 146 6E
39 Whitwell, Derby, England, U.K. 53 16N 1 11W
34 Whitwell, Isle of Wight, England, U.K. 50 35N 1 19W
163 Whitwell, U.S.A. 35 15N 85 30W
34 Whitwick, Eng., U.K. 52 45N 1 23W
38 Whitworth, Eng., U.K. 53 40N 2 11W
39 Whixley, England, U.K. 54 2N 1 19W
157 Wholdaia L., Canada .60 40N 104 20W
145 Whyalla, S. Australia 33 2S 137 30E
160 Wiarton, Canada 44 50N 81 10W
124 Wiawso, Ghana 6 10N 2 25W
42 Wiay I., Scotland, U.K. 57 24N 7 12W
164 Wibaux, U.S.A. 47 0N 104 13W
55 Wiblingwerde, Ger. ...51 19N 7 37E
165 Wichita Falls, U.S.A. .33 57N 98 30W
43 Wick, Scotland, U.K. 58 26N 3 5W
43 Wick R., Scot., U.K. .58 28N 3 14W
36 Wick, Wales, U.K. 51 24N 3 32W
167 Wickenburg, U.S.A. ...33 58N 112 45W
142 Wickepin, W. Australia 32 42S 117 33E
165 Wickett, U.S.A. 31 37N 102 58W
35 Wickford, Eng., U.K. 51 37N 0 31E
34 Wickham, Eng., U.K. 50 54N 1 11W
35 Wickham Market, England, U.K. 52 9N 1 21E
160 Wickliffe, U.S.A. 41 46N 81 29W
45 Wicklow, Ireland 53 0N 6 2W
45 Wicklow, co., Ireland .52 59N 6 25W
43 Wicklow Hd., Ireland 52 59N 6 3W
45 Wicklow Gap, Ireland 53 3N 6 23W
45 Wicklow Mts., Ireland 53 0N 6 30W
55 Wickrath, Germany ...51 8N 6 25E
36 Wickwar, Eng., U.K. .51 35N 2 23W
60 Widawa, Poland 51 27N 18 51E
41 Widdrington, Eng., U.K. 55 15N 1 35W
144 Wide B., Territory of New Guinea 4 52S 152 0E
43 Wide Firth, Scotland, U.K. 59 2N 8 0W
36 Widecombe, Eng., U.K. 50 34N 3 48W
36 Widemouth, Eng., U.K. 50 45N 4 34W
142 Widgemooltha, Austral. 31 29S 121 30E
38 Widnes, England, U.K. 53 22N 2 44W
55 Wiehl, Germany 50 57N 7 32E
56 Wiek, Germany 54 37N 13 17E
60 Wielbark, Poland 53 24N 20 55E
60 Wielen, Poland 52 53N 16 9E
59 Wieliczka, Poland 50 0N 20 5E
60 Wieluń, Poland 51 15N 18 40E
59 Wien (Vienna), Austria 48 12N 16 22
59 Wiener Neustadt, Aust. 47 49N 16 16E
60 Wieprz R., Koszalin, Poland 54 26N 16 35E
60 Wieprz R., Lublin, Pol. 51 15N 22 50E
54 Wierden, Netherlands 52 22N 6 35E
60 Wieruszów, Poland 51 19N 18 9E
57 Wiesbaden, Germany .50 7N 8 17E
14 Wiese, I., U.S.S.R. 77 5N 83 0E
57 Wiesental, Germany ...49 15N 8 30E
38 Wigan, England, U.K. 53 33N 2 38W
164 Wiggins, Colo., U.S.A. 40 16N 104 3W
165 Wiggins, Miss., U.S.A. 30 53N 89 9W
34 Wight, I. of, Eng., U.K. 50 40N 1 20W
34 Wigmore, Eng., U.K. .52 19N 2 51W
34 Wigston, England, U.K. 52 35N 1 6W
38 Wigton, Eng., U.K. ...54 50N 3 9W
40 Wigtown, Scot., U.K. 54 52N 4 27W
40 Wigtown, Co., Scot., U.K. 54 53N 4 45W
40 Wigtown B., Scot., U.K. 54 46N 4 15W
55 Wijchen, Netherlands 51 48N 5 44E
57 Wil, Switzerland 47 28N 9 3E
164 Wilber, U.S.A. 40 34N 96 59W
160 Wilberforce, Canada ...45 0N 78 15W
165 Wilburton, U.S.A. 34 55N 95 15W
143 Wilcannia, Australia .31 30S 143 26E
160 Wilcox, U.S.A. 41 34N 78 43W
57 Wildbad, Germany ...48 44N 8 32E
134 Wildebeespan, S. Afr. 29 36S 23 13E
134 Wilderness, The, C. Porv., S. Africa 34 0S 22 33E
56 Wildeshausen, Germany 52 54N 8 25E
58 Wildspitze, Mt., Austria 46 53N 10 53E
58 Wildon, Austria 46 52N 15 31E
164 Wildrose, U.S.A. 48 36N 103 17W
162 Wildwood, U.S.A. 39 5N 74 46W
135 Wilge R., OFS, S. Afr. 27 0S 28 15E
133 Wilge R., S. Africa 25 40S 29 10E
144 Wilhelm Mt., North-East New Guinea ... 5 57S 145 0E
15 Wilhelm II Coast, Antarctica 67 0S 90 0E
55 Wilhelmina Canal, Neth. 51 36N 5 7E
175 Wilhelmina Mt., Surinam 3 50N 56 30W
56 Wilhelm-Pieck Staat Guben, E. Germany 51 58N 14 45E
58 Wilhelmsburg, Austria 48 6N 15 36E
56 Wilhelmsburg, Germany 53 28N 10 1E
56 Wilhelmshaven, Ger. .53 30N 8 9E
15 Wilkes Land, Antarc .69 0S 120 0E
161 Wilkes-Barre, U.S.A. .41 15N 75 52W
163 Wilkesboro, U.S.A. 36 10N 81 9W
157 Wilkie, Canada 52 27N 108 42W
160 Wilkinsburg, U.S.A. ...40 26N 79 50W
166 Willamina, U.S.A. 45 9N 123 32W
166 Willapa, B., U.S.A. ...46 44N 124 0W
167 Willard, N.M., U.S.A. 34 35N 106 1W
166 Willard, Utah, U.S.A. 41 28N 112 1W
144 Willaumez Pen., Territory of New Guinea 5 3S 150 3E
167 Wilcox, U.S.A. 32 13N 109 52W
55 Willebroek, Belgium .51 4N 4 22E
55 Willemstad, Neth. 51 41N 4 27E
169 Willemstad, W. Indies 12 5N 69 0W
34 Willenhall, Eng., U.K. 52 36N 2 3W
35 Willesborough, England, U.K. 51 8N 0 55E
143 William Mt., Australia 37 11S 142 33E
142 Williams, W. Australia 33 0S 117 0E
167 Williams, Ariz., U.S.A. 35 16N 112 11W
156 Williams Lake, Canada 52 20N 122 10W
142 Williambury, Western Australia 23 45S 115 12E
163 Williamsburg, Ky., U.S.A. 36 45N 84 10W
160 Williamsburg, Pa., U.S.A. 40 27N 78 14W
162 Williamsburg, Va., U.S.A. 37 17N 76 44W
160 Williamson, N.Y., U.S.A. 43 14N 77 15W
162 Williamson, W. Va., U.S.A. 37 46N 82 17W
160 Williamsport, U.S.A. .41 18N 77 1W
163 Williamston, U.S.A. ...35 50N 77 5W
143 Williamstown, Austral. 37 46S 144 58E
46 Williamstown, Ireland 53 41N 8 34W
161 Williamstown, Mass., U.S.A. 42 41N 73 12W
161 Williamstown, N.Y., U.S.A. 43 25N 75 54W
165 Williamsville, Mo., U.S.A. 37 0N 90 33W
55 Willich, Germany 51 16N 6 32E
161 Willimantic, U.S.A. ...41 45N 72 12W
35 Willingdon, Eng., U.K. 50 47N 0 17E
39 Willington, Eng., U.K. 54 43N 1 41W
163 Williston, U.S.A. 29 25N 82 28W
164 Williston, U.S.A. 48 10N 103 35W
134 Williston, S. Africa ...31 20S 20 53E
36 Williton, England, U.K. 51 9N 3 20W
166 Willits, U.S.A. 39 28N 123 17W
164 Willmar, U.S.A. 45 5N 95 0W
39 Willoughby, Lincs., England, U.K. 53 14N 0 12E
34 Willoughby, Notts., England, U.K. 52 49N 1 3W
135 Willoughby, S. Africa 30 23S 26 11E
160 Willoughby, U.S.A. ...41 38N 81 26W
157 Willow Bunch, Canada 49 20N 105 35W
164 Willow Lake, U.S.A. .44 40N 97 40W
156 Willow River, Canada 54 6N 122 28W
165 Willow Springs, U.S.A. 37 0N 92 0W
143 Willow Tree, Australia 31 40S 150 45E
134 Willowmore, S. Africa 33 15S 23 30E
144 Willows, Australia ...23 45S 147 25E
166 Willows, U.S.A. 39 30N 122 10W
135 Willowvale, S. Africa .32 15S 28 31E
165 Wills Pt., U.S.A. 32 42N 95 57W
145 Willunga, S. Australia 35 15S 138 30E
162 Wilmette, Ill., U.S.A. 42 6N 87 44W
162 Wilmington, Del., U.S.A. 39 45N 75 32W
36 Wilmington, Eng., U.K. 50 46N 3 8W
162 Wilmington, Ill., U.S.A. 41 19N 88 10W
163 Wilmington, N.C., U.S.A. 34 14N 77 54W
162 Wilmington, Ohio, U.S.A. 39 29N 83 46W
38 Wilmslow, Eng., U.K. 53 19N 2 14W
34 Wilnecote, Eng., U.K. 52 36N 1 40W
166 Wilsall, U.S.A. 45 59N 110 44W
163 Wilson, N.C., U.S.A. .35 44N 77 54W
167 Wilson, Mt., U.S.A. ...37 55N 105 3W
143 Wilson's Prom., Austral. 39 5S 146 28E
56 Wilster, Germany 53 55N 9 23E
164 Wilton, U.S.A. 47 12N 100 53W
34 Wiltshire, co., Eng., U.K. 51 20N 2 0W
54 Wiltz, Luxembourg ...49 57N 5 55E
142 Wiluna, W. Australia .26 40S 120 25E
135 Wimblington, Eng., U.K. 52 31N 0 5E
134 Wimborne, Eng., U.K. 50 48N 2 0W
49 Wimereux, France 50 45N 1 37E
143 Wimmera, div., Austral. 36 30S 142 0E
143 Wimmera R., Australia 36 48S 142 50E
57 Wimpfen, Germany ...49 12N 9 10E
135 Winburg, O.F.S., S. Afr. 28 30S 27 2E
36 Wincanton, Eng., U.K. 51 3N 2 24W
161 Winch, U.S.A. 42 26N 71 9W
143 Winchelsea, Australia 38 10S 144 1E
35 Winchelsea, Eng., U.K. 50 55N 0 43E
161 Winchendon, U.S.A. .42 40N 72 3W
34 Winchester, Eng., U.K. 51 4N 1 19W
147 Winchester, N.Z. 44 11S 171 17E
161 Winchester, Conn., U.S.A. 41 53N 73 9W
166 Winchester, Idaho, U.S.A. 46 11N 116 32W
162 Winchester, Ind., U.S.A. 40 10N 84 56W
162 Winchester, Ky., U.S.A. 38 0N 84 8W
161 Winchester, N.H., U.S.A. 42 47N 72 22W
163 Winchester, Tenn., U.S.A. 35 11N 86 8W
162 Winchester, Va., U.S.A. 39 14N 78 8W
166 Wind R., U.S.A. 43 30N 109 30W
166 Wind River Range, Mts., U.S.A. 43 0N 109 30W
160 Windber, U.S.A. 40 14N 78 50W
109 Windehsi, Indonesia ... 2 30S 134 10E
163 Winder, U.S.A. 34 0N 83 40W
145 Windera, Australia 26 17S 151 51E
38 Windermere, Eng., U.K. 54 24N 2 56W
38 Windermere L., England, U.K. 54 20N 2 57W
129 Windhoek, S.W. Africa 22 35S 17 4E
58 Windischgarsten, Aust. 47 42N 14 21E
164 Windom, U.S.A. 43 48N 95 3W
145 Windorah, Australia .25 24S 142 36E
167 Window Rock, U.S.A. 35 47N 109 4W
34 Windrush R., Eng., U.K. 51 48N 1 35W
57 Windsheim, Germany 49 29N 10 25E
143 Windsor, N.S.W., Austral. 33 34S 150 44E
155 Windsor, N.S., Canada 44 59N 64 5W
154 Windsor, Ont., Canada 42 25N 83 0W
35 Windsor, England, U.K. 51 28N 0 36W
147 Windsor, New Zealand 44 59S 170 49E
164 Windsor, Col., U.S.A. 40 33N 104 55W
161 Windsor, Conn., U.S.A. 41 50N 72 40W
164 Windsor, Miss., U.S.A. 38 32N 93 31W
161 Windsor, N.Y., U.S.A. 42 5N 75 37W
161 Windsor, Vt., U.S.A. .43 30N 72 25W
133 Windsorton, S. Africa 28 16S 24 44E
133 Windsorton Rd., S Afr. 28 25S 24 50E
169 Windward Is., W. Ind. 13 0N 63 0W
169 Windward Passage, Caribbean 20 0N 74 0W
41 Windygates, Scot., U.K. 56 12N 3 1W
45 Windygap, Ireland 52 28N 7 24W
157 Winefred L., Canada .55 30N 110 30W
127 Winejok, Sudan 9 1N 27 30E
165 Winfield, Kans., U.S.A. 37 15N 97 0W
143 Wingen Mt., Australia 31 50S 150 58E
154 Wingham, Canada 43 55N 81 25W
35 Wingham, Eng., U.K. 51 16N 1 12E
143 Wingham, Australia ...31 48S 152 22E
166 Winifred, U.S.A. 47 30N 109 28W
154 Winisk L., Canada 52 55N 87 40W
154 Winisk, Canada 55 20N 85 15W
154 Winisk R., Canada 54 40N 87 0W
165 Wink, U.S.A. 31 49N 103 9W
36 Winkleigh, Eng., U.K. 50 49N 3 57W
157 Winkler, Canada 49 15N 98 0W
58 Winklern, Austria 46 52N 12 53E
125 Winneba, Ghana 5 25N 0 36W
164 Winnebago, U.S.A. 43 43N 94 8W
162 Winnebago L., U.S.A. 44 0N 88 20W
166 Winnemucca, U.S.A. .41 0N 117 45W
166 Winnenucca, L., U.S.A. 40 25N 119 21W
164 Winner, U.S.A. 43 23N 99 52W
162 Winnetka, U.S.A. 42 8N 87 46W
165 Winnfield, U.S.A. 31 57N 92 38W
166 Winnett, U.S.A. 47 2N 108 28W
164 Winnibigoshish L., U.S.A. 47 25N 94 12W
142 Winning Pool, Austral. 23 9S 114 30E
157 Winnipeg, Canada 49 50N 97 15W
157 Winnipeg, L., Canada 52 30N 98 0W
157 Winnipeg R., Canada .50 25N 95 30W
157 Winnipeg Beach, Can. 50 30N 96 58W
157 Winnipegosis, Canada 52 40N 100 0W
157 Winnipegosis L., Can. 52 40N 100 0W
165 Winnsboro, Lou, U.S.A. 32 10N 91 41W
163 Winnsboro, S.C., U.S.A. 34 23N 81 5W
165 Winnsboro, Tex., U.S.A. 32 56N 95 15W
155 Winokapau, L., Canada 53 15N 62 50W
165 Winona, Miss., U.S.A. 33 30N 89 42W
164 Winona, Wis., U.S.A. 44 3N 91 45W

MAP
161 Winooski, U.S.A. 44 31N 73 11W
54 Winschoten, Neth. 53 9N 7 3E
56 Winsen, Germany 52 40N 9 54E
56 Winsen, Ger. 53 21N 10 11E
38 Winsford, Ches., England, U.K. 53 12N 2 31W
36 Winsford, Som., England, U.K. 51 5N 3 35W
35 Winslow, Eng., U.K. .51 57N 0 52W
167 Winslow, U.S.A. 35 2N 110 41W
134 Winstead, S. Africa ...28 55S 22 11E
161 Winstead, U.S.A. 41 55N 73 5W
39 Winster, England, U.K. 53 9N 1 42W
163 Winston-Salem, U.S.A. 36 7N 80 15W
163 Winter Garden, U.S.A. 28 33N 81 35W
163 Winter Haven, U.S.A. 28 0N 81 42W
163 Winter Park, U.S.A. .28 34N 81 19W
56 Winterberg, N. Rhine-Westphalia, Germany 51 12N 8 30E
135 Winterberge Mts., C. Prov., S. Africa 32 20S 26 30E
36 Winterborne Abbas, England, U.K. 50 52N 2 30W
165 Winters, U.S.A. 31 58N 99 58W
133 Winter's Rush, S. Afr. 28 23S 24 22E
164 Winterset, U.S.A. 41 18N 94 0W
160 Wintersville, U.S.A. ...40 23N 80 38W
54 Winterswijk, Neth. 51 58N 6 43E
57 Winterthur, Switzerland 47 30N 8 44E
39 Winterton, Lincs., England, U.K. 53 39N 0 37W
35 Winterton, Norfolk, England, U.K. 52 43N 1 43E
135 Winterton, Nat., S. Afr. 28 46S 29 35E
164 Winthorp, U.S.A. 44 31N 94 25W
166 Winthrop, U.S.A. 48 27N 120 6W
144 Winton, Australia 22 21S 143 0E
147 Winton, New Zealand 46 8S 168 20E
163 Winton, N.C., U.S.A. .36 25N 76 58W
161 Winton, Pa., U.S.A. ...41 27N 75 33W
55 Wipperfürth, Germany 51 7N 7 24E
39 Wirksworth Eng., U.K. 53 5N 1 34W
29 Wirral, pen., Eng., U.K. 53 25N 3 0W
35 Wisbech, England, U.K. 52 39N 0 10E
35 Wisborough Green, England, U.K. 51 2N 0 30W
164 Wisconsin, st., U.S.A. 44 30N 90 0W
164 Wisconsin Dells, U.S.A. 43 38N 89 45W
164 Wisconsin R., U.S.A. .45 25N 89 45W
164 Wisconsin Rapids, U.S.A. 44 25N 89 50W
166 Wisdom, U.S.A. 45 36N 113 1W
41 Wishaw, Scot., U.K. .55 46N 3 55W
164 Wishek, U.S.A. 46 20N 99 35W
39 Wiske R., Eng., U.K. 54 26N 1 27W
60 Wisla, R., Poland 53 38N 18 47E
56 Wismar, Germany 53 53N 11 23E
56 Wismar B., Germany .54 0N 11 15E
164 Wisner, U.S.A. 42 0N 96 46W
49 Wissant, France 50 52N 1 40E
49 Wissembourg, France 49 2N 7 57E
55 Wissen, Germany 50 47N 7 45E
130 Wissmann Falls, Congo 5 22S 20 50E
59 Wistok, R., Poland ...50 7N 22 25E
59 Wistoka, R., Poland .49 50N 21 28E
133 Witbank, Trans., S. Afr. 25 51S 29 14E
165 Witchita, U.S.A. 37 40N 97 22W
134 Witdraai, S. Africa ...26 58S 20 48E
133 Witfontein, S. Africa .26 55S 26 7E
35 Witham, England, U.K. 51 48N 0 39E
39 Witham R., Eng., U.K. 53 3N 0 8W
39 Withern, Eng., U.K. .53 18N 0 9E
39 Withernsea, Eng., U.K. 53 43N 0 2W
135 Witlaagte, OFS, S. Afr. 28 40S 27 19E
35 Witley, England, U.K. 51 9N 0 39W
135 Witmos, C. Prov., S. Afr. 32 33S 25 45E
34 Witney, England, U.K. 51 47N 1 29W
133 Witpoort, S. Africa ...25 21S 29 51E
134 Witputs, S.W. Africa .27 37S 17 54E
133 Witrivier, S. Africa ...25 20S 31 0E
135 Witsieshoek, S. Africa 28 30S 28 46E
135 Witteberge, Mts., S. Afr. 30 37S 27 22E
135 Witteklip, S. Africa ...33 53S 25 19E
55 Wittem, Netherlands .50 48N 5 55E
56 Witten, Germany 51 26N 7 19E
56 Wittenberg, Germany 51 51N 12 39E
56 Wittenberge, Germany 53 0N 11 44E
56 Wittenburg, Germany 53 30N 11 4E
142 Wittenoom, W. Australia 22 15S 118 20E
35 Wittersham, Eng., U.K. 51 1N 0 42E
56 Wittingen, Germany ...52 43N 10 43E
57 Wittlich, Germany 50 0N 6 54E
56 Wittow, pen., Germany 54 37N 13 21E

MAP
56 Wittstock, Germany .53 10N 12 30E
131 Witu, Kenya 2 20S 40 20E
133 Witwatersrand, S. Afr. 26 0S 27 0E
56 Witzenhausen, Ger. ...51 20N 9 50E
36 Wiveliscombe, Eng. U.K. 51 2N 3 20W
35 Wivenhoe, Eng., U.K. 51 51N 0 59E
60 Wladyslawowo, Poland 52 6N 18 28E
109 Wlingi, Indonesia 8 5S 112 25E
60 Wloclawek, Poland ...52 40N 19 3E
60 Wloszczowa, Poland ...50 50N 19 55E
35 Woburn, England, U.K. 51 59N 0 37W
35 Woburn Sands, England, U.K. 51 1N 0 38W
161 Woburn, U.S.A. 42 31N 71 7W
143 Wodonga, Vic., Austral. 36 5S 146 50E
59 Wodzislaw, Poland ...50 1N 18 26E
49 Woerth, France 48 57N 7 45E
49 Woevre, dist., France 49 15N 5 45E
109 Wokam I., Indonesia . 5 45S 134 28E
156 Woking, Canada 55 35N 118 50W
35 Woking, England, U.K. 51 18N 0 33W
35 Wokingham, Eng., U.K. 51 25N 0 50W
60 Wolbrom, Poland 50 24N 19 45E
60 Wolczyn, Poland 51 1N 18 2E
56 Woldegk, Germany ...53 27N 13 35E
166 Wolf Creek, U.S.A. 47 1N 112 2W
164 Wolf Point, U.S.A. ...48 6N 105 40W
36 Wolf Rock, Eng., U.K. 49 56N 5 50W
161 Wolfe I., Canada 44 7N 76 27W
56 Wolfenbüttel, Germany 52 10N 10 33E
156 Wolfenden, Canada ...52 0N 119 25W
144 Wolfram, Australia ...17 6S 145 0E
37 Wolf's Castle, Wales, U.K. 51 53N 4 57W
58 Wolfsberg, Austria 46 50N 14 52E
56 Wolfsburg, Germany .52 27N 10 49E
56 Wolgast, Germany 54 3N 13 46E
57 Wolhusen, Switzerland 47 4N 8 4E
60 Wolin, Poland 53 40N 14 37E
176 Wollaston Is. Chile 55 40S 67 30W
157 Wollaston L., Canada 58 20N 103 30W
152 Wollaston Pen., Can. .69 30N 113 0W
143 Wollondilly, R., Austral. 34 0S 150 27E
143 Wollongong, Australia 34 25S 150 54E
133 Wolmaransstad, S. Afr. 27 12S 26 13E
56 Wolmirstedt, Germany 52 15N 11 35E
60 Wolomin, Poland 52 19N 21 15E
60 Wolow, Poland 51 20N 16 38E
157 Wolseley, Canada 50 25N 103 15W
134 Wolseley, S. Africa ...33 26S 19 7E
145 Wolseley, S. Australia 36 14S 140 58E
38 Wolsingham, Eng., U.K. 54 44N 1 52W
14 Wolstenholme Sound, Greenland 74 30N 75 0W
34 Wolverhampton, England, U.K. 52 35N 2 6W
35 Wolverton, Eng., U.K. 52 3N 0 48W
41 Wolviston, Eng., U.K. 54 39N 1 25W
135 Wolwehoek, S. Africa 26 55S 27 48E
127 Wombera, Ethiopia ...10 45N 35 49E
39 Wombwell, Eng., U.K. 53 31N 1 23W
143 Won Wron, Australia 38 23S 146 45E
145 Wondai, Australia ...26 20S 151 49E
135 Wonderkop, S. Africa 27 50S 27 26E
143 Wongallorroo L., N.S.W., Australia ...31 35S 144 2E
142 Wongan. W. Australia 30 51S 116 37E
142 Wongan Hills, W. Australia 30 53S 116 42E
142 Wongawal, W. Austral. 25 5S 121 55E
112 Wonju, South Korea .37 30N 127 59E
55 Wonk, Belgium 50 46N 5 38E
109 Wonosari, Indonesia . 7 38S 110 36E
112 Wŏnsan, North Korea 39 20N 127 25E
34 Wonston, Eng., U.K. .51 9N 1 18W
143 Wonthaggi, Australia .38 29S 145 31E
157 Wood, Mt., Canada ...49 13N 106 13W
164 Wood Lake, U.S.A. ...42 38N 100 14W
156 Wood Buffalo Pk., Can. 59 30N 113 0W
142 Woodanilling, Australia 33 31S 117 24E
160 Woodbridge, Canada .43 48N 79 35W
35 Woodbridge, Eng., U.K. 52 6N 1 19E
36 Woodbury, Eng., U.K. 50 40N 3 24W
45 Wooden Bridge, Ireland 52 50N 6 13W
143 Woodend, Vic., Austral. 37 20N 144 33E
44 Woodford, Ireland 53 3N 8 23W
39 Woodhall Spa., England, U.K. 53 10N 0 12W
35 Woodham Ferrers, England, U.K. 51 40N 0 37E
166 Woodland, U.S.A. 38 40N 121 50W
142 Woodlands, W. Austral. 24 42S 118 2E
144 Woodlark I., Territory of Papua . 9 1S 148 0E
35 Woodley, Eng., U.K. .51 26N 0 54W
156 Woodpecker, Canada .53 30N 122 40W

MAP
38 Woodplumpton, England, U.K. 53 47N 2 46W
157 Woodridge, Canada ...49 20N 96 20W
167 Woodruff, U.S.A. 34 51N 110 1W
166 Woodruff, U.S.A. 41 30N 111 4W
143 Woodside, Vic., Austral. 38 28S 146 53E
136 Woods L., Australia ...17 50S 133 30E
155 Woods, L., Canada 54 30N 65 0W
157 Woods, L., of the, Canada-U.S.A. 49 30N 94 30W
155 Woodstock, N.B., Can. 46 11N 67 37W
154 Woodstock, Ont., Can. 43 10N 80 45W
34 Woodstock, Eng., U.K. 51 51N 1 20W
144 Woodstock, Queens., Austral. 19 22S 142 45E
164 Woodstock, Ill., U.S.A. 42 17N 88 30W
101 Woodstock, N.H., U.S.A. 43 59N 71 41W
161 Woodstock, Vt., U.S.A. 43 37N 72 31W
161 Woodsville, U.S.A. ...44 10N 72 0W
146 Woodville, N.Z. 40 20S 175 53E
165 Woodville, U.S.A. 30 45N 94 25W
165 Woodward, U.S.A. 36 24N 99 28W
142 Woodward, Mt., S. Australia 26 0S 131 0E
36 Wookey, Eng., U.K. .51 13N 2 41W
36 Wookey Hole, Eng., U.K. 51 13N 2 41W
34 Wool, England, U.K. .50 41N 2 13W
36 Woolacombe, Eng., U.K. 51 10N 4 12W
143 Woolamai, C., Austral. 38 30S 145 23E
39 Wooler, England, U.K. 55 33N 2 0W
142 Woolgangie, W. Austral. 31 12S 120 35E
143 Woomargama, Austral. 35 45S 147 15E
145 Woombye, Australia .26 40S 152 55E
143 Woomelang, Australia 35 37S 142 40E
145 Woomera, S. Australia 31 9S 136 56E
143 Woonona, Australia ...34 32S 150 49E
161 Woonsocker, U.S.A. ...42 0N 71 30W
164 Woonsockett, U.S.A. .44 5N 98 15W
143 Wooramel, W. Australia 25 45S 114 40E
142 Wooramel, R., Austral. 25 30S 114 30E
143 Woorinen, Vic., Australia. 35 14S 143 27E
142 Wooroloo, W. Australia 31 45S 116 25E
145 Wooroorooka Austral. 29 0S 145 41E
160 Wooster, U.S.A. 40 38N 81 55W
34 Wootton Bassett, England, U.K. 51 32N 1 55W
34 Wootton Wawen, England, U.K. 52 16N 1 47W
34 Worcester, Eng., U.K. 52 12N 2 12W
134 Worcester, S. Africa ...33 39S 19 27E
161 Worcester, Mass., U.S.A. 42 14N 71 49W
161 Worcester, N.Y., U.S.A. 42 35N 74 45W
34 Worcester, co., Eng., U.K. 52 13N 2 10W
34 Worfield, England, U.K. 52 34N 2 22W
58 Wörgl, Austria 47 29N 12 3E
125 Worikambo, Ghana ...10 43N 0 11W
38 Workington, Eng., U.K. 54 39N 3 34W
39 Worksop, Eng., U.K. .53 19N 1 9W
54 Workum, Netherlands 52 59N 5 26E
166 Worland, U.S.A. 44 0N 107 59W
49 Wormhoudt, France ...50 52N 2 28E
41 Wormit, Scotland, U.K. 56 26N 2 59W
57 Worms, Germany 49 37N 8 21E
37 Worms Head, Wales, United Kingdom ...51 33N 4 19W
35 Worplesdon, Eng., U.K. 51 16N 0 36W
142 Worsley, W. Australia 33 15S 116 2E
35 Wortham, Eng., U.K. 52 22N 1 3E
165 Wortham, U.S.A. 31 48N 96 27W
58 Worther See, L., Aust. 46 37N 14 19E
35 Worthing, Eng., U.K. 50 49N 0 21W
164 Worthington, U.S.A. .43 35N 95 30W
109 Wosi, Indonesia 0 15S 128 0E
127 Wota (Shoa Ghimira), Ethiopia 7 4N 35 51E
34 Wotton-under-Edge, England, U.K. 51 37N 2 20W
55 Woudrichem, Neth. ...51 49N 5 0E
123 Wour, Chad. 21 14N 16 0E
55 Wouw, Netherlands ...51 31N 4 23E
109 Wowoni I., Indonesia 4 5S 123 5E
39 Wragby, England, U.K. 53 17N 0 18W
91 Wrangel I., U.S.S.R. .71 0N 180 0E
156 Wrangell, Alaska, U.S.A. 56 30N 132 25W
156 Wrangell, I., Alas., U.S.A. 56 20N 132 10W
152 Wrangell Mts., Alaska, U.S.A. 61 40N 143 30W
39 Wrangle, England, U.K. 53 3N 0 9E
42 Wrath, C., Scot., U.K. 58 38N 5 0W

MAP
164 Wray, U.S.A. 40 8N 102 18W
34 Wrekin, The, Mt., England, U.K. 52 41N 2 35W
163 Wrens, U.S.A. 33 13N 82 23W
35 Wrentham, Eng., U.K. 52 24N 1 39E
37 Wrexham, Wales, U.K. 53 5N 3 0W
56 Wriezen, Germany 52 43N 14 9E
156 Wright, Canada 51 45N 121 30W
109 Wright, Philippines 11 42N 125 2E
167 Wrightson, Mt., U.S.A. 31 49N 110 56W
152 Wrigley, Canada 63 0N 123 30W
36 Wrightlington, Eng. U.K. 51 18N 2 16W
35 Writtle, England, U.K. 51 44N 0 27E
60 Wroclaw (Breslau), Pol. 51 5N 17 5E
60 Wroclaw (Breslau), prov., Poland 51 0N 77 0E
60 Wronki, Poland 52 41N 16 21E
35 Wrotham, Eng., U.K. 51 18N 0 20E
34 Wroughton, Eng., U.K. 51 31N 1 47W
35 Wroxham, Eng., U.K. 52 42N 1 23E
60 Wrzesnia, Poland 52 21N 17 36E
60 Wschowa, Poland 51 48N 16 20E
142 Wubin, W. Australia .30 8S 116 30E
112 Wuchai, China 39 10N 111 36E
113 Wuchan, China 28 30N 108 10E
112 Wuchang, Heilungkiang, China 44 51N 127 10E
113 Wuchang, Hupei, China 30 34N 114 25E
112 Wuchen, China 41 10N 108 32E
113 Wuchow, China 23 26N 111 19E
112 Wuchung, China 38 4N 106 12E
113 Wuhan, China 30 32N 114 22E
113 Wuhu, China 31 21N 118 30E
113 Wukang, China 26 50N 110 15E
113 Wukang, China 30 35N 119 50E
125 Wukari, Nigeria 7 57N 9 42E
113 Wuki (Taning), China 31 27N 109 46E
125 Wulehe, Ghana 3 42N 0 0
55 Wülfrath, Germany ...51 18N 7 2E
109 Wuliaru, I., Indonesia 7 10S 131 0E
125 Wum, Cameroon 6 40N 10 2E
131 Wundanyi, Kenya 3 24S 38 22E
127 Wuneba, Sudan 4 49N 30 22E
113 Wuning, China 29 16N 115 0E
154 Wunnummin L., Can. 52 50N 89 20W
57 Wunsiedel, Germany .50 2N 12 0E
56 Wunstorf, Germany ...52 26N 9 29E
103 Wuntho, Burma 23 55N 95 45E
113 Wuping, China 25 5N 116 20E
55 Wupper R., Germany 51 7N 7 0E
56 Wuppertal, Germany .51 15N 7 8E
142 Wurarga W. Australia 28 15S 116 12E
55 Würm, Germany 51 2N 6 10E
55 Wurselen, Germany ...50 49N 6 8E
57 Würzburg, Germany .49 46N 9 55E
56 Wurzen, Germany 51 21N 12 45E
113 Wushan, China 31 3N 109 57E
113 Wusih, China 31 30N 120 30E
56 Wustrow, Germany ...54 4N 11 33E
111 Wusu, China 44 10N 84 55E
112 Wutai, China 41 16N 114 6E
113 Wutu, China 33 27N 104 37E
111 Wutunghlia, China 29 25N 104 0E
55 Wuustwezel, Belgium 51 23N 4 36E
111 Wuwei, China 38 0N 102 30E
112 Wuyi, China 37 54N 116 0E
113 Wuyi, China 28 45N 119 56E
113 Wuyi Shan, Mts., China 26 40N 116 30E
112 Wuying, China 48 10N 129 20E
125 Wuyo, Nigeria 10 23N 11 50E
113 Wuyuan, China 41 15N 108 30E
142 Wyalkatchem, Austral. 31 8S 117 22E
143 Wyalong, N.S.W., Austral. 35 45S 147 50E
161 Wyalusing, U.S.A. ...41 40N 76 16W
162 Wyandotte, U.S.A. ...42 14N 83 13W
145 Wyandra, Australia ...27 12S 145 56E
143 Wyangala Res., Austral. 34 6S 149 22E
143 Wycheproof, Australia 36 0N 143 17E
142 Wydgee, W. Australia 28 50S 117 45E
34 Wye, R., England, U.K. 52 0N 2 36W
142 Wyemandoo, Mt., Australia 28 28S 118 29E
37 Wylfa Hd., Wales, U.K. 53 25N 4 28W
143 Wymlet, Vic., Austral. 34 52S 142 10E
35 Wymondham, Leicester, England, U.K. 52 45N 0 42W
35 Wymondham, Norfolk, England, U.K. 52 34N 1 7E
164 Wymore, U.S.A. 40 10N 97 8W
134 Wynberg, S. Africa ...34 2S 18 28E
142 Wyndham, W. Austral. 15 33S 128 3E
147 Wyndham, N.Z. 46 20S 168 51E
165 Wynne, U.S.A. 35 15N 90 50W
37 Wynnstay, Wales, U.K. 52 36N 3 33W
145 Wynnum, Australia ...27 29S 152 58E
157 Wynyard, Canada 51 45N 104 10W
145 Wynyard, Tas., Austral. 40 59S 145 45E
160 Wyoming, U.S.A. 42 46N 78 4W
158 Wyoming, st., U.S.A. .42 48N 109 0W

MAP
143 Wyong, N.S.W., Austral. 33 14S 151 24E
43 Wyre, I., Scot., U.K. .59 7N 2 58W
38 Wyre, R., Eng., U.K. 53 58N 2 40W
60 Wyrzysk, Poland 53 10N 17 17E
60 Wyszków Poland 52 36N 21 25E
60 Wyszogród, Poland ...52 23N 20 9E
162 Wytheville, U.S.A. 37 0N 81 3W

X

56 Xanten, Germany 51 40N 6 27E
76 Xanthi, & pref., Greece 41 10N 24 58E
174 Xapuri, Brazil 10 35S 68 35W
162 Xenia, Ohio, U.S.A. ...39 42N 83 57W
107 Xieng Khouang Mt., Laos 19 17N 103 25E
77 Xilókastron, Greece ...38 4N 22 43E
133 Xinavane, Mozambique 25 2S 32 47E
77 Xiniás, L., Greece 39 2N 22 12E
175 Xingu R., Brazil 2 25S 52 35W
175 Xique-Xique, Brazil .10 40S 42 40W

Y

144 Yaamba, Queensland, Australia 23 8S 150 22E
111 Yaan, China 30 0N 102 59E
143 Yaapeet, Vic., Australia 35 38S 142 0E
98 Ya'bad, Jordan 32 27N 35 10E
127 Yaballo, Ethiopia 4 57N 38 8E
125 Yabassi, Cameroon 4 30N 9 57E
75 Yablanitsa, Bulgaria .43 2N 24 5E
91 Yablonovyy Ra., Siberia 53 0N 114 0E
172 Yacuiba, Bolivia 22 0S 63 25W
106 Yadgir, India 16 45N 77 5E
163 Yadkin R., U.S.A. ...36 15N 81 0W
87 Yadrin, U.S.S.R. 55 57N 46 6E
113 Yaeyama Rettō 24 30N 123 40E
125 Yagaba, Ghana 10 14N 1 20W
98 Yagur, Israel 32 45N 35 4E
114 Yahatahama, Japan ...33 25N 132 40E
156 Yahk, Canada 49 15N 116 10W
130 Yahuma, Congo 1 0N 22 5E
113 Yaicheng, China 18 14N 109 7E
125 Yajua, Nigeria 11 27N 12 49E
103 Yakiang, China 30 4N 101 15E
166 Yakima, U.S.A. 46 42N 120 30W
166 Yakima R., U.S.A. ...47 0N 120 30W
124 Yako, Upper Volta 12 59N 2 15W
75 Yakoruda, Bulgaria ...42 1N 23 29E
112 Yakoshih, China 49 13N 120 35E
114 Yaku-shima, I., Japan 30 20N 130 30E
91 Yakut, A.S.S.R., U.S.S.R. 62 0N 130 0E
152 Yakutat, Alaska, USA 59 50N 139 44W
91 Yakutsk, U.S.S.R. 62 5N 129 40E
107 Yala, Thailand 6 40N 101 12E
165 Yalabusha, R., U.S.A. 33 53N 89 50W
142 Yalbalgo, W. Australia 25 10S 114 45E
144 Yalboroo, Australia ...20 50S 148 30E
160 Yale, U.S.A. 43 9N 82 47W
142 Yalgoo, W. Australia .28 16S 116 39E
77 Yalikavak, Turkey ...37 6N 27 18E
121 Yalinga, Cent Afr. Rep. 6 20N 23 10E
168 Yalkubul, Punta, Mex. 21 32N 88 37W
144 Yalleroi, Australia ...24 3S 145 42E
143 Yallourn, Vic., Austral. 38 10S 146 18E
78 Yalpukh, Ozero, L., U.S.S.R. 45 30N 28 41E
88 Yalta, U.S.S.R. 44 30N 34 10E
112 Yalu R., China-Korea 41 30N 126 30E
112 Yalu R., China 47 45N 122 40E
111 Yalung, R., China 32 0N 100 0E
90 Yalutorovsk, U.S.S.R. 56 30N 65 40E
98 Yam Kinneret (L. Tiberias), Israel 32 49N 35 36E
160 Yamagata, Japan 38 20N 140 20E
114 Yamagata, pref., Japan 38 30N 140 0E
114 Yamaguchi, Japan ...34 10N 131 32E
114 Yamaguchi pref., Japan 34 20N 131 40E
90 Yamal Pen., U.S.S.R. 71 0N 70 0E
84 Yaman Tau, Mt. U.S.S.R. 54 20N 57 40E
100 Yamana, Si. Arab. 24 5N 47 30E
114 Yamanashi, pref. Jap. 35 40N 138 40E
89 Yamankhalinka, U.S.S.R. 47 43N 49 21E
145 Yamba, N.S.W., Austral. 29 30S 153 22E
127 Yambio, Sudan 4 35N 28 16E
75 Yambol, Bulgaria 42 30N 26 36E
111 Yamdrok Tso, L., Tibet, China 29 0N 90 40E
103 Yamèthin, Burma 20 30N 96 15E
113 Yamhsien, China 21 45N 108 31E
125 Yamil, Nigeria 12 53N 8 4E
145 Yamma Yamma L., Queens., Australia .26 16S 141 20E
166 Yampa R., U.S.A. 40 37N 108 0W
138 Yampi Sd., W. Austral. 15 15S 123 30E
88 Yampol, U.S.S.R. 48 15N 28 15E
125 Yamrat, Nigeria 10 11N 9 55E
75 Yamrukohal, Mt., Bulg. 42 44N 24 52E
98 Yamun, Jordan 32 29N 35 14E

MAP
104 Yamuna (Jumna), R., India 27 0N 78 30E
125 Yan, Nigeria 10 5N 12 11E
106 Yan Oya, R., Ceylon . 9 0N 81 10E
91 Yana R., U.S.S.R. 69 0N 134 0E
143 Yanac, Vic., Australia 36 0s 141 15E
106 Yanam, India 16 47N 82 15E
174 Yanaoca, Peru 14 10s 71 10w
84 Yanaul, U.S.S.R. 56 25N 55 0E
145 Yancannia, Australia .30 12s 142 35E
142 Yanchep, W. Australia 31 30s 115 45E
143 Yanco, N.S.W., Austral. 34 38s 146 27E
125 Yanda, Nigeria 11 32N 10 48E
144 Yandabome, North East New Guinea ... 7 1s 145 46E
142 Yandal, W. Australia .27 35s 121 10E
142 Yandanooka, Western Australia 29 18s 115 29E
142 Yandil, W. Australia .26 20s 119 50E
130 Yangambi, Congo 0 47N 24 20E
113 Yangchow, China 32 25N 119 25E
112 Yangchuan, China 38 0N 113 29E
90 Yangi-Yer, U.S.S.R. .40 17N 68 48E
112 Yangkao, China 40 20N 113 40E
113 Yangshui (Hinghwa), China 29 53N 115 3E
113 Yangso, China 24 36N 110 32E
112 Yangtsun, China 39 29N 117 4E
113 Yangtze, R., China 30 0N 116 30E
111 Yangtze (Kinsha), R., China 32 30N 98 30E
113 Yangtze Gorges, China 30 56N 109 30E
113 Yangtze Kiang, R., China 31 40N 122 0E
107 Yanhee Res., Thailand 17 30N 98 45E
164 Yankton, U.S.A. 42 55N 97 25w
145 Yanna, Australia 26 58s 146 0E
130 Yanonge, Congo 0 35N 24 38E
113 Yanping, China 22 25N 112 0E
75 Yantra, R., Bulgaria .43 35N 25 37E
121 Yao, Chad 12 56N 17 33E
113 Yao Shan, China 24 0N 110 0E
112 Yaomen, China 44 31N 125 8E
125 Yaoundé, Cameroon ... 3 50N 11 35E
136 Yap I., U.S. Pac. Is. Trust Terr. 9 30N 138 10E
168 Yaqui, R., Mexico 28 28N 109 30w
87 Yar, U.S.S.R. 58 14N 52 5E
145 Yaraka, Australia 24 53s 144 3E
87 Yaransk, U.S.S.R. 57 13N 47 56E
122 Yarboutenda, Gambia 13 20N 13 50w
36 Yarcombe, Eng., U.K. 50 51N 3 6w
121 Yarda, Chad 18 35N 19 0E
35 Yare R., England, U.K. 52 36N 1 28E
84 Yarensk, U.S.S.R. 61 10N 49 8E
126 Yarfa, Saudi Arabia ...24 40N 38 35E
174 Yari R., Colombia 1 0N 73 40w
142 Yaringa North, Austral. 25 53s 114 30E
142 Yaringa South, W Australia 26 3s 114 28E
111 Yarkand (Soche), China 38 24N 77 20E
161 Yarker, Canada 44 23N 76 26w
102 Yarkhun R., W. Pak. 36 30N 72 45E
35 Yarm, England, U.K. 54 31N 1 21w
155 Yarmouth, Canada 43 53N 65 45w
34 Yarmouth, I of W., England, U.K. 50 42N 1 29w
87 Yaroslavl, U.S.S.R. ...57 35N 39 55E
143 Yarra, R., Vic., Austral. 37 45s 143 21E
142 Yarra Yarra Lakes, Western Australia .29 12s 115 45E
144 Yarraden, Australia ...14 28s 143 15E
145 Yarram, Vic., Australia 38 29s 146 40E
145 Yarraman Cr., Austral. 26 46s 152 1E
145 Yarranvale, Australia 26 50s 145 20E
143 Yarrawonga, Australia 36 0s 146 0E
41 Yarrow, Scotland, U.K. 55 32N 3 0w
143 Yarto, Vic., Australia 35 28s 142 16E
91 Yartsevo, U.S.S.R. ...60 20N 90 0E
174 Yarumal, Colombia ... 6 58N 75 24w
86 Yaselda, R., U.S.S.R. 52 26N 25 30E
125 Yashi, Nigeria 12 23N 7 54E
88 Yasinovataya, U.S.S.R. 48 7N 37 57E
154 Yasinski, L., Canada .53 10N 77 0w
107 Yasothon, Thailand ...15 50N 104 10E
143 Yass & Res., Australia 34 50s 149 0E
98 Yas'ur, Israel 32 54N 35 10E
77 Yatagan, Turkey 37 20N 28 10E
36 Yate, England, U.K. .51 32N 2 26w
165 Yates Center, U.S.A. .37 53N 95 45w
147 Yates Pt., N.Z. 44 29s 167 49E
157 Yathkyed L., Canada 63 0N 98 0w
174 Yati, Bolivia 19 0s 62 23w
114 Yatsushiro, Japan ...32 30N 130 40E
98 Yatta, Jordan 31 27N 35 6E
36 Yatton, England, U.K. 51 23N 2 50w
86 Yaunelgava, U.S.S.R. 56 35N 25 0E
174 Yaupi, Ecuador 2 55s 78 0w
175 Yauri, Peru 14 50s 71 25w
174 Yauyos, Peru 12 10s 75 50w
104 Yaval, India 21 10N 75 42E
174 Yavari R., Peru 4 50s 72 0w
98 Yavneel, Israel 32 43N 35 34E
98 Yavne, Israel 31 52N 34 45E
86 Yavorov, U.S.S.R. ...49 55N 23 20E
124 Yawri B., Sierra Leone 8 22N 13 0w
35 Yaxley, England, U.K. 52 31N 0 14w
101 Yazd (Yezd), Iran ...31 55N 54 27E
101 Yazdan, Iran 33 30N 60 50E
165 Yazoo, R., U.S.A. 32 35N 90 50w
165 Yazoo City, U.S.A. 32 48N 90 28w
58 Ybbs, Austria 48 12N 15 4E
142 Yealering, W. Australia 32 35s 117 30E
36 Yealmpton, Eng., U.K. 50 21N 4 0w
123 Yebbi-Souma, Chad ...21 7N 17 54E
122 Yebel Jarris Tighzert, W., Morocco 23 10N 9 37w
103 Yebyu, Burma 14 15N 98 13E
65 Yecla, Spain 38 35N 1 5w
122 Yeddou, Spanish Sahara 28 5N 9 2w
87 Yefremov, U.S.S.R. ...53 15N 38 3E
89 Yegorlyk R., U.S.S.R. 46 15N 41 30E
89 Yegorlykskaya, USSR 46 5N 40 35E
87 Yegoryevsk, U.S.S.R. 55 27N 38 55E
172 Yegros, Paraguay 26 20s 56 25w
112 Yehsien, China 37 12N 119 58E
98 Yehud, Israel 32 3N 34 53E
127 Yei, Sudan 4 3N 30 40E
127 Yei R., Sudan 5 50N 30 20E
87 Yelan, U.S.S.R. 50 55N 43 43E
87 Yelan Kolenovski, U.S.S.R. 51 16N 40 45E
106 Yelandur, India 12 6N 77 0E
91 Yelanskoye, U.S.S.R. .61 25N 128 0E
145 Yelarbon, Australia ...28 33s 150 49E
87 Yelatma, U.S.S.R. ...55 0N 41 52E
87 Yelets, U.S.S.R. 52 40N 38 30E
124 Yelimané, Mali 15 9N 22 49E
42 Yell I., Scotland, U.K. 60 35N 1 5w
42 Yell Sd., Scotland, U.K. 60 33N 1 15w
106 Yellamanchilli (Elamanchili), India 17 26N 82 50E
113 Yellow River, *see* Hwang Ho 38 0N 117 20E
112 Yellow Sea, China 35 0N 123 0E
142 Yellowdine, W. Austral. 31 17s 119 40E
156 Yellowhead P., Canada 53 0N 118 30w
156 Yellowknife, Canada .62 30N 114 10w
152 Yellowknife R., Canada 63 30N 113 30w
166 Yellowstone L., U.S.A. 44 30N 110 20w
164 Yellowstone R., U.S.A. 46 35N 105 45w
166 Yellowstone National Park, U.S.A. 44 35N 110 0w
86 Yelnya, U.S.S.R. 54 35N 33 15E
86 Yelsk, U.S.S.R. 51 50N 29 3E
126 Yelwa, Nigeria 10 49N 8 41E
99 Yemen, king., Arabia .15 0N 44 0E
88 Yenakiyevo, U.S.S.R. 48 15N 38 5E
112 Yenan, China 36 55N 109 20E
103 Yenangyaung, Burma 20 30N 95 0E
100 Yenbo', Saudi Arabia 24 0N 38 5E
112 Yencheng, China 36 44N 110 2E
112 Yencheng, China 33 22N 120 12E
113 Yencheng, China 33 43N 114 10E
112 Yenchwan, China 37 0N 110 5E
143 Yenda, N.S.W., Australia 34 13s 146 14E
124 Yendéré, Ivory Coast .10 12N 4 59w
125 Yendi, Ghana 9 29N 0 1w
113 Yengchun, China 22 10N 111 27E
76 Yenisala, Greece 41 1N 24 57E
90 Yenisei G., U.S.S.R. .72 20N 81 0E
90 Yenisey, R., U.S.S.R. 68 0N 86 30E
91 Yeniseysk, U.S.S.R. ...58 39N 92 4E
112 Yenki, China 42 12N 86 30E
112 Yenki, China 43 12N 129 30E
112 Yenking, China 40 30N 116 0E
51 Yenne, France 45 43N 5 44E
89 Yenotyevka, U.S.S.R. 47 15N 47 0E
113 Yenshih, China 34 46N 112 58E
112 Yentai, China 37 33N 121 25E
91 Yenyuka, U.S.S.R. ...58 20N 121 30E
142 Yeo L., W. Australia .28 0s 124 30E
36 Yeo R., England, U.K. 51 1N 2 46w
106 Yeola, India 20 0N 74 30E
104 Yeotmal, India 20 20N 78 15E
143 Yeoval, N.S.W., Austral. 32 41s 148 39E
36 Yeovil, England, U.K. 50 57N 2 38w
62 Yepes, Spain 39 55N 3 39w
144 Yeppoon, Australia ...23 5s 150 47E
77 Yeraki, Greece 37 0N 22 42E
89 Yerevan, U.S.S.R. ...40 10N 44 20E
142 Yerilla, W. Australia .29 24s 121 47E
166 Yerington, U.S.A. 39 0N 119 11w
106 Yerla, R., India 17 35N 74 30E
91 Yermakovo, U.S.S.R. 52 35N 126 20E
167 Yermo, U.S.A. 34 58N 116 13w
84 Yermolayevo, U.S.S.R. 52 58N 56 12E
91 Yerofei Paulovich, U.S.S.R. 54 0N 122 0E
87 Yershov, U.S.S.R. ...51 15N 48 27E
48 Yerville, France 49 40N 0 53E
88 Yesil R., Turkey 41 0N 36 40E
165 Yeso, U.S.A. 34 29N 104 87w
89 Yessentuki, U.S.S.R. .44 0N 42 45E
65 Yeste, Spain 38 22N 2 19w
48 Yeu, I. d', France 46 42N 2 20w
113 Yeungchun, China ...22 15N 111 40E
113 Yeungkong, China ...21 55N 112 0E
113 Yeungshan, China ...24 27N 112 15E
89 Yevlakh, U.S.S.R. 40 39N 47 7E
88 Yevpatoriya, U.S.S.R. 45 15N 33 20E
91 Yevseyeva, U.S.S.R. .67 10N 153 5E
87 Yevstratovskiy, U.S.S.R. 50 11N 39 2E
89 Yeya R., U.S.S.R. ...46 40N 39 0E
88 Yeysk Staro, U.S.S.R. 46 40N 38 12E
90 Yezelovo, U.S.S.R. ...67 20N 74 5E
173 Yhu, Paraguay 25 0s 56 0w
126 Yi-allaq G., Egypt ...30 21N 33 31E
77 Yiali, I., Greece 36 41N 27 11E
77 Yialtra, Greece 38 51N 22 59E
77 Yianisadhes, I., Greece 35 20N 26 10E
76 Yiannitsa, Greece 40 46N 22 24E
99 Yibal, Muscat & Oman 22 10N 56 8E
112 Yicheng, China 35 31N 111 45E
76 Yidha, Greece 40 35N 22 53E
113 Yihsien, China 34 50N 117 50E
113 Yilan, Taiwan 24 47N 121 44E
113 Yincheng, China 31 0N 113 40E
112 Yinchwan, China 38 30N 106 20E
142 Yindarigooda, L., Western Australia .30 40s 121 52E
113 Yingcheng, China 31 0N 113 44E
112 Yingchow, China 39 45N 113 30E
112 Yingkow, China 40 43N 122 9E
113 Yingshan, China 30 50N 115 45E
113 Yingshang, China 32 36N 116 16E
113 Yingtak, China 24 10N 113 5E
113 Yingtan, China 28 12N 115 59E
113 Yingkiang, China 28 10N 108 40E
103 Yinmabin, Burma 22 10N 94 55E
142 Yinnietharra, Australia 24 36s 116 7E
76 Yioura, I., Greece 39 23N 24 10E
107 Yipang, China 22 15N 101 26E
128 Yirga Alem, Ethiopia 6 34N 38 29E
77 Yithion, Greece 36 46N 22 34E
112 Yitu, China 36 40N 118 25E
113 Yiyang, China 28 31N 112 3E
113 Yiyang, China 28 45N 112 16E
98 Yizre'el, Israel 32 34N 35 19E
82 Ylitornio, Finland ...66 10N 23 57E
81 Ylivieska, Finland ...64 5N 24 47E
81 Yngaren, L., Sweden .58 50N 16 30E
165 Yoakum, U.S.A. 29 20N 97 10w
109 Yog Pt., Philippines ...13 55N 124 20E
129 Yokadouma, Cameroon 3 35N 14 50E
114 Yokkaichi, Japan 35 0N 136 30E
125 Yoko, Cameroon 5 50N 12 20E
114 Yokohama, Japan ...35 30N 139 32E
114 Yokosuko, Japan ...35 20N 139 40E
125 Yola, Nigeria 9 10N 12 29E
169 Yolaina, Cordillera de, Nicaragua 11 30N 84 0w
143 Yolgali, N.S.W., Australia 34 20s 146 7E
107 Yom R., Thailand ...15 15N 100 20E
114 Yonago, Japan 35 25N 133 19E
114 Yonaguni, Is., Japan .24 28N 122 59E
107 Yong Peng, Malaysia . 2 0N 103 3E
112 Yongchon, South Korea 35 55N 138 55E
112 Yongwol, South Korea 37 18N 128 20E
124 Yonibana, Sierra Leone 8 30N 12 19w
157 Yonker, Canada 52 40N 109 40w
161 Yonkers, U.S.A. 40 57N 73 51w
49 Yonne, dépt., France 47 50N 3 40E
49 Yonne R., France 48 12N 3 13E
125 Yonov, Nigeria 7 33N 8 42E
98 Yoqne'am, Israel ...32 40N 35 6E
35 York, Eng., U.K. 53 58N 1 7w
163 York, Ala., U.S.A. ...32 30N 88 18w
164 York, Neb., U.S.A. ...40 55N 97 35w
162 York, Pa., U.S.A. 39 57N 76 43w
142 York, W. Australia ...31 52s 116 47E
144 York, C., Australia ...10 35s 142 30E
14 York, C., Greenland ...75 15N 67 30w
157 York Factory, Canada 57 0N 92 30w
138 York Sd., W. Australia 14 30s 125 0E
39 York, Vale of, Eng., U.K. 54 15N 1 25w
39 York Wolds, Eng., U.K. 54 0N 0 30w
145 Yorke Pen, S. Austral. 34 40s 137 35E
39 Yorkshire, co., Eng., U.K. 54 54N 1 0w
157 Yorkton, Canada 51 11N 102 28w
165 Yorktown, U.S.A. 29 0N 97 29w
142 Yornup, W. Australia 34 2s 116 10E
167 Yosemite National Park, U.S.A. 37 50N 119 30w
87 Yoshkar Ola, U.S.S.R. 56 49N 47 10E
113 Yosu, South Korea 34 47N 127 45E
113 Yotsing, China 28 10N 120 55E
142 Youanmi, W. Austral. 28 37s 118 49E
44 Youghal, Ireland 51 58N 7 51w
44 Youghal Bay, Ireland 51 55N 7 50w
124 Youkoukoun, Guinea .12 35N 13 11w
143 Young, NSW, Austral. 34 19s 148 18E
167 Young, U.S.A. 34 9N 110 56w
172 Young, Uruguay 32 44s 57 36w
147 Young Ra., N.Z. 44 10s 169 30E
145 Younghusband Pen., South Australia 34 45s 139 15E
157 Youngstown, Canada .51 35N 111 10w
160 Youngstown, N.Y., U.S.A. 43 16N 79 2w
160 Youngstown, Ohio, U.S.A. 41 7N 80 41w
160 Youngsville, U.S.A. 41 51N 79 12w
122 Youssoufia (Louis Gentil), Morocco ...32 16N 8 31w
142 Yoweragabbie, W. Australia 28 10s 117 30E
34 Yoxall, England, U.K. 52 45N 1 49w
36 Yoxford, Eng., U.K. .52 16N 1 30E
113 Yoyang, China 29 27N 113 10E
100 Yozgat, Turkey 39 51N 34 47E
48 Yport, France 49 45N 0 15E
54 Ypres, Belgium 50 50N 2 52E
162 Ypsilanti, U.S.A. 42 18N 83 40w
166 Yreka, U.S.A. 41 44N 122 40w
37 Ysbyty Ystwyth, Wales, United Kingdom 52 20N 3 50w
167 Ysleta, U.S.A. 31 45N 106 24w
51 Yssingeaux, France ...45 9N 4 8E
81 Ystad, Sweden 55 26N 13 50E
37 Ystalyfera, Wales, U.K. 51 46N 3 48w
37 Ystrad, Wales, U.K. .52 12N 4 8w
37 Ystradgynlais, Wales, United Kingdom ...51 47N 3 45w
37 Ystwyth R., Wales, UK 52 24N 4 2w
43 Ythan R., Scot., U.K. 57 26N 1 12w
79 Ytre Adal, Norway ...60 15N 10 14E
80 Ytterhogdal, Sweden .62 12N 14 45E
91 Ytyryk, U.S.S.R. 66 25N 151 0E
113 Yu Shan, Mt., Taiwan 23 30N 121 0E
113 Yuanling, China 28 30N 110 5E
111 Yuanyang, China 23 10N 102 58E
166 Yuba City, U.S.A. 39 12N 121 45w
114 Yubetsu, Japan 44 15N 143 40E
168 Yucatan, st., Mexico .21 30N 86 30w
16 Yucatán Basin, Caribbean Sea 20 0N 84 0w
169 Yucatan Channel, Caribbean Sea 22 0N 86 30w
167 Yucca, U.S.A. 34 56N 114 6w
112 Yucheng, China 36 55N 116 40E
90 Yudino, U.S.S.R. 55 10N 67 55E
90 Yuganskie, U.S.S.R. .66 0N 71 40E
69 Yugoslavia, rep., Eur. 44 0N 20 0E
112 Yuhsien, China 39 45N 114 33E
113 Yuhsien, China 34 4N 113 40E
113 Yuhwan, China 28 1N 121 12E
113 Yükan, China 28 43N 116 35E
86 Yukhnov, U.S.S.R. ...54 44N 35 15E
113 Yukikow, China 31 29N 118 17E
154 Yukon, terr., Canada .63 0N 135 0w
152 Yukon R., Alas./Canada 65 30N 150 0w
138 Yule R., W. Australia 21 10s 118 10E
126 Yuli, Nigeria 9 44N 10 12E
113 Yülin, Hainan, China .18 10N 109 31E
113 Yülin (Watlam), Kwangsi-Chuang, China 22 30N 110 50E
112 Yülin, Shensi, China .38 20N 109 15E
143 Yuluma, N.S.W., Austral. 35 6s 146 15E
167 Yuma, Ariz., U.S.A. ...32 45N 114 45w
164 Yuma, Colo., U.S.A. .40 10N 102 43w
131 Yumbe, Uganda 3 28N 31 15E
172 Yumbel, Chile 37 5s 72 40w
111 Yümen, China 41 13N 96 55E
143 Yundamindera, Western Australia .29 4s 122 3E
113 Yungan, China 25 50N 117 25E
174 Yungas, Bolivia 17 0s 66 0w
172 Yungay, Chile 37 10s 72 5w
113 Yungchun, China 25 20N 118 15E
143 Yungera Vic., Austral. 34 42s 143 3E
113 Yungfu, China 25 1N 109 58E
113 Yunghing, China 26 12N 113 3E
112 Yunghwo, China 36 58N 110 56E
113 Yungshun, China 29 3N 109 50E
113 Yungsin, China 26 55N 114 10E
113 Yungtsi, China 34 50N 110 25E
113 Yungyun, China 24 31N 113 28E
113 Yünhsien, China 32 30N 111 0E
113 Yunhwo, China 28 0N 119 32E
113 Yunlin, Taiwan 23 45N 120 30E
103 Yunlung, China 25 50N 99 25E
111 Yünnan, prov., China 25 0N 102 30E
142 Yunndaga, W. Austral. 29 45s 121 0E
64 Yunquera de Henares, Spain 40 47N 3 11w
113 Yunsiao, China 24 0N 117 20E
86 Yuratishki, U.S.S.R. .54 3N 25 52E
90 Yuribei, U.S.S.R. 71 20N 76 30E
174 Yurimaguas, Peru 5 55s 76 0w
87 Yurya, U.S.S.R. 59 1N 49 13E
87 Yuryev Polskiy, U.S.S.R. 56 30N 59 47E
87 Yuryevets, U.S.S.R. ...57 25N 43 2E
169 Yuscarán, Honduras .13 58N 86 51w
111 Yüshu China 32 50N 96 50E
112 Yushu, China 44 48N 126 37E
113 Yutu, China 26 0N 115 15E
112 Yütze, China 37 45N 112 45E
113 Yuyang, China 28 45N 108 35E
113 Yüyao, China 30 0N 121 20E
112 Yuyu, China 40 10N 112 20E
113 Yuyuan, China 24 58N 112 4E
87 Yuzha, U.S.S.R. 56 40N 42 10E
91 Yuzhno-Sakhalinsk, U.S.S.R. 47 5N 142 5E
49 Yvelines, dept., France 48 40N 1 45E
57 Yverdon, Switzerland 46 47N 6 39E
48 Yvetot, France 49 37N 0 44E

Z

122 Za, R., Morocco 34 5N 2 30w
54 Zaandam, Netherlands 52 26N 4 49E
123 Zab, Monts du, Algeria 34 55N 5 0E
74 Zabalj, Yugoslavia 45 21N 20 5E
74 Zabarj, Yugoslavia 45 23N 20 5E
74 Zabari, Yugoslavia 44 22N 21 15E
125 Zabéré, Upper Volta .11 12N 0 36w
60 Zabkowice Slaskie, Pol. 50 22N 19 17E
74 Zabljak, Yugoslavia ...42 19N 19 10E
101 Zābol, Iran 31 0N 61 25E
101 Zaboli, Iran 27 10N 61 35E
60 Zabrze, Poland 50 24N 18 50E
60 Zabludow, Poland 53 0N 23 19E
59 Zabno, Poland 50 9N 20 50E
168 Zacapa, Guatemala ...14 59N 89 31w
168 Zacatecas, Mexico 22 49N 102 34w
168 Zacatecas, st., Mexico 23 30N 103 0w
168 Zacatecoluea, Salvador 13 29N 88 51w
168 Zacoalco, Mexico 20 10N 103 40w
71 Zadar, Yugoslavia 44 8N 15 8E
125 Zadawa, Nigeria 11 33N 10 19E
107 Zadetkyi Kyun (St. Matthew's I), Burma 10 0N 98 25E
87 Zadonsk, U.S.S.R. ...52 25N 38 56E
98 Zafad, Israel 32 58N 35 29E
77 Zafora I., Greece 36 5N 26 24E
63 Zafra, Spain 38 26N 6 30w
60 Zagan, Poland 51 39N 15 22E
126 Zagazig, Egypt 30 40N 31 12E
123 Zaghouan, Tunisia ...36 19N 10 2E
76 Zaglivererion, Greece .40 36N 23 15E
122 Zaglou, Algeria 27 17N 0 3w
125 Zagnanado, Dahomey 7 18N 2 28E
76 Zagora, Greece 39 27N 23 6E
122 Zagora, Morocco 30 14N 5 51w
87 Zagorsk, U.S.S.R. 56 20N 38 10E
71 Zagreb, Yugoslavia ...45 50N 16 0E
101 Zagros Mts., Iran 33 45N 47 0E
74 Zagubica, Yugoslavia .44 15N 21 47E
101 Zahedan, Iran 29 30N 60 50E
106 Zahirabad, India 17 43N 77 37E
100 Zahlah, Lebanon 33 52N 35 50E
56 Zahna, Germany 51 54N 12 47E
122 Zahrez Chergui, Algeria 35 0N 3 30E
122 Zahrez Rharbi, Algeria 34 50N 2 55E
76 Zahrishtë, Albania ...42 10N 20 17E
122 Zair, Algeria 29 47N 5 51w
130 Zaire, dist., Angola ... 6 30s 13 30E
130 Zaire, st., Africa 3 0s 22 0E
74 Zaječar, Yugoslavia ...43 53N 22 18E
132 Zaka, Rhodesia 20 20s 31 28E
91 Zakamensk, U.S.S.R. .50 23N 103 17E
98 Zakariya, Israel 31 43N 34 57E
89 Zakataly, U.S.S.R. ...41 38N 46 35E
100 Zakhu, Iraq 37 10N 42 50E
77 Zakinthos, Greece 37 47N 20 54E
77 Zakinthos, I., Greece .37 45N 27 45E
59 Zakopane, Poland 49 18N 19 57E
59 Zala, co., Hungary 46 42N 16 50E
59 Zala R., Hungary 46 53N 17 6E
59 Zalaegerszeg, Hungary 46 53N 16 47E
59 Zalalovo, Hungary 46 51N 16 35E
63 Zalamea de la Serena, Spain 38 40N 5 38w
63 Zalamea la Real, Spain 37 41N 6 38w
125 Zalau, Nigeria 10 30N 8 58E
125 Zălău Rumania 47 12N 23 5E
71 Zalec, Yugoslavia 46 16N 15 10E
88 Zaleshchiki, U.S.S.R. 48 45N 25 45E
60 Zalew Wislany, U.S.S.R. and Poland 54 20N 19 50E
60 Zalewo, Poland 53 55N 19 41E
121 Zalingei, Sudan 13 5N 23 10E
123 Zaltan, Jabal, Libya ..28 46N 19 45E
55 Zaltbommel, Neth. ...51 48N 5 15E
132 Zambesi, Delta, Mozam. 18 46s 36 16E
132 Zambezi R., S.E. Africa 15 40s 29 15E
109 Zamboanga, Philippines 6 59N 122 3E
87 Zametchino, U.S.S.R. 53 30N 42 30E
168 Zamora, Mexico 20 0N 102 21w
62 Zamora, Spain 41 30N 5 45w
62 Zamora, prov., Spain ...41 30N 5 46w
60 Zamósc, Poland 50 50N 23 22E
123 Zamzam, W., Libya ...31 0N 14 30E
125 Zan, Ghana 9 26N 0 17w
90 Zanatas, U.S.S.R. 43 11N 81 18E
64 Zancara R., Spain 39 20N 3 0w
55 Zandhoven, Belgium .57 13N 4 40E
54 Zandvoort, Netherlands 52 21N 4 36E
160 Zanesville, U.S.A. 39 56N 82 2w
132 Zangue R., Mozambique 18 5s 35 10E
100 Zanjan, Iran 36 40N 48 35E
72 Zannone, I., Italy 40 58N 13 2E
142 Zanthus, W. Australia 30 55s 123 29E
131 Zanzibar, tn., Tanzania 6 12s 39 12E
131 Zanzibar Chan., Tanz. 6 0s 39 0E
131 Zanzibar & I., Tanzania 6 12s 39 12E
123 Zanzur, Libya 32 55N 13 1E
123 Zaouatalaz, Algeria ...24 57N 8 16E
123 Zaouiet El-Kahla (Ft. Flatters), Algeria ...27 10N 6 40E

MAP
122 Zaouiet Reggane (Reggan), Algeria ...26 32N 0 3E
74 Zapadna Morava, R., Yugoslavia 43 50N 20 15E
86 Zapadnaya Dvina, U.S.S.R. 56 15N 32 3E
59 Zapadné Beskydy, Mts., Europe 49 30N 19 0E
58 Zapadocesky, reg., Cz. 49 35N 13 0E
59 Zapadoslovensky, reg., Czechoslovakia 48 30N 17 30E
176 Zapala, Argentina 39 0S 70 5W
165 Zapata, U.S.A. 26 56N 92 17W
63 Zapaton, R., Spain 39 0N 6 49W
88 Zaporozhye, U.S.S.R. 47 50N 35 10E
73 Zapponeta, Italy 41 27N 15 57E
100 Zara, Turkey 39 58N 37 43E
64 Zaragoza, Spain 41 39N 0 53W
64 Zaragoza, Prov., Spain 41 35N 1 0W
168 Zaragoza, Coahuila, Mexico 28 30N 101 0W
168 Zaragoza, Nuevo Leon, Mexico 24 0N 99 36W
101 Zarand, Iran 30 46N 56 34E
78 Zarand, Munţii, Mts., Rumania 46 14N 22 7E
125 Zaranda, Nigeria 15 38S 9 34E
86 Zarasai, U.S.S.R. 55 40N 26 12E
172 Zarate, Argentina 34 7S 59 0W
87 Zaraysk, U.S.S.R. 54 48N 38 53E
174 Zaraza, Venezuela 9 21N 65 19W
157 Zarembo I., Alas., U.S.A. 56 20N 132 50W
125 Zari, Nigeria 13 8N 12 37E
125 Zaria, Nigeria 11 0N 7 40E
60 Zarki, Poland 50 38N 19 21E
60 Zarnów, Poland 51 16N 20 9E
98 Zarnuqa, Israel 31 53N 34 47E
98 Zarqa R., Jordan 32 10N 35 37E
174 Zaruma, Ecuador 3 40S 79 30W
62 Zarza de Granadilla, Sp. 40 14N 6 3W
123 Zarzaitine, Algeria 28 32N 9 5E
60 Zary, Poland 51 37N 15 10E
123 Zarzis, Tunisia 33 31N 11 2E
62 Zas, Spain 43 4N 8 53W
91 Zashiversk, U.S.S.R. .67 25N 142 40E
102 Zaskar Mountains, Kashmir 33 15N 77 30E
135 Zastron, O.F.S., S. Africa 30 18S 27 7E
58 Zatec, Czechoslovakia 50 20N 13 32E
91 Zatishe, U.S.S.R. 66 5N 158 55E
74 Zavala,. Yugoslavia ...42 50N 17 59E
101 Zavareh, Iran 33 35N 52 28E
55 Zavenaar, Netherlands 51 56N 6 5E
55 Zaventem, Belgium ...50 53N 4 28E
89 Zavetnoye, U.S.S.R. .47 13N 43 50E
74 Zavidovici, Yugoslavia 44 27N 18 13E
91 Zavitinsk, U.S.S.R. ...50 10N 129 20E
15 Zavodoski, I., Falk. Is. Dep. 56 0S 27 45W
126 Zaw Shammas, Egypt 31 25N 26 26E

MAP
126 Zaw Um el Rakham, Egypt 31 18N 27 1E
126 Zaw Ungelia, Egypt ...31 23N 26 42E
132 Zawi, Rhodesia 17 0S 30 10E
60 Zawiercie, Poland 50 30N 19 13E
101 Zayandeh R., Iran 32 35N 32 0E
123 Zazamt, W., Libya 30 29N 14 30E
59 Zazriva, Czechoslovakia 49 16N 19 7E
86 Zbarazh, U.S.S.R. 49 43N 25 44E
60 Zbaszyn, Poland 52 14N 15 56E
60 Zblewo, Poland 53 56N 18 19E
86 Zdolbunov, U.S.S.R. .50 30N 26 15E
74 Zdrelo, Yugoslavia 44 16N 21 28E
60 Zdunska Wola, Poland 51 37N 18 59E
156 Zeballos, Canada 49 57N 126 10W
125 Zebila, Ghana 11 1N 0 26W
133 Zebediela, S. Africa ...24 25S 29 25E
54 Zeebrugge, Belgium ...51 19N 3 12E
145 Zeehan, Tas., Austral. 41 52S 145 25E
135 Zeekoe R., S. Africa ...30 30S 24 55E
54 Zeeland, prov. Neth. .51 30N 3 50E
133 Zeerust, Trans., S. Afr. 25 31S 26 4E
122 Zegdou, Algeria 29 51N 4 53W
127 Zeghie, Ethiopia 11 43N 37 18E
124 Zegoua Mali 10 32N 5 35W
56 Zehdenick, Germany .52 59N 13 20E
99 Zeila, Somali Republic 11 15N 43 30E
54 Zeist, Netherlands 52 5N 5 15E
98 Zeita, Jordan 32 23N 35 2E
56 Zeita, Germany 51 3N 12 9E
74 Zelengora Ra., Y.-slav. 43 22N 18 30E
74 Zelenika, Yugoslavia .42 27N 18 37E
87 Zelendolsk, U.S.S.R. .55 55N 48 30E
86 Zelenogradsk, U.S.S.R. 54 53N 20 29E
89 Zelenokumsk, U.S.S.R. 44 30N 44 1E
89 Zelenovski, U.S.S.R. .48 6N 50 45E
74 Zelkin, Mt., Yugoslavia 43 30N 20 50E
57 Zell, Baden, Germany 47 42N 7 50E
58 Zell am See, Austria ...47 19N 12 47E
56 Zella Mehlis, Germany 50 40N 10 41E
122 Zeluan, Morocco 35 1N 2 58W
54 Zelzate, Belgium 51 13N 3 47E
123 Zembra I., Tunisia 37 5N 10 56E
122 Zemmora, Algeria 35 44N 0 51E
122 Zemoul, W., Algeria ...29 15N 7 30W
74 Zenica, Yugoslavia 44 10N 17 57E
122 Zenina, Algeria 34 30N 2 37E
130 Zenza, R., Angola 9 35S 13 20E
74 Zepce, Yugoslavia 44 28N 18 2E
56 Zerbst, Germany 51 59N 12 8E
122 Zerhamra, Algeria 29 58N 2 30W
57 Zermatt, Switzerland .46 2N 7 46E
57 Zernez, Switzerland ...46 42N 10 7E
123 Zeroud, R., Tunisia ...35 30N 9 30E
76 Zerqan, Albania 41 30N 20 20E
89 Zestafoni, U.S.S.R. 42 6N 43 0E
42 Zetland, co., Scot., U.K. 60 30N 0 15W
56 Zeulenroda, Germany 50 39N 12 0E
56 Zeven, Germany 53 17N 9 19E

MAP
55 Zevenbergen, Neth. ...51 38N 4 37E
70 Zevio, Italy 45 23N 11 10E
91 Zeya, U.S.S.R. 54 2N 127 20E
91 Zeya R., U.S.S.R. 53 30N 127 0E
62 Zezere, R., Portugal ...40 0N 7 55W
60 Zgierz, Poland 51 45N 19 27E
60 Zgorzelec, Poland 51 10N 15 0E
86 Zhabinka, U.S.S.R. ...52 13N 24 2E
86 Zhamensk, U.S.S.R. ...54 37N 21 17E
86 Zharkovskiy, U.S.S.R. 55 56N 32 19E
88 Zhashkov, U.S.S.R. ...49 15N 30 5E
88 Zhdanov, U.S.S.R. 47 5N 37 31E
87 Zherdevka, U.S.S.R. .51 56N 41 21E
91 Zhigansk, U.S.S.R. 66 35N 124 10E
87 Zhigulevsk, U.S.S.R. .53 28N 49 45E
87 Zhiguli Mts., U.S.S.R. 53 20N 48 45E
86 Zhitomir U.S.S.R. 50 20N 28 40E
86 Zhizdra, U.S.S.R. 53 45N 34 40E
86 Zhlobin, U.S.S.R. 52 55N 30 0E
88 Zhmerinka, U.S.S.R. .49 2N 28 10E
86 Zhukovka, U.S.S.R. ...53 35N 33 50E
91 Zhupanovo, U.S.S.R. .51 59N 15 9E
104 Ziarat, West Pakistan 30 25N 67 42E
60 Ziebice, Poland 50 37N 17 2E
138 Ziel, Mt., Australia 23 20S 132 30E
60 Zielona Góra, Poland .51 57N 15 31E
60 Zielona Góra, Prov., Pol. 51 57N 15 30E
54 Zierikzee, Netherlands 51 40N 3 55E
56 Ziesar, Germany 52 16N 12 19E
126 Zifta, Egypt 30 43N 31 14E
121 Ziguei, Chad 14 50N 15 50E
124 Ziguinchor, Senegal ...12 25N 16 20W
98 Zikhron Ya'Aqov, Israel 32 34N 34 56E
100 Zile, Turkey 40 15N 36 0E
100 Zilfi, Saudi Arabia......26 12N 44 52E
59 Zilina, Czechoslovakia 49 12N 18 42E
123 Zillah, Libya 28 40N 17 41E
58 Zillertaler Alpen, Aust. 47 6N 11 45E
111 Zilling Tso L., Tibet, China 31 40N 89 0E
91 Zima, U.S.S.R. 54 0N 102 5E
132 Zimane, Mozambique .22 9S 33 25E
122 Zimane, Adrar in, Alg. 22 10N 4 30E
168 Zimapan, Mexico 20 40N 99 20W
132 Zimba, Zambia 17 20S 26 25E
132 Zimbabwe Ruins, Rhod. 20 16S 31 0E
89 Zimovniki, U.S.S.R. ...47 10N 42 25E
125 Zinarie, Upper Volta .12 44N 1 10W
125 Zinder, Niger 13 48N 9 0E
130 Zinga, Cent. Afr. Rep. 3 49N 18 34E
56 Zingst, Germany 54 24N 12 45E
122 Zini, Yebel, Morocco .28 0N 11 0W
99 Zinjibar, S. Yemen 13 5N 46 0E
81 Zinkgruvan, Sweden .58 50N 15 15E
56 Zinnowitz, Germany .54 5N 13 54E
167 Zion Nat. Park, U.S.A. 37 25N 112 50W
174 Zipaquira, Colombia ... 5 0N 74 0W
59 Zirc Hungary 47 17N 17 42E
71 Ziri, Yugoslavia 47 17N 11 14E
71 Zirie I., Yugoslavia ...43 39N 15 42E

MAP
58 Zirl, Austria 47 17N 11 14E
59 Zisterdorf, Austria 48 33N 16 45E
168 Zitacuaro, Mexico 19 20N 100 30W
59 Zitava, R., Cz. 48 14N 18 21E
74 Ziltište, Yugoslavia ...45 30N 2 32E
76 Zitsa, Greece 39 47N 20 40E
56 Zittau, Germany 50 54N 14 47E
74 Zivinice, Yugoslavia ...44 27N 18 36E
122 Ziz. R., Morocco 31 40N 4 15W
100 Zizip, Turkey 37 5N 37 50E
71 Zlarin, Yugoslavia 43 42N 15 49E
71 Zlatar, Yugoslavia 46 5N 16 3E
74 Zlatar, Ra., Yugoslavia 42 55N 25 59E
75 Zlataritsa, Bulgaria ...43 2N 24 55E
74 Zlatibor Ra. Y.-slavia 43 45N 19 43E
75 Zlatica Bulgaria 42 41N 24 7E
78 Zlatna, Rumania 46 8N 23 11E
75 Zlatograd, Bulgaria ...41 22N 25 7E
84 Zlatoust, U.S.S.R. 55 10N 59 30E
74 Zletovo, Yugoslavia ...41 59N 22 17E
123 Zlitan, Libya 32 25N 14 35E
74 Zljeb, Mt., Yugoslavia 42 40N 20 17E
60 Zlocieniec, Poland 53 30N 16 1E
74 Zlot, Yugoslavia 44 1N 22 0E
60 Zlotoryja, Poland 51 8N 15 55E
60 Zlotów, Poland 53 22N 17 2E
60 Zmigród, Poland 51 28N 16 53E
88 Zmiyev, U.S.S.R. 49 45N 36 27E
88 Znamenka, U.S.S.R. .48 45N 32 30E
60 Znin, Poland 52 51N 17 44E
58 Znojmo, Czechoslovakia 48 50N 16 2E
132 Zóbuè, Mozambique ...15 38S 34 26E
55 Zoelen, Netherlands ...51 55N 5 24E
70 Zogno, Italy 45 49N 9 41E
86 Zolochev, U.S.S.R. 49 45N 24 58E
88 Zolotonosha, U.S.S.R. 49 45N 32 5E
132 Zomba, Malawi 15 30S 35 19E
130 Zongo, Congo 4 12N 18 0E
88 Zonguldak, Turkey 41 28N 31 50E
55 Zonhoven, Belgium ...50 59N 5 23E
125 Zorgo, Upper Volta ...12 22N 0 35W
63 Zorita, Spain 39 17N 5 39W
78 Zorleni, Rumania 46 14N 27 44E
75 Zornitsa, Bulgaria 42 23N 26 58E
168 Zorra Island, Panama Canal Zone 9 18N 79 52W
124 Zorzor, Liberia 7 46N 9 28W
174 Zorritos, Peru 3 50S 80 40W
56 Zossen, Germany 52 13N 13 28E
123 Zouar, Chad 20 30N 16 32E
120 Zouérabe, Mauritania 22 35N 12 30W
122 Zousfana, W., Algeria 31 51N 1 30W
54 Zoutkamp, Netherlands 53 20N 6 18E
60 Zqorzelec, Poland 51 9N 15 0E
74 Zrenjanin, Yugoslavia 45 22N 20 23E
125 Zuarungu, Ghana 10 49N 0 52W
125 Zuba Nigeria 9 11N 7 12E
63 Zubia, Spain 37 8N 3 33W
86 Zubtsov, U.S.S.R. 56 10N 34 34E
124 Zuénoula, Ivory Coast 7 34N 6 3W
64 Zuera, Spain 41 51N 0 49W
123 Zuetina, Libya 30 58N 20 7E

MAP
57 Zug, Switzerland 47 10N 8 31E
57 Zug, can., Switzerland 47 9N 8 35E
89 Zugdidi, U.S.S.R. 42 30N 41 48E
57 Zugersee, Switzerland 47 7N 8 35E
57 Zugspitze, Mt., Ger. ...47 25N 10 59E
55 Zuid Beijerland, Neth. 51 45N 4 22E
54 Zuid Holland, prov., Netherlands 52 0N 4 35E
54 Zuidhorn, Netherlands 53 15N 6 23E
65 Zujar, Spain 37 34N 2 50W
63 Zujar R., Spain 38 30N 5 30E
127 Zula, Ethiopia 15 17N 39 40E
56 Zülpich, Germany 50 41N 6 38E
135 Zululand, reg., S. Africa 28 0S 32 0E
64 Zumaya, Spain 43 19N 2 15W
132 Zumbo, Mozambique .15 35S 30 26E
125 Zummo, Nigeria 9 51N 12 59E
130 Zundi, Angola 16 26S 16 45E
132 Zune, Mozambique 18 59S 35 18E
174 Zunga, Ecuador 1 20S 78 5W
125 Zungur, Nigeria 10 4N 9 49E
135 Zungwini, Nat., S. Afr. 27 34S 30 53E
167 Zuni, U.S.A. 35 7N 108 57W
74 Zupanja, Yugoslavia .45 4N 18 43E
127 Zuqar I., Yemen 14 0N 42 40E
74 Zur, Yugoslavia 42 13N 20 34E
57 Zürich, Switzerland ...47 22N 8 32E
57 Zürich, can., Switz. ...47 26N 8 40E
57 Zürichsee, L., Switz. .47 18N 8 40E
60 Zuromin, Poland 53 4N 19 57E
125 Zuru, Nigeria 11 27N 5 4E
71 Zut, I., Yugoslavia 43 52N 15 17E
55 Zutendaal, Belgium ...50 56N 5 35E
54 Zutphen, Netherlands 52 9N 6 12E
123 Zuwarrah, Libya 32 58N 12 1E
87 Zuyevka, U.S.S.R. 58 27N 51 10E
71 Zuzemberk, Yugoslavia 45 52N 14 56E
88 Zvenigorodka, U.S.S.R. 49 4N 30 56E
90 Zverinogolovskoye, U.S.S.R. 55 0N 62 30E
90 Zverovo, U.S.S.R. 71 40N 83 20E
75 Zvezdets, Bulgaria 42 6N 27 26E
59 Zvolen, Czechoslovakia 48 33N 19 10E
74 Zvonce, Yugoslavia ...42 57N 22 34E
74 Zvornik, Yugoslavia ...44 26N 19 7E
127 Zwai L., Ethiopia 8 0N 38 50E
124 Zwedru (Tchien), Liberia 5 59N 8 15W
57 Zweibrücken, Germany 49 15N 7 20E
56 Zwenkau, Germany ...51 13N 12 19E
58 Zwettl, Austria 48 35N 15 9E
56 Zwickau, Germany 50 43N 12 30E
55 Zwijndrecht, Belgium 51 13N 4 20E
54 Zwolle, Netherlands ...52 31N 6 6E
165 Zwolle, U.S.A. 31 42N 93 40W
60 Zyrardów, Poland 52 3N 20 35E
89 Zyrya, U.S.S.R. 40 22N 50 18E
90 Zyryanovsk, U.S.S.R. 49 50N 84 57E
59 Zywiec, Poland 49 42N 19 12E

Printed in Great Britain by George Philip Printers, Limited, London MHL